COLLINS
ITALIAN
COLLEGE
DICTIONARY

COLLINS
ITALIAN
COLLEGE
DICTIONARY

ITALIAN-ENGLISH · ENGLISH-ITALIAN

HarperCollinsPublishers

COLLINS ITALIAN COLLEGE DICTIONARY

ITALIAN-ENGLISH ENGLISH-ITALIAN

HarperCollins*Publishers*

First published in this edition 1991

© HarperCollins Publishers 1991

Latest reprint 1992

ISBN 0 00 433343 8

Catherine E. Love, Michela Clari

editorial staff/segreteria di redazione
Angela Campbell, Vivian Marr,
Elspeth Anderson, Anne Marie Banks,
Anne Bradley, Susan Dunsmore

Printed in Great Britain by
HarperCollins Manufacturing, Glasgow

INDICE

CONTENTS

I marchi registrati

I termini che a nostro parere costituiscono un marchio registrato sono stati designati come tali. In ogni caso, né la presenza né l'assenza di tale designazione implicano alcuna valutazione del loro reale stato giuridico.

Note on trademarks

Words which we have reason to believe constitute trademarks have been designated as such. However, neither the presence nor the absence of such designation should be regarded as affecting the legal status of any trademark.

INTRODUZIONE

Per capire l'inglese

Questo nuovo ed aggiornatissimo dizionario si rivolge alle esigenze del mondo moderno, con un ampio lemmario che rispecchia la lingua inglese di oggi e comprende, naturalmente, anche la terminologia in uso nel mondo degli affari e dell'informatica, nonché un'ampia scelta di abbreviazioni, sigle, acronimi e termini geografici che compaiono di frequente nella stampa. Per una facile consultazione, le forme irregolari di verbi e sostantivi compaiono come lemmi principali con un rimando alla forma di partenza, dove viene fornita la traduzione.

Per esprimersi in inglese

Per aiutarvi ad esprimervi in un inglese corretto ed idiomatico, abbiamo inserito un sistema di indicatori, una preziosa "guida" al vostro servizio, per chiarirvi il senso e l'ambito d'uso di ciascuna traduzione ed orientarvi verso la scelta che più si adatta al vostro contesto. Tutti i termini d'uso corrente sono stati trattati in modo dettagliato ed esauriente ed illustrati da esempi tipici.

Un compagno di lavoro

L'attenzione e la cura che hanno accompagnato la creazione di questo nuovo dizionario Collins ne fanno uno strumento di facile consultazione, prezioso ed affidabile per lo studio ed il lavoro. Ci auguriamo che costituirà un fedele compagno al servizio di tutte le vostre esigenze linguistiche.

INTRODUCTION

Understanding Italian

This new and thoroughly up-to-date dictionary provides the user with wide-ranging, practical coverage of current usage, including terminology relevant to business and office automation, and a comprehensive selection of abbreviations, acronyms and geographical names commonly found in the press. You will also find, for ease of consultation, irregular forms of Italian verbs and nouns with a cross-reference to the basic form where a translation is given.

Self-expression in Italian

To help you express yourself correctly and idiomatically in Italian, numerous indications – think of them as signposts – guide you to the most appropriate translation for your context. All the most commonly used words are given detailed treatment, with many examples of typical usage.

A working companion

Much care has been taken to make this new Collins dictionary thoroughly reliable, easy to use and relevant to your work and study. We hope it will become a long-serving companion for all your foreign language needs.

ABBREVIAZIONI

ABBREVIATIONS

aggettivo	**a**	adjective
abbreviazione	**abbr**	abbreviation
avverbio	**ad**	adverb
amministrazione	**ADMIN**	administration
aeronautica, viaggi aerei	**AER**	flying, air travel
aggettivo	**ag**	adjective
agricoltura	**AGR**	agriculture
amministrazione	**AMM**	administration
anatomia	**ANAT**	anatomy
architettura	**ARCHIT**	architecture
astronomia, astrologia	**ASTR**	astronomy, astrology
l'automobile	**AUT**	the motor car and motoring
avverbio	**av**	adverb
aeronautica, viaggi aerei	**AVIAT**	flying, air travel
biologia	**BIOL**	biology
botanica	**BOT**	botany
inglese di Gran Bretagna	**Brit**	British English
consonante	**C**	consonant
chimica	**CHIM, CHEM**	chemistry
congiunzione	**cj**	conjunction
familiare (! da evitare)	**col(!)**	colloquial usage (! particularly offensive)
commercio, finanza, banca	**COMM**	commerce, finance, banking
informatica	**COMPUT**	computing
congiunzione	**cong**	conjunction
edilizia	**CONSTR**	building
sostantivo usato come aggettivo, non può essere usato né come attributo, né dopo il sostantivo qualificato	**cpd**	compound element: noun used as adjective and which cannot follow the noun it qualifies
cucina	**CUC, CULIN**	cookery
davanti a	**dav**	before
determinante: articolo, aggettivo dimostrativo o indefinito etc	**det**	determiner: article, demonstrative etc
diritto	**DIR**	law
economia	**ECON**	economics
edilizia	**EDIL**	building
elettricità, elettronica	**ELETTR, ELEC**	electricity, electronics
esclamazione, interiezione	**escl, excl**	exclamation, interjection
specialmente	**esp**	especially
femminile	**f**	feminine
familiare (! da evitare)	**fam(!)**	colloquial usage (! particularly offensive)
ferrovia	**FERR**	railways
figurato	**fig**	figurative use
fisiologia	**FISIOL**	physiology
fotografia	**FOT**	photography
(verbo inglese) la cui particella è inseparabile dal verbo	**fus**	(phrasal verb) where the particle cannot be separated from main verb
nella maggior parte dei sensi; generalmente	**gen**	in most or all senses; generally
geografia, geologia	**GEO**	geography, geology

ABBREVIAZIONI

ABBREVIATIONS

geometria	**GEOM**	geometry
impersonale	**impers**	impersonal
informatica	**INFORM**	computing
insegnamento, sistema scolastico e universitario	**INS**	schooling, schools and universities
invariabile	**inv**	invariable
irregolare	**irg**	irregular
grammatica, linguistica	**LING**	grammar, linguistics
maschile	**m**	masculine
matematica	**MAT(H)**	mathematics
termine medico, medicina	**MED**	medical term, medicine
il tempo, meteorologia	**METEOR**	the weather, meteorology
maschile o femminile, secondo il sesso	**m/f**	either masculine or feminine depending on sex
esercito, lingua militare	**MIL**	military matters
musica	**MUS**	music
sostantivo	**n**	noun
nautica	**NAUT**	sailing, navigation
numerale (aggettivo, sostantivo)	**num**	numeral adjective or noun
	o.s.	oneself
peggiorativo	**peg, pej**	derogatory, pejorative
fotografia	**PHOT**	photography
fisiologia	**PHYSIOL**	physiology
plurale	**pl**	plural
politica	**POL**	politics
participio passato	**pp**	past participle
preposizione	**prep**	preposition
psicologia, psichiatria	**PSIC, PSYCH**	psychology, psychiatry
tempo del passato	**pt**	past tense
sostantivo che non si usa al plurale	**q**	uncountable noun: not used in the plural
qualcosa	**qc**	
qualcuno	**qn**	
religione, liturgia	**REL**	religions, church service
sostantivo	**s**	noun
	sb	somebody
insegnamento, sistema scolastico e universitario	**SCOL**	schooling, schools and universities
singolare	**sg**	singular
soggetto (grammaticale)	**sog**	(grammatical) subject
	sth	something
congiuntivo	**sub**	subjunctive
soggetto (grammaticale)	**subj**	(grammatical) subject
termine tecnico, tecnologia	**TECN, TECH**	technical term, technology
telecomunicazioni	**TEL**	telecommunications
tipografia	**TIP**	typography, printing
televisione	**TV**	television
tipografia	**TYP**	typography, printing
inglese degli Stati Uniti	**US**	American English
vocale	**V**	vowel
verbo	**vb**	verb

ABBREVIAZIONI

ABBREVIATIONS

verbo o gruppo verbale con funzione intransitiva	**vi**	verb or phrasal verb used intransitively
verbo riflessivo	**vr**	reflexive verb
verbo o gruppo verbale con funzione transitiva	**vt**	verb or phrasal verb used transitively
zoologia	**ZOOL**	zoology
marchio registrato	**®**	registered trademark
introduce un'equivalenza culturale	**≈**	introduces a cultural equivalent

TRASCRIZIONE FONETICA

CONSONANTI

CONSONANTS

NB. **p, b, t, d, k, g** sono seguiti da un'aspirazione in inglese.

NB. **p, b, t, d, k, g** are not aspirated in Italian.

*p*adre	p	*p*uppy
*b*am*b*ino	b	*b*a*b*y
*tutt*o	t	*t*en*t*
*d*a*d*o	d	*d*ad*d*y
*c*ane *ch*e	k	*c*ork *k*iss *ch*ord
*g*ola *gh*iro	g	*g*a*g g*uess
*s*ano	s	*s*o ri*c*e ki*ss*
*s*vago e*s*ame	z	cou*s*in buz*z*
*sc*ena	ʃ	*sh*eep *s*ugar
	ʒ	plea*s*ure bei*g*e
pe*c*e lan*c*iare	tʃ	*ch*ur*ch*
*g*iro *g*ioco	dʒ	*j*u*dg*e *g*eneral
a*f*a *f*aro	f	*f*arm ra*ff*le
*v*ero bra*v*o	v	*v*ery re*v*
	θ	*th*in ma*th*s
	ð	*th*at o*th*er
*l*etto a*l*a	l	*l*itt*l*e ba*ll*
g*li*	ʎ	
re*t*e ar*c*o	r	*r*at b*r*at
*r*amo *m*adre	m	*m*u*mm*y co*mb*
*n*o fuma*n*te	n	*n*o ra*n*
*gn*omo	ɲ	
	ŋ	si*ng*ing ba*n*k
	h	*h*at re*h*eat
bu*i*o p*i*acere	j	*y*et
*u*omo g*u*aio	w	*w*all be*w*ail
	x	lo*ch*

VARIE

MISCELLANEOUS

per l'inglese: la "r" finale viene pronunciata se seguita da una vocale

★

precede la sillaba accentata

'

precedes the stressed syllable

Come regola generale, in tutte le voci la trascrizione fonetica in parentesi quadra segue il termine cui si riferisce. Tuttavia, dalla parte inglese-italiano del dizionario, per la pronuncia di composti che siano formati da più parole non unite da trattino che appaiono comunque nel dizionario, si veda la trascrizione fonetica di ciascuna di queste parole alla rispettiva posizione alfabetica.

PHONETIC TRANSCRIPTION

VOCALI

NB. La messa in equivalenza di
certi suoni indica solo una
rassomiglianza approssimativa.

VOWELS

NB. The pairing of some vowel
sounds only indicates
approximate equivalence.

vino idea	i i:	heel bead
	ɪ	hit pity
stella edera	e	
epoca eccetto	ɛ	set tent
mamma amore	a æ	apple bat
	ɑ:	after car calm
	ʌ	fun cousin
	ə	over above
	ə:	urn fern work
rosa occhio	ɔ	wash pot
	ɔ:	born cork
ponte ognuno	o	
utile zucca	u	full soot
	u:	boon lewd

DITTONGHI

DIPHTHONGS

	ɪə	beer tier
	ɛə	tear fair there
	eɪ	date plaice day
	aɪ	life buy cry
	au	owl foul now
	əu	low no
	ɔɪ	boil boy oily
	uə	poor tour

*In general, we give the pronunciation of each entry in square brackets after the word in
question. However, on the English-Italian side, where the entry is composed of two or
more unhyphenated words, each of which is given elsewhere in this dictionary, you will
find the pronunciation of each word in its alphabetical position.*

ITALIAN PRONUNCIATION

VOWELS

Where the vowel **e** or the vowel **o** appears in a stressed syllable it can be either open [ɛ], [ɔ] or closed [e], [o]. As the open or closed pronunciation of these vowels is subject to regional variation, the distinction is of little importance to the user of this dictionary. Phonetic transcription for headwords containing these vowels will therefore only appear where other pronunciation difficulties are present.

CONSONANTS

c before "e" or "i" is pronounced *tch*.

ch is pronounced like the "k" in "kit".

g before "e" or "i" is pronounced like the "j" in "jet".

gh is pronounced like the "g" in "get".

gl before "e" or "i" is normally pronounced like the "lli" in "million", and in a few cases only like the "gl" in "glove".

gn is pronounced like the "ny" in "canyon".

sc before "e" or "i" is pronounced *sh*.

z is pronounced like the "ts" in "stetson", or like the "d's" in "bird's-eye".

Headwords containing the above consonants and consonantal groups have been given full phonetic transcription in this dictionary.

NB. All double written consonants in Italian are fully sounded: e.g. the *tt* in "tutto" is pronounced as in "ha*t t*rick".

ITALIAN VERBS

1 Gerundio *2* Participio passato *3* Presente *4* Imperfetto *5* Passato remoto *6* Futuro *7* Condizionale *8* Congiuntivo presente *9* Congiuntivo passato *10* Imperativo

accadere *like* cadere
accedere *like* concedere
accendere *2* acceso *5* accesi, accendesti
accludere *like* alludere
accogliere *like* cogliere
accondiscendere *like* scendere
accorgersi *like* scorgere
accorrere *like* correre
accrescere *like* crescere
addirsi *like* dire
addurre *like* ridurre
affiggere *2* affisso *5* affissi, affiggesti
affliggere *2* afflitto *5* afflissi, affliggesti
aggiungere *like* giungere
alludere *2* alluso *5* allusi, alludesti
ammettere *like* mettere
andare *3* vado, vai, va, andiamo, andate, vanno *6* andrò *etc 8* vada *10* va'!, vada!, andate!, vadano!
annettere *2* annesso *5* annessi *or* annettei, annettesti
apparire *2* apparso *3* appaio, appari *o* apparisci, appare *o* apparisce, appaiono *o* appariscono *5* apparvi *o* apparsi, apparisti, apparve *o* apparì *o* apparse, apparvero *o* apparirono *o* apparsero *8* appaia *o* apparisca
appartenere *like* tenere
appendere *2* appeso *5* appesi, appendesti
apporre *like* porre
apprendere *like* prendere
aprire *2* aperto *3* apro *5* aprii *o* apersi, apristi *8* apra
ardere *2* arso *5* arsi, ardesti
ascendere *like* scendere
aspergere *2* asperso *5* aspersi, aspergesti
assalire *like* salire
assistere *2* assistito
assolvere *2* assolto *5* assolsi *o* assolvei *o* assolvetti, assolvesti
assumere *2* assunto *5* assunsi, assumesti
astenersi *like* tenere
attendere *like* tendere
attingere *like* tingere
AVERE *3* ho, hai, ha, abbiamo, avete, hanno *5* ebbi, avesti, ebbe, avemmo, aveste, ebbero *6* avrò *etc 8* abbia *etc 10* abbi!, abbia!, abbiate!, abbiano!
avvedersi *like* vedere
avvenire *like* venire
avvincere *like* vincere
avvolgere *like* volgere
benedire *like* dire
bere *1* bevendo *2* bevuto *3* bevo *etc 4* bevevo *etc 5* bevvi *o* bevetti, bevesti *6* berrò *etc 8* beva *etc 9* bevessi *etc*
cadere *5* caddi, cadesti *6* cadrò *etc*
chiedere *2* chiesto *5* chiesi, chiedesti
chiudere *2* chiuso *5* chiusi, chiudesti
cingere *2* cinto *5* cinsi, cingesti
cogliere *2* colto *3* colgo, colgono *5* colsi, cogliesti *8* colga
coincidere *2* coinciso *5* coincisi, coincidesti
coinvolgere *like* volgere
commettere *like* mettere
commuovere *like* muovere
comparire *like* apparire
compiacere *like* piacere
compiangere *like* piangere
comporre *like* porre
comprendere *like* prendere
comprimere *2* compresso *5* compressi, comprimesti
compromettere *like* mettere
concedere *2* concesso *o* conceduto *5* concessi *o* concedei *o* concedetti, concedesti
concludere *like* alludere
concorrere *like* correre
condurre *like* ridurre
confondere *like* fondere
congiungere *like* giungere
connettere *like* annettere
conoscere *2* conosciuto *5* conobbi, conoscesti
consistere *like* assistere
contendere *like* tendere
contenere *like* tenere
contorcere *like* torcere
contraddire *like* dire
contraffare *like* fare
contrarre *like* trarre
convenire *like* venire
convincere *like* vincere
coprire *like* aprire
correggere *like* reggere
correre *2* corso *5* corsi, corresti
corrispondere *like* rispondere
corrompere *like* rompere
costringere *like* stringere
costruire *5* costrussi, costruisti
crescere *2* cresciuto *5* crebbi, crescesti
cuocere *2* cotto *3* cuocio, cociamo, cuociono *5* cossi, cocesti
dare *3* do, dai, dà, diamo, date, danno *5* diedi *o* detti, desti *6* darò *etc 8* dia *etc 9* dessi *etc 10* da'!, dai!, date!, diano!
decidere *2* deciso *5* decisi, decidesti
decrescere *like* crescere
dedurre *like* ridurre

deludere *like* **alludere**
deporre *like* **porre**
deprimere *like* **comprimere**
deridere *like* **ridere**
descrivere *like* **scrivere**
desumere *like* **assumere**
detergere *like* **tergere**
devolvere *2* devoluto
difendere *2* difeso *5* difesi, difendesti
diffondere *like* **fondere**
dipendere *like* **appendere**
dipingere *like* **tingere**
dire *1* dicendo *2* detto *3* dico, dici, dice, diciamo, dite, dicono *4* dicevo *etc 5* dissi, dicesti *6* dirò *etc 8* dica, diciamo, diciate, dicano *9* dicessi *etc 10* di'!, dica!, dite!, dicano!
dirigere *2* diretto *5* diressi, dirigesti
discendere *like* **scendere**
dischiudere *like* **chiudere**
disciogliere *like* **sciogliere**
discorrere *like* **correre**
discutere *2* discusso *5* discussi, discutesti
disfare *like* **fare**
disilludere *like* **alludere**
disperdere *like* **perdere**
dispiacere *like* **piacere**
disporre *like* **porre**
dissolvere *2* dissolto *o* dissoluto *5* dissolsi *o* dissolvetti *o* dissolvei, dissolvesti
dissuadere *like* **persuadere**
distendere *like* **tendere**
distinguere *2* distinto *5* distinsi, distinguesti
distogliere *like* **togliere**
distrarre *like* **trarre**
distruggere *like* **struggere**
divenire *like* **venire**
dividere *2* diviso *5* divisi, dividesti
dolere *3* dolgo, duoli, duole, dolgono *5* dolsi, dolesti *6* dorrò *etc 8* dolga
DORMIRE *1 GERUNDIO* dormendo
2 PARTICIPIO PASSATO dormito
3 PRESENTE dormo, dormi, dorme, dormiamo, dormite, dormono
4 IMPERFETTO dormivo, dormivi, dormiva, dormivamo, dormivate, dormivano
5 PASSATO REMOTO dormii, dormisti, dormì, dormimmo, dormiste, dormirono
6 FUTURO dormirò, dormirai, dormirà, dormiremo, dormirete, dormiranno
7 CONDIZIONALE dormirei, dormiresti, dormirebbe, dormiremmo, dormireste, dormirebbero
8 CONGIUNTIVO PRESENTE dorma, dorma, dorma, dormiamo, dormiate, dormano
9 CONGIUNTIVO PASSATO dormissi, dormissi, dormisse, dormissimo, dormiste, dormissero
10 IMPERATIVO dormi!, dorma!, dormite!, dormano!

dovere *3* devo *o* debbo, devi, deve, dobbiamo, dovete, devono *o* debbono *6* dovrò *etc 8* debba, dobbiamo, dobbiate, devano *o* debbano
eccellere *2* eccelso *5* eccelsi, eccellesti
eludere *like* **alludere**
emergere *2* emerso *5* emersi, emergesti
emettere *like* **mettere**
erigere *like* **dirigere**
escludere *like* **alludere**
esigere *2* esatto
esistere *2* esistito
espellere *2* espulso *5* espulsi, espellesti
esplodere *2* esploso *5* esplosi, esplodesti
esporre *like* **porre**
esprimere *like* **comprimere**
ESSERE *2* stato *3* sono, sei, è, siamo, siete, sono *4* ero, eri, era, eravamo, eravate, erano *5* fui, fosti, fu, fummo, foste, furono *6* sarò *etc 8* sia *etc 9* fossi, fossi, fosse, fossimo, foste, fossero *10* sii!, sia!, siate!, siano!
estendere *like* **tendere**
estinguere *like* **distinguere**
estrarre *like* **trarre**
evadere *2* evaso *5* evasi, evadesti
evolvere *2* evoluto
fare *1* facendo *2* fatto *3* faccio, fai, fa, facciamo, fate, fanno *4* facevo *etc 5* feci, facesti *6* farò *etc 8* faccia *etc 9* facessi *etc 10* fa'!, faccia!, fate!, facciano!
fingere *like* **cingere**
FINIRE *1 GERUNDIO* finendo
2 PARTICIPIO PASSATO finito
3 PRESENTE finisco, finisci, finisce, finiamo, finite, finiscono
4 IMPERFETTO finivo, finivi, finiva, finivamo, finivate, finivano
5 PASSATO REMOTO finii, finisti, finì, finimmo, finiste, finirono
6 FUTURO finirò, finirai, finirà, finiremo, finirete, finiranno
7 CONDIZIONALE finirei, finiresti, finirebbe, finiremmo, finireste, finirebbero
8 CONGIUNTIVO PRESENTE finisca, finisca, finisca, finiamo, finiate, finiscano
9 CONGIUNTIVO PASSATO finissi, finissi, finisse, finissimo, finiste, finissero
10 IMPERATIVO finisci!, finisca!, finite!, finiscano!
flettere *2* flesso
fondere *2* fuso *5* fusi, fondesti
friggere *2* fritto *5* frissi, friggesti
fungere *2* funsi, fungesti
giacere *3* giaccio, giaci, giace, giac(c)iamo, giacete, giacciono *5* giacqui, giacesti *8* giaccia *etc 10* giaci!, giaccia!, giac(c)iamo!, giacete!, giacciano!
giungere *2* giunto *5* giunsi, giungesti
godere *6* godrò *etc*
illudere *like* **alludere**

xvi

immergere *like* emergere
immettere *like* mettere
imporre *like* porre
imprimere *like* comprimere
incidere *like* decidere
includere *like* alludere
incorrere *like* correre
incutere *like* discutere
indulgere 2 indulto 5 indulsi, indulgesti
indurre *like* ridurre
inferire¹ 2 inferto 5 infersi, inferisti
inferire² 2 inferito 5 inferii, inferisti
infliggere *like* affliggere
infrangere 2 infranto 5 infransi, infrangesti
infondere *like* fondere
insistere *like* assistere
intendere *like* tendere
interdire *like* dire
interporre *like* porre
interrompere *like* rompere
intervenire *like* venire
intraprendere *like* prendere
introdurre *like* ridurre
invadere *like* evadere
irrompere *like* rompere
iscrivere *like* scrivere
istruire *like* costruire
ledere 2 leso 5 lesi, ledesti
leggere 2 letto 5 lessi, leggesti
maledire *like* dire
mantenere *like* tenere
mettere 2 messo 5 misi, mettesti
mordere 2 morso 5 morsi, mordesti
morire 2 morto 3 muoio, muori, muore, moriamo, morite, muoiono 6 morirò *o* morrò *etc* 8 muoia
mungere 2 munto 5 munsi, mungesti
muovere 2 mosso 5 mossi, movesti
nascere 2 nato 5 nacqui, nascesti
nascondere 2 nascosto 5 nascosi, nascondesti
nuocere 2 nuociuto 3 nuoccio, nuoci, nuoce, nociamo *o* nuociamo, nuocete, nuocciono 4 nuocevo *etc* 5 nocqui, nuocesti 6 nuocerò *etc* 7 nuoccia
occorrere *like* correre
offendere *like* difendere
offrire 2 offerto 3 offro 5 offersi *o* offrii, offristi 8 offra
omettere *like* mettere
opporre *like* porre
opprimere *like* comprimere
ottenere *like* tenere
parere 2 parso 3 paio, paiamo, paiono 5 parvi *o* parsi, paresti 6 parrò *etc* 8 paia, paiamo, paiate, paiano
PARLARE *1* GERUNDIO parlando
2 PARTICIPIO PASSATO parlato
3 PRESENTE parlo, parli, parla, parliamo, parlate, parlano
4 IMPERFETTO parlavo, parlavi, parlava, parlavamo, parlavate, parlavano
5 PASSATO REMOTO parlai, parlasti, parlò, parlammo, parlaste, parlarono
6 FUTURO parlerò, parlerai, parlerà, parleremo, parlerete, parleranno
7 CONDIZIONALE parlerei, parleresti, parlerebbe, parleremmo, parlereste, parlerebbero
8 CONGIUNTIVO PRESENTE parli, parli, parli, parliamo, parliate, parlino
9 CONGIUNTIVO PASSATO parlassi, parlassi, parlasse, parlassimo, parlaste, parlassero
10 IMPERATIVO parla!, parli!, parlate!, parlino!
percorrere *like* correre
percuotere 2 percosso 5 percossi, percotesti
perdere 2 perso *o* perduto 5 persi *o* perdei *o* perdetti, perdesti
permettere *like* mettere
persuadere 2 persuaso 5 persuasi, persuadesti
pervenire *like* venire
piacere 2 piaciuto 3 piaccio, piacciamo, piacciono 5 piacqui, piacesti 8 piaccia *etc*
piangere 2 pianto 5 piansi, piangesti
piovere 5 piovve
porgere 2 porto 5 porsi, porgesti
porre *1* ponendo 2 posto 3 pongo, poni, pone, poniamo, ponete, pongono 4 ponevo *etc* 5 posi, ponesti 6 porrò *etc* 8 ponga, poniamo, poniate, pongano 9 ponessi *etc*
posporre *like* porre
possedere *like* sedere
potere 3 posso, puoi, può, possiamo, potete, possono 6 potrò *etc* 8 possa, possiamo, possiate, possano
prediligere 2 prediletto 5 predilessi, prediligesti
predire *like* dire
prefiggersi *like* affiggere
preludere *like* alludere
prendere 2 preso 5 presi, prendesti
preporre *like* porre
prescrivere *like* scrivere
presiedere *like* sedere
presumere *like* assumere
pretendere *like* tendere
prevalere *like* valere
prevedere *like* vedere
prevenire *like* venire
produrre *like* ridurre
proferire *like* inferire²
profondere *like* fondere
promettere *like* mettere
promuovere *like* muovere
proporre *like* porre
prorompere *like* rompere
proscrivere *like* scrivere

proteggere 2 protetto 5 protessi, proteg-
   gesti
provenire like **venire**
provvedere like **vedere**
pungere 2 punto 5 punsi, pungesti
racchiudere like **chiudere**
raccogliere like **cogliere**
radere 2 raso 5 rasi, radesti
raggiungere like **giungere**
rapprendere like **prendere**
ravvedersi like **vedere**
recidere like **decidere**
redigere 2 redatto
redimere 2 redento 5 redensi, redimesti
reggere 2 retto 5 ressi, reggesti
rendere 2 reso 5 resi, rendesti
reprimere like **comprimere**
rescindere like **scindere**
respingere like **spingere**
restringere like **stringere**
ricadere like **cadere**
richiedere like **chiedere**
riconoscere like **conoscere**
ricoprire like **coprire**
ricorrere like **correre**
ridere 2 riso 5 risi, ridesti
ridire like **dire**
ridurre 1 riducendo 2 ridotto 3 riduco etc 4
   riducevo etc 5 ridussi, riducesti 6 ridurrò
   etc 8 riduca etc 9 riducessi etc
riempire 1 riempiendo 3 riempio, riempi,
   riempie, riempiono
rifare like **fare**
riflettere 2 riflettuto o riflesso
rifrangere like **infrangere**
rimanere 2 rimasto 3 rimango, rimangono
   5 rimasi, rimanesti 6 rimarrò etc 8
   rimanga
rimettere like **mettere**
rimpiangere like **piangere**
rinchiudere like **chiudere**
rincrescere like **crescere**
rinvenire like **venire**
ripercuotere like **percuotere**
riporre like **porre**
riprendere like **prendere**
riprodurre like **ridurre**
riscuotere like **scuotere**
risolvere like **assolvere**
risorgere like **sorgere**
rispondere 2 risposto 5 risposi, rispon-
   desti
ritenere like **tenere**
ritrarre like **trarre**
riuscire like **uscire**
rivedere like **vedere**
rivivere like **vivere**
rivolgere like **volgere**
rodere 2 roso 5 rosi, rodesti
rompere 2 rotto 5 ruppi, rompesti
salire 3 salgo, sali, salgono 8 salga
sapere 3 so, sai, sa, sappiamo, sapete,

sanno 5 seppi, sapesti 6 saprò etc 8 sappia
   etc 10 sappi!, sappia!, sappiate!, sap-
   piano!
scadere like **cadere**
scegliere 2 scelto 3 scelgo, scegli, sceglie,
   scegliamo, scegliete, scelgono 5 scelsi,
   scegliesti 8 scelga, scegliamo, scegliate,
   scelgano 10 scegli!, scelga!, scegliamo!,
   scegliete!, scelgano!
scendere 2 sceso 5 scesi, scendesti
schiudere like **chiudere**
scindere 2 scisso 5 scissi, scindesti
sciogliere 2 sciolto 3 sciolgo, sciolgi,
   scioglie, sciogliamo, sciogliete, sciolgo-
   no 5 sciolsi, sciogliesti 8 sciolga, sciogliamo, sciogliate, sciolgano 10 sciogli!,
   sciolga!, sciogliamo!, sciogliete!, sciolgano!
scommettere like **mettere**
scomparire like **apparire**
scomporre like **porre**
sconfiggere 2 sconfitto 5 sconfissi, scon-
   figgesti
sconvolgere like **volgere**
scoprire like **aprire**
scorgere 2 scorto 5 scorsi, scorgesti
scorrere like **correre**
scrivere 2 scritto 5 scrissi, scrivesti
scuotere 2 scosso 3 scuoto, scuoti, scuote,
   scotiamo, scotete, scuotono 5 scossi,
   scotesti 6 scoterò etc 8 scuota, scotiamo,
   scotiate, scuotano 10 scuoti!, scuota!,
   scotiamo!, scotete!, scuotano!
sedere 3 siedo, siedi, siede, siedono 8
   sieda
seppellire 2 sepolto
smettere like **mettere**
smuovere like **muovere**
socchiudere like **chiudere**
soccorrere like **correre**
soddisfare like **fare**
soffriggere like **friggere**
soffrire 2 sofferto 5 soffersi o soffrii, sof-
   fristi
soggiungere like **giungere**
solere 2 solito 3 soglio, suoli, suole, so-
   gliamo, solete, sogliono 8 soglia, so-
   gliamo, sogliate, sogliano
sommergere like **emergere**
sopprimere like **comprimere**
sorgere 2 sorto 3 sorsi, sorgesti
sorprendere like **prendere**
sorreggere like **reggere**
sorridere like **ridere**
sospendere like **appendere**
sospingere like **spingere**
sostenere like **tenere**
sottintendere like **tendere**
spandere 2 spanto
spargere 2 sparso 5 sparsi, spargesti
sparire 5 sparii o sparvi, sparisti
spegnere 2 spento 3 spengo, spengono 5

spensi, spegnesti 8 spenga
spendere *2* speso *5* spesi, spendesti
spingere *2* spinto *5* spinsi, spingesti
sporgere *like* **porgere**
stare *2* stato *3* sto, stai, sta, stiamo, state, stanno *5* stetti, stesti *6* starò *etc 8* stia *etc 9* stessi *etc 10* sta'!, stia!, state!, stiano!
stendere *like* **tendere**
storcere *like* **torcere**
stringere *2* stretto *5* strinsi, stringesti
struggere *2* strutto *5* strussi, struggesti
succedere *like* **concedere**
supporre *like* **porre**
svenire *like* **venire**
svolgere *like* **volgere**
tacere *2* taciuto *3* taccio, tacciono *5* tacqui, tacesti *8* taccia
tendere *2* teso *5* tesi, tendesti *etc*
tenere *3* tengo, tieni, tiene, tengono *5* tenni, tenesti *6* terrò *etc 8* tenga
tingere *2* tinto *5* tinsi, tingesti
togliere *2* tolto *5* tolgo, togli, toglie, togliamo, togliete, tolgono *5* tolsi, togliesti *8* tolga, togliamo, togliate, tolgano *10* togli!, tolga!, togliamo!, togliete!, tolgano!
torcere *2* torto *5* torsi, torcesti
tradurre *like* **ridurre**
trafiggere *like* **sconfiggere**
transigere *like* **esigere**
trarre *1* traendo *2* tratto *3* traggo, trai, trae, traiamo, traete, traggono *4* traevo *etc 5* trassi, traesti *6* trarrò *etc 8* tragga *9* traessi *etc*
trascorrere *like* **correre**
trascrivere *like* **scrivere**
trasmettere *like* **mettere**
trasparire *like* **apparire**
trattenere *like* **tenere**

uccidere *2* ucciso *5* uccisi, uccidesti
udire *3* odo, odi, ode, odono *8* oda
ungere *2* unto *5* unsi, ungesti
uscire *3* esco, esci, esce, escono *8* esca
valere *2* valso *3* valgo, valgono *5* valsi, valesti *6* varrò *etc 8* valga
vedere *2* visto *o* veduto *5* vidi, vedesti *6* vedrò *etc*
VENDERE *1* GERUNDIO vendendo
2 PARTICIPIO PASSATO venduto
3 PRESENTE vendo, vendi, vende, vendiamo, vendete, vendono
4 IMPERFETTO vendevo, vendevi, vendeva, vendevamo, vendevate, vendevano
5 PASSATO REMOTO vendei *o* vendetti, vendesti, vendé *o* vendette, vendemmo, vendeste, venderono *o* vendettero
6 FUTURO venderò, venderai, venderà, venderemo, venderete, venderanno
7 CONDIZIONALE venderei, venderesti, venderebbe, venderemmo, vendereste, venderebbero
8 CONGIUNTIVO PRESENTE venda, venda, venda, vendiamo, vendiate, vendano
9 CONGIUNTIVO PASSATO vendessi, vendessi, vendesse, vendessimo, vendeste, vendessero
10 IMPERATIVO vendi!, venda!, vendete!, vendano!
venire *2* venuto *3* vengo, vieni, viene, vengono *5* venni, venisti *6* verrò *etc 8* venga
vincere *2* vinto *5* vinsi, vincesti
vivere *2* vissuto *5* vissi, vivesti
volere *3* voglio, vuoi, vuole, vogliamo, volete, vogliono *5* volli, volesti *6* vorrò *etc 8* voglia *etc 10* vogli!, voglia!, vogliate!, vogliano!
volgere *2* volto *5* volsi, volgesti

VERBI INGLESI

present	pt	pp	present	pt	pp
arise (arising)	arose	arisen	eat	ate	eaten
awake (awaking)	awoke	awaked	fall	fell	fallen
be (am, is, are, being)	was, were	been	feed	fed	fed
			feel	felt	felt
bear	bore	born(e)	fight	fought	fought
beat	beat	beaten	find	found	found
become (becoming)	became	become	flee	fled	fled
befall	befell	befallen	fling	flung	flung
begin (beginning)	began	begun	fly (flies)	flew	flown
behold	beheld	beheld	forbid (forbidding)	forbade	forbidden
bend	bent	bent	forecast	forecast	forecast
beseech	besought	besought	forego	forewent	foregone
beset (besetting)	beset	beset	foresee	foresaw	foreseen
bet (betting)	bet (also betted)	bet (also betted)	foretell	foretold	foretold
			forget (forgetting)	forgot	forgotten
bid (bidding)	bid (also bade)	bid (also bidden)	forgive (forgiving)	forgave	forgiven
bind	bound	bound	forsake (forsaking)	forsook	forsaken
bite (biting)	bit	bitten	freeze (freezing)	froze	frozen
bleed	bled	bled	get (getting)	got	got, (US) gotten
blow	blew	blown			
break	broke	broken	give (giving)	gave	given
breed	bred	bred	go (goes)	went	gone
bring	brought	brought	grind	ground	ground
build	built	built	grow	grew	grown
burn	burnt (also burned)	burnt (also burned)	hang	hung (also hanged)	hung (also hanged)
burst	burst	burst	have (has; having)	had	had
buy	bought	bought	hear	heard	heard
can	could	(been able)	hide (hiding)	hid	hidden
cast	cast	cast	hit (hitting)	hit	hit
catch	caught	caught	hold	held	held
choose (choosing)	chose	chosen	hurt	hurt	hurt
			keep	kept	kept
cling	clung	clung	kneel	knelt (also kneeled)	knelt (also kneeled)
come (coming)	came	come			
			know	knew	known
cost	cost	cost	lay	laid	laid
creep	crept	crept	lead	led	led
cut (cutting)	cut	cut	lean	leant (also leaned)	leant (also leaned)
deal	dealt	dealt			
dig (digging)	dug	dug	leap	leapt (also leaped)	leapt (also leaped)
do (3rd person: he/she/it/does)	did	done	learn	learnt (also learned)	learnt (also learned)
draw	drew	drawn	leave (leaving)	left	left
dream	dreamed (also dreamt)	dreamed also dreamt)	lend	lent	lent
			let (letting)	let	let
drink	drank	drunk	lie (lying)	lay	lain
drive (driving)	drove	driven	light	lit (also lighted)	lit (also lighted)
dwell	dwelt	dwelt	lose (losing)	lost	lost

present	pt	pp	present	pt	pp
make (making)	made	made	**speed**	sped (*also* speeded)	sped (*also* speeded)
may	might	—	**spell**	spelt (*also* spelled)	spelt (*also* spelled)
mean	meant	meant	**spend**	spent	spent
meet	met	met	**spill**	spilt (*also* spilled)	spilt (*also* spilled)
mistake (mistaking)	mistook	mistaken			
mow	mowed	mown (*also* mowed)	**spin (spinning)**	spun	spun
			spit (spitting)	spat	spat
must	(had to)	(had to)	**split (splitting)**	split	split
pay	paid	paid	**spoil**	spoiled (*also* spoilt)	spoiled (*also* spoilt)
put (putting)	put	put			
quit (quitting)	quit (*also* quitted)	quit (*also* quitted)	**spread**	spread	spread
			spring	sprang	sprung
read	read	read	**stand**	stood	stood
rend	rent	rent	**steal**	stole	stolen
rid (ridding)	rid	rid	**stick**	stuck	stuck
ride (riding)	rode	ridden	**sting**	stung	stung
ring	rang	rung	**stink**	stank	stunk
rise (rising)	rose	risen	**stride (striding)**	strode	stridden
run (running)	ran	run			
saw	sawed	sawn	**strike (striking)**	struck	struck (*also* stricken)
say	said	said			
see	saw	seen	**strive (striving)**	strove	striven
seek	sought	sought	**swear**	swore	sworn
sell	sold	sold	**sweep**	swept	swept
send	sent	sent	**swell**	swelled	swollen (*also* swelled)
set (setting)	set	set			
shake (shaking)	shook	shaken	**swim (swimming)**	swam	swum
shall	should	—	**swing**	swung	swung
shear	sheared	shorn (*also* sheared)	**take (taking)**	took	taken
			teach	taught	taught
shed (shedding)	shed	shed	**tear**	tore	torn
			tell	told	told
shine (shining)	shone	shone	**think**	thought	thought
			throw	threw	thrown
shoot	shot	shot	**thrust**	thrust	thrust
show	showed	shown	**tread**	trod	trodden
shrink	shrank	shrunk	**wake (waking)**	woke (*also* waked)	woken (*also* waked)
shut (shutting)	shut	shut			
sing	sang	sung	**waylay**	waylaid	waylaid
sink	sank	sunk	**wear**	wore	worn
sit (sitting)	sat	sat	**weave (weaving)**	wove (*also* weaved)	woven (*also* weaved)
slay	slew	slain			
sleep	slept	slept	**wed (wedding)**	wedded (*also* wed)	wedded (*also* wed)
slide (sliding)	slid	slid			
sling	slung	slung	**weep**	wept	wept
slit (slitting)	slit	slit	**win (winning)**	won	won
smell	smelt (*also* smelled)	smelt (*also* smelled)	**wind**	wound	wound
			withdraw	withdrew	withdrawn
sow	sowed	sown (*also* sowed)	**withhold**	withheld	withheld
			withstand	withstood	withstood
speak	spoke	spoken	**wring**	wrung	wrung
			write (writing)	wrote	written

I NUMERI

NUMBERS

uno(a)	1	one
due	2	two
tre	3	three
quattro	4	four
cinque	5	five
sei	6	six
sette	7	seven
otto	8	eight
nove	9	nine
dieci	10	ten
undici	11	eleven
dodici	12	twelve
tredici	13	thirteen
quattordici	14	fourteen
quindici	15	fifteen
sedici	16	sixteen
diciassette	17	seventeen
diciotto	18	eighteen
diciannove	19	nineteen
venti	20	twenty
ventuno	21	twenty-one
ventidue	22	twenty-two
ventitré	23	twenty-three
ventotto	28	twenty-eight
trenta	30	thirty
quaranta	40	forty
cinquanta	50	fifty
sessanta	60	sixty
settanta	70	seventy
ottanta	80	eighty
novanta	90	ninety
cento	100	a hundred, one hundred
cento uno	101	a hundred and one
duecento	200	two hundred
mille	1 000	a thousand, one thousand
milleduecentodue	1 202	one thousand two hundred and two
cinquemila	5 000	five thousand
un milione	1 000 000	a million, one million

I NUMERI

NUMBERS

primo(a), 1°	first, 1st
secondo(a), 2°	second, 2nd
terzo(a), 3°	third, 3rd
quarto(a)	fourth, 4th
quinto(a)	fifth, 5th
sesto(a)	sixth, 6th
settimo(a)	seventh
ottavo(a)	eighth
nono(a)	ninth
decimo(a)	tenth
undicesimo(a)	eleventh
dodicesimo(a)	twelfth
tredicesimo(a)	thirteenth
quattordicesimo(a)	fourteenth
quindicesimo(a)	fifteenth
sedicesimo(a)	sixteenth
diciassettesimo(a)	seventeenth
diciottesimo(a)	eighteenth
diciannovesimo(a)	nineteenth
ventesimo(a)	twentieth
ventunesimo(a)	twenty-first
ventiduesimo(a)	twenty-second
ventitreesimo(a)	twenty-third
ventottesimo(a)	twenty-eighth
trentesimo(a)	thirtieth
centesimo(a)	hundredth
centunesimo(a)	hundred-and-first
millesimo(a)	thousandth
milionesimo(a)	millionth

ALFABETO TELEFONICO   PHONETIC ALPHABET

Italia come	fonetica		phonetics	GB for	USA
Ancona	[a]	A	[eɪ]	Andrew	Able
Bologna	[bi]	B	[bi:]	Benjamin	Baker
Como	[tʃi]	C	[si:]	Charlie	Charlie
Domodossola	[di]	D	[di:]	David	Dog
Empoli	[e]	E	[i:]	Edward	Easy
Firenze	['effe]	F	[ɛf]	Frederick	Fox
Genova	[dʒi]	G	[dʒi:]	George	George
Hotel	['akka]	H	[eɪtʃ]	Harry	How
Imola	[i]	I	[aɪ]	Isaac	Item
Jersey	[i'lunga]	J	[dʒeɪ]	Jack	Jig
Kursaal	['kappa]	K	[keɪ]	King	King
Livorno	['ɛlle]	L	[ɛl]	Lucy	Love
Milano	['ɛmme]	M	[ɛm]	Mary	Mike
Napoli	['ɛnne]	N	[ɛn]	Nellie	Nan
Otranto	[ɔ]	O	[əu]	Oliver	Oboe
Padova	[pi]	P	[pi:]	Peter	Peter
Quarto	[ku]	Q	[kju:]	Queen	Queen
Roma	['ɛrre]	R	[ɑ:*]	Robert	Roger
Savona	['ɛsse]	S	[ɛs]	Sugar	Sugar
Taranto	[ti]	T	[ti:]	Tommy	Tommy
Udine	[u]	U	[ju:]	Uncle	Uncle
Venezia	[vi, vu]	V	[vi:]	Victor	Victor
Washington	['dɔppjovu]	W	['dʌblju:]	William	William
Xeres	[iks]	X	[ɛks]	Xmas	Xmas
Yacht	['ipsilon]	Y	[waɪ]	Yellow	Yoke
Zara	['dzɛta]	Z	[zɛd, (US) zi:]	Zebra	Zebra

ITALIANO-INGLESE
ITALIAN-ENGLISH

A

A, a [a] *sf o m inv* (*lettera*) A, a; **A come Ancona** ≈ A for Andrew (*Brit*), A for Able (*US*); **dalla a alla z** from a to z.

A *abbr* (= *altezza*) h; (= *area*) A; (= *autostrada*) ≈ M (*Brit*).

a *prep* (*a + il* = **al**, *a + lo* = **allo**, *a + l'* = **all'**, *a + la* = **alla**, *a + i* = **ai**, *a + gli* = **agli**, *a + le* = **alle**) (*stato in luogo, tempo*) at; in; (*moto a luogo, complemento di termine*) to; (*mezzo*) with, by; (*scopo, fine*) for, to; **essere ~ Roma/alla posta/~ casa** to be in Rome/at the post office/at home; **~ 18 anni** at 18 (years of age); **~ mezzanotte/Natale** at midnight/Christmas; **alle 3** at 3 (o'clock); **~ maggio** in May; **~ giorni** in a few days; **~ piedi/cavallo** on foot/horseback; **pagato ~ ore/giornata** paid by the hour/day; **una barca ~ motore** a motorboat; **alla milanese** the Milanese way, in the Milanese fashion; **~ 500 lire il chilo** 500 lire a *o* per kilo; **viaggiare ~ 100 chilometri l'ora** to travel at 100 kilometres an *o* per hour; **~ 10 chilometri da Firenze** 10 kilometres from Florence; **restare ~ cena** to stay for dinner; **~ domani!** see you tomorrow!; **~ uno ~ uno** one by one.

AA *sigla* = **Alto Adige**.

AAS *sigla f* = **Azienda Autonoma di Soggiorno**.

AA.VV. *abbr* = *autori vari*.

a'bate *sm* abbot.

abbacchi'ato, a [abbak'kjato] *ag* downhearted, in low spirits.

abbacin'are [abbatʃi'nare] *vt* to dazzle.

abbagli'ante [abbaʎ'ʎante] *ag* dazzling; **~i** *smpl* (*AUT*): **accendere gli ~i** to put one's headlights on full (*Brit*) *o* high (*US*) beam.

abbagli'are [abbaʎ'ʎare] *vt* to dazzle; (*illudere*) to delude.

ab'baglio [ab'baʎʎo] *sm* blunder; **prendere un ~** to blunder, make a blunder.

abbai'are *vi* to bark.

abba'ino *sm* dormer window; (*soffitta*) attic room.

abbando'nare *vt* to leave, abandon, desert; (*trascurare*) to neglect; (*rinunciare a*) to abandon, give up; **~rsi** *vr* to let o.s. go; **~ il campo** (*MIL*) to retreat; **~ la presa** to let go; **~rsi a** (*ricordi, vizio*) to give o.s. up to.

abbando'nato, a *ag* (*casa*) deserted; (*miniera*) disused; (*trascurato: terreno, podere*) neglected; (*bambino*) abandoned.

abban'dono *sm* abandoning; neglecting; (*stato*) abandonment; neglect; (*SPORT*) withdrawal; (*fig*) abandon; **in ~** (*edificio, giardino*) neglected.

abbarbi'carsi *vr*: **~ (a)** (*anche fig*) to cling (to).

abbassa'mento *sm* lowering; (*di pressione, livello dell'acqua*) fall; (*di prezzi*) reduction; **~ di temperatura** drop in temperature.

abbas'sare *vt* to lower; (*radio*) to turn down; **~rsi** *vr* (*chinarsi*) to stoop; (*livello, sole*) to go down; (*fig: umiliarsi*) to demean o.s.; **~ i fari** (*AUT*) to dip (*Brit*) *o* dim (*US*) one's lights; **~ le armi** (*MIL*) to lay down one's arms.

ab'basso *escl*: **~ il re!** down with the king!

abbas'tanza [abbas'tantsa] *av* (*a sufficienza*) enough; (*alquanto*) quite, rather, fairly; **non è ~ furbo** he's not shrewd enough; **un vino ~ dolce** quite a sweet wine, a fairly sweet wine; **averne ~ di qn/qc** to have had enough of sb/sth.

ab'battere *vt* (*muro, casa, ostacolo*) to knock down; (*albero*) to fell; (: *sog: vento*) to bring down; (*bestie da macello*) to slaughter; (*cane, cavallo*) to destroy, put down; (*selvaggina, aereo*) to shoot down; (*fig: sog: malattia, disgrazia*) to lay low; **~rsi** *vr* (*avvilirsi*) to lose heart; **~rsi a terra** *o* **al suolo** to fall to the ground; **~rsi su** (*sog: maltempo*) to beat down on; (: *disgrazia*) to hit, strike.

abbatti'mento *sm* knocking down; felling; (*di casa*) demolition; (*prostrazione: fisica*) exhaustion; (: *morale*) despondency.

abbat'tuto, a *ag* despondent, depressed.

abba'zia [abbat'tsia] *sf* abbey.

abbece'dario [abbetʃe'darjo] *sm* primer.

abbelli'mento *sm* embellishment.

abbel'lire *vt* to make beautiful; (*ornare*) to embellish.

abbeve'rare *vt* to water; **~rsi** *vr* to drink.

abbevera'toio *sm* drinking trough.

'abbi, 'abbia, abbi'amo, 'abbiano, abbi'ate *vb vedi* **avere**.

abbicci [abbit'tʃi] *sm inv* alphabet; (*sillabario*) primer; (*fig*) rudiments *pl*.

abbi'ente *ag* well-to-do, well-off.

abbi'etto, a *ag* = **abietto**.

abbiglia'mento [abbiʎʎa'mento] *sm* dress *q*; (*indumenti*) clothes *pl*; (*industria*) clothing industry.

abbigli'are [abbiʎ'ʎare] vt to dress up.

abbina'mento sm combination; linking; matching.

abbi'nare vt: ~ (con o a) (gen) to combine (with); (nomi) to link (with); ~ **qc a qc** (colori etc) to match sth with sth.

abbindo'lare vt (fig) to cheat, trick.

abbocca'mento sm (colloquio) talks pl, meeting; (TECN: di tubi) connection.

abboc'care vt (tubi, canali) to connect, join up ♦ vi (pesce) to bite; (tubi) to join; ~ (all'amo) (fig) to swallow the bait.

abboc'cato, a ag (vino) sweetish.

abbona'mento sm subscription; (alle ferrovie etc) season ticket; **in** ~ for subscribers only; for season ticket holders only; **fare l'**~ (a) to take out a subscription (to); to buy a season ticket (for).

abbo'nare vt (cifra) to deduct; (fig: perdonare) to forgive; ~**rsi** vr: ~**rsi a un giornale** to take out a subscription to a newspaper; ~**rsi al teatro/alle ferrovie** to take out a season ticket for the theatre/ the train.

abbo'nato, a sm/f subscriber; season-ticket holder; **elenco degli** ~**i** telephone directory.

abbon'dante ag abundant, plentiful; (giacca) roomy.

abbon'danza [abbon'dantsa] sf abundance; plenty.

abbon'dare vi to abound, be plentiful; ~ **in** o **di** to be full of, abound in.

abbor'dabile ag (persona) approachable; (prezzo) reasonable.

abbor'dare vt (nave) to board; (persona) to approach; (argomento) to tackle; ~ **una curva** to take a bend.

abbotto'nare vt to button up, do up; ~**rsi** vr to button (up).

abbotto'nato, a ag (camicia etc) buttoned (up); (fig) reserved.

abbottona'tura sf buttons pl; **questo cappotto ha l'**~ **da uomo/da donna** this coat buttons on the man's/woman's side.

abboz'zare [abbot'tsare] vt to sketch, outline; (SCULTURA) to rough-hew; ~ **un sorriso** to give a hint of a smile.

ab'bozzo [ab'bɔttso] sm sketch, outline; (DIR) draft.

abbracci'are [abbrat'tʃare] vt to embrace; (persona) to hug, embrace; (professione) to take up; (contenere) to include; ~**rsi** vr to hug o embrace (one another).

ab'braccio [ab'brattʃo] sm hug, embrace.

abbrevi'are vt to shorten; (parola) to abbreviate, shorten.

abbreviazi'one [abbrevjat'tsjone] sf abbreviation.

abbron'zante [abbron'dzante] ag tanning, sun cpd.

abbron'zare [abbron'dzare] vt (pelle) to tan; (metalli) to bronze; ~**rsi** vr to tan, get a tan.

abbron'zato, a [abbron'dzato] ag (sun)tanned.

abbronza'tura [abbrondza'tura] sf tan, suntan.

abbrusto'lire vt (pane) to toast; (caffè) to roast.

abbruti'mento sm exhaustion; degradation.

abbru'tire vt (snervare, stancare) to exhaust; (degradare) to degrade; **essere abbrutito dall'alcool** to be ruined by drink.

abbuf'farsi vr (fam): ~ **(di qc)** to stuff o.s. (with sth).

abbuf'fata sf (fam) nosh-up; **farsi un'**~ to stuff o.s.

abbuo'nare vt = **abbonare**.

abbu'ono sm (COMM) allowance, discount; (SPORT) handicap.

abdi'care vi to abdicate; ~ **a** to give up, renounce.

abdicazi'one [abdikat'tsjone] sf abdication.

aberrazi'one [aberrat'tsjone] sf aberration.

abe'taia sf fir wood.

a'bete sm fir (tree); ~ **bianco** silver fir; ~ **rosso** spruce.

abi'etto, a ag despicable, abject.

'abile ag (idoneo): ~ **(a qc/a fare qc)** fit (for sth/to do sth); (capace) able; (astuto) clever; (accorto) skilful; ~ **al servizio militare** fit for military service.

abilità sf inv ability; cleverness; skill.

abili'tante ag qualifying; **corsi** ~**i** (INS) ≈ teacher training sg.

abili'tare vt: ~ **qn a qc/a fare qc** to qualify sb for sth/to do sth; **è stato abilitato all'insegnamento** he has qualified as a teacher.

abili'tato, a ag qualified; (TEL) which has an outside line.

abilitazi'one [abilitat'tsjone] sf qualification.

abis'sale ag abysmal; (fig: senza limiti) profound.

abis'sino, a ag, sm/f Abyssinian.

a'bisso sm abyss, gulf.

abitabilità sf: **licenza di** ~ document stating that a property is fit for habitation.

abi'tacolo sm (AER) cockpit; (AUT) inside; (di camion) (driver's) cab.

abi'tante sm/f inhabitant.

abi'tare vt to live in, dwell in ♦ vi: ~ **in campagna/a Roma** to live in the country/in Rome.

abi'tato, a ag inhabited; lived in ♦ sm (anche: **centro** ~) built-up area.

abitazi'one [abitat'tsjone] sf residence; house.

'abito sm dress q; (da uomo) suit; (da donna) dress; (abitudine, disposizione, REL) habit; ~**i** smpl (vestiti) clothes; **in** ~ **da**

cerimonia in formal dress; **in** ~ **da sera** in evening dress; **"è gradito l'~ scuro"** "dress formal"; ~ **mentale** way of thinking.

abitu'ale *ag* usual, habitual; (*cliente*) regular.

abitual'mente *av* usually, normally.

abitu'are *vt:* ~ **qn a** to get sb used *o* accustomed to; ~**rsi a** to get used to, accustom o.s. to.

abitudi'nario, a *ag* of fixed habits ♦ *sm/f* creature of habit.

abi'tudine *sf* habit; **aver l'~ di fare qc** to be in the habit of doing sth; **d'~** usually; **per** ~ from *o* out of habit.

abiu'rare *vt* to renounce.

abnegazi'one [abnegat'tsjone] *sf* (self-) abnegation, self-denial.

ab'norme *ag* (*enorme*) extraordinary; (*anormale*) abnormal.

abo'lire *vt* to abolish; (*DIR*) to repeal.

abolizi'one [abolit'tsjone] *sf* abolition; repeal.

abomi'nevole *ag* abominable.

abo'rigeno [abo'ridʒeno] *sm* aborigine.

abor'rire *vt* to abhor, detest.

abor'tire *vi* (*MED: accidentalmente*) to miscarry, have a miscarriage; (: *deliberatamente*) to have an abortion; (*fig*) to miscarry, fail.

a'borto *sm* miscarriage; abortion; (*fig*) freak; ~ **clandestino** backstreet abortion.

abrasi'one *sf* abrasion.

abra'sivo, a *ag, sm* abrasive.

abro'gare *vt* to repeal, abrogate.

abrogazi'one [abrogat'tsjone] *sf* repeal.

abruz'zese [abrut'tsese] *ag* of (*o* from) the Abruzzi.

A'bruzzo [a'bruttso] *sm:* **l'~, gli ~i** the Abruzzi.

'abside *sf* apse.

'Abu 'Dhabi *sf* Abu Dhabi.

a'bulico, a, ci, che *ag* lacking in willpower.

abu'sare *vi:* ~ **di** to abuse, misuse; (*approfittare, violare*) to take advantage of; ~ **dell'alcool/dei cibi** to drink/eat to excess.

abusi'vismo *sm* (*anche:* ~ **edilizio**) unlawful building, building without planning permission (*Brit*).

abu'sivo, a *ag* unauthorized, unlawful; (**occupante**) ~ (*di una casa*) squatter.

a'buso *sm* abuse, misuse; excessive use; **fare** ~ **di** (*stupefacenti, medicine*) to abuse.

a.C. *abbr av* (= *avanti Cristo*) BC.

'acca *sf* letter H; **non capire un'~** not to understand a thing.

ac'cadde *vb vedi* **accadere**.

acca'demia *sf* (*società*) learned society; (*scuola: d'arte, militare*) academy; ~ **di Belle Arti** art school.

acca'demico, a, ci, che *ag* academic ♦ *sm* academician.

acca'dere *vi* to happen, occur.

acca'duto *sm* event; **raccontare l'~** to describe what has happened.

accalappia'cani *sm inv* dog-catcher.

accalappi'are *vt* to catch; (*fig*) to trick, dupe.

accal'care *vt,* ~**rsi** *vr* to crowd, throng.

accal'darsi *vr* to grow hot.

accalo'rarsi *vr* (*fig*) to get excited.

accampa'mento *sm* camp.

accam'pare *vt* to encamp; (*fig*) to put forward, advance; ~**rsi** *vr* to camp; ~ **scuse** to make excuses.

accani'mento *sm* fury; (*tenacia*) tenacity, perseverance.

acca'nirsi *vr* (*infierire*) to rage; (*ostinarsi*) to persist.

accanita'mente *av* fiercely; assiduously.

acca'nito, a *ag* (*odio, gelosia*) fierce, bitter; (*lavoratore*) assiduous; (*giocatore*) inveterate; (*tifoso, sostenitore*) keen; **fumatore** ~ chain smoker.

ac'canto *av* near, nearby; ~ **a** *prep* near, beside, close to; **la casa** ~ the house next door.

accanto'nare *vt* (*problema*) to shelve; (*somma*) to set aside.

accaparra'mento *sm* (*COMM*) cornering, buying up.

accapar'rare *vt* (*COMM*) to corner, buy up; (*versare una caparra*) to pay a deposit on; ~**rsi** *vr:* ~**rsi qc** (*fig: simpatia, voti*) to secure sth (for o.s.).

accapigli'arsi [akkapiʎ'ʎarsi] *vr* to come to blows; (*fig*) to quarrel.

accappa'toio *sm* bathrobe.

accappo'nare *vi:* **far** ~ **la pelle a qn** (*fig*) to bring sb out in goosepimples.

accarez'zare [akkaret'tsare] *vt* to caress, stroke, fondle; (*fig*) to toy with.

accartocci'are [akkartot'tʃare] *vt* (*carta*) to roll up, screw up; ~**rsi** *vr* (*foglie*) to curl up.

acca'sarsi *vr* to set up house; to get married.

accasci'arsi [akkaʃ'ʃarsi] *vr* to collapse; (*fig*) to lose heart.

accatas'tare *vt* to stack, pile.

accatto'naggio [akkatto'naddʒo] *sm* begging.

accat'tone, a *sm/f* beggar.

accaval'lare *vt* (*gambe*) to cross; ~**rsi** *vr* (*sovrapporsi*) to overlap; (*addensarsi*) to gather.

acce'care [attʃe'kare] *vt* to blind ♦ *vi* to go blind.

ac'cedere [at'tʃɛdere] *vi:* ~ **a** to enter; (*richiesta*) to grant, accede to; (*fonte*) to gain access to.

accele'rare [attʃele'rare] *vt* to speed up ♦ *vi* (*AUT*) to accelerate; ~ **il passo** to quicken one's pace.

accele'rato, a [attʃele'rato] *ag* quick, rapid ♦ *sm* (*FERR*) local train, stopping train.

accelera'tore [attʃelera'tore] *sm* (*AUT*) accelerator.

accelerazi'one [attʃelerat'tsjone] *sf* acceleration.

ac'cendere [at'tʃendere] *vt* (*fuoco, sigaretta*) to light; (*luce, televisione*) to put *o* switch *o* turn on; (*AUT: motore*) to switch on; (*COMM: conto*) to open; (: *debito*) to contract; (: *ipoteca*) to raise; (*fig: suscitare*) to inflame, stir up; ~**rsi** *vr* (*luce*) to come *o* go on; (*legna*) to catch fire, ignite; (*fig: lotta, conflitto*) to break out.

accen'dino [attʃen'dino], **accendi'sigaro** [attʃendi'sigaro] *sm* (*cigarette*) lighter.

accen'nare [attʃen'nare] *vt* to indicate, point out; (*MUS*) to pick out the notes of; to hum ♦ *vi*: ~ **a** (*fig: alludere a*) to hint at; (: *far atto di*) to make as if; ~ **un saluto** (*con la mano*) to make as if to wave; (*col capo*) to half nod; ~ **un sorriso** to half smile; **accenna a piovere** it looks as if it's going to rain.

ac'cenno [at'tʃenno] *sm* (*cenno*) sign; nod; (*allusione*) hint.

accensi'one [attʃen'sjone] *sf* (*vedi accendere*) lighting; switching on; opening; (*AUT*) ignition.

accen'tare [attʃen'tare] *vt* (*parlando*) to stress; (*scrivendo*) to accent.

accentazi'one [attʃentat'tsjone] *sf* accentuation; stressing.

ac'cento [at'tʃento] *sm* accent; (*FONETICA, fig*) stress; (*inflessione*) tone (of voice).

accentra'mento [attʃentra'mento] *sm* centralization.

accen'trare [attʃen'trare] *vt* to centralize.

accentra'tore, 'trice [attʃentra'tore] *ag* (*persona*) unwilling to delegate; **politica** ~**trice** policy of centralization.

accentu'are [attʃentu'are] *vt* to stress, emphasize; ~**rsi** *vr* to become more noticeable.

accerchi'are [attʃer'kjare] *vt* to surround, encircle.

accerta'mento [attʃerta'mento] *sm* check; assessment.

accer'tare [attʃer'tare] *vt* to ascertain; (*verificare*) to check; (*reddito*) to assess; ~**rsi** *vr*: ~**rsi (di qc/che)** to make sure (of sth/that).

ac'ceso, a [at'tʃeso] *pp di* **accendere** ♦ *ag* lit; on; open; (*colore*) bright; ~ **di** (*ira, entusiasmo etc*) burning with.

acces'sibile [attʃes'sibile] *ag* (*luogo*) accessible; (*persona*) approachable; (*prezzo*) reasonable; (*idea*): ~ **a qn** within the reach of sb.

ac'cesso [at'tʃesso] *sm* (*anche INFORM*) access; (*MED*) attack, fit; (*impulso*

violento) fit, outburst; **programmi dell'**~ (*TV*) educational programmes; **tempo di** ~ (*INFORM*) access time; ~ **casuale/seriale/sequenziale** (*INFORM*) random/serial/sequential access.

accessori'ato, a [attʃesso'rjato] *ag* with accessories.

acces'sorio, a [attʃes'sɔrjo] *ag* secondary, of secondary importance; ~**i** *smpl* accessories.

ac'cetta [at'tʃetta] *sf* hatchet.

accet'tabile [attʃet'tabile] *ag* acceptable.

accet'tare [attʃet'tare] *vt* to accept; ~ **di fare qc** to agree to do sth.

accettazi'one [attʃettat'tsjone] *sf* acceptance; (*locale di servizio pubblico*) reception; ~ **bagagli** (*AER*) check-in (desk); ~ **con riserva** qualified acceptance.

ac'cetto, a [at'tʃetto] *ag* (*persona*) welcome; (**ben**) ~ **a tutti** well-liked by everybody.

accezi'one [attʃet'tsjone] *sf* meaning.

acchiap'pare [akkjap'pare] *vt* to catch; (*afferrare*) to seize.

ac'chito [ak'kito] *sm*: **a primo** ~ at first sight.

acciac'cato, a [attʃak'kato] *ag* (*persona*) full of aches and pains; (*abito*) crushed.

acci'acco, chi [at'tʃakko] *sm* ailment; ~**chi** *smpl* aches and pains.

acciaie'ria [attʃaje'ria] *sf* steelworks *sg*.

acci'aio [at'tʃajo] *sm* steel; ~ **inossidabile** stainless steel.

acciden'tale [attʃiden'tale] *ag* accidental.

accidental'mente [attʃidental'mente] *av* (*per caso*) by chance; (*non deliberatamente*) accidentally, by accident.

acciden'tato, a [attʃiden'tato] *ag* (*terreno etc*) uneven.

acci'dente [attʃi'dente] *sm* (*caso imprevisto*) accident; (*disgrazia*) mishap; ~**i!** (*fam: per rabbia*) damn (it)!; (: *per meraviglia*) good heavens!; ~**i a lui!** damn him!; **non vale un** ~ it's not worth a damn; **non capisco un** ~ it's as clear as mud to me; **mandare un** ~ **a qn** to curse sb.

ac'cidia [at'tʃidja] *sf* (*REL*) sloth.

accigli'ato, a [attʃiʎ'ʎato] *ag* frowning.

ac'cingersi [at'tʃindʒersi] *vr*: ~ **a fare** to be about to do.

acciotto'lato [attʃotto'lato] *sm* cobbles *pl*.

acciuf'fare [attʃuf'fare] *vt* to seize, catch.

acci'uga, ghe [at'tʃuga] *sf* anchovy; **magro come un'**~ as thin as a rake.

accla'mare *vt* (*applaudire*) to applaud; (*eleggere*) to acclaim.

acclamazi'one [akklamat'tsjone] *sf* applause; acclamation.

acclima'tare *vt* to acclimatize; ~**rsi** *vr* to become acclimatized.

acclimatazi'one [akklimatat'tsjone] *sf* acclimatization.

ac'cludere *vt* to enclose.

ac'cluso, a pp di **accludere ♦** ag enclosed.

accocco'larsi vr to crouch.

acco'darsi vr to follow, tag on (behind).

accogli'ente [akkoʎ'ʎɛnte] ag welcoming, friendly.

accogli'enza [akkoʎ'ʎɛntsa] sf reception; welcome; **fare una buona ~ a qn** to welcome sb.

ac'cogliere [ak'kɔʎʎere] vt (ricevere) to receive; (dare il benvenuto) to welcome; (approvare) to agree to, accept; (contenere) to hold, accommodate.

ac'colgo etc vb vedi **accogliere**.

accol'lare vt (fig): **~ qc a qn** to force sth on sb; **~rsi** vr: **~rsi qc** to take sth upon o.s., shoulder sth.

accol'lato, a ag (vestito) high-necked.

ac'colsi etc vb vedi **accogliere**.

accoltel'lare vt to knife, stab.

ac'colto, a pp di **accogliere.**

accoman'dita sf (DIR) limited partnership.

accomia'tare vt to dismiss; **~rsi** vr: **~rsi (da)** to take one's leave (of).

accomoda'mento sm agreement, settlement.

accomo'dante ag accommodating.

accomo'dare vt (aggiustare) to repair, mend; (riordinare) to tidy; (sistemare: questione, lite) to settle; **~rsi** vr (sedersi) to sit down; (fig: risolversi: situazione) to work out; **si accomodi!** (venga avanti) come in!; (si sieda) take a seat!

accompagna'mento [akkompaɲɲa'mento] sm (MUS) accompaniment; (COMM): **lettera di ~** accompanying letter.

accompa'gnare [akkompaɲ'ɲare] vt to accompany, come o go with; (MUS) to accompany; (unire) to couple; **~rsi** vr (armonizzarsi) to go well together; **~ qn a casa** to see sb home; **~ qn alla porta** to show sb out; **~ un regalo con un biglietto** to put in o send a card with a present; **~ qn con lo sguardo** to follow sb with one's eyes; **~ la porta** to close the door gently; **~rsi a** (frequentare) to frequent; (colori) to go with, match; (cibi) to go with.

accompagna'tore, 'trice [akkompaɲɲa'tore] sm/f companion, escort; (guida turistica) courier; (MUS) accompanist; (SPORT) team manager.

accomu'nare vt to pool, share; (avvicinare) to unite.

acconcia'tura [akkontʃa'tura] sf hairstyle.

accondiscen'dente [akkondiʃʃen'dɛnte] ag affable.

accondi'scendere [akkondiʃ'ʃendere] vi: **~ a** to agree o consent to.

accondi'sceso, a [akkondiʃ'ʃeso] pp di **accondiscendere.**

acconsen'tire vi: **~ (a)** to agree o consent (to); **chi tace acconsente** silence means consent.

acconten'tare vt to satisfy; **~rsi** vr: **~rsi di** to be satisfied with, content o.s. with; **chi si accontenta gode** there's no point in complaining.

ac'conto sm part payment; **pagare una somma in ~** to pay a sum of money as a deposit; **~ di dividendo** interim dividend.

accoppia'mento sm pairing off; mating; (ELETTR, INFORM) coupling.

accoppi'are vt to couple, pair off; (BIOL) to mate; **~rsi** vr to pair off; to mate.

accoppia'tore sm (TECN) coupler; **~ acustico** (INFORM) acoustic coupler.

acco'rato, a ag heartfelt.

accorci'are [akkor'tʃare] vt to shorten; **~rsi** vr to become shorter; (vestiti: nel lavaggio) to shrink.

accor'dare vt to reconcile; (colori) to match; (MUS) to tune; (LING): **~ qc con qc** to make sth agree with sth; (DIR) to grant; **~rsi** vr to agree, come to an agreement; (colori) to match.

ac'cordo sm agreement; (armonia) harmony; (MUS) chord; **essere d'~** to agree; **andare d'~** to get on well together; **d'~!** all right!, agreed!; **mettersi d'~ (con qn)** to agree o come to an agreement with sb; **prendere ~i con** to reach an agreement with; **~ commerciale** trade agreement; **A~ generale sulle tariffe ed il commercio** General Agreement on Tariffs and Trade, GATT.

ac'corgersi [ak'kɔrdʒersi] vr: **~ di** to notice; (fig) to realize.

accorgi'mento [akkordʒi'mento] sm shrewdness q; (espediente) trick, device.

ac'correre vi to run up.

ac'corsi vb vedi **accorgersi**; **accorrere.**

ac'corso, a pp di **accorrere.**

accor'tezza [akkor'tettsa] sf (avvedutezza) good sense; (astuzia) shrewdness.

ac'corto, a pp di **accorgersi ♦** ag shrewd; **stare ~** to be on one's guard.

accosta'mento sm (di colori etc) combination.

accos'tare vt (avvicinarsi a) to approach; (socchiudere: imposte) to half-close; (: porta) to leave ajar ♦ vi: **~ (a)** (NAUT) to come alongside; (AUT) to draw up (at); **~rsi** vr: **~rsi a** to draw near, approach; (somigliare) to be like, resemble; (fede, religione) to turn to; (idee politiche) to come to agree with; **~ qc a** (avvicinare) to bring sth near to, put sth near to; (colori, stili) to match sth with; (appoggiare: scala etc) to lean sth against.

accovacci'arsi [akkovat'tʃarsi] vr to crouch.

accoz'zaglia [akkot'tsaʎʎa] sf (peg: di idee, oggetti) jumble, hotchpotch; (: di persone) odd assortment.

ac'crebbi etc vb vedi **accrescere.**

accredi'tare vt (notizia) to confirm the

truth of; (*COMM*) to credit; (*diplomatico*) to accredit; ~**rsi** *vr* (*fig*) to gain credit.

ac'credito *sm* (*COMM*: *atto*) crediting; (: *effetto*) credit.

ac'crescere [ak'kreʃʃere] *vt* to increase; ~**rsi** *vr* to increase, grow.

accresci'mento [akkreʃʃi'mento] *sm* increase, growth.

accresci'tivo, a [akkreʃʃi'tivo] *ag, sm* (*LING*) augmentative.

accresci'uto, a [akkreʃ'ʃuto] *pp di* **accrescere**.

accucci'arsi [akkut'tʃarsi] *vr* (*cane*) to lie down; (*persona*) to crouch down.

accu'dire *vi*: ~ **a**, *vt* to attend to; to look after.

acculturazi'one [akkulturat'tsjone] *sf* (*SOCIOLOGIA*) integration.

accumu'lare *vt* to accumulate; ~**rsi** *vr* to accumulate; (*FINANZA*) to accrue.

accumula'tore *sm* (*ELETTR*) accumulator.

accumulazi'one [akkumulat'tsjone] *sf* accumulation.

ac'cumulo *sm* accumulation.

accura'tezza [akkura'tettsa] *sf* care; accuracy.

accu'rato, a *ag* (*diligente*) careful; (*preciso*) accurate.

ac'cusa *sf* accusation; (*DIR*) charge; l'~, **la pubblica** ~ (*DIR*) the prosecution; **mettere qn sotto** ~ to indict sb; **in stato di** ~ committed for trial.

accu'sabile *ag* (*DIR*) chargeable.

accu'sare *vt* (*sentire*: *dolore*) to feel; ~ **qn di qc** to accuse sb of sth; (*DIR*) to charge sb with sth; ~ **ricevuta di** (*COMM*) to acknowledge receipt of; ~ **la fatica** to show signs of exhaustion; **ha accusato il colpo** (*anche fig*) you could see that he had felt the blow.

accu'sato, a *sm/f* accused.

accusa'tore, 'trice *ag* accusing ♦ *sm/f* accuser ♦ *sm* (*DIR*) prosecutor.

a'cerbo, a [a'tʃerbo] *ag* bitter; (*frutta*) sour, unripe; (*persona*) immature.

'acero ['atʃero] *sm* maple.

a'cerrimo, a [a'tʃerrimo] *ag* very fierce.

ace'tato [atʃe'tato] *sm* acetate.

a'ceto [a'tʃeto] *sm* vinegar; **mettere sotto** ~ to pickle.

ace'tone [atʃe'tone] *sm* nail varnish remover.

'A.C.I. ['atʃi] *sigla m* (= *Automobile Club d'Italia*) ≈ AA (*Brit*), AAA (*US*).

acidità [atʃidi'ta] *sf* acidity; sourness; ~ **(di stomaco)** heartburn.

'acido, a ['atʃido] *ag* (*sapore*) acid, sour; (*CHIM*) acid ♦ *sm* (*CHIM*) acid.

a'cidulo, a [a'tʃidulo] *ag* slightly sour, slightly acid.

'acino ['atʃino] *sm* berry; ~ **d'uva** grape.

'ACLI *sigla fpl* (= *Associazioni Cristiane dei*

Lavoratori Italiani) *Christian Trade Union Association*.

'acme *sf* (*fig*) acme, peak; (*MED*) crisis.

'acne *sf* acne.

'acqua *sf* water; (*pioggia*) rain; ~**e** *sfpl* waters; **fare** ~ (*NAUT*) to leak, take in water; **essere con** *o* **avere l'**~ **alla gola** to be in great difficulty; **tirare** ~ **al proprio mulino** to feather one's own nest; **navigare in cattive** ~**e** (*fig*) to be in deep water; ~ **in bocca!** mum's the word!; ~ **corrente** running water; ~ **dolce** fresh water; ~ **di mare** sea water; ~ **minerale** mineral water; ~ **ossigenata** hydrogen peroxide; ~ **piovana** rain water; ~ **potabile** drinking water; ~ **salata** *o* **salmastra** salt water; ~ **tonica** tonic water.

acqua'forte, *pl* **acque'forti** *sf* etching.

a'cquaio *sm* sink.

acqua'ragia [akkwa'radʒa] *sf* turpentine.

a'cquario *sm* aquarium; (*dello zodiaco*): **A**~ Aquarius; **essere dell'A**~ to be Aquarius.

acquartie'rare *vt* (*MIL*) to quarter.

acqua'santa *sf* holy water.

a'cquatico, a, ci, che *ag* aquatic; (*sport, sci*) water *cpd*.

acquat'tarsi *vr* to crouch (down).

acqua'vite *sf* brandy.

acquaz'zone [akkwat'tsone] *sm* cloudburst, heavy shower.

acque'dotto *sm* aqueduct; waterworks *pl*, water system.

'acqueo, a *ag*: **vapore** ~ water vapour (*Brit*) *o* vapor (*US*); **umore** ~ aqueous humour (*Brit*) *o* humor (*US*).

acque'rello *sm* watercolour (*Brit*), watercolor (*US*).

acque'rugiola [akkwe'rudʒola] *sf* drizzle.

acquie'tare *vt* to appease; (*dolore*) to ease; ~**rsi** *vr* to calm down.

acqui'rente *sm/f* purchaser, buyer.

acqui'sire *vt* to acquire.

acquisizi'one [akkwizit'tsjone] *sf* acquisition.

acquis'tare *vt* to purchase, buy; (*fig*) to gain ♦ *vi* to improve; ~ **in bellezza** to become more beautiful; **ha acquistato in salute** his health has improved.

a'cquisto *sm* purchase; **fare** ~**i** to go shopping; **ufficio** ~**i** (*COMM*) purchasing department; ~ **rateale** instalment purchase, hire purchase (*Brit*).

acqui'trino *sm* bog, marsh.

acquo'lina *sf*: **far venire l'**~ **in bocca a qn** to make sb's mouth water.

a'cquoso, a *ag* watery.

'acre *ag* acrid, pungent; (*fig*) harsh, biting.

a'credine *sf* (*fig*) bitterness.

a'crilico, a, ci, che *ag, sm* acrylic.

a'crobata, i, e *sm/f* acrobat.

acro'batico, a, ci, che *ag* (*ginnastica*) acrobatic; (*AER*) aerobatic ♦ *sf* acrobatics *sg*.

acroba'zia [akrobat'tsia] *sf* acrobatic feat; ~**e aeree** aerobatics.

a'cronimo *sm* acronym.

a'cropoli *sf inv*: **l'A**~ the Acropolis.

acu'ire *vt* to sharpen; ~**rsi** *vr* (*gen*) to increase; (*crisi*) to worsen.

a'culeo *sm* (*ZOOL*) sting; (*BOT*) prickle.

a'cume *sm* acumen, perspicacity.

acumi'nato, a *ag* sharp.

a'custico, a, ci, che *ag* acoustic ♦ *sf* (*scienza*) acoustics *sg*; (*di una sala*) acoustics *pl*; **apparecchio** ~ hearing aid; **cornetto** ~ ear trumpet.

acu'tezza [aku'tettsa] *sf* sharpness; shrillness; acuteness; high pitch; intensity; keenness.

acutiz'zare [akutid'dzare] *vt* (*fig*) to intensify; ~**rsi** *vr* (*fig*: *crisi, malattia*) to become worse, worsen.

a'cuto, a *ag* (*appuntito*) sharp, pointed; (*suono, voce*) shrill, piercing; (*MAT, LING, MED*) acute; (*MUS*) high-pitched; (*fig*: *dolore, desiderio*) intense; (: *perspicace*) acute, keen ♦ *sm* (*MUS*) high note.

ad *prep* (*dav V*) = **a**.

adagi'are [ada'dʒare] *vt* to lay *o* set down carefully; ~**rsi** *vr* to lie down, stretch out.

a'dagio [a'dadʒo] *av* slowly ♦ *sm* (*MUS*) adagio; (*proverbio*) adage, saying.

ada'mitico, a, ci, che *ag*: **in costume** ~ in one's birthday suit.

adat'tabile *ag* adaptable.

adattabilità *sf* adaptability.

adatta'mento *sm* adaptation; **avere spirito di** ~ to be adaptable.

adat'tare *vt* to adapt; (*sistemare*) to fit; ~**rsi** *vr*: ~**rsi (a)** (*ambiente, tempi*) to adapt (to); (*essere adatto*) to be suitable (for); (*accontentarsi*): ~**rsi a qc/a fare qc** to make the best of sth/of doing sth.

adatta'tore *sm* (*ELETTR*) adapter, adaptor.

a'datto, a *ag*: ~ **(a)** suitable (for), right (for).

addebi'tare *vt*: ~ **qc a qn** to debit sb with sth; (*fig*: *incolpare*) to blame sb for sth.

ad'debito *sm* (*COMM*) debit.

addensa'mento *sm* thickening; gathering.

adden'sare *vt* to thicken; ~**rsi** *vr* to thicken; (*nuvole*) to gather.

adden'tare *vt* to bite into.

adden'trarsi *vr*: ~ **in** to penetrate, go into.

ad'dentro *av* (*fig*): **essere molto** ~ **in qc** to be well-versed in sth.

addestra'mento *sm* training; ~ **aziendale** company training.

addes'trare *vt*, ~**rsi** *vr* to train; ~**rsi in qc** to practise (*Brit*) *o* practice (*US*) sth.

ad'detto, a *ag*: ~ **a** (*persona*) assigned to; (*oggetto*) intended for ♦ *sm* employee; (*funzionario*) attaché; ~ **commerciale/ stampa** commercial/press attaché; ~ **al telex** telex operator; **gli** ~**i ai lavori**

authorized personnel; (*fig*) those in the know; **"vietato l'ingresso ai non** ~**i ai lavori"** "authorized personnel only".

addì *av* (*AMM*): ~ **3 luglio 1989** on the 3rd of July 1989 (*Brit*), on July 3rd 1989 (*US*).

addi'accio [ad'djattʃo] *sm* (*MIL*) bivouac; **dormire all'**~ to sleep in the open.

addi'etro *av* (*indietro*) behind; (*nel passato, prima*) before, ago.

ad'dio *sm, escl* goodbye, farewell.

addirit'tura *av* (*veramente*) really, absolutely; (*perfino*) even; (*direttamente*) directly, right away.

ad'dirsi *vr*: ~ **a** to suit, be suitable for.

'Addis A'beba *sf* Addis Ababa.

addi'tare *vt* to point out; (*fig*) to expose.

addi'tivo *sm* additive.

addizio'nale [addittsjo'nale] *ag* additional ♦ *sf* (*anche*: **imposta** ~) surtax.

addizio'nare [addittsjo'nare] *vt* (*MAT*) to add (up).

addizi'one [addit'tsjone] *sf* addition.

addob'bare *vt* to decorate.

ad'dobbo *sm* decoration.

addol'cire [addol'tʃire] *vt* (*caffè etc*) to sweeten; (*acqua, fig*: *carattere*) to soften; ~**rsi** *vr* (*fig*) to mellow, soften; ~ **la pillola** (*fig*) to sugar the pill.

addolo'rare *vt* to pain, grieve; ~**rsi** *vr*: ~**rsi (per)** to be distressed (by).

addolo'rato, a *ag* distressed, upset; **l'A**~**a** (*REL*) Our Lady of Sorrows.

ad'dome *sm* abdomen.

addomesti'care *vt* to tame.

addomi'nale *ag* abdominal; (**muscoli** *mpl*) ~**i** stomach muscles.

addormen'tare *vt* to put to sleep; ~**rsi** *vr* to fall asleep, go to sleep.

addormen'tato, a *ag* sleeping, asleep; (*fig*: *tardo*) stupid, dopey.

addos'sare *vt* (*appoggiare*): ~ **qc a qc** to lean sth against sth; (*fig*): ~ **la colpa a qn** to lay the blame on sb; ~**rsi** *vr*: ~**rsi qc** (*responsabilità etc*) to shoulder sth.

ad'dosso *av* (*sulla persona*) on; ~ **a** *prep* (*sopra*) on; (*molto vicino*) right next to; **mettersi** ~ **il cappotto** to put one's coat on; **andare** (*o* **venire**) ~ **a** (*AUT*: *altra macchina*) to run into; (: *pedone*) to run over; **non ho soldi** ~ I don't have any money on me; **stare** ~ **a qn** (*fig*) to breathe down sb's neck; **dare** ~ **a qn** (*fig*) to attack sb; **mettere gli occhi** ~ **a qn/qc** to take quite a fancy to sb/sth; **mettere le mani** ~ **a qn** (*picchiare*) to hit sb; (*catturare*) to seize sb; (*molestare*: *donna*) to touch sb up.

ad'dotto, a *pp di* **addurre**.

ad'duco *etc vb vedi* **addurre**.

ad'durre *vt* (*DIR*) to produce; (*citare*) to cite.

ad'dussi *etc vb vedi* **addurre**.

adegu'are *vt*: ~ **qc a** to adjust sth to; ~**rsi**

vr to adapt.

adegua'tezza [adegwa'tettsa] *sf* adequacy; suitability; fairness.

adegu'ato, a *ag* adequate; (*conveniente*) suitable; (*equo*) fair.

a'dempiere *vt* to fulfil (*Brit*), fulfill (*US*), carry out; (*comando*) to carry out.

adempi'mento *sm* fulfilment (*Brit*), fulfillment (*US*); carrying out; **nell'~ del proprio dovere** in the performance of one's duty.

adem'pire *vt* = **adempiere.**

'Aden: il golfo di ~ *sm* the Gulf of Aden.

ade'noidi *sfpl* adenoids.

a'depto *sm* disciple, follower.

ade'rente *ag* adhesive; (*vestito*) close-fitting ♦ *sm/f* follower.

ade'renza [ade'rɛntsa] *sf* adhesion; **~e** *sfpl* (*fig*) connections, contacts.

ade'rire *vi* (*stare attaccato*) to adhere, stick; **~ a** to adhere to, stick to; (*fig: società, partito*) to join; (: *opinione*) to support; (*richiesta*) to agree to.

ades'care *vt* (*attirare*) to lure, entice; (*TECN: pompa*) to prime.

adesi'one *sf* adhesion; (*fig: assenso*) agreement, acceptance; (*appoggio*) support.

ade'sivo, a *ag, sm* adhesive.

a'desso *av* (*ora*) now; (*or ora, poco fa*) just now; (*tra poco*) any moment now; **da ~ in poi** from now on; **per ~** for the moment, for now.

adia'cente [adja'tʃɛnte] *ag* adjacent.

adi'bire *vt* (*usare*): **~ qc a** to turn sth into.

'Adige ['adidʒe] *sm*: **l'~** the Adige.

'adipe *sm* fat.

adi'rarsi *vr*: **~ (con** *o* **contro qn per qc)** to get angry (with sb over sth).

adi'rato, a *ag* angry.

a'dire *vt* (*DIR*): **~ le vie legali** to take legal proceedings; **~ un'eredità** to take legal possession of an inheritance.

'adito *sm*: **dare ~ a** (*sospetti*) to give rise to.

ADN *sigla m* (= *acido deossiribonucleico*) DNA.

adocchi'are [adok'kjare] *vt* (*scorgere*) to catch sight of; (*occhieggiare*) to eye.

adole'scente [adoleʃ'ʃɛnte] *ag, sm/f* adolescent.

adole'scenza [adoleʃ'ʃɛntsa] *sf* adolescence.

adolescenzi'ale [adoleʃʃen'tsjale] *ag* adolescent.

adom'brare *vt* (*fig*) to veil, conceal; **~rsi** *vr* (*cavallo*) to shy; (*persona*) to grow suspicious; (: *aversene a male*) to be offended.

adope'rare *vt* to use; **~rsi** *vr* to strive; **~rsi per qn/qc** to do one's best for sb/sth.

ado'rare *vt* to adore; (*REL*) to adore, worship.

adorazi'one [adorat'tsjone] *sf* adoration; worship.

ador'nare *vt* to adorn.

a'dorno, a *ag*: **~ (di)** adorned (with).

adot'tare *vt* to adopt; (*decisione, provvedimenti*) to pass.

adot'tivo, a *ag* (*genitori*) adoptive; (*figlio, patria*) adopted.

adozi'one [adot'tsjone] *sf* adoption.

adri'atico, a, ci, che *ag* Adriatic ♦ *sm*: **l'A~, il mare A~** the Adriatic, the Adriatic Sea.

adu'lare *vt* to flatter.

adula'tore, 'trice *sm/f* flatterer.

adula'torio, a *ag* flattering.

adulazi'one [adulat'tsjone] *sf* flattery.

adulte'rare *vt* to adulterate.

adul'terio *sm* adultery.

a'dultero, a *ag* adulterous ♦ *sm/f* adulterer/adulteress.

a'dulto, a *ag* adult; (*fig*) mature ♦ *sm* adult, grown-up.

adu'nanza [adu'nantsa] *sf* assembly, meeting.

adu'nare *vt*, **~rsi** *vr* to assemble, gather.

adu'nata *sf* (*MIL*) parade, muster.

a'dunco, a, chi, che *ag* hooked.

AEDA *sigla mpl* (= *Autori Editori Associati*) *association of authors and publishers*.

aerazi'one [aerat'tsjone] *sf* ventilation; (*TECN*) aeration.

a'ereo, a *ag* air *cpd*; (*radice*) aerial ♦ *sm* aerial; (*aeroplano*) plane; **~ da caccia** fighter (plane); **~ di linea** airliner; **~ a reazione** jet (plane).

ae'robica *sf* aerobics *sg*.

aerodi'namico, a, ci, che *ag* aerodynamic; (*affusolato*) streamlined ♦ *sf* aerodynamics *sg*.

aeromo'dello *sm* model aircraft.

aero'nautica *sf* (*scienza*) aeronautics *sg*; **~ militare** air force.

aerona'vale *ag* (*forze, manovre*) air and sea *cpd*.

aero'plano *sm* (aero)plane (*Brit*), (air)plane (*US*).

aero'porto *sm* airport.

aeroportu'ale *ag* airport *cpd*.

aeros'calo *sm* airstrip.

aero'sol *sm inv* aerosol.

aerospazi'ale [aerospat'tsjale] *ag* aerospace.

aeros'tatico, a, ci, che *ag* aerostatic; **pallone ~** air balloon.

A.F. *abbr* (= *alta frequenza*) HF; (*AMM*) = **assegni familiari.**

'afa *sf* sultriness.

af'fabile *ag* affable.

affabilità *sf* affability.

affaccen'darsi [affattʃen'darsi] *vr*: **~ intorno a qc** to busy o.s. with sth.

affaccen'dato, a [affattʃen'dato] *ag* busy.

affacci'arsi [affat'tʃarsi] *vr*: **~ (a)** to appear (at); **~ alla vita** to come into the world.

affa'mato, a *ag* starving; (*fig*): **~ (di)**

eager (for).

affan'nare *vt* to leave breathless; (*fig*) to worry; **~rsi** *vr*: **~rsi per qn/qc** to worry about sb/sth.

af'fanno *sm* breathlessness; (*fig*) anxiety, worry.

affannosa'mente *av* with difficulty; anxiously.

affan'noso, a *ag* (*respiro*) difficult; (*fig*) troubled, anxious.

af'fare *sm* (*faccenda*) matter, affair; (*COMM*) piece of business, (business) deal; (*occasione*) bargain; (*DIR*) case; (*fam: cosa*) thing; **~i** *smpl* (*COMM*) business *sg*; **~ fatto!** done!, it's a deal!; **sono ~i miei** that's my business; **bada agli ~i tuoi!** mind your own business!; **uomo d'~i** businessman; **ministro degli A~i Esteri** Foreign Secretary (*Brit*), Secretary of State (*US*).

affa'rista, i *sm* profiteer, unscrupulous businessman.

affasci'nante [affaʃʃi'nante] *ag* fascinating.

affasci'nare [affaʃʃi'nare] *vt* to bewitch; (*fig*) to charm, fascinate.

affatica'mento *sm* tiredness.

affati'care *vt* to tire; **~rsi** *vr* (*durar fatica*) to tire o.s. out.

af'fatto *av* completely; **non ... ~** not ... at all; **niente ~** not at all.

affer'mare *vi* (*dire di sì*) to say yes ♦ *vt* (*dichiarare*) to maintain, affirm; **~rsi** *vr* to assert o.s., make one's name known.

affermativa'mente *av* in the affirmative, affirmatively.

afferma'tivo, a *ag* affirmative.

affermazi'one [affermat'tsjone] *sf* affirmation, assertion; (*successo*) achievement.

affer'rare *vt* to seize, grasp; (*fig: idea*) to grasp; **~rsi** *vr*: **~rsi a** to cling to.

Aff. Est. *abbr* = *Affari Esteri*.

affet'tare *vt* (*tagliare a fette*) to slice; (*ostentare*) to affect.

affet'tato, a *ag* sliced; affected ♦ *sm* sliced cold meat.

affetta'trice [affetta'tritʃe] *sf* meat slicer.

affettazi'one [affettat'tsjone] *sf* affectation.

affet'tivo, a *ag* emotional, affective.

af'fetto, a *ag*: **essere ~ da** to suffer from ♦ *sm* affection; **gli ~i familiari** one's nearest and dearest.

affettuosa'mente *av* affectionately; (*nelle lettere*): (**ti saluto**) **~, Maria** love, Maria.

affettuosità *sf inv* affection; **~** *sfpl* (*manifestazioni*) demonstrations of affection.

affettu'oso, a *ag* affectionate.

affezio'narsi [affettsjo'narsi] *vr*: **~ a** to grow fond of.

affezio'nato, a [affettsjo'nato] *ag*: **~ a qn/qc** fond of sb/sth; (*attaccato*) attached to sb/sth.

affezi'one [affet'tsjone] *sf* (*affetto*) affection; (*MED*) ailment, disorder.

affian'care *vt* to place side by side; (*MIL*) to flank; (*fig*) to support; **~ qc a qc** to place sth next to *o* beside sth; **~rsi** *vr*: **~rsi a qn** to stand beside sb.

affiata'mento *sm* understanding.

affia'tarsi *vr* to get on well together.

affibbi'are *vt* to buckle, do up; (*fig: dare*) to give.

affidabilità *sf* reliability.

affida'mento *sm* (*DIR: di bambino*) custody; (*fiducia*): **fare ~** to rely on sb; **non dà nessun ~** he's not to be trusted.

affi'dare *vt*: **~ qc** *o* **qn a qn** to entrust sth *o* sb to sb; **~rsi** *vr*: **~rsi a** to place one's trust in.

affievo'lirsi *vr* to grow weak.

af'figgere [af'fiddʒere] *vt* to stick up, post up.

affi'lare *vt* to sharpen.

affi'lato, a *ag* (*gen*) sharp; (*volto, naso*) thin.

affili'are *vt* to affiliate; **~rsi** *vr*: **~rsi a** to become affiliated to.

affi'nare *vt* to sharpen.

affinché [affin'ke] *cong* in order that, so that.

af'fine *ag* similar.

affinità *sf inv* affinity.

affio'rare *vi* to emerge.

af'fissi *etc vb vedi* **affiggere.**

affissi'one *sf* billposting.

af'fisso, a *pp di* **affiggere** ♦ *sm* bill, poster; (*LING*) affix.

affitta'camere *sm/f inv* landlord/landlady.

affit'tare *vt* (*dare in affitto*) to let, rent (out); (*prendere in affitto*) to rent.

af'fitto *sm* rent; (*contratto*) lease; **dare in ~** to rent (out), let; **prendere in ~** to rent.

affittu'ario *sm* lessee.

af'fliggere [af'fliddʒere] *vt* to torment; **~rsi** *vr* to grieve.

af'flissi *etc vb vedi* **affliggere.**

af'flitto, a *pp di* **affliggere.**

afflizi'one [afflit'tsjone] *sf* distress, torment.

afflosci'arsi [affloʃ'ʃarsi] *vr* to go limp; (*frutta*) to go soft.

afflu'ente *sm* tributary.

afflu'enza [afflu'ɛntsa] *sf* flow; (*di persone*) crowd.

afflu'ire *vi* to flow; (*fig: merci, persone*) to pour in.

af'flusso *sm* influx.

affo'gare *vt, vi* to drown; **~rsi** *vr* to drown; (*deliberatamente*) to drown o.s.

affo'gato, a *ag* drowned; (*CUC: uova*) poached.

affolla'mento *sm* crowding; (*folla*) crowd.

affol'lare *vt*, **~rsi** *vr* to crowd.

affol'lato, a *ag* crowded.

affonda'mento *sm* (*di nave*) sinking.

affon'dare *vt* to sink.

affran'care *vt* to free, liberate; (*AMM*) to redeem; (*lettera*) to stamp; (: *meccanicamente*) to frank (*Brit*), meter (*US*); **~rsi** *vr* to free o.s.

affranca'trice [affranka'tritʃe] *sf* franking machine (*Brit*), postage meter (*US*).

affranca'tura *sf* (*di francobollo*) stamping; franking (*Brit*), metering (*US*); (*tassa di spedizione*) postage; **~ a carico del destinatario** postage paid.

af'franto, a *ag* (*esausto*) worn out; (*abbattuto*) overcome.

af'fresco, schi *sm* fresco.

affret'tare *vt* to quicken, speed up; **~rsi** *vr* to hurry; **~rsi a fare qc** to hurry o hasten to do sth.

affret'tato, a *ag* (*veloce: passo, ritmo*) quick, fast; (*frettoloso: decisione*) hurried, hasty; (: *lavoro*) rushed.

affron'tare *vt* (*pericolo etc*) to face; (*assalire: nemico*) to confront; **~rsi** *vr* (*reciproco*) to confront each other.

af'fronto *sm* affront, insult; **fare un ~ a qn** to insult sb.

affumi'care *vt* to fill with smoke; to blacken with smoke; (*alimenti*) to smoke.

affuso'lato, a *ag* tapering.

af'gano, a *ag, sm/f* Afghan.

Af'ghanistan [af'ganistan] *sm*: **l'~** Afghanistan.

a.f.m. *abbr* (*COMM*: = *a fine mese*) e.o.m. (= *end of month*).

a'foso, a *ag* sultry, close.

'Africa *sf*: **l'~** Africa.

afri'cander *sm inv* Afrikaner.

afri'cano, a *ag, sm/f* African.

afroasi'atico a, ci, che *ag* Afro-Asian.

afrodi'siaco, a, ci, che *ag, sm* aphrodisiac.

AG *sigla* = *Agrigento*.

a'genda [a'dʒɛnda] *sf* diary; **~ tascabile/da tavolo** pocket/desk diary.

a'gente [a'dʒɛnte] *sm* agent; **~ di cambio** stockbroker; **~ di custodia** prison officer; **~ marittimo** shipping agent; **~ di polizia** police officer; **~ provocatore** agent provocateur; **~ delle tasse** tax inspector; **~ di vendita** sales agent; **resistente agli ~i atmosferici** weather-resistant.

agen'zia [adʒen'tsia] *sf* agency; (*succursale*) branch; **~ di collocamento** employment agency; **~ immobiliare** estate agent's (office) (*Brit*), real estate office (*US*); **A~ Internazionale per l'Energia Atomica (AIEA)** International Atomic Energy Agency (IAEA); **~ matrimoniale** marriage bureau; **~ pubblicitaria** advertising agency; **~ di stampa** press agency; **~ viaggi** travel agency.

agevo'lare [adʒevo'lare] *vt* to facilitate, make easy.

agevolazi'one [adʒevolat'sjone] *sf* (*facilitazione economica*) facility; **~ di pagamento** payment on easy terms; **~i creditizie** credit facilities; **~i fiscali** tax concessions.

a'gevole [a'dʒevole] *ag* easy; (*strada*) smooth.

agganci'are [aggan'tʃare] *vt* to hook up; (*FERR*) to couple; **~rsi** *vr*: **~rsi a** to hook up to; (*fig: pretesto*) to seize on.

ag'gancio [ag'gantʃo] *sm* (*TECN*) coupling; (*fig: conoscenza*) contact.

ag'geggio [ad'dʒeddʒo] *sm* gadget, contraption.

agget'tivo [addʒet'tivo] *sm* adjective.

agghiacciante [aggjat'tʃante] *ag* (*fig*) chilling.

agghiacci'are [aggjat'tʃare] *vt* to freeze; (*fig*) to make one's blood run cold; **~rsi** *vr* to freeze.

agghin'darsi [aggin'darsi] *vr* to deck o.s. out.

aggio'gare [addʒo'gare] *vt* (*buoi*) to yoke; (*popolo*) to subjugate.

aggiorna'mento [addʒorna'mento] *sm* updating; revision; postponement; **corso di ~** refresher course.

aggior'nare [addʒor'nare] *vt* (*opera, manuale*) to bring up-to-date; (: *rivedere*) to revise; (*listino*) to maintain, up-date; (*seduta etc*) to postpone; **~rsi** *vr* to bring (o keep) o.s. up-to-date.

aggior'nato, a [addʒor'nato] *ag* up-to-date.

aggio'taggio [addʒo'taddʒo] *sm* (*ECON*) rigging the market.

aggi'rare [addʒi'rare] *vt* to go round; (*fig: ingannare*) to trick; **~rsi** *vr* to wander about; **il prezzo s'aggira sul milione** the price is around the million mark.

aggiudi'care [addʒudi'kare] *vt* to award; (*all'asta*) to knock down; **~rsi qc** to win sth.

ag'giungere [ad'dʒundʒere] *vt* to add.

aggi'unsi [ad'dʒunsi] *etc vb vedi* **aggiungere**.

aggi'unto, a [ad'dʒunto] *pp di* **aggiungere** ♦ *ag* assistant *cpd* ♦ *sm* assistant ♦ *sf* addition; **sindaco ~** deputy mayor; **in ~a ...** what's more ....

aggius'tare [addʒus'tare] *vt* (*accomodare*) to mend, repair; (*riassettare*) to adjust; (*fig: lite*) to settle; **~rsi** *vr* (*arrangiarsi*) to make do; (*con senso reciproco*) to come to an agreement; **ti aggiusto io!** I'll fix you!

agglome'rato *sm* (*di rocce*) conglomerate; (*di legno*) chipboard; **~ urbano** built-up area.

aggrap'parsi *vr*: **~ a** to cling to.

aggrava'mento *sm* worsening.

aggra'vante *ag* (*DIR*) aggravating ♦ *sf* aggravation.

aggra'vare *vt* (*aumentare*) to increase; (*appesantire: anche fig*) to weigh down, make heavy; (*fig: pena*) to make worse; **~rsi** *vr* (*fig*) to worsen, become worse.

ag'gravio *sm*: ~ **di costi** increase in costs.

aggrazi'ato, a [aggrat'tsjato] *ag* graceful.

aggre'dire *vt* to attack, assault.

aggre'gare *vt*: ~ **qn a qc** to admit sb to sth; ~**rsi** *vr* to join; ~**rsi a** to join, become a member of.

aggre'gato, a *ag* associated ♦ *sm* aggregate; ~ **urbano** built-up area.

aggressi'one *sf* aggression; (*atto*) attack, assault; ~ **a mano armata** armed assault.

aggressività *sf* aggressiveness.

aggres'sivo, a *ag* aggressive.

aggres'sore *sm* aggressor, attacker.

aggrot'tare *vt*: ~ **le sopracciglia** to frown.

aggrovigli'are [aggroviʎ'ʎare] *vt* to tangle; ~**rsi** *vr* (*fig*) to become complicated.

agguan'tare *vt* to catch, seize.

aggu'ato *sm* trap; (*imboscata*) ambush; **tendere un** ~ **a qn** to set a trap for sb.

agguer'rito, a *ag* (*sostenitore, nemico*) fierce.

agia'tezza [adʒa'tettsa] *sf* prosperity.

agi'ato, a [a'dʒato] *ag* (*vita*) easy; (*persona*) well-off, well-to-do.

'agile ['adʒile] *ag* agile, nimble.

agilità [adʒili'ta] *sf* agility, nimbleness.

'agio ['adʒo] *sm* ease, comfort; ~**i** *smpl* comforts; **mettersi a proprio** ~ to make o.s. at home *o* comfortable; **dare** ~ **a qn di fare qc** to give sb the chance of doing sth.

a'gire [a'dʒire] *vi* to act; (*esercitare un'azione*) to take effect; (*TECN*) to work, function; ~ **contro qn** (*DIR*) to take action against sb.

agi'tare [adʒi'tare] *vt* (*bottiglia*) to shake; (*mano, fazzoletto*) to wave; (*fig: turbare*) to disturb; (*: incitare*) to stir (up); ~**rsi** *vr* (*mare*) to be rough; (*malato, dormitore*) to toss and turn; (*bambino*) to fidget; (*emozionarsi*) to get upset; (*POL*) to agitate.

agi'tato, a [adʒi'tato] *ag* rough; restless; fidgety; upset, perturbed.

agita'tore, 'trice [adʒita'tore] *sm/f* (*POL*) agitator.

agitazi'one [adʒitat'tsjone] *sf* agitation; (*POL*) unrest, agitation; **mettere in** ~ **qn** to upset *o* distress sb.

'agit-'prop ['adʒit'prɔp] *abbr m* (= *agitatore-propagandista*) communist agitator.

'agli ['aʎʎi] *prep + det vedi* **a**.

'aglio ['aʎʎo] *sm* garlic.

a'gnello [aɲ'ɲello] *sm* lamb.

a'gnostico, a, ci, che [aɲ'ɲɔstiko] *ag*, *sm/f* agnostic.

'ago, pl 'aghi *sm* needle; ~ **da calza** knitting needle.

ago. *abbr* (= *agosto*) Aug.

ago'nia *sf* agony.

ago'nistico, a, ci, che *ag* athletic; (*fig*) competitive.

agoniz'zante [agonid'dzante] *ag* dying.

agoniz'zare [agonid'dzare] *vi* to be dying.

agopun'tura *sf* acupuncture.

a'gosto *sm* August; *per fraseologia vedi* luglio.

a'grario, a *ag* agrarian, agricultural; (*riforma*) land *cpd* ♦ *sm* landowner ♦ *sf* agriculture.

a'gricolo, a *ag* agricultural, farm *cpd*.

agricol'tore *sm* farmer.

agricol'tura *sf* agriculture, farming.

agri'foglio [agri'fɔʎʎo] *sm* holly.

agrimen'sore *sm* land surveyor.

agritu'rismo *sm* farm holidays *pl*.

'agro, a *ag* sour, sharp.

agro'dolce [agro'doltʃe] *ag* bittersweet; (*salsa*) sweet and sour.

a'grume *sm* (*spesso al pl: pianta*) citrus; (*: frutto*) citrus fruit.

agru'meto *sm* citrus grove.

aguz'zare [agut'tsare] *vt* to sharpen; ~ **gli orecchi** to prick up one's ears; ~ **l'ingegno** to use one's wits.

aguz'zino, a [agud'dzino] *sm/f* jailer; (*fig*) tyrant.

a'guzzo, a [a'guttso] *ag* sharp.

'ahi *escl* (*dolore*) ouch!

ahimè *escl* alas!

'ai *prep + det vedi* **a**.

'Aia *sf*: L'~ The Hague.

'aia *sf* threshing-floor.

AIDDA *sigla f* (= *Associazione Imprenditrici Donne Dirigenti d'Azienda*) association of women entrepreneurs and managers.

AIE *sigla f* (= *Associazione Italiana degli Editori*) publishers' association.

AIEA *sigla f vedi* **Agenzia Internazionale per l'Energia Atomica**.

AIED *sigla f* (= *Associazione Italiana Educazione Demografica*) ≈ FPA (= *Family Planning Association*).

AIG *sigla f* (= *Associazione Italiana Alberghi per la Gioventù*) ≈ YHA (*Brit*).

ai'ola *sf* = **aiuola**.

AIPI *sigla f* = *Associazione Italiana Protezione Infanzia*.

ai'rone *sm* heron.

ai'tante *ag* robust.

aiu'ola *sf* flower bed.

aiu'tante *sm/f* assistant ♦ *sm* (*MIL*) adjutant; (*NAUT*) master-at-arms; ~ **di campo** aide-de-camp.

aiu'tare *vt* to help; ~ **qn (a fare)** to help sb (to do).

ai'uto *sm* help, assistance, aid; (*aiutante*) assistant; **venire in** ~ **di qn** to come to sb's aid; ~ **chirurgo** assistant surgeon.

aiz'zare [ait'tsare] *vt* to incite; ~ **i cani contro qn** to set the dogs on sb.

al *prep + det vedi* **a**.

a.l. *abbr* = **anno luce**.

'ala, pl 'ali *sf* wing; **fare** ~ to fall back, make way; ~ **destra/sinistra** (*SPORT*) right/left wing.

ala'bastro *sm* alabaster.

'alacre *ag* quick, brisk.

alacrità *sf* promptness, speed.

alam'bicco, chi *sm* still (*CHIM*).

a'lano *sm* Great Dane.

a'lare *ag* wing *cpd*; **~i** *smpl* firedogs.

A'laska *sf*: **l'~** Alaska.

a'lato, a *ag* winged.

'alba *sf* dawn; **all'~** at dawn.

alba'nese *ag*, *sm/f*, *sm* Albanian.

Alba'nia *sf*: **l'~** Albania.

'albatro *sm* albatross.

albeggi'are [albed'dʒare] *vi*, *vb impers* to dawn.

albe'rato, a *ag* (*viale, piazza*) lined with trees, tree-lined.

albera'tura *sf* (*NAUT*) masts *pl*.

alber'gare *vt* (*dare albergo*) to accommodate ♦ *vi* (*poetico*) to dwell.

alberga'tore, 'trice *sm/f* hotelier, hotel-keeper.

alberghi'ero, a [alber'gjɛro] *ag* hotel *cpd*.

al'bergo, ghi *sm* hotel; **~ diurno** *public toilets with washing and shaving facilities etc*; **~ della gioventù** youth hostel.

'albero *sm* tree; (*NAUT*) mast; (*TECN*) shaft; **~ a camme** camshaft; **~ genealogico** family tree; **~ a gomiti** crankshaft; **~ maestro** mainmast; **~ di Natale** Christmas tree; **~ di trasmissione** transmission shaft.

albi'cocca, che *sf* apricot.

albi'cocco, chi *sm* apricot tree.

'albo *sm* (*registro*) register, roll; (*AMM*) notice board.

'album *sm* album; **~ da disegno** sketch book.

al'bume *sm* albumen; (*bianco d'uovo*) egg white.

albu'mina *sf* albumin.

'alce ['altʃe] *sm* elk.

al'chimia [al'kimja] *sf* alchemy.

alchi'mista, i [alki'mista] *sm* alchemist.

'alcol *sm inv* = **alcool**.

alcolicità [alkolitʃi'ta] *sf* alcohol(ic) content.

al'colico, a, ci, che *ag* alcoholic ♦ *sm* alcoholic drink.

alco'lismo *sm* alcoholism.

alco'lista, i, e *sm/f* alcoholic.

alcoliz'zato, a [alkolid'dzato] *sm/f* alcoholic.

'alcool *sm inv* alcohol; **~ denaturato** methylated spirits *pl* (*Brit*), wood alcohol (*US*); **~ etilico** ethyl alcohol; **~ metilico** methyl alcohol.

alco'test *sm inv* Breathalyser ® (*Brit*), Breathalyzer ® (*US*).

al'cova *sf* alcove.

al'cuno, a *det* (*dav sm*: **alcun** + *C, V*, **alcuno** + *s impura, gn, pn, ps, x, z*; *dav sf*: **alcuna** + *C*, **alcun'** +*V*) (*nessuno*): **non ... ~** no, not any; **~i(e)** *det pl*, *pronome pl* some, a

few; **non c'è ~a fretta** there's no hurry, there isn't any hurry; **senza alcun riguardo** without any consideration.

aldilà *sm inv*: **l'~** the next life, the afterlife.

alea'torio, a *ag* (*incerto*) uncertain.

aleggi'are [aled'dʒare] *vi* (*fig*: *profumo, sospetto*) to be in the air.

Ales'sandria *sf* (*anche*: **~ d'Egitto**) Alexandria.

a'letta *sf* (*TECN*) fin; tab.

Aleu'tine *sfpl*: **le isole ~** the Aleutian Islands.

alfa'betico, a, ci, che *ag* alphabetical.

alfa'beto *sm* alphabet.

alfanu'merico, a, ci, che *ag* alphanumeric.

alfi'ere *sm* standard-bearer; (*SCACCHI*) bishop.

al'fine *av* finally, in the end.

'alga, ghe *sf* seaweed *q*, alga.

'algebra ['aldʒebra] *sf* algebra.

Al'geri [al'dʒeri] *sf* Algiers.

Alge'ria [aldʒe'ria] *sf*: **l'~** Algeria.

alge'rino, a [aldʒe'rino] *ag*, *sm/f* Algerian.

algo'ritmo *sm* algorithm.

ALI *sigla f* (= *Associazione Librai Italiani*) *booksellers' association*.

ali'ante *sm* (*AER*) glider.

'alibi *sm inv* alibi.

a'lice [a'litʃe] *sf* anchovy.

alie'nare *vt* (*DIR*) to transfer; (*rendere ostile*) to alienate; **~rsi qn** to alienate sb.

alie'nato, a *ag* alienated; transferred; (*fuor di senno*) insane ♦ *sm* lunatic, insane person.

alienazi'one [aljenat'tsjone] *sf* alienation; transfer; insanity.

ali'eno, a *ag* (*avverso*): **~ (da)** opposed (to), averse (to) ♦ *sm/f* alien.

alimen'tare *vt* to feed; (*TECN*) to feed, supply; (*fig*) to sustain ♦ *ag* food *cpd*; **~i** *smpl* foodstuffs; (*anche*: **negozio di ~i**) grocer's shop; **regime ~** diet.

alimentazi'one [alimentat'tsjone] *sf* feeding; (*cibi*) diet; **~ di fogli** (*INFORM*) sheet feed.

ali'mento *sm* food; **~i** *smpl* food *sg*; (*DIR*) alimony.

a'liquota *sf* share; **~ d'imposta** tax rate; **~ minima** (*FISCO*) basic rate.

alis'cafo *sm* hydrofoil.

'alito *sm* breath.

all., alleg. *abbr* (= *allegato*) enc., encl.

'alla *prep* + *det vedi* **a**.

allaccia'mento [allattʃa'mento] *sm* (*TECN*) connection.

allacci'are [allat'tʃare] *vt* (*scarpe*) to tie, lace (up); (*cintura*) to do up, fasten; (*due località*) to link; (*luce, gas*) to connect; (*amicizia*) to form; **~rsi** *vr* (*vestito*) to fasten; **~ o ~rsi la cintura** to fasten one's belt.

allaccia'tura [allattʃa'tura] *sf* fastening.

allaga'mento *sm* flooding *q*; flood.
alla'gare *vt*, **~rsi** *vr* to flood.
allampa'nato, a *ag* lanky.
allar'gare *vt* to widen; (*vestito*) to let out; (*aprire*) to open; (*fig: dilatare*) to extend; **~rsi** *vr* (*gen*) to widen; (*scarpe, pantaloni*) to stretch; (*fig: problema, fenomeno*) to spread.
allar'mare *vt* to alarm; **~rsi** *vr* to become alarmed.
al'larme *sm* alarm; **mettere qn in ~** to alarm sb; **~ aereo** air-raid warning.
allar'mismo *sm* scaremongering.
allar'mista, i, e *sm/f* scaremonger, alarmist.
allat'tare *vt* (*sog: donna*) to (breast-)feed; (: *animale*) to suckle; **~ artificialmente** to bottle-feed.
'alle *prep* + *det vedi* **a**.
alle'anza [alle'antsa] *sf* alliance.
alle'arsi *vr* to form an alliance.
alle'ato, a *ag* allied ♦ *sm/f* ally.
alle'gare *vt* (*accludere*) to enclose; (*DIR: citare*) to cite, adduce; (*denti*) to set on edge.
alle'gato, a *ag* enclosed ♦ *sm* enclosure; **in ~** enclosed; **in ~ Vi inviamo ...** please find enclosed ....
allegge'rire [alleddʒe'rire] *vt* to lighten, make lighter; (*fig: sofferenza*) to alleviate, lessen; (: *lavoro, tasse*) to reduce.
allego'ria *sf* allegory.
alle'gria *sf* gaiety, cheerfulness.
al'legro, a *ag* cheerful, merry; (*un po' brillo*) merry, tipsy; (*vivace: colore*) bright ♦ *sm* (*MUS*) allegro.
allena'mento *sm* training.
alle'nare *vt*, **~rsi** *vr* to train.
allena'tore *sm* (*SPORT*) trainer, coach.
allen'tare *vt* to slacken; (*disciplina*) to relax; **~rsi** *vr* to become slack; (*ingranaggio*) to work loose.
aller'gia, 'gie [aller'dʒia] *sf* allergy.
al'lergico, a, ci, che [al'lɛrdʒiko] *ag* allergic.
allesti'mento *sm* preparation, setting up; **in ~** in preparation.
alles'tire *vt* (*cena*) to prepare; (*esercito, nave*) to equip, fit out; (*spettacolo*) to stage.
allet'tante *ag* attractive, alluring.
allet'tare *vt* to lure, entice.
alleva'mento *sm* breeding, rearing; (*luogo*) stock farm; **pollo d'~** battery hen.
alle'vare *vt* (*animale*) to breed, rear; (*bambino*) to bring up.
alleva'tore *sm* breeder.
allevi'are *vt* to alleviate.
alli'bire *vi* to turn pale; (*essere turbato*) to be disconcerted.
alli'bito, a *ag* pale; disconcerted.
allibra'tore *sm* bookmaker.
allie'tare *vt* to cheer up, gladden.

alli'evo *sm* pupil; (*apprendista*) apprentice; **~ ufficiale** cadet.
alliga'tore *sm* alligator.
allinea'mento *sm* alignment.
alline'are *vt* (*persone, cose*) to line up; (*TIP*) to align; (*fig: economia, salari*) to adjust, align; **~rsi** *vr* to line up; (*fig: a idee*): **~rsi a** to come into line with.
alline'ato, a *ag* aligned, in line; **paesi non ~i** (*POL*) non-aligned countries.
'allo *prep* + *det vedi* **a**.
al'locco, a, chi, che *sm* tawny owl ♦ *sm/f* oaf.
allocuzi'one [allokut'tsjone] *sf* address, solemn speech.
al'lodola *sf* (sky)lark.
allogg'iare [allod'dʒare] *vt* to accommodate ♦ *vi* to live.
al'loggio [al'lɔddʒo] *sm* lodging, accommodation (*Brit*), accommodations (*US*); (*appartamento*) flat (*Brit*), apartment (*US*).
allontana'mento *sm* removal; dismissal; estrangement.
allonta'nare *vt* to send away, send off; (*impiegato*) to dismiss; (*pericolo*) to avert, remove; (*estraniare*) to alienate; **~rsi** *vr*: **~rsi (da)** to go away (from); (*estraniarsi*) to become estranged (from).
al'lora *av* (*in quel momento*) then ♦ *cong* (*in questo caso*) well then; (*dunque*) well then, so; **la gente d'~** people then *o* in those days; **da ~ in poi** from then on; **e ~?** (*che fare?*) what now?; (*e con ciò?*) so what?
allor'ché [allor'ke] *cong* (*formale*) when, as soon as.
al'loro *sm* laurel; **riposare** *o* **dormire sugli ~i** to rest on one's laurels.
'alluce ['allutʃe] *sm* big toe.
alluci'nante [allutʃi'nante] *ag* (*scena, spettacolo*) awful, terrifying; (*fam: incredibile*) amazing.
alluci'nato, a [allutʃi'nato] *ag* terrified; (*fuori di sé*) bewildered, confused.
allucinazi'one [allutʃinat'tsjone] *sf* hallucination.
al'ludere *vi*: **~ a** to allude to, hint at.
allu'minio *sm* aluminium (*Brit*), aluminum (*US*).
allu'naggio [allu'naddʒo] *sm* moon landing.
allu'nare *vi* to land on the moon.
allun'gare *vt* to lengthen; (*distendere*) to prolong, extend; (*diluire*) to water down; **~rsi** *vr* to lengthen; (*ragazzo*) to stretch, grow taller; (*sdraiarsi*) to lie down, stretch out; **~ le mani** (*rubare*) to pick pockets; **gli allungò uno schiaffo** he took a swipe at him.
al'lusi *etc vb vedi* **alludere**.
allusi'one *sf* hint, allusion.
al'luso, a *pp di* **alludere**.
alluvi'one *sf* flood.

alma'nacco, chi sm almanac.

al'meno av at least ♦ cong: **(se)** ~ if only; **(se)** ~ **piovesse!** if only it would rain!

a'logeno, a [a'lɔdʒeno] ag: **lampada** ~**a** halogen lamp.

a'lone sm halo.

al'pestre ag (delle alpi) alpine; (montuoso) mountainous.

'Alpi sfpl: **le** ~ the Alps.

alpi'nismo sm mountaineering, climbing.

alpi'nista, i, e sm/f mountaineer, climber.

al'pino, a ag Alpine; mountain cpd; ~**i** smpl (MIL) Italian Alpine troops.

al'quanto av rather, a little; ~, **a** det a certain amount of, some ♦ pronome a certain amount, some; ~**i(e)** det pl, pronome pl several, quite a few.

Al'sazia [al'sattsja] sf Alsace.

alt escl halt!, stop! ♦ sm: **dare l'**~ to call a halt.

alta'lena sf (a funi) swing; (in bilico, anche fig) seesaw.

al'tare sm altar.

alte'rare vt to alter, change; (cibo) to adulterate; (registro) to falsify; (persona) to irritate; ~**rsi** vr to alter; (cibo) to go bad; (persona) to lose one's temper.

alterazi'one [alterat'tsjone] sf alteration, change; adulteration; falsification; annoyance.

al'terco, chi sm altercation, wrangle.

alter'nanza [alter'nantsa] sf alternation; (AGR) rotation.

alter'nare vt, ~**rsi** vr to alternate.

alterna'tivo, a ag alternative ♦ sf alternative; **non abbiamo** ~**e** we have no alternative.

alter'nato, a ag alternate; (ELETTR) alternating.

alterna'tore sm alternator.

al'terno, a ag alternate; **a giorni** ~**i** on alternate days, every other day.

al'tero, a ag proud.

al'tezza [al'tettsa] sf (di edificio, persona) height; (di tessuto) width, breadth; (di acqua, pozzo) depth; (di suono) pitch; (GEO) latitude; (titolo) highness; (fig: nobiltà) greatness; **essere all'**~ **di** to be on a level with; (fig) to be up to o equal to; **all'**~ **della farmacia** near the chemist's.

altez'zoso, a [altet'tsoso] ag haughty.

al'ticcio, a, ci, ce [al'tittʃo] ag tipsy.

altipi'ano sm = **altopiano.**

altiso'nante ag (fig) high-sounding, pompous.

alti'tudine sf altitude.

'alto, a ag high; (persona) tall; (tessuto) wide, broad; (sonno, acque) deep; (suono) high(-pitched); (GEO) upper; (: settentrionale) northern ♦ sm top (part) ♦ av high; (parlare) aloud, loudly; **il palazzo è** ~ **20 metri** the building is 20 metres high;

il tessuto è ~ **70 cm** the material is 70 cm wide; **ad** ~**a voce** aloud; **a notte** ~**a** in the dead of night; **in** ~ up, upwards; at the top; **mani in** ~! hands up!; **dall'**~ **in** o **al basso** up and down; **degli** ~**i e bassi** (fig) ups and downs; **andare a testa** ~**a** (fig) to carry one's head high; **essere in** ~ **mare** (fig) to be far from a solution; ~**a fedeltà** high fidelity, hi-fi; ~**a moda** haute couture; **l'A**~ **Medioevo** the Early Middle Ages; **l'**~ **Po** the upper reaches of the Po.

altoate'sino, a ag of (o from) the Alto Adige.

alto'forno sm blast furnace.

altolo'cato, a ag of high rank, highly placed.

altopar'lante sm loudspeaker.

altopi'ano, pl **alti'piani** sm upland plain, plateau.

'Alto 'Volta sm: **l'**~ Upper Volta.

altret'tanto, a ag, pronome as much; (pl) as many ♦ av equally; **tanti auguri!** — **grazie,** ~ all the best! — thank you, the same to you.

'altri pronome inv (qualcuno) somebody; (: in espressioni negative) anybody; (un'altra persona) another (person).

altri'menti av otherwise.

'altro, a det other; **un** ~ **libro** (supplementare) another book, one more book; (diverso) another book, a different book; **un** ~ another (one); **l'**~ the other (one); **gli** ~**i** (la gente) others, other people; **desidera** ~? do you want anything else?; **aiutarsi l'un l'**~ to help one another; **l'uno e l'**~ both (of them); **l'**~ **giorno** the other day; **l'**~ **ieri** the day before yesterday; **domani l'**~ the day after tomorrow; **quest'**~ **mese** next month; **da un giorno all'**~ from day to day; (qualsiasi giorno) any day now; **d'**~**a parte** on the other hand; **tra l'**~ among other things; **ci mancherebbe** ~! that's all we need!; **non faccio** ~ **che studiare** I do nothing but study; **sei contento?** — ~ **che!/tutt'**~! are you pleased? — and how!/on the contrary!; **noi/voi** ~**i** us/you (lot).

altroché [altro'ke] escl certainly!, and how!

al'tronde av: **d'**~ on the other hand.

al'trove av elsewhere, somewhere else.

al'trui ag inv other people's ♦ sm: **l'**~ other people's belongings pl.

altru'ismo sm altruism.

altru'ista, i, e ag altruistic ♦ sm/f altruist.

al'tura sf (rialto) height, high ground; (alto mare) open sea; **pesca d'**~ deep-sea fishing.

a'lunno, a sm/f pupil.

alve'are sm hive.

'alveo sm riverbed.

alzabandi'era [altsaban'djera] sm inv (MIL): **l'**~ the raising of the flag.

al'zare [al'tsare] *vt* to raise, lift; (*issare*) to hoist; (*costruire*) to build, erect; ~**rsi** *vr* to rise; (*dal letto*) to get up; (*crescere*) to grow tall (*o* taller); ~ **le spalle** to shrug one's shoulders; ~ **le carte** to cut the cards; ~ **il gomito** to drink too much; ~ **le mani su qn** to raise one's hand to sb; ~ **i tacchi** to take to one's heels; ~**rsi in piedi** to stand up, get to one's feet; ~**rsi col piede sbagliato** to get out of bed on the wrong side.

al'zata [al'tsata] *sf* lifting, raising; **un'**~ **di spalle** a shrug.

A.M. *abbr* = **aeronautica militare**.

a'mabile *ag* lovable; (*vino*) sweet.

'AMAC *sigla f* = *Aeronautica Militare-Aviazione Civile*.

a'maca, che *sf* hammock.

amalga'mare *vt*, ~**rsi** *vr* to amalgamate.

a'mante *ag*: ~ **di** (*musica etc*) fond of ♦ *sm/f* lover/mistress.

ama'ranto *sm* (*BOT*) love-lies-bleeding ♦ *ag inv*: **color** ~ reddish purple.

a'mare *vt* to love; (*amico, musica, sport*) to like.

amareggi'are [amared'dʒare] *vt* to sadden, upset; ~**rsi** *vr* to get upset; ~**rsi la vita** to make one's life a misery.

amareggi'ato, a [amared'dʒato] *ag* upset, saddened.

ama'rena *sf* sour black cherry.

ama'retto *sm* (*dolce*) macaroon; (*liquore*) bitter liqueur made with almonds.

ama'rezza [ama'rettsa] *sf* bitterness.

a'maro, a *ag* bitter ♦ *sm* bitterness; (*liquore*) bitters *pl*.

ama'rognolo, a [ama'roɲɲolo] *ag* slightly bitter.

a'mato, a *ag* beloved, loved, dear ♦ *sm/f* loved one.

ama'tore, 'trice *sm/f* (*amante*) lover; (*intenditore*: *di vini etc*) connoisseur; (*dilettante*) amateur.

a'mazzone [a'maddzone] *sf* (*MITOLOGIA*) Amazon; (*cavallerizza*) horsewoman; (*abito*) riding habit; **cavalcare all'**~ to ride sidesaddle; **il Rio delle A**~**i** the (river) Amazon.

amaz'zonico, a, ci, che [amad'dzɔniko] *ag* Amazonian; Amazon *cpd*.

ambasce'ria [ambaʃʃe'ria] *sf* embassy.

ambasci'ata [ambaʃ'ʃata] *sf* embassy; (*messaggio*) message.

ambascia'tore, 'trice [ambaʃʃa'tore] *sm/f* ambassador/ambassadress.

ambe'due *ag inv*: ~ **i ragazzi** both boys ♦ *pronome inv* both.

ambi'destro, a *ag* ambidextrous.

ambien'tale *ag* environmental; (*temperatura*) ambient *cpd*.

ambien'tare *vt* to acclimatize; (*romanzo, film*) to set; ~**rsi** *vr* to get used to one's surroundings.

ambientazi'one [ambjentat'tsjone] *sf* setting.

ambi'ente *sm* environment; (*fig: insieme di persone*) milieu; (*stanza*) room.

ambiguità *sf inv* ambiguity.

am'biguo, a *ag* ambiguous; (*persona*) shady.

am'bire *vt* (*anche: vi:* ~ **a**) to aspire to; **un premio molto ambito** a much sought-after prize.

'ambito *sm* sphere, field.

ambiva'lente *ag* ambivalent; **questo apparecchio è** ~ this is a dual-purpose device.

ambizi'one [ambit'tsjone] *sf* ambition.

ambizi'oso, a [ambit'tsjoso] *ag* ambitious.

'ambo *ag inv* both.

'ambra *sf* amber; ~ **grigia** ambergris.

ambu'lante *ag* travelling, itinerant.

ambu'lanza [ambu'lantsa] *sf* ambulance.

ambulatori'ale *ag* (*MED*) outpatients *cpd*; **operazione** ~ operation as an outpatient; **visita** ~ visit to the doctor's surgery (*Brit*) *o* office (*US*).

ambula'torio *sm* (*studio medico*) surgery (*Brit*), doctor's office (*US*).

'AMDI *sigla f* = *Associazione Medici Dentisti Italiani*.

'AME *sigla m* = *Accordo Monetario Europeo*.

a'meba *sf* amoeba (*Brit*), ameba (*US*).

amenità *sf inv* pleasantness *q*; (*facezia*) pleasantry.

a'meno, a *ag* pleasant; (*strano*) funny, strange; (*spiritoso*) amusing.

A'merica *sf*: **l'**~ America; **l'**~ **latina** Latin America; **l'**~ **del sud** South America.

america'nata *sf* (*peg*): **le Olimpiadi sono state una vera** ~ the Olympics were a typically vulgar American extravaganza.

america'nismo *sm* Americanism; (*ammirazione*) love of America.

ameri'cano, a *ag, sm/f* American.

ame'tista *sf* amethyst.

ami'anto *sm* asbestos.

a'mica *sf vedi* **amico**.

ami'chevole [ami'kevole] *ag* friendly.

ami'cizia [ami'tʃittsja] *sf* friendship; ~**e** *sfpl* (*amici*) friends; **fare** ~ **con qn** to make friends with sb.

a'mico, a, ci, che *sm/f* friend; (*amante*) boyfriend/girlfriend; ~ **del cuore** *o* **intimo** bosom friend; ~ **d'infanzia** childhood friend.

'amido *sm* starch.

ammac'care *vt* (*pentola*) to dent; (*persona*) to bruise; ~**rsi** *vr* to bruise.

ammacca'tura *sf* dent; bruise.

ammaes'trare *vt* (*animale*) to train; (*persona*) to teach.

ammai'nare *vt* to lower, haul down.

amma'larsi *vr* to fall ill.

amma'lato, a *ag* ill, sick ♦ *sm/f* sick

person; (*paziente*) patient.
ammali'are *vt* (*fig*) to enchant, charm.
ammalia'tore, 'trice *sm/f* enchanter/
enchantress.
am'manco, chi *sm* (*ECON*) deficit.
ammanet'tare *vt* to handcuff.
ammanica'tura *sf* string-pulling.
amman'sire *vt* (*animale*) to tame; (*fig*:
persona) to calm down, placate.
amman'tarsi *vr*: ~ **di** (*persona*) to wrap
o.s. in; (*fig*: *prato etc*) to be covered in.
amma'raggio [amma'raddʒo] *sm* (sea) landing; splashdown.
amma'rare *vi* (*AER*) to make a sea landing; (*astronave*) to splash down.
ammas'sare *vt* (*ammucchiare*) to amass;
(*raccogliere*) to gather together; ~**rsi** *vr* to
pile up; to gather.
am'masso *sm* mass; (*mucchio*) pile, heap;
(*ECON*) stockpile.
ammat'tire *vi* to go mad.
ammaz'zare [ammat'tsare] *vt* to kill; ~**rsi** *vr*
(*uccidersi*) to kill o.s.; (*rimanere ucciso*) to
be killed; ~**rsi di lavoro** to work o.s. to
death.
am'menda *sf* amends *pl*; (*DIR*, *SPORT*) fine;
fare ~ **di qc** to make amends for sth.
am'messo, a *pp di* **ammettere ♦** *cong*: ~
che supposing that.
am'mettere *vt* to admit; (*riconoscere:*
fatto) to acknowledge, admit; (*permettere*)
to allow, accept; (*supporre*) to suppose;
ammettiamo che ... let us suppose that ....
ammez'zato [ammed'dzato] *sm* (*anche*: **piano**
~) entresol, mezzanine.
ammic'care *vi*: ~ **(a)** to wink (at).
amminis'trare *vt* to run, manage; (*REL*,
DIR) to administer.
amministra'tivo, a *ag* administrative.
amministra'tore *sm* administrator;
(*COMM*) director; ~ **aggiunto** associate
director; ~ **delegato** managing director;
~ **fiduciario** trustee; ~ **unico** sole director.
amministrazi'one [amministrat'tsjone] *sf*
management; administration; **consiglio**
d'~ board of directors; **l'**~ **comunale** local
government; ~ **fiduciaria** trust.
ammi'raglia [ammi'raʎʎa] *sf* flagship.
ammiragli'ato [ammiraʎ'ʎato] *sm* admiralty.
ammi'raglio [ammi'raʎʎo] *sm* admiral.
ammi'rare *vt* to admire.
ammira'tore, 'trice *sm/f* admirer.
ammirazi'one [ammirat'tsjone] *sf* admiration.
am'misi *etc vb vedi* **ammettere**.
ammis'sibile *ag* admissible, acceptable.
ammissi'one *sf* admission; (*approvazione*)
acknowledgment.
Amm.ne *abbr* = **amministrazione**.
ammobili'are *vt* to furnish.
ammoder'nare *vt* to modernize.
am'modo, a 'modo *av* properly ♦ *ag inv*
respectable, nice.

ammogli'are [ammoʎ'ʎare] *vt* to find a wife
for; ~**rsi** *vr* to marry, take a wife.
am'mollo *sm*: **lasciare in** ~ to leave to
soak.
ammo'niaca *sf* ammonia.
ammoni'mento *sm* warning; admonish-
ment.
ammo'nire *vt* (*avvertire*) to warn;
(*rimproverare*) to admonish; (*DIR*) to caution.
ammonizi'one [ammonit'tsjone] *sf* (*monito*:
anche SPORT) warning; (*rimprovero*) reprimand; (*DIR*) caution.
ammon'tare *vi*: ~ **a** to amount to ♦ *sm*
(total) amount.
ammonticchi'are [ammontik'kjare] *vt* to pile
up, heap up.
ammor'bare *vt* (*diffondere malattia*) to infect; (*sog*: *odore*) to taint, foul.
ammorbi'dente *sm* fabric softener.
ammorbi'dire *vt* to soften.
ammorta'mento *sm* redemption; amortization; ~ **fiscale** capital allowance.
ammor'tare *vt* (*FINANZA*: *debito*) to pay
off, redeem; (: *spese d'impianto*) to write
off.
ammortiz'zare [ammortid'dzare] *vt*
(*FINANZA*) to pay off, redeem; (: *spese*
d'impianto) to write off; (*AUT*, *TECN*) to
absorb, deaden.
ammortizza'tore [ammortiddza'tore] *sm*
(*AUT*, *TECN*) shock absorber.
Amm.re *abbr* = **amministratore**.
ammucchi'are [ammuk'kjare] *vt*, ~**rsi** *vr* to
pile up, accumulate.
ammuf'fire *vi* to go mouldy (*Brit*) *o* moldy
(*US*).
ammutina'mento *sm* mutiny.
ammuti'narsi *vr* to mutiny.
ammuti'nato, a *ag* mutinous ♦ *sm*
mutineer.
ammuto'lire *vi* to be struck dumb.
amne'sia *sf* amnesia.
amnis'tia *sf* amnesty.
'amo *sm* (*PESCA*) hook; (*fig*) bait.
amo'rale *ag* amoral.
a'more *sm* love; ~**i** *smpl* love affairs; **il tuo**
bambino è un ~ your baby's a darling;
fare l'~ *o* **all'**~ to make love; **andare d'**~ **e**
d'accordo con qn to get on like a house on
fire with sb; **per** ~ *o* **per forza** by hook or
by crook; **amor proprio** self-esteem, pride.
amoreggi'are [amored'dʒare] *vi* to flirt.
amo'revole *ag* loving, affectionate.
a'morfo, a *ag* amorphous; (*fig*: *persona*)
lifeless.
amo'rino *sm* cupid.
amo'roso, a *ag* (*affettuoso*) loving,
affectionate; (*d'amore: sguardo*) amorous;
(: *poesia, relazione*) love *cpd*.
am'pere [ã'pɛr] *sm inv* amp(ère).
ampi'ezza [am'pjettsa] *sf* width, breadth;

spaciousness; (*fig: importanza*) scale, size; ~ **di vedute** broad-mindedness.

'ampio, a *ag* wide, broad; (*spazioso*) spacious; (*abbondante: vestito*) loose; (*: gonna*) full; (*: spiegazione*) ample, full.

am'plesso *sm* (*sessuale*) intercourse.

amplia'mento *sm* (*di strada*) widening; (*di aeroporto*) expansion; (*fig*) broadening.

ampli'are *vt* (*allargare*) to widen; (*fig: discorso*) to enlarge on; ~**rsi** *vr* to grow, increase; ~ **la propria cultura** to broaden one's mind.

amplifi'care *vt* to amplify; (*magnificare*) to extol.

amplifica'tore *sm* (*TECN, MUS*) amplifier.

amplificazi'one [amplifikat'tsjone] *sf* amplification.

am'polla *sf* (*vasetto*) cruet.

ampol'loso, a *ag* bombastic, pompous.

ampu'tare *vt* (*MED*) to amputate.

amputazi'one [amputat'tsjone] *sf* amputation.

'Amsterdam *sf* Amsterdam.

AN *sigla* = *Ancona*.

'ANA *sigla f* (*MIL*) = *Associazione Nazionale Alpini*.

ANAAO *sigla f* (= *Associazione Nazionale Aiuti e Assistenti Ospedalieri*) *trade union for hospital workers*.

anabbagli'ante [anabbaʎ'ʎante] *ag* (*AUT*) dipped (*Brit*), dimmed (*US*); ~**i** *smpl* dipped o dimmed headlights.

anacro'nismo *sm* anachronism.

a'nagrafe *sf* (*registro*) register of births, marriages and deaths; (*ufficio*) registry office (*Brit*), office of vital statistics (*US*).

ana'grafico, a, ci, che *ag* (*AMM*): **dati** ~**ci** personal data; **comune di residenza** ~**a** district where resident.

ana'gramma, i *sm* anagram.

anal'colico, a, ci, che *ag* non-alcoholic ♦ *sm* soft drink; **bevanda** ~**a** soft drink.

analfa'beta, i, e *ag*, *sm/f* illiterate.

analfabe'tismo *sm* illiteracy.

anal'gesico, a, ci, che [anal'dʒɛziko] *ag, sm* analgesic.

a'nalisi *sf inv* analysis; (*MED: esame*) test; **in ultima** ~ in conclusion, in the final analysis; ~ **grammaticale** parsing; ~ **del sangue** blood test; ~ **dei sistemi/costi** systems/cost analysis.

ana'lista, i, e *sm/f* analyst; (*PSIC*) (psycho)analyst; ~ **finanziario** financial analyst; ~ **di sistemi** systems analyst.

ana'litico, a, ci, che *ag* analytic(al).

analiz'zare [analid'dzare] *vt* to analyse (*Brit*), analyze (*US*); (*MED*) to test.

analo'gia, 'gie [analo'dʒia] *sf* analogy.

ana'logico, a, ci, che [ana'lɔdʒiko] *ag* analogical; (*calcolatore, orologio*) analog(ue).

a'nalogo, a, ghi, ghe *ag* analogous.

'ananas *sm inv* pineapple.

anar'chia [anar'kia] *sf* anarchy.

a'narchico, a, ci, che [a'narkiko] *ag* anarchic(al) ♦ *sm/f* anarchist.

'A.N.A.S. *sigla f* (= *Azienda Nazionale Autonoma delle Strade*) *national roads department*.

ana'tema, i *sm* anathema.

anato'mia *sf* anatomy.

ana'tomico, a, ci, che *ag* anatomical; (*sedile*) contoured.

'anatra *sf* duck; ~ **selvatica** mallard.

ana'troccolo *sm* duckling.

'ANCA *sigla f* = *Associazione Nazionale Cooperative Agricole*.

'anca, che *sf* (*ANAT*) hip; (*ZOOL*) haunch.

'ANCAB *sigla f* (= *Associazione Nazionale delle Cooperative di Abitazione*) *national association of housing cooperatives*.

ANCC *sigla f* = *Associazione Nazionale Carabinieri*.

'ANCE ['antʃe] *sigla f* (= *Associazione Nazionale Costruttori Edili*) *national association of builders*.

'anche ['anke] *cong* also; (*perfino*) even; **vengo anch'io!** I'm coming too!; ~ **se** even if; ~ **volendo, non finiremmo in tempo** even if we wanted to, we wouldn't finish in time.

ancheggi'are [anked'dʒare] *vi* to wiggle (one's hips).

anchilo'sato, a [ankilo'zato] *ag* stiff.

'ANCI ['antʃi] *sigla f* (= *Associazione Nazionale dei Comuni Italiani*) *national confederation of local authorities*.

ancone'tano, a *ag* of (o from) Ancona.

an'cora *av* still; (*di nuovo*) again; (*di più*) some more; (*persino*): ~ **più forte** even stronger; **non** ~ not yet; ~ **una volta** once more, once again; ~ **un po'** a little more; (*di tempo*) a little longer.

'ancora *sf* anchor; **gettare/levare l'**~ to cast/weigh anchor; ~ **di salvezza** (*fig*) last hope.

anco'raggio [anko'raddʒo] *sm* anchorage.

anco'rare *vt*, ~**rsi** *vr* to anchor.

ANCR *sigla f* (= *Associazione Nazionale Combattenti e Reduci*) *servicemen's and ex-servicemen's association*.

Andalu'sia *sf*: l'~ Andalusia.

anda'luso, a *ag, sm/f* Andalusian.

anda'mento *sm* (*di strada, malattia*) course; (*del mercato*) state.

an'dante *ag* (*corrente*) current; (*di poco pregio*) cheap, second-rate ♦ *sm* (*MUS*) andante.

an'dare *sm*: **a lungo** ~ in the long run; **con l'andar del tempo** with the passing of time; **racconta storie a tutto** ~ she's forever talking rubbish ♦ *vi* (*gen*) to go; (*essere adatto*): ~ **a** to suit; (*piacere*): **il suo comportamento non mi va** I don't like the way he behaves; **ti va di ~ al cinema?** do you feel like going to the cinema?; **~ a cavallo** to ride; **~ in macchina/aereo** to go by car/plane; **~ a fare qc** to go and do sth; **~ a pescare/sciare** to go fishing/skiing; **andarsene** to go away; **vado e vengo** I'll be back in a minute; **~ per i 50** (*età*) to be getting on for 50; **~ a male** to go bad; **~ fiero di qc/qn** to be proud of sth/sb; **~ perduto** to be lost; **come va?** (*lavoro, progetto*) how are things?; **come va? — bene, grazie!** how are you? — fine, thanks!; **va fatto entro oggi** it's got to be done today; **ne va della nostra vita** our lives are at stake; **se non vado errato** if I'm not mistaken; **le mele vanno molto** apples are selling well; **va da sé** (*è naturale*) it goes without saying; **per questa volta vada** let's say no more about it this time.

an'data *sf* (*viaggio*) outward journey; **biglietto di sola ~** single (*Brit*) *o* one-way ticket; **biglietto di ~ e ritorno** return (*Brit*) *o* round-trip (*US*) ticket.

anda'tura *sf* (*modo di andare*) walk, gait; (*SPORT*) pace; (*NAUT*) tack.

an'dazzo [an'dattso] *sm* (*peg*): **prendere un brutto ~** to take a turn for the worse.

'Ande *sfpl*: **le ~** the Andes.

an'dino, a *ag* Andean.

andirivi'eni *sm inv* coming and going.

'andito *sm* corridor, passage.

An'dorra *sf* Andorra.

andrò *etc vb vedi* **andare**.

an'drone *sm* entrance hall.

ANDS *sigla f* (= *Associazione Nazionale Docenti Subalterni*) teachers' union.

'ANDU *sigla f* (= *Associazione Nazionale Docenti Universitari*) association of university teachers.

a'neddoto *sm* anecdote.

ane'lare *vi*: **~ a** (*fig*) to long for, yearn for.

a'nelito *sm* (*fig*): **~ di** longing *o* yearning for.

a'nello *sm* ring; (*di catena*) link.

ane'mia *sf* anaemia (*Brit*), anemia (*US*).

a'nemico, a, ci, che *ag* anaemic (*Brit*), anemic (*US*).

a'nemone *sm* anemone.

aneste'sia *sf* anaesthesia (*Brit*), anesthesia (*US*).

aneste'sista, i, e *sm/f* anaesthetist (*Brit*), anesthetist (*US*).

anes'tetico, a, ci, che *ag, sm* anaesthetic (*Brit*), anesthetic (*US*).

anestetiz'zare [anestetid'dzare] *vt* to anaesthetize (*Brit*), anesthetize (*US*).

an'fibio, a *ag* amphibious ♦ *sm* amphibious vehicle.

anfite'atro *sm* amphitheatre (*Brit*), amphitheater (*US*).

anfitri'one *sm* host.

'anfora *sf* amphora.

an'fratto *sm* ravine.

an'gelico, a, ci, che [an'dʒɛliko] *ag* angelic(al).

'angelo ['andʒelo] *sm* angel; **~ custode** guardian angel; **l'~ del focolare** (*fig*) the perfect housewife.

anghe'ria [ange'ria] *sf* vexation.

an'gina [an'dʒina] *sf* tonsillitis; **~ pectoris** angina.

angli'cano, a *ag* Anglican.

angli'cismo [angli'tʃizmo] *sm* anglicism.

an'glofilo, a *ag* anglophilic ♦ *sm/f* anglophile.

anglo'sassone *ag* Anglo-Saxon.

An'gola *sf*: **l'~** Angola.

ango'lano, a *ag, sm/f* Angolan.

ango'lare *ag* angular.

angola'tura *sf* angle.

angolazi'one [angolat'tsjone] *sf* (*di angolo*) angulation; (*FOT, CINEMA, TV, fig*) angle.

'angolo *sm* corner; (*MAT*) angle; **~ cottura** (*di appartamento etc*) cooking area; **fare ~ con** (*strada*) to run into; **dietro l'~** (*anche fig*) round the corner.

ango'loso, a *ag* (*oggetto*) angular; (*volto, corpo*) angular, bony.

an'goscia, sce [an'gɔʃʃa] *sf* deep anxiety, anguish *q*.

angosci'are [angoʃ'ʃare] *vt* to cause anguish to; **~rsi** *vr*: **~rsi (per)** (*preoccuparsi*) to become anxious (about); (*provare angoscia*) to get upset (about *o* over).

angosci'oso, a [angoʃ'ʃoso] *ag* (*d'angoscia*) anguished; (*che dà angoscia*) distressing, painful.

angu'illa *sf* eel.

an'guria *sf* watermelon.

an'gustia *sf* (*ansia*) anguish, distress; (*povertà*) poverty, want.

angusti'are *vt* to distress; **~rsi** *vr*: **~rsi (per)** to worry (about).

an'gusto, a *ag* (*stretto*) narrow; (*fig*) mean, petty.

'anice ['anitʃe] *sm* (*CUC*) aniseed; (*BOT*) anise; (*liquore*) anisette.

ani'dride *sf* (*CHIM*): **~ carbonica/solforosa** carbon/sulphur dioxide.

'anima *sf* soul; (*abitante*) inhabitant; **~ gemella** soul mate; **un'~ in pena** (*anche fig*) a tormented soul; **non c'era ~ viva** there wasn't a living soul; **volere un bene dell'~ a qn** to be extremely fond of sb; **rompere l'~ a qn** to drive sb mad; **il nonno buon'~ ...** Grandfather, God rest his soul ....

ani'male *sm, ag* animal.

anima'lesco, a, schi, sche *ag* (*gesto, atteggiamento*) animal-like.

ani'mare *vt* to give life to, liven up; (*incoraggiare*) to encourage; **~rsi** *vr* to become animated, come to life.

ani'mato, a *ag* animate; (*vivace*) lively, animated; (: *strada*) busy.

anima'tore, 'trice *sm/f* guiding spirit; (*CINEMA*) animator; (*di festa*) life and soul.

animazi'one [animat'tsjone] *sf* liveliness; (*di strada*) bustle; (*CINEMA*) animation; ~ **teatrale** amateur dramatics.

'animo *sm* (*mente*) mind; (*cuore*) heart; (*coraggio*) courage; (*disposizione*) character, disposition; **avere in** ~ **di fare qc** to intend *o* have a mind to do sth; **farsi** ~ to pluck up courage; **fare qc di buon/mal** ~ to do sth willingly/unwillingly; **perdersi d'**~ to lose heart.

animosità *sf* animosity.

A'NITA *sigla f* = *Associazione Nazionale dell'Industria dei Trasporti Automobilistici*; *Associazione Naturista Italiana*.

'anitra *sf* = **anatra**.

'Ankara *sf* Ankara.

ANM *sigla f* (= *Associazione Nazionale dei Magistrati*) *national association of magistrates*.

ANMI *sigla f* (= *Associazione Nazionale Marinai d'Italia*) *national association of seamen*.

ANMIG *sigla f* (= *Associazione Nazionale fra Mutilati e Invalidi di Guerra*) *national association for disabled ex-servicemen*.

anna'cquare *vt* to water down, dilute.

annaffi'are *vt* to water.

annaffia'toio *sm* watering can.

an'nali *smpl* annals.

annas'pare *vi* (*nell'acqua*) to flounder; (*fig*: *nel buio, nell'incertezza*) to grope.

an'nata *sf* year; (*importo annuo*) annual amount; **vino di** ~ vintage wine.

annebbi'are *vt* (*fig*) to cloud; **~rsi** *vr* to become foggy; (*vista*) to become dim.

annega'mento *sm* drowning.

anne'gare *vt, vi* to drown; **~rsi** *vr* (*accidentalmente*) to drown; (*deliberatamente*) to drown o.s.

anne'rire *vt* to blacken ♦ *vi* to become black.

annessi'one *sf* (*POL*) annexation.

an'nesso, a *pp di* **annettere** ♦ *ag* attached; (*POL*) annexed; ... **e tutti gli** ~**i e connessi** ... and so on and so forth.

an'nettere *vt* (*POL*) to annex; (*accludere*) to attach.

annichi'lare, annichi'lire [anniki'lare, anniki'lire] *vt* to annihilate.

anni'darsi *vr* to nest.

annienta'mento *sm* annihilation, destruction.

annien'tare *vt* to annihilate, destroy.

anniver'sario *sm* anniversary.

'anno *sm* year; **quanti** ~**i hai?** — **ho 40** ~**i** how old are you? — I'm 40 (years old); **gli** ~**i 20** the 20s; **porta bene gli** ~**i** she

doesn't look her age; **porta male gli** ~**i** she looks older than she is; ~ **commerciale** business year; ~ **giudiziario** legal year; ~ **luce** light year; **gli** ~**i di piombo** *the Seventies in Italy, characterized by terrorist attacks and killings*.

anno'dare *vt* to knot, tie; (*fig*: *rapporto*) to form.

annoi'are *vt* to bore; (*seccare*) to annoy; **~rsi** *vr* to be bored; to be annoyed.

an'noso, a *ag* (*albero*) old; (*fig*: *problema etc*) age-old.

anno'tare *vt* (*registrare*) to note, note down (*Brit*); (*commentare*) to annotate.

annotazi'one [annotat'tsjone] *sf* note; annotation.

annove'rare *vt* to number.

annu'ale *ag* annual.

annual'mente *av* annually, yearly.

annu'ario *sm* yearbook.

annu'ire *vi* to nod; (*acconsentire*) to agree.

annulla'mento *sm* annihilation, destruction; cancellation; annulment; quashing.

annul'lare *vt* to annihilate, destroy; (*contratto, francobollo*) to cancel; (*matrimonio*) to annul; (*sentenza*) to quash; (*risultati*) to declare void.

an'nullo *sm* (*AMM*) cancelling.

annunci'are [annun'tʃare] *vt* to announce; (*dar segni rivelatori*) to herald.

annuncia'tore, 'trice [annuntʃa'tore] *sm/f* (*RADIO, TV*) announcer.

Annunciazi'one [annuntʃat'tsjone] *sf* (*REL*): **l'**~ the Annunciation.

an'nuncio [an'nuntʃo] *sm* announcement; (*fig*) sign; ~ **pubblicitario** advertisement; ~**i economici** classified advertisements, small ads; **piccoli** ~**i** small ads, classified ads; ~**i mortuari** (*colonna*) obituary column.

'annuo, a *ag* annual, yearly.

annu'sare *vt* to sniff, smell; ~ **tabacco** to take snuff.

annuvola'mento *sm* clouding (over).

annuvo'lare *vt* to cloud; **~rsi** *vr* to become cloudy, cloud over.

'ano *sm* anus.

'anodo *sm* anode.

anoma'lia *sf* anomaly.

a'nomalo, a *ag* anomalous.

anoni'mato *sm* anonymity; **conservare l'**~ to remain anonymous.

a'nonimo, a *ag* anonymous ♦ *sm* (*autore*) anonymous writer (*o* painter *etc*); **un tipo** ~ (*peg*) a colourless (*Brit*) *o* colorless (*US*) character.

anor'male *ag* abnormal ♦ *sm/f* subnormal person; (*eufemismo*) homosexual.

anormalità *sf inv* abnormality.

'ANSA *sigla f* (= *Agenzia Nazionale Stampa Associata*) *national press agency*.

'ansa *sf* (*manico*) handle; (*di fiume*) bend,

loop.

an'sante *ag* out of breath, panting.

'ANSEA *sigla f* (= *Associazione delle Nazioni del Sud-Est asiatico*) ASEAN.

'ansia *sf* anxiety; **stare in ~ (per qn/qc)** to be anxious (about sb/sth).

ansietà *sf* anxiety.

ansi'mare *vi* to pant.

ansi'oso, a *ag* anxious.

'anta *sf* (*di finestra*) shutter; (*di armadio*) door.

antago'nismo *sm* antagonism.

antago'nista, i, e *sm/f* antagonist.

an'tartico, a, ci, che *ag* Antarctic ♦ *sm*: **l'A~** the Antarctic.

An'tartide *sf*: **l'~** Antarctica.

ante'bellico, a, ci, che *ag* prewar *cpd*.

antece'dente [antetʃe'dɛnte] *ag* preceding, previous.

ante'fatto *sm* previous events *pl*; previous history.

antegu'erra *sm* pre-war period.

ante'nato *sm* ancestor, forefather.

an'tenna *sf* (*RADIO, TV*) aerial; (*ZOOL*) antenna, feeler; **rizzare le ~e** (*fig*) to prick up one's ears.

ante'porre *vt*: **~ qc a qc** to place *o* put sth before sth.

ante'posto, a *pp di* **anteporre**.

ante'prima *sf* preview.

anteri'ore *ag* (*ruota, zampa*) front *cpd*; (*fatti*) previous, preceding.

antesi'gnano [antesiɲ'ɲano] *sm* (*STORIA*) standard-bearer; (*fig*) forerunner.

antia'ereo, a *ag* anti-aircraft *cpd*.

antia'tomico, a, ci, che *ag* anti-nuclear; **rifugio ~** fallout shelter.

antibi'otico, a, ci, che *ag, sm* antibiotic.

anti'caglia [anti'kaʎʎa] *sf* junk *q*.

anti'camera *sf* anteroom; **fare ~** to be kept waiting; **non mi passerebbe neanche per l'~ del cervello** it wouldn't even cross my mind.

anti'carie *ag inv* which fights tooth decay.

antichità [antiki'ta] *sf inv* antiquity; (*oggetto*) antique.

antici'clone [antitʃi'klone] *sm* anticyclone.

antici'pare [antitʃi'pare] *vt* (*consegna, visita*) to bring forward, anticipate; (*somma di denaro*) to pay in advance; (*notizia*) to disclose ♦ *vi* to be ahead of time.

antici'pato, a [antitʃi'pato] *ag* (*prima del previsto*) early; **pagamento ~** payment in advance.

anticipazi'one [antitʃipat'tsjone] *sf* anticipation; (*di notizia*) advance information; (*somma di denaro*) advance.

an'ticipo [an'titʃipo] *sm* anticipation; (*di denaro*) advance; **in ~** early, in advance; **con un sensibile ~** well in advance.

an'tico, a, chi, che *ag* (*quadro, mobili*) antique; (*dell'antichità*) ancient; **all'~a** old-fashioned.

anticoncezio'nale [antikontʃettsjo'nale] *sm* contraceptive.

anticonfor'mista, i, e *ag, sm/f* nonconformist.

anticonge'lante [antikondʒe'lante] *ag, sm* antifreeze.

anticongiuntu'rale [antikondʒuntu'rale] *ag* (*ECON*): **misure ~i** measures to remedy the economic situation.

anti'corpo *sm* antibody.

anticostituzio'nale [antikostituttsjo'nale] *ag* unconstitutional.

anti'doping *sm inv* (*SPORT*) dope test.

an'tidoto *sm* antidote.

anti'droga *ag inv* anti-drugs *cpd*.

antie'stetico, a, ci, che *ag* unsightly.

an'tifona *sf* (*MUS, REL*) antiphon; **capire l'~** (*fig*) to take the hint.

anti'furto *sm* anti-theft device.

anti'gelo [anti'dʒɛlo] *ag inv* antifreeze *cpd* ♦ *sm* (*per motore*) antifreeze; (*per cristalli*) de-icer.

antigi'enico, a, ci, che [anti'dʒɛniko] *ag* unhygienic.

An'tille *sfpl*: **le ~** the West Indies.

an'tilope *sf* antelope.

anti'mafia *ag inv* anti-mafia *cpd*.

antin'cendio [antin'tʃendjo] *ag inv* fire *cpd*; **bombola ~** fire extinguisher.

anti'nebbia *sm inv* (*anche:* **faro ~**: *AUT*) fog lamp.

antine'vralgico, a, ci, che [antine'vraldʒiko] *ag* painkilling ♦ *sm* painkiller.

antio'rario *ag*: **in senso ~** in an anticlockwise (*Brit*) *o* counterclockwise (*US*) direction, anticlockwise, counterclockwise.

anti'pasto *sm* hors d'œuvre.

antipa'tia *sf* antipathy, dislike.

anti'patico, a, ci, che *ag* unpleasant, disagreeable.

An'tipodi *smpl*: **gli ~** the Antipodes; **essere agli a~** (*fig*) to be poles apart.

antiquari'ato *sm* antique trade; **un pezzo d'~** an antique.

anti'quario *sm* antique dealer.

anti'quato, a *ag* antiquated, old-fashioned.

antiri'flesso *ag inv* (*schermo*) non-glare *cpd*.

anti'ruggine [anti'ruddʒine] *ag* anti-rust *cpd* ♦ *sm inv* rust-preventer.

antise'mita, i, e *ag* anti-semitic.

antisemi'tismo *sm* anti-semitism.

anti'settico, a, ci, che *ag, sm* antiseptic.

antista'minico, a, ci, che *ag, sm* antihistamine.

anti'stante *ag* opposite.

antiterro'rismo *sm* anti-terrorist measures *pl*.

an'titesi *sf* antithesis.

antolo'gia, 'gie [antolo'dʒia] *sf* anthology.

antono'masia *sf* antonomasia; **per ~** par excellence.

'antro *sm* cavern.

antro'pofago, gi *sm* cannibal.

antropolo'gia [antropolo'dʒia] *sf* anthropology.

antropo'logico, a, ci, che [antropo'lɔdʒiko] *ag* anthropological.

antro'pologo, a, gi, ghe *sm/f* anthropologist.

anu'lare *ag* ring *cpd* ♦ *sm* ring finger.

An'versa *sf* Antwerp.

'anzi ['antsi] *av* (*invece*) on the contrary; (*o meglio*) or rather, or better still.

anzianità [antsjani'ta] *sf* old age; (*AMM*) seniority.

anzi'ano, a [an'tsjano] *ag* old; (*AMM*) senior ♦ *sm/f* old person; senior member.

anziché [antsi'ke] *cong* rather than.

anzi'tempo [antsi'tɛmpo] *av* (*in anticipo*) early.

anzi'tutto [antsi'tutto] *av* first of all.

AO *sigla* = *Aosta*.

aos'tano, a *ag* of (*o* from) Aosta.

AP *sigla* = *Ascoli Piceno*.

a'partheid [a'partheit] *sm* apartheid.

apar'titico, a, ci, che *ag* (*POL*) non-party *cpd*.

apa'tia *sf* apathy, indifference.

a'patico, a, ci, che *ag* apathetic, indifferent.

a.p.c. *abbr* = **a pronta cassa**.

'ape *sf* bee.

aperi'tivo *sm* aperitif.

aperta'mente *av* openly.

a'perto, a *pp di* aprire ♦ *ag* open ♦ *sm*: **all'~** in the open (air); **rimanere a bocca ~a** (*fig*) to be taken aback.

aper'tura *sf* opening; (*ampiezza*) width, spread; (*POL*) approach; (*FOT*) aperture; **~ alare** wing span; **~ mentale** open-mindedness; **~ di credito** (*COMM*) granting of credit.

API *sigla f* = *Associazione Piccole e Medie Industrie*.

'apice ['apitʃe] *sm* apex; (*fig*) height.

apicol'tore *sm* beekeeper.

apicol'tura *sf* beekeeping.

ap'nea *sf*: **immergersi in ~** to dive without breathing apparatus.

apoca'lisse *sf* apocalypse.

a'polide *ag* stateless.

apo'litico, a, ci, che *ag* (*neutrale*) non-political; (*indifferente*) apolitical.

apoples'sia *sf* (*MED*) apoplexy.

a'postolo *sm* apostle.

apostro'fare *vt* (*parola*) to write with an apostrophe; (*persona*) to address.

a'postrofo *sm* apostrophe.

app. *abbr* (= *appendice*) app.

appaga'mento *sm* satisfaction; fulfilment.

appa'gare *vt* to satisfy; (*desiderio*) to fulfil; **~rsi** *vr*: **~rsi di** to be satisfied with.

appai'are *vt* to couple, pair.

ap'paio *etc vb vedi* **apparire**.

Appa'lachi [appa'laki] *smpl*: **i Monti ~** the Appalachian Mountains.

appallotto'lare *vt* (*carta, foglio*) to screw into a ball; **~rsi** *vr* (*gatto*) to roll up into a ball.

appalta'tore *sm* contractor.

ap'palto *sm* (*COMM*) contract; **dare/prendere in ~ un lavoro** to let out/undertake a job on contract.

appan'naggio [appan'naddʒo] *sm* (*compenso*) annuity; (*fig*) privilege, prerogative.

appan'nare *vt* (*vetro*) to mist; (*metallo*) to tarnish; (*vista*) to dim; **~rsi** *vr* to mist over; to tarnish; to grow dim.

appa'rato *sm* equipment, machinery; (*ANAT*) apparatus; **~ scenico** (*TEATRO*) props *pl*.

apparecchi'are [apparek'kjare] *vt* to prepare; (*tavola*) to set ♦ *vi* to set the table.

apparecchia'tura [apparekkja'tura] *sf* equipment; (*macchina*) machine, device.

appa'recchio [appa'rekkjo] *sm* piece of apparatus, device; (*aeroplano*) aircraft *inv*; **~i sanitari** bathroom *o* sanitary appliances; **~ televisivo/telefonico** television set/telephone.

appa'rente *ag* apparent.

apparente'mente *av* apparently.

appa'renza [appa'rɛntsa] *sf* appearance; **in** *o* **all'~** apparently, to all appearances.

appa'rire *vi* to appear; (*sembrare*) to seem, appear.

appari'scente [appariʃ'ʃɛnte] *ag* (*colore*) garish, gaudy; (*bellezza*) striking.

apparizi'one [apparit'tsjone] *sf* apparition.

ap'parso, a *pp di* **apparire**.

apparta'mento *sm* flat (*Brit*), apartment (*US*).

appar'tarsi *vr* to withdraw.

appar'tato, a *ag* (*luogo*) secluded.

apparte'nenza [apparte'nɛntsa] *sf*: **~ (a)** (*gen*) belonging (to); (*a un partito, club*) membership (of).

apparte'nere *vi*: **~ a** to belong to.

ap'parvi *etc vb vedi* **apparire**.

appassio'nante *ag* thrilling, exciting.

appassio'nare *vt* to thrill; (*commuovere*) to move; **~rsi** *vr*: **~rsi a qc** to take a great interest in sth; to be deeply moved by sth.

appassio'nato, a *ag* passionate; (*entusiasta*): **~ (di)** keen (on).

appas'sire *vi* to wither.

appel'larsi *vr* (*ricorrere*): **~ a** to appeal to; (*DIR*): **~ contro** to appeal against.

ap'pello *sm* roll-call; (*implorazione, DIR*) appeal; (*sessione d'esame*) exam session; **fare ~ a** to appeal to; **fare l'~** (*INS*) to call the register *o* roll; (*MIL*) to call the roll.

ap'pena *av* (*a stento*) hardly, scarcely; (*solamente, da poco*) just ♦ *cong* as soon as; **(non) ~ furono arrivati ...** as soon as they had arrived ...; ~ ... **che** o **quando** no sooner ... than.

ap'pendere vt to hang (up).

appendi'abiti sm inv hook, peg; (mobile) hall stand (Brit), hall tree (US).

appen'dice [appen'ditʃe] sf appendix; **romanzo d'~** popular serial.

appendi'cite [appendi'tʃite] sf appendicitis.

Appen'nini smpl: **gli ~** the Apennines.

appesan'tire vt to make heavy; **~rsi** vr to grow stout.

ap'peso, a pp di **appendere**.

appe'tito sm appetite.

appeti'toso, a ag appetising; (fig) attractive, desirable.

appezza'mento [appettsa'mento] sm (anche: ~ **di terreno**) plot, piece of ground.

appia'nare vt to level; (fig) to smooth away, iron out; **~rsi** vr (divergenze) to be ironed out.

appiat'tire vt to flatten; **~rsi** vr to become flatter; (farsi piatto) to flatten o.s.; **~rsi al suolo** to lie flat on the ground.

appic'care vt: ~ **il fuoco a** to set fire to, set on fire.

appicci'care [appittʃi'kare] vt to stick; (fig): ~ **qc a qn** to palm sth off on sb; **~rsi** vr to stick; (fig: persona) to cling.

appiccica'ticcio, a, ci, ce [appittʃika'tittʃo] ag, **appicci'coso, a** [appittʃi'koso] ag sticky; (fig: persona): **essere ~** to cling like a leech.

appie'dato, a ag: **rimanere ~** to be left without means of transport.

appi'eno av fully.

appigli'arsi [appiʎ'ʎarsi] vr: ~ **a** (afferrarsi) to take hold of; (fig) to cling to.

ap'piglio [ap'piʎʎo] sm hold; (fig) pretext.

appiop'pare vt: ~ **qc a qn** (nomignolo) to pin sth on sb; (compito difficile) to saddle sb with sth; **gli ha appioppato un pugno sul muso** he punched him in the face.

appiso'larsi vr to doze off.

applau'dire vt, vi to applaud.

ap'plauso sm applause no pl.

appli'cabile ag: ~ **(a)** applicable (to).

appli'care vt to apply; (regolamento) to enforce; **~rsi** vr to apply o.s.

appli'cato, a ag (arte, scienze) applied ◆ sm (AMM) clerk.

applicazi'one [applikat'tsjone] sf application; enforcement; **~i tecniche** (INS) practical subjects.

appoggi'are [appod'dʒare] vt (mettere contro): ~ **qc a qc** to lean o rest sth against sth; (fig: sostenere) to support; **~rsi** vr: **~rsi a** to lean against; (fig) to rely upon.

ap'poggio [ap'pɔddʒo] sm support.

appollai'arsi vr (anche fig) to perch.

ap'pongo, ap'poni etc vb vedi **apporre**.

ap'porre vt to affix.

appor'tare vt to bring.

ap'porto sm (gen, FINANZA) contribution.

ap'posi etc vb vedi **apporre**.

apposita'mente av (apposta) on purpose; (specialmente) specially.

ap'posito, a ag appropriate.

ap'posta av on purpose, deliberately; **neanche a farlo ~**, ... by sheer coincidence, ...

appos'tare vt to lie in wait for; **~rsi** vr to lie in wait.

ap'posto, a pp di **apporre**.

ap'prendere vt (imparare) to learn; (comprendere) to grasp.

apprendi'mento sm learning.

appren'dista, i, e sm/f apprentice.

apprendi'stato sm apprenticeship.

apprensi'one sf apprehension.

appren'sivo, a ag apprehensive.

ap'preso, a pp di **apprendere**.

ap'presso av (accanto, vicino) close by, near; (dietro) behind; (dopo, più tardi) after, later ◆ ag inv (dopo): **il giorno ~** the next day; ~ **a** prep (vicino a) near, close to.

appres'tare vt to prepare, get ready; **~rsi** vr: **~rsi a fare qc** to prepare o get ready to do sth.

ap'pretto sm starch.

apprez'zabile [appret'tsabile] ag (notevole) noteworthy, significant; (percepibile) appreciable.

apprezza'mento [apprettsa'mento] sm appreciation; (giudizio) opinion; (commento) comment.

apprez'zare [appret'tsare] vt to appreciate.

ap'proccio [ap'prɔttʃo] sm approach.

appro'dare vi (NAUT) to land; (fig): **non ~ a nulla** to come to nothing.

ap'prodo sm landing; (luogo) landing-place.

approfit'tare vi: ~ **di** (persona, situazione) to take advantage of; (occasione, opportunità) to make the most of, profit by.

approfon'dire vt to deepen; (fig) to study in depth; **~rsi** vr (gen, fig) to deepen; (peggiorare) to get worse.

appron'tare vt to prepare, get ready.

appropri'arsi vr: ~ **di qc** to appropriate sth, take possession of sth; ~ **indebitamente di** to embezzle.

appropri'ato, a ag appropriate.

appropriazi'one [approprjat'tsjone] sf appropriation; ~ **indebita** (DIR) embezzlement.

approssi'mare vt (cifra): ~ **per eccesso/per difetto** to round up/down; **~rsi** vr: **~rsi a** to approach, draw near.

approssima'tivo, a ag approximate, rough; (impreciso) inexact, imprecise.

approssimazi'one [approssimat'tsjone] sf approximation; **per ~** approximately, roughly.

appro'vare vt (condotta, azione) to approve

of; (*candidato*) to pass; (*progetto di legge*) to approve.

approvazi'one [approvat'tsjone] *sf* approval.

approvvigiona'mento [approvvidʒona'mento] *sm* supplying; stocking up; ~**i** *smpl* (*MIL*) supplies.

approvvigio'nare [approvvidʒo'nare] *vt* to supply; ~**rsi** *vr* to lay in provisions, stock up; ~ **qn di qc** to supply sb with sth.

appunta'mento *sm* appointment; (*amoroso*) date; **darsi** ~ to arrange to meet (one another).

appun'tare *vt* (*rendere aguzzo*) to sharpen; (*fissare*) to pin, fix; (*annotare*) to note down.

appun'tato *sm* (*CARABINIERI*) corporal.

appun'tino *av* perfectly.

appun'tire *vt* to sharpen.

ap'punto *sm* note; (*rimprovero*) reproach ♦ *av* (*proprio*) exactly, just; **per l'**~**!**, ~**!** exactly!

appu'rare *vt* to check, verify.

apr. *abbr* (= *aprile*) Apr.

apribot'tiglie [apribot'tiλλe] *sm inv* bottleopener.

a'prile *sm* April; **pesce d'**~**!** April Fool!; *per fraseologia vedi* **luglio**.

a'prire *vt* to open; (*via, cadavere*) to open up; (*gas, luce, acqua*) to turn on ♦ *vi* to open; ~**rsi** *vr* to open; ~ **le ostilità** (*MIL*) to start up *o* begin hostilities; ~ **una sessione** (*INFORM*) to log on; ~**rsi a qn** to confide in sb, open one's heart to sb; **mi si è aperto lo stomaco** I feel rather peckish; **apriti cielo!** heaven forbid!

apris'catole *sm inv* tin (*Brit*) *o* can opener.

APT *sigla f* (= *Azienda di Promozione Turistica*) = tourist board.

AQ *sigla* = *Aquila*.

a'quario *sm* = **acquario**.

'aquila *sf* (*ZOOL*) eagle; (*fig*) genius.

aqui'lone *sm* (*giocattolo*) kite; (*vento*) North wind.

AR *sigla* = *Arezzo*.

A'rabia Sau'dita *sf*: **l'**~ Saudi Arabia.

a'rabico, a, ci, che *ag*: **il Deserto** ~ the Arabian Desert.

a'rabile *ag* arable.

'arabo, a *ag*, *sm/f* Arab ♦ *sm* (*LING*) Arabic; **parlare** ~ (*fig*) to speak double Dutch (*Brit*).

a'rachide [a'rakide] *sf* peanut.

ara'gosta *sf* spiny lobster.

a'raldica *sf* heraldry.

a'raldo *sm* herald.

aran'ceto [aran'tʃeto] *sm* orange grove.

a'rancia, ce [a'rantʃa] *sf* orange.

aranci'ata [aran'tʃata] *sf* orangeade.

a'rancio [a'rantʃo] *sm* (*BOT*) orange tree; (*colore*) orange ♦ *ag inv* (*colore*) orange; **fiori di** ~ orange blossom *sg*.

aranci'one [aran'tʃone] *ag inv*: (**color**) ~

bright orange.

a'rare *vt* to plough (*Brit*), plow (*US*).

ara'tore *sm* ploughman (*Brit*), plowman (*US*).

a'ratro *sm* plough (*Brit*), plow (*US*).

ara'tura *sf* ploughing (*Brit*), plowing (*US*).

a'razzo [a'rattso] *sm* tapestry.

arbi'traggio [arbi'traddʒo] *sm* (*SPORT*) refereeing; umpiring; (*DIR*) arbitration; (*COMM*) arbitrage.

arbi'trare *vt* (*SPORT*) to referee; to umpire; (*DIR*) to arbitrate.

arbi'trario, a *ag* arbitrary.

arbi'trato *sm* arbitration.

ar'bitrio *sm* will; (*abuso, sopruso*) arbitrary act.

'arbitro *sm* arbiter, judge; (*DIR*) arbitrator; (*SPORT*) referee; (*: TENNIS, CRICKET*) umpire.

arbo'scello [arboʃ'ʃɛllo] *sm* sapling.

ar'busto *sm* shrub.

'arca, che *sf* (*sarcofago*) sarcophagus; **l'**~ **di Noè** Noah's ark.

ar'caico, a, ci, che *ag* archaic.

ar'cangelo [ar'kandʒelo] *sm* archangel.

ar'cano, a *ag* arcane, mysterious ♦ *sm* mystery.

ar'cata *sf* (*ARCHIT, ANAT*) arch; (*ordine di archi*) arcade.

archeolo'gia [arkeolo'dʒia] *sf* arch(a)eology.

archeo'logico, a, ci, che [arkeo'lɔdʒiko] *ag* arch(a)eological.

archeologo, a, gi, ghe [arke'ɔlogo] *sm/f* arch(a)eologist.

ar'chetipo [ar'kɛtipo] *sm* archetype.

ar'chetto [ar'ketto] *sm* (*MUS*) bow.

architet'tare [arkitet'tare] *vt* (*fig: ideare*) to devise; (*: macchinare*) to plan, concoct.

archi'tetto [arki'tetto] *sm* architect.

architet'tonico, a, ci, che [arkitet'tɔniko] *ag* architectural.

architet'tura [arkitet'tura] *sf* architecture.

archivi'are [arki'vjare] *vt* (*documenti*) to file; (*DIR*) to dismiss.

archiviazi'one [arkivjat'tsjone] *sf* filing; dismissal.

ar'chivio [ar'kivjo] *sm* archives *pl*; (*INFORM*) file; ~ **principale** (*INFORM*) master file.

archi'vista, i, e [arki'vista] *sm/f* (*AMM*) archivist; (*in ufficio*) filing clerk.

'ARCI ['artʃi] *sigla f* (= *Associazione Ricreativa Culturale Italiana*) *cultural society*.

arci'ere [ar'tʃɛre] *sm* archer.

ar'cigno, a [ar'tʃiɲɲo] *ag* grim, severe.

arci'one [ar'tʃone] *sm* saddlebow.

Arcip. *abbr* = **arcipelago**.

arci'pelago, ghi [artʃi'pelago] *sm* archipelago.

arci'vescovo [artʃi'veskovo] *sm* archbishop.

'arco, chi *sm* (*arma, MUS*) bow; (*ARCHIT*) arch; (*MAT*) arc; **nell'**~ **di 3 settimane** within the space of 3 weeks; ~ **co-**

stituzionale *political parties involved in formulating Italy's post-war constitution.*

arcoba'leno *sm* rainbow.

arcu'ato, a *ag* curved, bent; **dalle gambe** ~e bow-legged.

ar'dente *ag* burning; (*fig*) burning, ardent.

'ardere *vt, vi* to burn; **legna da** ~ firewood.

ar'desia *sf* slate.

ardi'mento *sm* daring.

ar'dire *vi* to dare ♦ *sm* daring.

ar'dito, a *ag* brave, daring, bold; (*sfacciato*) bold.

ar'dore *sm* blazing heat; (*fig*) ardour, fervour.

'arduo, a *ag* arduous, difficult.

'area *sf* area; (*EDIL*) land, ground; **nell'~ dei partiti di sinistra** among the parties of the left; ~ **fabbricabile** building land; ~ **di rigore** (*SPORT*) penalty area; ~ **di servizio** (*AUT*) service area.

a'rena *sf* arena; (*per corride*) bullring; (*sabbia*) sand.

are'naria *sf* sandstone.

are'narsi *vr* to run aground; (*fig: trattative*) to come to a standstill.

areo'plano *sm* = **aeroplano.**

are'tino, a *ag* of (*o* from) Arezzo.

'argano *sm* winch.

argen'tato, a [ardʒen'tato] *ag* silver-plated; (*colore*) silver, silvery; (*capelli*) silver(-grey).

ar'genteo, a [ar'dʒenteo] *ag* silver, silvery.

argente'ria [ardʒente'ria] *sf* silverware, silver.

argenti'ere [ardʒen'tjere] *sm* silversmith.

Argen'tina [ardʒen'tina] *sf:* **l'~** Argentina.

argen'tino, a [ardʒen'tino] *ag, sm/f* (*dell'Argentina*) Argentinian ♦ *sf* crewneck sweater.

ar'gento [ar'dʒento] *sm* silver; ~ **vivo** quicksilver; **avere l'~ (vivo) addosso** (*fig*) to be fidgety.

ar'gilla [ar'dʒilla] *sf* clay.

argi'nare [ardʒi'nare] *vt* (*fiume, acque*) to embank; (*: con diga*) to dyke up; (*fig: inflazione, corruzione*) to check; (*: spese*) to limit.

'argine ['ardʒine] *sm* embankment, bank; (*diga*) dyke, dike; **far** ~ **a, porre un** ~ **a** (*fig*) to check, hold back.

argomen'tare *vi* to argue.

argo'mento *sm* argument; (*materia, tema*) subject; **tornare sull'~** to bring the matter up again.

argu'ire *vt* to deduce.

ar'guto, a *ag* sharp, quick-witted; (*spiritoso*) witty.

ar'guzia [ar'guttsja] *sf* wit; (*battuta*) witty remark.

'aria *sf* air; (*espressione, aspetto*) air, look; (*MUS: melodia*) tune; (*: di opera*) aria; **all'~ aperta** in the open (air); **manca l'~**

it's stuffy; **andare all'~** (*piano, progetto*) to come to nothing; **mandare all'~ qc** to ruin *o* upset sth; **darsi delle ~e** to put on airs and graces; **ha la testa per** ~ his head is in the clouds; **che** ~ **tira?** (*fig: atmosfera*) what's the atmosphere like?

aridità *sf* aridity, dryness; (*fig*) lack of feeling.

'arido, a *ag* arid.

arieggi'are [arjed'dʒare] *vt* (*cambiare aria*) to air; (*imitare*) to imitate.

ari'ete *sm* ram; (*MIL*) battering ram; (*dello zodiaco*): **A~** Aries; **essere dell'A~** to be Aries.

a'ringa, ghe *sf* herring *inv*; ~ **affumicata** smoked herring, kipper; ~ **marinata** pickled herring.

'arista *sf* (*CUC*) chine of pork.

aristo'cratico, a, ci, che *ag* aristocratic.

aristocra'zia [aristokrat'tsia] *sf* aristocracy.

arit'metica *sf* arithmetic.

arlec'chino [arlek'kino] *sm* harlequin.

'arma, i *sf* weapon, arm; (*parte dell'esercito*) arm; **alle** ~**i!** to arms!; **chiamare alle** ~**i** to call up (*Brit*), draft (*US*); **sotto le** ~**i** in the army (*o* forces); **combattere ad** ~**i pari** (*anche fig*) to fight on equal terms; **essere alle prime** ~**i** (*fig*) to be a novice; **passare qn per le** ~**i** to execute sb; **battersi all'~ bianca** to fight with blades; ~ **a doppio taglio** (*anche fig*) double-edged weapon; ~ **da fuoco** firearm.

ar'madio *sm* cupboard; (*per abiti*) wardrobe; ~ **a muro** built-in cupboard.

armamen'tario *sm* equipment, instruments *pl.*

arma'mento *sm* (*MIL*) armament; (*: materiale*) arms *pl*, weapons *pl*; (*NAUT*) fitting out; manning; **la corsa agli** ~**i** the arms race.

ar'mare *vt* to arm; (*arma da fuoco*) to cock; (*NAUT: nave*) to rig, fit out; to man; (*EDIL: volta, galleria*) to prop up, shore up; ~**rsi** *vr* to arm o.s.; (*MIL*) to take up arms.

ar'mato, a *ag:* ~ (**di**) (*anche fig*) armed (with) ♦ *sf* (*MIL*) army; (*NAUT*) fleet; **rapina a mano** ~**a** armed robbery.

arma'tore *sm* shipowner.

arma'tura *sf* (*struttura di sostegno*) framework; (*impalcatura*) scaffolding; (*STORIA*) armour *q* (*Brit*), armor *q* (*US*), suit of armo(u)r.

armeggi'are [armed'dʒare] *vi* (*affaccendarsi*): ~ (**intorno a qc**) to mess about (with sth).

Ar'menia *sf:* **l'~** Armenia.

ar'meno, a *ag, sm/f, sm* Armenian.

arme'ria *sf* (*deposito*) armoury (*Brit*), armory (*US*); (*collezione*) collection of arms.

armis'tizio [armis'tittsjo] *sm* armistice.

armo'nia *sf* harmony.

ar'monico, a, ci, che *ag* harmonic; (*fig*)

harmonious ♦ *sf* (*MUS*) harmonica; ~a a
bocca mouth organ.
armoni'oso, a *ag* harmonious.
armoniz'zare [armonid'dzare] *vt* to
harmonize; (*colori, abiti*) to match ♦ *vi* to
be in harmony; to match.
ar'nese *sm* tool, implement; (*oggetto in-
determinato*) thing, contraption; **male in** ~
(*malvestito*) badly dressed; (*di salute mal-
ferma*) in poor health; (*di condizioni
economiche*) down-at-heel.
'arnia *sf* hive.
a'roma, i *sm* aroma; fragrance; ~i *smpl*
herbs and spices; ~i **naturali/artificiali**
natural/artificial flavouring *sg* (*Brit*) o
flavoring *sg* (*US*).
aro'matico, a, ci, che *ag* aromatic; (*cibo*)
spicy.
aromatiz'zare [aromatid'dzare] *vt* to season,
flavour (*Brit*), flavor (*US*).
'arpa *sf* (*MUS*) harp.
ar'peggio [ar'pedd3o] *sm* (*MUS*) arpeggio.
ar'pia *sf* (*anche fig*) harpy.
arpi'one *sm* (*gancio*) hook; (*cardine*) hinge;
(*PESCA*) harpoon.
arrabat'tarsi *vr* to do all one can, strive.
arrabbi'are *vi* (*cane*) to be affected with
rabies; ~rsi *vr* (*essere preso dall'ira*) to get
angry, fly into a rage.
arrabbi'ato, a *ag* (*cane*) rabid, with rabies;
(*persona*) furious, angry.
arrabbia'tura *sf*: **prendersi un'**~ (**per qc**) to
become furious (over sth).
arraf'fare *vt* to snatch, seize; (*sottrarre*) to
pinch.
arrampi'carsi *vr* to climb (up); ~ **sui vetri**
o **sugli specchi** (*fig*) to clutch at straws.
arrampi'cata *sf* climb.
arrampica'tore, 'trice *sm/f* (*gen, SPORT*)
climber; ~ **sociale** (*fig*) social climber.
arran'care *vi* to limp, hobble; (*fig*) to
struggle along.
arran'giare [arran'd3are] *vt* to arrange; ~rsi
vr to manage, do the best one can.
arre'care *vt* to bring; (*causare*) to cause.
arreda'mento *sm* (*studio*) interior design;
(*mobili etc*) furnishings *pl*.
arre'dare *vt* to furnish.
arreda'tore, 'trice *sm/f* interior designer.
ar'redo *sm* fittings *pl*, furnishings *pl*; ~ **per
uffici** office furnishings.
arrem'baggio [arrem'badd3o] *sm* (*NAUT*)
boarding.
ar'rendersi *vr* to surrender; ~ **all'evidenza
(dei fatti)** to face (the) facts.
arren'devole *ag* (*persona*) yielding,
compliant.
arrendevo'lezza [arrendevo'lettsa] *sf*
compliancy.
ar'reso, a *pp di* **arrendersi**.
arres'tare *vt* (*fermare*) to stop, halt;
(*catturare*) to arrest; ~rsi *vr* (*fermarsi*) to
stop.
arres'tato, a *sm/f* person under arrest.
ar'resto *sm* (*cessazione*) stopping; (*fermata*)
stop; (*cattura, MED*) arrest; (*COMM: in
produzione*) stoppage; **subire un** ~ to come
to a stop o standstill; **mettere agli** ~i to
place under arrest; ~i **domiciliari** (*DIR*)
house arrest.
arre'trare *vt, vi* to withdraw.
arre'trato, a *ag* (*lavoro*) behind schedule;
(*paese, bambino*) backward; (*numero di
giornale*) back *cpd*; ~i *smpl* arrears; **gli** ~i
dello stipendio back pay *sg*.
arricchi'mento [arrikki'mento] *sm* enrich-
ment.
arric'chire [arrik'kire] *vt* to enrich; ~rsi *vr* to
become rich.
arric'chito, a [arrik'kito] *sm/f* nouveau riche.
arricci'are [arrit'tʃare] *vt* to curl; ~ **il naso** to
turn up one's nose.
ar'ridere *vi*: ~ **a qn** (*fortuna, successo*) to
smile on sb.
ar'ringa, ghe *sf* harangue; (*DIR*) address
by counsel.
arrischi'are [arris'kjare] *vt* to risk; ~rsi *vr* to
venture, dare.
arrischi'ato, a [arris'kjato] *ag* risky; (*teme-
rario*) reckless, rash.
ar'riso, a *pp di* **arridere**.
arri'vare *vi* to arrive; (*avvicinarsi*) to
come; (*accadere*) to happen, occur; ~ **a**
(*livello, grado etc*) to reach; **lui arriva a
Roma alle 7** he gets to o arrives at Rome
at 7; ~ **a fare qc** to manage to do sth,
succeed in doing sth; **non ci arrivo** I can't
reach it; (*fig: non capisco*) I can't understand it.
arri'vato, a *ag* (*persona: di successo*)
successful ♦ *sm/f*: **essere un** ~ to have
made it; **nuovo** ~ newcomer; **ben** ~! welcome!; **non sono l'ultimo** ~! (*fig*) I'm no
fool!
arrive'derci [arrive'dertʃi] *escl* goodbye!
arrive'derla *escl* (*forma di cortesia*) goodbye!
arri'vismo *sm* (*ambizione*) ambitiousness;
(*sociale*) social climbing.
arri'vista, i, e *sm/f* go-getter.
ar'rivo *sm* arrival; (*SPORT*) finish, finishing
line.
arro'gante *ag* arrogant.
arro'ganza [arro'gantsa] *sf* arrogance.
arro'gare *vt*: ~rsi **il diritto di fare qc** to
assume the right to do sth; ~rsi **il merito
di qc** to claim credit for sth.
arro'lare *vb* = **arruolare**.
arrossa'mento *sm* reddening.
arros'sare *vt* (*occhi, pelle*) to redden, make
red; ~rsi *vr* to go o become red.
arros'sire *vi* (*per vergogna, timidezza*) to
blush; (*per gioia*) to flush, blush.
arros'tire *vt* to roast; (*pane*) to toast; (*ai

ferri) to grill.

ar'rosto *sm, ag inv* roast; ~ **di manzo** roast beef.

arro'tare *vt* to sharpen; (*investire con un veicolo*) to run over.

arro'tino *sm* knife-grinder.

arroto'lare *vt* to roll up.

arroton'dare *vt* (*forma, oggetto*) to round; (*stipendio*) to add to; (*somma*) to round off.

arrovel'larsi *vr* (*anche*: ~ **il cervello**) to rack one's brains.

arroven'tato, a *ag* red-hot.

arruf'fare *vt* to ruffle; (*fili*) to tangle; (*fig: questione*) to confuse.

arruggi'nire [arruddʒi'nire] *vt* to rust; ~**rsi** *vr* to rust; (*fig*) to become rusty.

arruola'mento *sm* (*MIL*) enlistment.

arruo'lare *vt* (*MIL*) to enlist; ~**rsi** *vr* to enlist, join up.

arse'nale *sm* (*MIL*) arsenal; (*cantiere navale*) dockyard.

ar'senico *sm* arsenic.

'arsi *vb vedi* **ardere**.

'arso, a *pp di* **ardere** ♦ *ag* (*bruciato*) burnt; (*arido*) dry.

ar'sura *sf* (*calore opprimente*) burning heat; (*siccità*) drought.

art. *abbr* (= *articolo*) art.

'arte *sf* art; (*abilità*) skill; **a regola d'**~ (*fig*) perfectly; **senz'**~ **né parte** penniless and out of a job.

arte'fatto, a *ag* (*stile, modi*) affected; (*cibo*) adulterated.

ar'tefice [ar'tefitʃe] *sm/f* craftsman/woman; (*autore*) author.

ar'teria *sf* artery.

arterioscle'rosi *sf* arteriosclerosis, hardening of the arteries.

arteri'oso, a *ag* arterial.

'artico, a, ci, che *ag* Arctic ♦ *sm*: **l'A**~ the Arctic; **il Circolo polare** ~ the Arctic Circle; **l'Oceano** ~ the Arctic Ocean.

artico'lare *ag* (*ANAT*) of the joints, articular ♦ *vt* to articulate; (*suddividere*) to divide, split up; ~**rsi** *vr*: ~**rsi in** (*discorso, progetto*) to be divided into.

artico'lato, a *ag* (*linguaggio*) articulate; (*AUT*) articulated.

articolazi'one [artikolat'tsjone] *sf* (*ANAT, TECN*) joint; (*di voce, concetto*) articulation.

ar'ticolo *sm* article; ~ **di fondo** (*STAMPA*) leader, leading article; ~**i di marca** branded goods; **un bell'**~ (*fig*) a real character.

'Artide *sm*: **l'**~ the Arctic.

artifici'ale [artifi'tʃale] *ag* artificial.

artifici'ere [artifi'tʃɛre] *sm* (*MIL*) artificer; (: *per disinnescare bombe*) bomb-disposal expert.

arti'ficio [arti'fitʃo] *sm* (*espediente*) trick,

artifice; (*ricerca di effetto*) artificiality.

artifici'oso, a [artifi'tʃoso] *ag* cunning; (*non spontaneo*) affected.

artigia'nale [artidʒa'nale] *ag* craft *cpd*.

artigia'nato [artidʒa'nato] *sm* craftsmanship; craftsmen *pl*.

artigi'ano, a [arti'dʒano] *sm/f* craftsman/woman.

artigli'ere [artiʎ'ʎɛre] *sm* artilleryman.

artiglie'ria [artiʎʎe'ria] *sf* artillery.

ar'tiglio [ar'tiʎʎo] *sm* claw; (*di rapaci*) talon; **sfoderare gli** ~**i** (*fig*) to show one's claws.

ar'tista, i, e *sm/f* artist; **un lavoro da** ~ (*fig*) a professional piece of work.

ar'tistico, a, ci, che *ag* artistic.

'arto *sm* (*ANAT*) limb.

ar'trite *sf* (*MED*) arthritis.

ar'trosi *sf* osteoarthritis.

arzigogo'lato, a [ardzigogo'lato] *ag* tortuous.

arzi'gogolo [ardzi'gɔgolo] *sm* tortuous expression.

ar'zillo, a [ar'dzillo] *ag* lively, sprightly.

a'scella [aʃ'ʃɛlla] *sf* (*ANAT*) armpit.

ascen'dente [aʃʃen'dɛnte] *sm* ancestor; (*fig*) ascendancy; (*ASTR*) ascendant.

a'scendere [aʃ'ʃendere] *vi*: ~ **al trono** to ascend the throne.

ascensi'one [aʃʃen'sjone] *sf* (*ALPINISMO*) ascent; (*REL*): **l'A**~ the Ascension; **isola dell'A**~ Ascension Island.

ascen'sore [aʃʃen'sore] *sm* lift.

a'scesa [aʃ'ʃesa] *sf* ascent; (*al trono*) accession; (*al potere*) rise.

a'scesi [aʃ'ʃezi] *sf* asceticism.

a'sceso, a [aʃ'ʃeso] *pp di* **ascendere**.

a'scesso [aʃ'ʃesso] *sm* (*MED*) abscess.

a'sceta, i [aʃ'ʃeta] *sm* ascetic.

'ascia, pl 'asce ['aʃʃa] *sf* axe.

asciugaca'pelli [aʃʃugaka'pelli] *sm* hair-drier.

asciuga'mano [aʃʃuga'mano] *sm* towel.

asciu'gare [aʃʃu'gare] *vt* to dry; ~**rsi** *vr* to dry o.s.; (*diventare asciutto*) to dry.

asciuga'trice [aʃʃuga'tritʃe] *sf* spin-dryer.

asciut'tezza [aʃʃut'tettsa] *sf* dryness; leanness; curtness.

asci'utto, a [aʃ'ʃutto] *ag* dry; (*fig: magro*) lean; (: *burbero*) curt ♦ *sm*: **restare all'**~ (*fig*) to be left penniless; **restare a bocca** ~**a** (*fig*) to be disappointed.

asco'lano, a *ag* of (*o* from) Ascoli.

ascol'tare *vt* to listen to; ~ **il consiglio di qn** to listen to *o* heed sb's advice.

ascolta'tore, 'trice *sm/f* listener.

as'colto *sm*: **essere** *o* **stare in** ~ to be listening; **dare** *o* **prestare** ~ **(a)** to pay attention (to); **indice di** ~ (*TV, RADIO*) audience rating.

AS. COM. *sigla f* = *Associazione Commercianti*.

as'critto, a *pp di* **ascrivere**.

as'crivere *vt* (*attribuire*): ~ **qc a qn** to

attribute sth to sb; ~ **qc a merito di qn** to give sb credit for sth.

a'**settico, a, ci, che** *ag* aseptic.

asfal'**tare** *vt* to asphalt.

as'**falto** *sm* asphalt.

asfis'**sia** *sf* asphyxia, asphyxiation.

asfissi'**ante** *ag* (*gas*) asphyxiating; (*fig: calore, ambiente*) stifling, suffocating; (: *persona*) tiresome.

asfissi'**are** *vt* to asphyxiate, suffocate; (*fig: opprimere*) to stifle; (: *infastidire*) to get on sb's nerves ♦ *vi* to suffocate, asphyxiate.

'**Asia** *sf*: **l'~** Asia.

asi'**atico, a, ci, che** *ag, sm/f* Asiatic, Asian.

a'**silo** *sm* refuge, sanctuary; **~ (d'infanzia)** nursery(-school); **~ nido** crèche; **~ politico** political asylum.

asim'**metrico, a, ci, che** *ag* asymmetric(al).

'**asino** *sm* donkey, ass; **la bellezza dell'~** (*fig: di ragazza*) the beauty of youth; **qui casca l'~!** there's the rub!

'**asma** *sf* asthma.

as'**matico, a, ci, che** *ag, sm/f* asthmatic.

asoci'**ale** [aso'tʃale] *ag* antisocial.

'**asola** *sf* buttonhole.

as'**parago, gi** *sm* asparagus *q*.

as'**pergere** [as'pɛrdʒere] *vt*: **~ (di o con)** to sprinkle (with).

as'**persi** *etc vb vedi* **aspergere**.

as'**perso, a** *pp di* **aspergere**.

aspet'**tare** *vt* to wait for; (*anche COMM*) to await; (*aspettarsi*) to expect; (*essere in serbo: notizia, evento etc*) to be in store for, lie ahead of ♦ *vi* to wait; **~rsi qc** to expect sth; **~ un bambino** to be expecting (a baby); **questo non me l'aspettavo** I wasn't expecting this; **me l'aspettavo!** I thought as much!

aspetta'**tiva** *sf* expectation; **inferiore all'~** worse than expected; **essere/mettersi in ~** (*AMM*) to be on/take leave of absence.

as'**petto** *sm* (*apparenza*) aspect, appearance, look; (*punto di vista*) point of view; **di bell'~** good-looking.

aspi'**rante** *ag* (*attore etc*) aspiring ♦ *sm/f* candidate, applicant.

aspira'**polvere** *sm inv* vacuum cleaner.

aspi'**rare** *vt* (*respirare*) to breathe in, inhale; (*sog: apparecchi*) to suck (up) ♦ *vi*: **~ a** to aspire to.

aspira'**tore** *sm* extractor fan.

aspirazi'**one** [aspirat'tsjone] *sf* (*TECN*) suction; (*anelito*) aspiration.

aspi'**rina** *sf* aspirin.

aspor'**tare** *vt* (*anche MED*) to remove, take away.

as'**prezza** [as'prettsa] *sf* sourness, tartness; pungency; harshness; roughness; rugged

nature.

'**aspro, a** *ag* (*sapore*) sour, tart; (*odore*) acrid, pungent; (*voce, clima, fig*) harsh; (*superficie*) rough; (*paesaggio*) rugged.

Ass. *abbr* = **assicurazione; assicurata; assegno.**

assaggi'**are** [assad'dʒare] *vt* to taste.

assag'**gini** [assad'dʒini] *smpl* (*CUC*) selection *of first courses*.

as'**saggio** [as'saddʒo] *sm* tasting; (*piccola quantità*) taste; (*campione*) sample.

as'**sai** *av* (*molto*) a lot, much; (: *con ag*) very; (*a sufficienza*) enough ♦ *ag inv* (*quantità*) a lot of, much; (*numero*) a lot of, many; **~ contento** very pleased.

as'**salgo** *etc vb vedi* **assalire.**

assa'**lire** *vt* to attack, assail.

assali'**tore, 'trice** *sm/f* attacker, assailant.

assal'**tare** *vt* (*MIL*) to storm; (*banca*) to raid; (*treno, diligenza*) to hold up.

as'**salto** *sm* attack, assault; **prendere d'~** (*fig: negozio, treno*) to storm; (: *personalità*) to besiege; **d'~** (*editoria, giornalista etc*) aggressive.

assapo'**rare** *vt* to savour (*Brit*), savor (*US*).

assassi'**nare** *vt* to murder; (*POL*) to assassinate; (*fig*) to ruin.

assas'**sinio** *sm* murder; assassination.

assas'**sino, a** *ag* murderous ♦ *sm/f* murderer; assassin.

'**asse** *sm* (*TECN*) axle; (*MAT*) axis ♦ *sf* board; **~ da stiro** ironing board.

assecon'**dare** *vt*: **~ qn (in qc)** to go along with sb (in sth); **~ i desideri di qn** to go along with sb's wishes; **~ i capricci di qn** to give in to sb's whims.

assedi'**are** *vt* to besiege.

as'**sedio** *sm* siege.

asse'**gnare** [assep'ɲare] *vt* to assign, allot; (*premio*) to award.

assegna'**tario** [assepɲa'tarjo] *sm* (*DIR*) assignee; (*COMM*) recipient; **l'~ del premio** the person awarded the prize.

assegnazi'**one** [assepɲat'tsjone] *sf* (*di casa, somma*) allocation; (*di carica*) assignment; (*di premio, borsa di studio*) awarding.

as'**segno** [as'seɲɲo] *sm* allowance; (*anche:* **~ bancario**) cheque (*Brit*), check (*US*); **contro ~** cash on delivery; **~ circolare** bank draft; **~ di invalidità** o **di malattia** injury o sickness benefit; **~ post-datato** post-dated cheque; **~ sbarrato** crossed cheque; **~ non sbarrato** uncrossed cheque; **~ di studio** study grant; "**~ non trasferibile**" "account payee only"; **~ di viaggio** travel(l)er's cheque; **~ a vuoto** dud cheque; **~i alimentari** alimony *sg*; **~i familiari** ≈ child benefit *sg*.

assem'**blaggio** [assem'bladdʒo] *sm* (*IN-DUSTRIA*) assembly.

assem'**blare** *vt* to assemble.

assem'blea *sf* assembly; (*raduno, adunanza*) meeting.

assembra'mento *sm* public gathering; **divieto di** ~ ban on public meetings.

assen'nato, a *ag* sensible.

as'senso *sm* assent, consent.

assen'tarsi *vr* to go out.

as'sente *ag* absent; (*fig*) faraway, vacant ♦ *sm/f* absentee.

assente'ismo *sm* absenteeism.

assente'ista, i, e *sm/f* (*dal lavoro*) absentee.

assen'tire *vi*: ~ (a) to agree (to), assent (to).

as'senza [as'sɛntsa] *sf* absence.

asse'rire *vt* to maintain, assert.

asserragli'arsi [asserraʎ'ʎarsi] *vr*: ~ (in) to barricade o.s. (in).

asser'vire *vt* to enslave; (*fig*: *animo, passioni*) to subdue; ~rsi *vr*: ~rsi (a) to submit (to).

asserzi'one [asser'tsjone] *sf* assertion.

assesso'rato *sm* councillorship.

asses'sore *sm* councillor.

assesta'mento *sm* (*sistemazione*) arrangement; (*EDIL, GEO*) settlement.

asses'tare *vt* (*mettere in ordine*) to put in order, arrange; ~rsi *vr* to settle in; (*GEO*) to settle; ~ **un colpo a qn** to deal sb a blow.

asse'tato, a *ag* thirsty, parched.

as'setto *sm* order, arrangement; (*NAUT, AER*) trim; **in** ~ **di guerra** on a war footing; ~ **territoriale** country planning.

assicu'rare *vt* (*accertare*) to ensure; (*infondere certezza*) to assure; (*fermare, legare*) to make fast, secure; (*fare un contratto di assicurazione*) to insure; ~rsi *vr* (*accertarsi*): ~rsi (di) to make sure (of); (*contro il furto etc*): ~rsi (contro) to insure o.s. (against).

assicu'rato, a *ag* insured ♦ *sf* (*anche*: **lettera** ~a) registered letter.

assicura'tore, 'trice *ag* insurance *cpd* ♦ *sm/f* insurance agent; **società** ~trice insurance company.

assicurazi'one [assikurat'tsjone] *sf* assurance; insurance; ~ **multi-rischio** comprehensive insurance.

assidera'mento *sm* exposure.

asside'rare *vt* to freeze; ~rsi *vr* to freeze; **morire assiderato** to die of exposure.

as'siduo, a *ag* (*costante*) assiduous; (*regolare*) regular.

assi'eme *av* (*insieme*) together ♦ *prep*: ~ **a** (together) with.

assil'lante *ag* (*dubbio, pensiero*) nagging; (*creditore*) pestering.

assil'lare *vt* to pester, torment.

as'sillo *sm* (*fig*) worrying thought.

assimi'lare *vt* to assimilate.

assimilazi'one [assimilat'tsjone] *sf* assimilation.

assi'oma, i *sm* axiom.

assio'matico, a, ci, che *ag* axiomatic.

as'sise *sfpl* (*DIR*) assizes (*Brit*); **corte** *f* **d'**~ court of assizes, ≈ crown court (*Brit*).

assis'tente *sm/f* assistant; ~ **sociale** social worker; ~ **universitario** (assistant) lecturer; ~ **di volo** (*AER*) steward/stewardess.

assis'tenza [assis'tɛntsa] *sf* assistance; ~ **legale** legal aid; ~ **ospedaliera** free hospital treatment; ~ **sanitaria** health service; ~ **sociale** welfare services *pl*.

assistenzi'ale [assisten'tsjale] *ag* (*ente, organizzazione*) welfare *cpd*; (*opera*) charitable.

assistenzia'lismo [assistentsja'lizmo] *sm* (*peg*) excessive state aid.

as'sistere *vt* (*aiutare*) to assist, help; (*curare*) to treat ♦ *vi*: ~ (a qc) (*essere presente*) to be present (at sth), attend (sth).

assis'tito, a *pp di* **assistere**.

'asso *sm* ace; **piantare qn in** ~ to leave sb in the lurch.

associ'are [asso'tʃare] *vt* to associate; (*rendere partecipe*): ~ **qn a** (*affari*) to take sb into partnership in; (*partito*) to make sb a member of; ~rsi *vr* to enter into partnership; ~rsi **a** to become a member of, join; (*dolori, gioie*) to share in; ~ **qn alle carceri** to take sb to prison.

associazi'one [assotʃat'tsjone] *sf* association; ~ **di categoria** trade association; ~ **a** *o* **per delinquere** (*DIR*) criminal association; **A**~ **Europea di Libero Scambio** European Free Trade Association, EFTA; ~ **in partecipazione** (*COMM*) joint venture.

asso'dare *vt* (*muro, posizione*) to strengthen; (*fatti, verità*) to ascertain.

asso'dato, a *ag* well-founded.

assogget'tare [assoddʒet'tare] *vt* to subject, subjugate; ~rsi *vr*: ~rsi **a** to submit to.

asso'lato, a *ag* sunny.

assol'dare *vt* to recruit.

as'solsi *etc vb vedi* **assolvere**.

as'solto, a *pp di* **assolvere**.

assoluta'mente *av* absolutely.

asso'luto, a *ag* absolute.

assoluzi'one [assolut'tsjone] *sf* (*DIR*) acquittal; (*REL*) absolution.

as'solvere *vt* (*DIR*) to acquit; (*REL*) to absolve; (*adempiere*) to carry out, perform.

assomigli'are [assomiʎ'ʎare] *vi*: ~ **a** to resemble, look like.

asson'nato, a *ag* sleepy.

asso'pirsi *vr* to doze off.

assor'bente *ag* absorbent ♦ *sm*: ~ **igienico** sanitary towel; ~ **interno** tampon.

assor'bire *vt* to absorb; (*fig: far proprio*) to assimilate.

assor'dare *vt* to deafen.

assorti'mento *sm* assortment.

assor'tito, a *ag* assorted; (*colori*) matched, matching.

as'sorto, a *ag* absorbed, engrossed.

assottigli'are [assottiʎ'ʎare] *vt* to make thin, thin; (*aguzzare*) to sharpen; (*ridurre*) to reduce; ~**rsi** *vr* to grow thin; (*fig: ridursi*) to be reduced.

A.S.S.T. *sigla f* (= *Azienda di Stato per i Servizi Telefonici*) state-run telecommunications company.

assue'fare *vt* to accustom; ~**rsi** *vr*: ~**rsi a** to get used to, accustom o.s. to.

assue'fatto, a *pp di* **assuefare**.

assuefazi'one [assuefat'tsjone] *sf* (*MED*) addiction.

as'sumere *vt* (*impiegato*) to take on, engage; (*responsabilità*) to assume, take upon o.s.; (*contegno, espressione*) to assume, put on; (*droga*) to consume.

as'sunsi *etc vb vedi* **assumere**.

as'sunto, a *pp di* **assumere** ♦ *sm* (*tesi*) proposition.

assunzi'one [assun'tsjone] *sf* (*di impiegati*) employment, engagement; (*REL*): **l'A~** the Assumption.

assurdità *sf inv* absurdity; **dire delle** ~ to talk nonsense.

as'surdo, a *ag* absurd.

'asta *sf* pole; (*modo di vendita*) auction.

as'tante *sm* bystander.

astante'ria *sf* casualty department.

as'temio, a *ag* teetotal ♦ *sm/f* teetotaller.

aste'nersi *vr*: ~ **(da)** to abstain (from), refrain (from); (*POL*) to abstain (from).

astensi'one *sf* abstention.

astensio'nista, i, e *sm/f* (*POL*) abstentionist.

aste'risco, schi *sm* asterisk.

aste'roide *sm* asteroid.

'astice ['astitʃe] *sm* lobster.

astigi'ano, a [asti'dʒano] *ag* of (*o* from) Asti.

asti'nenza [asti'nɛntsa] *sf* abstinence; **essere in crisi di** ~ to suffer from withdrawal symptoms.

'astio *sm* rancour, resentment.

astrat'tismo *sm* (*ARTE*) abstract art.

as'tratto, a *ag* abstract.

'astro *sm* star.

astrolo'gia [astrolo'dʒia] *sf* astrology.

astro'logico, a, ci, che [astro'lɔdʒiko] *ag* astrological.

as'trologo, a, ghi, ghe *sm/f* astrologer.

astro'nauta, i, e *sm/f* astronaut.

astro'nautica *sf* astronautics *sg*.

astro'nave *sf* space ship.

astrono'mia *sf* astronomy.

astro'nomico, a, ci, che *ag* astronomic(al).

as'tronomo *sm* astronomer.

as'tuccio [as'tuttʃo] *sm* case, box, holder.

as'tuto, a *ag* astute, cunning, shrewd.

as'tuzia [as'tuttsja] *sf* astuteness, shrewdness; (*azione*) trick.

AT *sigla* = *Asti*.

A.T. *abbr* (= *alta tensione*) HT.

ATA *sigla f* = *Associazione Turistica Albergatori*.

a'tavico, a, ci, che *ag* atavistic.

ate'ismo *sm* atheism.

atelier [atə'lje] *sm inv* (*laboratorio*) workshop; (*studio*) studio; (*sartoria*) fashion house.

A'tene *sf* Athens.

ate'neo *sm* university.

ateni'ese *ag, sm/f* Athenian.

'ateo, a *ag, sm/f* atheist.

a'tipico, a, ci, che *ag* atypical.

at'lante *sm* atlas; **i Monti dell'A~** the Atlas Mountains.

at'lantico, a, ci, che *ag* Atlantic ♦ *sm*: **l'A~, l'Oceano A~** the Atlantic, the Atlantic Ocean.

at'leta, i, e *sm/f* athlete.

at'letica *sf* athletics *sg*; ~ **leggera** track and field events *pl*; ~ **pesante** weightlifting and wrestling.

ATM *sigla f* = *Azienda Tranviaria Municipale*.

atmos'fera *sf* atmosphere.

atmos'ferico, a, ci, che *ag* atmospheric.

a'tollo *sm* atoll.

a'tomico, a, ci, che *ag* atomic; (*nucleare*) atomic, atom *cpd*, nuclear.

atomizza'tore [atomiddza'tore] *sm* (*di acqua, lacca*) spray; (*di profumo*) atomizer.

'atomo *sm* atom.

'atono, a *ag* (*FONETICA*) unstressed.

'atrio *sm* entrance hall, lobby.

a'troce [a'trotʃe] *ag* (*che provoca orrore*) dreadful; (*terribile*) atrocious.

atrocità [atrotʃi'ta] *sf inv* atrocity.

atro'fia *sf* atrophy.

attacca'brighe [attakka'brige] *sm/f inv* quarrelsome person.

attacca'mento *sm* (*fig*) attachment, affection.

attacca'panni *sm* hook, peg; (*mobile*) hall stand.

attac'care *vt* (*unire*) to attach; (*cucendo*) to sew on; (*far aderire*) to stick (on); (*appendere*) to hang (up); (*assalire: anche fig*) to attack; (*iniziare*) to begin, start; (*fig: contagiare*) to pass on ♦ *vi* to stick, adhere; ~**rsi** *vr* to stick, adhere; (*trasmettersi per contagio*) to be contagious; (*afferrarsi*): ~**rsi (a)** to cling (to); (*fig: affezionarsi*): ~**rsi (a)** to become attached (to); ~ **discorso** to start a conversation; **con me non attacca!** that won't work with me!

attacca'ticcio, a, ci, ce [attakka'tittʃo] *ag* sticky.

attacca'tura *sf* (*di manica*) join; ~ **(dei capelli)** hairline.

at'tacco, chi *sm* (*azione offensiva: anche fig*) attack; (*MED*) attack, fit; (*SCI*) binding; (*ELETTR*) socket.

attanagli'are [attanaʎ'ʎare] *vt* (*anche fig*) to grip.

attar'darsi *vr*: ~ **a fare qc** (*fermarsi*) to stop to do sth; (*stare più a lungo*) to stay behind to do sth.

attec'chire [attek'kire] *vi* (*pianta*) to take root; (*fig*) to catch on.

atteggia'mento [atteddʒa'mento] *sm* attitude.

atteggi'arsi [atted'dʒarsi] *vr*: ~ **a** to pose as.

attem'pato, a *ag* elderly.

atten'dente *sm* (*MIL*) orderly, batman.

at'tendere *vt* to wait for, await ♦ *vi*: ~ **a** to attend to.

atten'dibile *ag* (*scusa, storia*) credible; (*fonte, testimone, notizia*) reliable; (*persona*) trustworthy.

atte'nersi *vr*: ~ **a** to keep *o* stick to.

atten'tare *vi*: ~ **a** to make an attempt on.

atten'tato *sm* attack; ~ **alla vita di qn** attempt on sb's life.

at'tento, a *ag* attentive; (*accurato*) careful, thorough ♦ *escl* be careful!; **stare** ~ **a qc** to pay attention to sth; ~**i!** (*MIL*) attention!; ~**i al cane** beware of the dog.

attenu'ante *sf* (*DIR*) extenuating circumstance.

attenu'are *vt* to alleviate, ease; (*diminuire*) to reduce; ~**rsi** *vr* to ease, abate.

attenuazi'one [attenuat'tsjone] *sf* alleviation; easing; reduction.

attenzi'one [atten'tsjone] *sf* attention ♦ *escl* watch out!, be careful!; **coprire qn di** ~**i** to lavish attention on sb.

atter'raggio [atter'raddʒo] *sm* landing; ~ **di fortuna** emergency landing.

atter'rare *vt* to bring down ♦ *vi* to land.

atter'rire *vt* to terrify.

at'tesa *sf vedi* **atteso**.

at'tesi *etc vb vedi* **attendere**.

at'teso, a *pp di* **attendere** ♦ *sf* waiting; (*tempo trascorso aspettando*) wait; **essere in** ~**a di qc** to be waiting for sth; **in** ~**a di una vostra risposta** (*COMM*) awaiting your reply; **restiamo in** ~**a di Vostre ulteriori notizie** (*COMM*) we look forward to hearing (further) from you.

attes'tare *vt*: ~ **qc/che** to testify to sth/(to the fact) that.

attes'tato *sm* certificate.

attestazi'one [attestat'tsjone] *sf* (*certificato*) certificate; (*dichiarazione*) statement.

'attico, ci *sm* attic.

at'tiguo, a *ag* adjacent, adjoining.

attil'lato, a *ag* (*vestito*) close-fitting, tight; (*persona*) dressed up.

'attimo *sm* moment; **in un** ~ in a moment.

atti'nente *ag*: ~ **a** relating to, concerning.

atti'nenza [atti'nentsa] *sf* connection.

at'tingere [at'tindʒere] *vt*: ~ **a** *o* **da** (*acqua*) to draw from; (*denaro, notizie*) to obtain from.

at'tinto, a *pp di* **attingere**.

atti'rare *vt* to attract; ~**rsi delle critiche** to incur criticism.

atti'tudine *sf* (*disposizione*) aptitude; (*atteggiamento*) attitude.

atti'vare *vt* to activate; (*far funzionare*) to set going, start.

atti'vista, i, e *sm/f* activist.

attività *sf inv* activity; (*COMM*) assets *pl*; ~ **liquide** (*COMM*) liquid assets.

at'tivo, a *ag* active; (*COMM*) profit-making ♦ *sm* (*COMM*) assets *pl*; **in** ~ in credit; **chiudere in** ~ to show a profit; **avere qc al proprio** ~ (*fig*) to have sth to one's credit.

attiz'zare [attit'tsare] *vt* (*fuoco*) to poke; (*fig*) to stir up.

attizza'toio [attittsa'tojo] *sm* poker.

'atto, a *ag*: ~ **a** fit for, capable of ♦ *sm* act; (*azione, gesto*) action, act, deed; (*DIR: documento*) deed, document; ~**i** *smpl* (*di congressi etc*) proceedings; **essere in** ~ to be under way; **mettere in** ~ to put into action; **fare** ~ **di fare qc** to make as if to do sth; **all'**~ **pratico** in practice; **dare** ~ **a qn di qc** to give sb credit for sth; ~ **di nascita/morte** birth/death certificate; ~ **di proprietà** title deed; ~ **pubblico** official document; ~ **di vendita** bill of sale; ~**i osceni (in luogo pubblico)** (*DIR*) indecent exposure; ~**i verbali** transactions.

at'tonito, a *ag* dumbfounded, astonished.

attorcigli'are [attortʃiʎ'ʎare] *vt*, ~**rsi** *vr* to twist.

at'tore, 'trice *sm/f* actor/actress.

attorni'are *vt* (*circondare*) to surround; ~**rsi** *vr*: ~**rsi di** to surround o.s. with.

at'torno *av*, ~ **a** *prep* round, around, about.

attrac'care *vt, vi* (*NAUT*) to dock, berth.

at'tracco, chi *sm* (*NAUT: manovra*) docking, berthing; (*luogo*) berth.

at'trae *etc vb vedi* **attrarre**.

attra'ente *ag* attractive.

at'traggo *etc vb vedi* **attrarre**.

at'trarre *vt* to attract.

at'trassi *etc vb vedi* **attrarre**.

attrat'tiva *sf* attraction, charm.

at'tratto, a *pp di* **attrarre**.

attraversa'mento *sm* crossing; ~ **pedonale** pedestrian crossing.

attraver'sare *vt* to cross; (*città, bosco, fig: periodo*) to go through; (*sog: fiume*) to run through.

attra'verso *prep* through; (*da una parte all'altra*) across.

attrazi'one [attrat'tsjone] *sf* attraction.

attrez'zare [attret'tsare] *vt* to equip; (*NAUT*) to rig.

attrezza'tura [attrettsa'tura] *sf* equipment *q*; rigging; ~**e per uffici** office equipment.

at'trezzo [at'trettso] *sm* tool, instrument; (*SPORT*) piece of equipment.

attribu'ire *vt*: ~ qc a qn (*assegnare*) to give *o* award sth to sb; (*quadro etc*) to attribute sth to sb.

attri'buto *sm* attribute.

at'trice [at'tritʃe] *sf vedi* **attore**.

at'trito *sm* (*anche fig*) friction.

attu'abile *ag* feasible.

attuabilità *sf* feasibility.

attu'ale *ag* (*presente*) present; (*di attualità*) topical; (*che è in atto*) actual.

attualità *sf inv* topicality; (*avvenimento*) current event; **notizie d'~** (*TV*) the news *sg*.

attualiz'zare [attualid'dzare] *vt* to update, bring up to date.

attual'mente *av* at the moment, at present.

attu'are *vt* to carry out; **~rsi** *vr* to be realized.

attuazi'one [attuat'tsjone] *sf* carrying out.

attu'tire *vt* to deaden, reduce; **~rsi** *vr* to die down.

A.U. *abbr* = **allievo ufficiale**.

au'dace [au'datʃe] *ag* audacious, daring, bold; (*provocante*) provocative; (*sfacciato*) impudent, bold.

au'dacia [au'datʃa] *sf* audacity, daring; boldness; provocativeness; impudence.

'audio *sm* (*TV, RADIO, CINEMA*) sound.

audiocas'setta *sf* (audio) cassette.

audio'leso, a *sm/f* person who is hard of hearing.

audiovi'sivo, a *ag* audiovisual.

audi'torio *sm* auditorium.

audizi'one [audit'tsjone] *sf* hearing; (*MUS*) audition.

'auge ['audʒe] *sf* (*della gloria, carriera*) height, peak; **essere in ~** to be at the top.

augu'rale *ag*: **messaggio ~** greeting; **biglietto ~** greetings card.

augu'rare *vt* to wish; **~rsi qc** to hope for sth.

au'gurio *sm* (*presagio*) omen; (*voto di benessere etc*) (good) wish; **essere di buon/cattivo ~** to be of good omen/be ominous; **fare gli ~i a qn** to give sb one's best wishes; **tanti ~i!** all the best!

'aula *sf* (*scolastica*) classroom; (*universitaria*) lecture theatre; (*di edificio pubblico*) hall; **~ magna** main hall; **~ del tribunale** courtroom.

aumen'tare *vt, vi* to increase; **~ di peso** (*persona*) to put on weight; **la produzione è aumentata del 50%** production has increased by 50%.

au'mento *sm* increase.

'aureo, a *ag* (*di oro*) gold *cpd*; (*fig: colore, periodo*) golden.

au'reola *sf* halo.

au'rora *sf* dawn.

ausili'are *ag, sm, sm/f* auxiliary.

au'silio *sm* aid.

auspi'cabile *ag* desirable.

auspi'care *vt* to call for, express a desire for.

aus'picio [aus'pitʃo] *sm* omen; (*protezione*) patronage; **sotto gli ~i di** under the auspices of; **è di buon ~** it augurs well.

austerità *sf inv* austerity.

aus'tero, a *ag* austere.

aus'trale *ag* southern.

Aus'tralia *sf*: **l'~** Australia.

australi'ano, a *ag, sm/f* Australian.

'Austria *sf*: **l'~** Austria.

aus'triaco, a, ci, che *ag, sm/f* Austrian.

au'tarchico, a, ci, che [au'tarkiko] *ag* (*sistema*) self-sufficient, autarkic; (*prodotto*) home *cpd*, home-produced.

'aut 'aut *sm inv* ultimatum.

autenti'care *vt* to authenticate.

autenticità [autentitʃi'ta] *sf* authenticity.

au'tentico, a, ci, che *ag* (*quadro, firma*) authentic, genuine; (*fatto*) true, genuine.

au'tista, i *sm* driver; (*personale*) chauffeur.

'auto *sf inv* car.

autoade'sivo, a *ag* self-adhesive ♦ *sm* sticker.

autoartico'lato *sm* articulated lorry (*Brit*), semi (trailer) (*US*).

autobiogra'fia *sf* autobiography.

autobio'grafico, a, ci, che *ag* autobiographic(al).

auto'blinda *sf* armoured (*Brit*) *o* armored (*US*) car.

auto'bomba *sf inv* car bomb.

auto'botte *sf* tanker.

'autobus *sm inv* bus.

auto'carro *sm* lorry (*Brit*), truck.

autocis'terna [autotʃis'tɛrna] *sf* tanker.

autoco'lonna *sf* convoy.

autocon'trollo *sm* self-control.

autocopia'tivo, a *ag*: **carta ~a** carbonless paper.

autocorri'era *sf* coach, bus.

auto'cratico, a, ci, che *ag* autocratic.

auto'critica, che *sf* self-criticism.

au'toctono, a *ag, sm/f* native.

autodemolizi'one [autodemolit'tsjone] *sf* breaker's yard (*Brit*).

autodi'datta, i, e *sm/f* autodidact, self-taught person.

autodi'fesa *sf* self-defence.

autoferrotranvi'ario, a *ag* public transport *cpd*.

autogesti'one [autodʒes'tjone] *sf* worker management.

autoges'tito, a [autodʒes'tito] *ag* under worker management.

au'tografo, a *ag, sm* autograph.

auto'grill *sm inv* motorway café (*Brit*), roadside restaurant (*US*).

autolesio'nismo *sm* (*fig*) self-destruction.

auto'linea *sf* bus route.

au'toma, i sm automaton.

auto'matico, a, ci, che ag automatic ♦ sm (bottone) snap fastener; (fucile) automatic; **selezione** ~**a** (TEL) direct dialling.

automazi'one [automat'tsjone] sf: ~ **delle procedure d'ufficio** office automation.

auto'mezzo [auto'mɛddzo] sm motor vehicle.

auto'mobile sf (motor) car; ~ **da corsa** racing car (Brit), race car (US).

automobi'lismo sm (gen) motoring; (SPORT) motor racing.

automobi'lista, i, e sm/f motorist.

automobi'listico, a, ci, che ag car cpd (Brit), automobile cpd (US); (sport) motor cpd.

autono'leggio [autono'leddʒo] sm car hire (Brit), car rental.

autono'mia sf autonomy; (di volo) range.

au'tonomo, a ag autonomous; (sindacato, pensiero) independent.

auto'parco, chi sm (parcheggio) car park (Brit), parking lot (US); (insieme di automezzi) transport fleet.

auto'pompa sf fire engine.

autop'sia sf post-mortem (examination), autopsy.

auto'radio sf inv (apparecchio) car radio; (autoveicolo) radio car.

au'tore, 'trice sm/f author; **l'**~ **del furto** the person who committed the robbery; **diritti d'**~ copyright sg; (compenso) royalties.

autoregolamentazi'one [autoregolamentat-'tsjone] sf self-regulation.

auto'revole ag authoritative; (persona) influential.

autorilevazi'one [autorilevat'tsjone] sf: ~ **di errori** (INFORM) automatic error detection.

autori'messa sf garage.

autorità sf inv authority.

autori'tratto sm self-portrait.

autoriz'zare [autorid'dzare] vt to authorize, give permission for.

autorizzazi'one [autoriddzat'tsjone] sf authorization.

autos'catto sm (FOT) timer.

autos'contro sm dodgem car (Brit), bumper car (US).

autoscu'ola sf driving school.

autosno'dato sm articulated vehicle.

autos'top sm hitchhiking.

autostop'pista, i, e sm/f hitchhiker.

autos'trada sf motorway (Brit), highway (US).

autosuffici'ente [autosuffi'tʃɛnte] ag self-sufficient.

autotassazi'one [autotassat'tsjone] sf system of taxation where individual himself assesses and pays tax due.

auto'treno sm articulated lorry (Brit), semi (trailer) (US).

autove'icolo sm motor vehicle.

autovet'tura sf (motor) car.

autun'nale ag (di autunno) autumn cpd; (da autunno) autumnal.

au'tunno sm autumn.

AV sigla = Avellino.

a/v abbr = **a vista**.

aval'lare vt (FINANZA) to guarantee; (fig: sostenere) to back; (: confermare) to confirm.

a'vallo sm (FINANZA) guarantee.

avam'braccio, pl(f) **-cia** [avam'brattʃo] sm forearm.

avam'posto sm (MIL) outpost.

A'vana sf: **l'**~ Havana.

a'vana sm inv (sigaro) Havana (cigar); (colore) Havana brown.

avan'guardia sf vanguard; (ARTE) avant-garde.

avansco'perta sf (MIL) reconnaissance; **andare in** ~ to reconnoitre.

a'vanti av (stato in luogo) in front; (moto: andare, venire) forward; (tempo: prima) before ♦ prep (luogo): ~ **a** before, in front of; (tempo): ~ **Cristo** before Christ ♦ escl (entrate) come (o go) in!; (MIL) forward!; (coraggio) come on! ♦ sm inv (SPORT) forward; **il giorno** ~ the day before; ~ **e indietro** backwards and forwards; **andare** ~ to go forward; (continuare) to go on; (precedere) to go (on) ahead; (orologio) to be fast; **essere** ~ **negli studi** to be well advanced with one's studies; **mandare** ~ **la famiglia** to provide for one's family; **mandare** ~ **un'azienda** to run a business; ~ **il prossimo!** next please!

avan'treno sm (AUT) front chassis.

avanza'mento [avantsa'mento] sm (gen) advance; (fig) progress; promotion.

avan'zare [avan'tsare] vt (spostare in avanti) to move forward, advance; (domanda) to put forward; (promuovere) to promote; (essere creditore): ~ **qc da qn** to be owed sth by sb ♦ vi (andare avanti) to move forward, advance; (fig: progredire) to make progress; (essere d'avanzo) to be left, remain; **basta e avanza** that's more than enough.

avan'zato, a [avan'tsato] ag (teoria, tecnica) advanced ♦ sf (MIL) advance; **in età** ~**a** advanced in years, up in years.

a'vanzo [a'vantso] sm (residuo) remains pl, left-overs pl; (MAT) remainder; (COMM) surplus; (eccedenza di bilancio) profit carried forward; **averne d'**~ **di qc** to have more than enough of sth; ~ **di cassa** cash in hand; ~ **di galera** (fig) jailbird.

ava'ria sf (guasto) damage; (: meccanico) breakdown.

avari'ato, a ag (merce) damaged; (cibo) off.

ava'rizia [ava'rittsja] sf avarice; **crepi l'**~**!** to hang with the expense!

a'varo, a ag avaricious, miserly ♦ sm miser.

a'vena *sf* oats *pl.*

a'vere *sm* (*COMM*) credit; **~i** *smpl* (*ricchezza*) wealth *sg*, possessions ♦ *vt*, *vb ausiliare* to have; **~ da mangiare/bere** to have something to eat/drink; **~ da** *o* **a fare qc** to have to do sth; **~** (**a**) **che fare** *o* **vedere con qn/qc** to have to do with sb/ sth; **ho 28 anni** I am 28 (years old); **cos'hai?** what's wrong *o* what's the matter (with you)?; **avercela con qn** to have something against sb; **quanti ne abbiamo oggi?** what's the date today?; **ne ha ancora per molto?** have you got much longer to go?; **averne fin sopra i capelli** *o* **piene le tasche** (*fam*) to be fed up to the teeth; *vedi anche* **fame, freddo** *etc.*

'avi *smpl* ancestors, forefathers.

avia'tore, 'trice *sm/f* aviator, pilot.

aviazi'one [avjat'tsjone] *sf* aviation; (*MIL*) air force; **~ civile** civil aviation.

avicol'tura *sf* bird breeding; (*di pollame*) poultry farming.

avidità *sf* eagerness; greed.

'avido, a *ag* eager; (*peg*) greedy.

avi'ere *sm* (*MIL*) airman.

avitami'nosi *sf* vitamin deficiency.

avo'cado *sm* avocado.

a'vorio *sm* ivory.

a'vulso, a *ag*: **parole ~e dal contesto** words out of context; **~ dalla società** (*fig*) cut off from society.

Avv. *abbr* = **avvocato.**

avva'lersi *vr*: **~ di** to avail o.s. of.

avvalla'mento *sm* sinking *q*; (*effetto*) depression.

avvalo'rare *vt* to confirm.

avvantaggi'are [avvantad'dʒare] *vt* to favour (*Brit*), favor (*US*); **~rsi** *vr* (*trarre vantaggio*): **~rsi di** to take advantage of; (*prevalere*): **~rsi negli affari/sui concorrenti** to get ahead in business/of one's competitors.

avve'dersi *vr*: **~ di qn/qc** to notice sb/sth.

avve'duto, a *ag* (*accorto*) prudent; (*scaltro*) astute.

avvelena'mento *sm* poisoning.

avvele'nare *vt* to poison.

avve'nente *ag* attractive, charming.

av'vengo *etc vb vedi* **avvenire.**

avveni'mento *sm* event.

avve'nire *vi*, *vb impers* to happen, occur ♦ *sm* future.

av'venni *etc vb vedi* **avvenire.**

avven'tarsi *vr*: **~ su** *o* **contro qn/qc** to hurl o.s. *o* rush at sb/sth.

avven'tato, a *ag* rash, reckless.

avven'tizio, a [avven'tittsjo] *ag* (*impiegato*) temporary; (*guadagno*) casual.

av'vento *sm* advent, coming; (*REL*): **l'A~** Advent.

avven'tore *sm* customer.

avven'tura *sf* adventure; (*amorosa*) affair; **avere spirito d'~** to be adventurous.

avventu'rarsi *vr* to venture.

avventuri'ero, a *sm/f* adventurer/ adventuress.

avventu'roso, a *ag* adventurous.

avve'nuto, a *pp di* **avvenire.**

avve'rarsi *vr* to come true.

av'verbio *sm* adverb.

avverrò *etc vb vedi* **avvenire.**

avver'sare *vt* to oppose.

avver'sario, a *ag* opposing ♦ *sm* opponent, adversary.

avversi'one *sf* aversion.

avversità *sf inv* adversity, misfortune.

av'verso, a *ag* (*contrario*) contrary; (*sfavorevole*) unfavourable (*Brit*), unfavorable (*US*).

avver'tenza [avver'tɛntsa] *sf* (*ammonimento*) warning; (*cautela*) care; (*premessa*) foreword; **~e** *sfpl* (*istruzioni per l'uso*) instructions.

avverti'mento *sm* warning.

avver'tire *vt* (*avvisare*) to warn; (*rendere consapevole*) to inform, notify; (*percepire*) to feel.

av'vezzo, a [av'vettso] *ag*: **~ a** used to.

avvia'mento *sm* (*atto*) starting; (*effetto*) start; (*AUT*) starting; (: *dispositivo*) starter; (*COMM*) goodwill.

avvi'are *vt* (*mettere sul cammino*) to direct; (*impresa, trattative*) to begin, start; (*motore*) to start; **~rsi** *vr* to set off, set out.

avvicenda'mento [avvitʃenda'mento] *sm* alternation; (*AGR*) rotation; **c'è molto ~ di personale** there is a high turnover of staff.

avvicen'dare [avvitʃen'dare] *vt*, **~rsi** *vr* to alternate.

avvicina'mento [avvitʃina'mento] *sm* approach.

avvici'nare [avvitʃi'nare] *vt* to bring near; (*trattare con: persona*) to approach; **~rsi** *vr*: **~rsi (a qn/qc)** to approach (sb/sth), draw near (to sb/sth); (*somigliare*) to be similar (to sb/sth), be close (to sb/sth).

avvi'lente *ag* (*umiliante*) humiliating; (*scoraggiante*) discouraging, disheartening.

avvili'mento *sm* humiliation; disgrace; discouragement.

avvi'lire *vt* (*umiliare*) to humiliate; (*degradare*) to disgrace; (*scoraggiare*) to dishearten, discourage; **~rsi** *vr* (*abbattersi*) to lose heart.

avvilup'pare *vt* (*avvolgere*) to wrap up; (*ingarbugliare*) to entangle.

avvinaz'zato, a [avvinat'tsato] *ag* drunk.

av'vincere [av'vintʃere] *vt* to charm, enthral.

avvinghi'are [avvin'gjare] *vt* to clasp; **~rsi** *vr*: **~rsi a** to cling to.

av'vinsi *etc vb vedi* **avvincere.**

av'vinto, a *pp di* **avvincere.**

av'vio *sm* start, beginning; **dare l'~ a qc** to start sth off; **prendere l'~** to get going, get under way.

avvi'saglia [avvi'zaʎʎa] *sf* (*sintomo: di temporale etc*) sign; (*di malattia*) manifestation, sign, symptom; (*scaramuccia*) skirmish.

avvi'sare *vt* (*far sapere*) to inform; (*mettere in guardia*) to warn.

avvisa'tore *sm* (*apparecchio d'allarme*) alarm; **~ acustico** horn; **~ d'incendio** fire alarm.

av'viso *sm* warning; (*annuncio*) announcement; (*affisso*) notice; (*inserzione pubblicitaria*) advertisement; **a mio ~** in my opinion; **mettere qn sull'~** to put sb on their guard; **fino a nuovo ~** until further notice; **~ di consegna/spedizione** (*COMM*) delivery/consignment note; **~ di pagamento** (*COMM*) payment advice.

avvis'tare *vt* to sight.

avvi'tare *vt* to screw down (*o* in).

avviz'zire [avvit'tsire] *vi* to wither.

avvo'cato, 'essa *sm/f* (*DIR*) barrister (*Brit*), lawyer; (*fig*) defender, advocate; **~ di parte civile** counsel for the plaintiff; **~ difensore** counsel for the defence.

av'volgere [av'vɔldʒere] *vt* to roll up; (*bobina*) to wind up; (*avviluppare*) to wrap up; **~rsi** *vr* (*avvilupparsi*) to wrap o.s. up.

avvol'gibile [avvol'dʒibile] *sm* roller blind (*Brit*), blind.

avvolgi'mento [avvoldʒi'mento] *sm* winding.

av'volsi *etc vb vedi* **avvolgere**.

av'volto, a *pp di* **avvolgere**.

avvol'toio *sm* vulture.

aza'lea [addza'lɛa] *sf* azalea.

azi'enda [ad'dzjɛnda] *sf* business, firm, concern; **~ agricola** farm; **~ (autonoma) di soggiorno** tourist board; **~ a partecipazione statale** *business in which the State has a financial interest*; **~e pubbliche** public corporations.

azien'dale [addzjen'dale] *ag* company *cpd*; **organizzazione ~** business administration.

azio'nare [attsjo'nare] *vt* to activate.

azio'nario, a [attsjo'narjo] *ag* share *cpd*; **capitale ~** share capital; **mercato ~** stock market.

azi'one [at'tsjone] *sf* action; (*COMM*) share; **~ sindacale** industrial action; **~i preferenziali** preference shares (*Brit*), preferred stock *sg* (*US*).

azio'nista, i, e [attsjo'nista] *sm/f* (*COMM*) shareholder.

a'zoto [ad'dzɔto] *sm* nitrogen.

az'teco, a, ci, che [as'tɛko] *ag, sm/f* Aztec.

azzan'nare [attsan'nare] *vt* to sink one's teeth into.

azzar'dare [addzar'dare] *vt* (*soldi, vita*) to risk, hazard; (*domanda, ipotesi*) to hazard,

venture; **~rsi** *vr*: **~rsi a fare** to dare (to) do.

azzar'dato, a [addzar'dato] *ag* (*impresa*) risky; (*risposta*) rash.

az'zardo [ad'dzardo] *sm* risk; **gioco d'~** game of chance.

azzec'care [attsek'kare] *vt* (*bersaglio*) to hit, strike; (*risposta, pronostico*) to get right; (*fig: indovinare*) to guess.

azzera'mento [addzera'mento] *sm* (*INFORM*) reset.

azze'rare [addze'rare] *vt* (*MAT, FISICA*) to make equal to zero, reduce to zero; (*TECN: strumento*) to (re)set to zero.

'azzimo, a ['addzimo] *ag* unleavened ♦ *sm* unleavened bread.

azzop'pare [attsop'pare] *vt* to lame, make lame.

Az'zorre [ad'dzorre] *sfpl*: **le ~** the Azores.

azzuf'farsi [attsuf'farsi] *vr* to come to blows.

az'zurro, a [ad'dzurro] *ag* blue ♦ *sm* (*colore*) blue; **gli ~i** (*SPORT*) the Italian national team.

azzur'rognolo, a [addzur'roɲɲolo] *ag* bluish.

B

B, b [bi] *sf o m inv* (*lettera*) B, b; **~ come Bologna** ≈ B for Benjamin (*Brit*), B for Baker (*US*).

BA *sigla* = Bari.

ba'bau *sm inv* ogre, bogey man.

bab'beo *sm* simpleton.

'babbo *sm* (*fam*) dad, daddy; **B~ Natale** Father Christmas.

bab'buccia, ce [bab'buttʃa] *sf* slipper; (*per neonati*) bootee.

babbu'ino *sm* baboon.

ba'bordo *sm* (*NAUT*) port side.

ba'cato, a *ag* worm-eaten, rotten; (*fig: mente*) diseased; (: *persona*) corrupt.

'bacca, che *sf* berry.

baccalà *sm* dried salted cod; (*fig: peg*) dummy.

bac'cano *sm* din, clamour (*Brit*), clamor (*US*).

bac'cello [bat'tʃello] *sm* pod.

bac'chetta [bak'ketta] *sf* (*verga*) stick, rod; (*di direttore d'orchestra*) baton; (*di tamburo*) drumstick; **comandare a ~** to rule with a rod of iron; **~ magica** magic wand.

ba'checa, che [ba'kɛka] *sf* (*mobile*) showcase, display case; (*UNIVERSITÀ, in ufficio*) notice board (*Brit*), bulletin board (*US*).

bacia'mano [batʃa'mano] *sm*: **fare il ~ a qn** to kiss sb's hand.

baci'are [ba'tʃare] *vt* to kiss; **~rsi** *vr* to kiss (one another).

ba'cillo [ba'tʃillo] *sm* bacillus, germ.

baci'nella [batʃi'nɛlla] *sf* basin.

ba'cino [ba'tʃino] *sm* basin; (*MINERALOGIA*) field, bed; (*ANAT*) pelvis; (*NAUT*) dock; **~ carbonifero** coalfield; **~ di carenaggio** dry dock; **~ petrolifero** oilfield.

'bacio ['batʃo] *sm* kiss.

'baco, chi *sm* worm; **~ da seta** silkworm.

'bada *sf*: **tenere qn a ~** (*tener d'occhio*) to keep an eye on sb; (*tenere a distanza*) to hold sb at bay.

ba'dare *vi* (*fare attenzione*) to take care, be careful; **~ a** (*occuparsi di*) to look after, take care of; (*dar ascolto*) to pay attention to; **è un tipo che non bada a spese** money is no object to him; **bada ai fatti tuoi!** mind your own business!

ba'dia *sf* abbey.

ba'dile *sm* shovel.

'baffi *smpl* moustache *sg*, mustache *sg* (*US*); (*di animale*) whiskers; **leccarsi i ~** to lick one's lips; **ridere sotto i ~** to laugh up one's sleeve.

bagagli'aio [bagaʎ'ʎajo] *sm* luggage van (*Brit*) *o* car (*US*); (*AUT*) boot (*Brit*), trunk (*US*).

ba'gaglio [ba'gaʎʎo] *sm* luggage *q*, baggage *q*; **fare/disfare i ~i** to pack/unpack; **~ a mano** hand luggage.

bagat'tella *sf* trifle, trifling matter.

Bag'dad *sf* Baghdad.

baggia'nata [baddʒa'nata] *sf* foolish action; **dire ~e** to talk nonsense.

bagli'ore [baʎ'ʎore] *sm* flash, dazzling light; **un ~ di speranza** a sudden ray of hope.

ba'gnante [baɲ'ɲante] *sm/f* bather.

ba'gnare [baɲ'ɲare] *vt* to wet; (*inzuppare*) to soak; (*innaffiare*) to water; (*sog: fiume*) to flow through; (*: mare*) to wash, bathe; (*brindare*) to drink to, toast; **~rsi** *vr* (*al mare*) to go swimming *o* bathing; (*in vasca*) to have a bath.

ba'gnato, a [baɲ'ɲato] *ag* wet; **era come un pulcino ~** he looked like a drowned rat.

ba'gnino [baɲ'ɲino] *sm* lifeguard.

'bagno ['baɲɲo] *sm* bath; (*locale*) bathroom; **~i** *smpl* (*stabilimento*) baths; **fare il ~** to have a bath; (*nel mare*) to go swimming *o* bathing; **fare il ~ a qn** to give sb a bath; **mettere a ~** to soak; **~ (di) schiuma** bubble bath.

bagnoma'ria [baɲɲoma'ria] *sm*: **cuocere a ~** to cook in a double saucepan (*Brit*) *o* double boiler (*US*).

Ba'hama [ba'ama] *sfpl*: **le ~** the Bahamas.

Bah'rein [ba'rein] *sm*: **il ~** Bahrain *o* Bahrein.

'baia *sf* bay.

baio'netta *sf* bayonet.

'baita *sf* mountain hut.

balaus'trata *sf* balustrade.

balbet'tare *vi* to stutter, stammer; (*bimbo*) to babble ♦ *vt* to stammer out.

bal'buzie [bal'buttsje] *sf* stammer.

balbuzi'ente [balbut'tsjɛnte] *ag* stuttering, stammering.

Bal'cani *smpl*: **i ~** the Balkans.

bal'canico, a, ci, che *ag* Balkan.

bal'cone *sm* balcony.

baldac'chino [baldak'kino] *sm* canopy; **letto a ~** four-poster (bed).

bal'danza [bal'dantsa] *sf* self-confidence; boldness.

'baldo, a *ag* bold, daring.

bal'doria *sf*: **fare ~** to have a riotous time.

Bale'ari *sfpl*: **le isole ~** the Balearic Islands.

ba'lena *sf* whale.

bale'nare *vb impers*: **balena** there's lightning ♦ *vi* to flash; **mi balenò un'idea** an idea flashed through my mind.

baleni'era *sf* (*per la caccia*) whaler, whaling ship.

ba'leno *sm* flash of lightning; **in un ~** in a flash.

ba'lera *sf* (*locale*) dance hall; (*pista*) dance floor.

ba'lestra *sf* crossbow.

'balia *sf* wet-nurse; **~ asciutta** nanny.

ba'lia *sf*: **in ~ di** at the mercy of; **essere lasciato in ~ di se stesso** to be left to one's own devices.

ba'lilla *sm inv* (*STORIA*) *member of Fascist youth group*.

ba'listico, a, ci, che *ag* ballistic ♦ *sf* ballistics *sg*; **perito ~** ballistics expert.

'balla *sf* (*di merci*) bale; (*fandonia*) (tall) story.

bal'labile *sm* dance number, dance tune.

bal'lare *vt, vi* to dance.

bal'lata *sf* ballad.

balla'toio *sm* (*terrazzina*) gallery.

balle'rina *sf* dancer; ballet dancer; (*scarpa*) pump; **~ di rivista** chorus girl.

balle'rino *sm* dancer; ballet dancer.

bal'letto *sm* ballet.

'ballo *sm* dance; (*azione*) dancing *q*; **~ in maschera** *o* **mascherato** fancy-dress ball; **essere in ~** (*fig: persona*) to be involved; (*: cosa*) to be at stake; **tirare in ~ qc** to bring sth up, raise sth.

ballot'taggio [ballot'taddʒo] *sm* (*POL*) second ballot.

balne'are *ag* seaside *cpd*; (*stagione*) bathing.

ba'locco, chi *sm* toy.

ba'lordo, a *ag* stupid, senseless.

bal'samico, a, ci, che *ag* (*aria, brezza*) balmy; **pomata ~a** balsam.

'**balsamo** *sm* (*aroma*) balsam; (*lenimento, fig*) balm.
'**baltico, a, ci, che** *ag* Baltic; **il (mar) B~** the Baltic (Sea).
balu'ardo *sm* bulwark.
'**balza** ['baltsa] *sf* (*dirupo*) crag; (*di stoffa*) frill.
bal'zano, a [bal'tsano] *ag* (*persona, idea*) queer, odd.
bal'zare [bal'tsare] *vi* to bounce; (*lanciarsi*) to jump, leap; **la verità balza agli occhi** the truth of the matter is obvious.
'**balzo** ['baltso] *sm* bounce; jump, leap; (*del terreno*) crag; **prendere la palla al ~** (*fig*) to seize one's opportunity.
bam'bagia [bam'badʒa] *sf* (*ovatta*) cotton wool (*Brit*), absorbent cotton (*US*); (*cascame*) cotton waste; **tenere qn nella ~** (*fig*) to mollycoddle sb.
bam'bina *sf vedi* **bambino**.
bambi'naia *sf* nanny, nurse(maid).
bam'bino, a *sm/f* child; **fare il ~** to behave childishly.
bam'boccio [bam'bɔttʃo] *sm* plump child; (*pupazzo*) rag doll.
'**bambola** *sf* doll.
bambo'lotto *sm* male doll.
bambù *sm* bamboo.
ba'nale *ag* banal, commonplace.
banalità *sf inv* banality.
ba'nana *sf* banana.
ba'nano *sm* banana tree.
'**banca, che** *sf* bank; **~ d'affari** merchant bank; **~ (di) dati** data bank.
banca'rella *sf* stall.
ban'cario, a *ag* banking, bank *cpd* ♦ *sm* bank clerk.
banca'rotta *sf* bankruptcy; **fare ~** to go bankrupt.
bancarotti'ere *sm* bankrupt.
ban'chetto [ban'ketto] *sm* banquet.
banchi'ere [ban'kjɛre] *sm* banker.
ban'china [ban'kina] *sf* (*di porto*) quay; (*per pedoni, ciclisti*) path; (*di stazione*) platform; **~ cedevole** (*AUT*) soft verge (*Brit*) o shoulder (*US*); **~ spartitraffico** (*AUT*) central reservation (*Brit*), median (strip) (*US*).
ban'chisa [ban'kiza] *sf* pack ice.
'**banco, chi** *sm* bench; (*di negozio*) counter; (*di mercato*) stall; (*di officina*) (work-) bench; (*GEO, banca*) bank; **sotto ~** (*fig*) under the counter; **tenere il ~** (*nei giochi*) to be (the) banker; **tener ~** (*fig*) to monopolize the conversation; **~ di chiesa** pew; **~ di corallo** coral reef; **~ degli imputati** dock; **~ del Lotto** lottery-ticket office; **~ di prova** (*fig*) testing ground; **~ dei testimoni** witness box (*Brit*) o stand (*US*).
banco'giro [banko'dʒiro] *sm* credit transfer.
'**Bancomat** ® *sm inv* automated banking; (*tessera*) cash card.

banco'nota *sf* banknote.
'**banda** *sf* band; (*di stoffa*) band, stripe; (*lato, parte*) side; (*di calcolatore*) tape; **~ perforata** punch tape.
banderu'ola *sf* (*METEOR*) weathercock, weathervane; **essere una ~** (*fig*) to be fickle.
bandi'era *sf* flag, banner; **battere ~ italiana** (*nave etc*) to fly the Italian flag; **cambiare ~** (*fig*) to change sides; **~ di comodo** flag of convenience.
ban'dire *vt* to proclaim; (*esiliare*) to exile; (*fig*) to dispense with.
ban'dito *sm* outlaw, bandit.
bandi'tore *sm* (*di aste*) auctioneer.
'**bando** *sm* proclamation; (*esilio*) exile, banishment; **mettere al ~ qn** to exile sb; (*fig*) to freeze sb out; **~ alle ciance!** that's enough talk!
'**bandolo** *sm* (*di matassa*) end; **trovare il ~ della matassa** (*fig*) to find the key to the problem.
Bang'kok [ban'kɔk] *sf* Bangkok.
Bangla'desh [bangla'dɛʃ] *sm*: **il ~** Bangladesh.
bar *sm inv* bar.
'**bara** *sf* coffin.
ba'racca, che *sf* shed, hut; (*peg*) hovel; **mandare avanti la ~** to keep things going; **piantare ~ e burattini** to throw everything up.
barac'cato, a *sm/f person living in temporary camp.*
barac'chino [barak'kino] *sm* (*chiosco*) stall; (*apparecchio*) CB radio.
barac'cone *sm* booth, stall; **~i** *smpl* (*luna park*) funfair *sg* (*Brit*), amusement park; **fenomeno da ~** circus freak.
barac'copoli *sf inv* shanty town.
bara'onda *sf* hubbub, bustle.
ba'rare *vi* to cheat.
'**baratro** *sm* abyss.
barat'tare *vt*: **~ qc con** to barter sth for, swap sth for.
ba'ratto *sm* barter.
ba'rattolo *sm* (*di latta*) tin; (*di vetro*) jar; (*di coccio*) pot.
'**barba** *sf* beard; **farsi la ~** to shave; **farla in ~ a qn** (*fig*) to fool sb; **servire qn di ~ e capelli** (*fig*) to teach sb a lesson; **che ~!** what a bore!
barbabi'etola *sf* beetroot (*Brit*), beet (*US*); **~ da zucchero** sugar beet.
Bar'bados *sfpl*: **le ~** Barbados *sg*.
bar'barico, a, ci, che *ag* (*invasione*) barbarian; (*usanze, metodi*) barbaric.
bar'barie *sf* barbarity.
'**barbaro, a** *ag* barbarous; **~i** *smpl* barbarians.
'**barbecue** ['ba:bikju:] *sm inv* barbecue.
barbi'ere *sm* barber.
barbi'turico, a, ci, che *ag* barbituric ♦ *sm*

barbiturate.

bar'bone *sm* (*cane*) poodle; (*vagabondo*) tramp.

bar'buto, a *ag* bearded.

'barca, che *sf* boat; **una ~ di** (*fig*) heaps of, tons of; **mandare avanti la ~** (*fig*) to keep things going; **~ a remi** rowing boat (*Brit*), rowboat (*US*); **~ a vela** sailing boat (*Brit*), sailboat (*US*).

barcai'olo *sm* boatman.

barcame'narsi *vr* (*nel lavoro*) to get by; (*a parole*) to beat about the bush.

Barcel'lona [bartʃelˈlona] *sf* Barcelona.

barcol'lare *vi* to stagger.

bar'cone *sm* (*per ponti di barche*) pontoon.

ba'rella *sf* (*lettiga*) stretcher.

'Barents: il mar di ~ *sm* the Barents Sea.

ba'rese *ag* of (*o* from) Bari.

bari'centro [bariˈtʃɛntro] *sm* centre (*Brit*) *o* center (*US*) of gravity.

ba'rile *sm* barrel, cask.

ba'rista, i, e *sm/f* barman/barmaid; bar owner.

ba'ritono *sm* baritone.

bar'lume *sm* glimmer, gleam.

'baro *sm* (*CARTE*) cardsharp.

ba'rocco, a, chi, che *ag, sm* baroque.

ba'rometro *sm* barometer.

ba'rone *sm* baron; **i ~i della medicina** (*fig peg*) the top brass in the medical faculty.

baro'nessa *sf* baroness.

'barra *sf* bar; (*NAUT*) helm; (*segno grafico*) stroke.

barri'care *vt* to barricade.

barri'cata *sf* barricade; **essere dall'altra parte della ~** (*fig*) to be on the other side of the fence.

barri'era *sf* barrier; (*GEO*) reef; **la Grande B~ Corallina** the Great Barrier Reef.

bar'roccio [barˈrɔttʃo] *sm* cart.

ba'ruffa *sf* scuffle; **fare ~** to squabble.

barzel'letta [bardzelˈletta] *sf* joke, funny story.

basa'mento *sm* (*parte inferiore, piedestallo*) base; (*TECN*) bed, base plate.

ba'sare *vt* to base, found; **~rsi** *vr*: **~rsi su** (*sog: fatti, prove*) to be based *o* founded on; (: *persona*) to base one's arguments on.

'basco, a, schi, sche *ag* Basque ♦ *sm/f* Basque ♦ *sm* (*lingua*) Basque; (*copricapo*) beret.

bas'culla *sf* weighing machine, weighbridge.

'base *sf* base; (*fig: fondamento*) basis; (*POL*) rank and file; **di ~** basic; **in ~ a** on the basis of, according to; **in ~ a ciò ...** on that basis ...; **a ~ di caffè** coffee-based; **essere alla ~ di qc** to be at the root of sth; **gettare le ~i per qc** to lay the basis *o* foundations for sth; **avere buone ~i** (*INS*) to have a sound educational background.

'baseball [ˈbeisbɔːl] *sm* baseball.

ba'setta *sf* sideburn.

basi'lare *ag* basic, fundamental.

Basi'lea *sf* Basle.

ba'silica, che *sf* basilica.

ba'silico *sm* basil.

bas'sezza [basˈsettsa] *sf* (*d'animo, di sentimenti*) baseness; (*azione*) base action.

'basso, a *ag* low; (*di statura*) short; (*meridionale*) southern ♦ *sm* bottom, lower part; (*MUS*) bass; **a occhi ~i** with eyes lowered; **a ~ prezzo** cheap; **scendere da ~** to go downstairs; **cadere in ~** (*fig*) to come down in the world; **la ~a Italia** southern Italy; **il ~ Medioevo** the late Middle Ages.

basso'fondo, *pl* **bassi'fondi** *sm* (*GEO*) shallows *pl*; **i bassifondi** (*della città*) the seediest parts of the town.

bassorili'evo *sm* bas-relief.

bas'sotto, a *ag* squat ♦ *sm* (*cane*) dachshund.

bas'tardo, a *ag* (*animale, pianta*) hybrid, crossbreed; (*persona*) illegitimate, bastard (*peg*) ♦ *sm/f* illegitimate child, bastard (*peg*); (*cane*) mongrel.

bas'tare *vi, vb impers* to be enough, be sufficient; **~ a qn** to be enough for sb; **~ a se stesso** to be self-sufficient; **basta chiedere** *o* **che chieda a un vigile** you have only to *o* need only ask a policeman; **basti dire che ...** suffice it to say that ...; **basta!** that's enough!, that will do!; **punto e basta!** and that's that!

basti'an *sm*: **~ contrario** awkward customer.

basti'mento *sm* ship, vessel.

basto'nare *vt* to beat, thrash; **avere l'aria di un cane bastonato** to look crestfallen.

basto'nata *sf* blow (with a stick); **prendere qn a ~e** to give sb a good beating.

baston'cino [bastonˈtʃino] *sm* (*piccolo bastone*) small stick; (*TECN*) rod; (*SCI*) ski pole; **~i di pesce** (*CUC*) fish fingers (*Brit*), fish sticks (*US*).

bas'tone *sm* stick; **~i** *smpl* (*CARTE*) suit in Neapolitan pack of cards; **~ da passeggio** walking stick; **mettere i ~i fra le ruote a qn** to put a spoke in sb's wheel.

bat'taglia [batˈtaʎʎa] *sf* battle.

bat'taglio [batˈtaʎʎo] *sm* (*di campana*) clapper; (*di porta*) knocker.

battagli'one [battaʎˈʎone] *sm* battalion.

bat'tello *sm* boat.

bat'tente *sm* (*imposta: di porta*) wing, flap; (: *di finestra*) shutter; (*per bussare*) knocker; (*di orologio*) hammer; **chiudere i ~i** (*fig*) to shut up shop.

'battere *vt* to beat; (*grano*) to thresh; (*percorrere*) to scour; (*rintoccare: le ore*) to strike ♦ *vi* (*bussare*) to knock; (*urtare*): ~ **contro** to hit *o* strike against; (*pioggia, sole*) to beat down; (*cuore*) to beat; (*TENNIS*) to serve; ~**rsi** *vr* to fight; ~ **le mani** to clap; ~ **i piedi** to stamp one's feet; ~ **su un argomento** to hammer home an argument; ~ **a macchina** to type; ~ **il marciapiede** (*peg*) to walk the streets, be on the game; ~ **un rigore** (*CALCIO*) to take a penalty; ~ **in testa** (*AUT*) to knock; **in un batter d'occhio** in the twinkling of an eye; **senza** ~ **ciglio** without batting an eyelid; **battersela** to run off.

bat'teri *smpl* bacteria.

batte'ria *sf* battery; (*MUS*) drums *pl*; ~ **da cucina** pots and pans *pl*.

batteriolo'gia [batterjolo'dʒia] *sf* bacteriology.

bat'tesimo *sm* (*sacramento*) baptism; (*rito*) baptism, christening; **tenere qn a** ~ to be godfather (*o* godmother) to sb.

battez'zare [batted'dzare] *vt* to baptize; to christen.

battiba'leno *sm*: **in un** ~ in a flash.

batti'becco, chi *sm* squabble.

batticu'ore *sm* palpitations *pl*; **avere il** ~ to be frightened to death.

bat'tigia [bat'tidʒa] *sf* water's edge.

batti'mano *sm* applause.

batti'panni *sm inv* carpet-beater.

battis'tero *sm* baptistry.

battis'trada *sm inv* (*di pneumatico*) tread; (*di gara*) pacemaker.

battitap'peto *sm inv* upright vacuum cleaner.

'battito *sm* beat, throb; ~ **cardiaco** heartbeat; ~ **della pioggia/dell'orologio** beating of the rain/ticking of the clock.

batti'tore *sm* (*CRICKET*) batsman; (*BASEBALL*) batter; (*CACCIA*) beater.

batti'tura *sf* (*anche*: ~ **a macchina**) typing; (*del grano*) threshing.

bat'tuta *sf* blow; (*di macchina da scrivere*) stroke; (*MUS*) bar; beat; (*TEATRO*) cue; (*di caccia*) beating; (*POLIZIA*) combing, scouring; (*TENNIS*) service; **fare una** ~ to crack a joke, make a witty remark; **aver la** ~ **pronta** (*fig*) to have a ready answer; **è ancora alle prime** ~**e** it's just started.

ba'tuffolo *sm* wad.

ba'ule *sm* trunk; (*AUT*) boot (*Brit*), trunk (*US*).

bau'xite [bauk'site] *sf* bauxite.

'bava *sf* (*di animale*) slaver, slobber; (*di lumaca*) slime; (*di vento*) breath.

bava'glino [bavaʎ'ʎino] *sm* bib.

ba'vaglio [ba'vaʎʎo] *sm* gag.

bava'rese *ag*, *sm/f* Bavarian.

'bavero *sm* collar.

Bavi'era *sf* Bavaria.

ba'zar [bad'dzar] *sm inv* bazaar.

baz'zecola [bad'dzɛkola] *sf* trifle.

bazzi'care [battsi'kare] *vt* (*persona*) to hang about with; (*posto*) to hang about ♦ *vi*: ~ **in/con** to hang about/hang about with.

be'arsi *vr*: ~ **di qc/a fare qc** to delight in sth/in doing sth; ~ **alla vista di** to enjoy looking at.

beati'tudine *sf* bliss.

be'ato, a *ag* blessed; (*fig*) happy; ~ **te!** lucky you!

bebè *sm inv* baby.

bec'caccia, ce [bek'kattʃa] *sf* woodcock.

bec'care *vt* to peck; (*fig: raffreddore*) to pick up, catch; ~**rsi** *vr* (*fig*) to squabble.

bec'cata *sf* peck.

becheggi'are [bekked'dʒare] *vi* to pitch.

beccherò *etc* [bekke'rɔ] *vb vedi* **beccare**.

bec'chime [bek'kime] *sm* birdseed.

bec'chino [bek'kino] *sm* gravedigger.

'becco, chi *sm* beak, bill; (*di caffettiera etc*) spout; lip; (*fig fam*) cuckold; **mettere** ~ (*fam*) to butt in; **chiudi il** ~! (*fam*) shut your mouth!, shut your trap!; **non ho il** ~ **di un quattrino** (*fam*) I'm broke.

Be'fana *sf* old woman who, according to legend, brings children their presents at the Epiphany; (*Epifania*) Epiphany; (*donna brutta*): **b**~ hag, witch.

'beffa *sf* practical joke; **farsi** ~ *o* ~**e di qn** to make a fool of sb.

bef'fardo, a *ag* scornful, mocking.

bef'fare *vt* (*anche*: ~**rsi di**) to make a fool of, mock.

'bega, ghe *sf* quarrel.

'begli ['bɛʎʎi], **'bei** *ag vedi* **bello**.

beige [bɛʒ] *ag inv* beige.

Bei'rut *sf* Beirut.

bel *ag vedi* **bello**.

be'lare *vi* to bleat.

be'lato *sm* bleating.

'belga, gi, ghe *ag*, *sm/f* Belgian.

'Belgio ['bɛldʒo] *sm*: **il** ~ Belgium.

Bel'grado *sf* Belgrade.

'bella *sf vedi* **bello**.

bel'lezza [bel'lettsa] *sf* beauty; **chiudere** *o* **finire qc in** ~ to finish sth with a flourish; **che** ~! fantastic!; **ho pagato la** ~ **di 60.000 lire** I paid 60,000 lire, no less.

belli'coso, a *ag* warlike.

bellige'rante [bellidʒe'rante] *ag* belligerent.

bellim'busto *sm* dandy.

'bello, a *ag* (*dav sm* **bel** +*C*, **bell'** +*V*, **bello** + *s impura*, *gn*, *pn*, *ps*, *x*, *z*, *pl* **bei** +*C*, **begli** + *s impura etc o V*) beautiful, fine, lovely; (*uomo*) handsome ♦ *sm* (*bellezza*) beauty; (*tempo*) fine weather ♦ *sf* beauty, belle; (*innamorata*) sweetheart; (*anche*: ~**a copia**) fair copy; (*SPORT, CARTE*) deciding match ♦ *av*: **fa** ~ the weather is fine, it's fine; **una** ~**a cifra** a considerable sum of money; **un bel niente** absolutely nothing; **è una truffa** ~**a e buona!** it's a real fraud!; **è bell'e finito** it's already finished; **adesso**

viene il ~ now comes the best bit; **proprio sul più** ~ at that very moment; **farsi** ~ **di qc** (*vantarsi*) to show off about sth; **fare la** ~**a vita** to lead an easy life; **cosa fa di** ~? are you doing anything interesting?; **alla bell'e meglio** somehow or other; **oh** ~**a!, anche questa è** ~**a!** (*ironico*) that's nice!; **le B**~**e Arti** fine arts.

bellu'nese *ag* of (*o* from) Belluno.

'**belva** *sf* wild animal.

belve'dere *sm inv* panoramic viewpoint.

benché [ben'ke] *cong* although.

'**benda** *sf* bandage; (*per gli occhi*) blindfold.

ben'dare *vt* to bandage; to blindfold.

bendis'posto, a *ag*: ~ **a qn/qc** well-disposed towards sb/sth.

'**bene** *av* well; (*completamente, affatto*): **è ben difficile** it's very difficult ♦ *ag inv*: **gente** ~ well-to-do people ♦ *sm* good; (*COMM*) asset; ~**i** *smpl* (*averi*) property *sg*, estate *sg*; **io sto** ~**/poco** ~ I'm well/not very well; **va** ~ all right; **ben più lungo/ caro** much longer/more expensive; **lo spero** ~ I certainly hope so; **volere un** ~ **dell'anima a qn** to love sb very much; **un uomo per** ~ a respectable man; **fare** ~ to do the right thing; **fare** ~ **a** (*salute*) to be good for; **fare del** ~ **a qn** to do sb a good turn; **di** ~ **in meglio** better and better; ~**i ambientali** environmental assets; ~**i di consumo** consumer goods; ~**i di consumo durevole** consumer durables; ~**i culturali** cultural heritage; ~**i immateriali** immaterial *o* intangible assets; ~**i patrimoniali** fixed assets; ~**i privati** private property *sg*; ~**i pubblici** public property *sg*; ~**i reali** tangible assets.

bene'detto, a *pp di* **benedire** ♦ *ag* blessed, holy.

bene'dire *vt* to bless; to consecrate; **l'ho mandato a farsi** ~ (*fig*) I told him to go to hell.

benedizi'one [benedit'tsjone] *sf* blessing.

benedu'cato, a *ag* well-mannered.

benefat'tore, '**trice** *sm/f* benefactor/ benefactress.

benefi'cenza [benefi'tʃɛntsa] *sf* charity.

benefici'are [benefi'tʃare] *vi*: ~ **di** to benefit by, benefit from.

benefici'ario, a [benefi'tʃarjo] *ag, sm/f* beneficiary.

bene'ficio [bene'fitʃo] *sm* benefit; **con** ~ **d'inventario** (*fig*) with reservations.

be'nefico, a, ci, che *ag* beneficial; charitable.

'**Benelux** *sm*: **il** ~ Benelux, the Benelux countries.

beneme'renza [beneme'rɛntsa] *sf* merit.

bene'merito, a *ag* meritorious.

bene'placito [bene'platʃito] *sm* (*approvazione*) approval; (*permesso*) permission.

be'nessere *sm* well-being.

benes'tante *ag* well-to-do.

benes'tare *sm* consent, approval.

benevo'lenza [benevo'lɛntsa] *sf* benevolence.

be'nevolo, a *ag* benevolent.

ben'godi *sm* land of plenty.

benia'mino, a *sm/f* favourite (*Brit*), favorite (*US*).

be'nigno, a [be'niɲɲo] *ag* kind, kindly; (*critica etc*) favourable (*Brit*), favorable (*US*); (*MED*) benign.

benintenzio'nato, a [benintentsjo'nato] *ag* well-meaning.

benin'teso *av* of course; ~ **che** *cong* provided that.

benpen'sante *sm/f* conformist.

benser'vito *sm*: **dare il** ~ **a qn** (*sul lavoro*) to give sb the sack, fire sb; (*fig*) to send sb packing.

bensì *cong* but (rather).

benve'nuto, a *ag, sm* welcome; **dare il** ~ **a qn** to welcome sb.

ben'visto, a *ag*: **essere** ~ **(da)** to be well thought of (by).

benvo'lere *vt*: **farsi** ~ **da tutti** to win everybody's affection; **prendere a** ~ **qn/qc** to take a liking to sb/sth.

ben'zina [ben'dzina] *sf* petrol (*Brit*), gas (*US*); **fare** ~ to get petrol *o* gas; **rimanere senza** ~ to run out of petrol *o* gas.

benzi'naio [bendzi'najo] *sm* petrol (*Brit*) *o* gas (*US*) pump attendant.

be'one *sm* heavy drinker.

'**bere** *vt* to drink; (*assorbire*) to soak up; **questa volta non me la dai a** ~! I won't be taken in this time!

berga'masco, a, schi, sche *ag* of (*o* from) Bergamo.

'**Bering** ['beriŋ]: **il mar di** ~ *sm* the Bering Sea.

ber'lina *sf* (*AUT*) saloon (car) (*Brit*), sedan (*US*); **mettere alla** ~ (*fig*) to hold up to ridicule.

Ber'lino *sf* Berlin; ~ **est/ovest** East/West Berlin.

Ber'muda *sfpl*: **le** ~ Bermuda *sg*.

ber'muda *smpl* (*calzoncini*) Bermuda shorts.

'**Berna** *sf* Bern.

ber'noccolo *sm* bump; (*inclinazione*) flair.

ber'retto *sm* cap.

berrò *etc vb vedi* **bere**.

bersagli'are [bersaʎ'ʎare] *vt* to shoot at; (*colpire ripetutamente, fig*) to bombard; **bersagliato dalla sfortuna** dogged by ill fortune.

bersagli'ere [bersaʎ'ʎɛre] *sm member of rifle regiment in Italian army*.

ber'saglio [ber'saʎʎo] *sm* target.

bes'temmia *sf* curse; (*REL*) blasphemy.

bestemmi'are *vi* to curse, swear; to blaspheme ♦ *vt* to curse, swear at; to blaspheme; ~ **come un turco** to swear like a trooper.

'**bestia** *sf* animal; **lavorare come una** ~ to work like a dog; **andare in** ~ (*fig*) to fly into a rage; **una** ~ **rara** (*fig: persona*) an oddball; ~ **da soma** beast of burden.

besti'ale *ag* bestial, brutish; (*fam*): **fa un caldo** ~ it's terribly hot; **fa un freddo** ~ it's bitterly cold.

bestialità *sf inv* (*qualità*) bestiality; **dire/ fare una** ~ **dopo l'altra** to say/do one idiotic thing after another.

besti'ame *sm* livestock; (*bovino*) cattle *pl*.

Bet'lemme *sf* Bethlehem.

betoni'era *sf* cement mixer.

'**bettola** *sf* (*peg*) dive.

be'tulla *sf* birch.

be'vanda *sf* drink, beverage.

bevi'tore, 'trice *sm/f* drinker.

'**bevo** *etc vb vedi* **bere**.

be'vuto, a *pp di* **bere** ♦ *sf* drink.

'**bevvi** *etc vb vedi* **bere**.

BG *sigla* = Bergamo.

BI *sigla f* = Banca d'Italia.

bi'ada *sf* fodder.

bianche'ria [bjanke'ria] *sf* linen; ~ **intima** underwear; ~ **da donna** ladies' underwear, lingerie.

bi'anco, a, chi, che *ag* white; (*non scritto*) blank ♦ *sm* white; (*intonaco*) whitewash ♦ *sm/f* white, white man/woman; **in** ~ (*foglio, assegno*) blank; **in** ~ **e nero** (*TV, FOT*) black and white; **mangiare in** ~ to follow a bland diet; **pesce in** ~ boiled fish; **andare in** ~ (*non riuscire*) to fail; (*in amore*) to be rejected; **notte** ~**a o in** ~ sleepless night; **voce** ~**a** (*MUS*) treble (voice); **votare scheda** ~**a** to return a blank voting slip; ~ **dell'uovo** egg-white.

bianco'segno [bjanko'seɲɲo] *sm* signature to a blank document.

biancos'pino *sm* hawthorn.

biasci'care [bjaʃʃi'kare] *vt* to mumble.

biasi'mare *vt* to disapprove of, censure.

bi'asimo *sm* disapproval, censure.

'**bibbia** *sf* bible.

bibe'ron *sm inv* feeding bottle.

'**bibita** *sf* (soft) drink.

bibliogra'fia *sf* bibliography.

biblio'teca, che *sf* library; (*mobile*) bookcase.

bibliote'cario, a *sm/f* librarian.

bicame'rale *ag* (*POL*) two-chamber *cpd*.

bicarbo'nato *sm*: ~ (**di sodio**) bicarbonate (of soda).

bicchi'ere [bik'kjɛre] *sm* glass; **è** (**facile**) **come bere un bicchier d'acqua** it's as easy as pie.

bici'cletta [bitʃi'kletta] *sf* bicycle; **andare in** ~ to cycle.

bi'cipite [bi'tʃipite] *sm* bicep.

bidé *sm inv* bidet.

bi'dello, a *sm/f* (*INS*) janitor.

bidirezio'nale [bidirettsjo'nale] *ag* bidirectional.

bido'nare *vt* (*fam: piantare in asso*) to let down; (: *imbrogliare*) to cheat, swindle.

bido'nata *sf* (*fam*) swindle.

bi'done *sm* drum, can; (*anche:* ~ **dell'immondizia**) (dust)bin; (*fam: truffa*) swindle; **fare un** ~ **a qn** (*fam*) to let sb down; to cheat sb.

bidon'ville [bidɔ̃'vil] *sf inv* shanty town.

bi'eco, a, chi, che *ag* sinister.

bi'ella *sf* (*TECN*) connecting rod.

bien'nale *ag* biennial ♦ *sf*: **la B**~ **di Venezia** the Venice Arts Festival.

bi'ennio *sm* period of two years.

bi'erre *sm/f* member of the Red Brigades.

bi'etola *sf* beet.

bifo'cale *ag* bifocal.

bi'folco, a, chi, che *sm/f* (*peg*) bumpkin, yokel.

'**bifora** *sf* (*ARCHIT*) mullioned window.

bifor'carsi *vr* to fork.

biforcazi'one [biforkat'tsjone] *sf* fork.

bifor'cuto, a *ag* (*anche fig*) forked.

biga'mia *sf* bigamy.

'**bigamo, a** *ag* bigamous ♦ *sm/f* bigamist.

bighello'nare [bigello'nare] *vi* to loaf (about).

bighel'lone, a [bigel'lone] *sm/f* loafer.

bigiotte'ria [bidʒotte'ria] *sf* costume jewellery (*Brit*) o jewelry (*US*); (*negozio*) jeweller's (shop) (*Brit*) o jewelry store (*US*) (*selling only costume jewellery*).

bigli'ardo [biʎ'ʎardo] *sm* = **biliardo**.

bigliet'taio, a [biʎʎet'tajo] *sm/f* (*nei treni*) ticket inspector; (*in autobus etc*) conductor/conductress; (*CINEMA, TEATRO*) box-office attendant.

bigliette'ria [biʎʎette'ria] *sf* (*di stazione*) ticket office; booking office; (*di teatro*) box office.

bigli'etto [biʎ'ʎetto] *sm* (*per viaggi, spettacoli etc*) ticket; (*cartoncino*) card; (*anche:* ~ **di banca**) (bank)note; ~ **d'auguri/da visita** greetings/visiting card; ~ **d'andata e ritorno** return (*Brit*) o round-trip (*US*) ticket; ~ **omaggio** complimentary ticket.

bignè [biɲ'ɲɛ] *sm inv* cream puff.

bigo'dino *sm* roller, curler.

bi'gotto, a *ag* over-pious ♦ *sm/f* church fiend.

bi'kini *sm inv* bikini.

bi'lancia, ce [bi'lantʃa] *sf* (*pesa*) scales *pl*; (: *di precisione*) balance; (*dello zodiaco*): **B**~ Libra; **essere della B**~ to be Libra; ~ **commerciale/dei pagamenti** balance of trade/payments.

bilanci'are [bilan'tʃare] *vt* (*pesare*) to weigh; (: *fig*) to weigh up; ~ **le uscite e le entrate** (*COMM*) to balance expenditure and revenue.

bi'lancio [bi'lantʃo] *sm* (*COMM*) balance(-sheet); (*statale*) budget; **far quadrare il ~** to balance the books; **chiudere il ~ in attivo/passivo** to make a profit/loss; **fare il ~ di** (*fig*) to assess; **~ consolidato** consolidated balance; **~ consuntivo** (final) balance; **~ preventivo** budget; **~ pubblico** national budget; **~ di verifica** trial balance.

'bile *sf* bile; (*fig*) rage, anger.

bili'ardo *sm* billiards *sg*; (*tavolo*) billiard table.

'bilico, chi *sm*: **essere in ~** to be balanced; (*fig*) to be undecided; **tenere qn in ~** to keep sb in suspense.

bi'lingue *ag* bilingual.

bili'one *sm* (*mille milioni*) thousand million, billion (*US*); (*milione di milioni*) billion (*Brit*), trillion (*US*).

'bimbo, a *sm/f* little boy/girl.

bimen'sile *ag* fortnightly.

bimes'trale *ag* two-monthly, bimonthly.

bi'mestre *sm* two-month period; **ogni ~** every two months.

bi'nario, a *ag* binary ♦ *sm* (railway) track *o* line; (*piattaforma*) platform; **~ morto** dead-end track.

bi'nocolo *sm* binoculars *pl*.

bio... *prefisso* bio....

bio'chimica [bio'kimika] *sf* biochemistry.

biodegra'dabile *ag* biodegradable.

bio'fisica *sf* biophysics *sg*.

biogra'fia *sf* biography.

bio'grafico, a, ci, che *ag* biographical.

bi'ografo, a *sm/f* biographer.

biolo'gia [biolo'dʒia] *sf* biology.

bio'logico, a, ci, che [bio'lɔdʒiko] *ag* biological.

bi'ologo, a, ghi, ghe *sm/f* biologist.

bi'ondo, a *ag* blond, fair.

bi'onica *sf* bionics *sg*.

biop'sia *sf* biopsy.

bio'ritmo *sm* biorhythm.

bipar'tito, a *ag* (*POL*) two-party *cpd* ♦ *sm* (*POL*) two-party alliance.

'birba *sf* rascal, rogue.

bir'bante *sm* rascal, rogue.

birbo'nata *sf* naughty trick.

bir'bone, a *ag* (*bambino*) naughty ♦ *sm/f* little rascal.

biri'chino, a [biri'kino] *ag* mischievous ♦ *sm/f* scamp, little rascal.

bi'rillo *sm* skittle (*Brit*), pin (*US*); **~i** *smpl* (*gioco*) skittles *sg* (*Brit*), bowling *q* (*US*).

Bir'mania *sf*: **la ~** Burma.

bir'mano, a *ag, sm/f* Burmese (*inv*).

'biro ® *sf inv* biro ®.

'birra *sf* beer; **~ scura** stout; **a tutta ~** (*fig*) at top speed.

birre'ria *sf* (*locale*) ≈ bierkeller; (*fabbrica*) brewery.

bis *escl, sm inv* encore ♦ *ag inv* (*treno, auto-*

bus) relief *cpd* (*Brit*), additional; (*numero*): **12 ~ 12a.**

bi'saccia, ce [bi'zattʃa] *sf* knapsack.

Bi'sanzio [bi'zantsjo] *sf* Byzantium.

bis'betico, a, ci, che *ag* ill-tempered, crabby.

bisbigli'are [bizbiʎ'ʎare] *vt, vi* to whisper.

bis'biglio [biz'biʎʎo] *sm* whisper; (*notizia*) rumour (*Brit*), rumor (*US*).

bisbi'glio [bizbiʎ'ʎio] *sm* whispering.

bis'boccia, ce [biz'bɔttʃa] *sf* binge, spree; **fare ~** to have a binge.

'bisca, sche *sf* gambling house.

Bis'caglia [bis'kaʎʎa] *sf*: **il golfo di ~** the Bay of Biscay.

'bischero ['biskero] *sm* (*MUS*) peg; (*fam: toscano*) fool, idiot.

'biscia, sce ['biʃʃa] *sf* snake; **~ d'acqua** water snake.

biscot'tato, a *ag* crisp; **fette ~e** rusks.

bis'cotto *sm* biscuit.

bises'tile *ag*: **anno ~** leap year.

bisezi'one [biset'tsjone] *sf* dichotomy.

bis'lacco, a, chi, che *ag* odd, weird.

bis'lungo, a, ghi, ghe *ag* oblong.

bis'nonno, a *sm/f* great-grandfather/grandmother.

biso'gnare [bizoɲ'ɲare] *vb impers*: **bisogna che tu parta/lo faccia** you'll have to go/do it; **bisogna parlargli** we'll (*o* I'll) have to talk to him ♦ *vi* (*esser utile*) to be necessary.

bi'sogno [bi'zoɲɲo] *sm* need; **~i** *smpl* (*necessità corporali*): **fare i propri ~i** to relieve o.s.; **avere ~ di qc/di fare qc** to need sth/to do sth; **al ~, in caso di ~** if need be.

biso'gnoso, a [bizoɲ'ɲoso] *ag* needy, poor; **~ di** in need of, needing.

bi'sonte *sm* (*ZOOL*) bison.

bis'tecca, che *sf* steak, beefsteak; **~ al sangue/ai ferri** rare/grilled steak.

bisticci'are [bistit'tʃare] *vi*, **~rsi** *vr* to quarrel, bicker.

bis'ticcio [bis'tittʃo] *sm* quarrel, squabble; (*gioco di parole*) pun.

bistrat'tare *vt* to maltreat.

'bisturi *sm inv* scalpel.

bi'sunto, a *ag* very greasy.

bi'torzolo [bi'tortsolo] *sm* (*sulla testa*) bump; (*sul corpo*) lump.

'bitter *sm inv* bitters *pl*.

bivac'care *vi* (*MIL*) to bivouac; (*fig*) to bed down.

bi'vacco, chi *sm* bivouac.

'bivio *sm* fork; (*fig*) dilemma.

bizan'tino, a [biddzan'tino] *ag* Byzantine.

'bizza ['biddza] *sf* tantrum; **fare le ~e** to throw a tantrum.

biz'zarro, a [bid'dzarro] *ag* bizarre, strange.

biz'zeffe [bid'dzɛffe]: **a ~** *av* in plenty, galore.

BL *sigla* = Belluno.

blan'dire *vt* to soothe; to flatter.

'blando, a *ag* mild, gentle.

blas'femo, a *ag* blasphemous ♦ *sm/f* blasphemer.

bla'sone *sm* coat of arms.

blate'rare *vi* to chatter, blether.

'blatta *sf* cockroach.

blin'dato, a *ag* armoured (*Brit*), armored (*US*); **camera ~a** strongroom; **vetro ~** bulletproof glass.

bloc'care *vt* to block; (*isolare*) to isolate, cut off; (*porto*) to blockade; (*prezzi, beni*) to freeze; (*meccanismo*) to jam; **~rsi** *vr* (*motore*) to stall; (*freni, porta*) to jam, stick; (*ascensore*) to get stuck, stop; **ha bloccato la macchina** (*AUT*) he jammed on the brakes.

bloccas'terzo [blokkas'tɛrtso] *sm* (*AUT*) steering lock.

bloccherò *etc* [blokke'rɔ] *vb vedi* **bloccare**.

bloc'chetto [blok'ketto] *sm* notebook.

'blocco, chi *sm* block; (*MIL*) blockade; (*dei fitti*) restriction; (*quadernetto*) pad; (*fig: unione*) coalition; (*il bloccare*) blocking; isolating, cutting-off; blockading; freezing; jamming; **in ~** (*nell'insieme*) as a whole; (*COMM*) in bulk; **~ cardiaco** cardiac arrest.

bloc-'notes [blɔk'nɔt] *sm inv* notebook, notepad.

blu *ag inv, sm inv* dark blue.

bluf'fare *vi* (*anche fig*) to bluff.

'blusa *sf* (*camiciotto*) smock; (*camicetta*) blouse.

BMT *sigla m* = **bollettino meteorologico**.

BN *sigla* = Benevento.

BO *sigla* = Bologna.

'boa *sm inv* (*ZOOL*) boa constrictor; (*sciarpa*) feather boa ♦ *sf* buoy.

bo'ato *sm* rumble, roar.

bob [bɔb] *sm inv* bobsleigh.

bo'bina *sf* reel, spool; (*di pellicola*) spool; (*di film*) reel; (*ELETTR*) coil.

'bocca, che *sf* mouth; **essere di buona ~** to be a hearty eater; (*fig*) to be easily satisfied; **essere sulla ~ di tutti** (*persona, notizia*) to be the talk of the town; **rimanere a ~ asciutta** to have nothing to eat; (*fig*) to be disappointed; **in ~ al lupo!** good luck!; **~ di leone** (*BOT*) snapdragon.

boc'caccia, ce [bok'kattʃa] *sf* (*malalingua*) gossip; (*smorfia*): **fare le ~ce** to pull faces.

boc'caglio [bok'kaʎʎo] *sm* (*TECN*) nozzle; (*di respiratore*) mouthpiece.

boc'cale *sm* jug; **~ da birra** tankard.

bocca'scena [bokkaʃ'ʃɛna] *sm inv* proscenium.

boc'cata *sf* mouthful; (*di fumo*) puff; **prendere una ~ d'aria** to go out for a breath of (fresh) air.

boc'cetta [bot'tʃetta] *sf* small bottle.

boccheggi'are [bokked'dʒare] *vi* to gasp.

boc'chino [bok'kino] *sm* (*di sigaretta, sigaro: cannella*) cigarette-holder; cigar-holder; (*di pipa, strumenti musicali*) mouthpiece.

'boccia, ce ['bottʃa] *sf* bottle; (*da vino*) decanter, carafe; (*palla di legno, metallo*) bowl; **gioco delle ~ce** bowls *sg*.

bocci'are [bot'tʃare] *vt* (*proposta, progetto*) to reject; (*INS*) to fail; (*BOCCE*) to hit.

boccia'tura [bottʃa'tura] *sf* failure.

bocci'olo [bot'tʃɔlo] *sm* bud.

'boccolo *sm* curl.

boc'cone *sm* mouthful, morsel; **mangiare un ~** to have a bite to eat.

boc'coni *av* face downwards.

Bo'emia *sf* Bohemia.

bo'emo, a *ag, sm/f* Bohemian.

bofonchi'are [bofon'kjare] *vi* to grumble.

Bogotá *sf* Bogotá.

'boia *sm inv* executioner; hangman; **fa un freddo ~** (*fam*) it's cold as hell; **mondo ~!**, **~ d'un mondo ladro!** (*fam*) damn!, blast!

boi'ata *sf* botch.

boicot'taggio [boikot'taddʒo] *sm* boycott.

boicot'tare *vt* to boycott.

'bolgia, ge ['bɔldʒa] *sf* (*fig*): **c'era una tale ~ al cinema** the cinema was absolutely mobbed.

'bolide *sm* (*ASTR*) meteor; (*macchina: da corsa*) racing car (*Brit*), race car (*US*); (: *elaborata*) performance car; **come un ~** like a flash, at top speed; **entrare/uscire come un ~** to charge in/out.

Bo'livia *sf*: **la ~** Bolivia.

bolivi'ano, a *ag, sm/f* Bolivian.

'bolla *sf* bubble; (*MED*) blister; (*COMM*) bill, receipt; **finire in una ~ di sapone** (*fig*) to come to nothing; **~ di accompagnamento** waybill; **~ di consegna** delivery note; **~ papale** papal bull.

bol'lare *vt* to stamp; (*fig*) to brand.

bol'lente *ag* boiling; boiling hot; **calmare i ~i spiriti** to sober up, calm down.

bol'letta *sf* bill; (*ricevuta*) receipt; **essere in ~** to be hard up; **~ di consegna** delivery note; **~ doganale** clearance certificate; **~ di trasporto aereo** air waybill.

bollet'tino *sm* bulletin; (*COMM*) note; **~ meteorologico** weather forecast; **~ di ordinazione** order form; **~ di spedizione** consignment note.

bol'lire *vt, vi* to boil; **qualcosa bolle in pentola** (*fig*) there's something brewing.

bol'lito *sm* (*CUC*) boiled meat.

bolli'tore *sm* (*TECN*) boiler; (*CUC: per acqua*) kettle; (: *per latte*) milk pan.

bolli'tura *sf* boiling.

'bollo *sm* stamp; **imposta di ~** stamp duty; **~ auto** road tax; **~ per patente** driving licence tax; **~ postale** postmark.

bol'lore *sm*: **dare un ~ a qc** to bring sth to

the boil (*Brit*) *o* a boil (*US*); **i ~i della gioventù** youthful enthusiasm *sg.*

bolo'gnese [boloɲ'ɲese] *ag* Bolognese; **spaghetti alla ~** spaghetti bolognese.

'**bomba** *sf* bomb; **tornare a ~** (*fig*) to get back to the point; **sei stato una ~!** you were tremendous!; **~ atomica** atom bomb; **~ a mano** hand grenade; **~ ad orologeria** time bomb.

bombarda'mento *sm* bombardment; bombing.

bombar'dare *vt* to bombard; (*da aereo*) to bomb.

bombardi'ere *sm* bomber.

bom'betta *sf* bowler (hat) (*Brit*), derby (*US*).

'**bombola** *sf* cylinder; **~ del gas** gas cylinder.

bomboni'era *sf* box of sweets (*as souvenir at weddings, first communions etc*).

bo'naccia, ce [bo'nattʃa] *sf* dead calm.

bonacci'one, a [bonat'tʃone] *ag* good-natured, easy-going ♦ *sm/f* good-natured sort.

bo'nario, a *ag* good-natured, kind.

bo'nifica, che *sf* reclamation; reclaimed land.

bo'nifico, ci *sm* (*riduzione, abbuono*) discount; (*versamento a terzi*) credit transfer.

Bonn *sf* Bonn.

bontà *sf* goodness; (*cortesia*) kindness; **aver la ~ di fare qc** to be good *o* kind enough to do sth.

'**bonus-'malus** *sm inv* ≈ no-claims bonus.

bor'bonico, a, ci, che *ag* Bourbon; (*fig*) backward, out of date.

borbot'tare *vi* to mumble; (*stomaco*) to rumble.

borbot'tio, ii *sm* mumbling; rumbling.

'**borchia** ['borkja] *sf* stud.

borda'tura *sf* (*SARTORIA*) border, trim.

bor'deaux [bor'dɔ] *sm* (*colore*) burgundy, maroon; (*vino*) Bordeaux.

bor'dello *sm* brothel.

'**bordo** *sm* (*NAUT*) ship's side; (*orlo*) edge; (*striscia di guarnizione*) border, trim; **a ~ di** (*nave, aereo*) aboard, on board; (*macchina*) in; **sul ~ della strada** at the roadside; **persona d'alto ~** (*fig*) VIP.

bor'dura *sf* border.

bor'gata *sf* hamlet; (*a Roma*) working-class suburb.

bor'ghese [bor'geze] *ag* (*spesso peg*) middleclass; bourgeois; **abito ~** civilian dress; **poliziotto in ~** plainclothes policeman.

borghe'sia [borge'zia] *sf* middle classes *pl*; bourgeoisie.

'**borgo, ghi** *sm* (*paesino*) village; (*quartiere*) district; (*sobborgo*) suburb.

'**boria** *sf* self-conceit, arrogance.

bori'oso, a *ag* arrogant.

bor'lotto *sm* kidney bean.

'**Borneo** *sm*: **il ~** Borneo.

boro'talco *sm* talcum powder.

bor'raccia, ce [bor'rattʃa] *sf* canteen, waterbottle.

'**borsa** *sf* bag; (*anche*: **~ da signora**) handbag; (*ECON*): **la B~ (valori)** the Stock Exchange; **~ dell'acqua calda** hot-water bottle; **B~ merci** commodity exchange; **~ nera** black market; **~ della spesa** shopping bag; **~ di studio** grant.

borsai'olo *sm* pickpocket.

bor'seggio [bor'seddʒo] *sm* pickpocketing.

borsel'lino *sm* purse.

bor'sello *sm* gent's handbag.

bor'setta *sf* handbag.

bor'sista, i, e *sm/f* (*ECON*) speculator; (*INS*) grant-holder.

bos'caglia [bos'kaʎʎa] *sf* woodlands *pl*.

boscai'olo *sm* woodcutter; forester.

bos'chetto [bos'ketto] *sm* copse, grove.

'**bosco, schi** *sm* wood.

bos'coso, a *ag* wooded.

'**bossolo** *sm* cartridge case.

Bot, bot *sigla m inv vedi* **buono ordinario del Tesoro**.

bo'tanico, a, ci, che *ag* botanical ♦ *sm* botanist ♦ *sf* botany.

'**botola** *sf* trap door.

Bots'wana [bots'vana] *sm*: **il ~** Botswana.

'**botta** *sf* blow; (*rumore*) bang; **dare (un sacco di) ~e a qn** to give sb a good thrashing; **~ e risposta** (*fig*) cut and thrust.

'**botte** *sf* barrel, cask; **essere in una ~ di ferro** (*fig*) to be as safe as houses; **volere la ~ piena e la moglie ubriaca** to want to have one's cake and eat it.

bot'tega, ghe *sf* shop; (*officina*) workshop; **stare a ~ (da qn)** to serve one's apprenticeship (with sb); **le B~ghe Oscure** headquarters of the Italian Communist party.

botte'gaio, a *sm/f* shopkeeper.

botte'ghino [botte'gino] *sm* ticket office; (*del lotto*) public lottery office.

bot'tiglia [bot'tiʎʎa] *sf* bottle.

bottiglie'ria [bottiʎʎe'ria] *sf* wine shop.

bot'tino *sm* (*di guerra*) booty; (*di rapina, furto*) loot; **fare ~ di qc** (*anche fig*) to make off with sth.

'**botto** *sm* bang; crash; **di ~** suddenly; **d'un ~** (*fam*) in a flash.

bot'tone *sm* button; (*BOT*) bud; **stanza dei ~i** control room; (*fig*) nerve centre; **attaccare (un) ~ a o con qn** to buttonhole sb; **botton d'oro** buttercup.

bo'vino, a *ag* bovine; **~i** *smpl* cattle.

box [bɔks] *sm inv* (*per cavalli*) horsebox; (*per macchina*) lock-up; (*per macchina da corsa*) pit; (*per bambini*) playpen.

boxe [bɔks] *sf* boxing.

'**bozza** ['bɔttsa] *sf* draft; (*TIP*) proof; **~ di stampa/impaginata** galley/page proof.

boz'zetto [bot'tsetto] *sm* sketch.

'bozzolo ['bɔttsolo] *sm* cocoon.

BR *sigla fpl* = **Brigate Rosse** ♦ *sigla* = *Brindisi*.

'braca, che *sf* (*gamba di pantalone*) trouser leg; **~che** *sfpl* (*fam*) trousers, pants (*US*); (*mutandoni*) drawers; **calare le ~che** (*fig fam*) to chicken out.

brac'care *vt* to hunt.

brac'cetto [brat't∫etto] *sm*: **a ~** arm in arm.

braccherò *etc* [brakke'rɔ] *vb vedi* **braccare**.

bracci'ale [brat't∫ale] *sm* bracelet; (*distintivo*) armband.

braccia'letto [brattʃa'letto] *sm* bracelet, bangle.

bracci'ante [brat't∫ante] *sm* (*AGR*) day labourer.

bracci'ata [brat't∫ata] *sf* armful; (*nel nuoto*) stroke.

'braccio ['bratt∫o] *sm* (*pl*(*f*) **braccia**: *ANAT*) arm; (*pl*(*m*) **bracci**: *di gru, fiume*) arm; (*: di edificio*) wing; **camminare sotto ~** to walk arm in arm; **è il suo ~ destro** he's his right-hand man; **~ di ferro** (*anche fig*) trial of strength; **~ di mare** sound.

bracci'olo [brat't∫ɔlo] *sm* (*appoggio*) arm.

'bracco, chi *sm* hound.

bracconi'ere *sm* poacher.

'brace ['brat∫e] *sf* embers *pl*.

braci'ere [bra't∫ere] *sm* brazier.

braci'ola [bra't∫ɔla] *sf* (*CUC*) chop.

'bradipo *sm* (*ZOOL*) sloth.

'brado, a *ag*: **allo stato ~** in the wild *o* natural state.

'brama *sf*: **~** (**di/di fare**) longing (for/to do), yearning (for/to do).

bra'mare *vt*: **~** (**qc/di fare qc**) to long (for sth/to do sth), yearn (for sth/to do sth).

bramo'sia *sf*: **~** (**di**) longing (for), yearning (for).

'branca, che *sf* branch.

'branchia ['brankja] *sf* (*ZOOL*) gill.

'branco, chi *sm* (*di cani, lupi*) pack; (*di uccelli, pecore*) flock; (*peg: di persone*) gang, pack.

branco'lare *vi* to grope, feel one's way.

'branda *sf* camp bed.

bran'dello *sm* scrap, shred; **a ~i** in tatters, in rags; **fare a ~i** to tear to shreds.

bran'dina *sf* camp bed (*Brit*), cot (*US*).

bran'dire *vt* to brandish.

'brano *sm* piece; (*di libro*) passage.

bra'sare *vt* to braise.

bra'sato *sm* braised meat.

Bra'sile *sm*: **il ~** Brazil.

Bra'silia *sf* Brasilia.

brasili'ano, a *ag*, *sm/f* Brazilian.

bra'vata *sf* (*azione spavalda*) act of bravado.

'bravo, a *ag* (*abile*) clever, capable, skilful; (*buono*) good, honest; (*: bambino*) good; (*coraggioso*) brave; **~!** well done!; (*al tea-*

tro) bravo!; **su da ~!** (*fam*) there's a good boy!; **mi sono fatto le mie ~e 8 ore di lavoro** I put in a full 8 hours' work.

bra'vura *sf* cleverness, skill.

'breccia, ce ['brett∫a] *sf* breach; **essere sulla ~** (*fig*) to be going strong; **fare ~ nell'animo** *o* **nel cuore di qn** to find the way to sb's heart.

'Brema *sf* Bremen.

bre'saola *sf* kind of dried salted beef.

bresci'ano, a [bre∫'∫ano] *ag* of (*o* from) Brescia.

Bre'tagna [bre'taɲɲa] *sf*: **la ~** Brittany.

bre'tella *sf* (*AUT*) link; **~e** *sfpl* braces.

'brettone *ag*, *sm/f* Breton.

'breve *ag* brief, short; **in ~** in short; **per farla ~** to cut a long story short; **a ~** (*COMM*) short-term.

brevet'tare *vt* to patent.

bre'vetto *sm* patent; **~ di pilotaggio** pilot's licence (*Brit*) *o* license (*US*).

brevità *sf* brevity.

'brezza ['breddza] *sf* breeze.

'bricco, chi *sm* jug; **~ del caffè** coffeepot.

bricco'nata *sf* mischievous trick.

bric'cone, a *sm/f* rogue, rascal.

'briciola ['brit∫ola] *sf* crumb.

'briciolo ['brit∫olo] *sm* (*specie fig*) bit.

bridge [bridʒ] *sm* bridge.

'briga, ghe *sf* (*fastidio*) trouble, bother; **attaccar ~** to start a quarrel; **pigliarsi la ~ di fare qc** to take the trouble to do sth.

brigadi'ere *sm* (*dei carabinieri etc*) ≈ sergeant.

bri'gante *sm* bandit.

bri'gata *sf* (*MIL*) brigade; (*gruppo*) group, party; **le B~e Rosse** (*POL*) the Red Brigades.

briga'tismo *sm* *phenomenon of the Red Brigades*.

briga'tista, i, e *sm/f* (*POL*) *member of the Red Brigades*.

'briglia ['briʎʎa] *sf* rein; **a ~ sciolta** at full gallop; (*fig*) at full speed.

bril'lante *ag* bright; (*anche fig*) brilliant; (*che luccica*) shining ♦ *sm* diamond.

brillan'tina *sf* brilliantine.

bril'lare *vi* to shine; (*mina*) to blow up ♦ *vt* (*mina*) to set off.

'brillo, a *ag* merry, tipsy.

'brina *sf* hoarfrost.

brin'dare *vi*: **~ a qn/qc** to drink to *o* toast sb/sth.

'brindisi *sm inv* toast.

'brio *sm* liveliness, go.

bri'oche [bri'ɔʃ] *sf inv* brioche (bun).

bri'oso, a *ag* lively.

'briscola *sf* type of card game; (*seme vincente*) trump(s); (*carta*) trump card.

bri'tannico, a, ci, che *ag* British ♦ *sm/f* Briton; **i B~ci** the British *pl*.

'brivido *sm* shiver; (*di ribrezzo*) shudder;

(*fig*) thrill; **racconti del** ~ suspense stories.

brizzo'lato, a [brittso'lato] *ag* (*persona*) going grey; (*barba, capelli*) greying.

'**brocca, che** *sf* jug.

broc'cato *sm* brocade.

'**broccolo** *sm* broccoli *q*.

bro'daglia [bro'daʎʎa] *sf* (*peg*) dishwater.

'**brodo** *sm* broth; (*per cucinare*) stock; ~ **ristretto** consommé; **lasciare** (**cuocere**) **qn nel suo** ~ to let sb stew (in his own juice); **tutto fa** ~ every little bit helps.

brogli'accio [broʎ'ʎattʃo] *sm* scribbling pad.

'**broglio** ['brɔʎʎo] *sm*: ~ **elettorale** gerrymandering; ~**i** *smpl* (*DIR*) malpractices.

bron'chite [bron'kite] *sf* (*MED*) bronchitis.

'**broncio** ['brontʃo] *sm* sulky expression; **tenere il** ~ to sulk.

'**bronco, chi** *sm* bronchial tube.

bronto'lare *vi* to grumble; (*tuono, stomaco*) to rumble.

bronto'lone, a *ag* grumbling ♦ *sm/f* grumbler.

bron'zina [bron'dzina] *sf* (*TECN*) bush.

'**bronzo** ['brondzo] *sm* bronze; **che faccia di** ~**!** what a brass neck!

bross. *abbr* = **in brossura.**

bros'sura *sf*: **in** ~ (*libro*) limpback.

bru'care *vt* to browse on, nibble at.

brucherà *etc* [bruke'ra] *vb vedi* **brucare.**

bruciacchi'are [brutʃak'kjare] *vt* to singe, scorch; ~**rsi** *vr* to become singed *o* scorched.

brucia'pelo [brutʃa'pelo]: **a** ~ *av* point-blank.

bruci'are [bru'tʃare] *vt* to burn; (*scottare*) to scald ♦ *vi* to burn; ~ **gli avversari** (*SPORT, fig*) to leave the rest of the field behind; ~ **le tappe** *o* **i tempi** (*SPORT, fig*) to shoot ahead; ~**rsi la carriera** to put an end to one's career.

brucia'tore [brutʃa'tore] *sm* burner.

brucia'tura [brutʃa'tura] *sf* (*atto*) burning *q*; (*segno*) burn; (*scottatura*) scald.

bruci'ore [bru'tʃore] *sm* burning *o* smarting sensation.

'**bruco, chi** *sm* grub; (*di farfalla*) caterpillar.

'**brufolo** *sm* pimple, spot.

brughi'era [bru'gjɛra] *sf* heath, moor.

bruli'care *vi* to swarm.

'**brullo, a** *ag* bare, bleak.

'**bruma** *sf* mist.

'**bruno, a** *ag* brown, dark; (*persona*) dark(-haired).

'**brusco, a, schi, sche** *ag* (*sapore*) sharp; (*modi, persona*) brusque, abrupt; (*movimento*) abrupt, sudden.

bru'sio *sm* buzz, buzzing.

bru'tale *ag* brutal.

brutalità *sf inv* brutality.

'**bruto, a** *ag* (*forza*) brute *cpd* ♦ *sm* brute.

'**brutta** *sf vedi* **brutto.**

brut'tezza [brut'tettsa] *sf* ugliness.

'**brutto, a** *ag* ugly; (*cattivo*) bad; (*malattia, strada, affare*) nasty, bad ♦ *sm*: **guardare qn di** ~ to give sb a nasty look ♦ *sf* rough copy, first draft; ~ **tempo** bad weather; **passare un** ~ **quarto d'ora** to have a nasty time of it; **vedersela** ~**a** (*per un attimo*) to have a nasty moment; (*per un periodo*) to have a bad time of it.

brut'tura *sf* (*cosa brutta*) ugly thing; (*sudiciume*) filth; (*azione meschina*) mean action.

Bru'xelles [bry'sɛl] *sf* Brussels.

BS *sigla* = *Brescia.*

B.T. *abbr* (= *bassa tensione*) LT ♦ *sigla m inv* = **buono del Tesoro.**

btg *abbr* = **battaglione.**

'**buca, che** *sf* hole; (*avvallamento*) hollow; ~ **delle lettere** letterbox.

buca'neve *sm inv* snowdrop.

bu'care *vt* (*forare*) to make a hole (*o* holes) in; (*pungere*) to pierce; (*biglietto*) to punch; ~**rsi** *vr* (*con eroina*) to mainline; ~ **una gomma** to have a puncture; **avere le mani bucate** (*fig*) to be a spendthrift.

'**Bucarest** *sf* Bucharest.

bu'cato *sm* (*operazione*) washing; (*panni*) wash, washing.

'**buccia, ce** ['buttʃa] *sf* skin, peel; (*corteccia*) bark.

bucherel'lare [bukerel'lare] *vt* to riddle with holes.

bucherò *etc* [buke'rɔ] *vb vedi* **bucare.**

'**buco, chi** *sm* hole; **fare un** ~ **nell'acqua** to fail, draw a blank; **farsi un** ~ (*fam: drogarsi*) to have a fix.

'**Budapest** *sf* Budapest.

bud'dismo *sm* Buddhism.

bu'dello *sm* intestine; (*fig: tubo*) tube; (*vicolo*) alley; ~**a** *sfpl* bowels, guts.

bu'dino *sm* pudding.

'**bue, pl bu'oi** *sm* ox; (*anche: carne di* ~) beef; **uovo all'occhio di** ~ fried egg.

Bu'enos 'Aires *sf* Buenos Aires.

'**bufalo** *sm* buffalo.

bu'fera *sf* storm.

buf'fetto *sm* flick.

'**buffo, a** *ag* funny; (*TEATRO*) comic.

buffo'nata *sf* (*azione*) prank, jest; (*parola*) jest.

buf'fone *sm* buffoon.

bugge'rare [buddʒe'rare] *vt* to swindle, cheat.

bu'gia, 'gie [bu'dʒia] *sf* lie; (*candeliere*) candleholder.

bugi'ardo, a [bu'dʒardo] *ag* lying, deceitful ♦ *sm/f* liar.

bugi'gattolo [budʒi'gattolo] *sm* poky little room.

'**buio, a** *ag* dark ♦ *sm* dark, darkness; **fa** ~ **pesto** it's pitch-dark.

'**bulbo** *sm* (*BOT*) bulb; ~ **oculare** eyeball.

Bulga'ria *sf*: la ~ Bulgaria.
'bulgaro, a *ag*, *sm/f*, *sm* Bulgarian.
'bullo *sm* (*persona*) tough.
bul'lone *sm* bolt.
bu'oi *smpl di* **bue**.
buona'fede *sf* good faith.
buon'anima *sf* = **buon'anima**; *vedi* **anima**.
buona'notte *escl* good night! ♦ *sf*: **dare la** ~ **a** to say good night to.
buona'sera *escl* good evening!
buoncos'tume *sm* public morality; **la (squadra del)** ~ (*POLIZIA*) the vice squad.
buondi *escl* hello!
buongi'orno [bwonˈdʒorno] *escl* good morning (*o* afternoon)!
buon'grado *av*: **di** ~ willingly.
buongus'taio, a *sm/f* gourmet.
buon'gusto *sm* good taste.
bu'ono, a *ag* (*dav sm* **buon** + *C o V*, **buono** + *s impura, gn, pn, ps, x, z*; *dav sf* **buona** + *C*, **buon'** + *V*) good; (*benevolo*): ~ **(con)** good (to), kind (to); (*adatto*): ~ **a/da** fit for/to ♦ *sm* good; (*COMM*) voucher, coupon; **alla buona** *ag* simple ♦ *av* in a simple way, without any fuss; **è un tipo alla buona** he's an easy-going sort; **che Dio ce la mandi buona!** here's hoping!; **accetterà con le buone o con le cattive** he'll have to accept whether he wants to or not; **essere un poco di** ~ to be a nasty piece of work; **buon compleanno!** happy birthday!; **buon divertimento!** have a nice time!; **buona fortuna!** good luck!; **buon riposo!** sleep well!; **buon viaggio!** bon voyage!, have a good trip!; **tante buone cose!** all the best!; ~ **d'acquisto** credit note, credit slip; ~ **di cassa** cash voucher; ~ **di consegna** delivery note; **ad ogni buon conto** in any case; ~ **fruttifero** interest-bearing bond; ~ **d'imbarco** shipping note; ~ **d'imposta** *special credit instrument for tax-relief purposes*; **di buon mattino** early in the morning; **a buon mercato** cheap; **di buon'ora** early; ~ **a nulla** good-for-nothing; ~ **ordinario del Tesoro (Bot, bot)** short-term treasury bond; ~ **postale fruttifero** interest-bearing bond (*issued by Italian Post Office*); **buon senso** common sense; ~ **del Tesoro** treasury bill; **deciditi una buona volta!** make up your mind once and for all!; **fare buon viso a cattivo gioco** to put a good face on things.
buon'senso *sm* = **buon senso**.
buontem'pone, a *sm/f* jovial person.
buonu'scita [bwonuʃˈʃita] *sf* (*INDUSTRIA*) golden handshake; (*di affitti*) *sum paid for the relinquishing of tenancy rights*.
burat'tino *sm* puppet.
'burbero, a *ag* surly, gruff.
'burla *sf* prank, trick.
bur'lare *vt*: ~ **qc/qn**, **~rsi di qc/qn** to make fun of sth/sb.

bu'rocrate *sm* bureaucrat.
buro'cratico, a, ci, che *ag* bureaucratic.
burocra'zia [burokratˈtsia] *sf* bureaucracy.
bur'rasca, sche *sf* storm.
burras'coso, a *ag* stormy.
'burro *sm* butter.
bur'rone *sm* ravine.
bus'care *vt* (*anche*: **~rsi**: *raffreddore*) to get, catch; **buscarle** (*fam*) to get a hiding.
buscherò *etc* [buskeˈrɔ] *vb vedi* **buscare**.
bus'sare *vi* to knock; ~ **a quattrini** (*fig*) to ask for money.
'bussola *sf* compass; **perdere la** ~ (*fig*) to lose one's bearings.
'busta *sf* (*da lettera*) envelope; (*astuccio*) case; **in** ~ **aperta/chiusa** in an unsealed/sealed envelope; ~ **paga** pay packet.
busta'rella *sf* bribe, backhander.
bus'tina *sf* (*piccola busta*) envelope; (*di cibi, farmaci*) sachet; (*MIL*) forage cap; ~ **di tè** tea bag.
'busto *sm* bust; (*indumento*) corset, girdle; **a mezzo** ~ (*fotografia, ritratto*) half-length.
bu'tano *sm* butane.
but'tare *vt* to throw; (*anche*: ~ **via**) throw away; **~rsi** *vr* (*saltare*) to jump; ~ **giù** (*scritto*) to scribble down, dash off; (*cibo*) to gulp down; (*edificio*) to pull down, demolish; (*pasta, verdura*) to put into boiling water; **ho buttato là una frase** I mentioned it in passing; **buttiamoci!** (*saltiamo*) let's jump!; (*rischiamo*) let's have a go!; **~rsi dalla finestra** to jump out of the window.
'buzzo ['buddzo] *sm* (*fam*: *pancia*) belly, paunch; **di** ~ **buono** (*con impegno*) with a will.

C

C, c [tʃi] *sf o m inv* (*lettera*) C, c ♦ *abbr* (*GEO*) = **capo**; (= *Celsius, centigrado*) C; (= *conto*) a/c; ~ **come Como** ≈ C for Charlie.
CA *sigla* = Cagliari.
c.a. *abbr* (*ELETTR*) *vedi* **corrente alternata**; (*COMM*) = *corrente anno*.
cab. *abbr* = **cablogramma**.
caba'ret [kabaˈrɛ] *sm inv* cabaret.
ca'bina *sf* (*di nave*) cabin; (*da spiaggia*) beach hut; (*di autocarro, treno*) cab; (*di aereo*) cockpit; (*di ascensore*) cage; ~ **di proiezione** (*CINEMA*) projection booth; ~ **di registrazione** recording booth; ~ **telefonica** callbox, (tele)phone box *o* booth.

cabi'nato *sm* cabin cruiser.
ca'blaggio [ka'bladdʒo] *sm* wiring.
cablo'gramma *sm* cable(gram).
ca'cao *sm* cocoa.
'cacca *sf (fam: anche fig)* shit *(!)*.
'caccia ['kattʃa] *sf* hunting; *(con fucile)* shooting; *(inseguimento)* chase; *(cacciagione)* game ♦ *sm inv (aereo)* fighter; *(nave)* destroyer; **andare a ~** to go hunting; **andare a ~ di guai** to be asking for trouble; **~ grossa** big-game hunting; **~ all'uomo** manhunt.
cacciabombardi'ere [kattʃabombar'djɛre] *sm* fighter-bomber.
cacciagi'one [kattʃa'dʒone] *sf* game.
cacci'are [kat'tʃare] *vt* to hunt; *(mandar via)* to chase away; *(ficcare)* to shove, stick ♦ *vi* to hunt; **~rsi** *vr (fam: mettersi)*: **~rsi tra la folla** to plunge into the crowd; **dove s'è cacciata la mia borsa?** where has my bag got to?; **~rsi nei guai** to get into trouble; **~ fuori qc** to whip *o* pull sth out; **~ un urlo** to let out a yell.
caccia'tora [kattʃa'tora] *sf (giacca)* hunting jacket; *(CUC):* **pollo** *etc* **alla ~** chicken *etc* chasseur.
caccia'tore [kattʃa'tore] *sm* hunter; **~ di frodo** poacher; **~ di dote** fortune-hunter.
cacciatorpedini'ere [kattʃatorpedi'njɛre] *sm* destroyer.
caccia'vite [kattʃa'vite] *sm inv* screwdriver.
cache'mire [kaʃ'mir] *sm inv* cashmere.
ca'chet [ka'ʃɛ] *sm (MED)* capsule; *(: compressa)* tablet; *(compenso)* fee; *(colorante per capelli)* rinse.
'cachi ['kaki] *sm inv (albero, frutto)* persimmon; *(colore)* khaki ♦ *ag inv* khaki.
'cacio ['katʃo] *sm* cheese; **essere come il ~ sui maccheroni** *(fig)* to turn up at the right moment.
'cactus *sm inv* cactus.
ca'davere *sm* (dead) body, corpse.
cada'verico, a, ci, che *ag (fig)* deathly pale.
'caddi *etc vb vedi* **cadere.**
ca'dente *ag* falling; *(casa)* tumbledown; *(persona)* decrepit.
ca'denza [ka'dɛntsa] *sf* cadence; *(andamento ritmico)* rhythm; *(MUS)* cadenza.
ca'dere *vi* to fall; *(denti, capelli)* to fall out; *(tetto)* to fall in; **questa gonna cade bene** this skirt hangs well; **lasciar ~** *(anche fig)* to drop; **~ dal sonno** to be falling asleep on one's feet; **~ ammalato** to fall ill; **~ dalle nuvole** *(fig)* to be taken aback.
ca'detto *sm* cadet.
cadrò *etc vb vedi* **cadere.**
ca'duto, a *ag (morto)* dead ♦ *sm* dead soldier ♦ *sf* fall; **monumento ai ~i** war memorial; **~a di temperatura** drop in temperature; **la ~a dei capelli** hair loss; **~a del sistema** *(INFORM)* system failure.

caffè *sm inv* coffee; *(locale)* café; **~ corretto** coffee with liqueur; **~ in grani** coffee beans; **~ macchiato** coffee with a dash of milk; **~ macinato** ground coffee.
caffe'ina *sf* caffeine.
caffel'latte *sm inv* white coffee.
caffette'ria *sf* coffee shop.
caffetti'era *sf* coffeepot.
ca'fone *sm (contadino)* peasant; *(peg)* boor.
cagio'nare [kadʒo'nare] *vt* to cause, be the cause of.
cagio'nevole [kadʒo'nevole] *ag* delicate, weak.
cagli'are [kaʎ'ʎare] *vi* to curdle.
cagliari'tano, a [kaʎʎari'tano] *ag* of *(o* from*)* Cagliari.
'cagna ['kaɲɲa] *sf (ZOOL, peg)* bitch.
ca'gnara [kaɲ'ɲara] *sf (fig)* uproar.
ca'gnesco, a, schi, sche [kaɲ'ɲesko] *ag (fig)*: **guardare qn in ~** to scowl at sb.
CAI *sigla m* = **Club Alpino Italiano.**
'Cairo *sm*: **il ~** Cairo.
cala'brese *ag, sm/f* Calabrian.
cala'brone *sm* hornet.
Cala'hari [kala'ari]: **il Deserto di ~** *sm* the Kalahari Desert.
cala'maio *sm* inkpot; inkwell.
cala'maro *sm* squid.
cala'mita *sf* magnet.
calamità *sf inv* calamity, disaster; **~ naturale** natural disaster.
ca'lare *vt (far discendere)* to lower; *(MAGLIA)* to decrease ♦ *vi (discendere)* to go *(o* come*)* down; *(tramontare)* to set, go down; **~ di peso** to lose weight.
ca'lata *sf (invasione)* invasion.
'calca *sf* throng, press.
cal'cagno [kal'kaɲɲo] *sm* heel.
cal'care *sm* limestone ♦ *vt (premere coi piedi)* to tread, press down; *(premere con forza)* to press down; *(mettere in rilievo)* to stress; **~ la mano** to overdo it, exaggerate; **~ le scene** *(fig)* to be on the stage; **~ le orme di qn** *(fig)* to follow in sb's footsteps.
'calce ['kaltʃe] *sm*: **in ~** at the foot of the page ♦ *sf* lime; **~ viva** quicklime.
calces'truzzo [kaltʃes'truttso] *sm* concrete.
calcherò *etc* [kalke'rɔ] *vb vedi* **calcare.**
calci'are [kal'tʃare] *vt, vi* to kick.
calcia'tore [kaltʃa'tore] *sm* footballer *(Brit)*, (football) player.
cal'cina [kal'tʃina] *sf* (lime) mortar.
calci'naccio [kaltʃi'nattʃo] *sm* flake of plaster.
'calcio ['kaltʃo] *sm (pedata)* kick; *(sport)* football, soccer; *(di pistola, fucile)* butt; *(CHIM)* calcium; **~ d'angolo** *(SPORT)* corner (kick); **~ di punizione** *(SPORT)* free kick.
'calco, chi *sm (ARTE)* casting, moulding *(Brit)*, molding *(US)*; cast, mo(u)ld.

calco'lare *vt* to calculate, work out, reckon; (*ponderare*) to weigh (up).

calcola'tore, 'trice *ag* calculating ♦ *sm* calculator; (*fig*) calculating person ♦ *sf* (*anche*: **macchina calcolatrice**) calculator; ~ **digitale** digital computer; ~ **elettronico** computer; ~ **da tavolo** desktop computer.

'calcolo *sm* (*anche MAT*) calculation; (*infinitesimale etc*) calculus; (*MED*) stone; **fare il** ~ **di qc** to work sth out; **fare i propri** ~**i** (*fig*) to weigh the pros and cons; **per** ~ out of self-interest.

cal'daia *sf* boiler.

caldar'rosta *sf* roast chestnut.

caldeggi'are [kalded'dʒare] *vt* to support.

'caldo, a *ag* warm; (*molto* ~) hot; (*fig: appassionato*) keen ♦ *sm* heat; **ho** ~ I'm warm; I'm hot; **fa** ~ it's warm; it's hot; **non mi fa né** ~ **né freddo** I couldn't care less; **a** ~ (*fig*) in the heat of the moment.

caleidos'copio *sm* kaleidoscope.

calen'dario *sm* calendar.

ca'lende *sfpl* calends; **rimandare qc alle** ~ **greche** to put sth off indefinitely.

ca'lesse *sm* gig.

'calibro *sm* (*di arma*) calibre, bore; (*TECN*) callipers *pl*; (*fig*) calibre; **di grosso** ~ (*fig*) prominent.

'calice ['kalitʃe] *sm* goblet; (*REL*) chalice.

ca'ligine [ka'lidʒine] *sf* fog; (*mista con fumo*) smog.

calligra'fia *sf* (*scrittura*) handwriting; (*arte*) calligraphy.

'callo *sm* callus; (*ai piedi*) corn; **fare il** ~ **a qc** to get used to sth.

'calma *sf* calm; **faccia con** ~ take your time.

cal'mante *sm* sedative, tranquillizer.

cal'mare *vt* to calm; (*lenire*) to soothe; ~**rsi** *vr* to grow calm, calm down; (*vento*) to abate; (*dolori*) to ease.

calmi'ere *sm* controlled price.

'calmo, a *ag* calm, quiet.

'calo *sm* (*COMM: di prezzi*) fall; (*: di volume*) shrinkage; (*: di peso*) loss.

ca'lore *sm* warmth; (*intenso, FISICA*) heat; **essere in** ~ (*ZOOL*) to be on heat.

calo'ria *sf* calorie.

calo'rifero *sm* radiator.

calo'roso, a *ag* warm; **essere** ~ not to feel the cold.

calpes'tare *vt* to tread on, trample on; "**è vietato** ~ **l'erba**" "keep off the grass".

ca'lunnia *sf* slander; (*scritta*) libel.

cal'vario *sm* (*fig*) affliction, cross.

cal'vizie [kal'vittsje] *sf* baldness.

'calvo, a *ag* bald.

'calza ['kaltsa] *sf* (*da donna*) stocking; (*da uomo*) sock; **fare la** ~ to knit; ~**e di nailon** nylons, (nylon) stockings.

calza'maglia [kaltsa'maʎʎa] *sf* tights *pl*; (*per danza, ginnastica*) leotard.

cal'zare [kal'tsare] *vt* (*scarpe, guanti: mettersi*) to put on; (*: portare*) to wear ♦ *vi* to fit; ~ **a pennello** to fit like a glove.

calza'tura [kaltsa'tura] *sf* footwear.

calzaturi'ficio [kaltsaturi'fitʃo] *sm* shoe o footwear factory.

cal'zetta [kal'tsetta] *sf* ankle sock; **una mezza** ~ (*fig*) a nobody.

calzet'tone [kaltset'tone] *sm* heavy knee-length sock.

cal'zino [kal'tsino] *sm* sock.

calzo'laio [kaltso'lajo] *sm* shoemaker; (*che ripara scarpe*) cobbler.

calzole'ria [kaltsole'ria] *sf* (*negozio*) shoe shop; (*arte*) shoemaking.

calzon'cini [kaltson'tʃini] *smpl* shorts; ~ **da bagno** (swimming) trunks.

cal'zone [kal'tsone] *sm* trouser leg; (*CUC*) savoury turnover made with pizza dough; ~**i** *smpl* trousers (*Brit*), pants (*US*).

camale'onte *sm* chameleon.

cambi'ale *sf* bill (of exchange); (*pagherò cambiario*) promissory note; ~ **di comodo** o **di favore** accommodation bill.

cambia'mento *sm* change.

cambi'are *vt* to change; (*modificare*) to alter, change; (*barattare*): ~ **(qc con qn/ qc)** to exchange (sth with sb/for sth) ♦ *vi* to change, alter; ~**rsi** *vr* (*variare abito*) to change; ~ **casa** to move (house); ~ **idea** to change one's mind; ~ **treno** to change trains; ~ **le carte in tavola** (*fig*) to change one's tune; ~ **(l')aria in una stanza** to air a room; **è ora di** ~ **aria** (*andarsene*) it's time to move on.

cambiava'lute *sm inv* exchange office.

'cambio *sm* change; (*modifica*) alteration, change; (*scambio, COMM*) exchange; (*corso dei cambi*) rate (of exchange); (*TECN, AUT*) gears *pl*; **in** ~ **di** in exchange for; **dare il** ~ **a qn** to take over from sb; **fare il** o **un** ~ to change (over); ~ **a termine** (*COMM*) forward exchange.

'Cambital *sigla m* = Ufficio Italiano dei Cambi.

Cam'bogia [kam'bɔdʒa] *sf*: **la** ~ Cambodia.

cambogi'ano, a [kambo'dʒano] *ag, sm/f* Cambodian.

cam'busa *sf* storeroom.

'camera *sf* room; (*anche:* ~ **da letto**) bedroom; (*POL*) chamber, house; ~ **ardente** mortuary chapel; ~ **d'aria** inner tube; (*di pallone*) bladder; ~ **blindata** strongroom; **C~ di Commercio** Chamber of Commerce; **C~ dei Deputati** Chamber of Deputies, ≈ House of Commons (*Brit*), ≈ House of Representatives (*US*); ~ **a gas** gas chamber; ~ **del lavoro** trades union centre (*Brit*), labor union center (*US*); ~ **a un letto/a due letti/matrimoniale** single/twin-bedded/double room; ~ **oscura** (*FOT*) dark room; ~ **da pranzo** dining room.

came'rata, i, e *sm/f* companion, mate ♦ *sf* dormitory.

camera'tismo *sm* comradeship.

cameri'era *sf* (*domestica*) maid; (*che serve a tavola*) waitress; (*che fa le camere*) chambermaid.

cameri'ere *sm* (man)servant; (*di ristorante*) waiter.

came'rino *sm* (*TEATRO*) dressing room.

'Camerun *sm*: **il** ~ Cameroon.

'camice ['kamitʃe] *sm* (*REL*) alb; (*per medici etc*) white coat.

cami'cetta [kami'tʃetta] *sf* blouse.

ca'micia, cie [ka'mitʃa] *sf* (*da uomo*) shirt; (*da donna*) blouse; **nascere con la** ~ (*fig*) to be born lucky; **sudare sette** ~**cie** (*fig*) to have a hell of a time; ~ **di forza** straitjacket; ~ **da notte** (*da donna*) nightdress; (*da uomo*) nightshirt; **C**~ **nera** (*fascista*) Blackshirt.

camici'aio, a [kami'tʃajo] *sm/f* (*sarto*) shirtmaker; (*che vende camicie*) shirtseller.

camici'ola [kami'tʃɔla] *sf* vest.

camici'otto [kami'tʃɔtto] *sm* casual shirt; (*per operai*) smock.

cami'netto *sm* hearth, fireplace.

ca'mino *sm* chimney; (*focolare*) fireplace, hearth.

'camion *sm inv* lorry (*Brit*), truck (*US*).

camion'cino [kamjon'tʃino] *sm* van.

camio'netta *sf* jeep.

camio'nista, i *sm* lorry driver (*Brit*), truck driver (*US*).

'camma *sf* cam; **albero a** ~**e** camshaft.

cam'mello *sm* (*ZOOL*) camel; (*tessuto*) camel hair.

cam'meo *sm* cameo.

cammi'nare *vi* to walk; (*funzionare*) to work, go; ~ **a carponi** *o* **a quattro zampe** to go on all fours.

cammi'nata *sf* walk; **fare una** ~ to go for a walk.

cam'mino *sm* walk; (*sentiero*) path; (*itinerario, direzione, tragitto*) way; **mettersi in** ~ to set *o* start off; **cammin facendo** on the way; **riprendere il** ~ to continue on one's way.

camo'milla *sf* camomile; (*infuso*) camomile tea.

ca'morra *sf* Camorra; (*fig*) racket.

camor'rista, i, e *sm/f* member of the Camorra; (*fig*) racketeer.

ca'moscio [ka'mɔʃʃo] *sm* chamois.

cam'pagna [kam'paɲɲa] *sf* country, countryside; (*POL, COMM, MIL*) campaign; **in** ~ in the country; **andare in** ~ to go to the country; **fare una** ~ to campaign; ~ **promozionale vendite** sales campaign.

campa'gnolo, a [kampaɲ'ɲɔlo] *ag* country *cpd* ♦ *sf* (*AUT*) cross-country vehicle.

cam'pale *ag* field *cpd*; (*fig*): **una giornata** ~ a hard day.

cam'pana *sf* bell; (*anche:* ~ **di vetro**) bell jar; **sordo come una** ~ as deaf as a doorpost; **sentire l'altra** ~ (*fig*) to hear the other side of the story.

campa'nella *sf* small bell; (*di tenda*) curtain ring.

campa'nello *sm* (*all'uscio, da tavola*) bell.

campa'nile *sm* bell tower, belfry.

campani'lismo *sm* parochialism.

cam'pano, a *ag* of (*o* from) Campania.

cam'pare *vi* to live; (*tirare avanti*) to get by, manage; ~ **alla giornata** to live from day to day.

cam'pato, a *ag*: ~ **in aria** unsound, unfounded.

campeggi'are [kamped'dʒare] *vi* to camp; (*risaltare*) to stand out.

campeggia'tore, 'trice [kampeddʒa'tore] *sm/f* camper.

cam'peggio [kam'peddʒo] *sm* camping; (*terreno*) camp site; **fare (del)** ~ to go camping.

cam'pestre *ag* country *cpd*, rural; **corsa** ~ cross-country race.

'camping ['kæmpiŋ] *sm inv* camp site.

campio'nario, a *ag*: **fiera** ~**a** trade fair ♦ *sm* collection of samples.

campio'nato *sm* championship.

campiona'tura *sf* (*COMM*) production of samples; (*STATISTICA*) sampling.

campi'one, 'essa *sm/f* (*SPORT*) champion ♦ *sm* (*COMM*) sample; ~ **gratuito** free sample; **prelievi di** ~ product samples.

'campo *sm* (*gen*) field; (*MIL*) field; (*: accampamento*) camp; (*spazio delimitato: sportivo etc*) ground; field; (*di quadro*) background; **i** ~**i** (*campagna*) the countryside; **padrone del** ~ (*fig*) victor; ~ **da aviazione** airfield; ~ **di concentramento** concentration camp; ~ **di golf** golf course; ~ **lungo** (*CINEMA, TV, FOT*) long shot; ~ **da tennis** tennis court; ~ **visivo** field of vision.

campo'santo, *pl* campi'santi *sm* cemetery.

camuf'fare *vt* to disguise; ~**rsi** *vr*: ~**rsi (da)** to disguise o.s. (as); (*per ballo in maschera*) to dress up (as).

CAN *abbr* (= *Costo, Assicurazione e Nolo*) CIF.

Can. *abbr* (*GEO*) = **canale**.

'Canada *sm*: **il** ~ Canada.

cana'dese *ag, sm/f* Canadian ♦ *sf* (*anche:* **tenda** ~) ridge tent.

ca'naglia [ka'naʎʎa] *sf* rabble; mob; (*persona*) scoundrel, rogue.

ca'nale *sm* (*anche fig*) channel; (*artificiale*) canal.

'canapa *sf* hemp; ~ **indiana** cannabis.

Ca'narie *sfpl*: **le (isole)** ~ the Canary Islands, the Canaries.

cana'rino *sm* canary.

Can'berra *sf* Canberra.

cancel'lare |kantʃel'lare| vt (con la gomma) to rub out, erase; (con la penna) to strike out; (annullare) to annul, cancel; (disdire) to cancel.

cancel'lata |kantʃel'lata| sf railing(s) (pl).

cancelle'ria |kantʃelle'ria| sf chancery; (quanto necessario per scrivere) stationery.

cancelli'ere |kantʃel'ljɛre| sm chancellor; (di tribunale) clerk of the court.

can'cello |kan'tʃello| sm gate.

cance'rogeno, a |kantʃe'rɔdʒeno| ag carcinogenic ♦ sm carcinogen.

cance'rologo, a, gi, ghe |kantʃe'rɔlogo| sm/f cancer specialist.

cance'roso, a |kantʃe'roso| ag cancerous ♦ sm/f cancer patient.

can'crena sf gangrene.

'cancro sm (MED) cancer; (dello zodiaco): C~ Cancer; **essere del C~** to be Cancer.

candeggi'are |kanded'dʒare| vt to bleach.

candeg'gina |kanded'dʒina| sf bleach.

can'dela sf candle; ~ **(di accensione)** (AUT) spark(ing) plug; **una lampadina da 100** ~e (ELETTR) a 100 watt bulb; **a lume di** ~ by candlelight; **tenere la** ~ (fig) to play gooseberry (Brit), act as chaperone.

cande'labro sm candelabra.

candeli'ere sm candlestick.

cande'lotto sm candle; ~ **di dinamite** stick of dynamite; ~ **lacrimogeno** tear gas grenade.

candi'darsi vr: ~ **(per)** (POL) to present o.s. as candidate (for).

candi'dato, a sm/f candidate; (aspirante a una carica) applicant.

candida'tura sf candidature; application.

'candido, a ag white as snow; (puro) pure; (sincero) sincere, candid.

can'dito, a ag candied.

can'dore sm brilliant white; purity; sincerity, candour (Brit), candor (US).

'cane sm dog; (di pistola, fucile) cock; **fa un freddo** ~ it's bitterly cold; **non c'era un** ~ there wasn't a soul; **quell'attore è un** ~ he's a rotten actor; ~ **da caccia** hunting dog; ~ **da guardia** guard dog; ~ **lupo** alsatian; ~ **da salotto** lap dog; ~ **da slitta** husky.

ca'nestro sm basket; **fare un** ~ (SPORT) to shoot a basket.

cangi'ante |kan'dʒante| ag iridescent; **seta** ~ shot silk.

can'guro sm kangaroo.

ca'nicola sf scorching heat.

ca'nile sm kennel; (di allevamento) kennels pl; ~ **municipale** dog pound.

ca'nino, a ag, sm canine.

'canna sf (pianta) reed; (: indica, da zucchero) cane; (bastone) stick, cane; (di fucile) barrel; (di organo) pipe; (DROGA: gergo) joint; ~ **fumaria** chimney flue; ~ **da pesca** (fishing) rod; ~ **da zucchero** sugar cane.

can'nella sf (CUC) cinnamon; (di conduttura, botte) tap.

cannel'loni smpl pasta tubes stuffed with sauce and baked.

can'neto sm bed of reeds.

can'nibale sm cannibal.

cannocchi'ale |kannok'kjale| sm telescope.

canno'nata sf: **è una vera** ~! (fig) it's (o he's etc) fantastic!

can'none sm (MIL) gun; (: STORIA) cannon; (tubo) pipe, tube; (piega) box pleat; (fig) ace; **donna** ~ fat woman.

cannoni'ere sm (NAUT) gunner; (CALCIO) goal scorer.

can'nuccia, ce |kan'nuttʃa| sf (drinking) straw.

ca'noa sf canoe.

'canone sm canon, criterion; (mensile, annuo) rent; fee; **legge dell'equo** ~ fair rent act.

ca'nonica, che sf presbytery.

ca'nonico, ci sm (REL) canon.

canoniz'zare |kanonid'dzare| vt to canonize.

ca'noro, a ag (uccello) singing, song cpd.

canot'taggio |kanot'taddʒo| sm rowing.

canotti'era sf vest (Brit), undershirt (US).

ca'notto sm small boat, dinghy; canoe.

cano'vaccio |kano'vattʃo| sm (tela) canvas; (strofinaccio) duster; (trama) plot.

can'tante sm/f singer.

can'tare vt, vi to sing; ~ **vittoria** to crow; **fare** ~ **qn** (fig) to make sb talk.

cantas'torie sm/f inv storyteller.

cantau'tore, 'trice sm/f singer-composer.

canterel'lare vt, vi to hum, sing to o.s.

canticchi'are |kantik'kjare| vt, vi to hum, sing to o.s.

canti'ere sm (EDIL) (building) site; (anche: ~ navale) shipyard.

canti'lena sf (filastrocca) lullaby; (fig) sing-song voice.

can'tina sf (locale) cellar; (bottega) wine shop.

'canto sm song; (arte) singing; (REL) chant; chanting; (poesia) poem, lyric; (parte di una poesia) canto; (parte, lato): **da un** ~ on the one hand; **d'altro** ~ on the other hand.

canto'nata sf (di edificio) corner; **prendere una** ~ (fig) to blunder.

can'tone sm (in Svizzera) canton.

cantoni'era ag: **(casa)** ~ road inspector's house.

can'tuccio |kan'tuttʃo| sm corner, nook.

ca'nuto, a ag white, whitehaired.

canzo'nare |kantso'nare| vt to tease.

canzona'tura |kantsona'tura| sf teasing; (beffa) joke.

can'zone |kan'tsone| sf song; (POESIA) canzone.

canzoni'ere |kantso'njɛre| sm (MUS) songbook; (*LETTERATURA*) collection of poems.

'caos *sm inv* chaos.

ca'otico, a, ci, che *ag* chaotic.

CAP *sigla m vedi* **codice di avviamento postale.**

cap. *abbr* (= *capitolo*) ch.

ca'pace [ka'patʃe] *ag* able, capable; (*ampio, vasto*) large, capacious; **sei ~ di farlo?** can you *o* are you able to do it?; **~ d'intendere e di volere** (*DIR*) in full possession of one's faculties.

capacità [kapatʃi'ta] *sf inv* ability; (*DIR, di recipiente*) capacity; **~ produttiva** production capacity.

capaci'tarsi [kapatʃi'tarsi] *vr:* **~ di** to make out, understand.

ca'panna *sf* hut.

capan'nello *sm* knot (of people).

ca'panno *sm* (*di cacciatori*) hide; (*da spiaggia*) bathing hut.

capan'none *sm* (*AGR*) barn; (*fabbricato industriale*) (factory) shed.

caparbietà *sf* stubbornness.

ca'parbio, a *ag* stubborn.

ca'parra *sf* deposit, down payment.

capa'tina *sf:* **fare una ~ da qn/in centro** to pop in on sb/into town.

capeggi'are [kaped'dʒare] *vt* (*rivolta etc*) to head, lead.

ca'pello *sm* hair; **~i** *smpl* (*capigliatura*) hair *sg*; **averne fin sopra i ~i di qc/qn** to be fed up to the (back) teeth with sth/sb; **mi ci hanno tirato per i ~i** (*fig*) they dragged me into it; **tirato per i ~i** (*spiegazione*) farfetched.

capel'lone, a *sm/f* hippie.

capel'luto, a *ag:* **cuoio ~** scalp.

capez'zale [kapet'tsale] *sm* bolster; (*fig*) bedside.

ca'pezzolo [ka'pettsolo] *sm* nipple.

capi'ente *ag* capacious.

capi'enza [ka'pjentsa] *sf* capacity.

capiglia'tura [kapiʎʎa'tura] *sf* hair.

ca'pire *vt* to understand; **~ al volo** to catch on straight away; **si capisce!** (*certamente!*) of course!, certainly!

capi'tale *ag* (*mortale*) capital; (*fondamentale*) main *cpd*, chief *cpd* ♦ *sf* (*città*) capital ♦ *sm* (*ECON*) capital; **~ azionario** equity capital, share capital; **~ d'esercizio** working capital; **~ fisso** capital assets, fixed capital; **~ immobile** real estate; **~ liquido** cash assets *pl*; **~ mobile** movables *pl*; **~ di rischio** risk capital; **~ sociale** (*di società*) authorized capital; (*di club*) funds *pl*; **~ di ventura** venture capital, risk capital.

capita'lismo *sm* capitalism.

capita'lista, i, e *ag, sm/f* capitalist.

capitaliz'zare [kapitalid'dzare] *vt* to capitalize.

capitalizzazi'one [kapitaliddzat'tsjone] *sf* capitalization.

capita'nare *vt* to lead; (*CALCIO*) to captain.

capitane'ria *sf:* **~ (di porto)** port authorities *pl.*

capi'tano *sm* captain; **~ di lungo corso** master mariner; **~ di ventura** (*STORIA*) mercenary leader.

capi'tare *vi* (*giungere casualmente*) to happen to go, find o.s.; (*accadere*) to happen; (*presentarsi: cosa*) to turn up, present itself ♦ *vb impers* to happen; **~ a proposito/bene/male** to turn up at the right moment/at a good time/at a bad time; **mi è capitato un guaio** I've had a spot of trouble.

capi'tello *sm* (*ARCHIT*) capital.

capito'lare *vi* to capitulate.

capitolazi'one [kapitolat'tsjone] *sf* capitulation.

ca'pitolo *sm* chapter; **~i** *smpl* (*COMM*) items; **non ho voce in ~** (*fig*) I have no say in the matter.

capi'tombolo *sm* headlong fall, tumble.

'capo *sm* (*ANAT*) head; (*persona*) head, leader; (*: in ufficio*) head, boss; (*: in tribù*) chief; (*estremità: di tavolo, scale*) head, top; (*: di filo*) end; (*GEO*) cape; **andare a ~** to start a new paragraph; **"punto a ~"** "full stop — new paragraph"; **da ~** over again; **in ~ a** (*tempo*) within; **da un ~ all'altro** from one end to the other; **fra ~ e collo** (*all'improvviso*) out of the blue; **un discorso senza né ~ né coda** a senseless *o* meaningless speech; **~ d'accusa** (*DIR*) charge; **~ di bestiame** head *inv* of cattle; **C~ di Buona Speranza** Cape of Good Hope; **~ di vestiario** item of clothing.

capo'banda, *pl* **capi'banda** *sm* (*MUS*) bandmaster; (*di malviventi, fig*) gang leader.

ca'poccia [ka'pɔttʃa] *sm inv* (*di lavoranti*) overseer; (*peg: capobanda*) boss.

capo'classe, *pl(m)* **capi'classe,** *pl(f) inv sm/f* (*INS*) ≈ form captain (*Brit*), class president (*US*).

capocu'oco, chi *sm* head cook.

Capo'danno *sm* New Year.

capofa'miglia, *pl(m)* **capifa'miglia,** *pl(f) inv* [kapofa'miʎʎa] *sm/f* head of the family.

capo'fitto: **a ~** *av* headfirst, headlong.

capo'giro [kapo'dʒiro] *sm* dizziness *q*; **da ~** (*fig*) astonishing, staggering.

capo'gruppo, *pl(m)* **capi'gruppo,** *pl(f) inv sm/f* group leader.

capola'voro, i *sm* masterpiece.

capo'linea, *pl* **capi'linea** *sm* terminus.

capo'lino *sm:* **far ~** to peep out (*o* in *etc*).

capo'lista, *pl(m)* **capi'lista,** *pl(f) inv sm/f* (*POL*) top candidate on electoral list.

capolu'ogo, *pl* **ghi** *o* **capilu'oghi** *sm* chief town, administrative centre (*Brit*) *o* center (US).

capo'mastro, *pl* **i** *o* **capi'mastri** *sm* master builder.

capo'rale *sm* (*MIL*) lance corporal (*Brit*), private first class (*US*).

capore'parto, *pl(m)* **capire'parto,** *pl(f)* *inv sm/f* (*di operai*) foreman; (*di ufficio, negozio*) head of department.

capo'sala *sf inv* (*MED*) ward sister.

capo'saldo, *pl* **capi'saldi** *sm* stronghold; (*fig: fondamento*) basis, cornerstone.

capo'squadra, *pl* **capi'squadra** *sm* (*di operai*) foreman, ganger; (*MIL*) squad leader; (*SPORT*) team captain.

capostazi'one, *pl* **capistazi'one** [kapo-stat'tsjone] *sm* station master.

capos'tipite *sm* progenitor; (*fig*) earliest example.

capo'tavola, *pl(m)* **capi'tavola,** *pl(f)* *inv sm/f* (*persona*) head of the table; **sedere a** ~ to sit at the head of the table.

ca'pote [ka'pɔt] *sf inv* (*AUT*) hood (*Brit*), soft top.

capo'treno, *pl* **capi'treno** *o* **capo'treni** *sm* guard.

capouf'ficio, *pl(m)* **capiuf'ficio,** *pl(f)* *inv* [kapouf'fitʃo] *sm/f* head clerk.

'Capo 'Verde *sm*: **il** ~ Cape Verde.

capo'verso *sm* (*di verso, periodo*) first line; (*TIP*) indent; (*paragrafo*) paragraph; (*DIR: comma*) section.

capo'volgere [kapo'voldʒere] *vt* to overturn; (*fig*) to reverse; **~rsi** *vr* to overturn; (*barca*) to capsize; (*fig*) to be reversed.

capovolgi'mento [kapovoldʒi'mento] *sm* (*fig*) reversal, complete change.

capo'volto, a *pp di* **capovolgere** ♦ *ag* upside down; (*barca*) capsized.

'cappa *sf* (*mantello*) cape, cloak; (*del camino*) hood.

cap'pella *sf* (*REL*) chapel.

cappel'lano *sm* chaplain.

cap'pello *sm* hat; **ti faccio tanto di** ~! (*fig*) I take my hat off to you!; ~ **a bombetta** bowler (hat), derby (*US*); ~ **a cilindro** top hat.

'cappero *sm* caper.

cap'pone *sm* capon.

cappot'tare *vi* (*AUT*) to overturn.

cap'potto *sm* (over)coat.

cappuc'cino [kapput'tʃino] *sm* (*frate*) Capuchin monk; (*bevanda*) frothy white coffee.

cap'puccio [kap'puttʃo] *sm* (*copricapo*) hood; (*della biro*) cap.

'capra *sf* (she-)goat.

ca'prese *ag* from (*o* of) Capri.

ca'pretto *sm* kid.

ca'priccio [ka'prittʃo] *sm* caprice, whim; (*bizza*) tantrum; **fare i** ~**i** to be very naughty; ~ **della sorte** quirk of fate.

capricci'oso, a [kaprit'tʃoso] *ag* capricious,

whimsical; naughty.

Capri'corno *sm* Capricorn; **essere del** ~ (*dello zodiaco*) to be Capricorn.

capri'foglio [kapri'fɔʎʎo] *sm* honeysuckle.

capri'ola *sf* somersault.

capri'olo *sm* roe deer.

'capro *sm* billy-goat; ~ **espiatorio** (*fig*) scapegoat.

ca'prone *sm* billy-goat.

'capsula *sf* capsule; (*di arma, per bottiglie*) cap.

cap'tare *vt* (*RADIO, TV*) to pick up; (*cattivarsi*) to gain, win.

CAR *sigla m* = *Centro Addestramento Reclute*.

cara'bina *sf* rifle.

carabini'ere *sm* member of Italian military police force.

Ca'racas *sf* Caracas.

ca'raffa *sf* carafe.

Ca'raibi *smpl*: **il mar dei** ~ the Caribbean (Sea).

cara'ibico, a, ci, che *ag* Caribbean.

cara'mella *sf* sweet.

cara'mello *sm* caramel.

ca'rato *sm* (*di oro, diamante etc*) carat.

ca'rattere *sm* character; (*caratteristica*) characteristic, trait; **avere un buon** ~ to be good-natured; **informazione di** ~ **tecnico/confidenziale** information of a technical/confidential nature; **essere in** ~ **con qc** (*intonarsi*) to be in harmony with sth.

caratte'rino *sm* difficult nature *o* character.

caratte'ristico, a, ci, che *ag* characteristic ♦ *sf* characteristic, feature; **segni** ~**ci** (*su passaporto etc*) distinguishing marks.

caratteriz'zare [karatterid'dzare] *vt* to characterize, distinguish.

carboi'drato *sm* carbohydrate.

carbo'naio *sm* (*chi fa carbone*) charcoal-burner; (*commerciante*) coalman, coal merchant.

car'bone *sm* coal; ~ **fossile** (pit) coal; **essere** *o* **stare sui** ~**i ardenti** to be like a cat on hot bricks.

car'bonio *sm* (*CHIM*) carbon.

carboniz'zare [karbonid'dzare] *vt* (*legna*) to carbonize; (: *parzialmente*) to char; **morire carbonizzato** to be burned to death.

carbu'rante *sm* (motor) fuel.

carbura'tore *sm* carburettor.

car'cassa *sf* carcass; (*fig: peg: macchina etc*) (old) wreck.

carce'rato, a [kartʃe'rato] *sm/f* prisoner.

'carcere ['kartʃere] *sm* prison; (*pena*) imprisonment; ~ **di massima sicurezza** top-security prison.

carceri'ere, a [kartʃe'rjere] *sm/f* (*anche fig*) jailer.

carci'ofo [kar'tʃɔfo] *sm* artichoke.

cardel'lino *sm* goldfinch.

car'diaco, a, ci, che *ag* cardiac, heart *cpd.*
cardi'nale *ag, sm* cardinal.
'cardine *sm* hinge.
cardiolo'gia [kardjolo'dʒia] *sf* cardiology.
cardi'ologo, gi *sm* heart specialist, cardiologist.
'cardo *sm* thistle.
ca'rente *ag*: ~ **di** lacking in.
ca'renza [ka'rentsa] *sf* lack, scarcity; (*vitaminica*) deficiency.
cares'tia *sf* famine; (*penuria*) scarcity, dearth.
ca'rezza [ka'rettsa] *sf* caress; **dare** *o* **fare una** ~ **a** (*persona*) to caress; (*animale*) to stroke, pat.
carez'zare [karet'tsare] *vt* to caress, stroke, fondle.
carez'zevole [karet'tsevole] *ag* sweet, endearing.
'cargo, ghi *sm* (*nave*) cargo boat, freighter; (*aereo*) freighter.
cari'arsi *vr* (*denti*) to decay.
'carica *sf vedi* **carico**.
caricabatte'rie *sm inv* (*ELETTR*) battery charger.
cari'care *vt* to load; (*aggravare: anche fig*) to weigh down; (*orologio*) to wind up; (*batteria, MIL*) to charge; **~rsi** *vr*: **~rsi di** to burden *o* load o.s. with; (*fig: di responsabilità, impegni*) to burden o.s. with.
carica'tura *sf* caricature.
'carico, a, chi, che *ag* (*che porta un peso*): ~ **di** loaded *o* laden with; (*fucile*) loaded; (*orologio*) wound up; (*batteria*) charged; (*colore*) deep; (*caffè, tè*) strong ♦ *sm* (*il caricare*) loading; (*ciò che si carica*) load; (*COMM*) shipment; (*fig: peso*) burden, weight ♦ *sf* (*mansione ufficiale*) office, position; (*MIL, TECN, ELETTR*) charge; ~ **di debiti** up to one's ears in debt; **persona a** ~ dependent; **essere a** ~ **di qn** (*spese etc*) to be charged to sb; (*accusa, prova*) to be against sb; **testimone a** ~ witness for the prosecution; **farsi** ~ **di** (*problema, responsabilità*) to take on; **a** ~ **del cliente** at the customer's expense; ~ **di lavoro** (*di ditta, reparto*) workload; ~ **utile** payload; **capacità di** ~ cargo capacity; **entrare/essere in** ~a to come into/be in office; **ricoprire** *o* **rivestire una** ~a to hold a position; **uscire di** ~a to leave office; **dare la** ~a a (*orologio*) to wind up; (*fig: persona*) to back up; **tornare alla** ~a (*fig*) to insist, persist; **ha una forte** ~a **di simpatia** he's very likeable.
'carie *sf* (*dentaria*) decay.
ca'rino, a *ag* lovely, pretty, nice; (*simpatico*) nice.
ca'risma [ka'rizma] *sm* charisma.
carità *sf* charity; **per** ~! (*escl di rifiuto*) good heavens, no!
carita'tevole *ag* charitable.

carnagi'one [karna'dʒone] *sf* complexion.
car'nale *ag* (*amore*) carnal; (*fratello*) blood *cpd.*
'carne *sf* flesh; (*bovina, ovina etc*) meat; **in** ~ **e ossa** in the flesh, in person; **essere (bene) in** ~ to be well padded, be plump; **non essere né** ~ **né pesce** (*fig*) to be neither fish nor fowl; ~ **di manzo/maiale/pecora** beef/pork/mutton; ~ **in scatola** tinned *o* canned meat; ~ **tritata** mince (*Brit*), hamburger meat (*US*), minced (*Brit*) *o* ground (*US*) meat.
car'nefice [kar'nefitʃe] *sm* executioner; hangman.
carnefi'cina [karnefi'tʃina] *sf* carnage; (*fig*) disaster.
carne'vale *sm* carnival.
car'nivoro, a *ag* carnivorous.
car'noso, a *ag* fleshy; (*pianta, frutto, radice*) pulpy; (*labbra*) full.
'caro, a *ag* (*amato*) dear; (*costoso*) dear, expensive; **se ti è** ~**a la vita** if you value your life.
ca'rogna [ka'roɲɲa] *sf* carrion; (*fig fam*) swine.
caro'sello *sm* merry-go-round.
ca'rota *sf* carrot.
caro'vana *sf* caravan.
caro'vita *sm* high cost of living.
'carpa *sf* carp.
Car'pazi [kar'patsi] *smpl*: **i** ~ the Carpathian Mountains.
carpente'ria *sf* carpentry.
carpenti'ere *sm* carpenter.
car'pire *vt*: ~ **qc a qn** (*segreto etc*) to get sth out of sb.
car'poni *av* on all fours.
car'rabile *ag* suitable for vehicles; **"passo** ~**"** "keep clear".
car'raio, a *ag*: **passo** ~ vehicle entrance.
carreggi'ata [karred'dʒata] *sf* carriageway (*Brit*), roadway; **rimettersi in** ~ (*fig: recuperare*) to catch up; **tenersi in** ~ (*fig*) to keep to the right path.
carrel'lata *sf* (*CINEMA, TV: tecnica*) tracking; (: *scena*) running shot; ~ **di successi** medley of hit tunes.
car'rello *sm* trolley; (*AER*) undercarriage; (*CINEMA*) dolly; (*di macchina da scrivere*) carriage.
car'retta *sf*: **tirare la** ~ (*fig*) to plod along.
car'retto *sm* handcart.
carri'era *sf* career; **fare** ~ to get on; **ufficiale di** ~ (*MIL*) regular officer; **a gran** ~ at full speed.
carri'ola *sf* wheelbarrow.
'carro *sm* cart, wagon; **il Gran/Piccolo C**~ (*ASTR*) the Great/Little Bear; **mettere il** ~ **avanti ai buoi** (*fig*) to put the cart before the horse; ~ **armato** tank; ~ **attrezzi** (*AUT*) breakdown van (*Brit*), tow truck (*US*); ~ **funebre** hearse; ~ **merci/bestiame**

(*FERR*) goods/animal wagon.

car'rozza [kar'rɔttsa] *sf* carriage, coach; ~ **letto** (*FERR*) sleeper; ~ **ristorante** (*FERR*) dining car.

carroz'zella [karrot'tsɛlla] *sf* (*per bambini*) pram (*Brit*), baby carriage (*US*); (*per invalidi*) wheelchair.

carrozze'ria [karrottse'ria] *sf* body, coachwork (*Brit*); (*officina*) coachbuilder's workshop (*Brit*), body shop.

carrozzi'ere [karrot'tsjɛre] *sm* (*AUT*: *progettista*) car designer; (: *meccanico*) coachbuilder.

carroz'zina [karrot'tsina] *sf* pram (*Brit*), baby carriage (*US*).

carroz'zone [karrot'tsone] *sm* (*da circo, di zingari*) caravan.

car'rucola *sf* pulley.

'carta *sf* paper; (*al ristorante*) menu; (*GEO*) map; plan; (*documento, da gioco*) card; (*costituzione*) charter; ~**e** *sfpl* (*documenti*) papers, documents; **alla** ~ (*al ristorante*) à la carte; **cambiare le** ~**e in tavola** (*fig*) to shift one's ground; **fare** ~**e false** (*fig*) to go to great lengths; ~ **assegni** bank card; ~ **assorbente** blotting paper; ~ **bollata** *o* **da bollo** (*AMM*) official stamped paper; ~ **di credito** credit card; ~ **di debito** cash card; ~ (**geografica**) map; ~ **d'identità** identity card; ~ **igienica** toilet paper; ~ **d'imbarco** (*AER, NAUT*) boarding card, boarding pass; ~ **da lettere** writing paper; ~ **libera** (*AMM*) unstamped paper; ~ **millimetrata** graph paper; ~ **oleata** waxed paper; ~ **da pacchi,** ~ **da imballo** wrapping paper, brown paper; ~ **da parati** wallpaper; ~ **verde** (*AUT*) green card; ~ **vetrata** sandpaper; ~ **da visita** visiting card.

cartacar'bone, *pl* **cartecar'bone** *sf* carbon paper.

car'taccia, ce [kar'tattʃa] *sf* waste paper.

cartamo'neta *sf* paper money.

carta'pecora *sf* parchment.

carta'pesta *sf* papier-mâché.

cartas'traccia [kartas'trattʃa] *sf* waste paper.

car'teggio [kar'teddʒo] *sm* correspondence.

car'tella *sf* (*scheda*) card; (*custodia: di cartone*) folder; (: *di uomo d'affari etc*) briefcase; (: *di scolaro*) schoolbag, satchel; ~ **clinica** (*MED*) case sheet.

cartel'lino *sm* (*etichetta*) label; (*su porta*) notice; (*scheda*) card; **timbrare il** ~ (*all'entrata*) to clock in; (*all'uscita*) to clock out; ~ **di presenza** clock card, timecard.

car'tello *sm* sign; (*pubblicitario*) poster; (*stradale*) sign, signpost; (*in dimostrazioni*) placard; (*ECON*) cartel.

cartel'lone *sm* (*pubblicitario*) advertising poster; (*della tombola*) scoring frame; (*TEATRO*) playbill; **tenere il** ~ (*spettacolo*) to have a long run.

carti'era *sf* paper mill.

carti'lagine [karti'ladʒine] *sf* cartilage.

car'tina *sf* (*AUT, GEO*) map.

car'toccio [kar'tɔttʃo] *sm* paper bag; **cuocere al** ~ (*CUC*) to bake in tinfoil.

cartogra'fia *sf* cartography.

carto'laio, a *sm/f* stationer.

cartole'ria *sf* stationer's (shop (*Brit*)).

carto'lina *sf* postcard; ~ **di auguri** greetings card; ~ **precetto** *o* **rosa** (*MIL*) call-up card.

carto'mante *sm/f* fortune-teller (*using cards*).

carton'cino [karton'tʃino] *sm* (*materiale*) thin cardboard; (*biglietto*) card; ~ **della società** compliments slip.

car'tone *sm* cardboard; (*del latte, dell'aranciata*) carton; (*ARTE*) cartoon; ~**i animati** (*CINEMA*) cartoons.

car'tuccia, ce [kar'tuttʃa] *sf* cartridge; ~ **a salve** blank cartridge; **mezza** ~ (*fig: persona*) good-for-nothing.

'casa *sf* house; (*specialmente la propria* ~) home; (*COMM*) firm, house; **essere a** ~ to be at home; **vado a** ~ **mia/tua** I'm going home/to your house; ~ **di correzione** ≈ community home (*Brit*), reformatory (*US*); ~ **di cura** nursing home; ~ **editrice** publishing house; ~ **dello studente** student hostel; ~ **di tolleranza,** ~ **d'appuntamenti** brothel; ~**e popolari** ≈ council houses (*o* flats) (*Brit*), ≈ public housing units (*US*).

Casa'blanca *sf* Casablanca.

ca'sacca, che *sf* military coat; (*di fantino*) blouse.

ca'sale *sm* (*gruppo di case*) hamlet; (*casa di campagna*) farmhouse.

casa'lingo, a, ghi, ghe *ag* household, domestic; (*fatto a casa*) home-made; (*semplice*) homely; (*amante della casa*) home-loving ♦ *sf* housewife; ~**ghi** *smpl* (*oggetti*) household articles; **cucina** ~**a** plain home cooking.

ca'sata *sf* family lineage.

ca'sato *sm* family name.

Casc. *abbr* (*GEO*) = **cascata.**

casca'morto *sm* woman-chaser; **fare il** ~ to chase women.

cas'care *vi* to fall; ~ **bene/male** (*fig*) to land lucky/unlucky; ~ **dalle nuvole** (*fig*) to be taken aback; ~ **dal sonno** to be falling asleep on one's feet; **caschi il mondo** no matter what; **non cascherà il mondo se** ... it won't be the end of the world if ....

cas'cata *sf* fall; (*d'acqua*) cascade, waterfall.

cascherò *etc* [kaske'rɔ] *vb vedi* **cascare.**

ca'scina [kaʃ'ʃina] *sf* farmstead.

casci'nale [kaʃʃi'nale] *sm* (*casolare*) farmhouse; (*cascina*) farmstead.

'casco, schi *sm* helmet; (*del parrucchiere*) hair-dryer; (*di banane*) bunch; **i** ~**schi blu** the UN peace-keeping troops.

caseggi'ato [kased'dʒato] *sm* (*edificio*) large block of flats (*Brit*) *o* apartment building (*US*); (*gruppo di case*) group of houses.
casei'ficio [kazei'fitʃo] *sm* creamery.
ca'sella *sf* pigeonhole; ~ **postale (C.P.)** post office box (P.O. box).
casel'lario *sm* (*mobile*) filing cabinet; (*raccolta di pratiche*) files *pl*; ~ **giudiziale** court records *pl*; ~ **penale** police files *pl*.
ca'sello *sm* (*di autostrada*) tollgate.
case'reccio, a, ci, ce [kase'rettʃo] *ag* homemade.
ca'serma *sf* barracks *pl*.
caser'tano, a *ag* of (*o* from) Caserta.
ca'sino *sm* (*confusione*) row, racket; (*casa di prostituzione*) brothel.
casinò *sm inv* casino.
ca'sistica *sf* (*MED*) record of cases; **secondo la ~ degli incidenti stradali** according to road accident data.
'caso *sm* chance; (*fatto, vicenda*) event, incident; (*possibilità*) possibility; (*MED, LING*) case; **a ~** at random; **per ~** by chance, by accident; **in ogni ~, in tutti i ~i** in any case, at any rate; **in ~ contrario** otherwise; **al ~** should the opportunity arise; **nel ~ che** in case; **~ mai** if by chance; **far ~ a qc/qn** to pay attention to sth/sb; **fare** *o* **porre** *o* **mettere il ~ che** to suppose that; **guarda ~ ...** strangely enough ...; **è il ~ che ce ne andiamo** we'd better go; ~ **limite** borderline case.
caso'lare *sm* cottage.
'Caspio *sm*: **il mar ~** the Caspian Sea.
'caspita *escl* (*di sorpresa*) good heavens!; (*di impazienza*) for goodness' sake!
'cassa *sf* case, crate, box; (*bara*) coffin; (*mobile*) chest; (*involucro: di orologio etc*) case; (*macchina*) cash register; (*luogo di pagamento*) cash desk, checkout (counter); (*fondo*) fund; (*istituto bancario*) bank; **battere ~** (*fig*) to come looking for money; ~ **automatica prelievi** automatic telling machine, cash dispenser; ~ **continua** night safe; **mettere in ~ integrazione** ≈ to lay off; **C~ del Mezzogiorno** development fund for the South of Italy; ~ **mutua** *o* **malattia** health insurance scheme; ~ **di risonanza** (*MUS*) soundbox; (*fig*) platform; ~ **di risparmio** savings bank; ~ **rurale e artigiana** credit institution (*serving farmers and craftsmen*); ~ **toracica** (*ANAT*) chest.
cassa'forte, *pl* **casse'forti** *sf* safe.
cassa'panca, *pl* **cassa'panche** *o* **casse'panche** *sf* settle.
casseru'ola, casse'rola *sf* saucepan.
cas'setta *sf* box; (*per registratore*) cassette; (*CINEMA, TEATRO*) box-office takings *pl*; **pane a** *o* **in ~** toasting loaf; **film di ~** (*commerciale*) box-office draw; **far ~** to be a box-office success; ~ **delle lettere** letter-box; ~ **di sicurezza** strongbox.
cas'setto *sm* drawer.
casset'tone *sm* chest of drawers.
cassi'ere, a *sm/f* cashier; (*di banca*) teller.
cassinte'grato, a *sm/f* person who has been laid off.
cas'sone *sm* (*cassa*) large case, large chest.
Cast. *abbr* = **castello**.
'casta *sf* caste.
cas'tagna [kas'taɲɲa] *sf* chestnut; **prendere qn in ~** (*fig*) to catch sb in the act.
cas'tagno [kas'taɲɲo] *sm* chestnut (tree).
cas'tano, a *ag* chestnut (brown).
cas'tello *sm* castle; (*TECN*) scaffolding.
casti'gare *vt* to punish.
casti'gato, a *ag* (*casto, modesto*) pure, chaste; (*emendato: prosa, versione*) expurgated, amended.
cas'tigo, ghi *sm* punishment.
castità *sf* chastity.
'casto, a *ag* chaste, pure.
cas'toro *sm* beaver.
cas'trante *ag* frustrating.
cas'trare *vt* to castrate; to geld; to doctor (*Brit*), fix (*US*); (*fig: iniziativa*) to frustrate.
castrone'ria *sf* (*fam*): **dire ~e** to talk rubbish.
casu'ale *ag* chance *cpd*.
ca'supola *sf* simple little cottage.
cata'comba *sf* catacomb.
cata'fascio [kata'faʃʃo] *sm*: **andare a ~** to collapse; **mandare a ~** to wreck.
catalizza'tore [kataliddza'tore] *sm* (*anche fig*) catalyst.
ca'talogo, ghi *sm* catalogue; ~ **dei prezzi** price list.
Cata'lonia *sf*: **la ~** Catalonia.
cata'nese *ag* of (*o* from) Catania.
cata'pecchia [kata'pekkja] *sf* hovel.
cata'pulta *sf* catapult.
catarifran'gente [katarifran'dʒente] *sm* (*AUT*) reflector.
ca'tarro *sm* catarrh.
ca'tasta *sf* stack, pile.
ca'tasto *sm* land register; land registry office.
ca'tastrofe *sf* catastrophe, disaster.
catas'trofico, a, ci, che *ag* (*evento*) catastrophic; (*persona, previsione*) pessimistic.
cate'chismo [kate'kizmo] *sm* catechism.
catego'ria *sf* category; (*di albergo*) class.
cate'gorico, a, ci, che *ag* categorical.
ca'tena *sf* chain; **reazione a ~** chain reaction; **susseguirsi a ~** to happen in quick succession; ~ **di montaggio** assembly line; ~**e da neve** (*AUT*) snow chains.
cate'naccio [kate'nattʃo] *sm* bolt.
cate'nella *sf* (*ornamento*) chain; (*di orologio*) watch chain; (*di porta*) door chain.

cate'ratta *sf* cataract; (*chiusa*) sluice gate.
ca'terva *sf* (*di cose*) loads *pl*, heaps *pl*; (*di persone*) horde.
cate'tere *sm* (*MED*) catheter.
cati'nella *sf*: **piovere a ~e** to pour, rain cats and dogs.
ca'tino *sm* basin.
ca'todico, a, ci, che *ag*: **tubo a raggi ~ci** cathode-ray tube.
ca'torcio [ka'tɔrtʃo] *sm* (*peg*) old wreck.
ca'trame *sm* tar.
'cattedra *sf* teacher's desk; (*di università*) chair; **salire** *o* **montare in ~** (*fig*) to pontificate.
catte'drale *sf* cathedral.
catte'dratico, a, ci, che *ag* (*insegnamento*) university *cpd*; (*ironico*) pedantic ♦ *sm/f* professor.
catti'veria *sf* (*qualità*) wickedness; (*di bambino*) naughtiness; (*azione*) wicked action; **fare una ~** to do something wicked; to be naughty.
cattività *sf* captivity.
cat'tivo, a *ag* bad; (*malvagio*) bad, wicked; (*turbolento: bambino*) bad, naughty; (: *mare*) rough; (*odore, sapore*) nasty, bad ♦ *sm/f* bad *o* wicked person; **farsi ~ sangue** to worry, get in a state; **farsi un ~ nome** to earn o.s. a bad reputation; **i ~i** (*nei film*) the baddies (*Brit*), the bad guys (*US*).
cattoli'cesimo [kattoli'tʃezimo] *sm* Catholicism.
cat'tolico, a, ci, che *ag*, *sm/f* (Roman) Catholic.
cat'tura *sf* capture.
cattu'rare *vt* to capture.
cau'casico, a, ci, che *ag*, *sm/f* Caucasian.
'Caucaso *sm*: **il ~** the Caucasus.
caucciù [kaut'tʃu] *sm* rubber.
'causa *sf* cause; (*DIR*) lawsuit, case, action; **a ~ di** because of; **per ~ sua** because of him; **fare** *o* **muovere ~ a qn** to take legal action against sb; **parte in ~** litigant.
cau'sale *ag* (*LING*) causal ♦ *sf* cause, reason.
cau'sare *vt* to cause.
'caustico, a, ci, che *ag* caustic.
cau'tela *sf* caution, prudence.
caute'lare *vt* to protect; **~rsi** *vr*: **~rsi (da** *o* **contro)** to take precautions (against).
'cauto, a *ag* cautious, prudent.
cauzio'nare [kauttsjo'nare] *vt* to guarantee.
cauzi'one [kaut'tsjone] *sf* security; (*DIR*) bail; **rilasciare dietro ~** to release on bail.
cav. *abbr* = **cavaliere**.
'cava *sf* quarry.
caval'care *vt* (*cavallo*) to ride; (*muro*) to sit astride; (*sog: ponte*) to span.
caval'cata *sf* ride; (*gruppo di persone*) riding party.

cavalca'via *sm inv* flyover.
cavalci'oni [kaval'tʃoni]: **a ~ di** *prep* astride.
cavali'ere *sm* rider; (*feudale, titolo*) knight; (*soldato*) cavalryman; (*al ballo*) partner.
cavalle'resco, a, schi, sche *ag* chivalrous.
cavalle'ria *sf* chivalry; (*milizia a cavallo*) cavalry.
cavalle'rizzo, a [kavalle'rittso] *sm/f* riding instructor; circus rider.
caval'letta *sf* grasshopper; (*dannosa*) locust.
caval'letto *sm* (*FOT*) tripod; (*da pittore*) easel.
caval'lina *sf* (*GINNASTICA*) horse; (*gioco*) leap-frog; **correre la ~** (*fig*) to sow one's wild oats.
ca'vallo *sm* horse; (*SCACCHI*) knight; (*AUT: anche: ~ vapore*) horsepower; (*dei pantaloni*) crotch; **a ~** on horseback; **a ~ di** astride, straddling; **siamo a ~** (*fig*) we've made it; **da ~** (*fig: dose*) drastic; (: *febbre*) raging; **vivere a ~ tra due periodi** to straddle two periods; **~ di battaglia** (*TEATRO*) tour de force; (*fig*) hobbyhorse; **~ da corsa** racehorse; **~ a dondolo** rocking horse; **~ da sella** saddle horse; **~ da soma** packhorse.
ca'vare *vt* (*togliere*) to draw out, extract, take out; (: *giacca, scarpe*) to take off; (: *fame, sete, voglia*) to satisfy; **~rsi** *vr*: **~rsi da** (*guai, problemi*) to get out of; **cavarsela** to get away with it; to manage, get on all right; **non ci caverà un bel nulla** you'll get nothing out of it (*o* him *etc*).
cava'tappi *sm inv* corkscrew.
ca'verna *sf* cave.
caver'noso, a *ag* (*luogo*) cavernous; (*fig: voce*) deep; (: *tosse*) raucous.
ca'vezza [ka'vettsa] *sf* halter.
'cavia *sf* guinea pig.
cavi'ale *sm* caviar.
ca'viglia [ka'viʎʎa] *sf* ankle.
cavil'lare *vi* to quibble.
ca'villo *sm* quibble.
cavil'loso, a *ag* quibbling, hair-splitting.
cavità *sf inv* cavity.
'cavo, a *ag* hollow ♦ *sm* (*ANAT*) cavity; (*grossa corda*) rope, cable; (*ELETTR, TEL*) cable.
cavo'lata *sf* (*fam*) stupid thing, foolish thing.
cavolfi'ore *sm* cauliflower.
'cavolo *sm* cabbage; **non m'importa un ~** (*fam*) I don't give a hoot; **che ~ vuoi?** (*fam*) what the heck do you want?; **~ di Bruxelles** Brussels sprout.
caz'zata [kat'tsata] *sf* (*fam!*: *stupidaggine*) stupid thing, something stupid.
'cazzo [kattso] *sm* (*fam!*: *pene*) prick (!); **non gliene importa un ~** (*fig fam!*) he doesn't give a damn about it; **fatti i ~i tuoi** (*fig fam!*) mind your own damn busi-

ness.

caz'zotto [kat'tsɔtto] *sm* punch; **fare a ~i** to have a punch-up.

cazzu'ola [kat'tswɔla] *sf* trowel.

CB *sigla* = *Campobasso*.

CC *abbr* = *Carabinieri*.

cc *abbr* (= *centimetro cubico*) cc.

C.C. *abbr* = **codice civile**.

c.c. *abbr* (= *conto corrente*) c/a, a/c; (*ELETTR*) *vedi* **corrente continua**.

c/c *abbr* (= *conto corrente*) c/a, a/c.

CCI *sigla f* (= *Camera di Commercio Internazionale*) ICC (= *International Chamber of Commerce*).

CCIAA *sigla f* = *Camera di Commercio Industria, Agricoltura e Artigianato*.

CCT *sigla m vedi* **certificato di credito del Tesoro**.

C.D. *abbr* (= *Corpo Diplomatico*) CD.

c.d. *abbr* = **cosiddetto**.

c.d.d. *abbr* (= *come dovevasi dimostrare*) QED (= *quod erat demonstrandum*).

C.d.M. *abbr* = **Cassa del Mezzogiorno**.

CE *sigla* = *Caserta*.

ce [tʃe] *pronome, av vedi* **ci**.

C.E. *sigla* = **Consiglio d'Europa**.

CECA *sigla f* (= *Comunità Europea del Carbone e dell'Acciaio*) ECSC (= *European Coal and Steel Community*).

cec'chino [tʃek'kino] *sm* sniper; (*POL*) *member of parliament who votes against his own party*.

'cece ['tʃetʃe] *sm* chickpea, garbanzo (*esp US*).

cecità [tʃetʃi'ta] *sf* blindness.

'ceco, a, chi, che ['tʃeko] *ag, sm/f, sm* Czech.

Cecoslo'vacchia [tʃekozlo'vakkja] *sf*: **la ~** Czechoslovakia.

cecoslo'vacco, a, chi, che [tʃekozlo'vakko] *ag, sm/f* Czechoslovakian.

CED [tʃed] *sigla m* = **centro elaborazione dati**.

'cedere ['tʃedere] *vt* (*concedere: posto*) to give up; (*DIR*) to transfer, make over ♦ *vi* (*cadere*) to give way, subside; **~ (a)** to surrender (to), yield (to), give in (to); **~ il passo (a qn)** to let (sb) pass in front; **~ il passo a qc** (*fig*) to give way to sth; **~ la parola (a qn)** to hand over (to sb).

ce'devole [tʃe'devole] *ag* (*terreno*) soft; (*fig*) yielding.

'cedola ['tʃedola] *sf* (*COMM*) coupon; voucher.

ce'drata [tʃe'drata] *sf* citron juice.

'cedro ['tʃedro] *sm* cedar; (*albero da frutto, frutto*) citron.

'CEE ['tʃee] *sigla f vedi* **Comunità Economica Europea**.

'ceffo ['tʃeffo] *sm* (*peg*) ugly mug.

cef'fone [tʃef'fone] *sm* slap, smack.

ce'lare [tʃe'lare] *vt* to conceal; **~rsi** *vr* to

hide.

cele'brare [tʃele'brare] *vt* to celebrate; (*cerimonia*) to hold; **~ le lodi di qc/qn** to sing the praises of sth/sb.

celebrazi'one [tʃelebrat'tsjone] *sf* celebration.

'celebre ['tʃelebre] *ag* famous, celebrated.

celebrità [tʃelebri'ta] *sf inv* fame; (*persona*) celebrity.

'celere ['tʃelere] *ag* fast, swift; (*corso*) crash *cpd* ♦ *sf* (*POLIZIA*) riot police.

ce'leste [tʃe'leste] *ag* celestial; heavenly; (*colore*) sky-blue.

'celia [tʃelja] *sf* joke; **per ~** for a joke.

celi'bato [tʃeli'bato] *sm* celibacy.

'celibe ['tʃelibe] *ag* single, unmarried ♦ *sm* bachelor.

'cella ['tʃella] *sf* cell; **~ di rigore** punishment cell.

cello'phane ® [selo'fan] *sm* cellophane ®.

'cellula ['tʃellula] *sf* (*BIOL, ELETTR, POL*) cell.

cellu'lare [tʃellu'lare] *ag* cellular ♦ *sm* (*furgone*) police van; **segregazione ~** (*DIR*) solitary confinement.

cellu'lite [tʃellu'lite] *sf* cellulitis.

'celta ['tʃelta] *sm/f* Celt.

'celtico, a, ci, che ['tʃeltiko] *ag, sm* Celtic.

'cembalo ['tʃembalo] *sm* (*MUS*) harpsichord.

cemen'tare [tʃemen'tare] *vt* (*anche fig*) to cement.

ce'mento [tʃe'mento] *sm* cement; **~ armato** reinforced concrete.

'cena ['tʃena] *sf* dinner; (*leggera*) supper.

ce'nacolo [tʃe'nakolo] *sm* (*circolo*) coterie, circle; (*REL, dipinto*) Last Supper.

ce'nare [tʃe'nare] *vi* to dine, have dinner.

'cencio ['tʃentʃo] *sm* piece of cloth, rag; (*per spolverare*) duster; **essere bianco come un ~** to be as white as a sheet.

'cenere ['tʃenere] *sf* ash.

Cene'rentola [tʃene'rentola] *sf* (*anche fig*) Cinderella.

'cenno ['tʃenno] *sm* (*segno*) sign, signal; (*gesto*) gesture; (*col capo*) nod; (*con la mano*) wave; (*allusione*) hint, mention; (*breve esposizione*) short account; **far ~ di si/no** to nod (one's head)/shake one's head; **~ d'intesa** sign of agreement; **~i di storia dell'arte** an outline of the history of art.

censi'mento [tʃensi'mento] *sm* census.

'CENSIS ['tʃensis] *sigla m* (= *Centro Studi Investimenti Sociali*) *independent institute carrying out research on Italy's social and cultural welfare*.

cen'sore [tʃen'sore] *sm* censor.

cen'sura [tʃen'sura] *sf* censorship; censor's office; (*fig*) censure.

censu'rare [tʃensu'rare] *vt* to censor; to censure.

cent. *abbr* = **centesimo**.

centelli'nare [tʃentelli'nare] *vt* to sip; (*fig*) to savour (*Brit*), savor (*US*).

cente'nario, a [tʃente'narjo] *ag (che ha cento anni)* hundred-year-old; *(che ricorre ogni cento anni)* centennial, centenary *cpd* ♦ *sm/f* centenarian ♦ *sm* centenary.

cen'tesimo, a [tʃen'tezimo] *ag, sm* hundredth; **essere senza un ~** to be penniless.

cen'tigrado, a [tʃen'tigrado] *ag* centigrade; **20 gradi ~i** 20 degrees centigrade.

cen'tilitro [tʃen'tilitro] *sm* centilitre.

cen'timetro [tʃen'timetro] *sm* centimetre *(Brit)*, centimeter *(US)*; *(nastro)* measuring tape *(in centimetres)*.

centi'naio, *pl(f)* **-aia** [tʃenti'najo] *sm:* **un ~ (di)** a hundred; about a hundred.

'cento ['tʃento] *num* a hundred, one hundred; **per ~** per cent; **al ~ per ~** a hundred per cent; **~ di questi giorni!** many happy returns (of the day)!

centodi'eci [tʃento'djɛtʃi] *num* one hundred and ten; **laurearsi con ~ e lode** *(UNIVERSITÀ)* ≈ to graduate with first-class honours.

cento'mila [tʃento'mila] *num* a *o* one hundred thousand; **te l'ho detto ~ volte** *(fig)* I've told you a thousand times.

Cen'trafrica [tʃen'trafrika] *sm:* **il ~** the Central African Republic.

cen'trale [tʃen'trale] *ag* central ♦ *sf:* **~ elettrica** electric power station; **~ del latte** dairy; **~ di polizia** police headquarters *pl*; **telefonica** (telephone) exchange; **sede ~** head office.

centrali'nista [tʃentrali'nista] *sm/f* operator.

centra'lino [tʃentra'lino] *sm* (telephone) exchange; *(di albergo etc)* switchboard.

centraliz'zare [tʃentralid'dzare] *vt* to centralize.

cen'trare [tʃen'trare] *vt* to hit the centre *(Brit) o* center *(US)* of; *(TECN)* to centre; **~ una risposta** to get the right answer; **ha centrato il problema** you've hit the nail on the head.

centra'vanti [tʃentra'vanti] *sm inv* centre forward.

cen'trifuga [tʃen'trifuga] *sf* spin-dryer.

'centro ['tʃentro] *sm* centre *(Brit)*, center *(US)*; **fare ~** to hit the bull's eye; *(CALCIO)* to score; *(fig)* to hit the nail on the head; **~ balneare** seaside resort; **~ commerciale** shopping centre; *(città)* commercial centre; **~ di costo** cost centre; **~ elaborazione dati** data-processing unit; **~ ospedaliero** hospital complex; **~ sociale** community centre; **~i vitali** *(anche fig)* vital organs.

centromedi'ano [tʃentrome'djano] *sm (CALCIO)* centre half.

'ceppo ['tʃeppo] *sm (di albero)* stump; *(pezzo di legno)* log.

'cera ['tʃera] *sf* wax; *(aspetto)* appearance, look; **~ per pavimenti** floor polish.

cera'lacca [tʃera'lakka] *sf* sealing wax.

ce'ramica, che [tʃe'ramika] *sf* ceramic; *(ARTE)* ceramics *sg*.

cerbi'atto [tʃer'bjatto] *sm* fawn.

'cerca ['tʃerka] *sf:* **in** *o* **alla ~ di** in search of.

cercaper'sone [tʃerkaper'sone] *sm inv* bleeper.

cer'care [tʃer'kare] *vt* to look for, search for ♦ **di fare qc** to try to do sth.

cercherò *etc* [tʃerke'rɔ] *vb vedi* **cercare**.

'cerchia ['tʃerkja] *sf* circle.

cerchi'ato, a [tʃer'kjato] *ag:* **occhiali ~i d'osso** horn-rimmed spectacles; **avere gli occhi ~i** to have dark rings under one's eyes.

'cerchio ['tʃerkjo] *sm* circle; *(giocattolo, di botte)* hoop; **dare un colpo al ~ e uno alla botte** *(fig)* to keep two things going at the same time.

cerchi'one [tʃer'kjone] *sm* (wheel) rim.

cere'ale [tʃere'ale] *sm* cereal.

cere'brale [tʃere'brale] *ag* cerebral.

ceri'monia [tʃeri'mɔnja] *sf* ceremony; **senza tante ~e** *(senza formalità)* informally; *(bruscamente)* unceremoniously, without so much as a by-your-leave.

cerimoni'ale [tʃerimoni'njale] *sm* etiquette; ceremonial.

cerimoni'ere [tʃerimoni'njɛre] *sm* master of ceremonies.

cerimoni'oso, a [tʃerimo'njoso] *ag* formal, ceremonious.

ce'rino [tʃe'rino] *sm* wax match.

CERN [tʃern] *sigla m* (= *Comitato Europeo di Ricerche Nucleari)* CERN.

'cernia ['tʃɛrnja] *sf (ZOOL)* stone bass.

cerni'era [tʃer'njɛra] *sf* hinge; **~ lampo** zip (fastener) *(Brit)*, zipper *(US)*.

'cernita ['tʃernita] *sf* selection; **fare una ~ di** to select.

'cero ['tʃero] *sm* (church) candle.

ce'rone [tʃe'rone] *sm (trucco)* greasepaint.

ce'rotto [tʃe'rɔtto] *sm* sticking plaster.

certa'mente [tʃerta'mente] *av* certainly, surely.

cer'tezza [tʃer'tettsa] *sf* certainty.

certifi'care [tʃertifi'kare] *vt* to certify.

certifi'cato [tʃertifi'kato] *sm* certificate; **~ medico/di nascita** medical/birth certificate; **~ di credito del Tesoro (CCT)** treasury bill.

certificazi'one [tʃertifikat'tsjone] *sf* certification; **~ di bilancio** *(COMM)* external audit.

'certo, a ['tʃerto] *ag* certain; *(sicuro)*: **~ (di/che)** certain *o* sure (of/that) ♦ *det* certain ♦ *av* certainly, of course; **~i** *pronome pl* some; **un ~ non so che** an indefinable something; **di una ~a età** past one's prime, not so young; **sì ~** yes indeed; **no ~** certainly not; **di ~** certainly.

certo'sino [tʃerto'zino] *sm* Carthusian monk; *(liquore)* chartreuse; **è un lavoro da ~** it's a pernickety job.

cer'tuni [tʃer'tuni] *pronome pl* some (people).

ce'rume [ʃʃe'rume] *sm* (ear) wax.

cer'vello, *pl* **i** *(anche: pl(f))* **a** *o* **e)** [tʃer'vɛllo] *sm* brain; ~ **elettronico** computer; **avere il** *o* **essere un** ~ **fino** to be sharp-witted; **è uscito di** ~, **gli è dato di volta il** ~ he's gone off his head.

cervi'cale [tʃervi'kale] *ag* cervical.

'cervo, a ['tʃervo] *sm/f* stag/hind ♦ *sm* deer; ~ **volante** stag beetle.

cesel'lare [tʃezel'lare] *vt* to chisel; *(incidere)* to engrave.

ce'sello [tʃe'zɛllo] *sm* chisel.

'CESIS ['tʃesis] *sigla m* (= *Comitato Esecutivo per i Servizi di Informazione e di Sicurezza) committee on intelligence and security matters, reporting to the Prime Minister.*

ce'soie [tʃe'zoje] *sfpl* shears.

ces'puglio [tʃes'puʎʎo] *sm* bush.

ces'sare [tʃes'sare] *vi, vt* to stop, cease; ~ **di fare qc** to stop doing sth; **"cessato allarme"** "all clear".

ces'sate il fu'oco [tʃes'sate-] *sm* ceasefire.

cessazi'one [tʃessat'tsjone] *sf* cessation; *(interruzione)* suspension.

cessi'one [tʃes'sjone] *sf* transfer.

'cesso ['tʃɛsso] *sm* (*fam: gabinetto*) bog.

'cesta ['tʃesta] *sf* (large) basket.

ces'tello [tʃes'tɛllo] *sm* (*per bottiglie*) crate; *(di lavatrice)* drum.

cesti'nare [tʃesti'nare] *vt* to throw away; *(fig: proposta)* to turn down; (: *romanzo*) to reject.

ces'tino [tʃes'tino] *sm* basket; *(per la carta straccia)* wastepaper basket; ~ **da viaggio** *(FERR)* packed lunch (*o* dinner).

'cesto ['tʃesto] *sm* basket.

ce'sura [tʃe'zura] *sf* caesura.

ce'taceo [tʃe'tatʃeo] *sm* sea mammal.

'ceto ['tʃeto] *sm* (social) class.

'cetra ['tʃetra] *sf* zither; *(fig: di poeta)* lyre.

cetrio'lino [tʃetrio'lino] *sm* gherkin.

cetri'olo [tʃetri'ɔlo] *sm* cucumber.

Cf., Cfr. *abbr* (= *confronta*) cf.

CFS *sigla m* (= *Corpo Forestale dello Stato) body responsible for the planting and management of forests.*

cg *abbr* (= *centigrammo*) cg.

C.G.I.L. *sigla f* (= *Confederazione Generale Italiana del Lavoro) trades union organization.*

CH *sigla* = *Chieti.*

cha'let [ʃa'lɛ] *sm inv* chalet.

cham'pagne [ʃã'paɲ] *sm inv* champagne.

chance [ʃãs] *sf inv* chance.

charme [ʃarm] *sm* charm.

'charter ['tʃa:tər] *ag inv (volo)* charter *cpd*; *(aereo)* chartered ♦ *sm inv* chartered plane.

che [ke] *pronome (relativo: persona: soggetto)* who; (: *oggetto)* whom; (: *cosa*) which,

that; *(interrogativo, esclamativo)* what; **l'uomo** ~ **io vedo** the man (whom) I see; **il libro** ~ **è sul tavolo** the book which *o* that is on the table; **il giorno** ~... the day (that)...; **la sera** ~ **ti ho visto** the evening I saw you; ~ **(cosa) fai?** what are you doing?; **a** ~ **(cosa) pensi?** what are you thinking about?; **non sa** ~ **fare** he doesn't know what to do ♦ *det* what; *(di numero limitato)* which; ~ **vestito ti vuoi mettere?** what (*o* which) dress do you want to put on?; ~ **tipo di film hai visto?** what sort of film did you see?; ~ **bel vestito!** what a lovely dress!; ~ **buono!** how delicious! ♦ *cong* that; **so** ~ **tu c'eri** I know (that) you were there; **voglio** ~ **tu studi** I want you to study; *(affinché)*: **vieni qua,** ~ **ti veda** come here, so that I can see you; *(temporale)*: **arrivai** ~ **eri già partito** you had already left when I arrived; **sono anni** ~ **non lo vedo** I haven't seen him in years; *(in frasi imperative)*: ~ **venga pure** let him come by all means; **non** ~ **sia stupido** not that he's stupid; ~ **tu venga o no, noi partiamo lo stesso** we're leaving whether you come or not; *vedi* **non, più, meno** *etc.*

'checca, che ['kekka] *sf (fam: omosessuale)* fairy.

chef [ʃɛf] *sm inv* chef.

chero'sene [kero'zɛne] *sm* kerosene.

cheru'bino [keru'bino] *sm* cherub.

che'tare [ke'tare] *vt* to hush, silence; ~**rsi** *vr* to quieten down, fall silent.

cheti'chella [keti'kɛlla]: **alla** ~ *av* stealthily, unobtrusively; **andarsene alla** ~ to slip away.

'cheto, a ['keto] *ag* quiet, silent.

chi [ki] *pronome (interrogativo: soggetto)* who; (: *oggetto)*: **di** ~ **è questo libro?** whose book is this?; **con** ~ **parli?** to whom are you talking?, who are you talking to?; *(relativo: colui/colei che)* he/she who; (: *complemento)*: **dillo a** ~ **vuoi** tell it to whoever you like; ~ **dice una cosa** ~ **un'altra** some say one thing some another; **lo riferirò a** ~ **di dovere** I'll pass it on to the relevant person; **so io di** ~ **parlo** I'm naming no names; ~ **si somiglia si piglia** birds of a feather flock together; **si salvi** ~ **può** every man for himself.

chiacchie'rare [kjakkje'rare] *vi* to chat; *(discorrere futilmente)* to chatter; *(far pettegolezzi)* to gossip.

chiacchie'rata [kjakkje'rata] *sf* chat; **farsi una** ~ to have a chat.

chi'acchiere ['kjakkjere] *sfpl* chatter *q*; gossip *q*; **fare due** *o* **quattro** ~ to have a chat; **perdersi in** ~ to waste time talking.

chiacchie'rone, a [kjakkje'rone] *ag* talkative, chatty; gossipy ♦ *sm/f* chatterbox; gossip.

chia'mare [kja'mare] *vt* to call; *(rivolgersi a qn)* to call (in), send for; ~**rsi** *vr* (*aver* *nome*) to be called; **mi chiamo Paolo** my name is Paolo, I'm called Paolo; **mandare a ~ qn** to send for sb, call sb in; **~ alle armi** to call up; **~ in giudizio** to summon; **~ qn da parte** to take sb aside.

chia'mata [kja'mata] *sf (TEL)* call; *(MIL)* call-up; **~ interurbana** long-distance call; **~ con preavviso** person-to-person call; **~ alle urne** *(POL)* election.

chi'appa ['kjappa] *sf (fam: natica)* cheek; **~e** *sfpl* bottom *sg*.

chi'ara ['kjara] *sf* egg white.

chia'rezza [kja'rettsa] *sf* clearness; clarity.

chiarifi'care [kjarifi'kare] *vt (anche fig)* to clarify.

chiarificazi'one [kjarifikat'tsjone] *sf* clarification.

chiari'mento [kjari'mento] *sm* clarification *q*, explanation.

chia'rire [kja'rire] *vt* to make clear; *(fig: spiegare)* to clear up, explain; **~rsi** *vr* to become clear; **si sono chiariti** they've sorted things out.

chi'aro, a ['kjaro] *ag* clear; *(luminoso)* clear, bright; *(colore)* pale, light ♦ *av (parlare, vedere)* clearly; **si sta facendo ~** the day is dawning; **sia ~a una cosa** let's get one thing straight; **mettere in ~ qc** *(fig)* to clear sth up; **parliamoci ~** let's be frank.

chia'rore [kja'rore] *sm (diffuse)* light.

chiaroveg'gente [kjaroved'dʒɛnte] *sm/f* clairvoyant.

chi'asso ['kjasso] *sm* uproar, row; **far ~** to make a din; *(fig)* to make a fuss; *(: scalpore)* to cause a stir.

chias'soso, a [kjas'soso] *ag* noisy, rowdy; *(vistoso)* showy, gaudy.

'chiatta ['kjatta] *sf* barge.

chi'ave ['kjave] *sf* key ♦ *ag inv* key *cpd*; **chiudere a ~** to lock; **~ d'accensione** *(AUT)* ignition key; **~ a forcella** fork spanner; **~ inglese** monkey wrench; **in ~ politica** in political terms; **~ di volta** *(anche fig)* keystone; **~i in mano** *(contratto)* turn-key *cpd*; **prezzo ~i in mano** *(di macchina)* on-the-road price.

chiavis'tello [kjavis'tɛllo] *sm* bolt.

chi'azza ['kjattsa] *sf* stain, splash.

chiaz'zare [kjat'tsare] *vt* to stain, splash.

chic [ʃik] *ag inv* chic, elegant.

chicches'sia [kikkes'sia] *pronome* anyone, anybody.

'chicco, chi ['kikko] *sm (di cereale, riso)* grain; *(di caffè)* bean; **~ di grandine** hailstone; **~ d'uva** grape.

chi'edere ['kjɛdere] *vt (per sapere)* to ask; *(per avere)* to ask for ♦ *vi*: **~ di qn** to ask after sb; *(al telefono)* to ask for *o* want sb; **~rsi** *vr*: **~rsi (se)** to wonder (whether); **~ qc a qn** to ask sb sth; to ask sb for sth; **~ scusa a qn** to apologize to sb; **~ l'elemosina** to beg; **non chiedo altro**

that's all I want.

chieri'chetto [kjeri'ketto] *sm* altar boy.

chi'erico, ci ['kjɛriko] *sm* cleric; altar boy.

chi'esa ['kjɛza] *sf* church.

chi'esi *etc* ['kjɛzi] *vb vedi* **chiedere**.

chi'esto, a ['kjɛsto] *pp di* **chiedere**.

'Chigi ['kidʒi]: **palazzo ~** *sm (POL) offices of the Italian Prime Minister*.

'chiglia ['kiʎʎa] *sf* keel.

'chilo ['kilo] *sm* kilo.

chilo'grammo [kilo'grammo] *sm* kilogram(me).

chilome'traggio [kilome'traddʒo] *sm (AUT)* ≈ mileage.

chilo'metrico, a, ci, che [kilo'mɛtriko] *ag* kilometric; *(fig)* endless.

chi'lometro [ki'lɔmetro] *sm* kilometre *(Brit)*, kilometer *(US)*.

'chimico, a, ci, che ['kimiko] *ag* chemical ♦ *sm/f* chemist ♦ *sf* chemistry.

chi'mono [ki'mɔno] *sm inv* kimono.

'china ['kina] *sf (pendio)* slope, descent; *(BOT)* cinchona; **(inchiostro di) ~** Indian ink; **risalire la ~** *(fig)* to be on the road to recovery.

chi'nare [ki'nare] *vt* to lower, bend; **~rsi** *vr* to stoop, bend.

chincaglie'ria [kinkaʎʎe'ria] *sf* fancy-goods shop; **~e** *sfpl* fancy goods, knick-knacks.

chi'nino [ki'nino] *sm* quinine.

'chino, a ['kino] *ag*: **a capo ~, a testa ~a** head bent *o* bowed.

chi'occia, ce ['kjɔttʃa] *sf* brooding hen.

chi'occio, a, ci, ce ['kjɔttʃo] *ag (voce)* clucking.

chi'occiola ['kjɔttʃola] *sf* snail; **scala a ~** spiral staircase.

chi'odo ['kjɔdo] *sm* nail; *(fig)* obsession; **~ scaccia ~** *(proverbio)* one problem drives away another; **roba da ~i!** it's unbelievable!; **~ di garofano** *(CUC)* clove.

chi'oma ['kjɔma] *sf (capelli)* head of hair; *(di albero)* foliage.

chi'osco, schi ['kjɔsko] *sm* kiosk, stall.

chi'ostro ['kjɔstro] *sm* cloister.

chiro'mante [kiro'mante] *sm/f* palmist; *(indovino)* fortune-teller.

chirur'gia [kirur'dʒia] *sf* surgery.

chi'rurgico, a, ci, che [ki'rurdʒiko] *ag* surgical.

chi'rurgo, ghi *o* **gi** [ki'rurgo] *sm* surgeon.

chissà [kis'sa] *av* who knows, I wonder.

chi'tarra [ki'tarra] *sf* guitar.

chitar'rista, i, e [kitar'rista] *sm/f* guitarist, guitar player.

chi'udere ['kjudere] *vt* to close, shut; *(luce, acqua)* to put off, turn off; *(definitivamente: fabbrica)* to close down, shut down; *(strada)* to close; *(recingere)* to enclose; *(porre termine)* to end ♦ *vi* to close, shut; to close down, shut down; to end; **~rsi** *vr* to shut, close; *(ritirarsi: an-*

che fig) to shut o.s. away; (*ferita*) to close up; ~ **un occhio su** (*fig*) to turn a blind eye to; **chiudi la bocca!** *o* **il becco!** (*fam*) shut up!

chi'unque [ki'unkwe] *pronome* (*relativo*) whoever; (*indefinito*) anyone, anybody; ~ **sia** whoever it is.

'**chiusi** *etc* ['kjusi] *vb vedi* **chiudere**.

chi'uso, a ['kjuso] *pp di* **chiudere** ♦ *ag* (*porta*) shut, closed; (: *a chiave*) locked; (*senza uscita: strada etc*) blocked off; (*rubinetto*) off; (*persona*) uncommunicative; (*ambiente, club*) exclusive ♦ *sm*: **stare al ~** (*fig*) to be shut up ♦ *sf* (*di corso d'acqua*) sluice, lock; (*recinto*) enclosure; (*di discorso etc*) conclusion, ending; "~" (*negozio etc*) "closed"; "~ **al pubblico**" "no admittance to the public".

chiu'sura [kju'sura] *sf* closing; shutting; closing *o* shutting down; enclosing; putting *o* turning off; ending; (*dispositivo*) catch; fastening; fastener; **orario di ~** closing time; ~ **lampo** ® zip (fastener) (*Brit*), zipper (*US*).

ci [tʃi] (*dav lo, la, li, le, ne diventa* **ce**) *pronome* (*personale*) us; (: *complemento di termine*) (to) us; (: *riflessivo*) ourselves; (: *reciproco*) one another; (*dimostrativo: di ciò, su ciò, in ciò etc*) about (*o* on *o* of) it ♦ *av* (*qui*) here; (*lì*) there; ~ **siamo divertiti** we enjoyed ourselves; ~ **amiamo** we love one another; **non so cosa far~** I don't know what to do about it; **che c'entro io?** what have I got to do with it?; ~ **puoi giurare,** ~ **puoi scommettere** you can bet on it; ~ **puoi contare** you can depend on it; ~ **sei?** (*sei pronto*) are you ready?; (*hai capito*) do you follow?; **esser~** *vedi* **essere**.

C.ia *abbr* (= *compagnia*) Co.

cia'batta [tʃa'batta] *sf* mule, slipper.

ciabat'tino [tʃabat'tino] *sm* cobbler.

ciac [tʃak] *sm* (*CINEMA*) clapper board; ~**, si gira!** action!

Ci'ad [tʃad] *sm*: **il ~** Chad.

ci'alda ['tʃalda] *sf* (*CUC*) wafer.

cial'trone [tʃal'trone] *sm* good-for-nothing.

ciam'bella [tʃam'bɛlla] *sf* (*CUC*) ring-shaped cake; (*salvagente*) rubber ring.

ci'ancia, ce ['tʃantʃa] *sf* gossip *q*, tittle-tattle *q*.

cianfru'saglie [tʃanfru'zaʎʎe] *sfpl* bits and pieces.

cia'nuro [tʃa'nuro] *sm* cyanide.

ci'ao ['tʃao] *escl* (*all'arrivo*) hello!; (*alla partenza*) cheerio! (*Brit*), bye!

ciar'lare [tʃar'lare] *vi* to chatter; (*peg*) to gossip.

ciarla'tano [tʃarla'tano] *sm* charlatan.

cias'cuno, a [tʃas'kuno] (*dav sm*: **ciascun** +*C, V,* **ciascuno** +*s impura, gn, pn, ps, x, z*; *dav sf*: **ciascuna** +*C,* **ciascun'** +*V*) *det, pronome* each.

ci'barsi [tʃi'barsi] *vr*: ~ **di** (*anche fig*) to live on.

ciber'netica [tʃiber'nɛtika] *sf* cybernetics *sg*.

'**cibo** ['tʃibo] *sm* food.

ci'cala [tʃi'kala] *sf* cicada.

cica'trice [tʃika'tritʃe] *sf* scar.

cicatriz'zarsi [tʃikatrid'dzarsi] *vr* to form a scar, heal (up).

'**cicca, che** ['tʃikka] *sf* cigarette end; (*fam: sigaretta*) fag; **non vale una ~** (*fig*) it's worthless.

'**ciccia** ['tʃittʃa] *sf* (*fam: carne*) meat; (: *grasso umano*) fat, flesh.

cicci'one, a [tʃit'tʃone] *sm/f* (*fam*) fatty.

cice'rone [tʃitʃe'rone] *sm* guide.

cicla'mino [tʃikla'mino] *sm* cyclamen.

ci'clismo [tʃi'klizmo] *sm* cycling.

ci'clista, i, e [tʃi'klista] *sm/f* cyclist.

'**ciclo** ['tʃiklo] *sm* cycle; (*di malattia*) course.

ciclomo'tore [tʃiklomo'tore] *sm* moped.

ci'clone [tʃi'klone] *sm* cyclone.

ciclos'tile [tʃiklos'tile] *sm* cyclostyle (*Brit*).

ci'cogna [tʃi'koɲɲa] *sf* stork.

ci'coria [tʃi'kɔrja] *sf* chicory.

'**CIDA** ['tʃida] *sigla f* = *Confederazione Italiana Dirigenti d'Azienda.*

ci'eco, a, chi, che ['tʃɛko] *ag* blind ♦ *sm/f* blind man/woman; **alla** ~**a** (*anche fig*) blindly.

ci'elo ['tʃɛlo] *sm* sky; (*REL*) heaven; **toccare il ~ con un dito** (*fig*) to walk on air; **per amor del** ~! for heavens' sake!

'**cifra** ['tʃifra] *sf* (*numero*) figure, numeral; (*somma di denaro*) sum, figure; (*monogramma*) monogram, initials *pl*; (*codice*) code, cipher.

ci'frare [tʃi'frare] *vt* (*messaggio*) to code; (*lenzuola etc*) to embroider with a monogram.

'**ciglio** ['tʃiʎʎo] *sm* (*margine*) edge, verge; (*pl(f)* **ciglia**: *delle palpebre*) (eye)lash; (*sopracciglio*) eyebrow; **non ha battuto ~** (*fig*) he didn't bat an eyelid.

'**cigno** ['tʃiɲɲo] *sm* swan.

cigo'lante [tʃigo'lante] *ag* squeaking, creaking.

cigo'lare [tʃigo'lare] *vi* to squeak, creak.

CIIS *sigla m* (= *Comitato Interparlamentare per l'Informazione e la Sicurezza*) all-party committee on intelligence and security.

'**Cile** ['tʃile] *sm*: **il ~** Chile.

ci'lecca [tʃi'lekka] *sf*: **far ~** to fail.

ci'leno, a [tʃi'lɛno] *ag, sm/f* Chilean.

cili'egia, gie *o* **ge** [tʃi'ljɛdʒa] *sf* cherry.

cili'egio [tʃi'ljɛdʒo] *sm* cherry tree.

cilin'drata [tʃilin'drata] *sf* (*AUT*) (cubic) capacity; **una macchina di grossa ~** a big-engined car.

ci'lindro [tʃi'lindro] *sm* cylinder; (*cappello*) top hat.

CIM [tʃim] *sigla m* = *centro d'igiene mentale.*

'**cima** ['tʃima] *sf* (*sommità*) top; (*di monte*)

top, summit; (*estremità*) end; (*fig: persona*) genius; **in ~ a** at the top of; **da ~ a fondo** from top to bottom; (*fig*) from beginning to end.

ci'melio [tʃi'mɛljo] *sm* relic.

cimen'tare [tʃimen'tare] *vt* to put to the test; **~rsi** *vr*: **~rsi in qc** to undertake sth.

'cimice ['tʃimitʃe] *sf* (*ZOOL*) bug; (*puntina*) drawing pin (*Brit*), thumbtack (*US*).

cimini'era [tʃimi'njɛra] *sf* chimney; (*di nave*) funnel.

cimi'tero [tʃimi'tɛro] *sm* cemetery.

ci'murro [tʃi'murro] *sm* (*di cani*) distemper.

'Cina ['tʃina] *sf*: **la ~** China.

cin'cin, cin cin [tʃin'tʃin] *escl* cheers!

cincischi'are [tʃintʃis'kjare] *vi* to mess about, fiddle about.

'cine ['tʃine] *sm inv* (*fam*) cinema.

cine'asta, i, e [tʃine'asta] *sm/f* person in the film industry; film-maker.

cinegior'nale [tʃinedʒor'nale] *sm* newsreel.

'cinema ['tʃinema] *sm inv* cinema; **~ muto** silent films; **~ d'essai** (*locale*) avant-garde cinema, experimental cinema.

cine'presa [tʃine'presa] *sf* cine-camera.

ci'nese [tʃi'nese] *ag*, *sm/f*, *sm* Chinese *inv*.

cine'teca, che [tʃine'tɛka] *sf* (*collezione*) film collection, film library; (*locale*) film library.

ci'netico, a, ci, che [tʃi'nɛtiko] *ag* kinetic.

'cingere ['tʃindʒere] *vt* (*attorniare*) to surround, encircle; **~ la vita con una cintura** to put a belt round one's waist; **~ d'assedio** to besiege, lay siege to.

'cinghia ['tʃingja] *sf* strap; (*cintura, TECN*) belt; **tirare la ~** (*fig*) to tighten one's belt.

cinghi'ale [tʃin'gjale] *sm* wild boar.

cinguet'tare [tʃingwet'tare] *vi* to twitter.

'cinico, a, ci, che ['tʃiniko] *ag* cynical ♦ *sm/f* cynic.

ci'nismo [tʃi'nizmo] *sm* cynicism.

cin'quanta [tʃin'kwanta] *num* fifty.

cinquante'nario [tʃinkwante'narjo] *sm* fiftieth anniversary.

cinquan'tenne [tʃinkwan'tɛnne] *sm/f* fifty-year-old man/woman.

cinquan'tesimo, a [tʃinkwan'tɛzimo] *num* fiftieth.

cinquan'tina [tʃinkwan'tina] *sf* (*serie*): **una ~ (di)** about fifty; (*età*): **essere sulla ~** to be about fifty.

'cinque ['tʃinkwe] *num* five; **avere ~ anni** to be five (years old); **il ~ dicembre 1988** the fifth of December 1988; **alle ~ (***ora***)** at five (o'clock); **siamo in ~** there are five of us.

cinquecen'tesco, a, schi, sche [tʃinkwe-tʃen'tesko] *ag* sixteenth-century.

cinque'cento [tʃinkwe'tʃento] *num* five hundred ♦ *sm*: **il C~** the sixteenth century.

cinque'mila [tʃinkwe'mila] *num* five thousand.

'cinsi *etc* ['tʃinsi] *vb vedi* cingere.

'cinta ['tʃinta] *sf* (*anche*: **~ muraria**) city walls *pl*; **muro di ~** (*di giardino etc*) surrounding wall.

cin'tare [tʃin'tare] *vt* to enclose.

'cinto, a ['tʃinto] *pp di* cingere.

'cintola ['tʃintola] *sf* (*cintura*) belt; (*vita*) waist.

cin'tura [tʃin'tura] *sf* belt; **~ di salvataggio** lifebelt (*Brit*), life preserver (*US*); **~ di sicurezza** (*AUT, AER*) safety o seat belt.

cintu'rino [tʃintu'rino] *sm* strap; **~ dell'orologio** watch strap.

CIO *sigla m* (= *Comitato Internazionale Olimpico*) IOC (= *International Olympic Committee*).

ciò [tʃɔ] *pronome* this; that; **~ che** what; **~ nonostante** o **nondimeno** nevertheless, in spite of that; **con tutto ~** for all that, in spite of everything.

ci'occa, che ['tʃɔkka] *sf* (*di capelli*) lock.

ciocco'lata [tʃokko'lata] *sf* chocolate; (*bevanda*) (hot) chocolate; **~ al latte/fondente** milk/plain chocolate.

cioccola'tino [tʃokkola'tino] *sm* chocolate.

ciocco'lato [tʃokko'lato] *sm* chocolate.

cioè [tʃo'ɛ] *av* that is (to say).

ciondo'lare [tʃondo'lare] *vt* (*far dondolare*) to dangle, swing ♦ *vi* to dangle; (*fig*) to loaf (about).

ci'ondolo ['tʃondolo] *sm* pendant; **~ portafortuna** charm.

ciondo'loni [tʃondo'loni] *av*: **con le braccia/gambe ~** with arms/legs dangling.

ciononos'tante [tʃononos'tante] *av* nonetheless, nevertheless.

ci'otola ['tʃɔtola] *sf* bowl.

ci'ottolo ['tʃɔttolo] *sm* pebble; (*di strada*) cobble(stone).

ci'piglio [tʃi'piʎʎo] *sm* frown.

ci'polla [tʃi'polla] *sf* onion; (*di tulipano etc*) bulb.

ci'presso [tʃi'prɛsso] *sm* cypress (tree).

'cipria ['tʃiprja] *sf* (face) powder.

cipri'ota, i, e [tʃipri'ɔta] *ag*, *sm/f* Cypriot.

'Cipro ['tʃipro] *sm* Cyprus.

'circa ['tʃirka] *av* about, roughly ♦ *prep* about, concerning; **a mezzogiorno ~** about midday.

'circo, chi ['tʃirko] *sm* circus.

circo'lare [tʃirko'lare] *vi* to circulate; (*AUT*) to drive (along), move (along) ♦ *ag* circular ♦ *sf* (*AMM*) circular; (*di autobus*) circle (line); **circola voce che ...** there is a rumour going about that ...; **assegno ~** banker's draft.

circolazi'one [tʃirkolat'tsjone] *sf* circulation; (*AUT*): **la ~** (the) traffic; **libretto di ~** log book, registration book; **tassa di ~** road tax.

'circolo ['tʃirkolo] *sm* circle; **entrare in ~** (*ANAT*) to enter the bloodstream.

circoncisi'one [tʃirkontʃi'tsjone] *sf* circumcision.

circon'dare [tʃirkon'dare] *vt* to surround.

circondari'ale [tʃirkonda'rjale] *ag*: **casa di pena** ~ district prison.

circon'dario [tʃirkon'darjo] *sm* (*DIR*) administrative district; (*zona circostante*) neighbourhood (*Brit*), neighborhood (*US*).

circonfe'renza [tʃirkonfe'rentsa] *sf* circumference.

circonvallazi'one [tʃirkonvallat'tsjone] *sf* ring road (*Brit*), beltway (*US*); (*per evitare una città*) by-pass.

circos'critto, a [tʃirkos'kritto] *pp di* **circoscrivere**.

circos'crivere [tʃirkos'krivere] *vt* to circumscribe; (*fig*) to limit, restrict.

circoscrizi'one [tʃirkoskrit'tsjone] *sf* (*AMM*) district, area; ~ **elettorale** constituency.

circos'petto, a [tʃirkos'petto] *ag* circumspect, cautious.

circos'tante [tʃirkos'tante] *ag* surrounding, neighbouring (*Brit*), neighboring (*US*).

circos'tanza [tʃirkos'tantsa] *sf* circumstance; (*occasione*) occasion; **parole di** ~ words suited to the occasion.

circu'ire [tʃirku'ire] *vt* (*fig*) to fool, take in.

cir'cuito [tʃir'kuito] *sm* circuit; **andare in** *o* **fare corto** ~ to short-circuit; ~ **integrato** integrated circuit.

ci'rillico, a, ci, che [tʃi'rilliko] *ag* Cyrillic.

'C.I.S.A.L. ['tʃisal] *sigla f* (= *Confederazione Italiana Sindacati Autonomi dei Lavoratori*) trades union organization.

C.I.S.L. [tʃisl] *sigla f* (= *Confederazione Italiana Sindacati Lavoratori*) trades union organization.

'C.I.S.N.A.L. ['tʃisnal] *sigla f* (= *Confederazione Italiana Sindacati Nazionali dei Lavoratori*) trades union organization.

'ciste ['tʃiste] *sf* = **cisti.**

cis'terna [tʃis'terna] *sf* tank, cistern.

'cisti ['tʃisti] *sf inv* cyst.

cis'tite [tʃis'tite] *sf* cystitis.

C.I.T. [tʃit] *sigla f* = *Compagnia Italiana Turismo*.

cit. *abbr* (= *citato, citata*) cit.

ci'tare [tʃi'tare] *vt* (*DIR*) to summon; (*autore*) to quote; (*a esempio, modello*) to cite; ~ **qn per danni** to sue sb.

citazi'one [tʃitat'tsjone] *sf* summons *sg*; quotation; (*di persona*) mention.

ci'tofono [tʃi'tofono] *sm* entry phone; (*in uffici*) intercom.

cito'logico, a, ci, che [tʃito'lɔdʒiko] *ag*: **esame** ~ *test for detection of cancerous cells.*

'citrico, a, ci, che ['tʃitriko] *ag* citric.

città [tʃit'ta] *sf inv* town; (*importante*) city; ~ **universitaria** university campus; **C**~ **del Capo** Cape Town.

citta'della [tʃitta'dɛlla] *sf* citadel, stronghold.

cittadi'nanza [tʃittadi'nantsa] *sf* citizens *pl*,

inhabitants *pl* of a town (*o* city); (*DIR*) citizenship.

citta'dino, a [tʃitta'dino] *ag* town *cpd*; city *cpd* ♦ *sm/f* (*di uno Stato*) citizen; (*abitante di città*) town dweller, city dweller.

ci'uccio ['tʃuttʃo] *sm* (*fam*) comforter, dummy (*Brit*), pacifier (*US*).

ci'uco, a, chi, che ['tʃuko] *sm/f* ass.

ci'uffo ['tʃuffo] *sm* tuft.

ci'urma ['tʃurma] *sf* (*di nave*) crew.

ci'vetta [tʃi'vetta] *sf* (*ZOOL*) owl; (*fig: donna*) coquette, flirt ♦ *ag inv*: **auto/nave** ~ decoy car/ship; **fare la** ~ **con qn** to flirt with sb.

civet'tare [tʃivet'tare] *vt* to flirt.

civette'ria [tʃivette'ria] *sf* coquetry, coquettishness.

civettu'olo, a [tʃivet'twɔlo] *ag* flirtatious.

'civico, a, ci, che ['tʃiviko] *ag* civic; (*museo*) municipal, town *cpd*; **guardia** ~**a** town policeman; **senso** ~ public spirit.

ci'vile [tʃi'vile] *ag* civil; (*non militare*) civilian; (*nazione*) civilized ♦ *sm* civilian; **stato** ~ marital status; **abiti** ~**i** civvies.

civi'lista, i, e [tʃivi'lista] *sm/f* (*avvocato*) civil lawyer; (*studioso*) expert in civil law.

civiliz'zare [tʃivilid'dzare] *vt* to civilize.

civilizzazi'one [tʃiviliddzat'tsjone] *sf* civilization.

civiltà [tʃivil'ta] *sf* civilization; (*cortesia*) civility.

ci'vismo [tʃi'vizmo] *sm* public spirit.

CL *sigla* = *Caltanissetta*.

cl *abbr* (= *centilitro*) cl.

'clacson *sm inv* (*AUT*) horn.

cla'more *sm* (*frastuono*) din, uproar, clamour (*Brit*), clamor (*US*); (*fig*) outcry.

clamo'roso, a *ag* noisy; (*fig*) sensational.

clandestinità *sf* (*di attività*) secret nature; **vivere nella** ~ to live in hiding; (*ricercato politico*) to live underground.

clandes'tino, a *ag* clandestine; (*POL*) underground, clandestine ♦ *sm/f* stowaway.

clari'netto *sm* clarinet.

'classe *sf* class; **di** ~ (*fig*) with class; of excellent quality; ~ **turistica** (*AER*) economy class.

classi'cismo [klassi'tʃizmo] *sm* classicism.

'classico, a, ci, che *ag* classical; (*tradizionale: moda*) classic(al) ♦ *sm* classic; classical author; (*anche*: **liceo** ~) secondary school with emphasis on the humanities.

clas'sifica, che *sf* classification; (*SPORT*) placings *pl*; (*di dischi*) charts *pl*, hit parade.

classifi'care *vt* to classify; (*candidato, compito*) to grade; ~**rsi** *vr* to be placed.

classifica'tore *sm* filing cabinet.

classificazi'one [klassifikat'tsjone] *sf* classification; grading.

clas'sista, i, e *ag* class-conscious ♦ *sm/f*

class-conscious person.
claudi'cante *ag* (*zoppo*) lame; (*fig*: *prosa*) halting.
'clausola *sf* (*DIR*) clause.
clau'sura *sf* (*REL*): **monaca di ~** nun belonging to an enclosed order; **fare una vita di ~** (*fig*) to lead a cloistered life.
'clava *sf* club.
clavi'cembalo [klavi'tʃembalo] *sm* harpsichord.
cla'vicola *sf* (*ANAT*) collarbone.
cle'mente *ag* merciful; (*clima*) mild.
cle'menza [kle'mentsa] *sf* mercy, clemency; mildness.
clep'tomane *sm/f* kleptomaniac.
cleri'cale *ag* clerical.
'clero *sm* clergy.
cles'sidra *sf* (*a sabbia*) hourglass; (*ad acqua*) water clock.
cliché [kli'ʃe] *sm inv* (*TIP*) plate; (*fig*) cliché.
cli'ente *sm/f* customer, client.
clien'tela *sf* customers *pl*, clientèle.
cliente'lismo *sm*: **~ politico** political nepotism.
'clima, i *sm* climate.
cli'matico, a, ci, che *ag* climatic; **stazione ~a** health resort.
climatizzazi'one [klimatiddzat'tsjone] *sf* air conditioning.
'clinico, a, ci, che *ag* clinical ♦ *sm* (*medico*) clinician ♦ *sf* (*scienza*) clinical medicine; (*casa di cura*) clinic, nursing home; (*settore d'ospedale*) clinic; **quadro ~** anamnesis; **avere l'occhio ~** (*fig*) to have an expert eye.
clis'tere *sm* (*MED*) enema; (: *apparecchio*) *device used to give an enema*.
clo'aca, che *sf* sewer.
cloche [klɔʃ] *sf inv* (*AER*) control stick, joystick; **cambio a ~** (*AUT*) floor-mounted gear lever.
'cloro *sm* chlorine.
cloro'filla *sf* chlorophyll.
cloro'formio *sm* chloroform.
club *sm inv* club.
cm *abbr* (= *centimetro*) cm.
c.m. *abbr* (= *corrente mese*) inst.
CN *sigla* = *Cuneo*.
c/n *abbr* = *conto nuovo*.
CNEN *sigla m* (= *Comitato Nazionale per l'Energia Nucleare*) ≈ AEA (*Brit*), AEC (*US*).
CNIOP *sigla m* = *Centro Nazionale per l'Istruzione e l'Orientamento Professionale*.
CNR *sigla m* (= *Consiglio Nazionale delle Ricerche*) science research council.
CNRN *sigla m* = *Comitato Nazionale Ricerche Nucleari*.
CO *sigla* = *Como*.
Co. *abbr* (= *compagnia*) Co.
coabi'tare *vi* to live together, live under the same roof.

coagu'lare *vt* to coagulate ♦ *vi*, **~rsi** *vr* to coagulate; (*latte*) to curdle.
coalizi'one [koalit'tsjone] *sf* coalition.
co'atto, a *ag* (*DIR*) compulsory, forced; **condannare al domicilio ~** to place under house arrest.
'COBAS *sigla mpl* (= *Comitati di base*) independent trades unions.
'cobra *sm inv* cobra.
coca'ina *sf* cocaine.
coc'carda *sf* cockade.
cocchi'ere [kok'kjere] *sm* coachman.
'cocchio ['kɔkkjo] *sm* (*carrozza*) coach; (*biga*) chariot.
cocci'nella [kottʃi'nɛlla] *sf* ladybird (*Brit*), ladybug (*US*).
'coccio ['kɔttʃo] *sm* earthenware; (*vaso*) earthenware pot; **~i** *smpl* fragments (of pottery).
cocciu'taggine [kottʃu'taddʒine] *sf* stubbornness, pig-headedness.
cocci'uto, a [kot'tʃuto] *ag* stubborn, pigheaded.
'cocco, chi *sm* (*pianta*) coconut palm; (*frutto*): **noce di ~** coconut ♦ *sm/f* (*fam*) darling; **è il ~ della mamma** he's mummy's darling.
cocco'drillo *sm* crocodile.
cocco'lare *vt* to cuddle, fondle.
co'cente [ko'tʃente] *ag* (*anche fig*) burning.
cocerò *etc* [kotʃe'rɔ] *vb vedi* **cuocere**.
co'comero *sm* watermelon.
co'cuzzolo [ko'kuttsolo] *sm* top; (*di capo, cappello*) crown.
cod. *abbr* = *codice*.
'coda *sf* tail; (*fila di persone, auto*) queue (*Brit*), line (*US*); (*di abiti*) train; **con la ~ dell'occhio** out of the corner of one's eye; **mettersi in ~** to queue (up) (*Brit*), line up (*US*); to join the queue *o* line; **~ di cavallo** (*acconciatura*) ponytail; **avere la ~ di paglia** (*fig*) to have a guilty conscience; **~ di rospo** (*CUC*) frogfish tail.
co'dardo, a *ag* cowardly ♦ *sm/f* coward.
co'desto, a *ag, pronome* (*poetico*) this; that.
'codice ['kɔditʃe] *sm* code; (*manoscritto antico*) codex; **~ di avviamento postale (CAP)** postcode (*Brit*), zip code (*US*); **~ a barre** bar code; **~ civile** civil code; **~ fiscale** tax code; **~ penale** penal code; **~ della strada** highway code.
co'difica *sf* codification; (*INFORM*: *di programma*) coding.
codifi'care *vt* (*DIR*) to codify; (*cifrare*) to code.
codificazi'one [kodifikat'tsjone] *sf* coding.
coercizi'one [koertʃit'tsjone] *sf* coercion.
coe'rente *ag* coherent.
coe'renza [koe'rentsa] *sf* coherence.
coesi'one *sf* cohesion.
coe'sistere *vi* to coexist.
coe'taneo, a *ag, sm/f* contemporary; **essere**

~ **di qn** to be the same age as sb.
cofa'netto *sm* casket; ~ **dei gioielli** jewel case.
'cofano *sm* (*AUT*) bonnet (*Brit*), hood (*US*); (*forziere*) chest.
'coffa *sf* (*NAUT*) top.
'cogli ['kɔʎʎi] *prep* + *det vedi* **con**.
'cogliere ['kɔʎʎere] *vt* (*fiore, frutto*) to pick, gather; (*sorprendere*) to catch, surprise; (*bersaglio*) to hit; (*fig: momento opportuno etc*) to grasp, seize, take; (: *capire*) to grasp; ~ **l'occasione (per fare)** to take the opportunity (to do); ~ **sul fatto** *o* **in flagrante/alla sprovvista** to catch red-handed/unprepared; ~ **nel segno** (*fig*) to hit the nail on the head.
cogli'one [koʎ'ʎone] *sm* (*fam!*: *testicolo*): ~**i** balls (!); (: *fig: persona sciocca*) jerk; **rompere i** ~**i a qn** to get on sb's tits (!).
co'gnac [kɔ'ɲak] *sm inv* cognac.
co'gnato, a [koɲ'ɲato] *sm/f* brother-/sister-in-law.
cognizi'one [koɲɲit'tsjone] *sf* knowledge; **con** ~ **di causa** with full knowledge of the facts.
co'gnome [koɲ'ɲome] *sm* surname.
'coi *prep* + *det vedi* **con**.
coi'bente *ag* insulating.
coinci'denza [kointʃi'dɛntsa] *sf* coincidence; (*FERR, AER, di autobus*) connection.
coin'cidere [koin'tʃidere] *vi* to coincide.
coin'ciso, a [koin'tʃizo] *pp di* **coincidere**.
coinqui'lino *sm* fellow tenant.
cointeres'senza [kointeres'sɛntsa] *sf* (*COMM*): **avere una** ~ **in qc** to own shares in sth; ~ **dei lavoratori** profit-sharing.
coin'volgere [koin'vɔldʒere] *vt*: ~ **in** to involve in.
coinvolgi'mento [koinvoldʒi'mento] *sm* involvement.
coin'volto, a *pp di* **coinvolgere**.
col *prep* + *det vedi* **con**.
Col. *abbr* (= *colonnello*) Col.
colà *av* there.
cola'brodo *sm inv* strainer.
cola'pasta *sm inv* colander.
co'lare *vt* (*liquido*) to strain; (*pasta*) to drain; (*oro fuso*) to pour ♦ *vi* (*sudore*) to drip; (*botte*) to leak; (*cera*) to melt; ~ **a picco** *vt, vi* (*nave*) to sink.
co'lata *sf* (*di lava*) flow; (*FONDERIA*) casting.
colazi'one [kolat'tsjone] *sf* (*anche*: **prima** ~) breakfast; (*anche*: **seconda** ~) lunch; **fare** ~ to have breakfast (*o* lunch); ~ **di lavoro** working lunch.
Coldi'retti *abbr f* (= *Confederazione nazionale coltivatori diretti*) *federation of Italian farmers*.
co'lei *pronome vedi* **colui**.
co'lera *sm* (*MED*) cholera.
coleste'rolo *sm* cholesterol.

COLF *abbr f* = **collaboratrice familiare**.
'colgo *etc vb vedi* **cogliere**.
colibrì *sm* hummingbird.
'colica *sf* (*MED*) colic.
co'lino *sm* strainer.
'colla *prep* + *det vedi* **con** ♦ *sf* glue; (*di farina*) paste.
collabo'rare *vi* to collaborate; ~ **a** to collaborate on; (*giornale*) to contribute to.
collabora'tore, 'trice *sm/f* collaborator; contributor; ~ **esterno** freelance; ~**trice familiare** home help.
collaborazi'one [kollaborat'tsjone] *sf* collaboration; contribution.
col'lana *sf* necklace; (*collezione*) collection, series.
col'lant [kɔ'lã] *sm inv* tights *pl*.
col'lare *sm* collar.
col'lasso *sm* (*MED*) collapse.
collate'rale *ag* collateral; **effetti** ~**i** side effects.
collau'dare *vt* to test, try out.
col'laudo *sm* testing *q*; test.
'colle *prep* + *det vedi* **con** ♦ *sm* hill.
col'lega, ghi, ghe *sm/f* colleague.
collega'mento *sm* connection; (*MIL*) liaison; (*RADIO*) link(-up); **ufficiale di** ~ liaison officer.
colle'gare *vt* to connect, join, link; ~**rsi** *vr* (*RADIO, TV*) to link up; ~**rsi con** (*TEL*) to get through to.
collegi'ale [kolle'dʒale] *ag* (*riunione, decisione*) collective; (*INS*) boarding school *cpd* ♦ *sm/f* boarder; (*fig: persona timida e inesperta*) schoolboy/girl.
col'legio [kol'ledʒo] *sm* college; (*convitto*) boarding school; ~ **elettorale** (*POL*) constituency.
'collera *sf* anger; **andare in** ~ to get angry.
col'lerico, a, ci, che *ag* quick-tempered, irascible.
col'letta *sf* collection.
collettività *sf* community.
collet'tivo, a *ag* collective; (*interesse*) general, everybody's; (*biglietto, visita etc*) group *cpd* ♦ *sm* (*POL*) (political) group; **società in nome** ~ (*COMM*) partnership.
col'letto *sm* collar; ~**i bianchi** (*fig*) white-collar workers.
collezio'nare [kollettsjo'nare] *vt* to collect.
collezi'one [kollet'tsjone] *sf* collection.
colli'mare *vi* to correspond, coincide.
col'lina *sf* hill.
colli'nare *ag* hill *cpd*.
col'lirio *sm* eyewash.
collisi'one *sf* collision.
'collo *prep* + *det vedi* **con** ♦ *sm* neck; (*di abito*) neck, collar; (*pacco*) parcel; ~ **del piede** instep.
colloca'mento *sm* (*impiego*) employment; (*disposizione*) placing, arrangement; **ufficio di** ~ ≈ Jobcentre (*Brit*), state (*o* federal)

employment agency (*US*); ~ **a riposo** retirement.

collo'care *vt* (*libri, mobili*) to place; (*persona: trovare un lavoro per*) to find a job for, place; (*COMM: merce*) to find a market for; ~ **qn a riposo** to retire sb.

collocazi'one [kollokat'tsjone] *sf* placing; (*di libro*) classification.

colloqui'ale *ag* (*termine etc*) colloquial; (*tono*) informal.

col'loquio *sm* conversation, talk; (*ufficiale, per un lavoro*) interview; (*INS*) preliminary oral exam; **avviare un ~ con qn** (*POL etc*) to start talks with sb.

col'loso, a *ag* sticky.

col'lottola *sf* nape *o* scruff of the neck; **afferrare qn per la ~** to grab sb by the scruff of the neck.

collusi'one *sf* (*DIR*) collusion.

colluttazi'one [kolluttat'tsjone] *sf* scuffle.

col'mare *vt*: ~ **di** (*anche fig*) to fill with; (*dare in abbondanza*) to load *o* overwhelm with; ~ **un divario** (*fig*) to bridge a gap.

'**colmo, a** *ag*: ~ **(di)** full (of) ♦ *sm* summit, top; (*fig*) height; **al ~ della disperazione** in the depths of despair; **è il ~!** it's the last straw!; **e per ~ di sfortuna** ... and to cap it all ....

co'lomba *sf vedi* **colombo**.

Co'lombia *sf*: **la ~** Colombia.

colombi'ano, a *ag, sm/f* Colombian.

co'lombo, a *sm/f* dove; pigeon; ~**i** (*fig fam*) lovebirds.

Co'lonia *sf* Cologne.

co'lonia *sf* colony; (*per bambini*) holiday camp; (**acqua di**) ~ (eau de) cologne.

coloni'ale *ag* colonial ♦ *sm/f* colonist, settler.

co'lonico, a, ci, che *ag*: **casa ~a** farmhouse.

coloniz'zare [kolonid'dzare] *vt* to colonize.

co'lonna *sf* column; ~ **sonora** (*CINEMA*) sound track; ~ **vertebrale** spine, spinal column.

colon'nello *sm* colonel.

co'lono *sm* (*coltivatore*) tenant farmer.

colo'rante *sm* colouring (*Brit*), coloring (*US*).

colo'rare *vt* to colour (*Brit*), color (*US*); (*disegno*) to colo(u)r in.

co'lore *sm* colour (*Brit*), color (*US*); (*CARTE*) suit; **a ~i** in colo(u)r, colo(u)r *cpd*; **la gente di ~** colo(u)red people; **diventare di tutti i ~i** to turn scarlet; **farne di tutti i ~i** to get up to all sorts of mischief; **passarne di tutti i ~i** to go through all sorts of problems.

colo'rito, a *ag* coloured (*Brit*), colored (*US*); (*viso*) rosy, pink; (*linguaggio*) colourful (*Brit*), colorful (*US*) ♦ *sm* (*tinta*) colour (*Brit*), color (*US*); (*carnagione*) complexion.

co'loro *pronome pl vedi* **colui**.

colos'sale *ag* colossal, enormous.

co'losso *sm* colossus.

'**colpa** *sf* fault; (*biasimo*) blame; (*colpevolezza*) guilt; (*azione colpevole*) offence; (*peccato*) sin; **di chi è la ~?** whose fault is it?; **è ~ sua** it's his fault; **per ~ di** through, owing to; **senso di ~** sense of guilt; **dare la ~ a qn di qc** to blame sb for sth.

col'pevole *ag* guilty.

colpevoliz'zare [kolpevolid'dzare] *vt*: ~ **qn** to make sb feel guilty.

col'pire *vt* to hit, strike; (*fig*) to strike; **rimanere colpito da qc** to be amazed *o* struck by sth; **è stato colpito da ordine di cattura** there is a warrant out for his arrest; ~ **nel segno** (*fig*) to hit the nail on the head, be spot on (*Brit*).

'**colpo** *sm* (*urto*) knock; (*fig: affettivo*) blow, shock; (*: aggressivo*) blow; (*di pistola*) shot; (*MED*) stroke; (*furto*) raid; **di ~, tutto d'un ~** suddenly; **fare ~** to make a strong impression; **il motore perde ~i** (*AUT*) the engine is misfiring; **è morto sul ~** he died instantly; **mi hai fatto venire un ~!** what a fright you gave me!; **ti venisse un ~!** (*fam*) drop dead!; ~ **d'aria** chill; ~ **in banca** bank job *o* raid; ~ **basso** (*PUGILATO, fig*) punch below the belt; ~ **di fulmine** love at first sight; ~ **di grazia** coup de grâce; (*fig*) finishing blow; **a ~ d'occhio** at a glance; ~ **di scena** (*TEATRO*) coup de théâtre; (*fig*) dramatic turn of events; ~ **di sole** sunstroke; ~**i di sole** (*nei capelli*) highlights; ~ **di Stato** coup d'état; ~ **di telefono** phone call; ~ **di testa** (sudden) impulse *o* whim; ~ **di vento** gust (of wind).

col'poso, a *ag*: **omicidio ~** manslaughter.

'**colsi** *etc vb vedi* **cogliere**.

coltel'lata *sf* stab.

col'tello *sm* knife; **avere il ~ dalla parte del manico** (*fig*) to have the whip hand; ~ **a serramanico** clasp knife.

colti'vare *vt* to cultivate; (*verdura*) to grow, cultivate.

coltiva'tore *sm* farmer; ~ **diretto** small independent farmer.

coltivazi'one [koltivat'tsjone] *sf* cultivation; growing; ~ **intensiva** intensive farming.

'**colto, a** *pp di* **cogliere** ♦ *ag* (*istruito*) cultured, educated.

'**coltre** *sf* blanket.

col'tura *sf* cultivation; ~ **alternata** crop rotation.

co'lui, co'lei, *pl* **co'loro** *pronome* the one; ~ **che parla** the one *o* the man *o* the person who is speaking; **colei che amo** the one *o* the woman *o* the person (whom) I love.

com. *abbr* = **comunale; commissione**.

'**coma** *sm inv* coma.

comanda'mento *sm* (*REL*) commandment.

coman'dante *sm* (*MIL*) commander, commandant; (*di reggimento*) commanding officer; (*NAUT, AER*) captain.

coman'dare *vi* to be in command ♦ *vt* to command; (*imporre*) to order, command; ~ **a qn di fare** to order sb to do.

co'mando *sm* (*ingiunzione*) order, command; (*autorità*) command; (*TECN*) control; ~ **generale** general headquarters *pl*; ~ **a distanza** remote control.

co'mare *sf* (*madrina*) godmother; (*donna pettegola*) gossip.

co'masco, a, schi, sche *ag* of (*o* from) Como.

combaci'are [komba't∫are] *vi* to meet; (*fig*: *coincidere*) to coincide, correspond.

combat'tente *ag* fighting ♦ *sm* combatant; **ex-~** ex-serviceman.

com'battere *vt* to fight; (*fig*) to combat, fight against ♦ *vi* to fight.

combatti'mento *sm* fight; fighting *q*; (*di pugilato*) match; **mettere fuori** ~ to knock out.

combat'tivo, a *ag* pugnacious.

combat'tuto, a *ag* (*incerto*: *persona*) uncertain, undecided; (*gara, partita*) hard fought.

combi'nare *vt* to combine; (*organizzare*) to arrange; (*fam*: *fare*) to make, cause ♦ *vi* (*corrispondere*): ~ (**con**) to correspond (with).

combinazi'one [kombinat'tsjone] *sf* combination; (*caso fortuito*) coincidence; **per** ~ by chance.

com'briccola *sf* (*gruppo*) party; (*banda*) gang.

combus'tibile *ag* combustible ♦ *sm* fuel.

combusti'one *sf* combustion.

com'butta *sf* (*peg*) gang; **in** ~ in league.

'come *av* (*gen*) like; (*in qualità di*) as; (*interrogativo, esclamativo*) how; (*che cosa, prego*): ~**?** pardon?, sorry? ♦ *cong* as; (*che, in quale modo*) how; (*appena che, quando*) as soon as; ~ **sta?** how are you?; ~ **sei cresciuto!** how you've grown!; ~ **se** as if, as though; **ora** ~ **ora** right now; **oggi** ~ **oggi** at the present time; ~ **mai?** how come?; **com'è il tuo amico?** what's your friend like?; **attento a** ~ **parli!** mind your tongue!; ~ **non detto** let's forget it; **com'è vero Dio** as God is my witness; *vedi* **così.**

'COMECON *abbr m* (= *Consiglio di Mutua Assistenza Economica*) COMECON.

come'done *sm* blackhead.

co'meta *sf* comet.

'comico, a, ci, che *ag* (*TEATRO*) comic; (*buffo*) comical ♦ *sm* (*attore*) comedian, comic actor; (*comicità*) comic spirit, comedy.

co'mignolo [ko'miɲɲolo] *sm* chimney top.

cominci'are [komin't∫are] *vt, vi* to begin, start; ~ **a fare/col fare** to begin to do/by doing; **cominciamo bene!** (*ironico*) we're off to a fine start!

comi'tato *sm* committee; ~ **direttivo** steering committee; ~ **di gestione** works council.

comi'tiva *sf* party, group.

co'mizio [ko'mittsjo] *sm* (*POL*) meeting, assembly; ~ **elettorale** election rally.

'comma, i *sm* (*DIR*) subsection.

com'mando *sm inv* commando (squad).

com'media *sf* comedy; (*opera teatrale*) play; (*: che fa ridere*) comedy; (*fig*) playacting *q*.

commedi'ante *sm/f* (*peg*) third-rate actor/ actress; (*: fig*) sham.

commedi'ografo, a *sm/f* (*autore*) comedy writer.

commemo'rare *vt* to commemorate.

commemorazi'one [kommemorat'tsjone] *sf* commemoration.

commenda'tore *sm* official title awarded for services to one's country.

commen'sale *sm/f* table companion.

commen'tare *vt* to comment on; (*testo*) to annotate; (*RADIO, TV*) to give a commentary on.

commenta'tore, 'trice *sm/f* commentator.

com'mento *sm* comment; (*a un testo, RADIO, TV*) commentary; ~ **musicale** (*CINEMA*) background music.

commerci'ale [kommer't∫ale] *ag* commercial, trading; (*peg*) commercial.

commercia'lista, i, e [kommert∫a'lista] *sm/f* (*laureato*) graduate in economics and commerce; (*consulente*) business consultant.

commercializ'zare [kommert∫alid'dzare] *vt* to market.

commercializzazi'one [kommert∫aliddzat-'tsjone] *sf* marketing.

commerci'ante [kommer't∫ante] *sm/f* trader, dealer; (*negoziante*) shopkeeper; ~ **all'ingrosso** wholesaler; ~ **in proprio** sole trader.

commerci'are [kommer't∫are] *vi*: ~ **in**, *vt* to deal *o* trade in.

com'mercio [kom'mɛrt∫o] *sm* trade, commerce; **essere in** ~ (*prodotto*) to be on the market *o* on sale; **essere nel** ~ (*persona*) to be in business; ~ **all'ingrosso/al minuto** wholesale/retail trade.

com'messo, a *pp di* **commettere** ♦ *sm/f* shop assistant (*Brit*), sales clerk (*US*) ♦ *sm* (*impiegato*) clerk ♦ *sf* (*COMM*) order; ~ **viaggiatore** commercial traveller.

commes'tibile *ag* edible; ~**i** *smpl* foodstuffs.

com'mettere *vt* to commit; (*ordinare*) to commission, order.

commi'ato *sm* leave-taking; **prendere ~ da qn** to take one's leave of sb.

commi'nare *vt* (*DIR*) to make provision for.

commise'rare *vt* to sympathize with, commiserate with.

commiserazi'one [kommizerat'tsjone] *sf* commiseration.

com'misi *etc vb vedi* **commettere**.

commissari'ato *sm* (*AMM*) commissionership; (*: sede*) commissioner's office; (*: di polizia*) police station.

commis'sario *sm* commissioner; (*di pubblica sicurezza*) ≈ (police) superintendent (*Brit*), (police) captain (*US*); (*SPORT*) steward; (*membro di commissione*) member of a committee *o* board; **alto ~** high commissioner; **~ di bordo** (*NAUT*) purser; **~ d'esame** member of an examining board; **~ di gara** race official; **~ tecnico** (*SPORT*) national coach.

commissio'nare *vt* to order, place an order for.

commissio'nario *sm* (*COMM*) agent, broker.

commissi'one *sf* (*incarico*) errand; (*comitato*, *percentuale*) commission; (*COMM*: *ordinazione*) order; **~i** *sfpl* (*acquisti*) shopping *sg*; **~ d'esame** examining board; **~ d'inchiesta** committee of enquiry; **~ permanente** standing committee; **~i bancarie** bank charges.

commit'tente *sm/f* (*COMM*) purchaser, customer.

com'mosso, a *pp di* **commuovere**.

commo'vente *ag* moving.

commozi'one [kommot'tsjone] *sf* emotion, deep feeling; **~ cerebrale** (*MED*) concussion.

commu'overe *vt* to move, affect; **~rsi** *vr* to be moved.

commu'tare *vt* (*pena*) to commute; (*ELETTR*) to change *o* switch over.

commutazi'one [kommutat'tsjone] *sf* (*DIR*, *ELETTR*) commutation.

comò *sm inv* chest of drawers.

como'dino *sm* bedside table.

comodità *sf inv* comfort; convenience.

'comodo, a *ag* comfortable; (*facile*) easy; (*conveniente*) convenient; (*utile*) useful, handy ♦ *sm* comfort; convenience; **con ~** at one's convenience *o* leisure; **fare il proprio ~** to do as one pleases; **far ~** to be useful *o* handy; **stia ~!** don't bother to get up!

compae'sano, a *sm/f* fellow-countryman/woman; person from the same town.

com'pagine [kom'padʒine] *sf* (*squadra*) team.

compa'gnia [kompaɲ'ɲia] *sf* company; (*gruppo*) gathering; **fare ~ a qn** to keep sb company; **essere di ~** to be sociable.

com'pagno, a [kom'paɲɲo] *sm/f* (*di classe*,

gioco) companion; (*POL*) comrade; **~ di lavoro** workmate; **~ di scuola** schoolfriend; **~ di viaggio** fellow traveller.

com'paio *etc vb vedi* **comparire**.

compa'rare *vt* to compare.

compara'tivo, a *ag*, *sm* comparative.

comparazi'one [komparat'tsjone] *sf* comparison.

com'pare *sm* (*padrino*) godfather; (*complice*) accomplice; (*fam: amico*) old pal, old mate.

compa'rire *vi* to appear; **~ in giudizio** (*DIR*) to appear before the court.

comparizi'one [komparit'tsjone] *sf* (*DIR*) appearance; **mandato di ~** summons *sg*.

com'parso, a *pp di* **comparire** ♦ *sf* appearance; (*TEATRO*) walk-on; (*CINEMA*) extra.

comparteci'pare [kompartetʃi'pare] *vi* (*COMM*): **~ a** to have a share in.

compartecipazi'one [kompartetʃipat'tsjone] *sf* sharing; (*quota*) share; **~ agli utili** profit-sharing; **in ~** jointly.

comparti'mento *sm* compartment; (*AMM*) district.

com'parvi *etc vb vedi* **comparire**.

compas'sato, a *ag* (*persona*) composed; **freddo e ~** cool and collected.

compassi'one *sf* compassion, pity; **avere ~ di qn** to feel sorry for sb, pity sb; **fare ~** to arouse pity.

compassio'nevole *ag* compassionate.

com'passo *sm* (pair of) compasses *pl*; callipers *pl*.

compa'tibile *ag* (*scusabile*) excusable; (*conciliabile*, *INFORM*) compatible.

compati'mento *sm* compassion; indulgence; **con aria di ~** with a condescending air.

compa'tire *vt* (*aver compassione di*) to sympathize with, feel sorry for; (*scusare*) to make allowances for.

compatri'ota, i, e *sm/f* compatriot.

compat'tezza [kompat'tettsa] *sf* (*solidità*) compactness; (*fig: unità*) solidarity.

com'patto, a *ag* compact; (*roccia*) solid; (*folla*) dense; (*fig: gruppo*, *partito*) united, close-knit.

com'pendio *sm* summary; (*libro*) compendium.

compen'sare *vt* (*equilibrare*) to compensate for, make up for; **~rsi** *vr* (*reciproco*) to balance each other out; **~ qn di** (*rimunerare*) to pay *o* remunerate sb for; (*risarcire*) to pay compensation to sb for; (*fig: fatiche*, *dolori*) to reward sb for.

compen'sato *sm* (*anche*: **legno ~**) plywood.

com'penso *sm* compensation; payment, remuneration; reward; **in ~** (*d'altra parte*) on the other hand.

'compera *sf* purchase; **fare le ~e** to do the shopping.

compe'rare _vt_ = **comprare**.

compe'tente _ag_ competent; _(mancia)_ apt, suitable; _(capace)_ qualified; **rivolgersi all'ufficio** ~ to apply to the office concerned.

compe'tenza [kompe'tɛntsa] _sf_ competence; _(DIR: autorità)_ jurisdiction; _(TECN, COMM)_ expertise; ~**e** _sfpl (onorari)_ fees; **definire le** ~**e** to establish responsibilities.

com'petere _vi_ to compete, vie; _(DIR: spettare)_: ~ **a** to lie within the competence of.

competi'tore, 'trice _sm/f_ competitor.

competizi'one [kompetit'tsjone] _sf_ competition; **spirito di** ~ competitive spirit.

compia'cente [kompja'tʃɛnte] _ag_ courteous, obliging.

compia'cenza [kompja'tʃɛntsa] _sf_ courtesy.

compia'cere [kompja'tʃere] _vi_: ~ **a** to gratify, please ♦ _vt_ to please; ~**rsi** _vr (provare soddisfazione)_: ~**rsi di** _o_ **per qc** to be delighted at sth; _(rallegrarsi)_: ~**rsi con qn** to congratulate sb; _(degnarsi)_: ~**rsi di fare** to be so good as to do.

compiaci'mento [kompjatʃi'mento] _sm_ satisfaction.

compiaci'uto, a [kompja'tʃuto] _pp di_ **compiacere**.

compi'angere [kom'pjandʒere] _vt_ to sympathize with, feel sorry for.

compi'anto, a _pp di_ **compiangere** ♦ _ag_: **il** ~ **presidente** the late lamented president ♦ _sm_ mourning, grief.

'compiere _vt (concludere)_ to finish, complete; _(adempiere)_ to carry out, fulfil; ~**rsi** _vr (avverarsi)_ to be fulfilled, come true; ~ **gli anni** to have one's birthday.

compi'lare _vt_ to compile; _(modulo)_ to complete, fill in _(Brit)_, fill out _(US)_.

compila'tore, 'trice _sm/f_ compiler.

compilazi'one [kompilat'tsjone] _sf_ compilation; completion.

compi'mento _sm (termine, conclusione)_ completion, fulfilment; **portare a** ~ **qc** to conclude sth, bring sth to a conclusion.

com'pire _vb_ = **compiere**.

compi'tare _vt_ to spell out.

'compito _sm (incarico)_ task, duty; _(dovere)_ duty; _(INS)_ exercise; _(: a casa)_ piece of homework; **fare i** ~**i** to do one's homework.

com'pito, a _ag_ well-mannered, polite.

compiu'tezza [kompju'tettsa] _sf (completezza)_ completeness; _(perfezione)_ perfection.

compi'uto, a _pp di_ **compiere** ♦ _ag_: **a 20 anni** ~**i** at 20 years of age, at age 20; **un fatto** ~ a fait accompli.

comple'anno _sm_ birthday.

complemen'tare _ag_ complementary; _(INS: materia)_ subsidiary.

comple'mento _sm_ complement; _(MIL)_ reserve (troops); ~ **oggetto** _(LING)_ direct object.

comples'sato, a _ag, sm/f_: **essere (un)** ~ to be full of complexes _o_ hang-ups _(fam)_.

complessità _sf_ complexity.

complessiva'mente _av (nell'insieme)_ on the whole; _(in tutto)_ altogether.

comples'sivo, a _ag (globale)_ comprehensive, overall; _(totale: cifra)_ total; **visione** ~**a** overview.

com'plesso, a _ag_ complex ♦ _sm (PSIC, EDIL)_ complex; _(MUS: corale)_ ensemble; _(: orchestrina)_ band; _(: di musica pop)_ group; **in** _o_ **nel** ~ on the whole.

completa'mento _sm_ completion.

comple'tare _vt_ to complete.

com'pleto, a _ag_ complete; _(teatro, autobus)_ full ♦ _sm_ suit; **al** ~ full; _(tutti presenti)_ all present; **essere al** ~ _(teatro)_ to be sold out; ~ **da sci** ski suit.

compli'care _vt_ to complicate; ~**rsi** _vr_ to become complicated.

complicazi'one [komplikat'tsjone] _sf_ complication; **salvo** ~**i** unless any difficulties arise.

'complice ['kɔmplitʃe] _sm/f_ accomplice.

complimen'tarsi _vr_: ~ **con** to congratulate.

compli'mento _sm_ compliment; ~**i** _smpl (cortesia eccessiva)_ ceremony _sg_; ~**i!** congratulations!; **senza** ~**i!** don't stand on ceremony!; make yourself at home!; help yourself!

complot'tare _vi_ to plot, conspire.

com'plotto _sm_ plot, conspiracy.

com'pone _etc vb vedi_ **comporre**.

compo'nente _sm/f_ member ♦ _sm_ component.

com'pongo _etc vb vedi_ **comporre**.

compo'nibile _ag (mobili, cucina)_ fitted.

componi'mento _sm (DIR)_ settlement; _(INS)_ composition; _(poetico, teatrale)_ work.

com'porre _vt (musica, testo)_ to compose; _(mettere in ordine)_ to arrange; _(DIR: lite)_ to settle; _(TIP)_ to set; _(TEL)_ to dial; **comporsi** _vr_: **comporsi di** to consist of, be composed of.

comportamen'tale _ag_ behavioural _(Brit)_, behavioral _(US)_.

comporta'mento _sm_ behaviour _(Brit)_, behavior _(US)_; _(di prodotto)_ performance.

compor'tare _vt (implicare)_ to involve, entail; _(consentire)_ to permit, allow (of); ~**rsi** _vr (condursi)_ to behave.

com'posi _etc vb vedi_ **comporre**.

composi'tore, 'trice _sm/f_ composer; _(TIP)_ compositor, typesetter.

composizi'one [kompozit'tsjone] _sf_ composition; _(DIR)_ settlement.

com'posta _sf vedi_ **composto**.

compos'tezza [kompos'tettsa] _sf_ composure; decorum.

com'posto, a _pp di_ **comporre** ♦ _ag (persona)_

composed, self-possessed; (: *decoroso*) dignified; (*formato da più elementi*) compound *cpd* ♦ *sm* compound; (*CUC etc*) mixture ♦ *sf* (*CUC*) stewed fruit *q*; (*AGR*) compost.

com'prare *vt* to buy; (*corrompere*) to bribe.

compra'tore, 'trice *sm/f* buyer, purchaser.

compra'vendita *sf* (*COMM*) (contract of) sale; **un atto di** ~ a deed of sale.

com'prendere *vt* (*contenere*) to comprise, consist of; (*capire*) to understand.

compren'donio *sm*: **essere duro di** ~ to be slow on the uptake.

compren'sibile *ag* understandable.

comprensi'one *sf* understanding.

compren'sivo, a *ag* (*prezzo*): ~ **di** inclusive of; (*indulgente*) understanding.

compren'sorio *sm* area, territory; (*AMM*) district.

com'preso, a *pp di* **comprendere** ♦ *ag* (*incluso*) included; **tutto** ~ all inclusive, all in.

com'pressa *sf vedi* **compresso**.

compressi'one *sf* compression.

com'presso, a *pp di* **comprimere** ♦ *ag* (*vedi comprimere*) pressed; compressed; repressed ♦ *sf* (*MED*: *garza*) compress; (: *pastiglia*) tablet.

compres'sore *sm* compressor; (*anche*: **rullo** ~) steamroller.

compri'mario, a *sm/f* (*TEATRO*) supporting actor/actress.

com'primere *vt* (*premere*) to press; (*FISICA*) to compress; (*fig*) to repress.

compro'messo, a *pp di* **compromettere** ♦ *sm* compromise.

compro'mettere *vt* to compromise; ~**rsi** *vr* to compromise o.s.

comproprietà *sf* (*DIR*) joint ownership.

compro'vare *vt* to confirm.

com'punto, a *ag* contrite; **con fare** ~ with a solemn air.

compunzi'one [kompun'tsjone] *sf* contrition; solemnity.

compu'tare *vt* to calculate; (*addebitare*): ~ **qc a qn** to debit sb with sth.

com'puter [kəm'pju:tər] *sm inv* computer.

computeriz'zato, a [komputerid'dzato] *ag* computerized.

computiste'ria *sf* accounting, book-keeping.

'computo *sm* calculation; **fare il** ~ **di** to count.

comu'nale *ag* municipal, town *cpd*; **consiglio/palazzo** ~ town council/hall; **è un impiegato** ~ he works for the local council.

co'mune *ag* common; (*consueto*) common, everyday; (*di livello medio*) average; (*ordinario*) ordinary ♦ *sm* (*AMM*) town council; (: *sede*) town hall ♦ *sf* (*di persone*) commune; **fuori del** ~ out of the ordinary; **avere in** ~ to have in common,

share; **mettere in** ~ to share; **un nostro** ~ **amico** a mutual friend of ours; **fare cassa** ~ to pool one's money.

comuni'care *vt* (*notizia*) to pass on, convey; (*malattia*) to pass on; (*ansia etc*) to communicate; (*trasmettere*: *calore etc*) to transmit, communicate; (*REL*) to administer communion to ♦ *vi* to communicate; ~**rsi** *vr* (*propagarsi*): ~**rsi a** to spread to; (*REL*) to receive communion.

comunica'tivo, a *ag* (*sentimento*) infectious; (*persona*) communicative ♦ *sf* communicativeness.

comuni'cato *sm* communiqué; ~ **stampa** press release.

comunicazi'one [komunikat'tsjone] *sf* communication; (*annuncio*) announcement; (*TEL*): ~ **(telefonica)** (telephone) call; **dare la** ~ **a qn** to put sb through; **ottenere la** ~ to get through; **salvo** ~**i contrarie da parte Vostra** unless we hear from you to the contrary.

comuni'one *sf* communion; ~ **dei beni** (*DIR*: *tra coniugi*) joint ownership of property.

comu'nismo *sm* communism.

comu'nista, i, e *ag*, *sm/f* communist.

comunità *sf inv* community; **C~ Economica Europea (CEE)** European Economic Community (EEC).

comuni'tario, a *ag* community *cpd*.

co'munque *cong* however, no matter how ♦ *av* (*in ogni modo*) in any case; (*tuttavia*) however, nevertheless.

con *prep* (*nei seguenti casi* **con** *può fondersi con l'articolo definito*: con + il = **col**, con + la = **colla**, con + gli = **cogli**, con + i = **coi**, con + le = **colle**) with; **partire col treno** to leave by train; ~ **mio grande stupore** to my great astonishment; ~ **la forza** by force; ~ **questo freddo** in this cold weather; ~ **il 1° di ottobre** as of October 1st; ~ **tutto ciò** in spite of that, for all that; ~ **tutto che era arrabbiato** even though he was angry, in spite of the fact that he was angry; **e** ~ **questo?** so what?

co'nato *sm*: ~ **di vomito** retching.

'conca, che *sf* (*GEO*) valley.

concate'nare *vt* to link up, connect; ~**rsi** *vr* to be connected.

'concavo, a *ag* concave.

con'cedere [kon'tʃɛdere] *vt* (*accordare*) to grant; (*ammettere*) to admit, concede; ~**rsi qc** to treat o.s. to sth, allow o.s. sth.

concentra'mento [kontʃentra'mento] *sm* concentration.

concen'trare [kontʃen'trare] *vt*, ~**rsi** *vr* to concentrate.

concen'trato [kontʃen'trato] *sm* concentrate; ~ **di pomodoro** tomato purée.

concentrazi'one [kontʃentrat'tsjone] *sf* concentration; ~ **orizzontale/verticale** (*ECON*) horizontal/vertical integration.

con'centrico, a, ci, che [kon'tʃɛntriko] *ag* concentric.

conce'pibile [kontʃe'pibile] *ag* conceivable.

concepi'mento [kontʃepi'mento] *sm* conception.

conce'pire [kontʃe'pire] *vt* (*bambino*) to conceive; (*progetto, idea*) to conceive (of); (*metodo, piano*) to devise; (*situazione*) to imagine, understand.

con'cernere [kon'tʃɛrnere] *vt* to concern; **per quanto mi concerne** as far as I'm concerned.

concer'tare [kontʃer'tare] *vt* (*MUS*) to harmonize; (*ordire*) to devise, plan; ~**rsi** *vr* to agree.

concer'tista, i, e [kontʃer'tista] *sm/f* (*MUS*) concert performer.

con'certo [kon'tʃɛrto] *sm* (*MUS*) concert; (: *componimento*) concerto.

con'cessi *etc* [kon'tʃɛssi] *vb vedi* **concedere**.

concessio'nario [kontʃessjo'narjo] *sm* (*COMM*) agent, dealer; ~ **esclusivo (di)** sole agent (for).

concessi'one [kontʃes'sjone] *sf* concession.

con'cesso, a [kon'tʃɛsso] *pp di* **concedere**.

con'cetto [kon'tʃɛtto] *sm* (*pensiero, idea*) concept; (*opinione*) opinion; **è un impiegato di** ~ ≈ he's a white-collar worker.

concezi'one [kontʃet'tsjone] *sf* conception; (*idea*) view, idea.

con'chiglia [kon'kiʎʎa] *sf* shell.

'concia ['kontʃa] *sf* (*di pelli*) tanning; (*di tabacco*) curing; (*sostanza*) tannin.

conci'are [kon'tʃare] *vt* (*pelli*) to tan; (*tabacco*) to cure; (*fig: ridurre in cattivo stato*) to beat up; ~**rsi** *vr* (*sporcarsi*) to get in a mess; (*vestirsi male*) to dress badly; **ti hanno conciato male** *o* **per le feste!** they've really beaten you up!

concili'abile [kontʃi'ljabile] *ag* compatible.

concili'abolo [kontʃi'ljabolo] *sm* secret meeting.

concili'ante [kontʃi'ljante] *ag* conciliatory.

concili'are [kontʃi'ljare] *vt* to reconcile; (*contravvenzione*) to pay on the spot; (*favorire: sonno*) to be conducive to, induce; (*procurare: simpatia*) to gain; ~**rsi qc** to gain *o* win sth (for o.s.); ~**rsi qn** to win sb over; ~**rsi con** to be reconciled with.

conciliazi'one [kontʃiljat'tsjone] *sf* reconciliation; (*DIR*) settlement; **la C**~ (*STORIA*) the Lateran Pact.

con'cilio [kon'tʃiljo] *sm* (*REL*) council.

conci'mare [kontʃi'mare] *vt* to fertilize; (*con letame*) to manure.

con'cime [kon'tʃime] *sm* manure; (*chimico*) fertilizer.

concisi'one [kontʃi'zjone] *sf* concision, conciseness.

con'ciso, a [kon'tʃizo] *ag* concise, succinct.

conci'tato, a [kontʃi'tato] *ag* excited, emotional.

concitta'dino, a [kontʃitta'dino] *sm/f* fellow citizen.

con'clave *sm* conclave.

con'cludere *vt* to conclude; (*portare a compimento*) to conclude, finish, bring to an end; (*operare positivamente*) to achieve ♦ *vi* (*essere convincente*) to be conclusive; ~**rsi** *vr* to come to an end, close.

conclusi'one *sf* conclusion; (*risultato*) result.

conclu'sivo, a *ag* conclusive; (*finale*) final.

con'cluso, a *pp di* **concludere**.

concomi'tanza [konkomi'tantsa] *sf* (*di circostanze, fatti*) combination.

concor'danza [konkor'dantsa] *sf* (*anche LING*) agreement.

concor'dare *vt* (*prezzo*) to agree on; (*LING*) to make agree ♦ *vi* to agree; ~ **una tregua** to agree to a truce.

concor'dato *sm* agreement; (*REL*) concordat.

con'corde *ag* (*d'accordo*) in agreement; (*simultaneo*) simultaneous.

con'cordia [kon'kɔrdja] *sf* harmony, concord.

concor'rente *ag* competing; (*MAT*) concurrent ♦ *sm/f* (*SPORT, COMM*) competitor; (*a un concorso di bellezza*) contestant.

concor'renza [konkor'rentsa] *sf* competition; ~ **sleale** unfair competition; **a prezzi di** ~ at competitive prices.

concorrenzi'ale [konkorren'tsjale] *ag* competitive.

con'correre *vi*: ~ **(in)** (*MAT*) to converge *o* meet (in); ~ **(a)** (*competere*) to compete (for); (: *INS: a una cattedra*) to apply (for); (*partecipare: a un'impresa*) to take part (in), contribute (to).

con'corso, a *pp di* **concorrere** ♦ *sm* competition; (*esame*) competitive examination; ~ **di bellezza** beauty contest; ~ **di circostanze** combination of circumstances; ~ **di colpa** (*DIR*) contributory negligence; **un** ~ **ippico** a showjumping event; ~ **in reato** (*DIR*) complicity in a crime; ~ **per titoli** competitive examination for qualified candidates.

con'creto, a *ag* concrete ♦ *sm*: **in** ~ in reality.

concu'bina *sf* concubine ♦ *sm*: **sono** ~**i** they are living together.

concussi'one *sf* (*DIR*) extortion.

con'danna *sf* condemnation; sentence; conviction; ~ **a morte** death sentence.

condan'nare *vt* (*disapprovare*) to condemn; (*DIR*): ~ **a** to sentence to; ~ **per** to convict of.

condan'nato, a *sm/f* convict.

conden'sare *vt*, ~**rsi** *vr* to condense.

condensa'tore *sm* capacitor.

condensazi'one [kondensat'tsjone] *sf* condensation.

condi'mento *sm* seasoning; dressing.

con'dire *vt* to season; (*insalata*) to dress.

condiscen'dente [kondiʃʃen'dɛnte] *ag* obliging; compliant.

condiscen'denza [kondiʃʃen'dɛntsa] *sf* (*disponibilità*) obligingness; (*arrendevolezza*) compliance.

condi'scendere [kondiʃ'ʃendere] *vi*: ~ **a** to agree to.

condi'sceso, a [kondiʃ'ʃeso] *pp di* **condiscendere**.

condi'videre *vt* to share.

condi'viso, a *pp di* **condividere**.

condizio'nale [kondittsjo'nale] *ag* conditional ♦ *sm* (*LING*) conditional ♦ *sf* (*DIR*) suspended sentence.

condiziona'mento [kondittsjona'mento] *sm* conditioning; ~ **d'aria** air conditioning.

condizio'nare [kondittsjo'nare] *vt* to condition; **ad aria condizionata** air-conditioned.

condizi'one [kondit'tsjone] *sf* condition; ~**i** *sfpl* (*di pagamento etc*) terms, conditions; **a ~ che** on condition that, provided that; **a nessuna ~** on no account; ~**i a convenirsi** terms to be arranged; ~**i di lavoro** working conditions; ~**i di vendita** sales terms.

condogli'anze [kondoʎ'ʎantse] *sfpl* condolences.

condomini'ale *ag*: **riunione ~** residents' meeting; **spese ~i** common charges.

condo'minio *sm* joint ownership; (*edificio*) jointly-owned building.

con'domino *sm* joint owner.

condo'nare *vt* (*DIR*) to remit.

con'dono *sm* remission; ~ **fiscale** *conditional amnesty for people evading tax*.

con'dotta *sf vedi* **condotto**.

con'dotto, a *pp di* **condurre** ♦ *ag*: **medico ~** local authority doctor (*in country district*) ♦ *sm* (*canale, tubo*) pipe, conduit; (*ANAT*) duct ♦ *sf* (*modo di comportarsi*) conduct, behaviour (*Brit*), behavior (*US*); (*di un affare etc*) handling; (*di acqua*) piping; (*incarico sanitario*) *country medical practice controlled by a local authority*.

condu'cente [kondu'tʃɛnte] *sm* driver.

con'duco *etc vb vedi* **condurre**.

con'durre *vt* to conduct; (*azienda*) to manage; (*accompagnare: bambino*) to take; (*automobile*) to drive; (*trasportare: acqua, gas*) to convey, conduct; (*fig*) to lead ♦ *vi* to lead; **condursi** *vr* to behave, conduct o.s.; ~ **a termine** to conclude.

con'dussi *etc vb vedi* **condurre**.

condut'tore, 'trice *ag*: **filo ~** (*fig*) thread; **motivo ~** leitmotiv ♦ *sm* (*di mezzi pubblici*) driver; (*FISICA*) conductor.

condut'tura *sf* (*gen*) pipe; (*di acqua, gas*) main.

conduzi'one [kondut'tsjone] *sf* (*di affari, ditta*) management; (*DIR*: *locazione*) lease; (*FISICA*) conduction.

confabu'lare *vi* to confab.

confa'cente [konfa'tʃɛnte] *ag*: ~ **a qn/qc** suitable for sb/sth; **clima ~ alla salute** healthy climate.

Confagricol'tura *abbr f* (= *Confederazione generale dell'Agricoltura Italiana*) *confederation of Italian farmers*.

CON'FAPI *sigla f* = *Confederazione Nazionale della Piccola Industria*.

con'farsi *vr*: ~ **a** to suit, agree with.

Confartigia'nato [konfartidʒa'nato] *abbr f* = *Confederazione Generale dell'Artigianato Italiano*.

con'fatto, a *pp di* **confarsi**.

Confcom'mercio [konfkom'mɛrtʃo] *abbr f* = *Confederazione Generale del Commercio*.

confederazi'one [konfederat'tsjone] *sf* confederation; ~ **imprenditoriale** employers' association.

confe'renza [konfe'rɛntsa] *sf* (*discorso*) lecture; (*riunione*) conference; ~ **stampa** press conference.

conferenzi'ere, a [konferen'tsjɛre] *sm/f* lecturer.

conferi'mento *sm* conferring, awarding.

confe'rire *vt*: ~ **qc a qn** to give sth to sb, confer sth on sb ♦ *vi* to confer.

con'ferma *sf* confirmation.

confer'mare *vt* to confirm.

confes'sare *vt*, ~**rsi** *vr* to confess; **andare a ~rsi** (*REL*) to go to confession.

confessio'nale *ag*, *sm* confessional.

confessi'one *sf* confession; (*setta religiosa*) denomination.

con'fesso, a *ag*: **essere reo ~** to have pleaded guilty.

confes'sore *sm* confessor.

con'fetto *sm* sugared almond; (*MED*) pill.

confet'tura *sf* (*gen*) jam; (*di arance*) marmalade.

confezio'nare [konfettsjo'nare] *vt* (*vestito*) to make (up); (*merci, pacchi*) to package.

confezi'one [konfet'tsjone] *sf* (*di abiti: da uomo*) tailoring; (: *da donna*) dressmaking; (*imballaggio*) packaging; ~ **regalo** gift pack; ~ **risparmio** economy size; ~ **da viaggio** travel pack; ~**i per signora** ladies' wear *q*; ~**i da uomo** menswear *q*.

confic'care *vt*: ~ **qc in** to hammer o drive sth into; ~**rsi** *vr* to stick.

confi'dare *vi*: ~ **in** to confide in, rely on ♦ *vt* to confide; ~**rsi con qn** to confide in sb.

confi'dente *sm/f* (*persona amica*) confidant/confidante; (*informatore*) informer.

confi'denza [konfi'dɛntsa] *sf* (*familiarità*) intimacy, familiarity; (*fiducia*) trust, confidence; (*rivelazione*) confidence; **prendersi (troppe) ~e** to take liberties; **fare una ~ a qn** to confide something to sb.

confidenzi'ale [konfiden'tsjale] *ag* familiar,

friendly; (*segreto*) confidential; **in via ~** confidentially.

configu'rarsi *vr*: **~ a** to assume the shape *o* form of.

configurazi'one [konfigurat'tsjone] *sf* configuration.

confi'nante *ag* neighbouring (*Brit*), neighboring (*US*).

confi'nare *vi*: **~ con** to border on ♦ *vt* (*POL*) to intern; (*fig*) to confine; **~rsi** *vr* (*isolarsi*): **~rsi in** to shut o.s. up in.

confi'nato, a *ag* interned ♦ *sm/f* internee.

Confin'dustria *sigla f* (= *Confederazione Generale dell'Industria Italiana*) *employers' association*, ≈ CBI (*Brit*).

con'fine *sm* boundary; (*di paese*) border, frontier; **territorio di ~** border zone.

con'fino *sm* internment.

con'fisca *sf* confiscation.

confis'care *vt* to confiscate.

conflagrazi'one [konflagrat'tsjone] *sf* conflagration.

con'flitto *sm* conflict; **essere in ~ con qc** to clash with sth; **essere in ~ con qn** to be at loggerheads with sb.

conflittu'ale *ag*: **rapporto ~** relationship based on conflict.

conflittualità *sf* conflicts *pl*.

conflu'enza [konflu'ɛntsa] *sf* (*di fiumi*) confluence; (*di strade*) junction.

conflu'ire *vi* (*fiumi*) to flow into each other, meet; (*strade*) to meet.

con'fondere *vt* to mix up, confuse; (*imbarazzare*) to embarrass; **~rsi** *vr* (*mescolarsi*) to mingle; (*turbarsi*) to be confused; (*sbagliare*) to get mixed up; **~ le idee a qn** to mix sb up, confuse sb.

confor'mare *vt* (*adeguare*): **~ a** to adapt *o* conform to; **~rsi** *vr*: **~rsi (a)** to conform (to).

con'forme *ag*: **~ a** (*simile*) similar to; (*corrispondente*) in keeping with.

conforme'mente *av* accordingly; **~ a** in accordance with.

confor'mismo *sm* conformity.

confor'mista, i, e *sm/f* conformist.

conformità *sf* conformity; **in ~ a** in conformity with.

confor'tare *vt* to comfort, console.

confor'tevole *ag* (*consolante*) comforting; (*comodo*) comfortable.

con'forto *sm* (*consolazione, sollievo*) comfort, consolation; (*conferma*) support; **a ~ di qc** in support of sth; **i ~i (religiosi)** the last sacraments.

confra'ternita *sf* brotherhood.

confron'tare *vt* to compare; **~rsi** *vr* (*scontrarsi*) to have a confrontation.

con'fronto *sm* comparison; (*DIR, MIL, POL*) confrontation; **in *o* a ~ di** in comparison with, compared to; **nei miei (*o* tuoi *etc*) ~i** towards me (*o* you *etc*).

con'fusi *etc vb vedi* **confondere**.

confusi'one *sf* confusion; (*imbarazzo*) embarrassment; **far ~** (*disordine*) to make a mess; (*chiasso*) to make a racket; (*confondere*) to confuse things.

con'fuso, a *pp di* **confondere** ♦ *ag* (*vedi confondere*) confused; embarrassed.

confu'tare *vt* to refute.

conge'dare [kondʒe'dare] *vt* to dismiss; (*MIL*) to demobilize; **~rsi** *vr* to take one's leave.

con'gedo [kon'dʒedo] *sm* (*anche MIL*) leave; **prendere ~ da qn** to take one's leave of sb; **~ assoluto** (*MIL*) discharge.

conge'gnare [kondʒeɲ'ɲare] *vt* to construct, put together.

con'gegno [kon'dʒeɲɲo] *sm* device, mechanism.

congela'mento [kondʒela'mento] *sm* (*gen*) freezing; (*MED*) frostbite; **~ salariale** wage freeze.

conge'lare [kondʒe'lare] *vt*, **~rsi** *vr* to freeze.

congela'tore [kondʒela'tore] *sm* freezer.

con'genito, a [kon'dʒɛnito] *ag* congenital.

con'gerie [kon'dʒɛrje] *sf inv* (*di oggetti*) heap; (*di idee*) muddle, jumble.

congestio'nare [kondʒestjo'nare] *vt* to congest; **essere congestionato** (*persona, viso*) to be flushed; (*zona: per traffico*) to be congested.

congesti'one [kondʒes'tjone] *sf* congestion.

conget'tura [kondʒet'tura] *sf* conjecture, supposition.

con'giungere [kon'dʒundʒere] *vt*, **~rsi** *vr* to join (together).

congiunti'vite [kondʒunti'vite] *sf* conjunctivitis.

congiun'tivo [kondʒun'tivo] *sm* (*LING*) subjunctive.

congi'unto, a [kon'dʒunto] *pp di* **congiungere** ♦ *ag* (*unito*) joined ♦ *sm/f* (*parente*) relative.

congiun'tura [kondʒun'tura] *sf* (*giuntura*) junction, join; (*ANAT*) joint; (*circostanza*) juncture; (*ECON*) economic situation.

congiuntu'rale [kondʒuntu'rale] *ag* of the economic situation; **crisi ~** economic crisis.

congiunzi'one [kondʒun'tsjone] *sf* (*LING*) conjunction.

congi'ura [kon'dʒura] *sf* conspiracy.

congiu'rare [kondʒu'rare] *vi* to conspire.

conglome'rato *sm* (*GEO*) conglomerate; (*fig*) conglomeration; (*EDIL*) concrete.

'Congo *sm*: **il ~** the Congo.

congo'lese *ag*, *sm/f* Congolese *inv*.

congratu'larsi *vr*: **~ con qn per qc** to congratulate sb on sth.

congratulazi'oni [kongratulat'tsjoni] *sfpl* congratulations.

con'grega, ghe *sf* band, bunch.

congregazi'one [kongregat'tsjone] *sf* congregation.

congres'sista, i, e *sm/f* participant at a congress.

con'gresso *sm* congress.

'congruo, a *ag* (*prezzo, compenso*) adequate, fair; (*ragionamento*) coherent, consistent.

conguagli'are [kongwaʎ'ʎare] *vt* to balance; (*stipendio*) to adjust.

congu'aglio [kon'gwaʎʎo] *sm* balancing; adjusting; (*somma di denaro*) balance; **fare il ~ di** to balance; to adjust.

coni'are *vt* to mint, coin; (*fig*) to coin.

coniazi'one [konjat'tsjone] *sf* mintage.

'conico, a, ci, che *ag* conical.

co'nifera *sf* conifer.

conigli'era [koniʎ'ʎera] *sf* (*gabbia*) rabbit hutch; (*più grande*) rabbit run.

conigli'etto [koniʎ'ʎetto] *sm* bunny.

co'niglio [ko'niʎʎo] *sm* rabbit; **sei un ~!** (*fig*) you're chicken!

coniu'gale *ag* (*amore, diritti*) conjugal; (*vita*) married, conjugal.

coniu'gare *vt* (*LING*) to conjugate; **~rsi** *vr* to get married.

coniu'gato, a *ag* (*AMM*) married.

coniugazi'one [konjugat'tsjone] *sf* (*LING*) conjugation.

'coniuge ['kɔnjudʒe] *sm/f* spouse.

connatu'rato, a *ag* inborn.

connazio'nale [konnattsjo'nale] *sm/f* fellow-countryman/woman.

connessi'one *sf* connection.

con'nesso, a *pp di* **connettere**.

con'nettere *vt* to connect, join ♦ *vi* (*fig*) to think straight.

connet'tore *sm* (*ELETTR*) connector.

conni'vente *ag* conniving.

conno'tati *smpl* distinguishing marks; **rispondere ai ~i** to fit the description; **cambiare i ~i a qn** (*fam*) to beat sb up.

con'nubio *sm* (*matrimonio*) marriage; (*fig*) union.

'cono *sm* cone; **~ gelato** ice-cream cone.

co'nobbi *etc vb vedi* **conoscere**.

cono'scente [konoʃ'ʃɛnte] *sm/f* acquaintance.

cono'scenza [konoʃ'ʃɛntsa] *sf* (*il sapere*) knowledge *q*; (*persona*) acquaintance; (*facoltà sensoriale*) consciousness *q*; **essere a ~ di qc** to know sth; **portare qn a ~ di qc** to inform sb of sth; **per vostra ~** for your information; **fare la ~ di qn** to make sb's acquaintance; **perdere ~** to lose consciousness; **~ tecnica** know-how.

co'noscere [ko'noʃʃere] *vt* to know; **ci siamo conosciuti a Firenze** we (first) met in Florence; **~ qn di vista** to know sb by sight; **farsi ~** (*fig*) to make a name for o.s.

conosci'tore, 'trice [konoʃʃi'tore] *sm/f* connoisseur.

conosci'uto, a [konoʃ'ʃuto] *pp di* **conoscere** ♦

ag well-known.

con'quista *sf* conquest.

conquis'tare *vt* to conquer; (*fig*) to gain, win.

conquista'tore, 'trice *sm/f* (*in guerra*) conqueror ♦ *sm* (*seduttore*) lady-killer.

cons. *abbr* = **consiglio**.

consa'crare *vt* (*REL*) to consecrate; (*: sacerdote*) to ordain; (*dedicare*) to dedicate; (*fig: uso etc*) to sanction; **~rsi a** to dedicate o.s. to.

consangu'ineo, a *sm/f* blood relation.

consa'pevole *ag*: **~ di** aware *o* conscious of.

consapevo'lezza [konsapevo'lettsa] *sf* awareness, consciousness.

'conscio, a, sci, sce ['kɔnʃo] *ag*: **~ di** aware *o* conscious of.

consecu'tivo, a *ag* consecutive; (*successivo: giorno*) following, next.

con'segna [kon'seɲɲa] *sf* delivery; (*merce consegnata*) consignment; (*custodia*) care, custody; (*MIL: ordine*) orders *pl*; (*: punizione*) confinement to barracks; **alla ~** on delivery; **dare qc in ~ a qn** to entrust sth to sb; **passare le ~e a qn** to hand over to sb; **~ a domicilio** home delivery; **~ in contrassegno, pagamento alla ~** cash on delivery; **~ sollecita** prompt delivery.

conse'gnare [konse'ɲɲare] *vt* to deliver; (*affidare*) to entrust, hand over; (*MIL*) to confine to barracks.

consegna'tario [konseɲɲa'tarjo] *sm* consignee.

consegu'ente *ag* consequent.

conseguente'mente *av* consequently.

consegu'enza [konse'gwentsa] *sf* consequence; **per** *o* **di ~** consequently.

consegui'mento *sm* (*di scopo, risultato etc*) achievement, attainment; **al ~ della laurea** on graduation.

consegu'ire *vt* to achieve ♦ *vi* to follow, result; **~ la laurea** to graduate, obtain one's degree.

con'senso *sm* approval, consent.

consensu'ale *ag* (*DIR*) by mutual consent.

consen'tire *vi*: **~ a** to consent *o* agree to ♦ *vt* to allow, permit; **mi si consenta di ringraziare ...** I would like to thank ....

consenzi'ente [konsen'tsjɛnte] *ag* (*gen, DIR*) consenting.

con'serto, a *ag*: **a braccia ~e** with one's arms folded.

con'serva *sf* (*CUC*) preserve; **~ di frutta** jam; **~ di pomodoro** tomato purée; **~e alimentari** tinned (*o* canned *o* bottled) foods.

conser'vare *vt* (*CUC*) to preserve; (*custodire*) to keep; (*: dalla distruzione etc*) to preserve, conserve; **~rsi** *vr* to keep.

conserva'tore, 'trice *ag, sm/f* (*POL*) conservative.

conserva'torio *sm* (*di musica*) conservatory.

conservato'rismo *sm* (*POL*) conservatism.

conservazi'one [konservat'tsjone] *sf* preservation; conservation; **istinto di ~** instinct for self-preservation; **a lunga ~** (*latte, panna*) long-life *cpd*.

con'sesso *sm* (*assemblea*) assembly; (*riunione*) meeting.

conside'rabile *ag* worthy of consideration.

conside'rare *vt* to consider; (*reputare*) to consider, regard; **~ molto qn** to think highly of sb.

conside'rato, a *ag* (*prudente*) cautious, careful; (*stimato*) highly thought of, esteemed.

considerazi'one [konsiderat'tsjone] *sf* (*esame, riflessione*) consideration; (*stima*) regard, esteem; (*pensiero, osservazione*) observation; **prendere in ~** to take into consideration.

conside'revole *ag* considerable.

consigli'abile [konsiʎ'ʎabile] *ag* advisable.

consigli'are [konsiʎ'ʎare] *vt* (*persona*) to advise; (*metodo, azione*) to recommend, advise, suggest; **~rsi** *vr*: **~rsi con qn** to ask sb for advice.

consigli'ere, a [konsiʎ'ʎɛre] *sm/f* adviser ♦ *sm*: **~ d'amministrazione** board member; **~ comunale** town councillor; **~ delegato** (*COMM*) managing director.

con'siglio [kon'siʎʎo] *sm* (*suggerimento*) advice *q*, piece of advice; (*assemblea*) council; **~ d'amministrazione** board; **C~ d'Europa** Council of Europe; **~ di fabbrica** works council; **il C~ dei Ministri** (*POL*) ≈ the Cabinet; **C~ di stato** *advisory body to the Italian government on administrative matters and their legal implications*; **C~ superiore della magistratura** *state body responsible for judicial appointments and regulations*.

con'simile *ag* similar.

consis'tente *ag* solid; (*fig*) sound, valid.

consis'tenza [konsis'tɛntsa] *sf* (*di impasto*) consistency; (*di stoffa*) texture; **senza ~** (*sospetti, voci*) ill-founded, groundless; **~ di cassa/di magazzino** cash/stock in hand; **~ patrimoniale** financial solidity.

con'sistere *vi*: **~ in** to consist of.

consis'tito, a *pp di* **consistere**.

'CONSOB *sigla f* (= *Commissione nazionale per le società e la borsa*) *regulatory body for the Italian Stock Exchange*.

consoci'arsi [konso'tʃarsi] *vr* to go into partnership.

consoci'ato, a [konso'tʃato] *ag* associated ♦ *sm/f* associate.

conso'lante *ag* consoling, comforting.

conso'lare *ag* consular ♦ *vt* (*confortare*) to console, comfort; (*rallegrare*) to cheer up; **~rsi** *vr* to be comforted; to cheer up.

conso'lato *sm* consulate.

consolazi'one [konsolat'tsjone] *sf* consolation, comfort.

'console *sm* consul ♦ *sf* [kɔ̃'sɔl] (*quadro di comando*) console.

consolida'mento *sm* strengthening; consolidation.

consoli'dare *vt* to strengthen, reinforce; (*MIL, terreno*) to consolidate; **~rsi** *vr* to consolidate.

consolidazi'one [konsolidat'tsjone] *sf* strengthening; consolidation.

consommé [kɔ̃sɔ'me] *sm inv* consommé.

conso'nante *sf* consonant.

conso'nanza [konso'nantsa] *sf* consonance.

'consono, a *ag*: **~ a** consistent with, consonant with.

con'sorte *sm/f* consort.

con'sorzio [kon'sɔrtsjo] *sm* consortium; **~ agrario** farmers' cooperative; **~ di garanzia** (*COMM*) underwriting syndicate.

con'stare *vi*: **~ di** to consist of ♦ *vb impers*: **mi consta che** it has come to my knowledge that, it appears that; **a quanto mi consta** as far as I know.

consta'tare *vt* to establish, verify; (*notare*) to notice, observe.

constatazi'one [konstatat'tsjone] *sf* observation; **~ amichevole** (*in incidenti*) *jointly-agreed statement for insurance purposes*.

consu'eto, a *ag* habitual, usual ♦ *sm*: **come di ~** as usual.

consuetudi'nario, a *ag*: **diritto ~** (*DIR*) common law.

consue'tudine *sf* habit; (*usanza*) custom.

consu'lente *sm/f* consultant; **~ aziendale/tecnico** management/technical consultant.

consu'lenza [konsu'lɛntsa] *sf* consultancy; **~ medica/legale** medical/legal advice; **ufficio di ~** consultancy office; **~ fiscale** tax consultancy office; **~ tecnica** technical consultancy *o* advice.

consul'tare *vt* to consult; **~rsi** *vr*: **~rsi con qn** to seek the advice of sb.

consultazi'one [konsultat'tsjone] *sf* consultation; **~i** *sfpl* (*POL*) talks, consultations; **libro di ~** reference book.

consul'tivo, a *ag* consultative.

consul'torio *sm*: **~ familiare** *o* **matrimoniale** marriage guidance centre; **~ pediatrico** children's clinic.

consu'mare *vt* (*logorare: abiti, scarpe*) to wear out; (*usare*) to consume, use up; (*mangiare, bere*) to consume; (*DIR*) to consummate; **~rsi** *vr* to wear out; to be used up; (*anche fig*) to be consumed; (*combustibile*) to burn out.

consu'mato, a *ag* (*vestiti, scarpe, tappeto*) worn; (*persona: esperto*) accomplished.

consuma'tore *sm* consumer.

consumazi'one [konsumat'tsjone] *sf* (*bibita*) drink; (*spuntino*) snack; (*DIR*) consummation.

consu'mismo *sm* consumerism.

con'sumo *sm* consumption; wear; use; **generi** *o* **beni di** ~ consumer goods; **beni di largo** ~ basic commodities; **imposta sui** ~**i** tax on consumer goods.

consun'tivo *sm* (*ECON*) final balance.

con'sunto, a *ag* worn-out; (*viso*) wasted.

'conta *sf* (*nei giochi*): **fare la** ~ to see who is going to be "it".

con'tabile *ag* accounts *cpd*, accounting ♦ *sm/f* accountant.

contabilità *sf* (*attività, tecnica*) accounting, accountancy; (*insieme dei libri etc*) books *pl*, accounts *pl*; (**ufficio**) ~ accounts department; ~ **finanziaria** financial accounting; ~ **di gestione** management accounting.

contachi'lometri [kontaki'lɔmetri] *sm inv* ≈ mileometer.

conta'dino, a *sm/f* countryman/woman; farm worker; (*peg*) peasant.

contagi'are [konta'dʒare] *vt* to infect.

con'tagio [kon'tadʒo] *sm* infection; (*per contatto diretto*) contagion; (*epidemia*) epidemic.

contagi'oso, a [konta'dʒoso] *ag* infectious; contagious.

conta'giri [konta'dʒiri] *sm inv* (*AUT*) rev counter.

conta'gocce [konta'gottʃe] *sm inv* dropper.

contami'nare *vt* to contaminate.

contaminazi'one [kontaminat'tsjone] *sf* contamination.

con'tante *sm* cash; **pagare in** ~**i** to pay cash.

con'tare *vt* to count; (*considerare*) to consider ♦ *vi* to count, be of importance; ~ **su qn** to count *o* rely on sb; ~ **di fare qc** to intend to do sth; **ha i giorni contati, ha le ore contate** his days are numbered; **la gente che conta** people who matter.

contas'catti *sm inv* telephone meter.

conta'tore *sm* meter.

contat'tare *vt* to contact.

con'tatto *sm* contact; **essere in** ~ **con qn** to be in touch with sb; **fare** ~ (*ELETTR: fili*) to touch.

'conte *sm* count.

con'tea *sf* (*STORIA*) earldom; (*AMM*) county.

conteggi'are [konted'dʒare] *vt* to charge, put on the bill.

con'teggio [kon'tedd͡ʒo] *sm* calculation.

con'tegno [kon'teɲɲo] *sm* (*comportamento*) behaviour (*Brit*), behavior (*US*); (*atteggiamento*) attitude; **darsi un** ~ (*ostentare disinvoltura*) to act nonchalant; (*ricomporsi*) to pull o.s. together.

conte'gnoso, a [konteɲ'noso] *ag* reserved, dignified.

contem'plare *vt* to contemplate, gaze at; (*DIR*) to make provision for.

contempla'tivo, a *ag* contemplative.

contemplazi'one [kontemplat'tsjone] *sf* contemplation.

con'tempo *sm*: **nel** ~ meanwhile, in the meantime.

contemporanea'mente *av* simultaneously; at the same time.

contempo'raneo, a *ag, sm/f* contemporary.

conten'dente *sm/f* opponent, adversary.

con'tendere *vi* (*competere*) to compete; (*litigare*) to quarrel ♦ *vt*: ~ **qc a qn** to contend with *o* be in competition with sb for sth.

conte'nere *vt* to contain; ~**rsi** *vr* to contain o.s.

conteni'tore *sm* container.

conten'tabile *ag*: **difficilmente** ~ difficult to please.

conten'tare *vt* to please, satisfy; ~**rsi** *vr*: ~**rsi di** to be satisfied with, content o.s. with; **si contenta di poco** he is easily satisfied.

conten'tezza [konten'tettsa] *sf* contentment.

conten'tino *sm* sop.

con'tento, a *ag* pleased, glad; ~ **di** pleased with.

conte'nuto *ag* (*ira, entusiasmo*) restrained, suppressed; (*forza*) contained ♦ *sm* contents *pl*; (*argomento*) content.

contenzi'oso, a [konten'tsjoso] *ag* (*DIR*) contentious ♦ *sm* (*AMM*): **ufficio** ~ legal department.

con'teso, a *pp di* **contendere** ♦ *sf* dispute, argument.

con'tessa *sf* countess.

contes'tare *vt* (*DIR*) to notify; (*fig*) to dispute; ~ **il sistema** to protest against the system.

contesta'tore, 'trice *ag* anti-establishment ♦ *sm/f* protester.

contestazi'one [kontestat'tsjone] *sf* (*DIR: disputa*) dispute; (: *notifica*) notification; (*POL*) anti-establishment activity; **in caso di** ~ if there are any objections.

con'testo *sm* context.

con'tiguo, a *ag*: ~ **(a)** adjacent (to).

continen'tale *ag* continental.

conti'nente *ag* continent ♦ *sm* (*GEO*) continent; (: *terra ferma*) mainland.

conti'nenza [konti'nɛntsa] *sf* continence.

contin'gente [kontin'dʒɛnte] *ag* contingent ♦ *sm* (*COMM*) quota; (*MIL*) contingent.

contin'genza [kontin'dʒɛntsa] *sf* circumstance; (**indennità di**) ~ cost-of-living allowance.

continua'mente *av* (*senza interruzione*) continuously, nonstop; (*ripetutamente*) continually.

continu'are *vt* to continue (with), go on with ♦ *vi* to continue, go on; ~ **a fare qc** to go on *o* continue doing sth; **continua a nevicare/a fare freddo** it's still snowing/

cold.

continua'tivo, a *ag (occupazione)* permanent; *(periodo)* consecutive.

continuazi'one [kontinuat'tsjone] *sf* continuation.

continuità *sf* continuity.

con'tinuo, a *ag (numerazione)* continuous; *(pioggia)* continual, constant; *(ELETTR: corrente)* direct; **di ~** continually.

'conto *sm (calcolo)* calculation; *(COMM, ECON)* account; *(di ristorante, albergo)* bill; *(fig: stima)* consideration, esteem; **avere un ~ in sospeso (con qn)** to have an outstanding account (with sb); *(fig)* to have a score to settle (with sb); **fare i ~i con qn** to settle one's account with sb; **fare ~ su qn** to count *o* rely on sb; **fare ~ che** *(supporre)* to suppose that; **rendere ~ a qn di qc** to be accountable to sb for sth; **rendersi ~ di qc/che** to realize sth/that; **tener ~ di qn/qc** to take sb/sth into account; **tenere qc da ~** to take great care of sth; **ad ogni buon ~** in any case; **di poco/nessun ~** of little/no importance; **per ~ di** on behalf of; **per ~ mio** as far as I'm concerned; *(da solo)* on my own; **a ~i fatti, in fin dei ~i** all things considered; **mi hanno detto strane cose sul suo ~** I've heard some strange things about him; **~ capitale** capital account; **~ cifrato** numbered account; **~ corrente** current account *(Brit)*, checking account *(US)*; **~ corrente postale** Post Office account; **~ economico** profit and loss account; **~ in partecipazione** joint account; **~ passivo** account payable; **~ profitti e perdite** profit and loss account; **~ alla rovescia** countdown; **~ valutario** foreign currency account.

con'torcere [kon'tɔrtʃere] *vt* to twist; *(panni)* to wring (out); **~rsi** *vr* to twist, writhe.

contor'nare *vt* to surround; **~rsi** *vr*: **~rsi di** to surround o.s. with.

con'torno *sm (linea)* outline, contour; *(ornamento)* border; *(CUC)* vegetables *pl*; **fare da ~** a to surround.

contorsi'one *sf* contortion.

con'torto, a *pp di* contorcere.

contrabban'dare *vt* to smuggle.

contrabbandi'ere, a *sm/f* smuggler.

contrab'bando *sm* smuggling, contraband; **merce di ~** contraband, smuggled goods *pl*.

contrab'basso *sm (MUS)* (double) bass.

contraccambi'are *vt (favore etc)* to return; **vorrei ~** I'd like to show my appreciation.

contraccet'tivo, a [kontrattʃet'tivo] *ag, sm* contraceptive.

contrac'colpo *sm* rebound; *(di arma da fuoco)* recoil; *(fig)* repercussion.

con'trada *sf* street; district.

contrad'detto, a *pp di* contraddire.

contrad'dire *vt* to contradict; **~rsi** *vr* to contradict o.s.; *(uso reciproco: persone)* to contradict each other *o* one another; *(: testimonianze etc)* to be contradictory.

contraddis'tinguere *vt (merce)* to mark; *(fig: atteggiamento, persona)* to distinguish.

contraddis'tinto, a *pp di* contraddistinguere.

contraddit'torio, a *ag* contradictory; *(sentimenti)* conflicting ♦ *sm (DIR)* crossexamination.

contraddizi'one [kontraddit'tsjone] *sf* contradiction; **cadere in ~** to contradict o.s.; **essere in ~** *(tesi, affermazioni)* to contradict one another; **spirito di ~** argumentativeness.

con'trae *etc vb vedi* contrarre.

contra'ente *sm* contractor.

contra'erea *sf (MIL)* anti-aircraft artillery.

contraf'fare *vt (persona)* to mimic; *(voce)* to disguise; *(firma)* to forge, counterfeit.

contraf'fatto, a *pp di* contraffare ♦ *ag* counterfeit.

contraffazi'one [kontraffat'tsjone] *sf* mimicking *q*; disguising *q*; forging *q*; *(cosa contraffatta)* forgery.

contraf'forte *sm (ARCHIT)* buttress; *(GEO)* spur.

con'traggo *etc vb vedi* contrarre.

con'tralto *sm (MUS)* contralto.

contrap'pello *sm (MIL)* second roll call.

contrappe'sare *vt* to counterbalance; *(fig: decisione)* to weigh up.

contrap'peso *sm* counterbalance, counterweight.

contrap'porre *vt*: **~ qc a qc** to counter sth with sth; *(paragonare)* to compare sth with sth; **contrapporsi** *vr*: **contrapporsi a qc** to contrast with sth, be opposed to sth.

contrap'posto, a *pp di* contrapporre.

contraria'mente *av*: **~ a** contrary to.

contrari'are *vt (contrastare)* to thwart, oppose; *(irritare)* to annoy, bother; **~rsi** *vr* to get annoyed.

contrari'ato, a *ag* annoyed.

contrarietà *sf* adversity; *(fig)* aversion.

con'trario, a *ag* opposite; *(sfavorevole)* unfavourable *(Brit)*, unfavorable *(US)* ♦ *sm* opposite; **essere ~ a qc** *(persona)* to be against sth; **al ~** on the contrary; **in caso ~** otherwise; **avere qualcosa in ~** to have some objection; **non ho niente in ~** I have no objection.

con'trarre *vt (malattia, debito)* to contract; *(muscoli)* to tense; *(abitudine, vizio)* to pick up; *(accordo, patto)* to enter into; **contrarsi** *vr* to contract; **~ matrimonio** to marry.

contrasse'gnare [kontrasseɲ'ɲare] *vt* to mark.

contras'segno [kontras'seɲɲo] *sm (distintivo)* distinguishing mark; **spedire in ~** *(COMM)*

to send COD.
con'trassi *etc vb vedi* **contrarre**.
contras'tante *ag* contrasting.
contras'tare *vt* (*avversare*) to oppose; (*impedire*) to bar; (*negare: diritto*) to contest, dispute ♦ *vi*: ~ **(con)** (*essere in disaccordo*) to contrast (with); (*lottare*) to struggle (with).
con'trasto *sm* contrast; (*conflitto*) conflict; (*litigio*) dispute.
contrat'tacco *sm* counterattack; **passare al** ~ (*fig*) to fight back.
contrat'tare *vt*, *vi* to negotiate.
contrat'tempo *sm* hitch.
con'tratto, a *pp di* **contrarre** ♦ *sm* contract; ~ **di acquisto** purchase agreement; ~ **di affitto**, ~ **di locazione** lease; ~ **collettivo di lavoro** collective agreement; ~ **di lavoro** contract of employment; ~ **a termine** forward contract.
contrattu'ale *ag* contractual; **forza** ~ (*di sindacato*) bargaining power.
contravve'nire *vi*: ~ **a** (*legge*) to contravene; (*obbligo*) to fail to meet.
contravven'tore, 'trice *sm/f* offender.
contravve'nuto, a *pp di* **contravvenire**.
contravvenzi'one [kontravven'tsjone] *sf* contravention; (*ammenda*) fine.
contrazi'one [kontrat'tsjone] *sf* contraction; (*di prezzi etc*) reduction.
contribu'ente *sm/f* taxpayer; ratepayer (*Brit*), property tax payer (*US*).
contribu'ire *vi* to contribute.
contribu'tivo, a *ag* contributory.
contri'buto *sm* contribution; (*sovvenzione*) subsidy, contribution; (*tassa*) tax; ~**i previdenziali** ≈ national insurance (*Brit*) *o* welfare (*US*) contributions; ~**i sindacali** trade union dues.
con'trito, a *ag* contrite, penitent.
'contro *prep* against; ~ **di me/lui** against me/him; **pastiglie** ~ **la tosse** throat lozenges; ~ **pagamento** (*COMM*) on payment; ~ **ogni mia aspettativa** contrary to my expectations; **per** ~ on the other hand.
contro'battere *vt* (*fig: a parole*) to answer back; (: *confutare*) to refute.
controbilanci'are [kontrobilan'tʃare] *vt* to counterbalance.
controcor'rente *av*: **andare** ~ (*anche fig*) to swim against the tide.
controcul'tura *sf* counterculture.
controffen'siva *sf* counteroffensive.
controfi'gura *sf* (*CINEMA*) double.
controfir'mare *vt* to countersign.
control'lare *vt* (*accertare*) to check; (*sorvegliare*) to watch, control; (*tenere nel proprio potere, fig: dominare*) to control; ~**rsi** *vr* to control o.s.
control'lata *sf* (*COMM: società*) associated company.
con'trollo *sm* check; watch; control; **base**

di ~ (*AER*) ground control; **telefono sotto** ~ tapped telephone; **visita di** ~ (*MED*) checkup; ~ **doganale** customs inspection; ~ **di gestione** management control; ~ **delle nascite** birth control; ~ **di qualità** quality control.
control'lore *sm* (*FERR, AUTOBUS*) (ticket) inspector; ~ **di volo** *o* **del traffico aereo** air traffic controller.
contro'luce [kontro'lutʃe] *sf inv* (*FOT*) backlit shot ♦ *av*: **(in)** ~ against the light; (*fotografare*) into the light.
contro'mano *av*: **guidare** ~ to drive on the wrong side of the road; (*in un senso unico*) to drive the wrong way up a one-way street.
contropar'tita *sf* (*fig: compenso*): **come** ~ in return.
contropi'ede *sm* (*SPORT*): **azione di** ~ sudden counter-attack; **prendere qn in** ~ (*fig*) to catch sb off his (*o* her) guard.
controprodu'cente [kontroprodu'tʃente] *ag* counterproductive.
con'trordine *sm* counter-order; **salvo** ~ unless I (*o* you *etc*) hear to the contrary.
contro'senso *sm* (*contraddizione*) contradiction in terms; (*assurdità*) nonsense.
controspio'naggio [kontrospio'naddʒo] *sm* counterespionage.
controva'lore *sm* equivalent (value).
contro'vento *av* against the wind; **navigare** ~ (*NAUT*) to sail to windward.
contro'versia *sf* controversy; (*DIR*) dispute; ~ **sindacale** industrial dispute.
contro'verso, a *ag* controversial.
contro'voglia [kontro'vɔʎʎa] *av* unwillingly.
contu'mace [kontu'matʃe] *ag* (*DIR*): **rendersi** ~ to default, fail to appear in court ♦ *sm/f* (*DIR*) defaulter.
contu'macia [kontu'matʃa] *sf* (*DIR*) default.
contun'dente *ag*: **corpo** ~ blunt instrument.
contur'bante *ag* (*sguardo, bellezza*) disturbing.
contur'bare *vt* to disturb, upset.
contusi'one *sf* (*MED*) bruise.
convale'scente [konvaleʃ'ʃente] *ag*, *sm/f* convalescent.
convale'scenza [konvaleʃ'ʃentsa] *sf* convalescence.
convali'dare *vt* (*AMM*) to validate; (*fig: sospetto, dubbio*) to confirm.
con'vegno [kon'veɲɲo] *sm* (*incontro*) meeting; (*congresso*) convention, congress; (*luogo*) meeting place.
conve'nevoli *smpl* civilities.
conveni'ente *ag* suitable; (*vantaggioso*) profitable; (: *prezzo*) cheap.
conveni'enza [konve'njentsa] *sf* suitability; advantage; cheapness; ~**e** *sfpl* social conventions.
conve'nire *vt* to agree upon ♦ *vi* (*riunirsi*)

to gather, assemble; (*concordare*) to agree; (*tornare utile*) to be worthwhile ♦ *vb impers*: **conviene fare questo** it is advisable to do this; **conviene andarsene** we should go; **ne convengo** I agree; **come convenuto** as agreed; **in data da ~** on a date to be agreed; **come (si) conviene ad una signorina** as befits a young lady.

conven'ticola *sf* (*cricca*) clique; (*riunione*) secret meeting.

con'vento *sm* (*di frati*) monastery; (*di suore*) convent.

conve'nuto, a *pp di* **convenire** ♦ *sm* (*cosa pattuita*) agreement ♦ *sm/f* (*DIR*) defendant; **i ~i** (*i presenti*) those present.

convenzio'nale [konventsjo'nale] *ag* conventional.

convenzio'nato, a [konventsjo'nato] *ag* (*ospedale, clinica*) providing free health care, ≈ National Health Service *cpd* (*Brit*).

convenzi'one [konven'tsjone] *sf* (*DIR*) agreement; (*nella società*) convention; **le ~i (sociali)** social conventions.

conver'gente [konver'dʒɛnte] *ag* convergent.

conver'genza [konver'dʒɛntsa] *sf* convergence.

con'vergere [kon'vɛrdʒere] *vi* to converge.

con'versa *sf* (*REL*) lay sister.

conver'sare *vi* to have a conversation, converse.

conversazi'one [konversat'tsjone] *sf* conversation; **fare ~** (*chiacchierare*) to chat, have a chat.

conversi'one *sf* conversion; **~ ad U** (*AUT*) U-turn.

con'verso, a *pp di* **convergere; per ~** *av* conversely.

conver'tire *vt* (*trasformare*) to change; (*POL, REL*) to convert; **~rsi** *vr*: **~rsi (a)** to be converted (to).

conver'tito, a *sm/f* convert.

converti'tore *sm* (*ELETTR*) converter.

con'vesso, a *ag* convex.

convin'cente [konvin'tʃɛnte] *ag* convincing.

con'vincere [kon'vintʃere] *vt* to convince; **~ qn di qc** to convince sb of sth; (*DIR*) to prove sb guilty of sth; **~ qn a fare qc** to persuade sb to do sth.

con'vinto, a *pp di* **convincere** ♦ *ag*: **reo ~** (*DIR*) convicted criminal.

convinzi'one [konvin'tsjone] *sf* conviction, firm belief.

convis'suto, a *pp di* **convivere**.

convi'tato, a *sm/f* guest.

con'vitto *sm* (*INS*) boarding school.

convi'venza [konvi'vɛntsa] *sf* living together; (*DIR*) cohabitation.

con'vivere *vi* to live together.

convivi'ale *ag* convivial.

convo'care *vt* to call, convene; (*DIR*) to summon.

convocazi'one [konvokat'tsjone] *sf* meeting; summons *sg*; **lettera di ~** (letter of) notification to appear *o* attend.

convogli'are [konvoʎ'ʎare] *vt* to convey; (*dirigere*) to direct, send.

con'voglio [kon'vɔʎʎo] *sm* (*di veicoli*) convoy; (*FERR*) train; **~ funebre** funeral procession.

convo'lare *vi*: **~ a (giuste) nozze** (*scherzoso*) to tie the knot.

convulsi'one *sf* convulsion.

con'vulso, a *ag* (*pianto*) violent, convulsive; (*attività*) feverish.

COOP. *abbr f* = **cooperativa**.

coope'rare *vi*: **~ (a)** to cooperate (in).

coopera'tiva *sf* cooperative.

cooperazi'one [kooperat'tsjone] *sf* cooperation.

coordi'nare *vt* to coordinate.

coordi'nate *sfpl* (*MAT, GEO*) coordinates.

coordi'nati *smpl* (*MODA*) coordinates.

coordinazi'one [koordinat'tsjone] *sf* coordination.

Copen'hagen [kopen'agen] *sf* Copenhagen.

co'perchio [ko'perkjo] *sm* cover; (*di pentola*) lid.

co'perta *sf* cover; (*di lana*) blanket; (*da viaggio*) rug; (*NAUT*) deck.

coper'tina *sf* (*STAMPA*) cover, jacket.

co'perto, a *pp di* **coprire** ♦ *ag* covered; (*cielo*) overcast ♦ *sm* place setting; (*posto a tavola*) place; (*al ristorante*) cover charge; **~ di** covered in *o* with.

coper'tone *sm* (*telo impermeabile*) tarpaulin; (*AUT*) rubber tyre.

coper'tura *sf* (*anche ECON, MIL*) cover; (*di edificio*) roofing; **fare un gioco di ~** (*SPORT*) to play a defensive game; **~ assicurativa** insurance cover.

'copia *sf* copy; (*FOT*) print; **brutta/bella ~** rough/final copy; **~ conforme** (*DIR*) certified copy; **~ omaggio** presentation copy.

copi'are *vt* to copy.

copia'trice [kopja'tritʃe] *sf* copier, copying machine.

copi'one *sm* (*CINEMA, TEATRO*) script.

'coppa *sf* (*bicchiere*) goblet; (*per frutta, gelato*) dish; (*trofeo*) cup, trophy; **~e** *sfpl* (*CARTE*) suit in Neapolitan pack of cards; **~ dell'olio** oil sump (*Brit*) *o* pan (*US*).

'coppia *sf* (*di persone*) couple; (*di animali, SPORT*) pair.

copri'capo *sm* headgear; (*cappello*) hat.

coprifu'oco, chi *sm* curfew.

copri'letto *sm* bedspread.

co'prire *vt* to cover; (*occupare: carica, posto*) to hold; **~rsi** *vr* (*cielo*) to cloud over; (*vestirsi*) to wrap up, cover up; (*ECON*) to cover o.s.; **~rsi di** (*macchie, muffa*) to become covered in; **~ qn di baci** to smother sb with kisses; **~ le spese** to break even; ~**rsi le spalle** (*fig*) to cover o.s.

coque [kɔk] *sf*: **uovo alla** ~ boiled egg.

co'raggio [ko'raddʒo] *sm* courage, bravery; ~**!** (*forza!*) come on!; (*animo!*) cheer up!; **farsi** ~ to pluck up courage; **hai un bel** ~**!** (*sfacciataggine*) you've got a nerve *o* a cheek!

coraggi'oso, a [korad'dʒoso] *ag* courageous, brave.

co'rale *ag* choral; (*approvazione*) unanimous.

co'rallo *sm* coral; **il mar dei C**~**i** the Coral Sea.

co'rano *sm* (*REL*) Koran.

co'razza [ko'rattsa] *sf* armour (*Brit*), armor (*US*); (*di animali*) carapace, shell; (*MIL*) armo(u)r(-plating).

coraz'zato, a [korat'tsato] *ag* (*MIL*) armoured (*Brit*), armored (*US*) ♦ *sf* battleship.

corazzi'ere [korat'tsjɛre] *sm* (*STORIA*) cuirassier; (*guardia presidenziale*) carabiniere *of the President's guard*.

corbelle'ria *sf* stupid remark; ~**e** *sfpl* (*sciocchezze*) nonsense *q*.

'corda *sf* cord; (*fune*) rope; (*spago, MUS*) string; **dare** ~ **a qn** (*fig*) to let sb have his (*o* her) way; **tenere sulla** ~ **qn** (*fig*) to keep sb on tenterhooks; **tagliare la** ~ (*fig*) to slip away, sneak off; **essere giù di** ~ to feel down; ~**e vocali** vocal cords.

cor'data *sf* (*ALPINISMO*) roped party.

cordi'ale *ag* cordial, warm ♦ *sm* (*bevanda*) cordial.

cordialità *sf inv* warmth, cordiality; ~ *sfpl* (*saluti*) best wishes.

cor'doglio [kor'dɔʎʎo] *sm* grief; (*lutto*) mourning.

cor'done *sm* cord, string; (*linea: di polizia*) cordon; ~ **ombelicale** umbilical cord; ~ **sanitario** quarantine line.

Co'rea *sf*: **la** ~ Korea; **la** ~ **del Nord/Sud** North/South Korea.

core'ano, a *ag*, *sm/f* Korean.

coreogra'fia *sf* choreography.

core'ografo, a *sm/f* choreographer.

cori'aceo, a [ko'rjatʃeo] *ag* (*BOT, ZOOL*) coriaceous; (*fig*) tough.

cori'andolo *sm* (*BOT*) coriander; ~**i** *smpl* (*per carnevale etc*) confetti *q*.

cori'care *vt* to put to bed; ~**rsi** *vr* to go to bed.

coricherò *etc* [korike'rɔ] *vb vedi* **coricare**.

Co'rinto *sf* Corinth.

co'rista, i, e *sm/f* (*REL*) choir member, chorister; (*TEATRO*) member of the chorus.

'corna *sfpl vedi* **corno**.

cor'nacchia [kor'nakkja] *sf* crow.

corna'musa *sf* bagpipes *pl*.

'cornea *sf* (*ANAT*) cornea.

'corner *sm inv* (*CALCIO*) corner (kick); **salvarsi in** ~ (*fig: in gara, esame etc*) to get through by the skin of one's teeth.

cor'netta *sf* (*MUS*) cornet; (*TEL*) receiver.

cor'netto *sm* (*CUC*) croissant; ~ **acustico** ear trumpet.

cor'nice [kor'nitʃe] *sf* frame; (*fig*) background, setting.

cornici'one [korni'tʃone] *sm* (*di edificio*) ledge; (*ARCHIT*) cornice.

'corno *sm* (*ZOOL*: *pl(f)* ~**a**, *MUS*) horn; (*fam*): **fare le** ~**a a qn** to be unfaithful to sb; **dire peste e** ~**a di qn** to call sb every name under the sun; **un** ~**!** not on your life!

Corno'vaglia [korno'vaʎʎa] *sf*: **la** ~ Cornwall.

cor'nuto, a *ag* (*con corna*) horned; (*fam!*: *marito*) cuckolded ♦ *sm* (*fam!*) cuckold; (: *insulto*) bastard (!).

'coro *sm* chorus; (*REL*) choir.

corol'lario *sm* corollary.

co'rona *sf* crown; (*di fiori*) wreath.

corona'mento *sm* (*di impresa*) completion; (*di carriera*) crowning achievement; **il** ~ **dei propri sogni** the fulfilment of one's dreams.

coro'nare *vt* to crown.

coro'naria *sf* coronary artery.

'corpo *sm* body; (*cadavere*) (dead) body; (*militare, diplomatico*) corps *inv*; (*di opere*) corpus; **prendere** ~ to take shape; **darsi anima e** ~ **a** to give o.s. heart and soul to; **a** ~ **a** ~ hand-to-hand; ~ **d'armata** army corps; ~ **di ballo** corps de ballet; ~ **dei carabinieri** ≈ police force; ~ **celeste** heavenly body; ~ **di guardia** (*soldati*) guard; (*locale*) guardroom; ~ **insegnante** teaching staff; ~ **del reato** material evidence.

corpo'rale *ag* bodily; (*punizione*) corporal.

corpora'tura *sf* build, physique.

corporazi'one [korporat'tsjone] *sf* corporation.

cor'poreo, a *ag* bodily, physical.

cor'poso, a *ag* (*vino*) full-bodied.

corpu'lento, a *ag* stout, corpulent.

corpu'lenza [korpu'lɛntsa] *sf* stoutness, corpulence.

cor'puscolo *sm* corpuscle.

corre'dare *vt*: ~ **di** to provide *o* furnish with; **domanda corredata dai seguenti documenti** application accompanied by the following documents.

cor'redo *sm* equipment; (*di sposa*) trousseau.

cor'reggere [kor'rɛddʒere] *vt* to correct; (*compiti*) to correct, mark.

cor'rente *ag* (*fiume*) flowing; (*acqua del rubinetto*) running; (*moneta, prezzo*) current; (*comune*) everyday ♦ *sm*: **essere al** ~ **(di)** to be well-informed (about) ♦ *sf* (*movimento di liquido*) current, stream; (*spiffero*) draught; (*ELETTR*, *METEOR*) current; (*fig*) trend, tendency; **mettere al ~ (di)** to inform (of); **la vostra lettera del 5 ~ mese** (*in lettere commerciali*) in your letter of the 5th inst.; **articoli di qualità ~** average-quality products; **~ alternata (c.a.)** alternating current (AC); **~ continua (c.c.)** direct current (DC).

corrente'mente *av* (*comunemente*) commonly; **parlare una lingua ~** to speak a language fluently.

corren'tista, i, e *sm/f* (current (*Brit*) o checking (*US*)) account holder.

cor'reo, a *sm/f* (*DIR*) accomplice.

'correre *vi* to run; (*precipitarsi*) to rush; (*partecipare a una gara*) to race, run; (*fig: diffondersi*) to go round ♦ *vt* (*SPORT: gara*) to compete in; (*rischio*) to run; (*pericolo*) to face; **~ dietro a qn** to run after sb; **corre voce che ...** it is rumoured that ....

corresponsabilità *sf* joint responsibility; (*DIR*) joint liability.

corresponsi'one *sf* payment.

cor'ressi *etc vb vedi* **correggere**.

corret'tezza [korret'tettsa] *sf* (*di comportamento*) correctness; (*SPORT*) fair play.

cor'retto, a *pp di* **correggere** ♦ *ag* (*comportamento*) correct, proper; **caffè ~ al cognac** coffee laced with brandy.

corret'tore, 'trice *sm/f:* **~ di bozze** proof-reader ♦ *sm:* (**liquido**) **~ correction** fluid.

correzi'one [korret'tsjone] *sf* correction; marking; **~ di bozze** proofreading.

cor'rida *sf* bullfight.

corri'doio *sm* corridor; **manovre di ~** (*POL*) lobbying *sg*.

corri'dore *sm* (*SPORT*) runner; (*: su veicolo*) racer.

corri'era *sf* coach (*Brit*), bus.

corri'ere *sm* (*diplomatico, di guerra*) courier; (*posta*) mail, post; (*spedizioniere*) carrier.

corri'mano *sm* handrail.

corrispet'tivo *sm* amount due; **versare a qn il ~ di una prestazione** to pay sb the amount due for his (o her) services.

corrispon'dente *ag* corresponding ♦ *sm/f* correspondent.

corrispon'denza [korrispon'dɛntsa] *sf* correspondence; **~ in arrivo/partenza** incoming/outgoing mail.

corris'pondere *vi* (*equivalere*): **~ (a)** to correspond (to); (*per lettera*): **~ con** to correspond with ♦ *vt* (*stipendio*) to pay; (*fig: amore*) to return.

corris'posto, a *pp di* **corrispondere**.

corrobo'rare *vt* to strengthen, fortify; (*fig*) to corroborate, bear out.

cor'rodere *vt*, **~rsi** *vr* to corrode.

cor'rompere *vt* to corrupt; (*comprare*) to

bribe.

corrosi'one *sf* corrosion.

corro'sivo, a *ag* corrosive.

cor'roso, a *pp di* **corrodere**.

cor'rotto, a *pp di* **corrompere** ♦ *ag* corrupt.

corrucci'arsi [korrut'tʃarsi] *vr* to grow angry o vexed.

corru'gare *vt* to wrinkle; **~ la fronte** to knit one's brows.

cor'ruppi *etc vb vedi* **corrompere**.

corrut'tela *sf* corruption, depravity.

corruzi'one [korrut'tsjone] *sf* corruption; bribery; **~ di minorenne** (*DIR*) corruption of a minor.

'corsa *sf* running *q*; (*gara*) race; (*di autobus, taxi*) journey, trip; **fare una ~** to run, dash; (*SPORT*) to run a race; **andare o essere di ~** to be in a hurry; **~ ad ostacoli** (*IPPICA*) steeplechase; (*ATLETICA*) hurdles race.

cor'saro, a *ag:* **nave ~a** privateer ♦ *sm* privateer.

'corsi *etc vb vedi* **correre**.

cor'sia *sf* (*AUT, SPORT*) lane; (*di ospedale*) ward; **~ preferenziale** ≈ bus lane; **~ di sorpasso** (*AUT*) overtaking lane.

'Corsica *sf:* **la ~** Corsica.

cor'sivo *sm* cursive (writing); (*TIP*) italics *pl*.

'corso, a *pp di* **correre** ♦ *ag*, *sm/f* Corsican ♦ *sm* course; (*strada cittadina*) main street; (*di unità monetaria*) circulation; (*di titoli, valori*) rate, price; **dar libero ~ a** to give free expression to; **in ~** in progress, under way; (*annata*) current; **~ d'acqua** river; stream; (*artificiale*) waterway; **~ serale** evening class; **aver ~ legale** to be legal tender.

'corte *sf* (court)yard; (*DIR, regale*) court; **fare la ~ a qn** to court sb; **~ d'appello** court of appeal; **~ di cassazione** final court of appeal; **C~ dei Conti** *State audit court;* **C~ Costituzionale** *special court dealing with constitutional and ministerial matters;* **~ marziale** court-martial.

cor'teccia, ce [kor'tettʃa] *sf* bark.

corteggia'mento [korteddʒa'mento] *sm* courtship.

corteggi'are [korted'dʒare] *vt* to court.

corteggia'tore [korteddʒa'tore] *sm* suitor.

cor'teo *sm* procession; **~ funebre** funeral cortège.

cor'tese *ag* courteous.

corte'sia *sf* courtesy; **fare una ~ a qn** to do sb a favour; **per ~, dov'è ...?** excuse me, please, where is ...?

cortigi'ano, a [korti'dʒano] *sm/f* courtier ♦ *sf* courtesan.

cor'tile *sm* (court)yard.

cor'tina *sf* curtain; (*anche fig*) screen.

corti'sone *sm* cortisone.

'corto, a *ag* short ♦ *av:* **tagliare ~** to come

straight to the point; **essere a ~ di qc** to be short of sth; **essere a ~ di parole** to be at a loss for words; **la settimana ~a** the 5-day week; **~ circuito** short-circuit.

cortocir'cuito |kortotʃir'kuito| *sm* = **corto circuito**.

cortome'traggio |kortome'traddʒo| *sm* short (feature film).

cor'vino, a *ag* (*capelli*) jet-black.

'corvo *sm* raven.

'cosa *sf* thing; (*faccenda*) affair, matter, business *q*; **(che) ~?** what?; **(che) cos'è?** what is it?; **a ~ pensi?** what are you thinking about?; **tante belle ~e!** all the best!; **ormai è ~ fatta!** (*positivo*) it's in the bag!; (*negativo*) it's done now!; **a ~e fatte** when it's all over.

'cosca, sche *sf* (*di mafiosi*) clan.

'coscia, sce |'kɔʃʃa| *sf* thigh; **~ di pollo** (*CUC*) chicken leg.

cosci'ente |koʃ'ʃɛnte| *ag* conscious; **~ di** conscious *o* aware of.

cosci'enza |koʃ'ʃɛntsa| *sf* conscience; (*consapevolezza*) consciousness; **~ politica** political awareness.

coscienzi'oso, a |koʃʃɛn'tsjoso| *ag* conscientious.

cosci'otto |koʃ'ʃɔtto| *sm* (*CUC*) leg.

cos'critto *sm* (*MIL*) conscript.

coscrizi'one |koskrit'tsjone| *sf* conscription.

così *av* so; (*in questo modo*) like this, like that ♦ *ag inv* (*tale*): **non ho mai visto un film ~** I've never seen such a film ♦ *cong* (*perciò*) so, therefore; **~ lontano** so far away; **un ragazzo ~ intelligente** such an intelligent boy; **~ ... come** as ... as; **non è ~ bravo come te** he's not as good as you; **come stai? — ~ ~** how are you? — so-so; **non ho detto ~** I didn't say that; **e ~ via** and so on; **per ~ dire** so to speak.

cosicché |kosik'ke| *cong* so (that).

cosid'detto, a *ag* so-called.

cos'mesi *sf* (*scienza*) cosmetics *sg*; (*prodotti*) cosmetics *pl*; (*trattamento*) beauty treatment.

cos'metico, a, ci, che *ag, sm* cosmetic.

'cosmico, a, ci, che *ag* cosmic.

'cosmo *sm* cosmos.

cosmo'nauta, i, e *sm/f* cosmonaut.

cosmopo'lita, i, e *ag* cosmopolitan.

'coso *sm* (*fam: oggetto*) thing, thingumajig; (: *aggeggio*) contraption; (: *persona*) what's his name, thingumajig.

cos'pargere |kos'pardʒere| *vt*: **~ di** to sprinkle with.

cos'parso, a *pp di* **cospargere**.

cos'petto *sm*: **al ~ di** in front of; in the presence of.

cospicuità *sf* vast quantity.

cos'picuo, a *ag* considerable, large.

cospi'rare *vi* to conspire.

cospira'tore, 'trice *sm/f* conspirator.

cospirazi'one |kospirat'tsjone| *sf* conspiracy.

'cossi *etc vb vedi* **cuocere**.

Cost. *abbr* = **costituzione**.

'costa *sf* (*tra terra e mare*) coast(line); (*litorale*) shore; (*pendio*) slope; (*ANAT*) rib; **navigare sotto ~** to hug the coast; **la C~ Azzurra** the French Riviera; **la C~ d'Avorio** the Ivory Coast; **velluto a ~e** corduroy.

costà *av* there.

cos'tante *ag* constant; (*persona*) steadfast ♦ *sf* constant.

cos'tanza |kos'tantsa| *sf* (*gen*) constancy; (*fermezza*) constancy, steadfastness; **il Lago di C~** Lake Constance.

cos'tare *vi, vt* to cost; **~ caro** to be expensive, cost a lot; **~ un occhio della testa** to cost a fortune; **costi quel che costi** no matter what.

'Costa 'Rica *sf*: **la ~** Costa Rica.

cos'tata *sf* (*CUC*: *di manzo*) large chop.

cos'tato *sm* (*ANAT*) ribs *pl*.

costeggi'are |kosted'dʒare| *vt* to be close to; to run alongside.

cos'tei *pronome vedi* **costui**.

costellazi'one |kostellat'tsjone| *sf* constellation.

coster'nare *vt* to dismay.

coster'nato, a *ag* dismayed.

costernazi'one |kosternat'tsjone| *sf* dismay, consternation.

costi'ero, a *ag* coastal, coast *cpd* ♦ *sf* stretch of coast.

costi'pato, a *ag* (*stitico*) constipated.

costitu'ire *vt* (*comitato, gruppo*) to set up, form; (*collezione*) to put together, build up; (*sog: elementi, parti: comporre*) to make up, constitute; (*rappresentare*) to constitute; (*DIR*) to appoint; **~rsi** *vr*: **~rsi (alla polizia)** to give o.s. up (to the police); **~rsi parte civile** (*DIR*) to associate in an action with the public prosecutor for damages; **il fatto non costituisce reato** this is not a crime.

costitu'tivo, a *ag* constituent, component; **atto ~** (*DIR: di società*) memorandum of association.

costituzio'nale |kostituttsjo'nale| *ag* constitutional.

costituzi'one |kostitut'tsjone| *sf* setting up; building up; constitution.

'costo *sm* cost; **sotto ~** for less than cost price; **a ogni *o* qualunque ~, a tutti i ~i** at all costs; **~i di esercizio** running costs; **~i fissi** fixed costs; **~i di gestione** operating costs; **~i di produzione** production costs.

'costola *sf* (*ANAT*) rib; **ha la polizia alle ~e** the police are hard on his heels.

costo'letta *sf* (*CUC*) cutlet.

cos'toro *pronome pl vedi* **costui**.

cos'toso, a *ag* expensive, costly.

cos'tretto, a *pp di* **costringere**.

cos'tringere [kos'trindʒere] *vt:* ~ **qn a fare qc** to force sb to do sth.

costrit'tivo, a *ag* coercive.

costrizi'one [kostrit'tsjone] *sf* coercion.

costru'ire *vt* to construct, build.

costrut'tivo, a *ag* (*EDIL*) building *cpd;* (*fig*) constructive.

costruzi'one [kostrut'tsjone] *sf* construction, building; **di** ~ **inglese** British-made.

cos'tui, cos'tei, *pl* **cos'toro** *pronome* (*soggetto*) he/she; *pl* they; (*complemento*) him/her; *pl* them; **si può sapere chi è** ~? (*peg*) just who is that fellow?

cos'tume *sm* (*uso*) custom; (*foggia di vestire, indumento*) costume; **il buon** ~ public morality; **donna di facili** ~**i** woman of easy morals; ~ **da bagno** bathing *o* swimming costume (*Brit*), swimsuit; (*da uomo*) bathing *o* swimming trunks *pl.*

costu'mista, i, e *sm/f* costume maker, costume designer.

co'tenna *sf* bacon rind.

co'togna [ko'toɲɲa] *sf* quince.

coto'letta *sf* (*di maiale, montone*) chop; (*di vitello, agnello*) cutlet.

coto'nare *vt* (*capelli*) to backcomb.

co'tone *sm* cotton; ~ **idrofilo** cotton wool (*Brit*), absorbent cotton (*US*).

cotoni'ficio [kotoni'fitʃo] *sm* cotton mill.

'cotta *sf* (*REL*) surplice; (*fam: innamoramento*) crush.

'cottimo *sm:* **lavorare a** ~ to do piecework.

'cotto, a *pp di* **cuocere** ♦ *ag* cooked; (*fam: innamorato*) head-over-heels in love ♦ *sm* brickwork; ~ **a puntino** cooked to perfection; **dirne di** ~**e e di crude a qn** to call sb every name under the sun; **farne di** ~**e e di crude** to get up to all kinds of mischief; **mattone di** ~ fired brick; **pavimento in** ~ tile floor.

cot'tura *sf* cooking; (*in forno*) baking; (*in umido*) stewing; ~ **a fuoco lento** simmering; **angolo** (**di**) ~ cooking area.

co'vare *vt* to hatch; (*fig: malattia*) to be sickening for; (*: odio, rancore*) to nurse ♦ *vi* (*fuoco, fig*) to smoulder (*Brit*), smolder (*US*).

co'vata *sf* (*anche fig*) brood.

'covo *sm* den; ~ **di terroristi** terrorist base.

co'vone *sm* sheaf.

'cozza ['kɔttsa] *sf* mussel.

coz'zare [kot'tsare] *vi:* ~ **contro** to bang into, collide with.

'cozzo ['kɔttso] *sm* collision.

C.P. *abbr* (= *cartolina postale*) pc; (*POSTA*) *vedi* **casella postale**; (*NAUT*) = **capitaneria (di porto)**; (*DIR*) = **codice penale**.

Cra'covia *sf* Cracow.

'crampo *sm* cramp.

'cranio *sm* skull.

cra'tere *sm* crater.

cra'vatta *sf* tie; ~ **a farfalla** bow tie.

cravat'tino *sm* bow tie.

cre'anza [kre'antsa] *sf* manners *pl;* **per buona** ~ out of politeness.

cre'are *vt* to create.

creatività *sf* creativity.

cre'ato *sm* creation.

crea'tore, 'trice *ag* creative ♦ *sm/f* creator; **un** ~ **di alta moda** fashion designer; **andare al C**~ to go to meet one's maker.

crea'tura *sf* creature; (*bimbo*) baby, infant.

creazi'one [kreat'tsjone] *sf* creation; (*fondazione*) foundation, establishment.

'crebbi *etc vb vedi* **crescere**.

cre'dente *sm/f* (*REL*) believer.

cre'denza [kre'dɛntsa] *sf* belief; (*armadio*) sideboard.

credenzi'ali [kreden'tsjali] *sfpl* credentials.

'credere *vt* to believe ♦ *vi:* ~ **in,** ~ **a** to believe in; ~ **qn onesto** to believe sb (to be) honest; ~ **che** to believe *o* think that; ~**rsi furbo** to think one is clever; **lo credo bene!** I can well believe it!; **fai quello che credi** *o* **come credi** do as you please.

cre'dibile *ag* credible, believable.

credibilità *sf* credibility.

credi'tizio, a [kredi'tittsjo] *ag* credit.

'credito *sm* (*anche COMM*) credit; (*reputazione*) esteem, repute; **comprare a** ~ to buy on credit; ~ **agevolato** easy credit terms; ~ **d'imposta** tax credit.

credi'tore, 'trice *sm/f* creditor.

'credo *sm inv* creed.

'credulo, a *ag* credulous.

credu'lone, a *sm/f* simpleton, sucker (*fam*).

'crema *sf* cream; (*con uova, zucchero etc*) custard; ~ **idratante** moisturizing cream; ~ **pasticciera** confectioner's custard; ~ **solare** sun cream.

cre'mare *vt* to cremate.

crema'torio *sm* crematorium.

cremazi'one [kremat'tsjone] *sf* cremation.

'cremisi *ag inv, sm inv* crimson.

Crem'lino *sm:* **il** ~ the Kremlin.

cremo'nese *ag of* (*o* from) Cremona.

cre'moso, a *ag* creamy.

'crepa *sf* crack.

cre'paccio [kre'pattʃo] *sm* large crack, fissure; (*di ghiacciaio*) crevasse.

crepacu'ore *sm* broken heart.

crepa'pelle *av:* **ridere a** ~ to split one's sides laughing.

cre'pare *vi* (*fam: morire*) to snuff it (*Brit*), kick the bucket; ~ **dalle risa** to split one's sides laughing; ~ **dall'invidia** to be green with envy.

crepi'tare *vi* (*fuoco*) to crackle; (*pioggia*) to patter.

crepi'tio, ii *sm* crackling; pattering.

cre'puscolo *sm* twilight, dusk.

cre'scendo [kreʃ'ʃɛndo] *sm* (*MUS*) crescendo.

cre'scente [kreʃ'ʃɛnte] *ag* (*gen*) growing, increasing; (*luna*) waxing.

'crescere ['kreʃʃere] *vi* to grow ♦ *vt* (*figli*) to raise.

cre'scione [kreʃ'ʃone] *sm* watercress.

'crescita ['kreʃʃita] *sf* growth.

cresci'uto, a [kreʃ'ʃuto] *pp di* **crescere**.

'cresima *sf* (*REL*) confirmation.

cresi'mare *vt* to confirm.

'crespo, a *ag* (*capelli*) frizzy; (*tessuto*) puckered ♦ *sm* crêpe.

'cresta *sf* crest; (*di polli, uccelli*) crest, comb; **alzare la ~** (*fig*) to become cocky; **abbassare la ~** (*fig*) to climb down; **essere sulla ~ dell'onda** (*fig*) to be riding high.

'Creta *sf* Crete.

'creta *sf* (*gesso*) chalk; (*argilla*) clay.

cre'tese *ag, sm/f* Cretan.

creti'nata *sf* (*fam*): **dire/fare una ~** to say/do a stupid thing.

cre'tino, a *ag* stupid ♦ *sm/f* idiot, fool.

CRI *sigla f* = *Croce Rossa Italiana.*

cric *sm inv* (*TECN*) jack.

'cricca, che *sf* clique.

'cricco, chi *sm* = **cric.**

cri'ceto [kri'tʃeto] *sm* hamster.

crimi'nale *ag, sm/f* criminal.

'Criminalpol. *abbr* = **polizia criminale.**

'crimine *sm* (*DIR*) crime.

criminolo'gia [kriminolo'dʒia] *sf* criminology.

crimi'noso, a *ag* criminal.

cri'nale *sm* ridge.

'crine *sm* horsehair.

crini'era *sf* mane.

'cripta *sf* crypt.

crisan'temo *sm* chrysanthemum.

'crisi *sf inv* crisis; (*MED*) attack, fit; **essere in ~** (*partito, impresa etc*) to be in a state of crisis; **~ energetica** energy crisis; **~ di nervi** attack *o* fit of nerves.

cristalle'ria *sf* (*fabbrica*) crystal glassworks *sg*; (*oggetti*) crystalware.

cristal'lino, a *ag* (*MINERALOGIA*) crystalline; (*fig: suono, acque*) crystal clear ♦ *sm* (*ANAT*) crystalline lens.

cristalliz'zare [kristallid'dzare] *vi*, **~rsi** *vr* to crystallize; (*fig*) to become fossilized.

cris'tallo *sm* crystal.

cristia'nesimo *sm* Christianity.

cristianità *sf* Christianity; (*i cristiani*) Christendom.

cristi'ano, a *ag, sm/f* Christian; **un povero ~** (*fig*) a poor soul *o* beggar; **comportarsi da ~** (*fig*) to behave in a civilized manner.

'cristo *sm*: **C~** Christ; **(un) povero ~** (a) poor beggar.

cri'terio *sm* criterion; (*buon senso*) (common) sense.

'critica, che *sf vedi* **critico.**

criti'care *vt* to criticize.

'critico, a, ci, che *ag* critical ♦ *sm* critic ♦ *sf* criticism; **la ~a** (*attività*) criticism; (*persone*) the critics *pl*.

criti'cone, a *sm/f* faultfinder.

crivel'lare *vt*: **~ (di)** to riddle (with).

cri'vello *sm* riddle.

croc'cante *ag* crisp, crunchy ♦ *sm* (*CUC*) almond crunch.

'crocchia ['krɔkkja] *sf* chignon, bun.

'crocchio ['krɔkkjo] *sm* (*di persone*) small group, cluster.

'croce ['krotʃe] *sf* cross; **in ~** (*di traverso*) crosswise; (*fig*) on tenterhooks; **mettere in ~** (*anche fig: criticare*) to crucify; (: *tormentare*) to nag to death; **la C~ Rossa** the Red Cross; **~ uncinata** swastika.

croce'figgere *etc* [krotʃe'fiddʒere] = **crocifiggere** *etc*.

croceros'sina [krotʃeros'sina] *sf* Red Cross nurse.

croce'via [krotʃe'via] *sm inv* crossroads *sg*.

croci'ato, a [kro'tʃato] *ag* cross-shaped ♦ *sm* (*anche fig*) crusader ♦ *sf* crusade.

cro'cicchio [kro'tʃikkjo] *sm* crossroads *sg*.

croci'era [kro'tʃera] *sf* (*viaggio*) cruise; (*ARCHIT*) transept; **altezza di ~** (*AER*) cruising height; **velocità di ~** (*AER, NAUT*) cruising speed.

croci'figgere [krotʃi'fiddʒere] *vt* to crucify.

crocifissi'one [krotʃifis'sjone] *sf* crucifixion.

croci'fisso, a [krotʃi'fisso] *pp di* **crocifiggere** ♦ *sm* crucifix.

crogio'larsi [krodʒo'larsi] *vr*: **~ al sole** to bask in the sun.

crogi'olo [kro'dʒɔlo] *sm* crucible; (*fig*) melting pot.

crol'lare *vi* to collapse.

'crollo *sm* collapse; (*di prezzi*) slump, sudden fall.

'croma *sf* (*MUS*) quaver (*Brit*), eighth note (*US*).

cro'mato, a *ag* chromium-plated.

'cromo *sm* chrome, chromium.

cromo'soma, i *sm* chromosome.

'cronaca, che *sf* chronicle; (*STAMPA*) news *sg*; (: *rubrica*) column; (*TV, RADIO*) commentary; **fatto *o* episodio di ~** news item; **~ nera** crime news *sg*; crime column.

'cronico, a, ci, che *ag* chronic.

cro'nista, i *sm* (*STAMPA*) reporter, columnist.

cronis'toria *sf* chronicle; (*fig: ironico*) blow-by-blow account.

cronolo'gia [kronolo'dʒia] *sf* chronology.

cronome'trare *vt* to time.

cro'nometro *sm* chronometer; (*a scatto*) stopwatch.

'crosta *sf* crust; (*MED*) scab; (*ZOOL*) shell; (*di ghiaccio*) layer; (*fig peg: quadro*) daub.

cros'tacei [kros'tatʃei] *smpl* shellfish.

cros'tata *sf* (*CUC*) tart.

cros'tino *sm* (*CUC*) croûton; (: *da antipasto*) canapé.

crucci'are [krut'tʃare] *vt* to torment, worry; **~rsi** *vr*: **~rsi per** to torment o.s. over.

'**cruccio** ['kruttʃo] *sm* worry, torment.
cruci'ale [kru'tʃale] *ag* crucial.
cruci'verba [krutʃi'vɛrba] *sm inv* crossword (puzzle).
cru'dele *ag* cruel.
crudeltà *sf* cruelty.
'**crudo, a** *ag* (*non cotto*) raw; (*aspro*) harsh, severe.
cru'ento, a *ag* bloody.
cru'miro *sm* (*peg*) blackleg (*Brit*), scab.
'**cruna** *sf* eye (of a needle).
'**crusca** *sf* bran.
crus'cotto *sm* (*AUT*) dashboard.
CS *sigla* = Cosenza.
C.S. *sigla* (*MIL*) = *comando supremo*; (*AUT*) = **codice della strada.**
c.s. *abbr* = *come sopra*.
CT *sigla* = Catania.
c.t. *abbr* = **commissario tecnico.**
'**Cuba** *sf* Cuba.
cu'bano, a *ag*, *sm/f* Cuban.
cu'betto *sm* (small) cube; ~ **di ghiaccio** ice cube.
'**cubico, a, ci, che** *ag* cubic.
'**cubo, a** *ag* cubic ♦ *sm* cube; **elevare al** ~ (*MAT*) to cube.
cuc'cagna [kuk'kaɲɲa] *sf*: **paese della** ~ land of plenty; **albero della** ~ greasy pole (*fig*).
cuc'cetta [kut'tʃetta] *sf* (*FERR*) couchette; (*NAUT*) berth.
cucchiai'ata [kukkja'jata] *sf* spoonful; tablespoonful.
cucchia'ino [kukkja'ino] *sm* teaspoon; coffee spoon.
cucchi'aio [kuk'kjajo] *sm* spoon; (*da tavola*) tablespoon; (*cucchiaiata*) spoonful; tablespoonful.
'**cuccia, ce** ['kuttʃa] *sf* dog's bed; **a** ~**!** down!
cuccio'lata [kuttʃo'lata] *sf* litter.
'**cucciolo** ['kuttʃolo] *sm* cub; (*di cane*) puppy.
cu'cina [ku'tʃina] *sf* (*locale*) kitchen; (*arte culinaria*) cooking, cookery; (*le vivande*) food, cooking; (*apparecchio*) cooker; **di** ~ (*libro, lezione*) cookery *cpd*; ~ **componibile** fitted kitchen; ~ **economica** kitchen range.
cuci'nare [kutʃi'nare] *vt* to cook.
cuci'nino [kutʃi'nino] *sm* kitchenette.
cu'cire [ku'tʃire] *vt* to sew, stitch; ~ **la bocca a qn** (*fig*) to shut sb up.
cu'cito, a [ku'tʃito] *sm* sewing; (*INS*) sewing, needlework.
cuci'trice [kutʃi'tritʃe] *sf* (*TIP*: *per libri*) stitching machine; (*per fogli*) stapler.
cuci'tura [kutʃi'tura] *sf* sewing, stitching; (*costura*) seam.
cucù *sm inv*, **cu'culo** *sm* cuckoo.
'**cuffia** *sf* bonnet, cap; (*da infermiera*) cap; (*da bagno*) (bathing) cap; (*per ascoltare*) headphones *pl*, headset.

cu'gino, a [ku'dʒino] *sm/f* cousin.
'**cui** *pronome* (*nei complementi indiretti*): **la persona a** ~ **accennava** the person you were referring to *o* to whom you referred; **il libro di** ~ **parlavo** the book I was talking about *o* about which I was talking; **il quartiere in** ~ **abito** the district where I live; (*inserito tra l'articolo e il sostantivo*) whose; **il** ~ **nome** whose name; **la** ~ **madre** whose mother; **per** ~ (*perciò*) therefore, so.
culi'naria *sf* cookery.
'**culla** *sf* cradle.
cul'lare *vt* to rock; (*fig*: *idea, speranza*) to cherish; ~**rsi** *vr* (*gen*) to sway; ~**rsi in vane speranze** (*fig*) to cherish fond hopes; ~**rsi nel dolce far niente** (*fig*) to sit back and relax.
culmi'nante *ag*: **posizione** ~ (*ASTR*) highest point; **punto** *o* **momento** ~ (*fig*) climax.
culmi'nare *vi*: ~ **in** *o* **con** to culminate in.
'**culmine** *sm* top, summit.
'**culo** *sm* (*fam!*) arse (*Brit!*), ass (*US!*); (: *fig*: *fortuna*): **aver** ~ to have the luck of the devil; **prendere qn per il** ~ to take the piss out of sb (*!*).
'**culto** *sm* (*religione*) religion; (*adorazione*) worship, adoration; (*venerazione*: *anche fig*) cult.
cul'tura *sf* (*gen*) culture; (*conoscenza*) education, learning; **di** ~ (*persona*) cultured; (*istituto*) cultural, of culture; ~ **generale** general knowledge; ~ **di massa** mass culture.
cultu'rale *ag* cultural.
cultu'rismo *sm* body-building.
cumu'lare *vt* to accumulate, amass.
cumula'tivo, a *ag* cumulative; (*prezzo*) inclusive; (*biglietto*) group *cpd*.
'**cumulo** *sm* (*mucchio*) pile, heap; (*METEOR*) cumulus; ~ **dei redditi** (*FISCO*) combined incomes; ~ **delle pene** (*DIR*) consecutive sentences.
'**cuneo** *sm* wedge.
cu'netta *sf* (*di strada etc*) bump; (*scolo*: *nelle strade di città*) gutter; (: *di campagna*) ditch.
cu'nicolo *sm* (*galleria*) tunnel; (*di miniera*) pit, shaft; (*di talpa*) hole.
cu'oca *sf vedi* **cuoco.**
cu'ocere ['kwɔtʃere] *vt* (*alimenti*) to cook; (*mattoni etc*) to fire ♦ *vi* to cook; ~ **in umido/a vapore/in padella** to stew/steam/fry; ~ **al forno** (*pane*) to bake; (*arrosto*) to roast.
cu'oco, a, chi, che *sm/f* cook; (*di ristorante*) chef.
cuoi'ame *sm* leather goods *pl*.
cu'oio *sm* leather; ~ **capelluto** scalp; **tirare le** ~**a** (*fam*) to kick the bucket.
cu'ore *sm* heart; ~**i** *smpl* (*CARTE*) hearts; **avere buon** ~ to be kind-hearted; **stare a**

~ **a qn** to be important to sb; **un grazie di** ~ heartfelt thanks; **ringraziare di** ~ to thank sincerely; **nel profondo del** ~ in one's heart of hearts; **avere la morte nel** ~ to be sick at heart.

cupi'digia [kupi'didʒa] *sf* greed, covetousness.

'**cupo, a** *ag* dark; (*suono*) dull; (*fig*) gloomy, dismal.

'**cupola** *sf* dome; (*più piccola*) cupola.

'**cura** *sf* care; (*MED: trattamento*) (course of) treatment; **aver** ~ **di** (*occuparsi di*) to look after; **a** ~ **di** (*libro*) edited by; **fare una** ~ to follow a course of treatment; ~ **dimagrante** diet.

cu'rabile *ag* curable.

cu'rante *ag:* **medico** ~ doctor (in charge of a patient).

cu'rare *vt* (*malato, malattia*) to treat; (: *guarire*) to cure; (*aver cura di*) to take care of; (*testo*) to edit; ~**rsi** *vr* to take care of o.s.; (*MED*) to follow a course of treatment; ~**rsi di** to pay attention to; (*occuparsi di*) to look after.

cu'rato *sm* parish priest; (*protestante*) vicar, minister.

cura'tore, 'trice *sm/f* (*DIR*) trustee; (*di antologia etc*) editor; ~ **fallimentare** (official) receiver.

'**curia** *sf* (*REL*): **la** ~ **romana** the Roman curia; ~ **notarile** notaries' association *o* guild.

curio'saggine [kurjo'saddʒine] *sf* nosiness.

curio'sare *vi* to look round, wander round; (*tra libri*) to browse; ~ **nei negozi** to look *o* wander round the shops; ~ **nelle faccende altrui** to poke one's nose into other people's affairs.

curiosità *sf inv* curiosity; (*cosa rara*) curio, curiosity.

curi'oso, a *ag* (*che vuol sapere*) curious, inquiring; (*ficcanaso*) curious, inquisitive; (*bizzarro*) strange, curious ♦ *sm/f* busybody, nosy parker; **essere** ~ **di** to be curious about; **una folla di** ~**i** a crowd of onlookers.

cur'riculum *sm inv:* ~ **(vitae)** curriculum vitae.

cur'sore *sm* (*INFORM*) cursor.

'**curva** *sf* curve; (*stradale*) bend, curve.

cur'vare *vt* to bend ♦ *vi* (*veicolo*) to take a bend; (*strada*) to bend, curve; ~**rsi** *vr* to bend; (*legno*) to warp.

'**curvo, a** *ag* curved; (*piegato*) bent.

CUS *sigla m = Centro Universitario Sportivo*.

cusci'netto [kuʃʃi'netto] *sm* pad; (*TECN*) bearing ♦ *ag inv*: **stato** ~ buffer state; ~ **a sfere** ball bearing.

cu'scino [kuʃ'ʃino] *sm* cushion; (*guanciale*) pillow.

'**cuspide** *sf* (*ARCHIT*) spire.

cus'tode *sm/f* (*di museo*) keeper, custodian;

(*di parco*) warden; (*di casa*) concierge; (*di fabbrica, carcere*) guard.

cus'todia *sf* care; (*DIR*) custody; (*astuccio*) case, holder; **avere qc in** ~ to look after sth; **dare qc in** ~ **a qn** to entrust sth to sb's care; **agente di** ~ prison warder; ~ **delle carceri** prison security; ~ **cautelare** (*DIR*) custody.

custo'dire *vt* (*conservare*) to keep; (*assistere*) to look after, take care of; (*fare la guardia*) to guard.

'**cute** *sf* (*ANAT*) skin.

cu'ticola *sf* cuticle.

C.V. *abbr* = **cavallo vapore**.

c.v.d. *abbr* (= *come volevasi dimostrare*) QED (= *quod erat demonstrandum*).

c.vo *abbr* = **corsivo**.

CZ *sigla* = *Catanzaro*.

D

D, d [di] *sf o m inv* (*lettera*) D, d; **D come Domodossola** ≈ D for David (*Brit*), D for Dog (*US*).

D *abbr* (= *destra*) R; (*FERR*) = **diretto**.

da *prep* (*da + il* = **dal**, *da + lo* = **dallo**, *da + l'* = **dall'**, *da + la* = **dalla**, *da + i* = **dai**, *da + gli* = **dagli**, *da + le* = **dalle**) (*agente*) by; (*provenienza*) from; (*causale*) with; (*moto a luogo: riferito a persone*): **vado** ~ **Pietro/dal giornalaio** I'm going to Pietro's (house)/to the newsagent's; (*stato in luogo: riferito a persone*): **sono** ~ **Pietro** I'm at Pietro's (house); (*moto per luogo*) through; (*fuori da*) out of, from; (*tempo*): **vivo qui** ~ **un anno** I have been living here for a year; **è dalle 3 che ti aspetto** I've been waiting for you since 3 (o'clock); ~ **bambino piangevo molto** I cried a lot as a *o* when I was a child; **qualcosa** ~ **bere/mangiare** something to drink/eat; **comportarsi** ~ **bambino** to behave like a child; **una ragazza dai capelli biondi** a girl with blonde hair; **un vestito** ~ **100.000 lire** a 100,000 lire dress; **è una cosa** ~ **poco** it's nothing special; ~ **... a** from ... to; ~ **oggi in poi** from today onwards; **d'ora in poi** *o* **in avanti** from now on; **l'ho fatto** ~ **me** I did it myself; **non è** ~ **lui** it's not like him; **macchina** ~ **corsa** racing car.

dà *vb vedi* **dare**.

dab'bene *ag inv* honest, decent.

'**Dacca** *sf* Dacca.

dac'capo, da 'capo *av* (*di nuovo*) (once) again; (*dal principio*) all over again, from

the beginning.
dacché |dak'ke| *cong* since.
'dado *sm* (*da gioco*) dice *o* die (*pl* dice); (*CUC*) stock cube (*Brit*), bouillon cube (*US*); (*TECN*) (screw) nut; ~i *smpl* (game of) dice.
daf'fare, da 'fare *sm* work, toil; **avere un gran** ~ to be very busy.
'dagli |'daʎʎi|, **'dai** *prep* + *det vedi* **da**.
'daino *sm* (fallow) deer *inv*; (*pelle*) buckskin.
Da'kar *sf* Dakar.
dal *prep* + *det vedi* **da**.
dal. *abbr* (= *decalitro*) dal.
dall', 'dalla, 'dalle, 'dallo *prep* + *det vedi* **da**.
dal'tonico, a, ci, che *ag* colour-blind (*Brit*), colorblind (*US*).
dam. *abbr* (= *decametro*) dam.
'dama *sf* lady; (*nei balli*) partner; (*gioco*) draughts *sg* (*Brit*), checkers *sg* (*US*); **far** ~ (*nel gioco*) to make a crown; ~ **di compagnia** lady's companion; ~ **di corte** lady-in-waiting.
Da'masco *sf* Damascus.
dami'gella |dami'dʒella| *sf* (*STORIA*) damsel; (: *titolo*) mistress; ~ **d'onore** (*di sposa*) bridesmaid.
damigi'ana |dami'dʒana| *sf* demijohn.
dam'meno *ag inv*: **per non essere** ~ **di qn** so as not to be outdone by sb.
DAMS *sigla m* (= *Disciplina delle Arti, della Musica, dello Spettacolo*) *study of the performing arts*.
da'naro *sm* = **denaro**.
dana'roso, a *ag* wealthy.
da'nese *ag* Danish ♦ *sm/f* Dane ♦ *sm* (*LING*) Danish.
Dani'marca *sf*: **la** ~ Denmark.
dan'nare *vt* (*REL*) to damn; ~**rsi** *vr*: ~**rsi** (**per**) (*fig: tormentarsi*) to be worried to death (by); **far** ~ **qn** to drive sb mad; ~**rsi l'anima per qc** (*affannarsi*) to work o.s. to death for sth; (*tormentarsi*) to worry o.s. to death over sth.
dan'nato, a *ag* damned.
dannazi'one |dannat'tsjone| *sf* damnation.
danneggi'are |danned'dʒare| *vt* to damage; (*rovinare*) to spoil; (*nuocere*) to harm; **la parte danneggiata** (*DIR*) the injured party.
'danno *vb vedi* **dare** ♦ *sm* damage; (*a persona*) harm, injury; ~**i** *smpl* (*DIR*) damages; **a** ~ **di qn** to sb's detriment; **chiedere/risarcire i** ~**i** to sue for/pay damages.
dan'noso, a *ag*: ~ (**a** *o* **per**) harmful (to), bad (for).
dan'tesco, a schi, sche *ag* Dantesque; **l'opera** ~**a** Dante's work.
Da'nubio *sm*: **il** ~ the Danube.
'danza |'dantsa| *sf*: **la** ~ dancing; **una** ~ a dance.
dan'zante |dan'tsante| *ag* dancing; **serata** ~ dance.
dan'zare |dan'tsare| *vt, vi* to dance.
danza'tore, 'trice |dantsa'tore| *sm/f* dancer.
dapper'tutto *av* everywhere.
dap'poco *ag inv* inept; worthless.
dap'prima *av* at first.
Darda'nelli *smpl*: **i** ~ the Dardanelles.
'dardo *sm* dart.
'dare *sm* (*COMM*) debit ♦ *vt* to give; (*produrre: frutti, suono*) to produce ♦ *vi* (*guardare*): ~ **su** to look (out) onto; ~**rsi** *vr*: ~**rsi a** to dedicate o.s. to; **quanti anni mi dai?** how old do you think I am?; **danno ancora quel film?** is that film still showing?; ~ **da mangiare a qn** to give sb something to eat; ~ **per certo qc** to consider sth certain; ~ **ad intendere a qn che** ... to lead sb to believe that ...; ~ **per morto qn** to give sb up for dead; ~ **qc per scontato** to take sth for granted; ~**rsi ammalato** to report sick; ~**rsi alla bella vita** to have a good time; ~**rsi al bere** to take to drink; ~**rsi al commercio** to go into business; ~**rsi da fare per fare qc** to go to a lot of bother to do sth; ~**rsi per vinto** to give in; **può** ~**rsi** maybe, perhaps; **si dà il caso che** ... it so happens that ...; **darsela a gambe** to take to one's heels; **il** ~ **e l'avere** (*ECON*) debits and credits *pl*.
Dar-es-Sa'laam *sf* Dar-es-Salaam.
'darsena *sf* dock.
'data *sf* date; **in** ~ **da destinarsi** on a date still to be announced; **in** ~ **odierna** as of today; **amicizia di lunga** *o* **vecchia** ~ longstanding friendship; ~ **di emissione** date of issue; ~ **di nascita** date of birth; ~ **di scadenza** expiry date.
da'tare *vt* to date ♦ *vi*: ~ **da** to date from.
da'tato, a *ag* dated.
'dato, a *ag* (*stabilito*) given ♦ *sm* datum; ~**i** *smpl* data *pl*; ~ **che** given that; **in** ~**i casi** in certain cases; **è un** ~ **di fatto** it's a fact.
da'tore, 'trice *sm/f*: ~ **di lavoro** employer.
'dattero *sm* date (*BOT*).
dattilogra'fare *vt* to type.
dattilogra'fia *sf* typing.
datti'lografo, a *sm/f* typist.
dattilos'critto *sm* typescript.
da'vanti *av* in front; (*dirimpetto*) opposite ♦ *ag inv* front ♦ *sm* front; ~ **a** *prep* in front of; (*dirimpetto a*) facing, opposite; (*in presenza di*) before, in front of.
davan'zale |davan'tsale| *sm* windowsill.
da'vanzo, d'a'vanzo |da'vantso| *av* more than enough.
dav'vero *av* really, indeed; **dico** ~ I mean it.
dazi'ario, a |dat'tsjarjo| *ag* excise *cpd*.
'dazio |'dattsjo| *sm* (*somma*) duty; (*luogo*) customs *pl*; ~ **d'importazione** import duty.
db *abbr* (= *decibel*) dB.

DC *sigla f* = **Democrazia Cristiana**.
d.C. *av abbr* (= *dopo Cristo*) A.D.
DD *abbr* (*FERR*) = **direttissimo**.
D.D.T. *abbr m* (= *dicloro-difenil-tricloroetano*) D.D.T.
'dea *sf* goddess.
'debbo *etc vb vedi* **dovere**.
debel'lare *vt* to overcome, conquer.
debili'tare *vt* to debilitate.
debita'mente *av* duly, properly.
'debito, a *ag* due, proper ♦ *sm* debt; (*COMM: dare*) debit; **a tempo** ~ at the right time; **portare a** ~ **di qn** to debit sb with; ~ **consolidato** consolidated debt; ~ **d'imposta** tax liability; ~ **pubblico** national debt.
debi'tore, 'trice *sm/f* debtor.
'debole *ag* weak, feeble; (*suono*) faint; (*luce*) dim ♦ *sm* weakness.
debo'lezza [debo'lettsa] *sf* weakness.
debut'tante *sm/f* (*gen*) beginner, novice; (*TEATRO*) actor/actress at the beginning of his (*o* her) career.
debut'tare *vi* to make one's début.
de'butto *sm* début.
'decade *sf* period of ten days.
deca'dente *ag* decadent.
deca'denza [deka'dentsa] *sf* decline; (*DIR*) loss, forfeiture.
deca'duto, a *ag* (*persona*) impoverished; (*norma*) lapsed.
decaffei'nato, a *ag* decaffeinated.
de'calogo *sm* (*fig*) rulebook.
de'cano *sm* (*REL*) dean.
decan'tare *vt* (*virtù, bravura etc*) to praise; (*persona*) to sing the praises of.
decapi'tare *vt* to decapitate, behead.
decappot'tabile *ag, sf* convertible.
dece'duto, a [detʃe'duto] *ag* deceased.
decele'rare [detʃele'rare] *vt, vi* to decelerate, slow down.
decen'nale [detʃen'nale] *ag* (*che dura 10 anni*) ten-year *cpd*; (*che ricorre ogni 10 anni*) ten-yearly, every ten years ♦ *sm* (*ricorrenza*) tenth anniversary.
de'cenne [de'tʃɛnne] *ag*: **un bambino** ~ a ten-year-old child, a child of ten.
de'cennio [de'tʃɛnnjo] *sm* decade.
de'cente [de'tʃɛnte] *ag* decent, respectable, proper; (*accettabile*) satisfactory, decent.
decentraliz'zare [detʃentralid'dzare] *vt* (*AMM*) to decentralize.
decentra'mento [detʃentra'mento] *sm* decentralization.
decen'trare [detʃen'trare] *vt* to decentralize, move out of *o* away from the centre.
de'cenza [de'tʃɛntsa] *sf* decency, propriety.
de'cesso [de'tʃɛsso] *sm* death; **atto di** ~ death certificate.
de'cidere [de'tʃidere] *vi* to decide, make up one's mind ♦ *vt*: ~ **qc** to decide on sth; (*questione, lite*) to settle sth; ~**rsi** *vr*: ~**rsi**

(a fare) to decide (to do), make up one's mind (to do); ~ **di fare/che** to decide to do/that; ~ **di qc** (*sog: cosa*) to determine sth.
deci'frare [detʃi'frare] *vt* to decode; (*fig*) to decipher, make out.
de'cilitro [de'tʃilitro] *sm* decilitre (*Brit*), deciliter (*US*).
deci'male [detʃi'male] *ag* decimal.
deci'mare [detʃi'mare] *vt* to decimate.
'decimo, a ['dɛtʃimo] *num* tenth.
de'cina [de'tʃina] *sf* ten; (*circa dieci*): **una** ~ **(di)** about ten.
de'cisi [de'tʃizi] *etc vb vedi* **decidere**.
decisio'nale [detʃizjo'nale] *ag* decision-making *cpd*.
decisi'one [detʃi'zjone] *sf* decision; **prendere una** ~ to make a decision; **con** ~ decisively, resolutely.
deci'sivo, a [detʃi'zivo] *ag* (*gen*) decisive; (*fattore*) deciding.
de'ciso, a [de'tʃizo] *pp di* **decidere** ♦ *ag* (*persona, carattere*) determined; (*tono*) firm, resolute.
declas'sare *vt* to downgrade; to lower in status; **1ª declassata** (*FERR*) *first-class carriage which may be used by second-class passengers*.
decli'nare *vi* (*pendio*) to slope down; (*fig: diminuire*) to decline; (*tramontare*) to set, go down ♦ *vt* to decline; ~ **le proprie generalità** (*fig*) to give one's particulars; ~ **ogni responsabilità** to disclaim all responsibility.
declinazi'one [deklinat'tsjone] *sf* (*LING*) declension.
de'clino *sm* decline.
de'clivio *sm* (*downward*) slope.
decodifi'care *vt* to decode.
decol'lare *vi* (*AER*) to take off.
décolleté [dekol'te] *ag inv* (*abito*) low-necked, low-cut ♦ *sm* (*di abito*) low neckline; (*di donna*) cleavage.
de'collo *sm* take-off.
decolo'rare *vt* to bleach.
decom'porre *vt*, **decomporsi** *vr* to decompose.
decomposizi'one [dekompozit'tsjone] *sf* decomposition.
decom'posto, a *pp di* **decomporre**
decompressi'one *sf* decompression.
deconge'lare [dekondʒe'lare] *vt* to defrost.
decongestio'nare [dekondʒestjo'nare] *vt* (*MED, traffico*) to relieve congestion in.
deco'rare *vt* to decorate.
decora'tivo, a *ag* decorative.
decora'tore, 'trice *sm/f* (interior) decorator.
decorazi'one [dekorat'tsjone] *sf* decoration.
de'coro *sm* decorum.
deco'roso, a *ag* decorous, dignified.
decor'renza [dekor'rɛntsa] *sf*: **con** ~ **da** (as)

from.

de'correre *vi* to pass, elapse; *(avere effetto)* to run, have effect.

de'corso, a *pp di* **decorrere** ♦ *sm (evoluzione: anche* MED*)* course.

de'crebbi *etc vb vedi* **decrescere**.

de'crepito, a *ag* decrepit.

de'crescere [de'kreʃʃere] *vi (diminuire)* to decrease, diminish; *(acque)* to subside, go down; *(prezzi)* to go down.

decresci'uto, a [dekreʃ'ʃuto] *pp di* **decrescere**.

decre'tare *vt (norma)* to decree; *(mobilitazione)* to order; ~ **lo stato d'emergenza** to declare a state of emergency; ~ **la nomina di qn** to decide on the appointment of sb.

de'creto *sm* decree; ~ **legge** *decree with the force of law*; ~ **di sfratto** eviction order.

decur'tare *vt (debito, somma)* to reduce.

decurtazi'one [dekurtat'tsjone] *sf* reduction.

'dedalo *sm* maze, labyrinth.

'dedica, che *sf* dedication.

dedi'care *vt* to dedicate; ~**rsi** *vr:* ~**rsi a** *(votarsi)* to devote o.s. to.

dedicherò *etc* [dedike'rɔ] *vb vedi* **dedicare**.

'dedito, a *ag:* ~ **a** *(studio etc)* dedicated *o* devoted to; *(vizio)* addicted to.

de'dotto, a *pp di* **dedurre**.

de'duco *etc vb vedi* **dedurre**.

de'durre *vt (concludere)* to deduce; *(defalcare)* to deduct.

de'dussi *etc vb vedi* **dedurre**.

deduzi'one [dedut'tsjone] *sf* deduction.

defal'care *vt* to deduct.

defenes'trare *vt* to throw out of the window; *(fig)* to remove from office.

defe'rente *ag* respectful, deferential.

defe'rire *vt (*DIR*):* ~ **a** to refer to.

defezi'one [defet'tsjone] *sf* defection, desertion.

defici'ente [defi'tʃɛnte] *ag (mancante):* ~ **di** deficient in; *(insufficiente)* insufficient ♦ *sm/f* mental defective; *(peg: cretino)* idiot.

defici'enza [defi'tʃɛntsa] *sf* deficiency; *(carenza)* shortage; *(fig: lacuna)* weakness.

'deficit ['dɛfitʃit] *sm inv (*ECON*)* deficit.

defi'nire *vt* to define; *(risolvere)* to settle; *(questione)* to finalize.

defini'tivo, a *ag* definitive, final ♦ *sf:* **in** ~**a** *(dopotutto)* when all is said and done; *(dunque)* well then.

defi'nito, a *ag* definite; **ben** ~ clear, clear cut.

definizi'one [definit'tsjone] *sf (gen)* definition; *(di disputa, vertenza)* settlement; *(di tempi, obiettivi)* establishment.

deflagrazi'one [deflagrat'tsjone] *sf* explosion.

deflazi'one [deflat'tsjone] *sf (*ECON*)* deflation.

deflet'tore *sm (*AUT*)* quarterlight *(Brit)*, deflector *(US)*.

deflu'ire *vi:* ~ **da** *(liquido)* to flow away

from; *(fig: capitali)* to flow out of.

de'flusso *sm (della marea)* ebb.

defor'mare *vt (alterare)* to put out of shape; *(corpo)* to deform; *(pensiero, fatto)* to distort; ~**rsi** *vr* to lose its shape.

deformazi'one [deformat'tsjone] *sf (*MED*)* deformation; **questa è** ~ **professionale!** that's force of habit because of your *(o his etc)* job!

de'forme *ag* deformed; disfigured.

deformità *sf inv* deformity.

defrau'dare *vt:* ~ **qn di qc** to defraud sb of sth, cheat sb out of sth.

de'funto, a *ag* late *cpd* ♦ *sm/f* deceased.

degene'rare [dedʒene'rare] *vi* to degenerate.

degenerazi'one [dedʒenerat'tsjone] *sf* degeneration.

de'genere [de'dʒenere] *ag* degenerate.

de'gente [de'dʒɛnte] *sm/f* bedridden person; *(ricoverato in ospedale)* in-patient.

de'genza [de'dʒɛntsa] *sf* confinement to bed; ~ **ospedaliera** period in hospital.

'degli ['deʎʎi] *prep + det vedi* **di**.

deglu'tire *vt* to swallow.

de'gnarsi [deɲ'ɲarsi] *vr:* ~ **di fare** to deign *o* condescend to do.

'degno, a ['deɲɲo] *ag* dignified; ~ **di** worthy of; ~ **di lode** praiseworthy.

degra'dare *vt (*MIL*)* to demote; *(privare della dignità)* to degrade; ~**rsi** *vr* to demean o.s.

de'grado *sm:* ~ **urbano** urban decline.

degus'tare *vt* to sample, taste.

degustazi'one [degustat'tsjone] *sf* sampling, tasting; ~ **di vini** *(locale)* specialist wine bar; ~ **di caffè** *(locale)* specialist coffee shop.

'dei *smpl di* **dio** ♦ *prep + det vedi* **di**.

del *prep + det vedi* **di**.

dela'tore, 'trice *sm/f* police informer.

'delega, ghe *sf (procura)* proxy; **per** ~ **notarile** ≈ through a solicitor *(Brit) o* lawyer.

dele'gare *vt* to delegate.

dele'gato *sm* delegate.

delegazi'one [delegat'tsjone] *sf* delegation.

delegherò *etc* [delege'rɔ] *vb vedi* **delegare**.

dele'terio, a *ag* deleterious, noxious.

del'fino *sm (*ZOOL*)* dolphin; *(*STORIA*)* dauphin; *(fig)* probable successor.

'Delhi ['dɛli] *sf* Delhi.

de'libera *sf* decision.

delibe'rare *vt* to come to a decision on ♦ *vi (*DIR*):* ~ **(su qc)** to rule (on sth).

delica'tezza [delika'tettsa] *sf* delicacy; frailty; thoughtfulness; tactfulness.

deli'cato, a *ag* delicate; *(salute)* delicate, frail; *(fig: gentile)* thoughtful, considerate; *(: che dimostra tatto)* tactful.

delimi'tare *vt (anche fig)* to delimit.

deline'are *vt* to outline; ~**rsi** *vr* to be outlined; *(fig)* to emerge.

delin'quente *sm/f* criminal, delinquent.

delin'quenza [delin'kwɛntsa] *sf* criminality, delinquency; ~ **minorile** juvenile delinquency.

de'liquio *sm* (*MED*) swoon; **cadere in** ~ to swoon.

deli'rante *ag* (*MED*) delirious; (*fig: folla*) frenzied; (: *discorso, mente*) insane.

deli'rare *vi* to be delirious, rave; (*fig*) to rave.

de'lirio *sm* delirium; (*ragionamento insensato*) raving; (*fig*): **andare/mandare in** ~ to go/send into a frenzy.

de'litto *sm* crime; ~ **d'onore** *crime committed to avenge one's honour*.

delittu'oso, a *ag* criminal.

de'lizia [de'littsja] *sf* delight.

delizi'are [delit'tsjare] *vt* to delight; ~**rsi** *vr*: ~**rsi di qc/a fare qc** to take delight in sth/in doing sth.

delizi'oso, a [delit'tsjoso] *ag* delightful; (*cibi*) delicious.

dell', 'della, 'delle, 'dello *prep + det vedi* **di**.

'delta *sm inv* delta.

delta'plano *sm* hang-glider; **volo col** ~ hang-gliding.

delucidazi'one [delutʃidat'tsjone] *sf* clarification *q*.

delu'dente *ag* disappointing.

de'ludere *vt* to disappoint.

de'lusi *etc vb vedi* **deludere**.

delusi'one *sf* disappointment.

de'luso, a *pp di* **deludere** ♦ *ag* disappointed.

dema'gogico, a, ci, che [dema'gɔdʒiko] *ag* popularity-seeking, demagogic.

dema'gogo, ghi *sm* demagogue.

de'manio *sm* state property.

de'mente *ag* (*MED*) demented, mentally deranged; (*fig*) crazy, mad.

de'menza [de'mɛntsa] *sf* dementia; madness; ~ **senile** senile dementia.

demenzi'ale [demen'tsjale] *ag* insane.

'demmo *vb vedi* **dare**.

demo'cratico, a, ci, che *ag* democratic.

democra'zia [demokrat'tsia] *sf* democracy; **la D~ Cristiana** the Christian Democrat Party.

democristi'ano, a *ag, sm/f* Christian Democrat.

demogra'fia *sf* demography.

demo'grafico, a, ci, che *ag* demographic; **incremento** ~ increase in population.

demo'lire *vt* to demolish.

demolizi'one [demolit'tsjone] *sf* demolition.

'demone *sm* demon.

de'monio *sm* demon, devil; **il D~** the Devil.

demoraliz'zare [demoralid'dzare] *vt* to demoralize; ~**rsi** *vr* to become demoralized.

demoti'vare *vt*: ~ **qn** to take away sb's motivation.

demoti'vato, a *ag* unmotivated, lacking motivation.

de'naro *sm* money; ~**i** *smpl* (*CARTE*) suit in Neapolitan pack of cards.

denatu'rato, a *ag vedi* **alcool**.

deni'grare *vt* to denigrate, run down.

denomi'nare *vt* to name; ~**rsi** *vr* to be named *o* called.

denomina'tore *sm* (*MAT*) denominator.

denominazi'one [denominat'tsjone] *sf* name; denomination; ~ **di origine controllata** (**D.O.C.**) *label guaranteeing the quality and origin of a wine*.

deno'tare *vt* to denote, indicate.

densità *sf inv* density; (*di nebbia*) thickness, denseness; **ad alta/bassa** ~ **di popolazione** densely/sparsely populated.

'denso, a *ag* thick, dense.

den'tale *ag* dental.

den'tario, a *ag* dental.

denta'tura *sf* set of teeth, teeth *pl*; (*TECN: di ruota*) serration.

'dente *sm* tooth; (*di forchetta*) prong; (*GEO: cima*) jagged peak; **al** ~ (*CUC: pasta*) cooked so as to be firm when eaten; **mettere i** ~**i** to teethe; **mettere qc sotto i** ~**i** to have a bite to eat; **avere il** ~ **avvelenato contro** *o* **con qn** to bear sb a grudge; ~ **di leone** (*BOT*) dandelion; ~**i del giudizio** wisdom teeth.

'dentice ['dɛntitʃe] *sm* (*ZOOL*) sea bream.

denti'era *sf* (set of) false teeth *pl*.

denti'fricio [denti'fritʃo] *sm* toothpaste.

den'tista, i, e *sm/f* dentist.

'dentro *av* inside; (*in casa*) indoors; (*fig: nell'intimo*) inwardly ♦ *prep*: ~ (**a**) in; **piegato in** ~ folded over; **qui/là** ~ in here/there; ~ **di sé** (*pensare, brontolare*) to oneself; **tenere tutto** ~ to keep everything bottled up (inside o.s.); **darci** ~ (*fig fam*) to slog away, work hard.

denucleariz'zato, a [denuklearid'dzato] *ag* denuclearized, nuclear-free.

denu'dare *vt* (*persona*) to strip; (*parte del corpo*) to bare; ~**rsi** *vr* to strip.

de'nuncia, ce *o* **cie** [de'nuntʃa], **de'nunzia** [de'nuntsja] *sf* denunciation; declaration; **fare una** ~ *o* **sporgere** ~ **contro qn** (*DIR*) to report sb to the police; ~ **del reddito** (*income*) tax return.

denunci'are [denun'tʃare], **denunzi'are** [denun'tsjare] *vt* to denounce; (*dichiarare*) to declare; ~ **qn/qc (alla polizia)** to report sb/sth to the police.

denu'trito, a *ag* undernourished.

denutrizi'one [denutrit'tsjone] *sf* malnutrition.

deodo'rante *sm* deodorant.

deontolo'gia [deontolo'dʒia] *sf* (*professionale*) professional code of conduct.

depenalizzazi'one [depenaliddzat'tsjone] *sf* decriminalization.

dépen'dance [depã'dãs] *sf inv* outbuilding.

depe'ribile *ag* perishable; **merce** ~ perishables *pl*, perishable goods *pl*.

deperi'mento *sm* (*di persona*) wasting away; (*di merci*) deterioration.

depe'rire *vi* to waste away.

depila'torio, a *ag* hair-removing, depilatory ♦ *sm* hair remover, depilatory.

depilazi'one [depilat'tsjone] *sf* hair removal, depilation.

dépli'ant [depli'ã] *sm inv* leaflet; (*opuscolo*) brochure.

deplo'rare *vt* to deplore; to lament.

deplo'revole *ag* deplorable.

de'pone, de'pongo *etc vb vedi* **deporre**.

de'porre *vt* (*depositare*) to put down; (*rimuovere: da una carica*) to remove; (: *re*) to depose; (*DIR*) to testify; ~ **le armi** (*MIL*) to lay down arms; ~ **le uova** to lay eggs.

depor'tare *vt* to deport.

depor'tato, a *sm/f* deportee.

deportazi'one [deportat'tsjone] *sf* deportation.

de'posi *etc vb vedi* **deporre**.

deposi'tante *sm* (*COMM*) depositor.

deposi'tare *vt* (*gen, GEO, ECON*) to deposit; (*lasciare*) to leave; (*merci*) to store; ~**rsi** *vr* (*sabbia, polvere*) to settle.

deposi'tario *sm* (*COMM*) depository.

de'posito *sm* deposit; (*luogo*) warehouse; depot; (: *MIL*) depot; ~ **bagagli** left-luggage office; ~ **di munizioni** ammunition dump.

deposizi'one [depozit'tsjone] *sf* deposition; (*da una carica*) removal; **rendere una falsa** ~ to perjure o.s.

de'posto, a *pp di* **deporre**.

depra'vare *vt* to corrupt, pervert.

depra'vato, a *ag* depraved ♦ *sm/f* degenerate.

depre'care *vt* to deprecate, deplore.

depre'dare *vt* to rob, plunder.

depressi'one *sf* depression; **area** *o* **zona di** ~ (*METEOR*) area of low pressure; (*ECON*) depressed area.

de'presso, a *pp di* **deprimere** ♦ *ag* depressed.

deprezza'mento [deprettsa'mento] *sm* depreciation.

deprez'zare [depret'tsare] *vt* (*ECON*) to depreciate.

depri'mente *ag* depressing.

de'primere *vt* to depress.

depu'rare *vt* to purify.

depura'tore *sm*: ~ **d'acqua** water purifier; ~ **di gas** scrubber.

depu'tato, a *o* **'essa** *sm/f* (*POL*) deputy, ≈ Member of Parliament (*Brit*), ≈ Congressman/woman (*US*).

deputazi'one [deputat'tsjone] *sf* deputation; (*POL*) position of deputy, ≈ parliamentary seat (*Brit*), ≈ seat in Congress (*US*).

deraglia'mento [deraʎʎa'mento] *sm* derailment.

deragli'are [deraʎ'ʎare] *vi* to be derailed; **far** ~ to derail.

dera'pare *vi* (*veicolo*) to skid; (*SCI*) to sideslip.

derattizzazi'one [derattiddzat'tsjone] *sf* rodent control.

deregolamen'tare *vt* to deregulate.

deregolamentazi'one [deregolamentat'tsjone] *sf* deregulation.

dere'litto, a *ag* derelict.

dere'tano *sm* (*fam*) bottom, buttocks *pl*.

de'ridere *vt* to mock, deride.

de'risi *etc vb vedi* **deridere**.

derisi'one *sf* derision, mockery.

de'riso, a *pp di* **deridere**.

deri'sorio, a *ag* (*gesto, tono*) mocking.

de'riva *sf* (*NAUT, AER*) drift; (*dispositivo*: *AER*) fin; (: *NAUT*) centre-board (*Brit*), centerboard (*US*); **andare alla** ~ (*anche fig*) to drift.

deri'vare *vi*: ~ **da** to derive from ♦ *vt* to derive; (*corso d'acqua*) to divert.

deri'vato, a *ag* derived ♦ *sm* (*CHIM, LING*) derivative; (*prodotto*) by-product.

derivazi'one [derivat'tsjone] *sf* derivation; diversion.

derma'tite *sf* dermatitis.

dermatolo'gia [dermatolo'dʒia] *sf* dermatology.

derma'tologo, a, gi, ghe *sm/f* dermatologist.

'deroga, ghe *sf* (special) dispensation; **in** ~ **a** as a (special) dispensation to.

dero'gare *vi*: ~ **a** (*DIR*) to repeal in part.

der'rate *sfpl* commodities; ~ **alimentari** foodstuffs.

deru'bare *vt* to rob.

des'critto, a *pp di* **descrivere**.

des'crivere *vt* to describe.

descrizi'one [deskrit'tsjone] *sf* description.

de'serto, a *ag* deserted ♦ *sm* (*GEO*) desert; **isola** ~**a** desert island.

deside'rabile *ag* desirable.

deside'rare *vt* to want, wish for; (*sessualmente*) to desire; ~ **fare/che qn faccia** to want *o* wish to do/sb to do; **desidera fare una passeggiata?** would you like to go for a walk?; **farsi** ~ (*fare il prezioso*) to play hard to get; (*farsi aspettare*) to take one's time; **lascia molto a** ~ it leaves a lot to be desired.

desi'derio *sm* wish; (*più intenso, carnale*) desire.

deside'roso, a *ag*: ~ **di** longing *o* eager for.

desi'gnare [desiɲ'ɲare] *vt* to designate, appoint; (*data*) to fix; **la vittima designata** the intended victim.

designazi'one [desiɲɲat'tsjone] *sf* designation, appointment.

desi'nare *vi* to dine, have dinner ♦ *sm* dinner.

desi'nenza [dezi'nɛntsa] *sf* (*LING*) ending, inflexion.

de'sistere *vi*: ~ **da** to give up, desist from.

desis'tito, a *pp di* **desistere**.

deso'lante *ag* distressing.

deso'lato, a *ag* (*paesaggio*) desolate; (*persona: spiacente*) sorry.

desolazi'one [dezolat'tsjone] *sf* desolation.

'despota, i *sm* despot.

'dessi *etc vb vedi* **dare**.

destabiliz'zare [destabilid'dzare] *vt* to destabilize.

des'tare *vt* to wake (up); (*fig*) to awaken, arouse; ~**rsi** *vr* to wake (up).

'deste *etc vb vedi* **dare**.

desti'nare *vt* to destine; (*assegnare*) to appoint, assign; (*indirizzare*) to address; ~ **qc a qn** to intend to give sth to sb, intend sb to have sth.

destina'tario, a *sm/f* (*di lettera*) addressee; (*di merce*) consignee; (*di mandato*) payee.

destinazi'one [destinat'tsjone] *sf* destination; (*uso*) purpose.

des'tino *sm* destiny, fate.

destitu'ire *vt* to dismiss, remove.

destituzi'one [destitut'tsjone] *sf* dismissal, removal.

'desto, a *ag* (wide) awake.

'destra *sf vedi* **destro**.

destreggi'arsi [destred'dʒarsi] *vr* to manoeuvre (*Brit*), maneuver (*US*).

des'trezza [des'trettsa] *sf* skill, dexterity.

'destro, a *ag* right, right-hand; (*abile*) skilful (*Brit*), skillful (*US*), adroit ♦ *sf* (*mano*) right hand; (*parte*) right (side); (*POL*): **la** ~**a** the right ♦ *sm* (*BOXE*) right; **a** ~**a** (*essere*) on the right; (*andare*) to the right; **tenere la** ~**a** to keep to the right.

de'sumere *vt* (*dedurre*) to infer, deduce; (*trarre: informazioni*) to obtain.

de'sunto, a *pp di* **desumere**.

detas'sare *vt* to remove the duty (*o* tax) from.

dete'nere *vt* (*incarico, primato*) to hold; (*proprietà*) to have, possess; (*in prigione*) to detain, hold.

de'tengo, de'tenni *etc vb vedi* **detenere**.

deten'tivo, a *ag*: **mandato** ~ imprisonment order; **pena** ~**a** prison sentence.

deten'tore, 'trice *sm/f* (*di titolo, primato etc*) holder.

dete'nuto, a *sm/f* prisoner.

detenzi'one [deten'tsjone] *sf* holding; possession; detention.

deter'gente [deter'dʒɛnte] *ag* detergent; (*crema, latte*) cleansing ♦ *sm* detergent.

de'tergere [de'tɛrdʒere] *vt* (*gen*) to clean; (*pelle, viso*) to cleanse; (*sudore*) to wipe (away).

deteriora'mento *sm*: ~ (**di**) deterioration

(in).

deterio'rare *vt* to damage; ~**rsi** *vr* to deteriorate.

deteri'ore *ag* (*merce*) second-rate; (*significato*) pejorative; (*tradizione letteraria*) lesser, minor.

determi'nante *ag* decisive, determining.

determi'nare *vt* to determine.

determina'tivo, a *ag* determining; **articolo** ~ (*LING*) definite article.

determi'nato, a *ag* (*gen*) certain; (*particolare*) specific; (*risoluto*) determined, resolute.

determinazi'one [determinat'tsjone] *sf* determination; (*decisione*) decision.

deter'rente *ag, sm* deterrent.

deterrò *etc vb vedi* **detenere**.

deter'sivo *sm* detergent; (*per bucato: in polvere*) washing powder (*Brit*), soap powder.

de'terso, a *pp di* **detergere**.

detes'tare *vt* to detest, hate.

deti'ene *etc vb vedi* **detenere**.

deto'nare *vi* to detonate.

detona'tore *sm* detonator.

detonazi'one [detonat'tsjone] *sf* (*di esplosivo*) detonation, explosion; (*di arma*) bang; (*di motore*) pinking (*Brit*), knocking.

de'trae, de'traggo *etc vb vedi* **detrarre**.

de'trarre *vt*: ~ (**da**) to deduct (from), take away (from).

de'trassi *etc vb vedi* **detrarre**.

de'tratto, a *pp di* **detrarre**.

detrazi'one [detrat'tsjone] *sf* deduction; ~ **d'imposta** tax allowance.

detri'mento *sm* detriment, harm; **a** ~ **di** to the detriment of.

de'trito *sm* (*GEO*) detritus.

detroniz'zare [detronid'dzare] *vt* to dethrone.

'detta *sf*: **a** ~ **di** according to.

dettagli'ante [dettaʎ'ʎante] *sm/f* (*COMM*) retailer.

dettagli'are [dettaʎ'ʎare] *vt* to detail, give full details of.

dettagliata'mente [dettaʎʎata'mente] *av* in detail.

det'taglio [det'taʎʎo] *sm* detail; (*COMM*): **il** ~ retail; **al** ~ (*COMM*) retail; separately.

det'tame *sm* dictate, precept.

det'tare *vt* to dictate; ~ **legge** (*fig*) to lay down the law.

det'tato *sm* dictation.

detta'tura *sf* dictation.

'detto, a *pp di* **dire** ♦ *ag* (*soprannominato*) called, known as; (*già nominato*) abovementioned ♦ *sm* saying; ~ **fatto** no sooner said than done; **presto** ~! it's easier said than done!

detur'pare *vt* to disfigure; (*moralmente*) to sully.

devas'tante *ag* (*anche fig*) devastating.

devas'tare *vt* to devastate; (*fig*) to ravage.

devastazi'one [devastat'tsjone] *sf* devastation, destruction.

devi'are *vi*: ~ **(da)** to turn off (from) ♦ *vt* to divert.

deviazi'one [devjat'tsjone] *sf* (*anche AUT*) diversion; **fare una** ~ to make a detour.

'devo *etc vb vedi* **dovere.**

devo'luto, a *pp di* **devolvere.**

devoluzi'one [devolut'tsjone] *sf* (*DIR*) devolution, transfer.

de'volvere *vt* (*DIR*) to transfer, devolve; ~ **qc in beneficenza** to give sth to charity.

de'voto, a *ag* (*REL*) devout, pious; (*affezionato*) devoted.

devozi'one [devot'tsjone] *sf* devoutness; (*anche REL*) devotion.

dg *abbr* (= *decigrammo*) dg.

di *prep* (*di* + *il* = **del**, *di* + *lo* = **dello**, *di* + *l'* = **dell'**, *di* + *la* = **della**, *di* + *i* = **dei**, *di* + *gli* = **degli**, *di* + *le* = **delle**) of; (*causa*) with; for; of; (*mezzo*) with; (*provenienza*) from ♦ *det*: **del pane** (some) bread; **dei libri** (some) books; **la sorella** ~ **mio padre** my father's sister; **un sacchetto** ~ **plastica/orologio d'oro** a plastic bag/gold watch; **tremare** ~ **paura** to tremble with fear; **un bambino** ~ **tre anni** a child of three, a three-year-old child; **una commedia** ~ **Goldoni** a comedy by Goldoni; **il nome** ~ **Maria** the name Mary; ~ **primavera/giugno** in spring/June; ~ **mattina/sera** in the morning/evening; ~ **notte** by night; at night; in the night; ~ **domenica** on Sundays; ~ ... **in** from ... to; *vedi* **più, meno** *etc.*

dì *sm* day; **buon** ~! hallo!; **a** ~ = **addì.**

dia'bete *sm* diabetes *sg.*

dia'betico, a, ci, che *ag, sm/f* diabetic.

dia'bolico, a, ci, che *ag* diabolical.

di'acono *sm* (*REL*) deacon.

dia'dema, i *sm* diadem; (*di donna*) tiara.

dia'framma, i *sm* (*divisione*) screen; (*ANAT, FOT, contraccettivo*) diaphragm.

di'agnosi [di'aɲɲozi] *sf* diagnosis *sg.*

diagnosti'care [diaɲɲosti'kare] *vt* to diagnose.

dia'gnostico, a, ci, che [diaɲ'ɲɔstiko] *ag* diagnostic; **aiuti** ~**ci** (*INFORM*) debugging aids.

diago'nale *ag, sf* diagonal.

dia'gramma, i *sm* diagram; ~ **a barre** bar chart; ~ **di flusso** flow chart.

dialet'tale *ag* dialectal; **poesia** ~ poetry in dialect.

dia'letto *sm* dialect.

di'alisi *sf* dialysis.

dialo'gante *ag*: **unità** ~ (*INFORM*) interactive terminal.

dialo'gare *vi*: ~ **(con)** to have a dialogue (with); (*conversare*) to converse (with) ♦ *vt* (*scena*) to write the dialogue for.

di'alogo, ghi *sm* dialogue.

dia'mante *sm* diamond.

di'ametro *sm* diameter.

di'amine *escl*: **che** ~ ...? what on earth ...?

diaposi'tiva *sf* transparency, slide.

di'aria *sf* daily (expense) allowance.

di'ario *sm* diary; ~ **di bordo** (*NAUT*) log(book); ~ **di classe** (*INS*) class register; ~ **degli esami** (*INS*) exam timetable.

diar'rea *sf* diarrhoea.

dia'triba *sf* diatribe.

diavole'ria *sf* (*azione*) act of mischief; (*aggeggio*) weird contraption.

di'avolo *sm* devil; **è un buon** ~ he's a good sort; **avere un** ~ **per capello** to be in a foul temper; **avere una fame/un freddo del** ~ to be ravenously hungry/frozen stiff; **mandare qn al** ~ (*fam*) to tell sb to go to hell; **fare il** ~ **a quattro** to kick up a fuss.

di'battere *vt* to debate, discuss; ~**rsi** *vr* to struggle.

dibatti'mento *sm* (*dibattito*) debate, discussion; (*DIR*) hearing.

di'battito *sm* debate, discussion.

dic. *abbr* (= *dicembre*) Dec.

dicas'tero *sm* ministry.

'dice ['ditʃe] *vb vedi* **dire.**

di'cembre [di'tʃɛmbre] *sm* December; *per fraseologia vedi* **luglio.**

dicem'brino, a [ditʃem'brino] *ag* December *cpd.*

dice'ria [ditʃe'ria] *sf* rumour (*Brit*), rumor (*US*), piece of gossip.

dichia'rare [dikja'rare] *vt* to declare; ~**rsi** *vr* to declare o.s.; (*innamorato*) to declare one's love; **si dichiara che** ... it is hereby declared that ...; ~**rsi vinto** to acknowledge defeat.

dichia'rato, a [dikja'rato] *ag* (*nemico, ateo*) avowed.

dichiarazi'one [dikjarat'tsjone] *sf* declaration; ~ **dei redditi** statement of income; (*modulo*) tax return.

dician'nove [ditʃan'nɔve] *num* nineteen.

dicianno'venne [ditʃanno'vɛnne] *ag, sm/f* nineteen-year-old.

dicias'sette [ditʃas'sɛtte] *num* seventeen.

diciasset'tenne [ditʃasset'tɛnne] *ag, sm/f* seventeen-year-old.

diciot'tenne [ditʃot'tɛnne] *ag, sm/f* eighteen-year-old.

dici'otto [di'tʃɔtto] *num* eighteen ♦ *sm inv* (*INS*) *minimum satisfactory mark awarded in Italian universities.*

dici'tura [ditʃi'tura] *sf* words *pl*, wording.

'dico *etc vb vedi* **dire.**

didasca'lia *sf* (*di illustrazione*) caption; (*CINEMA*) subtitle; (*TEATRO*) stage directions *pl.*

di'dattico, a, ci, che *ag* didactic; (*metodo, programma*) teaching; (*libro*) educational ♦ *sf* didactics *sg*; teaching methodology.

di'dentro *av* inside, indoors.

didi'etro *av* behind ♦ *ag inv* (*ruota, giardino*) back, rear *cpd* ♦ *sm* (*di casa*) rear; (*fam: sedere*) backside.

di'eci ['djɛtʃi] *num* ten.

dieci'mila [djɛtʃi'mila] *num* ten thousand.

die'cina [dje'tʃina] *sf* = **decina**.

di'edi *etc vb vedi* **dare**.

'diesel ['di:zəl] *sm inv* diesel engine.

di'eta *sf* diet; **essere a ~** to be on a diet.

die'tologo, a, gi, ghe *sm/f* dietician.

di'etro *av* behind; (*in fondo*) at the back ♦ *prep* behind; (*tempo: dopo*) after ♦ *sm* (*di foglio, giacca*) back; (*di casa*) back, rear ♦ *ag inv* back *cpd*; **le zampe di ~** the hind legs; **~ ricevuta** against receipt; **~ richiesta** on demand; (*scritta*) on application; **andare ~ a** (*anche fig*) to follow; **stare ~ a qn** (*sorvegliare*) to keep an eye on sb; (*corteggiare*) to hang around sb; **portarsi ~ qn/qc** to bring sb/sth with one, bring sb/sth along; **gli hanno riso/parlato ~** they laughed at/talked about him behind his back.

di'etro 'front *escl* about turn! (*Brit*), about face! (*US*) ♦ *sm* (*MIL*) about-turn, about-face; (*fig*) volte-face, about-turn, about-face; **fare ~** (*MIL, fig*) to about-turn, about-face; (*tornare indietro*) to turn round.

di'fatti *cong* in fact, as a matter of fact.

di'fendere *vt* to defend; **~rsi** *vr* (*cavarsela*) to get by; **~rsi da/contro** to defend o.s. from/against; **~rsi dal freddo** to protect o.s. from the cold; **sapersi ~** to know how to look after o.s.

difen'sivo, a *ag* defensive ♦ *sf*: **stare sulla ~a** (*anche fig*) to be on the defensive.

difen'sore, a *sm/f* defender; **avvocato ~** counsel for the defence (*Brit*) *o* defense (*US*).

di'fesa *sf vedi* **difeso**.

di'fesi *etc vb vedi* **difendere**.

di'feso, a *pp di* **difendere** ♦ *sf* defence (*Brit*), defense (*US*); **prendere le ~e di qn** to defend sb, take sb's part.

difet'tare *vi* to be defective; **~ di** to be lacking in, lack.

difet'tivo, a *ag* defective.

di'fetto *sm* (*mancanza*): **~ di** lack of; (*di fabbricazione*) fault, flaw, defect; (*morale*) fault, failing, defect; (*fisico*) defect; **far ~** to be lacking; **in ~** at fault; **in the wrong**.

difet'toso, a *ag* defective, faulty.

diffa'mare *vt* (*a parole*) to slander; (*per iscritto*) to libel.

diffama'torio, a *ag* slanderous; libellous.

diffamazi'one [diffamat'tsjone] *sf* slander; libel.

diffe'rente *ag* different.

diffe'renza [diffe'rɛntsa] *sf* difference; **a ~ di** unlike; **non fare ~ (tra)** to make no distinction (between).

differenzi'ale [differen'tsjale] *ag, sm* differential; **classi ~i** (*INS*) special classes (*for backward children*).

differenzi'are [differen'tsjare] *vt* to differentiate; **~rsi da** to differentiate o.s. from; to differ from.

diffe'rire *vt* to postpone, defer ♦ *vi* to be different.

dif'ficile [dif'fitʃile] *ag* difficult; (*persona*) hard to please, difficult (to please); (*poco probabile*): **è ~ che sia libero** it is unlikely that he'll be free ♦ *sm/f*: **fare il(la) ~** to be difficult, be awkward ♦ *sm* difficult part; difficulty; **essere ~ nel mangiare** to be fussy about one's food.

diffici'lmente [diffitʃil'mente] *av* (*con difficoltà*) with difficulty; **~ verrà** he's unlikely to come.

difficoltà *sf inv* difficulty.

difficol'toso, a *ag* (*compito*) difficult, hard; (*persona*) difficult, hard to please; **digestione ~a** poor digestion.

dif'fida *sf* (*DIR*) warning, notice.

diffi'dare *vi*: **~ di** to be suspicious *o* distrustful of ♦ *vt* (*DIR*) to warn; **~ qn dal fare qc** to warn sb not to do sth, caution sb against doing sth.

diffi'dente *ag* suspicious, distrustful.

diffi'denza [diffi'dɛntsa] *sf* suspicion, distrust.

dif'fondere *vt* (*luce, calore*) to diffuse; (*notizie*) to spread, circulate; **~rsi** *vr* to spread.

dif'fusi *etc vb vedi* **diffondere**.

diffusi'one *sf* diffusion; spread; (*anche di giornale*) circulation; (*FISICA*) scattering.

dif'fuso, a *pp di* **diffondere** ♦ *ag* (*FISICA*) diffuse; (*notizia, malattia etc*) widespread; **è opinione ~a che ...** it's widely held that ....

difi'lato *av* (*direttamente*) straight, directly; (*subito*) straight away.

difte'rite *sf* diphtheria.

'diga, ghe *sf* dam; (*portuale*) breakwater.

dige'rente [didʒe'rɛnte] *ag* (*apparato*) digestive.

dige'rire [didʒe'rire] *vt* to digest.

digesti'one [didʒes'tjone] *sf* digestion.

diges'tivo, a [didʒes'tivo] *ag* digestive ♦ *sm* (after-dinner) liqueur.

Digi'one [di'dʒone] *sf* Dijon.

digi'tale [didʒi'tale] *ag* digital; (*delle dita*) finger *cpd*, digital ♦ *sf* (*BOT*) foxglove.

digi'tare [didʒi'tare] *vt* (*dati*) to key (in); (*tasto*) to press.

digiu'nare [didʒu'nare] *vi* to starve o.s.; (*REL*) to fast.

digi'uno, a [di'dʒuno] *ag*: **essere ~** not to have eaten ♦ *sm* fast; **a ~** on an empty stomach.

dignità [diɲɲi'ta] *sf inv* dignity.

digni'tario [diɲɲi'tarjo] *sm* dignitary.

digni'toso, a [diɲɲi'toso] *ag* dignified.

'DIGOS *sigla f* (= *Divisione Investigazioni Generali e Operazioni Speciali*) *police department dealing with political security.*

digressi'one *sf* digression.

digri'gnare [digriɲ'ɲare] *vt*: ~ **i denti** to grind one's teeth.

dila'gare *vi* to flood; *(fig)* to spread.

dilani'are *vt* to tear to pieces.

dilapi'dare *vt* to squander, waste.

dila'tare *vt* to dilate; *(gas)* to cause to expand; *(passaggio, cavità)* to open (up); ~**rsi** *vr* to dilate; *(FISICA)* to expand.

dilatazi'one [dilatat'tsjone] *sf* (*ANAT*) dilation; *(di gas, metallo)* expansion.

dilazio'nare [dilattsjo'nare] *vt* to delay, defer.

dilazi'one [dilat'tsjone] *sf* deferment.

dileggi'are [diled'dʒare] *vt* to mock, deride.

dilegu'are *vi*, ~**rsi** *vr* to vanish, disappear.

di'lemma, i *sm* dilemma.

dilet'tante *sm/f* dilettante; *(anche SPORT)* amateur.

dilet'tare *vt* to give pleasure to, delight; ~**rsi** *vr*: ~**rsi di** to take pleasure in, enjoy.

dilet'tevole *ag* delightful.

di'letto, a *ag* dear, beloved ♦ *sm* pleasure, delight.

dili'gente [dili'dʒɛnte] *ag* (*scrupoloso*) diligent; *(accurato)* careful, accurate.

dili'genza [dili'dʒɛntsa] *sf* diligence; care; *(carrozza)* stagecoach.

dilu'ire *vt* to dilute.

dilun'garsi *vr* (*fig*): ~ **su** to talk at length on *o* about.

diluvi'are *vb impers* to pour (down).

di'luvio *sm* downpour; *(inondazione, fig)* flood; **il** ~ **universale** the Flood.

dima'grante *ag* slimming *cpd*.

dima'grire *vi* to get thinner, lose weight.

dime'nare *vt* to wave, shake; ~**rsi** *vr* to toss and turn; *(fig)* to struggle; ~ **la coda** *(sog: cane)* to wag its tail.

dimensi'one *sf* dimension; *(grandezza)* size; **considerare un discorso nella sua** ~ **politica** to look at a speech in terms of its political significance.

dimenti'canza [dimenti'kantsa] *sf* forgetfulness; *(errore)* oversight, slip; **per** ~ inadvertently.

dimenti'care *vt* to forget; ~**rsi** *vr*: ~**rsi di qc** to forget sth.

dimentica'toio *sm* (*scherzoso*): **cadere/ mettere nel** ~ to sink into/consign to oblivion.

di'mentico, a, chi, che *ag*: ~ **di** (*che non ricorda*) forgetful of; *(incurante)* oblivious of, unmindful of.

di'messo, a *pp di* **dimettere** ♦ *ag* (*voce*) subdued; *(uomo, abito)* modest, humble.

dimesti'chezza [dimesti'kettsa] *sf* familiarity.

di'mettere *vt*: ~ **qn da** to dismiss sb from; *(dall'ospedale)* to discharge sb from; ~**rsi**

vr: ~**rsi (da)** to resign (from).

dimez'zare [dimed'dzare] *vt* to halve.

diminu'ire *vt* to reduce, diminish; *(prezzi)* to bring down, reduce ♦ *vi* to decrease, diminish; *(rumore)* to die down, die away; *(prezzi)* to fall, go down.

diminu'tivo, a *ag, sm* diminutive.

diminuzi'one [diminut'tsjone] *sf* decreasing, diminishing; **in** ~ on the decrease; ~ **della produttività** fall in productivity.

di'misi *etc vb vedi* **dimettere.**

dimissio'nario, a *ag* outgoing, resigning.

dimissi'oni *sfpl* resignation *sg*; **dare** *o* **presentare le** ~ to resign, hand in one's resignation.

di'mora *sf* residence; **senza fissa** ~ of no fixed address *o* abode.

dimo'rare *vi* to reside.

dimos'trante *sm/f* (*POL*) demonstrator.

dimos'trare *vt* to demonstrate, show; *(provare)* to prove, demonstrate; ~**rsi** *vr*: ~**rsi molto abile** to show o.s. *o* prove to be very clever; **non dimostra la sua età** he doesn't look his age; **dimostra 30 anni** he looks about 30 (years old).

dimostra'tivo, a *ag* (*anche LING*) demonstrative.

dimostrazi'one [dimostrat'tsjone] *sf* demonstration; proof.

di'namico, a, ci, che *ag* dynamic ♦ *sf* dynamics *sg*.

dina'mismo *sm* dynamism.

dinami'tardo, a *ag*: **attentato** ~ dynamite attack ♦ *sm/f* dynamiter.

dina'mite *sf* dynamite.

'dinamo *sf inv* dynamo.

di'nanzi [di'nantsi]: ~ **a** *prep* in front of.

dinas'tia *sf* dynasty.

dini'ego, ghi *sm* (*rifiuto*) refusal; *(negazione)* denial.

dinocco'lato, a *ag* lanky; **camminare** ~ to walk with a slouch.

dino'sauro *sm* dinosaur.

din'torno *av* round, (round) about; ~**i** *smpl* outskirts; **nei** ~**i di** in the vicinity *o* neighbourhood of.

'dio, *pl* 'dei *sm* god; **D**~ God; **gli dei** the gods; **si crede un** ~ he thinks he's wonderful; **D**~ **mio!** my God!; **D**~ **ce la mandi buona!** let's hope for the best; **D**~ **ce ne scampi e liberi!** God forbid!

di'ocesi [di'ɔtʃezi] *sf inv* diocese.

dios'sina *sf* dioxin.

dipa'nare *vt* (*lana*) to wind into a ball; *(fig)* to disentangle, sort out.

diparti'mento *sm* department.

dipen'dente *ag* dependent ♦ *sm/f* employee.

dipen'denza [dipen'dɛntsa] *sf* dependence; **essere alle** ~**e di qn** to be employed by sb *o* in sb's employ.

di'pendere *vi*: ~ **da** to depend on; *(finanziariamente)* to be dependent on; *(derivare)* to come from, be due to.

di'pesi etc vb vedi **dipendere**.

di'peso, a pp di **dipendere**.

di'pingere [di'pindʒere] vt to paint.

di'pinsi etc vb vedi **dipingere**.

di'pinto, a pp di **dipingere** ♦ sm painting.

di'ploma, i sm diploma.

diplo'mare vt to award a diploma to, graduate (US) ♦ vi to obtain a diploma, graduate (US).

diplo'matico, a, ci, che ag diplomatic ♦ sm diplomat.

diplo'mato, a ag qualified ♦ sm/f qualified person, holder of a diploma.

diploma'zia [diplomat'tsia] sf diplomacy.

di'porto sm: **imbarcazione** f **da** ~ pleasure craft.

dira'dare vt to thin (out); (visite) to reduce, make less frequent; ~**rsi** vr to disperse; (nebbia) to clear (up).

dira'mare vt to issue ♦ vi, ~**rsi** vr (strade) to branch.

'dire vt to say; (segreto, fatto) to tell; ~ **qc a qn** to tell sb sth; ~ **a qn di fare qc** to tell sb to do sth; ~ **di sì/no** to say yes/no; **si dice che** ... they say that ...; **mi si dice che** ... I am told that ...; **si direbbe che** ... it looks (o sounds) as though ...; **dica, signora?** (in un negozio) yes, Madam, can I help you?; **sa quello che dice** he knows what he's talking about; **lascialo** ~ (esprimersi) let him have his say; (ignoralo) just ignore him; **come sarebbe a** ~? what do you mean?; **che ne diresti di andarcene?** how about leaving?; **chi l'avrebbe mai detto!** who would have thought it!; **si dicono esperti** they say they are experts; **per così** ~ so to speak; **a dir poco** to say the least; **non c'è che** ~ there's no doubt about it; **non dico di no** I can't deny it; **il che è tutto** ~ need I say more?

di'ressi etc vb vedi **dirigere**.

diretta'mente av (immediatamente) directly, straight; (personalmente) directly; (senza intermediari) direct, straight.

diret'tissima sf (tragitto) most direct route; (DIR): **processo per** ~ summary trial.

diret'tissimo sm (FERR) fast (through) train.

diret'tivo, a ag (POL, AMM) executive; (COMM) managerial, executive ♦ sm leadership, leaders pl ♦ sf directive, instruction.

di'retto, a pp di **dirigere** ♦ ag direct ♦ sm (FERR) through train ♦ sf: **in (linea)** ~**a** (RADIO, TV) live; **il mio** ~ **superiore** my immediate superior.

diret'tore, 'trice sm/f (di azienda) director; manager/ess; (di scuola elementare) head (teacher) (Brit), principal (US); ~

amministrativo company secretary (Brit), corporate executive secretary (US); ~ **del carcere** prison governor (Brit) o warden (US); ~ **di filiale** branch manager; ~ **d'orchestra** conductor; ~ **di produzione** (CINEMA) producer; ~ **sportivo** team manager; ~ **tecnico** (SPORT) trainer, coach.

direzi'one [diret'tsjone] sf (senso: anche fig) direction; (conduzione: gen) running; (: di partito) leadership; (: di società) management; (: di giornale) editorship; (direttori) management; **in** ~ **di** in the direction of, towards.

diri'gente [diri'dʒente] ag managerial ♦ sm/f executive; (POL) leader; **classe** ~ ruling class.

diri'genza [diri'dʒentsa] sf management; (POL) leadership.

dirigenzi'ale [diridʒen'tsjale] ag managerial.

di'rigere [di'ridʒere] vt to direct; (impresa) to run, manage; (MUS) to conduct; ~**rsi** vr: ~**rsi verso** o **a** to make o head for; ~ **i propri passi verso** to make one's way towards; **il treno era diretto a Pavia** the train was heading for Pavia.

diri'gibile [diri'dʒibile] sm airship.

dirim'petto av opposite; ~ **a** prep opposite, facing.

di'ritto, a ag straight; (onesto) straight, upright ♦ av straight, directly ♦ sm right side; (TENNIS) forehand; (MAGLIA) plain stitch, knit stitch; (prerogativa) right; (leggi, scienza): **il** ~ law; **stare** ~ to stand up straight; **aver** ~ **a qc** to be entitled to sth; **punto** ~ plain (stitch); **andare** ~ to go straight on; **a buon** ~ quite rightly; ~**i (d'autore)** royalties; ~ **di successione** right of succession.

dirit'tura sf (SPORT) straight; (fig) rectitude.

diroc'cato, a ag tumbledown, in ruins.

dirom'pente ag (anche fig) explosive.

dirotta'mento sm: ~ **(aereo)** hijack.

dirot'tare vt (nave, aereo) to change the course of; (aereo: sotto minaccia) to hijack; (traffico) to divert ♦ vi (nave, aereo) to change course.

dirotta'tore, 'trice sm/f hijacker.

di'rotto, a ag (pioggia) torrential; (pianto) unrestrained; **piovere a** ~ to pour, rain cats and dogs; **piangere a** ~ to cry one's heart out.

di'rupo sm crag, precipice.

disabi'tato, a ag uninhabited.

disabitu'arsi vr: ~ **a** to get out of the habit of.

disac'cordo sm disagreement.

disadat'tato, a ag (PSIC) maladjusted.

disa'dorno, a ag plain, unadorned.

disaffezi'one [dizaffet'tsjone] sf disaffection.

disa'gevole [disa'dʒevole] ag (scomodo) uncomfortable; (*difficile*) difficult.

disagi'ato, a [diza'dʒato] *ag* poor, needy; (*vita*) hard.

di'sagio [di'zadʒo] *sm* discomfort; (*disturbo*) inconvenience; (*fig: imbarazzo*) embarrassment; ∼**i** *smpl* hardship *sg*, poverty *sg*; **essere a** ∼ to be ill at ease.

di'samina *sf* close examination.

disappro'vare *vt* to disapprove of.

disapprovazi'one [dizapprovat'tsjone] *sf* disapproval.

disap'punto *sm* disappointment.

disarcio'nare [dizartʃo'nare] *vt* to unhorse.

disar'mante *ag* (*fig*) disarming.

disar'mare *vt*, *vi* to disarm.

di'sarmo *sm* (*MIL*) disarmament.

di'sastro *sm* disaster.

disas'troso, a *ag* disastrous.

disat'tento, a *ag* inattentive.

disattenzi'one [dizatten'tsjone] *sf* carelessness, lack of attention.

disatti'vare *vt* (*bomba*) to de-activate, defuse.

disa'vanzo [diza'vantso] *sm* (*ECON*) deficit.

disavven'tura *sf* misadventure, mishap.

dis'brigo, ghi *sm* (prompt) clearing up *o* settlement.

dis'capito *sm*: **a** ∼ **di** to the detriment of.

dis'carica, che *sf* (*di rifiuti*) rubbish tip *o* dump.

discen'dente [diʃʃen'dɛnte] *ag* descending ♦ *sm/f* descendant.

di'scendere [diʃ'ʃendere] *vt* to go (*o* come) down ♦ *vi* to go (*o* come) down; (*smontare*) to get off; ∼ **da** (*famiglia*) to be descended from; ∼ **dalla macchina/dal treno** to get out of the car/out of *o* off the train; ∼ **da cavallo** to dismount, get off one's horse.

di'scepolo, a [diʃ'ʃepolo] *sm/f* disciple.

di'scernere [diʃ'ʃernere] *vt* to discern.

discerni'mento [diʃʃerni'mento] *sm* discernment.

di'sceso, a [diʃ'ʃeso] *pp di* **discendere** ♦ *sf* descent; (*pendio*) slope; **in** ∼**a** (*strada*) downhill *cpd*, sloping; ∼**a libera** (*SCI*) downhill race.

dischi'udere [dis'kjudere] *vt* (*aprire*) to open; (*fig: rivelare*) to disclose, reveal.

dischi'usi etc [dis'kjusi] *vb vedi* **dischiudere**.

dischi'uso, a [dis'kjuso] *pp di* **dischiudere**.

di'scinto, a [diʃ'ʃinto] *ag* (*anche:* **in abiti** ∼**i**) half-undressed.

disci'ogliere [diʃ'ʃɔʎʎere] *vt*, ∼**rsi** *vr* to dissolve; (*fondere*) to melt.

disci'olto, a [diʃ'ʃɔlto] *pp di* **disciogliere**.

disci'plina [diʃʃi'plina] *sf* discipline.

discipli'nare [diʃʃipli'nare] *ag* disciplinary ♦ *vt* to discipline.

'disco, schi *sm* disc, disk; (*SPORT*) discus; (*fonografico*) record; (*INFORM*) disk; ∼ **magnetico** (*INFORM*) magnetic disk; ∼

orario (*AUT*) parking disc; ∼ **rigido** (*INFORM*) hard disk; ∼ **volante** flying saucer.

discogra'fia *sf* (*tecnica*) recording, record-making; (*industria*) record industry.

disco'grafico, a, ci, che *ag* record *cpd*, recording *cpd* ♦ *sm* record producer; **casa** ∼**a** record(ing) company.

'discolo, a *ag* (*bambino*) undisciplined, unruly ♦ *sm/f* rascal.

discol'pare *vt* to clear of blame; ∼**rsi** *vr* to clear o.s., prove one's innocence; (*giustificarsi*) to excuse o.s.

disco'noscere [disko'noʃʃere] *vt* (*figlio*) to disown; (*meriti*) to ignore, disregard.

disconosci'uto, a [diskonoʃ'ʃuto] *pp di* **disconoscere**.

discon'tinuo, a *ag* (*linea*) broken; (*rendimento, stile*) irregular; (*interesse*) sporadic.

dis'corde *ag* conflicting, clashing.

dis'cordia *sf* discord; (*dissidio*) disagreement, clash.

dis'correre *vi*: ∼ **(di)** to talk (about).

dis'corso, a *pp di* **discorrere** ♦ *sm* speech; (*conversazione*) conversation, talk.

dis'costo, a *ag* faraway, distant ♦ *av* far away; ∼ **da** *prep* far from.

disco'teca, che *sf* (*raccolta*) record library; (*luogo di ballo*) disco(thèque).

discre'panza [diskre'pantsa] *sf* discrepancy.

dis'creto, a *ag* discreet; (*abbastanza buono*) reasonable, fair.

discrezi'one [diskret'tsjone] *sf* discretion; (*giudizio*) judgment, discernment; **a** ∼ **di** at the discretion of.

discrimi'nante *ag* (*fattore, elemento*) decisive ♦ *sf* (*DIR*) extenuating circumstance.

discrimi'nare *vt* to discrimate.

discriminazi'one [diskriminat'tsjone] *sf* discrimination.

dis'cussi etc *vb vedi* **discutere**.

discussi'one *sf* discussion; (*litigio*) argument; **mettere in** ∼ to bring into question; **fuori** ∼ out of the question.

dis'cusso, a *pp di* **discutere**.

dis'cutere *vt* to discuss, debate; (*contestare*) to question, dispute ♦ *vi* (*conversare*): ∼ **(di)** to discuss; (*litigare*) to argue.

discu'tibile *ag* questionable.

disde'gnare [dizdeɲ'ɲare] *vt* to scorn.

dis'degno [diz'deɲɲo] *sm* scorn, disdain.

disde'gnoso, a [dizdeɲ'ɲoso] *ag* disdainful, scornful.

dis'detto, a *pp di* **disdire** ♦ *sf* cancellation; (*sfortuna*) bad luck.

disdi'cevole [dizdi'tʃevole] *ag* improper, unseemly.

dis'dire *vt* (*prenotazione*) to cancel; ∼ **un contratto d'affitto** (*DIR*) to give notice (to quit).

dise'gnare [diseɲ'ɲare] *vt* to draw; (*progettare*) to design; (*fig*) to outline.

disegna'tore, 'trice [diseɲɲa'tore] *sm/f* designer.

di'segno [di'zeɲɲo] *sm* drawing; (*su stoffa etc*) design; (*fig: schema*) outline; ~ **industriale** industriale design; ~ **di legge** (*DIR*) bill.

diser'bante *sm* weed-killer.

disere'dare *vt* to disinherit.

diser'tare *vt, vi* to desert.

diser'tore *sm* (*MIL*) deserter.

diserzi'one [dizer'tsjone] *sf* (*MIL*) desertion.

disfaci'mento [disfatʃi'mento] *sm* (*di cadavere*) decay; (*fig: di istituzione, impero, società*) decline, decay; **in** ~ in decay.

dis'fare *vt* to undo; (*valigie*) to unpack; (*meccanismo*) to take to pieces; (*lavoro, paese*) to destroy; (*neve*) to melt; **~rsi** *vr* to come undone; (*neve*) to melt; ~ **il letto** to strip the bed; **~rsi di qn** (*liberarsi*) to get rid of sb.

dis'fatta *sf vedi* **disfatto**.

disfat'tista, i, e *sm/f* defeatist.

dis'fatto, a *pp di* **disfare** ♦ *ag* (*gen*) undone, untied; (*letto*) unmade; (*persona: sfinito*) exhausted, worn-out; (: *addolorato*) grief-stricken ♦ *sf* (*sconfitta*) rout.

disfunzi'one [disfun'tsjone] *sf* (*MED*) dysfunction; ~ **cardiaca** heart trouble.

disge'lare [dizdʒe'lare] *vt, vi,* **~rsi** *vr* to thaw.

dis'gelo [diz'dʒelo] *sm* thaw.

dis'grazia [diz'grattsja] *sf* (*sventura*) misfortune; (*incidente*) accident, mishap.

disgrazi'ato, a [dizgrat'tsjato] *ag* unfortunate ♦ *sm/f* wretch.

disgre'gare *vt,* **~rsi** *vr* to break up.

disgu'ido *sm* hitch; ~ **postale** error in postal delivery.

disgus'tare *vt* to disgust; **~rsi** *vr:* **~rsi di** to be disgusted by.

dis'gusto *sm* disgust.

disgus'toso, a *ag* disgusting.

disidra'tare *vt* to dehydrate.

disidra'tato, a *ag* dehydrated.

disil'ludere *vt* to disillusion, disenchant.

disillusi'one *sf* disillusion, disenchantment.

disimpa'rare *vt* to forget.

disimpe'gnare [dizimpeɲ'ɲare] *vt* (*persona: da obblighi*): ~ **da** to release from; (*oggetto dato in pegno*) to redeem, get out of pawn; **~rsi** *vr:* **~rsi da** (*obblighi*) to release o.s. from, free o.s. from.

disincagli'are [dizinkaʎ'ʎare] *vt* (*barca*) to refloat; **~rsi** *vr* to get afloat again.

disincan'tato, a *ag* disenchanted, disillusioned.

disincenti'vare [dizintʃenti'vare] *vt* to discourage.

disinfes'tare *vt* to disinfest.

disinfestazi'one [dizinfestat'tsjone] *sf* disinfestation.

disinfet'tante *ag, sm* disinfectant.

disinfet'tare *vt* to disinfect.

disinfezi'one [dizinfet'tsjone] *sf* disinfection.

disingan'nare *vt* to disillusion.

disin'ganno *sm* disillusion.

disini'bito, a *ag* uninhibited.

disinnes'care *vt* to defuse.

disinnes'tare *vt* (*marcia*) to disengage.

disinqui'nare *vt* to free from pollution.

disinte'grare *vt, vi* to disintegrate.

disinteres'sarsi *vr:* ~ **di** to take no interest in.

disinte'resse *sm* indifference; (*generosità*) unselfishness.

disintossi'care *vt* (*alcolizzato, drogato*) to treat for alcoholism (*o* drug addiction); **~rsi** *vr* to clear out one's system; (*alcolizzato, drogato*) to be treated for alcoholism (*o* drug addiction).

disintossicazi'one [dizintossikat'tsjone] *sf* treatment for alcoholism (*o* drug addiction).

disin'volto, a *ag* casual, free and easy.

disinvol'tura *sf* casualness, ease.

disles'sia *sf* dyslexia.

disli'vello *sm* difference in height; (*fig*) gap.

dislo'care *vt* to station, position.

dismi'sura *sf* excess; **a** ~ to excess, excessively.

disobbe'dire *etc* = **disubbidire** *etc.*

disoccu'pato, a *ag* unemployed ♦ *sm/f* unemployed person.

disoccupazi'one [dizokkupat'tsjone] *sf* unemployment.

disonestà *sf* dishonesty.

diso'nesto, a *ag* dishonest.

disono'rare *vt* to dishonour (*Brit*), dishonor (*US*), bring disgrace upon.

diso'nore *sm* dishonour (*Brit*), dishonor (*US*), disgrace.

di'sopra *av* (*con contatto*) on top; (*senza contatto*) above; (*al piano superiore*) upstairs ♦ *ag inv* (*superiore*) upper ♦ *sm inv* top, upper part; **la gente** ~ the people upstairs; **il piano** ~ the floor above.

disordi'nare *vt* to mess up, disarrange; (*MIL*) to throw into disorder.

disordi'nato, a *ag* untidy; (*privo di misura*) irregular, wild.

di'sordine *sm* (*confusione*) disorder, confusion; (*sregolatezza*) debauchery; **~i** *smpl* (*POL etc*) disorder *sg*; (*tumulti*) riots.

disor'ganico, a, ci, che *ag* incoherent, disorganized.

disorienta'mento *sm* (*fig*) confusion, bewilderment.

disorien'tare *vt* to disorientate; **~rsi** *vr* (*fig*) to get confused, lose one's bearings.

disorien'tato, a *ag* disorientated.

disos'sare vt (CUC) to bone.

di'sotto av below, underneath; (in fondo) at the bottom; (al piano inferiore) downstairs ♦ ag inv (inferiore) lower; bottom cpd ♦ sm inv (parte inferiore) lower part; bottom; **la gente** ~ the people downstairs; **il piano** ~ the floor below.

dis'paccio [dis'pattʃo] sm dispatch.

dispa'rato, a ag disparate.

'dispari ag inv odd, uneven.

disparità sf inv disparity.

dis'parte: in ~ av (da lato) aside, apart; **tenersi** o **starsene in** ~ to keep to o.s., hold aloof.

dis'pendio sm (di denaro, energie) expenditure; (: spreco) waste.

dispendi'oso, a ag expensive.

dis'pensa sf pantry, larder; (mobile) sideboard; (DIR) exemption; (REL) dispensation; (fascicolo) number, issue.

dispen'sare vt (elemosine, favori) to distribute; (esonerare) to exempt.

dispe'rare vi: ~ (di) to despair (of); ~**rsi** vr to despair.

dispe'rato, a ag (persona) in despair; (caso, tentativo) desperate.

disperazi'one [disperat'tsjone] sf despair.

dis'perdere vt (disseminare) to disperse; (MIL) to scatter, rout; (fig: consumare) to waste, squander; ~**rsi** vr to disperse; to scatter.

dispersi'one sf dispersion, dispersal; (FISICA, CHIM) dispersion.

disper'sivo, a ag (lavoro etc) disorganized.

dis'perso, a pp di disperdere ♦ sm/f missing person; (MIL) missing soldier.

dis'petto sm spite q, spitefulness q; **fare un** ~ **a qn** to play a (nasty) trick on sb; **a** ~ **di** in spite of; **con suo grande** ~ much to his annoyance.

dispet'toso, a ag spiteful.

dispia'cere [dispja'tʃere] sm (rammarico) regret, sorrow; (dolore) grief ♦ vi: ~ **a** to displease ♦ vb impers: **mi dispiace (che)** I am sorry (that); ~**i** smpl (preoccupazioni) troubles, worries; **se non le dispiace, me ne vado adesso** if you don't mind, I'll go now.

dispiaci'uto, a [dispja'tʃuto] pp di dispiacere ♦ ag sorry.

dis'pone, dis'pongo etc vb vedi disporre.

dispo'nibile ag available.

dis'porre vt (sistemare) to arrange; (preparare) to prepare; (DIR) to order; (persuadere): ~ **qn a** to incline o dispose sb towards ♦ vi (decidere) to decide; (usufruire): ~ **di** to use, have at one's disposal; (essere dotato): ~ **di** to have; **disporsi** vr (ordinarsi) to place o.s., arrange o.s.; **disporsi a fare** to get ready to do; **disporsi all'attacco** to prepare for an attack; **disporsi in cerchio** to form a circle.

dis'posi etc vb vedi disporre.

disposi'tivo sm (meccanismo) device; (DIR) pronouncement; ~ **di controllo** o **di comando** control device; ~ **di sicurezza** (gen) safety device; (di arma da fuoco) safety catch.

disposizi'one [dispozit'tsjone] sf arrangement, layout; (stato d'animo) mood; (tendenza) bent, inclination; (comando) order; (DIR) provision, regulation; **a** ~ **di qn** at sb's disposal; **per** ~ **di legge** by law; ~ **testamentaria** provisions of a will.

dis'posto, a pp di disporre ♦ ag (incline): ~ **a fare** disposed o prepared to do.

dis'potico, a, ci, che ag despotic.

dispo'tismo sm despotism.

disprez'zare [dispret'tsare] vt to despise.

dis'prezzo [dis'prettso] sm contempt; **con** ~ **del pericolo** with a total disregard for the danger involved.

'disputa sf dispute, quarrel.

dispu'tare vt (contendere) to dispute, contest; (SPORT: partita) to play; (: gara) to take part in ♦ vi to quarrel; ~ **di** to discuss; ~**rsi qc** to fight for sth.

dissa'crare vt to desecrate.

dissangua'mento sm loss of blood.

dissangu'are vt (fig: persona) to bleed white; (: patrimonio) to suck dry; ~**rsi** vr (MED) to lose blood; (fig) to ruin o.s.; **morire dissanguato** to bleed to death.

dissa'pore sm slight disagreement.

'disse vb vedi dire.

disse'care vt to dissect.

dissec'care vt, ~**rsi** vr to dry up.

dissemi'nare vt to scatter; (fig: notizie) to spread.

dis'senso sm dissent; (disapprovazione) disapproval.

dissente'ria sf dysentery.

dissen'tire vi: ~ (da) to disagree (with).

disseppel'lire vt (esumare: cadavere) to disinter, exhume; (dissotterrare: anche fig) to dig up, unearth; (: rancori) to resurrect.

dissertazi'one [dissertat'tsjone] sf dissertation.

disser'vizio [disser'vittsjo] sm inefficiency.

disses'tare vt (ECON) to ruin.

disses'tato, a ag (fondo stradale) uneven; (economia, finanze) shaky; **"strada** ~**a"** (per lavori in corso) "road up" (Brit), "road out" (US).

dis'sesto sm (financial) ruin.

disse'tante ag refreshing.

disse'tare vt to quench the thirst of; ~**rsi** vr to quench one's thirst.

dissezi'one [disset'tsjone] sf dissection.

'dissi vb vedi dire.

dissi'dente ag, sm/f dissident.

dis'sidio sm disagreement.

dis'simile ag different, dissimilar.

dissimu'lare vt (fingere) to dissemble;

(*nascondere*) to conceal.

dissimula'tore, 'trice *sm/f* dissembler.

dissimulazi'one [dissimulat'tsjone] *sf* dissembling; concealment.

dissi'pare *vt* to dissipate; (*scialacquare*) to squander, waste.

dissipa'tezza [dissipa'tettsa] *sf* dissipation.

dissi'pato, a *ag* dissolute, dissipated.

dissipazi'one [dissipat'tsjone] *sf* squandering.

dissoci'are [dissot'tʃare] *vt* to dissociate.

dis'solto, a *pp di* **dissolvere**.

disso'lubile *ag* soluble.

dissolu'tezza [dissolu'tettsa] *sf* dissoluteness.

dissolu'tivo, a *ag* (*forza*) divisive; **processo** ~ (*anche fig*) process of dissolution.

disso'luto, a *pp di* **dissolvere** ♦ *ag* dissolute, licentious.

dissol'venza [dissol'vɛntsa] *sf* (*CINEMA*) fading.

dis'solvere *vt* to dissolve; (*neve*) to melt; (*fumo*) to disperse; ~**rsi** *vr* to dissolve; to melt; to disperse.

disso'nante *ag* discordant.

disso'nanza [disso'nantsa] *sf* (*fig: di opinioni*) clash.

dissotter'rare *vt* (*cadavere*) to disinter, exhume; (*tesori, rovine*) to dig up, unearth; (*fig: sentimenti, odio*) to bring up again, resurrect.

dissu'adere *vt*: ~ **qn da** to dissuade sb from.

dissuasi'one *sf* dissuasion.

dissu'aso, a *pp di* **dissuadere**.

distacca'mento *sm* (*MIL*) detachment.

distac'care *vt* to detach, separate; (*SPORT*) to leave behind; ~**rsi** *vr* to be detached; (*fig*) to stand out; ~**rsi da** (*fig: allontanarsi*) to grow away from.

dis'tacco, chi *sm* (*separazione*) separation; (*fig: indifferenza*) detachment; (*SPORT*): **vincere con un** ~ **di ...** to win by a distance of ....

dis'tante *av* far away ♦ *ag* distant, far away; **essere** ~ **(da)** to be a long way (from); **è** ~ **da qui?** is it far from here?; **essere** ~ **nel tempo** to be in the distant past.

dis'tanza [dis'tantsa] *sf* distance; **comando a** ~ remote control; **a** ~ **di 2 giorni** 2 days later; **tener qn a** ~ to keep sb at arm's length; **prendere le** ~**e da qc/qn** to dissociate o.s. from sth/sb; **tenere** *o* **mantenere le** ~**e** to keep one's distance; ~ **focale** focal length; ~ **di sicurezza** safe distance; (*AUT*) braking distance; ~ **di tiro** range; ~ **di visibilità** visibility.

distanzi'are [distan'tsjare] *vt* to space out, place at intervals; (*SPORT*) to outdistance; (*fig: superare*) to outstrip, surpass.

dis'tare *vi*: **distiamo pochi chilometri da Roma** we are only a few kilometres (away) from Rome; **dista molto da qui?** is

it far (away) from here?; **non dista molto** it's not far (away).

dis'tendere *vt* (*coperta*) to spread out; (*gambe*) to stretch (out); (*mettere a giacere*) to lay; (*rilassare: muscoli, nervi*) to relax; ~**rsi** *vr* (*rilassarsi*) to relax; (*sdraiarsi*) to lie down.

distensi'one *sf* stretching; relaxation; (*POL*) détente.

disten'sivo, a *ag* (*gen*) relaxing, restful; (*farmaco*) tranquillizing; (*POL*) conciliatory.

dis'teso, a *pp di* **distendere** ♦ *ag* (*allungato: persona, gamba*) stretched out; (*rilassato: persona, atmosfera*) relaxed ♦ *sf* expanse, stretch; **avere un volto** ~ to look relaxed.

distil'lare *vt* to distil.

distil'lato *sm* distillate.

distillazi'one [distillat'tsjone] *sf* distillation.

distille'ria *sf* distillery.

dis'tinguere *vt* to distinguish; ~**rsi** *vr* (*essere riconoscibile*) to be distinguished; (*emergere*) to stand out, be conspicuous, distinguish o.s.; **un vino che si distingue per il suo aroma** a wine with a distinctive bouquet.

dis'tinguo *sm inv* distinction.

dis'tinta *sf* (*nota*) note; (*elenco*) list; ~ **di pagamento** receipt; ~ **di versamento** payin slip.

distin'tivo, a *ag* distinctive; distinguishing ♦ *sm* badge.

dis'tinto, a *pp di* **distinguere** ♦ *ag* (*dignitoso ed elegante*) distinguished; ~**i saluti** (*in lettera*) yours faithfully.

distinzi'one [distin'tsjone] *sf* distinction; **non faccio** ~**i** (*tra persone*) I don't discriminate; (*tra cose*) it's all one to me; **senza** ~ **di razza/religione ...** no matter what one's race/creed ....

dis'togliere [dis'tɔʎʎere] *vt*: ~ **da** to take away from; (*fig*) to dissuade from.

dis'tolto, a *pp di* **distogliere**.

dis'torcere [dis'tɔrtʃere] *vt* to twist; (*fig*) to twist, distort; ~**rsi** *vr* (*contorcersi*) to twist.

distorsi'one *sf* (*MED*) sprain; (*FISICA, OTTICA*) distortion.

dis'torto, a *pp di* **distorcere**.

dis'trarre *vt* to distract; (*divertire*) to entertain, amuse; **distrarsi** *vr* (*non fare attenzione*) to be distracted, let one's mind wander; (*svagarsi*) to amuse *o* enjoy o.s.; ~ **lo sguardo** to look away; **non distrarti!** pay attention!

distratta'mente *av* absent-mindedly, without thinking.

dis'tratto, a *pp di* **distrarre** ♦ *ag* absent-minded; (*disattento*) inattentive.

distrazi'one [distrat'tsjone] *sf* absent-mindedness; inattention; (*svago*) distraction, entertainment; **errori di** ~ careless mistakes.

dis'tretto *sm* district.

distribu'ire *vt* to distribute; (*CARTE*) to deal (out); (*consegnare: posta*) to deliver; (*lavoro*) to allocate, assign; (*ripartire*) to share out.

distribu'tore *sm* (*di benzina*) petrol (*Brit*) o gas (*US*) pump; (*AUT, ELETTR*) distributor; (*automatico*) vending machine.

distribuzi'one [distribut'tsjone] *sf* distribution; delivery; allocation, assignment; sharing out.

distri'care *vt* to disentangle, unravel; ~rsi *vr* (*tirarsi fuori*): ~rsi da to get out of, disentangle o.s. from; (*fig: cavarsela*) to manage, get by.

distro'fia *sf* dystrophy.

dis'truggere [dis'truddʒere] *vt* to destroy.

distrut'tivo, a *ag* destructive.

dis'trutto, a *pp di* **distruggere**.

distruzi'one [distrut'tsjone] *sf* destruction.

distur'bare *vt* to disturb, trouble; (*sonno, lezioni*) to disturb, interrupt; ~rsi *vr* to put o.s. out; **non si disturbi** please don't bother.

dis'turbo *sm* trouble, bother, inconvenience; (*indisposizione*) (slight) disorder, ailment; ~i *smpl* (*RADIO, TV*) static *sg*; ~ **della quiete pubblica** (*DIR*) disturbance of the peace; ~i **di stomaco** stomach trouble *sg*.

disubbidi'ente *ag* disobedient.

disubbidi'enza [dizubbi'djɛntsa] *sf* disobedience; ~ **civile** civil disobedience.

disubbi'dire *vi*: ~ **(a qn)** to disobey (sb).

disuguagli'anza [dizugwaʎ'ʎantsa] *sf* inequality.

disugu'ale *ag* unequal; (*diverso*) different; (*irregolare*) uneven.

disumanità *sf* inhumanity.

disu'mano, a *ag* inhuman; **un grido** ~ a terrible cry.

disuni'one *sf* disunity.

disu'nire *vt* to divide, disunite.

di'suso *sm*: **andare** o **cadere in** ~ to fall into disuse.

'dita *sfpl di* **dito**.

di'tale *sm* thimble.

di'tata *sf* (*colpo*) jab (with one's finger); (*segno*) fingermark.

'dito, *pl(f)* **'dita** *sm* finger; (*misura*) finger, finger's breadth; ~ **(del piede)** toe; **mettersi le** ~**a nel naso** to pick one's nose; **mettere il** ~ **sulla piaga** (*fig*) to touch a sore spot; **non ha mosso un** ~ **(per aiutarmi)** he didn't lift a finger (to help me); **ormai è segnato a** ~ everyone knows about him now.

'ditta *sf* firm, business; **macchina della** ~ company car.

dit'tafono *sm* Dictaphone ®.

ditta'tore *sm* dictator.

ditta'tura *sf* dictatorship.

dit'tongo, ghi *sm* diphthong.

di'urno, a *ag* day *cpd*, daytime *cpd* ♦ *sm* (*anche:* **albergo** ~) *public toilets with washing and shaving facilities etc*; **ore** ~**e** daytime *sg*; **spettacolo** ~ matinee; **turno** ~ day shift.

'diva *sf vedi* **divo**.

diva'gare *vi* to digress.

divagazi'one [divagat'tsjone] *sf* digression; ~i **sul tema** variations on a theme.

divam'pare *vi* to flare up, blaze up.

di'vano *sm* sofa; (*senza schienale*) divan; ~ **letto** bed settee, sofa bed.

divari'care *vt* to open wide.

di'vario *sm* difference.

di'vengo *etc vb vedi* **divenire**.

dive'nire *vi* = **diventare**.

di'venni *etc vb vedi* **divenire**.

diven'tare *vi* to become; ~ **famoso/ professore** to become famous/a teacher; ~ **vecchio** to grow old; **c'è da** ~ **matti** it's enough to drive you mad.

dive'nuto, a *pp di* **divenire**.

di'verbio *sm* altercation.

diver'gente [diver'dʒɛnte] *ag* divergent.

diver'genza [diver'dʒɛntsa] *sf* divergence; ~ **d'opinioni** difference of opinion.

di'vergere [di'vɛrdʒere] *vi* to diverge.

diverrò *etc vb vedi* **divenire**.

diversa'mente *av* (*in modo differente*) differently; (*altrimenti*) otherwise; ~ **da quanto stabilito** contrary to what had been decided.

diversifi'care *vt* to diversify, vary; ~rsi *vr*: ~rsi **(per)** to differ (in).

diversificazi'one [diversifikat'tsjone] *sf* diversification; difference.

diversi'one *sf* diversion.

diversità *sf inv* difference, diversity; (*varietà*) variety.

diver'sivo, a *ag* diversionary ♦ *sm* diversion, distraction; **fare un'azione** ~**a** to create a diversion.

di'verso, a *ag* (*differente*): ~ **(da)** different (from) ♦ *sm* (*omosessuale*) homosexual; ~i, **e** *det pl* several, various; (*COMM*) sundry ♦ *pronome pl* several (people), many (people).

diver'tente *ag* amusing.

diverti'mento *sm* amusement, pleasure; (*passatempo*) pastime, recreation; **buon** ~! enjoy yourself!

diver'tire *vt* to amuse, entertain; ~rsi *vr* to amuse o enjoy o.s.; **divertiti!** enjoy yourself, have a good time!; ~rsi **alle spalle di qn** to have a laugh at sb's expense.

diver'tito, a *ag* amused.

divez'zare [divet'tsare] *vt* (*anche fig*): ~ **(da)** to wean (from).

divi'dendo *sm* dividend.

di'videre vt (anche MAT) to divide; (distribuire, ripartire) to divide (up), split (up); ~**rsi** vr (persone) to separate, part; (coppia) to separate; ~**rsi (in)** (scindersi) to divide (into), split up (into); (ramificarsi) to fork; **è diviso dalla moglie** he's separated from his wife; **si divide tra casa e lavoro** he divides his time between home and work.

divi'eto sm prohibition; "~ **di accesso**" "no entry"; "~ **di caccia**" "no hunting"; "~ **di parcheggio**" "no parking"; "~ **di sosta**" (AUT) "no waiting".

divinco'larsi vr to wriggle, writhe.

divinità sf inv divinity.

di'vino, a ag divine.

di'visa sf (MIL etc) uniform; (COMM) foreign currency.

di'visi etc vb vedi **dividere**.

divisi'one sf division; ~ **in sillabe** syllable division; (a fine riga) hyphenation.

di'vismo sm (esibizionismo) playing to the crowd.

di'viso, a pp di **dividere**.

divi'sorio, a ag (siepe, muro esterno) dividing; (muro interno) dividing, partition cpd ♦ sm (in una stanza) partition.

'divo, a sm/f star; **come una** ~**a** like a prima donna.

divo'rare vt to devour; ~ **qc con gli occhi** to eye sth greedily.

divorzi'are [divor'tsjare] vi: ~ **(da qn)** to divorce (sb).

divorzi'ato, a [divor'tsjato] ag divorced ♦ sm/f divorcee.

di'vorzio [di'vɔrtsjo] sm divorce.

divul'gare vt to divulge, disclose; (rendere comprensibile) to popularize; ~**rsi** vr to spread.

divulgazi'one [divulgat'tsjone] sf (vedi vb) disclosure; popularization; spread.

dizio'nario [dittsjo'narjo] sm dictionary.

dizi'one [dit'tsjone] sf diction; pronunciation.

Dja'karta [dʒa'karta] sf Djakarta.

dl abbr (= decilitro) dl.

dm abbr (= decimetro) dm.

DNA sigla m (BIOL) DNA.

do sm (MUS) C; (: solfeggiando la scala) do(h).

dobbi'amo vb vedi **dovere**.

D.O.C. [dɔk] sigla vedi **denominazione di origine controllata**.

doc. abbr = **documento**.

'doccia, ce ['dottʃa] sf (bagno) shower; (condotto) pipe; **fare la** ~ to have a shower; ~ **fredda** (fig) slap in the face.

do'cente [do'tʃente] ag teaching ♦ sm/f teacher; (di università) lecturer.

do'cenza [do'tʃentsa] sf university teaching o lecturing; **ottenere la libera** ~ to become a lecturer.

D.O.C.G. sigla (= denominazione di origine controllata e garantita) label guaranteeing the quality and origin of a wine.

'docile ['dɔtʃile] ag docile.

documen'tare vt to document; ~**rsi** vr: ~**rsi (su)** to gather information o material (about).

documen'tario, a ag, sm documentary.

documentazi'one [dokumentat'tsjone] sf documentation.

docu'mento sm document; ~**i** smpl (d'identità etc) papers.

Dodeca'neso sm: **le Isole del** ~ the Dodecanese Islands.

dodi'cenne [dodi'tʃɛnne] ag, sm/f twelve-year-old.

dodi'cesimo, a [dodi'tʃɛzimo] num twelfth.

'dodici ['doditʃi] num twelve.

do'gana sf (ufficio) customs pl; (tassa) (customs) duty; **passare la** ~ to go through customs.

doga'nale ag customs cpd.

dogani'ere sm customs officer.

'doglie ['dɔʎʎe] sfpl (MED) labour sg (Brit), labor sg (US), labo(u)r pains.

'dogma, i sm dogma.

dog'matico, a, ci, che ag dogmatic.

'dolce ['doltʃe] ag sweet; (colore) soft; (carattere, persona) gentle, mild; (fig: mite: clima) mild; (non ripido: pendio) gentle ♦ sm (sapore ~) sweetness, sweet taste; (CUC: portata) sweet, dessert; (: torta) cake; **il** ~ **far niente** sweet idleness.

dol'cezza [dol'tʃettsa] sf sweetness; softness; mildness; gentleness.

dolci'ario, a [dol'tʃarjo] ag confectionery cpd.

dolci'astro, a [dol'tʃastro] ag (sapore) sweetish.

dolcifi'cante [doltʃifi'kante] ag sweetening ♦ sm sweetener.

dolci'umi [dol'tʃumi] smpl sweets.

do'lente ag sorrowful, sad.

do'lere vi to be sore, hurt, ache; ~**rsi** vr to complain; (essere spiacente): ~**rsi di** to be sorry for; **mi duole la testa** my head aches, I've got a headache.

'dolgo etc vb vedi **dolere**.

'dollaro sm dollar.

'dolo sm (DIR) malice; (frode) fraud, deceit.

Dolo'miti sfpl: **le** ~ the Dolomites.

dolo'rante ag aching, sore.

do'lore sm (fisico) pain; (morale) sorrow, grief; **se lo scoprono sono** ~**i!** if they find out there'll be trouble!

dolo'roso, a ag painful; sorrowful, sad.

do'loso, a ag (DIR) malicious; **incendio** ~ arson.

'dolsi etc vb vedi **dolere**.

dom. abbr (= domenica) Sun.

do'manda sf (interrogazione) question; (richiesta) demand; (: cortese) request;

(*DIR: richiesta scritta*) application; (*ECON*): **la ~** demand; **fare una ~ a qn** to ask sb a question; **fare ~ (per un lavoro)** to apply (for a job); **far regolare ~ (di qc)** to apply through the proper channels (for sth); **fare ~ all'autorità giudiziaria** to apply to the courts; **~ di divorzio** divorce petition; **~ di matrimonio** proposal.

doman'dare *vt* (*per avere*) to ask for; (*per sapere*) to ask; (*esigere*) to demand; **~rsi** *vr* to wonder, ask o.s.; **~ qc a qn** to ask sb for sth; to ask sb sth.

do'mani *av* tomorrow ♦ *sm* (*l'indomani*) next day, following day; **il ~** (*il futuro*) the future; (*il giorno successivo*) the next day; **un ~** some day; **~ l'altro** the day after tomorrow; **~ (a) otto** tomorrow week, a week tomorrow; **a ~!** see you tomorrow!

do'mare *vt* to tame.

doma'tore, 'trice *sm/f* (*gen*) tamer; **~ di cavalli** horsebreaker; **~ di leoni** lion tamer.

domat'tina *av* tomorrow morning.

do'menica, che *sf* Sunday; *per fraseologia vedi* **martedì**.

domeni'cale *ag* Sunday *cpd*.

domeni'cano, a *ag, sm/f* Dominican.

do'mestica, che *sf vedi* **domestico**.

do'mestico, a, ci, che *ag* domestic ♦ *sm/f* servant, domestic; **le pareti ~che** one's own four walls; **animale** *m* **~** pet; **una ~a a ore** a daily (woman).

domicili'are [domitʃi'ljare] *ag vedi* **arresto**.

domicili'arsi [domitʃi'ljarsi] *vr* to take up residence.

domi'cilio [domi'tʃiljo] *sm* (*DIR*) domicile, place of residence; **visita a ~** (*MED*) house call; **"recapito a ~"** "deliveries"; **violazione di ~** (*DIR*) breaking and entering.

domi'nante *ag* (*colore, nota*) dominant; (*opinione*) prevailing; (*idea*) main *cpd*, chief *cpd*; (*posizione*) dominating *cpd*; (*classe, partito*) ruling *cpd*.

domi'nare *vt* to dominate; (*fig: sentimenti*) to control, master ♦ *vi* to be in the dominant position; **~rsi** *vr* (*controllarsi*) to control o.s.; **~ su** (*fig*) to surpass, outclass.

domina'tore, 'trice *ag* ruling *cpd* ♦ *sm/f* ruler.

dominazi'one [dominat'tsjone] *sf* domination.

domini'cano, a *ag*: **la Repubblica D~a** the Dominican Republic.

do'minio *sm* dominion; (*fig: campo*) field, domain; **~i coloniali** colonies; **essere di ~ pubblico** (*notizia etc*) to be common knowledge.

do'nare *vt* to give, present; (*per beneficenza etc*) to donate ♦ *vi* (*fig*): **~ a** to suit, become; **~ sangue** to give blood.

dona'tore, 'trice *sm/f* donor; **~ di sangue/**

di organi blood/organ donor.

donazi'one [donat'tsjone] *sf* donation; **atto di ~** (*DIR*) deed of gift.

'donde *av* (*poetico*) whence.

dondo'lare *vt* (*cullare*) to rock; **~rsi** *vr* to swing, sway.

'dondolo *sm*: **sedia/cavallo a ~** rocking chair/horse.

dongio'vanni [dondʒo'vanni] *sm* Don Juan, ladies' man.

'donna *sf* woman; (*titolo*) Donna; (*CARTE*) queen; **figlio di buona ~!** (*fam*) son of a bitch!; **~ di casa** housewife; **~ a ore** daily (help *o* woman); **~ delle pulizie** cleaning lady, cleaner; **~ di servizio** maid; **~ di vita** *o* **di strada** prostitute, streetwalker.

donnai'olo *sm* ladykiller.

don'nesco, a, schi, sche *ag* women's, woman's.

'donnola *sf* weasel.

'dono *sm* gift.

'dopo *av* (*tempo*) afterwards; (: *più tardi*) later; (*luogo*) after, next ♦ *prep* after ♦ *cong* (*temporale*): **~ aver studiato** after having studied ♦ *ag inv*: **il giorno ~** the following day; **~ mangiato va a dormire** after having eaten *o* after a meal he goes for a sleep; **un anno ~** a year later; **~ di me/lui** after me/him; **~ che** = **dopoché**.

dopo'barba *sm inv* after-shave.

dopoché [dopo'ke] *cong* after, when.

dopodiché [dopodi'ke] *av* after which.

dopodo'mani *av* the day after tomorrow.

dopogu'erra *sm* postwar years *pl*.

dopola'voro *sm* recreational club.

dopo'pranzo [dopo'prandzo] *av* after lunch (*o* dinner).

doposcì [dopoʃ'ʃi] *sm inv* après-ski outfit.

doposcu'ola *sm inv* school club offering extra tuition and recreational facilities.

dopo'tutto *av* after all.

doppi'aggio [dop'pjaddʒo] *sm* (*CINEMA*) dubbing.

doppi'are *vt* (*NAUT*) to round; (*SPORT*) to lap; (*CINEMA*) to dub.

doppia'tore, 'trice *sm/f* dubber.

doppi'etta *sf* (*fucile*) double-barrelled (*Brit*) *o* double-barreled (*US*) shotgun; (*sparo*) shot from both barrels; (*CALCIO*) double; (*PUGILATO*) one-two; (*AUT*) double-declutch (*Brit*), double-clutch (*US*).

doppi'ezza [dop'pjettsa] *sf* (*fig: di persona*) duplicity, double-dealing.

'doppio, a *ag* double; (*fig: falso*) double-dealing, deceitful ♦ *sm* (*quantità*): **il ~ (di)** twice as much (*o* many), double the amount (*o* number) of; (*SPORT*) doubles *pl* ♦ *av* double; **battere una lettera in ~a copia** to type a letter with a carbon copy; **fare il ~ gioco** (*fig*) to play a double game; **chiudere a ~a mandata** to double-lock; **~ senso** double entendre; **frase a ~**

senso sentence with a double meaning; **un utensile a ~ uso** a dual-purpose utensil.

doppio'fondo *sm* (*di valigia*) false bottom; (*NAUT*) double hull.

doppi'one *sm* duplicate (copy).

doppio'petto *sm* double-breasted jacket.

dop'pista *sm/f* (*TENNIS*) doubles player.

do'rare *vt* to gild; (*CUC*) to brown; **~ la pillola** (*fig*) to sugar the pill.

do'rato, a *ag* golden; (*ricoperto d'oro*) gilt, gilded.

dora'tura *sf* gilding.

dormicchi'are [dormik'kjare] *vi* to doze.

dormi'ente *ag* sleeping ♦ *sm/f* sleeper.

dormigli'one, a [dormiʎ'ʎone] *sm/f* sleepy-head.

dor'mire *vi* to sleep; (*essere addormentato*) to be asleep, be sleeping; **il caffè non mi fa ~** coffee keeps me awake; **~ come un ghiro** to sleep like a log; **~ della grossa** to sleep soundly, be dead to the world; **~ in piedi** (*essere stanco*) to be asleep on one's feet.

dor'mita *sf*: **farsi una ~** to have a good sleep.

dormi'torio *sm* dormitory; **~ pubblico** doss house (*Brit*) *o* flophouse (*US*) (*run by local authority*).

dormi'veglia [dormi'veʎʎa] *sm* drowsiness.

dorrò *etc vb vedi* **dolere**.

dor'sale *ag*: **spina ~** backbone, spine.

'dorso *sm* back; (*di montagna*) ridge, crest; (*di libro*) spine; (*NUOTO*) backstroke; **a ~ di cavallo** on horseback.

do'saggio [do'zaddʒo] *sm* (*atto*) measuring out; **sbagliare il ~** to get the proportions wrong.

do'sare *vt* to measure out; (*MED*) to dose.

'dose *sf* quantity, amount; (*MED*) dose.

dossi'er [do'sje] *sm inv* dossier, file.

'dosso *sm* (*rilievo*) rise; (*: di strada*) bump; (*dorso*): **levarsi di ~ i vestiti** to take one's clothes off; **levarsi un peso di ~** (*fig*) to take a weight off one's mind.

do'tare *vt*: **~ di** to provide *o* supply with; (*fig*) to endow with.

do'tato, a *ag*: **~ di** (*attrezzature*) equipped with; (*bellezza, intelligenza*) endowed with; **un uomo ~** a gifted man.

dotazi'one [dotat'tsjone] *sf* (*insieme di beni*) endowment; (*di macchine etc*) equipment; **dare qc in ~ a qn** to issue sb with sth, issue sth to sb; **i macchinari in ~ alla fabbrica** the machinery in use in the factory.

'dote *sf* (*di sposa*) dowry; (*assegnata a un ente*) endowment; (*fig*) gift, talent.

Dott. *abbr* (= *dottore*) Dr.

'dotto, a *ag* (*colto*) learned ♦ *sm* (*sapiente*) scholar; (*ANAT*) duct.

dotto'rato *sm* degree; **~ di ricerca** doctor-ate, doctor's degree.

dot'tore, 'essa *sm/f* doctor.

dot'trina *sf* doctrine.

Dott.ssa *abbr* (= *dottoressa*) Dr.

double-'face [dubl'fas] *ag inv* reversible.

'dove *av* where; (*in cui*) where, in which; (*dovunque*) wherever ♦ *sm*: **per ogni ~** everywhere; **di dov'è?** where are you from?; **da ~ abito vedo tutta la città** I can see the whole city from where I live; **per ~ si passa?** which way should we go?; **ti dò una mano fin ~ posso** I'll help you as much as I can.

do'vere *sm* (*obbligo*) duty ♦ *vt* (*essere debitore*): **~ qc (a qn)** to owe (sb) sth ♦ *vi* (*seguito dall'infinito: obbligo*) to have to; **lui deve farlo** he has to do it, he must do it; **è dovuto partire** he had to leave; **ha dovuto pagare** he had to pay; (*: intenzione*): **devo partire domani** I'm (due) to leave tomorrow; (*: probabilità*): **dev'essere tardi** it must be late; **doveva accadere** it was bound to happen; **avere il senso del ~** to have a sense of duty; **rivolgersi a chi di ~** to apply to the appropriate authority *o* person; **a ~** (*bene*) properly; (*debitamente*) as he (*o* she *etc*) deserves; **come si deve** (*bene*) properly; (*meritatamente*) properly, as he (*o* she *etc*) deserves; **una persona come si deve** a respectable person.

dove'roso, a *ag* (right and) proper.

dovrò *etc vb vedi* **dovere**.

do'vunque *av* (*in qualunque luogo*) wher-ever; (*dappertutto*) everywhere; **~ io vada** wherever I go.

dovuta'mente *av* (*debitamente*: *redigere, compilare*) correctly; (*: rimproverare*) as he (*o* she *etc*) deserves.

do'vuto, a *ag* (*causato*): **~ a** due to ♦ *sm* due; **nel modo ~** in the proper way; **ho lavorato più del ~** I worked more than was necessary.

doz'zina [dod'dzina] *sf* dozen; **una ~ di uova** a dozen eggs; **di** *o* **da ~** (*scrittore, spettacolo*) second-rate.

dozzi'nale [doddzi'nale] *ag* cheap, second-rate.

DP *sigla f* (= *Democrazia Proletaria*) political party.

'draga, ghe *sf* dredger.

dra'gare *vt* to dredge.

dragherò *etc* [drage'rɔ] *vb vedi* **dragare**.

'drago, ghi *sm* dragon; (*fig fam*) genius.

'dramma, i *sm* drama; **fare un ~ di qc** to make a drama out of sth.

dram'matico, a, ci, che *ag* dramatic.

drammatiz'zare [drammatid'dzare] *vt* to dramatize.

dramma'turgo, ghi *sm* playwright, drama-tist.

drappeggi'are [drapped'dʒare] *vt* to drape.

drap'peggio [drap'peddʒo] *sm* (*tessuto*) drapery; (*di abito*) folds.

drap'pello *sm* (*MIL*) squad; (*gruppo*) band, group.

'drappo *sm* cloth.

'drastico, a, ci, che *ag* drastic.

dre'naggio [dre'nadd͡ʒo] *sm* drainage.

dre'nare *vt* to drain.

'Dresda *sf* Dresden.

drib'blare *vi* (*CALCIO*) to dribble ♦ *vt* (*avversario*) to dodge, avoid.

'dritto, a *ag*, *av* = **diritto** ♦ *sm/f* (*fam: furbo*): **è un** ~ he's a crafty *o* sly one ♦ *sf* (*destra*) right, right hand; (*NAUT*) starboard; **a ~a e a manca** (*fig*) on all sides, right, left and centre.

driz'zare [drit'tsare] *vt* (*far tornare diritto*) to straighten; (*volgere: sguardo, occhi*) to turn, direct; (*innalzare: antenna, muro*) to erect; **~rsi** *vr* to stand up; ~ **le orecchie** to prick up one's ears; **~rsi in piedi** to rise to one's feet; **~rsi a sedere** to sit up.

'droga, ghe *sf* (*sostanza aromatica*) spice; (*stupefacente*) drug; **~ghe pesanti/leggere** hard/soft drugs.

dro'gare *vt* to season, spice; to drug, dope; **~rsi** *vr* to take drugs.

dro'gato, a *sm/f* drug addict.

droghe'ria [droge'ria] *sf* grocer's (shop) (*Brit*), grocery (store) (*US*).

drogherò *etc* [droge'rɔ] *vb vedi* **drogare**.

droghi'ere, a [dro'gjɛre] *sm/f* grocer.

drome'dario *sm* dromedary.

D.T. *abbr* = **direttore tecnico**.

'dubbio, a *ag* (*incerto*) doubtful, dubious; (*ambiguo*) dubious ♦ *sm* (*incertezza*) doubt; **avere il** ~ **che** to be afraid that, suspect that; **essere in** ~ **fra** to hesitate between; **mettere in** ~ **qc** to question sth; **nutrire seri ~i su qc** to have grave doubts about sth; **senza** ~ doubtless, no doubt.

dubbi'oso, a *ag* doubtful, dubious.

dubi'tare *vi*: ~ **di** (*onestà*) to doubt; (*risultato*) to be doubtful of; ~ **di qn** to mistrust sb; ~ **di sé** to be unsure of o.s.

Du'blino *sf* Dublin.

'duca, chi *sm* duke.

'duce ['dut͡ʃe] *sm* (*STORIA*) captain; (*: del fascismo*) duce.

du'chessa [du'kessa] *sf* duchess.

'due *num* two; **a** ~ **a** ~ two at a time, two by two; **dire** ~ **parole** to say a few words; **ci metto** ~ **minuti** I'll have it done in a tick (*Brit*) *o* jiffy.

duecen'tesco, a, schi, sche [duet͡ʃen'tesko] *ag* thirteenth-century.

due'cento [due't͡ʃɛnto] *num* two hundred ♦ *sm*: **il D~** the thirteenth century.

duel'lare *vi* to fight a duel.

du'ello *sm* duel.

due'mila *num* two thousand ♦ *sm inv*: **il** ~ the year two thousand.

due'pezzi [due'pɛttsi] *sm* (*costume da bagno*) two-piece swimsuit; (*abito femminile*) two-piece suit.

du'etto *sm* duet.

'dulcis in 'fundo ['dult͡ʃisin'fundo] *av* to cap it all.

'duna *sf* dune.

'dunque *cong* (*perciò*) so, therefore; (*riprendendo il discorso*) well (then) ♦ *sm inv*: **venire al** ~ to come to the point.

'duo *sm inv* (*MUS*) duet; (*TEATRO, CINEMA, fig*) duo.

du'ole *etc vb vedi* **dolere**.

du'omo *sm* cathedral.

'duplex *sm inv* (*TEL*) party line.

dupli'cato *sm* duplicate.

'duplice ['duplit͡ʃe] *ag* double, twofold; **in** ~ **copia** in duplicate.

duplicità [duplit͡ʃi'ta] *sf* (*fig*) duplicity.

du'rante *prep* during; **vita natural** ~ for life.

du'rare *vi* to last; **non può** ~**!** this can't go on any longer!; ~ **fatica a** to have difficulty in; ~ **in carica** to remain in office.

du'rata *sf* length (of time); duration; **per tutta la** ~ **di** throughout; ~ **media della vita** life expectancy.

du'rezza [du'rettsa] *sf* hardness; stubbornness; harshness; toughness.

'duro, a *ag* (*pietra, lavoro, materasso, problema*) hard; (*persona: ostinato*) stubborn, obstinate; (*: severo*) harsh, hard; (*voce*) harsh; (*carne*) tough ♦ *sm/f* (*persona*) tough one ♦ *av*: **tener** ~ (*resistere*) to stand firm, hold out; **avere la pelle ~a** (*fig: persona*) to be tough; **fare il** ~ to act tough; ~ **di comprendonio** slow-witted; ~ **d'orecchi** hard of hearing.

du'rone *sm* hard skin.

'duttile *ag* (*sostanza*) malleable; (*fig: carattere*) docile, biddable; (*: stile*) adaptable.

D.V. *abbr* (= *Deo volente*) DV.

E

E, e [e] *sf o m inv* (*lettera*) E, e; **E come Empoli** ≈ E for Edward (*Brit*), E for Easy (*US*).

E *abbr* (= *est*) E; (*AUT*) = *itinerario europeo*.

e, *dav V spesso* **ed** *cong* and; (*avversativo*) but; (*eppure*) and yet; ~ **lui?** what about him?; ~ **compralo!** well buy it then!

è *vb vedi* **essere**.

E.A. *abbr* = *ente autonomo*.
E.A.D. *sigla f vedi* **elaborazione automatica dei dati**.
ebaniste'ria *sf* cabinet-making; (*negozio*) cabinet-maker's shop.
'ebano *sm* ebony.
eb'bene *cong* well (then).
'ebbi *etc vb vedi* **avere**.
eb'brezza [eb'brettsa] *sf* intoxication.
'ebbro, a *ag* drunk; ~ **di** (*gioia etc*) beside o.s. *o* wild with.
'ebete *ag* stupid, idiotic.
ebe'tismo *sm* stupidity.
ebollizi'one [ebollit'tsjone] *sf* boiling; **punto di** ~ boiling point.
e'braico, a, ci, che *ag* Hebrew, Hebraic ♦ *sm* (*LING*) Hebrew.
e'breo, a *ag* Jewish ♦ *sm/f* Jew/Jewess.
'Ebridi *sfpl*: **le (isole)** ~ the Hebrides.
e'burneo, a *ag* ivory *cpd*.
E/C *abbr* = **estratto conto**.
eca'tombe *sf* (*strage*) slaughter, massacre.
ecc *abbr av* (= *eccetera*) etc.
ecce'dente [ettʃe'dɛnte] *sm* surplus.
ecce'denza [ettʃe'dɛntsa] *sf* excess, surplus; (*INFORM*) overflow.
ec'cedere [et'tʃedere] *vt* to exceed ♦ *vi* to go too far; ~ **nel bere/mangiare** to indulge in drink/food to excess.
eccel'lente [ettʃel'lɛnte] *ag* excellent.
eccel'lenza [ettʃel'lɛntsa] *sf* excellence; (*titolo*): **Sua E~** His Excellency.
ec'cellere [et'tʃellere] *vi*: ~ **(in)** to excel (at); ~ **su tutti** to surpass everyone.
ec'celso, a [et'tʃelso] *pp di* **eccellere** ♦ *ag* (*cima, montagna*) high; (*fig: ingegno*) great, exceptional.
ec'centrico, a, ci, che [et'tʃɛntriko] *ag* eccentric.
ecces'sivo, a [ettʃes'sivo] *ag* excessive.
ec'cesso [et'tʃɛsso] *sm* excess; **all'~** (*gentile, generoso*) to excess, excessively; **dare in** ~**i** to fly into a rage; ~ **di velocità** (*AUT*) speeding; ~ **di zelo** overzealousness.
ec'cetera [et'tʃetera] *av* et cetera, and so on.
ec'cetto [et'tʃetto] *prep* except, with the exception of; ~ **che** *cong* except, other than; ~ **che (non)** unless.
eccettu'are [ettʃettu'are] *vt* to except; **eccettuati i presenti** present company excepted.
eccezio'nale [ettʃettsjo'nale] *ag* exceptional; **in via del tutto** ~ in this instance, exceptionally.
eccezi'one [ettʃet'tsjone] *sf* exception; (*DIR*) objection; **a** ~ **di** with the exception of, except for; **d'~** exceptional; **fare un'~ alla regola** to make an exception to the rule.
ec'chimosi [ek'kimozi] *sf inv* bruise.
ec'cidio [et'tʃidjo] *sm* massacre.
ecci'tante [ettʃi'tante] *ag* (*gen*) exciting; (*sostanza*) stimulating ♦ *sm* stimulant.

ecci'tare [ettʃi'tare] *vt* (*curiosità, interesse*) to excite, arouse; (*folla*) to incite; ~**rsi** *vr* to get excited; (*sessualmente*) to become aroused.
eccitazi'one [ettʃitat'tsjone] *sf* excitement.
ecclesi'astico, a, ci, che *ag* ecclesiastical, church *cpd*; clerical ♦ *sm* ecclesiastic.
'ecco *av* (*per dimostrare*): ~ **il treno!** here's *o* here comes the train!; (*dav pronome*): ~**mi!** here I am!; ~**ne uno!** here's one (of them)!; (*dav pp*): ~ **fatto!** there, that's it done!
ec'come *av* rather; **ti piace?** — ~! do you like it? — I'll say! *o* and how! *o* rather! (*Brit*).
ECG *sigla m* = **elettrocardiogramma**.
echeggi'are [eked'dʒare] *vi* to echo.
e'clettico, a, ci, che *ag, sm/f* eclectic.
eclet'tismo *sm* eclecticism.
eclis'sare *vt* to eclipse; (*fig*) to eclipse, overshadow; ~**rsi** *vr* (*persona: scherzoso*) to slip away.
e'clissi *sf* eclipse.
'eco, pl(m) 'echi *sm o f* echo; **suscitò** *o* **ebbe una profonda** ~ it caused quite a stir.
ecogra'fia *sf* (*MED*) ultrasound.
ecolo'gia [ekolo'dʒia] *sf* ecology.
eco'logico, a, ci, che [eko'lɔdʒiko] *ag* ecological.
e'cologo, a, gi, ghe *sm/f* ecologist.
econo'mato *sm* (*INS*) bursar's office.
econo'mia *sf* economy; (*scienza*) economics *sg*; (*risparmio: azione*) saving; **fare** ~ to economize, make economies; **l'~ sommersa** the black (*Brit*) *o* underground (*US*) economy.
eco'nomico, a, ci, che *ag* economic; (*poco costoso*) economical; **edizione** ~**a** economy edition.
econo'mista, i *sm* economist.
economiz'zare [ekonomid'dzare] *vt, vi* to save.
e'conomo, a *ag* thrifty ♦ *sm/f* (*INS*) bursar.
'ECU *abbr m inv* (= *European Currency Unit*) ECU.
'Ecuador *sm*: **l'~** Ecuador.
ecu'menico, a, ci, che *ag* ecumenical.
ec'zema [ek'dzɛma] *sm* eczema.
ed *cong vedi* **e**.
Ed. *abbr* = **editore**.
ed. *abbr* = **edizione**.
'edera *sf* ivy.
e'dicola *sf* newspaper kiosk *o* stand (*US*).
edico'lante *sm/f* news vendor (*in kiosk*).
edifi'cante *ag* edifying.
edifi'care *vt* to build; (*fig: teoria, azienda*) to establish; (*indurre al bene*) to edify.
edi'ficio [edi'fitʃo] *sm* building; (*fig*) structure.
e'dile *ag* building *cpd*.
edi'lizio, a [edi'littsjo] *ag* building *cpd* ♦ *sf* building, building trade.

Edim'burgo *sf* Edinburgh.
'edito, a *ag* published.
edi'tore, 'trice *ag* publishing *cpd* ♦ *sm/f* publisher; (*curatore*) editor.
edito'ria *sf* publishing.
editori'ale *ag* publishing *cpd* ♦ *sm* (*articolo di fondo*) editorial, leader.
e'ditto *sm* edict.
edizi'one [edit'tsjone] *sf* edition; (*tiratura*) printing; ~ **a tiratura limitata** limited edition.
edo'nismo *sm* hedonism.
e'dotto, a *ag* informed; **rendere qn ~ su qc** to inform sb about sth.
edu'canda *sf* boarder.
edu'care *vt* to educate; (*gusto, mente*) to train; ~ **qn a fare** to train sb to do.
educa'tivo, a *ag* educational.
edu'cato, a *ag* polite, well-mannered.
educazi'one [edukat'tsjone] *sf* education; (*familiare*) upbringing; (*comportamento*) (good) manners *pl*; **per ~** out of politeness; **questa è pura mancanza d'~!** this is sheer bad manners!; ~ **fisica** (*INS*) physical training *o* education.
educherò *etc* [eduke'rɔ] *vb vedi* **educare**.
E.E.D. *sigla f vedi* **elaborazione elettronica dei dati**.
EEG *sigla m* = **elettroencefalogramma**.
e'felide *sf* freckle.
effemi'nato, a *ag* effeminate.
effe'rato, a *ag* brutal, savage.
efferve'scente [efferveʃ'ʃɛnte] *ag* effervescent.
effettiva'mente *av* (*in effetti*) in fact; (*a dire il vero*) really, actually.
effet'tivo, a *ag* (*reale*) real, actual; (*impiegato, professore*) permanent; (*MIL*) regular ♦ *sm* (*MIL*) strength; (*di patrimonio etc*) sum total.
ef'fetto *sm* effect; (*COMM: cambiale*) bill; (*fig: impressione*) impression; **far ~** (*medicina*) to take effect, (start to) work; **cercare l'~** to seek attention; **in ~i** in fact; **~i attivi** (*COMM*) bills receivable; **~i passivi** (*COMM*) bills payable; **~i personali** personal effects, personal belongings.
effettu'are *vt* to effect, carry out.
effi'cace [effi'katʃe] *ag* effective.
effi'cacia [effi'katʃa] *sf* effectiveness.
effici'ente [effi'tʃɛnte] *ag* efficient.
efficien'tismo [effitʃen'tizmo] *sm* maximum efficiency.
effici'enza [effi'tʃɛntsa] *sf* efficiency.
effigi'are [effi'dʒare] *vt* to represent, portray.
ef'figie [ef'fidʒe] *sf inv* effigy.
ef'fimero, a *ag* ephemeral.
ef'fluvio *sm* (*anche peg, ironico*) scent, perfume.
effusi'one *sf* effusion.
e.g. *abbr* (= *exempli gratia*) e.g.
egemo'nia [edʒemo'nia] *sf* hegemony.

E'geo [e'dʒɛo] *sm*: **l'~, il mare ~** the Aegean (Sea).
'egida ['ɛdʒida] *sf*: **sotto l'~ di** under the aegis of.
E'gitto [e'dʒitto] *sm*: **l'~** Egypt.
egizi'ano, a [edʒit'tsjano] *ag, sm/f* Egyptian.
e'gizio, a [e'dʒittsjo] *ag, sm/f* (ancient) Egyptian.
'egli ['eʎʎi] *pronome* he; ~ **stesso** he himself.
'ego *sm inv* (*PSIC*) ego.
ego'centrico, a, ci, che [ego'tʃentriko] *ag* egocentric(al) ♦ *sm/f* self-centred (*Brit*) *o* self-centered (*US*) person.
egocen'trismo [egotʃen'trizmo] *sm* egocentricity.
ego'ismo *sm* selfishness, egoism.
ego'ista, i, e *ag* selfish, egoistic ♦ *sm/f* egoist.
ego'istico, a, ci, che *ag* egoistic, selfish.
ego'tismo *sm* egotism.
ego'tista, i, e *ag* egotistic ♦ *sm/f* egotist.
Egr. *abbr* = **Egregio**.
e'gregio, a, gi, gie [e'grɛdʒo] *ag* distinguished; (*nelle lettere*): **E~ Signore** Dear Sir.
eguagli'anza *etc* [egwaʎ'ʎantsa] *vedi* **uguaglianza** *etc*.
eguali'tario, a *ag, sm/f* egalitarian.
E.I. *abbr* = *Esercito Italiano*.
elabo'rare *vt* (*progetto*) to work out, elaborate; (*dati*) to process; (*digerire*) to digest.
elabora'tore *sm* (*INFORM*): ~ **elettronico** computer.
elaborazi'one [elaborat'tsjone] *sf* elaboration; processing; digestion; ~ **automatica dei dati (E.A.D.)** (*INFORM*) automatic data processing (A.D.P.); ~ **elettronica dei dati (E.E.D.)** (*INFORM*) electronic data processing (E.D.P.); ~ **testi** (*INFORM*) text processing.
elar'gire [elar'dʒire] *vt* to hand out.
elargizi'one [elardʒit'tsjone] *sf* donation.
elasticiz'zato, a [elastitʃid'dzato] *ag* (*tessuto*) stretch *cpd*.
e'lastico, a, ci, che *ag* elastic; (*fig: andatura*) springy; (: *decisione, vedute*) flexible ♦ *sm* (*gommino*) rubber band; (*per il cucito*) elastic *q*.
ele'fante *sm* elephant.
ele'gante *ag* elegant.
ele'ganza [ele'gantsa] *sf* elegance.
e'leggere [e'lɛddʒere] *vt* to elect.
elemen'tare *ag* elementary; **le (scuole) ~i** primary (*Brit*) *o* grade (*US*) school; **prima ~** first year of primary school, ≈ infants' class (*Brit*), ≈ 1st grade (*US*).
ele'mento *sm* element; (*parte componente*) element, component, part; **~i** *smpl* (*della scienza etc*) elements, rudiments.
ele'mosina *sf* charity, alms *pl*; **chiedere l'~**

to beg.

elemosi'nare *vt* to beg for, ask for ♦ *vi* to beg.

elen'care *vt* to list.

elencherò *etc* [elenke'rɔ] *vb vedi* **elencare**.

e'lenco, chi *sm* list; ~ **nominativo** list of names; ~ **telefonico** telephone directory.

e'lessi *etc vb vedi* **eleggere**.

elet'tivo, a *ag* (*carica etc*) elected.

e'letto, a *pp di* **eleggere** ♦ *sm/f* (*nominato*) elected member.

eletto'rale *ag* electoral, election *cpd*.

eletto'rato *sm* electorate.

elet'tore, 'trice *sm/f* voter, elector.

elet'trauto *sm inv* workshop for car electrical repairs; (*tecnico*) car electrician.

elettri'cista, i [elettri'tʃista] *sm* electrician.

elettricità [elettritʃi'ta] *sf* electricity.

e'lettrico, a, ci, che *ag* electric(al).

elettrifi'care *vt* to electrify.

elettriz'zante [elettrid'dzante] *ag* (*fig*) electrifying, thrilling.

elettriz'zare [elettrid'dzare] *vt* to electrify; ~**rsi** *vr* to become charged with electricity; (*fig: persona*) to be thrilled.

e'lettro... *prefisso* electro....

elettrocardio'gramma, i *sm* electrocardiogram.

e'lettrodo *sm* electrode.

elettrodo'mestico, a, ci, che *ag*: **apparecchi** ~**ci** domestic (electrical) appliances.

elettroencefalo'gramma, i [elettroentʃefalo-'gramma] *sm* electroencephalogram.

elet'trogeno, a [elet'trɔdʒeno] *ag*: **gruppo** ~ generator.

elet'trolisi *sf* electrolysis.

elettroma'gnetico, a, ci, che [elet-tromaɲ'ɲetiko] *ag* electromagnetic.

elettromo'trice [elettromo'tritʃe] *sf* electric train.

elet'trone *sm* electron.

elet'tronico, a, ci, che *ag* electronic ♦ *sf* electronics *sg*.

elettro'shock [elettroʃ'ʃɔk] *sm inv* (electro)shock treatment.

elettro'tecnico, a, ci, che *ag* electrotechnical ♦ *sm* electrical engineer.

ele'vare *vt* to raise; (*edificio*) to erect; (*multa*) to impose; ~ **un numero al quadrato** to square a number.

eleva'tezza [eleva'tettsa] *sf* (*altezza*) elevation; (*di animo, pensiero*) loftiness.

ele'vato, a *ag* (*gen*) high; (*cime*) high, lofty; (*fig: stile, sentimenti*) lofty.

elevazi'one [elevat'tsjone] *sf* elevation; (*l'elevare*) raising.

elezi'one [elet'tsjone] *sf* election; ~**i** *sfpl* (*POL*) election(s); **patria d'**~ chosen country.

'elica, che *sf* propeller.

eli'cottero *sm* helicopter.

e'lidere *vt* (*FONETICA*) to elide; ~**rsi** *vr*

(*forze*) to cancel each other out, neutralize each other.

elimi'nare *vt* to eliminate.

elimina'toria *sf* eliminating round.

eliminazi'one [eliminat'tsjone] *sf* elimination.

'elio *sm* helium.

eli'porto *sm* heliport.

elisabetti'ano, a *ag* Elizabethan.

eli'sir *sm inv* elixir.

e'liso, a *pp di* **elidere**.

eli'tario, a *ag* elitist.

é'lite [e'lit] *sf inv* élite.

'ella *pronome* she; (*forma di cortesia*) you; ~ **stessa** she herself; you yourself.

el'lisse *sf* ellipse.

el'littico, a, ci, che *ag* elliptic(al).

el'metto *sm* helmet.

'elmo *sm* helmet.

elogi'are [elo'dʒare] *vt* to praise.

elogia'tivo, a [elodʒa'tivo] *ag* laudatory.

e'logio [e'lɔdʒo] *sm* (*discorso, scritto*) eulogy; (*lode*) praise; ~ **funebre** funeral oration.

elo'quente *ag* eloquent; **questi dati sono** ~**i** these facts speak for themselves.

elo'quenza [elo'kwentsa] *sf* eloquence.

e'loquio *sm* speech, language.

elucu'brare *vt* (*piano*) to ponder about, ponder over.

elucubrazi'oni [elukubrat'tsjoni] *sfpl* (*anche ironico*) cogitations, ponderings.

e'ludere *vt* to evade.

e'lusi *etc vb vedi* **eludere**.

elusi'one *sf*: ~ **d'imposta** tax evasion.

elu'sivo, a *ag* evasive.

e'luso, a *pp di* **eludere**.

el'vetico, a, ci, che *ag* Swiss.

emaci'ato, a [ema'tʃato] *ag* emaciated.

ema'nare *vt* to send out, give off; (*fig: leggi*) to promulgate; (: *decreti*) to issue ♦ *vi*: ~ **da** to come from.

emanazi'one [emanat'tsjone] *sf* (*di raggi, calore*) emanation; (*di odori*) exhalation; (*di legge*) promulgation; (*di ordine, circolare*) issuing.

emanci'pare [emantʃi'pare] *vt* to emancipate; ~**rsi** *vr* (*fig*) to become liberated *o* emancipated.

emancipazi'one [emantʃipat'tsjone] *sf* emancipation.

emargi'nare [emardʒi'nare] *vt* (*fig: socialmente*) to cast out.

emargi'nato, a [emardʒi'nato] *sm/f* outcast.

ematolo'gia [ematolo'dʒia] *sf* haematology (*Brit*), hematology (*US*).

ema'toma, i *sm* haematoma (*Brit*), hematoma (*US*).

em'blema, i *sm* emblem.

emble'matico, a, ci, che *ag* emblematic; (*fig: atteggiamento, parole*) symbolic.

embo'lia *sf* embolism.

embri'one *sm* embryo.

emenda'mento *sm* amendment.
emen'dare *vt* to amend.
emer'gente [emer'dʒɛnte] *ag* emerging.
emer'genza [emer'dʒɛntsa] *sf* emergency; **in caso di ~** in an emergency.
e'mergere [e'mɛrdʒere] *vi* to emerge; *(sommergibile)* to surface; *(fig: distinguersi)* to stand out.
e'merito, a *ag (insigne)* distinguished; **è un ~ cretino!** he's a complete idiot!
e'mersi *etc vb vedi* **emergere**.
e'merso, a *pp di* **emergere** ♦ *ag (GEO)*: **terre ~e** lands above sea level.
e'messo, a *pp di* **emettere**.
e'mettere *vt (suono, luce)* to give out, emit; *(onde radio)* to send out; *(assegno, francobollo, ordine)* to issue; *(fig: giudizio)* to express, voice; **~ la sentenza** *(DIR)* to pass sentence.
emi'crania *sf* migraine.
emi'grante *ag*, *sm/f* emigrant.
emi'grare *vi* to emigrate.
emi'grato, a *ag* emigrant ♦ *sm/f* emigrant; *(STORIA)* émigré.
emigrazi'one [emigrat'tsjone] *sf* emigration.
emili'ano, a *ag* of *(o* from) Emilia.
emi'nente *ag* eminent, distinguished.
emi'nenza [emi'nɛntsa] *sf* eminence; **~ grigia** *(fig)* éminence grise.
emi'rato *sm* emirate; **gli E~i Arabi Uniti** the United Arab Emirates.
emis'fero *sm* hemisphere; **~ boreale/australe** northern/southern hemisphere.
e'misi *etc vb vedi* **emettere**.
emis'sario *sm (GEO)* outlet, effluent; *(inviato)* emissary.
emissi'one *sf (vedi* **emettere**) emission; sending out; issue; *(RADIO)* broadcast.
emit'tente *ag (banca)* issuing; *(RADIO)* broadcasting, transmitting ♦ *sf (RADIO)* transmitter.
emofi'lia *sf* haemophilia *(Brit)*, hemophilia *(US)*.
emofi'liaco, a, ci, che *ag*, *sm/f* haemophiliac *(Brit)*, hemophiliac *(US)*.
emoglo'bina *sf* haemoglobin *(Brit)*, hemoglobin *(US)*.
emorra'gia, 'gie [emorra'dʒia] *sf* haemorrhage *(Brit)*, hemorrhage *(US)*.
emor'roidi *sfpl* haemorrhoids *(Brit)*, hemorrhoids *(US)*.
emos'tatico, a, ci, che *ag* haemostatic *(Brit)*, hemostatic *(US)*; **laccio ~** tourniquet; **matita ~a** styptic pencil.
emotività *sf* emotionalism.
emo'tivo, a *ag* emotional.
emozio'nante [emottsjo'nante] *ag* exciting, thrilling.
emozio'nare [emottsjo'nare] *vt (appassionare)* to thrill, excite; *(commuovere)* to move; *(innervosire)* to upset; **~rsi** *vr* to be excited; to be moved; to be upset.

emozi'one [emot'tsjone] *sf* emotion; *(agitazione)* excitement.
'empio, a *ag (sacrilego)* impious; *(spietato)* cruel, pitiless; *(malvagio)* wicked, evil.
em'porio *sm* general store.
emu'lare *vt* to emulate.
'emulo, a *sm/f* imitator.
emulsi'one *sf* emulsion.
EN *sigla* = *Enna*.
en'ciclica, che [en'tʃiklika] *sf (REL)* encyclical.
enciclope'dia [entʃiklope'dia] *sf* encyclop(a)edia.
encomi'abile *ag* commendable, praiseworthy.
encomi'are *vt* to commend, praise.
en'comio *sm* commendation; **~ solenne** *(MIL)* mention in dispatches.
endove'noso, a *ag (MED)* intravenous ♦ *sf* intravenous injection.
E'NEA *sigla f* = *Comitato nazionale per la ricerca e lo sviluppo dell'Energia Nucleare e delle Energie Alternative*.
'E.N.E.L. *sigla m* (= *Ente Nazionale per l'Energia Elettrica)* national electricity company.
ener'getico, a, ci, che [ener'dʒetiko] *ag (risorse, crisi)* energy *cpd*; *(sostanza, alimento)* energy-giving.
ener'gia, 'gie [ener'dʒia] *sf (FISICA)* energy; *(fig)* energy, strength, vigour *(Brit)*, vigor *(US)*.
e'nergico, a, ci, che [e'nɛrdʒiko] *ag* energetic, vigorous.
'enfasi *sf* emphasis; *(peg)* bombast, pomposity.
en'fatico, a, ci, che *ag* emphatic; pompous.
enfatiz'zare [enfatid'dzare] *vt* to emphasize, stress.
enfi'sema *sm* emphysema.
'ENI *sigla m* = *Ente Nazionale Idrocarburi*.
e'nigma, i *sm* enigma.
enig'matico, a, ci, che *ag* enigmatic.
'ENIT *sigla m* (= *Ente Nazionale Italiano per il Turismo)* Italian tourist authority.
en'nesimo, a *ag (MAT, fig)* nth; **per l'~a volta** for the umpteenth time.
enolo'gia [enolo'dʒia] *sf* oenology *(Brit)*, enology *(US)*.
e'nologo, gi *sm* wine expert.
e'norme *ag* enormous, huge.
enormità *sf inv* enormity, huge size; *(assurdità)* absurdity; **non dire ~!** don't talk nonsense!
eno'teca, che *sf (negozio)* wine bar.
'E.N.P.A. *sigla m* (= *Ente Nazionale Protezione Animali)* ≈ RSPCA *(Brit)*, ≈ SPCA *(US)*.
'E.N.P.A.S. *sigla m* (= *Ente Nazionale di Previdenza e Assistenza per i Dipendenti Statali) welfare organization for State*

employees.

'ente *sm* (*istituzione*) body, board, corporation; (*FILOSOFIA*) being; ~ **locale** local authority (*Brit*), local government (*US*); ~ **pubblico** public body; ~ **di ricerca** research organization.

ente'rite *sf* enteritis.

entità *sf* (*FILOSOFIA*) entity; (*di perdita, danni, investimenti*) extent; (*di popolazione*) size; **di molta/poca** ~ (*avvenimento, incidente*) of great/little importance.

en'trambi, e *pronome pl* both (of them) ◊ *ag pl*: ~ **i ragazzi** both boys, both of the boys.

en'trante *ag* (*prossimo: mese, anno*) next, coming.

en'trare *vi* to enter, go (*o* come) in; ~ **in** (*luogo*) to enter, go (*o* come) into; (*trovar posto, poter stare*) to fit into; (*essere ammesso a: club etc*) to join, become a member of; ~ **in automobile** to get into the car; **far** ~ **qn** (*visitatore etc*) to show sb in; ~ **in società/in commercio con qn** to go into partnership/business with sb; **questo non c'entra** (*fig*) that's got nothing to do with it.

en'trata *sf* entrance, entry; ~**e** *sfpl* (*COMM*) receipts, takings; (*ECON*) income *sg*; "~ **libera"** "admission free"; **con l'**~ **in vigore dei nuovi provvedimenti** ... once the new measures come into effect ...; ~**e tributarie** tax revenue *sg*.

'entro *prep* (*temporale*) within; ~ **domani** by tomorrow; ~ **e non oltre il 25 aprile** no later than 25th April.

entro'terra *sm inv* hinterland.

entusias'mante *ag* exciting.

entusias'mare *vt* to excite, fill with enthusiasm; ~**rsi** *vr*: ~**rsi (per qc/qn)** to become enthusiastic (about sth/sb).

entusi'asmo *sm* enthusiasm.

entusi'asta, i, e *ag* enthusiastic ◊ *sm/f* enthusiast.

entusi'astico, a, ci, che *ag* enthusiastic.

enucle'are *vt* (*formale: chiarire*) to explain.

enume'rare *vt* to enumerate, list.

enunci'are [enun'tʃare] *vt* (*teoria*) to enunciate, set out.

en'zima, i *sm* enzyme.

e'patico, a, ci, che *ag* hepatic; **cirrosi** ~**a** cirrhosis of the liver.

epa'tite *sf* hepatitis.

'epico, a, ci, che *ag* epic.

epide'mia *sf* epidemic.

epi'dermico, a, ci, che *ag* (*ANAT*) skin *cpd*; (*fig: interesse, impressioni*) superficial.

epi'dermide *sf* skin, epidermis.

Epifa'nia *sf* Epiphany.

e'pigono *sm* imitator.

e'pigrafe *sf* epigraph; (*su libro*) dedication.

epiles'sia *sf* epilepsy.

epi'lettico, a, ci, che *ag, sm/f* epileptic.

e'pilogo, ghi *sm* conclusion.

epi'sodico, a, ci, che *ag* (*romanzo, narrazione*) episodic; (*fig: occasionale*) occasional.

epi'sodio *sm* episode; **sceneggiato a** ~**i** serial.

e'pistola *sf* epistle.

episto'lare *ag* epistolary; **essere in rapporto o relazione** ~ **con qn** to correspond *o* be in correspondence with sb.

e'piteto *sm* epithet.

'epoca, che *sf* (*periodo storico*) age, era; (*tempo*) time; (*GEO*) age; **mobili d'**~ period furniture; **fare** ~ (*scandalo*) to cause a stir; (*cantante, moda*) to mark a new era.

epo'pea *sf* (*anche fig*) epic.

ep'pure *cong* and yet, nevertheless.

EPT *sigla m* (= *Ente Provinciale per il Turismo*) district tourist bureau.

epu'rare *vt* (*POL*) to purge.

equ'anime *ag* (*imparziale*) fair, impartial.

equa'tore *sm* equator.

equazi'one [ekwat'tsjone] *sf* (*MAT*) equation.

e'questre *ag* equestrian.

equi'latero, a *ag* equilateral.

equili'brare *vt* to balance.

equili'brato, a *ag* (*carico, fig: giudizio*) balanced; (*vita*) well-regulated; (*persona*) stable, well-balanced.

equi'librio *sm* balance, equilibrium; **perdere l'**~ to lose one's balance; **stare in** ~ **su** (*persona*) to balance on; (*oggetto*) to be balanced on.

equili'brismo *sm* tightrope walking; (*fig*) juggling.

e'quino, a *ag* horse *cpd*, equine.

equi'nozio [ekwi'nɔttsjo] *sm* equinox.

equipaggia'mento [ekwipaddʒa'mento] *sm* (*operazione: di nave*) equipping, fitting out; (*: di spedizione, esercito*) equipping, kitting out; (*attrezzatura*) equipment.

equipaggi'are [ekwipad'dʒare] *vt* to equip; ~**rsi** *vr* to equip o.s.

equi'paggio [ekwi'paddʒo] *sm* crew.

equipa'rare *vt* to make equal.

é'quipe [e'kip] *sf* (*SPORT, gen*) team.

equità *sf* equity, fairness.

equitazi'one [ekwitat'tsjone] *sf* (horse-)riding.

equiva'lente *ag, sm* equivalent.

equiva'lenza [ekwiva'lɛntsa] *sf* equivalence.

equiva'lere *vi*: ~ **a** to be equivalent to; ~**rsi** *vr* (*forze etc*) to counterbalance each other; (*soluzioni*) to amount to the same thing; **equivale a dire che** ... that is the same as saying that ....

equi'valso, a *pp di* **equivalere**.

equivo'care *vi* to misunderstand.

e'quivoco, a, ci, che *ag* equivocal, ambiguous; (*sospetto*) dubious ◊ *sm* misunderstanding; **a scanso di** ~**ci** to avoid any misunderstanding; **giocare sull'**~ to equivocate.

'**equo, a** *ag* fair, just.

'**era** *sf* era.

'**era** *etc vb vedi* **essere**.

erari'ale *ag*: **ufficio** ~ ≈ tax office; **imposte** ~**i** revenue taxes; **spese** ~**i** public expenditure *sg*.

e'rario *sm*: **l'**~ ≈ the Treasury.

'**erba** *sf* grass; (*aromatica, medicinale*) herb; **in** ~ (*fig*) budding; **fare di ogni** ~ **un fascio** (*fig*) to lump everything (*o* everybody) together.

er'baccia, ce [er'battʃa] *sf* weed.

er'bette *sfpl* beet tops.

erbo'rista, i, e *sm/f* herbalist.

erboriste'ria *sf* (*scienza*) study of medicinal herbs; (*negozio*) herbalist's (shop).

er'boso, a *ag* grassy.

e'rede *sm/f* heir; ~ **legittimo** heir-at-law.

eredità *sf* (*DIR*) inheritance; (*BIOL*) heredity; **lasciare qc in** ~ **a qn** to leave *o* bequeath sth to sb.

eredi'tare *vt* to inherit.

eredi'tario, a *ag* hereditary.

erediti'era *sf* heiress.

ere'mita, i *sm* hermit.

eremi'taggio [eremi'taddʒo] *sm* hermitage.

'**eremo** *sm* hermitage; (*fig*) retreat.

ere'sia *sf* heresy.

e'ressi *etc vb vedi* **erigere**.

e'retico, a, ci, che *ag* heretical ♦ *sm/f* heretic.

e'retto, a *pp di* **erigere** ♦ *ag* erect, upright.

erezi'one [eret'tsjone] *sf* (*FISIOL*) erection.

ergasto'lano, a *sm/f* prisoner serving a life sentence, lifer (*fam*).

er'gastolo *sm* (*DIR*: *pena*) life imprisonment; (*: luogo di pena*) prison (*for those serving life sentences*).

ergo'nomico, a, ci, che *ag* ergonomic(al).

'**erica** *sf* heather.

e'rigere [e'ridʒere] *vt* to erect, raise; (*fig: fondare*) to found.

eri'tema *sm* (*MED*) inflammation, erythema; ~ **solare** sunburn.

ermel'lino *sm* ermine.

er'metico, a, ci, che *ag* hermetic.

'**ernia** *sf* (*MED*) hernia; ~ **del disco** slipped disc.

'**ero** *vb vedi* **essere**.

e'rodere *vt* to erode.

e'roe *sm* hero.

ero'gare *vt* (*somme*) to distribute; (*gas, servizi*) to supply.

erogazi'one [erogat'tsjone] *sf* distribution; supply.

e'roico, a, ci, che *ag* heroic.

ero'ina *sf* heroine; (*droga*) heroin.

ero'ismo *sm* heroism.

erosi'one *sf* erosion.

e'roso, a *pp di* **erodere**.

e'rotico, a, ci, che *ag* erotic.

ero'tismo *sm* eroticism.

'**erpete** *sm* herpes *sg*.

'**erpice** ['erpitʃe] *sm* (*AGR*) harrow.

er'rare *vi* (*vagare*) to wander, roam; (*sbagliare*) to be mistaken.

er'roneo, a *ag* erroneous, wrong.

er'rore *sm* error, mistake; (*morale*) error; **per** ~ by mistake; ~ **giudiziario** miscarriage of justice.

'**erto, a** *ag* (very) steep ♦ *sf* steep slope; **stare all'**~**a** to be on the alert.

eru'dire *vt* to teach, educate.

eru'dito, a *ag* learned, erudite.

erut'tare *vt* (*sog: vulcano*) to throw out, belch.

eruzi'one [erut'tsjone] *sf* eruption; (*MED*) rash.

E.S. *sigla m* (= *elettroshock*) ECT.

esacer'bare [ezatʃer'bare] *vt* to exacerbate.

esage'rare [ezadʒe'rare] *vt* to exaggerate ♦ *vi* to exaggerate; (*eccedere*) to go too far; **senza** ~ without exaggeration.

esage'rato, a [ezadʒe'rato] *ag* (*notizia, proporzioni*) exaggerated; (*curiosità, pignoleria*) excessive; (*prezzo*) exorbitant ♦ *sm/f*: **sei il solito** ~ you are exaggerating as usual.

esagerazi'one [esadʒerat'tsjone] *sf* exaggeration.

esago'nale *ag* hexagonal.

e'sagono *sm* hexagon.

esa'lare *vt* (*odori*) to give off ♦ *vi*: ~ **(da)** to emanate (from); ~ **l'ultimo respiro** (*fig*) to breathe one's last.

esalazi'one [ezalat'tsjone] *sf* (*emissione*) exhalation; (*odore*) fumes *pl*.

esal'tante *ag* exciting.

esal'tare *vt* to exalt; (*entusiasmare*) to excite, stir; ~**rsi** *vr*: ~**rsi (per qc)** to grow excited (about sth).

esal'tato, a *sm/f* fanatic.

esaltazi'one [ezaltat'tsjone] *sf* (*elogio*) extolling, exalting; (*nervosa*) intense excitement; (*mistica*) exaltation.

e'same *sm* examination; (*INS*) exam, examination; **fare** *o* **dare un** ~ to sit *o* take an exam; **fare un** ~ **di coscienza** to search one's conscience; ~ **di guida** driving test; ~ **del sangue** blood test.

esami'nare *vt* to examine.

e'sangue *ag* bloodless; (*fig: pallido*) pale, wan; (*: privo di vigore*) lifeless.

e'sanime *ag* lifeless.

esaspe'rare *vt* to exasperate; (*situazione*) to exacerbate; ~**rsi** *vr* to become annoyed *o* exasperated.

esasperazi'one [ezasperat'tsjone] *sf* exasperation.

esatta'mente *av* exactly; accurately, precisely.

esat'tezza [ezat'tettsa] *sf* exactitude, accuracy, precision; **per l'~** to be precise.

e'satto, a *pp di* **esigere** ♦ *ag* (*calcolo, ora*) correct, right, exact; (*preciso*) accurate, precise; (*puntuale*) punctual.

esat'tore *sm* (*di imposte etc*) collector.

esatto'ria *sf*: **~ comunale** district rates office (*Brit*) *o* assessor's office (*US*).

esau'dire *vt* to grant, fulfil (*Brit*), fulfill (*US*).

esauri'ente *ag* exhaustive.

esauri'mento *sm* exhaustion; **~ nervoso** nervous breakdown; **svendita (fino) ad ~ della merce** clearance sale.

esau'rire *vt* (*stancare*) to exhaust, wear out; (*provviste, miniera*) to exhaust; **~rsi** *vr* to exhaust o.s., wear o.s. out; (*provviste*) to run out.

esau'rito, a *ag* exhausted; (*merci*) sold out; (*libri*) out of print; **essere ~** (*persona*) to be run down; **registrare il tutto ~** (*TEATRO*) to have a full house.

e'sausto, a *ag* exhausted.

esauto'rare *vt* (*dirigente, funzionario*) to deprive of authority.

esazi'one [ezat'tsjone] *sf* collection (of taxes).

'esca, *pl* **'esche** *sf* bait.

escamo'tage [ɛskamɔ'taʒ] *sm* subterfuge.

escande'scenza [eskandeʃ'ʃɛntsa] *sf*: **dare in ~e** to lose one's temper, fly into a rage.

'esce ['ɛʃʃe] *vb vedi* **uscire**.

eschi'mese [eski'mese] *ag, sm/f, sm* Eskimo.

'esci ['ɛʃʃi] *vb vedi* **uscire**.

escl. *abbr* (= *escluso*) excl.

escla'mare *vi* to exclaim, cry out.

esclamazi'one [esklamat'tsjone] *sf* exclamation.

es'cludere *vt* to exclude.

es'clusi *etc vb vedi* **escludere**.

esclusi'one *sf* exclusion; **a ~ di, fatta ~ per** except (for), apart from; **senza ~ (alcuna)** without exception; **procedere per ~** to follow a process of elimination; **senza ~ di colpi** (*fig*) with no holds barred.

esclu'siva *sf vedi* **esclusivo**.

esclusiva'mente *av* exclusively, solely.

esclu'sivo, a *ag* exclusive ♦ *sf* (*DIR, COMM*) exclusive *o* sole rights *pl*.

es'cluso, a *pp di* **escludere** ♦ *ag*: **nessuno ~** without exception; **IVA ~a** excluding VAT, exclusive of VAT.

'esco *vb vedi* **uscire**.

escogi'tare [eskodʒi'tare] *vt* to devise, think up.

'escono *vb vedi* **uscire**.

escoriazi'one [eskorjat'tsjone] *sf* abrasion, graze.

escre'menti *smpl* excrement *sg*, faeces.

escursi'one *sf* (*gita*) excursion, trip; (: *a piedi*) hike, walk; (*METEOR*): **~ termica** temperature range.

escursio'nista, i, e *sm/f* (*gitante*) (day) tripper; (: *a piedi*) hiker, walker.

ese'crare *vt* to loathe, abhor.

esecu'tivo, a *ag, sm* executive.

esecu'tore, 'trice *sm/f* (*MUS*) performer; (*DIR*) executor.

esecuzi'one [ezekut'tsjone] *sf* execution, carrying out; (*MUS*) performance; **~ capitale** execution.

ese'geta, i [eze'dʒɛta] *sm* commentator.

esegu'ire *vt* to carry out, execute; (*MUS*) to perform, execute.

e'sempio *sm* example; **per ~** for example, for instance; **fare un ~** to give an example.

esem'plare *ag* exemplary ♦ *sm* example; (*copia*) copy; (*BOT, ZOOL, GEO*) specimen.

esemplifi'care *vt* to exemplify.

esen'tare *vt*: **~ qn/qc da** to exempt sb/sth from.

esen'tasse *ag inv* tax-free.

e'sente *ag*: **~ da** (*dispensato da*) exempt from; (*privo di*) free from.

esenzi'one [ezen'tsjone] *sf* exemption.

e'sequie *sfpl* funeral rites; funeral service *sg*.

eser'cente [ezer'tʃɛnte] *sm/f* trader, dealer; shopkeeper.

eserci'tare [ezertʃi'tare] *vt* (*professione*) to practise (*Brit*), practice (*US*); (*allenare: corpo, mente*) to exercise, train; (*diritto*) to exercise; (*influenza, pressione*) to exert; **~rsi** *vr* to practise; **~rsi nella guida** to practise one's driving.

esercitazi'one [ezertʃitat'tsjone] *sf* (*scolastica, militare*) exercise; **~i di tiro** target practice *sg*.

e'sercito [e'zɛrtʃito] *sm* army.

eser'cizio [ezer'tʃittsjo] *sm* practice; (*compito, movimento*) exercise; (*azienda*) business, concern; (*ECON*): **~ finanziario** financial year; **in ~** (*medico etc*) practising (*Brit*), practicing (*US*); **nell'~ delle proprie funzioni** in the execution of one's duties.

esi'bire *vt* to exhibit, display; (*documenti*) to produce, present; **~rsi** *vr* (*attore*) to perform; (*fig*) to show off.

esibizi'one [ezibit'tsjone] *sf* exhibition; (*di documento*) presentation; (*spettacolo*) show, performance.

esibizio'nista, i, e [ezibittsjo'nista] *sm/f* exhibitionist.

esi'gente [ezi'dʒɛnte] *ag* demanding.

esi'genza [ezi'dʒɛntsa] *sf* demand, requirement.

e'sigere [e'zidʒere] *vt* (*pretendere*) to demand; (*richiedere*) to demand, require; (*imposte*) to collect.

e'siguo, a *ag* small, slight.

esila'rante *ag* hilarious; **gas ~** laughing gas.

'**esile** *ag* (*persona*) slender, slim; (*stelo*) thin; (*voce*) faint.
esili'are *vt* to exile.
esili'ato, a *ag* exiled ♦ *sm/f* exile.
e'silio *sm* exile.
e'simere *vt*: ~ **qn/qc da** to exempt sb/sth from; ~**rsi** *vr*: ~**rsi da** to get out of.
esis'tente *ag* existing; (*attuale*) present, current.
esis'tenza [ezis'tɛntsa] *sf* existence.
esistenzia'lismo [ezistentsja'lizmo] *sm* existentialism.
e'sistere *vi* to exist.
esis'tito, a *pp di* **esistere**.
esi'tante *ag* hesitant; (*voce*) faltering.
esi'tare *vi* to hesitate.
esitazi'one [ezitat'tsjone] *sf* hesitation.
'**esito** *sm* result, outcome.
'**eskimo** *sm* (*giaccone*) parka.
'**esodo** *sm* exodus.
e'sofago, gi *sm* oesophagus (*Brit*), esophagus (*US*).
esone'rare *vt*: ~ **qn da** to exempt sb from.
esorbi'tante *ag* exorbitant, excessive.
esor'cismo [ezor'tʃizmo] *sm* exorcism.
esorciz'zare [ezortʃid'dzare] *vt* to exorcize.
esordi'ente *sm/f* beginner.
e'sordio *sm* debut.
esor'dire *vi* (*nel teatro*) to make one's debut; (*fig*) to start out, begin (one's career); **esordì dicendo che** ... he began by saying (that) ....
esor'tare *vt*: ~ **qn a fare** to urge sb to do.
esortazi'one [ezortat'tsjone] *sf* exhortation.
e'soso, a *ag* (*prezzo*) exorbitant; (*persona*: *avido*) grasping.
eso'terico, a, ci, che *ag* esoteric.
e'sotico, a, ci, che *ag* exotic.
es'pandere *vt* to expand; (*confini*) to extend; (*influenza*) to extend, spread; ~**rsi** *vr* to expand.
espansi'one *sf* expansion.
espansività *sf* expansiveness.
espan'sivo, a *ag* expansive, communicative.
es'panso, a *pp di* **espandere**.
espatri'are *vi* to leave one's country.
es'patrio *sm* expatriation; **permesso di** ~ authorization to leave the country.
espedi'ente *sm* expedient; **vivere di** ~**i** to live by one's wits.
es'pellere *vt* to expel.
esperi'enza [espe'rjɛntsa] *sf* experience; (*SCIENZA: prova*) experiment; **parlare per** ~ to speak from experience.
esperi'mento *sm* experiment; **fare un** ~ to carry out *o* do an experiment.
es'perto, a *ag*, *sm/f* expert.
espi'are *vt* to atone for.
espiazi'one [espiat'tsjone] *sf*: ~ (**di**) expiation (of), atonement (for).
espi'rare *vt*, *vi* to breathe out.

espleta'mento *sm* (*AMM*) carrying out.
esple'tare *vt* (*AMM*) to carry out.
espli'care *vt* (*attività*) to carry out, perform.
esplica'tivo, a *ag* explanatory.
es'plicito, a [es'plitʃito] *ag* explicit.
es'plodere *vi* (*anche fig*) to explode ♦ *vt* to fire.
esplo'rare *vt* to explore.
esplora'tore, 'trice *sm/f* explorer; (*anche*: **giovane** ~) (boy) scout/(girl) guide (*Brit*) *o* scout (*US*) ♦ *sm* (*NAUT*) scout (ship).
esplorazi'one [esplorat'tsjone] *sf* exploration; **mandare qn in** ~ (*MIL*) to send sb to scout ahead.
esplosi'one *sf* explosion.
esplo'sivo, a *ag*, *sm* explosive.
es'ploso, a *pp di* **esplodere**.
es'pone *etc vb vedi* **esporre**.
espo'nente *sm/f* (*rappresentante*) representative.
esponenzi'ale [esponen'tsjale] *ag* (*MAT*) exponential.
es'pongo, es'poni *etc vb vedi* **esporre**.
es'porre *vt* (*merci*) to display; (*quadro*) to exhibit, show; (*fatti, idee*) to explain, set out; (*porre in pericolo, FOT*) to expose; **esporsi** *vr*: **esporsi a** (*sole, pericolo*) to expose o.s. to; (*critiche*) to lay o.s. open to.
espor'tare *vt* to export.
esporta'tore, 'trice *ag* exporting ♦ *sm* exporter.
esportazi'one [esportat'tsjone] *sf* (*azione*) exportation, export; (*insieme di prodotti*) exports *pl*.
es'pose *etc vb vedi* **esporre**.
espo'simetro *sm* exposure meter.
esposizi'one [espozit'tsjone] *sf* displaying; exhibiting; setting out; (*anche FOT*) exposure; (*mostra*) exhibition; (*narrazione*) explanation, exposition.
es'posto, a *pp di* **esporre** ♦ *ag*: ~ **a nord** facing north, north-facing ♦ *sm* (*AMM*) statement, account; (: *petizione*) petition.
espressi'one *sf* expression.
espres'sivo, a *ag* expressive.
es'presso, a *pp di* **esprimere** ♦ *ag* express ♦ *sm* (*lettera*) express letter; (*anche*: **treno** ~) express train; (*anche*: **caffè** ~) espresso.
es'primere *vt* to express; ~**rsi** *vr* to express o.s.
espropri'are *vt* (*terreni, edifici*) to place a compulsory purchase order on; (*persona*) to dispossess.
espropriazi'one [esproprjat'tsjone] *sf*, **es'proprio** *sm* expropriation; ~ **per pubblica utilità** compulsory purchase.
espu'gnare [espuɲ'ɲare] *vt* to take by force, storm.
es'pulsi *etc vb vedi* **espellere**.

espulsi'one *sf* expulsion.
es'pulso, a *pp di* **espellere**.
'essa *pronome f*, **'esse** *pronome fpl vedi* **esso**.
es'senza [es'sɛntsa] *sf* essence.
essenzi'ale [essen'tsjale] *ag* essential ♦ *sm*: **l'~** the main *o* most important thing.
'essere *sm* being; **~ umano** human being ♦ *vi, vb con attributo* to be ♦ *vb ausiliare* to have (*o qualche volta* be); **è giovane/ professore** he is young/a teacher; **è l'una** it's one o'clock; **sono le otto** it's eight o'clock; **esserci: c'è/ci sono** there is/there are; **che c'è?** what's wrong?; **ci siamo!** here we are!; (*fig*) this is it!; (*: siamo alle solite*) here we go again!; **~ di** (*appartenenza*) to belong to; (*origine*) to be from; **è di mio fratello** it belongs to my brother, it's my brother's; **è venuto?** has he come?, did he come?; **è stato fabbricato in India** it was made in India; **è da fare subito** it must be *o* is to be done immediately; **non è da te** it's not like you; **sarà quel che sarà** what will be will be; **come se niente fosse** as if nothing had happened; **sia quel che sia, io me ne vado** whatever happens I'm off; **c'era una volta ... ** once upon a time there was ....
'essi *pronome mpl vedi* **esso**.
essic'care *vt* (*gen*) to dry; (*legname*) to season; (*cibi*) to desiccate; (*bacino, palude*) to drain; **~rsi** *vr* (*fiume, pozzo*) to dry up; (*vernice*) to dry (out).
'esso, a *pronome* it; (*riferito a persona: soggetto*) he/she; (*: complemento*) him/her; **~i, e** *pronome pl* they; (*complemento*) them.
est *sm* east; **i paesi dell'E~** the Eastern bloc *sg*.
'estasi *sf* ecstasy.
estasi'are *vt* to send into raptures; **~rsi** *vr*: **~rsi (davanti a)** to go into ecstasies (over), go into raptures (over).
es'tate *sf* summer.
es'tatico, a, ci, che *ag* ecstatic.
estempo'raneo, a *ag* (*discorso*) extempore, impromptu; (*brano musicale*) impromptu.
es'tendere *vt* to extend; **~rsi** *vr* (*diffondersi*) to spread; (*territorio, confini*) to extend.
estensi'one *sf* extension; (*di superficie*) expanse; (*di voce*) range.
estenu'ante *ag* wearing, tiring.
estenu'are *vt* (*stancare*) to wear out, tire out.
esteri'ore *ag* outward, external.
esteriorità *sf inv* outward appearance.
esterioriz'zare [esterjorid'dzare] *vt* (*gioia etc*) to show.
ester'nare *vt* to express; **~ un sospetto** to voice a suspicion.
es'terno, a *ag* (*porta, muro*) outer, outside;

(*scala*) outside; (*alunno, impressione*) external ♦ *sm* outside, exterior ♦ *sm/f* (*allievo*) day pupil; **"per uso ~"** "for external use only"; **gli ~i sono stati girati a Glasgow** (*CINEMA*) the location shots were taken in Glasgow.
'estero, a *ag* foreign ♦ *sm*: **all'~** abroad; **Ministero degli E~i, gli E~i** Ministry for Foreign Affairs, ≈ Foreign Office (*Brit*), ≈ State Department (*US*).
esterofi'lia *sf* excessive love of foreign things.
esterre'fatto, a *ag* (*costernato*) horrified; (*sbalordito*) astounded.
es'tesi *etc vb vedi* **estendere**.
es'teso, a *pp di* **estendere** ♦ *ag* extensive, large; **scrivere per ~** to write in full.
es'tetico, a, ci, che *ag* aesthetic ♦ *sf* (*disciplina*) aesthetics *sg*; (*bellezza*) attractiveness; **chirurgia ~a** cosmetic surgery; **cura ~a** beauty treatment.
este'tista, i, e *sm/f* beautician.
'estimo *sm* valuation; (*disciplina*) surveying.
es'tinguere *vt* to extinguish, put out; (*debito*) to pay off; (*conto*) to close; **~rsi** *vr* to go out; (*specie*) to become extinct.
es'tinsi *etc vb vedi* **estinguere**.
es'tinto, a *pp di* **estinguere**.
estin'tore *sm* (fire) extinguisher.
estinzi'one [estin'tsjone] *sf* putting out; (*di specie*) extinction; (*di debito*) payment; (*di conto*) closing.
estir'pare *vt* (*pianta*) to uproot, pull up; (*dente*) to extract; (*tumore*) to remove; (*fig: vizio*) to eradicate.
es'tivo, a *ag* summer *cpd*.
Es'tonia *sf*: **l'~** Estonia.
es'torcere [es'tɔrtʃere] *vt*: **~ qc (a qn)** to extort sth (from sb).
estorsi'one *sf* extortion.
es'torto, a *pp di* **estorcere**.
estra'dare *vt* to extradite.
estradizi'one [estradit'tsjone] *sf* extradition.
es'trae, es'traggo *etc vb vedi* **estrarre**.
es'traneo, a *ag* foreign; (*discorso*) extraneous, unrelated ♦ *sm/f* stranger; **rimanere ~ a qc** to take no part in sth; **sentirsi ~ a** (*famiglia, società*) to feel alienated from; **"ingresso vietato agli ~i"** "no admittance to unauthorized personnel".
estrani'arsi *vr*: **~ (da)** to cut o.s. off (from).
es'trarre *vt* to extract; (*minerali*) to mine; (*sorteggiare*) to draw; **~ a sorte** to draw lots.
es'trassi *etc vb vedi* **estrarre**.
es'tratto, a *pp di* **estrarre** ♦ *sm* extract; (*di documento*) abstract; **~ conto** (bank) statement; **~ di nascita** birth certificate.
estrazi'one [estrat'tsjone] *sf* extraction; mining; drawing *q*; draw.
estrema'mente *av* extremely.

estre'mista, i, e *sm/f* extremist.

estremità *sf inv* extremity, end ♦ *sfpl* (*ANAT*) extremities.

es'tremo, a *ag* extreme; (*ultimo: ora, tentativo*) final, last ♦ *sm* extreme; (*di pazienza, forza*) limit, end; **~i** *smpl* (*DIR*) essential elements; (*AMM: dati essenziali*) details, particulars; **l'E~ Oriente** the Far East.

estrinse'care *vt* to express, show.

'estro *sm* (*capriccio*) whim, fancy; (*ispirazione creativa*) inspiration.

estro'messo, a *pp di* **estromettere**.

estro'mettere *vt*: **~ (da)** (*partito, club etc*) to expel (from); (*discussione*) to exclude (from).

estromissi'one *sf* expulsion.

es'troso, a *ag* whimsical, capricious; inspired.

estro'verso, a *ag, sm* extrovert.

estu'ario *sm* estuary.

esube'rante *ag* exuberant; (*COMM*) redundant (*Brit*), laid-off.

esube'ranza [ezube'rantsa] *sf* (*di persona*) exuberance; **~ di personale** (*COMM*) overmanning (*Brit*), over-staffing (*US*).

esu'lare *vi*: **~ da** (*competenza*) to be beyond; (*compiti*) not to be part of.

'esule *sm/f* exile.

esul'tanza [ezul'tantsa] *sf* exultation.

esul'tare *vi* to exult.

esu'mare *vt* (*salma*) to exhume, disinter; (*fig*) to unearth.

età *sf inv* age; **all'~ di 8 anni** at the age of 8, at 8 years of age; **ha la mia ~** he (*o* she) is the same age as me *o* as I am; **di mezza ~** middle-aged; **raggiungere la maggiore ~** to come of age; **essere in ~ minore** to be under age; **in ~ avanzata** advanced in years.

eta'nolo *sm* ethanol.

'etere *sm* ether.

e'tereo, a *ag* ethereal.

eternità *sf* eternity.

e'terno, a *ag* eternal; (*interminabile: lamenti, attesa*) never-ending; **in ~** for ever, eternally.

etero'geneo, a [etero'dʒɛneo] *ag* heterogeneous.

'etica *sf vedi* **etico**.

eti'chetta [eti'ketta] *sf* label; (*cerimoniale*): **l'~** etiquette.

'etico, a, ci, che *ag* ethical ♦ *sf* ethics *sg*.

etimolo'gia, 'gie [etimolo'dʒia] *sf* etymology.

e'tiope *ag, sm/f* Ethiopian.

Eti'opia *sf*: **l'~** Ethiopia.

eti'opico, a, ci, che *ag, sm* (*LING*) Ethiopian.

'Etna *sm*: **l'~** Etna.

'etnico, a, ci, che *ag* ethnic.

e'trusco, a, schi, sche *ag, sm/f* Etruscan.

'ettaro *sm* hectare (= *10,000 m²*).

'etto *sm abbr* = **ettogrammo**.

etto'grammo *sm* hectogram(me) (= *100 grams*).

et'tolitro *sm* hectolitre (*Brit*), hectoliter (*US*).

EU *abbr* = **Europa**.

euca'lipto *sm* eucalyptus.

Eucaris'tia *sf*: **l'~** the Eucharist.

eufe'mismo *sm* euphemism.

eufo'ria *sf* euphoria.

Eu'rasia *sf* Eurasia.

eurasi'atico, a, ci, che *ag, sm/f* Eurasian.

Eura'tom *sigla f* (= *Comunità Europea dell'Energia Atomica*) Euratom.

eurodepu'tato *sm* Euro MP.

eurodi'visa *sf* Eurocurrency.

euro'dollaro *sm* Eurodollar.

euromer'cato *sm* Euromarket.

Eu'ropa *sf*: **l'~** Europe.

euro'peo, a *ag, sm/f* European.

eutana'sia *sf* euthanasia.

E.V. *abbr* = *Eccellenza Vostra*.

evacu'are *vt* to evacuate.

evacuazi'one [evakuat'tsjone] *sf* evacuation.

e'vadere *vi* (*fuggire*): **~ da** to escape from ♦ *vt* (*sbrigare*) to deal with, dispatch; (*tasse*) to evade.

evan'gelico, a, ci, che [evan'dʒɛliko] *ag* evangelical.

evange'lista, i [evandʒe'lista] *sm* evangelist.

evapo'rare *vi* to evaporate.

evaporazi'one [evaporat'tsjone] *sf* evaporation.

e'vasi *etc vb vedi* **evadere**.

evasi'one *sf* (*vedi evadere*) escape; dispatch; **dare ~ ad un ordine** to carry out *o* execute an order; **letteratura d'~** escapist literature; **~ fiscale** tax evasion.

eva'sivo, a *ag* evasive.

e'vaso, a *pp di* **evadere** ♦ *sm* escapee.

eva'sore *sm*: **~ (fiscale)** tax evader.

eveni'enza [eve'njɛntsa] *sf*: **nell'~ che ciò succeda** should that happen; **essere pronto ad ogni ~** to be ready for anything *o* any eventuality.

e'vento *sm* event.

eventu'ale *ag* possible.

eventualità *sf inv* eventuality, possibility; **nell'~ di** in the event of.

eventual'mente *av* if need be, if necessary.

'Everest *sm*: **l'~, il Monte ~** (Mount) Everest.

eversi'one *sf* subversion.

ever'sivo, a *ag* subversive.

evi'dente *ag* evident, obvious.

evidente'mente *av* evidently; (*palesemente*) obviously, evidently.

evi'denza [evi'dɛntsa] *sf* obviousness; **mettere in ~** to point out, highlight; **tenere in ~ qc** to bear sth in mind.

evidenzia'tore [evidentsja'tore] *sm* (*penna*)

highlighter.
evi'rare *vt* to castrate.
evi'tabile *ag* avoidable.
evi'tare *vt* to avoid; ~ **di fare** to avoid doing; ~ **qc a qn** to spare sb sth.
'evo *sm* age, epoch.
evo'care *vt* to evoke.
evoca'tivo, a *ag* evocative.
evocherò *etc* [evoke'rɔ] *vb vedi* **evocare**.
evolu'tivo, a *ag* (*gen*, BIOL) evolutionary; (MED) progressive.
evo'luto, a *pp di* **evolversi** ♦ *ag* (*popolo, civiltà*) (highly) developed, advanced; (*persona: emancipato*) independent; (: *senza pregiudizi*) broad-minded.
evoluzi'one [evolut'tsjone] *sf* evolution.
e'volversi *vr* to evolve; **con l'~ della situazione** as the situation develops.
ev'viva *escl* hurrah!; ~ **il re!** long live the king!, hurrah for the king!
ex *prefisso* ex-, former ♦ *sm/f inv* ex-boyfriend/girlfriend.
ex 'aequo [ɛg'zɛkwo] *av*: **classificarsi primo** ~ to come joint first, come equal first.
'extra *ag inv, sm inv* extra.
extraconiu'gale *ag* extramarital.
extraparlamen'tare *ag* extra-parliamentary.
extrasensori'ale *ag*: **percezione** *f* ~ extrasensory perception.
extraur'bano, a *ag* suburban.

F

F, f ['ɛffe] *sf o m inv* (*lettera*) F, f; **F come Firenze** ≈ F for Frederick (*Brit*), F for Fox (US).
F *abbr* (= *Fahrenheit*) F.
F. *abbr* (= *fiume*) R.
fa *vb vedi* **fare** ♦ *sm inv* (MUS) F; (: *solfeggiando la scala*) fa ♦ *av*: **10 anni** ~ **10** years ago.
fabbi'sogno [fabbi'zoɲɲo] *sm* needs *pl*, requirements *pl*; **il** ~ **nazionale di petrolio** the country's oil requirements; ~ **del settore pubblico** public sector borrowing requirement (*Brit*), government debt borrowing (US).
'fabbrica *sf* factory.
fabbri'cante *sm* manufacturer, maker.
fabbri'care *vt* to build; (*produrre*) to manufacture, make; (*fig*) to fabricate, invent.
fabbri'cato *sm* building.
fabbricazi'one [fabbrikat'tsjone] *sf* building,

fabrication; making, manufacture, manufacturing.
'fabbro *sm* (black)smith.
fac'cenda [fat'tʃɛnda] *sf* matter, affair; (*cosa da fare*) task, chore; **le** ~**e domestiche** the housework *sg*.
fac'cetta [fat'tʃetta] *sf* (*di pietra preziosa*) facet.
fac'chino [fak'kino] *sm* porter.
'faccia, ce ['fattʃa] *sf* face; (*di moneta, medaglia*) side; ~ **a** ~ face to face; **di** ~ **a** opposite, facing; **avere la** ~ **(tosta) di dire/fare qc** to have the cheek *o* nerve to say/do sth; **fare qc alla** ~ **di qn** to do sth to spite sb; **leggere qc in** ~ **a qn** to see sth written all over sb's face.
facci'ata [fat'tʃata] *sf* façade; (*di pagina*) side.
'faccio *etc* ['fattʃo] *vb vedi* **fare**.
fa'cente [fa'tʃɛnte]: ~ **funzione** *sm* (AMM) deputy.
fa'cessi *etc* [fa'tʃessi] *vb vedi* **fare**.
fa'ceto, a [fa'tʃeto] *ag* witty, humorous.
fa'cevo *etc* [fa'tʃevo] *vb vedi* **fare**.
fa'cezia [fa'tʃɛttsja] *sf* witticism, witty remark.
fa'chiro [fa'kiro] *sm* fakir.
'facile ['fatʃile] *ag* easy; (*affabile*) easygoing; (*disposto*): ~ **a** inclined to, prone to; (*probabile*): **è** ~ **che piova** it's likely to rain; **donna di** ~**i costumi** woman of easy virtue, loose woman.
facilità [fatʃili'ta] *sf* easiness; (*disposizione, dono*) aptitude.
facili'tare [fatʃili'tare] *vt* to make easier.
facilitazi'one [fatʃilitat'tsjone] *sf* (*gen*) facilities *pl*; ~**i di pagamento** easy terms, credit facilities.
facil'mente [fatʃil'mente] *av* (*gen*) easily; (*probabilmente*) probably.
faci'lone, a [fatʃi'lone] *sm/f* (*peg*) happy-go-lucky person.
facino'roso, a [fatʃino'roso] *ag* violent.
facoltà *sf inv* faculty; (CHIM) property; (*autorità*) power.
facolta'tivo, a *ag* optional; (*fermata d'autobus*) request *cpd*.
facol'toso, a *ag* wealthy, rich.
fac'simile *sm* facsimile.
'faggio ['faddʒo] *sm* beech.
fagi'ano [fa'dʒano] *sm* pheasant.
fagio'lino [fadʒo'lino] *sm* French (*Brit*) *o* string bean.
fagi'olo [fa'dʒolo] *sm* bean; **capitare a** ~ to come at the right time.
fagoci'tare [fagotʃi'tare] *vt* (*fig: industria etc*) to absorb, swallow up; (*scherzoso: cibo*) to devour.
fa'gotto *sm* bundle; (MUS) bassoon; **far** ~ (*fig*) to pack up and go.
'fai *vb vedi* **fare**.
'faida *sf* feud.

fa'ina *sf* (*ZOOL*) stone marten.

'Fahrenheit ['fa:rənheit] *sm* Fahrenheit.

fa'lange [fa'landʒe] *sf* (*ANAT, MIL*) phalanx.

fal'cata *sf* stride.

'falce ['faltʃe] *sf* scythe; ~ **e martello** (*POL*) hammer and sickle.

fal'cetto [fal'tʃetto] *sm* sickle.

falci'are [fal'tʃare] *vt* to cut; (*fig*) to mow down.

falcia'trice [faltʃa'tritʃe] *sf* (*per fieno*) reaping machine; (*per erba*) mowing machine.

'falco, chi *sm* hawk.

fal'cone *sm* falcon.

'falda *sf* (*GEO*) layer, stratum; (*di cappello*) brim; (*di cappotto*) tails *pl*; (*di monte*) lower slope; (*di tetto*) pitch; (*di neve*) flake; **abito a ~e** tails *pl*.

fale'gname [faleɲ'ɲame] *sm* joiner.

fa'lena *sf* (*ZOOL*) moth.

'Falkland ['falkland] *sfpl*: **le isole** ~ the Falkland Islands.

fal'lace [fal'latʃe] *ag* misleading, deceptive.

'fallico, a, ci, che *ag* phallic.

fallimen'tare *ag* (*COMM*) bankruptcy *cpd*; **bilancio** ~ negative balance, deficit; **diritto** ~ bankruptcy law.

falli'mento *sm* failure; bankruptcy.

fal'lire *vi* (*non riuscire*): ~ (**in**) to fail (in); (*DIR*) to go bankrupt ♦ *vt* (*colpo, bersaglio*) to miss.

fal'lito, a *ag* unsuccessful; bankrupt ♦ *sm/f* bankrupt.

'fallo *sm* error, mistake; (*imperfezione*) defect, flaw; (*SPORT*) foul; fault; (*ANAT*) phallus; **senza** ~ without fail; **cogliere qn in** ~ to catch sb out; **mettere il piede in** ~ to slip.

fal'locrate *sm* male chauvinist.

falò *sm inv* bonfire.

fal'sare *vt* to distort, misrepresent.

falsa'riga, ghe *sf* lined page, ruled page; **sulla** ~ **di ...** (*fig*) along the lines of ....

fal'sario *sm* forger; counterfeiter.

falsifi'care *vt* to forge; (*monete*) to forge, counterfeit.

falsità *sf inv* (*di persona, notizia*) falseness; (*bugia*) falsehood, lie.

'falso, a *ag* false; (*errato*) wrong; (*falsificato*) forged; fake; (: *oro, gioielli*) imitation *cpd* ♦ *sm* forgery; **essere un** ~ **magro** to be heavier than one looks; **giurare il** ~ to commit perjury; ~ **in atto pubblico** forgery (of a legal document).

'fama *sf* fame; (*reputazione*) reputation, name.

'fame *sf* hunger; **aver** ~ to be hungry; **fare la** ~ (*fig*) to starve, exist at subsistence level.

fa'melico, a, ci, che *ag* ravenous.

famige'rato, a [famidʒe'rato] *ag* notorious, ill-famed.

fa'miglia [fa'miʎʎa] *sf* family.

famili'are *ag* (*della famiglia*) family *cpd*; (*ben noto*) familiar; (*rapporti, atmosfera*) friendly; (*LING*) informal, colloquial ♦ *sm/f* relative, relation; **una vettura** ~ a family car.

familiarità *sf* familiarity; friendliness; informality.

familiariz'zare [familjarid'dzare] *vi*: ~ **con qn** to get to know sb; **abbiamo familiarizzato subito** we got on well together from the start.

fa'moso, a *ag* famous, well-known.

fa'nale *sm* (*AUT*) light, lamp (*Brit*); (*luce stradale, NAUT*) light; (*di faro*) beacon.

fa'natico, a, ci, che *ag* fanatical; (*del teatro, calcio etc*): ~ **di** *o* **per** mad *o* crazy about ♦ *sm/f* fanatic; (*tifoso*) fan.

fanciul'lezza [fantʃul'lettsa] *sf* childhood.

fanci'ullo, a [fan'tʃullo] *sm/f* child.

fan'donia *sf* tall story; ~**e** *sfpl* nonsense *sg*.

fan'fara *sf* brass band; (*musica*) fanfare.

fanfa'rone *sm* braggart.

fan'ghiglia [fan'giʎʎa] *sf* mire, mud.

'fango, ghi *sm* mud; **fare i** ~**ghi** (*MED*) to take a course of mud baths.

fan'goso, a *ag* muddy.

'fanno *vb vedi* **fare**.

fannul'lone, a *sm/f* idler, loafer.

fantasci'enza [fantaʃ'ʃɛntsa] *sf* science fiction.

fanta'sia *sf* fantasy, imagination; (*capriccio*) whim, caprice ♦ *ag inv*: **vestito** ~ patterned dress.

fantasi'oso, a *ag* (*dotato di fantasia*) imaginative; (*bizzarro*) fanciful, strange.

fan'tasma, i *sm* ghost, phantom.

fantasti'care *vi* to daydream.

fantastiche'ria [fantastike'ria] *sf* daydream.

fan'tastico, a, ci, che *ag* fantastic; (*potenza, ingegno*) imaginative.

'fante *sm* infantryman; (*CARTE*) jack, knave (*Brit*).

fante'ria *sf* infantry.

fan'tino *sm* jockey.

fan'toccio [fan'tɔttʃo] *sm* puppet.

fanto'matico, a, ci, che *ag* (*nave, esercito*) phantom *cpd*; (*personaggio*) mysterious.

FAO *sigla f* FAO (= *Food and Agriculture Organization*).

fara'butto *sm* crook.

fara'ona *sf* guinea fowl.

fara'one *sm* (*STORIA*) Pharaoh.

fara'onico, a, ci, che *ag* of the Pharaohs; (*fig*) enormous, huge.

far'cire [far'tʃire] *vt* (*carni, peperoni etc*) to stuff; (*torte*) to fill.

fard [far] *sm inv* blusher.

far'dello *sm* bundle; (*fig*) burden.

'fare *vt* to make; (*operare, agire*) to do; (*TEATRO*) to act; ~ **l'avvocato/il medico** to be a lawyer/doctor; ~ **del tennis** to play tennis; ~ **il morto/l'ignorante** to act dead/

the fool; **non fa niente** it doesn't matter; **2 più 2 fa 4** 2 and 2 are *o* make 4; **farcela** to succeed, manage; **non ce la faccio più** I can't go on any longer; **farla a qn** to get the better of sb; **farla finita con qc** to have done with sth; **ti facevo più intelligente** I thought you were more intelligent ♦ *vi* (*essere adatto*) to be suitable; (*stare per*): **fece per parlare quando ...** he was about to speak when ...; **~ in modo di** to act in such a way that; **faccia pure!** go ahead!; **~ da** (*~ le funzioni di*) to act as; **ci sa ~** he's very capable; **fa proprio al caso nostro** it's just what we need; **"davvero?"** — **fece** "really?" — he said ♦ *vb impers*: *vedi* **bello, freddo** *etc*; **~ piangere/ridere qn** to make sb cry/laugh; **~ venire qn** to send for sb; **fammi vedere** let me see; **~rsi** *vr* (*diventare*) to become; **~rsi la macchina** to get a car for o.s.; **~rsi avanti** to come forward; **~rsi notare** to get o.s. noticed; **fatti più in là!** move along a bit!

fa'retra *sf* quiver.

far'falla *sf* butterfly.

farfugli'are [farfuʎ'ʎare] *vt, vi* to mumble, mutter.

fa'rina *sf* flour; **~ gialla** maize (*Brit*) *o* corn (*US*) flour; **~ integrale** wholemeal (*Brit*) *o* whole-wheat (*US*) flour; **questa non è ~ del tuo sacco** (*fig*) this isn't your own idea (*o* work).

fari'nacei [fari'natʃei] *smpl* starches.

fa'ringe [fa'rindʒe] *sf* (*ANAT*) pharynx.

fari'noso, a *ag* (*patate*) floury; (*neve, mela*) powdery.

farma'ceutico, a, ci, che [farma'tʃeutiko] *ag* pharmaceutical.

farma'cia, 'cie [farma'tʃia] *sf* pharmacy; (*negozio*) chemist's (shop) (*Brit*), pharmacy.

farma'cista, i, e [farma'tʃista] *sm/f* chemist (*Brit*), pharmacist.

'farmaco, ci *o* **chi** *sm* drug, medicine.

farneti'care *vi* to rave, be delirious.

'faro *sm* (*NAUT*) lighthouse; (*AER*) beacon; (*AUT*) headlight, headlamp (*Brit*).

farragi'noso, a [farradʒi'noso] *ag* (*stile*) muddled, confused.

'farsa *sf* farce.

far'sesco, a, schi, sche *ag* farcical.

fasc. *abbr* = **fascicolo**.

'fascia, sce ['faʃʃa] *sf* band, strip; (*MED*) bandage; (*di sindaco, ufficiale*) sash; (*parte di territorio*) strip, belt; (*di contribuenti etc*) group, band; **essere in ~sce** (*anche fig*) to be in one's infancy; **~ oraria** time band.

fasci'are [faʃ'ʃare] *vt* to bind; (*MED*) to bandage; (*bambino*) to put a nappy (*Brit*) *o* diaper (*US*) on.

fascia'tura [faʃʃa'tura] *sf* (*azione*) bandaging; (*fascia*) bandage.

fa'scicolo [faʃ'ʃikolo] *sm* (*di documenti*) file, dossier; (*di rivista*) issue, number; (*opuscolo*) booklet, pamphlet.

'fascino ['faʃʃino] *sm* charm, fascination.

'fascio ['faʃʃo] *sm* bundle, sheaf; (*di fiori*) bunch; (*di luce*) beam; (*POL*): **il F~** the Fascist Party.

fa'scismo [faʃ'ʃizmo] *sm* fascism.

fa'scista, i, e [faʃ'ʃista] *ag, sm/f* fascist.

'fase *sf* phase; (*TECN*) stroke; **in ~ di espansione** in a period of expansion; **essere fuori ~** (*motore*) to be rough (*Brit*), run roughly; (*fig*) to feel rough (*Brit*) *o* rotten.

fas'tidio *sm* bother, trouble; **dare ~ a qn** to bother *o* annoy sb; **sento ~ allo stomaco** my stomach's upset; **avere ~i con la polizia** to have trouble *o* bother with the police.

fastidi'oso, a *ag* annoying, tiresome; (*schifiltoso*) fastidious.

'fasto *sm* pomp, splendour (*Brit*), splendor (*US*).

fas'toso, a *ag* sumptuous, lavish.

fa'sullo, a *ag* (*gen*) fake; (*dichiarazione, persona*) false; (*pretesto*) bogus.

'fata *sf* fairy.

fa'tale *ag* fatal; (*inevitabile*) inevitable; (*fig*) irresistible.

fata'lismo *sm* fatalism.

fatalità *sf inv* inevitability; (*avversità*) misfortune; (*fato*) fate, destiny.

fa'tato, a *ag* (*spada, chiave*) magic; (*castello*) enchanted.

fa'tica, che *sf* hard work, toil; (*sforzo*) effort; (*di metalli*) fatigue; **a ~** with difficulty; **respirare a ~** to have difficulty (in) breathing; **fare ~ a fare qc** to find it difficult to do sth; **animale da ~** beast of burden.

fati'caccia, ce [fati'kattʃa] *sf*: **fu una ~** it was hard work, it was a hell of a job (*fam*).

fati'care *vi* to toil; **~ a fare qc** to have difficulty doing sth.

fati'cata *sf* hard work.

fa'tichi *etc* [fa'tiki] *vb vedi* **faticare**.

fati'coso, a *ag* (*viaggio, camminata*) tiring, exhausting; (*lavoro*) laborious.

fa'tidico, a, ci, che *ag* fateful.

'fato *sm* fate, destiny.

Fatt. *abbr* (= *fattura*) inv.

fat'taccio [fat'tattʃo] *sm* foul deed.

fat'tezze [fat'tettse] *sfpl* features.

fat'tibile *ag* feasible, possible.

fattis'pecie [fattis'petʃe] *sf*: **nella** *o* **in ~** in this case *o* instance.

'fatto, a *pp di* **fare** ♦ *ag*: **un uomo ~** a grown man ♦ *sm* fact; (*azione*) deed; (*avvenimento*) event, occurrence; (*di romanzo, film*) action, story; **~ a mano/in casa** hand-/home-made; **è ben ~a** she has a nice figure; **cogliere qn sul** ~ to catch sb red-handed; **il** ~ **sta** o **è che** the fact remains o is that; **in** ~ **di** as for, as far as ... is concerned; **fare i** ~**i propri** to mind one's own business; **è uno che sa il** ~ **suo** he knows what he's about; **gli ho detto il** ~ **suo** I told him what I thought of him; **porre qn di fronte al** ~ **compiuto** to present sb with a fait accompli.

fat'tore sm (AGR) farm manager; (MAT: elemento costitutivo) factor.

fatto'ria sf farm; (casa) farmhouse.

fatto'rino sm errand boy; (di ufficio) office boy; (d'albergo) porter.

fattucchi'era [fattuk'kjɛra] sf witch.

fat'tura sf (COMM) invoice; (di abito) tailoring; (malia) spell; **pagamento contro presentazione** ~ payment on invoice.

fattu'rare vt (COMM) to invoice; (prodotto) to produce; (vino) to adulterate.

fattu'rato sm (COMM) turnover.

fatturazi'one [fatturat'tsjone] sf billing, invoicing.

'fatuo, a ag vain, fatuous; **fuoco** ~ (anche fig) will-o'-the-wisp.

'fauci ['fautʃi] sfpl (di leone etc) jaws; (di vulcano) mouth sg.

'fauna sf fauna.

'fausto, a ag (formale) happy; **un** ~ **presagio** a good omen.

fau'tore, 'trice sm/f advocate, supporter.

'fava sf broad bean.

fa'vella sf speech.

fa'villa sf spark.

'favo sm (di api) honeycomb.

'favola sf (fiaba) fairy tale; (d'intento morale) fable; (fandonia) yarn; **essere la** ~ **del paese** (oggetto di critica) to be the talk of the town; (zimbello) to be a laughing stock.

favo'loso, a ag fabulous; (incredibile) incredible.

fa'vore sm favour (Brit), favor (US); **per** ~ please; **prezzo/trattamento di** ~ preferential price/treatment; **condizioni di** ~ (COMM) favo(u)rable terms; **fare un** ~ **a qn** to do sb a favo(u)r; **col** ~ **delle tenebre** under cover of darkness.

favoreggia'mento [favoreddʒa'mento] sm (DIR) aiding and abetting.

favo'revole ag favourable (Brit), favorable (US).

favo'rire vt to favour (Brit), favor (US); (il commercio, l'industria, le arti) to promote, encourage; **vuole** ~**?** won't you help yourself?; **favorisca in salotto** please come into the sitting room; **mi favorisca i documenti** please may I see your papers?

favori'tismo sm favouritism (Brit), favoritism (US).

favo'rito, a ag, sm/f favourite (Brit), favorite (US).

fazi'one [fat'tsjone] sf faction.

faziosità [fattsjosi'ta] sf sectarianism.

fazzo'letto [fattso'letto] sm handkerchief; (per la testa) (head)scarf.

F.C. abbr = **fuoricorso**.

f.co abbr = **franco**.

FE sigla = Ferrara.

febb. abbr (= febbraio) Feb.

feb'braio sm February; per fraseologia vedi **luglio**.

'febbre sf fever; **aver la** ~ to have a high temperature; ~ **da fieno** hay fever.

feb'brile ag (anche fig) feverish.

'feccia, ce ['fettʃa] sf dregs pl.

'feci ['fetʃi] sfpl faeces, excrement sg.

'feci etc ['fetʃi] vb vedi **fare**.

'fecola sf potato flour.

fecon'dare vt to fertilize.

fecondazi'one [fekondat'tsjone] sf fertilization; ~ **artificiale** artificial insemination.

fecondità sf fertility.

fe'condo, a ag fertile.

'Fedcom sigla m = Fondo Europeo di Cooperazione Monetaria.

'fede sf (credenza) belief, faith; (REL) faith; (fiducia) faith, trust; (fedeltà) loyalty; (anello) wedding ring; (attestato) certificate; **aver** ~ **in qn** to have faith in sb; **tener** ~ **a** (ideale) to remain loyal to; (giuramento, promessa) to keep; **in buona/cattiva** ~ in good/bad faith; **"in** ~**"** (DIR) "in witness whereof".

fe'dele ag (leale): ~ **(a)** faithful (to); (veritiero) true, accurate ♦ sm/f follower; **i** ~**i** (REL) the faithful.

fedeltà sf faithfulness; (coniugale) fidelity; (esattezza: di copia, traduzione) accuracy; **alta** ~ (RADIO) high fidelity.

'federa sf pillowslip, pillowcase.

fede'rale ag federal.

federazi'one [federat'tsjone] sf federation.

Feder'caccia [feder'kattʃa] abbr f (= Federazione Italiana della Caccia) hunting federation.

Feder'calcio [feder'kaltʃo] abbr m (= Federazione Italiana Gioco Calcio) Italian football association.

Federcon'sorzi [federkon'sɔrtsi] abbr f (= Federazione Italiana dei Consorzi Agrari) federation of farmers' cooperatives.

fe'difrago, a, ghi, ghe ag faithless, perfidious.

fe'dina sf (DIR): ~ **(penale)** record; **avere la** ~ **penale sporca** to have a police record.

'fegato sm liver; (fig) guts pl, nerve; **mangiarsi** o **rodersi il** ~ to be consumed with rage.

'felce ['feltʃe] sf fern.

fe'lice [fe'litʃe] ag happy; (fortunato) lucky.

felicità [felitʃi'ta] sf happiness.

felici'tarsi [felitʃi'tarsi] vr (congratularsi): ~ **con qn per qc** to congratulate sb on sth.

felicitazi'oni [felitʃitat'tsjoni] *sfpl* congratulations.

fe'lino, a *ag*, *sm* feline.

fel'pato, a *ag* (*tessuto*) brushed; (*passo*) stealthy; **con passo** ~ stealthily.

'feltro *sm* felt.

'femmina *sf* (*ZOOL*, *TECN*) female; (*figlia*) girl, daughter; (*spesso peg*) woman.

femmi'nile *ag* feminine; (*sesso*) female; (*lavoro*, *giornale*) woman's, women's; (*moda*) women's ♦ *sm* (*LING*) feminine.

femminilità *sf* femininity.

femmi'nismo *sm* feminism.

femmi'nista, i, e *ag*, *sm/f* feminist.

'femore *sm* thighbone, femur.

'fendere *vt* to cut through.

fendi'nebbia *sm* (*AUT*) fog lamp.

fendi'tura *sf* (*gen*) crack; (*di roccia*) cleft, crack.

fe'nomeno *sm* phenomenon.

'feretro *sm* coffin.

feri'ale *ag*: **giorno** ~ weekday, working day.

'ferie *sfpl* holidays (*Brit*), vacation *sg* (*US*); **andare in** ~ to go on holiday *o* vacation; **25 giorni di** ~ **pagate** 25 days' holiday *o* vacation with pay.

feri'mento *sm* wounding.

fe'rire *vt* to injure; (*deliberatamente*: *MIL etc*) to wound; (*colpire*) to hurt; **~rsi** *vr* to hurt o.s., injure o.s.

fe'rito, a *sm/f* wounded *o* injured man/woman ♦ *sf* injury; wound.

feri'toia *sf* slit.

'ferma *sf* (*MIL*) (period of) service; (*CACCIA*): **cane da** ~ pointer.

ferma'carte *sm inv* paperweight.

fermacra'vatta *sm inv* tiepin (*Brit*), tie tack (*US*).

fer'maglio [fer'maʎʎo] *sm* clasp; (*gioiello*) brooch; (*per documenti*) clip.

ferma'mente *av* firmly.

fer'mare *vt* to stop, halt; (*POLIZIA*) to detain, hold; (*bottone etc*) to fasten, fix ♦ *vi* to stop; **~rsi** *vr* to stop, halt; **~rsi a fare qc** to stop to do sth.

fer'mata *sf* stop; ~ **dell'autobus** bus stop.

fermentazi'one [fermentat'tsjone] *sf* fermentation.

fer'mento *sm* (*anche fig*) ferment; (*lievito*) yeast.

fer'mezza [fer'mettsa] *sf* (*fig*) firmness, steadfastness.

'fermo, a *ag* still, motionless; (*veicolo*) stationary; (*orologio*) not working; (*saldo*: *anche fig*) firm; (*voce*, *mano*) steady ♦ *escl* stop!; keep still! ♦ *sm* (*chiusura*) catch, lock; (*DIR*): ~ **di polizia** police detention; ~ **restando che** ... it being understood that ....

'fermo 'posta *av*, *sm inv* poste restante (*Brit*), general delivery (*US*).

fe'roce [fe'rɔtʃe] *ag* (*animale*) wild, fierce, ferocious; (*persona*) cruel, fierce; (*fame*, *dolore*) raging.

fe'rocia, cie [fe'rɔtʃa] *sf* ferocity.

Ferr. *abbr* = **ferrovia**.

fer'raglia [fer'raʎʎa] *sf* scrap iron.

ferra'gosto *sm* (*festa*) feast of the Assumption; (*periodo*) August holidays *pl* (*Brit*) *o* vacation (*US*).

ferra'menta *sfpl* ironmongery *sg* (*Brit*), hardware *sg*; **negozio di** ~ ironmonger's (*Brit*), hardware shop *o* store (*US*).

fer'rare *vt* (*cavallo*) to shoe.

fer'rato, a *ag* (*FERR*): **strada** ~**a** railway line (*Brit*), railroad line (*US*); (*fig*): **essere** ~ **in** (*materia*) to be well up in.

ferra'vecchio [ferra'vɛkkjo] *sm* scrap merchant.

'ferreo, a *ag* iron *cpd*.

ferri'era *sf* ironworks *sg o pl*.

'ferro *sm* iron; **una bistecca ai** ~**i** a grilled steak; **mettere a** ~ **e fuoco** to put to the sword; **essere ai** ~**i corti** (*fig*) to be at daggers drawn; **tocca** ~! touch wood!; ~ **battuto** wrought iron; ~ **di cavallo** horseshoe; ~ **da stiro** iron; ~**i da calza** knitting needles; **i** ~**i del mestiere** the tools of the trade.

ferrotranvi'ario, a *ag* public transport *cpd*.

Ferrotranvi'eri *abbr f* (= *Federazione Nazionale Lavoratori Autoferrotranvieri e Internavigatori*) *transport workers' union*.

ferro'via *sf* railway (*Brit*), railroad (*US*).

ferrovi'ario, a *ag* railway *cpd* (*Brit*), railroad *cpd* (*US*).

ferrovi'ere *sm* railwayman (*Brit*), railroad man (*US*).

'fertile *ag* fertile.

fertilità *sf* fertility.

fertiliz'zante [fertilid'dzante] *sm* fertilizer.

fertiliz'zare [fertilid'dzare] *vt* to fertilize.

fer'vente *ag* fervent, ardent.

'fervere *vi*: **fervono i preparativi per** ... they are making feverish preparations for ....

'fervido, a *ag* fervent, ardent.

fer'vore *sm* fervour (*Brit*), fervor (*US*), ardour (*Brit*), ardor (*US*); (*punto culminante*) height.

'fesa *sf* (*CUC*) rump of veal.

fesse'ria *sf* stupidity; **dire** ~**e** to talk nonsense.

'fesso, a *pp di* **fendere** ♦ *ag* (*fam*: *sciocco*) crazy, cracked.

fes'sura *sf* crack, split; (*per gettone*, *moneta*) slot.

'festa *sf* (*religiosa*) feast; (*pubblica*) holiday; (*compleanno*) birthday; (*onomastico*) name day; (*ricevimento*) celebration, party; **far** ~ to have a holiday; (*far baldoria*) to live it up; **far** ~ **a qn** to give sb a warm welcome; **essere vestito a** ~ to be dressed up to the nines; ~ **comandata** (*REL*) holiday of obligation; **la** ~ **della**

mamma/del papà Mother's/Father's Day.

festeggia'menti [festeddʒa'menti] *smpl* celebrations.

festeggi'are [fested'dʒare] *vt* to celebrate; *(persona)* to have a celebration for.

fes'tino *sm* party; *(con balli)* ball.

fes'tivo, a *ag (atmosfera)* festive; **giorno** ~ holiday.

fes'toso, a *ag* merry, joyful.

fe'tente *ag (puzzolente)* fetid; *(comportamento)* disgusting ♦ *sm/f (fam)* stinker, rotter *(Brit)*.

fe'ticcio [fe'tittʃo] *sm* fetish.

'feto *sm* foetus *(Brit)*, fetus *(US)*.

fe'tore *sm* stench, stink.

'fetta *sf* slice.

fet'tuccia, ce [fet'tuttʃa] *sf* tape, ribbon.

fettuc'cine [fettut'tʃine] *sfpl (CUC)* ribbon-shaped pasta.

feu'dale *ag* feudal.

'feudo *sm (STORIA)* fief; *(fig)* stronghold.

ff *abbr (AMM)* = **facente funzione**; (= *fogli*) pp.

FF.AA *abbr* = **forze armate**.

FF.SS. *abbr* (= *Ferrovie dello Stato*) *Italian railways*.

FG *sigla* = *Foggia*.

FI *sigla* = *Firenze*.

fi'aba *sf* fairy tale.

fia'besco, a, schi, sche *ag* fairy-tale *cpd*.

fi'acca *sf* weariness; *(svogliatezza)* listlessness; **battere la** ~ to shirk.

fiac'care *vt* to weaken.

fiaccherò *etc* [fjakke'rɔ] *vb vedi* **fiaccare**.

fi'acco, a, chi, che *ag (stanco)* tired, weary; *(svogliato)* listless; *(debole)* weak; *(mercato)* slack.

fi'accola *sf* torch.

fiacco'lata *sf* torchlight procession.

fi'ala *sf* phial.

fi'amma *sf* flame; *(NAUT)* pennant.

fiam'mante *ag (colore)* flaming; **nuovo** ~ brand new.

fiam'mata *sf* blaze.

fiammeggi'are [fjammed'dʒare] *vi* to blaze.

fiam'mifero *sm* match.

fiam'mingo, a, ghi, ghe *ag* Flemish ♦ *sm/f* Fleming ♦ *sm (LING)* Flemish; *(ZOOL)* flamingo; **i F~ghi** the Flemish.

fian'cata *sf (di nave etc)* side; *(NAUT)* broadside.

fiancheggi'are [fjanked'dʒare] *vt* to border; *(fig)* to support, back (up); *(MIL)* to flank.

fi'anco, chi *sm* side; *(di persona)* hip; *(MIL)* flank; **di** ~ sideways, from the side; **a** ~ **a** ~ side by side; **prestare il proprio** ~ **alle critiche** to leave o.s. open to criticism; ~ **destr/sinistr!** *(MIL)* right/left turn!

Fi'andre *sfpl:* **le** ~ Flanders *sg*.

fiaschette'ria [fjaskette'ria] *sf* wine shop.

fi'asco, schi *sm* flask; *(fig)* fiasco; **fare** ~ to be a fiasco.

fia'tare *vi (fig: parlare)*: **senza** ~ without saying a word.

fi'ato *sm* breath; *(resistenza)* stamina; **~i** *smpl (MUS)* wind instruments; **avere il** ~ **grosso** to be out of breath; **prendere** ~ to catch one's breath; **bere qc tutto d'un** ~ to drink sth in one go *o* gulp.

'fibbia *sf* buckle.

'fibra *sf* fibre, fiber *(US)*; *(fig)* constitution; ~ **ottica** optical fibre; ~ **di vetro** fibreglass *(Brit)*, fiberglass *(US)*.

ficca'naso, ** *pl(m)* **~i, *pl(f)* *inv sm/f* busybody, nos(e)y parker.

fic'care *vt* to push, thrust, drive; **~rsi** *vr (andare a finire)* to get to; ~ **il naso negli affari altrui** *(fig)* to poke *o* stick one's nose into other people's business; **~rsi nei pasticci** *o* **nei guai** to get into hot water *o* a fix.

ficcherò *etc* [fikke'rɔ] *vb vedi* **ficcare**.

fiche [fiʃ] *sf inv (nei giochi d'azzardo)* chip.

'fico, chi *sm (pianta)* fig tree; *(frutto)* fig; ~ **d'India** prickly pear; ~ **secco** dried fig.

fidanza'mento [fidantsa'mento] *sm* engagement.

fidan'zarsi [fidan'tsarsi] *vr* to get engaged.

fidan'zato, a [fidan'tsato] *sm/f* fiancé/fiancée.

fi'darsi *vr:* ~ **di** to trust; **~rsi è bene non ~rsi è meglio** *(proverbio)* better safe than sorry.

fi'dato, a *ag* reliable, trustworthy.

fideius'sore *sm (DIR)* guarantor.

'fido, a *ag* faithful, loyal ♦ *sm (COMM)* credit.

fi'ducia [fi'dutʃa] *sf* confidence, trust; **incarico di** ~ position of trust, responsible position; **persona di** ~ reliable person; **è il mio uomo di** ~ he is my right-hand man; **porre la questione di** ~ *(POL)* to ask for a vote of confidence.

fiduci'oso, a [fidu'tʃoso] *ag* trusting.

fi'ele *sm (MED)* bile; *(fig)* bitterness.

fie'nile *sm* hayloft.

fi'eno *sm* hay.

fi'era *sf* fair; *(animale)* wild beast; ~ **di beneficenza** charity bazaar; ~ **campionaria** trade fair.

fie'rezza [fje'rettsa] *sf* pride.

fi'ero, a *ag* proud; *(crudele)* fierce, cruel; *(audace)* bold.

fi'evole *ag (luce)* dim; *(suono)* weak.

'fifa *sf (fam)*: **aver** ~ to have the jitters.

fi'fone, a *sm/f (fam, scherzoso)* coward.

fig. *abbr* (= *figura*) fig.

FIGC *sigla f* (= *Federazione Italiana Gioco Calcio*) *Italian football association*.

'Figi ['fidʒi] *sfpl:* **le isole** ~ Fiji, the Fiji Islands.

'figlia ['fiʎʎa] *sf* daughter; *(COMM)* counterfoil *(Brit)*, stub.

figli'are [fiʎ'ʎare] *vi* to give birth.

figli'astro, a [fiʎ'ʎastro] *sm/f* stepson/

daughter.

'figlio ['fiʎʎo] *sm* son; (*senza distinzione di sesso*) child; ~ **d'arte: essere** ~ **d'arte** to come from a theatrical (*o* musical *etc*) family; ~ **di puttana** (*fam!*) son of a bitch (*!*); ~ **unico** only child.

figli'occio, a, ci, ce [fiʎ'ʎɔttʃo] *sm/f* godchild, godson/daughter.

figli'ola [fiʎ'ʎɔla] *sf* daughter; (*fig*: *ragazza*) girl.

figli'olo [fiʎ'ʎɔlo] *sm* (*anche fig*: *ragazzo*) son.

fi'gura *sf* figure; (*forma, aspetto esterno*) form, shape; (*illustrazione*) picture, illustration; **far** ~ to look smart; **fare una brutta** ~ to make a bad impression; **che** ~**!** how embarrassing!

figu'raccia, ce [figu'rattʃa] *sf*: **fare una** ~ to create a bad impression.

figu'rare *vi* to appear ♦ *vt*: **~rsi qc** to imagine sth; **~rsi** *vr*: **figurati!** imagine that!; **ti do noia?** — **ma figurati!** am I disturbing you? — not at all!

figura'tivo, a *ag* figurative.

figu'rina *sf* (*statuetta*) figurine; (*cartoncino*) picture card.

figuri'nista, i, e *sm/f* dress designer.

figu'rino *sm* fashion sketch.

fi'guro *sm*: **un losco** ~ a suspicious character.

figu'rone *sm*: **fare un** ~ (*persona, oggetto*) to look terrific; (*persona: con un discorso etc*) to make an excellent impression.

'fila *sf* row, line; (*coda*) queue; (*serie*) series, string; **di** ~ in succession; **fare la** ~ to queue; **in** ~ **indiana** in single file.

fila'mento *sm* filament.

fi'lanca ® *sf stretch material.*

fi'landa *sf* spinning mill.

fi'lante *ag*: **stella** ~ (*stella cadente*) shooting star; (*striscia di carta*) streamer.

filantro'pia *sf* philanthropy.

filan'tropico, a, ci, che *ag* philanthropic (al).

fi'lantropo *sm* philanthropist.

fi'lare *vt* to spin; (*NAUT*) to pay out ♦ *vi* (*baco, ragno*) to spin; (*formaggio fuso*) to go stringy; (*liquido*) to trickle; (*discorso*) to hang together; (*fam: amoreggiare*) to go steady; (*muoversi a forte velocità*) to go at full speed; (*andarsene lentamente*) to make o.s. scarce ♦ *sm* (*di alberi etc*) row, line; ~ **diritto** (*fig*) to toe the line.

filar'monico, a, ci, che *ag* philharmonic.

filas'trocca, che *sf* nursery rhyme.

filate'lia *sf* philately, stamp collecting.

fi'lato, a *ag* spun ♦ *sm* yarn ♦ *av*: **vai dritto** ~ **a casa** go straight home; **3 giorni** ~**i** 3 days running *o* on end.

fila'tura *sf* spinning; (*luogo*) spinning mill.

fi'letto *sm* (*ornamento*) braid, trimming; (*di vite*) thread; (*di carne*) fillet.

fili'ale *ag* filial ♦ *sf* (*di impresa*) branch.

filibusti'ere *sm* pirate; (*fig*) adventurer.

fili'grana *sf* (*in oreficeria*) filigree; (*su carta*) watermark.

fi'lippica *sf* invective.

Filip'pine *sfpl*: **le** ~ the Philippines.

filip'pino, a *ag, sm/f* Filipino.

film *sm inv* film.

fil'mare *vt* to film.

fil'mato *sm* short film.

fil'mina *sf* film strip.

'filo *sm* (*anche fig*) thread; (*filato*) yarn; (*metallico*) wire; (*di lama, rasoio*) edge; **con un** ~ **di voce** in a whisper; **un** ~ **d'aria** (*fig*) a breath of air; **dare del** ~ **da torcere a qn** to create difficulties for sb, make life difficult for sb; **fare il** ~ **a qn** (*corteggiare*) to be after sb, chase sb; **per** ~ **e per segno** in detail; ~ **d'erba** blade of grass; ~ **di perle** string of pearls; ~ **di Scozia** fine cotton yarn; ~ **spinato** barbed wire.

filoameri'cano, a *ag* pro-American.

'filobus *sm inv* trolley bus.

filodiffusi'one *sf* rediffusion.

filodram'matico, a, ci, che *ag*: **(compagnia)** ~**a** amateur dramatic society ♦ *sm/f* amateur actor/actress.

filon'cino [filon'tʃino] *sm* ≈ French stick.

fi'lone *sm* (*di minerali*) seam, vein; (*pane*) ≈ Vienna loaf; (*fig*) trend.

filoso'fia *sf* philosophy.

filo'sofico, a, ci, che *ag* philosophical.

fi'losofo, a *sm/f* philosopher.

filosovi'etico, a, ci, che *ag* pro-Soviet.

filo'via *sf* (*linea*) trolley line; (*bus*) trolley bus.

fil'trare *vt, vi* to filter.

'filtro *sm* filter; (*pozione*) potion; ~ **dell'olio** (*AUT*) oil filter.

'filza ['filtsa] *sf* (*anche fig*) string.

FIN *sigla f* = Federazione Italiana Nuoto.

fin *av, prep* = **fino**.

fi'nale *ag* final ♦ *sm* (*di libro, film*) end, ending; (*MUS*) finale ♦ *sf* (*SPORT*) final.

fina'lista, i, e *sm/f* finalist.

finalità *sf* (*scopo*) aim, purpose.

finaliz'zare [finalid'dzare] *vt*: ~ **a** to direct towards.

final'mente *av* finally, at last.

fi'nanza [fi'nantsa] *sf* finance; ~**e** *sfpl* (*di individuo, Stato*) finances; **(Guardia di)** ~ (*di frontiera*) ≈ Customs and Excise (*Brit*), ≈ Customs Service (*US*); **(Intendenza di)** ~ ≈ Inland Revenue (*Brit*), ≈ Internal Revenue Service (*US*); **Ministro delle** ~**e** Minister of Finance, ≈ Chancellor of the Exchequer (*Brit*), ≈ Secretary of the Treasury (*US*).

finanzia'mento [finantsja'mento] *sm* (*azione*) financing; (*denaro fornito*) funds *pl*.

finanzi'are [finan'tsjare] *vt* to finance, fund.

finanzi'ario, a [finan'tsjarjo] *ag* financial ♦ *sf*

(*anche*: **società ~a**) investment company.

finanzia'tore, **'trice** *ag*: **ente ~**, **società ~trice** backer ♦ *sm/f* backer.

finanzi'ere [finan'tsjɛre] *sm* financier; (*guardia di finanza: doganale*) customs officer; (: *tributaria*) Inland Revenue official (*Brit*), Internal Revenue official (*US*).

finché [fin'ke] *cong* (*per tutto il tempo che*) as long as; (*fino al momento in cui*) until; **~ vorrai** as long as you like; **aspetta ~ non esca** wait until he goes (*o* comes) out.

'**fine** *ag* (*lamina, carta*) thin; (*capelli, polvere*) fine; (*vista, udito*) keen, sharp; (*persona: raffinata*) refined, distinguished; (*osservazione*) subtle ♦ *sf* end ♦ *sm* aim, purpose; (*esito*) result, outcome; **in** *o* **alla ~** in the end, finally; **alla fin ~** at the end of the day, in the end; **che ~ ha fatto?** what became of him?; **buona ~ e buon principio!** (*augurio*) happy New Year!; **a fin di bene** with the best of intentions; **al ~ di fare qc** (in order) to do sth; **condurre qc a buon ~** to bring sth to a successful conclusion; **secondo ~** ulterior motive.

'**fine setti'mana** *sm o f inv* weekend.

fi'nestra *sf* window.

fines'trino *sm* (*di treno, auto*) window.

fi'nezza [fi'nettsa] *sf* thinness; fineness; keenness, sharpness; refinement; subtlety.

'**fingere** ['findʒere] *vt* to feign; (*supporre*) to imagine, suppose; **~rsi** *vr*: **~rsi ubriaco/pazzo** to pretend to be drunk/crazy; **~ di fare** to pretend to do.

fini'menti *smpl* (*di cavallo etc*) harness *sg*.

fini'mondo *sm* pandemonium.

fi'nire *vt* to finish ♦ *vi* to finish, end ♦ *sm*: **sul ~ della festa** towards the end of the party; **~ di fare** (*compiere*) to finish doing; (*smettere*) to stop doing; **~ in galera** to end up *o* finish up in prison; **farla finita** (*con la vita*) to put an end to one's life; **com'è andata a ~?** what happened in the end?; **finiscila!** stop it!

fini'tura *sf* finish.

finlan'dese *ag* Finnish ♦ *sm/f* Finn ♦ *sm* (*LING*) Finnish.

Fin'landia *sf*: **la ~** Finland.

'**fino**, **a** *ag* (*capelli, seta*) fine; (*oro*) pure; (*fig: acuto*) shrewd ♦ *av* (*spesso troncato in* **fin**: *pure, anche*) even ♦ *prep* (*spesso troncato in* **fin**: *tempo*): **fin quando?** till when?; (: *luogo*): **fin qui** as far as here; **~ a** (*tempo*) until, till; (*luogo*) as far as, (up) to; **fin da domani** from tomorrow onwards; **fin da ieri** since yesterday; **fin dalla nascita** from *o* since birth.

fi'nocchio [fi'nɔkkjo] *sm* fennel; (*fam peg*: *pederasta*) queer.

fi'nora *av* up till now.

'**finsi** *etc vb vedi* **fingere**.

'**finto**, **a** *pp di* **fingere** ♦ *ag* (*capelli, dente*) false; (*fiori*) artificial; (*cuoio, pelle*) imitation *cpd*; (*fig: simulato: pazzia etc*) feigned, sham ♦ *sf* pretence (*Brit*), pretense (*US*), sham; (*SPORT*) feint; **far ~a (di fare)** to pretend (to do); **l'ho detto per ~a** I was only pretending; (*per scherzo*) I was only kidding.

finzi'one [fin'tsjone] *sf* pretence (*Brit*), pretense (*US*), sham.

fioc'care *vi* (*neve*) to fall; (*fig: insulti etc*) to fall thick and fast.

fi'occo, chi *sm* (*di nastro*) bow; (*di stoffa, lana*) flock; (*di neve*) flake; (*NAUT*) jib; **coi ~chi** (*fig*) first-rate; **~chi di granoturco** cornflakes.

fi'ocina ['fjɔtʃina] *sf* harpoon.

fi'oco, a, chi, che *ag* faint, dim.

fi'onda *sf* catapult.

fio'raio, a *sm/f* florist.

fiorda'liso *sm* (*BOT*) cornflower.

fi'ordo *sm* fjord.

fi'ore *sm* flower; **~i** *smpl* (*CARTE*) clubs; **nel ~ degli anni** in one's prime; **a fior d'acqua** on the surface of the water; **a fior di labbra** in a whisper; **aver i nervi a fior di pelle** to be on edge; **fior di latte** cream; **è costato fior di soldi** it cost a pretty penny; **il fior ~ della società** the cream of society; **~i di campo** wild flowers.

fio'rente *ag* (*industria, paese*) flourishing; (*salute*) blooming; (*petto*) ample.

fioren'tino, a *ag, sm/f* Florentine ♦ *sf* (*CUC*) T-bone steak.

fio'retto *sm* (*SCHERMA*) foil.

fio'rire *vi* (*rosa*) to flower; (*albero*) to blossom; (*fig*) to flourish.

fio'rista, i, e *sm/f* florist.

fiori'tura *sf* (*di pianta*) flowering, blooming; (*di albero*) blossoming; (*fig: di commercio, arte*) flourishing; (*insieme dei fiori*) flowers *pl*; (*MUS*) fioritura.

fi'otto *sm* (*di lacrime*) flow, flood; (*di sangue*) gush, spurt.

'**FIPE** *sigla f* = *Federazione Italiana Pubblici Esercizi.*

Fi'renze [fi'rɛntse] *sf* Florence.

'**firma** *sf* signature; (*reputazione*) name.

firma'mento *sm* firmament.

fir'mare *vt* to sign.

firma'tario, a *sm/f* signatory.

fisar'monica *sf* accordion.

fis'cale *ag* fiscal, tax *cpd*; (*meticoloso*) punctilious; **medico ~** *doctor employed by Social Security to verify cases of sick leave.*

fisca'lista, i, e *sm/f* tax consultant.

fiscaliz'zare [fiskalid'dzare] *vt* to exempt from taxes.

fischi'are [fis'kjare] *vi* to whistle ♦ *vt* to whistle; (*attore*) to boo, hiss; **mi fischian le orecchie** my ears are singing; (*fig*) my ears are burning.

fischiet'tare [fiskjet'tare] *vi, vt* to whistle.

fischi'etto [fis'kjetto] *sm (strumento)* whistle.

'fischio ['fiskjo] *sm* whistle; **prendere ~i per fiaschi** to get hold of the wrong end of the stick.

'fisco *sm* tax authorities *pl*, ≈ Inland Revenue *(Brit)*, ≈ Internal Revenue Service *(US)*.

'fisica *sf vedi* **fisico**.

fisica'mente *av* physically.

'fisico, a, ci, che *ag* physical ♦ *sm/f* physicist ♦ *sm* physique ♦ *sf* physics *sg*.

'fisima *sf* fixation.

fisiolo'gia [fizjolo'dʒia] *sf* physiology.

fisiono'mia *sf* face, physiognomy.

fisiotera'pia *sf* physiotherapy.

fis'saggio [fis'saddʒo] *sm (FOT)* fixing.

fis'sare *vt* to fix, fasten; *(guardare intensamente)* to stare at; *(data, condizioni)* to fix, establish, set; *(prenotare)* to book; **~rsi** *vr*: **~rsi su** *(sog: sguardo, attenzione)* to focus on; *(fig: idea)* to become obsessed with.

fissazi'one [fissat'tsjone] *sf (PSIC)* fixation.

fissi'one *sf* fission.

'fisso, a *ag* fixed; *(stipendio, impiego)* regular ♦ *av*: **guardar ~ qn/qc** to stare at sb/ sth; **avere un ragazzo ~** to have a steady boyfriend; **senza ~a dimora** of no fixed abode.

'fitta *sf vedi* **fitto**.

fit'tavolo *sm* tenant.

fit'tizio, a [fit'tittsjo] *ag* fictitious, imaginary.

'fitto, a *ag* thick, dense; *(pioggia)* heavy ♦ *sm (affitto, pigione)* rent ♦ *sf* sharp pain; **una ~a al cuore** *(fig)* a pang of grief; **nel ~ del bosco** in the heart *o* depths of the wood.

fiu'mana *sf* torrent; *(fig)* stream, flood.

fi'ume *sm* river ♦ *ag inv*: **processo ~** long-running trial; **scorrere a ~i** *(acqua, sangue)* to flow in torrents.

fiu'tare *vt* to smell, sniff; *(sog: animale)* to scent; *(fig: inganno)* to get wind of, smell; **~ tabacco** to take snuff; **~ cocaina** to snort cocaine.

fi'uto *sm* (sense of) smell; *(fig)* nose.

'flaccido, a ['flattʃido] *ag* flabby.

fla'cone *sm* bottle.

flagel'lare [fladʒel'lare] *vt* to flog, scourge; *(sog: onde)* to beat against.

fla'gello [fla'dʒello] *sm* scourge.

fla'grante *ag* flagrant; **cogliere qn in ~** to catch sb red-handed.

fla'nella *sf* flannel.

flash [flaʃ] *sm inv (FOT)* flash; *(giornalistico)* newsflash.

'flauto *sm* flute.

'flebile *ag* faint, feeble.

'flemma *sf (calma)* coolness, phlegm; *(MED)* phlegm.

flem'matico, a, ci, che *ag* phlegmatic, cool.

fles'sibile *ag* pliable; *(fig: che si adatta)* flexible.

flessi'one *sf (gen)* bending; *(GINNASTICA: a terra)* sit-up; *(: in piedi)* forward bend; *(: sulle gambe)* knee-bend; *(diminuzione)* slight drop, slight fall; *(LING)* inflection; **fare una ~** to bend; **una ~ economica** a downward trend in the economy.

'flesso, a *pp di* **flettere**.

flessu'oso, a *ag* supple, lithe; *(andatura)* flowing, graceful.

'flettere *vt* to bend.

'flipper ['flipper] *sm inv* pinball machine.

flirt [flə:t] *sm inv* brief romance, flirtation.

F.lli *abbr (= fratelli)* Bros.

'flora *sf* flora.

'florido, a *ag* flourishing; *(fig)* glowing with health.

'floscio, a, sci, sce ['floʃʃo] *ag (cappello)* floppy, soft; *(muscoli)* flabby.

'flotta *sf* fleet.

'fluido, a *ag, sm* fluid.

flu'ire *vi* to flow.

fluore'scente [fluoreʃ'ʃente] *ag* fluorescent.

flu'oro *sm* fluorine.

fluo'ruro *sm* fluoride.

'flusso *sm* flow; *(FISICA, MED)* flux; **~ e riflusso** ebb and flow; **~ di cassa** *(COMM)* cash flow.

fluttu'are *vi* to rise and fall; *(ECON)* to fluctuate.

fluvi'ale *ag* river *cpd*, fluvial.

FM *abbr vedi* **modulazione di frequenza**.

FMI *sigla m vedi* **Fondo Monetario Internazionale**.

FO *sigla = Forlì*.

fo'bia *sf* phobia.

'foca, che *sf (ZOOL)* seal.

fo'caccia, ce [fo'kattʃa] *sf kind of pizza*; *(dolce)* bun; **rendere pan per ~** to get one's own back, give tit for tat.

fo'cale *ag* focal.

focaliz'zare [fokalid'dzare] *vt (FOT: immagine)* to get into focus; *(fig: situazione)* to get into perspective; **~ l'attenzione su** to focus one's attention on.

'foce ['fotʃe] *sf (GEO)* mouth.

fo'chista, i [fo'kista] *sm (FERR)* stoker, fireman.

foco'laio *sm (MED)* centre *(Brit)* o center *(US)* of infection; *(fig)* hotbed.

foco'lare *sm* hearth, fireside; *(TECN)* furnace.

fo'coso, a *ag* fiery; *(cavallo)* mettlesome, fiery.

'fodera *sf (di vestito)* lining; *(di libro, poltrona)* cover.

fode'rare *vt* to line; to cover.

'fodero *sm (di spada)* scabbard; *(di pugnale)* sheath; *(di pistola)* holster.

'foga *sf* enthusiasm, ardour *(Brit)*, ardor *(US)*.

'**foggia, ge** ['fɔddʒa] *sf* (*maniera*) style; (*aspetto*) form, shape; (*moda*) fashion, style.

foggi'are [fod'dʒare] *vt* to shape; to style.

'**foglia** ['fɔʎʎa] *sf* leaf; **ha mangiato la ~** (*fig*) he's caught on; **~ d'argento/d'oro** silver/gold leaf.

fogli'ame [foʎ'ʎame] *sm* foliage, leaves *pl*.

fogli'etto [foʎ'ʎetto] *sm* (*piccolo foglio*) slip of paper, piece of paper; (*manifestino*) leaflet, handout.

'**foglio** ['fɔʎʎo] *sm* (*di carta*) sheet (of paper); (*di metallo*) sheet; (*documento*) document; (*banconota*) (bank)note; **~ rosa** (*AUT*) provisional licence; **~ di via** (*DIR*) expulsion order; **~ volante** pamphlet.

'**fogna** ['foɲɲa] *sf* drain, sewer.

fogna'tura [foɲɲa'tura] *sf* drainage, sewerage.

föhn [føːn] *sm inv* hair-dryer.

fo'lata *sf* gust.

fol'clore *sm* folklore.

folgo'rare *vt* (*sog: fulmine*) to strike down; (*: alta tensione*) to electrocute.

folgorazi'one [folgorat'tsjone] *sf* electrocution; **ebbe una ~** (*fig: idea*) he had a brainwave.

'**folgore** *sf* thunderbolt.

'**folla** *sf* crowd, throng.

'**folle** *ag* mad, insane; (*TECN*) idle; **in ~** (*AUT*) in neutral.

folleggi'are [folled'dʒare] *vi* (*divertirsi*) to paint the town red.

fol'letto *sm* elf.

fol'lia *sf* folly, foolishness; foolish act; (*pazzia*) madness, lunacy; **amare qn alla ~** to love sb to distraction; **costare una ~** to cost the earth.

'**folto, a** *ag* thick.

fomen'tare *vt* to stir up, foment.

fon *sm inv* = **föhn**.

fon'dale *sm* (*del mare*) bottom; (*TEATRO*) backdrop; **il ~ marino** the sea bed.

fondamen'tale *ag* fundamental, basic.

fonda'mento *sm* foundation; **~a** *sfpl* (*EDIL*) foundations.

fon'dare *vt* to found; (*fig: dar base*): **~ qc su** to base sth on; **~rsi** *vr* (*teorie*): **~rsi (su)** to be based (on).

fonda'tezza [fonda'tettsa] *sf* soundness.

fondazi'one [fondat'tsjone] *sf* foundation.

'**fondere** *vt* (*neve*) to melt; (*metallo*) to fuse, melt; (*fig: colori*) to merge, blend; (*: imprese, gruppi*) to merge ♦ *vi* to melt; **~rsi** *vr* to melt; (*fig: partiti, correnti*) to unite, merge.

fonde'ria *sf* foundry.

fondi'ario, a *ag* land *cpd*.

fon'dina *sf* (*piatto fondo*) soup plate; (*portapistola*) holster.

'**fondo, a** *ag* deep ♦ *sm* (*di recipiente, pozzo*) bottom; (*di stanza*) back; (*quantità di liquido che resta, deposito*) dregs *pl*; (*sfondo*) background; (*unità immobiliare*) property, estate; (*somma di denaro*) fund; (*SPORT*) long-distance race; **~i** *smpl* (*denaro*) funds; **a notte ~a** at dead of night; **in ~ a** at the bottom of; at the back of; (*strada*) at the end of; **laggiù in ~** (*lontano*) over there; (*in profondità*) down there; **in ~** (*fig*) after all, all things considered; **andare fino in ~ a** (*fig*) to examine thoroughly; **andare a ~** (*nave*) to sink; **conoscere a ~** to know inside out; **dar ~ a** (*fig: provvisti, soldi*) to use up; **toccare il ~** (*fig*) to plumb the depths; **a ~ perduto** (*COMM*) without security; **~ comune di investimento** investment trust; **F~ Monetario Internazionale (FMI)** International Monetary Fund (IMF); **~ di previdenza** social insurance fund; **~ di riserva** reserve fund; **~ tinta** (*cosmetico*) foundation; **~ urbano** town property; **~i di caffè** coffee grounds; **~i d'esercizio** working capital *sg*; **~i liquidi** ready money *sg*, liquid assets; **~i di magazzino** old *o* unsold stock *sg*; **~i neri** slush fund *sg*.

fo'netica *sf* phonetics *sg*.

fon'tana *sf* fountain.

fonta'nella *sf* drinking fountain.

'**fonte** *sf* spring, source; (*fig*) source ♦ *sm*: **~ battesimale** (*REL*) font.

'**footing** ['futiŋ] *sm* jogging.

fo'raggio [fo'raddʒo] *sm* fodder, forage.

fo'rare *vt* to pierce, make a hole in; (*pallone*) to burst; (*pneumatico*) to puncture; (*biglietto*) to punch; **~rsi** *vr* (*gen*) to develop a hole; (*AUT, pallone, timpano*) to burst; **~ una gomma** to burst a tyre (*Brit*) *o* tire (*US*).

fora'tura *sf* piercing; bursting; puncturing; punching.

'**forbici** ['fɔrbitʃi] *sfpl* scissors.

forbi'cina [forbi'tʃina] *sf* earwig.

for'bito, a *ag* (*stile, modi*) polished.

'**forca, che** *sf* (*AGR*) fork, pitchfork; (*patibolo*) gallows *sg*.

for'cella [for'tʃella] *sf* (*TECN*) fork; (*di monte*) pass.

for'chetta [for'ketta] *sf* fork; **essere una buona ~** to enjoy one's food.

for'cina [for'tʃina] *sf* hairpin.

'**forcipe** ['fɔrtʃipe] *sm* forceps *pl*.

for'cone *sm* pitchfork.

fo'rense *ag* (*linguaggio*) legal; **avvocato ~** barrister (*Brit*), lawyer.

fo'resta *sf* forest; **la F~ Nera** the Black Forest.

fores'tale *ag* forest *cpd*; **guardia ~** forester.

foreste'ria *sf* (*di convento, palazzo etc*) guest rooms *pl*, guest quarters *pl*.

foresti'ero, a *ag* foreign ♦ *sm/f* foreigner.

for'fait [fɔr'fɛ] *sm inv*: (**prezzo a**) **~** fixed price, set price; **dichiarare ~** (*SPORT*) to withdraw; (fig) to give up.

forfe'tario, a ag: **prezzo** ~ (da pagare) fixed o set price; (da ricevere) lump sum.

'forfora sf dandruff.

'forgia, ge ['fɔrdʒa] sf forge.

forgi'are [for'dʒare] vt to forge.

'forma sf form; (aspetto esteriore) form, shape; (DIR: procedura) procedure; (per calzature) last; (stampo da cucina) mould (Brit), mold (US); ~e sfpl (del corpo) figure, shape; **le ~e** (convenzioni) appearances; **errori di** ~ stylistic errors; **essere in** ~ to be in good shape; **tenersi in** ~ to keep fit; **in** ~ **ufficiale/privata** officially/privately; **una** ~ **di formaggio** a (whole) cheese.

formag'gino [formad'dʒino] sm processed cheese.

for'maggio [for'maddʒo] sm cheese.

for'male ag formal.

formalità sf inv formality.

formaliz'zare [formalid'dzare] vt to formalize.

for'mare vt to form, shape, make; (numero di telefono) to dial; (fig: carattere) to form, mould (Brit), mold (US); ~**rsi** vr to form, take shape; **il treno si forma a Milano** the train starts from Milan.

for'mato sm format, size.

formattazi'one [formattat'tsjone] sf (INFORM) formatting.

formazi'one [format'tsjone] sf formation; (fig: educazione) training; ~ **professionale** vocational training.

for'mica, che sf ant.

formi'caio sm anthill.

formico'lare vi (gamba, braccio) to tingle; (brulicare: anche fig): ~ **di** to be swarming with; **mi formicola la gamba** I've got pins and needles in my leg, my leg's tingling.

formico'lio sm pins and needles pl; swarming.

formi'dabile ag powerful, formidable; (straordinario) remarkable.

for'moso, a ag shapely.

'formula sf formula; ~ **di cortesia** (nelle lettere) letter ending.

formu'lare vt to formulate.

for'nace [for'natʃe] sf (per laterizi etc) kiln; (per metalli) furnace.

for'naio sm baker.

for'nello sm (elettrico, a gas) ring; (di pipa) bowl.

for'nire vt: ~ **qn di qc,** ~ **qc a qn** to provide o supply sb with sth, supply sth to sb; ~**rsi** vr: ~**rsi di** (procurarsi) to provide o.s. with.

for'nito, a ag: **ben** ~ (negozio) well-stocked.

forni'tore, 'trice ag: **ditta** ~**trice di ...** company supplying ... ♦ sm/f supplier.

forni'tura sf supply.

'forno sm (di cucina) oven; (panetteria) bakery; (TECN: per calce etc) kiln; (: per metalli) furnace; **fare i** ~**i** (MED) to undergo heat treatment.

'foro sm (buco) hole; (STORIA) forum; (tribunale) (law) court.

'forse av perhaps, maybe; (circa) about; **essere in** ~ to be in doubt.

forsen'nato, a ag mad, crazy, insane.

'forte ag strong; (suono) loud; (spesa) considerable, great ♦ av strongly; (velocemente) fast; (a voce alta) loud(ly); (violentemente) hard ♦ sm (edificio) fort; (specialità) forte, strong point; **piatto** ~ (CUC) main dish; **avere un** ~ **mal di testa/raffreddore** to have a bad headache/cold; **essere** ~ **in qc** to be good at sth; **farsi** ~ **di qc** to make use of o avail o.s. of sth; **dare man** ~ **a qn** to back sb up, support sb; **usare le maniere** ~**i** to use strong-arm tactics.

for'tezza [for'tettsa] sf (morale) strength; (luogo fortificato) fortress.

fortifi'care vt to fortify, strengthen.

for'tuito, a ag fortuitous, chance cpd.

for'tuna sf (destino) fortune, luck; (buona sorte) success, fortune; (eredità, averi) fortune; **per** ~ luckily, fortunately; **di** ~ makeshift, improvised; **atterraggio di** ~ emergency landing.

fortu'nale sm storm.

fortunata'mente av luckily, fortunately.

fortu'nato, a ag lucky, fortunate; (coronato da successo) successful.

fortu'noso, a ag (vita) eventful; (avvenimento) unlucky.

fo'runcolo sm (MED) boil.

forvi'are vt, vi = **fuorviare.**

'forza ['fɔrtsa] sf strength; (potere) power; (FISICA) force ♦ escl come on!; ~**e** sfpl (fisiche) strength sg; (MIL) forces; **per** ~ against one's will; (naturalmente) of course; **per** ~ **di cose** by force of circumstances; **a viva** ~ by force; **a** ~ **di** by dint of; **farsi** ~ (coraggio) to pluck up one's courage; **bella** ~! (ironico) how clever of you (o him etc)!; ~ **lavoro** work force, manpower; **per causa di** ~ **maggiore** (DIR) by reason of an act of God; (per estensione) due to circumstances beyond one's control; **la** ~ **pubblica** the police pl; ~ **di vendita** (COMM) sales force; ~ **di volontà** willpower; **le** ~**e armate** the armed forces.

for'zare [for'tsare] vt to force; (cassaforte, porta) to force (open); (voce) to strain; ~ **qn a fare** to force sb to do.

for'zato, a [for'tsato] ag forced ♦ sm (DIR) prisoner sentenced to hard labour (Brit) o labor (US).

forzi'ere [for'tsjɛre] sm strongbox; (di pirati) treasure chest.

for'zuto, a [for'tsuto] *ag* big and strong.
fos'chia [fos'kia] *sf* mist, haze.
'fosco, a, schi, sche *ag* dark, gloomy; **dipingere qc a tinte ~sche** (*fig*) to paint a gloomy picture of sth.
fos'fato *sm* phosphate.
fosfore'scente [fosforeʃ'ʃɛnte] *ag* phosphorescent; (*lancetta dell'orologio etc*) luminous.
'fosforo *sm* phosphorous.
'fossa *sf* pit; (*di cimitero*) grave; **~ biologica** septic tank; **~ comune** mass grave.
fos'sato *sm* ditch; (*di fortezza*) moat.
fos'setta *sf* dimple.
'fossi *etc vb vedi* **essere**.
'fossile *ag, sm* fossil (*cpd*).
'fosso *sm* ditch; (*MIL*) trench.
'foste *etc vb vedi* **essere**.
'foto *sf inv* photo; **~ ricordo** souvenir photo; **~ tessera** passport(-type) photo.
foto... *prefisso* photo....
fotocomposi'tore *sm* filmsetter.
fotocomposizi'one [fotokompozit'tsjone] *sf* film setting.
foto'copia *sf* photocopy.
fotocopi'are *vt* to photocopy.
foto'genico, a, ci, che [foto'dʒɛniko] *ag* photogenic.
fotogra'fare *vt* to photograph.
fotogra'fia *sf* (*procedimento*) photography; (*immagine*) photograph; **fare una ~** to take a photograph; **una ~ a colori/in bianco e nero** a colour/black and white photograph.
foto'grafico, a, ci, che *ag* photographic; **macchina ~a** camera.
fo'tografo, a *sm/f* photographer.
foto'gramma, i *sm* (*CINEMA*) frame.
fotomo'dello, a *sm/f* fashion model.
fotomon'taggio [fotomon'taddʒo] *sm* photomontage.
fotore'porter *sm/f inv* newspaper (*o* magazine) photographer.
fotoro'manzo [fotoro'mandzo] *sm* romantic picture story.
foto'sintesi *sf* photosynthesis.
'fottere *vt* (*fam!: avere rapporti sessuali*) to fuck(*!*), screw(*!*); (: *rubare*) to pinch, swipe; (: *fregare*): **mi hanno fottuto** they played a dirty trick on me; **vai a farti ~!** fuck off! (*!*)
fot'tuto, a *ag* (*fam!*) bloody, fucking(*!*).
fou'lard [fu'lar] *sm inv* scarf.
FR *sigla* = *Frosinone*.
fr. *abbr* (*COMM*) = **franco**.
fra *prep* = **tra**.
fracas'sare *vt* to shatter, smash; **~rsi** *vr* to shatter, smash; (*veicolo*) to crash.
fra'casso *sm* smash; crash; (*baccano*) din, racket.
'fradicio, a, ci, ce ['fraditʃo] *ag* (*guasto*)

rotten; (*molto bagnato*) soaking (wet); **ubriaco ~** blind drunk.
'fragile ['fradʒile] *ag* fragile; (*salute*) delicate; (*nervi, vetro*) brittle.
fragilità [fradʒili'ta] *sf* (*vedi ag*) fragility; delicacy; brittleness.
'fragola *sf* strawberry.
fra'gore *sm* (*di cascate, carro armato*) roar; (*di tuono*) rumble.
frago'roso, a *ag* deafening; **ridere in modo ~** to roar with laughter.
fra'grante *ag* fragrant.
frain'tendere *vt* to misunderstand.
frain'teso, a *pp di* **fraintendere**.
fram'mento *sm* fragment.
fram'misto, a *ag*: **~ a** interspersed with, mixed with.
'frana *sf* landslide; (*fig: persona*): **essere una ~** to be useless, be a walking disaster area.
fra'nare *vi* to slip, slide down.
franca'mente *av* frankly.
fran'cese [fran'tʃeze] *ag* French ♦ *sm/f* Frenchman/woman ♦ *sm* (*LING*) French; **i F~i** the French.
fran'chezza [fran'kettsa] *sf* frankness, openness.
fran'chigia, gie [fran'kidʒa] *sf* (*AMM*) exemption; (*DIR*) franchise; (*NAUT*) shore leave; **~ doganale** exemption from customs duty.
'Francia ['frantʃa] *sf*: **la ~** France.
'franco, a, chi, che *ag* (*COMM*) free; (*sincero*) frank, open, sincere ♦ *sm* (*moneta*) franc; **farla ~a** (*fig*) to get off scot-free; **~ a bordo** free on board; **~ di dogana** duty-free; **~ a domicilio** delivered free of charge; **~ fabbrica** ex factory, ex works; **prezzo ~ fabbrica** ex-works price; **~ magazzino** ex warehouse; **~ di porto** carriage free; **~ vagone** free on rail; **~ tiratore** *sm* sniper; (*POL*) *member of parliament who votes against his own party.*
franco'bollo *sm* (postage) stamp.
franco-cana'dese *ag, sm/f* French Canadian.
Franco'forte *sf* Frankfurt.
fran'gente [fran'dʒɛnte] *sm* (*onda*) breaker; (*scoglio emergente*) reef; (*circostanza*) situation, circumstance.
'frangia, ge ['frandʒa] *sf* fringe.
frangi'flutti [frandʒi'flutti] *sm inv* breakwater.
frangi'vento [frandʒi'vɛnto] *sm* windbreak.
fran'toio *sm* (*AGR*) olive press; (*TECN*) crusher.
frantu'mare *vt*, **~rsi** *vr* to break into pieces, shatter.
fran'tumi *smpl* pieces, bits; (*schegge*) splinters; **andare in ~, mandare in ~** to shatter, smash to pieces *o* smithereens.
frappé *sm* (*CUC*) milk shake.
fra'sario *sm* (*gergo*) vocabulary, language.

'**frasca, sche** *sf* (leafy) branch; **saltare di palo in** ~ to jump from one subject to another.

'**frase** *sf* (*LING*) sentence; (*locuzione, espressione, MUS*) phrase; ~ **fatta** set phrase.

fraseolo'gia [frazeolo'dʒia] *sf* phraseology.

'**frassino** *sm* ash (tree).

frastagli'ato, a [frastaʎ'ʎato] *ag* (*costa*) indented, jagged.

frastor'nare *vt* (*intontire*) to daze; (*confondere*) to bewilder, befuddle.

frastor'nato, a *ag* dazed; bewildered.

frastu'ono *sm* hubbub, din.

'**frate** *sm* friar, monk.

fratel'lanza [fratel'lantsa] *sf* brotherhood; (*associazione*) fraternity.

fratel'lastro *sm* stepbrother.

fra'tello *sm* brother; ~**i** *smpl* brothers; (*nel senso di fratelli e sorelle*) brothers and sisters.

fra'terno, a *ag* fraternal, brotherly.

fratri'cida, i, e [fratri'tʃida] *ag* fratricidal ♦ *sm/f* fratricide; **guerra** ~ civil war.

frat'taglie [frat'taʎʎe] *sfpl* (*CUC: gen*) offal *sg*; (: *di pollo*) giblets.

frat'tanto *av* in the meantime, meanwhile.

frat'tempo *sm*: **nel** ~ in the meantime, meanwhile.

frat'tura *sf* fracture; (*fig*) split, break.

fraudo'lento, a *ag* fraudulent.

fraziona'mento [frattsjona'mento] *sm* division, splitting up.

frazi'one [frat'tsjone] *sf* fraction; (*borgata*): ~ **di comune** hamlet.

'**freccia, ce** ['frettʃa] *sf* arrow; ~ **di direzione** (*AUT*) indicator.

frec'ciata [fret'tʃata] *sf*: **lanciare una** ~ to make a cutting remark.

fred'dare *vt* to shoot dead.

fred'dezza [fred'dettsa] *sf* coldness.

'**freddo, a** *ag, sm* cold; **fa** ~ it's cold; **aver** ~ to be cold; **soffrire il** ~ to feel the cold; **a** ~ (*fig*) deliberately.

freddo'loso, a *ag* sensitive to the cold.

fred'dura *sf* pun.

fre'gare *vt* to rub; (*fam: truffare*) to take in, cheat; (: *rubare*) to swipe, pinch; **fregarsene** (*fam!*): **chi se ne frega?** who gives a damn (about it)?

fre'gata *sf* rub; (*fam*) swindle; (*NAUT*) frigate.

frega'tura *sf* (*fam: imbroglio*) rip-off; (: *delusione*) let-down.

fregherò *etc* [frege'rɔ] *vb vedi* **fregare**.

'**fregio** ['fredʒo] *sm* (*ARCHIT*) frieze; (*ornamento*) decoration.

'**fremere** *vi*: ~ **di** to tremble *o* quiver with; ~ **d'impazienza** to be champing at the bit.

'**fremito** *sm* tremor, quiver.

fre'nare *vt* (*veicolo*) to slow down; (*cavallo*) to rein in; (*lacrime*) to restrain, hold back

♦ *vi* to brake; ~**rsi** *vr* (*fig*) to restrain o.s., control o.s.

fre'nata *sf*: **fare una** ~ to brake.

frene'sia *sf* frenzy.

fre'netico, a, ci, che *ag* frenetic.

'**freno** *sm* brake; (*morso*) bit; **tenere a** ~ (*passioni etc*) to restrain; **tenere a** ~ **la lingua** to hold one's tongue; ~ **a disco** disc brake; ~ **a mano** handbrake.

frequen'tare *vt* (*scuola, corso*) to attend; (*locale, bar*) to go to, frequent; (*persone*) to see (often).

frequen'tato, a *ag* (*locale*) busy.

fre'quente *ag* frequent; **di** ~ frequently.

fre'quenza [fre'kwɛntsa] *sf* frequency; (*INS*) attendance.

fre'sare *vt* (*TECN*) to mill.

fres'chezza [fres'kettsa] *sf* freshness.

'**fresco, a, schi, sche** *ag* fresh; (*temperatura*) cool; (*notizia*) recent, fresh ♦ *sm*: **godere il** ~ to enjoy the cool air; ~ **di bucato** straight from the wash, newly washed; **stare** ~ (*fig*) to be in for it; **mettere al** ~ to put in a cool place; (*fig: in prigione*) to put inside *o* in the cooler.

fres'cura *sf* cool.

'**fresia** *sf* freesia.

'**fretta** *sf* hurry, haste; **in** ~ in a hurry; **in** ~ **e furia** in a mad rush; **aver** ~ to be in a hurry; **far** ~ **a qn** to hurry sb.

frettolosa'mente *av* hurriedly, in a rush.

fretto'loso, a *ag* (*persona*) in a hurry; (*lavoro etc*) hurried, rushed.

fri'abile *ag* (*terreno*) friable; (*pasta*) crumbly.

'**friggere** ['friddʒere] *vt* to fry ♦ *vi* (*olio etc*) to sizzle; **vai a farti** ~! (*fam*) get lost!

frigidità [fridʒidi'ta] *sf* frigidity.

'**frigido, a** ['fridʒido] *ag* (*MED*) frigid.

fri'gnare [friɲ'ɲare] *vi* to whine, snivel.

fri'gnone, a [friɲ'ɲone] *sm/f* whiner, sniveller.

'**frigo, ghi** *sm* fridge.

frigo'rifero, a *ag* refrigerating ♦ *sm* refrigerator; **cella** ~**a** cold store.

fringu'ello *sm* chaffinch.

'**frissi** *etc vb vedi* **friggere**.

frit'tata *sf* omelet(te); **fare una** ~ (*fig*) to make a mess of things.

frit'tella *sf* (*CUC*) pancake; (: *ripiena*) fritter.

'**fritto, a** *pp di* **friggere** ♦ *ag* fried ♦ *sm* fried food; **ormai siamo** ~**i**! (*fig fam*) now we've had it!; **è un argomento** ~ **e rifritto** that's old hat; ~ **misto** mixed fry.

frit'tura *sf* (*cibo*) fried food; ~ **di pesce** mixed fried fish.

friu'lano, a *ag* of (*o* from) Friuli.

'**frivolo, a** *ag* frivolous.

frizi'one [frit'tsjone] *sf* friction; (*di pelle*) rub, rub-down; (*AUT*) clutch.

friz'zante [frid'dzante] *ag* (*anche fig*) sparkling.

'**frizzo** ['friddzo] *sm* witticism.

fro'dare *vt* to defraud, cheat.

'**frode** *sf* fraud; ~ **fiscale** tax evasion.

'**frodo** *sm*: **di** ~ illegal, contraband; **pescatore di** ~, **cacciatore di** ~ poacher.

'**frogia, gie** ['frɔdʒa] *sf* (*di cavallo etc*) nostril.

'**frollo, a** *ag* (*carne*) tender; (: *di selvaggina*) high; (*fig: persona*) soft; **pasta** ~**a** short(crust) pastry.

'**fronda** *sf* (leafy) branch; (*di partito politico*) internal opposition; ~**e** *sfpl* (*di albero*) foliage *sg*.

fron'tale *ag* frontal; (*scontro*) head-on.

'**fronte** *sf* (*ANAT*) forehead; (*di edificio*) front, façade ♦ *sm* (*MIL, POL, METEOR*) front; **a** ~, **di** ~ facing, opposite; **di** ~ **a** (*posizione*) opposite, facing, in front of; (*a paragone di*) compared with; **far** ~ **a** (*nemico, problema*) to confront; (*responsabilità*) to face up to; (*spese*) to cope with.

fronteggi'are [fronted'dʒare] *vt* (*avversari, difficoltà*) to face, stand up to; (*spese*) to cope with.

frontes'pizio [frontes'pittsjo] *sm* (*ARCHIT*) frontispiece; (*di libro*) title page.

fronti'era *sf* border, frontier.

fron'tone *sm* pediment.

'**fronzolo** ['frondzolo] *sm* frill.

'**frotta** *sf* crowd; **in** ~, **a** ~**e** in their hundreds, in droves.

'**frottola** *sf* fib; **raccontare un sacco di** ~**e** to tell a pack of lies.

fru'gale *ag* frugal.

fru'gare *vi* to rummage ♦ *vt* to search.

frugherò *etc* [fruge'rɔ] *vb vedi* **frugare**.

frui'tore *sm* user.

fruizi'one [fruit'tsjone] *sf* use.

frul'lare *vt* (*CUC*) to whisk ♦ *vi* (*uccelli*) to flutter; **cosa ti frulla in mente?** what is going on in that mind of yours?

frul'lato *sm* (*CUC*) milk shake; (: *con solo frutta*) fruit drink.

frulla'tore *sm* electric mixer.

frul'lino *sm* whisk.

fru'mento *sm* wheat.

frusci'are [fruʃ'ʃare] *vi* to rustle.

fru'scio [fruʃ'ʃio] *sm* rustle; rustling.

'**frusta** *sf* whip; (*CUC*) whisk.

frus'tare *vt* to whip.

frus'tata *sf* lash.

frus'tino *sm* riding crop.

frus'trare *vt* to frustrate.

frustrazi'one [frustrat'tsjone] *sf* frustration.

'**frutta** *sf* fruit; (*portata*) dessert; ~ **candita/secca** candied/dried fruit.

frut'tare *vi* (*investimenti, deposito*) to bear dividends, give a return; **il mio deposito in banca (mi) frutta il 10%** my bank deposits bring (me) in 10%; **quella gara gli fruttò la**

medaglia d'oro he won the gold medal in that competition.

frut'teto *sm* orchard.

frutticol'tura *sf* fruit growing.

frut'tifero, a *ag* (*albero etc*) fruit-bearing; (*fig: che frutta*) fruitful, profitable; **deposito** ~ interest-bearing deposit.

frutti'vendolo, a *sm/f* greengrocer (*Brit*), produce dealer (*US*).

'**frutto** *sm* fruit; (*fig: risultato*) result(s); (*ECON: interesse*) interest; (: *reddito*) income; **è** ~ **della tua immaginazione** it's a figment of your imagination; ~**i di mare** seafood *sg*.

fruttu'oso, a *ag* fruitful, profitable.

FS *abbr* (= *Ferrovie dello Stato*) Italian railways.

f.t. *abbr* = **fuori testo**.

f.to *abbr* (= *firmato*) signed.

fu *vb vedi* **essere** ♦ *ag inv*: **il** ~ **Paolo Bianchi** the late Paolo Bianchi.

fuci'lare [futʃi'lare] *vt* to shoot.

fuci'lata [futʃi'lata] *sf* rifle shot.

fucilazi'one [futʃilat'tsjone] *sf* execution (by firing squad).

fu'cile [fu'tʃile] *sm* rifle, gun; (*da caccia*) shotgun, gun; ~ **a canne mozze** sawn-off shotgun.

fu'cina [fu'tʃina] *sf* forge.

'**fuco, chi** *sm* drone.

'**fucsia** *sf* fuchsia.

'**fuga, ghe** *sf* escape, flight; (*di gas, liquidi*) leak; (*MUS*) fugue; **mettere qn in** ~ to put sb to flight; ~ **di cervelli** brain drain.

fu'gace [fu'gatʃe] *ag* fleeting, transient.

fu'gare *vt* (*dubbi, incertezze*) to dispel, drive out.

fug'gevole [fud'dʒevole] *ag* fleeting.

fuggi'asco, a, schi, sche [fud'dʒasko] *ag*, *sm/f* fugitive.

fuggi'fuggi [fuddʒi'fuddʒi] *sm* scramble, stampede.

fug'gire [fud'dʒire] *vi* to flee, run away; (*fig: passar veloce*) to fly ♦ *vt* to avoid.

fuggi'tivo, a [fuddʒi'tivo] *sm/f* fugitive, runaway.

'**fui** *vb vedi* **essere**.

ful'gore *sm* brilliance, splendour (*Brit*), splendor (*US*).

fu'liggine [fu'liddʒine] *sf* soot.

fulmi'nare *vt* (*sog: elettricità*) to electrocute; (*con arma da fuoco*) to shoot dead; ~**rsi** *vr* (*lampadina*) to go, blow; (*fig: con lo sguardo*): **mi fulminò (con uno sguardo)** he looked daggers at me.

'**fulmine** *sm* bolt of lightning; ~**i** *smpl* lightning *sg*; ~ **a ciel sereno** bolt from the blue.

ful'mineo, a *ag* (*fig: scatto*) rapid; (: *minaccioso*) threatening.

'**fulvo, a** *ag* tawny.

fumai'olo *sm* (*di nave*) funnel; (*di fabbrica*)

chimney.

fu'mante *ag* (*piatto etc*) steaming.

fu'mare *vi* to smoke; (*emettere vapore*) to steam ♦ *vt* to smoke.

fu'mario, a *ag*: **canna ~a** flue.

fu'mata *sf* (*segnale*) smoke signal; **farsi una ~** to have a smoke; **~ bianca/nera** (*in Vaticano*) *signal that a new pope has/has not been elected.*

fuma'tore, 'trice *sm/f* smoker.

fu'metto *sm* comic strip; **giornale** *m* **a ~i** comic.

'fummo *vb vedi* **essere**.

'fumo *sm* smoke; (*vapore*) steam; (*il fumare tabacco*) smoking; **~i** *smpl* (*industriali etc*) fumes; **vendere ~** to deceive, cheat; **è tutto ~ e niente arrosto** it has no substance to it; **i ~i dell'alcool** (*fig*) the after-effects of drink.

fu'mogeno, a [fu'mɔdʒɛno] *ag* (*candelotto*) smoke *cpd* ♦ *sm* smoke bomb; **cortina ~a** smoke screen.

fu'moso, a *ag* smoky; (*fig*) muddled.

fu'nambolo, a *sm/f* tightrope walker.

'fune *sf* rope, cord; (*più grossa*) cable.

'funebre *ag* (*rito*) funeral; (*aspetto*) gloomy, funereal.

fune'rale *sm* funeral.

fu'nesto, a *ag* (*incidente*) fatal; (*errore, decisione*) fatal, disastrous; (*atmosfera*) gloomy, dismal.

'fungere ['fundʒere] *vi*: **~ da** to act as.

'fungo, ghi *sm* fungus; (*commestibile*) mushroom; **~ velenoso** toadstool; **crescere come i ~ghi** (*fig*) to spring up overnight.

funico'lare *sf* funicular railway.

funi'via *sf* cable railway.

'funsi *etc vb vedi* **fungere**.

'funto, a *pp di* **fungere**.

funzio'nare [funtsjo'nare] *vi* to work, function; (*fungere*): **~ da** to act as.

funzio'nario [funtsjo'narjo] *sm* official; **~ statale** civil servant.

funzi'one [fun'tsjone] *sf* function; (*carica*) post, position; (*REL*) service; **in ~** (*meccanismo*) in operation; **in ~ di** (*come*) as; **vive in ~ dei figli** he lives for his children; **far ~ di** to act as; **fare la ~ di qn** (*farne le veci*) to take sb's place.

fu'oco, chi *sm* fire; (*fornello*) ring; (*FOT, FISICA*) focus; **dare ~ a qc** to set fire to sth; **far ~** (*sparare*) to fire; **prendere ~** to catch fire; **~ d'artificio** firework; **~ di paglia** flash in the pan; **~ sacro** *o* **di Sant'Antonio** (*MED fam*) shingles *sg*.

fuorché [fwor'ke] *cong, prep* except.

FU'ORI *sigla m* (= *Fronte Unitario Omosessuale Rivoluzionario Italiano*) *gay liberation movement.*

fu'ori *av* outside; (*all'aperto*) outdoors, outside; (*~ di casa, SPORT*) out; (*esclamativo*) get out! ♦ *prep*: **~ (di)** out of, outside ♦ *sm*

outside; **essere in ~** (*sporgere*) to stick out; **lasciar ~ qc/qn** to leave sth/sb out; **far ~** (*fam: soldi*) to spend; (: *cioccolatini*) to eat up; (: *rubare*) to nick; **far ~ qn** (*fam*) to kill sb, do sb in; **essere tagliato ~** (*da un gruppo, ambiente*) to be excluded; **essere ~ di sé** to be beside oneself; **~ luogo** (*inopportuno*) out of place, uncalled for; **~ mano** out of the way, remote; **~ pasto** between meals; **~ pericolo** out of danger; **~ dai piedi!** get out of the way!; **~ servizio** out of order; **~ stagione** out of season; **illustrazione ~ testo** (*STAMPA*) plate; **~ uso** out of use.

fuori'bordo *sm inv* speedboat (with outboard motor); outboard motor.

fuori'busta *sm inv* unofficial payment.

fuori'classe *sm/f inv* (undisputed) champion.

fuori'corso *ag inv* (*moneta*) no longer in circulation; (*INS*): (**studente**) **~** *undergraduate who has not completed a course in due time.*

fuorigi'oco [fwori'dʒɔko] *sm* offside.

fuori'legge [fwori'leddʒe] *sm/f inv* outlaw.

fuori'serie *ag inv* (*auto etc*) custom-built ♦ *sf* custom-built car.

fuoris'trada *sm* (*AUT*) cross-country vehicle.

fuoru'scito, a, fuoriu'scito, a [fwor(i)uʃ'ʃito] *sm/f* exile ♦ *sf* (*di gas*) leakage, escape; (*di sangue, linfa*) seepage.

fuorvi'are *vt* to mislead; (*fig*) to lead astray ♦ *vi* to go astray.

furbacchi'one, a [furbak'kjone] *sm/f* cunning old devil.

fur'bizia [fur'bittsja] *sf* (*vedi ag*) cleverness; cunning; **una ~** a cunning trick.

'furbo, a *ag* clever, smart; (*peg*) cunning ♦ *sm/f*: **fare il ~** to (try to) be clever *o* smart; **fatti ~!** show a bit of sense!

fu'rente *ag*: **~ (contro)** furious (with).

fure'ria *sf* (*MIL*) orderly room.

fu'retto *sm* ferret.

fur'fante *sm* rascal, scoundrel.

furgon'cino [furgon'tʃino] *sm* small van.

fur'gone *sm* van.

'furia *sf* (*ira*) fury, rage; (*fig: impeto*) fury, violence; (*fretta*) rush; **a ~ di** by dint of; **andare su tutte le ~e** to fly into a rage.

furi'bondo, a *ag* furious.

furi'ere *sm* quartermaster.

furi'oso, a *ag* furious; (*mare, vento*) raging.

'furono *vb vedi* **essere**.

fu'rore *sm* fury; (*esaltazione*) frenzy; **far ~** to be all the rage.

fur'tivo, a *ag* furtive.

'furto *sm* theft; **~ con scasso** burglary.

'fusa *sfpl*: **fare le ~** to purr.

fu'scello [fuʃ'ʃello] *sm* twig.

'fusi *etc vb vedi* **fondere**.

fu'sibile *sm* (*ELETTR*) fuse.

fusi'one sf (di metalli) fusion, melting; (colata) casting; (COMM) merger; (fig) merging.
'fuso, a pp di **fondere** ♦ sm (FILATURA) spindle; **diritto come un ~** as stiff as a ramrod; **~ orario** time zone.
fusoli'era sf (AER) fusillage.
fus'tagno [fus'taɲɲo] sm corduroy.
fus'tella sf (su scatola di medicinali) tear-off tab.
fusti'gare vt (frustare) to flog; (fig: costumi) to censure, denounce.
fus'tino sm (di detersivo) tub.
'fusto sm stem; (ANAT, di albero) trunk; (recipiente) drum, can; (fam) he-man.
'futile ag vain, futile.
futilità sf inv futility.
futu'rismo sm futurism.
fu'turo, a ag, sm future.

G

G, g [dʒi] sf o m inv (lettera) G, g; **G come Genova** ≈ G for George.
g. abbr (= grammo) g.
gabar'dine [gabar'din] sm (tessuto) gabardine; (soprabito) gabardine raincoat.
gab'bare vt to take in, dupe; **~rsi** vr: **~rsi di qn** to make fun of sb.
'gabbia sf cage; (DIR) dock; (da imballaggio) crate; **la ~ degli accusati** (DIR) the dock; **~ dell'ascensore** lift (Brit) o elevator (US) shaft; **~ toracica** (ANAT) rib cage.
gabbi'ano sm (sea)gull.
gabi'netto sm (MED etc) consulting room; (POL) ministry; (di decenza) toilet, lavatory; (INS: di fisica etc) laboratory.
Ga'bon sm: **il ~** Gabon.
ga'elico, a, ci, che ag, sm Gaelic.
gaffe [gaf] sf inv blunder, boob (fam).
gagli'ardo, a [gaʎ'ʎardo] ag strong, vigorous.
gai'ezza [ga'jettsa] sf gaiety, cheerfulness.
'gaio, a ag cheerful.
'gala sf (sfarzo) pomp; (festa) gala.
ga'lante ag gallant, courteous; (avventura, poesia) amorous.
galante'ria sf gallantry.
galantu'omo, pl galantu'omini sm gentleman.
ga'lassia sf galaxy.
gala'teo sm (good) manners pl, etiquette.
gale'otto sm (rematore) galley slave; (carcerato) convict.

ga'lera sf (NAUT) galley; (prigione) prison.
'galla sf: **a ~** afloat; **venire a ~** to surface, come to the surface; (fig: verità) to come out.
galleggia'mento [galleddʒa'mento] sm floating; **linea di ~** (di nave) waterline.
galleggi'ante [galled'dʒante] ag floating ♦ sm (natante) barge; (di pescatore, lenza, TECN) float.
galleggi'are [galled'dʒare] vi to float.
galle'ria sf (traforo) tunnel; (ARCHIT, d'arte) gallery; (TEATRO) circle; (strada coperta con negozi) arcade; **~ del vento** o **aerodinamica** (AER) wind tunnel.
'Galles sm: **il ~** Wales.
gal'lese ag Welsh ♦ sm/f Welshman/woman ♦ sm (LING) Welsh; **i G~i** the Welsh.
gal'letta sf cracker; (NAUT) ship's biscuit.
gal'letto sm young cock, cockerel; (fig) cocky young man; **fare il ~** to play the gallant.
'Gallia sf: **la ~** Gaul.
gal'lina sf hen; **andare a letto con le ~e** to go to bed early.
gal'lismo sm machismo.
'gallo sm cock; **al canto del ~** at daybreak, at cockcrow; **fare il ~** to play the gallant.
gal'lone sm piece of braid; (MIL) stripe; (unità di misura) gallon.
galop'pare vi to gallop.
galop'pino sm errand boy; (POL) canvasser.
ga'loppo sm gallop; **al** o **di ~** at a gallop.
galvaniz'zare [galvanid'dzare] vt to galvanize.
'gamba sf leg; (asta: di lettera) stem; **in ~** (in buona salute) well; (bravo, sveglio) bright, smart; **prendere qc sotto ~** (fig) to treat sth too lightly; **scappare a ~e levate** to take to one's heels; **~e!** scatter!
gam'bale sm legging.
gambe'retto sm shrimp.
'gambero sm (di acqua dolce) crayfish; (di mare) prawn.
'Gambia sf: **la ~** the Gambia.
'gambo sm stem; (di frutta) stalk.
ga'mella sf mess tin.
'gamma sf (MUS) scale; (di colori, fig) range; **~ di prodotti** product range.
ga'nascia, sce [ga'naʃʃa] sf jaw; **~sce del freno** (AUT) brake shoes.
'gancio ['gantʃo] sm hook.
'Gange ['gandʒe] sm: **il ~** the Ganges.
'gangheri ['gangeri] smpl: **uscire dai ~** (fig) to fly into a temper.
gan'grena sf = **cancrena**.
'gara sf competition; (SPORT) competition; contest; match; (: corsa) race; **fare a ~** to compete, vie; **~ d'appalto** (COMM) tender.
ga'rage [ga'raʒ] sm inv garage.
ga'rante sm/f guarantor.

garan'tire *vt* to guarantee; *(debito)* to stand surety for; *(dare per certo)* to assure.

garan'tismo *sm* protection of civil liberties.

garan'zia [garan'tsia] *sf* guarantee; *(pegno)* security; **in ~** under guarantee.

gar'bare *vi*: **non mi garba** I don't like it (*o* him *etc*).

garba'tezza [garba'tettsa] *sf* courtesy, politeness.

gar'bato, a *ag* courteous, polite.

'garbo *sm* *(buone maniere)* politeness, courtesy; *(di vestito etc)* grace, style.

gar'buglio [gar'buʎʎo] *sm* tangle; *(fig)* muddle, mess.

gareggi'are [gared'dʒare] *vi* to compete.

garga'nella *sf*: **a ~** from the bottle.

garga'rismo *sm* gargle; **fare i ~i** to gargle.

ga'ritta *sf* *(di caserma)* sentry box.

ga'rofano *sm* carnation; **chiodo di ~** clove.

gar'retto *sm* hock.

gar'rire *vi* to chirp.

'garrulo, a *ag* *(uccello)* chirping; *(persona: loquace)* garrulous, talkative.

'garza ['gardza] *sf* *(per bende)* gauze.

gar'zone [gar'dzone] *sm* *(di negozio)* boy.

gas *sm inv* gas; **a tutto ~** at full speed; **dare ~** *(AUT)* to accelerate; **~ lacrimogeno** tear gas; **~ naturale** natural gas.

ga'sare *etc* = **gassare** *etc*.

ga'sato, a *sm/f* *(fam: persona)* freak.

gas'dotto *sm* gas pipeline.

ga'solio *sm* diesel (oil).

ga's(s)are *vt* to aerate, carbonate; *(asfissiare)* to gas; **~rsi** *vr* *(fam)* to get excited.

ga's(s)ato, a *ag* *(bibita)* aerated, fizzy.

gas'soso, a *ag* gaseous; gassy ♦ *sf* fizzy drink.

'gastrico, a, ci, che *ag* gastric.

gastroente'rite *sf* gastroenteritis.

gastrono'mia *sf* gastronomy.

gas'tronomo, a *sm/f* gourmet, gastronome.

'gatta *sf* cat, she-cat; **una ~ da pelare** *(fam)* a thankless task; **qui ~ ci cova!** I smell a rat!, there's something fishy going on here!

gatta'buia *sf* *(fam scherzoso: prigione)* clink.

gat'tino *sm* kitten.

'gatto *sm* cat, tomcat; **~ delle nevi** *(AUT, SCI)* snowcat; **~ a nove code** cat-o'-nine-tails; **~ selvatico** wildcat.

gatto'pardo *sm*: **~ africano** serval; **~ americano** ocelot.

gat'tuccio [gat'tuttʃo] *sm* dogfish.

gau'dente *sm/f* pleasure-seeker.

'gaudio *sm* joy, happiness.

ga'vetta *sf* *(MIL)* mess tin; **venire dalla ~** *(MIL, fig)* to rise from the ranks.

'gazza ['gaddza] *sf* magpie.

gaz'zarra [gad'dzarra] *sf* racket, din.

gaz'zella [gad'dzɛlla] *sf* gazelle; *(dei ca-*

rabinieri) (high-speed) police car.

gaz'zetta [gad'dzetta] *sf* news sheet; **G~ Ufficiale** *official publication containing details of new laws.*

gaz'zoso, a [gad'dzoso] *ag* = **gassoso.**

Gazz. Uff. *abbr* = **Gazzetta Ufficiale.**

GB *sigla* (= *Gran Bretagna*) GB.

G.C. *abbr* = **genio civile.**

G.d.F. *abbr* = **guardia di finanza.**

GE *sigla* = *Genova.*

gel [dʒɛl] *sm inv* gel.

ge'lare [dʒe'lare] *vt, vi, vb impers* to freeze; **mi ha gelato il sangue** *(fig)* it made my blood run cold.

ge'lata [dʒe'lata] *sf* frost.

gelate'ria [dʒelate'ria] *sf* ice-cream shop.

gela'tina [dʒela'tina] *sf* gelatine; **~ esplosiva** gelignite; **~ di frutta** fruit jelly.

gelati'noso, a [dʒelati'noso] *ag* gelatinous, jelly-like.

ge'lato, a [dʒe'lato] *ag* frozen ♦ *sm* ice cream.

'gelido, a ['dʒɛlido] *ag* icy, ice-cold.

'gelo ['dʒɛlo] *sm* *(temperatura)* intense cold; *(brina)* frost; *(fig)* chill.

ge'lone [dʒe'lone] *sm* chilblain.

gelo'sia [dʒelo'sia] *sf* jealousy.

ge'loso, a [dʒe'loso] *ag* jealous.

'gelso ['dʒɛlso] *sm* mulberry (tree).

gelso'mino [dʒelso'mino] *sm* jasmine.

gemel'laggio [dʒemel'laddʒo] *sm* twinning.

gemel'lare [dʒemel'lare] *ag* twin *cpd* ♦ *vt* *(città)* to twin.

ge'mello, a [dʒe'mɛllo] *ag, sm/f* twin; **~i** *smpl* *(di camicia)* cufflinks; *(dello zodiaco)*: **G~i** Gemini *sg*; **essere dei G~i** to be Gemini.

'gemere ['dʒɛmere] *vi* to moan, groan; *(cigolare)* to creak; *(gocciolare)* to drip, ooze.

'gemito ['dʒɛmito] *sm* moan, groan.

'gemma ['dʒɛmma] *sf* *(BOT)* bud; *(pietra preziosa)* gem.

Gen *abbr* (*MIL*: = *generale*) Gen.

gen. *abbr* (= *generale, generalmente*) gen.

gen'darme [dʒen'darme] *sm* policeman; *(fig)* martinet.

'gene ['dʒɛne] *sm* gene.

genealo'gia, 'gie [dʒenealo'dʒia] *sf* genealogy.

genea'logico, a, ci, che [dʒenea'lɔdʒiko] *ag* genealogical; **albero ~** family tree.

gene'rale [dʒene'rale] *ag, sm* general; **in ~** *(per sommi capi)* in general terms; *(di solito)* usually, in general; **a ~ richiesta** by popular request.

generalità [dʒenerali'ta] *sfpl* *(dati d'identità)* particulars.

generaliz'zare [dʒeneralid'dzare] *vt, vi* to generalize.

generalizzazi'one [dʒeneraliddzat'tsjone] *sf* generalization.

general'mente [dʒeneral'mente] *av* generally.

gene'rare [dʒene'rare] *vt* (*dar vita*) to give birth to; (*produrre*) to produce; (*causare*) to arouse; (*TECN*) to produce, generate.

genera'tore [dʒenera'tore] *sm* (*TECN*) generator.

generazi'one [dʒenerat'tsjone] *sf* generation.

'genere ['dʒɛnere] *sm* kind, type, sort; (*BIOL*) genus; (*merce*) article, product; (*LING*) gender; (*ARTE, LETTERATURA*) genre; **in** ~ generally, as a rule; **cose del** *o* **di questo** ~ such things; **il** ~ **umano** mankind; **~i alimentari** foodstuffs; **~i di consumo** consumer goods; **~i di prima necessità** basic essentials.

ge'nerico, a, ci, che [dʒe'nɛriko] *ag* generic; (*vago*) vague, imprecise; **medico** ~ general practitioner.

'genero ['dʒɛnero] *sm* son-in-law.

generosità [dʒenerosi'ta] *sf* generosity.

gene'roso, a [dʒene'roso] *ag* generous.

'genesi ['dʒɛnezi] *sf* genesis.

ge'netico, a, ci, che [dʒe'nɛtiko] *ag* genetic
♦ *sf* genetics *sg*.

gen'giva [dʒen'dʒiva] *sf* (*ANAT*) gum.

ge'nia [dʒe'nia] *sf* (*peg*) mob, gang.

geni'ale [dʒe'njale] *ag* (*persona*) of genius; (*idea*) ingenious, brilliant.

'genio ['dʒɛnjo] *sm* genius; (*attitudine, talento*) talent, flair, genius; **andare a** ~ **a qn** to be to sb's liking, appeal to sb; ~ **civile** civil engineers *pl*; **il** ~ **(militare)** the Engineers.

geni'tale [dʒeni'tale] *ag* genital; **~i** *smpl* genitals.

geni'tore [dʒeni'tore] *sm* parent, father *o* mother; **~i** *smpl* parents.

genn. *abbr* (= *gennaio*) Jan.

gen'naio [dʒen'najo] *sm* January; *per fraseologia vedi* **luglio.**

geno'cidio [dʒeno'tʃidjo] *sm* genocide.

'Genova ['dʒɛnova] *sf* Genoa.

geno'vese [dʒeno'vese] *ag, sm/f* Genoese (*pl inv*).

gen'taglia [dʒen'taʎʎa] *sf* (*peg*) rabble.

'gente ['dʒɛnte] *sf* people *pl*.

gen'tile [dʒen'tile] *ag* (*persona, atto*) kind; (: *garbato*) courteous, polite; (*nelle lettere*): **G~ Signore** Dear Sir; (: *sulla busta*): **G~ Signor Fernando Villa** Mr Fernando Villa.

genti'lezza [dʒenti'lettsa] *sf* kindness; courtesy, politeness; **per** ~ (*per favore*) please.

gentilu'omo, pl gentilu'omini [dʒenti'lwɔmo] *sm* gentleman.

genuflessi'one [dʒenufles'sjone] *sf* genuflection.

genu'ino, a [dʒenu'ino] *ag* (*prodotto*) natural; (*persona, sentimento*) genuine, sincere.

geogra'fia [dʒeogra'fia] *sf* geography.

geo'grafico, a, ci, che [dʒeo'grafiko] *ag* geographical.

ge'ografo, a [dʒe'ɔgrafo] *sm/f* geographer.

geolo'gia [dʒeolo'dʒia] *sf* geology.

geo'logico, a, ci, che [dʒeo'lɔdʒiko] *ag* geological.

ge'ometra, i, e [dʒe'ɔmetra] *sm/f* (*professionista*) surveyor.

geome'tria [dʒeome'tria] *sf* geometry.

geo'metrico, a, ci, che [dʒeo'mɛtriko] *ag* geometric(al).

geopo'litico, a, ci, che [dʒeopo'litiko] *ag* geopolitical.

ge'ranio [dʒe'ranjo] *sm* geranium.

ge'rarca, chi [dʒe'rarka] *sm* (*STORIA*: *nel fascismo*) party official.

gerar'chia [dʒerar'kia] *sf* hierarchy.

ge'rarchico, a, ci, che [dʒe'rarkiko] *ag* hierarchical.

ge'rente [dʒe'rɛnte] *sm/f* manager/manageress.

ge'renza [dʒe'rɛntsa] *sf* management.

'gergo, ghi ['dʒɛrgo] *sm* jargon; slang.

geria'tria [dʒerja'tria] *sf* geriatrics *sg*.

geri'atrico, a, ci, che [dʒe'rjatriko] *ag* geriatric.

'gerla ['dʒɛrla] *sf* conical wicker basket.

Ger'mania [dʒer'manja] *sf*: **la** ~ Germany; **la** ~ **occidentale/orientale** West/East Germany.

'germe ['dʒɛrme] *sm* germ; (*fig*) seed.

germinazi'one [dʒerminat'tsjone] *sf* germination.

germogli'are [dʒermoʎ'ʎare] *vi* (*emettere germogli*) to sprout; (*germinare*) to germinate.

ger'moglio [dʒer'moʎʎo] *sm* shoot; (*gemma*) bud.

gero'glifico, ci [dʒero'glifiko] *sm* hieroglyphic.

geron'tologo, a, gi, ghe [dʒeron'tɔlogo] *sm/f* specialist in geriatrics.

ge'rundio [dʒe'rundjo] *sm* gerund.

Gerusa'lemme [dʒeruza'lɛmme] *sf* Jerusalem.

'gesso ['dʒɛsso] *sm* chalk; (*SCULTURA, MED, EDIL*) plaster; (*statua*) plaster figure; (*minerale*) gypsum.

'gesta ['dʒɛsta] *sfpl* (*letterario*) deeds, feats.

ges'tante [dʒes'tante] *sf* expectant mother.

gestazi'one [dʒestat'tsjone] *sf* gestation.

gestico'lare [dʒestiko'lare] *vi* to gesticulate.

gestio'nale [dʒestjo'nale] *ag* administrative, management *cpd*.

gesti'one [dʒes'tjone] *sf* management; ~ **di magazzino** stock control; ~ **patrimoniale** investment management.

ges'tire [dʒes'tire] *vt* to run, manage.

'gesto ['dʒɛsto] *sm* gesture.

ges'tore [dʒes'tore] *sm* manager.

Gesù [dʒe'zu] *sm* Jesus; ~ **bambino** the Christ Child.

gesu'ita, i [dʒezu'ita] *sm* Jesuit.

get'tare [dʒet'tare] *vt* to throw; (*anche:* ~ **via**) to throw away *o* out; (*SCULTURA*) to cast; (*EDIL*) to lay; (*acqua*) to spout; (*grido*) to utter; ~**rsi** *vr:* ~**rsi in** (*impresa*) to throw o.s. into; (*mischia*) to hurl o.s. into; (*sog: fiume*) to flow into; ~ **uno sguardo su** to take a quick look at.

get'tata [dʒet'tata] *sf* (*di cemento, gesso, metalli*) cast; (*diga*) jetty.

'gettito ['dʒettito] *sm* revenue.

'getto ['dʒetto] *sm* (*di gas, liquido, AER*) jet; (*BOT*) shoot; **a ~ continuo** uninterruptedly; **di ~** (*fig*) straight off, in one go.

get'tone [dʒet'tone] *sm* token; (*per giochi*) counter; (: *roulette etc*) chip; ~ **di presenza** attendance fee; ~ **telefonico** telephone token.

gettoni'era [dʒetto'njera] *sf* telephone-token dispenser.

'geyser ['gaizə] *sm inv* geyser.

'Ghana ['gana] *sm:* **il** ~ Ghana.

'ghenga, ghe ['genga] *sf* (*fam*) gang, crowd.

ghe'pardo [ge'pardo] *sm* cheetah.

gher'mire [ger'mire] *vt* to grasp, clasp, clutch.

'ghetta ['getta] *sf* (*gambale*) gaiter.

ghettiz'zare [gettid'dzare] *vt* to segregate.

'ghetto ['getto] *sm* ghetto.

ghiacci'aia [gjat'tʃaja] *sf* (*anche fig*) icebox.

ghiacci'aio [gjat'tʃajo] *sm* glacier.

ghiacci'are [gjat'tʃare] *vt* to freeze; (*fig*): ~ **qn** to make sb's blood run cold ♦ *vi* to freeze, ice over.

ghiacci'ato, a [gjat'tʃato] *ag* frozen; (*bevanda*) ice-cold.

ghi'accio ['gjattʃo] *sm* ice.

ghiacci'olo [gjat'tʃɔlo] *sm* icicle; (*tipo di gelato*) ice lolly (*Brit*), popsicle (*US*).

ghi'aia ['gjaja] *sf* gravel.

ghi'anda ['gjanda] *sf* (*BOT*) acorn.

ghi'andola ['gjandola] *sf* gland.

ghiando'lare [gjando'lare] *ag* glandular.

ghigliot'tina [giʎʎot'tina] *sf* guillotine.

ghi'gnare [giɲ'ɲare] *vi* to sneer.

'ghigno ['giɲɲo] *sm* (*espressione*) sneer; (*risata*) mocking laugh.

'ghingheri ['gingeri] *smpl:* **in** ~ all dolled up; **mettersi in** ~ to put on one's Sunday best.

ghi'otto, a ['gjotto] *ag* greedy; (*cibo*) delicious, appetizing.

ghiot'tone, a [gjot'tone] *sm/f* glutton.

ghiottone'ria [gjottone'ria] *sf* greed, gluttony; (*cibo*) delicacy, titbit (*Brit*), tidbit (*US*).

ghiri'bizzo [giri'biddzo] *sm* whim.

ghiri'goro [giri'gɔro] *sm* scribble, squiggle.

ghir'landa [gir'landa] *sf* garland, wreath.

'ghiro ['giro] *sm* dormouse.

'ghisa ['giza] *sf* cast iron.

G.I. *abbr* = **giudice istruttore**.

già [dʒa] *av* already; (*ex, in precedenza*) for-

merly ♦ *escl* of course!, yes indeed!; ~ **che ci sei ...** while you are at it ....

gi'acca, che ['dʒakka] *sf* jacket; ~ **a vento** windcheater (*Brit*), windbreaker (*US*).

giacché [dʒak'ke] *cong* since, as.

giac'chetta [dʒak'ketta] *sf* (*light*) jacket.

'giaccio *etc* ['dʒattʃo] *vb vedi* **giacere**.

giac'cone [dʒak'kone] *sm* heavy jacket.

gia'cenza [dʒa'tʃentsa] *sf:* **merce in** ~ goods in stock; **capitale in** ~ uninvested capital; ~**e di magazzino** unsold stock.

gia'cere [dʒa'tʃere] *vi* to lie.

giaci'mento [dʒatʃi'mento] *sm* deposit.

gia'cinto [dʒa'tʃinto] *sm* hyacinth.

giaci'uto, a [dʒa'tʃuto] *pp di* **giacere**.

gi'acqui *etc* ['dʒakkwi] *vb vedi* **giacere**.

gi'ada ['dʒada] *sf* jade.

giaggi'olo [dʒad'dʒɔlo] *sm* iris.

giagu'aro [dʒa'gwaro] *sm* jaguar.

gial'lastro, a [dʒal'lastro] *ag* yellowish; (*carnagione*) sallow.

gi'allo ['dʒallo] *ag* yellow; (*carnagione*) sallow ♦ *sm* yellow; (*anche: romanzo* ~) detective novel; (*anche: film* ~) detective film; ~ **dell'uovo** yolk; **il mar G~** the Yellow Sea.

gial'lognolo, a [dʒal'loɲɲolo] *ag* yellowish, dirty yellow.

Gia'maica [dʒa'maika] *sf:* **la** ~ Jamaica.

giamai'cano, a [dʒamai'kano] *ag, sm/f* Jamaican.

giam'mai [dʒam'mai] *av* never.

Giap'pone [dʒap'pone] *sm:* **il** ~ Japan.

giappo'nese [dʒappo'nese] *ag, sm/f, sm* Japanese *inv*.

gi'ara ['dʒara] *sf* jar.

giardi'naggio [dʒardi'naddʒo] *sm* gardening.

giardi'netta [dʒardi'netta] *sf* estate car (*Brit*), station wagon (*US*).

giardini'ere, a [dʒardi'njere] *sm/f* gardener ♦ *sf* (*misto di sottaceti*) mixed pickles *pl*; (*automobile*) = **giardinetta**.

giar'dino [dʒar'dino] *sm* garden; ~ **d'infanzia** nursery school; ~ **pubblico** public gardens *pl*, (public) park; ~ **zoologico** zoo.

giarretti'era [dʒarret'tjera] *sf* garter.

Gi'ava ['dʒava] *sf* Java.

giavel'lotto [dʒavel'lɔtto] *sm* javelin.

gib'boso, a [dʒib'boso] *ag* (*superficie*) bumpy; (*naso*) crooked.

Gibil'terra [dʒibil'terra] *sf* Gibraltar.

gi'gante, 'essa [dʒi'gante] *sm/f* giant ♦ *ag* giant, gigantic; (*COMM*) giant-size.

gigan'tesco, a, schi, sche [dʒigan'tesko] *ag* gigantic.

gigantogra'fia [dʒigantogra'fia] *sf* (*FOT*) blow-up.

'giglio ['dʒiʎʎo] *sm* lily.

gilè [dʒi'lɛ] *sm inv* waistcoat.

gin [dʒin] *sm inv* gin.

gin'cana [dʒin'kana] *sf* gymkhana.

ginecolo'gia [dʒinekolo'dʒia] *sf* gynaecology

(*Brit*), gynecology (*US*).

gine'cologo, a, gi, ghe [dʒine'kɔlogo] *sm/f* gynaecologist (*Brit*), gynecologist (*US*).

gi'nepro [dʒi'nepro] *sm* juniper.

gi'nestra [dʒi'nɛstra] *sf* (*BOT*) broom.

Gi'nevra [dʒi'nevra] *sf* Geneva; **il Lago di ~** Lake Geneva.

gingil'larsi [dʒindʒil'larsi] *vr* to fritter away one's time; (*giocare*): **~ con** to fiddle with.

gin'gillo [dʒin'dʒillo] *sm* plaything.

gin'nasio [dʒin'nazjo] *sm the 4th and 5th year of secondary school in Italy.*

gin'nasta, i, e [dʒin'nasta] *sm/f* gymnast.

gin'nastica [dʒin'nastika] *sf* gymnastics *sg*; (*esercizio fisico*) keep-fit exercises *pl*; (*INS*) physical education.

'ginnico, a, ci, che ['dʒinnko] *ag* gymnastic.

gi'nocchio [dʒi'nɔkkjo], *pl(m)* **gi'nocchi** *o pl(f)* **gi'nocchia** *sm* knee; **stare in ~** to kneel, be on one's knees; **mettersi in ~** to kneel (down).

ginocchi'oni [dʒinok'kjoni] *av* on one's knees.

gio'care [dʒo'kare] *vt* to play; (*scommettere*) to stake, wager, bet; (*ingannare*) to take in ♦ *vi* to play; (*a roulette etc*) to gamble; (*fig*) to play a part, be important; (*TECN*: *meccanismo*) to be loose; **~ a** (*gioco, sport*) to play; (*cavalli*) to bet on; **~ d'astuzia** to be crafty; **~rsi la carriera** to put one's career at risk; **~rsi tutto** to risk everything; **a che gioco giochiamo?** what are you playing at?

gioca'tore, 'trice [dʒoka'tore] *sm/f* player; gambler.

gio'cattolo [dʒo'kattolo] *sm* toy.

giocherel'lare [dʒokerel'lare] *vi*: **~ con** (*giocattolo*) to play with; (*distrattamente*) to fiddle with.

giocherò *etc* [dʒoke'rɔ] *vb vedi* **giocare.**

gio'chetto [dʒo'ketto] *sm* (*gioco*) game; (*tranello*) trick; (*fig*): **è un ~** it's child's play.

gi'oco, chi ['dʒɔko] *sm* game; (*divertimento, TECN*) play; (*al casinò*) gambling; (*CARTE*) hand; (*insieme di pezzi etc necessari per un gioco*) set; **per ~** for fun; **fare il doppio ~ con qn** to double-cross sb; **prendersi ~ di qn** to pull sb's leg; **stare al ~ di qn** to play along with sb; **è in ~ la mia reputazione** my reputation is at stake; **~ d'azzardo** game of chance; **~ della palla** ball game; **~ degli scacchi** chess set; **i G~chi Olimpici** the Olympic Games.

gioco'forza [dʒoko'fɔrtsa] *sm*: **essere ~** to be inevitable.

giocoli'ere [dʒoko'ljɛre] *sm* juggler.

gio'coso, a [dʒo'koso] *ag* playful, jesting.

gio'gaia [dʒo'gaja] *sf* (*GEO*) range of mountains.

gi'ogo, ghi ['dʒogo] *sm* yoke.

gi'oia ['dʒɔja] *sf* joy, delight; (*pietra preziosa*) jewel, precious stone.

gioielle'ria [dʒojelle'ria] *sf* jeweller's (*Brit*) o jeweler's (*US*) craft; (*negozio*) jewel(l)er's (shop).

gioielli'ere, a [dʒojel'ljɛre] *sm/f* jeweller (*Brit*), jeweler (*US*).

gioi'ello [dʒo'jɛllo] *sm* jewel, piece of jewellery (*Brit*) o jewelry (*US*); **~i** *smpl* (*gioie*) jewel(l)ery *sg*.

gioi'oso, a [dʒo'joso] *ag* joyful.

Gior'dania [dʒor'danja] *sf*: **la ~** Jordan.

Gior'dano [dʒor'dano] *sm*: **il ~** the Jordan.

gior'dano, a [dʒor'dano] *ag, sm/f* Jordanian.

giorna'laio, a [dʒorna'lajo] *sm/f* newsagent (*Brit*), newsdealer (*US*).

gior'nale [dʒor'nale] *sm* (news)paper; (*diario*) journal, diary; (*COMM*) journal; **~ di bordo** (*NAUT*) ship's log; **~ radio** radio news *sg*.

giorna'letto [dʒorna'letto] *sm* (children's) comic.

giornali'ero, a [dʒorna'ljɛro] *ag* daily; (*che varia: umore*) changeable ♦ *sm* day labourer (*Brit*) o laborer (*US*).

giorna'lino [dʒorna'lino] *sm* children's comic.

giorna'lismo [dʒorna'lizmo] *sm* journalism.

giorna'lista, i, e [dʒorna'lista] *sm/f* journalist.

giorna'listico, a, ci, che [dʒorna'listiko] *ag* journalistic; **stile ~** journalese.

giornal'mente [dʒornal'mente] *av* daily.

gior'nata [dʒor'nata] *sf* day; (*paga*) day's wages, day's pay; **durante la ~ di ieri** yesterday; **fresco di ~** (*uovo*) freshly laid; **vivere alla ~** to live from day to day; **~ lavorativa** working day.

gi'orno ['dʒorno] *sm* day; (*opposto alla notte*) day, daytime; (*luce del ~*) daylight; **al ~** per day; **di ~** by day; **~ per ~** day by day; **al ~ d'oggi** nowadays; **tutto il santo ~** all day long.

gi'ostra ['dʒɔstra] *sf* (*per bimbi*) merry-go-round; (*torneo storico*) joust.

gios'trare [dʒos'trare] *vi* (*STORIA*) to joust, tilt; **~rsi** *vr* to manage.

giov. *abbr* (= *giovedì*) Thur(s).

giova'mento [dʒova'mento] *sm* benefit, help.

gi'ovane ['dʒovane] *ag* young; (*aspetto*) youthful ♦ *sm/f* youth/girl, young man/woman; **i ~i** young people; **è ~ del mestiere** he's new to the job.

giova'netto, a [dʒova'netto] *sm/f* young man/woman.

giova'nile [dʒova'nile] *ag* youthful; (*scritti*) early; (*errore*) of youth.

giova'notto [dʒova'nɔtto] *sm* young man.

gio'vare [dʒo'vare] *vi*: **~ a** (*essere utile*) to be useful to; (*far bene*) to be good for ♦ *vb impers* (*essere bene, utile*) to be useful; **~rsi** *vr*: **~rsi di qc** to make use of sth; **a**

che giova prendersela? what's the point of getting upset?

Gi'ove ['dʒɔve] *sm* (*MITOLOGIA*) Jove; (*ASTR*) Jupiter.

giovedì [dʒove'di] *sm inv* Thursday; *per fraseologia vedi* **martedì**.

gio'venca, che [dʒo'vɛnka] *sf* heifer.

gioventù [dʒoven'tu] *sf* (*periodo*) youth; (*i giovani*) young people *pl*, youth.

giovi'ale [dʒo'vjale] *ag* jovial, jolly.

giovi'nastro [dʒovi'nastro] *sm* young thug.

giovin'cello [dʒovin'tʃello] *sm* young lad.

giovi'nezza [dʒovi'nettsa] *sf* youth.

gira'dischi [dʒira'diski] *sm inv* record player.

gi'raffa [dʒi'raffa] *sf* giraffe; (*TV, CINEMA, RADIO*) boom.

gira'mento [dʒira'mento] *sm*: ~ **di testa** fit of dizziness.

gira'mondo [dʒira'mondo] *sm/f inv* globetrotter.

gi'randola [dʒi'randola] *sf* (*fuoco d'artificio*) Catherine wheel; (*giocattolo*) toy windmill; (*banderuola*) weather vane, weathercock.

gi'rante [dʒi'rante] *sm/f* (*chi gira un assegno*) endorser.

gi'rare [dʒi'rare] *vt* (*far ruotare*) to turn; (*percorrere, visitare*) to go round; (*CINEMA*) to shoot; (: *film: come regista*) to make; (*COMM*) to endorse ♦ *vi* to turn; (*più veloce*) to spin; (*andare in giro*) to wander, go around; **~rsi** *vr* to turn; ~ **attorno a** to go round; to revolve round; **si girava e rigirava nel letto** he tossed and turned in bed; **far ~ la testa a qn** to make sb dizzy; (*fig*) to turn sb's head; **gira al largo** keep your distance; **girala come ti pare** (*fig*) look at it whichever way you like; **gira e rigira ...** after a lot of driving (*o walking*) about ...; (*fig*) whichever way you look at it; **cosa ti gira?** (*fam*) what's got into you?; **mi ha fatto ~ le scatole** (*fam*) he drove me crazy.

girar'rosto [dʒirar'rosto] *sm* (*CUC*) spit.

gira'sole [dʒira'sole] *sm* sunflower.

gi'rata [dʒi'rata] *sf* (*passeggiata*) stroll; (*con veicolo*) drive; (*COMM*) endorsement.

gira'tario, a [dʒira'tarjo] *sm/f* endorsee.

gira'volta [dʒira'vɔlta] *sf* twirl, turn; (*curva*) sharp bend; (*fig*) about-turn.

gi'rello [dʒi'rɛllo] *sm* (*di bambino*) Babywalker ® (*Brit*), go-cart (*US*); (*taglio di carne*) topside (*Brit*), top round (*US*).

gi'retto [dʒi'retto] *sm* (*passeggiata*) walk, stroll; (: *in macchina*) drive, spin; (: *in bicicletta*) ride.

gi'revole [dʒi'revole] *ag* revolving, turning.

gi'rino [dʒi'rino] *sm* tadpole.

'giro ['dʒiro] *sm* (*circuito, cerchio*) circle; (*di chiave, manovella*) turn; (*viaggio*) tour, excursion; (*passeggiata*) stroll, walk; (*in macchina*) drive; (*in bicicletta*) ride;

(*SPORT*: *della pista*) lap; (*di denaro*) circulation; (*CARTE*) hand; (*TECN*) revolution; **fare un** ~ to go for a walk (*o a drive o a ride*); **fare il** ~ **di** (*parco, città*) to go round; **andare in** ~ (*a piedi*) to go about, walk around; **guardarsi in** ~ to look around; **prendere in** ~ **qn** (*fig*) to take sb for a ride; **a stretto** ~ **di posta** by return of post; **nel** ~ **di un mese** in a month's time; **essere nel** ~ (*fig*) to belong to a circle (of friends); ~ **d'affari** (*viaggio*) business tour; (*COMM*) turnover; ~ **di parole** circumlocution; ~ **di prova** (*AUT*) test drive; ~ **turistico** sightseeing tour; ~ **vita** waist measurement.

giro'collo [dʒiro'kɔllo] *sm*: **a** ~ crewneck *cpd*.

giro'conto [dʒiro'konto] *sm* (*ECON*) credit transfer.

gi'rone [dʒi'rone] *sm* (*SPORT*) series of games; ~ **di andata/ritorno** (*CALCIO*) first/second half of the season.

gironzo'lare [dʒirondzo'lare] *vi* to stroll about.

giro'tondo [dʒiro'tondo] *sm* ring-a-ring-o'-roses (*Brit*), ring-around-the-rosey (*US*); **in** ~ in a circle.

girova'gare [dʒirova'gare] *vi* to wander about.

gi'rovago, a, ghi, ghe [dʒi'rɔvago] *sm/f* (*vagabondo*) tramp; (*venditore*) peddler; **una compagnia di** ~**ghi** (*attori*) a company of strolling actors.

'gita ['dʒita] *sf* excursion, trip; **fare una** ~ to go for a trip, go on an outing.

gi'tano, a [dʒi'tano] *sm/f* gipsy.

gi'tante [dʒi'tante] *sm/f* member of a tour.

giù [dʒu] *av* down; (*dabbasso*) downstairs; **in** ~ downwards, down; **la mia casa è un po' più in** ~ my house is a bit further on; ~ **di lì** (*pressappoco*) thereabouts; **bambini dai 6 anni in** ~ children aged 6 and under; **cadere** ~ **per le scale** to fall down the stairs; ~ **le mani!** hands off!; **essere** ~ (*fig: di salute*) to be run down; (: *di spirito*) to be depressed; **quel tipo non mi va** ~ I can't stand that guy.

gi'ubba ['dʒubba] *sf* jacket.

giub'botto [dʒub'bɔtto] *sm* jerkin; ~ **antiproiettile** bulletproof vest.

giubi'lare [dʒubi'lare] *vi* to rejoice.

gi'ubilo ['dʒubilo] *sm* rejoicing.

giudi'care [dʒudi'kare] *vt* to judge; (*accusato*) to try; (*lite*) to arbitrate in; ~ **qn/qc bello** to consider sb/sth (to be) beautiful.

giudi'cato [dʒudi'kato] *sm* (*DIR*): **passare in** ~ to pass final judgment.

gi'udice ['dʒuditʃe] *sm* judge; ~ **collegiale** member of the court; ~ **conciliatore** justice of the peace; ~ **istruttore** examining (*Brit*) *o* committing (*US*) magistrate;

~ **popolare** member of a jury.
giudizi'ale [dʒudit'tsjale] *ag* judicial.
giudizi'ario, a [dʒudit'tsjarjo] *ag* legal, judicial.
giu'dizio [dʒu'dittsjo] *sm* judgment; (*opinione*) opinion; (*DIR*) judgment, sentence; (: *processo*) trial; (: *verdetto*) verdict; **aver** ~ to be wise *o* prudent; **essere in attesa di** ~ to be awaiting trial; **citare in** ~ to summons; **l'imputato è stato rinviato a** ~ the accused has been committed for trial.
giudizi'oso, a [dʒudit'tsjoso] *ag* prudent, judicious.
gi'uggiola ['dʒuddʒola] *sf*: **andare in brodo di** ~**e** (*fam*) to be over the moon.
gi'ugno ['dʒuɲɲo] *sm* June; *per fraseologia vedi* **luglio**.
giu'livo, a [dʒu'livo] *ag* merry.
giul'lare [dʒul'lare] *sm* jester.
giu'menta [dʒu'menta] *sf* mare.
gi'unco, chi ['dʒunko] *sm* (*BOT*) rush.
gi'ungere ['dʒundʒere] *vi* to arrive ♦ *vt* (*mani etc*) to join; ~ **a** to arrive at, reach; ~ **nuovo a qn** to come as news to sb; ~ **in porto** to reach harbour; (*fig*) to be brought to a successful outcome.
gi'ungla ['dʒungla] *sf* jungle.
gi'unsi *etc* ['dʒunsi] *vb vedi* **giungere**.
gi'unto, a ['dʒunto] *pp di* **giungere** ♦ *sm* (*TECN*) coupling, joint ♦ *sf* addition; (*organo esecutivo, amministrativo*) council, board; **per** ~**a** into the bargain, in addition; ~**a militare** military junta.
giun'tura [dʒun'tura] *sf* joint.
giuo'care [dʒwo'kare] *vt, vi* = **giocare**.
giu'oco ['dʒwɔko] *sm* = **gioco**.
giura'mento [dʒura'mento] *sm* oath; ~ **falso** perjury.
giu'rare [dʒu'rare] *vt* to swear ♦ *vi* to swear, take an oath; **gliel'ho giurata** I swore I would get even with him.
giu'rato, a [dʒu'rato] *ag*: **nemico** ~ sworn enemy ♦ *sm/f* juror, juryman/woman.
giu'ria [dʒu'ria] *sf* jury.
giu'ridico, a, ci, che [dʒu'ridiko] *ag* legal.
giurisdizi'one [dʒurizdit'tsjone] *sf* jurisdiction.
giurispru'denza [dʒurispru'dɛntsa] *sf* jurisprudence.
giu'rista, i, e [dʒu'rista] *sm/f* jurist.
giustap'porre [dʒustap'porre] *vt* to juxtapose.
giustapposizi'one [dʒustappozit'tsjone] *sf* juxtaposition.
giustap'posto, a [dʒustap'posto] *pp di* **giustappore**.
giustifi'care [dʒustifi'kare] *vt* to justify; ~**rsi** *vr*: ~**rsi di** *o* **per qc** to justify *o* excuse o.s. for sth.
giustifica'tivo, a [dʒustifika'tivo] *ag* (*AMM*): **nota** *o* **pezza** ~**a** receipt.

giustificazi'one [dʒustifikat'tsjone] *sf* justification; (*INS*) (note of) excuse.
gius'tizia [dʒus'tittsja] *sf* justice; **farsi** ~ (**da sé**) (*vendicarsi*) to take the law into one's own hands.
giustizi'are [dʒustit'tsjare] *vt* to execute, put to death.
giustizi'ere [dʒustit'tsjɛre] *sm* executioner.
gi'usto, a ['dʒusto] *ag* (*equo*) fair, just; (*vero*) true, correct; (*adatto*) right, suitable; (*preciso*) exact, correct ♦ *av* (*esattamente*) exactly, precisely; (*per l'appunto, appena*) just; **arrivare** ~ to arrive just in time; **ho** ~ **bisogno di te** you're just the person I need.
'glabro, a *ag* hairless.
glaci'ale [gla'tʃale] *ag* glacial.
gla'diolo *sm* gladiolus.
'glandola *sf* = **ghiandola**.
'glassa *sf* (*CUC*) icing.
gli [ʎi] *det mpl* (*dav V, s impura, gn, pn, ps, x, z*) the ♦ *pronome* (*a lui*) to him; (*a esso*) to it; (*in coppia con lo, la, li, le, ne: a lui, a lei, a loro etc*): **gliele do** I'm giving them to him (*o her o* them); **gliene ho parlato** I spoke to him (*o her o* them) about it; *vedi anche* **il**.
glice'rina [glitʃe'rina] *sf* glycerine.
'glicine ['glitʃine] *sm* wistaria.
gli'ela *etc* ['ʎela] *vedi* **gli**.
glo'bale *ag* overall; (*vista*) global.
'globo *sm* globe.
'globulo *sm* (*ANAT*): ~ **rosso/bianco** red/white corpuscle.
'gloria *sf* glory; **farsi** ~ **di qc** to pride o.s. on sth, take pride in sth.
glori'arsi *vr*: ~ **di qc** to pride o.s. on sth, glory *o* take pride in sth.
glorifi'care *vt* to glorify.
glori'oso, a *ag* glorious.
glos'sario *sm* glossary.
glu'cosio *sm* glucose.
'gluteo *sm* gluteus; ~**i** *smpl* buttocks.
GM *abbr* = **genio militare**.
GN *abbr* = **gratifica natalizia**.
G.N. *abbr* = **gas naturale**.
'gnocchi ['ɲɔkki] *smpl* (*CUC*) small dumplings made of semolina potato or potato.
'gnomo ['ɲomo] *sm* gnome.
'gnorri ['ɲorri] *sm/f inv*: **non fare lo** ~**!** stop acting as if you didn't know anything about it!
GO *sigla* = **Gorizia**.
'goal ['goul] *sm inv* (*SPORT*) goal.
'gobba *sf* (*ANAT*) hump; (*protuberanza*) bump.
'gobbo, a *ag* hunchbacked; (*ricurvo*) round-shouldered ♦ *sm/f* hunchback.
'Gobi *smpl*: **il Deserto dei** ~ the Gobi Desert.
'goccia, ce ['gottʃa] *sf* drop; ~ **di rugiada** dewdrop; **somigliarsi come due** ~**ce**

d'acqua to be as like as two peas in a pod; **è la ~ che fa traboccare il vaso!** it's the last straw!

'goccio ['gottʃo] *sm* drop, spot.

goccio'lare [gottʃo'lare] *vi, vt* to drip.

goccio'lio [gottʃo'lio] *sm* dripping.

go'dere *vi* (*compiacersi*): **~ (di)** to be delighted (at), rejoice (at); (*trarre vantaggio*): **~ di** to enjoy, benefit from ♦ *vt* to enjoy; **~rsi la vita** to enjoy life; **godersela** to have a good time, enjoy o.s.

godi'mento *sm* enjoyment.

godrò *etc vb vedi* **godere**.

gof'faggine [gof'faddʒine] *sf* clumsiness.

'goffo, a *ag* clumsy, awkward.

'gogna ['goɲɲa] *sf* pillory.

gol *sm inv* = **goal**.

'gola *sf* (*ANAT*) throat; (*golosità*) gluttony, greed; (*di camino*) flue; (*di monte*) gorge; **fare ~** (*anche fig*) to tempt; **ricacciare il pianto** *o* **le lacrime in ~** to swallow one's tears.

go'letta *sf* (*NAUT*) schooner.

golf *sm inv* (*SPORT*) golf; (*maglia*) cardigan.

'golfo *sm* gulf.

goli'ardico, a, ci, che *ag* (*canto, vita*) student *cpd*.

go'loso, a *ag* greedy.

'golpe *sm inv* (*POL*) coup.

gomi'tata *sf*: **dare una ~ a qn** to elbow sb; **farsi avanti a** (**forza** *o* **furia di**) **~e** to elbow one's way through; **fare a ~e per qc** to fight to get sth.

'gomito *sm* elbow; (*di strada etc*) sharp bend.

go'mitolo *sm* ball.

'gomma *sf* rubber; (*colla*) gum; (*per cancellare*) rubber, eraser; (*di veicolo*) tyre (*Brit*), tire (*US*); **~ da masticare** chewing gum; **~ a terra** flat tyre.

gommapi'uma ® *sf* foam rubber.

gom'mino *sm* rubber tip; (*rondella*) rubber washer.

gom'mista, i, e *sm/f* tyre (*Brit*) *o* tire (*US*) specialist; (*rivenditore*) tyre *o* tire merchant.

gom'mone *sm* rubber dinghy.

gom'moso, a *ag* rubbery.

'gondola *sf* gondola.

gondoli'ere *sm* gondolier.

gonfa'lone *sm* banner.

gonfi'are *vt* (*pallone*) to blow up, inflate; (*dilatare, ingrossare*) to swell; (*fig: notizia*) to exaggerate; **~rsi** *vr* to swell; (*fiume*) to rise.

'gonfio, a *ag* swollen; (*stomaco*) bloated; (*palloncino, gomme*) inflated, blown up; (*con pompa*) pumped up; (*vela*) full; **occhi ~i di pianto** eyes swollen with tears; **~ di orgoglio** (*persona*) puffed up (with pride); **avere il portafoglio ~** to have a bulging wallet.

gonfi'ore *sm* swelling.

gongo'lare *vi* to look pleased with o.s.; **~ di gioia** to be overjoyed.

'gonna *sf* skirt; **~ pantalone** culottes *pl*.

'gonzo ['gondzo] *sm* simpleton, fool.

gorgheggi'are [gorged'dʒare] *vi* to warble; to trill.

gor'gheggio [gor'geddʒo] *sm* (*MUS, di uccello*) trill.

'gorgo, ghi *sm* whirlpool.

gorgogli'are [gorgoʎ'ʎare] *vi* to gurgle.

gorgo'glio [gorgoʎ'ʎio] *sm* gurgling.

go'rilla *sm inv* gorilla; (*guardia del corpo*) bodyguard.

'gotico, a, ci, che *ag, sm* Gothic.

'gotta *sf* gout.

gover'nante *sm/f* ruler ♦ *sf* (*di bambini*) governess; (*donna di servizio*) housekeeper.

gover'nare *vt* (*stato*) to govern, rule; (*pilotare, guidare*) to steer; (*bestiame*) to tend, look after.

governa'tivo, a *ag* (*politica, decreto*) government *cpd*, governmental; (*stampa*) pro-government.

governa'tore *sm* governor.

go'verno *sm* government.

'gozzo ['gottso] *sm* (*ZOOL*) crop; (*MED*) goitre; (*fig fam*) throat.

gozzovigli'are [gottsoviʎ'ʎare] *vi* to make merry, carouse.

gpm *abbr* (= *giri per minuto*) rpm.

GR *sigla* = **Grosseto** ♦ *sigla m* = **giornale radio**.

gracchi'are [grak'kjare] *vi* to caw.

graci'dare [gratʃi'dare] *vi* to croak.

graci'dio, ii [gratʃi'dio] *sm* croaking.

'gracile ['gratʃile] *ag* frail, delicate.

gra'dasso *sm* boaster.

gradata'mente *av* gradually, by degrees.

gradazi'one [gradat'tsjone] *sf* (*sfumatura*) gradation; **~ alcolica** alcoholic content, strength.

gra'devole *ag* pleasant, agreeable.

gradi'mento *sm* pleasure, satisfaction; **essere di mio** (*o* **tuo** *etc*) **~** to be to my (*o* your *etc*) liking.

gradi'nata *sf* flight of steps; (*in teatro, stadio*) tiers *pl*.

gra'dino *sm* step; (*ALPINISMO*) foothold.

gra'dire *vt* (*accettare con piacere*) to accept; (*desiderare*) to wish, like; **gradisce una tazza di tè?** would you like a cup of tea?

gra'dito, a *ag* welcome.

'grado *sm* (*MAT, FISICA etc*) degree; (*stadio*) degree, level; (*MIL, sociale*) rank; **essere in ~ di fare** to be in a position to do; **di buon ~** willingly; **per ~i** by degrees; **un cugino di primo/secondo ~** a first/second cousin; **subire il terzo ~** (*anche fig*) to be given the third degree.

gradu'ale *ag* gradual.

gradu'are vt to grade.

gradu'ato, a ag (esercizi) graded; (scala, termometro) graduated ♦ sm (MIL) noncommissioned officer.

gradua'toria sf (di concorso) list; (per la promozione) order of seniority.

graduazi'one [graduat'tsjone] sf graduation.

'graffa sf (gancio) clip; (segno grafico) brace.

graf'fetta sf paper clip.

graffi'are vt to scratch.

graffia'tura sf scratch.

'graffio sm scratch.

graf'fiti smpl graffiti.

gra'fia sf spelling; (scrittura) handwriting.

'grafico, a, ci, che ag graphic ♦ sm graph; (persona) graphic designer ♦ sf graphic arts pl; ~ **a torta** pie chart.

gra'migna [gra'miɲɲa] sf weed; couch grass.

gram'matica, che sf grammar.

grammati'cale ag grammatical.

'grammo sm gram(me).

'gramo, a ag (vita) wretched.

gran ag vedi **grande**.

'grana sf (granello, di minerali, corpi spezzati) grain; (fam: seccatura) trouble; (: soldi) cash ♦ sm inv cheese similar to Parmesan.

gra'naglie [gra'naʎʎe] sfpl corn sg, seed sg.

gra'naio sm granary, barn.

gra'nata sf (frutto) pomegranate; (pietra preziosa) garnet; (proiettile) grenade.

granati'ere sm (MIL) grenadier; (fig) fine figure of a man.

Gran Bre'tagna [granbre'taɲɲa] sf: **la** ~ Great Britain.

gran'cassa sf (MUS) bass drum.

'granchio ['grankjo] sm crab; (fig) blunder; **prendere un** ~ (fig) to blunder.

grandango'lare sm wide-angle lens sg.

'grande ag (qualche volta **gran** +C, **grand'** +V) (grosso, largo, vasto) big, large; (alto) tall; (lungo) long; (in sensi astratti) great ♦ sm/f (persona adulta) adult, grown-up; (chi ha ingegno e potenza) great man/woman; **mio fratello più** ~ my big o older brother; **il gran pubblico** the general public; **di gran classe** (prodotto) high-class; **cosa farai da** ~**?** what will you be o do when you grow up?; **fare le cose in** ~ to do things in style; **fare il** ~ (strafare) to act big; **una gran bella donna** a very beautiful woman; **non è una gran cosa** o **un gran che** it's nothing special; **non ne so gran che** I don't know very much about it.

grandeggi'are [granded'dʒare] vi (emergere per grandezza): ~ **su** to tower over; (darsi arie) to put on airs.

gran'dezza [gran'dettsa] sf (dimensione) size; (fig) greatness; **in** ~ **naturale** lifesize; **manie di** ~ delusions of grandeur.

grandi'nare vb impers to hail.

'grandine sf hail.

grandi'oso, a ag grand, grandiose.

gran'duca, chi sm grand duke.

grandu'cato sm grand duchy.

grandu'chessa [grandu'kessa] sf grand duchess.

gra'nello sm (di cereali, uva) seed; (di frutta) pip; (di sabbia, sale etc) grain.

gra'nita sf kind of water ice.

gra'nito sm granite.

'grano sm (in quasi tutti i sensi) grain; (frumento) wheat; (di rosario, collana) bead; ~ **di pepe** peppercorn.

gran'turco sm maize.

'granulo sm granule; (MED) pellet.

'grappa sf rough, strong brandy.

'grappolo sm bunch, cluster.

'graspo sm bunch (of grapes).

gras'setto sm (TIP) bold (type) (Brit), bold face.

'grasso, a ag fat; (cibo) fatty; (pelle) greasy; (terreno) rich; (fig: guadagno, annata) plentiful; (: volgare) coarse, lewd ♦ sm (di persona, animale) fat; (sostanza che unge) grease.

gras'soccio, a, ci, ce [gras'sɔttʃo] ag plump.

gras'sone, a sm/f (fam: persona) dumpling.

'grata sf grating.

gra'ticcio [gra'tittʃo] sm trellis; (stuoia) mat.

gra'ticola sf grill.

gra'tifica, che sf bonus; ~ **natalizia** Christmas bonus.

gratificazi'one [gratifikat'tsjone] sf (soddisfazione) satisfaction, reward.

grati'nare vt (CUC) to cook au gratin.

'gratis av free, for nothing.

grati'tudine sf gratitude.

'grato, a ag grateful.

gratta'capo sm worry, headache.

gratta'cielo [gratta'tʃɛlo] sm skyscraper.

grat'tare vt (pelle) to scratch; (raschiare) to scrape; (pane, formaggio, carote) to grate; (fam: rubare) to pinch ♦ vi (stridere) to grate; (AUT) to grind; ~**rsi** vr to scratch o.s.; ~**rsi la pancia** (fig) to twiddle one's thumbs.

grat'tata sf scratch; **fare una** ~ (AUT: fam) to grind the gears.

grat'tugia, gie [grat'tudʒa] sf grater.

grattugi'are [grattu'dʒare] vt to grate; **pane** m **grattugiato** breadcrumbs pl.

gratuità sf (fig) gratuitousness.

gra'tuito, a ag free; (fig) gratuitous.

gra'vame sm tax; (fig) burden, weight.

gra'vare vt to burden ♦ vi: ~ **su** to weigh on.

'grave ag (danno, pericolo, peccato etc) grave, serious; (responsabilità) heavy, grave; (contegno) grave, solemn; (voce, suono) deep, low-pitched; (LING): **accento** ~ grave accent ♦ sm (FISICA) (heavy) body; **un malato** ~ a person who is seriously ill.

gravi'danza [gravi'dantsa] *sf* pregnancy.

'gravido, a *ag* pregnant.

gravità *sf* seriousness; (*anche* FISICA) gravity.

gravi'tare *vi* (FISICA): ~ **intorno a** to gravitate round.

gra'voso, a *ag* heavy, onerous.

'grazia ['grattsja] *sf* grace; (*favore*) favour (*Brit*), favor (*US*); (*DIR*) pardon; **di** ~ (*ironico*) if you please; **troppa** ~! (*ironico*) you're too generous!; **quanta** ~ **di Dio!** what abundance!; **entrare nelle** ~**e di qn** to win sb's favour; **Ministero di G**~ **e Giustizia** Ministry of Justice, ≈ Lord Chancellor's Office (*Brit*), ≈ Department of Justice (*US*).

grazi'are [grat'tsjare] *vt* (DIR) to pardon.

'grazie ['grattsje] *escl* thank you!; ~ **mille!** *o* **tante!** *o* **infinite!** thank you very much!; ~ **a** thanks to.

grazi'oso, a [grat'tsjoso] *ag* charming, delightful; (*gentile*) gracious.

'Grecia ['grɛtʃa] *sf*: **la** ~ Greece.

'greco, a, ci, che *ag*, *sm/f*, *sm* Greek.

gre'gario *sm* (CICLISMO) supporting rider.

'gregge, *pl* (*f*) **i** ['greddʒe] *sm* flock.

'greggio, a, gi, ge ['greddʒo] *ag* raw, unrefined; (*diamante*) rough, uncut; (*tessuto*) unbleached ♦ *sm* (*anche*: **petrolio** ~) crude (oil).

grembi'ule *sm* apron; (*sopravveste*) overall.

'grembo *sm* lap; (*ventre della madre*) womb.

gre'mito, a *ag*: ~ **(di)** packed *o* crowded (with).

'greto *sm* (exposed) gravel bed of a river.

'gretto, a *ag* mean, stingy; (*fig*) narrow-minded.

'greve *ag* heavy.

'grezzo, a ['greddzo] *ag* = **greggio**.

gri'dare *vi* (*per chiamare*) to shout, cry (out); (*strillare*) to scream, yell ♦ *vt* to shout (out), yell (out); ~ **aiuto** to cry *o* shout for help.

'grido, *pl* (*m*) **i** *o* *pl* (*f*) **a** *sm* shout, cry; scream, yell; (*di animale*) cry; **di** ~ **famoso**; **all'ultimo** ~ in the latest style.

'grigio, a, gi, gie ['gridʒo] *ag*, *sm* grey (*Brit*), gray (*US*).

'griglia ['griʎʎa] *sf* (*per arrostire*) grill; (ELETTR) grid; (*inferriata*) grating; **alla** ~ (CUC) grilled.

grigli'ata [griʎ'ʎata] *sf* (CUC) grill.

gril'letto *sm* trigger.

'grillo *sm* (ZOOL) cricket; (*fig*) whim; **ha dei** ~**i per la testa** his head is full of nonsense.

grimal'dello *sm* picklock.

'grinfia *sf*: **cadere nelle** ~**e di qn** (*fig*) to fall into sb's clutches.

'grinta *sf* grim expression; (SPORT) fighting spirit; **avere molta** ~ to be very determined.

'grinza ['grintsa] *sf* crease, wrinkle; (*ruga*) wrinkle; **il tuo ragionamento non fa una** ~ your argument is faultless.

grin'zoso, a [grin'tsoso] *ag* wrinkled; creased.

grip'pare *vi* (TECN) to seize.

gris'sino *sm* bread-stick.

groenlan'dese *ag* Greenland *cpd* ♦ *sm/f* Greenlander.

Groen'landia *sf*: **la** ~ Greenland.

'gronda *sf* eaves *pl*.

gron'daia *sf* gutter.

gron'dante *ag* dripping.

gron'dare *vi* to pour; (*essere bagnato*): ~ **di** to be dripping with ♦ *vt* to drip with.

'groppa *sf* (*di animale*) back, rump; (*fam*: *dell'uomo*) back, shoulders *pl*.

'groppo *sm* tangle; **avere un** ~ **alla gola** (*fig*) to have a lump in one's throat.

'grossa *sf* (*unità di misura*) gross.

gros'sezza [gros'settsa] *sf* size; thickness.

gros'sista, i, e *sm/f* (COMM) wholesaler.

'grosso, a *ag* big, large; (*di spessore*) thick; (*grossolano*: *anche fig*) coarse; (*grave*, *insopportabile*) serious, great; (*tempo*, *mare*) rough ♦ *sm*: **il** ~ **di** the bulk of; **un pezzo** ~ (*fig*) a VIP, a bigwig; **farla** ~**a** to do something very stupid; **dirle** ~**e** to tell tall stories (*Brit*) *o* tales (*US*); **questa è** ~**a!** that's a good one!; **sbagliarsi di** ~ to be completely wrong; **dormire della** ~**a** to sleep like a log.

grossolanità *sf* coarseness.

grosso'lano, a *ag* rough, coarse; (*fig*) coarse, crude; (: *errore*) stupid.

grosso'modo *av* roughly.

'grotta *sf* cave; grotto.

grot'tesco, a, schi, sche *ag* grotesque.

grovi'era *sm o f* gruyère (cheese).

gro'viglio [gro'viʎʎo] *sm* tangle; (*fig*) muddle.

gru *sf inv* crane.

'gruccia, ce ['gruttʃa] *sf* (*per camminare*) crutch; (*per abiti*) coat-hanger.

gru'gnire [gruɲ'ɲire] *vi* to grunt.

gru'gnito [gruɲ'ɲito] *sm* grunt.

'grugno ['gruɲɲo] *sm* snout; (*fam*: *faccia*) mug.

'grullo, a *ag* silly, stupid.

'grumo *sm* (*di sangue*) clot; (*di farina etc*) lump.

gru'moso, a *ag* lumpy.

'gruppo *sm* group; ~ **sanguigno** blood group.

gruvi'era *sm o f* = **groviera**.

'gruzzolo ['gruttsolo] *sm* (*di denaro*) hoard.

GT *abbr* (AUT: = *gran turismo*) GT.

G.U. *abbr* = **Gazzetta Ufficiale**.

guada'gnare [gwadaɲ'ɲare] *vt* (*ottenere*) to

gain; (*soldi, stipendio*) to earn; (*vincere*) to win; (*raggiungere*) to reach; **tanto di guadagnato!** so much the better!

gua'dagno [gwa'daɲɲo] *sm* earnings *pl*; (*COMM*) profit; (*vantaggio, utile*) advantage, gain; ~ **di capitale** capital gains *pl*; ~ **lordo/netto** gross/net earnings *pl*.

gua'dare *vt* to ford.

gu'ado *sm* ford; **passare a** ~ to ford.

gu'ai *escl*: ~ **a te** (*o lui etc*)! woe betide you (*o him etc*)!

gua'ina *sf* (*fodero*) sheath; (*indumento per donna*) girdle.

gu'aio *sm* trouble, mishap; (*inconveniente*) trouble, snag.

gua'ire *vi* to whine, yelp.

gua'ito *sm* (*di cane*) yelp, whine; (*il guaire*) yelping, whining.

gu'ancia, ce ['gwantʃa] *sf* cheek.

guanci'ale [gwan'tʃale] *sm* pillow; **dormire fra due ~i** (*fig*) to sleep easy, have no worries.

gu'anto *sm* glove; **trattare qn con i ~i** (*fig*) to handle sb with kid gloves; **gettare/raccogliere il ~** (*fig*) to throw down/take up the gauntlet.

guan'tone *sm* boxing glove.

guarda'boschi [gwarda'bɔski] *sm inv* forester.

guarda'caccia [gwarda'kattʃa] *sm inv* gamekeeper.

guarda'coste *sm inv* coastguard; (*nave*) coastguard patrol vessel.

guarda'linee *sm inv* (*SPORT*) linesman.

guarda'macchine [gwarda'makkine] *sm/f inv* car-park (*Brit*) *o* parking lot (*US*) attendant.

guar'dare *vt* (*con lo sguardo: osservare*) to look at; (*film, televisione*) to watch; (*custodire*) to look after, take care of ♦ *vi* to look; (*badare*): ~ **a** to pay attention to; (*luoghi: esser orientato*): ~ **a** to face; **~rsi** *vr* to look at o.s.; ~ **di** to try to; **~rsi da** (*astenersi*) to refrain from; (*stare in guardia*) to beware of; **~rsi da fare** to take care not to do; **ma guarda un po'!** good heavens!; **e guarda caso ...** as if by coincidence ...; ~ **qn dall'alto in basso** to look down on sb; **non ~ in faccia a nessuno** (*fig*) to have no regard for anybody; ~ **di traverso** to scowl *o* frown at; ~ **a vista qn** to keep a close watch on sb.

guarda'roba *sm inv* wardrobe; (*locale*) cloakroom.

guardarobi'ere, a *sm/f* cloakroom attendant.

guardasi'gilli [gwardasi'dʒilli] *sm inv* ≈ Lord Chancellor (*Brit*), ≈ Attorney General (*US*).

gu'ardia *sf* (*individuo, corpo*) guard; (*sorveglianza*) watch; **fare la ~ a qc/qn** to guard sth/sb; **stare in ~** (*fig*) to be on one's guard; **il medico di** ~ the doctor on call; **il fiume ha raggiunto il livello di** ~ the river has reached the high-water mark; ~ **carceraria** (prison) warder (*Brit*) *o* guard (*US*); ~ **del corpo** bodyguard; ~ **di finanza** (*corpo*) customs *pl*; (*persona*) customs officer; ~ **forestale** forest ranger; ~ **giurata** security guard; ~ **medica** emergency doctor service; ~ **municipale** town policeman; ~ **notturna** night security guard; ~ **di pubblica sicurezza** policeman.

guardi'ano, a *sm/f* (*di carcere*) warder (*Brit*), guard (*US*); (*di villa etc*) caretaker; (*di museo*) custodian; (*di zoo*) keeper; ~ **notturno** night watchman.

guar'dina *sf* cell.

guar'dingo, a, ghi, ghe *ag* wary, cautious.

guardi'ola *sf* porter's lodge; (*MIL*) look-out tower.

guarigi'one [gwari'dʒone] *sf* recovery.

gua'rire *vt* (*persona, malattia*) to cure; (*ferita*) to heal ♦ *vi* to recover, be cured; to heal (up).

guarnigi'one [gwarni'dʒone] *sf* garrison.

guar'nire *vt* (*ornare: abiti*) to trim; (*CUC*) to garnish.

guarnizi'one [gwarnit'tsjone] *sf* trimming; garnish; (*TECN*) gasket.

guasta'feste *sm/f inv* spoilsport.

guas'tare *vt* to spoil, ruin; (*meccanismo*) to break; **~rsi** *vr* (*cibo*) to go bad; (*meccanismo*) to break down; (*tempo*) to change for the worse; (*amici*) to quarrel, fall out.

gu'asto, a *ag* (*non funzionante*) broken; (: *telefono etc*) out of order; (*andato a male*) bad, rotten; (: *dente*) decayed, bad; (*fig: corrotto*) depraved ♦ *sm* breakdown; (*avaria*) failure; ~ **al motore** engine failure.

Guate'mala *sm*: **il** ~ Guatemala.

guatemal'teco, a, ci, che *ag, sm/f* Guatemalan.

gu'azza ['gwattsa] *sf* heavy dew.

guazza'buglio [gwattsa'buʎʎo] *sm* muddle.

gu'ercio, a, ci, ce ['gwertʃo] *ag* cross-eyed.

gu'erra *sf* war; (*tecnica: atomica, chimica etc*) warfare; **fare la ~ (a)** to wage war (against); ~ **mondiale** world war.

guerrafon'daio *sm* warmonger.

guerreggi'are [gwerred'dʒare] *vi* to wage war.

guer'resco, a, schi, sche *ag* (*di guerra*) war *cpd*; (*incline alla guerra*) warlike.

guerri'ero, a *ag* warlike ♦ *sm* warrior.

guer'riglia [gwer'riʎʎa] *sf* guerrilla warfare.

guerrigli'ero [gwerriʎ'ʎero] *sm* guerrilla.

'gufo *sm* owl.

'guglia ['guʎʎa] *sf* (*ARCHIT*) spire; (*di roccia*) needle.

Gui'ana *sf*: **la ~ francese** French Guiana.

gu'ida *sf* guide; (*comando, direzione*) guidance, direction; (*AUT*) driving; (:

sterzo) steering; (*tappeto*, *di tenda*, *cassetto*) runner; ~ **a destra/sinistra** (*AUT*) right-/left-hand drive; **essere alla ~ di** (*governo*) to head; (*spedizione*, *paese*) to lead; **far da ~ a qn** (*mostrare la strada*) to show sb the way; (*in una città*) to show sb (a)round; ~ **telefonica** telephone directory.

gui'dare *vt* to guide; (*condurre a capo*) to lead; (*auto*) to drive; (*aereo*, *nave*) to pilot; **sa ~?** can you drive?

guida'tore, 'trice *sm/f* (*conducente*) driver.

Gui'nea *sf*: **la Repubblica di ~** the Republic of Guinea; **la ~ Equatoriale** Equatorial Guinea.

guin'zaglio [gwin'tsaʎʎo] *sm* leash, lead.

gu'isa *sf*: **a ~ di** like, in the manner of.

guiz'zare [gwit'tsare] *vi* to dart; to flicker; to leap; ~ **via** (*fuggire*) to slip away.

gu'izzo ['gwittso] *sm* (*di animali*) dart; (*di fulmine*) flash.

'guscio ['guʃʃo] *sm* shell.

gus'tare *vt* (*cibi*) to taste; (: *assaporare con piacere*) to enjoy, savour (*Brit*), savor (*US*); (*fig*) to enjoy, appreciate ♦ *vi*: ~ **a** to please; **non mi gusta affatto** I don't like it at all.

gusta'tivo, a *ag*: **papille** *fpl* ~**e** taste buds.

'gusto *sm* (*senso*) taste; (*sapore*) taste, flavour (*Brit*), flavor (*US*); (*godimento*) enjoyment; **al ~ di fragola** strawberry-flavo(u)red; **di ~ barocco** in the baroque style; **mangiare di ~** to eat heartily; **prenderci ~: ci ha preso ~** he's acquired a taste for it, he's got to like it.

gus'toso, a *ag* tasty; (*fig*) agreeable.

guttu'rale *ag* guttural.

Gu'yana [gu'jana] *sf*: **la ~** Guyana.

H

H, h ['akka] *sf o m inv* (*lettera*) H, h ♦ *abbr* (= *ora*) hr; (= *etto*, *altezza*) h; **H come hotel** ≈ H for Harry (*Brit*), H for How (*US*).

ha, 'hai [a, ai] *vb vedi* **avere**.

Ha'iti [a'iti] *sf* Haiti.

haiti'ano, a [ai'tjano] *ag*, *sm/f* Haitian.

hall [hɔːl] *sf inv* hall, foyer.

'handicap ['handikap] *sm inv* handicap.

handicap'pato, a [andikap'pato] *ag* handicapped ♦ *sm/f* handicapped person, disabled person.

'hanno ['anno] *vb vedi* **avere**.

ha'scisc [aʃ'ʃiʃ] *sm* hashish.

hawai'ano, a [ava'jano] *ag*, *sm/f* Hawaiian.

Ha'waii [a'vai] *sfpl*: **le ~** Hawaii *sg*.

'Helsinki ['ɛlsinki] *sf* Helsinki.

'herpes ['ɛrpes] *sm* (*MED*) herpes *sg*; ~ **zoster** shingles *sg*.

hg *abbr* (= *ettogrammo*) hg.

'hi-fi ['haifai] *sf inv*, *ag inv* hi-fi.

Hima'laia [ima'laja] *sm*: **l'~** the Himalayas *pl*.

hl *abbr* (= *ettolitro*) hl.

ho [ɔ] *vb vedi* **avere**.

'hobby ['hɔbi] *sm inv* hobby.

'hockey ['hɔki] *sm* hockey; ~ **su ghiaccio** ice hockey.

'holding ['houldiŋ] *sf inv* holding company.

Hon'duras [on'duras] *sm* Honduras.

'Hong Kong ['ɔkɔg] *sf* Hong Kong.

Hono'lulu [ono'lulu] *sf* Honolulu.

'hostess ['houstis] *sf inv* air hostess (*Brit*) *o* stewardess.

ho'tel [o'tɛl] *sm inv* hotel.

Hz *abbr* (= *hertz*) Hz.

I

I, i [i] *sf o m inv* (*lettera*) I, i; **I come Imola** ≈ I for Isaac (*Brit*), I for Item (*US*).

i *det mpl* the; *vedi anche* **il**.

IACP *sigla m* (= *Istituto Autonomo per le Case Popolari*) *public housing association*.

i'ato *sm* hiatus.

i'berico, a, ci, che *ag* Iberian; **la Penisola I~a** the Iberian Peninsula.

iber'nare *vi* to hibernate ♦ *vt* (*MED*) to induce hypothermia in.

ibernazi'one [ibernat'tsjone] *sf* hibernation.

ibid. *abbr* (= *ibidem*) ib(id).

'ibrido, a *ag*, *sm* hybrid.

'ICE ['itʃe] *sigla m* (= *Istituto nazionale per il Commercio Estero*) *overseas trade board*.

i'cona *sf* icon.

id *abbr* (= *idem*) do.

Id'dio *sm* God.

i'dea *sf* idea; (*opinione*) opinion, view; (*ideale*) ideal; **avere le ~e chiare** to know one's mind; **cambiare ~** to change one's mind; **dare l'~ di** to seem, look like; **neanche** *o* **neppure per ~!** certainly not!, no way!; ~ **fissa** obsession.

ide'ale *ag*, *sm* ideal.

idea'lismo *sm* idealism.

idea'lista, i, e *sm/f* idealist.

idea'listico, a, ci, che *ag* idealistic.

idealiz'zare [idealid'dzare] *vt* to idealize.

ide'are *vt* (*immaginare*) to think up, con-

ceive; (*progettare*) to plan.
idea'tore, 'trice *sm/f* author.
i'dentico, a, ci, che *ag* identical.
identifi'care *vt* to identify.
identificazi'one [identifikat'tsjone] *sf* identification.
identità *sf inv* identity.
ideolo'gia, 'gie [ideolo'dʒia] *sf* ideology.
ideo'logico, a, ci, che [ideo'lɔdʒiko] *ag* ideological.
i'dillico, a, ci, che *ag* idyllic.
i'dillio *sm* idyll; **tra di loro è nato un ~** they have fallen in love.
idi'oma, i *sm* idiom, language.
idio'matico, a, ci, che *ag* idiomatic; **frase** *f* **~a** idiom.
idiosincra'sia *sf* idiosyncrasy.
idi'ota, i, e *ag* idiotic ♦ *sm/f* idiot.
idio'zia [idjot'tsia] *sf* idiocy; (*atto, discorso*) idiotic thing to do (*o* say).
ido'latra, i, e *ag* idolatrous ♦ *sm/f* idolater.
idola'trare *vt* to worship; (*fig*) to idolize.
idola'tria *sf* idolatry.
'idolo *sm* idol.
idoneità *sf* suitability; **esame** *m* **di ~** qualifying examination.
i'doneo, a *ag*: **~ a** suitable for, fit for; (*MIL*) fit for; (*qualificato*) qualified for.
i'drante *sm* hydrant.
idra'tante *ag* (*crema*) moisturizing ♦ *sm* moisturizer.
idra'tare *vt* (*pelle*) to moisturize.
idratazi'one [idratat'tsjone] *sf* moisturizing.
i'draulico, a, ci, che *ag* hydraulic ♦ *sm* plumber ♦ *sf* hydraulics *sg*.
'idrico, a, ci, che *ag* water *cpd*.
idrocar'buro *sm* hydrocarbon.
idroe'lettrico, a, ci, che *ag* hydroelectric.
i'drofilo, a *ag*: **cotone** *m* **~** cotton wool (*Brit*), absorbent cotton (*US*).
idrofo'bia *sf* rabies *sg*.
i'drofobo, a *ag* rabid; (*fig*) furious.
i'drogeno [i'drɔdʒeno] *sm* hydrogen.
idro'porto *sm* (*AER*) seaplane base.
idrorepel'lente *ag* water-repellent.
idros'calo *sm* = **idroporto**.
idrovo'lante *sm* seaplane.
i'ella *sf* bad luck.
iel'lato, a *ag* plagued by bad luck.
i'ena *sf* hyena.
ie'ratico, a, ci, che *ag* (*REL*: *scrittura*) hieratic; (*fig*: *atteggiamento*) solemn.
i'eri *av*, *sm* yesterday; **il giornale di ~** yesterday's paper; **~ l'altro** the day before yesterday; **~ sera** yesterday evening.
ietta'tore, 'trice *sm/f* jinx.
igi'ene [i'dʒɛne] *sf* hygiene; **norme d'~** sanitary regulations; **ufficio d'~** public health office; **~ mentale** mental health; **~ pubblica** public health.
igi'enico, a, ci, che [i'dʒɛniko] *ag* hygienic; (*salubre*) healthy.

IGM *sigla m* (= *Ispettorato Generale della Motorizzazione*) road traffic inspectorate.
i'gnaro, a [iɲ'ɲaro] *ag*: **~ di** unaware of, ignorant of.
i'gnifugo, a, ghi, ghe [iɲ'ɲifugo] *ag* flame-resistant, fireproof.
i'gnobile [iɲ'ɲɔbile] *ag* despicable, vile.
igno'minia [iɲɲo'minja] *sf* ignominy.
igno'rante [iɲɲo'rante] *ag* ignorant.
igno'ranza [iɲɲo'rantsa] *sf* ignorance.
igno'rare [iɲɲo'rare] *vt* (*non sapere, conoscere*) to be ignorant *o* unaware of, not to know; (*fingere di non vedere, sentire*) to ignore.
i'gnoto, a [iɲ'ɲɔto] *ag* unknown ♦ *sm/f*: **figlio di ~i** child of unknown parentage; **il Milite l~** the Unknown Soldier.
il *det m* (*pl*(*m*) **i**; *diventa* **lo** (*pl* **gli**) *davanti a s impura, gn, pn, ps, x, z; f* **la** (*pl* **le**)) (*gen*) the; (*generalizzazione, l'astrazione*) *generalmente non tradotto;* **~ libro/lo studente/l'acqua** the book/the student/the water; **~ coraggio/l'amore/la giovinezza** courage/love/youth; **~ venerdì** *etc* (*abitualmente*) on Fridays *etc*; (*quel giorno*) on (the) Friday *etc*; **la settimana prossima** next week; **2.500 lire ~ chilo/paio** 2,500 lire a *o* per kilo/pair; **rompersi la gamba** to break one's leg; **avere i capelli neri/il naso rosso** to have dark hair/a red nose.
'ilare *ag* cheerful.
ilarità *sf* hilarity, mirth.
ill. *abbr* (= *illustrazione*; *illustrato*) ill.
illangui'dire *vi* to grow weak *o* feeble.
illazi'one [illat'tsjone] *sf* inference, deduction.
il'lecito, a [il'letʃito] *ag* illicit.
ille'gale *ag* illegal.
illegalità *sf* illegality.
illeg'gibile [illed'dʒibile] *ag* illegible.
illegittimità [illedʒittimi'ta] *sf* illegitimacy.
ille'gittimo, a [ille'dʒittimo] *ag* illegitimate.
il'leso, a *ag* unhurt, unharmed.
illiba'tezza [illiba'tettsa] *sf* (*di donna*) virginity.
illi'bato, a *ag*: **donna ~a** virgin.
illimi'tato, a *ag* boundless; unlimited.
illi'vidire *vi* (*volto, mani*) to turn livid; (*cielo*) to grow leaden.
ill.mo *abbr* = **illustrissimo**.
il'logico, a, ci, che [il'lɔdʒiko] *ag* illogical.
il'ludere *vt* to deceive, delude; **~rsi** *vr* to deceive o.s., delude o.s.
illumi'nare *vt* to light up, illuminate; (*fig*) to enlighten; **~rsi** *vr* to light up; **~ a giorno** (*con riflettori*) to floodlight.
illumi'nato, a *ag* (*fig*: *sovrano, spirito*) enlightened.
illuminazi'one [illuminat'tsjone] *sf* lighting; illumination; floodlighting; (*fig*) flash of

inspiration.

illumi'nismo *sm* (*STORIA*): **l'l~** the Enlightenment.

il'lusi *etc vb vedi* **illudere.**

illusi'one *sf* illusion; **farsi delle ~i** to delude o.s.

illusio'nismo *sm* conjuring.

illusio'nista, i, e *sm/f* conjurer.

il'luso, a *pp di* **illudere.**

illu'sorio, a *ag* illusory.

illus'trare *vt* to illustrate.

illustra'tivo, a *ag* illustrative.

illustrazi'one [illustrat'tsjone] *sf* illustration.

il'lustre *ag* eminent, renowned.

illus'trissimo, a *ag* (*negli indirizzi*) very revered.

'ILOR *sigla f vedi* **imposta locale sui redditi.**

IM *sigla* = *Imperia.*

imbacuc'care *vt*, **~rsi** *vr* to wrap up.

imbaldan'zire [imbaldan'tsire] *vt* to give confidence to; **~rsi** *vr* to grow bold.

imbal'laggio [imbal'laddʒo] *sm* packing *q*.

imbal'lare *vt* to pack; (*AUT*) to race; **~rsi** *vr* (*AUT*) to race.

imbalsa'mare *vt* to embalm.

imbambo'lato, a *ag* (*sguardo, espressione*) vacant, blank.

imban'dire *vt*: **~ un banchetto** to prepare a lavish feast.

imban'dito, a *ag*: **tavola ~a** lavishly o sumptuously decked table.

imbaraz'zante [imbarat'tsante] *ag* embarrassing, awkward.

imbaraz'zare [imbarat'tsare] *vt* (*mettere a disagio*) to embarrass; (*ostacolare: movimenti*) to hamper; (: *stomaco*) to lie heavily on; **~rsi** *vr* to become embarrassed.

imbaraz'zato, a [imbarat'tsato] *ag* embarrassed; **avere lo stomaco ~** to have an upset stomach.

imba'razzo [imba'rattso] *sm* (*disagio*) embarrassment; (*perplessità*) puzzlement, bewilderment; **essere o trovarsi in ~** to be in an awkward situation o predicament; **mettere in ~** to embarrass; **~ di stomaco** indigestion.

imbarca'dero *sm* landing stage.

imbar'care *vt* (*passeggeri*) to embark; (*merci*) to load; **~rsi** *vr*: **~rsi su** to board; **~rsi per l'America** to sail for America; **~rsi in** (*fig: affare*) to embark on.

imbarcazi'one [imbarkat'tsjone] *sf* (small) boat, (small) craft *inv*; **~ di salvataggio** lifeboat.

im'barco, chi *sm* embarkation; loading; boarding; (*banchina*) landing stage; **carta d'~** boarding pass (*Brit*), boarding card.

imbastar'dire *vt* to bastardize, debase; **~rsi** *vr* to degenerate, become debased.

imbas'tire *vt* (*cucire*) to tack; (*fig: abbozzare*) to sketch, outline.

im'battersi *vr*: **~ in** (*incontrare*) to bump o run into.

imbat'tibile *ag* unbeatable, invincible.

imbavagli'are [imbavaʎ'ʎare] *vt* to gag.

imbec'care *vt* (*uccelli*) to feed; (*fig*) to prompt, put words into sb's mouth.

imbec'cata *sf* (*TEATRO*) prompt; **dare l'~ a qn** to prompt sb; (*fig*) to give sb their cue.

imbe'cille [imbe'tʃille] *ag* idiotic ♦ *sm/f* idiot; (*MED*) imbecile.

imbecillità [imbetʃilli'ta] *sf inv* (*MED, fig*) imbecility, idiocy; **dire ~** to talk nonsense.

imbellet'tare *vt* (*viso*) to make up, put make-up on; **~rsi** *vr* to make o.s. up, put on one's make-up.

imbel'lire *vt* to adorn, embellish ♦ *vi* to grow more beautiful.

im'berbe *ag* beardless; **un giovanotto ~** a callow youth.

imbestia'lire *vt* to infuriate; **~rsi** *vr* to become infuriated, fly into a rage.

im'bevere *vt* to soak; **~rsi** *vr*: **~rsi di** to soak up, absorb.

imbian'care *vt* to whiten; (*muro*) to whitewash ♦ *vi* to become o turn white.

imbianca'tura *sf* (*di muro: con bianco di calce*) whitewashing; (: *con altre pitture*) painting.

imbian'chino [imbjan'kino] *sm* (house) painter, painter and decorator.

imbion'dire *vt* (*capelli*) to lighten; (*CUC: cipolla*) to brown; **~rsi** *vr* (*capelli*) to lighten, go blonde, go fair; (*messi*) to turn golden, ripen.

imbizzar'rirsi [imbiddzar'rirsi] *vr* (*cavallo*) to become frisky.

imboc'care *vt* (*bambino*) to feed; (*entrare: strada*) to enter, turn into ♦ *vi*: **~ in** (*sog: strada*) to lead into; (: *fiume*) to flow into.

imbocca'tura *sf* mouth; (*di strada, porto*) entrance; (*MUS, del morso*) mouthpiece.

im'bocco, chi *sm* entrance.

imboni'tore *sm* (*di spettacolo, circo*) barker.

imborghe'sirsi [imborge'zirsi] *vr* to become bourgeois.

imbos'care *vt* to hide; **~rsi** *vr* (*MIL*) to evade military service.

imbos'cata *sf* ambush.

imbos'cato *sm* draft dodger (*US*).

imboschi'mento [imboski'mento] *sm* afforestation.

imbottigli'are [imbottiʎ'ʎare] *vt* to bottle; (*NAUT*) to blockade; (*MIL*) to hem in; **~rsi** *vr* to be stuck in a traffic jam.

imbot'tire *vt* to stuff; (*giacca*) to pad; **~rsi** *vr*: **~rsi di** (*rimpinzarsi*) to stuff o.s. with.

imbot'tito, a *ag* (*sedia*) upholstered; (*giacca*) padded ♦ *sf* quilt.

imbotti'tura *sf* stuffing; padding.

imbracci'are [imbrat'tʃare] *vt* (*fucile*) to

shoulder; (*scudo*) to grasp.

imbra'nato, a *ag* clumsy, awkward ♦ *sm/f* clumsy person.

imbratta'carte *sm/f* (*peg*) scribbler.

imbrat'tare *vt* to dirty, smear, daub; **~rsi** *vr*: **~rsi (di)** to dirty o.s. (with).

imbratta'tele *sm/f* (*peg*) dauber.

imbrigli'are [imbriʎ'ʎare] *vt* to bridle.

imbroc'care *vt* (*fig*) to guess correctly.

imbrogli'are [imbroʎ'ʎare] *vt* to mix up; (*fig: raggirare*) to deceive, cheat; (: *confondere*) to confuse, mix up; **~rsi** *vr* to get tangled; (*fig*) to become confused.

im'broglio [im'brɔʎʎo] *sm* (*groviglio*) tangle; (*situazione confusa*) mess; (*truffa*) swindle, trick.

imbrogli'one, a [imbroʎ'ʎone] *sm/f* cheat, swindler.

imbronci'are [imbron'tʃare] *vi* (*anche*: **~rsi**) to sulk.

imbronci'ato, a [imbron'tʃato] *ag* (*persona*) sulky; (*cielo*) cloudy, threatening.

imbru'nire *vi*, *vb impers* to grow dark; **all'~** at dusk.

imbrut'tire *vt* to make ugly ♦ *vi* to become ugly.

imbu'care *vt* to post.

imbur'rare *vt* to butter.

imbuti'forme *ag* funnel-shaped.

im'buto *sm* funnel.

i'mene *sm* hymen.

imi'tare *vt* to imitate; (*riprodurre*) to copy; (*assomigliare*) to look like.

imita'tore, 'trice *sm/f* (*gen*) imitator; (*TEATRO*) impersonator, impressionist.

imitazi'one [imitat'tsjone] *sf* imitation.

immaco'lato, a *ag* spotless; immaculate.

immagazzi'nare [immagaddzi'nare] *vt* to store.

immagi'nabile [immadʒi'nabile] *ag* imaginable.

immagi'nare [immadʒi'nare] *vt* to imagine; (*supporre*) to suppose; (*inventare*) to invent; **s'immagini!** don't mention it!, not at all!

immagi'nario, a [immadʒi'narjo] *ag* imaginary.

immagina'tiva [immadʒina'tiva] *sf* imagination.

immaginazi'one [immadʒinat'tsjone] *sf* imagination; (*cosa immaginata*) fancy.

im'magine [im'madʒine] *sf* image; (*rappresentazione grafica, mentale*) picture.

immagi'noso, a [immadʒi'noso] *ag* (*linguaggio, stile*) fantastic.

immalinco'nire *vt* to sadden, depress; **~rsi** *vr* to become depressed, become melancholy.

imman'cabile *ag* unfailing.

immancabil'mente *av* without fail, unfailingly.

imma'nente *ag* (*FILOSOFIA*) inherent,

immanent.

immangi'abile [imman'dʒabile] *ag* inedible.

immatrico'lare *vt* to register; **~rsi** *vr* (*INS*) to matriculate, enrol.

immatricolazi'one [immatrikolat'tsjone] *sf* registration; matriculation, enrolment.

immaturità *sf* immaturity.

imma'turo, a *ag* (*frutto*) unripe; (*persona*) immature; (*prematuro*) premature.

immedesi'marsi *vr*: **~ in** to identify with.

immediata'mente *av* immediately, at once.

immedia'tezza [immedja'tettsa] *sf* immediacy.

immedi'ato, a *ag* immediate.

immemo'rabile *ag* immemorial; **da tempo ~** from time immemorial.

im'memore *ag*: **~ di** forgetful of.

immensità *sf* immensity.

im'menso, a *ag* immense.

im'mergere [im'mɛrdʒere] *vt* to immerse, plunge; **~rsi** *vr* to plunge; (*sommergibile*) to dive, submerge; (*dedicarsi a*): **~rsi in** to immerse o.s. in.

immeri'tato, a *ag* undeserved.

immeri'tevole *ag* undeserving, unworthy.

immersi'one *sf* immersion; (*di sommergibile*) submersion, dive; (*di palombaro*) dive; **linea di ~** (*NAUT*) water line.

im'merso, a *pp di* **immergere**.

im'messo, a *pp di* **immettere**.

im'mettere *vt*: **~ (in)** to introduce (into); **~ dati in un computer** to enter data on a computer.

immi'grante *ag*, *sm/f* immigrant.

immi'grare *vi* to immigrate.

immi'grato, a *sm/f* immigrant.

immigrazi'one [immigrat'tsjone] *sf* immigration.

immi'nente *ag* imminent.

immi'nenza [immi'nɛntsa] *sf* imminence.

immischi'are [immis'kjare] *vt*: **~ qn in** to involve sb in; **~rsi** *vr*: **~rsi in** to interfere *o* meddle in.

immiseri'mento *sm* impoverishment.

immis'sario *sm* (*GEO*) affluent, tributary.

immissi'one *sf* (*gen*) introduction; (*di aria, gas*) intake; **~ di dati** (*INFORM*) data entry.

im'mobile *ag* motionless, still; (**beni**) **~i** *smpl* real estate *sg*.

immobili'are *ag* (*DIR*) property *cpd*; **patrimonio ~** real estate; **società ~** property company.

immobi'lismo *sm* inertia.

immobilità *sf* immobility.

immobiliz'zare [immobilid'dzare] *vt* to immobilize; (*ECON*) to lock up.

immobi'lizzo [immobi'liddzo] *sm*: **spese d'~** capital expenditure.

immo'destia *sf* immodesty.

immo'desto, a *ag* immodest.

immo'lare *vt* to sacrifice.

immondez'zaio [immondet'tsajo] *sm* rubbish dump.

immon'dizia [immon'dittsja] *sf* dirt, filth; (*spesso al pl: spazzatura, rifiuti*) rubbish *q*, refuse *q*.

im'mondo, a *ag* filthy, foul.

immo'rale *ag* immoral.

immoralità *sf* immorality.

immorta'lare *vt* to immortalize.

immor'tale *ag* immortal.

immortalità *sf* immortality.

im'mune *ag* (*esente*) exempt; (*MED, DIR*) immune.

immunità *sf* immunity; ~ **parlamentare** parliamentary privilege.

immuniz'zare [immunid'dzare] *vt* (*MED*) to immunize.

immunizzazi'one [immuniddzat'tsjone] *sf* immunization.

immuno'logico, a, ci, che [immuno'lɔdʒiko] *ag* immunological.

immu'tabile *ag* immutable; unchanging.

impac'care *vt* to pack.

impacchet'tare [impakket'tare] *vt* to pack up.

impacci'are [impat'tʃare] *vt* to hinder, hamper.

impacci'ato, a [impat'tʃato] *ag* awkward, clumsy; (*imbarazzato*) embarrassed.

im'paccio [im'pattʃo] *sm* obstacle; (*imbarazzo*) embarrassment; (*situazione imbarazzante*) awkward situation.

im'pacco, chi *sm* (*MED*) compress.

impadro'nirsi *vr*: ~ **di** to seize, take possession of; (*fig: apprendere a fondo*) to master.

impa'gabile *ag* priceless.

impagi'nare [impadʒi'nare] *vt* (*TIP*) to paginate, page (up).

impaginazi'one [impadʒinat'tsjone] *sf* pagination.

impagli'are [impaʎ'ʎare] *vt* to stuff (with straw).

impa'lato, a *ag* (*fig*) stiff as a board.

impalca'tura *sf* scaffolding; (*anche fig*) framework.

impalli'dire *vi* to turn pale; (*fig*) to fade.

impa'nare *vt* (*CUC*) to dip (*o* roll) in breadcrumbs, bread (*US*).

impanta'narsi *vr* to sink (in the mud); (*fig*) to get bogged down.

impape'rarsi *vr* to stumble over a word.

impappi'narsi *vr* to stammer, falter.

impa'rare *vt* to learn; **così impari!** that'll teach you!

impara'ticcio [impara'tittʃo] *sm* half-baked notions *pl*.

impareggi'abile [impared'dʒabile] *ag* incomparable.

imparen'tarsi *vr*: ~ **con** to marry into.

'impari *ag inv* (*disuguale*) unequal; (*dispari*) odd.

impar'tire *vt* to bestow, give.

imparzi'ale [impar'tsjale] *ag* impartial, unbiased.

imparzialità [impartsjali'ta] *sf* impartiality.

impas'sibile *ag* impassive.

impas'tare *vt* (*pasta*) to knead; (*colori*) to mix.

impastic'carsi *vr* to pop pills.

im'pasto *sm* (*l'impastare: di pane*) kneading; (: *di cemento*) mixing; (*pasta*) dough; (*anche fig*) mixture.

im'patto *sm* impact.

impau'rire *vt* to scare, frighten ♦ *vi* (*anche:* ~**rsi**) to become scared *o* frightened.

im'pavido, a *ag* intrepid, fearless.

impazi'ente [impat'tsjɛnte] *ag* impatient.

impazi'enza [impat'tsjɛntsa] *sf* impatience.

impaz'zata [impat'tsata] *sf*: **all'**~ (*precipitosamente*) at breakneck speed; (*colpire*) wildly.

impaz'zire [impat'tsire] *vi* to go mad; ~ **per qn/qc** to be crazy about sb/sth.

impec'cabile *ag* impeccable.

impedi'mento *sm* obstacle, hindrance.

impe'dire *vt* (*vietare*): ~ **a qn di fare** to prevent sb from doing; (*ostruire*) to obstruct; (*impacciare*) to hamper, hinder.

impe'gnare [impeɲ'ɲare] *vt* (*dare in pegno*) to pawn; (*onore etc*) to pledge; (*prenotare*) to book, reserve; (*obbligare*) to oblige; (*occupare*) to keep busy; (*MIL: nemico*) to engage; ~**rsi** *vr* (*vincolarsi*): ~**rsi a fare** to undertake to do; (*mettersi risolutamente*): ~**rsi in qc** to devote o.s. to sth; ~**rsi con qn** (*accordarsi*) to come to an agreement with sb.

impegna'tivo, a [impeɲɲa'tivo] *ag* binding; (*lavoro*) demanding, exacting.

impe'gnato, a [impeɲ'ɲato] *ag* (*occupato*) busy; (*fig: romanzo, autore*) committed, engagé.

im'pegno [im'peɲɲo] *sm* (*obbligo*) obligation; (*promessa*) promise, pledge; (*zelo*) diligence, zeal; (*compito, d'autore*) commitment; ~**i di lavoro** business commitments.

impego'larsi *vr* (*fig*): ~ **in** to get heavily involved in.

impela'garsi *vr* = **impegolarsi.**

impel'lente *ag* pressing, urgent.

impene'trabile *ag* impenetrable.

impen'narsi *vr* (*cavallo*) to rear up; (*AER*) to go into a climb; (*fig*) to bridle.

impen'nata *sf* (*di cavallo*) rearing up; (*di aereo*) climb, nose-up; (*fig: scatto d'ira*) burst of anger.

impen'sabile *ag* (*inaccettabile*) unthinkable; (*difficile da concepire*) inconceivable.

impen'sato, a *ag* unforeseen, unexpected.

impensie'rire *vt*, ~**rsi** *vr* to worry.

impe'rante *ag* prevailing.

impe'rare vi (anche fig) to reign, rule.
impera'tivo, a ag, sm imperative.
impera'tore, 'trice sm/f emperor/empress.
impercet'tibile [impertʃet'tibile] ag imperceptible.
imperdo'nabile ag unforgivable, unpardonable.
imper'fetto, a ag imperfect ♦ sm (LING) imperfect (tense).
imperfezi'one [imperfet'tsjone] sf imperfection.
imperi'ale ag imperial.
imperia'lismo sm imperialism.
imperi'oso, a ag (persona) imperious; (motivo, esigenza) urgent, pressing.
imperi'turo, a ag everlasting.
impe'rizia [impe'rittsja] sf lack of experience.
imperma'lirsi vr to take offence.
imperme'abile ag waterproof ♦ sm raincoat.
imperni'are vt: ~ qc su to hinge sth on; (fig: discorso, relazione etc) to base sth on; ~rsi vr (fig): ~rsi su to be based on.
im'pero sm empire; (forza, autorità) rule, control.
imperscru'tabile ag inscrutable.
imperso'nale ag impersonal.
imperso'nare vt to personify; (TEATRO) to play, act (the part of); ~rsi vr: ~rsi in un ruolo to get into a part, live a part.
imper'territo, a ag unperturbed.
imperti'nente ag impertinent.
imperti'nenza [imperti'nɛntsa] sf impertinence.
impertur'babile ag imperturbable.
imperver'sare vi to rage.
im'pervio, a ag (luogo) inaccessible; (strada) impassable.
'impeto sm (moto, forza) force, impetus; (assalto) onslaught; (fig: impulso) impulse; (: slancio) transport; **con ~** (parlare) forcefully, energetically.
impe'trare vt to beg for, beseech.
impet'tito, a ag stiff, erect; **camminare ~** to strut.
impetu'oso, a ag (vento) strong, raging; (persona) impetuous.
impian'tare vt (motore) to install; (azienda, discussione) to establish, start.
impian'tistica sf plant design and installation.
impi'anto sm (installazione) installation; (apparecchiature) plant; (sistema) system; **~ elettrico** wiring; **~ sportivo** sports complex; **~i di risalita** (SCI) ski lifts.
impias'trare, impiastricci'are [impjastrit-'tʃare] vt to smear, dirty.
impi'astro sm poultice; (fig fam: persona) nuisance.
impiccagi'one [impikka'dʒone] sf hanging.
impic'care vt to hang; ~rsi vr to hang o.s.
impicci'are [impit'tʃare] vt to hinder, hamper; ~rsi vr to meddle, interfere; **impicciati degli affari tuoi!** mind your own business!
im'piccio [im'pittʃo] sm (ostacolo) hindrance; (seccatura) trouble, bother; (affare imbrogliato) mess; **essere d'~** to be in the way; **cavare o togliere qn dagli ~i** to get sb out of trouble.
impicci'one, a [impit'tʃone] sm/f busybody.
impie'gare vt (usare) to use, employ; (assumere) to employ, take on; (spendere: denaro, tempo) to spend; (investire) to invest; ~rsi vr to get a job, obtain employment; **impiego un quarto d'ora per andare a casa** it takes me o I take a quarter of an hour to get home.
impiega'tizio, a [impjega'tittsjo] ag clerical, white-collar cpd; **lavoro/ceto ~** clerical o white-collar work/workers pl.
impie'gato, a sm/f employee; **~ statale** state employee.
impi'ego, ghi sm (uso) use; (occupazione) employment; (posto di lavoro) (regular) job, post; (ECON) investment; **~ pubblico** job in the public sector.
impieto'sire vt to move to pity; ~rsi vr to be moved to pity.
impie'toso, a ag pitiless, cruel.
impie'trire vt (anche fig) to petrify.
impigli'are [impiʎ'ʎare] vt to catch, entangle; ~rsi vr to get caught up o entangled.
impi'grire vt to make lazy ♦ vi (anche: ~rsi) to grow lazy.
impingu'are vt (maiale etc) to fatten; (fig: tasche, casse dello Stato) to stuff with money.
impiom'bare vt (pacco) to seal (with lead); (dente) to fill.
impla'cabile ag implacable.
impli'care vt to imply; (coinvolgere) to involve; ~rsi vr: ~rsi (in) to become involved (in).
implicazi'one [implikat'tsjone] sf implication.
im'plicito, a [im'plitʃito] ag implicit.
implo'rare vt to implore.
impolve'rare vt to cover with dust; ~rsi vr to get dusty.
impoma'tare vt (pelle) to put ointment on; (capelli) to pomade; (baffi) to wax; ~rsi vr (fam) to get spruced up.
im'pone etc vb vedi **imporre**.
impo'nente ag imposing, impressive.
im'pongo etc vb vedi **imporre**.
impo'nibile ag taxable ♦ sm taxable income.
impopo'lare ag unpopular.
impopolarità sf unpopularity.
im'porre vt to impose; (costringere) to force, make; (far valere) to impose, enforce; **imporsi** vr (persona) to assert o.s.; (cosa: rendersi necessario) to become

necessary; (*aver successo*: *moda, attore*) to become popular; ~ **a qn di fare** to force sb to do, make sb do.

impor'tante *ag* important.

impor'tanza [impor'tantsa] *sf* importance; **dare** ~ **a qc** to attach importance to sth; **darsi** ~ to give o.s. airs.

impor'tare *vt* (*introdurre dall'estero*) to import ♦ *vi* to matter, be important ♦ *vb impers* (*essere necessario*) to be necessary; (*interessare*) to matter; **non importa!** it doesn't matter!; **non me ne importa!** I don't care!

importa'tore, 'trice *ag* importing ♦ *sm/f* importer.

importazi'one [importat'tsjone] *sf* importation; (*merci importate*) imports *pl*.

im'porto *sm* (total) amount.

importu'nare *vt* to bother.

impor'tuno, a *ag* irksome, annoying.

im'posi *etc vb vedi* **imporre.**

imposizi'one [impozit'tsjone] *sf* imposition; (*ordine*) order, command; (*onere, imposta*) tax.

imposses'sarsi *vr*: ~ **di** to seize, take possession of.

impos'sibile *ag* impossible; **fare l'**~ to do one's utmost, do all one can.

impossibilità *sf* impossibility; **essere nell'**~ **di fare qc** to be unable to do sth.

impossibili'tato, a *ag*: **essere** ~ **a fare qc** to be unable to do sth.

im'posta *sf* (*di finestra*) shutter; (*tassa*) tax; ~ **indiretta sui consumi** excise duty *o* tax; ~ **locale sui redditi** (**ILOR**) tax on unearned income; ~ **patrimoniale** property tax; ~ **sul reddito** income tax; ~ **sul reddito delle persone fisiche** (**IRPEF**) personal income tax; ~ **di successione** capital transfer tax (*Brit*), inheritance tax (*US*); ~ **sugli utili** tax on profits; ~ **sul valore aggiunto** (**I.V.A.**) value added tax (VAT) (*Brit*), sales tax (*US*).

impos'tare *vt* (*imbucare*) to post; (*servizio, organizzazione*) to set up; (*lavoro*) to organize, plan; (*resoconto, rapporto*) to plan; (*problema*) to set out, formulate; (*TIP*: *pagina*) to lay out; ~ **la voce** (*MUS*) to pitch one's voice.

impostazi'one [impostat'tsjone] *sf* (*di lettera*) posting (*Brit*), mailing (*US*); (*di problema, questione*) formulation, statement; (*di lavoro*) organization, planning; (*di attività*) setting up; (*MUS*: *di voce*) pitch.

im'posto, a *pp di* **imporre.**

impos'tore, a *sm/f* impostor.

impo'tente *ag* weak, powerless; (*anche MED*) impotent.

impo'tenza [impo'tɛntsa] *sf* weakness, powerlessness; impotence.

impove'rire *vt* to impoverish ♦ *vi* (*anche*: ~**rsi**) to become poor.

imprati'cabile *ag* (*strada*) impassable; (*campo da gioco*) unplayable.

imprati'chire [imprati'kire] *vt* to train; ~**rsi** *vr*: ~**rsi in qc** to practise (*Brit*) *o* practice (*US*) sth.

impre'care *vi* to curse, swear; ~ **contro** to hurl abuse at.

impreci'sato, a [impretʃi'zato] *ag* (*non preciso*: *quantità, numero*) indeterminate.

imprecisi'one [impretʃi'zjone] *sf* imprecision; inaccuracy.

impre'ciso, a [impre'tʃizo] *ag* imprecise, vague; (*calcolo*) inaccurate.

impre'gnare [impreɲ'ɲare] *vt*: ~ **(di)** (*imbevere*) to soak *o* impregnate (with); (*riempire*: *anche fig*) to fill (with).

imprendi'tore *sm* (*industriale*) entrepreneur; (*appaltatore*) contractor; **piccolo** ~ small businessman.

imprendito'ria *sf* enterprise; (*imprenditori*) entrepreneurs *pl*.

imprenditori'ale *ag* (*ceto, classe*) entrepreneurial.

imprepa'rato, a *ag*: ~ **(a)** (*gen*) unprepared (for); (*lavoratore*) untrained (for); **cogliere qn** ~ to catch sb unawares.

impreparazi'one [impreparat'tsjone] *sf* lack of preparation.

im'presa *sf* (*iniziativa*) enterprise; (*azione*) exploit; (*azienda*) firm, concern; ~ **familiare** family firm; ~ **pubblica** state-owned enterprise.

impre'sario *sm* (*TEATRO*) manager, impresario; ~ **di pompe funebri** funeral director.

imprescin'dibile [impreʃʃin'dibile] *ag* not to be ignored.

im'pressi *etc vb vedi* **imprimere.**

impressio'nante *ag* impressive; upsetting.

impressio'nare *vt* to impress; (*turbare*) to upset; (*FOT*) to expose; ~**rsi** *vr* to be easily upset.

impressi'one *sf* impression; (*fig*: *sensazione*) sensation, feeling; (*stampa*) printing; **fare** ~ (*colpire*) to impress; (*turbare*) to frighten, upset; **fare buona/cattiva** ~ **a** to make a good/bad impression on.

im'presso, a *pp di* **imprimere.**

impres'tare *vt*: ~ **qc a qn** to lend sth to sb.

impreve'dibile *ag* unforeseeable; (*persona*) unpredictable.

imprevi'dente *ag* lacking in foresight.

imprevi'denza [imprevi'dɛntsa] *sf* lack of foresight.

impre'visto, a *ag* unexpected, unforeseen ♦ *sm* unforeseen event; **salvo** ~**i** unless anything unexpected happens.

imprezio'sire [imprettsjo'sire] *vt*: ~ **di** to embellish with.

imprigiona'mento [impridʒona'mento] *sm* imprisonment.

imprigio'nare [imprid3o'nare] *vt* to imprison.

im'primere *vt* (*anche fig*) to impress, stamp; (*comunicare: movimento*) to transmit, give.

impro'babile *ag* improbable, unlikely.

'improbo, a *ag* (*fatica, lavoro*) hard, laborious.

im'pronta *sf* imprint, impression, sign; (*di piede, mano*) print; (*fig*) mark, stamp; ~ **digitale** fingerprint.

impro'perio *sm* insult.

impropo'nibile *ag* which cannot be proposed *o* suggested.

im'proprio, a *ag* improper; **arma** ~**a** offensive weapon.

improro'gabile *ag* (*termine*) that cannot be extended.

improvvisa'mente *av* suddenly; unexpectedly.

improvvi'sare *vt* to improvise; ~**rsi** *vr*: ~**rsi cuoco** to (decide to) act as cook.

improvvi'sata *sf* (pleasant) surprise.

improvvisazi'one [improvvizat'tsjone] *sf* improvisation; **spirito d'**~ spirit of invention.

improv'viso, a *ag* (*imprevisto*) unexpected; (*subitaneo*) sudden; **all'**~ unexpectedly; suddenly.

impru'dente *ag* foolish, imprudent; (*osservazione*) unwise.

impru'denza [impru'dɛntsa] *sf* foolishness, imprudence; **è stata un'**~ that was a foolish *o* an imprudent thing to do.

impu'dente *ag* impudent.

impu'denza [impu'dɛntsa] *sf* impudence.

impudi'cizia [impudi'tʃittsja] *sf* immodesty.

impu'dico, a, chi, che *ag* immodest.

impu'gnare [impuɲ'ɲare] *vt* to grasp, grip; (*DIR*) to contest.

impugna'tura [impuɲɲa'tura] *sf* grip, grasp; (*manico*) handle; (: *di spada*) hilt.

impulsività *sf* impulsiveness.

impul'sivo, a *ag* impulsive.

im'pulso *sm* impulse; **dare un** ~ **alle vendite** to boost sales.

impune'mente *av* with impunity.

impunità *sf* impunity.

impu'nito, a *ag* unpunished.

impun'tarsi *vr* to stop dead, refuse to budge; (*fig*) to be obstinate.

impurità *sf inv* impurity.

im'puro, a *ag* impure.

impu'tare *vt* (*ascrivere*): ~ **qc a** to attribute sth to; (*DIR: accusare*): ~ **qn di** to charge sb with, accuse sb of.

impu'tato, a *sm/f* (*DIR*) accused, defendant.

imputazi'one [imputat'tsjone] *sf* (*DIR*) charge; (*di spese*) allocation.

imputri'dire *vi* to rot.

in *prep* (*in + il* = **nel**, *in + lo* = **nello**, *in + l'* = **nell'**, *in + la* = **nella**, *in + i* = **nei**,

in + gli = **negli**, *in + le* = **nelle**) in; (*moto a luogo*) to; (: *dentro*) into; (*mezzo*): ~ **autobus/treno** by bus/train; (*composizione*): ~ **marmo** made of marble, marble *cpd*; **essere** ~ **casa** to be at home; **andare** ~ **Austria** to go to Austria; **Maria Bianchi** ~ **Rossi** Maria Rossi née Bianchi; **siamo** ~ **quattro** there are four of us.

i'nabile *ag*: ~ **a** incapable of; (*fisicamente, MIL*) unfit for.

inabilità *sf*: ~ **(a)** unfitness (for).

inabi'tabile *ag* uninhabitable.

inabi'tato, a *ag* uninhabited.

inacces'sibile [inattʃes'sibile] *ag* (*luogo*) inaccessible; (*persona*) unapproachable; (*mistero*) unfathomable.

inaccet'tabile [inattʃet'tabile] *ag* unacceptable.

inacer'bire [inatʃer'bire] *vt* to exacerbate; ~**rsi** *vr* (*persona*) to become embittered.

inaci'dire [inatʃi'dire] *vt* (*persona, carattere*) to embitter; ~**rsi** *vr* (*latte*) to go sour; (*fig: persona, carattere*) to become sour, become embittered.

ina'datto, a *ag*: ~ **(a)** unsuitable *o* unfit (for).

inadegu'ato, a *ag* inadequate.

inadempi'ente *ag* defaulting ♦ *sm/f* defaulter.

inadempi'enza [inadem'pjɛntsa] *sf*: ~ **a un contratto** non-fulfilment of a contract; **dovuto alle** ~**e dei funzionari** due to negligence on the part of the officials.

inadempi'mento *sm* non-fulfilment.

inaffer'rabile *ag* elusive; (*concetto, senso*) difficult to grasp.

'INAIL *sigla m* (= *Istituto Nazionale per l'Assicurazione contro gli Infortuni sul Lavoro*) state body providing sickness benefit in the event of accidents at work.

ina'lare *vt* to inhale.

inala'tore *sm* inhaler.

inalazi'one [inalat'tsjone] *sf* inhalation.

inalbe'rare *vt* (*NAUT*) to hoist; raise; ~**rsi** *vr* (*fig*) to flare up, fly off the handle.

inalte'rabile *ag* unchangeable; (*colore*) fast, permanent; (*affetto*) constant.

inalte'rato, a *ag* unchanged.

inami'dare *vt* to starch.

inami'dato, a *ag* starched.

inammis'sibile *ag* inadmissible.

inani'mato, a *ag* inanimate; (*senza vita: corpo*) lifeless.

inappa'gabile *ag* insatiable.

inappel'labile *ag* (*decisione*) final, irrevocable; (*DIR*) final, not open to appeal.

inappe'tenza [inappe'tɛntsa] *sf* (*MED*) lack of appetite.

inappun'tabile *ag* irreproachable, flawless.

inar'care *vt* (*schiena*) to arch; (*sopracciglia*) to raise; ~**rsi** *vr* to arch.

inaridi'mento *sm* (*anche fig*) drying up.

inari'dire *vt* to make arid, dry up ♦ *vi* (*anche:* ~**rsi**) to dry up, become arid.

inarres'tabile *ag* (*processo*) irreversible; (*emorragia*) that cannot be stemmed; (*corsa del tempo*) relentless.

inascol'tato, a *ag* unheeded, unheard.

inaspettata'mente *av* unexpectedly.

inaspet'tato, a *ag* unexpected.

inas'prire *vt* (*disciplina*) to tighten up, make harsher; (*carattere*) to embitter; (*rapporti*) to make worse; ~**rsi** *vr* to become harsher; to become bitter; to become worse.

inattac'cabile *ag* (*anche fig*) unassailable; (*alibi*) cast-iron.

inatten'dibile *ag* unreliable.

inat'teso, a *ag* unexpected.

inat'tivo, a *ag* inactive, idle; (*CHIM*) inactive.

inattu'abile *ag* impracticable.

inau'dito, a *ag* unheard of.

inaugu'rale *ag* inaugural.

inaugu'rare *vt* to inaugurate, open; (*monumento*) to unveil.

inaugurazi'one [inaugurat'tsjone] *sf* inauguration; unveiling.

inavve'duto, a *ag* careless, inadvertent.

inavver'tenza [inavver'tɛntsa] *sf* carelessness, inadvertence.

inavvertita'mente *av* inadvertently, unintentionally.

inavvici'nabile [inavvitʃi'nabile] *ag* unapproachable.

'Inca *ag inv, sm/f inv* Inca.

incagli'are [inkaʎ'ʎare] *vi* (*NAUT: anche:* ~**rsi**) to run aground.

incalco'labile *ag* incalculable.

incal'lito, a *ag* calloused; (*fig*) hardened, inveterate; (: *insensibile*) hard.

incal'zante [inkal'tsante] *ag* urgent, insistent; (*crisi*) imminent.

incal'zare [inkal'tsare] *vt* to follow *o* pursue closely; (*fig*) to press ♦ *vi* (*urgere*) to be pressing; (*essere imminente*) to be imminent.

iname'rare *vt* (*DIR*) to expropriate.

incammi'nare *vt* (*fig: avviare*) to start up; ~**rsi** *vr* to set off.

incana'lare *vt* (*anche fig*) to channel; ~**rsi** *vr* (*folla*): ~**rsi verso** to converge on.

incancre'nirsi *vr* to become gangrenous.

incande'scente [inkandeʃ'ʃɛnte] *ag* incandescent, white-hot.

incan'tare *vt* to enchant, bewitch; ~**rsi** *vr* (*rimanere intontito*) to be spellbound; to be in a daze; (*meccanismo: bloccarsi*) to jam.

incanta'tore, 'trice *ag* enchanting, bewitching ♦ *sm/f* enchanter/enchantress.

incan'tesimo *sm* spell, charm.

incan'tevole *ag* charming, enchanting.

in'canto *sm* spell, charm, enchantment; (*asta*) auction; **come per** ~ as if by magic; **ti sta d'**~! (*vestito etc*) it really suits you!; **mettere all'**~ to put up for auction.

incanu'tire *vi* to go white.

inca'pace [inka'patʃe] *ag* incapable.

incapacità [inkapatʃi'ta] *sf* inability; (*DIR*) incapacity; ~ **d'intendere e di volere** diminished responsibility.

incapo'nirsi *vr* to be stubborn, be determined.

incap'pare *vi*: ~ **in qc/qn** (*anche fig*) to run into sth/sb.

incappucci'are [inkapput'tʃare] *vt* to put a hood on; ~**rsi** *vr* (*persona*) to put on a hood.

incapricci'arsi [inkaprit'tʃarsi] *vr*: ~ **di** to take a fancy to *o* for.

incapsu'lare *vt* (*dente*) to crown.

incarce'rare [inkartʃe'rare] *vt* to imprison.

incari'care *vt*: ~ **qn di fare** to give sb the responsibility of doing; ~**rsi** *vr*: ~**rsi di** to take care *o* charge of.

incari'cato, a *ag*: ~ (**di**) in charge (of), responsible (for) ♦ *sm/f* delegate, representative; **docente** ~ (*di università*) lecturer without tenure; ~ **d'affari** (*POL*) chargé d'affaires.

in'carico, chi *sm* task, job; (*INS*) temporary post.

incar'nare *vt* to embody; ~**rsi** *vr* to be embodied; (*REL*) to become incarnate.

incarnazi'one [inkarnat'tsjone] *sf* incarnation; (*fig*) embodiment.

incarta'mento *sm* dossier, file.

incartapeco'rito, a *ag* (*pelle*) wizened, shrivelled (*Brit*), shriveled (*US*).

incar'tare *vt* to wrap (in paper).

incasel'lare *vt* (*posta*) to sort; (*fig: nozioni*) to pigeonhole.

incas'sare *vt* (*merce*) to pack (in cases); (*gemma: incastonare*) to set; (*ECON: riscuotere*) to collect; (*PUGILATO: colpi*) to take, stand up to.

in'casso *sm* cashing, encashment; (*introito*) takings *pl*.

incasto'nare *vt* to set.

incastona'tura *sf* setting.

incas'trare *vt* to fit in, insert; (*fig: intrappolare*) to catch; ~**rsi** *vr* (*combaciare*) to fit together; (*restare bloccato*) to become stuck.

in'castro *sm* slot, groove; (*punto di unione*) joint; **gioco a** ~ interlocking puzzle.

incate'nare *vt* to chain up.

incatra'mare *vt* to tar.

incatti'vire *vt* to make wicked; ~**rsi** *vr* to turn nasty.

in'cauto, a *ag* imprudent, rash.

inca'vare *vt* to hollow out.

inca'vato, a *ag* hollow; (*occhi*) sunken.

in'cavo *sm* hollow; (*solco*) groove.

incavo'larsi *vr* (*fam*) to lose one's temper,

get annoyed.

incaz'zarsi [inkat'tsarsi] *vr* (*fam!*) to get steamed up.

in'cedere [in'tʃedere] *vi* (*poetico*) to advance solemnly ♦ *sm* solemn gait.

incendi'are [intʃen'djare] *vt* to set fire to; ~**rsi** *vr* to catch fire, burst into flames.

incendi'ario, a [intʃen'djarjo] *ag* incendiary ♦ *sm/f* arsonist.

in'cendio [in'tʃendjo] *sm* fire.

incene'rire [intʃene'rire] *vt* to burn to ashes, incinerate; (*cadavere*) to cremate; ~**rsi** *vr* to be burnt to ashes.

inceneri'tore [intʃeneri'tore] *sm* incinerator.

in'censo [in'tʃenso] *sm* incense.

incensu'rato, a [intʃensu'rato] *ag* (*DIR*): **essere** ~ to have a clean record.

incenti'vare [intʃenti'vare] *vt* (*produzione, vendite*) to boost; (*persona*) to motivate.

incen'tivo [intʃen'tivo] *sm* incentive.

incen'trarsi [intʃen'trarsi] *vr*: ~ **su** (*fig*) to centre (*Brit*) *o* center (*US*) on.

incep'pare [intʃep'pare] *vt* to obstruct, hamper; ~**rsi** *vr* to jam.

ince'rata [intʃe'rata] *sf* (*tela*) tarpaulin; (*impermeabile*) oilskins *pl*.

incer'tezza [intʃer'tettsa] *sf* uncertainty.

in'certo, a [in'tʃerto] *ag* uncertain; (*irresoluto*) undecided, hesitating ♦ *sm* uncertainty; **gli** ~**i del mestiere** the risks of the job.

incespi'care [intʃespi'kare] *vi*: ~ (**in qc**) to trip (over sth).

inces'sante [intʃes'sante] *ag* incessant.

in'cesto [in'tʃesto] *sm* incest.

in'cetta [in'tʃetta] *sf* buying up; **fare** ~ **di qc** to buy up sth.

inchi'esta [in'kjesta] *sf* investigation, inquiry.

inchi'nare [inki'nare] *vt* to bow; ~**rsi** *vr* to bend down; (*per riverenza*) to bow; (: *donna*) to curtsy.

in'chino [in'kino] *sm* bow; curtsy.

inchio'dare [inkjo'dare] *vt* to nail (down); ~ **la macchina** (*AUT*) to jam on the brakes.

inchi'ostro [in'kjɔstro] *sm* ink; ~ **simpatico** invisible ink.

inciam'pare [intʃam'pare] *vi* to trip, stumble.

inci'ampo [in'tʃampo] *sm* obstacle; **essere d'**~ **a qn** (*fig*) to be in sb's way.

inciden'tale [intʃiden'tale] *ag* incidental.

incidental'mente [intʃidental'mente] *av* (*per caso*) by chance; (*per inciso*) incidentally, by the way.

inci'dente [intʃi'dɛnte] *sm* accident; (*episodio*) incident; **e con questo l'**~ **è chiuso** and that is the end of the matter; ~ **d'auto** car accident; ~ **diplomatico** diplomatic incident.

inci'denza [intʃi'dɛntsa] *sf* incidence; **avere una forte** ~ **su qc** to affect sth greatly.

in'cidere [in'tʃidere] *vi*: ~ **su** to bear upon,

affect ♦ *vt* (*tagliare incavando*) to cut into; (*ARTE*) to engrave; to etch; (*canzone*) to record.

in'cinta [in'tʃinta] *ag f* pregnant.

incipi'ente [intʃi'pjente] *ag* incipient.

incipri'are [intʃi'prjare] *vt* to powder.

in'circa [in'tʃirka] *av*: **all'**~ more or less, very nearly.

in'cisi *etc* [in'tʃizi] *vb vedi* **incidere**.

incisi'one [intʃi'zjone] *sf* cut; (*disegno*) engraving; etching; (*registrazione*) recording; (*MED*) incision.

inci'sivo, a [intʃi'zivo] *ag* incisive; (*ANAT*): (**dente**) ~ incisor.

in'ciso, a [in'tʃizo] *pp di* **incidere** ♦ *sm*: **per** ~ incidentally, by the way.

inci'sore [intʃi'zore] *sm* (*ARTE*) engraver.

incita'mento [intʃita'mento] *sm* incitement.

inci'tare [intʃi'tare] *vt* to incite.

inci'vile [intʃi'vile] *ag* uncivilized; (*villano*) impolite.

incivi'lire [intʃivi'lire] *vt* to civilize.

inciviltà [intʃivil'ta] *sf* (*di popolazione*) barbarism; (*fig*: *di trattamento*) barbarity; (: *maleducazione*) incivility, rudeness.

incl. *abbr* (= *incluso*) encl.

incle'mente *ag* (*giudice, sentenza*) severe, harsh; (*fig*: *clima*) harsh; (: *tempo*) inclement.

incle'menza [inkle'mentsa] *sf* severity; harshness; inclemency.

incli'nabile *ag* (*schienale*) reclinable.

incli'nare *vt* to tilt ♦ *vi* (*fig*): ~ **a qc/a fare** to incline towards sth/doing; to tend towards sth/to do; ~**rsi** *vr* (*barca*) to list; (*aereo*) to bank.

incli'nato, a *ag* sloping.

inclinazi'one [inklinat'tsjone] *sf* slope; (*fig*) inclination, tendency.

in'cline *ag*: ~ **a** inclined to.

in'cludere *vt* to include; (*accludere*) to enclose.

inclusi'one *sf* inclusion.

inclu'sivo, a *ag*: ~ **di** inclusive of.

in'cluso, a *pp di* **includere** ♦ *ag* included; enclosed.

incoe'rente *ag* incoherent; (*contraddittorio*) inconsistent.

incoe'renza [inkoe'rentsa] *sf* incoherence; inconsistency.

in'cognito, a [in'kɔɲɲito] *ag* unknown ♦ *sm*: **in** ~ incognito ♦ *sf* (*MAT, fig*) unknown quantity.

incol'lare *vt* to glue, gum; (*unire con colla*) to stick together; ~ **gli occhi addosso a qn** (*fig*) to fix one's eyes on sb.

incolla'tura *sf* (*IPPICA*): **vincere/perdere di un'**~ to win/lose by a head.

incolon'nare *vt* to draw up in columns.

inco'lore *ag* colourless (*Brit*), colorless (*US*).

incol'pare *vt*: ~ **qn di** to charge sb with.

in'colto, a ag (terreno) uncultivated; (trascurato: capelli) neglected; (persona) uneducated.

in'colume ag safe and sound, unhurt.

incolumità sf safety.

incom'bente ag (pericolo) imminent, impending.

incom'benza [inkom'bɛntsa] sf duty, task.

in'combere vi (sovrastare minacciando): ~ su to threaten, hang over.

incominci'are [inkomin'tʃare] vi, vt to begin, start.

incomo'dare vt to trouble, inconvenience; ~rsi vr to put o.s. out.

in'comodo, a ag uncomfortable; (inopportuno) inconvenient ♦ sm inconvenience, bother.

incompa'tibile ag incompatible.

incompatibilità sf incompatibility; ~ di carattere (mutual) incompatibility.

incompe'tente ag incompetent.

incompe'tenza [inkompe'tɛntsa] sf incompetence.

incompi'uto, a ag unfinished, incomplete.

incom'pleto, a ag incomplete.

incompren'sibile ag incomprehensible.

incomprensi'one sf incomprehension.

incom'preso, a ag not understood; misunderstood.

inconce'pibile [inkontʃe'pibile] ag inconceivable.

inconcili'abile [inkontʃi'ljabile] ag irreconcilable.

inconclu'dente ag inconclusive; (persona) ineffectual.

incondizio'nato, a [inkondittsjo'nato] ag unconditional.

inconfes'sabile ag (pensiero, peccato) unmentionable.

inconfon'dibile ag unmistakable.

inconfu'tabile ag irrefutable.

incongru'ente ag inconsistent.

incongru'enza [inkongru'ɛntsa] sf inconsistency.

in'congruo, a ag incongruous.

inconsa'pevole ag: ~ di unaware of, ignorant of.

inconsapevo'lezza [inkonsapevo'lettsa] sf ignorance, lack of awareness.

in'conscio, a, sci, sce [in'kɔnʃo] ag unconscious ♦ sm (PSIC): l'~ the unconscious.

inconsis'tente ag (patrimonio) insubstantial; (dubbio) unfounded; (ragionamento, prove) tenuous, flimsy.

inconsis'tenza [inkonsis'tɛntsa] sf insubstantial nature; lack of foundation; flimsiness.

inconso'labile ag inconsolable.

inconsu'eto, a ag unusual.

incon'sulto, a ag rash.

inconten'tabile ag (desiderio, avidità) insatiable; (persona: capriccioso) hard to please, very demanding.

incontes'tabile ag incontrovertible, indisputable.

inconti'nenza [inkonti'nɛntsa] sf incontinence.

incon'trare vt to meet; (difficoltà) to meet with; ~rsi vr to meet.

incon'trario av: all'~ (sottosopra) upside down; (alla rovescia) back to front; (all'indietro) backwards; (nel senso contrario) the other way round.

incontras'tabile ag incontrovertible, indisputable.

incontras'tato, a ag (successo, vittoria, verità) uncontested, undisputed.

in'contro av: ~ a (verso) towards ♦ sm meeting; (SPORT) match; meeting; (fortuito) encounter; **venire ~ a** (richieste, esigenze) to comply with; ~ di calcio football match (Brit), soccer game (US).

incontrol'labile ag uncontrollable.

inconveni'ente sm drawback, snag.

incoraggia'mento [inkoraddʒa'mento] sm encouragement; **premio d'~** consolation prize.

incoraggi'are [inkorad'dʒare] vt to encourage.

incor'nare vt to gore.

incornici'are [inkorni'tʃare] vt to frame.

incoro'nare vt to crown.

incoronazi'one [inkoronat'tsjone] sf coronation.

incorpo'rare vt to incorporate; (fig: annettere) to annex.

incorreg'gibile [inkorred'dʒibile] ag incorrigible.

in'correre vi: ~ in to meet with, run into.

incorrut'tibile ag incorruptible.

in'corso, a pp di **incorrere**.

incosci'ente [inkoʃ'ʃɛnte] ag (inconscio) unconscious; (irresponsabile) reckless, thoughtless.

incosci'enza [inkoʃ'ʃɛntsa] sf unconsciousness; recklessness, thoughtlessness.

incos'tante ag (studente, impiegato) inconsistent; (carattere) fickle, inconstant; (rendimento) sporadic.

incos'tanza [inkos'tantsa] sf inconstancy, fickleness.

incostituzio'nale [inkostituttsjo'nale] ag unconstitutional.

incre'dibile ag incredible, unbelievable.

incredulità sf incredulity.

in'credulo, a ag incredulous, disbelieving.

incremen'tare vt to increase; (dar sviluppo a) to promote.

incre'mento sm (sviluppo) development; (aumento numerico) increase, growth.

incresci'oso, a [inkreʃ'ʃoso] ag (spiacevole) unpleasant; regrettable.

incres'parsi vr (acqua) to ripple; (capelli) to go frizzy; (pelle, tessuto) to wrinkle.

incrimi'nare *vt* (*DIR*) to charge.

incriminazi'one [inkriminat'tsjone] *sf* (*atto d'accusa*) indictment, charge.

incri'nare *vt* to crack; (*fig*: *rapporti, amicizia*) to cause to deteriorate; **~rsi** *vr* to crack; to deteriorate.

incrina'tura *sf* crack; (*fig*) rift.

incroci'are [inkro'tʃare] *vt* to cross; (*incontrare*) to meet ♦ *vi* (*NAUT, AER*) to cruise; **~rsi** *vr* (*strade*) to cross, intersect; (*persone, veicoli*) to pass each other; **~ le braccia/le gambe** to fold one's arms/cross one's legs.

incrocia'tore [inkrotʃa'tore] *sm* cruiser.

in'crocio [in'krotʃo] *sm* (*anche FERR*) crossing; (*di strade*) crossroads.

incrol'labile *ag* (*fede*) unshakeable, firm.

incros'tare *vt* to encrust; **~rsi** *vr*: **~rsi di** to become encrusted with.

incrostazi'one [inkrostat'tsjone] *sf* encrustation; (*di calcare*) scale; (*nelle tubature*) fur (*Brit*), scale.

incru'ento, a *ag* (*battaglia*) without bloodshed, bloodless.

incuba'trice [inkuba'tritʃe] *sf* incubator.

incubazi'one [inkubat'tsjone] *sf* incubation.

'incubo *sm* nightmare.

in'cudine *sf* anvil; **trovarsi** *o* **essere tra l'~ e il martello** (*fig*) to be between the devil and the deep blue sea.

incul'care *vt*: **~ qc in** to inculcate sth into, instill sth into.

incune'are *vt* to wedge.

incu'rabile *ag* incurable.

incu'rante *ag*: **~ (di)** heedless (of), careless (of).

in'curia *sf* negligence.

incurio'sire *vt* to make curious; **~rsi** *vr* to become curious.

incursi'one *sf* raid.

incur'vare *vt*, **~rsi** *vr* to bend, curve.

in'cusso, a *pp di* **incutere.**

incusto'dito, a *ag* unguarded, unattended; **passaggio a livello ~** unmanned level crossing.

in'cutere *vt* to arouse; **~ timore/rispetto a qn** to strike fear into sb/command sb's respect.

'indaco *sm* indigo.

indaffa'rato, a *ag* busy.

inda'gare *vt* to investigate.

indaga'tore, 'trice *ag* (*sguardo, domanda*) searching; (*mente*) inquiring.

in'dagine [in'dadʒine] *sf* investigation, inquiry; (*ricerca*) research, study; **~ di mercato** market survey.

indebita'mente *av* (*immeritatamente*) undeservedly; (*erroneamente*) wrongfully.

indebi'tarsi *vr* to run *o* get into debt.

in'debito, a *ag* undeserved; wrongful.

indeboli'mento *sm* weakening; (*debolezza*) weakness.

indebo'lire *vt, vi* (*anche:* **~rsi**) to weaken.

inde'cente [inde'tʃɛnte] *ag* indecent.

inde'cenza [inde'tʃɛntsa] *sf* indecency; **è un'~!** (*vergogna*) it's scandalous!, it's a disgrace!

indeci'frabile [indetʃi'frabile] *ag* indecipherable.

indecisi'one [indetʃi'zjone] *sf* indecisiveness; indecision.

inde'ciso, a [inde'tʃizo] *ag* indecisive; (*irresoluto*) undecided.

indeco'roso, a *ag* (*comportamento*) indecorous, unseemly.

inde'fesso, a *ag* untiring, indefatigable.

indefi'nibile *ag* indefinable.

indefi'nito, a *ag* (*anche LING*) indefinite; (*impreciso, non determinato*) undefined.

indefor'mabile *ag* crushproof.

in'degno, a [in'deɲɲo] *ag* (*atto*) shameful; (*persona*) unworthy.

inde'lebile *ag* indelible.

indelica'tezza [indelika'tettsa] *sf* tactlessness.

indeli'cato, a *ag* (*domanda*) indiscreet, tactless.

indemoni'ato, a *ag* possessed (by the devil).

in'denne *ag* unhurt, uninjured.

indennità *sf inv* (*rimborso: di spese*) allowance; (*: di perdita*) compensation, indemnity; **~ di contingenza** cost-of-living allowance; **~ di fine rapporto** severance payment (*on retirement, redundancy or when taking up other employment*); **~ di trasferta** travel expenses *pl*.

indenniz'zare [indennid'dzare] *vt* to compensate.

inden'nizzo [inden'niddzo] *sm* (*somma*) compensation, indemnity.

indero'gabile *ag* binding.

indescri'vibile *ag* indescribable.

indeside'rabile *ag* undesirable.

indeside'rato, a *ag* unwanted.

indetermina'tezza [indetermina'tettsa] *sf* vagueness.

indetermina'tivo, a *ag* (*LING*) indefinite.

indetermi'nato, a *ag* indefinite, indeterminate.

in'detto, a *pp di* **indire.**

'India *sf*: **l'~** India; **le ~e occidentali** the West Indies.

indi'ano, a *ag* Indian ♦ *sm/f* (*d'India*) Indian; (*d'America*) Red Indian; **l'Oceano I~** the Indian Ocean.

indiavo'lato, a *ag* possessed (by the devil); (*vivace, violento*) wild.

indi'care *vt* (*mostrare*) to show, indicate; (*: col dito*) to point to, point out; (*consigliare*) to suggest, recommend.

indica'tivo, a *ag* indicative ♦ *sm* (*LING*) indicative (mood).

indi'cato, a *ag* (*consigliato*) advisable; (*adatto*): **~ per** suitable for, appropriate for.

indica'tore, 'trice *ag* indicating ♦ *sm* (*elenco*) guide; directory; (*TECN*) gauge; indicator; **cartello** ~ sign; ~ **della benzina** petrol (*Brit*) *o* gas (*US*) gauge, fuel gauge; ~ **di velocità** (*AUT*) speedometer; (*AER*) airspeed indicator.

indicazi'one [indikat'tsjone] *sf* indication; (*informazione*) piece of information; ~**i per l'uso** instructions for use.

'indice ['inditʃe] *sm* (*ANAT:* *dito*) index finger, forefinger; (*lancetta*) needle, pointer; (*fig: indizio*) sign; (*TECN, MAT, nei libri*) index; ~ **azionario** share index; ~ **di gradimento** (*RADIO, TV*) popularity rating; ~ **dei prezzi al consumo** ≈ retail price index.

indicherò *etc* [indike'rɔ] *vb vedi* **indicare.**

indi'cibile [indi'tʃibile] *ag* inexpressible.

indiciz'zare [inditʃid'dzare] *vt:* ~ **al costo della vita** to index-link (*Brit*), index (*US*).

indiciz'zato, a [inditʃid'dzato] *ag* (*polizza, salario etc*) index-linked (*Brit*), indexed (*US*).

indicizzazi'one [inditʃiddzat'tsjone] *sf* indexing.

indietreggi'are [indjetred'dʒare] *vi* to draw back, retreat.

indi'etro *av* back; (*guardare*) behind, back; (*andare, cadere: anche:* **all'**~) backwards; **rimanere** ~ to be left behind; **essere** ~ (*col lavoro*) to be behind; (*orologio*) to be slow; **rimandare qc** ~ to send sth back; **non vado né avanti né** ~ (*fig*) I'm not getting anywhere, I'm getting nowhere.

indi'feso, a *ag* (*città, confine*) undefended; (*persona*) defenceless (*Brit*), defenseless (*US*), helpless.

indiffe'rente *ag* indifferent ♦ *sm*: **fare l'**~ to pretend to be indifferent, be *o* act casual; (*fingere di non vedere o sentire*) to pretend not to notice.

indiffe'renza [indiffe'rɛntsa] *sf* indifference.

in'digeno, a [in'didʒeno] *ag* indigenous, native ♦ *sm/f* native.

indi'gente [indi'dʒɛnte] *ag* poverty-stricken, destitute.

indi'genza [indi'dʒɛntsa] *sf* extreme poverty.

indigesti'one [indidʒes'tjone] *sf* indigestion.

indi'gesto, a [indi'dʒesto] *ag* indigestible.

indi'gnare [indiɲ'ɲare] *vt* to fill with indignation; ~**rsi** *vr* to be (*o* get) indignant.

indignazi'one [indiɲɲat'tsjone] *sf* indignation.

indimenti'cabile *ag* unforgettable.

'indio, a *ag, sm/f* (South American) Indian.

indipen'dente *ag* independent.

indipendente'mente *av* independently; ~ **dal fatto che gli piaccia o meno, verrà!** he's coming, whether he likes it or not!

indipen'denza [indipen'dɛntsa] *sf* independence.

in'dire *vt* (*concorso*) to announce; (*elezioni*) to call.

indi'retto, a *ag* indirect.

indiriz'zare [indirit'tsare] *vt* (*dirigere*) to direct; (*mandare*) to send; (*lettera*) to address; ~ **la parola a qn** to address sb.

indiriz'zario [indirit'tsarjo] *sm* mailing list.

indi'rizzo [indi'rittso] *sm* address; (*direzione*) direction; (*avvio*) trend, course; ~ **assoluto** (*INFORM*) absolute address.

indisci'plina [indiʃʃi'plina] *sf* indiscipline.

indiscipli'nato, a [indiʃʃipli'nato] *ag* undisciplined, unruly.

indis'creto, a *ag* indiscreet.

indiscrezi'one [indiskret'tsjone] *sf* indiscretion.

indiscrimi'nato, a *ag* indiscriminate.

indis'cusso, a *ag* unquestioned.

indiscu'tibile *ag* indisputable, unquestionable.

indispen'sabile *ag* indispensable, essential.

indispet'tire *vt* to irritate, annoy ♦ *vi* (*anche:* ~**rsi**) to get irritated *o* annoyed.

indispo'nente *ag* irritating, annoying.

indis'porre *vt* to antagonize.

indisposizi'one [indispozit'tsjone] *sf* (slight) indisposition.

indis'posto, a *pp di* **indisporre** ♦ *ag* indisposed, unwell.

indisso'lubile *ag* indissoluble.

indistinta'mente *av* (*senza distinzioni*) indiscriminately, without exception; (*in modo indefinito:* *vedere, sentire*) vaguely, faintly.

indis'tinto, a *ag* indistinct.

indistrut'tibile *ag* indestructible.

in'divia *sf* endive.

individu'ale *ag* individual.

individua'lismo *sm* individualism.

individua'lista, i, e *sm/f* individualist.

individualità *sf* individuality.

individual'mente *av* individually.

individu'are *vt* (*dar forma distinta a*) to characterize; (*determinare*) to locate; (*riconoscere*) to single out.

indi'viduo *sm* individual.

indivi'sibile *ag* indivisible; **quei due sono** ~**i** (*fig*) those two are inseparable.

indi'viso, a *ag* undivided.

indizi'are [indit'tsjare] *vt:* ~ **qn di qc** to cast suspicion on sb for sth.

indizi'ato, a [indit'tsjato] *ag* suspected ♦ *sm/f* suspect.

in'dizio [in'dittsjo] *sm* (*segno*) sign, indication; (*POLIZIA*) clue; (*DIR*) piece of evidence.

Indo'cina [indo'tʃina] *sf:* **l'**~ Indochina.

'indole *sf* nature, character.

indo'lente *ag* indolent.

indo'lenza [indo'lɛntsa] *sf* indolence.

indolen'zire [indolen'tsire] *vt* (*gambe, braccia etc*) to make stiff, cause to ache; (: *in-*

torpidire) to numb; ~**rsi** *vr* to become stiff; to go numb.

indolen'zito, a [indolen'tsito] *ag* stiff, aching; (*intorpidito*) numb.

indo'lore *ag* painless.

indo'mani *sm*: **l'~** the next day, the following day.

Indo'nesia *sf*: **l'~** Indonesia.

indonesi'ano, a *ag*, *sm/f*, *sm* Indonesian.

indo'rare *vt* (*rivestire in oro*) to gild; (*CUC*) to dip in egg yolk; ~ **la pillola** (*fig*) to sugar the pill.

indos'sare *vt* (*mettere indosso*) to put on; (*avere indosso*) to have on.

indossa'tore, 'trice *sm/f* model.

in'dotto, a *pp di* **indurre**.

indottri'nare *vt* to indoctrinate.

indovi'nare *vt* (*scoprire*) to guess; (*immaginare*) to imagine, guess; (*il futuro*) to foretell; **tirare a** ~ to make a shot in the dark.

indovi'nato, a *ag* successful; (*scelta*) inspired.

indovi'nello *sm* riddle.

indo'vino, a *sm/f* fortuneteller.

indù *ag*, *sm/f* Hindu.

indubbia'mente *av* undoubtedly.

in'dubbio, a *ag* certain, undoubted.

in'duco *etc vb vedi* **indurre**.

indugi'are [indu'dʒare] *vi* to take one's time, delay.

in'dugio [in'dudʒo] *sm* (*ritardo*) delay; **senza** ~ without delay.

indul'gente [indul'dʒɛnte] *ag* indulgent; (*giudice*) lenient.

indul'genza [indul'dʒɛntsa] *sf* indulgence; leniency.

in'dulgere [in'duldʒere] *vi*: ~ **a** (*accondiscendere*) to comply with; (*abbandonarsi*) to indulge in.

in'dulto, a *pp di* **indulgere** ♦ *sm* (*DIR*) pardon.

indu'mento *sm* article of clothing, garment; ~**i** *smpl* (*vestiti*) clothes; ~**i intimi** underwear *sg*.

induri'mento *sm* hardening.

indu'rire *vt* to harden ♦ *vi* (*anche*: ~**rsi**) to harden, become hard.

in'durre *vt*: ~ **qn a fare qc** to induce *o* persuade sb to do sth; ~ **qn in errore** to mislead sb; ~ **in tentazione** to lead into temptation.

in'dussi *etc vb vedi* **indurre**.

in'dustria *sf* industry; **la piccola/grande** ~ small/big business.

industri'ale *ag* industrial ♦ *sm* industrialist.

industrializ'zare [industrjalid'dzare] *vt* to industrialize.

industrializzazi'one [industrjaliddzat'tsjone] *sf* industrialization.

industri'arsi *vr* to do one's best, try hard.

industri'oso, a *ag* industrious, hard-working.

induzi'one [indut'tsjone] *sf* induction.

inebe'tito, a *ag* dazed, stunned.

inebri'are *vt* (*anche fig*) to intoxicate; ~**rsi** *vr* to become intoxicated.

inecce'pibile [inettʃe'pibile] *ag* unexceptionable.

i'nedia *sf* starvation.

i'nedito, a *ag* unpublished.

ineffi'cace [ineffi'katʃe] *ag* ineffective.

ineffi'cacia [ineffi'katʃa] *sf* inefficacy, ineffectiveness.

ineffici'ente [ineffi'tʃɛnte] *ag* inefficient.

ineffici'enza [ineffi'tʃɛntsa] *sf* inefficiency.

ineguagli'abile [inegwaʎ'ʎabile] *ag* incomparable, matchless.

ineguagli'anza [inegwaʎ'ʎantsa] *sf* (*sociale*) inequality; (*di superficie, livello*) unevenness.

inegu'ale *ag* unequal; (*irregolare*) uneven.

inelut'tabile *ag* inescapable.

ineluttabilità *sf* inescapability.

inenar'rabile *ag* unutterable.

inequivo'cabile *ag* unequivocal.

ine'rente *ag*: ~ **a** concerning, regarding.

i'nerme *ag* unarmed, defenceless (*Brit*), defenseless (*US*).

inerpi'carsi *vr*: ~ (**su**) to clamber (up).

i'nerte *ag* inert; (*inattivo*) indolent, sluggish.

i'nerzia [i'nɛrtsja] *sf* inertia; indolence, sluggishness.

inesat'tezza [inezat'tettsa] *sf* inaccuracy.

ine'satto, a *ag* (*impreciso*) inaccurate, inexact; (*erroneo*) incorrect; (*AMM*: *non riscosso*) uncollected.

inesau'ribile *ag* inexhaustible.

inesis'tente *ag* non-existent.

ineso'rabile *ag* inexorable, relentless.

inesorabil'mente *av* inexorably.

inesperi'enza [inespe'rjɛntsa] *sf* inexperience.

ines'perto, a *ag* inexperienced.

inespli'cabile *ag* inexplicable.

inesplo'rato, a *ag* unexplored.

ines'ploso, a *ag* unexploded.

inespres'sivo, a *ag* (*viso*) expressionless, inexpressive.

ines'presso, a *ag* unexpressed.

inespri'mibile *ag* inexpressible.

inespu'gnabile [inespuɲ'ɲabile] *ag* (*fortezza, torre etc*) impregnable.

ineste'tismo *sm* beauty problem.

inesti'mabile *ag* inestimable; (*valore*) incalculable.

inestir'pabile *ag* ineradicable.

inetti'tudine *sf* ineptitude.

i'netto, a *ag* (*incapace*) inept; (*che non ha attitudine*): ~ (**a**) unsuited (to).

ine'vaso, a *ag* (*ordine, corrispondenza*) outstanding.

inevi'tabile *ag* inevitable.

inevitabil'mente *av* inevitably.

i'nezia [i'nɛttsja] *sf* trifle, thing of no importance.

infagot'tare *vt* to bundle up, wrap up; **~rsi** *vr* to wrap up.

infal'libile *ag* infallible.

infallibilità *sf* infallibility.

infa'mante *ag* (*accusa*) defamatory, slanderous.

infa'mare *vt* to defame.

in'fame *ag* infamous; (*fig: cosa, compito*) awful, dreadful.

in'famia *sf* infamy.

infan'tile *ag* child *cpd*; childlike; (*adulto, azione*) childish; **letteratura** ~ children's books *pl*.

in'fanzia [in'fantsja] *sf* childhood; (*bambini*) children *pl*; **prima** ~ babyhood, infancy.

infari'nare *vt* to cover with (*o* sprinkle with *o* dip in) flour; ~ **di zucchero** to sprinkle with sugar.

infarina'tura *sf* (*fig*) smattering.

in'farto *sm* (*MED*): ~ (**cardiaco**) coronary.

infasti'dire *vt* to annoy, irritate; **~rsi** *vr* to get annoyed *o* irritated.

infati'cabile *ag* tireless, untiring.

in'fatti *cong* as a matter of fact, in fact, actually.

infatu'arsi *vr*: ~ **di** *o* **per** to become infatuated with, fall for.

infatuazi'one [infatuat'tsjone] *sf* infatuation.

in'fausto, a *ag* unpropitious, unfavourable (*Brit*), unfavorable (*US*).

infecondità *sf* infertility.

infe'condo, a *ag* infertile.

infe'dele *ag* unfaithful.

infedeltà *sf* infidelity.

infe'lice [infe'litʃe] *ag* unhappy; (*sfortunato*) unlucky, unfortunate; (*inopportuno*) inopportune, ill-timed; (*mal riuscito: lavoro*) bad, poor.

infelicità [infelitʃi'ta] *sf* unhappiness.

infel'trire *vi*, **~rsi** *vr* (*lana*) to become matted.

infe'renza [infe'rɛntsa] *sf* inference.

inferi'ore *ag* lower; (*per intelligenza, qualità*) inferior ♦ *sm/f* inferior; ~ **a** (*numero, quantità*) less *o* smaller than; (*meno buono*) inferior to; ~ **alla media** below average.

inferiorità *sf* inferiority.

infe'rire *vt* (*dedurre*) to infer, deduce.

inferme'ria *sf* infirmary; (*di scuola, nave*) sick bay.

infermi'ere, a *sm/f* nurse.

infermità *sf inv* illness; infirmity; ~ **di mente** mental illness.

in'fermo, a *ag* (*ammalato*) ill; (*debole*) infirm; ~ **di mente** mentally ill.

infer'nale *ag* infernal; (*proposito, complotto*) diabolical; **un tempo** ~ (*fam*) hellish weather.

in'ferno *sm* hell; **soffrire le pene dell'~** (*fig*)

to go through hell.

infero'cire [infero'tʃire] *vt* to make fierce ♦ *vi*, **~rsi** *vr* to become fierce.

inferri'ata *sf* grating.

infervo'rare *vt* to arouse enthusiasm in; **~rsi** *vr* to get excited, get carried away.

infes'tare *vt* to infest.

infet'tare *vt* to infect; **~rsi** *vr* to become infected.

infet'tivo, a *ag* infectious.

in'fetto, a *ag* infected; (*acque*) polluted, contaminated.

infezi'one [infet'tsjone] *sf* infection.

infiac'chire [infjak'kire] *vt* to weaken ♦ *vi* (*anche:* **~rsi**) to grow weak.

infiam'mabile *ag* inflammable.

infiam'mare *vt* to set alight; (*fig, MED*) to inflame; **~rsi** *vr* to catch fire; (*MED*) to become inflamed; (*fig*): **~rsi di** to be fired with.

infiammazi'one [infjammat'tsjone] *sf* (*MED*) inflammation.

infias'care *vt* to bottle.

infici'are [infi'tʃare] *vt* (*DIR*: *atto, dichiarazione*) to challenge.

in'fido, a *ag* unreliable, treacherous.

infie'rire *vi*: ~ **su** (*fisicamente*) to attack furiously; (*verbalmente*) to rage at; (*epidemia*) to rage over.

in'figgere [in'fiddʒere] *vt*: ~ **qc in** to thrust *o* drive sth into.

infi'lare *vt* (*ago*) to thread; (*mettere: chiave*) to insert; (: *vestito*) to slip *o* put on; (*strada*) to turn into, take; **~rsi** *vr*: **~rsi in** to slip into; (*indossare*) to slip on; ~ **un anello al dito** to slip a ring on one's finger; ~ **l'uscio** to slip in; to slip out; **~rsi la giacca** to put on one's jacket.

infil'trarsi *vr* to penetrate, seep through; (*MIL*) to infiltrate.

infil'trato, a *sm/f* infiltrator.

infiltrazi'one [infiltrat'tsjone] *sf* infiltration.

infil'zare [infil'tsare] *vt* (*infilare*) to string together; (*trafiggere*) to pierce.

'infimo, a *ag* lowest; **un albergo di** ~ **ordine** a third-rate hotel.

in'fine *av* finally; (*insomma*) in short.

infin'gardo, a *ag* lazy ♦ *sm/f* slacker.

infinità *sf* infinity; (*in quantità*): **un'~ di** an infinite number of.

infinitesi'male *ag* infinitesimal.

infi'nito, a *ag* infinite; (*LING*) infinitive ♦ *sm* infinity; (*LING*) infinitive; **all'~** (*senza fine*) endlessly; (*LING*) in the infinitive.

infinocchi'are [infinok'kjare] *vt* (*fam*) to hoodwink.

infiore'scenza [infjoreʃ'ʃɛntsa] *sf* inflorescence.

infir'mare *vt* (*DIR*) to invalidate.

infischi'arsi [infis'kjarsi] *vr*: ~ **di** not to care about.

in'fisso, a *pp di* **infiggere** ♦ *sm* fixture; (*di*

porta, finestra) frame.
infit'tire *vt, vi* (*anche:* ~**rsi**) to thicken.
inflazio'nare [inflattsjo'nare] *vt* to inflate.
inflazi'one [inflat'tsjone] *sf* inflation.
inflazio'nistico, a, ci, che [inflattsjo'nistiko] *ag* inflationary.
infles'sibile *ag* inflexible; (*ferreo*) unyielding.
inflessi'one *sf* inflexion.
in'fliggere [in'fliddʒere] *vt* to inflict.
in'flissi *etc vb vedi* **infliggere**.
in'flitto, a *pp di* **infliggere**.
influ'ente *ag* influential.
influ'enza [influ'entsa] *sf* influence; (*MED*) influenza, flu.
influen'zare [influen'tsare] *vt* to influence, have an influence on.
influ'ire *vi*: ~ **su** to influence.
in'flusso *sm* influence.
INFN *sigla m* = *Istituto Nazionale di Fisica Nucleare*.
info'cato, a *ag* (*metallo etc*) red-hot; (*sabbia, guance*) burning; (*discorso*) heated, passionate.
info'gnarsi [infoɲ'ɲarsi] *vr* (*fam*) to get into a mess; ~ **in un mare di debiti** to be up to one's *o* the eyes in debt.
infol'tire *vt, vi* to thicken.
infon'dato, a *ag* unfounded, groundless.
in'fondere *vt*: ~ **qc in qn** to instill sth in sb; ~ **fiducia in qn** to inspire sb with confidence.
infor'care *vt* to fork (up); (*bicicletta, cavallo*) to get on; (*occhiali*) to put on.
infor'male *ag* informal.
infor'mare *vt* to inform, tell; ~**rsi** *vr*: ~**rsi** (**di** *o* **su**) to inquire (about); **tenere informato qn** to keep sb informed.
infor'matico, a, ci, che *ag* (*settore*) computer *cpd* ♦ *sf* computer science.
informa'tivo, a *ag* informative; **a titolo** ~ for information only.
informatiz'zare [informatid'dzare] *vt* to computerize.
informa'tore *sm* informer.
informazi'one [informat'tsjone] *sf* piece of information; ~**i** *sfpl* information *sg*; **chiedere un'**~ to ask for (some) information.
in'forme *ag* shapeless.
informico'larsi *vr*, **informico'lirsi** *vr*: **mi si è informicolata una gamba** I've got pins and needles in my leg.
infor'nare *vt* to put in the oven.
infor'nata *sf* (*anche fig*) batch.
infortu'narsi *vr* to injure o.s., have an accident.
infortu'nato, a *ag* injured, hurt ♦ *sm/f* injured person.
infor'tunio *sm* accident; ~ **sul lavoro** industrial accident, accident at work.
infortu'nistica *sf* study of (industrial) accidents.

infos'sarsi *vr* (*terreno*) to sink; (*guance*) to become hollow.
infos'sato, a *ag* hollow; (*occhi*) deep-set; (*: per malattia*) sunken.
infradici'are [infradi'tʃare] *vt* (*inzuppare*) to soak, drench; (*marcire*) to rot; ~**rsi** *vr* to get soaked, get drenched; to rot.
in'frangere [in'frandʒere] *vt* to smash; (*fig: legge, patti*) to break; ~**rsi** *vr* to smash, break.
infran'gibile [infran'dʒibile] *ag* unbreakable.
in'franto, a *pp di* **infrangere** ♦ *ag* broken.
infra'rosso, a *ag, sm* infrared.
infrasettima'nale *ag* midweek *cpd*.
infrastrut'tura *sf* infrastructure.
infrazi'one [infrat'tsjone] *sf*: ~ **a** breaking of, violation of.
infredda'tura *sf* slight cold.
infreddo'lito, a *ag* cold, chilled.
infre'quente *ag* infrequent, rare.
infrol'lire *vi*, ~**rsi** *vr* (*selvaggina*) to become high.
infruttu'oso, a *ag* fruitless.
infu'ori *av* out; **all'**~ outwards; **all'**~ **di** (*eccetto*) except, with the exception of.
infuri'are *vi* to rage; ~**rsi** *vr* to fly into a rage.
infusi'one *sf* infusion.
in'fuso, a *pp di* **infondere** ♦ *ag*: **scienza** ~**a** (*anche ironico*) innate knowledge ♦ *sm* infusion; ~ **di camomilla** camomile tea.
Ing. *abbr* = **ingegnere**.
ingaggi'are [ingad'dʒare] *vt* (*assumere con compenso*) to take on, hire; (*SPORT*) to sign on; (*MIL*) to engage.
in'gaggio [in'gaddʒo] *sm* hiring; signing on.
ingagliar'dire [ingaʎʎar'dire] *vt* to strengthen, invigorate ♦ *vi* (*anche:* ~**rsi**) to grow stronger.
ingan'nare *vt* to deceive; (*coniuge*) to be unfaithful to; (*fisco*) to cheat; (*eludere*) to dodge, elude; (*fig: tempo*) to while away ♦ *vi* (*apparenza*) to be deceptive; ~**rsi** *vr* to be mistaken, be wrong.
inganna'tore, 'trice *ag* deceptive; (*persona*) deceitful.
ingan'nevole *ag* deceptive.
in'ganno *sm* deceit, deception; (*azione*) trick; (*menzogna, frode*) cheat, swindle; (*illusione*) illusion.
ingarbugli'are [ingarbuʎ'ʎare] *vt* to tangle; (*fig*) to confuse, muddle; ~**rsi** *vr* to become confused *o* muddled.
ingarbu'gliato, a [ingarbuʎ'ʎato] *ag* tangled; confused, muddled.
inge'gnarsi [indʒeɲ'ɲarsi] *vr* to do one's best, try hard; ~ **per vivere** to live by one's wits; **basta** ~ **un po'** you just need a bit of ingenuity.
inge'gnere [indʒeɲ'ɲere] *sm* engineer; ~ **civile/navale** civil/naval engineer.
ingegne'ria [indʒeɲɲe'ria] *sf* engineering.

in'gegno [in'dʒeɲɲo] *sm* (*intelligenza*) intelligence, brains *pl*; (*capacità creativa*) ingenuity; (*disposizione*) talent.

ingegnosità [indʒeɲɲosi'ta] *sf* ingenuity.

inge'gnoso, a [indʒeɲ'ɲoso] *ag* ingenious, clever.

ingelo'sire [indʒelo'sire] *vt* to make jealous ♦ *vi* (*anche:* ~rsi) to become jealous.

in'gente [in'dʒɛnte] *ag* huge, enormous.

ingenti'lire [indʒenti'lire] *vt* to refine, civilize; ~rsi *vr* to become more refined, become more civilized.

ingenuità [indʒenui'ta] *sf* ingenuousness.

in'genuo, a [in'dʒɛnuo] *ag* ingenuous, naïve.

inge'renza [indʒe'rɛntsa] *sf* interference.

inge'rire [indʒe'rire] *vt* to ingest.

inges'sare [indʒes'sare] *vt* (*MED*) to put in plaster.

ingessa'tura [indʒessa'tura] *sf* plaster.

Inghil'terra [ingil'tɛrra] *sf*: l'~ England.

inghiot'tire [ingjot'tire] *vt* to swallow.

in'ghippo [in'gippo] *sm* trick.

ingial'lire [indʒal'lire] *vi* to go yellow.

ingigan'tire [indʒigan'tire] *vt* to enlarge, magnify ♦ *vi* to become gigantic *o* enormous.

inginocchi'arsi [indʒinok'kjarsi] *vr* to kneel (down).

inginocchia'toio [indʒinokkja'tojo] *sm* priedieu.

ingioiel'lare [indʒojel'lare] *vt* to bejewel, adorn with jewels.

ingiù [in'dʒu] *av* down, downwards.

ingi'ungere [in'dʒundʒere] *vt*: ~ a qn di fare qc to enjoin *o* order sb to do sth.

ingi'unto, a [in'dʒunto] *pp di* **ingiungere**.

ingiunzi'one [indʒun'tsjone] *sf* injunction, command; ~ di pagamento final demand.

ingi'uria [in'dʒurja] *sf* insult; (*fig: danno*) damage.

ingiuri'are [indʒu'rjare] *vt* to insult, abuse.

ingiuri'oso, a [indʒu'rjoso] *ag* insulting, abusive.

ingiusta'mente [indʒusta'mente] *av* unjustly.

ingiustifi'cabile [indʒustifi'kabile] *ag* unjustifiable.

ingiustifi'cato, a [indʒustifi'kato] *ag* unjustified.

ingius'tizia [indʒus'tittsja] *sf* injustice.

ingi'usto, a [in'dʒusto] *ag* unjust, unfair.

in'glese *ag* English ♦ *sm/f* Englishman/woman ♦ *sm* (*LING*) English; gli l~i the English; andarsene *o* filare all'~ to take French leave.

ingob'bire *vi*, ~rsi *vr* to become stooped.

ingoi'are *vt* to gulp (down); (*fig*) to swallow (up); ha dovuto ~ il rospo (*fig*) he had to accept the situation.

ingol'fare *vt*, ~rsi *vr* (*motore*) to flood.

ingolo'sire *vt*: ~ qn to make sb's mouth water; (*fig*) to attract sb ♦ *vi* (*anche:* ~rsi): ~ (di) (*anche fig*) to become greedy (for).

ingom'brante *ag* cumbersome.

ingom'brare *vt* (*strada*) to block; (*stanza*) to clutter up.

in'gombro, a *ag*: ~ di (*strada*) blocked by; (*stanza*) cluttered up with ♦ *sm* obstacle; essere d'~ to be in the way; per ragioni di ~ for reasons of space.

ingor'digia [ingor'didʒa] *sf*: ~ (di) greed (for); avidity (for).

in'gordo, a *ag*: ~ di greedy for; (*fig*) greedy *o* avid for ♦ *sm/f* glutton.

ingor'gare *vt* to block; ~rsi *vr* to be blocked up, be choked up.

in'gorgo, ghi *sm* blockage, obstruction; (*anche:* ~ stradale) traffic jam.

ingoz'zare [ingot'tsare] *vt* (*animali*) to fatten; (*fig: persona*) to stuff; ~rsi *vr*: ~rsi (di) to stuff o.s. (with).

ingra'naggio [ingra'naddʒo] *sm* (*TECN*) gear; (*di orologio*) mechanism; gli ~i della burocrazia the bureaucratic machinery.

ingra'nare *vi* to mesh, engage ♦ *vt* to engage; ~ la marcia to get into gear.

ingrandi'mento *sm* enlargement; extension; magnification; growth; expansion.

ingran'dire *vt* (*anche FOT*) to enlarge; (*estendere*) to extend; (*OTTICA, fig*) to magnify ♦ *vi* (*anche:* ~rsi) to become larger *o* bigger; (*aumentare*) to grow, increase; (*espandersi*) to expand.

ingrandi'tore *sm* (*FOT*) enlarger.

ingras'saggio [ingras'saddʒo] *sm* greasing.

ingras'sare *vt* to make fat; (*animali*) to fatten; (*AGR: terreno*) to manure; (*lubrificare*) to grease ♦ *vi* (*anche:* ~rsi) to get fat, put on weight.

ingrati'tudine *sf* ingratitude.

in'grato, a *ag* ungrateful; (*lavoro*) thankless, unrewarding.

ingrazi'are [ingrat'tsjare] *vt*: ~rsi qn to ingratiate o.s. with sb.

ingredi'ente *sm* ingredient.

in'gresso *sm* (*porta*) entrance; (*atrio*) hall; (*l'entrare*) entrance, entry; (*facoltà di entrare*) admission; "~ libero" "admission free"; ~ principale main entrance; ~ di servizio tradesmen's entrance.

ingros'sare *vt* to increase; (*folla, livello*) to swell ♦ *vi* (*anche:* ~rsi) to increase; to swell.

in'grosso *av*: all'~ (*COMM*) wholesale; (*all'incirca*) roughly, about.

ingru'gnato, a [ingruɲ'ɲato] *ag* grumpy.

inguai'arsi *vr* to get into trouble.

inguai'nare *vt* to sheathe.

ingual'cibile [ingwal'tʃibile] *ag* creaseresistant.

ingua'ribile *ag* incurable.

'inguine *sm* (*ANAT*) groin.

ingurgi'tare [ingurdʒi'tare] *vt* to gulp down.

ini'bire *vt* to forbid, prohibit; (*PSIC*) to inhibit.

ini'bito, a *ag* inhibited ♦ *sm/f* inhibited person.

inibi'torio, a *ag* (*PSIC*) inhibitory, inhibitive; (*provvedimento, misure*) restrictive.

inibizi'one [inibit'tsjone] *sf* prohibition; inhibition.

iniet'tare *vt* to inject; ~**rsi** *vr*: ~**rsi di sangue** (*occhi*) to become bloodshot.

iniezi'one [injet'tsjone] *sf* injection.

inimi'care *vt* to alienate, make hostile; ~**rsi** *vr*: ~**rsi con qn** to fall out with sb; **si è inimicato gli amici di un tempo** he has alienated his old friends.

inimi'cizia [inimi'tʃittsja] *sf* animosity.

inimi'tabile *ag* inimitable.

inimmagi'nabile [inimmadʒi'nabile] *ag* unimaginable.

ininfiam'mabile *ag* non-flammable.

inintelli'gibile [inintelli'dʒibile] *ag* unintelligible.

ininterrotta'mente *av* non-stop, continuously.

ininter'rotto, a *ag* (*fila*) unbroken; (*rumore*) uninterrupted.

iniquità *sf inv* iniquity; (*atto*) wicked action.

i'niquo, a *ag* iniquitous.

inizi'ale [init'tsjale] *ag*, *sf* initial.

inizializ'zare [inittsjalid'dzare] *vt* (*INFORM*) to boot.

inizial'mente [inittsjal'mente] *av* initially, at first.

inizi'are [init'tsjare] *vi*, *vt* to begin, start; ~ **qn a** to initiate sb into; (*pittura etc*) to introduce sb to; ~ **a fare qc** to start doing sth.

inizia'tiva [inittsja'tiva] *sf* initiative; ~ **privata** private enterprise.

inizia'tore, 'trice [inittsja'tore] *sm/f* initiator.

i'nizio [i'nittsjo] *sm* beginning; **all'**~ at the beginning, at the start; **dare** ~ **a qc** to start sth, get sth going; **essere agli** ~**i** (*progetto, lavoro etc*) to be in the initial stages.

innaffi'are *etc* = **annaffiare** *etc.*

innal'zare [innal'tsare] *vt* (*sollevare, alzare*) to raise; (*rizzare*) to erect; ~**rsi** *vr* to rise.

innamora'mento *sm* falling in love.

innamo'rare *vt* to enchant, charm; ~**rsi** *vr*: ~**rsi (di qn)** to fall in love (with sb).

innamo'rato, a *ag* (*che nutre amore*): ~ **(di)** in love (with); (*appassionato*): ~ **di** very fond of ♦ *sm/f* lover; (*anche scherzoso*) sweetheart.

in'nanzi [in'nantsi] *av* (*stato in luogo*) in front, ahead; (*moto a luogo*) forward, on; (*tempo: prima*) before ♦ *prep* (*prima*) before; ~ **a** in front of; **d'ora** ~ from now on; **farsi** ~ to step forward; ~ **tempo** ahead of time; ~ **tutto** above all.

in'nato, a *ag* innate.

innatu'rale *ag* unnatural.

inne'gabile *ag* undeniable.

inneggi'are [inned'dʒare] *vi*: ~ **a** to sing hymns to; (*fig*) to sing the praises of.

innervo'sire *vt*: ~ **qn** to get on sb's nerves; ~**rsi** *vr* to get irritated *o* upset.

innes'care *vt* to prime.

in'nesco, schi *sm* primer.

innes'tare *vt* (*BOT, MED*) to graft; (*TECN*) to engage; (*inserire: presa*) to insert.

in'nesto *sm* graft; grafting *q*; (*TECN*) clutch; (*ELETTR*) connection.

'inno *sm* hymn; ~ **nazionale** national anthem.

inno'cente [inno'tʃɛnte] *ag* innocent.

inno'cenza [inno'tʃɛntsa] *sf* innocence.

in'nocuo, a *ag* innocuous, harmless.

innomi'nato, a *ag* unnamed.

inno'vare *vt* to change, make innovations in.

innova'tivo, a *ag* innovative.

innovazi'one [innovat'tsjone] *sf* innovation.

innume'revole *ag* innumerable.

inocu'lare *vt* (*MED*) to inoculate.

ino'doro, a *ag* odourless (*Brit*), odorless (*US*).

inoffen'sivo, a *ag* harmless.

inol'trare *vt* (*AMM*) to pass on, forward; ~**rsi** *vr* (*addentrarsi*) to advance, go forward.

inol'trato, a *ag*: **a notte** ~**a** late at night; **a primavera** ~**a** late in the spring.

i'noltre *av* besides, moreover.

i'noltro *sm* (*AMM*) forwarding.

inon'dare *vt* to flood.

inondazi'one [inondat'tsjone] *sf* flooding *q*; flood.

inope'roso, a *ag* inactive, idle.

inopi'nato, a *ag* unexpected.

inoppor'tuno, a *ag* untimely, ill-timed; (*poco adatto*) inappropriate; (*momento*) inopportune.

inoppu'gnabile [inoppuɲ'ɲabile] *ag* incontrovertible.

inor'ganico, a, ci, che *ag* inorganic.

inorgo'glire [inorgoʎ'ʎire] *vt* to make proud ♦ *vi* (*anche*: ~**rsi**) to become proud; ~**rsi di qc** to pride o.s. on sth.

inor'ridire *vt* to horrify ♦ *vi* to be horrified.

inospi'tale *ag* inhospitable.

inosser'vante *ag*: **essere** ~ **di** to fail to comply with.

inosser'vato, a *ag* (*non notato*) unobserved; (*non rispettato*) not observed, not kept; **passare** ~ to go unobserved, escape notice.

inossi'dabile *ag* stainless.

INPS *sigla m* (= *Istituto Nazionale Previdenza Sociale*) social security service.

inqua'drare *vt* (*foto, immagine*) to frame; (*fig*) to situate, set.

inquadra'tura *sf* (*CINEMA, FOT*: *atto*) framing; (: *immagine*) shot; (: *sequenza*) sequence.

inqualifi'cabile *ag* unspeakable.

inquie'tante *ag* disturbing, worrying.

inquie'tare *vt* (*turbare*) to disturb, worry; **~rsi** *vr* to worry, become anxious; (*impazientirsi*) to get upset.

inqui'eto, a *ag* restless; (*preoccupato*) worried, anxious.

inquie'tudine *sf* anxiety, worry.

inqui'lino, a *sm/f* tenant.

inquina'mento *sm* pollution.

inqui'nare *vt* to pollute.

inqui'rente *ag* (*DIR*): **magistrato ~** examining (*Brit*) *o* committing (*US*) magistrate; **commissione ~** commission of inquiry.

inqui'sire *vt, vi* to investigate.

inquisi'tore, 'trice *ag* (*sguardo*) inquiring.

inquisizi'one [inkwizit'tsjone] *sf* inquisition.

insabbia'mento *sm* (*fig*) shelving.

insabbi'are *vt* (*fig: pratica*) to shelve; **~rsi** *vr* (*barca*) to run aground; (*fig: pratica*) to be shelved.

insac'care *vt* (*grano, farina etc*) to bag, put into sacks; (*carne*) to put into sausage skins.

insac'cati *smpl* (*CUC*) sausages.

insa'lata *sf* salad; (*pianta*) lettuce; **~ mista** mixed salad.

insalati'era *sf* salad bowl.

insa'lubre *ag* unhealthy.

insa'nabile *ag* (*piaga*) which cannot be healed; (*situazione*) irremediable; (*odio*) implacable.

insangui'nare *vt* to stain with blood.

in'sania *sf* insanity.

insapo'nare *vt* to soap; **~rsi le mani** to soap one's hands.

insapo'nata *sf*: **dare un'~ a qc** to give sth a (quick) soaping.

insapo'rire *vt* to flavour (*Brit*), flavor (*US*); (*con spezie*) to season; **~rsi** *vr* to acquire flavo(u)r.

insa'poro, a *ag* tasteless, insipid.

insa'puta *sf*: **all'~ di qn** without sb knowing.

insazi'abile [insat'tsjabile] *ag* insatiable.

inscato'lare *vt* (*frutta, carne*) to can.

insce'nare [inʃe'nare] *vt* (*TEATRO*) to stage, put on; (*fig*) to stage.

inscin'dibile [inʃin'dibile] *ag* (*fattori*) inseparable; (*legame*) indissoluble.

insec'chire [insek'kire] *vt* (*seccare*) to dry up; (: *piante*) to wither ♦ *vi* to dry up, become dry; to wither.

insedia'mento *sm* (*AMM: in carica, ufficio*) installation; (*villaggio, colonia*) settlement.

insedi'are *vt* (*AMM*) to install; **~rsi** *vr* (*AMM*) to take up office; (*colonia, profughi etc*) to settle; (*MIL*) to take up positions.

in'segna [in'seɲɲa] *sf* sign; (*emblema*) sign, emblem; (*bandiera*) flag, banner; **~e** *sfpl* (*decorazioni*) insignia *pl*.

insegna'mento [inseɲɲa'mento] *sm* teaching; **trarre ~ da un'esperienza** to learn from an experience, draw a lesson from an experience; **che ti serva da ~** let this be a lesson to you.

inse'gnante [inseɲ'ɲante] *ag* teaching ♦ *sm/f* teacher.

inse'gnare [inseɲ'ɲare] *vt, vi* to teach; **~ a qn qc** to teach sb sth; **~ a qn a fare qc** to teach sb (how) to do sth; **come lei ben m'insegna ...** (*ironico*) as you will doubtless be aware ....

insegui'mento *sm* pursuit, chase; **darsi all'~ di qn** to give chase to sb.

insegu'ire *vt* to pursue, chase.

insegui'tore, 'trice *sm/f* pursuer.

insel'lare *vt* to saddle.

inselvati'chire [inselvati'kire] *vt* (*persona*) to make unsociable ♦ *vi* (*anche:* **~rsi**) to grow wild; (*persona*) to become unsociable.

inseminazi'one [inseminat'tsjone] *sf* insemination.

insena'tura *sf* inlet, creek.

insen'sato, a *ag* senseless, stupid.

insen'sibile *ag* (*anche fig*) insensitive.

insensibilità *sf* insensitivity, insensibility.

insepa'rabile *ag* inseparable.

inse'polto, a *ag* unburied.

inseri'mento *sm* (*gen*) insertion; **problemi di ~** (*di persona*) adjustment problems.

inse'rire *vt* to insert; (*ELETTR*) to connect; (*allegare*) to enclose; **~rsi** *vr* (*fig*): **~rsi in** to become part of; **~ un annuncio sul giornale** to put *o* place an advertisement in the newspaper.

in'serto *sm* (*pubblicazione*) insert; **~ filmato** (film) clip.

inser'vibile *ag* useless.

inservi'ente *sm/f* attendant.

inserzi'one [inser'tsjone] *sf* insertion; (*avviso*) advertisement; **fare un'~ sul giornale** to put an advertisement in the newspaper.

inserzio'nista, i, e [insertsjo'nista] *sm/f* advertiser.

insetti'cida, i [insetti'tʃida] *sm* insecticide.

in'setto *sm* insect.

insicu'rezza [insiku'rettsa] *sf* insecurity.

insi'curo, a *ag* insecure.

in'sidia *sf* snare, trap; (*pericolo*) hidden danger; **tendere un'~ a qn** to lay *o* set a trap for sb.

insidi'are *vt* (*MIL*) to harass; **~ la vita di qn** to make an attempt on sb's life.

insidi'oso, a *ag* insidious.

insi'eme *av* together; (*contemporaneamente*) at the same time ♦ *prep*: **~ a** *o* **con** together with ♦ *sm* whole; (*MAT, servizio, assortimento*) set; (*MODA*) ensemble, outfit; **tutti ~** all together; **tutto ~** all together; (*in una volta*) at one go; **nell'~** on the whole; **d'~** (*veduta etc*) overall.

in'signe [in'siɲɲe] *ag* (*persona*) famous, distinguished, eminent; (*città, monumento*) notable.

insignifi'cante [insiɲɲifi'kante] *ag* insignificant.

insi'gnire [insiɲ'ɲire] *vt*: ~ **qn di** to honour (*Brit*) *o* honor (*US*) sb with, decorate sb with.

insin'cero, a [insin'tʃero] *ag* insincere.

insinda'cabile *ag* unquestionable.

insinu'ante *ag* (*osservazione, sguardo*) insinuating; (*maniere*) ingratiating.

insinu'are *vt* (*introdurre*): ~ **qc in** to slip *o* slide sth into; (*fig*) to insinuate, imply; **~rsi** *vr*: **~rsi in** to seep into; (*fig*) to creep into; to worm one's way into.

insinuazi'one [insinuat'tsjone] *sf* (*fig*) insinuation.

in'sipido, a *ag* insipid.

insis'tente *ag* insistent; (*pioggia, dolore*) persistent.

insis'tenza [insis'tɛntsa] *sf* insistence; persistence.

in'sistere *vi*: ~ **su qc** to insist on sth; ~ **in qc/a fare** (*perseverare*) to persist in sth/in doing.

insis'tito, a *pp di* **insistere**.

'insito, a *ag*: ~ **(in)** inherent (in).

insoddis'fatto, a *ag* dissatisfied.

insoddisfazi'one [insoddisfat'tsjone] *sf* dissatisfaction.

insoffe'rente *ag* intolerant.

insoffe'renza [insoffe'rɛntsa] *sf* impatience.

insolazi'one [insolat'tsjone] *sf* (*MED*) sunstroke.

inso'lente *ag* insolent.

insolen'tire *vi* to grow insolent ♦ *vt* to insult, be rude to.

inso'lenza [inso'lɛntsa] *sf* insolence.

in'solito, a *ag* unusual, out of the ordinary.

inso'lubile *ag* insoluble.

inso'luto, a *ag* (*non risolto*) unsolved; (*non pagato*) unpaid, outstanding.

insol'vente *ag* (*DIR*) insolvent.

insol'venza [insol'vɛntsa] *sf* (*DIR*) insolvency.

insol'vibile *ag* insolvent.

in'somma *av* (*in breve, in conclusione*) in short; (*dunque*) well ♦ *escl* for heaven's sake!

inson'dabile *ag* unfathomable.

in'sonne *ag* sleepless.

in'sonnia *sf* insomnia, sleeplessness.

insonno'lito, a *ag* sleepy, drowsy.

insonorizzazi'one [insonoriddzat'tsjone] *sf* soundproofing.

insoppor'tabile *ag* unbearable.

insoppri'mibile *ag* insuppressible.

insor'genza [insor'dʒɛntsa] *sf* (*di malattia*) onset.

in'sorgere [in'sordʒere] *vi* (*ribellarsi*) to rise

up, rebel; (*apparire*) to come up, arise.

insormon'tabile *ag* (*ostacolo*) insurmountable, insuperable.

in'sorsi *etc vb vedi* **insorgere**.

in'sorto, a *pp di* **insorgere** ♦ *sm/f* rebel, insurgent.

insospet'tabile *ag* (*al di sopra di ogni sospetto*) above suspicion; (*inatteso*) unsuspected.

insospet'tato, a *ag* unsuspected.

insospet'tire *vt* to make suspicious ♦ *vi* (*anche*: **~rsi**) to become suspicious.

insoste'nibile *ag* (*posizione, teoria*) untenable; (*dolore, situazione*) intolerable, unbearable; **le spese di manutenzione sono ~i** the maintenance costs are excessive.

insostitu'ibile *ag* (*persona*) irreplaceable; (*aiuto, presenza*) invaluable.

insoz'zare [insot'tsare] *vt* (*pavimento*) to make dirty; (*fig: reputazione, memoria*) to tarnish, sully; **~rsi** *vr* to get dirty.

inspe'rabile *ag*: **la guarigione/salvezza era ~** there was no hope of a cure/of rescue; **abbiamo ottenuto risultati ~i** the results we achieved were far better than we had hoped.

inspe'rato, a *ag* unhoped-for.

inspie'gabile *ag* inexplicable.

inspi'rare *vt* to breathe in, inhale.

in'stabile *ag* (*carico, indole*) unstable; (*tempo*) unsettled; (*equilibrio*) unsteady.

instabilità *sf* instability; (*di tempo*) changeability.

instal'lare *vt* to install; **~rsi** *vr* (*sistemarsi*): **~rsi in** to settle in.

installazi'one [installat'tsjone] *sf* installation.

instan'cabile *ag* untiring, indefatigable.

instau'rare *vt* to introduce, institute.

instil'lare *vt* to instil.

instra'dare *vt* = **istradare**.

insù *av* up, upwards; **guardare all'~** to look up *o* upwards; **naso all'~** turned-up nose.

insubordinazi'one [insubordinat'tsjone] *sf* insubordination.

insuc'cesso [insut'tʃɛsso] *sm* failure, flop.

insudici'are [insudi'tʃare] *vt* to dirty; **~rsi** *vr* to get dirty.

insuffici'ente [insuffi'tʃɛnte] *ag* insufficient; (*compito, allievo*) inadequate.

insuffici'enza [insuffi'tʃɛntsa] *sf* insufficiency; inadequacy; (*INS*) fail; ~ **di prove** (*DIR*) lack of evidence.

insu'lare *ag* insular.

insu'lina *sf* insulin.

in'sulso, a *ag* (*sciocco*) inane, silly; (*persona*) dull, insipid.

insul'tare *vt* to insult, affront.

in'sulto *sm* insult, affront.

insupe'rabile *ag* (*ostacolo, difficoltà*) insuperable, insurmountable; (*eccellente: qualità, prodotto*) unbeatable; (: *persona, interpretazione*) unequalled.

insuper'bire *vt* to make proud, make arrogant; ~**rsi** *vr* to become arrogant.

insurrezi'one [insurret'tsjone] *sf* revolt, insurrection.

insussis'tente *ag* non-existent.

intac'care *vt* (*fare tacche*) to cut into; (*corrodere*) to corrode; (*fig: cominciare ad usare: risparmi*) to break into; (*: ledere*) to damage.

intagli'are [intaʎ'ʎare] *vt* to carve.

intaglia'tore, 'trice [intaʎʎa'tore] *sm/f* engraver.

in'taglio [in'taʎʎo] *sm* carving.

intan'gibile [intan'dʒibile] *ag* (*bene, patrimonio*) untouchable; (*fig: diritto*) inviolable.

in'tanto *av* (*nel frattempo*) meanwhile, in the meantime; (*per cominciare*) just to begin with; ~ **che** *cong* while.

in'tarsio *sm* inlaying *q*, marquetry *q*; inlay.

intasa'mento *sm* (*ostruzione*) blockage, obstruction; (*AUT: ingorgo*) traffic jam.

inta'sare *vt* to choke (up), block (up); (*AUT*) to obstruct, block; ~**rsi** *vr* to become choked *o* blocked.

intas'care *vt* to pocket.

in'tatto, a *ag* intact; (*puro*) unsullied.

intavo'lare *vt* to start, enter into.

inte'gerrimo, a [inte'dʒɛrrimo] *ag* honest, upright.

inte'grale *ag* complete; (*pane, farina*) wholemeal (*Brit*), wholewheat (*US*); **film in versione** ~ uncut version of a film; **calcolo** ~ (*MAT*) integral calculus; **edizione** ~ unabridged edition.

inte'grante *ag*: **parte** *f* ~ integral part.

inte'grare *vt* to complete; (*MAT*) to integrate; ~**rsi** *vr* (*persona*) to become integrated.

integra'tivo, a *ag* (*assegno*) supplementary; (*INS*): **esame** ~ assessment test sat when changing schools.

integrazi'one [integrat'tsjone] *sf* integration.

integrità *sf* integrity.

'integro, a *ag* (*intatto, intero*) complete, whole; (*retto*) upright.

intelaia'tura *sf* frame; (*fig*) structure, framework.

intel'letto *sm* intellect.

intellettu'ale *ag, sm/f* intellectual.

intellettua'loide (*peg*) *ag* pseudo-intellectual ♦ *sm/f* pseudo-intellectual, would-be intellectual.

intelli'gente [intelli'dʒente] *ag* intelligent.

intelli'genza [intelli'dʒentsa] *sf* intelligence.

intelli'ghenzia [intelli'gentsja] *sf* intelligentsia.

intelli'gibile [intelli'dʒibile] *ag* intelligible.

inteme'rato, a *ag* (*persona, vita*) blameless, irreproachable; (*coscienza*) clear; (*fama*) unblemished.

intempe'rante *ag* intemperate, immoderate.

intempe'ranza [intempe'rantsa] *sf* intemperance; ~**e** *sfpl* (*eccessi*) excesses.

intem'perie *sfpl* bad weather *sg*.

intempes'tivo, a *ag* untimely.

inten'dente *sm*: ~ **di Finanza** inland (*Brit*) *o* internal (*US*) revenue officer.

inten'denza [inten'dɛntsa] *sf*: ~ **di Finanza** inland (*Brit*) *o* internal (*US*) revenue office.

in'tendere *vt* (*avere intenzione*): ~ **fare qc** to intend *o* mean to do sth; (*comprendere*) to understand; (*udire*) to hear; (*significare*) to mean; ~**rsi** *vr* (*conoscere*): ~**rsi di** to know a lot about, be a connoisseur of; (*accordarsi*) to get on (well); ~**rsi con qn su qc** to come to an agreement with sb about sth; **intendersela con qn** (*avere una relazione amorosa*) to have an affair with sb; **mi ha dato a** ~ **che ...** he led me to believe that ...; **non vuole** ~ **ragione** he won't listen to reason; **s'intende!** naturally!, of course!; **intendiamoci** let's get it quite clear; **ci siamo intesi?** is that clear?, is that understood?

intendi'mento *sm* (*intelligenza*) understanding; (*proposito*) intention.

intendi'tore, 'trice *sm/f* connoisseur, expert; **a buon intenditor poche parole** (*proverbio*) a word is enough to the wise.

intene'rire *vt* (*fig*) to move (to pity); ~**rsi** *vr* (*fig*) to be moved.

intensifi'care *vt*, ~**rsi** *vr* to intensify.

intensità *sf* intensity; (*del vento*) force, strength.

inten'sivo, a *ag* intensive.

in'tenso, a *ag* (*luce, profumo*) strong; (*colore*) intense, deep.

inten'tare *vt* (*DIR*): ~ **causa contro qn** to start *o* institute proceedings against sb.

inten'tato, a *ag*: **non lasciare nulla d'**~ to leave no stone unturned, try everything.

in'tento, a *ag* (*teso, assorto*): ~ **(a)** intent (on), absorbed (in) ♦ *sm* aim, purpose; **fare qc con l'**~ **di** to do sth with the intention of; **riuscire nell'**~ to achieve one's aim.

intenzio'nale [intentsjo'nale] *ag* intentional; (*DIR: omicidio*) premeditated; **fallo** ~ (*SPORT*) deliberate foul.

intenzio'nato, a [intentsjo'nato] *ag*: **essere** ~ **a fare qc** to intend to do sth, have the intention of doing sth; **ben** ~ well-meaning, well-intentioned; **mal** ~ ill-intentioned.

intenzi'one [inten'tsjone] *sf* intention; (*DIR*) intent; **avere** ~ **di fare qc** to intend to do sth, have the intention of doing sth.

intera'gire [intera'dʒire] *vi* to interact.

intera'mente *av* entirely, completely.

interat'tivo, a *ag* interactive.

interazi'one [interat'tsjone] *sf* interaction.

interca'lare *sm* pet phrase, stock phrase ♦ *vt* to insert.

interca'pedine *sf* gap, cavity.

inter'cedere [inter'tʃɛdere] *vi* to intercede.

intercessi'one [intertʃes'sjone] *sf* intercession.

intercet'tare [intertʃet'tare] *vt* to intercept.

intercettazi'one [intertʃettat'tsjone] *sf*: ~ **telefonica** telephone tapping.

intercon'nettere *vt* to interconnect.

inter'correre *vi* (*esserci*) to exist; (*passare: tempo*) to elapse.

inter'corso, a *pp di* **intercorrere**.

inter'detto, a *pp di* **interdire** ♦ *ag* forbidden, prohibited; (*sconcertato*) dumbfounded ♦ *sm* (*REL*) interdict; **rimanere** ~ to be taken aback.

inter'dire *vt* to forbid, prohibit, ban; (*REL*) to interdict; (*DIR*) to deprive of civil rights.

interdizi'one [interdit'tsjone] *sf* prohibition, ban.

interessa'mento *sm* interest; (*intervento*) intervention, good offices *pl*.

interes'sante *ag* interesting; **essere in stato** ~ to be expecting (a baby).

interes'sare *vt* to interest; (*concernere*) to concern, be of interest to; (*far intervenire*): ~ **qn a** to draw sb's attention to ♦ *vi*: ~ **a** to interest, matter to; ~**rsi** *vr* (*mostrare interesse*): ~**rsi a** to take an interest in, be interested in; (*occuparsi*): ~**rsi di** to take care of; **precipitazioni che interessano le regioni settentrionali** rainfall affecting the north; **si è interessato di farmi avere quei biglietti** he took the trouble to get me those tickets.

interes'sato, a *ag* (*coinvolto*) interested, involved; (*peg*): **essere** ~ to act out of pure self-interest ♦ *sm/f* (*coinvolto*) person concerned; **a tutti gli** ~**i** to all those concerned, to all interested parties.

inte'resse *sm* (*anche COMM*) interest; (*tornaconto*): **fare qc per** ~ to do sth out of self-interest; ~ **maturato** (*ECON*) accrued interest; ~ **privato in atti di ufficio** (*AMM*) abuse of public office.

interes'senza [interes'sɛntsa] *sf* (*ECON*) profit-sharing.

inter'faccia, ce [inter'fattʃa] *sf* (*INFORM*) interface; ~ **utente** user interface.

interfe'renza [interfe'rɛntsa] *sf* interference.

interfe'rire *vi* to interfere.

inter'fono *sm* intercom; (*apparecchio*) internal phone.

interiezi'one [interjet'tsjone] *sf* exclamation, interjection.

'interim *sm inv* (*periodo*) interim, interval; **ministro ad** ~ acting *o* interim minister; (*incarico*) temporary appointment.

interi'ora *sfpl* entrails.

interi'ore *ag* inner *cpd*; **parte** *f* ~ inside.

interiorità *sf* inner being.

interioriz'zare [interjorid'dzare] *vt* to internalize.

inter'linea *sf* (*DATTILOGRAFIA*) spacing; (*TIP*) leading; **doppia** ~ double spacing.

interlocu'tore, 'trice *sm/f* speaker.

interlocu'torio, a *ag* interlocutory.

inter'ludio *sm* (*MUS*) interlude.

intermedi'ario, a *ag, sm/f* intermediary.

intermediazi'one [intermedjat'tsjone] *sf* mediation.

inter'medio, a *ag* intermediate.

inter'mezzo [inter'meddzo] *sm* (*intervallo*) interval; (*breve spettacolo*) intermezzo.

intermi'nabile *ag* interminable, endless.

intermit'tente *ag* intermittent.

intermit'tenza [intermit'tɛntsa] *sf*: **ad** ~ intermittent.

interna'mento *sm* internment; confinement (to a mental hospital).

inter'nare *vt* (*arrestare*) to intern; (*MED*) to confine to a mental hospital.

inter'nato, a *ag* interned; confined (to a mental hospital) ♦ *sm/f* internee; inmate (of a mental hospital) ♦ *sm* (*collegio*) boarding school; (*MED*) period as a houseman (*Brit*) *o* an intern (*US*).

internazio'nale [internattsjo'nale] *ag* international.

inter'nista, i, e *sm/f* specialist in internal medicine.

in'terno, a *ag* (*di dentro*) internal, interior, inner; (: *mare*) inland; (*nazionale*) domestic; (*allievo*) boarding ♦ *sm* inside, interior; (*di paese*) interior; (*fodera*) lining; (*di appartamento*) flat (*Brit*) *o* apartment (*US*) (number); (*TEL*) extension ♦ *sm/f* (*INS*) boarder; ~**i** *smpl* (*CINEMA*) interior shots; **commissione** ~**a** (*INS*) internal examination board; **"per uso** ~**"** (*MED*) "to be taken internally"; **all'**~ inside; **Ministero degli I**~**i** Ministry of the Interior, ≈ Home Office (*Brit*), ≈ Department of the Interior (*US*); **notizie dall'**~ (*STAMPA*) home news.

in'tero, a *ag* (*integro, intatto*) whole, entire; (*completo, totale*) complete; (*numero*) whole; (*non ridotto: biglietto*) full.

interpel'lanza [interpel'lantsa] *sf*: **presentare un'**~ (*POL*) to ask a (parliamentary) question; ~ **parlamentare** interpellation.

interpel'lare *vt* to consult; (*POL*) to question.

Inter'pol *sf* Interpol.

inter'porre *vt* (*ostacolo*): ~ **qc a qc** to put sth in the way of sth; (*influenza*) to use; **interporsi** *vr* to intervene; ~ **appello** (*DIR*) to appeal; **interporsi fra** (*mettersi in mezzo*) to come between.

inter'posto, a *pp di* **interporre**.

interpre'tare *vt* (*spiegare, tradurre*) to interpret; (*MUS, TEATRO*) to perform;

(*personaggio, sonata*) to play; (*canzone*) to sing.

interpretari'ato *sm* interpreting.

interpretazi'one [interpretat'tsjone] *sf* interpretation.

in'terprete *sm/f* interpreter; (*TEATRO*) actor/actress, performer; (*MUS*) performer; **farsi ~ di** to act as a spokesman for.

interpunzi'one [interpun'tsjone] *sf* punctuation; **segni di ~** punctuation marks.

inter'rare *vt* (*seme, pianta*) to plant; (*tubature etc*) to lay underground; (*MIL*: *pezzo d'artiglieria*) to dig in; (*riempire di terra: canale*) to fill in.

interro'gare *vt* to question; (*INS*) to test.

interroga'tivo, a *ag* (*occhi, sguardo*) questioning, inquiring; (*LING*) interrogative ♦ *sm* question; (*fig*) mystery.

interroga'torio, a *ag* interrogatory, questioning ♦ *sm* (*DIR*) questioning *q*.

interrogazi'one [interrogat'tsjone] *sf* questioning *q*; (*INS*) oral test; (*POL*): **~ (parlamentare)** question.

inter'rompere *vt* to interrupt; (*studi, trattative*) to break off, interrupt; **~rsi** *vr* to break off, stop.

inter'rotto, a *pp di* **interrompere**.

interrut'tore *sm* switch.

interruzi'one [interrut'tsjone] *sf* (*vedi interrompere*) interruption; break; **~ di gravidanza** termination of pregnancy.

interse'care *vt*, **~rsi** *vr* to intersect.

inter'stizio [inter'stittsjo] *sm* interstice, crack.

interur'bano, a *ag* inter-city; (*TEL*: *chiamata*) trunk *cpd* (*Brit*), long-distance; (*: telefono*) long-distance ♦ *sf* trunk call (*Brit*), long-distance call.

inter'vallo *sm* interval; (*spazio*) space, gap; **~ pubblicitario** (*TV*) commercial break.

interve'nire *vi* (*partecipare*): **~ a** to take part in; (*intromettersi: anche POL*) to intervene; (*MED: operare*) to operate.

inter'vento *sm* participation; (*intromissione*) intervention; (*MED*) operation; (*breve discorso*) speech; **fare un ~ nel corso di** (*dibattito, programma*) to take part in.

interve'nuto, a *pp di* **intervenire** ♦ *sm*: **gli ~i** those present.

inter'vista *sf* interview.

intervis'tare *vt* to interview.

intervista'tore, 'trice *sm/f* interviewer.

in'teso, a *pp di* **intendere** ♦ *ag* agreed ♦ *sf* understanding; (*accordo*) agreement, understanding; **resta ~ che ...** it is understood that ...; **non darsi per ~ di qc** to take no notice of sth; **uno sguardo d'~a** a knowing look.

intes'tare *vt* (*lettera*) to address;

(*proprietà*): **~ a** to register in the name of; **~ un assegno a qn** to make out a cheque to sb.

intesta'tario, a *sm/f* holder.

intestazi'one [intestat'tsjone] *sf* heading; (*su carta da lettere*) letterhead; (*registrazione*) registration.

intesti'nale *ag* intestinal.

intes'tino, a *ag* (*lotte*) internal, civil ♦ *sm* (*ANAT*) intestine.

intiepi'dire *vt* (*riscaldare*) to warm (up); (*raffreddare*) to cool (down); (*fig: amicizia etc*) to cool; **~rsi** *vr* to warm (up); to cool (down); to cool.

intima'mente *av* intimately; **sono ~ convinto che ...** I'm firmly *o* deeply convinced that ...; **i due fatti sono ~ connessi** the two events are closely connected.

inti'mare *vt* to order, command; **~ la resa a qn** (*MIL*) to call upon sb to surrender.

intimazi'one [intimat'tsjone] *sf* order, command.

intima'torio, a *ag* threatening.

intimidazi'one [intimidat'tsjone] *sf* intimidation.

intimi'dire *vt* to intimidate ♦ *vi* (*anche: ~rsi*) to grow shy.

intimità *sf* intimacy; privacy; (*familiarità*) familiarity.

'intimo, a *ag* intimate; (*affetti, vita*) private; (*fig: profondo*) inmost ♦ *sm* (*persona*) intimate *o* close friend; (*dell'animo*) bottom, depths *pl*; **parti ~e** (*ANAT*) private parts; **rapporti ~i** (*sessuali*) intimate relations.

intimo'rire *vt* to frighten; **~rsi** *vr* to become frightened.

in'tingere [in'tindʒere] *vt* to dip.

in'tingolo *sm* sauce; (*pietanza*) stew.

in'tinto, a *pp di* **intingere**.

intiriz'zire [intirid'dzire] *vt* to numb ♦ *vi* (*anche: ~rsi*) to go numb.

intito'lare *vt* to give a title to; (*dedicare*) to dedicate; **~rsi** *vr* (*libro, film*) to be called.

intolle'rabile *ag* intolerable.

intolle'rante *ag* intolerant.

intolle'ranza [intolle'rantsa] *sf* intolerance.

intona'care *vt* to plaster.

in'tonaco, ci *o* **chi** *sm* plaster.

into'nare *vt* (*canto*) to start to sing; (*armonizzare*) to match; **~rsi** *vr* (*colori*) to go together; **~rsi a** (*carnagione*) to suit; (*abito*) to go with, match.

intonazi'one [intonat'tsjone] *sf* intonation.

inton'tire *vt* to stun, daze ♦ *vi*, **~rsi** *vr* to be stunned *o* dazed.

inton'tito, a *ag* stunned, dazed; **~ dal sonno** stupid with sleep.

in'toppo *sm* stumbling block, obstacle.

intorbi'dare *vt* (*liquido*) to make turbid; (*mente*) to cloud; **~ le acque** (*fig*) to muddy the waters.

in'torno *av* around; ~ **a** *prep* (*attorno a*) around; (*riguardo, circa*) about.

intorpi'dire *vt* to numb; (*fig*) to make sluggish ♦ *vi* (*anche:* ~**rsi**) to grow numb; (*fig*) to become sluggish.

intossi'care *vt* to poison.

intossicazi'one [intossikat'tsjone] *sf* poisoning.

intradu'cibile [intradu'tʃibile] *ag* untranslatable.

intralci'are [intral'tʃare] *vt* to hamper, hold up.

in'tralcio [in'traltʃo] *sm* hitch.

intrallaz'zare [intrallat'tsare] *vi* to intrigue, scheme.

intral'lazzo [intral'lattso] *sm* (*POL*) intrigue, manoeuvre (*Brit*), maneuver (*US*); (*traffico losco*) racket.

intramon'tabile *ag* timeless.

intramusco'lare *ag* intramuscular.

intransi'gente [intransi'dʒɛnte] *ag* intransigent, uncompromising.

intransi'genza [intransi'dʒɛntsa] *sf* intransigence.

intransi'tivo, a *ag, sm* intransitive.

intrappo'lare *vt* to trap; **rimanere intrappolato** to be trapped; **farsi** ~ to get caught.

intrapren'dente *ag* enterprising, go-ahead; (*con le donne*) forward, bold.

intrapren'denza [intrapren'dɛntsa] *sf* audacity, initiative; (*con le donne*) boldness.

intra'prendere *vt* to undertake; (*carriera*) to embark (up)on.

intra'preso, a *pp di* **intraprendere**.

intrat'tabile *ag* intractable.

intratte'nere *vt* (*divertire*) to entertain; (*chiacchierando*) to engage in conversation; (*rapporti*) to have, maintain; ~**rsi** *vr* to linger; ~**rsi su qc** to dwell on sth.

intratteni'mento *sm* entertainment.

intrave'dere *vt* to catch a glimpse of; (*fig*) to foresee.

intrecci'are [intret'tʃare] *vt* (*capelli*) to plait, braid; (*intessere: anche fig*) to weave, interweave, intertwine; ~**rsi** *vr* to intertwine, become interwoven; ~ **le mani** to clasp one's hands; ~ **una relazione amorosa** (*fig*) to begin an affair.

in'treccio [in'trettʃo] *sm* (*fig: trama*) plot, story.

in'trepido, a *ag* fearless, intrepid.

intri'care *vt* (*fili*) to tangle; (*fig: faccenda*) to complicate; ~**rsi** *vr* to become tangled; to become complicated.

in'trico, chi *sm* (*anche fig*) tangle.

intri'gante *ag* scheming ♦ *sm/f* schemer, intriguer.

intri'gare *vi* to manoeuvre (*Brit*), maneuver (*US*), scheme.

in'trigo, ghi *sm* plot, intrigue.

in'trinseco, a, ci, che *ag* intrinsic.

in'triso, a *ag:* ~ (**di**) soaked (in).

intris'tire *vi* (*persona: diventare triste*) to grow sad; (*pianta*) to wilt.

intro'dotto, a *pp di* **introdurre**.

intro'durre *vt* to introduce; (*chiave etc*): ~ **qc in** to insert sth into; (*persona: far entrare*) to show in; **introdursi** *vr* (*moda, tecniche*) to be introduced; **introdursi in** (*persona: penetrare*) to enter; (: *entrare furtivamente*) to steal *o* slip into.

introduzi'one [introdut'tsjone] *sf* introduction.

in'troito *sm* income, revenue.

intro'messo, a *pp di* **intromettersi**.

intro'mettersi *vr* to interfere, meddle; (*interporsi*) to intervene.

intromissi'one *sf* interference, meddling; intervention.

introspezi'one [introspet'tsjone] *sf* introspection.

intro'vabile *ag* (*persona, oggetto*) who (*o* which) cannot be found; (*libro etc*) unobtainable.

intro'verso, a *ag* introverted ♦ *sm/f* introvert.

intrufo'larsi *vr:* ~ (**in**) (*stanza*) to sneak in(to), slip in(to); (*conversazione*) to butt in (on).

in'truglio [in'truʎʎo] *sm* concoction.

intrusi'one *sf* intrusion; interference.

in'truso, a *sm/f* intruder.

intu'ire *vt* to perceive by intuition; (*rendersi conto*) to realize.

in'tuito *sm* intuition; (*perspicacia*) perspicacity.

intuizi'one [intuit'tsjone] *sf* intuition.

inturgi'dire [inturdʒi'dire] *vi,* ~**rsi** *vr* to swell.

inumanità *sf inv* inhumanity.

inu'mano, a *ag* inhuman.

inu'mare *vt* (*seppellire*) to bury, inter.

inumazi'one [inumat'tsjone] *sf* burial, interment.

inumi'dire *vt* to dampen, moisten; ~**rsi** *vr* to become damp *o* wet.

inurba'mento *sm* urbanization.

inusi'tato, a *ag* unusual.

i'nutile *ag* useless; (*superfluo*) pointless, unnecessary; **è stato tutto** ~**!** it was all in vain!

inutilità *sf* uselessness; pointlessness.

inutiliz'zabile [inutilid'dzabile] *ag* unusable.

inutil'mente *av* (*senza risultato*) fruitlessly; (*senza utilità, scopo*) unnecessarily, needlessly; **l'ho cercato** ~ I looked for him in vain; **ti preoccupi** ~ there's nothing for you to worry about, there's no need for you to worry.

inva'dente *ag* (*fig*) intrusive.

inva'denza [inva'dɛntsa] *sf* intrusiveness.

in'vadere *vt* to invade; (*affollare*) to swarm into, overrun; (*sog: acque*) to flood.

invadi'trice [invadi'tritʃe] *ag f vedi* **invasore**.

inva'ghirsi [inva'girsi] *vr*: ~ **di** to take a fancy to.

invali'cabile *ag* (*montagna*) impassable.

invali'dare *vt* to invalidate.

invalidità *sf* infirmity; disability; (*DIR*) invalidity.

in'valido, a *ag* (*infermo*) infirm; (*al lavoro*) disabled; (*DIR*: *nullo*) invalid ♦ *sm/f* invalid; disabled person; ~ **di guerra** disabled ex-serviceman; ~ **del lavoro** industrially disabled person.

in'valso, a *ag* (*diffuso*) established.

in'vano *av* in vain.

invari'abile *ag* invariable.

invari'ato, a *ag* unchanged.

inva'sare *vt* (*pianta*) to pot.

inva'sato, a *ag* possessed (by the devil) ♦ *sm/f* person possessed by the devil; **urlare come un** ~ to shout like a madman.

invasi'one *sf* invasion.

in'vaso, a *pp di* **invadere**.

inva'sore, invadi'trice [invadi'tritʃe] *ag* invading ♦ *sm* invader.

invecchia'mento [invekkja'mento] *sm* growing old; ageing; **questo whisky ha un ~ di 12 anni** this whisky has been matured for 12 years.

invecchi'are [invek'kjare] *vi* (*persona*) to grow old; (*vino, popolazione*) to age; (*moda*) to become dated ♦ *vt* to age; (*far apparire più vecchio*) to make look older; **lo trovo invecchiato** I find he has aged.

in'vece [in'vetʃe] *av* instead; (*al contrario*) on the contrary; ~ **di** *prep* instead of.

inve'ire *vi*: ~ **contro** to rail against.

invele'nire *vt* to embitter; ~**rsi** *vr* to become bitter.

inven'duto, a *ag* unsold.

inven'tare *vt* to invent; (*pericoli, pettegolezzi*) to make up, invent.

inventari'are *vt* to make an inventory of, inventory.

inven'tario *sm* inventory; (*COMM*) stocktaking *q*.

inven'tivo, a *ag* inventive ♦ *sf* inventiveness.

inven'tore, 'trice *sm/f* inventor.

invenzi'one [inven'tsjone] *sf* invention; (*bugia*) lie, story.

invere'condia *sf* shamelessness, immodesty.

inver'nale *ag* winter *cpd*; (*simile all'inverno*) wintry.

in'verno *sm* winter; **d'~** in (the) winter.

invero'simile *ag* unlikely ♦ *sm*: **ha dell'~** it's hard to believe, it's incredible.

inversi'one *sf* inversion; **"divieto d'~"** (*AUT*) "no U-turns".

in'verso, a *ag* opposite; (*MAT*) inverse ♦ *sm* contrary, opposite; **in senso ~** in the opposite direction; **in ordine ~** in reverse order.

inverte'brato, a *ag, sm* invertebrate.

inver'tire *vt* to invert; (*disposizione, posti*) to change; (*ruoli*) to exchange; ~ **la marcia** (*AUT*) to do a U-turn; ~ **la rotta** (*NAUT*) to go about; (*fig*) to do a U-turn.

inver'tito, a *sm/f* homosexual.

investi'gare *vt*, *vi* to investigate.

investiga'tivo, a *ag*: **squadra ~a** detective squad.

investiga'tore, 'trice *sm/f* investigator, detective.

investigazi'one [investigat'tsjone] *sf* investigation, inquiry.

investi'mento *sm* (*ECON*) investment; (*di veicolo*) crash, collision; (*di pedone*) knocking down.

inves'tire *vt* (*denaro*) to invest; (*sog: veicolo: pedone*) to knock down; (*: altro veicolo*) to crash into; (*apostrofare*) to assail; (*incaricare*): ~ **qn di** to invest sb with; ~**rsi** *vr* (*fig*): ~**rsi di una parte** to enter thoroughly into a role.

investi'tore, 'trice *sm/f* driver responsible for an accident.

investi'tura *sf* investiture.

invete'rato, a *ag* inveterate.

invet'tiva *sf* invective.

invi'are *vt* to send.

invi'ato, a *sm/f* envoy; (*STAMPA*) correspondent.

in'vidia *sf* envy; **fare ~ a qn** to make sb envious.

invidi'are *vt*: ~ **qn (per qc)** to envy sb (for sth); ~ **qc a qn** to envy sb sth; **non aver nulla da ~ a nessuno** to be as good as the next one.

invidi'oso, a *ag* envious.

invin'cibile [invin'tʃibile] *ag* invincible.

in'vio, 'vii *sm* sending; (*insieme di merci*) consignment.

invio'labile *ag* inviolable.

invio'lato, a *ag* (*diritto, segreto*) inviolate; (*foresta*) virgin *cpd*; (*montagna, vetta*) unscaled.

invipe'rire *vi*, ~**rsi** *vr* to become furious, fly into a temper.

invipe'rito, a *ag* furious.

invis'chiare [invis'kjare] *vt* (*fig*): ~ **qn in qc** to involve sb in sth, mix sb up in sth; ~**rsi** *vr*: ~**rsi (con qn/in qc)** to get mixed up *o* involved (with sb/in sth).

invi'sibile *ag* invisible.

in'viso, a *ag*: ~ **a** unpopular with.

invi'tante *ag* (*proposta, odorino*) inviting; (*sorriso*) appealing, attractive.

invi'tare *vt* to invite; ~ **qn a fare** to invite sb to do.

invi'tato, a *sm/f* guest.

in'vito *sm* invitation; **dietro ~ del sig. Rossi** at Mr Rossi's invitation.

invo'care *vt* (*chiedere: aiuto, pace*) to cry out for; (*appellarsi: la legge, Dio*) to appeal to, invoke.

invogli'are [invoʎ'ʎare] *vt*: ~ qn a fare to tempt sb to do, induce sb to do.

involon'tario, a *ag* (*errore*) unintentional; (*gesto*) involuntary.

invol'tino *sm* (*CUC*) roulade.

in'volto *sm* (*pacco*) parcel; (*fagotto*) bundle.

in'volucro *sm* cover, wrapping.

involu'tivo, a *ag*: subire un processo ~ to regress.

invo'luto, a *ag* involved, intricate.

involuzi'one [involut'tsjone] *sf* (*di stile*) convolutedness; (*regresso*): subire un'~ to regress.

invulne'rabile *ag* invulnerable.

inzacche'rare [intsakke'rare] *vt* to spatter with mud; ~rsi *vr* to get muddy.

inzup'pare [intsup'pare] *vt* to soak; ~rsi *vr* to get soaked; inzuppò i biscotti nel latte he dipped the biscuits in the milk.

'io *pronome* I ♦ *sm inv*: l'~ the ego, the self; ~ stesso(a) I myself; sono ~ it's me.

i'odio *sm* iodine.

i'ogurt *sm inv* = yoghurt.

i'one *sm* ion.

l'onio *sm*: lo ~, il mar ~ the Ionian (Sea).

'iosa: a ~ *av* in abundance, in great quantity.

'IPAB *sigla fpl* (= *Istituzioni pubbliche di Assistenza e Beneficenza*) charitable institutions.

i'perbole *sf* (*LETTERATURA*) hyperbole; (*MAT*) hyperbola.

iper'bolico, a, ci, che *ag* (*LETTERATURA, MAT*) hyperbolic(al); (*fig: esagerato*) exaggerated.

ipermer'cato *sm* hypermarket.

ipersen'sibile *ag* (*persona*) hypersensitive; (*FOT: lastra, pellicola*) hypersensitized.

ipertensi'one *sf* high blood pressure, hypertension.

ip'nosi *sf* hypnosis.

ip'notico, a, ci, che *ag* hypnotic.

ipno'tismo *sm* hypnotism.

ipnotiz'zare [ipnotid'dzare] *vt* to hypnotize.

ipoal'lergico, a, ci, che [ipoal'lɛrdʒiko] *ag* hypoallergenic.

ipocon'dria *sf* hypochondria.

ipocon'driaco, a, ci, che *ag, sm/f* hypochondriac.

ipocri'sia *sf* hypocrisy.

i'pocrita, i, e *ag* hypocritical ♦ *sm/f* hypocrite.

ipo'teca, che *sf* mortgage.

ipote'care *vt* to mortgage.

i'potesi *sf inv* hypothesis; facciamo l'~ che ..., ammettiamo per ~ che ... let's suppose o assume that ...; nella peggiore/migliore delle ~i at worst/best; nell'~ che venga should he come, if he comes; se per ~ io

partissi ... just supposing I were to leave ....

ipo'tetico, a, ci, che *ag* hypothetical.

ipotiz'zare [ipotid'dzare] *vt*: ~ che to form the hypothesis that.

'ippico, a, ci, che *ag* horse *cpd* ♦ *sf* horse-racing.

ippocas'tano *sm* horse chestnut.

ip'podromo *sm* racecourse.

ippo'potamo *sm* hippopotamus.

'ipsilon *sf o m inv* (*lettera*) Y, y; (: *dell'alfabeto greco*) upsilon.

IP'SOA *sigla m* (= *Istituto Post-Universitario per lo Studio dell'Organizzazione Aziendale*) postgraduate institute of business administration.

'ira *sf* anger, wrath.

ira'cheno, a [ira'kɛno] *ag, sm/f* Iraqi.

l'ran *sm*: l'~ Iran.

irani'ano, a *ag, sm/f* Iranian.

l'raq *sm*: l'~ Iraq.

'IRCE ['irtʃe] *sigla m* = Istituto per le relazioni culturali con l'Estero.

'IRI *sigla m* (= *Istituto per la Ricostruzione Industriale*) state-controlled industrial investment office.

'iride *sf* (*arcobaleno*) rainbow; (*ANAT, BOT*) iris.

Ir'landa *sf*: l'~ Ireland; l'~ del Nord Northern Ireland, Ulster; la Repubblica d'~ Eire, the Republic of Ireland; il mar d'~ the Irish Sea.

irlan'dese *ag* Irish ♦ *sm/f* Irishman/woman; gli l~i the Irish.

iro'nia *sf* irony.

i'ronico, a, ci, che *ag* ironic(al).

ironiz'zare [ironid'dzare] *vt, vi*: ~ su to be ironical about.

i'roso, a *ag* (*sguardo, tono*) angry, wrathful; (*persona*) irascible.

'IRPEF *sigla f vedi* imposta sul reddito delle persone fisiche.

ir'pino, a *ag* of (*o* from) Irpinia.

irradi'are *vt* to radiate; (*sog: raggi di luce: illuminare*) to shine on ♦ *vi* (*diffondersi: anche*: ~rsi) to radiate.

irradiazi'one [irradjat'tsjone] *sf* radiation.

irraggiun'gibile [irraddʒun'dʒibile] *ag* unreachable; (*fig: meta*) unattainable.

irragio'nevole [irradʒo'nevole] *ag* (*privo di ragione*) irrational; (*fig: persona, pretese, prezzo*) unreasonable.

irrazio'nale [irrattsjo'nale] *ag* irrational.

irre'ale *ag* unreal.

irrealiz'zabile [irrealid'dzabile] *ag* (*sogno, desiderio*) unattainable, unrealizable; (*progetto*) unworkable, impracticable.

irrealtà *sf* unreality.

irrecupe'rabile *ag* (*gen*) irretrievable; (*fig: persona*) irredeemable.

irrecu'sabile *ag* (*offerta*) not to be refused; (*prova*) irrefutable.

irreden'tista, i, e *ag*, *sm/f* (*STORIA*) Irredentist.

irrefre'nabile *ag* uncontrollable.

irrefu'tabile *ag* irrefutable.

irrego'lare *ag* irregular; (*terreno*) uneven.

irregolarità *sf inv* irregularity; unevenness *q*.

irremo'vibile *ag* (*fig*) unshakeable, unyielding.

irrepa'rabile *ag* irreparable; (*fig*) inevitable.

irrepe'ribile *ag* nowhere to be found.

irrepren'sibile *ag* irreproachable.

irrequi'eto, a *ag* restless.

irresis'tibile *ag* irresistible.

irreso'luto, a *ag* irresolute.

irrespi'rabile *ag* (*aria*) unbreathable; (*fig*: *opprimente*) stifling, oppressive; (*: malsano*) unhealthy.

irrespon'sabile *ag* irresponsible.

irrestrin'gibile [irrestrin'dʒibile] *ag* unshrinkable, non-shrink (*Brit*).

irrever'sibile *ag* irreversible.

irrevo'cabile *ag* irrevocable.

irricono'scibile [irrikonoʃ'ʃibile] *ag* unrecognizable.

irridu'cibile [irridu'tʃibile] *ag* irreducible; (*fig*) unshakeable.

irrifles'sivo, a *ag* thoughtless.

irri'gare *vt* (*annaffiare*) to irrigate; (*sog: fiume etc*) to flow through.

irrigazi'one [irrigat'tsjone] *sf* irrigation.

irrigidi'mento [irridʒidi'mento] *sm* stiffening; hardening; tightening.

irrigi'dire [irridʒi'dire] *vt* to stiffen; (*disciplina*) to tighten; **~rsi** *vr* to stiffen; (*posizione, atteggiamento*) to harden.

irriguar'doso, a *ag* disrespectful.

ir'riguo, a *ag* (*terreno*) irrigated; (*acque*) irrigation *cpd*.

irrile'vante *ag* (*trascurabile*) insignificant.

irrinunci'abile [irrinun'tʃabile] *ag* vital; which cannot be abandoned.

irripe'tibile *ag* unrepeatable.

irri'solto, a *ag* (*problema*) unresolved.

irri'sorio, a *ag* derisory.

irrispet'toso, a *ag* disrespectful.

irri'tabile *ag* irritable.

irri'tante *ag* (*atteggiamento*) irritating, annoying; (*MED*) irritant.

irri'tare *vt* (*mettere di malumore*) to irritate, annoy; (*MED*) to irritate; **~rsi** *vr* (*stizzirsi*) to become irritated *o* annoyed; (*MED*) to become irritated.

irritazi'one [irritat'tsjone] *sf* irritation; annoyance.

irrive'rente *ag* irreverent.

irrobus'tire *vt* (*persona*) to make stronger, make more robust; (*muscoli*) to strengthen; **~rsi** *vr* to become stronger.

ir'rompere *vi*: **~ in** to burst into.

irro'rare *vt* to sprinkle; (*AGR*) to spray.

ir'rotto, a *pp di* **irrompere**.

irru'ente *ag* (*fig*) impetuous, violent.

irru'enza [irru'entsa] *sf* impetuousness; **con ~** impetuously.

ir'ruppi *etc vb vedi* **irrompere**.

irruvi'dire *vt* to roughen ♦ *vi* (*anche*: **~rsi**) to become rough.

irruzi'one [irrut'tsjone] *sf*: **fare ~ in** to burst into; (*sog: polizia*) to raid.

ir'suto, a *ag* (*petto*) hairy; (*barba*) bristly.

'irto, a *ag* bristly; **~ di** bristling with.

Is. *abbr* (= *isola*) I.

is'crissi *etc vb vedi* **iscrivere**.

is'critto, a *pp di* **iscrivere** ♦ *sm/f* member; **gli ~i alla gara** the competitors; **per** *o* **in ~** in writing.

is'crivere *vt* to register, enter; (*persona*): **~ (a)** to register (in), enrol (in); **~rsi** *vr*: **~rsi (a)** (*club, partito*) to join; (*università*) to register *o* enrol (at); (*esame, concorso*) to register *o* enter (for).

iscrizi'one [iskrit'tsjone] *sf* (*epigrafe etc*) inscription; (*a scuola, società etc*) enrolment; registration.

'ISEF *sigla m* = *Istituto Superiore di Educazione Fisica*.

Is'lam *sm*: **l'~** Islam.

is'lamico, a, ci, che *ag* Islamic.

Is'landa *sf*: **l'~** Iceland.

islan'dese *ag* Icelandic ♦ *sm/f* Icelander ♦ *sm* (*LING*) Icelandic.

'isola *sf* island; **~ pedonale** (*AUT*) pedestrian precinct.

isola'mento *sm* isolation; (*TECN*) insulation; **essere in cella di ~** to be in solitary confinement; **~ acustico** soundproofing; **~ termico** thermal insulation.

iso'lano, a *ag* island *cpd* ♦ *sm/f* islander.

iso'lante *ag* insulating ♦ *sm* insulator.

iso'lare *vt* to isolate; (*TECN*) to insulate; (*: acusticamente*) to soundproof.

iso'lato, a *ag* isolated; insulated ♦ *sm* (*edificio*) block.

isolazio'nismo [isolattsjo'nismo] *sm* isolationism.

i'sotopo *sm* isotope.

ispessi'mento *sm* thickening.

ispes'sire *vt* to thicken; **~rsi** *vr* to get thicker, thicken.

ispetto'rato *sm* inspectorate.

ispet'tore, 'trice *sm/f* inspector; (*COMM*) supervisor; **~ di zona** (*COMM*) area supervisor *o* manager; **~ di reparto** shop walker (*Brit*), floor walker (*US*).

ispezio'nare [ispettsjo'nare] *vt* to inspect.

ispezi'one [ispet'tsjone] *sf* inspection.

'ispido, a *ag* bristly, shaggy.

ispi'rare *vt* to inspire; **~rsi** *vr*: **~rsi a** to draw one's inspiration from; (*conformarsi*) to be based on; **l'idea m'ispira** the idea appeals to me.

ispira'tore, 'trice *ag* inspiring ♦ *sm/f* inspirer; (*di ribellione*) instigator.

ispirazi'one [ispirat'tsjone] *sf* inspiration; **secondo l'~ del momento** according to the mood of the moment.

Isra'ele *sm*: **l'~** Israel.

israeli'ano, a *ag*, *sm/f* Israeli.

israe'lita, i, e *sm/f* Jew/Jewess; (*STORIA*) Israelite.

israe'litico, a, ci, che *ag* Jewish.

is'sare *vt* to hoist; **~ l'ancora** to weigh anchor.

'Istanbul *sf* Istanbul.

istan'taneo, a *ag* instantaneous ♦ *sf* (*FOT*) snapshot.

is'tante *sm* instant, moment; **all'~, sull'~** instantly, immediately.

is'tanza [is'tantsa] *sf* petition, request; **giudice di prima ~** (*DIR*) judge of the court of first instance; **giudizio di seconda ~** judgment on appeal; **in ultima ~** (*fig*) finally; **~ di divorzio** petition for divorce.

'ISTAT *sigla m* = *Istituto Centrale di Statistica*.

'ISTEL *sigla f* = *Indagine sull'ascolto delle televisioni in Italia*.

is'terico, a, ci, che *ag* hysterical.

isteri'lire *vt* (*terreno*) to render infertile; (*fig*: *fantasia*) to dry up; **~rsi** *vr* to become infertile; to dry up.

iste'rismo *sm* hysteria.

isti'gare *vt* to incite.

istigazi'one [istigat'tsjone] *sf* instigation; **~ a delinquere** (*DIR*) incitement to crime.

istin'tivo, a *ag* instinctive.

is'tinto *sm* instinct.

istitu'ire *vt* (*fondare*) to institute, found; (*porre*: *confronto*) to establish; (*intraprendere*: *inchiesta*) to set up.

isti'tuto *sm* institute; (*di università*) department; (*ente*, *DIR*) institution; **~ di bellezza** beauty salon; **~ di credito** bank, banking institution; **~ tecnico commerciale** ≈ commercial college; **~ tecnico industriale statale** ≈ technical college.

istitu'tore, 'trice *sm/f* (*fondatore*) founder; (*precettore*) tutor/governess.

istituzi'one [istitut'tsjone] *sf* institution; **~i** *sfpl* (*DIR*) institutes; **lotta alle ~i** struggle against the Establishment.

'istmo *sm* (*GEO*) isthmus.

isto'gramma, i *sm* histogram.

istra'dare *vt* (*fig*: *persona*): **~ (a/verso)** to direct (to/towards).

istri'ano, a *ag*, *sm/f* Istrian.

'istrice ['istritʃe] *sm* porcupine.

istri'one *sm* (*peg*) ham (actor).

istru'ire *vt* (*insegnare*) to teach; (*ammaestrare*) to train; (*informare*) to instruct, inform; (*DIR*) to prepare.

istru'ito, a *ag* educated.

istrut'tivo, a *ag* instructive.

istrut'tore, 'trice *sm/f* instructor ♦ *ag*:

giudice ~ examining (*Brit*) o committing (*US*) magistrate.

istrut'toria *sf* (*DIR*) (preliminary) investigation and hearing; **formalizzare un'~** to proceed to a formal hearing.

istruzi'one [istrut'tsjone] *sf* (*gen*) training; (*INS*, *cultura*) education; (*direttiva*) instruction; (*DIR*) = **istruttoria**; **Ministero della Pubblica I~** Ministry of Education; **~i di spedizione** forwarding instructions; **~i per l'uso** instructions (for use).

istupi'dire *vt* (*sog*: *colpo*) to stun, daze; (: *droga*, *stanchezza*) to stupefy; **~rsi** *vr* to become stupid.

'ISVE *sigla m* (= *Istituto di Studi per lo Sviluppo Economico*) *institute for research into economic development*.

l'talia *sf*: **l'~** Italy.

itali'ano, a *ag* Italian ♦ *sm/f* Italian ♦ *sm* (*LING*) Italian; **gli I~i** the Italians.

ITC *sigla m* = **istituto tecnico commerciale**.

'iter *sm* passage, course; **l'~ burocratico** the bureaucratic process.

itine'rante *ag* wandering, itinerant; **mostra ~** touring exhibition; **spettacolo ~** travelling (*Brit*) o traveling (*US*) show, touring show.

itine'rario *sm* itinerary.

'ITIS *sigla m* = **istituto tecnico industriale statale**.

itte'rizia [itte'rittsja] *sf* (*MED*) jaundice.

'ittico, a, ci, che *ag* fish *cpd*; fishing *cpd*.

Iugos'lavia *sf* = **Jugoslavia**.

iugos'lavo, a *ag*, *sm/f* = **jugoslavo, a**.

i'uta *sf* jute.

'I.V.A. *sigla f* *vedi* **imposta sul valore aggiunto**.

'ivi *av* (*formale*, *poetico*) therein; (*nelle citazioni*) ibid.

J

J, j [i'lunga] *sm* o *f inv* (*lettera*) J, j; **~ come Jersey** ≈ J for Jack (*Brit*), J for Jig (*US*).

jazz [dʒaz] *sm* jazz.

jaz'zista, i [dʒad'dzista] *sm* jazz player.

jeans [dʒinz] *smpl* jeans.

jeep [dʒip] *sm inv* jeep.

'jersey ['dʒɛrzi] *sm inv* jersey (cloth).

'jockey ['dʒɔki] *sm inv* (*CARTE*) jack; (*fantino*) jockey.

'jogging ['dʒɔgiŋ] *sm* jogging; **fare ~** to go jogging.

'jolly ['dʒɔli] *sm inv* joker.

jr. *abbr* (= *junior*) Jr., jr.

ju'do [dʒu'dɔ] *sm* judo.
Jugos'lavia [jugoz'lavja] *sf*: **la** ~ Yugoslavia.
jugos'lavo, a *ag, sm/f* Yugoslav(ian).
'juke 'box ['dʒuk'bɔks] *sm inv* jukebox.
'juta ['juta] *sf* = **iuta**.

K

K, k ['kappa] *sf o m inv* (*lettera*) K, k ♦ *abbr*
(= *kilo-, chilo-*) k; (*INFORM*) K; **K come**
Kursaal ≈ K for King.
Kam'pala *sf* Kampala.
kara'kiri *sm* harakiri.
karatè [kara'tɛ] *sm* karate.
'Kashmir ['kaʃmir] *sm*: **il** ~ Kashmir.
ka'yak [ka'jak] *sm inv* kayak.
keni'ano, a, keni'ota, i, e *ag, sm/f* Kenyan.
'Kenya ['kenja] *sm*: **il** ~ Kenya.
kero'sene [kero'zɛne] *sm* = **cherosene**.
kg *abbr* (= *chilogrammo*) kg.
kib'butz [kib'buts] *sm inv* kibbutz.
Kilimangi'aro [kiliman'dʒaro] *sm*: **il** ~
Kilimanjaro.
'killer ['killer] *sm inv* gunman, hired gun.
'kilo *etc* = **chilo** *etc*.
kilt [kilt] *sm inv* kilt.
ki'mono [ki'mɔno] *sm* = **chimono**.
kitsch [kitʃ] *sm* kitsch.
km *abbr* (= *chilometro*) km.
kmq *abbr* (= *chilometro quadrato*) km².
ko'ala [ko'ala] *sm inv* koala (bear).
'krapfen ['krapfən] *sm inv* doughnut.
Ku'ala Lum'pur *sf* Kuala Lumpur.
Ku'wait [ku'vait] *sm*: **il** ~ Kuwait.
kW *abbr* (= *kilowatt, chilowatt*) kW.
kWh *abbr* (= *kilowattora*) kW/h.

L

L, l ['ɛlle] *sf o m inv* (*lettera*) L, l ♦ *abbr* (=
lira) L; **L come Livorno** ≈ L for Lucy
(*Brit*), L for Love (*US*).
l' *det vedi* **la, lo**.
la *det f* (*dav V l'*) the ♦ *pronome* (*dav V l'*)
(*oggetto: persona*) her; (: *cosa*) it; (:
forma di cortesia) you ♦ *sm inv* (*MUS*) A; (:
solfeggiando la scala) la; *vedi anche* **il**.
là *av* there; **di** ~ (*da quel luogo*) from there;

(*in quel luogo*) in there; (*dall'altra parte*)
over there; **di** ~ **di** beyond; **per di** ~ that
way; **più in** ~ further on; (*tempo*) later
on; ~ **dentro/sopra/sotto** in/up (*o* on)/
under there; ~ **per** ~ (*sul momento*) there
and then; **essere in** ~ **con gli anni** to be
getting on (in years); **essere più di** ~ **che**
di qua to be more dead than alive; **va'** ~!
come off it!; **stavolta è andato troppo in** ~
this time he's gone too far; *vedi anche*
quello.
'labbro *sm* (*pl(f)*: **labbra**: *solo nel senso*
ANAT) lip.
'labile *ag* fleeting, ephemeral.
labi'rinto *sm* labyrinth, maze.
labora'torio *sm* (*di ricerca*) laboratory; (*di*
arti, mestieri) workshop; ~ **linguistico**
language laboratory.
labori'oso, a *ag* (*faticoso*) laborious;
(*attivo*) hard-working.
labu'rista, i, e *ag* Labour *cpd* (*Brit*) ♦ *sm/f*
Labour Party member (*Brit*).
'lacca, che *sf* lacquer; (*per unghie*) nail
varnish (*Brit*), nail polish.
lac'care *vt* (*mobili*) to varnish, lacquer.
'laccio ['lattʃo] *sm* noose; (*legaccio, tirante*)
lasso; (*di scarpa*) lace; ~ **emostatico**
(*MED*) tourniquet.
lace'rante [latʃe'rante] *ag* (*suono*) piercing,
shrill.
lace'rare [latʃe'rare] *vt* to tear to shreds,
lacerate; ~**rsi** *vr* to tear.
'lacero, a ['latʃero] *ag* (*logoro*) torn,
tattered; (*MED*) lacerated; **ferita** ~-
contusa injury with lacerations and bruis-
ing.
la'conico, a, ci, che *ag* laconic, brief.
'lacrima *sf* tear; (*goccia*) drop; **in** ~**e** in
tears.
lacri'mare *vi* to water.
lacri'mevole *ag* heartrending, pitiful.
lacri'mogeno, a [lakri'mɔdʒeno] *ag*: **gas** ~
tear gas.
lacri'moso, a *ag* tearful.
la'cuna *sf* (*fig*) gap.
la'custre *ag* lake *cpd*.
lad'dove *cong* whereas.
'ladro *sm* thief; **al** ~! stop thief!
ladro'cinio [ladro'tʃinjo] *sm* theft, robbery.
la'druncolo, a *sm/f* petty thief.
laggiù [lad'dʒu] *av* down there; (*di là*) over
there.
'lagna ['laɲɲa] *sf* (*fam: persona, cosa*) drag,
bore; **fare la** ~ to whine, moan.
la'gnanza [laɲ'ɲantsa] *sf* complaint.
la'gnarsi [laɲ'ɲarsi] *vr*: ~ **(di)** to complain
(about).
'lago, ghi *sm* lake.
'Lagos ['lagos] *sf* Lagos.
'lagrima *etc* = **lacrima** *etc*.
la'guna *sf* lagoon.
lagu'nare *ag* lagoon *cpd*.

'laico, a, ci, che *ag* (*apostolato*) lay; (*vita*) secular; (*scuola*) non-denominational ♦ *sm/f* layman/woman ♦ *sm* lay brother.

'laido, a *ag* filthy, foul; (*fig*: *osceno*) obscene, filthy.

'lama *sf* blade ♦ *sm inv* (*ZOOL*) llama; (*REL*) lama.

lambic'care *vt* to distil; **~rsi il cervello** to rack one's brains.

lam'bire *vt* (*fig*: *sog*: *fiamme*) to lick; (: *acqua*) to lap.

lam'bretta ® *sf* scooter.

la'mella *sf* (*di metallo etc*) thin sheet, thin strip; (*di fungo*) gill.

lamen'tare *vt* to lament; **~rsi** *vr* (*emettere lamenti*) to moan, groan; (*rammaricarsi*): **~rsi (di)** to complain (about).

lamen'tela *sf* complaining *q*.

lamen'tevole *ag* (*voce*) complaining, plaintive; (*stato*) lamentable, pitiful.

la'mento *sm* moan, groan; (*per la morte di qn*) lament.

lamen'toso, a *ag* plaintive.

la'metta *sf* razor blade.

lami'era *sf* sheet metal.

'lamina *sf* (*lastra sottile*) thin sheet (*o* layer *o* plate); **~ d'oro** gold leaf; gold foil.

lami'nare *vt* to laminate.

lami'nato, a *ag* laminated; (*tessuto*) lamé ♦ *sm* laminate.

'lampada *sf* lamp; **~ a petrolio/a gas** oil/gas lamp; **~ a spirito** blowlamp (*Brit*), blowtorch; **~ a stelo** standard lamp (*Brit*), floor lamp; **~ da tavolo** table lamp.

lampa'dario *sm* chandelier.

lampa'dina *sf* light bulb; **~ tascabile** pocket torch (*Brit*), flashlight (*US*).

lam'pante *ag* (*fig*: *evidente*) crystal clear, evident.

lam'para *sf* fishing lamp; (*barca*) boat for fishing by lamplight (*in Mediterranean*).

lampeggi'are [lamped'dʒare] *vi* (*luce, fari*) to flash ♦ *vb impers*: **lampeggia** there's lightning.

lampeggia'tore [lampeddʒa'tore] *sm* (*AUT*) indicator.

lampi'one *sm* street light *o* lamp (*Brit*).

'lampo *sm* (*METEOR*) flash of lightning; (*di luce, fig*) flash ♦ *ag inv*: **cerniera ~** zip (*fastener*) (*Brit*), zipper (*US*); **guerra ~** blitzkrieg; **~i** *smpl* (*METEOR*) lightning *q*; **passare come un ~** to flash past *o* by.

lam'pone *sm* raspberry.

'lana *sf* wool; **~ d'acciaio** steel wool; **pura ~ vergine** pure new wool; **~ di vetro** glass wool.

lan'cetta [lan'tʃetta] *sf* (*indice*) pointer, needle; (*di orologio*) hand.

'lancia, ce ['lantʃa] *sf* (*arma*) lance; (: *picca*) spear; (*di pompa antincendio*) nozzle; (*imbarcazione*) launch; **partire ~ in resta** (*fig*) to set off ready for battle;

spezzare una ~ in favore di qn (*fig*) to come to sb's defence; **~ di salvataggio** lifeboat.

lancia'bombe [lantʃa'bombe] *sm inv* (*MIL*) mortar.

lanciafi'amme [lantʃa'fjamme] *sm inv* flamethrower.

lancia'missili [lantʃa'missili] *ag inv* missile-launching ♦ *sm inv* missile launcher.

lancia'razzi [lantʃa'raddzi] *ag inv* rocket-launching ♦ *sm inv* rocket launcher.

lanci'are [lan'tʃare] *vt* to throw, hurl, fling; (*SPORT*) to throw; (*far partire: automobile*) to get up to full speed; (*bombe*) to drop; (*razzo, prodotto, moda*) to launch; (*emettere: grido*) to give out; **~rsi** *vr*: **~rsi contro/su** to throw *o* hurl *o* fling o.s. against/on; **~rsi in** (*fig*) to embark on; **~ un cavallo** to give a horse his head; **~ il disco** (*SPORT*) to throw the discus; **~ il peso** (*SPORT*) to put the shot; **~rsi all'inseguimento di qn** to set off in pursuit of sb; **~rsi col paracadute** to parachute.

lanciasi'luri [lantʃasi'luri] *sm inv* torpedo tube.

lanci'ato, a [lan'tʃato] *ag* (*affermato: attore, prodotto*) well-known, famous; (*veicolo*) speeding along, racing along.

lanci'nante [lantʃi'nante] *ag* (*dolore*) shooting, throbbing; (*grido*) piercing.

'lancio ['lantʃo] *sm* throwing *q*; throw; dropping *q*; drop; launching *q*; launch; **~ del disco** (*SPORT*) throwing the discus; **~ del peso** (*SPORT*) putting the shot.

'landa *sf* (*GEO*) moor.

'languido, a *ag* (*fiacco*) languid, weak; (*tenero, malinconico*) languishing.

langu'ire *vi* to languish; (*conversazione*) to flag.

langu'ore *sm* weakness, languor.

lani'ero, a *ag* wool *cpd*, woollen (*Brit*), woolen (*US*).

lani'ficio [lani'fitʃo] *sm* woollen (*Brit*) *o* woolen (*US*) mill.

lano'lina *sf* lanolin(e).

la'noso, a *ag* woolly.

lan'terna *sf* lantern; (*faro*) lighthouse.

lanter'nino *sm*: **cercarsele col ~** to be asking for trouble.

la'nugine [la'nudʒine] *sf* down.

'Laos *sm* Laos.

lapalissi'ano, a *ag* self-evident.

La 'Paz [la'pas] *sf* La Paz.

lapi'dare *vt* to stone.

lapi'dario, a *ag* (*fig*) terse.

'lapide *sf* (*di sepolcro*) tombstone; (*commemorativa*) plaque.

la'pin [la'pɛ̃] *sm inv* coney.

'lapis *sm inv* pencil.

'lappone *ag, sm/f, sm* Lapp.

Lap'ponia *sf*: **la ~** Lapland.

'lapsus *sm inv* slip.

'lardo *sm* bacon fat, lard.

lar'ghezza [lar'gettsa] *sf* width; breadth; looseness; generosity; ~ **di vedute** broad-mindedness.

lar'gire [lar'dʒire] *vt* to give generously.

'largo, a, ghi, ghe *ag* wide, broad; (*maniche*) wide; (*abito: troppo ampio*) loose; (*fig*) generous ♦ *sm* width; breadth; (*mare aperto*): **il ~** the open sea ♦ *sf*: **stare** *o* **tenersi alla ~a (da qn/qc)** to keep one's distance (from sb/sth), keep away (from sb/sth); ~ **due metri** two metres wide; ~ **di spalle** broad-shouldered; **di ~ghe vedute** broad-minded; **in ~a misura** to a great *o* large extent; **su ~a scala** on a large scale; **di manica ~a** generous, open-handed; **al ~ di Genova** off (the coast of) Genoa; **farsi ~ tra la folla** to push one's way through the crowd.

'larice ['laritʃe] *sm* (*BOT*) larch.

la'ringe [la'rindʒe] *sf* larynx.

larin'gite [larin'dʒite] *sf* laryngitis.

laringoi'atra, i, e *sm/f* (*medico*) throat specialist.

'larva *sf* larva; (*fig*) shadow.

la'sagne [la'zaɲɲe] *sfpl* lasagna *sg*.

lasciapas'sare [laʃʃapas'sare] *sm inv* pass, permit.

lasci'are [laʃ'ʃare] *vt* to leave; (*abbandonare*) to leave, abandon, give up; (*cessare di tenere*) to let go of ♦ *vb ausiliare*: ~ **qn fare qc** to let sb do sth ♦ *vi*: ~ **di fare** (*smettere*) to stop doing; **~rsi andare/ truffare** to let o.s. go/be cheated; ~ **andare** *o* **correre** *o* **perdere** to let things go their own way; ~ **stare qc/qn** to leave sth/sb alone; ~ **qn erede** to make sb one's heir; ~ **la presa** to lose one's grip; ~ **il segno (su qc)** to leave a mark (on sth); (*fig*) to leave one's mark (on sth); ~ **(molto) a desiderare** to leave much to be desired; **ci ha lasciato la vita** it cost him his life.

'lascito ['laʃʃito] *sm* (*DIR*) legacy.

la'scivia [laʃ'ʃivja] *sf* lust, lasciviousness.

la'scivo, a [laʃ'ʃivo] *ag* lascivious.

'laser ['lazer] *ag, sm inv*: **(raggio)** ~ laser (beam).

lassa'tivo, a *ag, sm* laxative.

las'sismo *sm* laxity.

'lasso *sm*: ~ **di tempo** interval, lapse of time.

lassù *av* up there.

'lastra *sf* (*di pietra*) slab; (*di metallo, FOT*) plate; (*di ghiaccio, vetro*) sheet; (*radio-grafica*) X-ray (plate).

lastri'care *vt* to pave.

lastri'cato *sm* paving.

'lastrico, ci *o* **chi** *sm* paving; **essere sul ~** (*fig*) to be penniless; **gettare qn sul ~** (*fig*) to leave sb destitute.

las'trone *sm* (*ALPINISMO*) sheer rock face.

la'tente *ag* latent.

late'rale *ag* lateral, side *cpd*; (*uscita, ingresso etc*) side *cpd* ♦ *sm* (*CALCIO*) half-back.

lateral'mente *av* sideways.

late'rizio [late'rittsjo] *sm* (perforated) brick.

latifon'dista, i, e *sm/f* large agricultural landowner.

lati'fondo *sm* large estate.

la'tino, a *ag, sm* Latin.

la'tinoameri'cano, a *ag, sm/f* Latin-American.

lati'tante *sm/f* fugitive (from justice).

lati'tanza [lati'tantsa] *sf*: **darsi alla ~** to go into hiding.

lati'tudine *sf* latitude.

'lato, a *ag*: **in senso ~** broadly speaking ♦ *sm* side; (*fig*) aspect, point of view; **d'altro ~** (*d'altra parte*) on the other hand.

la'trare *vi* to bark.

la'trina *sf* public lavatory.

latro'cinio [latro'tʃinjo] *sm* = **ladrocinio.**

'latta *sf* tin (plate); (*recipiente*) tin, can.

lat'taio, a *sm/f* (*distributore*) milkman/ woman; (*commerciante*) dairyman/woman.

lat'tante *ag* unweaned ♦ *sm/f* breast-fed baby.

'latte *sm* milk; **fratello di ~** foster brother; **avere ancora il ~ alla bocca** (*fig*) to be still wet behind the ears; **tutto ~ e miele** (*fig*) all smiles; ~ **detergente** cleansing milk *o* lotion; ~ **intero** full-cream milk; ~ **magro** *o* **scremato** skimmed milk; ~ **secco** *o* **in polvere** dried *o* powdered milk.

'latteo, a *ag* milky; (*dieta, prodotto*) milk *cpd*.

latte'ria *sf* dairy.

latti'cini [latti'tʃini] *smpl* dairy products.

lat'tina *sf* (*di birra etc*) can.

lat'tuga, ghe *sf* lettuce.

'laurea *sf* degree.

laure'ando, a *sm/f* final-year student.

laure'are *vt* to confer a degree on; **~rsi** *vr* to graduate.

laure'ato, a *ag, sm/f* graduate.

'lauro *sm* laurel.

'lauto, a *ag* (*pranzo, mancia*) lavish; **~i guadagni** handsome profits.

'lava *sf* lava.

lavabianche'ria [lavabjanke'ria] *sf inv* washing machine.

la'vabo *sm* washbasin.

la'vaggio [la'vaddʒo] *sm* washing *q*; ~ **del cervello** brainwashing *q*.

la'vagna [la'vaɲɲa] *sf* (*GEO*) slate; (*di scuola*) blackboard; ~ **luminosa** overhead projector.

la'vanda *sf* (*anche MED*) wash; (*BOT*) lavender; **fare una ~ gastrica a qn** to pump sb's stomach.

lavan'daia *sf* washerwoman.

lavande'ria *sf* (*di ospedale, caserma etc*) laundry; ~ **automatica** launderette; ~ **a**

secco dry-cleaner's.
lavan'dino sm sink; (del bagno) washbasin.
lavapi'atti sm/f dishwasher.
la'vare vt to wash; **~rsi** vr to wash, have a wash; **~ a secco** to dry-clean; **~ i panni sporchi in pubblico** (fig) to wash one's dirty linen in public; **~rsi le mani/i denti** to wash one's hands/clean one's teeth.
lava'secco sm o f inv dry-cleaner's.
lavasto'viglie [lavasto'viʎʎe] sm o f inv (macchina) dishwasher.
la'vata sf wash; (fig): **dare una ~ di capo a qn** to give sb a good telling-off.
lava'tivo sm (clistere) enema; (buono a nulla) good-for-nothing, idler.
lava'toio sm (public) washhouse.
lava'trice [lava'tritʃe] sf washing machine.
lava'tura sf washing q; **~ di piatti** dishwater.
la'vello sm (kitchen) sink.
la'vina sf snowslide.
lavo'rante sm/f worker.
lavo'rare vi to work; (fig: bar, studio etc) to do good business ♦ vt to work; **~ a** to work on; **~ a maglia** to knit; **~ di fantasia** (suggestionarsi) to imagine things; (fantasticare) to let one's imagination run free; **~rsi qn** (fig: convincere) to work on sb.
lavora'tivo, a ag working.
lavora'tore, 'trice sm/f worker ♦ ag working.
lavorazi'one [lavorat'tsjone] sf (gen) working; (di legno, pietra) carving; (di film) making; (di prodotto) manufacture; (modo di esecuzione) workmanship.
lavo'rio sm intense activity.
la'voro sm work; (occupazione) job, work q; (opera) piece of work, job; (ECON) labour (Brit), labor (US); **Ministero del L~** Department of Employment (Brit), Department of Labor (US); **(fare) i ~i di casa** (to do) the housework sg; **~i forzati** hard labour sg; **i ~i del parlamento** the parliamentary session sg; **~i pubblici** public works.
lazi'ale [lat'tsjale] ag of (o from) Lazio.
lazza'retto [laddza'retto] sm leper hospital.
lazza'rone [laddza'rone] sm scoundrel.
'lazzo ['laddzo] sm jest.
LE sigla = Lecce.
le det fpl the ♦ pronome (oggetto) them; (: a lei, a essa) (to) her; (: forma di cortesia) (to) you; vedi anche **il**.
le'ale ag loyal; (sincero) sincere; (onesto) fair.
lea'lista, i, e sm/f loyalist.
lealtà sf loyalty; sincerity; fairness.
'leasing ['li:ziŋ] sm leasing; lease.
'lebbra sf leprosy.
leb'broso, a ag leprous ♦ sm/f leper.
'lecca 'lecca sm inv lollipop.

leccapi'edi sm/f inv (peg) toady, bootlicker.
lec'care vt to lick; (sog: gatto: latte etc) to lick o lap up; (fig) to flatter; **~rsi** vr (fig) to preen o.s.; **~rsi i baffi** to lick one's lips.
lec'cato, a ag affected ♦ sf lick.
leccherò etc [lekke'rɔ] vb vedi **leccare**.
'leccio ['lettʃo] sm holm oak, ilex.
leccor'nia sf titbit, delicacy.
'lecito, a ['lɛtʃito] ag permitted, allowed; **se mi è ~** if I may; **mi sia ~ far presente che** ... may I point out that ....
'ledere vt to damage, injure; **~ gli interessi di qn** to be prejudicial to sb's interests.
'lega, ghe sf league; (di metalli) alloy; **metallo di bassa ~** base metal; **gente di bassa ~** common o vulgar people.
le'gaccio [le'gattʃo] sm string, lace.
le'gale ag legal ♦ sm lawyer; **corso ~ delle monete** official exchange rate; **medicina ~** forensic medicine; **studio ~** lawyer's office.
legalità sf legality, lawfulness.
legaliz'zare [legalid'dzare] vt to authenticate; (regolarizzare) to legalize.
le'game sm (corda, fig: affettivo) tie, bond; (nesso logico) link, connection; **~ di sangue** o **di parentela** family tie.
le'gare vt (prigioniero, capelli, cane) to tie (up); (libro) to bind; (CHIM) to alloy; (fig: collegare) to bind, join ♦ vi (far lega) to unite; (fig) to get on well; **è pazzo da ~** (fam) he should be locked up.
lega'tario, a sm/f (DIR) legatee.
le'gato sm (REL) legate; (DIR) legacy, bequest.
lega'toria sf (attività) bookbinding; (negozio) bookbinder's.
lega'tura sf (di libro) binding; (MUS) ligature.
legazi'one [legat'tsjone] sf legation.
le'genda [le'dʒɛnda] sf (di carta geografica etc) = **leggenda**.
'legge ['leddʒe] sf law; **~ procedurale** procedural law.
leg'genda [led'dʒɛnda] sf (narrazione) legend; (di carta geografica etc) key, legend.
leggen'dario, a [leddʒen'darjo] ag legendary.
'leggere ['leddʒere] vt, vi to read; **~ il pensiero di qn** to read sb's mind o thoughts.
legge'rezza [leddʒe'rettsa] sf lightness; thoughtlessness; fickleness.
leg'gero [led'dʒero] ag light; (agile, snello) nimble, agile, light; (tè, caffè) weak; (fig: non grave, piccolo) slight; (: spensierato) thoughtless; (: incostante) fickle; free and easy; **una ragazza ~a** (fig) a flighty girl; **alla ~a** thoughtlessly.
leggi'adro, a [led'dʒadro] ag pretty, lovely; (movimenti) graceful.
leg'gibile [led'dʒibile] ag legible; (libro)

readable, worth reading.

leg'gio, 'gii [led'dʒio] sm lectern; (MUS) music stand.

legherò etc [lege'rɔ] vb vedi **legare**.

legife'rare [ledʒife'rare] vi to legislate.

legio'nario [ledʒo'narjo] sm (romano) legionary; (volontario) legionnaire.

legi'one [le'dʒone] sf legion; ~ **straniera** foreign legion.

legisla'tivo, a [ledʒizla'tivo] ag legislative.

legisla'tore [ledʒizla'tore] sm legislator.

legisla'tura [ledʒizla'tura] sf legislature.

legislazi'one [ledʒizlat'tsjone] sf legislation.

legitti'mare [ledʒitti'mare] vt (figlio) to legitimize; (comportamento etc) to justify.

legittimità [ledʒittimi'ta] sf legitimacy.

le'gittimo, a [le'dʒittimo] ag legitimate; (fig: giustificato, lecito) justified, legitimate; ~**a difesa** (DIR) self-defence (Brit), self-defense (US).

'legna ['leɲɲa] sf firewood.

le'gnaia [leɲ'ɲaja] sf woodshed.

legnai'olo [leɲɲa'jɔlo] sm woodcutter.

le'gname [leɲ'ɲame] sm wood, timber.

le'gnata [leɲ'ɲata] sf blow with a stick; **dare a qn un sacco di** ~**e** to give sb a good hiding.

'legno ['leɲɲo] sm wood; (pezzo di ~) piece of wood; **di** ~ wooden; ~ **compensato** plywood.

le'gnoso, a [leɲ'ɲoso] ag (di legno) wooden; (come il legno) woody; (carne) tough.

le'gumi smpl (BOT) pulses.

'lei pronome (soggetto) she; (oggetto: per dare rilievo, con preposizione) her; (forma di cortesia: anche: **L**~) you ♦ sf inv: **la mia** ~ my beloved ♦ sm: **dare del** ~ **a qn** to address sb as "lei"; ~ **stessa** she herself; you yourself; **è** ~ it's her.

'lembo sm (di abito, strada) edge; (striscia sottile: di terra) strip.

'lemma, i sm headword.

'lemme 'lemme av (very) very slowly.

'lena sf (fig) energy, stamina; **di buona** ~ (lavorare, camminare) at a good pace.

Lenin'grado sf Leningrad.

le'nire vt to soothe.

'lente sf (OTTICA) lens sg; ~ **d'ingrandimento** magnifying glass; ~**i a contatto**, ~**i corneali** contact lenses.

len'tezza [len'tettsa] sf slowness.

len'ticchia [len'tikkja] sf (BOT) lentil.

len'tiggine [len'tiddʒine] sf freckle.

'lento, a ag slow; (molle: fune) slack; (non stretto: vite, abito) loose ♦ sm (ballo) slow dance.

'lenza ['lentsa] sf fishing line.

lenzu'olo [len'tswɔlo] sm sheet; ~**a** sfpl pair of sheets; ~ **funebre** shroud.

leon'cino [leon'tʃino] sm lion cub.

le'one sm lion; (dello zodiaco): **L**~ Leo; **essere del L**~ to be Leo.

leo'pardo sm leopard.

lepo'rino, a ag: **labbro** ~ harelip.

'lepre sf hare.

'lercio, a, ci, ce ['lɛrtʃo] ag filthy.

lerci'ume [ler'tʃume] sm filth.

'lesbico, a, ci, che ag, sf lesbian.

'lesi etc vb vedi **ledere**.

lesi'nare vt to be stingy with ♦ vi: ~ **(su)** to skimp (on), be stingy (with).

lesi'one sf (MED) lesion; (DIR) injury, damage; (EDIL) crack.

le'sivo, a ag: ~ **(di)** damaging (to), detrimental (to).

'leso, a pp di **ledere** ♦ ag (offeso) injured; **parte** ~**a** (DIR) injured party; ~**a maestà** lese-majesty.

Le'sotho [le'soto] sm Lesotho.

les'sare vt (CUC) to boil.

'lessi etc vb vedi **leggere**.

lessi'cale ag lexical.

'lessico, ci sm vocabulary; (dizionario) lexicon.

lessicogra'fia sf lexicography.

'lesso, a ag boiled ♦ sm boiled meat.

'lesto, a ag quick; (agile) nimble; ~ **di mano** (per rubare) light-fingered; (per picchiare) free with one's fists.

lesto'fante sm swindler, con man.

le'tale ag lethal, deadly.

leta'maio sm dunghill.

le'tame sm manure, dung.

le'targo, ghi sm lethargy; (ZOOL) hibernation.

le'tizia [le'tittsja] sf joy, happiness.

'letta sf: **dare una** ~ **a qc** to glance o look through sth.

'lettera sf letter; ~**e** sfpl (letteratura) literature sg; (studi umanistici) arts (subjects); **alla** ~ literally; **in** ~**e** in words, in full; **diventar** ~ **morta** (legge) to become a dead letter; **restar** ~ **morta** (consiglio, invito) to go unheeded; ~ **di accompagnamento** accompanying letter; ~ **assicurata** registered letter; ~ **di cambio** (COMM) bill of exchange; ~ **di credito** (COMM) letter of credit; ~ **di intenti** letter of intent; ~ **di presentazione** o **raccomandazione** letter of introduction; ~ **raccomandata** recorded delivery (Brit) o certified (US) letter; ~ **di trasporto aereo** (COMM) air waybill.

lette'rale ag literal.

letteral'mente av literally.

lette'rario, a ag literary.

lette'rato, a ag well-read, scholarly.

lettera'tura sf literature.

let'tiga, ghe sf (portantina) litter; (barella) stretcher.

let'tino sm cot (Brit), crib (US).

'letto, a pp di **leggere** ♦ sm bed; **andare a** ~ to go to bed; ~ **a castello** bunk beds pl; ~ **a una piazza/a due piazze** o **matrimoniale**

single/double bed.

Let'tonia *sf:* **la ~** Latvia.

lettorato *sm* (*INS*) lectorship, assistantship; (*REL*) lectorate.

let'tore, 'trice *sm/f* reader; (*INS*) (foreign language) assistant (*Brit*), (foreign) teaching assistant (*US*) ♦ *sm:* **~ ottico (di caratteri)** optical character reader.

let'tura *sf* reading.

leuce'mia [leutʃe'mia] *sf* leukaemia.

'leva *sf* lever; (*MIL*) conscription; **far ~ su qn** to work on sb; **essere di ~** to be due for call-up; **~ del cambio** (*AUT*) gear lever.

le'vante *sm* east; (*vento*) East wind; **il L~** the Levant.

le'vare *vt* (*occhi, braccio*) to raise; (*sollevare, togliere: tassa, divieto*) to lift; (: *indumenti*) to take off, remove; (*rimuovere*) to take away; (: *dal di sopra*) to take off; (: *dal di dentro*) to take out; **~rsi** *vr* to get up; (*sole*) to rise; **~ le tende** (*fig*) to pack up and leave; **~rsi il pensiero** to put one's mind at rest; **levati di mezzo** *o* **di lì** *o* **di torno!** get out of my way!

le'vata *sf* (*di posta*) collection.

leva'taccia, ce [leva'tattʃa] *sf* early rise.

leva'toio, a *ag:* **ponte ~** drawbridge.

leva'trice [leva'tritʃe] *sf* midwife.

leva'tura *sf* intelligence, mental capacity.

levi'gare *vt* to smooth; (*con carta vetrata*) to sand.

levi'gato, a *ag* (*superficie*) smooth; (*fig: stile*) polished; (: *viso*) flawless.

levità *sf* lightness.

levri'ere *sm* greyhound.

lezi'one [let'tsjone] *sf* lesson; (*all'università, sgridata*) lecture; **fare ~** to teach; to lecture.

lezi'oso, a [let'tsjoso] *ag* affected; simpering.

'lezzo ['leddzo] *sm* stench, stink.

lg *abbr* (= *lira sterlina*) £.

LI *sigla* = *Livorno*.

li *pronome pl* (*oggetto*) them.

lì *av* there; **di** *o* **da ~** from there; **per di ~** that way; **di ~ a pochi giorni** a few days later; **~ per ~** there and then; at first; **essere ~ (~) per fare** to be on the point of doing, be about to do; **~ dentro** in there; **~ sotto** under there; **~ sopra** on there; up there; **tutto ~** that's all; *vedi anche* **quello**.

libagi'one [liba'dʒone] *sf* libation.

liba'nese *ag, sm/f* Lebanese *inv.*

Li'bano *sm:* **il ~** the Lebanon.

'libbra *sf* (*peso*) pound.

li'beccio [li'bettʃo] *sm* south-west wind.

li'bello *sm* libel.

li'bellula *sf* dragonfly.

libe'rale *ag, sm/f* liberal.

liberaliz'zare [liberalid'dzare] *vt* to liberalize.

libe'rare *vt* (*rendere libero: prigioniero*) to release; (: *popolo*) to free, liberate; (*sgombrare: passaggio*) to clear; (: *stanza*) to vacate; (*produrre: energia*) to release; **~rsi** *vr:* **~rsi di qc/qn** to get rid of sth/sb.

libera'tore, 'trice *ag* liberating ♦ *sm/f* liberator.

liberazi'one [liberat'tsjone] *sf* liberation; release; freeing.

li'bercolo *sm* (*peg*) worthless book.

Li'beria *sf:* **la ~** Liberia.

liberi'ano, a *ag, sm/f* Liberian.

libe'rismo *sm* (*ECON*) laissez-faire.

'libero, a *ag* free; (*strada*) clear; (*non occupato: posto etc*) vacant, free; (*TEL*) not engaged; **~ di fare qc** free to do sth; **~ da** free from; **una donna dai ~i costumi** a woman of loose morals; **avere via ~a** to have a free hand; **dare via ~a a qn** to give sb the go-ahead; **via ~a!** all clear!; **~ arbitrio** free will; **~ professionista** self-employed professional person; **~ scambio** free trade; **~a uscita** (*MIL*) leave.

liberoscam'bismo *sm* (*ECON*) free trade.

libertà *sf inv* freedom; (*tempo disponibile*) free time ♦ *sfpl* (*licenza*) liberties; **essere in ~ provvisoria/vigilata** to be released without bail/be on probation; **~ di riunione** right to hold meetings.

liber'tario, a *ag* libertarian.

liber'tino, a *ag, sm/f* libertine.

'liberty ['liberti] *ag inv, sm* art nouveau.

'Libia *sf:* **la ~** Libya.

'libico, a, ci, che *ag, sm/f* Libyan.

li'bidine *sf* lust.

libidi'noso, a *ag* lustful, libidinous.

li'bido *sf* libido.

li'braio *sm* bookseller.

li'brario, a *ag* book *cpd.*

li'brarsi *vr* to hover.

libre'ria *sf* (*bottega*) bookshop; (*stanza*) library; (*mobile*) bookcase.

li'bretto *sm* booklet; (*taccuino*) notebook; (*MUS*) libretto; **~ degli assegni** chequebook (*Brit*), checkbook (*US*); **~ di circolazione** (*AUT*) logbook; **~ di deposito** (bank) deposit book; **~ di risparmio** (savings) bankbook, passbook; **~ universitario** student's report book.

'libro *sm* book; **~ bianco** (*POL*) white paper; **~ di cassa** cash book; **~ di consultazione** reference book; **~ mastro** ledger; **~ paga** payroll; **~ tascabile** paperback; **~ di testo** textbook; **~i contabili** (account) books; **~i sociali** company records.

li'cantropo *sm* werewolf.

lice'ale [litʃe'ale] *ag* secondary school *cpd* (*Brit*), high school *cpd* (*US*) ♦ *sm/f* secondary school *o* high school pupil.

li'cenza [li'tʃentsa] *sf* (*permesso*) permission, leave; (*di pesca, caccia, circolazione*) permit, licence (*Brit*), license (*US*); (*MIL*) leave; (*INS*) school-leaving certificate; (*libertà*) liberty; (*sfrenatezza*) licentiousness; **andare in** ~ (*MIL*) to go on leave; **su** ~ **di ...** (*COMM*) under licence from ...; ~ **di esportazione** export licence; ~ **di fabbricazione** manufacturer's licence; ~ **poetica** poetic licence.

licenzia'mento [litʃentsja'mento] *sm* dismissal.

licenzi'are [litʃen'tsjare] *vt* (*impiegato*) to dismiss; (*INS*) to award a certificate to; ~**rsi** *vr* (*impiegato*) to resign, hand in one's notice; (*INS*) to obtain one's school-leaving certificate.

licenziosità [litʃentsjosi'ta] *sf* licentiousness.

licenzi'oso, a [litʃen'tsjoso] *ag* licentious.

li'ceo [li'tʃɛo] *sm* (*INS*) secondary (*Brit*) o high (*US*) school (*for 14- to 19-year-olds*); ~ **classico/scientifico** secondary or high school specializing in classics/scientific subjects.

li'chene [li'kɛne] *sm* (*BOT*) lichen.

'lido *sm* beach, shore.

'Liechtenstein ['liktənstain] *sm*: **il** ~ Liechtenstein.

li'eto, a *ag* happy, glad; "**molto** ~" (*nelle presentazioni*) "pleased to meet you''; **a** ~ **fine** with a happy ending.

li'eve *ag* light; (*di poco conto*) slight; (*sommesso: voce*) faint, soft.

lievi'tare *vi* (*anche fig*) to rise ♦ *vt* to leaven.

li'evito *sm* yeast; ~ **di birra** brewer's yeast.

'ligio, a, gi, gie ['lidʒo] *ag* faithful, loyal.

li'gnaggio [liɲ'naddʒo] *sm* descent, lineage.

'ligure *ag* Ligurian; **la Riviera L**~ the Italian Riviera.

'lilla, lillà *sm inv* lilac.

'Lima *sf* Lima.

'lima *sf* file; ~ **da unghie** nail file.

limacci'oso, a [limat'tʃoso] *ag* muddy.

li'mare *vt* to file (down); (*fig*) to polish.

'limbo *sm* (*REL*) limbo.

li'metta *sf* nail file.

limi'tare *vt* to limit, restrict; (*circoscrivere*) to bound, surround.

limitata'mente *av* to a limited extent; ~ **alle mie possibilità** in so far as I am able.

limita'tivo, a *ag* limiting, restricting.

limi'tato, a *ag* limited, restricted.

limitazi'one [limitat'tsjone] *sf* limitation, restriction.

'limite *sm* limit; (*confine*) border, boundary ♦ *ag inv*: **caso** ~ extreme case; **al** ~ if the worst comes to the worst (*Brit*), if worst comes to worst (*US*); ~ **di velocità** speed limit.

li'mitrofo, a *ag* neighbouring (*Brit*), neighboring (*US*).

'limo *sm* mud, slime; (*GEO*) silt.

limo'nata *sf* lemonade (*Brit*), (lemon) soda (*US*); (*spremuta*) lemon squash (*Brit*), lemonade (*US*).

li'mone *sm* (*pianta*) lemon tree; (*frutto*) lemon.

limpi'dezza [limpi'dettsa] *sf* clearness; (*di discorso*) clarity.

'limpido, a *ag* (*acqua*) limpid, clear; (*cielo*) clear; (*fig: discorso*) clear, lucid.

'lince ['lintʃe] *sf* lynx.

linci'are [lin'tʃare] *vt* to lynch.

'lindo, a *ag* tidy, spick and span; (*biancheria*) clean.

'linea *sf* (*gen*) line; (*di mezzi pubblici di trasporto: itinerario*) route; (: *servizio*) service; (*di prodotto: collezione*) collection; (: *stile*) style; **a grandi** ~**e** in outline; **mantenere la** ~ to look after one's figure; **è caduta la** ~ (*TEL*) I (*o* you *etc*) have been cut off; **di** ~: **aereo di** ~ airliner; **nave di** ~ liner; **volo di** ~ scheduled flight; **in** ~ **diretta da** (*TV, RADIO*) coming to you direct from; ~ **aerea** airline; ~ **continua** solid line; ~ **di partenza/d'arrivo** (*SPORT*) starting/finishing line; ~ **punteggiata** dotted line; ~ **di tiro** line of fire.

linea'menti *smpl* features; (*fig*) outlines.

line'are *ag* linear; (*fig*) coherent, logical.

line'etta *sf* (*trattino*) dash; (*d'unione*) hyphen.

'linfa *sf* (*BOT*) sap; (*ANAT*) lymph; ~ **vitale** (*fig*) lifeblood.

lin'gotto *sm* ingot, bar.

'lingua *sf* (*ANAT, CUC*) tongue; (*idioma*) language; **mostrare la** ~ to stick out one's tongue; **di** ~ **italiana** Italian-speaking; ~ **madre** mother tongue; **una** ~ **di terra** a spit of land.

lingu'accia [lin'gwattʃa] *sf* (*fig*) spiteful gossip.

linguacci'uto, a [lingwat'tʃuto] *ag* gossipy.

lingu'aggio [lin'gwaddʒo] *sm* language; ~ **giuridico** legal language; ~ **macchina** (*INFORM*) machine language; ~ **di programmazione** (*INFORM*) programming language.

lingu'etta *sf* (*di strumento*) reed; (*di scarpa, TECN*) tongue; (*di busta*) flap.

lingu'ista, i, e *sm/f* linguist.

lingu'istico, a, ci, che *ag* linguistic ♦ *sf* linguistics *sg*.

lini'mento *sm* liniment.

'lino *sm* (*pianta*) flax; (*tessuto*) linen.

li'noleum *sm inv* linoleum, lino.

liofiliz'zare [liofilid'dzare] *vt* to freeze-dry.

liofiliz'zati [liofilid'dzati] *smpl* freeze-dried foods.

Li'one *sf* Lyons.

'LIPU *sigla f* (= *Lega Italiana Protezione Uccelli*) *society for the protection of birds.*

liqu'ame *sm* liquid sewage.

lique'fare *vt* (*render liquido*) to liquefy; (*fondere*) to melt; ~**rsi** *vr* to liquefy; to melt.

lique'fatto, a *pp di* **liquefare**.

liqui'dare *vt* (*società, beni*; *persona*: *uccidere*) to liquidate; (*persona*: *sbarazzarsene*) to get rid of; (*conto, problema*) to settle; (*COMM*: *merce*) to sell off, clear.

liquidazi'one [likwidat'tsjone] *sf* (*di società, persona*) liquidation; (*di conto*) settlement; (*di problema*) settling; (*COMM*: *di merce*) clearance sale; (*AMM*) severance pay (*on retirement, redundancy, or when taking up other employment*).

liquidità *sf* liquidity.

'liquido, a *ag, sm* liquid; **denaro** ~ cash, ready money; ~ **per freni** brake fluid.

liqui'gas ® *sm inv* Calor gas ® (*Brit*), butane.

liqui'rizia [likwi'rittsja] *sf* liquorice.

li'quore *sm* liqueur.

liquo'roso, a *ag*: **vino** ~ dessert wine.

'lira *sf* (*unità monetaria*) lira; (*MUS*) lyre; ~ **sterlina** pound sterling.

'lirico, a, ci, che *ag* lyric(al); (*MUS*) lyric ♦ *sf* (*poesia*) lyric poetry; (*componimento poetico*) lyric; (*MUS*) opera; **cantante/ teatro** ~ opera singer/house.

li'rismo *sm* lyricism.

Lis'bona *sf* Lisbon.

'lisca, sche *sf* (*di pesce*) fishbone.

lisci'are [liʃ'ʃare] *vt* to smooth; (*fig*) to flatter; ~**rsi i capelli** to straighten one's hair.

'liscio, a, sci, sce ['liʃʃo] *ag* smooth; (*capelli*) straight; (*mobile*) plain; (*bevanda alcolica*) neat; (*fig*) straightforward, simple ♦ *av*: **andare** ~ to go smoothly; **passarla** ~**a** to get away with it.

li'seuse [li'zøz] *sf inv* bed jacket.

'liso, a *ag* worn out, threadbare.

'lista *sf* (*striscia*) strip; (*elenco*) list; ~ **elettorale** electoral roll; ~ **delle vivande** menu.

lis'tare *vt*: ~ **(di)** to edge (with), border (with).

lis'tino *sm* list; ~ **di borsa** the Stock Exchange list; ~ **dei cambi** (foreign) exchange rate; ~ **dei prezzi** price list.

lita'nia *sf* litany.

'lite *sf* quarrel, argument; (*DIR*) lawsuit.

liti'gare *vi* to quarrel; (*DIR*) to litigate.

li'tigio [li'tidʒo] *sm* quarrel.

litigi'oso, a [liti'dʒoso] *ag* quarrelsome; (*DIR*) litigious.

litogra'fia *sf* (*sistema*) lithography; (*stampa*) lithograph.

lito'grafico, a, ci, che *ag* lithographic.

lito'rale, a *ag* coastal, coast *cpd* ♦ *sm* coast.

lito'raneo, a *ag* coastal.

'litro *sm* litre (*Brit*), liter (*US*).

lit'torio, a *ag* (*STORIA*) lictorial; **fascio** ~ fasces *pl*.

Litu'ania *sf*: **la** ~ Lithuania.

litur'gia, 'gie [litur'dʒia] *sf* liturgy.

li'uto *sm* lute.

li'vella *sf* level; ~ **a bolla d'aria** spirit level.

livel'lare *vt* to level, make level; ~**rsi** *vr* to become level; (*fig*) to level out, balance out.

livella'trice [livella'tritʃe] *sf* steamroller.

li'vello *sm* level; (*fig*) level, standard; **ad alto** ~ (*fig*) high-level; **a** ~ **mondiale** world-wide; **a** ~ **di confidenza** confidentially; ~ **di magazzino** stock level; ~ **del mare** sea level; **sul** ~ **del mare** above sea level; ~ **occupazionale** level of employment; ~ **retributivo** salary level.

'livido, a *ag* livid; (*per percosse*) bruised, black and blue; (*cielo*) leaden ♦ *sm* bruise.

li'vorre *sm* malice, spite.

Li'vorno *sf* Livorno, Leghorn.

li'vrea *sf* livery.

'lizza ['littsa] *sf* lists *pl*; **essere in** ~ **per** (*fig*) to compete for; **scendere in** ~ (*anche fig*) to enter the lists.

lo *det m* (*dav s impura, gn, pn, ps, x, z*; *dav V* **l'**) the ♦ *pronome* (*dav V* **l'**) (*oggetto*: *persona*) him; (: *cosa*) it; ~ **sapevo** I knew it; ~ **so** I know; **sii buono, anche se lui non** ~ **è** be good, even if he isn't; *vedi anche* **il**.

'lobbia *sf* homburg.

lob'bista, i, e *sm/f* lobbyist.

'lobo *sm* lobe; ~ **dell'orecchio** ear lobe.

lo'cale *ag* local ♦ *sm* room; (*luogo pubblico*) premises *pl*; ~ **notturno** nightclub.

località *sf inv* locality.

localiz'zare [lokalid'dzare] *vt* (*circoscrivere*) to confine, localize; (*accertare*) to locate, place.

lo'canda *sf* inn.

locandi'ere, a *sm/f* innkeeper.

locan'dina *sf* (*TEATRO*) poster.

lo'care *vt* (*casa*) to rent out, let; (*macchina*) to hire out (*Brit*), rent (out).

loca'tario, a *sm/f* tenant.

loca'tivo, a *ag* (*DIR*) rentable.

loca'tore, 'trice *sm/f* landlord/lady.

locazi'one [lokat'tsjone] *sf* (*da parte del locatario*) renting *q*; (*da parte del locatore*) renting out *q*, letting *q*; (*contratto di*) ~ lease; (*canone di*) ~ rent; **dare in** ~ to rent out, let.

locomo'tiva *sf* locomotive.

locomo'tore *sm* electric locomotive.

locomozi'one [lokomot'tsjone] *sf* locomotion; **mezzi di** ~ vehicles, means of transport.

'loculo *sm* burial recess.

lo'custa *sf* locust.

locuzi'one [lokut'tsjone] *sf* phrase, expression.

lo'dare *vt* to praise.

'lode *sf* praise; (*INS*): **laurearsi con 110 e** ~ ≈ to graduate with first-class honours (*Brit*), ≈ to graduate summa cum laude (*US*).

'loden *sm inv* (*stoffa*) loden; (*cappotto*)

loden overcoat.

lo'devole *ag* praiseworthy.

loga'ritmo *sm* logarithm.

'loggia, ge ['lɔddʒa] *sf* (*ARCHIT*) loggia; (*circolo massonico*) lodge.

loggi'one [lod'dʒone] *sm* (*di teatro*): **il ~** the Gods *sg*.

logica'mente [lodʒika'mente] *av* naturally, obviously.

logicità [lodʒitʃi'ta] *sf* logicality.

'logico, a, ci, che ['lɔdʒiko] *ag* logical ♦ *sf* logic.

lo'gistica [lo'dʒistika] *sf* logistics *sg*.

'logo *sm inv* logo.

logora'mento *sm* (*di vestiti etc*) wear.

logo'rante *ag* exhausting.

logo'rare *vt* to wear out; (*sciupare*) to waste; **~rsi** *vr* to wear out; (*fig*) to wear o.s. out.

logo'rio *sm* wear and tear; (*fig*) strain.

'logoro, a *ag* (*stoffa*) worn out, threadbare; (*persona*) worn out.

'Loira *sf*: **la ~** the Loire.

lom'baggine [lom'baddʒine] *sf* lumbago.

Lombar'dia *sf*: **la ~** Lombardy.

lom'bardo, a *ag, sm/f* Lombard.

lom'bare *ag* (*ANAT, MED*) lumbar.

lom'bata *sf* (*taglio di carne*) loin.

'lombo *sm* (*ANAT*) loin.

lom'brico, chi *sm* earthworm.

londi'nese *ag* London *cpd* ♦ *sm/f* Londoner.

'Londra *sf* London.

lon'ganime *ag* forbearing.

longevità [londʒevi'ta] *sf* longevity.

lon'gevo, a [lon'dʒevo] *ag* long-lived.

longi'lineo, a [londʒi'lineo] *ag* long-limbed.

longi'tudine [londʒi'tudine] *sf* longitude.

lontana'mente *av* remotely; **non ci pensavo neppure ~** it didn't even occur to me.

lonta'nanza [lonta'nantsa] *sf* distance; absence.

lon'tano, a *ag* (*distante*) distant, faraway; (*assente*) absent; (*vago: sospetto*) slight, remote; (*tempo: remoto*) far-off, distant; (*parente*) distant, remote ♦ *av* far; **è ~a la casa?** is it far to the house?, is the house far from here?; **è ~ un chilometro** it's a kilometre away *o* a kilometre from here; **più ~** farther; **da** *o* **di ~** from a distance; **~ da** a long way from; **alla ~a** slightly, vaguely.

'lontra *sf* otter.

lo'quace [lo'kwatʃe] *ag* talkative, loquacious; (*fig: gesto etc*) eloquent.

'lordo, a *ag* dirty, filthy; (*peso, stipendio*) gross; **~ d'imposta** pre-tax.

Lo'rena *sf* (*GEO*) Lorraine.

'loro *pronome pl* (*oggetto, con preposizione*) them; (*complemento di termine*) to them; (*soggetto*) they; (*forma di cortesia: anche:* **L~**) you; to you; **il(la) ~, i(le) ~** *det* their;

(*forma di cortesia: anche:* **L~**) your ♦ *pronome* theirs; (*forma di cortesia: anche:* **L~**) yours ♦ *sm inv*: **il ~** their (*o* your) money ♦ *sf inv*: **la ~** (*opinione*) their (*o* your) view; **i ~** (*famiglia*) their (*o* your) family; (*amici etc*) their (*o* your) own people; **un ~ amico** a friend of theirs; **è dalla ~** he's on their (*o* your) side; **ne hanno fatto un'altra delle ~** they've (*o* you've) done it again; **~ stessi(e)** they themselves; you yourselves.

lo'sanga, ghe *sf* diamond, lozenge.

Lo'sanna *sf* Lausanne.

'losco, a, schi, sche *ag* (*fig*) shady, suspicious.

'lotta *sf* struggle, fight; (*SPORT*) wrestling; **essere in ~ (con)** to be in conflict (with); **fare la ~ (con)** to wrestle (with); **~ armata** armed struggle; **~ di classe** (*POL*) class struggle; **~ libera** (*SPORT*) all-in wrestling (*Brit*), freestyle.

lot'tare *vi* to fight, struggle; to wrestle.

lotta'tore, 'trice *sm/f* wrestler.

lotte'ria *sf* lottery; (*di gara ippica*) sweepstake.

lottiz'zare [lottid'dzare] *vt* to divide into plots.

lottizzazi'one [lottiddzat'tsjone] *sf* division into plots.

'lotto *sm* (*gioco*) (state) lottery; (*parte*) lot; (*EDIL*) site; **vincere un terno al ~** (*anche fig*) to hit the jackpot.

lozi'one [lot'tsjone] *sf* lotion.

L.st. *abbr* (= *lire sterline*) £.

LT *sigla* = *Latina*.

LU *sigla* = *Lucca*.

lubrifi'cante *sm* lubricant.

lubrifi'care *vt* to lubricate.

lu'cano, a *ag* of (*o* from) Lucania.

luc'chetto [luk'ketto] *sm* padlock.

lucci'care [luttʃi'kare] *vi* to sparkle; (*oro*) to glitter; (*stella*) to twinkle; (*occhi*) to glisten.

lucci'chio [luttʃi'kio] *sm* sparkling; glittering; twinkling; glistening.

lucci'cone [luttʃi'kone] *sm*: **avere i ~i agli occhi** to have tears in one's eyes.

'luccio ['luttʃo] *sm* (*ZOOL*) pike.

'lucciola ['luttʃola] *sf* (*ZOOL*) firefly; glowworm.

'luce ['lutʃe] *sf* light; (*finestra*) window; **alla ~ di** by the light of; **fare qc alla ~ del sole** (*fig*) to do sth in the open; **dare alla ~** (*bambino*) to give birth to; **fare ~ su qc** (*fig*) to shed *o* throw light on sth; **~ del sole/della luna** sun/moonlight.

lu'cente [lu'tʃente] *ag* shining.

lucen'tezza [lutʃen'tettsa] *sf* shine.

lu'cerna [lu'tʃerna] *sf* oil lamp.

lucer'nario [lutʃer'narjo] *sm* skylight.

lu'certola [lu'tʃertola] *sf* lizard.

luci'dare [lutʃi'dare] *vt* to polish; (*ricalcare*)

to trace.

lucida'trice [lutʃida'tritʃe] *sf* floor polisher.

lucidità [lutʃidi'ta] *sf* lucidity.

'**lucido, a** ['lutʃido] *ag* shining, bright; (*lucidato*) polished; (*fig*) lucid ♦ *sm* shine, lustre (*Brit*), luster (*US*); (*per scarpe etc*) polish; (*disegno*) tracing.

lu'cignolo [lu'tʃiɲɲolo] *sm* wick.

lucra'tivo, a *ag* lucrative; **a scopo** ~ for gain.

'**lucro** *sm* profit, gain; **a scopo di** ~ for gain; **organizzazione senza scopo di** ~ non-profit-making (*Brit*) *o* non-profit (*US*) organization.

lu'croso, a *ag* lucrative, profitable.

luculli'ano, a *ag* (*pasto*) sumptuous.

lu'dibrio *sm* mockery *q*; (*oggetto di scherno*) laughing stock.

'**lue** *sf* syphilis.

'**luglio** ['luʎʎo] *sm* July; **nel mese di** ~ in July, in the month of July; **il primo** ~ the first of July; **arrivare il 2** ~ to arrive on the 2nd of July; **all'inizio/alla fine di** ~ at the beginning/at the end of July; **durante il mese di** ~ during July; **a** ~ **del prossimo anno** in July of next year; **ogni anno a** ~ every July; **che fai a** ~? what are you doing in July?; **ha piovuto molto a** ~ **quest'anno** July was very wet this year.

'**lugubre** *ag* gloomy.

'**lui** *pronome* (*soggetto*) he; (*oggetto: per dare rilievo, con preposizione*) him ♦ *sm inv*: **il mio** ~ my beloved; ~ **stesso** he himself; **è** ~ it's him.

lu'maca, che *sf* slug; (*chiocciola*) snail.

luma'cone *sm* (large) slug; (*fig*) slowcoach (*Brit*), slowpoke (*US*).

'**lume** *sm* light; (*lampada*) lamp; ~ **a olio** oil lamp; **chiedere** ~**i a qn** (*fig*) to ask sb for advice; **a** ~ **di naso** (*fig*) by rule of thumb.

lumi'cino [lumi'tʃino] *sm* small *o* faint light; **essere (ridotto) al** ~ (*fig*) to be at death's door.

lumi'era *sf* chandelier.

lumi'nare *sm* luminary.

lumi'naria *sf* (*per feste*) illuminations *pl*.

lumine'scente [luminJ'Jɛnte] *ag* luminescent.

lu'mino *sm* small light; ~ **da notte** nightlight; ~ **per i morti** candle for the dead.

lumi'noso, a *ag* (*che emette luce*) luminous; (*cielo, colore, stanza*) bright; (*sorgente*) of light, light *cpd*; (*fig: sorriso*) bright, radiant; **insegna** ~**a** illuminated sign.

lun. *abbr* (= *lunedì*) Mon.

'**luna** *sf* moon; ~ **nuova/piena** new/full moon; **avere la** ~ to be in a bad mood; ~ **di miele** honeymoon.

'**luna park** *sm inv* amusement park, funfair.

lu'nare *ag* lunar, moon *cpd*.

lu'nario *sm* almanac; **sbarcare il** ~ to make ends meet.

lu'natico, a, ci, che *ag* whimsical, temperamental.

lunedì *sm inv* Monday; *per fraseologia vedi* **martedì**.

lun'gaggine [lun'gaddʒine] *sf* slowness; ~**i della burocrazia** red tape.

lunga'mente *av* (*a lungo*) for a long time; (*estesamente*) at length.

lun'garno *sm* embankment along the Arno.

lun'ghezza [lun'gettsa] *sf* length; ~ **d'onda** (*FISICA*) wavelength.

'**lungi** ['lundʒi] *av*: ~ **da** *prep* far from.

lungimi'rante [lundʒimi'rante] *ag* far-sighted.

'**lungo, a, ghi, ghe** *ag* long; (*lento: persona*) slow; (*diluito: caffè, brodo*) weak, watery, thin ♦ *sm* length ♦ *prep* along; ~ **3 metri** 3 metres long; **avere la barba** ~**a** to be unshaven; **a** ~ for a long time; **a** ~ **andare** in the long run; **di gran** ~**a** (*molto*) by far; **andare in** ~ *o* **per le lunghe** to drag on; **saperla** ~**a** to know what's what; **in** ~ **e in largo** far and wide, all over; ~ **il corso dei secoli** throughout the centuries; **navigazione di** ~ **corso** ocean-going navigation.

lungofi'ume *sm* embankment.

lungo'lago *sm* road round a lake.

lungo'mare *sm* promenade.

lungome'traggio [lungome'traddʒo] *sm* (*CINEMA*) feature film.

lungo'tevere *sm* embankment along the Tiber.

lu'notto *sm* (*AUT*) rear *o* back window; ~ **termico** heated rear window.

lu'ogo, ghi *sm* place; (*posto: di incidente etc*) scene, site; (*punto, passo di libro*) passage; **in** ~ **di** instead of; **in primo** ~ in the first place; **aver** ~ to take place; **dar** ~ **a** to give rise to; ~ **comune** commonplace; ~ **del delitto** scene of the crime; ~ **geometrico** locus; ~ **di nascita** birthplace; (*AMM*) place of birth; ~ **di pena** prison, penitentiary; ~ **di provenienza** place of origin.

luogote'nente *sm* (*MIL*) lieutenant.

lupacchi'otto [lupak'kjɔtto] *sm* (*ZOOL*) (wolf) cub.

lu'para *sf* sawn-off shotgun.

lu'petto *sm* (*ZOOL*) (wolf) cub; (*negli scouts*) cub scout.

'**lupo, a** *sm/f* wolf/she-wolf; **cane** ~ alsatian (dog) (*Brit*), German shepherd (dog); **tempo da** ~**i** filthy weather.

'**luppolo** *sm* (*BOT*) hop.

'**lurido, a** *ag* filthy.

luri'dume *sm* filth.

lu'singa, ghe *sf* (*spesso al pl*) flattery *q*.

lusin'gare *vt* to flatter.

lusinghi'ero, a [luzin'gjɛro] *ag* flattering, gratifying.

lus'sare vt (MED) to dislocate.

lussazi'one [lussat'tsjone] sf (MED) dislocation.

lussembur'ghese [lussembur'gese] ag of (o from) Luxembourg ♦ sm/f native (o inhabitant) of Luxembourg.

Lussem'burgo sm (stato): **il** ~ Luxembourg ♦ sf (città) Luxembourg.

'lusso sm luxury; **di** ~ luxury cpd.

lussu'oso, a ag luxurious.

lussureggi'are [lussured'dʒare] vi to be luxuriant.

lus'suria sf lust.

lussuri'oso, a ag lascivious, lustful.

lus'trare vt to polish, shine.

lustras'carpe sm/f inv shoeshine.

lus'trino sm sequin.

'lustro, a ag shiny; (pelliccia) glossy ♦ sm shine, gloss; (fig) prestige, glory; (quinquennio) five-year period.

'lutto sm mourning; **essere in/portare il** ~ to be in/wear mourning.

luttu'oso, a ag mournful, sad.

M

M, m ['ɛmme] sf o m inv (lettera) M, m; **M come Milano** ≈ M for Mary (Brit), M for Mike (US).

m. abbr = **mese; metro; miglia; monte.**

ma cong but; ~ **insomma!** for goodness sake!; ~ **no!** of course not!

'macabro, a ag gruesome, macabre.

macché [mak'ke] escl not at all!, certainly not!

macche'roni [makke'roni] smpl macaroni sg.

'macchia ['makkja] sf stain, spot; (chiazza di diverso colore) spot; splash, patch; (tipo di boscaglia) scrub; ~ **d'inchiostro** ink stain; **estendersi a** ~ **d'olio** (fig) to spread rapidly; **darsi/vivere alla** ~ (fig) to go into/live in hiding.

macchi'are [mak'kjare] vt (sporcare) to stain, mark; ~**rsi** vr (persona) to get dirty; (stoffa) to stain; to get stained o marked; ~**rsi di un delitto** to be guilty of a crime.

macchi'ato, a [mak'kjato] ag (pelle, pelo) spotted; ~ **di** stained with; **caffè** ~ coffee with a dash of milk.

macchi'etta [mak'kjetta] sf (disegno) sketch, caricature; (TEATRO) caricature; (fig: persona) character.

'macchina ['makkina] sf machine; (motore, locomotiva) engine; (automobile) car; (fig: meccanismo) machinery; **andare in** ~ (AUT) to go by car; (STAMPA) to go to press; **salire in** ~ to get into the car; **venire in** ~ to come by car; **sala** ~**e** (NAUT) engine room; ~ **da cucire** sewing machine; ~ **fotografica** camera; ~ **da presa** cine o movie camera; ~ **da scrivere** typewriter; ~ **utensile** machine tool; ~ **a vapore** steam engine.

macchinal'mente [makkinal'mente] av mechanically.

macchi'nare [makki'nare] vt to plot.

macchi'nario [makki'narjo] sm machinery.

macchinazi'one [makkinat'tsjone] sf plot, machination.

macchi'netta [makki'netta] sf (fam: caffettiera) percolator; (: accendino) lighter.

macchi'nista, i [makki'nista] sm (di treno) engine-driver; (di nave) engineer; (TEATRO, TV) stagehand.

macchi'noso, a [makki'noso] ag complex, complicated.

mace'donia [matʃe'dɔnja] sf fruit salad.

macel'laio [matʃel'lajo] sm butcher.

macel'lare [matʃel'lare] vt to slaughter, butcher.

macellazi'one [matʃellat'tsjone] sf slaughtering, butchering.

macelle'ria [matʃelle'ria] sf butcher's (shop).

ma'cello [ma'tʃɛllo] sm (mattatoio) slaughterhouse, abattoir (Brit); (fig) slaughter, massacre; (: disastro) shambles sg.

mace'rare [matʃe'rare] vt to macerate; (CUC) to marinate; ~**rsi** vr to waste away; (fig): ~**rsi in** to be consumed with.

macerazi'one [matʃerat'tsjone] sf maceration.

ma'cerie [ma'tʃɛrje] sfpl rubble sg, debris sg.

'macero ['matʃero] sm (operazione) pulping; (stabilimento) pulping mill; **carta da** ~ paper for pulping.

machia'vellico, a, ci, che [makja'vɛlliko] ag (anche fig) Machiavellian.

ma'cigno [ma'tʃiɲɲo] sm (masso) rock, boulder.

maci'lento, a [matʃi'lɛnto] ag emaciated.

'macina ['matʃina] sf (pietra) millstone; (macchina) grinder.

macinacaffè [matʃinakaf'fɛ] sm inv coffee grinder.

macina'pepe [matʃina'pepe] sm inv peppermill.

maci'nare [matʃi'nare] vt to grind; (carne) to mince (Brit), grind (US).

maci'nato [matʃi'nato] sm meal, flour; (carne) minced (Brit) o ground (US) meat.

maci'nino [matʃi'nino] sm (per caffè) coffee grinder; (per pepe) peppermill; (scherzoso: macchina) old banger (Brit), clunker (US).

maciul'lare [matʃul'lare] vt (canapa, lino) to brake; (fig: braccio etc) to crush.

'macro... prefisso macro....

macu'lato, a ag (pelo) spotted.

Ma'dama: palazzo ~ sm (POL) seat of the Italian Chamber of Senators.

Ma'dera sf (GEO) Madeira ♦ sm inv (vino) Madeira.

'madido, a ag: ~ **(di)** wet o moist (with).

Ma'donna sf (REL) Our Lady.

mador'nale ag enormous, huge.

'madre sf mother; (matrice di bolletta) counterfoil ♦ ag inv mother cpd; **ragazza** ~ unmarried mother; **scena** ~ (TEATRO) principal scene; (fig) terrible scene.

madre'lingua sf mother tongue, native language.

madre'patria sf mother country, native land.

madre'perla sf mother-of-pearl.

Ma'drid sf Madrid.

madri'gale sm madrigal.

madri'leno, a ag of (o from) Madrid ♦ sm/f person from Madrid.

ma'drina sf godmother.

maestà sf inv majesty; **Sua M**~ **la Regina** Her Majesty the Queen.

maestosità sf majesty.

maes'toso, a ag majestic.

ma'estra sf vedi **maestro**.

maes'trale sm north-west wind.

maes'tranze [maes'trantse] sfpl workforce sg.

maes'tria sf mastery, skill.

ma'estro, a sm/f (INS: anche: ~ **di scuola** o **elementare**) primary (Brit) o grade school (US) teacher; (esperto) expert ♦ sm (artigiano, fig: guida) master; (MUS) maestro ♦ ag (principale) main; (di grande abilità) masterly, skilful (Brit), skillful (US); **un colpo da** ~ (fig) a masterly move; **muro** ~ main wall; **strada** ~**a** main road; ~**a d'asilo** nursery teacher; ~ **di ballo** dancing master; ~ **di cerimonie** master of ceremonies; ~ **d'orchestra** conductor, director (US); ~ **di scherma** fencing master; ~ **di sci** ski instructor.

'mafia sf Mafia.

mafi'oso sm member of the Mafia.

'maga, ghe sf sorceress.

ma'gagna [ma'gaɲɲa] sf defect, flaw, blemish; (noia, guaio) problem.

ma'gari escl (esprime desiderio): ~ **fosse vero!** if only it were true!; **ti piacerebbe andare in Scozia?** — ~**!** would you like to go to Scotland? — and how! ♦ av (anche) even; (forse) perhaps.

magazzi'naggio [magaddzi'naddʒo] sm: **(spese di)** ~ storage charges pl, warehousing charges pl.

magazzini'ere [magaddzi'njɛre] sm warehouseman.

magaz'zino [magad'dzino] sm warehouse;

grande ~ department store; ~ **doganale** bonded warehouse.

'maggio ['maddʒo] sm May; per fraseologia vedi **luglio**.

maggio'rana [maddʒo'rana] sf (BOT) (sweet) marjoram.

maggio'ranza [maddʒo'rantsa] sf majority; **nella** ~ **dei casi** in most cases.

maggio'rare [maddʒo'rare] vt to increase, raise.

maggiorazi'one [maddʒorat'tsjone] sf (COMM) rise, increase.

maggior'domo [maddʒor'dɔmo] sm butler.

maggi'ore [mad'dʒore] ag (comparativo: più grande) bigger, larger, taller; greater; (: più vecchio: sorella, fratello) older, elder; (: di grado superiore) senior; (: più importante, MIL, MUS) major; (superlativo) biggest, largest; tallest; greatest; oldest, eldest ♦ sm/f (di grado) superior; (di età) elder; (MIL) major; (: AER) squadron leader; **la maggior parte** the majority; **andare per la** ~ (cantante, attore etc) to be very popular, be "in".

maggio'renne [maddʒo'rɛnne] ag of age ♦ sm/f person who has come of age.

maggiori'tario, a [maddʒori'tarjo] ag majority cpd.

maggior'mente [maddʒor'mente] av much more; (con senso superlativo) most.

ma'gia [ma'dʒia] sf magic.

'magico, a, ci, che ['madʒiko] ag magic; (fig) fascinating, charming, magical.

'magio ['madʒo] sm (REL): **i re Magi** the Magi, the Three Wise Men.

magis'tero [madʒis'tɛro] sm teaching; (fig: maestria) skill; (INS): **Facoltà di M**~ ≈ teachers' training college.

magis'trale [madʒis'trale] ag primary (Brit) o grade school (US) teachers', primary o grade school teaching cpd; (abile) skilful (Brit), skillful (US); **istituto** ~ secondary school for the training of primary teachers.

magis'trato [madʒis'trato] sm magistrate.

magistra'tura [madʒistra'tura] sf magistrature; (magistrati): **la** ~ the Bench.

'maglia ['maʎʎa] sf stitch; (lavoro ai ferri) knitting q; (tessuto, SPORT) jersey; (maglione) jersey, sweater; (di catena) link; (di rete) mesh; **avviare/diminuire le** ~**e** to cast on/cast off; **lavorare a** ~, **fare la** ~ to knit; ~ **diritta/rovescia** plain/purl.

magli'aia [maʎ'ʎaja] sf knitter.

maglie'ria [maʎʎe'ria] sf knitwear; (negozio) knitwear shop; **macchina per** ~ knitting machine.

magli'etta [maʎ'ʎetta] sf (canottiera) vest; (tipo camicia) T-shirt.

magli'ficio [maʎʎi'fitʃo] sm knitwear factory.

ma'glina [maʎ'ʎina] sf (tessuto) jersey.

'maglio ['maʎʎo] sm mallet; (macchina) power hammer.

magli'one [maʎ'ʎone] *sm* jersey, sweater.

'magma *sm* magma; *(fig)* mass.

ma'gnaccia [maɲ'ɲattʃa] *sm inv (peg)* pimp.

magnanimità [maɲɲanimi'ta] *sf* magnanimity.

ma'gnanimo, a [maɲ'ɲanimo] *ag* magnanimous.

ma'gnate [maɲ'ɲate] *sm* tycoon, magnate.

ma'gnesia [maɲ'ɲɛzja] *sf (CHIM)* magnesia.

ma'gnesio [maɲ'ɲɛzjo] *sm (CHIM)* magnesium; **al ~** *(lampada, flash)* magnesium *cpd*.

ma'gnete [maɲ'ɲɛte] *sm* magnet.

ma'gnetico, a, ci, che [maɲ'ɲɛtiko] *ag* magnetic.

magne'tismo [maɲɲe'tizmo] *sm* magnetism.

magnetiz'zare [maɲɲetid'dzare] *vt (FISICA)* to magnetize; *(fig)* to mesmerize.

magne'tofono [maɲɲe'tɔfono] *sm* tape recorder.

magnifica'mente [maɲɲifika'mente] *av* magnificently, extremely well.

magnifi'cenza [maɲɲifi'tʃɛntsa] *sf* magnificence, splendour *(Brit)*, splendor *(US)*.

ma'gnifico, a, ci, che [maɲ'ɲifiko] *ag* magnificent, splendid; *(ospite)* generous.

'magno, a ['maɲɲo] *ag:* **aula ~a** main hall.

ma'gnolia [maɲ'ɲɔlja] *sf* magnolia.

'mago, ghi *sm (stregone)* magician, wizard; *(illusionista)* magician.

ma'grezza [ma'grettsa] *sf* thinness.

'magro, a *ag* (very) thin, skinny; *(carne)* lean; *(formaggio)* low-fat; *(fig: scarso, misero)* meagre *(Brit)*, meager *(US)*, poor; *(: meschino: scusa)* poor, lame; **mangiare di ~** not to eat meat.

'mai *av (nessuna volta)* never; *(talvolta)* ever; **non ... ~** never; **~ più** never again; **come ~?** why *(o how)* on earth?; **chi/ dove/quando ~?** whoever/wherever/whenever?

mai'ale *sm (ZOOL)* pig; *(carne)* pork.

mai'olica *sf* majolica.

maio'nese *sf* mayonnaise.

Mai'orca *sf* Majorca.

'mais *sm* maize *(Brit)*, corn *(US)*.

mai'uscolo, a *ag (lettera)* capital ♦ *sf* capital letter ♦ *sm* capital letters *pl*; *(TIP)* upper case; **scrivere tutto (in) ~** to write everything in capitals *o* in capital letters.

mal *av, sm vedi* **male**.

'mala *sf (gergo)* underworld.

malac'corto, a *ag* rash, careless.

mala'fede *sf* bad faith.

malaf'fare: di ~ *ag (gente)* shady, dishonest; **donna di ~** prostitute.

mala'gevole [mala'dʒevole] *ag* difficult, hard.

mala'grazia [mala'grattsja] *sf:* **con ~** with bad grace, impolitely.

mala'lingua, *pl* **male'lingue** *sf* gossip *(person)*.

mala'mente *av* badly; *(sgarbatamente)* rudely.

malan'dato, a *ag (persona: di salute)* in poor health; *(: di condizioni finanziarie)* badly off; *(trascurato)* shabby.

ma'lanimo *sm* ill will, malevolence; **di ~** unwillingly.

ma'lanno *sm (disgrazia)* misfortune; *(malattia)* ailment.

mala'pena *sf:* **a ~** hardly, scarcely.

ma'laria *sf* malaria.

ma'larico, a, ci, che *ag* malarial.

mala'sorte *sf* bad luck.

mala'ticcio, a [mala'tittʃo] *ag* sickly.

ma'lato, a *ag* ill, sick; *(gamba)* bad; *(pianta)* diseased ♦ *sm/f* sick person; *(in ospedale)* patient; **darsi ~** *(sul lavoro etc)* to go sick.

malat'tia *sf (infettiva etc)* illness, disease; *(cattiva salute)* illness, sickness; *(di pianta)* disease; **mettersi in ~** to go on sick leave; **fare una ~ di qc** *(fig: disperarsi)* to get in a state about sth.

malaugu'rato, a *ag* ill-fated, unlucky.

malau'gurio *sm* bad *o* ill omen; **uccello del ~** bird of ill omen.

mala'vita *sf* underworld.

malavi'toso, a *sm/f* gangster.

mala'voglia [mala'vɔʎʎa]: **di ~** *av* unwillingly, reluctantly.

Ma'lawi [ma'lavi] *sm:* **il ~** Malawi.

Ma'lysia *sf* Malaysia.

malaysi'ano, a *ag, sm/f* Malaysian.

malcapi'tato, a *ag* unlucky, unfortunate ♦ *sm/f* unfortunate person.

mal'concio, a, ci, ce [mal'kontʃo] *ag* in a sorry state.

malcon'tento *sm* discontent.

malcos'tume *sm* immorality.

mal'destro, a *ag (inabile)* inexpert, inexperienced; *(goffo)* awkward.

maldi'cente [maldi'tʃɛnte] *ag* slanderous.

maldi'cenza [maldi'tʃɛntsa] *sf* malicious gossip.

maldis'posto, a *ag:* **~ (verso)** ill-disposed (towards).

Mal'dive *sfpl:* **le ~** the Maldives.

'male *av* badly ♦ *sm (ciò che è ingiusto, disonesto)* evil; *(danno, svantaggio)* harm; *(sventura)* misfortune; *(dolore fisico, morale)* pain, ache; **sentirsi ~** to feel ill; **aver mal di cuore/fegato** to have a heart/liver complaint; **aver mal di denti/d'orecchi/di testa** to have toothache/earache/a headache; **aver mal di gola** to have a sore throat; **aver ~ ai piedi** to have sore feet; **far ~** *(dolere)* to hurt; **far ~ alla salute** to be bad for one's health; **far del ~ a qn** to hurt *o* harm sb; **parlar ~ di qn** to speak ill of sb; **restare** *o* **rimanere ~** to be sorry; to be disappointed; to be hurt; **trattar ~ qn** to ill-treat sb; **andare a ~** to go off *o* bad;

come va? — **non c'è** ~ how are you? — not bad; **di** ~ **in peggio** from bad to worse; **per** ~ **che vada** however badly things go; **non avertene a** ~, **non prendertela a** ~ don't take it to heart; **mal comune mezzo gaudio** (*proverbio*) a trouble shared is a trouble halved; **mal d'auto** carsickness; **mal di mare** seasickness.

male'detto, a *pp di* **maledire** ♦ *ag* cursed, damned; (*fig fam*) damned, blasted.

male'dire *vt* to curse.

maledizi'one [maledit'tsjone] *sf* curse; ~! damn it!

maledu'cato, a *ag* rude, ill-mannered.

maleducazi'one [maledukat'tsjone] *sf* rudeness.

male'fatta *sf* misdeed.

male'ficio [male'fitʃo] *sm* witchcraft.

ma'lefico, a, ci, che *ag* (*aria, cibo*) harmful, bad; (*influsso, azione*) evil.

ma'lese *ag, sm/f* Malay(an) ♦ *sm* (*LING*) Malay.

Ma'lesia *sf* Malaya.

ma'lessere *sm* indisposition, slight illness; (*fig*) uneasiness.

malevo'lenza [malevo'lɛntsa] *sf* malevolence.

ma'levolo, a *ag* malevolent.

malfa'mato, a *ag* notorious.

mal'fatto, a *ag* (*persona*) deformed; (*oggetto*) badly made; (*lavoro*) badly done.

malfat'tore, 'trice *sm/f* wrongdoer.

mal'fermo, a *ag* unsteady, shaky; (*salute*) poor, delicate.

malformazi'one [malformat'tsjone] *sf* malformation.

'malga, ghe *sf* Alpine hut.

malgo'verno *sm* maladministration.

mal'grado *prep* in spite of, despite ♦ *cong* although; **mio** (*o* **tuo** *etc*) ~ against my (*o* your *etc*) will.

ma'lia *sf* spell; (*fig: fascino*) charm.

mali'ardo, a *ag* (*occhi, sorriso*) bewitching ♦ *sf* enchantress.

maligna'mente [maliɲɲa'mente] *av* maliciously.

mali'gnare [maliɲ'ɲare] *vi:* ~ **su** to malign, speak ill of.

malignità [maliɲɲi'ta] *sf inv* (*qualità*) malice, spite; (*osservazione*) spiteful remark; **con** ~ spitefully, maliciously.

ma'ligno, a [ma'liɲɲo] *ag* (*malvagio*) malicious, malignant; (*MED*) malignant.

malinco'nia *sf* melancholy, gloom.

malin'conico, a, ci, che *ag* melancholy.

malincu'ore: **a** ~ *av* reluctantly, unwillingly.

malinfor'mato, a *ag* misinformed.

malintenzio'nato, a [malintentsjo'nato] *ag* ill-intentioned.

malin'teso, a *ag* misunderstood; (*riguardo,*

senso del dovere) mistaken, wrong ♦ *sm* misunderstanding.

ma'lizia [ma'littsja] *sf* (*malignità*) malice; (*furbizia*) cunning; (*espediente*) trick.

malizi'oso, a [malit'tsjoso] *ag* malicious; cunning; (*vivace, birichino*) mischievous.

malle'abile *ag* malleable.

malleva'dore *sm* guarantor.

malleve'ria *sf* guarantee, surety.

mal'loppo *sm* (*fam: refurtiva*) loot.

malme'nare *vt* to beat up; (*fig*) to ill-treat.

mal'messo, a *ag* shabby.

malnu'trito, a *ag* undernourished.

malnutrizi'one [malnutrit'tsjone] *sf* malnutrition.

'malo, a *ag:* **in** ~ **modo** badly.

ma'locchio [ma'lɔkkjo] *sm* evil eye.

ma'lora *sf* (*fam*): **andare in** ~ to go to the dogs; **va in** ~! go to hell!

ma'lore *sm* (sudden) illness.

malri'dotto, a *ag* (*abiti, scarpe, persona*) in a sorry state; (*casa, macchina*) dilapidated, in a poor state of repair.

mal'sano, a *ag* unhealthy.

malsi'curo, a *ag* unsafe.

'Malta *sf* Malta.

'malta *sf* (*EDIL*) mortar.

mal'tempo *sm* bad weather.

malte'nuto, a *ag* badly looked after, badly kept.

mal'tese *ag, sm/f, sm* Maltese *inv.*

'malto *sm* malt.

mal'tolto *sm* ill-gotten gains *pl.*

maltratta'mento *sm* ill treatment.

maltrat'tare *vt* to ill-treat.

malu'more *sm* bad mood; (*irritabilità*) bad temper; (*discordia*) ill feeling; **di** ~ in a bad mood.

'malva *sf* (*BOT*) mallow ♦ *ag, sm inv* mauve.

mal'vagio, a, gi, gie [mal'vadʒo] *ag* wicked, evil.

malvagità [malvadʒi'ta] *sf inv* (*qualità*) wickedness; (*azione*) wicked deed.

malversazi'one [malversat'tsjone] *sf* (*DIR*) embezzlement.

malves'tito, a *ag* badly dressed, ill-clad.

mal'visto, a *ag:* ~ (**da**) disliked (by), unpopular (with).

malvi'vente *sm* criminal.

malvolenti'eri *av* unwillingly, reluctantly.

malvo'lere *vt:* **farsi** ~ **da qn** to make o.s. unpopular with sb ♦ *sm:* **prendere qn a** ~ to take a dislike to sb.

'mamma *sf* mum(my) (*Brit*), mom (*US*); ~ **mia!** my goodness!

mam'mario, a *ag* (*ANAT*) mammary.

mam'mella *sf* (*ANAT*) breast; (*di vacca, capra etc*) udder.

mam'mifero *sm* mammal.

mam'mismo *sm* excessive attachment to one's mother.

'mammola *sf* (*BOT*) violet.

'manager ['mænidʒə] *sm inv* manager.
manageri'ale [manadʒe'rjale] *ag* managerial.
ma'nata *sf* (*colpo*) slap; (*quantità*) handful.
'manca *sf* left (hand); **a destra e a ~ left**, right and centre, on all sides.
manca'mento *sm* (*di forze*) (feeling of) faintness, weakness.
man'canza [man'kantsa] *sf* lack; (*carenza*) shortage, scarcity; (*fallo*) fault; (*imperfezione*) failing, shortcoming; **per ~ di tempo** through lack of time; **in ~ di meglio** for lack of anything better; **sentire la ~ di qc/qn** to miss sth/sb.
man'care *vi* (*essere insufficiente*) to be lacking; (*venir meno*) to fail; (*sbagliare*) to be wrong, make a mistake; (*non esserci*) to be missing, not to be there; (*essere lontano*): **~ (da)** to be away (from) ♦ *vt* to miss; **~ di** to lack; **~ a** (*promessa*) to fail to keep; **tu mi manchi** I miss you; **mancò poco che morisse** he very nearly died; **mancano ancora 10 sterline** we're still £10 short; **manca un quarto alle 6** it's a quarter to 6; **non mancherò** I won't forget, I'll make sure I do; **ci mancherebbe altro!** of course I (*o you etc*) will!; **~ da casa** to be away from home; **~ di rispetto a** *o* **verso qn** to be lacking in respect towards sb, be disrespectful towards sb; **~ di parola** not to keep one's word, go back on one's word; **sentirsi ~** to feel faint.
man'cato, a *ag* (*tentativo*) unsuccessful; (*artista*) failed.
manche [mãʃ] *sf inv* (*SPORT*) heat.
mancherò *etc* [manke'rɔ] *vb vedi* **mancare**.
man'chevole [man'kevole] *ag* (*insufficiente*) inadequate, insufficient.
manchevo'lezza [mankevo'lettsa] *sf* (*scorrettezza*) fault, shortcoming.
'mancia, ce ['mantʃa] *sf* tip; **~ competente** reward.
manci'ata [man'tʃata] *sf* handful.
man'cino, a [man'tʃino] *ag* (*braccio*) left; (*persona*) left-handed; (*fig*) underhand.
'manco *av* (*nemmeno*): **~ per sogno** *o* **per idea!** not on your life!
man'dante *sm/f* (*DIR*) principal; (*istigatore*) instigator.
manda'rancio [manda'rantʃo] *sm* clementine.
man'dare *vt* to send; (*far funzionare: macchina*) to drive; (*emettere*) to send out; (*: grido*) to give, utter, let out; **~ avanti** (*persona*) to send ahead; (*fig: famiglia*) to provide for; (*: ditta*) to look after, run; (*: pratica*) to attend to; **~ a chiamare qn** to send for sb; **~ giù** to send down; (*anche fig*) to swallow; **~ in onda** (*RADIO, TV*) to broadcast; **~ in rovina** to ruin; **~ via** to send away; (*licenziare*) to fire.
manda'rino *sm* mandarin (orange); (*cinese*) mandarin.
man'data *sf* (*quantità*) lot, batch; (*di*

chiave) turn; **chiudere a doppia ~** to double-lock.
manda'tario *sm* (*DIR*) representative, agent.
man'dato *sm* (*incarico*) commission; (*DIR: provvedimento*) warrant; (*di deputato etc*) mandate; (*ordine di pagamento*) postal *o* money order; **~ d'arresto, ~ di cattura** warrant for arrest; **~ di comparizione** summons *sg*; **~ di perquisizione** search warrant.
man'dibola *sf* mandible, jaw.
mando'lino *sm* mandolin(e).
'mandorla *sf* almond.
mandor'lato *sm* nut brittle.
'mandorlo *sm* almond tree.
'mandria *sf* herd.
mandri'ano *sm* cowherd, herdsman.
man'drino *sm* (*TECN*) mandrel.
maneg'gevole [maned'dʒevole] *ag* easy to handle.
maneggi'are [maned'dʒare] *vt* (*creta, cera*) to mould (*Brit*), mold (*US*), work, fashion; (*arnesi, utensili*) to handle; (*: adoperare*) to use; (*fig: persone, denaro*) to handle, deal with.
ma'neggio [ma'neddʒo] *sm* moulding (*Brit*), molding (*US*); handling; use; (*intrigo*) plot, scheme; (*per cavalli*) riding school.
ma'nesco, a, schi, sche *ag* free with one's fists.
ma'nette *sfpl* handcuffs.
manga'nello *sm* club.
manga'nese *sm* manganese.
mange'reccio, a, ci, ce [mandʒe'rettʃo] *ag* edible.
mangi'abile [man'dʒabile] *ag* edible, eatable.
mangia'dischi [mandʒa'diski] *sm inv* record player.
mangia'nastri [mandʒa'nastri] *sm inv* cassette-recorder.
mangi'are [man'dʒare] *vt* to eat; (*intaccare*) to eat into *o* away; (*CARTE, SCACCHI etc*) to take ♦ *vi* to eat ♦ *sm* eating; (*cibo*) food; (*cucina*) cooking; **fare da ~** to do the cooking; **~rsi le parole** to mumble; **~rsi le unghie** to bite one's nails.
mangia'soldi [mandʒa'sɔldi] *ag inv* (*fam*): **macchinetta ~** one-armed bandit.
mangia'toia [mandʒa'toja] *sf* feeding-trough.
man'gime [man'dʒime] *sm* fodder.
mangiucchi'are [mandʒuk'kjare] *vt* to nibble.
'mango, ghi *sm* mango.
ma'nia *sf* (*PSIC*) mania; (*fig*) obsession, craze; **avere la ~ di fare qc** to have a habit of doing sth; **~ di persecuzione** persecution complex *o* mania.
mania'cale *ag* (*PSIC*) maniacal; (*fanatico*) fanatical.
ma'niaco, a, ci, che *ag* suffering from a mania; **~ (di)** obsessed (by), crazy (about).

'**manica, che** *sf* sleeve; (*fig: gruppo*) gang, bunch; (*GEO*): **la M~, il Canale della M~** the (English) Channel; **senza ~che** sleeveless; **essere in ~che di camicia** to be in one's shirt sleeves; **essere di ~ larga/ stretta** to be easy-going/strict; **~ a vento** (*AER*) wind sock.

manica'retto *sm* titbit (*Brit*), tidbit (*US*).

mani'chetta [mani'ketta] *sf* (*TECN*) hose.

mani'chino [mani'kino] *sm* (*di sarto, vetrina*) dummy.

'**manico, ci** *sm* handle; (*MUS*) neck; **~ di scopa** broomstick.

mani'comio *sm* mental hospital; (*fig*) madhouse.

mani'cotto *sm* muff; (*TECN*) coupling; sleeve.

mani'cure *sm* o *f inv* manicure ♦ *sf inv* manicurist.

mani'era *sf* way, manner; (*stile*) style, manner; **~e** *sfpl* manners; **in ~ che** so that; **in ~ da** so as to; **alla ~ di** in o after the style of; **in una ~ o nell'altra** one way or another; **in tutte le ~e** at all costs; **usare buone ~e con qn** to be polite to sb; **usare le ~e forti** to use strong-arm tactics.

manie'rato, a *ag* affected.

mani'ero *sm* manor.

manifat'tura *sf* (*lavorazione*) manufacture; (*stabilimento*) factory.

manifatturi'ero, a *ag* manufacturing.

manifes'tante *sm/f* demonstrator.

manifes'tare *vt* to show, display; (*esprimere*) to express; (*rivelare*) to reveal, disclose ♦ *vi* to demonstrate; **~rsi** *vr* to show o.s.; **~rsi amico** to prove o.s. (to be) a friend.

manifestazi'one [manifestat'tsjone] *sf* show, display; expression; (*sintomo*) sign, symptom; (*dimostrazione pubblica*) demonstration; (*cerimonia*) event.

manifes'tino *sm* leaflet.

mani'festo, a *ag* obvious, evident ♦ *sm* poster, bill; (*scritto ideologico*) manifesto.

ma'niglia [ma'niʎʎa] *sf* handle; (*sostegno: negli autobus etc*) strap.

Ma'nila *sf* Manila.

manipo'lare *vt* to manipulate; (*alterare: vino*) to adulterate.

manipolazi'one [manipolat'tsjone] *sf* manipulation; adulteration.

ma'nipolo *sm* (*drappello*) handful.

manis'calco, chi *sm* blacksmith, farrier (*Brit*).

'**manna** *sf* (*REL*) manna.

man'naia *sf* (*del boia*) (executioner's) axe o ax (*US*); (*per carni*) cleaver.

man'naro, a *ag*: **lupo ~** werewolf.

'**mano, i** *sf* hand; (*strato: di vernice etc*) coat; **a ~** by hand; **cucito a ~** hand-sewn; **fatto a ~** handmade; **alla ~** (*persona*) easy-going; **fuori ~** out of the way; **di prima ~** (*notizia*) first-hand; **di seconda ~** second-hand; **man ~** little by little, gradually; **man ~ che** as; **a piene ~i** (*fig*) generously; **avere le ~i bucate** to spend money like water; **aver le ~i in pasta** to be in the know; **avere qc per le ~i** (*progetto, lavoro*) to have sth in hand; **dare una ~ a qn** to lend sb a hand; **dare una ~ di vernice a qc** to give sth a coat of paint; **darsi** o **stringersi la ~** to shake hands; **forzare la ~** to go too far; **mettere ~ a qc** to have a hand in sth; **mettere le ~i avanti** (*fig*) to safeguard o.s.; **restare a ~i vuote** to be left empty-handed; **venire alle ~i** to come to blows; **~i in alto!** hands up!

mano'dopera *sf* labour (*Brit*), labor (*US*).

mano'messo, a *pp di* **manomettere**.

mano'mettere *vt* (*alterare*) to tamper with; (*aprire indebitamente*) to break open illegally.

manomissi'one *sf* (*di prove etc*) tampering; (*di lettera*) opening.

ma'nopola *sf* (*dell'armatura*) gauntlet; (*guanto*) mitt; (*di impugnatura*) hand-grip; (*pomello*) knob.

manos'critto, a *ag* handwritten ♦ *sm* manuscript.

manova'lanza [manova'lantsa] *sf* unskilled workers *pl*.

mano'vale *sm* labourer (*Brit*), laborer (*US*).

mano'vella *sf* handle; (*TECN*) crank.

ma'novra *sf* manoeuvre (*Brit*), maneuver (*US*); (*FERR*) shunting; **~e di corridoio** palace intrigues.

mano'vrare *vt* (*veicolo*) to manoeuvre (*Brit*), maneuver (*US*); (*macchina, congegno*) to operate; (*fig: persona*) to manipulate ♦ *vi* to manoeuvre.

manro'vescio [manro'vɛʃʃo] *sm* slap (*with back of hand*).

man'sarda *sf* attic.

mansi'one *sf* task, duty, job.

mansu'eto, a *ag* (*animale*) tame; (*persona*) gentle, docile.

mansue'tudine *sf* tameness; gentleness, docility.

man'tello *sm* cloak; (*fig: di neve etc*) blanket, mantle; (*TECN: involucro*) casing, shell; (*ZOOL*) coat.

mante'nere *vt* to maintain; (*adempiere: promesse*) to keep, abide by; (*provvedere a*) to support, maintain; **~rsi** *vr*: **~rsi calmo/giovane** to stay calm/young; **~ i contatti con qn** to keep in touch with sb.

manteni'mento *sm* maintenance.

mante'nuto, a *sm/f* gigolo/kept woman.

'**mantice** ['mantitʃe] *sm* bellows *pl*; (*di carrozza, automobile*) hood.

'**manto** *sm* cloak; **~ stradale** road surface.

'**Mantova** *sf* Mantua.

manto'vano, a *ag* of (*o* from) Mantua.

manu'ale *ag* manual ♦ *sm* (*testo*) manual, handbook.

manua'listico, a, ci, che *ag* textbook *cpd*.

manual'mente *av* manually, by hand.

ma'nubrio *sm* handle; (*di bicicletta etc*) handlebars *pl*; (*SPORT*) dumbbell.

manu'fatto *sm* manufactured article; ~**i** *smpl* manufactured goods.

manutenzi'one [manuten'tsjone] *sf* maintenance, upkeep; (*d'impianti*) maintenance, servicing.

'manzo ['mandzo] *sm* (*ZOOL*) steer; (*carne*) beef.

Mao'metto *sm* Mohammed.

'mappa *sf* (*GEO*) map.

mappa'mondo *sm* map of the world; (*globo girevole*) globe.

ma'rasma, i *sm* (*fig*) decay, decline.

mara'tona *sf* marathon.

'marca, che *sf* mark; (*bollo*) stamp; (*COMM: di prodotti*) brand; (*contrassegno, scontrino*) ticket, check; **prodotti di (gran)** ~ high-class products; ~ **da bollo** official stamp.

mar'care *vt* (*munire di contrassegno*) to mark; (*a fuoco*) to brand; (*SPORT: gol*) to score; (: *avversario*) to mark; (*accentuare*) to stress; ~ **visita** (*MIL*) to report sick.

mar'cato, a *ag* (*lineamenti, accento etc*) pronounced.

'Marche ['marke] *sfpl*: **le** ~ the Marches (*region of central Italy*).

marcherò *etc* [marke'rɔ] *vb vedi* **marcare**.

mar'chese, a [mar'keze] *sm/f* marquis *o* marquess/marchioness.

marchi'ano, a [mar'kjano] *ag* (*errore*) glaring, gross.

marchi'are [mar'kjare] *vt* to brand.

marchigi'ano, a [marki'dʒano] *ag* of (*o* from) the Marches.

'marchio ['markjo] *sm* (*di bestiame*, COMM, *fig*) brand; ~ **depositato** registered trademark; ~ **di fabbrica** trademark.

'marcia, ce ['martʃa] *sf* (*anche* MUS, MIL) march; (*funzionamento*) running; (*il camminare*) walking; (AUT) gear; **mettere in** ~ to start; **mettersi in** ~ to get moving; **far** ~ **indietro** (AUT) to reverse; (*fig*) to back-pedal; ~ **forzata** forced march; ~ **funebre** funeral march.

marciapi'ede [martʃa'pjɛde] *sm* (*di strada*) pavement (*Brit*), sidewalk (*US*); (FERR) platform.

marci'are [mar'tʃare] *vi* to march; (*andare: treno, macchina*) to go; (*funzionare*) to run, work.

'marcio, a, ci, ce ['martʃo] *ag* (*frutta, legno*) rotten, bad; (MED) festering; (*fig*) corrupt, rotten ♦ *sm*: **c'è del** ~ **in questa storia** (*fig*) there's something fishy about

this business; **avere torto** ~ to be utterly wrong.

mar'cire [mar'tʃire] *vi* (*andare a male*) to go bad, rot; (*suppurare*) to fester; (*fig*) to rot.

marci'ume [mar'tʃume] *sm* (*parte guasta: di cibi etc*) rotten part, bad part; (*di radice, pianta*) rot; (*fig: corruzione*) rottenness, corruption.

'marco, chi *sm* (*unità monetaria*) mark.

'mare *sm* sea; **di** ~ (*brezza, acqua, uccelli, pesce*) sea *cpd*; **in** ~ at sea; **per** ~ by sea; **sul** ~ (*barca*) on the sea; (*villaggio, località*) by *o* beside the sea; **andare al** ~ (*in vacanza etc*) to go to the seaside; **il mar Caspio** the Caspian Sea; **il mar Morto** the Dead Sea; **il mar Nero** the Black Sea; **il** ~ **del Nord** the North Sea; **il mar Rosso** the Red Sea; **il mar dei Sargassi** the Sargasso Sea; **i** ~**i del Sud** the South Seas.

ma'rea *sf* tide; **alta/bassa** ~ high/low tide.

mareggi'ata [mared'dʒata] *sf* heavy sea.

ma'remma *sf* (GEO) maremma, swampy coastal area.

marem'mano, a *ag* (*zona, macchia*) swampy; (*della Maremma*) of (*o* from) the Maremma.

mare'moto *sm* seaquake.

maresci'allo [mareʃ'ʃallo] *sm* (MIL) marshal; (: *sottufficiale*) warrant officer.

marez'zato, a [mared'dzato] *ag* (*seta etc*) watered, moiré; (*legno*) veined; (*carta*) marbled.

marga'rina *sf* margarine.

marghe'rita [marge'rita] *sf* (ox-eye) daisy, marguerite; (*di stampante*) daisy wheel.

margheri'tina [margeri'tina] *sf* daisy.

margi'nale [mardʒi'nale] *ag* marginal.

'margine ['mardʒine] *sm* margin; (*di bosco, via*) edge, border; **avere un buon** ~ **di tempo/denaro** to have plenty of time/money; ~ **di guadagno** *o* **di utile** profit margin; ~ **di sicurezza** safety margin.

mariju'ana [mæri'wa:nə] *sf* marijuana.

ma'rina *sf* navy; (*costa*) coast; (*quadro*) seascape; ~ **mercantile** merchant navy (*Brit*) *o* marine (*US*); ~ **militare (M.M.)** ≈ Royal Navy (RN) (*Brit*), Navy (*US*).

mari'naio *sm* sailor.

mari'nare *vt* (CUC) to marinate; ~ **la scuola** to play truant.

mari'naro, a *ag* (*tradizione, popolo*) seafaring; (CUC) with seafood; **alla** ~**a** (*vestito, cappello*) sailor *cpd*; **borgo** ~ district where fishing folk live.

mari'nata *sf* marinade.

ma'rino, a *ag* sea *cpd*, marine.

mario'netta *sf* puppet.

mari'tare *vt* to marry; ~**rsi** *vr*: ~**rsi a** *o* **con qn** to marry sb, get married to sb.

mari'tato, a *ag* married.

ma'rito *sm* husband; **prendere** ~ to get

married; **ragazza (in età) da** ~ girl of marriageable age.

ma'rittimo, a *ag* maritime, sea *cpd.*

mar'maglia [mar'maʎʎa] *sf* mob, riff-raff.

marmel'lata *sf* jam; (*di agrumi*) marmalade.

mar'mitta *sf* (*recipiente*) pot; (*AUT*) silencer.

'marmo *sm* marble.

mar'mocchio [mar'mɔkkjo] *sm* (*fam*) (little) kid.

mar'motta *sf* (*ZOOL*) marmot.

maroc'chino, a [marok'kino] *ag, sm/f* Moroccan.

Ma'rocco *sm*: **il** ~ Morocco.

ma'roso *sm* breaker.

'marra *sf* hoe.

Marra'kesh [marra'keʃ] *sf* Marrakesh.

mar'rone *ag inv* brown ♦ *sm* (*BOT*) chestnut.

mar'sala *sm inv* (*vino*) Marsala (wine).

Mar'siglia [mar'siʎʎa] *sf* Marseilles.

mar'sina *sf* tails *pl*, tail coat.

mar'supio *sm* (*ZOOL*) pouch, marsupium.

mart. *abbr* (= *martedì*) Tue(s).

'Marte *sm* (*ASTR, MITOLOGIA*) Mars.

martedì *sm inv* Tuesday; **di** *o* **il** ~ on Tuesdays; **oggi è** ~ **3 aprile** (the date) today is Tuesday 3rd April; ~ **stavo male** I wasn't well on Tuesday; **il giornale di** ~ Tuesday's newspaper; ~ **grasso** Shrove Tuesday.

martel'lante *ag* (*fig: dolore*) throbbing.

martel'lare *vt* to hammer ♦ *vi* (*pulsare*) to throb; (: *cuore*) to thump.

martel'letto *sm* (*di pianoforte*) hammer; (*di macchina da scrivere*) typebar; (*di giudice, nelle vendite all'asta*) gavel; (*MED*) percussion hammer.

mar'tello *sm* hammer; (*di uscio*) knocker; **suonare a** ~ (*fig: campane*) to sound the tocsin; ~ **pneumatico** pneumatic drill.

marti'netto *sm* (*TECN*) jack.

martin'gala *sf* (*di giacca*) half-belt; (*di cavallo*) martingale.

'martire *sm/f* martyr.

mar'tirio *sm* martyrdom; (*fig*) agony, torture.

'martora *sf* marten.

martori'are *vt* to torment, torture.

mar'xismo *sm* Marxism.

mar'xista, i, e *ag, sm/f* Marxist.

marza'pane [martsa'pane] *sm* marzipan.

marzi'ale [mar'tsjale] *ag* martial.

'marzo ['martso] *sm* March; *per fraseologia vedi* **luglio**.

marzo'lino, a [martso'lino] *ag* March *cpd.*

mascalzo'nata [maskaltso'nata] *sf* dirty trick.

mascal'zone [maskal'tsone] *sm* rascal, scoundrel.

mas'cara *sm inv* mascara.

mascar'pone *sm soft cream cheese often* used in desserts.

ma'scella [maʃ'ʃɛlla] *sf* (*ANAT*) jaw.

'maschera ['maskera] *sf* mask; (*travestimento*) disguise; (: *per un ballo etc*) fancy dress; (*TEATRO, CINEMA*) usher/usherette; (*personaggio del teatro*) stock character; **in** ~ (*mascherato*) masked; **ballo in** ~ fancy-dress ball; **gettare la** ~ (*fig*) to reveal o.s.; ~ **antigas/subacquea** gas/diving mask; ~ **di bellezza** face pack.

masche'rare [maske'rare] *vt* to mask; (*travestire*) to disguise; to dress up; (*fig: celare*) to hide, conceal; (*MIL*) to camouflage; ~**rsi** *vr*: ~**rsi da** to disguise o.s. as; to dress up as; (*fig*) to masquerade as.

masche'rina [maske'rina] *sf* (*piccola maschera*) mask; (*di animale*) patch; (*di scarpe*) toe-cap; (*AUT*) radiator grill.

mas'chile [mas'kile] *ag* masculine; (*sesso, popolazione*) male; (*abiti*) men's; (*per ragazzi: scuola*) boys'.

'maschio, a ['maskjo] *ag* (*BIOL*) male; (*virile*) manly ♦ *sm* (*anche ZOOL, TECN*) male; (*uomo*) man; (*ragazzo*) boy; (*figlio*) son.

masco'lino, a *ag* masculine.

mas'cotte [mas'kɔt] *sf inv* mascot.

maso'chismo [mazo'kizmo] *sm* masochism.

maso'chista, i, e [mazo'kista] *ag* masochistic ♦ *sm/f* masochist.

'massa *sf* mass; (*di errori etc*): **una** ~ **di** heaps of, masses of; (*di gente*) mass, multitude; (*ELETTR*) earth; **in** ~ (*COMM*) in bulk; (*tutti insieme*) en masse; **adunata in** ~ mass meeting; **manifestazione/cultura di** ~ mass demonstration/culture; **produrre in** ~ to mass-produce; **la** ~ **(del popolo)** the masses *pl.*

massa'crante *ag* exhausting, gruelling.

massa'crare *vt* to massacre, slaughter.

mas'sacro *sm* massacre, slaughter; (*fig*) mess, disaster.

massaggi'are [massad'dʒare] *vt* to massage.

massaggia'tore, 'trice [massaddʒa'tore] *sm/f* masseur/masseuse.

mas'saggio [mas'saddʒo] *sm* massage.

mas'saia *sf* housewife.

masse'ria *sf* large farm.

masse'rizie [masse'rittsje] *sfpl* (household) furnishings.

mas'siccio, a, ci, ce [mas'sittʃo] *ag* (*oro, legno*) solid; (*palazzo*) massive; (*corporatura*) stout ♦ *sm* (*GEO*) massif.

'massima *sf vedi* **massimo**.

massi'male *sm* maximum; (*COMM*) ceiling, limit.

'massimo, a *ag, sm* maximum ♦ *sf* (*sentenza, regola*) maxim; (*METEOR*) maximum temperature; **in linea di** ~**a** generally speaking; **arrivare entro il tempo** ~ to arrive within the time limit; **al** ~ at (the) most; **sfruttare qc al** ~ to make full use of sth; **arriverò al ~ alle 5** I'll arrive at 5 at the latest; **erano presenti le ~e autorità** all the most important dignitaries were there; **il ~ della pena** (*DIR*) the maximum penalty.

mas'sivo, a *ag* (*intervento*) en masse; (*emigrazione*) mass; (*emorragia*) massive.

'masso *sm* rock, boulder.

mas'sone *sm* freemason.

massone'ria *sf* freemasonry.

mas'sonico, a, ci, che *ag* masonic.

mas'tello *sm* tub.

masti'care *vt* to chew.

'mastice ['mastitʃe] *sm* mastic; (*per vetri*) putty.

mas'tino *sm* mastiff.

masturbazi'one [masturbat'tsjone] *sf* masturbation.

ma'tassa *sf* skein.

mate'matico, a, ci, che *ag* mathematical ♦ *sm/f* mathematician ♦ *sf* mathematics *sg*.

materas'sino *sm* mat; **~ gonfiabile** air bed.

mate'rasso *sm* mattress; **~ a molle** spring *o* interior-sprung mattress.

ma'teria *sf* (*FISICA*) matter; (*TECN, COMM*) material, matter *q*; (*disciplina*) subject; (*argomento*) subject matter, material; **prima di entrare in ~** ... before discussing the matter in hand ...; **un esperto in ~** (**di musica** *etc*) an expert on the subject (of music *etc*); **sono ignorante in ~** I know nothing about it; **~ grassa** fat; **~ grigia** (*anche fig*) grey matter; **~e plastiche** plastics; **~e prime** raw materials.

materi'ale *ag* material; (*fig: grossolano*) rough, rude ♦ *sm* material; (*insieme di strumenti etc*) equipment *q*, materials *pl*; **~ da costruzione** building materials *pl*.

materia'lista, i, e *ag* materialistic ♦ *sm/f* materialist.

materializ'zarsi [materjalid'dzarsi] *vr* to materialize.

material'mente *av* (*fisicamente*) materially; (*economicamente*) financially.

materni'tà *sf* motherhood, maternity; (*clinica*) maternity hospital; **in (congedo di) ~** on maternity leave.

ma'terno, a *ag* (*amore, cura etc*) maternal, motherly; (*nonno*) maternal; (*lingua, terra*) mother *cpd*; **scuola ~a** nursery school.

ma'tita *sf* pencil; **~e colorate** crayons; **~ per gli occhi** eyeliner (pencil).

ma'trice [ma'tritʃe] *sf* matrix; (*COMM*) counterfoil; (*fig: origine*) background.

ma'tricola *sf* (*registro*) register; (*numero*) registration number; (*nell'università*) freshman, fresher (*Brit fam*).

ma'trigna [ma'trinɲa] *sf* stepmother.

matrimoni'ale *ag* matrimonial, marriage *cpd*; **camera/letto ~** double room/bed.

matri'monio *sm* marriage, matrimony; (*durata*) marriage, married life; (*cerimonia*) wedding.

ma'trona *sf* (*fig*) matronly woman.

matta'toio *sm* abattoir (*Brit*), slaughterhouse.

mat'tina *sf* morning; **la** *o* **alla** *o* **di ~** in the morning; **di prima ~, la ~ presto** early in the morning; **dalla ~ alla sera** (*continuamente*) from morning to night; (*improvvisamente: cambiare*) overnight.

matti'nata *sf* morning; (*spettacolo*) matinée, afternoon performance; **in ~** in the course of the morning; **nella ~** in the morning; **nella tarda ~** at the end of the morning; **nella tarda ~ di sabato** late on Saturday morning.

mattini'ero, a *ag*: **essere ~** to be an early riser.

mat'tino *sm* morning; **di buon ~** early in the morning.

'matto, a *ag* mad, crazy; (*fig: falso*) false, imitation; (: *opaco*) matt, dull ♦ *sm/f* madman/woman; **avere una voglia ~a di qc** to be dying for sth; **far diventare ~ qn** to drive sb mad *o* crazy; **una gabbia di ~i** (*fig*) a madhouse.

mat'tone *sm* brick; (*fig*): **questo libro/film è un ~** this book/film is heavy going.

matto'nella *sf* tile.

mattu'tino, a *ag* morning *cpd*.

matu'rare *vi* (*anche: ~rsi*) (*frutta, grano*) to ripen; (*ascesso*) to come to a head; (*fig: persona, idea, ECON*) to mature ♦ *vt* to ripen; to (make) mature; **~ una decisione** to come to a decision.

maturi'tà *sf* maturity; (*di frutta*) ripeness, maturity; (*INS*) school-leaving examination, ≈ GCE A-levels (*Brit*).

ma'turo, a *ag* mature; (*frutto*) ripe, mature.

ma'tusa *sm/f inv* (*scherzoso*) old fogey.

Mauri'tania *sf*: **la ~** Mauritania.

Mau'rizio [mau'rittsjo] *sf*: (**l'isola di**) **~** Mauritius.

mauso'leo *sm* mausoleum.

max. *abbr* (= *massimo*) max.

'maxi... *prefisso* maxi....

'mazza ['mattsa] *sf* (*bastone*) club; (*martello*) sledge-hammer; (*SPORT: da golf*) club; (: *da baseball, cricket*) bat.

maz'zata [mat'tsata] *sf* (*anche fig*) heavy blow.

maz'zetta [mat'tsetta] *sf* (*di banconote etc*) bundle.

'mazzo ['mattso] *sm* (*di fiori, chiavi etc*) bunch; (*di carte da gioco*) pack.

MC *sigla* = *Macerata*.

ME *sigla* = *Messina*.

me *pronome* me; **sei bravo quanto ~** you are as clever as I (am) *o* as me.

me'andro *sm* meander.

M.E.C. [mɛk] *abbr m* = **Mercato Comune Europeo**.

'Mecca *sf (anche fig)*: **La** ~ Mecca.

meccanica'mente *av* mechanically.

mec'canico, a, ci, che *ag* mechanical ♦ *sm* mechanic ♦ *sf* mechanics *sg*; *(attività tecnologica)* mechanical engineering; *(meccanismo)* mechanism; **officina** ~**a** garage.

mecca'nismo *sm* mechanism.

meccaniz'zare [mekkanid'dzare] *vt* to mechanize.

meccanizzazi'one [mekkaniddzat'tsjone] *sf* mechanization.

meccanogra'fia *sf* (mechanical) data processing.

meccano'grafico, a, ci, che *ag*: **centro** ~ data processing department.

mece'nate [metʃe'nate] *sm* patron.

mèche [mɛʃ] *sf inv* streak; **farsi le** ~ to have one's hair streaked.

me'daglia [me'daʎʎa] *sf* medal; ~ **d'oro** *(oggetto)* gold medal; *(persona)* gold medallist *(Brit)* o medalist *(US)*.

medagli'one [medaʎ'ʎone] *sm* *(ARCHIT)* medallion; *(gioiello)* locket.

me'desimo, a *ag* same; *(in persona)*: **io** ~ I myself.

'media *sf vedi* **medio**.

media'mente *av* on average.

medi'ano, a *ag* median; *(valore)* mean ♦ *sm* *(CALCIO)* half-back.

medi'ante *prep* by means of.

medi'are *vt* *(fare da mediatore)* to act as mediator in; *(MAT)* to average.

medi'ato, a *ag* indirect.

media'tore, 'trice *sm/f* mediator; *(COMM)* middle man, agent; **fare da** ~ **fra** to mediate between.

mediazi'one [medjat'tsjone] *sf* mediation; *(COMM: azione, compenso)* brokerage.

medica'mento *sm* medicine, drug.

medi'care *vt* to treat; *(ferita)* to dress.

medi'cato, a *ag* *(garza, shampoo)* medicated.

medicazi'one [medikat'tsjone] *sf* treatment, medication; dressing; **fare una** ~ **a qn** to dress sb's wounds.

medi'cina [medi'tʃina] *sf* medicine; ~ **legale** forensic medicine.

medici'nale [meditʃi'nale] *ag* medicinal ♦ *sm* drug, medicine.

'medico, a, ci, che *ag* medical ♦ *sm* doctor; ~ **di bordo** ship's doctor; ~ **di famiglia** family doctor; ~ **fiscale** *doctor who examines patients signed off sick for a lengthy period by their private doctor*; ~ **generico** general practitioner, GP.

medie'vale *ag* medieval.

'medio, a *ag* average; *(punto, ceto)* middle; *(altezza, statura)* medium ♦ *sm* *(dito)* middle finger ♦ *sf* average; *(MAT)* mean;

(INS: voto) end-of-term average; ~**e** *sfpl*, **scuola** ~**a** *first 3 years of secondary school*; **licenza** ~**a** *leaving certificate awarded at the end of 3 years of secondary education*; **in** ~**a** on average; **al di sopra/sotto della** ~**a** above/below average; **viaggiare ad una** ~**a di ...** to travel at an average speed of ...; **il M**~ **Oriente** the Middle East.

medi'ocre *ag* *(gen)* mediocre; *(qualità, stipendio)* poor.

mediocrità *sf* mediocrity; poorness.

medioe'vale *ag* = **medievale**.

Medio'evo *sm* Middle Ages *pl*.

medita'bondo, a *ag* thoughtful.

medi'tare *vt* to ponder over, meditate on; *(progettare)* to plan, think out ♦ *vi* to meditate.

medi'tato, a *ag* *(gen)* meditated; *(parole)* carefully-weighed; *(vendetta)* premeditated; **ben** ~ *(piano)* well worked-out, neat.

meditazi'one [meditat'tsjone] *sf* meditation.

mediter'raneo, a *ag* Mediterranean; **il (mare) M**~ the Mediterranean (Sea).

'medium *sm/f inv* medium.

me'dusa *sf* *(ZOOL)* jellyfish.

me'gafono *sm* megaphone.

mega'lomane *ag, sm/f* megalomaniac.

me'gera [me'dʒɛra] *sf* *(peg: donna)* shrew.

'meglio ['mɛʎʎo] *av, ag inv* better; *(con senso superlativo)* best ♦ *sm* *(la cosa migliore)*: **il** ~ the best (thing); **faresti** ~ **ad andartene** you had better leave; **alla** ~ as best one can; **andar di bene in** ~ to get better and better; **fare del proprio** ~ to do one's best; **per il** ~ for the best; **aver la** ~ **su qn** to get the better of sb.

'mela *sf* apple; ~ **cotogna** quince.

mela'grana *sf* pomegranate.

melan'zana [melan'dzana] *sf* aubergine *(Brit)*, eggplant *(US)*.

me'lassa *sf* molasses *sg*, treacle.

me'lenso, a *ag* dull, stupid.

mel'lifluo, a *ag* *(peg)* sugary, honeyed.

'melma *sf* mud, mire.

'melo *sm* apple tree.

melo'dia *sf* melody.

me'lodico, a, ci, che *ag* melodic.

melodi'oso, a *ag* melodious.

melo'dramma, i *sm* melodrama.

me'lone *sm* (musk) melon.

'membra *sfpl vedi* **membro**.

mem'brana *sf* membrane.

'membro *sm* member; *(pl(f)* ~**a**: *arto)* limb.

memo'rabile *ag* memorable.

memo'randum *sm inv* memorandum.

'memore *ag*: ~ **di** *(ricordando)* mindful of; *(riconoscente)* grateful for.

me'moria *sf* *(anche INFORM)* memory; ~**e** *sfpl* *(opera autobiografica)* memoirs; **a** ~ *(imparare, sapere)* by heart; **a** ~ **d'uomo**

within living memory; ~ **di sola lettura** (*INFORM*) read-only memory; ~ **tampone** (*INFORM*) buffer.

memori'ale *sm* (*raccolta di memorie*) memoirs *pl*; (*DIR*) memorial.

memoriz'zare [memorid'dzare] *vt* (*gen*) to memorize; (*INFORM*) to store.

memorizzazi'one [memoriddzat'tsjone] *sf* memorization; storage.

'mena *sf* scheme.

mena'dito: a ~ *av* perfectly, thoroughly; **sapere qc a ~** to have sth at one's fingertips.

mena'gramo *sm/f inv* jinx, Jonah.

me'nare *vt* to lead; (*picchiare*) to hit, beat; (*dare: colpi*) to deal; ~ **la coda** (*cane*) to wag its tail; ~ **qc per le lunghe** to drag sth out; ~ **il can per l'aia** (*fig*) to beat about (*Brit*) *o* around (*US*) the bush.

mendi'cante *sm/f* beggar.

mendi'care *vt* to beg for ♦ *vi* to beg.

menefre'ghismo [menefre'gizmo] *sm* (*fam*) couldn't-care-less attitude.

me'ninge [me'nindʒe] *sf* (*MED*) meninx; **spremersi le ~i** to rack one's brains.

menin'gite [menin'dʒite] *sf* meningitis.

me'nisco *sm* (*ANAT, MAT, FISICA*) meniscus.

'meno *av* less; (*in frasi comparative*): ~ **freddo che** not as cold as, less cold than; (: *seguito da nome, pronome*): ~ **alto di** not as tall as, less tall than; (*in frasi superlative*): **il(la) ~ bravo(a)** the least clever; (*di temperatura*) below (zero), minus; (*MAT*) minus, less; (*l'ora*): **sono le 8 ~ un quarto** it's a quarter to eight (*Brit*) *o* of eight (*US*) ♦ *ag inv* (*tempo, denaro*) less; (*errori, persone*) fewer ♦ *prep* except (for) ♦ *sm inv* (*la parte minore*): **il ~** the least; (*MAT*) minus; **i ~** (*la minoranza*) the minority; **a ~ che** *cong* unless; **essere da ~ di** to be outdone by; **fare a ~ di qc** (*privarsene*) to do without sth; (*rinunciarvi*) to give up; **fare a ~ di fumare** to give up smoking; **non potevo fare a ~ di ridere** I couldn't help laughing; **mille lire in ~ a** thousand lire less; ~ **male** so much the better; thank goodness.

meno'mare *vt* (*danneggiare*) to maim, disable.

meno'mato, a *ag* (*persona*) disabled ♦ *sm/f* disabled person.

menomazi'one [menomat'tsjone] *sf* disablement.

meno'pausa *sf* menopause.

'mensa *sf* (*locale*) canteen; (: *MIL*) mess; (: *nelle università*) refectory.

men'sile *ag* monthly ♦ *sm* (*periodico*) monthly (magazine); (*stipendio*) monthly salary.

mensil'mente *av* (*ogni mese*) every month; (*una volta al mese*) monthly.

'mensola *sf* bracket; (*ripiano*) shelf;

(*ARCHIT*) corbel.

'menta *sf* mint; (*anche*: ~ **piperita**) peppermint; (*bibita*) peppermint cordial; (*caramella*) mint, peppermint.

men'tale *ag* mental.

mentalità *sf inv* mentality.

mental'mente *av* mentally.

'mente *sf* mind; **imparare/sapere qc a ~** to learn/know sth by heart; **avere in ~ qc** to have sth in mind; **avere in ~ di fare qc** to intend to do sth; **fare venire in ~ qc a qn** to remind sb of sth; **mettersi in ~ di fare qc** to make up one's mind to do sth; **passare di ~ a qn** to slip sb's mind; **tenere a ~ qc** to bear sth in mind; **a ~ fredda** objectively; **lasciami fare ~ locale** let me think.

mente'catto, a *ag* half-witted ♦ *sm/f* half-wit, imbecile.

men'tire *vi* to lie.

men'tito, a *ag*: **sotto ~e spoglie** under false pretences (*Brit*) *o* pretenses (*US*).

'mento *sm* chin; **doppio ~** double chin.

men'tolo *sm* menthol.

'mentre *cong* (*temporale*) while; (*avversativo*) whereas ♦ *sm*: **in quel ~** at that very moment.

menù *sm inv* (set) menu; ~ **turistico** standard *o* tourists' menu.

menzio'nare [mentsjo'nare] *vt* to mention.

menzi'one [men'tsjone] *sf* mention; **fare ~ di** to mention.

men'zogna [men'tsoɲɲa] *sf* lie.

menzo'gnero, a [mentsoɲ'ɲero] *ag* false, untrue.

mera'viglia [mera'viʎʎa] *sf* amazement, wonder; (*persona, cosa*) marvel, wonder; **a ~** perfectly, wonderfully.

meravigli'are [meraviʎ'ʎare] *vt* to amaze, astonish; ~**rsi** *vr*: ~**rsi (di)** to marvel (at); (*stupirsi*) to be amazed (at), be astonished (at); **mi meraviglio di te!** I'm surprised at you!; **non c'è da ~rsi** it's not surprising.

meravigli'oso, a [meraviʎ'ʎoso] *ag* wonderful, marvellous (*Brit*), marvelous (*US*).

merc. *abbr* (= *mercoledì*) Wed.

mer'cante *sm* merchant; ~ **d'arte** art dealer; ~ **di cavalli** horse dealer.

mercanteggi'are [merkanted'dʒare] *vt* (*onore, voto*) to sell ♦ *vi* to bargain, haggle.

mercan'tile *ag* commercial, mercantile; (*nave, marina*) merchant *cpd* ♦ *sm* (*nave*) merchantman.

mercan'zia [merkan'tsia] *sf* merchandise, goods *pl*.

merca'tino *sm* (*rionale*) local street market; (*ECON*) unofficial stock market.

mer'cato *sm* market; **di ~** (*economia, prezzo, ricerche*) market *cpd*; **mettere** *o* **lanciare qc sul ~** to launch sth on the market; **a buon ~** *ag, av* cheap; ~ **dei cambi** exchange market; **M~ Comune**

(Europeo) (European) Common Market; ~ **del lavoro** labour market, job market; ~ **nero** black market; ~ **al rialzo/al ribasso** (*BORSA*) sellers'/buyers' market; ~ **a termine** forward market, futures market.

'**merce** ['mɛrtʃe] *sf* goods *pl*, merchandise; ~ **deperibile** perishable goods *pl*.

mercé [mer'tʃe] *sf* mercy; **essere alla ~ di qn** to be at sb's mercy.

merce'nario, a [mertʃe'narjo] *ag*, *sm* mercenary.

merce'ria [mertʃe'ria] *sf* (*articoli*) haberdashery (*Brit*), notions *pl* (*US*); (*bottega*) haberdasher's shop (*Brit*), notions store (*US*).

mercoledì *sm inv* Wednesday; ~ **delle Ceneri** Ash Wednesday; *per fraseologia vedi* **martedì**.

mer'curio *sm* mercury.

'**merda** *sf* (*fam!*) shit (*!*).

me'renda *sf* afternoon snack.

meridi'ano, a *ag* (*di mezzogiorno*) midday *cpd*, noonday ♦ *sm* meridian ♦ *sf* (*orologio*) sundial.

meridio'nale *ag* southern ♦ *sm/f* southerner.

meridi'one *sm* south.

me'ringa, ghe *sf* (*CUC*) meringue.

meri'tare *vt* to deserve, merit ♦ *vb impers* (*valere la pena*): **merita andare** it is worth going; **non merita neanche parlarne** it's not worth talking about; **per quel che merita** for what it's worth.

meri'tevole *ag* worthy.

'**merito** *sm* merit; (*valore*) worth; **dare ~ a qn di** to give sb credit for; **finire a pari ~** to finish joint first (*o second etc*); to tie; **in ~ a** as regards, with regard to; **entrare nel ~ di una questione** to go into a matter; **non so niente in ~** I don't know anything about it.

meritocra'zia [meritokrat'tsia] *sf* meritocracy.

meri'torio, a *ag* praiseworthy.

mer'letto *sm* lace.

'**merlo** *sm* (*ZOOL*) blackbird; (*ARCHIT*) battlement.

mer'luzzo [mer'luttso] *sm* (*ZOOL*) cod.

'**mescere** ['meʃʃere] *vt* to pour (out).

meschinità [meskini'ta] *sf* wretchedness; meagreness; meanness; narrow-mindedness.

mes'chino, a [mes'kino] *ag* wretched; (*scarso*) meagre (*Brit*), meager (*US*); (*persona*: *gretta*) mean; (: *limitata*) narrow-minded, petty; **fare una figura ~a** to cut a poor figure.

'**mescita** ['meʃʃita] *sf* wine shop.

mesci'uto, a [meʃ'ʃuto] *pp di* **mescere**.

mesco'lanza [mesko'lantsa] *sf* mixture.

mesco'lare *vt* to mix; (*vini, colori*) to blend; (*mettere in disordine*) to mix up, muddle up; (*carte*) to shuffle; ~**rsi** *vr* to mix; to blend; to get mixed up; (*fig*): ~**rsi in** to get mixed up in, meddle in.

'**mese** *sm* month; **il ~ scorso** last month; **il corrente ~** this month.

'**messa** *sf* (*REL*) mass; (*il mettere*): ~ **a fuoco** focusing; ~ **in moto** starting; ~ **in piega** (*acconciatura*) set; ~ **a punto** (*TECN*) adjustment; (*AUT*) tuning; (*fig*) clarification; ~ **in scena** = **messinscena**.

messagge'rie [messaddʒe'rie] *sfpl* (*ditta: di distribuzione*) distributors; (: *di trasporto*) freight company.

messag'gero [messad'dʒero] *sm* messenger.

mes'saggio [mes'saddʒo] *sm* message.

mes'sale *sm* (*REL*) missal.

'**messe** *sf* harvest.

Mes'sia *sm inv* (*REL*): **il ~** the Messiah.

messi'cano, a *ag*, *sm/f* Mexican.

'**Messico** *sm*: **il ~** Mexico; **Città del ~** Mexico City.

messin'scena [messin'ʃena] *sf* (*TEATRO*) production.

'**messo, a** *pp di* **mettere** ♦ *sm* messenger.

mestie'rante *sm/f* (*peg*) money-grubber; (: *scrittore*) hack.

mesti'ere *sm* (*professione*) job; (: *manuale*) trade; (: *artigianale*) craft; (*fig: abilità nel lavoro*) skill, technique; **di ~** by *o* to trade; **essere del ~** to know the tricks of the trade.

mes'tizia [mes'tittsja] *sf* sadness, melancholy.

'**mesto, a** *ag* sad, melancholy.

'**mestola** *sf* (*CUC*) ladle; (*EDIL*) trowel.

'**mestolo** *sm* (*CUC*) ladle.

mestru'ale *ag* menstrual.

mestruazi'one [mestruat'tsjone] *sf* menstruation; **avere le ~i** to have one's period.

'**meta** *sf* destination; (*fig*) aim, goal.

metà *sf inv* half; (*punto di mezzo*) middle; **dividere qc a *o* per ~** to divide sth in half, halve sth; **fare a ~ (di qc con qn)** to go halves (with sb in sth); **a ~ prezzo** at half price; **a ~ settimana** midweek; **a ~ strada** halfway; **verso la ~ del mese** halfway through the month, towards the middle of the month; **dire le cose a ~** to leave some things unsaid; **fare le cose a ~** to leave things half-done; **la mia dolce ~** (*fam scherzoso*) my better half.

metabo'lismo *sm* metabolism.

meta'fisica *sf* metaphysics *sg*.

me'tafora *sf* metaphor.

me'tallico, a, ci, che *ag* (*di metallo*) metal *cpd*; (*splendore, rumore etc*) metallic.

metalliz'zato, a [metallid'dzato] *ag* (*verniciatura*) metallic.

me'tallo *sm* metal; **di ~** metal *cpd*.

metallur'gia [metallur'dʒia] *sf* metallurgy.

metalmec'canico, a, ci, che *ag* engineering *cpd* ♦ *sm* engineering worker.

meta'morfosi *sf* metamorphosis.

me'tano *sm* methane.

me'teora *sf* meteor.

meteo'rite *sm* meteorite.

meteorolo'gia [meteorolo'dʒia] *sf* meteorology.

meteoro'logico, a, ci, che [meteoro'lɔdʒiko] *ag* meteorological, weather *cpd*.

meteo'rologo, a, ghi, ghe *sm/f* meteorologist.

me'ticcio, a, ci, ce [me'tittʃo] *sm/f* half-caste, half-breed.

metico'loso, a *ag* meticulous.

me'todico, a, ci, che *ag* methodical.

'metodo *sm* method; (*manuale*) tutor (*Brit*), manual; **far qc con/senza** ~ to do sth methodically/unmethodically.

me'traggio [me'traddʒo] *sm* (*SARTORIA*) length; (*CINEMA*) footage; **film a lungo** ~ feature film; **film a corto** ~ short film.

metra'tura *sf* length.

'metrico, a, ci, che *ag* metric; (*POESIA*) metrical ♦ *sf* metrics *sg*.

'metro *sm* metre (*Brit*), meter (*US*); (*nastro*) tape measure; (*asta*) (metre) rule.

metrò *sm inv* underground (*Brit*), subway (*US*).

metro'notte *sm inv* night security guard.

me'tropoli *sf* metropolis.

metropoli'tano, a *ag* metropolitan ♦ *sf* underground (*Brit*), subway (*US*).

'mettere *vt* to put; (*abito*) to put on; (: *portare*) to wear; (*installare: telefono*) to put in; (*fig: provocare*): ~ **fame/allegria a qn** to make sb hungry/happy; (*supporre*): **mettiamo che** ... let's suppose *o* say that ...; ~**rsi** *vr* (*persona*) to put o.s.; (*oggetto*) to go; (*disporsi: faccenda*) to turn out; ~**rsi a piangere/ridere** to start crying/laughing, start *o* begin to cry/laugh; ~**rsi a sedere** to sit down; ~**rsi al lavoro** to set to work; ~**rsi a letto** to get into bed; (*per malattia*) to take to one's bed; ~**rsi il cappello** to put on one's hat; ~**rsi sotto** to get down to things; ~**rsi in società** to set up in business; **si sono messi insieme** (*coppia*) they've started going out together (*Brit*) *o* dating (*US*); ~**rci**: ~**rci molta cura/molto tempo** to take a lot of care/a lot of time; **mettercela tutta** to do one's best; **ci ho messo 3 ore per venire** it's taken me 3 hours to get here; ~ **un annuncio sul giornale** to place an advertisement in the paper; ~ **a confronto** to compare; ~ **in conto** (*somma etc*) to put on account; ~ **in luce** (*problemi, errori*) to stress, highlight; ~ **a tacere qn/qc** to keep sb/sth quiet; ~ **su casa** to set up house; ~ **su un negozio** to start a shop; ~ **su peso** to put on weight; ~ **via** to put away.

mez'zadro [med'dzadro] *sm* (*AGR*) sharecropper.

mezza'luna [meddza'luna], *pl* **mezze'lune** *sf* half-moon; (*dell'islamismo*) crescent; (*coltello*) (semicircular) chopping knife.

mezza'nino [meddza'nino] *sm* mezzanine (floor).

mez'zano, a [med'dzano] *ag* (*medio*) average, medium; (*figlio*) middle *cpd* ♦ *sm/f* (*intermediario*) go-between; (*ruffiano*) pimp.

mezza'notte [meddza'nɔtte] *sf* midnight.

'mezzo, a ['meddzo] *ag* half; **un** ~ **litro/panino** half a litre/roll ♦ *av* half-; ~ **morto** half-dead ♦ *sm* (*metà*) half; (*parte centrale: di strada etc*) middle; (*per raggiungere un fine*) means *sg*; (*veicolo*) vehicle; (*nell'indicare l'ora*): **le nove e** ~ half past nine; **mezzogiorno e** ~ half past twelve ♦ *sf*: **la** ~**a** half-past twelve (in the afternoon); ~**i** *smpl* (*possibilità economiche*) means; **di** ~**a età** middle-aged; **aver una** ~**a idea di fare qc** to have half a mind to do sth; **è stato un** ~ **scandalo** it almost caused a scandal; **un soprabito di** ~**a stagione** a spring (*o* autumn) coat; **a** ~**a voce** in an undertone; **una volta e** ~ **più grande** one and a half times bigger; **di** ~ middle, in the middle; **andarci di** ~ (*patir danno*) to suffer; **esserci di** ~ (*ostacolo*) to be in the way; **levarsi** *o* **togliersi di** ~ to get out of the way; **mettersi di** ~ to interfere; **togliere di** ~ (*persona, cosa*) to get rid of; (*fam: uccidere*) to bump off; **non c'è una via di** ~ there's no middle course; **in** ~ **a** in the middle of; **nel bel** ~ (**di**) right in the middle (of); **per** *o* **a** ~ **di** by means of; **a** ~ **corriere** by carrier; ~**i di comunicazione di massa** mass media *pl*; ~**i pubblici** public transport *sg*; ~**i di trasporto** means of transport.

mezzogi'orno [meddzo'dʒorno] *sm* midday, noon; (*GEO*) south; **a** ~ at 12 (o'clock) *o* midday *o* noon; **il** ~ **d'Italia** southern Italy.

mez'z'ora, mez'zora [med'dzora] *sf* half-hour, half an hour.

MI *sigla* = *Milano*.

mi *pronome* (*dav lo, la, li, le, ne diventa* **me**) (*oggetto*) me; (*complemento di termine*) (to) me; (*riflessivo*) myself ♦ *sm* (*MUS*) E; (: *solfeggiando la scala*) mi; ~ **aiuti?** will you help me?; **me ne ha parlato** he spoke to me about it, he told me about it; ~ **servo da solo** I'll help myself.

'mia *vedi* **mio**.

miago'lare *vi* to miaow, mew.

'mica *sf* (*CHIM*) mica ♦ *av* (*fam*): **non ...** ~ not ... at all; **non sono** ~ **stanco** I'm not a bit tired; **non sarà** ~ **partito?** he wouldn't have left, would he?; ~ **male** not bad.

'miccia, ce ['mittʃa] *sf* fuse.

micidi'ale [mitʃi'djale] *ag* fatal;

(*dannosissimo*) deadly.

'**micio, a, ci, cie** ['mitʃo] *sm/f* pussy (cat).

microbiolo'gia [mikrobiolo'dʒia] *sf* microbiology.

'**microbo** *sm* microbe.

microcir'cuito [mikrotʃir'kuito] *sm* microcircuit.

micro'film *sm inv* microfilm.

mi'crofono *sm* microphone.

microinfor'matica *sf* microcomputing.

micro'onda *sf* microwave.

microproces'sore [mikroprotʃes'sore] *sm* microprocessor.

micros'copico, a, ci, che *ag* microscopic.

micros'copio *sm* microscope.

micro'solco, chi *a* (*solco*) microgroove; (*disco*: *a 33 giri*) long-playing record, LP; (: *a 45 giri*) extended-play record, EP.

micros'pia *sf* hidden microphone, bug (*fam*).

mi'dollo, *pl*(*f*) ~**a** *sm* (ANAT) marrow; ~ **spinale** spinal cord.

'**mie, mi'ei** *vedi* mio.

mi'ele *sm* honey.

mi'etere *vt* (AGR) to reap, harvest; (*fig*: *vite*) to take, claim.

mietitrebbia'trice [mjetitrebbja'tritʃe] *sf* combine harvester.

mieti'trice [mjeti'tritʃe] *sf* (*macchina*) harvester.

mieti'tura *sf* (*raccolto*) harvest; (*lavoro*) harvesting; (*tempo*) harvest-time.

'**miglia** ['miʎʎa] *sfpl di* miglio.

migli'aio [miʎ'ʎajo], *pl*(*f*) ~**a** *sm* thousand; **un** ~ (**di**) about a thousand; **a** ~**a** by the thousand, in thousands.

'**miglio** ['miʎʎo] *sm* (BOT) millet; (*pl*(*f*) ~**a**: *unità di misura*) mile; ~ **marino** *o* **nautico** nautical mile.

migliora'mento [miʎʎora'mento] *sm* improvement.

miglio'rare [miʎʎo'rare] *vt, vi* to improve.

migli'ore [miʎ'ʎore] *ag* (*comparativo*) better; (*superlativo*) best ♦ *sm*: **il** ~ **the best** (thing) ♦ *sm/f*: **il(la)** ~ **the best** (person); **il miglior vino di questa regione** the best wine in this area; **i** ~**i auguri** best wishes.

miglio'ria [miʎʎo'ria] *sf* improvement.

'**mignolo** ['miɲɲolo] *sm* (ANAT) little finger, pinkie; (: *dito del piede*) little toe.

mi'grare *vi* to migrate.

migrazi'one [migrat'tsjone] *sf* migration.

'**mila** *pl di* mille.

mila'nese *ag* Milanese ♦ *sm/f* person from Milan; **i** ~**i** the Milanese; **cotoletta alla** ~ (CUC) Wiener schnitzel; **risotto alla** ~ (CUC) *risotto with saffron*.

Mi'lano *sf* Milan.

miliar'dario, a *ag, sm/f* millionaire.

mili'ardo *sm* thousand million (*Brit*), billion (*US*).

mili'are *ag*: **pietra** ~ milestone.

milio'nario, a *ag, sm/f* millionaire.

mili'one *sm* million; **un** ~ **di lire** a million lire.

mili'tante *ag, sm/f* militant.

mili'tanza [mili'tantsa] *sf* militancy.

mili'tare *vi* (MIL) to be a soldier, serve; (*fig*: *in un partito*) to be a militant ♦ *ag* military ♦ *sm* serviceman; **fare il** ~ to do one's military service; ~ **di carriera** regular (soldier).

milita'resco, a, schi, sche *ag* (*portamento*) military *cpd*.

'**milite** *sm* soldier.

mi'lizia [mi'littsja] *sf* (*corpo armato*) militia.

milizi'ano [milit'tsjano] *sm* militiaman.

millanta'tore, 'trice *sm/f* boaster.

millante'ria *sf* (*qualità*) boastfulness.

'**mille** *num* (*pl* **mila**) *a o* one thousand; **dieci-mila** ten thousand.

mille'foglie [mille'fɔʎʎe] *sm inv* (CUC) cream *o* vanilla slice.

mil'lennio *sm* millennium.

millepi'edi *sm inv* centipede.

mil'lesimo, a *ag, sm* thousandth.

milli'grammo *sm* milligram(me).

mil'lilitro *sm* millilitre (*Brit*), milliliter (*US*).

mil'limetro *sm* millimetre (*Brit*), millimeter (*US*).

'**milza** ['miltsa] *sf* (ANAT) spleen.

mi'metico, a, ci, che *ag* (*arte*) mimetic; **tuta** ~**a** (MIL) camouflage.

mimetiz'zare [mimetid'dzare] *vt* to camouflage; ~**rsi** *vr* to camouflage o.s.

'**mimica** *sf* (*arte*) mime.

'**mimo** *sm* (*attore, componimento*) mime.

mi'mosa *sf* mimosa.

min. *abbr* (= *minuto, minimo*) min.

'**mina** *sf* (*esplosiva*) mine; (*di matita*) lead.

mi'naccia, ce [mi'nattʃa] *sf* threat; **sotto la** ~ **di** under threat of.

minacci'are [minat'tʃare] *vt* to threaten; ~ **qn di morte** to threaten to kill sb; ~ **di fare qc** to threaten to do sth; **minaccia di piovere** it looks like rain.

minacci'oso, a [minat'tʃoso] *ag* threatening.

mi'nare *vt* (MIL) to mine; (*fig*) to undermine.

mina'tore *sm* miner.

mina'torio, a *ag* threatening.

minchi'one, a [min'kjone] (*fam*) *ag* idiotic ♦ *sm/f* idiot.

mine'rale *ag, sm* mineral.

mineralo'gia [mineralo'dʒia] *sf* mineralogy.

mine'rario, a *ag* (*delle miniere*) mining; (*dei minerali*) ore *cpd*.

mi'nestra *sf* soup; ~ **in brodo** noodle soup; ~ **di verdura** vegetable soup.

mines'trone *sm* thick vegetable and pasta soup.

mingher'lino, a [minger'lino] *ag* thin, slender.

'mini *ag inv* mini ♦ *sf inv* miniskirt.

minia'tura *sf* miniature.

minielabora'tore *sm* minicomputer.

mini'era *sf* mine; **~ di carbone** coalmine; (*impresa*) colliery (*Brit*), coalmine.

mini'gonna *sf* miniskirt.

minimiz'zare [minimid'dzare] *vt* to minimize.

'minimo, a *ag* minimum, least, slightest; (*piccolissimo*) very small, slight; (*il più basso*) lowest, minimum ♦ *sm* minimum; **al ~** at least; **girare al ~** (*AUT*) to idle; **il ~ indispensabile** the bare minimum; **il ~ della pena** the minimum sentence.

minis'tero *sm* (*POL*, *REL*) ministry; (*governo*) government; (*DIR*): **Pubblico M~** State Prosecutor; **~ delle Finanze** Ministry of Finance, ≈ Treasury.

mi'nistro *sm* (*POL*, *REL*) minister; **~ delle Finanze** Minister of Finance, ≈ Chancellor of the Exchequer (*Brit*).

mino'ranza [mino'rantsa] *sf* minority; **essere in ~** to be in the minority.

mino'rato, a *ag* handicapped ♦ *sm/f* physically (*o* mentally) handicapped person.

minorazi'one [minorat'tsjone] *sf* handicap.

Mi'norca *sf* Minorca.

mi'nore *ag* (*comparativo*) less; (: *più piccolo*) smaller; (: *numero*) lower; (: *inferiore*) lower, inferior; (: *meno importante*) minor; (: *più giovane*) younger; (*superlativo*) least; smallest; lowest; least important; youngest ♦ *sm/f* (*minorenne*) minor, person under age; **in misura ~** to a lesser extent; **questo è il male ~** this is the lesser evil.

mino'renne *ag* under age ♦ *sm/f* minor, person under age.

mino'rile *ag* juvenile; **carcere ~** young offenders' institution; **delinquenza ~** juvenile delinquency.

minori'tario, a *ag* minority *cpd*.

mi'nuscolo, a *ag* (*scrittura, carattere*) small; (*piccolissimo*) tiny ♦ *sf* small letter ♦ *sm* small letters *pl*; (*TIP*) lower case; **scrivere tutto (in) ~** to write everything in small letters.

mi'nuta *sf* rough copy, draft.

mi'nuto, a *ag* tiny, minute; (*pioggia*) fine; (*corporatura*) delicate, fine; (*lavoro*) detailed ♦ *sm* (*unità di misura*) minute; **al ~** (*COMM*) retail; **avere i ~i contati** to have very little time.

mi'nuzia [mi'nuttsja] *sf* (*cura*) meticulousness; (*particolare*) detail.

minuziosa'mente [minuttsjosa'mente] *av* meticulously; in minute detail.

minuzi'oso, a [minut'tsjoso] *ag* (*persona, descrizione*) meticulous; (*esame*) minute.

'mio, 'mia, mi'ei, 'mie *det*: **il ~, la mia** etc my ♦ *pronome*: **il ~, la mia** etc mine ♦ *sm*:

ho speso del ~ I spent my own money ♦ *sf*: **la mia** (*opinione*) my view; **i miei** my family; **un ~ amico** a friend of mine; **per amor ~** for my sake; **è dalla mia** he is on my side; **anch'io ho avuto le mie** (*disavventure*) I've had my problems too; **ne ho fatta una delle mie!** (*sciocchezze*) I've done it again!; **cerco di stare sulle mie** I try to keep myself to myself.

'miope *ag* short-sighted.

mio'pia *sf* short-sightedness, myopia; (*fig*) short-sightedness.

'mira *sf* (*anche fig*) aim; **avere una buona/cattiva ~** to be a good/bad shot; **prendere la ~** to take aim; **prendere di ~ qn** (*fig*) to pick on sb.

mi'rabile *ag* admirable, wonderful.

mi'racolo *sm* miracle.

miraco'loso, a *ag* miraculous.

mi'raggio [mi'raddʒo] *sm* mirage.

mi'rare *vi*: **~ a** to aim at.

mi'riade *sf* myriad.

mi'rino *sm* (*TECN*) sight; (*FOT*) viewer, viewfinder.

mir'tillo *sm* bilberry (*Brit*), blueberry (*US*), whortleberry.

'mirto *sm* myrtle.

mi'santropo, a *sm/f* misanthropist.

mi'scela [miʃ'ʃela] *sf* mixture; (*di caffè*) blend.

miscel'lanea [miʃʃel'lanea] *sf* miscellany.

'mischia ['miskja] *sf* scuffle; (*RUGBY*) scrum, scrummage.

mischi'are [mis'kjare] *vt*, **~rsi** *vr* to mix, blend.

misco'noscere [misko'noʃʃere] *vt* (*qualità, coraggio etc*) to fail to appreciate.

miscre'dente *ag* (*REL*) misbelieving; (: *incredulo*) unbelieving ♦ *sm/f* misbeliever; unbeliever.

mis'cuglio [mis'kuʎʎo] *sm* mixture, hotchpotch, jumble.

'mise *vb vedi* **mettere**.

mise'rabile *ag* (*infelice*) miserable, wretched; (*povero*) poverty-stricken; (*di scarso valore*) miserable.

mi'seria *sf* extreme poverty; (*infelicità*) misery; **~e** *sfpl* (*del mondo etc*) misfortunes, troubles; **costare una ~** to cost next to nothing; **piangere ~** to plead poverty; **ridursi in ~** to be reduced to poverty; **porca ~!** (*fam*) (bloody) hell!

miseri'cordia *sf* mercy, pity.

misericordi'oso, a *ag* merciful.

'misero, a *ag* miserable, wretched; (*povero*) poverty-stricken; (*insufficiente*) miserable.

mis'fatto *sm* misdeed, crime.

'misi *vb vedi* **mettere**.

mi'sogino [mi'zɔdʒino] *sm* misogynist.

'missile *sm* missile; **~ cruise** *o* **di crociera** cruise missile; **~ terra-aria** surface-to-air

missile.
missio'nario, a *ag, sm/f* missionary.
missi'one *sf* mission.
misteri'oso, a *ag* mysterious.
mis'tero *sm* mystery; **fare ~ di qc** to make a mystery out of sth; **quanti ~i!** why all the mystery?
'**mistico, a, ci, che** *ag* mystic(al) ♦ *sm* mystic.
mistifi'care *vt* to fool, bamboozle.
'**misto, a** *ag* mixed; (*scuola*) mixed, coeducational ♦ *sm* mixture; **un tessuto in ~ lino** a linen mix.
mis'tura *sf* mixture.
mi'sura *sf* measure; (*misurazione, dimensione*) measurement; (*taglia*) size; (*provvedimento*) measure, step; (*moderazione*) moderation; (*MUS*) time; (: *divisione*) bar; (*fig: limite*) bounds *pl*, limit; **in ~ di** in accordance with, according to; **nella ~ in cui** inasmuch as, insofar as; **in giusta ~** moderately; **oltre ~** beyond measure; **su ~** made to measure; **in ugual ~** equally, in the same way; **a ~ d'uomo** on a human scale; **passare la ~** to overstep the mark, go too far; **prendere le ~e a qn** to take sb's measurements, measure sb; **prendere le ~e di qc** to measure sth; **ho preso le mie ~e** I've taken the necessary steps; **non ha il senso della ~** he doesn't know when to stop; **~ di lunghezza/capacità** measure of length/capacity; **~e di sicurezza/prevenzione** safety/precautionary measures.
misu'rare *vt* (*ambiente, stoffa*) to measure; (*terreno*) to survey; (*abito*) to try on; (*pesare*) to weigh; (*fig: parole etc*) to weigh up; (: *spese, cibo*) to limit ♦ *vi* to measure; **~rsi** *vr*: **~rsi con qn** to have a confrontation with sb; (*competere*) to compete with sb.
misu'rato, a *ag* (*ponderato*) measured; (*prudente*) cautious; (*moderato*) moderate.
misurazi'one [mizurat'tsjone] *sf* measuring; (*di terreni*) surveying.
'**mite** *ag* mild; (*prezzo*) moderate, reasonable.
'**mitico, a, ci, che** *ag* mythical.
miti'gare *vt* to mitigate, lessen; (*lenire*) to soothe, relieve; **~rsi** *vr* (*odio*) to subside; (*tempo*) to become milder.
'**mitilo** *sm* mussel.
'**mito** *sm* myth.
mitolo'gia, 'gie [mitolo'dʒia] *sf* mythology.
mito'logico, a, ci, che [mito'lɔdʒiko] *ag* mythological.
'**mitra** *sf* (*REL*) mitre (*Brit*), miter (*US*) ♦ *sm inv* (*arma*) sub-machine gun.
mitragli'are [mitraʎ'ʎare] *vt* to machine-gun.
mitraglia'tore, 'trice [mitraʎʎa'tore] *ag*: **fucile** *m* **~** sub-machine gun ♦ *sf* machine gun.

mitteleuro'peo, a *ag* Central European.
mit'tente *sm/f* sender.
ml *abbr* (= *millilitro*) ml.
MLD *sigla m vedi* **Movimento per la Liberazione della Donna.**
MM *abbr* = *Metropolitana Milanese.*
mm *abbr* (= *millimetro*) mm.
M.M. *abbr vedi* **marina militare.**
MN *sigla* = *Mantova.*
M/N, m/n *abbr* (= *motonave*) MV.
MO *sigla* = *Modena.*
M.O. *abbr* = **Medio Oriente.**
mo' *sm*: **a ~ di** *prep* like; **a ~ di esempio** by way of example.
'**mobile** *ag* mobile; (*parte di macchina*) moving; (*DIR: bene*) movable, personal ♦ *sm* (*arredamento*) piece of furniture; **~i** *smpl* furniture *sg*.
mo'bilia *sf* furniture.
mobili'are *ag* (*DIR*) personal, movable.
mo'bilio *sm* = **mobilia.**
mobilità *sf* mobility.
mobili'tare *vt* to mobilize; **~ l'opinione pubblica** to rouse public opinion.
mobilitazi'one [mobilitat'tsjone] *sf* mobilization.
mocas'sino *sm* moccasin.
mocci'oso, a [mot'tʃoso] *sm/f* (*bambino piccolo*) little kid; (*peg*) snotty-nosed kid.
'**moccolo** *sm* (*di candela*) candle end; (*fam: bestemmia*) oath; (: *moccio*) snot; **reggere il ~** to play gooseberry (*Brit*), act as chaperon(e).
'**moda** *sf* fashion; **alla ~, di ~** fashionable, in fashion.
modalità *sf inv* formality; **seguire attentamente le ~ d'uso** to follow the instructions carefully; **~ giuridiche** legal procedures; **~ di pagamento** method of payment.
mo'della *sf* model.
model'lare *vt* (*creta*) to model, shape; **~rsi** *vr*: **~rsi su** to model o.s. on.
mo'dello *sm* model; (*stampo*) mould (*Brit*), mold (*US*) ♦ *ag inv* model *cpd*.
'**modem** *sm inv* modem.
mode'nese *ag* of (o from) Modena.
mode'rare *vt* to moderate; **~rsi** *vr* to restrain o.s.; **~ la velocità** to reduce speed; **~ i termini** to weigh one's words.
mode'rato, a *ag* moderate.
modera'tore, 'trice *sm/f* moderator.
moderazi'one [moderat'tsjone] *sf* moderation.
moderniz'zare [modernid'dzare] *vt* to bring up to date, modernize; **~rsi** *vr* to get up to date.
mo'derno, a *ag* modern.
mo'destia *sf* modesty; **~ a parte ...** in all modesty ..., though I say it myself ....
mo'desto, a *ag* modest.
'**modico, a, ci, che** *ag* reasonable, moder-

ate.

mo'difica, che *sf* modification; **subire delle ~che** to undergo some modifications.

modifi'care *vt* to modify, alter; **~rsi** *vr* to alter, change.

mo'dista *sf* milliner.

'modo *sm* way, manner; (*mezzo*) means, way; (*occasione*) opportunity; (*LING*) mood; (*MUS*) mode; **~i** *smpl* (*maniere*) manners; **a suo ~, a ~ suo** in his own way; **ad** *o* **in ogni ~** anyway; **di** *o* **in ~ che** so that; **in ~ da** so as to; **in tutti i ~i** at all costs; (*comunque sia*) anyway; (*in ogni caso*) in any case; **in un certo qual ~** in a way, in some ways; **in qualche ~** somehow or other; **oltre ~** extremely; **~ di dire** turn of phrase; **per ~ di dire** so to speak; **fare a ~ proprio** to do as one likes; **fare le cose a ~** to do things properly; **una persona a ~** a well-mannered person; **c'è ~ e ~ di farlo** there's a right way and a wrong way of doing it.

modu'lare *vt* to modulate ♦ *ag* modular.

modulazi'one [modulat'tsjone] *sf* modulation; **~ di frequenza** (**FM**) frequency modulation (FM).

'modulo *sm* (*modello*) form; (*ARCHIT, lunare, di comando*) module; **~ di domanda** application form; **~ d'iscrizione** enrolment form; **~ di versamento** deposit slip.

Moga'discio [moga'diʃʃo] *sm* Mogadishu.

'mogano *sm* mahogany.

'mogio, a, gi, gie ['mɔdʒo] *ag* down in the dumps, dejected.

'moglie ['moʎʎe] *sf* wife.

mo'hair [mɔ'ɛr] *sm* mohair.

mo'ine *sfpl* cajolery *sg*; (*leziosità*) affectation *sg*; **fare le ~ a qn** to cajole sb.

'mola *sf* millstone; (*utensile abrasivo*) grindstone.

mo'lare *vt* to grind ♦ *ag* (*pietra*) mill *cpd* ♦ *sm* (*dente*) molar.

'mole *sf* mass; (*dimensioni*) size; (*edificio grandioso*) massive structure; **una ~ di lavoro** masses (*Brit*) *o* loads of work.

mo'lecola *sf* molecule.

moles'tare *vt* to bother, annoy.

mo'lestia *sf* annoyance, bother; **recar ~ a qn** to bother sb.

mo'lesto, a *ag* annoying.

moli'sano, a *ag* of (*o* from) Molise.

'molla *sf* spring; **~e** *sfpl* (*per camino*) tongs; **prendere qn con le ~e** to treat sb with kid gloves.

mol'lare *vt* to release, let go; (*NAUT*) to ease; (*fig: ceffone*) to give ♦ *vi* (*cedere*) to give in; **~ gli ormeggi** (*NAUT*) to cast off; **~ la presa** to let go.

'molle *ag* soft; (*muscoli*) flabby; (*fig: debole*) weak, feeble.

molleggi'ato, a [molled'dʒato] *ag* (*letto*) sprung; (*auto*) with good suspension.

mol'leggio [mol'leddʒo] *sm* (*per veicoli*) suspension; (*elasticità*) springiness; (*GINNASTICA*) knee-bends *pl.*

mol'letta *sf* (*per capelli*) hairgrip; (*per panni stesi*) clothes peg (*Brit*) *o* pin (*US*); **~e** *sfpl* (*per zucchero*) tongs.

mol'lezza [mol'lettsa] *sf* softness; flabbiness; weakness, feebleness; **~e** *sfpl*: **vivere nelle ~e** to live in the lap of luxury.

mol'lica, che *sf* crumb, soft part.

mol'liccio, a, ci, ce [mol'littʃo] (*terreno, impasto*) soggy; (*frutta*) soft; (*floscio: mano*) limp; (: *muscolo*) flabby.

mol'lusco, schi *sm* mollusc.

'molo *sm* jetty, pier.

mol'teplice [mol'teplitʃe] *ag* (*formato di più elementi*) complex; **~i** *pl* (*svariati: interessi, attività*) numerous, various.

molteplicità [molteplitʃi'ta] *sf* multiplicity.

moltipli'care *vt* to multiply; **~rsi** *vr* to multiply; (*richieste*) to increase in number.

moltiplica'tore *sm* multiplier.

moltiplicazi'one [moltiplikat'tsjone] *sf* multiplication.

molti'tudine *sf* multitude; **una ~ di** a vast number *o* a multitude of.

'molto, a *det* much, a lot of; (*con sostantivi al plurale*): **~i(e)** many, a lot of; (*lungo: tempo*) long ♦ *av* a lot; (*in frasi negative*) much; (*intensivo*) very ♦ *pronome* much, a lot; **~i(e)** *pronome pl* many, a lot; **~ meglio** much *o* a lot better; **~ buono** very good; **~a gente** a lot of people, many people; **per ~ (tempo)** for a long time; **ci vuole ~ (tempo)?** will it take long?; **arriverà fra non ~** he'll arrive soon.

momentanea'mente *av* at the moment, at present.

momen'taneo, a *ag* momentary, fleeting.

mo'mento *sm* moment; **da un ~ all'altro** at any moment; (*all'improvviso*) suddenly; **al ~ di fare** just as I was (*o* you were *o* he was *etc*) doing; **a ~i** (*da un ~ all'altro*) any time *o* moment now; (*quasi*) nearly; **per il ~** for the time being; **dal ~ che** ever since; (*dato che*) since; **~ culminante** climax.

'monaca, che *sf* nun.

'Monaco *sf* Monaco; **~ (di Baviera)** Munich.

'monaco, ci *sm* monk.

mo'narca, chi *sm* monarch.

monar'chia [monar'kia] *sf* monarchy.

mo'narchico, a, ci, che [mo'narkiko] *ag* (*stato, autorità*) monarchic; (*partito, fede*) monarchist ♦ *sm/f* monarchist.

monas'tero *sm* (*di monaci*) monastery; (*di monache*) convent.

mo'nastico, a, ci, che *ag* monastic.

'monco, a, chi, che *ag* maimed; (*fig*) incomplete; **~ d'un braccio** one-armed.

mon'cone *sm* stump.

mon'dana *sf* prostitute.
mondanità *sf* (*frivolezza*) worldliness; **le ~** (*piaceri*) the pleasures of the world.
mon'dano, a *ag* (*anche fig*) worldly; (*dell'alta società*) society *cpd*; fashionable.
mon'dare *vt* (*frutta, patate*) to peel; (*piselli*) to shell; (*pulire*) to clean.
mondez'zaio [mondet'tsajo] *sm* rubbish (*Brit*) *o* garbage (*US*) dump.
mondi'ale *ag* (*campionato, popolazione*) world *cpd*; (*influenza*) world-wide; **di fama ~** world famous.
'mondo *sm* world; (*grande quantità*): **un ~ di** lots of, a host of; **il gran** *o* **bel ~** high society; **per niente al ~, per nessuna cosa al ~** not for all the world; **da che ~ è ~** since time *o* the world began; **mandare qn all'altro ~** to kill sb; **mettere/venire al ~** to bring/come into the world; **vivere fuori dal ~** to be out of touch with the real world; **(sono) cose dell'altro ~!** it's incredible!; **com'è piccolo il ~!** it's a small world!
mone'gasco, a, schi, sche *ag, sm/f* Monegasque.
mo'nello, a *sm/f* street urchin; (*ragazzo vivace*) scamp, imp.
mo'neta *sf* coin; (*ECON: valuta*) currency; (*denaro spicciolo*) (small) change; **~ estera** foreign currency; **~ legale** legal tender.
mone'tario, a *ag* monetary.
Mon'golia *sf*: **la ~** Mongolia.
mon'golico, a, ci, che *ag* Mongolian.
mongo'lismo *sm* mongolism, Down's syndrome.
'mongolo, a *ag* Mongolian ♦ *sm/f, sm* Mongol, Mongolian.
mongo'loide *ag, sm/f* (*MED*) mongol.
'monito *sm* warning.
'monitor *sm inv* (*TECN, TV*) monitor.
mo'nocolo *sm* (*lente*) monocle, eyeglass.
monoco'lore *ag* (*POL*): **governo ~** one-party government.
monoga'mia *sf* monogamy.
mo'nogamo, a *ag* monogamous ♦ *sm* monogamist.
monogra'fia *sf* monograph.
mono'gramma, i *sm* monogram.
mono'lingue *ag* monolingual.
mo'nologo, ghi *sm* monologue.
mono'pattino *sm* scooter.
mono'polio *sm* monopoly; **~ di stato** government monopoly.
monopoliz'zare [monopolid'dzare] *vt* to monopolize.
mono'sillabo, a *ag* monosyllabic ♦ *sm* monosyllable.
monoto'nia *sf* monotony.
mo'notono, a *ag* monotonous.
monsi'gnore [monsiɲ'ɲore] *sm* (*REL: titolo*) Your (*o* His) Grace.
mon'sone *sm* monsoon.

monta'carichi [monta'kariki] *sm inv* hoist, goods lift.
mon'taggio [mon'taddʒo] *sm* (*TECN*) assembly; (*CINEMA*) editing.
mon'tagna [mon'taɲɲa] *sf* mountain; (*zona montuosa*): **la ~** the mountains *pl*; **andare in ~** to go to the mountains; **aria/strada di ~** mountain air/road; **casa di ~** house in the mountains; **~e russe** roller coaster *sg*, big dipper *sg* (*Brit*).
monta'gnoso, a [montaɲ'ɲoso] *ag* mountainous.
monta'naro, a *ag* mountain *cpd* ♦ *sm/f* mountain dweller.
mon'tano, a *ag* mountain *cpd*.
mon'tante *sm* (*di porta*) jamb; (*di finestra*) upright; (*CALCIO: palo*) post; (*PUGILATO*) upper cut; (*COMM*) total amount.
mon'tare *vt* to go (*o* come) up; (*cavallo*) to ride; (*apparecchiatura*) to set up, assemble; (*CUC*) to whip; (*ZOOL*) to cover; (*incastonare*) to mount, set; (*CINEMA*) to edit; (*FOT*) to mount ♦ *vi* to go (*o* come) up; (*a cavallo*): **~ bene/male** to ride well/badly; (*aumentare di livello, volume*) to rise; **~rsi** *vr* to become bigheaded; **~ qc** to exaggerate sth; **~ qn** *o* **la testa a qn** to turn sb's head; **~rsi la testa** to become big-headed; **~ in bicicletta/ macchina/treno** to get on a bicycle/ into a car/on a train; **~ a cavallo** to get on *o* mount a horse; **~ la guardia** (*MIL*) to mount guard.
monta'tura *sf* assembling *q*; (*di occhiali*) frames *pl*; (*di gioiello*) mounting, setting; (*fig*): **~ pubblicitaria** publicity stunt.
montavi'vande *sm inv* dumbwaiter.
'monte *sm* mountain; **a ~** upstream; **andare a ~** (*fig*) to come to nothing; **mandare a ~ qc** (*fig*) to upset sth, cause sth to fail; **il M~ Bianco** Mont Blanc; **il M~ Everest** Mount Everest; **~ di pietà** pawnshop; **~ premi** prize.
Monteci'torio [montetʃi'torjo] *sm*: **palazzo ~** (*POL*) seat of the Italian Chamber of Deputies.
mont'gomery [mənt'gʌməri] *sm inv* duffel coat.
mon'tone *sm* (*ZOOL*) ram; (*anche*: **giacca di ~**) sheepskin (jacket); **carne di ~** mutton.
montuosità *sf* mountainous nature.
montu'oso, a *ag* mountainous.
monu'mento *sm* monument.
mo'quette [mɔ'kɛt] *sf* fitted carpet.
'mora *sf* (*del rovo*) blackberry; (*del gelso*) mulberry; (*DIR*) delay; (*: somma*) arrears *pl*.
mo'rale *ag* moral ♦ *sf* (*scienza*) ethics *sg*, moral philosophy; (*complesso di norme*) moral standards *pl*, morality; (*condotta*) morals *pl*; (*insegnamento morale*) moral ♦

sm morale; **la ~ della favola** the moral of the tale; **essere giù di ~** to be feeling down; **aver il ~ alto/a terra** to be in good/ low spirits.

mora'lista, i, e *ag* moralistic ♦ *sm/f* moralist.

moralità *sf* morality; (*condotta*) morals *pl*.

mora'toria *sf* (*DIR*) moratorium.

morbi'dezza [morbi'dettsa] *sf* softness; smoothness; tenderness.

'morbido, a *ag* soft; (*pelle*) soft, smooth; (*carne*) tender.

mor'billo *sm* (*MED*) measles *sg*.

'morbo *sm* disease.

mor'boso, a *ag* (*fig*) morbid.

'morchia ['mɔrkja] *sf* (*residuo grasso*) dregs *pl*; oily deposit.

mor'dace [mor'datʃe] *ag* biting, cutting.

mor'dente *sm* (*fig: di satira, critica*) bite; (: *di persona*) drive.

'mordere *vt* to bite; (*addentare*) to bite into; (*corrodere*) to eat into.

mordicchi'are [mordik'kjare] *vt* (*gen*) to chew at.

mo'rente *ag* dying ♦ *sm/f* dying man/ woman.

mor'fina *sf* morphine.

mo'ria *sf* high mortality.

mori'bondo, a *ag* dying, moribund.

morige'rato, a [moridʒe'rato] *ag* of good morals.

mo'rire *vi* to die; (*abitudine, civiltà*) to die out; **~ di dolore** to die of a broken heart; **~ di fame** to die of hunger; (*fig*) to be starving; **~ di freddo** to freeze to death; (*fig*) to be frozen; **~ d'invidia** to be green with envy; **~ di noia/paura** to be bored/ scared to death; **~ dalla voglia di fare qc** to be dying to do sth; **fa un caldo da ~** it's terribly hot.

mormo'rare *vi* to murmur; (*brontolare*) to grumble; **si mormora che ...** it's rumoured (*Brit*) *o* rumored (*US*) that ...; **la gente mormora** people are talking.

mormo'rio *sm* murmuring; grumbling.

'moro, a *ag* dark(-haired); dark(-complexioned); **i M~i** *smpl* (*STORIA*) the Moors.

mo'roso, a *ag* in arrears ♦ *sm/f* (*fam: innamorato*) sweetheart.

'morsa *sf* (*TECN*) vice (*Brit*), vise (*US*); (*fig: stretta*) grip.

mor'setto *sm* (*TECN*) clamp; (*ELETTR*) terminal.

morsi'care *vt* to nibble (at), gnaw (at); (*sog: insetto*) to bite.

'morso, a *pp di* **mordere** ♦ *sm* bite; (*di insetto*) sting; (*parte della briglia*) bit; **dare un ~ a qc/qn** to bite sth/sb; **i ~i della fame** pangs of hunger.

morta'della *sf* (*CUC*) mortadella (*type of salted pork meat*).

mor'taio *sm* mortar.

mor'tale *ag*, *sm* mortal.

mortalità *sf* mortality; (*STATISTICA*) mortality, death rate.

'morte *sf* death; **in punto di ~** at death's door; **ferito a ~** (*soldato*) mortally wounded; (*in incidente*) fatally injured; **essere annoiato a ~** to be bored to death *o* to tears; **avercela a ~ con qn** to be bitterly resentful of sb; **avere la ~ nel cuore** to have a heavy heart.

mortifi'care *vt* to mortify.

'morto, a *pp di* **morire** ♦ *ag* dead ♦ *sm/f* dead man/woman; **i ~i** the dead; **fare il ~** (*nell'acqua*) to float on one's back; **un ~ di fame** (*fig peg*) a down-and-out; **le campane suonavano a ~** the funeral bells were tolling.

mor'torio *sm* (*anche fig*) funeral.

mo'saico, ci *sm* mosaic; **l'ultimo tassello del ~** (*fig*) the last piece of the puzzle.

'Mosca *sf* Moscow.

'mosca, sche *sf* fly; **rimanere** *o* **restare con un pugno di ~sche** (*fig*) to be left empty-handed; **non si sentiva una ~** (*fig*) you could have heard a pin drop; **~ cieca** blind-man's buff.

mos'cato *sm* muscatel (wine).

mosce'rino [moʃʃe'rino] *sm* midge, gnat.

mos'chea [mos'kɛa] *sf* mosque.

mos'chetto [mos'ketto] *sm* musket.

moschet'tone [mosket'tone] *sm* (*gancia*) spring clip; (*ALPINISMO*) karabiner, snap-link.

moschi'cida, i, e [moski'tʃida] *ag* fly *cpd*; **carta ~** flypaper.

'moscio, a, sci, sce ['moʃʃo] *ag* (*fig*) lifeless; **ha la "r" ~a** he can't roll his "r"'s.

mos'cone *sm* (*ZOOL*) bluebottle; (*barca*) pedalo; (: *a remi*) *kind of pedalo with oars.*

mosco'vita, i, e *ag*, *sm/f* Muscovite.

'mossa *sf* movement; (*nel gioco*) move; **darsi una ~** (*fig*) to give o.s. a shake; **prendere le ~e da qc** to come about as the result of sth.

'mossi *etc vb vedi* **muovere**.

'mosso, a *pp di* **muovere** ♦ *ag* (*mare*) rough; (*capelli*) wavy; (*FOT*) blurred; (*ritmo, prosa*) animated.

mos'tarda *sf* mustard.

'mosto *sm* must.

'mostra *sf* exhibition, show; (*ostentazione*) show; **in ~** on show; **far ~ di** (*fingere*) to pretend; **far ~ di sé** to show off; **mettersi in ~** to draw attention to o.s.

mos'trare *vt* to show ♦ *vi*: **~ di fare** to pretend to do; **~rsi** *vr* to appear; **~ la lingua** to stick out one's tongue.

'mostro *sm* monster.

mostru'oso, a *ag* monstrous.

mo'tel *sm inv* motel.

moti'vare *vt* (*causare*) to cause;

(giustificare) to justify, account for.
motivazi'one [motivat'tsjone] *sf* justification; *(PSIC)* motivation.

mo'tivo *sm (causa)* reason, cause; *(movente)* motive; *(letterario)* (central) theme; *(disegno)* motif, design, pattern; *(MUS)* motif; **per quale ~?** why?, for what reason?; **per ~i di salute** for health reasons, on health grounds; **~i personali** personal reasons.

'moto *sm (anche FISICA)* motion; *(movimento, gesto)* movement; *(esercizio fisico)* exercise; *(sommossa)* rising, revolt; *(commozione)* feeling, impulse ♦ *sf inv (motocicletta)* motorbike; **fare del ~** to take some exercise; **un ~ d'impazienza** an impatient gesture; **mettere in ~** to set in motion; *(AUT)* to start up.

moto'carro *sm* three-wheeler van.
motoci'cletta [mototʃi'kletta] *sf* motorcycle.
motoci'clismo [mototʃi'klizmo] *sm* motorcycling, motorcycle racing.
motoci'clista, i, e [mototʃi'klista] *sm/f* motorcyclist.
moto'nave *sf* motor vessel.
motopesche'reccio [motopeske'rettʃo] *sm* motor fishing vessel.

mo'tore, 'trice *ag* motor; *(TECN)* driving ♦ *sm* engine, motor ♦ *sf (TECN)* engine, motor; **albero ~** drive shaft; **forza ~trice** driving force; **a ~** motor *cpd*, power-driven; **~ a combustione interna/a reazione** internal combustion/jet engine.

moto'rino *sm* moped; **~ di avviamento** *(AUT)* starter.

motoriz'zato, a [motorid'dzato] *ag (truppe)* motorized; *(persona)* having a car *o* transport.

motorizzazi'one [motoriddzat'tsjone] *sf (ufficio tecnico e organizzativo):* **(ufficio della)** ~ road traffic office.

motos'cafo *sm* motorboat.
motove'detta *sf* motor patrol vessel.
mo'trice [mo'tritʃe] *sf vedi* **motore**.
mot'teggio [mot'teddʒo] *sm* banter.

'motto *sm (battuta scherzosa)* witty remark; *(frase emblematica)* motto, maxim.
mo'vente *sm* motive.
mo'venza [mo'vɛntsa] *sf* movement.
movimen'tare *vt* to liven up.
movimen'tato, a *ag (festa, partita)* lively; *(riunione)* animated; *(strada, vita)* busy; *(soggiorno)* eventful.

movi'mento *sm* movement; *(fig)* activity, hustle and bustle; *(MUS)* tempo, movement; **essere sempre in ~** to be always on the go; **fare un po' di ~** *(esercizio fisico)* to take some exercise; **c'è molto ~ in città** the town is very busy; **~ di capitali** movement of capital; **M~ per la Liberazione della Donna (MLD)** Women's Movement.

movi'ola *sf* moviola; **rivedere qc alla ~** to see an action *(Brit) o* instant *(US)* replay of sth.

Mozam'bico [moddzam'biko] *sm:* **il ~** Mozambique.

mozi'one [mot'tsjone] *sf (POL)* motion; **~ d'ordine** *(POL)* point of order.

mozzafi'ato [mottsa'fjato] *ag inv* breathtaking.

moz'zare [mot'tsare] *vt* to cut off; *(coda)* to dock; **~ il fiato** *o* **il respiro a qn** *(fig)* to take sb's breath away.

mozza'rella [mottsa'rella] *sf* mozzarella *(a moist Neapolitan curd cheese).*

mozzi'cone [mottsi'kone] *sm* stub, butt, end; *(anche:* **~ di sigaretta)** cigarette end.

'mozzo *sm* ['mɔddzo] *(MECCANICA)* hub; ['mottso] *(NAUT)* ship's boy; **~ di stalla** stable boy.

mq *abbr (= metro quadro)* sq.m.
MS *sigla = Massa Carrara.*
ms. *abbr (= manoscritto)* ms.
Mti *abbr = monti.*
'mucca, che *sf* cow.
'mucchio ['mukkjo] *sm* pile, heap; *(fig):* **un ~ di** lots of, heaps of.
'muco, chi *sm* mucus.
mu'cosa *sf* mucous membrane.
'muffa *sf* mould *(Brit)*, mold *(US)*, mildew; **fare la ~** to go mouldy *(Brit) o* moldy *(US).*
mugghi'are [mug'gjare] *vi (fig: mare, tuono)* to roar; *(: vento)* to howl.
mug'gire [mud'dʒire] *vi (vacca)* to low, moo; *(toro)* to bellow; *(fig)* to roar.
mug'gito [mud'dʒito] *sm* low, moo; bellow; roar.
mu'ghetto [mu'getto] *sm* lily of the valley.
mu'gnaio, a [muɲ'ɲajo] *sm/f* miller.
mugo'lare *vi (cane)* to whimper, whine; *(fig: persona)* to moan.
mugu'gnare [muguɲ'ɲare] *vi (fam)* to mutter, mumble.
mulatti'era *sf* mule track.
mu'latto, a *ag, sm/f* mulatto.
muli'nare *vi* to whirl, spin (round and round).
muli'nello *sm (moto vorticoso)* eddy, whirl; *(di canna da pesca)* reel; *(NAUT)* windlass.
mu'lino *sm* mill; **~ a vento** windmill.
'mulo *sm* mule.
'multa *sf* fine.
mul'tare *vt* to fine.
multico'lore *ag* multicoloured *(Brit)*, multicolored *(US).*
multi'forme *ag (paesaggio, attività, interessi)* varied; *(ingegno)* versatile.
multimedi'ale *ag* multimedia *cpd.*
multinazio'nale [multinattsjo'nale] *ag, sf* multinational.
'multiplo, a *ag, sm* multiple.
multiu'tenza [multiu'tɛntsa] *sf (INFORM)* time sharing.

'mummia *sf* mummy.

'mungere ['mundʒere] *vt* (*anche fig*) to milk.

mungi'tura [mundʒi'tura] *sf* milking.

munici'pale [munitʃi'pale] *ag* (*gen*) municipal; **palazzo ~** town hall; **autorità ~i** local authorities (*Brit*), local government *sg*.

muni'cipio [muni'tʃipjo] *sm* town council; (*edificio*) town hall; **sposarsi in ~** ≈ to get married in a registry office (*Brit*), have a civil marriage.

mu'nifico, a, ci, che *ag* munificent, generous.

mu'nire *vt*: **~ qc/qn di** to equip sth/sb with; **~ di firma** (*documento*) to sign.

munizi'oni [munit'tsjoni] *sfpl* (*MIL*) ammunition *sg*.

'munsi *etc vb vedi* **mungere**.

'munto, a *pp di* **mungere**.

mu'oio *etc vb vedi* **morire**.

mu'overe *vt* to move; (*ruota, macchina*) to drive; (*sollevare: questione, obiezione*) to raise, bring up; (: *accusa*) to make, bring forward; **~rsi** *vr* to move; **~ causa a qn** (*DIR*) to take legal action against sb; **~ a compassione** to move to pity; **~ guerra a** *o* **contro qn** to wage war against sb; **~ mari e monti** to move heaven and earth; **~ al pianto** to move to tears; **~ i primi passi** to take one's first steps; (*fig*) to be starting out; **muoviti!** hurry up!, get a move on!

'mura *sfpl vedi* **muro**.

mu'raglia [mu'raʎʎa] *sf* (high) wall.

mu'rale *ag* wall *cpd*; mural.

mu'rare *vt* (*persona, porta*) to wall up.

mu'rario, a *ag* building *cpd*; **arte ~a** masonry.

mura'tore *sm* (*con pietre*) mason; (*con mattoni*) bricklayer.

mura'tura *sf* (*lavoro murario*) masonry; **casa in ~** (*di pietra*) stonebuilt house; (*di mattoni*) brick house.

'muro *sm* wall; **~a** *sfpl* (*cinta cittadina*) walls; **a ~** wall *cpd*; (*armadio etc*) built-in; **mettere al ~** (*fucilare*) to shoot *o* execute (by firing squad); **~ di cinta** surrounding wall; **~ divisorio** dividing wall; **~ del suono** sound barrier.

'musa *sf* muse.

'muschio ['muskjo] *sm* (*ZOOL*) musk; (*BOT*) moss.

musco'lare *ag* muscular, muscle *cpd*.

muscola'tura *sf* muscle structure.

'muscolo *sm* (*ANAT*) muscle.

mu'seo *sm* museum.

museru'ola *sf* muzzle.

'musica *sf* music; **~ da ballo/camera** dance/chamber music.

musi'cale *ag* musical.

musicas'setta *sf* (pre-recorded) cassette.

musi'cista, i, e [muzi'tʃista] *sm/f* musician.

musi'comane *sm/f* music lover.

'muso *sm* muzzle; (*di auto, aereo*) nose; **tenere il ~** to sulk.

mu'sone, a *sm/f* sulky person.

'mussola *sf* muslin.

mus(s)ul'mano, a *ag*, *sm/f* Muslim, Moslem.

'muta *sf* (*di animali*) moulting (*Brit*), molting (*US*); (*di serpenti*) sloughing; (*per immersioni subacquee*) diving suit; (*gruppo di cani*) pack.

mu'tabile *ag* changeable.

muta'mento *sm* change.

mu'tande *sfpl* (*da uomo*) (under)pants.

mutan'dine *sfpl* (*da donna, bambino*) pants (*Brit*), briefs; **~ di plastica** plastic pants.

mu'tare *vt*, *vi* to change, alter.

mutazi'one [mutat'tsjone] *sf* change, alteration; (*BIOL*) mutation.

mu'tevole *ag* changeable.

muti'lare *vt* to mutilate, maim; (*fig*) to mutilate, deface.

muti'lato, a *sm/f* disabled person (*through loss of limbs*); **~ di guerra** disabled ex-serviceman (*Brit*) *o* war veteran (*US*).

mutilazi'one [mutilat'tsjone] *sf* mutilation.

mu'tismo *sm* (*MED*) mutism; (*atteggiamento*) (stubborn) silence.

'muto, a *ag* (*MED*) dumb; (*emozione, dolore, CINEMA*) silent; (*LING*) silent, mute; (*carta geografica*) blank; **~ per lo stupore** *etc* speechless with amazement *etc*; **ha fatto scena ~a** he didn't utter a word.

'mutua *sf* (*anche*: **cassa ~**) health insurance scheme; **medico della ~** ≈ National Health Service doctor (*Brit*).

mutu'are *vt* (*fig*) to borrow.

mutu'ato, a *sm/f* member of a health insurance scheme.

'mutuo, a *ag* (*reciproco*) mutual ♦ *sm* (*ECON*) (long-term) loan; **~ ipotecario** mortgage.

N

N, n ['ɛnne] *sf o m* (*lettera*) N, n; **N come Napoli** ≈ N for Nellie (*Brit*), N for Nan (*US*).

N *abbr* (= *nord*) N.

n *abbr* (= *numero*) no.

NA *sigla* = *Napoli*.

na'babbo *sm* (*anche fig*) nabob.

'nacchere ['nakkere] *sfpl* castanets.

NAD *sigla m* = **nucleo anti-droga**.

na'dir *sm* (*ASTR*) nadir.

'nafta *sf* naphtha; (*per motori diesel*) diesel

oil.

nafta'lina *sf* (*CHIM*) naphthalene; (*tarmicida*) mothballs *pl*.

'naia *sf* (*ZOOL*) cobra; (*MIL*) *slang term for national service*.

na'if [na'if] *ag inv* naïve.

'nailon *sm* = **nylon**.

Nai'robi *sf* Nairobi.

'nanna *sf* (*linguaggio infantile*): **andare a ~** to go to beddy-byes.

'nano, a *ag*, *sm/f* dwarf.

napole'tano, a *ag*, *sm/f* Neapolitan ♦ *sf* (*macchinetta da caffè*) Neapolitan coffee pot.

'Napoli *sf* Naples.

'nappa *sf* tassel.

nar'ciso [nar'tʃizo] *sm* narcissus.

nar'cosi *sf* general anaesthesia, narcosis.

nar'cotico, ci *sm* narcotic.

na'rice [na'ritʃe] *sf* nostril.

nar'rare *vt* to tell the story of, recount.

narra'tivo, a *ag* narrative ♦ *sf* (*branca letteraria*) fiction.

narra'tore, 'trice *sm/f* narrator.

narrazi'one [narrat'tsjone] *sf* narration; (*racconto*) story, tale.

na'sale *ag* nasal.

na'scente [naʃ'ʃɛnte] *ag* (*sole, luna*) rising.

'nascere ['naʃʃɛre] *vi* (*bambino*) to be born; (*pianta*) to come o spring up; (*fiume*) to rise, have its source; (*sole*) to rise; (*dente*) to come through; (*fig: derivare, conseguire*): **~ da** to arise from, be born out of; **è nata nel 1952** she was born in 1952; **da cosa nasce cosa** one thing leads to another.

'nascita ['naʃʃita] *sf* birth.

nasci'turo, a [naʃʃi'turo] *sm/f* future child; **come si chiamerà il ~?** what's the baby going to be called?

nas'condere *vt* to hide, conceal; **~rsi** *vr* to hide.

nascon'diglio [naskon'diʎʎo] *sm* hiding place.

nascon'dino *sm* (*gioco*) hide-and-seek.

nas'cosi *etc vb vedi* **nascondere**.

nas'costo, a *pp di* **nascondere** ♦ *ag* hidden; **di ~** secretly.

na'sello *sm* (*ZOOL*) hake.

'naso *sm* nose.

Nas'sau *sf* Nassau.

'nastro *sm* ribbon; (*magnetico, isolante, SPORT*) tape; **~ adesivo** adhesive tape; **~ trasportatore** conveyor belt.

nas'turzio [nas'turtsjo] *sm* nasturtium.

na'tale *ag* of one's birth ♦ *sm* (*REL*): **N~** Christmas; (*giorno della nascita*) birthday; **~i** *smpl*: **di illustri/umili ~i** of noble/humble birth.

natalità *sf* birth rate.

nata'lizio, a [nata'littsjo] *ag* (*del Natale*) Christmas *cpd*.

na'tante *sm* craft *inv*, boat.

'natica, che *sf* (*ANAT*) buttock.

na'tio, a, 'tii, 'tie *ag* native.

Natività *sf* (*REL*) Nativity.

na'tivo, a *ag*, *sm/f* native.

'nato, a *pp di* **nascere** ♦ *ag*: **un attore ~** a born actor; **~a Pieri** née Pieri.

'N.A.T.O. *sigla f* NATO (= *North Atlantic Treaty Organization*).

na'tura *sf* nature; **pagare in ~** to pay in kind; **~ morta** still life.

natu'rale *ag* natural ♦ *sm*: **al ~** (*alimenti*) served plain; (*ritratto*) life-size; **(ma) è ~!** (*in risposte*) of course!; **a grandezza ~** life-size; **acqua ~** spring water.

natura'lezza [natura'lettsa] *sf* naturalness.

natura'lista, i, e *sm/f* naturalist.

naturaliz'zare [naturalid'dzare] *vt* to naturalize.

natural'mente *av* naturally; (*certamente, sì*) of course.

natu'rismo *sm* naturism, nudism.

natu'rista, i, e *ag*, *sm/f* naturist, nudist.

naufra'gare *vi* (*nave*) to be wrecked; (*persona*) to be shipwrecked; (*fig*) to fall through.

nau'fragio [nau'fradʒo] *sm* shipwreck; (*fig*) ruin, failure.

'naufrago, ghi *sm* castaway, shipwreck victim.

'nausea *sf* nausea; **avere la ~** to feel sick (*Brit*) o ill (*US*); **fino alla ~** ad nauseam.

nausea'bondo, a *ag*, **nause'ante** *ag* nauseating, sickening.

nause'are *vt* to nauseate, make (feel) sick (*Brit*) o ill (*US*).

'nautico, a, ci, che *ag* nautical ♦ *sf* (art of) navigation; **salone ~** (*mostra*) boat show.

na'vale *ag* naval; **battaglia ~** naval battle; (*gioco*) battleships *pl*.

na'vata *sf* (*anche:* **~ centrale**) nave; (*anche:* **~ laterale**) aisle.

'nave *sf* ship, vessel; **~ da carico** cargo ship, freighter; **~ cisterna** tanker; **~ da guerra** warship; **~ di linea** liner; **~ passeggeri** passenger ship; **~ portaerei** aircraft carrier; **~ spaziale** spaceship.

na'vetta *sf* shuttle; (*servizio di collegamento*) shuttle (service).

navi'cella [navi'tʃɛlla] *sf* (*di aerostato*) gondola; **~ spaziale** spaceship.

navi'gabile *ag* navigable.

navi'gante *sm* sailor, seaman.

navi'gare *vi* to sail; **~ in cattive acque** (*fig*) to be in deep water.

navi'gato, a *ag* (*fig: esperto*) experienced.

naviga'tore, 'trice *sm/f* (*gen*) navigator; **~ solitario** single-handed sailor.

navigazi'one [navigat'tsjone] *sf* navigation; **dopo una settimana di ~** after a week at sea.

na'viglio [na'viʎʎo] *sm* fleet, ships *pl*;

(canale artificiale) canal; ~ **da pesca** fishing fleet.

'Nazaret(h) ['naddzaret] *sf* Nazareth.

nazio'nale [nattsjo'nale] *ag* national ♦ *sf* (*SPORT*) national team.

naziona'lismo [nattsjona'lizmo] *sm* nationalism.

naziona'lista, i, e [nattsjona'lista] *ag, sm/f* nationalist.

nazionalità [nattsjonali'ta] *sf inv* nationality.

nazionaliz'zare [nattsjonalid'dzare] *vt* to nationalize.

nazionalizzazi'one [nattsjonaliddzat'tsjone] *sf* nationalization.

nazi'one [nat'tsjone] *sf* nation.

na'zismo [nat'tsizmo] *sm* Nazism.

na'zista, i, e [nat'tsista] *ag, sm/f* Nazi.

NB *abbr* (= *nota bene*) NB.

N.d.A. *abbr* (= *nota dell'autore*) author's note.

N.d.D. *abbr* = *nota della direzione*.

N.d.E. *abbr* (= *nota dell'editore*) publisher's note.

N.d.R. *abbr* (= *nota della redazione*) editor's note.

N.d.T. *abbr* (= *nota del traduttore*) translator's note.

ne *av* (*moto da luogo*) from there ♦ *pronome* of him/her/it/them; about him/her/it/them; ~ **riconosco la voce** I recognize his (*o* her) voice; **non parliamone più!** let's not talk about him (*o* her *o* it *o* them) any more!; ~ **deduco che l'avete trovato** I gather you've found it; ~ **consegue che ...** it follows therefore that ...; (*con valore partitivo*): **hai dei libri?** — **si,** ~ **ho** have you any books? — yes, I have (some); **hai del pane?** — **no, non** ~ **ho** have you any bread? — no, I don't have any; **quanti anni hai?** — ~ **ho 17** how old are you? — I'm 17.

né *cong*: ~ **...** ~ neither ... nor; ~ **l'uno** ~ **l'altro lo vuole** neither of them wants it; ~ **più** ~ **meno** no more no less; **non parla** ~ **l'italiano** ~ **il tedesco** he speaks neither Italian nor German, he doesn't speak either Italian or German; **non piove** ~ **nevica** it isn't raining or snowing.

N.E. *abbr* (= *nordest*) NE.

ne'anche [ne'anke] *av, cong* not even; **non ...** ~ not even; ~ **se volesse potrebbe venire** he couldn't come even if he wanted to; **non l'ho visto** — **neanch'io** I didn't see him — neither did I *o* I didn't either; ~ **per idea** *o* **sogno!** not on your life!; **non ci penso** ~! I wouldn't dream of it!; ~ **a pagarlo lo farebbe** he wouldn't do it even if you paid him.

'nebbia *sf* fog; (*foschia*) mist.

nebbi'oso, a *ag* foggy; misty.

nebulizza'tore [nebuliddza'tore] *sm* atomizer.

nebu'losa *sf* nebula.

nebulosità *sf* haziness.

nebu'loso, a *ag* (*atmosfera, cielo*) hazy; (*fig*) hazy, vague.

néces'saire [nese'ser] *sm inv*: ~ **da viaggio** overnight case *o* bag.

necessaria'mente [netʃessarja'mente] *av* necessarily.

neces'sario, a [netʃes'sarjo] *ag* necessary ♦ *sm*: **fare il** ~ to do what is necessary; **lo stretto** ~ the bare essentials *pl*.

necessità [netʃessi'ta] *sf inv* necessity; (*povertà*) need, poverty; **trovarsi nella** ~ **di fare qc** to be forced *o* obliged to do sth, have to do sth.

necessi'tare [netʃessi'tare] *vt* to require ♦ *vi* (*aver bisogno*): ~ **di** to need.

necro'logio [nekro'lɔdʒo] *sm* obituary notice; (*registro*) register of deaths.

ne'fando, a *ag* infamous, wicked.

ne'fasto, a *ag* inauspicious, ill-omened.

ne'gare *vt* to deny; (*rifiutare*) to deny, refuse; ~ **di aver fatto/che** to deny having done/that.

negativa'mente *av* negatively; **rispondere** ~ to give a negative response.

nega'tivo, a *ag, sf, sm* negative.

negazi'one [negat'tsjone] *sf* negation.

negherò *etc* [nege'rɔ] *vb vedi* **negare**.

ne'gletto, a [ne'gletto] *ag* (*trascurato*) neglected.

'negli ['neʎʎi] *prep + det vedi* **in**.

négli'gé [negli'ʒe] *sm inv* negligee.

negli'gente [negli'dʒɛnte] *ag* negligent, careless.

negli'genza [negli'dʒɛntsa] *sf* negligence, carelessness.

negozi'abile [negot'tsjabile] *ag* negotiable.

negozi'ante [negot'tsjante] *sm/f* trader, dealer; (*bottegaio*) shopkeeper (*Brit*), storekeeper (*US*).

negozi'are [negot'tsjare] *vt* to negotiate ♦ *vi*: ~ **in** to trade *o* deal in.

negozi'ato [negot'tsjato] *sm* negotiation.

negozia'tore, 'trice [negottsja'tore] *sm/f* negotiator.

ne'gozio [ne'gɔttsjo] *sm* (*locale*) shop (*Brit*), store (*US*); (*affare*) (piece of) business *q*; (*DIR*): ~ **giuridico** legal transaction.

'negro, a *ag, sm/f* Negro.

negro'mante *sm/f* necromancer.

negroman'zia [negroman'tsia] *sf* necromancy.

'nei, nel, nell', 'nella, 'nelle, 'nello *prep + det vedi* **in**.

'nembo *sm* (*METEOR*) nimbus.

ne'mico, a, ci, che *ag* hostile; (*MIL*) enemy *cpd* ♦ *sm/f* enemy; **essere** ~ **di** to be strongly averse *o* opposed to.

nem'meno *av, cong* = **neanche**.

'nenia *sf* dirge; (*motivo monotono*) monotonous tune.

'neo *sm* mole; (*fig*) (slight) flaw.

'**neo**... *prefisso* neo....

neofa'scista, i, e [neofaʃ'ʃista] *sm/f* neofascist.

neolo'gismo [neolo'dʒizmo] *sm* neologism.

'**neon** *sm* (*CHIM*) neon.

neo'nato, a *ag* newborn ♦ *sm/f* newborn baby.

neozelan'dese [neoddzelan'dese] *ag* New Zealand *cpd* ♦ *sm/f* New Zealander.

Ne'pal *sm*: **il** ~ Nepal.

nep'pure *av*, *cong* = **neanche**.

ner'bata *sf* (*colpo*) blow; (*sferzata*) whiplash.

'**nerbo** *sm* lash; (*fig*) strength, backbone.

nerbo'ruto, a *ag* muscular; robust.

ne'retto *sm* (*TIP*) bold type.

'**nero, a** *ag* black; (*scuro*) dark ♦ *sm* black; **nella miseria più** ~**a** in utter *o* abject poverty; **essere di umore** ~, **essere** ~ to be in a filthy mood; **mettere qc** ~ **su bianco** to put sth down in black and white; **vedere tutto** ~ to look on the black side (of things).

nero'fumo *sm* lampblack.

nerva'tura *sf* (*ANAT*) nervous system; (*BOT*) veining; (*ARCHIT*, *TECN*) rib.

'**nervo** *sm* (*ANAT*) nerve; (*BOT*) vein; **avere i** ~**i** to be on edge; **dare sui** ~**i a qn** to get on sb's nerves; **tenere/avere i** ~**i saldi** to keep/be calm; **che** ~**i!** damn (it)!

nervo'sismo *sm* (*PSIC*) nervousness; (*irritazione*) irritability.

ner'voso, a *ag* nervous; (*irritabile*) irritable ♦ *sm* (*fam*): **far venire il** ~ **a qn** to get on sb's nerves; **farsi prendere dal** ~ to let o.s. get irritated.

'**nespola** *sf* (*BOT*) medlar; (*fig*) blow, punch.

'**nespolo** *sm* medlar tree.

'**nesso** *sm* connection, link.

nes'suno, a *det* (*dav sm* **nessun** + *C*, *V*, **nessuno** + *s impura*, *gn*, *pn*, *ps*, *x*, *z*; *dav sf* **nessuna** + *C*, **nessun'** + *V*) (*non uno*) no, *espressione negativa* + any; (*qualche*) any ♦ *pronome* (*non uno*) no one, nobody, *espressione negativa* + any(one); (: *cosa*) none, *espressione negativa* + any; (*qualcuno*) anyone, anybody; (*qualcosa*) anything; **non c'è nessun libro** there isn't any book, there is no book; **hai** ~**a obiezione?** do you have any objections?; ~ **è venuto, non è venuto** ~ nobody came; **nessun altro** no one else, nobody else; **nessun'altra cosa** nothing else; **in nessun luogo** nowhere.

net'tare *vt* to clean ♦ *sm* ['nɛttare] nectar.

net'tezza [net'tettsa] *sf* cleanness, cleanliness; ~ **urbana** cleansing department (*Brit*), department of sanitation (*US*).

'**netto, a** *ag* (*pulito*) clean; (*chiaro*) clear, clear-cut; (*deciso*) definite; (*ECON*) net; **tagliare qc di** ~ to cut sth clean off; **taglio**

~ **col passato** (*fig*) clean break with the past.

nettur'bino *sm* dustman (*Brit*), garbage collector (*US*).

neurochirur'gia [neurokirur'dʒia] *sf* neurosurgery.

neurolo'gia [neurolo'dʒia] *sf* neurology.

neuro'logico, a, ci, che [neuro'lɔdʒiko] *ag* neurological.

neu'rologo a, gi, ghe *sm/f* neurologist.

neu'rosi *sf inv* = **nevrosi**.

neu'trale *ag* neutral.

neutralità *sf* neutrality.

neutraliz'zare [neutralid'dzare] *vt* to neutralize.

'**neutro, a** *ag* neutral; (*LING*) neuter ♦ *sm* (*LING*) neuter.

neu'trone *sm* neutron.

ne'vaio *sm* snowfield.

'**neve** *sf* snow; **montare a** ~ (*CUC*) to whip up; ~ **carbonica** dry ice.

nevi'care *vb impers* to snow.

nevi'cata *sf* snowfall.

ne'vischio [ne'viskjo] *sm* sleet.

ne'voso, a *ag* snowy; snow-covered.

nevral'gia [nevral'dʒia] *sf* neuralgia.

ne'vralgico, a, ci, che [ne'vraldʒiko] *ag*: **punto** ~ (*MED*) nerve centre; (*fig*) crucial point.

nevras'tenico, a, ci, che *ag* (*MED*) neurasthenic; (*fig*) hot-tempered ♦ *sm/f* neurasthenic; hot-tempered person.

ne'vrosi *sf inv* neurosis.

ne'vrotico, a, ci, che *ag*, *sm/f* (*anche fig*) neurotic.

Nia'gara *sm*: **le cascate del** ~ the Niagara Falls.

'**nibbio** *sm* (*ZOOL*) kite.

Nica'ragua *sm*: **il** ~ Nicaragua.

nicaragu'ense *ag*, *sm/f* Nicaraguan.

'**nicchia** ['nikkja] *sf* niche; (*naturale*) cavity, hollow; ~ **di mercato** (*COMM*) niche market.

nicchi'are [nik'kjare] *vi* to shilly-shally, hesitate.

'**nichel** ['nikel] *sm* nickel.

nichi'lismo [niki'lizmo] *sm* nihilism.

Nico'sia *sf* Nicosia.

nico'tina *sf* nicotine.

nidi'ata *sf* (*di uccelli, fig*: *di bambini*) brood; (*di altri animali*) litter.

nidifi'care *vi* to nest.

'**nido** *sm* nest ♦ *ag inv*: **asilo** ~ day nursery, crèche; **a** ~ **d'ape** (*tessuto etc*) honeycomb *cpd*.

ni'ente *pronome* (*nessuna cosa*) nothing; (*qualcosa*) anything; **non** ... ~ nothing, *espressione negativa* + anything ♦ *sm* nothing ♦ *av* (*in nessuna misura*): **non è** ~ **buono** it's not good at all; **una cosa da** ~ a trivial thing; **poco o** ~ next to nothing; ~ **affatto** not at all, not in the least;

nient'altro nothing else; **nient'altro che** nothing but; just, only; ~ **di** ~ absolutely nothing; **per** ~ (*invano, gratuitamente*) for nothing; **non ... per** ~ not ... at all; ~ **male!** not bad at all!; ~ **paura!** never fear!; **e** ~ **scuse!** don't try to make excuses!; **basta un** ~ **per farla piangere** the slightest thing is enough to make her cry.

nientedi'meno, niente'meno *av* actually, even ♦ *escl* really!, I say!

'Niger ['nidʒer] *sm*: **il** ~ Niger; (*fiume*) the Niger.

Ni'geria [ni'dʒɛrja] *sf* Nigeria.

nigeri'ano, a [nidʒe'rjano] *ag, sm/f* Nigerian.

'Nilo *sm*: **il** ~ the Nile.

'nimbo *sm* halo.

'ninfa *sf* nymph.

nin'fea *sf* water lily.

nin'fomane *sf* nymphomaniac.

ninna'nanna *sf* lullaby.

'ninnolo *sm* (*balocco*) plaything; (*gingillo*) knick-knack.

ni'pote *sm/f* (*di zii*) nephew/niece; (*di nonni*) grandson/daughter, grandchild.

nip'ponico, a, ci, che *ag* Japanese.

niti'dezza [niti'dettsa] *sf* (*gen*) clearness; (*di stile*) clarity; (*FOT, TV*) sharpness.

'nitido, a *ag* clear; (*immagine*) sharp, well-defined.

ni'trato *sm* nitrate.

'nitrico, a, ci, che *ag* nitric.

ni'trire *vi* to neigh.

ni'trito *sm* (*di cavallo*) neighing *q*; neigh; (*CHIM*) nitrite.

nitroglice'rina [nitroglitʃe'rina] *sf* nitroglycerine.

'niveo, a *ag* snow-white.

'Nizza ['nittsa] *sf* Nice.

nn *abbr* (= *numeri*) nos.

NO *sigla* = Novara.

no *av* (*risposta*) no; **vieni o** ~**?** are you coming or not?; **come** ~**!** of course!, certainly!; **perché** ~**?** why not?

N.O. *abbr* (= *nordovest*) NW.

nobil'donna *sf* noblewoman.

'nobile *ag* noble ♦ *sm/f* noble, nobleman/woman.

nobili'are *ag* noble.

nobili'tare *vt* (*anche fig*) to ennoble; ~**rsi** *vr* (*rendersi insigne*) to distinguish o.s.

nobiltà *sf* nobility; (*di azione etc*) nobleness.

nobilu'omo *sm, pl* **-u'omini** nobleman.

'nocca, che *sf* (*ANAT*) knuckle.

'noccio *etc* ['nottʃo] *vb vedi* **nuocere.**

nocci'ola [not'tʃɔla] *sf* hazelnut ♦ *ag inv* (*anche*: **color** ~) hazel, light brown.

noccio'lina [nottʃo'lina] *sf* (*anche*: ~ **americana**) peanut.

'nocciolo ['nottʃolo] *sm* (*di frutto*) stone; (*fig*) heart, core; [not'tʃɔlo] (*albero*) hazel.

'noce ['notʃe] *sm* (*albero*) walnut tree ♦ *sf* (*frutto*) walnut; **una** ~ **di burro** (*CUC*) a

knob of butter (*Brit*), a dab of butter (*US*); ~ **di cocco** coconut; ~ **moscata** nutmeg.

noce'pesca, sche [notʃe'pɛska] *sf* nectarine.

no'cevo *etc* [no'tʃevo] *vb vedi* **nuocere.**

noci'uto [no'tʃuto] *pp di* **nuocere.**

no'civo, a [no'tʃivo] *ag* harmful, noxious.

'nocqui *etc vb vedi* **nuocere.**

'nodo *sm* (*di cravatta, legname, NAUT*) knot; (*AUT, FERR*) junction; (*MED, ASTR, BOT*) node; (*fig: legame*) bond, tie; (: *punto centrale*) heart, crux; **avere un** ~ **alla gola** to have a lump in one's throat; **tutti i** ~**i vengono al pettine** (*proverbio*) your sins will find you out.

no'doso, a *ag* (*tronco*) gnarled.

'nodulo *sm* (*ANAT, BOT*) nodule.

'noi *pronome* (*soggetto*) we; (*oggetto: per dare rilievo, con preposizione*) us; ~ **stessi(e)** we ourselves; (*oggetto*) ourselves; **da** ~ (*nel nostro paese*) in our country, where we come from; (*a casa nostra*) at our house.

'noia *sf* boredom; (*disturbo, impaccio*) bother *q*, trouble *q*; **avere qn/qc a** ~ not to like sb/sth; **mi è venuto a** ~ I'm tired of it; **dare** ~ **a** to annoy; **avere delle** ~**e con qn** to have trouble with sb.

noi'altri *pronome* we.

noi'oso, a *ag* boring; (*fastidioso*) annoying, troublesome.

noleggi'are [noled'dʒare] *vt* (*prendere a noleggio*) to hire (*Brit*), rent; (*dare a noleggio*) to hire out (*Brit*), rent out; (*aereo, nave*) to charter.

noleggia'tore, 'trice [noleddʒa'tore] *sm/f* hirer (*Brit*), renter; charterer.

no'leggio [no'leddʒo] *sm* hire (*Brit*), rental; charter.

no'lente *ag*: **volente o** ~ whether one likes it or not, willy-nilly.

'nolo *sm* hire (*Brit*), rental; charter; (*per trasporto merci*) freight; **prendere/dare a** ~ **qc** to hire/hire out sth (*Brit*), rent/rent out sth.

'nomade *ag* nomadic ♦ *sm/f* nomad.

noma'dismo *sm* nomadism.

'nome *sm* name; (*LING*) noun; **in** *o* **a** ~ **di** in the name of; **di** *o* **per** ~ (*chiamato*) called, named; **conoscere qn di** ~ to know sb by name; **fare il** ~ **di qn** to name sb; **faccia pure il mio** ~ feel free to mention my name; ~ **d'arte** stage name; ~ **di battesimo** Christian name; ~ **depositato** trade name; ~ **di famiglia** surname; ~ **da ragazza** maiden name; ~ **da sposata** married name.

no'mea *sf* notoriety.

no'mignolo [no'miɲɲolo] *sm* nickname.

'nomina *sf* appointment.

nomi'nale *ag* nominal; (*LING*) noun *cpd*.

nomi'nare *vt* to name; (*eleggere*) to

appoint; (*citare*) to mention; **non l'ho mai sentito ~** I've never heard of it (*o* him).

nomina'tivo, a *ag* (*LING*) nominative; (*COMM*) registered ♦ *sm* (*LING: anche:* **caso ~**) nominative (case); (*COMM, AMM*) name.

non *av* not ♦ *prefisso* non-; **grazie — ~ c'è di che** thank you — don't mention it; **i ~ credenti** the unbelievers; *vedi* **affatto, appena** *etc*.

nonché [non'ke] *cong* (*tanto più, tanto meno*) let alone; (*e inoltre*) as well as.

nonconfor'mista, i, e *ag, sm/f* nonconformist.

noncu'rante *ag*: **~ (di)** careless (of), indifferent (to); **con fare ~** with a nonchalant air.

noncu'ranza [nonku'rantsa] *sf* carelessness, indifference; **un'aria di ~** a nonchalant air.

nondi'meno *cong* (*tuttavia*) however; (*nonostante*) nevertheless.

'nonno, a *sm/f* grandfather/mother; (*in senso più familiare*) grandma/grandpa; **~i** *smpl* grandparents.

non'nulla *sm inv*: **un ~** nothing, a trifle.

'nono, a *num* ninth.

nonos'tante *prep* in spite of, notwithstanding ♦ *cong* although, even though.

non plus 'ultra *sm inv*: **il ~ (di)** the last word (in).

nontiscordardimé *sm inv* (*BOT*) forget-me-not.

nord *sm* north ♦ *ag inv* north; (*regione*) northern; **verso ~** north, northwards; **l'America del N~** North America.

nor'dest *sm* north-east.

'nordico, a, ci, che *ag* nordic, northern European.

nor'dista, i, e *ag, sm/f* Yankee.

nor'dovest *sm* north-west.

Norim'berga *sf* Nuremberg.

'norma *sf* (*principio*) norm; (*regola*) regulation, rule; (*consuetudine*) custom, rule; **~ normally**; **a ~ di legge** according to law, as laid down by law; **al di sopra della ~** above average, above the norm; **per sua ~ e regola** for your information; **proporsi una ~ di vita** to set o.s. rules to live by; **~e di sicurezza** safety regulations; **~e per l'uso** instructions for use.

nor'male *ag* normal.

normalità *sf* normality.

normaliz'zare [normalid'dzare] *vt* to normalize, bring back to normal.

normal'mente *av* normally.

Norman'dia *sf*: **la ~** Normandy.

nor'manno, a *ag, sm/f* Norman.

norma'tivo, a *ag* normative ♦ *sf* regulations *pl*.

norve'gese [norve'dʒese] *ag, sm/f, sm* Norwegian.

Nor'vegia [nor'vedʒa] *sf*: **la ~** Norway.

noso'comio *sm* hospital.

nostal'gia [nostal'dʒia] *sf* (*di casa, paese*) homesickness; (*del passato*) nostalgia.

nos'talgico, a, ci, che [nos'taldʒiko] *ag* homesick; nostalgic ♦ *sm/f* (*POL*) person *who hopes for the return of Fascism*.

nos'trano, a *ag* local; (*pianta, frutta*) home-produced.

'nostro, a *det*: **il(la) ~(a)** *etc* our ♦ *pronome*: **il(la) ~(a)** *etc* ours ♦ *sm*: **abbiamo speso del ~** we spent our own money ♦ *sf*: **la ~a** (*opinione*) our view; **i ~i** our family; our own people; **è dei ~i** he's one of us; **è dalla ~a** (*parte*) he's on our side; **anche noi abbiamo avuto le ~e** (*disavventure*) we've had our problems too; **alla ~a!** (*brindisi*) to us!

nos'tromo *sm* boatswain.

'nota *sf* (*segno*) mark; (*comunicazione scritta, MUS*) note; (*fattura*) bill; (*elenco*) list; **prendere ~ di qc** to note sth, make a note of sth, write sth down; (*fig: fare attenzione*) to note sth, take note of sth; **degno di ~** noteworthy, worthy of note; **~e caratteristiche** distinguishing marks *o* features; **~e a piè di pagina** footnotes.

no'tabile *ag* notable; (*persona*) important ♦ *sm* prominent citizen.

no'taio *sm* notary.

no'tare *vt* (*segnare: errori*) to mark; (*registrare*) to note (down), write down; (*rilevare, osservare*) to note, notice; **farsi ~** to get o.s. noticed.

nota'rile *ag*: **atto ~** legal document (*authorized by a notary*); **studio ~** notary's office.

notazi'one [notat'tsjone] *sf* (*MUS*) notation.

no'tevole *ag* (*talento*) notable, remarkable; (*peso*) considerable.

no'tifica, che *sf* notification.

notifi'care *vt* (*DIR*): **~ qc a qn** to notify sb of sth, give sb notice of sth.

notificazi'one [notifikat'tsjone] *sf* notification.

no'tizia [no'tittsja] *sf* (*piece of*) news *sg*; (*informazione*) piece of information; **~e** *sfpl* news *sg*; information *sg*.

notizi'ario [notit'tsjarjo] *sm* (*RADIO, TV, STAMPA*) news *sg*.

'noto, a *ag* (well-)known.

notorietà *sf* fame; notoriety.

no'torio, a *ag* well-known; (*peg*) notorious.

not'tambulo, a *sm/f* night-bird (*fig*).

not'tata *sf* night.

'notte *sf* night; **di ~** at night; (*durante la ~*) in the night, during the night; **questa ~** (*passata*) last night; (*che viene*) tonight; **nella ~ dei tempi** in the mists of time; **come va? — peggio che andar di ~** how are things? — worse than ever; **~ bianca** sleepless night.

notte'tempo *av* at night; during the night.

'nottola *sf* (*ZOOL*) noctule.

not'turno, a *ag* nocturnal; (*servizio, guardiano*) night *cpd* ♦ *sf* (*SPORT*) evening fixture (*Brit*) *o* match.

nov. *abbr* (= *novembre*) Nov.

no'vanta *num* ninety.

novan'tenne *ag, sm/f* ninety-year-old.

novan'tesimo, a *num* ninetieth.

novan'tina *sf*: **una** ~ (**di**) about ninety.

'nove *num* nine.

novecen'tesco, a, schi, sche [novetʃen'tesko] *ag* twentieth-century.

nove'cento [nove'tʃento] *num* nine hundred ♦ *sm*: **il N**~ the twentieth century.

no'vella *sf* (*LETTERATURA*) short story.

novel'lino, a *ag* (*pivello*) green, inexperienced.

novel'lista, i, e *sm/f* short-story writer.

novel'listica *sf* (*arte*) short-story writing; (*insieme di racconti*) short stories *pl*.

no'vello, a *ag* (*piante, patate*) new; (*insalata, verdura*) early; (*sposo*) newly-married.

no'vembre *sm* November; *per fraseologia vedi* **luglio**.

novem'brino, a *ag* November *cpd*.

nove'mila *num* nine thousand.

noven'nale *ag* (*che dura 9 anni*) nine-year *cpd*; (*ogni 9 anni*) nine-yearly.

novi'lunio *sm* (*ASTR*) new moon.

novità *sf inv* novelty; (*innovazione*) innovation; (*cosa originale, insolita*) something new; (*notizia*) (piece of) news *sg*; **le** ~ **della moda** the latest fashions.

novizi'ato [novit'tsjato] *sm* (*REL*) novitiate; (*tirocinio*) apprenticeship.

no'vizio, a [no'vittsjo] *sm/f* (*REL*) novice; (*tirocinante*) beginner, apprentice.

nozi'one [not'tsjone] *sf* notion, idea; ~**i** *sfpl* (*rudimenti*) basic knowledge *sg*, rudiments.

nozio'nismo [nottsjo'nizmo] *sm* superficial knowledge.

nozio'nistico, a, ci, che [nottsjo'nistiko] *ag* superficial.

'nozze ['nottse] *sfpl* wedding *sg*, marriage *sg*; ~ **d'argento/d'oro** silver/golden wedding *sg*.

N.P.A. *abbr* = **nave portaerei**.

ns. *abbr* (*COMM*) = **nostro**.

NU *sigla* = *Nuoro*.

N.U. *sigla* (= *Nazioni Unite*) UN.

'nube *sf* cloud.

nubi'fragio [nubi'fradʒo] *sm* cloudburst.

'nubile *ag* (*donna*) unmarried, single.

'nuca, che *sf* nape of the neck.

nucle'are *ag* nuclear.

'nucleo *sm* nucleus; (*gruppo*) team, unit, group; (*MIL, POLIZIA*) squad; ~ **antidroga** anti-drugs squad; **il** ~ **familiare** the family unit.

nu'dismo *sm* nudism.

nu'dista, i, e *sm/f* nudist.

nudità *sf inv* nudity, nakedness; (*di paesaggio*) bareness ♦ *sfpl* (*parti nude del corpo*) nakedness *sg*.

'nudo, a *ag* (*persona*) bare, naked, nude; (*membra*) bare, naked; (*montagna*) bare ♦ *sm* (*ARTE*) nude; **a occhio** ~ to the naked eye; **a piedi** ~**i** barefoot; **mettere a** ~ (*cuore, verità*) to lay bare; **gli ha detto** ~ **e crudo che** ... he told him bluntly that ....

'nugolo *sm*: **un** ~ **di** a whole host of.

'nulla *pronome, av* = **niente** ♦ *sm*: **il** ~ nothing; **svanire nel** ~ to vanish into thin air; **basta un** ~ **per farlo arrabbiare** he gets annoyed over the slightest thing.

nulla'osta *sm inv* authorization.

nulla'tenente *ag*: **essere** ~ to own nothing ♦ *sm/f* person with no property.

nullità *sf inv* nullity; (*persona*) nonentity.

'nullo, a *ag* useless, worthless; (*DIR*) null (and void); (*SPORT*): **incontro** ~ draw.

nume'rale *ag, sm* numeral.

nume'rare *vt* to number.

numerazi'one [numerat'tsjone] *sf* numbering; (*araba, decimale*) notation.

nu'merico, a, ci, che *ag* numerical.

'numero *sm* number; (*romano, arabo*) numeral; (*di spettacolo*) act, turn; **dare i** ~**i** (*farneticare*) not to be all there; **tanto per fare** ~ **invitiamo anche lui** why don't we invite him to make up the numbers?; **ha tutti i** ~**i per riuscire** he's got what it takes to succeed; **che** ~ **tuo fratello!** your brother is a real character!; ~ **civico** house number; ~ **chiuso** (*UNIVERSITÀ*) selective entry system; ~ **doppio** (*di rivista*) issue with supplement; ~ **di scarpe** size of shoe.

nume'roso, a *ag* numerous, many; (*folla, famiglia*) large.

'nunzio ['nuntsjo] *sm* (*REL*) nuncio.

nu'occio *etc* ['nwɔttʃo] *vb vedi* **nuocere**.

nu'ocere ['nwɔtʃere] *vi*: ~ **a** to harm, damage; **il tentar non nuoce** (*proverbio*) there's no harm in trying.

nuoci'uto, a [nwo'tʃuto] *pp di* **nuocere**.

nu'ora *sf* daughter-in-law.

nuo'tare *vi* to swim; (*galleggiare: oggetti*) to float; ~ **a rana/sul dorso** to do the breast stroke/backstroke.

nuo'tata *sf* swim.

nuota'tore, 'trice *sm/f* swimmer.

nu'oto *sm* swimming.

nuova'mente *av* again.

Nu'ova York *sf* New York.

Nu'ova Ze'landa [-dze'landa] *sf*: **la** ~ New Zealand.

nu'ovo, a *ag* new ♦ *sf* (*notizia*) (piece of) news *sg*; **come** ~ as good as new; **di** ~ again; **fino a** ~ **ordine** until further notice; **il suo volto non mi è** ~ I know his face;

rimettere a ~ (*cosa, macchina*) to do up like new; **anno** ~, **vita** ~**a!** it's time to turn over a new leaf!; ~ **fiammante** *o* **di zecca** brand-new; **la N~a Guinea** New Guinea; **la N~a Inghilterra** New England; **la N~a Scozia** Nova Scotia.

nu'trice [nu'tritʃe] *sf* wet nurse.

nutri'ente *ag* nutritious, nourishing.

nutri'mento *sm* food, nourishment.

nu'trire *vt* to feed; (*fig: sentimenti*) to harbour (*Brit*), harbor (*US*), nurse.

nutri'tivo, a *ag* nutritional; (*alimento*) nutritious.

nu'trito, a *ag* (*numeroso*) large; (*fitto*) heavy; **ben/mal** ~ well/poorly fed.

nutrizi'one [nutrit'tsjone] *sf* nutrition.

'**nuvolo, a** *ag* cloudy ♦ *sf* cloud.

nuvolosità *sf* cloudiness.

nuvo'loso, a *ag* cloudy.

nuzi'ale [nut'tsjale] *ag* nuptial; wedding *cpd*.

'**nylon** ['nailən] *sm* nylon.

O

O, o [ɔ] *sf o m inv* (*lettera*) O, o; ~ **come Otranto** ≈ O for Oliver (*Brit*), O for Oboe (*US*).

o *cong* (*dav V spesso* **od**) or; ~ ... ~ either ... or; ~ **l'uno** ~ **l'altro** either (of them); ~ **meglio** or rather.

O. *abbr* (= *ovest*) W.

'**oasi** *sf inv* oasis.

obbedi'ente *etc vedi* **ubbidiente** *etc.*

obbiet'tare *etc vedi* **obiettare** *etc.*

obbli'gare *vt* (*costringere*): ~ **qn a fare** to force *o* oblige sb to do; (*DIR*) to bind; ~**rsi** *vr*: ~**rsi a fare** to undertake to do; ~**rsi per qn** (*DIR*) to stand surety for sb, act as guarantor for sb.

obbliga'tissimo, a *ag* (*ringraziamento*): ~**!** much obliged!

obbli'gato, a *ag* (*costretto, grato*) obliged; (*percorso, tappa*) set, fixed; **passaggio** ~ (*fig*) essential requirement.

obbliga'torio, a *ag* compulsory, obligatory.

obbligazi'one [obbligat'tsjone] *sf* obligation; (*COMM*) bond, debenture; ~ **dello Stato** government bond; ~**i convertibili** convertible loan stock, convertible debentures.

obbligazio'nista, i, e [obbligattsjo'nista] *sm/f* bond-holder.

'**obbligo, ghi** *sm* obligation; (*dovere*) duty; **avere l'**~ **di fare, essere nell'**~ **di fare** to be obliged to do; **essere d'**~ (*discorso, applauso*) to be called for; **avere degli** ~**ghi**

con *o* **verso qn** to be under an obligation to sb, be indebted to sb; **le formalità d'**~ the necessary formalities.

obb.mo *abbr* = **obbligatissimo**.

ob'brobrio *sm* disgrace; (*fig*) mess, eyesore.

obe'lisco, schi *sm* obelisk.

obe'rato, a *ag*: ~ **di** (*lavoro*) overloaded *o* overburdened with; (*debiti*) crippled with.

obesità *sf* obesity.

o'beso, a *ag* obese.

obiet'tare *vt*: ~ **che** to object that; ~ **su qc** to object to sth, raise objections concerning sth.

obiettiva'mente *av* objectively.

obiettività *sf* objectivity.

obiet'tivo, a *ag* objective ♦ *sm* (*OTTICA, FOT*) lens *sg*, objective; (*MIL, fig*) objective.

obiet'tore *sm* objector; ~ **di coscienza** conscientious objector.

obiezi'one [objet'tsjone] *sf* objection.

obi'torio *sm* morgue.

o'bliquo, a *ag* oblique; (*inclinato*) slanting; (*fig*) devious, underhand; **sguardo** ~ sidelong glance.

oblite'rare *vt* (*francobollo*) to cancel; (*biglietto*) to stamp.

oblitera'trice [oblitera'tritʃe] *sf* (*anche:* **macchina** ~) cancelling machine; stamping machine.

oblò *sm inv* porthole.

o'blungo, a, ghi, ghe *ag* oblong.

'**oboe** *sm* oboe.

obsole'scenza [obsoleʃ'ʃentsa] *sf* (*ECON*) obsolescence.

obso'leto, a *ag* obsolete.

OC *abbr* (= *onde corte*) SW.

'**oca, pl** '**oche** *sf* goose.

o'caggine [o'kaddʒine] *sf* silliness, stupidity.

occasio'nale *ag* (*incontro*) chance; (*cliente, guadagni*) casual, occasional.

occasi'one *sf* (*caso favorevole*) opportunity; (*causa, motivo, circostanza*) occasion; (*COMM*) bargain; **all'**~ should the need arise; **alla prima** ~ at the first opportunity; **d'**~ (*a buon prezzo*) bargain *cpd*; (*usato*) secondhand.

occhi'aia [ok'kjaja] *sf* eye socket; ~**e** *sfpl* (*sotto gli occhi*) shadows (under the eyes).

occhi'ali [ok'kjali] *smpl* glasses, spectacles; ~ **da sole** sunglasses.

occhi'ata [ok'kjata] *sf* look, glance; **dare un'**~ **a** to have a look at.

occhieggi'are [okkjed'dʒare] *vi* (*apparire qua e là*) to peep (out).

occhi'ello [ok'kjello] *sm* buttonhole; (*asola*) eyelet.

'**occhio** ['ɔkkjo] *sm* eye; ~**!** careful!, watch out!; **a** ~ **nudo** with the naked eye; **a quattr'**~**i** privately, in private; **avere** ~ to have a good eye; **chiudere un** ~ **(su)** (*fig*) to turn a blind eye (to), shut one's eyes (to); **costare un ~ della testa** to cost a fortune; **dare all'~** o **nell'~ a qn** to catch sb's eye; **fare l'~ a qc** to get used to sth; **tenere d'~ qn** to keep an eye on sth; **vedere di buon/mal ~ qc** to look favourably/unfavourably on sth.

occhio'lino [okkjo'lino] *sm:* **fare l'~ a qn** to wink at sb.

occiden'tale [ottʃiden'tale] *ag* western ♦ *sm/f* Westerner.

occi'dente [ottʃi'dente] *sm* west; (*POL*): **l'O~** the West; **a ~** in the west.

oc'cipite [ot'tʃipite] *sm* back of the head, occiput (*ANAT*).

oc'cludere *vt* to block.

occlusi'one *sf* blockage, obstruction.

oc'cluso, a *pp di* occludere.

occor'rente *ag* necessary ♦ *sm* all that is necessary.

occor'renza [okkor'rentsa] *sf* necessity, need; **all'~** in case of need.

oc'correre *vi* to be needed, be required ♦ *vb impers:* **occorre farlo** it must be done; **occorre che tu parta** you must leave, you'll have to leave; **mi occorrono i soldi** I need the money.

oc'corso, a *pp di* occorrere.

occulta'mento *sm* concealment.

occul'tare *vt* to hide, conceal.

oc'culto, a *ag* hidden, concealed; (*scienze, forze*) occult.

occu'pante *sm/f* (*di casa*) occupier, occupant; **~ abusivo** squatter.

occu'pare *vt* to occupy; (*manodopera*) to employ; (*ingombrare*) to occupy, take up; **~rsi** *vr* to occupy o.s., keep o.s. busy; (*impiegarsi*) to get a job; **~rsi di** (*interessarsi*) to take an interest in; (*prendersi cura di*) to look after, take care of.

occu'pato, a *ag* (*MIL, POL*) occupied; (*persona: affaccendato*) busy; (*posto, sedia*) taken; (*toilette, TEL*) engaged.

occupazio'nale [okkupattsjo'nale] *ag* employment *cpd*, of employment.

occupazi'one [okkupat'tsjone] *sf* occupation; (*impiego, lavoro*) job; (*ECON*) employment.

Oce'ania [otʃe'anja] *sf:* **l'~** Oceania.

o'ceano [o'tʃɛano] *sm* ocean.

'ocra *sf* ochre.

'OCSE *sigla f* (= *Organizzazione per la Cooperazione e lo Sviluppo Economico*) OECD (= *Organization for Economic Cooperation and Development*).

ocu'lare *ag* ocular, eye *cpd*; **testimone ~** eye witness.

ocula'tezza [okula'tettsa] *sf* caution; shrewdness.

ocu'lato, a *ag* (*attento*) cautious, prudent; (*accorto*) shrewd.

ocu'lista, i, e *sm/f* eye specialist, oculist.

od *cong vedi* o.

'ode *sf* ode.

'ode *etc vb vedi* **udire**.

odi'are *vt* to hate, detest.

odi'erno, a *ag* today's, of today; (*attuale*) present; **in data ~a** (*formale*) today.

'odio *sm* hatred; **avere in ~ qc/qn** to hate o detest sth/sb.

odi'oso, a *ag* hateful, odious; **rendersi ~ (a)** to make o.s. unpopular (with).

'odo *etc vb vedi* **udire**.

odontoi'atra, i, e *sm/f* dentist, dental surgeon.

odontoia'tria *sf* dentistry.

odonto'tecnico, ci *sm* dental technician.

odo'rare *vt* (*annusare*) to smell; (*profumare*) to perfume, scent ♦ *vi:* **~ (di)** to smell (of).

odo'rato *sm* sense of smell.

o'dore *sm* smell; **gli ~i** *smpl* (*CUC*) (aromatic) herbs; **sentire ~ di qc** to smell sth; **morire in ~ di santità** (*REL*) to die in the odour (*Brit*) o odor (*US*) of sanctity.

odo'roso, a *ag* sweet-smelling.

of'fendere *vt* to offend; (*violare*) to break, violate; (*insultare*) to insult; (*ferire*) to hurt; **~rsi** *vr* (*con senso reciproco*) to insult one another; (*risentirsi*): **~rsi (di)** to take offence (at), be offended (by).

offen'sivo, a *ag, sf* offensive.

offen'sore *sm* offender; (*MIL*) aggressor.

offe'rente *sm* (*in aste*): **al migliore ~** to the highest bidder.

of'ferto, a *pp di* **offrire** ♦ *sf* offer; (*donazione, anche REL*) offering; (*in gara d'appalto*) tender; (*in aste*) bid; (*ECON*) supply; **fare un'~a** to make an offer; (*per appalto*) to tender; (*ad un'asta*) to bid; **~a pubblica d'acquisto (OPA)** takeover bid; **~a pubblica di vendita (OPV)** public offer for sale; **~a reale** tender; **"~e d'impiego"** (*STAMPA*) "situations vacant" (*Brit*), "help wanted" (*US*).

of'feso, a *pp di* **offendere** ♦ *ag* offended; (*fisicamente*) hurt, injured ♦ *sm/f* offended party ♦ *sf* insult, affront; (*MIL*) attack; (*DIR*) offence (*Brit*), offense (*US*); **essere ~ con qn** to be annoyed with sb; **parte ~a** (*DIR*) plaintiff.

offi'cina [offi'tʃina] *sf* workshop.

of'frire *vt* to offer; **~rsi** *vr* (*proporsi*) to offer (o.s.), volunteer; (*occasione*) to present itself; (*esporsi*): **~rsi a** to expose o.s. to; **ti offro da bere** I'll buy you a drink; **"offresi posto di segretaria"** "secretarial vacancy", "vacancy for secretary"; **"segretaria offresi"** "secretary seeks post".

offus'care *vt* to obscure, darken; (*fig: intelletto*) to dim, cloud; (: *fama*) to obscure, overshadow; **~rsi** *vr* to grow dark; to cloud, grow dim; to be obscured.

of'talmico, a, ci, che *ag* ophthalmic.

oggettività [oddʒettivi'ta] *sf* objectivity.

ogget'tivo, a [oddʒet'tivo] *ag* objective.

og'getto [od'dʒetto] *sm* object; *(materia, argomento)* subject (matter); *(in lettere commerciali)*: ~ ... re ...; **essere ~ di** *(critiche, controversia)* to be the subject of; *(odio, pietà etc)* to be the object of; **essere ~ di scherno** to be a laughing stock; **in ~ a quanto detto** *(in lettere)* as regards the matter mentioned above; **~i preziosi** valuables, articles of value; **~i smarriti** lost property *sg* (*Brit*), lost and found *sg* (*US*).

'oggi ['ɔddʒi] *av, sm* today; **~ stesso** today, this very day; **~ come ~** at present, as things stand; **dall' ~ al domani** from one day to the next; **a tutt'~** up till now, till today; **le spese a tutt'~ sono ...** expenses to date are ...; **~ a otto** a week today.

oggigi'orno [oddʒi'dʒorno] *av* nowadays.

o'giva [o'dʒiva] *sf* ogive, pointed arch.

'ogni ['oɲɲi] *det* every, each; *(tutti)* all; *(con valore distributivo)* every; **~ uomo è mortale** all men are mortal; **viene ~ due giorni** he comes every two days; **~ cosa** everything; **ad ~ costo** at all costs, at any price; **in ~ luogo** everywhere; **~ tanto** every so often; **~ volta che** every time that.

Ognis'santi [oɲɲis'santi] *sm* All Saints' Day.

o'gnuno [oɲ'ɲuno] *pronome* everyone, everybody.

'ohi *escl* oh!; *(esprimente dolore)* ow!

ohimè *escl* oh dear!

'OIL *sigla f* (= *Organizzazione Internazionale del Lavoro*) ILO.

OL *abbr* (= *onde lunghe*) LW.

O'landa *sf*: **l'~** Holland.

olan'dese *ag* Dutch ♦ *sm* (*LING*) Dutch ♦ *sm/f* Dutchman/woman; **gli O~i** the Dutch.

ole'andro *sm* oleander.

ole'ato, a *ag*: **carta ~a** greaseproof paper (*Brit*), wax paper (*US*).

oleo'dotto *sm* oil pipeline.

ole'oso, a *ag* oily; *(che contiene olio)* oil *cpd*.

ol'fatto *sm* sense of smell.

oli'are *vt* to oil.

olia'tore *sm* oil can, oiler.

oli'era *sf* oil cruet.

olim'piadi *sfpl* Olympic Games.

o'limpico, a, ci, che *ag* Olympic.

'olio *sm* oil; *(PITTURA)*: **un (quadro a) ~** an oil painting; **sott'~** (*CUC*) in oil; **~ di fegato di merluzzo** cod liver oil; **~ d'oliva** olive oil; **~ santo** holy oil; **~ di semi** vegetable oil; **~ solare** suntan oil.

o'liva *sf* olive.

oli'vastro, a *ag* olive(-coloured) (*Brit*), olive(-colored) (*US*); *(carnagione)* sallow.

oli'veto *sm* olive grove.

o'livo *sm* olive tree.

'olmo *sm* elm.

olo'causto *sm* holocaust.

OLP *sigla f* (= *Organizzazione per la Liberazione della Palestina*) PLO.

oltraggi'are [oltrad'dʒare] *vt* to offend, insult.

ol'traggio [ol'traddʒo] *sm* offence (*Brit*), offense (*US*), insult; *(DIR)*: **~ al pudore** indecent behaviour (*Brit*) *o* behavior (*US*); **~ alla corte** contempt of court.

oltraggi'oso, a [oltrad'dʒoso] *ag* offensive.

ol'tralpe *av* beyond the Alps.

ol'tranza [ol'trantsa] *sf*: **a ~** to the last, to the bitter end; **sciopero ad ~** all-out strike.

oltran'zismo [oltran'tsizmo] *sm* (*POL*) extremism.

oltran'zista, i, e [oltran'tsista] *sm/f* (*POL*) extremist.

'oltre *av* (*più in là*) further; *(di più: aspettare)* longer, more ♦ *prep* (*di là da*) beyond, over, on the other side of; *(più di)* more than, over; *(in aggiunta a)* besides; *(eccetto)*: **~ a** except, apart from; **~ a tutto** on top of all that.

oltrecor'tina *av* behind the Iron Curtain; **paesi d'~** Iron Curtain countries.

oltre'manica *av* across the Channel.

oltre'mare *av* overseas.

oltre'modo *av* extremely, greatly.

oltreo'ceano [oltreo'tʃeano] *av* overseas ♦ *sm*: **paesi d'~** overseas countries.

oltrepas'sare *vt* to go beyond, exceed.

OM *abbr* (= *onde medie*) MW; (*MIL*) = *ospedale militare*.

o'maggio [o'maddʒo] *sm* (*dono*) gift; (*segno di rispetto*) homage, tribute; **~i** *smpl* (*complimenti*) respects; **in ~** (*copia, biglietto*) complimentary; **rendere ~ a** to pay homage *o* tribute to; **presentare i propri ~i a qn** (*formale*) to pay one's respects to sb.

'Oman *sm*: **l'~** Oman.

ombeli'cale *ag* umbilical.

ombe'lico, chi *sm* navel.

'ombra *sf* (*zona non assolata, fantasma*) shade; (*sagoma scura*) shadow ♦ *ag inv*: **bandiera ~** flag of convenience; **governo ~** (*POL*) shadow cabinet; **sedere all'~** to sit in the shade; **nell'~** (*tramare, agire*) secretly; **restare nell'~** (*fig: persona*) to remain in obscurity; **senza ~ di dubbio** without the shadow of a doubt.

ombreggi'are [ombred'dʒare] *vt* to shade.

om'brello *sm* umbrella; **~ da sole** parasol, sunshade.

ombrel'lone *sm* beach umbrella.

om'bretto *sm* eyeshadow.

om'broso, a *ag* shady, shaded; (*cavallo*) nervous, skittish; (*persona*) touchy, easily offended.

ome'lette [ɔmə'lɛt] *sf inv* omelet(te).

ome'lia *sf* (*REL*) homily, sermon.

omeopa'tia *sf* homoeopathy (*Brit*), homeopathy (*US*).

omeo'patico, a, ci, che *ag* homoeopathic (*Brit*), homeopathic (*US*) ♦ *sm* homoeopath (*Brit*), homeopath (*US*).

omertà *sf* conspiracy of silence.

o'messo, a *pp di* **omettere.**

o'mettere *vt* to omit, leave out; ~ **di fare** to omit *o* fail to do.

omi'cida, i, e [omi'tʃida] *ag* homicidal, murderous ♦ *sm/f* murderer/murderess.

omi'cidio [omi'tʃidjo] *sm* murder; ~ **colposo** (*DIR*) culpable homicide; ~ **premeditato** (*DIR*) murder.

o'misi *etc vb vedi* **omettere.**

omissi'one *sf* omission; **reato d'~** criminal negligence; ~ **di atti d'ufficio** negligence (*by a public employee*); ~ **di denuncia** failure to report a crime; ~ **di soccorso** (*DIR*) failure to stop and give assistance.

omogeneiz'zato [omodʒeneid'dzato] *sm* baby food.

omo'geneo, a [omo'dʒɛneo] *ag* homogeneous.

omolo'gare *vt* (*DIR*) to approve, recognize; (*ratificare*) to ratify.

omologazi'one [omologat'tsjone] *sf* approval; ratification.

o'mologo, a, ghi, ghe *ag* homologous, corresponding.

o'monimo, a *sm/f* namesake ♦ *sm* (*LING*) homonym.

omosessu'ale *ag*, *sm/f* homosexual.

O.M.S. *sigla f vedi* **Organizzazione Mondiale della Sanità.**

On. *abbr* (*POL*) = **onorevole.**

'oncia, ce ['ontʃa] *sf* ounce.

'onda *sf* wave; **mettere** *o* **mandare in** ~ (*RADIO, TV*) to broadcast; **andare in** ~ (*RADIO, TV*) to go on the air; **~e corte/medie/lunghe** short/medium/long wave *sg*; **l'~ verde** (*AUT*) synchronized traffic lights *pl*.

on'data *sf* wave, billow; (*fig*) wave, surge; **a ~e** in waves; ~ **di caldo** heatwave; ~ **di freddo** cold spell *o* snap.

'onde *cong* (*affinché: col congiuntivo*) so that, in order that; (*: con l'infinito*) so as to, in order to.

ondeggi'are [onded'dʒare] *vi* (*acqua*) to ripple; (*muoversi sulle onde: barca*) to rock, roll; (*fig: muoversi come le onde, barcollare*) to sway; (*: essere incerto*) to waver.

on'doso, a *ag* (*moto*) of the waves.

ondu'lato, a *ag* (*capelli*) wavy; (*terreno*) undulating; **cartone** ~ corrugated paper; **lamiera ~a** sheet of corrugated iron.

ondula'torio, a *ag* undulating; (*FISICA*) undulatory, wave *cpd*.

ondulazi'one [ondulat'tsjone] *sf* undulation; (*acconciatura*) wave.

one'rato, a *ag*: ~ **di** burdened with, loaded with.

'onere *sm* burden; ~ **finanziario** financial charge; **~i fiscali** taxes.

one'roso, a *ag* (*fig*) heavy, onerous.

onestà *sf* honesty.

onesta'mente *av* honestly; fairly; virtuously; (*in verità*) honestly, frankly.

o'nesto, a *ag* (*probo, retto*) honest; (*giusto*) fair; (*casto*) chaste, virtuous.

'onice ['ɔnitʃe] *sf* onyx.

o'nirico, a, ci, che *ag* dreamlike, dream *cpd.*

onnipo'tente *ag* omnipotent.

onnipre'sente *ag* omnipresent; (*scherzoso*) ubiquitous.

onnisci'ente [onniʃ'ʃɛnte] *ag* omniscient.

onniveg'gente [onnived'dʒɛnte] *ag* all-seeing.

ono'mastico, ci *sm* name day.

ono'ranze [ono'rantse] *sfpl* honours (*Brit*), honors (*US*).

ono'rare *vt* to honour (*Brit*), honor (*US*); (*far onore a*) to do credit to; **~rsi** *vr*: **~rsi di qc/di fare** to feel hono(u)red by sth/to do.

ono'rario, a *ag* honorary ♦ *sm* fee.

o'nore *sm* honour (*Brit*), honor (*US*); **in** ~ **di** in hono(u)r of; **fare gli ~i di casa** to play host (*o* hostess); **fare** ~ **a** to hono(u)r; (*pranzo*) to do justice to; (*famiglia*) to be a credit to; **farsi** ~ to distinguish o.s.; **posto d'~** place of hono(u)r; **a onor del vero** ... to tell the truth ....

ono'revole *ag* honourable (*Brit*), honorable (*US*) ♦ *sm/f* (*POL*) ≈ Member of Parliament (*Brit*), ≈ Congressman/woman (*US*).

onorifi'cenza [onorifi'tʃentsa] *sf* honour (*Brit*), honor (*US*); decoration.

ono'rifico, a, ci, che *ag* honorary.

'onta *sf* shame, disgrace; **ad** ~ **di** despite, notwithstanding.

on'tano *sm* alder.

'O.N.U. *sigla f* (= *Organizzazione delle Nazioni Unite*) UN, UNO.

OO.PP. *abbr vedi* **opere pubbliche.**

'OPA *sigla f vedi* **offerta pubblica d'acquisto.**

o'paco, a, chi, che *ag* (*vetro*) opaque; (*metallo*) dull, matt.

o'pale *sm o f* opal.

'opera *sf* (*gen*) work; (*azione rilevante*) action, deed, work; (*MUS*) work; opus; (*: melodramma*) opera; (*: teatro*) opera house; (*ente*) institution, organization; **per** ~ **sua** thanks to him; **fare** ~ **di persuasione presso qn** to try to convince sb; **mettersi/essere all'~** to get down to/be at work; ~ **d'arte** work of art; ~ **buffa** comic opera; ~ **lirica** (grand) opera; ~ **pia** religious charity; **~e pubbliche (OO.PP.)** public works; **~e di restauro/di scavo** restoration/excavation work sg.

ope'raio, a ag working-class; workers'; (ZOOL: ape, formica) worker cpd ♦ sm/f worker; **classe ~a** working class; **~ di fabbrica** factory worker; **~ di giornata** day labourer (Brit) o laborer (US); **~ specializzato** o **qualificato** skilled worker; **~ non specializzato** semi-skilled worker.

ope'rare vt to carry out, make; (MED) to operate on ♦ vi to operate, work; (rimedio) to act, work; (MED) to operate; **~rsi** vr to occur, take place; (MED) to have an operation; **~rsi d'appendicite** to have one's appendix out; **~ qn d'urgenza** to perform an emergency operation on sb.

opera'tivo, a ag operative, operating; **piano ~** (MIL) plan of operations.

ope'rato sm (comportamento) actions pl.

opera'tore, 'trice sm/f operator; (TV, CINEMA) cameraman; **aperto solo agli ~i** (COMM) open to the trade only; **~ di borsa** dealer on the stock exchange; **~ economico** agent, broker; **~ del suono** sound recordist; **~ turistico** tour operator.

opera'torio, a ag (MED) operating.

operazi'one [operat'tsjone] sf operation.

ope'retta sf (MUS) operetta, light opera.

operosità sf industry.

ope'roso, a ag industrious, hard-working.

opi'ficio [opi'fitʃo] sm factory, works pl.

opi'nabile ag (discutibile) debatable, questionable; **è ~** it is a matter of opinion.

opini'one sf opinion; **avere il coraggio delle proprie ~i** to have the courage of one's convictions; **l'~ pubblica** public opinion.

op là escl (per far saltare) hup!; (a bimbo che è caduto) upsy-daisy!

'oppio sm opium.

oppi'omane sm/f opium addict.

oppo'nente ag opposing ♦ sm/f opponent.

op'pongo etc vb vedi **opporre**.

op'porre vt to oppose; **opporsi** vr: **opporsi (a qc)** to oppose (sth); to object (to sth); **~ resistenza/un rifiuto** to offer resistance/ to refuse.

opportu'nista, i, e sm/f opportunist.

opportunità sf inv opportunity; (convenienza) opportuneness, timeliness.

oppor'tuno, a ag timely, opportune; (giusto) right, appropriate; **a tempo ~** at the right o the appropriate time.

op'posi etc vb vedi **opporre**.

opposi'tore, 'trice sm/f opposer, opponent.

opposizi'one [oppozit'tsjone] sf opposition; (DIR) objection; **essere in netta ~** (idee, opinioni) to clash, be in complete opposition; **fare ~ a qn/qc** to oppose sb/sth.

op'posto, a pp di **opporre** ♦ ag opposite; (opinioni) conflicting ♦ sm opposite, contrary; **all'~** on the contrary.

oppressi'one sf oppression.

oppres'sivo, a ag oppressive.

op'presso, a pp di **opprimere**.

oppres'sore sm oppressor.

oppri'mente ag (caldo, noia) oppressive; (persona) tiresome; (: deprimente) depressing.

op'primere vt (premere, gravare) to weigh down; (estenuare: sog: caldo) to suffocate, oppress; (tiranneggiare: popolo) to oppress.

oppu'gnare [oppuɲ'ɲare] vt (fig) to refute.

op'pure cong or (else).

op'tare vi: **~ per** (scegliere) to opt for, decide upon; (BORSA) to take (out) an option on.

'optimum sm inv optimum.

opu'lento, a ag (ricco) rich, wealthy, affluent; (: arredamento etc) opulent.

opu'lenza [opu'lentsa] sf (vedi ag) richness, wealth, affluence; opulence.

o'puscolo sm booklet, pamphlet.

OPV sigla f vedi **offerta pubblica di vendita**.

opzio'nale [optsjo'nale] ag optional.

opzi'one [op'tsjone] sf option.

OR sigla = Oristano.

'ora sf (60 minuti) hour; (momento) time; **che ~ è?, che ~e sono?** what time is it?; **domani a quest'~** this time tomorrow; **non veder l'~ di fare** to long to do, look forward to doing; **fare le ~e piccole** to stay up till the early hours (of the morning) o the small hours; **è ~ di partire** it's time to go; **di buon' ~** early; **alla buon'~!** at last!; **~ legale** o **estiva** summer time (Brit), daylight saving time (US); **~ locale** local time; **~ di pranzo** lunchtime; **~ di punta** (AUT) rush hour ♦ av (adesso) now; (poco fa): **è uscito proprio ~** he's just gone out; (tra poco) presently, in a minute; (correlativo): **~ ... ~** now ... now; **d'~ in avanti** o **poi** from now on; **or ~** just now, a moment ago; **~ come ~** right now, at present; **10 anni or sono** 10 years ago.

o'racolo sm oracle.

'orafo sm goldsmith.

o'rale ag, sm oral.

oral'mente av orally.

ora'mai av = **ormai**.

o'rario, a ag hourly; (fuso, segnale) time cpd; (velocità) per hour ♦ sm timetable, schedule; (di visite etc) hours pl, time(s pl); **~ di apertura/chiusura** opening/closing time; **~ di apertura degli sportelli** bank opening hours; **~ elastico** o **flessibile** (INDUSTRIA) flexitime; **~ ferroviario** railway timetable; **~ di lavoro/d'ufficio** working/ office hours.

o'rata sf sea bream.

ora'tore, 'trice sm/f speaker; orator.

ora'torio, a ag oratorical ♦ sm (REL) oratory; (MUS) oratorio ♦ sf (arte) oratory.

orazi'one [orat'tsjone] *sf* (*REL*) prayer; (*discorso*) speech, oration.

or'bene *cong* so, well (then).

'orbita *sf* (*ASTR, FISICA*) orbit; (*ANAT*) (eye-) socket.

orbi'tare *vi* to orbit.

'Orcadi *sfpl:* **le (isole)** ~ the Orkney Islands, the Orkneys.

or'chestra [or'kɛstra] *sf* orchestra.

orches'trale [orkes'trale] *ag* orchestral ♦ *sm/f* orchestra player.

orches'trare [orkes'trare] *vt* to orchestrate; (*fig*) to stage-manage.

orchi'dea [orki'dɛa] *sf* orchid.

'orcio ['ortʃo] *sm* jar.

'orco, chi *sm* ogre.

'orda *sf* horde.

or'digno [or'diɲɲo] *sm:* ~ **esplosivo** explosive device.

ordi'nale *ag, sm* ordinal.

ordina'mento *sm* order, arrangement; (*regolamento*) regulations *pl*, rules *pl*; ~ **scolastico/giuridico** education/legal system.

ordi'nanza [ordi'nantsa] *sf* (*DIR, MIL*) order; (*AMM: decreto*) decree; (*persona: MIL*) orderly, batman; **d'~** (*MIL*) regulation *cpd*; **ufficiale d'~** orderly; ~ **municipale** by(e)-law.

ordi'nare *vt* (*mettere in ordine*) to arrange, organize; (*COMM*) to order; (*prescrivere: medicina*) to prescribe; (*comandare*): ~ **a qn di fare qc** to order *o* command sb to do sth; (*REL*) to ordain.

ordi'nario, a *ag* (*comune*) ordinary; (*grossolano*) coarse, common ♦ *sm* ordinary; (*di università*) full professor.

ordina'tivo, a *ag* regulating, governing ♦ *sm* (*COMM*) order.

ordi'nato, a *ag* tidy, orderly.

ordinazi'one [ordinat'tsjone] *sf* (*COMM*) order; (*REL*) ordination; **fare un'~ di qc** to put in an order for sth, order sth; **eseguire qc su** ~ to make sth to order.

'ordine *sm* order; (*carattere*): **d'~ pratico** of a practical nature; **all'~** (*COMM: assegno*) to order; **di prim'~** first-class; **fino a nuovo** ~ until further notice; **essere in** ~ (*documenti*) to be in order; (*persona, stanza*) to be tidy; **mettere in** ~ to put in order, tidy (up); **richiamare all'~** to call to order; **le forze dell'~** the forces of law and order; ~ **d'acquisto** purchase order; **l'~ degli avvocati** ≈ the Bar; ~ **del giorno** (*di seduta*) agenda; (*MIL*) order of the day; **l'~ dei medici** ≈ the Medical Association; ~ **di pagamento** standing order (*Brit*), automatic payment (*US*); **l'~ pubblico** law and order; **~i (sacri)** (*REL*) holy orders.

or'dire *vt* (*fig*) to plot, scheme.

or'dito *sm* (*di tessuto*) warp.

orecchi'abile [orek'kjabile] *ag* (*canzone*) catchy.

orec'chino [orek'kino] *sm* earring.

o'recchio [o'rekkjo], *pl(f)* **o'recchie** *sm* (*ANAT*) ear; **avere** ~ to have a good ear (for music); **venire all'~ di qn** to come to sb's attention; **fare ~e da mercante (a)** to turn a deaf ear (to).

orecchi'oni [orek'kjoni] *smpl* (*MED*) mumps *sg.*

o'refice [o'refitʃe] *sm* goldsmith; jeweller (*Brit*), jeweler (*US*).

orefice'ria [orefitʃe'ria] *sf* (*arte*) goldsmith's art; (*negozio*) jeweller's (shop) (*Brit*), jewelry store (*US*).

'orfano, a *ag* orphan(ed) ♦ *sm/f* orphan; ~ **di padre/madre** fatherless/motherless.

orfano'trofio *sm* orphanage.

orga'netto *sm* barrel organ; (*fam: armonica a bocca*) mouth organ; (: *fisarmonica*) accordion.

or'ganico, a, ci, che *ag* organic ♦ *sm* personnel, staff.

organi'gramma, i *sm* organization chart; (*INFORM*) computer flow chart.

orga'nismo *sm* (*BIOL*) organism; (*ANAT, AMM*) body, organism.

orga'nista, i, e *sm/f* organist.

organiz'zare [organid'dzare] *vt* to organize; **~rsi** *vr* to get organized.

organizza'tivo, a [organiddza'tivo] *ag* organizational.

organizza'tore, 'trice [organiddza'tore] *ag* organizing ♦ *sm/f* organizer.

organizzazi'one [organiddzat'tsjone] *sf* (*azione*) organizing, arranging; (*risultato*) organization; **O~ Mondiale della Sanità (O.M.S.)** World Health Organization (WHO).

'organo *sm* organ; (*di congegno*) part; (*portavoce*) spokesman/woman, mouthpiece; **~i di trasmissione** (*TECN*) transmission (unit) *sg.*

or'gasmo *sm* (*FISIOL*) orgasm; (*fig*) agitation, anxiety.

'orgia, ge ['ɔrdʒa] *sf* orgy.

or'goglio [or'goʎʎo] *sm* pride.

orgogli'oso, a [orgoʎ'ʎoso] *ag* proud.

orien'tabile *ag* adjustable.

orien'tale *ag* (*paese, regione*) eastern; (*tappeti, lingua, civiltà*) oriental.

orienta'mento *sm* positioning; orientation; direction; **senso di** ~ sense of direction; **perdere l'~** to lose one's bearings; ~ **professionale** careers guidance.

orien'tare *vt* (*situare*) to position; (*carta, bussola*) to orientate; (*fig*) to direct; **~rsi** *vr* to find one's bearings; (*fig: tendere*) to tend, lean; (: *indirizzarsi*): **~rsi verso** to take up, go in for.

orienta'tivo, a *ag* indicative, for guidance; **a scopo** ~ for guidance.

ori'ente *sm* east; **l'O~** the East, the Orient; **il Medio/l'Estremo O~** the Middle/Far

East; **a ~** in the east.
ori'ficio [ori'fitʃo], **ori'fizio** [ori'fittsjo] *sm*
(*apertura*) opening; (: *di tubo*) mouth;
(*ANAT*) orifice.
o'rigano *sm* oregano.
origi'nale [oridʒi'nale] *ag* original; (*bizzarro*)
eccentric ♦ *sm* original.
originalità [oridʒinali'ta] *sf* originality;
eccentricity.
origi'nare [oridʒi'nare] *vt* to bring about,
produce ♦ *vi:* **~ da** to arise *o* spring from.
origi'nario, a [oridʒi'narjo] *ag* original;
essere ~ di to be a native of; (*animale,
pianta*) to be indigenous to, be native to.
o'rigine [o'ridʒine] *sf* origin; **all'~** originally;
d'~ inglese of English origin; **avere ~ da**
to originate from; **dare ~ a** to give rise to.
origli'are [oriʎ'ʎare] *vi:* **~ (a)** to eavesdrop
(on).
o'rina *sf* urine.
ori'nale *sm* chamberpot.
ori'nare *vi* to urinate ♦ *vt* to pass.
orina'toio *sm* (public) urinal.
ori'undo, a *ag:* **essere ~ di Milano** *etc* to be
of Milanese *etc* extraction *o* origin ♦ *sm/f*
person of foreign extraction *o* origin.
orizzon'tale [oriddzon'tale] *ag* horizontal.
oriz'zonte [orid'dzonte] *sm* horizon.
ORL *sigla f* (*MED*: = *otorinolaringoiatria*)
ENT.
or'lare *vt* to hem.
orla'tura *sf* (*azione*) hemming *q*; (*orlo*)
hem.
'orlo *sm* edge, border; (*di recipiente*) rim,
brim; (*di vestito etc*) hem; **pieno fino all'~**
full to the brim, brimful; **sull'~ della
pazzia/della rovina** on the brink *o* verge of
madness/ruin; **~ a giorno** hemstitch.
'orma *sf* (*di persona*) footprint; (*di animale*)
track; (*impronta, traccia*) mark, trace;
seguire *o* **calcare le ~e di qn** to follow in
sb's footsteps.
or'mai *av* by now, by this time; (*adesso*)
now; (*quasi*) almost, nearly.
ormeggi'are [ormed'dʒare] *vt*, **~rsi** *vr*
(*NAUT*) to moor.
or'meggio [or'meddʒo] *sm* (*atto*) mooring *q*;
(*luogo*) moorings *pl*; **posto d'~** berth.
or'mone *sm* hormone.
ornamen'tale *ag* ornamental, decorative.
orna'mento *sm* ornament, decoration.
or'nare *vt* to adorn, decorate; **~rsi** *vr:* **~rsi
(di)** to deck o.s. (out) (with).
or'nato, a *ag* ornate.
ornitolo'gia [ornitolo'dʒia] *sf* ornithology.
orni'tologo, a, gi, ghe *sm/f* ornithologist.
'oro *sm* gold; **d'~, in ~** gold *cpd*; **d'~**
(*colore, occasione*) golden; (*persona*)
marvellous (*Brit*), marvelous (*US*); **un
affare d'~** a real bargain; **prendere qc per
~ colato** to take sth as gospel (truth); **~
zecchino** pure gold.

orologe'ria [orolodʒe'ria] *sf* watchmaking *q*;
watchmaker's (shop); clockmaker's
(shop); **bomba a ~** time bomb.
orologi'aio [orolo'dʒajo] *sm* watchmaker;
clockmaker.
oro'logio [oro'lɔdʒo] *sm* clock; (*da tasca, da
polso*) watch; **~ da polso** wristwatch; **~ al
quarzo** quartz watch; **~ a sveglia** alarm
clock.
o'roscopo *sm* horoscope.
or'rendo, a *ag* (*spaventoso*) horrible, awful;
(*bruttissimo*) hideous.
or'ribile *ag* horrible.
'orrido, a *ag* fearful, horrid.
orripi'lante *ag* hair-raising, horrifying.
or'rore *sm* horror; **avere in ~ qn/qc** to
loathe *o* detest sb/sth; **mi fanno ~** I loathe
o detest them.
orsacchi'otto [orsak'kjɔtto] *sm* teddy bear.
'orso *sm* bear; **~ bruno/bianco** brown/polar
bear.
orsù *escl* come now!
or'taggio [or'taddʒo] *sm* vegetable.
or'tensia *sf* hydrangea.
or'tica, che *sf* (stinging) nettle.
orti'caria *sf* nettle rash.
orticol'tura *sf* horticulture.
'orto *sm* vegetable garden, kitchen garden;
(*AGR*) market garden (*Brit*), truck farm
(*US*); **~ botanico** botanical garden(s *pl*).
orto'dosso, a *ag* orthodox.
ortofrut'ticolo, a *ag* fruit and vegetable
cpd.
ortogo'nale *ag* perpendicular.
ortogra'fia *sf* spelling.
orto'lano, a *sm/f* (*venditore*) greengrocer
(*Brit*), produce dealer (*US*).
ortope'dia *sf* orthopaedics *sg* (*Brit*),
orthopedics *sg* (*US*).
orto'pedico, a, ci, che *ag* orthopaedic
(*Brit*), orthopedic (*US*) ♦ *sm* orthopaedic
specialist (*Brit*), orthopedist (*US*).
orzai'olo [ordza'jɔlo] *sm* (*MED*) stye.
or'zata [or'dzata] *sf* barley water.
'orzo ['ɔrdzo] *sm* barley.
'OSA *sigla f* (= *Organizzazione degli Stati
Americani*) OAS (= *Organization of
American States*).
o'sare *vt, vi* to dare; **~ fare** to dare (to)
do; **come osi?** how dare you?
oscenità [oʃʃeni'ta] *sf inv* obscenity.
o'sceno, a [oʃ'ʃeno] *ag* obscene;
(*ripugnante*) ghastly.
oscil'lare [oʃʃil'lare] *vi* (*pendolo*) to swing;
(*dondolare: al vento etc*) to rock; (*variare*)
to fluctuate; (*TECN*) to oscillate; (*fig*): **~
fra** to waver between.
oscillazi'one [oʃʃillat'tsjone] *sf* oscillation;
(*di prezzi, temperatura*) fluctuation.
oscura'mento *sm* darkening; obscuring;
(*in tempo di guerra*) blackout.
oscu'rare *vt* to darken, obscure; (*fig*) to

obscure; **~rsi** vr (cielo) to darken, cloud over; (persona): **si oscurò in volto** his face clouded over.

oscurità sf (vedi ag) darkness; obscurity; gloominess.

os'curo, a ag dark; (fig: incomprensibile) obscure; (: umile: vita, natali) humble, obscure; (: triste: pensiero) gloomy, sombre ♦ sm: **all'~** in the dark; **tenere qn all'~ di qc** to keep sb in the dark about sth.

'Oslo sf Oslo.

ospe'dale sm hospital.

ospedali'ero, a ag hospital cpd.

ospi'tale ag hospitable.

ospitalità sf hospitality.

ospi'tare vt to give hospitality to; (sog: albergo) to accommodate.

'ospite sm/f (persona che ospita) host/ hostess; (persona ospitata) guest.

os'pizio [os'pittsjo] sm (per vecchi etc) home.

'ossa sfpl vedi osso.

ossa'tura sf (ANAT) skeletal structure, frame; (TECN, fig) framework.

'osseo, a ag bony; (tessuto etc) bone cpd.

osse'quente ag: ~ **alla legge** law-abiding.

os'sequio sm deference, respect; **~i** smpl (saluto) respects, regards; **porgere i propri ~i a qn** (formale) to pay one's respects to sb; **~i alla signora!** (give my) regards to your wife!

ossequi'oso, a ag obsequious.

osser'vanza [osser'vantsa] sf observance.

osser'vare vt to observe, watch; (esaminare) to examine; (notare, rilevare) to notice, observe; (DIR: la legge) to observe, respect; (mantenere: silenzio) to keep, observe; **far ~ qc a qn** to point sth out to sb.

osserva'tore, 'trice ag observant, perceptive ♦ sm/f observer.

osserva'torio sm (ASTR) observatory; (MIL) observation post.

osservazi'one [osservat'tsjone] sf observation; (di legge etc) observance; (considerazione critica) observation, remark; (rimprovero) reproof; **in ~** under observation; **fare un'~** to make a remark; to raise an objection; **fare un'~ a qn** to criticize sb.

ossessio'nare vt to obsess, haunt; (tormentare) to torment, harass.

ossessi'one sf obsession; (seccatura) nuisance.

osses'sivo, a ag obsessive, haunting; troublesome.

os'sesso, a ag (spiritato) possessed.

os'sia cong that is, to be precise.

ossi'buchi [ossi'buki] smpl di **ossobuco**.

ossi'dare vt, **~rsi** vr to oxidize.

ossidazi'one [ossidat'tsjone] sf oxidization, oxidation.

'ossido sm oxide; ~ **di carbonio** carbon monoxide.

ossige'nare [ossid3e'nare] vt to oxygenate; (decolorare) to bleach; **acqua ossigenata** hydrogen peroxide.

os'sigeno [os'sid3eno] sm oxygen.

'osso sm (pl(f) **ossa** nel senso ANAT) bone; **d'~** (bottone etc) of bone, bone cpd; **avere le ~a rotte** to be dead o dog tired; **bagnato fino all'~** soaked to the skin; **essere ridotto all'~** (fig: magro) to be just skin and bone; (: senza soldi) to be in dire straits; **rompersi l'~ del collo** to break one's neck; **rimetterci l'~ del collo** (fig) to ruin o.s., lose everything; **un ~ duro** (persona, impresa) a tough number; ~ **di seppia** cuttlebone.

osso'buco, pl **ossi'buchi** sm (CUC) marrowbone; (: piatto) stew made with knuckle of veal in tomato sauce.

os'suto, a ag bony.

ostaco'lare vt to block, obstruct.

os'tacolo sm obstacle; (EQUITAZIONE) hurdle, jump; **essere di ~ a qn/qc** (fig) to stand in the way of sb/sth.

os'taggio [os'tadd3o] sm hostage.

'oste, os'tessa sm/f innkeeper.

osteggi'are [osted'd3are] vt to oppose, be opposed to.

os'tello sm: ~ **della gioventù** youth hostel.

osten'sorio sm (REL) monstrance.

osten'tare vt to make a show of, flaunt.

ostentazi'one [ostentat'tsjone] sf ostentation, show.

oste'ria sf inn.

os'tessa sf vedi **oste**.

os'tetrico, a, ci, che ag obstetric ♦ sm obstetrician ♦ sf midwife.

'ostia sf (REL) host; (per medicinali) wafer.

'ostico, a, ci, che ag difficult, tough.

os'tile ag hostile.

ostilità sf hostility ♦ sfpl (MIL) hostilities.

osti'narsi vr to insist, dig one's heels in; ~ **a fare** to persist (obstinately) in doing.

osti'nato, a ag (caparbio) obstinate; (tenace) persistent, determined.

ostinazi'one [ostinat'tsjone] sf obstinacy; persistence.

ostra'cismo [ostra'tʃizmo] sm ostracism.

'ostrica, che sf oyster.

ostru'ire vt to obstruct, block.

ostruzi'one [ostrut'tsjone] sf obstruction, blockage.

ostruzio'nismo [ostruttsjo'nizmo] sm (POL) obstructionism; (SPORT) obstruction; **fare dell'~ a** (progetto, legge) to obstruct; ~ **sindacale** work-to-rule (Brit), slowdown (US).

o'tite sf ear infection.

oto'rino(laringoi'atra), i, e sm/f ear, nose and throat specialist.

'otre sm (recipiente) goatskin.

ott. *abbr* (= *ottobre*) Oct.

ottago'nale *ag* octagonal.

ot'tagono *sm* octagon.

ot'tano *sm* octane; **numero di** ~**i** octane rating.

ot'tanta *num* eighty.

ottan'tenne *ag* eighty-year-old ♦ *sm/f* octogenarian.

ottan'tesimo, a *num* eightieth.

ottan'tina *sf*: **una** ~ **(di)** about eighty.

ot'tavo, a *num* eighth ♦ *sf* octave.

ottempe'ranza [ottempe'rantsa] *sf*: **in** ~ **a** (*AMM*) in accordance with, in compliance with.

ottempe'rare *vi*: ~ **a** to comply with, obey.

ottene'brare *vt* to darken; (*fig*) to cloud.

otte'nere *vt* to obtain, get; (*risultato*) to achieve, obtain.

'ottico, a, ci, che *ag* (*della vista: nervo*) optic; (*dell'ottica*) optical ♦ *sm* optician ♦ *sf* (*scienza*) optics *sg*; (*FOT: lenti, prismi etc*) optics *pl*.

otti'male *ag* optimal, optimum.

ottima'mente *av* excellently, very well.

otti'mismo *sm* optimism.

otti'mista, i, e *sm/f* optimist.

'ottimo, a *ag* excellent, very good.

'otto *num* eight.

ot'tobre *sm* October; *per fraseologia vedi* **luglio.**

otto'brino, a *ag* October *cpd*.

ottocen'tesco, a, schi, sche [ottotʃen'tesko] *ag* nineteenth-century.

otto'cento [otto'tʃɛnto] *num* eight hundred ♦ *sm*: **l'O**~ the nineteenth century.

otto'mila *num* eight thousand.

ot'tone *sm* brass; **gli** ~**i** (*MUS*) the brass.

ottuage'nario, a [ottuadʒe'narjo] *ag, sm/f* octogenarian.

ot'tundere *vt* (*fig*) to dull.

ottu'rare *vt* to close (up); (*dente*) to fill.

ottura'tore *sm* (*FOT*) shutter; (*nelle armi*) breechblock.

otturazi'one [otturat'tsjone] *sf* closing (up); (*dentaria*) filling.

ot'tuso, a *pp di* **ottundere** ♦ *ag* (*MAT, fig*) obtuse; (*suono*) dull.

o'vaia *sf*, **o'vaio** *sm* (*ANAT*) ovary.

o'vale *ag, sm* oval.

o'vatta *sf* cotton wool; (*per imbottire*) padding, wadding.

ovat'tare *vt* (*imbottire*) to pad; (*fig: smorzare*) to muffle.

ovazi'one [ovat'tsjone] *sf* ovation.

'ovest *sm* west; **a** ~ **(di)** west (of); **verso** ~ westward(s).

o'vile *sm* pen, enclosure; **tornare all'**~ (*fig*) to return to the fold.

o'vino, a *ag* sheep *cpd*, ovine.

'O.V.N.I. *sigla m* (= *oggetto volante non identificato*) UFO.

ovulazi'one [ovulat'tsjone] *sf* ovulation.

'ovulo *sm* (*FISIOL*) ovum.

o'vunque *av* = **dovunque.**

ov'vero *cong* (*ossia*) that is, to be precise; (*oppure*) or (else).

ovvi'are *vi*: ~ **a** to obviate.

'ovvio, a *ag* obvious.

ozi'are [ot'tsjare] *vi* to laze around.

'ozio ['ɔttsjo] *sm* idleness; (*tempo libero*) leisure; **ore d'**~ leisure time; **stare in** ~ to be idle.

ozi'oso, a [ot'tsjoso] *ag* idle.

o'zono [od'dzɔno] *sm* ozone.

P

P, p [pi] *sf o m inv* (*lettera*) P, p; **P come Padova** ≈ P for Peter.

P *abbr* (= *peso*) wt; (= *posteggio*) P.

p *abbr* (= *pagina*) p.

PA *sigla* = Palermo.

P.A. *abbr* = **pubblica amministrazione.**

paca'tezza [paka'tettsa] *sf* quietness, calmness.

pa'cato, a *ag* quiet, calm.

'pacca, che *sf* slap.

pac'chetto [pak'ketto] *sm* packet; ~ **applicativo** (*INFORM*) applications package; ~ **azionario** (*FINANZA*) shareholding; ~ **software** (*INFORM*) software package; ~ **turistico** package holiday (*Brit*) o tour.

pacchi'ano, a [pak'kjano] *ag* (*colori*) garish; (*abiti, arredamento*) vulgar, garish.

'pacco, chi *sm* parcel; (*involto*) bundle; ~ **postale** parcel.

paccot'tiglia [pakkot'tiʎʎa] *sf* trash, junk.

'pace ['patʃe] *sf* peace; **darsi** ~ to resign o.s.; **fare (la)** ~ **con qn** to make it up with sb.

pachis'tano, a [pakis'tano] *ag, sm/f* Pakistani.

pacifi'care [patʃifi'kare] *vt* (*riconciliare*) to reconcile, make peace between; (*mettere in pace*) to pacify.

pa'cifico, a, ci, che [pa'tʃifiko] *ag* (*persona*) peaceable; (*vita*) peaceful; (*fig: indiscusso*) indisputable; (*: ovvio*) obvious, clear ♦ *sm*: **il P**~, **l'Oceano P**~ the Pacific (Ocean).

paci'fismo [patʃi'fizmo] *sm* pacifism.

paci'fista, i, e [patʃi'fista] *sm/f* pacifist.

pa'dano, a *ag* of the Po; **la pianura** ~**a** the Lombardy plain.

pa'della *sf* frying pan; (*per infermi*) bedpan.

padigli'one [padiʎ'ʎone] *sm* pavilion.

'Padova sf Padua.

pado'vano, a ag of (o from) Padua.

'padre sm father; **~i** smpl (antenati) fore-fathers.

Padre'terno sm: **il ~** God the Father.

pa'drino sm godfather.

padro'nale ag (scala, entrata) main, principal; **casa ~** country house.

padro'nanza [padro'nantsa] sf command, mastery.

padro'nato sm: **il ~** the ruling class.

pa'drone, a smf master/mistress; (proprietario) owner; (datore di lavoro) employer; **essere ~ di sé** to be in control of o.s.; **~/a di casa** master/mistress of the house; (per gli inquilini) landlord/lady.

padroneggi'are [padroned'dʒare] vt (fig: sentimenti) to master, control; (: materia) to master, know thoroughly; **~rsi** vr to control o.s.

pae'saggio [pae'zaddʒo] sm landscape.

paesag'gista, i, e [paezad'dʒista] smf (pittore) landscape painter.

pae'sano, a ag country cpd ♦ smf villager; countryman/woman.

pa'ese sm (nazione) country, nation; (terra) country, land; (villaggio) village; **~ di provenienza** country of origin; **i P~i Bassi** the Netherlands.

paf'futo, a ag chubby, plump.

'paga, ghe sf pay, wages pl; **giorno di ~** pay day.

pa'gabile ag payable; **~ alla consegna/a vista** payable on delivery/on demand.

pa'gaia sf paddle.

paga'mento sm payment; **~ anticipato** payment in advance; **~ alla consegna** payment on delivery; **~all'ordine** cash with order.

pa'gano, a ag, smf pagan.

pa'gare vt to pay; (acquisto, fig: colpa) to pay for; (contraccambiare) to repay, pay back ♦ vi to pay; **quanto l'ha pagato?** how much did you pay for it?; **~ con carta di credito** to pay by credit card; **~ in contanti** to pay cash; **~ di persona** (fig) to suffer the consequences; **l'ho pagata cara** (fig) I paid dearly for it.

pa'gella [pa'dʒella] sf (INS) school report (Brit), report card (US).

'paggio ['paddʒo] sm page(boy).

pagherò [page'rɔ] vb vedi **pagare** ♦ sm inv IOU; **~ cambiario** promissory note.

'pagina ['padʒina] sf page.

'paglia ['paʎʎa] sf straw; **avere la coda di ~** (fig) to have a guilty conscience; **fuoco di ~** (fig) flash in the pan.

pagliac'cetto [paʎʎat'tʃetto] sm (per bambini) rompers pl.

pagli'accio [paʎ'ʎattʃo] sm clown.

pagli'aio [paʎ'ʎajo] sm haystack.

paglie'riccio [paʎʎe'rittʃo] sm straw mattress.

pagli'etta [paʎ'ʎetta] sf (cappello per uomo) (straw) boater; (per tegami etc) steel wool.

pagli'uzza [paʎ'ʎuttsa] sf (blade of) straw; (d'oro etc) tiny particle, speck.

pa'gnotta [paɲ'ɲɔtta] sf round loaf.

pa'goda sf pagoda.

pail'lette [pa'jɛt] sf inv sequin.

'paio, pl (f) 'paia sm pair; **un ~ di occhiali** a pair of glasses; **un ~ di** (alcuni) a couple of; **è un altro ~ di maniche** (fig) that's another kettle of fish.

'paio etc vb vedi **parere**.

pai'olo, paiu'olo sm (copper) pot.

'Pakistan sm: **il ~** Pakistan.

pakis'tano, a ag, smf = **pachistano**.

pal. abbr = **palude**.

'pala sf shovel; (di remo, ventilatore, elica) blade; (di ruota) paddle.

palan'drana sf (scherzoso: abito lungo e largo) tent.

pa'lato sm palate.

pa'lazzo [pa'lattso] sm (reggia) palace; (edificio) building; **~ di giustizia** courthouse; **~ dello sport** sports stadium.

pal'chetto [pal'ketto] sm shelf.

'palco, chi sm (TEATRO) box; (tavolato) platform, stand; (ripiano) layer.

palco'scenico, ci [palkoʃ'ʃɛniko] sm (TEATRO) stage.

palermi'tano, a ag of (o from) Palermo ♦ smf person from Palermo.

Pa'lermo sf Palermo.

pale'sare vt to reveal, disclose; **~rsi** vr to reveal o show o.s.

pa'lese ag clear, evident.

Pales'tina sf: **la ~** Palestine.

palesti'nese ag, smf Palestinian.

pa'lestra sf gymnasium; (esercizio atletico) exercise, training; (fig) training ground, school.

pa'letta sf spade; (per il focolare) shovel; (del capostazione) signalling disc.

pa'letto sm stake, peg; (spranga) bolt.

palin'sesto sm (STORIA) palimpsest; (TV, RADIO) programme (Brit) o program (US) schedule.

'palio sm (gara): **il P~** horserace run at Siena; **mettere qc in ~** to offer sth as a prize.

palis'sandro sm rosewood.

paliz'zata [palit'tsata] sf palisade.

'palla sf ball; (pallottola) bullet; **prendere la ~ al balzo** (fig) to seize one's opportunity.

pallaca'nestro sm basketball.

pallanu'oto sm water polo.

palla'volo sf volleyball.

palleggi'are [palled'dʒare] vi (CALCIO) to practise (Brit) o practice (US) with the ball; (TENNIS) to knock up.

pallia'tivo sm palliative; (fig) stopgap

measure.

'pallido, a *ag* pale.

pal'lina *sf* (*bilia*) marble.

pal'lino *sm* (*BILIARDO*) cue ball; (*BOCCE*) jack; (*proiettile*) pellet; (*pois*) dot; **bianco a ~i blu** white with blue dots; **avere il ~ di** (*fig*) to be crazy about.

pallon'cino [pallon'tʃino] *sm* balloon; (*lampioncino*) Chinese lantern.

pal'lone *sm* (*palla*) ball; (*CALCIO*) football; (*aerostato*) balloon; **gioco del ~** ball game.

pal'lore *sm* pallor, paleness.

pal'lottola *sf* pellet; (*proiettile*) bullet.

'palma *sf* (*ANAT*) = **palmo**; (*BOT*) palm; **~ da datteri** date palm.

pal'mato, a *ag* (*ZOOL*: *piede*) webbed; (*BOT*) palmate.

pal'mipede *ag* web-footed.

pal'mizio [pal'mittsjo] *sm* (*palma*) palm tree; (*ramo*) palm.

'palmo *sm* (*ANAT*) palm; **essere alto un ~** (*fig*) to be tiny; **restare con un ~ di naso** (*fig*) to be badly disappointed.

'palo *sm* (*legno appuntito*) stake; (*sostegno*) pole; **fare da** *o* **il ~** (*fig*) to act as look-out; **saltare di ~ in frasca** (*fig*) to jump from one topic to another.

palom'baro *sm* diver.

pa'lombo *sm* (*pesce*) dogfish.

pal'pare *vt* to feel, finger.

'palpebra *sf* eyelid.

palpi'tare *vi* (*cuore*, *polso*) to beat; (: *più forte*) to pound, throb; (*fremere*) to quiver.

palpitazi'one [palpitat'tsjone] *sf* palpitation.

'palpito *sm* (*del cuore*) beat; (*fig: d'amore etc*) throb.

paltò *sm inv* overcoat.

pa'lude *sf* marsh, swamp.

palu'doso, a *ag* marshy, swampy.

pa'lustre *ag* marsh *cpd*, swamp *cpd*.

'pampino *sm* vine leaf.

pana'cea [pana'tʃɛa] *sf* panacea.

'Panama *sf* Panama; **il canale di ~** the Panama Canal.

pana'mense *ag*, *sm/f* Panamanian.

'panca, che *sf* bench.

pan'cetta [pan'tʃetta] *sf* (*CUC*) bacon.

pan'chetto [pan'ketto] *sm* stool; footstool.

pan'china [pan'kina] *sf* garden seat; (*di giardino pubblico*) (park) bench.

'pancia, ce ['pantʃa] *sf* belly, stomach; **mettere** *o* **fare ~** to be getting a paunch; **avere mal di ~** to have stomach ache *o* a sore stomach.

panci'era [pan'tʃɛra] *sf* corset.

panci'olle [pan'tʃɔlle] *av*: **stare in ~** to lounge about (*Brit*) *o* around.

panci'otto [pan'tʃɔtto] *sm* waistcoat.

'pancreas *sm inv* pancreas.

'panda *sm inv* panda.

pande'monio *sm* pandemonium.

pan'doro *sm type of sponge cake eaten at Christmas.*

'pane *sm* bread; (*pagnotta*) loaf (of bread); (*forma*): **un ~ di burro/cera** *etc* a pat of butter/bar of wax *etc*; **guadagnarsi il ~** to earn one's living; **dire ~ al ~, vino al vino** (*fig*) to call a spade a spade; **rendere pan per focaccia** (*fig*) to give tit for tat; **~ casereccio** homemade bread; **~ a cassetta** sliced bread; **~ integrale** wholemeal bread; **~ di segale** rye bread; **pan di Spagna** sponge cake; **~ tostato** toast.

panette'ria *sf* (*forno*) bakery; (*negozio*) baker's (shop), bakery.

panetti'ere, a *sm/f* baker.

panet'tone *sm a kind of spiced brioche with sultanas, eaten at Christmas.*

pan'forte *sm* Sienese nougat-type delicacy.

pangrat'tato *sm* breadcrumbs *pl*.

'panico, a, ci, che *ag*, *sm* panic; **essere in preda al ~** to be panic-stricken; **lasciarsi prendere dal ~** to panic.

pani'ere *sm* basket.

pani'ficio [pani'fitʃo] *sm* (*forno*) bakery; (*negozio*) baker's (shop), bakery.

pa'nino *sm* roll; **~ imbottito** filled roll; sandwich.

panino'teca, che *sf* sandwich bar.

'panna *sf* (*CUC*) cream; (*AUT*) = **panne; ~ di cucina** cooking cream; **~ montata** whipped cream.

'panne [pan] *sf inv* (*AUT*) breakdown; **essere in ~** to have broken down.

pan'nello *sm* panel; **~ di controllo** control panel.

'panno *sm* cloth; **~i** *smpl* (*abiti*) clothes; **mettiti nei miei ~i** (*fig*) put yourself in my shoes.

pan'nocchia [pan'nɔkkja] *sf* (*di mais etc*) ear.

panno'lino *sm* (*per bambini*) nappy (*Brit*), diaper (*US*).

pano'rama, i *sm* panorama.

pano'ramico, a, ci, che *ag* panoramic; **strada ~a** scenic route.

panta'loni *smpl* trousers (*Brit*), pants (*US*), pair *sg* of trousers *o* pants.

pan'tano *sm* bog.

pan'tera *sf* panther.

pan'tofola *sf* slipper.

panto'mima *sf* pantomime.

pan'zana [pan'tsana] *sf* fib, tall story.

pao'nazzo, a [pao'nattso] *ag* purple.

'papa, i *sm* pope.

papà *sm inv* dad(dy); **figlio di ~** spoilt young man.

pa'pale *ag* papal.

pa'pato *sm* papacy.

pa'pavero *sm* poppy.

'papero, a *sm/f* (*ZOOL*) gosling ♦ *sf* (*fig*) slip of the tongue, blunder.

papi'llon [papi'jɔ̃] *sm inv* bow tie.

pa'piro *sm* papyrus.

'pappa *sf* baby cereal.

pappa'gallo *sm* parrot; *(fig: uomo)* Romeo, wolf.

pappa'gorgia, ge [pappa'gɔrdʒa] *sf* double chin.

pap'pare *vt (fam: anche: ~rsi)* to gobble up.

par. *abbr* (= *paragrafo*) par.

'para *sf:* **suole di** ~ crepe soles.

parà *abbr m inv* (= *paracadutista*) para.

pa'rabola *sf (MAT)* parabola; *(REL)* parable.

para'brezza [para'breddza] *sm inv (AUT)* windscreen *(Brit)*, windshield *(US)*.

paracadu'tare *vt,* ~rsi *vr* to parachute.

paraca'dute *sm inv* parachute.

paracadu'tismo *sm* parachuting.

paracadu'tista, i, e *sm/f* parachutist; *(MIL)* paratrooper.

para'carro *sm* kerbstone *(Brit)*, curbstone *(US)*.

para'diso *sm* paradise.

parados'sale *ag* paradoxical.

para'dosso *sm* paradox.

para'fango, ghi *sm* mudguard.

paraf'fina *sf* paraffin, paraffin wax.

parafra'sare *vt* to paraphrase.

pa'rafrasi *sf inv* paraphrase.

para'fulmine *sm* lightning conductor.

pa'raggi [pa'raddʒi] *smpl:* **nei** ~ in the vicinity, in the neighbourhood *(Brit)* o neighborhood *(US)*.

parago'nare *vt:* ~ **con/a** to compare with/to.

para'gone *sm* comparison; *(esempio analogo)* analogy, parallel; **reggere al** ~ to stand comparison.

para'grafo *sm* paragraph.

paraguai'ano, a *ag, sm/f* Paraguayan.

Paragu'ay [para'gwai] *sm:* **il** ~ Paraguay.

pa'ralisi *sf inv* paralysis.

para'litico, a, ci, che *ag, sm/f* paralytic.

paraliz'zare [paralid'dzare] *vt* to paralyze.

parallela'mente *av* in parallel.

paral'lelo, a *ag* parallel ♦ *sm (GEO)* parallel; *(comparazione)*: **fare un** ~ **tra** to draw a parallel between ♦ *sf* parallel (line); ~**e** *sfpl (attrezzo ginnico)* parallel bars.

para'lume *sm* lampshade.

para'medico, a, ci, che *ag* paramedical.

para'menti *smpl (REL)* vestments.

pa'rametro *sm* parameter.

paramili'tare *ag* paramilitary.

pa'ranco, chi *sm* hoist.

para'noia *sf* paranoia.

para'noico, a, ci, che *ag, sm/f* paranoid.

paranor'male *ag* paranormal.

para'occhi [para'ɔkki] *smpl* blinkers *(Brit)*, blinders *(US)*.

para'petto *sm* parapet.

para'piglia [para'piʎʎa] *sm* commotion, uproar.

parapsicolo'gia [parapsikolo'dʒia] *sf* parapsychology.

pa'rare *vt (addobbare)* to adorn, deck; *(proteggere)* to shield, protect; *(scansare: colpo)* to parry; *(CALCIO)* to save ♦ *vi:* **dove vuole andare a** ~? what are you driving at?; ~**rsi** *vr (presentarsi)* to appear, present o.s.

parasco'lastico, a, ci, che *ag (attività)* extracurricular.

para'sole *sm inv* parasol, sunshade.

paras'sita, i *sm* parasite.

parassi'tario, a *ag* parasitic.

parasta'tale *ag* state-controlled.

paras'tato *sm* employees in the state-controlled sector.

pa'rata *sf (SPORT)* save; *(MIL)* review, parade.

pa'rati *smpl* hangings *pl;* **carta da** ~ wallpaper.

para'tia *sf (di nave)* bulkhead.

para'urti *sm inv (AUT)* bumper.

para'vento *sm* folding screen; **fare da** ~ **a qn** *(fig)* to shield sb.

par'cella [par'tʃella] *sf* fee.

parcheggi'are [parked'dʒare] *vt* to park.

par'cheggio [par'keddʒo] *sm* parking *q;* *(luogo)* car park *(Brit)*, parking lot *(US)*; *(singolo posto)* parking space.

par'chimetro [par'kimetro] *sm* parking meter.

'parco, chi *sm* park; *(spazio per deposito)* depot; *(complesso di veicoli)* fleet.

'parco, a, chi, che *ag:* ~ **(in)** *(sobrio)* moderate (in); *(avaro)* sparing (with).

pa'recchio, a [pa'rekkjo] *det* quite a lot of; *(tempo)* quite a lot of, a long; ~**i(e)** *det pl* quite a lot of, several ♦ *pronome* quite a lot, quite a bit; *(tempo)* quite a while, a long time; ~**i(e)** *pronome pl* quite a lot, several ♦ *av (con ag)* quite, rather; *(con vb)* quite a lot, quite a bit.

pareggi'are [pared'dʒare] *vt* to make equal; *(terreno)* to level, make level; *(bilancio, conti)* to balance ♦ *vi (SPORT)* to draw.

pa'reggio [pa'reddʒo] *sm (ECON)* balance; *(SPORT)* draw.

paren'tado *sm* relatives *pl,* relations *pl.*

pa'rente *sm/f* relative, relation.

paren'tela *sf (vincolo di sangue, fig)* relationship; *(insieme dei parenti)* relations *pl,* relatives *pl.*

pa'rentesi *sf (segno grafico)* bracket, parenthesis; *(frase incisa)* parenthesis; *(digressione)* parenthesis, digression; **tra** ~ in brackets; *(fig)* incidentally.

pa'rere *sm (opinione)* opinion; *(consiglio)* advice, opinion; **a mio** ~ in my opinion ♦ *vi* to seem, appear ♦ *vb impers:* **pare che** it seems o appears that; they say that; **mi**

pare che it seems to me that; **mi pare di si/no** I think so/don't think so; **fai come ti pare** do as you like; **che ti pare del mio libro?** what do you think of my book?

pa'rete *sf* wall.

'pari *ag inv (uguale)* equal, same; *(in giochi)* equal; drawn, tied; *(MAT)* even ♦ *sm inv (POL: di Gran Bretagna)* peer ♦ *sm/f inv* peer, equal; **copiato ~** ~ copied word for word; **siamo ~** *(fig)* we are quits *o* even; **alla ~** on the same level; *(BORSA)* at par; **ragazza alla ~** au pair (girl); **mettersi alla ~ con** to place o.s. on the same level as; **mettersi in ~ con** to catch up with; **andare di ~ passo con qn** to keep pace with sb.

parifi'care *vt (scuola)* to recognize officially.

parifi'cato, a *ag:* **scuola ~a** *officially recognized private school.*

Pa'rigi [pa'ridʒi] *sf* Paris.

pari'gino, a [pari'dʒino] *ag, sm/f* Parisian.

pa'riglia [pa'riʎʎa] *sf* pair; **rendere la ~** to give tit for tat.

parità *sf* parity, equality; *(SPORT)* draw, tie.

pari'tetico, a, ci, che *ag:* **commissione ~a** joint committee; **rapporto ~** equal relationship.

parlamen'tare *ag* parliamentary ♦ *sm/f* ≈ Member of Parliament *(Brit)*, ≈ Congressman/woman *(US)* ♦ *vi* to negotiate, parley.

parla'mento *sm* parliament.

parlan'tina *sf (fam)* talkativeness; **avere una buona ~** to have the gift of the gab.

par'lare *vi* to speak, talk; *(confidare cose segrete)* to talk ♦ *vt* to speak; **~ (a qn) di** to speak *o* talk (to sb) about; **~ chiaro** to speak one's mind; **~ male di qn/qc** to speak ill of sb/sth; **~ del più e del meno** to talk of this and that; **ne ho sentito ~** I have heard it mentioned; **non parliamone più** let's just forget about it; **i dati parlano** *(fig)* the facts speak for themselves.

par'lata *sf (dialetto)* dialect.

parla'tore, 'trice *sm/f* speaker.

parla'torio *sm (di carcere etc)* visiting room; *(REL)* parlour *(Brit)*, parlor *(US)*.

parlot'tare *vi* to mutter.

parmigi'ano, a [parmi'dʒano] *ag* Parma *cpd,* of *(o* from*)* Parma ♦ *sm (grana)* Parmesan (cheese); **alla ~a** *(CUC)* with Parmesan cheese.

paro'dia *sf* parody.

pa'rola *sf* word; *(facoltà)* speech; **~e** *sfpl (chiacchiere)* talk *sg;* **chiedere la ~** to ask permission to speak; **dare la ~ a qn** to call on sb to speak; **dare la propria ~ a qn** to give sb one's word; **mantenere la ~** to keep one's word; **mettere una buona ~ per qn** to put in a good word for sb; **passare**

dalle ~e ai fatti to get down to business; **prendere la ~** to take the floor; **rimanere senza ~e** to be speechless; **rimangiarsi la ~** to go back on one's word; **non ho ~e per ringraziarla** I don't know how to thank you; **rivolgere la ~ a qn** to speak to sb; **non è detta l'ultima ~** that's not the end of the matter; **è una persona di ~** he is a man of his word; **in ~e povere** in plain English; **~ d'onore** word of honour; **~ d'ordine** *(MIL)* password; **~e incrociate** crossword (puzzle) *sg.*

paro'laccia, ce [paro'lattʃa] *sf* bad word, swearword.

paros'sismo *sm* paroxysm.

par'quet [par'kɛ] *sm* parquet (flooring).

parrò *etc vb vedi* **parere.**

par'rocchia [par'rɔkkja] *sf* parish; *(chiesa)* parish church.

parrocchi'ano, a [parrok'kjano] *sm/f* parishioner.

'parroco, ci *sm* parish priest.

par'rucca, che *sf* wig.

parrucchi'ere, a [parruk'kjɛre] *sm/f* hairdresser ♦ *sm* barber.

parruc'cone *sm (peg)* old fogey.

parsi'monia *sf* frugality, thrift.

parsimoni'oso, a *ag* frugal, thrifty.

'parso, a *pp di* **parere.**

'parte *sf* part; *(lato)* side; *(quota spettante a ciascuno)* share; *(direzione)* direction; *(POL)* party; faction; *(DIR)* party; **a ~** *ag* separate ♦ *av* separately; **scherzi a ~** joking aside; **a ~ ciò** apart from that; **inviare a ~** *(campioni etc)* to send under separate cover; **da ~** *(in disparte)* to one side, aside; **mettere/prendere da ~** to put/take aside; **d'altra ~** on the other hand; **da ~ di** *(per conto di)* on behalf of; **da ~ mia** as far as I'm concerned, as for me; **da ~ di madre** on his *(o* her *etc)* mother's side; **essere dalla ~ della ragione** to be in the right; **da ~ a ~** right through; **da qualche ~** somewhere; **da nessuna ~** nowhere; **da questa ~** *(in questa direzione)* this way; **da ogni ~** on all sides, everywhere; *(moto da luogo)* from all sides; **fare ~ di qc** to belong to sth; **prendere ~ a qc** to take part in sth; **prendere le ~i di qn** to take sb's side; **mettere qn a ~ di qc** to inform sb of sth; **costituirsi ~ civile contro qn** *(DIR)* to associate in an action with the public prosecutor against sb; **la ~ lesa** *(DIR)* the injured party; **le ~i in causa** the parties concerned.

parteci'pante [partetʃi'pante] *sm/f:* **~ (a)** *(a riunione, dibattito)* participant (in); *(a gara sportiva)* competitor (in); *(a concorso)* entrant (to).

parteci'pare [partetʃi'pare] *vi:* **~ a** to take part in, participate in; *(utili etc)* to share in; *(spese etc)* to contribute to; *(dolore,* *successo di qn*) to share (in) ♦ *vt:* ~ **le nozze (a)** to announce one's wedding (to).

partecipazi'one [partetʃipat'tsjone] *sf* participation; sharing; (*ECON*) interest; ~ **a banda armata** (*DIR*) belonging to an armed gang; ~ **di maggioranza/minoranza** controlling/minority interest; ~ **agli utili** profit-sharing; ~**i di nozze** *wedding announcement card*; **ministro delle P**~**i statali** *minister responsible for companies in which the state has a financial interest.*

par'tecipe [par'tetʃipe] *ag* participating; **essere** ~ **di** to take part in, participate in; (*gioia, dolore*) to share (in); (*consapevole*) to be aware of.

parteggi'are [parted'dʒare] *vi:* ~ **per** to side with, be on the side of.

par'tenza [par'tɛntsa] *sf* departure; (*SPORT*) start; **essere in** ~ to be about to leave, be leaving; **passeggeri in** ~ **per** passengers travelling (*Brit*) o traveling (*US*) to; **siamo tornati al punto di** ~ (*fig*) we are back where we started; **falsa** ~ (*anche fig*) false start.

parti'cella [parti'tʃɛlla] *sf* particle.

parti'cipio [parti'tʃipjo] *sm* participle.

partico'lare *ag* (*specifico*) particular; (*proprio*) personal, private; (*speciale*) special, particular; (*caratteristico*) distinctive; (*fuori dal comune*) peculiar ♦ *sm* detail, particular; **in** ~ in particular, particularly; **entrare nei** ~**i** to go into details.

particolareggi'ato, a [partikolared'dʒato] *ag* (extremely) detailed.

particolarità *sf inv* (*carattere eccezionale*) peculiarity; (*dettaglio*) particularity, detail; (*caratteristica*) characteristic, feature.

partigi'ano, a [parti'dʒano] *ag* partisan ♦ *sm* (*fautore*) supporter, champion; (*MIL*) partisan.

par'tire *vi* to go, leave; (*allontanarsi*) to go o (*o drive etc*) away o off; (*petardo, colpo*) to go off; (*fig: avere inizio, SPORT*) to start; **sono partita da Roma alle 7** I left Rome at 7; **il volo parte da Ciampino** the flight leaves from Ciampino; **a** ~ **da** from; **la seconda a** ~ **da destra** the second from the right; ~ **in quarta** to drive off at top speed; (*fig*) to be very enthusiastic.

par'tita *sf* (*COMM*) lot, consignment; (*ECON: registrazione*) entry, item; (*CARTE, SPORT: gioco*) game; (: *competizione*) match, game; ~ **di caccia** hunting party; ~ **IVA** VAT account; ~ **semplice/doppia** (*COMM*) single-/double-entry book-keeping.

par'tito *sm* (*POL*) party; (*decisione*) decision, resolution; (*persona da maritare*) match; **per** ~ **preso** on principle; **mettere la testa a** ~ to settle down.

parti'tura *sf* (*MUS*) score.

'parto *sm* (*MED*) labour (*Brit*), labor (*US*); **sala** ~ labo(u)r room; **morire di** ~ to die in childbirth.

partori'ente *sf* woman in labour (*Brit*) o labor (*US*).

parto'rire *vt* to give birth to; (*fig*) to produce.

par'venza [par'vɛntsa] *sf* semblance.

'parvi *etc vb vedi* **parere.**

parzi'ale [par'tsjale] *ag* (*limitato*) partial; (*non obiettivo*) biased, partial.

parzialità [partsjali'ta] *sf:* ~ **(a favore di)** partiality (for), bias (towards); ~ **(contro)** bias (against).

'pascere ['paʃʃere] *vi* to graze ♦ *vt* (*brucare*) to graze on; (*far pascolare*) to graze, pasture.

pasci'uto, a [paʃ'ʃuto] *pp di* **pascere** ♦ *ag:* **ben** ~ plump.

pasco'lare *vt, vi* to graze.

'pascolo *sm* pasture.

'Pasqua *sf* Easter; **isola di** ~ Easter Island.

pas'quale *ag* Easter *cpd.*

pasqu'etta *sf* Easter Monday.

pas'sabile *ag* fairly good, passable.

pas'saggio [pas'saddʒo] *sm* passing *q*, passage; (*traversata*) crossing *q*, passage; (*luogo, prezzo della traversata, brano di libro etc*) passage; (*su veicolo altrui*) lift (*Brit*), ride; (*SPORT*) pass; **di** ~ (*persona*) passing through; ~ **pedonale/a livello** pedestrian/level (*Brit*) o grade (*US*) crossing; ~ **di proprietà** transfer of ownership.

passamane'ria *sf* braid, trimming.

passamon'tagna [passamon'taɲɲa] *sm inv* balaclava.

pas'sante *sm/f* passer-by ♦ *sm* loop.

passa'porto *sm* passport.

pas'sare *vi* (*andare*) to go; (*veicolo, pedone*) to pass (by), go by; (*fare una breve sosta: postino etc*) to come, ,call; (: *amico: per fare una visita*) to call o drop in; (*sole, aria, luce*) to get through; (*trascorrere: giorni, tempo*) to pass, go by; (*fig: proposta di legge*) to be passed; (: *dolore*) to pass, go away; (*CARTE*) to pass ♦ *vt* (*attraversare*) to cross; (*trasmettere: messaggio*): ~ **qc a qn** to pass sth on to sb; (*dare*): ~ **qc a qn** to pass sth to sb, give sb sth; (*trascorrere: tempo*) to spend; (*superare: esame*) to pass; (*triturare: verdura*) to strain; (*approvare*) to pass, approve; (*oltrepassare, sorpassare: anche fig*) to go beyond, pass; (*fig: subire*) to go through; ~ **da ... a** to pass from ... to; ~ **di padre in figlio** to be handed down o to pass from father to son; ~ **per** (*anche fig*) to go through; ~ **per stupido/un genio** to be taken for a fool/a genius; ~ **sopra** (*anche fig*) to pass over; ~ **attraverso** (*anche fig*) to go through; ~ **ad altro** to change the subject; (*in una riunione*) to discuss the next item; ~ **in banca/ufficio** to call (in) at the bank/office; ~ **alla storia** to pass into history; ~ **a un esame** to go up (to the next class) after an exam; ~ **di moda** to go out of fashion; ~ **a prendere qc/qn** to call and pick sth/sb up; **le passo il Signor X** (*al telefono*) here is Mr X, I'm putting you through to Mr X; **farsi** ~ **per** to pass o.s. off as, pretend to be; **lasciar** ~ **qn/qc** to let sb/sth through; **col** ~ **degli anni** (*riferito al presente*) as time goes by; (*riferito al passato*) as time passed o went by; **il peggio è passato** the worst is over; **30 anni e passa** well over 30 years ago; ~ **una mano di vernice su qc** to give sth a coat of paint; **passarsela: come te la passi?** how are you getting on o along?

pas'sata *sf*: **dare una** ~ **di vernice a qc** to give sth a coat of paint; **dare una** ~ **al giornale** to have a look at the paper, skim through the paper.

passa'tempo *sm* pastime, hobby.

pas'sato, a *ag* (*scorso*) last; (*finito: gloria, generazioni*) past; (*usanze*) out of date; (*sfiorito*) faded ♦ *sm* past; (*LING*) past (tense); **l'anno** ~ last year; **nel corso degli anni** ~i over the past years; **nei tempi** ~i in the past; **sono le 8** ~**e** it's past o after 8 o'clock; **è acqua** ~**a** (*fig*) it's over and done with; ~ **prossimo** (*LING*) present perfect; ~ **remoto** (*LING*) past historic; ~ **di verdura** (*CUC*) vegetable purée.

passa'tutto *sm inv*, **passaver'dura** *sm inv* vegetable mill.

passeg'gero, a [passed'dʒero] *ag* passing ♦ *sm/f* passenger.

passeggi'are [passed'dʒare] *vi* to go for a walk; (*in veicolo*) to go for a drive.

passeggi'ata [passed'dʒata] *sf* walk; drive; (*luogo*) promenade; **fare una** ~ to go for a walk (o drive).

passeg'gino [passed'dʒino] *sm* pushchair (*Brit*), stroller (*US*).

pas'seggio [pas'seddʒo] *sm* walk, stroll; (*luogo*) promenade; **andare a** ~ to go for a walk o a stroll.

passe'rella *sf* footbridge; (*di nave, aereo*) gangway; (*pedana*) catwalk.

'passero *sm* sparrow.

pas'sibile *ag*: ~ **di** liable to.

passio'nale *ag* (*temperamento*) passionate; **delitto** ~ crime of passion.

passi'one *sf* passion.

passività *sf* (*qualità*) passivity, passiveness; (*COMM*) liability.

pas'sivo, a *ag* passive ♦ *sm* (*LING*) passive; (*ECON*) debit; (: *complesso dei debiti*) liabilities *pl*.

'passo *sm* step; (*andatura*) pace; (*rumore*) (foot)step; (*orma*) footprint; (*passaggio, fig: brano*) passage; (*valico*) pass; **a** ~ **d'uomo** at walking pace; (*AUT*) dead

slow; ~ **(a)** ~ step by step; **fare due** o **quattro** ~**i** to go for a walk o a stroll; **andare al** ~ **coi tempi** to keep up with the times; **di questo** ~ (*fig*) at this rate; **fare i primi** ~**i** (*anche fig*) to take one's first steps; **fare il gran** ~ (*fig*) to take the plunge; **fare un** ~ **falso** (*fig*) to make the wrong move; **tornare sui propri** ~**i** to retrace one's steps; **"~ carraio"** "vehicle entrance — keep clear".

'pasta *sf* (*CUC*) dough; (: *impasto per dolce*) pastry; (: *anche:* ~ **alimentare**) pasta; (*massa molle di materia*) paste; (*fig: indole*) nature; ~**e** *sfpl* (*pasticcini*) pastries; ~ **in brodo** noodle soup; ~ **sfoglia** puff pastry o paste (*US*).

pastasci'utta [pasta∫'∫utta] *sf* pasta.

pasteggi'are [pasted'dʒare] *vi*: ~ **a vino/ champagne** to have wine/champagne with one's meal.

pas'tella *sf* batter.

pas'tello *sm* pastel.

pas'tetta *sf* (*CUC*) = **pastella**.

pas'ticca, che *sf* = **pastiglia**.

pasticce'ria [pastitt∫e'ria] *sf* (*pasticcini*) pastries *pl*, cakes *pl*; (*negozio*) cake shop; (*arte*) confectionery.

pasticci'are [pastit't∫are] *vt* to mess up, make a mess of ♦ *vi* to make a mess.

pasticci'ere, a [pastit't∫ɛre] *sm/f* pastrycook; confectioner.

pastic'cino [pastit't∫ino] *sm* petit four.

pas'ticcio [pas'tittʃo] *sm* (*CUC*) pie; (*lavoro disordinato, imbroglio*) mess; **trovarsi nei** ~**i** to get into trouble.

pasti'ficio [pasti'fitʃo] *sm* pasta factory.

pas'tiglia [pas'tiʎʎa] *sf* pastille, lozenge.

pas'tina *sf* small pasta shapes used in soup.

pasti'naca, che *sf* parsnip.

'pasto *sm* meal; **vino da** ~ table wine.

pas'toia *sf* (*fig*): ~ **burocratica** red tape.

pasto'rale *ag* pastoral.

pas'tore *sm* shepherd; (*REL*) pastor, minister; (*anche:* **cane** ~) sheepdog; ~ **scozzese** (*ZOOL*) collie; ~ **tedesco** (*ZOOL*) Alsatian (dog) (*Brit*), German shepherd (dog).

pasto'rizia [pasto'rittsja] *sf* sheep-rearing, sheep farming.

pastoriz'zare [pastorid'dzare] *vt* to pasteurize.

pas'toso, a *ag* doughy; pasty; (*fig: voce, colore*) mellow, soft.

pas'trano *sm* greatcoat.

pas'tura *sf* pasture.

pa'tacca, che *sf* (*distintivo*) medal, decoration; (*fig: macchia*) grease spot, grease mark.

pa'tata *sf* potato; ~**e fritte** chips (*Brit*), French fries.

pata'tine *sfpl* (potato) crisps (*Brit*) o chips (*US*).

pata'trac *sm* (*crollo: anche fig*) crash.
pâté [pa'te] *sm inv* pâté; ~ **di fegato d'oca** pâté de foie gras.
pa'tella *sf* (*ZOOL*) limpet.
pa'tema, i *sm* anxiety, worry.
paten'tato, a *ag* (*munito di patente*) licensed, certified; (*fig scherzoso: qualificato*) utter, thorough.
pa'tente *sf* licence (*Brit*), license (*US*); (*anche*: ~ **di guida**) driving licence (*Brit*), driver's license (*US*).
paten'tino *sm* temporary licence (*Brit*) *o* license (*US*).
paternità *sf* paternity, fatherhood.
pa'terno, a *ag* (*affetto, consigli*) fatherly; (*casa, autorità*) paternal.
pa'tetico, a, ci, che *ag* pathetic; (*commovente*) moving, touching.
'pathos ['patos] *sm* pathos.
pa'tibolo *sm* gallows *sg*, scaffold.
pati'mento *sm* suffering.
'patina *sf* (*su rame etc*) patina; (*sulla lingua*) fur, coating.
pa'tire *vt, vi* to suffer.
pa'tito, a *sm/f* enthusiast, fan, lover.
patolo'gia [patolo'dʒia] *sf* pathology.
pato'logico, a, ci, che [pato'lɔdʒiko] *ag* pathological.
pa'tologo, a, gi, ghe *sm/f* pathologist.
'patria *sf* homeland; **amor di** ~ patriotism.
patri'arca, chi *sm* patriarch.
pa'trigno [pa'triɲɲo] *sm* stepfather.
patri'monio *sm* estate, property; (*fig*) heritage; **mi è costato un** ~ (*fig*) it cost me a fortune, I paid a fortune for it; ~ **spirituale/culturale** spiritual/cultural heritage; ~ **ereditario** (*fig*) hereditary characteristics *pl*; ~ **pubblico** public property.
'patrio, a, ii, ie *ag* (*di patria*) native *cpd*, of one's country; (*DIR*): ~**a potestà** parental authority; **amor** ~ love of one's country.
patri'ota, i, e *sm/f* patriot.
patri'ottico, a, ci, che *ag* patriotic.
patriot'tismo *sm* patriotism.
patroci'nare [patrotʃi'nare] *vt* (*DIR: difendere*) to defend; (*sostenere*) to sponsor, support.
patro'cinio [patro'tʃinjo] *sm* defence (*Brit*), defense (*US*); support, sponsorship.
patro'nato *sm* patronage; (*istituzione benefica*) charitable institution *o* society.
pa'trono *sm* (*REL*) patron saint; (*socio di patronato*) patron; (*DIR*) counsel.
'patta *sf* flap; (*dei pantaloni*) fly.
patteggi'are [patted'dʒare] *vt, vi* to negotiate.
patti'naggio [patti'naddʒo] *sm* skating.
patti'nare *vi* to skate; ~ **sul ghiaccio** to ice-skate.
pattina'tore, 'trice *sm/f* skater.
'pattino *sm* skate; (*di slitta*) runner; (*AER*) skid; (*TECN*) sliding block; ~**i** (**da**

ghiaccio) (ice) skates; ~**i a rotelle** roller skates.
pat'tino *sm* (*barca*) kind of pedalo with oars.
'patto *sm* (*accordo*) pact, agreement; (*condizione*) term, condition; **a** ~ **che** on condition that; **a nessun** ~ under no circumstances; **venire** *o* **scendere a** ~**i** (**con**) to come to an agreement (with).
pat'tuglia [pat'tuʎʎa] *sf* (*MIL*) patrol.
pattugli'are [pattuʎ'ʎare] *vt* to patrol.
pattu'ire *vt* to reach an agreement on.
pattumi'era *sf* (dust)bin (*Brit*), ashcan (*US*).
pa'ura *sf* fear; **aver** ~ **di/di fare/che** to be frightened *o* afraid of/of doing/that; **far** ~ **a** to frighten; **per** ~ **di/che** for fear of/that; **ho** ~ **di sì/no** I am afraid so/not.
pau'roso, a *ag* (*che fa paura*) frightening; (*che ha paura*) fearful, timorous.
'pausa *sf* (*sosta*) break; (*nel parlare, MUS*) pause.
paven'tato, a *ag* much-feared.
pa'vese *ag* of (*o* from) Pavia.
'pavido, a *ag* (*letterario*) fearful.
pavimen'tare *vt* (*stanza*) to floor; (*strada*) to pave.
pavimentazi'one [pavimentat'tsjone] *sf* flooring; paving.
pavi'mento *sm* floor.
pa'vone *sm* peacock.
pavoneggi'arsi [pavoned'dʒarsi] *vr* to strut about, show off.
pazien'tare [pattsjen'tare] *vi* to be patient.
pazi'ente [pat'tsjɛnte] *ag, sm/f* patient.
pazi'enza [pat'tsjɛntsa] *sf* patience; **perdere la** ~ to lose (one's) patience.
pazza'mente [pattsa'mente] *av* madly; **essere** ~ **innamorato** to be madly in love.
paz'zesco, a, schi, sche [pat'tsesko] *ag* mad, crazy.
paz'zia [pat'tsia] *sf* (*MED*) madness, insanity; (*di azione, decisione*) madness, folly; **è stata una** ~! it was sheer madness!
'pazzo, a ['pattso] *ag* (*MED*) mad, insane; (*strano*) wild, mad ♦ *sm/f* madman/woman; ~ **di** (*gioia, amore etc*) mad *o* crazy with; ~ **per qc/qn** mad *o* crazy about sth/sb; **essere** ~ **da legare** to be raving mad *o* a raving lunatic.
PC *sigla* = *Piacenza*.
P.C. *abbr* = **polizza di carico**.
p.c. *abbr* = *per condoglianze*; *per conoscenza*.
PCI *sigla m* = *Partito Comunista Italiano*.
PCUS *sigla m* = *Partito Comunista dell'Unione Sovietica*.
PD *sigla* = *Padova*.
P.D. *abbr* = **partita doppia**.
PE *sigla* = *Pescara*.
'pecca, che *sf* defect, flaw, fault.
peccami'noso, a *ag* sinful.

pec'care *vi* to sin; (*fig*) to err.

pec'cato *sm* sin; **è un ~ che** it's a pity that; **che ~!** what a shame *o* pity!; **un ~ di gioventù** (*fig*) a youthful error *o* indiscretion.

pecca'tore, 'trice *sm/f* sinner.

peccherò *etc* [pekke'rɔ] *vb vedi* **peccare**.

'pece ['petʃe] *sf* pitch.

pechi'nese [peki'nese] *ag, sm/f* Pekin(g)ese (*inv*) ♦ *sm* (*anche:* **cane ~**) Pekin(g)ese *inv*, Peke.

Pe'chino [pe'kino] *sf* Beijing, Peking.

'pecora *sf* sheep; **~ nera** (*fig*) black sheep.

peco'raio *sm* shepherd.

peco'rella *sf* lamb; **la ~ smarrita** the lost sheep; **cielo a ~e** (*fig: nuvole*) mackerel sky.

peco'rino *sm* sheep's milk cheese.

pecu'lato *sm* (*DIR*) embezzlement.

peculi'are *ag*: **~ di** peculiar to.

pecuni'ario, a *ag* financial, money *cpd*.

pe'daggio [pe'daddʒo] *sm* toll.

pedago'gia [pedago'dʒia] *sf* pedagogy, educational methods *pl*.

peda'gogico, a, ci, che [peda'gɔdʒiko] *ag* pedagogic(al).

peda'lare *vi* to pedal; (*andare in bicicletta*) to cycle.

pe'dale *sm* pedal.

pe'dana *sf* footboard; (*SPORT: nel salto*) springboard; (*: nella scherma*) piste.

pe'dante *ag* pedantic ♦ *sm/f* pedant.

pe'data *sf* (*impronta*) footprint; (*colpo*) kick; **prendere a ~e qn/qc** to kick sb/sth.

pede'rasta, i *sm* pederast.

pe'destre *ag* prosaic, pedestrian.

pedi'atra, i, e *sm/f* paediatrician (*Brit*), pediatrician (*US*).

pedia'tria *sf* paediatrics *sg* (*Brit*), pediatrics *sg* (*US*).

pedi'cure *sm/f inv* chiropodist (*Brit*), podiatrist (*US*).

pedi'luvio *sm* footbath.

pe'dina *sf* (*della dama*) draughtsman (*Brit*), draftsman (*US*); (*fig*) pawn.

pedi'nare *vt* to shadow, tail.

pedo'nale *ag* pedestrian.

pe'done, a *sm/f* pedestrian ♦ *sm* (*SCACCHI*) pawn.

'peggio ['peddʒo] *av, ag inv* worse ♦ *sm o f*: **il** *o* **la ~** the worst; **cambiare in ~** to get *o* become worse; **alla ~** at worst, if the worst comes to the worst; **tirare avanti alla meno ~** to get along as best one can; **avere la ~** to come off worse, get the worst of it.

peggiora'mento [peddʒora'mento] *sm* worsening.

peggio'rare [peddʒo'rare] *vt* to make worse, worsen ♦ *vi* to grow worse, worsen.

peggiora'tivo, a [peddʒora'tivo] *ag* pejorative.

peggi'ore [ped'dʒore] *ag* (*comparativo*) worse; (*superlativo*) worst ♦ *sm/f*: **il(la) ~** the worst (person); **nel ~ dei casi** if the worst comes to the worst.

'pegno ['peɲɲo] *sm* (*DIR*) security, pledge; (*nei giochi di società*) forfeit; (*fig*) pledge, token; **dare in ~ qc** to pawn sth; **in ~ d'amicizia** as a token of friendship; **banco dei ~i** pawnshop.

pe'lame *sm* (*di animale*) coat, fur.

pelapa'tate *sm inv* potato peeler.

pe'lare *vt* (*spennare*) to pluck; (*spellare*) to skin; (*sbucciare*) to peel; (*fig*) to make pay through the nose; **~rsi** *vr* to go bald.

pe'lato, a *ag* (*sbucciato*) peeled; (*calvo*) bald; (**pomodori) ~i** peeled tomatoes.

pel'lame *sm* skins *pl*, hides *pl*.

'pelle *sf* skin; (*di animale*) skin, hide; (*cuoio*) leather; **essere ~ ed ossa** to be skin and bone; **avere la ~ d'oca** to have goose pimples *o* goose flesh; **avere i nervi a fior di ~** to be edgy; **non stare più nella ~ dalla gioia** to be beside o.s. with delight; **lasciarci la ~** to lose one's life; **amici per la ~** firm *o* close friends.

pellegri'naggio [pellegri'naddʒo] *sm* pilgrimage.

pelle'grino, a *sm/f* pilgrim.

pelle'rossa, pelli'rossa, *pl* **pelli'rosse** *sm/f* Red Indian.

pellette'ria *sf* (*articoli*) leather goods *pl*; (*negozio*) leather goods shop.

pelli'cano *sm* pelican.

pellicce'ria [pellittʃe'ria] *sf* (*negozio*) furrier's (shop); (*quantità di pellicce*) furs *pl*.

pel'liccia, ce [pel'littʃa] *sf* (*mantello di animale*) coat, fur; (*indumento*) fur coat.

pellicci'aio [pellit'tʃajo] *sm* furrier.

pel'licola *sf* (*membrana sottile*) film, layer; (*FOT, CINEMA*) film.

pelli'rossa *sm/f* = **pellerossa**.

'pelo *sm* hair; (*pelame*) coat, hair; (*pelliccia*) fur; (*di tappeto*) pile; (*di liquido*) surface; **per un ~**: **per un ~ non ho perduto il treno** I very nearly missed the train; **c'è mancato un ~ che affogasse** he narrowly escaped drowning; **cercare il ~ nell'uovo** (*fig*) to pick holes, split hairs; **non aver ~i sulla lingua** (*fig*) to speak one's mind.

pe'loso, a *ag* hairy.

'peltro *sm* pewter.

pe'luche [pə'lyʃ] *sm* plush; **giocattoli di ~** soft toys.

pe'luria *sf* down.

'pena *sf* (*DIR*) sentence; (*punizione*) punishment; (*sofferenza*) sadness *q*, sorrow; (*fatica*) trouble *q*, effort; (*difficoltà*) difficulty; **far ~** to be pitiful; **mi fai ~** I feel sorry for you; **essere** *o* **stare in ~ (per qc/qn)** to worry *o* be anxious (about sth/sb); **prendersi** *o* **darsi la ~ di fare** to go to the trouble of doing; **vale la ~ farlo** it's worth doing, it's worth it; **non ne vale la ~** it's not worth the effort, it's not worth it; **~ di morte** death sentence; **~ pecuniaria** fine.

pe'nale *ag* penal ♦ *sf* (*anche:* **clausola ~**) penalty clause; **causa ~** criminal trial; **diritto ~** criminal law; **pagare la ~** to pay the penalty.

pena'lista, i, e *sm/f* (*avvocato*) criminal lawyer.

penalità *sf inv* penalty.

penaliz'zare [penalid'dzare] *vt* (*SPORT*) to penalize.

pe'nare *vi* (*patire*) to suffer; (*faticare*) to struggle.

pen'dente *ag* hanging; leaning ♦ *sm* (*ciondolo*) pendant; (*orecchino*) drop earring.

pen'denza [pen'dɛntsa] *sf* slope, slant; (*grado d'inclinazione*) gradient; (*ECON*) outstanding account.

'pendere *vi* (*essere appeso*): **~ da** to hang from; (*essere inclinato*) to lean; (*fig: incombere*): **~ su** to hang over.

pen'dio, ii *sm* slope, slant; (*luogo in pendenza*) slope.

'pendola *sf* pendulum clock.

pendo'lare *ag* pendulum *cpd*, pendular ♦ *sm/f* commuter.

pendola'rismo *sm* commuting.

'pendolo *sm* (*peso*) pendulum; (*anche:* **orologio a ~**) pendulum clock.

'pene *sm* penis.

pene'trante *ag* piercing, penetrating.

pene'trare *vi* to come *o* get in ♦ *vt* to penetrate; **~ in** to enter; (*sog: proiettile*) to penetrate; (: *acqua, aria*) to go *o* come into.

penicil'lina [penitʃil'lina] *sf* penicillin.

peninsu'lare *ag* peninsular; **l'Italia ~** mainland Italy.

pe'nisola *sf* peninsula.

peni'tente *sm/f* penitent.

peni'tenza [peni'tɛntsa] *sf* penitence; (*punizione*) penance.

penitenzi'ario [peniten'tsjarjo] *sm* prison.

'penna *sf* (*di uccello*) feather; (*per scrivere*) pen; **~e** *sfpl* (*CUC*) quills (*type of pasta*); **~ a feltro/stilografica/a sfera** felt-tip/fountain/ballpoint pen.

pen'nacchio [pen'nakkjo] *sm* (*ornamento*) plume; **un ~ di fumo** (*fig*) a plume *o* spiral of smoke.

penna'rello *sm* felt(-tip) pen.

pennel'lare *vi* to paint.

pen'nello *sm* brush; (*per dipingere*) (paint)brush; **a ~** (*perfettamente*) to perfection, perfectly; **~ per la barba** shaving brush.

Pen'nini *smpl*: **i ~** the Pennines.

pen'nino *sm* nib.

pen'none *sm* (*NAUT*) yard; (*stendardo*) banner, standard.

pe'nombra *sf* half-light, dim light.

pe'noso, a *ag* painful, distressing; (*faticoso*) tiring, laborious.

pen'sare *vi* to think ♦ *vt* to think; (*inventare, escogitare*) to think out; **~ a** to think of; (*amico, vacanze*) to think of *o* about; (*problema*) to think about; **~ di fare qc** to think of doing sth; **~ bene/male di qn** to think well/badly of sb, have a good/bad opinion of sb; **penso di sì** I think so; **penso di no** I don't think so; **a pensarci bene** ... on second thoughts (*Brit*) *o* thought (*US*) ...; **non voglio nemmeno pensarci** I don't even want to think about it; **ci penso io** I'll see to *o* take care of it.

pen'sata *sf* (*trovata*) idea, thought.

pensa'tore, 'trice *sm/f* thinker.

pensie'rino *sm* (*dono*) little gift; (*pensiero*): **ci farò un ~** I'll think about it.

pensi'ero *sm* thought; (*modo di pensare, dottrina*) thinking *q*; (*preoccupazione*) worry, care, trouble; **darsi ~ per qc** to worry about sth; **stare in ~ per qn** to be worried about sb; **un ~ gentile** (*anche fig: dono etc*) a kind thought.

pensie'roso, a *ag* thoughtful.

'pensile *ag* hanging.

pensiona'mento *sm* retirement; **~ anticipato** early retirement.

pensio'nante *sm/f* (*presso una famiglia*) lodger; (*di albergo*) guest.

pensio'nato, a *sm/f* pensioner ♦ *sm* (*istituto*) hostel.

pensi'one *sf* (*al prestatore di lavoro*) pension; (*vitto e alloggio*) board and lodging; (*albergo*) boarding house; **andare in ~** to retire; **mezza ~** half board; **~ completa** full board; **~ d'invalidità** disablement pension; **~ per la vecchiaia** old-age pension.

pensio'nistico, a, ci, che *ag* pension *cpd*.

pen'soso, a *ag* thoughtful, pensive, lost in thought.

pen'tagono *sm* pentagon.

pentapar'tito *sm* (*POL*) five-party coalition government.

Pente'coste *sf* Pentecost, Whit Sunday (*Brit*).

penti'mento *sm* repentance, contrition.

pen'tirsi *vr*: **~ di** to repent of; (*rammaricarsi*) to regret, be sorry for.

penti'tismo *sm* confessions from terrorists and members of organized crime rackets.

pen'tito, a *sm/f* ≈ supergrass (*Brit*), terrorist/criminal who turns police informer.

'pentola *sf* pot; **~ a pressione** pressure cooker.

pe'nultimo, a *ag* last but one (*Brit*), next to last, penultimate.

pe'nuria *sf* shortage.

penzo'lare [pendzo'lare] *vi* to dangle, hang

loosely.

penzo'loni [pɛndzo'loni] *av* dangling, hanging down; **stare ~** to dangle, hang down.

pe'pato, a *ag* (*condito con pepe*) peppery, hot; (*fig: pungente*) sharp.

'pepe *sm* pepper; **~ macinato/in grani** ground/whole pepper.

pepero'nata *sf stewed peppers, tomatoes and onions.*

peperon'cino [peperon'tʃino] *sm* chilli pepper.

pepe'rone *sm*: **~ (rosso)** red pepper, capsicum; **~ (verde)** green pepper, capsicum; **rosso come un ~** as red as a beetroot (*Brit*), fire-engine red (*US*); **~i ripieni** stuffed peppers.

pe'pita *sf* nugget.

per *prep* for; (*moto attraverso luogo*) through; (*mezzo, modo*) by; (*causa*) because of, owing to ♦ *cong*: **~ fare** (so as) to do, in order to do; **~ aver fatto** for having done; **partire ~ l'Inghilterra** to leave for England; **proseguire ~ Londra** to go on to London; **sedere ~ terra** to sit on the ground; **~ lettera/ferrovia** by letter/rail; **~ tutta l'estate** all through the summer, throughout the summer, all summer long; **~ abitudine** out of habit, from habit; **assentarsi ~ malattia** to be off because of *o* through *o* owing to illness; **giorno ~ giorno** day by day; **uno ~ uno** one by one; **uno ~ volta** one at a time; **~ persona** per person; **moltiplicare/dividere 9 ~ 3** to multiply/divide 9 by 3; **~ cento** per cent; **~ poco che sia** however little it may be, little though it may be.

'pera *sf* pear.

pe'raltro *av* moreover, what's more.

per'bacco *escl* by Jove!

per'bene *ag inv* respectable, decent ♦ *av* (*con cura*) properly, well.

perbe'nismo *sm* (so-called) respectability.

percentu'ale [pertʃentu'ale] *sf* percentage; (*commissione*) commission.

perce'pire [pertʃe'pire] *vt* (*sentire*) to perceive; (*ricevere*) to receive.

percet'tibile [pertʃet'tibile] *ag* perceptible.

percezi'one [pertʃet'tsjone] *sf* perception.

perché [per'ke] *av* why ♦ *cong* (*causale*) because; (*finale*) in order that, so that; (*consecutivo*): **è troppo forte ~ si possa batterlo** he's too strong to be beaten ♦ *sm inv* (*motivo*) reason; **non c'è un vero ~** there's no real reason for it; **i ~ sono tanti** there are many reasons for it.

perciò [per'tʃɔ] *cong* so, for this (*o* that) reason.

per'correre *vt* (*luogo*) to go all over; (: *paese*) to travel up and down, go all over; (*distanza*) to cover.

percor'ribile *ag* (*strada*) which can be followed.

per'corso, a *pp di* **percorrere** ♦ *sm* (*tragitto*) journey; (*tratto*) route.

per'cosso, a *pp di* **percuotere** ♦ *sf* blow.

percu'otere *vt* to hit, strike.

percussi'one *sf* percussion; **strumenti a ~** (*MUS*) percussion instruments.

per'dente *ag* losing ♦ *sm/f* loser.

'perdere *vt* to lose; (*lasciarsi sfuggire*) to miss; (*sprecare: tempo, denaro*) to waste; (*mandare in rovina: persona*) to ruin ♦ *vi* to lose; (*serbatoio etc*) to leak; **~rsi** *vr* (*smarrirsi*) to get lost; (*svanire*) to disappear, vanish; **saper ~** to be a good loser; **lascia ~!** forget it!, never mind!; **non ho niente da ~** (*fig*) I've got nothing to lose; **è un'occasione da non ~** it's a marvellous opportunity; (*affare*) it's a great bargain; **è fatica persa** it's a waste of effort; **~ al gioco** to lose money gambling; **~ di vista qn** (*anche fig*) to lose sight of sb; **~rsi di vista** to lose sight of each other; (*fig*) to lose touch; **~rsi alla vista** to disappear from sight; **~rsi in chiacchiere** to waste time talking.

perdifi'ato: a ~ *av* (*correre*) at breathtaking speed; (*gridare*) at the top of one's voice.

perdigi'orno [perdi'dʒorno] *sm/f inv* idler, waster.

'perdita *sf* loss; (*spreco*) waste; (*fuoriuscita*) leak; **siamo in ~** (*COMM*) we are running at a loss; **a ~ d'occhio** as far as the eye can see.

perdi'tempo *sm/f inv* waster, idler.

perdizi'one [perdit'tsjone] *sf* (*REL*) perdition, damnation; **luogo di ~** place of ill repute.

perdo'nare *vt* to pardon, forgive; (*scusare*) to excuse, pardon; **per farsi ~** in order to be forgiven; **perdona la domanda ... if you don't mind my asking ...; **vogliate ~ il (mio) ritardo** my apologies for being late; **un male che non perdona** an incurable disease.

per'dono *sm* forgiveness; (*DIR*) pardon; **chiedere ~ a qn (per)** to ask for sb's forgiveness (for); (*scusarsi*) to apologize to sb (for).

perdu'rare *vi* to go on, last; (*perseverare*) to persist.

perduta'mente *av* desperately, passionately.

per'duto, a *pp di* **perdere** ♦ *ag* (*gen*) lost; **sentirsi *o* vedersi ~** (*fig*) to realize the hopelessness of one's position; **una donna ~a** (*fig*) a fallen woman.

peregri'nare *vi* to wander, roam.

pe'renne *ag* eternal, perpetual, perennial; (*BOT*) perennial.

peren'torio, a *ag* peremptory; (*definitivo*) final.

perfetta'mente *av* perfectly; **sai ~ che ...** you know perfectly well that ....

per'fetto, a *ag* perfect ♦ *sm* (*LING*) perfect (tense).

perfeziona'mento [perfettsjona'mento] *sm*: ~ **(di)** improvement (in), perfection (of); **corso di** ~ proficiency course.

perfezio'nare [perfettsjo'nare] *vt* to improve, perfect; ~**rsi** *vr* to improve.

perfezi'one [perfet'tsjone] *sf* perfection.

perfezio'nismo [perfettsjo'nizmo] *sm* perfectionism.

perfezio'nista, i, e [perfettsjo'nista] *sm/f* perfectionist.

per'fidia *sf* perfidy.

'perfido, a *ag* perfidious, treacherous.

per'fino *av* even.

perfo'rare *vt* to pierce; (*MED*) to perforate; (*banda, schede*) to punch; (*trivellare*) to drill.

perfora'tore, 'trice *sm/f* punch-card operator ♦ *sm* (*utensile*) punch; (*INFORM*): ~ **di schede** card punch ♦ *sf* (*TECN*) boring *o* drilling machine; (*INFORM*) card punch.

perforazi'one [perforat'tsjone] *sf* piercing; perforation; punching; drilling.

perga'mena *sf* parchment.

perico'lante *ag* precarious.

pe'ricolo *sm* danger; **essere fuori** ~ to be out of danger; (*MED*) to be off the danger list; **mettere in** ~ to endanger, put in danger.

perico'loso, a *ag* dangerous.

perife'ria *sf* periphery; (*di città*) outskirts *pl*.

peri'ferico, a, ci, che *ag* (*ANAT, INFORM*) peripheral; (*zona*) outlying.

pe'rifrasi *sf inv* circumlocution.

pe'rimetro *sm* perimeter.

peri'odico, a, ci, che *ag* periodic(al); (*MAT*) recurring ♦ *sm* periodical.

pe'riodo *sm* period; ~ **contabile** accounting period; ~ **di prova** trial period.

peripe'zie [peripet'tsie] *sfpl* ups and downs, vicissitudes.

'periplo *sm* circumnavigation.

pe'rire *vi* to perish, die.

peris'copio *sm* periscope.

pe'rito, a *ag* expert, skilled ♦ *sm/f* expert; (*agronomo, navale*) surveyor; **un** ~ **chimico** a qualified chemist.

perito'nite *sf* peritonitis.

pe'rizia [pe'rittsja] *sf* (*abilità*) ability; (*giudizio tecnico*) expert opinion; expert's report; ~ **psichiatrica** psychiatrist's report.

'perla *sf* pearl.

per'lina *sf* bead.

perlo'meno *av* (*almeno*) at least.

perlopiù *av* (*quasi sempre*) in most cases, usually.

perlus'trare *vt* to patrol.

perlustrazi'one [perlustrat'tsjone] *sf* patrol, reconnaissance; **andare in** ~ to go on patrol.

perma'loso, a *ag* touchy.

perma'nente *ag* permanent ♦ *sf* permanent wave, perm.

perma'nenza [perma'nentsa] *sf* permanence; (*soggiorno*) stay; **buona** ~**!** enjoy your stay!

perma'nere *vi* to remain.

per'mango, per'masi *etc vb vedi* **permanere.**

perme'abile *ag* permeable.

perme'are *vt* to permeate.

per'messo, a *pp di* **permettere** ♦ *sm* (*autorizzazione*) permission, leave; (*dato a militare, impiegato*) leave; (*licenza*) licence (*Brit*), license (*US*), permit; (*MIL: foglio*) pass; ~**?, è** ~**?** (*posso entrare?*) may I come in?; (*posso passare?*) excuse me; ~ **di lavoro/pesca** work/fishing permit.

per'mettere *vt* to allow, permit; ~ **a qn qc/di fare qc** to allow sb sth/to do sth; ~**rsi** *vr*: ~**rsi qc/di fare qc** (*concedersi*) to allow o.s. sth/to do sth; (*avere la possibilità*) to afford sth/to do sth; **permettete che mi presenti** let me introduce myself, may I introduce myself?; **mi sia permesso di sottolineare che ...** may I take the liberty of pointing out that ....

per'misi *etc vb vedi* **permettere.**

permis'sivo, a *ag* permissive.

'permuta *sf* (*DIR*) transfer; (*COMM*) trade-in; **accettare qc in** ~ to take sth as a trade-in; **valore di** ~ (*di macchina etc*) trade-in value.

per'nacchia [per'nakkja] *sf* (*fam*): **fare una** ~ to blow a raspberry.

per'nice [per'nitʃe] *sf* partridge.

pernici'oso, a [perni'tʃoso] *ag* pernicious.

'perno *sm* pivot.

pernot'tare *vi* to spend the night, stay overnight.

'pero *sm* pear tree.

però *cong* (*ma*) but; (*tuttavia*) however, nevertheless.

pero'rare *vt* (*DIR, fig*): ~ **la causa di qn** to plead sb's case.

perpendico'lare *ag, sf* perpendicular.

perpen'dicolo *sm*: **a** ~ perpendicularly.

perpe'trare *vt* to perpetrate.

perpetu'are *vt* to perpetuate.

per'petuo, a *ag* perpetual.

perplessità *sf inv* perplexity.

per'plesso, a *ag* perplexed, puzzled.

perqui'sire *vt* to search.

perquisizi'one [perkwizit'tsjone] *sf* (police) search; **mandato di** ~ search warrant.

'perse *etc vb vedi* **perdere.**

persecu'tore *sm* persecutor.

persecuzi'one [persekut'tsjone] *sf* persecution.

persegu'ibile *ag* (*DIR*): **essere** ~ **per legge** to be liable to prosecution.

persegu'ire *vt* to pursue; (*DIR*) to

prosecute.
persegui'tare vt to persecute.
perseve'rante ag persevering.
perseve'ranza [perseve'rantsa] sf perseverance.
perseve'rare vi to persevere.
'persi etc vb vedi **perdere**.
'Persia sf: la ~ Persia.
persi'ano, a ag, sm/f Persian ♦ sf shutter;
~a avvolgibile roller blind.
'persico, a, ci, che ag: il golfo P~ the
Persian Gulf; pesce ~ perch.
per'sino av = perfino.
persis'tente ag persistent.
persis'tenza [persis'tɛntsa] sf persistence.
per'sistere vi to persist; ~ a fare to persist
in doing.
persis'tito, a pp di **persistere**.
'perso, a pp di **perdere** ♦ ag (smarrito: anche fig) lost; (sprecato) wasted; **fare qc a
tempo** ~ to do sth in one's spare time; ~
per ~ I've (o we've etc) got nothing
further to lose.
per'sona sf person; (qualcuno): **una** ~
someone, somebody, espressione interrogativa + anyone o anybody; ~e sfpl people
pl; **non c'è** ~ **che** ... there's nobody who
..., there isn't anybody who ...; **in** ~, **di** ~
in person; **per interposta** ~ through an
intermediary o a third party; ~ **giuridica**
(DIR) legal person.
perso'naggio [perso'naddʒo] sm (persona
ragguardevole) personality, figure; (tipo)
character, individual; (LETTERATURA)
character.
perso'nale ag personal ♦ sm staff,
personnel; (figura fisica) build ♦ sf
(mostra) one-man (o one-woman) exhibition.
personalità sf inv personality.
personaliz'zato, a [personalid'dzato] ag
personalized.
personal'mente av personally.
personifi'care vt to personify; to embody.
perspi'cace [perspi'katʃe] ag shrewd, discerning.
perspi'cacia [perspi'katʃa] sf perspicacity,
shrewdness.
persu'adere vt: ~ **qn (di qc/a fare)** to
persuade sb (of sth/to do).
persuasi'one sf persuasion.
persua'sivo, a ag persuasive.
persu'aso, a pp di **persuadere**.
per'tanto cong (quindi) so, therefore.
'pertica, che sf pole.
perti'nace [perti'natʃe] ag determined;
persistent.
perti'nente ag: ~ **(a)** relevant (to),
pertinent (to).
perti'nenza [perti'nɛntsa] sf (attinenza)
pertinence, relevance; (competenza):
essere di ~ **di qn** to be sb's business.

per'tosse sf whooping cough.
per'tugio [per'tudʒo] sm hole, opening.
pertur'bare vt to disrupt; (persona) to disturb, perturb.
perturbazi'one [perturbat'tsjone] sf disruption; disturbance.
Perù sm: il ~ Peru.
peru'gino, a [peru'dʒino] ag of (o from) Perugia.
peruvi'ano, a ag, sm/f Peruvian.
per'vadere vt to pervade.
per'vaso, a pp di **pervadere**.
perve'nire vi: ~ **a** to reach, arrive at,
come to; (venire in possesso): **gli pervenne
una fortuna** he inherited a fortune; **far** ~
qc a to have sth sent to.
perve'nuto, a pp di **pervenire**.
perversi'one sf perversion.
perversità sf perversity.
per'verso, a ag perverted.
perver'tire vt to pervert.
pervi'cace [pervi'katʃe] ag stubborn,
obstinate.
pervi'cacia [pervi'katʃa] sf stubbornness,
obstinacy.
p.es. abbr (= per esempio) e.g.
'pesa sf weighing q; weighbridge.
pe'sante ag heavy; (fig: noioso) dull, boring.
pesan'tezza [pesan'tettsa] sf (anche fig)
heaviness; **avere** ~ **di stomaco** to feel
bloated.
pesaper'sone ag inv: (**bilancia**) ~ (weighing) scales pl; (automatica) weighing
machine.
pe'sare vt to weigh ♦ vi (avere un peso) to
weigh; (essere pesante) to be heavy; (fig)
to carry weight; ~ **su** (fig) to lie heavy
on; to influence; to hang over; **mi pesa
sgridarlo** I find it hard to scold him; **tutta
la responsabilità pesa su di lui** all the responsibility rests on his shoulders; **è una
situazione che mi pesa** it's a difficult situation for me; **il suo parere pesa molto** his
opinion counts for a lot; ~ **le parole** to
weigh one's words.
'pesca sf (pl **pesche**: frutto) peach; (il
pescare) fishing; **andare a** ~ to go fishing;
~ **di beneficenza** (lotteria) lucky dip; ~
con la lenza angling; ~ **subacquea** underwater fishing.
pes'caggio [pes'kaddʒo] sm (NAUT) draught
(Brit), draft (US).
pes'care vt (pesce) to fish for; to catch; (qc
nell'acqua) to fish out; (fig: trovare) to get
hold of, find.
pesca'tore sm fisherman; (con lenza)
angler.
'pesce ['peʃʃe] sm fish gen inv; **P~i** (dello
zodiaco) Pisces; **essere dei P~i** to be
Pisces; **non saper che ~i prendere** (fig) not
to know which way to turn; ~ **d'aprile!**

April Fool!; ~ **martello** hammerhead; ~ **rosso** goldfish; ~ **spada** swordfish.

pesce'cane [peʃʃe'kane] *sm* shark.

pesche'reccio [peske'rettʃo] *sm* fishing boat.

pesche'ria [peske'ria] *sf* fishmonger's (shop) (*Brit*), fish store (*US*).

pescherò *etc* [peske'rɔ] *vb vedi* **pescare**.

peschi'era [pes'kjɛra] *sf* fishpond.

pesci'vendolo, a [peʃʃi'vendolo] *sm/f* fishmonger (*Brit*), fish merchant (*US*).

'pesco, schi *sm* peach tree.

pes'coso, a *ag* teeming with fish.

'peso *sm* weight; (*SPORT*) shot; **dar ~ a qc** to attach importance to sth; **essere di ~ a qn** (*fig*) to be a burden to sb; **rubare sul ~** to give short weight; **lo portarono via di ~** they carried him away bodily; **avere due ~i e due misure** (*fig*) to have double standards; **~ lordo/netto** gross/net weight; **~ piuma/mosca/gallo/medio/massimo** (*PUGILATO*) feather/fly/bantam/middle/heavyweight.

pessi'mismo *sm* pessimism.

pessi'mista, i, e *ag* pessimistic ♦ *sm/f* pessimist.

'pessimo, a *ag* very bad, awful; **di ~a qualità** of very poor quality.

pes'tare *vt* to tread on, trample on; (*sale, pepe*) to grind; (*uva, aglio*) to crush; (*fig: picchiare*): **~ qn** to beat sb up; **~ i piedi** to stamp one's feet; **~ i piedi a qn** (*anche fig*) to tread on sb's toes.

'peste *sf* plague; (*persona*) nuisance, pest.

pes'tello *sm* pestle.

pes'tifero, a *ag* (*anche fig*) pestilential, pestiferous; (*odore*) noxious.

pesti'lenza [pesti'lɛntsa] *sf* pestilence; (*fetore*) stench.

'pesto, a *ag*: **c'è buio ~** it's pitch dark ♦ *sm* (*CUC*) sauce made with basil, garlic, cheese and oil; **occhio ~** black eye.

'petalo *sm* (*BOT*) petal.

pe'tardo *sm* firecracker, banger (*Brit*).

petizi'one [petit'tsjone] *sf* petition; **fare una ~ a** to petition.

'peto *sm* (*fam!*) fart (*!*).

petrol'chimica [petrol'kimika] *sf* petro-chemical industry.

petroli'era *sf* (*nave*) oil tanker.

petroli'ere *sm* (*industriale*) oilman; (*tecnico*) worker in the oil industry.

petroli'ero, a *ag* oil *cpd*.

petro'lifero, a *ag* oil *cpd*.

pe'trolio *sm* oil, petroleum; (*per lampada, fornello*) paraffin (*Brit*), kerosene (*US*); **lume a ~** oil *o* paraffin *o* kerosene lamp; **~ grezzo** crude oil.

pettego'lare *vi* to gossip.

pettego'lezzo [pettego'leddzo] *sm* gossip *q*; **fare ~i** to gossip.

pet'tegolo, a *ag* gossipy ♦ *sm/f* gossip.

petti'nare *vt* to comb (the hair of); **~rsi** *vr*

to comb one's hair.

pettina'tura *sf* (*acconciatura*) hairstyle.

'pettine *sm* comb; (*ZOOL*) scallop.

petti'rosso *sm* robin.

'petto *sm* chest; (*seno*) breast, bust; (*CUC: di carne bovina*) brisket; (: *di pollo etc*) breast; **prendere qn/qc di ~** to face up to sb/sth; **a doppio ~** (*abito*) double-breasted.

petto'rale *ag* pectoral.

petto'ruto, a *ag* broad-chested; full-breasted.

petu'lante *ag* insolent.

'pezza ['pɛttsa] *sf* piece of cloth; (*toppa*) patch; (*cencio*) rag, cloth; (*AMM*): **~ d'appoggio** *o* **giustificativa** voucher; **trattare qn come una ~ da piedi** to treat sb like a doormat.

pez'zato, a [pet'tsato] *ag* piebald.

pez'zente [pet'tsɛnte] *sm/f* beggar.

'pezzo ['pɛttso] *sm* (*gen*) piece; (*brandello, frammento*) piece, bit; (*di macchina, arnese etc*) part; (*STAMPA*) article; (*di tempo*): **aspettare un ~** to wait quite a while *o* some time; **andare a ~i** to break into pieces; **essere a ~i** (*oggetto*) to be in pieces *o* bits; (*fig: persona*) to be shattered; **un bel ~ d'uomo** a fine figure of a man; **abito a due ~i** two-piece suit; **essere tutto d'un ~** (*fig*) to be a man (*o* woman) of integrity; **~ di cronaca** (*STAMPA*) report; **~ grosso** (*fig*) bigwig; **~ di ricambio** spare part.

P.F. *abbr* = **per favore; prossimo futuro**.

PG *sigla* = *Perugia*.

P.G. *abbr* = **procuratore generale**.

PI *sigla* = *Pisa*.

P.I. *abbr* = **Pubblica Istruzione**.

pi'accio *etc* ['pjattʃo] *vb vedi* **piacere**.

pia'cente [pja'tʃɛnte] *ag* attractive, pleasant.

pia'cere [pja'tʃere] *vi* to please; ♦ *sm* pleasure; (*favore*) favour (*Brit*), favor (*US*); **una ragazza che piace** (*piacevole*) a likeable girl; (*attraente*) an attractive girl; **~ a: mi piace** I like it; **quei ragazzi non mi piacciono** I don't like those boys; **gli piacerebbe andare al cinema** he would like to go to the cinema; **il suo discorso è piaciuto molto** his speech was well received; **"~!"** (*nelle presentazioni*) "pleased to meet you!"; **con ~** certainly, with pleasure; **per ~** please; **fare un ~ a qn** to do sb a favour; **mi fa ~ per lui** I am pleased for him; **mi farebbe ~ rivederlo** I would like to see him again.

pia'cevole [pja'tʃevole] *ag* pleasant, agreeable.

piaci'mento [pjatʃi'mento] *sm*: **a ~** (*a volontà*) as much as one likes, at will; **lo farà a suo ~** he'll do it when it suits him.

piaci'uto, a [pja'tʃuto] *pp di* **piacere**.

pi'acqui *etc vb vedi* **piacere**.

pi'aga, ghe *sf* (*lesione*) sore; (*ferita: anche*

fig) wound; (*fig: flagello*) scourge, curse; (: *persona*) pest, nuisance.

piagnis'teo [pjaɲɲis'tɛo] *sm* whining, whimpering.

piagnuco'lare [pjaɲɲuko'lare] *vi* to whimper.

piagnuco'lio, ii [pjaɲɲuko'lio] *sm* whimpering.

piagnuco'loso, a [pjaɲɲuko'loso] *ag* whiny, whimpering, moaning.

pi'alla *sf* (*arnese*) plane.

pial'lare *vt* to plane.

pialla'trice [pjalla'tritʃe] *sf* planing machine.

pi'ana *sf* stretch of level ground; (*più esteso*) plain.

pianeggi'ante [pjaned'dʒante] *ag* flat, level.

piane'rottolo *sm* landing.

pia'neta *sm* (*ASTR*) planet.

pi'angere ['pjandʒere] *vi* to cry, weep; (*occhi*) to water ♦ *vt* to cry, weep; (*lamentare*) to bewail, lament; ~ **la morte di qn** to mourn sb's death.

pianifi'care *vt* to plan.

pianificazi'one [pjanifikat'tsjone] *sf* (*ECON*) planning; ~ **aziendale** corporate planning.

pia'nista, i, e *sm/f* pianist.

pi'ano, a *ag* (*piatto*) flat, level; (*MAT*) plane; (*facile*) straightforward, simple; (*chiaro*) clear, plain ♦ *av* (*adagio*) slowly; (*a bassa voce*) softly; (*con cautela*) slowly, carefully ♦ *sm* (*MAT*) plane; (*GEO*) plain; (*livello*) level, plane; (*di edificio*) floor; (*programma*) plan; (*MUS*) piano; **pian** ~ very slowly; (*poco a poco*) little by little; **una casa di 3 ~i** a 3-storey (*Brit*) o 3-storied (*US*) house; **al ~ di sopra/di sotto** on the floor above/below; **all'ultimo** ~ on the top floor; **al ~ terra** on the ground floor; **in primo/secondo** ~ (*FOT, CINEMA etc*) in the foreground/background; **fare un primo** ~ (*FOT, CINEMA*) to take a close-up; **di primo** ~ (*fig*) prominent, high-ranking; **un fattore di secondo** ~ a secondary o minor factor; **passare in secondo** ~ to become less important; **mettere tutto sullo stesso** ~ to lump everything together, give equal importance to everything; **tutto secondo i ~i** all according to plan; ~ **di lavoro** (*superficie*) worktop; (*programma*) work plan; ~ **regolatore** (*URBANISTICA*) town-planning scheme; ~ **stradale** road surface.

piano'forte *sm* piano, pianoforte.

piano'terra *sm inv* = **piano terra**.

pi'ansi *etc vb vedi* **piangere**.

pi'anta *sf* (*BOT*) plant; (*ANAT: anche*: ~ **del piede**) sole (of the foot); (*grafico*) plan; (*cartina topografica*) map; **ufficio a** ~ **aperta** open-plan office; **in** ~ **stabile** on the permanent staff; ~ **stradale** street map, street plan.

piantagi'one [pjanta'dʒone] *sf* plantation.

pianta'grane *sm/f inv* troublemaker.

pian'tare *vt* to plant; (*conficcare*) to drive o hammer in; (*tenda*) to put up, pitch; (*fig: lasciare*) to leave, desert; ~**rsi** *vr*: ~**rsi davanti a qn** to plant o.s. in front of sb; ~ **qn in asso** to leave sb in the lurch; ~ **grane** (*fig*) to cause trouble; **piantala!** (*fam*) cut it out!

pian'tato, a *ag*: **ben** ~ (*persona*) well-built.

pianta'tore *sm* planter.

pianter'reno *sm* ground floor.

pi'anto, a *pp di* **piangere** ♦ *sm* tears *pl*, crying.

pianto'nare *vt* to guard, watch over.

pian'tone *sm* (*vigilante*) sentry, guard; (*soldato*) orderly; (*AUT*) steering column.

pia'nura *sf* plain.

pi'astra *sf* plate; (*di pietra*) slab; (*di fornello*) hotplate; **panino alla** ~ ≈ toasted sandwich; ~ **di registrazione** tape deck.

pias'trella *sf* tile.

piastrel'lare *vt* to tile.

pias'trina *sf* (*ANAT*) platelet; (*MIL*) identity disc (*Brit*) o tag (*US*).

piatta'forma *sf* (*anche fig*) platform; ~ **continentale** (*GEO*) continental shelf; ~ **girevole** (*TECN*) turntable; ~ **di lancio** (*MIL*) launching pad o platform; ~ **rivendicativa** document prepared by the unions in an industry which sets out their claims.

piat'tello *sm* clay pigeon; **tiro al** ~ clay-pigeon shooting (*Brit*), trapshooting.

piat'tino *sm* (*di tazza*) saucer.

pi'atto, a *ag* flat; (*fig: scialbo*) dull ♦ *sm* (*recipiente, vivanda*) dish; (*portata*) course; (*parte piana*) flat (part); ~**i** *smpl* (*MUS*) cymbals; **un** ~ **di minestra** a plate of soup; ~ **fondo** soup dish; ~ **forte** main course; ~ **del giorno** dish of the day, plat du jour; ~ **del giradischi** turntable; ~**i già pronti** (*CUC*) ready-cooked dishes.

pi'azza ['pjattsa] *sf* square; (*COMM*) market; (*letto, lenzuolo*): **a una** ~ single; **a due** ~**e** double; **far** ~ **pulita** to make a clean sweep; **mettere in** ~ (*fig: rendere pubblico*) to make public; **scendere in** ~ (*fig*) to take to the streets, demonstrate; ~ **d'armi** (*MIL*) parade ground.

piazza'forte [pjattsa'forte], *pl* **piazze'forti** *sf* (*MIL*) stronghold.

piaz'zale [pjat'tsale] *sm* (large) square.

piazza'mento [pjattsa'mento] *sm* (*SPORT*) place, placing.

piaz'zare [pjat'tsare] *vt* to place; (*COMM*) to market, sell; ~**rsi** *vr* (*SPORT*) to be placed; ~**rsi bene** to finish with the leaders o in a good position.

piaz'zista, i [pjat'tsista] *sm* (*COMM*) commercial traveller.

piaz'zola [pjat'tsɔla] *sf* (*AUT*) lay-by (*Brit*), (roadside) stopping place.

'picca, che *sf* pike; ~**che** *sfpl* (*CARTE*)

spades; **rispondere ~che a qn** (*fig*) to give sb a flat refusal.

pic'cante *ag* hot, pungent; (*fig*) racy.

pic'carsi *vr*: **~ di fare** to pride o.s. on one's ability to do; **~ per qc** to take offence (*Brit*) *o* offense (*US*) at sth.

picchet'taggio [pikket'taddʒo] *sm* picketing.

picchet'tare [pikket'tare] *vt* to picket.

pic'chetto [pik'ketto] *sm* (*MIL, di scioperanti*) picket.

picchi'are [pik'kjare] *vt* (*persona: colpire*) to hit, strike; (: *prendere a botte*) to beat (up); (*battere*) to beat; (*sbattere*) to bang ♦ *vi* (*bussare*) to knock; (: *con forza*) to bang; (*colpire*) to hit, strike; (*sole*) to beat down.

picchi'ata [pik'kjata] *sf* knock; bang; blow; (*percosse*) beating, thrashing; (*AER*) dive; **scendere in ~** to (nose-)dive.

picchiet'tare [pikkjet'tare] *vt* (*punteggiare*) to spot, dot; (*colpire*) to tap.

'picchio ['pikkjo] *sm* woodpecker.

pic'cino, a [pit'tʃino] *ag* tiny, very small.

picci'olo [pit'tʃɔlo] *sm* (*BOT*) stalk.

piccio'naia [pittʃo'naja] *sf* pigeon-loft; (*TEATRO*): **la ~** the gods *sg* (*Brit*), the gallery.

picci'one [pit'tʃone] *sm* pigeon; **pigliare due ~i con una fava** (*fig*) to kill two birds with one stone.

'picco, chi *sm* peak; **a ~** vertically; **colare a ~** (*NAUT, fig*) to sink.

picco'lezza [pikko'lettsa] *sf* (*dimensione*) smallness; (*fig: grettezza*) meanness, pettiness; (: *inezia*) trifle.

'piccolo, a *ag* small; (*oggetto, mano, di età: bambino*) small, little (*dav sostantivo*); (*di breve durata: viaggio*) short; (*fig*) mean, petty ♦ *sm/f* child, little one ♦ *sm*: **nel mio ~** in my own small way; **~i** *smpl* (*di animale*) young *pl*; **in ~** in miniature; **la ~a borghesia** the lower middle classes; (*peg*) the petty bourgeoisie.

pic'cone *sm* pick(-axe).

pic'cozza [pik'kɔttsa] *sf* ice-axe.

pic'nic *sm inv* picnic; **fare un ~** to have a picnic.

pi'docchio [pi'dɔkkjo] *sm* louse.

pidocchi'oso, a [pidok'kjoso] *ag* (*infestato*) lousy; (*fig: taccagno*) mean, stingy, tight.

piè *sm inv*: **a ogni ~ sospinto** (*fig*) at every step; **saltare a ~ pari** (*omettere*) to skip; **a ~ di pagina** at the foot of the page; **note a ~ di pagina** footnotes.

pi'ede *sm* foot; (*di mobile*) leg; **in ~i** standing; **a ~i** on foot; **a ~i nudi** barefoot; **su due ~i** (*fig*) at once; **mettere qc in ~i** (*azienda etc*) to set sth up; **prendere ~** (*fig*) to gain ground, catch on; **puntare i ~i** (*fig*) to dig one's heels in; **sentirsi mancare la terra sotto i ~i** to feel lost; **non sta in ~i** (*persona*) he can't stand; (*fig: scusa etc*) it doesn't hold water; **tenere in ~i** (*persona*)

to keep on his (*o* her) feet; (*fig: ditta etc*) to keep going; **a ~ libero** (*DIR*) on bail; **sul ~ di guerra** (*MIL*) ready for action; **~ di porco** crowbar.

piedis'tallo, piedes'tallo *sm* pedestal.

pi'ega, ghe *sf* (*piegatura, GEO*) fold; (*di gonna*) pleat; (*di pantaloni*) crease; (*grinza*) wrinkle, crease; **prendere una brutta** *o* **cattiva ~** (*fig: persona*) to get into bad ways; (: *situazione*) to take a turn for the worse; **non fa una ~** (*fig: ragionamento*) it's faultless; **non ha fatto una ~** (*fig: persona*) he didn't bat an eye(-lid) (*Brit*) *o* an eye(lash) (*US*).

piega'mento *sm* folding; bending; **~ sulle gambe** (*GINNASTICA*) kneebend.

pie'gare *vt* to fold; (*braccia, gambe, testa*) to bend ♦ *vi* to bend; **~rsi** *vr* to bend; (*fig*): **~rsi (a)** to yield (to), submit (to).

piega'tura *sf* folding *q*; bending *q*; fold; bend.

piegherò *etc* [pjege'rɔ] *vb vedi* **piegare**.

pieghet'tare [pjeget'tare] *vt* to pleat.

pie'ghevole [pje'gevole] *ag* pliable, flexible; (*porta*) folding; (*fig*) yielding, docile.

Pie'monte *sm*: **il ~** Piedmont.

piemon'tese *ag, sm/f* Piedmontese.

pi'ena *sf vedi* **pieno**.

pie'nezza [pje'nettsa] *sf* fullness.

pi'eno, a *ag* full; (*muro, mattone*) solid ♦ *sm* (*colmo*) height, peak; (*carico*) full load ♦ *sf* (*di fiume*) flood, spate; (*gran folla*) crowd, throng; **~ di** full of; **a ~e mani** abundantly; **a tempo ~** full-time; **a ~i voti** (*eleggere*) unanimously; **laurearsi a ~i voti** to graduate with full marks; **in ~ giorno** in broad daylight; **in ~ inverno** in the depths of winter; **in ~a notte** in the middle of the night; **in ~a stagione** at the height of the season; **in ~** (*completamente: sbagliare*) completely; (*colpire, centrare*) bang *o* right in the middle; **avere ~i poteri** to have full powers; **nel ~ possesso delle sue facoltà** in full possession of his faculties; **fare il ~ (di benzina)** to fill up (with petrol).

pietà *sf* pity; (*REL*) piety; **senza ~** (*agire*) ruthlessly; (*persona*) pitiless, ruthless; **avere ~ di** (*compassione*) to pity, feel sorry for; (*misericordia*) to have pity *o* mercy on; **far ~** to arouse pity; (*peg*) to be terrible.

pie'tanza [pje'tantsa] *sf* dish, course.

pie'toso, a *ag* (*compassionevole*) pitying, compassionate; (*che desta pietà*) pitiful.

pi'etra *sf* stone; **mettiamoci una ~ sopra** (*fig*) let bygones be bygones; **~ preziosa** precious stone, gem; **~ dello scandalo** (*fig*) cause of scandal.

pie'traia *sf* (*terreno*) stony ground.

pietrifi'care *vt* to petrify; (*fig*) to transfix, paralyze.

pie'trisco, schi _sm_ crushed stone, road metal.

pi'eve _sf_ parish church.

'piffero _sm_ (_MUS_) pipe.

pigi'ama [pi'dʒama] _sm_ pyjamas _pl._

'pigia 'pigia ['pidʒa'pidʒa] _sm_ crowd, press.

pigi'are [pi'dʒare] _vt_ to press.

pigia'trice [pidʒa'tritʃe] _sf_ (_macchina_) wine press.

pigi'one [pi'dʒone] _sf_ rent.

pigli'are [piʎ'ʎare] _vt_ to take, grab; (_afferrare_) to catch.

'piglio ['piʎʎo] _sm_ look, expression.

pig'mento _sm_ pigment.

pig'meo, a _sm/f_ pygmy.

'pigna ['piɲɲa] _sf_ pine cone.

pignole'ria [piɲɲole'ria] _sf_ fastidiousness, fussiness.

pi'gnolo, a [piɲ'ɲɔlo] _ag_ pernickety.

pigno'rare [piɲɲo'rare] _vt_ (_DIR_) to distrain.

pigo'lare _vi_ to cheep, chirp.

pigo'lio _sm_ cheeping, chirping.

pi'grizia [pi'grittsja] _sf_ laziness.

'pigro, a _ag_ lazy; (_fig: ottuso_) slow, dull.

PIL _sigla m vedi_ **prodotto interno lordo**.

'pila _sf_ (_catasta, di ponte_) pile; (_ELETTR_) battery; (_fam: torcia_) torch (_Brit_), flashlight; **a ~, a ~e** battery-operated.

pi'lastro _sm_ pillar.

'pillola _sf_ pill; **prendere la ~** (_contraccettivo_) to be on the pill.

pi'lone _sm_ (_di ponte_) pier; (_di linea elettrica_) pylon.

pi'lota, i, e _sm/f_ pilot; (_AUT_) driver ♦ _ag inv_ pilot _cpd_; **~ automatico** automatic pilot.

pilo'taggio [pilo'taddʒo] _sm_: **cabina di ~** flight deck.

pilo'tare _vt_ to pilot; to drive.

piluc'care _vt_ to nibble at.

pi'mento _sm_ pimento, allspice.

pim'pante _ag_ lively, full of beans.

pinaco'teca, che _sf_ art gallery.

pi'neta _sf_ pinewood.

ping-'pong [piŋ'pɔŋ] _sm_ table tennis.

'pingue _ag_ fat, corpulent.

pingu'edine _sf_ corpulence.

pingu'ino _sm_ (_ZOOL_) penguin.

'pinna _sf_ fin; (_di pinguino, spatola di gomma_) flipper.

pin'nacolo _sm_ pinnacle.

'pino _sm_ pine (tree).

pi'nolo _sm_ pine kernel.

'pinta _sf_ pint.

'pinza ['pintsa] _sf_ pliers _pl_; (_MED_) forceps _pl_; (_ZOOL_) pincer.

pinzette [pin'tsette] _sfpl_ tweezers.

'pio, a, 'pii, 'pie _ag_ pious; (_opere, istituzione_) charitable, charity _cpd_.

piogge'rella [pjoddʒe'rella] _sf_ drizzle.

pi'oggia, ge ['pjɔddʒa] _sf_ rain; (_fig: di regali, fiori_) shower; (_di insulti_) hail; **sotto la ~** in the rain; **~ acida** acid rain.

pi'olo _sm_ peg; (_di scala_) rung.

piom'bare _vi_ to fall heavily; (_gettarsi con impeto_): **~ su** to fall upon, assail ♦ _vt_ (_dente_) to fill.

piomba'tura _sf_ (_di dente_) filling.

piom'bino _sm_ (_sigillo_) (lead) seal; (_del filo a piombo_) plummet; (_PESCA_) sinker.

pi'ombo _sm_ (_CHIM_) lead; (_sigillo_) (lead) seal; (_proiettile_) (lead) shot; **a ~** (_cadere_) straight down; (_muro etc_) plumb; **andare con i piedi di ~** (_fig_) to tread carefully.

pioni'ere, a _sm/f_ pioneer.

pi'oppo _sm_ poplar.

pio'vano, a _ag_: **acqua ~a** rainwater.

pi'overe _vb impers_ to rain ♦ _vi_ (_fig: scendere dall'alto_) to rain down; (: _affluire in gran numero_): **~ in** to pour into; **non ci piove sopra** (_fig_) there's no doubt about it.

pioviggi'nare [pjoviddʒi'nare] _vb impers_ to drizzle.

piovosità _sf_ rainfall.

pio'voso, a _ag_ rainy.

pi'ovra _sf_ octopus.

pi'ovve _etc vb vedi_ **piovere**.

'pipa _sf_ pipe.

pipì _sf_ (_fam_): **fare ~** to have a wee (wee).

pipis'trello _sm_ (_ZOOL_) bat.

pi'ramide _sf_ pyramid.

pi'rata, i _sm_ pirate; **~ della strada** hit-and-run driver.

Pire'nei _smpl_: **i ~** the Pyrenees.

'pirico, a, ci, che _ag_: **polvere ~a** gunpowder.

pi'rite _sf_ pyrite.

piro'etta _sf_ pirouette.

pi'rofilo, a _ag_ heat-resistant ♦ _sf_ heat-resistant glass; (_tegame_) heat-resistant dish.

pi'roga, ghe _sf_ dug-out canoe.

pi'romane _sm/f_ arsonist.

pi'roscafo _sm_ steamer, steamship.

pi'sano, a _ag_ Pisan.

pisci'are [piʃ'ʃare] _vi_ (_fam!_) to piss (!), pee (!).

pi'scina [piʃ'ʃina] _sf_ (swimming) pool.

pi'sello _sm_ pea.

piso'lino _sm_ nap; **fare un ~** to have a nap.

'pista _sf_ (_traccia_) track, trail; (_di stadio_) track; (_di pattinaggio_) rink; (_da sci_) run; (_AER_) runway; (_di circo_) ring; **~ da ballo** dance floor; **~ ciclabile** cycle track; **~ di lancio** launch(ing) pad; **~ di rullaggio** (_AER_) taxiway; **~ di volo** (_AER_) runway.

pis'tacchio [pis'takkjo] _sm_ pistachio (tree); pistachio (nut).

pis'tillo _sm_ (_BOT_) pistil.

pis'tola _sf_ pistol, gun; **~ a spruzzo** spray gun; **~ a tamburo** revolver.

pis'tone _sm_ piston.

pi'tocco, chi _sm_ skinflint, miser.

pi'tone _sm_ python.

pit'tore, 'trice _sm/f_ painter.

pitto'resco, a, schi, sche *ag* picturesque.

pit'torico, a, ci, che *ag* of painting, pictorial.

pit'tura *sf* painting; ~ **fresca** wet paint.

pittu'rare *vt* to paint.

più *av* more; (*in frasi comparative*) more, *aggettivo corto* + ...er; (*in frasi superlative*) most, *aggettivo corto* + ...est; (*negativo*): **non** ... ~ no more, *espressione negativa* + any more; no longer; (*di temperatura*) above zero; (*MAT*) plus ♦ *prep* plus, besides ♦ *ag inv* more; (*parecchi*) several ♦ *sm inv* (*la parte maggiore*): **il** ~ the most; (*MAT*) plus (sign); **i** ~ the majority; ~ **che/di** more than; ~ **che altro** above all; ~ **che mai** more than ever; ~ **grande che** bigger than; ~ **di 10 persone/te** more than 10 people/you; **il** ~ **intelligente/grande** the most intelligent/the biggest; **di** ~ more; **e per di** ~ (*inoltre*) and what's more, moreover; **3 ore/litri di** ~ **che** 3 hours/litres more than; **una volta di** ~ once more; **3 chili in** ~ 3 kilos more, 3 extra kilos; **a** ~ **non posso** as much as possible; **al** ~ **presto** as soon as possible; **al** ~ **tardi** at the latest; ~ **o meno** more or less; **né** ~ **né meno** no more, no less; **non lavora** ~ he doesn't work any more, he no longer works; **non ce n'è** ~ there isn't any left; **non c'è** ~ **nessuno** there's no one left; **non c'è** ~ **niente da fare** there's nothing more to be done; **si fa sempre** ~ **difficile** it is getting more and more difficult; **chi** ~ **chi meno hanno tutti contribuito** everybody made a contribution of some sort; **il** ~ **delle volte** more often than not, generally; **tutt'al** ~, **al** ~ if the worst comes to the worst.

piuccheper'fetto [pjukkeper'fɛtto] *sm* (*LING*) pluperfect, past perfect.

pi'uma *sf* feather; ~**e** *sfpl* down *sg*; (*piumaggio*) plumage *sg*, feathers.

piu'maggio [pju'maddʒo] *sm* plumage, feathers *pl*.

piu'mino *sm* (eider)down; (*per letto*) eiderdown; (: *tipo danese*) duvet, continental quilt; (*giacca*) quilted jacket (*with goose-feather padding*); (*per cipria*) powder puff; (*per spolverare*) feather duster.

piut'tosto *av* rather; ~ **che** (*anziché*) rather than.

pi'vello, a *sm/f* greenhorn.

'pizza ['pittsa] *sf* (*CUC*) pizza; (*CINEMA*) reel.

pizze'ria [pittse'ria] *sf place where pizzas are made, sold or eaten.*

pizzi'cagnolo, a [pittsi'kaɲɲolo] *sm/f* specialist grocer.

pizzi'care [pittsi'kare] *vt* (*stringere*) to nip, pinch; (*pungere*) to sting; to bite; (*MUS*) to pluck ♦ *vi* (*prudere*) to itch, be itchy; (*cibo*) to be hot *o* spicy.

pizziche'ria [pittsike'ria] *sf* delicatessen

(shop).

'pizzico, chi ['pittsiko] *sm* (*pizzicotto*) pinch, nip; (*piccola quantità*) pinch, dash; (*d'insetto*) sting; bite.

pizzi'cotto [pittsi'kɔtto] *sm* pinch, nip.

'pizzo ['pittso] *sm* (*merletto*) lace; (*barbetta*) goatee beard.

pla'care *vt* to placate, soothe; ~**rsi** *vr* to calm down.

'placca, che *sf* plate; (*con iscrizione*) plaque; (*anche*: ~ **dentaria**) (dental) plaque.

plac'care *vt* to plate; **placcato in oro/argento** gold-/silver-plated.

pla'centa [pla'tʃɛnta] *sf* placenta.

placidità [platʃidi'ta] *sf* calm, peacefulness.

'placido, a ['platʃido] *ag* placid, calm.

plafoni'era *sf* ceiling light.

plagi'are [pla'dʒare] *vt* (*copiare*) to plagiarize; (*DIR*: *influenzare*) to coerce.

'plagio ['pladʒo] *sm* plagiarism; (*DIR*) duress.

plaid [plɛd] *sm inv* (travelling) rug (*Brit*), lap robe (*US*).

pla'nare *vi* (*AER*) to glide.

'plancia, ce ['plantʃa] *sf* (*NAUT*) bridge; (*AUT*: *cruscotto*) dashboard.

'plancton *sm inv* plankton.

plane'tario, a *ag* planetary ♦ *sm* (*locale*) planetarium.

'plasma *sm* plasma.

plas'mare *vt* to mould (*Brit*), mold (*US*), shape.

'plastico, a, ci, che *ag* plastic ♦ *sm* (*rappresentazione*) relief model; (*esplosivo*): **bomba al** ~ plastic bomb ♦ *sf* (*arte*) plastic arts *pl*; (*MED*) plastic surgery; (*sostanza*) plastic; **in materiale** ~ plastic.

plasti'lina ® *sf* plasticine ®.

'platano *sm* plane tree.

pla'tea *sf* (*TEATRO*) stalls *pl* (*Brit*), orchestra (*US*).

plate'ale *ag* (*gesto, atteggiamento*) theatrical.

plateal'mente *av* theatrically.

'platino *sm* platinum.

pla'tonico, a, ci, che *ag* platonic.

plau'dire *vi*: ~ **a** to applaud.

plau'sibile *ag* plausible.

'plauso *sm* (*fig*) approval.

ple'baglia [ple'baʎʎa] *sf* (*peg*) rabble, mob.

'plebe *sf* common people.

ple'beo, a *ag* plebeian; (*volgare*) coarse, common.

plebi'scito [plebiʃ'ʃito] *sm* plebiscite.

ple'nario, a *ag* plenary.

pleni'lunio *sm* full moon.

'plettro *sm* plectrum.

pleu'rite *sf* pleurisy.

PLI *sigla m* (*POL*) = Partito Liberale Italiano.

'plico, chi *sm* (*pacco*) parcel; **in** ~ **a parte**

(*COMM*) under separate cover.

plo'tone *sm* (*MIL*) platoon; ~ **d'esecuzione** firing squad.

'plumbeo, a *ag* leaden.

plu'rale *ag*, *sm* plural.

plura'lismo *sm* pluralism.

pluralità *sf* plurality; (*maggioranza*) majority.

plusva'lenza [pluzva'lɛntsa] *sf* capital gain.

plusva'lore *sm* (*ECON*) surplus.

plu'tonio *sm* plutonium.

pluvi'ale *ag* rain *cpd*.

pluvi'ometro *sm* rain gauge.

P.M. *abbr* (*POL*) = **Pubblico Ministero**; (= *Polizia Militare*) MP (= *Military Police*).

pm *abbr* = *peso molecolare*.

PN *sigla* = *Pordenone*.

pneu'matico, a, ci, che *ag* inflatable; (*TECN*) pneumatic ♦ *sm* (*AUT*) tyre (*Brit*), tire (*US*).

PNL *sigla m vedi* **prodotto nazionale lordo**.

Po *sm*: **il** ~ the Po.

po' *av*, *sm vedi* **poco**.

P.O. *abbr* = **posta ordinaria**.

po'chezza [po'kettsa] *sf* insufficiency, shortage; (*fig*: *meschinità*) meanness, smallness.

'poco, a, chi, che *ag* (*quantità*) little, *negazione* + (very) much; (*numero*) few, *negazione* + (very) many ♦ *av* little, *espressione negativa* + much; (*con ag*) *espressione negativa* + very ♦ *pronome* (very) little; ~**chi(che)** *pronome pl* few ♦ *sm*: **il** ~ **che guadagna** ... what little he earns ...; **con** ~**a spesa** for a small outlay; **a** ~ **prezzo** at a low price, cheap; **è un tipo di** ~**che parole** he's a man of few words; **un po'** a little, a bit; **sono un po' stanco** I'm a bit tired; **un po' di soldi/pane** a little money/bread; **sta** ~ **bene** he's not very well; ~ **prima/dopo** shortly before/afterwards; ~ **fa** a short time ago; **a** ~ **a** ~ little by little; **fra** ~ **o un po'** in a little while; **a dir** ~ to say the least; **è una cosa da** ~ it's nothing, it's of no importance.

po'dere *sm* (*AGR*) farm.

pode'roso, a *ag* powerful.

podestà *sm inv* (*nel fascismo*) podestà, mayor.

'podio *sm* dais, platform; (*MUS*) podium.

po'dismo *sm* (*SPORT*: *marcia*) walking; (: *corsa*) running.

po'dista, i, e *sm/f* walker; runner.

po'ema, i *sm* poem.

poe'sia *sf* (*arte*) poetry; (*componimento*) poem.

po'eta, 'essa *sm/f* poet/poetess.

poe'tare *vi* to write poetry.

po'etico, a, ci, che *ag* poetic(al).

poggi'are [pod'dʒare] *vt* to lean, rest; (*posare*) to lay, place.

poggia'testa [poddʒa'tɛsta] *sm inv* (*AUT*) headrest.

'poggio ['pɔddʒo] *sm* hillock, knoll.

'poi *av* then; (*alla fine*) finally, at last ♦ *sm*: **pensare al** ~ to think of the future; **e** ~ (*inoltre*) and besides; **questa** ~ **(è bella)** (*ironico*) that's a good one!; **d'ora in** ~ from now on; **da domani in** ~ from tomorrow onwards.

poiché [poi'ke] *cong* since, as.

'poker *sm* poker.

po'lacco, a, chi, che *ag* Polish ♦ *sm/f* Pole.

po'lare *ag* polar.

'polca, che *sf* polka.

po'lemico, a, ci, che *ag* polemic(al), controversial ♦ *sf* controversy; **fare** ~**che** to be contentious.

polemiz'zare [polemid'dzare] *vi*: ~ **(su qc)** to argue (about sth).

po'lenta *sf* (*CUC*) sort of thick porridge made with maize flour.

polen'tone, a *sm/f* slowcoach (*Brit*), slowpoke (*US*).

pole'sano, a *ag* of (*o* from) Polesine (*area between the Po and the Adige*).

POL'FER *abbr f* = *Polizia Ferroviaria*.

'poli... *prefisso* poly....

poliambula'torio *sm* (*MED*) health clinic.

poli'clinico, ci *sm* general hospital, polyclinic.

poli'estere *sm* polyester.

poliga'mia *sf* polygamy.

po'ligono *sm* polygon; ~ **di tiro** rifle range.

Poli'nesia *sf*: **la** ~ Polynesia.

polinesi'ano, a *ag*, *sm/f* Polynesian.

'polio(mie'lite) *sf* polio(myelitis).

'polipo *sm* polyp.

polisti'rolo *sm* polystyrene.

poli'tecnico, ci *sm* postgraduate technical college.

po'litica, che *sf vedi* **politico**.

politi'cante *sm/f* (*peg*) petty politician.

politiciz'zare [politit∫id'dzare] *vt* to politicize.

po'litico, a, ci, che *ag* political ♦ *sm/f* politician ♦ *sf* politics *sg*; (*linea di condotta*) policy; **elezioni** ~**che** parliamentary (*Brit*) *o* congressional (*US*) election(s); **uomo** ~ politician; **darsi alla** ~**a** to go into politics; **fare** ~**a** (*militante*) to be a political activist; (*come professione*) to be in politics; **la** ~**a del governo** the government's policies; ~**a aziendale** company policy; ~**a estera** foreign policy; ~**a dei prezzi** prices policy; ~**a dei redditi** incomes policy.

poliva'lente *ag* multi-purpose.

poli'zia [polit'tsia] *sf* police; ~ **giudiziaria** ≈ Criminal Investigation Department (CID) (*Brit*), Federal Bureau of Investigation (FBI) (*US*); ~ **sanitaria/tributaria** health/tax inspectorate; ~ **stradale** traffic police.

polizi'esco, a, schi, sche [polit'tsjesko] *ag* police *cpd*; (*film, romanzo*) detective *cpd*.

polizi'otto [polit'tsjɔtto] *sm* policeman; **cane** ~ police dog; **donna** ~ policewoman.

'polizza ['pɔlittsa] *sf* (*COMM*) bill; ~ **di assicurazione** insurance policy; ~ **di carico** bill of lading.

pol'laio *sm* henhouse.

pollai'olo, a *sm/f* poulterer (*Brit*), poultryman.

pol'lame *sm* poultry.

pol'lastro *sm* (*ZOOL*) cockerel.

'pollice ['pɔllitʃe] *sm* thumb; (*unità di misura*) inch.

'polline *sm* pollen.

polli'vendolo, a *sm/f* poulterer (*Brit*), poultryman.

'pollo *sm* chicken; **far ridere i** ~**i** (*situazione, persona*) to be utterly ridiculous.

polmo'nare *ag* lung *cpd*, pulmonary.

pol'mone *sm* lung.

polmo'nite *sf* pneumonia.

'polo *sm* (*GEO, FISICA*) pole; (*gioco*) polo; **il P**~ **sud/nord** the South/North Pole.

Po'lonia *sf*: **la** ~ Poland.

'polpa *sf* flesh, pulp; (*carne*) lean meat.

pol'paccio [pol'pattʃo] *sm* (*ANAT*) calf.

polpas'trello *sm* fingertip.

pol'petta *sf* (*CUC*) meatball.

polpet'tone *sm* (*CUC*) meatloaf.

'polpo *sm* octopus.

pol'poso, a *ag* fleshy.

pol'sino *sm* cuff.

'polso *sm* (*ANAT*) wrist; (*pulsazione*) pulse; (*fig: forza*) drive, vigour (*Brit*), vigor (*US*); **avere** ~ (*fig*) to be strong; **un uomo di** ~ a man of nerve.

pol'tiglia [pol'tiʎʎa] *sf* (*composto*) mash, mush; (*di fango e neve*) slush.

pol'trire *vi* to laze about.

pol'trona *sf* armchair; (*TEATRO: posto*) seat in the front stalls (*Brit*) *o* the orchestra (*US*).

poltron'cina [poltron'tʃina] *sf* (*TEATRO*) seat in the back stalls (*Brit*) *o* the orchestra (*US*).

pol'trone *ag* lazy, slothful.

'polvere *sf* dust; (*anche:* ~ **da sparo**) (gun)powder; (*sostanza ridotta minutissima*) powder, dust; **caffè in** ~ instant coffee; **latte in** ~ dried *o* powdered milk; **sapone in** ~ soap powder; ~ **di ferro** iron filings *pl*; ~ **d'oro** gold dust; ~ **pirica** *o* **da sparo** gunpowder.

polveri'era *sf* powder magazine.

polve'rina *sf* (*gen, MED*) powder; (*gergo: cocaina*) snow.

polveriz'zare [polverid'dzare] *vt* to pulverize; (*nebulizzare*) to atomize; (*fig*) to crush, pulverize; (*: record*) to smash.

polve'rone *sm* thick cloud of dust.

polve'roso, a *ag* dusty.

po'mata *sf* ointment, cream.

po'mello *sm* knob.

pomeridi'ano, a *ag* afternoon *cpd*; **nelle ore** ~**e** in the afternoon.

pome'riggio [pome'riddʒo] *sm* afternoon; **nel primo/tardo** ~ in the early/late afternoon.

'pomice ['pomitʃe] *sf* pumice.

pomici'are [pomi'tʃare] *vi* (*fam: sbaciucchiarsi*) to neck.

'pomo *sm* (*mela*) apple; (*ornamentale*) knob; (*di sella*) pommel; ~ **d'Adamo** (*ANAT*) Adam's apple.

pomo'doro *sm* tomato.

'pompa *sf* pump; (*sfarzo*) pomp (and ceremony); ~ **antincendio** fire hose; ~ **di benzina** petrol (*Brit*) *o* gas (*US*) pump; (*distributore*) filling *o* gas (*US*) station; (**impresa di**) ~**e funebri** funeral parlour *sg* (*Brit*), undertaker's *sg*, mortician's (*US*).

pom'pare *vt* to pump; (*trarre*) to pump out; (*gonfiare d'aria*) to pump up.

pompei'ano, a *ag* of (*o* from) Pompei.

pom'pelmo *sm* grapefruit.

pompi'ere *sm* fireman.

pom'poso, a *ag* pompous.

ponde'rare *vt* to ponder over, consider carefully.

ponde'roso, a *ag* (*anche fig*) weighty.

po'nente *sm* west.

'pongo, 'poni *etc vb vedi* **porre**.

'ponte *sm* bridge; (*di nave*) deck; (*: anche:* ~ **di comando**) bridge; (*impalcatura*) scaffold; **vivere sotto i** ~**i** to be a tramp; **fare il** ~ (*fig*) to take the extra day off (*between 2 public holidays*); **governo** ~ interim government; ~ **aereo** airlift; ~ **di barche** (*MIL*) pontoon bridge; ~ **di coperta** (*NAUT*) upper deck; ~ **levatoio** drawbridge; ~ **radio** radio link; ~ **sospeso** suspension bridge.

pon'tefice [pon'tefitʃe] *sm* (*REL*) pontiff.

ponti'cello [ponti'tʃɛllo] *sm* (*di occhiali, MUS*) bridge.

pontifi'care *vi* (*anche fig*) to pontificate.

pontifi'cato *sm* pontificate.

ponti'ficio, a, ci, cie [ponti'fitʃo] *ag* papal; **Stato P**~ Papal State.

pon'tile *sm* jetty.

'popeline ['pɔpelin] *sm* poplin.

popo'lano, a *ag* popular, of the people ♦ *sm/f* man/woman of the people.

popo'lare *ag* popular; (*quartiere, clientela*) working-class ♦ *vt* (*rendere abitato*) to populate; ~**rsi** *vr* to fill with people, get crowded; **manifestazione** ~ mass demonstration; **repubblica** ~ people's republic.

popolarità *sf* popularity.

popolazi'one [popolat'tsjone] *sf* population.

'popolo *sm* people.

popo'loso, a *ag* densely populated.

po'pone *sm* melon.

'poppa *sf* (*di nave*) stern; (*mammella*) breast; **a** ~ aft, astern.

pop'pante *sm/f* unweaned infant; *(fig:* ine*sperto)* whippersnapper.

pop'pare *vt* to suck.

pop'pata *sf (allattamento)* feed.

poppa'toio *sm* (feeding) bottle.

popu'lista, i, e *ag* populist.

por'caio *sm (anche fig)* pigsty.

porcel'lana [portʃel'lana] *sf* porcelain, china; *(oggetto)* piece of porcelain.

porcel'lino, a [portʃel'lino] *sm/f* piglet; ~ **d'India** guinea pig.

porche'ria [porke'ria] *sf* filth, muck; *(fig: oscenità)* obscenity; *(: azione disonesta)* dirty trick; *(: cosa mal fatta)* rubbish.

por'chetta [por'ketta] *sf* roast sucking pig.

por'cile [por'tʃile] *sm* pigsty.

por'cino, a [por'tʃino] *ag* of pigs, pork *cpd* ♦ *sm (fungo) type of edible mushroom.*

'porco, ci *sm* pig; *(carne)* pork.

porcos'pino *sm* porcupine.

'porgere ['pɔrdʒere] *vt* to hand, give; *(tendere)* to hold out.

pornogra'fia *sf* pornography.

porno'grafico, a, ci, che *ag* pornographic.

'poro *sm* pore.

po'roso, a *ag* porous.

'porpora *sf* purple.

'porre *vt (mettere)* to put; *(collocare)* to place; *(posare)* to lay (down), put (down); *(fig: supporre)*: **poniamo (il caso) che** ... let's suppose that ...; **porsi** *vr (mettersi)*: **porsi a sedere/in cammino** to sit down/set off; ~ **le basi di** *(fig)* to lay the foundations of, establish; ~ **una domanda a qn** to ask sb a question, put a question to sb; ~ **la propria fiducia in qn** to place one's trust in sb; ~ **fine** *o* **termine a qc** to put an end *o* a stop to sth; **posto che** ... supposing that ..., on the assumption that ...; **porsi in salvo** to save o.s.

'porro *sm (BOT)* leek; *(MED)* wart.

'porsi *etc vb vedi* **porgere.**

'porta *sf* door; *(SPORT)* goal; *(INFORM)* port; ~**e** *sfpl (di città)* gates; **mettere qn alla** ~ to throw sb out; **sbattere** *o* **chiudere la** ~ **in faccia a qn** *(anche fig)* to slam the door in sb's face; **trovare tutte le** ~**e chiuse** *(fig)* to find the way barred; **a** ~**e chiuse** *(DIR)* in camera; **l'inverno è alle** ~**e** *(fig)* winter is upon us; **vendita** ~ **a** ~ door-to-door selling; ~ **di servizio** tradesmen's entrance; ~ **di sicurezza** emergency exit; ~ **stagna** watertight door.

portaba'gagli [portaba'gaʎʎi] *sm inv (facchino)* porter; *(AUT, FERR)* luggage rack.

portabandi'era *sm inv* standard bearer.

porta'borse *sm inv (peg)* lackey.

porta'cenere [porta'tʃenere] *sm inv* ashtray.

portachi'avi [porta'kjavi] *sm inv* keyring.

porta'cipria [porta'tʃiprja] *sm inv* powder compact.

porta'erei *sf inv (nave)* aircraft carrier ♦ *sm inv (aereo)* aircraft transporter.

portafi'nestra, *pl* **portefi'nestre** *sf* French window.

porta'foglio [porta'fɔʎʎo] *sm (busta)* wallet; *(cartella)* briefcase; *(POL, BORSA)* portfolio; ~ **titoli** investment portfolio.

portafor'tuna *sm inv* lucky charm; mascot.

portagi'oie [porta'dʒɔje] *sm inv*, **portagioi'elli** [portadʒo'jelli] *sm inv* jewellery *(Brit) o* jewelry *(US)* box.

por'tale *sm* portal.

porta'lettere *sm/f inv* postman/woman *(Brit)*, mailman/woman *(US)*.

porta'mento *sm* carriage, bearing.

portamo'nete *sm inv* purse.

por'tante *ag (muro etc)* supporting, load-bearing.

portan'tina *sf* sedan chair; *(per ammalati)* stretcher.

portaom'brelli *sm inv* umbrella stand.

porta'pacchi [porta'pakki] *sm inv (di moto, bicicletta)* luggage rack.

por'tare *vt (sostenere, sorreggere: peso, bambino, pacco)* to carry; *(indossare: abito, occhiali)* to wear; *(: capelli lunghi)* to have; *(avere: nome, titolo)* to have, bear; *(recare)*: ~ **qc a qn** to take *(o* bring) sth to sb; *(fig: sentimenti)* to bear; ~**rsi** *vr (recarsi)* to go; ~ **avanti** *(discorso, idea)* to pursue; ~ **via** to take away; *(rubare)* to take; ~ **i bambini a spasso** to take the children for a walk; ~ **fortuna** to bring good luck; ~ **qc alla bocca** to lift *o* put sth to one's lips; **porta bene i suoi anni** he's wearing well; **dove porta questa strada?** where does this road lead?, where does this road take you?; **il documento porta la tua firma** the document has *o* bears your signature; **non gli porto rancore** I don't bear him a grudge; **la polizia si è portata sul luogo del disastro** the police went to the scene of the disaster.

portari'viste *sm inv* magazine rack.

portasa'pone *sm inv* soap dish.

portasiga'rette *sm inv* cigarette case.

portas'pilli *sm inv* pincushion.

por'tata *sf (vivanda)* course; *(AUT)* carrying *(o* loading) capacity; *(di arma)* range; *(volume d'acqua)* (rate of) flow; *(fig: limite)* scope, capability; *(: importanza)* impact, import; **alla** ~ **di tutti** *(conoscenza)* within everybody's capabilities; *(prezzo)* within everybody's means; **a/fuori** ~ **(di)** within/out of reach (of); **a** ~ **di mano** within (arm's) reach; **di grande** ~ of great importance.

por'tatile *ag* portable.

por'tato, a *ag (incline)*: ~ **a** inclined *o* apt to.

porta'tore, 'trice *sm/f (anche COMM)* bearer; (*MED*) carrier; **pagabile al** ~ payable to the bearer.

portatovagli'olo [portatovaʎ'ʎɔlo] *sm* napkin ring.

portau'ovo *sm inv* eggcup.

porta'voce [porta'votʃe] *sm/f inv* spokesman/ woman.

por'tello *sm* (*di portone*) door; (*NAUT*) hatch.

por'tento *sm* wonder, marvel.

porten'toso, a *ag* wonderful, marvellous (*Brit*), marvelous (*US*).

porti'cato *sm* portico.

'portico, ci *sm* portico; (*riparo*) lean-to.

porti'era *sf* (*AUT*) door.

porti'ere *sm* (*portinaio*) concierge, caretaker; (*di hotel*) porter; (*nel calcio*) goalkeeper.

porti'naio, a *sm/f* concierge, caretaker.

portine'ria *sf* caretaker's lodge.

'porto, a *pp di* **porgere** ♦ *sm* (*NAUT*) harbour (*Brit*), harbor (*US*), port; (*spesa di trasporto*) carriage ♦ *sm inv* port (wine); **andare** *o* **giungere in** ~ (*fig*) to come to a successful conclusion; **condurre qc in** ~ to bring sth to a successful conclusion; ~ **d'armi** gun licence (*Brit*) *o* license (*US*); ~ **fluviale** river port; ~ **franco** free port; ~ **marittimo** seaport; ~ **militare** naval base; ~ **pagato** carriage paid, post free *o* paid; ~ **di scalo** port of call.

Porto'gallo *sm*: **il** ~ Portugal.

porto'ghese [porto'gese] *ag*, *sm/f*, *sm* Portuguese *inv*.

por'tone *sm* main entrance, main door.

portori'cano, a *ag*, *sm/f* Puerto Rican.

Porto'rico *sf* Puerto Rico.

portu'ale *ag* harbour *cpd* (*Brit*), harbor *cpd* (*US*), port *cpd* ♦ *sm* dock worker.

porzi'one [por'tsjone] *sf* portion, share; (*di cibo*) portion, helping.

'posa *sf* (*FOT*) exposure; (*atteggiamento, di modello*) pose; (*riposo*): **lavorare senza** ~ to work without a break; **mettersi in** ~ to pose; **teatro di** ~ photographic studio.

posa'cenere [posa'tʃenere] *sm inv* ashtray.

po'sare *vt* to put (down), lay (down) ♦ *vi* (*ponte, edificio, teoria*): ~ **su** to rest on; (*FOT, atteggiarsi*) to pose; ~**rsi** *vr* (*ape, aereo*) to land; (*uccello*) to alight; (*sguardo*) to settle.

po'sata *sf* piece of cutlery; ~**e** *sfpl* cutlery *sg*.

posa'tezza [posa'tettsa] *sf* (*di persona*) composure; (*di discorso*) balanced nature.

po'sato, a *ag* steady; (*discorso*) balanced.

pos'critto *sm* postscript.

'posi *etc vb vedi* **porre**.

posi'tivo, a *ag* positive.

posizi'one [pozit'tsjone] *sf* position; **farsi una** ~ to make one's way in the world; **prendere** ~ (*fig*) to take a stand; **luci di** ~

(*AUT*) sidelights.

posolo'gia, 'gie [pozolo'dʒia] *sf* dosage, directions *pl* for use.

pos'porre *vt* to place after; (*differire*) to postpone, defer.

pos'posto, a *pp di* **posporre**.

posse'dere *vt* to own, possess; (*qualità, virtù*) to have, possess; (*conoscere a fondo: lingua etc*) to have a thorough knowledge of; (*sog: ira etc*) to possess.

possedi'mento *sm* possession.

pos'sente *ag* strong, powerful.

posses'sivo, a *ag* possessive.

pos'sesso *sm* possession; **essere in** ~ **di qc** to be in possession of sth; **prendere** ~ **di qc** to take possession of sth; **entrare in** ~ **dell'eredità** to come into one's inheritance.

posses'sore *sm* owner.

pos'sibile *ag* possible ♦ *sm*: **fare tutto il** ~ to do everything possible; **nei limiti del** ~ as far as possible; **al più tardi** ~ as late as possible; **vieni prima** ~ come as soon as possible.

possibi'lista, i, e *ag*: **essere** ~ to keep an open mind.

possibilità *sf inv* possibility ♦ *sfpl* (*mezzi*) means; **aver la** ~ **di fare** to be in a position to do; to have the opportunity to do; **nei limiti delle nostre** ~ in so far as we can.

possibil'mente *av* if possible.

possi'dente *sm/f* landowner.

possi'edo *etc vb vedi* **possedere**.

'posso *etc vb vedi* **potere**.

post ... *prefisso* post ....

'posta *sf* (*servizio*) post, postal service; (*corrispondenza*) post, mail; (*ufficio postale*) post office; (*nei giochi d'azzardo*) stake; (*CACCIA*) hide (*Brit*), blind (*US*); ~**e** *sfpl* (*amministrazione*) post office; **fare la** ~ **a qn** (*fig*) to lie in wait for sb; **la** ~ **in gioco è troppo alta** (*fig*) there's too much at stake; **a bella** ~ (*apposta*) on purpose; **piccola** ~ (*su giornale*) letters to the editor, letters page; ~ **aerea** airmail; ~ **elettronica** electronic mail; ~ **ordinaria** ≈ second-class mail; **P**~**e e Telecomunicazioni (PP.TT.)** *postal and telecommunications service*; **ministro delle P**~**e e Telecomunicazioni** Postmaster General.

posta'giro [posta'dʒiro] *sm* post office cheque (*Brit*) *o* check (*US*), postal giro (*Brit*).

pos'tale *ag* postal, post office *cpd* ♦ *sm* (*treno*) mail train; (*nave*) mail boat; (*furgone*) mail van; **timbro** ~ postmark.

postazi'one [postat'tsjone] *sf* (*MIL*) emplacement.

post'bellico, a, ci, che *ag* postwar.

posteggi'are [posted'dʒare] *vt*, *vi* to park.

posteggia'tore, 'trice [posteddʒa'tore] *sm/f*

car-park attendant (*Brit*), parking-lot attendant (*US*).

pos'teggio [pos'teddʒo] *sm* car park (*Brit*), parking lot (*US*); (*di taxi*) rank (*Brit*), stand (*US*).

postelegra'fonico, a, ci, che *ag* postal and telecommunications *cpd*.

'posteri *smpl* posterity *sg*; **i nostri ~** our descendants.

posteri'ore *ag* (*dietro*) back; (*dopo*) later ♦ *sm* (*fam: sedere*) behind.

posteri'ori: a ~ *ag inv* after the event (*dopo sostantivo*) ♦ *av* looking back.

posterità *sf* posterity.

pos'ticcio, a, ci, ce [pos'tittʃo] *ag* false ♦ *sm* hairpiece.

postici'pare [postitʃi'pare] *vt* to defer, postpone.

pos'tilla *sf* marginal note.

pos'tino *sm* postman (*Brit*), mailman (*US*).

'posto, a *pp di* **porre** ♦ *sm* (*sito, posizione*) place; (*impiego*) job; (*spazio libero*) room, space; (*di parcheggio*) space; (*sedile: al teatro, in treno etc*) seat; (*MIL*) post; **a ~** (*in ordine*) in place, tidy; (*fig*) settled; (: *persona*) reliable; **mettere a ~** (*riordinare*) to tidy (up), put in order; (*faccende: sistemare*) to straighten out; **prender ~** to take a seat; **al ~ di** in place of; **sul ~** on the spot; **~ di blocco** roadblock; **~ di lavoro** job; **~ di polizia** police station; **~ telefonico pubblico (P.T.P.)** public telephone; **~ di villeggiatura** holiday (*Brit*) o tourist spot; **~i in piedi** (*TEATRO, in autobus*) standing room.

postopera'torio, a *ag* (*MED*) postoperative.

pos'tribolo *sm* brothel.

post'scriptum *sm inv* postscript.

'postumo, a *ag* posthumous; (*tardivo*) belated; **~i** *smpl* (*conseguenze*) aftereffects, consequences.

po'tabile *ag* drinkable; **acqua ~** drinking water.

po'tare *vt* to prune.

po'tassio *sm* potassium.

pota'tura *sf* pruning.

po'tente *ag* (*nazione*) strong, powerful; (*veleno, farmaco*) potent, strong.

po'tenza [po'tɛntsa] *sf* power; (*forza*) strength; **all'ennesima ~** to the nth degree; **le Grandi P~e** the Great Powers; **~ militare** military might o strength.

potenzi'ale [poten'tsjale] *ag, sm* potential.

potenzia'mento [potentsja'mento] *sm* development.

potenzi'are [poten'tsjare] *vt* to develop.

po'tere *vb + infinito* can; (*sog: persona*) can, to be able to; (*autorizzazione*) can, may; (*possibilità, ipotesi*) may ♦ *vb impers*: **può darsi** perhaps; **può darsi che** perhaps, it may be that ♦ *sm* power; **avresti potuto dirmelo!** you could o might have told me!;

non ne posso più! I can't take any more!; **essere al ~** (*POL*) to be in power o in office; **~ d'acquisto** purchasing power; **~ esecutivo** executive power.

potestà *sf* (*potere*) power; (*DIR*) authority.

potrò *etc vb vedi* **potere**.

pove'raccio, a, ci, ce [pove'rattʃo] *sm/f* poor devil.

'povero, a *ag* poor; (*disadorno*) plain, bare ♦ *sm/f* poor man/woman; **i ~i** the poor; **~ di** lacking in, having little; **minerale ~ di ferro** ore with a low iron content; **paese ~ di risorse** country short of o lacking in resources.

povertà *sf* poverty.

pozi'one [pot'tsjone] *sf* potion.

'pozza ['pottsa] *sf* pool.

poz'zanghera [pot'tsangera] *sf* puddle.

'pozzo ['pottso] *sm* well; (*cava: di carbone*) pit; (*di miniera*) shaft; **~ nero** cesspit; **~ petrolifero** oil well.

pp. *abbr* (= *pagine*) pp.

p.p. *abbr* (= *per procura*) pp.

PP.SS. *abbr* = **partecipazioni statali**.

PP.TT. *abbr* = **Poste e Telecomunicazioni**; *vedi* **posta**.

PR *sigla* = *Parma* ♦ *sigla m* (*POL*) = *Partito Radicale*.

P.R. *abbr* = **piano regolatore; procuratore della Repubblica**.

'Praga *sf* Prague.

prag'matico, a, ci, che *ag* pragmatic.

pram'matica *sf* custom; **essere di ~** to be customary.

pran'zare [pran'dzare] *vi* to dine, have dinner; to lunch, have lunch.

'pranzo ['prandzo] *sm* dinner; (*a mezzogiorno*) lunch.

'prassi *sf* usual procedure.

'pratica, che *sf* practice; (*esperienza*) experience; (*conoscenza*) knowledge, familiarity; (*tirocinio*) training, practice; (*AMM: affare*) matter, case; (: *incartamento*) file, dossier; (*praticamente*) in practice; **mettere in ~** to put into practice; **fare le ~che per** (*AMM*) to do the paperwork for; **~ restrittiva** restrictive practice; **~che illecite** dishonest practices.

prati'cabile *ag* (*progetto*) practicable, feasible; (*luogo*) passable, practicable.

pratica'mente *av* (*in modo pratico*) in a practical way, practically; (*quasi*) practically, almost.

prati'cante *sm/f* apprentice, trainee; (*REL*) (regular) churchgoer.

prati'care *vt* to practise (*Brit*), practice (*US*); (*SPORT: tennis etc*) to play; (: *nuoto, scherma etc*) to go in for; (*eseguire: apertura, buco*) to make; **~ uno sconto** to give a discount.

praticità [pratitʃi'ta] *sf* practicality,

practicalness; **per** ~ for practicality's sake.

'pratico, a, ci, che *ag* practical; ~ **di** (*esperto*) experienced *o* skilled in; (*familiare*) familiar with; **all'atto** ~ in practice; **è** ~ **del mestiere** he knows his trade; **mi è più** ~ **venire di pomeriggio** it's more convenient for me to come in the afternoon.

'prato *sm* meadow; (*di giardino*) lawn.

preal'larme *sm* warning (signal).

preal'pino, a *ag* of the Pre-Alps.

pre'ambolo *sm* preamble; **senza tanti** ~**i** without beating about (*Brit*) *o* around (*US*) the bush.

preannunci'are [preannun'tʃare], **preannunzi'are** [preannun'tsjare] *vt* to give advance notice of.

preavvi'sare *vt* to give advance notice of.

preav'viso *sm* notice; **telefonata con** ~ personal *o* person to person call.

pre'bellico, a, ci, che *ag* prewar *cpd*.

precari'ato *sm* temporary employment.

precarietà *sf* precariousness.

pre'cario, a *ag* precarious; (*INS*) temporary, without tenure.

precauzio'nale [prekauttsjo'nale] *ag* precautionary.

precauzi'one [prekaut'tsjone] *sf* caution, care; (*misura*) precaution; **prendere** ~**i** to take precautions.

prece'dente [pretʃe'dɛnte] *ag* previous ♦ *sm* precedent; **il discorso/film** ~ the previous *o* preceding speech/film; **senza** ~**i** unprecedented; ~**i penali** (*DIR*) criminal record *sg*.

prece'denza [pretʃe'dɛntsa] *sf* priority, precedence; (*AUT*) right of way; **dare** ~ **assoluta a qc** to give sth top priority.

pre'cedere [pre'tʃɛdere] *vt* to precede, go (*o* come) before.

pre'cetto [pre'tʃɛtto] *sm* precept; (*MIL*) call-up notice.

precet'tore [pretʃet'tore] *sm* (private) tutor.

precipi'tare [pretʃipi'tare] *vi* (*cadere*) to fall headlong; (*fig: situazione*) to get out of control ♦ *vt* (*gettare dall'alto in basso*) to hurl, fling; (*fig: affrettare*) to rush; ~**rsi** *vr* (*gettarsi*) to hurl *o* fling o.s.; (*affrettarsi*) to rush.

precipi'tato, a [pretʃipi'tato] *ag* hasty ♦ *sm* (*CHIM*) precipitate.

precipitazi'one [pretʃipitat'tsjone] *sf* (*METEOR*) precipitation; (*fig*) haste.

precipi'toso, a [pretʃipi'toso] *ag* (*caduta, fuga*) headlong; (*fig: avventato*) rash, reckless; (: *affrettato*) hasty, rushed.

preci'pizio [pretʃi'pittsjo] *sm* precipice; **a** ~ (*fig: correre*) headlong.

pre'cipuo, a [pre'tʃipuo] *ag* principal, main.

precisa'mente [pretʃiza'mente] *av* (*gen*) precisely; (*con esattezza*) exactly.

preci'sare [pretʃi'zare] *vt* to state, specify; (*spiegare*) to explain (in detail); **vi preciseremo la data in seguito** we'll let you know the exact date later; **tengo a** ~ **che** ... I must point out that ....

precisazi'one [pretʃizat'tsjone] *sf* clarification.

precisi'one [pretʃi'zjone] *sf* precision; accuracy; **strumenti di** ~ precision instruments.

pre'ciso, a [pre'tʃizo] *ag* (*esatto*) precise; (*accurato*) accurate, precise; (*deciso: idea*) precise, definite; (*uguale*): **2 vestiti** ~**i** 2 dresses exactly the same; **sono le 9** ~**e** it's exactly 9 o'clock.

pre'cludere *vt* to block, obstruct.

pre'cluso, a *pp di* **precludere**.

pre'coce [pre'kɔtʃe] *ag* early; (*bambino*) precocious; (*vecchiaia*) premature.

precocità [prekotʃi'ta] *sf* (*di morte*) untimeliness; (*di bambino*) precociousness.

precon'cetto, a [prekon'tʃetto] *ag* preconceived ♦ *sm* preconceived idea, prejudice.

pre'correre *vt* to anticipate; ~ **i tempi** to be ahead of one's time.

precorri'tore, 'trice *sm/f* precursor, forerunner.

pre'corso, a *pp di* **precorrere**.

precur'sore *sm* forerunner, precursor.

'preda *sf* (*bottino*) booty; (*animale, fig*) prey; **essere** ~ **di** to fall prey to; **essere in** ~ **a** to be prey to.

pre'dare *vt* to plunder.

preda'tore *sm* predator.

predeces'sore, a [predetʃes'sore] *sm/f* predecessor.

pre'della *sf* platform, dais; altar-step.

predesti'nare *vt* to predestine.

predestinazi'one [predestinat'tsjone] *sf* predestination.

pre'detto, a *pp di* **predire** ♦ *ag* aforesaid, aforementioned.

'predica, che *sf* sermon; (*fig*) lecture, talking-to.

predi'care *vt, vi* to preach.

predica'tivo, a *ag* predicative.

predi'cato *sm* (*LING*) predicate.

predi'letto, a *pp di* **prediligere** ♦ *ag, sm/f* favourite (*Brit*), favorite (*US*).

predilezi'one [predilet'tsjone] *sf* fondness, partiality; **avere una** ~ **per qc/qn** to be partial to sth/fond of sb.

predi'ligere [predi'lidʒere] *vt* to prefer, have a preference for.

pre'dire *vt* to foretell, predict.

predis'porre *vt* to get ready, prepare; ~ **qn a qc** to predispose sb to sth.

predisposizi'one [predispozit'tsjone] *sf* (*MED*) predisposition; (*attitudine*) bent, aptitude; **avere** ~ **alla musica** to have a bent for music.

predis'posto, a *pp di* **predisporre.**
predizi'one [predit'tsjone] *sf* prediction.
predomi'nante *ag* predominant.
predomi'nare *vi* (*prevalere*) to predominate; (*eccellere*) to excel.
predo'minio *sm* predominance; supremacy.
preesis'tente *ag* pre-existent.
pree'sistere *vi* to pre-exist.
preesis'tito, a *pp di* **preesistere.**
prefabbri'cato, a *ag* (*EDIL*) prefabricated.
prefazi'one [prefat'tsjone] *sf* preface, foreword.
prefe'renza [prefe'rɛntsa] *sf* preference; **a ~ di** rather than; **di ~** preferably, by preference; **non ho ~e** I have no preferences either way, I don't mind.
preferenzi'ale [preferen'tsjale] *ag* preferential; **corsia ~** (*AUT*) bus and taxi lane.
prefe'ribile *ag*: **~ (a)** preferable (to), better (than); **sarebbe ~ andarsene** it would be better to go.
preferibil'mente *av* preferably.
prefe'rire *vt* to prefer, like better; **~ il caffè al tè** to prefer coffee to tea, like coffee better than tea.
pre'fetto *sm* prefect.
prefet'tura *sf* prefecture.
pre'figgersi [pre'fiddʒersi] *vr*: **~rsi uno scopo** to set o.s. a goal.
prefigu'rare *vt* (*simboleggiare*) to foreshadow; (*prevedere*) to foresee.
pre'fisso, a *pp di* **prefiggersi** ♦ *sm* (*LING*) prefix; (*TEL*) dialling (*Brit*) *o* dial (*US*) code.
Preg. *abbr* = **pregiatissimo.**
pre'gare *vi* to pray ♦ *vt* (*REL*) to pray to; (*implorare*) to beg; (*chiedere*): **~ qn di fare** to ask sb to do; **farsi ~** to need coaxing *o* persuading.
pre'gevole [pre'dʒevole] *ag* valuable.
pregherò *etc* [prege'rɔ] *vb vedi* **pregare.**
preghi'era [pre'gjɛra] *sf* (*REL*) prayer; (*domanda*) request.
pregi'arsi [pre'dʒarsi] *vr*: **mi pregio di farle sapere che ...** I am pleased to inform you that ....
pregia'tissimo, a [predʒa'tissimo] *ag* (*in lettere*): **~ Signor G. Agnelli** G. Agnelli Esquire.
pregi'ato, a [pre'dʒato] *ag* (*opera*) valuable; (*tessuto*) fine; (*valuta*) strong; **vino ~** vintage wine.
'pregio ['predʒo] *sm* (*stima*) esteem, regard; (*qualità*) (good) quality, merit; (*valore*) value, worth; **il ~ di questo sistema è ...** the merit of this system is ...; **oggetto di ~** valuable object.
pregiudi'care [predʒudi'kare] *vt* to prejudice, harm, be detrimental to.
pregiudi'cato, a [predʒudi'kato] *sm/f* (*DIR*) previous offender.

pregiu'dizio [predʒu'dittsjo] *sm* (*idea errata*) prejudice; (*danno*) harm *q*.
'pregno, a ['prɛɲɲo] *ag* (*saturo*): **~ di** full of, saturated with.
'prego *escl* (*a chi ringrazia*) don't mention it!; (*invitando qn ad accomodarsi*) please sit down!; (*invitando qn ad andare prima*) after you!
pregus'tare *vt* to look forward to.
preis'toria *sf* prehistory.
preis'torico, a, ci, che *ag* prehistoric.
pre'lato *sm* prelate.
prela'vaggio [prela'vaddʒo] *sm* pre-wash.
prelazi'one [prelat'tsjone] *sf* (*DIR*) preemption; **avere il diritto di ~ su qc** to have the first option on sth.
preleva'mento *sm* (*BANCA*) withdrawal; (*di merce*) picking up, collection.
prele'vare *vt* (*denaro*) to withdraw; (*campione*) to take; (*merce*) to pick up, collect; (*sog: polizia*) to take, capture.
preli'bato, a *ag* delicious.
preli'evo *sm* (*BANCA*) withdrawal; (*MED*): **fare un ~ (di)** to take a sample (of).
prelimi'nare *ag* preliminary; **~i** *smpl* preliminary talks; preliminaries.
pre'ludere *vi*: **~ a** (*preannunciare: crisi, guerra, temporale*) to herald, be a sign of; (*introdurre: dibattito etc*) to introduce, be a prelude to.
pre'ludio *sm* prelude.
pre'luso, a *pp di* **preludere.**
pré-ma'man [prema'mã] *sm inv* maternity dress.
prematrimoni'ale *ag* premarital.
prema'turo, a *ag* premature.
premedi'tare *vt* to premeditate, plan.
premeditazi'one [premeditat'tsjone] *sf* (*DIR*) premeditation; **con ~** *ag* premeditated ♦ *av* with intent.
'premere *vt* to press ♦ *vi*: **~ su** to press down on; (*fig*) to put pressure on; **~ a** (*fig: importare*) to matter to; **~ il grilletto** to pull the trigger.
pre'messo, a *pp di* **premettere** ♦ *sf* introductory statement, introduction; **mancano le ~e per una buona riuscita** we lack the basis for a successful outcome.
pre'mettere *vt* to put before; (*dire prima*) to start by saying, state first; **premetto che ...** I must say first of all that ...; **premesso che ...** given that ...; **ciò premesso ...** that having been said ....
premi'are *vt* to give a prize to; (*fig: merito, onestà*) to reward.
premiazi'one [premjat'tsjone] *sf* prize-giving.
premi'nente *ag* pre-eminent.
'premio *sm* prize; (*ricompensa*) reward; (*COMM*) premium; (*AMM*: *indennità*) bonus; **in ~ per** as a prize (*o* reward) for; **~ d'ingaggio** (*SPORT*) signing-on fee; **~ di produzione** productivity bonus.

pre'misi *etc vb vedi* **premettere.**

premoni'tore, 'trice *ag* premonitory.

premonizi'one [premonit'tsjone] *sf* premonition.

premu'nirsi *vr*: ~ **di** to provide o.s. with; ~ **contro** to protect o.s. from, guard o.s. against.

pre'mura *sf* (*fretta*) haste, hurry; (*riguardo*) attention, care; **aver** ~ to be in a hurry; **far** ~ **a qn** to hurry sb; **usare ogni** ~ **nei riguardi di qn, circondare qn di** ~**e** to be very attentive to sb.

premu'roso, a *ag* thoughtful, considerate.

prena'tale *ag* antenatal.

'prendere *vt* to take; (*andare a prendere*) to get, fetch; (*ottenere*) to get; (*guadagnare*) to get, earn; (*catturare: ladro, pesce*) to catch; (*collaboratore, dipendente*) to take on; (*passeggero*) to pick up; (*chiedere: somma, prezzo*) to charge, ask; (*trattare: persona*) to handle ♦ *vi* (*colla, cemento*) to set; (*pianta*) to take; (*fuoco: nel camino*) to catch; (*voltare*): ~ **a destra** to turn (to the) right; ~**rsi** *vr* (*azzuffarsi*): ~**rsi a pugni** to come to blows; **prende qualcosa?** (*da bere, da mangiare*) would you like something to eat (*o* drink)?; **prendo un caffè** I'll have a coffee; ~ **a fare qc** to start doing sth; ~ **qn/qc per** (*scambiare*) to take sb/sth for; ~ **l'abitudine di** to get into the habit of; ~ **fuoco** to catch fire; ~ **le generalità di qn** to take down sb's particulars; ~ **nota di** to take note of; ~ **parte a** to take part in; ~**rsi cura di qn/qc** to look after sb/sth; ~**rsi un impegno** to take on a commitment; **prendersela** (*adirarsi*) to get annoyed; (*preoccuparsi*) to get upset, worry.

prendi'sole *sm inv* sundress.

preno'tare *vt* to book, reserve.

prenotazi'one [prenotat'tsjone] *sf* booking, reservation.

preoccu'pante *ag* worrying.

preoccu'pare *vt* to worry; ~**rsi** *vr*: ~**rsi di qn/qc** to worry about sb/sth; ~**rsi per qn** to be anxious for sb.

preoccupazi'one [preokkupat'tsjone] *sf* worry, anxiety.

preordi'nato, a *ag* preordained.

prepa'rare *vt* to prepare; (*esame, concorso*) to prepare for; ~**rsi** *vr* (*vestirsi*) to get ready; ~**rsi a qc/a fare** to get ready *o* prepare (o.s.) for sth/to do; ~ **da mangiare** to prepare a meal.

prepara'tivi *smpl* preparations.

prepa'rato, a *ag* (*gen*) prepared; (*pronto*) ready ♦ *sm* (*prodotto*) preparation.

prepara'torio, a *ag* preparatory.

preparazi'one [preparat'tsjone] *sf* preparation; **non ha la necessaria** ~ **per svolgere questo lavoro** he lacks the qualifications necessary for the job.

prepensiona'mento *sm* early retirement.

preponde'rante *ag* predominant.

pre'porre *vt* to place before; (*fig*) to prefer.

preposizi'one [prepozit'tsjone] *sf* (*LING*) preposition.

pre'posto, a *pp di* **preporre.**

prepo'tente *ag* (*persona*) domineering, arrogant; (*bisogno, desiderio*) overwhelming, pressing ♦ *sm/f* bully.

prepo'tenza [prepo'tentsa] *sf* arrogance; (*comportamento*) arrogant behaviour (*Brit*) *o* behavior (*US*).

pre'puzio [pre'puttsjo] *sm* (*ANAT*) foreskin.

preroga'tiva *sf* prerogative.

'presa *sf* taking *q*; catching *q*; (*di città*) capture; (*indurimento: di cemento*) setting; (*appiglio*, SPORT) hold; (*di acqua, gas*) (supply) point; (ELETTR): ~ (**di corrente**) socket; (: *al muro*) point; (*piccola quantità: di sale etc*) pinch; (CARTE) trick; **far** ~ (*colla*) to set; **ha fatto** ~ **sul pubblico** (*fig*) it caught the public's imagination; **a** ~ **rapida** (*cemento*) quick-setting; **di forte** ~ (*fig*) with wide appeal; **essere alle** ~**e con qc** (*fig*) to be struggling with sth; **macchina da** ~ (CINEMA) cine camera (*Brit*), movie camera (*US*); ~ **d'aria** air inlet; ~ **diretta** (AUT) direct drive; ~ **in giro** leg-pull (*Brit*), joke; ~ **di posizione** stand.

pre'sagio [pre'zadʒo] *sm* omen.

presa'gire [preza'dʒire] *vt* to foresee.

presa'lario *sm* (INS) grant.

'presbite *ag* long-sighted.

presbiteri'ano, a *ag*, *sm/f* Presbyterian.

presbi'terio *sm* presbytery.

pre'scindere [preʃ'ʃindere] *vi*: ~ **da** to leave out of consideration; **a** ~ **da** apart from.

pre'scisso, a [preʃ'ʃisso] *pp di* **prescindere.**

presco'lastico, a, ci, che *ag* pre-school *cpd.*

pres'critto, a *pp di* **prescrivere.**

pres'crivere *vt* to prescribe.

prescrizi'one [preskrit'tsjone] *sf* (MED, DIR) prescription; (*norma*) rule, regulation.

'prese *etc vb vedi* **prendere.**

presen'tare *vt* to present; (*far conoscere*): ~ **qn (a)** to introduce sb (to); (AMM: *inoltrare*) to submit; ~**rsi** *vr* (*recarsi, farsi vedere*) to present o.s., appear; (*farsi conoscere*) to introduce o.s.; (*occasione*) to arise; ~ **qc in un'esposizione** to show *o* display sth at an exhibition; ~ **qn in società** to introduce sb into society; ~**rsi come candidato** (POL) to stand (*Brit*) *o* run (*US*) as a candidate; ~**rsi bene/male** to have a good/poor appearance; **la situazione si presenta difficile** things aren't looking too good, things look a bit tricky.

presentazi'one [prezentat'tsjone] *sf* presentation; introduction.

pre'sente *ag* present; (*questo*) this ♦ *sm*

present ♦ *sf* (*lettera*): **con la ~ vi comunico ... this is to inform you that ...** ♦ *sm/f* person present; **i ~i** those present; **aver ~ qc/qn** to remember sth/sb; **essere ~ a una riunione** to be present at *o* attend a meeting; **tener ~ qn/qc** to keep sb/sth in mind; **esclusi i ~i** present company excepted.

presenti'mento *sm* premonition.

pre'senza [pre'zɛntsa] *sf* presence; (*aspetto esteriore*) appearance; **in ~ di** in (the) presence of; **di bella ~** of good appearance; **~ di spirito** presence of mind.

presenzi'are [prezen'tsjare] *vi*: **~ a** to be present at, attend.

pre'sepio, pre'sepe *sm* crib.

preser'vare *vt* to protect.

preserva'tivo *sm* sheath, condom.

'presi *etc vb vedi* **prendere**.

'preside *sm/f* (*INS*) head (teacher) (*Brit*), principal (*US*); (*di facoltà universitaria*) dean.

presi'dente *sm* (*POL*) president; (*di assemblea, COMM*) chairman; **il P~ della Camera** (*POL*) ≈ the Speaker; **P~ del Consiglio (dei Ministri)** Prime Minister.

presiden'tessa *sf* president; (*moglie*) president's wife; (*di assemblea, COMM*) chairwoman.

presi'denza [presi'dɛntsa] *sf* presidency; office of president; chairmanship; **assumere la ~** to become president; to take the chair; **essere alla ~** to be president (*o* chairman); **candidato alla ~** presidential candidate; candidate for the chairmanship.

presidenzi'ale [presiden'tsjale] *ag* presidential.

presidi'are *vt* to garrison.

pre'sidio *sm* garrison.

presi'edere *vt* to preside over ♦ *vi*: **~ a** to direct, be in charge of.

'preso, a *pp di* **prendere**.

'pressa *sf* (*TECN*) press.

pres'sante *ag* (*bisogno, richiesta*) urgent, pressing.

pressap'poco *av* about, roughly, approximately.

pressi'one *sf* pressure; **far ~ su qn** to put pressure on sb; **subire forti ~i** to be under strong pressure; **~ sanguigna** blood pressure.

'presso *av* (*vicino*) nearby, close at hand ♦ *prep* (*vicino a*) near; (*accanto a*) beside, next to; (*in casa di*): **~ qn** at sb's home; (*nelle lettere*) care of (*abbr* c/o); (*alle dipendenze di*): **lavora ~ di noi** he works for *o* with us ♦ *smpl*: **nei ~i di** near, in the vicinity of; **ha avuto grande successo ~ i giovani** it has been a hit with young people.

pressoché [presso'ke] *av* nearly, almost.

pressuriz'zare [pressurid'dzare] *vt* to pressur-

ize.

prestabi'lire *vt* to arrange beforehand, arrange in advance.

presta'nome *sm/f inv* (*peg*) figurehead.

pres'tante *ag* good-looking.

pres'tanza [pres'tantsa] *sf* (robust) good looks *pl*.

pres'tare *vt*: **~ (qc a qn)** to lend (sb sth *o* sth to sb); **~rsi** *vr* (*offrirsi*): **~rsi a fare** to offer to do; (*essere adatto*): **~rsi a** to lend itself to, be suitable for; **~ aiuto** to lend a hand; **~ ascolto** *o* **orecchio** to listen; **~ attenzione** to pay attention; **~ fede a qc/qn** to give credence to sth/sb; **~ giuramento** to take an oath; **la frase si presta a molteplici interpretazioni** the phrase lends itself to numerous interpretations.

prestazi'one [prestat'tsjone] *sf* (*TECN, SPORT*) performance, **~i** *sfpl* (*di persona: servizi*) services.

prestigia'tore, 'trice [prestidʒa'tore] *sm/f* conjurer.

pres'tigio [pres'tidʒo] *sm* (*potere*) prestige; (*illusione*): **gioco di ~** conjuring trick.

prestigi'oso, a [presti'dʒoso] *ag* prestigious.

'prestito *sm* lending *q*; loan; **dar in ~** to lend; **prendere in ~** to borrow; **~ bancario** bank loan; **~ pubblico** public borrowing.

'presto *av* (*tra poco*) soon; (*in fretta*) quickly; (*di buon'ora*) early; **a ~** see you soon; **~ o tardi** sooner or later; **fare ~ a fare qc** to hurry up and do sth; (*non costare fatica*) to have no trouble doing sth; **si fa ~ a criticare** it's easy to criticize; **è ancora ~ per decidere** it's still too early *o* too soon to decide.

pre'sumere *vt* to presume, assume.

presu'mibile *ag* (*dati, risultati*) likely.

pre'sunsi *etc vb vedi* **presumere**.

pre'sunto, a *pp di* **presumere** ♦ *ag*: **il ~ colpevole** the alleged culprit.

presuntu'oso, a *ag* presumptuous.

presunzi'one [prezun'tsjone] *sf* presumption.

presup'porre *vt* to suppose, to presuppose.

presup'posto, a *pp di* **presupporre** ♦ *sm* (*premessa*) supposition, premise; **partendo dal ~ che ...** assuming that ...; **mancano i ~i necessari** the necessary conditions are lacking.

'prete *sm* priest.

preten'dente *sm/f* pretender ♦ *sm* (*corteggiatore*) suitor.

pre'tendere *vt* (*esigere*) to demand, require; (*sostenere*): **~ che** to claim that; **pretende di aver sempre ragione** he thinks he's always right.

pretenzi'oso, a [preten'tsjoso] *ag* pretentious.

preterintenzio'nale [preterintentsjo'nale] *ag* (*DIR*): **omicidio ~** manslaughter.

pre'teso, a *pp di* **pretendere** ♦ *sf* (*esigenza*) claim, demand; (*presunzione, sfarzo*) pretentiousness; **avanzare una ~a** to put forward a claim o demand; **senza ~e** *ag* unpretentious ♦ *av* unpretentiously.

pre'testo *sm* pretext, excuse; **con il ~ di** on the pretext of.

pretestu'oso, a *ag* (*data, motivo*) used as an excuse.

pre'tore *sm* magistrate.

pre'tura *sf* (*DIR: sede*) magistrates' court (*Brit*), circuit o superior court (*US*); (: *magistratura*) magistracy.

preva'lente *ag* prevailing.

prevalente'mente *av* mainly, for the most part.

preva'lenza [preva'lɛntsa] *sf* predominance.

preva'lere *vi* to prevail.

pre'valso, a *pp di* **prevalere**.

prevari'care *vi* (*abusare del potere*) to abuse one's power.

prevaricazi'one [prevarikat'tsjone] *sf* (*abuso di potere*) abuse of power.

preve'dere *vt* (*indovinare*) to foresee; (*presagire*) to foretell; (*considerare*) to make provision for; **nulla lasciava ~ che ...** there was nothing to suggest o to make one think that ...; **come previsto** as expected; **spese previste** anticipated expenditure; **previsto per martedì** scheduled for Tuesday.

preve'dibile *ag* predictable; **non era assolutamente ~ che ...** no one could have foreseen that ....

prevedibil'mente *av* as one would expect.

preve'nire *vt* (*anticipare: obiezione*) to forestall; (: *domanda*) to anticipate; (*evitare*) to avoid, prevent; (*avvertire*): **~ qn (di)** to warn sb (of); to inform sb (of).

preventi'vare *vt* (*COMM*) to estimate.

preven'tivo, a *ag* preventive ♦ *sm* (*COMM*) estimate; **fare un ~** to give an estimate; **bilancio ~** budget; **carcere ~** custody (*pending trial*).

preve'nuto, a *ag* (*mal disposto*): **~ (contro qc/qn)** prejudiced (against sth/sb).

prevenzi'one [preven'tsjone] *sf* prevention; (*preconcetto*) prejudice.

previ'dente *ag* showing foresight; prudent.

previ'denza [previ'dɛntsa] *sf* foresight; **istituto di ~** provident institution; **~ sociale** social security (*Brit*), welfare (*US*).

pre'vidi *etc vb vedi* **prevedere**.

'previo, a *ag* (*COMM*): **~ avviso** upon notice; **~ pagamento** upon payment.

previsi'one *sf* forecast, prediction; **~i meteorologiche** o **del tempo** weather forecast *sg*.

pre'visto, a *pp di* **prevedere** ♦ *sm*: **più/meno del ~** more/less than expected; **prima del ~** earlier than expected.

prezi'oso, a *ag* [pret'tsjoso] *ag* precious; (*aiuto, consiglio*) invaluable ♦ *sm* jewel; valuable.

prez'zemolo [pret'tsemolo] *sm* parsley.

'prezzo ['prɛttso] *sm* price; **a ~ di costo** at cost, at cost price (*Brit*); **tirare sul ~** to bargain, haggle; **il ~ pattuito è 1.000.000 di lire** the agreed price is 1,000,000 lire; **~ d'acquisto/di vendita** buying/selling price; **~ di fabbrica** factory price; **~ di mercato** market price; **~ scontato** reduced price; **~ unitario** unit price.

PRI *sigla m* (*POL*) = *Partito Repubblicano Italiano*.

prigi'one [pri'dʒone] *sf* prison.

prigio'nia [pridʒo'nia] *sf* imprisonment.

prigioni'ero, a [pridʒo'njɛro] *ag* captive ♦ *sm/f* prisoner.

'prima *sf vedi* **primo** ♦ *av* before; (*in anticipo*) in advance, beforehand; (*per l'addietro*) at one time, formerly; (*più presto*) sooner, earlier; (*in primo luogo*) first ♦ *cong*: **~ di fare/che parta** before doing/he leaves; **~ di** *prep* before; **~ o poi** sooner or later; **due giorni ~** two days before o earlier; **~ d'ora** before now.

pri'mario, a *ag* primary; (*principale*) chief, leading, primary ♦ *sm/f* (*medico*) head physician, chief physician.

pri'mate *sm* (*REL, ZOOL*) primate.

prima'tista, i, e *sm/f* (*SPORT*) record holder.

pri'mato *sm* supremacy; (*SPORT*) record.

prima'vera *sf* spring.

primave'rile *ag* spring *cpd*.

primeggi'are [primed'dʒare] *vi* to excel, be one of the best.

primi'tivo, a *ag* (*gen*) primitive; (*significato*) original.

pri'mizie [pri'mittsje] *sfpl* early produce *sg*.

'primo, a *ag* first; (*fig*) initial; basic; prime ♦ *sm/f* first (one) ♦ *sm* (*CUC*) first course; (*in date*): **il ~ luglio** the first of July ♦ *sf* (*TEATRO*) first night; (*CINEMA*) première; (*AUT*) first (gear); **le ~e ore del mattino** the early hours of the morning; **di ~a mattina** early in the morning; **in ~a pagina** (*STAMPA*) on the front page; **ai ~i freddi** at the first sign of cold weather; **ai ~i di maggio** at the beginning of May; **i ~i del Novecento** the early twentieth century; **viaggiare in ~a** to travel first-class; **per ~a cosa** firstly; **in ~ luogo** first of all, in the first place; **di ~'ordine** o **~a qualità** first-class, first-rate; **in un ~ tempo** o **momento** at first; **~a donna** leading lady; (*di opera lirica*) prima donna.

primo'genito, a [primo'dʒenito] *ag, sm/f* firstborn.

pri'mordi *smpl* beginnings.

primordi'ale *ag* primordial.

'primula *sf* primrose.

princi'pale [printʃi'pale] *ag* main, principal ♦ *sm* manager, boss; **sede ~** head office.

principal'mente [printʃipal'mente] *av* mainly, principally.

princi'pato [printʃi'pato] *sm* principality.

'principe ['printʃipe] *sm* prince; ~ **ereditario** crown prince.

princi'pesco, a, schi, sche [printʃi'pesko] *ag* (*anche fig*) princely.

princi'pessa [printʃi'pessa] *sf* princess.

principi'ante [printʃi'pjante] *sm/f* beginner.

principi'are [printʃi'pjare] *vt, vi* to start, begin.

prin'cipio [prin'tʃipjo] *sm* (*inizio*) beginning, start; (*origine*) origin, cause; (*concetto, norma*) principle; **al** *o* **in** ~ at first; **fin dal** ~ right from the start; **per** ~ on principle; **una questione di** ~ a matter of principle; **una persona di sani ~i morali** a person of sound moral principles; ~ **attivo** active ingredient.

pri'ore *sm* (*REL*) prior.

pri'ori: a ~ *ag inv* prior; **a priori ♦** *av* at first glance; initially; a priori.

priorità *sf* priority; **avere la** ~ **(su)** to have priority (over).

priori'tario, a *ag* having priority, of utmost importance.

'prisma, i *sm* prism.

pri'vare *vt*: ~ **qn di** to deprive sb of; **~rsi** *vr*: **~rsi di** to go *o* do without.

priva'tiva *sf* (*ECON*) monopoly.

pri'vato, a *ag* private **♦** *sm/f* (*anche:* ~ **cittadino**) private citizen; **in** ~ in private; **diritto** ~ (*DIR*) civil law; **ritirarsi a vita ~a** to withdraw from public life; **"non vendiamo a ~i"** "wholesale only".

privazi'one [privat'tsjone] *sf* privation, hardship.

privilegi'are [privile'dʒare] *vt* to favour (*Brit*), favor (*US*).

privilegi'ato, a [privile'dʒato] *ag* (*individuo, classe*) privileged; (*trattamento, COMM: credito*) preferential; **azioni ~e** preference shares (*Brit*), preferred stock (*US*).

privi'legio [privi'lɛdʒo] *sm* privilege; **avere il** ~ **di fare** to have the privilege of doing, be privileged to do.

'privo, a *ag*: ~ **di** without, lacking.

pro *prep* for, on behalf of **♦** *sm inv* (*utilità*) advantage, benefit; **a che ~?** what's the use?; **il** ~ **e il contro** the pros and cons.

pro'babile *ag* probable, likely.

probabilità *sf inv* probability; **con molta** ~ very probably, in all probability.

probabil'mente *av* probably.

pro'bante *ag* convincing.

pro'blema, i *sm* problem.

proble'matico, a, ci, che *ag* problematic; (*incerto*) doubtful **♦** *sf* problems *pl*.

pro'boscide [pro'bɔʃʃide] *sf* (*di elefante*) trunk.

procacci'are [prokat'tʃare] *vt* to get, obtain.

procaccia'tore [prokattʃa'tore] *sm*: ~ **d'affari**

sales executive.

pro'cace [pro'katʃe] *ag* (*donna, aspetto*) provocative.

pro'cedere [pro'tʃedere] *vi* to proceed; (*comportarsi*) to behave; (*iniziare*): ~ **a** to start; ~ **contro** (*DIR*) to start legal proceedings against; ~ **oltre** to go on ahead; **prima di** ~ **oltre** before going any further; **gli affari procedono bene** business is going well; **bisogna** ~ **con cautela** we have to proceed cautiously; **non luogo a** ~ (*DIR*) nonsuit.

procedi'mento [protʃedi'mento] *sm* (*modo di condurre*) procedure; (*di avvenimenti*) course; (*TECN*) process; ~ **penale** (*DIR*) criminal proceedings *pl*.

proce'dura [protʃe'dura] *sf* (*DIR*) procedure.

proces'sare [protʃes'sare] *vt* (*DIR*) to try.

processi'one [protʃes'sjone] *sf* procession.

pro'cesso [pro'tʃesso] *sm* (*DIR*) trial; proceedings *pl*; (*metodo*) process; **essere sotto** ~ to be on trial; **mettere sotto** ~ (*anche fig*) to put on trial; ~ **di fabbricazione** manufacturing process.

processu'ale [protʃessu'ale] *ag* (*DIR*): **atti ~i** records of a trial; **spese ~i** legal costs.

Proc. Gen. *abbr* = **procuratore generale.**

pro'cinto [pro'tʃinto] *sm*: **in** ~ **di fare** about to do, on the point of doing.

proci'one [pro'tʃone] *sm* raccoon.

pro'clama, i *sm* proclamation.

procla'mare *vt* to proclaim.

proclamazi'one [proklamat'tsjone] *sf* proclamation, declaration.

procrasti'nare *vt* (*data*) to postpone; (*pagamento*) to defer.

procre'are *vt* to procreate.

pro'cura *sf* (*DIR*) proxy, power of attorney; (*ufficio*) attorney's office; **per** ~ by proxy; **la P~ della Repubblica** the Public Prosecutor's Office.

procu'rare *vt*: ~ **qc a qn** (*fornire*) to get *o* obtain sth for sb; (*causare: noie etc*) to bring *o* give sb sth.

procura'tore, 'trice *sm/f* (*DIR*) ≈ solicitor; (*: chi ha la procura*) holder of power of attorney; ~ **generale** (*in corte d'appello*) public prosecutor; (*in corte di cassazione*) Attorney General; ~ **legale** ≈ solicitor (*Brit*), lawyer; ~ **della Repubblica** (*in corte d'assise, tribunale*) public prosecutor.

prodi'gare *vt* to be lavish with; **~rsi** *vr*: **~rsi per qn** to do all one can for sb.

pro'digio [pro'didʒo] *sm* marvel, wonder; (*persona*) prodigy.

prodigi'oso, a [prodi'dʒoso] *ag* prodigious; phenomenal.

'prodigo, a, ghi, ghe *ag* lavish, extravagant.

pro'dotto, a *pp di* **produrre ♦** *sm* product; ~ **di base** primary product; ~ **finale** end product; ~ **interno lordo (PIL)** gross

domestic product (GDP); ~ **nazionale
lordo (PNL)** gross national product (GNP);
~**i agricoli** farm produce *sg*; ~**i di bellezza**
cosmetics; ~**i chimici** chemicals.
pro'duco *etc vb vedi* **produrre**.
pro'durre *vt* to produce.
pro'dussi *etc vb vedi* **produrre**.
produttività *sf* productivity.
produt'tivo, a *ag* productive.
produt'tore, 'trice *ag* producing *cpd* ♦ *sm/f*
producer; **paese ~ di petrolio** oil-
producing country.
produzi'one [produt'tsjone] *sf* production;
(*rendimento*) output; ~ **in serie** mass
production.
pro'emio *sm* introduction, preface.
Prof. *abbr* (= *professore*) Prof.
profa'nare *vt* to desecrate.
pro'fano, a *ag* (*mondano*) secular, profane;
(*sacrilego*) profane.
profe'rire *vt* to utter.
profes'sare *vt* to profess; (*medicina etc*) to
practise (*Brit*), practice (*US*).
professio'nale *ag* professional; **scuola ~**
training college.
professi'one *sf* profession; **di ~** professional, by profession; **libera ~** profession.
professio'nista, i, e *sm/f* professional.
profes'sore, 'essa *sm/f* (*INS*) teacher; (*: di
università*) lecturer; (*: titolare di cattedra*)
professor; ~ **d'orchestra** member of an
orchestra.
pro'feta, i *sm* prophet.
pro'fetico, a, ci, che *ag* prophetic.
profetiz'zare [profetid'dzare] *vt* to prophesy.
profe'zia [profet'tsia] *sf* prophecy.
pro'ficuo, a *ag* useful, profitable.
profi'lare *vt* to outline; (*ornare: vestito*) to
edge; ~**rsi** *vr* to stand out, be silhouetted;
to loom up.
profi'lassi *sf* (*MED*) preventive treatment,
prophylaxis.
profi'lattico, a, ci, che *ag* prophylactic ♦
sm (*anticoncezionale*) sheath, condom.
pro'filo *sm* profile; (*breve descrizione*)
sketch, outline; **di ~** in profile.
profit'tare *vi*: ~ **di** (*trarre profitto*) to profit
by; (*approfittare*) to take advantage of.
pro'fitto *sm* advantage, profit, benefit; (*fig:
progresso*) progress; (*COMM*) profit;
ricavare un ~ da to make a profit from *o*
out of; **vendere con ~** to sell at a profit;
conto ~i e perdite profit and loss account.
pro'fondere *vt* (*lodi*) to lavish; (*denaro*) to
squander; ~**rsi** *vr*: ~**rsi in** to be profuse
in.
profondità *sf inv* depth.
pro'fondo, a *ag* deep; (*rancore,
meditazione*) profound ♦ *sm* depth(s *pl*);
bottom; ~ **8 metri** 8 metres deep.
pro'forma *ag* routine *cpd* ♦ *sm inv* formality
♦ *av*: **fare qc ~** to do sth as a formality.

'**profugo, a, ghi, ghe** *sm/f* refugee.
profu'mare *vt* to perfume ♦ *vi* to be fragrant; ~**rsi** *vr* to put on perfume *o* scent.
profumata'mente *av*: **pagare qc ~** to pay
through the nose for sth.
profu'mato, a *ag* (*fiore, aria*) fragrant;
(*fazzoletto, saponetta*) scented; (*pelle*)
sweet-smelling; (*persona*) with perfume
on.
profume'ria *sf* perfumery; (*negozio*)
perfume shop.
pro'fumo *sm* (*prodotto*) perfume, scent;
(*fragranza*) scent, fragrance.
profusi'one *sf* profusion; **a ~** in plenty.
pro'fuso, a *pp di* **profondere**.
progeni'tore, 'trice [prodʒeni'tore] *sm/f*
ancestor.
proget'tare [prodʒet'tare] *vt* to plan; (*TECN:
edificio*) to plan, design; ~ **di fare qc** to
plan to do sth.
progettazi'one [prodʒettat'tsjone] *sf* planning; **in corso di ~** at the planning stage.
proget'tista, i, e [prodʒet'tista] *sm/f*
designer.
pro'getto [pro'dʒetto] *sm* plan; (*idea*) plan,
project; **avere in ~ di fare qc** to be planning to do sth; ~ **di legge** (*POL*) bill.
'**prognosi** ['proɲɲozi] *sf* (*MED*) prognosis;
essere in ~ riservata to be on the danger
list.
pro'gramma, i *sm* programme (*Brit*), program (*US*); (*TV, RADIO*) program(me)s
pl; (*INS*) syllabus, curriculum; (*INFORM*)
program; **avere in ~ di fare qc** to be planning to do sth; ~ **applicativo** (*INFORM*)
application program.
program'mare *vt* (*TV, RADIO*) to put on;
(*INFORM*) to program; (*ECON*) to plan.
programma'tore, 'trice *sm/f* (*INFORM*)
computer programmer (*Brit*) *o* programer
(*US*).
programmazi'one [programmat'tsjone] *sf*
programming (*Brit*), programing (*US*);
planning.
progre'dire *vi* to progress, make progress.
progressi'one *sf* progression.
progres'sista, i, e *ag, sm/f* progressive.
progressiva'mente *av* progressively.
progres'sivo, a *ag* progressive.
pro'gresso *sm* progress *q*; **fare ~i** to make
progress.
proi'bire *vt* to forbid, prohibit; ~ **a qn di
fare qc** (*vietare*) to forbid sb to do sth;
(*impedire*) to prevent sb from doing sth.
proibi'tivo, a *ag* prohibitive.
proi'bito, a *ag* forbidden; "**è ~ l'accesso**"
"no admittance"; "**è ~ fumare**" "no
smoking".
proibizi'one [proibit'tsjone] *sf* prohibition.
proiet'tare *vt* (*gen, GEOM, CINEMA*) to
project; (*: presentare*) to show, screen;
(*luce, ombra*) to throw, cast, project.

proi'ettile *sm* projectile, bullet (*o* shell *etc*).
proiet'tore *sm* (*CINEMA*) projector; (*AUT*) headlamp; (*MIL*) searchlight.
proiezi'one [projet'tsjone] *sf* (*CINEMA*) projection; showing.
'prole *sf* children *pl*, offspring.
proletari'ato *sm* proletariat.
prole'tario, a *ag, sm/f* proletarian.
prolife'rare *vi* (*fig*) to proliferate.
pro'lifico, a, ci, che *ag* prolific.
pro'lisso, a *ag* verbose.
'prologo, ghi *sm* prologue.
pro'lunga, ghe *sf* (*di cavo elettrico etc*) extension.
prolunga'mento *sm* (*gen*) extension; (*di strada*) continuation.
prolun'gare *vt* (*discorso, attesa*) to prolong; (*linea, termine*) to extend.
prome'moria *sm inv* memorandum.
pro'messa *sf* promise; **fare/mantenere una ~** to make/keep a promise.
pro'messo, a *pp di* **promettere.**
promet'tente *ag* promising.
pro'mettere *vt* to promise ♦ *vi* to be *o* look promising; **~ a qn di fare** to promise sb that one will do.
promi'nente *ag* prominent.
promi'nenza [promi'nɛntsa] *sf* prominence.
promiscuità *sf* promiscuousness.
pro'miscuo, a *ag*: **matrimonio ~** mixed marriage; **nome ~** (*LING*) common-gender noun.
pro'misi *etc vb vedi* **promettere.**
promon'torio *sm* promontory, headland.
pro'mosso, a *pp di* **promuovere.**
promo'tore, 'trice *sm/f* promoter, organizer.
promozio'nale [promottsjo'nale] *ag* promotional; **"vendita ~"** "special offer".
promozi'one [promot'tsjone] *sf* promotion; **~ delle vendite** sales promotion.
promul'gare *vt* to promulgate.
promulgazi'one [promulgat'tsjone] *sf* promulgation.
promu'overe *vt* to promote.
proni'pote *sm/f* (*di nonni*) great-grandchild, great-grandson/granddaughter; (*di zii*) great-nephew/niece; **~i** *smpl* (*discendenti*) descendants.
pro'nome *sm* (*LING*) pronoun.
pronomi'nale *ag* pronominal.
pronosti'care *vt* to foretell, predict.
pro'nostico, ci *sm* forecast.
pron'tezza [pron'tɛttsa] *sf* readiness; quickness, promptness; **~ di riflessi** quick reflexes; **~ di spirito/mente** readiness of wit/mind.
'pronto, a *ag* ready; (*rapido*) fast, quick, prompt; **~!** (*TEL*) hello!; **essere ~ a fare qc** to be ready to do sth; **~ all'ira** quick-tempered; **a ~a cassa** (*COMM*) cash (*Brit*) *o* collect (*US*) on delivery; **~a consegna**

(*COMM*) prompt delivery; **~ soccorso** first aid.
prontu'ario *sm* manual, handbook.
pro'nuncia [pro'nuntʃa] *sf* pronunciation.
pronunci'are [pronun'tʃare] *vt* (*parola, sentenza*) to pronounce; (*dire*) to utter; (*discorso*) to deliver; **~rsi** *vr* to declare one's opinion; **~rsi a favore di/contro** to pronounce o.s. in favour of/against; **non mi pronuncio** I'm not prepared to comment.
pronunci'ato, a [pronun'tʃato] *ag* (*spiccato*) pronounced, marked; (*sporgente*) prominent.
pro'nunzia *etc* [pro'nuntsja] = **pronuncia** *etc*.
propa'ganda *sf* propaganda.
propagan'dare *vt* (*idea*) to propagandize; (*prodotto, invenzione*) to push, plug (*fam*).
propa'gare *vt* (*notizia, malattia*) to spread; (*REL, BIOL*) to propagate; **~rsi** *vr* to spread; to propagate; (*FISICA*) to be propagated.
prope'deutico, a, ci, che *ag* (*corso, trattato*) introductory.
pro'pendere *vi*: **~ per** to favour (*Brit*), favor (*US*), lean towards.
propensi'one *sf* inclination, propensity; **avere ~ a credere che ...** to be inclined to think that ....
pro'penso, a *pp di* **propendere** ♦ *ag*: **essere ~ a qc** to be in favour (*Brit*) *o* favor (*US*) of sth; **essere ~ a fare qc** to be inclined to do sth.
propi'nare *vt* to administer.
pro'pizio, a [pro'pittsjo] *ag* favourable (*Brit*), favorable (*US*).
pro'porre *vt* (*suggerire*): **~ qc (a qn)** to suggest sth (to sb); (*candidato*) to put forward; (*legge, brindisi*) to propose; **~ di fare** to suggest *o* propose doing; **proporsi di fare** to propose *o* intend to do; **proporsi una meta** to set o.s. a goal.
proporzio'nale [proportsjo'nale] *ag* proportional.
proporzio'nato, a [proportsjo'nato] *ag*: **~ a** proportionate to, proportional to; **ben ~** well-proportioned.
proporzi'one [propor'tsjone] *sf* proportion; **in ~ a** in proportion to.
pro'posito *sm* (*intenzione*) intention, aim; (*argomento*) subject, matter; **a ~ di** regarding, with regard to; **a questo ~** on this subject; **di ~** (*apposta*) deliberately, on purpose; **a ~** by the way; **capitare a ~** (*cosa, persona*) to turn up at the right time.
proposizi'one [propozit'tsjone] *sf* (*LING*) clause; (: *periodo*) sentence.
pro'posto, a *pp di* **proporre** ♦ *sf* proposal; (*suggerimento*) suggestion; **fare una ~a to** put forward a proposal; to make a suggestion; **~a di legge** (*POL*) bill.

propria'mente *av (correttamente)* properly, correctly; *(in modo specifico)* specifically; ~ **detto** in the strict sense of the word.

proprietà *sf inv (ciò che si possiede)* property *gen q*, estate; *(caratteristica)* property; *(correttezza)* correctness; **essere di ~ di qn** to belong to sb; ~ **edilizia** (developed) property; ~ **privata** private property.

proprie'tario, a *sm/f* owner; *(di albergo etc)* proprietor, owner; *(per l'inquilino)* landlord/lady; ~ **terriero** landowner.

'proprio, a *ag (possessivo)* own; (: *impersonale)* one's; *(esatto)* exact, correct, proper; *(senso, significato)* literal; *(LING: nome)* proper; *(particolare)*: ~ **di** characteristic of, peculiar to ♦ *av (precisamente)* just, exactly; *(davvero)* really; *(affatto)*: **non ... ~ not ... at all ♦ *sm (COMM)*: **mettersi in ~** to set up on one's own; **l'ha visto con i (suoi) ~i occhi** he saw it with his own eyes.

propu'gnare [propuɲ'ɲare] *vt* to support.

propulsi'one *sf* propulsion; **a ~ atomica** atomic-powered.

propul'sore *sm (TECN)* propeller.

'prora *sf (NAUT)* bow(s *pl)*, prow.

'proroga, ghe *sf* extension; postponement.

proro'gare *vt* to extend; *(differire)* to postpone, defer.

pro'rompere *vi* to burst out.

pro'rotto, a *pp di* **prorompere**.

pro'ruppi *etc vb vedi* **prorompere**.

'prosa *sf* prose; *(TEATRO)*: **la stagione della ~** the theatre season; **attore di ~** theatre actor; **compagnia di ~** theatrical company.

pro'saico, a, ci, che *ag (fig)* prosaic, mundane.

pro'sciogliere [proʃ'ʃɔʎʎere] *vt* to release; *(DIR)* to acquit.

prosciogli'mento [proʃʃɔʎʎi'mento] *sm* acquittal.

prosci'olto, a [proʃ'ʃɔlto] *pp di* **prosciogliere**.

prosciu'gare [proʃʃu'gare] *vt (terreni)* to drain, reclaim; ~**rsi** *vr* to dry up.

prosci'utto [proʃ'ʃutto] *sm* ham.

pros'critto, a *pp di* **proscrivere** ♦ *sm/f* exile; outlaw.

pros'crivere *vt* to exile, banish.

prosecuzi'one [prosekut'tsjone] *sf* continuation.

prosegui'mento *sm* continuation; **buon ~!** all the best!; *(a chi viaggia)* enjoy the rest of your journey!

prosegu'ire *vt* to carry on with, continue ♦ *vi* to carry on, go on.

pro'selito *sm (REL, POL)* convert.

prospe'rare *vi* to thrive.

prosperità *sf* prosperity.

'prospero, a *ag (fiorente)* flourishing, thriving, prosperous.

prospe'roso, a *ag (robusto)* hale and hearty; (: *ragazza)* buxom.

prospet'tare *vt (esporre)* to point out, show; *(ipotesi)* to advance; *(affare)* to outline; ~**rsi** *vr* to look, appear.

prospet'tiva *sf (ARTE)* perspective; *(veduta)* view; *(fig: previsione, possibilità)* prospect.

pros'petto *sm (DISEGNO)* elevation; *(veduta)* view, prospect; *(facciata)* façade, front; *(tabella)* table; *(sommario)* summary.

prospici'ente [prospi'tʃɛnte] *ag*: ~ **qc** facing *o* overlooking sth.

prossima'mente *av* soon.

prossimità *sf* nearness, proximity; **in ~ di** near (to), close to; **in ~ delle feste natalizie** as Christmas approaches.

'prossimo, a *ag (vicino)*: ~ **a** near (to), close to; *(che viene subito dopo)* next; *(parente)* close ♦ *sm* neighbour *(Brit)*, neighbor *(US)*, fellow man; **nei ~i giorni** in the next few days; **in un ~ futuro** in the near future; ~ **venturo (pv)** *(AMM)*: **venerdì ~ venturo** next Friday.

'prostata *sf* prostate (gland).

prosti'tuta *sf* prostitute.

prostituzi'one [prostitut'tsjone] *sf* prostitution.

pros'trare *vt (fig)* to exhaust, wear out; ~**rsi** *vr (fig)* to humble o.s.; **prostrato dal dolore** overcome *o* prostrate with grief.

prostrazi'one [prostrat'tsjone] *sf* prostration.

protago'nista, i, e *sm/f* protagonist.

pro'teggere [pro'tɛddʒere] *vt* to protect.

pro'teico, a, ci, che *ag* protein *cpd*; **altamente ~** high in protein.

prote'ina *sf* protein.

pro'tendere *vt* to stretch out.

pro'teso, a *pp di* **protendere**.

pro'testa *sf* protest.

protes'tante *ag, sm/f* Protestant.

protes'tare *vt, vi* to protest; ~**rsi** *vr*: ~**rsi innocente** *etc* to protest one's innocence *o* that one is innocent *etc*.

pro'testo *sm (DIR)* protest; **mandare una cambiale in ~** to dishonour *(Brit) o* dishonor *(US)* a bill.

protet'tivo, a *ag* protective.

pro'tetto, a *pp di* **proteggere**.

protetto'rato *sm* protectorate.

protet'tore, 'trice *sm/f* protector; *(sostenitore)* patron ♦ *ag (REL)*: **santo ~** patron saint; **società ~trice dei consumatori** consumer protection society.

protezi'one [protet'tsjone] *sf* protection; *(patrocinio)* patronage; **misure di ~** protective measures; ~ **civile** civil defence *(Brit) o* defense *(US)*.

protezio'nismo [protettsjo'nizmo] *sm* protectionism.

protocol'lare *vt* to register ♦ *ag* formal; of

protocol.
proto'collo sm protocol; (registro) register of documents ♦ ag inv: **foglio** ~ foolscap; **numero di** ~ reference number.
pro'tone sm proton.
pro'totipo sm prototype.
pro'trarre vt (prolungare) to prolong; **protrarsi** vr to go on, continue.
pro'tratto, a pp di **protrarre**.
protube'ranza [protube'rantsa] sf protuberance, bulge.
Prov. abbr (= provincia) Prov.
'prova sf (esperimento, cimento) test, trial; (tentativo) attempt, try; (MAT, testimonianza etc) proof q; (DIR) evidence q, proof q; (INS) exam, test; (TEATRO) rehearsal; (di abito) fitting; **a** ~ **di** (in testimonianza di) as proof of; **a** ~ **di fuoco** fireproof; **assumere in** ~ (per lavoro) to employ on a trial basis; **essere in** ~ (persona: per lavoro) to be on trial; **mettere alla** ~ to put to the test; **giro di** ~ test o trial run; **fino a** ~ **contraria** until (it's) proved otherwise; ~ **a carico/a discarico** (DIR) evidence for the prosecution/for the defence; ~ **documentale** (DIR) documentary evidence; ~ **generale** (TEATRO) dress rehearsal; ~ **testimoniale** (DIR) testimonial evidence.
pro'vare vt (sperimentare) to test; (tentare) to try, attempt; (assaggiare) to try, taste; (sperimentare in sé) to experience; (sentire) to feel; (cimentare) to put to the test; (dimostrare) to prove; (abito) to try on; ~**rsi** vr: ~**rsi (a fare)** to try o attempt (to do); ~ **a fare** to try o attempt to do.
proveni'enza [prove'njɛntsa] sf origin, source.
prove'nire vi: ~ **da** to come from.
pro'venti smpl revenue sg.
prove'nuto, a pp di **provenire**.
Pro'venza [pro'ventsa] sf: **la** ~ Provence.
proven'zale [proven'tsale] ag Provençal.
pro'verbio sm proverb.
pro'vetta sf test tube; **bambino in** ~ testtube baby.
pro'vetto, a ag skilled, experienced.
pro'vincia, ce o **cie** [pro'vintʃa] sf province.
provinci'ale [provin'tʃale] ag provincial; **(strada)** ~ main road (Brit), highway (US).
pro'vino sm (CINEMA) screen test; (campione) specimen.
provo'cante ag (attraente) provocative.
provo'care vt (causare) to cause, bring about; (eccitare: riso, pietà) to arouse; (irritare, sfidare) to provoke.
provoca'tore, 'trice sm/f agitator ♦ ag: **agente** ~ agent provacateur.
provoca'torio, a ag provocative.
provocazi'one [provokat'tsjone] sf provocation.

provve'dere vi (disporre): ~ **(a)** to provide (for); (prendere un provvedimento) to take steps, act ♦ vt: ~ **qc a qn** to supply sth to sb; ~**rsi** vr: ~**rsi di** to provide o.s. with.
provvedi'mento sm measure; (di previdenza) precaution; ~ **disciplinare** disciplinary measure.
provvedito'rato sm (AMM): ~ **agli studi** divisional education offices pl.
provvedi'tore sm (AMM): ~ **agli studi** divisional director of education.
provvi'denza [provvi'dɛntsa] sf: **la** ~ providence.
provvidenzi'ale [provviden'tsjale] ag providential.
provvigi'one [provvi'dʒone] sf (COMM) commission; **lavoro/stipendio a** ~ job/salary on a commission basis.
provvi'sorio, a ag temporary; (governo) temporary, provisional.
prov'visto, a pp di **provvedere** ♦ sf provision, supply; **fare** ~**e** to take in supplies.
'prua sf (NAUT) = **prora**.
pru'dente ag cautious, prudent; (assennato) sensible, wise.
pru'denza [pru'dɛntsa] sf prudence, caution; wisdom; **per** ~ as a precaution, to be on the safe side.
'prudere vi to itch, be itchy.
'prugna ['pruɲɲa] sf plum; ~ **secca** prune.
prurigi'noso, a [pruridʒi'noso] ag itchy.
pru'rito sm itchiness q; itch.
PS sigla = Pesaro.
P.S. abbr (= postscriptum) P.S.; (COMM) = **partita semplice** ♦ sigla f vedi **Pubblica Sicurezza**.
PSDI sigla m (POL) = Partito Socialista Democratico Italiano.
pseu'donimo sm pseudonym.
PSI sigla m (POL) = Partito Socialista Italiano.
psica'nalisi sf psychoanalysis.
psicana'lista, i, e sm/f psychoanalyst.
psicanaliz'zare [psikanalid'dzare] vt to psychoanalyse.
'psiche ['psike] sf psyche.
psiche'delico, a, ci, che [psike'dɛliko] ag psychedelic.
psichi'atra, i, e [psi'kjatra] sm/f psychiatrist.
psichia'tria [psikja'tria] sf psychiatry.
psichi'atrico, a, ci, che [psi'kjatriko] ag (caso) psychiatric; (reparto, ospedale) psychiatric, mental.
'psichico, a, ci, che ['psikiko] ag psychological.
psico'farmaco, ci sm (MED) drug used in treatment of mental conditions.
psicolo'gia [psikolo'dʒia] sf psychology.
psico'logico, a, ci, che [psiko'lɔdʒiko] ag psychological.
psi'cologo, a, gi, ghe sm/f psychologist.
psico'patico, a, ci, che ag psychopathic ♦

sm/f psychopath.

psi'cosi *sf inv* (*MED*) psychosis; (*fig*) obsessive fear.

psicoso'matico, a, ci, che *ag* psychosomatic.

PT *sigla* = Pistoia.

Pt. *abbr* (*GEO*: = *punta*) Pt.

P.T. *abbr* (= *Posta e Telegrafi*) ≈ PO (= *Post Office*); (*FISCO*) = **polizia tributaria.**

P.T.P. *abbr vedi* **posto telefonico pubblico.**

pubbli'care *vt* to publish.

pubblicazi'one [pubblikat'tsjone] *sf* publication; ~ **periodica** periodical; ~**i (matrimoniali)** *sfpl* (marriage) banns.

pubbli'cista, i, e [pubbli'tʃista] *sm/f* (*STAMPA*) freelance journalist.

pubblicità [pubblitʃi'ta] *sf* (*diffusione*) publicity; (*attività*) advertising; (*annunci nei giornali*) advertisements *pl*; **fare ~ a qc** to advertise sth.

pubblici'tario, a [pubblitʃi'tarjo] *ag* advertising *cpd*; (*trovata, film*) publicity *cpd* ♦ *sm* advertising agent; **annuncio** *o* **avviso ~** advertisement.

'pubblico, a, ci, che *ag* public; (*statale: scuola etc*) state *cpd* ♦ *sm* public; (*spettatori*) audience; **in ~** in public; **la ~a amministrazione** public administration; **un ~ esercizio** a catering (*o* hotel *o* entertainment) business; ~ **funzionario** civil servant; **Ministero della P~a Istruzione** ≈ Department of Education and Science (*Brit*), ≈ Department of Health, Education and Welfare (*US*); **P~ Ministero** Public Prosecutor's Office; **la P~a Sicurezza (P.S.)** the police.

'pube *sm* (*ANAT*) pubis.

pubertà *sf* puberty.

'pudico, a, ci, che *ag* modest.

pu'dore *sm* modesty.

puericul'tura *sf* infant care.

pue'rile *ag* childish.

pu'erpera *sf woman who has just given birth.*

pugi'lato [pudʒi'lato] *sm* boxing.

'pugile ['pudʒile] *sm* boxer.

pugli'ese [puʎ'ʎese] *ag* of (*o* from) Puglia.

pugna'lare [puɲɲa'lare] *vt* to stab.

pu'gnale [puɲ'ɲale] *sm* dagger.

'pugno ['puɲɲo] *sm* fist; (*colpo*) punch; (*quantità*) fistful; **avere qn in ~** to have sb in the palm of one's hand; **tenere la situazione in ~** to have control of the situation; **scrivere qc di proprio ~** to write sth in one's own hand.

'pulce ['pultʃe] *sf* flea.

pul'cino [pul'tʃino] *sm* chick.

pu'ledro, a *sm/f* colt/filly.

pu'leggia, ge [pu'leddʒa] *sf* pulley.

pu'lire *vt* to clean; (*lucidare*) to polish; **far ~ qc** to have sth cleaned; ~ **a secco** to dry-clean.

pu'lito, a *ag* (*anche fig*) clean; (*ordinato*) neat, tidy ♦ *sf* quick clean; **avere la coscienza ~a** to have a clear conscience.

puli'tura *sf* cleaning; ~ **a secco** dry cleaning.

puli'zia [pulit'tsia] *sf* (*atto*) cleaning; (*condizione*) cleanness; **fare le ~e** to do the cleaning, do the housework.

'pullman *sm inv* coach (*Brit*), bus.

pul'lover *sm inv* pullover, jumper.

pullu'lare *vi* to swarm, teem.

pul'mino *sm* minibus.

'pulpito *sm* pulpit.

pul'sante *sm* (push-)button.

pul'sare *vi* to pulsate, beat.

pulsazi'one [pulsat'tsjone] *sf* beat.

pul'viscolo *sm* fine dust.

'puma *sm inv* puma.

pun'gente [pun'dʒente] *ag* prickly; stinging; (*anche fig*) biting.

'pungere ['pundʒere] *vt* to prick; (*sog: insetto, ortica*) to sting; (: *freddo*) to bite; ~ **qn sul vivo** (*fig*) to cut sb to the quick.

pungigli'one [pundʒiʎ'ʎone] *sm* sting.

pungo'lare *vt* to goad.

pu'nire *vt* to punish.

puni'tivo, a *ag* punitive.

punizi'one [punit'tsjone] *sf* punishment; (*SPORT*) penalty.

'punsi *etc vb vedi* **pungere.**

'punta *sf* point; (*parte terminale*) tip, end; (*di monte*) peak; (*di costa*) promontory; (*minima parte*) touch, trace; **in ~ di piedi** on tiptoe; **ore di ~** peak hours; **uomo di ~** (*SPORT, POL*) front-rank *o* leading man.

pun'tare *vt* (*piedi a terra, gomiti sul tavolo*) to plant; (*dirigere: pistola*) to point; (*scommettere*): ~ **su** to bet on ♦ *vi* (*mirare*): ~ **a** to aim at; (*avviarsi*): ~ **su** to head *o* make for; (*fig: contare*): ~ **su** to count *o* rely on.

puntas'pilli *sm inv* = **portaspilli.**

pun'tata *sf* (*gita*) short trip; (*scommessa*) bet; (*parte di opera*) instalment (*Brit*), installment (*US*); **farò una ~ a Parigi** I'll pay a flying visit to Paris; **romanzo a ~e** serial.

punteggi'are [punted'dʒare] *vt* to punctuate.

punteggia'tura [punteddʒa'tura] *sf* punctuation.

pun'teggio [pun'teddʒo] *sm* score.

puntel'lare *vt* to support.

pun'tello *sm* prop, support.

punteru'olo *sm* (*TECN*) punch; (: *per stoffa*) bodkin.

pun'tiglio [pun'tiʎʎo] *sm* obstinacy, stubbornness.

puntigli'oso, a [puntiʎ'ʎoso] *ag* punctilious.

pun'tina *sf*: ~ **da disegno** drawing pin (*Brit*), thumb tack (*US*); ~**e** *sfpl* (*AUT*) points.

pun'tino *sm* dot; **fare qc a ~** to do sth properly; **arrivare a ~** to arrive just at the right moment; **cotto a ~** cooked to perfection; **mettere i ~i sulle "i"** (*fig*) to dot the i's and cross the t's.

'**punto, a** *pp di* **pungere ♦** *sm* (*segno, macchiolina*) dot; (*LING*) full stop; (*MAT, momento*, *di punteggio, fig*: *argomento*) point; (*posto*) spot; (*a scuola*) mark; (*nel cucire, nella maglia*, *MED*) stitch **♦** *av*: **non ... ~** not ... at all; **due ~i** *sm inv* (*LING*) colon; **ad un certo ~** at a certain point; **fino ad un certo ~** (*fig*) to a certain extent; **sul ~ di fare** (just) about to do; **fare il ~** (*NAUT*) to take a bearing; **fare il ~ della situazione** (*analisi*) to take stock of the situation; (*riassunto*) to sum up the situation; **alle 6 in ~** at 6 o'clock sharp *o* on the dot; **essere a buon ~** to have reached a satisfactory stage; **mettere a ~** to adjust; (*motore*) to tune; (*cannocchiale*) to focus; (*fig*) to settle; **venire al ~** to come to the point; **vestito di tutto ~** all dressed up; **di ~ in bianco** point-blank; **~ d'arrivo** arrival point; **~ cardinale** point of the compass, cardinal point; **~ debole** weak point; **~ esclamativo/interrogativo** exclamation/question mark; **~ d'incontro** meeting place, meeting point; **~ morto** standstill; (*comedone*) **~ nero** blackhead; **~ nevralgico** (*anche fig*) nerve centre (*Brit*) *o* center (*US*); **~ di partenza** (*anche fig*) starting point; **~ di riferimento** landmark; (*fig*) point of reference; **~ di vendita** retail outlet; **~ e virgola** semicolon; **~ di vista** (*fig*) point of view; **~i di sospensione** suspension points.

puntu'ale *ag* punctual.

puntualità *sf* punctuality.

puntualiz'zare [puntualid'dzare] *vt* to make clear.

puntual'mente *av* (*gen*) on time; (*ironico*: *al solito*) as usual.

pun'tura *sf* (*di ago*) prick; (*di insetto*) sting, bite; (*MED*) puncture; (: *iniezione*) injection; (*dolore*) sharp pain.

punzecchi'are [puntsek'kjare] *vt* to prick; (*fig*) to tease.

punzo'nare [puntso'nare] *vt* (*TECN*) to stamp.

pun'zone [pun'tsone] *sm* (*per metalli*) stamp, die.

può, pu'oi *vb vedi* **potere**.

'**pupa** *sf* doll.

pu'pazzo [pu'pattso] *sm* puppet.

pu'pillo, a *sm/f* (*DIR*) ward; (*prediletto*) favourite (*Brit*), favorite (*US*), pet **♦** *sf* (*ANAT*) pupil.

purché [pur'ke] *cong* provided that, on condition that.

'**pure** *cong* (*tuttavia*) and yet, nevertheless; (*anche se*) even if **♦** *av* (*anche*) too, also; **pur di** (*al fine di*) just to; **faccia ~!** go ahead!, please do!

purè *sm*, **pu'rea** *sf* (*CUC*) purée; (: *di patate*) mashed potatoes.

pu'rezza [pu'rettsa] *sf* purity.

'**purga, ghe** *sf* (*MED*) purging *q*; purge; (*POL*) purge.

pur'gante *sm* (*MED*) purgative, purge.

pur'gare *vt* (*MED, POL*) to purge; (*pulire*) to clean.

purga'torio *sm* purgatory.

purifi'care *vt* to purify; (*metallo*) to refine.

purificazi'one [purifikat'tsjone] *sf* purification; refinement.

puri'tano, a *ag, sm/f* puritan.

'**puro, a** *ag* pure; (*acqua*) clear, limpid; (*vino*) undiluted; **di razza ~a** thoroughbred; **per ~ caso** by sheer chance, purely by chance.

puro'sangue *sm/f inv* thoroughbred.

pur'troppo *av* unfortunately.

pus *sm* pus.

pusil'lanime *ag* cowardly.

'**pustola** *sf* pimple.

puta'caso *av* just supposing, suppose.

puti'ferio *sm* rumpus, row.

putre'fare *vi* to putrefy, rot.

putre'fatto, a *pp di* **putrefare**.

putrefazi'one [putrefat'tsjone] *sf* putrefaction.

'**putrido, a** *ag* putrid, rotten.

put'tana *sf* (*fam!*) whore (*!*).

'**putto** *sm* cupid.

'**puzza** ['puttsa] *sf* = **puzzo**.

puz'zare [put'tsare] *vi* to stink; **la faccenda puzza (d'imbroglio)** the whole business stinks.

'**puzzo** ['puttso] *sm* stink, foul smell.

'**puzzola** ['puttsola] *sf* polecat.

puzzo'lente [puttso'lente] *ag* stinking.

PV *sigla* = *Pavia*.

pv *abbr vedi* **prossimo venturo**.

PZ *sigla* = *Potenza*.

Q

Q, q [ku] *sf o m inv* (*lettera*) Q, q; **Q come Quarto** ≈ Q for Queen.

q *abbr* (= *quintale*) q.

Qa'tar [ka'tar] *sm*: **il ~** Qatar.

Q.G. *abbr* = **quartier generale**.

Q.I. *abbr vedi* **quoziente d'intelligenza**.

qua *av* here; **in ~** (*verso questa parte*) this way; **~ dentro/sotto** *etc* in/under here *etc*; **da un anno in ~** for a year now; **da quando in ~?** since when?; **per di ~** (*passare*) this way; **al di ~ di** (*fiume*, *strada*) on this side of; *vedi* **questo.**

'quacchero, a ['kwakkero] *sm/f* Quaker.

qua'derno *sm* notebook; (*per scuola*) exercise book.

qua'drangolo *sm* quadrangle.

qua'drante *sm* quadrant; (*di orologio*) face.

qua'drare *vi* (*bilancio*) to balance, tally; (*fig: corrispondere*): ~ **(con)** to correspond (with) ♦ *vt* (*MAT*) to square; **far ~ il bilancio** to balance the books; **non mi quadra** I don't like it.

qua'drato, a *ag* square; (*fig: equilibrato*) level-headed, sensible; (: *peg*) square ♦ *sm* (*MAT*) square; (*PUGILATO*) ring; **5 al ~** 5 squared.

quadret'tato, a *ag* (*foglio*) squared; (*tessuto*) checked.

qua'dretto *sm*: **a ~i** (*tessuto*) checked; (*foglio*) squared.

quadrien'nale *ag* (*che dura 4 anni*) four-year *cpd*; (*che avviene ogni 4 anni*) four-yearly.

quadri'foglio [kwadri'fɔʎʎo] *sm* four-leaf clover.

quadri'mestre *sm* (*periodo*) four-month period; (*INS*) term.

'quadro *sm* (*pittura*) painting, picture; (*quadrato*) square; (*tabella*) table, chart; (*TECN*) board, panel; (*TEATRO*) scene; (*fig: scena, spettacolo*) sight; (: *descrizione*) outline, description; **~i** *smpl* (*POL*) party organizers; (*COMM*) managerial staff; (*MIL*) cadres; (*CARTE*) diamonds; **a ~i** (*disegno*) checked; **fare un ~ della situazione** to outline the situation; **~ clinico** (*MED*) case history; **~ di comando** control panel; **~i intermedi** middle management *sg*.

qua'drupede *sm* quadruped.

quadrupli'care *vt* to quadruple.

'quadruplo, a *ag, sm* quadruple.

quaggiù [kwad'dʒu] *av* down here.

'quaglia ['kwaʎʎa] *sf* quail.

'qualche ['kwalke] *det* some; (*alcuni*) a few; (*in espressioni interrogative*) any; (*uno*): **c'è ~ medico?** is there a doctor?; **ho comprato ~ libro** I've bought some *o* a few books; **ha ~ sigaretta?** have you any cigarettes?; **una persona di ~ rilievo** a person of some importance; **~ cosa** = **qualcosa**; **in ~ modo** somehow; **~ volta** sometimes.

qualche'duno [kwalke'duno] *pronome* = **qualcuno.**

qual'cosa *pronome* something; (*in espressioni interrogative*) anything; **qualcos'altro** something else; anything else; **~ di nuovo** something new; anything new; **~ da mangiare** something to eat; anything to eat; **c'è ~ che non va?** is there something *o* anything wrong?

qual'cuno *pronome* (*persona*) someone, somebody; (: *in espressioni interrogative*) anyone, anybody; (*alcuni*) some; **~ è favorevole a noi** some are on our side; **qualcun altro** someone *o* somebody else; anyone *o* anybody else.

'quale *det* what; (*discriminativo*) which; (*come*) as ♦ *pronome* (*interrogativo*) which; (*relativo*): **il(la) ~** (*persona: soggetto*) who; (: *oggetto, con preposizione*) whom; (*cosa*) which; (*possessivo*): **la signora della ~ ammiriamo la bellezza** the lady whose beauty we admire ♦ *av* (*in qualità di*) as; **~ disgrazia!** what a misfortune!; **in un certo qual modo** in some way or other, somehow or other; **per la qual cosa** for which reason; **accetterò ~i che siano le condizioni** I'll accept whatever the conditions; **a tutti coloro i ~i fossero interessati ...** to whom it may concern ...; **~ legale della signora** as the lady's lawyer.

qua'lifica, che *sf* qualification; (*titolo*) title.

qualifi'care *vt* to qualify; (*definire*): **~ qn/qc come** to describe sb/sth as; **~rsi** *vr* (*anche SPORT*) to qualify; **~rsi a un concorso** to pass a competitive exam.

qualifica'tivo, a *ag* qualifying.

qualifi'cato, a *ag* (*dotato di qualifica*) qualified; (*esperto, abile*) skilled; **non mi ritengo ~ per questo lavoro** I don't think I'm qualified for this job; **è un medico molto ~** he is a very distinguished doctor.

qualificazi'one [kwalifikat'tsjone] *sf* qualification; **gara di ~** (*SPORT*) qualifying event.

qualità *sf inv* quality; **di ottima** *o* **prima ~** top quality; **in ~ di** in one's capacity as; **in ~ di amica** as a friend; **articoli di ogni ~** all sorts of goods; **controllo (di) ~** quality control; **prodotto di ~** quality product.

qualita'tivo, a *ag* qualitative.

qua'lora *cong* in case, if.

qual'siasi, qua'lunque *det inv* any; (*quale che sia*) whatever; (*discriminativo*) whichever; (*posposto: mediocre*) poor, indifferent; ordinary; **mettiti un vestito ~** put on any old dress; **~ cosa** anything; **~ cosa accada** whatever happens; **a ~ costo** at any cost, whatever the cost; **l'uomo ~** the man in the street; **~ persona** anyone, anybody.

qualunqu'ista, i, e *sm/f* person indifferent to politics.

'quando *cong, av* when; **~ sarò ricco** when I'm rich; **da ~** (*dacché*) since; (*interrogativo*): **da ~ sei qui?** how long have you been here?; **di ~ in ~** from time to time; **quand'anche** even if.

quantifi'care *vt* to quantify.

quantità *sf inv* quantity; (*gran numero*): **una ~ di** a great deal of; a lot of; **in grande ~** in large quantities.

quantita'tivo, a *ag* quantitative ♦ *sm* (*COMM: di merce*) amount, quantity.

'**quanto, a** det (interrogativo: quantità) how much; (: numero) how many; (esclamativo) what a lot of, how much (o many); (relativo) as much … as; as many … as ♦ pronome (interrogativo) how much; how many; (: tempo) how long; (relativo) as much as; as many as; ~i(e) pronome pl (persone) all those who ♦ av (interrogativo: con ag, av) how; (: con vb) how much; (esclamativo: con ag, av) how; (: con vb) how much, what a lot; (con valore relativo) as much as; **ho ~ denaro mi occorre** I have as much money as I need; **studierò ~ posso** I'll study as much as o all I can; **~i ne abbiamo oggi?** what is the date today?; **~i anni hai?** how old are you?; **~ costa?, quant'è?** how much does it cost?, how much is it?; **in ~** (in qualità di) as; (poiché) since, as; **(in) ~ a** as for; **a ~ dice lui** according to him; **per ~ sia brava, fa degli errori** however good she may be, she makes mistakes; **per ~ io sappia** as far as I know; **~ prima** as soon as possible; **~ tempo?** how long?, how much time?; **~ più … tanto meno** the more … the less; **~ più … tanto più** the more … the more; **saranno scelti ~i hanno fatto la richiesta in tempo** all those whose applications arrived in time will be selected; **in risposta a ~ esposto nella sua lettera …** in answer to the points raised in your letter ….

quan'**tunque** cong although, though.
qua'**ranta** num forty.
quaran'**tena** sf quarantine.
quaran'**tenne** ag, sm/f forty-year-old.
quaran'**tennio** sm (period of) forty years.
quaran'**tesimo, a** num fortieth.
quaran'**tina** sf: **una ~ (di)** about forty.
quaran'**totto** sm inv forty-eight; **fare un ~** (fam) to raise hell.
qua'**resima** sf: **la ~** Lent.
'**quarta** sf vedi quarto.
quar'**tetto** sm quartet(te).
quarti'**ere** sm district, area; (MIL) quarters pl; **~ generale (Q.G.)** headquarters pl (HQ); **~ residenziale** residential area o district; **i ~i alti** the smart districts.
'**quarto, a** ag fourth ♦ sm fourth; (quarta parte) quarter ♦ sf (AUT) fourth (gear); (INS: elementare) fourth year of primary school; (: superiore) seventh year of secondary school; **un ~ di vino** a quarter-litre (Brit) o quarter-liter (US) bottle of wine; **le 6 e un ~** a quarter past (Brit) o after (US) 6; **~ d'ora** quarter of an hour; **tre ~i d'ora** three quarters of an hour; **le otto e tre ~i, le nove meno un ~ (a)** quarter to (Brit) o of (US) nine; **passare un brutto ~ d'ora** (fig) to have a bad o nasty time of it; **~i di finale** (SPORT) quarter finals.

'**quarzo** ['kwartso] sm quartz.
'**quasi** av almost, nearly ♦ cong (anche: ~ che) as if; **(non) … ~ mai** hardly ever; **~ ~ me ne andrei** I've half a mind to leave.
quas'**sù** av up here.
'**quatto, a** ag crouched, squatting; (silenzioso) silent; **~ ~** very quietly; stealthily.
quattordi'**cenne** [kwattordi'tʃɛnne] ag, sm/f fourteen-year-old.
quat'**tordici** [kwat'torditʃi] num fourteen.
quat'**trini** smpl money sg, cash sg.
'**quattro** num four; **in ~ e quattr'otto** in less than no time; **dirne ~ a qn** to give sb a piece of one's mind; **fare il diavolo a ~** to kick up a rumpus; **fare ~ chiacchiere** to have a chat; **farsi in ~ per qn** to go out of one's way for sb, put o.s. out for sb.
quat'**trocchi** [kwat'trɔkki] sm inv (fig fam: persona con occhiali) four-eyes; **a ~** av (tra 2 persone) face to face; (privatamente) in private.
quattrocen'**tesco, a, schi, sche** [kwat-trotʃen'tesko] ag fifteenth-century.
quattro'**cento** [kwattro'tʃɛnto] num four hundred ♦ sm: **il Q~** the fifteenth century.
quattro'**mila** num four thousand.
'**quello, a** det (dav sm **quel** + C, **quell'** + V, **quello** + s impura, gn, pn, ps, x, z; pl **quei** + C, **quegli** + V o s impura, gn, pn, ps, x, z; dav sf **quella** + C, **quell'** + V; pl **quelle**) that; those pl ♦ pronome that (one); those (ones) pl; (ciò) that; **~(a) che** the one who; **~i(e) che** those who; **ho fatto ~ che potevo** I did what I could; **~(a) … lì o là** det that; **quell'uomo lì** that man; **~(a) lì o là** pronome that one; **~ bianco** the white one; **da ~ che ho sentito** from what I've heard; **in quel di Milano** in the Milan area o region.
'**quercia, ce** ['kwɛrtʃa] sf oak (tree); (legno) oak.
que'**rela** sf (DIR) (legal) action.
quere'**lare** vt to bring an action against.
que'**sito** sm question, query; problem.
'**questi** pronome (poetico) this person.
questio'**nario** sm questionnaire.
questi'**one** sf problem, question; (controversia) issue; (litigio) quarrel; **in ~** in question; **il caso in ~** the matter at hand; **la persona in ~** the person involved; **non voglio essere chiamato in ~** I don't want to be dragged into the argument; **fuor di ~** out of the question; **è ~ di tempo** it's a matter o question of time.
'**questo, a** det this; these pl ♦ pronome this (one); those (ones) pl; (ciò) this; **~(a) … qui o qua** det this; **~ ragazzo qui** this boy; **~(a) qui o qua** pronome this one; **io prendo ~ cappotto, tu prendi quello** I'll take this coat, you take that one; **preferisce ~i o quelli?** do you prefer these (ones) or those

(ones)?; **vengono Paolo e Mario: ~ da Roma, quello da Palermo** Paolo and Mario are coming: the latter from Rome, the former from Palermo; **quest'oggi** today; **e con ~?** so what?; **e con ~ se n'è andato** and with that he left; **con tutto ~** in spite of this, despite all this; **~ è quanto** that's all.

ques'tore sm ≈ chief constable (*Brit*), ≈ police commissioner (*US*).

'questua sf collection (of alms).

ques'tura sf police headquarters pl.

questu'rino sm (*fam*: poliziotto) cop.

qui av here; **da o di ~** from here; **di ~ in avanti** from now on; **di ~ a poco/una settimana** in a little while/a week's time; **~ dentro/sopra/vicino** in/up/near here; vedi **questo**.

quie'scenza [kwjeʃ'ʃɛntsa] sf (*AMM*): **porre qn in ~** to retire sb.

quie'tanza [kwje'tantsa] sf receipt.

quie'tare vt to calm, soothe.

qui'ete sf quiet, quietness; calmness; stillness; peace; **turbare la ~ pubblica** (*DIR*) to disturb the peace.

qui'eto, a ag quiet; (*notte*) calm, still; (*mare*) calm; **l'ho fatto per il ~ vivere** I did it for a quiet life.

'quindi av then ♦ cong therefore, so.

quindi'cenne [kwindi'tʃɛnne] ag, sm/f fifteen-year-old.

'quindici ['kwinditʃi] num fifteen; **~ giorni** a fortnight (*Brit*), two weeks.

quindi'cina [kwindi'tʃina] sf (*serie*): **una ~ (di)** about fifteen; **fra una ~ di giorni** in a fortnight (*Brit*) o two weeks.

quindici'nale [kwinditʃi'nale] ag fortnightly (*Brit*), semimonthly (*US*) ♦ sm (*rivista*) fortnightly magazine (*Brit*), semimonthly (*US*).

quinquen'nale ag (*che dura 5 anni*) five-year cpd; (*che avviene ogni 5 anni*) five-yearly.

quin'quennio sm period of five years.

quinta sf vedi **quinto**.

quin'tale sm quintal (*100 kg*).

quin'tetto sm quintet(te).

'quinto, a num fifth ♦ sf (*AUT*) fifth (gear); (*INS*: elementare) *fifth year of primary school*; (: superiore) *final year of secondary school*; (*TEATRO*) wing; **un ~ della popolazione** a fifth of the population; **tre ~i** three fifths; **in ~a pagina** on the fifth page, on page five.

qui pro quo sm inv misunderstanding.

'Quito sf Quito.

quiz [kwidz] sm inv (*domanda*) question; (*anche*: **gioco a ~**) quiz game.

'quorum sm quorum.

'quota sf (*parte*) quota, share; (*AER*) height, altitude; (*IPPICA*) odds pl; **prendere/perdere ~** (*AER*) to gain/lose

height o altitude; **~ imponibile** taxable income; **~ d'iscrizione** (*INS*) enrolment fee; (*ad una gara*) entry fee; (*ad un club*) membership fee; **~ di mercato** market share.

quo'tare vt (*BORSA*) to quote; (*valutare*: anche fig) to value; **è un pittore molto quotato** he is rated highly as a painter.

quotazi'one [kwotat'tsjone] sf quotation.

quotidi'ana'mente av daily, every day.

quotidi'ano, a ag daily; (*banale*) everyday ♦ sm (*giornale*) daily (paper).

quozi'ente [kwot'tsjɛnte] sm (*MAT*) quotient; **~ di crescita zero** zero growth rate; **~ d'intelligenza (Q.I.)** intelligence quotient (IQ).

R

R, r ['ɛrre] sf o m (*lettera*) R, r; **R come Roma** ≈ R for Robert (*Brit*), R for Roger (*US*).

R abbr (*POSTA*) = **raccomandata**; (*FERR*) = **rapido**.

RA sigla = Ravenna.

ra'barbaro sm rhubarb.

Ra'bat sf Rabat.

rabberci'are [rabber'tʃare] vt (*anche* fig) to patch up.

'rabbia sf (*ira*) anger, rage; (*accanimento, furia*) fury; (*MED*: idrofobia) rabies sg.

rab'bino sm rabbi.

rabbi'oso, a ag angry, furious; (*facile all'ira*) quick-tempered; (*forze, acqua etc*) furious, raging; (*MED*) rabid, mad.

rabbo'nire vt, **~rsi** vr to calm down.

rabbrivi'dire vi to shudder, shiver.

rabbui'arsi vr to grow dark.

rabdo'mante sm water diviner.

racc. abbr (*POSTA*) = **raccomandata**.

raccapez'zarsi [rakkapet'tsarsi] vr: **non ~** to be at a loss.

raccapricci'ante [rakkaprit'tʃante] ag horrifying.

racca'priccio [rakka'prittʃo] sm horror.

raccatta'palle sm inv (*SPORT*) ballboy.

raccat'tare vt to pick up.

rac'chetta [rak'ketta] sf (*per tennis*) racket; (*per ping-pong*) bat; **~ da neve** snowshoe; **~ da sci** ski stick.

'racchio, a ['rakkjo] ag (*fam*) ugly.

racchi'udere [rak'kjudere] vt to contain.

racchi'uso, a [rak'kjuso] pp di **racchiudere**.

rac'cogliere [rak'kɔʎʎere] vt to collect; (*raccattare*) to pick up; (*frutti, fiori*) to pick, pluck; (*AGR*) to harvest; (*approvazione, voti*) to win; (*profughi*) to take in; (*vele*) to furl; (*capelli*) to put up; ~**rsi** *vr* to gather; (*fig*) to gather one's thoughts; to meditate; **non ha raccolto** (*allusione*) he didn't take the hint; (*frecciata*) he took no notice of it; ~ **i frutti del proprio lavoro** (*fig*) to reap the benefits of one's work; ~ **le idee** (*fig*) to gather one's thoughts.

raccogli'mento [rakkoʎʎi'mento] *sm* meditation.

raccogli'tore [rakkoʎʎi'tore] *sm* (*cartella*) folder, binder; ~ **a fogli mobili** loose-leaf binder.

rac'colto, a *pp di* **raccogliere** ♦ *ag* (*persona: pensoso*) thoughtful; (*luogo: appartato*) secluded, quiet ♦ *sm* (*AGR*) crop, harvest ♦ *sf* collecting *q*; collection; (*AGR*) harvesting *q*, gathering *q*; harvest, crop; **fare la** ~**a di qc** to collect sth; **chiamare a** ~**a** to gather together.

raccoman'dabile *ag* (highly) commendable; **è un tipo poco** ~ he is not to be trusted.

raccoman'dare *vt* to recommend; (*affidare*) to entrust; ~**rsi** *vr*: ~**rsi a qn** to commend o.s. to sb; ~ **a qn di fare qc** to recommend that sb does sth; ~ **a qn di non fare qc** to tell *o* warn sb not to do sth; ~ **qn a qn/alle cure di qn** to entrust sb to sb/to sb's care; **mi raccomando!** don't forget!

raccoman'dato, a *ag* (*lettera, pacco*) recorded-delivery (*Brit*), certified (*US*); (*candidato*) recommended ♦ *sm/f*: **essere un(a)** ~**(a) di ferro** to have friends in high places ♦ *sf* (*anche:* **lettera** ~**a**) recorded-delivery letter; ~**a con ricevuta di ritorno (Rrr)** recorded-delivery letter with advice of receipt.

raccomandazi'one [rakkomandat'tsjone] *sf* recommendation; **lettera di** ~ letter of introduction.

raccomo'dare *vt* (*riparare*) to repair, mend.

raccon'tare *vt*: ~ **(a qn)** (*dire*) to tell (sb); (*narrare*) to relate (to sb), tell (sb) about; **a me non la racconti** don't try and kid me; **cosa mi racconti di nuovo?** what's new?

rac'conto *sm* telling *q*, relating *q*; (*fatto raccontato*) story, tale; (*genere letterario*) short story; ~**i per bambini** children's stories.

raccorci'are [rakkor'tʃare] *vt* to shorten.

raccor'dare *vt* to link up, join.

rac'cordo *sm* (*TECN: giunzione*) connection, joint; (*AUT: di autostrada*) slip road (*Brit*), entrance (*o* exit) ramp (*US*); ~ **anulare** (*AUT*) ring road (*Brit*), beltway (*US*).

ra'chitico, a, ci, che [ra'kitiko] *ag* suffering from rickets; (*fig*) scraggy, scrawny.

rachi'tismo [raki'tizmo] *sm* (*MED*) rickets *sg*.

racimo'lare [ratʃimo'lare] *vt* (*fig*) to scrape together, glean.

'rada *sf* (natural) harbour (*Brit*) *o* harbor (*US*).

'radar *sm inv* radar.

raddol'cire [raddol'tʃire] *vt* (*persona, carattere*) to soften; ~**rsi** *vr* (*tempo*) to grow milder; (*persona*) to soften, mellow.

raddoppia'mento *sm* doubling.

raddoppi'are *vt, vi* to double.

rad'doppio *sm* (*gen*) doubling; (*BILIARDO*) double; (*EQUITAZIONE*) gallop.

raddriz'zare [raddrit'tsare] *vt* to straighten; (*fig: correggere*) to put straight, correct.

'radere *vt* (*barba*) to shave off; (*mento*) to shave; (*fig: rasentare*) to graze; to skim; ~**rsi** *vr* to shave (o.s.); ~ **al suolo** to raze to the ground.

radi'ale *ag* radial.

radi'ante *ag* (*calore, energia*) radiant.

radi'are *vt* to strike off.

radia'tore *sm* radiator.

radiazi'one [radjat'tsjone] *sf* (*FISICA*) radiation; (*cancellazione*) striking off.

radi'cale *ag* radical ♦ *sm* (*LING*) root; (*MAT, POL*) radical.

radi'cato, a *ag* (*pregiudizio, credenza*) deep-seated, deeply-rooted.

ra'dicchio [ra'dikkjo] *sm variety of chicory.*

ra'dice [ra'ditʃe] *sf* root; **segno di** ~ (*MAT*) radical sign; **colpire alla** ~ (*fig*) to strike at the root; **mettere** ~**i** (*idee, odio etc*) to take root; (*persona*) to put down roots; ~ **quadrata** (*MAT*) square root.

'radio *sf inv* radio ♦ *sm* (*CHIM*) radium; **trasmettere per** ~ to broadcast; **stazione/ ponte** ~ radio station/link; ~ **ricevente/ trasmittente** receiver/transmitter.

radioabbo'nato, a *sm/f* radio subscriber.

radioama'tore, 'trice *sm/f* amateur radio operator, ham (*fam*).

radioascolta'tore, 'trice *sm/f* (radio) listener.

radioattività *sf* radioactivity.

radioat'tivo, a *ag* radioactive.

radiocoman'dare *vt* to operate by remote control.

radiocoman'dato, a *ag* remote-controlled.

radioco'mando *sm* remote control.

radiocomunicazi'one [radjokomunikat'tsjone] *sf* radio message.

radio'cronaca, che *sf* radio commentary.

radiocro'nista, i, e *sm/f* radio commentator.

radiodiffusi'one *sf* (radio) broadcasting.

radio'fonico, a, ci, che *ag* radio *cpd*.

radiogra'fare *vt* to X-ray.

radiogra'fia *sf* radiography; (*foto*) X-ray photograph.

radio'lina *sf* portable radio, transistor (radio).

radiolo'gia [radjolo'dʒia] *sf* radiology.

radi'ologo, a, gi, ghe *sm/f* radiologist.

radiorice'vente [radjoritʃe'vɛnte] *sf* (*anche*: **apparecchio ~**) receiver.

radi'oso, a *ag* radiant.

radiostazi'one [radjostat'tsjone] *sf* radio station.

radios'veglia [radjoz'veʎʎa] *sf* radio alarm.

radio'tecnico, a, ci, che *ag* radio engineering *cpd* ♦ *sm* radio engineer.

radiotelegra'fista, i, e *sm/f* radiotelegrapher.

radiotera'pia *sf* radiotherapy.

radiotrasmit'tente *ag* (radio) broadcasting *cpd* ♦ *sf* (radio) broadcasting station.

'rado, a *ag* (*capelli*) sparse, thin; (*visite*) infrequent; **di ~** rarely; **non di ~** not uncommonly.

radu'nare *vt*, **~rsi** *vr* to gather, assemble.

radu'nata *sf* (*MIL*) muster.

ra'duno *sm* gathering, meeting.

ra'dura *sf* clearing.

'rafano *sm* horseradish.

raffazzo'nare [raffattso'nare] *vt* to patch up.

raf'fermo, a *ag* stale.

'raffica, che *sf* (*METEOR*) gust (of wind); **~ di colpi** (*di fucile*) burst of gunfire.

raffigu'rare *vt* to represent.

raffi'nare *vt* to refine.

raffina'tezza [raffina'tettsa] *sf* refinement.

raffi'nato, a *ag* refined.

raffine'ria *sf* refinery.

raffor'zare [raffor'tsare] *vt* to reinforce.

rafforza'tivo, a [raffortsa'tivo] *ag* (*LING*) intensifying ♦ *sm* (*LING*) intensifier.

raffredda'mento *sm* cooling.

raffred'dare *vt* to cool; (*fig*) to dampen, have a cooling effect on; **~rsi** *vr* to grow cool *o* cold; (*prendere un raffreddore*) to catch a cold; (*fig*) to cool (off).

raffred'dato, a *ag* (*MED*): **essere ~** to have a cold.

raffred'dore *sm* (*MED*) cold.

raffron'tare *vt* to compare.

raf'fronto *sm* comparison.

'rafia *sf* (*fibra*) raffia.

raga'nella *sf* (*ZOOL*) tree frog.

ra'gazzo, a [ra'gattso] *sm/f* boy/girl; (*fam: fidanzato*) boyfriend/girlfriend; **nome da ~a** maiden name; **~a madre** unmarried mother; **~a squillo** call girl.

ragge'lare [raddʒe'lare] *vt*, *vi*, **~rsi** *vr* to freeze.

raggi'ante [rad'dʒante] *ag* radiant, shining; **~ di gioia** beaming *o* radiant with joy.

raggi'era [rad'dʒɛra] *sf* (*di ruota*) spokes *pl*; **a ~** with a sunburst pattern.

'raggio ['raddʒo] *sm* (*di sole etc*) ray; (*MAT, distanza*) radius; (*di ruota etc*) spoke; **nel ~ di 20 km** within a radius of 20 km *o* a 20-km radius; **a largo ~** (*esplorazione, incursione*) wide-ranging; **~ d'azione** range;

~ laser laser beam; **~i X** X-rays.

raggi'rare [raddʒi'rare] *vt* to take in, trick.

rag'giro [rad'dʒiro] *sm* trick.

raggi'ungere [rad'dʒundʒere] *vt* to reach; (*persona: riprendere*) to catch up (with); (*bersaglio*) to hit; (*fig: meta*) to achieve; **~ il proprio scopo** to reach one's goal, achieve one's aim; **~ un accordo** to come to *o* reach an agreement.

raggi'unto, a [rad'dʒunto] *pp di* **raggiungere**.

raggomito'larsi *vr* to curl up.

raggranel'lare *vt* to scrape together.

raggrin'zare [raggrin'tsare] *vt*, *vi* (*anche*: **~rsi**) to wrinkle.

raggru'mare *vt*, **~rsi** *vr* (*sangue, latte*) to clot.

raggruppa'mento *sm* (*azione*) grouping; (*gruppo*) group; (: *MIL*) unit.

raggrup'pare *vt* to group (together).

ragguagli'are [raggwaʎ'ʎare] *vt* (*paragonare*) to compare; (*informare*) to inform.

raggu'aglio [rag'gwaʎʎo] *sm* comparison; (*informazione, relazione*) piece of information.

ragguar'devole *ag* (*degno di riguardo*) distinguished, notable; (*notevole: somma*) considerable.

'ragia ['radʒa] *sf*: **acqua ~** turpentine.

ragiona'mento [radʒona'mento] *sm* reasoning *q*; argument.

ragio'nare [radʒo'nare] *vi* (*usare la ragione*) to reason; (*discorrere*): **~ (di)** to argue (about); **cerca di ~** try and be reasonable.

ragi'one [ra'dʒone] *sf* reason; (*dimostrazione, prova*) argument, reason; (*diritto*) right; **aver ~** to be right; **aver ~ di qn** to get the better of sb; **dare ~ a qn** (*sog: persona*) to side with sb; (: *fatto*) to prove sb right; **farsi una ~ di qc** to accept sth, come to terms with sth; **in ~ di** at the rate of; **a** *o* **con ~** rightly, justly; **perdere la ~** to become insane; (*fig*) to take leave of one's senses; **a ragion veduta** after due consideration; **per ~i di famiglia** for family reasons; **~ di scambio** terms of trade; **~ sociale** (*COMM*) corporate name; **ragion di stato** reason of State.

ragione'ria [radʒone'ria] *sf* accountancy; (*ufficio*) accounts department.

ragio'nevole [radʒo'nevole] *ag* reasonable.

ragioni'ere, a [radʒo'njere] *sm/f* accountant.

ragli'are [raʎ'ʎare] *vi* to bray.

ragna'tela [raɲɲa'tela] *sf* cobweb, spider's web.

'ragno ['raɲɲo] *sm* spider; **non cavare un ~ dal buco** (*fig*) to draw a blank.

ragù *sm inv* (*CUC*) meat sauce (*for pasta*).

RAI-TV [raiti'vu] *sigla f* = *Radio televisione italiana*.

rallegra'menti *smpl* congratulations.

ralle'grare *vt* to cheer up; **~rsi** *vr* to cheer

up; (*provare allegrezza*) to rejoice; ~**rsi con qn** to congratulate sb.

rallenta'mento *sm* slowing down; slackening.

rallen'tare *vt, vi* to slow down; ~ **il passo** to slacken one's pace.

rallenta'tore *sm* (*CINEMA*) slow-motion camera; **al** ~ (*anche fig*) in slow motion.

raman'zina [raman'dzina] *sf* lecture, telling-off.

ra'mare *vt* (*superficie*) to copper, coat with copper; (*AGR: vite*) to spray with copper sulphate.

ra'marro *sm* green lizard.

ra'mato, a *ag* (*oggetto: rivestito di rame*) copper-coated, coppered; (*capelli, barba*) coppery, copper-coloured (*Brit*), copper-colored (*US*).

'rame *sm* (*CHIM*) copper; **di** ~ copper *cpd*; **incisione su** ~ copperplate.

ramifi'care *vi* (*BOT*) to put out branches; ~**rsi** *vr* (*diramarsi*) to branch out; (*MED: tumore, vene*) to ramify; ~**rsi in** (*biforcarsi*) to branch into.

ramificazi'one [ramifikat'tsjone] *sf* ramification.

ra'mingo, a, ghi, ghe *ag* (*poetico*): **andare** ~ to go wandering, wander.

ra'mino *sm* (*CARTE*) rummy.

rammari'carsi *vr*: ~ (**di**) (*rincrescersi*) to be sorry (about), regret; (*lamentarsi*) to complain (about).

ram'marico, chi *sm* regret.

rammen'dare *vt* to mend; (*calza*) to darn.

ram'mendo *sm* mending *q*; darning *q*; mend; darn.

rammen'tare *vt* to remember, recall; ~**rsi** *vr*: ~**rsi (di qc)** to remember (sth); ~ **qc a qn** to remind sb of sth.

rammol'lire *vt* to soften ♦ *vi* (*anche:* ~**rsi**) to go soft.

rammol'lito, a *ag* weak ♦ *sm/f* weakling.

'ramo *sm* branch; (*di commercio*) field; **non è il mio** ~ it's not my field *o* line.

ramo'scello [ramoʃ'ʃello] *sm* twig.

'rampa *sf* flight (of stairs); ~ **di lancio** launching pad.

rampi'cante *ag* (*BOT*) climbing.

ram'pino *sm* (*gancio*) hook; (*NAUT*) grapnel.

ram'pollo *sm* (*di acqua*) spring; (*BOT: germoglio*) shoot; (*fig: discendente*) descendant.

ram'pone *sm* harpoon; (*ALPINISMO*) crampon.

'rana *sf* frog; ~ **pescatrice** angler fish.

'rancido, a ['rantʃido] *ag* rancid.

'rancio ['rantʃo] *sm* (*MIL*) mess; **ora del** ~ mess time.

ran'core *sm* rancour (*Brit*), rancor (*US*), resentment; **portare** ~ **a qn, provare** ~ **per** *o* **verso qn** to bear sb a grudge.

ran'dagio, a, gi, gie *o* **ge** [ran'daddʒo] *ag* (*gatto, cane*) stray.

ran'dello *sm* club, cudgel.

'rango, ghi *sm* (*grado*) rank; (*condizione sociale*) station, social standing; **persone di** ~ **inferiore** people of lower standing; **uscire dai** ~**ghi** to fall out; (*fig*) to step out of line.

Ran'gun *sf* Rangoon.

rannicchi'arsi [rannik'kjarsi] *vr* to crouch, huddle.

rannuvo'larsi *vr* to cloud over, become overcast.

ra'nocchio [ra'nɔkkjo] *sm* (edible) frog.

ranto'lare *vi* to wheeze.

ranto'lio *sm* (*il respirare affannoso*) wheezing; (: *di agonizzante*) death rattle.

'rantolo *sm* wheeze; death rattle.

ra'nuncolo *sm* (*BOT*) buttercup.

'rapa *sf* (*BOT*) turnip.

ra'pace [ra'patʃe] *ag* (*animale*) predatory; (*fig*) rapacious, grasping ♦ *sm* bird of prey.

ra'pare *vt* (*capelli*) to crop, cut very short.

'rapida *sf vedi* **rapido**.

rapida'mente *av* quickly, rapidly.

rapidità *sf* speed.

'rapido, a *ag* fast; (*esame, occhiata*) quick, rapid ♦ *sm* (*FERR*) express (train) ♦ *sf* (*di fiume*) rapid.

rapi'mento *sm* kidnapping; (*fig*) rapture.

ra'pina *sf* robbery; ~ **in banca** bank robbery; ~ **a mano armata** armed robbery.

rapi'nare *vt* to rob.

rapina'tore, 'trice *sm/f* robber.

ra'pire *vt* (*cose*) to steal; (*persone*) to kidnap; (*fig*) to enrapture, delight.

ra'pito, a *ag* (*persona*) kidnapped; (*fig: in estasi*): **ascoltare** ~ **qn** to be captivated by sb's words ♦ *sm/f* kidnapped person.

rapi'tore, 'trice *sm/f* kidnapper.

rappacifi'care [rappatʃifi'kare] *vt* (*riconciliare*) to reconcile; ~**rsi** *vr* (*uso reciproco*) to be reconciled, make it up (*fam*).

rappacificazi'one [rappatʃifikat'tsjone] *sf* reconciliation.

rappez'zare [rappet'tsare] *vt* to patch.

rappor'tare *vt* (*confrontare*) to compare; (*riprodurre*) to reproduce.

rap'porto *sm* (*resoconto*) report; (*legame*) relationship; (*MAT, TECN*) ratio; ~**i** *smpl* (*fra persone, paesi*) relations; **in** ~ **a quanto è successo** with regard to *o* in relation to what happened; **fare** ~ **a qn su qc** to report sth to sb; **andare a** ~ **da qn** to report to sb; **chiamare qn a** ~ (*MIL*) to summon sb; **essere in buoni/cattivi** ~**i con qn** to be on good/bad terms with sb; ~ **d'affari**, ~ **di lavoro** business relations; ~ **di compressione** (*TECN*) pressure ratio; ~ **coniugale** marital relationship; ~ **di tra-**

smissione (*TECN*) gear; ~**i sessuali** sexual intercourse *sg*.

rap'prendersi *vr* to coagulate, clot; (*latte*) to curdle.

rappre'saglia [rappre'saʎʎa] *sf* reprisal, retaliation.

rappresen'tante *sm/f* representative; ~ **di commercio** sales representative, sales rep (*fam*); ~ **sindacale** union delegate *o* representative.

rappresen'tanza [rapprezen'tantsa] *sf* delegation, deputation; (*COMM*: *ufficio, sede*) agency; **in** ~ **di qn** on behalf of sb; **spese di** ~ entertainment expenses; **macchina di** ~ official car; **avere la** ~ **di** to be the agent for; ~ **esclusiva** sole agency; **avere la** ~ **esclusiva** to be sole agent.

rappresen'tare *vt* to represent; (*TEATRO*) to perform; **farsi** ~ **dal proprio legale** to be represented by one's lawyer.

rappresenta'tivo, a *ag* representative ♦ *sf* (*di partito, sindacale*) representative group; (*SPORT*: *squadra*) representative (team).

rappresentazi'one [rapprezentat'tsjone] *sf* representation; performing *q*; (*spettacolo*) performance; **prima** ~ **assoluta** world première.

rap'preso, a *pp di* **rapprendere**.

rapso'dia *sf* rhapsody.

'raptus *sm inv*: ~ **di follia** fit of madness.

rara'mente *av* seldom, rarely.

rare'fare *vt*, ~**rsi** *vr* to rarefy.

rare'fatto, a *pp di* **rarefare** ♦ *ag* rarefied.

rarefazi'one [rarefat'tsjone] *sf* rarefaction.

rarità *sf inv* rarity.

'raro, a *ag* rare.

ra'sare *vt* (*barba etc*) to shave off; (*siepi, erba*) to trim, cut; ~**rsi** *vr* to shave (o.s.).

ra'sato, a *ag* (*erba*) trimmed, cut; (*tessuto*) smooth; **avere la barba** ~**a** to be clean-shaven.

rasa'tura *sf* shave.

raschia'mento [raskja'mento] *sm* (*MED*) curettage; ~ **uterino** D and C.

raschi'are [ras'kjare] *vt* to scrape; (*macchia, fango*) to scrape off ♦ *vi* to clear one's throat.

rasen'tare *vt* (*andar rasente*) to keep close to; (*sfiorare*) to skim along (*o* over); (*fig*) to border on.

ra'sente *prep*: ~ **(a)** close to, very near.

'raso, a *pp di* **radere** ♦ *ag* (*barba*) shaved; (*capelli*) cropped; (*con misure di capacità*) level; (*pieno*: *bicchiere*) full to the brim ♦ *sm* (*tessuto*) satin; ~ **terra** close to the ground; **volare** ~ **terra** to hedgehop; **un cucchiaio** ~ a level spoonful.

ra'soio *sm* razor; ~ **elettrico** electric shaver *o* razor.

'raspo *sm* (*di uva*) grape stalk.

ras'segna [ras'seɲɲa] *sf* (*MIL*) inspection, review; (*esame*) inspection; (*resoconto*) review, survey; (*pubblicazione letteraria etc*) review; (*mostra*) exhibition, show; **passare in** ~ (*MIL, fig*) to review.

rasse'gnare [rasseɲ'ɲare] *vt*: ~ **le dimissioni** to resign, hand in one's resignation; ~**rsi** *vr* (*accettare*): ~**rsi (a qc/a fare)** to resign o.s. (to sth/to doing).

rassegnazi'one [rasseɲɲat'tsjone] *sf* resignation.

rasse're'nare *vt* (*persona*) to cheer up; ~**rsi** *vr* (*tempo*) to clear up.

rasset'tare *vt* to tidy, put in order; (*aggiustare*) to repair, mend.

rassicu'rante *ag* reassuring.

rassicu'rare *vt* to reassure; ~**rsi** *vr* to take heart, recover one's confidence.

rassicurazi'one [rassikurat'tsjone] *sf* reassurance.

rasso'dare *vt* to harden, stiffen; (*fig*) to strengthen, consolidate.

rassomigli'anza [rassomiʎ'ʎantsa] *sf* resemblance.

rassomigli'are [rassomiʎ'ʎare] *vi*: ~ **a** to resemble, look like.

rastrella'mento *sm* (*MIL, di polizia*) (thorough) search.

rastrel'lare *vt* to rake; (*fig: perlustrare*) to comb.

rastrelli'era *sf* rack; (*per piatti*) dish rack.

ras'trello *sm* rake.

'rata *sf* (*quota*) instalment, installment (*US*); **pagare a** ~**e** to pay by instal(l)ments *o* on hire purchase (*Brit*); **comprare/vendere a** ~**e** to buy/sell on hire purchase (*Brit*) *o* on the installment plan (*US*).

rate'ale *ag*: **pagamento** ~ payment by instal(l)ments; **vendita** ~ hire purchase (*Brit*), installment plan (*US*).

rate'are, rateiz'zare [rateid'dzare] *vt* to divide into instal(l)ments.

rateazi'one [rateat'tsjone] *sf* division into instal(l)ments.

'rateo *sm* (*COMM*) accrual.

ra'tifica, che *sf* ratification.

ratifi'care *vt* (*DIR*) to ratify.

'ratto *sm* (*DIR*) abduction; (*ZOOL*) rat.

rattop'pare *vt* to patch.

rat'toppo *sm* patching *q*; patch.

rattrap'pire *vt* to make stiff; ~**rsi** *vr* to be stiff.

rattris'tare *vt* to sadden; ~**rsi** *vr* to become sad.

rau'cedine [rau't ʃedine] *sf* hoarseness.

'rauco, a, chi, che *ag* hoarse.

rava'nello *sm* radish.

raven'nate *ag* (*o* from) Ravenna.

ravi'oli *smpl* ravioli *sg*.

ravve'dersi *vr* to mend one's ways.

ravvi'are *vt* (*capelli*) to tidy; ~**rsi i capelli** to tidy one's hair.

ravvicina'mento [ravvitʃina'mento] *sm* (*tra persone*) reconciliation; (*POL*: *tra paesi etc*) rapprochement.

ravvici'nare [ravvitʃi'nare] *vt* (*avvicinare*): ~ **qc a** to bring sth nearer to; (*oggetti*) to bring closer together; (*fig*: *persone*) to reconcile, bring together; ~**rsi** *vr* to be reconciled.

ravvi'sare *vt* to recognize.

ravvi'vare *vt* to revive; (*fig*) to brighten up, enliven; ~**rsi** *vr* to revive; to brighten up.

Rawal'pindi [raval'pindi] *sf* Rawalpindi.

razio'cinio [rattsjo'tʃinjo] *sm* reasoning *q*; reason; (*buon senso*) common sense.

razio'nale [rattsjo'nale] *ag* rational.

razionalità [rattsjonali'ta] *sf* rationality; (*buon senso*) common sense.

raziona'mento [rattsjona'mento] *sm* rationing.

razio'nare [rattsjo'nare] *vt* to ration.

razi'one [rat'tsjone] *sf* ration; (*porzione*) portion, share.

'razza ['rattsa] *sf* race; (*ZOOL*) breed; (*discendenza*, *stirpe*) stock, race; (*sorta*) sort, kind.

raz'zia [rat'tsia] *sf* raid, foray.

razzi'ale [rat'tsjale] *ag* racial.

raz'zismo [rat'tsizmo] *sm* racism, racialism.

raz'zista, i, e [rat'tsista] *ag*, *sm/f* racist, racialist.

'razzo ['raddzo] *sm* rocket; ~ **di segnalazione** flare; ~ **vettore** vector rocket.

razzo'lare [rattso'lare] *vi* (*galline*) to scratch about.

RC *sigla* = *Reggio Calabria*.

RDT *sigla f vedi* **Repubblica Democratica Tedesca**.

RE *sigla* = *Reggio Emilia*.

re *sm inv* (*sovrano*) king; (*MUS*) D; (*: solfeggiando la scala*) re.

rea'gente [rea'dʒente] *sm* reagent.

rea'gire [rea'dʒire] *vi* to react.

re'ale *ag* real; (*di, da re*) royal ♦ *sm*: **il** ~ reality; **i R~i** the Royal family.

rea'lismo *sm* realism.

rea'lista, i, e *sm/f* realist; (*POL*) royalist.

rea'listico, a, ci, che *ag* realistic.

realiz'zare [realid'dzare] *vt* (*progetto etc*) to realize, carry out; (*sogno, desiderio*) to realize, fulfil; (*scopo*) to achieve; (*COMM*: *titoli etc*) to realize; (*CALCIO etc*) to score; ~**rsi** *vr* to be realized.

realizzazi'one [realiddzat'tsjone] *sf* realization; fulfilment; achievement; ~ **scenica** stage production.

rea'lizzo [rea'liddzo] *sm* (*conversione in denaro*) conversion into cash; (*vendita forzata*) clearance sale.

real'mente *av* really, actually.

realtà *sf inv* reality; **in** ~ (*in effetti*) in fact; (*a dire il vero*) really.

re'ame *sm* kingdom, realm; (*fig*) realm.

re'ato *sm* offence (*Brit*), offense (*US*).

reat'tore *sm* (*FISICA*) reactor; (*AER*: *aereo*) jet; (*: motore*) jet engine.

reazio'nario, a [reattsjo'narjo] *ag*, *sm/f* (*POL*) reactionary.

reazi'one [reat'tsjone] *sf* reaction; **motore/aereo a** ~ jet engine/plane; **forze della** ~ reactionary forces; ~ **a catena** (*anche fig*) chain reaction.

'rebbio *sm* prong.

'rebus *sm inv* rebus; (*fig*) puzzle; enigma.

recapi'tare *vt* to deliver.

re'capito *sm* (*indirizzo*) address; (*consegna*) delivery; **ha un** ~ **telefonico?** do you have a telephone number where you can be reached?; ~ **a domicilio** home delivery (service).

re'care *vt* (*portare*) to bring; (*avere su di sé*) to carry, bear; (*cagionare*) to cause, bring; ~**rsi** *vr* to go; ~ **danno a qn** to harm sb, cause harm to sb.

re'cedere [re'tʃɛdere] *vi* to withdraw.

recensi'one [retʃen'sjone] *sf* review.

recen'sire [retʃen'sire] *vt* to review.

recen'sore, a [retʃen'sore] *sm/f* reviewer.

re'cente [re'tʃɛnte] *ag* recent; **di** ~ recently; **più** ~ latest, most recent.

recente'mente [retʃɛnte'mente] *av* recently.

rece'pire [retʃe'pire] *vt* to understand, take in.

recessi'one [retʃes'sjone] *sf* (*ECON*) recession.

re'cesso [re'tʃɛsso] *sm* (*azione*) recession, receding; (*DIR*) withdrawal; (*luogo*) recess.

recherò *etc* [reke'rɔ] *vb vedi* **recare**.

re'cidere [re'tʃidere] *vt* to cut off, chop off.

reci'divo, a [retʃi'divo] *sm/f* (*DIR*) second (*o* habitual) offender, recidivist.

recin'tare [retʃin'tare] *vt* to enclose, fence off.

re'cinto [re'tʃinto] *sm* enclosure; (*ciò che recinge*) fence; surrounding wall.

recinzi'one [retʃin'tsjone] *sf* (*azione*) enclosure, fencing-off; (*recinto*: *di legno*) fence; (*: di mattoni*) wall; (*: reticolato*) wire fencing; (*: a sbarre*) railings *pl*.

recipi'ente [retʃi'pjɛnte] *sm* container.

re'ciproco, a, ci, che [re'tʃiproko] *ag* reciprocal.

re'ciso, a [re'tʃizo] *pp di* **recidere**.

'recita ['rɛtʃita] *sf* performance.

'recital ['rɛtʃital] *sm inv* recital.

reci'tare [retʃi'tare] *vt* (*poesia, lezione*) to recite; (*dramma*) to perform; (*ruolo*) to play *o* act (the part of).

recitazi'one [retʃitat'tsjone] *sf* recitation; (*di attore*) acting; **scuola di** ~ drama school.

recla'mare *vi* to complain ♦ *vt* (*richiedere*) to demand.

ré'clame [re'klam] *sf inv* advertising *q*; advertisement, advert (*Brit*), ad (*fam*).

reclamiz'zare [reklamid'dzare] *vt* to

advertise.

re'clamo *sm* complaint; **sporgere** ~ **a** to complain to, make a complaint to.

recli'nabile *ag* (*sedile*) reclining.

recli'nare *vt* (*capo*) to bow, lower; (*sedile*) to tilt.

reclusi'one *sf* (*DIR*) imprisonment.

re'cluso, a *sm/f* prisoner.

'recluta *sf* recruit.

recluta'mento *sm* recruitment.

reclu'tare *vt* to recruit.

re'condito, a *ag* secluded; (*fig*) secret, hidden.

'record *ag inv* record *cpd* ♦ *sm inv* record; **in tempo** ~, **a tempo di** ~ in record time; **detenere il** ~ **di** to hold the record for; ~ **mondiale** world record.

recrimi'nare *vi*: ~ (**su qc**) to complain (about sth).

recriminazi'one [rekriminat'tsjone] *sf* recrimination.

recrude'scenza [rekrudeʃ'ʃɛntsa] *sf* fresh outbreak.

recupe'rare *etc* = **ricuperare** *etc*.

redargu'ire *vt* to rebuke.

re'dassi *etc vb vedi* **redigere.**

re'datto, a *pp di* **redigere.**

redat'tore, 'trice *sm/f* (*STAMPA*) editor; (: *di articolo*) writer; (*di dizionario etc*) compiler; ~ **capo** chief editor.

redazi'one [redat'tsjone] *sf* editing; writing; (*sede*) editorial office(s); (*personale*) editorial staff; (*versione*) version.

reddi'tizio, a [reddi'tittsjo] *ag* profitable.

'reddito *sm* income; (*dello Stato*) revenue; (*di un capitale*) yield; ~ **complessivo** gross income; ~ **disponibile** disposable income; ~ **fisso** fixed income; ~ **imponibile/non imponibile** taxable/non-taxable income; ~ **da lavoro** earned income; ~ **nazionale** national income; ~ **pubblico** public revenue.

re'densi *etc vb vedi* **redimere.**

re'dento, a *pp di* **redimere.**

reden'tore *sm*: **il R~** the Redeemer.

redenzi'one [reden'tsjone] *sf* redemption.

re'digere [re'didʒere] *vt* to write; (*contratto*) to draw up.

re'dimere *vt* to deliver; (*REL*) to redeem.

'redini *sfpl* reins.

redi'vivo, a *ag* returned to life, reborn.

'reduce ['rɛdutʃe] *ag* (*gen*): ~ **da** returning from, back from ♦ *sm/f* survivor; (*veterano*) veteran; **essere** ~ **da** (*esame, colloquio*) to have been through; (*malattia*) to be just over.

'refe *sm* thread.

refe'rendum *sm inv* referendum.

refe'renza [refe'rɛntsa] *sf* reference.

re'ferto *sm* medical report.

refet'torio *sm* refectory.

refezi'one [refet'tsjone] *sf* (*INS*) school meal.

refrat'tario, a *ag* refractory; (*fig*): **essere** ~

alla matematica to have no aptitude for mathematics.

refrige'rante [refridʒe'rante] *ag* (*TECN*) cooling, refrigerating; (*bevanda*) refreshing ♦ *sm* (*CHIM: fluido*) coolant; (*TECN: apparecchio*) refrigerator.

refrige'rare [refridʒe'rare] *vt* to refrigerate; (*rinfrescare*) to cool, refresh.

refrigerazi'one [refridʒerat'tsjone] *sf* refrigeration; (*TECN*) cooling; ~ **ad acqua** (*AUT*) water-cooling.

refri'gerio [refri'dʒɛrjo] *sm*: **trovare** ~ to find somewhere cool.

refur'tiva *sf* stolen goods *pl*.

Reg. *abbr* (= *reggimento*) Regt; (*AMM*) = *regolamento*.

rega'lare *vt* to give (as a present), make a present of.

re'gale *ag* regal.

re'galo *sm* gift, present ♦ *ag inv*: **confezione** ~ gift pack; **fare un** ~ **a qn** to give sb a present; **"articoli da** ~**"** "gifts".

re'gata *sf* regatta.

reg'gente [red'dʒɛnte] *ag* (*proposizione*) main; (*sovrano*) reigning ♦ *sm/f* regent; **principe** ~ prince regent.

reg'genza [red'dʒɛntsa] *sf* regency.

'reggere ['reddʒere] *vt* (*tenere*) to hold; (*sostenere*) to support, bear, hold up; (*portare*) to carry, bear; (*resistere*) to withstand; (*dirigere: impresa*) to manage, run; (*governare*) to rule, govern; (*LING*) to take, be followed by ♦ *vi* (*resistere*): ~ **a** to stand up to, hold out against; (*sopportare*): ~ **a** to stand; (*durare*) to last; (*fig: teoria etc*) to hold water; ~**rsi** *vr* (*stare ritto*) to stand; (*fig: dominarsi*) to control o.s.; ~**rsi sulle gambe** *o* **in piedi** to stand up.

'reggia, ge ['reddʒa] *sf* royal palace.

reggi'calze [reddʒi'kaltse] *sm inv* suspender belt.

reggi'mento [reddʒi'mento] *sm* (*MIL*) regiment.

reggi'petto [reddʒi'pɛtto] *sm*, **reggi'seno** [reddʒi'seno] *sm* bra.

re'gia, 'gie [re'dʒia] *sf* (*TV, CINEMA etc*) direction.

re'gime [re'dʒime] *sm* (*POL*) regime; (*DIR: aureo, patrimoniale etc*) system; (*MED*) diet; (*TECN*) (*engine*) speed; ~ **di giri** (*di motore*) revs *pl* per minute; ~ **vegetariano** vegetarian diet.

re'gina [re'dʒina] *sf* queen.

'regio, a, gi, gie ['rɛdʒo] *ag* royal.

regio'nale [redʒo'nale] *ag* regional.

regi'one [re'dʒone] *sf* (*gen*) region; (*territorio*) region, area.

re'gista, i, e [re'dʒista] *sm/f* (*TV, CINEMA etc*) director.

regis'trare [redʒis'trare] *vt* (*AMM*) to register; (*COMM*) to enter; (*notare*) to report, note; (*canzone, conversazione, sog*: *strumento di misura*) to record; (*mettere a punto*) to adjust, regulate; ~ **i bagagli** (*AER*) to check in one's luggage; ~ **i freni** (*TECN*) to adjust the brakes.

registra'tore [redʒistra'tore] *sm* (*strumento*) recorder, register; (*magnetofono*) tape recorder; ~ **di cassa** cash register; ~ **a cassette** cassette recorder; ~ **di volo** (*AER*) flight recorder, black box (*fam*).

registrazi'one [redʒistrat'tsjone] *sf* registration; entry; reporting; recording; adjustment; ~ **bagagli** (*AER*) check-in.

re'gistro [re'dʒistro] *sm* (*libro*) register; (*DIR*) registry; (*MUS, TECN*) register; (*COMM*): ~ **(di cassa)** ledger; **ufficio del** ~ registrar's office; ~ **di bordo** logbook; ~**i contabili** (account) books.

re'gnante [reɲ'ɲante] *ag* reigning, ruling ♦ *sm/f* ruler.

re'gnare [reɲ'ɲare] *vi* to reign, rule; (*fig*) to reign.

'regno ['reɲɲo] *sm* kingdom; (*periodo*) reign; (*fig*) realm; **il** ~ **animale/vegetale** the animal/vegetable kingdom; **il R**~ **Unito** the United Kingdom.

'regola *sf* rule; **a** ~ **d'arte** duly; perfectly; **essere in** ~ (*dipendente*) to be a registered employee; (*fig: essere pulito*) to be clean; **fare le cose in** ~ to do things properly; **avere le carte in** ~ (*gen*) to have one's papers in order; (*fig: essere adatto*) to be the right person; **per tua (norma e)** ~ for your information; **un'eccezione alla** ~ an exception to the rule.

rego'labile *ag* adjustable.

regolamen'tare *ag* (*distanza, velocità*) regulation *cpd*, proper; (*disposizione*) statutory ♦ *vt* (*gen*) to control; **entro il tempo** ~ within the time allowed, within the prescribed time.

regola'mento *sm* (*complesso di norme*) regulations *pl*; (*di debito*) settlement; ~ **di conti** (*fig*) settling of scores.

rego'lare *ag* regular; (*velocità*) steady; (*superficie*) even; (*passo*) steady, even; (*in regola: documento*) in order ♦ *vt* to regulate, control; (*apparecchio*) to adjust, regulate; (*questione, conto, debito*) to settle; ~**rsi** *vr* (*moderarsi*): ~**rsi nel bere/ nello spendere** to control one's drinking/ spending; (*comportarsi*) to behave, act; **presentare** ~ **domanda** to apply through the proper channels; ~ **i conti** (*fig*) to settle old scores.

regolarità *sf inv* regularity; steadiness; evenness; (*nel pagare*) punctuality.

regolariz'zare [regolarid'dzare] *vt* (*posizione*) to regularize; (*debito*) to settle.

rego'lata *sf*: **darsi una** ~ to pull o.s. together.

regola'tezza [regola'tettsa] *sf* (*ordine*)

orderliness; (*moderazione*) moderation.

rego'lato, a *ag* (*ordinato*) orderly; (*moderato*) moderate.

regola'tore *sm* (*TECN*) regulator; ~ **di frequenza/di volume** frequency/volume control.

'regolo *sm* ruler; ~ **calcolatore** slide rule.

regre'dire *vi* to regress.

regressi'one *sf* regression.

re'gresso *sm* (*fig: declino*) decline.

rei'etto, a *sm/f* outcast.

reincarnazi'one [reinkarnat'tsjone] *sf* reincarnation.

reinte'grare *vt* (*produzione*) to restore; (*energie*) to recover; (*dipendente*) to reinstate.

reintegrazi'one [reintegrat'tsjone] *sf* (*di produzione*) restoration; (*di dipendente*) reinstatement.

relativa'mente *av* relatively.

relatività *sf* relativity.

rela'tivo, a *ag* relative; (*attinente*) relevant; (*rispettivo*) respective; ~ **a** (*che concerne*) relating to, concerning; (*proporzionato*) in proportion to.

rela'tore, 'trice *sm/f* (*gen*) spokesman/ woman; (*INS: di tesi*) supervisor.

re'lax *sm* relaxation.

relazi'one [relat'tsjone] *sf* (*fra cose, persone*) relation(ship); (*resoconto*) report, account; ~**i** *sfpl* (*conoscenze*) connections; **essere in** ~ to be connected; **mettere in** ~ (*fatti, elementi*) to make the connection between; **in** ~ **a quanto detto prima** with regard to what has already been said; **essere in buone** ~**i con qn** to be on good terms with sb; **fare una** ~ to make a report, give an account; ~**i pubbliche (RP)** public relations (PR).

rele'gare *vt* to banish; (*fig*) to relegate.

religi'one [reli'dʒone] *sf* religion.

religi'oso, a [reli'dʒoso] *ag* religious ♦ *sm/f* monk/nun.

re'liquia *sf* relic.

re'litto *sm* wreck; (*fig*) down-and-out.

re'mainder [ri'meində] *sm inv* (*libro*) remainder.

re'mare *vi* to row.

remini'scenze [reminiʃ'ʃentse] *sfpl* reminiscences.

remissi'one *sf* remission; (*deferenza*) submissiveness, compliance; ~ **del debito** remission of debt; ~ **di querela** (*DIR*) withdrawal of an action.

remissività *sf* submissiveness.

remis'sivo, a *ag* submissive, compliant.

'remo *sm* oar.

'remora *sf* (*poetico: indugio*) hesitation.

re'moto, a *ag* remote.

remune'rare *etc* = **rimunerare** *etc*.

'rena *sf* sand.

re'nale *ag* kidney *cpd*.

'**rendere** *vt* (*ridare*) to return, give back; (: *saluto etc*) to return; (*produrre*) to yield, bring in; (*esprimere*, *tradurre*) to render; (*far diventare*): ~ **qc possibile** to make sth possible ♦ *vi* (*fruttare*: *ditta*) to be profitable; (: *investimento*, *campo*) to yield, be productive; ~ **grazie a qn** to thank sb; ~ **omaggio a qn** to honour sb; ~ **un servizio a qn** to do sb a service; ~ **una testimonianza** to give evidence; ~ **la visita** to pay a return visit; **non so se rendo l'idea** I don't know whether I'm making myself clear; ~**rsi utile** to make o.s. useful; ~**rsi conto di qc** to realize sth.

rendi'conto *sm* (*rapporto*) report, account; (*AMM*, *COMM*) statement of account.

rendi'mento *sm* (*reddito*) yield; (*di manodopera*, *TECN*) efficiency; (*capacità di produrre*) output; (*di studenti*) performance.

'**rendita** *sf* (*di individuo*) private o unearned income; (*COMM*) revenue; ~ **annua** annuity; ~ **vitalizia** life annuity.

'**rene** *sm* kidney.

'**reni** *sfpl* back *sg*.

reni'tente *ag* reluctant, unwilling; ~ **ai consigli di qn** unwilling to follow sb's advice; **essere** ~ **alla leva** (*MIL*) to fail to report for military service.

'**renna** *sf* reindeer *inv*.

'**Reno** *sm*: **il** ~ the Rhine.

'**reo, a** *sm/f* (*DIR*) offender.

re'parto *sm* department, section; (*MIL*) detachment; ~ **acquisti** purchasing office.

repel'lente *ag* repulsive; (*CHIM*: *insettifugo*): **liquido** ~ (liquid) repellant.

repen'taglio [repen'taʎʎo] *sm*: **mettere a** ~ to jeopardize, risk.

repen'tino, a *ag* sudden, unexpected.

repe'ribile *ag* available.

repe'rire *vt* to find, trace.

re'perto *sm* (*ARCHEOLOGIA*) find; (*MED*) report; (*anche*: ~ **giudiziario**) exhibit.

reper'torio *sm* (*TEATRO*) repertory; (*elenco*) index, (alphabetical) list.

'**replica, che** *sf* repetition; reply, answer; (*obiezione*) objection; (*TEATRO*, *CINEMA*) repeat performance; (*copia*) replica.

repli'care *vt* (*ripetere*) to repeat; (*rispondere*) to answer, reply.

repressi'one *sf* repression.

repres'sivo, a *ag* repressive.

re'presso, a *pp di* **reprimere**.

re'primere *vt* to suppress, repress.

re'pubblica, che *sf* republic; **la R~ Democratica Tedesca (RDT)** the German Democratic Republic (GDR); **la R~ Federale Tedesca (RFT)** the Federal Republic of Germany (FRG).

repubbli'cano, a *ag*, *sm/f* republican.

repu'tare *vt* to consider, judge.

reputazi'one [reputat'tsjone] *sf* reputation;

farsi una cattiva ~ to get o.s. a bad name.

'**requie** *sf* rest; **dare** ~ **a qn** to give sb some peace; **senza** ~ unceasingly.

requi'sire *vt* to requisition.

requi'sito *sm* requirement; **avere i** ~**i necessari per un lavoro** to have the necessary qualifications for a job.

requi'sitoria *sf* (*DIR*) closing speech (for the prosecution).

requisizi'one [rekwizit'tsjone] *sf* requisition.

'**resa** *sf* (*l'arrendersi*) surrender; (*restituzione*, *rendimento*) return; ~ **dei conti** rendering of accounts; (*fig*) day of reckoning.

re'scindere [reʃ'ʃindere] *vt* (*DIR*) to rescind, annul.

re'scisso, a [reʃ'ʃisso] *pp di* **rescindere**.

'**resi** *etc vb vedi* **rendere**.

resi'dente *ag* resident.

resi'denza [resi'dɛntsa] *sf* residence.

residenzi'ale [residen'tsjale] *ag* residential.

residu'ale *ag* residual.

re'siduo, a *ag* residual, remaining ♦ *sm* remainder; (*CHIM*) residue; ~**i industriali** industrial waste *sg*.

'**resina** *sf* resin.

resis'tente *ag* (*che resiste*): ~ **a** resistant to; (*forte*) strong; (*duraturo*) long-lasting, durable; ~ **all'acqua** waterproof; ~ **al caldo** heat-resistant; ~ **al fuoco** fireproof; ~ **al gelo** frost-resistant.

resis'tenza [resis'tɛntsa] *sf* (*gen*, *ELETTR*) resistance; (*di persona*: *fisica*) stamina, endurance; (: *mentale*) endurance, resistance; **opporre** ~ **(a)** to offer o put up resistance (to); (*decisione*, *scelta*) to show opposition (to).

re'sistere *vi* to resist; ~ **a** (*assalto*, *tentazioni*) to resist; (*dolore*, *sog*: *pianta*) to withstand; (*non patir danno*) to be resistant to.

resis'tito, a *pp di* **resistere**.

'**reso, a** *pp di* **rendere**.

reso'conto *sm* report, account.

respin'gente [respin'dʒɛnte] *sm* (*FERR*) buffer.

res'pingere [res'pindʒere] *vt* to drive back, repel; (*rifiutare*: *pacco*, *lettera*) to return; (: *invito*) to refuse; (: *proposta*) to reject, turn down; (*INS*: *bocciare*) to fail.

res'pinto, a *pp di* **respingere**.

respi'rare *vi* to breathe; (*fig*) to get one's breath; to breathe again ♦ *vt* to breathe (in), inhale.

respira'tore *sm* respirator.

respira'torio, a *ag* respiratory.

respirazi'one [respirat'tsjone] *sf* breathing; ~ **artificiale** artificial respiration; ~ **bocca a bocca** mouth-to-mouth resuscitation, kiss of life (*fam*).

res'piro *sm* breathing *q*; (*singolo atto*) breath; (*fig*) respite, rest; **mandare un** ~

di sollievo to give a sigh of relief; **trattenere il** ~ to hold one's breath; **lavorare senza** ~ to work non-stop; **di ampio** ~ (*opera, lavoro*) far-reaching.

respon'sabile *ag* responsible ♦ *sm/f* person responsible; (*capo*) person in charge; ~ **di** responsible for; (*DIR*) liable for.

responsabilità *sf inv* responsibility; (*legale*) liability; **assumere la** ~ **di** to take on the responsibility for; **affidare a qn la** ~ **di qc** to make sb responsible for sth; ~ **patrimoniale** debt liability; ~ **penale** criminal liability.

responsabiliz'zare [responsabilid'dzare] *vt*: ~ **qn** to make sb feel responsible.

res'ponso *sm* answer; (*DIR*) verdict.

'ressa *sf* crowd, throng.

'ressi *etc vb vedi* **reggere**.

res'tare *vi* (*rimanere*) to remain, stay; (*diventare*): ~ **orfano/cieco** to become *o* be left an orphan/become blind; (*trovarsi*): ~ **sorpreso** to be surprised; (*avanzare*) to be left, remain; ~ **d'accordo** to agree; **non resta più niente** there's nothing left; **restano pochi giorni** there are only a few days left; **che resti tra di noi** this is just between ourselves; ~ **in buoni rapporti** to remain on good terms; ~ **senza parole** to be left speechless.

restau'rare *vt* to restore.

restaura'tore, 'trice *sm/f* restorer.

restaurazi'one [restaurat'tsjone] *sf* (*POL*) restoration.

res'tauro *sm* (*di edifici etc*) restoration; **in** ~ under repair; **sotto** ~ (*dipinto*) being restored; **chiuso per** ~**i** closed for repairs.

res'tio, a, 'tii, 'tie *ag* restive; (*persona*): ~ **a** reluctant to.

restitu'ire *vt* to return, give back; (*energie, forze*) to restore.

restituzi'one [restitut'tsjone] *sf* return; (*di soldi*) repayment.

'resto *sm* remainder, rest; (*denaro*) change; (*MAT*) remainder; ~**i** *smpl* leftovers; (*di città*) remains; **del** ~ moreover, besides; ~**i mortali** (mortal) remains.

res'tringere [res'trindʒere] *vt* to reduce; (*vestito*) to take in; (*stoffa*) to shrink; (*fig*) to restrict, limit; ~**rsi** *vr* (*strada*) to narrow; (*stoffa*) to shrink.

restrit'tivo, a *ag* restrictive.

restrizi'one [restrit'tsjone] *sf* restriction.

resurrezi'one [resurret'tsjone] *sf* = **risurrezione**.

resusci'tare [resuʃʃi'tare] *vt, vi* = **risuscitare**.

re'tata *sf* (*PESCA*) haul, catch; **fare una** ~ **di** (*fig: persone*) to round up.

'rete *sf* net; (*di recinzione*) wire netting; (*AUT, FERR, di spionaggio etc*) network; (*fig*) trap, snare; **segnare una** ~ (*CALCIO*) to score a goal; ~ **ferroviaria/stradale/di distribuzione** railway/road/distribution net-

work; ~ **del letto** (sprung) bed base; ~ **da pesca** fishing net; ~ (**televisiva**) (*sistema*) network; (*canale*) channel.

reti'cente [reti'tʃɛnte] *ag* reticent.

reti'cenza [reti'tʃɛntsa] *sf* reticence.

retico'lato *sm* grid; (*rete metallica*) wire netting; (*di filo spinato*) barbed wire fence.

'retina *sf* (*ANAT*) retina.

re'torico, a, ci, che *ag* rhetorical ♦ *sf* rhetoric.

retribu'ire *vt* to pay; (*premiare*) to reward; **un lavoro mal retribuito** a poorly-paid job.

retribu'tivo, a *ag* pay *cpd*.

retribuzi'one [retribut'tsjone] *sf* payment; reward.

re'trivo, a *ag* (*fig*) reactionary.

'retro *sm inv* back ♦ *av* (*dietro*): **vedi** ~ see over(leaf).

retroattività *sf* retroactivity.

retroat'tivo, a *ag* (*DIR: legge*) retroactive; (*AMM: salario*) backdated.

retrobot'tega, ghe *sf* back shop.

retro'cedere [retro'tʃedere] *vi* to withdraw ♦ *vt* (*CALCIO*) to relegate; (*MIL*) to degrade; (*AMM*) to demote.

retrocessi'one [retrotʃes'sjone] *sf* (*di impiegato*) demotion.

retro'cesso, a [retro'tʃɛsso] *pp di* **retrocedere**.

retroda'tare *vt* (*AMM*) to backdate.

re'trogrado, a *ag* (*fig*) reactionary, backward-looking.

retrogu'ardia *sf* (*anche fig*) rearguard.

retro'marcia [retro'martʃa] *sf* (*AUT*) reverse; (: *dispositivo*) reverse gear.

retro'scena [retroʃ'ʃena] *sm inv* (*TEATRO*) backstage; ~ *smpl* (*fig*) behind-the-scenes activity *sg*.

retrospet'tivo, a *ag* retrospective ♦ *sf* (*ARTE*) retrospective exhibition.

retros'tante *ag*: ~ (**a**) at the back (of).

retro'terra *sm* hinterland.

retro'via *sf* (*MIL*) zone behind the front; **mandare nelle** ~**e** to send to the rear.

retrovi'sore *sm* (*AUT*) (rear-view) mirror.

'retta *sf* (*MAT*) straight line; (*di convitto*) charge for bed and board; (*fig: ascolto*): **dar** ~ **a** to listen to, pay attention to.

rettango'lare *ag* rectangular.

ret'tangolo, a *ag* right-angled ♦ *sm* rectangle.

ret'tifica, che *sf* rectification, correction.

rettifi'care *vt* (*curva*) to straighten; (*fig*) to rectify, correct.

'rettile *sm* reptile.

retti'lineo, a *ag* rectilinear.

retti'tudine *sf* rectitude, uprightness.

'retto, a *pp di* **reggere** ♦ *ag* straight; (*MAT*): **angolo** ~ right angle; (*onesto*) honest, upright; (*giusto, esatto*) correct, proper, right.

ret'tore *sm* (*REL*) rector; (*di università*) ≈

chancellor.

reuma'tismo *sm* rheumatism.

Rev. *abbr* (= *Reverendo*) Rev(d).

reve'rendo, a *ag*: **il ~ padre Belli** the Reverend Father Belli.

reve'rente *ag* = **riverente**.

reve'renza [reve'rɛntsa] *sf* = **riverenza**.

rever'sibile *ag* reversible.

revisio'nare *vt* (*conti*) to audit; (*TECN*) to overhaul, service; (*DIR: processo*) to review; (*componimento*) to revise.

revisi'one *sf* auditing *q*; audit; servicing *q*; overhaul; review; revision; **~ di bilancio** audit; **~ di bozze** proofreading; **~ contabile interna** internal audit.

revi'sore *sm*: **~ di conti/bozze** auditor/ proofreader.

'revoca *sf* revocation.

revo'care *vt* to revoke.

re'volver *sm inv* revolver.

revolve'rata *sf* revolver shot.

'Reykjavik ['reikjavik] *sf* Reykjavik.

RFT *sigla f vedi* **Repubblica Federale Tedesca**.

ri'abbia *etc vb vedi* **riavere**.

riabili'tare *vt* to rehabilitate; (*fig*) to restore to favour (*Brit*) *o* favor (*US*).

riabilitazi'one [riabilitat'tsjone] *sf* rehabilitation.

riac'cendere [riat'tʃɛndere] *vt* (*sigaretta, fuoco, gas*) to light again; (*luce, radio, TV*) to switch on again; (*fig: sentimenti, interesse*) to rekindle, revive; **~rsi** *vr* (*fuoco*) to catch again; (*luce, radio, TV*) to come back on again; (*fig: sentimenti*) to revive, be rekindled.

riac'ceso, a [riat'tʃeso] *pp di* **riaccendere**.

riacqui'stare *vt* (*gen*) to buy again; (*ciò che si era venduto*) to buy back; (*fig: buonumore, sangue freddo, libertà*) to regain; **~ la salute** to recover (one's health); **~ le forze** to regain one's strength.

Ri'ad *sf* Riyadh.

riaddormen'tare *vt* to put to sleep again; **~rsi** *vr* to fall asleep again.

rial'zare [rial'tsare] *vt* to raise, lift; (*alzare di più*) to heighten, raise; (*aumentare: prezzi*) to increase, raise ♦ *vi* (*prezzi*) to rise, increase.

rial'zista, i [rial'tsista] *sm* (*BORSA*) bull.

ri'alzo [ri'altso] *sm* (*di prezzi*) increase, rise; (*sporgenza*) rise; **giocare al ~** (*BORSA*) to bull.

rian'dare *vi*: **~ (in)**, **~ (a)** to go back (to), return (to).

riani'mare *vt* (*MED*) to resuscitate; (*fig: rallegrare*) to cheer up; (: *dar coraggio*) to give heart to; **~rsi** *vr* to recover consciousness; to cheer up; to take heart.

rianimazi'one [rianimat'tsjone] *sf* (*MED*) resuscitation; **centro di ~** intensive care

unit.

ria'perto, a *pp di* **riaprire**.

riaper'tura *sf* reopening.

riappa'rire *vi* to reappear.

riap'parso, a *pp di* **riapparire**.

riap'pendere *vt* to rehang; (*TEL*) to hang up.

ria'prire *vt*, **~rsi** *vr* to reopen, open again.

ri'armo *sm* (*MIL*) rearmament.

ri'arso, a *ag* (*terreno*) arid; (*gola*) parched; (*labbra*) dry.

rias'setto *sm* (*di stanza etc*) rearrangement; (*ordinamento*) reorganization.

rias'sumere *vt* (*riprendere*) to resume; (*impiegare di nuovo*) to re-employ; (*sintetizzare*) to summarize.

rias'sunto, a *pp di* **riassumere** ♦ *sm* summary.

riattac'care *vt* (*attaccare di nuovo*): **~ (a)** (*manifesto, francobollo*) to stick back (on); (*bottone*) to sew back (on); (*quadro, chiavi*) to hang back up (on); **~ (il telefono o il ricevitore)** to hang up (the receiver).

ria'vere *vt* to have again; (*avere indietro*) to get back; (*riacquistare*) to recover; **~rsi** *vr* to recover; (*da svenimento, stordimento*) to come round.

riba'dire *vt* (*fig*) to confirm.

ri'balta *sf* (*sportello*) flap; (*TEATRO: proscenio*) front of the stage; (: *apparecchio d'illuminazione*) footlights *pl*; (*fig*) limelight; **tornare alla ~** (*personaggio*) to make a comeback; (*problema*) to come up again.

ribal'tabile *ag* (*sedile*) tip-up.

ribal'tare *vt*, *vi* (*anche:* **~rsi**) to turn over, tip over.

ribas'sare *vt* to lower, bring down ♦ *vi* to come down, fall.

ribas'sista, i *sm* (*BORSA*) bear.

ri'basso *sm* reduction, fall; **essere in ~** (*azioni, prezzi*) to be down; (*fig: popolarità*) to be on the decline; **giocare al ~** (*BORSA*) to bear.

ri'battere *vt* (*battere di nuovo*) to beat again; (*con macchina da scrivere*) to type again; (*palla*) to return; (*confutare*) to refute; **~ che** to retort that.

ribattez'zare [ribatted'dzare] *vt* to rename.

ribel'larsi *vr*: **~ (a)** to rebel (against).

ri'belle *ag* (*soldati*) rebel; (*ragazzo*) rebellious ♦ *sm/f* rebel.

ribelli'one *sf* rebellion.

'ribes *sm inv* currant; **~ nero** blackcurrant; **~ rosso** redcurrant.

ribol'lire *vi* (*fermentare*) to ferment; (*fare bolle*) to bubble, boil; (*fig*) to seethe.

ri'brezzo [ri'breddzo] *sm* disgust, loathing; **far ~ a** to disgust.

ribut'tante *ag* disgusting, revolting.

ricacci'are [rikat'tʃare] *vt* (*respingere*) to

drive back; ~ **qn fuori** to throw sb out.

rica'dere vi to fall again; (*scendere a terra*, *fig*: *nel peccato etc*) to fall back; (*vestiti*, *capelli etc*) to hang (down); (*riversarsi*: *fatiche*, *colpe*): ~ **su** to fall on.

rica'duta sf (*MED*) relapse.

rical'care vt (*disegni*) to trace; (*fig*) to follow faithfully.

ricalci'trare [rikaltʃi'trare] vi (*cavalli*, *asini*, *muli*) to kick.

rica'mare vt to embroider.

ricambi'are vt to change again; (*contraccambiare*) to return.

ri'cambio sm exchange, return; (*FISIOL*) metabolism; ~**i** smpl, **pezzi di** ~ spare parts; ~ **della manodopera** labour turnover.

ri'camo sm embroidery; **senza** ~**i** (*fig*) without frills.

ricapito'lare vt to recapitulate, sum up.

ricapitolazi'one [rikapitolat'tsjone] sf recapitulation, summary.

ricari'care vt (*arma*, *macchina fotografica*) to reload; (*penna*) to refill; (*orologio*, *giocattolo*) to rewind; (*ELETTR*) to recharge.

ricat'tare vt to blackmail.

ricatta'tore, **'trice** sm/f blackmailer.

ri'catto sm blackmail; **fare un** ~ **a qn** to blackmail sb; **subire un** ~ to be blackmailed.

rica'vare vt (*estrarre*) to draw out, extract; (*ottenere*) to obtain, gain.

rica'vato sm (*di vendite*) proceeds pl.

ri'cavo sm proceeds pl; (*CONTABILITÀ*) revenue.

ric'chezza [rik'kettsa] sf wealth; (*fig*) richness; ~**e** sfpl (*beni*) wealth sg, riches; ~**e naturali** natural resources.

'riccio, **a** ['rittʃo] ag curly ♦ sm (*ZOOL*) hedgehog; (: *anche*: ~ **di mare**) sea urchin.

'ricciolo ['rittʃolo] sm curl.

ricci'uto, **a** [rit'tʃuto] ag curly.

'ricco, **a**, **chi**, **che** ag rich; (*persona*, *paese*) rich, wealthy ♦ sm/f rich man/woman; **i** ~**chi** the rich; ~ **di** (*idee*, *illustrazioni etc*) full of; (*risorse*, *fauna etc*) rich in.

ri'cerca, **che** [ri'tʃerka] sf search; (*indagine*) investigation, inquiry; (*studio*): **la** ~ research; **una** ~ piece of research; **mettersi alla** ~ **di** to go in search of, look o search o hunt for; **essere alla** ~ **di** to be searching for, be looking for; ~ **di mercato** market research; ~ **operativa** operational research.

ricer'care [ritʃer'kare] vt (*motivi*, *cause*) to look for, try to determine; (*successo*, *piacere*) to pursue; (*onore*, *gloria*) to seek.

ricerca'tezza [ritʃerka'tettsa] sf (*raffinatezza*) refinement; (: *peg*) affectation.

ricer'cato, **a** [ritʃer'kato] ag (*apprezzato*)

much sought-after; (*affettato*) studied, affected ♦ sm/f (*POLIZIA*) wanted man/woman.

ricerca'tore, **'trice** [ritʃerka'tore] sm/f (*INS*) researcher.

ri'cetta [ri'tʃetta] sf (*MED*) prescription; (*CUC*) recipe; (*fig*: *antidoto*): ~ **contro** remedy for.

ricet'tacolo [ritʃet'takolo] sm (*peg*: *luogo malfamato*) den.

ricet'tario [ritʃet'tarjo] sm (*MED*) prescription pad; (*CULIN*) recipe book.

ricetta'tore, **'trice** [ritʃetta'tore] sm/f (*DIR*) receiver (of stolen goods).

ricettazi'one [ritʃettat'tsjone] sf (*DIR*) receiving (stolen goods).

ricet'tivo, **a** [ritʃet'tivo] ag receptive.

rice'vente [ritʃe'vɛnte] ag (*RADIO*, *TV*) receiving ♦ sm/f (*COMM*) receiver.

ri'cevere [ri'tʃevere] vt to receive; (*stipendio*, *lettera*) to get, receive; (*accogliere*: *ospite*) to welcome; (*vedere*: *cliente*, *rappresentante etc*) to see; **"confermiamo di aver ricevuto tale merce"** (*COMM*) "we acknowledge receipt of these goods".

ricevi'mento [ritʃevi'mento] sm receiving q; (*trattenimento*) reception; **al** ~ **della merce** on receipt of the goods.

ricevi'tore [ritʃevi'tore] sm (*TECN*) receiver; ~ **delle imposte** tax collector.

ricevito'ria [ritʃevito'ria] sf (*FISCO*): ~ (**delle imposte**) Inland Revenue (*Brit*) or Internal Revenue (*US*) Office; ~ **del lotto** lottery office.

rice'vuta [ritʃe'vuta] sf receipt; **accusare** ~ **di qc** (*COMM*) to acknowledge receipt of sth; ~ **fiscale** official receipt (for tax purposes); ~ **di ritorno** (*POSTA*) advice of receipt; ~ **di versamento** receipt of payment.

ricezi'one [ritʃet'tsjone] sf (*RADIO*, *TV*) reception.

richia'mare [rikja'mare] vt (*chiamare indietro*, *ritelefonare*) to call back; (*ambasciatore*, *truppe*) to recall; (*rimproverare*) to reprimand; (*attirare*) to attract, draw; ~**rsi** vr: ~**rsi a** (*riferirsi a*) to refer to; ~ **qn all'ordine** to call sb to order; **desidero** ~ **la vostra attenzione su** ... I would like to draw your attention to ....

richi'amo [ri'kjamo] sm call; recall; reprimand; attraction.

richie'dente [rikje'dɛnte] sm/f applicant.

richi'edere [ri'kjedere] vt to ask again for; (*chiedere indietro*): ~ **qc** to ask for sth back; (*chiedere*: *per sapere*) to ask; (: *per avere*) to ask for; (*AMM*: *documenti*) to apply for; (*esigere*) to need, require; **essere molto richiesto** to be in great demand.

richi'esto, **a** [ri'kjɛsto] pp di **richiedere** ♦ sf (*domanda*) request; (*AMM*) application, request; (*esigenza*) demand, request; **a** ~**a** on request.

rici'clare [ritʃi'klare] *vt* (*vetro, carta, bottiglie*) to recycle; (*fig: personale*) to retrain.

'**ricino** ['ritʃino] *sm*: **olio di** ~ castor oil.

ricogni'tore [rikoɲɲi'tore] *sm* (*AER*) reconnaissance aircraft.

ricognizi'one [rikoɲɲit'tsjone] *sf* (*MIL*) reconnaissance; (*DIR*) recognition, acknowledgement.

ricolle'gare *vt* (*collegare nuovamente: gen*) to join again, link again; (*connettere: fatti*): ~ **(a, con)** to connect (with); ~**rsi** *vr*: ~**rsi a** (*sog: fatti: connettersi*) to be connected to; (: *persona: riferirsi*) to refer to.

ri'colmo, a *ag*: ~ **(di)** (*bicchiere*) full to the brim (with); (*stanza*) full (of).

ricominci'are [rikomin'tʃare] *vt, vi* to start again, begin again; ~ **a fare qc** to begin doing *o* to do sth again, start doing *o* to do sth again.

ricom'pensa *sf* reward.

ricompen'sare *vt* to reward.

ricom'porsi *vr* to compose o.s., regain one's composure.

ricom'posto, a *pp di* **ricomporsi**.

riconcili'are [rikontʃi'ljare] *vt* to reconcile; ~**rsi** *vr* to be reconciled.

riconciliazi'one [rikontʃiliat'tsjone] *sf* reconciliation.

ricon'dotto, a *pp di* **ricondurre**.

ricon'durre *vt* to bring (*o* take) back.

ricon'ferma *sf* reconfirmation.

riconfer'mare *vt* to reconfirm.

ricono'scente [rikonoʃ'ʃɛnte] *ag* grateful.

ricono'scenza [rikonoʃ'ʃɛntsa] *sf* gratitude.

rico'noscere [riko'noʃʃere] *vt* to recognize; (*DIR: figlio, debito*) to acknowledge; (*ammettere: errore*) to admit, acknowledge; ~ **qn colpevole** to find sb guilty.

riconosci'mento [rikonoʃʃi'mento] *sm* recognition; acknowledgement; (*identificazione*) identification; **come** ~ **dei servizi resi in** recognition of services rendered; **documento di** ~ means of identification; **segno di** ~ distinguishing mark.

riconosci'uto, a [rikonoʃ'ʃuto] *pp di* **riconoscere**.

riconquis'tare *vt* (*MIL*) to reconquer; (*libertà, stima*) to win back.

rico'perto, a *pp di* **ricoprire**.

ricopi'are *vt* to copy.

rico'prire *vt* to re-cover; (*coprire*) to cover; (*occupare: carica*) to hold.

ricor'dare *vt* to remember, recall; (*richiamare alla memoria*): ~ **qc a qn** to remind sb of sth; ~**rsi** *vr*: ~**rsi (di)** to remember; ~**rsi di qc/di aver fatto** to remember sth/having done.

ri'cordo *sm* memory; (*regalo*) keepsake, souvenir; (*di viaggio*) souvenir; ~**i** *smpl* (*memorie*) memoirs.

ricor'rente *ag* recurrent, recurring.

ricor'renza [rikor'rɛntsa] *sf* recurrence; (*festività*) anniversary.

ri'correre *vi* (*ripetersi*) to recur; ~ **a** (*rivolgersi*) to turn to; (: *DIR*) to appeal to; (*servirsi di*) to have recourse to; ~ **in appello** to lodge an appeal.

ri'corso, a *pp di* **ricorrere** ♦ *sm* recurrence; (*DIR*) appeal; **far** ~ **a** = **ricorrere a**.

ricostitu'ente *ag* (*MED*): **cura** ~ tonic treatment ♦ *sm* (*MED*) tonic.

ricostitu'ire *vt* (*società*) to build up again; (*governo, partito*) to re-form; ~**rsi** *vr* (*gruppo etc*) to re-form.

ricostru'ire *vt* (*casa*) to rebuild; (*fatti*) to reconstruct.

ricostruzi'one [rikostrut'tsjone] *sf* rebuilding *q*; reconstruction.

ri'cotta *sf* soft white unsalted cheese made from sheep's milk.

ricove'rare *vt* to give shelter to; ~ **qn in ospedale** to admit sb to hospital.

ricove'rato, a *sm/f* patient.

ri'covero *sm* shelter, refuge; (*MIL*) shelter; (*MED*) admission (to hospital); ~ **antiaereo** air-raid shelter.

ricre'are *vt* to recreate; (*rinvigorire*) to restore; (*fig: distrarre*) to amuse.

ricrea'tivo, a *ag* recreational.

ricreazi'one [rikreat'tsjone] *sf* recreation, entertainment; (*INS*) break.

ri'credersi *vr* to change one's mind.

ricupe'rare *vt* (*rientrare in possesso di*) to recover, get back; (*tempo perduto*) to make up for; (*NAUT*) to salvage; (: *naufraghi*) to rescue; (*delinquente*) to rehabilitate; ~ **lo svantaggio** (*SPORT*) to close the gap.

ri'cupero *sm* (*gen*) recovery; (*di relitto etc*) salvaging; **capacità di** ~ resilience.

ricu'sare *vt* to refuse.

ridacchi'are [ridak'kjare] *vi* to snigger.

ri'dare *vt* to return, give back.

'**ridda** *sf* (*di ammiratori etc*) swarm; (*di pensieri*) jumble.

ri'dente *ag* (*occhi, volto*) smiling; (*paesaggio*) delightful.

'**ridere** *vi* to laugh; (*deridere, beffare*): ~ **di** to laugh at, make fun of; **non c'è niente da** ~, **c'è poco da** ~ it's not a laughing matter.

rides'tare *vt* (*fig: ricordi, passioni*) to reawaken.

ri'detto, a *pp di* **ridire**.

ridico'laggine [ridiko'laddʒine] *sf* (*di situazione*) absurdity; (*cosa detta o fatta*) nonsense *q*.

ridicoliz'zare [ridikolid'dzare] *vt* to ridicule.

ri'dicolo, a *ag* ridiculous, absurd ♦ *sm*:

cadere nel ~ to become ridiculous; **rendersi** ~ to make a fool of o.s.

ridimensiona'mento *sm* reorganization; (*di fatto storico*) reappraisal.

ridimensio'nare *vt* to reorganize; (*fig*) to see in the right perspective.

ri'dire *vt* to repeat; (*criticare*) to find fault with; to object to; **trova sempre qualcosa da** ~ he always manages to find fault.

ridon'dante *ag* redundant.

ri'dosso *sm*: **a** ~ **di** (*dietro*) behind; (*contro*) against.

ri'dotto, a *pp di* **ridurre.**

ri'duco *etc vb vedi* **ridurre.**

ri'durre *vt* (*anche* CHIM, MAT) to reduce; (*prezzo, spese*) to cut, reduce; (*accorciare*: *opera letteraria*) to abridge; (: RADIO, TV) to adapt; **ridursi** *vr* (*diminuirsi*) to be reduced, shrink; **ridursi a** to be reduced to; **ridursi a pelle e ossa** to be reduced to skin and bone.

ri'dussi *etc vb vedi* **ridurre.**

ridut'tore *sm* (TECN, CHIM, ELETTR) reducer.

riduzi'one [ridut'tsjone] *sf* reduction; abridgement; adaptation.

ri'ebbi *etc vb vedi* **riavere.**

riedu'care *vt* (*persona, arto*) to re-educate; (*malato*) to rehabilitate.

rieducazi'one [riedukat'tsjone] *sf* re-education; rehabilitation; **centro di** ~ rehabilitation centre.

rie'leggere [rie'lɛddʒere] *vt* to re-elect.

rie'letto, a *pp di* **rieleggere.**

riempi'mento *sm* filling (up).

riem'pire *vt* to fill (up); (*modulo*) to fill in o out; **~rsi** *vr* to fill (up); (*mangiare troppo*) to stuff o.s.; ~ **qc di** to fill sth (up) with.

riempi'tivo, a *ag* filling ♦ *sm* (*anche fig*) filler.

rien'tranza [rien'trantsa] *sf* recess; indentation.

rien'trare *vi* (*entrare di nuovo*) to go (o come) back in; (*tornare*) to return; (*fare una rientranza*) to go in, curve inwards; to be indented; (*riguardare*): ~ **in** to be included among, form part of; ~ **(a casa)** to get back home; **non rientriamo nelle spese** we are not within our budget.

ri'entro *sm* (*ritorno*) return; (*di astronave*) re-entry.

riepilo'gare *vt* to summarize ♦ *vi* to recapitulate.

rie'pilogo, ghi *sm* recapitulation; **fare un** ~ **di qc** to summarize sth.

rie'same *sm* re-examination.

riesami'nare *vt* to re-examine.

ri'esco *etc vb vedi* **riuscire.**

ri'essere *vi*: **ci risiamo!** (*fam*) we're back to this again!

rievo'care *vt* (*passato*) to recall; (*commemorare*: *figura, meriti*) to commemorate.

rifaci'mento [rifatʃi'mento] *sm* (*di film*) remake; (*di opera letteraria*) rehashing.

ri'fare *vt* to do again; (*ricostruire*) to make again; (*nodo*) to tie again, do up again; (*imitare*) to imitate, copy; **~rsi** *vr* (*risarcirsi*): **~rsi di** to make up for; (*vendicarsi*): **~rsi di qc su qn** to get one's own back on sb for sth; (*riferirsi*): **~rsi a** (*periodo, fenomeno storico*) to go back to; ~ **il letto** to make the bed; **~rsi una vita** to make a new life for o.s.

ri'fatto, a *pp di* **rifare.**

riferi'mento *sm* reference; **in** o **con** ~ **a** with reference to; **far** ~ **a** to refer to.

rife'rire *vt* (*riportare*) to report; (*ascrivere*): ~ **qc a** to attribute sth to ♦ *vi* to do a report; **~rsi** *vr*: **~rsi a** to refer to; **riferirò** I'll pass on the message.

rifi'lare *vt* (*tagliare a filo*) to trim; (*fam*: *affibbiare*): ~ **qc a qn** to palm sth off on sb.

rifi'nire *vt* to finish off, put the finishing touches to.

rifini'tura *sf* finishing touch; **~e** *sfpl* (*di mobile, auto*) finish *sg*.

rifiu'tare *vt* to refuse; ~ **di fare** to refuse to do.

rifi'uto *sm* refusal; **~i** *smpl* (*spazzatura*) rubbish *sg*, refuse *sg*.

riflessi'one *sf* (FISICA) reflection; (*il pensare*) thought, reflection; (*osservazione*) remark.

rifles'sivo, a *ag* (*persona*) thoughtful, reflective; (LING) reflexive.

ri'flesso, a *pp di* **riflettere** ♦ *sm* (*di luce, su specchio*) reflection; (FISIOL) reflex; (*su capelli*) light; (*fig*) effect; **di** o **per** ~ indirectly; **avere i** **~i pronti** to have quick reflexes.

ri'flettere *vt* to reflect ♦ *vi* to think; **~rsi** *vr* to be reflected; (*ripercuotersi*): **~rsi su** to have repercussions on; ~ **su** to think over.

riflet'tore *sm* reflector; (*proiettore*) floodlight; (: MIL) searchlight.

ri'flusso *sm* flowing back; (*della marea*) ebb; **un'epoca di** ~ an era of nostalgia.

rifocil'larsi [rifotʃil'larsi] *vr* (*poetico*) to take refreshment.

ri'fondere *vt* (*rimborsare*) to refund, repay; ~ **le spese a qn** to refund sb's expenses; ~ **i danni a qn** to compensate sb for damages.

ri'forma *sf* reform; (MIL) declaration of unfitness for service; discharge (*on health grounds*); **la R~** (REL) the Reformation.

rifor'mare *vt* to re-form; (*cambiare, innovare*) to reform; (MIL: *recluta*) to declare unfit for service; (: *soldato*) to invalid out, discharge.

riforma'tore, 'trice *ag* reforming ♦ *sm/f* reformer.

riforma'torio *sm* (DIR) community home

(*Brit*), reformatory (*US*).

rifor'mista, i, e *ag*, *sm/f* reformist.

riforni'mento *sm* supplying, providing; restocking; (*di carburante*) refuelling; ~**i** *smpl* supplies, provisions; **fare** ~ **di** (*viveri*) to stock up with; (*benzina*) to fill up with; **posto di** ~ filling *o* gas (*US*) station.

rifor'nire *vt* (*provvedere*): ~ **di** to supply *o* provide with; (*fornire di nuovo: casa etc*) to restock.

ri'frangere [ri'frandʒere] *vt* to refract.

ri'fratto, a *pp di* **rifrangere**.

rifrazi'one [rifrat'tsjone] *sf* refraction.

rifug'gire [rifud'dʒire] *vi* to escape again; (*fig*): ~ **da** to shun.

rifugi'arsi [rifu'dʒarsi] *vr* to take refuge.

rifugi'ato, a [rifu'dʒato] *sm/f* refugee.

ri'fugio [ri'fudʒo] *sm* refuge, shelter; (*in montagna*) shelter; ~ **antiaereo** air-raid shelter.

ri'fuso, a *pp di* **rifondere**.

'riga, ghe *sf* line; (*striscia*) stripe; (*di persone, cose*) line, row; (*regolo*) ruler; (*scriminatura*) parting; **mettersi in** ~ to line up; **a** ~**ghe** (*foglio*) lined; (*vestito*) striped; **buttare giù due** ~**ghe** (*note*) to jot down a few notes; **mandami due** ~**ghe appena arrivi** drop me a line as soon as you arrive.

ri'gagnolo [ri'gaɲɲolo] *sm* rivulet.

ri'gare *vt* (*foglio*) to rule ♦ *vi*: ~ **diritto** (*fig*) to toe the line.

riga'toni *smpl* (*CUC*) *short, ridged pasta shapes.*

rigatti'ere *sm* junk dealer.

riga'tura *sf* (*di pagina, quaderno*) lining, ruling; (*di fucile*) rifling.

rigene'rare [ridʒene'rare] *vt* (*gen, TECN*) to regenerate; (*forze*) to restore; (*gomma*) to retread; ~**rsi** *vr* (*gen*) to regenerate; (*ramo, tumore*) to regenerate, grow again; **gomma rigenerata** retread.

rigenerazi'one [ridʒenerat'tsjone] *sf* regeneration.

riget'tare [ridʒet'tare] *vt* (*gettare indietro*) to throw back; (*fig: respingere*) to reject; (*vomitare*) to bring *o* throw up.

ri'getto [ri'dʒetto] *sm* (*anche MED*) rejection.

ri'ghello [ri'gello] *sm* ruler.

righerò etc [rige'rɔ] *vb vedi* **rigare**.

rigi'dezza [ridʒi'dettsa], **rigidità** [ridʒidi'ta] *sf* rigidity; stiffness; severity, rigours *pl* (*Brit*), rigors *pl* (*US*); strictness.

'rigido, a ['ridʒido] *ag* rigid, stiff; (*membra etc: indurite*) stiff; (*METEOR*) harsh, severe; (*fig*) strict.

rigi'rare [ridʒi'rare] *vt* to turn; ~**rsi** *vr* to turn round; (*nel letto*) to turn over; ~ **qc tra le mani** to turn sth over in one's hands; ~ **il discorso** to change the subject.

'rigo, ghi *sm* line; (*MUS*) staff, stave.

rigogli'oso, a [rigoʎ'ʎoso] *ag* (*pianta*) luxuriant; (*fig: commercio, sviluppo*) thriving.

rigonfia'mento *sm* (*ANAT*) swelling; (*su legno, intonaco etc*) bulge.

ri'gonfio, a *ag* swollen; (*grembiule, sporta*): ~ **di** bulging with.

ri'gore *sm* (*METEOR*) harshness, rigours *pl* (*Brit*), rigors *pl* (*US*); (*fig*) severity, strictness; (*anche:* **calcio di** ~) penalty; **di** ~ compulsory; **"è di** ~ **l'abito da sera"** "evening dress"; **area di** ~ (*CALCIO*) penalty box (*Brit*); **a rigor di termini** strictly speaking.

rigorosità *sf* strictness; rigour (*Brit*), rigor (*US*).

rigo'roso, a *ag* (*severo: persona, ordine*) strict; (*preciso*) rigorous.

rigover'nare *vt* to wash (up).

riguar'dare *vt* to look at again; (*considerare*) to regard, consider; (*concernere*) to regard, concern; ~**rsi** *vr* (*aver cura di sé*) to look after o.s.; **per quel che mi riguarda** as far as I'm concerned; **sono affari che non ti riguardano** it's none of your business.

rigu'ardo *sm* (*attenzione*) care; (*considerazione*) regard, respect; ~ **a** concerning, with regard to; **per** ~ **a** out of respect for; **ospite/persona di** ~ very important guest/ person; **non aver** ~**i nell'agire/nel parlare** to act/speak freely.

riguar'doso, a *ag* (*rispettoso*) respectful; (*premuroso*) considerate, thoughtful.

rigurgi'tare [rigurdʒi'tare] *vi* (*liquido*): ~ **da** to gush out from; (*recipiente: traboccare*): ~ **di** to overflow with.

ri'gurgito [ri'gurdʒito] *sm* (*MED*) regurgitation; (*fig: ritorno, risveglio*) revival.

rilanci'are [rilan'tʃare] *vt* (*lanciare di nuovo: gen*) to throw again; (: *moda*) to bring back; (: *prodotto*) to re-launch; ~ **un'offerta** (*asta*) to make a higher bid.

ri'lancio [ri'lantʃo] *sm* (*CARTE, di offerta*) raising.

rilasci'are [rilaʃ'ʃare] *vt* (*rimettere in libertà*) to release; (*AMM: documenti*) to issue; (*intervista*) to give; ~ **delle dichiarazioni** to make a statement.

ri'lascio [ri'laʃʃo] *sm* release; issue.

rilassa'mento *sm* (*gen, MED*) relaxation.

rilas'sare *vt* to relax; ~**rsi** *vr* to relax; (*fig: disciplina*) to become slack.

rilassa'tezza [rilassa'tettsa] *sf* (*fig: di costumi, disciplina*) laxity.

rilas'sato, a *ag* (*persona, muscoli*) relaxed; (*disciplina, costumi*) lax.

rile'gare *vt* (*libro*) to bind.

rilega'tura *sf* binding.

ri'leggere [ri'lɛddʒere] *vt* to reread, read again; (*rivedere*) to read over.

ri'lento: a ~ *av* slowly.

ri'letto, a *pp di* **rileggere**.

rileva'mento sm (topografico, statistico) survey; (NAUT) bearing.

rile'vante ag considerable; important.

rile'vanza [rile'vantsa] sf importance.

rile'vare vt (ricavare) to find; (notare) to notice; (mettere in evidenza) to point out; (venire a conoscere: notizia) to learn; (raccogliere: dati) to gather, collect; (TOPOGRAFIA) to survey; (MIL) to relieve; (COMM) to take over.

rilevazi'one [rilevat'tsjone] sf survey.

rili'evo sm (ARTE, GEO) relief; (fig: rilevanza) importance; (osservazione) point, remark; (TOPOGRAFIA) survey; **dar ~ a** o **mettere in ~ qc** (fig) to bring sth out, highlight sth; **di poco/nessun ~** (fig) of little/no importance; **un personaggio di ~** an important person.

rilut'tante ag reluctant.

rilut'tanza [rilut'tantsa] sf reluctance.

'rima sf rhyme; (verso) verse; **far ~ con** to rhyme with; **rispondere a qn per le ~e** to give sb tit for tat.

riman'dare vt to send again; (restituire, rinviare) to send back, return; (differire): **~ qc (a)** to postpone sth o put sth off (till); (fare riferimento): **~ qn a** to refer sb to; **essere rimandato** (INS) to have to resit one's exams.

ri'mando sm (rinvio) return; (dilazione) postponement; (riferimento) cross-reference.

rimaneggi'are [rimaned'dʒare] vt (testo) to reshape, recast; (POL) to reshuffle.

rima'nente ag remaining ♦ sm rest, remainder; **i ~i** (persone) the rest of them, the others.

rima'nenza [rima'nɛntsa] sf rest, remainder; **~e** sfpl (COMM) unsold stock sg.

rima'nere vi (restare) to remain, stay; (avanzare) to be left, remain; (restare stupito) to be amazed; (restare, mancare): **rimangono poche settimane a Pasqua** there are only a few weeks left till Easter; (diventare): **~ vedovo** to be left a widower; (trovarsi): **~ confuso/sorpreso** to be confused/surprised; **rimane da vedere se** it remains to be seen whether.

rimangi'are [riman'dʒare] vt to eat again; **~rsi la parola/una promessa** (fig) to go back on one's word/one's promise.

ri'mango etc vb vedi **rimanere**.

ri'mare vt, vi to rhyme.

rimargi'nare [rimardʒi'nare] vt, vi (anche: **~rsi**) to heal.

ri'masto, a pp di **rimanere**.

rima'sugli [rima'suʎʎi] smpl leftovers.

rimbal'zare [rimbal'tsare] vi to bounce back, rebound; (proiettile) to ricochet.

rim'balzo [rim'baltso] sm rebound; ricochet.

rimbam'bire vi to be in one's dotage; (rincretinire) to grow foolish.

rimbam'bito, a ag senile, gaga (fam); **un vecchio ~** a doddering old man.

rimbec'care vt (persona) to answer back; (offesa) to return.

rimbecil'lire [rimbetʃil'lire] vi, **~rsi** vr to become stupid.

rimboc'care vt (orlo) to turn up; (coperta) to tuck in; (maniche, pantaloni) to turn o roll up.

rimbom'bare vi to resound.

rimbor'sare vt to pay back, repay; **~ qc a qn** to reimburse sb for sth.

rim'borso sm repayment; (di spese, biglietto) refund; **~ d'imposta** tax rebate.

rimboschi'mento [rimboski'mento] sm re-afforestation.

rimbos'chire [rimbos'kire] vt to reafforest.

rimbrot'tare vt to reproach.

rim'brotto sm reproach.

rimedi'are vi: **~ a** to remedy ♦ vt (fam: procurarsi) to get o scrape together; **~ da vivere** to scrape a living.

ri'medio sm (medicina) medicine; (cura, fig) remedy, cure; **porre ~ a qc** to remedy sth; **non c'è ~** there's no way out, there's nothing to be done about it.

rimesco'lare vt to mix well, stir well; (carte) to shuffle; **sentirsi ~ il sangue** (per rabbia) to feel one's blood boil.

ri'messa sf (locale: per veicoli) garage; (: per aerei) hangar; (COMM: di merce) consignment; (: di denaro) remittance; (TENNIS) return; (CALCIO: anche: **~ in gioco**) throw-in.

ri'messo, a pp di **rimettere**.

rimes'tare vt (mescolare) to mix well, stir well; (fig: passato) to drag up again.

ri'mettere vt (mettere di nuovo) to put back; (indossare di nuovo): **~ qc** to put sth back on, put sth on again; (restituire) to return, give back; (affidare) to entrust; (: decisione) to refer; (condonare) to remit; (COMM: merci) to deliver; (: denaro) to remit; (vomitare) to bring up; (perdere: anche: **rimetterci**) to lose; **~rsi** vr: **~rsi a** (affidarsi) to trust; **~ a nuovo** (casa etc) to do up (Brit) o over (US); **rimetterci di tasca propria** to be out of pocket; **~rsi al bello** (tempo) to clear up; **~rsi in cammino** to set off again; **~rsi al lavoro** to start working again; **~rsi in salute** to get better, recover one's health.

ri'misi etc vb vedi **rimettere**.

'rimmel ® sm inv mascara.

rimoderna'mento sm modernization.

rimoder'nare vt to modernize.

ri'monta sf (SPORT, gen) recovery.

rimon'tare vt (meccanismo) to reassemble; (tenda) to put up again ♦ vi (salire di nuovo): **~ in** (macchina, treno) to get back into; (SPORT) to close the gap.

rimorchi'are [rimor'kjare] vt to tow; (fig:

ragazza) to pick up.

rimorchia'tore [rimorkja'tore] *sm* (*NAUT*) tug(boat).

ri'morchio [ri'mɔrkjo] *sm* tow; (*veicolo*) trailer; **andare a ~** to be towed; **prendere a ~** to tow; **cavo da ~** towrope; **autocarro con ~** articulated lorry (*Brit*), semi(trailer) (*US*).

ri'morso *sm* remorse; **avere il ~ di aver fatto qc** to deeply regret having done sth.

ri'mosso, a *pp di* **rimuovere.**

rimos'tranza [rimos'trantsa] *sf* protest, complaint; **fare le proprie ~e a qn** to remonstrate with sb.

rimozi'one [rimot'tsjone] *sf* removal; (*da un impiego*) dismissal; (*PSIC*) repression; "*~ forzata*" "illegally parked vehicles will be removed at owner's expense".

rimpas'tare *vt* (*POL: ministero*) to reshuffle.

rim'pasto *sm* (*POL*) reshuffle; **~ ministeriale** cabinet reshuffle.

rimpatri'are *vi* to return home ♦ *vt* to repatriate.

rim'patrio *sm* repatriation.

rimpi'angere [rim'pjandʒere] *vt* to regret; (*persona*) to miss; **~ di (non) aver fatto qc** to regret (not) having done sth.

rimpi'anto, a *pp di* **rimpiangere** ♦ *sm* regret.

rimpiat'tino *sm* hide-and-seek.

rimpiaz'zare [rimpjat'tsare] *vt* to replace.

rimpiccio'lire [rimpittʃo'lire] *vt* to make smaller ♦ *vi* (*anche:* **~rsi**) to become smaller.

rimpin'zare [rimpin'tsare] *vt:* **~ di** to cram o stuff with.

rimprove'rare *vt* to rebuke, reprimand.

rim'provero *sm* rebuke, reprimand; **di ~** (*tono, occhiata*) reproachful; (*parole*) of reproach.

rimugi'nare [rimudʒi'nare] *vt* (*fig*) to turn over in one's mind.

rimune'rare *vt* (*retribuire*) to remunerate; (*ricompensare: sacrificio etc*) to reward; **un lavoro ben rimunerato** a well-paid job.

rimunera'tivo, a *ag* (*lavoro, attività*) remunerative, profitable.

rimunerazi'one [rimunerat'tsjone] *sf* remuneration; (*premio*) reward.

rimu'overe *vt* to remove; (*destituire*) to dismiss; (*fig: distogliere*) to dissuade.

rinascimen'tale [rinaʃʃimen'tale] *ag* Renaissance *cpd,* of the Renaissance.

Rinasci'mento [rinaʃʃi'mento] *sm:* **il ~** the Renaissance.

ri'nascita [ri'naʃʃita] *sf* rebirth, revival.

rincal'zare [rinkal'tsare] *vt* (*palo, albero*) to support, prop up; (*lenzuola*) to tuck in.

rin'calzo [rin'kaltso] *sm* support, prop; (*rinforzo*) reinforcement; (*SPORT*) reserve (player); **~i** *smpl* (*MIL*) reserves.

rinca'rare *vt* to increase the price of ♦ *vi* to go up, become more expensive; **~ la dose**

(*fig*) to pile it on.

rin'caro *sm:* **~ (di)** (*prezzi, costo della vita*) increase (in); (*prodotto*) increase in the price (of).

rinca'sare *vi* to go home.

rinchi'udere [rin'kjudere] *vt* to shut (*o* lock) up; **~rsi** *vr:* **~rsi in** to shut o.s. up in; **~rsi in se stesso** to withdraw into o.s.

rinchi'uso, a [rin'kjuso] *pp di* **rinchiudere.**

rincitrul'lirsi [rintʃitrul'lirsi] *vr* to grow foolish.

rin'correre *vt* to chase, run after.

rin'corso, a *pp di* **rincorrere** ♦ *sf* short run.

rin'crescere [rin'kreʃʃere] *vb impers:* **mi rincresce che/di non poter fare** I'm sorry that/I can't do, I regret that/being unable to do.

rincresci'mento [rinkreʃʃi'mento] *sm* regret.

rincresci'uto, a [rinkreʃ'ʃuto] *pp di* **rincrescere.**

rincu'lare *vi* to draw back; (*arma*) to recoil.

rinfacci'are [rinfat'tʃare] *vt* (*fig*): **~ qc a qn** to throw sth in sb's face.

rinfoco'lare *vt* (*fig: odio, passioni*) to rekindle; (: *risentimento, rabbia*) to stir up.

rinfor'zare [rinfor'tsare] *vt* to reinforce, strengthen ♦ *vi* (*anche:* **~rsi**) to grow stronger.

rin'forzo [rin'fɔrtso] *sm:* **mettere un ~ a** to strengthen; **~i** *smpl* (*MIL*) reinforcements; **di ~** (*asse, sbarra*) strengthening; (*esercito*) supporting; (*personale*) extra, additional.

rinfran'care *vt* to encourage, reassure.

rinfres'cante *ag* (*bibita*) refreshing.

rinfres'care *vt* (*atmosfera, temperatura*) to cool (down); (*abito, pareti*) to freshen up ♦ *vi* (*tempo*) to grow cooler; **~rsi** *vr* (*ristorarsi*) to refresh o.s.; (*lavarsi*) to freshen up; **~ la memoria a qn** to refresh sb's memory.

rin'fresco, schi *sm* (*festa*) party; **~schi** *smpl* (*cibi e bevande*) refreshments.

rin'fusa *sf:* **alla ~** in confusion, higgledypiggledy.

ringhi'are [rin'gjare] *vi* to growl, snarl.

ringhi'era [rin'gjɛra] *sf* railing; (*delle scale*) banister(s *pl*).

'ringhio ['ringjo] *sm* growl, snarl.

ringhi'oso, a [rin'gjoso] *ag* growling, snarling.

ringiova'nire [rindʒova'nire] *vt* (*sog: vestito, acconciatura etc*): **~ qn** to make sb look younger; (: *vacanze etc*) to rejuvenate ♦ *vi* (*anche:* **~rsi**) to become (*o* look) younger.

ringrazia'mento [ringrattsja'mento] *sm* thanks *pl;* **lettera/biglietto di ~** thank you letter/card.

ringrazi'are [ringrat'tsjare] *vt* to thank; **~ qn di qc** to thank sb for sth; **~ qn per aver fatto qc** to thank sb for doing sth.

rinne'gare *vt* (*fede*) to renounce; (*figlio*) to disown, repudiate.

rinne'gato, a *sm/f* renegade.

rinnova'mento *sm* renewal; (*economico*) revival.

rinno'vare *vt* to renew; (*ripetere*) to repeat, renew; ~**rsi** *vr* (*fenomeno*) to be repeated, recur.

rin'novo *sm* (*di contratto*) renewal; "**chiuso per ~ (dei) locali**" (*negozio*) "closed for alterations".

rinoce'ronte [rinotʃe'ronte] *sm* rhinoceros.

rino'mato, a *ag* renowned, celebrated.

rinsal'dare *vt* to strengthen.

rinsa'vire *vi* to come to one's senses.

rinsec'chito, a [rinsek'kito] *ag* (*vecchio, albero*) thin, gaunt.

rinta'narsi *vr* (*animale*) to go into its den; (*persona: nascondersi*) to hide.

rintoc'care *vi* (*campana*) to toll; (*orologio*) to strike.

rin'tocco, chi *sm* toll.

rintracci'are [rintrat'tʃare] *vt* to track down; (*persona scomparsa, documento*) to trace.

rintro'nare *vi* to boom, roar ♦ *vt* (*assordare*) to deafen; (*stordire*) to stun.

rintuz'zare [rintut'tsare] *vt* (*fig: sentimento*) to check, repress; (: *accusa*) to refute.

ri'nuncia [ri'nuntʃa] *sf* renunciation; ~ **a** (*carica*) resignation from; (*eredità*) relinquishment of; ~ **agli atti del giudizio** (*DIR*) abandonment of a claim.

rinunci'are [rinun'tʃare] *vi*: ~ **a** to give up, renounce; ~ **a fare qc** to give up doing sth.

rinuncia'tario, a [rinuntʃa'tarjo] *ag* defeatist.

ri'nunzia *etc* [ri'nuntsja] = **rinuncia** *etc*.

rinva'sare *vt* to re-pot.

rinveni'mento *sm* (*ritrovamento*) recovery; (*scoperta*) discovery; (*METALLURGIA*) tempering.

rinve'nire *vt* to find, recover; (*scoprire*) to discover, find out ♦ *vi* (*riprendere i sensi*) to come round; (*riprendere l'aspetto naturale*) to revive.

rinve'nuto, a *pp di* **rinvenire**.

rinver'dire *vi* (*bosco, ramo*) to become green again.

rinvi'are *vt* (*rimandare indietro*) to send back, return; (*differire*): ~ **qc (a)** to postpone sth *o* put sth off (till); (: *seduta*) to adjourn sth (till); (*fare un rimando*): ~ **qn a** to refer sb to; ~ **a giudizio** (*DIR*) to commit for trial.

rinvigo'rire *vt* to strengthen.

rin'vio, 'vii *sm* (*rimando*) return; (*differimento*) postponement; (: *di seduta*) adjournment; (*in un testo*) cross-reference.

riò *etc vb vedi* **riavere**.

'Rio de Ja'neiro ['riodedʒa'neiro] *sf* Rio de Janeiro.

rio'nale *ag* (*mercato, cinema*) local, district *cpd*.

ri'one *sm* district, quarter.

riordina'mento *sm* (*di ente, azienda*) re-organization.

riordi'nare *vt* (*rimettere in ordine*) to tidy; (*riorganizzare*) to reorganize.

riorganiz'zare [riorganid'dzare] *vt* to reorganize.

riorganizzazi'one [riorganiddzat'tsjone] *sf* reorganization.

ripa'gare *vt* to repay.

ripa'rare *vt* (*proteggere*) to protect, defend; (*correggere: male, torto*) to make up for; (: *errore*) to put right; (*aggiustare*) to repair ♦ *vi* (*mettere rimedio*): ~ **a** to make up for; ~**rsi** *vr* (*rifugiarsi*) to take refuge *o* shelter.

ripa'rato, a *ag* (*posto*) sheltered.

riparazi'one [riparat'tsjone] *sf* (*di un torto*) reparation; (*di guasto, scarpe*) repairing *q*; repair; (*risarcimento*) compensation; (*INS*): **esame di ~** resit (*Brit*), test retake (*US*).

ri'paro *sm* (*protezione*) shelter, protection; (*rimedio*) remedy; **al ~ da** (*sole, vento*) sheltered from; **mettersi al ~** to take shelter; **correre ai ~i** (*fig*) to take remedial action.

ripar'tire *vt* (*dividere*) to divide up; (*distribuire*) to share out, distribute ♦ *vi* to leave again; (*motore*) to start again.

ripartizi'one [ripartit'tsjone] *sf* division; sharing out, distribution; (*AMM: dipartimento*) department.

ripas'sare *vi* to come (*o* go) back ♦ *vt* (*scritto, lezione*) to go over (again).

ri'passo *sm* (*di lezione*) revision (*Brit*), review (*US*).

ripensa'mento *sm* second thoughts *pl* (*Brit*), change of mind; **avere un ~** to have second thoughts, change one's mind.

ripen'sare *vi* to think; (*cambiare idea*) to change one's mind; (*tornare col pensiero*): ~ **a** to recall; **a ripensarci** ... on thinking it over ....

riper'correre *vt* (*itinerario*) to travel over again; (*strada*) to go along again; (*fig: ricordi, passato*) to go back over.

riper'corso, a *pp di* **ripercorrere**.

riper'cosso, a *pp di* **ripercuotersi**.

ripercu'otersi *vr*: ~ **su** (*fig*) to have repercussions on.

ripercussi'one *sf* (*fig*): **avere una ~** *o* **delle ~i su** to have repercussions on.

ripes'care *vt* (*pesce*) to catch again; (*persona, cosa*) to fish out; (*fig: ritrovare*) to dig out.

ripe'tente *sm/f* student repeating the year, repeater (*US*).

ri'petere *vt* to repeat; (*ripassare*) to go over.

ripeti'tore sm (RADIO, TV) relay.

ripetizi'one [ripetit'tsjone] sf repetition; (di lezione) revision; ~i sfpl (INS) private tutoring o coaching sg; **fucile a ~** repeating rifle.

ripetuta'mente av repeatedly, again and again.

ripi'ano sm (GEO) terrace; (di mobile) shelf.

ri'picca sf: **per ~** out of spite.

'ripido, a ag steep.

ripiega'mento sm (MIL) retreat.

ripie'gare vt to refold; (piegare più volte) to fold (up) ♦ vi (MIL) to retreat, fall back; (fig: accontentarsi): **~ su** to make do with; **~rsi** vr to bend.

ripi'ego, ghi sm expedient; **una soluzione di ~** a makeshift solution.

ripi'eno, a ag full; (CUC) stuffed; (: panino) filled ♦ sm (CUC) stuffing.

ri'pone, ri'pongo etc vb vedi **riporre**.

ri'porre vt (porre al suo posto) to put back, replace; (mettere via) to put away; (fiducia, speranza): **~ qc in qn** to place o put sth in sb.

ripor'tare vt (portare indietro) to bring (o take) back; (riferire) to report; (citare) to quote; (ricevere) to receive, get; (vittoria) to gain; (successo) to have; (MAT) to carry; (COMM) to carry forward; **~rsi** vr: **~rsi a** (anche fig) to go back to; (riferirsi a) to refer to; **~ danni** to suffer damage; **ha riportato gravi ferite** he was seriously injured.

ri'porto sm amount carried over; amount carried forward.

ripo'sante ag (gen) restful; (musica, colore) soothing.

ripo'sare vt (bicchiere, valigia) to put down; (dare sollievo) to rest ♦ vi to rest; **~rsi** vr to rest; **qui riposa ...** (su tomba) here lies ....

ripo'sato, a ag (viso, aspetto) rested; (mente) fresh.

ri'posi etc vb vedi **riporre**.

ri'poso sm rest; (MIL): **~!** at ease!; **a ~** (in pensione) retired; **giorno di ~** day off; **"oggi ~"** (CINEMA, TEATRO) "no performance today"; (ristorante) "closed today".

ripos'tiglio [ripos'tiʎʎo] sm lumber room (Brit), storage room (US).

ri'posto, a pp di **riporre** ♦ ag (fig: senso, significato) hidden.

ri'prendere vt (prigioniero, fortezza) to recapture; (prendere indietro) to take back; (ricominciare: lavoro) to resume; (andare a prendere) to fetch, come back for; (assumere di nuovo: impiegati) to take on again, re-employ; (rimproverare) to tell off; (restringere: abito) to take in; (CINEMA) to shoot; **~rsi** vr to recover;

(correggersi) to correct o.s.; **~ a fare qc** to start doing sth again; **~ il cammino** to set off again; **~ i sensi** to recover consciousness; **~ sonno** to go back to sleep.

ripresen'tare vt (certificato) to submit again; (domanda) to put forward again; (persona) to introduce again; **~rsi** vr (ritornare: persona) to come back; (: occasione) to arise again; **~rsi a** (esame) to sit (Brit) o take (US) again; (concorso) to enter again; **~rsi come candidato** (POL) to stand (Brit) o run (US) again (as a candidate).

ri'preso, a pp di **riprendere** ♦ sf recapture; resumption; (economica, da malattia, emozione) recovery; (AUT) acceleration q; (TEATRO, CINEMA) rerun; (CINEMA: presa) shooting q; shot; (SPORT) second half; (: PUGILATO) round; **a più ~e** on several occasions, several times.

ripristi'nare vt to restore.

ri'pristino sm (gen) restoration; (di tradizioni) revival.

ripro'dotto, a pp di **riprodurre**.

ripro'durre vt to reproduce; **riprodursi** vr (BIOL) to reproduce; (riformarsi) to form again.

riprodut'tivo, a ag reproductive.

riprodut'tore, 'trice ag (organo) reproductive ♦ sm: **~ acustico** pick-up; **~ a cassetta** cassette player.

riproduzi'one [riprodut'tsjone] sf reproduction; **~ vietata** all rights reserved.

ripro'messo, a pp di **ripromettersi**.

ripro'mettersi vt (aspettarsi): **~ qc da** to expect sth from; (intendere): **~ di fare qc** to intend to do sth.

ripro'porre vt: **riproporsi di fare qc** to intend to do sth.

ripro'posto, a pp di **riproporre**.

ri'prova sf confirmation; **a ~ di** as confirmation of.

ripro'vare vt (provare di nuovo: gen) to try again; (: vestito) to try on again; (: sensazione) to experience again ♦ vi (tentare): **~ (a fare qc)** to try (to do sth) again; **riproverò più tardi** I'll try again later.

ripro'vevole ag reprehensible.

ripudi'are vt to repudiate, disown.

ri'pudio sm repudiation, disowning.

ripu'gnante [ripuɲ'ɲante] ag disgusting, repulsive.

ripu'gnanza [ripuɲ'ɲantsa] sf repugnance, disgust.

ripu'gnare [ripuɲ'ɲare] vi: **~ a qn** to repel o disgust sb.

ripu'lire vt to clean up; (sog: ladri) to clean out; (perfezionare) to polish, refine.

ripulsi'one sf (FISICA, fig) repulsion.

ri'quadro sm square; (ARCHIT) panel.

ri'sacca, che sf backwash.

ri'saia *sf* paddy field.

risa'lire *vi* (*ritornare in su*) to go back up; ~ **a** (*ritornare con la mente*) to go back to; (*datare da*) to date back to, go back to.

risa'lita *sf*: **mezzi di** ~ (*SCI*) ski lifts.

risal'tare *vi* (*fig: distinguersi*) to stand out; (*ARCHIT*) to project, jut out.

ri'salto *sm* prominence; (*sporgenza*) projection; **mettere** *o* **porre in** ~ **qc** to make sth stand out.

risana'mento *sm* (*economico*) improvement; (*bonifica*) reclamation; ~ **del bilancio** reorganization of the budget; ~ **edilizio** building improvement.

risa'nare *vt* (*guarire*) to heal, cure; (*palude*) to reclaim; (*economia*) to improve; (*bilancio*) to reorganize.

risa'pere *vt*: ~ **qc** to come to know of sth.

risa'puto, a *ag*: **è** ~ **che** ... everyone knows that ..., it's common knowledge that ....

risarci'mento [risartʃi'mento] *sm*: ~ **(di)** compensation (for); **aver diritto al** ~ **dei danni** to be entitled to damages.

risar'cire [risar'tʃire] *vt* (*cose*) to pay compensation for; (*persona*): ~ **qn di qc** to compensate sb for sth; ~ **i danni a qn** to pay sb damages.

ri'sata *sf* laugh.

riscalda'mento *sm* heating; ~ **centrale** central heating.

riscal'dare *vt* (*scaldare*) to heat; (: *mani, persona*) to warm; (*minestra*) to reheat; ~**rsi** *vr* to warm up.

riscat'tare *vt* (*prigioniero*) to ransom, pay a ransom for; (*DIR*) to redeem; ~**rsi** *vr* (*da disonore*) to redeem o.s.

ris'catto *sm* ransom; redemption.

rischia'rare [riskja'rare] *vt* (*illuminare*) to light up; (*colore*) to make lighter; ~**rsi** *vr* (*tempo*) to clear up; (*cielo*) to clear; (*fig: volto*) to brighten up; ~**rsi la voce** to clear one's throat.

rischi'are [ris'kjare] *vt* to risk ♦ *vi*: ~ **di fare qc** to risk *o* run the risk of doing sth.

'rischio ['riskjo] *sm* risk; **a proprio** ~ **e pericolo** at one's own risk; **correre il** ~ **di fare qc** to run the risk of doing sth; ~ **del mestiere** occupational hazard.

rischi'oso, a [ris'kjoso] *ag* risky, dangerous.

risciac'quare [riʃʃak'kware] *vt* to rinse.

risci'acquo [riʃ'ʃakkwo] *sm* rinse.

riscon'trare *vt* (*confrontare: due cose*) to compare; (*esaminare*) to check, verify; (*rilevare*) to find.

ris'contro *sm* comparison; check, verification; (*AMM: lettera di risposta*) reply; **mettere a** ~ to compare; **in attesa di un vostro cortese** ~ we look forward to your reply.

risco'perto, a *pp di* **riscoprire**.

risco'prire *vt* to rediscover.

riscossi'one *sf* collection.

ris'cosso, a *pp di* **riscuotere** ♦ *sf* (*riconquista*) recovery, reconquest.

riscu'otere *vt* (*ritirare una somma dovuta*) to collect; (: *stipendio*) to draw, collect; (*fig: successo etc*) to win, earn; ~**rsi** *vr*: ~**rsi (da)** to shake o.s. (out of), rouse o.s. (from); ~ **un assegno** to cash a cheque.

'rise *etc vb vedi* **ridere**.

risenti'mento *sm* resentment.

risen'tire *vt* to hear again; (*provare*) to feel ♦ *vi*: ~ **di** to feel (*o* show) the effects of; ~**rsi** *vr*: ~**rsi di** *o* **per** to take offence (*Brit*) *o* offense (*US*) at, resent.

risen'tito, a *ag* resentful.

ri'serbo *sm* reserve.

ri'serva *sf* reserve; (*di caccia, pesca*) preserve; (*restrizione, di indigeni*) reservation; **fare** ~ **di** (*cibo*) to get in a supply of; **tenere di** ~ to keep in reserve; **con le dovute** ~**e** with certain reservations; **ha accettato con la** ~ **di potersi ritirare** he accepted with the proviso that he could pull out.

riser'vare *vt* (*tenere in serbo*) to keep, put aside; (*prenotare*) to book, reserve; ~**rsi** *vr*: ~**rsi di fare qc** to intend to do sth; ~**rsi il diritto di fare qc** to reserve the right to do sth.

riserva'tezza [riserva'tettsa] *sf* reserve.

riser'vato, a *ag* (*prenotato, fig: persona*) reserved; (*confidenziale*) confidential; (*lettera, informazione*) confidential.

'risi *etc vb vedi* **ridere**.

ri'sibile *ag* laughable.

risi'edere *vi*: ~ **a** *o* **in** to reside in.

'risma *sf* (*di carta*) ream; (*fig*) kind, sort.

'riso, a *pp di* **ridere** ♦ *sm* (*pianta*) rice; (*pl(f)* ~**a**: *il ridere*): **un** ~ a laugh; **il** ~ laughter; **uno scoppio di** ~**a** a burst of laughter.

riso'lino *sm* snigger.

risolle'vare *vt* (*sollevare di nuovo: testa*) to raise again, lift up again; (*fig: questione*) to raise again, bring up again; (: *morale*) to raise; ~**rsi** *vr* (*da terra*) to rise again; (*fig: da malattia*) to recover; ~ **le sorti di qc** to improve the chances of sth.

ri'solsi *etc vb vedi* **risolvere**.

ri'solto, a *pp di* **risolvere**.

risolu'tezza [risolu'tettsa] *sf* determination.

risolu'tivo, a *ag* (*determinante*) decisive; (*che risolve*): **arrivare ad una formula** ~**a** to come up with a formula to resolve a situation.

riso'luto, a *ag* determined, resolute.

risoluzi'one [risolut'tsjone] *sf* solving *q*; (*MAT*) solution; (*decisione, di immagine*) resolution; (*DIR: di contratto*) annulment, cancellation.

ri'solvere *vt* (*difficoltà, controversia*) to resolve; (*problema*) to solve; (*decidere*): ~ **di fare** to resolve to do; ~**rsi** *vr* (*decidersi*): ~**rsi a fare** to make up one's mind to do; (*andare a finire*): ~**rsi in** to end up, turn out; ~**rsi in nulla** to come to nothing.

risol'vibile *ag* solvable.

riso'nanza [riso'nantsa] *sf* resonance; **aver vasta** ~ (*fig*: *fatto etc*) to be known far and wide.

riso'nare *vt, vi* = **risuonare**.

ri'sorgere [ri'sordʒere] *vi* to rise again.

risorgimen'tale [risordʒimen'tale] *ag* of the Risorgimento.

risorgi'mento [risordʒi'mento] *sm* revival; **il R~** (*STORIA*) the Risorgimento.

ri'sorsa *sf* expedient, resort; ~**e** *sfpl* (*naturali, finanziarie etc*) resources; **persona piena di** ~**e** resourceful person.

ri'sorsi *etc vb vedi* **risorgere**.

ri'sorto, a *pp di* **risorgere**.

ri'sotto *sm* (*CUC*) risotto.

risparmi'are *vt* to save; (*non uccidere*) to spare ♦ *vi* to save; ~ **qc a qn** to spare sb sth; ~ **fatica/fiato** to save one's energy/breath; **risparmiati il disturbo** *o* **la fatica** (*anche ironico*) save yourself the trouble.

risparmia'tore, 'trice *sm/f* saver.

ris'parmio *sm* saving *q*; (*denaro*) savings *pl*.

rispecchi'are [rispek'kjare] *vt* to reflect; ~**rsi** *vr* to be reflected.

rispe'dire *vt* to send back; ~ **qc a qn** to send sth back to sb.

rispet'tabile *ag* respectable; (*considerevole*: *somma*) sizeable, considerable.

rispettabilità *sf* respectability.

rispet'tare *vt* to respect; (*legge*) to obey, comply with, abide by; (*promessa*) to keep; **farsi** ~ to command respect; ~ **le distanze** to keep one's distance; ~ **i tempi** to keep to schedule; **ogni medico che si rispetti** every self-respecting doctor.

rispettiva'mente *av* respectively.

rispet'tivo, a *ag* respective.

ris'petto *sm* respect; ~**i** *smpl* (*saluti*) respects, regards; ~ **a** (*in paragone a*) compared to; (*in relazione a*) as regards, as for; ~ (**di** *o* **per**) (*norme, leggi*) observance (of), compliance (with); **portare** ~ **a qn/qc** to have *o* feel respect for sb/sth; **mancare di** ~ **a qn** to be disrespectful to sb; **con** ~ **parlando** with respect, if you will excuse my saying so; (**porga**) **i miei** ~**i alla signora** (give) my regards to your wife.

rispet'toso, a *ag* respectful.

risplen'dente *ag* (*giornata, sole*) bright, shining; (*occhi*) sparkling.

ris'plendere *vi* to shine.

rispon'dente *ag*: ~ **a** in keeping *o* conformity with.

rispon'denza [rispon'dɛntsa] *sf* correspondence.

ris'pondere *vi* to answer, reply; (*freni*) to respond; ~ **a** (*domanda*) to answer, reply to; (*persona*) to answer; (*invito*) to reply to; (*provocazione, sog*: *veicolo, apparecchio*) to respond to; (*corrispondere a*) to correspond to; (: *speranze, bisogno*) to answer; ~ **a qn di qc** (*essere responsabile*) to be answerable to sb for sth.

rispo'sarsi *vr* to get married again, remarry.

ris'posto, a *pp di* **rispondere** ♦ *sf* answer, reply; **in** ~**a a** in reply to; **dare una** ~**a** to give an answer; **diamo** ~**a alla vostra lettera del** ... in reply to your letter of ....

'rissa *sf* brawl.

ris'soso, a *ag* quarrelsome.

rist. *abbr* = **ristampa**.

ristabi'lire *vt* to re-establish, restore; (*persona*: *sog*: *riposo etc*) to restore to health; ~**rsi** *vr* to recover.

rista'gnare [rista'ɲɲare] *vi* (*acqua*) to become stagnant; (*sangue*) to cease flowing; (*fig*: *industria*) to stagnate.

ris'tagno [ris'taɲɲo] *sm* stagnation; **c'è un** ~ **delle vendite** business is slack.

ris'tampa *sf* reprinting *q*; reprint.

ristam'pare *vt* to reprint.

risto'rante *sm* restaurant.

risto'rarsi *vr* to have something to eat and drink; (*riposarsi*) to rest, have a rest.

ristora'tore, 'trice *ag* refreshing, reviving ♦ *sm* (*gestore di ristorante*) restaurateur.

ris'toro *sm* (*bevanda, cibo*) refreshment; **posto di** ~ (*FERR*) buffet, snack bar; **servizio di** ~ (*FERR*) refreshments *pl*.

ristret'tezza [ristret'tettsa] *sf* (*strettezza*) narrowness; (*fig*: *scarsezza*) scarcity, lack; (: *meschinità*) meanness; ~**e** *sfpl* (*povertà*) poverty *sg*.

ris'tretto, a *pp di* **restringere** ♦ *ag* (*racchiuso*) enclosed, hemmed in; (*angusto*) narrow; (*limitato*): ~ (**a**) restricted *o* limited (to); (*CUC*: *brodo*) thick; (: *caffè*) extra strong.

ristruttu'rare *vt* (*azienda*) to reorganize; (*edificio*) to restore; (*appartamento*) to alter.

ristrutturazi'one [ristrutturat'tsjone] *sf* reorganization; restoration; alteration.

risucchi'are [risuk'kjare] *vt* to suck in.

ri'succhio [ri'sukkjo] *sm* (*di acqua*) undertow, pull; (*di aria*) suction.

risul'tare *vi* (*dimostrarsi*) to prove (to be), turn out (to be); (*riuscire*): ~ **vincitore** to emerge as the winner; ~ **da** (*provenire*) to result from, be the result of; **mi risulta che** ... I understand that ..., as far as I know ...; (**ne**) **risulta che** ... it follows that ...; **non mi risulta** not as far as I know.

risul'tato *sm* result.

risuo'nare *vi* (*rimbombare*) to resound.

risurrezi'one [risurret'tsjone] *sf* (*REL*) resurrection.

risusci'tare [risuʃʃi'tare] *vt* to resuscitate, restore to life; (*fig*) to revive, bring back ♦ *vi* to rise (from the dead).

risvegli'are [rizveʎ'ʎare] *vt* (*gen*) to wake up, waken; (*fig: interesse*) to stir up, arouse; (: *curiosità*) to arouse; (*fig: dall'inerzia etc*): ~ **qn (da)** to rouse sb (from); **~rsi** *vr* to wake up, awaken; (*fig: interesse, curiosità*) to be aroused.

ris'veglio [riz'veʎʎo] *sm* waking up; (*fig*) revival.

ris'volto *sm* (*di giacca*) lapel; (*di pantaloni*) turn-up (*Brit*), cuff (*US*); (*di manica*) cuff; (*di tasca*) flap; (*di libro*) inside flap; (*fig*) implication.

ritagli'are [ritaʎ'ʎare] *vt* (*tagliar via*) to cut out.

ri'taglio [ri'taʎʎo] *sm* (*di giornale*) cutting, clipping; (*di stoffa etc*) scrap; **nei ~i di tempo** in one's spare time.

ritar'dare *vi* (*persona, treno*) to be late; (*orologio*) to be slow ♦ *vt* (*rallentare*) to slow down; (*impedire*) to delay, hold up; (*differire*) to postpone, delay; ~ **il pagamento** to defer payment.

ritarda'tario, a *sm/f* latecomer.

ritar'dato, a *ag* (*PSIC*) retarded.

ri'tardo *sm* delay; (*di persona aspettata*) lateness *q*; (*fig: mentale*) backwardness; **in** ~ late.

ri'tegno [ri'teɲɲo] *sm* restraint.

ritem'prare *vt* (*forze, spirito*) to restore.

rite'nere *vt* (*trattenere*) to hold back; (: *somma*) to deduct; (*giudicare*) to consider, believe.

ri'tengo, ri'tenni *etc vb vedi* **ritenere**.

riten'tare *vt* to try again, make another attempt at.

rite'nuta *sf* (*sul salario*) deduction; ~ **d'acconto** advance deduction of tax; ~ **alla fonte** (*FISCO*) taxation at source.

riterrò, riti'ene *etc vb vedi* **ritenere**.

riti'rare *vt* to withdraw; (*POL: richiamare*) to recall; (*andare a prendere: pacco etc*) to collect, pick up; **~rsi** *vr* to withdraw; (*da un'attività*) to retire; (*stoffa*) to shrink; (*marea*) to recede; **gli hanno ritirato la patente** they disqualified him from driving (*Brit*), they took away his licence (*Brit*) *o* license (*US*); **~rsi a vita privata** to withdraw from public life.

riti'rata *sf* (*MIL*) retreat; (*latrina*) lavatory.

riti'rato, a *ag* secluded; **fare vita ~a** to live in seclusion.

ri'tiro *sm* (*di truppe, candidati, soldi*) withdrawal; (*di pacchi*) collection; (*di passaporto*) confiscation; (*da attività*) retirement; (*luogo appartato*) retreat.

rit'mato, a *ag* rhythmic(al).

'ritmico, a, ci, che *ag* rhythmic(al).

'ritmo *sm* rhythm; (*fig*) rate; (: *della vita*)

pace, tempo; **al** ~ **di** at a speed *o* rate of; **ballare al** ~ **di valzer** to waltz.

'rito *sm* rite; **di** ~ usual, customary.

ritoc'care *vt* (*disegno, fotografia*) to touch up; (*testo*) to alter.

ri'tocco, chi *sm* touching up *q*; alteration.

ri'torcere [ri'tɔrtʃere] *vt* (*filato*) to twist; (*fig: accusa, insulto*) to throw back; **~rsi** *vr* (*tornare a danno di*): **~rsi contro** to turn against.

ritor'nare *vi* to return, go (*o* come) back; (*ripresentarsi*) to recur; (*ridiventare*): ~ **ricco** to become rich again ♦ *vt* (*restituire*) to return, give back.

ritor'nello *sm* refrain.

ri'torno *sm* return; **durante il (viaggio di)** ~ on the return trip, on the way back; **al** ~ (*tornando*) on the way back; **essere di** ~ to be back; **far** ~ to return; **avere un** ~ **di fiamma** (*AUT*) to backfire; (*fig: persona*) to be back in love again.

ritorsi'one *sf* (*rappresaglia*) retaliation.

ri'torto, a *pp di* **ritorcere** ♦ *ag* (*cotone, corda*) twisted.

ri'trarre *vt* (*trarre indietro, via*) to withdraw; (*distogliere: sguardo*) to turn away; (*rappresentare*) to portray, depict; (*ricavare*) to get, obtain; **ritrarsi** *vr* to move back.

ritrat'tare *vt* (*disdire*) to retract, take back; (*trattare nuovamente*) to deal with again.

ritrattazi'one [ritrattat'tsjone] *sf* withdrawal.

ritrat'tista, i, e *sm/f* portrait painter.

ri'tratto, a *pp di* **ritrarre** ♦ *sm* portrait.

ritro'sia *sf* (*riluttanza*) reluctance, unwillingness; (*timidezza*) shyness.

ri'troso, a *ag* (*restio*): ~ **(a)** reluctant (to); (*schivo*) shy; **andare a** ~ to go backwards.

ritrova'mento *sm* (*di cadavere, oggetto smarrito etc*) finding; (*oggetto ritrovato*) find.

ritro'vare *vt* to find; (*salute*) to regain; (*persona*) to find; to meet again; **~rsi** *vr* (*essere, capitare*) to find o.s.; (*raccapezzarsi*) to find one's way; (*con senso reciproco*) to meet (again).

ritro'vato *sm* discovery.

ri'trovo *sm* meeting place; ~ **notturno** night club.

'ritto, a *ag* (*in piedi*) standing, on one's feet; (*levato in alto*) erect, raised; (: *capelli*) standing on end; (*posto verticalmente*) upright.

ritu'ale *ag, sm* ritual.

riuni'one *sf* (*adunanza*) meeting; (*riconciliazione*) reunion; **essere in** ~ to be at a meeting.

riu'nire *vt* (*ricongiungere*) to join (together); (*riconciliare*) to reunite, bring together (again); **~rsi** *vr* (*adunarsi*) to meet; (*tornare a stare insieme*) to be reunited; **siamo qui riuniti per festeggiare il**

vostro anniversario we are gathered here to celebrate your anniversary.

riu'scire [riuʃ'ʃire] vi (uscire di nuovo) to go out again, go back out; (aver esito: fatti, azioni) to go, turn out; (aver successo) to succeed, be successful; (essere, apparire) to be, prove; (raggiungere il fine) to manage, succeed; ~ **a fare qc** to manage o be able to do sth; **questo mi riesce nuovo** this is new to me.

riu'scita [riuʃ'ʃita] sf (esito) result, outcome; (buon esito) success.

riutiliz'zare [riutilid'dzare] vt to use again, re-use.

'riva sf (di fiume) bank; (di lago, mare) shore; **in ~ al mare** on the (sea) shore.

ri'vale ag rival cpd ♦ sm/f rival; **non avere ~i** (anche fig) to be unrivalled.

rivaleggi'are [rivaled'dʒare] vi to compete, vie.

rivalità sf rivalry.

ri'valsa sf (rivincita) revenge; (risarcimento) compensation; **prendersi una ~ su qn** to take revenge on sb.

rivalu'tare vt (ECON) to revalue.

rivalutazi'one [rivalutat'tsjone] sf (ECON) re-valuation; (fig) re-evaluation.

rivan'gare vt (ricordi etc) to dig up (again).

rive'dere vt to see again; (ripassare) to revise; (verificare) to check.

rivedrò etc vb vedi **rivedere**.

rive'lare vt to reveal; (divulgare) to reveal, disclose; (dare indizio) to reveal, show; **~rsi** vr (manifestarsi) to be revealed; **~rsi onesto** etc to prove to be honest etc.

rivela'tore, 'trice ag revealing ♦ sm (TECN) detector; (FOT) developer.

rivelazi'one [rivelat'tsjone] sf revelation.

ri'vendere vt (vendere: di nuovo) to resell, sell again; (: al dettaglio) to retail, sell retail.

rivendi'care vt to claim, demand.

rivendicazi'one [rivendikat'tsjone] sf claim; **~i salariali** wage claims.

ri'vendita sf (bottega) retailer's (shop); ~ **di tabacchi** tobacconist's (shop).

rivendi'tore, 'trice sm/f retailer; ~ **autorizzato** authorized dealer.

riverbe'rare vt to reflect.

ri'verbero sm (di luce, calore) reflection; (di suono) reverberation.

rive'rente ag reverent, respectful.

rive'renza [rive'rentsa] sf reverence; (inchino) bow; curtsey.

rive'rire vt (rispettare) to revere; (salutare) to pay one's respects to.

river'sare vt (anche fig) to pour; **~rsi** vr (fig: persone) to pour out.

rivesti'mento sm covering; coating.

rives'tire vt to dress again; (ricoprire) to cover; (: con vernice) to coat; (fig: carica) to hold; **~rsi** vr to get dressed again; to

change (one's clothes); ~ **di piastrelle** to tile.

ri'vidi etc vb vedi **rivedere**.

rivi'era sf coast; **la ~ italiana** the Italian Riviera.

ri'vincita [ri'vintʃita] sf (SPORT) return match; (fig) revenge; **prendersi la ~ (su qn)** to take o get one's revenge (on sb).

rivis'suto, a pp di **rivivere**.

ri'vista sf review; (periodico) magazine, review; (TEATRO) revue; variety show.

ri'visto, a pp di **rivedere**.

rivitaliz'zare [rivitalid'dzare] vt to revitalize.

ri'vivere vi (riacquistare forza) to come alive again; (tornare in uso) to be revived ♦ vt to relive.

'rivo sm stream.

ri'volgere [ri'vɔldʒere] vt (attenzione, sguardo) to turn, direct; (parole) to address; **~rsi** vr to turn round; (fig: dirigersi per informazioni): **~rsi a** to go and see, go and speak to; ~ **un'accusa/una critica a qn** to accuse/criticize sb; **~rsi all'ufficio competente** to apply to the office concerned.

rivolgi'mento [rivoldʒi'mento] sm upheaval.

ri'volsi etc vb vedi **rivolgere**.

ri'volta sf revolt, rebellion.

rivol'tante ag revolting, disgusting.

rivol'tare vt to turn over; (con l'interno all'esterno) to turn inside out; (disgustare: stomaco) to upset, turn; (: fig) to revolt, disgust; **~rsi** vr (ribellarsi): **~rsi (a)** to rebel (against).

rivol'tella sf revolver.

ri'volto, a pp di **rivolgere**.

rivol'toso, a ag rebellious ♦ sm/f rebel.

rivoluzio'nare [rivoluttsjo'nare] vt to revolutionize.

rivoluzio'nario, a [rivoluttsjo'narjo] ag, sm/f revolutionary.

rivoluzi'one [rivolut'tsjone] sf revolution.

riz'zare [rit'tsare] vt to raise, erect; **~rsi** vr to stand up; (capelli) to stand on end; **~rsi in piedi** to stand up, get to one's feet.

RNA sigla m RNA (= ribonucleic acid).

RO sigla = Rovigo.

'roba sf stuff, things pl; (possessi, beni) belongings pl, things pl, possessions pl; ~ **da mangiare** things to eat, food; ~ **da matti!** it's sheer madness o lunacy!

robi'vecchi [robi'vɛkki] sm/f inv junk dealer.

'robot sm inv robot.

ro'botica sf robotics sg.

robus'tezza [robus'tettsa] sf (di persona, pianta) robustness, sturdiness; (di edificio, ponte) soundness.

ro'busto, a ag robust, sturdy; (solido: catena) strong; (: edificio, ponte) sound, solid; (vino) full-bodied.

'rocca, che sf fortress.

rocca'forte sf stronghold.

roc'chetto [rok'ketto] *sm* reel, spool.

'roccia, ce ['rɔttʃa] *sf* rock; **fare ~** (*SPORT*) to go rock climbing.

roccia'tore, 'trice [rottʃa'tore] *sm/f* rock climber.

rocci'oso, a [rot'tʃoso] *ag* rocky; **le Montagne R~e** the Rocky Mountains.

'roco, a, chi, che *ag* hoarse.

ro'daggio [ro'daddʒo] *sm* running (*Brit*) *o* breaking (*US*) in; **in ~** running *o* breaking in; **periodo di ~** (*fig*) period of adjustment.

'Rodano *sm*: **il ~** the Rhone.

ro'dare *vt* (*AUT, TECN*) to run (*Brit*) *o* break (*US*) in.

ro'deo *sm* rodeo.

'rodere *vt* to gnaw (at); (*distruggere poco a poco*) to eat into.

'Rodi *sf* Rhodes.

rodi'tore *sm* (*ZOOL*) rodent.

rodo'dendro *sm* rhododendron.

'rogito ['rɔdʒito] *sm* (*DIR*) (notary's) deed.

'rogna ['rɔɲɲa] *sf* (*MED*) scabies *sg*; (*di animale*) mange; (*fig*) bother, nuisance.

ro'gnone [roɲ'ɲone] *sm* (*CUC*) kidney.

ro'gnoso, a [roɲ'ɲoso] *ag* (*persona*) scabby; (*animale*) mangy; (*fig*) troublesome.

'rogo, ghi *sm* (*per cadaveri*) (funeral) pyre; (*supplizio*): **il ~** the stake.

rol'lare *vi* (*NAUT, AER*) to roll.

rol'lio *sm* roll(ing).

'Roma *sf* Rome.

roma'gnolo, a [romaɲ'ɲɔlo] *ag* of (*o* from) Romagna.

roma'nesco, a, schi, sche *ag* Roman ♦ *sm* Roman dialect.

Roma'nia *sf*: **la ~** Romania.

ro'manico, a, ci, che *ag* Romanesque.

ro'mano, a *ag*, *sm/f* Roman.

romantiche'ria [romantike'ria] *sf* sentimentality.

romanti'cismo [romanti'tʃizmo] *sm* romanticism.

ro'mantico, a, ci, che *ag* romantic.

ro'manza [ro'mandza] *sf* (*MUS, LETTERATURA*) romance.

roman'zare [roman'dzare] *vt* to romanticize.

roman'zesco, a, schi, sche [roman'dzesko] *ag* (*stile, personaggi*) fictional; (*fig*) storybook *cpd*.

romanzi'ere [roman'dzjere] *sm* novelist.

ro'manzo, a [ro'mandzo] *ag* (*LING*) romance *cpd* ♦ *sm* (*medievale*) romance; (*moderno*) novel; **~ d'amore** love story; **~ d'appendice** serial (story); **~ cavalleresco** tale of chivalry; **~ poliziesco, ~ giallo** detective story; **~ rosa** romantic novel.

rom'bare *vi* to rumble, thunder, roar.

'rombo *sm* rumble, thunder, roar; (*MAT*) rhombus; (*ZOOL*) turbot.

ro'meno, a *ag*, *sm/f*, *sm* = **rumeno**.

'rompere *vt* to break; (*conversazione*,

fidanzamento) to break off ♦ *vi* to break; **~rsi** *vr* to break; **mi rompe le scatole** (*fam*) he (*o* she) is a pain in the neck; **~rsi un braccio** to break an arm.

rompi'capo *sm* worry, headache; (*indovinello*) puzzle; (*in enigmistica*) brainteaser.

rompi'collo *sm* daredevil.

rompighi'accio [rompi'gjattʃo] *sm* (*NAUT*) icebreaker.

rompis'catole *sm/f inv* (*fam*) pest, pain in the neck.

'ronda *sf* (*MIL*) rounds *pl*, patrol.

ron'della *sf* (*TECN*) washer.

'rondine *sf* (*ZOOL*) swallow.

ron'done *sm* (*ZOOL*) swift.

ron'fare *vi* (*russare*) to snore.

ron'zare [ron'dzare] *vi* to buzz, hum.

ron'zino [ron'dzino] *sm* (*peg: cavallo*) nag.

ron'zio, ii [ron'dzio] *sm* buzzing, humming.

'rosa *sf* rose; (*fig: gruppo*): **~ dei candidati** list of candidates ♦ *ag inv*, *sm* pink.

ro'saio *sm* (*pianta*) rosebush, rose tree; (*giardino*) rose garden.

ro'sario *sm* (*REL*) rosary.

ro'sato, a *ag* pink, rosy ♦ *sm* (*vino*) rosé (wine).

ro'seo, a *ag* (*anche fig*) rosy.

ro'seto *sm* rose garden.

ro'setta *sf* (*diamante*) rose-cut diamond; (*rondella*) washer.

'rosi *vb vedi* **rodere**.

rosicchi'are [rosik'kjare] *vt* to gnaw (at); (*mangiucchiare*) to nibble (at).

rosma'rino *sm* rosemary.

'roso, a *pp di* **rodere**.

roso'lare *vt* (*CUC*) to brown.

roso'lia *sf* (*MED*) German measles *sg*, rubella.

ro'sone *sm* rosette; (*vetrata*) rose window.

'rospo *sm* (*ZOOL*) toad; **mandar giù** *o* **ingoiare un** *o* **il ~** (*fig*) to swallow a bitter pill; **sputa il ~!** out with it!

ros'setto *sm* (*per labbra*) lipstick; (*per guance*) rouge.

ros'siccio, a, ci, ce [ros'sittʃo] *ag* reddish.

'rosso, a *ag*, *sm*, *sm/f* red; **diventare ~ (per la vergogna)** to blush *o* go red (with *o* for shame); **il mar R~** the Red Sea; **~ d'uovo** egg yolk.

ros'sore *sm* flush, blush.

rosticce'ria [rostittʃe'ria] *sf* shop selling roast meat and other cooked food.

'rostro *sm* rostrum; (*becco*) beak.

ro'tabile *ag* (*percorribile*): **strada ~** roadway; (*FERR*): **materiale ~** rolling stock.

ro'taia *sf* rut, track; (*FERR*) rail.

ro'tare *vt, vi* to rotate.

rota'tivo, a *ag* rotating, rotation *cpd*.

rotazi'one [rotat'tsjone] *sf* rotation.

rote'are *vt, vi* to whirl; **~ gli occhi** to roll one's eyes.

ro'tella sf small wheel; (di mobile) castor.
roto'calco, chi sm (TIP) rotogravure;
(rivista) illustrated magazine.
roto'lare vt, vi to roll; ~**rsi** vr to roll
(about).
roto'lio sm rolling.
'rotolo sm (di carta, stoffa) roll; (di corda)
coil; **andare a** ~**i** (fig) to go to rack and
ruin; **mandare a** ~**i** (fig) to ruin.
ro'tondo, a ag round ♦ sf rotunda.
ro'tore sm rotor.
'rotta sf (AER, NAUT) course, route; (MIL)
rout; **a** ~ **di collo** at breakneck speed;
essere in ~ **con qn** to be on bad terms
with sb; **fare** ~ **su** o **per** o **verso** to head
for o towards; **cambiare** ~ (anche fig) to
change course; **in** ~ **di collisione** on a
collision course; **ufficiale di** ~ navigator,
navigating officer.
rot'tame sm fragment, scrap, broken bit;
~**i** smpl (di nave, aereo etc) wreckage sg;
~**i di ferro** scrap iron sg.
'rotto, a pp di **rompere** ♦ ag broken;
(calzoni) torn, split; (persona: pratico, resistente): ~ **a** accustomed o inured to ♦
sm: **per il** ~ **della cuffia** by the skin of
one's teeth; ~**i** smpl: **20.000 lire e** ~**i**
20,000-odd lire.
rot'tura sf (azione) breaking q; (di rapporti)
breaking off; (MED) fracture, break.
rou'lotte [ru'lɔt] sf inv caravan.
ro'vente ag red-hot.
'rovere sm oak.
ro'vescia [ro'veʃʃa] sf: **alla** ~ upside-down;
inside-out; **oggi mi va tutto alla** ~ everything is going wrong (for me) today.
rovesci'are [roveʃ'ʃare] vt (versare in giù) to
pour; (: accidentalmente) to spill;
(capovolgere) to turn upside down;
(gettare a terra) to knock down; (: fig:
governo) to overthrow; (piegare
all'indietro: testa) to throw back; ~**rsi** vr
(sedia, macchina) to overturn; (barca) to
capsize; (liquido) to spill; (fig: situazione)
to be reversed.
ro'vescio, sci [ro'veʃʃo] sm other side,
wrong side; (della mano) back; (di moneta) reverse; (pioggia) sudden downpour;
(fig) setback; (MAGLIA: anche: **punto** ~)
purl (stitch); (TENNIS) backhand (stroke);
a ~ (sottosopra) upside-down; (con
l'esterno all'interno) inside-out; **capire qc a**
~ to misunderstand sth; ~ **di fortuna** setback.
ro'vina sf ruin; ~**e** sfpl ruins; **andare in** ~
(andare a pezzi) to collapse; (fig) to go to
rack and ruin; **mandare qc/qn in** ~ to ruin
sth/sb.
rovi'nare vi to collapse, fall down ♦ vt (far
cadere giù: casa) to demolish;
(danneggiare, fig) to ruin.
rovi'nato, a ag ruined, damaged; (fig:

persona) ruined.
rovi'noso, a ag ruinous.
rovis'tare vt (casa) to ransack; (tasche) to
rummage in (o through).
'rovo sm (BOT) blackberry bush, bramble
bush.
roz'zezza [rod'dzettsa] sf roughness, coarseness.
'rozzo, a ['roddzo] ag rough, coarse.
RP sigla fpl vedi **relazioni pubbliche**.
R.R. abbr (POSTA) = **ricevuta di ritorno**.
Rrr abbr (POSTA) = **raccomandata con
ricevuta di ritorno**.
RSVP abbr (= répondez s'il vous plaît)
RSVP.
'ruba sf: **andare a** ~ to sell like hot cakes.
rubacu'ori sm inv ladykiller.
ru'bare vt to steal; ~ **qc a qn** to steal sth
from sb.
rubi'condo, a ag ruddy.
rubi'netto sm tap, faucet (US).
ru'bino sm ruby.
ru'bizzo, a [ru'bittso] ag lively, sprightly.
'rublo sm rouble.
ru'brica, che sf (di giornale: colonna)
column; (: pagina) page; (quadernetto) index book; (: per indirizzi) address book.
'rude ag tough, rough.
'rudere sm (rovina) ruins pl.
rudimen'tale ag rudimentary, basic.
rudi'menti smpl rudiments; basic
principles.
ruffi'ano sm pimp.
'ruga, ghe sf wrinkle.
'ruggine ['ruddʒine] sf rust.
rug'gire [rud'dʒire] vi to roar.
rug'gito [rud'dʒito] sm roar.
rugi'ada [ru'dʒada] sf dew.
ru'goso, a ag wrinkled; (scabro: superficie
etc) rough.
rul'lare vi (tamburo, nave) to roll; (aereo)
to taxi.
rul'lino sm (FOT) roll of film, spool.
rul'lio, ii sm (di tamburi) roll.
'rullo sm (di tamburi) roll; (arnese cilindrico,
TIP) roller; ~ **compressore** steam roller;
~ **di pellicola** roll of film.
rum sm rum.
ru'meno, a ag, sm/f, sm Romanian.
rumi'nante sm (ZOOL) ruminant.
rumi'nare vt (ZOOL) to ruminate; (fig) to
ruminate on o over, chew over.
ru'more sm: **un** ~ a noise, a sound; **il** ~
noise; **fare** ~ to make a noise; **un** ~ **di
passi** the sound of footsteps; **la notizia ha
fatto molto** ~ (fig) the news aroused great
interest.
rumoreggi'are [rumored'dʒare] vi (tuono etc)
to rumble; (fig: folla) to clamour (Brit),
clamor (US).
rumo'roso, a ag noisy.
ru'olo sm (TEATRO, fig) role, part; (elenco)

roll, register, list; **di** ~ permanent, on the permanent staff; **professore di** ~ (*INS*) ≈ lecturer with tenure; **fuori** ~ (*personale, insegnante*) temporary.

ru'ota *sf* wheel; **a** ~ (*forma*) circular; ~ **anteriore/posteriore** front/back wheel; **andare a** ~ **libera** to freewheel; **parlare a** ~ **libera** (*fig*) to speak freely; ~ **di scorta** spare wheel.

ruo'tare *vt, vi* = **rotare**.

'rupe *sf* cliff, rock.

ru'pestre *ag* rocky.

'ruppi *etc vb vedi* **rompere**.

ru'rale *ag* rural, country *cpd*.

ru'scello [ruʃˈʃɛllo] *sm* stream.

'ruspa *sf* excavator.

rus'pante *ag* (*pollo*) free-range.

rus'sare *vi* to snore.

'Russia *sf*: **la** ~ Russia.

'russo, a *ag, sm/f, sm* Russian.

'rustico, a, ci, che *ag* country *cpd*, rural; (*arredamento*) rustic; (*fig*) rough, unrefined ♦ *sm* (*fabbricato: per attrezzi*) shed; (*per abitazione*) farm labourer's (*Brit*) o farmhand's cottage.

'ruta *sf* (*BOT*) rue.

rut'tare *vi* to belch.

'rutto *sm* belch.

'ruvido, a *ag* rough, coarse.

ruzzo'lare [ruttsoˈlare] *vi* to tumble down.

ruzzo'loni [ruttsoˈloni] *av*: **cadere** ~ to tumble down; **fare le scale** ~ to tumble down the stairs.

S

S, s [ˈɛsse] *sf o m* (*lettera*) S, s; **S come Savona** ≈ S for Sugar.

s *abbr* (= *secondo*) sec.

S. *abbr* (= *sud*) S; (= *santo*) St.

SA *sigla* = *Salerno* ♦ *abbr vedi* **società anonima**.

sa *vb vedi* **sapere**.

sab. *abbr* (= *sabato*) Sat.

'sabato *sm* Saturday; *per fraseologia vedi* **martedì**.

'sabbia *sf* sand; ~**e mobili** quicksand(s *pl*).

sabbia'tura *sf* (*MED*) sand bath; (*TECN*) sand-blasting; **fare le** ~**e** to take sand baths.

sabbi'oso, a *ag* sandy.

sabo'taggio [saboˈtaddʒo] *sm* sabotage.

sabo'tare *vt* to sabotage.

sabota'tore, 'trice *sm/f* saboteur.

'sacca, che *sf* bag; (*bisaccia*) haversack;

(*insenatura*) inlet; ~ **d'aria** air pocket; ~ **da viaggio** travelling bag.

sacca'rina *sf* saccharin(e).

sac'cente [satˈtʃɛnte] *sm/f* know-all (*Brit*), know-it-all (*US*).

saccheggi'are [sakkedˈdʒare] *vt* to sack, plunder.

sac'cheggio [sakˈkeddʒo] *sm* sack(ing).

sac'chetto [sakˈketto] *sm* (small) bag; (small) sack; ~ **di carta/di plastica** paper/plastic bag.

'sacco, chi *sm* bag; (*per carbone etc*) sack; (*ANAT, BIOL*) sac; (*tela*) sacking; (*saccheggio*) sack(ing); (*fig: grande quantità*): **un** ~ **di** lots of, heaps of; **cogliere** o **prendere qn con le mani nel** ~ to catch sb red-handed; **vuotare il** ~ to confess, spill the beans; **mettere qn nel** ~ to cheat sb; **colazione** *f* **al** ~ packed lunch; ~ **a pelo** sleeping bag; ~ **per i rifiuti** bin bag (*Brit*), garbage bag (*US*).

sacer'dote [satʃerˈdɔte] *sm* priest.

sacer'dozio [satʃerˈdɔttsjo] *sm* priesthood.

sacra'mento *sm* sacrament.

sa'crario *sm* memorial chapel.

sacres'tano *sm* = **sagrestano**.

sacres'tia *sf* = **sagrestia**.

sacrifi'care *vt* to sacrifice; ~**rsi** *vr* to sacrifice o.s.; (*privarsi di qc*) to make sacrifices.

sacri'ficio [sakriˈfitʃo] *sm* sacrifice.

sacri'legio [sacriˈlɛdʒo] *sm* sacrilege.

sa'crilego, a, ghi, ghe *ag* (*REL*) sacrilegious.

'sacro, a *ag* sacred.

sacro'santo, a *ag* sacrosanct.

'sadico, a, ci, che *ag* sadistic ♦ *sm/f* sadist.

sa'dismo *sm* sadism.

sa'etta *sf* arrow; (*fulmine: anche fig*) thunderbolt.

sa'fari *sm inv* safari.

sa'gace [saˈgatʃe] *ag* shrewd, sagacious.

sa'gacia [saˈgatʃa] *sf* sagacity, shrewdness.

sag'gezza [sadˈdʒettsa] *sf* wisdom.

saggi'are [sadˈdʒare] *vt* (*metalli*) to assay; (*fig*) to test.

'saggio, a, gi, ge [ˈsaddʒo] *ag* wise ♦ *sm* (*persona*) sage; (*operazione sperimentale*) test; (: *dell'oro*) assay; (*fig: prova*) proof; (*campione indicativo*) sample; (*scritto: letterario*) essay; (: *INS*) written test; **dare** ~ **di** to give proof of; **in** ~ as a sample.

sag'gistica [sadˈdʒistika] *sf* ≈ non-fiction.

Sagit'tario [sadʒitˈtarjo] *sm* Sagittarius; **essere del** ~ to be Sagittarius.

'sagoma *sf* (*profilo*) outline, profile; (*forma*) form, shape; (*TECN*) template; (*bersaglio*) target; (*fig: persona*) character.

'sagra *sf* festival.

sa'grato *sm* churchyard.

sagres'tano *sm* sacristan; sexton.

sagres'tia *sf* sacristy; (*culto protestante*)

vestry.

Sa'hara [sa'ara] *sm*: **il (Deserto del)** ~ the Sahara (Desert).

sahari'ana [saa'rjana] *sf* bush jacket.

'sai *vb vedi* **sapere**.

Sai'gon *sf* Saigon.

'sala *sf* hall; (*stanza*) room; ~ **d'aspetto** waiting room; ~ **da ballo** ballroom; ~ **(dei) comandi** control room; ~ **per concerti** concert hall; ~ **per conferenze** (*INS*) lecture hall; (*in aziende*) conference room; ~ **da gioco** gaming room; ~ **macchine** (*NAUT*) engine room; ~ **operatoria** (*MED*) operating theatre (*Brit*) o room (*US*); ~ **da pranzo** dining room; ~ **per ricevimenti** banqueting hall; ~ **delle udienze** (*DIR*) courtroom.

sa'lace [sa'latʃe] *ag* (*spinto, piccante*) salacious, saucy; (*mordace*) cutting, biting.

sala'mandra *sf* salamander.

sa'lame *sm* salami *q*, salami sausage.

sala'moia *sf* (*CUC*) brine.

sa'lare *vt* to salt.

salari'ale *ag* wage *cpd*, pay *cpd*; **aumento** ~ wage *o* pay increase (*Brit*) o raise (*US*).

salari'ato, a *sm/f* wage-earner.

sa'lario *sm* pay, wages *pl*; ~ **base** basic wage; ~ **minimo garantito** guaranteed minimum wage.

salas'sare *vt* (*MED*) to bleed.

sa'lasso *sm* (*MED*) bleeding, bloodletting; (*fig: forte spesa*) drain.

sala'tino *sm* cracker, salted biscuit.

sa'lato, a *ag* (*sapore*) salty; (*CUC*) salted, salt *cpd*; (*fig: discorso etc*) biting, sharp; (: *prezzi*) steep, stiff.

sal'dare *vt* (*congiungere*) to join, bind; (*parti metalliche*) to solder; (: *con saldatura autogena*) to weld; (*conto*) to settle, pay.

salda'tore *sm* (*operaio*) solderer; welder; (*utensile*) soldering iron.

salda'trice [salda'tritʃe] *sf* (*macchina*) welder, welding machine; ~ **ad arco** arc welder.

salda'tura *sf* soldering; welding; (*punto saldato*) soldered joint; weld; ~ **autogena** welding; ~ **dolce** soft soldering.

sal'dezza [sal'dettsa] *sf* firmness, strength.

'saldo, a *ag* (*resistente, forte*) strong, firm; (*fermo*) firm, steady, stable; (*fig*) firm, steadfast ♦ *sm* (*svendita*) sale; (*di conto*) settlement; (*ECON*) balance; **pagare a** ~ to pay in full; ~ **attivo** credit; ~ **passivo** deficit; ~ **da riportare** balance carried forward.

'sale *sm* salt; (*fig*) wit; ~**i** *smpl* (*Med: da annusare*) smelling salts; **sotto** ~ salted; **restare di** ~ (*fig*) to be dumbfounded; **ha poco** ~ **in zucca** he doesn't have much sense; ~ **da cucina**, ~ **grosso** cooking salt;

~ **da tavola**, ~ **fino** table salt; ~**i da bagno** bath salts; ~**i minerali** mineral salts; ~**i e tabacchi** tobacconist's (shop).

sal'gemma [sal'dʒɛmma] *sm* rock salt.

'salgo *etc vb vedi* **salire**.

'salice ['salitʃe] *sm* willow; ~ **piangente** weeping willow.

sali'ente *ag* (*fig*) salient, main.

sali'era *sf* salt cellar.

sa'lino, a *ag* saline ♦ *sf* saltworks *sg*.

sa'lire *vi* to go (*o* come) up; (*aereo etc*) to climb, go up; (*passeggero*) to get on; (*sentiero, prezzi, livello*) to go up, rise ♦ *vt* (*scale, gradini*) to go (*o* come) up; ~ **su** to climb (up); ~ **sul treno/sull'autobus** to board the train/the bus; ~ **in macchina** to get into the car; ~ **a cavallo** to mount; ~ **al potere** to rise to power; ~ **al trono** to ascend the throne; ~ **alle stelle** (*prezzi*) to rocket.

sali'scendi [saliʃ'ʃendi] *sm inv* latch.

sa'lita *sf* climb, ascent; (*erta*) hill, slope; **in** ~ *ag, av* uphill.

sa'liva *sf* saliva.

'salma *sf* corpse.

sal'mastro, a *ag* (*acqua*) salt *cpd*; (*sapore*) ~ salty ♦ *sm* (*sapore*) salty taste; (*odore*) salty smell.

'salmo *sm* psalm.

sal'mone *sm* salmon.

salmo'nella *sf* salmonella.

Salo'mone: le isole ~ *sfpl* the Solomon Islands.

sa'lone *sm* (*stanza*) sitting room, lounge; (*in albergo*) lounge; (*di ricevimento*) reception room; (*su nave*) lounge, saloon; (*mostra*) show, exhibition; (*negozio: di parrucchiere*) hairdresser's (salon); ~ **dell'automobile** motor show; ~ **di bellezza** beauty salon.

salotti'ero, a *ag* mundane.

sa'lotto *sm* lounge, sitting room; (*mobilio*) lounge suite.

sal'pare *vi* (*NAUT*) to set sail; (*anche:* ~ **l'ancora**) to weigh anchor.

'salsa *sf* (*CUC*) sauce; **in tutte le** ~**e** (*fig*) in all kinds of ways; ~ **di pomodoro** tomato sauce.

sal'sedine *sf* (*del mare, vento*) saltiness; (*incrostazione*) (dried) salt.

sal'siccia, ce [sal'sittʃa] *sf* pork sausage.

salsi'era *sf* sauceboat (*Brit*), gravy boat.

sal'tare *vi* to jump, leap; (*esplodere*) to blow up, explode; (: *valvola*) to blow; (*venir via*) to pop off; (*non aver luogo: corso etc*) to be cancelled ♦ *vt* to jump (over), leap (over); (*fig: pranzo, capitolo*) to skip, miss (out); (*CUC*) to sauté; **far** ~ to blow up; (*serratura: forzare*) to break; **far** ~ **il banco** (*GIOCO*) to break the bank; **farsi** ~ **le cervella** to blow one's brains out; **ma che ti salta in mente?** what are you thinking of?; ~ **da un argomento all'altro** to jump from one subject to another; ~ **addosso a qn** (*aggredire*) to attack sb; ~ **fuori** to jump out, leap out; (*venire trovato*) to turn up; ~ **fuori con** (*frase, commento*) to come out with; ~ **giù da qc** to jump off sth, jump down from sth.

saltel'lare *vi* to skip; to hop.

sal'tello *sm* hop, little jump.

saltim'banco, chi *sm* acrobat.

'**salto** *sm* jump; (*SPORT*) jumping; (*dislivello*) drop; **fare un** ~ to jump, leap; **fare un** ~ **da qn** to pop over to sb's (place); ~ **in alto/lungo** high/long jump; ~ **con l'asta** pole vaulting; ~ **mortale** somersault; **un** ~ **di qualità** (*miglioramento*) significant improvement.

saltu'ario, a *ag* occasional, irregular.

sa'lubre *ag* healthy, salubrious.

salume'ria *sf* delicatessen.

sa'lumi *smpl* salted pork meats.

salumi'ere, a *sm/f* ≈ delicatessen owner.

salumi'ficio [salumi'fitʃo] *sm* cured pork meat factory.

salu'tare *ag* healthy; (*fig*) salutary, beneficial ♦ *vt* (*per dire buon giorno, fig*) to greet; (*per dire addio*) to say goodbye to; (*MIL*) to salute; **mi saluti sua moglie** my regards to your wife.

sa'lute *sf* health; ~**!** (*a chi starnutisce*) bless you!; (*nei brindisi*) cheers!; **bere alla** ~ **di qn** to drink (to) sb's health; **la** ~ **pubblica** public welfare; **godere di buona** ~ to be healthy, enjoy good health.

sa'luto *sm* (*gesto*) wave; (*parola*) greeting; (*MIL*) salute; **gli ha tolto il** ~ he no longer says hello to him; **cari** ~**i, tanti** ~**i** best regards; **vogliate gradire i nostri più distinti** ~**i** yours faithfully; **i miei** ~**i alla sua signora** my regards to your wife.

'**salva** *sf* salvo.

salvacon'dotto *sm* (*MIL*) safe-conduct.

salvada'naio *sm* moneybox, piggy bank.

salvado'regno, a [salvado'reɲɲo] *ag, sm/f* Salvadorean.

salva'gente [salva'dʒɛnte] *sm* (*NAUT*) lifebuoy; (*pl inv: stradale*) traffic island; ~ **a ciambella** lifebelt; ~ **a giubbotto** lifejacket (*Brit*), life preserver (*US*).

salvaguar'dare *vt* to safeguard.

salvagu'ardia *sf* safeguard; **a** ~ **di** for the safeguard of.

sal'vare *vt* to save; (*trarre da un pericolo*) to rescue; (*proteggere*) to protect; ~**rsi** *vr* to save o.s.; to escape; ~ **la vita a qn** to save sb's life; ~ **le apparenze** to keep up appearances.

salva'taggio [salva'taddʒo] *sm* rescue.

salva'tore, 'trice *sm/f* saviour (*Brit*), savior (*US*).

salvazi'one [salvat'tsjone] *sf* (*REL*) salvation.

'**salve** *escl* (*fam*) hi!

sal'vezza [sal'vettsa] *sf* salvation; (*sicurezza*) safety.

'**salvia** *sf* (*BOT*) sage.

salvi'etta *sf* napkin, serviette.

'**salvo, a** *ag* safe, unhurt, unharmed; (*fuori pericolo*) safe, out of danger ♦ *sm*: **in** ~ safe ♦ *prep* (*eccetto*) except; ~ **che** *cong* (*a meno che*) unless; (*eccetto che*) except (that); **mettere qc in** ~ to put sth in a safe place; **mettersi in** ~ to reach safety; **portare qn in** ~ to lead sb to safety; ~ **contrordini** barring instructions to the contrary; ~ **errori e omissioni** errors and omissions excepted; ~ **imprevisti** barring accidents.

sam'buco *sm* elder (tree).

sa'nare *vt* to heal, cure; (*economia*) to put right.

sana'torio *sm* sanatorium (*Brit*), sanitarium (*US*).

san'cire [san'tʃire] *vt* to sanction.

'**sandalo** *sm* (*BOT*) sandalwood; (*calzatura*) sandal.

'**sangue** *sm* blood; **farsi cattivo** ~ to fret, get worked up; **all'ultimo** ~ (*duello, lotta*) to the death; **non corre buon** ~ **tra di loro** there's bad blood between them; **buon** ~ **non mente!** blood will out!; ~ **freddo** (*fig*) sang-froid, calm; **a** ~ **freddo** in cold blood.

sangu'igno, a [san'gwiɲɲo] *ag* blood *cpd*; (*colore*) blood-red.

sangui'nante *ag* bleeding.

sangui'nare *vi* to bleed.

sangui'nario, a *ag* bloodthirsty.

sangui'noso, a *ag* bloody.

sangui'suga, ghe *sf* leech.

sanità *sf* health; (*salubrità*) healthiness; **Ministero della S**~ Department of Health; ~ **mentale** sanity; ~ **pubblica** public health.

sani'tario, a *ag* health *cpd*; (*condizioni*) sanitary ♦ *sm* (*AMM*) doctor; **Ufficiale S**~ Health Officer; (*impianti*) ~**i** *smpl* bathroom *o* sanitary fittings.

San Ma'rino *sf*: **la Repubblica di** ~ the Republic of San Marino.

'**sanno** *vb vedi* **sapere**.

'**sano, a** *ag* healthy; (*denti, costituzione*) healthy, sound; (*integro*) whole, unbroken; (*fig: politica, consigli*) sound; ~ **di mente** sane; **di** ~**a pianta** completely, entirely; ~ **e salvo** safe and sound.

Santi'ago *sf*: ~ **(del Cile)** Santiago (de Chile).

santifi'care *vt* to sanctify; (*feste*) to observe.

san'tino *sm* holy picture.

san'tissimo, a *ag*: **il S**~ **Sacramento** the Holy Sacrament; **il Padre S**~ (*papa*) the Holy Father.

santità *sf* sanctity; holiness; **Sua/Vostra** ~ (*titolo di papa*) His/Your Holiness.

'**santo, a** *ag* holy; *(fig)* saintly; *(seguito da nome proprio: dav sm* **san** + *C,* **sant'** + *V,* **santo** + *s impura, gn, pn, ps, x, z; dav sf* **santa** + *C,* **sant'** + *V)* saint ♦ *sm/f* saint; **parole ~e!** very true!; **tutto il ~ giorno** the whole blessed day, all day long; **non c'è ~ che tenga!** that's no excuse!; **la S~a Sede** the Holy See.

san'tone *sm* holy man.

santu'ario *sm* sanctuary.

sanzio'nare [santsjo'nare] *vt* to sanction.

sanzi'one [san'tsjone] *sf* sanction; *(penale, civile)* sanction, penalty; **~i economiche** economic sanctions.

sa'pere *vt* to know; *(essere capace di):* **so nuotare** I know how to swim, I can swim ♦ *vi:* **~ di** *(aver sapore)* to taste of; *(aver odore)* to smell of ♦ *sm* knowledge; **far ~ qc a qn** to inform sb about sth, let sb know sth; **venire a ~ qc (da qn)** to find out *o* hear about sth (from sb); **non ne vuole più ~ di lei** he doesn't want to have anything more to do with her; **mi sa che non sia vero** I don't think that's true.

sapi'ente *ag* (*dotto*) learned; (*che rivela abilità*) masterly ♦ *sm/f* scholar.

sapien'tone, a *sm/f (peg)* know-all *(Brit)*, know-it-all *(US)*.

sapi'enza [sa'pjentsa] *sf* wisdom.

sa'pone *sm* soap; **~ da barba** shaving soap; **~ da bucato** washing soap; **~ liquido** liquid soap; **~ in scaglie** soapflakes *pl.*

sapo'netta *sf* cake *o* bar *o* tablet of soap.

sa'pore *sm* taste, flavour *(Brit)*, flavor *(US)*.

sapo'rito, a *ag* tasty; *(fig: arguto)* witty; (*: piccante*) racy.

sappi'amo *vb vedi* **sapere**.

saprò *etc vb vedi* **sapere**.

sapu'tello, a *sm/f* know-all *(Brit)*, know-it-all *(US)*.

sarà *etc vb vedi* **essere**.

sara'banda *sf (fig)* uproar.

saraci'nesca, sche [saratʃi'neska] *sf (serranda)* rolling shutter.

sar'casmo *sm* sarcasm *q*; sarcastic remark.

sar'castico, a, ci, che *ag* sarcastic.

sarchi'are [sar'kjare] *vt* *(AGR)* to hoe.

sar'cofago, gi *o* **ghi** *sm* sarcophagus.

Sar'degna [sar'deɲɲa] *sf:* **la ~** Sardinia.

sar'dina *sf* sardine.

'**sardo, a** *ag, sm/f* Sardinian.

sar'donico, a, ci, che *ag* sardonic.

sa'rei *etc vb vedi* **essere**.

'**sarta** *sf vedi* **sarto**.

'**sartia** *sf (NAUT)* stay.

sarti'ame *sm (NAUT)* stays *pl.*

'**sarto, a** *sm/f* tailor/dressmaker; **~ d'alta moda** couturier.

sarto'ria *sf* tailor's (shop); dressmaker's (shop); *(casa di moda)* fashion house;

(arte) couture.

sas'sata *sf* blow with a stone; **tirare una ~ contro** *o* **a qc/qn** to throw a stone at sth/sb.

'**sasso** *sm* stone; *(ciottolo)* pebble; *(masso)* rock; **restare** *o* **rimanere di ~** to be dumbfounded.

sassofo'nista, i, e *sm/f* saxophonist.

sas'sofono *sm* saxophone.

sas'sone *ag, sm/f, sm* Saxon.

sas'soso, a *ag* stony; pebbly.

'**Satana** *sm* Satan.

sa'tanico, a, ci, che *ag* satanic, fiendish.

sa'tellite *sm, ag* satellite.

'**satira** *sf* satire.

satireggi'are [satired'dʒare] *vt* to satirize ♦ *vi (fare della satira)* to be satirical; *(scrivere satire)* to write satires.

sa'tirico, a, ci, che *ag* satiric(al).

sa'tollo, a *ag* full, replete.

satu'rare *vt* to saturate.

saturazi'one [saturat'tsjone] *sf* saturation.

'**saturo, a** *ag* saturated; *(fig):* **~ di** full of; **~ d'acqua** *(terreno)* waterlogged.

'**SAUB** *sigla f (= Struttura Amministrativa Unificata di Base)* state welfare system.

'**sauna** *sf* sauna; **fare la ~** to have *o* take a sauna.

sa'vana *sf* savannah.

'**savio, a** *ag* wise, sensible ♦ *sm* wise man.

Sa'voia *sf:* **la ~** Savoy.

savoi'ardo, a *ag* of Savoy, Savoyard ♦ *sm (biscotto)* sponge finger.

sazi'are [sat'tsjare] *vt* to satisfy, satiate; **~rsi** *vr (riempirsi di cibo):* **~rsi (di)** to eat one's fill (of); *(fig):* **~rsi di** to grow tired *o* weary of.

sazietà [sattsje'ta] *sf* satiety, satiation.

'**sazio, a** ['sattsjo] *ag:* **~ (di)** sated (with), full (of); *(fig: stufo)* fed up (with), sick (of).

sbada'taggine [zbada'taddʒine] *sf (sventatezza)* carelessness; *(azione)* oversight.

sba'dato, a *ag* careless, inattentive.

sbadigli'are [zbadiʎ'ʎare] *vi* to yawn.

sba'diglio [zba'diʎʎo] *sm* yawn; **fare uno ~** to yawn.

'**sbafo** *sm:* **a ~** at somebody else's expense.

sbagli'are [zbaʎ'ʎare] *vt* to make a mistake in, get wrong ♦ *vi (fare errori)* to make a mistake (*o* mistakes), be mistaken; *(ingannarsi)* to be wrong; *(operare in modo non giusto)* to err; **~rsi** *vr* to make a mistake, be mistaken, be wrong; **~ la mira/strada** to miss one's aim/take the wrong road; **scusi, ho sbagliato numero** *(TEL)* sorry, I've got the wrong number; **non c'è da ~rsi** there can be no mistake.

sbagli'ato, a [zbaʎ'ʎato] *ag (gen)* wrong; *(compito)* full of mistakes; *(conclusione)* erroneous.

'**sbaglio** ['zbaʎʎo] *sm* mistake, error; *(mo-*

error; **fare uno** ~ to make a mistake.

sbales'trato, a *ag* (*persona: scombussolato*) unsettled.

sbal'lare *vt* (*merce*) to unpack ♦ *vi* (*nel fare un conto*) to overestimate; (*DROGA: gergo*) to get high.

sbal'lato, a *ag* (*calcolo*) wrong; (*fam: ragionamento, persona*) screwy.

'sballo *sm* (*DROGA: gergo*) trip.

sballot'tare *vt* to toss (about).

sbalor'dire *vt* to stun, amaze ♦ *vi* to be stunned, be amazed.

sbalordi'tivo, a *ag* amazing; (*prezzo*) incredible, absurd.

sbal'zare [zbal'tsare] *vt* to throw, hurl; (*fig: da una carica*) to remove, dismiss ♦ *vi* (*balzare*) to bounce; (*saltare*) to leap, bound.

'sbalzo ['zbaltso] *sm* (*spostamento improvviso*) jolt, jerk; **a** ~i jerkily; (*fig*) in fits and starts; **uno** ~ **di temperatura** a sudden change in temperature.

sban'care *vt* (*nei giochi*) to break the bank at (*o* of); (*fig*) to ruin, bankrupt.

sbanda'mento *sm* (*NAUT*) list; (*AUT*) skid; (*fig: di persona*) confusion; **ha avuto un periodo di** ~ he went off the rails for a bit.

sban'dare *vi* (*NAUT*) to list; (*AUT*) to skid; ~**rsi** *vr* (*folla*) to disperse; (*truppe*) to scatter; (*fig: famiglia*) to break up.

sban'data *sf* (*AUT*) skid; (*NAUT*) list; **prendere una** ~ **per qn** (*fig*) to fall for sb.

sban'dato, a *sm/f* mixed-up person.

sbandie'rare *vt* (*bandiera*) to wave; (*fig*) to parade, show off.

'sbando *sm*: **essere allo** ~ to drift.

sbarac'care *vt* (*libri, piatti etc*) to clear (up).

sbaragli'are [zbaraʎˈʎare] *vt* (*MIL*) to rout; (*in gare sportive etc*) to beat, defeat.

sba'raglio [zbaˈraʎʎo] *sm*: **gettarsi allo** ~ (*soldato*) to throw o.s. into the fray; (*fig*) to risk everything.

sbaraz'zarsi [zbarat'tsarsi] *vr*: ~ **di** to get rid of, rid o.s. of.

sbaraz'zino, a [zbarat'tsino] *ag* impish, cheeky.

sbar'bare *vt*, ~**rsi** *vr* to shave.

sbarba'tello *sm* novice, greenhorn.

sbar'care *vt* (*passeggeri*) to disembark; (*merci*) to unload ♦ *vi* to disembark.

'sbarco *sm* disembarkation; unloading; (*MIL*) landing.

'sbarra *sf* bar; (*di passaggio a livello*) barrier; (*DIR*): **mettere/presentarsi alla** ~ to bring/appear before the court.

sbarra'mento *sm* (*stradale*) barrier; (*diga*) dam, barrage; (*MIL*) barrage.

sbar'rare *vt* (*bloccare*) to block, bar; (*cancellare: assegno*) to cross (*Brit*); ~ **il passo** to bar the way; ~ **gli occhi** to open

one's eyes wide.

sbar'rato, a *ag* (*porta*) barred; (*passaggio*) blocked, barred; (*strada*) blocked, obstructed; (*occhi*) staring; (*assegno*) crossed (*Brit*).

'sbattere *vt* (*porta*) to bang; (*tappeti, ali, CUC*) to beat; (*urtare*) to knock, hit ♦ *vi* (*porta, finestra*) to bang; (*agitarsi: ali, vele etc*) to flap; ~ **qn fuori/in galera** to throw sb out/into prison; **me ne sbatto!** (*fam*) I don't give a damn!

sbat'tuto, a *ag* (*viso, aria*) dejected, worn out; (*uovo*) beaten.

sba'vare *vi* to dribble; (*colore*) to smear, smudge.

sbava'tura *sf* (*di persone*) dribbling; (*di lumache*) slime; (*di rossetto, vernice*) smear.

sbelli'carsi *vr*: ~ **dalle risa** to split one's sides laughing.

'sberla *sf* slap.

sber'leffo *sm*: **fare uno** ~ **a qn** to make a face at sb.

sbia'dire *vi* (*anche:* ~**rsi**), *vt* to fade.

sbia'dito, a *ag* faded; (*fig*) colourless (*Brit*), colorless (*US*), dull.

sbian'care *vt* to whiten; (*tessuto*) to bleach ♦ *vi* (*impallidire*) to grow pale *o* white.

sbi'eco, a, chi, che *ag* (*storto*) squint, askew; **di** ~: **guardare qn di** ~ (*fig*) to look askance at sb; **tagliare una stoffa di** ~ to cut material on the bias.

sbigot'tire *vt* to dismay, stun ♦ *vi* (*anche:* ~**rsi**) to be dismayed.

sbilanci'are [zbilanˈtʃare] *vt* to throw off balance; ~**rsi** *vr* (*perdere l'equilibrio*) to overbalance, lose one's balance; (*fig: compromettersi*) to compromise o.s.

sbi'lenco, a, chi, che *ag* (*persona*) crooked, misshapen; (*fig: idea, ragionamento*) twisted.

sbirci'are [zbirˈtʃare] *vt* to cast sidelong glances at, eye.

sbirci'ata [zbirˈtʃata] *sf*: **dare una** ~ **a qc** to glance at sth, have a look at sth.

'sbirro *sm* (*peg*) cop.

sbizzar'rirsi [zbiddzarˈrirsi] *vr* to indulge one's whims.

sbloc'care *vt* to unblock, free; (*freno*) to release; (*prezzi, affitti*) to free from controls; ~**rsi** *vr* (*gen*) to become unblocked; (*passaggio, strada*) to clear, become unblocked; **la situazione si è sbloccata** things are moving again.

sboc'care *vi*: ~ **in** (*fiume*) to flow into; (*strada*) to lead into; (*persona*) to come (out) into; (*fig: concludersi*) to end (up) in.

sboc'cato, a *ag* (*persona*) foul-mouthed; (*linguaggio*) foul.

sbocci'are [zbotˈtʃare] *vi* (*fiore*) to bloom, open (out).

open (out).

'**sbocco, chi** sm (di fiume) mouth; (di strada) end; (di tubazione, COMM) outlet; (uscita: anche fig) way out; **una strada senza ~** a dead end; **siamo in una situazione senza ~chi** there's no way out of this for us.

sbocconcel'lare [zbokkontʃel'lare] vt: **~ (qc)** to nibble (at sth).

sbollen'tare vt (CUC) to parboil.

sbol'lire vi (fig) to cool down, calm down.

'**sbornia** sf (fam): **prendersi una ~** to get plastered.

sbor'sare vt (denaro) to pay out.

sbot'tare vi: **~ in una risata/per la collera** to burst out laughing/explode with anger.

sbotto'nare vt to unbutton, undo.

sbra'cato, a ag slovenly.

sbracci'arsi [zbrat'tʃarsi] vr to wave (one's arms about).

sbracci'ato, a [zbrat'tʃato] ag (camicia) sleeveless; (persona) bare-armed.

sbrai'tare vi to yell, bawl.

sbra'nare vt to tear to pieces.

sbricio'lare [zbritʃo'lare] vt, **~rsi** vr to crumble.

sbri'gare vt to deal with, get through; (cliente) to attend to, deal with; **~rsi** vr to hurry (up).

sbriga'tivo, a ag (persona, modo) quick, expeditious; (giudizio) hasty.

sbrina'mento sm defrosting.

sbri'nare vt to defrost.

sbrindel'lato, a ag tattered, in tatters.

sbrodo'lare vt to stain, dirty.

sbron'zarsi [zbron'tsarsi] vr (fam) to get sozzled.

'**sbronzo, a** ['zbrontso] (fam) ag sozzled ♦ sf: **prendersi una ~a** to get sozzled.

sbruf'fone, a sm/f boaster, braggart.

sbu'care vi (apparire) to pop out (o up).

sbucci'are [zbut'tʃare] vt (arancia, patata) to peel; (piselli) to shell; **~rsi un ginocchio** to graze one's knee.

sbucherò etc [zbuke'rɔ] vb vedi **sbucare**.

sbudel'larsi vr: **~ dalle risa** to split one's sides laughing.

sbuf'fare vi (persona, cavallo) to snort; (: ansimare) to puff, pant; (treno) to puff.

'**sbuffo** sm (di aria, fumo, vapore) puff; **maniche a ~** puff(ed) sleeves.

sc. abbr (TEATRO: = scena) sc.

S.C. abbr = **stato civile**; **Suprema Corte (di Cassazione)**.

'**scabbia** sf (MED) scabies sg.

'**scabro, a** ag rough, harsh; (fig) concise, terse.

sca'broso, a ag (fig: difficile) difficult, thorny; (: imbarazzante) embarrassing; (: sconcio) indecent.

scacchi'era [skak'kjɛra] sf chessboard.

scacchiere [skak'kjɛre] sm (MIL) sector; **S~**

(in Gran Bretagna) Exchequer.

scaccia'cani [skattʃa'kani] sm o f inv pistol with blanks.

scacciapensi'eri [skattʃapen'sjɛri] sm inv (MUS) jew's-harp.

scacci'are [skat'tʃare] vt to chase away o out, drive away o out; **~ qn di casa** to turn sb out of the house.

'**scacco, chi** sm (pezzo del gioco) chessman; (quadretto di scacchiera) square; (fig) setback, reverse; **~ch** smpl (gioco) chess sg; **a ~chi** (tessuto) check(ed); **subire uno ~** (fig: sconfitta) to suffer a setback.

scacco'matto sm checkmate; **dare ~ a qn** (anche fig) to checkmate sb.

'**scaddi** etc vb vedi **scadere**.

sca'dente ag shoddy, of poor quality.

sca'denza [ska'dɛntsa] sf (di cambiale, contratto) maturity; (di passaporto) expiry date; **a breve/lunga ~** short-/long-term; **data di ~** expiry date; **~ a termine** fixed deadline.

sca'dere vi (contratto etc) to expire; (debito) to fall due; (valore, forze, peso) to decline, go down.

sca'fandro sm (di palombaro) diving suit; (di astronauta) spacesuit.

scaffala'tura sf shelving, shelves pl.

scaf'fale sm shelf; (mobile) set of shelves.

'**scafo** sm (NAUT, AER) hull.

scagio'nare [skadʒo'nare] vt to exonerate, free from blame.

'**scaglia** ['skaʎʎa] sf (ZOOL) scale; (scheggia) chip, flake.

scagli'are [skaʎ'ʎare] vt (lanciare: anche fig) to hurl, fling; **~rsi su** o **contro** to hurl o fling o.s. at; (fig) to rail at.

scagliona'mento [skaʎʎona'mento] sm (MIL) arrangement in echelons.

scaglio'nare [skaʎʎo'nare] vt (pagamenti) to space out, spread out; (MIL) to echelon.

scagli'one [skaʎ'ʎone] sm (MIL) echelon; (GEO) terrace; **a ~i** in groups.

sca'gnozzo [skaɲ'ɲɔttso] sm (peg) lackey.

'**scala** sf (a gradini etc) staircase, stairs pl; (a pioli, di corda) ladder; (MUS, GEO, di colori, valori, fig) scale; **~e** sfpl (scalinata) stairs; **su larga** o **vasta ~** on a large scale; **su piccola ~**, **su ~ ridotta** on a small scale; **su ~ nazionale/mondiale** on a national/worldwide scale; **in ~ di 1 a 100.000** on a scale of 1 cm to 1 km; **riproduzione in ~** reproduction to scale; **~ a chiocciola** spiral staircase; **~ a libretto** stepladder; **~ di misure** system of weights and measures; **~ mobile** escalator; (ECON) sliding scale; **~ mobile (dei salari)** index-linked pay scale; **~ di sicurezza** (antincendio) fire escape.

sca'lare vt (ALPINISMO, muro) to climb, scale; (debito) to scale down, reduce; **questa somma vi viene scalata dal prezzo**

originale this sum is deducted from the original price.

sca'lata sf scaling q, climbing q; (arrampicata, fig) climb; **dare la ~ a** (fig) to make a bid for.

scala'tore, 'trice sm/f climber.

scalca'gnato, a [skalkaɲ'ɲato] ag (logoro) worn; (persona) shabby.

scalci'are [skal'tʃare] vi to kick.

scalci'nato, a [skaltʃi'nato] ag (fig peg) shabby.

scalda'bagno [skalda'baɲɲo] sm water heater.

scal'dare vt to heat; **~rsi** vr to warm up, heat up; (al fuoco, al sole) to warm o.s.; (fig) to get excited; **~ la sedia** (fig) to twiddle one's thumbs.

scaldavi'vande sm inv dish warmer.

scal'dino sm (per mani) hand-warmer; (per piedi) foot-warmer; (per letto) bed-warmer.

scal'fire vt to scratch.

scalfit'tura sf scratch.

scali'nata sf staircase.

sca'lino sm (anche fig) step; (di scala a pioli) rung.

scal'mana sf (hot) flush.

scalma'narsi vr (affaticarsi) to rush about, rush around; (agitarsi, darsi da fare) to get all hot and bothered; (arrabbiarsi) to get excited, get steamed up.

scalma'nato, a sm/f hothead.

'scalo sm (NAUT) slipway; (: porto d'approdo) port of call; (AER) stopover; **fare ~ (a)** (NAUT) to call (at), put in (at); (AER) to land (at), make a stop (at); **volo senza ~** non-stop flight; **~ merci** (FERR) goods (Brit) o freight yard.

sca'logna [ska'loɲɲa] sf (fam) bad luck.

scalo'gnato, a [skaloɲ'ɲato] ag (fam) unlucky.

scalop'pina sf (CUC) escalope.

scal'pello sm chisel.

scalpi'tare vi (cavallo) to paw the ground; (persona) to stamp one's feet.

scal'pore sm noise, row; **far ~** (notizia) to cause a sensation o a stir.

'scaltro, a ag cunning, shrewd.

scal'zare [skal'tsare] vt (albero) to bare the roots of; (muro, fig: autorità) to undermine.

'scalzo, a ['skaltso] ag barefoot.

scambi'are vt to exchange; (confondere): **~ qn/qc per** to take o mistake sb/sth for; **mi hanno scambiato il cappello** they've given me the wrong hat.

scambi'evole ag mutual, reciprocal.

'scambio sm exchange; (COMM) trade; (FERR) points pl; **fare (uno) ~** to make a swap; **libero ~** free trade; **~i con l'estero** foreign trade.

scamosci'ato, a [skamoʃ'ʃato] ag suede.

scampa'gnata [skampaɲ'ɲata] sf trip to the country.

scampa'nare vi to peal.

scam'pare vt (salvare) to rescue, save; (evitare: morte, prigione) to escape ♦ vi: **~ (a qc)** to survive (sth), escape (sth); **scamparla bella** to have a narrow escape.

'scampo sm (salvezza) escape; (ZOOL) prawn; **cercare ~ nella fuga** to seek safety in flight; **non c'è (via di) ~** there's no way out.

'scampolo sm remnant.

scanala'tura sf (incavo) channel, groove.

scandagli'are [skandaʎ'ʎare] vt (NAUT) to sound; (fig) to sound out; to probe.

scanda'listico, a, ci, che ag (settimanale etc) sensational.

scandaliz'zare [skandalid'dzare] vt to shock, scandalize; **~rsi** vr to be shocked.

'scandalo sm scandal; **dare ~** to cause a scandal.

scanda'loso, a ag scandalous, shocking.

Scandi'navia sf: **la ~** Scandinavia.

scandi'navo, a ag, sm/f Scandinavian.

scan'dire vt (versi) to scan; (parole) to articulate, pronounce distinctly; **~ il tempo** (MUS) to beat time.

scan'nare vt (animale) to butcher, slaughter; (persona) to cut o slit the throat of.

'scanno sm seat, bench.

scansafa'tiche [skansafa'tike] sm/f inv idler, loafer.

scan'sare vt (rimuovere) to move (aside), shift; (schivare: schiaffo) to dodge; (sfuggire) to avoid; **~rsi** vr to move aside.

scan'sia sf shelves pl; (per libri) bookcase.

'scanso sm: **a ~ di** in order to avoid, as a precaution against; **a ~ di equivoci** to avoid (any) misunderstanding.

scanti'nato sm basement.

scanto'nare vi to turn the corner; (svignarsela) to sneak off.

scanzo'nato, a [skantso'nato] ag easy-going.

scapacci'one [skapat'tʃone] sm clout, slap.

scapes'trato, a ag dissolute.

'scapito sm (perdita) loss; (danno) damage, detriment; **a ~ di** to the detriment of.

'scapola sf shoulder blade.

'scapolo sm bachelor.

scappa'mento sm (AUT) exhaust.

scap'pare vi (fuggire) to escape; (andare via in fretta) to rush off; **~ di prigione** to escape from prison; **~ di mano** (oggetto) to slip out of one's hands; **~ di mente a qn** to slip sb's mind; **lasciarsi ~** (occasione, affare) to miss, let go by; (dettaglio) to overlook; (parola) to let slip; (prigioniero) to let escape; **mi scappò detto** I let it slip.

scap'pata sf quick visit o call.

scappa'tella sf escapade.

scappa'toia sf way out.

scara'beo *sm* beetle.

scarabocchi'are [skarabok'kjare] *vt* to scribble, scrawl.

scara'bocchio [skara'bɔkkjo] *sm* scribble, scrawl.

scara'faggio [skara'faddʒo] *sm* cockroach.

scaraman'zia [skaraman'tsia] *sf*: **per ~** for luck.

scara'muccia, ce [skara'muttʃa] *sf* skirmish.

scaraven'tare *vt* to fling, hurl.

scarce'rare [skartʃe'rare] *vt* to release (from prison).

scarcerazi'one [skartʃerat'tsjone] *sf* release (from prison).

scardi'nare *vt* to take off its hinges.

'scarica, che *sf* (*di più armi*) volley of shots; (*di sassi, pugni*) hail, shower; (*ELETTR*) discharge; **~ di mitra** burst of machine-gun fire.

scari'care *vt* (*merci, camion etc*) to unload; (*passeggeri*) to set down; (*arma*) to unload; (: *sparare, ELETTR*) to discharge; (*sog: corso d'acqua*) to empty, pour; (*fig: liberare da un peso*) to unburden, relieve; **~rsi** *vr* (*orologio*) to run *o* wind down; (*batteria, accumulatore*) to go flat (*Brit*) *o* dead; (*fig: rilassarsi*) to unwind; (: *sfogarsi*) to let off steam; **~ le proprie responsabilità su qn** to off-load one's responsibilities onto sb; **~ la colpa addosso a qn** to blame sb; **il fulmine si scaricò su un albero** the lightning struck a tree.

scarica'tore *sm* loader; (*di porto*) docker.

'scarico, a, chi, che *ag* unloaded; (*orologio*) run down; (*batteria, accumulatore*) dead, flat (*Brit*) ♦ *sm* (*di merci, materiali*) unloading; (*di immondizie*) dumping, tipping (*Brit*); (: *luogo*) rubbish dump; (*TECN: deflusso*) draining; (: *dispositivo*) drain; (*AUT*) exhaust; **~ del lavandino** waste outlet.

scarlat'tina *sf* scarlet fever.

scar'latto, a *ag* scarlet.

'scarno, a *ag* thin, bony.

'scarpa *sf* shoe; **fare le ~e a qn** (*fig*) to double-cross sb; **~e da ginnastica** gym shoes; **~e coi tacchi (alti)** high-heeled shoes; **~e col tacco basso** low-heeled shoes; **~e senza tacco** flat shoes; **~e da tennis** tennis shoes.

scar'pata *sf* escarpment.

scarpi'era *sf* shoe rack.

scar'pone *sm* boot; **~i da montagna** climbing boots; **~i da sci** ski-boots.

scarroz'zare [skarrot'tsare] *vt* to drive around.

scarseggi'are [skarsed'dʒare] *vi* to be scarce; **~ di** to be short of, lack.

scar'sezza [skar'settsa] *sf* scarcity, lack.

'scarso, a *ag* (*insufficiente*) insufficient, meagre (*Brit*), meager (*US*); (*povero: annata*) poor, lean; (*INS: voto*) poor; **~ di**

lacking in; **3 chili ~i** just under 3 kilos, barely 3 kilos.

scartabel'lare *vt* to skim through, glance through.

scarta'faccio [skarta'fattʃo] *sm* notebook.

scarta'mento *sm* (*FERR*) gauge; **~ normale/ridotto** standard/narrow gauge.

scar'tare *vt* (*pacco*) to unwrap; (*idea*) to reject; (*MIL*) to declare unfit for military service; (*carte da gioco*) to discard; (*CALCIO*) to dodge (past) ♦ *vi* to swerve.

'scarto *sm* (*cosa scartata, anche COMM*) reject; (*di veicolo*) swerve; (*differenza*) gap, difference; **~ salariale** wage differential.

scar'toffie *sfpl* (*peg*) papers *pl*.

scas'sare *vt* (*fam: rompere*) to wreck.

scassi'nare *vt* to break, force.

'scasso *sm vedi* **furto**.

scate'nare *vt* (*fig*) to incite, stir up; **~rsi** *vr* (*temporale*) to break; (*rivolta*) to break out; (*persona: infuriarsi*) to rage.

scate'nato, a *ag* wild.

'scatola *sf* box; (*di latta*) tin (*Brit*), can; **cibi in ~** tinned (*Brit*) *o* canned foods; **una ~ di cioccolatini** a box of chocolates; **comprare qc a ~ chiusa** to buy sth sight unseen; **~ cranica** cranium.

scat'tante *ag* quick off the mark; (*agile*) agile.

scat'tare *vt* (*fotografia*) to take ♦ *vi* (*congegno, molla etc*) to be released; (*balzare*) to spring up; (*SPORT*) to put on a spurt; (*fig: per l'ira*) to fly into a rage; (*legge, provvedimento*) to come into effect; **~ in piedi** to spring to one's feet; **far ~** to release.

'scatto *sm* (*dispositivo*) release; (: *di arma da fuoco*) trigger mechanism; (*rumore*) click; (*balzo*) jump, start; (*SPORT*) spurt; (*fig: di ira etc*) fit; (: *di stipendio*) increment; **di ~** suddenly; **serratura a ~** spring lock.

scatu'rire *vi* to gush, spring.

scaval'care *vt* (*ostacolo*) to pass (*o* climb) over; (*fig*) to get ahead of, overtake.

sca'vare *vt* (*terreno*) to dig; (*legno*) to hollow out; (*pozzo, galleria*) to bore; (*città sepolta etc*) to excavate.

scava'trice [skava'tritʃe] *sf* (*macchina*) excavator.

scavezza'collo [skavettsa'kɔllo] *sm* daredevil.

'scavo *sm* excavating *q*; excavation.

scazzot'tare [skattsot'tare] *vt* (*fam*) to beat up, give a thrashing to.

'scegliere ['ʃeʎʎere] *vt* (*gen*) to choose; (*candidato, prodotto*) to choose, select; **~ di fare** to choose to do.

sce'icco, chi [ʃe'ikko] *sm* sheik.

'scelgo *etc* ['ʃelgo] *vb vedi* **scegliere**.

scelle'rato, a [ʃelle'rato] *ag* wicked, evil.

scel'lino [ʃel'lino] *sm* shilling.

'scelto, a ['ʃelto] *pp di* **scegliere** ♦ *ag*

(*gruppo*) carefully selected; (*frutta, verdura*) choice, top quality; (*MIL*: *specializzato*) crack *cpd*, highly skilled ♦ *sf* choice; (*selezione*) selection, choice; **frutta o formaggi a** ~**a** a choice of fruit or cheese; **fare una** ~**a** to make a choice, choose; **non avere** ~**a** to have no choice *o* option; **di prima** ~**a** top grade *o* quality.

sce'**mare** [ʃe'mare] *vt*, *vi* to diminish.

sce'**menza** [ʃe'mɛntsa] *sf* stupidity *q*; stupid thing (to do *o* say).

'**scemo, a** ['ʃemo] *ag* stupid, silly.

'**scempio** ['ʃempjo] *sm* slaughter, massacre; (*fig*) ruin; **far** ~ **di** (*fig*) to play havoc with, ruin.

'**scena** ['ʃena] *sf* (*gen*) scene; (*palcoscenico*) stage; **le** ~**e** (*fig*: *teatro*) the stage; **andare in** ~ to be staged *o* put on *o* performed; **mettere in** ~ to stage; **uscire di** ~ to leave the stage; (*fig*) to leave the scene; **fare una** ~ (*fig*) to make a scene; **ha fatto** ~ **muta** (*fig*) he didn't open his mouth.

sce'**nario** [ʃe'narjo] *sm* scenery; (*di film*) scenario.

sce'**nata** [ʃe'nata] *sf* row, scene.

'**scendere** ['ʃendere] *vi* to go (*o* come) down; (*strada, sole*) to go down; (*notte*) to fall; (*passeggero: fermarsi*) to get out, alight; (*fig: temperatura, prezzi*) to fall, drop ♦ *vt* (*scale, pendio*) to go (*o* come) down; ~ **dalle scale** to go (*o* come) down the stairs; ~ **dal treno** to get off *o* out of the train; ~ **dalla macchina** to get out of the car; ~ **da cavallo** to dismount, get off one's horse; ~ **ad un albergo** to put up *o* stay at a hotel.

sceneggi'**ato** [ʃened'dʒato] *sm* television drama.

sceneggia'**tore, 'trice** [ʃeneddʒa'tore] *sm/f* script-writer.

sceneggia'**tura** [ʃenedʒa'tura] *sf* (*TEATRO*) scenario; (*CINEMA*) screenplay, scenario.

'**scenico, a, ci, che** ['ʃeniko] *ag* stage *cpd*.

scenogra'**fia** [ʃenogra'fia] *sf* (*TEATRO*) stage design; (*CINEMA*) set design; (*elementi scenici*) scenery.

sce'**nografo, a** [ʃe'nɔgrafo] *sm/f* set designer.

sce'**riffo** [ʃe'riffo] *sm* sheriff.

scervel'**larsi** [ʃervel'larsi] *vr*: ~ (**su qc**) to rack one's brains (over sth).

scervel'**lato, a** [ʃervel'lato] *ag* feather-brained, scatterbrained.

'**sceso, a** ['ʃeso] *pp di* **scendere**.

scetti'**cismo** [ʃetti'tʃizmo] *sm* scepticism (*Brit*), skepticism (*US*).

'**scettico, a, ci, che** ['ʃettiko] *ag* sceptical (*Brit*), skeptical (*US*).

'**scettro** ['ʃettro] *sm* sceptre (*Brit*), scepter (*US*).

'**scheda** ['skeda] *sf* (index) card; ~ **a circuito stampato** printed-circuit board; ~ **elettorale** ballot paper; ~ **perforata** punch card.

sche'**dare** [ske'dare] *vt* (*dati*) to file; (*libri*) to catalogue; (*registrare: anche POLIZIA*) to put on one's files.

sche'**dario** [ske'darjo] *sm* file; (*mobile*) filing cabinet.

sche'**dato, a** [ske'dato] *ag* with a (police) record ♦ *sm/f* person with a (police) record.

sche'**dina** [ske'dina] *sf* pools coupon (*Brit*).

'**scheggia, ge** ['skeddʒa] *sf* splinter, sliver.

'**scheletro** ['skeletro] *sm* skeleton.

'**schema, i** ['skema] *sm* (*diagramma*) diagram, sketch; (*progetto, abbozzo*) outline, plan; **ribellarsi agli** ~**i** to rebel against traditional values; **secondo gli** ~**i tradizionali** in accordance with traditional values.

sche'**matico, a, ci, che** [ske'matiko] *ag* schematic.

schematiz'**zare** [skematid'dzare] *vt* to schematize.

'**scherma** ['skerma] *sf* fencing.

scher'**maglia** [sker'maʎʎa] *sf* (*fig*) skirmish.

scher'**mirsi** [sker'mirsi] *vr* to defend o.s., protect o.s.

'**schermo** ['skermo] *sm* shield, screen; (*CINEMA, TV*) screen.

schermogra'**fia** [skermogra'fia] *sf* X-rays *pl*.

scher'**nire** [sker'nire] *vt* to mock, sneer at.

'**scherno** ['skerno] *sm* mockery, derision; **farsi** ~ **di** to sneer at; **essere oggetto di** ~ to be a laughing stock.

scher'**zare** [sker'tsare] *vi* to joke.

'**scherzo** ['skertso] *sm* joke; (*tiro*) trick; (*MUS*) scherzo; **è uno** ~! (*una cosa facile*) it's child's play!, it's easy!; **per** ~ for a joke *o* a laugh; **fare un brutto** ~ **a qn** to play a nasty trick on sb; ~**i a parte** seriously, joking apart.

scher'**zoso, a** [sker'tsoso] *ag* (*tono, gesto*) playful; (*osservazione*) facetious; **è un tipo** ~ he likes a joke.

schiaccia'**noci** [skjattʃa'notʃi] *sm inv* nutcracker.

schiacci'**ante** [skjat'tʃante] *ag* overwhelming.

schiacci'**are** [skjat'tʃare] *vt* (*dito*) to crush; (*noci*) to crack; ~ **un pisolino** to have a nap.

schiaffeggi'**are** [skjaffed'dʒare] *vt* to slap.

schi'**affo** ['skjaffo] *sm* slap; **prendere qn a** ~**i** to slap sb's face; **uno** ~ **morale** a slap in the face, a rebuff.

schiamaz'**zare** [skjamat'tsare] *vi* to squawk, cackle.

schia'**mazzo** [skja'mattso] *sm* (*fig: chiasso*) din, racket.

schian'**tare** [skjan'tare] *vt* to break, tear apart; ~**rsi** *vr* to break (up), shatter; ~**rsi al suolo** (*aereo*) to crash (to the ground).

schi'**anto** ['skjanto] *sm* (*rumore*) crash; tearing sound; **è uno** ~! (*fam*) it's (*o* he's *o* she's) terrific!; **di** ~ all of a sudden.

schia'rire [skja'rire] *vt* to lighten, make lighter ♦ *vi* (*anche:* ~**rsi**) to grow lighter; (*tornar sereno*) to clear, brighten up; ~**rsi la voce** to clear one's throat.

schia'rita [skja'rita] *sf* (*METEOR*) bright spell; (*fig*) improvement, turn for the better.

schiat'tare [skjat'tare] *vi* to burst; ~ **d'invidia** to be green with envy; ~ **di rabbia** to be beside o.s. with rage.

schiavitù [skjavi'tu] *sf* slavery.

schiaviz'zare [skjavid'dzare] *vt* to enslave.

schi'avo, a ['skjavo] *sm/f* slave.

schi'ena ['skjɛna] *sf* (*ANAT*) back.

schie'nale [skje'nale] *sm* (*di sedia*) back.

schi'era ['skjɛra] *sf* (*MIL*) rank; (*gruppo*) group, band.

schiera'mento [skjera'mento] *sm* (*MIL, SPORT*) formation; (*fig*) alliance.

schie'rare [skje'rare] *vt* (*esercito*) to line up, draw up, marshal; ~**rsi** *vr* to line up; (*fig*): ~**rsi con** *o* **dalla parte di/contro qn** to side with/oppose sb.

schi'etto, a ['skjɛtto] *ag* (*puro*) pure; (*fig*) frank, straightforward.

schi'fare [ski'fare] *vt* to disgust.

schi'fezza [ski'fettsa] *sf*: **essere una** ~ (*cibo, bibita etc*) to be disgusting; (*film, libro*) to be dreadful.

schifil'toso, a [skifil'toso] *ag* fussy, difficult.

'schifo ['skifo] *sm* disgust; **fare** ~ (*essere fatto male, dare pessimi risultati*) to be awful; **mi fa** ~ it makes me sick, it's disgusting; **quel libro è uno** ~ that book's rotten.

schi'foso, a [ski'foso] *ag* disgusting, revolting; (*molto scadente*) rotten, lousy.

schioc'care [skjok'kare] *vt* (*frusta*) to crack; (*dita*) to snap; (*lingua*) to click; ~ **le labbra** to smack one's lips.

schioppet'tata [skjoppet'tata] *sf* gunshot.

schi'oppo ['skjɔppo] *sm* rifle, gun.

schi'udere ['skjudere] *vt,* ~**rsi** *vr* to open.

schi'uma ['skjuma] *sf* foam; (*di sapone*) lather; (*di latte*) froth.

schiu'mare [skju'mare] *vt* to skim ♦ *vi* to foam.

schi'uso, a ['skjuso] *pp di* **schiudere.**

schi'vare [ski'vare] *vt* to dodge, avoid.

'schivo, a ['skivo] *ag* (*ritroso*) stand-offish, reserved; (*timido*) shy.

schizofre'nia [skiddzofre'nia] *sf* schizophrenia.

schizo'frenico, a, ci, che [skiddzo'frɛniko] *ag* schizophrenic.

schiz'zare [skit'tsare] *vt* (*spruzzare*) to spurt, squirt; (*sporcare*) to splash, spatter; (*fig: abbozzare*) to sketch ♦ *vi* to spurt, squirt; (*saltar fuori*) to dart up (*o* off *etc*); ~ **via** (*animale, persona*) to dart away; (*macchina, moto*) to accelerate away.

schizzi'noso, a [skittsi'noso] *ag* fussy, finicky.

'schizzo ['skittso] *sm* (*di liquido*) spurt; splash, spatter; (*abbozzo*) sketch.

sci [ʃi] *sm inv* (*attrezzo*) ski; (*attività*) skiing; ~ **di fondo** cross-country skiing, ski touring (*US*); ~ **nautico** water-skiing.

'scia, *pl* **'scie** ['ʃia] *sf* (*di imbarcazione*) wake; (*di profumo*) trail.

scià [ʃa] *sm inv* shah.

sci'abola ['ʃabola] *sf* sabre (*Brit*), saber (*US*).

scia'callo [ʃa'kallo] *sm* jackal; (*fig peg: profittatore*) shark, profiteer; (: *ladro*) looter.

sciac'quare [ʃak'kware] *vt* to rinse.

scia'gura [ʃa'gura] *sf* disaster, calamity.

sciagu'rato, a [ʃagu'rato] *ag* unfortunate; (*malvagio*) wicked.

scialac'quare [ʃalak'kware] *vt* to squander.

scia'lare [ʃa'lare] *vi* to throw one's money around.

sci'albo, a ['ʃalbo] *ag* pale, dull; (*fig*) dull, colourless (*Brit*), colorless (*US*).

sci'alle ['ʃalle] *sm* shawl.

sci'alo ['ʃalo] *sm* squandering, waste.

scia'luppa [ʃa'luppa] *sf* (*NAUT*) sloop; (*anche:* ~ **di salvataggio**) lifeboat.

scia'mare [ʃa'mare] *vi* to swarm.

sci'ame ['ʃame] *sm* swarm.

scian'cato, a [ʃan'kato] *ag* lame; (*mobile*) rickety.

sci'are [ʃi'are] *vi* to ski; **andare a** ~ to go skiing.

sci'arpa ['ʃarpa] *sf* scarf; (*fascia*) sash.

scia'tore, 'trice [ʃia'tore] *sm/f* skier.

sciat'tezza [ʃat'tettsa] *sf* slovenliness.

sci'atto, a ['ʃatto] *ag* (*persona: nell'aspetto*) slovenly, unkempt; (: *nel lavoro*) sloppy, careless.

'scibile ['ʃibile] *sm* knowledge.

scien'tifico, a, ci, che [ʃen'tifiko] *ag* scientific; **la (polizia)** ~**a** the forensic department.

sci'enza ['ʃentsa] *sf* science; (*sapere*) knowledge; ~**e** *sfpl* (*INS*) science *sg*; ~**e naturali** natural sciences; ~**e politiche** political science *sg*.

scienzi'ato, a [ʃen'tsjato] *sm/f* scientist.

'Scilly ['ʃilli]: **le isole** ~ *sfpl* the Scilly Isles.

'scimmia ['ʃimmja] *sf* monkey.

scimmiot'tare [ʃimmjot'tare] *vt* to ape, mimic.

scimpanzé [ʃimpan'tse] *sm inv* chimpanzee.

scimu'nito, a [ʃimu'nito] *ag* silly, idiotic.

'scindere ['ʃindere] *vt,* ~**rsi** *vr* to split (up).

scin'tilla [ʃin'tilla] *sf* spark.

scintil'lare [ʃintil'lare] *vi* to spark; (*acqua, occhi*) to sparkle.

scintil'lio [ʃintil'lio] *sm* sparkling.

scioc'care [ʃok'kare] *vt* to shock.

scioc'chezza [ʃok'kettsa] *sf* stupidity *q*;

stupid *o* foolish thing; **dire** ~**e** to talk nonsense.

sci'occo, a, chi, che [ˈʃɔkko] *ag* stupid, foolish.

sci'ogliere [ˈʃɔʎʎere] *vt* (*nodo*) to untie; (*capelli*) to loosen; (*persona, animale*) to untie, release; (*fig: persona*): ~ **da** to release from; (*neve*) to melt; (*nell'acqua: zucchero etc*) to dissolve; (*fig: mistero*) to solve; (*porre fine a: contratto*) to cancel; (: *società, matrimonio*) to dissolve; (: *riunione*) to bring to an end; ~**rsi** *vr* to loosen, come untied; to melt; to dissolve; (*assemblea, corteo, duo*) to break up; ~ **i muscoli** to limber up; ~ **il ghiaccio** (*fig*) to break the ice; ~ **le vele** (*NAUT*) to set sail; ~**rsi dai legami** (*fig*) to free o.s. from all ties.

sci'olgo *etc* [ˈʃɔlgo] *vb vedi* **sciogliere**.

sciol'tezza [ʃolˈtettsa] *sf* agility; suppleness; ease.

sci'olto, a [ˈʃɔlto] *pp di* **sciogliere** ♦ *ag* loose; (*agile*) agile, nimble; (*disinvolto*) free and easy; **essere** ~ **nei movimenti** to be supple; **versi** ~**i** (*POESIA*) blank verse.

sciope'rante [ʃopeˈrante] *sm/f* striker.

sciope'rare [ʃopeˈrare] *vi* to strike, go on strike.

sci'opero [ˈʃɔpero] *sm* strike; **fare** ~ to strike; **entrare in** ~ to go on *o* come out on strike; ~ **bianco** work-to-rule (*Brit*), slowdown (*US*); ~ **della fame** hunger strike; ~ **selvaggio** wildcat strike; ~ **a singhiozzo** on-off strike; ~ **di solidarietà** sympathy strike.

sciori'nare [ʃoriˈnare] *vt* (*ostentare*) to show off, display.

scio'via [ʃioˈvia] *sf* ski lift.

sciovi'nismo [ʃoviˈnizmo] *sm* chauvinism.

sciovi'nista, i, e [ʃoviˈnista] *sm/f* chauvinist.

sci'pito, a [ʃiˈpito] *ag* insipid.

scip'pare [ʃipˈpare] *vt*: ~ **qn** to snatch sb's bag.

scippa'tore [ʃippaˈtore] *sm* bag-snatcher.

'scippo [ˈʃippo] *sm* bag-snatching.

sci'rocco [ʃiˈrɔkko] *sm* sirocco.

sci'roppo [ʃiˈrɔppo] *sm* syrup; ~ **per la tosse** cough syrup, cough mixture.

'scisma, i [ˈʃizma] *sm* (*REL*) schism.

scissi'one [ʃisˈsjone] *sf* (*anche fig*) split, division; (*FISICA*) fission.

'scisso, a [ˈʃisso] *pp di* **scindere**.

sciu'pare [ʃuˈpare] *vt* (*abito, libro, appetito*) to spoil, ruin; (*tempo, denaro*) to waste; ~**rsi** *vr* to get spoilt *o* ruined; (*rovinarsi la salute*) to ruin one's health.

scivo'lare [ʃivoˈlare] *vi* to slide *o* glide along; (*involontariamente*) to slip, slide.

'scivolo [ˈʃivolo] *sm* slide; (*TECN*) chute.

scivo'loso, a [ʃivoˈloso] *ag* slippery.

scle'rosi *sf* sclerosis.

scoc'care *vt* (*freccia*) to shoot ♦ *vi* (*guizzare*) to shoot up; (*battere: ora*) to strike.

scoccherò *etc* [skokkeˈrɔ] *vb vedi* **scoccare**.

scocci'are [skotˈtʃare] *vt* to bother, annoy; ~**rsi** *vr* to be bothered *o* annoyed.

scoccia'tore, 'trice [skotˈtʃaˈtore] *sm/f* nuisance, pest (*fam*).

scoccia'tura [skotˈtʃaˈtura] *sf* nuisance, bore.

sco'della *sf* bowl.

scodinzo'lare [skodintsoˈlare] *vi* to wag its tail.

scogli'era [skoʎˈʎɛra] *sf* reef; (*rupe*) cliff.

'scoglio [ˈskɔʎʎo] *sm* (*al mare*) rock; (*fig: ostacolo*) difficulty, stumbling block.

scogli'oso, a [skoʎˈʎoso] *ag* rocky.

scoi'attolo *sm* squirrel.

scola'pasta *sm inv* colander.

sco'lare *ag*: **età** ~ school age ♦ *vt* to drain ♦ *vi* to drip.

scola'resca *sf* schoolchildren *pl*, pupils *pl*.

sco'laro, a *sm/f* pupil, schoolboy/girl.

sco'lastico, a, ci, che *ag* (*gen*) scholastic; (*libro, anno, divisa*) school *cpd*.

scol'lare *vt* (*staccare*) to unstick; ~**rsi** *vr* to come unstuck.

scol'lato, a *ag* (*vestito*) low-cut, lownecked; (*donna*) wearing a low-cut dress (*o blouse etc*).

scolla'tura *sf* neckline.

'scolo *sm* drainage; (*sbocco*) drain; (*acqua*) waste water; **canale di** ~ drain; **tubo di** ~ drainpipe.

scolo'rire *vt* to fade; to discolour (*Brit*), discolor (*US*) ♦ *vi* (*anche:* ~**rsi**) to fade; to become discolo(u)red; (*impallidire*) to turn pale.

scol'pire *vt* to carve, sculpt.

scombi'nare *vt* to mess up, upset.

scombi'nato, a *ag* confused, muddled.

scombusso'lare *vt* to upset.

scom'messo, a *pp di* **scommettere** ♦ *sf* bet, wager; **fare una** ~**a** to bet.

scom'mettere *vt, vi* to bet.

scomo'dare *vt* to trouble, bother, disturb; (*fig: nome famoso*) to involve, drag in; ~**rsi** *vr* to put o.s. out; ~**rsi a fare** to go to the bother *o* trouble of doing.

scomodità *sf inv* (*di sedia, letto etc*) discomfort; (*di orario, sistemazione etc*) inconvenience.

'scomodo, a *ag* uncomfortable; (*sistemazione, posto*) awkward, inconvenient.

scompagi'nare [skompadʒiˈnare] *vt* to upset, throw into disorder.

scompa'rire *vi* (*sparire*) to disappear, vanish; (*fig*) to be insignificant.

scom'parso, a *pp di* **scomparire** ♦ *sf* disappearance; (*fig: morte*) passing away, death.

scomparti'mento *sm* (*FERR*) compartment; (*sezione*) division.

scom'parto *sm* compartment, division.

scom'penso *sm* imbalance, lack of balance.

scompigli'are [skompiʎ'ʎare] *vt* (*cassetto, capelli*) to mess up, disarrange; (*fig: piani*) to upset.

scom'piglio [skom'piʎʎo] *sm* mess, confusion.

scom'porre *vt* (*parola, numero*) to break up; (*CHIM*) to decompose; **scomporsi** *vr* (*CHIM*) to decompose; (*fig*) to get upset, lose one's composure; **senza scomporsi** unperturbed.

scom'posto, a *pp di* **scomporre** ♦ *ag* (*gesto*) unseemly; (*capelli*) ruffled, dishevelled.

sco'munica, che *sf* excommunication.

scomuni'care *vt* to excommunicate.

sconcer'tante [skontʃer'tante] *ag* disconcerting.

sconcer'tare [skontʃer'tare] *vt* to disconcert, bewilder.

'sconcio, a, ci, ce ['skontʃo] *ag* (*osceno*) indecent, obscene ♦ *sm* (*cosa riprovevole, mal fatta*) disgrace.

sconclusio'nato, a *ag* incoherent, illogical.

sconfes'sare *vt* to renounce, disavow; to repudiate.

scon'figgere [skon'fiddʒere] *vt* to defeat, overcome.

sconfi'nare *vi* to cross the border; (*in proprietà privata*) to trespass; (*fig*): ~ **da** to stray *o* digress from.

sconfi'nato, a *ag* boundless, unlimited.

scon'fitto, a *pp di* **sconfiggere** ♦ *sf* defeat.

sconfor'tante, a *ag* discouraging, disheartening.

sconfor'tare *vt* to discourage, dishearten; ~**rsi** *vr* to become discouraged, become disheartened, lose heart.

scon'forto *sm* despondency.

sconge'lare [skondʒe'lare] *vt* to defrost.

scongiu'rare [skondʒu'rare] *vt* (*implorare*) to beseech, implore; (*eludere: pericolo*) to ward off, avert.

scongi'uro [skon'dʒuro] *sm* (*esorcismo*) exorcism; **fare gli** ~**i** to touch wood (*Brit*), knock on wood (*US*).

scon'nesso, a *ag* (*fig: discorso*) incoherent, rambling.

sconosci'uto, a [skonoʃ'ʃuto] *ag* unknown; new, strange ♦ *sm/f* stranger, unknown person.

sconquas'sare *vt* to shatter, smash.

scon'quasso *sm* (*danno*) damage; (*fig*) confusion.

sconside'rato, a *ag* thoughtless, rash.

sconsigli'are [skonsiʎ'ʎare] *vt*: ~ **qc a qn** to advise sb against sth; ~ **qn dal fare qc** to advise sb not to do *o* against doing sth.

sconso'lato, a *ag* disconsolate.

scon'tare *vt* (*COMM: detrarre*) to deduct; (: *debito*) to pay off; (: *cambiale*) to discount; (*pena*) to serve; (*colpa, errori*) to

pay for, suffer for.

scon'tato, a *ag* (*previsto*) foreseen, taken for granted; (*prezzo, merce*) discounted, at a discount; **dare per** ~ **che** to take it for granted that.

sconten'tare *vt* to displease, dissatisfy.

sconten'tezza [skonten'tettsa] *sf* displeasure, dissatisfaction.

scon'tento, a *ag*: ~ **(di)** discontented *o* dissatisfied (with) ♦ *sm* discontent, dissatisfaction.

'sconto *sm* discount; **fare** *o* **concedere uno** ~ to give a discount; **uno** ~ **del 10%** a 10% discount.

scon'trarsi *vr* (*treni etc*) to crash, collide; (*venire ad uno scontro, fig*) to clash; ~ **con** to crash into, collide with.

scon'trino *sm* ticket.

'scontro *sm* (*MIL, fig*) clash; (*di veicoli*) crash, collision; ~ **a fuoco** shoot-out.

scon'troso, a *ag* sullen, surly; (*permaloso*) touchy.

sconveni'ente *ag* unseemly, improper.

sconvol'gente [skonvol'dʒente] *ag* (*notizia, brutta esperienza*) upsetting, disturbing; (*bellezza*) amazing; (*passione*) overwhelming.

scon'volgere [skon'vɔldʒere] *vt* to throw into confusion, upset; (*turbare*) to shake, disturb, upset.

scon'volto, a *pp di* **sconvolgere** ♦ *ag* (*persona*) distraught, very upset.

'scopa *sf* broom; (*CARTE*) Italian card game.

sco'pare *vt* to sweep; (*fam!*) to screw (!).

scoperchi'are [skoper'kjare] *vt* (*pentola, vaso*) to take the lid off, uncover; (*casa*) to take the roof off.

sco'perto, a *pp di* **scoprire** ♦ *ag* uncovered; (*capo*) uncovered, bare; (*macchina*) open; (*MIL*) exposed, without cover; (*conto*) overdrawn ♦ *sf* discovery ♦ *sm*: **allo** ~ (*dormire etc*) out in the open; **assegno** ~ uncovered cheque; **avere un conto** ~ to be overdrawn.

'scopo *sm* aim, purpose; **a che** ~? what for?; **adatto allo** ~ fit for its purpose; **allo** ~ **di fare qc** in order to do sth; **a** ~ **di lucro** for gain *o* money; **senza** ~ (*fare, cercare*) pointlessly.

scoppi'are *vi* (*spaccarsi*) to burst; (*esplodere*) to explode; (*fig*) to break out; ~ **in pianto** *o* **a piangere** to burst out crying; ~ **dalle risa** *o* **dal ridere** to split one's sides laughing; ~ **dal caldo** to be boiling; ~ **di salute** to be the picture of health.

scoppiet'tare *vi* to crackle.

'scoppio *sm* explosion; (*di tuono, arma etc*) crash, bang; (*di pneumatico*) bang; (*fig: di guerra*) outbreak; **a** ~ **ritardato** delayed-action; **reazione a** ~ **ritardato** delayed *o* slow reaction; **uno** ~ **di risa** a burst of laughter; **uno** ~ **di collera** an explosion of anger.

sco'prire vt to discover; (liberare da ciò che copre) to uncover; (: monumento) to unveil; ~**rsi** vr to put on lighter clothes; (fig) to give o.s. away.

scopri'tore, 'trice sm/f discoverer.

scoraggi'are [skorad'dʒare] vt to discourage; ~**rsi** vr to become discouraged, lose heart.

scor'butico, a, ci, che ag (fig) cantankerous.

scorcia'toia [skortʃa'toja] sf short cut.

'scorcio ['skortʃo] sm (ARTE) foreshortening; (di secolo, periodo) end, close; ~ **panoramico** vista.

scor'dare vt to forget; ~**rsi** vr: ~**rsi di qc/di fare** to forget sth/to do.

sco'reggia [sko'reddʒa] (fam!) sf fart (!).

scoreggi'are [skored'dʒare] (fam!) vi to fart (!).

'scorgere ['skɔrdʒere] vt to make out, distinguish, see.

sco'ria sf (di metalli) slag; (vulcanica) scoria; ~**e radioattive** (FISICA) radioactive waste sg.

'scorno sm ignominy, disgrace.

scorpacci'ata [skorpat'tʃata] sf: **fare una ~ (di)** to stuff o.s. (with), eat one's fill (of).

scorpi'one sm scorpion; (dello zodiaco): **S~** Scorpio; **essere dello S~** to be Scorpio.

scorraz'zare [skorrat'tsare] vi to run about.

'scorrere vt (giornale, lettera) to run o skim through ♦ vi (liquido, fiume) to run, flow; (fune) to run; (cassetto, porta) to slide easily; (tempo) to pass (by).

scorre'ria sf raid, incursion.

scorret'tezza [skorret'tettsa] sf incorrectness; lack of politeness, rudeness; unfairness; **commettere una ~** (essere sleale) to be unfair.

scor'retto, a ag (sbagliato) incorrect; (sgarbato) impolite; (sconveniente) improper; (sleale) unfair; (gioco) foul.

scor'revole ag (porta) sliding; (fig: stile) fluent, flowing.

scorri'banda sf (MIL) raid; (escursione) trip, excursion.

'scorsi etc vb vedi **scorgere**.

'scorso, a pp di **scorrere** ♦ ag last ♦ sf quick look, glance; **lo ~ mese** last month.

scor'soio, a ag: **nodo ~** noose.

'scorta sf (di personalità, convoglio) escort; (provvista) supply, stock; **sotto la ~ di due agenti** escorted by two policemen; **fare ~ di** to stock up with, get in a supply of; **di ~** (materiali) spare; **ruota di ~** spare wheel.

scor'tare vt to escort.

scor'tese ag discourteous, rude.

scorte'sia sf discourtesy, rudeness; (azione) discourtesy.

scorti'care vt to skin.

'scorto, a pp di **scorgere**.

'scorza ['skɔrdza] sf (di albero) bark; (di agrumi) peel, skin.

sco'sceso, a [skoʃ'ʃeso] ag steep.

'scosso, a pp di **scuotere** ♦ ag (turbato) shaken, upset ♦ sf jerk, jolt, shake; (ELETTR, fig) shock; **prendere la ~a** to get an electric shock; ~**a di terremoto** earth tremor.

scos'sone sm: **dare uno ~ a qn** to give sb a shake; **procedere a ~i** to jolt o jerk along.

scos'tante ag (fig) off-putting (Brit), unpleasant.

scos'tare vt to move (away), shift; ~**rsi** vr to move away.

scostu'mato, a ag immoral, dissolute.

scot'tante ag (fig: urgente) pressing; (: delicato) delicate.

scot'tare vt (ustionare) to burn; (: con liquido bollente) to scald ♦ vi to burn; (caffè) to be too hot.

scotta'tura sf burn; scald.

'scotto, a ag overcooked ♦ sm (fig): **pagare lo ~ (di)** to pay the penalty (for).

sco'vare vt to drive out, flush out; (fig) to discover.

'Scozia ['skɔttsja] sf: **la ~** Scotland.

scoz'zese [skot'tsese] ag Scottish ♦ sm/f Scot.

screan'zato, a [skrean'tsato] ag ill-mannered ♦ sm/f boor.

scredi'tare vt to discredit.

scre'mare vt to skim.

scre'mato, a ag skimmed.

screpo'lare vt, ~**rsi** vr to crack.

screpola'tura sf cracking q; crack.

screzi'ato, a [skret'tsjato] ag streaked.

'screzio ['skrettsjo] sm disagreement.

scribac'chino [skribak'kino] sm (peg: impiegato) penpusher; (: scrittore) hack.

scricchio'lare [skrikkjo'lare] vi to creak, squeak.

scricchio'lio [skrikkjo'lio] sm creaking.

'scricciolo ['skrittʃolo] sm wren.

'scrigno ['skriɲɲo] sm casket.

scrimina'tura sf parting.

'scrissi etc vb vedi **scrivere**.

'scritto, a pp di **scrivere** ♦ ag written ♦ sm writing; (lettera) letter, note ♦ sf inscription; ~**i** smpl (letterari etc) work(s), writings; **per o in ~** in writing.

scrit'toio sm writing desk.

scrit'tore, 'trice sm/f writer.

scrit'tura sf writing; (COMM) entry; (contratto) contract; (REL): **la Sacra S~** the Scriptures pl; ~**e** sfpl (COMM) accounts, books.

scrittu'rare vt (TEATRO, CINEMA) to sign up, engage; (COMM) to enter.

scriva'nia sf desk.

scri'vano sm (amanuense) scribe; (impiegato) clerk.

scri'vente sm/f writer.

'scrivere vt to write; **come si scrive?** how is

it spelt?, how do you write it?; ~ **qc a qn**
to write sth to sb; ~ **qc a macchina** to
type sth; ~ **a penna/matita** to write in
pen/pencil; ~ **qc maiuscolo/minuscolo** to
write sth in capital/small letters.

scroc'care *vt* (*fam*) to scrounge, cadge.

scroc'cone, a *sm/f* scrounger.

'**scrofa** *sf* (*ZOOL*) sow.

scrol'lare *vt* to shake; ~**rsi** *vr* (*anche fig*) to
give o.s. a shake; ~ **le spalle/il capo** to
shrug one's shoulders/shake one's head;
~**rsi qc di dosso** (*ache fig*) to shake sth off.

scrol'lata *sf* shake; ~ **di spalle** shrug (of
one's shoulders).

scrosci'ante [skroʃ'ʃante] *ag* (*pioggia*) pouring; (*fig*: *applausi*) thunderous.

scrosci'are [skroʃ'ʃare] *vi* (*pioggia*) to pour
down, pelt down; (*torrente*, *fig*: *applausi*)
to thunder, roar.

'**scroscio** ['skrɔʃʃo] *sm* pelting; thunder,
roar; (*di applausi*) burst.

scros'tare *vt* (*intonaco*) to scrape off, strip;
~**rsi** *vr* to peel off, flake off.

'**scrupolo** *sm* scruple; (*meticolosità*) care,
conscientiousness; **essere senza** ~**i** to be
unscrupulous.

scrupo'loso, a *ag* scrupulous; conscientious.

scru'tare *vt* to scrutinize; (*intenzioni*, *causa*)
to examine, scrutinize.

scruti'nare *vt* (*voti*) to count.

scru'tinio *sm* (*votazione*) ballot; (*insieme
delle operazioni*) poll; (*INS*) (*meeting for*)
*assignment of marks at end of a term or
year*.

scu'cire [sku'tʃire] *vt* (*orlo etc*) to unpick,
undo; ~**rsi** *vr* to come unstitched.

scude'ria *sf* stable.

scu'detto *sm* (*SPORT*) (championship)
shield; (*distintivo*) badge.

scu'discio [sku'diʃʃo] *sm* (*riding*) crop,
(riding) whip.

'**scudo** *sm* shield; **farsi** ~ **di** *o* **con qc** to
shield o.s. with sth; ~ **aereo/missilistico**
air/missile defence (*Brit*) *o* defense (*US*);
~ **termico** heat shield.

sculacci'are [skulat'tʃare] *vt* to spank.

sculacci'one [skulat'tʃone] *sm* spanking.

scul'tore, 'trice *sm/f* sculptor.

scul'tura *sf* sculpture.

scu'ola *sf* school; ~ **elementare** primary
(*Brit*) *o* grade (*US*) school; ~ **guida** driving school; ~ **materna** nursery school; ~
dell'obbligo compulsory education; ~
privata/pubblica private/state school; ~**e
serali** evening classes, night school *sg*; ~
tecnica technical college.

scu'otere *vt* to shake; ~**rsi** *vr* to jump, be
startled; (*fig*: *muoversi*) to rouse o.s., stir
o.s.; (: *turbarsi*) to be shaken.

'**scure** *sf* axe, ax (*US*).

scu'rire *vt* to darken, make darker.

'**scuro, a** *ag* dark; (*fig*: *espressione*) grim ♦
sm darkness; dark colour (*Brit*) *o* color
(*US*); (*imposta*) (window) shutter; **verde/
rosso** *etc* ~ dark green/red *etc*.

scur'rile *ag* scurrilous.

'**scusa** *sf* excuse; ~**e** *sfpl* apology *sg*,
apologies; **chiedere** ~ **a qn (per)** to
apologize to sb (for); **chiedo** ~ I'm sorry;
(*disturbando etc*) excuse me; **vi prego di
accettare le mie** ~**e** please accept my
apologies.

scu'sare *vt* to excuse; ~**rsi** *vr*: ~**rsi (di)** to
apologize (for); (**mi**) **scusi** I'm sorry; (*per
richiamare l'attenzione*) excuse me.

S.C.V. *sigla* = *Stato della Città del Vaticano.*

sdebi'tarsi *vt*: ~**rsi (con qn di** *o* **per qc)** (*anche fig*) to repay (sb for sth).

sde'gnare [zdeɲ'ɲare] *vt* to scorn, despise;
~**rsi** *vr* (*adirarsi*) to get angry.

sde'gnato, a [zdeɲ'ɲato] *ag* indignant, angry.

'**sdegno** ['zdeɲɲo] *sm* scorn, disdain.

sde'gnoso, a [zdeɲ'ɲoso] *ag* scornful, disdainful.

sdilin'quirsi *vr* (*illanguidirsi*) to become
sentimental.

sdoga'nare *vt* (*COMM*) to clear through
customs.

sdolci'nato, a [zdoltʃi'nato] *ag* mawkish,
oversentimental.

sdoppia'mento *sm* (*CHIM*: *di composto*)
splitting; (*PSIC*): ~ **della personalità** split
personality.

sdoppi'are *vt* (*dividere*) to divide *o* split in
two.

sdrai'arsi *vr* to stretch out, lie down.

'**sdraio** *sm*: **sedia a** ~ deck chair.

sdrammatiz'zare [zdrammatid'dzare] *vt* to
play down, minimize.

sdruccio'lare [zdruttʃo'lare] *vi* to slip, slide.

sdruccio'levole [zdruttʃo'levole] *ag* slippery.

sdru'cito, a [zdru'tʃito] *ag* (*strappato*) torn;
(*logoro*) threadbare.

se *pronome vedi* **si** ♦ *cong* if; (*in frasi
interrogative indirette*) if, whether; **non so**
~ **scrivere o telefonare** I don't known
whether *o* if I should write or phone; ~
mai if, if ever; (*caso mai*) in case; ~ **solo**
o **solamente** if only; ~ **fossi in te** if I were
you; ~ **no** otherwise, or else; ~ **non** (*anzi*)
if not; (*tranne*) except; **come** ~ as if.

S.E. *abbr* (= *sud-est*) SE; (= *Sua Eccellenza*)
HE.

sé *pronome* (*gen*) oneself; (*esso, essa, lui, lei,
loro*) itself; himself; herself; themselves; ~
stesso(a) *pronome* oneself; itself;
himself; herself; ~ **stessi(e)** *pronome pl*
themselves; **di per** ~ **non è un problema**
it's no problem in itself; **parlare tra** ~ **e** ~
to talk to oneself; **va da** ~ **che** ... it goes
without saying that ..., it's obvious that

..., it stands to reason that ...; **è un caso a ~ o a ~ stante** it's a special case.

seb'bene *cong* although, though.

'sebo *sm* sebum.

sec. *abbr* (= *secolo*) c.

'secca *sf vedi* **secco**.

sec'care *vt* to dry; (*prosciugare*) to dry up; (*fig: importunare*) to annoy, bother ♦ *vi* to dry; to dry up; **~rsi** *vr* to dry; to dry up; (*fig*) to grow annoyed; **si è seccato molto** he was very annoyed.

sec'cato, a *ag* (*fig: infastidito*) bothered, annoyed; (: *stufo*) fed up.

secca'tore, 'trice *sm/f* nuisance, bother.

secca'tura *sf* (*fig*) bother *q*, trouble *q*.

seccherò *etc* [sekke'rɔ] *vb vedi* **seccare**.

'secchia ['sekkja] *sf* bucket, pail.

secchi'ello [sek'kjɛllo] *sm* (*per bambini*) pail, bucket.

'secchio ['sekkjo] *sm* bucket, pail; **~ della spazzatura** *o* **delle immondizie** dustbin (*Brit*), garbage can (*US*).

'secco, a, chi, che *ag* dry; (*fichi, pesce*) dried; (*foglie, ramo*) withered; (*magro: persona*) thin, skinny; (*fig: risposta, modo di fare*) curt, abrupt; (: *colpo*) clean, sharp ♦ *sm* (*siccità*) drought ♦ *sf* (*del mare*) shallows *pl*; **restarci ~** (*fig: morire sul colpo*) to drop dead; **avere la gola ~a** to feel dry, be parched; **lavare a ~** to dry-clean; **tirare a ~** (*barca*) to beach.

secen'tesco, a, schi, sche [setʃen'tesko] *ag* = **seicentesco**.

se'cernere [se'tʃɛrnere] *vt* to secrete.

seco'lare *ag* age-old, centuries-old; (*laico, mondano*) secular.

'secolo *sm* century; (*epoca*) age.

se'conda *sf vedi* **secondo**.

secondaria'mente *av* secondly.

secon'dario, a *ag* secondary; **scuola/istruzione ~a** secondary school/education.

secon'dino *sm* prison officer, warder (*Brit*).

se'condo, a *ag* second ♦ *sm* second; (*di pranzo*) main course ♦ *sf* (*AUT*) second (gear); (*FERR*) second class ♦ *prep* according to; (*nel modo prescritto*) in accordance with; **~ me** in my opinion, to my mind; **~ la legge/quanto si era deciso** in accordance with the law/the decision taken; **di ~a classe** second-class; **di ~a mano** second-hand; **viaggiare in ~a** to travel second-class; **comandante** *m* **in ~a** second-in-command; **a ~a di** *prep* according to; in accordance with.

secondo'genito, a [sekondo'dʒɛnito] *sm/f* second-born.

secrezi'one [sekret'tsjone] *sf* secretion.

'sedano *sm* celery.

se'dare *vt* (*dolore*) to soothe; (*rivolta*) to put down, suppress.

seda'tivo, a *ag*, *sm* sedative.

'sede *sf* (*luogo di residenza*) (place of) residence; (*di ditta: principale*) head office; (: *secondaria*) branch (office); (*di organizzazione*) headquarters *pl*; (*di governo, parlamento*) seat; (*REL*) see; **in ~ di** (*in occasione di*) during; **in altra ~** on another occasion; **in ~ legislativa** in legislative sitting; **prendere ~** to take up residence; **un'azienda con diverse ~i in città** a firm with several branches in the city; **~ centrale** head office; **~ sociale** registered office.

seden'tario, a *ag* sedentary.

se'dere *vi* to sit, be seated; **~rsi** *vr* to sit down ♦ *sm* (*deretano*) bottom; **posto a ~** seat.

'sedia *sf* chair; **~ elettrica** electric chair; **~ a rotelle** wheelchair.

sedi'cenne [sedi'tʃɛnne] *ag*, *sm/f* sixteen-year-old.

sedi'cente [sedi'tʃɛnte] *ag* self-styled.

sedi'cesimo, a [sedi'tʃɛzimo] *num* sixteenth.

'sedici ['seditʃi] *num* sixteen.

se'dile *sm* seat; (*panchina*) bench.

sedi'mento *sm* sediment.

sedizi'one [sedit'tsjone] *sf* revolt, rebellion.

sedizi'oso, a [sedit'tsjoso] *ag* seditious.

se'dotto, a *pp di* **sedurre**.

sedu'cente [sedu'tʃɛnte] *ag* seductive; (*proposta*) very attractive.

se'durre *vt* to seduce.

se'duta *sf* session, sitting; (*riunione*) meeting; **essere in ~** to be in session, be sitting; **~ stante** (*fig*) immediately; **~ spiritica** seance.

sedut'tore, 'trice *sm/f* seducer/seductress.

seduzi'one [sedut'tsjone] *sf* seduction; (*fascino*) charm, appeal.

SEeO *abbr* (= *salvo errori e omissioni*) E and OE.

'sega, ghe *sf* saw; **~ circolare** circular saw; **~ a mano** handsaw.

'segale *sf* rye.

se'gare *vt* to saw; (*recidere*) to saw off.

sega'tura *sf* (*residuo*) sawdust.

'seggio ['sɛddʒo] *sm* seat; **~ elettorale** polling station.

'seggiola ['sɛddʒola] *sf* chair.

seggio'lino [seddʒo'lino] *sm* seat; (*per bambini*) child's chair; **~ di sicurezza** (*AUT*) child safety seat.

seggio'lone [seddʒo'lone] *sm* (*per bambini*) highchair.

seggio'via [seddʒo'via] *sf* chairlift.

seghe'ria [sege'ria] *sf* sawmill.

segherò *etc* [sege'rɔ] *vb vedi* **segare**.

seghet'tato, a [seget'tato] *ag* serrated.

se'ghetto [se'getto] *sm* hacksaw.

seg'mento *sm* segment.

segna'lare [seɲɲa'lare] *vt* (*essere segno di*) to indicate, be a sign of; (*avvertire*) to signal; (*menzionare*) to indicate; (: *fatto,* *risultato, aumento*) to report; (: *errore, dettaglio*) to point out; (*AUT*) to signal, indicate; ~**rsi** *vr* (*distinguersi*) to distinguish o.s.; ~ **qn a qn** (*per lavoro etc*) to bring sb to sb's attention.

segnalazi'one [seɲɲalat'tsjone] *sf* (*azione*) signalling; (*segnale*) signal; (*annuncio*) report; (*raccomandazione*) recommendation.

se'gnale [seɲ'ɲale] *sm* signal; (*cartello*): ~ **stradale** road sign; ~ **acustico** acoustic *o* sound signal; ~ **d'allarme** alarm; (*FERR*) communication cord; ~ **di linea libera** (*TEL*) dialling (*Brit*) *o* dial (*US*) tone; ~ **luminoso** light signal; ~ **di occupato** (*TEL*) engaged tone (*Brit*), busy signal (*US*); ~ **orario** (*RADIO*) time signal.

segna'letica [seɲɲa'lɛtika] *sf* signalling, signposting; ~ **stradale** road signs *pl*.

segna'libro [seɲɲa'libro] *sm* bookmark(er).

segna'punti [seɲɲa'punti] *sm/f inv* scorer, scorekeeper.

se'gnare [seɲ'ɲare] *vt* to mark; (*prendere nota*) to note; (*indicare*) to indicate, mark; (*SPORT: goal*) to score; ~**rsi** *vr* (*REL*) to make the sign of the cross, cross o.s.

'segno ['seɲɲo] *sm* sign; (*impronta, contrassegno*) mark; (*bersaglio*) target; **fare ~ di si/no** to nod (one's head)/shake one's head; **fare ~ a qn di fermarsi** to motion (to) sb to stop; **cogliere** *o* **colpire nel ~** (*fig*) to hit the mark; **in** *o* **come ~ d'amicizia** as a mark *o* token of friendship; **"~i particolari"** (*su documento etc*) "distinguishing marks".

segre'gare *vt* to segregate, isolate.

segregazi'one [segregat'tsjone] *sf* segregation.

se'greta *sf vedi* **segreto**.

segre'tario, a *sm/f* secretary; ~ **comunale** town clerk; ~ **del partito** party leader; ~ **di Stato** Secretary of State.

segrete'ria *sf* (*di ditta, scuola*) (secretary's) office; (*d'organizzazione internazionale*) secretariat; (*POL etc: carica*) office of Secretary; ~ **telefonica** answering service.

segre'tezza [segre'tettsa] *sf* secrecy; **notizie della massima ~** confidential information; **in tutta ~** in secret; (*confidenzialmente*) in confidence.

se'greto, a *ag* secret ♦ *sm* secret ♦ *sf* dungeon; **in ~** in secret, secretly; **il ~ professionale** professional secrecy; **un ~ professionale** a professional secret.

segu'ace [se'gwatʃe] *sm/f* follower, disciple.

segu'ente *ag* following, next; **nel modo ~** as follows, in the following way.

se'gugio [se'gudʒo] *sm* hound, hunting dog; (*fig*) private eye, sleuth.

segu'ire *vt* to follow; (*frequentare: corso*) to attend ♦ *vi* to follow; (*continuare: testo*) to continue; ~ **i consigli di qn** to follow *o* to

take sb's advice; ~ **gli avvenimenti di attualità** to follow *o* keep up with current events; **come segue** as follows; **"segue"** "to be continued".

segui'tare *vt* to continue, carry on with ♦ *vi* to continue, carry on.

'seguito *sm* (*scorta*) suite, retinue; (*discepoli*) followers *pl*; (*serie*) sequence, series *sg*; (*continuazione*) continuation; (*conseguenza*) result; **di ~** at a stretch, on end; **in ~** later on; **in ~ a, a ~ di** following; (*a causa di*) as a result of, owing to; **essere al ~ di qn** to be among sb's suite, be one of sb's retinue; **non aver ~** (*conseguenze*) to have no repercussions; **facciamo ~ alla lettera del ...** further to *o* in answer to your letter of ....

'sei *vb vedi* **essere** ♦ *num* six.

Sei'celle [sei'tʃelle] *sfpl*: **le ~** the Seychelles.

seicen'tesco, a, schi, sche [seitʃen'tesko] *ag* seventeenth-century.

sei'cento [sei'tʃento] *num* six hundred ♦ *sm*: **il S~** the seventeenth century.

sei'mila *num* six thousand.

'selce ['seltʃe] *sf* flint, flintstone.

selci'ato [sel'tʃato] *sm* cobbled surface.

selet'tivo, a *ag* selective.

selet'tore *sm* (*TECN*) selector.

selezio'nare [selettsjo'nare] *vt* to select.

selezi'one [selet'tsjone] *sf* selection; **fare una ~** to make a selection *o* choice.

'sella *sf* saddle.

sel'lare *vt* to saddle.

sel'lino *sm* saddle.

seltz *sm inv* soda (water).

'selva *sf* (*bosco*) wood; (*foresta*) forest.

selvag'gina [selvad'dʒina] *sf* (*animali*) game.

sel'vaggio, a, gi, ge [sel'vaddʒo] *ag* wild; (*tribù*) savage, uncivilized; (*fig*) savage, brutal ♦ *sm/f* savage.

sel'vatico, a, ci, che *ag* wild.

S.Em. *abbr* (= *Sua Eminenza*) HE.

se'maforo *sm* (*AUT*) traffic lights *pl*.

sembi'anza [sem'bjantsa] *sf* (*poetico: aspetto*) appearance; ~**e** *pl* (*lineamenti*) features; (*fig: falsa apparenza*) semblance.

sem'brare *vi* to seem ♦ *vb impers*: **sembra che** it seems that; **mi sembra che** it seems to me that; (*penso che*) I think (that); ~ **di essere** to seem to be; **non mi sembra vero!** I can't believe it!

'seme *sm* seed; (*sperma*) semen; (*CARTE*) suit.

se'mente *sf* seed.

semes'trale *ag* (*che dura 6 mesi*) six-month *cpd*; (*che avviene ogni 6 mesi*) six-monthly.

se'mestre *sm* half-year, six-month period.

'semi... *prefisso* semi....

semi'cerchio [semi'tʃerkjo] *sm* semicircle.

semicondut'tore *sm* semiconductor.

semidetenzi'one [semideten'tsjone] *sf* custodial sentence whereby individual must *spend a minimum of 10 hours per day in prison.*

semifi'nale *sf* semifinal.

semi'freddo, a *ag* (*CUC*) chilled ♦ *sm* ice-cream cake.

semilibertà *sf custodial sentence which allows prisoner to study or work outside prison for part of the day.*

'semina *sf* (*AGR*) sowing.

semi'nare *vt* to sow.

semi'nario *sm* seminar; (*REL*) seminary.

semi'nato *sm*: **uscire dal** ~ (*fig*) to wander off the point.

seminter'rato *sm* basement; (*appartamento*) basement flat (*Brit*) *o* apartment (*US*).

semi'ologo, a, gi, ghe *sm/f* semiologist.

se'mitico, a, ci, che *ag* semitic.

sem'mai = **se mai.**

'semola *sf* bran; ~ **di grano duro** durum wheat.

semo'lato *ag*: **zucchero** ~ caster sugar.

semo'lino *sm* semolina.

'semplice ['semplitʃe] *ag* simple; (*di un solo elemento*) single; **è una** ~ **formalità** it's a mere formality.

semplice'mente [semplitʃe'mente] *av* simply.

sempli'cistico, a, ci, che [sempli'tʃistiko] *ag* simplistic.

semplicità [semplitʃi'ta] *sf* simplicity.

semplifi'care *vt* to simplify.

semplificazi'one [semplifikat'tsjone] *sf* simplification; **fare una** ~ **di** to simplify.

'sempre *av* always; (*ancora*) still; **posso** ~ **tentare** I can always *o* still try; **da** ~ always; **per** ~ forever; **una volta per** ~ once and for all; ~ **che** *cong* provided (that); ~ **più** more and more; ~ **meno** less and less; **va** ~ **meglio** things are getting better and better; **è** ~ **meglio che niente** it's better than nothing; **è (pur)** ~ **tuo fratello** he is still your brother (however); **c'è** ~ **la possibilità che** ... there's still a chance that ..., there's always the possibility that ....

sempre'verde *ag, sm o f* (*BOT*) evergreen.

Sen. *abbr* (= *senatore*) Sen.

'senape *sf* (*CUC*) mustard.

se'nato *sm* senate.

sena'tore, 'trice *sm/f* senator.

'Senegal *sm*: **il** ~ Senegal.

senega'lese *ag, sm/f* Senegalese *inv*.

se'nese *ag* of (*o* from) Siena.

se'nile *ag* of senile.

'Senna *sf*: **la** ~ the Seine.

'senno *sm* judgment, (common) sense; **col** ~ **di poi** with hindsight.

sennò *av* = **se no.**

'seno *sm* (*ANAT*: *petto, mammella*) breast; (: *grembo, fig*) womb; (: *cavità*) sinus; (*GEO*) inlet, creek; (*MAT*) sine; **in** ~ **al partito/all'organizzazione** within the party/

the organization.

sen'sale *sm* (*COMM*) agent.

sensa'tezza [sensa'tettsa] *sf* good sense, good judgment.

sen'sato, a *ag* sensible.

sensazio'nale [sensattsjo'nale] *ag* sensational.

sensazi'one [sensat'tsjone] *sf* feeling, sensation; **fare** ~ to cause a sensation, create a stir; **avere la** ~ **che** to have a feeling that.

sen'sibile *ag* sensitive; (*ai sensi*) perceptible; (*rilevante, notevole*) appreciable, noticeable; ~ **a** sensitive to.

sensibilità *sf* sensitivity.

sensibiliz'zare [sensibilid'dzare] *vt* (*fig*) to make aware, awaken.

'senso *sm* (*FISIOL, istinto*) sense; (*impressione, sensazione*) feeling, sensation; (*significato*) meaning, sense; (*direzione*) direction; ~**i** *smpl* (*coscienza*) consciousness *sg*; (*sensualità*) senses; **perdere/riprendere i** ~**i** to lose/regain consciousness; **avere** ~ **pratico** to be practical; **avere un sesto** ~ to have a sixth sense; **fare** ~ **a** (*ripugnare*) to disgust, repel; **ciò non ha** ~ **that** doesn't make sense; **senza** *o* **privo di** ~ meaningless; **nel** ~ **che** in the sense that; **nel vero** ~ **della parola** in the true sense of the word; **nel** ~ **della lunghezza** lengthwise, lengthways; **nel** ~ **della larghezza** widthwise; **ho dato disposizioni in quel** ~ I've given instructions to that end *o* effect; ~ **comune** common sense; ~ **del dovere** sense of duty; **in** ~ **opposto** in the opposite direction; **in** ~ **orario/antiorario** clockwise/anticlockwise; ~ **dell'umorismo** sense of humour; **a** ~ **unico** one-way; "~ **vietato**" (*AUT*) "no entry".

sensu'ale *ag* sensual; sensuous.

sensualità *sf* sensuality; sensuousness.

sen'tenza [sen'tentsa] *sf* (*DIR*) sentence; (*massima*) maxim.

sentenzi'are [senten'tsjare] *vi* (*DIR*) to pass judgment.

senti'ero *sm* path.

sentimen'tale *ag* sentimental; (*vita, avventura*) love *cpd*.

senti'mento *sm* feeling.

senti'nella *sf* sentry.

sen'tire *vt* (*percepire al tatto, fig*) to feel; (*udire*) to hear; (*ascoltare*) to listen to; (*odore*) to smell; (*avvertire con il gusto, assaggiare*) to taste ♦ *vi*: ~ **di** (*avere sapore*) to taste of; (*avere odore*) to smell of; ~**rsi** *vr* (*uso reciproco*) to be in touch; ~**rsi bene/male** to feel well/unwell *o* ill; ~**rsi di fare qc** (*essere disposto*) to feel like doing sth; ~ **la mancanza di qn** to miss sb; **ho sentito dire che** ... I have heard that ...; **a** ~ **lui** ... to hear him talk ...; **fatti** ~ keep in touch; **intendo** ~ **il mio legale/il parere di un medico** I'm going to consult my lawyer/a doctor.

sentita'mente *av* sincerely; **ringraziare** ~ to thank sincerely.

sen'tito, a *ag* (*sincero*) sincere, warm; **per** ~ **dire** by hearsay.

sen'tore *sm* rumour (*Brit*), rumor (*US*), talk; **aver** ~ **di qc** to hear about sth.

'senza ['sɛntsa] *prep, cong* without; ~ **dir nulla** without saying a word; ~ **dire che ...** not to mention the fact that ...; ~ **contare che ...** without considering that ...; **fare** ~ **qc** to do without sth; ~ **di me** without me; ~ **che io lo sapessi** without me *o* my knowing; ~ **amici** friendless; **senz'altro** of course, certainly; ~ **dubbio** no doubt; ~ **scrupoli** unscrupulous.

senza'tetto [sɛntsa'tɛtto] *sm/f inv* homeless person; **i** ~ the homeless.

sepa'rare *vt* to separate; (*dividere*) to divide; (*tenere distinto*) to distinguish; ~**rsi** *vr* (*coniugi*) to separate, part; (*amici*) to part; ~**rsi da** (*coniuge*) to separate *o* part from; (*amico, socio*) to part company with; (*oggetto*) to part with.

separata'mente *av* separately.

sepa'rato, a *ag* (*letti, conto etc*) separate; (*coniugi*) separated.

separazi'one [separat'tsjone] *sf* separation; ~ **dei beni** division of property.

séparé [sepa're] *sm inv* screen.

se'polcro *sm* sepulchre (*Brit*), sepulcher (*US*).

se'polto, a *pp di* **seppellire**.

sepol'tura *sf* burial; **dare** ~ **a qn** to bury sb.

seppel'lire *vt* to bury.

'seppi *etc vb vedi* **sapere**.

'seppia *sf* cuttlefish ♦ *ag inv* sepia.

sep'pure *cong* even if.

se'quela *sf* (*di avvenimenti*) series, sequence; (*di offese, ingiurie*) string.

se'quenza [se'kwɛntsa] *sf* sequence.

sequenzi'ale [sekwen'tsjale] *ag* sequential.

seques'trare *vt* (*DIR*) to impound; (*rapire*) to kidnap; (*costringere in un luogo*) to keep, confine.

se'questro *sm* (*DIR*) impoundment; ~ **di persona** kidnapping.

se'quoia *sf* sequoia.

'sera *sf* evening; **di** ~ in the evening; **domani** ~ tomorrow evening, tomorrow night; **questa** ~ this evening, tonight.

se'rale *ag* evening *cpd*; **scuola** ~ evening classes *pl*, night school.

se'rata *sf* evening; (*ricevimento*) party.

ser'bare *vt* to keep; (*mettere da parte*) to put aside; ~ **rancore/odio verso qn** to bear sb a grudge/hate sb.

serba'toio *sm* tank; (*cisterna*) cistern.

'serbo *ag* Serbian ♦ *sm/f* Serbian, Serb ♦ *sm* (*LING*) Serbian; (*il serbare*): **mettere/ tenere** *o* **avere in** ~ **qc** to put/keep sth aside.

serbocro'ato, a *ag, sm* Serbo-Croat.

sere'nata *sf* (*MUS*) serenade.

serenità *sf* serenity.

se'reno, a *ag* (*tempo, cielo*) clear; (*fig*) serene, calm ♦ *sm* (*tempo*) good weather; **un fulmine a ciel** ~ (*fig*) a bolt from the blue.

serg. *abbr* (= *sergente*) Sgt.

ser'gente [ser'dʒɛnte] *sm* (*MIL*) sergeant.

'serie *sf inv* (*successione*) series *inv*; (*gruppo, collezione*: *di chiavi etc*) set; (*SPORT*) division; league; (*COMM*): **modello di** ~**/fuori** ~ standard/custom-built model; **in** ~ in quick succession; (*COMM*) mass *cpd*; **tutta una** ~ **di problemi** a whole string *o* series of problems.

serietà *sf* seriousness; reliability.

'serio, a *ag* serious; (*impiegato*) responsible, reliable; (*ditta, cliente*) reliable, dependable; **sul** ~ (*davvero*) really, truly; (*seriamente*) seriously, in earnest; **dico sul** ~ I'm serious; **faccio sul** ~ I mean it; **prendere qc/qn sul** ~ to take sth/sb seriously.

ser'mone *sm* sermon.

'serpe *sf* snake; (*fig peg*) viper.

serpeggi'are [serped'dʒare] *vi* to wind; (*fig*) to spread.

ser'pente *sm* snake; ~ **a sonagli** rattlesnake.

'serra *sf* greenhouse; hothouse; (*GEO*) sierra.

serra'manico *sm*: **coltello a** ~ jack-knife.

ser'randa *sf* roller shutter.

ser'rare *vt* to close, shut; (*a chiave*) to lock; (*stringere*) to tighten; (*premere: nemico*) to close in on; ~ **i pugni/i denti** to clench one's fists/teeth; ~ **le file** to close ranks.

ser'rata *sf* (*INDUSTRIA*) lockout.

ser'rato, a *ag* (*veloce*): **a ritmo** ~ quickly, fast.

serra'tura *sf* lock.

'serva *sf vedi* **servo**.

ser'vigio [ser'vidʒo] *sm* favour (*Brit*), favor (*US*), service.

ser'vire *vt* to serve; (*clienti: al ristorante*) to wait on; (*: al negozio*) to serve, attend to; (*fig: giovare*) to aid, help; (*CARTE*) to deal ♦ *vi* (*TENNIS*) to serve; (*essere utile*): ~ **a qn** to be of use to sb; ~ **a qc/a fare** (*utensile etc*) to be used for sth/for doing; ~ **(a qn) da** to serve as (for sb); ~**rsi** *vr* (*usare*): ~**rsi di** to use; (*prendere: cibo*): ~**rsi (di)** to help o.s. (to); (*essere cliente abituale*): ~**rsi da** to be a regular customer at, go to; **non mi serve più** I don't need it any more; **non serve che lei vada** you don't need to go.

servitù *sf* servitude; slavery; (*personale di servizio*) servants *pl*, domestic staff.

servizi'evole [servit'tsjevole] *ag* obliging, willing to help.

ser'vizio [ser'vittsjo] *sm* service; (*al risto-rante*: *sul conto*) service (charge); (*STAMPA, TV, RADIO*) report; (*da tè, caffè etc*) set, service; ~**i** *smpl* (*di casa*) kitchen and bathroom; (*ECON*) services; **essere di** ~ to be on duty; **fuori** ~ (*telefono etc*) out of order; ~ **compreso/escluso** service included/not included; **entrata di** ~ service *o* tradesman's (*Brit*) entrance; **casa con doppi** ~**i** house with two bathrooms; ~ **assistenza clienti** after-sales service; ~ **in diretta** (*TV, RADIO*) live coverage; ~ **foto-grafico** (*STAMPA*) photo feature; ~ **militare** military service; ~ **d'ordine** (*POLIZIA*) police patrol; (*di manifestanti*) team of stewards (*responsible for crowd control*); ~**i segreti** secret service *sg;* ~**i di sicurezza** security forces.

'servo, a *sm/f* servant.

servo'freno *sm* (*AUT*) servo brake.

servos'terzo [servos'tɛrtso] *sm* (*AUT*) power steering.

'sesamo *sm* (*BOT*) sesame.

ses'santa *num* sixty.

sessan'tenne *ag, sm/f* sixty-year-old.

sessan'tesimo, a *num* sixtieth.

sessan'tina *sf*: **una** ~ (**di**) about sixty.

sessi'one *sf* session.

'sesso *sm* sex; **il** ~ **debole/forte** the weaker/stronger sex.

sessu'ale *ag* sexual, sex *cpd*.

sessualità *sf* sexuality.

sessu'ologo, a, gi, ghe *sm/f* sexologist, sex specialist.

ses'tante *sm* sextant.

'sesto, a *num* sixth ♦ *sm*: **rimettere in** ~ (*aggiustare*) to put back in order; (*fig: persona*) to put back on his (*o* her) feet; **rimettersi in** ~ (*riprendersi*) to recover, get well; (*riassettarsi*) to tidy o.s. up.

'seta *sf* silk.

setacci'are [setat'tʃare] *vt* (*farina etc*) to sift, sieve; (*fig: zona*) to search, comb.

se'taccio [se'tattʃo] *sm* sieve; **passare al** ~ (*fig*) to search, comb.

'sete *sf* thirst; **avere** ~ to be thirsty; ~ **di potere** thirst for power.

seti'ficio [seti'fitʃo] *sm* silk factory.

'setola *sf* bristle.

sett. *abbr* (= *settembre*) Sept.

'setta *sf* sect.

set'tanta *num* seventy.

settan'tenne *ag, sm/f* seventy-year-old.

settan'tesimo, a *num* seventieth.

settan'tina *sf*: **una** ~ (**di**) about seventy.

'sette *num* seven.

settecen'tesco, a, schi, sche [settetʃen'tesko] *ag* eighteenth-century.

sette'cento [sette'tʃɛnto] *num* seven hundred ♦ *sm*: **il S**~ the eighteenth century.

set'tembre *sm* September; *per fraseologia vedi* **luglio**.

sette'mila *num* seven thousand.

settentrio'nale *ag* northern ♦ *sm/f* north-erner.

settentri'one *sm* north.

'settico, a, ci, che *ag* (*MED*) septic.

setti'mana *sf* week; **la** ~ **scorsa/prossima** last/next week; **a metà** ~ in the middle of the week.

settima'nale *ag, sm* weekly.

'settimo, a *num* seventh.

set'tore *sm* sector; ~ **privato/pubblico** private/public sector; ~ **terziario** service industries *pl*.

Se'ul *sf* Seoul.

severità *sf* severity.

se'vero, a *ag* severe.

sevizi'are [sevit'tsjare] *vt* to torture.

se'vizie [se'vittsje] *sfpl* torture *sg*.

sez. *abbr* = **sezione**.

sezio'nare [settsjo'nare] *vt* to divide into sec-tions; (*MED*) to dissect.

sezi'one [set'tsjone] *sf* section; (*MED*) dissec-tion.

sfaccen'dato, a [sfattʃen'dato] *ag* idle.

sfaccetta'tura [sfattʃetta'tura] *sf* (*azione*) faceting; (*parte sfaccettata, fig*) facet.

sfacchi'nare [sfakki'nare] *vi* (*fam*) to toil, drudge.

sfacchi'nata [sfakki'nata] *sf* (*fam*) chore, drudgery *q*.

sfaccia'taggine [sfattʃa'taddʒine] *sf* in-solence, cheek.

sfacci'ato, a [sfat'tʃato] *ag* (*maleducato*) cheeky, impudent; (*vistoso*) gaudy.

sfa'celo [sfa'tʃɛlo] *sm* (*fig*) ruin, collapse.

sfal'darsi *vr* to flake (off).

sfal'sare *vt* to offset.

sfa'mare *vt* (*nutrire*) to feed; (*soddisfare la fame*): ~ **qn** to satisfy sb's hunger; ~**rsi** *vr* to satisfy one's hunger, fill o.s. up.

sfarfal'lio *sm* (*CINEMA, TV*) flickering.

'sfarzo ['sfartso] *sm* pomp, splendour (*Brit*), splendor (*US*).

sfar'zoso, a [sfar'tsoso] *ag* splendid, magnificent.

sfasa'mento *sm* (*ELETTR*) phase displace-ment; (*fig*) confusion, bewilderment.

sfa'sato, a *ag* (*ELETTR, motore*) out of phase; (*fig: persona*) confused, bewildered.

sfasci'are [sfaʃ'ʃare] *vt* (*ferita*) to unband-age; (*distruggere: porta*) to smash, shatter; ~**rsi** *vr* (*rompersi*) to smash, shatter.

sfa'tare *vt* (*leggenda*) to explode.

sfati'cato, a *sm/f* idler, loafer.

'sfatto, a *ag* (*letto*) unmade; (*orlo etc*) un-done; (*gelato, neve*) melted; (*frutta*) over-ripe; (*riso, pasta etc*) overdone, over-cooked; (*fam: persona, corpo*) flabby.

sfavil'lare *vi* to spark, send out sparks; (*risplendere*) to sparkle.

sfa'vore sm disfavour (Brit), disfavor (US), disapproval.

sfavo'revole ag unfavourable (Brit), unfavorable (US).

sfega'tato, a ag fanatical.

'sfera sf sphere.

'sferico, a, ci, che ag spherical.

sfer'rare vt (fig: colpo) to land, deal; (: attacco) to launch.

sfer'zante [sfer'tsante] ag (critiche, parole) stinging.

sfer'zare [sfer'tsare] vt to whip; (fig) to lash out at.

sfian'care vt to wear out, exhaust; ~rsi vr to exhaust o.s., wear o.s. out.

sfia'tare vi to allow air (o gas etc) to escape.

sfiata'toio sm blowhole; (TECN) vent.

sfi'brante ag exhausting, energy-sapping.

sfi'brare vt (indebolire) to exhaust, enervate.

sfi'brato, a ag exhausted, worn out.

'sfida sf challenge.

sfi'dante ag challenging ♦ sm/f challenger.

sfi'dare vt to challenge; (fig) to defy, brave; ~ qn a fare qc to challenge sb to do sth; ~ un pericolo to brave a danger; sfido che ... I dare say (that) ....

sfi'ducia [sfi'dutʃa] sf distrust, mistrust; avere ~ in qn/qc to distrust sb/sth.

sfigu'rare vt (persona) to disfigure; (quadro, statua) to deface ♦ vi (far cattiva figura) to make a bad impression.

sfilacci'are [sfilat'tʃare] vt, vi, ~rsi vr to fray.

sfi'lare vt (ago) to unthread; (abito, scarpe) to slip off ♦ vi (truppe) to march past, parade; (manifestanti) to march; ~rsi vr (perle etc) to come unstrung; (orlo, tessuto) to fray; (calza) to run, ladder.

sfi'lata sf (MIL) parade; (di manifestanti) march; ~ di moda fashion show.

'sfilza ['sfiltsa] sf (di case) row; (di errori) series inv.

'sfinge ['sfindʒe] sf sphinx.

sfini'mento sm exhaustion.

sfi'nito, a ag exhausted.

sfio'rare vt to brush (against); (argomento) to touch upon; ~ la velocità di 150 km/h to touch 150 km/h.

sfio'rire vi to wither, fade.

'sfitto, a ag vacant, empty.

sfo'cato, a ag (FOT) out of focus.

sfoci'are [sfo'tʃare] vi: ~ in to flow into; (fig: malcontento) to develop into.

sfode'rato, a ag (vestito) unlined.

sfo'gare vt to vent, pour out; ~rsi vr (sfogare la propria rabbia) to give vent to one's anger; (confidarsi): ~rsi (con) to pour out one's feelings (to); non sfogarti su di me! don't take your bad temper out on me!

sfoggi'are [sfod'dʒare] vt, vi to show off.

'sfoggio ['sfɔddʒo] sm show, display; fare ~ di to show off, display.

sfogherò etc [sfoge'rɔ] vb vedi sfogare.

'sfoglia ['sfɔʎʎa] sf sheet of pasta dough; pasta ~ (CUC) puff pastry.

sfogli'are [sfoʎ'ʎare] vt (libro) to leaf through.

'sfogo, ghi sm outlet; (eruzione cutanea) rash; (fig) outburst; dare ~ a (fig) to give vent to.

sfolgo'rante ag (luce) blazing; (fig: vittoria) brilliant.

sfolgo'rare vi to blaze.

sfolla'gente [sfolla'dʒente] sm inv truncheon (Brit), billy (US).

sfol'lare vt to empty, clear ♦ vi to disperse; ~ da (città) to evacuate.

sfol'lato, a ag evacuated ♦ sm/f evacuee.

sfol'tire vt, ~rsi vr to thin (out).

sfon'dare vt (porta) to break down; (scarpe) to wear a hole in; (cesto, scatola) to burst, knock the bottom out of; (MIL) to break through ♦ vi (riuscire) to make a name for o.s.

sfon'dato, a ag (scarpe) worn out; (scatola) burst; (sedia) broken, damaged; essere ricco ~ to be rolling in it.

'sfondo sm background.

sfor'mare vt to put out of shape, knock out of shape; ~rsi vr to lose shape, get out of shape.

sfor'mato, a ag (che ha perso forma) shapeless ♦ sm (CUC) type of soufflé.

sfor'nare vt (pane) to take out of the oven; (fig) to churn out.

sfor'nito, a ag: ~ di lacking in, without; (negozio) out of.

sfor'tuna sf misfortune, ill luck q; avere ~ to be unlucky; che ~! how unfortunate!

sfortu'nato, a ag unlucky; (impresa, film) unsuccessful.

sfor'zare [sfor'tsare] vt to force; (voce, occhi) to strain; ~rsi vr: ~rsi di o a o per fare to try hard to do.

'sforzo ['sfɔrtso] sm effort; (tensione eccessiva, TECN) strain; fare uno ~ to make an effort; essere sotto ~ (motore, macchina, fig: persona) to be under stress.

'sfottere vt (fam) to tease.

sfracel'lare [sfratʃel'lare] vt, ~rsi vr to smash.

sfrat'tare vt to evict.

'sfratto sm eviction; dare lo ~ a qn to give sb notice to quit.

sfrecci'are [sfret'tʃare] vi to shoot o flash past.

sfre'gare vt (strofinare) to rub; (graffiare) to scratch; ~rsi le mani to rub one's hands; ~ un fiammifero to strike a match.

sfregi'are [sfre'dʒare] vt to slash, gash; (persona) to disfigure; (quadro) to deface.

'sfregio ['sfredʒo] sm gash; scar; (fig) insult.

sfre'nato, a *ag* (*fig*) unrestrained, unbridled.

sfron'dare *vt* (*albero*) to prune, thin out; (*fig: discorso, scritto*) to prune (down).

sfronta'tezza [sfronta'tettsa] *sf* impudence, cheek.

sfron'tato, a *ag* impudent, cheeky.

sfrutta'mento *sm* exploitation.

sfrut'tare *vt* (*terreno*) to overwork, exhaust; (*miniera*) to exploit, work; (*fig: operai, occasione, potere*) to exploit.

sfrutta'tore, 'trice *sm/f* exploiter.

sfug'gente [sfud'dʒɛnte] *ag* (*fig: sguardo*) elusive; (*mento*) receding.

sfug'gire [sfud'dʒire] *vi* to escape; ~ **a** (*custode*) to escape (from); (*morte*) to escape; ~ **a qn** (*dettaglio, nome*) to escape sb; ~ **di mano a qn** to slip out of sb's hand (*o* hands); **lasciarsi** ~ **un'occasione** to let an opportunity go by; ~ **al controllo** (*macchina*) to go out of control; (*situazione*) to be no longer under control.

sfug'gita [sfud'dʒita] *sf*: **di** ~ (*rapidamente, in fretta*) in passing.

sfu'mare *vt* (*colori, contorni*) to soften, shade off ♦ *vi* to shade (off), fade; (*fig: svanire*) to vanish, disappear; (*: speranze*) to come to nothing.

sfuma'tura *sf* shading off *q*; (*tonalità*) shade, tone; (*fig*) touch, hint.

sfuri'ata *sf* (*scatto di collera*) fit of anger; (*rimprovero*) sharp rebuke.

'sfuso, a *ag* (*caramelle etc*) loose, unpacked; (*vino*) unbottled; (*birra*) draught (*Brit*), draft (*US*).

sg. *abbr* = **seguente**.

S.G. *abbr* = *Sua Grazia*.

sga'bello *sm* stool.

sgabuz'zino [zgabud'dzino] *sm* lumber room.

sgambet'tare *vi* to kick one's legs about.

sgam'betto *sm*: **far lo** ~ **a qn** to trip sb up; (*fig*) to oust sb.

sganasci'arsi [zganaʃ'ʃarsi] *vr*: ~ **dalle risa** to roar with laughter.

sganci'are [zgan'tʃare] *vt* to unhook; (*chiusura*) to unfasten, undo; (*FERR*) to uncouple; (*bombe: da aereo*) to release, drop; (*fig: fam: soldi*) to fork out; ~**rsi** *vr* to come unhooked; to come unfastened, come undone; to uncouple; (*fig*): ~**rsi (da)** to get away (from).

sganghe'rato, a [zgange'rato] *ag* (*porta*) off its hinges; (*auto*) ramshackle; (*riso*) wild, boisterous.

sgar'bato, a *ag* rude, impolite.

'sgarbo *sm*: **fare uno** ~ **a qn** to be rude to sb.

sgargi'ante [zgar'dʒante] *ag* gaudy, showy.

sgar'rare *vi* (*persona*) to step out of line; (*orologio: essere avanti*) to gain; (*: essere indietro*) to lose.

'sgarro *sm* inaccuracy.

sgattaio'lare *vi* to sneak away *o* off.

sge'lare [zdʒe'lare] *vi, vt* to thaw.

'sghembo, a ['zgembo] *ag* (*obliquo*) slanting; (*storto*) crooked.

sghignaz'zare [zgiɲɲat'tsare] *vi* to laugh scornfully.

sghignaz'zata [zgiɲɲat'tsata] *sf* scornful laugh.

sgob'bare *vi* (*fam: scolaro*) to swot; (*: operaio*) to slog.

sgoccio'lare [zgottʃo'lare] *vt* (*vuotare*) to drain (to the last drop) ♦ *vi* (*acqua*) to drip; (*recipiente*) to drain.

'sgoccioli ['zgottʃoli] *smpl*: **essere agli** ~ (*lavoro, provviste etc*) to be nearly finished; (*periodo*) to be nearly over; **siamo agli** ~ we've nearly finished, the end is in sight.

sgo'larsi *vr* to talk (*o* shout *o* sing) o.s. hoarse.

sgomb(e)'rare *vt* to clear; (*andarsene da: stanza*) to vacate; (*evacuare*) to evacuate.

'sgombro, a *ag*: ~ **(di)** clear (of), free (from) ♦ *sm* (*ZOOL*) mackerel; (*anche*: **sgombero**) clearing; vacating; evacuation; (*: trasloco*) removal.

sgomen'tare *vt* to dismay; ~**rsi** *vr* to be dismayed.

sgo'mento, a *ag* dismayed ♦ *sm* dismay, consternation.

sgomi'nare *vt* (*nemico*) to rout; (*avversario*) to defeat; (*fig: epidemia*) to overcome.

sgonfi'are *vt* to let down, deflate; ~**rsi** *vr* to go down.

'sgonfio, a *ag* (*pneumatico, pallone*) flat.

'sgorbio *sm* blot; scribble.

sgor'gare *vi* to gush (out).

sgoz'zare [zgot'tsare] *vt* to cut the throat of.

sgra'devole *ag* unpleasant, disagreeable.

sgra'dito, a *ag* unpleasant, unwelcome.

sgraffi'gnare [zgraffiɲ'ɲare] *vt* (*fam*) to pinch, swipe.

sgrammati'cato, a *ag* ungrammatical.

sgra'nare *vt* (*piselli*) to shell; ~ **gli occhi** to open one's eyes wide.

sgran'chirsi [zgran'kirsi] *vr* to stretch; ~ **le gambe** to stretch one's legs.

sgranocchi'are [zgranok'kjare] *vt* to munch.

sgras'sare *vt* to remove the grease from.

'sgravio *sm*: ~ **fiscale** *o* **contributivo** tax relief.

sgrazi'ato, a [zgrat'tsjato] *ag* clumsy, ungainly.

sgreto'lare *vt* to cause to crumble; ~**rsi** *vr* to crumble.

sgri'dare *vt* to scold.

sgri'data *sf* scolding.

sguai'ato, a *ag* coarse, vulgar.

sguai'nare *vt* to draw, unsheathe.

sgual'cire [zgwal'tʃire] *vt* to crumple (up),

crease.

sgual'drina *sf* (*peg*) slut.

sgu'ardo *sm* (*occhiata*) look, glance; (*espressione*) look (in one's eye); **dare uno ~ a qc** to glance at sth, cast a glance *o* an eye over sth; **alzare** *o* **sollevare lo ~** to raise one's eyes, look up; **cercare qc/qn con lo ~** to look (a)round for sth/sb.

'sguattero, a *sm/f* scullery boy/maid.

sguaz'zare [zgwat'tsare] *vi* (*nell'acqua*) to splash about; (*nella melma*) to wallow; **~ nell'oro** to be rolling in money.

sguinzagli'are [zgwintsaʎ'ʎare] *vt* to let off the leash; (*fig: persona*): **~ qn dietro a qn** to set sb on sb.

sgusci'are [zguʃ'ʃare] *vt* to shell ♦ *vi* (*sfuggire di mano*) to slip; **~ via** to slip *o* slink away.

'shampoo ['ʃampo] *sm inv* shampoo.

shock [ʃɔk] *sm inv* shock.

SI *sigla* = Siena.

si *pronome* (*dav lo, la, li, le, ne diventa* **se**) (*riflessivo*) oneself, *m* himself, *f* herself, *soggetto non umano* itself; *pl* themselves; (*reciproco*) one another, each other; (*passivante*): **lo ~ ripara facilmente** it is easily repaired; (*possessivo*): **lavarsi le mani** to wash one's hands; (*impersonale*): **~ vede che è felice** one *o* you can see that he's happy; (*noi*): **tra poco ~ parte** we're leaving soon; (*la gente*): **~ dice che** they *o* people say that; **mi ~ dice che ...** I am told that ... ♦ *sm* (*MUS*) B; (*: solfeggiando la scala*) ti.

sì *av* yes ♦ *sm*: **non mi aspettavo un ~** I didn't expect him (*o* her *etc*) to say yes; **per me è ~** I should think so, I expect so; **saranno stati ~ e no in 20** there must have been about 20 of them; **uno ~ e uno no** every other one; **un giorno ~ e uno no** every other day; **dire di ~** to say yes; **spero/penso di ~** I hope/think so; **fece di ~ col capo** he nodded (his head); **e ~ che ...** and to think that ....

'sia *cong*: **~ ... ~** (*o ... o*): **~ che lavori, ~ che non lavori** whether he works or not; (*tanto ... quanto*): **verranno ~ Luigi ~ suo fratello** both Luigi and his brother will be coming.

'sia *etc vb vedi* **essere**.

SIAE *sigla f* = *Società Italiana Autori ed Editori*.

Si'am *sm*: **il ~** Siam.

sia'mese *ag, sm/f* siamese *inv*.

si'amo *vb vedi* **essere**.

Si'beria *sf*: **la ~** Siberia.

sibi'lare *vi* to hiss; (*fischiare*) to whistle.

'sibilo *sm* hiss; whistle.

si'cario *sm* hired killer.

sicché [sik'ke] *cong* (*perciò*) so (that), therefore; (*e quindi*) (and) so.

siccità [sittʃi'ta] *sf* drought.

sic'come *cong* since, as.

Si'cilia [si'tʃilja] *sf*: **la ~** Sicily.

sicili'ano, a [sitʃi'ljano] *ag, sm/f* Sicilian.

sico'moro *sm* sycamore.

'siculo, a *ag, sm/f* Sicilian.

si'cura *sf* (*di arma, spilla*) safety catch; (*di portiera*) safety lock.

sicu'rezza [siku'rettsa] *sf* safety; security; confidence; certainty; **di ~** safety *cpd*; **~ stradale** road safety; **avere la ~ di qc** to be sure *o* certain of sth; **lo so con ~** I am quite certain; **ha risposto con molta ~** he answered very confidently.

si'curo, a *ag* safe; (*ben difeso*) secure; (*fiducioso*) confident; (*certo*) sure, certain; (*notizia, amico*) reliable; (*esperto*) skilled ♦ *av* (*anche*: **di ~**) certainly ♦ *sm*: **andare sul ~** to play safe; **essere/mettere al ~** to be safe/put in a safe place; **~ di sé** self-confident, sure of o.s.; **sentirsi ~** to feel safe *o* secure; **essere ~ di/che** to be sure of/that; **da fonte ~a** from reliable sources.

siderur'gia [siderur'dʒia] *sf* iron and steel industry.

side'rurgico, a, ci, che [side'rurdʒiko] *ag* iron and steel *cpd*.

'sidro *sm* cider.

si'edo *etc vb vedi* **sedere**.

si'epe *sf* hedge.

si'ero *sm* (*MED*) serum; **~ antivipera** snake bite serum; **~ del latte** whey.

sieroposi'tivo, a *ag* HIV positive.

si'erra *sf* (*GEO*) sierra.

Si'erra Le'one *sf*: **la ~** Sierra Leone.

si'esta *sf* siesta, (afternoon) nap.

si'ete *vb vedi* **essere**.

si'filide *sf* syphilis.

si'fone *sm* siphon.

Sig. *abbr* (= *signore*) Mr.

siga'retta *sf* cigarette.

'sigaro *sm* cigar.

Sigg. *abbr* (= *signori*) Messrs.

sigil'lare [sidʒil'lare] *vt* to seal.

si'gillo [si'dʒillo] *sm* seal.

'sigla *sf* (*iniziali*) initials *pl*; (*abbreviazione*) acronym, abbreviation; **~ automobilistica** *abbreviation of province on vehicle number plate;* **~ musicale** signature tune.

si'glare *vt* to initial.

Sig.na *abbr* (= *signorina*) Miss.

signifi'care [siɲɲifi'kare] *vt* to mean; **cosa significa?** what does this mean?

significa'tivo, a [siɲɲifika'tivo] *ag* significant.

signifi'cato [siɲɲifi'kato] *sm* meaning.

si'gnora [siɲ'ɲora] *sf* lady; **la ~ X** Mrs ['mɪsɪz] X; **buon giorno S~/Signore/Signorina** good morning; (*deferente*) good morning Madam/Sir/Madam; (*quando si conosce il nome*) good morning Mrs/Mr/Miss X; **Gentile S~/Signore/Signorina** (*in una lettera*) Dear Madam/Sir/Madam;

Gentile (*o* **Cara**) **S~ Rossi** Dear Mrs Rossi; **Gentile S~ Anna Rossi** (*sulle buste*) Mrs Anna Rossi; **il signor Rossi e ~** Mr Rossi and his wife; **~e e signori** ladies and gentlemen; **le presento la mia ~** may I introduce my wife?

si'gnore [siɲ'ɲore] *sm* gentleman; (*padrone*) lord, master; (*REL*): **il S~** the Lord; **il signor X** Mr ['mɪstə*] X; **signor Presidente** Mr Chairman; **Gentile** (*o Caro*) **Signor Rossi** (*in lettere*) Dear Mr Rossi; **Gentile Signor Paolo Rossi** (*sulle buste*) Mr Paolo Rossi; **i ~i Bianchi** (*coniugi*) Mr and Mrs Bianchi; *vedi anche* **signora.**

signo'ria [siɲɲo'ria] *sf* (*STORIA*) seignory, signoria; **S~ Vostra (S.V.)** (*AMM*) you.

signo'rile [siɲɲo'rile] *ag* refined.

signorilità [siɲɲorili'ta] *sf* (*raffinatezza*) refinement; (*eleganza*) elegance.

signo'rina [siɲɲo'rina] *sf* young lady; **la ~ X** Miss X; **Gentile** (*o Cara*) **S~ Rossi** (*in lettere*) Dear Miss Rossi; **Gentile S~ Anna Rossi** (*sulle buste*) Miss Anna Rossi; *vedi anche* **signora.**

signo'rino [siɲɲo'rino] *sm* young master.

Sig.ra *abbr* (= *signora*) Mrs.

silenzia'tore [silentsja'tore] *sm* silencer.

si'lenzio [si'lɛntsjo] *sm* silence; **fare ~** to be quiet, stop talking; **far passare qc sotto ~** to keep quiet about sth, hush sth up.

silenzi'oso, a [silen'tsjoso] *ag* silent, quiet.

'silice ['silitʃe] *sf* silica.

si'licio [si'litʃo] *sm* silicon; **piastrina di ~** silicon chip.

'sillaba *sf* syllable.

silu'rare *vt* to torpedo; (*fig: privare del comando*) to oust.

si'luro *sm* torpedo.

simbi'osi *sf* (*BIOL, fig*) symbiosis.

simboleggi'are [simboled'dʒare] *vt* to symbolize.

sim'bolico, a, ci, che *ag* symbolic(al).

simbo'lismo *sm* symbolism.

'simbolo *sm* symbol.

simi'lare *ag* similar.

'simile *ag* (*analogo*) similar; (*di questo tipo*): **un uomo ~** such a man, a man like this ♦ *sm* (*persona*) fellow man; **libri ~i** such books; **~ a** similar to; **non ho mai visto niente di ~** I've never seen anything like that; **è insegnante o qualcosa di ~** he's a teacher or something like that; **vendono vasi e ~i** they sell vases and things like that; **i suoi ~i** one's fellow men; one's peers.

simili'tudine *sf* (*LING*) simile.

simme'tria *sf* symmetry.

sim'metrico, a, ci, che *ag* symmetric(al).

simpa'tia *sf* (*qualità*) pleasantness; (*inclinazione*) liking; **avere ~ per qn** to like sb, have a liking for sb; **con ~** (*su lettera etc*) with much affection.

sim'patico, a, ci, che *ag* (*persona*) nice, pleasant, likeable; (*casa, albergo etc*) nice, pleasant.

simpatiz'zante [simpatid'dzante] *sm/f* sympathizer.

simpatiz'zare [simpatid'dzare] *vi:* **~ con** to take a liking to.

sim'posio *sm* symposium.

simu'lare *vt* to sham, simulate; (*TECN*) to simulate.

simulazi'one [simulat'tsjone] *sf* shamming, simulation.

simul'taneo, a *ag* simultaneous.

sin. *abbr* (= *sinistra*) L.

sina'goga, ghe *sf* synagogue.

sincera'mente [sintʃera'mente] *av* (*gen*) sincerely; (*francamente*) honestly, sincerely.

since'rarsi [sintʃe'rarsi] *vr:* **~ (di qc)** to make sure (of sth).

sincerità [sintʃeri'ta] *sf* sincerity.

sin'cero, a [sin'tʃero] *ag* (*genuino*) sincere; (*onesto*) genuine.

'sincope *sf* syncopation; (*MED*) blackout.

sin'cronico, a, ci, che *ag* synchronic.

sincroniz'zare [sinkronid'dzare] *vt* to synchronize.

sinda'cale *ag* (trade-)union *cpd.*

sindaca'lista, i, e *sm/f* trade unionist.

sinda'care *vt* (*controllare*) to inspect; (*fig: criticare*) to criticize.

sinda'cato *sm* (*di lavoratori*) (trade) union; **~ dei datori di lavoro** employers' association.

'sindaco, ci *sm* mayor.

'sindrome *sf* (*MED*) syndrome.

sinfo'nia *sf* (*MUS*) symphony.

sin'fonico, a, ci, che *ag* symphonic; (*orchestra*) symphony *cpd.*

singa'lese *ag, sm/f, sm* Sin(g)halese *inv.*

Singa'pore *sf* Singapore.

singhioz'zare [singjot'tsare] *vi* to sob; to hiccup.

singhi'ozzo [sin'gjottso] *sm* (*di pianto*) sob; (*MED*) hiccup; **avere il ~** to have the hiccups; **a ~** (*fig*) by fits and starts.

singo'lare *ag* (*insolito*) remarkable, singular; (*LING*) singular ♦ *sm* (*LING*) singular; (*TENNIS*): **~ maschile/femminile** men's/women's singles.

singolar'mente *av* (*separatamente*) individually, one at a time; (*in modo strano*) strangely, peculiarly, oddly.

'singolo, a *ag* single, individual ♦ *sm* (*persona*) individual; (*TENNIS*) = **singolare; ogni ~ individuo** each individual; **camera ~a** single room.

sinis'trato, a *ag* damaged ♦ *sm/f* disaster victim; **zona ~a** disaster area.

si'nistro, a *ag* left, left-hand; (*fig*) sinister ♦ *sm* (*incidente*) accident ♦ *sf* (*POL*) left (wing); **a ~a** on the left; (*direzione*) to the left; **a ~a di** to the left of; **di ~a** left-wing; **tenere la ~a** to keep to the left; **guida a ~a** left-hand drive.

'sino *prep* = **fino**.

si'nonimo, a *ag* synonymous ♦ *sm* synonym; **~ di** synonymous with.

sin'tassi *sf* syntax.

sin'tattico, a, ci, che *ag* syntactic.

'sintesi *sf* synthesis; *(riassunto)* summary, résumé; **in ~** in brief, in short.

sin'tetico, a, ci, che *ag* synthetic; *(conciso)* brief, concise.

sintetiz'zare [sintetid'dzare] *vt* to synthesize; *(riassumere)* to summarize.

sintetizza'tore [sintetiddza'tore] *sm* (*MUS*) synthesizer; **~ di voce** voice synthesizer.

sinto'matico, a, ci, che *ag* symptomatic.

'sintomo *sm* symptom.

sinto'nia *sf* (*RADIO*) tuning; **essere in ~ con qn** *(fig)* to be on the same wavelength as sb.

sintoniz'zare [sintonid'dzare] *vt* to tune (in); **~rsi** *vr*: **~rsi su** to tune in to.

sintonizza'tore [sintoniddza'tore] *sm* tuner.

sinu'oso, a *ag* (*strada*) winding.

sinu'site *sf* sinusitis.

SIP *sigla f* (= *Società Italiana per l'esercizio telefonico*) Italian telephone company.

si'pario *sm* (*TEATRO*) curtain.

si'rena *sf* (*apparecchio*) siren; *(nella mitologia, fig)* siren, mermaid; **~ d'allarme** *(per incendio)* fire alarm; *(per furto)* burglar alarm.

'Siria *sf*: **la ~** Syria.

siri'ano, a *ag, sm/f* Syrian.

si'ringa, ghe *sf* syringe.

'sisma, i *sm* earthquake.

'SISMI *sigla m* (= *Servizio per l'Informazione e la Sicurezza Militari*) *military security service*.

'sismico, a, ci, che *ag* seismic; *(zona)* earthquake *cpd*.

sis'mografo *sm* seismograph.

sissi'gnore [sissiɲ'ɲore] *av* *(a un superiore)* yes, sir; *(enfatico)* yes indeed, of course.

sis'tema, i *sm* system; *(metodo)* method, way; **trovare il ~ per fare qc** to find a way to do sth; **~ decimale/metrico** decimal/metric system; **~ operativo** (*INFORM*) operating system; **~ solare** solar system; **~ di vita** way of life.

siste'mare *vt* *(mettere a posto)* to tidy, put in order; *(risolvere: questione)* to sort out, settle; *(procurare un lavoro a)* to find a job for; *(dare un alloggio a)* to settle, find accommodation *(Brit)* o accommodations *(US)* for; **~rsi** *vr* *(problema)* to be settled; *(persona: trovare alloggio)* to find accommodation(s); (: *trovarsi un lavoro*) to get fixed up with a job; **ti sistemo io!** I'll soon sort you out!; **~ qn in un albergo** to fix sb up with a hotel.

siste'matico, a, ci, che *ag* systematic.

sistemazi'one [sistemat'tsjone] *sf* arrangement, order; settlement; employment; accommodation *(Brit)*, accommodations *(US)*.

'sito, a *ag* (*AMM*) situated ♦ *sm* *(letterario)* place.

situ'are *vt* to site, situate.

situ'ato, a *ag*: **~ a/su** situated at/on.

situazi'one [situat'tsjone] *sf* situation; **vista la sua ~ familiare** given your family situation o circumstances; **nella sua ~** in your position o situation; **mi trovo in una ~ critica** I'm in a very difficult situation o position.

'skai ® *sm* Leatherette ®.

slacci'are [zlat'tʃare] *vt* to undo, unfasten.

slanci'arsi [zlan'tʃarsi] *vr* to dash, fling o.s.

slanci'ato, a [zlan'tʃato] *ag* slender.

'slancio ['zlantʃo] *sm* dash, leap; *(fig)* surge; **in uno ~ d'affetto** in a burst o rush of affection; **di ~** impetuously.

sla'vato, a *ag* faded, washed out; *(fig: viso, occhi)* pale, colourless *(Brit)*, colorless *(US)*.

sla'vina *sf* snowslide.

'slavo, a *ag* Slav(onic), Slavic.

sle'ale *ag* disloyal; *(concorrenza etc)* unfair.

slealtà *sf* disloyalty; unfairness.

sle'gare *vt* to untie.

'slitta *sf* sledge; *(trainata)* sleigh.

slitta'mento *sm* slipping; skidding; postponement; **~ salariale** wage drift.

slit'tare *vi* to slip, slide; (*AUT*) to skid; *(incontro, conferenza)* to be put off, be postponed.

s.l.m. *abbr* (= *sul livello del mare*) a.s.l.

slo'gare *vt* (*MED*) to dislocate; (: *caviglia, polso*) to sprain.

sloga'tura *sf* dislocation; sprain.

sloggi'are [zlod'dʒare] *vt* (*inquilino*) to turn out; *(nemico)* to drive out, dislodge ♦ *vi* to move out.

S.M. *abbr* (*MIL*) = **Stato Maggiore**; (= *Sua Maestà*) HM.

smacchi'are [zmak'kjare] *vt* to remove stains from.

smacchia'tore [zmakkja'tore] *sm* stain remover.

'smacco, chi *sm* humiliating defeat.

smagli'ante [zmaʎ'ʎante] *ag* brilliant, dazzling.

smagli'are [zmaʎ'ʎare] *vt*, **~rsi** *vr* (*calza*) to ladder.

smaglia'tura [zmaʎʎa'tura] *sf* (*su maglia, calza*) ladder *(Brit)*, run; (*MED: sulla pelle*) stretch mark.

sma'grito, a *ag*: **essere ~** to have lost a lot of weight.

smalizi'ato, a [zmalit'tsjato] *ag* shrewd, cunning.

smal'tare *vt* to enamel; *(ceramica)* to glaze; *(unghie)* to varnish.

smal'tire *vt* (*merce*) to sell off; (*rifiuti*) to dispose of; (*cibo*) to digest; (*peso*) to lose; (*rabbia*) to get over; ~ **la sbornia** to sober up.

'smalto *sm* (*anche di denti*) enamel; (*per ceramica*) glaze; ~ **per unghie** nail varnish.

smance'rie [zmantʃe'rie] *sfpl* mawkishness *sg*.

'smania *sf* agitation, restlessness; (*fig*): ~ **di** thirst for, craving for; **avere la ~ addosso** to have the fidgets; **avere la ~ di fare** to long *o* yearn to do.

smani'are *vi* (*agitarsi*) to be restless *o* agitated; (*fig*): ~ **di fare** to long *o* yearn to do.

smantella'mento *sm* dismantling.

smantel'lare *vt* to dismantle.

smargi'asso [zmar'dʒasso] *sm* show-off.

smarri'mento *sm* loss; (*fig*) bewilderment; dismay.

smar'rire *vt* to lose; (*non riuscire a trovare*) to mislay; ~**rsi** *vr* (*perdersi*) to lose one's way, get lost; (*: oggetto*) to go astray.

smar'rito, a *ag* (*oggetto*) lost; (*fig: confuso: persona*) bewildered, nonplussed; (*: sguardo*) bewildered; **ufficio oggetti ~i** lost property office (*Brit*), lost and found (*US*).

smasche'rare [zmaske'rare] *vt* to unmask.

SME *abbr* = *Stato Maggiore Esercito* ♦ *sigla m* (= *Sistema Monetario Europeo*) EMS (= *European Monetary System*).

smem'brare *vt* (*gruppo, partito etc*) to split; ~**rsi** *vr* to split up.

smemo'rato, a *ag* forgetful.

smen'tire *vt* (*negare*) to deny; (*testimonianza*) to refute; (*reputazione*) to give the lie to; ~**rsi** *vr* to be inconsistent.

smen'tita *sf* denial; refutation.

sme'raldo *sm, ag inv* emerald.

smerci'are [zmer'tʃare] *vt* (*COMM*) to sell; (*: svendere*) to sell off.

'smercio ['zmɛrtʃo] *sm* sale; **avere poco/molto ~** to have poor/good sales.

smerigli'ato, a [zmeriʎ'ʎato] *ag*: **carta ~a** emery paper; **vetro ~** frosted glass.

sme'riglio [zme'riʎʎo] *sm* emery.

'smesso, a *pp di* **smettere** ♦ *ag*: **abiti** *mpl* ~**i** cast-offs.

'smettere *vt* to stop; (*vestiti*) to stop wearing ♦ *vi* to stop, cease; ~ **di fare** to stop doing.

smidol'lato, a *ag* spineless ♦ *sm/f* spineless person.

smilitarizzazi'one [zmilitariddzat'tsjone] *sf* demilitarization.

'smilzo, a [zmiltso] *ag* thin, lean.

sminu'ire *vt* to diminish, lessen; (*fig*) to belittle; ~ **l'importanza di qc** to play sth down.

sminuz'zare [zminut'tsare] *vt* to break into small pieces; to crumble.

'smisi *etc vb vedi* **smettere**.

smista'mento *sm* (*di posta*) sorting; (*FERR*) shunting.

smis'tare *vt* (*pacchi etc*) to sort; (*FERR*) to shunt.

smisu'rato, a *ag* boundless, immeasurable; (*grandissimo*) immense, enormous.

smitiz'zare [zmitid'dzare] *vt* to debunk.

smobili'tare *vt* to demobilize.

smobi'lizzo [zmobi'liddzo] *sm* (*COMM*) disinvestment.

smo'dato, a *ag* excessive, unrestrained.

smode'rato, a *ag* immoderate.

'smoking ['smoukiŋ] *sm inv* dinner jacket (*Brit*), tuxedo (*US*).

smon'tare *vt* (*mobile, macchina etc*) to take to pieces, dismantle; (*fig: scoraggiare*) to dishearten ♦ *vi* (*scendere: da cavallo*) to dismount; (*: da treno*) to get off; (*terminare il lavoro*) to stop (work); ~**rsi** *vr* to lose heart; to lose one's enthusiasm.

'smorfia *sf* grimace; (*atteggiamento lezioso*) simpering; **fare ~e** to make faces; to simper.

smorfi'oso, a *ag* simpering.

'smorto, a *ag* (*viso*) pale, wan; (*colore*) dull.

smor'zare [zmor'tsare] *vt* (*suoni*) to deaden; (*colori*) to tone down; (*luce*) to dim; (*sete*) to quench; (*entusiasmo*) to dampen; ~**rsi** *vr* (*suono, luce*) to fade; (*entusiasmo*) to dampen.

'smosso, a *pp di* **smuovere**.

smotta'mento *sm* landslide.

'smunto, a *ag* haggard, pinched.

smu'overe *vt* to move, shift; (*fig: commuovere*) to move; (*: dall'inerzia*) to rouse, stir; ~**rsi** *vr* to move, shift.

smus'sare *vt* (*angolo*) to round off, smooth; (*lama etc*) to blunt; ~**rsi** *vr* to become blunt.

s.n. *abbr* = *senza numero*.

snatu'rato, a *ag* inhuman, heartless.

snazionaliz'zare [znattsjonalid'dzare] *vt* to denationalize.

snelli'mento *sm* (*di traffico*) speeding up; (*di procedura*) streamlining.

snel'lire *vt* (*persona*) to make slim; (*traffico*) to speed up; (*procedura*) to streamline; ~**rsi** *vr* (*persona*) to (get) slim; (*traffico*) to speed up.

'snello, a *ag* (*agile*) agile; (*svelto*) slender, slim.

sner'vante *ag* (*attesa, lavoro*) exasperating.

sner'vare *vt* to enervate, wear out; ~**rsi** *vr* to become enervated.

sni'dare *vt* to drive out, flush out.

snob'bare *vt* to snub.

sno'bismo *sm* snobbery.

snoccio'lare [znottʃo'lare] *vt* (*frutta*) to stone; (*fig: orazioni*) to rattle off; (*: verità*) to blab; (*: fam: soldi*) to shell out.

sno'dabile *ag* (*lampada*) adjustable; (*tubo, braccio*) hinged; **rasoio con testina** ~ swivel-head razor.

sno'dare *vt* to untie, undo; (*rendere agile, mobile*) to loosen; **~rsi** *vr* to come loose; (*articolarsi*) to bend; (*strada, fiume*) to wind.

SO *sigla* = Sondrio.

so *vb vedi* **sapere.**

S.O. *abbr* (= *sudovest*) SW.

so'ave *ag* (*voce, maniera*) gentle; (*volto*) delicate, sweet; (*musica*) soft, sweet; (*profumo*) delicate.

soavità *sf* gentleness; delicacy; sweetness; softness.

sobbal'zare [sobbal'tsare] *vi* to jolt, jerk; (*trasalire*) to jump, start.

sob'balzo [sob'baltso] *sm* jerk, jolt; jump, start.

sobbar'carsi *vr*: ~ **a** to take on, undertake.

sob'borgo, ghi *sm* suburb.

sobil'lare *vt* to stir up, incite.

'sobrio, a *ag* sober.

Soc. *abbr* (= *società*) Soc.

socchi'udere [sok'kjudere] *vt* (*porta*) to leave ajar; (*occhi*) to half-close.

socchi'uso, a [sok'kjuso] *pp di* **socchiudere ♦** *ag* (*porta, finestra*) ajar; (*occhi*) half-closed.

soc'combere *vi* to succumb, give way.

soc'correre *vt* to help, assist.

soccorri'tore, 'trice *sm/f* rescuer.

soc'corso, a *pp di* **soccorrere ♦** *sm* help, aid, assistance; **~i** *smpl* relief *sg*, aid *sg*; **prestare** ~ **a qn** to help *o* assist sb; **venire in** ~ **di qn** to help sb, come to sb's aid; **operazioni di** ~ rescue operations; ~ **stradale** breakdown service.

socialdemo'cratico, a, ci, che [sotʃaldemo'kratiko] *sm/f* Social Democrat.

soci'ale [so'tʃale] *ag* social; (*di associazione*) club *cpd*, association *cpd*.

socia'lismo [sotʃa'lizmo] *sm* socialism.

socia'lista, i, e [sotʃa'lista] *ag, sm/f* socialist.

socializ'zare [sotʃalid'dzare] *vi* to socialize.

società [sotʃe'ta] *sf inv* society; (*sportiva*) club; (*COMM*) company; **in** ~ **con qn** in partnership with sb; **mettersi in** ~ **con qn** to go into business with sb; **l'alta** ~ high society; ~ **anonima (SA)** ≈ limited (*Brit*) *o* incorporated (*US*) company; ~ **per azioni (S.p.A.)** joint-stock company; ~ **di comodo** shell company; ~ **fiduciaria** trust company; ~ **di mutuo soccorso** friendly society (*Brit*), benefit society (*US*); ~ **a responsabilità limitata (S.r.l.)** *type of limited liability company*.

soci'evole [so'tʃevole] *ag* sociable.

socievo'lezza [sotʃevo'lettsa] *sf* sociableness.

'socio ['sɔtʃo] *sm* (*DIR, COMM*) partner; (*membro di associazione*) member.

sociolo'gia [sotʃolo'dʒia] *sf* sociology.

soci'ologo, a, gi, ghe [so'tʃɔlogo] *sm/f* sociologist.

'soda *sf* (*CHIM*) soda; (*acqua gassata*) soda (water).

soda'lizio [soda'littsjo] *sm* association, society.

soddisfa'cente [soddisfa'tʃɛnte] *ag* satisfactory.

soddis'fare *vt, vi*: ~ **a** to satisfy; (*impegno*) to fulfil; (*debito*) to pay off; (*richiesta*) to meet, comply with; (*offesa*) to make amends for.

soddis'fatto, a *pp di* **soddisfare ♦** *ag* satisfied, pleased; **essere** ~ **di** to be satisfied *o* pleased with.

soddisfazi'one [soddisfat'tsjone] *sf* satisfaction.

'sodio *sm* (*CHIM*) sodium.

'sodo, a *ag* firm, hard ♦ *sm*: **venire al** ~ to come to the point ♦ *av* (*picchiare, lavorare*) hard; **dormire** ~ to sleep soundly.

sofà *sm inv* sofa.

soffe'renza [soffe'rɛntsa] *sf* suffering; (*COMM*): **in** ~ unpaid.

sof'ferto, a *pp di* **soffrire ♦** *ag* (*vittoria*) hard-fought; (*distacco, decisione*) painful.

soffi'are *vt* to blow; (*notizia, segreto*) to whisper ♦ *vi* to blow; (*sbuffare*) to puff (and blow); **~rsi il naso** to blow one's nose; ~ **qc/qn a qn** (*fig*) to pinch *o* steal sth/sb from sb; ~ **via qc** to blow sth away.

soffi'ata *sf* (*fam*) tip-off; **fare una** ~ **alla polizia** to tip off the police.

'soffice ['sɔffitʃe] *ag* soft.

soffi'etto *sm* (*MUS, per fuoco*) bellows *pl*; **porta a** ~ folding door.

'soffio *sm* (*di vento*) breath; (*di fumo*) puff; (*MED*) murmur.

soffi'one *sm* (*BOT*) dandelion.

sof'fitta *sf* attic.

sof'fitto *sm* ceiling.

soffo'cante *ag* suffocating, stifling.

soffo'care *vi* (*anche*: **~rsi**) to suffocate, choke ♦ *vt* to suffocate, choke; (*fig*) to stifle, suppress.

soffocazi'one [soffokat'tsjone] *sf* suffocation.

sof'friggere [sof'friddʒere] *vt* to fry lightly.

sof'frire *vt* to suffer, endure; (*sopportare*) to bear, stand ♦ *vi* to suffer; to be in pain; ~ **(di) qc** (*MED*) to suffer from sth.

sof'fritto, a *pp di* **soffriggere ♦** *sm* (*CUC*) *fried mixture of herbs, bacon and onions.*

So'fia *sf* (*GEO*) Sofia.

sofisti'care *vt* (*vino, cibo*) to adulterate.

sofisti'cato, a *ag* sophisticated; (*vino*) adulterated.

sofisticazi'one [sofistikat'tsjone] *sf* adulteration.

'software ['sɔftwɛa] *sm*: ~ **applicativo** applications package.

sogget'tivo, a [soddʒet'tivo] *ag* subjective.

sog'getto, a [sod'dʒetto] *ag*: ~ **a** (*sot-*

tomesso) subject to; (*esposto: a variazioni, danni etc*) subject *o* liable to ♦ *sm* subject; ~ **a tassa** taxable; **recitare a** ~ (*TEATRO*) to improvise.

soggezi'one [soddʒet'tsjone] *sf* subjection; (*timidezza*) awe; **avere** ~ **di qn** to be ill at ease in sb's presence.

sogghi'gnare [soggiɲ'ɲare] *vi* to sneer.

sog'ghigno [sog'giɲɲo] *sm* sneer.

soggia'cere [soddʒa'tʃere] *vi:* ~ **a** to be subjected to.

soggio'gare [soddʒo'gare] *vt* to subdue, subjugate.

soggior'nare [soddʒor'nare] *vi* to stay.

soggi'orno [sod'dʒorno] *sm* (*invernale, marino*) stay; (*stanza*) living room.

soggi'ungere [sod'dʒundʒere] *vt* to add.

soggi'unto, a [sod'dʒunto] *pp di* **soggiungere.**

'soglia ['sɔʎʎa] *sf* doorstep; (*anche fig*) threshold.

'sogliola ['sɔʎʎola] *sf* (*ZOOL*) sole.

so'gnante [soɲ'ɲante] *ag* dreamy.

so'gnare [soɲ'ɲare] *vt, vi* to dream; ~ **a occhi aperti** to daydream.

sogna'tore, 'trice [soɲɲa'tore] *sm/f* dreamer.

'sogno ['soɲɲo] *sm* dream.

'soia *sf* (*BOT*) soya.

sol *sm* (*MUS*) G; (*: solfeggiando la scala*) so(h).

so'laio *sm* (*soffitta*) attic.

sola'mente *av* only, just.

so'lare *ag* solar, sun *cpd*.

sol'care *vt* (*terreno, fig: mari*) to plough (*Brit*), plow (*US*).

'solco, chi *sm* (*scavo, fig: ruga*) furrow; (*incavo*) rut, track; (*di disco*) groove; (*scia*) wake.

sol'dato *sm* soldier; ~ **di leva** conscript; ~ **semplice** private.

'soldo *sm* (*fig*): **non avere un** ~ to be penniless; **non vale un** ~ it's not worth a penny; **~i** *smpl* (*denaro*) money *sg*.

'sole *sm* sun; (*luce*) sun(light); (*tempo assolato*) sun(shine); **prendere il** ~ to sunbathe.

soleggi'ato, a [soled'dʒato] *ag* sunny.

so'lenne *ag* solemn.

solennità *sf* solemnity; (*festività*) holiday, feast day.

so'lere *vt:* ~ **fare qc** to be in the habit of doing sth ♦ *vb impers:* **come suole accadere** as is usually the case, as usually happens; **come si suol dire** as they say.

so'lerte *ag* diligent.

so'lerzia [so'lɛrtsja] *sf* diligence.

so'letta *sf* (*per scarpe*) insole.

sol'fato *sm* sulphate (*Brit*), sulfate (*US*).

sol'forico, a, ci, che *ag* sulphuric (*Brit*), sulfuric (*US*); **acido** ~ sulphuric *o* sulfuric acid.

sol'furo *sm* sulphur (*Brit*), sulfur (*US*).

soli'dale *ag* in agreement; **essere** ~ **con qn** (*essere d'accordo*) to be in agreement with sb; (*appoggiare*) to be behind sb.

solidarietà *sf* solidarity.

solidifi'care *vt, vi* (*anche:* ~**rsi**) to solidify.

solidità *sf* solidity.

'solido, a *ag* solid; (*forte, robusto*) sturdy, solid; (*fig: ditta*) sound, solid ♦ *sm* (*MAT*) solid.

soli'loquio *sm* soliloquy.

so'lista, i, e *ag* solo ♦ *sm/f* soloist.

solita'mente *av* usually, as a rule.

soli'tario, a *ag* (*senza compagnia*) solitary, lonely; (*solo, isolato*) solitary, lone; (*deserto*) lonely ♦ *sm* (*gioiello, gioco*) solitaire.

'solito, a *ag* usual; **essere** ~ **fare** to be in the habit of doing; **di** ~ usually; **più tardi del** ~ later than usual; **come al** ~ as usual; **siamo alle** ~**e!** (*fam*) here we go again!

soli'tudine *sf* solitude.

sollaz'zare [sollat'tsare] *vt* to entertain; ~**rsi** *vr* to amuse o.s.

sol'lazzo [sol'lattso] *sm* amusement.

solleci'tare [solletʃi'tare] *vt* (*lavoro*) to speed up; (*persona*) to urge on; (*chiedere con insistenza*) to press for, request urgently; (*stimolare*): ~ **qn a fare** to urge sb to do; (*TECN*) to stress.

sollecitazi'one [solletʃitat'tsjone] *sf* entreaty, request; (*fig*) incentive; (*TECN*) stress; **lettera di** ~ (*COMM*) reminder.

sol'lecito, a [sol'letʃito] *ag* prompt, quick ♦ *sm* (*COMM*) reminder; ~ **di pagamento** payment reminder.

solleci'tudine [solletʃi'tudine] *sf* promptness, speed.

solleti'care *vt* to tickle.

sol'letico *sm* tickling; **soffrire il** ~ to be ticklish.

solleva'mento *sm* raising; lifting; (*ribellione*) revolt; ~ **pesi** (*sport*) weight-lifting.

solle'vare *vt* to lift, raise; (*fig: persona: alleggerire*): ~ (**da**) to relieve (of); (*: dar conforto*) to comfort, relieve; (*: questione*) to raise; (*: far insorgere*) to stir (to revolt); ~**rsi** *vr* to rise; (*fig: riprendersi*) to recover; (*: ribellarsi*) to rise up; ~**rsi da terra** (*persona*) to get up from the ground; (*aereo*) to take off; **sentirsi sollevato** to feel relieved.

solli'evo *sm* relief; (*conforto*) comfort; **con mio grande** ~ to my great relief.

'solo, a *ag* alone; (*in senso spirituale: isolato*) lonely; (*unico*): **un** ~ **libro** only one book, a single book; (*con ag numerale*): **veniamo noi tre** ~**i** just *o* only the three of us are coming ♦ *av* (*soltanto*) only, just; ~ **che** *cong* but; **è il** ~ **pro-**

prietario he's the sole proprietor; **l'incontrò due ~e volte** he only met him twice; **non ~ ... ma anche** not only ... but also; **fare qc da ~** to do sth (all) by oneself; **vive (da) ~** he lives on his own; **possiamo vederci da ~i?** can I see you in private?

sol'stizio [sol'stittsjo] *sm* solstice.

sol'tanto *av* only.

so'lubile *ag* (*sostanza*) soluble; **caffè ~** instant coffee.

soluzi'one [solut'tsjone] *sf* solution; **senza ~ di continuità** uninterruptedly.

sol'vente *ag*, *sm* solvent; **~ per unghie** nail polish remover; **~ per vernici** paint remover.

sol'venza [sol'vɛntsa] *sf* (*COMM*) solvency.

'soma *sf* load, burden; **bestia da ~** beast of burden.

So'malia *sf*: **la ~** Somalia.

'somalo, a *ag*, *sm/f*, *sm* Somali.

so'maro *sm* ass, donkey.

so'matico, a, ci, che *ag* somatic.

somigli'anza [somiʎ'ʎantsa] *sf* resemblance.

somigli'are [somiʎ'ʎare] *vi*: **~ a** to be like, resemble; (*nell'aspetto fisico*) to look like; **~rsi** *vr* to be (*o* look) alike.

'somma *sf* (*MAT*) sum; (*di denaro*) sum (of money); (*complesso di varie cose*) whole amount, sum total; **tirare le ~e** (*fig*) to sum up; **tirate le ~e** (*fig*) all things considered.

som'mare *vt* to add up; (*aggiungere*) to add; **tutto sommato** all things considered.

som'mario, a *ag* (*racconto, indagine*) brief; (*giustizia*) summary ♦ *sm* summary.

som'mergere [som'mɛrdʒere] *vt* to submerge.

sommer'gibile [sommer'dʒibile] *sm* submarine.

som'merso, a *pp di* **sommergere**.

som'messo, a *ag* (*voce*) soft, subdued.

somminis'trare *vt* to give, administer.

sommità *sf inv* summit, top; (*fig*) height.

'sommo, a *ag* highest; (*rispetto*) highest, greatest; (*poeta, artista*) great, outstanding ♦ *sm* (*fig*) height; **per ~i capi** in short, in brief.

som'mossa *sf* uprising.

sommozza'tore [sommottsa'tore] *sm* (deepsea) diver; (*MIL*) frogman.

so'naglio [so'naʎʎo] *sm* (*di mucche etc*) bell; (*per bambini*) rattle.

so'nante *ag*: **denaro** *o* **moneta ~** (ready) cash.

so'nare *etc* = **suonare** *etc*.

'sonda *sf* (*MED, METEOR, AER*) probe; (*MINERALOGIA*) drill ♦ *ag inv*: **pallone** *m* **~** weather balloon.

son'daggio [son'daddʒo] *sm* sounding; probe; boring, drilling; (*indagine*) survey; **~ d'opinioni** opinion poll.

son'dare *vt* (*NAUT*) to sound; (*atmosfera,*

piaga) to probe; (*MINERALOGIA*) to bore, drill; (*fig: opinione etc*) to survey, poll.

so'netto *sm* sonnet.

son'nambulo, a *sm/f* sleepwalker.

sonnecchi'are [sonnek'kjare] *vi* to doze, nod.

sonnel'lino *sm* nap.

son'nifero *sm* sleeping drug (*o* pill).

'sonno *sm* sleep; **aver ~** to be sleepy; **prendere ~** to fall asleep.

sonno'lento, a *ag* sleepy, drowsy; (*movimenti*) sluggish.

sonno'lenza [sonno'lɛntsa] *sf* sleepiness, drowsiness.

'sono *vb vedi* **essere**.

so'noro, a *ag* (*ambiente*) resonant; (*voce*) sonorous, ringing; (*onde, film*) sound *cpd* ♦ *sm*: **il ~** (*CINEMA*) the talkies *pl*.

sontu'oso, a *ag* sumptuous.

so'pire *vt* (*fig: dolore, tensione*) to soothe.

so'pore *sm* drowsiness.

sopo'rifero, a *ag* soporific.

soppe'rire *vi*: **~ a** to provide for; **~ alla mancanza di qc** to make up for the lack of sth.

soppe'sare *vt* to weigh in one's hand(s), feel the weight of; (*fig*) to weigh up.

soppian'tare *vt* to supplant.

soppi'atto *av*: **di ~** secretly; furtively.

soppor'tabile *ag* tolerable, bearable.

soppor'tare *vt* (*reggere*) to support; (*subire: perdita, spese*) to bear, sustain; (*soffrire: dolore*) to bear, endure; (*sog: cosa: freddo*) to withstand; (: *persona: freddo, vino*) to take; (*tollerare*) to put up with, tolerate.

sopportazi'one [sopportat'tsjone] *sf* patience; **avere spirito di ~, avere capacità di ~** to be long-suffering.

soppressi'one *sf* aboliton; withdrawal; suppression; deletion; elimination, liquidation.

sop'presso, a *pp di* **sopprimere**.

sop'primere *vt* (*carica, privilegi etc*) to abolish, do away with; (*servizio*) to withdraw; (*pubblicazione*) to suppress; (*parola, frase*) to delete; (*uccidere*) to eliminate, liquidate.

'sopra *prep* (*gen*) on; (*al di sopra di, più in alto di*) above; over; (*riguardo a*) on, about ♦ *av* on top; (*attaccato, scritto*) on it; (*al di sopra*) above; (*al piano superiore*) upstairs; **donne ~ i 30 anni** women over 30 (years of age); **100 metri ~ il livello del mare** 100 metres above sea level; **5 gradi ~ lo zero** 5 degrees above zero; **abito di ~** I live upstairs; **essere al di ~ di ogni sospetto** to be above suspicion; **per i motivi ~ illustrati** for the above-mentioned reasons, for the reasons shown above; **dormirci ~** (*fig*) to sleep on it; **passar ~ a qc** (*anche fig*) to pass over sth.

so'prabito *sm* overcoat.

sopraccen'nato, a [soprattʃen'nato] *ag* above-mentioned.

soprac'ciglio [soprat'tʃiʎʎo], *pl(f)* **soprac-'ciglia** *sm* eyebrow.

sopracco'perta *sf* (*di letto*) bedspread; (*di libro*) jacket.

soprad'detto, a *ag* aforesaid.

sopraf'fare *vt* to overcome, overwhelm.

sopraf'fatto, a *pp di* **sopraffare**.

sopraffazi'one [sopraffat'tsjone] *sf* overwhelming, overpowering.

sopraf'fino, a *ag* (*pranzo, vino*) excellent; (*fig*) masterly.

sopraggi'ungere [soprad'dʒundʒere] *vi* (*giungere all'improvviso*) to arrive (unexpectedly); (*accadere*) to occur (unexpectedly).

sopraggi'unto, a [soprad'dʒunto] *pp di* **sopraggiungere**.

soprallu'ogo, ghi *sm* (*di esperti*) inspection; (*di polizia*) on-the-spot investigation.

sopram'mobile *sm* ornament.

soprannatu'rale *ag* supernatural.

sopran'nome *sm* nickname.

soprannomi'nare *vt* to nickname.

sopran'numero *av*: **in ~** in excess.

so'prano, a *sm/f* (*persona*) soprano ♦ *sm* (*voce*) soprano.

soprappensi'ero *av* lost in thought.

soprappiù *sm.* surplus, extra; **in ~** extra, surplus; (*per giunta*) besides, in addition.

sopras'salto *sm*: **di ~** with a start, with a jump.

soprasse'dere *vi*: **~ a** to delay, put off.

soprat'tassa *sf* surtax.

soprat'tutto *av* (*anzitutto*) above all; (*specialmente*) especially.

sopravvalu'tare *vt* (*persona, capacità*) to overestimate.

sopravve'nire *vi* to arrive, appear; (*fatto*) to occur.

soprav'vento *sm*: **avere/prendere il ~ su qn** to have/get the upper hand over sb.

sopravvis'suto, a *pp di* **sopravvivere** ♦ *sm/f* survivor.

sopravvi'venza [sopravvi'ventsa] *sf* survival.

soprav'vivere *vi* to survive; (*continuare a vivere*): **~ (in)** to live on (in); **~ a** (*incidente etc*) to survive; (*persona*) to outlive.

soprele'vata *sf* (*di strada, ferrovia*) elevated section.

soprinten'dente *sm/f* supervisor; (*statale*: *di belle arti etc*) keeper.

soprinten'denza [soprinten'dentsa] *sf* supervision; (*ente*): **~ alle Belle Arti** *government department responsible for monuments and artistic treasures*.

soprin'tendere *vi*: **~ a** to superintend, supervise.

soprin'teso, a *pp di* **soprintendere**.

so'pruso *sm* abuse of power; **subire un ~** to

be abused.

soq'quadro *sm*: **mettere a ~** to turn upside-down.

sor'betto *sm* sorbet, water ice (*Brit*).

sor'bire *vt* to sip; (*fig*) to put up with.

'sorcio ['sortʃo] *sm* mouse.

'sordido, a *ag* sordid; (*fig*: *gretto*) stingy.

sor'dina *sf*: **in ~** softly; (*fig*) on the sly.

sordità *sf* deafness.

'sordo, a *ag* deaf; (*rumore*) muffled; (*dolore*) dull; (*lotta*) silent, hidden; (*odio, rancore*) veiled ♦ *sm/f* deaf person.

sordo'muto, a *ag* deaf-and-dumb ♦ *sm/f* deaf-mute.

so'rella *sf* sister.

sorel'lastra *sf* stepsister.

sor'gente [sor'dʒente] *sf* (*acqua che sgorga*) spring; (*di fiume, FISICA, fig*) source; **acqua di ~** spring water; **~ di calore** source of heat; **~ termale** thermal spring.

'sorgere ['sordʒere] *vi* to rise; (*scaturire*) to spring, rise; (*fig*: *difficoltà*) to arise ♦ *sm*: **al ~ del sole** at sunrise.

sori'ano, a *ag, sm/f* tabby.

sormon'tare *vt* (*fig*) to overcome, surmount.

sorni'one, a *ag* sly.

sorpas'sare *vt* (*AUT*) to overtake; (*fig*) to surpass; (: *eccedere*) to exceed, go beyond; **~ in altezza** to be higher than; (*persona*) to be taller than.

sorpas'sato, a *ag* (*metodo, moda*) outmoded, old-fashioned; (*macchina*) obsolete.

sor'passo *sm* (*AUT*) overtaking.

sorpren'dente *ag* surprising; (*eccezionale, inaspettato*) astonishing, amazing.

sor'prendere *vt* (*cogliere: in flagrante etc*) to catch; (*stupire*) to surprise; **~rsi** *vr*: **~rsi (di)** to be surprised (at).

sor'preso, a *pp di* **sorprendere** ♦ *sf* surprise; **fare una ~a a qn** to give sb a surprise; **prendere qn di ~a** to take sb by surprise *o* unawares.

sor'reggere [sor'reddʒere] *vt* to support, hold up; (*fig*) to sustain.

sor'retto, a *pp di* **sorreggere**.

sor'ridere *vi* to smile.

sor'riso, a *pp di* **sorridere** ♦ *sm* smile.

sor'sata *sf* gulp; **bere a ~e** to gulp.

sorseggi'are [sorsed'dʒare] *vt* to sip.

'sorsi *etc vb vedi* **sorgere**.

'sorso *sm* sip; **d'un ~, in un ~ solo** at one gulp.

'sorta *sf* sort, kind; **di ~** whatever, of any kind, at all; **ogni ~ di** all sorts of; **di ogni ~** of every kind.

'sorte *sf* (*fato*) fate, destiny; (*evento fortuito*) chance; **tirare a ~** to draw lots; **tentare la ~** to try one's luck.

sorteggi'are [sorted'dʒare] *vt* to draw for.

sor'teggio [sor'teddʒo] *sm* draw.

sorti'legio [sorti'lɛdʒo] *sm* witchcraft *q*; (*incantesimo*) spell; **fare un ~ a qn** to cast a spell on sb.

sor'tire *vr* (*ottenere*) to produce.

sor'tita *sf* (*MIL*) sortie.

'sorto, a *pp di* **sorgere.**

sorvegli'ante [sorveʎ'ʎante] *sm/f* (*di carcere*) guard, warder (*Brit*); (*di fabbrica etc*) supervisor.

sorvegli'anza [sorveʎ'ʎantsa] *sf* watch; supervision; (*POLIZIA, MIL*) surveillance.

sorvegli'are [sorveʎ'ʎare] *vt* (*bambino, bagagli, prigioniero*) to watch, keep an eye on; (*malato*) to watch over; (*territorio, casa*) to watch *o* keep watch over; (*lavori*) to supervise.

sorvo'lare *vt* (*territorio*) to fly over ♦ *vi*: **~ su** (*fig*) to skim over.

S.O.S. *sigla m* mayday, SOS.

'sosia *sm inv* double.

sos'pendere *vt* (*appendere*) to hang (up); (*interrompere, privare di una carica*) to suspend; (*rimandare*) to defer; **~ un quadro al muro/un lampadario al soffitto** to hang a picture on the wall/a chandelier from the ceiling; **~ qn dal suo incarico** to suspend sb from office.

sospensi'one *sf* (*anche CHIM, AUT*) suspension; deferment; **~ condizionale della pena** (*DIR*) suspended sentence.

sos'peso, a *pp di* **sospendere** ♦ *ag* (*appeso*): **~ a** hanging on (*o* from); (*treno, autobus*) cancelled; **in ~** in abeyance; (*conto*) outstanding; **tenere in ~** (*fig*) to keep in suspense; **col fiato ~** with bated breath.

sospet'tare *vt* to suspect ♦ *vi*: **~ di** to suspect; (*diffidare*) to be suspicious of.

sos'petto, a *ag* suspicious ♦ *sm* suspicion; **destare ~i** to arouse suspicion.

sospet'toso, a *ag* suspicious.

sos'pingere [sos'pindʒere] *vt* to drive, push.

sos'pinto, a *pp di* **sospingere.**

sospi'rare *vi* to sigh ♦ *vt* to long for, yearn for.

sos'piro *sm* sigh; **~ di sollievo** sigh of relief.

'sosta *sf* (*fermata*) stop, halt; (*pausa*) pause, break; **senza ~** non-stop, without a break.

sostanti'vato, a *ag* (*LING*): **aggettivo ~** adjective used as a noun.

sostan'tivo *sm* noun, substantive.

sos'tanza [sos'tantsa] *sf* substance; **~e** *sfpl* (*ricchezze*) wealth *sg*, possessions; **in ~** in short, to sum up; **la ~ del discorso** the essence of the speech.

sostanzi'ale [sostan'tsjale] *ag* substantial.

sostanzi'oso, a [sostan'tsjoso] *ag* (*cibo*) nourishing, substantial.

sos'tare *vi* (*fermarsi*) to stop (for a while), stay; (*fare una pausa*) to take a break.

sos'tegno [sos'teɲɲo] *sm* support; **a ~ di** in support of; **muro di ~** supporting wall.

soste'nere *vt* to support; (*prendere su di sé*) to take on, bear; (*resistere*) to withstand, stand up to; (*affermare*): **~ che** to maintain that; **~rsi** *vr* to hold o.s. up, support o.s.; (*fig*) to keep up one's strength; **~ qn** (*moralmente*) to be a support to sb; (*difendere*) to stand up for sb, take sb's part; **~ gli esami** to sit exams; **~ il confronto** to bear *o* stand comparison.

soste'nibile *ag* (*tesi*) tenable; (*spese*) bearable.

sosteni'tore, 'trice *sm/f* supporter.

sostenta'mento *sm* maintenance, support; **mezzi di ~** means of support.

soste'nuto, a *ag* (*stile*) elevated; (*velocità, ritmo*) sustained; (*prezzo*) high ♦ *sm/f*: **fare il(la) ~(a)** to be standoffish, keep one's distance.

sostitu'ire *vt* (*mettere al posto di*): **~ qn/qc a** to substitute sb/sth for; (*prendere il posto di*) to replace, take the place of.

sostitu'tivo, a *ag* (*AMM: documento, certificato*) equivalent.

sosti'tuto, a *sm/f* substitute; **~ procuratore della Repubblica** (*DIR*) deputy public prosecutor.

sostituzi'one [sostitut'tsjone] *sf* substitution; **in ~ di** as a substitute for, in place of.

sotta'ceti [sotta'tʃeti] *smpl* pickles.

sot'tana *sf* (*sottoveste*) underskirt; (*gonna*) skirt; (*REL*) soutane, cassock.

sot'tecchi [sot'tekki] *av*: **guardare di ~** to steal a glance at.

sotter'fugio [sotter'fudʒo] *sm* subterfuge.

sotter'raneo, a *ag* underground ♦ *sm* cellar.

sotter'rare *vt* to bury.

sottigli'ezza [sottiʎ'ʎettsa] *sf* thinness; slimness; (*fig: acutezza*) subtlety; shrewdness; **~e** *sfpl* (*pedanteria*) quibbles.

sot'tile *ag* thin; (*figura, caviglia*) thin, slim, slender; (*fine: polvere, capelli*) fine; (*fig: leggero*) light; (*: vista*) sharp, keen; (*: olfatto*) fine, discriminating; (*: mente*) subtle; shrewd ♦ *sm*: **non andare per il ~** not to mince matters.

sottiliz'zare [sottilid'dzare] *vi* to split hairs.

sottin'tendere *vt* (*intendere qc non espresso*) to understand; (*implicare*) to imply; **lasciare ~ che** to let it be understood that.

sottin'teso, a *pp di* **sottintendere** ♦ *sm* allusion; **parlare senza ~i** to speak plainly.

'sotto *prep* (*gen*) under; (*più in basso di*) below ♦ *av* underneath, beneath; (*al piano inferiore*): **(al piano) di ~** downstairs; **~ il monte** at the foot of the mountain; **~ la pioggia/il sole** in the rain/sun(shine); **tutti quelli ~ i 18 anni** all those under 18 (years of age) (*Brit*) *o* under age 18 (*US*); **~ il livello del mare** below sea level; **~ il chilo** under *o* less than a kilo; **ha 5 impiegati ~ di sé** he has 5 clerks under him; **siamo ~ Natale/Pasqua** it's nearly Christmas/Easter; **~ un certo punto di vista** in a sense; **~ forma di** in the form of; **~ falso nome** under a false name; **~ terra** underground; **~ voce** in a low voice; **chiuso ~ vuoto** vacuum packed.

sotto'banco *av* (*di nascosto*: *vendere, comprare*) under the counter; (*agire*) in an underhand way.

sottobicchi'ere [sottobik'kjɛre] *sm* mat, coaster.

sotto'bosco, schi *sm* undergrowth *q*.

sotto'braccio [sotto'brattʃo] *av* by the arm; **prendere qn ~** to take sb by the arm; **camminare ~ a qn** to walk arm in arm with sb.

sottochi'ave [sotto'kjave] *av* under lock and key.

sottoco'perta *av* (*NAUT*) below deck.

sotto'costo *av* below cost (price).

sottocu'taneo, a *ag* subcutaneous.

sottoes'posto, a *ag* (*fotografia, pellicola*) underexposed.

sotto'fondo *sm* background; **~ musicale** background music.

sotto'gamba *av*: **prendere qc ~** not to take sth seriously.

sotto'gonna *sf* underskirt.

sottogo'verno *sm* political patronage.

sotto'gruppo *sm* subgroup; (*di partito*) faction.

sottoline'are *vt* to underline; (*fig*) to emphasize, stress.

sot't'olio *av, ag inv* in oil.

sotto'mano *av* (*a portata di mano*) within reach, to hand; (*di nascosto*) secretly.

sottoma'rino, a *ag* (*flora*) submarine; (*cavo, navigazione*) underwater ♦ *sm* (*NAUT*) submarine.

sotto'messo, a *pp di* **sottomettere** ♦ *ag* submissive.

sotto'mettere *vt* to subdue, subjugate; **~rsi** *vr* to submit.

sottomissi'one *sf* submission.

sottopas'saggio [sottopas'saddʒo] *sm* (*AUT*) underpass; (*pedonale*) subway, underpass.

sotto'porre *vt* (*costringere*) to subject; (*fig: presentare*) to submit; **sottoporsi** *vr* to submit; **sottoporsi a** (*subire*) to undergo.

sotto'posto, a *pp di* **sottoporre**.

sottopro'dotto *sm* by-product.

sottoproduzi'one [sottoprodut'tsjone] *sf* underproduction.

sottoproletari'ato *sm*: **il ~** the underprivileged class.

sot'tordine *av*: **passare in ~** to become of minor importance.

sottos'cala *sm inv* (*ripostiglio*) cupboard (*Brit*) o closet (*US*) under the stairs; (*stanza*) room under the stairs.

sottos'critto, a *pp di* **sottoscrivere** ♦ *sm/f*: **io ~, il ~** the undersigned.

sottos'crivere *vt* to sign ♦ *vi*: **~ a** to subscribe to.

sottoscrizi'one [sottoskrit'tsjone] *sf* signing; subscription.

sottosegre'tario *sm*: **S~ di Stato** Under-Secretary of State (*Brit*), Assistant Secretary of State (*US*).

sotto'sopra *av* upside-down.

sottos'tante *ag* (*piani*) lower; **nella valle ~** in the valley below.

sottos'tare *vi*: **~ a** (*assoggettarsi a*) to submit to; (: *richieste*) to give in to; (*subire: prova*) to undergo.

sottosu'olo *sm* subsoil.

sottosvilup'pato, a *ag* underdeveloped.

sottosvi'luppo *sm* underdevelopment.

sottote'nente *sm* (*MIL*) second lieutenant.

sotto'terra *av* underground.

sotto'tetto *sm* attic.

sotto'titolo *sm* subtitle.

sottovalu'tare *vt* (*persona, prova*) to underestimate, underrate.

sotto'vento *av* (*NAUT*) leeward(s) ♦ *ag inv* (*lato*) leeward, lee.

sotto'veste *sf* underskirt.

sotto'voce [sotto'votʃe] *av* in a low voice.

sottovu'oto *av*: **confezionare ~** to vacuum-pack ♦ *ag*: **confezione** *f* **~** vacuum pack.

sot'trarre *vt* (*MAT*) to subtract, take away; **sottrarsi** *vr*: **sottrarsi a** (*sfuggire*) to escape; (*evitare*) to avoid; **~ qn/qc a** (*togliere*) to remove sb/sth from; (*salvare*) to save o rescue sb/sth from; **~ qc a qn** (*rubare*) to steal sth from sb; **sottratte le spese** once expenses have been deducted.

sot'tratto, a *pp di* **sottrarre**.

sottrazi'one [sottrat'tsjone] *sf* (*MAT*) subtraction; (*furto*) removal.

sottuffici'ale [sottuffi'tʃale] *sm* (*MIL*) non-commissioned officer; (*NAUT*) petty officer.

so'vente *av* often.

soverchi'are [sover'kjare] *vt* to overpower, overwhelm.

soverchie'ria [soverkje'ria] *sf* (*prepotenza*) abuse (of power).

sovi'etico, a, ci, che *ag* Soviet ♦ *sm/f* Soviet citizen.

sovrabbon'dante *ag* overabundant.

sovrabbon'danza [sovrabbon'dantsa] *sf* overabundance; **in ~** in excess.

sovraccari'care *vt* to overload.

sovrac'carico, a, chi, che *ag*: **~ (di)** overloaded (with) ♦ *sm* excess load; **~ di lavoro** extra work.

sovraesposizi'one [sovraespozit'tsjone] *sf* (*FOT*) overexposure.

sovraffol'lato, a *ag* overcrowded.

sovraimmagazzi'nare [sovraimmagaddzi'nare] *vt* to overstock.

sovranità *sf* sovereignty; *(fig: superiorità)* supremacy.

sovrannatu'rale *ag* = **soprannaturale.**

so'vrano, a *ag* sovereign; *(fig: sommo)* supreme ♦ *sm/f* sovereign, monarch.

sovrappopolazi'one [sovrappopolat'tsjone] *sf* overpopulation.

sovrap'porre *vt* to place on top of, put on top of; *(FOT, GEOM)* to superimpose; **sovrapporsi** *vr (fig: aggiungersi)* to be added; *(FOT)* to be superimposed.

sovrapposizi'one [sovrapposit'tsjone] *sf* superimposition.

sovrap'posto, a *pp di* **sovrapporre.**

sovrapproduzi'one [sovrapprodut'tsjone] *sf* overproduction.

sovras'tare *vi*: ~ **a**, *vt (vallata, fiume)* to overhang; *(fig)* to hang over, threaten.

sovrastrut'tura *sf* superstructure.

sovrecci'tare [sovrettʃi'tare] *vt* to overexcite.

sovrimpressi'one *sf (FOT, CINEMA)* double exposure; **immagini in** ~ superimposed images.

sovrinten'dente *etc* = **soprintendente** *etc.*

sovru'mano, a *ag* superhuman.

sovve'nire *vi (venire in mente)*: ~ **a** to occur to.

sovvenzio'nare [sovventsjo'nare] *vt* to subsidize.

sovvenzi'one [sovven'tsjone] *sf* subsidy, grant.

sovver'sivo, a *ag* subversive.

sovverti'mento *sm* subversion, undermining.

sovver'tire *vt (POL: ordine, stato)* to subvert, undermine.

'sozzo, a ['sottso] *ag* filthy, dirty.

SP *sigla* = La Spezia.

S.P. *abbr* = **strada provinciale;** *vedi* **provinciale.**

S.p.A. *abbr vedi* **società per azioni.**

spac'care *vt* to split, break; *(legna)* to chop; ~**rsi** *vr* to split, break.

spacca'tura *sf* split.

spaccherò [spakke'rɔ] *etc vb vedi* **spaccare.**

spacci'are [spat'tʃare] *vt (vendere)* to sell (off); *(mettere in circolazione)* to circulate; *(droga)* to peddle, push; ~**rsi** *vr*: ~**rsi per** *(farsi credere)* to pass o.s. off as, pretend to be.

spacci'ato, a [spat'tʃato] *ag (fam: malato, fuggiasco)*: **essere** ~ to be done for.

spaccia'tore, 'trice [spattʃa'tore] *sm/f (di droga)* pusher; *(di denaro falso)* dealer.

'spaccio ['spattʃo] *sm (di merce rubata, droga)*: ~ **(di)** trafficking (in); *(di denaro falso)*: ~ **(di)** passing (of); *(vendita)* sale; *(bottega)* shop.

'spacco, chi *sm (fenditura)* split, crack; *(strappo)* tear; *(di gonna)* slit.

spac'cone *sm/f* boaster, braggart.

'spada *sf* sword.

spadroneggi'are [spadroned'dʒare] *vi* to swagger.

spae'sato, a *ag* disorientated, lost.

spaghet'tata [spaget'tata] *sf* spaghetti meal.

spa'ghetti [spa'getti] *smpl (CUC)* spaghetti *sg.*

'Spagna ['spaɲɲa] *sf*: **la** ~ Spain.

spa'gnolo, a [spaɲ'ɲɔlo] *ag* Spanish ♦ *sm/f* Spaniard ♦ *sm (LING)* Spanish; **gli S~i** the Spanish.

'spago, ghi *sm* string, twine; **dare** ~ **a qn** *(fig)* to let sb have his *(o* her) way.

spai'ato, a *ag (calza, guanto)* odd.

spalan'care *vt,* ~**rsi** *vr* to open wide.

spa'lare *vt* to shovel.

'spalla *sf* shoulder; *(fig: TEATRO)* stooge; ~**e** *sfpl (dorso)* back; **di** ~**e** from behind; **seduto alle mie** ~**e** sitting behind me; **prendere/colpire qn alle** ~**e** to take/hit sb from behind; **mettere qn con le** ~**e al muro** *(fig)* to put sb with his *(o* her) back to the wall; **vivere alle** ~**e di qn** *(fig)* to live off sb.

spalleggi'are [spalled'dʒare] *vt* to back up, support.

spal'letta *sf (parapetto)* parapet.

spalli'era *sf (di sedia etc)* back; *(di letto: da capo)* head(board); *(: da piedi)* foot(board); *(GINNASTICA)* wall bars *pl.*

spal'lina *sf (MIL)* epaulette; *(di sottoveste, maglietta)* strap; **senza** ~**e** strapless.

spal'mare *vt* to spread.

'spalti *smpl (di stadio)* terraces *(Brit),* ≈ bleachers *(US).*

'spandere *vt* to spread; *(versare)* to pour (out); ~**rsi** *vr* to spread; ~ **lacrime** to shed tears.

'spanto, a *pp di* **spandere.**

spa'rare *vt* to fire ♦ *vi (far fuoco)* to fire; *(tirare)* to shoot; ~ **a qn/qc** to shoot sb/sth, fire at sb/sth.

spa'rato *sm (di camicia)* dicky.

spara'tore *sm* gunman.

spara'toria *sf* exchange of shots.

sparecchi'are [sparek'kjare] *vt*: ~ **(la tavola)** to clear the table.

spa'reggio [spa'reddʒo] *sm (SPORT)* play-off.

'spargere ['spardʒere] *vt (sparpagliare)* to scatter; *(versare: vino)* to spill; *(: lacrime, sangue)* to shed; *(diffondere)* to spread; *(emanare)* to give off *(o* out); ~**rsi** *vr (voce, notizia)* to spread; *(persone)* to scatter; **si è sparsa una voce sul suo conto** there is a rumour going round about him.

spargi'mento [spardʒi'mento] *sm* scattering; spilling; shedding; ~ **di sangue** bloodshed.

spa'rire *vi* to disappear, vanish; ~ **dalla circolazione** *(fig fam)* to lie low, keep a low profile.

sparizi'one [sparit'tsjone] *sf* disappearance.

spar'lare *vi*: ~ **di** to run down, speak ill of.

'sparo *sm* shot.

sparpagli'are [sparpaʎ'ʎare] *vt,* **~rsi** *vr* to scatter.

'sparso, a *pp di* **spargere** ♦ *ag* scattered; (*sciolto*) loose; **in ordine ~** (*MIL*) in open order.

sparti'acque *sm* (*GEO*) watershed.

sparti'neve *sm inv* snowplough (*Brit*), snowplow (*US*).

spar'tire *vt* (*eredità, bottino*) to share out; (*avversari*) to separate.

spar'tito *sm* (*MUS*) score.

sparti'traffico *sm inv* (*AUT*) central reservation (*Brit*), median (strip) (*US*).

spartizi'one [spartit'tsjone] *sf* division.

spa'ruto, a *ag* (*viso etc*) haggard.

sparvi'ero *sm* (*ZOOL*) sparrowhawk.

spasi'mante *sm* suitor.

spasi'mare *vi* to be in agony; **~ di fare** (*fig*) to yearn to do; **~ per qn** to be madly in love with sb.

'spasimo *sm* pang.

'spasmo *sm* (*MED*) spasm.

spas'modico, a, ci, che *ag* (*angoscioso*) agonizing; (*MED*) spasmodic.

spas'sarsela *vi* to enjoy o.s., have a good time.

spassio'nato, a *ag* dispassionate, impartial.

'spasso *sm* (*divertimento*) amusement, enjoyment; **andare a ~** to go out for a walk; **essere a ~** (*fig*) to be out of work; **mandare qn a ~** (*fig*) to give sb the sack.

spas'soso, a *ag* amusing, entertaining.

'spastico, a, ci, che *ag, sm/f* spastic.

'spatola *sf* spatula.

spau'racchio [spau'rakkjo] *sm* scarecrow.

spau'rire *vt* to frighten, terrify.

spavalde'ria *sf* boldness, arrogance.

spa'valdo, a *ag* arrogant, bold.

spaventa'passeri *sm inv* scarecrow.

spaven'tare *vt* to frighten, scare; **~rsi** *vr* to become frightened, become scared.

spa'vento *sm* fear, fright; **far ~ a qn** to give sb a fright.

spaven'toso, a *ag* frightening, terrible; (*fig fam*) tremendous, fantastic.

spazi'ale [spat'tsjale] *ag* (*volo, nave, tuta*) space *cpd*; (*ARCHIT, GEOM*) spatial.

spazia'tura [spattsja'tura] *sf* (*TIP*) spacing.

spazien'tire [spattsjen'tire] *vi* (*anche:* **~rsi**) to lose one's patience.

'spazio ['spattsjo] *sm* space; (*posto*) room, space; **fare ~ per qc/qn** to make room for sth/sb; **nello ~ di un'ora** within an hour, in the space of an hour; **dare ~ a** (*fig*) to make room for; **~ aereo** airspace.

spazi'oso, a [spat'tsjoso] *ag* spacious.

spazzaca'mino [spattsaka'mino] *sm* chimney sweep.

spazza'neve [spattsa'neve] *sm inv* (*spartineve, SCI*) snowplough (*Brit*), snowplow (*US*).

spaz'zare [spat'tsare] *vt* to sweep; (*foglie etc*) to sweep up; (*cacciare*) to sweep away.

spazza'tura [spattsa'tura] *sf* sweepings *pl*; (*immondizia*) rubbish.

spaz'zino [spat'tsino] *sm* street sweeper.

'spazzola ['spattsola] *sf* brush; **capelli a ~** crew cut *sg*; **~ per abiti** clothesbrush; **~ da capelli** hairbrush.

spazzo'lare [spattso'lare] *vt* to brush.

spazzo'lino [spattso'lino] *sm* (small) brush; **~ da denti** toothbrush.

specchi'arsi [spek'kjarsi] *vr* to look at o.s. in a mirror; (*riflettersi*) to be mirrored, be reflected.

specchi'era [spek'kjɛra] *sf* large mirror; (*mobile*) dressing table.

specchi'etto [spek'kjetto] *sm* (*tabella*) table, chart; **~ da borsetta** pocket mirror; **~ retrovisore** (*AUT*) rear-view mirror.

'specchio ['spɛkkjo] *sm* mirror; (*tabella*) table, chart; **uno ~ d'acqua** a sheet of water.

speci'ale [spe'tʃale] *ag* special; **in special modo** especially; **inviato ~** (*RADIO, TV, STAMPA*) special correspondent; **offerta ~** special offer; **poteri/leggi ~i** (*POL*) emegency powers/legislation.

specia'lista, i, e [spetʃa'lista] *sm/f* specialist.

specia'listico, a, ci, che [spetʃa'listiko] *ag* (*conoscenza, preparazione*) specialized.

specialità [spetʃali'ta] *sf inv* speciality; (*branca di studio*) special field, speciality.

specializ'zare [spetʃalid'dzare] *vt* (*industria*) to make more specialized; **~rsi** *vr:* **~rsi (in)** to specialize (in).

specializ'zato, a [spetʃalid'dzato] *ag* (*manodopera*) skilled; **operaio non ~** semiskilled worker; **essere ~ in** to be a specialist in.

specializzazi'one [spetʃaliddzat'tsjone] *sf* specialization; **prendere la ~ in** to specialize in.

special'mente [spetʃal'mente] *av* especially, particularly.

'specie ['spetʃe] *sf inv* (*BIOL, BOT, ZOOL*) species *inv*; (*tipo*) kind, sort ♦ *av* especially, particularly; **una ~ di** a kind of; **fare ~ a qn** to surprise sb; **la ~ umana** mankind.

spe'cifica, che [spe'tʃifika] *sf* specification.

specifi'care [spetʃifi'kare] *vt* to specify, state.

spe'cifico, a, ci, che [spe'tʃifiko] *ag* specific.

specu'lare *vi:* **~ su** (*COMM*) to speculate in; (*sfruttare*) to exploit; (*meditare*) to speculate on.

specula'tore, 'trice *sm/f* (*COMM*) speculator.

speculazi'one [spekulat'tsjone] *sf* speculation.

spe'dire *vt* to send; (*COMM*) to dispatch, forward; **~ per posta** to post (*Brit*), mail (*US*); **~ per mare** to ship.

spedita'mente *av* quickly; **camminare** ~ to walk at a brisk pace.

spe'dito, a *ag* (*gen*) quick; **con passo** ~ at a brisk pace.

spedizi'one [spedit'tsjone] *sf* sending; (*collo*) consignment; (*scientifica etc*) expedition; (*COMM*) forwarding; shipping; **fare una** ~ to send a consignment; **agenzia di** ~ forwarding agency; **spese di** ~ postal charges; (*COMM*) forwarding charges.

spedizioni'ere [spedittsjo'njɛre] *sm* forwarding agent, shipping agent.

'spegnere ['spɛɲɲere] *vt* (*fuoco, sigaretta*) to put out, extinguish; (*apparecchio elettrico*) to turn *o* switch off; (*gas*) to turn off; (*fig: suoni, passioni*) to stifle; (*debito*) to extinguish; ~**rsi** *vr* to go out; to go off; (*morire*) to pass away.

speleolo'gia [speleolo'dʒia] *sf* (*studio*) speleology; (*pratica*) potholing (*Brit*), speleology.

spele'ologo, a, gi, ghe *sm/f* speleologist; potholer.

spel'lare *vt* (*scuoiare*) to skin; (*scorticare*) to graze; ~**rsi** *vr* to peel.

'spendere *vt* to spend; ~ **una buona parola per qn** (*fig*) to put in a good word for sb.

'spengo *etc vb vedi* **spegnere**.

spen'nare *vt* to pluck.

'spensi *etc vb vedi* **spegnere**.

spensiera'tezza [spensjera'tettsa] *sf* carefreeness, lightheartedness.

spensie'rato, a *ag* carefree.

'spento, a *pp di* **spegnere** ♦ *ag* (*suono*) muffled; (*colore*) dull; (*sigaretta*) out; (*civiltà, vulcano*) extinct.

spe'ranza [spe'rantsa] *sf* hope; **nella** ~ **di rivederti** hoping to see *o* in the hope of seeing you again; **pieno di** ~**e** hopeful; **senza** ~ (*situazione*) hopeless; (*amare*) without hope.

speran'zoso, a [speran'tsoso] *ag* hopeful.

spe'rare *vt* to hope for ♦ *vi*: ~ **in** to trust in; ~ **che/di fare** to hope that/to do; **lo spero, spero di sì** I hope so; **tutto fa** ~ **per il meglio** everything leads one to hope for the best.

sper'duto, a *ag* (*isolato*) out-of-the-way; (*persona: smarrita, a disagio*) lost.

spergiu'ro, a [sper'dʒuro] *sm/f* perjurer ♦ *sm* perjury.

sperico'lato, a *ag* fearless, daring; (*guidatore*) reckless.

sperimen'tale *ag* experimental; **fare qc in via** ~ to try sth out.

sperimen'tare *vt* to experiment with, test; (*fig*) to test, put to the test.

sperimentazi'one [sperimentat'tsjone] *sf* experimentation.

'sperma, i *sm* (*BIOL*) sperm.

spermato'zoo, i [spermatod'dzɔo] *sm* spermatozoon.

spe'rone *sm* spur.

sperpe'rare *vt* to squander.

'sperpero *sm* (*di denaro*) squandering, waste; (*di cibo, materiali*) waste.

'spesa *sf* (*soldi spesi*) expense; (*costo*) cost; (*acquisto*) purchase; (*fam: acquisto del cibo quotidiano*) shopping; ~**e** *sfpl* expenses; (*COMM*) costs; charges; **ridurre le** ~**e** (*gen*) to cut down; (*COMM*) to reduce expenditure; **fare la** ~ to do the shopping; **fare le** ~**e di qc** (*fig*) to pay the price for sth; **a** ~**e di** (*a carico di*) at the expense of; **con la modica** ~ **di un milione di lire** for the modest sum *o* outlay of one million lire; ~ **pubblica** public expenditure; ~**e accessorie** incidental expenses; ~**e generali** overheads; ~**e di gestione** operating expenses; ~**e d'impianto** initial outlay; ~**e legali** legal costs; ~**e di manutenzione, ~e di mantenimento** maintenance costs; ~**e postali** postage *sg*; ~**e di sbarco e sdoganamento** landing charges; ~**e di trasporto** handling charge; ~**e di viaggio** travelling (*Brit*) *o* traveling (*US*) expenses.

spe'sare *vt*: **viaggio tutto spesato** all-expenses-paid trip.

'speso, a *pp di* **spendere**.

'spesso, a *ag* (*fitto*) thick; (*frequente*) frequent ♦ *av* often; ~**e volte** frequently, often.

spes'sore *sm* thickness; **ha uno** ~ **di 20 cm** it is 20 cm thick.

Spett. *abbr vedi* **spettabile**.

spet'tabile *ag* (*abbr: Spett.: in lettere*): ~ **ditta X** Messrs X and Co; **avvertiamo la** ~ **clientela ...** we inform our customers ....

spettaco'lare *ag* spectacular.

spet'tacolo *sm* (*rappresentazione*) performance, show; (*vista, scena*) sight; **dare** ~ **di sé** to make an exhibition *o* a spectacle of o.s.

spettaco'loso, a *ag* spectacular.

spet'tanza [spet'tantsa] *sf* (*competenza*) concern; **non è di mia** ~ it's no concern of mine.

spet'tare *vi*: ~ **a** (*decisione*) to be up to; (*stipendio*) to be due to; **spetta a lei decidere** it's up to you to decide.

spetta'tore, 'trice *sm/f* (*CINEMA, TEATRO*) member of the audience; (*di avvenimento*) onlooker, witness.

spettego'lare *vi* to gossip.

spetti'nare *vt*: ~ **qn** to ruffle sb's hair; ~**rsi** *vr* to get one's hair in a mess.

spet'trale *ag* spectral, ghostly.

'spettro *sm* (*fantasma*) spectre (*Brit*), specter (*US*); (*FISICA*) spectrum.

'spezie ['spettsje] *sfpl* (*CUC*) spices.

spez'zare [spet'tsare] *vt* (*rompere*) to break; (*fig: interrompere*) to break up; ~**rsi** *vr* to break.

spezza'tino [spettsa'tino] *sm* (*CUC*) stew.

spez'zato, a [spet'tsato] *ag* (*unghia, ramo, braccio*) broken ♦ *sm* (*abito maschile*) co-ordinated jacket and trousers (*Brit*) *o* pants (*US*); **fare orario ~** to work a split shift.

spezzet'tare [spettset'tare] *vt* to break up (*o* chop) into small pieces.

spez'zino, a [spet'tsino] *ag* of (*o* from) La Spezia.

spez'zone [spet'tsone] *sm* (*CINEMA*) clip.

'spia *sf* spy; (*confidente della polizia*) in-former; (*ELETTR*) indicating light; warn-ing light; (*fessura*) peephole; (*fig: sintomo*) sign, indication; **~ dell'olio** (*AUT*) oil warning light.

spia'cente [spja'tʃɛnte] *ag* sorry; **essere ~ di qc/di fare qc** to be sorry about sth/for doing sth; **siamo ~i di dovervi annunciare che ...** we regret to announce that ....

spia'cevole [spja'tʃevole] *ag* unpleasant, dis-agreeable.

spi'aggia, ge ['spjaddʒa] *sf* beach.

spia'nare *vt* (*terreno*) to level, make level; (*edificio*) to raze to the ground; (*pasta*) to roll out; (*rendere liscio*) to smooth (out).

spi'ano *sm*: **a tutto ~** (*lavorare*) non-stop, without a break; (*spendere*) lavishly.

spian'tato, a *ag* penniless, ruined.

spi'are *vt* to spy on; (*occasione etc*) to watch *o* wait for.

spi'ata *sf* tip-off.

spiattel'lare *vt* (*fam: verità, segreto*) to blurt out.

spi'azzo ['spjattso] *sm* open space; (*radura*) clearing.

spic'care *vt* (*assegno, mandato di cattura*) to issue ♦ *vi* (*risaltare*) to stand out; **~ il volo** to fly off; (*fig*) to spread one's wings; **~ un balzo** to jump, leap.

spic'cato, a *ag* (*marcato*) marked, strong; (*notevole*) remarkable.

spiccherò *etc* [spikke'rɔ] *vb vedi* **spiccare**.

'spicchio ['spikkjo] *sm* (*di agrumi*) segment; (*di aglio*) clove; (*parte*) piece, slice.

spicci'arsi [spit'tʃarsi] *vr* to hurry up.

spiccio'lata [spittʃo'lata] *av*: **alla ~** in dribs and drabs, a few at a time.

'spicciolo, a ['spittʃolo] *ag*: **moneta ~a, ~i** *smpl* (small) change.

'spicco, chi *sm*: **fare ~** to stand out; **di ~** outstanding, prominent; (*tema*) main, principal.

spie'dino *sm* (*utensile*) skewer; (*cibo*) kebab.

spi'edo *sm* (*CUC*) spit; **pollo allo ~** spit-roasted chicken.

spiega'mento *sm* (*MIL*): **~ di forze** deploy-ment of forces.

spie'gare *vt* (*far capire*) to explain; (*tovaglia*) to unfold; (*vele*) to unfurl; **~rsi** *vr* to explain o.s., make o.s. clear; **~ qc a**

qn to explain sth to sb; **il problema si spiega** one can understand the problem; **non mi spiego come ...** I can't understand how ....

spiegazi'one [spjegat'tsjone] *sf* explanation; **avere una ~ con qn** to have it out with sb.

spiegaz'zare [spjegat'tsare] *vt* to crease, crumple.

spiegherò *etc* [spjege'rɔ] *vb vedi* **spiegare**.

spie'tato, a *ag* ruthless, pitiless.

spiffe'rare *vt* (*fam*) to blurt out, blab.

'spiffero *sm* draught (*Brit*), draft (*US*).

'spiga, ghe *sf* (*BOT*) ear.

spigli'ato, a [spiʎ'ʎato] *ag* self-possessed, self-confident.

spigo'lare *vt* (*anche fig*) to glean.

'spigolo *sm* corner; (*GEOM*) edge.

spigo'loso, a *ag* (*mobile*) angular; (*persona, carattere*) difficult.

'spilla *sf* brooch; (*da cravatta, cappello*) pin.

spil'lare *vt* (*vino, fig*) to tap; **~ denaro/ notizie a qn** to tap sb for money/ information.

'spillo *sm* pin; (*spilla*) brooch; **tacco a ~** stiletto heel (*Brit*), spike heel (*US*); **~ di sicurezza** *o* **da balia** safety pin; **~ di sicurezza** (*MIL*) (safety) pin.

spilorce'ria [spilortʃe'ria] *sf* meanness, stingi-ness.

spi'lorcio, a, ci, ce [spi'lortʃo] *ag* mean, stingy.

spilun'gone *sm/f* beanpole.

'spina *sf* (*BOT*) thorn; (*ZOOL*) spine, prickle; (*di pesce*) bone; (*ELETTR*) plug; (*di botte*) bunghole; **birra alla ~** draught beer; **stare sulle ~e** (*fig*) to be on tenter-hooks; **~ dorsale** (*ANAT*) backbone.

spi'nacio [spi'natʃo] *sm* spinach *q*; (*CUC*): **~i** spinach *sg*.

spi'nale *ag* (*ANAT*) spinal.

spi'nato, a *ag* (*fornito di spine*): **filo ~** barbed wire; (*tessuto*) herringbone *cpd*.

spi'nello *sm* (*DROGA: gergo*) joint.

'spingere ['spindʒere] *vt* to push; (*condurre: anche fig*) to drive; (*stimolare*): **~ qn a fare** to urge *o* press sb to do; **~rsi** *vr* (*inol-trarsi*) to push on, carry on; **~rsi troppo lontano** (*anche fig*) to go too far.

'spino *sm* (*BOT*) thorn bush.

spi'noso, a *ag* thorny, prickly.

'spinsi *etc vb vedi* **spingere**.

spinte'rogeno [spinte'rɔdʒeno] *sm* (*AUT*) coil ignition.

'spinto, a *pp di* **spingere** ♦ *sf* (*urto*) push; (*FISICA*) thrust; (*fig: stimolo*) incentive, spur; (: *appoggio*) string-pulling *q*; **dare una ~a a qn** (*fig*) to pull strings for sb.

spin'tone *sm* push, shove.

spio'naggio [spio'naddʒo] *sm* espionage, spy-ing.

spion'cino [spion'tʃino] *sm* peephole.

spio'nistico, a, ci, che *ag* (*organizzazione*)

spy *cpd*; **rete** ~**a** spy ring.
spi'overe *vi* (*scorrere*) to flow down; (*ricadere*) to hang down, fall.
'spira *sf* coil.
spi'raglio [spiˈraʎʎo] *sm* (*fessura*) chink, narrow opening; (*raggio di luce, fig*) glimmer, gleam.
spi'rale *sf* spiral; (*contraccettivo*) coil; **a** ~ spiral(-shaped); ~ **inflazionistica** inflationary spiral.
spi'rare *vi* (*vento*) to blow; (*morire*) to expire, pass away.
spiri'tato, a *ag* possessed; (*fig: persona, espressione*) wild.
spiri'tismo *sm* spiritualism.
'spirito *sm* (*REL, CHIM, disposizione d'animo, di legge etc, fantasma*) spirit; (*pensieri, intelletto*) mind; (*arguzia*) wit; (*umorismo*) humour, wit; **in buone condizioni di** ~ in the right frame of mind; **è una persona di** ~ he has a sense of humour (*Brit*) *o* humor (*US*); **battuta di** ~ joke; ~ **di classe** class consciousness; **non ha** ~ **di parte** he never takes sides; **lo S**~ **Santo** the Holy Spirit *o* Ghost.
spirito'saggine [spiritoˈsaddʒine] *sf* witticism; (*peg*) wisecrack.
spiri'toso, a *ag* witty.
spiritu'ale *ag* spiritual.
splen'dente *ag* (*giornata*) bright, sunny; (*occhi*) shining; (*pavimento*) shining, gleaming.
'splendere *vi* to shine.
'splendido, a *ag* splendid; (*splendente*) shining; (*sfarzoso*) magnificent, splendid.
splen'dore *sm* splendour (*Brit*), splendor (*US*); (*luce intensa*) brilliance, brightness.
spodes'tare *vt* to deprive of power; (*sovrano*) to depose.
'spoglia [ˈspɔʎʎa] *sf vedi* **spoglio**.
spogli'are [spoʎˈʎare] *vt* (*svestire*) to undress; (*privare, fig: depredare*): ~ **qn di qc** to deprive sb of sth; (*togliere ornamenti: anche fig*): ~ **qn/qc di** to strip sb/sth of; ~**rsi** *vr* to undress, strip; ~**rsi di** (*ricchezze etc*) to deprive o.s. of, give up; (*pregiudizi*) to rid o.s. of.
spoglia'rello [spoʎʎaˈrello] *sm* striptease.
spoglia'toio [spoʎʎaˈtojo] *sm* dressing room; (*di scuola etc*) cloakroom; (*SPORT*) changing room.
'spoglio, a [ˈspɔʎʎo] *ag* (*pianta, terreno*) bare; (*privo*): ~ **di** stripped of; lacking in, without ♦ *sm* (*di voti*) counting ♦ *sf* (*ZOOL*) skin, hide; (: *di rettile*) slough; ~**e** *sfpl* (*salma*) remains; (*preda*) spoils, booty *sg*.
'spola *sf* shuttle; (*bobina*) spool; **fare la** ~ **(fra)** to go to and fro *o* shuttle (between).
spo'letta *sf* (*CUCITO*: *bobina*) spool; (*di bomba*) fuse.
spol'pare *vt* to strip the flesh off.
spolve'rare *vt* (*anche CUC*) to dust; (*con*

spazzola) to brush; (*con battipanni*) to beat; (*fig: mangiare*) to polish off ♦ *vi* to dust.
'sponda *sf* (*di fiume*) bank; (*di mare, lago*) shore; (*bordo*) edge.
sponsoriz'zare [sponsoridˈdzare] *vt* to sponsor.
sponsorizzazi'one [sponsoriddzatˈtsjone] *sf* sponsorship.
spon'taneo, a *ag* spontaneous; (*persona*) unaffected, natural; **di sua** ~**a volontà** of his own free will.
spopo'lare *vt* to depopulate ♦ *vi* (*attirare folla*) to draw the crowds; ~**rsi** *vr* to become depopulated.
spo'radico, a, ci, che *ag* sporadic.
sporcacci'one, a [sporkatˈtʃone] *sm/f* (*peg*) pig, filthy person.
spor'care *vt* to dirty, make dirty; (*fig*) to sully, soil; ~**rsi** *vr* to get dirty.
spor'cizia [sporˈtʃittsja] *sf* (*stato*) dirtiness; (*sudiciume*) dirt, filth; (*fig: cosa oscena*) obscenity.
'sporco, a, chi, che *ag* dirty, filthy; **avere la coscienza** ~**a** to have a guilty conscience.
spor'genza [sporˈdʒentsa] *sf* projection.
'sporgere [ˈspɔrdʒere] *vt* to put out, stretch out ♦ *vi* (*venire in fuori*) to stick out; ~**rsi** *vr* to lean out; ~ **querela contro qn** (*DIR*) to take legal action against sb.
'sporsi *etc vb vedi* **sporgere**.
sport *sm inv* sport.
'sporta *sf* shopping bag.
spor'tello *sm* (*di treno, auto etc*) door; (*di banca, ufficio*) window, counter; ~ **automatico** (*BANCA*) cash dispenser, automated telling machine.
spor'tivo, a *ag* (*gara, giornale*) sports *cpd*; (*persona*) sporty; (*abito*) casual; (*spirito, atteggiamento*) sporting ♦ *sm/f* sportsman/woman; **campo** ~ playing field; **giacca** ~**a** sports (*Brit*) *o* sport (*US*) jacket.
'sporto, a *pp di* **sporgere**.
'sposa *sf* bride; (*moglie*) wife; **abito** *o* **vestito da** ~ wedding dress.
sposa'lizio [spozaˈlittsjo] *sm* wedding.
spo'sare *vt* to marry; (*fig: idea, fede*) to espouse; ~**rsi** *vr* to get married, marry; ~**rsi con qn** to marry sb, get married to sb.
spo'sato, a *ag* married.
'sposo *sm* (*bride*)groom; (*marito*) husband; **gli** ~**i** the newlyweds.
spos'sante *ag* exhausting.
spossa'tezza [spossaˈtettsa] *sf* exhaustion.
spos'sato, a *ag* exhausted, weary.
sposta'mento *sm* movement, change of position.
spos'tare *vt* to move, shift; (*cambiare: orario*) to change; ~**rsi** *vr* to move; **hanno spostato la partenza di qualche giorno** they

postponed *o* put off their departure by a few days.

'**spranga, ghe** *sf* (*sbarra*) bar; (*catenaccio*) bolt.

spran'gare *vt* to bar; to bolt.

'**sprazzo** ['sprattso] *sm* (*di sole etc*) flash; (*fig: di gioia etc*) burst.

spre'care *vt* to waste; **~rsi** *vr* (*persona*) to waste one's energy.

'**spreco, chi** *sm* waste.

spre'gevole [spre'dʒevole] *ag* contemptible, despicable.

'**spregio** ['sprɛdʒo] *sm* scorn, disdain.

spregiudi'cato, a [spredʒudi'kato] *ag* unprejudiced, unbiased; (*peg*) unscrupulous.

'**spremere** *vt* to squeeze; **~rsi le meningi** (*fig*) to rack one's brains.

spre'muta *sf* fresh fruit juice; **~ d'arancia** fresh orange juice.

sprez'zante [spret'tsante] *ag* scornful, contemptuous.

'**sprezzo** ['sprɛttso] *sm* contempt, scorn, disdain.

sprigio'nare [spridʒo'nare] *vt* to give off, emit; **~rsi** *vr* to emanate; (*uscire con impeto*) to burst out.

spriz'zare [sprit'tsare] *vt, vi* to spurt; **~ gioia/salute** to be bursting with joy/health.

sprofon'dare *vi* to sink; (*casa*) to collapse; (*suolo*) to give way, subside; **~rsi** *vr*: **~rsi in** (*poltrona*) to sink into; (*fig*) to become immersed *o* absorbed in.

sproloqui'are *vi* to ramble on.

spro'loquio *sm* rambling speech.

spro'nare *vt* to spur (on).

'**sprone** *sm* (*sperone, fig*) spur.

sproporzio'nato, a [sproportsjo'nato] *ag* disproportionate, out of all proportion.

sproporzi'one [spropor'tsjone] *sf* disproportion.

sproposi'tato, a *ag* (*lettera, discorso*) full of mistakes; (*fig: costo*) excessive, enormous.

spro'posito *sm* blunder; **a ~** at the wrong time; (*rispondere, parlare*) irrelevantly.

sprovve'duto, a *ag* inexperienced, naïve.

sprov'visto, a *ag* (*mancante*): **~ di** lacking in, without; **ne siamo ~i** (*negozio*) we are out of it (*o* them); **alla ~a** unawares.

spruz'zare [sprut'tsare] *vt* (*a nebulizzazione*) to spray; (*aspergere*) to sprinkle; (*inzaccherare*) to splash.

spruzza'tore [spruttsa'tore] *sm* (*per profumi*) spray, atomizer; (*per biancheria*) sprinkler, spray.

'**spruzzo** ['spruttso] *sm* spray; splash; **verniciatura a ~** spray painting.

spudora'tezza [spudora'tettsa] *sf* shamelessness.

spudo'rato, a *ag* shameless.

'**spugna** ['spuɲɲa] *sf* (*ZOOL*) sponge; (*tessuto*) towelling.

spu'gnoso, a [spuɲ'ɲoso] *ag* spongy.

spulci'are [spul'tʃare] *vt* (*animali*) to rid of fleas; (*fig: testo, compito*) to examine thoroughly.

'**spuma** *sf* (*schiuma*) foam; (*bibita*) fizzy drink.

spu'mante *sm* sparkling wine.

spumeggi'ante [spumed'dʒante] *ag* (*vino, fig*) sparkling; (*birra, mare*) foaming.

spu'mone *sm* (*CUC*) mousse.

spun'tare *sm*: **allo ~ del sole** at sunrise; **allo ~ del giorno** at daybreak ♦ *vt* (*coltello*) to break the point of; (*capelli*) to trim; (*elenco*) to tick off (*Brit*), check off (*US*) ♦ *vi* (*uscire: germogli*) to sprout; (: *capelli*) to begin to grow; (: *denti*) to come through; (*apparire*) to appear (suddenly); **~rsi** *vr* to become blunt, lose its point; **spuntarla** (*fig*) to make it, win through.

spun'tino *sm* snack.

'**spunto** *sm* (*TEATRO, MUS*) cue; (*fig*) starting point; **dare lo ~ a** to give rise to; **prendere ~ da qc** to take sth as one's starting point.

spur'gare *vt* (*fogna*) to clean, clear; **~rsi** *vr* (*MED*) to expectorate.

spu'tare *vt* to spit out; (*fig*) to belch (out) ♦ *vi* to spit.

'**sputo** *sm* spittle *q*, spit *q*.

sputta'nare *vt* (*fam*) to bad-mouth.

'**squadra** *sf* (*strumento*) (set) square; (*gruppo*) team, squad; (*di operai*) gang, squad; (*MIL*) squad; (: *AER, NAUT*) squadron; (*SPORT*) team; **lavoro a ~e** teamwork; **~ mobile/del buon costume** (*POLIZIA*) flying/vice squad.

squa'drare *vt* to square, make square; (*osservare*) to look at closely.

squa'driglia [skwa'driʎʎa] *sf* (*AER*) flight; (*NAUT*) squadron.

squa'drone *sm* squadron.

squagli'arsi [skwaʎ'ʎarsi] *vr* to melt; (*fig*) to sneak off.

squa'lifica, che *sf* disqualification.

squalifi'care *vt* to disqualify.

'**squallido, a** *ag* wretched, bleak.

squal'lore *sm* wretchedness, bleakness.

'**squalo** *sm* shark.

'**squama** *sf* scale.

squa'mare *vt* to scale; **~rsi** *vr* to flake *o* peel (off).

squarcia'gola [skwartʃa'gola]: **a ~** *av* at the top of one's voice.

squarci'are [skwar'tʃare] *vt* (*muro, corpo*) to rip open; (*tessuto*) to rip; (*fig: tenebre, silenzio*) to split; (: *nuvole*) to pierce.

'**squarcio** ['skwartʃo] *sm* (*ferita*) gash; (*in lenzuolo, abito*) rip; (*in un muro*) breach; (*in una nave*) hole; (*brano*) passage, excerpt; **uno ~ di sole** a burst of sunlight.

squar'tare *vt* to quarter, cut up; (*cadavere*)

to dismember.

squattri'nato, a *ag* penniless ♦ *sm/f* pauper.

squili'brare *vt* to unbalance.

squili'brato, a *ag* (*PSIC*) unbalanced ♦ *sm/f* deranged person.

squi'librio *sm* (*differenza, sbilancio*) imbalance; (*PSIC*) derangement.

squil'lante *ag* (*suono*) shrill, sharp; (*voce*) shrill.

squil'lare *vi* (*campanello, telefono*) to ring (out); (*tromba*) to blare.

'squillo *sm* ring, ringing *q*; blare ♦ *sf inv* (*anche*: **ragazza** ~) call girl.

squi'sito, a *ag* exquisite; (*cibo*) delicious; (*persona*) delightful.

squit'tire *vi* (*uccello*) to squawk; (*topo*) to squeak.

SR *sigla* = Siracusa.

sradi'care *vt* to uproot; (*fig*) to eradicate.

sragio'nare [zradʒo'nare] *vi* to talk nonsense, rave.

sregola'tezza [zregola'tettsa] *sf* (*nel mangiare, bere*) lack of moderation; (*di vita*) dissoluteness, dissipation.

srego'lato, a *ag* (*senza ordine: vita*) disorderly; (*smodato*) immoderate; (*dissoluto*) dissolute.

Sri 'Lanka [sri'lanka] *sm*: **il** ~ Sri Lanka.

S.r.l. *abbr vedi* **società a responsabilità limitata**.

sroto'lare *vt*, ~**rsi** *vr* to unroll.

SS *sigla* = Sassari.

S.S. *abbr* (*REL*) = Sua Santità; Santa Sede; santi, santissimo; (*AUT*) = **strada statale**; *vedi* **statale**.

sta *etc vb vedi* **stare**.

'stabbio *sm* (*recinto*) pen, fold; (*di maiali*) pigsty; (*letame*) manure.

'stabile *ag* stable, steady; (*tempo: non variabile*) settled; (*TEATRO*: *compagnia*) resident ♦ *sm* (*edificio*) building; **teatro** ~ civic theatre.

stabili'mento *sm* (*edificio*) establishment; (*fabbrica*) plant, factory; ~ **balneare** bathing establishment; ~ **tessile** textile mill.

stabi'lire *vt* to establish; (*fissare: prezzi, data*) to fix; (*decidere*) to decide; ~**rsi** (*prendere dimora*) to settle; **resta stabilito che ...** it is agreed that ....

stabilità *sf* stability.

stabiliz'zare [stabilid'dzare] *vt* to stabilize.

stabilizza'tore [stabiliddza'tore] *sm* stabilizer.

stabilizzazi'one [stabiliddzat'tsjone] *sf* stabilization.

staccano'vista, i, e *sm/f* (*ironico*) eager beaver.

stac'care *vt* (*levare*) to detach, remove; (*separare: anche fig*) to separate, divide; (*strappare*) to tear off (*o* out); (*scandire: parole*) to pronounce clearly; (*SPORT*) to leave behind; ~**rsi** *vr* (*bottone etc*) to come off; (*scostarsi*): ~**rsi (da)** to move away

(from); (*fig: separarsi*): ~**rsi da** to leave; **non** ~ **gli occhi da qn** not to take one's eyes off sb; ~ **la televisione/il telefono** to disconnect the television/the phone; ~ **un assegno** to write a cheque.

staccio'nata [stattʃo'nata] *sf* (*gen*) fence; (*IPPICA*) hurdle.

'stacco, chi *sm* (*intervallo*) gap; (: *tra due scene*) break; (*differenza*) difference; (*SPORT*: *nel salto*) takeoff.

sta'dera *sf* lever scales *pl*.

'stadio *sm* (*SPORT*) stadium; (*periodo, fase*) phase, stage.

'staffa *sf* (*di sella, TECN*) stirrup; **perdere le** ~**e** (*fig*) to fly off the handle.

staf'fetta *sf* (*messo*) dispatch rider; (*SPORT*) relay race.

stagflazi'one [stagflat'tsjone] *sf* (*ECON*) stagflation.

stagio'nale [stadʒo'nale] *ag* seasonal ♦ *sm/f* seasonal worker.

stagio'nare [stadʒo'nare] *vt* (*legno*) to season; (*formaggi, vino*) to mature.

stagio'nato, a [stadʒo'nato] *ag* (*vedi vb*) seasoned; matured; (*scherzoso: attempato*) getting on in years.

stagi'one [sta'dʒone] *sf* season; **alta/bassa** ~ high/low season.

stagli'arsi [staʎ'ʎarsi] *vr* to stand out, be silhouetted.

sta'gnante [staɲ'ɲante] *ag* stagnant.

sta'gnare [staɲ'ɲare] *vt* (*vaso, tegame*) to tin-plate; (*barca, botte*) to make watertight; (*sangue*) to stop ♦ *vi* to stagnate.

sta'gnino [staɲ'ɲino] *sm* tinsmith.

'stagno, a ['staɲɲo] *ag* (*a tenuta d'acqua*) watertight; (*a tenuta d'aria*) airtight ♦ *sm* (*acquitrino*) pond; (*CHIM*) tin.

sta'gnola [staɲ'ɲola] *sf* tinfoil.

stalag'mite *sf* stalagmite.

stalat'tite *sf* stalactite.

'stalla *sf* (*per bovini*) cowshed; (*per cavalli*) stable.

stalli'ere *sm* groom, stableboy.

'stallo *sm* stall, seat; (*SCACCHI*) stalemate; (*AER*) stall; **situazione di** ~ (*fig*) stalemate.

stal'lone *sm* stallion.

sta'mani, stamat'tina *av* this morning.

stam'becco, chi *sm* ibex.

stam'berga, ghe *sf* hovel.

'stampa *sf* (*TIP, FOT*: *tecnica*) printing; (*impressione, copia fotografica*) print; (*insieme di quotidiani, giornalisti etc*): **la** ~ the press; **andare in** ~ to go to press; **mandare in** ~ to pass for press; **errore di** ~ printing error; **prova di** ~ print sample; **libertà di** ~ freedom of the press; "~**e**" "printed matter".

stam'pante *sf* (*INFORM*) printer; ~ **seriale/termica** serial/thermal printer.

stam'pare *vt* to print; (*pubblicare*) to publish; (*coniare*) to strike, coin; (*imprimere*: anche *fig*) to impress.

stampa'tello *sm* block letters *pl*.

stam'pato, a *ag* printed ♦ *sm* (*opuscolo*) leaflet; (*modulo*) form; ~**i** *smpl* printed matter *sg*.

stam'pella *sf* crutch.

stampigli'are [stampiʎ'ʎare] *vt* to stamp.

stampiglia'tura [stampiʎʎa'tura] *sf* (*atto*) stamping; (*marchio*) stamp.

'stampo *sm* mould; (*fig*: *indole*) type, kind, sort.

sta'nare *vt* to drive out.

stan'care *vt* to tire, make tired; (*annoiare*) to bore; (*infastidire*) to annoy; ~**rsi** *vr* to get tired, tire o.s. out; ~**rsi (di)** (*stufarsi*) to grow weary (of), grow tired (of).

stan'chezza [stan'kettsa] *sf* tiredness, fatigue.

'stanco, a, chi, che *ag* tired; ~ **di** tired of, fed up with.

standardiz'zare [standardid'dzare] *vt* to standardize.

stan'dista, i, e *sm/f* (*in una fiera etc*) person responsible for a stand.

'stanga, ghe *sm* bar; (*di carro*) shaft.

stan'gata *sf* (*colpo*: anche *fig*) blow; (*cattivo risultato*) poor result; (*CALCIO*) shot.

stan'ghetta [stan'getta] *sf* (*di occhiali*) leg; (*MUS, di scrittura*) bar.

'stanno *vb vedi* **stare**.

sta'notte *av* tonight; (*notte passata*) last night.

'stante *prep* owing to, because of; **a sé** ~ (*appartamento, casa*) independent, separate.

stan'tio, a, 'tii, 'tie *ag* stale; (*burro*) rancid; (*fig*) old.

stan'tuffo *sm* piston.

'stanza ['stantsa] *sf* room; (*POESIA*) stanza; **essere di** ~ **a** (*MIL*) to be stationed in; ~ **da bagno** bathroom; ~ **da letto** bedroom.

stanzia'mento [stantsja'mento] *sm* allocation.

stanzi'are [stan'tsjare] *vt* to allocate.

stan'zino [stan'tsino] *sm* (*ripostiglio*) storeroom; (*spogliatoio*) changing room (*Brit*), locker room (*US*).

stap'pare *vt* to uncork; (*tappo a corona*) to uncap.

'stare *vi* (*restare in un luogo*) to stay, remain; (*abitare*) to stay, live; (*essere situato*) to be, be situated; (*anche*: ~ **in piedi**) to stand; (*essere, trovarsi*) to be; (*dipendere*): **se stesse in me** if it were up to me, if it depended on me; (*seguito da gerundio*): **sta studiando** he's studying; ~ **per fare qc** to be about to do sth; **starci** (*esserci spazio*): **nel baule non ci sta più niente** there's no more room in the boot; (*accettare*): **ci stai?** is that okay with you?; ~ **a** (*attenersi a*) to follow, stick to; (*seguito dall'infinito*): ~ **a sentire** to listen;

staremo a vedere let's wait and see; **stiamo a discutere** we're talking; (*toccare a*): **sta a te giocare** it's your turn to play; **sta a te decidere** it's up to you to decide; ~ **a qn** (*abiti etc*) to fit sb; **queste scarpe mi stanno strette** these shoes are tight for me; **il rosso ti sta bene** red suits you; **come sta?** how are you?; **io sto bene/male** I'm very well/not very well; ~ **fermo** to keep *o* stay still; ~ **seduto** to sit, be sitting; ~ **zitto** to keep quiet; **stando così le cose** given the situation; **stando a ciò che dice lui** according to him *o* to his version.

starnaz'zare [starnat'tsare] *vi* to squawk.

starnu'tire *vi* to sneeze.

star'nuto *sm* sneeze.

sta'sera *av* this evening, tonight.

'stasi *sf* (*MED, fig*) stasis.

sta'tale *ag* state *cpd*, government *cpd* ♦ *sm/f* state employee; (*nell'amministrazione*) ≈ civil servant; **bilancio** ~ national budget; **strada** ~ ≈ trunk (*Brit*) *o* main road.

stataliz'zare [statalid'dzare] *vt* to nationalize, put under state control.

'statico, a, ci, che *ag* (*ELETTR, fig*) static.

sta'tista, i *sm* statesman.

sta'tistico, a, ci, che *ag* statistical ♦ *sf* statistic; (*scienza*) statistics *sg*; **fare una** ~**a** to carry out a statistical examination.

'stato, a *pp di* **essere, stare** ♦ *sm* (*condizione*) state, condition; (*POL*) state; (*DIR*) status; **essere in** ~ **d'accusa** (*DIR*) to be committed for trial; **essere in** ~ **d'arresto** (*DIR*) to be under arrest; **essere in** ~ **interessante** to be pregnant; ~ **d'assedio/ d'emergenza** state of siege/emergency; ~ **civile** (*AMM*) marital status; ~ **di famiglia** (*AMM*) certificate giving details of a household and its dependents; ~ **maggiore** (*MIL*) general staff; ~ **patrimoniale** (*COMM*) statement of assets and liabilities; **gli S~i Uniti (d'America)** the United States (of America).

'statua *sf* statue.

statuni'tense *ag* United States *cpd*, of the United States.

sta'tura *sf* (*ANAT*) height; (*fig*) stature; **essere alto/basso di** ~ to be tall/short *o* small.

sta'tuto *sm* (*DIR*) statute; **regione a** ~ **speciale** Italian region with political autonomy in certain matters; ~ **della società** (*COMM*) articles *pl* of association.

sta'volta *av* this time.

staziona'mento [stattsjona'mento] *sm* (*AUT*) parking; (: *sosta*) waiting; **freno di** ~ handbrake.

stazio'nare [stattsjo'nare] *vi* (*veicoli*) to be parked.

stazio'nario, a [stattsjo'narjo] *ag* stationary; (*fig*) unchanged.

stazi'one [stat'tsjone] *sf* station; (*balneare, invernale etc*) resort; ~ **degli autobus** bus station; ~ **balneare** seaside resort; ~ **climatica** health resort; ~ **ferroviaria** railway (*Brit*) *o* railroad (*US*) station; ~ **invernale** winter sports resort; ~ **di lavoro** work station; ~ **di polizia** police station (*in small town*); ~ **di servizio** service *o* petrol (*Brit*) *o* filling station; ~ **termale** spa.

'stazza ['stattsa] *sf* tonnage.

st. civ. *abbr* = **stato civile**.

'stecca, che *sf* stick; (*di ombrello*) rib; (*di sigarette*) carton; (*MED*) splint; (*stonatura*): **fare una** ~ to sing (*o* play) a wrong note.

stec'cato *sm* fence.

stec'chito, a [stek'kito] *ag* dried up; (*persona*) skinny; **lasciar** ~ **qn** (*fig*) to leave sb flabbergasted; **morto** ~ stone dead.

'stella *sf* star; ~ **alpina** (*BOT*) edelweiss; ~ **cadente** *o* **filante** shooting star; ~ **di mare** (*ZOOL*) starfish.

stel'lato, a *ag* (*cielo, notte*) starry.

'stelo *sm* stem; (*asta*) rod; **lampada a** ~ standard lamp (*Brit*), floor lamp.

'stemma, i *sm* coat of arms.

'stemmo *vb vedi* **stare**.

stempe'rare *vt* (*calce, colore*) to dissolve.

stempi'ato, a *ag* with a receding hairline.

stempia'tura *sf* receding hairline.

sten'dardo *sm* standard.

'stendere *vt* (*braccia, gambe*) to stretch (out); (*tovaglia*) to spread (out); (*bucato*) to hang out; (*mettere a giacere*) to lay (down); (*spalmare: colore*) to spread; (*mettere per iscritto*) to draw up; **~rsi** *vr* (*coricarsi*) to stretch out, lie down; (*estendersi*) to extend, stretch.

stendibianche'ria [stendibjanke'ria] *sm inv* clotheshorse.

stendi'toio *sm* (*locale*) drying room; (*stendibiancheria*) clotheshorse.

stenodattilogra'fia *sf* shorthand typing (*Brit*), stenography (*US*).

stenodatti'lografo, a *sm/f* shorthand typist (*Brit*), stenographer (*US*).

stenogra'fare *vt* to take down in shorthand.

stenogra'fia *sf* shorthand.

ste'nografo, a *sm/f* stenographer.

sten'tare *vi*: ~ **a fare** to find it hard to do, have difficulty doing.

sten'tato, a *ag* (*compito, stile*) laboured (*Brit*), labored (*US*); (*sorriso*) forced.

'stento *sm* (*fatica*) difficulty; **~i** *smpl* (*privazioni*) hardship *sg*, privation *sg*; **a** ~ *av* with difficulty, barely.

'steppa *sf* steppe.

'sterco *sm* dung.

stereofo'nia *sf* stereophony.

'stereo('fonico, a, ci, che) *ag* stereo(phonic).

stereoti'pato, a *ag* stereotyped.

stere'otipo *sm* stereotype; **pensare per ~i** to think in clichés.

'sterile *ag* sterile; (*terra*) barren; (*fig*) futile, fruitless.

sterilità *sf* sterility.

steriliz'zare [sterilid'dzare] *vt* to sterilize.

sterilizzazi'one [steriliddzat'tsjone] *sf* sterilization.

ster'lina *sf* pound (sterling).

stermi'nare *vt* to exterminate, wipe out.

stermi'nato, a *ag* immense, endless.

ster'minio *sm* extermination, destruction; **campo di** ~ death camp.

'sterno *sm* (*ANAT*) breastbone.

ster'paglia [ster'paʎʎa] *sf* brushwood.

'sterpo *sm* dry twig.

ster'rare *vt* to excavate.

ster'zare [ster'tsare] *vt, vi* (*AUT*) to steer.

'sterzo ['stertso] *sm* steering; (*volante*) steering wheel.

'steso, a *pp di* **stendere**.

'stessi *etc vb vedi* **stare**.

'stesso, a *ag* same; (*rafforzativo: in persona, proprio*): **il re** ~ the king himself *o* in person ♦ *pronome*: **lo(la) ~(a)** the same (one); **quello** ~ **giorno** that very day; **i suoi ~i avversari lo ammirano** even his enemies admire him; **fa lo** ~ it doesn't matter; **parto lo** ~ I'm going all the same; **per me è lo** ~ it's all the same to me, it doesn't matter to me; *vedi* **io, tu** *etc*.

ste'sura *sf* (*azione*) drafting *q*, drawing up *q*; (*documento*) draft.

stetos'copio *sm* stethoscope.

'stetti *etc vb vedi* **stare**.

'stia *sf* hutch.

'stia *etc vb vedi* **stare**.

'stigma, i *sm* stigma.

'stigmate *sfpl* (*REL*) stigmata.

sti'lare *vt* to draw up, draft.

'stile *sm* style; (*classe*) style, class; (*SPORT*): ~ **libero** freestyle; **mobili in** ~ period furniture; **in grande** ~ in great style; **è proprio nel suo** ~ (*fig*) it's just like him.

sti'lismo *sm* concern for style.

sti'lista, i, e *sm/f* designer.

sti'listico, a, ci, che *ag* stylistic.

stiliz'zato, a [stilid'dzato] *ag* stylized.

stil'lare *vi* (*trasudare*) to ooze; (*gocciolare*) to drip.

stilli'cidio [stilli'tʃidjo] *sm* (*fig*) continual pestering (*o* moaning *etc*).

stilo'grafica, che *sf* (*anche*: **penna** ~) fountain pen.

Stim. *abbr* = **stimata**.

'stima *sf* esteem; valuation; assessment, estimate; **avere** ~ **di qn** to have respect for sb; **godere della** ~ **di qn** to enjoy sb's respect; **fare la** ~ **di qc** to estimate the value of sth.

sti'mare *vt* (*persona*) to esteem, hold in high regard; (*terreno, casa etc*) to value; (*stabilire in misura approssimativa*) to estimate, assess; (*ritenere*): ~ **che** to consider that; ~**rsi fortunato** to consider o.s. (to be) lucky.

Stim.ma *abbr* = *stimatissima*.

stimo'lante *ag* stimulating ♦ *sm* (*MED*) stimulant.

stimo'lare *vt* to stimulate; (*incitare*): ~ **qn (a fare)** to spur sb on (to do).

stimolazi'one [stimolat'tsjone] *sf* stimulation.

'stimolo *sm* (*anche fig*) stimulus.

'stinco, chi *sm* shin; shinbone.

'stingere ['stindʒere] *vt, vi* (*anche:* ~**rsi**) to fade.

'stinto, a *pp di* **stingere**.

sti'pare *vt* to cram, pack; ~**rsi** *vr* (*accalcarsi*) to crowd, throng.

stipendi'are *vt* (*pagare*) to pay (a salary to).

stipendi'ato, a *ag* salaried ♦ *sm/f* salaried worker.

sti'pendio *sm* salary.

'stipite *sm* (*di porta, finestra*) jamb.

stipu'lare *vt* (*redigere*) to draw up.

stipulazi'one [stipulat'tsjone] *sf* (*di contratto: stesura*) drafting; (: *firma*) signing.

stiracchi'are [stirak'kjare] *vt* (*fig: significato di una parola*) to stretch, force; ~**rsi** *vr* (*persona*) to stretch.

stira'mento *sm* (*MED*) sprain.

sti'rare *vt* (*abito*) to iron; (*distendere*) to stretch; (*strappare: muscolo*) to strain; ~**rsi** *vr* (*fam*) to stretch (o.s.).

stira'tura *sf* ironing.

'stirpe *sf* birth, stock; descendants *pl*.

stiti'chezza [stiti'kettsa] *sf* constipation.

'stitico, a, ci, che *ag* constipated.

'stiva *sf* (*di nave*) hold.

sti'vale *sm* boot.

stiva'letto *sm* ankle boot.

sti'vare *vt* to stow, load.

'stizza ['stittsa] *sf* anger, vexation.

stiz'zire [stit'tsire] *vt* to irritate ♦ *vi*, ~**rsi** *vr* to become irritated, become vexed.

stiz'zoso, a [stit'tsoso] *ag* (*persona*) quick-tempered, irascible; (*risposta*) angry.

stocca'fisso *sm* stockfish, dried cod.

Stoc'carda *sf* Stuttgart.

stoc'cata *sf* (*colpo*) stab, thrust; (*fig*) gibe, cutting remark.

Stoc'colma *sf* Stockholm.

'stoffa *sf* material, fabric; (*fig*): **aver la ~ di** to have the makings of; **avere della ~** to have what it takes.

stoi'cismo [stoi'tʃizmo] *sm* stoicism.

'stoico, a, ci, che *ag* stoic(al).

sto'ino *sm* doormat.

'stola *sf* stole.

stol'tezza [stol'tettsa] *sf* stupidity; (*azione*)

foolish action.

'stolto, a *ag* stupid, foolish.

'stomaco, chi *sm* stomach; **dare di ~** to vomit, be sick.

sto'nare *vt* to sing (*o* play) out of tune ♦ *vi* to be out of tune, sing (*o* play) out of tune; (*fig*) to be out of place, jar; (: *colori*) to clash.

sto'nato, a *ag* (*persona*) off-key; (*strumento*) off-key, out of tune.

stona'tura *sf* (*suono*) false note.

stop *sm inv* (*TELEGRAFIA*) stop; (*AUT: cartello*) stop sign; (: *fanalino d'arresto*) brake-light (*Brit*), stoplight.

'stoppa *sf* tow.

'stoppia *sf* (*AGR*) stubble.

stop'pino *sm* (*di candela*) wick; (*miccia*) fuse.

'storcere ['stɔrtʃere] *vt* to twist; ~**rsi** *vr* to writhe, twist; ~ **il naso** (*fig*) to turn up one's nose; ~**rsi la caviglia** to twist one's ankle.

stordi'mento *sm* (*gen*) dizziness; (*da droga*) stupefaction.

stor'dire *vt* (*intontire*) to stun, daze; ~**rsi** *vr*: ~**rsi col bere** to dull one's senses with drink.

stor'dito, a *ag* stunned; (*sventato*) scatter-brained, heedless.

'storia *sf* (*scienza, avvenimenti*) history; (*racconto, bugia*) story; (*faccenda, questione*) business *q*; (*pretesto*) excuse, pretext; ~**e** *sfpl* (*smancerie*) fuss *sg*; **passare alla ~** to go down in history; **non ha fatto ~e** he didn't make a fuss.

storicità [storitʃi'ta] *sf* historical authenticity.

'storico, a, ci, che *ag* historic(al) ♦ *sm/f* historian.

storiogra'fia *sf* historiography.

stori'one *sm* (*ZOOL*) sturgeon.

stor'mire *vi* to rustle.

'stormo *sm* (*di uccelli*) flock.

stor'nare *vt* (*COMM*) to transfer.

stor'nello *sm kind of folk song*.

'storno *sm* starling.

storpi'are *vt* to cripple, maim; (*fig: parole*) to mangle; (: *significato*) to twist.

storpia'tura *sf* (*fig: di parola*) twisting, distortion.

'storpio, a *ag* crippled, maimed.

'storsi *etc vb vedi* **storcere**.

'storto, a *pp di* **storcere** ♦ *ag* (*chiodo*) twisted, bent; (*gamba, quadro*) crooked; (*fig: ragionamento*) false, wrong ♦ *sf* (*distorsione*) sprain, twist; (*recipiente*) retort ♦ *av*: **guardare ~ qn** (*fig*) to look askance at sb; **andar ~** to go wrong.

sto'viglie [sto'viʎʎe] *sfpl* dishes *pl*, crockery.

str. *abbr* (*GEO*) = **stretto**.

'strabico, a, ci, che *ag* squint-eyed; (*occhi*) squint.

strabili'ante *ag* astonishing, amazing.
strabili'are *vi* to astonish, amaze.
stra'bismo *sm* squinting.
strabuz'zare [strabud'dzare] *vt*: ~ **gli occhi** to open one's eyes wide.
stra'carico, a, chi, che *ag* overloaded.
strac'chino [strak'kino] *sm* *type of soft cheese*.
stracci'are [strat'tʃare] *vt* to tear.
'straccio, a, ci, ce ['strattʃo] *ag*: **carta** ~**a** waste paper ♦ *sm* rag; (*per pulire*) cloth, duster.
stracci'one, a [strat'tʃone] *sm/f* ragamuffin.
stracci'vendolo [strattʃi'vendolo] *sm* ragman.
'stracco, a, chi, che *ag*: ~ **(morto)** exhausted, dead tired.
stra'cotto, a *ag* overcooked ♦ *sm* (*CUC*) beef stew.
'strada *sf* road; (*di città*) street; (*cammino, via, fig*) way; ~ **facendo** on the way; **tre ore di** ~ **(a piedi)/(in macchina)** three hours' walk/drive; **essere sulla buona** ~ (*nella vita*) to be on the right road *o* path; (*con indagine etc*) to be on the right track; **essere fuori** ~ (*fig*) to be on the wrong track; **fare** *o* **farsi** ~ (*fig: persona*) to get on in life; **portare qn sulla cattiva** ~ to lead sb astray; **donna di** ~ (*fig peg*) streetwalker; **ragazzo di** ~ (*fig peg*) street urchin; ~ **ferrata** railway (*Brit*), railroad (*US*); ~ **principale** main road; ~ **senza uscita** dead end, cul-de-sac.
stra'dale *ag* road *cpd*; (*polizia, regolamento*) traffic *cpd*.
stra'dario *sm* street guide.
stra'dino *sm* road worker.
strafalci'one [strafal'tʃone] *sm* blunder, howler.
stra'fare *vi* to overdo it.
stra'fatto, a *pp di* **strafare**.
stra'foro: di ~ *av* (*di nascosto*) on the sly.
strafot'tente *ag*: **è** ~ he doesn't give a damn, he couldn't care less.
strafot'tenza [strafot'tentsa] *sf* arrogance.
'strage ['stradʒe] *sf* massacre, slaughter.
stra'grande *ag*: **la** ~ **maggioranza** the overwhelming majority.
stralci'are [stral'tʃare] *vt* to remove.
'stralcio ['straltʃo] *sm* (*COMM*): **vendere in** ~ to sell off (at bargain prices) ♦ *ag inv*: **legge** ~ abridged version of an act.
stralu'nato, a *ag* (*occhi*) rolling; (*persona*) beside o.s., very upset.
stramaz'zare [stramat'tsare] *vi* to fall heavily.
strambe'ria *sf* eccentricity.
'strambo, a *ag* strange, queer.
strampa'lato, a *ag* odd, eccentric.
stra'nezza [stra'nettsa] *sf* strangeness.
strango'lare *vt* to strangle; ~**rsi** *vr* to choke.

strani'ero, a *ag* foreign ♦ *sm/f* foreigner.
stra'nito, a *ag* dazed.
'strano, a *ag* strange, odd.
straordi'nario, a *ag* extraordinary; (*treno etc*) special ♦ *sm* (*lavoro*) overtime.
strapaz'zare [strapat'tsare] *vt* to ill-treat; ~**rsi** *vr* to tire o.s. out, overdo things.
stra'pazzo [stra'pattso] *sm* strain, fatigue; **da** ~ (*fig*) third-rate.
strapi'eno, a *ag* full to overflowing.
strapi'ombo *sm* overhanging rock; **a** ~ overhanging.
strapo'tere *sm* excessive power.
strappa'lacrime *ag inv* (*fam*): **romanzo** (*o* **film** *etc*) ~ tear-jerker.
strap'pare *vt* (*gen*) to tear, rip; (*pagina etc*) to tear off, tear out; (*sradicare*) to pull up; (*togliere*): ~ **qc a qn** to snatch sth from sb; (*fig*) to wrest sth from sb; ~**rsi** *vr* (*lacerarsi*) to rip, tear; (*rompersi*) to break; ~**rsi un muscolo** to tear a muscle.
'strappo *sm* (*strattone*) pull, tug; (*lacerazione*) tear, rip; (*fig fam: passaggio*) lift (*Brit*), ride (*US*); **fare uno** ~ **alla regola** to make an exception to the rule; ~ **muscolare** torn muscle.
strapun'tino *sm* jump *o* foldaway seat.
strari'pare *vi* to overflow.
Stras'burgo *sf* Strasbourg.
strasci'care [straʃʃi'kare] *vt* to trail; (*piedi*) to drag; ~ **le parole** to drawl.
'strascico, chi ['straʃʃiko] *sm* (*di abito*) train; (*conseguenza*) after-effect.
strata'gemma, i [strata'dʒemma] *sm* stratagem.
stra'tega, ghi *sm* strategist.
strate'gia, 'gie [strate'dʒia] *sf* strategy.
stra'tegico, a, ci, che [stra'tedʒiko] *ag* strategic.
'strato *sm* layer; (*rivestimento*) coat, coating; (*GEO, fig*) stratum; (*METEOR*) stratus.
stratos'fera *sf* stratosphere.
strat'tone *sm* tug, jerk; **dare uno** ~ **a qc** to tug *o* jerk sth, give sth a tug *o* jerk.
stravac'cato, a *ag* sprawling.
strava'gante *ag* odd, eccentric.
strava'ganza [strava'gantsa] *sf* eccentricity.
stra'vecchio, a [stra'vekkjo] *ag* very old.
strave'dere *vi*: ~ **per qn** to dote on sb.
stra'visto, a *pp di* **stravedere**.
stra'vizio [stra'vittsjo] *sm* excess.
stra'volgere [stra'vɔldʒere] *vt* (*volto*) to contort; (*fig: animo*) to trouble deeply; (: *verità*) to twist, distort.
stra'volto, a *pp di* **stravolgere** ♦ *ag* (*persona: per stanchezza etc*) in a terrible state; (: *per sofferenza*) distraught.
strazi'ante [strat'tsjante] *ag* (*scena*) harrowing; (*urlo*) bloodcurdling; (*dolore*) excruciating.
strazi'are [strat'tsjare] *vt* to torture, torment.
'strazio ['strattsjo] *sm* torture; (*fig: cosa fatta*

male): **essere uno** ~ to be appalling; **fare** ~ **di** (*corpo, vittima*) to mutilate.

'strega, ghe *sf* witch.

stre'gare *vt* to bewitch.

stre'gone *sm* (*mago*) wizard; (*di tribù*) witch doctor.

stregone'ria *sf* (*pratica*) witchcraft; **fare una** ~ to cast a spell.

'stregua *sf*: **alla** ~ **di** by the same standard as.

stre'mare *vt* to exhaust.

'stremo *sm*: **essere allo** ~ to be at the end of one's tether.

'strenna *sf*: ~ **natalizia** (*regalo*) Christmas present; (*libro*) *book published for the Christmas market*.

'strenuo, a *ag* brave, courageous.

strepi'tare *vi* to yell and shout.

'strepito *sm* (*di voci, folla*) clamour (*Brit*), clamor (*US*); (*di catene*) clanking, rattling.

strepi'toso, a *ag* clamorous, deafening; (*fig: successo*) resounding.

stres'sante *ag* stressful.

stres'sare *vt* to put under stress.

stres'sato, a *ag* under stress.

'stretta *sf vedi* **stretto**.

stretta'mente *av* tightly; (*rigorosamente*) strictly.

stret'tezza [stret'tettsa] *sf* narrowness; ~**e** *sfpl* (*povertà*) poverty *sg*, straitened circumstances.

'stretto, a *pp di* **stringere** ♦ *ag* (*corridoio, limiti*) narrow; (*gonna, scarpe, nodo, curva*) tight; (*intimo: parente, amico*) close; (*rigoroso: osservanza*) strict; (*preciso: significato*) precise, exact ♦ *sm* (*braccio di mare*) strait ♦ *sf* (*di mano*) grasp; (*finanziaria*) squeeze; (*fig: dolore, turbamento*) pang; **a denti** ~**i** with clenched teeth; **lo** ~ **necessario** the bare minimum; **una** ~**a di mano** a handshake; **una** ~**a al cuore** a sudden sadness; **essere alle** ~**e** to have one's back to the wall.

stret'toia *sf* bottleneck; (*fig*) tricky situation.

stri'ato, a *ag* streaked.

stria'tura *sf* (*atto*) streaking; (*effetto*) streaks *pl*.

stric'nina *sf* strychnine.

'strida *sfpl* screaming *sg*.

stri'dente *ag* strident.

'stridere *vi* (*porta*) to squeak; (*animale*) to screech, shriek; (*colori*) to clash.

'strido, *pl*(*f*) **strida** *sm* screech, shriek.

stri'dore *sm* screeching, shrieking.

'stridulo, a *ag* shrill.

'striglia ['strix ka] *sf* currycomb.

strigli'are [striʎ'ʎare] *vt* (*cavallo*) to curry.

strigli'ata [striʎ'ʎata] *sf* (*di cavallo*) currying; (*fig*): **dare una** ~ **a qn** to give sb a scolding.

stril'lare *vt, vi* to scream, shriek.

'strillo *sm* scream, shriek.

stril'lone *sm* newspaper seller.

strimin'zito, a [strimin'tsito] *ag* (*misero*) shabby; (*molto magro*) skinny.

strimpel'lare *vt* (*MUS*) to strum.

'stringa, ghe *sf* lace.

strin'gare *vt* (*fig: discorso*) to condense.

strin'gato, a *ag* (*fig*) concise.

'stringere ['strindʒere] *vt* (*avvicinare due cose*) to press (together), squeeze (together); (*tenere stretto*) to hold tight, clasp, clutch; (*pugno, mascella, denti*) to clench; (*labbra*) to compress; (*avvitare*) to tighten; (*abito*) to take in; (*sog: scarpe*) to pinch, be tight for; (*fig: concludere: patto*) to make; (: *accelerare: passo*) to quicken ♦ *vi* (*incalzare*) to be pressing; ~**rsi** *vr* (*accostarsi*): ~**rsi a** to press o.s. up against; ~ **la mano a qn** to shake sb's hand; ~ **gli occhi** to screw up one's eyes; ~ **amicizia con qn** to make friends with sb; **stringi stringi** in conclusion; **il tempo stringe** time is short.

'strinsi *etc vb vedi* **stringere**.

'striscia, sce ['striʃʃa] *sf* (*di carta, tessuto etc*) strip; (*riga*) stripe; ~**sce (pedonali)** zebra crossing *sg*; **a** ~**sce** striped.

strisci'ante [striʃ'ʃante] *ag* (*fig peg*) unctuous; (*ECON: inflazione*) creeping.

strisci'are [striʃ'ʃare] *vt* (*piedi*) to drag; (*muro, macchina*) to graze ♦ *vi* to crawl, creep.

'striscio ['striʃʃo] *sm* graze; (*MED*) smear; **colpire di** ~ to graze.

strisci'one [striʃ'ʃone] *sm* banner.

strito'lare *vt* to grind.

striz'zare [strit'tsare] *vt* (*arancia*) to squeeze; (*panni*) to wring (out); ~ **l'occhio** to wink.

striz'zata [strit'tsata] *sf*: **dare una** ~ **a qc** to give sth a wring; **una** ~ **d'occhio** a wink.

'strofa *sf*, **'strofe** *sf inv* strophe.

strofi'naccio [strofi'nattʃo] *sm* duster, cloth; (*per piatti*) dishcloth; (*per pavimenti*) floorcloth.

strofi'nare *vt* to rub.

stron'care *vt* to break off; (*fig: ribellione*) to suppress, put down; (: *film, libro*) to tear to pieces.

'stronzo ['strontso] *sm* (*sterco*) turd; (*fig fam!: persona*) shit (*!*).

stropicci'are [stropit'tʃare] *vt* to rub.

stroz'zare [strot'tsare] *vt* (*soffocare*) to choke, strangle; ~**rsi** *vr* to choke.

strozza'tura [strottsa'tura] *sf* (*restringimento*) narrowing; (*di strada etc*) bottleneck.

stroz'zino, a [strot'tsino] *sm/f* (*usuraio*) usurer; (*fig*) shark.

struc'care *vt* to remove make-up from; ~**rsi** *vr* to remove one's make-up.

'struggere ['struddʒere] *vt* (*fig*) to consume; ~**rsi** *vr* (*fig*): ~**rsi di** to be consumed with.

struggi'mento [struddʒi'mento] *sm* (*deside-rio*) yearning.

strumen'tale *ag* (*MUS*) instrumental.

strumentaliz'zare [strumentalid'dzare] *vt* to exploit, use to one's own ends.

strumentazi'one [strumentat'tsjone] *sf* (*MUS*) orchestration; (*TECN*) instrumentation.

stru'mento *sm* (*arnese, fig*) instrument, tool; (*MUS*) instrument; ~ **a corda** *o* **ad arco/a fiato** string(ed)/wind instrument.

'strussi *etc vb vedi* **struggere.**

'strutto *sm* lard.

strut'tura *sf* structure.

struttu'rare *vt* to structure.

'struzzo ['struttso] *sm* ostrich; **fare lo ~, fare la politica dello** ~ to bury one's head in the sand.

stuc'care *vt* (*muro*) to plaster; (*vetro*) to putty; (*decorare con stucchi*) to stucco.

stucca'tore, 'trice *sm/f* plasterer; (*artista*) stucco worker.

stuc'chevole [stuk'kevole] *ag* nauseating; (*fig*) tedious, boring.

'stucco, chi *sm* plaster; (*da vetri*) putty; (*ornamentale*) stucco; **rimanere di** ~ (*fig*) to be dumbfounded.

stu'dente, 'essa *sm/f* student; (*scolaro*) pupil, schoolboy/girl.

studen'tesco, a, schi, sche *ag* student *cpd.*

studi'are *vt* to study; ~**rsi** *vr* (*sforzarsi*): ~**rsi di fare** to try *o* endeavour (*Brit*) *o* endeavor (*US*) to do.

studi'ato, a *ag* (*modi, sorriso*) affected.

'studio *sm* studying; (*ricerca, saggio, stanza*) study; (*di professionista*) office; (*di artista, CINEMA, TV, RADIO*) studio; (*di medico*) surgery (*Brit*), office (*US*); ~**i** *smpl* (*INS*) studies; **alla fine degli** ~**i** at the end of one's course (of studies); **secondo recenti** ~**i, appare che** ... recent research indicates that ...; **la proposta è allo** ~ the proposal is under consideration; ~ **legale** lawyer's office.

studi'oso, a *ag* studious, hardworking ♦ *sm/f* scholar.

'stufa *sf* stove; ~ **elettrica** electric fire *o* heater; ~ **a legna/carbone** wood-burning/coal stove.

stu'fare *vt* (*CUC*) to stew; (*fig fam*) to bore.

stu'fato *sm* (*CUC*) stew.

'stufo, a *ag* (*fam*): **essere** ~ **di** to be fed up with, be sick and tired of.

stu'oia *sf* mat.

stu'olo *sm* crowd, host.

stupefa'cente [stupefa'tʃɛnte] *ag* stunning, astounding ♦ *sm* drug, narcotic.

stupe'fare *vt* to stun, astound.

stupe'fatto, a *pp di* **stupefare.**

stupefazi'one [stupefat'tsjone] *sf* astonish-ment.

stu'pendo, a *ag* marvellous, wonderful.

stupi'daggine [stupi'daddʒine] *sf* stupid thing (to do *o* say).

stupidità *sf* stupidity.

'stupido, a *ag* stupid.

stu'pire *vt* to amaze, stun ♦ *vi* (*anche:* ~**rsi**): ~ (**di**) to be amazed (at), be stunned (by); **non c'è da** ~**rsi** that's not surprising.

stu'pore *sm* amazement, astonishment.

stu'prare *vt* to rape.

stupra'tore *sm* rapist.

'stupro *sm* rape.

stu'rare *vt* (*lavandino*) to clear.

stuzzica'denti [stuttsika'dɛnti] *sm* toothpick.

stuzzi'cante [stuttsi'kante] *ag* (*gen*) stimula-ting; (*appetitoso*) appetizing.

stuzzi'care [stuttsi'kare] *vt* (*ferita etc*) to poke (at), prod (at); (*fig*) to tease; (: *appetito*) to whet; (: *curiosità*) to stimulate; ~ **i denti** to pick one's teeth.

su *prep* (*su + il* = **sul**, *su + lo* = **sullo**, *su + l'* = **sull'**, *su + la* = **sulla**, *su + i* = **sui**, *su + gli* = **sugli**, *su + le* = **sulle**) on; (*moto a luogo*) on, on to; (*addosso, sopra*) over; (*intorno a, riguardo a*) about, on; (*approssimazione: circa*) about, around ♦ *av* up; (*sopra*) (up) above; (*al piano supe-riore*) upstairs ♦ *escl* come on!; **è sulla de-stra** it's on the right; **100 metri sul livello del mare** 100 metres above sea level; **fecero rotta** ~ **Palermo** they set out towards Palermo; **sul vestito indossava un golf rosso** she was wearing a red sweater over her dress; **una ragazza sui 17 anni** a girl of about 17 (years of age); **in 3 casi** ~ **10** in 3 cases out of 10; **spedire qc** ~ **richie-sta** to send sth on request; **sta sulle sue** he keeps to himself; **dai 20 anni in** ~ from the age of 20 onwards; **prezzi dalle mille lire in** ~ prices from 1000 lire (upwards); **andare** ~ **e giù** to go up and down.

'sua *vedi* **suo.**

sua'dente *ag* persuasive.

sub *sm/f inv* skin-diver.

su'bacqueo, a *ag* underwater ♦ *sm* skin-diver.

subaffit'tare *vt* to sublet.

subaf'fitto *sm* (*contratto*) sublet.

subal'terno, a *ag, sm* subordinate; (*MIL*) subaltern.

subappal'tare *vt* to subcontract.

subap'palto *sm* subcontract.

sub'buglio [sub'buʎʎo] *sm* confusion, turmoil; **essere/mettere in** ~ to be in/throw into a turmoil.

sub'conscio, a [sub'kɔnʃo], **subcosci'ente** [subkoʃ'ʃɛnte] *ag, sm* subconscious.

'subdolo, a *ag* underhand, sneaky.

suben'trare *vi*: ~ **a qn in qc** to take over sth from sb; **sono subentrati altri problemi** other problems arose.

su'bire *vt* to suffer, endure.

subis'sare *vt* (*fig*): ~ **di** to overwhelm with, load with.

subi'taneo, a *ag* sudden.

'subito *av* immediately, at once, straight away.

su'blime *ag* sublime.

sublo'care *vt* to sublease.

sublocazi'one [sublokat'tsjone] *sf* sublease.

subnor'male *ag* subnormal ♦ *sm/f* mentally handicapped person.

subodo'rare *vt* (*insidia etc*) to smell, suspect.

subordi'nare *vt* to subordinate.

subordi'nato, a *ag* subordinate; (*dipendente*): ~ **a** dependent on, subject to.

subordinazi'one [subordinat'tsjone] *sf* subordination.

su'bordine *sm*: **in** ~ secondarily.

subur'bano, a *ag* suburban.

succe'daneo [suttʃe'daneo] *sm* substitute.

suc'cedere [sut'tʃɛdere] *vi* (*prendere il posto di qn*): ~ **a** to succeed; (*venire dopo*): ~ **a** to follow; (*accadere*) to happen; **~rsi** *vr* to follow each other; ~ **al trono** to succeed to the throne; **sono cose che succedono** these things happen.

successi'one [suttʃes'sjone] *sf* succession; **tassa di** ~ death duty (*Brit*), inheritance tax (*US*).

successiva'mente [suttʃessiva'mente] *av* subsequently.

succes'sivo, a [suttʃes'sivo] *ag* successive; **il giorno** ~ the following day; **in un momento** ~ subsequently.

suc'cesso, a [sut'tʃɛsso] *pp di* **succedere** ♦ *sm* (*esito*) outcome; (*buona riuscita*) success; **di** ~ (*libro, personaggio*) successful; **avere** ~ (*persona*) to be successful; (*idea*) to be well received.

succes'sore [suttʃes'sore] *sm* successor.

succhi'are [suk'kjare] *vt* to suck (up).

succhi'otto [suk'kjɔtto] *sm* dummy (*Brit*), pacifier (*US*), comforter (*US*).

suc'cinto, a [sut'tʃinto] *ag* (*discorso*) succinct; (*abito*) brief.

'succo, chi *sm* juice; (*fig*) essence, gist; ~ **di frutta/pomodoro** fruit/tomato juice.

suc'coso, a *ag* juicy; (*fig*) pithy.

'succube *sm/f* victim; **essere** ~ **di qn** to be dominated by sb.

succu'lento, a *ag* succulent.

succur'sale *sf* branch (office).

sud *sm* south ♦ *ag inv* south; (*regione*) southern; **verso** ~ south, southwards; **l'Italia del S**~ Southern Italy; **l'America del S**~ South America.

Su'dafrica *sm*: **il** ~ South Africa.

sudafri'cano, a *ag, sm/f* South African.

Suda'merica *sm*: **il** ~ South America.

sudameri'cano, a *ag, sm/f* South American.

Su'dan *sm*: **il** ~ (the) Sudan.

suda'nese *ag, sm/f* Sudanese *inv*.

su'dare *vi* to perspire, sweat; ~ **freddo** to come out in a cold sweat.

su'dato, a *ag* (*persona, mani*) sweaty; (*fig: denaro*) hard-earned ♦ *sf* (*anche fig*) sweat; **una vittoria** ~**a** a hard-won victory; **ho fatto una bella** ~**a per finirlo in tempo** it was a real sweat to get it finished in time.

sud'detto, a *ag* above-mentioned.

suddi'tanza [suddi'tantsa] *sf* subjection; (*cittadinanza*) citizenship.

sud'dito, a *sm/f* subject.

suddi'videre *vt* to subdivide.

suddivisi'one *sf* subdivision.

suddi'viso, a *pp di* **suddividere**.

su'dest *sm* south-east; **vento di** ~ south-easterly wind; **il** ~ **asiatico** South-East Asia.

sudice'ria [suditʃe'ria] *sf* (*qualità*) filthiness, dirtiness; (*cosa sporca*) dirty thing.

'sudicio, a, ci, ce ['suditʃo] *ag* dirty, filthy.

sudici'ume [sudi'tʃume] *sm* dirt, filth.

su'dore *sm* perspiration, sweat.

su'dovest *sm* south-west; **vento di** ~ south-westerly wind.

'sue *vedi* **suo**.

'Suez ['suez] *sm*: **il Canale di** ~ the Suez Canal.

suffici'ente [suffi'tʃɛnte] *ag* enough, sufficient; (*borioso*) self-important; (*INS*) satisfactory.

suffici'enza [suffi'tʃɛntsa] *sf* (*INS*) pass mark; **con un'aria di** ~ (*fig*) with a condescending air; **a** ~ enough; **ne ho avuto a** ~! I've had enough of this!

suf'fisso *sm* (*LING*) suffix.

suffra'gare *vt* to support.

suf'fragio [suf'fradʒo] *sm* (*voto*) vote; ~ **universale** universal suffrage.

suggel'lare [suddʒel'lare] *vt* (*fig*) to seal.

suggeri'mento [suddʒeri'mento] *sm* suggestion; (*consiglio*) piece of advice, advice *q*; **dietro suo** ~ on his advice.

sugge'rire [suddʒe'rire] *vt* (*risposta*) to tell; (*consigliare*) to advise; (*proporre*) to suggest; (*TEATRO*) to prompt; ~ **a qn di fare qc** to suggest to sb that he (*o* she) do sth.

suggeri'tore, 'trice [suddʒeri'tore] *sm/f* (*TEATRO*) prompter.

suggestio'nare [suddʒestjo'nare] *vt* to influence.

suggesti'one [suddʒes'tjone] *sf* (*PSIC*) suggestion; (*istigazione*) instigation.

sugges'tivo, a [suddʒes'tivo] *ag* (*paesaggio*) evocative; (*teoria*) interesting, attractive.

'sughero ['sugero] *sm* cork.

'sugli ['suʎʎi] *prep + det vedi* **su**.

'sugo, ghi *sm* (*succo*) juice; (*di carne*) gravy; (*condimento*) sauce; (*fig*) gist, essence.

su'goso, a *ag* (*frutto*) juicy; (*fig: articolo*

etc) pithy.

'sui *prep* + *det vedi* **su**.

sui'cida, i, e [sui'tʃida] *ag* suicidal ♦ *sm/f* suicide.

suici'darsi [suitʃi'darsi] *vr* to commit suicide.

sui'cidio [sui'tʃidjo] *sm* suicide.

su'ino, a *ag*: **carne** ~**a** pork ♦ *sm* pig; ~**i** *smpl* swine *pl*.

sul, sull', 'sulla, 'sulle, 'sullo *prep* + *det vedi* **su**.

sulta'nina *sf*: (**uva**) ~ sultana.

sul'tano, a *sm/f* sultan/sultana.

Su'matra *sf* Sumatra.

sunnomi'nato, a *ag* aforesaid *cpd*.

'sunto *sm* summary.

'suo, 'sua, 'sue, su'oi *det*: **il** ~, **la sua** *etc* (*di lui*) his; (*di lei*) her; (*di esso*) its; (*con valore indefinito*) one's, his/her; (*forma di cortesia: anche:* **S**~) your ♦ *pronome*: **il** ~, **la sua** *etc* his; hers; yours ♦ *sm*: **ha speso del** ~ he (*o* she *etc*) spent his (*o* her *etc*) own money ♦ *sf*: **la** ~**a** (*opinione*) his (*o* her *etc*) view; **i suoi** (*parenti*) his (*o* her *etc*) family; **un** ~ **amico** a friend of his (*o* hers *etc*); **è dalla** ~**a** he's on his (*o* her *etc*) side; **anche lui ha avuto le** ~**e** (*disavventure*) he's had his problems too.

su'ocero, a ['swɔtʃero] *sm/f* father/mother-in-law; **i** ~**i** *smpl* father- and mother-in-law.

su'oi *vedi* **suo**.

su'ola *sf* (*di scarpa*) sole.

su'olo *sm* (*terreno*) ground; (*terra*) soil.

suo'nare *vt* (*MUS*) to play; (*campana*) to ring; (*ore*) to strike; (*clacson, allarme*) to sound ♦ *vi* to play; (*telefono, campana*) to ring; (*ore*) to strike; (*clacson, fig: parole*) to sound.

suo'nato, a *ag* (*compiuto*): **ha cinquant'anni** ~**i** he is well over fifty.

suona'tore, 'trice *sm/f* player; ~ **ambulante** street musician.

suone'ria *sf* alarm.

su'ono *sm* sound.

su'ora *sf* (*REL*) nun; **Suor Maria** Sister Maria.

'super *ag inv*: (**benzina**) ~ ≈ four-star (petrol) (*Brit*), premium (*US*).

supera'mento *sm* (*di ostacolo*) overcoming; (*di montagna*) crossing.

supe'rare *vt* (*oltrepassare: limite*) to exceed, surpass; (*attraversare: fiume*) to cross; (*sorpassare: veicolo*) to overtake; (*fig: essere più bravo di*) to surpass, outdo; (: *difficoltà*) to overcome; (: *esame*) to get through; ~ **qn in altezza/peso** to be taller/heavier than sb; **ha superato la cinquantina** he's over fifty (years of age); ~ **i limiti di velocità** to exceed the speed limit; **stavolta ha superato se stesso** this time he has surpassed himself.

supe'rato, a *ag* outmoded.

su'perbia *sf* pride.

su'perbo, a *ag* proud; (*fig*) magnificent, superb.

superfici'ale [superfi'tʃale] *ag* superficial.

superficialità [superfitʃali'ta] *sf* superficiality.

super'ficie, ci [super'fitʃe] *sf* surface; **tornare in** ~ (*a galla*) to return to the surface; (*fig: problemi etc*) to resurface; ~ **alare** (*AER*) wing area; ~ **velica** (*NAUT*) sail area.

su'perfluo, a *ag* superfluous.

superi'ora *sf* (*REL: anche:* **madre** ~) mother superior.

superi'ore *ag* (*piano, arto, classi*) upper; (*più elevato: temperatura, livello*): ~ (**a**) higher (than); (*migliore*): ~ (**a**) superior (to) ♦ *sfpl*: **le** ~**i** (*INS*) ≈ senior comprehensive school (*Brit*), senior high (school) (*US*); **il corso** ~ **di un fiume** the upper reaches of a river.

superiorità *sf* superiority.

superla'tivo, a *ag, sm* superlative.

superla'voro *sm* overwork.

supermer'cato *sm* supermarket.

superpo'tenza [superpo'tentsa] *sf* (*POL*) superpower.

super'sonico, a, ci, che *ag* supersonic.

su'perstite *ag* surviving ♦ *sm/f* survivor.

superstizi'one [superstit'tsjone] *sf* superstition.

superstizi'oso, a [superstit'tsjoso] *ag* superstitious.

super'strada *sf* ≈ expressway.

supervisi'one *sf* supervision.

supervi'sore *sm* supervisor.

su'pino, a *ag* supine; **accettazione** ~**a** (*fig*) blind acceptance.

suppel'lettile *sf* furnishings *pl*.

suppergiù [supper'dʒu] *av* more or less, roughly.

suppl. *abbr* (= *supplemento*) suppl(l).

supplemen'tare *ag* extra; (*treno*) relief *cpd*; (*entrate*) additional.

supple'mento *sm* supplement.

sup'plente *ag* temporary; (*insegnante*) supply *cpd* (*Brit*), substitute *cpd* (*US*) ♦ *sm/f* temporary member of staff; supply (*o* substitute) teacher.

supp'lenza [sup'plɛntsa] *sf*: **fare** ~ to do supply (*Brit*) *o* substitute (*US*) teaching.

supple'tivo, a *ag* (*gen*) supplementary; (*sessione d'esami*) extra.

'supplica, che *sf* (*preghiera*) plea; (*domanda scritta*) petition, request.

suppli'care *vt* to implore, beseech.

suppli'chevole [suppli'kevole] *ag* imploring.

sup'plire *vi*: ~ **a** to make up for, compensate for.

sup'plizio [sup'plittsjo] *sm* torture.

sup'pongo, sup'poni *etc vb vedi* **supporre**.

sup'porre *vt* to suppose; **supponiamo che ...** let's *o* just suppose that ....

sup'porto *sm* (*sostegno*) support.
supposizi'one [suppozit'tsjone] *sf* supposition.
sup'posta *sf* (*MED*) suppository.
sup'posto, a *pp di* **supporre.**
suppu'rare *vi* to suppurate.
suprema'zia [supremat'tsia] *sf* supremacy.
su'premo, a *ag* supreme; **S~a Corte (di Cassazione)** Supreme Court.
surclas'sare *vt* to outclass.
surge'lare [surdʒe'lare] *vt* to (deep-)freeze.
surge'lato, a [surdʒe'lato] *ag* (deep-)frozen ♦ *smpl*: **i ~i** frozen food *sg*.
surme'nage [syrmə'naʒ] *sm* (*fisico*) overwork; (*mentale*) mental strain; (*SPORT*) overtraining.
sur'plus *sm inv* (*ECON*) surplus; **~ di manodopera** overmanning.
surre'ale *ag* surrealistic.
surriscalda'mento *sm* (*gen*, *TECN*) overheating.
surriscal'dare *vt* to overheat.
surro'gato *sm* substitute.
suscet'tibile [suʃʃet'tibile] *ag* (*sensibile*) touchy, sensitive; (*soggetto*): **~ di miglioramento** that can be improved, open to improvement.
suscettibilità [suʃʃettibili'ta] *sf* touchiness; **urtare la ~ di qn** to hurt sb's feelings.
susci'tare [suʃʃi'tare] *vt* to provoke, arouse.
su'sina *sf* plum.
su'sino *sm* plum (tree).
sussegu'ire *vt* to follow; **~rsi** *vr* to follow one another.
sussidi'ario, a *ag* subsidiary; (*treno*) relief *cpd*; (*fermata*) extra.
sus'sidio *sm* subsidy; (*aiuto*) aid; **~i didattici/audiovisivi** teaching/audiovisual aids; **~ di disoccupazione** unemployment benefit (*Brit*) *o* benefits (*US*); **~ per malattia** sickness benefit.
sussi'ego *sm* haughtiness; **con aria di ~** haughtily.
sussis'tenza [sussis'tɛntsa] *sf* subsistence.
sus'sistere *vi* to exist; (*essere fondato*) to be valid *o* sound.
sussul'tare *vi* to shudder.
sus'sulto *sm* start.
sussur'rare *vt*, *vi* to whisper, murmur; **si sussurra che** ... it's rumoured (*Brit*) *o* rumored (*US*) that ....
sus'surro *sm* whisper, murmur.
su'tura *sf* (*MED*) suture.
sutu'rare *vt* to stitch up, suture.
suv'via *escl* come on!
SV *sigla* = **Savona.**
S.V. *abbr vedi* **Signoria Vostra.**
sva'gare *vt* (*divertire*) to amuse; (*distrarre*): **~ qn** to take sb's mind off things; **~rsi** *vr* to amuse o.s.; to take one's mind off things.
'svago, ghi *sm* (*riposo*) relaxation;

(*ricreazione*) amusement; (*passatempo*) pastime.
svaligi'are [zvali'dʒare] *vt* to rob, burgle (*Brit*), burglarize (*US*).
svaligia'tore, 'trice [zvalidʒa'tore] *sm/f* (*di banca*) robber; (*di casa*) burglar.
svalu'tare *vt* (*ECON*) to devalue; (*fig*) to belittle; **~rsi** *vr* (*ECON*) to be devalued.
svalutazi'one [zvalutat'tsjone] *sf* devaluation.
svam'pito, a *ag* absent-minded ♦ *sm/f* absent-minded person.
sva'nire *vi* to disappear, vanish.
sva'nito, a *ag* (*fig*: *persona*) absent-minded.
svantaggi'ato, a [zvantad'dʒato] *ag* at a disadvantage.
svan'taggio [zvan'taddʒo] *sm* disadvantage; (*inconveniente*) drawback, disadvantage; **tornerà a suo ~** it will work against you.
svantaggi'oso, a [zvantad'dʒoso] *ag* disadvantageous; **è un'offerta ~a per me** it's not in my interest to accept this offer; **è un prezzo ~** it is not an attractive price.
svapo'rare *vi* to evaporate.
svapo'rato, a *ag* (*bibita*) flat.
svari'ato, a *ag* (*vario*, *diverso*) varied; (*numeroso*) various.
'svastica, che *sf* swastika.
sve'dese *ag* Swedish ♦ *sm/f* Swede ♦ *sm* (*LING*) Swedish.
'sveglia ['zveʎʎa] *sf* waking up; (*orologio*) alarm (clock); **suonare la ~** (*MIL*) to sound the reveille; **~ telefonica** alarm call.
svegli'are [zveʎ'ʎare] *vt* to wake up; (*fig*) to awaken, arouse; **~rsi** *vr* to wake up; (*fig*) to be revived, reawaken.
'sveglio, a ['zveʎʎo] *ag* awake; (*fig*) alert, quick-witted.
sve'lare *vt* to reveal.
svel'tezza [zvel'tettsa] *sf* (*gen*) speed; (*mentale*) quick-wittedness.
svel'tire *vt* (*gen*) to speed up; (*procedura*) to streamline.
'svelto, a *ag* (*passo*) quick; (*mente*) quick, alert; (*linea*) slim, slender; **alla ~a** quickly.
'svendere *vt* to sell off, clear.
'svendita *sf* (*COMM*) (clearance) sale.
sve'nevole *ag* mawkish.
'svengo *etc vb vedi* **svenire.**
sveni'mento *sm* fainting fit, faint.
sve'nire *vi* to faint.
sven'tare *vt* to foil, thwart.
sventa'tezza [zventa'tettsa] *sf* (*distrazione*) absent-mindedness; (*mancanza di prudenza*) rashness.
sven'tato, a *ag* (*distratto*) scatterbrained; (*imprudente*) rash.
svento'lare *vt*, *vi* to wave, flutter.
sven'trare *vt* to disembowel.
sven'tura *sf* misfortune.
sventu'rato, a *ag* unlucky, unfortunate.

sve'nuto, a *pp di* **svenire.**

svergo'gnare [zvergoɲ'ɲare] *vt* to shame.

svergo'gnato, a [zvergoɲ'ɲato] *ag* shameless ♦ *sm/f* shameless person.

sver'nare *vi* to spend the winter.

sverrò *etc vb vedi* **svenire.**

sves'tire *vt* to undress; **~rsi** *vr* to get undressed.

'Svezia ['zvɛttsja] *sf*: **la ~** Sweden.

svez'zare [zvet'tsare] *vt* to wean.

svi'are *vt* to divert; (*fig*) to lead astray; **~rsi** *vr* to go astray.

svico'lare *vi* to slip down an alley; (*fig*) to sneak off.

svi'gnarsela [zviɲ'ɲarsela] *vr* to slip away, sneak off.

svili'mento *sm* debasement.

svi'lire *vt* to debase.

svilup'pare *vt*, **~rsi** *vr* to develop.

svi'luppo *sm* development; (*di industria*) expansion; **in via di ~** in the process of development; **paesi in via di ~** developing countries.

svinco'lare *vt* to free, release; (*merce*) to clear.

'svincolo *sm* (*COMM*) clearance; (*stradale*) motorway (*Brit*) *o* expressway (*US*) intersection.

svisce'rare [zviʃʃe'rare] *vt* (*fig: argomento*) to examine in depth.

svisce'rato, a [zviʃʃe'rato] *ag* (*amore, odio*) passionate.

'svista *sf* oversight.

svi'tare *vt* to unscrew.

'Svizzera ['zvittsera] *sf*: **la ~** Switzerland.

'svizzero, a ['zvittsero] *ag*, *sm/f* Swiss.

svoglia'tezza [zvoʎʎa'tettsa] *sf* listlessness; indolence.

svogli'ato, a [zvoʎ'ʎato] *ag* listless; (*pigro*) lazy, indolent.

svolaz'zare [zvolat'tsare] *vi* to flutter.

'svolgere ['zvɔldʒere] *vt* to unwind; (*srotolare*) to unroll; (*fig: argomento*) to develop; (: *piano, programma*) to carry out; **~rsi** *vr* to unwind; to unroll; (*fig: aver luogo*) to take place; (: *procedere*) to go on; **tutto si è svolto secondo i piani** everything went according to plan.

svolgi'mento [zvoldʒi'mento] *sm* development; carrying out; (*andamento*) course.

'svolsi *etc vb vedi* **svolgere.**

'svolta *sf* (*atto*) turning *q*; (*curva*) turn, bend; (*fig*) turning-point; **essere ad una ~ nella propria vita** to be at a crossroads in one's life.

svol'tare *vi* to turn.

'svolto, a *pp di* **svolgere.**

svuo'tare *vt* to empty (out).

'Swaziland ['swadziland] *sm*: **lo ~** Swaziland.

'Sydney ['sidnei] *sf* Sydney.

T

T, t [ti] *sf o m inv* (*lettera*) T, t; **T come Taranto** ≈ T for Tommy.

T *abbr* = **tabaccheria.**

t *abbr* = **tara; tonnellata.**

TA *sigla* = *Taranto.*

tabac'caio, a *sm/f* tobacconist.

tabacche'ria [tabakke'ria] *sf* tobacconist's (shop).

tabacchi'era [tabak'kjɛra] *sf* snuffbox.

ta'bacco, chi *sm* tobacco.

ta'bella *sf* (*tavola*) table; (*elenco*) list; **~ di marcia** schedule; **~ dei prezzi** price list.

tabel'lone *sm* (*per pubblicità*) billboard; (*per informazioni*) notice board (*Brit*), bulletin board (*US*); (: *in stazione*) timetable board.

taber'nacolo *sm* tabernacle.

tabù *ag*, *sm inv* taboo.

'tabula 'rasa *sf* tabula rasa; **fare ~** (*fig*) to make a clean sweep.

tabu'lare *vt* to tabulate.

tabu'lato *sm* (*INFORM*) printout.

tabula'tore *sm* tabulator.

TAC *sigla f* (*MED*: = *Tomografia Assiale Computerizzata*) CAT.

'tacca, che *sf* notch, nick; **di mezza ~** (*fig*) mediocre.

taccagne'ria [takkaɲɲe'ria] *sf* meanness, stinginess.

tac'cagno, a [tak'kaɲɲo] *ag* mean, stingy.

tac'cheggio [tak'keddʒo] *sm* shoplifting.

tac'chino [tak'kino] *sm* turkey.

'taccia, ce ['tattʃa] *sf* bad reputation.

tacci'are [tat'tʃare] *vt*: **~ qn di** (*vigliaccheria etc*) to accuse sb of.

'taccio *etc* ['tattʃo] *vb vedi* **tacere.**

'tacco, chi *sm* heel.

taccu'ino *sm* notebook.

ta'cere [ta'tʃere] *vi* to be silent *o* quiet; (*smettere di parlare*) to fall silent ♦ *vt* to keep to oneself, say nothing about; **far ~ qn** to make sb be quiet; (*fig*) to silence sb; **mettere a ~ qc** to hush sth up.

ta'chimetro [ta'kimetro] *sm* speedometer.

'tacito, a ['tatʃito] *ag* silent; (*sottinteso*) tacit, unspoken.

taci'turno, a [tatʃi'turno] *ag* taciturn.

taci'uto, a [ta'tʃuto] *pp di* **tacere.**

'tacqui *etc vb vedi* **tacere.**

ta'fano *sm* horsefly.

taffe'ruglio [taffe'ruʎʎo] *sm* brawl, scuffle.

taffettà *sm* taffeta.

'taglia ['taʎʎa] *sf* (*statura*) height; (*misura*) size; (*riscatto*) ransom; (*ricompensa*) reward; ~**e forti** (*ABBIGLIAMENTO*) outsize.

taglia'boschi [taʎʎa'bɔski] *sm inv* woodcutter.

taglia'carte [taʎʎa'karte] *sm inv* paperknife.

taglia'legna [taʎʎa'leɲɲa] *sm inv* woodcutter.

tagli'ando [taʎ'ʎando] *sm* coupon.

tagli'are [taʎ'ʎare] *vt* to cut; (*recidere, interrompere*) to cut off; (*intersecare*) to cut across, intersect; (*carne*) to carve; (*vini*) to blend ♦ *vi* to cut; (*prendere una scorciatoia*) to take a short-cut; ~ **la strada a qn** to cut across in front of sb; ~ **corto** (*fig*) to cut short.

taglia'telle [taʎʎa'tɛlle] *sfpl* tagliatelle *pl*.

tagli'ato, a [taʎ'ʎato] *ag*: **essere ~ per qc** (*fig*) to be cut out for sth.

taglia'trice [taʎʎa'tritʃe] *sf* (*TECN*) cutter.

taglia'unghie [taʎʎa'ungje] *sm inv* nail clippers *pl*.

taglieggi'are [taʎʎed'dʒare] *vt* to exact a tribute from.

tagli'ente [taʎ'ʎɛnte] *ag* sharp.

tagli'ere [taʎ'ʎɛre] *sm* chopping board; (*per il pane*) bread board.

'taglio ['taʎʎo] *sm* cutting *q*; cut; (*parte tagliente*) cutting edge; (*di abito*) cut; (*di stoffa: lunghezza*) length; (*di vini*) blending; **di ~** on edge, edgeways; **banconote di piccolo/grosso ~** notes of small/large denomination.

tagli'ola [taʎ'ʎɔla] *sf* trap, snare.

tagli'one [taʎ'ʎone] *sm*: **la legge del ~** the concept of an eye for an eye and a tooth for a tooth.

tagliuz'zare [taʎʎut'tsare] *vt* to cut into small pieces.

Ta'hiti [ta'iti] *sf* Tahiti.

tailan'dese *ag, sm/f, sm* Thai.

Tai'landia *sf*: **la ~** Thailand.

tai'lleur [ta'jœr] *sm inv* lady's suit.

Tai'wan [tai'wan] *sm*: **il ~** Taiwan.

'talamo *sm* (*poetico*) marriage bed.

'talco *sm* talcum powder.

'tale *det* such; (*intensivo*): **un ~/~i** ... such (a)/such ... ♦ *pronome* (*questa, quella persona già menzionata*) the one, the person; (*indefinito*): **un(una) ~** someone; **il ~ giorno alla ~ ora** on such and such a day at such and such a time; ~ **quale: il tuo vestito è ~ quale il mio** your dress is just *o* exactly like mine; **quel/quella ~** that person, that man/woman; **il tal dei ~i** what's-his-name.

ta'lento *sm* talent.

talis'mano *sm* talisman.

tallo'nare *vt* to pursue; ~ **il pallone** (*CALCIO, RUGBY*) to heel the ball.

tallon'cino [tallon'tʃino] *sm* counterfoil (*Brit*), stub; ~ **del prezzo** (*di medicinali*)

tear-off tag.

tal'lone *sm* heel.

tal'mente *av* so.

ta'lora *av* = **talvolta**.

'talpa *sf* (*ZOOL*) mole.

tal'volta *av* sometimes, at times.

tambu'rello *sm* tambourine.

tambu'rino *sm* drummer boy.

tam'buro *sm* drum; **freni a ~** drum brakes; **pistola a ~** revolver; **a ~ battente** (*fig*) immediately, at once.

Ta'migi [ta'midʒi] *sm*: **il ~** the Thames.

tampona'mento *sm* (*AUT*) collision; ~ **a catena** pile-up.

tampo'nare *vt* (*otturare*) to plug; (*urtare: macchina*) to crash *o* ram into.

tam'pone *sm* (*MED*) wad, pad; (*per timbri*) ink-pad; (*respingente*) buffer; ~ **assorbente** tampon.

'tana *sf* lair, den; (*fig*) den, hideout.

'tanfo *sm* (*di muffa*) musty smell; (*puzza*) stench.

tan'gente [tan'dʒɛnte] *ag* (*MAT*): ~ **a** tangential *o* ♦ *sf* tangent; (*quota*) share; (*denaro estorto*) rake-off (*fam*), cut.

tangenzi'ale [tandʒen'tsjale] *sf* (*strada*) by-pass.

'Tangeri ['tandʒeri] *sf* Tangiers.

tan'gibile [tan'dʒibile] *ag* tangible.

'tango, ghi *sm* tango.

'tanica, che *sf* jerry can.

tan'nino *sm* tannin.

tan'tino: un ~ *av* a little, a bit.

'tanto, a *det* (*pane, acqua, soldi*) so much; (*persone, libri*) so many ♦ *pronome* so much (*o* many) ♦ *av* (*con ag, av*) so; (*con vb*) so much, such a lot; (: *così a lungo*) so long; **due volte ~** twice as much; ~ ... **quanto: ho ~i libri quanti (ne hanno) loro** I have as many books as they have *o* as them; **conosco ~ Carlo quanto suo padre** I know both Carlo and his father; **è ~ bella quanto buona** she is as beautiful as she is good; ~ **più** ... ~ **più** the more ... the more; ~ ... **da** so ... as; **un ~:** **costa un ~ al metro** it costs so much per metre; **guardare con ~ d'occhi** to gaze wide-eyed at; ~ **per cambiare** just for a change; **una volta ~** just once; ~ **è inutile** in any case it's useless; ~ **vale che** ... you may *o* might as well ...; **di ~ in ~, ogni ~** every so often.

Tanza'nia [tandza'nia] *sf*: **la ~** Tanzania.

tapi'oca *sf* tapioca.

'tappa *sf* (*luogo di sosta*, *fermata*) stop, halt; (*parte di un percorso*) stage, leg; (*SPORT*) lap; **a ~e** in stages; **bruciare le ~e** (*fig*) to be a whizz kid.

tappa'buchi [tappa'buki] *sm inv* stopgap; **fare da ~** to act as a stopgap.

tap'pare *vt* to plug, stop up; (*bottiglia*) to cork.

tappa'rella *sf* rolling shutter.

tap'peto *sm* carpet; (*anche:* **tappetino**) rug; (*di tavolo*) cloth; (*SPORT*): **andare al ~** to go down for the count; **mettere sul ~** (*fig*) to bring up for discussion.

tappez'zare [tappet'tsare] *vt* (*con carta*) to paper; (*rivestire*): **~ qc (di)** to cover sth (with).

tappezze'ria [tappettse'ria] *sf* (*arredamento*) soft furnishings *pl*; (*carta da parati*) wall covering; (*di automobile*) upholstery; **far da ~** (*fig*) to be a wallflower.

tappezzi'ere [tappet'tsjere] *sm* upholsterer.

'tappo *sm* stopper; (*in sughero*) cork; **~ a corona** bottle top; **~ a vite** screw top.

TAR *sigla m* = *Tribunale Amministrativo Regionale*.

'tara *sf* (*peso*) tare; (*MED*) hereditary defect; (*difetto*) flaw.

ta'rantola *sf* tarantula.

ta'rare *vt* (*COMM*) to tare; (*TECN*) to calibrate.

ta'rato, a *ag* (*COMM*) tared; (*MED*) with a hereditary defect.

tara'tura *sf* (*COMM*) taring; (*TECN*) calibration.

tarchi'ato, a [tar'kjato] *ag* stocky, thickset.

tar'dare *vi* to be late ♦ *vt* to delay; **~ a fare** to delay doing.

'tardi *av* late; **più ~** later (on); **al più ~** at the latest; **sul ~** (*verso sera*) late in the day; **far ~** to be late; (*restare alzato*) to stay up late.

tar'divo, a *ag* (*primavera*) late; (*rimedio*) belated, tardy; (*fig: bambino*) retarded.

'tardo, a *ag* (*lento, fig: ottuso*) slow; (*tempo: avanzato*) late.

tar'dona *sf* (*peg*): **essere una ~** to be mutton dressed as lamb.

'targa, ghe *sf* plate; (*AUT*) number (*Brit*) o license (*US*) plate.

tar'gare *vt* (*AUT*) to register.

ta'riffa *sf* (*gen*) rate, tariff; (*di trasporti*) fare; (*elenco*) price list; tariff; **la ~ in vigore** the going rate; **~ normale/ridotta** standard/reduced rate; (*su mezzi di trasporto*) full/concessionary fare; **~ salariale** wage rate; **~ unica** flat rate; **~e doganali** customs rates o tariff; **~e postali/telefoniche** postal/telephone charges.

tarif'fario, ii *ag*: **aumento ~** increase in charges o rates ♦ *sm* tariff, table of charges.

'tarlo *sm* woodworm.

'tarma *sf* moth.

tarmi'cida, i [tarmi'tʃida] *ag, sm* moth-killer.

ta'rocco, chi *sm* tarot card; **~chi** *smpl* (*gioco*) tarot *sg*.

tar'pare *vt* (*fig*): **~ le ali a qn** to clip sb's wings.

tartagli'are [tartaʎ'ʎare] *vi* to stutter, stammer.

'tartaro, a *ag, sm* (*in tutti i sensi*) tartar.

tarta'ruga, ghe *sf* tortoise; (*di mare*) turtle; (*materiale*) tortoiseshell.

tartas'sare *vt* (*fam*): **~ qn** to give sb the works; **~ qn a un esame** to give sb a grilling at an exam.

tar'tina *sf* canapé.

tar'tufo *sm* (*BOT*) truffle.

'tasca, sche *sf* pocket; **da ~** pocket *cpd*; **fare i conti in ~ a qn** (*fig*) to meddle in sb's affairs.

tas'cabile *ag* (*libro*) pocket *cpd*.

tasca'pane *sm* haversack.

tas'chino [tas'kino] *sm* breast pocket.

Tas'mania *sf*: **la ~** Tasmania.

'tassa *sf* (*imposta*) tax; (*doganale*) duty; (*per iscrizione: a scuola etc*) fee; **~ di circolazione/di soggiorno** road/tourist tax.

tas'sametro *sm* taximeter.

tas'sare *vt* to tax; to levy a duty on.

tassa'tivo, a *ag* peremptory.

tassazi'one [tassat'tsjone] *sf* taxation; **soggetto a ~** taxable.

tas'sello *sm* (*di legno, pietra*) plug; (*assaggio*) wedge.

tassì *sm inv* = **taxi**.

tas'sista, i, e *sm/f* taxi driver.

'tasso *sm* (*di natalità, d'interesse etc*) rate; (*BOT*) yew; (*ZOOL*) badger; **~ di cambio/d'interesse** rate of exchange/interest; **~ di crescita** growth rate.

tas'tare *vt* to feel; **~ il terreno** (*fig*) to see how the land lies.

tasti'era *sf* keyboard.

tastie'rino *sm*: **~ numerico** numeric keypad.

'tasto *sm* key; (*tatto*) touch, feel; **toccare un ~ delicato** (*fig*) to touch on a delicate subject; **toccare il ~ giusto** (*fig*) to strike the right note; **~ funzione** (*INFORM*) function key; **~ delle maiuscole** (*su macchina da scrivere etc*) shift key.

tas'toni *av*: **procedere (a) ~** to grope one's way forward.

'tata *sf* (*linguaggio infantile*) nanny.

'tattico, a, ci, che *ag* tactical ♦ *sf* tactics *pl*.

'tatto *sm* (*senso*) touch; (*fig*) tact; **duro al ~** hard to the touch; **aver ~** to be tactful, have tact.

tatu'aggio [tatu'addʒo] *sm* tattooing; (*disegno*) tattoo.

tatu'are *vt* to tattoo.

ta'verna *sf* (*osteria*) tavern.

'tavola *sf* table; (*asse*) plank, board; (*lastra*) tablet; (*quadro*) panel (painting); (*illustrazione*) plate; **~ calda** snack bar; **~ pieghevole** folding table.

tavo'lata *sf* company at table.

tavo'lato *sm* boarding; (*pavimento*) wooden floor.

tavo'letta *sf* tablet, bar; **a ~** (*AUT*) flat out.

tavo'lino *sm* small table; (*scrivania*) desk; ~ **da tè/gioco** coffee/card table; **mettersi a** ~ **to** get down to work; **decidere qc a** ~ (*fig*) to decide sth on a theoretical level.

'tavolo *sm* table; ~ **da disegno** drawing board; ~ **da lavoro** desk; (*TECN*) workbench; ~ **operatorio** (*MED*) operating table.

tavo'lozza [tavo'lɔttsa] *sf* (*ARTE*) palette.

'taxi *sm inv* taxi.

'tazza ['tattsa] *sf* cup; ~ **da caffè/tè** coffee/tea cup; **una** ~ **di caffè/tè** a cup of coffee/tea.

taz'zina [tat'tsina] *sf* coffee cup.

TBC *abbr f* (= *tubercolosi*) TB.

TCI *sigla m* = *Touring Club Italiano*.

TE *sigla* = *Teramo*.

te *pronome* (*soggetto: in forme comparative, oggetto*) you.

tè *sm inv* tea; (*trattenimento*) tea party.

tea'trale *ag* theatrical.

te'atro *sm* theatre; ~ **comico** comedy; ~ **di posa** film studio.

'tecnico, a, ci, che *ag* technical ♦ *sm/f* technician ♦ *sf* technique; (*tecnologia*) technology.

tecnolo'gia [teknolo'dʒia] *sf* technology; **alta** ~ high technology, hi-tech.

tecno'logico, a, ci, che [tekno'lɔdʒiko] *ag* technological.

te'desco, a, schi, sche *ag, sm/f, sm* German; ~ **orientale/occidentale** East/West German.

tedi'are *vt* (*infastidire*) to bother, annoy; (*annoiare*) to bore.

'tedio *sm* tedium, boredom.

tedi'oso, a *ag* tedious, boring.

te'game *sm* (*CUC*) pan; **al** ~ fried.

'teglia ['teʎʎa] *sf* (*CUC: per dolci*) (baking) tin (*Brit*), cake pan (*US*); (*: per arrosti*) (roasting) tin.

'tegola *sf* tile.

Teh'ran *sf* Tehran.

tei'era *sf* teapot.

tel. *abbr* (= *telefono*) tel.

'tela *sf* (*tessuto*) cloth; (*per vele, quadri*) canvas; (*dipinto*) canvas, painting; **di** ~ (*calzoni*) (heavy) cotton *cpd*; (*scarpe, borsa*) canvas *cpd*; ~ **cerata** oilcloth; ~ **di ragno** spider's web.

te'laio *sm* (*apparecchio*) loom; (*struttura*) frame.

Tel A'viv *sf* Tel Aviv.

teleabbo'nato *sm* television licence holder.

tele'camera *sf* television camera.

telecoman'dare *vt* to operate by remote control.

teleco'mando *sm* remote control; (*dispositivo*) remote-control device.

telecomunicazi'oni [telekomunikat'tsjoni] *sfpl* telecommunications.

tele'cronaca, che *sf* television report.

telecro'nista, i, e *sm/f* (television) commentator.

tele'ferica, che *sf* cableway.

tele'film *sm inv* television film.

telefo'nare *vi* to telephone, ring; (*fare una chiamata*) to make a phone call ♦ *vt* to telephone; ~ **a qn** to telephone sb, phone o ring o call sb (up).

telefo'nata *sf* (telephone) call; ~ **urbana/interurbana** local/long-distance call; ~ **a carico del destinatario** reverse charge (*Brit*) o collect (*US*) call; ~ **con preavviso** person-to-person call.

telefonica'mente *av* by (tele)phone.

tele'fonico, a, ci, che *ag* (tele)phone *cpd*.

telefo'nista, i, e *sm/f* telephonist; (*d'impresa*) switchboard operator.

te'lefono *sm* telephone; **avere il** ~ to be on the (tele)phone; ~ **a gettoni** ≈ pay phone; ~ **interno** internal phone; ~ **pubblico** public phone, call box (*Brit*).

telegior'nale [teledʒor'nale] *sm* television news (programme).

telegra'fare *vt, vi* to telegraph, cable.

telegra'fia *sf* telegraphy.

tele'grafico, a, ci, che *ag* telegraph *cpd*, telegraphic.

telegra'fista, i, e *sm/f* telegraphist, telegraph operator.

te'legrafo *sm* telegraph; (*ufficio*) telegraph office.

tele'gramma, i *sm* telegram.

tele'matica *sf* data transmission; telematics *sg*.

teleobiet'tivo *sm* telephoto lens *sg*.

telepa'tia *sf* telepathy.

teles'chermo [teles'kɛrmo] *sm* television screen.

teles'copio *sm* telescope.

telescri'vente *sf* teleprinter (*Brit*), teletypewriter (*US*).

teleselet'tivo, a *ag*: **prefisso** ~ dialling code (*Brit*), dial code (*US*).

teleselezi'one [teleselet'tsjone] *sf* direct dialling.

telespetta'tore, 'trice *sm/f* (television) viewer.

tele'taxe ® [tele'taks] *sm inv* telephone meter.

tele'video *sm videotext* service.

televisi'one *sf* television.

televi'sore *sm* television set.

'telex *sm inv* telex.

'telo *sm* length of cloth.

te'lone *sm* (*per merci etc*) tarpaulin; (*sipario*) drop curtain.

'tema, i *sm* theme; (*INS*) essay, composition.

te'matica *sf* basic themes *pl*.

teme'rario, a *ag* rash, reckless.

te'mere *vt* to fear, be afraid of; (*essere sensibile a: freddo, calore*) to be sensitive to ♦ *vi* to be afraid; (*essere preoccupato*): ~ **per** to worry about, fear for; ~ **di/che** to be afraid of/that.

temperama'tite *sm inv* pencil sharpener.

tempera'mento *sm* temperament.

tempe'rante *ag* moderate.

tempe'rare *vt* (*aguzzare*) to sharpen; (*fig*) to moderate, control, temper.

tempe'rato, a *ag* moderate, temperate; (*clima*) temperate.

tempera'tura *sf* temperature; ~ **ambiente** room temperature.

tempe'rino *sm* penknife.

tem'pesta *sf* storm; ~ **di sabbia/neve** sand/snowstorm.

tempes'tare *vt* (*percuotere*): ~ **qn di colpi** to rain blows on sb; (*bombardare*): ~ **qn di domande** to bombard sb with questions; (*ornare*) to stud.

tempestività *sf* timeliness.

tempes'tivo, a *ag* timely.

tempes'toso, a *ag* stormy.

'tempia *sf* (*ANAT*) temple.

'tempio *sm* (*edificio*) temple.

tem'pismo *sm* sense of timing.

tem'pistiche [tem'pistike] *sfpl* (*COMM*) time and motion.

'tempo *sm* (*METEOR*) weather; (*cronologico*) time; (*epoca*) time, times *pl*; (*di film, gioco: parte*) part; (*MUS*) time; (: *battuta*) beat; (*LING*) tense; **un ~** once; **da ~ for a long time now**; ~ **fa** some time ago; **poco ~ dopo** not long after; **a ~ e luogo** at the right time and place; **ogni cosa a suo ~** we'll (*o* you'll *etc*) deal with it in due course; **al ~ stesso** *o* **a un ~** at the same time; **per ~** early; **per qualche ~** for a while; **trovare il ~ di fare qc** to find the time to do sth; **aver fatto il proprio ~** to have had its (*o* his *etc*) day; **primo/secondo ~** (*TEATRO*) first/second part; (*SPORT*) first/second half; **rispettare i ~i** to keep to the timetable; **stringere i ~i** to speed things up; **con i ~i che corrono** these days; **in questi ultimi ~i** of late; **ai miei ~i** in my day; ~ **di cottura** cooking time; **in ~ utile** in due time *o* course; ~**i di esecuzione** (*COMM*) time scale *sg*; ~**i di lavorazione** (*COMM*) throughput time *sg*; ~**i morti** (*COMM*) downtime *sg*, idle time *sg*.

tempo'rale *ag* temporal ♦ *sm* (*METEOR*) (thunder)storm.

tempora'lesco, a, schi, sche *ag* stormy.

tempo'raneo, a *ag* temporary.

temporeggi'are [tempored'dʒare] *vi* to play for time, temporize.

'tempra *sf* (*TECN*: *atto*) tempering, hardening; (: *effetto*) temper; (*fig*: *costituzione fisica*) constitution; (: *intellettuale*) temperament.

tem'prare *vt* to temper.

te'nace [te'natʃe] *ag* strong, tough; (*fig*) tenacious.

te'nacia [te'natʃa] *sf* tenacity.

te'naglie [te'naʎʎe] *sfpl* pincers *pl*.

'tenda *sf* (*riparo*) awning; (*di finestra*) curtain; (*per campeggio etc*) tent.

ten'daggio [ten'daddʒo] *sm* curtaining, curtains *pl*, drapes *pl* (*US*).

ten'denza [ten'dɛntsa] *sf* tendency; (*orientamento*) trend; **avere** ~ **a** *o* **per qc** to have a bent for sth; ~ **al rialzo/ribasso** (*BORSA*) upward/downward trend.

tendenziosità [tendentsjosi'ta] *sf* tendentiousness.

tendenzi'oso, a [tenden'tsjoso] *ag* tendentious, bias(s)ed.

'tendere *vt* (*allungare al massimo*) to stretch, draw tight; (*porgere: mano*) to hold out; (*fig: trappola*) to lay, set ♦ *vi*: ~ **a qc/a fare** to tend towards sth/to do; **tutti i nostri sforzi sono tesi a …** all our efforts are geared towards …; ~ **l'orecchio** to prick up one's ears; **il tempo tende al caldo** the weather is getting hot; **un blu che tende al verde** a greenish blue.

ten'dina *sf* curtain.

'tendine *sm* tendon, sinew.

ten'done *sm* (*da circo*) big top.

ten'dopoli *sf inv* (large) camp.

'tenebre *sfpl* darkness *sg*.

tene'broso, a *ag* dark, gloomy.

te'nente *sm* lieutenant.

te'nere *vt* to hold; (*conservare, mantenere*) to keep; (*ritenere, considerare*) to consider; (*spazio: occupare*) to take up, occupy; (*seguire: strada*) to keep to; (*dare: lezione, conferenza*) to give ♦ *vi* to hold; (*colori*) to be fast; (*dare importanza*): ~ **a** to care about; ~ **a fare** to want to do, be keen to do; ~**rsi** *vr* (*stare in una determinata posizione*) to stand; (*stimarsi*) to consider o.s.; (*aggrapparsi*): ~**rsi a** to hold on to; (*attenersi*): ~**rsi a** to stick to; ~ **in gran conto** *o* **considerazione qn** to have a high regard for sb, think highly of sb; ~ **conto di qc** to take sth into consideration; ~ **presente qc** to bear sth in mind; **non ci sono scuse che tengano** I'll take no excuses; ~**rsi per la mano** (*uso reciproco*) to hold hands; ~**rsi in piedi** to stay on one's feet.

tene'rezza [tene'rettsa] *sf* tenderness.

'tenero, a *ag* tender; (*pietra, cera, colore*) soft; (*fig*) tender, loving ♦ *sm*: **tra quei due c'è del ~** there's a romance budding between those two.

'tengo *etc vb vedi* **tenere**.

'tenia *sf* tapeworm.

'tenni *etc vb vedi* **tenere**.

'tennis *sm* tennis; ~ **da tavolo** table tennis.

ten'nista, i, e *smf* tennis player.

te'nore *sm* (*tono*) tone; (*MUS*) tenor; ~ **di**

vita way of life; *(livello)* standard of living.

tensi'one *sf* tension; **ad alta ~** *(ELETTR)* high-voltage *cpd*, high-tension *cpd*.

ten'tacolo *sm* tentacle.

ten'tare *vt (indurre)* to tempt; *(provare)*: **~ qc/di fare** to attempt *o* try sth/to do; **~ la sorte** to try one's luck.

tenta'tivo *sm* attempt.

tentazi'one [tentat'tsjone] *sf* temptation; **aver la ~ di fare** to be tempted to do.

tentenna'mento *sm (fig)* hesitation, wavering; **dopo molti ~i** after much hesitation.

tenten'nare *vi* to shake, be unsteady; *(fig)* to hesitate, waver ♦ *vt*: **~ il capo** to shake one's head.

ten'toni *av*: **andare a ~** *(anche fig)* to grope one's way.

'tenue *ag (sottile)* fine; *(colore)* soft; *(fig)* slender, slight.

te'nuta *sf (capacità)* capacity; *(divisa)* uniform; *(abito)* dress; *(AGR)* estate; **a ~ d'aria** airtight; **~ di strada** roadholding power; **in ~ da lavoro** in one's working clothes; **in ~ da sci** in a skiing outfit.

teolo'gia [teolo'dʒia] *sf* theology.

teo'logico, a, ci, che [teo'lɔdʒiko] *ag* theological.

te'ologo, gi *sm* theologian.

teo'rema, i *sm* theorem.

teo'ria *sf* theory; **in ~** in theory, theoretically.

te'orico, a, ci, che *ag* theoretic(al) ♦ *sm* theorist, theoretician; **a livello ~, in linea ~a** theoretically.

teoriz'zare [teorid'dzare] *vt* to theorize.

'tepido, a *ag* = **tiepido**.

te'pore *sm* warmth.

'teppa *sf* mob, hooligans *pl*.

tep'paglia [tep'paʎʎa] *sf* hooligans *pl*.

tep'pismo *sm* hooliganism.

tep'pista, i *sm* hooligan.

tera'peutico, a, ci, che *ag* therapeutic.

tera'pia *sf* therapy.

tera'pista, i, e *sm/f* therapist.

tergicris'tallo [terdʒikris'tallo] *sm* windscreen *(Brit) o* windshield *(US)* wiper.

tergiver'sare [terdʒiver'sare] *vi* to shilly-shally.

'tergo *sm*: **a ~** behind; **vedi a ~** please turn over.

'terital ® *sm inv* Terylene ®.

ter'male *ag* thermal.

'terme *sfpl* thermal baths.

'termico, a, ci, che *ag* thermal; **centrale ~a** thermal power station.

termi'nale *ag (fase, parte)* final; *(MED)* terminal ♦ *sm* terminal; **tratto ~** *(di fiume)* lower reaches *pl*.

termi'nare *vt* to end; *(lavoro)* to finish ♦ *vi* to end.

terminazi'one [terminat'tsjone] *sf (fine)* end;

(LING) ending; **~i nervose** *(ANAT)* nerve endings.

'termine *sm* term; *(fine, estremità)* end; *(di territorio)* boundary, limit; **fissare un ~** to set a deadline; **portare a ~ qc** to bring sth to a conclusion; **contratto a ~** *(COMM)* forward contract; **a breve/lungo ~** short-/long-term; **ai ~i di legge** by law; **in altri ~i** in other words; **parlare senza mezzi ~i** to talk frankly, not to mince one's words.

terminolo'gia [terminolo'dʒia] *sf* terminology.

'termite *sf* termite.

termoco'perta *sf* electric blanket.

ter'mometro *sm* thermometer.

termonucle'are *ag* thermonuclear.

'termos *sm inv* = **thermos**.

termosi'fone *sm* radiator; **(riscaldamento a) ~** central heating.

ter'mostato *sm* thermostat.

'terna *sf* set of three; *(lista di tre nomi)* list of three candidates.

'terno *sm (al lotto etc)* (set of) three winning numbers; **vincere un ~ al lotto** *(fig)* to hit the jackpot.

'terra *sf (gen, ELETTR)* earth; *(sostanza)* soil, earth; *(opposto al mare)* land *q*; *(regione, paese)* land; *(argilla)* clay; **~e** *sfpl (possedimento)* lands, land *sg*; **a o per ~** *(stato)* on the ground *(o* floor); *(moto)* to the ground, down; **mettere a ~** *(ELETTR)* to earth; **essere a ~** *(fig: depresso)* to be at rock bottom; **via ~** *(viaggiare)* by land, overland; **strada in ~ battuta** dirt track; **~ di nessuno** no man's land; **la T~ Santa** the Holy Land; **~ di Siena** sienna; **~ ~** *(fig: persona, argomento)* prosaic, pedestrian.

terra'cotta *sf* terracotta; **vasellame di ~** earthenware.

terra'ferma *sf* dry land, terra firma; *(continente)* mainland.

ter'raglia [ter'raʎʎa] *sf* pottery; **~e** *pl (oggetti)* crockery *sg*, earthenware *sg*.

Terra'nova *sf*: **la ~** Newfoundland.

terrapi'eno *sm* embankment, bank.

ter'razza [ter'rattsa] *sf*, **ter'razzo** [ter'rattso] *sm* terrace.

terremo'tato, a *ag (zona)* devastated by an earthquake ♦ *sm/f* earthquake victim.

terre'moto *sm* earthquake.

ter'reno, a *ag (vita, beni)* earthly ♦ *sm (suolo, fig)* ground; *(COMM)* land *q*, plot (of land); site; *(SPORT, MIL)* field; **perdere ~** *(anche fig)* to lose ground; **un ~ montuoso** a mountainous terrain; **~ alluvionale** *(GEO)* alluvial soil.

'terreo, a *ag (viso, colorito)* wan.

ter'restre *ag (superficie)* of the earth, earth's; *(di terra: battaglia, animale)* land *cpd*; *(REL)* earthly, worldly.

ter'ribile *ag* terrible, dreadful.

ter'riccio [ter'rittʃo] *sm* soil.

terri'ero, a *ag*: **proprietà** ~**a** landed property; **proprietario** ~ landowner.

terrifi'cante *ag* terrifying.

ter'rina *sf* (*zuppiera*) tureen.

territori'ale *ag* territorial.

terri'torio *sm* territory.

ter'rone, a *sm/f derogatory term used by Northern Italians to describe Southern Italians.*

ter'rore *sm* terror; **avere il** ~ **di qc** to be terrified of sth.

terro'rismo *sm* terrorism.

terro'rista, i, e *sm/f* terrorist.

terroriz'zare [terrorid'dzare] *vt* to terrorize.

'terso, a *ag* clear.

ter'zetto [ter'tsetto] *sm* (*MUS*) trio, terzetto; (*di persone*) trio.

terzi'ario, a [ter'tsjarjo] *ag* (*GEO, ECON*) tertiary.

ter'zino [ter'tsino] *sm* (*CALCIO*) fullback, back.

'terzo, a ['tɛrtso] *ag* third ♦ *sm* (*frazione*) third; (*DIR*) third party ♦ *sf* (*gen*) third; (*AUT*) third (gear); (*di trasporti*) third class; (*INS: elementare*) *3rd year at primary school*; (: *media*) *third year at secondary school*; (: *superiore*) *sixth year at secondary school*; ~**i** *smpl* (*altri*) others, other people; **agire per conto di** ~**i** to act on behalf of a third party; **assicurazione contro** ~**i** third-party insurance (*Brit*), liability insurance (*US*); **la** ~**a età** old age; **il** ~ **mondo** the Third World; **di terz'ordine** third rate; **la** ~**a pagina** (*STAMPA*) the Arts page.

'tesa *sf* brim; **a larghe** ~**e** wide-brimmed.

'teschio ['tɛskjo] *sm* skull.

'tesi *sf inv* thesis; ~ **di laurea** degree thesis.

'tesi *etc vb vedi* **tendere**.

'teso, a *pp di* **tendere** ♦ *ag* (*tirato*) taut, tight; (*fig*) tense.

tesore'ria *sf* treasury.

tesori'ere *sm* treasurer.

te'soro *sm* treasure; **il Ministero del T**~ the Treasury; **far** ~ **dei consigli di qn** to take sb's advice to heart.

'tessera *sf* (*documento*) card; (*di abbonato*) season ticket; (*di giornalista*) pass; **ha la** ~ **del partito** he's a party member.

tesse'rare *vt* (*iscrivere*) to give a membership card to.

tesse'rato, a *sm/f* (*di società sportiva etc*) (fully paid-up) member; (*POL*) (card-carrying) member.

'tessere *vt* to weave; ~ **le lodi di qn** (*fig*) to sing sb's praises.

'tessile *ag, sm* textile.

tessi'tore, 'trice *sm/f* weaver.

tessi'tura *sf* weaving.

tes'suto *sm* fabric, material; (*BIOL*) tissue; (*fig*) web.

'testa *sf* head; (*di cose: estremità, parte anteriore*) head, front; **5.000 lire a** ~ 5,000 lire apiece *o* a head *o* per person; **a** ~ **alta** with one's head held high; **a** ~ **bassa** (*correre*) headlong; (*con aria dimessa*) with head bowed; **di** ~ *ag* (*vettura etc*) front; **dare alla** ~ to go to one's head; **fare di** ~ **propria** to go one's own way; **in** ~ (*SPORT*) in the lead; **essere in** ~ **alla classifica** (*corridore*) to be number one; (*squadra*) to be at the top of the league table; (*disco*) to be top of the charts, be number one; **essere alla** ~ **di qc** (*società*) to be the head of; (*esercito*) to be at the head of; **tenere** ~ **a qn** (*nemico etc*) to stand up to sb; **una** ~ **d'aglio** a bulb of garlic; ~ **o croce?** heads or tails?; **avere la** ~ **dura** to be stubborn; ~ **di serie** (*TENNIS*) seed, seeded player.

'testa-'coda *sm inv* (*AUT*) spin.

testamen'tario, a *ag* (*DIR*) testamentary; **le sue disposizioni** ~**e** the provisions of his will.

testa'mento *sm* (*atto*) will, testament; **l'Antico/il Nuovo T**~ (*REL*) the Old/New Testament.

testar'daggine [testar'daddʒine] *sf* stubbornness, obstinacy.

tes'tardo, a *ag* stubborn, pig-headed.

tes'tare *vt* to test.

tes'tata *sf* (*parte anteriore*) head; (*intestazione*) heading; **missile a** ~ **nucleare** missile with a nuclear warhead.

'teste *sm/f* witness.

tes'ticolo *sm* testicle.

testi'era *sf* (*del letto*) headboard; (*di cavallo*) headpiece.

testi'mone *sm/f* (*DIR*) witness; **fare da** ~ **alle nozze di qn** to be a witness at sb's wedding; ~ **oculare** eye witness.

testimoni'anza [testimo'njantsa] *sf* (*atto*) deposition; (*effetto*) evidence; (*fig: prova*) proof; **accusare qn di falsa** ~ to accuse sb of perjury; **rilasciare una** ~ to give evidence.

testimoni'are *vt* to testify; (*fig*) to bear witness to, testify to ♦ *vi* to give evidence, testify; ~ **il vero** to tell the truth; ~ **il falso** to perjure o.s.

tes'tina *sf* (*di giradischi, registratore*) head.

'testo *sm* text; **fare** ~ (*opera, autore*) to be authoritative; (*fig: dichiarazione*) to carry weight.

testu'ale *ag* textual; **le sue parole** ~**i** his (*o* her) actual words.

tes'tuggine [tes'tuddʒine] *sf* tortoise; (*di mare*) turtle.

'tetano *sm* (*MED*) tetanus.

'tetro, a *ag* gloomy.

'tetta *sf* (*fam*) boob, tit.

tetta'rella *sf* teat.

'tetto *sm* roof; **abbandonare il** ~ **coniugale**

to desert one's family; ~ **a cupola** dome.
tet'toia *sf* roofing; canopy.
'Tevere *sm*: **il** ~ the Tiber.
TG, Tg *abbr m* = **telegiornale**.
'thermos ® ['tɛrmos] *sm inv* vacuum *o* Thermos ® flask.
'thriller ['θrilə], **'thrilling** ['θriliŋ] *sm inv* thriller.
ti *pronome* (*dav lo, la, li, le, ne diventa* **te**) (*oggetto*) you; (*complemento di termine*) (to) you; (*riflessivo*) yourself; ~ **aiuto?** can I give you a hand?; **te lo ha dato?** did he give it to you?; ~ **sei lavato?** have you washed?
ti'ara *sf* (*REL*) tiara.
'Tibet *sm*: **il** ~ Tibet.
tibe'tano, a *ag, smf* Tibetan.
'tibia *sf* tibia, shinbone.
tic *sm inv* tic, (nervous) twitch; (*fig*) mannerism.
ticchet'tio [tikket'tio] *sm* (*di macchina da scrivere*) clatter; (*di orologio*) ticking; (*della pioggia*) patter.
'ticchio ['tikkjo] *sm* (*ghiribizzo*) whim; (*tic*) tic, (nervous) twitch.
'ticket *sm inv* (*MED*) prescription charge (*Brit*).
ti'ene *etc vb vedi* **tenere**.
ti'epido, a *ag* lukewarm, tepid.
ti'fare *vi*: ~ **per** to be a fan of; (*parteggiare*) to side with.
'tifo *sm* (*MED*) typhus; (*fig*): **fare il** ~ **per** to be a fan of.
tifoi'dea *sf* typhoid.
ti'fone *sm* typhoon.
ti'foso, a *sm/f* (*SPORT etc*) fan.
tight ['tait] *sm inv* morning suit.
'tiglio ['tiʎʎo] *sm* lime (tree), linden (tree).
'tigna ['tiɲɲa] *sf* (*MED*) ringworm.
ti'grato, a *ag* striped.
'tigre *sf* tiger.
tilt *sm*: **andare in** ~ (*fig*) to go haywire.
tim'ballo *sm* (*strumento*) kettledrum; (*CUC*) timbale.
tim'brare *vt* to stamp; (*annullare: francobolli*) to postmark; ~ **il cartellino** to clock in.
'timbro *sm* stamp; (*MUS*) timbre, tone.
timi'dezza [timi'dettsa] *sf* shyness, timidity.
'timido, a *ag* shy, timid.
'timo *sm* thyme.
ti'mone *sm* (*NAUT*) rudder.
timoni'ere *sm* helmsman.
timo'rato, a *ag* conscientious; ~ **di Dio** God-fearing.
ti'more *sm* (*paura*) fear; (*rispetto*) awe; **avere** ~ **di qc/qn** (*paura*) to be afraid of sth/sb.
timo'roso, a *ag* timid, timorous.
'timpano *sm* (*ANAT*) eardrum; (*MUS*): ~**i** kettledrums, timpani.
ti'nello *sm* small dining room.

'tingere ['tindʒere] *vt* to dye.
'tino *sm* vat.
ti'nozza [ti'nɔttsa] *sf* tub.
'tinsi *etc vb vedi* **tingere**.
'tinta *sf* (*materia colorante*) dye; (*colore*) colour (*Brit*), color (*US*), shade.
tinta'rella *sf* (*fam*) (sun)tan.
tintin'nare *vi* to tinkle.
tintin'nio *sm* tinkling.
'tinto, a *pp di* **tingere**.
tinto'ria *sf* (*officina*) dyeworks *sg*; (*lavasecco*) dry cleaner's (shop).
tin'tura *sf* (*operazione*) dyeing; (*colorante*) dye; ~ **di iodio** tincture of iodine.
'tipico, a, ci, che *ag* typical.
'tipo *sm* type; (*genere*) kind, type; (*fam*) chap, fellow; **vestiti di tutti i** ~**i** all kinds of clothes; **sul** ~ **di questo** of this sort; **sei un bel** ~**!** you're a fine one!
tipogra'fia *sf* typography.
tipo'grafico, a, ci, che *ag* typographic(al).
ti'pografo *sm* typographer.
'tira e 'molla *sm inv* tug-of-war.
ti'raggio [ti'raddʒo] *sm* (*di camino etc*) draught (*Brit*), draft (*US*).
Ti'rana *sf* Tirana.
tiranneggi'are [tiranned'dʒare] *vt* to tyrannize.
tiran'nia *sf* tyranny.
ti'ranno, a *ag* tyrannical ♦ *sm* tyrant.
ti'rante *sm* (*NAUT, di tenda etc*) guy; (*EDIL*) brace.
tirapi'edi *sm/f inv* hanger-on.
ti'rare *vt* (*gen*) to pull; (*estrarre*): ~ **qc da** to take *o* pull sth out of; to get sth out of; to extract sth from; (*chiudere: tenda etc*) to draw, pull; (*tracciare, disegnare*) to draw, trace; (*lanciare: sasso, palla*) to throw; (*stampare*) to print; (*pistola, freccia*) to fire ♦ *vi* (*vento*) to blow; (*abito*) to be tight; (*fare fuoco*) to fire; (*fare del tiro, CALCIO*) to shoot; ~ **qn da parte** to take *o* draw sb aside; ~ **un sospiro (di sollievo)** to heave a sigh (of relief); ~ **a indovinare** to take a guess; ~ **sul prezzo** to bargain; ~ **avanti** *vi* to struggle on ♦ *vt* (*famiglia*) to provide for; (*ditta*) to look after; ~ **fuori** to take out, pull out; ~ **giù** to pull down; ~ **su** to pull up; (*capelli*) to put up; (*fig: bambino*) to bring up; ~**rsi indietro** to move back; (*fig*) to back out; ~**rsi su** to pull o.s. up; (*fig*) to cheer o.s. up.
tira'tore *sm* gunman; **un buon** ~ a good shot; ~ **scelto** marksman.
tira'tura *sf* (*azione*) printing; (*di libro*) (print) run; (*di giornale*) circulation.
tirchie'ria [tirkje'ria] *sf* meanness, stinginess.
'tirchio, a ['tirkjo] *ag* mean, stingy.
tiri'tera *sf* drivel, hot air.
'tiro *sm* shooting *q*, firing *q*; (*colpo, sparo*) shot; (*di palla: lancio*) throwing *q*; throw;

(fig) trick; **essere a ~** to be in range; **giocare un brutto ~ o un ~ mancino a qn** to play a dirty trick on s.b.; **cavallo da ~** draught *(Brit)* o draft *(US)* horse; **~ a segno** target shooting; *(luogo)* shooting range.

tiroci'nante [tirotʃi'nante] *ag, sm/f* apprentice *(cpd)*; trainee *(cpd)*.

tiro'cinio [tiro'tʃinjo] *sm* apprenticeship; *(professionale)* training.

ti'roide *sf* thyroid (gland).

tiro'lese *ag, sm/f* Tyrolean, Tyrolese *inv*.

Ti'rolo *sm*: **il ~** the Tyrol.

tir'rennico, a, ci, che *ag* Tyrrhenian.

Tir'reno *sm*: **il (mar) ~** the Tyrrhenian Sea.

ti'sana *sf* herb tea.

'tisi *sf (MED)* consumption.

'tisico, a, ci, che *ag (MED)* consumptive; *(fig: gracile)* frail ♦ *sm/f* consumptive (person).

ti'tanico, a, ci, che *ag* gigantic, enormous.

ti'tano *sm (MITOLOGIA, fig)* titan.

tito'lare *ag* appointed; *(sovrano)* titular ♦ *sm/f* incumbent; *(proprietario)* owner; *(CALCIO)* regular player.

tito'lato, a *ag (persona)* titled.

'titolo *sm* title; *(di giornale)* headline; *(diploma)* qualification; *(COMM)* security; *(: azione)* share; **a che ~?** for what reason?; **a ~ di amicizia** out of friendship; **a ~ di cronaca** for your information; **a ~ di premio** as a prize; **~ di credito** share; **~ obbligazionario** bond; **~ al portatore** bearer bond; **~ di proprietà** title deed; **~i di stato** government securities; **~i di testa** *(CINEMA)* credits.

titu'bante *ag* hesitant, irresolute.

tivù *sf inv (fam)* telly *(Brit)*, TV.

'tizio, a ['tittsjo] *sm/f* fellow, chap.

tiz'zone [tit'tsone] *sm* brand.

T.M.G. *abbr (= tempo medio di Greenwich)* GMT.

TN *sigla = Trento*.

TNT *sigla m (= trinitrotoluolo)* TNT.

TO *sigla = Torino*.

toast [toust] *sm inv* toasted sandwich.

toc'cante *ag* touching.

toc'care *vt* to touch; *(tastare)* to feel; *(fig: riguardare)* to concern; *(: commuovere)* to touch, move; *(: pungere)* to hurt, wound; *(: far cenno a: argomento)* to touch on, mention ♦ *vi*: **~ a** *(accadere)* to happen to; *(spettare)* to be up to; **tocca a te difenderci** it's up to you to defend us; **a chi tocca?** whose turn is it?; **mi toccò pagare** I had to pay; **~ il fondo** *(in acqua)* to touch the bottom; *(fig)* to touch rock bottom; **~ con mano** *(fig)* to find out for o.s.; **~ qn sul vivo** to cut sb to the quick.

tocca'sana *sm inv* cure-all, panacea.

toccherò *etc* [tokke'rɔ] *vb vedi* **toccare**.

'tocco, chi *sm* touch; *(ARTE)* stroke, touch.

'toga, ghe *sf* toga; *(di magistrato, professore)* gown.

'togliere ['tɔʎʎere] *vt (rimuovere)* to take away *(o off)*, remove; *(riprendere, non concedere più)* to take away, remove; *(MAT)* to take away, subtract; *(liberare)* to free; **~ qc a qn** to take sth (away) from sb; **ciò non toglie che** ... nevertheless ..., be that as it may ...; **~rsi il cappello** to take off one's hat.

'Togo *sm*: **il ~** Togo.

toilette [twa'lɛt] *sf inv (gabinetto)* toilet; *(cosmesi)* make-up; *(abbigliamento)* gown, dress; *(mobile)* dressing table; **fare ~** to get made up, make o.s. beautiful.

'Tokyo *sf* Tokyo.

to'letta *sf* = **toilette**.

'tolgo *etc vb vedi* **togliere**.

tolle'rante *ag* tolerant.

tolle'ranza [tolle'rantsa] *sf* tolerance; **casa di ~** brothel.

tolle'rare *vt* to tolerate; **non tollero repliche** I won't stand for objections; **non sono tollerati i ritardi** lateness will not be tolerated.

To'losa *sf* Toulouse.

'tolsi *etc vb vedi* **togliere**.

'tolto, a *pp di* **togliere**.

to'maia *sf (di scarpa)* upper.

'tomba *sf* tomb.

tom'bale *ag*: **pietra ~** tombstone, gravestone.

tom'bino *sm* manhole cover.

'tombola *sf (gioco)* tombola; *(ruzzolone)* tumble.

'tomo *sm* volume.

'tonaca, che *sf (REL)* habit.

to'nare *vi* = **tuonare**.

'tondo, a *ag* round.

'tonfo *sm* splash; *(rumore sordo)* thud; *(caduta)*: **fare un ~** to take a tumble.

'tonico, a, ci, che *ag* tonic ♦ *sm* tonic; *(cosmetico)* toner.

tonifi'cante *ag* invigorating, bracing.

tonifi'care *vt (muscoli, pelle)* to tone up; *(irrobustire)* to invigorate, brace.

ton'nara *sf* tuna-fishing nets *pl*.

tonnel'laggio [tonnel'laddʒo] *sm (NAUT)* tonnage.

tonnel'lata *sf* ton.

'tonno *sm* tuna (fish).

'tono *sm (gen, MUS)* tone; *(di colore)* shade, tone; **rispondere a ~** *(a proposito)* to answer to the point; *(nello stesso modo)* to answer in kind; *(per le rime)* to answer back.

ton'silla *sf* tonsil.

tonsil'lite *sf* tonsillitis.

ton'sura *sf* tonsure.

'tonto, a *ag* dull, stupid ♦ *sm/f* blockhead, dunce; **fare il finto ~** to play dumb.

to'paia *sf (di topo)* mousehole; *(di ratto)*

rat's nest; (*fig*: *casa etc*) hovel, dump.

to'pazio [to'pattsjo] *sm* topaz.

topi'cida, i [topi'tʃida] *sm* rat poison.

'topless ['tɔplis] *sm inv* topless bathing costume.

'topo *sm* mouse; ~ **d'albergo** (*fig*) hotel thief; ~ **di biblioteca** (*fig*) bookworm.

topogra'fia *sf* topography.

'toppa *sf* (*serratura*) keyhole; (*pezza*) patch.

to'race [to'ratʃe] *sm* chest.

'torba *sf* peat.

'torbido, a *ag* (*liquido*) cloudy; (: *fiume*) muddy; (*fig*) dark; troubled ♦ *sm*: **pescare nel** ~ (*fig*) to fish in troubled waters.

'torcere ['tɔrtʃere] *vt* to twist; (*biancheria*) to wring (out); **~rsi** *vr* to twist, writhe; **dare del filo da** ~ **a qn** to make life *o* things difficult for sb.

torchi'are [tor'kjare] *vt* to press.

'torchio ['tɔrkjo] *sm* press; **mettere qn sotto il** ~ (*fig fam*: *interrogare*) to grill sb; ~ **tipografico** printing press.

'torcia, ce ['tɔrtʃa] *sf* torch; ~ **elettrica** torch (*Brit*), flashlight (*US*).

torci'collo [tortʃi'kɔllo] *sm* stiff neck.

'tordo *sm* thrush.

to'rero *sm* bullfighter, toreador.

tori'nese *ag* of (*o* from) Turin ♦ *sm/f* person from Turin.

To'rino *sf* Turin.

tor'menta *sf* snowstorm.

tormen'tare *vt* to torment; **~rsi** *vr* to fret, worry o.s.

tor'mento *sm* torment.

torna'conto *sm* advantage, benefit.

tor'nado *sm* tornado.

tor'nante *sm* hairpin bend (*Brit*) *o* curve (*US*).

tor'nare *vi* to return, go (*o* come) back; (*ridiventare*: *anche fig*) to become (again); (*riuscire giusto, esatto*: *conto*) to work out; (*risultare*) to turn out (to be), prove (to be); ~ **al punto di partenza** to start again; ~ **a casa** to go (*o* come) home; **i conti tornano** the accounts balance; ~ **utile** to prove *o* turn out (to be) useful.

torna'sole *sm inv* litmus.

tor'neo *sm* tournament.

'tornio *sm* lathe.

tor'nire *vt* (*TECN*) to turn (on a lathe); (*fig*) to shape, polish.

tor'nito, a *ag* (*gambe, caviglie*) well-shaped.

'toro *sm* bull; (*dello zodiaco*): **T~** Taurus; **essere del T~** to be Taurus.

tor'pedine *sf* torpedo.

torpedini'era *sf* torpedo boat.

tor'pore *sm* torpor.

'torre *sf* tower; (*SCACCHI*) rook, castle; ~ **di controllo** (*AER*) control tower.

torrefazi'one [torrefat'tsjone] *sf* roasting.

torreggi'are [torred'dʒare] *vi*: ~ **(su)** to

tower (over).

tor'rente *sm* torrent.

torren'tizio, a [torren'tittsjo] *ag* torrential.

torrenzi'ale [torren'tsjale] *ag* torrential.

tor'retta *sf* turret.

'torrido, a *ag* torrid.

torri'one *sm* keep.

tor'rone *sm* nougat.

'torsi *etc vb vedi* **torcere**.

torsi'one *sf* twisting; (*TECN*) torsion.

'torso *sm* torso, trunk; (*ARTE*) torso; **a** ~ **nudo** bare-chested.

'torsolo *sm* (*di cavolo etc*) stump; (*di frutta*) core.

'torta *sf* cake.

torti'era *sf* cake tin (*Brit*), cake pan (*US*).

'torto, a *pp di* **torcere** ♦ *ag* (*ritorto*) twisted; (*storto*) twisted, crooked ♦ *sm* (*ingiustizia*) wrong; (*colpa*) fault; **a** ~ wrongly; **a** ~ **o a ragione** rightly or wrongly; **aver** ~ to be wrong; **fare un** ~ **a qn** to wrong sb; **essere/passare dalla parte del** ~ to be/put o.s. in the wrong; **lui non ha tutti i** ~**i** there's something in what he says.

'tortora *sf* turtle dove.

tortu'oso, a *ag* (*strada*) twisting; (*fig*) tortuous.

tor'tura *sf* torture.

tortu'rare *vt* to torture.

'torvo, a *ag* menacing, grim.

tosa'erba *sm o f inv* (lawn)mower.

to'sare *vt* (*pecora*) to shear; (*cane*) to clip; (*siepe*) to clip, trim.

tosa'tura *sf* (*di pecore*) shearing; (*di cani*) clipping; (*di siepi*) trimming, clipping.

Tos'cana *sf*: **la** ~ Tuscany.

tos'cano, a *ag*, *sm/f* Tuscan ♦ *sm* (*anche*: **sigaro** ~) strong Italian cigar.

'tosse *sf* cough.

tossicità [tossitʃi'ta] *sf* toxicity.

'tossico, a, ci, che *ag* toxic.

tossicodipen'dente *sm/f* drug addict.

tossicodipen'denza [tossikodipen'dɛntsa] *sf* drug addiction.

tossi'comane *sm/f* drug addict.

tossicoma'nia *sf* drug addiction.

tos'sina *sf* toxin.

tos'sire *vi* to cough.

tosta'pane *sm inv* toaster.

tos'tare *vt* to toast; (*caffè*) to roast.

tosta'tura *sf* (*di pane*) toasting; (*di caffè*) roasting.

'tosto, a *ag*: **faccia ~a** cheek ♦ *av* at once, immediately; ~ **che** as soon as.

to'tale *ag*, *sm* total.

totalità *sf*: **la** ~ **di** all of, the total amount (*o* number) of; **the whole** + *sg*.

totali'tario, a *ag* totalitarian; (*totale*) complete, total; **adesione ~a** complete support.

totalita'rismo *sm* (*POL*) totalitarianism.

totaliz'zare [totalid'dzare] *vt* to total;

(*SPORT*: *punti*) to score.

totalizza'tore [totaliddza'tore] *sm* (*TECN*) totalizator; (*IPPICA*) totalizator, tote (*fam*).

toto'calcio [toto'kaltʃo] *sm gambling pool betting on football results*, ≈ (football) pools *pl* (*Brit*).

tour'née [tur'ne] *sf* tour; **essere in** ~ to be on tour.

to'vaglia [to'vaʎʎa] *sf* tablecloth.

tovagli'olo [tovaʎ'ʎɔlo] *sm* napkin.

'tozzo, a ['tɔttso] *ag* squat ♦ *sm*: ~ **di pane** crust of bread.

TP *sigla* = *Trapani*.

TR *sigla* = *Terni*.

Tr *abbr* (*COMM*) = **tratta**.

tra *prep* (*di due persone, cose*) between; (*di più persone, cose*) among(st); (*tempo: entro*) within, in; **prendere qn** ~ **le braccia** to take sb in one's arms; **litigano** ~ **(di) loro** they're fighting amongst themselves; ~ **5 giorni** in 5 days' time; ~ **breve** *o* **poco** soon; ~ **sé e sé** (*parlare etc*) to oneself; **sia detto** ~ **noi** ... between you and me ...; ~ **una cosa e l'altra** what with one thing and another.

trabal'lante *ag* shaky.

trabal'lare *vi* to stagger, totter.

tra'biccolo *sm* (*peg*: *auto*) old banger (*Brit*), jalopy.

traboc'care *vi* to overflow.

traboc'chetto [trabok'ketto] *sm* (*fig*) trap ♦ *ag inv* trap *cpd*; **domanda** ~ trick question.

traca'gnotto, a [trakaɲ'ɲɔtto] *ag* dumpy ♦ *sm/f* dumpy person.

tracan'nare *vt* to gulp down.

'traccia, ce ['trattʃa] *sf* (*segno, striscia*) trail, track; (*orma*) tracks *pl*; (*testimonianza*) trace, sign; (*abbozzo*) outline; **essere sulle** ~**ce di qn** to be on sb's trail.

tracci'are [trat'tʃare] *vt* to trace, mark (out); (*disegnare*) to draw; (*fig: abbozzare*) to outline; ~ **un quadro della situazione** to outline the situation.

tracci'ato [trat'tʃato] *sm* (*grafico*) layout, plan; ~ **di gara** (*SPORT*) race route.

tra'chea [tra'kɛa] *sf* windpipe, trachea.

tra'colla *sf* shoulder strap; **portare qc a** ~ to carry sth over one's shoulder; **borsa a** ~ shoulder bag.

tra'collo *sm* (*fig*) collapse, ruin; ~ **finanziario** crash; **avere un** ~ (*MED*) to have a setback; (*COMM*) to collapse.

traco'tante *ag* overbearing, arrogant.

traco'tanza [trako'tantsa] *sf* arrogance.

trad. *abbr* = **traduzione**.

tradi'mento *sm* betrayal; (*DIR*, *MIL*) treason; **a** ~ by surprise; **alto** ~ high treason.

tra'dire *vt* to betray; (*coniuge*) to be unfaithful to; (*doveri: mancare*) to fail in;

(*rivelare*) to give away, reveal; **ha tradito le attese di tutti** he let everyone down.

tradi'tore, 'trice *sm/f* traitor.

tradizio'nale [tradittsjo'nale] *ag* traditional.

tradizi'one [tradit'tsjone] *sf* tradition.

tra'dotto, a *pp di* **tradurre** ♦ *sf* (*MIL*) troop train.

tra'durre *vt* to translate; (*spiegare*) to render, convey; (*DIR*): ~ **qn in carcere/ tribunale** to take sb to prison/court; ~ **in cifre** to put into figures; ~ **in atto** (*fig*) to put into effect.

tradut'tore, 'trice *sm/f* translator.

traduzi'one [tradut'tsjone] *sf* translation; (*DIR*) transfer.

'trae *vb vedi* **trarre**.

tra'ente *sm/f* (*ECON*) drawer.

trafe'lato, a *ag* out of breath.

traffi'cante *sm/f* dealer; (*peg*) trafficker.

traffi'care *vi* (*commerciare*): ~ **(in)** to trade (in), deal (in); (*affaccendarsi*) to busy o.s. ♦ *vt* (*peg*) to traffic in.

traffi'cato, a *ag* (*strada, zona*) busy.

'traffico, ci *sm* traffic; (*commercio*) trade, traffic; ~ **aereo/ferroviario** air/rail traffic; ~ **di droga** drug trafficking; ~ **stradale** traffic.

tra'figgere [tra'fiddʒere] *vt* to run through, stab; (*fig*) to pierce.

tra'fila *sf* procedure.

trafi'letto *sm* (*di giornale*) short article.

tra'fitto, a *pp di* **trafiggere**.

trafo'rare *vt* to bore, drill.

tra'foro *sm* (*azione*) boring, drilling; (*galleria*) tunnel.

trafu'gare *vt* to purloin.

tra'gedia [tra'dʒɛdja] *sf* tragedy.

'traggo *etc vb vedi* **trarre**.

traghet'tare [traget'tare] *vt* to ferry.

tra'ghetto [tra'getto] *sm* crossing; (*barca*) ferry(boat).

tragicità [tradʒitʃi'ta] *sf* tragedy.

'tragico, a, ci, che ['tradʒiko] *ag* tragic ♦ *sm* (*autore*) tragedian; **prendere tutto sul** ~ (*fig*) to take everything far too seriously.

tragi'comico, a, ci, che [tradʒi'kɔmiko] *ag* tragicomic.

tra'gitto [tra'dʒitto] *sm* (*passaggio*) crossing; (*viaggio*) journey.

tragu'ardo *sm* (*SPORT*) finishing line; (*fig*) goal, aim.

'trai *etc vb vedi* **trarre**.

traiet'toria *sf* trajectory.

trai'nare *vt* to drag, haul; (*rimorchiare*) to tow.

'traino *sm* (*carro*) wagon; (*slitta*) sledge; (*carico*) load.

tralasci'are [tralaʃ'ʃare] *vt* (*studi*) to neglect; (*dettagli*) to leave out, omit.

'tralcio ['traltʃo] *sm* (*BOT*) shoot.

tra'liccio [tra'littʃo] *sm* (*tela*) ticking; (*struttura*) trellis; (*ELETTR*) pylon.

tram *sm inv* tram *(Brit)*, streetcar *(US)*.
'trama *sf (filo)* weft, woof; *(fig: argomento, maneggio)* plot.
traman'dare *vt* to pass on, hand down.
tra'mare *vt (fig)* to scheme, plot.
tram'busto *sm* turmoil.
trames'tio *sm* bustle.
tramez'zino [tramed'dzino] *sm* sandwich.
tra'mezzo [tra'mɛddzo] *sm* partition.
'tramite *prep* through ♦ *sm* means *pl*; **agire/fare da** ~ to act as/be a go-between.
tramon'tana *sf (METEOR)* north wind.
tramon'tare *vi* to set, go down.
tra'monto *sm* setting; *(del sole)* sunset.
tramor'tire *vi* to faint ♦ *vt* to stun.
trampo'lino *sm (per tuffi)* springboard, diving board; *(per lo sci)* ski-jump.
'trampolo *sm* stilt.
tramu'tare *vt*: ~ **in** to change into, turn into.
'trancia, ce ['trantʃa] *sf* slice; *(cesoia)* shearing machine.
tranci'are [tran'tʃare] *vt (TECN)* to shear.
'trancio ['trantʃo] *sm* slice.
tra'nello *sm* trap; **tendere un** ~ **a qn** to set a trap for sb; **cadere in un** ~ to fall into a trap.
trangugi'are [trangu'dʒare] *vt* to gulp down.
'tranne *prep* except (for), but (for); ~ **che** *cong* unless; **tutti i giorni** ~ **il venerdì** every day except *o* with the exception of Friday.
tranquil'lante *sm (MED)* tranquillizer.
tranquillità *sf* calm, stillness; quietness; peace of mind.
tranquilliz'zare [trankwillid'dzare] *vt* to reassure.
tran'quillo, a *ag* calm, quiet; *(bambino, scolaro)* quiet; *(sereno)* with one's mind at rest; **sta'** ~ don't worry.
transat'lantico, a, ci, che *ag* transatlantic ♦ *sm* transatlantic liner.
tran'satto, a *pp di* **transigere**.
transazi'one [transat'tsjone] *sf (DIR)* settlement; *(COMM)* transaction, deal.
tran'senna *sf* barrier.
tran'setto *sm* transept.
transiberi'ano, a *ag* trans-Siberian.
tran'sigere [tran'sidʒere] *vi (DIR)* to reach a settlement; *(venire a patti)* to compromise, come to an agreement.
tran'sistor *sm inv*, **transis'tore** *sm* transistor.
transi'tabile *ag* passable.
transi'tare *vi* to pass.
transi'tivo, a *ag* transitive.
'transito *sm* transit; **di** ~ *(merci)* in transit; *(stazione)* transit *cpd*; **"divieto di** ~**"** "no entry"; **"**~ **interrotto"** "road closed".
transi'torio, a *ag* transitory, transient; *(provvisorio)* provisional.

transizi'one [transit'tsjone] *sf* transition.
tran 'tran *sm* routine; **il solito** ~ the same old routine.
tran'via *sf* tramway *(Brit)*, streetcar line *(US)*.
tranvi'ario, a *ag* tram *cpd (Brit)*, streetcar *cpd (US)*; **linea** ~**a** tramline, streetcar line.
tranvi'ere *sm (conducente)* tram driver *(Brit)*, streetcar driver *(US)*; *(bigliettaio)* tram *o* streetcar conductor.
trapa'nare *vt (TECN)* to drill.
'trapano *sm (utensile)* drill; *(: MED)* trepan.
trapas'sare *vt* to pierce.
trapas'sato *sm (LING)* past perfect.
tra'passo *sm* passage; ~ **di proprietà** *(di case)* conveyancing; *(di auto etc)* legal transfer.
trape'lare *vi* to leak, drip; *(fig)* to leak out.
tra'pezio [tra'pɛttsjo] *sm (MAT)* trapezium; *(attrezzo ginnico)* trapeze.
trape'zista, i, e [trapet'tsista] *sm/f* trapeze artist.
trapian'tare *vt* to transplant.
trapi'anto *sm* transplanting; *(MED)* transplant.
'trappola *sf* trap.
tra'punta *sf* quilt.
'trarre *vt* to draw, pull; *(prendere, tirare fuori)* to take (out), draw; *(derivare)* to obtain; ~ **beneficio** *o* **profitto da qc** to benefit from sth; ~ **le conclusioni** to draw one's own conclusions; ~ **esempio da qn** to follow sb's example; ~ **guadagno** to make a profit; ~ **qn d'impaccio** to get sb out of an awkward situation; ~ **origine da qc** to have its origins *o* originate in sth; ~ **in salvo** to rescue.
trasa'lire *vi* to start, jump.
trasan'dato, a *ag* shabby.
trasbor'dare *vt* to transfer; *(NAUT)* to tran(s)ship ♦ *vi (NAUT)* to change ship; *(AER)* to change plane; *(FERR)* to change (trains).
trascenden'tale [traʃʃenden'tale] *ag* transcendental.
tra'scendere [traʃ'ʃendere] *vt (FILOSOFIA, REL)* to transcend; *(fig: superare)* to surpass, go beyond.
tra'sceso, a [traʃ'ʃeso] *pp di* **trascendere**.
trasci'nare [traʃʃi'nare] *vt* to drag; ~**rsi** *vr* to drag o.s. along; *(fig)* to drag on.
tras'correre *vt (tempo)* to spend, pass ♦ *vi* to pass.
tras'corso, a *pp di* **trascorrere** ♦ *ag* past ♦ *sm* mistake.
tras'critto, a *pp di* **trascrivere**.
tras'crivere *vt* to transcribe.
trascrizi'one [traskrit'tsjone] *sf* transcription.
trascu'rare *vt* to neglect; *(non considerare)* to disregard.

trascura'tezza [traskura'tettsa] *sf* carelessness, negligence.

trascu'rato, a *ag.* *(casa)* neglected; *(persona)* careless, negligent.

traseco'lato, a *ag* astounded, amazed.

trasferi'mento *sm* transfer; *(trasloco)* removal, move.

trasfe'rire *vt* to transfer; **~rsi** *vr* to move.

tras'ferta *sf* transfer; *(indennità)* travelling expenses *pl*; *(SPORT)* away game.

trasfigu'rare *vt* to transfigure.

trasfor'mare *vt* to transform, change.

trasforma'tore *sm* transformer.

trasformazi'one [trasformat'tsjone] *sf* transformation.

trasfusi'one *sf* *(MED)* transfusion.

trasgre'dire *vt* to break, infringe; *(ordini)* to disobey.

trasgressi'one *sf* breaking, infringement; disobeying.

trasgres'sore, trasgredi'trice [trazgredi'tritʃe] *sm/f* *(DIR)* transgressor.

tras'lato, a *ag* metaphorical, figurative.

traslo'care *vt* to move, transfer; **~rsi** *vr* to move.

tras'loco, chi *sm* removal.

tras'messo, a *pp di* **trasmettere**.

tras'mettere *vt* *(passare)*: **~ qc a qn** to pass sth on to sb; *(mandare)* to send; *(TECN, TEL, MED)* to transmit; *(TV, RADIO)* to broadcast.

trasmetti'tore *sm* transmitter.

trasmissi'one *sf* *(gen, FISICA, TECN)* transmission; *(passaggio)* transmission, passing on; *(TV, RADIO)* broadcast.

trasmit'tente *sf* transmitting *o* broadcasting station.

traso'gnato, a [trasoɲ'ɲato] *ag* dreamy.

traspa'rente *ag* transparent.

traspa'renza [traspa'rentsa] *sf* transparency; **guardare qc in ~** to look at sth against the light.

traspa'rire *vi* to show (through).

tras'parso, a *pp di* **trasparire**.

traspi'rare *vi* to perspire; *(fig)* to come to light, leak out.

traspirazi'one [traspirat'tsjone] *sf* perspiration.

tras'porre *vt* to transpose.

traspor'tare *vt* to carry, move; *(merce)* to transport, convey; **lasciarsi ~ (da qc)** *(fig)* to let o.s. be carried away (by sth).

tras'porto *sm* transport; *(fig)* rapture, passion; **con ~** passionately; **compagnia di ~** carriers *pl*; *(per strada)* hauliers *pl* (*Brit*), haulers *pl* (*US*); **mezzi di ~** means of transport; **nave/aereo da ~** transport ship/aircraft; **~ (funebre)** funeral procession; **~ marittimo/aereo** sea/air transport; **~ stradale** (road) haulage; **i ~i pubblici** public transport.

tras'posto, a *pp di* **trasporre**.

'trassi *etc vb vedi* **trarre**.

trastul'lare *vt* to amuse; **~rsi** *vr* to amuse o.s.

tras'tullo *sm* game.

trasu'dare *vi* *(filtrare)* to ooze; *(sudare)* to sweat ♦ *vt* to ooze with.

trasver'sale *ag* *(taglio, sbarra)* cross(-); *(retta)* transverse; **via ~** side street.

trasvo'lare *vt* to fly over.

'tratta *sf* *(ECON)* draft; *(di persone)*: **la ~ delle bianche** the white slave trade; **~ documentaria** documentary bill of exchange.

tratta'mento *sm* treatment; *(servizio)* service; **ricevere un buon ~** *(cliente)* to get good service; **~ di fine rapporto** *(COMM)* severance pay.

trat'tare *vt* *(gen)* to treat; *(commerciare)* to deal in; *(svolgere: argomento)* to discuss, deal with; *(negoziare)* to negotiate ♦ *vi:* **~ di** to deal with; **~ con** *(persona)* to deal with; **si tratta di ...** it's about ...; **si tratterebbe solo di poche ore** it would just be a matter of a few hours.

tratta'tive *sfpl* negotiations; **essere in ~ con qn** to negotiate with sb.

trat'tato *sm* *(testo)* treatise; *(accordo)* treaty; **~ commerciale** trade agreement; **~ di pace** peace treaty.

trattazi'one [trattat'tsjone] *sf* treatment.

tratteggi'are [tratted'dʒare] *vt* *(disegnare: a tratti)* to sketch, outline; *(: col tratteggio)* to hatch.

trat'teggio [trat'teddʒo] *sm* hatching.

tratte'nere *vt* *(far rimanere: persona)* to detain; *(tenere, frenare, reprimere)* to hold back, keep back; *(astenersi dal consegnare)* to hold, keep; *(detrarre: somma)* to deduct; **~rsi** *vr* *(astenersi)* to restrain o.s., stop o.s.; *(soffermarsi)* to stay, remain; **sono stato trattenuto in ufficio** I was delayed at the office.

tratteni'mento *sm* entertainment; *(festa)* party.

tratte'nuta *sf* deduction.

trat'tino *sm* dash; *(in parole composte)* hyphen.

'tratto, a *pp di* **trarre** ♦ *sm* *(di penna, matita)* stroke; *(parte)* part, piece; *(di strada)* stretch; *(di mare, cielo)* expanse; *(di tempo)* period (of time); **~i** *smpl* *(caratteristiche)* features; *(modo di fare)* ways, manners; **a un ~, d'un ~** suddenly.

trat'tore *sm* tractor.

tratto'ria *sf* (small) restaurant.

'trauma, i *sm* trauma; **~ cranico** concussion.

trau'matico, a, ci, che *ag* traumatic.

traumatiz'zare [traumatid'dzare] *vt* *(MED)* to traumatize; *(fig: impressionare)* to shock.

tra'vaglio [tra'vaʎʎo] *sm* *(angoscia)* pain, suffering; *(MED)* pains *pl*; **~ di parto**

labour pains.

trava'sare vt to pour; (vino) to decant.

tra'vaso sm pouring; decanting.

trava'tura sf beams pl.

'trave sf beam.

tra'veggole sfpl: **avere le ~** to be seeing things.

tra'versa sf (trave) crosspiece; (via) side-street; (FERR) sleeper (Brit), (railroad) tie (US); (CALCIO) crossbar.

traver'sare vt to cross.

traver'sata sf crossing; (AER) flight, trip.

traver'sie sfpl mishaps, misfortunes.

traver'sina sf (FERR) sleeper (Brit), (railroad) tie (US).

tra'verso, a ag oblique; **di ~** ag askew ♦ av sideways; **andare di ~** (cibo) to go down the wrong way; **messo di ~** sideways on; **guardare di ~** to look askance at; **via ~a** side road; **ottenere qc per vie ~e** (fig) to obtain sth in an underhand way.

travesti'mento sm disguise.

traves'tire vt to disguise; **~rsi** vr to disguise o.s.

traves'tito sm transvestite.

travi'are vt (fig) to lead astray.

travi'sare vt (fig) to distort, misrepresent.

travol'gente [travol'dʒɛnte] ag overwhelming.

tra'volgere [tra'vɔldʒere] vt to sweep away, carry away; (fig) to overwhelm.

tra'volto, a pp di **travolgere**.

trazi'one [trat'tsjone] sf traction; **~ anteriore/posteriore** (AUT) front-wheel/rear-wheel drive.

tre num three.

tre'alberi sm inv (NAUT) three-master.

'trebbia sf (AGR: operazione) threshing; (: stagione) threshing season.

trebbi'are vt to thresh.

trebbia'trice [trebbja'tritʃe] sf threshing machine.

'treccia, ce ['trettʃa] sf plait, braid; **lavorato a ~ce** (pullover etc) cable-knit.

trecen'tesco, a, schi, sche [tretʃen'tesko] ag fourteenth-century.

tre'cento [tre'tʃɛnto] num three hundred ♦ sm: **il T~** the fourteenth century.

tredi'cenne [tredi'tʃɛnne] ag, sm/f thirteen-year-old.

tredi'cesimo, a [tredi'tʃɛzimo] num thirteenth ♦ sf Christmas bonus of a month's pay.

'tredici ['treditʃi] num thirteen ♦ sm inv: **fare ~** (TOTOCALCIO) to win the pools (Brit).

'tregua sf truce; (fig) respite; **senza ~** non-stop, without stopping, uninterruptedly.

tre'mante ag trembling, shaking.

tre'mare vi to tremble, shake; **~ di** (freddo etc) to shiver o tremble with; (paura, rabbia) to shake o tremble with.

trema'rella sf shivers pl.

tre'mendo, a ag terrible, awful.

tremen'tina sf turpentine.

tre'mila num three thousand.

'tremito sm trembling q; shaking q; shivering q.

tremo'lare vi to tremble; (luce) to flicker; (foglie) to quiver.

tre'more sm tremor.

'treno sm train; (AUT): **~ di gomme** set of tyres; **~ locale/diretto/espresso** local/fast/express train; **~ merci** goods (Brit) o freight train; **~ rapido** express (train) (for which supplement must be paid); **~ straordinario** special train; **~ viaggiatori** passenger train.

'trenta num thirty ♦ sm inv (INS): **~ e lode** full marks plus distinction o cum laude.

tren'tenne ag, sm/f thirty-year-old.

tren'tennio sm period of thirty years.

tren'tesimo, a num thirtieth.

tren'tina sf: **una ~ (di)** thirty or so, about thirty.

trepi'dante ag anxious.

trepi'dare vi to be anxious; **~ per qn** to be anxious about sb.

'trepido, a ag anxious.

treppi'ede sm tripod; (CUC) trivet.

tre'quarti sm inv three-quarter-length coat.

'tresca, sche sf (fig) intrigue; (: relazione amorosa) affair.

'trespolo sm trestle.

trevigi'ano, a [trevi'dʒano] ag of (o from) Treviso.

triango'lare ag triangular.

tri'angolo sm triangle.

tribo'lare vi (patire) to suffer; (fare fatica) to have a lot of trouble.

tribolazi'one [tribolat'tsjone] sf suffering, tribulation.

tri'bordo sm (NAUT) starboard.

tribù sf inv tribe.

tri'buna sf (podio) platform; (in aule etc) gallery; (di stadio) stand; **~ della stampa/riservata al pubblico** press/public gallery.

tribu'nale sm court; **presentarsi** o **comparire in ~** to appear in court; **~ militare** military tribunal; **~ supremo** supreme court.

tribu'tare vt to bestow; **~ gli onori dovuti a qn** to pay tribute to sb.

tribu'tario, a ag (imposta) fiscal, tax cpd; (GEO): **essere ~ di** to be a tributary of.

tri'buto sm tax; (fig) tribute.

tri'checo, chi [tri'kɛko] sm (ZOOL) walrus.

tri'ciclo [tri'tʃiklo] sm tricycle.

trico'lore ag three-coloured (Brit), three-colored (US) ♦ sm tricolo(u)r; (bandiera italiana) Italian flag.

tri'dente sm trident.

trien'nale ag (che dura 3 anni) three-year cpd; (che avviene ogni 3 anni) three-yearly.

tri'ennio *sm* period of three years.
tries'tino, a *ag* of (*o* from) Trieste.
tri'fase *ag* (*ELETTR*) three-phase.
tri'foglio [tri'fɔʎʎo] *sm* clover.
trifo'lato, a *ag* (*CUC*) *cooked in oil, garlic and parsley.*
'triglia ['triʎʎa] *sf* red mullet.
trigonome'tria *sf* trigonometry.
tril'lare *vi* (*MUS*) to trill.
tri'mestre *sm* period of three months; (*INS*) term, quarter (*US*); (*COMM*) quarter.
trimo'tore *sm* (*AER*) three-engined plane.
'trina *sf* lace.
trin'cea [trin'tʃea] *sf* trench.
trince'rare [trintʃe'rare] *vt* to entrench.
trinci'are [trin'tʃare] *vt* to cut up.
'Trinidad *sm*: ~ **e Tobago** Trinidad and Tobago.
Trinità *sf* (*REL*) Trinity.
'trio, *pl* **'trii** *sm* trio.
trion'fale *ag* triumphal, triumphant.
trion'fante *ag* triumphant.
trion'fare *vi* to triumph, win; ~ **su** to triumph over, overcome.
tri'onfo *sm* triumph.
tripli'care *vt* to triple.
'triplice ['triplitʃe] *ag* triple; **in ~ copia** in triplicate.
'triplo, a *ag* triple, treble ♦ *sm*: **il ~ (di)** three times as much (as); **la spesa è ~a** it costs three times as much.
'tripode *sm* tripod.
'Tripoli *sf* Tripoli.
'trippa *sf* (*CUC*) tripe.
tri'pudio *sm* triumph, jubilation; (*fig: di colori*) galaxy.
tris *sm inv* (*CARTE*): ~ **d'assi/di re** *etc* three aces/kings *etc*.
'triste *sf* sad; (*luogo*) dreary, gloomy.
tris'tezza [tris'tettsa] *sf* sadness; gloominess.
'tristo, a *ag* (*cattivo*) wicked, evil; (*meschino*) sorry, poor.
trita'carne *sm inv* mincer, grinder (*US*).
trita'ghiaccio [trita'gjattʃo] *sm inv* ice crusher.
tri'tare *vt* to mince, grind (*US*).
trita'tutto *sm inv* mincer, grinder (*US*).
'trito, a *ag* (*tritato*) minced, ground (*US*); ~ **e ritrito** (*idee, argomenti, frasi*) trite, hackneyed.
tri'tolo *sm* trinitrotoluene.
'trittico, ci *sm* (*ARTE*) triptych.
tritu'rare *vt* to grind.
tri'vella *sf* drill.
trivel'lare *vt* to drill.
trivellazi'one [trivellat'tsjone] *sf* drilling; **torre di ~** derrick.
trivi'ale *ag* vulgar, low.
trivialità *sf inv* (*volgarità*) coarseness, crudeness; (: *osservazione*) coarse *o* crude remark.
tro'feo *sm* trophy.

'trogolo *sm* (*per maiali*) trough.
'troia *sf* (*ZOOL*) sow; (*fig peg*) whore.
'tromba *sf* (*MUS*) trumpet; (*AUT*) horn; ~ **d'aria** whirlwind; ~ **delle scale** stairwell.
trombet'tista, i, e *sm/f* trumpeter, trumpet (player).
trom'bone *sm* trombone.
trom'bosi *sf* thrombosis.
tron'care *vt* to cut off; (*spezzare*) to break off.
'tronco, a, chi, che *ag* cut off; broken off; (*LING*) truncated ♦ *sm* (*BOT, ANAT*) trunk; (*fig: tratto*) section; (: *pezzo: di lancia*) stump; **licenziare qn in ~** (*fig*) to fire sb on the spot.
troneggi'are [troned'dʒare] *vi:* ~ **(su)** to tower (over).
'tronfio, a *ag* conceited.
'trono *sm* throne.
tropi'cale *ag* tropical.
'tropico, ci *sm* tropic; ~ **del Cancro/Capricorno** Tropic of Cancer/Capricorn; **i ~ci** the tropics.
'troppo, a *det, pronome* (*quantità*) too much; (*numero*) too many ♦ *av* (*con vb*) too much; (*con ag, av*) too; **di ~**: **qualche tazza di ~** a few cups too many, a few extra cups; **3000 lire di ~** 3000 lire too much; **essere di ~** to be in the way; ~ **buono da parte tua!** (*anche ironico*) you're too kind!
'trota *sf* trout.
trot'tare *vi* to trot.
trotterel'lare *vi* to trot along; (*bambino*) to toddle.
'trotto *sm* trot.
'trottola *sf* spinning top.
tro'vare *vt* to find; (*giudicare*): **trovo che** I find *o* think that; ~**rsi** *vr* (*reciproco: incontrarsi*) to meet; (*essere, stare*) to be; (*arrivare, capitare*) to find o.s.; **andare a ~ qn** to go and see sb; ~ **qn colpevole** to find sb guilty; **trovo giusto/sbagliato che** ... I think/don't think it's right that ...; ~**rsi bene/male** (*in un luogo, con qn*) to get on well/badly; ~**rsi d'accordo con qn** to be in agreement with sb.
tro'vata *sf* good idea; ~ **pubblicitaria** advertising gimmick.
trova'tello, a *sm/f* foundling.
truc'care *vt* (*falsare*) to fake; (*attore etc*) to make up; (*travestire*) to disguise; (*SPORT*) to fix; (*AUT*) to soup up; ~**rsi** *vr* to make up (one's face).
trucca'tore, 'trice *sm/f* (*CINEMA, TEATRO*) make-up artist.
'trucco, chi *sm* trick; (*cosmesi*) make-up; **i ~chi del mestiere** the tricks of the trade.
'truce ['trutʃe] *ag* fierce.
truci'dare [trutʃi'dare] *vt* to slaughter.
'truciolo ['trutʃolo] *sm* shaving.
'truffa *sf* fraud, swindle.

truf'fare *vt* to swindle, cheat.

truffa'tore, 'trice *sm/f* swindler, cheat.

'truppa *sf* troop.

TS *sigla* = Trieste.

tu *pronome* you; ~ **stesso(a)** you yourself; **dare del ~ a qn** to address sb as "tu"; **trovarsi a ~ per ~ con qn** to find o.s. face to face with sb.

'tua *vedi* **tuo.**

'tuba *sf* (*MUS*) tuba; (*cappello*) top hat.

tu'bare *vi* to coo.

tuba'tura *sf*, **tubazi'one** [tubat'tsjone] *sf* piping *q*, pipes *pl*.

tuberco'losi *sf* tuberculosis.

tu'betto *sm* tube.

tu'bino *sm* (*cappello*) bowler (*Brit*), derby (*US*); (*abito da donna*) sheath dress.

'tubo *sm* tube; (*per conduttore*) pipe; ~ **digerente** (*ANAT*) alimentary canal, digestive tract; ~ **di scappamento** (*AUT*) exhaust pipe.

tubo'lare *ag* tubular ♦ *sm* tubeless tyre (*Brit*) *o* tire (*US*).

'tue *vedi* **tuo.**

tuf'fare *vt* to plunge; (*intingere*) to dip; ~rsi *vr* to plunge, dive.

tuffa'tore, 'trice *sm/f* (*SPORT*) diver.

'tuffo *sm* dive; (*breve bagno*) dip.

tu'gurio *sm* hovel.

tuli'pano *sm* tulip.

tume'farsi *vr* (*MED*) to swell.

'tumido, a *ag* swollen.

tu'more *sm* (*MED*) tumour (*Brit*), tumor (*US*).

tumulazi'one [tumulat'tsjone] *sf* burial.

tu'multo *sm* uproar, commotion; (*sommossa*) riot; (*fig*) turmoil.

tumultu'oso, a *ag* rowdy, unruly; (*fig*) turbulent, stormy.

tungs'teno *sm* tungsten.

'tunica, che *sf* tunic.

'Tunisi *sf* Tunis.

Tuni'sia *sf*: **la ~** Tunisia.

tuni'sino, a *ag*, *sm/f* Tunisian.

'tunnel *sm inv* tunnel.

'tuo, 'tua, tu'oi, 'tue *det*: **il ~, la tua** *etc* your ♦ *pronome*: **il ~, la tua** *etc* yours ♦ *sm*: **hai speso del ~?** did you spend your own money? ♦ *sf*: **la ~a** (*opinione*) your view; **i tuoi** (*genitori, famiglia*) your family; **una ~a amica** a friend of yours; **è dalla ~a** he is on your side; **alla ~a!** (*brindisi*) your health!; **ne hai fatta una delle ~e!** (*sciocchezze*) you've done it again!

tuo'nare *vi* to thunder; **tuona** it is thundering, there's some thunder.

tu'ono *sm* thunder.

tu'orlo *sm* yolk.

tu'racciolo [tu'rattʃolo] *sm* cap, top; (*di sughero*) cork.

tu'rare *vt* to stop, plug; (*con sughero*) to

cork; ~**rsi il naso** to hold one's nose.

'turba *sf* (*folla*) crowd, throng; (: *peg*) mob; ~**e** *sfpl* disorder(s); **soffrire di ~e psichiche** to suffer from a mental disorder.

turba'mento *sm* disturbance; (*di animo*) anxiety, agitation.

tur'bante *sm* turban.

tur'bare *vt* to disturb, trouble; ~ **la quiete pubblica** (*DIR*) to disturb the peace.

tur'bina *sf* turbine.

turbi'nare *vi* to whirl.

'turbine *sm* whirlwind; ~ **di neve** swirl of snow; ~ **di polvere/sabbia** dust/sandstorm.

turbi'noso, a *ag* (*vento, danza etc*) whirling.

turbo'lento, a *ag* turbulent; (*ragazzo*) boisterous, unruly.

turbo'lenza [turbo'lɛntsa] *sf* turbulence.

turboreat'tore *sm* turbojet engine.

tur'chese [tur'kese] *ag, sm, sf* turquoise.

Tur'chia [tur'kia] *sf*: **la ~** Turkey.

tur'chino, a [tur'kino] *ag* deep blue.

'turco, a, chi, che *ag* Turkish ♦ *sm/f* Turk/ Turkish woman ♦ *sm* (*LING*) Turkish; **parlare ~** (*fig*) to talk double Dutch.

'turgido, a ['turdʒido] *ag* swollen.

tu'rismo *sm* tourism.

tu'rista, i, e *sm/f* tourist.

tu'ristico, a, ci, che *ag* tourist *cpd*.

tur'nista, i, e *sm/f* shift worker.

'turno *sm* turn; (*di lavoro*) shift; **di ~** (*soldato, medico, custode*) on duty; **a ~** (*rispondere*) in turn; (*lavorare*) in shifts; **fare a ~ a fare qc** to take turns to do sth; **è il suo ~** it's your (*o his etc*) turn.

'turpe *ag* filthy, vile.

turpi'loquio *sm* obscene language.

'tuta *sf* overalls *pl*; (*SPORT*) tracksuit; ~ **mimetica** (*MIL*) camouflage clothing; ~ **spaziale** spacesuit; ~ **subacquea** wetsuit.

tu'tela *sf* (*DIR*: *di minore*) guardianship; (: *protezione*) protection; (*difesa*) defence (*Brit*), defense (*US*); ~ **dell'ambiente** environmental protection; ~ **del consumatore** consumer protection.

tute'lare *vt* to protect, defend ♦ *ag* (*DIR*): **giudice ~** *judge with responsibility for guardianship cases.*

tu'tore, 'trice *sm/f* (*DIR*) guardian.

tutta'via *cong* nevertheless, yet.

'tutto, a *det* all ♦ *pronome* everything, all; ~**i(e)** *pronome pl* all (of them); (*ognuno*) everyone ♦ *av* (*completamente*) completely, quite ♦ *sm* whole; (*l'intero*): **il ~** all of it, the whole lot; ~ **il latte** all the milk, the whole of the milk; ~**a la sera** all evening, the whole evening; ~**a una bottiglia** a whole bottle; ~**i i ragazzi** all the boys; ~**e le sere** every evening; ~**i e due** both *o* each of us (*o* them); ~**i e cinque** all five of us (*o* them); **a ~a velocità** at full *o* top speed; **famoso in ~ il mondo** world-famous, famous the world over; **~e le volte che** every time (that); **a tutt'oggi** so far, up till now; **questo è ~, ecco ~** that's all; **~ compreso** inclusive, all-in (*Brit*); **~ considerato** all things considered; **in ~** in all; **in ~ e per ~** (*completamente*) entirely, completely; **con ~ che** (*malgrado*) although; **del ~** competely; **... che è ~ dire** ... and that's saying a lot; **tutt'altro** on the contrary; (*affatto*) not at all; **tutt'altro che felice** anything but happy; **tutt'al più** at (the) most; (*al più tardi*) at the latest; **tutt'al più possiamo prendere un treno** if the worst comes to the worst we can catch a train; **tutt'intorno** all around.

tutto'fare *ag inv*: **domestica ~** general maid; **ragazzo ~** office boy ♦ *sm/f inv* handyman/woman.

tut'tora *av* still.

tutù *sm inv* tutu, ballet skirt.

TV [ti'vu] *sf inv* (= *televisione*) TV ♦ *sigla* = *Treviso*.

U

U, u [u] *sf o m inv* (*lettera*) U, u; **U come Udine** ≈ U for Uncle; **inversione ad U** U-turn.

ub'bia *sf* (*letterario*) irrational fear.

ubbidi'ente *ag* obedient.

ubbidi'enza [ubbi'djɛntsa] *sf* obedience.

ubbi'dire *vi* to obey; **~ a** to obey; (*sog: veicolo, macchina*) to respond to.

ubicazi'one [ubikat'tsjone] *sf* site, location.

ubiquità *sf*: **non ho il dono dell'~** I can't be everywhere at once.

ubria'care *vt*: **~ qn** to get sb drunk; (*sog: alcool*) to make sb drunk; (*fig*) to make sb's head spin *o* reel; **~rsi** *vr* to get drunk; **~rsi di** (*fig*) to become intoxicated with.

ubria'chezza [ubria'kettsa] *sf* drunkenness.

ubri'aco, a, chi, che *ag, sm/f* drunk.

ubria'cone *sm* drunkard.

uccellagi'one [uttʃella'dʒone] *sf* bird catching.

uccella'tore [uttʃella'tore] *sm* bird catcher.

uccelli'era [uttʃel'ljɛra] *sf* aviary.

uccel'lino [uttʃel'lino] *sm* baby bird, chick.

uc'cello [ut'tʃello] *sm* bird.

uc'cidere [ut'tʃidere] *vt* to kill; **~rsi** *vr* (*suicidarsi*) to kill o.s.; (*perdere la vita*) to be killed.

uccisi'one [uttʃi'zjone] *sf* killing.

uc'ciso, a [ut'tʃizo] *pp di* **uccidere**.

ucci'sore [uttʃi'zore] *sm* killer.

UD *sigla* = *Udine*.

u'dibile *ag* audible.

udi'enza [u'djɛntsa] *sf* audience; (*DIR*) hearing; **dare ~ (a)** to grant an audience (to); **~ a porte chiuse** hearing in camera.

u'dire *vt* to hear.

udi'tivo, a *ag* auditory.

u'dito *sm* (sense of) hearing.

udi'tore, 'trice *sm/f* listener; (*INS*) unregistered student (*attending lectures*).

udi'torio *sm* (*persone*) audience.

U.E. *abbr* = *uso esterno*.

UEFA *sigla f* UEFA (= *Union of European Football Associations*).

'uffa *escl* tut!

uffici'ale [uffi'tʃale] *ag* official ♦ *sm* (*AMM*) official, officer; (*MIL*) officer; **pubblico ~** public official; **~ giudiziario** clerk of the court; **~ di marina** naval officer; **~ sanitario** health inspector; **~ di stato civile** registrar.

ufficializ'zare [uffitʃalid'dzare] *vt* to make official.

uf'ficio [uf'fitʃo] *sm* (*gen*) office; (*dovere*) duty; (*mansione*) task, function, job; (*agenzia*) agency, bureau; (*REL*) service; **d'~** *ag* office *cpd*; official ♦ *av* officially; **provvedere d'~** to act officially; **convocare d'~** (*DIR*) to summons; **difensore o avvocato d'~** (*DIR*) court-appointed counsel for the defence; **~ brevetti** patent office; **~ di collocamento** employment office; **~ informazioni** information bureau; **~ oggetti smarriti** lost property office (*Brit*), lost and found (*US*); **~ postale** post office; **~ vendite/del personale** sales/personnel department.

uffici'oso, a [uffi'tʃoso] *ag* unofficial.

'UFO *sm inv* UFO.

'ufo: a ~ *av* free, for nothing.

U'ganda *sf*: **l'~** Uganda.

'uggia ['uddʒa] *sf* (*noia*) boredom; (*fastidio*) bore; **avere/prendere qn in ~** to dislike/take a dislike to sb.

uggi'oso, a [ud'dʒoso] *ag* tiresome; (*tempo*) dull.

'ugola *sf* uvula.

uguagli'anza [ugwaʎ'ʎantsa] *sf* equality.

uguagli'are [ugwaʎ'ʎare] *vt* to make equal; (*essere uguale*) to equal, be equal to; (*livellare*) to level; **~rsi** *vr*: **~rsi a o con qn** (*paragonarsi*) to compare o.s. to sb.

ugu'ale *ag* equal; (*identico*) identical, the same; (*uniforme*) level, even ♦ *av*: **costano ~** they cost the same; **sono bravi ~** they're equally good.

ugual'mente *av* equally; (*lo stesso*) all the same.

U.I. *abbr* = *uso interno*.

UIL *sigla f* (= *Unione Italiana del Lavoro*) *trade union federation*.

'ulcera ['ultʃera] *sf* ulcer.

ulcerazi'one [ultʃerat'tsjone] *sf* ulceration.

u'liva *etc* = **oliva** *etc*.

ulteri'ore *ag* further.

ultima'mente *av* lately, of late.

ulti'mare *vt* to finish, complete.

ulti'matum *sm inv* ultimatum.

ulti'missime *sfpl* latest news *sg*.

'ultimo, a *ag* (*finale*) last; (*estremo*) farthest, utmost; (*recente: notizia, moda*) latest; (*fig: sommo, fondamentale*) ultimate ♦ *sm/f* last (one); **fino all'~** to the last, until the end; **da ~, in ~** in the end; **per ~** (*entrare, arrivare*) last; **abitare all'~ piano** to live on the top floor; **in ~a pagina** (*di giornale*) on the back page; **negli ~i tempi** recently; **all'~ momento** at the last minute; ... **la vostra lettera del 7 aprile ~ scorso** ... your letter of April 7th last; **in ~a analisi** in the final *o* last analysis; **in ~ luogo** finally.

ultrasi'nistra *sf* (*POL*) extreme left.

ultrasu'ono *sm* ultrasound.

ultravio'letto, a *ag* ultraviolet.

ulu'lare *vi* to howl.

ulu'lato *sm* howling *q*; howl.

umana'mente *av* (*con umanità*) humanely; (*nei limiti delle capacità umane*) humanly.

uma'nesimo *sm* humanism.

umanità *sf* humanity.

umani'tario, a *ag* humanitarian.

umaniz'zare [umanid'dzare] *vt* to humanize.

u'mano, a *ag* human; (*comprensivo*) humane.

umbi'lico *sm* = **ombelico**.

'umbro, a *ag* of (*o* from) Umbria.

umet'tare *vt* to dampen, moisten.

umi'diccio, a, ci, ce [umi'dittʃo] *ag* (*terreno*) damp; (*mano*) moist, clammy.

umidifi'care *vt* to humidify.

umidifica'tore *sm* humidifier.

umidità *sf* dampness; moistness; humidity.

'umido, a *ag* damp; (*mano, occhi*) moist; (*clima*) humid ♦ *sm* dampness, damp; **carne in ~** stew.

'umile *ag* humble.

umili'ante *ag* humiliating.

umili'are *vt* to humiliate; **~rsi** *vr* to humble o.s.

umiliazi'one [umiljat'tsjone] *sf* humiliation.

umiltà *sf* humility, humbleness.

u'more *sm* (*disposizione d'animo*) mood; (*carattere*) temper; **di buon/cattivo ~** in a good/bad mood.

umo'rismo *sm* humour (*Brit*), humor (*US*); **avere il senso dell'~** to have a sense of humo(u)r.

umo'rista, i, e *sm/f* humorist.

umo'ristico, a, ci, che *ag* humorous, funny.

un, un', una *vedi* **uno**.

u'nanime *ag* unanimous.

unanimità *sf* unanimity; **all'~** unanimously.

'una 'tantum *ag* one-off *cpd* ♦ *sf* (*imposta*) one-off tax.

unci'nato, a [untʃi'nato] *ag* (*amo*) barbed; (*ferro*) hooked; **croce ~a** swastika.

unci'netto [untʃi'netto] *sm* crochet hook.

un'cino [un'tʃino] *sm* hook.

undi'cenne [undi'tʃɛnne] *ag*, *sm/f* eleven-year-old.

undi'cesimo, a [undi'tʃɛzimo] eleventh.

'undici ['unditʃi] *num* eleven.

'ungere ['undʒere] *vt* to grease, oil; (*REL*) to anoint; (*fig*) to flatter, butter up; **~rsi** *vr* (*sporcarsi*) to get covered in grease; **~rsi con la crema** to put on cream.

unghe'rese [unge'rese] *ag*, *sm/f*, *sm* Hungarian.

Unghe'ria [unge'ria] *sf*: **l'~** Hungary.

'unghia ['ungja] *sf* (*ANAT*) nail; (*di animale*) claw; (*di rapace*) talon; (*di cavallo*) hoof; **pagare sull'~** (*fig*) to pay on the nail.

unghi'ata [un'gjata] *sf* (*graffio*) scratch.

ungu'ento *sm* ointment.

unica'mente *av* only.

'unico, a, ci, che *ag* (*solo*) only; (*ineguagliabile*) unique; (*singolo: binario*) single; **è figlio ~** he's an only child; **atto ~** (*TEATRO*) one-act play; **agente ~** (*COMM*) sole agent.

uni'corno *sm* unicorn.

unifi'care *vt* to unite, unify; (*sistemi*) to standardize.

unificazi'one [unifikat'tsjone] *sf* unification; standardization.

unifor'mare *vt* (*terreno, superficie*) to level; **~rsi** *vr*: **~rsi a** to conform to; **~ qc a** to adjust *o* relate sth to.

uni'forme *ag* uniform; (*superficie*) even ♦ *sf* (*divisa*) uniform; **alta ~** dress uniform.

uniformità *sf* uniformity; evenness.

unilate'rale *ag* one-sided; (*DIR, POL*) unilateral.

uni'one *sf* union; (*fig: concordia*) unity, harmony; **l'U~ Sovietica** the Soviet Union.

u'nire *vt* to unite; (*congiungere*) to join, connect; (*: ingredienti, colori*) to combine; (*in matrimonio*) to unite, join together; **~rsi** *vr* to unite; (*in matrimonio*) to be joined together; **~ qc a** to unite sth with; to join *o* connect sth with; to combine sth with; **~rsi a** (*gruppo, società*) to join.

u'nisono *sm*: **all'~** in unison.

unità *sf inv* (*unione, concordia*) unity; (*MAT, MIL, COMM, di misura*) unit; **~ centrale (di elaborazione)** (*INFORM*) central processing unit; **~ disco** (*INFORM*) disk drive; **~ monetaria** monetary unit.

uni'tario, a *ag* unitary; **prezzo ~** price per unit.

u'nito, a *ag* (*paese*) united; (*amici, famiglia*) close; **in tinta ~a** plain, self-coloured (*Brit*), self-colored (*US*).

univer'sale *ag* universal; general.
universalità *sf* universality.
universal'mente *av* universally.
università *sf inv* university.
universi'tario, a *ag* university *cpd* ♦ *sm/f* (*studente*) university student; (*insegnante*) academic, university lecturer.
uni'verso *sm* universe.
u'nivoco, a, ci, che *ag* unambiguous.
'uno, a *det, num* (*dav sm* **un** + *C, V,* **uno** + *s impura, gn, pn, ps, x, z; dav sf* **un'** + *V,* **una** + *C*) *det* a, an + *vocale* ♦ *num* one ♦ *pronome* (*un tale*) someone, somebody; (*con valore impersonale*) one, you ♦ *sf:* **è l'~a** it's one o'clock; **facciamo metà per ~** let's go halves; **a ~ a ~** one by one.
'unsi *etc vb vedi* **ungere**.
'unto, a *pp di* **ungere** ♦ *ag* greasy, oily ♦ *sm* grease.
untu'oso, a *ag* greasy, oily.
unzi'one [un'tsjone] *sf:* **l'Estrema U~** (*REL*) Extreme Unction.
u'omo, *pl* **u'omini** *sm* man; **da ~** (*abito, scarpe*) men's, for men; **a memoria d'~** since the world began; **a passo d'~** at walking pace; **~ d'affari** businessman; **~ d'azione** man of action; **~ di fiducia** right-hand man; **~ di mondo** man of the world; **~ di paglia** stooge; **~ rana** frogman; **l'~ della strada** the man in the street.
u'opo *sm:* **all'~** if necessary.
u'ovo, *pl(f)* **u'ova** *sm* egg; **cercare il pelo nell'~** (*fig*) to split hairs; **~ affogato** *o* **in camicia** poached egg; **~ bazzotto/sodo** soft-/hard-boiled egg; **~ alla coque** boiled egg; **~ di Pasqua** Easter egg; **~ al tegame** *o* **all'occhio di bue** fried egg; **uova strapazzate** scrambled eggs.
ura'gano *sm* hurricane.
U'rali *smpl:* **gli ~, i Monti ~** the Urals, the Ural Mountains.
u'ranio *sm* uranium.
urba'nesimo *sm* urbanization.
urba'nista, i, e *sm/f* town planner.
urba'nistica *sf* town planning.
urbanità *sf* urbanity.
ur'bano, a *ag* urban, city *cpd*, town *cpd*; (*TEL: chiamata*) local; (*fig*) urbane.
ur'gente [ur'dʒɛnte] *ag* urgent.
ur'genza [ur'dʒɛntsa] *sf* urgency; **in caso d'~** in (case of) an emergency; **d'~** *ag* emergency ♦ *av* urgently, as a matter of urgency; **non c'è ~** there's no hurry; **questo lavoro va fatto con ~** this work is urgent.
'urgere ['urdʒere] *vi* to be needed urgently.
u'rina *etc* = **orina** *etc*.
ur'lare *vi* (*persona*) to scream, yell; (*animale, vento*) to howl ♦ *vt* to scream, yell.
'urlo, *pl(m)* **'urli,** *pl(f)* **'urla** *sm* scream, yell; howl.

'urna *sf* urn; (*elettorale*) ballot box; **andare alle ~e** to go to the polls.
urrà *escl* hurrah!
U.R.S.S. *sigla f* (= *Unione delle Repubbliche Socialiste Sovietiche*): **l'~** the USSR.
ur'tare *vt* to bump into, knock against; (*fig: irritare*) to annoy ♦ *vi:* **~ contro** *o* **in** to bump into, knock against; (*fig: imbattersi*) to come up against; **~rsi** *vr* (*reciproco: scontrarsi*) to collide; (*: fig*) to clash; (*irritarsi*) to get annoyed.
'urto *sm* (*colpo*) knock, bump; (*scontro*) crash, collision; (*fig*) clash; **terapia d'~** (*MED*) shock treatment.
uruguai'ano, a *ag, sm/f* Uruguayan.
Urugu'ay *sm:* **l'~** Uruguay.
u.s. *abbr* = **ultimo scorso**.
'USA *smpl:* **gli ~** the USA.
u'sanza [u'zantsa] *sf* custom; (*moda*) fashion.
u'sare *vt* to use, employ ♦ *vi* (*essere di moda*) to be fashionable; (*servirsi*): **~ di** to use; (*: diritto*) to exercise; (*essere solito*): **~ fare** to be in the habit of doing, be accustomed to doing ♦ *vb impers:* **qui usa così** it's the custom round here; **~ la massima cura nel fare qc** to exercise great care when doing sth.
u'sato, a *ag* used; (*consumato*) worn; (*di seconda mano*) used, second-hand ♦ *sm* second-hand goods *pl*.
u'scente [uʃ'ʃɛnte] *ag* (*AMM*) outgoing.
usci'ere [uʃ'ʃɛre] *sm* usher.
'uscio ['uʃʃo] *sm* door.
u'scire [uʃ'ʃire] *vi* (*gen*) to come out; (*partire, andare a passeggio, a uno spettacolo etc*) to go out; (*essere sorteggiato: numero*) to come up; **~ da** (*gen*) to leave; (*posto*) to go (*o* come) out of, leave; (*solco, vasca etc*) to come out of; (*muro*) to stick out of; (*competenza etc*) to be outside; (*infanzia, adolescenza*) to leave behind; (*famiglia nobile etc*) to come from; **~ da** *o* **di casa** to go out; (*fig*) to leave home; **~ in automobile** to go out in the car, go for a drive; **~ di strada** (*AUT*) to go off *o* leave the road.
u'scita [uʃ'ʃita] *sf* (*passaggio, varco*) exit, way out; (*per divertimento*) outing; (*ECON: somma*) expenditure; (*fig: battuta*) witty remark; **"vietata l'~"** "no exit"; **~ di sicurezza** emergency exit.
usi'gnolo [uziɲ'ɲɔlo] *sm* nightingale.
U.S.L. [uzl] *sigla f* (= *unità sanitaria locale*) local health centre.
'uso *sm* (*utilizzazione*) use; (*esercizio*) practice (*Brit*), practise (*US*); (*abitudine*) custom; **fare ~ di qc** to use sth; **con l'~** with practice; **a ~ di** for (the use of); **d'~** (*corrente*) in use; **fuori ~** out of use; **essere in ~** to be in common *o* current use.

ustio'nare *vt* to burn; ~**rsi** *vr* to burn o.s.
usti'one *sf* burn.
usu'ale *ag* common, everyday.
usufru'ire *vi*: ~ **di** (*giovarsi di*) to take advantage of, make use of.
usu'frutto *sm* (*DIR*) usufruct.
u'sura *sf* usury; (*logoramento*) wear (and tear).
usu'raio *sm* usurer.
usur'pare *vt* to usurp.
usurpa'tore, 'trice *sm/f* usurper.
uten'sile *sm* tool, implement ♦ *ag*: **macchina** ~ machine tool; ~**i da cucina** kitchen utensils.
utensile'ria *sf* (*utensili*) tools *pl*; (*reparto*) tool room.
u'tente *sm/f* user; (*di gas etc*) consumer; (*del telefono*) subscriber; ~ **finale** end user.
'utero *sm* uterus, womb.
'utile *ag* useful ♦ *sm* (*vantaggio*) advantage, benefit; (*ECON: profitto*) profit; **rendersi** ~ to be helpful; **in tempo** ~ **per** in time for; **unire l'**~ **al dilettevole** to combine business with pleasure; **partecipare agli** ~**i** (*ECON*) to share in the profits.
utilità *sf* usefulness *q*; use; (*vantaggio*) benefit; **essere di grande** ~ to be very useful.
utili'tario, a *ag* utilitarian ♦ *sf* (*AUT*) economy car.
utiliz'zare [utilid'dzare] *vt* to use, make use of, utilize.
utilizzazi'one [utiliddzat'tsjone] *sf* utilization, use.
uti'lizzo [uti'liddzo] *sm* (*AMM*) utilization; (*BANCA: di credito*) availment.
util'mente *av* usefully, profitably.
uto'pia *sf* utopia; **è pura** ~ that's sheer utopianism.
uto'pistico, a, ci, che *ag* utopian.
UVA *abbr* = ultravioletto prossimo.
'uva *sf* grapes *pl*; ~ **passa** raisins *pl*; ~ **spina** gooseberry.
u'vetta *sf* raisins *pl*.

V

V, v [vi, vu] *sf o m inv* (*lettera*) V, v; **V come Venezia** ≈ V for Victor.
V *abbr* (= volt) V.
v. *abbr* (= vedi, verso, versetto) v.
VA *sigla* = Varese.
va, va' *vb vedi* andare.
va'cante *ag* vacant.

va'canza [va'kantsa] *sf* (*l'essere vacante*) vacancy; (*riposo, ferie*) holiday(s *pl*) (*Brit*), vacation (*US*); (*giorno di permesso*) day off, holiday; ~**e** *sfpl* (*periodo di ferie*) holidays, vacation *sg*; **essere/andare in** ~ to be/go on holiday *o* vacation; **far** ~ to have a holiday; ~**e estive** summer holiday(s) *o* vacation.
'vacca, che *sf* cow.
vacci'nare [vattʃi'nare] *vt* to vaccinate; **farsi** ~ to have a vaccination, get vaccinated.
vaccinazi'one [vattʃinat'tsjone] *sf* vaccination.
vac'cino [vat'tʃino] *sm* (*MED*) vaccine.
vacil'lante [vatʃil'lante] *ag* (*edificio, vecchio*) shaky, unsteady; (*fiamma*) flickering; (*salute, memoria*) shaky, failing.
vacil'lare [vatʃil'lare] *vi* to sway; (*fiamma*) to flicker; (*fig: memoria, coraggio*) to be failing, falter.
'vacuo, a *ag* (*fig*) empty, vacuous ♦ *sm* vacuum.
'vado *etc vb vedi* andare.
vagabon'daggio [vagabon'daddʒo] *sm* wandering, roaming; (*DIR*) vagrancy.
vagabon'dare *vi* to roam, wander.
vaga'bondo, a *sm/f* tramp, vagrant; (*fannullone*) idler, loafer.
va'gare *vi* to wander.
vagheggi'are [vaged'dʒare] *vt* to long for, dream of.
vagherò *etc* [vage'rɔ] *vb vedi* vagare.
va'ghezza [va'gettsa] *sf* vagueness.
va'gina [va'dʒina] *sf* vagina.
va'gire [va'dʒire] *vi* to whimper.
va'gito [va'dʒito] *sm* cry, wailing.
'vaglia ['vaʎʎa] *sm inv* money order; ~ **cambiario** promissory note; ~ **postale** postal order.
vagli'are [vaʎ'ʎare] *vt* to sift; (*fig*) to weigh up.
'vaglio ['vaʎʎo] *sm* sieve; **passare al** ~ (*fig*) to examine closely.
'vago, a, ghi, ghe *ag* vague.
va'gone *sm* (*FERR: per passeggeri*) carriage (*Brit*), car (*US*); (: *per merci*) truck, wagon; ~ **letto** sleeper, sleeping car; ~ **ristorante** dining *o* restaurant car.
'vai *vb vedi* andare.
vai'olo *sm* smallpox.
val. *abbr* = valuta.
va'langa, ghe *sf* avalanche.
va'lente *ag* able, talented.
va'lere *vi* (*avere forza, potenza*) to have influence; (*essere valido*) to be valid; (*avere vigore, autorità*) to hold, apply; (*essere capace: poeta, studente*) to be good, be able ♦ *vt* (*prezzo, sforzo*) to be worth; (*corrispondere*) to correspond to; (*procurare*): ~ **qc a qn** to earn sb sth; ~**rsi** *vr*: ~**rsi di** to make use of, take advantage of; **far** ~ (*autorità etc*) to assert; **far** ~ **le pro-**

prie ragioni to make o.s. heard; **farsi ~** to make o.s. appreciated *o* respected; **vale a dire** that is to say; **~ la pena** to be worth the effort *o* worth it; **l'uno vale l'altro** the one is as good as the other, they amount to the same thing; **non vale niente** it's worthless; **~rsi dei consigli di qn** to take sb's advice, act upon sb's advice.

va'levole *ag* valid.

'valgo *etc vb vedi* **valere.**

vali'care *vt* to cross.

'valico, chi *sm* (*passo*) pass.

validità *sf* validity.

'valido, a *ag* valid; (*rimedio*) effective; (*persona*) worthwhile; **essere di ~ aiuto a qn** to be a great help to sb.

valige'ria [validʒe'ria] *sf* (*assortimento*) leather goods *pl*; (*fabbrica*) leather goods factory; (*negozio*) leather goods shop.

va'ligia, gie *o* **ge** [va'lidʒa] *sf* (suit)case; **fare le ~gie** to pack (up); **~ diplomatica** diplomatic bag.

val'lata *sf* valley.

'valle *sf* valley; **a ~** (*di fiume*) downstream; **scendere a ~** to go downhill.

val'letto *sm* valet.

valligi'ano, a [valli'dʒano] *sm/f* inhabitant of a valley.

va'lore *sm* (*gen*, *COMM*) value; (*merito*) merit, worth; (*coraggio*) valour (*Brit*), valor (*US*); (*FINANZA*: *titolo*) security; **~i** *smpl* (*oggetti preziosi*) valuables; **crescere/diminuire di ~** to go up/down in value, gain/lose in value; **è di gran ~** it's worth a lot, it's very valuable; **privo di ~** worthless; **~ contabile** book value; **~ effettivo** real value; **~ nominale** *o* **facciale** nominal value; **~ di realizzo** break-up value; **~ di riscatto** surrender value; **~i bollati** (revenue) stamps.

valoriz'zare [valorid'dzare] *vt* (*terreno*) to develop; (*fig*) to make the most of.

valo'roso, a *ag* courageous.

'valso, a *pp di* **valere.**

va'luta *sf* currency, money; (*BANCA*): **~ 15 gennaio** interest to run from January 15th; **~ estera** foreign currency.

valu'tare *vt* (*casa*, *gioiello*, *fig*) to value; (*stabilire: peso, entrate, fig*) to estimate.

valu'tario, a *ag* (*FINANZA*: *norme*) currency *cpd*.

valutazi'one [valutat'tsjone] *sf* valuation; estimate.

'valva *sf* (*ZOOL*, *BOT*) valve.

'valvola *sf* (*TECN*, *ANAT*) valve; (*ELETTR*) fuse; **~ a farfalla del carburatore** (*AUT*) throttle; **~ di sicurezza** safety valve.

'valzer ['valtser] *sm inv* waltz.

vam'pata *sf* (*di fiamma*) blaze; (*di calore*) blast; (: *al viso*) flush.

vam'piro *sm* vampire.

vana'gloria *sf* boastfulness.

van'dalico, a, ci, che *ag* vandal *cpd*; **atto ~** act of vandalism.

vanda'lismo *sm* vandalism.

'vandalo *sm* vandal.

vaneggia'mento [vaneddʒa'mento] *sm* raving, delirium.

vaneggi'are [vaned'dʒare] *vi* to rave.

va'nesio, a *ag* vain, conceited.

'vanga, ghe *sf* spade.

van'gare *vt* to dig.

van'gelo [van'dʒelo] *sm* gospel.

vanifi'care *vt* to nullify.

va'niglia [va'niʎʎa] *sf* vanilla.

vanità *sf* vanity; (*di promessa*) emptiness; (*di sforzo*) futility.

vani'toso, a *ag* vain, conceited.

'vanno *vb vedi* **andare.**

'vano, a *ag* vain ♦ *sm* (*spazio*) space; (*apertura*) opening; (*stanza*) room; **il ~ della porta** the doorway; **il ~ portabagagli** (*AUT*) the boot (*Brit*), the trunk (*US*).

van'taggio [van'taddʒo] *sm* advantage; **trarre ~ da qc** to benefit from sth; **essere/portarsi in ~** (*SPORT*) to be in/take the lead.

vantaggi'oso, a [vantad'dʒoso] *ag* advantageous, favourable (*Brit*), favorable (*US*).

van'tare *vt* to praise, speak highly of; **~rsi** *vr*: **~rsi (di/di aver fatto)** to boast *o* brag (about/about having done).

vante'ria *sf* boasting.

'vanto *sm* boasting; (*merito*) virtue, merit; (*gloria*) pride.

'vanvera *sf*: **a ~** haphazardly; **parlare a ~** to talk nonsense.

va'pore *sm* vapour (*Brit*), vapor (*US*); (*anche: ~ acqueo*) steam; (*nave*) steamer; **a ~** (*turbina etc*) steam *cpd*; **al ~** (*CUC*) steamed.

vapo'retto *sm* steamer.

vapori'era *sf* (*FERR*) steam engine.

vaporiz'zare [vaporid'dzare] *vt* to vaporize.

vaporizza'tore [vaporiddza'tore] *sm* spray.

vaporizzazi'one [vaporiddzat'tsjone] *sf* vaporization.

vapo'roso, a *ag* (*tessuto*) filmy; (*capelli*) soft and full.

va'rare *vt* (*NAUT*, *fig*) to launch; (*DIR*) to pass.

var'care *vt* to cross.

'varco, chi *sm* passage; **aprirsi un ~ tra la folla** to push one's way through the crowd.

vare'china [vare'kina] *sf* bleach.

vari'abile *ag* variable; (*tempo*, *umore*) changeable, variable ♦ *sf* (*MAT*) variable.

vari'ante *sf* (*gen*) variation, change; (*LING*) variant; (*SPORT*) alternative route.

vari'are *vt*, *vi* to vary; **~ di opinione** to change one's mind.

variazi'one [varjat'tsjone] *sf* variation, change; (*MUS*) variation; **una ~ di programma** a change of plan.

va'rice [va'ritʃe] sf varicose vein.
vari'cella [vari'tʃella] sf chickenpox.
vari'coso, a ag varicose.
varie'gato, a ag variegated.
varietà sf inv variety ♦ sm inv variety show.
'vario, a ag varied; (parecchi: col sostantivo al pl) various; (mutevole: umore) changeable; ~**e** sfpl: ~**e ed eventuali** (nell'ordine del giorno) any other business.
vario'pinto, a ag multicoloured (Brit), multicolored (US).
'varo sm (NAUT, fig) launch; (di leggi) passing.
varrò etc vb vedi **valere**.
Var'savia sf Warsaw.
va'saio sm potter.
'vasca, sche sf basin; (anche: ~ **da bagno**) bathtub, bath.
va'scello [vaʃ'ʃɛllo] sm (NAUT) vessel, ship.
vas'chetta [vas'ketta] sf (per gelato) tub; (per sviluppare fotografie) dish.
vase'lina sf vaseline.
vasel'lame sm (stoviglie) crockery; (: di porcellana) china; ~ **d'oro/d'argento** gold/silver plate.
'vaso sm (recipiente) pot; (: barattolo) jar; (: decorativo) vase; (ANAT) vessel; ~ **da fiori** vase; (per piante) flowerpot.
vas'soio sm tray.
vastità sf vastness.
'vasto, a ag vast, immense; **di** ~**e proporzioni** (incendio) huge; (fenomeno, rivolta) widespread; **su** ~**a scala** on a vast o huge scale.
Vati'cano sm: **il** ~ the Vatican; **la Città del** ~ the Vatican City.
VC sigla = Vercelli.
VE sigla = Venezia ♦ abbr = Vostra Eccellenza.
ve pronome, av vedi **vi**.
vecchi'aia [vek'kjaja] sf old age.
'vecchio, a ['vɛkkjo] ag old ♦ sm/f old man/woman; **i** ~**i** the old; **è un mio** ~ **amico** he's an old friend of mine; **è un uomo** ~ **stile** o **stampo** he's an old-fashioned man; **è** ~ **del mestiere** he's an old hand at the job.
'vece ['vetʃe] sf: **in** ~ **di** in the place of, for; **fare le** ~**i di qn** to take sb's place; **firma del padre o di chi ne fa le** ~**i** signature of the father or guardian.
ve'dere vt, vi to see; ~**rsi** vr to meet, see one another; ~ **di fare qc** to see (to it) that sth is done, make sure that sth is done; **avere a che** ~ **con** to have to do with; **far** ~ **qc a qn** to show sb sth; **farsi** ~ to show o.s.; (farsi vivo) to show one's face; **farsi** ~ **da un medico** to go and see a doctor; **modo di** ~ outlook, view of things; **vedi pagina 8** (rimando) see page 8; **è da** ~ **se ...** it remains to be seen whether ...; **non vedo la ragione di farlo** I can't see any

reason to do it; **si era visto costretto a ...** he found himself forced to ...; **non (ci) si vede** (è buio etc) you can't see a thing; **ci vediamo domani!** see you tomorrow!; **non lo posso** ~ (fig) I can't stand him.
ve'detta sf (sentinella, posto) look-out; (NAUT) patrol boat.
ve'dette [və'dɛt] sf inv (attrice) star.
'vedovo, a sm/f widower/widow; **rimaner** ~ to be widowed.
vedrò etc vb vedi **vedere**.
ve'duta sf view; **di larghe** o **ampie** ~**e** broad-minded; **di** ~**e limitate** narrowminded.
vee'mente ag (discorso, azione) vehement; (assalto) vigorous; (passione) overwhelming.
vee'menza [vee'mɛntsa] sf vehemence; **con** ~ vehemently.
vege'tale [vedʒe'tale] ag, sm vegetable.
vege'tare [vedʒe'tare] vi (fig) to vegetate.
vegetari'ano, a [vedʒeta'rjano] ag, sm/f vegetarian.
vegetazi'one [vedʒetat'tsjone] sf vegetation.
'vegeto, a ['vɛdʒeto] ag (pianta) thriving; (persona) strong, vigorous.
veg'gente [ved'dʒɛnte] sm/f (indovino) clairvoyant.
'veglia ['veʎʎa] sf (sorveglianza) watch; (trattenimento) evening gathering; **tra la** ~ **e il sonno** half awake; **fare la** ~ **a un malato** to watch over a sick person; ~ **funebre** wake.
vegli'are [veʎ'ʎare] vi to stay o sit up; (stare vigile) to watch; to keep watch ♦ vt (malato, morto) to watch over, sit up with.
vegli'one [veʎ'ʎone] sm ball, dance.
ve'icolo sm vehicle; ~ **spaziale** spacecraft inv.
'vela sf (NAUT: tela) sail; (sport) sailing; **tutto va a gonfie** ~**e** (fig) everything is going perfectly.
ve'lare vt to veil; ~**rsi** vr (occhi, luna) to mist over; (voce) to become husky; ~**rsi il viso** to cover one's face (with a veil).
ve'lato, a ag veiled.
vela'tura sf (NAUT) sails pl.
veleggi'are [veled'dʒare] vi to sail; (AER) to glide.
ve'leno sm poison.
vele'noso, a ag poisonous.
ve'letta sf (di cappello) veil.
veli'ero sm sailing ship.
ve'lina sf (anche: **carta** ~: per imballare) tissue paper; (: per copie) flimsy paper; (copia) carbon copy.
ve'lista, i, e sm/f yachtsman/woman.
ve'livolo sm aircraft.
velleità sf inv vain ambition, vain desire.
vellei'tario, a ag unrealistic.
'vello sm fleece.
vellu'tato, a ag (stoffa, pesca, colore)

velvety; (*voce*) mellow.

vel'luto *sm* velvet; ~ **a coste** cord.

'velo *sm* veil; (*tessuto*) voile.

ve'loce [ve'lotʃe] *ag* fast, quick ♦ *av* fast, quickly.

velo'cista, i, e [velo'tʃista] *sm/f* (*SPORT*) sprinter.

velocità [velotʃi'ta] *sf* speed; **a forte** ~ at high speed; ~ **di crociera** cruising speed.

ve'lodromo *sm* velodrome.

ven. *abbr* (*REL*) = **venerabile**; (= *venerdì*) Fri.

'vena *sf* (*gen*) vein; (*filone*) vein, seam; (*fig: ispirazione*) inspiration; (: *umore*) mood; **essere in ~ di qc** to be in the mood for sth.

ve'nale *ag* (*prezzo, valore*) market *cpd*; (*fig*) venal; mercenary.

venalità *sf* venality.

ve'nato, a *ag* (*marmo*) veined, streaked; (*legno*) grained.

vena'torio, a *ag* hunting; **la stagione** ~**a** the hunting season.

vena'tura *sf* (*di marmo*) vein, streak; (*di legno*) grain.

ven'demmia *sf* (*raccolta*) grape harvest; (*quantità d'uva*) grape crop, grapes *pl*; (*vino ottenuto*) vintage.

vendemmi'are *vt* to harvest ♦ *vi* to harvest the grapes.

'vendere *vt* to sell; ~ **all'ingrosso/al dettaglio** *o* **minuto** to sell wholesale/retail; ~ **all'asta** to auction, sell by auction; **"vendesi"** "for sale".

ven'detta *sf* revenge.

vendi'care *vt* to avenge; ~**rsi** *vr*: ~**rsi (di)** to avenge o.s. (for); (*per rancore*) to take one's revenge (for); ~**rsi su qn** to revenge o.s. on sb.

vendica'tivo, a *ag* vindictive.

'vendita *sf* sale; **la** ~ (*attività*) selling; (*smercio*) sales *pl*; **in** ~ on sale; **mettere in** ~ to put on sale; **in** ~ **presso** on sale at; **contratto di** ~ sales agreement; **reparto** ~**e** sales department; ~ **all'asta** sale by auction; ~ **al dettaglio** *o* **minuto** retail; ~ **all'ingrosso** wholesale.

vendi'tore, 'trice *sm/f* seller, vendor; (*gestore di negozio*) trader, dealer.

ve'nefico, a, ci, che *ag* poisonous.

vene'rabile *ag*, **vene'rando, a** *ag* venerable.

vene'rare *vt* to venerate.

venerazi'one [venerat'tsjone] *sf* veneration.

venerdì *sm inv* Friday; **V~ Santo** Good Friday; *per fraseologia vedi* **martedì**.

'Venere *sm*, *sf* Venus.

ve'nereo, a *ag* venereal.

'veneto, a *ag* of (*o* from) the Veneto.

'veneto-giuli'ano, a ['vɛnetodʒu'ljano] *ag* of (*o* from) Venezia-Giulia.

Ve'nezia [ve'nɛttsja] *sf* Venice.

venezi'ano, a [venet'tsjano] *ag*, *sm/f*

Venetian.

Venezu'ela [venettsu'ɛla] *sm*: **il** ~ Venezuela.

venezue'lano, a [venettsue'lano] *ag*, *sm/f* Venezuelan.

'vengo *etc vb vedi* **venire**.

veni'ale *ag* venial.

ve'nire *vi* to come; (*riuscire: dolce, fotografia*) to turn out; (*come ausiliare: essere*): **viene ammirato da tutti** he is admired by everyone; ~ **da** to come from; **quanto viene?** how much does it cost?; **far** ~ (*mandare a chiamare*) to send for; (*medico*) to call, send for; ~ **a capo di qc** to unravel sth, sort sth out; ~ **al dunque** *o* **nocciolo** *o* **fatto** to come to the point; ~ **fuori** to come out; ~ **giù** to come down; ~ **meno** (*svenire*) to faint; ~ **meno a qc** not to fulfil sth; ~ **su** to come up; ~ **via** to come away; ~ **a sapere qc** to learn sth; ~ **a trovare qn** to come and see sb; **negli anni a** ~ in the years to come, in future; **è venuto il momento di ...** the time has come to ....

'venni *etc vb vedi* **venire**.

ven'taglio [ven'taʎʎo] *sm* fan.

ven'tata *sf* gust (of wind).

venten'nale *ag* (*che dura 20 anni*) twenty-year *cpd*; (*che ricorre ogni 20 anni*) which takes place every twenty years.

ven'tenne *ag*, *sm/f* twenty-year-old.

ven'tennio *sm* period of twenty years; **il** ~ **fascista** the Fascist period.

ven'tesimo, a *num* twentieth.

'venti *num* twenty.

venti'lare *vt* (*stanza*) to air, ventilate; (*fig: idea, proposta*) to air.

venti'lato, a *ag* (*camera, zona*) airy; **poco** ~ airless.

ventila'tore *sm* fan; (*su parete, finestra*) ventilator, fan.

ventilazi'one [ventilat'tsjone] *sf* ventilation.

ven'tina *sf*: **una** ~ **(di)** around twenty, twenty or so.

ventiquat'tr'ore *sfpl* (*periodo*) twenty-four hours ♦ *sf inv* (*SPORT*) twenty-four-hour race; (*valigetta*) overnight case.

venti'sette *num* twenty-seven; **il** ~ (*giorno di paga*) (monthly) pay day.

ventitré *num* twenty-three ♦ *sfpl*: **portava il cappello sulle** ~ he wore his hat at a jaunty angle.

'vento *sm* wind; **c'è** ~ it's windy; **un colpo di** ~ a gust of wind; **contro** ~ against the wind; ~ **contrario** (*NAUT*) headwind.

'ventola *sf* (*AUT*, *TECN*) fan.

ven'tosa *sf* (*ZOOL*) sucker; (*di gomma*) suction pad.

ven'toso, a *ag* windy.

ven'totto *num* twenty-eight.

'ventre *sm* stomach.

ven'triloquo *sm* ventriloquist.

ven'tuno *num* twenty-one.

ven'tura *sf*: **andare alla ~** to trust to luck; **soldato di ~** mercenary.

ven'turo, a *ag* next, coming.

ve'nuto, a *pp di* venire ♦ *sm/f*: **il(la) primo(a) ~(a)** the first person who comes along ♦ *sf* coming, arrival.

ver. *abbr* = **versamento.**

'vera *sf* wedding ring.

ve'race [ve'ratʃe] *ag* (*testimone*) truthful; (*testimonianza*) accurate; (*cibi*) real, genuine.

vera'mente *av* really.

ve'randa *sf* veranda(h).

ver'bale *ag* verbal ♦ *sm* (*di riunione*) minutes *pl*; **accordo ~** verbal agreement; **mettere a ~** to place in the minutes *o* on record.

'verbo *sm* (*LING*) verb; (*parola*) word; (*REL*): **il V~** the Word.

ver'boso, a *ag* verbose, wordy.

ver'dastro, a *ag* greenish.

'verde *ag, sm* green; **essere al ~** (*fig*) to be broke; **~ bottiglia/oliva** *ag inv* bottle/olive green; **i V~i** (*POL*) the Greens.

verdeggi'ante [verded'dʒante] *ag* green, verdant.

verde'rame *sm* verdigris.

ver'detto *sm* verdict.

ver'dura *sf* vegetables *pl*.

vere'condia *sf* modesty.

vere'condo, a *ag* modest.

'verga, ghe *sf* rod.

ver'gato a *ag* (*foglio*) ruled.

vergi'nale [verdʒi'nale] *ag* virginal.

'vergine ['verdʒine] *sf* virgin; (*dello zodiaco*): **V~** Virgo ♦ *ag* virgin; (*ragazza*): **essere ~** to be a virgin; **essere della V~** (*dello zodiaco*) to be Virgo; **pura lana ~** pure new wool; **olio ~ d'oliva** unrefined olive oil.

verginità [verdʒini'ta] *sf* virginity.

ver'gogna [ver'goɲɲa] *sf* shame; (*timidezza*) shyness, embarrassment.

vergo'gnarsi [vergoɲ'ɲarsi] *vr*: **~ (di)** to be *o* feel ashamed (of); to be shy (about), be embarrassed (about).

vergo'gnoso, a [vergoɲ'ɲoso] *ag* ashamed; (*timido*) shy, embarrassed; (*causa di vergogna: azione*) shameful.

veridicità [veriditʃi'ta] *sf* truthfulness.

ve'ridico, a, ci, che *ag* truthful.

ve'rifica, che *sf* checking *q*; check; **fare una ~ di** (*freni, testimonianza, firma*) to check; **~ contabile** (*FINANZA*) audit.

verifi'care *vt* (*controllare*) to check; (*confermare*) to confirm, bear out; (*FINANZA*) to audit.

verità *sf inv* truth; **a dire la ~, per la ~** truth to tell, actually.

veriti'ero, a *ag* (*che dice la verità*) truthful; (*conforme a verità*) true.

'verme *sm* worm.

vermi'celli [vermi'tʃelli] *smpl* vermicelli *sg*.

ver'miglio [ver'miʎʎo] *sm* vermilion, scarlet.

'vermut *sm inv* vermouth.

ver'nacolo *sm* vernacular.

ver'nice [ver'nitʃe] *sf* (*colorazione*) paint; (*trasparente*) varnish; (*pelle*) patent leather; **"~ fresca"** "wet paint".

vernici'are [verni'tʃare] *vt* to paint; to varnish.

vernicia'tura [vernitʃa'tura] *sf* painting; varnishing.

'vero, a *ag* (*veridico: fatti, testimonianza*) true; (*autentico*) real ♦ *sm* (*verità*) truth; (*realtà*) (real) life; **un ~ e proprio delinquente** a real criminal, an out and out criminal; **tant'è ~ che ...** so much so that ...; **a onor del ~, a dire il ~** to tell the truth.

vero'nese *ag* of (*o* from) Verona.

vero'simile *ag* likely, probable.

verrò *etc vb vedi* venire.

ver'ruca, che *sf* wart.

versa'mento *sm* (*pagamento*) payment; (*deposito di denaro*) deposit.

ver'sante *sm* slopes *pl*, side.

ver'sare *vt* (*fare uscire: vino, farina*) to pour (out); (*spargere: lacrime, sangue*) to shed; (*rovesciare*) to spill; (*ECON*) to pay; (: *depositare*) to deposit, pay in ♦ *vi*: **~ in gravi difficoltà** to find o.s. with serious problems; **~rsi** *vr* (*rovesciarsi*) to spill; (*fiume, folla*): **~rsi (in)** to pour (into).

versa'tile *ag* versatile.

versatilità *sf* versatility.

ver'sato, a *ag*: **~ in** to be (well-)versed in.

ver'setto *sm* (*REL*) verse.

versi'one *sf* version; (*traduzione*) translation.

'verso *sm* (*di poesia*) verse, line; (*di animale, uccello, venditore ambulante*) cry; (*direzione*) direction; (*modo*) way; (*di foglio di carta*) verso; (*di moneta*) reverse; **~i** *smpl* (*poesia*) verse *sg*; **per un ~ o per l'altro** one way or another; **prendere qn/qc per il ~ giusto** to approach sb/sth the right way; **rifare il ~ a qn** (*imitare*) to mimic sb; **non c'è ~ di persuaderlo** there's no way of persuading him, he can't be persuaded ♦ *prep* (*in direzione di*) toward(s); (*nei pressi di*) near, around (about); (*nei confronti di*) for; **~ di me** towards me; **~ l'alto** upwards; **~ il basso** downwards; **~ sera** towards evening.

'vertebra *sf* vertebra.

verte'brale *ag* vertebral; **colonna ~** spinal column, spine.

verte'brato, a *ag, sm* vertebrate.

ver'tenza [ver'tentsa] *sf* (*lite*) lawsuit, case; (*sindacale*) dispute.

'vertere *vi*: **~ su** to deal with, be about.

verti'cale *ag, sf* vertical.

'**vertice** ['vertitʃe] *sm* summit, top; (*MAT*) vertex; **conferenza al ~** (*POL*) summit conference.

ver'**tigine** [ver'tidʒine] *sf* dizziness *q*; dizzy spell; (*MED*) vertigo; **avere le ~i** to feel dizzy.

vertigi'**noso, a** [vertidʒi'noso] *ag* (*altezza*) dizzy; (*fig*) breathtakingly high (*o* deep *etc*).

'**verza** ['verdza] *sf* Savoy cabbage.

ve'**scica, che** [veʃ'ʃika] *sf* (*ANAT*) bladder; (*MED*) blister.

vesco'**vile** *ag* episcopal.

'**vescovo** *sm* bishop.

'**vespa** *sf* wasp; (®: *veicolo*) (motor) scooter.

ves'**paio** *sm* wasps' nest; **suscitare un ~** (*fig*) to stir up a hornets' nest.

vespasi'**ano** *sm* urinal.

'**vespro** *sm* (*REL*) vespers *pl*.

ves'**sare** *vt* to oppress.

vessazi'**one** [vessat'tsjone] *sf* oppression.

ves'**sillo** *sm* standard; (*bandiera*) flag.

ves'**taglia** [ves'taʎʎa] *sf* dressing gown, robe (*US*).

'**veste** *sf* garment; (*rivestimento*) covering; (*qualità, facoltà*) capacity; **~i** *sfpl* clothes, clothing *sg*; **in ~ ufficiale** (*fig*) in an official capacity; **in ~ di** in the guise of, as; **~ da camera** dressing gown, robe (*US*); **~ editoriale** layout.

vesti'**ario** *sm* wardrobe, clothes *pl*; **capo di ~** article of clothing, garment.

ves'**tibolo** *sm* (*entrance*) hall.

ves'**tigia** [ves'tidʒa] *sfpl* (*tracce*) vestiges, traces; (*rovine*) ruins, remains.

ves'**tire** *vt* (*bambino, malato*) to dress; (*avere indosso*) to have on, wear; **~rsi** *vr* to dress, get dressed; **~rsi da** (*negozio, sarto*) to buy *o* get one's clothes at.

ves'**tito, a** *ag* dressed ♦ *sm* garment; (*da donna*) dress; (*da uomo*) suit; **~i** *smpl* (*indumenti*) clothes; **~ di bianco** dressed in white.

Ve'**suvio** *sm*: **il ~** Vesuvius.

vete'**rano, a** *ag, sm/f* veteran.

veteri'**nario, a** *ag* veterinary ♦ *sm* veterinary surgeon (*Brit*), veterinarian (*US*), vet ♦ *sf* veterinary medicine.

'**veto** *sm inv* veto; **porre il ~ a qc** to veto sth.

ve'**traio** *sm* glassmaker; (*per finestre*) glazier.

ve'**trato, a** *ag* (*porta, finestra*) glazed; (*che contiene vetro*) glass ♦ *sf* glass door (*o* window); (*di chiesa*) stained glass window; **carta ~a** sandpaper.

vetre'**ria** *sf* (*stabilimento*) glassworks *sg*; (*oggetti di vetro*) glassware.

ve'**trina** *sf* (*di negozio*) (shop) window; (*armadio*) display cabinet.

vetri'**nista, i, e** *sm/f* window dresser.

ve'**trino** *sm* slide.

vetri'**olo** *sm* vitriol.

'**vetro** *sm* glass; (*per finestra, porta*) pane (of glass); **~ blindato** bulletproof glass; **~ infrangibile** shatterproof glass; **~ di sicurezza** safety glass; **i ~i di Murano** Murano glassware *sg*.

ve'**troso, a** *ag* vitreous.

'**vetta** *sf* peak, summit, top.

vet'**tore** *sm* (*MAT, FISICA*) vector; (*chi trasporta*) carrier.

vetto'**vaglie** [vetto'vaʎʎe] *sfpl* supplies.

vet'**tura** *sf* (*carrozza*) carriage; (*FERR*) carriage (*Brit*), car (*US*); (*auto*) car (*Brit*), automobile (*US*); **~ di piazza** hackney carriage.

vettu'**rino** *sm* coach driver, coachman.

vezzeggi'**are** [vettsed'dʒare] *vt* to fondle, caress.

vezzeggia'**tivo** [vettseddʒa'tivo] *sm* (*LING*) term of endearment.

'**vezzo** ['vettso] *sm* habit; **~i** *smpl* (*smancerie*) affected ways; (*leggiadria*) charms.

vez'**zoso, a** [vet'tsoso] *ag* (*grazioso*) charming, pretty; (*lezioso*) affected.

V.F. *abbr* = **vigili del fuoco**.

V.G. *abbr* = *Vostra Grazia*.

VI *sigla* = *Vicenza*.

vi (*dav lo, la, li, le, ne diventa* **ve**) *pronome* (*oggetto*) you; (*complemento di termine*) (to) you; (*riflessivo*) yourselves; (*reciproco*) each other ♦ *av* (*lì*) there; (*qui*) here; (*per questo/quel luogo*) through here/there; **~ è/sono** there is/are.

'**via** *sf* (*gen*) way; (*strada*) street; (*sentiero, pista*) path, track; (*AMM: procedimento*) channels *pl* ♦ *prep* (*passando per*) via, by way of ♦ *av* away ♦ *escl* go away!; (*suvvia*) come on!; (*SPORT*) go! ♦ *sm* (*SPORT*) starting signal; **per ~ di** (*a causa di*) because of, on account of; **in o per ~** on the way; **in ~ di guarigione** (*fig*) on the road to recovery; **per ~ aerea** by air; (*lettere*) by airmail; **~ satellite** by satellite; **andare/essere ~** to go/be away; **~ ~** (*pian piano*) gradually; **~ ~ che** (*a mano a mano*) as; **e ~ dicendo, e ~ di questo passo** and so on (and so forth); **dare il ~** (*SPORT*) to give the starting signal; **dare il ~ a un progetto** to give the green light to a project; **hanno dato il ~ ai lavori** they've begun *o* started work; **in ~ amichevole** in a friendly manner; **comporre una disputa in ~ amichevole** (*DIR*) to settle a dispute out of court; **in ~ eccezionale** as an exception; **in ~ privata o confidenziale** (*dire etc*) in confidence; **in ~ provvisoria** provisionally; **V~ lattea** (*ASTR*) Milky Way; **~ di mezzo** middle course; **non c'è ~ di scampo o d'uscita** there's no way out; **~e di comunicazione** communication routes.

viabilità sf (di strada) practicability; (rete stradale) roads pl, road network.
via'dotto sm viaduct.
viaggi'are [viad'dʒare] vi to travel; **le merci viaggiano via mare** the goods go o are sent by sea.
viaggia'tore, 'trice [viaddʒa'tore] ag travelling (Brit), traveling (US) ♦ sm traveller (Brit), traveler (US); (passeggero) passenger.
vi'aggio [vi'addʒo] sm travel(ling); (tragitto) journey, trip; **buon ~!** have a good trip!; **~ d'affari** business trip; **~ di nozze** honeymoon; **~ organizzato** package tour o holiday.
vi'ale sm avenue.
vian'dante sm/f vagrant.
vi'atico, ci sm (REL) viaticum; (fig) encouragement.
via'vai sm coming and going, bustle.
vi'brare vi to vibrate; (agitarsi): **~ (di)** to quiver (with).
vibrazi'one [vibrat'tsjone] sf vibration.
vi'cario sm (apostolico etc) vicar.
'vice ['vitʃe] sm/f deputy ♦ prefisso vice.
vice'console [vitʃe'kɔnsole] sm vice-consul.
vicediret'tore, 'trice [vitʃediret'tore] sm/f assistant manager/manageress; (di giornale etc) deputy editor.
vi'cenda [vi'tʃɛnda] sf event; **~e** sfpl (sorte) fortunes; **a ~** in turn; **con alterne ~e** with mixed fortunes.
vicen'devole [vitʃen'devole] ag mutual, reciprocal.
vicen'tino, a [vitʃen'tino] ag of (o from) Vicenza.
vicepresi'dente [vitʃepresi'dɛnte] sm vice-president, vice-chairman.
vice'versa [vitʃe'vɛrsa] av vice versa; **da Roma a Pisa e ~** from Rome to Pisa and back.
vi'chingo, a, ghi, ghe [vi'kingo] ag, sm/f Viking.
vici'nanza [vitʃi'nantsa] sf nearness, closeness; **~e** sfpl (paraggi) neighbourhood (Brit), neighborhood (US), vicinity.
vici'nato [vitʃi'nato] sm neighbourhood (Brit), neighborhood (US); (vicini) neighbo(u)rs pl.
vi'cino, a [vi'tʃino] ag (gen) near; (nello spazio) near, nearby; (accanto) next; (nel tempo) near, close at hand ♦ sm/f neighbour (Brit), neighbor (US) ♦ av near, close; **da ~** (guardare) close up; (esaminare, seguire) closely; (conoscere) well, intimately; **~ a** prep near (to), close to; (accanto a) beside; **mi sono stati molto ~i** (fig) they were very supportive towards me; **~ di casa** neighbo(u)r.
vicissi'tudini [vitʃissi'tudini] sfpl trials and tribulations.
'vicolo sm alley; **~ cieco** blind alley.

'video sm inv (TV: schermo) screen.
videocas'setta sf videocassette.
videogi'oco, chi [video'dʒɔko] sm video game.
videoregistra'tore [videoredʒistra'tore] sm (apparecchio) video (recorder).
videotermi'nale sm visual display unit.
'vidi etc vb vedi **vedere.**
vidi'mare vt (AMM) to authenticate.
vidimazi'one [vidimat'tsjone] sf (AMM) authentication.
Vi'enna sf Vienna.
vien'nese ag, sm/f Viennese inv.
vie'tare vt to forbid; (AMM) to prohibit; (libro) to ban; **~ a qn di fare** to forbid sb to do; to prohibit sb from doing.
vie'tato, a ag (vedi vb) forbidden; prohibited; banned; **"~ fumare/l'ingresso"** "no smoking/admittance"; **~ ai minori di 14/18 anni** prohibited to children under 14/18; **"senso ~"** (AUT) "no entry"; **"sosta ~a"** (AUT) "no parking".
Viet'nam sm: **il ~** Vietnam.
vietna'mita, i, e ag, sm/f, sm Vietnamese inv.
vi'eto, a ag worthless.
vi'gente [vi'dʒɛnte] ag in force.
'vigere ['vidʒere] vi (difettivo: si usa solo alla terza persona) to be in force; **in casa mia vige l'abitudine di ...** at home we are in the habit of ....
vigi'lante [vidʒi'lante] ag vigilant, watchful.
vigi'lanza [vidʒi'lantsa] sf vigilance; (sorveglianza: di operai, alunni) supervision; (: di sospetti, criminali) surveillance; **~ notturna** night-watchman service.
vigi'lare [vidʒi'lare] vt to watch over, keep an eye on; **~ che** to make sure that, see to it that.
vigi'lato, a [vidʒi'lato] sm/f (DIR) person under police surveillance.
vigila'trice [vidʒila'tritʃe] sf: **~ d'infanzia** nursery-school teacher; **~ scolastica** school health officer.
'vigile ['vidʒile] ag watchful ♦ sm (anche: ~ urbano) policeman (in towns); **~ del fuoco** fireman.
vigi'lessa [vidʒi'lessa] sf (traffic) policewoman.
vi'gilia [vi'dʒilja] sf (giorno antecedente) eve; **la ~ di Natale** Christmas Eve.
vigliacche'ria [viʎʎakke'ria] sf cowardice.
vigli'acco, a, chi, che [viʎ'ʎakko] ag cowardly ♦ sm/f coward.
'vigna ['viɲɲa] sf, **vi'gneto** [viɲ'ɲeto] sm vineyard.
vi'gnetta [viɲ'ɲetta] sf cartoon.
vi'gogna [vi'ɡoɲɲa] sf vicuña.
vi'gore sm vigour (Brit), vigor (US); (DIR): **essere/entrare in ~** to be in/come into force; **non è più in ~** it is no longer in force, it no longer applies.

vigo'roso, a *ag* vigorous.

'vile *ag* (*spregevole*) low, mean, base; (*codardo*) cowardly.

vili'pendere *vt* to despise, scorn.

vili'pendio *sm* contempt, scorn.

vili'peso, a *pp di* vilipendere.

'villa *sf* villa.

vil'laggio [vil'laddʒo] *sm* village; ~ **turistico** holiday village.

villa'nia *sf* rudeness, lack of manners; **fare** (*o* **dire**) **una** ~ **a qn** to be rude to sb.

vil'lano, a *ag* rude, ill-mannered ♦ *sm/f* boor.

villeggi'ante [villed'dʒante] *sm/f* holiday-maker (*Brit*), vacationer (*US*).

villeggi'are [villed'dʒare] *vi* to holiday, spend one's holidays (*Brit*), vacation (*US*).

villeggia'tura [villeddʒa'tura] *sf* holiday(s *pl*) (*Brit*), vacation (*US*); **luogo di** ~ (holiday) resort.

vil'letta *sf,* **vil'lino** *sm* small house (with a garden), cottage.

vil'loso, a *ag* hairy.

viltà *sf* cowardice *q*; (*gesto*) cowardly act.

'vimine *sm* wicker; **mobili di** ~**i** wicker furniture *sg*.

vi'naio *sm* wine merchant.

'vincere ['vintʃere] *vt* (*in guerra, al gioco, a una gara*) to defeat, beat; (*premio, guerra, partita*) to win; (*fig*) to overcome, conquer ♦ *vi* to win; ~ **qn in** (*abilità, bellezza*) to surpass sb in.

'vincita ['vintʃita] *sf* win; (*denaro vinto*) winnings *pl.*

vinci'tore, 'trice [vintʃi'tore] *sm/f* winner; (*MIL*) victor.

vinco'lante *ag* binding.

vinco'lare *vt* to bind; (*COMM: denaro*) to tie up.

vinco'lato, a *ag:* **deposito** ~ (*COMM*) fixed deposit.

'vincolo *sm* (*fig*) bond, tie; (*DIR*) obligation.

vi'nicolo, a *ag* wine *cpd*; **regione** ~**a** wine-producing area.

vinificazi'one [vinifikat'tsjone] *sf* wine-making.

'vino *sm* wine; ~ **bianco/rosso** white/red wine.

'vinsi *etc vb vedi* vincere.

'vinto, a *pp di* vincere ♦ *ag:* **darla** ~**a a qn** to let sb have his (*o* her) way; **darsi per** ~ to give up, give in.

vi'ola *sf* (*BOT*) violet; (*MUS*) viola ♦ *ag, sm inv* (*colore*) purple.

vio'lare *vt* (*chiesa*) to desecrate, violate; (*giuramento, legge*) to violate.

violazi'one [violat'tsjone] *sf* desecration; violation; ~ **di domicilio** (*DIR*) breaking and entering.

violen'tare *vt* to use violence on; (*donna*) to rape.

vio'lento, a *ag* violent.

vio'lenza [vio'lɛntsa] *sf* violence; ~ **carnale** rape.

vio'letto, a *ag, sm* (*colore*) violet ♦ *sf* (*BOT*) violet.

violi'nista, i, e *sm/f* violinist.

vio'lino *sm* violin.

violoncel'lista, i, e [violontʃel'lista] *sm/f* cellist, cello player.

violon'cello [violon'tʃello] *sm* cello.

vi'ottolo *sm* path, track.

VIP *sm/f inv* VIP.

'vipera *sf* viper, adder.

vi'raggio [vi'raddʒo] *sm* (*NAUT, AER*) turn; (*FOT*) toning.

vi'rale *ag* viral.

vi'rare *vi* (*NAUT*) to come about; (*AER*) to turn; (*FOT*) to tone; ~ **di bordo** to change course.

vi'rata *sf* coming about; turning; change of course.

'virgola *sf* (*LING*) comma; (*MAT*) point.

virgo'lette *sfpl* inverted commas, quotation marks.

vi'rile *ag* (*proprio dell'uomo*) masculine; (*non puerile, da uomo*) manly, virile.

virilità *sf* masculinity; manliness; (*sessuale*) virility.

virtù *sf inv* virtue; **in** *o* **per** ~ **di** by virtue of, by.

virtu'ale *ag* virtual.

virtu'oso, a *ag* virtuous ♦ *sm/f* (*MUS etc*) virtuoso.

viru'lento, a *ag* virulent.

'virus *sm inv* virus.

visa'gista, i, e [viza'dʒista] *sm/f* beautician.

visce'rale [viʃʃe'rale] *ag* (*MED*) visceral; (*fig*) profound, deep-rooted.

'viscere ['viʃʃere] *sm* (*ANAT*) internal organ ♦ *sfpl* (*di animale*) entrails *pl*; (*fig*) depths *pl*, bowels *pl.*

'vischio ['viskjo] *sm* (*BOT*) mistletoe; (*pania*) birdlime.

vischi'oso, a [vis'kjoso] *ag* sticky.

viscidità [viʃʃidi'ta] *sf* sliminess.

'viscido, a ['viʃʃido] *ag* slimy.

vis'conte, 'essa *sm/f* viscount/viscountess.

viscosità *sf* viscosity.

vis'coso, a *ag* viscous.

vi'sibile *ag* visible.

visi'bilio *sm:* **andare in** ~ to go into raptures.

visibilità *sf* visibility.

visi'era *sf* (*di elmo*) visor; (*di berretto*) peak.

visio'nare *vt* (*gen*) to look at, examine; (*CINEMA*) to screen.

visio'nario, a *ag, sm/f* visionary.

visi'one *sf* vision; **prendere** ~ **di qc** to examine sth, look sth over; **prima/seconda** ~ (*CINEMA*) first/second showing.

'visita *sf* visit; (*MED*) visit, call; (*: esame*) examination; **far** ~ **a qn, andare in** ~ **da**

qn to visit sb, pay sb a visit; **in ~ ufficiale in Italia** on an official visit to Italy; **orario di ~e** (*ospedale*) visiting hours; **~ di controllo** (*MED*) checkup; **~ a domicilio** house call; **~ guidata** guided tour; **~ sanitaria** sanitary inspection.

visi'tare *vt* to visit; (*MED*) to visit, call on; (*: esaminare*) to examine.

visita'tore, 'trice *sm/f* visitor.

vi'sivo, a *ag* visual.

'viso *sm* face; **fare buon ~ a cattivo gioco** to make the best of things.

vi'sone *sm* mink.

vi'sore *sm* (*FOT*) viewer.

'vispo, a *ag* quick, lively.

'vissi *etc vb vedi* **vivere**.

vis'suto, a *pp di* **vivere** ♦ *ag* (*aria, modo di fare*) experienced.

'vista *sf* (*facoltà*) (eye)sight; (*fatto di vedere*): **la ~ di** the sight of; (*veduta*) view; **con ~ sul lago** with a view over the lake; **sparare a ~** to shoot on sight; **pagabile a ~** payable on demand; **in ~ in** sight; **avere in ~ qc** to have sth in view; **mettersi in ~** to draw attention to o.s.; (*peg*) to show off; **perdere qn di ~** to lose sight of sb; (*fig*) to lose touch with sb; **far ~ di fare** to pretend to do; **a ~ d'occhio** as far as the eye can see; (*fig*) before one's very eyes.

vis'tare *vt* to approve; (*AMM: passaporto*) to visa.

'visto, a *pp di* **vedere** ♦ *sm* visa; **~ che** *cong* seeing (that); **~ d'ingresso/di transito** entry/transit visa; **~ permanente/di soggiorno** permanent/tourist visa.

vis'toso, a *ag* gaudy, garish; (*ingente*) considerable.

visu'ale *ag* visual.

visualiz'zare [vizualid'dzare] *vt* to visualize.

visualizza'tore [vizualiddza'tore] *sm* (*INFORM*) visual display unit, VDU.

visualizzazi'one [vizualiddzat'tsjone] *sf* (*INFORM*) display.

'vita *sf* life; (*ANAT*) waist; **essere in ~** to be alive; **pieno di ~** full of life; **a ~** for life; **membro a ~** life member.

vi'tale *ag* vital.

vitalità *sf* vitality.

vita'lizio, a [vita'littsjo] *ag* life *cpd* ♦ *sm* life annuity.

vita'mina *sf* vitamin.

'vite *sf* (*BOT*) vine; (*TECN*) screw; **giro di ~** (*anche fig*) turn of the screw.

vi'tello *sm* (*ZOOL*) calf; (*carne*) veal; (*pelle*) calfskin.

vi'ticcio [vi'tittʃo] *sm* (*BOT*) tendril.

viticol'tore *sm* wine grower.

viticol'tura *sf* wine growing.

'vitreo, a *ag* vitreous; (*occhio, sguardo*) glassy.

'vittima *sf* victim.

vitti'mismo *sm* self-pity.

'vitto *sm* food; (*in un albergo etc*) board; **~ e alloggio** board and lodging.

vit'toria *sf* victory.

vittori'ano, a *ag* Victorian.

vittori'oso, a *ag* victorious.

vitupe'rare *vt* to rail at *o* against.

vi'uzza [vi'uttsa] *sf* (*in città*) alley.

'viva *escl*: **~ il re!** long live the king!

vivacchi'are [vivak'kjare] *vi* to scrape a living.

vi'vace [vi'vatʃe] *ag* (*vivo, animato*) lively; (*: mente*) lively, sharp; (*colore*) bright.

vivacità [vivatʃi'ta] *sf* liveliness; brightness.

vivaciz'zare [vivatʃid'dzare] *vt* to liven up.

vi'vaio *sm* (*di pesci*) hatchery; (*AGR*) nursery.

viva'mente *av* (*commuoversi*) deeply, profoundly; (*ringraziare etc*) sincerely, warmly.

vi'vanda *sf* food; (*piatto*) dish.

vi'vente *ag* living, alive; **i ~i** the living.

'vivere *vi* to live ♦ *vt* to live; (*passare: brutto momento*) to live through, go through; (*sentire: gioie, pene di qn*) to share ♦ *sm* life; (*anche: modo di ~*) way of life; **~i** *smpl* food *sg*, provisions; **~ di** to live on.

vi'veur [vi'vœr] *sm inv* pleasure-seeker.

'vivido, a *ag* (*colore*) vivid, bright.

vivifi'care *vt* to enliven, give life to; (*piante etc*) to revive.

vivisezi'one [viviset'tsjone] *sf* vivisection.

'vivo, a *ag* (*vivente*) alive, living; (*fig*) lively; (*: colore*) bright, brilliant ♦ *sm*: **entrare nel ~ di una questione** to get to the heart of a matter; **i ~i** the living; **esperimenti su animali ~i** experiments on live *o* living animals; **~ e vegeto** hale and hearty; **farsi ~** (*fig*) to show one's face; to keep in touch; **con ~ rammarico** with deep regret; **congratulazioni vivissime** heartiest congratulations; **con i più ~i ringraziamenti** with deepest *o* warmest thanks; **ritrarre dal ~** to paint from life; **pungere qn nel ~** (*fig*) to cut sb to the quick.

vivrò *etc vb vedi* **vivere**.

vizi'are [vit'tsjare] *vt* (*bambino*) to spoil; (*corrompere moralmente*) to corrupt; (*DIR*) to invalidate.

vizi'ato, a [vit'tsjato] *ag* spoilt; (*aria, acqua*) polluted; (*DIR*) invalid, invalidated.

'vizio [vittsjo] *sm* (*morale*) vice; (*cattiva abitudine*) bad habit; (*imperfezione*) flaw, defect; (*errore*) fault, mistake; **~ di forma** legal flaw *o* irregularity; **~ procedurale** procedural error.

vizi'oso, a [vit'tsjoso] *ag* depraved; (*inesatto*) incorrect, wrong; **circolo ~** vicious circle.

V.le *abbr* = **viale**.

vocabo'lario *sm* (*dizionario*) dictionary;

(*lessico*) vocabulary.
vo'cabolo *sm* word.
vo'cale *ag* vocal ♦ *sf* vowel.
vocazi'one [vokat'tsjone] *sf* vocation; (*fig*) natural bent.
'voce ['votʃe] *sf* voice; (*diceria*) rumour (*Brit*), rumor (*US*); (*di un elenco, in bilancio*) item; (*di dizionario*) entry; **parlare a alta/bassa** ~ to speak in a loud/low *o* soft voice; **fare la** ~ **grossa** to raise one's voice; **dar** ~ **a qc** to voice sth, give voice to sth; **a gran** ~ in a loud voice, loudly; **te lo dico a** ~ I'll tell you when I see you; **a una** ~ unanimously; **aver** ~ **in capitolo** (*fig*) to have a say in the matter; ~**i di corridoio** rumours.
voci'are [vo'tʃare] *vi* to shout, yell.
vocife'rante [votʃife'rante] *ag* noisy.
vo'cio [vo'tʃio] *sm* shouting.
'vodka *sf inv* vodka.
'voga *sf* (*NAUT*) rowing; (*usanza*): **essere in** ~ to be in fashion *o* in vogue.
vo'gare *vi* to row.
voga'tore, 'trice *sm/f* oarsman/woman ♦ *sm* rowing machine.
vogherò *etc* [voge'rɔ] *vb vedi* **vogare**.
'voglia ['vɔʎʎa] *sf* desire, wish; (*macchia*) birthmark; **aver** ~ **di qc/di fare** to feel like sth/like doing; (*più forte*) to want sth/to do; **di buona** ~ willingly.
'voglio *etc* ['vɔʎʎo] *vb vedi* **volere**.
vogli'oso, a [voʎ'ʎoso] *ag* (*sguardo etc*) longing; (*più forte*) full of desire.
'voi *pronome* you; ~ **stessi(e)** you yourselves.
voi'altri *pronome* you.
vol. *abbr* (= *volume*) vol.
vo'lano *sm* (*SPORT*) shuttlecock; (*TECN*) flywheel.
vo'lant [vɔ'lã] *sm inv* frill.
vo'lante *ag* flying ♦ *sm* (steering) wheel ♦ *sf* (*POLIZIA: anche*: **squadra** ~) flying squad.
volanti'naggio [volanti'naddʒo] *sm* leafleting.
volan'tino *sm* leaflet.
vo'lare *vi* (*uccello, aereo, fig*) to fly; (*cappello*) to blow away *o* off, fly away *o* off; ~ **via** to fly away *o* off.
vo'lata *sf* flight; (*d'uccelli*) flock, flight; (*corsa*) rush; (*SPORT*) final sprint; **passare di** ~ **da qn** to drop in on sb briefly.
vo'latile *ag* (*CHIM*) volatile ♦ *sm* (*ZOOL*) bird.
volatiliz'zarsi [volatilid'dzarsi] *vr* (*CHIM*) to volatilize; (*fig*) to vanish, disappear.
vo'lente *ag*: **verrai** ~ **o nolente** you'll come whether you like it or not.
volente'roso, a *ag* willing, keen.
volenti'eri *av* willingly; "~" "with pleasure", "I'd be glad to".
vo'lere *sm* will; ~**i** *smpl* wishes; **contro il** ~ **di** against the wishes of; **per** ~ **del padre** in obedience to his father's will *o* wishes ♦ *vt* to want; (*esigere, richiedere*) to demand, require; **vuole un po' di formaggio?** would you like some cheese?; **voglio una risposta da voi** I want an answer from you; **che lei lo voglia o no** whether you like it or not; **come vuole** as you like; **voler fare qc** to want to do sth; **volevo parlartene** I meant to talk to you about it; **vuole o vorrebbe essere così gentile da ...?** would you be so kind as to ...?; ~ **che qn faccia** to want sb to do; **vorrei questo** I would like this; ~**rci** (*essere necessario*): **quanto ci vuole per andare da Roma a Firenze?** how long does it take to go from Rome to Florence?; **ci vogliono 4 metri di stoffa** 4 metres of material are required, you will need 4 metres of material; **è quel che ci vuole** it's just what is needed; ~ **bene a qn** to love sb; ~ **male a qn** to dislike sb; **volerne a qn** to bear sb a grudge; ~ **dire (che)** to mean (that); **voglio dire ...** (*per correggersi*) I mean ...; **volevo ben dire!** I thought as much!; **senza** ~ without meaning to, unintentionally; **la tradizione vuole che ...** custom requires that ...; **la leggenda vuole che ...** legend has it that ...; **te la sei voluta** you asked for it.
vol'gare *ag* vulgar.
volgarità *sf* vulgarity.
volgariz'zare [volgarid'dzare] *vt* to popularize.
volgar'mente *av* (*in modo volgare*) vulgarly, coarsely; (*del popolo*) commonly, popularly.
'volgere ['vɔldʒere] *vt* to turn ♦ *vi* to turn; (*tendere*): ~ **a**: **il tempo volge al brutto/al bello** the weather is breaking/is setting fair; **un rosso che volge al viola** a red verging on purple; ~**rsi** *vr* to turn; ~ **al peggio** to take a turn for the worse; ~ **al termine** to draw to an end.
'volgo *sm* common people.
voli'era *sf* aviary.
voli'tivo, a *ag* strong-willed.
'volli *etc vb vedi* **volere**.
'volo *sm* flight; **ci sono due ore di** ~ **da Londra a Milano** it's a two-hour flight between London and Milan; **al** ~: **colpire qc al** ~ to hit sth as it flies past; **prendere al** ~ (*autobus, treno*) to catch at the last possible moment; (*palla*) to catch as it flies past; (*occasione*) to seize; **capire al** ~ to understand straight away; **veduta a** ~ **d'uccello** bird's-eye view; ~ **di linea** scheduled flight.
volontà *sf inv* will; **a** ~ (*mangiare, bere*) as much as one likes; **buona/cattiva** ~ goodwill/lack of goodwill; **le sue ultime** ~ (*testamento*) his last will and testament *sg*.

volontaria'mente *av* voluntarily.
volontari'ato *sm* (*MIL*) voluntary service; (*lavoro*) voluntary work.
volon'tario, a *ag* voluntary ♦ *sm* (*MIL*) volunteer.
'volpe *sf* fox.
vol'pino, a *ag* (*pelo, coda*) fox's; (*aspetto, astuzia*) fox-like ♦ *sm* (*cane*) Pomeranian.
vol'pone, a *sm/f* (*fig*) old fox.
'volsi *etc vb vedi* **volgere.**
volt *sm inv* (*ELETTR*) volt.
'volta *sf* (*momento, circostanza*) time; (*turno, giro*) turn; (*curva*) turn, bend; (*ARCHIT*) vault; (*direzione*): **partire alla ~ di** to set off for; **a mia** (*o* **tua** *etc*) **~ in** turn; **una ~** once; **una ~ sola** only once; **c'era una ~** once upon a time there was; **le cose di una ~** the things of the past; **due ~e** twice; **tre ~e** three times; **una cosa per ~** one thing at a time; **una ~ o l'altra** one of these days; **una ~ per tutte** once and for all; **una ~ tanto** just for once; **lo facciamo un'altra ~** we'll do it another time *o* some other time; **a ~e** at times, sometimes; **di ~ in ~** from time to time; **una ~ che** (*temporale*) once; (*causale*) since; **3 ~e 4** 3 times 4; **ti ha dato di ~ il cervello?** have you gone out of your mind?
volta'faccia [volta'fattʃa] *sm inv* (*fig*) volteface.
vol'taggio [vol'taddʒo] *sm* (*ELETTR*) voltage.
vol'tare *vt* to turn; (*girare: moneta*) to turn over; (*rigirare*) to turn round ♦ *vi* to turn; **~rsi** *vr* to turn; to turn over; to turn round.
voltas'tomaco *sm* nausea; (*fig*) disgust.
volteggi'are [volted'dʒare] *vi* (*volare*) to circle; (*in equitazione*) to do trick riding; (*in ginnastica*) to vault.
'volto, a *pp di* **volgere** ♦ *ag* (*inteso a*): **il mio discorso è ~ a spiegare ...** in my speech I intend to explain ... ♦ *sm* face.
vo'lubile *ag* changeable, fickle.
vo'lume *sm* volume.
volumi'noso, a *ag* voluminous, bulky.
vo'luta *sf* (*gen*) spiral; (*ARCHIT*) volute.
voluttà *sf* sensual pleasure *o* delight.
voluttu'oso, a *ag* voluptuous.
vomi'tare *vt, vi* to vomit.
'vomito *sm* vomit; **ho il ~** I feel sick.
'vongola *sf* clam.
vo'race [vo'ratʃe] *ag* voracious, greedy.
voracità [voratʃi'ta] *sf* voracity, voraciousness.
vo'ragine [vo'radʒine] *sf* abyss, chasm.
vorrò *etc vb vedi* **volere.**
'vortice ['vortitʃe] *sm* whirl, vortex; (*fig*) whirl.
vorti'coso, a *ag* whirling.
'vostro, a *det*: **il(la) ~(a)** *etc* your ♦ *pronome*: **il(la) ~(a)** *etc* yours ♦ *sm*: **avete**

speso del ~? did you spend your own money? ♦ *sf*: **la ~a** (*opinione*) your view; **i ~i** (*famiglia*) your family; **un ~ amico** a friend of yours; **è dei ~i, è dalla ~a** he's on your side; **l'ultima ~a** (*COMM: lettera*) your most recent letter; **alla ~a!** (*brindisi*) here's to you!, your health!
vo'tante *sm/f* voter.
vo'tare *vi* to vote ♦ *vt* (*sottoporre a votazione*) to take a vote on; (*approvare*) to vote for; (*REL*): **~ qc a** to dedicate sth to; **~rsi** *vr*: to devote o.s. to.
votazi'one [votat'tsjone] *sf* vote, voting; **~i** *sfpl* (*POL*) votes; (*INS*) marks.
'voto *sm* (*POL*) vote; (*INS*) mark (*Brit*), grade (*US*); (*REL*) vow; (*: offerta*) votive offering; **aver ~i belli/brutti** (*INS*) to get good/bad marks *o* grades; **prendere i ~i** to take one's vows; **~ di fiducia** vote of confidence.
V.P. *abbr* (= *vicepresidente*) VP.
VR *sigla* = *Verona*.
v.r. *abbr* (= *vedi retro*) PTO.
V.S. *abbr* = *Vostra Santità, Vostra Signoria*.
vs. *abbr* (= *vostro*) yr.
v.s. *abbr* = *vedi sopra*.
VT *sigla* = *Viterbo*.
V.U. *abbr* = **vigile urbano.**
vul'canico, a, ci, che *ag* volcanic.
vulcanizzazi'one [vulkaniddzat'tsjone] *sf* vulcanization.
vul'cano *sm* volcano.
vulne'rabile *ag* vulnerable.
vulnerabilità *sf* vulnerability.
vu'oi, vu'ole *vb vedi* **volere.**
vuo'tare *vt,* **~rsi** *vr* to empty.
vu'oto, a *ag* empty; (*fig: privo*): **~ di** (*senso etc*) devoid of ♦ *sm* empty space, gap; (*spazio in bianco*) blank; (*FISICA*) vacuum; (*fig: mancanza*) gap, void; **a mani ~e** empty-handed; **assegno a ~** dud cheque (*Brit*), bad check (*US*); **~ d'aria** air pocket; **"~ a perdere"** "no deposit"; **"~ a rendere"** "returnable bottle".
v.v. *abbr* (= *vostro*) yr.

W

W, w ['dɔppjovu] *sf o m inv* (*lettera*) W, w; **W come Washington** ≈ W for William.
W *abbr* = **viva, evviva.**
'wafer ['vafer] *sm inv* (*CUC, ELETTR*) wafer.
wagon-'lit [vagɔ̃'li] *sm inv* (*FERR*) sleeping car.
'water 'closet ['wɔːtə'klɔzɪt] *sm inv* toilet,

lavatory.
watt [vat] *sm inv* (*ELETTR*) watt.
wat'tora [vat'tora] *sm inv* (*ELETTR*) watt-hour.
WC *sm inv* WC.
'weekend ['wi:kɛnd] *sm inv* weekend.
'western ['wɛstern] *ag* (*CINEMA*) cowboy *cpd*
♦ *sm inv* western, cowboy film; ~
all'italiana spaghetti western.
'whisky ['wiski] *sm inv* whisky.
'würstel ['vyrstəl] *sm inv* frankfurter.

X

X, x [iks] *sf o m inv* (*lettera*) X, x; **X come**
Xeres ≈ X for Xmas.
xenofo'bia [ksenofo'bia] *sf* xenophobia.
xe'nofobo, a [kse'nɔfobo] *ag* xenophobic ♦
sm/f xenophobe.
'xeres ['ksɛres] *sm inv* sherry.
xero'copia [ksero'kɔpja] *sf* xerox ®, photo-copy.
xerocopi'are [kseroko'pjare] *vt* to photocopy.
xi'lofono [ksi'lɔfono] *sm* xylophone.

Y

Y, y ['ipsilon] *sf o m inv* (*lettera*) Y, y; **Y**
come Yacht ≈ Y for Yellow (*Brit*), Y for
Yoke (*US*).
yacht [jɔt] *sm inv* yacht.
'yankee ['jæŋki] *sm/f inv* Yank, Yankee.
Y.C.I. *abbr* = *Yacht Club d'Italia*.
'Yemen ['jemen] *sm*: **lo** ~ Yemen.
'yiddish ['jidiʃ] *ag inv, sm inv* Yiddish.
'yoga ['jɔga] *ag inv, sm* yoga (*cpd*).
'yoghurt ['jɔgurt] *sm inv* yog(h)ourt.

Z

Z, z ['dzɛta] *sf o m inv* (*lettera*) Z, z; **Z come**
Zara ≈ Z for Zebra.
zabai'one [dzaba'jone] *sm dessert made of*
egg yolks, sugar and marsala.
zaf'fata [tsaf'fata] *sf* (*tanfo*) stench.
zaffe'rano [dzaffe'rano] *sm* saffron.
zaf'firo [dzaf'firo] *sm* sapphire.
'zagara ['dzagara] *sf* orange blossom.
'zaino ['dzaino] *sm* rucksack.
Za'ire [dza'ire] *sm*: **lo** ~ Zaire.
'Zambia ['dzambja] *sm*: **lo** ~ Zambia.
'zampa ['tsampa] *sf* (*di animale: gamba*) leg;
(*: piede*) paw; **a quattro** ~**e** on all fours;
~**e di gallina** (*calligrafia*) scrawl; (*rughe*)
crow's feet.
zam'pata [tsam'pata] *sf* (*di cane, gatto*) blow
with a paw.
zampet'tare [tsampet'tare] *vi* to scamper.
zampil'lare [tsampil'lare] *vi* to gush, spurt.
zam'pillo [tsam'pillo] *sm* gush, spurt.
zam'pino [tsam'pino] *sm* paw; **qui c'è sotto il**
suo ~ (*fig*) he's had a hand in this.
zam'pogna [tsam'poɲɲa] *sf instrument*
similar to bagpipes.
'zanna ['tsanna] *sf* (*di elefante*) tusk; (*di*
carnivori) fang.
zan'zara [dzan'dzara] *sf* mosquito.
zanzari'era [dzandza'rjɛra] *sf* mosquito net.
'zappa ['tsappa] *sf* hoe.
zap'pare [tsap'pare] *vt* to hoe.
zappa'tore [tsappa'tore] *sm* (*AGR*) hoer.
zappa'tura [tsappa'tura] *sf* (*AGR*) hoeing.
zar, za'rina [tsar, tsa'rina] *sm/f* tsar/tsarina.
'zattera ['dzattera] *sf* raft.
za'vorra [dza'vorra] *sf* ballast.
'zazzera ['tsattsera] *sf* shock of hair.
'zebra ['dzɛbra] *sf* zebra; ~**e** *sfpl* (*AUT*) zeb-ra crossing *sg* (*Brit*), crosswalk *sg* (*US*).
ze'brato, a [dze'brato] *ag* with black and
white stripes; **strisce** ~**e, attraversamento**
~ (*AUT*) zebra crossing (*Brit*), crosswalk
(*US*).
'zecca, che ['tsekka] *sf* (*ZOOL*) tick; (*officina*
di monete) mint.
zec'chino [tsek'kino] *sm* gold coin; **oro** ~
pure gold.
ze'lante [dze'lante] *ag* zealous.
'zelo ['dzɛlo] *sm* zeal.
'zenit ['dzɛnit] *sm* zenith.
'zenzero ['dzendzero] *sm* ginger.
'zeppa ['tseppa] *sf* wedge.
'zeppo, a ['tseppo] *ag*: ~ **di** crammed *o*

packed with.

zer'bino [dzer'bino] *sm* doormat.

'zero ['dzɛro] *sm* zero, nought; **vincere per tre a** ~ (*SPORT*) to win three-nil.

'zeta ['dzɛta] *sm o f* zed, (the letter) z.

'zia ['tsia] *sf* aunt.

zibel'lino [dzibel'lino] *sm* sable.

zi'gano, a [tsi'gano] *ag, sm/f* gypsy.

'zigomo ['dzigomo] *sm* cheekbone.

zigri'nare [dzigri'nare] *vt* (*gen*) to knurl; (*pellame*) to grain; (*monete*) to mill.

zig'zag [dzig'dzag] *sm inv* zigzag; **andare a** ~ to zigzag.

Zim'babwe [tsim'babwe] *sm*: **lo** ~ Zimbabwe.

zim'bello [dzim'bɛllo] *sm* (*oggetto di burle*) laughing-stock.

'zinco ['dzinko] *sm* zinc.

zinga'resco, a, schi, sche [dzinga'resko] *ag* gypsy *cpd*.

'zingaro, a ['dzingaro] *sm/f* gipsy.

'zio ['tsio], *pl* **'zii** *sm* uncle; **zii** *smpl* (*zio e zia*) uncle and aunt.

zi'tella [dzi'tɛlla] *sf* spinster; (*peg*) old maid.

zit'tire [tsit'tire] *vt* to silence, hush *o* shut up ♦ *vi* to hiss.

'zitto, a ['tsitto] *ag* quiet, silent; **sta'** ~! be quiet!

ziz'zania [dzid'dzanja] *sf* (*BOT*) darnel; (*fig*) discord; **gettare** *o* **seminare** ~ to sow discord.

'zoccolo ['tsɔkkolo] *sm* (*calzatura*) clog; (*di cavallo etc*) hoof; (*ARCHIT*) plinth; (*di parete*) skirting (board); (*di armadio*) base.

zodia'cale [dzodia'kale] *ag* zodiac *cpd*; **segno** ~ sign of the zodiac.

zo'diaco [dzo'diako] *sm* zodiac.

zolfa'nello [tsolfa'nɛllo] *sm* (sulphur) match.

'zolfo ['tsolfo] *sm* sulphur (*Brit*), sulfur (*US*).

'zolla ['dzolla] *sf* clod (of earth).

zol'letta [dzol'letta] *sf* sugar lump.

'zona ['dzɔna] *sf* zone, area; ~ **di depressione** (*METEOR*) trough of low pressure; ~ **pedonale** pedestrian precinct; ~ **verde** (*di abitato*) green area.

'zonzo ['dzondzo]: **a** ~ *av*: **andare a** ~ to wander about, stroll about.

'zoo ['dzɔo] *sm inv* zoo.

zoolo'gia [dzoolo'dʒia] *sf* zoology.

zoo'logico, a, ci, che [dzoo'lɔdʒiko] *ag* zoological.

zo'ologo, a, gi, ghe [dzo'ɔlogo] *sm/f* zoologist.

zoosa'fari [dzoosa'fari] *sm inv* safari park.

zoo'tecnico, a, ci, che [dzoo'tɛkniko] *ag* zootechnical; **il patrimonio** ~ **di un paese** a country's livestock resources.

zoppi'care [tsoppi'kare] *vi* to limp; (*fig: mobile*) to be shaky, rickety.

'zoppo, a ['tsɔppo] *ag* lame; (*fig: mobile*) shaky, rickety.

zoti'cone [dzoti'kone] *sm* lout.

zu'ava [dzu'ava] *sf*: **pantaloni** *mpl* **alla** ~ knickerbockers.

'zucca, che ['tsukka] *sf* (*BOT*) marrow (*Brit*), vegetable marrow (*US*); pumpkin; (*scherzoso*) head.

zucche'rare [tsukke'rare] *vt* to put sugar in.

zucche'rato, a [tsukke'rato] *ag* sweet, sweetened.

zuccheri'era [tsukke'rjɛra] *sf* sugar bowl.

zuccheri'ficio [tsukkeri'fitʃo] *sm* sugar refinery.

zucche'rino, a [tsukke'rino] *ag* sugary, sweet.

'zucchero ['tsukkero] *sm* sugar; ~ **di canna** cane sugar; ~ **caramellato** caramel; ~ **filato** candy floss, cotton candy (*US*); ~ **a velo** icing sugar (*Brit*), confectioner's sugar (*US*).

zucche'roso, a [tsukke'roso] *ag* sugary.

zuc'china [tsuk'kina] *sf*, **zuc'chino** [tsuk'kino] *sm* courgette (*Brit*), zucchini (*US*).

zuc'cotto [tsuk'kɔtto] *sm* ice-cream sponge.

'zuffa ['tsuffa] *sf* brawl.

zufo'lare [tsufo'lare] *vt, vi* to whistle.

'zuppa ['tsuppa] *sf* soup; (*fig*) mixture, muddle; ~ **inglese** (*CUC*) *dessert made with sponge cake, custard and chocolate,* ≈ trifle (*Brit*).

zuppi'era [tsup'pjɛra] *sf* soup tureen.

'zuppo, a ['tsuppo] *ag*: ~ **(di)** drenched (with), soaked (with).

Zu'rigo [dzu'rigo] *sf* Zurich.

ENGLISH-ITALIAN
INGLESE-ITALIANO

A

A, a [eɪ] *n* (*letter*) A, a *f or m inv*; (*SCOL*: *mark*) ≈ 10 (*ottimo*); (*MUS*): **A** la *m*; **A for Andrew**, (*US*) **A for Able** ≈ A come Ancona; **A road** *n* (*Brit AUT*) ≈ strada statale; **A shares** *npl* (*Brit STOCK EXCHANGE*) azioni *fpl* senza diritto di voto.

a, an [eɪ, ə, æn, ən, n] *indefinite article* un (uno + *s impure, gn, pn, ps, x, z*), *f* una (un' + *vowel*); ~ **mirror** uno specchio; **an apple** una mela; **I haven't got** ~ **car** non ho la macchina; **he's** ~ **doctor** è medico, fa il medico; **3** ~ **day/week** 3 al giorno/la *or* alla settimana; **10 km an hour** 10 km all'ora.

a. *abbr* = **acre.**

AA *n abbr* (*Brit*: = *Automobile Association*) ≈ A.C.I. *m* (= *Automobile Club d'Italia*); (*US*: = *Associate in/of Arts*) titolo di studio; (= *Alcoholics Anonymous*) A.A. *f* (= *Anonima Alcolisti*); (*MIL*) = **anti-aircraft.**

AAA *n abbr* (= *American Automobile Association*) ≈ A.C.I. *m* (= *Automobile Club d'Italia*); (*Brit*) = *Amateur Athletics Association*.

AAUP *n abbr* (= *American Association of University Professors*) *associazione dei professori universitari.*

AB *abbr* (*Brit*) *see* **able-bodied seaman;** (*Canada*) = *Alberta.*

aback [ə'bæk] *ad*: **to be taken** ~ essere sbalordito(a).

abacus, *pl* **abaci** ['æbəkəs, -saɪ] *n* pallottoliere *m*, abaco.

abandon [ə'bændən] *vt* abbandonare ♦ *n* abbandono; **to** ~ **ship** abbandonare la nave.

abandoned [ə'bændənd] *a* (*child, house etc*) abbandonato(a); (*unrestrained: manner*) disinvolto(a).

abase [ə'beɪs] *vt*: **to** ~ **o.s. (so far as to do)** umiliarsi *or* abbassarsi (al punto di fare).

abashed [ə'bæʃt] *a* imbarazzato(a).

abate [ə'beɪt] *vi* calmarsi.

abatement [ə'beɪtmənt] *n* (*of pollution, noise*) soppressione *f*, eliminazione *f*; **noise** ~ **society** associazione *f* per la lotta contro i rumori.

abattoir ['æbətwɑ:*] *n* (*Brit*) mattatoio.

abbey ['æbɪ] *n* abbazia, badia.

abbot ['æbət] *n* abate *m*.

abbreviate [ə'bri:vɪeɪt] *vt* abbreviare.

abbreviation [əbri:vɪ'eɪʃən] *n* abbreviazione *f*.

ABC *n abbr* (= *American Broadcasting Company*) *rete televisiva americana*.

abdicate ['æbdɪkeɪt] *vt* abdicare a ♦ *vi* abdicare.

abdication [æbdɪ'keɪʃən] *n* abdicazione *f*.

abdomen ['æbdəmən] *n* addome *m*.

abdominal [æb'dɔmɪnl] *a* addominale.

abduct [æb'dʌkt] *vt* rapire.

abduction [æb'dʌkʃən] *n* rapimento.

Aberdonian [æbə'dəunɪən] *a* di Aberdeen ♦ *n* abitante *m/f* di Aberdeen; originario/a di Aberdeen.

aberration [æbə'reɪʃən] *n* aberrazione *f*.

abet [ə'bɛt] *vt see* **aid.**

abeyance [ə'beɪəns] *n*: **in** ~ in sospeso.

abhor [əb'hɔ:*] *vt* aborrire.

abhorrent [əb'hɔrənt] *a* odioso(a).

abide [ə'baɪd] *vt* sopportare.

  abide by *vt fus* conformarsi a.

ability [ə'bɪlɪtɪ] *n* abilità *f inv*; **to the best of my** ~ con il massimo impegno.

abject ['æbdʒɛkt] *a* (*poverty*) abietto(a); (*apology*) umiliante; (*coward*) indegno(a), vile.

ablaze [ə'bleɪz] *a* in fiamme; ~ **with light** risplendente di luce.

able ['eɪbl] *a* capace; **to be** ~ **to do sth** essere capace di fare qc, poter fare qc.

able-bodied ['eɪbl'bɔdɪd] *a* robusto(a).

able-bodied seaman (AB) *n* (*Brit*) marinaio scelto.

ably ['eɪblɪ] *ad* abilmente.

ABM *n abbr* (= *anti-ballistic missile*) ABM *m*.

abnormal [æb'nɔ:məl] *a* anormale.

abnormality [æbnɔ:'mælɪtɪ] *n* (*condition*) anormalità; (*instance*) anomalia.

aboard [ə'bɔ:d] *ad* a bordo ♦ *prep* a bordo di; ~ **the train** in *or* sul treno.

abode [ə'bəud] *n* (*old*) dimora; (*LAW*) domicilio, dimora; **of no fixed** ~ senza fissa dimora.

abolish [ə'bɔlɪʃ] *vt* abolire.

abolition [æbəu'lɪʃən] *n* abolizione *f*.

abominable [ə'bɔmɪnəbl] *a* abominevole.

aborigine [æbə'rɪdʒɪnɪ] *n* aborigeno/a.

abort [ə'bɔ:t] *vt* (*MED, fig*) abortire; (*COMPUT*) interrompere l'esecuzione di.

abortion [ə'bɔ:ʃən] *n* aborto; **to have an** ~ avere un aborto, abortire.

abortive [ə'bɔ:tɪv] *a* abortivo(a).

abound [ə'baund] *vi* abbondare; **to** ~ **in** abbondare in.

about [ə'baut] *prep* intorno a, riguardo a ♦ *ad* circa; (*here and there*) qua e là; **do something** ~ **it!** fai qualcosa!; **it takes** ~ **10 hours** ci vogliono circa 10 ore; **at** ~ **2 o'clock** verso le due; **it's just** ~ **finished** è quasi finito; **is Paul** ~? (*Brit*) hai visto Paul in giro?; **it's the other way** ~ (*Brit*) è il contrario; **it's** ~ **here** è qui dintorno; **to walk** ~ **the town** camminare per la città; **to run** ~ (*Brit*) correre qua e là; **they left all their things lying** ~ hanno lasciato tutta la loro roba in giro; **to be** ~ **to**: he was ~ **to cry** stava per piangere; **I'm not** ~ **to do all that for nothing** non ho intenzione di fare tutto questo per niente; **what** *or* **how** ~ **doing this?** che ne pensa di fare questo?

about-face [ə'baut'feɪs] *n*, **about-turn** [ə'baut'tə:n] *n* (*MIL*) dietro front *m inv*.

above [ə'bʌv] *ad, prep* sopra; **mentioned** ~ suddetto; **costing** ~ **£10** più caro di 10 sterline; **he's not** ~ **a bit of blackmail** non rifuggirebbe dal ricatto; ~ **all** soprattutto.

aboveboard [ə'bʌv'bɔːd] *a* aperto(a); onesto(a).

abrasion [ə'breɪʒən] *n* abrasione *f*.

abrasive [ə'breɪzɪv] *a* abrasivo(a).

abreast [ə'brɛst] *ad* di fianco; **3** ~ per 3 di fronte; **to keep** ~ **of** tenersi aggiornato su.

abridge [ə'brɪdʒ] *vt* ridurre.

abroad [ə'brɔːd] *ad* all'estero; **there is a rumour** ~ **that ...** (*fig*) si sente dire in giro che ..., circola la voce che ....

abrupt [ə'brʌpt] *a* (*steep*) erto(a); (*sudden*) improvviso(a); (*gruff, blunt*) brusco(a).

abscess ['æbsɪs] *n* ascesso.

abscond [əb'skɔnd] *vi* scappare.

absence ['æbsəns] *n* assenza; **in the** ~ **of** (*person*) in assenza di; (*thing*) in mancanza di.

absent ['æbsənt] *a* assente; **to be** ~ **without leave (AWOL)** (*MIL etc*) essere assente ingiustificato.

absentee [æbsən'tiː] *n* assente *m/f*.

absenteeism [æbsən'tiːɪzəm] *n* assenteismo.

absent-minded ['æbsənt'maɪndɪd] *a* distratto(a).

absent-mindedness ['æbsənt'maɪndɪdnɪs] *n* distrazione *f*.

absolute ['æbsəluːt] *a* assoluto(a).

absolutely [æbsə'luːtlɪ] *ad* assolutamente.

absolve [əb'zɔlv] *vt*: **to** ~ **sb (from)** (*sin etc*) assolvere qn (da); **to** ~ **sb from** (*oath*) sciogliere qn da.

absorb [əb'sɔːb] *vt* assorbire; **to be** ~**ed in a book** essere immerso(a) in un libro.

absorbent [əb'sɔːbənt] *a* assorbente.

absorbent cotton *n* (*US*) cotone *m* idrofilo.

absorbing [əb'sɔːbɪŋ] *a* avvincente, molto interessante.

absorption [əb'sɔːpʃən] *n* assorbimento.

abstain [əb'steɪn] *vi*: **to** ~ **(from)** astenersi (da).

abstemious [əb'stiːmɪəs] *a* astemio(a).

abstention [əb'stɛnʃən] *n* astensione *f*.

abstinence ['æbstɪnəns] *n* astinenza.

abstract ['æbstrækt] *a* astratto(a) ♦ *n* (*summary*) riassunto ♦ *vt* [æb'strækt] estrarre.

absurd [əb'sɔːd] *a* assurdo(a).

absurdity [əb'sɔːdɪtɪ] *n* assurdità *f inv*.

ABTA ['æbtə] *n abbr* = *Association of British Travel Agents*.

Abu Dhabi ['æbuː'dɑːbɪ] *n* Abu Dhabi *f*.

abundance [ə'bʌndəns] *n* abbondanza.

abundant [ə'bʌndənt] *a* abbondante.

abuse *n* [ə'bjuːs] abuso; (*insults*) ingiurie *fpl* ♦ *vt* [ə'bjuːz] abusare di; **open to** ~ che si presta ad abusi.

abusive [ə'bjuːsɪv] *a* ingiurioso(a).

abysmal [ə'bɪzməl] *a* spaventoso(a).

abyss [ə'bɪs] *n* abisso.

AC *n abbr* (*US*) = *athletic club*.

a/c *abbr* (*BANKING etc*: = *account, account current*) c.

academic [ækə'dɛmɪk] *a* accademico(a); (*pej: issue*) puramente formale ♦ *n* universitario/a.

academic year *n* anno accademico.

academy [ə'kædəmɪ] *n* (*learned body*) accademia; (*school*) scuola privata; **military/naval** ~ scuola militare/navale; ~ **of** music conservatorio.

ACAS ['eɪkæs] *n abbr* (*Brit*: = *Advisory, Conciliation and Arbitration Service*) comitato governativo per il miglioramento della contrattazione collettiva.

accede [æk'siːd] *vi*: **to** ~ **to** (*request*) accedere a; (*throne*) ascendere a.

accelerate [æk'sɛləreɪt] *vt, vi* accelerare.

acceleration [æksɛlə'reɪʃən] *n* accelerazione *f*.

accelerator [æk'sɛləreɪtə*] *n* acceleratore *m*.

accent ['æksɛnt] *n* accento.

accentuate [æk'sɛntjueɪt] *vt* (*syllable*) accentuare; (*need, difference etc*) accentuare, mettere in risalto *or* in evidenza.

accept [ək'sɛpt] *vt* accettare.

acceptable [ək'sɛptəbl] *a* accettabile.

acceptance [ək'sɛptəns] *n* accettazione *f*; **to meet with general** ~ incontrare il favore *or* il consenso generale.

access ['æksɛs] *n* accesso ♦ *vt* (*COMPUT*) accedere a; **to have** ~ **to** avere accesso a; **the burglars gained** ~ **through a window** i ladri sono riusciti a penetrare da *or* attraverso una finestra.

accessible [æk'sɛsəbl] *a* accessibile.

accession [æk'sɛʃən] *n* (*addition*) aggiunta; (*to library*) accessione *f*, acquisto; (*of king*) ascesa *or* salita al trono.

accessory [æk'sɛsərɪ] *n* accessorio; **toilet accessories** *npl* (*Brit*) articoli *mpl* da toilette.

access road *n* strada d'accesso; (*to motorway*) raccordo di entrata.

access time *n* (*COMPUT*) tempo di accesso.

accident ['æksɪdənt] *n* incidente *m*; (*chance*) caso; **to meet with** *or* **to have an** ~ avere un incidente; ~**s at work** infortuni *mpl* sul lavoro; **by** ~ per caso.

accidental [æksɪ'dɛntl] *a* accidentale.

accidentally [æksɪ'dɛntəlɪ] *ad* per caso.

accident insurance *n* assicurazione *f* contro gli infortuni.

accident-prone ['æksɪdənt'prəun] *a*: he's **very** ~ è un vero passaguai.

acclaim [ə'kleɪm] *vt* acclamare ♦ *n* acclamazione *f.*

acclamation [æklə'meɪʃən] *n* (*approval*) acclamazione *f;* (*applause*) applauso.

acclimatize [ə'klaɪmətaɪz], (*US*) **acclimate** [ə'klaɪmeɪt] *vt:* **to become ~d** acclimatarsi.

accolade ['ækəleɪd] *n* encomio.

accommodate [ə'kɔmədeɪt] *vt* alloggiare; (*oblige, help*) favorire; **this car ~s 4 people comfortably** quest'auto può trasportare comodamente 4 persone.

accommodating [ə'kɔmədeɪtɪŋ] *a* compiacente.

accommodation, (*US*) **accommodations** [əkɔmə'deɪʃən(z)] *n*(*pl*) alloggio; **seating ~** (*Brit*) posti a sedere; **"~ to let"** (*Brit*) "camere in affitto"; **have you any ~?** avete posto?

accompaniment [ə'kʌmpənɪmənt] *n* accompagnamento.

accompanist [ə'kʌmpənɪst] *n* (*MUS*) accompagnatore/trice.

accompany [ə'kʌmpənɪ] *vt* accompagnare.

accomplice [ə'kʌmplɪs] *n* complice *m/f.*

accomplish [ə'kʌmplɪʃ] *vt* compiere; (*achieve*) ottenere.

accomplished [ə'kʌmplɪʃt] *a* (*person*) esperto(a).

accomplishment [ə'kʌmplɪʃmənt] *n* compimento; (*thing achieved*) risultato; **~s** *npl* (*skills*) doti *fpl.*

accord [ə'kɔːd] *n* accordo ♦ *vt* accordare; **of his own ~** di propria iniziativa; **with one ~** all'unanimità, di comune accordo.

accordance [ə'kɔːdəns] *n:* **in ~ with** in conformità con.

according [ə'kɔːdɪŋ]: **~ to** *prep* secondo; **it went ~ to plan** è andata secondo il previsto.

accordingly [ə'kɔːdɪŋlɪ] *ad* in conformità.

accordion [ə'kɔːdɪən] *n* fisarmonica.

accost [ə'kɔst] *vt* avvicinare.

account [ə'kaunt] *n* (*COMM*) conto; (*report*) descrizione *f;* **~s** *npl* (*COMM*) conti; **"~ payee only"** (*Brit*) "assegno non trasferibile"; **to keep an ~ of** tenere nota di; **to bring sb to ~ for sth/for having done sth** chiedere a qn di render conto di qc/per aver fatto qc; **by all ~s** a quanto si dice; **of little ~** di poca importanza; **on ~** in acconto; **to buy sth on ~** comprare qc a credito; **on no ~** per nessun motivo; **on ~ of** a causa di; **to take into ~, take ~ of** tener conto di.

account for *vt fus* (*explain*) spiegare; giustificare; **all the children were ~ed for** nessun bambino mancava all'appello.

accountability [ə'kauntə'bɪlɪtɪ] *n* responsabilità.

accountable [ə'kauntəbl] *a* responsabile.

accountancy [ə'kauntənsɪ] *n* ragioneria.

accountant [ə'kauntənt] *n* ragioniere/a.

accounting [ə'kauntɪŋ] *n* contabilità.

accounting period *n* esercizio finanziario, periodo contabile.

account number *n* numero di conto.

account payable *n* conto passivo.

account receivable *n* conto da esigere.

accredited [ə'krɛdɪtɪd] *a* accreditato(a).

accretion [ə'kriːʃən] *n* accrescimento.

accrue [ə'kruː] *vi* (*mount up*) aumentare; **to ~ to** derivare a; **~d charges** ratei *mpl* passivi; **~d interest** interesse *m* maturato.

accumulate [ə'kjuːmjuleɪt] *vt* accumulare ♦ *vi* accumularsi.

accumulation [əkjuːmju'leɪʃən] *n* accumulazione *f.*

accuracy ['ækjurəsɪ] *n* precisione *f.*

accurate ['ækjurɪt] *a* preciso(a).

accurately ['ækjurɪtlɪ] *ad* precisamente.

accusation [ækju'zeɪʃən] *n* accusa.

accusative [ə'kjuːzətɪv] *n* (*LING*) accusativo.

accuse [ə'kjuːz] *vt* accusare.

accused [ə'kjuːzd] *n* accusato/a.

accustom [ə'kʌstəm] *vt* abituare; **to ~ o.s. to sth** abituarsi a qc.

accustomed [ə'kʌstəmd] *a* (*usual*) abituale; **~ to** abituato(a) a.

AC/DC *abbr* (= *alternating current/direct current*) c.a./c.c.

ACE [eɪs] *n abbr* = *American Council on Education.*

ace [eɪs] *n* asso; **within an ~ of** (*Brit*) a un pelo da.

acerbic [ə'sɔːbɪk] *a* (*also fig*) acido(a).

acetate ['æsɪteɪt] *n* acetato.

ache [eɪk] *n* male *m*, dolore *m* ♦ *vi* (*be sore*) far male, dolere; (*yearn*): **to ~ to do sth** morire dalla voglia di fare qc; **I've got stomach ~** *or* (*US*) **a stomach ~** ho mal di stomaco; **my head ~s** mi fa male la testa; **I'm aching all over** mi duole dappertutto.

achieve [ə'tʃiːv] *vt* (*aim*) raggiungere; (*victory, success*) ottenere; (*task*) compiere.

achievement [ə'tʃiːvmənt] *n* compimento; successo.

acid ['æsɪd] *a* acido(a) ♦ *n* acido.

acidity [ə'sɪdɪtɪ] *n* acidità.

acid rain *n* pioggia acida.

acknowledge [ək'nɔlɪdʒ] *vt* riconoscere; (*letter: also:* **~ receipt of**) accusare ricevuta di.

acknowledgement [ək'nɔlɪdʒmənt] *n* riconoscimento; (*of letter*) conferma; **~s** (*in book*) ringraziamenti *mpl.*

ACLU *n abbr* (= *American Civil Liberties Union*) unione americana per le libertà civili.

acme ['ækmɪ] *n* culmine *m*, acme *m.*

acne ['æknɪ] *n* acne *f.*

acorn ['eɪkɔːn] *n* ghianda.

acoustic [ə'kuːstɪk] *a* acustico(a); *see also* **acoustics.**

acoustic coupler [-'kʌplə*] *n* (*COMPUT*) accoppiatore *m* acustico.

acoustics [ə'kuːstɪks] *n, npl* acustica.

acoustic screen *n* schermo acustico.

acquaint [ə'kweɪnt] *vt:* **to ~ sb with sth** far sapere qc a qn; **to be ~ed with** (*person*) conoscere.

acquaintance [ə'kweɪntəns] *n* conoscenza; (*person*) conoscente *m/f;* **to make sb's ~**

fare la conoscenza di qn.

acquiesce [ækwɪ'ɛs] *vi* (*agree*): **to ~ (in)** acconsentire (a).

acquire [ə'kwaɪə*] *vt* acquistare.

acquired [ə'kwaɪəd] *a* acquisito(a); **it's an ~ taste** è una cosa che si impara ad apprezzare.

acquisition [ækwɪ'zɪʃən] *n* acquisto.

acquisitive [ə'kwɪzɪtɪv] *a* a cui piace accumulare le cose.

acquit [ə'kwɪt] *vt* assolvere; **to ~ o.s. well** comportarsi bene.

acquittal [ə'kwɪtl] *n* assoluzione *f*.

acre ['eɪkə*] *n* acro (= 4047 *m²*).

acreage ['eɪkərɪdʒ] *n* superficie *f* in acri.

acrid ['ækrɪd] *a* (*smell*) acre, pungente; (*fig*) pungente.

acrimonious [ækrɪ'məʊnɪəs] *a* astioso(a).

acrobat ['ækrəbæt] *n* acrobata *m/f*.

acrobatic [ækrə'bætɪk] *a* acrobatico(a).

acrobatics [ækrə'bætɪks] *n* acrobatica ♦ *npl* acrobazie *fpl*.

Acropolis [ə'krɒpəlɪs] *n*: **the ~** l'Acropoli *f*.

across [ə'krɒs] *prep* (*on the other side*) dall'altra parte di; (*crosswise*) attraverso ♦ *ad* dall'altra parte; in larghezza; **to walk ~ (the road)** attraversare (la strada); **to take sb ~ the road** far attraversare la strada a qn; **~ from** di fronte a; **the lake is 12 km ~** il lago ha una larghezza di 12 km *or* è largo 12 km; **to get sth ~ to sb** (*fig*) far capire qc a qn.

acrylic [ə'krɪlɪk] *a* acrilico(a) ♦ *n* acrilico.

ACT *n abbr* (= *American College Test*) esame di ammissione a college.

act [ækt] *n* atto; (*in music-hall etc*) numero; (*LAW*) decreto ♦ *vi* agire; (*THEATRE*) recitare; (*pretend*) fingere ♦ *vt* (*part*) recitare; **to catch sb in the ~** cogliere qn in flagrante *or* sul fatto; **it's only an ~** è tutta scena, è solo una messinscena; **~ of God** (*LAW*) calamità *f inv* naturale; **to ~ Hamlet** (*Brit*) recitare la parte di Amleto; **to ~ the fool** (*Brit*) fare lo stupido; **to ~ as** agire da; **it ~s as a deterrent** serve da deterrente; **~ing in my capacity as chairman, I ...** in qualità di presidente, io ....

act on *vt*: **to ~ on sth** agire in base a qc.

act out *vt* (*event*) ricostruire; (*fantasies*) dare forma concreta a.

acting ['æktɪŋ] *a* che fa le funzioni di ♦ *n* (*of actor*) recitazione *f*; (*activity*): **to do some ~** fare del teatro (*or* del cinema); **he is the ~ manager** fa le veci del direttore.

action ['ækʃən] *n* azione *f*; (*MIL*) combattimento; (*LAW*) processo; **to take ~** agire; **to put a plan into ~** realizzare un piano; **out of ~** fuori combattimento; (*machine etc*) fuori servizio; **killed in ~** (*MIL*) ucciso in combattimento; **to bring an ~ against sb** (*LAW*) intentare causa contro qn.

action replay *n* (*Brit TV*) replay *m inv*.

activate ['æktɪveɪt] *vt* (*mechanism*) fare funzionare; (*CHEM*, *PHYSICS*) rendere

attivo(a).

active ['æktɪv] *a* attivo(a); **to play an ~ part in** partecipare attivamente a.

active duty (AD) *n* (*US MIL*) = **active service**.

actively ['æktɪvlɪ] *ad* attivamente.

active partner *n* (*COMM*) socio effettivo.

active service *n* (*Brit MIL*): **to be on ~** prestar servizio in zona di operazioni.

activist ['æktɪvɪst] *n* attivista *m/f*.

activity [æk'tɪvɪtɪ] *n* attività *f inv*.

actor ['æktə*] *n* attore *m*.

actress ['æktrɪs] *n* attrice *f*.

ACTT *n abbr* (*Brit*: = *Association of Cinematographic, Television and Allied Technicians*) sindacato dei tecnici cinematografici, televisivi e affini.

actual ['æktjuəl] *a* reale, vero(a).

actually ['æktjuəlɪ] *ad* veramente; (*even*) addirittura.

actuary ['æktjuərɪ] *n* attuario/a.

actuate ['æktjueɪt] *vt* attivare.

acuity [ə'kju:ɪtɪ] *n* acutezza.

acumen ['ækjumən] *n* acume *m;* **business ~** fiuto negli affari.

acupuncture ['ækjupʌŋktʃə*] *n* agopuntura.

acute [ə'kju:t] *a* acuto(a).

AD *ad abbr* (= *Anno Domini*) d. C. ♦ *n abbr* (*US MIL*) *see* **active duty**.

ad [æd] *n abbr* = **advertisement**.

adamant ['ædəmənt] *a* irremovibile.

Adam's apple ['ædəmz-] *n* pomo di Adamo.

adapt [ə'dæpt] *vt* adattare ♦ *vi*: **to ~ (to)** adattarsi (a).

adaptability [ədæptə'bɪlɪtɪ] *n* adattabilità.

adaptable [ə'dæptəbl] *a* (*device*) adattabile; (*person*) che sa adattarsi.

adaptation [ædæp'teɪʃən] *n* adattamento.

adapter, adaptor [ə'dæptə*] *n* (*ELEC*) adattatore *m*.

ADC *n abbr* (*MIL*) = **aide-de-camp**; (*US*: = *Aid to Dependent Children*) sussidio per figli a carico.

add [æd] *vt* aggiungere; (*figures*) addizionare ♦ *vi*: **to ~ to** (*increase*) aumentare.

add on *vt* aggiungere.

add up *vt* (*figures*) addizionare ♦ *vi* (*fig*): **it doesn't ~ up** non ha senso; **it doesn't ~ up to much** non è un granché.

adder ['ædə*] *n* vipera.

addict ['ædɪkt] *n* tossicomane *m/f*; (*fig*) fanatico/a; **heroin ~** eroinomane *m/f*; **drug ~** tossicodipendente *m/f*, tossicomane *m/f*.

addicted [ə'dɪktɪd] *a*: **to be ~ to** (*drink etc*) essere dedito(a) a; (*fig: football etc*) essere tifoso(a) di.

addiction [ə'dɪkʃən] *n* (*MED*) tossicomania.

adding machine ['ædɪŋ-] *n* addizionatrice *f*.

Addis Ababa ['ædɪs'æbəbə] *n* Addis Abeba *f*.

addition [ə'dɪʃən] *n* addizione *f*; **in ~** inoltre; **in ~ to** oltre.

additional [ə'dɪʃənl] *a* supplementare.

additive ['ædɪtɪv] *n* additivo.

address [ə'drɛs] *n* (*gen, COMPUT*) indirizzo;

(*talk*) discorso ♦ *vt* indirizzare; (*speak to*) fare un discorso a; **form of** ~ (*gen*) formula di cortesia; (*in letters*) formula d'indirizzo *or* di intestazione; **to** ~ **o.s. to sth** indirizzare le proprie energie verso qc; **absolute/relative** ~ (*COMPUT*) indirizzo assoluto/relativo.

Aden ['eɪdən] *n*: **the Gulf of** ~ il golfo di Aden.

adenoids ['ædɪnɔɪdz] *npl* adenoidi *fpl*.

adept ['ædɛpt] *a*: ~ **at** esperto(a) in.

adequate ['ædɪkwɪt] *a* (*description*, *reward*) adeguato(a); (*amount*) sufficiente; **to feel** ~ **to a task** sentirsi all'altezza di un compito.

adequately ['ædɪkwɪtlɪ] *ad* adeguatamente; sufficientemente.

adhere [əd'hɪə*] *vi*: **to** ~ **to** aderire a; (*fig*: *rule*, *decision*) seguire.

adhesion [əd'hi:ʒən] *n* adesione *f*.

adhesive [əd'hi:zɪv] *a* adesivo(a) ♦ *n* adesivo; ~ **tape** (*Brit*: *for parcels etc*) nastro adesivo; (*US*: *MED*) cerotto adesivo.

ad hoc [æd'hɔk] *a* (*decision*) ad hoc *inv*; (*committee*) apposito(a).

ad infinitum ['ædɪnfɪ'naɪtəm] *ad* all'infinito.

adjacent [ə'dʒeɪsənt] *a* adiacente; ~ **to** accanto a.

adjective ['ædʒɛktɪv] *n* aggettivo.

adjoin [ə'dʒɔɪn] *vt* essere contiguo(a) *or* attiguo(a) a.

adjoining [ə'dʒɔɪnɪŋ] *a* accanto *inv*, adiacente ♦ *prep* accanto a.

adjourn [ə'dʒə:n] *vt* rimandare, aggiornare; (*US*: *end*) sospendere ♦ *vi* sospendere la seduta; (*PARLIAMENT*) sospendere i lavori; (*go*) spostarsi; **to** ~ **a meeting till the following week** aggiornare *or* rinviare un incontro alla settimana seguente; **they** ~**ed to the pub** (*col*) si sono trasferiti al pub.

adjournment [ə'dʒə:nmənt] *n* rinvio, aggiornamento; sospensione *f*.

Adjt *abbr* (*MIL*) = **adjutant**.

adjudicate [ə'dʒu:dɪkeɪt] *vt* (*contest*) giudicare; (*claim*) decidere su.

adjudication [ədʒu:dɪ'keɪʃən] *n* decisione *f*.

adjust [ə'dʒʌst] *vt* aggiustare; (*COMM*) rettificare ♦ *vi*: **to** ~ (**to**) adattarsi (a).

adjustable [ə'dʒʌstəbl] *a* regolabile.

adjuster [ə'dʒʌstə*] *n see* **loss adjuster**.

adjustment [ə'dʒʌstmənt] *n* adattamento; (*of prices*, *wages*) aggiustamento.

adjutant ['ædʒətənt] *n* aiutante *m*.

ad-lib [æd'lɪb] *vt*, *vi* improvvisare ♦ *n* improvvisazione *f* ♦ *ad*: **ad lib** a piacere, a volontà.

adman ['ædmæn] *n* (*col*) pubblicitario/a.

admin [æd'mɪn] *n abbr* (*col*) = **administration**.

administer [əd'mɪnɪstə*] *vt* amministrare; (*justice*) somministrare.

administration [ədmɪnɪs'treɪʃən] *n* amministrazione *f*; **the A**~ (*US*) il Governo.

administrative [əd'mɪnɪstrətɪv] *a* amministrativo(a).

administrator [əd'mɪnɪstreɪtə*] *n* ammini-

stratore/trice.

admirable ['ædmərəbl] *a* ammirevole.

admiral ['ædmərəl] *n* ammiraglio.

Admiralty ['ædmərəltɪ] *n* (*Brit*: *also*: ~ **Board**) Ministero della Marina.

admiration [ædmə'reɪʃən] *n* ammirazione *f*.

admire [əd'maɪə*] *vt* ammirare.

admirer [əd'maɪərə*] *n* ammiratore/trice.

admission [əd'mɪʃən] *n* ammissione *f*; (*to exhibition*, *night club etc*) ingresso; (*confession*) confessione *f*; **by his own** ~ per sua ammissione; "~ **free**", "**free** ~" "ingresso gratuito".

admit [əd'mɪt] *vt* ammettere; far entrare; (*agree*) riconoscere; "**children not** ~**ted**" "vietato l'ingresso ai bambini"; **this ticket** ~**s two** questo biglietto è valido per due persone; **I must** ~ **that ...** devo ammettere *or* confessare che ....

admit of *vt fus* lasciare adito a.

admit to *vt fus* riconoscere.

admittance [əd'mɪtəns] *n* ingresso; "**no** ~" "vietato l'ingresso".

admittedly [əd'mɪtɪdlɪ] *ad* bisogna pur riconoscere (che).

admonish [əd'mɔnɪʃ] *vt* ammonire.

ad nauseam [æd'nɔ:zɪæm] *ad* fino alla nausea, a non finire.

ado [ə'du:] *n*: **without (any) more** ~ senza più indugi.

adolescence [ædəu'lɛsns] *n* adolescenza.

adolescent [ædəu'lɛsnt] *a*, *n* adolescente (*m/f*).

adopt [ə'dɔpt] *vt* adottare.

adopted [ə'dɔptɪd] *a* adottivo(a).

adoption [ə'dɔpʃən] *n* adozione *f*.

adore [ə'dɔ:*] *vt* adorare.

adoringly [ə'dɔ:rɪŋlɪ] *ad* con adorazione.

adorn [ə'dɔ:n] *vt* ornare.

adornment [ə'dɔ:nmənt] *n* ornamento.

ADP *n abbr see* **automatic data processing**.

adrenalin [ə'drɛnəlɪn] *n* adrenalina; **it gets the** ~ **going** ti dà una carica.

Adriatic (Sea) [eɪdrɪ'ætɪk-] *n* Adriatico.

adrift [ə'drɪft] *ad* alla deriva; **to come** ~ (*boat*) andare alla deriva; (*wire*, *rope etc*) essersi staccato(a) *or* sciolto(a).

adroit [ə'drɔɪt] *a* abile, destro(a).

ADT *abbr* (*US*: = *Atlantic Daylight Time*) ora legale di New York.

adult ['ædʌlt] *n* adulto/a.

adult education *n* scuola per adulti.

adulterate [ə'dʌltəreɪt] *vt* adulterare.

adultery [ə'dʌltərɪ] *n* adulterio.

adulthood ['ædʌlthud] *n* età adulta.

advance [əd'vɑ:ns] *n* avanzamento; (*money*) anticipo ♦ *vt* avanzare; (*date*, *money*) anticipare ♦ *vi* avanzare; **in** ~ in anticipo; **to make** ~**s to sb** (*gen*) fare degli approcci a qn; (*amorously*) fare delle avances a qn.

advanced [əd'vɑ:nst] *a* avanzato(a); (*SCOL*: *studies*) superiore; ~ **in years** avanti negli anni.

advancement [əd'vɑ:nsmənt] *n* avanzamento.

advance notice n preavviso.

advantage [əd'va:ntɪdʒ] n (also TENNIS) vantaggio; **to take ~ of** approfittarsi di; **it's to our ~** è nel nostro interesse, torna a nostro vantaggio.

advantageous [ædvən'teɪdʒəs] a vantaggioso(a).

advent ['ædvənt] n avvento; **A~** (REL) Avvento.

Advent calendar n calendario dell'Avvento.

adventure [əd'ventʃə*] n avventura.

adventurous [əd'ventʃərəs] a avventuroso(a).

adverb ['ædvə:b] n avverbio.

adversary ['ædvəsərɪ] n avversario/a.

adverse ['ædvə:s] a avverso(a); **in ~ circumstances** nelle avversità; **~ to** contrario(a) a.

adversity [əd'və:sɪtɪ] n avversità.

advert ['ædvə:t] n abbr (Brit) = **advertisement**.

advertise ['ædvətaɪz] vi (vt) fare pubblicità or réclame (a); fare un'inserzione (per vendere); **to ~ for** (staff) cercare tramite annuncio.

advertisement [əd'və:tɪsmənt] n (COMM) réclame f inv, pubblicità f inv; (in classified ads) inserzione f.

advertiser ['ædvətaɪzə*] n azienda che reclamizza un prodotto; (in newspaper) inserzionista m/f.

advertising ['ædvətaɪzɪŋ] n pubblicità.

advertising agency n agenzia pubblicitaria or di pubblicità.

advertising campaign n campagna pubblicitaria.

advice [əd'vaɪs] n consigli mpl; (notification) avviso; **piece of ~** consiglio; **to ask (sb) for ~** chiedere il consiglio (di qn), chiedere un consiglio (a qn); **legal ~** consulenza legale.

advice note n (Brit) avviso di spedizione.

advisable [əd'vaɪzəbl] a consigliabile.

advise [əd'vaɪz] vt consigliare; **to ~ sb of sth** informare qn di qc; **to ~ sb against sth/against doing sth** sconsigliare qc a qn/a qn di fare qc; **you will be well/ill ~d to go** fareste bene/male ad andare.

advisedly [əd'vaɪzɪdlɪ] ad (deliberately) deliberatamente.

adviser [əd'vaɪzə*] n consigliere/a; (in business) consulente m/f, consigliere/a.

advisory [əd'vaɪzərɪ] a consultivo(a); **in an ~ capacity** in veste di consulente.

advocate n ['ædvəkɪt] (upholder) sostenitore/trice ♦ vt ['ædvəkeɪt] propugnare; **to be an ~ of** essere a favore di.

advt. abbr = **advertisement**.

AEA n abbr (Brit: = Atomic Energy Authority) ente di controllo sulla ricerca e lo sviluppo dell'energia atomica.

AEC n abbr (US: = Atomic Energy Commission) ente di controllo sulla ricerca e lo sviluppo dell'energia atomica.

Aegean (Sea) [i:'dʒi:ən-] n (mare m) Egeo.

aegis ['i:dʒɪs] n: **under the ~ of** sotto gli auspici di.

aeon ['i:ən] n eternità f inv.

aerial ['ɛərɪəl] n antenna ♦ a aereo(a).

aerobatics ['ɛərəu'bætɪks] npl acrobazia aerea sg; (stunts) acrobazie fpl aeree.

aerobics [ɛə'rəubɪks] n aerobica.

aerodrome ['ɛərədrəum] n (Brit) aerodromo.

aerodynamic ['ɛərəudaɪ'næmɪk] a aerodinamico(a).

aeronautics [ɛərə'nɔ:tɪks] n aeronautica.

aeroplane ['ɛərəpleɪn] n aeroplano.

aerosol ['ɛərəsɔl] n aerosol m inv.

aerospace industry ['ɛərəuspeɪs-] n industria aerospaziale.

aesthetic [ɪs'θɛtɪk] a estetico(a).

AEU n abbr (Brit: = Amalgamated Engineering Union) sindacato dei tecnici.

afar [ə'fa:*] ad lontano; **from ~** da lontano.

AFB n abbr (US) = Air Force Base.

AFDC n abbr (US: = Aid to Families with Dependent Children) ≈ A.F. (= assegni familiari).

affable ['æfəbl] a affabile.

affair [ə'fɛə*] n affare m; (also: **love ~**) relazione f amorosa; **~s** (business) affari; **the Watergate ~** il caso Watergate.

affect [ə'fɛkt] vt toccare; (feign) fingere.

affectation [æfɛk'teɪʃən] n affettazione f.

affected [ə'fɛktɪd] a affettato(a).

affection [ə'fɛkʃən] n affezione f.

affectionate [ə'fɛkʃənɪt] a affettuoso(a).

affectionately [ə'fɛkʃənɪtlɪ] ad affettuosamente.

affidavit [æfɪ'deɪvɪt] n (LAW) affidavit m inv.

affiliated [ə'fɪlɪeɪtɪd] a affiliato(a); **~ company** filiale f.

affinity [ə'fɪnɪtɪ] n affinità f inv.

affirm [ə'fə:m] vt affermare, asserire.

affirmation [æfə'meɪʃən] n affermazione f.

affirmative [ə'fə:mətɪv] a affermativo(a) ♦ n: **in the ~** affermativamente.

affix [ə'fɪks] vt apporre; attaccare.

afflict [ə'flɪkt] vt affliggere.

affliction [ə'flɪkʃən] n afflizione f.

affluence ['æfluəns] n ricchezza.

affluent ['æfluənt] a ricco(a); **the ~ society** la società del benessere.

afford [ə'fɔ:d] vt permettersi; (provide) fornire; **I can't ~ the time** non ho veramente il tempo; **can we ~ a car?** possiamo permetterci un'automobile?

affray [ə'freɪ] n (Brit LAW) rissa.

affront [ə'frʌnt] n affronto.

affronted [ə'frʌntɪd] a insultato(a).

Afghan ['æfgæn] a, n afgano(a).

Afghanistan [æf'gænɪstɑ:n] n Afganistan m.

afield [ə'fi:ld] ad: **far ~** lontano.

AFL-CIO n abbr (= American Federation of Labor and Congress of Industrial Organizations) confederazione sindacale.

afloat [ə'fləut] a, ad a galla.

afoot [ə'fut] ad: **there is something ~** si sta preparando qualcosa.

aforementioned [ə'fɔ:mɛnʃənd] a suddetto(a).

aforesaid [ə'fɔːsɛd] a suddetto(a), predetto(a).

afraid [ə'freɪd] a impaurito(a); **to be ~ of** aver paura di; **to be ~ of doing** or **to do** aver paura di fare; **I am ~ that I'll be late** mi dispiace, ma farò tardi; **I'm ~ so!** ho paura di sì!, temo proprio di sì!; **I'm ~ not** no, mi dispiace, purtroppo no.

afresh [ə'frɛʃ] ad di nuovo.

Africa ['æfrɪkə] n Africa.

African ['æfrɪkən] a, n africano(a).

Afrikaans [æfrɪ'kɑːns] n afrikaans m.

Afrikaner [æfrɪ'kɑːnə*] n africander m inv.

Afro-American ['æfrəuə'mɛrɪkən] a afro-americano(a).

AFT n abbr (= American Federation of Teachers) sindacato degli insegnanti.

aft [ɑːft] ad a poppa, verso poppa.

after ['ɑːftə*] prep, ad dopo; **~ dinner** dopo cena; **the day ~ tomorrow** dopodomani; **what/who are you ~?** che/chi cerca?; **the police are ~ him** è ricercato dalla polizia; **~ you!** prima lei!, dopo di lei!; **~ all** dopo tutto.

aftercare ['ɑːftəkɛə*] n (Brit MED) assistenza medica post-degenza.

after-effects ['ɑːftərɪfɛkts] npl conseguenze fpl; (of illness) postumi mpl.

afterlife ['ɑːftəlaɪf] n vita dell'al di là.

aftermath ['ɑːftəmæθ] n conseguenze fpl; **in the ~ of** nel periodo dopo.

afternoon ['ɑːftə'nuːn] n pomeriggio; **good ~!** buon giorno!

afters ['ɑːftəz] n (Brit col: dessert) dessert m inv.

after-sales service [ɑːftə'seɪlz-] n servizio assistenza clienti.

after-shave (lotion) ['ɑːftəʃeɪv-] n dopobarba m inv.

aftershock ['ɑːftəʃɔk] n scossa di assestamento.

afterthought ['ɑːftəθɔːt] n: **as an ~** come aggiunta.

afterwards ['ɑːftəwədz] ad dopo.

again [ə'gɛn] ad di nuovo; **to begin/see ~** ricominciare/rivedere; **he opened it ~** l'ha aperto di nuovo, l'ha riaperto; **not ... ~** non ... più; **~ and ~** ripetutamente; **now and ~** di tanto in tanto, a volte.

against [ə'gɛnst] prep contro; **~ a blue background** su uno sfondo azzurro; **leaning ~ the desk** appoggiato alla scrivania; **(as) ~** (Brit) in confronto a, contro.

age [eɪdʒ] n età f inv ♦ vt, vi invecchiare; **what ~ is he?** quanti anni ha?; **he is 20 years of ~** ha 20 anni; **under ~** minorenne; **to come of ~** diventare maggiorenne; **it's been ~s since ...** sono secoli che ....

aged ['eɪdʒd] a: **~ 10** di 10 anni; **the ~** ['eɪdʒɪd] npl (elderly) gli anziani.

age group n generazione f; **the 40 to 50 ~** le persone fra i 40 e i 50 anni.

ageless ['eɪdʒlɪs] a senza età.

age limit n limite m d'età.

agency ['eɪdʒənsɪ] n agenzia; **through** or **by**

the ~ of grazie a.

agenda [ə'dʒɛndə] n ordine m del giorno; **on the ~** all'ordine del giorno.

agent ['eɪdʒənt] n agente m.

aggravate ['ægrəveɪt] vt aggravare, peggiorare; (annoy) esasperare.

aggravation [ægrə'veɪʃən] n peggioramento; esasperazione f.

aggregate ['ægrɪgeɪt] n aggregato; **on ~** (SPORT) con punteggio complessivo.

aggression [ə'grɛʃən] n aggressione f.

aggressive [ə'grɛsɪv] a aggressivo(a).

aggressiveness [ə'grɛsɪvnɪs] n aggressività.

aggrieved [ə'griːvd] a addolorato(a).

aghast [ə'gɑːst] a sbigottito(a).

agile ['ædʒaɪl] a agile.

agitate ['ædʒɪteɪt] vt turbare; agitare ♦ vi: **to ~ for** agitarsi per.

agitator ['ædʒɪteɪtə*] n agitatore/trice.

AGM n abbr see **annual general meeting**.

agnostic [æg'nɔstɪk] a, n agnostico(a).

ago [ə'gəu] ad: **2 days ~** 2 giorni fa; **not long ~** poco tempo fa; **as long ~ as 1960** già nel 1960; **how long ~?** quanto tempo fa?

agog [ə'gɔg] a: **(all) ~ (for)** ansioso(a) (di), impaziente (di).

agonize ['ægənaɪz] vi: **to ~ (over)** angosciarsi (per).

agonizing ['ægənaɪzɪŋ] a straziante.

agony ['ægənɪ] n agonia; **I was in ~** avevo dei dolori atroci.

agony column n posta del cuore.

agree [ə'griː] vt (price) pattuire ♦ vi: **to ~ (with)** essere d'accordo (con); (LING) concordare (con); **to ~ to sth/to do sth** accettare qc/di fare qc; **to ~ that** (admit) ammettere che; **to ~ on sth** accordarsi su qc; **it was ~d that ...** è stato deciso (di comune accordo) che ...; **garlic doesn't ~ with me** l'aglio non mi va.

agreeable [ə'griːəbl] a gradevole; (willing) disposto(a); **are you ~ to this?** è d'accordo con questo?

agreed [ə'griːd] a (time, place) stabilito(a); **to be ~** essere d'accordo.

agreement [ə'griːmənt] n accordo; **in ~** d'accordo; **by mutual ~** di comune accordo.

agricultural [ægrɪ'kʌltʃərəl] a agricolo(a).

agriculture ['ægrɪkʌltʃə*] n agricoltura.

aground [ə'graund] ad: **to run ~** arenarsi.

ahead [ə'hɛd] ad avanti; davanti; **~ of** davanti a; (fig: schedule etc) in anticipo su; **~ of time** in anticipo; **go ~!** avanti!; **go right** or **straight ~** tiri diritto; **they were (right) ~ of us** erano (proprio) davanti a noi.

AI n abbr = **Amnesty International**; (COMPUT) see **artificial intelligence**.

AIB n abbr (Brit: = Accident Investigation Bureau) ufficio d'inchiesta per incidenti aerei e simili.

AID n abbr = artificial insemination by donor; (US: = Agency for International Development) A.I.D. f.

aid [eɪd] n aiuto ♦ vt aiutare; **with the ~ of**

con l'aiuto di; **in** ~ **of** a favore di; **to** ~ **and abet** (*LAW*) essere complice di.

aide [eɪd] *n* (*person*) aiutante *m*.

aide-de-camp (ADC) ['eɪddə'kɒŋ] *n* (*MIL*) aiutante *m* di campo.

AIDS [eɪdz] *n abbr* (= *acquired immune deficiency syndrome*) A.I.D.S. *f*.

AIH *n abbr* = *artificial insemination by husband*.

ailing ['eɪlɪŋ] *a* sofferente; (*fig: economy, industry etc*) in difficoltà.

ailment ['eɪlmənt] *n* indisposizione *f*.

aim [eɪm] *vt*: **to** ~ **sth at** (*gun*) mirare qc a, puntare qc a; (*camera, remark*) rivolgere qc a; (*missile*) lanciare qc contro; (*blow etc*) tirare qc a ♦ *vi* (*also*: **to take** ~) prendere la mira ♦ *n* mira; **to** ~ **at** mirare; **to** ~ **to do** aver l'intenzione di fare.

aimless ['eɪmlɪs] *a*, **aimlessly** ['eɪmlɪslɪ] *ad* senza scopo.

ain't [eɪnt] (*col*) = **am not; aren't; isn't**.

air [ɛə*] *n* aria ♦ *vt* (*room, bed*) arieggiare; (*clothes*) far prendere aria a; (*idea, grievance*) esprimere pubblicamente, manifestare; (*views*) far conoscere ♦ *cpd* (*currents*) d'aria; (*attack*) aereo(a); **by** ~ (*travel*) in aereo; **to be on the** ~ (*RADIO, TV: station*) trasmettere; (: *programme*) essere in onda.

air base *n* base *f* aerea.

airbed ['ɛəbɛd] *n* (*Brit*) materassino.

airborne ['ɛəbɔːn] *a* (*plane*) in volo; (*troops*) aerotrasportato(a); **as soon as the plane was** ~ appena l'aereo ebbe decollato.

air cargo *n* carico trasportato per via aerea.

air-conditioned ['ɛəkən'dɪʃənd] *a* con *or* ad aria condizionata.

air conditioning *n* condizionamento d'aria.

air-cooled ['ɛəkuːld] *a* raffreddato(a) ad aria.

aircraft ['ɛəkrɑːft] *n* (*pl inv*) apparecchio.

aircraft carrier *n* portaerei *f inv*.

air cushion *n* cuscino gonfiabile; (*TECH*) cuscino d'aria.

airfield ['ɛəfiːld] *n* campo d'aviazione.

Air Force *n* aviazione *f* militare.

air freight *n* spedizione *f* di merci per via aerea; (*goods*) carico spedito per via aerea.

airgun ['ɛəgʌn] *n* fucile *m* ad aria compressa.

air hostess *n* hostess *f inv*.

airily ['ɛərɪlɪ] *ad* con disinvoltura.

airing ['ɛərɪŋ] *n*: **to give an** ~ **to** (*linen*) far prendere aria a; (*room*) arieggiare; (*fig: ideas etc*) ventilare.

air letter *n* (*Brit*) aerogramma *m*.

airlift ['ɛəlɪft] *n* ponte *m* aereo.

airline ['ɛəlaɪn] *n* linea aerea.

airliner ['ɛəlaɪnə*] *n* aereo di linea.

airlock ['ɛəlɔk] *n* cassa d'aria.

air mail *n* posta aerea; **by** ~ per via *or* posta aerea.

air mattress *n* materassino gonfiabile.

airplane ['ɛəpleɪn] *n* (*US*) aeroplano.

airport ['ɛəpɔːt] *n* aeroporto.

air raid *n* incursione *f* aerea.

airsick ['ɛəsɪk] *a*: **to be** ~ soffrire di mal

d'aereo.

airspace ['ɛəspeɪs] *n* spazio aereo.

airstrip ['ɛəstrɪp] *n* pista d'atterraggio.

air terminal *n* air-terminal *m inv*.

airtight ['ɛətaɪt] *a* ermetico(a).

air traffic control *n* controllo del traffico aereo.

air traffic controller *n* controllore *m* del traffico aereo.

air waybill *n* (*COMM*) bolletta di trasporto aereo.

airy ['ɛərɪ] *a* arioso(a); (*manners*) noncurante.

aisle [aɪl] *n* (*of church*) navata laterale; navata centrale; (*of plane*) corridoio.

ajar [ə'dʒɑː*] *a* socchiuso(a).

AK *abbr* (*US POST*) = *Alaska*.

aka *abbr* (= *also known as*) alias.

akin [ə'kɪn] *prep* simile a.

AL *abbr* (*US POST*) = *Alabama*.

ALA *n abbr* = *American Library Association*.

à la carte [ɑːlɑː'kɑːt] *ad* alla carta.

alacrity [ə'lækrɪtɪ] *n*: **with** ~ con prontezza.

alarm [ə'lɑːm] *n* allarme *m* ♦ *vt* allarmare.

alarm clock *n* sveglia.

alarming [ə'lɑːmɪŋ] *a* allarmante, preoccupante.

alarmist [ə'lɑːmɪst] *n* allarmista *m/f*.

alas [ə'læs] *excl* ohimè!, ahimè!

Alaska [ə'læskə] *n* Alasca.

Albania [æl'beɪnɪə] *n* Albania.

Albanian [æl'beɪnɪən] *a* albanese ♦ *n* albanese *m/f*; (*LING*) albanese *m*.

albeit [ɔːl'biːɪt] *cj* sebbene + *sub*, benché + *sub*.

album ['ælbəm] *n* album *m inv*; (*L.P.*) 33 giri *m inv*, L.P. *m inv*.

albumen ['ælbjumɪn] *n* albume *m*.

alchemy ['ælkɪmɪ] *n* alchimia.

alcohol ['ælkəhɒl] *n* alcool *m*.

alcoholic [ælkə'hɒlɪk] *a* alcolico(a) ♦ *n* alcolizzato/a.

alcoholism ['ælkəhɒlɪzəm] *n* alcolismo.

alcove ['ælkəuv] *n* alcova.

Ald. *abbr* = **alderman**.

alderman ['ɔːldəmən] *n* consigliere *m* comunale.

ale [eɪl] *n* birra.

alert [ə'lɜːt] *a* a vivo(a); (*watchful*) vigile ♦ *n* allarme *m* ♦ *vt*: **to** ~ **sb (to sth)** avvisare qn (di qc), avvertire qn (di qc); **to** ~ **sb to the dangers of sth** mettere qn in guardia contro qc; **on the** ~ all'erta.

Aleutian Islands [ə'luːʃən-] *npl* isole *fpl* Aleutine.

Alexandria [ælɪg'zændrɪə] *n* Alessandria (d'Egitto).

alfresco [æl'frɛskəu] *a, ad* all'aperto.

algebra ['ældʒɪbrə] *n* algebra.

Algeria [æl'dʒɪərɪə] *n* Algeria.

Algerian [æl'dʒɪərɪən] *a, n* algerino(a).

Algiers [æl'dʒɪəz] *n* Algeri *f*.

algorithm ['ælgərɪðəm] *n* algoritmo.

alias ['eɪlɪəs] *ad* alias ♦ *n* pseudonimo, falso nome *m*.

alibi ['ælıbaı] *n* alibi *m inv.*

alien ['eılıən] *n* straniero/a ♦ *a*: ~ **(to)** estraneo(a) (a).

alienate ['eılıəneıt] *vt* alienare.

alienation [eılıə'neıʃən] *n* alienazione *f*.

alight [ə'laıt] *a* acceso(a) ♦ *vi* scendere; *(bird)* posarsi.

align [ə'laın] *vt* allineare.

alignment [ə'laınmənt] *n* allineamento; **out of** ~ **(with)** non allineato (con).

alike [ə'laık] *a* simile ♦ *ad* allo stesso modo; **to look** ~ assomigliarsi; **winter and summer** ~ sia d'estate che d'inverno.

alimony ['ælımənı] *n (payment)* alimenti *mpl.*

alive [ə'laıv] *a* vivo(a); *(active)* attivo(a); ~ **with** pieno(a) di; ~ **to** conscio(a) di.

alkali ['ælkəlaı] *n* alcali *m inv.*

all [ɔ:l] *a* tutto(a), tutti(e) *pl* ♦ *pronoun* tutto *m*; *(pl)* tutti(e) ♦ *ad* tutto; ~ **the time/his life** tutto il tempo/tutta la sua vita; ~ **five** tutti e cinque; ~ **five girls** tutt'e cinque le ragazze; ~ **of them** tutti(e); ~ **of it** tutto; ~ **of us went** ci siamo andati tutti; ~ **day** tutto il giorno; **is that** ~**?** non c'è altro?; *(in shop)* basta così?; **for** ~ **their efforts** nonostante tutti i loro sforzi; **it's not as hard** *etc* **as** ~ **that** non è mica così duro *etc*; **at** ~ : **not at** ~ *(in answer to question)* per niente, (niente) affatto; *(in answer to thanks)* prego!, s'immagini!, si figuri!; **I'm not at** ~ **tired** non sono affatto *or* per niente stanco; **anything at** ~ **will do** andrà bene qualsiasi cosa; ~ **but** quasi; **to be/feel** ~ **in** *(Brit col)* essere/sentirsi sfinito *or* distrutto; ~ **in** ~ tutto sommato; ~ **out** *ad*: **to go** ~ **out** mettercela tutta.

allay [ə'leı] *vt (fears)* dissipare.

all clear *n (MIL)* cessato allarme *m inv*; *(fig)* okay *m.*

allegation [ælı'geıʃən] *n* asserzione *f.*

allege [ə'lɛdʒ] *vt* asserire; **he is** ~**d to have said ...** avrebbe detto che ....

alleged [ə'lɛdʒd] *a* presunto(a).

allegedly [ə'lɛdʒıdlı] *ad* secondo quanto si asserisce.

allegiance [ə'li:dʒəns] *n* fedeltà.

allegory ['ælıgərı] *n* allegoria.

all-embracing ['ɔ:lım'breısıŋ] *a* universale.

allergic [ə'lɔ:dʒık] *a*: ~ **to** allergico(a) a.

allergy ['ælədʒı] *n* allergia.

alleviate [ə'li:vıeıt] *vt* alleviare.

alley ['ælı] *n* vicolo; *(in garden)* vialetto.

alliance [ə'laıəns] *n* alleanza.

allied ['ælaıd] *a* alleato(a).

alligator ['ælıgeıtə*] *n* alligatore *m.*

all-important ['ɔ:lım'pɔ:tənt] *a* importantissimo(a).

all-in ['ɔ:lın] *a (Brit: also ad: charge)* tutto compreso.

all-in wrestling *n (Brit)* lotta americana.

alliteration [əlıtə'reıʃən] *n* allitterazione *f.*

all-night ['ɔ:l'naıt] *a* aperto(a) *(or* che dura) tutta la notte.

allocate ['æləkeıt] *vt (share out)* distribuire; *(duties, sum, time)*: **to** ~ **sth to** assegnare qc a; **to** ~ **sth for** stanziare qc per.

allocation [æləu'keıʃən] *n*: ~ **(of money)** stanziamento.

allot [ə'lɔt] *vt (share out)* spartire; **to** ~ **sth to** *(time)* dare qc a; *(duties)* assegnare qc a; **in the** ~**ted time** nel tempo fissato *or* prestabilito.

allotment [ə'lɔtmənt] *n (share)* spartizione *f*; *(garden)* lotto di terra.

all-out ['ɔ:laut] *a (effort etc)* totale ♦ *ad*: **to go all out for** mettercela tutta per.

allow [ə'lau] *vt (practice, behaviour)* permettere; *(sum to spend etc)* accordare; *(sum, time estimated)* dare; *(concede)*: **to** ~ **that** ammettere che; **to** ~ **sb to do** permettere a qn di fare; **he is** ~**ed to (do it)** lo può fare; **smoking is not** ~**ed** è vietato fumare, non è permesso fumare; **we must** ~ **3 days for the journey** dobbiamo calcolare 3 giorni per il viaggio.

allow for *vt fus* tener conto di.

allowance [ə'lauəns] *n (money received)* assegno; *(for travelling, accommodation)* indennità *f inv*; *(TAX)* detrazione *f* di imposta; **to make** ~**(s) for** tener conto di; *(person)* scusare.

alloy ['ælɔı] *n* lega.

all right *ad (feel, work)* bene; *(as answer)* va bene.

all-round ['ɔ:l'raund] *a* completo(a).

all-rounder [ɔ:l'raundə*] *n (Brit)*: **to be a good** ~ essere bravo(a) in tutto.

allspice ['ɔ:lspaıs] *n* pepe *m* della Giamaica.

all-time ['ɔ:l'taım] *a (record)* assoluto(a).

allude [ə'lu:d] *vi*: **to** ~ **to** alludere a.

alluring [ə'ljuərıŋ] *a* seducente.

allusion [ə'lu:ʒən] *n* allusione *f.*

alluvium [ə'lu:vıəm] *n* materiale *m* alluvionale.

ally ['ælaı] *n* alleato ♦ *vt* [ə'laı]: **to** ~ **o.s. with** allearsi con.

almighty [ɔ:l'maıtı] *a* onnipotente.

almond ['ɑ:mənd] *n* mandorla.

almost ['ɔ:lməust] *ad* quasi; **he** ~ **fell** per poco non è caduto.

alms [ɑ:mz] *n* elemosina.

aloft [ə'lɔft] *ad* in alto; *(NAUT)* sull'alberatura.

alone [ə'ləun] *a*, *ad* solo(a); **to leave sb** ~ lasciare qn in pace; **to leave sth** ~ lasciare stare qc; **let** ~ **...** figuriamoci poi ..., tanto meno ....

along [ə'lɔŋ] *prep* lungo ♦ *ad*: **is he coming** ~**?** viene con noi?; **he was hopping/limping** ~ veniva saltellando/zoppicando; ~ **with** insieme con.

alongside [ə'lɔŋ'saıd] *prep* accanto a; lungo ♦ *ad* accanto; *(NAUT)* sottobordo; **we brought our boat** ~ *(of a pier/shore etc)* abbiamo accostato la barca (al molo/alla riva *etc*).

aloof [ə'lu:f] *a* distaccato(a) ♦ *ad* a distanza, in disparte; **to stand** ~ tenersi a distanza *or* in disparte.

aloofness [əˈluːfnɪs] n distacco, riserbo.
aloud [əˈlaud] ad ad alta voce.
alphabet [ˈælfəbɛt] n alfabeto.
alphabetical [ælfəˈbɛtɪkəl] a alfabetico(a); **in ~ order** in ordine alfabetico.
alphanumeric [ælfənjuːˈmɛrɪk] a alfanumerico(a).
alpine [ˈælpaɪn] a alpino(a); **~ hut** rifugio alpino; **~ pasture** pascolo alpestre; **~ skiing** sci alpino.
Alps [ælps] npl: **the ~** le Alpi.
already [ɔːlˈrɛdɪ] ad già.
alright [ˈɔːlˈraɪt] ad (Brit) = **all right**.
Alsatian [ælˈseɪʃən] n (Brit: dog) pastore m tedesco, (cane m) lupo.
also [ˈɔːlsəu] ad anche.
altar [ˈɔltə*] n altare m.
alter [ˈɔltə*] vt, vi alterare.
alteration [ɔltəˈreɪʃən] n modificazione f, alterazione f; **~s** (SEWING, ARCHIT) modifiche fpl; **timetable subject to ~** orario soggetto a variazioni.
alternate a [ɔlˈtəːnɪt] alterno(a) ♦ vi [ˈɔltəːneɪt] alternare; **on ~ days** ogni due giorni.
alternately [ɔlˈtəːnɪtlɪ] ad alternatamente.
alternating current [ˈɔltəneɪtɪŋ-] n corrente f alternata.
alternative [ɔlˈtəːnətɪv] a (solutions) alternativo(a); (solution) altro(a) ♦ n (choice) alternativa; (other possibility) altra possibilità.
alternatively [ɔlˈtəːnətɪvlɪ] ad altrimenti, come alternativa.
alternator [ˈɔltəːneɪtə*] n (AUT) alternatore m.
although [ɔːlˈðəu] cj benché + sub, sebbene + sub.
altitude [ˈæltɪtjuːd] n altitudine f.
alto [ˈæltəu] n contralto.
altogether [ɔːltəˈgɛðə*] ad del tutto, completamente; (on the whole) tutto considerato; (in all) in tutto; **how much is that ~?** quant'è in tutto?
altruistic [æltruˈɪstɪk] a altruistico(a).
aluminium [æljuˈmɪnɪəm], (US) **aluminum** [əˈluːmɪnəm] n alluminio.
always [ˈɔːlweɪz] ad sempre.
AM abbr (= amplitude modulation) AM.
am [æm] vb see **be**.
a.m. ad abbr (= ante meridiem) della mattina.
AMA n abbr = American Medical Assocation.
amalgam [əˈmælgəm] n amalgama m.
amalgamate [əˈmælgəmeɪt] vt amalgamare ♦ vi amalgamarsi.
amalgamation [əmælgəˈmeɪʃən] n amalgamazione f; (COMM) fusione f.
amass [əˈmæs] vt ammassare.
amateur [ˈæmətə*] n dilettante m/f ♦ a (SPORT) dilettante; **~ dramatics** n filodrammatica.
amateurish [ˈæmətərɪʃ] a (pej) da dilettante.
amaze [əˈmeɪz] vt stupire; **to be ~d (at)** essere sbalordito(a) (da).

amazement [əˈmeɪzmənt] n stupore m.
amazing [əˈmeɪzɪŋ] a sorprendente, sbalorditivo(a); (bargain, offer) sensazionale.
amazingly [əˈmeɪzɪŋlɪ] ad incredibilmente, sbalorditivamente.
Amazon [ˈæməzən] n (MYTHOLOGY) Amazzone f; (river): **the ~** il Rio delle Amazzoni ♦ cpd (basin, jungle) amazzonico(a).
Amazonian [æməˈzəunɪən] a amazzonico(a).
ambassador [æmˈbæsədə*] n ambasciatore/trice.
amber [ˈæmbə*] n ambra; **at ~** (Brit AUT) giallo.
ambidextrous [æmbɪˈdɛkstrəs] a ambidestro(a).
ambience [ˈæmbɪəns] n ambiente m.
ambiguity [æmbɪˈgjuɪtɪ] n ambiguità f inv.
ambiguous [æmˈbɪgjuəs] a ambiguo(a).
ambition [æmˈbɪʃən] n ambizione f; **to achieve one's ~** realizzare le proprie aspirazioni or ambizioni.
ambitious [æmˈbɪʃəs] a ambizioso(a).
ambivalent [æmˈbɪvələnt] a ambivalente.
amble [ˈæmbl] vi (gen: **to ~ along**) camminare tranquillamente.
ambulance [ˈæmbjuləns] n ambulanza.
ambush [ˈæmbuʃ] n imboscata ♦ vt fare un'imboscata a.
ameba [əˈmiːbə] n (US) = **amoeba**.
ameliorate [əˈmiːlɪəreɪt] vt migliorare.
amen [ɑːˈmɛn] excl così sia, amen.
amenable [əˈmiːnəbl] a: **~ to** (advice etc) ben disposto(a) a.
amend [əˈmɛnd] vt (law) emendare; (text) correggere ♦ vi emendarsi; **to make ~s** fare ammenda.
amendment [əˈmɛndmənt] n emendamento; correzione f.
amenities [əˈmiːnɪtɪz] npl attrezzature fpl ricreative e culturali.
amenity [əˈmiːnɪtɪ] n amenità f inv.
America [əˈmɛrɪkə] n America.
American [əˈmɛrɪkən] a, n americano(a).
americanize [əˈmɛrɪkənaɪz] vt americanizzare.
amethyst [ˈæmɪθɪst] n ametista.
Amex [ˈæmɛks] n abbr = American Stock Exchange.
amiable [ˈeɪmɪəbl] a amabile, gentile.
amicable [ˈæmɪkəbl] a amichevole.
amid(st) [əˈmɪd(st)] prep fra, tra, in mezzo a.
amiss [əˈmɪs] a, ad: **there's something ~** c'è qualcosa che non va bene; **don't take it ~** non avertene a male.
ammo [ˈæməu] n abbr (col) = **ammunition**.
ammonia [əˈməunɪə] n ammoniaca.
ammunition [æmjuˈnɪʃən] n munizioni fpl; (fig) arma.
ammunition dump n deposito di munizioni.
amnesia [æmˈniːzɪə] n amnesia.
amnesty [ˈæmnɪstɪ] n amnistia; **to grant an ~ to** concedere l'amnistia a, amnistiare.
amoeba, (US) **ameba** [əˈmiːbə] n ameba.
amok [əˈmɔk] ad: **to run ~** diventare pazzo(a)

furioso(a).

among(st) [ə'mʌŋ(st)] *prep* fra, tra, in mezzo a.

amoral [eɪ'mɒrəl] *a* amorale.

amorous ['æmərəs] *a* amoroso(a).

amorphous [ə'mɔ:fəs] *a* amorfo(a).

amortization [əmɔ:taɪ'zeɪʃən] *n* (*COMM*) ammortamento.

amount [ə'maunt] *n* (*sum of money*) somma; (*of bill etc*) importo; (*quantity*) quantità *f inv* ♦ *vi*: to ~ to (*total*) ammontare a; (*be same as*) essere come; this ~s to a refusal questo equivale a un rifiuto.

amp(ère) ['æmp(εə*)] *n* ampere *m inv*; a 13 ~ plug una spina con fusibile da 13 ampere.

ampersand ['æmpəsænd] *n* e *f* commerciale.

amphibian [æm'fɪbɪən] *n* anfibio.

amphibious [æm'fɪbɪəs] *a* anfibio(a).

amphitheatre, (*US*) **amphitheater** ['æmfɪθɪətə*] *n* anfiteatro.

ample ['æmpl] *a* ampio(a); spazioso(a); (*enough*): this is ~ questo è più che sufficiente; to have ~ time/room avere assai tempo/posto.

amplifier ['æmplɪfaɪə*] *n* amplificatore *m*.

amplify ['æmplɪfaɪ] *vt* amplificare.

amply ['æmplɪ] *ad* ampiamente.

ampoule, (*US*) **ampule** ['æmpu:l] *n* (*MED*) fiala.

amputate ['æmpjuteɪt] *vt* amputare.

Amsterdam [æmstə'dæm] *n* Amsterdam *f*.

amt *abbr* = amount.

amuck [ə'mʌk] *ad* = amok.

amuse [ə'mju:z] *vt* divertire; to ~ o.s. with sth/by doing sth divertirsi con qc/a fare qc; to be ~d at essere divertito da; he was not ~d non l'ha trovato divertente.

amusement [ə'mju:zmənt] *n* divertimento; much to my ~ con mio grande spasso.

amusement arcade *n* sala giochi (*solo con macchinette a gettoni*).

amusing [ə'mju:zɪŋ] *a* divertente.

an [æn, ən, n] *indefinite article see* a.

ANA *n abbr* = *American Newspaper Association; American Nurses Association.*

anachronism [ə'nækrənɪzəm] *n* anacronismo.

anaemia [ə'ni:mɪə] *n* anemia.

anaemic [ə'ni:mɪk] *a* anemico(a).

anaesthetic [ænɪs'θetɪk] *a* anestetico(a) ♦ *n* anestetico; local/general ~ anestesia locale/totale; under the ~ sotto anestesia.

anaesthetist [æ'ni:sθɪtɪst] *n* anestesista *m/f*.

anagram ['ænəgræm] *n* anagramma *m*.

analgesic [ænæl'dʒi:sɪk] *a* analgesico(a) ♦ *n* analgesico.

analog(ue) ['ænəlɒg] *a* (*watch, computer*) analogico(a).

analogy [ə'nælədʒɪ] *n* analogia; to draw an ~ between fare un'analogia tra.

analyse ['ænəlaɪz] *vt* (*Brit*) analizzare.

analysis, *pl* **analyses** [ə'næləsɪs, -si:z] *n* analisi *f inv*; in the last ~ in ultima analisi.

analyst ['ænəlɪst] *n* (*political* ~ *etc*) analista *m/f*; (*US*) (psic)analista *m/f*.

analytic(al) [ænə'lɪtɪk(l)] *a* analitico(a).

analyze ['ænəlaɪz] *vt* (*US*) = analyse.

anarchist ['ænəkɪst] *a, n* anarchico(a).

anarchy ['ænəkɪ] *n* anarchia.

anathema [ə'næθɪmə] *n*: it is ~ to him non ne vuol neanche sentir parlare.

anatomical [ænə'tɒmɪkl] *a* anatomico(a).

anatomy [ə'nætəmɪ] *n* anatomia.

ANC *n abbr* = *African National Congress.*

ancestor ['ænsɪstə*] *n* antenato/a.

ancestral [æn'sɛstrəl] *a* avito(a).

ancestry ['ænsɪstrɪ] *n* antenati *mpl*; ascendenza.

anchor ['æŋkə*] *n* ancora ♦ *vi* (*also*: to drop ~) gettare l'ancora ♦ *vt* ancorare; to weigh ~ salpare *or* levare l'ancora.

anchorage ['æŋkərɪdʒ] *n* ancoraggio.

anchovy ['æntʃəvɪ] *n* acciuga.

ancient ['eɪnʃənt] *a* antico(a); (*fig*) anziano(a); ~ monument monumento storico.

ancillary [æn'sɪlərɪ] *a* ausiliario(a).

and [ænd] *cj* e (*often* ed *before vowel*); ~ so on e così via; try ~ do it prova a farlo; come ~ sit here vieni a sedere qui; better ~ better sempre meglio; more ~ more sempre di più.

Andes ['ændi:z] *npl*: the ~ le Ande.

Andorra [æn'dɔ:rə] *n* Andorra.

anecdote ['ænɪkdəut] *n* aneddoto.

anemia [ə'ni:mɪə] *etc* = **anaemia** *etc*.

anemone [ə'nɛmənɪ] *n* (*BOT*) anemone *m*; (*sea* ~) anemone *m* di mare, attinia.

anesthetic [ænɪs'θetɪk] *etc* = **anaesthetic** *etc*.

anew [ə'nju:] *ad* di nuovo.

angel ['eɪndʒəl] *n* angelo.

anger ['æŋgə*] *n* rabbia ♦ *vt* arrabbiare.

angina [æn'dʒaɪnə] *n* angina pectoris.

angle ['æŋgl] *n* angolo ♦ *vi*: to ~ for (*fig*) cercare di avere; from their ~ dal loro punto di vista.

angler ['æŋglə*] *n* pescatore *m* con la lenza.

Anglican ['æŋglɪkən] *a, n* anglicano(a).

anglicize ['æŋglɪsaɪz] *vt* anglicizzare.

angling ['æŋglɪŋ] *n* pesca con la lenza.

Anglo- ['æŋgləu] *prefix* anglo...; ~Italian *a, n* italobritannico(a).

Anglo-Saxon ['æŋgləu'sæksən] *a, n* anglosassone (*m/f*).

Angola [æŋ'gəulə] *n* Angola.

Angolan [æŋ'gəulən] *a, n* angolano(a).

angrily ['æŋgrɪlɪ] *ad* con rabbia.

angry ['æŋgrɪ] *a* arrabbiato(a), furioso(a); to be ~ with sb/at sth essere in collera con qn/per qc; to get ~ arrabbiarsi; to make sb ~ fare arrabbiare qn.

anguish ['æŋgwɪʃ] *n* angoscia.

angular ['æŋgjulə*] *a* angolare.

animal ['ænɪməl] *a, n* animale (*m*).

animal spirits *npl* vivacità.

animate *vt* ['ænɪmeɪt] animare ♦ *a* ['ænɪmɪt] animato(a).

animated ['ænɪmeɪtɪd] *a* animato(a).

animosity [ænɪ'mɒsɪtɪ] *n* animosità.

aniseed ['ænɪsi:d] *n* semi *mpl* di anice.
Ankara ['æŋkərə] *n* Ankara.
ankle ['æŋkl] *n* caviglia.
ankle socks *npl* calzini *mpl.*
annex *n* ['ænɛks] (*also*: *Brit*: **annexe**) edificio annesso ♦ *vt* [ə'nɛks] annettere.
annexation [ænɛk'seɪʃən] *n* annessione *f.*
annihilate [ə'naɪəleɪt] *vt* annientare.
anniversary [ænɪ'vɔ:sərɪ] *n* anniversario.
anniversary dinner *n* cena commemorativa.
annotate ['ænəʊteɪt] *vt* annotare.
announce [ə'naʊns] *vt* annunciare; **he ~d that he wasn't going** ha dichiarato che non (ci) sarebbe andato.
announcement [ə'naʊnsmənt] *n* annuncio; (*letter*, *card*) partecipazione *f*; **I'd like to make an ~** ho una comunicazione da fare.
announcer [ə'naʊnsə*] *n* (*RADIO*, *TV*: *between programmes*) annunciatore/trice; (: *in a programme*) presentatore/trice.
annoy [ə'nɔɪ] *vt* dare fastidio a; **to be ~ed (at sth/with sb)** essere seccato *or* irritato (per qc/con qn); **don't get ~ed!** non irritarti!
annoyance [ə'nɔɪəns] *n* fastidio; (*cause of* ~) noia.
annoying [ə'nɔɪɪŋ] *a* irritante, seccante.
annual ['ænjʊəl] *a* annuale ♦ *n* (*BOT*) pianta annua; (*book*) annuario.
annual general meeting (AGM) *n* (*Brit*) assemblea generale.
annually ['ænjʊəlɪ] *ad* annualmente.
annual report *n* relazione *f* annuale.
annuity [ə'nju:ɪtɪ] *n* annualità *f inv*; **life ~** vitalizio.
annul [ə'nʌl] *vt* annullare; (*law*) rescindere.
annulment [ə'nʌlmənt] *n* annullamento; rescissione *f.*
annum ['ænəm] *n see* **per annum.**
Annunciation [ənʌnsɪ'eɪʃən] *n* Annunciazione *f.*
anode ['ænəʊd] *n* anodo.
anoint [ə'nɔɪnt] *vt* ungere.
anomalous [ə'nɔmələs] *a* anomalo(a).
anomaly [ə'nɔməlɪ] *n* anomalia.
anon. [ə'nɔn] *abbr* = **anonymous.**
anonymity [ænə'nɪmɪtɪ] *n* anonimato.
anonymous [ə'nɔnɪməs] *a* anonimo(a); **to remain ~** mantenere l'anonimato.
anorak ['ænəræk] *n* giacca a vento.
anorexia [ænə'rɛksɪə] *n* (*also*: ~ **nervosa**) anoressia.
another [ə'nʌðə*] *a*: ~ **book** (*one more*) un altro libro, ancora un libro; (*a different one*) un altro libro ♦ *pronoun* un altro(un'altra), ancora uno(a); ~ **drink?** ancora qualcosa da bere?; **in ~ 5 years** fra altri 5 anni; *see also* **one.**
ANSI *n abbr* (= *American National Standards Institute*) associazione per la normalizzazione.
answer ['ɑ:nsə*] *n* risposta; soluzione *f* ♦ *vi* rispondere ♦ *vt* (*reply to*) rispondere a; (*problem*) risolvere; (*prayer*) esaudire; **in ~ to your letter** in risposta alla sua lettera; **to ~**

the phone rispondere (al telefono); **to ~ the bell** rispondere al campanello; **to ~ the door** aprire la porta.
answer back *vi* ribattere.
answer for *vt fus* essere responsabile di.
answer to *vt fus* (*description*) corrispondere a.
answerable ['ɑ:nsərəbl] *a*: ~ **(to sb/for sth)** responsabile (verso qn/di qc); **I am ~ to no-one** non devo rispondere a nessuno.
answering machine ['ɑ:nsərɪŋ-] *n* segreteria (telefonica) automatica.
ant [ænt] *n* formica.
ANTA *n abbr* = *American National Theater and Academy.*
antagonism [æn'tægənɪzəm] *n* antagonismo.
antagonist [æn'tægənɪst] *n* antagonista *m/f.*
antagonistic [æntægə'nɪstɪk] *a* antagonistico(a).
antagonize [æn'tægənaɪz] *vt* provocare l'ostilità di.
Antarctic [ænt'ɑ:ktɪk] *n*: **the ~** l'Antartide *f* ♦ *a* antartico(a).
Antarctica [ænt'ɑ:ktɪkə] *n* Antartide *f.*
Antarctic Circle *n* Circolo polare antartico.
Antarctic Ocean *n* Oceano antartico.
ante ['æntɪ] *n* (*CARDS*, *fig*): **to up the ~** alzare la posta in palio.
ante... ['æntɪ] *prefix* anti..., ante..., pre....
anteater ['ænti:tə*] *n* formichiere *m.*
antecedent [æntɪ'si:dənt] *n* antecedente *m*, precedente *m.*
antechamber ['æntɪtʃeɪmbə*] *n* anticamera.
antelope ['æntɪləʊp] *n* antilope *f.*
antenatal ['æntɪ'neɪtl] *a* prenatale.
antenatal clinic *n* assistenza medica preparto.
antenna, *pl* **antennae** [æn'tɛnə, -ni:] *n* antenna.
anthem ['ænθəm] *n* antifona; **national ~** inno nazionale.
ant-hill ['ænthɪl] *n* formicaio.
anthology [æn'θɔlədʒɪ] *n* antologia.
anthropologist [ænθrə'pɔlədʒɪst] *n* antropologo/a.
anthropology [ænθrə'pɔlədʒɪ] *n* antropologia.
anti- ['æntɪ] *prefix* anti....
anti-aircraft ['æntɪ'ɛəkrɑ:ft] *a* antiaereo(a).
anti-aircraft defence *n* difesa antiaerea.
antiballistic ['æntɪbə'lɪstɪk] *a* antibalistico(a).
antibiotic ['æntɪbaɪ'ɔtɪk] *a* antibiotico(a) ♦ *n* antibiotico.
antibody ['æntɪbɔdɪ] *n* anticorpo.
anticipate [æn'tɪsɪpeɪt] *vt* prevedere; pregustare; (*wishes*, *request*) prevenire; **as ~d** come previsto; **this is worse than I ~d** è peggio di quel che immaginavo or pensavo.
anticipation [æntɪsɪ'peɪʃən] *n* anticipazione *f*; (*expectation*) aspettative *fpl*; **thanking you in ~** vi ringrazio in anticipo.
anticlimax ['æntɪ'klaɪmæks] *n*: **it was an ~** fu una completa delusione.
anticlockwise ['æntɪ'klɔkwaɪz] *a* in senso antiorario.

antics ['æntɪks] *npl* buffonerie *fpl*.
anticyclone ['æntɪ'saɪkləʊn] *n* anticiclone *m*.
antidote ['æntɪdəʊt] *n* antidoto.
antifreeze ['æntɪfriːz] *n* anticongelante *m*.
antihistamine [æntɪ'hɪstəmɪn] *n* antistaminico.
Antilles [æn'tɪliːz] *npl*: **the ~** le Antille.
antipathy [æn'tɪpəθɪ] *n* antipatia.
Antipodean [æntɪpə'diːən] *a* degli Antipodi.
Antipodes [æn'tɪpədiːz] *npl*: **the ~** gli Antipodi.
antiquarian [æntɪ'kwɛərɪən] *a*: **~ bookshop** libreria antiquaria ♦ *n* antiquario/a.
antiquated ['æntɪkweɪtɪd] *a* antiquato(a).
antique [æn'tiːk] *n* antichità *f inv* ♦ *a* antico(a).
antique dealer *n* antiquario/a.
antique shop *n* negozio d'antichità.
antiquity [æn'tɪkwɪtɪ] *n* antichità *f inv*.
anti-semitic ['æntɪsɪ'mɪtɪk] *a* antisemitico(a), antisemita.
anti-semitism ['æntɪ'sɛmɪtɪzəm] *n* antisemitismo.
antiseptic [æntɪ'sɛptɪk] *a* antisettico(a) ♦ *n* antisettico.
antisocial ['æntɪ'səʊʃəl] *a* asociale; *(against society)* antisociale.
antitank [æntɪ'tæŋk] *a* anticarro *inv*.
antithesis, *pl* **antitheses** [æn'tɪθɪsɪs, -siːz] *n* antitesi *f inv*; *(contrast)* carattere *m* antitetico.
anti-trust [æntɪ'trʌst] *a* *(COMM)*: **~ legislation** legislazione *f* antitrust *inv*.
antlers ['æntləz] *npl* palchi *mpl*.
Antwerp ['æntwəːp] *n* Anversa.
anus ['eɪnəs] *n* ano.
anvil ['ænvɪl] *n* incudine *f*.
anxiety [æŋ'zaɪətɪ] *n* ansia; *(keenness)*: **~ to do** smania di fare.
anxious ['æŋkʃəs] *a* ansioso(a), inquieto(a); *(keen)*: **~ to do/that** impaziente di fare/che + *sub*; **I'm very ~ about you** sono molto preoccupato or in pensiero per te.
anxiously ['æŋkʃəslɪ] *ad* ansiosamente, con ansia.
any ['ɛnɪ] *a* *(in negative and interrogative sentences = some)* del, dell', dello, dei, degli, della, delle; alcuno(a); qualche; nessuno(a); *(no matter which)* non importa che; *(each and every)* tutto(a), ogni; **I haven't ~ bread/books** non ho pane/libri; **have you ~ money?** hai (dei) soldi?, hai qualche soldo?; **without ~ difficulty** senza (nessuna *or* alcuna) difficoltà; **come (at) ~ time** vieni a qualsiasi ora; **at ~ moment** da un momento all'altro; **~ day now** da un giorno all'altro; **in ~ case** in ogni caso; **at ~ rate** ad ogni modo ♦ *pronoun* uno(a) qualsiasi; *(anybody)* chiunque; *(in negative and interrogative sentences)*: **I haven't ~** non ne ho; **have you got ~?** ne hai?; **can ~ of you sing?** c'è qualcuno che sa cantare? ♦ *ad* *(in negative sentences)* per niente; *(in interrogative and conditional constructions)*: **I can't hear him ~ more** non lo sento più; **are you feel-**
ing ~ better? ti senti un po' meglio?; **do you want ~ more soup?** vuoi ancora della minestra?
anybody ['ɛnɪbɔdɪ] *pronoun* qualsiasi persona; *(in interrogative sentences)* qualcuno; *(in negative sentences)*: **I don't see ~** non vedo nessuno.
anyhow ['ɛnɪhaʊ] *ad* in qualsiasi modo; *(haphazard)* come capita; **I shall go ~** ci andrò lo stesso *or* comunque.
anyone ['ɛnɪwʌn] *pronoun* = **anybody**.
anyplace ['ɛnɪpleɪs] *pronoun* *(US col)* = **anywhere**.
anything ['ɛnɪθɪŋ] *pronoun* qualsiasi cosa; *(in interrogative sentences)* qualcosa; *(in negative sentences)* non ... niente, non ... nulla; **~ else?** *(in shop)* basta (così)?; **it can cost ~ between £15 and £20** può costare qualcosa come 15 o 20 sterline.
anytime ['ɛnɪtaɪm] *ad* in qualunque momento; quando vuole.
anyway ['ɛnɪweɪ] *ad* in *or* ad ogni modo.
anywhere ['ɛnɪwɛə*] *ad* da qualsiasi parte; *(in interrogative sentences)* da qualche parte; **I don't see him ~** non lo vedo da nessuna parte; **~ in the world** dovunque nel mondo.
Anzac ['ænzæk] *n abbr* *(= Australia-New Zealand Army Corps)* A.N.Z.A.C. *m*; *(soldier)* soldato dell'A.N.Z.A.C.
apart [ə'pɑːt] *ad* *(to one side)* a parte; *(separately)* separatamente; **with one's legs ~** con le gambe divaricate; **10 miles/a long way ~** a 10 miglia di distanza/molto lontani l'uno dall'altro; **they are living ~** sono separati; **~ from** *prep* a parte, eccetto.
apartheid [ə'pɑːteɪt] *n* apartheid *f*.
apartment [ə'pɑːtmənt] *n* *(US)* appartamento; **~s** *npl* appartamento ammobiliato.
apartment building *n* *(US)* stabile *m*, caseggiato.
apathetic [æpə'θetɪk] *a* apatico(a).
apathy ['æpəθɪ] *n* apatia.
APB *n abbr* *(US: = all points bulletin: police expression)* espressione della polizia che significa "trovate e arrestate il sospetto".
ape [eɪp] *n* scimmia ♦ *vt* scimmiottare.
Apennines ['æpənaɪnz] *npl*: **the ~** gli Apennini.
aperitif [ə'perɪtiːf] *n* aperitivo.
aperture ['æpətʃjʊə*] *n* apertura.
APEX ['eɪpɛks] *n abbr* *(Brit: = Association of Professional, Executive, Clerical and Computer Staff)* associazione dei professionisti, dirigenti, impiegati ed informatici; *(AVIAT: = advance purchase excursion)* APEX *m inv*.
apex ['eɪpɛks] *n* apice *m*.
aphid ['æfɪd] *n* afide *f*.
aphrodisiac [æfrəʊ'dɪzɪæk] *a* afrodisiaco(a) ♦ *n* afrodisiaco.
API *n abbr* = *American Press Institute*.
apiece [ə'piːs] *ad* ciascuno(a).
aplomb [ə'plɔm] *n* disinvoltura.

APO n abbr (US: = Army Post Office) ufficio postale dell'esercito.

apocalypse [ə'pɔkəlɪps] n apocalisse f.

apolitical [eɪpə'lɪtɪkl] a apolitico(a).

apologetic [əpɔlə'dʒɛtɪk] a (tone, letter) di scusa; **to be very ~ about** scusarsi moltissimo di.

apologetically [əpɔlə'dʒɛtɪkəlɪ] ad per scusarsi.

apologize [ə'pɔlədʒaɪz] vi: **to ~ (for sth to sb)** scusarsi (di qc a qn), chiedere scusa (a qn per qc).

apology [ə'pɔlədʒɪ] n scuse fpl; **please accept my apologies** la prego di accettare le mie scuse.

apoplectic [æpə'plɛktɪk] a (MED) apoplettico(a); **~ with rage** (col) livido(a) per la rabbia.

apoplexy ['æpəplɛksɪ] n apoplessia.

apostle [ə'pɔsl] n apostolo.

apostrophe [ə'pɔstrəfɪ] n (sign) apostrofo.

appal [ə'pɔːl] vt atterrire; sgomentare.

Appalachian Mountains [æpə'leɪʃən-] npl: **the ~** i Monti Appalachi.

appalling [ə'pɔːlɪŋ] a spaventoso(a); **she's an ~ cook** è un disastro come cuoca.

apparatus [æpə'reɪtəs] n apparato.

apparel [ə'pærl] n (US) abbigliamento, confezioni fpl.

apparent [ə'pærənt] a evidente.

apparently [ə'pærəntlɪ] ad evidentemente, a quanto pare.

apparition [æpə'rɪʃən] n apparizione f.

appeal [ə'piːl] vi (LAW) appellarsi alla legge ♦ n (LAW) appello; (request) richiesta; (charm) attrattiva; **to ~ for** chiedere (con insistenza); **to ~ to** (subj: person) appellarsi a; (: thing) piacere a; **to ~ to sb for mercy** chiedere pietà a qn; **it doesn't ~ to me** mi dice poco; **right of ~** diritto d'appello.

appealing [ə'piːlɪŋ] a (moving) commovente; (attractive) attraente.

appear [ə'pɪə*] vi apparire; (LAW) comparire; (publication) essere pubblicato(a); (seem) sembrare; **it would ~ that** sembra che; **to ~ in Hamlet** recitare nell'Amleto; **to ~ on TV** presentarsi in televisione.

appearance [ə'pɪərəns] n apparizione f; (look, aspect) aspetto; **to put in or make an ~** fare atto di presenza; **by order of ~** (THEATRE) in ordine di apparizione; **to keep up ~s** salvare le apparenze; **to all ~s** a giudicar dalle apparenze.

appease [ə'piːz] vt calmare, appagare.

appeasement [ə'piːzmənt] n (POL) appeasement m inv.

append [ə'pɛnd] vt (COMPUT) aggiungere in coda.

appendage [ə'pɛndɪdʒ] n aggiunta.

appendicitis [əpɛndɪ'saɪtɪs] n appendicite f.

appendix, pl **appendices** [ə'pɛndɪks, -siːz] n appendice f; **to have one's ~ out** operarsi or farsi operare di appendicite.

appetite ['æpɪtaɪt] n appetito; **that walk has**

given me an ~ la passeggiata mi ha messo appetito.

appetizer ['æpɪtaɪzə*] n (food) stuzzichino; (drink) aperitivo.

appetizing ['æpɪtaɪzɪŋ] a appetitoso(a).

applaud [ə'plɔːd] vt, vi applaudire.

applause [ə'plɔːz] n applauso.

apple ['æpl] n mela; (also: ~ **tree**) melo; **the ~ of one's eye** la pupilla dei propri occhi.

apple turnover n sfogliatella alle mele.

appliance [ə'plaɪəns] n apparecchio; **electrical ~s** elettrodomestici mpl.

applicable [ə'plɪkəbl] a applicabile; **to be ~ to** essere valido per; **the law is ~ from January** la legge entrerà in vigore in gennaio.

applicant ['æplɪkənt] n candidato/a; (ADMIN: for benefit etc) chi ha fatto domanda or richiesta.

application [æplɪ'keɪʃən] n applicazione f; (for a job, a grant etc) domanda; **on ~** su richiesta.

application form n modulo di domanda.

application program n (COMPUT) programma applicativo.

applications package n (COMPUT) software m inv applicativo.

applied [ə'plaɪd] a applicato(a); **~ arts** arti fpl applicate.

apply [ə'plaɪ] vt: **to ~ (to)** (paint, ointment) dare (a); (theory, technique) applicare (a) ♦ vi: **to ~ to** (ask) rivolgersi a; (be suitable for, relevant to) riguardare, riferirsi a; **to ~ (for)** (permit, grant, job) fare domanda (per); **to ~ the brakes** frenare; **to ~ o.s. to** dedicarsi a.

appoint [ə'pɔɪnt] vt nominare.

appointee [əpɔɪn'tiː] n incaricato/a.

appointment [ə'pɔɪntmənt] n nomina; (arrangement to meet) appuntamento; **by ~** su or per appuntamento; **to make an ~ with sb** prendere un appuntamento con qn; (PRESS): **"~s (vacant)"** "offerte fpl di impiego".

apportion [ə'pɔːʃən] vt attribuire.

appraisal [ə'preɪzl] n valutazione f.

appraise [ə'preɪz] vt (value) valutare, fare una stima di; (situation etc) fare il bilancio di.

appreciable [ə'priːʃəbl] a apprezzabile.

appreciate [ə'priːʃɪeɪt] vt (like) apprezzare; (be grateful for) essere riconoscente di; (be aware of) rendersi conto di ♦ vi (COMM) aumentare; **I ~d your help** ti sono grato per l'aiuto.

appreciation [əpriːʃɪ'eɪʃən] n apprezzamento; (FINANCE) aumento del valore.

appreciative [ə'priːʃɪətɪv] a (person) sensibile; (comment) elogiativo(a).

apprehend [æprɪ'hɛnd] vt (arrest) arrestare; (understand) comprendere.

apprehension [æprɪ'hɛnʃən] n (fear) inquietudine f.

apprehensive [æprɪ'hɛnsɪv] a apprensivo(a).

apprentice [ə'prɛntɪs] *n* apprendista *m/f* ♦ *vt*:
to be ~d to lavorare come apprendista
presso.

apprenticeship [ə'prɛntɪsʃɪp] *n* apprendistato;
to serve one's ~ fare il proprio apprendistato *or* tirocinio.

appro. ['æprəu] *abbr* (*Brit COMM: col*) = approval.

approach [ə'prəutʃ] *vi* avvicinarsi ♦ *vt* (*come near*) avvicinarsi a; (*ask, apply to*) rivolgersi a; (*subject, passer-by*) avvicinare ♦ *n* approccio; accesso; (*to problem*) modo di affrontare; to ~ sb about sth rivolgersi a qn per qc.

approachable [ə'prəutʃəbl] *a* accessibile.

approach road *n* strada d'accesso.

approbation [æprə'beɪʃən] *n* approvazione *f*, benestare *m*.

appropriate *vt* [ə'prəuprieit] (*take*) appropriarsi di ♦ *a* [ə'prəupriɪt] appropriato(a);
adatto(a); it would not be ~ for me to comment non sta a me fare dei commenti.

appropriately [ə'prəupriɪtlɪ] *ad* in modo appropriato.

appropriation [əprəupri'eɪʃən] *n* stanziamento.

approval [ə'pru:vəl] *n* approvazione *f*; on ~ (*COMM*) in prova, in esame; to meet with sb's ~ soddisfare qn, essere di gradimento di qn.

approve [ə'pru:v] *vt, vi* approvare.

approve of *vt fus* approvare.

approved school *n* (*Brit: old*) riformatorio.

approvingly [ə'pru:vɪŋlɪ] *ad* in approvazione.

approx. *abbr* = approximately.

approximate *a* [ə'prɔksɪmɪt] approssimativo(a) ♦ *vt* [ə'prɔksɪmeɪt] essere un'approssimazione di, avvicinarsi a.

approximately [ə'prɔksɪmətlɪ] *ad* circa.

approximation [ə'prɔksɪ'meɪʃən] *n* approssimazione *f*.

apr *n abbr* (= *annual percentage rate*) tasso di percentuale annuo.

Apr. *abbr* (= *April*) apr.

apricot ['eɪprɪkɔt] *n* albicocca.

April ['eɪprəl] *n* aprile *m*; ~ fool! pesce d'aprile!; *for phrases see also* July.

April Fool's Day *n* il primo d'aprile.

apron ['eɪprən] *n* grembiule *m*; (*AVIAT*) area di stazionamento.

apse [æps] *n* (*ARCHIT*) abside *f*.

APT *n abbr* (*Brit*: = *advanced passenger train*) treno ad altissima velocità.

apt [æpt] *a* (*suitable*) adatto(a); (*able*) capace; (*likely*): to be ~ to do avere tendenza a fare.

Apt. *abbr* = apartment.

aptitude ['æptɪtju:d] *n* abilità *f inv*.

aptitude test *n* test *m inv* attitudinale.

aptly ['æptlɪ] *ad* appropriatamente, in modo adatto.

aqualung ['ækwəlʌŋ] *n* autorespiratore *m*.

aquarium [ə'kwɛərɪəm] *n* acquario.

Aquarius [ə'kwɛərɪəs] *n* Acquario; to be ~

essere dell'Acquario.

aquatic [ə'kwætɪk] *a* acquatico(a).

aqueduct ['ækwɪdʌkt] *n* acquedotto.

AR *abbr* (*US POST*) = *Arkansas*.

ARA *n abbr* (*Brit*) = *Associate of the Royal Academy*.

Arab ['ærəb] *a, n* arabo(a).

Arabia [ə'reɪbɪə] *n* Arabia.

Arabian [ə'reɪbɪən] *a* arabo(a).

Arabian Desert *n* Deserto arabico.

Arabian Sea *n* mare *m* Arabico.

Arabic ['ærəbɪk] *a* arabico(a) ♦ *n* arabo.

Arabic numerals *npl* numeri arabi *mpl*, numerazione *f* araba.

arable ['ærəbl] *a* arabile.

ARAM *n abbr* (*Brit*) = *Associate of the Royal Academy of Music*.

arbiter ['ɑ:bɪtə*] *n* arbitro.

arbitrary ['ɑ:bɪtrərɪ] *a* arbitrario(a).

arbitrate ['ɑ:bɪtreɪt] *vi* arbitrare.

arbitration [ɑ:bɪ'treɪʃən] *n* (*LAW*) arbitrato; (*INDUSTRY*) arbitraggio.

arbitrator ['ɑ:bɪtreɪtə*] *n* arbitro.

ARC *n abbr* (= *American Red Cross*) C.R.I. *f* (= *Croce Rossa Italiana*).

arc [ɑ:k] *n* arco.

arcade [ɑ:'keɪd] *n* portico; (*passage with shops*) galleria.

arch [ɑ:tʃ] *n* arco; (*of foot*) arco plantare ♦ *vt* inarcare ♦ *prefix*: ~(-) grande (*before n*); per eccellenza.

archaeological [ɑ:kɪə'lɔdʒɪkəl] *a* archeologico(a).

archaeologist [ɑ:kɪ'ɔlədʒɪst] *n* archeologo/a.

archaeology [ɑ:kɪ'ɔlədʒɪ] *n* archeologia.

archaic [ɑ:'keɪɪk] *a* arcaico(a).

archangel ['ɑ:keɪndʒəl] *n* arcangelo.

archbishop [ɑ:tʃ'bɪʃəp] *n* arcivescovo.

arched [ɑ:tʃt] *a* arcuato(a), ad arco.

arch-enemy ['ɑ:tʃ'ɛnɪmɪ] *n* arcinemico/a.

archeology *etc* [ɑ:kɪ'ɔlədʒɪ] = archaeology *etc*.

archer ['ɑ:tʃə*] *n* arciere *m*.

archery ['ɑ:tʃərɪ] *n* tiro all'arco.

archetypal ['ɑ:kɪtaɪpəl] *a* tipico(a).

archetype ['ɑ:kɪtaɪp] *n* archetipo.

archipelago [ɑ:kɪ'pɛlɪgəu] *n* arcipelago.

architect ['ɑ:kɪtɛkt] *n* architetto.

architectural [ɑ:kɪ'tɛktʃərəl] *a* architettonico(a).

architecture ['ɑ:kɪtɛktʃə*] *n* architettura.

archive file *n* (*COMPUT*) file *m inv* di archivio.

archives ['ɑ:kaɪvz] *npl* archivi *mpl*.

archivist ['ɑ:kɪvɪst] *n* archivista *m/f*.

archway ['ɑ:tʃweɪ] *n* arco.

ARCM *n abbr* (*Brit*) = *Associate of the Royal College of Music*.

Arctic ['ɑ:ktɪk] *a* artico(a) ♦ *n*: the ~ l'Artico.

Arctic Circle *n* Circolo polare artico.

Arctic Ocean *n* Oceano artico.

ARD *n abbr* (*US MED*) = *acute respiratory disease*.

ardent ['ɑ:dənt] *a* ardente.

ardour, (*US*) **ardor** ['ɑːdə*] *n* ardore *m*.
arduous ['ɑːdjuəs] *a* arduo(a).
are [ɑː*] *vb see* **be**.
area ['ɛərɪə] *n* (*GEOM*) area; (*zone*) zona; (: *smaller*) settore *m*; **dining** ~ zona pranzo; **the London** ~ la zona di Londra.
area code *n* (*US TEL*) prefisso.
arena [ə'riːnə] *n* arena.
aren't [ɑːnt] = **are not**.
Argentina [ɑːdʒən'tiːnə] *n* Argentina.
Argentinian [ɑːdʒən'tɪnɪən] *a, n* argentino(a).
arguable ['ɑːgjuəbl] *a* discutibile; **it is** ~ **whether** ... è una cosa discutibile se ... + *sub*.
arguably ['ɑːgjuəblɪ] *ad*: **it is** ~ ... si può sostenere che sia ....
argue ['ɑːgjuː] *vi* (*quarrel*) litigare; (*reason*) ragionare ♦ *vt* (*debate*: *case*, *matter*) dibattere; **to** ~ **that** sostenere che; **to** ~ **about sth (with sb)** litigare per *or* a proposito di qc (con qn).
argument ['ɑːgjumənt] *n* (*reasons*) argomento; (*quarrel*) lite *f*; (*debate*) discussione *f*; ~ **for/against** argomento a *or* in favore di/contro.
argumentative [ɑːgjuˈmɛntətɪv] *a* litigioso(a).
aria ['ɑːrɪə] *n* aria.
ARIBA *n abbr* (*Brit*) = *Associate of the Royal Institute of British Architects*.
arid ['ærɪd] *a* arido(a).
aridity [ə'rɪdɪtɪ] *n* aridità.
Aries ['ɛərɪz] *n* Ariete *m*; **to be** ~ essere dell'Ariete.
arise, *pt* **arose,** *pp* **arisen** [ə'raɪz, ə'rəuz, ə'rɪzn] *vi* alzarsi; (*opportunity*, *problem*) presentarsi; **to** ~ **from** risultare da; **should the need** ~ dovesse presentarsi la necessità, in caso di necessità.
aristocracy [ærɪs'tɔkrəsɪ] *n* aristocrazia.
aristocrat ['ærɪstəkræt] *n* aristocratico/a.
aristocratic [ærɪstə'krætɪk] *a* aristocratico(a).
arithmetic [ə'rɪθmətɪk] *n* aritmetica.
arithmetical [ærɪθ'mɛtɪkəl] *a* aritmetico(a).
ark [ɑːk] *n*: **Noah's A**~ l'arca di Noè.
arm [ɑːm] *n* braccio; (*MIL*: *branch*) arma ♦ *vt* armare; ~ **in** ~ a braccetto; *see also* **arms**.
armaments ['ɑːməmənts] *npl* (*weapons*) armamenti *mpl*.
armband ['ɑːmbænd] *n* bracciale *m*.
armchair ['ɑːmtʃɛə*] *n* poltrona.
armed [ɑːmd] *a* armato(a).
armed forces *npl* forze *fpl* armate.
armed robbery *n* rapina a mano armata.
Armenia [ɑːˈmiːnɪə] *n* Armenia.
Armenian [ɑːˈmiːnɪən] *a* armeno(a) ♦ *n* armeno/a; (*LING*) armeno.
armful ['ɑːmful] *n* bracciata.
armistice ['ɑːmɪstɪs] *n* armistizio.
armour, (*US*) **armor** ['ɑːmə*] *n* armatura; (*also*: ~-**plating**) corazza, blindatura; (*MIL*: *tanks*) mezzi *mpl* blindati.
armo(u)red car *n* autoblinda *f inv*.
armo(u)ry ['ɑːmərɪ] *n* arsenale *m*.
armpit ['ɑːmpɪt] *n* ascella.

armrest ['ɑːmrɛst] *n* bracciolo.
arms [ɑːmz] *npl* (*weapons*) armi *fpl*; (*HERALDRY*) stemma *m*.
arms control *n* controllo degli armamenti.
arms race *n* corsa agli armamenti.
army ['ɑːmɪ] *n* esercito.
aroma [ə'rəumə] *n* aroma.
aromatic [ærə'mætɪk] *a* aromatico(a).
arose [ə'rəuz] *pt of* **arise**.
around [ə'raund] *ad* attorno, intorno ♦ *prep* intorno a; (*fig*: *about*): ~ **£5/3 o'clock** circa 5 sterline/le 3; **is he** ~? è in giro?
arouse [ə'rauz] *vt* (*sleeper*) svegliare; (*curiosity*, *passions*) suscitare.
arrange [ə'reɪndʒ] *vt* sistemare; (*programme*) preparare ♦ *vi*: **we have** ~**d for a taxi to pick you up** la faremo venire a prendere da un taxi; **it was** ~**d that** ... è stato deciso *or* stabilito che ...; **to** ~ **to do sth** mettersi d'accordo per fare qc.
arrangement [ə'reɪndʒmənt] *n* sistemazione *f*; (*plans etc*): ~**s** progetti *mpl*, piani *mpl*; **by** ~ su richiesta; **to come to an** ~ **(with sb)** venire ad un accordo (con qn), mettersi d'accordo *or* accordarsi (con qn); **I'll make** ~**s for you to be met** darò disposizioni *or* istruzioni perché ci sia qualcuno ad incontrarla.
array [ə'reɪ] *n* fila; (*COMPUT*) array *m inv*, insiemi *mpl*.
arrears [ə'rɪəz] *npl* arretrati *mpl*; **to be in** ~ **with one's rent** essere in arretrato con l'affitto.
arrest [ə'rɛst] *vt* arrestare; (*sb's attention*) attirare ♦ *n* arresto; **under** ~ in arresto.
arresting [ə'rɛstɪŋ] *a* (*fig*) che colpisce.
arrival [ə'raɪvəl] *n* arrivo; (*person*) arrivato/a; **new** ~ nuovo venuto.
arrive [ə'raɪv] *vi* arrivare.
arrive at *vt fus* arrivare a.
arrogance ['ærəgəns] *n* arroganza.
arrogant ['ærəgənt] *a* arrogante.
arrow ['ærəu] *n* freccia.
arse [ɑːs] *n* (*Brit col!*) culo(!).
arsenal ['ɑːsɪnl] *n* arsenale *m*.
arsenic ['ɑːsnɪk] *n* arsenico.
arson ['ɑːsn] *n* incendio doloso.
art [ɑːt] *n* arte *f*; (*craft*) mestiere *m*; **work of** ~ opera d'arte; *see also* **arts**.
artefact, (*US*) **artifact** ['ɑːtɪfækt] *n* manufatto.
arterial [ɑːˈtɪərɪəl] *a* (*ANAT*) arterioso(a); (*road etc*) di grande comunicazione; ~ **roads** le (grandi *or* principali) arterie.
artery ['ɑːtərɪ] *n* arteria.
artful ['ɑːtful] *a* furbo(a).
art gallery *n* galleria d'arte.
arthritis [ɑːˈθraɪtɪs] *n* artrite *f*.
artichoke ['ɑːtɪtʃəuk] *n* carciofo; **Jerusalem** ~ topinambur *m inv*.
article ['ɑːtɪkl] *n* articolo; ~**s** *npl* (*Brit LAW*: *training*) contratto di tirocinio; ~**s of clothing** indumenti *mpl*.
articles of association *npl* (*COMM*) statuto sociale.

articulate a [ɑ:'tɪkjulɪt] (person) che si esprime forbitamente; (speech) articolato(a) ♦ vi [ɑ:'tɪkjuleɪt] articolare.

articulated lorry n (Brit) autotreno.

artifact ['ɑ:tɪfækt] n (US) = **artefact**.

artifice ['ɑ:tɪfɪs] n (cunning) abilità, destrezza; (trick) artificio.

artificial [ɑ:tɪ'fɪʃəl] a artificiale.

artificial insemination [-ɪnsɛmɪ'neɪʃən] n fecondazione f artificiale.

artificial intelligence (AI) n intelligenza artificiale (IA).

artificial respiration n respirazione f artificiale.

artillery [ɑ:'tɪlərɪ] n artiglieria.

artisan ['ɑ:tɪzæn] n artigiano/a.

artist ['ɑ:tɪst] n artista m/f.

artistic [ɑ:'tɪstɪk] a artistico(a).

artistry ['ɑ:tɪstrɪ] n arte f.

artless ['ɑ:tlɪs] a semplice, ingenuo(a).

arts [ɑ:ts] npl (SCOL) lettere fpl.

art school n scuola d'arte.

ARV n abbr (= American Revised Version) traduzione della Bibbia.

AS n abbr (US SCOL: = Associate in/of Sciences) titolo di studio ♦ abbr (US POST) = American Samoa.

as [æz, əz] cj (cause) siccome, poiché; (time: moment) come, quando; (: duration) mentre; (manner) come ♦ prep (in the capacity of) da; ~ **big** ~ tanto grande quanto; **twice** ~ **big** ~ due volte più grande che; **big** ~ **it is** grande com'è; **much** ~ **I like them**, ... per quanto mi siano simpatici, ...; ~ **the years went by** col passare degli anni; ~ **she said** come lei ha detto; **he gave it to me** ~ **a present** me lo ha regalato; ~ **if** or **though** come se + sub; ~ **for** or **to** quanto a; ~ or **so long** ~ cj finché; purché; ~ **much (~)** tanto(a) (... quanto(a)); ~ **many (~)** tanti(e) (... quanti(e)); ~ **soon** ~ cj appena; ~ **soon** ~ **possible** prima possibile; ~ **such** ad come tale; ~ **well** ad anche; ~ **well** ~ cj come pure; see also **so**, **such**.

ASA n abbr (= American Standards Association) associazione per la normalizzazione.

a.s.a.p. abbr (= as soon as possible) prima possibile.

asbestos [æz'bɛstəs] n asbesto, amianto.

ascend [ə'sɛnd] vt salire.

ascendancy [ə'sɛndənsɪ] n ascendente m.

ascendant [ə'sɛndənt] n: **to be in the** ~ essere in auge.

ascension [ə'sɛnʃən] n: **the A~** (REL) l'Ascensione f.

Ascension Island n isola dell'Ascensione.

ascent [ə'sɛnt] n salita.

ascertain [æsə'teɪn] vt accertare.

ascetic [ə'sɛtɪk] a ascetico(a).

asceticism [ə'sɛtɪsɪzəm] n ascetismo.

ASCII ['æski:] n abbr (= American Standard Code for Information Interchange) ASCII m.

ascribe [ə'skraɪb] vt: **to** ~ **sth to** attribuire qc a.

ASCU n abbr (US) = Association of State Colleges and Universities.

ASE n abbr = American Stock Exchange.

ASH [æʃ] n abbr (Brit: = Action on Smoking and Health) iniziativa contro il fumo.

ash [æʃ] n (dust) cenere f; ~ **(tree)** frassino.

ashamed [ə'ʃeɪmd] a vergognoso(a); **to be** ~ **of** vergognarsi di; **to be** ~ **(of o.s.) for having done** vergognarsi di aver fatto.

ashen ['æʃən] a (pale) livido(a).

ashore [ə'ʃɔ:*] ad a terra; **to go** ~ sbarcare.

ashtray ['æʃtreɪ] n portacenere m.

Ash Wednesday n Mercoledì m inv delle Ceneri.

Asia ['eɪʃə] n Asia.

Asia Minor n Asia minore.

Asian ['eɪʃən] a, n asiatico(a).

Asiatic [eɪsɪ'ætɪk] a asiatico(a).

aside [ə'saɪd] ad da parte ♦ n a parte m; **to take sb** ~ prendere qn da parte; ~ **from** (as well as) oltre a; (except for) a parte.

ask [ɑ:sk] vt (request) chiedere; (question) domandare; (invite) invitare; **to** ~ **about sth** informarsi su or di qc; **to** ~ **sb sth/sb to do sth** chiedere qc a qn/a qn di fare qc; **to** ~ **sb about sth** chiedere a qn di qc; **to** ~ **(sb) a question** fare una domanda (a qn); **to** ~ **sb the time** chiedere l'ora a qn; **to** ~ **sb out to dinner** invitare qn a mangiare fuori; **you should** ~ **at the information desk** dovreste rivolgervi all'ufficio informazioni.

ask after vt fus chiedere di.

ask for vt fus chiedere; **it's just** ~**ing for trouble** or **for it** è proprio (come) andarsele a cercare.

askance [ə'skɑ:ns] ad: **to look** ~ **at sb** guardare qn di traverso.

askew [ə'skju:] ad di traverso, storto.

asking price ['ɑ:skɪŋ-] n prezzo di partenza.

asleep [ə'sli:p] a addormentato(a); **to be** ~ dormire; **to fall** ~ addormentarsi.

ASLEF ['æzlɛf] n abbr (Brit: = Associated Society of Locomotive Engineers and Firemen) sindacato dei conducenti dei treni e dei pompieri.

asp [æsp] n cobra m inv egiziano.

asparagus [əs'pærəgəs] n asparagi mpl.

asparagus tips npl punte fpl d'asparagi.

ASPCA n abbr (= American Society for the Prevention of Cruelty to Animals) ≈ E.N.P.A. m (Ente Nazionale per la Protezione degli Animali).

aspect ['æspɛkt] n aspetto.

aspersions [əs'pə:ʃənz] npl: **to cast** ~ **on** diffamare.

asphalt ['æsfælt] n asfalto.

asphyxiate [æs'fɪksɪeɪt] vt asfissiare.

asphyxiation [æsfɪksɪ'eɪʃən] n asfissia.

aspiration [æspə'reɪʃən] n aspirazione f.

aspire [əs'paɪə*] vi: **to** ~ **to** aspirare a.

aspirin ['æsprɪn] n aspirina.

ass [æs] n asino; (US col!) culo(!).

assail [ə'seɪl] vt assalire.

assailant [ə'seɪlənt] n assalitore m.
assassin [ə'sæsɪn] n assassino.
assassinate [ə'sæsɪneɪt] vt assassinare.
assassination [əsæsɪ'neɪʃən] n assassinio.
assault [ə'sɔ:lt] n (MIL) assalto; (gen: attack) aggressione f; (LAW): ~ **(and battery)** minacce e vie di fatto fpl ♦ vt assaltare; aggredire; (sexually) violentare.
assemble [ə'sɛmbl] vt riunire; (TECH) montare ♦ vi riunirsi.
assembly [ə'sɛmblɪ] n (meeting) assemblea; (construction) montaggio.
assembly language n (COMPUT) linguaggio assemblativo.
assembly line n catena di montaggio.
assent [ə'sɛnt] n assenso, consenso ♦ vi assentire; **to** ~ **(to sth)** approvare (qc).
assert [ə'sɔ:t] vt asserire; (insist on) far valere; **to** ~ **o.s.** farsi valere.
assertion [ə'sɔ:ʃən] n asserzione f.
assertive [ə'sɔ:tɪv] a che sa imporsi.
assess [ə'sɛs] vt valutare.
assessment [ə'sɛsmənt] n valutazione f; (judgment): ~ **(of)** giudizio (su).
assessor [ə'sɛsə*] n perito; funzionario del fisco.
asset ['æsɛt] n vantaggio; (person) elemento prezioso; ~**s** npl (COMM) beni mpl; disponibilità fpl; attivo.
asset-stripping ['æsɛt'strɪpɪŋ] n (COMM) acquisto di una società in fallimento con lo scopo di rivenderne le attività.
assiduous [ə'sɪdjuəs] a assiduo(a).
assign [ə'saɪn] vt: **to** ~ **(to)** (task) assegnare (a); (resources) riservare (a); (cause, meaning) attribuire (a); **to** ~ **a date to sth** fissare la data di qc.
assignment [ə'saɪnmənt] n compito.
assimilate [ə'sɪmɪleɪt] vt assimilare.
assimilation [əsɪmɪ'leɪʃən] n assimilazione f.
assist [ə'sɪst] vt assistere, aiutare.
assistance [ə'sɪstəns] n assistenza, aiuto.
assistant [ə'sɪstənt] n assistente m/f; (Brit: also: **shop** ~) commesso/a.
assistant manager n vicedirettore m.
assizes [ə'saɪzɪz] npl assise fpl.
associate [ə'səʊʃɪɪt] a associato(a); (member) aggiunto(a) ♦ n collega m/f; (in business) socio/a ♦ vb [ə'səʊʃɪeɪt] vt associare ♦ vi: **to** ~ **with sb** frequentare qn.
associated company [ə'səʊsɪ'eɪtɪd-] n società collegata.
associate director n amministratore m aggiunto.
association [əsəʊsɪ'eɪʃən] n associazione f; **in** ~ **with** in collaborazione con.
association football n (Brit) (gioco del) calcio.
assorted [ə'sɔ:tɪd] a assortito(a); **in** ~ **sizes** in diverse taglie.
assortment [ə'sɔ:tmənt] n assortimento.
Asst. abbr = **assistant**.
assuage [ə'sweɪdʒ] vt alleviare.
assume [ə'sju:m] vt supporre; (responsibilities etc) assumere; (attitude, name) prendere.
assumed name n nome m falso.
assumption [ə'sʌmpʃən] n supposizione f, ipotesi f inv; **on the** ~ **that** ... partendo dal presupposto che ....
assurance [ə'ʃuərəns] n assicurazione f; (self-confidence) fiducia in se stesso; **I can give you no** ~**s** non posso assicurarle or garantirle niente.
assure [ə'ʃuə*] vt assicurare.
AST abbr (US: = Atlantic Standard Time) ora invernale di New York.
asterisk ['æstərɪsk] n asterisco.
astern [ə'stɔ:n] ad a poppa.
asteroid ['æstərɔɪd] n asteroide m.
asthma ['æsmə] n asma.
asthmatic [æs'mætɪk] a, n asmatico(a).
astigmatism [ə'stɪgmətɪzəm] n astigmatismo.
astir [ə'stɔ:*] ad in piedi; (excited) in fermento.
ASTMS ['æstəmz] n abbr (Brit: = Association of Scientific, Technical and Managerial Staffs) sindacato del personale scientifico, tecnico e manageriale.
astonish [ə'stɔnɪʃ] vt stupire.
astonishing [ə'stɔnɪʃɪŋ] a sorprendente, stupefacente; **I find it** ~ **that** ... mi stupisce che ....
astonishingly [ə'stɔnɪʃɪŋlɪ] ad straordinariamente, incredibilmente.
astonishment [ə'stɔnɪʃmənt] n stupore m; **to my** ~ con mia gran meraviglia, con mio grande stupore.
astound [ə'staund] vt sbalordire.
astray [ə'streɪ] ad: **to go** ~ smarrirsi; (fig) traviarsi; **to go** ~ **in one's calculations** sbagliare i calcoli.
astride [ə'straɪd] ad a cavalcioni ♦ prep a cavalcioni di.
astringent [əs'trɪndʒənt] a, n astringente (m).
astrologer [əs'trɔlədʒə*] n astrologo/a.
astrology [əs'trɔlədʒɪ] n astrologia.
astronaut ['æstrənɔ:t] n astronauta m/f.
astronomer [əs'trɔnəmə*] n astronomo/a.
astronomical [æstrə'nɔmɪkl] a astronomico(a).
astronomy [əs'trɔnəmɪ] n astronomia.
astrophysics ['æstrəu'fɪzɪks] n astrofisica.
astute [əs'tju:t] a astuto(a).
asunder [ə'sʌndə*] ad: **to tear** ~ strappare.
ASV n abbr (= American Standard Version) traduzione della Bibbia.
asylum [ə'saɪləm] n asilo; (lunatic ~) manicomio; **to seek political** ~ chiedere asilo politico.
asymmetric(al) [eɪsɪ'mɛtrɪk(əl)] a asimmetrico(a).
at [æt] prep a; (because of: following surprised, annoyed etc) di; con; ~ **the top** in cima; ~ **Paolo's** da Paolo; ~ **the baker's** dal panettiere; ~ **times** talvolta; ~ **4 o'clock** alle quattro; ~ **night** di notte; ~ **£1 a kilo** a 1 sterlina al chilo; **two** ~ **a time** due alla or per volta; ~ **full speed** a tutta velocità.

ate [eɪt] *pt of* **eat**.
atheism ['eɪθɪɪzəm] *n* ateismo.
atheist ['eɪθɪɪst] *n* ateo/a.
Athenian [ə'θi:nɪən] *a, n* ateniese *(m/f)*.
Athens ['æθɪnz] *n* Atene *f*.
athlete ['æθli:t] *n* atleta *m/f*.
athletic [æθ'lεtɪk] *a* atletico(a).
athletics [æθ'lεtɪks] *n* atletica.
Atlantic [ət'læntɪk] *a* atlantico(a) ♦ *n*: **the ~ (Ocean)** l'Atlantico, l'Oceano Atlantico.
atlas ['ætləs] *n* atlante *m*.
Atlas Mountains *npl*: **the ~** i Monti dell'Atlante.
A.T.M. *abbr* (= *automated telling machine*) cassa automatica prelievi, sportello automatico.
atmosphere ['ætməsfɪə*] *n* atmosfera; *(air)* aria.
atmospheric [ætməs'fεrɪk] *a* atmosferico(a).
atmospherics [ætməs'fεrɪks] *npl* *(RADIO)* scariche *fpl*.
atoll ['ætɔl] *n* atollo.
atom ['ætəm] *n* atomo.
atomic [ə'tɔmɪk] *a* atomico(a).
atom(ic) bomb *n* bomba atomica.
atomizer ['ætəmaɪzə*] *n* atomizzatore *m*.
atone [ə'təun] *vi*: **to ~ for** espiare.
atonement [ə'təunmənt] *n* espiazione *f*.
ATP *n* *abbr* = *Association of Tennis Professionals*.
atrocious [ə'trəuʃəs] *a* atroce, pessimo(a).
atrocity [ə'trɔsɪtɪ] *n* atrocità *f* *inv*.
atrophy ['ætrəfɪ] *n* atrofia ♦ *vi* atrofizzarsi.
attach [ə'tætʃ] *vt* attaccare; *(document, letter)* allegare; *(MIL: troops)* assegnare; **to be ~ed to sb/sth** *(to like)* essere affezionato(a) a qn/qc; **the ~ed letter** la lettera acclusa *or* allegata.
attaché [ə'tæʃeɪ] *n* addetto.
attaché case *n* valigetta per documenti.
attachment [ə'tætʃmənt] *n* *(tool)* accessorio; *(love)*: **~ (to)** affetto (per).
attack [ə'tæk] *vt* attaccare; *(task etc)* iniziare; *(problem)* affrontare ♦ *n* attacco; *(also:* **heart ~)** infarto.
attacker [ə'tækə*] *n* aggressore *m*, assalitore/trice.
attain [ə'teɪn] *vt* *(also:* **to ~ to)** arrivare a, raggiungere.
attainments [ə'teɪnmənts] *npl* cognizioni *fpl*.
attempt [ə'tεmpt] *n* tentativo ♦ *vt* tentare; **~ed murder** *(LAW)* tentato omicidio; **to make an ~ on sb's life** attentare alla vita di qn; **he made no ~ to help** non ha (neanche) tentato *or* cercato di aiutare.
attend [ə'tεnd] *vt* frequentare; *(meeting, talk)* andare a; *(patient)* assistere.
attend to *vt fus* *(needs, affairs etc)* prendersi cura di; *(customer)* occuparsi di.
attendance [ə'tεndəns] *n* *(being present)* presenza; *(people present)* gente *f* presente.
attendant [ə'tεndənt] *n* custode *m/f*; persona di servizio ♦ *a* concomitante.
attention [ə'tεnʃən] *n* attenzione *f*; **~s**

premure *fpl*, attenzioni *fpl*; **~!** *(MIL)* attenti!; **at ~** *(MIL)* sull'attenti; **for the ~ of** *(ADMIN)* per l'attenzione di; **it has come to my ~ that ...** sono venuto a conoscenza (del fatto) che ....
attentive [ə'tεntɪv] *a* attento(a); *(kind)* premuroso(a).
attentively [ə'tεntɪvlɪ] *ad* attentamente.
attenuate [ə'tεnjueɪt] *vt* attenuare ♦ *vi* attenuarsi.
attest [ə'tεst] *vi*: **to ~ to** attestare.
attic ['ætɪk] *n* soffitta.
attire [ə'taɪə*] *n* abbigliamento.
attitude ['ætɪtju:d] *n* *(behaviour)* atteggiamento; *(posture)* posa; *(view)*: **~ (to)** punto di vista (nei confronti di).
attorney [ə'tə:nɪ] *n* *(US: lawyer)* avvocato; *(having proxy)* mandatario; **power of ~** procura.
Attorney General *n* *(Brit)* Procuratore *m* Generale; *(US)* Ministro della Giustizia.
attract [ə'trækt] *vt* attirare.
attraction [ə'trækʃən] *n* *(gen pl: pleasant things)* attrattiva; *(PHYSICS, fig: towards sth)* attrazione *f*.
attractive [ə'træktɪv] *a* attraente; *(idea, offer, price)* allettante, interessante.
attribute *n* ['ætrɪbju:t] attributo ♦ *vt* [ə'trɪbju:t]: **to ~ sth to** attribuire qc a.
attrition [ə'trɪʃən] *n*: **war of ~** guerra di logoramento.
Atty. Gen. *abbr* = **Attorney General**.
ATV *n* *abbr* *(Brit:* = *Associated Television)* rete televisiva indipendente; *(MIL etc)* = *all terrain vehicle*.
aubergine ['əubəʒi:n] *n* melanzana.
auburn ['ɔ:bən] *a* tizianesco(a).
auction ['ɔ:kʃən] *n* *(also:* **sale by ~)** asta ♦ *vt* *(also:* **to sell by ~)** vendere all'asta; *(also:* **to put up for ~)** mettere all'asta.
auctioneer [ɔ:kʃə'nɪə*] *n* banditore *m*.
auction room *n* sala dell'asta.
audacious [ɔ:'deɪʃəs] *a* *(bold)* audace; *(impudent)* sfrontato(a).
audacity [ɔ:'dæsɪtɪ] *n* audacia.
audible ['ɔ:dɪbl] *a* udibile.
audience ['ɔ:dɪəns] *n* *(people)* pubblico; spettatori *mpl*; ascoltatori *mpl*; *(interview)* udienza.
audio-typist ['ɔ:dɪəu'taɪpɪst] *n* dattilografo/a che trascrive da nastro.
audiovisual [ɔ:dɪəu'vɪzjuəl] *a* audiovisivo(a); **~ aids** sussidi *mpl* audiovisivi.
audit ['ɔ:dɪt] *n* revisione *f*, verifica ♦ *vt* rivedere, verificare.
audition [ɔ:'dɪʃən] *n* *(THEATRE)* audizione *f*; *(CINEMA)* provino ♦ *vi* fare un'audizione *(or* un provino).
auditor ['ɔ:dɪtə*] *n* revisore *m*.
auditorium [ɔ:dɪ'tɔ:rɪəm] *n* sala, auditorio.
AUEW *n* *abbr* *(Brit:* = *Amalgamated Union of Engineering Workers)* sindacato dei metalmeccanici.
Aug. *abbr* (= *August*) ago., ag.

augment [ɔ:g'mɛnt] *vt, vi* aumentare.
augur ['ɔ:gə•] *vt (be a sign of)* predire ♦ *vi*: it
~**s well** promette bene.
August ['ɔ:gəst] *n* agosto; *for phrases see also*
July.
august [ɔ:'gʌst] *a* augusto(a).
aunt [ɑ:nt] *n* zia.
auntie, aunty ['ɑ:ntɪ] *n* zietta.
au pair ['əu'pɛə•] *n (also:* ~ **girl**) (ragazza *f*)
alla pari *inv.*
aura ['ɔ:rə] *n* aura.
auspices ['ɔ:spɪsɪz] *npl*: **under the** ~ **of** sotto
gli auspici di.
auspicious [ɔ:s'pɪʃəs] *a* propizio(a).
austere [ɔs'tɪə•] *a* austero(a).
austerity [ɔs'tɛrɪtɪ] *n* austerità *f inv.*
Australasia [ɔstrə'leɪzɪə] *n* Australasia.
Australia [ɔs'treɪlɪə] *n* Australia.
Australian [ɔs'treɪlɪən] *a, n* australiano(a).
Austria ['ɔstrɪə] *n* Austria.
Austrian ['ɔstrɪən] *a, n* austriaco(a).
AUT *n abbr (Brit: = Association of University
Teachers) associazione dei docenti
universitari.*
authentic [ɔ:'θɛntɪk] *a* autentico(a).
authenticate [ɔ:'θɛntɪkeɪt] *vt* autenticare.
authenticity [ɔ:θɛn'tɪsɪtɪ] *n* autenticità.
author ['ɔ:θə•] *n* autore/trice.
authoritarian [ɔ:θɔrɪ'tɛərɪən] *a* autoritario(a).
authoritative [ɔ:'θɔrɪtətɪv] *a (account etc)*
autorevole; *(manner)* autoritario(a).
authority [ɔ:'θɔrɪtɪ] *n* autorità *f inv*;
(permission) autorizzazione *f*; **the authorities**
npl le autorità; **to have** ~ **to do sth** avere
l'autorizzazione a fare *or* il diritto di fare qc.
authorization [ɔ:θərɑɪ'zeɪʃən] *n* autorizzazione
f.
authorize ['ɔ:θərɑɪz] *vt* autorizzare.
authorized capital *n* capitale *m* nominale.
authorship ['ɔ:θəʃɪp] *n* paternità *(letteraria
etc).*
autistic [ɔ:'tɪstɪk] *a* autistico(a).
auto ['ɔ:təu] *n (US)* auto *f inv.*
autobiography [ɔ:təbɑɪ'ɔgrəfɪ] *n* autobio-
grafia.
autocratic [ɔ:tə'krætɪk] *a* autocratico(a).
autograph ['ɔ:təgrɑ:f] *n* autografo ♦ *vt*
firmare.
automat ['ɔ:təmæt] *n (US) tavola calda fornita esclusivamente di distributori automatici.*
automated ['ɔ:təmeɪtɪd] *a* automatizzato(a).
automatic [ɔ:tə'mætɪk] *a* automatico(a) ♦ *n*
(gun) arma automatica; *(car)* automobile *f*
con cambio automatico; *(washing machine)*
lavatrice *f* automatica.
automatically [ɔ:tə'mætɪklɪ] *ad* automaticamente.
automatic data processing (ADP) *n*
elaborazione *f* automatica dei dati (EAD).
automation [ɔ:tə'meɪʃən] *n* automazione *f.*
automaton, *pl* **automata** [ɔ:'tɔmətən, -tə] *n*
automa *m.*
automobile ['ɔ:təməbi:l] *n (US)* automobile *f.*

autonomous [ɔ:'tɔnəməs] *a* autonomo(a).
autonomy [ɔ:'tɔnəmɪ] *n* autonomia.
autopsy ['ɔ:tɔpsɪ] *n* autopsia.
autumn ['ɔ:təm] *n* autunno.
auxiliary [ɔ:g'zɪlɪərɪ] *a* ausiliario(a) ♦ *n*
ausiliare *m/f.*
AV *n abbr (= Authorized Version) traduzione
inglese della Bibbia* ♦ *abbr* = **audiovisual.**
Av. *abbr* = **avenue.**
avail [ə'veɪl] *vt*: **to** ~ **o.s. of** servirsi di; approfittarsi di ♦ *n*: **to no** ~ inutilmente.
availability [əveɪlə'bɪlɪtɪ] *n* disponibilità.
available [ə'veɪləbl] *a* disponibile; **every** ~
means tutti i mezzi disponibili; **to make sth**
~ **to sb** mettere qc a disposizione di qn; **is
the manager** ~**?** è libero il direttore?
avalanche ['ævəlɑ:nʃ] *n* valanga.
avant-garde ['ævɑ̃ŋ'gɑ:d] *a* d'avanguardia.
avarice ['ævərɪs] *n* avarizia.
avaricious [ævə'rɪʃəs] *a* avaro(a).
avdp. *abbr (= avoirdupois) sistema ponde-
rale anglosassone basato su libbra, oncia e
multipli.*
Ave. *abbr* = **avenue.**
avenge [ə'vɛndʒ] *vt* vendicare.
avenue ['ævənju:] *n* viale *m.*
average ['ævərɪdʒ] *n* media ♦ *a* medio(a) ♦ *vt*
(also: ~ **out at)** aggirarsi in media su,
essere in media di; **on** ~ in media; **above/
below (the)** ~ sopra/sotto la media.
averse [ə'vɜ:s] *a*: **to be** ~ **to sth/doing** essere
contrario(a) a qc/a fare; **I wouldn't be** ~ **to
a drink** non avrei nulla in contrario a bere
qualcosa.
aversion [ə'vɜ:ʃən] *n* avversione *f.*
avert [ə'vɜ:t] *vt* evitare, prevenire; *(one's
eyes)* distogliere.
aviary ['eɪvɪərɪ] *n* voliera, uccelliera.
aviation [eɪvɪ'eɪʃən] *n* aviazione *f.*
avid ['ævɪd] *a* avido(a).
avidly ['ævɪdlɪ] *ad* avidamente.
avocado [ævə'kɑ:dəu] *n (also: Brit:* ~ **pear)**
avocado *m inv.*
avoid [ə'vɔɪd] *vt* evitare.
avoidable [ə'vɔɪdəbl] *a* evitabile.
avoidance [ə'vɔɪdəns] *n* l'evitare *m.*
avowed [ə'vaud] *a* dichiarato(a).
AVP *n abbr (US)* = *assistant vice-president.*
AWACS ['eɪwæks] *n abbr (= airborne warning
and control system) sistema di allarme e controllo in volo.*
await [ə'weɪt] *vt* aspettare; ~**ing attention**
(COMM: letter) in attesa di risposta; *(:
order)* in attesa di essere evaso; **long** ~**ed**
tanto atteso(a).
awake [ə'weɪk] *a* sveglio(a) ♦ *vb (pt* **awoke**
[ə'wəuk], *pp* **awoken** [ə'wəukən] *or* **awaked)**
vt svegliare ♦ *vi* svegliarsi; ~ **to** consapevole
di.
awakening [ə'weɪknɪŋ] *n* risveglio.
award [ə'wɔ:d] *n* premio; *(LAW)* decreto ♦ *vt*
assegnare; *(LAW: damages)* decretare.
aware [ə'wɛə•] *a*: ~ **of** *(conscious)* conscio(a)
di; *(informed)* informato(a) di; **to become** ~

of accorgersi di; **politically/socially** ~ politicamente/socialmente preparato; **I am fully** ~ **that** ... mi rendo perfettamente conto che ....
awareness [ə'wɛənɪs] n consapevolezza; coscienza; **to develop people's** ~ **(of)** sensibilizzare la gente (a).
awash [ə'wɔʃ] a: ~ **(with)** inondato(a) (da).
away [ə'weɪ] a, ad via; lontano(a); **two kilometres** ~ a due chilometri di distanza; **two hours** ~ **by car** a due ore di distanza in macchina; **the holiday was two weeks** ~ mancavano due settimane alle vacanze; ~ **from** lontano da; **he's** ~ **for a week** è andato via per una settimana; **he's** ~ **in Milan** è (andato) a Milano; **to take** ~ vt portare via; **he was working/pedalling** etc ~ la particella indica la continuità e l'energia dell'azione: lavorava/pedalava etc più che poteva; **to fade/wither** etc ~ la particella rinforza l'idea della diminuzione.
away game n (SPORT) partita fuori casa.
awe [ɔ:] n timore m.
awe-inspiring ['ɔ:ɪnspaɪərɪŋ], **awesome** ['ɔ:səm] a imponente.
awestruck ['ɔ:strʌk] a sgomento(a).
awful ['ɔ:fəl] a terribile; **an** ~ **lot of** (people, cars, dogs) un numero incredibile di; (jam, flowers) una quantità incredibile di.
awfully ['ɔ:flɪ] ad (very) terribilmente.
awhile [ə'waɪl] ad (per) un po'.
awkward ['ɔ:kwəd] a (clumsy) goffo(a); (inconvenient) scomodo(a); (embarrassing) imbarazzante; (difficult) delicato(a), difficile.
awkwardness ['ɔ:kwədnɪs] n goffaggine f; scomodità; imbarazzo; delicatezza, difficoltà.
awl ['ɔ:l] n punteruolo.
awning ['ɔ:nɪŋ] n (of tent) veranda; (of shop, hotel etc) tenda.
awoke [ə'wəuk] pt of **awake**.
awoken [ə'wəukən] pp of **awake**.
AWOL ['eɪwɔl] abbr (MIL etc) see **absent without leave**.
awry [ə'raɪ] ad di traverso ♦ a storto(a); **to go** ~ andare a monte.
axe, (US) **ax** [æks] n scure f ♦ vt (project etc) abolire; (jobs) sopprimere; **to have an** ~ **to grind** (fig) fare i propri interessi or il proprio tornaconto.
axiom ['æksɪəm] n assioma m.
axiomatic [æksɪəu'mætɪk] a assiomatico(a).
axis ['æksɪs], pl **axes** ['æksi:z] n asse m.
axle ['æksl] n (also: ~-**tree**) asse m.
ay(e) [aɪ] excl (yes) sì.
AYH n abbr = American Youth Hostels.
AZ abbr (US POST) = Arizona.
azalea [ə'zeɪlɪə] n azalea.
Azores [ə'zɔ:z] npl: **the** ~ le Azzorre.
Aztec ['æztɛk] a, n azteco(a).
azure ['eɪʒə*] a azzurro(a).

B

B, b [bi:] n (letter) B, b f or m inv; (SCOL: mark) ≈ 8 (buono); (MUS): **B** si m; **B for Benjamin**, (US) **B for Baker** ≈ B come Bologna; **B road** n (Brit AUT) ≈ strada secondaria.
b. abbr = **born**.
BA n abbr = British Academy; (SCOL) see **Bachelor of Arts**.
babble ['bæbl] vi cianciare; mormorare ♦ n ciance fpl; mormorio.
baboon [bə'bu:n] n babbuino.
baby ['beɪbɪ] n bambino/a.
baby carriage n (US) carrozzina.
baby grand n (also: ~ **piano**) pianoforte m a mezza coda.
babyhood ['beɪbɪhud] n prima infanzia.
babyish ['beɪbɪɪʃ] a infantile.
baby-minder ['beɪbɪ'maɪndə*] n (Brit) bambinaia (che tiene i bambini mentre la madre lavora).
baby-sit ['beɪbɪsɪt] vi fare il (or la) babysitter.
baby-sitter ['beɪbɪsɪtə*] n baby-sitter m/f inv.
bachelor ['bætʃələ*] n scapolo; **B~ of Arts/Science (BA/BSc)** ≈ laureato/a in lettere/scienze; **B~ of Arts/Science degree (BA/BSc)** n ≈ laurea in lettere/scienze.
bachelorhood ['bætʃələhud] n celibato.
bachelor party n (US) festa di addio al celibato.
back [bæk] n (of person, horse) dorso, schiena; (of hand) dorso; (of house, car) didietro; (of train) coda; (of chair) schienale m; (of page) rovescio; (FOOTBALL) difensore m; ~ **to front** all'incontrario; **to break the** ~ **of a job** (Brit) fare il grosso or il peggio di un lavoro; **to have one's** ~ **to the wall** (fig) essere or trovarsi con le spalle al muro ♦ vt (financially) finanziare; (candidate: also: ~ **up**) appoggiare; (horse: at races) puntare su; (car) guidare a marcia indietro ♦ vi indietreggiare; (car etc) fare marcia indietro ♦ a (in compounds) posteriore, di dietro; arretrato(a); ~ **seats/wheels** (AUT) sedili mpl/ruote fpl posteriori; ~ **payments/rent** arretrati mpl; ~ **garden/room** giardino/stanza sul retro (della casa); **to take a** ~ **seat** (fig) restare in secondo piano ♦ ad (not forward) indietro; (returned): **he's** ~ è tornato; **when will you be** ~? quando torni?; **he ran** ~ tornò indietro di corsa; (restitution): **throw the ball** ~ ritira la palla; **can I have it** ~? posso riaverlo?; (again): **he called** ~ ha richiamato.
back down vi (fig) fare marcia indietro.

back on to vt fus: **the house ~s on to the golf course** il retro della casa dà sul campo da golf.

back out vi (of promise) tirarsi indietro.

back up vt (support) appoggiare, sostenere; (COMPUT) fare una copia di riserva di.

backache ['bækeɪk] n mal m di schiena.

backbencher ['bæk'bɛntʃə*] n (Brit) membro del Parlamento senza potere amministrativo.

backbiting ['bækbaɪtɪŋ] n maldicenza.

backbone ['bækbəun] n spina dorsale; **the ~ of the organization** l'anima dell'organizzazione.

backchat ['bæktʃæt] n (Brit col) impertinenza.

back-cloth ['bækkləθ] n (Brit) scena di sfondo.

backcomb ['bækkəum] vt (Brit) cotonare.

backdate [bæk'deɪt] vt (letter) retrodatare; **~d pay rise** aumento retroattivo.

backdrop ['bækdrɔp] n = **backcloth**.

backer ['bækə*] n sostenitore/trice; (COMM) fautore m.

backfire ['bæk'faɪə*] vi (AUT) dar ritorni di fiamma; (plans) fallire.

backgammon ['bækgæmən] n tavola reale.

background ['bækgraund] n sfondo; (of events, COMPUT) background m inv; (basic knowledge) base f; (experience) esperienza ♦ cpd (noise, music) di fondo; **~ reading** letture fpl sull'argomento; **family ~** ambiente m familiare.

backhand ['bækhænd] n (TENNIS: also: **~ stroke**) rovescio.

backhanded [bæk'hændɪd] a (fig) ambiguo(a).

backhander ['bækhændə*] n (Brit: bribe) bustarella.

backing ['bækɪŋ] n (COMM) finanziamento; (MUS) accompagnamento; (fig) appoggio.

backlash ['bæklæʃ] n contraccolpo, ripercussione f.

backlog ['bæklɔg] n: **~ of work** lavoro arretrato.

back number n (of magazine etc) numero arretrato.

backpack ['bækpæk] n zaino.

backpacker ['bækpækə*] n chi viaggia con zaino e sacco a pelo.

back pay n arretrato di paga.

backpedal ['bækpedl] vi pedalare all'indietro; (fig) far marcia indietro.

backside [bæk'saɪd] n (col) sedere m.

backslash ['bækslæʃ] n backslash m inv, barra obliqua inversa.

backslide ['bækslaɪd] vi ricadere.

backspace ['bækspeɪs] vi (in typing) battere il tasto di ritorno.

backstage [bæk'steɪdʒ] ad nel retroscena.

back street n vicolo.

back-street ['bækstriːt] a: **~ abortionist** praticante m/f di aborti clandestini.

backstroke ['bækstrəuk] n nuoto sul dorso.

backtrack ['bæktræk] vi = **backpedal**.

backup ['bækʌp] a (train, plane) supplementare; (COMPUT) di riserva ♦ n (support) appoggio, sostegno; (COMPUT: also: **~ file**) file m inv di riserva.

backward ['bækwəd] a (movement) indietro inv; (person) tardivo(a); (country) arretrato(a); **~ and forward movement** movimento avanti e indietro.

backwards ['bækwədz] ad indietro; (fall, walk) all'indietro; **to know sth ~** or (US) **~ and forwards** (col) sapere qc a menadito.

backwater ['bækwɔːtə*] n (fig) posto morto.

back yard n cortile m sul retro.

bacon ['beɪkən] n pancetta.

bacteria [bæk'tɪərɪə] npl batteri mpl.

bacteriology [bæktɪərɪ'ɔlədʒɪ] n batteriologia.

bad [bæd] a cattivo(a); (child) cattivello(a); (meat, food) andato(a) a male; **his ~ leg** la sua gamba malata; **to go ~** (meat, food) andare a male; **to have a ~ time of it** passarsela male; **I feel ~ about it** (guilty) mi sento un po' in colpa; **~ debt** credito difficile da recuperare; **~ faith** malafede f.

bade [bæd] pt of **bid**.

badge [bædʒ] n insegna; (of policeman) stemma m; (stick-on) adesivo.

badger ['bædʒə*] n tasso ♦ vt tormentare.

badly ['bædlɪ] ad (work, dress etc) male; **things are going ~** le cose vanno male; **~ wounded** gravemente ferito; **he needs it ~** ne ha gran bisogno; **~ off** a povero(a).

bad-mannered [bæd'mænəd] a maleducato(a), sgarbato(a).

badminton ['bædmɪntən] n badminton m.

bad-tempered [bæd'tɛmpəd] a irritabile; (in bad mood) di malumore.

baffle ['bæfl] vt (puzzle) confondere.

baffling ['bæflɪŋ] a sconcertante.

bag [bæg] n sacco; (handbag etc) borsa; (of hunter) carniere m; bottino ♦ vt (col: take) mettersi in tasca; prendersi; **~s of** (col: lots of) un sacco di; **to pack one's ~s** fare le valigie; **~s under the eyes** borse sotto gli occhi.

bagful ['bægful] n sacco (pieno).

baggage ['bægɪdʒ] n bagagli mpl.

baggage car n (US) bagagliaio.

baggage claim n ritiro bagagli.

baggy ['bægɪ] a largo(a), sformato(a).

Baghdad [bæg'dæd] n Bagdad f.

bagpipes ['bægpaɪps] npl cornamusa.

bag-snatcher ['bægsnætʃə*] n (Brit) scippatore/trice.

bag-snatching ['bægsnætʃɪŋ] n (Brit) scippo.

Bahamas [bə'hɑːməz] npl: **the ~** le isole Bahama.

Bahrain [bɑː'reɪn] n Bahrein m.

bail [beɪl] n cauzione f ♦ vt (prisoner: gen: **to grant ~ to**) concedere la libertà provvisoria su cauzione a; (NAUT: also: **~ out**) see **bale out**; **to be released on ~** essere rilasciato(a) su cauzione.

bail out vt (prisoner) ottenere la libertà provvisoria su cauzione di; (fig) tirare fuori dai guai ♦ vi see **bale out**.

bailiff ['beɪlɪf] n usciere m; fattore m.

bait [beɪt] n esca ♦ vt (hook) innescare; (trap)

munire di esca; (*fig*) tormentare.
bake [beɪk] *vt* cuocere al forno ♦ *vi* cuocersi al forno.
baked beans *npl* fagioli *mpl* all'uccelletto.
baker ['beɪkə*] *n* fornaio/a, panettiere/a.
bakery ['beɪkərɪ] *n* panetteria.
baking ['beɪkɪŋ] *n* cottura (al forno).
baking powder *n* lievito in polvere.
baking tin *n* stampo, tortiera.
baking tray *n* teglia.
balaclava [bælə'klɑːvə] *n* (*also*: ~ **helmet**) passamontagna *m inv*.
balance ['bæləns] *n* equilibrio; (*COMM*: *sum*) bilancio; (*scales*) bilancia ♦ *vt* tenere in equilibrio; (*pros and cons*) soppesare; (*budget*) far quadrare; (*account*) pareggiare; (*compensate*) contrappesare; ~ **of trade/payments** bilancia commerciale/dei pagamenti; ~ **brought forward** saldo riportato; ~ **carried forward** saldo da riportare; **to** ~ **the books** fare il bilancio.
balanced ['bælənst] *a* (*personality*, *diet*) equilibrato(a).
balance sheet *n* bilancio.
balcony ['bælkənɪ] *n* balcone *m*.
bald [bɔːld] *a* calvo(a).
baldness ['bɔːldnɪs] *n* calvizie *f*.
bale [beɪl] *n* balla.
  bale out *vt* (*NAUT*: *water*) vuotare; (: *boat*) aggottare ♦ *vi* (*of a plane*) gettarsi col paracadute.
Balearic [bælɪ'ærɪk] *a*: **the** ~ **Islands** le (isole) Baleari.
baleful ['beɪlful] *a* funesto(a).
balk [bɔːlk] *vi*: **to** ~ **(at)** tirarsi indietro (davanti a); (*horse*) recalcitrare (davanti a).
Balkan ['bɔːlkən] *a* balcanico(a) ♦ *n*: **the** ~**s** i Balcani.
ball [bɔːl] *n* palla; (*football*) pallone *m*; (*for golf*) pallina; (*dance*) ballo; **to play** ~ **(with sb)** giocare a palla (con qn); (*fig*) stare al gioco (di qn); **to be on the** ~ (*fig*: *competent*) essere in gamba; (: *alert*) stare all'erta; **to start the** ~ **rolling** (*fig*) fare la prima mossa; **the** ~ **is in your court** (*fig*) a lei la prossima mossa; *see also* **balls**.
ballad ['bæləd] *n* ballata.
ballast ['bæləst] *n* zavorra.
ball bearing *n* cuscinetto a sfere.
ball cock *n* galleggiante *m*.
ballerina [bælə'riːnə] *n* ballerina.
ballet ['bæleɪ] *n* balletto.
ballet dancer *n* ballerino/a.
ballistic [bə'lɪstɪk] *a* balistico(a).
ballistics [bə'lɪstɪks] *n* balistica.
balloon [bə'luːn] *n* pallone *m*; (*in comic strip*) fumetto ♦ *vi* gonfiarsi.
balloonist [bə'luːnɪst] *n* aeronauta *m/f*.
ballot ['bælət] *n* scrutinio.
ballot box *n* urna (per le schede).
ballot paper *n* scheda.
ballpark ['bɔːlpɑːk] *n* (*US*) stadio di baseball.
ballpark figure *n* (*col*) cifra approssimativa.
ball-point pen ['bɔːlpɔɪnt-] *n* penna a sfera.

ballroom ['bɔːlrum] *n* sala da ballo.
balls [bɔːlz] *npl* (*col!*) coglioni *mpl* (*!*).
balm [bɑːm] *n* balsamo.
balmy ['bɑːmɪ] *a* (*breeze*, *air*) balsamico(a); (*Brit col*) = **barmy**.
BALPA ['bælpə] *n* *abbr* (= *British Airline Pilots' Association*) *sindacato dei piloti.*
balsam ['bɔːlsəm] *n* balsamo.
balsa (wood) ['bɔːlsə-] *n* (legno di) balsa.
Baltic ['bɔːltɪk] *a*, *n*: **the** ~ (**Sea**) il (mar) Baltico.
balustrade [bæləs'treɪd] *n* balaustrata.
bamboo [bæm'buː] *n* bambù *m*.
bamboozle [bæm'buːzl] *vt* (*col*) infinocchiare.
ban [bæn] *n* interdizione *f* ♦ *vt* interdire; **he was** ~**ned from driving** (*Brit*) gli hanno ritirato la patente.
banal [bə'nɑːl] *a* banale.
banana [bə'nɑːnə] *n* banana.
band [bænd] *n* banda; (*at a dance*) orchestra; (*MIL*) fanfara.
  band together *vi* collegarsi.
bandage ['bændɪdʒ] *n* benda.
bandaid ['bændeɪd] *n* (*US*) cerotto.
bandit ['bændɪt] *n* bandito.
bandstand ['bændstænd] *n* palco dell'orchestra.
bandwagon ['bændwægən] *n*: **to jump on the** ~ (*fig*) seguire la corrente.
bandy ['bændɪ] *vt* (*jokes*, *insults*) scambiare.
  bandy about *vt* far circolare.
bandy-legged ['bændɪ'lɛgɪd] *a* dalle gambe storte.
bane [beɪn] *n*: **it** (*or* **he** *etc*) **is the** ~ **of my life** è la mia rovina.
bang [bæŋ] *n* botta; (*of door*) lo sbattere; (*blow*) colpo ♦ *vt* battere (violentemente); (*door*) sbattere ♦ *vi* scoppiare; sbattere; **to** ~ **at the door** picchiare alla porta; **to** ~ **into sth** sbattere contro qc ♦ *ad*: **to be** ~ **on time** (*Brit col*) spaccare il secondo; *see also* **bangs**.
banger ['bæŋə*] *n* (*Brit*: *car*: *also*: **old** ~) macinino; (*Brit col*: *sausage*) salsiccia; (*firework*) mortaretto.
Bangkok ['bæŋkɔk] *n* Bangkok *f*.
Bangladesh [bɑːŋglə'dɛʃ] *n* Bangladesh *m*.
bangle ['bæŋgl] *n* braccialetto.
bangs [bæŋz] *npl* (*US*: *fringe*) frangia, frangetta.
banish ['bænɪʃ] *vt* bandire.
banister(s) ['bænɪstə(z)] *n*(*pl*) ringhiera.
banjo, ~**es** *or* ~**s** ['bændʒəu] *n* banjo *m inv*.
bank [bæŋk] *n* (*for money*) banca, banco; (*of river*, *lake*) riva, sponda; (*of earth*) banco ♦ *vi* (*AVIAT*) inclinarsi in virata; (*COMM*): **they** ~ **with Pitt's** sono clienti di Pitt's.
  bank on *vt fus* contare su.
bank account *n* conto in banca.
bank card *n* = **banker's card**.
bank charges *npl* (*Brit*) spese *fpl* bancarie.
bank draft *n* assegno circolare *or* bancario.
banker ['bæŋkə*] *n* banchiere *m*; ~**'s card** (*Brit*) carta assegni; ~**'s order** (*Brit*) ordine

m di banca.
bank giro *n* bancogiro.
Bank holiday *n* (*Brit*) giorno di festa (*in cui le banche sono chiuse*).
banking ['bæŋkɪŋ] *n* attività bancaria; professione *f* di banchiere.
banking hours *npl* orario di sportello.
bank loan *n* prestito bancario.
bank manager *n* direttore *m* di banca.
banknote ['bæŋknəut] *n* banconota.
bank rate *n* tasso bancario.
bankrupt ['bæŋkrʌpt] *a, n* fallito(a); **to go ~** fallire.
bankruptcy ['bæŋkrʌptsɪ] *n* fallimento.
bank statement *n* estratto conto.
banner ['bænə*] *n* bandiera.
bannister(s) ['bænɪstə(z)] *n(pl)* = **banister(s)**.
banns [bænz] *npl* pubblicazioni *fpl* di matrimonio.
banquet ['bæŋkwɪt] *n* banchetto.
bantam-weight ['bæntəmweɪt] *n* peso gallo.
banter ['bæntə*] *n* scherzi *mpl* bonari.
BAOR *n abbr* = *British Army of the Rhine*.
baptism ['bæptɪzəm] *n* battesimo.
Baptist ['bæptɪst] *a, n* battista (*m/f*).
baptize [bæp'taɪz] *vt* battezzare.
bar [bɑ:*] *n* barra; (*of window etc*) sbarra; (*of chocolate*) tavoletta; (*fig*) ostacolo; restrizione *f*; (*pub*) bar *m inv*; (*counter: in pub*) banco; (*MUS*) battuta ♦ *vt* (*road, window*) sbarrare; (*person*) escludere; (*activity*) interdire; **~ of soap** saponetta; **the B~** (*LAW*) l'Ordine *m* degli avvocati; **behind ~s** (*prisoner*) dietro le sbarre; **none** senza eccezione.
Barbados [bɑ:'beɪdɔs] *n* Barbados *fpl*.
barbaric [bɑ:'bærɪk], **barbarous** ['bɑ:bərəs] *a* barbaro(a); barbarico(a).
barbecue ['bɑ:bɪkju:] *n* barbecue *m inv*.
barbed wire ['bɑ:bd-] *n* filo spinato.
barber ['bɑ:bə*] *n* barbiere *m*.
barbiturate [bɑ:'bɪtjurɪt] *n* barbiturico.
Barcelona [bɑ:sɪ'ləunə] *n* Barcellona *f*.
bar chart *n* diagramma *m* di frequenza.
bar code *n* codice *m* a barre.
bare [bɛə*] *a* nudo(a) ♦ *vt* scoprire, denudare; (*teeth*) mostrare; **the ~ essentials** lo stretto necessario.
bareback ['bɛəbæk] *ad* senza sella.
barefaced ['bɛəfeɪst] *a* sfacciato(a).
barefoot ['bɛəfut] *a, ad* scalzo(a).
bareheaded [bɛə'hɛdɪd] *a, ad* a capo scoperto.
barely ['bɛəlɪ] *ad* appena.
Barents Sea ['bærənts-] *n*: **the ~** il mar di Barents.
bargain ['bɑ:gɪn] *n* (*transaction*) contratto; (*good buy*) affare *m* ♦ *vi* (*haggle*) tirare sul prezzo; (*trade*) contrattare; **into the ~** per giunta.
bargain for *vt fus* (*col*): **to ~ for sth** aspettarsi qc; **he got more than he ~ed for** gli è andata peggio di quel che si aspettasse.

bargaining ['bɑ:gənɪŋ] *n* contrattazione *f*.
barge [bɑ:dʒ] *n* chiatta.
barge in *vi* (*walk in*) piombare dentro; (*interrupt talk*) intromettersi a sproposito.
barge into *vt fus* urtare contro.
baritone ['bærɪtəun] *n* baritono.
barium meal ['bɛərɪəm-] *n* (pasto di) bario.
bark [bɑ:k] *n* (*of tree*) corteccia; (*of dog*) abbaio ♦ *vi* abbaiare.
barley ['bɑ:lɪ] *n* orzo.
barley sugar *n* zucchero d'orzo.
barmaid ['bɑ:meɪd] *n* cameriera al banco.
barman ['bɑ:mən] *n* barista *m*.
barmy ['bɑ:mɪ] *a* (*Brit col*) tocco(a).
barn [bɑ:n] *n* granaio; (*for animals*) stalla.
barnacle ['bɑ:nəkl] *n* cirripede *m*.
barometer [bə'rɔmɪtə*] *n* barometro.
baron ['bærən] *n* barone *m*; (*fig*) magnate *m*; **the oil ~s** i magnati del petrolio; **the press ~s** i baroni della stampa.
baroness ['bærənɪs] *n* baronessa.
baronet ['bærənɪt] *n* baronetto.
barracks ['bærəks] *npl* caserma.
barrage ['bærɑ:ʒ] *n* (*MIL*) sbarramento; **a ~ of questions** una raffica di *or* un fuoco di fila di domande.
barrel ['bærəl] *n* barile *m*; (*of gun*) canna.
barrel organ *n* organetto a cilindro.
barren ['bærən] *a* sterile; (*soil*) arido(a).
barricade [bærɪ'keɪd] *n* barricata ♦ *vt* barricare.
barrier ['bærɪə*] *n* barriera; (*Brit: also*: **crash ~**) guardrail *m inv*.
barrier cream *n* (*Brit*) crema protettiva.
barring ['bɑ:rɪŋ] *prep* salvo.
barrister ['bærɪstə*] *n* (*Brit*) avvocato/essa (*con diritto di parlare davanti a tutte le corti*).
barrow ['bærəu] *n* (*cart*) carriola.
barstool ['bɑ:stu:l] *n* sgabello.
Bart. *abbr* (*Brit*) = **baronet**.
bartender ['bɑ:tendə*] *n* (*US*) barista *m*.
barter ['bɑ:tə*] *n* baratto ♦ *vt*: **to ~ sth for** barattare qc con.
base [beɪs] *n* base *f* ♦ *a* vile ♦ *vt*: **to ~ sth on** basare qc su; **to ~ at** (*troops*) mettere di stanza a; **coffee-~d** a base di caffè; **a Paris-~d firm** una ditta con sede centrale a Parigi; **I'm ~d in London** sono di base *or* ho base a Londra.
baseball ['beɪsbɔ:l] *n* baseball *m*.
baseboard ['beɪsbɔ:d] *n* (*US*) zoccolo, battiscopa *m inv*.
base camp *n* campo *m* base *inv*.
Basel [bɑ:l] *n* = **Basle**.
basement ['beɪsmənt] *n* seminterrato; (*of shop*) sotterraneo.
base rate *n* tasso di base.
bases ['beɪsi:z] *npl* of **basis**; ['beɪsɪz] *npl* of **base**.
bash [bæʃ] *vt* (*col*) picchiare ♦ *n*: **I'll have a ~ (at it)** (*Brit col*) ci proverò; **~ed in** *a* sfondato(a).
bash up *vt* (*col: car*) sfasciare; (: *Brit*:

person) riempire di *or* prendere a botte.
bashful ['bæʃful] *a* timido(a).
bashing ['bæʃɪŋ] *n*: **Paki-/queer-~** atti *mpl* di violenza contro i pachistani/gli omosessuali.
BASIC ['beɪsɪk] *n* (*COMPUT*) BASIC *m*.
basic ['beɪsɪk] *a* (*principles, precautions, rules*) elementare; (*salary*) base *inv* (*after n*).
basically ['beɪsɪklɪ] *ad* fondamentalmente, sostanzialmente.
basic rate *n* (*of tax*) aliquota minima.
basil ['bæzl] *n* basilico.
basin ['beɪsn] *n* (*vessel, also GEO*) bacino; (*also:* **wash~**) lavabo; (*Brit: for food*) terrina.
basis, *pl* **bases** ['beɪsɪs, -siːz] *n* base *f*; **on the ~ of what you've said** in base alle sue asserzioni.
bask [bɑːsk] *vi*: **to ~ in the sun** crogiolarsi al sole.
basket ['bɑːskɪt] *n* cesta; (*smaller*) cestino; (*with handle*) paniere *m*.
basketball ['bɑːskɪtbɔːl] *n* pallacanestro *f*.
basketball player *n* cestista *m/f*.
Basle [bɑːl] *n* Basilea.
Basque [bæsk] *a, n* basco(a).
bass [beɪs] *n* (*MUS*) basso.
bass clef *n* chiave *f* di basso.
bassoon [bə'suːn] *n* fagotto.
bastard ['bɑːstəd] *n* bastardo/a; (*col!*) stronzo (*!*).
baste [beɪst] *vt* (*CULIN*) ungere con grasso; (*SEWING*) imbastire.
bastion ['bæstɪən] *n* bastione *m*; (*fig*) baluardo.
BASW *n abbr* (= *British Association of Social Workers*) sindacato degli assistenti sociali.
bat [bæt] *n* pipistrello; (*for baseball etc*) mazza; (*Brit: for table tennis*) racchetta; **off one's own ~** di propria iniziativa ♦ *vt*: **he didn't ~ an eyelid** non battè ciglio.
batch [bætʃ] *n* (*of bread*) infornata; (*of papers*) cumulo; (*of applicants, letters*) gruppo; (*of work*) sezione *f*; (*of goods*) partita, lotto.
batch processing *n* (*COMPUT*) elaborazione *f* a blocchi.
bated ['beɪtɪd] *a*: **with ~ breath** col fiato sospeso.
bath [bɑːθ, *pl* bɑːðz] *n* bagno; (*bathtub*) vasca da bagno ♦ *vt* far fare il bagno a; **to have a ~** fare un bagno; *see also* **baths**.
bathchair ['bɑːθtʃeə*] *n* (*Brit*) poltrona a rotelle.
bathe [beɪð] *vi* fare il bagno ♦ *vt* bagnare; (*wound etc*) lavare.
bather ['beɪðə*] *n* bagnante *m/f*.
bathing ['beɪðɪŋ] *n* bagni *mpl*.
bathing cap *n* cuffia da bagno.
bathing costume, (*US*) **bathing suit** *n* costume *m* da bagno.
bathmat ['bɑːθmæt] *n* tappetino da bagno.
bathrobe ['bɑːθrəub] *n* accappatoio.
bathroom ['bɑːθrum] *n* stanza da bagno.

baths [bɑːðz] *npl* bagni *mpl* pubblici.
bath towel *n* asciugamano da bagno.
bathtub ['bɑːθtʌb] *n* (vasca da) bagno.
batman ['bætmən] *n* (*Brit MIL*) attendente *m*.
baton ['bætən] *n* bastone *m*; (*MUS*) bacchetta.
battalion [bə'tælɪən] *n* battaglione *m*.
batten ['bætən] *n* (*CARPENTRY*) assicella, correntino; (*for flooring*) tavola per pavimenti; (*NAUT*) serretta; (: *on sail*) stecca.
batten down *vt* (*NAUT*): **to ~ down the hatches** chiudere i boccaporti.
batter ['bætə*] *vt* battere ♦ *n* pastetta.
battered ['bætəd] *a* (*hat*) sformato(a); (*pan*) ammaccato(a); **~ wife/baby** consorte *f*/bambino(a) maltrattato(a).
battering ram ['bætərɪŋ-] *n* ariete *m*.
battery ['bætərɪ] *n* batteria; (*of torch*) pila.
battery charger *n* caricabatterie *m inv*.
battery farming *n* allevamento intensivo.
battle ['bætl] *n* battaglia ♦ *vi* battagliare, lottare; **to fight a losing ~** (*fig*) battersi per una causa persa; **that's half the ~** (*col*) è già una mezza vittoria.
battle dress *n* uniforme *f* da combattimento.
battlefield ['bætlfiːld] *n* campo di battaglia.
battlements ['bætlmənts] *npl* bastioni *mpl*.
battleship ['bætlʃɪp] *n* nave *f* da guerra.
bauble ['bɔːbl] *n* ninnolo.
baud [bɔːd] *n* (*COMPUT*) baud *m inv*.
baulk [bɔːlk] *vi* = **balk**.
bauxite ['bɔːksaɪt] *n* bauxite *f*.
Bavaria [bə'vɛərɪə] *n* Bavaria.
Bavarian [bə'vɛərɪən] *a, n* bavarese (*m/f*).
bawdy ['bɔːdɪ] *a* piccante.
bawl [bɔːl] *vi* urlare.
bay [beɪ] *n* (*of sea*) baia; (*Brit: for parking*) piazzola di sosta; (*loading*) piazzale *m* di (sosta e) carico; **to hold sb at ~** tenere qn a bada.
bay leaf *n* foglia d'alloro.
bayonet ['beɪənɪt] *n* baionetta.
bay tree *n* alloro.
bay window *n* bovindo.
bazaar [bə'zɑː*] *n* bazar *m inv*; vendita di beneficenza.
bazooka [bə'zuːkə] *n* bazooka *m inv*.
BB *n abbr* (*Brit:* = *Boys' Brigade*) organizzazione giovanile a fine educativo.
B & B *n abbr see* **bed and breakfast**.
BBB *n abbr* (*US:* = *Better Business Bureau*) organismo per la difesa dei consumatori.
BBC *n abbr* (= *British Broadcasting Corporation*) rete nazionale di radiotelevisione in Gran Bretagna.
BBE *n abbr* (*US:* = *Benevolent and Protective Order of Elks*) organizzazione filantropica.
BC *ad abbr* (= *before Christ*) a.C. ♦ *abbr* (*Canada*) = *British Columbia*.
BCG *n abbr* (= *Bacillus Calmette-Guérin*) vaccino antitubercolare.
BD *n abbr* (= *Bachelor of Divinity*) titolo di studio.
B/D *abbr* = **bank draft**.

BDS *n abbr* (= *Bachelor of Dental Surgery*) *titolo di studio.*

be, *pt* **was, were,** *pp* **been** [bi:, wɔz, wə:*, bi:n] *vi* essere; **how are you?** come sta?; **I am warm** ho caldo; **it is cold** fa freddo; **how much is it?** quanto costa?; **it's 8 o'clock** sono le 8; **it's only me** sono solo io; **he is four (years old)** ha quattro anni; **2 and 2 are 4** 2 più 2 fa 4; **where have you been?** dov'è stato?; dov'è andato?; **what are you doing?** che fa?, che sta facendo?; **if I were you ...** se fossi in lei ...; **am I to understand that ...?** devo dedurre che ...?; **I've been waiting for her for 2 hours** l'aspetto da 2 ore; **he was to have come yesterday** sarebbe dovuto venire ieri; **to ~ killed** essere *or* venire ucciso; **he is nowhere to ~ found** non lo si trova da nessuna parte; **the car is to ~ sold** abbiamo (*or* hanno *etc*) intenzione di vendere la macchina.

B/E *abbr* = **bill of exchange.**

beach [bi:tʃ] *n* spiaggia ♦ *vt* tirare in secco.

beach buggy *n* dune buggy *f inv.*

beachcomber ['bi:tʃkəumə*] *n* vagabondo (che s'aggira sulla spiaggia).

beachwear ['bi:tʃwɛə*] *n* articoli *mpl* da spiaggia.

beacon ['bi:kən] *n* (*lighthouse*) faro; (*marker*) segnale *m;* (*radio ~*) radiofaro.

bead [bi:d] *n* perlina; (*of dew, sweat*) goccia; **~s** (*necklace*) collana.

beady ['bi:dɪ] *a:* **~ eyes** occhi *mpl* piccoli e penetranti.

beagle ['bi:gl] *n* cane *m* da lepre.

beak [bi:k] *n* becco.

beaker ['bi:kə*] *n* coppa.

beam [bi:m] *n* trave *f;* (*of light*) raggio; (*RADIO*) fascio (d'onde) ♦ *vi* brillare ♦ *vt* (*smile*): **to ~ at sb** rivolgere un radioso sorriso a qn; **to drive on full** *or* **main ~** *or* (*US*) **high ~** guidare con gli abbaglianti accesi.

beaming ['bi:mɪŋ] *a* (*sun, smile*) raggiante.

bean [bi:n] *n* fagiolo; (*of coffee*) chicco.

beanshoots ['bi:nʃu:ts], **beansprouts** ['bi:nsprauts] *npl* germogli *mpl* di soia.

bear [bɛə*] *n* orso; (*STOCK EXCHANGE*) ribassista *m/f* ♦ *vb* (*pt* **bore,** *pp* **borne** [bɔ:*, bɔ:n]) *vt* (*gen*) portare; (*produce: fruit*) produrre, dare; (*: traces, signs*) mostrare; (*COMM: interest*) fruttare; (*endure*) sopportare ♦ *vi:* **to ~ right/left** piegare a destra/sinistra; **to ~ the responsibility of** assumersi la responsabilità di; **to ~ comparison with** reggere al paragone con; **I can't ~ him** non lo posso soffrire *or* sopportare; **to bring pressure to ~ on sb** fare pressione su qn.

bear out *vt* (*theory, suspicion*) confermare, convalidare.

bear up *vi* farsi coraggio; **he bore up well under the strain** ha sopportato bene lo stress.

bear with *vt fus* (*sb's moods, temper*) sopportare (con pazienza); **~ with me a**

minute solo un attimo, prego.

bearable ['bɛərəbl] *a* sopportabile.

beard [bɪəd] *n* barba.

bearded ['bɪədɪd] *a* barbuto(a).

bearer ['bɛərə*] *n* portatore *m;* (*of passport*) titolare *m/f.*

bearing ['bɛərɪŋ] *n* portamento; (*connection*) rapporto; (**ball**) **~s** *npl* cuscinetti *mpl* a sfere; **to take a ~** fare un rilevamento; **to find one's ~s** orientarsi.

beast [bi:st] *n* bestia.

beastly ['bi:stlɪ] *a* meschino(a); (*weather*) da cani.

beat [bi:t] *n* colpo; (*of heart*) battito; (*MUS*) tempo; battuta; (*of policeman*) giro ♦ *vt* (*pt* **beat,** *pp* **beaten**) battere; **off the ~en track** fuori mano; **to ~ about the bush** menare il cane per l'aia; **to ~ time** battere il tempo; **that ~s everything!** (*col*) questo è il colmo!

beat down *vt* (*door*) abbattere, buttare giù; (*price*) far abbassare; (*seller*) far scendere ♦ *vi* (*rain*) scrosciare; (*sun*) picchiare.

beat off *vt* respingere.

beat up *vt* (*col: person*) picchiare; (*eggs*) sbattere.

beater ['bi:tə*] *n* (*for eggs, cream*) frullino.

beating ['bi:tɪŋ] *n* botte *fpl;* (*defeat*) batosta; **to take a ~** prendere una (bella) batosta.

beat-up [bi:t'ʌp] *a* (*col*) scassato(a).

beautician [bju:'tɪʃən] *n* estetista *m/f.*

beautiful ['bju:tɪful] *a* bello(a).

beautifully ['bju:tɪflɪ] *ad* splendidamente.

beautify ['bju:tɪfaɪ] *vt* abbellire.

beauty ['bju:tɪ] *n* bellezza; (*concept*) bello; **the ~ of it is that ...** il bello è che ....

beauty contest *n* concorso di bellezza.

beauty queen *n* miss *f inv,* reginetta di bellezza.

beauty salon *n* istituto di bellezza.

beauty spot *n* neo; (*Brit: TOURISM*) luogo pittoresco.

beaver ['bi:və*] *n* castoro.

becalmed [bɪ'kɑ:md] *a* in bonaccia.

became [bɪ'keɪm] *pt of* **become.**

because [bɪ'kɔz] *cj* perché; **~ of** *prep* a causa di.

beck [bɛk] *n:* **to be at sb's ~ and call** essere a completa disposizione di qn.

beckon ['bɛkən] *vt* (*also:* **~ to**) chiamare con un cenno.

become [bɪ'kʌm] *vt* (*irg: like* **come**) diventare; **to ~ fat/thin** ingrassarsi/ dimagrire; **to ~ angry** arrabbiarsi; **it became known that ...** si è venuto a sapere che ...; **what has ~ of him?** che gli è successo?

becoming [bɪ'kʌmɪŋ] *a* (*behaviour*) che si conviene; (*clothes*) grazioso(a).

BEd *n abbr* (= *Bachelor of Education*) *laurea con abilitazione all'insegnamento.*

bed [bɛd] *n* letto; (*of flowers*) aiuola; (*of coal, clay*) strato; (*of sea, lake*) fondo; **to go to ~** andare a letto.

bed down *vi* sistemarsi (per dormire).

bed and breakfast (B & B) *n* (*terms*) camera con colazione; (*place*) ≈ pensione *f* familiare.

bedbug ['bɛdbʌg] *n* cimice *f*.

bedclothes ['bɛdkləuðz] *npl* coperte e lenzuola *fpl*.

bedcover ['bɛdkʌvə*] *n* copriletto.

bedding ['bɛdɪŋ] *n* coperte e lenzuola *fpl*.

bedevil [bɪ'dɛvl] *vt* (*person*) tormentare; (*plans*) ostacolare continuamente.

bedfellow ['bɛdfɛləu] *n*: **they are strange ~s** (*fig*) fanno una coppia ben strana.

bedlam ['bɛdləm] *n* baraonda.

bedpan ['bɛdpæn] *n* padella.

bedpost ['bɛdpəust] *n* colonnina del letto.

bedraggled [bɪ'drægld] *a* fradicio(a).

bedridden ['bɛdrɪdən] *a* costretto(a) a letto.

bedrock ['bɛdrɔk] *n* (GEO) basamento; (*fig*) fatti *mpl* di base.

bedroom ['bɛdrum] *n* camera da letto.

Beds *abbr* (*Brit*) = *Bedfordshire*.

bedside ['bɛdsaɪd] *n*: **at sb's ~** al capezzale di qn.

bedside lamp *n* lampada da comodino.

bedsit(ter) ['bɛdsɪt(ə*)] *n* (*Brit*) monolocale *m*.

bedspread ['bɛdsprɛd] *n* copriletto.

bedtime ['bɛdtaɪm] *n*: **it's ~** è ora di andare a letto.

bee [bi:] *n* ape *f*; **to have a ~ in one's bonnet (about sth)** avere la fissazione (di qc).

beech [bi:tʃ] *n* faggio.

beef [bi:f] *n* manzo.

beef up *vt* (*col*) rinforzare.

beefburger ['bi:fbə:gə*] *n* hamburger *m inv*.

beefeater ['bi:fi:tə*] *n* guardia della Torre di Londra.

beehive ['bi:haɪv] *n* alveare *m*.

beeline ['bi:laɪn] *n*: **to make a ~ for** buttarsi a capo fitto verso.

been [bi:n] *pp of* **be**.

beer [bɪə*] *n* birra.

beer can *n* lattina di birra.

beetle ['bi:tl] *n* scarafaggio; coleottero.

beetroot ['bi:tru:t] *n* (*Brit*) barbabietola.

befall [bɪ'fɔ:l] *vi(vt)* (*irg: like* **fall**) accadere (a).

befit [bɪ'fɪt] *vt* addirsi a.

before [bɪ'fɔ:*] *prep* (*in time*) prima di; (*in space*) davanti a ♦ *cj* prima che + *sub*; prima di ♦ *ad* prima; **~ going** prima di andare; **~ she goes** prima che vada; **the week ~** la settimana prima; **I've seen it ~** l'ho già visto; **I've never seen it ~** è la prima volta che lo vedo.

beforehand [bɪ'fɔ:hænd] *ad* in anticipo.

befriend [bɪ'frɛnd] *vt* assistere; mostrarsi amico a.

befuddled [bɪ'fʌdld] *a* confuso(a).

beg [bɛg] *vi* chiedere l'elemosina ♦ *vt* chiedere in elemosina; (*favour*) chiedere; (*entreat*) pregare; **I ~ your pardon** (*apologising*) mi scusi; (*not hearing*) scusi?; **this ~s the**

question of ... questo presuppone che sia già risolto il problema di ....

began [bɪ'gæn] *pt of* **begin**.

beggar ['bɛgə*] *n* (*also*: **~man**, **~woman**) mendicante *m/f*.

begin, *pt* **began**, *pp* **begun** [bɪ'gɪn, bɪ'gæn, bɪ'gʌn] *vt*, *vi* cominciare; **to ~ doing** *or* **to do sth** incominciare *or* iniziare a fare qc; **I can't ~ to thank you** non so proprio come ringraziarla; **to ~ with**, **I'd like to know** ... tanto per cominciare vorrei sapere ...; **~ning from Monday** a partire da lunedì.

beginner [bɪ'gɪnə*] *n* principiante *m/f*.

beginning [bɪ'gɪnɪŋ] *n* inizio, principio; **right from the ~** fin dall'inizio.

begrudge [bɪ'grʌdʒ] *vt*: **to ~ sb sth** dare qc a qn a malincuore; invidiare qn per qc.

beguile [bɪ'gaɪl] *vt* (*enchant*) incantare.

beguiling [bɪ'gaɪlɪŋ] *a* (*charming*) allettante; (*deluding*) ingannevole.

begun [bɪ'gʌn] *pp of* **begin**.

behalf [bɪ'hɑ:f] *n*: **on ~ of**, (US) **in ~ of** per conto di; a nome di.

behave [bɪ'heɪv] *vi* comportarsi; (*well*: *also*: **~ o.s.**) comportarsi bene.

behaviour, (US) **behavior** [bɪ'heɪvjə*] *n* comportamento, condotta.

behead [bɪ'hɛd] *vt* decapitare.

beheld [bɪ'hɛld] *pt*, *pp of* **behold**.

behind [bɪ'haɪnd] *prep* dietro; (*followed by pronoun*) dietro di; (*time*) in ritardo con ♦ *ad* dietro; in ritardo **~ in** didietro; **we're ~ them in technology** siamo più indietro *or* più arretrati di loro nella tecnica; **~ the scenes** dietro le quinte; **to be ~ (schedule) with sth** essere indietro con qc; (*payments*) essere in arretrato con qc; **to leave sth ~** dimenticare di prendere qc.

behold [bɪ'həuld] *vt* (*irg: like* **hold**) vedere, scorgere.

beige [beɪʒ] *a* beige *inv*.

Beijing [beɪ'dʒɪŋ] *n* Pechino *f*.

being ['bi:ɪŋ] *n* essere *m*; **to come into ~** cominciare ad esistere.

Beirut [beɪ'ru:t] *n* Beirut *f*.

belated [bɪ'leɪtɪd] *a* tardo(a).

belch [bɛltʃ] *vi* ruttare ♦ *vt* (*gen*: **~ out**: *smoke etc*) eruttare.

beleaguered [bɪ'li:gəd] *a* (*city*) assediato(a); (*army*) accerchiato(a); (*fig*) assillato(a).

Belfast ['bɛlfɑ:st] *n* Belfast *f*.

belfry ['bɛlfrɪ] *n* campanile *m*.

Belgian ['bɛldʒən] *a*, *n* belga (*m/f*).

Belgium ['bɛldʒəm] *n* Belgio.

Belgrade [bɛl'greɪd] *n* Belgrado *f*.

belie [bɪ'laɪ] *vt* smentire; (*give false impression of*) nascondere.

belief [bɪ'li:f] *n* (*opinion*) opinione *f*, convinzione *f*; (*trust*, *faith*) fede *f*; (*acceptance as true*) credenza; **in the ~ that** nella convinzione che; **it's beyond ~** è incredibile.

believe [bɪ'li:v] *vt*, *vi* credere; **to ~ in** (*God*) credere in; (*ghosts*) credere a; (*method*) avere fiducia in; **I don't ~ in corporal punishment** sono contrario alle punizioni corporali; **he is ~d to be abroad** si pensa (che) sia all'estero.

believer [bɪ'li:və*] n (REL) credente m/f; (in idea, activity): **to be a ~ in** credere in.

belittle [bɪ'lɪtl] vt sminuire.

Belize [bɛ'li:z] n Belize m.

bell [bɛl] n campana; (small, on door, electric) campanello; **that rings a ~** (fig) mi ricorda qualcosa.

bell-bottoms ['bɛlbɔtəmz] npl calzoni mpl a zampa d'elefante.

bellboy ['bɛlbɔɪ], (US) **bellhop** ['bɛlhɔp] n ragazzo d'albergo, fattorino d'albergo.

belligerent [bɪ'lɪdʒərənt] a (at war) belligerante; (fig) bellicoso(a).

bellow ['bɛləu] vi muggire; (cry) urlare (a squarciagola) ♦ vt (orders) urlare (a squarciagola).

bellows ['bɛləuz] npl soffietto.

bell push n (Brit) pulsante m del campanello.

belly ['bɛli] n pancia.

bellyache ['bɛlɪeɪk] n mal m di pancia ♦ vi (col) mugugnare.

bellybutton ['bɛlɪbʌtn] n ombelico.

belong [bɪ'lɔŋ] vi: **to ~ to** appartenere a; (club etc) essere socio di; **this book ~s here** questo libro va qui.

belongings [bɪ'lɔŋɪŋz] npl cose fpl, roba; **personal ~** effetti mpl personali.

beloved [bɪ'lʌvɪd] a adorato(a).

below [bɪ'ləu] prep sotto, al di sotto di ♦ ad sotto, di sotto; giù; **see ~** vedi sotto or oltre; **temperatures ~ normal** temperature al di sotto del normale.

belt [bɛlt] n cintura; (TECH) cinghia ♦ vt (thrash) picchiare ♦ vi (Brit col) filarsela; **industrial ~** zona industriale.

belt out vt (song) cantare a squarciagola.

belt up vi (Brit col) chiudere la boccaccia.

beltway ['bɛltweɪ] n (US AUT) circonvallazione f; (: motorway) autostrada.

bemoan [bɪ'məun] vt lamentare.

bemused [bɪ'mju:zd] a perplesso(a), stupito(a).

bench [bɛntʃ] n panca; (in workshop) banco; **the B~** (LAW) la Corte.

bench mark n banco di prova.

bend [bɛnd] vb (pt, pp **bent** [bɛnt]) vt curvare; (leg, arm) piegare ♦ vi curvarsi; piegarsi ♦ n (Brit: in road) curva; (in pipe, river) gomito.

bend down vi chinarsi.

bend over vi piegarsi.

bends [bɛndz] npl (MED) embolia.

beneath [bɪ'ni:θ] prep sotto, al di sotto di; (unworthy of) indegno(a) di ♦ ad sotto, di sotto.

benefactor ['bɛnɪfæktə*] n benefattore m.

benefactress ['bɛnɪfæktrɪs] n benefattrice f.

beneficial [bɛnɪ'fɪʃəl] a che fa bene; vantaggioso(a); **~ to** che giova a.

beneficiary [bɛnɪ'fɪʃərɪ] n (LAW) beneficiario/

a.

benefit ['bɛnɪfɪt] n beneficio, vantaggio; (allowance of money) indennità f inv ♦ vt far bene a ♦ vi: **he'll ~ from it** ne trarrà beneficio or profitto.

benefit performance n spettacolo di beneficenza.

Benelux ['bɛnɪlʌks] n Benelux m.

benevolent [bɪ'nɛvələnt] a benevolo(a).

BEng n abbr (= Bachelor of Engineering) laurea in ingegneria.

benign [bɪ'naɪn] a benevolo(a); (MED) benigno(a).

bent [bɛnt] pt, pp of **bend** ♦ n inclinazione f ♦ a (wire, pipe) piegato(a), storto(a); (col: dishonest) losco(a); **to be ~ on** essere deciso(a) a.

bequeath [bɪ'kwi:ð] vt lasciare in eredità.

bequest [bɪ'kwɛst] n lascito.

bereaved [bɪ'ri:vd] a in lutto ♦ npl: **the ~ i** familiari in lutto.

bereavement [bɪ'ri:vmənt] n lutto.

beret ['bɛreɪ] n berretto.

Bering Sea ['bɛrɪŋ-] n: **the ~** il mar di Bering.

Berks abbr (Brit) = Berkshire.

Berlin [bə:'lɪn] n Berlino f; **East/West ~** Berlino est/ovest.

berm [bə:m] n (US AUT) corsia d'emergenza.

Bermuda [bə:'mju:də] n le Bermude.

Bermuda shorts npl bermuda mpl.

Bern [bə:n] n Berna f.

berry ['bɛrɪ] n bacca.

berserk [bə'sə:k] a: **to go ~** montare su tutte le furie.

berth [bə:θ] n (bed) cuccetta; (for ship) ormeggio ♦ vi (in harbour) entrare in porto; (at anchor) gettare l'ancora; **to give sb a wide ~** (fig) tenersi alla larga da qn.

beseech, pt, pp besought [bɪ'si:tʃ, bɪ'sɔ:t] vt implorare.

beset, pt, pp beset [bɪ'sɛt] vt assalire ♦ a: **a policy ~ with dangers** una politica irta or piena di pericoli.

besetting [bɪ'sɛtɪŋ] a: **his ~ sin** il suo più grande difetto.

beside [bɪ'saɪd] prep accanto a; (compared with) rispetto a, in confronto a; **to be ~ o.s. (with anger)** essere fuori di sé; **that's ~ the point** non c'entra.

besides [bɪ'saɪdz] ad inoltre, per di più ♦ prep oltre a; (except) a parte.

besiege [bɪ'si:dʒ] vt (town) assediare; (fig) tempestare.

besotted [bɪ'sɔtɪd] a (Brit): **~ with** infatuato(a) di.

besought [bɪ'sɔ:t] pt, pp of **beseech**.

bespectacled [bɪ'spɛktɪkld] a occhialuto(a).

bespoke [bɪ'spəuk] a (Brit: garment) su misura; **~ tailor** sarto.

best [bɛst] a migliore ♦ ad meglio; **the ~ thing to do is ...** la cosa migliore da fare or farsi è ...; **the ~ part of** (quantity) la maggior parte di; **at ~** tutt'al più; **to make**

the ~ of sth cavare il meglio possibile da qc; **to do one's** ~ fare del proprio meglio; **to the** ~ **of my knowledge** per quel che ne so; **to the** ~ **of my ability** al massimo delle mie capacità; **he's not exactly patient at the** ~ **of times** non è mai molto paziente.

best man n testimone m dello sposo.

bestow [bɪ'stəu] vt: **to** ~ **sth on sb** conferire qc a qn.

bestseller ['bɛst'sɛlə*] n bestseller m inv.

bet [bɛt] n scommessa ♦ vt, vi (pt, pp **bet** or **betted**) scommettere; **it's a safe** ~ (fig) è molto probabile.

Bethlehem ['bɛθlɪhɛm] n Betlemme f.

betray [bɪ'treɪ] vt tradire.

betrayal [bɪ'treɪəl] n tradimento.

better ['bɛtə*] a migliore ♦ ad meglio ♦ vt migliorare ♦ n: **to get the** ~ **of** avere la meglio su; **you had** ~ **do it** è meglio che lo faccia; **he thought** ~ **of it** cambiò idea; **to get** ~ migliorare; **a change for the** ~ un cambiamento in meglio; **that's** ~! così va meglio!; **I had** ~ **go** dovrei andare; ~ **off** a più ricco(a); (fig): **you'd be** ~ **off this way** starebbe meglio così.

betting ['bɛtɪŋ] n scommesse fpl.

betting shop n (Brit) ufficio dell'allibratore.

between [bɪ'twiːn] prep tra ♦ ad in mezzo, nel mezzo; **the road** ~ **here and London** la strada da qui a Londra; **we only had £5** ~ **us** fra tutti e due avevamo solo 5 sterline.

bevel ['bɛvl] n (also: ~**(led) edge**) profilo smussato.

beverage ['bɛvərɪdʒ] n bevanda.

bevy ['bɛvɪ] n: **a** ~ **of** una banda di.

bewail [bɪ'weɪl] vt lamentare.

beware [bɪ'wɛə*] vt, vi: **to** ~ (**of**) stare attento(a) (a).

bewildered [bɪ'wɪldəd] a sconcertato(a), confuso(a).

bewildering [bɪ'wɪldərɪŋ] a sconcertante, sbalorditivo(a).

bewitching [bɪ'wɪtʃɪŋ] a affascinante.

beyond [bɪ'jɔnd] prep (in space) oltre; (exceeding) al di sopra di ♦ ad di là; ~ **doubt** senza dubbio; ~ **repair** irreparabile.

b/f abbr see **brought forward**.

BFPO n abbr (= British Forces Post Office) recapito delle truppe britanniche all'estero.

bhp n abbr (AUT: = brake horsepower) c.v. (= cavallo vapore).

bi... [baɪ] prefix bi....

biannual [baɪ'ænjuəl] a semestrale.

bias ['baɪəs] n (prejudice) pregiudizio; (preference) preferenza.

bias(s)ed ['baɪəst] a parziale; **to be** ~ **against** essere prevenuto(a) contro.

bib [bɪb] n bavaglino.

Bible ['baɪbl] n Bibbia.

bibliography [bɪblɪ'ɔgrəfɪ] n bibliografia.

bicarbonate of soda [baɪ'kɑːbənɪt-] n bicarbonato (di sodio).

bicentenary [baɪsɛn'tiːnərɪ], **bicentennial** [baɪsɛn'tɛnɪəl] n bicentenario.

biceps ['baɪsɛps] n bicipite m.

bicker ['bɪkə*] vi bisticciare.

bicycle ['baɪsɪkl] n bicicletta.

bicycle path n, **bicycle track** n sentiero ciclabile.

bicycle pump n pompa della bicicletta.

bid [bɪd] n offerta; (attempt) tentativo ♦ vb (pt **bade** [bæd] or **bid**, pp **bidden** ['bɪdn] or **bid**) vi fare un'offerta ♦ vt fare un'offerta di; **to** ~ **sb good day** dire buon giorno a qn.

bidder ['bɪdə*] n: **the highest** ~ il maggior offerente.

bidding ['bɪdɪŋ] n offerte fpl.

bide [baɪd] vt: **to** ~ **one's time** aspettare il momento giusto.

bidet ['biːdeɪ] n bidè m inv.

bidirectional ['baɪdɪ'rɛkʃənl] a bidirezionale.

biennial [baɪ'ɛnɪəl] a biennale ♦ n (pianta) biennale f.

bier [bɪə*] n bara.

bifocals [baɪ'fəuklz] npl occhiali mpl bifocali.

big [bɪg] a grande; grosso(a); **my** ~ **brother** mio fratello maggiore; **to do things in a** ~ **way** fare le cose in grande.

bigamy ['bɪgəmɪ] n bigamia.

big dipper [-'dɪpə*] n montagne fpl russe, otto m inv volante.

big end n (AUT) testa di biella.

bigheaded ['bɪg'hɛdɪd] a presuntuoso(a).

big-hearted ['bɪg'hɑːtɪd] a generoso(a).

bigot ['bɪgət] n persona gretta.

bigoted ['bɪgətɪd] a gretto(a).

bigotry ['bɪgətrɪ] n grettezza.

big toe n alluce m.

big top n tendone m del circo.

big wheel n (at fair) ruota (panoramica).

bigwig ['bɪgwɪg] n (col) pezzo grosso.

bike [baɪk] n bici f inv.

bikini [bɪ'kiːnɪ] n bikini m inv.

bilateral [baɪ'lætərl] a bilaterale.

bile [baɪl] n bile f.

bilingual [baɪ'lɪŋgwəl] a bilingue.

bilious ['bɪlɪəs] a biliare; (fig) bilioso(a).

bill [bɪl] n (in hotel, restaurant) conto; (COMM) fattura; (for gas, electricity) bolletta, conto; (POL) atto; (US: banknote) banconota; (notice) avviso; (THEATRE): **on the** ~ in cartellone; (of bird) becco ♦ vt mandare il conto a; **may I have the** ~ **please?** posso avere il conto per piacere?; **"stick** or **post no** ~**s"** "divieto di affissione"; **to fit** or **fill the** ~ (fig) fare al caso; ~ **of exchange** cambiale f, tratta; ~ **of lading** polizza di carico; ~ **of sale** atto di vendita.

billboard ['bɪlbɔːd] n tabellone m.

billet ['bɪlɪt] n alloggio ♦ vt (troops etc) alloggiare.

billfold ['bɪlfəuld] n (US) portafoglio.

billiards ['bɪljədz] n biliardo.

billion ['bɪljən] n (Brit) bilione m; (US) miliardo.

billow ['bɪləu] n (of smoke) nuvola; (of sail) rigonfiamento ♦ vi (smoke) alzarsi in volute; (sail) gonfiarsi.

bills payable (B/P, b.p.) *npl* effetti *mpl* passivi.

bills receivable (B/R, b.r.) *npl* effetti *mpl* attivi.

billy goat ['bɪlɪgəut] *n* caprone *m*, becco.

bin [bɪn] *n* bidone *m*; (*Brit: also*: **dust~**) pattumiera; (: *also*: **litter ~**) cestino.

binary ['baɪnərɪ] *a* binario(a).

bind, *pt, pp* **bound** [baɪnd, baund] *vt* legare; (*oblige*) obbligare.

  bind over *vt* (*LAW*) dare la condizionale a.

  bind up *vt* (*wound*) fasciare, bendare; **to be bound up in** (*work, research etc*) essere completamente assorbito da; **to be bound up with** (*person*) dedicarsi completamente a.

binder ['baɪndə*] *n* (*file*) classificatore *m*.

binding ['baɪndɪŋ] *n* (*of book*) legatura ♦ *a* (*contract*) vincolante.

binge [bɪndʒ] *n* (*col*): **to go on a ~** fare baldoria.

bingo ['bɪŋgəu] *n* gioco simile alla tombola.

binoculars [bɪ'nɔkjuləz] *npl* binocolo.

biochemistry [baɪəu'kɛmɪstrɪ] *n* biochimica.

biodegradable ['baɪəudɪ'greɪdəbl] *a* biodegradabile.

biographer [baɪ'ɔgrəfə*] *n* biografo/a.

biographic(al) [baɪə'græfɪk(l)] *a* biografico(a).

biography [baɪ'ɔgrəfɪ] *n* biografia.

biological [baɪə'lɔdʒɪkl] *a* biologico(a).

biologist [baɪ'ɔlədʒɪst] *n* biologo/a.

biology [baɪ'ɔlədʒɪ] *n* biologia.

biophysics [baɪəu'fɪzɪks] *n* biofisica.

biopsy ['baɪɔpsɪ] *n* biopsia.

biotechnology [baɪəutɛk'nɔlədʒɪ] *n* biotecnologia.

birch [bə:tʃ] *n* betulla.

bird [bə:d] *n* uccello; (*Brit col: girl*) bambola.

bird's-eye view ['bə:dzaɪ-] *n* vista panoramica.

bird watcher *n* ornitologo/a dilettante.

Biro ® ['baɪrəu] *n* biro ® *f inv*.

birth [bə:θ] *n* nascita; **to give ~ to** dare alla luce; (*fig*) dare inizio a.

birth certificate *n* certificato di nascita.

birth control *n* controllo delle nascite; contraccezione *f*.

birthday ['bə:θdeɪ] *n* compleanno.

birthmark ['bə:θmɑ:k] *n* voglia.

birthplace ['bə:θpleɪs] *n* luogo di nascita.

birth rate *n* indice *m* di natalità.

Biscay ['bɪskeɪ] *n*: **the Bay of ~** il golfo di Biscaglia.

biscuit ['bɪskɪt] *n* (*Brit*) biscotto; (*US*) panino al latte.

bisect [baɪ'sɛkt] *vt* tagliare in due (parti); (*MATH*) bisecare.

bishop ['bɪʃəp] *n* vescovo; (*CHESS*) alfiere *m*.

bit [bɪt] *pt of* **bite** ♦ *n* pezzo; (*of tool*) punta; (*of horse*) morso; (*COMPUT*) bit *m inv*; (*US*: *coin*) ottavo di dollaro; **a ~ of** un po' di; **a ~ mad/dangerous** un po' matto/pericoloso; **~ by ~** a poco a poco; **to do one's ~** fare la propria parte; **to come to ~s** (*break*) andare a pezzi; **bring all your ~s and pieces**

porta tutte le tue cose.

bitch [bɪtʃ] *n* (*dog*) cagna; (*col!*) puttana (*!*).

bite [baɪt] *vt, vi* (*pt* **bit** [bɪt], *pp* **bitten** ['bɪtn]) mordere ♦ *n* morso; (*insect* ~) puntura; (*mouthful*) boccone *m*; **let's have a ~** (**to eat**) mangiamo un boccone; **to ~ one's nails** mangiarsi le unghie.

biting ['baɪtɪŋ] *a* pungente.

bit part *n* (*THEATRE*) particina.

bitten ['bɪtn] *pp of* **bite**.

bitter ['bɪtə*] *a* amaro(a); (*wind, criticism*) pungente; (*icy: weather*) gelido(a) ♦ *n* (*Brit: beer*) birra amara; **to the ~ end** a oltranza.

bitterly ['bɪtəlɪ] *ad* (*disappoint, complain, weep*) amaramente; (*oppose, criticise*) aspramente; (*jealous*) profondamente; **it's ~ cold** fa un freddo gelido.

bitterness ['bɪtənɪs] *n* amarezza; gusto amaro.

bittersweet ['bɪtəswi:t] *a* agrodolce.

bitty ['bɪtɪ] *a* (*Brit col*) frammentario(a).

bitumen ['bɪtjumɪn] *n* bitume *m*.

bivouac ['bɪvuæk] *n* bivacco.

bizarre [bɪ'za:*] *a* bizzarro(a).

bk *abbr* = **bank; book**.

BL *n abbr* (= *Bachelor of Law(s)*, *Bachelor of Letters*) *titolo di studio*; (*US*: = *Bachelor of Literature*) *titolo di studio*.

bl *abbr* = **bill of lading**.

blab [blæb] *vi* parlare troppo ♦ *vt* (*also*: ~ **out**) spifferare.

black [blæk] *a* nero(a) ♦ *n* nero; (*person*): **B~** negro/a ♦ *vt* (*Brit INDUSTRY*) boicottare; ~ **coffee** caffè *m inv* nero; **to give sb a ~ eye** fare un occhio nero a qn; **in the ~** (*in credit*) in attivo; **there it is in ~ and white** (*fig*) eccolo nero su bianco; ~ **and blue** *a* tutto(a) pesto(a).

  black out *vi* (*faint*) svenire.

black belt *n* (*SPORT*) cintura nera; (*US*: *area*): **the ~** *zona abitata principalmente da negri*.

blackberry ['blækbərɪ] *n* mora.

blackbird ['blækbə:d] *n* merlo.

blackboard ['blækbɔ:d] *n* lavagna.

black box *n* (*AVIAT*) scatola nera.

Black Country *n* (*Brit*): **the ~** *zona carbonifera del centro dell'Inghilterra*.

blackcurrant [blæk'kʌrənt] *n* ribes *m inv*.

black economy *n* (*Brit*) economia sommersa.

blacken ['blækn] *vt* annerire.

Black Forest *n*: **the ~** la Foresta Nera.

blackhead ['blækhɛd] *n* punto nero, comedone *m*.

black ice *n* strato trasparente di ghiaccio.

blackjack ['blækdʒæk] *n* (*CARDS*) ventuno; (*US*: *truncheon*) manganello.

blackleg ['blæklɛg] *n* (*Brit*) crumiro.

blacklist ['blæklɪst] *n* lista nera ♦ *vt* mettere sulla lista nera.

blackmail ['blækmeɪl] *n* ricatto ♦ *vt* ricattare.

blackmailer ['blækmeɪlə*] *n* ricattatore/trice.

black market *n* mercato nero.

blackout ['blækaut] *n* oscuramento; *(fainting)* svenimento; *(TV)* interruzione *f* delle trasmissioni.

Black Sea *n*: **the ~** il mar Nero.

black sheep *n* pecora nera.

blacksmith ['blæksmɪθ] *n* fabbro ferraio.

black spot *n* *(AUT)* luogo famigerato per gli incidenti.

bladder ['blædə*] *n* vescica.

blade [bleɪd] *n* lama; *(of oar)* pala; **~ of grass** filo d'erba.

blame [bleɪm] *n* colpa ♦ *vt*: **to ~ sb/sth for sth** dare la colpa di qc a qn/qc; **who's to ~?** chi è colpevole?; **I'm not to ~** non è colpa mia.

blameless ['bleɪmlɪs] *a* irreprensibile.

blanch [blɑ:ntʃ] *vi (person)* sbiancare in viso ♦ *vt (CULIN)* scottare.

bland [blænd] *a* mite; *(taste)* blando(a).

blank [blæŋk] *a* bianco(a); *(look)* distratto(a) ♦ *n* spazio vuoto; *(cartridge)* cartuccia a salve; **to draw a ~** *(fig)* non aver nessun risultato.

blank cheque, *(US)* **blank check** *n* assegno in bianco; **to give sb a ~ to do** *(fig)* dare carta bianca a qn per fare.

blanket ['blæŋkɪt] *n* coperta ♦ *a (statement, agreement)* globale.

blanket cover *n*: **to give ~** *(subj: insurance policy)* coprire tutti i rischi.

blare [blɛə*] *vi* strombettare; *(radio)* suonare a tutto volume.

blasé ['blɑ:zeɪ] *a* blasé *inv.*

blasphemous ['blæsfɪməs] *a* blasfemo(a).

blasphemy ['blæsfɪmɪ] *n* bestemmia.

blast [blɑ:st] *n (of wind)* raffica; *(of air, steam)* getto; *(bomb ~)* esplosione *f* ♦ *vt* far saltare ♦ *excl (Brit col)* mannaggia!; **(at) full ~** a tutta forza.

blast off *vi (SPACE)* essere lanciato(a).

blast-off ['blɑ:stɔf] *n (SPACE)* lancio.

blatant ['bleɪtənt] *a* flagrante.

blatantly ['bleɪtəntlɪ] *ad*: **it's ~ obvious** è lampante.

blaze [bleɪz] *n (fire)* incendio; *(glow: of fire, sun etc)* bagliore *m*; *(fig)* vampata ♦ *vi (fire)* ardere, fiammeggiare; *(fig)* infiammarsi ♦ *vt*: **to ~ a trail** *(fig)* tracciare una via nuova; **in a ~ of publicity** circondato da grande pubblicità.

blazer ['bleɪzə*] *n* blazer *m inv.*

bleach [bli:tʃ] *n (also: household ~)* varechina ♦ *vt (material)* candeggiare.

bleached ['bli:tʃt] *a (hair)* decolorato(a).

bleachers ['bli:tʃəz] *npl (US)* posti *mpl* di gradinata.

bleak [bli:k] *a (prospect, future)* tetro(a); *(landscape)* desolato(a); *(weather)* gelido(a); *(smile)* pallido(a).

bleary-eyed ['blɪərɪ'aɪd] *a* dagli occhi offuscati.

bleat [bli:t] *vi* belare.

bleed, *pt, pp* **bled** [bli:d, blɛd] *vt* dissanguare; *(brakes, radiator)* spurgare ♦ *vi* sanguinare;

my nose is ~ing mi viene fuori sangue dal naso.

bleeper ['bli:pə*] *n (of doctor etc)* cicalino.

blemish ['blɛmɪʃ] *n* macchia.

blend [blɛnd] *n* miscela ♦ *vt* mescolare ♦ *vi (colours etc)* armonizzare.

blender ['blɛndə*] *n (CULIN)* frullatore *m*.

bless, *pt, pp* **blessed** *or* **blest** [blɛs, blɛst] *vt* benedire; **~ you!** *(sneezing)* salute!; **to be ~ed with** godere di.

blessed ['blɛsɪd] *a (REL: holy)* benedetto(a); *(happy)* beato(a); **every ~ day** tutti i santi giorni.

blessing ['blɛsɪŋ] *n* benedizione *f*; fortuna; **to count one's ~s** ringraziare Iddio, ritenersi fortunato; **it was a ~ in disguise** in fondo è stato un bene.

blest [blɛst] *pt, pp of* **bless.**

blew [blu:] *pt of* **blow.**

blight [blaɪt] *n (of plants)* golpe *f* ♦ *vt (hopes etc)* deludere; *(life)* rovinare.

blimey ['blaɪmɪ] *excl (Brit col)* accidenti!

blind [blaɪnd] *a* cieco(a) ♦ *n (for window)* avvolgibile *m*; *(Venetian ~)* veneziana ♦ *vt* accecare; **to turn a ~ eye (on** *or* **to)** chiudere un occhio (su).

blind alley *n* vicolo cieco.

blind corner *n (Brit)* svolta cieca.

blinders ['blaɪndəz] *npl (US)* = **blinkers.**

blindfold ['blaɪndfəuld] *n* benda ♦ *a, ad* bendato(a) ♦ *vt* bendare gli occhi a.

blindly ['blaɪndlɪ] *ad* ciecamente.

blindness ['blaɪndnɪs] *n* cecità.

blind spot *n (AUT etc)* punto cieco; *(fig)* punto debole.

blink [blɪŋk] *vi* battere gli occhi; *(light)* lampeggiare ♦ *n*: **to be on the ~** *(col)* essere scassato(a).

blinkers ['blɪŋkəz] *npl (Brit)* paraocchi *mpl.*

blinking ['blɪŋkɪŋ] *a (Brit col)*: **this ~ ...** questo(a) maledetto(a) ....

bliss [blɪs] *n* estasi *f*.

blissful ['blɪsfəl] *a (event, day)* stupendo(a), meraviglioso(a); *(smile)* beato(a); **in ~ ignorance** nella (più) beata ignoranza.

blissfully ['blɪsfəlɪ] *a (sigh, smile)* beatamente; **~ happy** magnificamente felice.

blister ['blɪstə*] *n (on skin)* vescica; *(on paintwork)* bolla ♦ *vi (paint)* coprirsi di bolle.

blithe [blaɪð] *a* gioioso(a), allegro(a).

blithely ['blaɪðlɪ] *ad* allegramente.

blithering ['blɪðərɪŋ] *a (col)*: **this ~ idiot** questa razza d'idiota.

BLit(t) *n abbr* (= *Bachelor of Literature*) titolo di studio.

blitz [blɪts] *n* blitz *m*; **to have a ~ on sth** *(fig)* prendere d'assalto qc.

blizzard ['blɪzəd] *n* bufera di neve.

BLM *n abbr* (*US:* = *Bureau of Land Management*) ≈ il demanio.

bloated ['bləutɪd] *a* gonfio(a).

blob [blɔb] *n (drop)* goccia; *(stain, spot)* macchia.

bloc [blɔk] *n (POL)* blocco.

block [blɔk] n (gen, COMPUT) blocco; (in pipes) ingombro; (toy) cubo; (of buildings) isolato; ~ **of flats** caseggiato ♦ vt (gen, COMPUT) bloccare; **3** ~**s from here** a 3 isolati di distanza da qui; **mental** ~ blocco mentale.

block up vt bloccare; (pipe) ingorgare, intasare.

blockade [blɔ'keɪd] n blocco ♦ vt assediare.

blockage ['blɔkɪdʒ] n ostacolo.

block and tackle n (TECH) paranco.

block booking n prenotazione f in blocco.

blockbuster ['blɔkbʌstə*] n libro or film etc sensazionale.

block capitals npl stampatello.

blockhead ['blɔkhɛd] n testa di legno.

block letters npl stampatello.

block release n (Brit) periodo pagato concesso al tirocinante per effettuare studi superiori.

block vote n (Brit) voto per delega.

bloke [bləuk] n (Brit col) tizio.

blond [blɔnd] n (man) biondo ♦ a biondo(a).

blonde [blɔnd] n (woman) bionda ♦ a biondo(a).

blood [blʌd] n sangue m; **new** ~ (fig) nuova linfa.

bloodcurdling ['blʌdkə:dlɪŋ] a raccapricciante, da far gelare il sangue.

blood donor n donatore/trice di sangue.

blood group n gruppo sanguigno.

bloodhound ['blʌdhaund] n segugio.

bloodless ['blʌdlɪs] a (pale) smorto(a), esangue; (coup) senza spargimento di sangue.

bloodletting ['blʌdlɛtɪŋ] n (MED) salasso; (fig) spargimento di sangue.

blood poisoning n setticemia.

blood pressure n pressione f sanguigna; **to have high/low** ~ avere la pressione alta/bassa.

bloodshed ['blʌdʃɛd] n spargimento di sangue.

bloodshot ['blʌdʃɔt] a: ~ **eyes** occhi iniettati di sangue.

bloodstained ['blʌdsteɪnd] a macchiato(a) di sangue.

bloodstream ['blʌdstri:m] n flusso del sangue.

blood test n analisi f inv del sangue.

bloodthirsty ['blʌdθə:stɪ] a assetato(a) di sangue.

blood transfusion n trasfusione f di sangue.

blood vessel n vaso sanguigno.

bloody ['blʌdɪ] a sanguinoso(a); (Brit col!): **this** ~ ... questo maledetto ...; **a** ~ **awful day** (col!) una giornata di merda (!); ~ **good** (col!) maledettamente buono.

bloody-minded ['blʌdɪ'maɪndɪd] a (Brit col) indisponente.

bloom [blu:m] n fiore m ♦ vi essere in fiore.

blooming ['blu:mɪŋ] a (col): **this** ~ ... questo(a) dannato(a) ....

blossom ['blɔsəm] n fiore m; (with pl sense) fiori mpl ♦ vi essere in fiore; **to** ~ **into** (fig)

diventare.

blot [blɔt] n macchia ♦ vt macchiare; **to be a** ~ **on the landscape** rovinare il paesaggio; **to** ~ **one's copy book** (fig) farla grossa.

blot out vt (memories) cancellare; (view) nascondere; (nation, city) annientare.

blotchy ['blɔtʃɪ] a (complexion) coperto(a) di macchie.

blotter ['blɔtə*] n tampone m (di carta assorbente).

blotting paper ['blɔtɪŋ-] n carta assorbente.

blouse [blauz] n camicetta.

blow [bləu] n colpo ♦ vb (pt **blew**, pp **blown** [blu:, bləun]) vi soffiare ♦ vt (fuse) far saltare; **to come to** ~**s** venire alle mani; **to** ~ **one's nose** soffiarsi il naso; **to** ~ **a whistle** fischiare.

blow away vi volare via ♦ vt portare via.

blow down vt abbattere.

blow off vt far volare via; **to** ~ **off course** far uscire di rotta.

blow out vi scoppiare.

blow over vi calmarsi.

blow up vi saltare in aria ♦ vt far saltare in aria; (tyre) gonfiare; (PHOT) ingrandire.

blow-dry ['bləudraɪ] n (hairstyle) messa in piega a föhn ♦ vt asciugare con il föhn.

blowlamp ['bləulæmp] n (Brit) lampada a benzina per saldare.

blown [bləun] pp of **blow**.

blowout ['bləuaut] n (of tyre) scoppio; (col: big meal) abbuffata.

blowtorch ['bləutɔ:tʃ] n lampada a benzina per saldare.

blowzy ['blauzɪ] a trasandato(a).

BLS n abbr (US) = Bureau of Labor Statistics.

blubber ['blʌbə*] n grasso di balena ♦ vi (pej) piangere forte.

bludgeon ['blʌdʒən] vt prendere a randellate.

blue [blu:] a azzurro(a), celeste; (darker) blu inv; ~ **film/joke** film/barzelletta pornografico(a); **(only) once in a** ~ **moon** a ogni morte di papa; **out of the** ~ (fig) all'improvviso; see also **blues**.

blue baby n neonato cianotico.

bluebell ['blu:bɛl] n giacinto di bosco.

bluebottle ['blu:bɔtl] n moscone m.

blue cheese n formaggio tipo gorgonzola.

blue-chip ['blu:tʃɪp] a: ~ **investment** investimento sicuro.

blue-collar worker ['blu:kɔlə*-] n operaio/a.

blue jeans npl blue-jeans mpl.

blueprint ['blu:prɪnt] n cianografia; (fig): ~ **(for)** formula (di).

blues [blu:z] npl: **the** ~ (MUS) il blues; **to have the** ~ (col: feeling) essere a terra.

bluff [blʌf] vi bluffare ♦ n bluff m inv; (promontory) promontorio scosceso ♦ a (person) brusco(a); **to call sb's** ~ mettere alla prova il bluff di qn.

blunder ['blʌndə*] n abbaglio ♦ vi prendere un abbaglio; **to** ~ **into sb/sth** andare a sbattere contro qn/qc.

blunt [blʌnt] a (edge) smussato(a); (point)

spuntato(a); (*knife*) che non taglia; (*person*) brusco(a) ♦ *vt* smussare; spuntare; **this pencil is** ~ questa matita non ha più la punta; ~ **instrument** (*LAW*) corpo contundente.

bluntly ['blʌntlɪ] *ad* (*speak*) senza mezzi termini.

bluntness ['blʌntnɪs] *n* (*of person*) brutale franchezza.

blur [bləː*] *n* cosa offuscata ♦ *vt* offuscare.

blurb [bləːb] *n* trafiletto pubblicitario.

blurred [bləːd] *a* (*photo*) mosso(a); (*TV*) sfuocato(a).

blurt out [bləːt-] *vt* lasciarsi sfuggire.

blush [blʌʃ] *vi* arrossire ♦ *n* rossore *m*.

blusher ['blʌʃə*] *n* fard *m inv*.

bluster ['blʌstə*] *n* spaccoпate *fpl*; (*threats*) vuote minacce *fpl* ♦ *vi* fare lo spaccone; minacciare a vuoto.

blustering ['blʌstərɪŋ] *a* (*tone etc*) da spaccone.

blustery ['blʌstərɪ] *a* (*weather*) burrascoso(a).

Blvd *abbr* = **boulevard**.

BM *n abbr* = *British Museum*; (*SCOL*: = *Bachelor of Medicine*) titolo di studio.

BMA *n abbr* = *British Medical Association*.

BMJ *n abbr* = *British Medical Journal*.

BMus *n abbr* (= *Bachelor of Music*) titolo di studio.

BO *n abbr* (*col* = *body odour*) odori *mpl* sgradevoli (del corpo); (*US*) = **box office**.

boar [bɔː*] *n* cinghiale *m*.

board [bɔːd] *n* tavola; (*on wall*) tabellone *m*; (*for chess etc*) scacchiera; (*committee*) consiglio, comitato; (*in firm*) consiglio d'amministrazione; (*NAUT, AVIAT*): **on** ~ a bordo ♦ *vt* (*ship*) salire a bordo di; (*train*) salire su; **full** ~ (*Brit*) pensione *f* completa; **half** ~ (*Brit*) mezza pensione; ~ **and lodging** vitto e alloggio; **above** ~ (*fig*) regolare; **across the** ~ (*fig: ad*) per tutte le categorie; (: *a*) generale; **to go by the** ~ venir messo(a) da parte.

board up *vt* (*door*) chiudere con assi.

boarder ['bɔːdə*] *n* pensionante *m/f*; (*SCOL*) convittore/trice.

board game *n* gioco da tavolo.

boarding card ['bɔːdɪŋ-] *n* (*AVIAT, NAUT*) carta d'imbarco.

boarding house *n* pensione *f*.

boarding pass *n* (*Brit*) = **boarding card**.

boarding school *n* collegio.

board meeting *n* riunione *f* di consiglio.

board room *n* sala del consiglio.

boardwalk ['bɔːdwɔːk] *n* (*US*) passeggiata a mare.

boast [bəust] *vi*: **to** ~ (**about** *or* **of**) vantarsi (di) ♦ *vt* vantare ♦ *n* vanteria; vanto.

boastful ['bəustful] *a* vanaglorioso(a).

boastfulness ['bəustfulnɪs] *n* vanagloria.

boat [bəut] *n* nave *f*; (*small*) barca; **to go by** ~ andare in barca *or* in nave; **we're all in the same** ~ (*fig*) siamo tutti nella stessa barca.

boater ['bəutə*] *n* (*hat*) paglietta.

boating ['bəutɪŋ] *n* canottaggio.

boatswain ['bəusn] *n* nostromo.

bob [bɔb] *vi* (*boat, cork on water: also:* ~ **up and down**) andare su e giù ♦ *n* (*Brit col*) = **shilling**.

bob up *vi* saltare fuori.

bobbin ['bɔbɪn] *n* bobina; (*of sewing machine*) rocchetto.

bobby ['bɔbɪ] *n* (*Brit col*) ≈ poliziotto.

bobsleigh ['bɔbsleɪ] *n* bob *m inv*.

bode [bəud] *vi*: **to** ~ **well/ill (for)** essere di buon/cattivo auspicio (per).

bodice ['bɔdɪs] *n* corsetto.

bodily ['bɔdɪlɪ] *a* (*comfort, needs*) materiale; (*pain*) fisico(a) ♦ *ad* (*carry*) in braccio; (*lift*) di peso.

body ['bɔdɪ] *n* corpo; (*of car*) carrozzeria; (*of plane*) fusoliera; (*organization*) associazione *f*, organizzazione *f*; (*quantity*) quantità *f inv*; (*of speech, document*) parte *f* principale; **in a** ~ in massa; **ruling** ~ direttivo; **a wine with** ~ un vino corposo.

body-building ['bɔdɪ'bɪldɪŋ] *n* culturismo.

bodyguard ['bɔdɪgɑːd] *n* guardia del corpo.

body repairs *npl* (*AUT*) lavori *mpl* di carrozzeria.

bodywork ['bɔdɪwəːk] *n* carrozzeria.

boffin ['bɔfɪn] *n* scienziato.

bog [bɔg] *n* palude *f* ♦ *vt*: **to get** ~**ged down** (*fig*) impantanarsi.

bogey ['bəugɪ] *n* (*worry*) spauracchio; (*also:* ~ **man**) babau *m inv*.

boggle ['bɔgl] *vi*: **the mind** ~**s** è incredibile.

Bogotá [bəugə'tɑː] *n* Bogotà *f*.

bogus ['bəugəs] *a* falso(a); finto(a).

Bohemia [bəu'hiːmɪə] *n* Boemia.

Bohemian [bəu'hiːmɪən] *a, n* boemo(a).

boil [bɔɪl] *vt, vi* bollire ♦ *n* (*MED*) foruncolo; **to come to the** *or* (*US*) **a** ~ raggiungere l'ebollizione; **to bring to the** *or* (*US*) **a** ~ portare a ebollizione; ~**ed egg** uovo alla coque; ~**ed potatoes** patate *fpl* bollite *or* lesse.

boil down *vi* (*fig*): **to** ~ **down to** ridursi a.

boil over *vi* traboccare (bollendo).

boiler ['bɔɪlə*] *n* caldaia.

boiler suit *n* (*Brit*) tuta.

boiling ['bɔɪlɪŋ] *a* bollente; **I'm** ~ (**hot**) (*col*) sto morendo di caldo.

boiling point *n* punto di ebollizione.

boisterous ['bɔɪstərəs] *a* chiassoso(a).

bold [bəuld] *a* audace; (*child*) impudente; (*outline*) chiaro(a); (*colour*) deciso(a).

boldness ['bəuldnɪs] *n* audacia; impudenza.

bold type *n* (*TYP*) neretto, grassetto.

Bolivia [bə'lɪvɪə] *n* Bolivia.

Bolivian [bə'lɪvɪən] *a, n* boliviano(a).

bollard ['bɔləd] *n* (*NAUT*) bitta; (*Brit AUT*) colonnina luminosa.

bolster ['bəulstə*] *n* capezzale *m*.

bolster up *vt* sostenere.

bolt [bəult] *n* chiavistello; (*with nut*) bullone *m* ♦ *ad*: ~ **upright** diritto(a) come un fuso ♦

vt serrare; (*food*) mangiare in fretta ♦ *vi* scappare via; **a ~ from the blue** (*fig*) un fulmine a ciel sereno.

bomb [bɔm] *n* bomba ♦ *vt* bombardare.

bombard [bɔm'bɑːd] *vt* bombardare.

bombardment [bɔm'bɑːdmənt] *n* bombardamento.

bombastic [bɔm'bæstɪk] *a* ampolloso(a).

bomb disposal *n*: **~ expert** artificiere *m*; **~ unit** corpo degli artificieri.

bomber ['bɔmə*] *n* bombardiere *m*; (*terrorist*) dinamitardo/a.

bombing ['bɔmɪŋ] *n* bombardamento.

bombshell ['bɔmʃɛl] *n* (*fig*) notizia bomba.

bomb site *n* luogo bombardato.

bona fide ['bəunə'faɪdɪ] *a* sincero(a); (*offer*) onesto(a).

bonanza [bə'nænzə] *n* cuccagna.

bond [bɔnd] *n* legame *m*; (*binding promise*, *FINANCE*) obbligazione *f*; **in ~** (*of goods*) in attesa di sdoganamento.

bondage ['bɔndɪdʒ] *n* schiavitù *f*.

bonded warehouse ['bɔndɪd-] *n* magazzino doganale.

bone [bəun] *n* osso; (*of fish*) spina, lisca ♦ *vt* disossare; togliere le spine a.

bone china *n* porcellana fine.

bone-dry ['bəun'draɪ] *a* asciuttissimo(a).

bone idle *a*: **to be ~** essere un(a) fannullone(a).

boner ['bəunə*] *n* (*US*) gaffe *f inv*.

bonfire ['bɔnfaɪə*] *n* falò *m inv*.

Bonn [bɔn] *n* Bonn *f*.

bonnet ['bɔnɪt] *n* cuffia; (*Brit*: *of car*) cofano.

bonny ['bɔnɪ] *a* (*esp Scottish*) bello(a), carino(a).

bonus ['bəunəs] *n* premio; (*on wages*) gratifica.

bony ['bəunɪ] *a* (*thin*: *person*) ossuto(a), angoloso(a); (*arm*, *face*, *MED*: *tissue*) osseo(a); (*meat*) pieno(a) di ossi; (*fish*) pieno(a) di spine.

boo [buː] *excl* ba! ♦ *vt* fischiare ♦ *n* fischio.

boob [buːb] *n* (*col*: *breast*) tetta; (: *Brit*: *mistake*) gaffe *f inv*.

booby prize ['buːbɪ-] *n* premio per il peggior contendente.

booby trap ['buːbɪ-] *n* trabocchetto; (*bomb*) congegno che esplode al contatto.

booby-trapped ['buːbɪtræpt] *a*: **a ~ car** una macchina con dell'esplosivo a bordo.

book [buk] *n* libro; (*of stamps etc*) blocchetto ♦ *vt* (*ticket*, *seat*, *room*) prenotare; (*driver*) multare; (*football player*) ammonire; **~s** *npl* (*COMM*) conti *mpl*; **to keep the ~s** (*COMM*) tenere la contabilità; **by the ~** secondo le regole; **to throw the ~ at sb** incriminare qn seriamente or con tutte le aggravanti.

book in *vi* (*Brit*: *at hotel*) prendere una camera.

book up *vt* riservare, prenotare; **the hotel is ~ed up** l'albergo è al completo; **all seats are ~ed up** è tutto esaurito.

bookable ['bukəbl] *a*: **seats are ~** si possono prenotare i posti.

bookcase ['bukkeɪs] *n* scaffale *m*.

book ends *npl* reggilibri *mpl*.

booking ['bukɪŋ] *n* (*Brit*) prenotazione *f*.

booking office *n* (*Brit*) biglietteria.

book-keeping ['buk'kiːpɪŋ] *n* contabilità.

booklet ['buklɪt] *n* opuscolo, libretto.

bookmaker ['bukmeɪkə*] *n* allibratore *m*.

bookseller ['buksɛlə*] *n* libraio.

bookshop ['bukʃɔp] *n* libreria.

bookstall ['bukstɔːl] *n* bancarella di libri.

bookstore ['bukstɔː*] *n* = **bookshop**.

book token *n* buono *m* libri *inv*.

book value *n* valore *m* contabile.

boom [buːm] *n* (*noise*) rimbombo; (*busy period*) boom *m inv* ♦ *vi* rimbombare; andare a gonfie vele.

boomerang ['buːməræŋ] *n* boomerang *m inv* ♦ *vi* (*fig*) avere effetto contrario; **to ~ on sb** (*fig*) ritorcersi contro qn.

boom town *n* città *f inv* in rapidissima espansione.

boon [buːn] *n* vantaggio.

boorish ['buərɪʃ] *a* maleducato(a).

boost [buːst] *n* spinta ♦ *vt* spingere; (*increase*: *sales*, *production*) incentivare; **to give a ~ to** (*morale*) tirar su; **it gave a ~ to his confidence** è stata per lui un'iniezione di fiducia.

booster ['buːstə*] *n* (*ELEC*) amplificatore *m*; (*TV*) amplificatore *m* di segnale; (*also*: **~ rocket**) razzo vettore; (*MED*) richiamo.

booster seat *n* (*AUT*: *for children*) seggiolino di sicurezza.

boot [buːt] *n* stivale *m*; (*ankle ~*) stivaletto; (*for hiking*) scarpone *m* da montagna; (*for football etc*) scarpa; (*Brit*: *of car*) portabagagli *m inv* ♦ *vt* (*COMPUT*) inizializzare; **to ~** (*in addition*) per giunta, in più; **to give sb the ~** (*col*) mettere qn alla porta.

booth [buːð] *n* (*at fair*) baraccone *m*; (*of cinema*, *telephone etc*) cabina; (*also*: **voting ~**) cabina (elettorale).

bootleg ['buːtlɛg] *a* di contrabbando; **~ record** registrazione *f* pirata *inv*.

booty ['buːtɪ] *n* bottino.

booze [buːz] (*col*) *n* alcool *m* ♦ *vi* trincare.

boozer ['buːzə*] *n* (*col*: *person*) beone *m*; (*Brit col*: *pub*) osteria.

border ['bɔːdə*] *n* orlo; margine *m*; (*of a country*) frontiera; **the B~** la *frontiera tra l'Inghilterra e la Scozia*; **the B~s** la *zona di confine tra l'Inghilterra e la Scozia*.

border on *vt fus* confinare con.

borderline ['bɔːdəlaɪn] *n* (*fig*) linea di demarcazione ♦ *a*: **~ case** caso limite.

bore [bɔː*] *pt of* **bear** ♦ *vt* (*hole*) perforare; (*person*) annoiare ♦ *n* (*person*) seccatore/trice; (*of gun*) calibro; **he's ~d to tears** or **~d to death** or **~d stiff** è annoiato a morte, si annoia da morire.

boredom ['bɔːdəm] *n* noia.

boring ['bɔːrɪŋ] *a* noioso(a).

born [bɔːn] *a*: **to be ~** nascere; **I was ~ in**

1960 sono nato nel 1960; ~ **blind** cieco dalla nascita; **a ~ comedian** un comico nato.
borne [bɔːn] *pp of* **bear**.
Borneo ['bɔːnɪəu] *n* Borneo.
borough ['bʌrə] *n* comune *m*.
borrow ['bɔrəu] *vt*: **to ~ sth (from sb)** prendere in prestito qc (da qn); **may I ~ your car?** può prestarmi la macchina?
borrower ['bɔrəuə*] *n* (*gen*) chi prende a prestito; (*ECON*) mutuatario/a.
borrowing ['bɔrəuɪŋ] *n* prestito.
borstal ['bɔːstl] *n* (*Brit*) riformatorio.
bosom ['buzəm] *n* petto; (*fig*) seno.
bosom friend *n* amico/a del cuore.
boss [bɔs] *n* capo ♦ *vt* (*also*: ~ **about** *or* **around**) comandare a bacchetta; **stop ~ing everyone about!** smettila di dare ordini a tutti!
bossy ['bɔsɪ] *a* prepotente.
bosun ['bəusn] *n* nostromo.
botanical [bə'tænɪkl] *a* botanico(a).
botanist ['bɔtənɪst] *n* botanico/a.
botany ['bɔtənɪ] *n* botanica.
botch [bɔtʃ] *vt* fare un pasticcio di.
both [bəuθ] *a* entrambi(e), tutt'e due ♦ *pronoun*: ~ (**of them**) entrambi(e); ~ **of us went, we ~ went** ci siamo andati tutt'e due ♦ *ad*: **they sell ~ meat and poultry** vendono insieme la carne ed il pollame.
bother ['bɔðə*] *vt* (*worry*) preoccupare; (*annoy*) infastidire ♦ *vi* (*gen*: ~ **o.s.**) preoccuparsi ♦ *n*: **it is a ~ to have to do** è una seccatura dover fare ♦ *excl* uffa!, accidenti!; **to ~ doing sth** darsi la pena di fare qc; **I'm sorry to ~ you** mi dispiace disturbarla; **please don't ~** non si scomodi; **it's no ~** non c'è problema.
Botswana [bɔt'swɑːnə] *n* Botswana *m*.
bottle ['bɔtl] *n* bottiglia; (*of perfume, shampoo etc*) flacone *m*; (*baby's*) biberon *m inv* ♦ *vt* imbottigliare; ~ **of wine/milk** bottiglia di vino/latte; **wine/milk ~** bottiglia da vino/del latte.
bottle up *vt* contenere.
bottle-fed ['bɔtlfed] *a* allattato(a) artificialmente.
bottleneck ['bɔtlnek] *n* ingorgo.
bottle-opener ['bɔtləupnə*] *n* apribottiglie *m inv*.
bottom ['bɔtəm] *n* fondo; (*of mountain, tree, hill*) piedi *mpl*; (*buttocks*) sedere *m* ♦ *a* più basso(a); ultimo(a); **at the ~ of** in fondo a; **to get to the ~ of sth** (*fig*) andare al fondo di *or* in fondo a qc.
bottomless ['bɔtəmlɪs] *a* senza fondo.
bough [bau] *n* ramo.
bought [bɔːt] *pt, pp of* **buy**.
boulder ['bəuldə*] *n* masso (tondeggiante).
boulevard ['buːlvɑːd] *n* viale *m*.
bounce [bauns] *vi* (*ball*) rimbalzare; (*cheque*) essere restituito(a) ♦ *vt* far rimbalzare ♦ *n* (*rebound*) rimbalzo; **to ~ in** entrare di slancio *or* con foga; **he's got plenty of ~** (*fig*) è molto esuberante.

bouncer ['baunsə*] *n* buttafuori *m inv*.
bound [baund] *pt, pp of* **bind** ♦ *n* (*gen pl*) limite *m*; (*leap*) salto ♦ *vt* (*leap*) saltare; (*limit*) delimitare ♦ *a*: **to be ~ to do sth** (*obliged*) essere costretto(a) a fare qc; **he's ~ to fail** (*likely*) è certo di fallire; ~ **for** diretto(a) a; **out of ~s** il cui accesso è vietato.
boundary ['baundrɪ] *n* confine *m*.
boundless ['baundlɪs] *a* illimitato(a).
bountiful ['bauntɪful] *a* (*person*) munifico(a); (*God*) misericordioso(a); (*supply*) abbondante.
bounty ['bauntɪ] *n* (*generosity*) liberalità, munificenza; (*reward*) taglia.
bounty hunter *n* cacciatore *m* di taglie.
bouquet ['bukeɪ] *n* bouquet *m inv*.
bourbon ['buəbən] *n* (*US: also*: ~ **whiskey**) bourbon *m inv*.
bourgeois ['buəʒwɑː] *a, n* borghese (*m/f*).
bout [baut] *n* periodo; (*of malaria etc*) attacco; (*BOXING etc*) incontro.
boutique [buː'tiːk] *n* boutique *f inv*.
bow *n* [bəu] nodo; (*weapon*) arco; (*MUS*) archetto; (*NAUT: also*: ~**s**) prua; [bau] (*with body*) inchino ♦ *vi* [bau] inchinarsi; (*yield*): **to ~ to** *or* **before** sottomettersi a; **to ~ to the inevitable** rassegnarsi all'inevitabile.
bowels [bauəlz] *npl* intestini *mpl*; (*fig*) viscere *fpl*.
bowl [bəul] *n* (*for eating*) scodella; (*for washing*) bacino; (*ball*) boccia; (*of pipe*) fornello; (*US: stadium*) stadio ♦ *vi* (*CRICKET*) servire (la palla); *see also* **bowls**.
bowl over *vt* (*fig*) sconcertare.
bow-legged ['bəu'legɪd] *a* dalle gambe storte.
bowler ['bəulə*] *n* giocatore *m* di bocce; (*CRICKET*) giocatore che serve la palla; (*Brit: also*: ~ **hat**) bombetta.
bowling ['bəulɪŋ] *n* (*game*) gioco delle bocce; bowling *m*.
bowling alley *n* pista da bowling.
bowling green *n* campo di bocce.
bowls [bəulz] *n* gioco delle bocce.
bow tie *n* cravatta a farfalla.
box [bɔks] *n* scatola; (*also*: **cardboard** ~) (scatola di) cartone *m*; (*crate*; *also for money*) cassetta; (*THEATRE*) palco; (*Brit AUT*) area d'incrocio ♦ *vi* fare pugilato ♦ *vt* mettere in (una) scatola; (*SPORT*) combattere contro.
boxer ['bɔksə*] *n* (*person*) pugile *m*; (*dog*) boxer *m inv*.
boxing ['bɔksɪŋ] *n* (*SPORT*) pugilato.
Boxing Day *n* (*Brit*) Santo Stefano.
boxing gloves *npl* guantoni *mpl* da pugile.
boxing ring *n* ring *m inv*.
box number *n* (*for advertisements*) casella.
box office *n* biglietteria.
box room *n* ripostiglio.
boy [bɔɪ] *n* ragazzo; (*small*) bambino; (*son*) figlio; (*servant*) servo.
boycott ['bɔɪkɔt] *n* boicottaggio ♦ *vt* boicottare.

boyfriend ['bɔɪfrɛnd] n ragazzo.
boyish ['bɔɪʃ] a di or da ragazzo.
Bp abbr = **bishop**.
BR abbr see **British Rail**.
bra [brɑ:] n reggipetto, reggiseno.
brace [breɪs] n sostegno; (on teeth) apparecchio correttore; (tool) trapano; (TYP: also: ~ **bracket**) graffa ♦ vt rinforzare, sostenere; ~ **o.s.** (fig) farsi coraggio; see also **braces**.
bracelet ['breɪslɪt] n braccialetto.
braces ['breɪsɪz] npl (Brit) bretelle fpl.
bracing ['breɪsɪŋ] a invigorante.
bracken ['brækən] n felce f.
bracket ['brækɪt] n (TECH) mensola; (group) gruppo; (TYP) parentesi f inv ♦ vt mettere fra parentesi; (fig: also: ~ **together**) mettere insieme; in ~**s** tra parentesi; **round/square** ~**s** parentesi tonde/quadre; **income** ~ fascia di reddito.
brackish ['brækɪʃ] a (water) salmastro(a).
brag [bræg] vi vantarsi.
braid [breɪd] n (trimming) passamano; (of hair) treccia.
Braille [breɪl] n braille m.
brain [breɪn] n cervello; ~**s** npl cervella fpl; **he's got** ~**s** è intelligente.
brainchild ['breɪntʃaɪld] n creatura, creazione f.
brainless ['breɪnlɪs] a deficiente, stupido(a).
brainstorm ['breɪnstɔ:m] n (fig) attacco di pazzia; (US) = **brainwave**.
brainwash ['breɪnwɔʃ] vt fare un lavaggio di cervello a.
brainwave ['breɪnweɪv] n lampo di genio.
brainy ['breɪnɪ] a intelligente.
braise [breɪz] vt brasare.
brake [breɪk] n (on vehicle) freno ♦ vt, vi frenare.
brake light n (fanalino dello) stop m inv.
brake pedal n pedale m del freno.
bramble ['bræmbl] n rovo; (fruit) mora.
bran [bræn] n crusca.
branch [brɑ:ntʃ] n ramo; (COMM) succursale f, filiale f ♦ vi diramarsi.
branch out vi: **to** ~ **out into** intraprendere una nuova attività nel ramo di.
branch line n (RAIL) linea secondaria.
branch manager n direttore m di filiale.
brand [brænd] n marca ♦ vt (cattle) marcare (a ferro rovente); (fig: pej): **to** ~ **sb a communist** etc definire qn come comunista etc.
brandish ['brændɪʃ] vt brandire.
brand name n marca.
brand-new ['brænd'nju:] a nuovo(a) di zecca.
brandy ['brændɪ] n brandy m inv.
brash [bræʃ] a sfacciato(a).
Brasilia [brə'zɪljə] n Brasilia.
brass [brɑ:s] n ottone m; **the** ~ (MUS) gli ottoni.
brass band n fanfara.
brassière ['bræsɪə*] n reggipetto, reggiseno.
brass tacks npl: **to get down to** ~ (col) venire al sodo.

brat [bræt] n (pej) marmocchio, monello/a.
bravado [brə'vɑ:dəʊ] n spavalderia.
brave [breɪv] a coraggioso(a) ♦ n guerriero m pellerossa inv ♦ vt affrontare.
bravery ['breɪvərɪ] n coraggio.
bravo [brɑ:'vəʊ] excl bravo!, bene!
brawl [brɔ:l] n rissa ♦ vi azzuffarsi.
brawn [brɔ:n] n muscolo; (meat) carne f di testa di maiale.
brawny ['brɔ:nɪ] a muscoloso(a).
bray [breɪ] n raglio ♦ vi ragliare.
brazen ['breɪzn] a svergognato(a) ♦ vt: **to** ~ **it out** fare lo sfacciato.
brazier ['breɪzɪə*] n braciere m.
Brazil [brə'zɪl] n Brasile m.
Brazilian [brə'zɪljən] a, n brasiliano(a).
Brazil nut n noce f del Brasile.
breach [bri:tʃ] vt aprire una breccia in ♦ n (gap) breccia, varco; (estrangement) rottura; (of duty) abuso; (breaking): ~ **of contract** rottura di contratto; ~ **of the peace** violazione f dell'ordine pubblico; ~ **of trust** abuso di fiducia.
bread [brɛd] n pane m; (col: money) grana; **to earn one's daily** ~ guadagnarsi il pane; **to know which side one's** ~ **is buttered on** saper fare i propri interessi; ~ **and butter** n pane e burro; (fig) mezzi mpl di sussistenza.
breadbin ['brɛdbɪn] n (Brit) cassetta f portapane inv.
breadboard ['brɛdbɔ:d] n tagliere m (per il pane); (COMPUT) pannello per esperimenti.
breadbox ['brɛdbɔks] n (US) cassetta f portapane inv.
breadcrumbs ['brɛdkrʌmz] npl briciole fpl; (CULIN) pangrattato.
breadline ['brɛdlaɪn] n: **to be on the** ~ avere appena denaro per vivere.
breadth [brɛtθ] n larghezza.
breadwinner ['brɛdwɪnə*] n chi guadagna il pane per tutta la famiglia.
break [breɪk] vb (pt **broke** [brəʊk], pp **broken** ['brəʊkən]) vt rompere; (law) violare; (promise) mancare a ♦ vi rompersi; (weather) cambiare ♦ n (gap) breccia; (fracture) rottura; (rest, also SCOL) intervallo; (: short) pausa; (chance) possibilità f inv; (holiday) vacanza; **to** ~ **one's leg** etc rompersi la gamba etc; **to** ~ **a record** battere un primato; **to** ~ **the news to sb** comunicare per primo la notizia a qn; ~ **with sb** (fig) rompere con qn; **to** ~ **even** vi coprire le spese; **to** ~ **free** or **loose** liberarsi; **without a** ~ senza una pausa; **to have** or **take a** ~ (few minutes) fare una pausa; (holiday) prendere un po' di riposo; **a lucky** ~ un colpo di fortuna.
break down vt (figures, data) analizzare; (door etc) buttare giù, abbattere; (resistance) stroncare ♦ vi crollare; (MED) avere un esaurimento (nervoso); (AUT) guastarsi.
break in vt (horse etc) domare ♦ vi (burglar) fare irruzione.
break into vt fus (house) fare irruzione in.

break off vi (speaker) interrompersi; (branch) troncarsi ♦ vt (talks, engagement) rompere.

break open vt (door etc) sfondare.

break out vi evadere; **to ~ out in spots** coprirsi di macchie.

break through vi: **the sun broke through** il sole ha fatto capolino tra le nuvole ♦ vt (defences, barrier) sfondare, penetrare in; (crowd) aprirsi un varco in or tra, aprirsi un passaggio in or tra.

break up vi (partnership) sciogliersi; (friends) separarsi ♦ vt fare in pezzi, spaccare; (fight etc) interrompere, far cessare; (marriage) finire.

breakable ['breikəbl] a fragile; **~s** npl oggetti mpl fragili.

breakage ['breikidʒ] n rottura; **to pay for ~s** pagare i danni.

breakaway ['breikəwei] a (group etc) scissionista, dissidente.

break-dancing ['breikdɑ:nsiŋ] n breakdance f.

breakdown ['breikdaun] n (AUT) guasto; (in communications) interruzione f; (MED: also: **nervous ~**) esaurimento nervoso; (of payments etc) resoconto.

breakdown service n (Brit) servizio riparazioni.

breakdown van n carro m attrezzi inv.

breaker ['breikə*] n frangente m.

breakeven ['breik'i:vn] cpd: **~ chart** n diagramma m del punto di rottura or pareggio; **~ point** n punto di rottura or pareggio.

breakfast ['brekfəst] n colazione f.

breakfast cereal n fiocchi mpl d'avena or di mais etc.

break-in ['breikin] n irruzione f.

breaking point ['breikiŋ-] n punto di rottura.

breakthrough ['breikθru:] n (MIL) breccia; (fig) passo avanti.

break-up ['breikʌp] n (of partnership, marriage) rottura.

break-up value n (COMM) valore m di realizzo.

breakwater ['breikwɔ:tə*] n frangiflutti m inv.

breast [brest] n (of woman) seno; (chest) petto.

breast-feed ['brestfi:d] vt, vi (irg: like **feed**) allattare (al seno).

breast pocket n taschino.

breast-stroke ['breststrəuk] n nuoto a rana.

breath [breθ] n fiato; **out of ~** senza fiato; **to go out for a ~ of air** andare a prendere una boccata d'aria.

Breathalyser ® ['breθəlaizə*] n alcoltest m inv.

breathe [bri:ð] vt, vi respirare; **I won't ~ a word about it** non fiaterò.

breathe in vi inspirare ♦ vt respirare.

breathe out vt, vi espirare.

breather ['bri:ðə*] n attimo di respiro.

breathing ['bri:ðiŋ] n respiro, respirazione f.

breathing space n (fig) attimo di respiro.

breathless ['breθlis] a senza fiato; (with excitement) con il fiato sospeso.

breath-taking ['breθteikiŋ] a sbalorditivo(a).

-bred [bred] suffix: **to be well/ill~** essere ben educato(a)/maleducato(a).

breed [bri:d] vb (pt, pp **bred** [bred]) vt allevare; (fig: hate, suspicion) generare, provocare ♦ vi riprodursi ♦ n razza, varietà f inv.

breeder ['bri:də*] n (PHYSICS: also: **~ reactor**) reattore m autofertilizzante.

breeding ['bri:diŋ] n riproduzione f; allevamento.

breeze [bri:z] n brezza.

breeze block n (Brit) mattone composto di scorie di coke.

breezy ['bri:zi] a arioso(a); allegro(a).

Breton ['bretən] a, n brettone (m/f).

brevity ['breviti] n brevità.

brew [bru:] vt (tea) fare un infuso di; (beer) fare; (plot) tramare ♦ vi (tea) essere in infusione; (beer) essere in fermentazione; (fig) bollire in pentola.

brewer ['bru:ə*] n birraio.

brewery ['bru:əri] n fabbrica di birra.

briar ['braiə*] n (thorny bush) rovo; (wild rose) rosa selvatica.

bribe [braib] n bustarella ♦ vt comprare; **to ~ sb to do sth** pagare qn sottobanco perché faccia qc.

bribery ['braibəri] n corruzione f.

bric-a-brac ['brikəbræk] n bric-a-brac m.

brick [brik] n mattone m.

bricklayer ['brikleiə*] n muratore m.

brickwork ['brikwə:k] n muratura in mattoni.

brickworks ['brikwə:ks] n fabbrica di mattoni.

bridal ['braidl] a nuziale; **~ party** corteo nuziale.

bride [braid] n sposa.

bridegroom ['braidgru:m] n sposo.

bridesmaid ['braidzmeid] n damigella d'onore.

bridge [bridʒ] n ponte m; (NAUT) ponte di comando; (of nose) dorso; (CARDS, DENTISTRY) bridge m inv ♦ vt (river) fare un ponte sopra; (gap) colmare.

bridging loan ['bridʒiŋ-] n (Brit) anticipazione f sul mutuo.

bridle ['braidl] n briglia ♦ vt tenere a freno; (horse) mettere la briglia a ♦ vi (in anger etc) adombrarsi, adontarsi.

bridle path n sentiero (per cavalli).

brief [bri:f] a breve ♦ n (LAW) comparsa ♦ vt (MIL etc) dare istruzioni a; **in ~ ...** in breve ..., a farla breve ...; **to ~ sb (about sth)** mettere qn al corrente (di qc); see also **briefs**.

briefcase ['bri:fkeis] n cartella.

briefing ['bri:fiŋ] n istruzioni fpl.

briefly ['bri:fli] ad (speak, visit) brevemente; (glimpse) di sfuggita.

briefness ['bri:fnis] n brevità.

briefs [bri:fs] npl mutande fpl.

Brig. abbr = **brigadier**.

brigade [bri'geid] n (MIL) brigata.

brigadier [brigə'diə*] n generale m di brigata.

bright [braɪt] *a* luminoso(a); (*person*) sveglio(a); (*colour*) vivace; **to look on the ~ side** vedere il lato positivo delle cose.

brighten ['braɪtn] (*also:* **~ up**) *vt* (*room*) rendere luminoso(a); rallegrare ♦ *vi* schiarirsi; (*person*) rallegrarsi.

brightly ['braɪtlɪ] *ad* (*shine*) vivamente, intensamente; (*smile*) radiosamente; (*talk*) con animazione.

brilliance ['brɪljəns] *n* splendore *m*; (*fig: of person*) genialità, talento.

brilliant ['brɪljənt] *a* brillante; (*sunshine*) sfolgorante.

brim [brɪm] *n* orlo.

brimful ['brɪm'ful] *a* pieno(a) *or* colmo(a) fino all'orlo; (*fig*) pieno(a).

brine [braɪn] *n* acqua salmastra; (*CULIN*) salamoia.

bring, *pt, pp* **brought** [brɪŋ, brɔːt] *vt* portare; **to ~ sth to an end** mettere fine a qc; **I can't ~ myself to sack him** non so risolvermi a licenziarlo.

bring about *vt* causare.

bring back *vt* riportare.

bring down *vt* (*lower*) far scendere; (*shoot down*) abbattere; (*government*) far cadere.

bring forward *vt* portare avanti; (*in time*) anticipare; (*BOOK-KEEPING*) riportare.

bring in *vt* (*person*) fare entrare; (*object*) portare; (*POL: bill*) presentare; (: *legislation*) introdurre; (*LAW: verdict*) emettere; (*produce: income*) rendere.

bring off *vt* (*task, plan*) portare a compimento; (*deal*) concludere.

bring out *vt* (*meaning*) mettere in evidenza; (*new product*) lanciare; (*book*) pubblicare, fare uscire.

bring round *or* **to** *vt* (*unconscious person*) far rinvenire.

bring up *vt* allevare; (*question*) introdurre.

brink [brɪŋk] *n* orlo; **on the ~ of doing sth** sul punto di fare qc; **she was on the ~ of tears** era lì lì per piangere.

brisk [brɪsk] *a* (*person, tone*) spiccio(a), sbrigativo(a); (: *abrupt*) brusco(a); (*wind*) fresco(a); (*trade etc*) vivace, attivo(a); **to go for a ~ walk** fare una camminata di buon passo; **business is ~** gli affari vanno bene.

bristle ['brɪsl] *n* setola ♦ *vi* rizzarsi; **bristling with** irto(a) di.

bristly ['brɪslɪ] *a* (*chin*) ispido(a); (*beard, hair*) irsuto(a), setoloso(a).

Brit [brɪt] *n abbr* (*col:* = *British person*) britannico/a.

Britain ['brɪtən] *n* Gran Bretagna.

British ['brɪtɪʃ] *a* britannico(a); **the ~** *npl* i Britannici; **the ~ Isles** *npl* le Isole Britanniche.

British Rail (BR) *n compagnia ferroviaria britannica*, ≈ Ferrovie *fpl* dello Stato (F.S.).

Briton ['brɪtən] *n* britannico/a.

Brittany ['brɪtənɪ] *n* Bretagna.

brittle ['brɪtl] *a* fragile.

Br(o) *abbr* (*REL*) = **brother**.

broach [brəʊtʃ] *vt* (*subject*) affrontare.

broad [brɔːd] *a* largo(a); (*distinction*) generale; (*accent*) spiccato(a) ♦ *n* (*US col*) bellona; **~ hint** allusione *f* esplicita; **in ~ daylight** in pieno giorno; **the ~ outlines** le grandi linee.

broad bean *n* fava.

broadcast ['brɔːdkɑːst] *n* trasmissione *f* ♦ *vb* (*pt, pp* **broadcast**) *vt* trasmettere per radio (*or* per televisione) ♦ *vi* fare una trasmissione.

broadcasting ['brɔːdkɑːstɪŋ] *n* radiodiffusione *f*; televisione *f*.

broadcasting station *n* stazione *f* trasmittente.

broaden ['brɔːdn] *vt* allargare ♦ *vi* allargarsi.

broadly ['brɔːdlɪ] *ad* (*fig*) in generale.

broad-minded ['brɔːd'maɪndɪd] *a* di mente aperta.

broccoli ['brɔkəlɪ] *n* (*BOT*) broccolo; (*CULIN*) broccoli *mpl*.

brochure ['brəʊʃjʊə*] *n* dépliant *m inv*.

brogue [brəʊg] *n* (*shoe*) scarpa rozza in cuoio; (*accent*) accento irlandese.

broil [brɔɪl] *vt* cuocere a fuoco vivo.

broke [brəʊk] *pt of* **break** ♦ *a* (*col*) squattrinato(a); **to go ~** fare fallimento.

broken ['brəʊkən] *pp of* **break** ♦ *a* (*gen*) rotto(a); (*stick, promise, vow*) spezzato(a); (*marriage*) fallito(a); **he comes from a ~ home** i suoi sono divisi; **in ~ French/English** in un francese/inglese stentato.

broken-down ['brəʊkən'daʊn] *a* (*car*) in panne, rotto(a); (*machine*) guasto(a), fuori uso; (*house*) abbandonato(a), in rovina.

broken-hearted ['brəʊkən'hɑːtɪd] *a*: **to be ~** avere il cuore spezzato.

broker ['brəʊkə*] *n* agente *m*.

brokerage ['brəʊkərɪdʒ] *n* (*COMM*) commissione *f* di intermediazione.

brolly ['brɔlɪ] *n* (*Brit col*) ombrello.

bronchitis [brɔŋ'kaɪtɪs] *n* bronchite *f*.

bronze [brɔnz] *n* bronzo.

bronzed [brɔnzd] *a* abbronzato(a).

brooch [brəʊtʃ] *n* spilla.

brood [bruːd] *n* covata ♦ *vi* (*hen*) covare; (*person*) rimuginare.

broody ['bruːdɪ] *a* (*fig*) cupo(a) e taciturno(a).

brook [bruk] *n* ruscello.

broom [brum] *n* scopa.

broomstick ['brumstɪk] *n* manico di scopa.

Bros. *abbr* (*COMM:* = *brothers*) F.lli (= *Fratelli*).

broth [brɔθ] *n* brodo.

brothel ['brɔθl] *n* bordello.

brother ['brʌðə*] *n* fratello.

brotherhood ['brʌðəhud] *n* fratellanza; confraternità *f inv*.

brother-in-law ['brʌðərɪnlɔː] *n* cognato.

brotherly ['brʌðəlɪ] *a* fraterno(a).

brought [brɔːt] *pt, pp of* **bring**.

brought forward (**b/f**) *a* (*COMM*) riportato(a).

brow [brau] *n* fronte *f*; (*rare, gen:* **eye~**) so-

pracciglio; (of hill) cima.
browbeat ['braubi:t] vt intimidire.
brown [braun] a bruno(a), marrone; (hair) castano(a) ♦ n (colour) color m bruno or marrone ♦ vt (CULIN) rosolare; **to go** ~ (person) abbronzarsi; (leaves) ingiallire.
brown bread n pane m integrale, pane nero.
brownie ['braunɪ] n giovane esploratrice f.
brown paper n carta da pacchi or da imballaggio.
brown rice n riso greggio.
brown sugar n zucchero greggio.
browse [brauz] vi (animal) brucare; (in bookshop etc) curiosare ♦ n: **to have a** ~ **(around)** dare un'occhiata (in giro); **to** ~ **through a book** sfogliare un libro.
bruise [bru:z] n ammaccatura; (on person) livido ♦ vt ammaccare; (leg etc) farsi un livido a; (fig: feelings) urtare ♦ vi (fruit) ammaccarsi.
Brum [brʌm] n abbr, **Brummagem** ['brʌmədʒəm] n (col) = Birmingham.
Brummie ['brʌmɪ] n (col) abitante m/f di Birmingham; originario/a di Birmingham.
brunch [brʌntʃ] n ricca colazione consumata in tarda mattinata.
brunette [bru:'nɛt] n bruna.
brunt [brʌnt] n: **the** ~ **of** (attack, criticism etc) il peso maggiore di.
brush [brʌʃ] n spazzola; (quarrel) schermaglia ♦ vt spazzolare; (gen: ~ **past**, ~ **against**) sfiorare; **to have a** ~ **with sb** (verbally) avere uno scontro con qn; (physically) venire a diverbio or alle mani con qn; **to have a** ~ **with the police** avere delle noie con la polizia.
brush aside vt scostare.
brush up vt (knowledge) rinfrescare.
brushed [brʌʃt] a (TECH: steel, chrome etc) sabbiato(a); (nylon, denim etc) pettinato(a).
brush-off ['brʌʃɔf] n: **to give sb the** ~ dare il ben servito a qn.
brushwood ['brʌʃwud] n macchia.
brusque [bru:sk] a (person, manner) brusco(a); (tone) secco(a).
Brussels ['brʌslz] n Bruxelles f.
Brussels sprout n cavolo di Bruxelles.
brutal ['bru:tl] a brutale.
brutality [bru:'tælɪtɪ] n brutalità.
brute [bru:t] n bestia; **by** ~ **force** con la forza, a viva forza.
brutish ['bru:tɪʃ] a da bruto.
BS n abbr (US: = Bachelor of Science) titolo di studio.
bs abbr = **bill of sale**.
BSA n abbr (US) = Boy Scouts of America.
BSc n abbr see **Bachelor of Science**.
BSI n abbr (= British Standards Institution) associazione per la normalizzazione.
BST abbr (= British Summer Time) ora legale.
Bt. abbr (Brit) = **baronet**.
btu n abbr (= British thermal unit) Btu m (= 1054.2 joules).

bubble ['bʌbl] n bolla ♦ vi ribollire; (sparkle, fig) essere effervescente.
bubble bath n bagno m schiuma inv.
Bucharest [bu:kə'rɛst] n Bucarest f.
buck [bʌk] n maschio (di camoscio, caprone, coniglio etc); (US col) dollaro ♦ vi sgroppare; **to pass the** ~ (**to sb**) scaricare (su di qn) la propria responsabilità.
buck up vi (cheer up) rianimarsi ♦ vt: **to** ~ **one's ideas up** mettere la testa a partito.
bucket ['bʌkɪt] n secchio ♦ vi (Brit col): **the rain is** ~**ing (down)** piove a catinelle.
buckle ['bʌkl] n fibbia ♦ vt affibbiare; (warp) deformare.
buckle down vi mettersi sotto.
Bucks [bʌks] abbr (Brit) = Buckinghamshire.
bud [bʌd] n gemma; (of flower) boccio ♦ vi germogliare; (flower) sbocciare.
Budapest [bju:də'pɛst] n Budapest f.
Buddha ['budə] n Budda m.
Buddhism ['budɪzəm] n buddismo.
Buddhist ['budɪst] a, n buddista (m/f).
budding ['bʌdɪŋ] a (flower) in boccio; (poet etc) in erba.
buddy ['bʌdɪ] n (US) compagno.
budge [bʌdʒ] vt scostare ♦ vi spostarsi.
budgerigar ['bʌdʒərɪga:*] n pappagallino.
budget ['bʌdʒɪt] n bilancio preventivo ♦ vi: **to** ~ **for sth** fare il bilancio per qc; **I'm on a tight** ~ devo contare la lira; **she works out her** ~ **every month** fa il preventivo delle spese ogni mese.
budgie ['bʌdʒɪ] n = budgerigar.
Buenos Aires ['bweɪnɔs'aɪrɪz] n Buenos Aires f.
buff [bʌf] a color camoscio inv ♦ n (enthusiast) appassionato/a.
buffalo, pl ~ or ~**es** ['bʌfələu] n bufalo; (US) bisonte m.
buffer ['bʌfə*] n respingente m; (COMPUT) memoria tampone, buffer m inv.
buffering ['bʌfərɪŋ] n (COMPUT) bufferizzazione f, memorizzazione f transitoria.
buffer state n stato cuscinetto.
buffet n ['bufeɪ] (food, Brit: bar) buffet m inv ♦ vt ['bʌfɪt] schiaffeggiare; scuotere; urtare.
buffet car n (Brit RAIL) ≈ servizio ristoro.
buffet lunch n pranzo in piedi.
buffoon [bə'fu:n] n buffone m.
bug [bʌg] n (insect) cimice f; (: gen) insetto; (fig: germ) virus m inv; (spy device) microfono spia; (COMPUT) bug m inv, errore m nel programma ♦ vt mettere sotto controllo; (room) installare microfoni spia in; (annoy) scocciare; **I've got the travel** ~ (fig) mi è presa la mania dei viaggi.
bugbear ['bʌgbɛə*] n spauracchio.
bugger ['bʌgə*] (col!) n bastardo (!) ♦ vb: ~ **off!** vaffanculo! (!); ~ (**it**)! merda! (!).
bugle ['bju:gl] n tromba.
build [bɪld] n (of person) corporatura ♦ vt (pt, pp **built** [bɪlt]) costruire.
build on vt fus (fig) prendere il via da.

build up vt (establish: business) costruire; (: reputation) fare, consolidare; (increase: production) allargare, incrementare; **don't ~ your hopes up too soon** non sperarci troppo.
builder ['bɪldə*] n costruttore m.
building ['bɪldɪŋ] n costruzione f; edificio; (also: ~ **trade**) edilizia.
building contractor n costruttore m, imprenditore m (edile).
building industry n industria edilizia.
building site n cantiere m di costruzione.
building society n (Brit) società f inv immobiliare.
building trade = **building industry**.
build-up ['bɪldʌp] n (of gas etc) accumulo; (publicity): **to give sb/sth a good ~** fare buona pubblicità a qn/qc.
built [bɪlt] pt, pp of **build**; **well-~** robusto(a).
built-in ['bɪlt'ɪn] a (cupboard) a muro; (device) incorporato(a).
built-up area ['bɪltʌp-] n abitato.
bulb [bʌlb] n (BOT) bulbo; (ELEC) lampadina.
bulbous ['bʌlbəs] a bulboso(a).
Bulgaria [bʌl'gɛərɪə] n Bulgaria.
Bulgarian [bʌl'gɛərɪən] a bulgaro(a) ♦ n bulgaro/a; (LING) bulgaro.
bulge [bʌldʒ] n rigonfiamento; (in birth rate, sales) punta ♦ vi essere protuberante or rigonfio(a); **to be bulging with** essere pieno(a) or zeppo(a) di.
bulk [bʌlk] n massa, volume m; **the ~ of** il grosso di; **(to buy) in ~** (comprare) in grande quantità.
bulk buying n acquisto di merce in grande quantità.
bulkhead ['bʌlkhɛd] n paratia.
bulky ['bʌlkɪ] a grosso(a); voluminoso(a).
bull [bul] n toro; (STOCK EXCHANGE) rialzista m/f; (REL) bolla (papale).
bulldog ['buldɔg] n bulldog m inv.
bulldoze ['buldəuz] vt aprire or spianare col bulldozer; **I was ~d into doing it** (fig col) mi ci hanno costretto con la prepotenza.
bulldozer ['buldəuzə*] n bulldozer m inv.
bullet ['bulɪt] n pallottola.
bulletin ['bulɪtɪn] n bollettino.
bulletin board n (COMPUT) bulletin board m inv.
bullet-proof ['bulɪtpruːf] a a prova di proiettile; **~ vest** giubbotto antiproiettile.
bullfight ['bulfaɪt] n corrida.
bullfighter ['bulfaɪtə*] n torero.
bullfighting ['bulfaɪtɪŋ] n tauromachia.
bullion ['buljən] n oro or argento in lingotti.
bullock ['bulək] n giovenco.
bullring ['bulrɪŋ] n arena (per corride).
bull's-eye ['bulzaɪ] n centro del bersaglio.
bully ['bulɪ] n prepotente m ♦ vt angariare; (frighten) intimidire.
bullying ['bulɪŋ] n prepotenze fpl.
bum [bʌm] n (col: backside) culo; (tramp) vagabondo/a; (US: idler) fannullone/a.
bum around vi (col) fare il vagabondo.
bumblebee ['bʌmblbiː] n (ZOOL) bombo.

bumf [bʌmf] n (col: forms etc) scartoffie fpl.
bump [bʌmp] n (blow) colpo; (jolt) scossa; (noise) botto; (on road etc) protuberanza; (on head) bernoccolo ♦ vt battere; (car) urtare, sbattere.
bump along vi procedere sobbalzando.
bump into vt fus scontrarsi con; (col: meet) imbattersi in, incontrare per caso.
bumper ['bʌmpə*] n (Brit) paraurti m inv ♦ a: **~ harvest** raccolto eccezionale.
bumper cars npl (US) autoscontri mpl.
bumph [bʌmf] n = **bumf**.
bumptious ['bʌmpʃəs] a presuntuoso(a).
bumpy ['bʌmpɪ] a (road) dissestato(a); (journey, flight) movimentato(a).
bun [bʌn] n focaccia; (of hair) crocchia.
bunch [bʌntʃ] n (of flowers, keys) mazzo; (of bananas) ciuffo; (of people) gruppo; **~ of grapes** grappolo d'uva.
bundle ['bʌndl] n fascio ♦ vt (also: ~ **up**) legare in un fascio; (put): **to ~ sth/sb into** spingere qc/qn in.
bundle off vt (person) mandare via in gran fretta.
bundle out vt far uscire (senza tante cerimonie).
bun fight n (Brit: col) tè m inv (ricevimento).
bung [bʌŋ] n tappo ♦ vt (Brit: throw: also: ~ **into**) buttare; (also: ~ **up**: pipe, hole) tappare, otturare; **my nose is ~ed up** (col) ho il naso otturato.
bungalow ['bʌŋgələu] n bungalow m inv.
bungle ['bʌŋgl] vt abborracciare.
bunion ['bʌnjən] n callo (al piede).
bunk [bʌŋk] n cuccetta.
bunk beds npl letti mpl a castello.
bunker ['bʌŋkə*] n (coal store) ripostiglio per il carbone; (MIL, GOLF) bunker m inv.
bunny ['bʌnɪ] n (also: ~ **rabbit**) coniglietto.
bunny girl n coniglietta.
bunny hill n (US SKI) pista per principianti.
bunting ['bʌntɪŋ] n pavesi mpl, bandierine fpl.
buoy [bɔɪ] n boa.
buoy up vt tenere a galla; (fig) sostenere.
buoyancy ['bɔɪənsɪ] n (of ship) galleggiabilità.
buoyant ['bɔɪənt] a galleggiante; (fig) vivace; (COMM: market) sostenuto(a); (prices, currency) stabile.
burden ['bəːdn] n carico, fardello ♦ vt caricare; (oppress) opprimere; **to be a ~ to sb** essere di peso a qn.
bureau, pl **~x** ['bjuərəu, -z] n (Brit: writing desk) scrivania; (US: chest of drawers) cassettone m; (office) ufficio, agenzia.
bureaucracy [bjuə'rɔkrəsɪ] n burocrazia.
bureaucrat ['bjuərəkræt] n burocrate m/f.
bureaucratic [bjuərə'krætɪk] a burocratico(a).
burgeon ['bəːdʒən] vi svilupparsi rapidamente.
burglar ['bəːglə*] n scassinatore m.
burglar alarm n antifurto m inv.
burglarize ['bəːgləraɪz] vt (US) svaligiare.
burglary ['bəːglərɪ] n furto con scasso.

burgle ['bə:gl] *vt* svaligiare.
Burgundy ['bə:gəndɪ] *n* Borgogna.
burial ['bɛrɪəl] *n* sepoltura.
burial ground *n* cimitero.
burly ['bə:lɪ] *a* robusto(a).
Burma ['bə:mə] *n* Birmania.
Burmese [bə:'mi:z] *a* birmano(a) ♦ *n* (*pl inv*) birmano/a; (*LING*) birmano.
burn [bə:n] *vt, vi* (*pt, pp* **burned** *or* **burnt** [bə:nt]) bruciare ♦ *n* bruciatura, scottatura; (*MED*) ustione *f*; **I've ~t myself!** mi sono bruciato!; **the cigarette ~t a hole in her dress** si è fatta un buco nel vestito con la sigaretta.
burn down *vt* distruggere col fuoco.
burn out *vt* (*subj: writer etc*): **to ~ o.s. out** esaurirsi.
burner ['bə:nə*] *n* fornello.
burning ['bə:nɪŋ] *a* (*building, forest*) in fiamme; (*issue, question*) scottante.
burnish ['bə:nɪʃ] *vt* brunire.
burnt [bə:nt] *pt, pp of* **burn**.
burnt sugar *n* (*Brit*) caramello.
burp [bə:p] (*col*) *n* rutto ♦ *vi* ruttare.
burrow ['bʌrəu] *n* tana ♦ *vt* scavare.
bursar ['bə:sə*] *n* economo/a; (*Brit: student*) borsista *m/f*.
bursary ['bə:sərɪ] *n* (*Brit*) borsa di studio.
burst [bə:st] *vb* (*pt, pp* **burst**) *vt* far scoppiare *or* esplodere ♦ *vi* esplodere; (*tyre*) scoppiare ♦ *n* scoppio; (*also:* ~ **pipe**) rottura nel tubo, perdita; ~ **of energy/laughter** scoppio d'energia/di risa; **a ~ of applause** uno scroscio d'applausi; **a ~ of speed** uno scatto (di velocità); ~ **blood vessel** rottura di un vaso sanguigno; **the river has ~ its banks** il fiume ha rotto gli argini *or* ha straripato; **to ~ into flames/tears** scoppiare in fiamme/lacrime; **to be ~ing with** essere pronto a scoppiare di; **to ~ out laughing** scoppiare a ridere; **to ~ open** *vi* aprirsi improvvisamente; (*door*) spalancarsi.
burst into *vt fus* (*room etc*) irrompere in.
burst out of *vt fus* precipitarsi fuori da.
bury ['bɛrɪ] *vt* seppellire; **to ~ one's face in one's hands** nascondere la faccia tra le mani; **to ~ one's head in the sand** (*fig*) fare (la politica del)lo struzzo; **to ~ the hatchet** (*fig*) seppellire l'ascia di guerra.
bus, ~**es** [bʌs, 'bʌsɪz] *n* autobus *m inv*.
bush [buʃ] *n* cespuglio; (*scrub land*) macchia.
bushel ['buʃl] *n* staio.
bushy ['buʃɪ] *a* (*plant, tail, beard*) folto(a); (*eyebrows*) irsuto(a).
busily ['bɪzɪlɪ] *ad* con impegno, alacremente.
business ['bɪznɪs] *n* (*matter*) affare *m*; (*trading*) affari *mpl*; (*firm*) azienda; (*job, duty*) lavoro; **to be away on** ~ essere andato via per affari; **I'm here on** ~ sono qui per affari; **to do** ~ **with sb** fare affari con qn; **he's in the insurance** ~ lavora nel campo delle assicurazioni; **it's none of my** ~ questo non mi riguarda; **he means** ~ non scherza.

business address *n* indirizzo di lavoro *or* d'ufficio.
business card *n* biglietto da visita della ditta.
businesslike ['bɪznɪslaɪk] *a* serio(a); efficiente.
businessman ['bɪznɪsmən] *n* uomo d'affari.
business trip *n* viaggio d'affari.
businesswoman ['bɪznɪswumən] *n* donna d'affari.
busker ['bʌskə*] *n* (*Brit*) suonatore/trice ambulante.
bus lane *n* (*Brit*) corsia riservata agli autobus.
bus shelter *n* pensilina (*alla fermata dell'autobus*).
bus station *n* stazione *f* delle autolinee, autostazione *f*.
bus stop *n* fermata d'autobus.
bust [bʌst] *n* (*ART*) busto; (*bosom*) seno ♦ *a* (*broken*) rotto(a) ♦ *vt* (*col: POLICE: arrest*) pizzicare, beccare; **to go** ~ fallire.
bustle ['bʌsl] *n* movimento, attività ♦ *vi* darsi da fare.
bustling ['bʌslɪŋ] *a* (*person*) indaffarato(a); (*town*) animato(a).
bust-up ['bʌstʌp] *n* (*Brit col*) lite *f*.
busy ['bɪzɪ] *a* occupato(a); (*shop, street*) molto frequentato(a) ♦ *vt*: **to ~ o.s.** darsi da fare; **he's a ~ man** (*normally*) è un uomo molto occupato; (*temporarily*) ha molto da fare, è molto occupato.
busybody ['bɪzɪbɔdɪ] *n* ficcanaso *m/f inv*.
busy signal *n* (*US*) segnale *m* di occupato.
but [bʌt] *cj* ma ♦ *prep* eccetto, tranne; **no one ~ him** solo lui; **nothing ~** null'altro che; ~ **for** senza, se non fosse per; **the last ~ one** (*Brit*) il(la) penultimo(a); **all ~ finished** quasi finito; **anything ~ finished** tutt'altro che finito.
butane ['bju:teɪn] *n* (*also:* ~ **gas**) butano.
butcher ['butʃə*] *n* macellaio ♦ *vt* macellare; ~**'s (shop)** macelleria.
butler ['bʌtlə*] *n* maggiordomo.
butt [bʌt] *n* (*cask*) grossa botte *f*; (*thick end*) estremità *f inv* più grossa; (*of gun*) calcio; (*of cigarette*) mozzicone *m*; (*Brit fig: target*) oggetto ♦ *vt* cozzare.
butt in *vi* (*interrupt*) interrompere.
butter ['bʌtə*] *n* burro ♦ *vt* imburrare.
buttercup ['bʌtəkʌp] *n* ranuncolo.
butter dish *n* burriera.
butterfingers ['bʌtəfɪŋgəz] *n* (*col*) mani *fpl* di ricotta.
butterfly ['bʌtəflaɪ] *n* farfalla; (*SWIMMING: also:* ~ **stroke**) (nuoto a) farfalla.
buttocks ['bʌtəks] *npl* natiche *fpl*.
button ['bʌtn] *n* bottone *m* ♦ *vt* (*also:* ~ **up**) abbottonare ♦ *vi* abbottonarsi.
buttonhole ['bʌtnhəul] *n* asola, occhiello ♦ *vt* (*person*) attaccar bottone a.
buttress ['bʌtrɪs] *n* contrafforte *m*.
buxom ['bʌksəm] *a* formoso(a).
buy [baɪ] *vt* (*pt, pp* **bought** [bɔ:t]) comprare,

acquistare ♦ *n*: **a good/bad** ~ un buon/
cattivo acquisto *or* affare; **to** ~ **sb sth/sth
from sb** comprare qc per qn/qc da qn; **to** ~
sb a drink offrire da bere a qn.
buy back *vt* riprendersi, prendersi indietro.
buy in *vt* (*Brit: goods*) far provvista di.
buy into *vt fus* (*Brit COMM*) acquistare
delle azioni di.
buy off *vt* (*col: bribe*) comprare.
buy out *vt* (*business*) rilevare.
buy up *vt* accaparrare.
buyer ['baɪə*] *n* compratore/trice; ~'**s market**
mercato favorevole ai compratori.
buzz [bʌz] *n* ronzio; (*col: phone call*) colpo di
telefono ♦ *vi* ronzare ♦ *vt* (*call on intercom*)
chiamare al citofono; (: *with buzzer*)
chiamare col cicalino; (*AVIAT: plane,
building*) passare rasente; **my head is** ~**ing**
mi gira la testa.
buzz off *vi* (*Brit col*) filare, levarsi di torno.
buzzard ['bʌzəd] *n* poiana.
buzzer ['bʌzə*] *n* cicalino.
buzz word *n* (*col*) termine *m* in voga.
by [baɪ] *prep* da; (*beside*) accanto a; vicino a,
presso; (*before*): ~ **4 o'clock** entro le 4 ♦ *ad
see* **pass**, **go** *etc*; **surrounded** ~ **enemies**
circondato(a) da nemici; **a painting** ~
Picasso un quadro di Picasso; ~ **bus/car** in
autobus/macchina; **paid** ~ **the hour**
pagato(a) a ore; **to increase** *etc* ~ **the hour**
aumentare di ora in ora; **to pay** ~ **cheque**
pagare con (un) assegno; ~ **the kilo/metre** a
chili/metri; **a room 3 metres** ~ **4** una stanza
di 3 metri per 4; **it missed me** ~ **inches** mi
ha mancato per un millimetro; ~ **saving
hard, he** ... risparmiando molto, lui ...; **(all)**
~ **oneself** tutto(a) solo(a); ~ **the way** a
proposito; ~ **and large** nell'insieme; ~ **and**
~ di qui a poco *or* presto.
bye(-bye) ['baɪ('baɪ)] *excl* ciao!, arrivederci!
by(e)-law ['baɪlɔ:] *n* legge *f* locale.
by-election ['baɪɪlɛkʃən] *n* (*Brit*) elezione *f*
straordinaria.
bygone ['baɪɡɔn] *a* passato(a) ♦ *n*: **let** ~**s be**
~**s** mettiamoci una pietra sopra.
bypass ['baɪpɑːs] *n* circonvallazione *f*; (*MED*)
by-pass *m inv* ♦ *vt* fare una deviazione
intorno a.
by-product ['baɪprɔdʌkt] *n* sottoprodotto; (*fig*)
conseguenza secondaria.
byre ['baɪə*] *n* (*Brit*) stalla.
bystander ['baɪstændə*] *n* spettatore/trice.
byte [baɪt] *n* (*COMPUT*) byte *m inv*.
byway ['baɪweɪ] *n* strada secondaria.
byword ['baɪwəːd] *n*: **to be a** ~ **for** essere
sinonimo di.
by-your-leave ['baɪjɔː'liːv] *n*: **without so
much as a** ~ senza nemmeno chiedere il
permesso.

C

C, c [siː] *n* (*letter*) C, c *f or m inv*; (*SCOL:
mark*) ≈ 6 (*sufficiente*); (*MUS*): **C** do; ~ **for
Charlie** ≈ C come Como.
C *abbr* (= *Celsius, centigrade*) C.
c. *abbr* (= *century*) sec.; (= *circa*) c; (*US etc*)
= **cent(s)**.
CA *abbr* = **Central America**; (*US POST*) =
California ♦ *n abbr* (*Brit*) *see* **chartered
accountant**.
ca. *abbr* (= *circa*) ca.
c/a *abbr* = **capital account**; **credit account**;
current account.
CAA *n abbr* (*Brit*: = *Civil Aviation Authority*,
US: = *Civil Aeronautics Authority*)
organismo di controllo e di sviluppo
dell'aviazione civile.
CAB *n abbr* (*Brit*: = *Citizens' Advice Bureau*)
organizzazione per la tutela del consumatore.
cab [kæb] *n* taxi *m inv*; (*of train, truck*)
cabina; (*horsedrawn*) carrozza.
cabaret ['kæbəreɪ] *n* cabaret *m inv*.
cabbage ['kæbɪdʒ] *n* cavolo.
cabin ['kæbɪn] *n* capanna; (*on ship*) cabina.
cabin cruiser *n* cabinato.
cabinet ['kæbɪnɪt] *n* (*POL*) consiglio dei ministri; (*furniture*) armadietto; (*also*: **display**
~) vetrinetta; **cocktail** ~ mobile *m* bar *inv*.
cabinet-maker ['kæbɪnɪt'meɪkə*] *n* stipettaio.
cabinet minister *n* ministro (*membro del
Consiglio*).
cable ['keɪbl] *n* cavo; fune *f*; (*TEL*) cablogramma *m* ♦ *vt* telegrafare.
cable-car ['keɪblkɑː*] *n* funivia.
cablegram ['keɪblɡræm] *n* cablogramma *m*.
cable railway *n* funicolare *f*.
cable television *n* televisione *f* via cavo.
cache [kæʃ] *n* nascondiglio; **a** ~ **of food** *etc*
un deposito segreto di viveri *etc*.
cackle ['kækl] *vi* schiamazzare.
cactus, *pl* **cacti** ['kæktəs, -taɪ] *n* cactus *m inv*.
CAD *n abbr* (= *computer-aided design*)
progettazione *f* con l'ausilio dell'elaboratore.
caddie ['kædɪ] *n* caddie *m inv*.
cadet [kə'dɛt] *n* (*MIL*) cadetto; **police** ~
allievo poliziotto.
cadge [kædʒ] *vt* (*col*) scroccare; **to** ~ **a meal
(off sb)** scroccare un pranzo (a qn).
cadre ['kædrɪ] *n* quadro.
Caesarean, (*US*) **Cesarean** [siː'zɛərɪən] *a*: ~
(section) (*taglio*) cesareo.
CAF *abbr* (*Brit*: = *cost and freight*) Caf *m*.
café ['kæfeɪ] *n* caffè *m inv*.
cafeteria [kæfɪ'tɪərɪə] *n* self-service *m inv*.
caffein(e) ['kæfiːn] *n* caffeina.

cage [keɪdʒ] *n* gabbia ♦ *vt* mettere in gabbia.
cagey ['keɪdʒɪ] *a* (*col*) chiuso(a); guardingo(a).
cagoule [kə'gu:l] *n* K-way ® *m inv*.
CAI *n abbr* (= *computer-aided instruction*) istruzione *f* assistita dall'elaboratore.
Cairo ['kaɪərəu] *n* il Cairo.
cajole [kə'dʒəul] *vt* allettare.
cake [keɪk] *n* torta; ~ **of soap** saponetta; **it's a piece of** ~ (*col*) è una cosa da nulla; **he wants to have his** ~ **and eat it (too)** (*fig*) vuole la botte piena e la moglie ubriaca.
caked [keɪkt] *a*: ~ **with** incrostato(a) di.
cake shop *n* pasticceria.
calamitous [kə'læmɪtəs] *a* disastroso(a).
calamity [kə'læmɪtɪ] *n* calamità *f inv*.
calcium ['kælsɪəm] *n* calcio.
calculate ['kælkjuleɪt] *vt* calcolare; (*estimate: chances, effect*) valutare.
calculate on *vt fus*: **to** ~ **on sth/on doing sth** contare su qc/di fare qc.
calculated ['kælkjuleɪtɪd] *a* calcolato(a), intenzionale; **a** ~ **risk** un rischio calcolato.
calculating ['kælkjuleɪtɪŋ] *a* calcolatore(trice).
calculation [kælkju'leɪʃən] *n* calcolo.
calculator ['kælkjuleɪtə*] *n* calcolatrice *f*.
calculus ['kælkjuləs] *n* calcolo; **integral/differential** ~ calcolo integrale/differenziale.
calendar ['kæləndə*] *n* calendario.
calendar month *n* mese *m* (secondo il calendario).
calendar year *n* anno civile.
calf, *pl* **calves** [ka:f, ka:vz] *n* (*of cow*) vitello; (*of other animals*) piccolo; (*also*: ~**skin**) (pelle *f* di) vitello; (*ANAT*) polpaccio.
caliber ['kælɪbə*] *n* (*US*) = **calibre**.
calibrate ['kælɪbreɪt] *vt* (*gun etc*) calibrare; (*scale of measuring instrument*) tarare.
calibre, (*US*) **caliber** ['kælɪbə*] *n* calibro.
calico ['kælɪkəu] *n* tela grezza, cotone *m* grezzo; (*US*) cotonina stampata.
California [kælɪ'fɔ:nɪə] *n* California.
calipers ['kælɪpəz] *npl* (*US*) = **callipers**.
call [kɔ:l] *vt* (*gen, also TEL*) chiamare; (*announce: flight*) annunciare; (*meeting, strike*) indire, proclamare; ♦ *vi* chiamare; (*visit: also*: ~ **in**, ~ **round**) passare ♦ *n* (*shout*) grido, urlo; visita; (*summons: for flight etc*) chiamata; (*fig: lure*) richiamo; (*also*: **telephone** ~) telefonata; **to be on** ~ essere a disposizione; **to make a** ~ telefonare, fare una telefonata; **please give me a** ~ **at 7** per piacere mi chiami alle 7; **to pay a** ~ **on sb** fare (una) visita a qn; **there's not much** ~ **for these items** non c'è molta richiesta di questi articoli; **she's** ~**ed Jane** si chiama Jane; **who is** ~**ing?** (*TEL*) chi parla?; **London** ~**ing** (*RADIO*) qui Londra.
call at *vt fus* (*subj: ship*) fare scalo a; (*: train*) fermarsi a.
call back *vi* (*return*) ritornare; (*TEL*) ritelefonare, richiamare ♦ *vt* (*TEL*) ritelefonare a, richiamare.
call for *vt fus* (*demand: action etc*) ri-

chiedere; (*collect: person*) passare a prendere; (*: goods*) ritirare.
call in *vt* (*doctor, expert, police*) chiamare, far venire.
call off *vt* (*meeting, race*) disdire; (*deal*) cancellare; (*dog*) richiamare; **the strike was** ~**ed off** lo sciopero è stato revocato.
call on *vt fus* (*visit*) passare da; (*request*): **to** ~ **on sb to do** chiedere a qn di fare.
call out *vi* urlare ♦ *vt* (*doctor, police, troops*) chiamare.
call up *vt* (*MIL*) richiamare.
callbox ['kɔ:lbɔks] *n* (*Brit*) cabina telefonica.
caller ['kɔ:lə*] *n* persona che chiama; visitatore/trice; **hold the line,** ~! (*TEL*) rimanga in linea, signore (or signora)!
call girl *n* ragazza *f* squillo *inv*.
call-in ['kɔ:lɪn] *n* (*US*) = **phone-in**.
calling ['kɔ:lɪŋ] *n* vocazione *f*.
calling card *n* (*US*) biglietto da visita.
callipers, (*US*) **calipers** ['kælɪpəz] *npl* (*MED*) gambale *m*; (*MATH*) calibro.
callous ['kæləs] *a* indurito(a), insensibile.
callousness ['kæləsnɪs] *n* insensibilità.
callow ['kæləu] *a* immaturo(a).
calm [ka:m] *a* calmo(a) ♦ *n* calma ♦ *vt* calmare.
calm down *vi* calmarsi ♦ *vt* calmare.
calmly ['ka:mlɪ] *ad* con calma.
calmness ['ka:mnɪs] *n* calma.
Calor gas ® ['kælə*-] *n* (*Brit*) butano.
calorie ['kælərɪ] *n* caloria; **low-**~ **product** prodotto a basso contenuto di calorie.
calve [ka:v] *vi* figliare.
calves [ka:vz] *npl of* **calf**.
CAM *n abbr* (= *computer-aided manufacturing*) fabbricazione *f* con l'ausilio dell'elaboratore.
camber ['kæmbə*] *n* (*of road*) bombatura.
Cambodia [kæm'bəudjə] *n* Cambogia.
Cambodian [kæm'bəudɪən] *a*, *n* cambogiano(a).
Cambs *abbr* (*Brit*) = *Cambridgeshire*.
came [keɪm] *pt of* **come**.
camel ['kæməl] *n* cammello.
cameo ['kæmɪəu] *n* cammeo.
camera ['kæmərə] *n* macchina fotografica; (*CINEMA, TV*) telecamera; (*also*: **cine**~, **movie** ~) cinepresa; **in** ~ a porte chiuse.
cameraman ['kæmərəmæn] *n* cameraman *m inv*.
Cameroon, Cameroun ['kæməru:n] *n* Camerun *m*.
camouflage ['kæməfla:ʒ] *n* camuffamento; (*MIL*) mimetizzazione *f* ♦ *vt* camuffare; mimetizzare.
camp [kæmp] *n* campeggio; (*MIL*) campo ♦ *vi* campeggiare; accamparsi; **to go** ~**ing** andare in campeggio.
campaign [kæm'peɪn] *n* (*MIL, POL etc*) campagna ♦ *vi*: **to** ~ **(for/against)** (*also fig*) fare una campagna (per/contro).
campaigner [kæm'peɪnə*] *n*: ~ **for** fautore/trice di; ~ **against** oppositore/trice di.

campbed ['kæmp'bɛd] *n* (*Brit*) brandina.
camper ['kæmpə*] *n* campeggiatore/trice.
camping ['kæmpɪŋ] *n* campeggio.
camp(ing) site *n* campeggio.
campus ['kæmpəs] *n* campus *m inv.*
camshaft ['kæmʃɑːft] *n* albero a camme.
can [kæn] *auxiliary vb see next headword* ♦ *n* (*of milk*) scatola; (*of oil*) bidone *m*; (*of water*) tanica; (*tin*) scatola ♦ *vt* mettere in scatola; **a ~ of beer** una lattina di birra; **to carry the ~** (*Brit col*) prendere la colpa.
can [kæn] *n, vt see previous headword* ♦ *auxiliary vb* (*gen*) potere; (*know how to*) sapere; **I ~ speak French** so parlare francese; **I ~ swim** *etc* so nuotare *etc*; **I ~'t see you** non ti vedo; **~ you hear me?** mi senti?; **could I have a word with you?** potrei parlarti un attimo?; **he could be in the library** può darsi che sia in biblioteca; **they could have forgotten** potrebbero essersene dimenticati.
Canada ['kænədə] *n* Canada *m.*
Canadian [kə'neɪdɪən] *a, n* canadese (*m/f*).
canal [kə'næl] *n* canale *m.*
canary [kə'nɛərɪ] *n* canarino.
Canary Islands, Canaries [kə'nɛərɪz] *npl:* **the ~** le (isole) Canarie.
Canberra ['kænbərə] *n* Camberra.
cancel ['kænsəl] *vt* annullare; (*train*) sopprimere; (*cross out*) cancellare.
cancel out *vt* (*MATH*) semplificare; (*fig*) annullare; **they ~ each other out** (*also fig*) si annullano a vicenda.
cancellation [kænsə'leɪʃən] *n* annullamento; soppressione *f*; cancellazione *f*; (*TOURISM*) prenotazione *f* annullata.
cancer ['kænsə*] *n* cancro; **C~** (*sign*) Cancro; **to be C~** essere del Cancro.
cancerous ['kænsərəs] *a* canceroso(a).
cancer patient *n* malato/a di cancro.
cancer research *n* ricerca sul cancro.
C and F *abbr* (*Brit:* = *cost and freight*) Caf *m.*
candid ['kændɪd] *a* onesto(a).
candidacy ['kændɪdəsɪ] *n* candidatura.
candidate ['kændɪdeɪt] *n* candidato/a.
candidature ['kændɪdətʃə*] *n* (*Brit*) = **candidacy.**
candied ['kændɪd] *a* candito(a); **~ apple** (*US*) mela caramellata.
candle ['kændl] *n* candela.
candlelight ['kændl'laɪt] *n:* **by ~** a lume di candela.
candlestick ['kændlstɪk] *n* (*also:* **candle holder**) bugia; (*bigger, ornate*) candeliere *m.*
candour, (*US*) **candor** ['kændə*] *n* sincerità.
candy ['kændɪ] *n* zucchero candito; (*US*) caramella; caramelle *fpl.*
candy-floss ['kændɪflɔs] *n* (*Brit*) zucchero filato.
candy store *n* (*US*) ≈ pasticceria.
cane [keɪn] *n* canna; (*for baskets, chairs etc*) bambù *m*; (*SCOL*) verga; (*for walking*) bastone *m* (da passeggio) ♦ *vt* (*Brit SCOL*) punire a colpi di verga.

canine ['keɪnaɪn] *a* canino(a).
canister ['kænɪstə*] *n* scatola metallica.
cannabis ['kænəbɪs] *n* canapa indiana.
canned ['kænd] *a* (*food*) in scatola; (*col: recorded: music*) registrato(a); (*Brit col: drunk*) sbronzo(a); (*US col: worker*) licenziato(a).
cannibal ['kænɪbəl] *n* cannibale *m/f.*
cannibalism ['kænɪbəlɪzəm] *n* cannibalismo.
cannon, *pl* **~** *or* **~s** ['kænən] *n* (*gun*) cannone *m.*
cannonball ['kænənbɔːl] *n* palla di cannone.
cannon fodder *n* carne *f* da macello.
cannot ['kænɔt] = **can not.**
canny ['kænɪ] *a* furbo(a).
canoe [kə'nuː] *n* canoa; (*SPORT*) canotto.
canoeing [kə'nuːɪŋ] *n* (*sport*) canottaggio.
canoeist [kə'nuːɪst] *n* canottiere *m.*
canon ['kænən] *n* (*clergyman*) canonico; (*standard*) canone *m.*
canonize ['kænənaɪz] *vt* canonizzare.
can opener [-'əupnə*] *n* apriscatole *m inv.*
canopy ['kænəpɪ] *n* baldacchino.
cant [kænt] *n* gergo ♦ *vt* inclinare ♦ *vi* inclinarsi.
can't [kænt] = **can not.**
Cantab. *abbr* (*Brit:* = *cantabrigiensis*) *of Cambridge.*
cantankerous [kæn'tæŋkərəs] *a* stizzoso(a).
canteen [kæn'tiːn] *n* mensa; (*Brit: of cutlery*) portaposate *m inv.*
canter ['kæntə*] *n* piccolo galoppo ♦ *vi* andare al piccolo galoppo.
cantilever ['kæntɪliːvə*] *n* trave *f* a sbalzo.
canvas ['kænvəs] *n* tela; **under ~** (*camping*) sotto la tenda; (*NAUT*) sotto la vela.
canvass ['kænvəs] *vt* (*COMM: district*) fare un'indagine di mercato in; (: *citizens, opinions*) fare un sondaggio di; (*POL: district*) fare un giro elettorale di; (: *person*) fare propaganda elettorale a.
canvasser ['kænvəsə*] *n* (*COMM*) agente *m* viaggiatore, piazzista *m*; (*POL*) propagandista *m/f* (elettorale).
canvassing ['kænvəsɪŋ] *n* sollecitazione *f.*
canyon ['kænjən] *n* canyon *m inv.*
CAP *n abbr* (= *Common Agricultural Policy*) PAC *f.*
cap [kæp] *n* (*also FOOTBALL*) berretto; (*of pen*) coperchio; (*of bottle*) tappo; (*of swimming*) cuffia; (*Brit: contraceptive: also:* **Dutch ~**) diaframma *m* ♦ *vt* tappare; (*outdo*) superare; **~ped with** ricoperto(a) di; **and to ~ it all, he ...** (*Brit*) e per completare l'opera, lui ....
capability [keɪpə'bɪlɪtɪ] *n* capacità *f inv*, abilità *f inv.*
capable ['keɪpəbl] *a* capace; **~ of** capace di; suscettibile di.
capacious [kə'peɪʃəs] *a* capace.
capacity [kə'pæsɪtɪ] *n* capacità *f inv*; (*of lift etc*) capienza; **in his ~ as** nella sua qualità di; **to work at full ~** lavorare al massimo delle proprie capacità; **this work is beyond**

my ~ questo lavoro supera le mie possibilità; **filled to** ~ pieno zeppo; **in an advisory** ~ a titolo consultativo.

cape [keɪp] *n* (*garment*) cappa; (*GEO*) capo.

Cape of Good Hope *n* Capo di Buona Speranza.

caper ['keɪpə*] *n* (*CULIN*: *also*: ~s) cappero; (*leap*) saltello; (*escapade*) birichinata.

Cape Town *n* Città del Capo.

capita ['kæpɪtə] *see* **per capita**.

capital ['kæpɪtl] *n* (*also*: ~ **city**) capitale *f*; (*money*) capitale *m*; (*also*: ~ **letter**) (lettera) maiuscola.

capital account *n* conto capitale.

capital allowance *n* ammortamento fiscale.

capital assets *npl* capitale *m* fisso.

capital expenditure *n* spese *fpl* in capitale.

capital gains tax *n* imposta sulla plus-valenza.

capital goods *n* beni *mpl* d'investimento, beni *mpl* capitali.

capital-intensive ['kæpɪtlɪn'tɛnsɪv] *a* ad alta intensità di capitale.

capitalism ['kæpɪtəlɪzəm] *n* capitalismo.

capitalist ['kæpɪtəlɪst] *a, n* capitalista (*m/f*).

capitalize ['kæpɪtəlaɪz] *vt* (*provide with capital*) capitalizzare.

capitalize on *vt fus* (*fig*) trarre vantaggio da.

capital punishment *n* pena capitale.

capital transfer tax *n* (*Brit*) imposta sui trasferimenti di capitali.

capitulate [kə'pɪtjuleɪt] *vi* capitolare.

capitulation [kəpɪtju'leɪʃən] *n* capitolazione *f*.

capricious [kə'prɪʃəs] *a* capriccioso(a).

Capricorn ['kæprɪkɔːn] *n* Capricorno; **to be** ~ essere del Capricorno.

caps [kæps] *abbr* = **capital letters**.

capsize [kæp'saɪz] *vt* capovolgere ♦ *vi* capovolgersi.

capstan ['kæpstən] *n* argano.

capsule ['kæpsjuːl] *n* capsula.

Capt. *abbr* (= *captain*) Cap.

captain ['kæptɪn] *n* capitano ♦ *vt* capitanare.

caption ['kæpʃən] *n* leggenda.

captivate ['kæptɪveɪt] *vt* avvincere.

captive ['kæptɪv] *a, n* prigioniero(a).

captivity [kæp'tɪvɪtɪ] *n* prigionia; **in** ~ (*animal*) in cattività.

captor ['kæptə*] *n* (*lawful*) chi ha catturato; (*unlawful*) rapitore *m*.

capture ['kæptʃə*] *vt* catturare, prendere; (*attention*) attirare ♦ *n* cattura; (*data* ~) registrazione *f or* rilevazione *f* di dati.

car [kaː*] *n* macchina, automobile *f*; (*US RAIL*) carrozza; **by** ~ in macchina.

Caracas [kə'rækəs] *n* Caracas *f*.

carafe [kə'ræf] *n* caraffa.

carafe wine *n* (*in restaurant*) ≈ vino sfuso.

caramel ['kærəməl] *n* caramello.

carat ['kærət] *n* carato; **18** ~ **gold** oro a 18 carati.

caravan ['kærəvæn] *n* roulotte *f inv*.

caravan site *n* (*Brit*) campeggio per roulotte.

caraway ['kærəweɪ] *n*: ~ **seed** seme *m* di cumino.

carbohydrates [kaːbəu'haɪdreɪts] *npl* (*foods*) carboidrati *mpl*.

carbolic acid [kaː'bɔlɪk-] *n* acido fenico, fenolo.

carbon ['kaːbən] *n* carbonio.

carbonated ['kaːbəneɪtəd] *a* (*drink*) gassato(a).

carbon copy *n* copia *f* carbone *inv*.

carbon dioxide [-daɪ'ɔksaɪd] *n* diossido di carbonio.

carbon paper *n* carta carbone.

carbon ribbon *n* nastro carbonato.

carburettor, (*US*) **carburetor** [kaːbju'rɛtə*] *n* carburatore *m*.

carcass ['kaːkəs] *n* carcassa.

carcinogenic [kaːsɪnə'dʒɛnɪk] *a* cancerogeno(a).

card [kaːd] *n* carta; (*thin cardboard*) cartoncino; (*visiting* ~ *etc*) biglietto; (*membership* ~) tessera; (*Christmas* ~ *etc*) cartolina; **to play** ~s giocare a carte.

cardamom ['kaːdəməm] *n* cardamomo.

cardboard ['kaːdbɔːd] *n* cartone *m*.

cardboard box *n* (scatola di) cartone *m*.

card-carrying member ['kaːd'kærɪŋ-] *n* tesserato/a.

card game *n* gioco di carte.

cardiac ['kaːdɪæk] *a* cardiaco(a).

cardigan ['kaːdɪgən] *n* cardigan *m inv*.

cardinal ['kaːdɪnl] *a, n* cardinale (*m*).

card index *n* schedario.

Cards *abbr* (*Brit*) = *Cardiganshire*.

cardsharp ['kaːdʃaːp] *n* baro.

card vote *n* (*Brit*) voto (palese) per delega.

CARE [kɛə*] *n abbr* = *Cooperative for American Relief Everywhere*.

care [kɛə*] *n* cura, attenzione *f*; (*worry*) preoccupazione *f* ♦ *vi*: **to** ~ **about** interessarsi di; **would you** ~ **to/for ...?** le piacerebbe ...?; **I wouldn't** ~ **to do it** non lo vorrei fare; **in sb's** ~ alle cure di qn; **to take** ~ fare attenzione; **to take** ~ **of** curarsi di; (*details, arrangements*) occuparsi di; **I don't** ~ non me ne importa; **I couldn't** ~ **less** non me ne importa un bel niente; ~ **of** (*c/o*) (*on letter*) presso; **"with** ~**"** "fragile"; **the child has been taken into** ~ il bambino è stato preso in custodia.

care for *vt fus* aver cura di; (*like*) voler bene a.

careen [kə'riːn] *vi* (*ship*) sbandare ♦ *vt* carenare.

career [kə'rɪə*] *n* carriera; (*occupation*) professione *f* ♦ *vi* (*also*: ~ **along**) andare di (gran) carriera.

career girl *n* donna dedita alla carriera.

careers officer *n* consulente *m/f* d'orientamento professionale.

carefree ['kɛəfriː] *a* sgombro(a) di preoccupazioni.

careful ['kɛəful] *a* attento(a); (*cautious*) cauto(a); **(be)** ~! attenzione!; **he's very** ~

with his money bada molto alle spese.
carefully ['kɛəfəlɪ] *ad* con cura; cautamente.
careless ['kɛəlɪs] *a* negligente; *(remark)* privo(a) di tatto.
carelessly ['kɛəlɪslɪ] *ad* negligentemente; senza tatto; *(without thinking)* distrattamente.
carelessness ['kɛəlɪsnɪs] *n* negligenza; mancanza di tatto.
caress [kə'rɛs] *n* carezza ♦ *vt* accarezzare.
caretaker ['kɛəteɪkə•] *n* custode *m*.
caretaker government *n (Brit)* governo *m* ponte *inv*.
car-ferry ['kɑːfɛrɪ] *n* traghetto.
cargo, ~es ['kɑːgəu] *n* carico.
cargo boat *n* cargo.
cargo plane *n* aereo di linea da carico.
car hire *n (Brit)* autonoleggio.
Caribbean [kærɪ'biːən] *a* caraibico(a); **the ~ (Sea)** il Mar dei Caraibi.
caricature ['kærɪkətjuə•] *n* caricatura.
caring ['kɛərɪŋ] *a (person)* premuroso(a); *(society, organization)* umanitario(a).
carnage ['kɑːnɪdʒ] *n* carneficina.
carnal ['kɑːnl] *a* carnale.
carnation [kɑː'neɪʃən] *n* garofano.
carnival ['kɑːnɪvəl] *n (public celebration)* carnevale *m*; *(US: funfair)* luna park *m inv*.
carnivorous [kɑː'nɪvərəs] *a* carnivoro(a).
carol ['kærəl] *n*: **(Christmas) ~** canto di Natale.
carouse [kə'rauz] *vi* far baldoria.
carousel [kærə'sɛl] *n (US)* giostra.
carp [kɑːp] *n (fish)* carpa.
carp at *vt fus* trovare a ridire su.
car park *n* parcheggio.
carpenter ['kɑːpɪntə•] *n* carpentiere *m*.
carpentry ['kɑːpɪntrɪ] *n* carpenteria.
carpet ['kɑːpɪt] *n* tappeto; *(Brit: fitted ~)* moquette *f inv* ♦ *vt* coprire con tappeto.
carpet slippers *npl* pantofole *fpl*.
carpet sweeper *n* scopatappeti *m inv*.
car rental *n (US)* autonoleggio.
carriage ['kærɪdʒ] *n* vettura; *(of goods)* trasporto; *(of typewriter)* carrello; *(bearing)* portamento; **~ forward** porto assegnato; **~ free** franco di porto; **~ paid** porto pagato.
carriage return *n (on typewriter etc)* leva *(or* tasto*)* del ritorno a capo.
carriageway ['kærɪdʒweɪ] *n (Brit: part of road)* carreggiata.
carrier ['kærɪə•] *n (of disease)* portatore/trice; *(COMM)* impresa di trasporti; *(NAUT)* portaerei *f inv*.
carrier bag *n (Brit)* sacchetto.
carrier pigeon *n* colombo viaggiatore.
carrion ['kærɪən] *n* carogna.
carrot ['kærət] *n* carota.
carry ['kærɪ] *vt (subj: person)* portare; *(: vehicle)* trasportare; *(a motion, bill)* far passare; *(involve: responsibilities etc)* comportare; *(COMM: goods)* tenere; *(: interest)* avere; *(MATH: figure)* riportare ♦ *vi (sound)* farsi sentire; **this loan carries 10%**

interest questo prestito è sulla base di un interesse del 10%; **to be carried away** *(fig)* farsi trascinare.
carry forward *vt (MATH, COMM)* riportare.
carry on *vi*: **to ~ on with sth/doing** continuare qc/a fare ♦ *vt* mandare avanti.
carry out *vt (orders)* eseguire; *(investigation)* svolgere; *(accomplish etc: plan)* realizzare; *(perform, implement: idea, threat)* mettere in pratica.
carrycot ['kærɪkɔt] *n (Brit)* culla portabile.
carry-on [kærɪ'ɔn] *n (col: fuss)* casino, confusione *f*; *(: annoying behaviour)*: **I've had enough of your ~!** mi hai proprio scocciato!
cart [kɑːt] *n* carro ♦ *vt (col)* trascinare, scarrozzare.
carte blanche ['kɑːt'blɔnʃ] *n*: **to give sb ~** dare carta bianca a qn.
cartel [kɑː'tɛl] *n (COMM)* cartello.
cartilage ['kɑːtɪlɪdʒ] *n* cartilagine *f*.
cartographer [kɑː'tɔgrəfə•] *n* cartografo/a.
cartography [kɑː'tɔgrəfɪ] *n* cartografia.
carton ['kɑːtən] *n (box)* scatola di cartone; *(of yogurt)* cartone *m*; *(of cigarettes)* stecca.
cartoon [kɑː'tuːn] *n (in newspaper etc)* vignetta; *(CINEMA, TV)* cartone *m* animato; *(ART)* cartone.
cartoonist [kɑː'tuːnɪst] *n* vignettista *m/f*; cartonista *m/f*.
cartridge ['kɑːtrɪdʒ] *n (for gun, pen)* cartuccia; *(for camera)* caricatore *m*; *(music tape)* cassetta; *(of record player)* testina.
cartwheel ['kɑːtwiːl] *n*: **to turn a ~** *(SPORT etc)* fare la ruota.
carve [kɑːv] *vt (meat)* trinciare; *(wood, stone)* intagliare.
carve up *vt (meat)* tagliare; *(fig: country)* suddividere.
carving ['kɑːvɪŋ] *n (in wood etc)* scultura.
carving knife *n* trinciante *m*.
car wash *n* lavaggio auto.
Casablanca [kæsə'blæŋkə] *n* Casablanca.
cascade [kæs'keɪd] *n* cascata ♦ *vi* scendere a cascata.
case [keɪs] *n* caso; *(LAW)* causa, processo; *(box)* scatola; *(also:* **suit~**) valigia; *(TYP)*: **lower/upper ~** *(carattere m)* minuscolo/maiuscolo; **to have a good ~** avere pretese legittime; **there's a strong ~ for reform** ci sono validi argomenti a favore della riforma; **in ~ of** in caso di; **in ~ he** caso mai lui; **just in ~** in caso di bisogno.
case-hardened ['keɪs'hɑːdnd] *a* indurito(a) dall'esperienza.
case history *n (MED)* cartella clinica.
case study *n studio di un caso.*
cash [kæʃ] *n (coins, notes)* soldi *mpl*, denaro; *(col: money)* quattrini *mpl* ♦ *vt* incassare; **to pay (in) ~** pagare in contanti; **to be short of ~** essere a corto di soldi; **~ with order/on delivery (COD)** *(COMM)* pagamento all'ordinazione/alla consegna.

cash in vt (insurance policy etc) riscuotere, riconvertire.

cash in on vt fus: **to ~ in on sth** sfruttare qc.

cash account n conto m cassa inv.

cash-and-carry ['kæʃənd'kærɪ] n cash and carry m inv.

cashbook ['kæʃbuk] n giornale m di cassa.

cash box n cassetta per il denaro spicciolo.

cash card n carta per prelievi automatici.

cash desk n (Brit) cassa.

cash discount n sconto per contanti.

cash dispenser n sportello automatico.

cashew [kæ'ʃu:] n (also: ~ **nut**) anacardio.

cash flow n cash-flow m inv, liquidità f inv.

cashier [kæ'ʃɪə*] n cassiere/a ♦ vt (esp MIL) destituire.

cashmere ['kæʃmɪə*] n cachemire m.

cash payment n pagamento in contanti.

cash price n prezzo per contanti.

cash register n registratore m di cassa.

cash sale n vendita per contanti.

casing ['keɪsɪŋ] n rivestimento.

casino [kə'si:nəu] n casinò m inv.

cask [kɑ:sk] n botte f.

casket ['kɑ:skɪt] n cofanetto; (US: coffin) bara.

Caspian Sea ['kæspɪən-] n: **the ~** il mar Caspio.

casserole ['kæsərəul] n casseruola; (food): **chicken ~** pollo in casseruola.

cassette [kæ'sɛt] n cassetta.

cassette deck n piastra di registrazione.

cassette player n riproduttore m a cassette.

cassette recorder n registratore m a cassette.

cast [kɑ:st] vt (pt, pp **cast**) (throw) gettare; (shed) perdere; spogliarsi di; (metal) gettare, fondere ♦ n (THEATRE) complesso di attori; (mould) forma; (also: **plaster ~**) ingessatura; (THEATRE): **to ~ sb as Hamlet** scegliere qn per la parte di Amleto; **to ~ one's vote** votare, dare il voto.

cast aside vt (reject) mettere da parte.

cast off vi (NAUT) salpare; (KNITTING) diminuire, calare ♦ vt + adv (NAUT) disormeggiare; (KNITTING) diminuire, calare.

cast on vt (KNITTING) avviare ♦ vi avviare (le maglie).

castanets [kæstə'nɛts] npl castagnette fpl.

castaway ['kɑ:stəwəɪ] n naufrago/a.

caste [kɑ:st] n casta.

caster sugar ['kɑ:stə-] n zucchero semolato.

casting vote ['kɑ:stɪŋ-] n (Brit) voto decisivo.

cast iron n ghisa ♦ a: **cast-iron** (fig: will, alibi) di ferro, d'acciaio.

castle ['kɑ:sl] n castello; (fortified) rocca.

castor ['kɑ:stə*] n (wheel) rotella.

castor oil n olio di ricino.

castrate [kæs'treɪt] vt castrare.

casual ['kæʒjul] a (by chance) casuale, fortuito(a); (irregular: work etc) avventizio(a); (unconcerned) noncurante,

indifferente; ~ **wear** casual m.

casual labour n manodopera avventizia.

casually ['kæʒjulɪ] ad con disinvoltura; (by chance) casualmente.

casualty ['kæʒjultɪ] n ferito/a; (dead) morto/a, vittima; **heavy casualties** npl grosse perdite fpl.

casualty ward n (Brit) pronto soccorso.

cat [kæt] n gatto.

catacombs ['kætəku:mz] npl catacombe fpl.

catalogue, (US) catalog ['kætələɔg] n catalogo ♦ vt catalogare.

catalyst ['kætəlɪst] n catalizzatore m.

catapult ['kætəpʌlt] n catapulta; fionda.

cataract ['kætərækt] n (also MED) cateratta.

catarrh [kə'tɑ:*] n catarro.

catastrophe [kə'tæstrəfɪ] n catastrofe f.

catastrophic [kætə'strɔfɪk] a catastrofico(a).

catcall ['kætkɔ:l] n (at meeting etc) fischio.

catch [kætʃ] vb (pt, pp **caught** [kɔ:t]) vt (train, thief, cold) acchiappare; (ball) afferrare; (person: by surprise) sorprendere; (understand) comprendere; (get entangled) impigliare ♦ vi (fire) prendere ♦ n (fish etc caught) retata, presa; (trick) inganno; (TECH) gancio; **to ~ sb's attention** or **eye** attirare l'attenzione di qn; **to ~ fire** prendere fuoco; **to ~ sight of** scorgere.

catch on vi (become popular) affermarsi, far presa; (understand): **to ~ on (to sth)** capire (qc).

catch out vt (Brit fig: with trick question) cogliere in fallo.

catch up vi mettersi in pari ♦ vt (also: ~ **up with**) raggiungere.

catching ['kætʃɪŋ] a (MED) contagioso(a).

catchment area ['kætʃmənt-] n (Brit SCOL) circoscrizione f scolare; (GEO) bacino pluviale.

catch phrase n slogan m inv; frase f fatta.

catch-22 ['kætʃtwentɪ'tu:] n: **it's a ~ situation** non c'è via d'uscita.

catchy ['kætʃɪ] a orecchiabile.

catechism ['kætɪkɪzəm] n catechismo.

categoric(al) [kætɪ'gɔrɪk(l)] a categorico(a).

categorize ['kætɪgəraɪz] vt categorizzare.

category ['kætɪgərɪ] n categoria.

cater ['keɪtə*] vi (gen: ~ **for**) provvedere da mangiare (per).

cater for vt fus (Brit: needs) provvedere a; (: readers, consumers) incontrare i gusti di.

caterer ['keɪtərə*] n fornitore m.

catering ['keɪtərɪŋ] n approvvigionamento.

catering trade n settore m ristoranti.

caterpillar ['kætəpɪlə*] n (ZOOL) bruco ♦ cpd (vehicle) cingolato(a); ~ **track** cingolo.

cathedral [kə'θi:drəl] n cattedrale f, duomo.

cathode ['kæθəud] n catodo.

cathode ray tube n tubo a raggi catodici.

catholic ['kæθəlɪk] a universale; aperto(a); eclettico(a); **C~** a, n (REL) cattolico(a).

cat's-eye ['kæts'aɪ] n (Brit AUT) catarifrangente m.

catsup ['kætsəp] n (US) ketchup m inv.

cattle ['kætl] *npl* bestiame *m*, bestie *fpl*.
catty ['kætɪ] *a* maligno(a), dispettoso(a).
Caucasian [kɔː'keɪzɪən] *a, n* caucasico(a).
Caucasus ['kɔːkəsəs] *n* Caucaso.
caucus ['kɔːkəs] *n* (*US Pol*) (riunione *f* del) comitato elettorale; (*Brit* POL: *group*) comitato di dirigenti.
caught [kɔːt] *pt, pp of* **catch.**
cauliflower ['kɒlɪflaʊə*] *n* cavolfiore *m*.
cause [kɔːz] *n* causa ♦ *vt* causare; **there is no ~ for concern** non c'è ragione di preoccuparsi; **to ~ sb to do sth** far fare qc a qn; **to ~ sth to be done** far fare qc.
causeway ['kɔːzweɪ] *n* strada rialzata.
caustic ['kɔːstɪk] *a* caustico(a).
caution ['kɔːʃən] *n* prudenza; (*warning*) avvertimento ♦ *vt* ammonire.
cautious ['kɔːʃəs] *a* cauto(a), prudente.
cautiously ['kɔːʃəslɪ] *ad* prudentemente.
cautiousness ['kɔːʃəsnɪs] *n* cautela.
cavalier [kævə'lɪə*] *n* (*knight*) cavaliere *m* ♦ *a* (*pej: offhand*) brusco(a).
cavalry ['kævəlrɪ] *n* cavalleria.
cave [keɪv] *n* caverna, grotta ♦ *vi*: **to go caving** fare speleologia.
cave in *vi* (*roof etc*) crollare.
caveman ['keɪvmæn] *n* uomo delle caverne.
cavern ['kævən] *n* caverna.
caviar(e) ['kævɪɑː*] *n* caviale *m*.
cavity ['kævɪtɪ] *n* cavità *f inv*.
cavity wall insulation *n* isolamento per pareti a intercapedine.
cavort [kə'vɔːt] *vi* far capriole.
cayenne (pepper) [keɪ'ɛn-] *n* pepe *m* di Caienna.
CB *n abbr* (*Brit*: = *Companion (of the Order) of the Bath*) titolo; (= *Citizens' Band (Radio)*) C.B. *m*; **~ radio (set)** baracchino.
CBC *n abbr* = *Canadian Broadcasting Corporation*.
CBE *n abbr* (*Brit*: = *Companion (of the Order) of the British Empire*) titolo.
CBI *n abbr* (= *Confederation of British Industry*) ≈ CONFINDUSTRIA (= *Confederazione Generale dell'Industria Italiana*).
CBS *n abbr* (*US*) = *Columbia Broadcasting System*.
CC *abbr* (*Brit*) = *county council*.
cc *abbr* (= *cubic centimetre*) cc; (*on letter etc*) = **carbon copy.**
CCA *n abbr* (*US*: = *Circuit Court of Appeals*) corte *f* d'appello itinerante.
CCU *n abbr* (*US*: = *coronary care unit*) unità coronarica.
CD *n abbr* (= *compact disk*) compact disk *m inv*; (*MIL*) = *Civil Defence (Corps)* (*Brit*), *Civil Defense (US)* ♦ *abbr* (*Brit*: = *Corps Diplomatique*) C.D.
CDC *n abbr* (*US*) = *center for disease control*.
Cdr. *abbr* (= *commander*) Com.
CDT *abbr* (*US*: = *Central Daylight Time*) ora legale del centro.
CDW *n abbr see* **collision damage waiver.**
cease [siːs] *vt, vi* cessare.

ceasefire ['siːsfaɪə*] *n* cessate il fuoco *m inv*.
ceaseless ['siːslɪs] *a* incessante, continuo(a).
CED *n abbr* (*US*) = *Committee for Economic Development*.
cedar ['siːdə*] *n* cedro.
cede [siːd] *vt* cedere.
CEEB *n abbr* (*US*: = *College Entrance Examination Board*) commissione *f* per l'esame di ammissione al college.
ceiling ['siːlɪŋ] *n* soffitto; (*fig: upper limit*) tetto, limite *m* massimo.
celebrate ['sɛlɪbreɪt] *vt, vi* celebrare.
celebrated ['sɛlɪbreɪtɪd] *a* celebre.
celebration [sɛlɪ'breɪʃən] *n* celebrazione *f*.
celebrity [sɪ'lɛbrɪtɪ] *n* celebrità *f inv*.
celeriac [sə'lɛrɪæk] *n* sedano *m* rapa *inv*.
celery ['sɛlərɪ] *n* sedano.
celestial [sɪ'lɛstɪəl] *a* celeste.
celibacy ['sɛlɪbəsɪ] *n* celibato.
cell [sɛl] *n* cella; (*BIOL*) cellula; (*ELEC*) elemento (di batteria).
cellar ['sɛlə*] *n* sottosuolo, cantina.
'cellist ['tʃɛlɪst] *n* violoncellista *m/f*.
'cello ['tʃɛləu] *n* violoncello.
cellophane ® ['sɛləfeɪn] *n* cellophane ® *m*.
cellular ['sɛljulə*] *a* cellulare.
celluloid ['sɛljulɔɪd] *n* celluloide *f*.
cellulose ['sɛljuləus] *n* cellulosa.
Celsius ['sɛlsɪəs] *a* Celsius *inv*.
Celt [kɛlt, sɛlt] *n* celta *m/f*.
Celtic ['kɛltɪk, 'sɛltɪk] *a* celtico(a) ♦ *n* (LING) celtico.
cement [sə'mɛnt] *n* cemento ♦ *vt* cementare.
cement mixer *n* betoniera.
cemetery ['sɛmɪtrɪ] *n* cimitero.
cenotaph ['sɛnətɑːf] *n* cenotafio.
censor ['sɛnsə*] *n* censore *m* ♦ *vt* censurare.
censorship ['sɛnsəʃɪp] *n* censura.
censure ['sɛnʃə*] *vt* censurare.
census ['sɛnsəs] *n* censimento.
cent [sɛnt] *n* (*US: coin*) centesimo (= *1:100 di un dollaro*); *see also* **per cent.**
centenary [sɛn'tiːnərɪ], **centennial** [sɛn'tɛnɪəl] *n* centenario.
center ['sɛntə*] *n, vt* (*US*) = **centre.**
centigrade ['sɛntɪgreɪd] *a* centigrado(a).
centilitre, (*US*) **centiliter** ['sɛntɪliːtə*] *n* centilitro.
centimetre, (*US*) **centimeter** ['sɛntɪmiːtə*] *n* centimetro.
centipede ['sɛntɪpiːd] *n* centopiedi *m inv*.
central ['sɛntrəl] *a* centrale.
Central African Republic *n* Repubblica centrafricana.
Central America *n* America centrale.
central heating *n* riscaldamento centrale.
centralize ['sɛntrəlaɪz] *vt* accentrare.
central processing unit (CPU) *n* (*COMPUT*) unità *f inv* centrale di elaborazione.
central reservation *n* (*Brit* AUT) banchina *f* spartitraffico *inv*.
centre, (*US*) **center** ['sɛntə*] *n* centro ♦ *vt* (*concentrate*): **to ~ (on)** concentrare (su).
centrefold, (*US*) **centerfold** ['sɛntəfəuld] *n*

(*PRESS*) poster *m* (all'interno di rivista).

centre-forward ['sɛntə'fɔːwəd] *n* (*SPORT*) centroavanti *m inv*.

centre-half ['sɛntə'hɑːf] *n* (*SPORT*) centromediano.

centrepiece, (*US*) **centerpiece** ['sɛntəpiːs] *n* centrotavola *m*; (*fig*) punto centrale.

centre spread *n* (*Brit*) pubblicità a doppia pagina.

centrifugal [sɛn'trɪfjugəl] *a* centrifugo(a).

centrifuge ['sɛntrɪfjuːʒ] *n* centrifuga.

century ['sɛntjurɪ] *n* secolo; **in the twentieth** ~ nel ventesimo secolo.

CEO *n abbr* (*US*) *see* **chief executive officer**.

ceramic [sɪ'ræmɪk] *a* ceramico(a).

cereal ['siːrɪəl] *n* cereale *m*.

cerebral ['sɛrɪbrəl] *a* cerebrale.

ceremonial [sɛrɪ'məunɪəl] *n* cerimoniale *m*; (*rite*) rito.

ceremony ['sɛrɪmənɪ] *n* cerimonia; **to stand on** ~ fare complimenti.

cert [səːt] *n* (*Brit col*): **it's a dead** ~ non c'è alcun dubbio.

certain ['səːtən] *a* certo(a); **to make** ~ **of** assicurarsi di; **for** ~ per certo, di sicuro.

certainly ['səːtənlɪ] *ad* certamente, certo.

certainty ['səːtəntɪ] *n* certezza.

certificate [sə'tɪfɪkɪt] *n* certificato; diploma *m*.

certified letter ['səːtɪfaɪd-] *n* (*US*) lettera raccomandata.

certified public accountant (CPA) ['səːtɪfaɪd-] *n* (*US*) ≈ commercialista *m/f*.

certify ['səːtɪfaɪ] *vt* certificare ♦ *vi*: **to** ~ **to** attestare a.

cervical ['səːvɪkl] *a*: ~ **cancer** cancro della cervice, tumore *m* al collo dell'utero; ~ **smear** Pap-test *m inv*.

cervix ['səːvɪks] *n* cervice *f*.

Cesarean [siː'zɛərɪən] *a*, *n* (*US*) = **Caesarean**.

cessation [sə'seɪʃən] *n* cessazione *f*; arresto.

cesspit ['sɛspɪt] *n* pozzo nero.

CET *abbr* (= *Central European Time*) *fuso orario*.

Ceylon [sɪ'lɔn] *n* Ceylon *f*.

cf. *abbr* (= *compare*) cfr.

c/f *abbr* (*COMM*) = *carried forward*.

CG *n abbr* (*US*) = **coastguard**.

cg *abbr* (= *centigram*) cg.

CH *n abbr* (*Brit*: = *Companion of Honour*) titolo.

ch *abbr* (*Brit*) = **central heating**.

ch. *abbr* (= *chapter*) cap.

Chad [tʃæd] *n* Chad *m*.

chafe [tʃeɪf] *vt* fregare, irritare ♦ *vi* (*fig*): **to** ~ **against** scontrarsi con.

chaffinch ['tʃæfɪntʃ] *n* fringuello.

chagrin ['ʃægrɪn] *n* disappunto, dispiacere *m*.

chain [tʃeɪn] *n* catena ♦ *vt* (*also*: ~ **up**) incatenare.

chain reaction *n* reazione *f* a catena.

chain-smoke ['tʃeɪnsməuk] *vi* fumare una sigaretta dopo l'altra.

chain store *n* negozio a catena.

chair [tʃɛə*] *n* sedia; (*armchair*) poltrona; (*of*

university) cattedra ♦ *vt* (*meeting*) presiedere; **the** ~ (*US*: *electric* ~) la sedia elettrica.

chairlift ['tʃɛəlɪft] *n* seggiovia.

chairman ['tʃɛəmən] *n* presidente *m*.

chairperson ['tʃɛəpəːsn] *n* presidente/essa.

chairwoman ['tʃɛəwumən] *n* presidentessa.

chalet ['ʃæleɪ] *n* chalet *m inv*.

chalice ['tʃælɪs] *n* calice *m*.

chalk [tʃɔːk] *n* gesso.

chalk up *vt* scrivere col gesso; (*fig*: *success*) ottenere; (*: victory*) riportare.

challenge ['tʃælɪndʒ] *n* sfida ♦ *vt* sfidare; (*statement*, *right*) mettere in dubbio; **to** ~ **sb to a fight/game** sfidare qn a battersi/ad una partita; **to** ~ **sb to do** sfidare qn a fare.

challenger ['tʃælɪndʒə*] *n* (*SPORT*) sfidante *m/f*.

challenging ['tʃælɪndʒɪŋ] *a* sfidante; (*remark*, *look*) provocatorio(a).

chamber ['tʃeɪmbə*] *n* camera; ~ **of commerce** camera di commercio.

chambermaid ['tʃeɪmbəmeɪd] *n* cameriera.

chamber music *n* musica da camera.

chamberpot ['tʃeɪmbəpɔt] *n* vaso da notte.

chameleon [kə'miːlɪən] *n* camaleonte *m*.

chamois ['ʃæmwɑː] *n* camoscio.

chamois leather ['ʃæmɪ-] *n* pelle *f* di camoscio.

champagne [ʃæm'peɪn] *n* champagne *m inv*.

champion ['tʃæmpɪən] *n* campione/essa; (*of cause*) difensore *m* ♦ *vt* difendere, lottare per.

championship ['tʃæmpɪənʃɪp] *n* campionato.

chance [tʃɑːns] *n* caso; (*opportunity*) occasione *f*; (*likelihood*) possibilità *f inv* ♦ *vt*: **to** ~ **it** rischiare, provarci ♦ *a* fortuito(a); **there is little** ~ **of his coming** è molto improbabile che venga; **to take a** ~ rischiare; **by** ~ per caso; **it's the** ~ **of a lifetime** è un'occasione unica; **the** ~**s are that** ... probabilmente ..., è probabile che ... + *sub*; **to** ~ **to do sth** (*formal*: *happen*) fare per caso qc.

chance (up)on *vt fus* (*person*) incontrare per caso, imbattersi in; (*thing*) trovare per caso.

chancel ['tʃɑːnsəl] *n* coro.

chancellor ['tʃɑːnsələ*] *n* cancelliere *m*; (*of university*) rettore *m* (onorario); **C~ of the Exchequer** (*Brit*) Cancelliere *m* dello Scacchiere.

chandelier [ʃændə'lɪə*] *n* lampadario.

change [tʃeɪndʒ] *vt* cambiare; (*transform*): **to** ~ **sb into** trasformare qn in ♦ *vi* cambiarsi; (*be transformed*): **to** ~ **into** trasformarsi in ♦ *n* cambiamento; (*money*) resto; **to** ~ **one's mind** cambiare idea; **to** ~ **gear** (*AUT*) cambiare (marcia); **she** ~**d into an old skirt** si è cambiata e ha messo una vecchia gonna; **a** ~ **of clothes** un cambio (di vestiti); **for a** ~ tanto per cambiare; **small** ~ spiccioli *mpl*, moneta; **keep the** ~ tenga il resto; **can you give me** ~ **for £1?** mi può cambiare una sterlina?

changeable ['tʃeɪndʒəbl] a (weather) variabile; (person) mutevole.

change machine n distributore m automatico di monete.

changeover ['tʃeɪndʒəuvə*] n cambiamento, passaggio.

changing ['tʃeɪndʒɪŋ] a che cambia; (colours) cangiante.

changing room n (Brit: in shop) camerino; (: SPORT) spogliatoio.

channel ['tʃænl] n canale m; (of river, sea) alveo ♦ vt canalizzare; (fig: interest, energies): **to ~ into** concentrare su, indirizzare verso; **through the usual ~s** per le solite vie; **the (English) C~** la Manica; **green/red ~** (CUSTOMS) uscita "niente da dichiarare"/"merci da dichiarare".

Channel Islands npl: **the ~** le Isole Normanne.

chant [tʃɑ:nt] n canto; salmodia; (of crowd) slogan m inv ♦ vt cantare; salmodiare; **the demonstrators ~ed their disapproval** i dimostranti lanciavano slogan di protesta.

chaos ['keɪɔs] n caos m.

chaotic [keɪ'ɔtɪk] a caotico(a).

chap [tʃæp] n (Brit col: man) tipo ♦ vt (skin) screpolare; **old ~** vecchio mio.

chapel ['tʃæpl] n cappella.

chaperone ['ʃæpərəun] n accompagnatore/trice ♦ vt accompagnare.

chaplain ['tʃæplɪn] n cappellano.

chapped [tʃæpt] a (skin, lips) screpolato(a).

chapter ['tʃæptə*] n capitolo.

char [tʃɑ:*] vt (burn) carbonizzare ♦ vi (Brit: cleaner) lavorare come domestica (a ore) ♦ n (Brit) = **charlady**.

character ['kærɪktə*] n (gen, COMPUT) carattere m; (in novel, film) personaggio; (eccentric) originale m; **a person of good ~** una persona a modo.

character code n (COMPUT) codice m di carattere.

characteristic ['kærɪktə'rɪstɪk] a caratteristico(a) ♦ n caratteristica; **~ of** tipico(a) di.

characterize ['kærɪktəraɪz] vt caratterizzare; (describe): **to ~ (as)** descrivere (come).

charade [ʃə'rɑ:d] n sciarada.

charcoal ['tʃɑ:kəul] n carbone m di legna.

charge [tʃɑ:dʒ] n accusa; (cost) prezzo; (of gun, battery, MIL: attack) carica ♦ vt (gun, battery, MIL: enemy) caricare; (customer) fare pagare a; (sum) fare pagare; (LAW): **to ~ sb (with)** accusare qn (di) ♦ vi (gen with: up, along etc) lanciarsi; **~s** npl: **bank ~s** commissioni fpl bancarie; **labour ~s** costi mpl del lavoro; **to ~ in/out** precipitarsi dentro/fuori; **to ~ up/down** lanciarsi su/giù per; **is there a ~?** c'è da pagare?; **there's no ~** non c'è niente da pagare; **extra ~** supplemento; **to take ~ of** incaricarsi di; **to be in ~ of** essere responsabile per; **to have ~ of sb** aver cura di qn; **how much do you ~ for this repair?** quanto chiede per la riparazione?; **to ~ an expense (up) to sb** addebitare una spesa a qn; **~ it to my account** lo metta or addebiti sul mio conto.

charge account n conto.

charge card n carta di credito commerciale.

chargé d'affaires ['ʃɑ:ʒeɪdæ'feə*] n incaricato d'affari.

chargehand ['tʃɑ:dʒhænd] n (Brit) caposquadra m/f.

charger ['tʃɑ:dʒə*] n (also: **battery ~**) caricabatterie m inv; (old: warhorse) destriero.

chariot ['tʃærɪət] n carro.

charitable ['tʃærɪtəbl] a caritatevole.

charity ['tʃærɪtɪ] n carità; (organization) opera pia.

charlady ['tʃɑ:leɪdɪ] n (Brit) domestica a ore.

charlatan ['ʃɑ:lətən] n ciarlatano.

charm [tʃɑ:m] n fascino; (on bracelet) ciondolo ♦ vt affascinare, incantare.

charm bracelet n braccialetto con ciondoli.

charming ['tʃɑ:mɪŋ] a affascinante.

chart [tʃɑ:t] n tabella; grafico; (map) carta nautica; (weather ~) carta del tempo ♦ vt fare una carta nautica di; (sales, progress) tracciare il grafico di; **to be in the ~s** (record, pop group) essere in classifica.

charter ['tʃɑ:tə*] vt (plane) noleggiare ♦ n (document) statuto; **on ~** a nolo.

chartered accountant (CA) ['tʃɑ:təd-] n (Brit) ragioniere/a professionista.

charter flight n volo m charter inv.

charwoman ['tʃɑ:wumən] n = **charlady**.

chase [tʃeɪs] vt inseguire; (also: **~ away**) cacciare ♦ n caccia.

chase down vt (US) = **chase up**.

chase up vt (Brit: person) scovare; (: information) scoprire, raccogliere.

chasm ['kæzəm] n abisso.

chassis ['ʃæsɪ] n telaio.

chastened ['tʃeɪsnd] a abbattuto(a), provato(a).

chastening ['tʃeɪsnɪŋ] a che fa riflettere.

chastise [tʃæs'taɪz] vt punire, castigare.

chastity ['tʃæstɪtɪ] n castità.

chat [tʃæt] vi (also: **have a ~**) chiacchierare ♦ n chiacchierata.

chat up vt (Brit col: girl) abbordare.

chat show n (Brit) talk show m inv, conversazione f televisiva.

chattel ['tʃætl] n see **goods**.

chatter ['tʃætə*] vi (person) ciarlare ♦ n ciarle fpl; **her teeth were ~ing** batteva i denti.

chatterbox ['tʃætəbɔks] n chiacchierone/a.

chatty ['tʃætɪ] a (style) familiare; (person) chiacchierino(a).

chauffeur ['ʃəufə*] n autista m.

chauvinism ['ʃəuvɪnɪzəm] n (also: **male ~**) maschilismo; (nationalism) sciovinismo.

chauvinist ['ʃəuvɪnɪst] n (also: **male ~**) maschilista m; (nationalist) sciovinista m/f.

chauvinistic [ʃəuvɪ'nɪstɪk] a sciovinistico(a).

ChE abbr = **chemical engineer**.

cheap [tʃi:p] a a buon mercato; (reduced:

fare, ticket) ridotto(a); (*joke*) grossolano(a); (*poor quality*) di cattiva qualità ♦ *ad* a buon mercato; ~**er** meno caro; ~ **money** denaro a basso tasso di interesse.

cheapen ['tʃiːpn] *vt* ribassare; (*fig*) avvilire.

cheaply ['tʃiːplɪ] *ad* a buon prezzo, a buon mercato.

cheat [tʃiːt] *vi* imbrogliare; (*at school*) copiare ♦ *vt* ingannare; (*rob*) defraudare ♦ *n* imbroglione *m*; copione *m*; (*trick*) inganno; **he's been ~ing on his wife** ha tradito sua moglie.

cheating ['tʃiːtɪŋ] *n* imbrogliare *m*; copiare *m*.

check [tʃɛk] *vt* verificare; (*passport, ticket*) controllare; (*halt*) fermare; (*restrain*) contenere ♦ *vi* (*official etc*) informarsi ♦ *n* verifica; controllo; (*curb*) freno; (*bill*) conto; (*pattern: gen pl*) quadretti *mpl*; (*US*) = **cheque** ♦ *a* (*also*: ~**ed**: *pattern, cloth*) a scacchi, a quadretti; **to ~ with sb** chiedere a qn; **to keep a ~ on sb/sth** controllare qn/qc, fare attenzione a qn/qc.

check in *vi* (*in hotel*) registrare; (*at airport*) presentarsi all'accettazione ♦ *vt* (*luggage*) depositare.

check off *vt* segnare.

check out *vi* (*from hotel*) saldare il conto ♦ *vt* (*luggage*) ritirare; (*investigate: story*) controllare, verificare; (*: person*) prendere informazioni su.

check up *vi*: **to ~ up (on sth)** investigare (qc); **to ~ up on sb** informarsi sul conto di qn.

checkbook ['tʃɛkbuk] *n* (*US*) = **chequebook**.

checkered ['tʃɛkəd] *a* (*US*) = **chequered**.

checkers ['tʃɛkəz] *n* (*US*) dama.

check guarantee card *n* (*US*) carta *f* assegni *inv*.

check-in ['tʃɛkɪn] *n* (*also*: ~ **desk**: *at airport*) check-in *m inv*, accettazione *f* (bagagli *inv*).

checking account ['tʃɛkɪŋ-] *n* (*US*) conto corrente.

checklist ['tʃɛklɪst] *n* lista di controllo.

checkmate ['tʃɛkmeɪt] *n* scaccomatto.

checkout ['tʃɛkaut] *n* (*in supermarket*) cassa.

checkpoint ['tʃɛkpɔɪnt] *n* posto di blocco.

checkroom ['tʃɛkrum] *n* (*US*) deposito *m* bagagli *inv*.

checkup ['tʃɛkʌp] *n* (*MED*) controllo medico.

cheek [tʃiːk] *n* guancia; (*impudence*) faccia tosta.

cheekbone ['tʃiːkbəun] *n* zigomo.

cheeky ['tʃiːkɪ] *a* sfacciato(a).

cheep [tʃiːp] *n* (*of bird*) pigolio ♦ *vi* pigolare.

cheer [tʃɪə*] *vt* applaudire; (*gladden*) rallegrare ♦ *vi* applaudire ♦ *n* (*gen pl*) applausi *mpl*; evviva *mpl*; ~**s!** salute!

cheer on *vt* (*person etc*) incitare.

cheer up *vi* rallegrarsi, farsi animo ♦ *vt* rallegrare.

cheerful ['tʃɪəful] *a* allegro(a).

cheerfulness ['tʃɪəfulnɪs] *n* allegria.

cheerio ['tʃɪərɪ'əu] *excl* (*Brit*) ciao!

cheerless ['tʃɪəlɪs] *a* triste.

cheese [tʃiːz] *n* formaggio.

cheeseboard ['tʃiːzbɔːd] *n* piatto del (*or* per il) formaggio.

cheesecake ['tʃiːzkeɪk] *n* specie di torta di ricotta, a volte con frutta.

cheetah ['tʃiːtə] *n* ghepardo.

chef [ʃɛf] *n* capocuoco.

chemical ['kɛmɪkl] *a* chimico(a) ♦ *n* prodotto chimico.

chemical engineering *n* ingegneria chimica.

chemist ['kɛmɪst] *n* (*Brit: pharmacist*) farmacista *m/f*; (*scientist*) chimico/a; ~**'s shop** *n* (*Brit*) farmacia.

chemistry ['kɛmɪstrɪ] *n* chimica.

cheque, (*US*) **check** [tʃɛk] *n* assegno; **to pay by ~** pagare per assegno *or* con un assegno.

chequebook, (*US*) **checkbook** ['tʃɛkbuk] *n* libretto degli assegni.

cheque card *n* (*Brit*) carta *f* assegni *inv*.

chequered, (*US*) **checkered** ['tʃɛkəd] *a* (*fig*) movimentato(a).

cherish ['tʃɛrɪʃ] *vt* aver caro; (*hope etc*) nutrire.

cheroot [ʃə'ruːt] *n* sigaro spuntato.

cherry ['tʃɛrɪ] *n* ciliegia.

Ches *abbr* (*Brit*) = *Cheshire*.

chess [tʃɛs] *n* scacchi *mpl*.

chessboard ['tʃɛsbɔːd] *n* scacchiera.

chessman ['tʃɛsmæn] *n* pezzo degli scacchi.

chessplayer ['tʃɛspleɪə*] *n* scacchista *m/f*.

chest [tʃɛst] *n* petto; (*box*) cassa; **to get sth off one's ~** (*col*) sputare il rospo; ~ **of drawers** cassettone *m*.

chest measurement *n* giro *m* torace *inv*.

chestnut ['tʃɛsnʌt] *n* castagna; (*also*: ~ *tree*) castagno ♦ *a* castano(a).

chew [tʃuː] *vt* masticare.

chewing gum ['tʃuːɪŋ-] *n* chewing gum *m*.

chic [ʃiːk] *a* elegante.

chick [tʃɪk] *n* pulcino; (*US col*) pollastrella.

chicken ['tʃɪkɪn] *n* pollo; (*col: coward*) coniglio.

chicken out *vi* (*col*) avere fifa; **to ~ out of sth** tirarsi indietro da qc per fifa *or* paura.

chicken feed *n* (*fig*) miseria.

chickenpox ['tʃɪkɪnpɔks] *n* varicella.

chickpea ['tʃɪkpiː] *n* cece *m*.

chicory ['tʃɪkərɪ] *n* cicoria.

chide [tʃaɪd] *vt* rimproverare.

chief [tʃiːf] *n* capo ♦ *a* principale; **C~ of Staff** (*MIL*) Capo di Stato Maggiore.

chief constable *n* (*Brit*) ≈ questore *m*.

chief executive, (*US*) **chief executive officer (CEO)** *n* direttore *m* generale.

chiefly ['tʃiːflɪ] *ad* per lo più, soprattutto.

chiffon ['ʃɪfɔn] *n* chiffon *m inv*.

chilblain ['tʃɪlbleɪn] *n* gelone *m*.

child, *pl* ~**ren** [tʃaɪld, 'tʃɪldrən] *n* bambino/a.

childbirth ['tʃaɪldbəːθ] *n* parto.

childhood ['tʃaɪldhud] *n* infanzia.

childish ['tʃaɪldɪʃ] *a* puerile.

childless ['tʃaɪldlɪs] *a* senza figli.

childlike ['tʃaɪldlaɪk] *a* fanciullesco(a).

child minder *n* (*Brit*) bambinaia.

children ['tʃɪldrən] npl of **child**.
Chile ['tʃɪli] n Cile m.
Chilean ['tʃɪlɪən] a, n cileno(a).
chill [tʃɪl] n freddo; (MED) infreddatura ♦ a
freddo(a), gelido(a) ♦ vt raffreddare;
(CULIN) mettere in fresco; "**serve ~ed**"
"servire fresco".
chilli, (US) **chili** ['tʃɪlɪ] n peperoncino.
chilly ['tʃɪlɪ] a freddo(a), fresco(a); (sensitive
to cold) freddoloso(a); **to feel ~** sentirsi in-
freddolito(a).
chime [tʃaɪm] n carillon m inv ♦ vi suonare,
scampanare.
chimney ['tʃɪmnɪ] n camino.
chimney sweep n spazzacamino.
chimpanzee [tʃɪmpæn'zi:] n scimpanzé m inv.
chin [tʃɪn] n mento.
China ['tʃaɪnə] n Cina.
china ['tʃaɪnə] n porcellana.
Chinese [tʃaɪ'ni:z] a cinese ♦ n (pl inv) cinese
m/f; (LING) cinese m.
chink [tʃɪŋk] n (opening) fessura; (noise)
tintinnio.
chip [tʃɪp] n (gen pl: CULIN) patatina fritta; (:
US: also: **potato ~**) patatina; (of wood,
glass, stone) scheggia; (in gambling) fiche f
inv; (COMPUT: micro~) chip m inv ♦ vt
(cup, plate) scheggiare; **when the ~s are
down** (fig) al momento critico.
  chip in vi (col: contribute) contribuire; (:
  interrupt) intromettersi.
chipboard ['tʃɪpbɔ:d] n agglomerato.
chipmunk ['tʃɪpmʌŋk] n tamia m striato.
chippings ['tʃɪpɪŋz] npl: **loose ~** brecciame
m.
chiropodist [kɪ'rɔpədɪst] n (Brit) pedicure m/f
inv.
chiropody [kɪ'rɔpədɪ] n (Brit) mestiere m di
callista.
chirp [tʃə:p] n cinguettio; (of crickets) cri cri
m ♦ vi cinguettare.
chirpy ['tʃə:pɪ] a (col) frizzante.
chisel ['tʃɪzl] n cesello.
chit [tʃɪt] n biglietto.
chitchat ['tʃɪtʃæt] n (col) chiacchiere fpl.
chivalrous ['ʃɪvəlrəs] a cavalleresco(a).
chivalry ['ʃɪvəlrɪ] n cavalleria; cortesia.
chives [tʃaɪvz] npl erba cipollina.
chloride ['klɔ:raɪd] n cloruro.
chlorinate ['klɔrɪneɪt] vt clorare.
chlorine ['klɔ:ri:n] n cloro.
chock [tʃɔk] n zeppa.
chock-a-block ['tʃɔkə'blɔk], **chockfull**
['tʃɔk'ful] a pieno(a) zeppo(a).
chocolate ['tʃɔklɪt] n (substance) cioccolato,
cioccolata; (drink) cioccolata; (a sweet)
cioccolatino.
choice [tʃɔɪs] n scelta ♦ a scelto(a); **a wide ~**
un'ampia scelta; **I did it by** or **from ~** l'ho
fatto di mia volontà or per mia scelta.
choir ['kwaɪə*] n coro.
choirboy ['kwaɪəbɔɪ] n corista m fanciullo.
choke [tʃəuk] vi soffocare ♦ vt soffocare;
(block) ingombrare ♦ n (AUT) valvola

dell'aria.
cholera ['kɔlərə] n colera m.
cholesterol [kə'lɛstərɔl] n colesterolo.
choose, pt **chose**, pp **chosen** [tʃu:z, tʃəuz,
'tʃəuzn] vt scegliere; **to ~ to do** decidere di
fare; preferire fare; **to ~ between** scegliere
tra; **to ~ from** scegliere da or tra.
choosy ['tʃu:zɪ] a: (**to be**) **~** (fare lo(la))
schizzinoso(a).
chop [tʃɔp] vt (wood) spaccare; (CULIN: also:
~ up) tritare ♦ n colpo netto; (CULIN) costoletta; **to get the ~** (Brit col: project)
essere bocciato(a); (: person: be sacked)
essere licenziato(a); see also **chops**.
  chop down vt (tree) abbattere.
choppy ['tʃɔpɪ] a (sea) mosso(a).
chops [tʃɔps] npl (jaws) mascelle fpl.
chopsticks ['tʃɔpstɪks] npl bastoncini mpl
cinesi.
choral ['kɔ:rəl] a corale.
chord [kɔ:d] n (MUS) accordo.
chore [tʃɔ:*] n faccenda; **household ~s**
faccende fpl domestiche.
choreographer [kɔrɪ'ɔgrəfə*] n coreografo/a.
chorister ['kɔrɪstə*] n corista m/f.
chortle ['tʃɔ:tl] vi ridacchiare.
chorus ['kɔ:rəs] n coro; (repeated part of
song, also fig) ritornello.
chose [tʃəuz] pt of **choose**.
chosen ['tʃəuzn] pp of **choose**.
chowder ['tʃaudə*] n zuppa di pesce.
Christ [kraɪst] n Cristo.
christen ['krɪsn] vt battezzare.
christening ['krɪsnɪŋ] n battesimo.
Christian ['krɪstɪən] a, n cristiano(a).
Christianity [krɪstɪ'ænɪtɪ] n cristianesimo.
Christian name n nome m di battesimo.
Christmas ['krɪsməs] n Natale m; **happy** or
merry ~! Buon Natale!
Christmas card n cartolina di Natale.
Christmas Day n il giorno di Natale.
Christmas Eve n la vigilia di Natale.
Christmas Island n isola di Christmas.
Christmas tree n albero di Natale.
chrome [krəum] n = **chromium**.
chromium ['krəumɪəm] n cromo; (also:
plating) cromatura.
chromosome ['krəuməsəum] n cromosoma m.
chronic ['krɔnɪk] a cronico(a); (fig: liar,
smoker) incallito(a).
chronicle ['krɔnɪkl] n cronaca.
chronological [krɔnə'lɔdʒɪkl] a cronolo-
gico(a).
chrysanthemum [krɪ'sænθəməm] n crisan-
temo.
chubby ['tʃʌbɪ] a paffuto(a).
chuck [tʃʌk] vt buttare, gettare; **to ~ (up** or
in) (Brit: job, person) piantare.
  chuck out vt buttar fuori.
chuckle ['tʃʌkl] vi ridere sommessamente.
chug [tʃʌg] vi (also: **~ along:** train) muoversi
sbuffando.
chum [tʃʌm] n compagno/a.
chump [tʃʌmp] n (col) idiota m/f.

chunk [tʃʌŋk] *n* pezzo; (*of bread*) tocco.
chunky [tʃʌŋkı] *a* (*furniture etc*) basso(a) e largo(a); (*person*) ben piantato(a); (*knitwear*) di lana grossa.
church [tʃəːtʃ] *n* chiesa; **the C~ of England** la Chiesa anglicana.
churchyard ['tʃəːtʃjɑːd] *n* sagrato.
churlish ['tʃəːlıʃ] *a* rozzo(a), sgarbato(a).
churn [tʃəːn] *n* (*for butter*) zangola; (*also:* **milk ~**) bidone *m*.
churn out *vt* sfornare.
chute [ʃuːt] *n* cascata; (*also:* **rubbish ~**) canale *m* di scarico; (*Brit: children's slide*) scivolo.
chutney ['tʃʌtnı] *n* salsa piccante (di frutta, zucchero e spezie).
CIA *n abbr* (*US:* = *Central Intelligence Agency*) C.I.A. *f*.
CID *n abbr* (*Brit*) *see* **Criminal Investigation Department**.
cider ['saıdə*] *n* sidro.
CIF *abbr* (= *cost, insurance and freight*) C.I.F. *m*.
cigar [sı'gɑ:*] *n* sigaro.
cigarette [sıgə'rɛt] *n* sigaretta.
cigarette case *n* portasigarette *m inv*.
cigarette end *n* mozzicone *m*.
cigarette holder *n* bocchino.
C-in-C *abbr see* **commander-in-chief**.
cinch [sıntʃ] *n* (*col*): **it's a ~** è presto fatto; (*sure thing*) è una cosa sicura.
cinder ['sındə*] *n* cenere *f*.
Cinderella [sındə'rɛlə] *n* Cenerentola.
cine-camera ['sını'kæmərə] *n* (*Brit*) cinepresa.
cine-film ['sınıfılm] *n* (*Brit*) pellicola.
cinema ['sınəmə] *n* cinema *m inv*.
cine-projector ['sınıprə'dʒɛktə*] *n* (*Brit*) proiettore *m*.
cinnamon ['sınəmən] *n* cannella.
cipher ['saıfə*] *n* cifra; (*fig: faceless employee etc*) persona di nessun conto; **in ~** in codice.
circa ['səːkə] *prep* circa.
circle ['səːkl] *n* cerchio; (*of friends etc*) circolo; (*in cinema*) galleria ♦ *vi* girare in circolo ♦ *vt* (*surround*) circondare; (*move round*) girare intorno a.
circuit ['səːkıt] *n* circuito.
circuit board *n* (*COMPUT*) tavola dei circuiti.
circuitous [səː'kjuıtəs] *a* indiretto(a).
circular ['səːkjulə*] *a* circolare ♦ *n* (*letter*) circolare *f*; (*as advertisement*) volantino pubblicitario.
circulate ['səːkjuleıt] *vi* circolare; (*person: socially*) girare e andare un po' da tutti ♦ *vt* far circolare.
circulating capital ['səːkjuleıtıŋ-] *n* (*COMM*) capitale *m* d'esercizio.
circulation [səːkju'leıʃən] *n* circolazione *f*; (*of newspaper*) tiratura.
circumcise ['səːkəmsaız] *vt* circoncidere.
circumference [sə'kʌmfərəns] *n* circonferenza.
circumflex ['səːkəmflɛks] *n* (*also:* **~ accent**) accento circonflesso.
circumscribe ['səːkəmskraıb] *vt* circoscrivere;

(*fig: limit*) limitare.
circumspect ['səːkəmspɛkt] *a* circospetto(a).
circumstances ['səːkəmstənsız] *npl* circostanze *fpl*; (*financial condition*) condizioni *fpl* finanziarie; **in the ~s** date le circostanze; **under no ~s** per nessun motivo.
circumstantial ['səːkəm'stænʃəl] *a* (*report, statement*) circostanziato(a), dettagliato(a); **~ evidence** prova indiretta.
circumvent [səːkəm'vɛnt] *vt* (*rule etc*) aggirare.
circus ['səːkəs] *n* circo; (*also:* **C~**: *in place names*) piazza (di forma circolare).
cistern ['sıstən] *n* cisterna; (*in toilet*) serbatoio d'acqua.
citation [saı'teıʃən] *n* citazione *f*.
cite [saıt] *vt* citare.
citizen ['sıtızn] *n* (*POL*) cittadino/a; (*resident*): **the ~s of this town** gli abitanti di questa città.
citizenship ['sıtıznʃıp] *n* cittadinanza.
citric ['sıtrık] *a*: **~ acid** acido citrico.
citrus fruit ['sıtrəs-] *n* agrume *m*.
city ['sıtı] *n* città *f inv*; **the C~** la Città di Londra (*centro commerciale*).
city centre *n* centro della città.
civic ['sıvık] *a* civico(a).
civic centre *n* (*Brit*) centro civico.
civil ['sıvıl] *a* civile; (*polite*) educato(a), gentile.
civil disobedience *n* disubbidienza civile.
civil engineer *n* ingegnere *m* civile.
civil engineering *n* ingegneria civile.
civilian [sı'vılıən] *a, n* borghese (*m/f*).
civilization [sıvılaı'zeıʃən] *n* civiltà *f inv*.
civilized ['sıvılaızd] *a* civilizzato(a); (*fig*) cortese.
civil law *n* codice *m* civile; (*study*) diritto civile.
civil rights *npl* diritti *mpl* civili.
civil servant *n* impiegato/a statale.
Civil Service *n* amministrazione *f* statale.
civil war *n* guerra civile.
cl *abbr* (= *centilitre*) cl.
clad [klæd] *a*: **~ (in)** vestito(a) (di).
claim [kleım] *vt* (*rights etc*) rivendicare; (*damages*) richiedere; (*assert*) sostenere, pretendere ♦ *vi* (*for insurance*) fare una domanda d'indennizzo ♦ *n* rivendicazione *f*; pretesa; (*right*) diritto; **to ~ that/to be** sostenere che/di essere; (*insurance*) ~ domanda d'indennizzo; **to put in a ~ for sth** fare una richiesta di qc.
claimant ['kleımənt] *n* (*ADMIN, LAW*) richiedente *m/f*.
claim form *n* (*gen*) modulo di richiesta; (*for expenses*) modulo di rimborso spese.
clairvoyant [klɛə'vɔıənt] *n* chiaroveggente *m/f*.
clam [klæm] *n* vongola.
clam up *vi* (*col*) azzittirsi.
clamber ['klæmbə*] *vi* arrampicarsi.
clammy ['klæmı] *a* (*weather*) caldo(a) umido(a); (*hands*) viscido(a).
clamour, (*US*) **clamor** ['klæmə*] *n* (*noise*)

clamore *m*; (*protest*) protesta ♦ *vi*: **to ~ for sth** chiedere a gran voce qc.
clamp [klæmp] *n* pinza; morsa ♦ *vt* ammorsare.
clamp down *vt fus* (*fig*): **to ~ down (on)** dare un giro di vite (a).
clan [klæn] *n* clan *m inv*.
clandestine [klæn'destin] *a* clandestino(a).
clang [klæŋ] *n* fragore *m*, suono metallico.
clansman ['klænzmən] *n* membro di un clan.
clap [klæp] *vi* applaudire ♦ *vt*: **to ~ one's hands** battere le mani ♦ *n*: **a ~ of thunder** un tuono.
clapping ['klæpɪŋ] *n* applausi *mpl*.
claret ['klærət] *n* vino di Bordeaux.
clarification [klærɪfɪ'keɪʃən] *n* (*fig*) chiarificazione *f*, chiarimento.
clarify ['klærɪfaɪ] *vt* chiarificare, chiarire.
clarinet [klærɪ'net] *n* clarinetto.
clarity ['klærɪtɪ] *n* chiarezza.
clash [klæʃ] *n* frastuono; (*fig*) scontro ♦ *vi* (*MIL*, *fig*: *have an argument*) scontrarsi; (*colours*) stridere; (*dates*, *events*) coincidere.
clasp [klɑːsp] *n* fermaglio, fibbia ♦ *vt* stringere.
class [klɑːs] *n* classe *f*; (*group*, *category*) tipo, categoria ♦ *vt* classificare.
class-conscious ['klɑːskɔnʃəs] *a* che ha coscienza di classe.
class consciousness *n* coscienza di classe.
classic ['klæsɪk] *a* classico(a) ♦ *n* classico.
classical ['klæsɪkəl] *a* classico(a).
classics ['klæsɪks] *npl* (*SCOL*) studi *mpl* umanistici.
classification [klæsɪfɪ'keɪʃən] *n* classificazione *f*.
classified ['klæsɪfaɪd] *a* (*information*) segreto(a), riservato(a); **~ ads** annunci economici.
classify ['klæsɪfaɪ] *vt* classificare.
classmate ['klɑːsmeɪt] *n* compagno/a di classe.
classroom ['klɑːsrum] *n* aula.
clatter ['klætə*] *n* acciottolio; scalpitio ♦ *vi* acciottolare; scalpitare.
clause [klɔːz] *n* clausola; (*LING*) proposizione *f*.
claustrophobia [klɔːstrə'fəubɪə] *n* claustrofobia.
claw [klɔː] *n* tenaglia; (*of bird of prey*) artiglio; (*of lobster*) pinza ♦ *vt* graffiare; afferrare.
clay [kleɪ] *n* argilla.
clean [kliːn] *a* pulito(a); (*clear*, *smooth*) netto(a) ♦ *vt* pulire ♦ *ad*: **he ~ forgot** si è completamente dimenticato; **to come ~** (*col*: *admit guilt*) confessare; **to have a ~ driving licence** *or* (*US*) **record** non aver mai preso contravvenzioni; **to ~ one's teeth** (*Brit*) lavarsi i denti.
clean off *vt* togliere.
clean out *vt* ripulire.
clean up *vi* far pulizia ♦ *vt* (*also fig*) ripulire; (*fig*: *make profit*): **to ~ up on** fare una barca di soldi con.

clean-cut ['kliːn'kʌt] *a* (*man*) curato(a); (*situation etc*) ben definito(a).
cleaner ['kliːnə*] *n* (*person*) uomo/donna delle pulizie; (*also*: **dry ~**) tintore/a; (*product*) smacchiatore *m*.
cleaning ['kliːnɪŋ] *n* pulizia.
cleaning lady *n* donna delle pulizie.
cleanliness ['klenlɪnɪs] *n* pulizia.
cleanly ['kliːnlɪ] *ad* in modo netto.
cleanse [klenz] *vt* pulire; purificare.
cleanser ['klenzə*] *n* detergente *m*; (*cosmetic*) latte *m* detergente.
clean-shaven ['kliːn'ʃeɪvn] *a* sbarbato(a).
cleansing department ['klenzɪŋ-] *n* (*Brit*) nettezza urbana.
clean-up ['kliːnʌp] *n* pulizia.
clear [klɪə*] *a* chiaro(a); (*road*, *way*) libero(a); (*profit*, *majority*) netto(a) ♦ *vt* sgombrare; liberare; (*site*, *woodland*) spianare; (*COMM*: *goods*) liquidare; (*LAW*: *suspect*) discolpare; (*obstacle*) superare; (*cheque*) fare la compensazione di ♦ *vi* (*weather*) rasserenarsi; (*fog*) andarsene ♦ *ad*: **~ of** distante da ♦ *n*: **to be in the ~** (*out of debt*) essere in attivo; (*out of suspicion*) essere a posto; (*out of danger*) essere fuori pericolo; **to ~ the table** sparecchiare (la tavola); **to ~ one's throat** schiarirsi la gola; **to ~ a profit** avere un profitto netto; **to make o.s. ~** spiegarsi bene; **to make it ~ to sb that ...** far capire a qn che ...; **I have a ~ day tomorrow** (*Brit*) non ho impegni domani; **to keep ~ of sb/sth** tenersi lontano da qn/qc, stare alla larga da qn/qc.
clear off *vi* (*col*: *leave*) svignarsela.
clear up *vi* schiarirsi ♦ *vt* mettere in ordine; (*mystery*) risolvere.
clearance ['klɪərəns] *n* (*removal*) sgombro; (*free space*) spazio; (*permission*) autorizzazione *f*, permesso.
clearance sale *n* vendita di liquidazione.
clear-cut ['klɪə'kʌt] *a* ben delineato(a), distinto(a).
clearing ['klɪərɪŋ] *n* radura; (*Brit BANKING*) clearing *m*.
clearing bank *n* (*Brit*) banca che fa uso della camera di compensazione.
clearing house *n* (*COMM*) camera di compensazione.
clearly ['klɪəlɪ] *ad* chiaramente.
clearway ['klɪəweɪ] *n* (*Brit*) strada con divieto di sosta.
cleavage ['kliːvɪdʒ] *n* (*of woman*) scollatura.
cleaver ['kliːvə*] *n* mannaia.
clef [klef] *n* (*MUS*) chiave *f*.
cleft [kleft] *n* (*in rock*) crepa, fenditura.
clemency ['klemənsɪ] *n* clemenza.
clement ['klemənt] *a* (*weather*) mite, clemente.
clench [klentʃ] *vt* stringere.
clergy ['klɜːdʒɪ] *n* clero.
clergyman ['klɜːdʒɪmən] *n* ecclesiastico.
clerical ['klerɪkl] *a* d'impiegato; (*REL*) clericale.

clerk [klɑ:k, (US) klə:rk] n impiegato/a; (US: salesman/woman) commesso/a; **C~ of the Court** (LAW) cancelliere m.

clever ['klɛvə*] a (mentally) intelligente; (deft, skilful) abile; (device, arrangement) ingegnoso(a).

clew [klu:] n (US) = **clue**.

cliché ['kli:ʃeɪ] n cliché m inv.

click [klɪk] vi scattare ♦ vt: **to ~ one's tongue** schioccare la lingua; **to ~ one's heels** battere i tacchi.

client ['klaɪənt] n cliente m/f.

clientele [kli:ɑ:n'tɛl] n clientela.

cliff [klɪf] n scogliera scoscesa, rupe f.

cliffhanger ['klɪfhæŋə*] n (TV, fig) episodio (or situazione etc) ricco(a) di suspense.

climactic [klaɪ'mæktɪk] a culminante.

climate ['klaɪmɪt] n clima m.

climax ['klaɪmæks] n culmine m; (of play etc) momento più emozionante; (sexual ~) orgasmo.

climb [klaɪm] vi salire; (clamber) arrampicarsi; (plane) prendere quota ♦ vt salire; (CLIMBING) scalare ♦ n salita; arrampicata; scalata; **to ~ over a wall** scavalcare un muro.

  climb down vi scendere; (Brit fig) far marcia indietro.

climbdown ['klaɪmdaun] n (Brit) ritirata.

climber ['klaɪmə*] n (also: **rock ~**) rocciatore/trice; alpinista m/f.

climbing ['klaɪmɪŋ] n (also: **rock ~**) alpinismo.

clinch [klɪntʃ] vt (deal) concludere.

cling [klɪŋ], pt, pp **clung** [klʌŋ, klʌŋ] vi: **to ~ (to)** tenersi stretto(a) (a); (of clothes) aderire strettamente (a).

clinic ['klɪnɪk] n clinica; (session) seduta; serie f di sedute.

clinical ['klɪnɪkəl] a clinico(a); (fig) freddo(a), distaccato(a).

clink [klɪŋk] vi tintinnare.

clip [klɪp] n (for hair) forcina; (also: **paper ~**) graffetta; (Brit: also: **bulldog ~**) fermafogli m inv; (holding hose etc) anello d'attacco ♦ vt (also: **~ together**: papers) attaccare insieme; (hair, nails) tagliare; (hedge) tosare.

clippers ['klɪpəz] npl macchinetta per capelli; (also: **nail ~**) forbicine fpl per le unghie.

clipping ['klɪpɪŋ] n (from newspaper) ritaglio.

clique [kli:k] n cricca.

cloak [kləuk] n mantello ♦ vt avvolgere.

cloakroom ['kləukrum] n (for coats etc) guardaroba m inv; (Brit) W.C.) gabinetti mpl.

clock [klɔk] n orologio; (of taxi) tassametro; **around the ~** ventiquattr'ore su ventiquattro; **to sleep round the ~** or **the ~ round** dormire un giorno intero; **to work against the ~** lavorare in gara col tempo; **30,000 on the ~** (Brit AUT) 30.000 sul contachilometri.

  clock in, clock on vi (Brit) timbrare il cartellino (all'entrata).

clock off, clock out vi (Brit) timbrare il cartellino (all'uscita).

clock up vt (miles, hours etc) fare.

clockwise ['klɔkwaɪz] ad in senso orario.

clockwork ['klɔkwə:k] n movimento or meccanismo a orologeria ♦ a (toy, train) a molla.

clog [klɔg] n zoccolo ♦ vt intasare ♦ vi intasarsi, bloccarsi.

cloister ['klɔɪstə*] n chiostro.

clone [kləun] n clone m.

close a, ad and derivatives [kləus] a vicino(a); (writing, texture) fitto(a); (watch) stretto(a); (examination) attento(a); (weather) afoso(a) ♦ ad vicino, dappresso; **~ to** prep vicino a; **~ by, ~ at hand** qui (or lì) vicino; **how ~ is Edinburgh to Glasgow?** quanto dista Edimburgo da Glasgow?; **a ~ friend** un amico intimo; **to have a ~ shave** (fig) scamparla bella; **at ~ quarters** da vicino ♦ vb, n and derivatives [kləuz] vt chiudere; (bargain, deal) concludere ♦ vi (shop etc) chiudere; (lid, door etc) chiudersi; (end) finire ♦ n (end) fine f; **to bring sth to a ~** terminare qc.

  close down vt chiudere (definitivamente) ♦ vi cessare (definitivamente).

  close in vi (hunters) stringersi attorno; (evening, night, fog) calare; **to ~ in on sb** accerchiare qn; **the days are closing in** le giornate si accorciano.

  close off vt (area) chiudere.

closed [kləuzd] a chiuso(a).

closed-circuit ['kləuzd'sə:kɪt] a: **~ television** televisione f a circuito chiuso.

closed shop n azienda o fabbrica che impiega solo aderenti ai sindacati.

close-knit ['kləus'nɪt] a (family, community) molto unito(a).

closely ['kləuslɪ] ad (examine, watch) da vicino; **we are ~ related** siamo parenti stretti; **a ~ guarded secret** un assoluto segreto.

closet ['klɔzɪt] n (cupboard) armadio.

close-up ['kləusʌp] n primo piano.

closing ['kləuzɪŋ] a (stages, remarks) conclusivo(a), finale; **~ price** (STOCK EXCHANGE) prezzo di chiusura.

closure ['kləuʒə*] n chiusura.

clot [klɔt] n (also: **blood ~**) coagulo; (col: idiot) scemo/a ♦ vi coagularsi.

cloth [klɔθ] n (material) tessuto, stoffa; (Brit: also: **tea~**) strofinaccio; (also: **table~**) tovaglia.

clothe [kləuð] vt vestire.

clothes [kləuðz] npl abiti mpl, vestiti mpl; **to put one's ~ on** vestirsi; **to take one's ~ off** togliersi i vestiti, svestirsi.

clothes brush n spazzola per abiti.

clothes line n corda (per stendere il bucato).

clothes peg, (US) **clothes pin** n molletta.

clothing ['kləuðɪŋ] n = **clothes**.

clotted cream ['klɔtɪd-] n (Brit) panna rappresa.

cloud [klaud] n nuvola; (of dust, smoke, gas) nube f ♦ vt (liquid) intorbidire; **to ~ the issue** distogliere dal problema; **every ~ has a silver lining** (proverb) non tutto il male vien per nuocere.

cloud over vi rannuvolarsi; (fig) offuscarsi.

cloudburst ['klaudbə:st] n acquazzone m.

cloud-cuckoo-land ['klaud'kuku:'lænd] n (Brit) mondo dei sogni.

cloudy ['klaudɪ] a nuvoloso(a); (liquid) torbido(a).

clout [klaut] n (blow) colpo; (fig) influenza ♦ vt dare un colpo a.

clove [kləuv] n chiodo di garofano; **~ of garlic** spicchio d'aglio.

clover ['kləuvə*] n trifoglio.

cloverleaf ['kləuvəli:f] n foglia di trifoglio; (AUT) raccordo (a quadrifoglio).

clown [klaun] n pagliaccio ♦ vi (also: ~ **about, ~ around**) fare il pagliaccio.

cloying ['klɔɪɪŋ] a (taste, smell) nauseabondo(a).

club [klʌb] n (society) club m inv, circolo; (weapon, GOLF) mazza ♦ vt bastonare ♦ vi: **to ~ together** associarsi; **~s** npl (CARDS) fiori mpl.

club car n (US RAIL) carrozza or vagone m ristorante.

clubhouse ['klʌbhaus] n sede f del circolo.

cluck [klʌk] vi chiocciare.

clue [klu:] n indizio; (in crosswords) definizione f; **I haven't a ~** non ho la minima idea.

clued up, (US) **clued in** [klu:d-] a (col) (ben) informato(a).

clump [klʌmp] n: **~ of trees** folto d'alberi.

clumsy ['klʌmzɪ] a (person) goffo(a), maldestro(a); (object) malfatto(a), mal costruito(a).

clung [klʌŋ] pt, pp of **cling**.

cluster ['klʌstə*] n gruppo ♦ vi raggrupparsi.

clutch [klʌtʃ] n (grip, grasp) presa, stretta; (AUT) frizione f ♦ vt afferrare, stringere forte; **to ~ at** aggrapparsi a.

clutter ['klʌtə*] vt (also: ~ **up**) ingombrare ♦ n confusione f, disordine m.

CM abbr (US POST) = North Marianna Islands.

cm abbr (= centimetre) cm.

CNAA n abbr (Brit: = Council for National Academic Awards) organizzazione che conferisce premi accademici.

CND n abbr = Campaign for Nuclear Disarmament.

CO n abbr (= commanding officer) Com.; (Brit) = Commonwealth Office ♦ abbr (US POST) = Colorado.

Co. abbr = **county**; (= company) C., C.ia.

c/o abbr (= care of) c/o.

coach [kəutʃ] n (bus) pullman m inv; (horse-drawn, of train) carrozza; (SPORT) allenatore/trice ♦ vt allenare.

coach trip n viaggio in pullman.

coagulate [kəu'ægjuleɪt] vt coagulare ♦ vi coagularsi.

coal [kəul] n carbone m.

coalface ['kəulfeɪs] n fronte f.

coalfield ['kəulfi:ld] n bacino carbonifero.

coalition [kəuə'lɪʃən] n coalizione f.

coalman ['kəulmən], **coal merchant** n negoziante m di carbone.

coalmine ['kəulmaɪn] n miniera di carbone.

coalminer ['kəulmaɪnə*] n minatore m.

coalmining ['kəulmaɪnɪŋ] n estrazione f del carbone.

coarse [kɔ:s] a (salt, sand etc) grosso(a); (cloth, person) rozzo(a); (vulgar: character, laugh) volgare.

coast [kəust] n costa ♦ vi (with cycle etc) scendere a ruota libera.

coastal ['kəustəl] a costiero(a).

coaster ['kəustə*] n (NAUT) nave f da cabotaggio; (for glass) sottobicchiere m.

coastguard ['kəustgɑ:d] n guardia costiera.

coastline ['kəustlaɪn] n linea costiera.

coat [kəut] n cappotto; (of animal) pelo; (of paint) mano f ♦ vt coprire; **~ of arms** n stemma m.

coat hanger n attaccapanni m inv.

coating ['kəutɪŋ] n rivestimento.

co-author ['kəu'ɔ:θə*] n coautore/trice.

coax [kəuks] vt indurre (con moine).

cob [kɔb] n see **corn**.

cobbler ['kɔblə*] n calzolaio.

cobbles ['kɔblz], **cobblestones** ['kɔblstəunz] npl ciottoli mpl.

COBOL ['kəubɔl] n COBOL m.

cobra ['kəubrə] n cobra m inv.

cobweb ['kɔbwɛb] n ragnatela.

cocaine [kə'keɪn] n cocaina.

cock [kɔk] n (rooster) gallo; (male bird) maschio ♦ vt (gun) armare; **to ~ one's ears** (fig) drizzare le orecchie.

cock-a-hoop [kɔkə'hu:p] a euforico(a).

cockerel ['kɔkərəl] n galletto.

cock-eyed ['kɔkaɪd] a (fig) storto(a); strampalato(a).

cockle ['kɔkl] n cardio.

cockney ['kɔknɪ] n cockney m/f inv (abitante dei quartieri popolari dell'East End di Londra).

cockpit ['kɔkpɪt] n abitacolo.

cockroach ['kɔkrəutʃ] n blatta.

cocktail ['kɔkteɪl] n cocktail m inv; **prawn ~,** (US) **shrimp ~** cocktail m inv di gamberetti.

cocktail cabinet n mobile m bar inv.

cocktail party n cocktail m inv.

cocktail shaker n shaker m inv.

cocoa ['kəukəu] n cacao.

coconut ['kəukənʌt] n noce f di cocco.

cocoon [kə'ku:n] n bozzolo.

COD abbr see **cash on delivery, collect on delivery**.

cod [kɔd] n merluzzo.

code [kəud] n codice m; **~ of behaviour** regole fpl di condotta; **~ of practice** codice professionale.

codeine ['kəudi:n] n codeina.

codicil ['kɔdɪsɪl] *n* codicillo.
codify ['kəudɪfaɪ] *vt* codificare.
cod-liver oil ['kɔdlɪvə*-] *n* olio di fegato di merluzzo.
co-driver ['kəu'draɪvə*] *n* (*in race*) copilota *m*; (*of lorry*) secondo autista *m*.
co-ed ['kəu'ɛd] *a abbr* = **coeducational** ♦ *n abbr* (*US: female student*) studentessa presso un'università mista; (*Brit: school*) scuola mista.
coeducational ['kəuɛdju'keɪʃənl] *a* misto(a).
coerce [kəu'ɔːs] *vt* costringere.
coercion [kəu'ɔːʃən] *n* coercizione *f*.
coexistence ['kəuɪg'zɪstəns] *n* coesistenza.
C. of C. *n abbr* = **chamber of commerce**.
C of E *abbr* = **Church of England**.
coffee ['kɔfɪ] *n* caffè *m inv*; **white ~**, (*US*) **~ with cream** caffellatte *m*.
coffee bar *n* (*Brit*) caffè *m inv*.
coffee bean *n* grano *or* chicco di caffè.
coffee break *n* pausa per il caffè.
coffeecake ['kɔfɪkeɪk] *n* (*US*) panino dolce all'uva.
coffee cup *n* tazzina da caffè.
coffeepot ['kɔfɪpɔt] *n* caffettiera.
coffee table *n* tavolino da tè.
coffin ['kɔfɪn] *n* bara.
C of I *abbr* = **Church of Ireland**.
C of S *abbr* = **Church of Scotland**.
cog [kɔg] *n* dente *m*.
cogent ['kəudʒənt] *a* convincente.
cognac ['kɔnjæk] *n* cognac *m inv*.
cogwheel ['kɔgwiːl] *n* ruota dentata.
cohabit [kəu'hæbɪt] *vi* (*formal*): **to ~ (with sb)** coabitare (con qn).
coherent [kəu'hɪərənt] *a* coerente.
cohesion [kəu'hiːʒən] *n* coesione *f*.
cohesive [kəu'hiːsɪv] *a* (*fig*) unificante, coesivo(a).
COHSE ['kəuzɪ] *n abbr* (*Brit: = Confederation of Health Service Employees*) confederazione dei dipendenti del Servizio Sanitario.
COI *n abbr* (*Brit*) = *Central Office of Information*.
coil [kɔɪl] *n* rotolo; (*one loop*) anello; (*AUT, ELEC*) bobina; (*contraceptive*) spirale *f*; (*of smoke*) filo ♦ *vt* avvolgere.
coin [kɔɪn] *n* moneta ♦ *vt* (*word*) coniare.
coinage ['kɔɪnɪdʒ] *n* sisteina *m* monetario.
coin-box ['kɔɪnbɔks] *n* (*Brit*) cabina telefonica.
coincide [kəuɪn'saɪd] *vi* coincidere.
coincidence [kəu'ɪnsɪdəns] *n* combinazione *f*.
coin-operated ['kɔɪn'ɔpəreɪtɪd] *a* (*machine*) (che funziona) a monete.
Coke ® [kəuk] *n* (*Coca-Cola*) coca *f inv*.
coke [kəuk] *n* coke *m*.
Col. *abbr* = **colonel**.
COLA *n abbr* (*US:* = *cost-of-living adjustment*) ≈ scala mobile.
colander ['kɔləndə*] *n* colino.
cold [kəuld] *a* freddo(a) ♦ *n* freddo; (*MED*) raffreddore *m*; **it's ~** fa freddo; **to be ~** aver freddo; **to catch ~** prendere freddo; **to**

catch a ~ prendere un raffreddore; **in ~ blood** a sangue freddo; **to have ~ feet** avere i piedi freddi; (*fig*) aver la fifa; **to give sb the ~ shoulder** ignorare qn.
cold-blooded [kəuld'blʌdɪd] *a* (*ZOOL*) a sangue freddo.
cold cream *n* crema emolliente.
coldly ['kəuldlɪ] *ad* freddamente.
cold sore *n* erpete *m*.
coleslaw ['kəulslɔː] *n* insalata di cavolo bianco.
colic ['kɔlɪk] *n* colica.
collaborate [kə'læbəreɪt] *vi* collaborare.
collaboration [kəlæbə'reɪʃən] *n* collaborazione *f*.
collaborator [kə'læbəreɪtə*] *n* collaboratore/trice.
collage [kɔ'lɑːʒ] *n* (*ART*) collage *m inv*.
collagen ['kɔlədʒən] *n* collageno.
collapse [kə'læps] *vi* (*gen*) crollare; (*government*) cadere; (*MED*) avere un collasso; (*plans*) fallire ♦ *n* crollo; caduta; collasso; fallimento.
collapsible [kə'læpsəbl] *a* pieghevole.
collar ['kɔlə*] *n* (*of coat, shirt*) colletto; (*for dog*) collare *m*; (*TECH*) anello, fascetta ♦ *vt* (*col: person, object*) beccare.
collarbone ['kɔləbəun] *n* clavicola.
collate [kɔ'leɪt] *vt* collazionare.
collateral [kɔ'lætərəl] *n* garanzia.
collation [kɔ'leɪʃən] *n* collazione *f*.
colleague ['kɔliːg] *n* collega *m/f*.
collect [kə'lɛkt] *vt* (*gen*) raccogliere; (*as a hobby*) fare collezione di; (*Brit: call for*) prendere; (*money owed, pension*) riscuotere; (*donations, subscriptions*) fare una colletta di ♦ *vi* (*people*) adunarsi, riunirsi; (*rubbish etc*) ammucchiarsi ♦ *ad* (*US TEL*): **to call ~** fare una chiamata a carico del destinatario; **to ~ one's thoughts** raccogliere le idee; **~ on delivery (COD)** (*US COMM*) pagamento alla consegna.
collected [kə'lɛktɪd] *a*: **~ works** opere *fpl* raccolte.
collection [kə'lɛkʃən] *n* collezione *f*; raccolta; (*for money*) colletta; (*POST*) levata.
collective [kə'lɛktɪv] *a* collettivo(a) ♦ *n* collettivo.
collective bargaining *n* trattative *fpl* (sindacali) collettive.
collector [kə'lɛktə*] *n* collezionista *m/f*; (*of taxes*) esattore *m*; **~'s item** *or* **piece** pezzo da collezionista.
college ['kɔlɪdʒ] *n* (*Brit, US SCOL*) college *m inv*; (*of technology, agriculture etc*) istituto superiore; (*body*) collegio; **~ of education** ≈ facoltà *f inv* di Magistero.
collide [kə'laɪd] *vi*: **to ~ (with)** scontrarsi (con).
collie ['kɔlɪ] *n* (*dog*) collie *m inv*.
colliery ['kɔlɪərɪ] *n* (*Brit*) miniera di carbone.
collision [kə'lɪʒən] *n* collisione *f*, scontro; **to be on a ~ course** (*also fig*) essere in rotta di collisione.

collision damage waiver (CDW) *n*
(*INSURANCE*) *copertura per i danni alla
vettura.*
colloquial [kə'ləukwɪəl] *a* familiare.
collusion [kə'luːʒən] *n* collusione *f*; **in ~ with**
in accordo segreto con.
Cologne [kə'ləun] *n* Colonia.
cologne [kə'ləun] *n* (*also:* **eau de ~**) acqua di
colonia.
Colombia [kə'lɒmbɪə] *n* Colombia.
Colombian [kə'lɒmbɪən] *a, n* colombiano(a).
colon ['kəulən] *n* (*sign*) due punti *mpl*; (*MED*)
colon *m inv.*
colonel ['kɔːnl] *n* colonnello.
colonial [kə'ləunɪəl] *a* coloniale.
colonize ['kɔlənaɪz] *vt* colonizzare.
colony ['kɔlənɪ] *n* colonia.
color *etc* ['kʌlə*] (*US*) = **colour** *etc.*
Colorado beetle [kɔlə'rɑːdəu-] *n* dorifora.
colossal [kə'lɔsl] *a* colossale.
colour, (*US*) **color** ['kʌlə*] *n* colore *m* ♦ *vt*
colorare; (*tint, dye*) tingere; (*fig: affect*)
influenzare ♦ *vi* arrossire ♦ *cpd* (*film, photograph, television*) a colori; **~s** *npl* (*of party,
club*) emblemi *mpl.*
colo(u)r bar *n* discriminazione *f* razziale (*in
locali etc*).
colo(u)r-blind ['kʌləblaɪnd] *a* daltonico(a).
colo(u)red ['kʌləd] *a* colorato(a); (*photo*) a
colori ♦ *n:* **~s** gente *f* di colore.
colo(u)r film *n* (*for camera*) pellicola a
colori.
colo(u)rful ['kʌləful] *a* pieno(a) di colore, a
vivaci colori; (*personality*) colorato(a).
colo(u)ring ['kʌlərɪŋ] *n* colorazione *f*; (*complexion*) colorito.
colo(u)r scheme combinazione *f* di colori.
colour supplement *n* (*Brit PRESS*) supplemento a colori.
colo(u)r television *n* televisione *f* a colori.
colt [kəult] *n* puledro.
column ['kɔləm] *n* colonna; (*fashion ~, sports
~ etc*) rubrica; **the editorial ~** l'articolo di
fondo.
columnist ['kɔləmnɪst] *n* articolista *m/f.*
coma ['kəumə] *n* coma *m inv.*
comb [kəum] *n* pettine *m* ♦ *vt* (*hair*)
pettinare; (*area*) battere a tappeto.
combat ['kɔmbæt] *n* combattimento ♦ *vt*
combattere, lottare contro.
combination [kɔmbɪ'neɪʃən] *n* combinazione *f.*
combination lock *n* serratura a
combinazione.
combine *vb* [kəm'baɪn] *vt* combinare; (*one
quality with another*): **to ~ sth with sth**
unire qc a qc ♦ *vi* unirsi; (*CHEM*) combinarsi
♦ *n* ['kɔmbaɪn] lega; (*ECON*) associazione *f*; **a
~d effort** uno sforzo collettivo.
combine (harvester) *n* mietitrebbia.
combo ['kɔmbəu] *n* (*JAZZ etc*) gruppo.
combustible [kəm'bʌstɪbl] *a* combustibile.
combustion [kəm'bʌstʃən] *n* combustione *f.*
come, *pt* **came,** *pp* **come** [kʌm, keɪm] *vi*
venire; (*arrive*) venire, arrivare; **~ with me**

vieni con me; **we've just ~ from Paris** siamo
appena arrivati da Parigi; **nothing came of
it** non è saltato fuori niente; **to ~ into sight**
or **view** apparire; **to ~ to** (*decision etc*)
raggiungere; **to ~ undone/loose** slacciarsi/
allentarsi; **coming!** vengo!; **if it ~s to it**
nella peggiore delle ipotesi.
come about *vi* succedere.
come across *vt fus* trovare per caso; **to ~
across well/badly** fare una buona/cattiva impressione.
come along *vi* (*pupil, work*) fare progressi; **~ along!** avanti!, andiamo!, forza!
come apart *vi* andare in pezzi; (*become
detached*) staccarsi.
come away *vi* venire via; (*become detached*) staccarsi.
come back *vi* ritornare; (*reply: col*): **can I
~ back to you on that one?** possiamo
riparlarne più tardi?
come by *vt fus* (*acquire*) ottenere;
procurarsi.
come down *vi* scendere; (*prices*) calare;
(*buildings*) essere demolito(a).
come forward *vi* farsi avanti; presentarsi.
come from *vt fus* venire da; provenire da.
come in *vi* entrare.
come in for *vt fus* (*criticism etc*) ricevere.
come into *vt fus* (*money*) ereditare.
come off *vi* (*button*) staccarsi; (*stain*)
andar via; (*attempt*) riuscire.
come on *vi* (*lights, electricity*) accendersi;
(*pupil, undertaking*) fare progressi; **~ on!**
avanti!, andiamo!, forza!
come out *vi* uscire; (*strike*) entrare in
sciopero.
come over *vt fus*: **I don't know what's ~
over him!** non so cosa gli sia successo!
come round *vi* (*after faint, operation*) riprendere conoscenza, rinvenire.
come through *vi* (*survive*) sopravvivere,
farcela; **the call came through** ci hanno
passato la telefonata.
come to *vi* rinvenire ♦ *vt* (*add up to:
amount*): **how much does it ~ to?** quanto
costa?, quanto viene?
come under *vt fus* (*heading*) trovarsi
sotto; (*influence*) cadere sotto, subire.
come up *vi* venire su.
come up against *vt fus* (*resistance,
difficulties*) urtare contro.
come up to *vt fus* arrivare (fino) a; **the
film didn't ~ up to our expectations** il film
ci ha delusi.
come up with *vt fus*: **he came up with an
idea** venne fuori con un'idea.
come upon *vt fus* trovare per caso.
comeback ['kʌmbæk] *n* (*THEATRE etc*)
ritorno; (*reaction*) reazione *f*; (*response*)
risultato, risposta.
COMECON ['kɔmɪkɔn] *n abbr* (= *Council for
Mutual Economic Aid*) COMECON *m.*
comedian [kə'miːdɪən] *n* comico.
comedienne [kəmiːdɪ'ɛn] *n* attrice *f* comica.

comedown ['kʌmdaun] *n* rovescio.
comedy ['kɔmɪdɪ] *n* commedia.
comet ['kɔmɪt] *n* cometa.
comeuppance [kʌm'ʌpəns] *n*: **to get one's ~** ricevere ciò che si merita.
comfort ['kʌmfət] *n* comodità *f inv*, benessere *m*; (*solace*) consolazione *f*, conforto ♦ *vt* consolare, confortare; *see also* **comforts**.
comfortable ['kʌmfətəbl] *a* comodo(a); (*income, majority*) più che sufficiente; **I don't feel very ~ about it** non mi sento molto tranquillo.
comfortably ['kʌmfətəblɪ] *ad* (*sit*) comodamente; (*live*) bene.
comforter ['kʌmfətə*] *n* (*US*) trapunta.
comforts ['kʌmfəts] *npl* comforts *mpl*, comodità *fpl*.
comfort station *n* (*US*) gabinetti *mpl*.
comic ['kɔmɪk] *a* comico(a) ♦ *n* comico; (*magazine*) giornaletto.
comical ['kɔmɪkl] *a* divertente, buffo(a).
comic strip *n* fumetto.
coming ['kʌmɪŋ] *n* arrivo ♦ *a* (*next*) prossimo(a); (*future*) futuro(a); **in the ~ weeks** nelle prossime settimane.
coming(s) and going(s) *n(pl)* andirivieni *m inv*.
Comintern ['kɔmɪntə:n] *n* KOMINTERN *m*.
comma ['kɔmə] *n* virgola.
command [kə'mɑ:nd] *n* ordine *m*, comando; (*MIL: authority*) comando; (*mastery*) padronanza; (*COMPUT*) command *m inv*, comando ♦ *vt* comandare; **to ~ sb to do** ordinare a qn di fare; **to have/take ~ of** avere/prendere il comando di; **to have at one's ~** (*money, resources etc*) avere a propria disposizione.
commandeer [kɔmən'dɪə*] *vt* requisire.
commander [kə'mɑ:ndə*] *n* capo; (*MIL*) comandante *m*.
commander-in-chief (C-in-C) [kə'mɑ:ndər-ɪn'tʃi:f] *n* (*MIL*) comandante *m* in capo.
commanding [kə'mɑ:ndɪŋ] *a* (*appearance*) imponente; (*voice, tone*) autorevole; (*lead, position*) dominante.
commanding officer *n* comandante *m*.
commandment [kə'mɑ:ndmənt] *n* (*REL*) comandamento.
command module *n* (*SPACE*) modulo di comando.
commando [kə'mɑ:ndəu] *n* commando *m inv*; membro di un commando.
commemorate [kə'meməreɪt] *vt* commemorare.
commemoration [kəmemə'reɪʃən] *n* commemorazione *f*.
commemorative [kə'memərətɪv] *a* commemorativo(a).
commence [kə'mens] *vt, vi* cominciare.
commend [kə'mend] *vt* lodare; raccomandare.
commendable [kə'mendəbl] *a* lodevole.
commendation [kɔmen'deɪʃən] *n* lode *f*; raccomandazione *f*; (*for bravery etc*)

encomio.
commensurate [kə'menʃərɪt] *a*: **~ with** proporzionato(a) a.
comment ['kɔment] *n* commento ♦ *vi*: **to ~ (on)** fare commenti (su); **to ~ that** osservare che; **"no ~"** "niente da dire".
commentary ['kɔməntərɪ] *n* commentario; (*SPORT*) radiocronaca; telecronaca.
commentator ['kɔmənteɪtə*] *n* commentatore/trice; (*SPORT*) radiocronista *m/f*; telecronista *m/f*.
commerce ['kɔmə:s] *n* commercio.
commercial [kə'mə:ʃəl] *a* commerciale ♦ *n* (*TV: also:* **~ break**) pubblicità *f inv*.
commercial bank *n* banca commerciale.
commercial college *n* ≈ istituto commerciale.
commercialism [kə'mə:ʃəlɪzəm] *n* affarismo.
commercialize [kə'mə:ʃəlaɪz] *vt* commercializzare.
commercial television *n* televisione *f* commerciale.
commercial traveller *n* commesso viaggiatore.
commercial vehicle *n* veicolo commerciale.
commiserate [kə'mɪzəreɪt] *vi*: **to ~ with** condolersi con.
commission [kə'mɪʃən] *n* commissione *f*; (*for salesman*) commissione, provvigione *f* ♦ *vt* (*MIL*) nominare (al comando); (*work of art*) commissionare; **I get 10% ~** ricevo il 10% sulle vendite; **out of ~** (*NAUT*) in disarmo; (*machine*) fuori uso; **to ~ sb to do sth** incaricare qn di fare qc; **to ~ sth from sb** (*painting etc*) commissionare qc a qn; **~ of inquiry** (*Brit*) commissione *f* d'inchiesta.
commissionaire [kəmɪʃə'neə*] *n* (*Brit: at shop, cinema etc*) portiere *m* in livrea.
commissioner [kə'mɪʃənə*] *n* commissionario; (*POLICE*) questore *m*.
commit [kə'mɪt] *vt* (*act*) commettere; (*to sb's care*) affidare; **to ~ o.s. (to do)** impegnarsi (a fare); **to ~ suicide** suicidarsi; **to ~ sb for trial** rinviare qn a giudizio.
commitment [kə'mɪtmənt] *n* impegno.
committed [kə'mɪtɪd] *a* (*writer*) impegnato(a); (*Christian*) convinto(a).
committee [kə'mɪtɪ] *n* comitato; **to be on a ~** far parte di un comitato *or* di una commissione.
committee meeting *n* riunione *f* di comitato *or* di commissione.
commodity [kə'mɔdɪtɪ] *n* prodotto, articolo; (*food*) derrata.
commodity exchange *n* borsa *f* merci *inv*.
common ['kɔmən] *a* comune; (*pej*) volgare; (*usual*) normale ♦ *n* terreno comune; **in ~** in comune; **in ~ use** di uso comune; **it's ~ knowledge that** è di dominio pubblico che; **to the ~ good** nell'interesse generale, per il bene comune; *see also* **Commons**.
commoner ['kɔmənə*] *n* cittadino/a (non nobile).
common ground *n* (*fig*) terreno comune.

common law *n* diritto consuetudinario.

common-law ['kɔmənlɔ:] *a:* ~ **wife** convivente *f* more uxorio.

commonly ['kɔmənlɪ] *ad* comunemente, usualmente.

Common Market *n* Mercato Comune.

commonplace ['kɔmənpleɪs] *a* banale, ordinario(a).

commonroom ['kɔmənrum] *n* sala di riunione; (*SCOL*) sala dei professori.

Commons ['kɔmənz] *npl* (*Brit POL*): **the (House of)** ~ la Camera dei Comuni.

common sense *n* buon senso.

Commonwealth ['kɔmənwelθ] *n:* **the** ~ il Commonwealth.

commotion [kə'məuʃən] *n* confusione *f*, tumulto.

communal ['kɔmju:nl] *a* (*life*) comunale; (*for common use*) pubblico(a).

commune *n* ['kɔmju:n] (*group*) comune *f* ♦ *vi* [kə'mju:n]: **to** ~ **with** mettersi in comunione con.

communicate [kə'mju:nɪkeɪt] *vt* comunicare, trasmettere ♦ *vi:* **to** ~ **(with)** comunicare (con).

communication [kəmju:nɪ'keɪʃən] *n* comunicazione *f*.

communication cord *n* (*Brit*) segnale *m* d'allarme.

communications network *n* rete *f* delle comunicazioni.

communications satellite *n* satellite *m* per telecomunicazioni.

communicative [kə'mju:nɪkətɪv] *a* (*gen*) loquace.

communion [kə'mju:nɪən] *n* (*also:* **Holy C**~) comunione *f*.

communiqué [kə'mju:nɪkeɪ] *n* comunicato.

communism ['kɔmjunɪzəm] *n* comunismo.

communist ['kɔmjunɪst] *a, n* comunista (*m/f*).

community [kə'mju:nɪtɪ] *n* comunità *f inv*.

community centre *n* circolo ricreativo.

community chest *n* (*US*) fondo di beneficenza.

community health centre *n* centro socio-sanitario.

community home *n* (*Brit*) riformatorio.

community service *n* (*Brit*) ≈ lavoro sostitutivo.

community spirit *n* spirito civico.

commutation ticket [kɔmju'teɪʃən-] *n* (*US*) biglietto di abbonamento.

commute [kə'mju:t] *vi* fare il pendolare ♦ *vt* (*LAW*) commutare.

commuter [kə'mju:tə*] *n* pendolare *m/f*.

compact *a* [kəm'pækt] compatto(a) ♦ *n* ['kɔmpækt] (*also:* **powder** ~) portacipria *m inv*.

compact disk *n* compact disk *m inv*.

companion [kəm'pænjən] *n* compagno/a.

companionship [kəm'pænjənʃɪp] *n* compagnia.

companionway [kəm'pænjənweɪ] *n* (*NAUT*) scala.

company ['kʌmpənɪ] *n* (*also COMM*, *MIL*, *THEATRE*) compagnia; **he's good** ~ è di buona compagnia; **we have** ~ abbiamo ospiti; **to keep sb** ~ tenere compagnia a qn; **to part** ~ **with** separarsi da; **Smith and C**~ Smith e soci.

company car *n* macchina (di proprietà) della ditta.

company director *n* amministratore *m*, consigliere *m* di amministrazione.

company secretary *n* (*Brit COMM*) segretario/a generale.

comparable ['kɔmpərəbl] *a* comparabile.

comparative [kəm'pærətɪv] *a* (*freedom*, *cost*) relativo(a); (*adjective*, *adverb etc*) comparativo(a); (*literature*) comparato(a).

comparatively [kəm'pærətɪvlɪ] *ad* relativamente.

compare [kəm'pɛə*] *vt:* **to** ~ **sth/sb with/to** confrontare qc/qn con/a ♦ *vi:* **to** ~ **(with)** reggere il confronto (con); ~**d with** *or* **to** a paragone di, rispetto a; **how do the prices** ~? che differenza di prezzo c'è?

comparison [kəm'pærɪsn] *n* confronto; **in** ~ **(with)** a confronto (di).

compartment [kəm'pɑ:tmənt] *n* compartimento; (*RAIL*) scompartimento.

compass ['kʌmpəs] *n* bussola; **(a pair of)** ~**es** (*MATH*) compasso; **within the** ~ **of** entro i limiti di.

compassion [kəm'pæʃən] *n* compassione *f*.

compassionate [kəm'pæʃənɪt] *a* compassionevole; **on** ~ **grounds** per motivi personali.

compatibility [kəmpætɪ'bɪlɪtɪ] *n* compatibilità.

compatible [kəm'pætɪbl] *a* compatibile.

compel [kəm'pɛl] *vt* costringere, obbligare.

compelling [kəm'pɛlɪŋ] *a* (*fig: argument*) irresistibile.

compendium [kəm'pɛndɪəm] *n* compendio.

compensate ['kɔmpənseɪt] *vt* risarcire ♦ *vi:* **to** ~ **for** compensare.

compensation [kɔmpən'seɪʃən] *n* compensazione *f*; (*money*) risarcimento.

compère ['kɔmpɛə*] *n* presentatore/trice.

compete [kəm'pi:t] *vi* (*take part*) concorrere; (*vie*): **to** ~ **(with)** fare concorrenza (a).

competence ['kɔmpɪtəns] *n* competenza.

competent ['kɔmpɪtənt] *a* competente.

competition [kɔmpɪ'tɪʃən] *n* gara, concorso; (*SPORT*) gara; (*ECON*) concorrenza; **in** ~ **with** in concorrenza con.

competitive [kəm'pɛtɪtɪv] *a* (*sports*) agonistico(a); (*person*) che ha spirito di competizione; (*ECON*) concorrenziale.

competitive examination *n* concorso.

competitor [kəm'pɛtɪtə*] *n* concorrente *m/f*.

compile [kəm'paɪl] *vt* compilare.

complacency [kəm'pleɪsnsɪ] *n* compiacenza di sé.

complacent [kəm'pleɪsnt] *a* compiaciuto(a) di sé.

complain [kəm'pleɪn] *vi:* **to** ~ **(about)** lagnarsi (di); (*in shop etc*) reclamare (per).

complain of vt fus (MED) accusare.
complaint [kəm'pleɪnt] n lamento; reclamo; (MED) malattia.
complement n ['kɔmplɪmənt] complemento; (especially of ship's crew etc) effettivo ♦ vt ['kɔmplɪmɛnt] (enhance) accompagnarsi bene a.
complementary [kɔmplɪ'mɛntərɪ] a complementare.
complete [kəm'pliːt] a completo(a) ♦ vt completare; (a form) riempire; **it's a ~ disaster** è un vero disastro.
completely [kəm'pliːtlɪ] ad completamente.
completion [kəm'pliːʃən] n completamento; **to be nearing ~** essere in fase di completamento; **on ~ of contract** alla firma del contratto.
complex ['kɔmplɛks] a complesso(a) ♦ n (PSYCH, buildings etc) complesso.
complexion [kəm'plɛkʃən] n (of face) carnagione f; (of event etc) aspetto.
complexity [kəm'plɛksɪtɪ] n complessità f inv.
compliance [kəm'plaɪəns] n acquiescenza; **in ~ with** (orders, wishes etc) in conformità con.
compliant [kəm'plaɪənt] a acquiescente, arrendevole.
complicate ['kɔmplɪkeɪt] vt complicare.
complicated ['kɔmplɪkeɪtɪd] a complicato(a).
complication [kɔmplɪ'keɪʃən] n complicazione f.
compliment n ['kɔmplɪmənt] complimento ♦ vt ['kɔmplɪmɛnt] fare un complimento a; **~s** npl complimenti mpl; rispetti mpl; **to pay sb a ~** fare un complimento a qn; **to ~ sb (on sth/on doing sth)** congratularsi or complimentarsi con qn (per qc/per aver fatto qc).
complimentary [kɔmplɪ'mɛntərɪ] a complimentoso(a), elogiativo(a); (free) in omaggio.
complimentary ticket n biglietto d'omaggio.
compliments slip n cartoncino della società.
comply [kəm'plaɪ] vi: **to ~ with** assentire a; conformarsi a.
component [kəm'pəunənt] a, n componente (m).
compose [kəm'pəuz] vt comporre; **to ~ o.s.** ricomporsi; **~d of** composto(a) di.
composed [kəm'pəuzd] a calmo(a).
composer [kəm'pəuzə*] n (MUS) compositore/trice.
composite ['kɔmpəzɪt] a composito(a); (MATH) composto(a).
composition [kɔmpə'zɪʃən] n composizione f.
compost ['kɔmpɔst] n composta, concime m.
composure [kəm'pəuʒə*] n calma.
compound ['kɔmpaund] n (CHEM, LING) composto; (enclosure) recinto ♦ a composto(a) ♦ vt (fig: problem, difficulty) peggiorare.
compound fracture n frattura esposta.
compound interest n interesse m composto.
comprehend [kɔmprɪ'hɛnd] vt comprendere, capire.

comprehension [kɔmprɪ'hɛnʃən] n comprensione f.
comprehensive [kɔmprɪ'hɛnsɪv] a comprensivo(a).
comprehensive insurance policy n polizza multi-rischio inv.
comprehensive (school) n (Brit) scuola secondaria aperta a tutti.
compress vt [kəm'prɛs] comprimere ♦ n ['kɔmprɛs] (MED) compressa.
compression [kəm'prɛʃən] n compressione f.
comprise [kəm'praɪz] vt (also: **be ~d of**) comprendere.
compromise ['kɔmprəmaɪz] n compromesso ♦ vt compromettere ♦ vi venire a un compromesso ♦ cpd (decision, solution) di compromesso.
compulsion [kəm'pʌlʃən] n costrizione f; **under ~** sotto pressioni.
compulsive [kəm'pʌlsɪv] a (PSYCH) incontrollabile; **he's a ~ smoker** non riesce a controllarsi nel fumare.
compulsory [kəm'pʌlsərɪ] a obbligatorio(a).
compulsory purchase n espropriazione f.
compunction [kəm'pʌŋkʃən] n scrupolo; **to have no ~ about doing sth** non farsi scrupoli a fare qc.
computer [kəm'pjuːtə*] n computer m inv, elaboratore m elettronico.
computerization [kəmpjuːtəraɪ'zeɪʃən] n computerizzazione f.
computerize [kəm'pjuːtəraɪz] vt computerizzare.
computer language n linguaggio m macchina inv.
computer peripheral n unità periferica.
computer program n programma m di computer.
computer programmer n programmatore/trice.
computer programming n programmazione f di computer.
computer science n informatica.
computer scientist n informatico/a.
computing [kəm'pjuːtɪŋ] n informatica.
comrade ['kɔmrɪd] n compagno/a.
comradeship ['kɔmrɪdʃɪp] n cameratismo.
comsat ['kɔmsæt] n abbr = **communications satellite**.
con [kɔn] vt (col) truffare ♦ n truffa; **to ~ sb into doing sth** indurre qn a fare qc con raggiri.
concave ['kɔn'keɪv] a concavo(a).
conceal [kən'siːl] vt nascondere.
concede [kən'siːd] vt concedere ♦ vi fare una concessione.
conceit [kən'siːt] n presunzione f, vanità.
conceited [kən'siːtɪd] a presuntuoso(a), vanitoso(a).
conceivable [kən'siːvəbl] a concepibile; **it is ~ that ...** può anche darsi che ....
conceivably [kən'siːvəblɪ] ad: **he may ~ be right** può anche darsi che abbia ragione.
conceive [kən'siːv] vt concepire ♦ vi concepire

un bambino; **to ~ of sth/of doing sth** immaginare qc/di fare qc.

concentrate ['kɔnsəntreɪt] *vi* concentrarsi ♦ *vt* concentrare.

concentration [kɔnsən'treɪʃən] *n* concentrazione *f*.

concentration camp *n* campo di concentramento.

concentric [kɔn'sɛntrɪk] *a* concentrico(a).

concept ['kɔnsɛpt] *n* concetto.

conception [kən'sɛpʃən] *n* concezione *f*; (*idea*) idea, concetto.

concern [kən'sə:n] *n* affare *m*; (*COMM*) azienda, ditta; (*anxiety*) preoccupazione *f* ♦ *vt* riguardare; **to be ~ed** (*about*) preoccuparsi (di); **to be ~ed with** occuparsi di; **as far as I am ~ed** per quanto mi riguarda; **"to whom it may ~"** "a tutti gli interessati"; **the department ~ed** (*under discussion*) l'ufficio in questione; (*relevant*) l'ufficio competente.

concerning [kən'sə:nɪŋ] *prep* riguardo a, circa.

concert ['kɔnsət] *n* concerto; **in ~** di concerto.

concerted [kən'sə:tɪd] *a* concertato(a).

concert hall *n* sala da concerti.

concertina [kɔnsə'ti:nə] *n* piccola fisarmonica ♦ *vi* ridursi come una fisarmonica.

concerto [kən'tʃə:təu] *n* concerto.

concession [kən'sɛʃən] *n* concessione *f*.

concessionaire [kənsɛʃə'nɛə*] *n* concessionario.

concessionary [kən'sɛʃənərɪ] *a* (*ticket, fare*) a prezzo ridotto.

conciliation [kənsɪlɪ'eɪʃən] *n* conciliazione *f*.

conciliatory [kən'sɪlɪətrɪ] *a* conciliativo(a).

concise [kən'saɪs] *a* conciso(a).

conclave ['kɔnkleɪv] *n* riunione *f* segreta; (*REL*) conclave *m*.

conclude [kən'klu:d] *vt* concludere ♦ *vi* (*speaker*) concludere; (*events*): **to ~ (with)** concludersi (con).

conclusion [kən'klu:ʒən] *n* conclusione *f*; **to come to the ~ that** ... concludere che ..., arrivare alla conclusione che ....

conclusive [kən'klu:sɪv] *a* conclusivo(a).

concoct [kən'kɔkt] *vt* inventare.

concoction [kən'kɔkʃən] *n* (*food, drink*) miscuglio.

concord ['kɔŋkɔ:d] *n* (*harmony*) armonia, concordia; (*treaty*) accordo.

concourse ['kɔŋkɔ:s] *n* (*hall*) atrio.

concrete ['kɔŋkri:t] *n* calcestruzzo ♦ *a* concreto(a); (*CONSTR*) di calcestruzzo.

concrete mixer *n* betoniera.

concur [kən'kə:*] *vi* concordare.

concurrently [kən'kʌrntlɪ] *ad* simultaneamente.

concussion [kən'kʌʃən] *n* (*MED*) commozione *f* cerebrale.

condemn [kən'dɛm] *vt* condannare.

condemnation [kɔndɛm'neɪʃən] *n* condanna.

condensation [kɔndɛn'seɪʃən] *n* condensazione *f*.

condense [kən'dɛns] *vi* condensarsi ♦ *vt* condensare.

condensed milk *n* latte *m* condensato.

condescend [kɔndɪ'sɛnd] *vi* condiscendere; **to ~ to do sth** degnarsi di fare qc.

condescending [kɔndɪ'sɛndɪŋ] *a* condiscendente.

condition [kən'dɪʃən] *n* condizione *f*; (*disease*) malattia ♦ *vt* condizionare, regolare; **in good/poor ~** in buone/cattive condizioni; **to have a heart ~** soffrire di (mal di) cuore; **weather ~s** condizioni meteorologiche; **on ~ that** a condizione che + *sub*, a condizione di.

conditional [kən'dɪʃənl] *a* condizionale; **to be ~ upon** dipendere da.

conditioner [kən'dɪʃənə*] *n* (*for hair*) balsamo.

condo ['kɔndəu] *n* *abbr* (*US col*) = **condominium**.

condolences [kən'dəulənsɪz] *npl* condoglianze *fpl*.

condom ['kɔndəm] *n* preservativo.

condominium [kɔndə'mɪnɪəm] *n* (*US*) condominio.

condone [kən'dəun] *vt* condonare.

conducive [kən'dju:sɪv] *a*: **~ to** favorevole a.

conduct *n* ['kɔndʌkt] condotta ♦ *vt* [kən'dʌkt] condurre; (*manage*) dirigere; amministrare; (*MUS*) dirigere; **to ~ o.s.** comportarsi.

conducted tour *n* gita accompagnata.

conductor [kən'dʌktə*] *n* (*of orchestra*) direttore *m* d'orchestra; (*on bus*) bigliettaio; (*US RAIL*) controllore *m*; (*ELEC*) conduttore *m*.

conductress [kən'dʌktrɪs] *n* (*on bus*) bigliettaia.

conduit ['kɔndɪt] *n* condotto; tubo.

cone [kəun] *n* cono; (*BOT*) pigna.

confectioner [kən'fɛkʃənə*] *n*: **~'s (shop)** ≈ pasticceria.

confectionery [kən'fɛkʃənərɪ] *n* dolciumi *mpl*.

confederate [kən'fɛdərɪt] *a* confederato(a) ♦ *n* (*pej*) complice *m/f*; (*US HISTORY*) confederato.

confederation [kənfɛdə'reɪʃən] *n* confederazione *f*.

confer [kən'fə:*] *vt*: **to ~ sth on** conferire qc a ♦ *vi* conferire; **to ~ (with sb about sth)** consultarsi (con qn su qc).

conference ['kɔnfərns] *n* congresso; **to be in ~** essere in riunione.

conference room *n* sala *f* conferenze *inv*.

confess [kən'fɛs] *vt* confessare, ammettere ♦ *vi* confessarsi.

confession [kən'fɛʃən] *n* confessione *f*.

confessional [kən'fɛʃənl] *n* confessionale *m*.

confessor [kən'fɛsə*] *n* confessore *m*.

confetti [kən'fɛtɪ] *n* coriandoli *mpl*.

confide [kən'faɪd] *vi*: **to ~ in** confidarsi con.

confidence ['kɔnfɪdns] *n* confidenza; (*trust*) fiducia; (*also:* **self-~**) sicurezza di sé; **to tell sb sth in strict ~** dire qc a qn in via strettamente confidenziale; **to have (every) ~ that** ... essere assolutamente certo(a) che ...;

motion of no ~ mozione *f* di sfiducia.
confidence trick *n* truffa.
confident ['kɔnfɪdənt] *a* sicuro(a); (*also*: **self-**~) sicuro(a) di sé.
confidential [kɔnfɪ'dɛnʃəl] *a* riservato(a); (*secretary*) particolare.
confidentiality ['kɔnfɪdɛnʃɪ'ælɪtɪ] *n* riservatezza, carattere *m* confidenziale.
configuration [kən'fɪgju'reɪʃən] *n* (*COMPUT*) configurazione *f*.
confine [kən'faɪn] *vt* limitare; (*shut up*) rinchiudere; **to** ~ **o.s. to doing sth** limitarsi a fare qc; *see also* **confines**.
confined [kən'faɪnd] *a* (*space*) ristretto(a).
confinement [kən'faɪnmənt] *n* prigionia; (*MIL*) consegna; (*MED*) parto.
confines ['kɔnfaɪnz] *npl* confini *mpl*.
confirm [kən'fə:m] *vt* confermare; (*REL*) cresimare.
confirmation [kɔnfə'meɪʃən] *n* conferma; cresima.
confirmed [kən'fə:md] *a* inveterato(a).
confiscate ['kɔnfɪskeɪt] *vt* confiscare.
confiscation [kɔnfɪs'keɪʃən] *n* confisca.
conflagration [kɔnflə'greɪʃən] *n* conflagrazione *f*.
conflict *n* ['kɔnflɪkt] conflitto ♦ *vi* [kən'flɪkt] essere in conflitto.
conflicting [kən'flɪktɪŋ] *a* contrastante; (*reports*, *evidence*, *opinions*) contraddittorio(a).
conform [kən'fɔ:m] *vi*: **to** ~ (**to**) conformarsi (a).
conformist [kən'fɔ:mɪst] *n* conformista *m/f*.
confound [kən'faund] *vt* confondere; (*amaze*) sconcertare.
confounded [kən'faundɪd] *a* maledetto(a).
confront [kən'frʌnt] *vt* confrontare; (*enemy*, *danger*) affrontare.
confrontation [kɔnfrən'teɪʃən] *n* scontro.
confuse [kən'fju:z] *vt* imbrogliare; (*one thing with another*) confondere.
confused [kən'fju:zd] *a* confuso(a); **to get** ~ confondersi.
confusing [kən'fju:zɪŋ] *a* che fa confondere.
confusion [kən'fju:ʒən] *n* confusione *f*.
congeal [kən'dʒi:l] *vi* (*blood*) congelarsi.
congenial [kən'dʒi:nɪəl] *a* (*person*) simpatico(a); (*place*, *work*, *company*) piacevole.
congenital [kən'dʒenɪtl] *a* congenito(a).
conger eel ['kɔŋgər-] *n* grongo.
congested [kən'dʒestɪd] *a* congestionato(a); (*telephone lines*) sovraccarico(a).
congestion [kən'dʒestʃən] *n* congestione *f*.
conglomerate [kən'glɔmərɪt] *n* (*COMM*) conglomerato.
conglomeration [kənglɔmə'reɪʃən] *n* conglomerazione *f*.
Congo ['kɔŋgəu] *n* Congo.
congratulate [kən'grætjuleɪt] *vt*: **to** ~ **sb** (**on**) congratularsi con qn (per *o* di).
congratulations [kəngrætju'leɪʃənz] *npl*: ~ (**on**) congratulazioni *fpl* (per) ♦ *excl* congratulazioni!, rallegramenti!

congregate ['kɔŋgrɪgeɪt] *vi* congregarsi, riunirsi.
congregation [kɔŋgrɪ'geɪʃən] *n* congregazione *f*.
congress ['kɔŋgres] *n* congresso.
congressman ['kɔŋgresmən] *n* (*US*) membro del Congresso.
congresswoman ['kɔŋgreswumən] *n* (*US*) (donna) membro del Congresso.
conical ['kɔnɪkl] *a* conico(a).
conifer ['kɔnɪfə*] *n* conifero.
coniferous [kə'nɪfərəs] *a* (*forest*) di conifere.
conjecture [kən'dʒektʃə*] *n* congettura ♦ *vt*, *vi* congetturare.
conjugal ['kɔndʒugl] *a* coniugale.
conjugate ['kɔndʒugeɪt] *vt* coniugare.
conjugation [kɔndʒə'geɪʃən] *n* coniugazione *f*.
conjunction [kən'dʒʌŋkʃən] *n* congiunzione *f*; **in** ~ **with** in accordo con, insieme con.
conjunctivitis [kəndʒʌŋktɪ'vaɪtɪs] *n* congiuntivite *f*.
conjure ['kʌndʒə*] *vi* fare giochi di prestigio.
conjure up *vt* (*ghost*, *spirit*) evocare; (*memories*) rievocare.
conjurer ['kʌndʒərə*] *n* prestigiatore/trice, prestidigitatore/trice.
conjuring trick ['kʌndʒərɪŋ-] *n* gioco di prestigio.
conker ['kɔŋkə*] *n* (*Brit col*) castagna (d'ippocastano).
conk out [kɔŋk-] *vi* (*col*) andare in panne.
conman ['kɔnmæn] *n* truffatore *m*.
connect [kə'nekt] *vt* connettere, collegare; (*ELEC*) collegare; (*fig*) associare ♦ *vi* (*train*): **to** ~ **with** essere in coincidenza con; **to be** ~**ed with** aver rapporti con; essere imparentato(a) con; **I am trying to** ~ **you** (*TEL*) sto cercando di darle la linea.
connection [kə'nekʃən] *n* relazione *f*, rapporto; (*ELEC*) connessione *f*; (*TEL*) collegamento; (*train etc*) coincidenza; **in** ~ **with** con riferimento a, a proposito di; **what is the** ~ **between them?** in che modo sono legati?; **business** ~**s** rapporti d'affari; **to miss/get one's** ~ (*train etc*) perdere/ prendere la coincidenza.
connexion [kə'nekʃən] *n* (*Brit*) = **connection**.
conning tower ['kɔnɪŋ-] *n* torretta di comando.
connive [kə'naɪv] *vi*: **to** ~ **at** essere connivente in.
connoisseur [kɔnɪ'sə:*] *n* conoscitore/trice.
connotation [kɔnə'teɪʃən] *n* connotazione *f*.
connubial [kə'nju:bɪəl] *a* coniugale.
conquer ['kɔŋkə*] *vt* conquistare; (*feelings*) vincere.
conqueror ['kɔŋkərə*] *n* conquistatore *m*.
conquest ['kɔŋkwest] *n* conquista.
cons [kɔnz] *npl see* **pro, convenience**.
conscience ['kɔnʃəns] *n* coscienza; **in all** ~ onestamente, in coscienza.
conscientious [kɔnʃɪ'enʃəs] *a* coscienzioso(a).

conscientious objector *n* obiettore *m* di coscienza.

conscious ['kɔnʃəs] *a* consapevole; (*MED*) conscio(a); (*deliberate*: *insult*, *error*) intenzionale, voluto(a); **to become ~ of sth/that** rendersi conto di qc/che.

consciousness ['kɔnʃəsnɪs] *n* consapevolezza; (*MED*) coscienza; **to lose/regain ~** perdere/riprendere coscienza.

conscript ['kɔnskrɪpt] *n* coscritto.

conscription [kən'skrɪpʃən] *n* coscrizione *f*.

consecrate ['kɔnsɪkreɪt] *vt* consacrare.

consecutive [kən'sɛkjutɪv] *a* consecutivo(a); **on 3 ~ occasions** 3 volte di fila.

consensus [kən'sɛnsəs] *n* consenso; **the ~ of opinion** l'opinione *f* unanime *or* comune.

consent [kən'sɛnt] *n* consenso ♦ *vi*: **to ~ (to)** acconsentire (a); **age of ~** età legale (per avere rapporti sessuali); **by common ~** di comune accordo.

consequence ['kɔnsɪkwəns] *n* conseguenza, risultato; importanza; **in ~** di conseguenza.

consequently ['kɔnsɪkwəntlɪ] *ad* di conseguenza, dunque.

conservation [kɔnsə'veɪʃən] *n* conservazione *f*; (*also*: **nature ~**) tutela dell'ambiente; **energy ~** risparmio energetico.

conservationist [kɔnsə'veɪʃənɪst] *n* fautore/trice della tutela dell'ambiente.

conservative [kən'sə:vətɪv] *a* conservatore(trice); (*cautious*) cauto(a); **C~** *a*, *n* (*Brit POL*) conservatore(trice).

conservatory [kən'sə:vətrɪ] *n* (*greenhouse*) serra.

conserve [kən'sə:v] *vt* conservare ♦ *n* conserva.

consider [kən'sɪdə*] *vt* considerare; (*take into account*) tener conto di; **to ~ doing sth** considerare la possibilità di fare qc; **all things ~ed** tutto sommato *or* considerato; **~ yourself lucky** puoi dirti fortunato.

considerable [kən'sɪdərəbl] *a* considerevole, notevole.

considerably [kən'sɪdərəblɪ] *ad* notevolmente, decisamente.

considerate [kən'sɪdərɪt] *a* premuroso(a).

consideration [kənsɪdə'reɪʃən] *n* considerazione *f*; (*reward*) rimunerazione *f*; **out of ~ for** per riguardo a; **under ~** in esame; **my first ~ is my family** il mio primo pensiero è per la mia famiglia.

considering [kən'sɪdərɪŋ] *prep* in considerazione di; **~ (that)** se si considera (che).

consign [kən'saɪn] *vt* consegnare; (*send*: *goods*) spedire.

consignee [kɔnsaɪ'ni:] *n* consegnatario/a, destinatario/a.

consignment [kən'saɪnmənt] *n* consegna; spedizione *f*.

consignment note *n* (*COMM*) nota di spedizione.

consignor [kən'saɪnə*] *n* mittente *m/f*.

consist [kən'sɪst] *vi*: **to ~ of** constare di,

essere composto(a) di.

consistency [kən'sɪstənsɪ] *n* consistenza; (*fig*) coerenza.

consistent [kən'sɪstənt] *a* coerente; (*constant*) costante; **~ with** compatibile con.

consolation [kɔnsə'leɪʃən] *n* consolazione *f*.

console *vt* [kən'səul] consolare ♦ *n* ['kɔnsəul] quadro di comando.

consolidate [kən'sɔlɪdeɪt] *vt* consolidare.

consols ['kɔnsɔlz] *npl* (*STOCK EXCHANGE*) titoli *mpl* del debito consolidato.

consommé [kən'sɔmeɪ] *n* consommé *m inv*, brodo ristretto.

consonant ['kɔnsənənt] *n* consonante *f*.

consort ['kɔnsɔ:t] *n* consorte *m/f*; **prince ~** principe *m* consorte ♦ *vi* (*often pej*): **to ~ with sb** frequentare qn.

consortium [kən'sɔ:tɪəm] *n* consorzio.

conspicuous [kən'spɪkjuəs] *a* cospicuo(a); **to make o.s. ~** farsi notare.

conspiracy [kən'spɪrəsɪ] *n* congiura, cospirazione *f*.

conspiratorial [kənspɪrə'tɔ:rɪəl] *a* cospiratorio(a).

conspire [kən'spaɪə*] *vi* congiurare, cospirare.

constable ['kʌnstəbl] *n* (*Brit*: *also*: **police ~**) ≈ poliziotto, agente *m* di polizia.

constabulary [kən'stæbjulərɪ] *n* forze *fpl* dell'ordine.

constant ['kɔnstənt] *a* costante; continuo(a).

constantly ['kɔnstəntlɪ] *ad* costantemente; continuamente.

constellation [kɔnstə'leɪʃən] *n* costellazione *f*.

consternation [kɔnstə'neɪʃən] *n* costernazione *f*.

constipated ['kɔnstɪpeɪtɪd] *a* stitico(a).

constipation [kɔnstɪ'peɪʃən] *n* stitichezza.

constituency [kən'stɪtjuənsɪ] *n* collegio elettorale; (*people*) elettori *mpl* (del collegio).

constituency party *n* sezione *f* locale (del partito).

constituent [kən'stɪtjuənt] *n* elettore/trice; (*part*) elemento componente.

constitute ['kɔnstɪtju:t] *vt* costituire.

constitution [kɔnstɪ'tju:ʃən] *n* costituzione *f*.

constitutional [kɔnstɪ'tju:ʃənl] *a* costituzionale.

constrain [kən'streɪn] *vt* costringere.

constrained [kən'streɪnd] *a* costretto(a).

constraint [kən'streɪnt] *n* (*restraint*) limitazione *f*, costrizione *f*; (*embarrassment*) imbarazzo, soggezione *f*.

constrict [kən'strɪkt] *vt* comprimere; opprimere.

construct [kən'strʌkt] *vt* costruire.

construction [kən'strʌkʃən] *n* costruzione *f*; (*fig*: *interpretation*) interpretazione *f*; **under ~** in costruzione.

construction industry *n* edilizia, industria edile.

constructive [kən'strʌktɪv] *a* costruttivo(a).

construe [kən'stru:] *vt* interpretare.

consul ['kɔnsl] *n* console *m*.

consulate ['kɔnsjulıt] *n* consolato.
consult [kən'sʌlt] *vt*: **to ~ sb (about sth)** consultare qn (su *or* riguardo a qc).
consultancy [kən'sʌltənsı] *n* consulenza.
consultancy fee *n* onorario di consulenza.
consultant [kən'sʌltənt] *n* (*MED*) consulente *m* medico; (*other specialist*) consulente ♦ *cpd*: **~ engineer** *n* ingegnere *m* consulente; **~ paediatrician** *n* specialista *m/f* in pediatria; **legal/management ~** consulente legale/ gestionale.
consultation [kɔnsəl'teıʃən] *n* consultazione *f*; (*MED*, *LAW*) consulto; **in ~ with** consultandosi con.
consulting room [kən'sʌltıŋ-] *n* (*Brit*) ambulatorio.
consume [kən'sju:m] *vt* consumare.
consumer [kən'sju:mə*] *n* consumatore/trice; (*of electricity, gas etc*) utente *m/f*.
consumer credit *n* credito al consumatore.
consumer durables *npl* prodotti *mpl* di consumo durevole.
consumer goods *npl* beni *mpl* di consumo.
consumerism [kən'sju:mərızəm] *n* (*consumer protection*) tutela del consumatore; (*ECON*) consumismo.
consumer society *n* società dei consumi.
consummate ['kɔnsʌmeıt] *vt* consumare.
consumption [kən'sʌmpʃən] *n* consumo; (*MED*) consunzione *f*; **not fit for human ~** non commestibile.
cont. *abbr* (= *continued*) segue.
contact ['kɔntækt] *n* contatto; (*person*) cono-scenza ♦ *vt* mettersi in contatto con; **to be in ~ with sb/sth** essere in contatto con qn/qc; **business ~s** contatti *mpl* d'affari.
contact lenses *npl* lenti *fpl* a contatto.
contagious [kən'teıdʒəs] *a* contagioso(a).
contain [kən'teın] *vt* contenere; **to ~ o.s.** contenersi.
container [kən'teınə*] *n* recipiente *m*; (*for shipping etc*) container *m*.
containerize [kən'teınəraız] *vt* mettere in container.
contaminate [kən'tæmıneıt] *vt* contaminare.
contamination [kəntæmı'neıʃən] *n* contaminazione *f*.
cont'd *abbr* (= *continued*) segue.
contemplate ['kɔntəmpleıt] *vt* contemplare; (*consider*) pensare a (*or* di).
contemplation [kɔntəm'pleıʃən] *n* contem-plazione *f*.
contemporary [kən'tempərərı] *a* contempo-raneo(a); (*design*) moderno(a) ♦ *n* contempo-raneo/a; (*of the same age*) coetaneo/a.
contempt [kən'tempt] *n* disprezzo; **~ of court** (*LAW*) oltraggio alla Corte.
contemptible [kən'temptəbl] *a* spregevole, vergognoso(a).
contemptuous [kən'temptjuəs] *a* sdegnoso(a).
contend [kən'tend] *vt*: **to ~ that** sostenere che ♦ *vi*: **to ~ with** lottare contro; **he has a lot to ~ with** ha un sacco di guai.
contender [kən'tendə*] *n* contendente *m/f*;

concorrente *m/f*.
content [kən'tent] *a* contento(a), soddi-sfatto(a) ♦ *vt* contentare, soddisfare ♦ *n* ['kɔntent] contenuto; **~s** *npl* contenuto; (*of barrel etc*: *capacity*) capacità *f inv*; **(table of) ~s** indice *m*; **to be ~ with** essere contento di; **to ~ o.s. with sth/with doing sth** accontentarsi di qc/di fare qc.
contented [kən'tentıd] *a* contento(a), soddi-sfatto(a).
contentedly [kən'tentıdlı] *ad* con soddi-sfazione.
contention [kən'tenʃən] *n* contesa; (*assertion*) tesi *f inv*; **bone of ~** pomo della discordia.
contentious [kən'tenʃəs] *a* polemico(a).
contentment [kən'tentmənt] *n* contentezza.
contest *n* ['kɔntest] lotta; (*competition*) gara, concorso ♦ *vt* [kən'test] contestare; (*LAW*) impugnare; (*compete for*) contendere.
contestant [kən'testənt] *n* concorrente *m/f*; (*in fight*) avversario/a.
context ['kɔntekst] *n* contesto; **in/out of ~** nel/fuori dal contesto.
continent ['kɔntınənt] *n* continente *m*; **the C~** (*Brit*) l'Europa continentale; **on the C~** in Europa.
continental [kɔntı'nentl] *a* continentale ♦ *n* (*Brit*) abitante *m/f* dell'Europa continentale.
continental breakfast *n* colazione *f* all'europea.
continental quilt *n* (*Brit*) piumino.
contingency [kən'tındʒənsı] *n* eventualità *f inv*.
contingency plan *n* misura d'emergenza.
contingent [kən'tındʒənt] *n* contingenza ♦ *a*: **to be ~ upon** dipendere da.
continual [kən'tınjuəl] *a* continuo(a).
continually [kən'tınjuəlı] *ad* di continuo.
continuation [kəntınju'eıʃən] *n* continuazione *f*; (*after interruption*) ripresa; (*of story*) seguito.
continue [kən'tınju:] *vi* continuare ♦ *vt* continuare; (*start again*) riprendere; **to be ~d** (*story*) continua; **~d on page 10** segue *or* continua a pagina 10.
continuity [kɔntı'nju:ıtı] *n* continuità; (*CINEMA*) (ordine *m* della) sceneggiatura.
continuity girl *n* (*CINEMA*) segretaria di edizione.
continuous [kən'tınjuəs] *a* continuo(a), ininterrotto(a); **~ performance** (*CINEMA*) spettacolo continuato; **~ stationery** (*COMPUT*) carta a moduli continui.
continuously [kən'tınjuəslı] *ad* (*repeatedly*) continuamente; (*uninterruptedly*) ininterrot-tamente.
contort [kən'tɔ:t] *vt* contorcere.
contortion [kən'tɔ:ʃən] *n* contorcimento; (*of acrobat*) contorsione *f*.
contortionist [kən'tɔ:ʃənıst] *n* contorsionista *m/f*.
contour ['kɔntuə*] *n* contorno, profilo; (*also*: **~ line**) curva di livello.
contraband ['kɔntrəbænd] *n* contrabbando ♦ *a*

di contrabbando.

contraception [kɔntrə'sɛpʃən] *n* contraccezione *f*.

contraceptive [kɔntrə'sɛptɪv] *a* contraccettivo(a) ♦ *n* contraccettivo.

contract *n* ['kɔntrækt] contratto ♦ *cpd* ['kɔntrækt] (*price*, *date*) del contratto; (*work*) a contratto ♦ *vi* [kən'trækt] (*COMM*): **to ~ to do sth** fare un contratto per fare qc; (*become smaller*) contrarre; **to be under ~ to do sth** aver stipulato un contratto per fare qc; **~ of employment** contratto di lavoro.

contract in *vi* impegnarsi (con un contratto); (*BRIT ADMIN*) *scegliere di pagare i contributi per una pensione*.

contract out *vi*: **to ~ out (of)** ritirarsi (da); (*Brit ADMIN*) (*scegliere di*) *non pagare i contributi per una pensione*.

contraction [kən'trækʃən] *n* contrazione *f*.

contractor [kən'træktə*] *n* imprenditore *m*.

contractual [kən'træktjuəl] *a* contrattuale.

contradict [kɔntrə'dɪkt] *vt* contraddire.

contradiction [kɔntrə'dɪkʃən] *n* contraddizione *f*; **to be in ~ with** discordare con.

contradictory [kɔntrə'dɪktərɪ] *a* contraddittorio(a).

contralto [kən'træltəu] *n* contralto.

contraption [kən'træpʃən] *n* (*pej*) aggeggio.

contrary ['kɔntrərɪ] *a* contrario(a); (*unfavourable*) avverso(a), contrario(a); [kən'trɛərɪ] (*perverse*) bisbetico(a) ♦ *n* contrario; **on the ~** al contrario; **unless you hear to the ~** a meno che non si disdica; **~ to what we thought** a differenza di *or* contrariamente a quanto pensavamo.

contrast *n* ['kɔntrɑ:st] contrasto ♦ *vt* [kən'trɑ:st] mettere in contrasto; **in ~ to** *or* **with** a differenza di, contrariamente a.

contrasting [kən'trɑ:stɪŋ] *a* contrastante, di contrasto.

contravene [kɔntrə'vi:n] *vt* contravvenire.

contravention [kɔntrə'vɛnʃən] *n*: **~ (of)** contravvenzione *f* (a), infrazione *f* (di).

contribute [kən'trɪbju:t] *vi* contribuire ♦ *vt*: **to ~ £10/an article to** dare 10 sterline/un articolo a; **to ~ to** contribuire a; (*newspaper*) scrivere per; (*discussion*) partecipare a.

contribution [kɔntrɪ'bju:ʃən] *n* contribuzione *f*.

contributor [kən'trɪbjutə*] *n* (*to newspaper*) collaboratore/trice.

contributory [kən'trɪbjutərɪ] *a* (*cause*) che contribuisce; **it was a ~ factor in ...** quello ha contribuito a ....

contributory pension scheme *n* (*Brit*) *sistema di pensionamento finanziato congiuntamente dai contributi del lavoratore e del datore di lavoro.*

contrite ['kɔntraɪt] *a* contrito(a).

contrivance [kən'traɪvəns] *n* congegno; espediente *m*.

contrive [kən'traɪv] *vt* inventare; escogitare ♦ *vi*: **to ~ to do** fare in modo di fare.

control [kən'trəul] *vt* dominare; (*firm, opera-*

tion etc) dirigere; (*check*) controllare; (*disease, fire*) arginare, limitare ♦ *n* controllo; **~s** *npl* comandi *mpl*; **to take ~ of** assumere il controllo di; **to be in ~ of** aver autorità su; essere responsabile di; controllare; **to ~ o.s.** controllarsi; **everything is under ~** tutto è sotto controllo; **the car went out of ~** la macchina non rispondeva ai comandi; **circumstances beyond our ~** circostanze *fpl* che non dipendono da noi.

control key *n* (*COMPUT*) tasto di controllo.

controller [kən'trəulə*] *n* controllore *m*.

controlling interest [kən'trəulɪŋ-] *n* (*COMM*) maggioranza delle azioni.

control panel *n* (*on aircraft, ship, TV etc*) quadro dei comandi.

control point *n* punto di controllo.

control room *n* (*NAUT, MIL*) sala di comando; (*RADIO, TV*) sala di regia.

control tower *n* (*AVIAT*) torre *f* di controllo.

control unit *n* (*COMPUT*) unità *f inv* di controllo.

controversial [kɔntrə'və:ʃl] *a* controverso(a), polemico(a).

controversy ['kɔntrəvə:sɪ] *n* controversia, polemica.

conurbation [kɔnə:'beɪʃən] *n* conurbazione *f*.

convalesce [kɔnvə'lɛs] *vi* rimettersi in salute.

convalescence [kɔnvə'lɛsns] *n* convalescenza.

convalescent [kɔnvə'lɛsnt] *a, n* convalescente (*m/f*).

convector [kən'vɛktə*] *n* convettore *m*.

convene [kən'vi:n] *vt* convocare; (*meeting*) organizzare ♦ *vi* convenire, adunarsi.

convenience [kən'vi:nɪəns] *n* comodità *f inv*; **at your ~** a suo comodo; **at your earliest ~** (*COMM*) appena possibile; **all modern ~s**, (*Brit*) **all mod cons** tutte le comodità moderne.

convenience foods *npl* cibi *mpl* precotti.

convenient [kən'vi:nɪənt] *a* conveniente, comodo(a); **if it is ~ to you** se per lei va bene, se non la incomoda.

conveniently [kən'vi:nɪəntlɪ] *ad* (*happen*) a proposito; (*situated*) in un posto comodo.

convent ['kɔnvənt] *n* convento.

convention [kən'vɛnʃən] *n* convenzione *f*; (*meeting*) convegno.

conventional [kən'vɛnʃənl] *a* convenzionale.

convent school *n* scuola retta da suore.

converge [kən'və:dʒ] *vi* convergere.

conversant [kən'və:snt] *a*: **to be ~ with** essere al corrente di; essere pratico(a) di.

conversation [kɔnvə'seɪʃən] *n* conversazione *f*.

conversational [kɔnvə'seɪʃənl] *a* non formale; (*COMPUT*) conversazionale; **~ Italian** l'italiano parlato.

conversationalist [kɔnvə'seɪʃnəlɪst] *n* conversatore/trice.

converse *n* ['kɔnvə:s] contrario, opposto ♦ *vi* [kən'və:s]: **to ~ (with sb about sth)** conversare (con qn su qc).

conversely [kɔn'və:slɪ] *ad* al contrario, per

contro.

conversion [kən'və:ʃən] n conversione f; (Brit: of house) trasformazione f, rimodernamento.

conversion table n tavola di equivalenze.

convert vt [kən'və:t] (REL, COMM) convertire; (alter) trasformare ♦ n ['kɔnvə:t] convertito/a.

convertible [kən'və:təbl] n macchina decappottabile.

convex ['kɔnvɛks] a convesso(a).

convey [kən'veɪ] vt trasportare; (thanks) comunicare; (idea) dare.

conveyance [kən'veɪəns] n (of goods) trasporto; (vehicle) mezzo di trasporto.

conveyancing [kən'veɪənsɪŋ] n (LAW) redazione f di transazioni di proprietà.

conveyor belt n nastro trasportatore.

convict vt [kən'vɪkt] dichiarare colpevole ♦ n ['kɔnvɪkt] carcerato/a.

conviction [kən'vɪkʃən] n condanna; (belief) convinzione f.

convince [kən'vɪns] vt: to ~ sb (of sth/that) convincere qn (di qc/che), persuadere qn (di qc/che).

convincing [kən'vɪnsɪŋ] a convincente.

convincingly [kən'vɪnsɪŋlɪ] ad in modo convincente.

convivial [kən'vɪvɪəl] a allegro(a).

convoluted ['kɔnvəlu:tɪd] a (shape) attorcigliato(a), avvolto(a); (argument) involuto(a).

convoy ['kɔnvɔɪ] n convoglio.

convulse [kən'vʌls] vt sconvolgere; to be ~d with laughter contorcersi dalle risa.

convulsion [kən'vʌlʃən] n convulsione f.

coo [ku:] vi tubare.

cook [kuk] vt cucinare, cuocere; (meal) preparare ♦ vi cuocere; (person) cucinare ♦ n cuoco/a.

  cook up vt (col: excuse, story) improvvisare, inventare.

cookbook ['kukbuk] n = **cookery book**.

cooker ['kukə*] n fornello, cucina.

cookery ['kukərɪ] n cucina.

cookery book n (Brit) libro di cucina.

cookie ['kukɪ] n (US) biscotto.

cooking ['kukɪŋ] n cucina ♦ cpd (apples, chocolate) da cuocere; (utensils, salt, foil) da cucina.

cookout ['kukaut] n (US) pranzo (cucinato) all'aperto.

cool [ku:l] a fresco(a); (not afraid) calmo(a); (unfriendly) freddo(a); (impertinent) sfacciato(a) ♦ vt raffreddare, rinfrescare ♦ vi raffreddarsi, rinfrescarsi; it's ~ (weather) fa fresco; to keep sth ~ or in a ~ place tenere qc in fresco.

  cool down vi raffreddarsi; (fig: person, situation) calmarsi.

cool box, (US) **cooler** ['ku:lə*] n borsa termica.

cooling tower ['ku:lɪŋ-] n torre f di raffreddamento.

coolly ['ku:lɪ] ad (calmly) con calma,

tranquillamente; (audaciously) come se niente fosse; (unenthusiastically) freddamente.

coolness ['ku:lnɪs] n freschezza; sangue m freddo, calma.

coop [ku:p] n stia ♦ vt: to ~ up (fig) rinchiudere.

co-op ['kəuɔp] n abbr (= cooperative (society)) coop f.

cooperate [kəu'ɔpəreɪt] vi cooperare, collaborare.

cooperation [kəuɔpə'reɪʃən] n cooperazione f, collaborazione f.

cooperative [kəu'ɔpərətɪv] a cooperativo(a) ♦ n cooperativa.

coopt [kəu'ɔpt] vt: to ~ sb into sth cooptare qn per qc.

coordinate vt [kəu'ɔ:dɪneɪt] coordinare ♦ n [kəu'ɔ:dɪnət] (MATH) coordinata; ~s npl (clothes) coordinati mpl.

coordination [kəuɔ:dɪ'neɪʃən] n coordinazione f.

coot [ku:t] n folaga.

co-ownership [kəu'əunəʃɪp] n comproprietà.

cop [kɔp] n (col) sbirro.

cope [kəup] vi farcela; to ~ with (problems) far fronte a.

Copenhagen [kəupən'heɪgən] n Copenhagen f.

copier ['kɔpɪə*] n (also: **photo~**) (foto)copiatrice f.

co-pilot ['kəupaɪlət] n secondo pilota m.

copious ['kəupɪəs] a copioso(a), abbondante.

copper ['kɔpə*] n rame m; (col: policeman) sbirro; ~s npl spiccioli mpl.

coppice ['kɔpɪs], **copse** [kɔps] n bosco ceduo.

copulate ['kɔpjuleɪt] vi accoppiarsi.

copy ['kɔpɪ] n copia; (book etc) esemplare m; (material: for printing) materiale m, testo ♦ vt (gen, COMPUT) copiare; (imitate) imitare; rough/fair ~ brutta/bella (copia); to make good ~ (fig) fare notizia.

  copy out vt ricopiare, trascrivere.

copycat ['kɔpɪkæt] n (pej) copione m.

copyright ['kɔpɪraɪt] n diritto d'autore; ~ reserved tutti i diritti riservati.

copy typist n dattilografo/a.

copywriter ['kɔpɪraɪtə*] n redattore m pubblicitario.

coral ['kɔrəl] n corallo.

coral reef n barriera corallina.

Coral Sea n: the ~ il mar dei Coralli.

cord [kɔ:d] n corda; (ELEC) filo; (fabric) velluto a coste; ~s npl (trousers) calzoni mpl (di velluto) a coste.

cordial ['kɔ:dɪəl] a, n cordiale (m).

cordless ['kɔ:dlɪs] a senza cavo.

cordon ['kɔ:dn] n cordone m.

  cordon off vt fare cordone intorno a.

corduroy ['kɔ:dərɔɪ] n fustagno.

CORE [kɔ:*] n abbr (US) = Congress of Racial Equality.

core [kɔ:*] n (of fruit) torsolo; (TECH) centro; (of earth, nuclear reactor) nucleo; (of problem etc) cuore m, nocciolo ♦ vt estrarre il torsolo da; **rotten to the** ~ marcio fino al midollo.

Corfu [kɔ:'fu:] *n* Corfù *f*.

coriander [kɔrɪ'ændə*] *n* coriandolo.

cork [kɔ:k] *n* sughero; (*of bottle*) tappo.

corkage ['kɔ:kɪdʒ] *n* somma da pagare se il cliente porta il proprio vino.

corked [kɔ:kt], (*US*) **corky** ['kɔ:kɪ] *a* (*wine*) che sa di tappo.

corkscrew ['kɔ:kskru:] *n* cavatappi *m inv.*

corm [kɔ:m] *n* cormo.

cormorant ['kɔ:mərnt] *n* cormorano.

Corn *abbr* (*Brit*) = **Cornwall.**

corn [kɔ:n] *n* (*Brit: wheat*) grano; (*US: maize*) granturco; (*on foot*) callo; ~ **on the cob** (*CULIN*) pannocchia cotta.

cornea ['kɔ:nɪə] *n* cornea.

corned beef ['kɔ:nd-] *n* carne *f* di manzo in scatola.

corner ['kɔ:nə*] *n* angolo; (*AUT*) curva; (*FOOTBALL: also:* ~ **kick**) corner *m inv*, calcio d'angolo ♦ *vt* intrappolare; mettere con le spalle al muro; (*COMM: market*) accaparrare ♦ *vi* prendere una curva; **to cut** ~**s** (*fig*) prendere una scorciatoia.

corner flag *n* (*FOOTBALL*) bandierina d'angolo.

corner kick *n* (*FOOTBALL*) calcio d'angolo.

cornerstone ['kɔ:nəstəun] *n* pietra angolare.

cornet ['kɔ:nɪt] *n* (*MUS*) cornetta; (*Brit: of ice-cream*) cono.

cornflakes ['kɔ:nfleɪks] *npl* fiocchi *mpl* di granturco.

cornflour ['kɔ:nflauə*] *n* (*Brit*) ≈ fecola di patate.

cornice ['kɔ:nɪs] *n* cornicione *m*; cornice *f*.

Cornish ['kɔ:nɪʃ] *a* della Cornovaglia.

corn oil *n* olio di mais.

cornstarch ['kɔ:nstɑ:tʃ] *n* (*US*) = **cornflour.**

cornucopia [kɔ:nju'kəupɪə] *n* grande abbondanza.

Cornwall ['kɔ:nwəl] *n* Cornovaglia.

corny ['kɔ:nɪ] *a* (*col*) trito(a).

corollary [kə'rɔlərɪ] *n* corollario.

coronary ['kɔrənərɪ] *n:* ~ **(thrombosis)** trombosi *f* coronaria.

coronation [kɔrə'neɪʃən] *n* incoronazione *f*.

coroner ['kɔrənə*] *n* magistrato incaricato di indagare la causa di morte in circostanze sospette.

coronet ['kɔrənɪt] *n* diadema *m*.

Corp. *abbr* = **corporation.**

corporal ['kɔ:pərl] *n* caporalmaggiore *m* ♦ *a:* ~ **punishment** pena corporale.

corporate ['kɔ:pərɪt] *a* comune; (*COMM*) costituito(a) (in corporazione).

corporate identity, corporate image *n* (*of organization*) immagine *f* di marca.

corporation [kɔ:pə'reɪʃən] *n* (*of town*) consiglio comunale; (*COMM*) ente *m*.

corporation tax *n* ≈ imposta societaria.

corps [kɔ:*], *pl* **corps** [kɔ:z] *n* corpo; **press** ~ ufficio *m* stampa *inv*.

corpse [kɔ:ps] *n* cadavere *m*.

corpuscle ['kɔ:pʌsl] *n* corpuscolo.

corral [kə'rɑ:l] *n* recinto.

correct [kə'rɛkt] *a* (*accurate*) corretto(a), esatto(a); (*proper*) corretto(a) ♦ *vt* correggere; **you are** ~ ha ragione.

correction [kə'rɛkʃən] *n* correzione *f*.

correlate ['kɔrɪleɪt] *vt* mettere in correlazione ♦ *vi:* **to** ~ **with** essere in rapporto con.

correlation [kɔrɪ'leɪʃən] *n* correlazione *f*.

correspond [kɔrɪs'pɔnd] *vi* corrispondere.

correspondence [kɔrɪs'pɔndəns] *n* corrispondenza.

correspondence column *n* (*PRESS*) rubrica delle lettere (al direttore).

correspondence course *n* corso per corrispondenza.

correspondent [kɔrɪs'pɔndənt] *n* corrispondente *m/f*.

corridor ['kɔrɪdɔ:*] *n* corridoio.

corroborate [kə'rɔbəreɪt] *vt* corroborare, confermare.

corrode [kə'rəud] *vt* corrodere ♦ *vi* corrodersi.

corrosion [kə'rəuʒən] *n* corrosione *f*.

corrosive [kə'rəuzɪv] *a* corrosivo(a).

corrugated ['kɔrəgeɪtɪd] *a* increspato(a); ondulato(a).

corrugated iron *n* lamiera di ferro ondulata.

corrupt [kə'rʌpt] *a* corrotto(a) ♦ *vt* corrompere; ~ **practices** (*dishonesty, bribery*) pratiche *fpl* illecite.

corruption [kə'rʌpʃən] *n* corruzione *f*.

corset ['kɔ:sɪt] *n* busto.

Corsica ['kɔ:sɪkə] *n* Corsica.

Corsican ['kɔ:sɪkən] *a, n* corso(a).

cortège [kɔ:'teɪʒ] *n* corteo.

cortisone ['kɔ:tɪzəun] *n* cortisone *m*.

coruscating ['kɔrəskeɪtɪŋ] *a* scintillante.

c.o.s. *abbr* (= *cash on shipment*) pagamento alla spedizione.

cosh [kɔʃ] *n* (*Brit*) randello (corto).

cosignatory [kəu'sɪgnətərɪ] *n* cofirmatario/a.

cosiness ['kəuzɪnɪs] *n* intimità.

cos lettuce ['kɔs-] *n* lattuga romana.

cosmetic [kɔz'mɛtɪk] *n* cosmetico ♦ *a* (*preparation*) cosmetico(a); (*surgery*) estetico(a); (*fig: reforms*) ornamentale.

cosmic ['kɔzmɪk] *a* cosmico(a).

cosmonaut ['kɔzmənɔ:t] *n* cosmonauta *m/f*.

cosmopolitan [kɔzmə'pɔlɪtn] *a* cosmopolita.

cosmos ['kɔzmɔs] *n* cosmo.

cosset ['kɔsɪt] *vt* vezzeggiare.

cost [kɔst] *n* costo ♦ *vb* (*pt, pp* **cost**) *vi* costare ♦ *vt* stabilire il prezzo di; ~**s** *npl* (*LAW*) spese *fpl*; **it** ~**s £5/too much** costa 5 sterline/troppo; **it** ~ **him his life/job** gli costò la vita/il suo lavoro; **how much does it** ~? quanto costa?, quanto viene?; **what will it** ~ **to have it repaired?** quanto costerà farlo riparare?; ~ **of living** costo della vita; **at all** ~**s** a ogni costo.

cost accountant *n* analizzatore *m* dei costi.

co-star ['kəustɑ:*] *n* attore/trice della stessa importanza del protagonista.

Costa Rica ['kɔstə'ri:kə] *n* Costa Rica.

cost centre n centro di costo.
cost control n controllo dei costi.
cost-effective ['kɔstɪ'fɛktɪv] a (gen) conveniente, economico(a); (COMM) redditizio(a), conveniente.
cost-effectiveness ['kɔstɪ'fɛktɪvnɪs] n convenienza.
costing ['kɔstɪŋ] n (determinazione f dei) costi mpl.
costly ['kɔstlɪ] a costoso(a), caro(a).
cost-of-living ['kɔstəv'lɪvɪŋ] a: ~ **allowance** indennità f inv di contingenza; ~ **index** indice m della scala mobile.
cost price n (Brit) prezzo all'ingrosso.
costume ['kɔstjuːm] n costume m; (lady's suit) tailleur m inv; (Brit: also: **swimming** ~) costume da bagno.
costume jewellery n bigiotteria.
cosy, (US) cozy ['kəʊzɪ] a intimo(a); (room, atmosphere) accogliente.
cot [kɔt] n (Brit: child's) lettino; (US: folding bed) brandina.
Cotswolds ['kɔtswəʊldz] npl: **the** ~ zona collinare del Gloucestershire.
cottage ['kɔtɪdʒ] n cottage m inv.
cottage cheese n fiocchi mpl di latte magro.
cottage industry n industria artigianale basata sul lavoro a cottimo.
cottage pie n piatto a base di carne macinata in sugo e purè di patate.
cotton ['kɔtn] n cotone m; ~ **dress** etc vestito etc di cotone.
cotton on vi (col): **to** ~ **on (to sth)** afferrare (qc).
cotton wool n (Brit) cotone m idrofilo.
couch [kaʊtʃ] n sofà m inv; (in doctor's surgery) lettino ♦ vt esprimere.
couchette [kuːˈʃɛt] n cuccetta.
cough [kɔf] vi tossire ♦ n tosse f.
cough drop n pasticca per la tosse.
cough mixture, cough syrup n sciroppo per la tosse.
could [kʊd] pt of **can**.
couldn't ['kʊdnt] = **could not**.
council ['kaʊnsl] n consiglio; **city** or **town** ~ consiglio comunale; **C~ of Europe** Consiglio d'Europa.
council estate n (Brit) quartiere m di case popolari.
council house n (Brit) casa popolare.
council housing n alloggi mpl popolari.
councillor ['kaʊnsələ*] n consigliere/a.
counsel ['kaʊnsl] n avvocato; consultazione f ♦ vt: **to** ~ **sth/sb to do sth** consigliare qc/a qn di fare qc; ~ **for the defence/the prosecution** avvocato difensore/di parte civile.
counsellor, (US) counselor ['kaʊnslə*] n consigliere/a; (US: lawyer) avvocato/essa.
count [kaʊnt] vt, vi contare ♦ n conto; (nobleman) conte m; **to** ~ **(up) to 10** contare fino a 10; **to** ~ **the cost of** calcolare il costo di; **not** ~**ing the children** senza contare i bambini; **10** ~**ing him** 10 compreso lui; ~ **yourself lucky** considerati fortunato; **it** ~**s**

for very little non conta molto, non ha molta importanza; **to keep** ~ **of sth** tenere il conto di qc.
count on vt fus contare su; **to** ~ **on doing sth** contare di fare qc.
count up vt addizionare.
countdown ['kaʊntdaʊn] n conto alla rovescia.
countenance ['kaʊntɪnəns] n volto, aspetto ♦ vt approvare.
counter ['kaʊntə*] n banco; (position: in post office, bank) sportello; (in game) gettone m; (TECH) contatore m ♦ vt opporsi a; (blow) parare ♦ ad: ~ **to** contro; in opposizione a; **to buy under the** ~ (fig) comperare sottobanco; **to** ~ **sth with sth/by doing sth** rispondere a qc con qc/facendo qc.
counteract [kaʊntər'ækt] vt agire in opposizione a; (poison etc) annullare gli effetti di.
counterattack ['kaʊntərətæk] n contrattacco ♦ vi contrattaccare.
counterbalance ['kaʊntəbæləns] vt contrappesare.
counter-clockwise ['kaʊntə'klɔkwaɪz] ad in senso antiorario.
counter-espionage [kaʊntər'ɛspɪənɑːʒ] n controspionaggio.
counterfeit ['kaʊntəfɪt] n contraffazione f, falso ♦ vt contraffare, falsificare ♦ a falso(a).
counterfoil ['kaʊntəfɔɪl] n matrice f.
counterintelligence ['kaʊntərɪn'tɛlɪdʒəns] n = **counter-espionage**.
countermand ['kaʊntəmɑːnd] vt annullare.
countermeasure ['kaʊntəmɛʒə*] n contromisura.
counteroffensive ['kaʊntərə'fɛnsɪv] n controffensiva.
counterpane ['kaʊntəpeɪn] n copriletto m inv.
counterpart ['kaʊntəpɑːt] n (of document etc) copia; (of person) corrispondente m/f.
counterproductive ['kaʊntəprə'dʌktɪv] a controproducente.
counterproposal ['kaʊntəprə'pəʊzl] n controproposta.
countersign ['kaʊntəsaɪn] vt controfirmare.
countersink ['kaʊntəsɪŋk] vt (hole) svasare.
countess ['kaʊntɪs] n contessa.
countless ['kaʊntlɪs] a innumerevole.
countrified ['kʌntrɪfaɪd] a rustico(a), campagnolo(a).
country ['kʌntrɪ] n paese m; (native land) patria; (as opposed to town) campagna; (region) regione f; **in the** ~ in campagna; **mountainous** ~ territorio montagnoso.
country and western (music) n musica country e western, country m.
country dancing n (Brit) danza popolare.
country house n villa in campagna.
countryman ['kʌntrɪmən] n (national) compatriota m; (rural) contadino.
countryside ['kʌntrɪsaɪd] n campagna.
country-wide ['kʌntrɪ'waɪd] a diffuso(a) in tutto il paese ♦ ad in tutto il paese.

county ['kauntɪ] *n* contea.
county town *n* (*Brit*) capoluogo.
coup, ~s [ku:, -z] *n* (*also*: ~ **d'état**) colpo di Stato; (*triumph*) bel colpo.
coupé [ku:'peɪ] *n* coupé *m inv*.
couple ['kʌpl] *n* coppia ♦ *vt* (*carriages*) agganciare; (*TECH*) accoppiare; (*ideas, names*) associare; **a ~ of** un paio di.
couplet ['kʌplɪt] *n* distico.
coupling ['kʌplɪŋ] *n* (*RAIL*) agganciamento.
coupon ['ku:pɔn] *n* (*voucher*) buono; (*COMM*) coupon *m inv*.
courage ['kʌrɪdʒ] *n* coraggio.
courageous [kə'reɪdʒəs] *a* coraggioso(a).
courgette [kuə'ʒɛt] *n* (*Brit*) zucchina.
courier ['kurɪə*] *n* corriere *m*; (*for tourists*) guida.
course [kɔ:s] *n* corso; (*of ship*) rotta; (*for golf*) campo; (*part of meal*) piatto; **first ~** primo piatto; **of ~** *ad* senz'altro, naturalmente; (**no) of ~ not!** certo che no!, no di certo!; **in the ~ of the next few days** nel corso dei prossimi giorni; **in due ~** a tempo debito; **~ (of action)** modo d'agire; **the best ~ would be to ...** la cosa migliore sarebbe ...; **we have no other ~ but to ...** non possiamo far altro che ...; **~ of lectures** corso di lezioni; **a ~ of treatment** (*MED*) una cura.
court [kɔ:t] *n* corte *f*; (*TENNIS*) campo ♦ *vt* (*woman*) fare la corte a; (*fig*: *favour, popularity*) cercare di conquistare; (: *death, disaster*) sfiorare, rasentare; **out of ~** (*LAW*: *settle*) in via amichevole; **to take to ~** citare in tribunale; **~ of appeal** corte d'appello.
courteous ['kɔ:tɪəs] *a* cortese.
courtesan [kɔ:tɪ'zæn] *n* cortigiana.
courtesy ['kɔ:təsɪ] *n* cortesia; **by ~ of** per gentile concessione di.
courtesy coach *n* autobus *m inv* gratuito (*di hotel, aeroporto etc*).
courtesy light *n* (*AUT*) luce *f* interna.
court-house ['kɔ:thaus] *n* (*US*) palazzo di giustizia.
courtier ['kɔ:tɪə*] *n* cortigiano/a.
courtmartial, *pl* **courtsmartial** ['kɔ:t'mɑ:ʃəl] *n* corte *f* marziale.
courtroom ['kɔ:trum] *n* tribunale *m*.
court shoe *n* scarpa *f* décolleté *inv*.
courtyard ['kɔ:tjɑ:d] *n* cortile *m*.
cousin ['kʌzn] *n* cugino/a.
cove [kəuv] *n* piccola baia.
covenant ['kʌvənənt] *n* accordo ♦ *vt*: **to ~ to do sth** impegnarsi (per iscritto) a fare qc.
Coventry ['kɔvəntrɪ] *n*: **to send sb to ~** (*fig*) dare l'ostracismo a qn.
cover ['kʌvə*] *vt* (*gen*) coprire; (*distance*) coprire, percorrere; (*PRESS*: *report on*) fare un servizio su ♦ *n* (*of pan*) coperchio; (*over furniture*) fodera; (*of book*) copertina; (*shelter*) riparo; (*COMM, INSURANCE*) copertura; **to take ~** mettersi al coperto; **under ~** al riparo; **under ~ of darkness** protetto dall'oscurità; **under separate ~**

(*COMM*) a parte, in plico separato; **£10 will ~ everything** 10 sterline saranno sufficienti.
cover up *vt* (*child, object*): **to ~ up (with)** coprire (di); (*fig*: *hide*: *truth, facts*) nascondere ♦ *vi*: **to ~ up for sb** (*fig*) coprire qn.
coverage ['kʌvərɪdʒ] *n* (*PRESS, TV, RADIO*): **to give full ~ to** fare un ampio servizio su.
coveralls ['kʌvərɔ:lz] *npl* (*US*) tuta.
cover charge *n* coperto.
covering ['kʌvərɪŋ] *n* copertura.
covering letter, (*US*) **cover letter** *n* lettera d'accompagnamento.
cover note *n* (*INSURANCE*) polizza (di assicurazione) provvisoria.
cover price *n* prezzo di copertina.
covert ['kʌvət] *a* nascosto(a); (*glance*) di sottecchi, furtivo(a).
cover-up ['kʌvərʌp] *n* occultamento (di informazioni).
covet ['kʌvɪt] *vt* bramare.
cow [kau] *n* vacca ♦ *cpd* femmina ♦ *vt* intimidire; **~ elephant** *n* elefantessa.
coward ['kauəd] *n* vigliacco/a.
cowardice ['kauədɪs] *n* vigliaccheria.
cowardly ['kauədlɪ] *a* vigliacco(a).
cowboy ['kaubɔɪ] *n* cow-boy *m inv*.
cower ['kauə*] *vi* acquattarsi.
cowshed ['kauʃɛd] *n* stalla.
cowslip ['kauslɪp] *n* (*BOT*) primula (odorata).
coxswain ['kɔksn] *n* (*abbr*: **cox**) timoniere *m*.
coy [kɔɪ] *a* falsamente timido(a).
coyote [kɔɪ'əutɪ] *n* coyote *m inv*.
cozy ['kəuzɪ] *a* (*US*) = **cosy**.
CP *n abbr* (= *Communist Party*) P.C. *m*.
cp. *abbr* (= *compare*) cfr.
c/p *abbr* (*Brit*) = **carriage paid**.
CPA *n abbr* (*US*) *see* **certified public accountant**.
CPI *n abbr* (*US*: = *Consumer Price Index*) indice dei prezzi al consumo.
Cpl. *abbr* = **corporal**.
CP/M *n abbr* (= *Control Program for Microcomputers*) CP/M *m*.
c.p.s. *abbr* (= *characters per second*) c.p.s.
CPSA *n abbr* (*Brit*: = *Civil and Public Services Association*) sindacato dei servizi pubblici.
CPU *n abbr see* **central processing unit**.
cr. *abbr* = **credit**; **creditor**.
crab [kræb] *n* granchio.
crab apple *n* mela selvatica.
crack [kræk] *n* (*split, slit*) fessura, crepa; incrinatura; (*noise*) schiocco; (: *of gun*) scoppio; (*joke*) battuta; (*col*: *attempt*): **to have a ~ at sth** tentare qc; (*DRUGS*) crack *m inv* ♦ *vt* spaccare; incrinare; (*whip*) schioccare; (*nut*) schiacciare; (*case, mystery*: *solve*) risolvere; (*code*) decifrare ♦ *cpd* (*athlete*) di prim'ordine; **to ~ jokes** (*col*) dire battute, scherzare; **to get ~ing** (*col*) darsi una mossa.
crack down on *vt fus* prendere serie misure contro, porre freno a.

crack up *vi* crollare.

crackdown ['krækdaun] *n* repressione *f*.

cracked [krækt] *a* (*col*) matto(a).

cracker ['krækə*] *n* cracker *m inv*; (*firework*) petardo; (*Christmas* ~) mortaretto natalizio (con sorpresa); **a ~ of a** ... (*Brit col*) un(a) ... formidabile; **he's ~s** (*Brit col*) è tocco.

crackle ['krækl] *vi* crepitare.

crackling ['kræklɪŋ] *n* crepitio; (*on radio, telephone*) disturbo; (*of pork*) cotenna croccante (del maiale).

cradle ['kreɪdl] *n* culla ♦ *vt* (*child*) tenere fra le braccia; (*object*) reggere tra le braccia.

craft [krɑːft] *n* mestiere *m*; (*cunning*) astuzia; (*boat*) naviglio.

craftsman ['krɑːftsmən] *n* artigiano.

craftsmanship ['krɑːftsmənʃɪp] *n* abilità.

crafty ['krɑːftɪ] *a* furbo(a), astuto(a).

crag [kræg] *n* roccia.

cram [kræm] *vt* (*fill*): **to ~ sth with** riempire qc di; (*put*): **to ~ sth into** stipare qc in.

cramming ['kræmɪŋ] *n* (*fig: pej*) sgobbare *m*.

cramp [kræmp] *n* crampo ♦ *vt* soffocare, impedire.

cramped [kræmpt] *a* ristretto(a).

crampon ['kræmpən] *n* (*CLIMBING*) rampone *m*.

cranberry ['krænbərɪ] *n* mirtillo.

crane [kreɪn] *n* gru *f inv* ♦ *vt, vi*: **to ~ forward, to ~ one's neck** allungare il collo.

cranium, pl crania ['kreɪnɪəm, 'kreɪnɪə] *n* cranio.

crank [kræŋk] *n* manovella; (*person*) persona stramba.

crankshaft ['kræŋkʃɑːft] *n* albero a gomiti.

cranky ['kræŋkɪ] *a* eccentrico(a); (*bad-tempered*): **to be ~** avere i nervi.

cranny ['krænɪ] *n see* **nook**.

crap [kræp] *n* (*col!*) fesserie *fpl*; **to have a ~** cacare (*!*).

crash [kræʃ] *n* fragore *m*; (*of car*) incidente *m*; (*of plane*) caduta; (*of business*) fallimento; (*STOCK EXCHANGE*) crollo ♦ *vt* fracassare ♦ *vi* (*plane*) fracassarsi; (*car*) avere un incidente; (*two cars*) scontrarsi; (*fig*) fallire, andare in rovina; **to ~ into** scontrarsi con; **he ~ed the car into a wall** andò a sbattere contro un muro con la macchina.

crash barrier *n* (*Brit AUT*) guardrail *m inv*.

crash course *n* corso intensivo.

crash helmet *n* casco.

crash landing *n* atterraggio di fortuna.

crass [kræs] *a* crasso(a).

crate [kreɪt] *n* gabbia.

crater ['kreɪtə*] *n* cratere *m*.

cravat(e) [krə'væt] *n* fazzoletto da collo.

crave [kreɪv] *vi*: **to ~ for** desiderare ardentemente.

craving ['kreɪvɪŋ] *n*: **~ (for)** (*for food, cigarettes etc*) (gran) voglia (di).

crawl [krɔːl] *vi* strisciare carponi; (*child*) andare a gattoni; (*vehicle*) avanzare lentamente ♦ *n* (*SWIMMING*) crawl *m*; **to ~**

to sb (*col*: *suck up*) arruffianarsi qn.

crayfish ['kreɪfɪʃ] *n* (*pl inv*) gambero (d'acqua dolce).

crayon ['kreɪən] *n* matita colorata.

craze [kreɪz] *n* mania.

crazed [kreɪzd] *a* (*look, person*) folle, pazzo(a); (*pottery, glaze*) incrinato(a).

crazy ['kreɪzɪ] *a* matto(a); **to go ~** uscir di senno, impazzire; **to be ~ about sb** (*col*: *keen*) essere pazzo di qn; **to be ~ about sth** andare matto per qc.

crazy paving *n* (*Brit*) lastricato a mosaico irregolare.

creak [kriːk] *vi* cigolare, scricchiolare.

cream [kriːm] *n* crema; (*fresh*) panna ♦ *a* (*colour*) color crema *inv*; **whipped ~** panna montata.

cream off *vt* (*best talents, part of profits*) portarsi via.

cream cake *n* torta alla panna.

cream cheese *n* formaggio fresco.

creamery ['kriːmərɪ] *n* (*shop*) latteria; (*factory*) caseificio.

creamy ['kriːmɪ] *a* cremoso(a).

crease [kriːs] *n* grinza; (*deliberate*) piega ♦ *vt* sgualcire ♦ *vi* sgualcirsi.

crease-resistant ['kriːsrɪzɪstənt] *a* ingualcibile.

create [kriː'eɪt] *vt* creare; (*fuss, noise*) fare.

creation [kriː'eɪʃən] *n* creazione *f*.

creative [kriː'eɪtɪv] *a* creativo(a).

creativity [kriːeɪ'tɪvɪtɪ] *n* creatività.

creator [kriː'eɪtə*] *n* creatore/trice.

creature ['kriːtʃə*] *n* creatura.

crèche, creche [krɛʃ] *n* asilo infantile.

credence ['kriːdns] *n* credenza, fede *f*.

credentials [krɪ'dɛnʃlz] *npl* (*papers*) credenziali *fpl*; (*letters of reference*) referenze *fpl*.

credibility [krɛdɪ'bɪlɪtɪ] *n* credibilità.

credible ['krɛdɪbl] *a* credibile; (*witness, source*) attendibile.

credit ['krɛdɪt] *n* credito; onore *m*; (*SCOL: esp US*) certificato del compimento di una parte del corso universitario ♦ *vt* (*COMM*) accreditare; (*believe: also*: **give ~ to**) credere, prestar fede a; **to ~ £5 to sb** accreditare 5 sterline a qn; **to ~ sb with sth** (*fig*) attribuire qc a qn; **on ~** a credito; **to one's ~** a proprio onore; **to take the ~ for** farsi il merito di; **to be in ~** (*person*) essere creditore(trice); (*bank account*) essere coperto(a); **he's a ~ to his family** fa onore alla sua famiglia; *see also* **credits**.

creditable ['krɛdɪtəbl] *a* che fa onore, degno(a) di lode.

credit account *n* conto di credito.

credit agency *n* (*Brit*) agenzia di analisi di credito.

credit balance *n* saldo attivo.

credit bureau *n* (*US*) agenzia di analisi di credito.

credit card *n* carta di credito.

credit control *n* controllo dei crediti.

credit facilities *npl* agevolazioni *fpl* creditizie.

credit limit *n* limite *m* di credito.

credit note *n* (*Brit*) nota di credito.

creditor ['krɛdɪtə*] *n* creditore/trice.

credits ['krɛdɪts] *npl* (*CINEMA*) titoli *mpl*.

credit transfer *n* bancogiro, postagiro.

creditworthy ['krɛdɪt'wə:ðɪ] *a* autorizzabile al credito.

credulity [krɪ'dju:lɪtɪ] *n* credulità.

creed [kri:d] *n* credo; dottrina.

creek [kri:k] *n* insenatura; (*US*) piccolo fiume *m*.

creel ['kri:l] *n* cestino per il pesce; (*also*: **lobster** ~) nassa.

creep [kri:p] *vi* (*pt, pp* **crept** [krɛpt]) avanzare furtivamente (*or* pian piano); (*plant*) arrampicarsi ♦ *n* (*col*): **he's a** ~ è un tipo viscido; **it gives me the** ~**s** (*col*) mi fa venire la pelle d'oca; **to** ~ **up on sb** avvicinarsi quatto quatto a qn; (*fig*: *old age etc*) cogliere qn alla sprovvista.

creeper ['kri:pə*] *n* pianta rampicante.

creepers ['kri:pəz] *npl* (*US*: *rompers*) tutina.

creepy ['kri:pɪ] *a* (*frightening*) che fa accapponare la pelle.

creepy-crawly ['kri:pɪ'krɔ:lɪ] *n* (*col*) bestiolina, insetto.

cremate [krɪ'meɪt] *vt* cremare.

cremation [krɪ'meɪʃən] *n* cremazione *f*.

crematorium, *pl* **crematoria** [krɛmə'tɔ:rɪəm, -'tɔ:rɪə] *n* forno crematorio.

creosote ['krɪəsəut] *n* creosoto.

crêpe [kreɪp] *n* crespo.

crêpe bandage *n* (*Brit*) fascia elastica.

crêpe paper *n* carta crespa.

crêpe sole *n* suola di para.

crept [krɛpt] *pt, pp of* **creep**.

crescendo [krɪ'ʃɛndəu] *n* crescendo.

crescent ['krɛsnt] *n* (*shape*) mezzaluna; (*street*) strada semicircolare.

cress [krɛs] *n* crescione *m*.

crest [krɛst] *n* cresta; (*of helmet*) pennacchiera; (*of coat of arms*) cimiero.

crestfallen ['krɛstfɔ:lən] *a* mortificato(a).

Crete ['kri:t] *n* Creta.

crevasse [krɪ'væs] *n* crepaccio.

crevice ['krɛvɪs] *n* fessura, crepa.

crew [kru:] *n* equipaggio; (*CINEMA*) troupe *f inv*; (*gang*) banda, compagnia.

crew-cut ['kru:kʌt] *n*: **to have a** ~ avere i capelli a spazzola.

crew-neck ['kru:nɛk] *n* girocollo.

crib [krɪb] *n* culla; (*REL*) presepio ♦ *vt* (*col*) copiare.

cribbage ['krɪbɪdʒ] *n* tipo di gioco di carte.

crick [krɪk] *n* crampo; ~ **in the neck** torcicollo.

cricket ['krɪkɪt] *n* (*insect*) grillo; (*game*) cricket *m*.

cricketer ['krɪkɪtə*] *n* giocatore *m* di cricket.

crime [kraɪm] *n* (*in general*) criminalità; (*instance*) crimine *m*, delitto.

crime wave *n* ondata di criminalità.

criminal ['krɪmɪnl] *a, n* criminale (*m/f*); **C**~ **Investigation Department (CID)** ≈ polizia giudiziaria.

crimp [krɪmp] *vt* arricciare.

crimson ['krɪmzn] *a* color cremisi *inv*.

cringe [krɪndʒ] *vi* acquattarsi; (*fig*) essere servile.

crinkle ['krɪŋkl] *vt* arricciare, increspare.

cripple ['krɪpl] *n* zoppo/a ♦ *vt* azzoppare; (*ship, plane*) avariare; (*production, exports*) rovinare; ~**d with arthritis** sciancato(a) per l'artrite.

crippling ['krɪplɪŋ] *a* (*taxes, debts*) esorbitante; (*disease*) molto debilitante.

crisis, *pl* **crises** ['kraɪsɪs, -si:z] *n* crisi *f inv*.

crisp [krɪsp] *a* croccante; (*fig*) frizzante; vivace; deciso(a).

crisps [krɪsps] *npl* (*Brit*) patatine *fpl* fritte.

criss-cross ['krɪskrɔs] *a* incrociato(a) ♦ *vt* incrociarsi.

criterion, *pl* **criteria** [kraɪ'tɪərɪən, -'tɪərɪə] *n* criterio.

critic ['krɪtɪk] *n* critico/a.

critical ['krɪtɪkl] *a* critico(a); **to be** ~ **of sb/ sth** criticare qn/qc, essere critico verso qn/qc.

critically ['krɪtɪklɪ] *ad* criticamente; ~ **ill** gravemente malato.

criticism ['krɪtɪsɪzəm] *n* critica.

criticize ['krɪtɪsaɪz] *vt* criticare.

critique [krɪ'ti:k] *n* critica, saggio critico.

croak [krəuk] *vi* gracchiare.

crochet ['krəuʃeɪ] *n* lavoro all'uncinetto.

crock [krɔk] *n* coccio; (*col*: *person*: *also*: **old** ~) rottame *m*; (: *car etc*) caffettiera, rottame *m*.

crockery ['krɔkərɪ] *n* vasellame *m*; (*plates, cups etc*) stoviglie *fpl*.

crocodile ['krɔkədaɪl] *n* coccodrillo.

crocus ['krəukəs] *n* croco.

croft [krɔft] *n* (*Brit*) piccolo podere *m*.

crofter ['krɔftə*] *n* (*Brit*) affittuario di un piccolo podere.

crone [krəun] *n* strega.

crony ['krəunɪ] *n* (*col*) amicone/a.

crook [kruk] *n* truffatore *m*; (*of shepherd*) bastone *m*.

crooked ['krukɪd] *a* curvo(a), storto(a); (*person, action*) disonesto(a).

crop [krɔp] *n* raccolto; (*produce*) coltivazione *f*; (*of bird*) gozzo, ingluvie *f* ♦ *vt* (*cut*: *hair*) tagliare, rapare; (*subj*: *animals*: *grass*) brucare.

crop up *vi* presentarsi.

cropper ['krɔpə*] *n*: **to come a** ~ (*col*) fare fiasco.

crop spraying *n* spruzzatura di antiparassitari.

croquet ['krəukeɪ] *n* croquet *m*.

croquette [krə'kɛt] *n* crocchetta.

cross [krɔs] *n* croce *f*; (*BIOL*) incrocio ♦ *vt* (*street etc*) attraversare; (*arms, legs, BIOL*) incrociare; (*cheque*) sbarrare; (*thwart*: *person, plan*) contrastare, ostacolare ♦ *vi*: **the boat** ~**es from ... to ...** la barca fa la

traversata da ... a ... ♦ *a* di cattivo umore; **to ~ o.s.** fare il segno della croce, segnarsi; **we have a ~ed line** (*Brit: on telephone*) c'è un'interferenza; **they've got their lines ~ed** (*fig*) si sono fraintesi; **to be/get ~ with sb (about sth)** essere arrabbiato(a)/arrabbiarsi con qn (per qc).
cross out *vt* cancellare.
cross over *vi* attraversare.
crossbar ['krɔsbɑ:*] *n* traversa.
crossbreed ['krɔsbri:d] *n* incrocio.
cross-Channel ferry ['krɔs'tʃænl-] *n* traghetto che attraversa la Manica.
cross-check ['krɔstʃɛk] *n* controprova ♦ *vi* fare una controprova.
crosscountry (race) [krɔs'kʌntrɪ-] *n* crosscountry *m inv*.
cross-examination ['krɔsɪgzæmɪ'neɪʃən] *n* (*LAW*) interrogatorio in contraddittorio.
cross-examine ['krɔsɪg'zæmɪn] *vt* (*LAW*) interrogare in contraddittorio.
cross-eyed ['krɔsaɪd] *a* strabico(a).
crossfire ['krɔsfaɪə*] *n* fuoco incrociato.
crossing ['krɔsɪŋ] *n* incrocio; (*sea-passage*) traversata; (*also:* **pedestrian ~**) passaggio pedonale.
cross-purposes ['krɔs'pə:pəsɪz] *npl*: **to be at ~ with sb** (*misunderstand*) fraintendere qn; **to talk at ~** fraintendersi.
cross-reference ['krɔs'rɛfərəns] *n* rinvio, rimando.
crossroads ['krɔsrəudz] *n* incrocio.
cross section *n* (*BIOL*) sezione *f* trasversale; (*in population*) settore *m* rappresentativo.
crosswalk ['krɔswɔ:k] *n* (*US*) strisce *fpl* pedonali, passaggio pedonale.
crosswind ['krɔswɪnd] *n* vento di traverso.
crosswise ['krɔswaɪz] *ad* di traverso.
crossword ['krɔswə:d] *n* cruciverba *m inv*.
crotch [krɔtʃ] *n* (*ANAT*) inforcatura; (*of garment*) pattina.
crotchet ['krɔtʃɪt] *n* (*MUS*) semiminima.
crotchety ['krɔtʃɪtɪ] *a* (*person*) burbero(a).
crouch [krautʃ] *vi* acquattarsi; rannicchiarsi.
croup [kru:p] *n* (*MED*) crup *m*.
crouton ['kru:tɔn] *n* crostino.
crow [krəu] *n* (*bird*) cornacchia; (*of cock*) canto del gallo ♦ *vi* (*cock*) cantare; (*fig*) vantarsi; cantar vittoria.
crowbar ['krəubɑ:*] *n* piede *m* di porco.
crowd [kraud] *n* folla ♦ *vt* affollare, stipare ♦ *vi* affollarsi; **~s of people** un sacco di gente.
crowded ['kraudɪd] *a* affollato(a); **~ with** stipato(a) di.
crowd scene *n* (*CINEMA, THEATRE*) scena di massa.
crown [kraun] *n* corona; (*of head*) calotta cranica; (*of hat*) cocuzzolo; (*of hill*) cima ♦ *vt* incoronare; (*tooth*) incapsulare; **and to ~ it all ...** (*fig*) e per giunta ..., e come se non bastasse ....
crown court *n* (*Brit*) ≈ corte *f* d'assise.
crowning ['kraunɪŋ] *a* (*achievement, glory*) supremo(a).

crown jewels *npl* gioielli *mpl* della Corona.
crown prince *n* principe *m* ereditario.
crow's-feet ['krəuzfi:t] *npl* zampe *fpl* di gallina.
crow's-nest ['krəuznɛst] *n* (*on sailing-ship*) coffa.
crucial ['kru:ʃl] *a* cruciale, decisivo(a); **~ to** essenziale per.
crucifix ['kru:sɪfɪks] *n* crocifisso.
crucifixion [kru:sɪ'fɪkʃən] *n* crocifissione *f*.
crucify ['kru:sɪfaɪ] *vt* crocifiggere, mettere in croce; (*fig*) distruggere, fare a pezzi.
crude [kru:d] *a* (*materials*) greggio(a); non raffinato(a); (*fig: basic*) crudo(a), primitivo(a); (: *vulgar*) rozzo(a), grossolano(a).
crude (oil) *n* (petrolio) greggio.
cruel ['kruəl] *a* crudele.
cruelty ['kruəltɪ] *n* crudeltà *f inv*.
cruet ['kru:ɪt] *n* ampolla.
cruise [kru:z] *n* crociera ♦ *vi* andare a velocità di crociera; (*taxi*) circolare.
cruise missile *n* missile *m* cruise *inv*.
cruiser ['kru:zə*] *n* incrociatore *m*.
cruising speed ['kru:zɪŋ-] *n* velocità *f inv* di crociera.
crumb [krʌm] *n* briciola.
crumble ['krʌmbl] *vt* sbriciolare ♦ *vi* sbriciolarsi; (*plaster etc*) sgrettolarsi; (*land, earth*) franare; (*building, fig*) crollare.
crumbly ['krʌmblɪ] *a* friabile.
crummy ['krʌmɪ] *a* (*col: cheap*) di infima categoria; (: *depressed*) giù *inv*.
crumpet ['krʌmpɪt] *n* specie di frittella.
crumple ['krʌmpl] *vt* raggrinzare, spiegazzare.
crunch [krʌntʃ] *vt* sgranocchiare; (*underfoot*) scricchiolare ♦ *n* (*fig*) punto *or* momento cruciale.
crunchy ['krʌntʃɪ] *a* croccante.
crusade [kru:'seɪd] *n* crociata ♦ *vi* (*fig*): **to ~ for/against** fare una crociata per/contro.
crusader [kru:'seɪdə*] *n* crociato; (*fig*): **~ (for)** sostenitore/trice (di).
crush [krʌʃ] *n* folla; (*love*): **to have a ~ on sb** avere una cotta per qn; (*drink*): **lemon ~** spremuta di limone ♦ *vt* schiacciare; (*crumple*) sgualcire; (*grind, break up: garlic, ice*) tritare; (: *grapes*) pigiare.
crush barrier *n* (*Brit*) transenna.
crushing ['krʌʃɪŋ] *a* schiacciante.
crust [krʌst] *n* crosta.
crustacean [krʌs'teɪʃən] *n* crostaceo.
crusty ['krʌstɪ] *a* (*loaf*) croccante.
crutch [krʌtʃ] *n* (*MED*) gruccia; (*support*) sostegno; (*also:* **crotch**) pattina.
crux [krʌks] *n* nodo.
cry [kraɪ] *vi* piangere; (*shout: also:* **~ out**) urlare ♦ *n* urlo, grido; (*of animal*) verso; **to ~ for help** gridare aiuto; **what are you ~ing about?** perché piangi?; **she had a good ~** si è fatta un bel pianto; **it's a far ~ from ...** (*fig*) è tutt'un'altra cosa da ....
cry off *vi* ritirarsi.
crying ['kraɪɪŋ] *a* (*fig*) palese; urgente.
crypt [krɪpt] *n* cripta.

cryptic ['krɪptɪk] a ermetico(a).

crystal ['krɪstl] n cristallo.

crystal-clear ['krɪstl'klɪə*] a cristallino(a); (fig) chiaro(a) (come il sole).

crystallize ['krɪstəlaɪz] vi cristallizzarsi ♦ vt (fig) concretizzare, concretare; ~d fruits (Brit) frutta candita.

CSA n abbr = Confederate States of America.

CSC n abbr (= Civil Service Commission) commissione per il reclutamento dei funzionari statali.

CSE n abbr (Brit: = Certificate of Secondary Education) diploma di istruzione superiore.

CSEU n abbr (Brit: = Confederation of Shipbuilding and Engineering Unions) confederazione dei sindacati della costruzione navale e meccanica.

CS gas n (Brit) tipo di gas lacrimogeno.

CST abbr (US: = central standard time) fuso orario.

CSU n abbr (Brit: = Civil Service Union) sindacato dei dipendenti statali.

CT abbr (US POST) = Connecticut.

ct abbr = **carat**.

cu. abbr = **cubic**.

cub [kʌb] n cucciolo; (also: ~ **scout**) lupetto.

Cuba ['kju:bə] n Cuba.

Cuban ['kju:bən] a, n cubano(a).

cubbyhole ['kʌbɪhəul] n angolino.

cube [kju:b] n cubo ♦ vt (MATH) elevare al cubo.

cube root n radice f cubica.

cubic ['kju:bɪk] a cubico(a); ~ **metre** etc metro etc cubo; ~ **capacity** (AUT) cilindrata.

cubicle ['kju:bɪkl] n scompartimento separato; cabina.

cuckoo ['kuku:] n cucù m inv.

cuckoo clock n orologio a cucù.

cucumber ['kju:kʌmbə*] n cetriolo.

cud [kʌd] n: **to chew the** ~ ruminare.

cuddle ['kʌdl] vt abbracciare, coccolare ♦ vi abbracciarsi.

cuddly ['kʌdlɪ] a da coccolare.

cudgel ['kʌdʒl] n randello ♦ vt: **to** ~ **one's brains** scervellarsi, spremere le meningi.

cue [kju:] n stecca; (THEATRE etc) segnale m.

cuff [kʌf] n (of shirt, coat etc) polsino; (US: on trousers) = **turnup**; (blow) schiaffo ♦ vt dare uno schiaffo a; **off the** ~ ad improvvisando.

cufflink ['kʌflɪŋk] n gemello.

cu. ft. abbr = cubic feet.

cu. in. abbr = cubic inches.

cuisine [kwɪ'zi:n] n cucina.

cul-de-sac ['kʌldəsæk] n vicolo cieco.

culinary ['kʌlɪnərɪ] a culinario(a).

cull [kʌl] vt (kill selectively: animals) selezionare e abbattere.

culminate ['kʌlmɪneɪt] vi: **to** ~ **in** culminare con.

culmination [kʌlmɪ'neɪʃən] n culmine m.

culottes [kju:'lɒts] npl gonna f pantalone inv.

culpable ['kʌlpəbl] a colpevole.

culprit ['kʌlprɪt] n colpevole m/f.

cult [kʌlt] n culto.

cult figure n idolo.

cultivate ['kʌltɪveɪt] vt (also fig) coltivare.

cultivation [kʌltɪ'veɪʃən] n coltivazione f.

cultural ['kʌltʃərəl] a culturale.

culture ['kʌltʃə*] n (also fig) cultura.

cultured ['kʌltʃəd] a colto(a).

cumbersome ['kʌmbəsəm] a ingombrante.

cumin ['kʌmɪn] n (spice) cumino.

cumulative ['kju:mjulətɪv] a cumulativo(a).

cunning ['kʌnɪŋ] n astuzia, furberia ♦ a astuto(a), furbo(a); (clever: device, idea) ingegnoso(a).

cup [kʌp] n tazza; (prize) coppa; **a** ~ **of tea** una tazza di tè.

cupboard ['kʌbəd] n armadio.

cup final n (Brit FOOTBALL) finale f di coppa.

Cupid ['kju:pɪd] n Cupido; (figurine): **c**~ cupido.

cupidity [kju:'pɪdɪtɪ] n cupidigia.

cupola ['kju:pələ] n cupola.

cup-tie ['kʌptaɪ] n (Brit FOOTBALL) partita di coppa.

curable ['kjuərəbl] a curabile.

curate ['kjuərɪt] n cappellano.

curator [kjuə'reɪtə*] n direttore m (di museo etc).

curb [kə:b] vt tenere a freno; (expenditure) limitare ♦ n freno; (US) = **kerb**.

curd cheese [kə:d-] n cagliata.

curdle ['kə:dl] vi cagliare.

curds [kə:dz] npl latte m cagliato.

cure [kjuə*] vt guarire; (CULIN) trattare; affumicare; essiccare ♦ n rimedio; **to be** ~**d of sth** essere guarito(a) da qc.

cure-all ['kjuərɔ:l] n (also fig) panacea, toccasana m inv.

curfew ['kə:fju:] n coprifuoco.

curio ['kjuərɪəu] n curiosità f inv.

curiosity [kjuərɪ'ɒsɪtɪ] n curiosità.

curious ['kjuərɪəs] a curioso(a); **I'm** ~ **about him** m'incuriosisce.

curiously ['kjuərɪəslɪ] ad con curiosità; (strangely) stranamente; ~ **enough**, ... per quanto possa sembrare strano, ...

curl [kə:l] n riccio; (of smoke etc) anello ♦ vt ondulare; (tightly) arricciare ♦ vi arricciarsi. **curl up** vi avvolgersi a spirale; rannicchiarsi.

curler ['kə:lə*] n bigodino; (SPORT) giocatore/trice di curling.

curlew ['kə:lu:] n chiurlo.

curling ['kə:lɪŋ] n (SPORT) curling m.

curling tongs, (US) **curling irons** npl (for hair) arricciacapelli m inv.

curly ['kə:lɪ] a ricciuto(a).

currant ['kʌrnt] n uva passa.

currency ['kʌrnsɪ] n moneta; **foreign** ~ divisa estera; **to gain** ~ (fig) acquistare larga diffusione.

current ['kʌrnt] a corrente; (tendency, price, event) attuale ♦ n corrente f; **in** ~ **use** in uso corrente, d'uso comune; **the** ~ **issue of a magazine** l'ultimo numero di una rivista;

direct/alternating ~ (*ELEC*) corrente continua/alternata.

current account *n* (*Brit*) conto corrente.

current affairs *npl* attualità *fpl*.

current assets (*COMM*) attivo realizzabile e disponibile.

current liabilities *npl* (*COMM*) passività *fpl* correnti.

currently ['kʌrntlɪ] *ad* attualmente.

curriculum, *pl* ~s *or* **curricula** [kə'rɪkjuləm, -lə] *n* curriculum *m inv*.

curriculum vitae (CV) [-'viːtaɪ] *n* curriculum vitae *m inv*.

curry ['kʌrɪ] *n* curry *m inv* ♦ *vt*: **to ~ favour with** cercare di attirarsi i favori di; **chicken** ~ pollo al curry.

curry powder *n* curry *m*.

curse [kəːs] *vt* maledire ♦ *vi* bestemmiare ♦ *n* maledizione *f*; bestemmia.

cursor ['kəːsə*] *n* (*COMPUT*) cursore *m*.

cursory ['kəːsərɪ] *a* superficiale.

curt [kəːt] *a* secco(a).

curtail [kəː'teɪl] *vt* (*visit etc*) accorciare; (*expenses etc*) ridurre, decurtare.

curtain ['kəːtn] *n* tenda; (*THEATRE*) sipario; **to draw the** ~s (*together*) chiudere *or* tirare le tende; (*apart*) aprire le tende.

curtain call *n* (*THEATRE*) chinata alla ribalta.

curts(e)y ['kəːtsɪ] *n* inchino, riverenza ♦ *vi* fare un inchino *or* una riverenza.

curvature ['kəːvətʃə*] *n* curvatura.

curve [kəːv] *n* curva ♦ *vt* curvare ♦ *vi* curvarsi; (*road*) fare una curva.

curved [kəːvd] *a* curvo(a).

cushion ['kuʃən] *n* cuscino ♦ *vt* (*shock*) fare da cuscinetto a.

cushy ['kuʃɪ] *a* (*col*): **a** ~ **job** un lavoro di tutto riposo; **to have a** ~ **time** spassarsela.

custard ['kʌstəd] *n* (*for pouring*) crema.

custard powder *n* (*Brit*) crema pasticcera in polvere.

custodian [kʌs'təudɪən] *n* custode *m/f*; (*of museum etc*) soprintendente *m/f*.

custody ['kʌstədɪ] *n* (*of child*) custodia; (*for offenders*) arresto; **to take sb into** ~ mettere qn in detenzione preventiva; **in the** ~ **of** alla custodia di.

custom ['kʌstəm] *n* costume *m*, usanza; (*LAW*) consuetudine *f*; (*COMM*) clientela; *see also* **customs**.

customary ['kʌstəmərɪ] *a* consueto(a); **it is** ~ **to do** è consuetudine fare.

custom-built ['kʌstəm'bɪlt] *a* *see* **custom-made**.

customer ['kʌstəmə*] *n* cliente *m/f*; **he's an awkward** ~ (*col*) è un tipo incontentabile.

customer profile *n* profilo del cliente.

customized ['kʌstəmaɪzd] *a* personalizzato(a); (*car*) fuoriserie *inv*.

custom-made ['kʌstəm'meɪd] *a* (*clothes*) fatto(a) su misura; (*other goods*: *also*: **custom-built**) fatto(a) su ordinazione.

customs ['kʌstəmz] *npl* dogana; **to go through (the)** ~ passare la dogana.

Customs and Excise *n* (*Brit*) Ufficio Dazi e Dogana.

customs duty *n* dazio doganale.

customs officer *n* doganiere *m*.

cut [kʌt] *vb* (*pt*, *pp* **cut**) *vt* tagliare; (*shape*, *make*) intagliare; (*reduce*) ridurre; (*col*: *avoid*: *class*, *lecture*, *appointment*) saltare ♦ *vi* tagliare; (*intersect*) tagliarsi ♦ *n* taglio; (*in salary etc*) riduzione *f*; **cold** ~s *npl* (*US*) affettati *mpl*; **power** ~ mancanza di corrente elettrica; **to** ~ **one's finger** tagliarsi un dito; **to get one's hair** ~ farsi tagliare i capelli; **to** ~ **a tooth** mettere un dente; **to** ~ **sb/sth short** interrompere qn/qc; **to** ~ **sb dead** ignorare qn completamente.

cut back *vt* (*plants*) tagliare; (*production*, *expenditure*) ridurre.

cut down *vt* (*tree*) abbattere; (*consumption*, *expenses*) ridurre; **to** ~ **sb down to size** (*fig*) sgonfiare *or* ridimensionare qn.

cut down on *vt fus* ridurre.

cut in *vi* (*interrupt conversation*): **to** ~ **in (on)** intromettersi (in); (*AUT*) tagliare la strada (a).

cut off *vt* tagliare; (*fig*) isolare; **we've been** ~ **off** (*TEL*) è caduta la linea.

cut out *vt* tagliare; (*picture*) ritagliare.

cut up *vt* (*gen*) tagliare; (*chop*: *food*) sminuzzare.

cut-and-dried ['kʌtən'draɪd] *a* (*also*: **cut-and-dry**) assodato(a).

cutaway ['kʌtəweɪ] *a*, *n*: ~ **(drawing)** spaccato.

cutback ['kʌtbæk] *n* riduzione *f*.

cute [kjuːt] *a* grazioso(a); (*clever*) astuto(a).

cut glass *n* cristallo.

cuticle ['kjuːtɪkl] *n* (*on nail*) pellicina, cuticola.

cutlery ['kʌtlərɪ] *n* posate *fpl*.

cutlet ['kʌtlɪt] *n* costoletta.

cutoff ['kʌtɔf] *n* (*also*: ~ **point**) limite *m*.

cutoff switch *n* interruttore *m*.

cutout ['kʌtaut] *n* (*switch*) interruttore *m*; (*paper*, *cardboard figure*) ritaglio.

cut-price ['kʌt'praɪs], (*US*) **cut-rate** ['kʌt'reɪt] *a* a prezzo ridotto.

cutthroat ['kʌtθrəut] *n* assassino ♦ *a*: ~ **competition** concorrenza spietata.

cutting ['kʌtɪŋ] *a* tagliente; (*fig*) pungente ♦ *n* (*Brit*: *PRESS*) ritaglio (di giornale); (: *RAIL*) trincea; (*CINEMA*) montaggio.

cuttlefish ['kʌtlfɪʃ] *n* seppia.

cut-up ['kʌtʌp] *a* stravolto(a).

CV *n abbr see* **curriculum vitae**.

C & W *n abbr* = **country and western (music)**.

cwo *abbr* = **cash with order**.

cwt. *abbr* = **hundredweight**.

cyanide ['saɪənaɪd] *n* cianuro.

cybernetics [saɪbə'nɛtɪks] *n* cibernetica.

cyclamen ['sɪkləmən] *n* ciclamino.

cycle ['saɪkl] *n* ciclo; (*bicycle*) bicicletta ♦ *vi* andare in bicicletta.

cycle race *n* gara *or* corsa ciclistica.

cycle rack n portabiciclette m inv.
cycling ['saɪklɪŋ] n ciclismo; **to go on a ~ holiday** (Brit) fare una vacanza in bicicletta.
cyclist ['saɪklɪst] n ciclista m/f.
cyclone ['saɪkləun] n ciclone m.
cygnet ['sɪgnɪt] n cigno giovane.
cylinder ['sɪlɪndə*] n cilindro.
cylinder capacity n cilindrata.
cylinder head n testata.
cylinder head gasket n guarnizione f della testata del cilindro.
cymbals ['sɪmblz] npl cembali mpl.
cynic ['sɪnɪk] n cinico/a.
cynical ['sɪnɪkl] a cinico(a).
cynicism ['sɪnɪsɪzəm] n cinismo.
CYO n abbr (US) = Catholic Youth Organization.
cypress ['saɪprɪs] n cipresso.
Cypriot ['sɪprɪət] a, n cipriota (m/f).
Cyprus ['saɪprəs] n Cipro.
cyst [sɪst] n cisti f inv.
cystitis [sɪ'staɪtɪs] n cistite f.
CZ n abbr (US: = Canal Zone) zona del Canale di Panama.
czar [zɑː*] n zar m inv.
Czech [tʃɛk] a ceco/a ♦ n ceco/a; (LING) ceco.
Czechoslovak [tʃɛkə'sləuvæk] a, n = **Czechoslovakian**.
Czechoslovakia [tʃɛkəslə'vækɪə] n Cecoslovacchia.
Czechoslovakian [tʃɛkəslə'vækɪən] a, n cecoslovacco(a).

D

D, d [diː] n (letter) D, d f or m inv; (MUS): **D** re m; **D for David,** (US) **D for Dog** ≈ D come Domodossola.
D abbr (US POL) = **democrat(ic).**
d abbr (Brit: old) = **penny.**
d. abbr = **died.**
DA n abbr (US) see **district attorney.**
dab [dæb] vt (eyes, wound) tamponare; (paint, cream) applicare (con leggeri colpetti); **a ~ of paint** un colpetto di vernice.
dabble ['dæbl] vi: **to ~ in** occuparsi (da dilettante) di.
Dacca ['dækə] n Dacca f.
dachshund ['dækshund] n bassotto.
dad, daddy [dæd, 'dædɪ] n babbo, papà m inv.
daddy-long-legs [dædɪ'lɔŋlɛgz] n tipula, zanzarone m.
daffodil ['dæfədɪl] n trombone m, giunchiglia.
daft [dɑːft] a sciocco(a); **to be ~ about sb** perdere la testa per qn; **to be ~ about sth** andare pazzo per qc.

dagger ['dægə*] n pugnale m.
dahlia ['deɪljə] n dalia.
daily ['deɪlɪ] a quotidiano(a), giornaliero(a) ♦ n quotidiano; (Brit: servant) donna di servizio ♦ ad tutti i giorni; **twice ~** due volte al giorno.
dainty ['deɪntɪ] a delicato(a), grazioso(a).
dairy ['dɛərɪ] n (shop) latteria; (on farm) caseificio ♦ cpd caseario(a).
dairy cow n mucca da latte.
dairy farm n caseificio.
dairy produce n latticini mpl.
dais ['deɪɪs] n pedana, palco.
daisy ['deɪzɪ] n margherita.
daisy wheel n (on printer) margherita.
daisy-wheel printer n stampante f a margherita.
Dakar ['dækə*] n Dakar f.
dale [deɪl] n valle f.
dally ['dælɪ] vi trastullarsi.
dalmatian [dæl'meɪʃən] n (dog) dalmata m.
dam [dæm] n diga; (reservoir) bacino artificiale ♦ vt sbarrare; costruire dighe su.
damage ['dæmɪdʒ] n danno, danni mpl; (fig) danno ♦ vt danneggiare; (fig) recar danno a; **~ to property** danni materiali.
damages ['dæmɪdʒɪz] npl (LAW) danni mpl; **to pay £5000 in ~** pagare 5000 sterline di indennizzo.
damaging ['dæmɪdʒɪŋ] a: **~ (to)** nocivo(a) (a).
Damascus [də'mɑːskəs] n Damasco f.
dame [deɪm] n (title, US col) donna; (THEATRE) vecchia signora (ruolo comico di donna recitato da un uomo).
damn [dæm] vt condannare; (curse) maledire ♦ n (col): **I don't give a ~** non me ne importa un fico ♦ a (col): **this ~ ...** questo maledetto ...; **~ (it)!** accidenti!
damnable ['dæmnəbl] a (col: behaviour) vergognoso(a); (: weather) schifoso(a).
damnation [dæm'neɪʃən] n (REL) dannazione f ♦ excl (col) dannazione!, diavolo!
damning ['dæmɪŋ] a (evidence) schiacciante.
damp [dæmp] a umido(a) ♦ n umidità, umido ♦ vt (also: **~en**) (cloth, rag) inumidire, bagnare; (enthusiasm etc) spegnere.
dampcourse ['dæmpkɔːs] n strato m isolante antiumido inv.
damper ['dæmpə*] n (MUS) sordina; (of fire) valvola di tiraggio; **to put a ~ on sth** (fig: atmosphere) gelare; (: enthusiasm) far sbollire.
dampness ['dæmpnɪs] n umidità, umido.
damson ['dæmzən] n susina damaschina.
dance [dɑːns] n danza, ballo; (ball) ballo ♦ vi ballare; **to ~ about** saltellare.
dance hall n dancing m inv, sala da ballo.
dancer ['dɑːnsə*] n danzatore/trice; (professional) ballerino/a.
dancing ['dɑːnsɪŋ] n danza, ballo.
D and C n abbr (MED: = dilation and curettage) raschiamento.
dandelion ['dændɪlaɪən] n dente m di leone.

dandruff ['dændrəf] n forfora.
dandy ['dændɪ] n dandy m inv, elegantone m ♦ a (US col) fantastico(a).
Dane [deɪn] n danese m/f.
danger ['deɪndʒə*] n pericolo; **there is a ~ of fire** c'è pericolo di incendio; **in ~** in pericolo; **out of ~** fuori pericolo; **he was in ~ of falling** rischiava di cadere.
danger list n (MED): **on the ~ list** in prognosi riservata.
dangerous ['deɪndʒrəs] a pericoloso(a).
dangerously ['deɪndʒrəslɪ] ad: **~ ill** in pericolo di vita.
danger zone n area di pericolo.
dangle ['dæŋgl] vt dondolare; (fig) far balenare ♦ vi pendolare.
Danish ['deɪnɪʃ] a danese ♦ n (LING) danese m.
Danish pastry n dolce m di pasta sfoglia.
dank [dæŋk] a freddo(a) e umido(a).
Danube ['dænjuːb] n: **the ~** il Danubio.
dapper ['dæpə*] a lindo(a).
Dardanelles [dɑːdə'nelz] npl Dardanelli mpl.
dare [dɛə*] vt: **to ~ sb to do** sfidare qn a fare ♦ vi: **to ~ (to) do sth** osare fare qc; **I ~n't tell him** (Brit) non oso dirglielo; **I ~ say he'll turn up** immagino che spunterà.
daredevil ['dɛədevl] n scavezzacollo m/f.
Dar-es-Salaam ['dɑːrɛssə'lɑːm] n Dar-es-Salaam f.
daring ['dɛərɪŋ] a audace, ardito(a).
dark [dɑːk] a (night, room) buio(a), scuro(a); (colour, complexion) scuro(a); (fig) cupo(a), tetro(a), nero(a) ♦ n: **in the ~** al buio; **it is/is getting ~** è/si sta facendo buio; **in the ~ about** (fig) all'oscuro di; **after ~** a notte fatta; **~ chocolate** cioccolata amara.
darken ['dɑːkən] vt (room) oscurare; (photo, painting) far scuro(a) ♦ vi oscurarsi; imbrunirsi.
dark glasses npl occhiali mpl scuri.
darkly ['dɑːklɪ] ad (gloomily) cupamente, con aria cupa; (in a sinister way) minacciosamente.
darkness ['dɑːknɪs] n oscurità, buio.
darkroom ['dɑːkruːm] n camera oscura.
darling ['dɑːlɪŋ] a caro(a) ♦ n tesoro.
darn [dɑːn] vt rammendare.
dart [dɑːt] n freccetta ♦ vi: **to ~ towards** (also: **make a ~ towards**) precipitarsi verso; **to ~ along** passare come un razzo; **to ~ away** guizzare via; see also **darts**.
dartboard ['dɑːtbɔːd] n bersaglio (per freccette).
darts [dɑːts] n tiro al bersaglio (con freccette).
dash [dæʃ] n (sign) lineetta; (small quantity: of liquid) goccio, goccino; (: of soda) spruzzo ♦ vt (missile) gettare; (hopes) infrangere ♦ vi: **to ~ towards** (also: **make a ~ towards**) precipitarsi verso.
dash away vi scappare via.
dashboard ['dæʃbɔːd] n cruscotto.
dashing ['dæʃɪŋ] a ardito(a).
dastardly ['dæstədlɪ] a vile.

data ['deɪtə] npl dati mpl.
database ['deɪtəbeɪs] n database m, base f di dati.
data capture n registrazione f or rilevazione f di dati.
data processing n elaborazione f (elettronica) dei dati.
data transmission n trasmissione f di dati.
date [deɪt] n data; (appointment) appuntamento; (fruit) dattero ♦ vt datare; (col: girl etc) uscire con; **what's the ~ today?** quanti ne abbiamo oggi?; **~ of birth** data di nascita; **closing ~** scadenza, termine m; **to ~** ad fino a oggi; **out of ~** scaduto(a); (old-fashioned) passato(a) di moda; **up to ~** moderno(a); aggiornato(a); **to bring up to ~** (correspondence, information) aggiornare; (method) modernizzare; (person) aggiornare, mettere al corrente; **~d the 13th** datato il 13; **thank you for your letter ~d 5th July** or (US) **July 5th** la ringrazio per la sua lettera in data 5 luglio.
dated ['deɪtɪd] a passato(a) di moda.
dateline ['deɪtlaɪn] n linea del cambiamento di data.
date stamp n timbro datario.
daub [dɔːb] vt imbrattare.
daughter ['dɔːtə*] n figlia.
daughter-in-law ['dɔːtərɪnlɔː] n nuora.
daunt [dɔːnt] vt intimidire.
daunting ['dɔːntɪŋ] a non invidiabile.
dauntless ['dɔːntlɪs] a intrepido(a).
dawdle ['dɔːdl] vi bighellonare; **to ~ over one's work** gingillarsi con il lavoro.
dawn [dɔːn] n alba ♦ vi (day) spuntare; (fig) venire in mente; **at ~** all'alba; **from ~ to dusk** dall'alba al tramonto; **it ~ed on him that ...** gli è venuto in mente che ....
dawn chorus n (Brit) coro mattutino degli uccelli.
day [deɪ] n giorno; (as duration) giornata; (period of time, age) tempo, epoca; **the ~ before** il giorno avanti or prima; **the ~ after, the following ~** il giorno dopo, il giorno seguente; **the ~ before yesterday** l'altroieri; **the ~ after tomorrow** dopodomani; **(on) that ~** quel giorno; **(on) the ~ that ...** il giorno che or in cui ...; **to work an 8-hour ~** avere una giornata lavorativa di 8 ore; **by ~** di giorno; **~ by** giorno per giorno; **paid by the ~** pagato(a) a giornata; **these ~s, in the present ~** di questi tempi, oggigiorno.
daybook ['deɪbuk] n (Brit) brogliaccio.
day boy n (SCOL) alunno esterno.
daybreak ['deɪbreɪk] n spuntar m del giorno.
daydream ['deɪdriːm] n sogno a occhi aperti ♦ vi sognare a occhi aperti.
day girl n (SCOL) alunna esterna.
daylight ['deɪlaɪt] n luce f del giorno.
Daylight Saving Time n (US) ora legale.
day release n: **to be on ~** avere un giorno di congedo alla settimana per formazione professionale.
day return (ticket) n (Brit) biglietto

giornaliero di andata e ritorno.
day shift *n* turno di giorno.
daytime ['deɪtaɪm] *n* giorno.
day-to-day ['deɪtə'deɪ] *a* (*routine*)
quotidiano(a); (*expenses*) giornaliero(a); **on
a ~ basis** a giornata.
day trip *n* gita (di un giorno).
day tripper *n* gitante *m/f*.
daze [deɪz] *vt* (*subj*: *drug*) inebetire; (: *blow*)
stordire ♦ *n*: **in a ~** inebetito(a); stordito(a).
dazzle ['dæzl] *vt* abbagliare.
dazzling ['dæzlɪŋ] *a* (*light*) abbagliante;
(*colour*) violento(a); (*smile*) smagliante.
dB *abbr* (= *decibel*) db.
DC *abbr* (*ELEC*: = *direct current*) c.c.; (*US
POST*) = *District of Columbia*.
DD *n abbr* (= *Doctor of Divinity*) titolo di
studio.
dd. *abbr* (*COMM*) = *delivered*.
D/D *abbr* = **direct debit**.
D-day ['diːdeɪ] *n giorno dello sbarco alleato in
Normandia*.
DDS *n abbr* (*US*: = *Doctor of Dental Science*;
Doctor of Dental Surgery) titoli di studio.
DDT *n abbr* (= *dichlorodiphenyl
trichloroethane*) D.D.T. *m*.
DE *abbr* (*US POST*) = *Delaware*.
DEA *n abbr* (*US*: = *Drug Enforcement
Administration*) ≈ squadra narcotici.
deacon ['diːkən] *n* diacono.
dead [dɛd] *a* morto(a); (*numb*) intirizzito(a) ♦
ad assolutamente, perfettamente; **the ~** *npl* i
morti; **he was shot ~** fu colpito a morte; **~
on time** in perfetto orario; **~ tired** stanco(a)
morto(a); **to stop ~** fermarsi in tronco; **the
line has gone ~** (*TEL*) è caduta la linea.
deaden ['dɛdn] *vt* (*blow, sound*) ammortire;
(*make numb*) intirizzire.
dead end *n* vicolo cieco.
dead-end ['dɛdɛnd] *a*: **a ~ job** un lavoro
senza sbocchi.
dead heat *n* (*SPORT*): **to finish in a ~** finire
alla pari.
dead-letter office [dɛd'lɛtə-] *n* ufficio della
posta in giacenza.
deadline ['dɛdlaɪn] *n* scadenza; **to work to a
~** avere una scadenza.
deadlock ['dɛdlɔk] *n* punto morto.
dead loss *n* (*col*): **to be a ~** (*person, thing*)
non valere niente.
deadly ['dɛdlɪ] *a* mortale; (*weapon, poison*)
micidiale ♦ *ad*: **~ dull** di una noia micidiale.
deadpan ['dɛdpæn] *a* a faccia impassibile.
Dead Sea *n*: **the ~** il mar Morto.
dead season *n* (*TOURISM*) stagione *f* morta.
deaf [dɛf] *a* sordo(a); **to turn a ~ ear to sth**
fare orecchi da mercante a qc.
deaf-aid ['dɛfeɪd] *n* apparecchio per la sordità.
deaf-and-dumb ['dɛfən'dʌm] *a* (*person*)
sordomuto(a); (*alphabet*) dei sordomuti.
deafen ['dɛfn] *vt* assordare.
deafening ['dɛfnɪŋ] *a* fragoroso(a),
assordante.
deaf-mute ['dɛfmjuːt] *n* sordomuto/a.

deafness ['dɛfnɪs] *n* sordità.
deal [diːl] *n* accordo; (*business ~*) affare *m* ♦
vt (*pt, pp* **dealt** [dɛlt]) (*blow, cards*) dare; **to
strike a ~ with sb** fare un affare con qn; **it's
a ~!** (*col*) affare fatto!; **he got a bad/fair ~
from them** l'hanno trattato male/bene; **a
good ~ of, a great ~ of** molto(a).
  deal in *vt fus* (*COMM*) occuparsi di.
  deal with *vt fus* (*COMM*) fare affari con,
  trattare con; (*handle*) occuparsi di; (*be
  about: book etc*) trattare di.
dealer ['diːlə*] *n* commerciante *m/f*.
dealership ['diːləʃɪp] *n* rivenditore *m*.
dealings ['diːlɪŋz] *npl* rapporti *mpl*; (*in goods,
shares*) transazioni *fpl*.
dealt [dɛlt] *pt, pp of* **deal**.
dean [diːn] *n* (*REL*) decano; (*SCOL*) preside *m*
di facoltà (*or* di collegio).
dear [dɪə*] *a* caro(a) ♦ *n*: **my ~** caro mio/cara
mia; **~ me!** Dio mio!; **D~ Sir/Madam** (*in
letter*) Egregio Signore/Egregia Signora; **D~
Mr/Mrs X** Gentile Signor/Signora X.
dearly ['dɪəlɪ] *ad* (*love*) moltissimo; (*pay*) a
caro prezzo.
dear money *n* (*COMM*) denaro ad alto
interesse.
dearth [dɑːθ] *n* scarsità, carestia.
death [dɛθ] *n* morte *f*; (*ADMIN*) decesso.
deathbed ['dɛθbed] *n* letto di morte.
death certificate *n* atto di decesso.
death duty *n* (*Brit*) imposta *or* tassa di
successione.
deathly ['dɛθlɪ] *a* di morte ♦ *ad* come un
cadavere.
death penalty *n* pena di morte.
death rate *n* indice *m* di mortalità.
death sentence *n* condanna a morte.
deathtrap ['dɛθtræp] *n* trappola mortale.
deb [dɛb] *n abbr* (*col*) = **debutante**.
debacle [deɪ'bɑːkl] *n* (*defeat*) disfatta;
(*collapse*) sfacelo.
debar [dɪ'bɑː*] *vt*: **to ~ sb from a club** *etc*
escludere qn da un club *etc*; **to ~ sb from
doing** vietare a qn di fare.
debase [dɪ'beɪs] *vt* (*currency*) adulterare;
(*person*) degradare.
debatable [dɪ'beɪtəbl] *a* discutibile; **it is ~
whether ...** è in dubbio se ....
debate [dɪ'beɪt] *n* dibattito ♦ *vt* dibattere, discutere ♦ *vi* (*consider*): **to ~ whether**
riflettere se.
debauchery [dɪ'bɔːtʃərɪ] *n* dissolutezza.
debenture [dɪ'bɛntʃə*] *n* (*COMM*) obbligazione
f.
debilitate [dɪ'bɪlɪteɪt] *vt* debilitare.
debit ['dɛbɪt] *n* debito ♦ *vt*: **to ~ a sum to sb**
or **to sb's account** addebitare una somma a
qn.
debit balance *n* saldo debitore.
debit note *n* nota di addebito.
debonair [dɛbə'nɛə*] *a* gioviale e
disinvolto(a).
debrief [diː'briːf] *vt* chiamare a rapporto (a
operazione ultimata).

debriefing [di:'bri:fɪŋ] *n* rapporto.

debris ['dɛbri:] *n* detriti *mpl*.

debt [dɛt] *n* debito; **to be in** ~ essere indebitato(a); ~**s of £5000** debiti per 5000 sterline; **bad** ~ debito insoluto.

debt collector *n* agente *m* di recupero crediti.

debtor ['dɛtə•] *n* debitore/trice.

debug [di:'bʌg] *vt* (*COMPUT*) localizzare e rimuovere errori in.

debunk [di:'bʌŋk] *vt* (*col*: *theory*) demistificare; (: *claim*) smentire; (: *person, institution*) screditare.

debut ['deɪbju:] *n* debutto.

debutante ['dɛbjuta:nt] *n* debuttante *f*.

Dec. *abbr* (= *December*) dic.

decade ['dɛkeɪd] *n* decennio.

decadence ['dɛkədəns] *n* decadenza.

decadent ['dɛkədənt] *a* decadente.

decaffeinated [dɪ'kæfɪneɪtɪd] *a* decaffeinato(a).

decamp [dɪ'kæmp] *vi* (*col*) filarsela, levare le tende.

decant [dɪ'kænt] *vt* (*wine*) travasare.

decanter [dɪ'kæntə•] *n* caraffa.

decarbonize [di:'kɑ:bənaɪz] *vt* (*AUT*) decarburare.

decay [dɪ'keɪ] *n* decadimento; imputridimento; (*fig*) rovina; (*also*: **tooth** ~) carie *f* ♦ *vi* (*rot*) imputridire; (*fig*) andare in rovina.

decease [dɪ'si:s] *n* decesso.

deceased [dɪ'si:st] *n*: **the** ~ il(la) defunto(a).

deceit [dɪ'si:t] *n* inganno.

deceitful [dɪ'si:tful] *a* ingannevole, perfido(a).

deceive [dɪ'si:v] *vt* ingannare; **to** ~ **o.s.** illudersi, ingannarsi.

decelerate [di:'sɛləreɪt] *vt, vi* rallentare.

December [dɪ'sɛmbə•] *n* dicembre *m*; *for phrases see also* **July.**

decency ['di:sənsɪ] *n* decenza.

decent ['di:sənt] *a* decente; **they were very** ~ **about it** si sono comportati da signori riguardo a ciò.

decently ['di:səntlɪ] *ad* (*respectably*) decentemente, convenientemente; (*kindly*) gentilmente.

decentralization [di:sɛntrəlaɪ'zeɪʃən] *n* decentramento.

decentralize [di:'sɛntrəlaɪz] *vt* decentrare.

deception [dɪ'sɛpʃən] *n* inganno.

deceptive [dɪ'sɛptɪv] *a* ingannevole.

decibel ['dɛsɪbɛl] *n* decibel *m inv*.

decide [dɪ'saɪd] *vt* (*person*) far prendere una decisione a; (*question, argument*) risolvere, decidere ♦ *vi* decidere, decidersi; **to** ~ **to do/that** decidere di fare/che; **to** ~ **on** decidere per; **to** ~ **against doing sth** decidere di non fare qc.

decided [dɪ'saɪdɪd] *a* (*resolute*) deciso(a); (*clear, definite*) netto(a), chiaro(a).

decidedly [dɪ'saɪdɪdlɪ] *ad* indubbiamente; decisamente.

deciding [dɪ'saɪdɪŋ] *a* decisivo(a).

deciduous [dɪ'sɪdjuəs] *a* deciduo(a).

decimal ['dɛsɪməl] *a, n* decimale (*m*); **to 3** ~ **places** al terzo decimale.

decimalize ['dɛsɪməlaɪz] *vt* (*Brit*) convertire al sistema metrico decimale.

decimal point *n* ≈ virgola.

decimate ['dɛsɪmeɪt] *vt* decimare.

decipher [dɪ'saɪfə•] *vt* decifrare.

decision [dɪ'sɪʒən] *n* decisione *f*; **to make a** ~ prendere una decisione.

decisive [dɪ'saɪsɪv] *a* (*victory, factor*) decisivo(a); (*influence*) determinante; (*manner, person*) risoluto(a), deciso(a); (*reply*) deciso(a), categorico(a).

deck [dɛk] *n* (*NAUT*) ponte *m*; (*of cards*) mazzo; (*of bus*): **top** ~ imperiale *m*; **to go up on** ~ salire in coperta; **below** ~ sotto coperta; **cassette** ~ piastra (di registrazione); **record** ~ piatto (giradischi).

deckchair ['dɛktʃɛə•] *n* sedia a sdraio.

deck hand *n* marinaio.

declaration [dɛklə'reɪʃən] *n* dichiarazione *f*.

declare [dɪ'klɛə•] *vt* dichiarare.

declassify [di:'klæsɪfaɪ] *vt* rendere accessibile al pubblico.

decline [dɪ'klaɪn] *n* (*decay*) declino; (*lessening*) ribasso ♦ *vt* declinare; rifiutare ♦ *vi* declinare; diminuire; ~ **in living standards** abbassamento del tenore di vita; **to** ~ **to do sth** rifiutar(si) di fare qc.

declutch [di:'klʌtʃ] *vi* (*Brit*) premere la frizione.

decode [di:'kəud] *vt* decifrare.

decoder [di:'kəudə•] *n* decodificatore *m*.

decompose [di:kəm'pəuz] *vi* decomporre.

decomposition [di:kɔmpə'zɪʃən] *n* decomposizione *f*.

decompression [di:kəm'prɛʃən] *n* decompressione *f*.

decompression chamber *n* camera di decompressione.

decongestant [di:kən'dʒɛstənt] *n* decongestionante *m*.

decontaminate [di:kən'tæmɪneɪt] *vt* decontaminare.

decontrol [di:kən'trəul] *vt* (*trade*) liberalizzare; (*prices*) togliere il controllo governativo a.

decor ['deɪkɔ:•] *n* decorazione *f*.

decorate ['dɛkəreɪt] *vt* (*adorn, give a medal to*) decorare; (*paint and paper*) pitturare e tappezzare.

decoration [dɛkə'reɪʃən] *n* decorazione *f*.

decorative ['dɛkərətɪv] *a* decorativo(a).

decorator ['dɛkəreɪtə•] *n* decoratore/trice.

decorum [dɪ'kɔ:rəm] *n* decoro.

decoy ['di:kɔɪ] *n* zimbello; **they used him as a** ~ **for the enemy** l'hanno usato come esca per il nemico.

decrease *n* ['di:kri:s] diminuzione *f* ♦ *vt, vi* [di:'kri:s] diminuire; **to be on the** ~ essere in diminuzione.

decreasing [di:'kri:sɪŋ] *a* sempre meno *inv*.

decree [dɪ'kri:] *n* decreto ♦ *vt*: **to** ~ **(that)** decretare (che + *sub*); ~ **absolute** sentenza di divorzio definitiva; ~ **nisi** [-'naɪsaɪ] sentenza provvisoria di divorzio.

decrepit [dɪ'krɛpɪt] *a* decrepito(a); *(building)* cadente.

decry [dɪ'kraɪ] *vt* condannare, deplorare.

dedicate ['dɛdɪkeɪt] *vt* consacrare; *(book etc)* dedicare.

dedicated ['dɛdɪkeɪtɪd] *a* coscienzioso(a); *(COMPUT)* specializzato(a), dedicato(a).

dedication [dɛdɪ'keɪʃən] *n* *(devotion)* dedizione *f*; *(in book)* dedica.

deduce [dɪ'djuːs] *vt* dedurre.

deduct [dɪ'dʌkt] *vt*: **to ~ sth (from)** dedurre qc (da); *(from wage etc)* trattenere qc (da).

deduction [dɪ'dʌkʃən] *n* *(deducting)* deduzione *f*; *(from wage etc)* trattenuta; *(deducing)* deduzione *f*, conclusione *f*.

deed [diːd] *n* azione *f*, atto; *(LAW)* atto; **~ of covenant** atto di donazione.

deem [diːm] *vt* *(formal)* giudicare, ritenere; **to ~ it wise to do** ritenere prudente fare.

deep [diːp] *a* profondo(a) ♦ *ad*: **~ in snow** affondato(a) nella neve; **spectators stood 20 ~** c'erano 20 file di spettatori; **knee-~ in water** in acqua fino alle ginocchia; **4 metres ~** profondo(a) 4 metri; **he took a ~ breath** fece un respiro profondo.

deepen ['diːpn] *vt* *(hole)* approfondire ♦ *vi* approfondirsi; *(darkness)* farsi più intenso(a).

deep-freeze [diːp'friːz] *n* congelatore *m* ♦ *vt* congelare.

deep-fry ['diːp'fraɪ] *vt* friggere in olio abbondante.

deeply ['diːplɪ] *ad* profondamente; **to regret sth ~** rammaricarsi sinceramente di qc.

deep-rooted ['diːp'ruːtɪd] *a* *(prejudice)* profondamente radicato(a); *(affection)* profondo(a); *(habit)* inveterato(a).

deep-sea diver ['diːp'siː-] *n* palombaro.

deep-sea diving *n* immersione *f* in alto mare.

deep-sea fishing *n* pesca d'alto mare.

deep-seated ['diːp'siːtɪd] *a* *(beliefs)* radicato(a).

deep-set ['diːp'sɛt] *a* *(eyes)* infossato(a).

deer [dɪə*] *n* *(pl inv)*: **the ~** i cervidi *(ZOOL)*; **(red) ~** cervo; **(fallow) ~** daino; **(roe) ~** capriolo.

deerskin ['dɪəskɪn] *n* pelle *f* di daino.

deerstalker ['dɪəstɔːkə*] *n* berretto da cacciatore.

deface [dɪ'feɪs] *vt* imbrattare.

defamation [dɛfə'meɪʃən] *n* diffamazione *f*.

defamatory [dɪ'fæmətərɪ] *a* diffamatorio(a).

default [dɪ'fɔːlt] *vi* *(LAW)* essere contumace; *(gen)* essere inadempiente ♦ *n* *(COMPUT: also:* **~ value)** default *m inv*; **by ~** *(LAW)* in contumacia; *(SPORT)* per abbandono; **to ~ on a debt** non onorare un debito.

defaulter [dɪ'fɔːltə*] *n* *(on debt)* inadempiente *m/f*.

default option *n* *(COMPUT)* opzione *f* di default.

defeat [dɪ'fiːt] *n* sconfitta ♦ *vt* *(team,*

opponents) sconfiggere; *(fig: plans, efforts)* frustrare.

defeatism [dɪ'fiːtɪzəm] *n* disfattismo.

defeatist [dɪ'fiːtɪst] *a, n* disfattista *(m/f)*.

defect *n* ['diːfɛkt] difetto ♦ *vi* [dɪ'fɛkt]: **to ~ to the enemy/the West** passare al nemico/ all'Ovest; **physical ~** difetto fisico; **mental ~** anomalia mentale.

defective [dɪ'fɛktɪv] *a* difettoso(a).

defector [dɪ'fɛktə*] *n* rifugiato(a) politico(a).

defence, *(US)* defense [dɪ'fɛns] *n* difesa; **in ~ of** in difesa di; **the Ministry of D~,** *(US)* **the Department of Defense** il Ministero della Difesa; **witness for the ~** teste *m/f* a difesa.

defenceless [dɪ'fɛnslɪs] *a* senza difesa.

defend [dɪ'fɛnd] *vt* difendere; *(decision, action)* giustificare; *(opinion)* sostenere.

defendant [dɪ'fɛndənt] *n* imputato/a.

defender [dɪ'fɛndə*] *n* difensore/a.

defending champion *n* *(SPORT)* campione/ essa in carica.

defending counsel *n* *(LAW)* avvocato difensore.

defense [dɪ'fɛns] *n* *(US)* = **defence**.

defensive [dɪ'fɛnsɪv] *a* difensivo(a) ♦ *n* difensiva; **on the ~** sulla difensiva.

defer [dɪ'fəː*] *vt* *(postpone)* differire, rinviare ♦ *vi* *(submit)*: **to ~ to sb/sth** rimettersi a qn/qc.

deference ['dɛfərəns] *n* deferenza; riguardo; **out of** *or* **in ~ to** per riguardo a.

defiance [dɪ'faɪəns] *n* sfida; **in ~ of** a dispetto di.

defiant [dɪ'faɪənt] *a* *(attitude)* di sfida; *(person)* ribelle.

defiantly [dɪ'faɪəntlɪ] *ad* con aria di sfida.

deficiency [dɪ'fɪʃənsɪ] *n* deficienza; carenza; *(COMM)* ammanco.

deficiency disease *n* malattia da carenza.

deficient [dɪ'fɪʃənt] *a* deficiente; insufficiente; **to be ~ in** mancare di.

deficit ['dɛfɪsɪt] *n* disavanzo.

defile *vb* [dɪ'faɪl] *vt* contaminare ♦ *vi* sfilare ♦ *n* ['diːfaɪl] gola, stretta.

define [dɪ'faɪn] *vt* *(gen, COMPUT)* definire.

definite ['dɛfɪnɪt] *a* *(fixed)* definito(a), preciso(a); *(clear, obvious)* ben definito(a), esatto(a); *(LING)* determinativo(a); **he was ~ about it** ne era sicuro.

definitely ['dɛfɪnɪtlɪ] *ad* indubbiamente.

definition [dɛfɪ'nɪʃən] *n* definizione *f*.

definitive [dɪ'fɪnɪtɪv] *a* definitivo(a).

deflate [diː'fleɪt] *vt* sgonfiare; *(ECON)* deflazionare; *(pompous person)* fare abbassare la cresta a.

deflation [diː'fleɪʃən] *n* *(ECON)* deflazione *f*.

deflationary [diː'fleɪʃənrɪ] *a* *(ECON)* deflazionistico(a).

deflect [dɪ'flɛkt] *vt* deflettere, deviare.

defog ['diː'fɔg] *vt* *(US AUT)* sbrinare.

defogger ['diː'fɔgə*] *n* *(US AUT)* sbrinatore *m*.

deform [dɪ'fɔːm] *vt* deformare.

deformed [dɪ'fɔːmd] *a* deforme.

deformity [dɪ'fɔːmɪtɪ] *n* deformità *f inv*.

defraud [dɪ'frɔːd] vt: **to ~ (of)** defraudare (di).

defray [dɪ'freɪ] vt: **to ~ sb's expenses** sostenere le spese di qn.

defrost [diː'frɔst] vt (fridge) disgelare; (frozen food) scongelare.

deft [dɛft] a svelto(a), destro(a).

defunct [dɪ'fʌŋkt] a defunto(a).

defuse [diː'fjuːz] vt disinnescare; (fig) distendere.

defy [dɪ'faɪ] vt sfidare; (efforts etc) resistere a; (refuse to obey: person) rifiutare di obbedire a.

degenerate vi [dɪ'dʒɛnəreɪt] degenerare ♦ a [dɪ'dʒɛnərɪt] degenere.

degradation [dɛgrə'deɪʃən] n degradazione f.

degrade [dɪ'greɪd] vt degradare.

degrading [dɪ'greɪdɪŋ] a degradante.

degree [dɪ'griː] n grado; (SCOL) laurea (universitaria); **10 ~s below freezing** 10 gradi sotto zero; **a (first) ~ in maths** una laurea in matematica; **a considerable ~ of risk** una grossa percentuale di rischio; **by ~s** (gradually) gradualmente, a poco a poco; **to some ~, to a certain ~** fino a un certo punto, in certa misura.

dehydrated [diːhaɪ'dreɪtɪd] a disidratato(a); (milk, eggs) in polvere.

dehydration [diːhaɪ'dreɪʃən] n disidratazione f.

de-ice [diː'aɪs] vt (windscreen) disgelare.

de-icer ['diː'aɪsə*] n sbrinatore m.

deign [deɪn] vi: **to ~ to do** degnarsi di fare.

deity ['diːɪtɪ] n divinità f inv; dio/dea.

dejected [dɪ'dʒɛktɪd] a abbattuto(a), avvilito(a).

dejection [dɪ'dʒɛkʃən] n abbattimento, avvilimento.

del. abbr = **delete**.

delay [dɪ'leɪ] vt (journey, operation) ritardare, rinviare; (travellers, trains) ritardare; (payment) differire ♦ n ritardo; **without ~** senza ritardo.

delayed-action [dɪ'leɪd'ækʃən] a a azione ritardata.

delectable [dɪ'lɛktəbl] a delizioso(a).

delegate n ['dɛlɪgɪt] delegato/a ♦ vt ['dɛlɪgeɪt] delegare; **to ~ sth to sb/sb to do sth** delegare qc a qn/qn a fare qc.

delegation [dɛlɪ'geɪʃən] n delegazione f; (of work etc) delega.

delete [dɪ'liːt] vt (gen, COMPUT) cancellare.

Delhi ['dɛlɪ] n Delhi f.

deliberate a [dɪ'lɪbərɪt] (intentional) intenzionale; (slow) misurato(a) ♦ vi [dɪ'lɪbəreɪt] deliberare, riflettere.

deliberately [dɪ'lɪbərɪtlɪ] ad (on purpose) deliberatamente.

deliberation [dɪlɪbə'reɪʃən] n (consideration) riflessione f; (discussion) discussione f, deliberazione f.

delicacy ['dɛlɪkəsɪ] n delicatezza.

delicate ['dɛlɪkɪt] a delicato(a).

delicately ['dɛlɪkɪtlɪ] ad (gen) delicatamente;

(act, express) con delicatezza.

delicatessen [dɛlɪkə'tɛsn] n ≈ salumeria.

delicious [dɪ'lɪʃəs] a delizioso(a), squisito(a).

delight [dɪ'laɪt] n delizia, gran piacere m ♦ vt dilettare; **it is a ~ to the eyes** è un piacere guardarlo; **to take ~ in** divertirsi a; **to be the ~ of** essere la gioia di.

delighted [dɪ'laɪtɪd] a: **~ (at or with sth)** contentissimo(a) (di qc), felice (di qc); **to be ~ to do sth/that** essere felice di fare qc/che + sub; **I'd be ~** con grande piacere.

delightful [dɪ'laɪtful] a (person, place, meal) delizioso(a); (smile, manner) incantevole.

delimit [diː'lɪmɪt] vt delimitare.

delineate [dɪ'lɪnɪeɪt] vt delineare.

delinquency [dɪ'lɪŋkwənsɪ] n delinquenza.

delinquent [dɪ'lɪŋkwənt] a, n delinquente (m/f).

delirious [dɪ'lɪrɪəs] a (MED, fig) delirante, in delirio; **to be ~** delirare; (fig) farneticare.

delirium [dɪ'lɪrɪəm] n delirio.

deliver [dɪ'lɪvə*] vt (mail) distribuire; (goods) consegnare; (speech) pronunciare; (free) liberare; (MED) far partorire; **to ~ a message** fare un'ambasciata; **to ~ the goods** (fig) partorire.

deliverance [dɪ'lɪvrəns] n liberazione f.

delivery [dɪ'lɪvərɪ] n distribuzione f; consegna; (of speaker) dizione f; (MED) parto; **to take ~ of** prendere in consegna.

delivery note n bolla di consegna.

delivery van, (US) **delivery truck** n furgoncino (per le consegne).

delouse ['diː'laus] vt spidocchiare.

delta ['dɛltə] n delta m.

delude [dɪ'luːd] vt deludere, illudere.

deluge ['dɛljuːdʒ] n diluvio ♦ vt (fig): **to ~ (with)** subissare (di), inondare (di).

delusion [dɪ'luːʒən] n illusione f.

de luxe [də'lʌks] a di lusso.

delve [dɛlv] vi: **to ~ into** frugare in; (subject) far ricerche in.

Dem. abbr (US POL) = **democrat(ic)**.

demagogue ['dɛməgɔg] n demagogo.

demand [dɪ'maːnd] vt richiedere ♦ n richiesta; (ECON) domanda; **to ~ sth (from or of sb)** pretendere qc (da qn), esigere qc (da qn); **in ~** ricercato(a), richiesto(a); **on ~** a richiesta.

demand draft n (COMM) tratta a vista.

demanding [dɪ'maːndɪŋ] a (boss) esigente; (work) impegnativo(a).

demarcation [diːmaː'keɪʃən] n demarcazione f.

demarcation dispute n (INDUSTRY) controversia settoriale (or di categoria).

demean [dɪ'miːn] vt: **to ~ o.s.** umiliarsi.

demeanour, (US) **demeanor** [dɪ'miːnə*] n comportamento; contegno.

demented [dɪ'mɛntɪd] a demente, impazzito(a).

demilitarized zone [diː'mɪlɪtəraɪzd-] n zona smilitarizzata.

demise [dɪ'maɪz] n decesso.

demist [di:'mɪst] vt (Brit AUT) sbrinare.
demister [di:'mɪstə*] n (Brit AUT) sbrinatore m.
demo ['dɛməu] n abbr (col) = **demonstration**.
demobilize [di:'məubɪlaɪz] vt smobilitare.
democracy [dɪ'mɔkrəsɪ] n democrazia.
democrat ['dɛməkræt] n democratico/a.
democratic [dɛmə'krætɪk] a democratico(a).
demography [dɪ'mɔgrəfɪ] n demografia.
demolish [dɪ'mɔlɪʃ] vt demolire.
demolition [dɛmə'lɪʃən] n demolizione f.
demon ['di:mən] n (also fig) demonio ♦ cpd: **a ~ squash player** un mago dello squash; **a ~ driver** un guidatore folle.
demonstrate ['dɛmənstreɪt] vt dimostrare, provare ♦ vi: **to ~ (for/against)** dimostrare (per/contro), manifestare (per/contro).
demonstration [dɛmən'streɪʃən] n dimostrazione f; (POL) manifestazione f, dimostrazione; **to hold a ~** (POL) tenere una manifestazione, fare una dimostrazione.
demonstrative [dɪ'mɔnstrətɪv] a dimostrativo(a).
demonstrator ['dɛmənstreɪtə*] n (POL) dimostrante m/f; (COMM: sales person) dimostratore/trice (: car, computer etc) modello per dimostrazione.
demoralize [dɪ'mɔrəlaɪz] vt demoralizzare.
demote [dɪ'məut] vt far retrocedere.
demotion [dɪ'məuʃən] n retrocessione f, degradazione f.
demur [dɪ'mə:*] vi (formal): **to ~ (at)** sollevare obiezioni (a or su) ♦ n: **without ~** senza obiezioni.
demure [dɪ'mjuə*] a contegnoso(a).
demurrage [dɪ'mʌrɪdʒ] n diritti mpl di immagazzinaggio; spese fpl di controstallia.
den [dɛn] n tana, covo.
denationalization ['di:næʃnəlaɪ'zeɪʃən] n denazionalizzazione f.
denationalize [di:'næʃnəlaɪz] vt snazionalizzare.
denial [dɪ'naɪəl] n diniego; rifiuto.
denier ['dɛnɪə*] n denaro (di filati, calze).
denigrate ['dɛnɪgreɪt] vt denigrare.
denim ['dɛnɪm] n tessuto di cotone ritorto; see also **denims**.
denim jacket n giubbotto di jeans.
denims ['dɛnɪmz] npl blue jeans mpl.
denizen ['dɛnɪzən] n (inhabitant) abitante m/f; (foreigner) straniero(a) naturalizzato(a).
Denmark ['dɛnmɑ:k] n Danimarca.
denomination [dɪnɔmɪ'neɪʃən] n (money) valore m; (REL) confessione f.
denominator [dɪ'nɔmɪneɪtə*] n denominatore m.
denote [dɪ'nəut] vt denotare.
denounce [dɪ'nauns] vt denunciare.
dense [dɛns] a fitto(a); (stupid) ottuso(a), duro(a).
densely ['dɛnslɪ] ad: **~ wooded** fittamente boscoso(a); **~ populated** densamente popolato(a).

density ['dɛnsɪtɪ] n densità f inv; **single/double ~ disk** (COMPUT) disco a singola/doppia densità di registrazione.
dent [dɛnt] n ammaccatura ♦ vt (also: **make a ~ in**) ammaccare; (fig) intaccare.
dental ['dɛntl] a dentale.
dental surgeon n medico/a dentista.
dentist ['dɛntɪst] n dentista m/f; **~'s surgery** (Brit) gabinetto dentistico.
dentistry ['dɛntɪstrɪ] n odontoiatria.
denture(s) ['dɛntʃə(z)] n(pl) dentiera.
denunciation [dɪnʌnsɪ'eɪʃən] n denuncia.
deny [dɪ'naɪ] vt negare; (refuse) rifiutare; **he denies having said it** nega di averlo detto.
deodorant [di:'əudərənt] n deodorante m.
depart [dɪ'pɑ:t] vi partire; **to ~ from** (leave) allontanarsi da, partire da; (fig) deviare da.
department [dɪ'pɑ:tmənt] n (COMM) reparto; (SCOL) sezione f, dipartimento; (POL) ministero; **that's not my ~** (also fig) questo non è di mia competenza; **D~ of State** (US) Dipartimento di Stato.
departmental [di:pɑ:'tmɛntl] a (dispute) settoriale; (meeting) di sezione; **~ manager** caporeparto m/f.
department store n grande magazzino.
departure [dɪ'pɑ:tʃə*] n partenza; (fig): **~ from** deviazione f da; **a new ~** una novità.
departure lounge n sala d'attesa.
depend [dɪ'pɛnd] vi: **to ~ (up)on** dipendere da; (rely on) contare su; (be dependent on) dipendere (economicamente) da, essere a carico di; **it ~s** dipende; **~ing on the result ...** a seconda del risultato ....
dependable [dɪ'pɛndəbl] a fidato(a); (car etc) affidabile.
dependant [dɪ'pɛndənt] n persona a carico.
dependence [dɪ'pɛndəns] n dipendenza.
dependent [dɪ'pɛndənt] a: **to be ~ (on)** (gen) dipendere (da); (child, relative) essere a carico (di) ♦ n = **dependant**.
depict [dɪ'pɪkt] vt (in picture) dipingere; (in words) descrivere.
depilatory [dɪ'pɪlətərɪ] n (also: **~ cream**) crema depilatoria.
depleted [dɪ'pli:tɪd] a diminuito(a).
deplorable [dɪ'plɔ:rəbl] a deplorevole, lamentevole.
deplore [dɪ'plɔ:*] vt deplorare.
deploy [dɪ'plɔɪ] vt dispiegare.
depopulate [di:'pɔpjuleɪt] vt spopolare.
depopulation ['di:pɔpju'leɪʃən] n spopolamento.
deport [dɪ'pɔ:t] vt deportare; espellere.
deportation [di:pɔ:'teɪʃən] n deportazione f.
deportation order n foglio di via obbligatorio.
deportment [dɪ'pɔ:tmənt] n portamento.
depose [dɪ'pəuz] vt deporre.
deposit [dɪ'pɔzɪt] n (COMM, GEO) deposito; (of ore, oil) giacimento; (CHEM) sedimento; (part payment) acconto; (for hired goods etc) cauzione f ♦ vt depositare; dare in acconto; (luggage etc) mettere or lasciare in

deposito; **to put down a ~ of £50** versare una caparra di 50 sterline.

deposit account *n* conto vincolato.

depositor [dɪ'pɒzɪtə*] *n* depositante *m/f*.

depository [dɪ'pɒzɪtərɪ] *n* (*person*) depositario/a; (*place*) deposito.

depot ['dɛpəu] *n* deposito.

depraved [dɪ'preɪvd] *a* depravato(a).

depravity [dɪ'prævɪtɪ] *n* depravazione *f*.

deprecate ['dɛprɪkeɪt] *vt* deprecare.

deprecating ['dɛprɪkeɪtɪŋ] *a* (*disapproving*) di biasimo; (*apologetic*): **a ~ smile** un sorriso di scusa.

depreciate [dɪ'priːʃɪeɪt] *vt* svalutare ♦ *vi* svalutarsi.

depreciation [dɪpriːʃɪ'eɪʃən] *n* svalutazione *f*.

depress [dɪ'prɛs] *vt* deprimere; (*press down*) premere.

depressant [dɪ'prɛsnt] *n* (*MED*) sedativo.

depressed [dɪ'prɛst] *a* (*person*) depresso(a), abbattuto(a); (*area*) depresso(a); (*COMM*: *market, trade*) stagnante, in ribasso; **to get ~** deprimersi.

depressing [dɪ'prɛsɪŋ] *a* deprimente.

depression [dɪ'prɛʃən] *n* depressione *f*.

deprivation [dɛprɪ'veɪʃən] *n* privazione *f*; (*state*) indigenza; (*PSYCH*) carenza affettiva.

deprive [dɪ'praɪv] *vt*: **to ~ sb of** privare qn di.

deprived [dɪ'praɪvd] *a* disgraziato(a).

dept. *abbr* = **department**.

depth [dɛpθ] *n* profondità *f* *inv*; **at a ~ of 3 metres** a una profondità di 3 metri, a 3 metri di profondità; **in the ~s of** nel profondo di; **nel cuore di; in the ~s of winter** in pieno inverno; **to study sth in ~** studiare qc in profondità; **to be out of one's ~** (*Brit*: *swimmer*) essere dove non si tocca; (*fig*) non sentirsi all'altezza della situazione.

depth charge *n* carica di profondità.

deputation [dɛpju'teɪʃən] *n* deputazione *f*, delegazione *f*.

deputize ['dɛpjutaɪz] *vi*: **to ~ for** svolgere le funzioni di.

deputy ['dɛpjutɪ] *n* (*replacement*) supplente *m/f*; (*second in command*) vice *m/f* ♦ *cpd*: **~ chairman** vicepresidente *m*; **~ head** (*SCOL*) vicepreside *m/f*; **~ leader** (*Brit POL*) sottosegretario.

derail [dɪ'reɪl] *vt* far deragliare; **to be ~ed** deragliare.

derailment [dɪ'reɪlmənt] *n* deragliamento.

deranged [dɪ'reɪndʒd] *a*: **to be (mentally) ~** essere pazzo(a).

derby ['dəːbɪ] *n* (*US*) bombetta.

Derbys *abbr* (*Brit*) = **Derbyshire**.

deregulate [diː'rɛgjuleɪt] *vt* eliminare la regolamentazione di.

deregulation ['diːrɛgju'leɪʃən] *n* eliminazione *f* della regolamentazione.

derelict ['dɛrɪlɪkt] *a* abbandonato(a).

deride [dɪ'raɪd] *vt* deridere.

derision [dɪ'rɪʒən] *n* derisione *f*.

derisive [dɪ'raɪsɪv] *a* di derisione.

derisory [dɪ'raɪsərɪ] *a* (*sum*) irrisorio(a).

derivation [dɛrɪ'veɪʃən] *n* derivazione *f*.

derivative [dɪ'rɪvətɪv] *n* derivato ♦ *a* derivato(a).

derive [dɪ'raɪv] *vt*: **to ~ sth from** derivare qc da; trarre qc da ♦ *vi*: **to ~ from** derivare da.

dermatitis [dəːmə'taɪtɪs] *n* dermatite *f*.

dermatology [dəːmə'tɒlədʒɪ] *n* dermatologia.

derogatory [dɪ'rɒgətərɪ] *a* denigratorio(a).

derrick ['dɛrɪk] *n* gru *f* *inv*; (*for oil*) derrick *m* *inv*.

derv [dəːv] *n* (*Brit*) gasolio.

DES *n* *abbr* (*Brit*: = *Department of Education and Science*) ≈ ministero della Pubblica Istruzione.

desalination [diːsælɪ'neɪʃən] *n* desalinizzazione *f*, dissalazione *f*.

descend [dɪ'sɛnd] *vt*, *vi* discendere, scendere; **to ~ from** discendere da; **in ~ing order of importance** in ordine decrescente d'importanza.

descend on *vt* *fus* (*subj*: *enemy, angry person*) assalire, piombare su; (: *misfortune*) arrivare addosso a; (: *fig*: *gloom, silence*) scendere su; **visitors ~ed (up)on us** ci sono arrivate visite tra capo e collo.

descendant [dɪ'sɛndənt] *n* discendente *m/f*.

descent [dɪ'sɛnt] *n* discesa; (*origin*) discendenza, famiglia.

describe [dɪs'kraɪb] *vt* descrivere.

description [dɪs'krɪpʃən] *n* descrizione *f*; (*sort*) genere *m*, specie *f*; **of every ~** di ogni genere e specie.

descriptive [dɪs'krɪptɪv] *a* descrittivo(a).

desecrate ['dɛsɪkreɪt] *vt* profanare.

desert *n* ['dɛzət] deserto ♦ *vb* [dɪ'zəːt] *vt* lasciare, abbandonare ♦ *vi* (*MIL*) disertare; *see also* **deserts**.

deserter [dɪ'zəːtə*] *n* disertore *m*.

desertion [dɪ'zəːʃən] *n* diserzione *f*.

desert island *n* isola deserta.

deserts [dɪ'zəːts] *npl*: **to get one's just ~** avere ciò che si merita.

deserve [dɪ'zəːv] *vt* meritare.

deservedly [dɪ'zəːvɪdlɪ] *ad* meritatamente, giustamente.

deserving [dɪ'zəːvɪŋ] *a* (*person*) meritevole, degno(a); (*cause*) meritorio(a).

desiccated ['dɛsɪkeɪtɪd] *a* essiccato(a).

design [dɪ'zaɪn] *n* (*sketch*) disegno; (: *of dress, car*) modello; (*layout, shape*) linea; (*pattern*) fantasia; (*COMM*) disegno tecnico; (*intention*) intenzione *f* ♦ *vt* disegnare; progettare; **to have ~s on** aver mire su; **well-~ed** ben concepito(a); **industrial ~** disegno industriale.

designate *vt* ['dɛzɪgneɪt] designare ♦ *a* ['dɛzɪgnɪt] designato(a).

designation [dɛzɪg'neɪʃən] *n* designazione *f*.

designer [dɪ'zaɪnə*] *n* (*TECH*) disegnatore/trice, progettista *m/f*; (*of furniture*) designer *m/f* *inv*; (*fashion ~*) disegnatore/trice di moda; (*of theatre sets*) scenografo/a.

desirability [dɪzaɪərə'bɪlɪtɪ] *n* desiderabilità;

vantaggio.

desirable [dɪ'zaɪərəbl] *a* desiderabile; **it is ~ that** è opportuno che + *sub*.

desire [dɪ'zaɪə*] *n* desiderio, voglia ♦ *vt* desiderare, volere; **to ~ sth/to do sth/that** desiderare qc/di fare qc/che + *sub*.

desirous [dɪ'zaɪərəs] *a*: **~ of** desideroso(a) di.

desk [dɛsk] *n* (*in office*) scrivania; (*for pupil*) banco; (*Brit: in shop, restaurant*) cassa; (*in hotel*) ricevimento; (*at airport*) accettazione *f*.

desk job *n* lavoro d'ufficio.

desk-top publishing ['dɛsktɔp-] *n* editoria individuale.

desolate ['dɛsəlɪt] *a* desolato(a).

desolation [dɛsə'leɪʃən] *n* desolazione *f*.

despair [dɪs'pɛə*] *n* disperazione *f* ♦ *vi*: **to ~ of** disperare di; **in ~** disperato(a).

despatch [dɪs'pætʃ] *n, vt* = **dispatch**.

desperate ['dɛspərɪt] *a* disperato(a); (*measures*) estremo(a); (*fugitive*) capace di tutto; **we are getting ~** siamo sull'orlo della disperazione.

desperately ['dɛspərɪtlɪ] *ad* disperatamente; (*very*) terribilmente, estremamente; **~ ill** in pericolo di vita.

desperation [dɛspə'reɪʃən] *n* disperazione *f*; **in ~** per disperazione.

despicable [dɪs'pɪkəbl] *a* disprezzabile.

despise [dɪs'paɪz] *vt* disprezzare, sdegnare.

despite [dɪs'paɪt] *prep* malgrado, a dispetto di, nonostante.

despondent [dɪs'pɔndənt] *a* abbattuto(a), scoraggiato(a).

despot ['dɛspɔt] *n* despota *m*.

dessert [dɪ'zə:t] *n* dolce *m*; frutta.

dessertspoon [dɪ'zə:tspu:n] *n* cucchiaio da dolci.

destabilize [di:'steɪbɪlaɪz] *vt* privare di stabilità; (*fig*) destabilizzare.

destination [dɛstɪ'neɪʃən] *n* destinazione *f*.

destine ['dɛstɪn] *vt* destinare.

destined ['dɛstɪnd] *a*: **to be ~ to do sth** essere destinato(a) a fare qc; **~ for London** diretto a Londra, con destinazione Londra.

destiny ['dɛstɪnɪ] *n* destino.

destitute ['dɛstɪtju:t] *a* indigente, bisognoso(a); **~ of** privo(a) di.

destroy [dɪs'trɔɪ] *vt* distruggere.

destroyer [dɪs'trɔɪə*] *n* (*NAUT*) cacciatorpediniere *m*.

destruction [dɪs'trʌkʃən] *n* distruzione *f*.

destructive [dɪs'trʌktɪv] *a* distruttivo(a).

desultory ['dɛsəltərɪ] *a* (*reading*) disordinato(a); (*conversation*) sconnesso(a); (*contact*) saltuario(a), irregolare.

detach [dɪ'tætʃ] *vt* staccare, distaccare.

detachable [dɪ'tætʃəbl] *a* staccabile.

detached [dɪ'tætʃt] *a* (*attitude*) distante.

detached house *n* villa.

detachment [dɪ'tætʃmənt] *n* (*MIL*) distaccamento; (*fig*) distacco.

detail ['di:teɪl] *n* particolare *m*, dettaglio; (*MIL*) piccolo distaccamento ♦ *vt* dettagliare,

particolareggiare; (*MIL*): **to ~ sb (for)** assegnare qn (a); **in ~** nei particolari; **to go into ~(s)** scendere nei particolari.

detailed ['di:teɪld] *a* particolareggiato(a).

detain [dɪ'teɪn] *vt* trattenere; (*in captivity*) detenere.

detainee [di:teɪ'ni:] *n* detenuto/a.

detect [dɪ'tɛkt] *vt* scoprire, scorgere; (*MED, POLICE, RADAR etc*) individuare.

detection [dɪ'tɛkʃən] *n* scoperta; individuazione *f*; **crime ~** indagini *fpl* criminali; **to escape ~** (*criminal*) eludere le ricerche; (*mistake*) passare inosservato(a).

detective [dɪ'tɛktɪv] *n* investigatore/trice; **private ~** investigatore *m* privato.

detective story *n* giallo.

detector [dɪ'tɛktə*] *n* rivelatore *m*.

détente [deɪ'tɑ:nt] *n* distensione *f*.

detention [dɪ'tɛnʃən] *n* detenzione *f*; (*SCOL*) permanenza forzata per punizione.

deter [dɪ'tə:*] *vt* dissuadere.

detergent [dɪ'tə:dʒənt] *n* detersivo.

deteriorate [dɪ'tɪərɪəreɪt] *vi* deteriorarsi.

deterioration [dɪtɪərɪə'reɪʃən] *n* deterioramento.

determination [dɪtə:mɪ'neɪʃən] *n* determinazione *f*.

determine [dɪ'tə:mɪn] *vt* determinare; **to ~ to do sth** decidere di fare qc.

determined [dɪ'tə:mɪnd] *a* (*person*) risoluto(a), deciso(a); **to be ~ to do sth** essere determinato or deciso a fare qc; **a ~ effort** uno sforzo di volontà.

deterrence [dɪ'tɛrəns] *n* deterrenza.

deterrent [dɪ'tɛrənt] *n* deterrente *m*; **to act as a ~** fungere da deterrente.

detest [dɪ'tɛst] *vt* detestare.

detestable [dɪ'tɛstəbl] *a* detestabile, abominevole.

detonate ['dɛtəneɪt] *vi* detonare ♦ *vt* far detonare.

detonator ['dɛtəneɪtə*] *n* detonatore *m*.

detour ['di:tuə*] *n* deviazione *f*.

detract [dɪ'trækt] *vt*: **to ~ from** detrarre da.

detractor [dɪ'træktə*] *n* detrattore/trice.

detriment ['dɛtrɪmənt] *n*: **to the ~ of** a detrimento di; **without ~ to** senza danno a.

detrimental [dɛtrɪ'mɛntl] *a*: **~ to** dannoso(a) a, nocivo(a) a.

deuce [dju:s] *n* (*TENNIS*) quaranta pari *m inv*.

devaluation [di:vælju'eɪʃən] *n* svalutazione *f*.

devalue ['di:'vælju:] *vt* svalutare.

devastate ['dɛvəsteɪt] *vt* devastare; **he was ~d by the news** la notizia fu per lui un colpo terribile.

devastating ['dɛvəsteɪtɪŋ] *a* devastatore(trice).

devastation [dɛvə'steɪʃən] *n* devastazione *f*.

develop [dɪ'vɛləp] *vt* sviluppare; (*habit*) prendere (gradualmente) ♦ *vi* svilupparsi; (*facts, symptoms: appear*) manifestarsi, rivelarsi; **to ~ a taste for sth** imparare a gustare qc; **to ~ into** diventare.

developer [dɪ'vɛləpə*] *n* (*PHOT*) sviluppatore

m; **property** ~ costruttore *m* (edile).

developing country [dɪ'vɛləpɪŋ-] *n* paese *m* in via di sviluppo.

development [dɪ'vɛləpmənt] *n* sviluppo.

development area *n* area di sviluppo industriale.

deviant ['di:vɪənt] *a* deviante.

deviate ['di:vɪeɪt] *vi*: **to** ~ **(from)** deviare (da).

deviation [di:vɪ'eɪʃən] *n* deviazione *f*.

device [dɪ'vaɪs] *n* (*apparatus*) congegno; (*explosive* ~) ordigno esplosivo.

devil ['dɛvl] *n* diavolo; demonio.

devilish ['dɛvlɪʃ] *a* diabolico(a).

devil-may-care ['dɛvlmeɪ'kɛə*] *a* impudente.

devious ['di:vɪəs] *a* (*means*) indiretto(a), tortuoso(a); (*person*) subdolo(a).

devise [dɪ'vaɪz] *vt* escogitare, concepire.

devoid [dɪ'vɔɪd] *a*: ~ **of** privo(a) di.

devolution [di:və'lu:ʃən] *n* (*POL*) decentramento.

devolve [dɪ'vɔlv] *vi*: **to** ~ **(up)on** ricadere su.

devote [dɪ'vəut] *vt*: **to** ~ **sth to** dedicare qc a.

devoted [dɪ'vəutɪd] *a* devoto(a); **to be** ~ **to** essere molto attaccato(a) a.

devotee [dɛvəu'ti:] *n* (*REL*) adepto/a; (*MUS*, *SPORT*) appassionato/a.

devotion [dɪ'vəuʃən] *n* devozione *f*, attaccamento; (*REL*) atto di devozione, preghiera.

devour [dɪ'vauə*] *vt* divorare.

devout [dɪ'vaut] *a* pio(a), devoto(a).

dew [dju:] *n* rugiada.

dexterity [dɛks'tɛrɪtɪ] *n* destrezza.

dext(e)rous ['dɛkstrəs] *a* (*skilful*) destro(a), abile; (*movement*) agile.

dg *abbr* (= *decigram*) dg.

DH *n abbr* = **Department of Health**; *see* **health**.

DHSS *n abbr* (*Brit*: *old*) = *Department of Health and Social Security*.

diabetes [daɪə'bi:ti:z] *n* diabete *m*.

diabetic [daɪə'bɛtɪk] *a* diabetico(a); (*chocolate*, *jam*) per diabetici ♦ *n* diabetico/a.

diabolical [daɪə'bɔlɪkl] *a* diabolico(a); (*col*: *dreadful*) infernale, atroce.

diaerisis [daɪ'ɛrɪsɪs] *n* dieresi *f inv*.

diagnose [daɪəg'nəuz] *vt* diagnosticare.

diagnosis, *pl* **diagnoses** [daɪəg'nəusɪs, -si:z] *n* diagnosi *f inv*.

diagonal [daɪ'ægənl] *a, n* diagonale (*f*).

diagram ['daɪəgræm] *n* diagramma *m*.

dial ['daɪəl] *n* quadrante *m*; (*on telephone*) disco combinatore ♦ *vt* (*number*) fare; **to** ~ **a wrong number** sbagliare numero; **can I** ~ **London direct?** si può chiamare Londra in teleselezione?

dial. *abbr* = **dialect**.

dialect ['daɪəlɛkt] *n* dialetto.

dialling code ['daɪəlɪŋ-], (*US*) **dial code** *n* prefisso.

dialling tone ['daɪəlɪŋ-], (*US*) **dial tone** *n* segnale *m* di linea libera.

dialogue ['daɪəlɔg] *n* dialogo.

dialysis [daɪ'ælɪsɪs] *n* dialisi *f*.

diameter [daɪ'æmɪtə*] *n* diametro.

diametrically [daɪə'mɛtrɪklɪ] *ad*: ~ **opposed (to)** diametralmente opposto(a) (a).

diamond ['daɪəmənd] *n* diamante *m*; (*shape*) rombo; ~**s** *npl* (*CARDS*) quadri *mpl*.

diamond ring *n* anello di brillanti; (*with one diamond*) anello con brillante.

diaper ['daɪəpə*] *n* (*US*) pannolino.

diaphragm ['daɪəfræm] *n* diaframma *m*.

diarrhoea, (*US*) **diarrhea** [daɪə'ri:ə] *n* diarrea.

diary ['daɪərɪ] *n* (*daily account*) diario; (*book*) agenda; **to keep a** ~ tenere un diario.

diatribe ['daɪətraɪb] *n* diatriba.

dice [daɪs] *n* (*pl inv*) dado ♦ *vt* (*CULIN*) tagliare a dadini.

dicey ['daɪsɪ] *a* (*col*): **it's a bit** ~ è un po' un rischio.

dichotomy [daɪ'kɔtəmɪ] *n* dicotomia.

Dictaphone ® ['dɪktəfəun] *n* dittafono.

dictate *vt* [dɪk'teɪt] dettare ♦ *vi*: **to** ~ **to** (*person*) dare ordini a, dettar legge a ♦ *n* ['dɪkteɪt] dettame *m*; **I won't be** ~**d** to non ricevo ordini.

dictation [dɪk'teɪʃən] *n* dettato; (*to secretary etc*) dettatura; **at** ~ **speed** a velocità di dettatura.

dictator [dɪk'teɪtə*] *n* dittatore *m*.

dictatorship [dɪk'teɪtəʃɪp] *n* dittatura.

diction ['dɪkʃən] *n* dizione *f*.

dictionary ['dɪkʃənrɪ] *n* dizionario.

did [dɪd] *pt of* **do**.

didactic [daɪ'dæktɪk] *a* didattico(a).

didn't = **did not**.

die [daɪ] *n* (*pl*: **dies**) conio; matrice *f*; stampo ♦ *vi* morire; **to be dying** star morendo; **to be dying for sth/to do sth** morire dalla voglia di qc/di fare qc; **to** ~ **(of** *or* **from)** morire (di).

die away *vi* spegnersi a poco a poco.

die down *vi* abbassarsi.

die out *vi* estinguersi.

diehard ['daɪhɑ:d] *n* reazionario/a.

diesel ['di:zl] *n* diesel *m*.

diesel engine *n* motore *m* diesel *inv*.

diesel fuel, **diesel oil** *n* gasolio (per motori diesel).

diet ['daɪət] *n* alimentazione *f*; (*restricted food*) dieta ♦ *vi* (*also*: **be on a** ~) stare a dieta; **to live on a** ~ **of** nutrirsi di.

dietician [daɪə'tɪʃən] *n* dietologo/a.

differ ['dɪfə*] *vi*: **to** ~ **from sth** differire da qc; essere diverso(a) da qc; **to** ~ **from sb over sth** essere in disaccordo con qn su qc.

difference ['dɪfrəns] *n* differenza; (*quarrel*) screzio; **it makes no** ~ **to me** per me è lo stesso; **to settle one's** ~**s** risolvere la situazione.

different ['dɪfrənt] *a* diverso(a).

differential [dɪfə'rɛnʃəl] *n* (*AUT*, *wages*) differenziale *m*.

differentiate [dɪfə'rɛnʃɪeɪt] *vi* differenziarsi; **to** ~ **between** discriminare fra, fare

differenza fra.
differently ['dɪfrəntlɪ] *ad* diversamente.
difficult ['dɪfɪkəlt] *a* difficile; ~ **to understand** difficile da capire.
difficulty ['dɪfɪkəltɪ] *n* difficoltà *f inv*; **to have difficulties with** (*police, landlord etc*) avere noie con; **to be in** ~ essere *or* trovarsi in difficoltà.
diffidence ['dɪfɪdəns] *n* mancanza di sicurezza.
diffident ['dɪfɪdənt] *a* sfiduciato(a).
diffuse *a* [dɪ'fju:s] diffuso(a) ♦ *vt* [dɪ'fju:z] diffondere, emanare.
dig [dɪg] *vb* (*pt, pp* **dug** [dʌg]) *vt* (*hole*) scavare; (*garden*) vangare ♦ *vi* scavare ♦ *n* (*prod*) gomitata; (*fig*) frecciata; (*AR-CHAEOLOGY*) scavo, scavi *mpl*; **to** ~ **into** (*snow, soil*) scavare; **to** ~ **into one's pockets for sth** frugarsi le tasche cercando qc; **to** ~ **one's nails into** conficcare le unghie in; *see also* **digs**.
 dig in *vi* (*col: eat*) attaccare a mangiare; (*also:* ~ **o.s. in:** *MIL*) trincerarsi; (: *fig*) insediarsi, installarsi ♦ *vt* (*compost*) interrare; (*knife, claw*) affondare; **to** ~ **in one's heels** (*fig*) impuntarsi.
 dig out *vt* (*survivors, car from snow*) tirar fuori (scavando), estrarre (scavando).
 dig up *vt* scavare; (*tree etc*) sradicare.
digest [daɪ'dʒɛst] *vt* digerire.
digestible [dɪ'dʒɛstəbl] *a* digeribile.
digestion [dɪ'dʒɛstʃən] *n* digestione *f*.
digestive [dɪ'dʒɛstɪv] *a* digestivo(a); ~ **system** apparato digerente.
digit ['dɪdʒɪt] *n* cifra; (*finger*) dito.
digital ['dɪdʒɪtəl] *a* digitale.
dignified ['dɪgnɪfaɪd] *a* dignitoso(a).
dignitary ['dɪgnɪtərɪ] *n* dignitario.
dignity ['dɪgnɪtɪ] *n* dignità.
digress [daɪ'grɛs] *vi:* **to** ~ **from** divagare da.
digression [daɪ'grɛʃən] *n* digressione *f*.
digs [dɪgz] *npl* (*Brit col*) camera ammobiliata.
dilapidated [dɪ'læpɪdeɪtɪd] *a* cadente.
dilate [daɪ'leɪt] *vt* dilatare ♦ *vi* dilatarsi.
dilatory ['dɪlətərɪ] *a* dilatorio(a).
dilemma [daɪ'lɛmə] *n* dilemma *m*; **to be in a** ~ essere di fronte a un dilemma.
diligent ['dɪlɪdʒənt] *a* diligente.
dill [dɪl] *n* aneto.
dilly-dally ['dɪlɪdælɪ] *vi* gingillarsi.
dilute [daɪ'lu:t] *vt* diluire; (*with water*) annacquare ♦ *a* diluito(a).
dim [dɪm] *a* (*light, eyesight*) debole; (*memory, outline*) vago(a); (*stupid*) ottuso(a) ♦ *vt* (*light: also: US AUT*) abbassare; **to take a** ~ **view of sth** non vedere di buon occhio qc.
dime [daɪm] *n* (*US*) = 10 cents.
dimension [dɪ'mɛnʃən] *n* dimensione *f*.
-dimensional [dɪ'mɛnʃənl] *a suffix:* **two**~ bidimensionale.
diminish [dɪ'mɪnɪʃ] *vt, vi* diminuire.
diminished [dɪ'mɪnɪʃt] *a:* ~ **responsibility** (*LAW*) incapacità d'intendere e di volere.
diminutive [dɪ'mɪnjutɪv] *a* minuscolo(a) ♦ *n* (*LING*) diminutivo.

dimly ['dɪmlɪ] *ad* debolmente; indistintamente.
dimmers ['dɪməz] *npl* (*US AUT*) anabbaglianti *mpl*; (: *parking lights*) luci *fpl* di posizione.
dimple ['dɪmpl] *n* fossetta.
dim-witted ['dɪm'wɪtɪd] *a* (*col*) sciocco(a), stupido(a).
din [dɪn] *n* chiasso, fracasso ♦ *vt:* **to** ~ **sth into sb** (*col*) ficcare qc in testa a qn.
dine [daɪn] *vi* pranzare.
diner ['daɪnə*] *n* (*person: in restaurant*) cliente *m*; (*RAIL*) carrozza *or* vagone *m* ristorante; (*US: eating place*) tavola calda.
dinghy ['dɪŋgɪ] *n* battello pneumatico; (*also:* **sailing** ~) dinghy *m inv*.
dingy ['dɪndʒɪ] *a* grigio(a).
dining area ['daɪnɪŋ-] *n* zona pranzo *inv*.
dining car *n* vagone *m* ristorante.
dining room *n* sala da pranzo.
dinner ['dɪnə*] *n* pranzo; (*evening meal*) cena; (*public*) banchetto; ~'**s ready!** a tavola!
dinner jacket *n* smoking *m inv*.
dinner party *n* cena.
dinner service *n* servizio da tavola.
dinner time *n* ora di pranzo (*or* cena).
dinosaur ['daɪnəsɔ:*] *n* dinosauro.
dint [dɪnt] *n:* **by** ~ **of (doing) sth** a forza di (fare) qc.
diocese ['daɪəsɪs] *n* diocesi *f inv*.
dioxide [daɪ'ɔksaɪd] *n* biossido.
dip [dɪp] *n* (*slope*) discesa; (*in sea*) bagno ♦ *vt* immergere, bagnare; (*Brit AUT: lights*) abbassare ♦ *vi* (*road*) essere in pendenza; (*bird, plane*) abbassarsi.
Dip. *abbr* (*Brit*) = **diploma**.
diphtheria [dɪf'θɪərɪə] *n* difterite *f*.
diphthong ['dɪfθɔŋ] *n* dittongo.
diploma [dɪ'pləumə] *n* diploma *m*.
diplomacy [dɪ'pləuməsɪ] *n* diplomazia.
diplomat ['dɪpləmæt] *n* diplomatico.
diplomatic [dɪplə'mætɪk] *a* diplomatico(a); **to break off** ~ **relations** rompere le relazioni diplomatiche.
diplomatic corps *n* corpo diplomatico.
dipstick ['dɪpstɪk] *n* (*AUT*) indicatore *m* di livello dell'olio.
dipswitch ['dɪpswɪtʃ] *n* (*Brit AUT*) levetta dei fari.
dire [daɪə*] *a* terribile; estremo(a).
direct [daɪ'rɛkt] *a* diretto(a); (*manner, person*) franco(a), esplicito(a) ♦ *vt* dirigere; **to** ~ **sb to do sth** dare direttive a qn di fare qc; **can you** ~ **me to ...?** mi può indicare la strada per ...?
direct cost *n* (*COMM*) costo diretto.
direct current *n* (*ELEC*) corrente *f* continua.
direct debit *n* (*BANKING*) addebito effettuato per ordine di un cliente di banca.
direct dialling *n* (*TEL*) ≈ teleselezione *f*.
direct hit *n* (*MIL*) colpo diretto.
direction [dɪ'rɛkʃən] *n* direzione *f*; (*of play, film, programme*) regia; ~**s** *npl* (*advice*) chiarimenti *mpl*; (*instructions: to a place*) indicazioni *fpl*; ~**s for use** istruzioni *fpl*; **to**

ask for ~s chiedere la strada; **sense of** ~ senso dell'orientamento; **in the** ~ **of** in direzione di.

directive [dɪˈrɛktɪv] *n* direttiva, ordine *m*; **a government** ~ una disposizione governativa.

direct labour *n* manodopera diretta.

directly [dɪˈrɛktlɪ] *ad* (*in straight line*) direttamente; (*at once*) subito.

direct mail *n* pubblicità diretta.

direct mailshot *n* (*Brit*) materiale *m* pubblicitario ad approccio diretto.

directness [daɪˈrɛktnɪs] *n* (*of person, speech*) franchezza.

director [dɪˈrɛktə*] *n* direttore/trice; amministratore/trice; (*THEATRE*, *CINEMA*, *TV*) regista *m/f*; **D**~ **of Public Prosecutions (DPP)** (*Brit*) ≈ Procuratore *m* della Repubblica.

directory [dɪˈrɛktərɪ] *n* elenco; (*street* ~) stradario; (*trade* ~) repertorio del commercio; (*COMPUT*) directory *m inv*.

directory enquiries, (*US*) **directory assistance** *n* (*TEL*) servizio informazioni, informazioni *fpl* elenco abbonati.

dirt [dəːt] *n* sporcizia; immondizia; **to treat sb like** ~ trattare qn come uno straccio.

dirt-cheap [ˈdəːtˈtʃiːp] *a* da due soldi.

dirt road *n* strada non asfaltata.

dirty [ˈdəːtɪ] *a* sporco(a) ♦ *vt* sporcare; ~ **story** storia oscena; ~ **trick** brutto scherzo.

disability [dɪsəˈbɪlɪtɪ] *n* invalidità *f inv*; (*LAW*) incapacità *f inv*.

disability allowance *n* pensione *f* d'invalidità.

disable [dɪsˈeɪbl] *vt* (*subj: illness, accident*) rendere invalido(a); (*tank, gun*) mettere fuori uso.

disabled [dɪsˈeɪbld] *a* invalido(a); (*maimed*) mutilato(a); (*through illness, old age*) inabile.

disadvantage [dɪsədˈvɑːntɪdʒ] *n* svantaggio.

disadvantaged [dɪsədˈvɑːntɪdʒd] *a* (*person*) svantaggiato(a).

disadvantageous [dɪsædvəˈnˈteɪdʒəs] *a* svantaggioso(a).

disaffected [dɪsəˈfɛktɪd] *a*: ~ (**to or towards**) scontento(a) di, insoddisfatto(a) di.

disaffection [dɪsəˈfɛkʃən] *n* malcontento, insoddisfazione *f*.

disagree [dɪsəˈgriː] *vi* (*differ*) discordare; (*be against, think otherwise*): **to** ~ (**with**) essere in disaccordo (con), dissentire (da); **I** ~ **with you** non sono d'accordo con lei; **garlic** ~**s with me** l'aglio non mi va.

disagreeable [dɪsəˈgriːəbl] *a* sgradevole; (*person*) antipatico(a).

disagreement [dɪsəˈgriːmənt] *n* disaccordo; (*quarrel*) dissapore *m*; **to have a** ~ **with sb** litigare con qn.

disallow [ˈdɪsəˈlau] *vt* respingere; (*Brit FOOTBALL: goal*) annullare.

disappear [dɪsəˈpɪə*] *vi* scomparire.

disappearance [dɪsəˈpɪərəns] *n* scomparsa.

disappoint [dɪsəˈpɔɪnt] *vt* deludere.

disappointed [dɪsəˈpɔɪntɪd] *a* deluso(a).

disappointing [dɪsəˈpɔɪntɪŋ] *a* deludente.

disappointment [dɪsəˈpɔɪntmənt] *n* delusione *f*.

disapproval [dɪsəˈpruːvəl] *n* disapprovazione *f*.

disapprove [dɪsəˈpruːv] *vi*: **to** ~ **of** disapprovare.

disapproving [dɪsəˈpruːvɪŋ] *a* di disapprovazione.

disarm [dɪsˈɑːm] *vt* disarmare.

disarmament [dɪsˈɑːməmənt] *n* disarmo.

disarming [dɪsˈɑːmɪŋ] *a* (*smile*) disarmante.

disarray [dɪsəˈreɪ] *n*: **in** ~ (*troops*) in rotta; (*thoughts*) confuso(a); (*clothes*) in disordine; **to throw into** ~ buttare all'aria.

disaster [dɪˈzɑːstə*] *n* disastro.

disaster area *n* zona disastrata.

disastrous [dɪˈzɑːstrəs] *a* disastroso(a).

disband [dɪsˈbænd] *vt* sbandare; (*MIL*) congedare ♦ *vi* sciogliersi.

disbelief [ˈdɪsbəˈliːf] *n* incredulità; **in** ~ incredulo(a).

disbelieve [ˈdɪsbəˈliːv] *vt* (*person, story*) non credere a, mettere in dubbio; **I don't** ~ **you** vorrei poterle credere.

disc [dɪsk] *n* disco.

disc. *abbr* (*COMM*) = **discount**.

discard [dɪsˈkɑːd] *vt* (*old things*) scartare; (*fig*) abbandonare.

disc brake *n* freno a disco.

discern [dɪˈsəːn] *vt* discernere, distinguere.

discernible [dɪˈsəːnəbl] *a* percepibile.

discerning [dɪˈsəːnɪŋ] *a* perspicace.

discharge *vt* [dɪsˈtʃɑːdʒ] (*duties*) compiere; (*settle: debt*) pagare, estinguere; (*ELEC, waste etc*) scaricare; (*MED*) emettere; (*patient*) dimettere; (*employee*) licenziare; (*soldier*) congedare; (*defendant*) liberare ♦ *n* [ˈdɪstʃɑːdʒ] (*ELEC*) scarica; (*MED, of gas, chemicals*) emissione *f*; (*vaginal* ~) perdite *fpl* (bianche); (*dismissal*) licenziamento; congedo; liberazione *f*; **to** ~ **one's gun** fare fuoco.

discharged bankrupt [dɪsˈtʃɑːdʒd-] *n* fallito cui il tribunale ha concesso la riabilitazione.

disciple [dɪˈsaɪpl] *n* discepolo.

disciplinary [ˈdɪsɪplɪnərɪ] *a* disciplinare; **to take** ~ **action against sb** prendere un provvedimento disciplinare contro qn.

discipline [ˈdɪsɪplɪn] *n* disciplina ♦ *vt* disciplinare; (*punish*) punire; **to** ~ **o.s. to do sth** imporsi di fare qc.

disc jockey (DJ) *n* disc jockey *m inv*.

disclaim [dɪsˈkleɪm] *vt* negare, smentire.

disclaimer [dɪsˈkleɪmə*] *n* smentita; **to issue a** ~ pubblicare una smentita.

disclose [dɪsˈkləuz] *vt* rivelare, svelare.

disclosure [dɪsˈkləuʒə*] *n* rivelazione *f*.

disco [ˈdɪskəu] *n abbr* = **discothèque**.

discolour, (*US*) **discolor** [dɪsˈkʌlə*] *vt* scolorire; (*sth white*) ingiallire ♦ *vi* sbiadire, scolorirsi; (*sth white*) ingiallire.

discolo(u)ration [dɪskʌləˈreɪʃən] *n* scolorimento.

discolo(u)red [dɪs'kʌləd] *a* scolorito(a); ingiallito(a).

discomfort [dɪs'kʌmfət] *n* disagio; (*lack of comfort*) scomodità *f inv*.

disconcert [dɪskən'sə:t] *vt* sconcertare.

disconnect [dɪskə'nɛkt] *vt* sconnettere, staccare; (*ELEC, RADIO*) staccare; (*gas, water*) chiudere.

disconnected [dɪskə'nɛktɪd] *a* (*speech, thought*) sconnesso(a).

disconsolate [dɪs'kɔnsəlɪt] *a* sconsolato(a).

discontent [dɪskən'tɛnt] *n* scontentezza.

discontented [dɪskən'tɛntɪd] *a* scontento(a).

discontinue [dɪskən'tɪnju:] *vt* smettere, cessare; "~d" (*COMM*) "sospeso".

discord ['dɪskɔ:d] *n* disaccordo; (*MUS*) dissonanza.

discordant [dɪs'kɔ:dənt] *a* discordante; dissonante.

discothèque ['dɪskəutɛk] *n* discoteca.

discount *n* ['dɪskaunt] sconto ♦ *vt* [dɪs'kaunt] scontare; (*report etc*) non badare a; **at a ~** con uno sconto; **to give sb a ~ on sth** fare uno sconto a qn su qc; **~ for cash** sconto *m* cassa *inv*.

discount house *n* (*FINANCE*) casa di sconto, discount house *f inv*; (*COMM: also*: **discount store**) discount *m inv*.

discount rate *n* tasso di sconto.

discourage [dɪs'kʌrɪdʒ] *vt* scoraggiare; (*dissuade, deter*) tentare di dissuadere.

discouragement [dɪs'kʌrɪdʒmənt] *n* (*dissuasion*) disapprovazione *f*; (*depression*) scoraggiamento; **to act as a ~** to ostacolare.

discouraging [dɪs'kʌrɪdʒɪŋ] *a* scoraggiante.

discourteous [dɪs'kə:tɪəs] *a* scortese.

discover [dɪs'kʌvə*] *vt* scoprire.

discovery [dɪs'kʌvərɪ] *n* scoperta.

discredit [dɪs'krɛdɪt] *vt* screditare; mettere in dubbio ♦ *n* discredito.

discreet [dɪ'skri:t] *a* discreto(a).

discreetly [dɪ'skri:tlɪ] *ad* con discrezione.

discrepancy [dɪ'skrɛpənsɪ] *n* discrepanza.

discretion [dɪ'skrɛʃən] *n* discrezione *f*; **use your own ~** giudichi lei.

discretionary [dɪs'krɛʃənərɪ] *a* (*powers*) discrezionale.

discriminate [dɪ'skrɪmɪneɪt] *vi*: **to ~ between** distinguere tra; **to ~ against** discriminare contro.

discriminating [dɪs'krɪmɪneɪtɪŋ] *a* (*ear, taste*) fine, giudizioso(a); (*person*) esigente; (*tax, duty*) discriminante.

discrimination [dɪskrɪmɪ'neɪʃən] *n* discriminazione *f*; (*judgement*) discernimento; **racial/sexual ~** discriminazione razziale/sessuale.

discus ['dɪskəs] *n* disco.

discuss [dɪ'skʌs] *vt* discutere; (*debate*) dibattere.

discussion [dɪ'skʌʃən] *n* discussione *f*; **under ~** in discussione.

disdain [dɪs'deɪn] *n* disdegno.

disease [dɪ'zi:z] *n* malattia.

diseased [dɪ'zi:zd] *a* malato(a).

disembark [dɪsɪm'bɑ:k] *vt, vi* sbarcare.

disembarkation [dɪsɛmbɑ:'keɪʃən] *n* sbarco.

disembodied [dɪsɪm'bɔdɪd] *a* disincarnato(a).

disembowel [dɪsɪm'bauəl] *vt* sbudellare, sventrare.

disenchanted [dɪsɪn'tʃɑ:ntɪd] *a* disincantato(a); **~ (with)** deluso(a) (da).

disenfranchise [dɪsɪn'fræntʃaɪz] *vt* privare del diritto di voto; (*COMM*) revocare una condizione di privilegio commerciale a.

disengage [dɪsɪn'geɪdʒ] *vt* disimpegnare; (*TECH*) distaccare; (*AUT*) disinnestare.

disengagement [dɪsɪn'geɪdʒmənt] *n* (*POL*) disimpegno.

disentangle [dɪsɪn'tæŋgl] *vt* sbrogliare.

disfavour, (*US*) **disfavor** [dɪs'feɪvə*] *n* sfavore *m*; disgrazia.

disfigure [dɪs'fɪgə*] *vt* sfigurare.

disgorge [dɪs'gɔ:dʒ] *vt* (*subj: river*) riversare.

disgrace [dɪs'greɪs] *n* vergogna; (*disfavour*) disgrazia ♦ *vt* disonorare, far cadere in disgrazia.

disgraceful [dɪs'greɪsful] *a* scandaloso(a), vergognoso(a).

disgruntled [dɪs'grʌntld] *a* scontento(a), di cattivo umore.

disguise [dɪs'gaɪz] *n* travestimento ♦ *vt* travestire; (*voice*) contraffare; (*feelings etc*) mascherare; **to ~ o.s.** as travestirsi da; **in ~** travestito(a); **there's no disguising the fact that ...** non si può nascondere (il fatto) che ....

disgust [dɪs'gʌst] *n* disgusto, nausea ♦ *vt* disgustare, far schifo a.

disgusting [dɪs'gʌstɪŋ] *a* disgustoso(a).

dish [dɪʃ] *n* piatto; **to do** *or* **wash the ~es** fare i piatti.

dish out *vt* (*food*) servire; (*advice*) elargire; (*money*) tirare fuori; (*exam papers*) distribuire.

dish up *vt* (*food*) servire; (*facts, statistics*) presentare.

dishcloth ['dɪʃklɔθ] *n* strofinaccio dei piatti.

dishearten [dɪs'hɑ:tn] *vt* scoraggiare.

dishevelled, (*US*) **disheveled** [dɪ'ʃɛvəld] *a* arruffato(a); scapigliato(a).

dishonest [dɪs'ɔnɪst] *a* disonesto(a).

dishonesty [dɪs'ɔnɪstɪ] *n* disonestà.

dishonour, (*US*) **dishonor** [dɪs'ɔnə*] *n* disonore *m*.

dishono(u)rable [dɪs'ɔnərəbl] *a* disonorevole.

dish soap *n* (*US*) detersivo liquido (per stoviglie).

dishtowel ['dɪʃtauəl] *n* strofinaccio dei piatti.

dishwasher ['dɪʃwɔʃə*] *n* lavastoviglie *f inv*; (*person*) sguattero/a.

disillusion [dɪsɪ'lu:ʒən] *vt* disilludere, disingannare ♦ *n* disillusione *f*; **to become ~ed (with)** perdere le illusioni (su).

disillusionment [dɪsɪ'lu:ʒənmənt] *n* disillusione *f*.

disincentive [dɪsɪn'sɛntɪv] *n*: **to act as a ~ (to)** agire da freno (su); **to be a ~ to**

scoraggiare.

disinclined [dısın'klaınd] *a*: **to be ~ to do sth** essere poco propenso(a) a fare qc.

disinfect [dısın'fɛkt] *vt* disinfettare.

disinfectant [dısın'fɛktənt] *n* disinfettante *m*.

disinflation [dısın'fleıʃən] *n* disinflazione *f*.

disinherit [dısın'hɛrıt] *vt* diseredare.

disintegrate [dıs'ıntıgreıt] *vi* disintegrarsi.

disinterested [dıs'ıntrəstıd] *a* disinteressato(a).

disjointed [dıs'dʒɔıntıd] *a* sconnesso(a).

disk [dısk] *n* (*COMPUT*) disco; **single-/double-sided ~** disco *m* monofaccia *inv*/a doppia faccia.

disk drive *n* disk drive *m inv*, unità *f inv* a dischi magnetici.

disk operating system (DOS) *n* sistema *m* operativo a disco.

diskette [dıs'kɛt] *n* (*COMPUT*) dischetto.

dislike [dıs'laık] *n* antipatia, avversione *f* ♦ *vt*: **he ~s it** non gli piace; **I ~ the idea** l'idea non mi va; **to take a ~ to sb/sth** prendere in antipatia qn/qc.

dislocate ['dısləkeıt] *vt* (*MED*) slogare; (*fig*) disorganizzare; **he ~d his shoulder** si è lussato una spalla.

dislodge [dıs'lɔdʒ] *vt* rimuovere, staccare; (*enemy*) sloggiare.

disloyal [dıs'lɔıəl] *a* sleale.

dismal ['dızml] *a* triste, cupo(a).

dismantle [dıs'mæntl] *vt* smantellare, smontare; (*fort, warship*) disarmare.

dismast [dıs'mɑːst] *vt* disalberare.

dismay [dıs'meı] *n* costernazione *f* ♦ *vt* sgomentare; **much to my ~** con mio gran stupore.

dismiss [dıs'mıs] *vt* congedare; (*employee*) licenziare; (*idea*) scacciare; (*LAW*) respingere ♦ *vi* (*MIL*) rompere i ranghi.

dismissal [dıs'mısəl] *n* congedo; licenziamento.

dismount [dıs'maunt] *vi* scendere ♦ *vt* (*rider*) disarcionare.

disobedience [dısə'biːdıəns] *n* disubbidienza.

disobedient [dısə'diːənt] *a* disubbidiente.

disobey [dısə'beı] *vt* disubbidire; (*rule*) trasgredire.

disorder [dıs'ɔːdə*] *n* disordine *m*; (*rioting*) tumulto; (*MED*) disturbo; **civil ~** disordini *mpl* interni.

disorderly [dıs'ɔːdəlı] *a* disordinato(a); tumultuoso(a).

disorderly conduct *n* (*LAW*) comportamento atto a turbare l'ordine pubblico.

disorganize [dıs'ɔːgənaız] *vt* disorganizzare.

disorganized [dıs'ɔːgənaızd] *a* (*person, life*) disorganizzato(a); (*system, meeting*) male organizzato(a).

disorientated [dıs'ɔːrıenteıtıd] *a* disorientato(a).

disown [dıs'əun] *vt* ripudiare.

disparaging [dıs'pærıdʒıŋ] *a* spregiativo(a), sprezzante; **to be ~ about sb/sth** denigrare qn/qc.

disparate ['dıspərıt] *a* disparato(a).

disparity [dıs'pærıtı] *n* disparità *f inv*.

dispassionate [dıs'pæʃənət] *a* calmo(a), freddo(a); imparziale.

dispatch [dıs'pætʃ] *vt* spedire, inviare; (*deal with: business*) sbrigare ♦ *n* spedizione *f*, invio; (*MIL, PRESS*) dispaccio.

dispatch department *n* reparto spedizioni.

dispatch rider *n* (*MIL*) corriere *m*, portaordini *m inv*.

dispel [dıs'pɛl] *vt* dissipare, scacciare.

dispensary [dıs'pɛnsərı] *n* farmacia; (*in chemist's*) dispensario.

dispense [dıs'pɛns] *vt* distribuire, amministrare; (*medicine*) preparare e dare; **to ~ sb from** dispensare qn da.

dispense with *vt fus* fare a meno di; (*make unnecessary*) rendere superfluo(a).

dispenser [dıs'pɛnsə*] *n* (*container*) distributore *m*.

dispensing chemist *n* (*Brit*) farmacista *m/f*.

dispersal [dıs'pəːsl] *n* dispersione *f*.

disperse [dıs'pəːs] *vt* disperdere; (*knowledge*) disseminare ♦ *vi* disperdersi.

dispirited [dıs'pırıtıd] *a* scoraggiato(a), abbattuto(a).

displace [dıs'pleıs] *vt* spostare.

displaced person *n* (*POL*) profugo/a.

displacement [dıs'pleısmənt] *n* spostamento.

display [dıs'pleı] *n* mostra; esposizione *f*; (*of feeling etc*) manifestazione *f*; (*military ~*) parata (militare); (*computer ~*) display *m inv*; (*pej*) ostentazione *f* ♦ *vt* mostrare; (*goods*) esporre; (*results*) affiggere; (*departure times*) indicare; **on ~** (*gen*) in mostra; (*goods*) in vetrina.

display advertising *n* pubblicità tabellare.

displease [dıs'pliːz] *vt* dispiacere a, scontentare; **~d with** scontento(a) di.

displeasure [dıs'plɛʒə*] *n* dispiacere *m*.

disposable [dıs'pəuzəbl] *a* (*pack etc*) a perdere; (*income*) disponibile; **~ nappy** (*Brit*) pannolino di carta.

disposal [dıs'pəuzl] *n* (*of rubbish*) evacuazione *f*; distruzione *f*; (*of property etc: by selling*) vendita; (*: by giving away*) cessione *f*; **at one's ~** alla sua disposizione; **to put sth at sb's ~** mettere qc a disposizione di qn.

dispose [dıs'pəuz] *vt* disporre.

dispose of *vt fus* (*time, money*) disporre di; (*COMM: sell*) vendere; (*unwanted goods*) sbarazzarsi di; (*problem*) eliminare.

disposed [dıs'pəuzd] *a*: **~ to do** disposto(a) a fare.

disposition [dıspə'zıʃən] *n* disposizione *f*; (*temperament*) carattere *m*.

dispossess ['dıspə'zɛs] *vt*: **to ~ sb (of)** spossessare qn (di).

disproportion [dısprə'pɔːʃən] *n* sproporzione *f*.

disproportionate [dısprə'pɔːʃənət] *a* sproporzionato(a).

disprove [dıs'pruːv] *vt* confutare.

dispute [dıs'pjuːt] *n* disputa; (*also*: **industrial**

~) controversia (sindacale) ♦ *vt* contestare; (*matter*) discutere; (*victory*) disputare; **to be in** *or* **under** ~ (*matter*) essere in discussione; (*territory*) essere oggetto di contesa.

disqualification [dɪskwɔlɪfɪ'keɪʃən] *n* squalifica; ~ **(from driving)** (*Brit*) ritiro della patente.

disqualify [dɪs'kwɔlɪfaɪ] *vt* (*SPORT*) squalificare; **to** ~ **sb from sth/from doing** rendere qn incapace a qc/a fare; squalificare qn da qc/da fare; **to** ~ **sb from driving** (*Brit*) ritirare la patente a qn.

disquiet [dɪs'kwaɪət] *n* inquietudine *f*.

disquieting [dɪs'kwaɪətɪŋ] *a* inquietante, allarmante.

disregard [dɪsrɪ'gɑːd] *vt* non far caso a, non badare a ♦ *n* (*indifference*): ~ **(for)** (*feelings*) insensibilità (a), indifferenza (verso); (*danger*) noncuranza (di); (*money*) disprezzo (di).

disrepair [dɪsrɪ'pɛə*] *n* cattivo stato; **to fall into** ~ (*building*) andare in rovina; (*street*) deteriorarsi.

disreputable [dɪs'rɛpjutəbl] *a* (*person*) di cattiva fama; (*area*) malfamato(a), poco raccomandabile.

disrepute ['dɪsrɪ'pjuːt] *n* disonore *m*, vergogna; **to bring into** ~ rovinare la reputazione di.

disrespectful [dɪsrɪ'spɛktful] *a* che manca di rispetto.

disrupt [dɪs'rʌpt] *vt* (*meeting, lesson*) disturbare, interrompere; (*public transport*) creare scompiglio in; (*plans*) scombussolare.

disruption [dɪs'rʌpʃən] *n* disordine *m*; interruzione *f*.

disruptive [dɪs'rʌptɪv] *a* (*influence*) negativo(a), deleterio(a); (*strike action*) paralizzante.

dissatisfaction [dɪssætɪs'fækʃən] *n* scontentezza, insoddisfazione *f*.

dissatisfied [dɪs'sætɪsfaɪd] *a*: ~ **(with)** scontento(a) *or* insoddisfatto(a) (di).

dissect [dɪ'sɛkt] *vt* sezionare; (*fig*) sviscerare.

disseminate [dɪ'sɛmɪneɪt] *vt* disseminare.

dissent [dɪ'sɛnt] *n* dissenso.

dissenter [dɪ'sɛntə*] *n* (*REL, POL etc*) dissidente *m/f*.

dissertation [dɪsə'teɪʃən] *n* (*SCOL*) tesi *f* inv, dissertazione *f*.

disservice [dɪs'səːvɪs] *n*: **to do sb a** ~ fare un cattivo servizio a qn.

dissident ['dɪsɪdnt] *a* dissidente; (*speech, voice*) di dissenso ♦ *n* dissidente *m/f*.

dissimilar [dɪ'sɪmɪlə*] *a*: ~ **(to)** dissimile *or* diverso(a) (da).

dissipate ['dɪsɪpeɪt] *vt* dissipare.

dissipated ['dɪsɪpeɪtɪd] *a* dissipato(a).

dissociate [dɪ'səuʃɪeɪt] *vt* dissociare; **to** ~ **o.s. from** dichiarare di non avere niente a che fare con.

dissolute ['dɪsəluːt] *a* dissoluto(a), licenzioso(a).

dissolve [dɪ'zɔlv] *vt* dissolvere, sciogliere; (*COMM, POL, marriage*) sciogliere ♦ *vi* dissolversi, sciogliersi; (*fig*) svanire.

dissuade [dɪ'sweɪd] *vt*: **to** ~ **sb** (**from**) dissuadere qn (da).

distaff side ['dɪstɑːf-] *n* ramo femminile di una famiglia.

distance ['dɪstns] *n* distanza; **in the** ~ in lontananza; **what's the** ~ **to London?** quanto dista Londra?; **it's within walking** ~ ci si arriva a piedi; **at a** ~ **of 2 metres** a 2 metri di distanza.

distant ['dɪstnt] *a* lontano(a), distante; (*manner*) riservato(a), freddo(a).

distaste [dɪs'teɪst] *n* ripugnanza.

distasteful [dɪs'teɪstful] *a* ripugnante, sgradevole.

Dist. Atty. *abbr* (*US*) = **district attorney**.

distemper [dɪs'tɛmpə*] *n* (*paint*) tempera; (*of dogs*) cimurro.

distend [dɪs'tɛnd] *vt* dilatare ♦ *vi* dilatarsi.

distended [dɪs'tɛndɪd] *a* (*stomach*) dilatato(a).

distil, (*US*) **distill** [dɪs'tɪl] *vt* distillare.

distillery [dɪs'tɪlərɪ] *n* distilleria.

distinct [dɪs'tɪŋkt] *a* distinto(a); (*preference, progress*) definito(a); **as** ~ **from** a differenza di.

distinction [dɪs'tɪŋkʃən] *n* distinzione *f*; (*in exam*) lode *f*; **to draw a** ~ **between** fare distinzione tra; **a writer of** ~ uno scrittore di notevoli qualità.

distinctive [dɪs'tɪŋktɪv] *a* distintivo(a).

distinctly [dɪs'tɪŋktlɪ] *ad* distintamente; (*remember*) chiaramente; (*unhappy, better*) decisamente.

distinguish [dɪs'tɪŋgwɪʃ] *vt* distinguere; discernere ♦ *vi*: **to** ~ **(between)** distinguere (tra); **to** ~ **o.s.** distinguersi.

distinguished [dɪs'tɪŋgwɪʃt] *a* (*eminent*) eminente; (*career*) brillante; (*refined*) distinto(a), signorile.

distinguishing [dɪs'tɪŋgwɪʃɪŋ] *a* (*feature*) distinto(a), caratteristico(a).

distort [dɪs'tɔːt] *vt* (*also fig*) distorcere; (*account, news*) falsare; (*TECH*) deformare.

distortion [dɪs'tɔːʃən] *n* (*gen*) distorsione *f*; (*of truth etc*) alterazione *f*; (*of facts*) travisamento; (*TECH*) deformazione *f*.

distract [dɪs'trækt] *vt* distrarre.

distracted [dɪs'træktɪd] *a* distratto(a).

distraction [dɪs'trækʃən] *n* distrazione *f*; **to drive sb to** ~ spingere qn alla pazzia.

distraught [dɪs'trɔːt] *a* stravolto(a).

distress [dɪs'trɛs] *n* angoscia; (*pain*) dolore *m* ♦ *vt* affliggere; **in** ~ (*ship etc*) in pericolo, in difficoltà; **~ed area** (*Brit*) zona sinistrata.

distressing [dɪs'trɛsɪŋ] *a* doloroso(a), penoso(a).

distress signal *n* segnale *m* di pericolo.

distribute [dɪs'trɪbjuːt] *vt* distribuire.

distribution [dɪstrɪ'bjuːʃən] *n* distribuzione *f*.

distribution cost *n* costo di distribuzione.

distributor [dɪs'trɪbjutə*] *n* distributore *m*;

(*COMM*) concessionario.
district ['dıstrıkt] *n* (*of country*) regione *f*; (*of town*) quartiere *m*; (*ADMIN*) distretto.
district attorney (DA) *n* (*US*) ≈ sostituto procuratore *m* della Repubblica.
district council *n* (*Brit*) consiglio comunale.
district nurse *n* (*Brit*) infermiera di quartiere.
distrust [dıs'trʌst] *n* diffidenza, sfiducia ♦ *vt* non aver fiducia in.
distrustful [dıs'trʌstful] *a* diffidente.
disturb [dıs'tə:b] *vt* disturbare; (*inconvenience*) scomodare; **sorry to ~ you** scusi se la disturbo.
disturbance [dıs'tə:bəns] *n* disturbo; (*political etc*) tumulto; (*by drunks etc*) disordini *mpl*; **~ of the peace** disturbo della quiete pubblica; **to cause a ~** provocare disordini.
disturbed [dıs'tə:bd] *a* turbato(a); **to be emotionally ~** avere problemi emotivi; **to be mentally ~** essere malato(a) di mente.
disturbing [dıs'tə:bıŋ] *a* sconvolgente.
disuse [dıs'ju:s] *n*: **to fall into ~** cadere in disuso.
disused [dıs'ju:zd] *a* abbandonato(a).
ditch [dıtʃ] *n* fossa ♦ *vt* (*col*) piantare in asso.
dither ['dıðə*] *vi* vacillare.
ditto ['dıtəu] *ad* idem.
divan [dı'væn] *n* divano.
divan bed *n* divano letto *inv*.
dive [daıv] *n* tuffo; (*of submarine*) immersione *f*; (*AVIAT*) picchiata; (*pej*) buco ♦ *vi* tuffarsi.
diver ['daıvə*] *n* tuffatore/trice; (*deep-sea* ~) palombaro.
diverge [daı'və:dʒ] *vi* divergere.
divergent [daı'və:dʒənt] *a* divergente.
diverse [daı'və:s] *a* vario(a).
diversification [daıvə:sıfı'keıʃən] *n* diversificazione *f*.
diversify [daı'və:sıfaı] *vt* diversificare.
diversion [daı'və:ʃən] *n* (*Brit AUT*) deviazione *f*; (*distraction*) divertimento.
diversity [daı'və:sıtı] *n* diversità *f inv*, varietà *f inv*.
divert [daı'və:t] *vt* (*traffic, river*) deviare; (*train, plane*) dirottare; (*amuse*) divertire.
divest [daı'vest] *vt*: **to ~ sb of** spogliare qn di.
divide [dı'vaıd] *vt* dividere; (*separate*) separare ♦ *vi* dividersi; **to ~ (between or among)** dividere (tra), ripartire (tra); **40 ~d by 5** 40 diviso 5.
divide out *vt*: **to ~ out (between or among)** (*sweets etc*) distribuire (tra); (*tasks*) distribuire *or* ripartire (tra).
divided [dı'vaıdıd] *a* (*country*) diviso(a); (*opinions*) discordi.
divided highway *n* (*US*) strada a doppia carreggiata.
divided skirt *n* gonna *f* pantalone *inv*.
dividend ['dıvıdend] *n* dividendo.
dividend cover *n* rapporto dividendo profitti.
dividers [dı'vaıdəz] *npl* compasso a punte fisse.

divine [dı'vaın] *a* divino(a) ♦ *vt* (*future*) divinare, predire; (*truth*) indovinare; (*water, metal*) individuare tramite radioestesia.
diving ['daıvıŋ] *n* tuffo.
diving board *n* trampolino.
diving suit *n* scafandro.
divinity [dı'vınıtı] *n* divinità *f inv*; teologia.
division [dı'vıʒən] *n* divisione *f*; separazione *f*; (*Brit FOOTBALL*) serie *f inv*; **~ of labour** divisione *f* del lavoro.
divisive [dı'vaısıv] *a* che è causa di discordia.
divorce [dı'vɔ:s] *n* divorzio ♦ *vt* divorziare da.
divorced [dı'vɔ:st] *a* divorziato(a).
divorcee [dıvɔ:'si:] *n* divorziato/a.
divulge [daı'vʌldʒ] *vt* divulgare, rivelare.
D.I.Y. *a, n abbr* (*Brit*) *see* **do-it-yourself**.
dizziness ['dızınıs] *n* vertigini *fpl*.
dizzy ['dızı] *a* (*height*) vertiginoso(a); **to make sb ~** far girare la testa a qn; **to feel ~** avere il capogiro; **I feel ~** mi gira la testa, ho il capogiro.
DJ *n abbr see* **disc jockey**.
Djakarta [dʒə'kɑ:tə] *n* Djakarta.
DJIA *n abbr* (*US STOCK EXCHANGE*: = *Dow-Jones Industrial Average*) indice *m* Dow-Jones.
dl *abbr* (= *decilitre*) dl.
DLit(t) *n abbr* = *Doctor of Literature*; *Doctor of Letters*.
DLO *n abbr* = **dead-letter office**.
dm *abbr* (= *decimetre*) dm.
DMus *n abbr* = *Doctor of Music*.
DMZ *n abbr* (= *demilitarized zone*) zona smilitarizzata.
DNA *n abbr* (= *deoxyribonucleic acid*) DNA *m*.
do [du:] *vt, vi* (*pt* **did** [dıd], *pp* **done** [dʌn]) fare ♦ *n* (*col: party*) festa; (: *formal gathering*) occasione *f*; **he didn't laugh** non ha riso; **~ you want any?** ne vuole?; **~ you speak English?** parla inglese?; **he laughed, didn't he?** lui ha riso, vero?; **~ they?** ah sì?, vero?; **who broke it? - I** did chi l'ha rotto? - sono stato io; **~ you agree? - I ~** è d'accordo? - sì; **you speak better than I ~** parla meglio di me; **so does he** anche lui; **DO come!** dai, vieni!; **I DO wish I could ...** magari potessi ...; **but I DO like it!** mi piace proprio!; **I'll ~ all I can** farò tutto il possibile; **how ~ you like your steak done?** come preferisce la bistecca?; **well done** ben cotto; **what can I ~ for you?** (*in shop*) desidera?; **to ~ one's nails** farsi le unghie; **to ~ one's teeth** pulirsi i denti; **to ~ one's hair** pettinarsi; **will it ~?** andrà bene?; **he's ~ing well/badly at school** va bene/male a scuola; **that'll ~!** (*in annoyance*) ora basta!; **to ~ sb out of sth** fregare qc a qn; **to make ~ (with)** arrangiarsi (con); **to ~ without sth** fare a meno di qc; **what did he ~ with the cat?** che ne ha fatto del gatto?; **what has that got to ~ with it?** che c'entra?
do away with *vt fus* abolire; (*kill*) far fuori.

do for *vt fus* (*Brit col*: *clean for*) fare i servizi per.

do up *vt* abbottonare; allacciare; (*house etc*) rimettere a nuovo; **to ~ o.s. up** farsi bello(a).

do with *vt fus* (*with can, could*: *need*) avere bisogno di; **I could ~ with some help/a drink** un aiuto/un bicchierino non guasterebbe; **it could ~ with a wash** una lavata non gli farebbe male.

do. *abbr* = **ditto**.

DOA (= *dead on arrival*) morto(a) durante il trasporto.

d.o.b. *abbr* = **date of birth**.

docile ['dəʊsaɪl] *a* docile.

dock [dɔk] *n* bacino; (*wharf*) molo; (*LAW*) banco degli imputati ♦ *vi* entrare in bacino ♦ *vt* (*pay etc*) decurtare.

dock dues *npl* diritti *mpl* di banchina.

docker ['dɔkə*] *n* scaricatore *m*.

docket ['dɔkɪt] *n* (*on parcel etc*) etichetta, cartellino.

dockyard ['dɔkjɑːd] *n* cantiere *m* navale.

doctor ['dɔktə*] *n* medico, dottore/essa; (*Ph.D. etc*) dottore/essa ♦ *vt* (*interfere with*: *food*, *drink*) adulterare; (: *text*, *document*) alterare, manipolare; **~'s office** (*US*) gabinetto medico, ambulatorio; **D~ of Philosophy (PhD)** dottorato di ricerca; (*person*) titolare *m/f* di un dottorato di ricerca.

doctorate ['dɔktərɪt] *n* ≈ dottorato di ricerca.

doctrine ['dɔktrɪn] *n* dottrina.

document *n* ['dɔkjumənt] documento ♦ *vt* ['dɔkjumɛnt] documentare.

documentary [dɔkju'mɛntərɪ] *a* documentario(a); (*evidence*) documentato(a) ♦ *n* documentario.

documentation [dɔkjumən'teɪʃən] *n* documentazione *f*.

DOD *n abbr* (*US*) = **Department of Defense**; *see* **defence**.

doddering ['dɔdərɪŋ] *a* traballante.

Dodecanese Islands [dəʊdɪkə'niːz-] *npl* Isole *fpl* del Dodecanneso.

dodge [dɔdʒ] *n* trucco; schivata ♦ *vt* schivare, eludere ♦ *vi* scansarsi; (*SPORT*) fare una schivata; **to ~ out of the way** scansarsi; **to ~ through the traffic** destreggiarsi nel traffico.

dodgems ['dɔdʒəmz] *npl* (*Brit*) autoscontri *mpl*.

DOE *n abbr* (*Brit*: = *Department of the Environment*) ≈ Ministero dell'Ambiente; (*US*) = **Department of Energy**; *see* **energy**.

doe [dəʊ] *n* (*deer*) femmina di daino; (*rabbit*) coniglia.

does [dʌz] *see* **do**.

doesn't ['dʌznt] = **does not**.

dog [dɔg] *n* cane *m* ♦ *vt* (*follow closely*) pedinare; (*fig*: *memory etc*) perseguitare; **to go to the ~s** (*person*) ridursi male, lasciarsi andare; (*nation etc*) andare in malora.

dog biscuits *npl* biscotti *mpl* per cani.

dog collar *n* collare *m* di cane; (*fig*) collarino.

dog-eared ['dɔgɪəd] *a* (*book*) con orecchie.

dog food *n* cibo per cani.

dogged ['dɔgɪd] *a* ostinato(a), tenace.

dogma ['dɔgmə] *n* dogma *m*.

dogmatic [dɔg'mætɪk] *a* dogmatico(a).

do-gooder [duː'gudə*] *n* (*col pej*): **to be a ~** fare il filantropo.

dogsbody ['dɔgzbɔdɪ] *n* (*Brit*) factotum *m inv*.

doing ['duːɪŋ] *n*: **this is your ~** è opera tua, sei stato tu.

doings ['duːɪŋz] *npl* attività *fpl*.

do-it-yourself (DIY) ['duːɪtjɔː'sɛlf] *n* il far da sé.

doldrums ['dɔldrəmz] *npl* (*fig*): **to be in the ~** essere giù; (*business*) attraversare un momento difficile.

dole [dəʊl] *n* (*Brit*) sussidio di disoccupazione; **to be on the ~** vivere del sussidio.

dole out *vt* distribuire.

doleful ['dəʊlful] *a* triste, doloroso(a).

doll [dɔl] *n* bambola.

doll up *vt*: **to ~ o.s. up** farsi bello(a).

dollar ['dɔlə*] *n* dollaro.

dollar area *n* area del dollaro.

dolphin ['dɔlfɪn] *n* delfino.

domain [də'meɪn] *n* dominio; (*fig*) campo, sfera.

dome [dəʊm] *n* cupola.

domestic [də'mɛstɪk] *a* (*duty, happiness, animal*) domestico(a); (*policy, affairs, flights*) nazionale; (*news*) dall'interno.

domesticated [də'mɛstɪkeɪtɪd] *a* addomesticato(a); (*person*) casalingo(a).

domesticity [dəʊmɛs'tɪsɪtɪ] *n* vita di famiglia.

domestic servant *n* domestico/a.

domicile ['dɔmɪsaɪl] *n* domicilio.

dominant ['dɔmɪnənt] *a* dominante.

dominate ['dɔmɪneɪt] *vt* dominare.

domination [dɔmɪ'neɪʃən] *n* dominazione *f*.

domineering [dɔmɪ'nɪərɪŋ] *a* dispotico(a), autoritario(a).

Dominican Republic [də'mɪnɪkən-] *n* Repubblica Dominicana.

dominion [də'mɪnɪən] *n* dominio; sovranità; (*Brit POL*) dominion *m inv*.

domino, ~es ['dɔmɪnəʊ] *n* domino; **~es** *n* (*game*) gioco del domino.

don [dɔn] *n* (*Brit*) docente *m/f* universitario(a) ♦ *vt* indossare.

donate [də'neɪt] *vt* donare.

donation [də'neɪʃən] *n* donazione *f*.

done [dʌn] *pp of* **do**.

donkey ['dɔŋkɪ] *n* asino.

donkey-work ['dɔŋkɪwəːk] *n* (*Brit col*) lavoro ingrato.

donor ['dəʊnə*] *n* donatore/trice.

don't [dəʊnt] *vb* = **do not**.

donut ['dəʊnʌt] *n* (*US*) = **doughnut**.

doodle ['duːdl] *n* scarabocchio ♦ *vi* scarabocchiare.

doom [duːm] *n* destino; rovina ♦ *vt*: **to be**

~**ed** (**to failure**) essere predestinato(a) (a fallire).

doomsday ['du:mzdeɪ] *n* il giorno del Giudizio.

door [dɔ:*] *n* porta; (*of vehicle*) sportello, portiera; **from ~ to ~** di porta in porta.

doorbell ['dɔ:bɛl] *n* campanello.

door handle *n* maniglia.

doorman ['dɔ:mæn] *n* (*in hotel*) portiere *m* in livrea; (*in block of flats*) portinaio.

doormat ['dɔ:mæt] *n* stuoia della porta.

doorstep ['dɔ:stɛp] *n* gradino della porta.

door-to-door ['dɔ:tə'dɔ:*] *a*: ~ **selling** vendita porta a porta.

doorway ['dɔ:weɪ] *n* porta; **in the ~** nel vano della porta.

dope [dəup] *n* (*col: drugs*) roba; (: *information*) dati *mpl* ♦ *vt* (*horse etc*) drogare.

dopey ['dəupɪ] *a* (*col*) inebetito(a).

dormant ['dɔ:mənt] *a* inattivo(a); (*fig*) latente.

dormer ['dɔ:mə*] *n* (*also:* ~ **window**) abbaino.

dormice ['dɔ:maɪs] *npl of* **dormouse**.

dormitory ['dɔ:mɪtrɪ] *n* dormitorio; (*US: hall of residence*) casa dello studente.

dormouse, *pl* **dormice** ['dɔ:maus, -maɪs] *n* ghiro.

Dors *abbr* (*Brit*) = *Dorset.*

DOS [dɔs] *n abbr see* **disk operating system.**

dosage ['dəusɪdʒ] *n* (*on medicine bottle*) posologia.

dose [dəus] *n* dose *f*; (*Brit: bout*) attacco ♦ *vt*: **to ~ sb with sth** somministrare qc a qn; **a ~ of flu** una bella influenza.

doss house ['dɔs-] *n* (*Brit*) asilo notturno.

dossier ['dɔsɪeɪ] *n* dossier *m inv.*

DOT *n abbr* (*US*) = **Department of Transportation;** *see* **transportation.**

dot [dɔt] *n* punto; macchiolina ♦ *vt*: ~**ted with** punteggiato(a) di; **on the ~** in punto.

dot command *n* (*COMPUT*) dot command *m inv.*

dote [dəut]: **to ~ on** *vt fus* essere infatuato(a) di.

dot-matrix printer [dɔt'meɪtrɪks-] *n* stampante *f* a matrice a punti.

dotted line ['dɔtɪd-] *n* linea punteggiata; **to sign on the ~** firmare (nell'apposito spazio); (*fig*) accettare.

dotty ['dɔtɪ] *a* (*col*) strambo(a).

double ['dʌbl] *a* doppio(a) ♦ *ad* (*fold*) in due, doppio; (*twice*): **to cost ~** (**sth**) costare il doppio (di qc) ♦ *n* sosia *m inv*; (*CINEMA*) controfigura ♦ *vt* raddoppiare; (*fold*) piegare doppio *or* in due ♦ *vi* raddoppiarsi; **spelt with a ~ "l"** scritto con due elle *or* con doppia elle; ~ **five two six (5526)** (*Brit TEL*) cinque cinque due sei; **on the ~,** (*Brit*) **at the ~** a passo di corsa; **to ~ as** (*have two uses etc*) funzionare *or* servire anche da; *see also* **doubles.**

double back *vi* (*person*) tornare sui propri passi.

double up *vi* (*bend over*) piegarsi in due; (*share room*) dividere la stanza.

double bass *n* contrabbasso.

double bed *n* letto matrimoniale.

double bend *n* (*Brit*) doppia curva.

double-breasted ['dʌbl'brɛstɪd] *a* a doppio petto.

double-check ['dʌbl'tʃɛk] *vt, vi* ricontrollare.

double-clutch ['dʌbl'klʌtʃ] *vi* (*US*) fare la doppietta.

double cream *n* (*Brit*) doppia panna.

doublecross ['dʌbl'krɔs] *vt* fare il doppio gioco con.

doubledecker ['dʌbl'dɛkə*] *n* autobus *m inv* a due piani.

double declutch *vi* (*Brit*) fare la doppietta.

double exposure *n* (*PHOT*) sovrimpressione *f.*

double glazing *n* (*Brit*) doppi vetri *mpl.*

double-page ['dʌblpeɪdʒ] *a*: ~ **spread** pubblicità a doppia pagina.

double parking *n* parcheggio in doppia fila.

double room *n* camera per due.

doubles ['dʌblz] *n* (*TENNIS*) doppio.

double time *n* tariffa doppia per lavoro straordinario.

doubly ['dʌblɪ] *ad* doppiamente.

doubt [daut] *n* dubbio ♦ *vt* dubitare di; **to ~ that** dubitare che + *sub*; **without (a) ~** senza dubbio; **beyond ~** fuor di dubbio; **I ~ it very much** ho i miei dubbi, nutro seri dubbi in proposito.

doubtful ['dautful] *a* dubbioso(a), incerto(a); (*person*) equivoco(a); **to be ~ about sth** avere dei dubbi su qc, non essere convinto di qc; **I'm a bit ~** non ne sono sicuro.

doubtless ['dautlɪs] *ad* indubbiamente.

dough [dəu] *n* pasta, impasto; (*col: money*) grana.

doughnut, (*US*) **donut** ['dəunʌt] *n* bombolone *m.*

dour [duə*] *a* arcigno(a).

douse [daus] *vt* (*with water*) infradiciare; (*flames*) spegnere.

dove [dʌv] *n* colombo/a.

Dover ['dəuvə*] *n* Dover *f.*

dovetail ['dʌvteɪl] *n*: ~ **joint** incastro a coda di rondine ♦ *vi* (*fig*) combaciare.

dowager ['dauədʒə*] *n* vedova titolata.

dowdy ['daudɪ] *a* trasandato(a); malvestito(a).

Dow-Jones average ['dau'dʒəunz-] *n* (*US*) indice *m* Dow-Jones.

down [daun] *n* (*fluff*) piumino; (*hill*) collina, colle *m* ♦ *ad* giù, di sotto ♦ *prep* giù per ♦ *vt* (*col: drink*) scolarsi; ~ **there** laggiù, là in fondo; ~ **here** quaggiù; **I'll be ~ in a minute** scendo tra un minuto; **the price of meat is ~** il prezzo della carne è sceso; **I've got it ~ in my diary** ce l'ho sulla mia agenda; **to pay £2 ~** dare 2 sterline in acconto *or* di anticipo; **I've been ~ with flu** sono stato a letto con l'influenza; **England is two goals ~** l'Inghilterra sta perdendo per due goal; **to ~ tools** (*Brit*) incrociare le braccia; **~ with X!** abbasso X!

down-and-out ['daunəndaut] *n* (*tramp*) barbone *m*.

down-at-heel ['daunət'hi:l] *a* scalcagnato(a); (*fig*) trasandato(a).

downbeat ['daunbi:t] *n* (*MUS*) tempo in battere ♦ *a* (*col*) volutamente distaccato(a).

downcast ['daunkɑ:st] *a* abbattuto(a).

downer ['daunə*] *n* (*col*: *drug*) farmaco depressivo; **to be on a ~** (*depressed*) essere giù.

downfall ['daunfɔ:l] *n* caduta; rovina.

downgrade ['daungreɪd] *vt* (*job, hotel*) declassare; (*employee*) degradare.

downhearted [daun'hɑ:tɪd] *a* scoraggiato(a).

downhill ['daun'hɪl] *ad* verso il basso ♦ *n* (*SKI*: *also*: **~ race**) discesa libera; **to go ~** andare in discesa; (*business*) andare a rotoli.

Downing Street ['daunɪŋ-] *n* (*Brit*): **10 ~** *residenza del primo ministro*.

download ['daunləud] *vt* (*COMPUT*) trasferire (*per esempio da un grosso calcolatore ad un microcalcolatore*).

down-market ['daun'mɑ:kɪt] *a* rivolto(a) ad una fascia di mercato inferiore.

down payment *n* acconto.

downplay ['daunpleɪ] *vt* (*US*) minimizzare.

downpour ['daunpɔ:*] *n* scroscio di pioggia.

downright ['daunraɪt] *a* franco(a); (*refusal*) assoluto(a).

Downs [daunz] *npl* (*Brit*): **the ~** *colline ricche di gesso nel sud-est dell'Inghilterra.*

downstairs ['daun'steəz] *ad* di sotto; al piano inferiore; **to come ~, go ~** scendere giù.

downstream ['daun'stri:m] *ad* a valle.

downtime ['dauntaɪm] *n* (*COMM*) tempi *mpl* morti.

down-to-earth ['dauntu'ə:θ] *a* pratico(a).

downtown ['daun'taun] *ad* in città ♦ *a* (*US*): **~ Chicago** il centro di Chicago.

downtrodden ['dauntrɔdn] *a* oppresso(a).

down under *ad* agli antipodi.

downward ['daunwəd] *a* in giù, in discesa; **a ~ trend** una diminuzione progressiva.

downward(s) ['daunwəd(z)] *ad* in giù, in discesa.

dowry ['daurɪ] *n* dote *f*.

doz. *abbr* = **dozen**.

doze [dəuz] *vi* sonnecchiare.

doze off *vi* appisolarsi.

dozen ['dʌzn] *n* dozzina; **a ~ books** una dozzina di libri; **80p a ~** 80 pence la dozzina; **~s of times** centinaia *or* migliaia di volte.

DPh, DPhil *n abbr* (= *Doctor of Philosophy*) ≈ dottorato di ricerca.

DPP *n abbr* (*Brit*) *see* **Director of Public Prosecutions.**

DPT *n abbr* (*MED*: = *diphtheria, pertussis, tetanus*) vaccino.

DPW *n abbr* (*US*: = *Department of Public Works*) ≈ Ministero dei Lavori Pubblici.

Dr, Dr. *abbr* (= *doctor*) Dr, Dott./Dott.ssa.

dr *abbr* (*COMM*) = **debtor**.

Dr. *abbr* (*in street names*) = **drive**.

drab [dræb] *a* tetro(a), grigio(a).

draft [drɑ:ft] *n* abbozzo; (*COMM*) tratta; (*US MIL*) contingente *m*; (: *call-up*) leva ♦ *vt* abbozzare; (*document, report*) stendere (in versione preliminare); *see also* **draught**.

drag [dræg] *vt* trascinare; (*river*) dragare ♦ *vi* trascinarsi ♦ *n* (*AVIAT, NAUT*) resistenza (aerodinamica); (*col*: *person*) noioso/a; (: *task*) noia; (*women's clothing*): **in ~** travestito (da donna).

  drag away *vt*: **to ~ away (from)** tirare via (da).

  drag on *vi* tirar avanti lentamente.

dragnet ['drægnɛt] *n* giacchio; (*fig*) rastrellamento.

dragon ['drægən] *n* drago.

dragonfly ['drægənflaɪ] *n* libellula.

dragoon [drə'gu:n] *n* (*cavalryman*) dragone *m* ♦ *vt*: **to ~ sb into doing sth** (*Brit*) costringere qn a fare qc.

drain [dreɪn] *n* canale *m* di scolo; (*for sewage*) fogna; (*on resources*) salasso ♦ *vt* (*land, marshes*) prosciugare; (*vegetables*) scolare; (*reservoir etc*) vuotare ♦ *vi* (*water*) defluire; **to feel ~ed** sentirsi svuotato(a), sentirsi sfinito(a).

drainage ['dreɪnɪdʒ] *n* prosciugamento; fognatura.

draining board ['dreɪnɪŋ-], **drainboard** (*US*) ['dreɪnbɔ:d] *n* piano del lavello.

drainpipe ['dreɪnpaɪp] *n* tubo di scarico.

drake [dreɪk] *n* maschio dell'anatra.

dram [dræm] *n* bicchierino (di whisky *etc*).

drama ['drɑ:mə] *n* (*art*) dramma *m*, teatro; (*play*) commedia; (*event*) dramma.

dramatic [drə'mætɪk] *a* drammatico(a).

dramatically [drə'mætɪklɪ] *ad* in modo spettacolare.

dramatist ['dræmətɪst] *n* drammaturgo/a.

dramatize ['dræmətaɪz] *vt* (*events etc*) drammatizzare; (*adapt*: *novel*: *for TV*) ridurre *or* adattare per la televisione; (: *for cinema*) ridurre *or* adattare per lo schermo.

drank [dræŋk] *pt of* **drink**.

drape [dreɪp] *vt* drappeggiare; *see also* **drapes.**

draper ['dreɪpə*] *n* (*Brit*) negoziante *m/f* di stoffe.

drapes [dreɪps] *npl* (*US*) tende *fpl*.

drastic ['dræstɪk] *a* drastico(a).

drastically ['dræstɪklɪ] *ad* drasticamente.

draught, (*US*) draft [drɑ:ft] *n* corrente *f* d'aria; (*NAUT*) pescaggio; **on ~** (*beer*) alla spina; *see also* **draughts.**

draughtboard ['drɑ:ftbɔ:d] *n* scacchiera.

draughts [drɑ:fts] *n* (*Brit*) (gioco della) dama.

draughtsman, (*US*) draftsman ['drɑ:ftsmən] *n* disegnatore *m*.

draughtsmanship, (*US*) draftsmanship ['drɑ:ftsmənʃɪp] *n* disegno tecnico; (*skill*) arte *f* del disegno.

draw [drɔ:] *vb* (*pt* **drew**, *pp* **drawn** [dru:,

drɔ:n]) *vt* tirare; (*attract*) attirare; (*picture*) disegnare; (*line, circle*) tracciare; (*money*) ritirare; (*formulate: conclusion*) trarre, ricavare; (: *comparison, distinction*): **to ~ (between)** fare (tra) ♦ *vi* (*SPORT*) pareggiare ♦ *n* (*SPORT*) pareggio; (*in lottery*) estrazione *f*; (*attraction*) attrazione *f*; **to ~ to a close** avvicinarsi alla conclusione; **to ~ near** *vi* avvicinarsi.

draw back *vi*: **to ~ back (from)** indietreggiare (di fronte a), tirarsi indietro (di fronte a).

draw in *vi* (*Brit: car*) accostarsi; (: *train*) entrare in stazione.

draw on *vt* (*resources*) attingere a; (*imagination, person*) far ricorso a.

draw out *vi* (*lengthen*) allungarsi ♦ *vt* (*money*) ritirare.

draw up *vi* (*stop*) arrestarsi, fermarsi ♦ *vt* (*document*) compilare; (*plans*) formulare.

drawback ['drɔ:bæk] *n* svantaggio, inconveniente *m*.

drawbridge ['drɔ:brɪdʒ] *n* ponte *m* levatoio.

drawee [drɔ:'i:] *n* trattario.

drawer [drɔ:*] *n* cassetto; ['drɔ:ə*] (*of cheque*) riscuotitore/trice.

drawing ['drɔ:ɪŋ] *n* disegno.

drawing board *n* tavola da disegno.

drawing pin *n* (*Brit*) puntina da disegno.

drawing room *n* salotto.

drawl [drɔ:l] *n* pronuncia strascicata.

drawn [drɔ:n] *pp of* **draw** ♦ *a* (*haggard: with tiredness*) tirato(a); (: *with pain*) contratto(a) (dal dolore).

drawstring ['drɔ:strɪŋ] *n* laccio (*per stringere maglie, sacche etc*).

dread [drɛd] *n* terrore *m* ♦ *vt* tremare all'idea di.

dreadful ['drɛdful] *a* terribile; **I feel ~!** (*ill*) mi sento uno straccio!; (*ashamed*) vorrei scomparire (dalla vergogna)!

dream [dri:m] *n* sogno ♦ *vt, vi* (*pt, pp* **dreamed** *or* **dreamt** [drɛmt]) sognare; **to have a ~ about sb/sth** fare un sogno su qn/qc; **sweet ~s!** sogni d'oro!

dream up *vt* (*reason, excuse*) inventare; (*plan, idea*) escogitare.

dreamer ['dri:mə*] *n* sognatore/trice.

dreamt [drɛmt] *pt, pp of* **dream**.

dreamy ['dri:mɪ] *a* (*look, voice*) sognante; (*person*) distratto(a), sognatore(trice).

dreary ['drɪərɪ] *a* tetro(a); monotono(a).

dredge [drɛdʒ] *vt* dragare.

dredge up *vt* tirare alla superficie; (*fig: unpleasant facts*) rivangare.

dredger ['drɛdʒə*] *n* draga; (*Brit: also:* **sugar ~**) spargizucchero *m inv*.

dregs [drɛgz] *npl* feccia.

drench [drɛntʃ] *vt* inzuppare; **~ed to the skin** bagnato(a) fino all'osso, bagnato(a) fradicio(a).

dress [drɛs] *n* vestito; (*clothing*) abbigliamento ♦ *vt* vestire; (*wound*) fasciare; (*food*) condire; preparare; (*shop window*)

allestire ♦ *vi* vestirsi; **to ~ o.s., to get ~ed** vestirsi; **she ~es very well** veste molto bene.

dress up *vi* vestirsi a festa; (*in fancy dress*) vestirsi in costume.

dress circle *n* prima galleria.

dress designer *n* disegnatore/trice di moda.

dresser ['drɛsə*] *n* (*THEATRE*) assistente *m/f* del camerino; (*also:* **window ~**) vetrinista *m/f*; (*furniture*) credenza.

dressing ['drɛsɪŋ] *n* (*MED*) benda; (*CULIN*) condimento.

dressing gown *n* (*Brit*) vestaglia.

dressing room *n* (*THEATRE*) camerino; (*SPORT*) spogliatoio.

dressing table *n* toilette *f inv*.

dressmaker ['drɛsmeɪkə*] *n* sarta.

dressmaking ['drɛsmeɪkɪŋ] *n* sartoria; confezioni *fpl* per donna.

dress rehearsal *n* prova generale.

dress shirt *n* camicia da sera.

dressy ['drɛsɪ] *a* (*col*) elegante.

drew [dru:] *pt of* **draw**.

dribble ['drɪbl] *vi* gocciolare; (*baby*) sbavare; (*FOOTBALL*) dribblare ♦ *vt* dribblare.

dried [draɪd] *a* (*fruit, beans*) secco(a); (*eggs, milk*) in polvere.

drier ['draɪə*] *n* = **dryer**.

drift [drɪft] *n* (*of current etc*) direzione *f*; forza; (*of sand, snow*) cumulo; (*general meaning*) senso ♦ *vi* (*boat*) essere trasportato(a) dalla corrente; (*sand, snow*) ammucchiarsi; **to catch sb's ~** capire dove qn vuole arrivare; **to let things ~** lasciare che le cose vadano come vogliono; **to ~ apart** (*friends*) perdersi di vista; (*lovers*) allontanarsi l'uno dall'altro.

drifter ['drɪftə*] *n* persona che fa una vita da zingaro.

driftwood ['drɪftwud] *n* resti *mpl* della mareggiata.

drill [drɪl] *n* trapano; (*MIL*) esercitazione *f* ♦ *vt* trapanare; (*soldiers*) esercitare, addestrare; (*pupils: in grammar*) fare esercitare ♦ *vi* (*for oil*) fare trivellazioni.

drilling ['drɪlɪŋ] *n* (*for oil*) trivellazione *f*.

drilling rig *n* (*on land*) torre *f* di perforazione; (*at · sea*) piattaforma (per trivellazioni subacquee).

drily ['draɪlɪ] *ad* = **dryly**.

drink [drɪŋk] *n* bevanda, bibita ♦ *vt, vi* (*pt* **drank**, *pp* **drunk** [dræŋk, drʌŋk]) bere; **to have a ~** bere qualcosa; **a ~ of water** un bicchier d'acqua; **would you like something to ~?** vuole qualcosa da bere?; **we had ~s before lunch** abbiamo preso l'aperitivo.

drink in *vt* (*subj: person: fresh air*) aspirare; (: *story*) ascoltare avidamente; (: *sight*) ammirare, bersi con gli occhi.

drinkable ['drɪŋkəbl] *a* (*not poisonous*) potabile; (*palatable*) bevibile.

drinker ['drɪŋkə*] *n* bevitore/trice.

drinking ['drɪŋkɪŋ] *n* (*drunkenness*) il bere, alcoolismo.

drinking fountain *n* fontanella.

drinking water n acqua potabile.
drip [drɪp] n goccia; (~*ping*) sgocciolio; (*MED*) fleboclisi f *inv*; (*col: spineless person*) lavativo ♦ vi gocciolare; (*washing*) sgocciolare; (*wall*) trasudare.
drip-dry ['drɪp'draɪ] a (*shirt*) che non si stira.
drip-feed ['drɪpfi:d] vt alimentare mediante fleboclisi.
dripping ['drɪpɪŋ] n (*CULIN*) grasso d'arrosto ♦ a: ~ **wet** fradicio(a).
drive [draɪv] n passeggiata or giro in macchina; (*also:* ~**way**) viale m d'accesso; (*energy*) energia; (*PSYCH*) impulso; bisogno; (*push*) sforzo eccezionale; campagna; (*SPORT*) drive m *inv*; (*TECH*) trasmissione f; (*COMPUT: also:* **disk** ~) disk drive m *inv*, unità f *inv* a dischi magnetici ♦ vb (pt **drove**, pp **driven** [drəuv, 'drɪvn]) vt (*vehicle*) guidare; (*nail*) piantare; (*push*) cacciare, spingere; (*TECH: motor*) azionare; far funzionare ♦ vi (*AUT: at controls*) guidare; (: *travel*) andare in macchina; **to go for a** ~ andare a fare un giro in macchina; **it's 3 hours'** ~ **from London** è a 3 ore di macchina da Londra; **left-/right-hand** ~ (*AUT*) guida a sinistra/destra; **front-/rear-wheel** ~ (*AUT*) trazione f anteriore/posteriore; **to** ~ **sb to** (**do**) **sth** spingere qn a (fare) qc; **he** ~**s a taxi** fa il tassista; **to** ~ **at 50 km an hour** guidare or andare a 50 km all'ora.
drive at vt fus (*fig: intend, mean*) mirare a, voler dire.
drive on vi proseguire, andare (più) avanti ♦ vt (*incite, encourage*) sospingere, spingere.
drive-in ['draɪvɪn] a, n (*esp US*) drive-in (m *inv*).
drive-in window n (*US*) sportello di drive-in.
drivel ['drɪvl] n (*col: nonsense*) ciance fpl.
driven ['drɪvn] pp of **drive**.
driver ['draɪvə*] n conducente m/f; (*of taxi*) tassista m; (*of bus*) autista m.
driver's license n (*US*) patente f di guida.
driveway ['draɪvweɪ] n viale m d'accesso.
driving ['draɪvɪŋ] a: ~ **rain** pioggia sferzante ♦ n guida.
driving belt n cinghia di trasmissione.
driving force n forza trainante.
driving instructor n istruttore/trice di scuola guida.
driving lesson n lezione f di guida.
driving licence n (*Brit*) patente f di guida.
driving mirror n specchietto retrovisore.
driving school n scuola f guida *inv*.
driving test n esame m di guida.
drizzle ['drɪzl] n pioggerella ♦ vi piovigginare.
droll [drəul] a buffo(a).
dromedary ['drɔmədərɪ] n dromedario.
drone [drəun] n ronzio; (*male bee*) fuco ♦ vi (*bee, aircraft, engine*) ronzare; (*also:* ~ **on:** *person*) continuare a parlare (in modo monotono); (: *voice*) continuare a ronzare.
drool [dru:l] vi sbavare; **to** ~ **over sb/sth** (*fig*) andare in estasi per qn/qc.
droop [dru:p] vi abbassarsi; languire.

drop [drɔp] n goccia; (*fall: in price*) calo, ribasso; (: *in salary*) riduzione f, taglio; (*also:* **parachute** ~) lancio; (*steep incline*) salto ♦ vt lasciar cadere; (*voice, eyes, price*) abbassare; (*set down from car*) far scendere ♦ vi cascare; (*decrease: wind, temperature, price, voice*) calare; (*numbers, attendance*) diminuire; ~**s** npl (*MED*) gocce fpl; **cough** ~**s** pastiglie fpl per la tosse; **a** ~ **of 10%** un calo del 10%; **to** ~ **sb a line** mandare due righe a qn; **to** ~ **anchor** gettare l'ancora.
drop in vi (*col: visit*): **to** ~ **in (on)** fare un salto (da), passare (da).
drop off vi (*sleep*) addormentarsi ♦ vt: **to** ~ **sb off** far scendere qn.
drop out vi (*withdraw*) ritirarsi; (*student etc*) smettere di studiare.
droplet ['drɔplɪt] n gocciolina.
dropout ['drɔpaut] n (*from society/university*) chi ha abbandonato (la società/gli studi).
dropper ['drɔpə*] n (*MED etc*) contagocce m *inv*.
droppings ['drɔpɪŋz] npl sterco.
dross [drɔs] n scoria; scarto.
drought [draut] n siccità f *inv*.
drove [drəuv] pt of **drive** ♦ n: ~**s of people** una moltitudine di persone.
drown [draun] vt affogare; (*also:* ~ **out:** *sound*) coprire ♦ vi affogare.
drowse [drauz] vi sonnecchiare.
drowsy ['drauzɪ] a sonnolento(a), assonnato(a).
drudge [drʌdʒ] n (*person*) uomo/donna di fatica; (*job*) faticaccia.
drudgery ['drʌdʒərɪ] n fatica improba; **housework is sheer** ~ le faccende domestiche sono alienanti.
drug [drʌg] n farmaco; (*narcotic*) droga ♦ vt drogare; **he's on** ~**s** si droga; (*MED*) segue una cura.
drug addict n tossicomane m/f.
druggist ['drʌgɪst] n (*US*) farmacista m/f.
drug peddler n spacciatore/trice di droga.
drugstore ['drʌgstɔ:*] n (*US*) negozio di generi vari e di articoli di farmacia con un bar.
drum [drʌm] n tamburo; (*for oil, petrol*) fusto ♦ vt: **to** ~ **one's fingers on the table** tamburellare con le dita sulla tavola; ~**s** npl (*MUS*) batteria.
drum up vt (*enthusiasm, support*) conquistarsi.
drummer ['drʌmə*] n batterista m/f.
drum roll n rullio di tamburi.
drumstick ['drʌmstɪk] n (*MUS*) bacchetta; (*chicken leg*) coscia di pollo.
drunk [drʌŋk] pp of **drink** ♦ a ubriaco(a); ebbro(a) ♦ n ubriacone/a; **to get** ~ ubriacarsi, prendere una sbornia.
drunkard ['drʌŋkəd] n ubriacone/a.
drunken ['drʌŋkən] a ubriaco(a); da ubriaco; ~ **driving** guida in stato di ebbrezza.
drunkenness ['drʌŋkənnɪs] n ubriachezza; ebbrezza.
dry [draɪ] a secco(a); (*day, clothes, fig:*

humour) asciutto(a); (*uninteresting*: *lecture*, *subject*) poco avvincente ♦ *vt* seccare; (*clothes*, *hair*, *hands*) asciugare ♦ *vi* asciugarsi; **on ~ land** sulla terraferma; **to ~ one's hands/hair/eyes** asciugarsi le mani/i capelli/gli occhi.

dry up *vi* seccarsi; (*source of supply*) esaurirsi; (*fig*: *imagination etc*) inaridirsi; (*fall silent*: *speaker*) azzittirsi.

dry-clean [draɪ'kliːn] *vt* pulire *or* lavare a secco.

dry-cleaner's [draɪ'kliːnəz] *n* lavasecco *m inv*.

dry-cleaning [draɪ'kliːnɪŋ] *n* pulitura a secco.

dry dock *n* (*NAUT*) bacino di carenaggio.

dryer ['draɪə*] *n* (*for hair*) föhn *m inv*, asciugacapelli *m inv*; (*for clothes*) asciugabiancheria *m inv*.

dry goods *npl* (*COMM*) tessuti *mpl* e mercerie *fpl*.

dry goods store *n* (*US*) negozio di stoffe.

dry ice *n* ghiaccio secco.

dryly ['draɪlɪ] *ad* con fare asciutto.

dryness ['draɪnɪs] *n* secchezza; (*of ground*) aridità.

dry rot *n* fungo del legno.

dry run *n* (*fig*) prova.

dry ski slope *n* pista artificiale.

DSc *n abbr* (= *Doctor of Science*) titolo di studio.

DSS *n abbr* (*Brit*) = **Department of Social Security**; *see* **social security**.

DST *abbr* (*US*) = **Daylight Saving Time.**

DT *n abbr* (*COMPUT*) = **data transmission.**

DTI *n abbr* (*Brit*) = **Department of Trade and Industry**; *see* **trade.**

DT's *n abbr* (*col*) = *delirium tremens.*

dual ['djuəl] *a* doppio(a).

dual carriageway *n* (*Brit*) strada a doppia carreggiata.

dual-control ['djuəlkən'trəul] *a* con doppi comandi.

dual nationality *n* doppia nazionalità.

dual-purpose ['djuəl'pə:pəs] *a* a doppio uso.

dubbed [dʌbd] *a* (*CINEMA*) doppiato(a); (*nicknamed*) soprannominato(a).

dubious ['dju:bɪəs] *a* dubbio(a); (*character*, *manner*) ambiguo(a), equivoco(a); **I'm very ~ about it** ho i miei dubbi in proposito.

Dublin ['dʌblɪn] *n* Dublino *f*.

Dubliner ['dʌblɪnə*] *n* dublinese *m/f*.

duchess ['dʌtʃɪs] *n* duchessa.

duck [dʌk] *n* anatra ♦ *vi* abbassare la testa ♦ *vt* spingere sotto (acqua).

duckling ['dʌklɪŋ] *n* anatroccolo.

duct [dʌkt] *n* condotto; (*ANAT*) canale *m*.

dud [dʌd] *n* (*shell*) proiettile *m* che fa cilecca; (*object*, *tool*): **it's a ~** è inutile, non funziona ♦ *a* (*Brit*: *cheque*) a vuoto; (*note*, *coin*) falso(a).

due [dju:] *a* dovuto(a); (*expected*) atteso(a); (*fitting*) giusto(a) ♦ *n* dovuto ♦ *ad*: **~ north** diritto verso nord; **~s** *npl* (*for club*, *union*) quota; (*in harbour*) diritti *mpl* di porto; **in ~ course** a tempo debito; finalmente; **~ to**

dovuto a; a causa di; **the rent's ~ on the 30th** l'affitto scade il 30; **the train is ~ at 8** il treno è atteso per le 8; **she is ~ back tomorrow** dovrebbe essere di ritorno domani; **I am ~ 6 days' leave** mi spettano 6 giorni di ferie.

due date *n* data di scadenza.

duel ['djuəl] *n* duello.

duet [dju:'ɛt] *n* duetto.

duff [dʌf] *a* (*Brit col*) barboso(a).

duffelbag, duffle bag ['dʌflbæg] *n* sacca da viaggio di tela.

duffelcoat, duffle coat ['dʌflkəut] *n* montgomery *m inv*.

duffer ['dʌfə*] *n* (*col*) schiappa.

dug [dʌg] *pt*, *pp of* **dig.**

duke [dju:k] *n* duca *m*.

dull [dʌl] *a* (*boring*) noioso(a); (*slow-witted*) ottuso(a); (*sound*, *pain*) sordo(a); (*weather*, *day*) fosco(a), scuro(a); (*blade*) smussato(a) ♦ *vt* (*pain*, *grief*) attutire; (*mind*, *senses*) intorpidire.

duly ['dju:lɪ] *ad* (*on time*) a tempo debito; (*as expected*) debitamente.

dumb [dʌm] *a* muto(a); (*stupid*) stupido(a); **to be struck ~** (*fig*) ammutolire, restare senza parole.

dumbbell ['dʌmbɛl] *n* (*SPORT*) manubrio, peso.

dumbfounded [dʌm'faundɪd] *a* stupito(a), stordito(a).

dummy ['dʌmɪ] *n* (*tailor's model*) manichino; (*SPORT*) finto; (*Brit*: *for baby*) tettarella ♦ *a* falso(a), finto(a).

dummy run *n* giro di prova.

dump [dʌmp] *n* mucchio di rifiuti; (*place*) luogo di scarico; (*MIL*) deposito; (*COMPUT*) scaricamento, dump *m inv* ♦ *vt* (*put down*) scaricare; mettere giù; (*get rid of*) buttar via; (*COMM*: *goods*) svendere; (*COMPUT*) scaricare; **to be (down) in the ~s** (*col*) essere giù di corda.

dumping ['dʌmpɪŋ] *n* (*ECON*) dumping *m*; (*of rubbish*): **"no ~"** "vietato lo scarico".

dumpling ['dʌmplɪŋ] *n* specie di gnocco.

dumpy ['dʌmpɪ] *a* tracagnotto(a).

dunce [dʌns] *n* asino.

dune [dju:n] *n* duna.

dung [dʌŋ] *n* concime *m*.

dungarees [dʌŋgə'ri:z] *npl* tuta.

dungeon ['dʌndʒən] *n* prigione *f* sotterranea.

dunk [dʌŋk] *vt* inzuppare.

duo ['dju:əu] *n* (*gen*, *MUS*) duo *m inv*.

duodenal [dju:əu'di:nl] *a* (*ulcer*) duodenale.

duodenum [dju:əu'di:nəm] *n* duodeno.

dupe [dju:p] *vt* gabbare, ingannare.

duplex ['dju:plɛks] *n* (*US*: *also*: **~ apartment**) appartamento su due piani.

duplicate *n* ['dju:plɪkət] doppio; (*copy of letter etc*) duplicato ♦ *vt* ['dju:plɪkeɪt] raddoppiare; (*on machine*) ciclostilare ♦ *a* (*copy*) conforme, esattamente uguale; **in ~** in duplice copia; **~ key** duplicato (della chiave).

duplicating machine ['dju:plɪkeɪtɪŋ],

duplicator ['dju:plɪkeɪtə*] n duplicatore m.
duplicity [dju:'plɪsɪtɪ] n doppiezza, duplicità.
Dur abbr (Brit) = Durham.
durability [djuərə'bɪlɪtɪ] n durevolezza; resistenza.
durable ['djuərəbl] a durevole; (clothes, metal) resistente.
duration [djuə'reɪʃən] n durata.
duress [djuə'rɛs] n: **under** ~ sotto costrizione.
Durex ® ['djuərɛks] n (Brit) preservativo.
during ['djuərɪŋ] prep durante, nel corso di.
dusk [dʌsk] n crepuscolo.
dusky ['dʌskɪ] a scuro(a).
dust [dʌst] n polvere f ♦ vt (furniture) spolverare; (cake etc): **to** ~ **with** cospargere con.
  dust off vt rispolverare.
dustbin ['dʌstbɪn] n (Brit) pattumiera.
duster ['dʌstə*] n straccio per la polvere.
dust jacket n sopraccoperta.
dustman ['dʌstmən] n (Brit) netturbino.
dustpan ['dʌstpæn] n pattumiera.
dusty ['dʌstɪ] a polveroso(a).
Dutch [dʌtʃ] a olandese ♦ n (LING) olandese m ♦ ad: **to go** ~ or **d**~ fare alla romana; **the** ~ gli Olandesi.
Dutch auction n asta all'olandese.
Dutchman ['dʌtʃmən], **Dutchwoman** ['dʌtʃwumən] n olandese m/f.
dutiable ['dju:tɪəbl] a soggetto(a) a dazio.
dutiful ['dju:tɪful] a (child) rispettoso(a); (husband) premuroso(a); (employee) coscienzioso(a).
duty ['dju:tɪ] n dovere m; (tax) dazio, tassa; **duties** npl mansioni fpl; **on** ~ di servizio; (MED): **in hospital**) di guardia; **off** ~ libero(a), fuori servizio; **to make it one's** ~ **to do sth** assumersi l'obbligo di fare qc; **to pay** ~ **on sth** pagare il dazio su qc.
duty-free ['dju:tɪ'fri:] a esente da dazio; ~ **shop** duty free m inv.
duty officer n (MIL etc) ufficiale m di servizio.
duvet ['du:veɪ] n piumino, piumone m.
DV abbr (= Deo volente) D.V.
DVLC n abbr (Brit: = Driver and Vehicle Licensing Office) ≈ I.M.C.T.C. m (= Ispettorato Generale della Motorizzazione Civile e dei Trasporti in Concessione).
DVM n abbr (US: = Doctor of Veterinary Medicine) titolo di studio.
dwarf [dwɔ:f] n nano/a ♦ vt far apparire piccolo.
dwell, pt, pp **dwelt** [dwɛl, dwɛlt] vi dimorare.
  dwell on vt fus indugiare su.
dweller ['dwɛlə*] n abitante m/f; **city** ~ cittadino/a.
dwelling ['dwɛlɪŋ] n dimora.
dwelt [dwɛlt] pt, pp of **dwell**.
dwindle ['dwɪndl] vi diminuire, decrescere.
dwindling ['dwɪndlɪŋ] a (strength, interest) che si affievolisce; (resources, supplies) in diminuzione.
dye [daɪ] n colore m; (chemical) colorante m,

tintura ♦ vt tingere; **hair** ~ tinta per capelli.
dyestuffs ['daɪstʌfs] npl coloranti mpl.
dying ['daɪɪŋ] a morente, moribondo(a).
dyke [daɪk] n diga; (channel) canale m di scolo; (causeway) sentiero rialzato.
dynamic [daɪ'næmɪk] a dinamico(a).
dynamics [daɪ'næmɪks] n or npl dinamica.
dynamite ['daɪnəmaɪt] n dinamite f ♦ vt far saltare con la dinamite.
dynamo ['daɪnəməu] n dinamo f inv.
dynasty ['dɪnəstɪ] n dinastia.
dysentery ['dɪsntrɪ] n dissenteria.
dyslexia [dɪs'lɛksɪə] n dislessia.
dyslexic [dɪs'lɛksɪk] a, n dislessico(a).
dyspepsia [dɪs'pɛpsɪə] n dispepsia.
dystrophy ['dɪstrəfɪ] n distrofia; **muscular** ~ distrofia muscolare.

E

E, e [i:] n (letter) E, e f or m inv; (MUS): **E** mi m; **E for Edward**, (US) **E for Easy** ≈ E come Empoli.
E abbr (= east) E.
E111 n abbr (also: **form** ~) E111 (modulo CEE per rimborso spese mediche).
ea. abbr = **each**.
E.A. n abbr (US) = educational age.
each [i:tʃ] a ogni, ciascuno(a) ♦ pronoun ciascuno(a), ognuno(a); ~ **one** ognuno(a); ~ **other** si (or ci etc); **they hate** ~ **other** si odiano (l'un l'altro); **you are jealous of** ~ **other** siete gelosi l'uno dell'altro; ~ **day** ogni giorno; **they have 2 books** ~ hanno 2 libri ciascuno; **they cost £5** ~ costano 5 sterline l'uno; ~ **of us** ciascuno or ognuno di noi.
eager ['i:gə*] a impaziente; desideroso(a); ardente; (keen: pupil) appassionato(a), attento(a); **to be** ~ **to do sth** non veder l'ora di fare qc; essere desideroso di fare qc; **to be** ~ **for** essere desideroso di, aver gran voglia di.
eagle ['i:gl] n aquila.
E and OE abbr (= errors and omissions excepted) S.E.O.
ear [ɪə*] n orecchio; (of corn) pannocchia; **up to the** ~**s in debt** nei debiti fino al collo.
earache ['ɪəreɪk] n mal m d'orecchi.
eardrum ['ɪədrʌm] n timpano.
earl [ə:l] n conte m.
earlier ['ə:lɪə*] a (date etc) anteriore; (edition etc) precedente, anteriore ♦ ad prima; **I can't come any** ~ non posso venire prima.
early ['ə:lɪ] ad presto, di buon'ora; (ahead of time) in anticipo ♦ a precoce; anticipato(a); che si fa vedere di buon'ora; (man) primitivo(a); (Christians, settlers) primo(a);

~ **in the morning/afternoon** nelle prime ore del mattino/del pomeriggio; **you're** ~! sei in anticipo!; **have an** ~ **night/start** vada a letto/parta presto; **in the** ~ *or* ~ **in the spring/19th century** all'inizio della primavera/dell'Ottocento; **she's in her** ~ **forties** ha appena passato la quarantina; **at your earliest convenience** (*COMM*) non appena possibile.

early retirement *n* ritiro anticipato.

early warning system *n* sistema *m* del preallarme.

earmark ['ɪəmɑːk] *vt*: **to** ~ **sth for** destinare qc a.

earn [əːn] *vt* guadagnare; (*rest, reward*) meritare; (*COMM: yield*) maturare; **to** ~ **one's living** guadagnarsi da vivere; **this** ~ed **him much praise, he** ~ed **much praise for this** si è attirato grandi lodi per questo.

earned income *n* reddito da lavoro.

earnest ['əːnɪst] *a* serio(a) ♦ *n* (*also:* ~ **money**) caparra; **in** ~ *ad* sul serio.

earnings ['əːnɪŋz] *npl* guadagni *mpl*; (*of company etc*) proventi *mpl*; (*salary*) stipendio.

ear nose and throat specialist *n* otorinolaringoiatra *m/f*.

earphones ['ɪəfəunz] *npl* cuffia.

earplugs ['ɪəplʌgz] *npl* tappi *mpl* per le orecchie.

earring ['ɪərɪŋ] *n* orecchino.

earshot ['ɪəʃɔt] *n*: **out of/within** ~ fuori portata/a portata d'orecchio.

earth [əːθ] *n* (*gen, also Brit ELEC*) terra; (*of fox etc*) tana ♦ *vt* (*Brit ELEC*) mettere a terra.

earthenware ['əːθənwɛə*] *n* terracotta; stoviglie *fpl* di terracotta ♦ *a* di terracotta.

earthly ['əːθlɪ] *a* terreno(a); ~ **paradise** paradiso terrestre; **there is no** ~ **reason to think** ... non vi è ragione di pensare ....

earthquake ['əːθkweɪk] *n* terremoto.

earth tremor *n* scossa sismica.

earthworks ['əːθwəːks] *npl* lavori *mpl* di sterro.

earthworm ['əːθwəːm] *n* lombrico.

earthy ['əːθɪ] *a* (*fig*) grossolano(a).

earwax ['ɪəwæks] *n* cerume *m*.

earwig ['ɪəwɪg] *n* forbicina.

ease [iːz] *n* agio, comodo ♦ *vt* (*soothe*) calmare; (*loosen*) allentare ♦ *vi* (*situation*) allentarsi, distendersi; **life of** ~ vita comoda; **with** ~ senza difficoltà; **at** ~ a proprio agio; (*MIL*) a riposo; **to feel at** ~/**ill at** ~ sentirsi a proprio agio/a disagio; **to** ~ **sth out/in** tirare fuori/infilare qc con delicatezza; facilitare l'uscita/l'entrata di qc.

ease off, ease up *vi* diminuire; (*slow down*) rallentarsi; (*fig*) rilassarsi.

easel ['iːzl] *n* cavalletto.

easily ['iːzɪlɪ] *ad* facilmente.

easiness ['iːzɪnɪs] *n* facilità, semplicità; (*of manners*) disinvoltura.

east [iːst] *n* est *m* ♦ *a* dell'est ♦ *ad* a oriente;

the E~ l'Oriente *m*; (*POL*) i Paesi dell'Est.

Easter ['iːstə*] *n* Pasqua ♦ *a* (*holidays*) pasquale, di Pasqua.

Easter egg *n* uovo di Pasqua.

Easter Island *n* isola di Pasqua.

easterly ['iːstəlɪ] *a* dall'est, d'oriente.

Easter Monday *n* Pasquetta.

eastern ['iːstən] *a* orientale, d'oriente; **E~ Europe** l'Europa orientale; **the E~ bloc** (*POL*) i Paesi dell'Est.

Easter Sunday *n* domenica di Pasqua.

East Germany *n* Germania dell'Est.

eastward(s) ['iːstwəd(z)] *ad* verso est, verso levante.

easy ['iːzɪ] *a* facile; (*manner*) disinvolto(a); (*carefree: life*) agiato(a), tranquillo(a) ♦ *ad*: **to take it** *or* **things** ~ prendersela con calma; **I'm** ~ (*col*) non ho problemi; **easier said than done** tra il dire e il fare c'è di mezzo il mare; **payment on** ~ **terms** (*COMM*) facilitazioni *fpl* di pagamento.

easy chair *n* poltrona.

easy-going ['iːzɪ'gəuɪŋ] *a* accomodante.

eat, *pt* **ate,** *pp* **eaten** [iːt, eɪt, 'iːtn] *vt* mangiare.

eat away *vt* (*subj: sea*) erodere; (: *acid*) corrodere.

eat away at, eat into *vt fus* rodere.

eat out *vi* mangiare fuori.

eat up *vt* (*meal etc*) finire di mangiare; **it** ~**s up electricity** consuma un sacco di corrente.

eatable ['iːtəbl] *a* mangiabile; (*safe to eat*) commestibile.

eaten ['iːtn] *pp of* **eat**.

eau de Cologne ['əudəkə'ləun] *n* acqua di colonia.

eaves [iːvz] *npl* gronda.

eavesdrop ['iːvzdrɔp] *vi*: **to** ~ (**on a conversation**) origliare (una conversazione).

ebb [ɛb] *n* riflusso ♦ *vi* rifluire; (*fig: also:* ~ **away**) declinare; ~ **and flow** flusso e riflusso; **to be at a low** ~ (*fig: person, spirits*) avere il morale a terra; (: *business*) andar male.

ebb tide *n* marea discendente.

ebony ['ɛbənɪ] *n* ebano.

ebullient [ɪ'bʌlɪənt] *a* esuberante.

EC *n abbr* (= *European Community*) CE (= Comunità Europea).

eccentric [ɪk'sɛntrɪk] *a, n* eccentrico(a).

ecclesiastic [ɪkliːzɪ'æstɪk] *n* ecclesiastico.

ecclesiastic(al) [ɪkliːzɪ'æstɪk(əl)] *a* ecclesiastico(a).

ECG *n abbr see* **electrocardiogram**.

ECGD *n abbr* (= *Export Credits Guarantee Department*) servizio di garanzia finanziaria per l'esportazione.

echo, ~**es** ['ɛkəu] *n* eco *m or f* ♦ *vt* ripetere; fare eco a ♦ *vi* echeggiare; dare un eco.

éclair ['eɪklɛə*] *n* ≈ bignè *m inv*.

eclipse [ɪ'klɪps] *n* eclissi *f inv* ♦ *vt* eclissare.

ECM *n abbr* (*US*: = *European Common Market*) MEC *m*.

ecologist [ɪ'kɔlədʒɪst] *n* ecologo/a.
ecology [ɪ'kɔlədʒɪ] *n* ecologia.
economic [i:kə'nɔmɪk] *a* economico(a); (*profitable*: *price*) vantaggioso(a); (*business*) che rende.
economical [i:kə'nɔmɪkəl] *a* economico(a); (*person*) economo(a).
economically [i:kə'nɔmɪklɪ] *ad* con economia; (*regarding economics*) dal punto di vista economico.
economics [i:kə'nɔmɪks] *n* economia ♦ *npl* aspetto *or* lato economico.
economist [ɪ'kɔnəmɪst] *n* economista *m/f*.
economize [ɪ'kɔnəmaɪz] *vi* risparmiare, fare economia.
economy [ɪ'kɔnəmɪ] *n* economia; **economies of scale** (*COMM*) economie *fpl* di scala.
economy class *n* (*AVIAT etc*) classe *f* turistica.
economy size *n* confezione *f* economica.
ECSC *n abbr* (= *European Coal & Steel Community*) C.E.C.A. *f* (= *Comunità Europea del Carbone e dell'Acciaio*).
ecstasy ['ɛkstəsɪ] *n* estasi *f inv*; **to go into ecstasies over** andare in estasi davanti a.
ecstatic [ɛks'tætɪk] *a* estatico(a), in estasi.
ECT *n abbr see* **electroconvulsive therapy**.
ECU *n abbr* (= *European Currency Unit*) ECU *m inv*.
Ecuador ['ɛkwədɔ:*] *n* Ecuador *m*.
ecumenical [i:kju'mɛnɪkl] *a* ecumenico(a).
eczema ['ɛksɪmə] *n* eczema *m*.
eddy ['ɛdɪ] *n* mulinello.
edge [ɛdʒ] *n* margine *m*; (*of table, plate, cup*) orlo; (*of knife etc*) taglio ♦ *vt* bordare ♦ *vi*: **to ~ away from** sgattaiolare da; **to ~ past** passar rasente; **to ~ forward** avanzare a poco a poco; **on ~** (*fig*) = **edgy**; **to have the ~ on** essere in vantaggio su.
edgeways ['ɛdʒweɪz] *ad* di fianco; **he couldn't get a word in ~** non riuscì a dire una parola.
edging ['ɛdʒɪŋ] *n* bordo.
edgy ['ɛdʒɪ] *a* nervoso(a).
edible ['ɛdɪbl] *a* commestibile; (*meal*) mangiabile.
edict ['i:dɪkt] *n* editto.
edifice ['ɛdɪfɪs] *n* edificio.
edifying ['ɛdɪfaɪɪŋ] *a* edificante.
Edinburgh ['ɛdɪnbərə] *n* Edimburgo *f*.
edit ['ɛdɪt] *vt* curare; (*newspaper, magazine*) dirigere; (*COMPUT*) correggere e modificare, editare.
edition [ɪ'dɪʃən] *n* edizione *f*.
editor ['ɛdɪtə*] *n* (*in newspaper*) redattore/trice; redattore/trice capo; (*of sb's work*) curatore/trice; (*film ~*) responsabile *m/f* del montaggio.
editorial [ɛdɪ'tɔ:rɪəl] *a* redazionale, editoriale ♦ *n* editoriale *m*; **the ~ staff** la redazione.
EDP *n abbr see* **electronic data processing**.
EDT *abbr* (*US*: = *Eastern Daylight Time*) *ora legale di New York*.
educate ['ɛdjukeɪt] *vt* istruire; educare.

education [ɛdju'keɪʃən] *n* (*teaching*) insegnamento; istruzione *f*; (*knowledge, culture*) cultura; (*SCOL*: *subject etc*) pedagogia; **primary** *or* (*US*) **elementary/secondary ~** scuola primaria/secondaria.
educational [ɛdju'keɪʃənl] *a* pedagogico(a); scolastico(a); istruttivo(a); **~ technology** tecnologie *fpl* applicate alla didattica.
Edwardian [ɛd'wɔ:dɪən] *a* edoardiano(a).
EE *abbr* = **electrical engineer**.
EEC *n abbr* (= *European Economic Community*) C.E.E. *f* (= *Comunità Economica Europea*).
EEG *n abbr see* **electroencephalogram**.
eel [i:l] *n* anguilla.
EENT *n abbr* (*US MED*) = *eye, ear, nose and throat*.
EEOC *n abbr* (*US*) = **Equal Employment Opportunity Commission**.
eerie ['ɪərɪ] *a* che fa accapponare la pelle.
EET *abbr* (= *Eastern European Time*) *fuso orario*.
effect [ɪ'fɛkt] *n* effetto ♦ *vt* effettuare; **to take ~** (*law*) entrare in vigore; (*drug*) fare effetto; **to have an ~ on sb/sth** avere *or* produrre un effetto su qn/qc; **to put into ~** (*plan*) attuare; **in ~** effettivamente; **his letter is to the ~ that** ... il contenuto della sua lettera è che ...; *see also* **effects**.
effective [ɪ'fɛktɪv] *a* efficace; (*striking*: *display, outfit*) che fa colpo; **~ date** data d'entrata in vigore; **to become ~** (*LAW*) entrare in vigore.
effectively [ɪ'fɛktɪvlɪ] *ad* (*efficiently*) efficacemente; (*strikingly*) ad effetto; (*in reality*) di fatto; (*in effect*) in effetti.
effectiveness [ɪ'fɛktɪvnɪs] *n* efficacia.
effects [ɪ'fɛkts] *npl* (*THEATRE*) effetti *mpl* scenici; (*property*) effetti *mpl*.
effeminate [ɪ'fɛmɪnɪt] *a* effeminato(a).
effervescent [ɛfə'vɛsnt] *a* effervescente.
efficacy ['ɛfɪkəsɪ] *n* efficacia.
efficiency [ɪ'fɪʃənsɪ] *n* efficienza; rendimento effettivo.
efficiency apartment *n* (*US*) miniappartamento.
efficient [ɪ'fɪʃənt] *a* efficiente; (*remedy, product, system*) efficace; (*machine, car*) che ha un buon rendimento.
efficiently [ɪ'fɪʃəntlɪ] *ad* efficientemente; efficacemente.
effigy ['ɛfɪdʒɪ] *n* effigie *f*.
effluent ['ɛfluənt] *n* effluente *m*.
effort ['ɛfət] *n* sforzo; **to make an ~ to do sth** sforzarsi di fare qc.
effortless ['ɛfətlɪs] *a* senza sforzo, facile.
effrontery [ɪ'frʌntərɪ] *n* sfrontatezza.
effusive [ɪ'fju:sɪv] *a* (*person*) espansivo(a); (*welcome, letter*) caloroso(a); (*thanks, apologies*) interminabile.
EFL *n abbr* (*SCOL*) = *English as a foreign language*.
EFTA ['ɛftə] *n abbr* (= *European Free Trade Association*) E.F.T.A. *f*.

e.g. *ad abbr* (= *exempli gratia*: *for example*) p.es.

egalitarian [ɪgælɪ'tɛərɪən] *a* egualitario(a).

egg [ɛg] *n* uovo.

egg on *vt* incitare.

eggcup ['ɛgkʌp] *n* portauovo *m inv*.

eggplant ['ɛgplɑ:nt] *n* (*esp US*) melanzana.

eggshell ['ɛgʃɛl] *n* guscio d'uovo ♦ *a* (*colour*) guscio d'uovo *inv*.

egg white *n* albume *m*, bianco d'uovo.

egg yolk *n* tuorlo, rosso (d'uovo).

ego ['i:gəu] *n* ego *m inv*.

egoism ['ɛgəuɪzəm] *n* egoismo.

egoist ['ɛgəuɪst] *n* egoista *m/f*.

egotism ['ɛgəutɪzəm] *n* egotismo.

egotist ['ɛgəutɪst] *n* egotista *m/f*.

Egypt ['i:dʒɪpt] *n* Egitto.

Egyptian [ɪ'dʒɪpʃən] *a, n* egiziano(a).

eiderdown ['aɪdədaun] *n* piumino.

eight [eɪt] *num* otto.

eighteen ['eɪ'ti:n] *num* diciotto.

eighth [eɪtθ] *num* ottavo(a).

eighty [eɪtɪ] *num* ottanta.

Eire ['ɛərə] *n* Repubblica d'Irlanda.

EIS *n abbr* (= *Educational Institute of Scotland*) *principale sindacato degli insegnanti in Scozia.*

either ['aɪðə*] *a* l'uno(a) o l'altro(a); (*both, each*) ciascuno(a); **on ~ side** su ciascun lato ♦ *pronoun*: **~ (of them)** (o) l'uno(a) o l'altro(a); **I don't like ~** non mi piace né l'uno né l'altro ♦ *ad* neanche; **no, I don't ~** no, neanch'io ♦ *cj*: **~ good or bad** o buono o cattivo; **I haven't seen ~ one or the other** non ho visto né l'uno né l'altro.

ejaculation [ɪdʒækju'leɪʃən] *n* (*PHYSIOL*) eiaculazione *f*.

eject [ɪ'dʒɛkt] *vt* espellere; lanciare ♦ *vi* (*pilot*) catapultarsi.

ejector seat [ɪ'dʒɛktə-] *n* sedile *m* eiettabile.

eke [i:k]: **to ~ out** *vt* far durare; aumentare.

EKG *n abbr* (*US*) = **electrocardiogram.**

el [ɛl] *n abbr* (*US col*) *see* **elevated railroad.**

elaborate *a* [ɪ'læbərɪt] elaborato(a), minuzioso(a) ♦ *vb* [ɪ'læbəreɪt] *vt* elaborare ♦ *vi* entrare in dettagli.

elapse [ɪ'læps] *vi* trascorrere, passare.

elastic [ɪ'læstɪk] *a* elastico(a) ♦ *n* elastico.

elastic band *n* (*Brit*) elastico.

elasticity [ɪlæs'tɪsɪtɪ] *n* elasticità.

elated [ɪ'leɪtɪd] *a* pieno(a) di gioia.

elation [ɪ'leɪʃən] *n* gioia.

elbow ['ɛlbəu] *n* gomito ♦ *vt*: **to ~ one's way through the crowd** farsi largo tra la folla a gomitate.

elbowroom ['ɛlbəurum] *n* spazio.

elder ['ɛldə*] *a* maggiore, più vecchio(a) ♦ *n* (*tree*) sambuco; **one's ~s** i più anziani.

elderly ['ɛldəlɪ] *a* anziano(a) ♦ *npl*: **the ~** gli anziani.

eldest ['ɛldɪst] *a, n*: **the ~ (child)** il(la) maggiore (dei bambini).

elect [ɪ'lɛkt] *vt* eleggere; (*choose*): **to ~ to do** decidere di fare ♦ *a*: **the president ~** il

presidente designato.

election [ɪ'lɛkʃən] *n* elezione *f*; **to hold an ~** indire un'elezione.

election campaign *n* campagna elettorale.

electioneering [ɪlɛkʃə'nɪərɪŋ] *n* propaganda elettorale.

elector [ɪ'lɛktə*] *n* elettore/trice.

electoral [ɪ'lɛktərəl] *a* elettorale.

electoral college *n* collegio elettorale.

electoral roll *n* (*Brit*) registro elettorale.

electorate [ɪ'lɛktərɪt] *n* elettorato.

electric [ɪ'lɛktrɪk] *a* elettrico(a).

electrical [ɪ'lɛktrɪkəl] *a* elettrico(a).

electrical engineer *n* ingegnere *m* elettrotecnico.

electrical failure *n* guasto all'impianto elettrico.

electric blanket *n* coperta elettrica.

electric chair *n* sedia elettrica.

electric cooker *n* cucina elettrica.

electric current *n* corrente *f* elettrica.

electric fire *n* (*Brit*) stufa elettrica.

electrician [ɪlɛk'trɪʃən] *n* elettricista *m*.

electricity [ɪlɛk'trɪsɪtɪ] *n* elettricità; **to switch on/off the ~** attaccare/staccare la corrente.

electricity board *n* (*Brit*) ente *m* regionale per l'energia elettrica.

electric light *n* luce *f* elettrica.

electric shock *n* scossa (elettrica).

electrify [ɪ'lɛktrɪfaɪ] *vt* (*RAIL*) elettrificare; (*audience*) elettrizzare.

electro... [ɪ'lɛktrəu] *prefix* elettro....

electrocardiogram (ECG) [ɪ'lɛktrə-'kɑ:dɪəgræm] *n* elettrocardiogramma *m*.

electro-convulsive therapy (ECT) [ɪ'lɛktrəkən'vʌlsɪv-] *n* elettroshockterapia.

electrocute [ɪ'lɛktrəkju:t] *vt* fulminare.

electrode [ɪ'lɛktrəud] *n* elettrodo.

electroencephalogram (EEG) [ɪ'lɛktrəuɛn-'sɛfələgræm] *n* (*MED*) elettroencefalogramma *m* (EEG).

electrolysis [ɪlɛk'trɒlɪsɪs] *n* elettrolisi *f*.

electromagnetic [ɪ'lɛktrəumæg'nɛtɪk] *n* elettromagnetico(a).

electron [ɪ'lɛktrɒn] *n* elettrone *m*.

electronic [ɪlɛk'trɒnɪk] *a* elettronico(a); *see also* **electronics.**

electronic data processing (EDP) *n* elaborazione *f* elettronica di dati.

electronic mail *n* posta elettronica.

electronics [ɪlɛk'trɒnɪks] *n* elettronica.

electron microscope *n* microscopio elettronico.

electroplated [ɪ'lɛktrəu'pleɪtɪd] *a* galvanizzato(a).

electrotherapy [ɪ'lɛktrəu'θɛrəpɪ] *n* elettroterapia.

elegance ['ɛlɪgəns] *n* eleganza.

elegant ['ɛlɪgənt] *a* elegante.

element ['ɛlɪmənt] *n* elemento; (*of heater, kettle etc*) resistenza.

elementary [ɛlɪ'mɛntərɪ] *a* elementare.

elephant ['ɛlɪfənt] *n* elefante/essa.

elevate ['ɛlɪveɪt] vt elevare.
elevated railroad (el) n (US) (ferrovia) soprelevata.
elevation [ɛlɪ'veɪʃən] n elevazione f; (height) altitudine f.
elevator ['ɛlɪveɪtə*] n elevatore m; (US: lift) ascensore m.
eleven [ɪ'lɛvn] num undici.
elevenses [ɪ'lɛvnzɪz] npl (Brit) caffè m a metà mattina.
eleventh [ɪ'lɛvnθ] a undicesimo(a); **at the ~ hour** (fig) all'ultimo minuto.
elf, pl **elves** [ɛlf, ɛlvz] n elfo.
elicit [ɪ'lɪsɪt] vt: **to ~ (from)** trarre (da), cavare fuori (da); **to ~ sth (from sb)** strappare qc (a qn).
eligible ['ɛlɪdʒəbl] a eleggibile; (for membership) che ha i requisiti; **to be ~ for a pension** essere pensionabile.
eliminate [ɪ'lɪmɪneɪt] vt eliminare.
elimination [ɪlɪmɪ'neɪʃən] n eliminazione f; **by process of ~** per eliminazione.
élite [eɪ'liːt] n élite f inv.
elitist [eɪ'liːtɪst] a (pej) elitario(a).
elixir [ɪ'lɪksə*] n elisir m inv.
Elizabethan [ɪlɪzə'biːθən] n elisabettiano(a).
ellipse [ɪ'lɪps] n ellisse f.
elliptical [ɪ'lɪptɪkl] a ellittico(a).
elm [ɛlm] n olmo.
elocution [ɛlə'kjuːʃən] n elocuzione f.
elongated ['iːlɔŋgeɪtɪd] a allungato(a).
elope [ɪ'ləup] vi (lovers) scappare.
elopement [ɪ'ləupmənt] n fuga romantica.
eloquence ['ɛləkwəns] n eloquenza.
eloquent ['ɛləkwənt] a eloquente.
else [ɛls] ad altro; **something ~** qualcos'altro; **somewhere ~** altrove; **everywhere ~** in qualsiasi altro luogo; **where ~?** in quale altro luogo?; **little ~** poco altro; **everyone ~** tutti gli altri; **nothing ~** nient'altro; **or ~** (otherwise) altrimenti; **is there anything ~ I can do?** posso fare qualcos'altro?
elsewhere [ɛls'wɛə*] ad altrove.
ELT n abbr (SCOL) = English Language Teaching.
elucidate [ɪ'luːsɪdeɪt] vt delucidare.
elude [ɪ'luːd] vt eludere.
elusive [ɪ'luːsɪv] a elusivo(a); (answer) evasivo(a); **he is very ~** è proprio inafferrabile or irraggiungibile.
elves [ɛlvz] npl of **elf**.
emaciated [ɪ'meɪsɪeɪtɪd] a emaciato(a).
emanate ['ɛməneɪt] vi: **to ~ from** emanare da.
emancipate [ɪ'mænsɪpeɪt] vt emancipare.
emancipation [ɪmænsɪ'peɪʃən] n emancipazione f.
emasculate [ɪ'mæskjuleɪt] vt (fig) rendere impotente.
embalm [ɪm'baːm] vt imbalsamare.
embankment [ɪm'bæŋkmənt] n (of road, railway) massicciata; (riverside) argine m; (dyke) diga.
embargo [ɪm'baːgəu] n (pl ~es: COMM,

NAUT) embargo ♦ vt mettere l'embargo su; **to put an ~ on sth** mettere l'embargo su qc.
embark [ɪm'baːk] vi: **to ~ (on)** imbarcarsi (su) ♦ vt imbarcare; **to ~ on** (fig) imbarcarsi in; (journey) intraprendere.
embarkation [ɛmbaː'keɪʃən] n imbarco.
embarkation card n carta d'imbarco.
embarrass [ɪm'bærəs] vt imbarazzare; **to be ~ed** essere imbarazzato(a).
embarrassing [ɪm'bærəsɪŋ] a imbarazzante.
embarrassment [ɪm'bærəsmənt] n imbarazzo.
embassy ['ɛmbəsɪ] n ambasciata; **the Italian E~** l'ambasciata d'Italia.
embed [ɪm'bɛd] vt conficcare; incastrare.
embellish [ɪm'bɛlɪʃ] vt abbellire; **to ~ (with)** (fig: story, truth) infiorare (con).
embers ['ɛmbəz] npl braci fpl.
embezzle [ɪm'bɛzl] vt appropriarsi indebitamente di.
embezzlement [ɪm'bɛzlmənt] n appropriazione f indebita, malversazione f.
embezzler [ɪm'bɛzlə*] n malversatore/trice.
embitter [ɪm'bɪtə*] vt amareggiare; inasprire.
emblem ['ɛmbləm] n emblema m.
embodiment [ɪm'bɔdɪmənt] n personificazione f, incarnazione f.
embody [ɪm'bɔdɪ] vt (features) racchiudere, comprendere; (ideas) dar forma concreta a, esprimere.
embolden [ɪm'bəuldn] vt incitare.
embolism ['ɛmbəlɪzəm] n embolia.
embossed [ɪm'bɔst] a in rilievo; goffrato(a); **~ with ...** con in rilievo ....
embrace [ɪm'breɪs] vt abbracciare; (include) comprendere ♦ vi abbracciarsi ♦ n abbraccio.
embroider [ɪm'brɔɪdə*] vt ricamare; (fig: story) abbellire.
embroidery [ɪm'brɔɪdərɪ] n ricamo.
embroil [ɪm'brɔɪl] vt: **to become ~ed (in sth)** restare invischiato(a) (in qc).
embryo ['ɛmbrɪəu] n (also fig) embrione m.
emend [ɪ'mɛnd] vt (text) correggere, emendare.
emerald ['ɛmərəld] n smeraldo.
emerge [ɪ'məːdʒ] vi apparire, sorgere; **it ~s that** (Brit) risulta che.
emergence [ɪ'məːdʒəns] n apparizione f; (of nation) nascita.
emergency [ɪ'məːdʒənsɪ] n emergenza; **in an ~** in caso di emergenza; **to declare a state of ~** dichiarare lo stato di emergenza.
emergency exit n uscita di sicurezza.
emergency landing n atterraggio forzato.
emergency lane n (US AUT) corsia d'emergenza.
emergency road service n (US) servizio riparazioni.
emergency service n servizio di pronto intervento.
emergency stop n (Brit AUT) frenata improvvisa.
emergent [ɪ'məːdʒənt] a: **~ nation** paese m in via di sviluppo.
emery board ['ɛmərɪ-] n limetta di carta

smerigliata.
emery paper *n* carta smerigliata.
emetic [ɪ'mɛtɪk] *n* emetico.
emigrant ['emɪgrənt] *n* emigrante *m/f*.
emigrate ['emɪgreɪt] *vi* emigrare.
emigration [emɪ'greɪʃən] *n* emigrazione *f*.
émigré ['emɪgreɪ] *n* emigrato/a.
eminence ['emɪnəns] *n* eminenza.
eminent ['emɪnənt] *a* eminente.
eminently ['emɪnəntlɪ] *ad* assolutamente, perfettamente.
emirate [e'mɪərɪt] *n* emirato.
emission [ɪ'mɪʃən] *n* emissione *f*.
emit [ɪ'mɪt] *vt* emettere.
emolument [ɪ'mɔljumənt] *n* (*often pl: formal*) emolumento.
emotion [ɪ'məuʃən] *n* emozione *f*; (*love, jealousy etc*) sentimento.
emotional [ɪ'məuʃənl] *a* (*person*) emotivo(a); (*scene*) commovente; (*tone, speech*) carico(a) d'emozione.
emotionally [ɪ'məuʃnəlɪ] *ad* (*behave, be involved*) sentimentalmente; (*speak*) con emozione; ~ **disturbed** con turbe emotive.
emotive [ɪ'məutɪv] *a* emotivo(a); ~ **power** capacità di commuovere.
empathy ['empəθɪ] *n* immedesimazione *f*; **to feel** ~ **with sb** immedesimarsi con i sentimenti di qn.
emperor ['empərə*] *n* imperatore *m*.
emphasis, *pl* **-ases** ['emfəsɪs, -siːz] *n* enfasi *f inv*; importanza; **to lay** *or* **place** ~ **on sth** (*fig*) mettere in risalto *or* in evidenza qc; **the** ~ **is on sport** si dà molta importanza allo sport.
emphasize ['emfəsaɪz] *vt* (*word, point*) sottolineare; (*feature*) mettere in evidenza.
emphatic [ɪm'fætɪk] *a* (*strong*) vigoroso(a); (*unambiguous, clear*) netto(a); categorico(a).
emphatically [ɪm'fætɪkəlɪ] *ad* vigorosamente; nettamente.
emphysema [emfɪ'siːmə] *n* (*MED*) enfisema *m*.
empire ['empaɪə*] *n* impero.
empirical [em'pɪrɪkl] *a* empirico(a).
employ [ɪm'plɔɪ] *vt* (*make use of: thing, method, person*) impiegare, servirsi di; (*give job to*) dare lavoro a, impiegare; **he's** ~**ed in a bank** lavora in banca.
employee [ɪmplɔɪ'iː] *n* impiegato/a.
employer [ɪm'plɔɪə*] *n* principale *m/f*, datore *m* di lavoro.
employment [ɪm'plɔɪmənt] *n* impiego; **to find** ~ trovare impiego *or* lavoro; **without** ~ disoccupato(a); **place of** ~ posto di lavoro.
employment agency *n* agenzia di collocamento.
employment exchange *n* (*Brit*) ufficio *m* collocamento *inv*.
empower [ɪm'pauə*] *vt*: **to** ~ **sb to do** concedere autorità a qn di fare.
empress ['emprɪs] *n* imperatrice *f*.
emptiness ['emptɪnɪs] *n* vuoto.
empty ['emptɪ] *a* vuoto(a); (*street, area*)

deserto(a); (*threat, promise*) vano(a) ♦ *n* (*bottle*) vuoto ♦ *vt* vuotare ♦ *vi* vuotarsi; (*liquid*) scaricarsi; **on an** ~ **stomach** a stomaco vuoto; **to** ~ **into** (*river*) gettarsi in.
empty-handed [emptɪ'hændɪd] *a* a mani vuote.
empty-headed [emptɪ'hedɪd] *a* sciocco(a).
EMS *n abbr* (= *European Monetary System*) S.M.E. *m*.
EMT *n abbr* = *emergency medical technician*.
emulate ['emjuleɪt] *vt* emulare.
emulsion [ɪ'mʌlʃən] *n* emulsione *f*; (*also*: ~ **paint**) colore *m* a tempera.
enable [ɪ'neɪbl] *vt*: **to** ~ **sb to do** permettere a qn di fare.
enact [ɪn'ækt] *vt* (*law*) emanare; (*play, scene*) rappresentare.
enamel [ɪ'næməl] *n* smalto.
enamel paint *n* vernice *f* a smalto.
enamoured [ɪ'næməd] *a*: ~ **of** innamorato(a) di.
encampment [ɪn'kæmpmənt] *n* accampamento.
encased [ɪn'keɪst] *a*: ~ **in** racchiuso(a) in; rivestito(a) di.
encash [ɪn'kæʃ] *vt* (*Brit*) incassare.
enchant [ɪn'tʃɑːnt] *vt* incantare; (*subj: magic spell*) catturare.
enchanting [ɪn'tʃɑːntɪŋ] *a* incantevole, affascinante.
encircle [ɪn'sɜːkl] *vt* accerchiare.
enc(l). *abbr* (*on letters etc*: = *enclosed, enclosure*) all., alleg.
enclose [ɪn'kləuz] *vt* (*land*) circondare, recingere; (*letter etc*): **to** ~ (**with**) allegare (con); **please find** ~**d** trovi qui accluso.
enclosure [ɪn'kləuʒə*] *n* recinto; (*COMM*) allegato.
encoder [ɪn'kəudə*] *n* (*COMPUT*) codificatore *m*.
encompass [ɪn'kʌmpəs] *vt* comprendere.
encore [ɔŋ'kɔː*] *excl*, *n* bis (*m inv*).
encounter [ɪn'kauntə*] *n* incontro ♦ *vt* incontrare.
encourage [ɪn'kʌrɪdʒ] *vt* incoraggiare; (*industry, growth etc*) favorire; **to** ~ **sb to do sth** incoraggiare qn a fare qc.
encouragement [ɪn'kʌrɪdʒmənt] *n* incoraggiamento.
encouraging [ɪn'kʌrɪdʒɪŋ] *a* incoraggiante.
encroach [ɪn'krəutʃ] *vi*: **to** ~ (**up)on** (*rights*) usurpare; (*time*) abusare di; (*land*) oltrepassare i limiti di.
encrusted [ɪn'krʌstɪd] *a*: ~ **with** incrostato(a) di.
encumbered [ɪn'kʌmbəd] *a*: **to be** ~ (**with**) essere carico(a) di.
encyclop(a)edia [ensaɪkləu'piːdɪə] *n* enciclopedia.
end [end] *n* fine *f*; (*aim*) fine *m*; (*of table*) bordo estremo; (*of line, rope etc*) estremità *f inv*; (*of pointed object*) punta; (*of town*) parte *f* ♦ *vt* finire; (*also*: **bring to an** ~, **put an** ~ **to**) mettere fine a ♦ *vi* finire; **from** ~

to ~ da un'estremità all'altra; **to come to an** ~ arrivare alla fine, finire; **to be at an** ~ essere finito; **in the** ~ alla fine; **at the** ~ **of the street** in fondo alla strada; **at the** ~ **of the day** (*Brit fig*) in fin dei conti; **on** ~ (*object*) ritto(a); **to stand on** ~ (*hair*) rizzarsi; **for 5 hours on** ~ per 5 ore di fila; **for hours on** ~ per ore e ore; **to this** ~, **with this** ~ **in view** a questo fine; **to** ~ (**with**) concludere (con).

end up *vi*: **to** ~ **up in** finire in.

endanger [ɪn'deɪndʒə*] *vt* mettere in pericolo; **an** ~**ed species** una specie in via di estinzione.

endear [ɪn'dɪə*] *vt*: **to** ~ **o.s. to sb** accattivarsi le simpatie di qn.

endearing [ɪn'dɪərɪŋ] *a* accattivante.

endearment [ɪn'dɪəmənt] *n*: **to whisper** ~**s** sussurrare tenerezze; **term of** ~ vezzeggiativo, parola affettuosa.

endeavour, (*US*) **endeavor** [ɪn'devə*] *n* sforzo, tentativo ♦ *vi*: **to** ~ **to do** cercare *or* sforzarsi di fare.

endemic [ɛn'demɪk] *a* endemico(a).

ending ['ɛndɪŋ] *n* fine *f*, conclusione *f*; (*LING*) desinenza.

endive ['ɛndaɪv] *n* (*curly*) indivia (riccia); (*smooth, flat*) indivia belga.

endless ['ɛndlɪs] *a* senza fine; (*patience, resources*) infinito(a); (*possibilities*) illimitato(a).

endorse [ɪn'dɔ:s] *vt* (*cheque*) girare; (*approve*) approvare, appoggiare.

endorsee [ɪndɔ:'si:] *n* giratario/a.

endorsement [ɪn'dɔ:smənt] *n* (*approval*) approvazione *f*; (*signature*) firma; (*Brit: on driving licence*) contravvenzione registrata sulla patente.

endorser [ɪn'dɔ:sə*] *n* girante *m/f*.

endow [ɪn'dau] *vt* (*prize*) istituire; (*hospital*) fondare; (*provide with money*) devolvere denaro a; (*equip*): **to** ~ **with** fornire di, dotare di.

endowment [ɪn'daumənt] *n* istituzione *f*; fondazione *f*; (*amount*) donazione *f*.

endowment assurance *n* assicurazione *f* mista.

end product *n* (*INDUSTRY*) prodotto finito; (*fig*) risultato.

end result *n* risultato finale.

endurable [ɪn'djuərəbl] *a* sopportabile.

endurance [ɪn'djuərəns] *n* resistenza; pazienza.

endurance test *n* prova di resistenza.

endure [ɪn'djuə*] *vt* sopportare, resistere a ♦ *vi* durare.

enduring [ɪn'djuərɪŋ] *a* duraturo(a).

end user *n* (*COMPUT*) consumatore(trice) effettivo(a).

enema ['ɛnɪmə] *n* (*MED*) clistere *m*.

enemy ['ɛnəmɪ] *a*, *n* nemico(a); **to make an** ~ **of sb** inimicarsi qn.

energetic [ɛnə'dʒetɪk] *a* energico(a); attivo(a).

energy ['ɛnədʒɪ] *n* energia; **Department of E**~ Ministero dell'Energia.

energy crisis *n* crisi *f* energetica.

energy-saving ['ɛnədʒɪ'seɪvɪŋ] *a* (*policy*) del risparmio energetico; (*device*) che risparmia energia.

enervating ['ɛnə:veɪtɪŋ] *a* debilitante.

enforce [ɪn'fɔ:s] *vt* (*LAW*) applicare, far osservare.

enforced [ɪn'fɔ:st] *a* forzato(a).

enfranchise [ɪn'fræntʃaɪz] *vt* (*give vote to*) concedere il diritto di voto a; (*set free*) affrancare.

engage [ɪn'geɪdʒ] *vt* (*hire*) assumere; (*lawyer*) incaricare; (*attention, interest*) assorbire; (*MIL*) attaccare; (*TECH*): **to** ~ **gear/the clutch** innestare la marcia/la frizione ♦ *vi* (*TECH*) ingranare; **to** ~ **in** impegnarsi in; **he is** ~**d in research/a survey** si occupa di ricerca/di un'inchiesta; **to** ~ **sb in conversation** attaccare conversazione con qn.

engaged [ɪn'geɪdʒd] *a* (*Brit: busy, in use*) occupato(a); (*betrothed*) fidanzato(a); **to get** ~ fidanzarsi.

engaged tone *n* (*Brit TEL*) segnale *m* di occupato.

engagement [ɪn'geɪdʒmənt] *n* impegno, obbligo; appuntamento; (*to marry*) fidanzamento; (*MIL*) combattimento; **I have a previous** ~ ho già un impegno.

engagement ring *n* anello di fidanzamento.

engaging [ɪn'geɪdʒɪŋ] *a* attraente.

engender [ɪn'dʒendə*] *vt* produrre, causare.

engine ['ɛndʒɪn] *n* (*AUT*) motore *m*; (*RAIL*) locomotiva.

engine driver *n* (*Brit: of train*) macchinista *m*.

engineer [ɛndʒɪ'nɪə*] *n* ingegnere *m*; (*Brit: for domestic appliances*) tecnico; (*US RAIL*) macchinista *m*; **civil/mechanical** ~ ingegnere civile/meccanico.

engineering [ɛndʒɪ'nɪərɪŋ] *n* ingegneria ♦ *cpd* (*works, factory, worker etc*) metalmeccanico(a).

engine failure *n* guasto al motore.

engine trouble *n* panne *f*.

England ['ɪŋglənd] *n* Inghilterra.

English ['ɪŋglɪʃ] *a* inglese ♦ *n* (*LING*) inglese *m*; **the** ~ *npl* gli Inglesi; **to be an** ~ **speaker** essere anglofono(a).

English Channel *n*: **the** ~ il Canale della Manica.

Englishman ['ɪŋglɪʃmən], **Englishwoman** ['ɪŋglɪʃwumən] *n* inglese *m/f*.

English-speaking ['ɪŋglɪʃ'spi:kɪŋ] *a* di lingua inglese.

engrave [ɪn'greɪv] *vt* incidere.

engraving [ɪn'greɪvɪŋ] *n* incisione *f*.

engrossed [ɪn'grəust] *a*: ~ **in** assorbito(a) da, preso(a) da.

engulf [ɪn'gʌlf] *vt* inghiottire.

enhance [ɪn'hɑ:ns] *vt* accrescere; (*position, reputation*) migliorare.

enigma [ɪ'nɪgmə] n enigma m.
enigmatic [ɛnɪg'mætɪk] a enigmatico(a).
enjoy [ɪn'dʒɔɪ] vt godere; (have: success, fortune) avere; (have benefit of: health) godere (di); **I ~ dancing** mi piace ballare; **to ~ o.s.** godersela, divertirsi.
enjoyable [ɪn'dʒɔɪəbl] a piacevole.
enjoyment [ɪn'dʒɔɪmənt] n piacere m, godimento.
enlarge [ɪn'lɑːdʒ] vt ingrandire ♦ vi: **to ~ on** (subject) dilungarsi su.
enlarged [ɪn'lɑːdʒd] a (edition) ampliato(a); (MED: organ, gland) ingrossato(a).
enlargement [ɪn'lɑːdʒmənt] n (PHOT) ingrandimento.
enlighten [ɪn'laɪtn] vt illuminare; dare chiarimenti a.
enlightened [ɪn'laɪtnd] a illuminato(a).
enlightening [ɪn'laɪtnɪŋ] a istruttivo(a).
enlightenment [ɪn'laɪtnmənt] n progresso culturale; chiarimenti mpl; (HISTORY): **the E~** l'Illuminismo.
enlist [ɪn'lɪst] vt arruolare; (support) procurare ♦ vi arruolarsi; **~ed man** (US MIL) soldato semplice.
enliven [ɪn'laɪvn] vt (people) rallegrare; (events) ravvivare.
enmity ['ɛnmɪtɪ] n inimicizia.
ennoble [ɪ'nəʊbl] vt nobilitare; (with title) conferire un titolo nobiliare a.
enormity [ɪ'nɔːmɪtɪ] n enormità f inv.
enormous [ɪ'nɔːməs] a enorme.
enormously [ɪ'nɔːməslɪ] ad enormemente.
enough [ɪ'nʌf] a, n: **~ time/books** assai tempo/libri; **have you got ~?** ne ha abbastanza or a sufficienza? ♦ ad: **big ~** abbastanza grande; **he has not worked ~** non ha lavorato abbastanza; **~!** basta!; **it's hot ~ (as it is)!** fa abbastanza caldo così!; **will £5 be ~?** bastano 5 sterline?; **that's ~** basta; **I've had ~!** non ne posso più!; **he was kind ~ to lend me the money** è stato così gentile da prestarmi i soldi; **... which, funnily ~ ...** che, strano a dirsi.
enquire [ɪn'kwaɪə*] vt, vi = inquire.
enrage [ɪn'reɪdʒ] vt fare arrabbiare.
enrich [ɪn'rɪtʃ] vt arricchire.
enrol, (US) enroll [ɪn'rəʊl] vt iscrivere; (at university) immatricolare ♦ vi iscriversi.
enrol(l)ment [ɪn'rəʊlmənt] n iscrizione f.
en route [ɔn'ruːt] ad: **~ for/from/to** in viaggio per/da/a.
ensconced [ɪn'skɔnst] a: **~ in** ben sistemato(a) in.
ensemble [ɑ̃ːn'sɑ̃ːmbl] n (MUS) ensemble m inv.
enshrine [ɪn'ʃraɪn] vt conservare come una reliquia.
ensign n (NAUT) ['ɛnsən] bandiera; (MIL) ['ɛnsaɪn] portabandiera m inv.
enslave [ɪn'sleɪv] vt fare schiavo.
ensue [ɪn'sjuː] vi seguire, risultare.
ensure [ɪn'ʃuə*] vt assicurare; garantire; **to ~ that** assicurarsi che.

ENT n abbr (MED: = Ear, Nose & Throat) O.R.L.
entail [ɪn'teɪl] vt comportare.
entangle [ɪn'tæŋgl] vt (thread etc) impigliare; **to become ~d in sth** (fig) rimanere impegolato in qc.
enter ['ɛntə*] vt (gen) entrare in; (club) associarsi a; (profession) intraprendere; (army) arruolarsi in; (competition) partecipare a; (sb for a competition) iscrivere; (write down) registrare; (COMPUT: data) introdurre, inserire ♦ vi entrare.
enter for vt fus iscriversi a.
enter into vt fus (explanation) cominciare a dare; (debate) partecipare a; (agreement) concludere; (negotiations) prendere parte a.
enter (up)on vt fus cominciare.
enteritis [ɛntə'raɪtɪs] n enterite f.
enterprise ['ɛntəpraɪz] n (undertaking, company) impresa; (spirit) iniziativa.
enterprising ['ɛntəpraɪzɪŋ] a intraprendente.
entertain [ɛntə'teɪn] vt divertire; (invite) ricevere; (idea, plan) nutrire.
entertainer [ɛntə'teɪnə*] n comico/a.
entertaining [ɛntə'teɪnɪŋ] a divertente ♦ n: **to do a lot of ~** avere molti ospiti.
entertainment [ɛntə'teɪnmənt] n (amusement) divertimento; (show) spettacolo.
entertainment allowance n spese fpl di rappresentanza.
enthralled [ɪn'θrɔːld] a affascinato(a).
enthralling [ɪn'θrɔːlɪŋ] a avvincente.
enthuse [ɪn'θuːz] vi: **to ~ (about or over)** entusiasmarsi (per).
enthusiasm [ɪn'θuːzɪæzəm] n entusiasmo.
enthusiast [ɪn'θuːzɪæst] n entusiasta m/f; **a jazz etc ~** un appassionato di jazz etc.
enthusiastic [ɪnθuːzɪ'æstɪk] a entusiasta, entusiastico(a); **to be ~ about sth/sb** essere appassionato di qc/entusiasta di qn.
entice [ɪn'taɪs] vt allettare, sedurre.
enticing [ɪn'taɪsɪŋ] a allettante.
entire [ɪn'taɪə*] a intero(a).
entirely [ɪn'taɪəlɪ] ad completamente, interamente.
entirety [ɪn'taɪərətɪ] n: **in its ~** nel suo complesso.
entitle [ɪn'taɪtl] vt (give right): **to ~ sb to sth/to do** dare diritto a qn a qc/a fare.
entitled [ɪn'taɪtld] a (book) che si intitola; **to be ~ to sth/to do sth** avere diritto a qc/a fare qc.
entity ['ɛntɪtɪ] n entità f inv.
entrails ['ɛntreɪlz] npl interiora fpl.
entrance n ['ɛntrns] entrata, ingresso; (of person) entrata ♦ vt [ɪn'trɑːns] incantare, rapire; **to gain ~ to** (university etc) essere ammesso a.
entrance examination n (to school) esame m di ammissione.
entrance fee n tassa d'iscrizione; (to museum etc) prezzo d'ingresso.
entrance ramp n (US AUT) rampa di

accesso.

entrancing [ɪnˈtrɑːnsɪŋ] a incantevole.

entrant [ˈentrnt] n partecipante m/f; concorrente m/f; (Brit: in exam) candidato/a.

entreat [enˈtriːt] vt supplicare.

entreaty [ɪnˈtriːtɪ] n supplica, preghiera.

entrée [ˈɔntreɪ] n (CULIN) prima portata.

entrenched [enˈtrentʃt] a radicato(a).

entrepreneur [ˈɔntrəprəˈnəː*] n imprenditore m.

entrepreneurial [ˈɔntrəprəˈnəːrɪəl] a imprenditoriale.

entrust [ɪnˈtrʌst] vt: **to ~ sth to** affidare qc a.

entry [ˈentrɪ] n entrata; (way in) entrata, ingresso; (in dictionary) voce f; (in diary, ship's log) annotazione f; (in account book, ledger, list) registrazione f; **"no ~"** "vietato l'ingresso"; (AUT) "divieto di accesso"; **single/double ~ book-keeping** partita semplice/doppia.

entry form n modulo d'iscrizione.

entry phone n (Brit) citofono.

entwine [ɪnˈtwaɪn] vt intrecciare.

enumerate [ɪˈnjuːməreɪt] vt enumerare.

enunciate [ɪˈnʌnsɪeɪt] vt enunciare; pronunciare.

envelop [ɪnˈveləp] vt avvolgere, avviluppare.

envelope [ˈenvələup] n busta.

enviable [ˈenvɪəbl] a invidiabile.

envious [ˈenvɪəs] a invidioso(a).

environment [ɪnˈvaɪərənmənt] n ambiente m; **Department of the E~** (Brit) ≈ Ministero dell'Ambiente.

environmental [ɪnvaɪərənˈmentl] a ecologico(a); ambientale; **~ studies** (in school etc) ecologia.

environmentalist [ɪnˈvaɪərənˈmentəlɪst] n studioso/a della protezione dell'ambiente.

Environmental Protection Agency (EPA) n (US) ≈ Ministero dell'Ambiente.

envisage [ɪnˈvɪzɪdʒ] vt immaginare; prevedere.

envision [ɪnˈvɪʒən] vt concepire, prevedere.

envoy [ˈenvɔɪ] n inviato/a.

envy [ˈenvɪ] n invidia ♦ vt invidiare; **to ~ sb sth** invidiare qn per qc.

enzyme [ˈenzaɪm] n enzima m.

EPA n abbr (US) see **Environmental Protection Agency**.

ephemeral [ɪˈfemərəl] a effimero(a).

epic [ˈepɪk] n poema m epico ♦ a epico(a).

epicentre, (US) **epicenter** [ˈepɪsentə*] n epicentro.

epidemic [epɪˈdemɪk] n epidemia.

epilepsy [ˈepɪlepsɪ] n epilessia.

epileptic [epɪˈleptɪk] a, n epilettico(a).

epilogue [ˈepɪlɔg] n epilogo.

Epiphany [ɪˈpɪfənɪ] n Epifania.

episcopal [ɪˈpɪskəpəl] a episcopale.

episode [ˈepɪsəud] n episodio.

epistle [ɪˈpɪsl] n epistola.

epitaph [ˈepɪtɑːf] n epitaffio.

epithet [ˈepɪθet] n epiteto.

epitome [ɪˈpɪtəmɪ] n epitome f; quintessenza.

epitomize [ɪˈpɪtəmaɪz] vt (fig) incarnare.

epoch [ˈiːpɔk] n epoca.

epoch-making [ˈiːpɔkmeɪkɪŋ] a che fa epoca.

eponymous [ɪˈpɔnɪməs] a dello stesso nome.

equable [ˈekwəbl] a uniforme; (climate) costante; (character) equilibrato(a).

equal [ˈiːkwl] a, n uguale (m/f) ♦ vt uguagliare; **~ to** (task) all'altezza di.

equality [iːˈkwɔlɪtɪ] n uguaglianza.

equalize [ˈiːkwəlaɪz] vt, vi pareggiare.

equalizer [ˈiːkwəlaɪzə*] n punto del pareggio.

equally [ˈiːkwəlɪ] ad ugualmente; **they are ~ clever** sono intelligenti allo stesso modo.

Equal Opportunities Commission, (US) **Equal Employment Opportunity Commission** n commissione contro discriminazioni sessuali o razziali nel mondo del lavoro.

equal(s) sign n segno d'uguaglianza.

equanimity [ekwəˈnɪmɪtɪ] n serenità.

equate [ɪˈkweɪt] vt: **to ~ sth with** considerare qc uguale a; (compare) paragonare qc con; **to ~ A to B** mettere in equazione A e B.

equation [ɪˈkweɪʃən] n (MATH) equazione f.

equator [ɪˈkweɪtə*] n equatore m.

Equatorial Guinea [ekwəˈtɔːrɪəl-] n Guinea Equatoriale.

equestrian [ɪˈkwestrɪən] a equestre ♦ n cavaliere/amazzone.

equilibrium [iːkwɪˈlɪbrɪəm] n equilibrio.

equinox [ˈiːkwɪnɔks] n equinozio.

equip [ɪˈkwɪp] vt equipaggiare, attrezzare; **to ~ sb/sth with** fornire qn/qc di; (machinery etc) dotato(a) di; **he is well ~ped for the job** ha i requisiti necessari per quel lavoro.

equipment [ɪˈkwɪpmənt] n attrezzatura; (electrical etc) apparecchiatura.

equitable [ˈekwɪtəbl] a equo(a), giusto(a).

equities [ˈekwɪtɪz] npl (Brit COMM) azioni fpl ordinarie.

equity [ˈekwɪtɪ] n equità.

equity capital n capitale m azionario.

equivalent [ɪˈkwɪvələnt] a, n equivalente (m); **to be ~ to** equivalere a.

equivocal [ɪˈkwɪvəkl] a equivoco(a); (open to suspicion) dubbio(a).

equivocate [ɪˈkwɪvəkeɪt] vi esprimersi in modo equivoco.

equivocation [ɪkwɪvəˈkeɪʃən] n parole fpl equivoche.

ER abbr (Brit) = Elizabeth Regina.

ERA n abbr (US POL) = Equal Rights Amendment.

era [ˈɪərə] n era, età f inv.

eradicate [ɪˈrædɪkeɪt] vt sradicare.

erase [ɪˈreɪz] vt cancellare.

eraser [ɪˈreɪzə*] n gomma.

erect [ɪˈrekt] a eretto(a) ♦ vt costruire; (monument, tent) alzare.

erection [ɪˈrekʃən] n (also PHYSIOL) erezione f; (of building) costruzione f; (of machinery) montaggio.

ergonomics [əːgəˈnɔmɪks] n ergonomia.

ERISA *n abbr* (*US:* = *Employee Retirement Income Security Act*) legge relativa al pensionamento statale.

ermine ['ɜːmɪn] *n* ermellino.

ERNIE ['ɜːnɪ] *n abbr* (*Brit:* = *Electronic Random Number Indicator Equipment*) sistema che seleziona i numeri vincenti di buoni del Tesoro.

erode [ɪ'rəud] *vt* erodere; (*metal*) corrodere.

erosion [ɪ'rəuʒən] *n* erosione *f*.

erotic [ɪ'rɔtɪk] *a* erotico(a).

eroticism [ɪ'rɔtɪsɪzəm] *n* erotismo.

err [ə:*] *vi* errare; (*REL*) peccare.

errand ['ɛrənd] *n* commissione *f;* **to run ~s** fare commissioni; **~ of mercy** atto di carità.

errand boy *n* fattorino.

erratic [ɪ'rætɪk] *a* imprevedibile; (*person, mood*) incostante.

erroneous [ɪ'rəunɪəs] *a* erroneo(a).

error ['ɛrə*] *n* errore *m;* **typing/spelling ~** errore di battitura/di ortografia; **in ~** per errore; **~s and omissions excepted** salvo errori ed omissioni.

error message *n* (*COMPUT*) messaggio di errore.

erstwhile ['ə:stwaɪl] *ad* allora, un tempo ♦ *a* di allora.

erudite ['ɛrjudaɪt] *a* erudito(a).

erupt [ɪ'rʌpt] *vi* erompere; (*volcano*) mettersi (*or* essere) in eruzione.

eruption [ɪ'rʌpʃən] *n* eruzione *f;* (*of anger, violence*) esplosione *f*.

ESA *n abbr* (= *European Space Agency*) ESA *f*.

escalate ['ɛskəleɪt] *vi* intensificarsi; (*costs*) salire.

escalation [ɛskə'leɪʃən] *n* escalation *f;* (*of prices*) aumento.

escalation clause *n* clausola di revisione.

escalator ['ɛskəleɪtə*] *n* scala mobile.

escapade [ɛskə'peɪd] *n* scappatella; avventura.

escape [ɪ'skeɪp] *n* evasione *f;* fuga; (*of gas etc*) fuga, fuoriuscita ♦ *vi* fuggire; (*from jail*) evadere, scappare; (*fig*) fuggire; (*leak*) uscire ♦ *vt* sfuggire a; **to ~ from sb** sfuggire a qn; **to ~ to** (*another place*) fuggire in; (*freedom, safety*) fuggire verso; **to ~ notice** passare inosservato(a).

escape artist *n* mago della fuga.

escape clause *n* clausola scappatoia.

escape hatch *n* (*in submarine, space rocket*) portello di sicurezza.

escape key *n* (*COMPUT*) tasto di escape, tasto per cambio di codice.

escape route *n* percorso della fuga.

escapism [ɪs'keɪpɪzəm] *n* evasione *f* (dalla realtà).

escapist [ɪs'keɪpɪst] *a* d'evasione ♦ *n* persona che cerca di evadere dalla realtà.

escapologist [ɛskə'pɔlədʒɪst] *n* (*Brit*) = **escape artist**.

escarpment [ɪs'kɑ:pmənt] *n* scarpata.

eschew [ɪs'tʃu:] *vt* evitare.

escort *n* ['ɛskɔ:t] scorta; (*to dance etc*): **her ~** il suo cavaliere; **his ~** la sua dama ♦ *vt* [ɪ'skɔ:t] scortare; accompagnare.

escort agency *n* agenzia di hostess.

Eskimo ['ɛskɪməu] *a* eschimese ♦ *n* eschimese *m/f;* (*LING*) eschimese *m*.

ESL *n abbr* (*SCOL*) = *English as a Second Language*.

esophagus [iː'sɔfəgəs] *n* (*US*) = **oesophagus**.

esoteric [ɛsəu'tɛrɪk] *a* esoterico(a).

ESP *n abbr see* **extrasensory perception**.

esp. *abbr* (= *especially*) spec.

especially [ɪ'spɛʃlɪ] *ad* specialmente; (*above all*) soprattutto; (*specifically*) espressamente; (*particularly*) particolarmente.

espionage ['ɛspɪɒnɑːʒ] *n* spionaggio.

esplanade [ɛsplə'neɪd] *n* lungomare *m*.

espouse [ɪ'spauz] *vt* abbracciare.

Esquire [ɪ'skwaɪə*] *n* (*Brit: abbr* **Esq.**): J. Brown, ~ Signor J. Brown.

essay ['ɛseɪ] *n* (*SCOL*) composizione *f;* (*LITERATURE*) saggio.

essence ['ɛsns] *n* essenza; **in ~** in sostanza; **speed is of the ~** la velocità è di estrema importanza.

essential [ɪ'sɛnʃəl] *a* essenziale; (*basic*) fondamentale ♦ *n* elemento essenziale; **it is ~ that** è essenziale che + *sub*.

essentially [ɪ'sɛnʃəlɪ] *ad* essenzialmente.

EST *abbr* (*US:* = *Eastern Standard Time*) fuso orario.

est. *abbr* = *established; estimate(d)*.

establish [ɪ'stæblɪʃ] *vt* stabilire; (*business*) mettere su; (*one's power etc*) confermare; (*prove: fact, identity, sb's innocence*) dimostrare.

establishment [ɪs'tæblɪʃmənt] *n* stabilimento; (*business*) azienda; **the E~** la classe dirigente; l'establishment *m;* **a teaching ~** un istituto d'istruzione.

estate [ɪ'steɪt] *n* proprietà *f inv;* (*LAW*) beni *mpl*, patrimonio; (*Brit: also:* **housing ~**) complesso edilizio.

estate agency *n* (*Brit*) agenzia immobiliare.

estate agent *n* (*Brit*) agente *m* immobiliare.

estate car *n* (*Brit*) giardiniera.

esteem [ɪ'sti:m] *n* stima ♦ *vt* considerare; stimare; **I hold him in high ~** gode di tutta la mia stima.

esthetic [ɪs'θɛtɪk] *a* (*US*) = **aesthetic**.

estimate *n* ['ɛstɪmət] stima; (*COMM*) preventivo ♦ *vb* ['ɛstɪmeɪt] *vt* stimare, valutare ♦ *vi* (*Brit COMM*): **to ~ for** fare il preventivo per; **to give sb an ~ of** fare a qn una valutazione approssimativa (*or* un preventivo) di; **at a rough ~** approssimativamente.

estimation [ɛstɪ'meɪʃən] *n* stima; opinione *f;* **in my ~** a mio giudizio, a mio avviso.

estimator ['ɛstɪmeɪtə*] *n* perito stimatore.

Estonia [ɛ'stəunɪə] *n* Estonia.

estranged [ɪ'streɪndʒd] *a* separato(a).

estrangement [ɪs'treɪndʒmənt] *n* alienazione

f.

estrogen ['i:strəudʒən] *n (US)* = **oestrogen**.

estuary ['ɛstjuərɪ] *n* estuario.

ET *abbr (US: = Eastern Time) fuso orario.*

ETA *n abbr (= estimated time of arrival)* ora di arrivo prevista.

et al. *abbr (= et alii: and others)* ed altri.

etc. *abbr (= et cetera)* ecc., etc.

etch [ɛtʃ] *vt* incidere all'acquaforte.

etching ['ɛtʃɪŋ] *n* acquaforte *f.*

ETD *n abbr (= estimated time of departure)* ora di partenza prevista.

eternal [ɪ'tə:nl] *a* eterno(a).

eternity [ɪ'tə:nɪtɪ] *n* eternità.

ether ['i:θə*] *n* etere *m.*

ethereal [ɪ'θɪərɪəl] *a* etereo(a).

ethical ['ɛθɪkl] *a* etico(a), morale.

ethics ['ɛθɪks] *n* etica ♦ *npl* morale *f.*

Ethiopia [i:θɪ'əupɪə] *n* Etiopia.

Ethiopian [i:θɪ'əupɪən] *a, n* etiope *(m/f).*

ethnic ['ɛθnɪk] *a* etnico(a).

ethnology [ɛθ'nɔlədʒɪ] *n* etnologia.

ethos ['i:θɔs] *n (of culture, group)* norma di vita.

etiquette ['ɛtɪkɛt] *n* etichetta.

ETU *n abbr (Brit: = Electrical Trades Union) sindacato dei lavoratori dell'industria elettrica.*

ETV *n abbr (US) = Educational Television.*

etymology [ɛtɪ'mɔlədʒɪ] *n* etimologia.

eucalyptus [ju:kə'lɪptəs] *n* eucalipto.

eulogy ['ju:lədʒɪ] *n* elogio.

euphemism ['ju:fəmɪzəm] *n* eufemismo.

euphemistic [ju:fə'mɪstɪk] *a* eufemistico(a).

euphoria [ju:'fɔ:rɪə] *n* euforia.

Eurasia [juə'reɪʃə] *n* Eurasia.

Eurasian [juə'reɪʃən] *a, n* eurasiano(a).

Euratom [juə'rætəm] *n abbr (= European Atomic Energy Community)* EURATOM *f.*

Eurocheque ['juərəutʃɛk] *n* eurochèque *m inv.*

Eurocrat ['juərəukræt] *n* eurocrate *m/f.*

Eurodollar ['juərəudɔlə*] *n* eurodollaro.

Europe ['juərəp] *n* Europa.

European [juərə'pi:ən] *a, n* europeo(a).

European Court of Justice *n* Corte *f* di Giustizia della Comunità Europea.

euthanasia [ju:θə'neɪzɪə] *n* eutanasia.

evacuate [ɪ'vækjueɪt] *vt* evacuare.

evacuation [ɪvækju'eɪʃən] *n* evacuazione *f.*

evade [ɪ'veɪd] *vt* eludere; *(duties etc)* sottrarsi a.

evaluate [ɪ'væljueɪt] *vt* valutare.

evangelist [ɪ'vændʒəlɪst] *n* evangelista *m.*

evangelize [ɪ'vændʒəlaɪz] *vt* evangelizzare.

evaporate [ɪ'væpəreɪt] *vi* evaporare ♦ *vt* far evaporare.

evaporated milk *n* latte *m* concentrato.

evaporation [ɪvæpə'reɪʃən] *n* evaporazione *f.*

evasion [ɪ'veɪʒən] *n* evasione *f.*

evasive [ɪ'veɪsɪv] *a* evasivo(a).

eve [i:v] *n*: **on the ~ of** alla vigilia di.

even ['i:vn] *a* regolare; *(number)* pari *inv* ♦ *ad* anche, perfino; **~ if,** **~ though** anche se; **~ more** ancora di più; **he loves her ~ more**

la ama anche di più; **~ faster** ancora più veloce; **~ so** ciò nonostante; **not ~ ...** nemmeno ...; **to break ~** finire in pari *or* alla pari; **to get ~ with sb** dare la pari a qn.

even out *vi* pareggiare.

evening ['i:vnɪŋ] *n* sera; *(as duration, event)* serata; **in the ~** la sera; **this ~** stasera, questa sera; **tomorrow/yesterday ~** domani/ieri sera.

evening class *n* corso serale.

evening dress *n (woman's)* abito da sera; **in ~ (man)** in abito scuro; *(woman)* in abito lungo.

evenly ['i:vənlɪ] *ad (distribute, space, spread)* uniformemente; *(divide)* in parti uguali.

evensong ['i:vnsɔŋ] *n* ≈ vespro.

event [ɪ'vɛnt] *n* avvenimento; *(SPORT)* gara; **in the ~ of** in caso di; **at all ~s** *(Brit),* **in any ~** in ogni caso; **in the ~** in realtà, di fatto; **in the course of ~s** nel corso degli eventi.

eventful [ɪ'vɛntful] *a* denso(a) di eventi.

eventing [ɪ'vɛntɪŋ] *n (HORSERIDING)* concorso ippico.

eventual [ɪ'vɛntʃuəl] *a* finale.

eventuality [ɪvɛntʃu'ælɪtɪ] *n* possibilità *f inv,* eventualità *f inv.*

eventually [ɪ'vɛntʃuəlɪ] *ad* finalmente.

ever ['ɛvə*] *ad* mai; *(at all times)* sempre; **for ~** per sempre; **the best ~** il migliore che ci sia mai stato; **hardly ~** non ... quasi mai; **did you ~ meet him?** l'ha mai incontrato?; **have you ~ been there?** c'è mai stato?; **~ so pretty** così bello(a); **thank you ~ so much** grazie mille; **yours ~** *(Brit: in letters)* sempre tuo; **~ since** *ad* da allora ♦ *cj* sin da quando.

Everest ['ɛvərɪst] *n (also:* **Mount ~)** Everest *m.*

evergreen ['ɛvəgri:n] *n* sempreverde *m.*

everlasting [ɛvə'lɑ:stɪŋ] *a* eterno(a).

every ['ɛvrɪ] *a* ogni; **~ day** tutti i giorni, ogni giorno; **~ other/third day** ogni due/tre giorni; **~ other car** una macchina su due; **~ now and then** ogni tanto, di quando in quando; **I have ~ confidence in him** ho piena fiducia in lui.

everybody ['ɛvrɪbɔdɪ] *pronoun* ognuno, tutti *pl;* **~ else** tutti gli altri; **~ knows about it** lo sanno tutti.

everyday ['ɛvrɪdeɪ] *a* quotidiano(a); di ogni giorno; *(use, occurrence, experience)* comune; *(expression)* di uso corrente.

everyone ['ɛvrɪwʌn] = **everybody**.

everything ['ɛvrɪθɪŋ] *pronoun* tutto, ogni cosa; **~ is ready** è tutto pronto; **he did ~ possible** ha fatto tutto il possibile.

everywhere ['ɛvrɪwɛə*] *ad* in ogni luogo, dappertutto; *(wherever)* ovunque; **~ you go you meet ...** ovunque si vada si trova ....

evict [ɪ'vɪkt] *vt* sfrattare.

eviction [ɪ'vɪkʃən] *n* sfratto.

eviction notice *n* avviso di sfratto.

evidence ['ɛvɪdəns] *n (proof)* prova; *(of*

witness) testimonianza; (*sign*): **to show** ~ **of** dare segni di; **to give** ~ deporre; **in** ~ (*obvious*) in evidenza; in vista.
evident ['ɛvɪdənt] *a* evidente.
evidently ['ɛvɪdəntlɪ] *ad* evidentemente.
evil ['i:vl] *a* cattivo(a), maligno(a) ♦ *n* male *m*.
evince [ɪ'vɪns] *vt* manifestare.
evocative [ɪ'vɔkətɪv] *a* evocativo(a).
evoke [ɪ'vəuk] *vt* evocare; (*admiration*) suscitare.
evolution [i:və'lu:ʃən] *n* evoluzione *f*.
evolve [ɪ'vɔlv] *vt* elaborare ♦ *vi* svilupparsi, evolversi.
ewe [ju:] *n* pecora.
ex- [ɛks] *prefix* ex; (*out of*): **the price** ~ **works** il prezzo franco fabbrica.
exacerbate [ɪk'sæsəbeɪt] *vt* (*pain*) aggravare; (*fig*: *relations, situation*) esacerbare, esasperare.
exact [ɪg'zækt] *a* esatto(a) ♦ *vt*: **to** ~ **sth** (**from**) estorcere qc (da); esigere qc (da).
exacting [ɪg'zæktɪŋ] *a* esigente; (*work*) faticoso(a).
exactitude [ɪg'zæktɪtju:d] *n* esattezza, precisione *f*.
exactly [ɪg'zæktlɪ] *ad* esattamente; ~! esatto!
exaggerate [ɪg'zædʒəreɪt] *vt, vi* esagerare.
exaggeration [ɪgzædʒə'reɪʃən] *n* esagerazione *f*.
exalt [ɪg'zɔ:lt] *vt* esaltare; elevare.
exalted [ɪg'zɔ:ltɪd] *a* (*rank, person*) elevato(a); (*elated*) esaltato(a).
exam [ɪg'zæm] *n abbr* (*SCOL*) = **examination.**
examination [ɪgzæmɪ'neɪʃən] *n* (*SCOL*) esame *m*; (*MED*) controllo; **to take** *or* (*Brit*) **sit an** ~ sostenere *or* dare un esame; **the matter is under** ~ la questione è all'esame.
examine [ɪg'zæmɪn] *vt* esaminare; (*SCOL*: *orally, LAW*: *person*) interrogare; (*inspect*: *machine, premises*) ispezionare; (*luggage, passport*) controllare; (*MED*) visitare.
examiner [ɪg'zæmɪnə*] *n* esaminatore/trice.
example [ɪg'zɑ:mpl] *n* esempio; **for** ~ ad *or* per esempio; **to set a good/bad** ~ dare il buon/cattivo esempio.
exasperate [ɪg'zɑ:spəreɪt] *vt* esasperare; ~**d by** (*or* at *or* with) esasperato da.
exasperating [ɪg'zɑ:spəreɪtɪŋ] *a* esasperante.
exasperation [ɪgzɑ:spə'reɪʃən] *n* esasperazione *f*.
excavate ['ɛkskəveɪt] *vt* scavare.
excavation [ɛkskə'veɪʃən] *n* escavazione *f*.
excavator ['ɛkskəveɪtə*] *n* scavatore *m*, scavatrice *f*.
exceed [ɪk'si:d] *vt* superare; (*one's powers, time limit*) oltrepassare.
exceedingly [ɪk'si:dɪŋlɪ] *ad* eccessivamente.
excel [ɪk'sɛl] *vi* eccellere ♦ *vt* sorpassare; **to** ~ **o.s.** (*Brit*) superare se stesso.
excellence ['ɛksələns] *n* eccellenza.
Excellency ['ɛksələnsɪ] *n*: **His** ~ Sua Eccellenza.

excellent ['ɛksələnt] *a* eccellente.
except [ɪk'sɛpt] *prep* (*also*: ~ **for,** ~**ing**) salvo, all'infuori di, eccetto ♦ *vt* escludere; ~ **if/when** salvo se/quando; ~ **that** salvo che.
exception [ɪk'sɛpʃən] *n* eccezione *f*; **to take** ~ **to** trovare a ridire su; **with the** ~ **of** ad eccezione di.
exceptional [ɪk'sɛpʃənl] *a* eccezionale.
excerpt ['ɛksə:pt] *n* estratto.
excess [ɪk'sɛs] *n* eccesso; **in** ~ **of** al di sopra di.
excess baggage *n* bagaglio in eccedenza.
excess fare *n* supplemento.
excessive [ɪk'sɛsɪv] *a* eccessivo(a).
excess supply *n* eccesso di offerta.
exchange [ɪks'tʃeɪndʒ] *n* scambio; (*also*: **telephone** ~) centralino ♦ *vt*: **to** ~ (**for**) scambiare (con); **in** ~ **for** in cambio di; **foreign** ~ (*COMM*) cambio.
exchange control *n* controllo sui cambi.
exchange market *n* mercato dei cambi.
exchange rate *n* tasso di cambio.
Exchequer [ɪks'tʃɛkə*] *n*: **the** ~ (*Brit*) lo Scacchiere, ≈ il ministero delle Finanze.
excisable [ɪk'saɪzəbl] *a* soggetto(a) a dazio.
excise *n* ['ɛksaɪz] imposta, dazio ♦ *vt* [ɛk'saɪz] recidere.
excise duties *npl* dazi *mpl*.
excitable [ɪk'saɪtəbl] *a* eccitabile.
excite [ɪk'saɪt] *vt* eccitare; **to get** ~**d** eccitarsi.
excitement [ɪk'saɪtmənt] *n* eccitazione *f*; agitazione *f*.
exciting [ɪk'saɪtɪŋ] *a* avventuroso(a); (*film, book*) appassionante.
excl. *abbr* (= *excluding, exclusive (of)*) escl.
exclaim [ɪk'skleɪm] *vi* esclamare.
exclamation [ɛksklə'meɪʃən] *n* esclamazione *f*.
exclamation mark *n* punto esclamativo.
exclude [ɪk'sklu:d] *vt* escludere.
excluding [ɪk'sklu:dɪŋ] *prep*: ~ **VAT** IVA esclusa.
exclusion [ɪk'sklu:ʒən] *n* esclusione *f*; **to the** ~ **of** escludendo.
exclusion clause *n* clausola di esclusione.
exclusive [ɪk'sklu:sɪv] *a* esclusivo(a); (*club*) selettivo(a); (*district*) snob *inv* ♦ *ad* (*COMM*) non compreso; ~ **of VAT** IVA esclusa; ~ **of postage** spese postali escluse; ~ **of service** servizio escluso; **from 1st to 15th March** ~ dal 1° al 15 marzo esclusi; ~ **rights** *npl* (*COMM*) diritti *mpl* esclusivi.
exclusively [ɪk'sklu:sɪvlɪ] *ad* esclusivamente.
excommunicate [ɛkskə'mju:nɪkeɪt] *vt* scomunicare.
excrement ['ɛkskrəmənt] *n* escremento.
excruciating [ɪk'skru:ʃieɪtɪŋ] *a* straziante, atroce.
excursion [ɪk'skə:ʃən] *n* escursione *f*, gita.
excursion ticket *n* biglietto a tariffa escursionistica.
excusable [ɪk'skju:zəbl] *a* scusabile.
excuse *n* [ɪk'skju:s] scusa ♦ *vt* [ɪk'skju:z] scusare; (*justify*) giustificare; **to make** ~**s**

for sb trovare giustificazioni per qn; **to ~ sb from** (activity) dispensare qn da; **~ me!** mi scusi!; **now if you will ~ me, ...** ora, mi scusi ma ...; **to ~ o.s. (for (doing) sth)** giustificarsi (per (aver fatto) qc).

ex-directory ['ɛksdɪ'rɛktərɪ] a (Brit): **~ (phone) number** numero non compreso nell'elenco telefonico.

execrable ['ɛksɪkrəbl] a (gen) pessimo(a); (manners) esecrabile.

execute ['ɛksɪkjuːt] vt (prisoner) giustiziare; (plan etc) eseguire.

execution [ɛksɪ'kjuːʃən] n esecuzione f.

executioner [ɛksɪ'kjuːʃnə*] n boia m inv.

executive [ɪg'zɛkjutɪv] n (COMM) dirigente m; (POL) esecutivo ♦ a esecutivo(a); (secretary) di direzione; (offices, suite) della direzione; (car, plane) dirigenziale; (position, job, duties) direttivo(a).

executive director n amministratore/trice.

executor [ɪg'zɛkjutə*] n esecutore(trice) testamentario(a).

exemplary [ɪg'zɛmplərɪ] a esemplare.

exemplify [ɪg'zɛmplɪfaɪ] vt esemplificare.

exempt [ɪg'zɛmpt] a: **~ (from)** (person: from tax) esentato(a) (da); (: from military service etc) esonerato(a) (da); (goods) esente (da) ♦ vt: **to ~ sb from** esentare qn da.

exemption [ɪg'zɛmpʃən] n esenzione f.

exercise ['ɛksəsaɪz] n esercizio ♦ vt esercitare; (dog) portar fuori ♦ vi (also: **take ~**) fare del movimento or moto.

exercise book n quaderno.

exert [ɪg'zəːt] vt esercitare; (strength, force) impiegare; **to ~ o.s.** sforzarsi.

exertion [ɪg'zəːʃən] n sforzo.

ex gratia ['ɛks'greɪʃə] a: **~ payment** gratifica.

exhale [ɛks'heɪl] vt, vi espirare.

exhaust [ɪg'zɔːst] n (also: **~ fumes**) scappamento; (also: **~ pipe**) tubo di scappamento ♦ vt esaurire; **to ~ o.s.** sfiancarsi.

exhausted [ɪg'zɔːstɪd] a esaurito(a).

exhausting [ɪg'zɔːstɪŋ] a estenuante.

exhaustion [ɪg'zɔːstʃən] n esaurimento; **nervous ~** sovraffaticamento mentale.

exhaustive [ɪg'zɔːstɪv] a esauriente.

exhibit [ɪg'zɪbɪt] n (ART) oggetto esposto; (LAW) documento or oggetto esibito ♦ vt esporre; (courage, skill) dimostrare.

exhibition [ɛksɪ'bɪʃən] n mostra, esposizione f; (of rudeness etc) spettacolo; **to make an ~ of o.s.** dare spettacolo di sé.

exhibitionist [ɛksɪ'bɪʃənɪst] n esibizionista m/f.

exhibitor [ɪg'zɪbɪtə*] n espositore/trice.

exhilarating [ɪg'zɪləreɪtɪŋ] a esilarante; stimolante.

exhilaration [ɪgzɪlə'reɪʃən] n esaltazione f, ebbrezza.

exhort [ɪg'zɔːt] vt esortare.

exile ['ɛksaɪl] n esilio; (person) esiliato/a ♦ vt esiliare; **in ~** in esilio.

exist [ɪg'zɪst] vi esistere.

existence [ɪg'zɪstəns] n esistenza; **to be in ~** esistere.

existentialism [ɛgzɪs'tɛnʃəlɪzəm] n esistenzialismo.

existing [ɪg'zɪstɪŋ] a (laws, regime) attuale.

exit ['ɛksɪt] n uscita ♦ vi (COMPUT, THEATRE) uscire.

exit ramp n (US AUT) rampa di uscita.

exit visa n visto d'uscita.

exodus ['ɛksədəs] n esodo.

ex officio ['ɛksə'fɪʃɪəu] a, ad d'ufficio.

exonerate [ɪg'zɔnəreɪt] vt: **to ~ from** discolpare da.

exorbitant [ɪg'zɔːbɪtənt] a (price) esorbitante; (demands) spropositato(a).

exorcize ['ɛksɔːsaɪz] vt esorcizzare.

exotic [ɪg'zɔtɪk] a esotico(a).

expand [ɪk'spænd] vt (chest, economy etc) sviluppare; (market, operations) espandere; (influence) estendere; (horizons) allargare ♦ vi svilupparsi; (also gas) espandersi; (metal) dilatarsi; **to ~ on** (notes, story etc) ampliare.

expanse [ɪk'spæns] n distesa, estensione f.

expansion [ɪk'spænʃən] n (gen) espansione f; (of town, economy) sviluppo; (of metal) dilatazione f.

expansionism [ɪk'spænʃənɪzəm] n espansionismo.

expansionist [ɪk'spænʃənɪst] a espansionistico(a).

expatriate n [ɛks'pætrɪət] espatriato/a ♦ vt [ɛks'pætrɪeɪt] espatriare.

expect [ɪk'spɛkt] vt (anticipate) prevedere, aspettarsi, prevedere or aspettarsi che + sub; (count on) contare su; (hope for) sperare; (require) richiedere, esigere; (suppose) supporre; (await, also baby) aspettare ♦ vi: **to be ~ing** essere in stato interessante; **to ~ sb to do** aspettarsi che qn faccia; **to ~ to do sth** pensare or contare di fare qc; **as ~ed** come previsto; **I ~ so** credo di sì.

expectancy [ɪk'spɛktənsɪ] n attesa; **life ~** probabilità fpl di vita.

expectant [ɪk'spɛktənt] a pieno(a) di aspettative.

expectantly [ɪk'spɛktəntlɪ] ad (look, listen) con un'aria d'attesa.

expectant mother n gestante f.

expectation [ɛkspɛk'teɪʃən] n aspettativa; speranza; **in ~ of** in previsione di; **against** or **contrary to all ~(s)** contro ogni aspettativa; **to come** or **live up to sb's ~s** rispondere alle attese di qn.

expedience, expediency [ɪk'spiːdɪəns, ɪk'spiːdɪənsɪ] n convenienza; **for the sake of ~** per una questione di comodità.

expedient [ɪk'spiːdɪənt] a conveniente, vantaggioso(a) ♦ n espediente m.

expedite ['ɛkspədaɪt] vt sbrigare; facilitare.

expedition [ɛkspə'dɪʃən] n spedizione f.

expeditionary force [ɛkspə'dɪʃənərɪ-] n corpo

di spedizione.

expeditious [ɛkspə'dɪʃəs] *a* sollecito(a), rapido(a).

expel [ɪk'spɛl] *vt* espellere.

expend [ɪk'spɛnd] *vt* spendere; (*use up*) consumare.

expendable [ɪk'spɛndəbl] *a* sacrificabile.

expenditure [ɪk'spɛndɪtʃə*] *n* spesa; (*of time, effort*) dispendio.

expense [ɪk'spɛns] *n* spesa; (*high cost*) costo; ~s *npl* (*COMM*) spese *fpl*, indennità *fpl*; **to go to the** ~ **of** sobbarcarsi la spesa di; **at great** ~ con grande impiego di mezzi; **at the** ~ **of** a spese di.

expense account *n* conto *m* spese *inv*.

expensive [ɪk'spɛnsɪv] *a* caro(a), costoso(a); **she has** ~ **tastes** le piacciono le cose costose.

experience [ɪk'spɪərɪəns] *n* esperienza ♦ *vt* (*pleasure*) provare; (*hardship*) soffrire; **to learn by** ~ imparare per esperienza.

experienced [ɪk'spɪərɪənst] *a* che ha esperienza.

experiment *n* [ɪk'spɛrɪmənt] esperimento, esperienza ♦ *vi* [ɪk'spɛrɪmɛnt] fare esperimenti; **to perform** *or* **carry out an** ~ fare un esperimento; **as an** ~ a titolo di esperimento; **to** ~ **with a new vaccine** sperimentare un nuovo vaccino.

experimental [ɪkspɛrɪ'mɛntl] *a* sperimentale; **at the** ~ **stage** in via di sperimentazione.

expert ['ɛkspə:t] *a, n* esperto(a); ~ **witness** (*LAW*) esperto/a; ~ **in** *or* **at doing sth** esperto nel fare qc; **an** ~ **on sth** un esperto di qc.

expertise [ɛkspə:'ti:z] *n* competenza.

expire [ɪk'spaɪə*] *vi* (*period of time, licence*) scadere.

expiry [ɪk'spaɪərɪ] *n* scadenza.

explain [ɪk'spleɪn] *vt* spiegare.

explain away *vt* dar ragione di.

explanation [ɛksplə'neɪʃən] *n* spiegazione *f*; **to find an** ~ **for sth** trovare la spiegazione di qc.

explanatory [ɪk'splænətrɪ] *a* esplicativo(a).

explicit [ɪk'splɪsɪt] *a* esplicito(a); (*definite*) netto(a).

explode [ɪk'spləud] *vi* esplodere ♦ *vt* (*fig: theory*) demolire; **to** ~ **a myth** distruggere un mito.

exploit *n* ['ɛksplɔɪt] impresa ♦ *vt* [ɪk'splɔɪt] sfruttare.

exploitation [ɛksplɔɪ'teɪʃən] *n* sfruttamento.

exploration [ɛksplə'reɪʃən] *n* esplorazione *f*.

exploratory [ɪk'splɔrətrɪ] *a* (*fig: talks*) esplorativo(a); ~ **operation** (*MED*) intervento d'esplorazione.

explore [ɪk'splɔ:*] *vt* esplorare; (*possibilities*) esaminare.

explorer [ɪk'splɔ:rə*] *n* esploratore/trice.

explosion [ɪk'spləuʒən] *n* esplosione *f*.

explosive [ɪk'spləusɪv] *a* esplosivo(a) ♦ *n* esplosivo.

exponent [ɪk'spəunənt] *n* esponente *m/f*.

export *vt* [ɛk'spɔ:t] esportare ♦ *n* ['ɛkspɔ:t] esportazione *f*; articolo di esportazione ♦ *cpd* d'esportazione.

exportation [ɛkspɔ:'teɪʃən] *n* esportazione *f*.

exporter [ɪk'spɔ:tə*] *n* esportatore *m*.

export licence *n* licenza d'esportazione.

expose [ɪk'spəuz] *vt* esporre; (*unmask*) smascherare; **to** ~ **o.s.** (*LAW*) oltraggiare il pudore.

exposed [ɪk'spəuzd] *a* (*land, house*) esposto(a); (*ELEC: wire*) scoperto(a); (*pipe, beam*) a vista.

exposition [ɛkspə'zɪʃən] *n* esposizione *f*.

exposure [ɪk'spəuʒə*] *n* esposizione *f*; (*PHOT*) posa; (*MED*) assideramento; **to die of** ~ morire assiderato(a).

exposure meter *n* esposimetro.

expound [ɪk'spaund] *vt* esporre; (*theory, text*) spiegare.

express [ɪk'sprɛs] *a* (*definite*) chiaro(a), espresso(a); (*Brit: letter etc*) espresso *inv* ♦ *n* (*train*) espresso ♦ *ad*: **to send sth** ~ spedire qc per espresso ♦ *vt* esprimere; **to** ~ **o.s.** esprimersi.

expression [ɪk'sprɛʃən] *n* espressione *f*.

expressionism [ɪk'sprɛʃənɪzəm] *n* espressionismo.

expressive [ɪk'sprɛsɪv] *a* espressivo(a).

expressly [ɪk'sprɛslɪ] *ad* espressamente.

expressway [ɪk'sprɛsweɪ] *n* (*US*) autostrada che attraversa la città.

expropriate [ɛks'prəuprɪeɪt] *vt* espropriare.

expulsion [ɪk'spʌlʃən] *n* espulsione *f*.

exquisite [ɛk'skwɪzɪt] *a* squisito(a).

ex-serviceman ['ɛks'sə:vɪsmən] *n* ex combattente *m*.

ext. *abbr* (*TEL*: = *extension*) int. (= *interno*).

extemporize [ɪk'stɛmpəraɪz] *vi* improvvisare.

extend [ɪk'stɛnd] *vt* (*visit*) protrarre; (*road, deadline*) prolungare; (*building*) ampliare; (*offer*) offrire, porgere; (*COMM: credit*) accordare ♦ *vi* (*land*) estendersi.

extension [ɪk'stɛnʃən] *n* (*of road, term*) prolungamento; (*of contract, deadline*) proroga; (*building*) annesso; (*to wire, table*) prolunga; (*telephone*) interno; (: *in private house*) apparecchio supplementare; ~ **3718** (*TEL*) interno 3718.

extension cable *n* (*ELEC*) prolunga.

extensive [ɪk'stɛnsɪv] *a* esteso(a), ampio(a); (*damage*) su larga scala; (*alterations*) notevole; (*inquiries*) esauriente; (*use*) grande.

extensively [ɪk'stɛnsɪvlɪ] *ad* (*altered, damaged etc*) radicalmente; **he's travelled** ~ ha viaggiato molto.

extent [ɪk'stɛnt] *n* estensione *f*; (*of knowledge, activities, power*) portata; (*degree: of damage, loss*) proporzioni *fpl*; **to some** ~ fino a un certo punto; **to a certain/large** ~ in certa/larga misura; **to what** ~? fino a che punto?; **to such an** ~ **that** ... a tal punto che ....

extenuating [ɪk'stɛnjueɪtɪŋ] *a*: ~ **circum-**

stances attenuanti *fpl*.
exterior [ɛk'stɪərɪə*] *a* esteriore, esterno(a) ♦ *n* esteriore *m*, esterno; aspetto (esteriore).
exterminate [ɪk'stə:mɪneɪt] *vt* sterminare.
extermination [ɪkstə:mɪ'neɪʃən] *n* sterminio.
external [ɛk'stə:nl] *a* esterno(a), esteriore ♦ *n*: **the ~s** le apparenze; **for ~ use only** (*MED*) solo per uso esterno; **~ affairs** (*POL*) affari *mpl* esteri.
externally [ɛk'stə:nəlɪ] *ad* esternamente.
extinct [ɪk'stɪŋkt] *a* estinto(a).
extinction [ɪk'stɪŋkʃən] *n* estinzione *f*.
extinguish [ɪk'stɪŋgwɪʃ] *vt* estinguere.
extinguisher [ɪk'stɪŋgwɪʃə*] *n* estintore *m*.
extol, (*US*) **extoll** [ɪk'stəul] *vt* (*merits*, *virtues*) magnificare; (*person*) celebrare.
extort [ɪk'stɔ:t] *vt*: **to ~ sth** (**from**) estorcere qc (da).
extortion [ɪk'stɔ:ʃən] *n* estorsione *f*.
extortionate [ɪk'stɔ:ʃənɪt] *a* esorbitante.
extra ['ɛkstrə] *a* extra *inv*, supplementare ♦ *ad* (*in addition*) di più ♦ *n* supplemento; (*THEATRE*) comparso; **wine will cost ~** il vino è extra; **~ large sizes** taglie *fpl* forti.
extra... ['ɛkstrə] *prefix* extra....
extract *vt* [ɪk'strækt] estrarre; (*money*, *promise*) strappare ♦ *n* ['ɛkstrækt] estratto; (*passage*) brano.
extraction [ɪk'strækʃən] *n* estrazione *f*; (*descent*) origine *f*.
extracurricular [ɛkstrəkə'rɪkjulə*] *a* (*SCOL*) parascolastico(a).
extradite ['ɛkstrədaɪt] *vt* estradare.
extradition [ɛkstrə'dɪʃən] *n* estradizione *f*.
extramarital [ɛkstrə'mærɪtl] *a* extraconiugale.
extramural [ɛkstrə'mjuərl] *a* fuori dell'università.
extraneous [ɛk'streɪnɪəs] *a*: **~ to** estraneo(a) a.
extraordinary [ɪk'strɔ:dnrɪ] *a* straordinario(a); **the ~ thing is that** ... la cosa strana è che ....
extraordinary general meeting *n* assemblea straordinaria.
extrapolation [ɪkstræpə'leɪʃən] *n* estrapolazione *f*.
extrasensory perception (**ESP**) [ɛkstrə'sɛnsərɪ-] *n* percezione *f* extrasensoriale.
extra time *n* (*FOOTBALL*) tempo supplementare.
extravagance [ɪk'strævəgəns] *n* (*excessive spending*) sperpero; (*thing bought*) stravaganza.
extravagant [ɪk'strævəgənt] *a* stravagante; (*in spending: person*) prodigo(a); (: *tastes*) dispendioso(a).
extreme [ɪk'stri:m] *a* estremo(a) ♦ *n* estremo; **~s of temperature** eccessivi sbalzi *mpl* di temperatura; **the ~ left/right** (*POL*) l'estrema sinistra/destra.
extremely [ɪk'stri:mlɪ] *ad* estremamente.
extremist [ɪk'stri:mɪst] *a*, *n* estremista (*m/f*).
extremity [ɪk'strɛmɪtɪ] *n* estremità *f inv*.

extricate ['ɛkstrɪkeɪt] *vt*: **to ~ sth** (**from**) districare qc (da).
extrovert ['ɛkstrəvə:t] *n* estroverso/a.
exuberance [ɪg'zu:bərəns] *n* esuberanza.
exuberant [ɪg'zju:bərənt] *a* esuberante.
exude [ɪg'zju:d] *vt* trasudare; (*fig*) emanare.
exult [ɪg'zʌlt] *vi* esultare, gioire.
exultant [ɪg'zʌltənt] *a* (*person*, *smile*) esultante; (*shout*, *expression*) di giubilo.
exultation [ɛgzʌl'teɪʃən] *n* giubilo; **in ~** per la gioia.
eye [aɪ] *n* occhio; (*of needle*) cruna ♦ *vt* osservare; **to keep an ~ on** tenere d'occhio; **in the public ~** esposto(a) al pubblico; **as far as the ~ can see** a perdita d'occhio; **with an ~ to doing sth** (*Brit*) con l'idea di far qc; **to have an ~ for sth** avere occhio per qc; **there's more to this than meets the ~** non è così semplice come sembra.
eyeball ['aɪbɔ:l] *n* globo dell'occhio.
eyebath ['aɪbɑ:θ] *n* occhino.
eyebrow ['aɪbrau] *n* sopracciglio.
eyebrow pencil *n* matita per le sopracciglia.
eye-catching ['aɪkætʃɪŋ] *a* che colpisce l'occhio.
eye cup *n* (*US*) = **eyebath**.
eyedrops ['aɪdrɔps] *npl* gocce *fpl* oculari, collirio.
eyeglass ['aɪglɑ:s] *n* monocolo.
eyelash ['aɪlæʃ] *n* ciglio.
eyelet ['aɪlɪt] *n* occhiello.
eye-level ['aɪlɛvl] *a* all'altezza degli occhi.
eyelid ['aɪlɪd] *n* palpebra.
eyeliner ['aɪlaɪnə*] *n* eye-liner *m inv*.
eye-opener ['aɪəupnə*] *n* rivelazione *f*.
eyeshadow ['aɪʃædəu] *n* ombretto.
eyesight ['aɪsaɪt] *n* vista.
eyesore ['aɪsɔ:*] *n* pugno nell'occhio.
eyestrain ['aɪstreɪn] *n*: **to get ~** stancarsi gli occhi.
eye-tooth, *pl* **-teeth** ['aɪtu:θ, -ti:θ] *n* canino superiore; **to give one's eye-teeth for sth/to do sth** (*fig*) dare non so che cosa per qc/per fare qc.
eyewash ['aɪwɔʃ] *n* collirio; (*fig*) sciocchezze *fpl*.
eye witness *n* testimone *m/f* oculare.
eyrie ['ɪərɪ] *n* nido (d'aquila).

F

F, f [ɛf] *n* (*letter*) F, f *f or m inv*; (*MUS*): **F** fa *m*; **F for Frederick**, (*US*) **F for Fox** ≈ F come Firenze.
F. *abbr* (= *Fahrenheit*) F.
FA *n abbr* (*Brit*) = *Football Association*.
FAA *n abbr* (*US*) = *Federal Aviation Admin-*

istration.

fable ['feɪbl] *n* favola.

fabric ['fæbrɪk] *n* stoffa, tessuto; (*ARCHIT*) struttura.

fabricate ['fæbrɪkeɪt] *vt* fabbricare.

fabrication [fæbrɪ'keɪʃən] *n* fabbricazione *f*.

fabric ribbon *n* (*for typewriter*) dattilonastro di tessuto.

fabulous ['fæbjuləs] *a* favoloso(a); (*col: super*) favoloso(a), fantastico(a).

façade [fə'sɑːd] *n* facciata; (*fig*) apparenza.

face [feɪs] *n* faccia, viso, volto; (*expression*) faccia; (*grimace*) smorfia; (*of clock*) quadrante *m*; (*of building*) facciata; (*side, surface*) faccia; (*of mountain, cliff*) parete *f* ♦ *vt* fronteggiare; (*fig*) affrontare; ~ **down** (*person*) bocconi; (*object*) a faccia in giù; **to lose/save** ~ perdere/salvare la faccia; **to pull a** ~ fare una smorfia; **in the** ~ **of** (*difficulties etc*) di fronte a; **on the** ~ **of it** a prima vista; **to** ~ **the fact that** ... riconoscere *or* ammettere che ....

face up to *vt fus* affrontare, far fronte a.

face cloth *n* (*Brit*) guanto di spugna.

face cream *n* crema per il viso.

faceless ['feɪslɪs] *a* anonimo(a).

face lift *n* lifting *m inv*; (*of façade etc*) ripulita.

face powder *n* cipria.

face-saving ['feɪs'seɪvɪŋ] *a* che salva la faccia.

facet ['fæsɪt] *n* faccetta, sfaccettatura; (*fig*) sfaccettatura.

facetious [fə'siːʃəs] *a* faceto(a).

face-to-face ['feɪstə'feɪs] *ad* faccia a faccia.

face value ['feɪs'væljuː] *n* (*of coin*) valore *m* facciale *or* nominale; **to take sth at** ~ (*fig*) giudicare qc dalle apparenze.

facia ['feɪʃɪə] *n* = **fascia**.

facial ['feɪʃəl] *a* facciale ♦ *n* trattamento del viso.

facile ['fæsaɪl] *a* facile; superficiale.

facilitate [fə'sɪlɪteɪt] *vt* facilitare.

facility [fə'sɪlɪtɪ] *n* facilità; **facilities** *npl* attrezzature *fpl*; **credit facilities** facilitazioni *fpl* di credito.

facing ['feɪsɪŋ] *n* (*of wall etc*) rivestimento; (*SEWING*) paramontura.

facsimile [fæk'sɪmɪlɪ] *n* facsimile *m inv*.

facsimile machine *n* telecopiatrice *f*.

fact [fækt] *n* fatto; **in** ~ infatti; **to know for a** ~ **that** ... sapere per certo che ...; **the** ~ (**of the matter**) **is that** ... la verità è che ...; **the** ~**s of life** (*sex*) i fatti riguardanti la vita sessuale; (*fig*) le realtà della vita.

fact-finding ['fæktfaɪndɪŋ] *a*: **a** ~ **tour/ mission** un viaggio/una missione d'inchiesta.

faction ['fækʃən] *n* fazione *f*.

factor ['fæktə*] *n* fattore *m*; (*COMM: company*) *organizzazione specializzata nell'incasso di crediti per conto terzi*; (*: agent*) agente *m* depositario ♦ *vi* incassare crediti per conto terzi; **human** ~ elemento umano; **safety** ~ coefficiente *m* di sicurezza.

factory ['fæktərɪ] *n* fabbrica, stabilimento.

factory farming *n* (*Brit*) allevamento su scala industriale.

factory ship *n* nave *f* fattoria *inv*.

factual ['fæktjuəl] *a* che si attiene ai fatti.

faculty ['fækltɪ] *n* facoltà *f inv*; (*US: teaching staff*) corpo insegnante.

fad [fæd] *n* mania; capriccio.

fade [feɪd] *vi* sbiadire, sbiadirsi; (*light, sound, hope*) attenuarsi, affievolirsi; (*flower*) appassire.

fade in *vt* (*picture*) aprire in dissolvenza; (*sound*) aumentare gradualmente d'intensità.

fade out *vt* (*picture*) chiudere in dissolvenza; (*sound*) diminuire gradualmente d'intensità.

faeces, (*US*) **feces** ['fiːsiːz] *npl* feci *fpl*.

fag [fæg] *n* (*Brit col: cigarette*) cicca; (*: chore*) sfacchinata; (*US col: homosexual*) frocio.

fag end *n* (*Brit col*) mozzicone *m*.

fagged out ['fægd-] *a* (*Brit col*) stanco(a) morto(a).

fail [feɪl] *vt* (*exam*) non superare; (*candidate*) bocciare; (*subj: courage, memory*) mancare a ♦ *vi* fallire; (*student*) essere respinto(a); (*supplies*) mancare; (*eyesight, health, light: also:* **be** ~**ing**) venire a mancare; (*brakes*) non funzionare; **to** ~ **to do sth** (*neglect*) mancare di fare qc; (*be unable*) non riuscire a fare qc; **without** ~ senza fallo; certamente.

failing ['feɪlɪŋ] *n* difetto ♦ *prep* in mancanza di; ~ **that** se questo non è possibile.

failsafe ['feɪlseɪf] *a* (*device etc*) di sicurezza.

failure ['feɪljə*] *n* fallimento; (*person*) fallito/ a; (*mechanical etc*) guasto; (*in exam*) insuccesso, bocciatura; (*of crops*) perdita; **his** ~ **to come** il fatto che non sia venuto; **it was a complete** ~ è stato un vero fiasco.

faint [feɪnt] *a* debole; (*recollection*) vago(a); (*mark*) indistinto(a); (*smell, breeze, trace*) leggero(a) ♦ *vi* svenire; **to feel** ~ sentirsi svenire.

faint-hearted [feɪnt'hɑːtɪd] *a* pusillanime.

faintly ['feɪntlɪ] *ad* debolmente; vagamente.

faintness ['feɪntnɪs] *n* debolezza.

fair [fɛə*] *a* (*person, decision*) giusto(a), equo(a); (*hair etc*) biondo(a); (*skin, complexion*) bianco(a); (*weather*) bello(a), clemente; (*good enough*) assai buono(a); (*sizeable*) bello(a) ♦ *ad*: **to play** ~ giocare correttamente ♦ *n* fiera; (*Brit: funfair*) luna park *m inv*; (*also:* **trade** ~) fiera campionaria; **it's not** ~! non è giusto!; **a** ~ **amount of** un bel po' di.

fair copy *n* bella copia.

fair-haired [fɛə'hɛəd] *a* (*person*) biondo(a).

fairly ['fɛəlɪ] *ad* equamente; (*quite*) abbastanza.

fairness ['fɛənɪs] *n* equità, giustizia; **in all** ~ per essere giusti, a dire il vero.

fair play *n* correttezza.

fairy ['fɛərɪ] *n* fata.

fairy godmother *n* fata buona.

fairy lights npl (Brit) lanternine fpl colorate.
fairy tale n fiaba.
faith [feɪθ] n fede f; (trust) fiducia; (sect) religione f, fede f; **to have ~ in sb/sth** avere fiducia in qn/qc.
faithful ['feɪθful] a fedele.
faithfully ['feɪθfəlɪ] ad fedelmente; **yours ~** (Brit: in letters) distinti saluti.
faith healer n guaritore/trice.
fake [feɪk] n imitazione f; (picture) falso; (person) impostore/a ♦ a falso(a) ♦ vt (accounts) falsificare; (illness) fingere; (painting) contraffare; **his illness is a ~ fa** finta di essere malato.
falcon ['fɔ:lkən] n falco, falcone m.
Falkland Islands ['fɔ:lklənd-] npl: **the ~ le** isole Falkland.
fall [fɔ:l] n caduta; (decrease) diminuzione f, calo; (in temperature) abbassamento; (in price) ribasso; (US: autumn) autunno ♦ vi (pt **fell**, pp **fallen** [fɛl, 'fɔ:lən]) cadere; (temperature, price) abbassare; **a ~ of earth** uno smottamento; **a ~ of snow** (Brit) una nevicata; **to ~ in love (with sb/sth)** innamorarsi (di qn/qc); **to ~ short of** (sb's expectations) non corrispondere a; **to ~ flat** vi (on one's face) cadere bocconi; (joke) fare cilecca; (plan) fallire; see also **falls**.
fall apart vi cadere a pezzi.
fall back vi indietreggiare; (MIL) ritirarsi.
fall back on vt fus ripiegare su; **to have sth to ~ back on** avere qc di riserva.
fall behind vi rimanere indietro; (fig: with payments) essere in arretrato.
fall down vi (person) cadere; (building, hopes) crollare.
fall for vt fus (person) prendere una cotta per; **to ~ for a trick** (or **a story** etc) cascarci.
fall in vi crollare; (MIL) mettersi in riga.
fall in with vt fus (sb's plans etc) trovarsi d'accordo con.
fall off vi cadere; (diminish) diminuire, abbassarsi.
fall out vi (friends etc) litigare.
fall over vi cadere.
fall through vi (plan, project) fallire.
fallacy ['fæləsɪ] n errore m.
fallback ['fɔ:lbæk] a: **~ position** posizione f di ripiego.
fallen ['fɔ:lən] pp of **fall**.
fallible ['fælɪbl] a fallibile.
falling ['fɔ:lɪŋ] a: **~ market** (COMM) mercato in ribasso.
falling-off ['fɔ:lɪŋ'ɔf] n calo.
fallopian tube [fə'ləupɪən-] n (ANAT) tuba di Falloppio.
fallout ['fɔ:laut] n fall-out m.
fallout shelter n rifugio antiatomico.
fallow ['fæləu] a incolto(a); a maggese.
falls [fɔ:lz] npl (waterfall) cascate fpl.
false [fɔ:ls] a falso(a); **under ~ pretences** con l'inganno.
false alarm n falso allarme m.

falsehood ['fɔ:lshud] n menzogna.
falsely ['fɔ:lslɪ] ad (accuse) a torto.
false teeth npl (Brit) denti mpl finti.
falsify ['fɔ:lsɪfaɪ] vt falsificare; (figures) alterare.
falter ['fɔ:ltə*] vi esitare, vacillare.
fame [feɪm] n fama, celebrità.
familiar [fə'mɪlɪə*] a familiare; (common) comune; (close) intimo(a); **to be ~ with** (subject) conoscere; **to make o.s. ~ with** familiarizzarsi con; **to be on ~ terms with** essere in confidenza con.
familiarity [fəmɪlɪ'ærɪtɪ] n familiarità; intimità.
familiarize [fə'mɪlɪəraɪz] vt: **to ~ sb with sth** far conoscere qc a qn.
family ['fæmɪlɪ] n famiglia.
family allowance n (Brit) assegni mpl familiari.
family business n impresa familiare.
family doctor n medico di famiglia.
family life n vita familiare.
family planning clinic n consultorio familiare.
family tree n albergo genealogico.
famine ['fæmɪn] n carestia.
famished ['fæmɪʃt] a affamato(a); **I'm ~!** (col) ho una fame da lupo!
famous ['feɪməs] a famoso(a).
famously ['feɪməslɪ] ad (get on) a meraviglia.
fan [fæn] n (folding) ventaglio; (machine) ventilatore m; (person) ammiratore/trice; (SPORT) tifoso/a ♦ vt far vento a; (fire, quarrel) alimentare.
fan out vi spargersi (a ventaglio).
fanatic [fə'nætɪk] n fanatico/a.
fanatical [fə'nætɪkl] a fanatico(a).
fan belt n cinghia del ventilatore.
fancied ['fænsɪd] a immaginario(a).
fanciful ['fænsɪful] a fantasioso(a); (object) di fantasia.
fancy ['fænsɪ] n immaginazione f, fantasia; (whim) capriccio ♦ cpd (di) fantasia inv ♦ vt (feel like, want) aver voglia di; (imagine) immaginare, credere; **to take a ~ to** incapricciarsi di; **it took** or **caught my ~** mi è piaciuto; **when the ~ takes him** quando ne ha voglia; **to ~ that** immaginare che; **he fancies her** gli piace.
fancy dress n costume m (per maschera).
fancy-dress ball n ballo in maschera.
fancy goods npl articoli mpl di ogni genere.
fanfare ['fænfeə*] n fanfara.
fanfold paper ['fænfəuld-] n carta a moduli continui.
fang [fæŋ] n zanna; (of snake) dente m.
fan heater n (Brit) stufa ad aria calda.
fanlight ['fænlaɪt] n lunetta.
fantasize ['fæntəsaɪz] vi fantasticare, sognare.
fantastic [fæn'tæstɪk] a fantastico(a).
fantasy ['fæntəsɪ] n fantasia, immaginazione f; fantasticheria; chimera.
FAO n abbr (= Food and Agriculture Organization) FAO f.

FAQ *abbr* (= *free alongside quay*) franco lungo banchina.

far [fɑ:*] *a*: **the ~ side/end** l'altra parte/l'altro capo; **the ~ left/right** (*POL*) l'estrema sinistra/destra ♦ *ad* lontano; **is it ~ to London?** è lontana Londra?; **it's not ~ (from here)** non è lontano (da qui); **~ away**, **~ off** lontano, distante; **~ better** assai migliore; **~ from** lontano da; **by ~** di gran lunga; **as ~ back as the 13th century** già nel duecento; **go as ~ as the farm** vada fino alla fattoria; **as ~ as I know** per quel che so; **as ~ as possible** nei limiti del possibile; **how ~ have you got with your work?** dov'è arrivato con il suo lavoro?

faraway ['fɑ:rǝweɪ] *a* lontano(a); (*voice*, *look*) assente.

farce [fɑ:s] *n* farsa.

farcical ['fɑ:sɪkǝl] *a* farsesco(a).

fare [fɛǝ*] *n* (*on trains*, *buses*) tariffa; (*in taxi*) prezzo della corsa; (*food*) vitto, cibo ♦ *vi* passarsela.

Far East *n*: **the ~** l'Estremo Oriente *m*.

farewell [fɛǝ'wɛl] *excl*, *n* addio ♦ *cpd* (*party etc*) d'addio.

far-fetched ['fɑ:'fɛtʃt] *a* (*explanation*) stiracchiato(a), forzato(a); (*idea*, *scheme*, *story*) inverosimile.

farm [fɑ:m] *n* fattoria, podere *m* ♦ *vt* coltivare.

farm out *vt* (*work*) dare in consegna.

farmer ['fɑ:mǝ*] *n* coltivatore/trice; agricoltore/trice.

farmhand ['fɑ:mhænd] *n* bracciante *m* agricolo.

farmhouse ['fɑ:mhaus] *n* fattoria.

farming ['fɑ:mɪŋ] *n* agricoltura; **intensive ~** coltura intensiva; **sheep ~** allevamento di pecore.

farm labourer *n* = **farmhand**.

farmland ['fɑ:mlænd] *n* terreno da coltivare.

farm produce *n* prodotti *mpl* agricoli.

farm worker *n* = **farmhand**.

farmyard ['fɑ:mjɑ:d] *n* aia.

Faroe Islands ['fɛǝrǝu-], **Faroes** ['fɛǝrǝuz] *npl*: **the ~** le isole Faeroer.

far-reaching ['fɑ:'ri:tʃɪŋ] *a* di vasta portata.

far-sighted ['fɑ:'saɪtɪd] *a* presbite; (*fig*) lungimirante.

fart [fɑ:t] (*col!*) *n* scoreggia(!) ♦ *vi* scoreggiare (!).

farther ['fɑ:ðǝ*] *ad* più lontano ♦ *a* più lontano(a).

farthest ['fɑ:ðɪst] *superlative of* **far**.

FAS *abbr* (*Brit*: = *free alongside ship*) franco banchina nave.

fascia ['feɪʃɪǝ] *n* (*AUT*) cruscotto.

fascinate ['fæsɪneɪt] *vt* affascinare.

fascinating ['fæsɪneɪtɪŋ] *a* affascinante.

fascination [fæsɪ'neɪʃǝn] *n* fascino.

fascism ['fæʃɪzǝm] *n* fascismo.

fascist ['fæʃɪst] *a*, *n* fascista (*m/f*).

fashion ['fæʃǝn] *n* moda; (*manner*) maniera, modo ♦ *vt* foggiare, formare; **in ~** alla moda; **out of ~** passato(a) di moda; **after a**

~ (*finish*, *manage etc*) così così; **in the Greek ~** alla greca.

fashionable ['fæʃǝnǝbl] *a* alla moda, di moda; (*writer*) di grido.

fashion designer *n* disegnatore/trice di moda.

fashion show *n* sfilata di moda.

fast [fɑ:st] *a* rapido(a), svelto(a), veloce; (*clock*): **to be ~** andare avanti; (*dye*, *colour*) solido(a) ♦ *ad* rapidamente; (*stuck*, *held*) saldamente ♦ *n* digiuno ♦ *vi* digiunare; **~ asleep** profondamente addormentato; **as ~ as I can** più in fretta possibile; **my watch is 5 minutes ~** il mio orologio va avanti di 5 minuti; **to make a boat ~** (*Brit*) ormeggiare una barca.

fasten ['fɑ:sn] *vt* chiudere, fissare; (*coat*) abbottonare, allacciare ♦ *vi* chiudersi, fissarsi; abbottonarsi, allacciarsi.

fasten (up)on *vt fus* (*idea*) cogliere al volo.

fastener ['fɑ:snǝ*], **fastening** ['fɑ:snɪŋ] *n* fermaglio, chiusura; (*Brit*: *zip ~*) chiusura lampo.

fast food *n* fast food *m inv*.

fastidious [fæs'tɪdɪǝs] *a* esigente, difficile.

fast lane *n* (*AUT*) ≈ corsia di sorpasso.

fat [fæt] *a* grasso(a) ♦ *n* grasso; **to live off the ~ of the land** vivere nel lusso, avere ogni ben di Dio.

fatal ['feɪtl] *a* fatale; mortale; disastroso(a).

fatalism ['feɪtǝlɪzǝm] *n* fatalismo.

fatality [fǝ'tælɪtɪ] *n* (*road death etc*) morto/a, vittima.

fatally ['feɪtǝlɪ] *ad* a morte.

fate [feɪt] *n* destino; (*of person*) sorte *f*; **to meet one's ~** trovare la morte.

fated ['feɪtɪd] *a* (*governed by fate*) destinato(a); (*person*, *project etc*) destinato(a) a finire male.

fateful ['feɪtful] *a* fatidico(a).

father ['fɑ:ðǝ*] *n* padre *m*.

Father Christmas *n* Babbo Natale.

fatherhood ['fɑ:ðǝhu:d] *n* paternità.

father-in-law ['fɑ:ðǝrɪnlɔ:] *n* suocero.

fatherland ['fɑ:ðǝlænd] *n* patria.

fatherly ['fɑ:ðǝlɪ] *a* paterno(a).

fathom ['fæðǝm] *n* braccio (= *1828 mm*) ♦ *vt* (*mystery*) penetrare, sondare.

fatigue [fǝ'ti:g] *n* stanchezza; (*MIL*) corvé *f*; **metal ~** fatica del metallo.

fatness ['fætnɪs] *n* grassezza.

fatten ['fætn] *vt*, *vi* ingrassare; **chocolate is ~ing** la cioccolata fa ingrassare.

fatty ['fætɪ] *a* (*food*) grasso(a) ♦ *n* (*col*) ciccione/a.

fatuous ['fætjuǝs] *a* fatuo(a).

faucet ['fɔ:sɪt] *n* (*US*) rubinetto.

fault [fɔ:lt] *n* colpa; (*TENNIS*) fallo; (*defect*) difetto; (*GEO*) faglia ♦ *vt* criticare; **it's my ~** è colpa mia; **to find ~ with** trovare da ridire su; **at ~** in fallo; **generous to a ~** eccessivamente generoso.

faultless ['fɔ:ltlɪs] *a* perfetto(a); senza difetto; impeccabile.

faulty ['fɔ:ltɪ] *a* difettoso(a).

fauna ['fɔ:nə] *n* fauna.

faux pas [fəu'pɑ:] *n* gaffe *f inv*.

favour, (*US*) **favor** ['feɪvə*] *n* favore *m* ♦ *vt* (*proposition*) favorire, essere favorevole a; (*pupil etc*) favorire; (*team, horse*) dare per vincente; **to do sb a ~** fare un favore *or* una cortesia a qn; **in ~ of** in favore di; **to be in ~ of sth/of doing sth** essere favorevole a qc/a fare qc; **to find ~ with sb** (*subj: person*) entrare nelle buone grazie di qn; (: *suggestion*) avere l'approvazione di qn.

favo(u)rable ['feɪvərəbl] *a* favorevole.

favo(u)rably ['feɪvərəblɪ] *ad* favorevolmente.

favo(u)rite ['feɪvrɪt] *a, n* favorito(a).

favo(u)ritism ['feɪvrɪtɪzəm] *n* favoritismo.

fawn [fɔ:n] *n* daino ♦ *a* (*also:* **~-coloured**) marrone chiaro *inv* ♦ *vi:* **to ~ (up)on** adulare servilmente.

fax [fæks] *n* (*document, machine*) facsimile *m inv* ♦ *vt* teletrasmettere, spedire in facsimile.

FBI *n abbr* (*US*: *= Federal Bureau of Investigation*) FBI *f*.

FCC *n abbr* (*US*) *= Federal Communications Commission*.

FCO *n abbr* (*Brit:* = *Foreign and Commonwealth Office*) ≈ Ufficio affari esteri.

FD *n abbr* (*US*) *= fire department*.

FDA *n abbr* (*US*) *= Food and Drug Administration*.

fear [fɪə*] *n* paura, timore *m* ♦ *vt* aver paura di, temere ♦ *vi:* **to ~ for** temere per, essere in ansia per; **~ of heights** vertigini *fpl*; **for ~ of** per paura di; **to ~ that** avere paura di (*or* che + *sub*), temere di (*or* che + *sub*).

fearful ['fɪəful] *a* pauroso(a); (*sight, noise*) terribile, spaventoso(a); (*frightened*): **to be ~ of** temere.

fearfully ['fɪəfəlɪ] *ad* (*timidly*) timorosamente; (*col: very*) terribilmente, spaventosamente.

fearless ['fɪəlɪs] *a* intrepido(a), senza paura.

fearsome ['fɪəsəm] *a* (*opponent*) formidabile, terribile; (*sight*) terrificante.

feasibility [fi:zə'bɪlɪtɪ] *n* praticabilità.

feasibility study *n* studio delle possibilità di realizzazione.

feasible ['fi:zəbl] *a* possibile, realizzabile.

feast [fi:st] *n* festa, banchetto; (*REL: also:* **~ day**) festa ♦ *vi* banchettare; **to ~ on** godersi, gustare.

feat [fi:t] *n* impresa, fatto insigne.

feather ['fɛðə*] *n* penna ♦ *cpd* (*mattress, bed, pillow*) di piume ♦ *vt:* **to ~ one's nest** (*fig*) arricchirsi.

feather-weight ['fɛðəweɪt] *n* peso *m* piuma *inv*.

feature ['fi:tʃə*] *n* caratteristica; (*article*) articolo ♦ *vt* (*subj: film*) avere come protagonista ♦ *vi* figurare; **~s** *npl* (*of face*) fisionomia; **a (special) ~ on sth/sb** un servizio speciale su qc/qn; **it ~d prominently in ...** ha avuto un posto di prima importanza in ....

feature film *n* film *m inv* principale.

featureless ['fi:tʃəlɪs] *a* anonimo(a), senza caratteri distinti.

Feb. [fɛb] *abbr* (*= February*) feb.

February ['fɛbruərɪ] *n* febbraio; *for phrases see also* **July.**

feces ['fi:si:z] *npl* (*US*) *=* **faeces.**

feckless ['fɛklɪs] *a* irresponsabile, incosciente.

Fed [fɛd] *abbr* (*US*) *=* **federal; federation.**

fed [fɛd] *pt, pp* **feed; to be ~ up** essere stufo(a).

Fed. [fɛd] *n abbr* (*US col*) *=* **Federal Reserve Board.**

federal ['fɛdərəl] *a* federale.

Federal Republic of Germany (FRG) *n* Repubblica Federale Tedesca (RFT).

Federal Reserve Board (Fed.) *n* (*US*) *organo di controllo del sistema bancario statunitense.*

Federal Trade Commission (FTC) *n* (*US*) *organismo di protezione contro le pratiche commerciali abusive.*

federation [fɛdə'reɪʃən] *n* federazione *f*.

fee [fi:] *n* pagamento; (*of doctor, lawyer*) onorario; (*for examination*) tassa d'esame; **school ~s** tasse *fpl* scolastiche; **entrance ~, membership ~** quota d'iscrizione; **for a small ~** per una somma modesta.

feeble ['fi:bl] *a* debole.

feeble-minded [fi:bl'maɪndɪd] *a* deficiente.

feed [fi:d] *n* (*of baby*) pappa ♦ *vt* (*pt, pp* **fed** [fɛd]) nutrire; (*horse etc*) dare da mangiare a; (*fire, machine*) alimentare ♦ *vi* (*baby, animal*) mangiare; **to ~ material into sth** introdurre materiale in qc; **to ~ data/information into sth** inserire dati/informazioni in qc.

feed back *vt* (*results*) riferire.

feed on *vt fus* nutrirsi di.

feedback ['fi:dbæk] *n* feed-back *m*; (*from person*) reazioni *fpl*.

feeder ['fi:də*] *n* (*bib*) bavaglino.

feeding bottle ['fi:dɪŋ-] *n* (*Brit*) biberon *m inv*.

feel [fi:l] *n* sensazione *f*; (*sense of touch*) tatto; (*of substance*) consistenza ♦ *vt* (*pt, pp* **felt** [fɛlt]) toccare; palpare; tastare; (*cold, pain, anger*) sentire; (*grief*) provare; (*think, believe*): **to ~ (that)** pensare che; **I ~ that you ought to do it** penso che dovreste farlo; **to ~ hungry/cold** aver fame/freddo; **to ~ lonely/better** sentirsi solo/meglio; **I don't ~ well** non mi sento bene; **to ~ sorry for** dispiacersi per; **it ~s soft** è morbido al tatto; **it ~s colder out here** sembra più freddo qui fuori; **it ~s like velvet** sembra velluto (al tatto); **to ~ like** (*want*) aver voglia di; **to ~ about** *or* **around for** cercare a tastoni; **to ~ about** *or* **around in one's pocket for** frugarsi in tasca per cercare; **I'm still ~ing my way** (*fig*) sto ancora tastando il terreno; **to get the ~ of sth** (*fig*) abituarsi a qc.

feeler ['fi:lə*] *n* (*of insect*) antenna; **to put out ~s** (*fig*) fare un sondaggio.

feeling ['fi:lɪŋ] *n* sensazione *f*; sentimento;

(*impression*) senso, impressione *f*; **to hurt sb's** ~**s** offendere qn; **what are your** ~**s about the matter?** che cosa ne pensa?; **my** ~ **is that ...** ho l'impressione che ...; **I got the** ~ **that ...** ho avuto l'impressione che ...; ~**s ran high about it** la cosa aveva provocato grande eccitazione.

feet [fiːt] *npl of* **foot**.

feign [feɪn] *vt* fingere, simulare.

felicitous [fɪ'lɪsɪtəs] *a* felice.

fell [fɛl] *pt of* **fall** ♦ *vt* (*tree*) abbattere; (*person*) atterrare ♦ *a*: **with one** ~ **blow** con un colpo terribile; **at one** ~ **swoop** in un colpo solo ♦ *n* (*Brit: mountain*) monte *m*; (: *moorland*): **the** ~**s** la brughiera.

fellow ['fɛləu] *n* individuo, tipo; (*comrade*) compagno; (*of learned society*) membro; (*of university*) ≈ docente *m/f* ♦ *cpd*: **their** ~ **prisoners/students** i loro compagni di prigione/studio.

fellow citizen *n* concittadino/a.

fellow countryman *n* compatriota *m*.

fellow feeling *n* simpatia.

fellow men *npl* simili *mpl*.

fellowship ['fɛləuʃɪp] *n* associazione *f*; compagnia; (*SCOL*) *specie di borsa di studio universitaria*.

fellow traveller *n* compagno/a di viaggio; (*POL*) simpatizzante *m/f*.

fell-walking ['fɛlwɔ:kɪŋ] *n* (*Brit*) passeggiate *fpl* in montagna.

felon ['fɛlən] *n* (*LAW*) criminale *m/f*.

felony ['fɛlənɪ] *n* (*LAW*) reato, crimine *m*.

felt [fɛlt] *pt*, *pp of* **feel** ♦ *n* feltro.

felt-tip pen ['fɛlttɪp-] *n* pennarello.

female ['fiːmeɪl] *n* (*ZOOL*) femmina; (*pej: woman*) donna, femmina ♦ *a* femminile; (*BIOL*, *ELEC*) femmina *inv*; **male and** ~ **students** studenti e studentesse.

female impersonator *n* (*THEATRE*) *attore comico che fa parti da donna*.

feminine ['fɛmɪnɪn] *a*, *n* femminile (*m*).

femininity [fɛmɪ'nɪnɪtɪ] *n* femminilità.

feminism ['fɛmɪnɪzəm] *n* femminismo.

feminist ['fɛmɪnɪst] *n* femminista *m/f*.

fen [fɛn] *n* (*Brit*): **the F**~**s** la regione delle Fen.

fence [fɛns] *n* recinto; (*SPORT*) ostacolo; (*col: person*) ricettatore/trice ♦ *vt* (*also*: ~ **in**) recingere ♦ *vi* schermire; **to sit on the** ~ (*fig*) rimanere neutrale.

fencing ['fɛnsɪŋ] *n* (*SPORT*) scherma.

fend [fɛnd] *vi*: **to** ~ **for o.s.** arrangiarsi.

fend off *vt* (*attack*, *attacker*) respingere, difendersi da; (*blow*) parare; (*awkward question*) eludere.

fender ['fɛndə*] *n* parafuoco; (*US*) parafango; paraurti *m inv*.

fennel ['fɛnl] *n* finocchio.

ferment *vi* [fə'mɛnt] fermentare ♦ *n* ['fə:mɛnt] agitazione *f*, eccitazione *f*.

fermentation [fə:mɛn'teɪʃən] *n* fermentazione *f*.

fern [fə:n] *n* felce *f*.

ferocious [fə'rəuʃəs] *a* feroce.

ferocity [fə'rɔsɪtɪ] *n* ferocità.

ferret ['fɛrɪt] *n* furetto.

ferret about, **ferret around** *vi* frugare.

ferret out *vt* (*person*) scovare, scoprire; (*secret*, *truth*) scoprire.

ferry ['fɛrɪ] *n* (*small*) traghetto; (*large*: *also*: ~**boat**) nave *f* traghetto *inv* ♦ *vt* traghettare; **to** ~ **sth/sb across** *or* **over** traghettare qc/qn da una parte all'altra.

ferryman ['fɛrɪmən] *n* traghettatore *m*.

fertile ['fə:taɪl] *a* fertile; (*BIOL*) fecondo(a); ~ **period** periodo di fecondità.

fertility [fə'tɪlɪtɪ] *n* fertilità; fecondità.

fertility drug *n* farmaco fecondativo.

fertilize ['fə:tɪlaɪz] *vt* fertilizzare; fecondare.

fertilizer ['fə:tɪlaɪzə*] *n* fertilizzante *m*.

fervent ['fə:vənt] *a* ardente, fervente.

fervour, (*US*) **fervor** ['fə:və*] *n* fervore *m*, ardore *m*.

fester ['fɛstə*] *vi* suppurare.

festival ['fɛstɪvəl] *n* (*REL*) festa; (*ART*, *MUS*) festival *m inv*.

festive ['fɛstɪv] *a* di festa; **the** ~ **season** (*Brit*: *Christmas*) il periodo delle feste.

festivities [fɛs'tɪvɪtɪz] *npl* festeggiamenti *mpl*.

festoon [fɛ'stu:n] *vt*: **to** ~ **with** ornare di; decorare con.

fetch [fɛtʃ] *vt* andare a prendere; (*sell for*) essere venduto(a) per; **how much did it** ~**?** a *or* per quanto lo ha venduto?

fetch up *vi* (*Brit*) andare a finire.

fetching ['fɛtʃɪŋ] *a* attraente.

fête [feɪt] *n* festa.

fetid ['fɛtɪd] *a* fetido(a).

fetish ['fɛtɪʃ] *n* feticcio.

fetter ['fɛtə*] *vt* (*person*) incatenare; (*horse*) legare; (*fig*) ostacolare.

fetters ['fɛtəz] *npl* catene *fpl*.

fettle ['fɛtl] *n* (*Brit*): **in fine** ~ in gran forma.

fetus ['fi:təs] *n* (*US*) = **foetus**.

feud [fju:d] *n* contesa, lotta ♦ *vi* essere in lotta; **a family** ~ una lite in famiglia.

feudal ['fju:dl] *a* feudale.

feudalism ['fju:dəlɪzəm] *n* feudalesimo.

fever ['fi:və*] *n* febbre *f*; **he has a** ~ ha la febbre.

feverish ['fi:vərɪʃ] *a* (*also fig*) febbrile; (*person*) febbricitante.

few [fju:] *a* pochi(e) ♦ *pronoun* alcuni(e); ~ **succeed** pochi ci riescono; **they were** ~ erano pochi; **a** ~ **...** qualche ...; **I know a** ~ ne conosco alcuni; **a good** ~, **quite a** ~ parecchi; **in the next** ~ **days** nei prossimi giorni; **in the past** ~ **days** negli ultimi giorni, in questi ultimi giorni; **every** ~ **days/ months** ogni due o tre giorni/mesi; **a** ~ **more days** qualche altro giorno.

fewer ['fju:ə*] *a* meno *inv*; meno numerosi(e) ♦ *pronoun* meno; **they are** ~ **now** adesso ce ne sono di meno.

fewest ['fju:ɪst] *a* il minor numero di.

FFA *n abbr* = *Future Farmers of America*.

FH *abbr* (*Brit*) = **fire hydrant**.

FHA *n abbr* (*US*) = *Federal Housing Administration*.

fiancé [fɪ'ɑ̃:ŋseɪ] *n* fidanzato.

fiancée [fɪ'ɑ̃:ŋseɪ] *n* fidanzata.

fiasco [fɪ'æskəu] *n* fiasco.

fib [fɪb] *n* piccola bugia.

fibre, (*US*) **fiber** ['faɪbə*] *n* fibra.

fibreboard, (*US*) **fiberboard** ['faɪbəbɔ:d] *n* pannello di fibre.

fibre-glass, (*US*) **fiber-glass** ['faɪbəglɑ:s] *n* fibra di vetro.

fibrositis [faɪbrə'saɪtɪs] *n* cellulite *f*.

FICA *n abbr* (*US*) = *Federal Insurance Contributions Act*.

fickle ['fɪkl] *a* incostante, capriccioso(a).

fiction ['fɪkʃən] *n* narrativa; (*sth made up*) finzione *f*.

fictional ['fɪkʃənl] *a* immaginario(a).

fictionalize ['fɪkʃənəlaɪz] *vt* romanzare.

fictitious [fɪk'tɪʃəs] *a* fittizio(a).

fiddle ['fɪdl] *n* (*MUS*) violino; (*cheating*) imbroglio; truffa ♦ *vt* (*Brit: accounts*) falsificare, falsare; **tax ~** frode *f* fiscale; **to work a ~** fare un imbroglio.
  fiddle with *vt fus* gingillarsi con.

fiddler ['fɪdlə*] *n* violinista *m/f*.

fiddly ['fɪdlɪ] *a* (*task*) da certosino; (*object*) complesso(a).

fidelity [fɪ'delɪtɪ] *n* fedeltà; (*accuracy*) esattezza.

fidget ['fɪdʒɪt] *vi* agitarsi.

fidgety ['fɪdʒɪtɪ] *a* agitato(a).

fiduciary [fɪ'du:ʃɪərɪ] *n* fiduciario.

field [fi:ld] *n* (*gen*, *COMPUT*) campo; **to lead the ~** (*SPORT*, *COMM*) essere in testa, essere al primo posto; **to have a ~ day** (*fig*) divertirsi, spassarsela.

field glasses *npl* binocolo (da campagna).

field marshal (FM) *n* feldmaresciallo.

fieldwork ['fi:ldwə:k] *n* ricerche *fpl* esterne; (*ARCHEOLOGY*, *GEO*) lavoro sul campo.

fiend [fi:nd] *n* demonio.

fiendish ['fi:ndɪʃ] *a* demoniaco(a).

fierce [fɪəs] *a* (*look*, *fighting*) fiero(a); (*wind*) furioso(a); (*attack*) feroce; (*enemy*) acerrimo(a).

fiery ['faɪərɪ] *a* ardente, infocato(a).

FIFA ['fi:fə] *n abbr* (= *Fédération Internationale de Football Association*) F.I.F.A. *f*.

fifteen [fɪf'ti:n] *num* quindici.

fifth [fɪfθ] *num* quinto(a).

fiftieth ['fɪftɪθ] *num* cinquantesimo(a).

fifty ['fɪftɪ] *num* cinquanta.

fifty-fifty ['fɪftɪ'fɪftɪ] *a*, *ad*: **to go ~ with sb** fare a metà con qn; **we have a ~ chance of success** abbiamo una probabilità su due di successo.

fig [fɪg] *n* fico.

fight [faɪt] *n* zuffa, rissa; (*MIL*) battaglia, combattimento; (*against cancer etc*) lotta ♦ *vb* (*pt*, *pp* **fought** [fɔ:t]) *vt* combattere; (*cancer*, *alcoholism*) lottare contro, combattere; (*LAW: case*) difendere ♦ *vi* battersi, combattere; (*quarrel*): **to ~ (with**

sb) litigare (con qn); (*fig*): **to ~ (for/against)** lottare (per/contro).
  fight back *vi* difendersi; (*SPORT*, *after illness*) riprendersi ♦ *vt* (*tears*) ricacciare.
  fight down *vt* (*anger*, *anxiety*) vincere; (*urge*) reprimere.
  fight off *vt* (*attack*, *attacker*) respingere; (*disease*, *sleep*, *urge*) lottare contro.
  fight out *vt*: **to ~ it out** risolvere la questione a pugni.

fighter ['faɪtə*] *n* combattente *m*; (*plane*) aeroplano da caccia.

fighter-bomber ['faɪtəbɔmə*] *n* caccia-bombardiere *m*.

fighter pilot *n* pilota *m* di caccia.

fighting ['faɪtɪŋ] *n* combattimento; (*in streets*) scontri *mpl*.

figment ['fɪgmənt] *n*: **a ~ of the imagination** un parto della fantasia.

figurative ['fɪgjurətɪv] *a* figurato(a).

figure ['fɪgə*] *n* (*DRAWING*, *GEOM*, *person*) figura; (*number*, *cipher*) cifra; (*body*, *outline*) forma ♦ *vi* (*appear*) figurare; (*US: make sense*) spiegarsi; essere logico(a) ♦ *vt* (*US: think*, *calculate*) pensare, immaginare; **public ~** personaggio pubblico; **~ of speech** figura retorica.
  figure on *vt fus* (*US*) contare su.
  figure out *vt* riuscire a capire; calcolare.

figurehead ['fɪgəhed] *n* (*NAUT*) polena; (*pej*) prestanome *m/f inv*.

figure skating *n* pattinaggio artistico.

Fiji (Islands) ['fi:dʒi:-] *n*(*pl*) le (isole) Figi.

filament ['fɪləmənt] *n* filamento.

filch [fɪltʃ] *vt* (*col: steal*) grattare.

file [faɪl] *n* (*tool*) lima; (*for nails*) limetta; (*dossier*) incartamento; (*in cabinet*) scheda; (*folder*) cartellina; (*for loose leaf*) raccoglitore *m*; (*row*) fila; (*COMPUT*) archivio, file *m inv* ♦ *vt* (*nails*, *wood*) limare; (*papers*) archiviare; (*LAW: claim*) presentare ♦ *vi*: **to ~ in/out** entrare/uscire in fila; **to ~ past** marciare in fila davanti a; **to ~ a suit against sb** intentare causa contro qn.

file name *n* (*COMPUT*) nome *m* del file.

filibuster ['fɪlɪbʌstə*] (*esp US POL*) *n* (*also*: **~er**) ostruzionista *m/f* ♦ *vi* fare ostruzionismo.

filing ['faɪlɪŋ] *n* archiviare *m*; *see also* **filings**.

filing cabinet *n* casellario.

filing clerk *n* archivista *m/f*.

filings ['faɪlɪŋz] *npl* limatura.

Filipino [fɪlɪ'pi:nəu] *n* filippino/a; (*LING*) tagal *m*.

fill [fɪl] *vt* riempire; (*tooth*) otturare; (*job*) coprire; (*supply: order*, *requirements*, *need*) soddisfare ♦ *n*: **to eat one's ~** mangiare a sazietà; **we've already ~ed that vacancy** abbiamo già assunto qualcuno per quel posto.
  fill in *vt* (*hole*) riempire; (*form*) compilare; (*details*, *report*) completare ♦ *vi*: **to ~ in for sb** sostituire qn; **to ~ sb in on sth** (*col*) mettere qn al corrente di qc.
  fill out *vt* (*form*, *receipt*) riempire.

fill up vt riempire ♦ vi (AUT) fare il pieno; ~ **it up, please** (AUT) mi faccia il pieno, per piacere.

fillet ['fɪlɪt] n filetto.

fillet steak n bistecca di filetto.

filling ['fɪlɪŋ] n (CULIN) impasto, ripieno; (for tooth) otturazione f.

filling station n stazione f di rifornimento.

fillip ['fɪlɪp] n incentivo, stimolo.

filly ['fɪlɪ] n puledra.

film [fɪlm] n (CINEMA) film m inv; (PHOT) pellicola; (thin layer) velo ♦ vt (scene) filmare.

film script n copione m.

film star n divo/a dello schermo.

filmstrip ['fɪlmstrɪp] n filmina.

film studio n studio cinematografico.

filter ['fɪltə*] n filtro ♦ vt filtrare.

  filter in, filter through vi (news) trapelare.

filter coffee n caffè m da passare al filtro.

filter lane n (Brit AUT) corsia di svincolo.

filter tip n filtro.

filth [fɪlθ] n sporcizia; (fig) oscenità.

filthy ['fɪlθɪ] a lordo(a), sozzo(a); (language) osceno(a).

fin [fɪn] n (of fish) pinna.

final ['faɪnl] a finale, ultimo(a); definitivo(a) ♦ n (SPORT) finale f; ~**s** npl (SCOL) esami mpl finali; ~ **demand** ingiunzione f di pagamento.

finale [fɪ'nɑːlɪ] n finale m.

finalist ['faɪnəlɪst] n (SPORT) finalista m/f.

finality [faɪ'nælɪtɪ] n irrevocabilità; **with an air of** ~ con risolutezza.

finalize ['faɪnəlaɪz] vt mettere a punto.

finally ['faɪnəlɪ] ad (lastly) alla fine; (eventually) finalmente; (once and for all) definitivamente.

finance [faɪ'næns] n finanza; (funds) fondi mpl, capitale m ♦ vt finanziare; ~**s** npl finanze fpl.

financial [faɪ'nænʃəl] a finanziario(a); ~ **statement** estratto conto finanziario.

financially [faɪ'nænʃəlɪ] ad finanziariamente.

financial year n anno finanziario, esercizio finanziario.

financier [faɪ'nænsɪə*] n finanziatore m.

find [faɪnd] vt (pt, pp **found** [faund]) trovare; (lost object) ritrovare ♦ n trovata, scoperta; **to** ~ **(some) difficulty in doing sth** trovare delle difficoltà nel fare qc; **to** ~ **sb guilty** (LAW) giudicare qn colpevole.

  find out vt informarsi di; (truth, secret) scoprire; (person) cogliere in fallo ♦ vi: **to** ~ **out about** informarsi su; (by chance) venire a sapere.

findings ['faɪndɪŋz] npl (LAW) sentenza, conclusioni fpl; (of report) conclusioni.

fine [faɪn] a bello(a); ottimo(a); (thin, subtle) fine ♦ ad (well) molto bene; (small) finemente ♦ n (LAW) multa ♦ vt (LAW) multare; **he's** ~ sta bene; **the weather is** ~ il tempo è bello; **you're doing** ~ te la cavi benissimo; **to cut it** ~ (of time, money)

farcela per un pelo.

fine arts npl belle arti fpl.

finely ['faɪnlɪ] ad (splendidly) in modo stupendo; (chop) finemente; (adjust) con precisione.

finery ['faɪnərɪ] n abiti mpl eleganti.

finesse [fɪ'nɛs] n finezza.

fine-tooth comb ['faɪntuː:θ-] n: **to go through sth with a** ~ (fig) passare qc al setaccio.

finger ['fɪŋgə*] n dito ♦ vt toccare, tastare.

fingernail ['fɪŋgəneɪl] n unghia.

fingerprint ['fɪŋgəprɪnt] n impronta digitale ♦ vt (person) prendere le impronte digitali di.

fingerstall ['fɪŋgəstɔːl] n ditale m.

fingertip ['fɪŋgətɪp] n punta del dito; **to have sth at one's** ~**s** (fig) avere qc sulla punta delle dita.

finicky ['fɪnɪkɪ] a esigente, pignolo(a); minuzioso(a).

finish ['fɪnɪʃ] n fine f; (SPORT: place) traguardo; (polish etc) finitura ♦ vt finire; (use up) esaurire ♦ vi finire; (session) terminare; **to** ~ **doing sth** finire di fare qc; **to** ~ **first/second** (SPORT) arrivare primo/ secondo; **she's** ~**ed with him** ha chiuso con lui.

  finish off vt compiere; (kill) uccidere.

  finish up vi, vt finire.

finished ['fɪnɪʃt] a (product) finito(a); (performance) perfetto(a); (col: tired) sfinito(a).

finishing line ['fɪnɪʃɪŋ-] n linea d'arrivo.

finishing school n scuola privata di perfezionamento (per signorine).

finishing touches npl ultimi ritocchi mpl.

finite ['faɪnaɪt] a limitato(a); (verb) finito(a).

Finland ['fɪnlənd] n Finlandia.

Finn [fɪn] n finlandese m/f.

Finnish ['fɪnɪʃ] a finlandese ♦ n (LING) finlandese m.

fiord [fjɔːd] n fiordo.

fir [fəː*] n abete m.

fire [faɪə*] n fuoco; incendio ♦ vt (discharge): **to** ~ **a gun** scaricare un fucile; (fig) infiammare; (dismiss) licenziare ♦ vi sparare, far fuoco; **on** ~ in fiamme; **insured against** ~ assicurato contro gli incendi; **electric/gas** ~ stufa elettrica/a gas; **to set** ~ **to sth, set sth on** ~ dar fuoco a qc, incendiare qc; **to be/come under** ~ (from) essere/finire sotto il fuoco or il tiro (di).

fire alarm n allarme m d'incendio.

firearm ['faɪərɑːm] n arma da fuoco.

fire brigade n (Brit) (corpo dei) pompieri mpl.

fire chief n (US) = **fire master**.

fire department n (US) = **fire brigade**.

fire drill n esercitazione f antincendio.

fire engine n autopompa.

fire escape n scala di sicurezza.

fire extinguisher n estintore m.

fireguard ['faɪəgɑːd] n (Brit) parafuoco.

fire hazard n: **that's a** ~ comporta rischi in caso d'incendio.

fire hydrant n idrante m.
fire insurance n assicurazione f contro gli incendi.
fireman ['faɪəmən] n pompiere m.
fire master n (Brit) comandante m dei vigili del fuoco.
fireplace ['faɪəpleɪs] n focolare m.
fireplug ['faɪəplʌg] n (US) = **fire hydrant**.
fire practice n = **fire drill**.
fireproof ['faɪəpruːf] a resistente al fuoco.
fire regulations npl norme fpl antincendio.
fire screen n parafuoco.
fireside ['faɪəsaɪd] n angolo del focolare.
fire station n caserma dei pompieri.
firewood ['faɪəwud] n legna.
firework ['faɪəwɜːk] n fuoco d'artificio.
firing ['faɪərɪŋ] n (MIL) spari mpl, tiro.
firing line n linea del fuoco; **to be in the ~** (fig) essere sotto tiro.
firing squad n plotone m d'esecuzione.
firm [fɜːm] a fermo(a); (offer, decision) definitivo(a) ♦ n ditta, azienda; **to be a ~ believer in sth** credere fermamente in qc.
firmly ['fɜːmlɪ] ad fermamente.
firmness ['fɜːmnɪs] n fermezza.
first [fɜːst] a primo(a) ♦ ad (before others) il primo, la prima; (before other things) per primo; (for the first time) per la prima volta; (when listing reasons etc) per prima cosa ♦ n (person: in race) primo/a; (Brit SCOL) laurea con lode; (AUT) prima; **at ~** dapprima, all'inizio; **~ of all** prima di tutto; **in the ~ instance** prima di tutto, in primo luogo; **I'll do it ~ thing tomorrow** lo farò per prima cosa domani; **from the (very) ~** fin dall'inizio, fin dal primo momento; **the ~ of January** il primo (di) gennaio.
first aid n pronto soccorso.
first-aid kit ['fɜːst'eɪd-] n cassetta pronto soccorso.
first-class ['fɜːst'klɑːs] a di prima classe.
first-class mail n ≈ espresso.
first-hand ['fɜːst'hænd] a di prima mano; diretto(a).
first lady n (US) moglie f del presidente.
firstly ['fɜːstlɪ] ad in primo luogo.
first name n prenome m.
first night n (THEATRE) prima.
first-rate ['fɜːst'reɪt] a di prima qualità, ottimo(a).
fir tree n abete m.
FIS n abbr (Brit: = Family Income Supplement) ≈ A.F. (= assegni familiari).
fiscal ['fɪskəl] a fiscale; **~ year** anno fiscale.
fish [fɪʃ] n (pl inv) pesce m ♦ vt, vi pescare; **to ~ a river** pescare in un fiume; **to go ~ing** andare a pesca.
  fish out vt (from water) ripescare; (from box etc) tirare fuori.
fishbone ['fɪʃbəun] n lisca, spina.
fisherman ['fɪʃəmən] n pescatore m.
fishery ['fɪʃərɪ] n zona da pesca.
fish factory n (Brit) fabbrica per la lavorazione del pesce.

fish farm n vivaio.
fish fingers npl (Brit) bastoncini mpl di pesce (surgelati).
fish hook n amo.
fishing boat ['fɪʃɪŋ-] n barca da pesca.
fishing industry n industria della pesca.
fishing line n lenza.
fishing net n rete f da pesca.
fishing rod n canna da pesca.
fishing tackle n attrezzatura da pesca.
fish market n mercato del pesce.
fishmonger ['fɪʃmʌŋgə*] n pescivendolo; **~'s (shop)** pescheria.
fish slice n (Brit) posata per servire il pesce.
fish sticks npl (US) = **fish fingers**.
fishy ['fɪʃɪ] a (fig) sospetto(a).
fission ['fɪʃən] n fissione f; **atomic/nuclear ~** fissione atomica/nucleare.
fissure ['fɪʃə*] n fessura.
fist [fɪst] n pugno.
fistfight ['fɪstfaɪt] n scazzottata.
fit [fɪt] a (MED, SPORT) in forma; (proper) adatto(a), appropriato(a); conveniente ♦ vt (subj: clothes) stare bene a; (match: facts etc) concordare con; (: description) corrispondere a; (adjust) aggiustare; (put in, attach) mettere; installare; (equip) fornire, equipaggiare ♦ vi (clothes) stare bene; (parts) andare bene, adattarsi; (in space, gap) entrare ♦ n (MED) attacco; **~ to** in grado di; **~ for** adatto(a) a; degno(a) di; **to keep ~** tenersi in forma; **~ for work** (after illness) in grado di riprendere il lavoro; **do as you think or see ~** faccia come meglio crede; **this dress is a tight/good ~** questo vestito è stretto/sta bene; **~ of anger/ enthusiasm** accesso d'ira/d'entusiasmo; **to have a ~** (MED) avere un attacco di convulsioni; (col) andare su tutte le furie; **by ~s and starts** a sbalzi.
  fit in vi accordarsi; adattarsi ♦ vt (object) far entrare; (fig: appointment, visitor) trovare il tempo per; **to ~ in with sb's plans** adattarsi ai progetti di qn.
  fit out vt (Brit: also: ~ up) equipaggiare.
fitful ['fɪtful] a saltuario(a).
fitment ['fɪtmənt] n componibile m.
fitness ['fɪtnɪs] n (MED) forma fisica; (of remark) appropriatezza.
fitted ['fɪtɪd] a: **~ carpet** moquette f inv; **~ cupboards** armadi mpl a muro; **~ kitchen** (Brit) cucina componibile.
fitter ['fɪtə*] n aggiustatore m or montatore m meccanico; (DRESSMAKING) sarto/a.
fitting ['fɪtɪŋ] a appropriato(a) ♦ n (of dress) prova; (of piece of equipment) montaggio, aggiustaggio; see also **fittings**.
fitting room n (in shop) camerino.
fittings ['fɪtɪŋz] npl impianti mpl.
five [faɪv] num cinque.
five-day week ['faɪvdeɪ-] n settimana di 5 giorni (lavorativi).
fiver ['faɪvə*] n (col: Brit) biglietto da cinque sterline; (: US) biglietto da cinque dollari.

fix [fɪks] *vt* fissare; *(mend)* riparare; *(make ready: meal, drink)* preparare ♦ *n*: **to be in a ~** essere nei guai; **the fight was a ~** *(col)* l'incontro è stato truccato.

fix up *vt (arrange: date, meeting)* fissare, stabilire; **to ~ sb up with sth** procurare qc a qn.

fixation [fɪk'seɪʃən] *n (PSYCH, fig)* fissazione *f*, ossessione *f*.

fixed [fɪkst] *a (prices etc)* fisso(a); **there's a ~ charge** c'è una quota fissa; **how are you ~ for money?** *(col)* a soldi come stai?

fixed assets *npl* beni *mpl* patrimoniali.

fixture ['fɪkstʃə*] *n* impianto (fisso); *(SPORT)* incontro (del calendario sportivo).

fizz [fɪz] *vi* frizzare.

fizzle ['fɪzl] *vi* frizzare; *(also:* **~ out:** *enthusiasm, interest)* smorzarsi, svanire; *(: plan)* fallire.

fizzy ['fɪzɪ] *a* frizzante; gassato(a).

fjord [fjɔːd] *n* = **fiord**.

FL *abbr (US POST)* = *Florida*.

flabbergasted ['flæbəgɑːstɪd] *a* sbalordito(a).

flabby ['flæbɪ] *a* flaccido(a).

flag [flæg] *n* bandiera; *(also:* **~stone)** pietra da lastricare ♦ *vi* stancarsi; affievolirsi; **~ of convenience** bandiera di convenienza.

flag down *vt* fare segno (di fermarsi) a.

flagon ['flægən] *n* bottiglione *m*.

flagpole ['flægpəul] *n* albero.

flagrant ['fleɪgrənt] *a* flagrante.

flag stop *n (US: for bus)* fermata facoltativa, fermata a richiesta.

flair [flɛə*] *n (for business etc)* fiuto; *(for languages etc)* facilità.

flak [flæk] *n (MIL)* fuoco d'artiglieria; *(col: criticism)* critiche *fpl*.

flake [fleɪk] *n (of rust, paint)* scaglia; *(of snow, soap powder)* fiocco ♦ *vi (also:* **~ off)** sfaldarsi.

flaky ['fleɪkɪ] *a (paintwork)* scrostato(a); *(skin)* squamoso(a); **~ pastry** *(CULIN)* pasta sfoglia.

flamboyant [flæm'bɔɪənt] *a* sgargiante.

flame [fleɪm] *n* fiamma; **old ~** *(col)* vecchia fiamma.

flamingo [flə'mɪŋgəu] *n* fenicottero, fiammingo.

flammable ['flæməbl] *a* infiammabile.

flan [flæn] *n (Brit)* flan *m inv*.

Flanders ['flɑːndəz] *n* Fiandre *fpl*.

flange [flændʒ] *n* flangia; *(on wheel)* suola.

flank [flæŋk] *n* fianco.

flannel ['flænl] *n (Brit: also:* **face ~)** guanto di spugna; *(fabric)* flanella; **~s** *npl* pantaloni *mpl* di flanella.

flannelette [flænə'lɛt] *n* flanella di cotone.

flap [flæp] *n (of pocket)* patta; *(of envelope)* lembo; *(AVIAT)* flap *m inv* ♦ *vt (wings)* battere ♦ *vi (sail, flag)* sbattere; *(col: also:* **be in a ~)** essere in agitazione.

flapjack ['flæpdʒæk] *n (US: pancake)* frittella; *(Brit: biscuit)* biscotto di avena.

flare [flɛə*] *n* razzo; *(in skirt etc)* svasatura.

flare up *vi* andare in fiamme; *(fig: person)* infiammarsi di rabbia; *(: revolt)* scoppiare.

flared ['flɛəd] *a (trousers)* svasato(a).

flash [flæʃ] *n* vampata; *(also:* **news ~)** notizia *f* lampo *inv*; *(PHOT)* flash *m inv*; *(US: torch)* torcia elettrica, lampadina tascabile ♦ *vt* accendere e spegnere; *(send: message)* trasmettere; *(flaunt)* ostentare ♦ *vi* brillare; *(light on ambulance, eyes etc)* lampeggiare; **in a ~** in un lampo; **~ of inspiration** lampo di genio; **to ~ one's headlights** lampeggiare; **he ~ed by or past** ci passò davanti come un lampo.

flashback ['flæʃbæk] *n* flashback *m inv*.

flashbulb ['flæʃbʌlb] *n* cubo *m* flash *inv*.

flash card *n (SCOL)* scheda didattica.

flashcube ['flæʃkjuːb] *n* flash *m inv*.

flasher ['flæʃə*] *n (AUT)* lampeggiatore *m*.

flashlight ['flæʃlaɪt] *n (torch)* lampadina tascabile.

flashpoint ['flæʃpɔɪnt] *n* punto di infiammabilità; *(fig)* livello critico.

flashy ['flæʃɪ] *a (pej)* vistoso(a).

flask [flɑːsk] *n* fiasco; *(CHEM)* beuta; *(also:* **vacuum ~)** thermos ® *m inv*.

flat [flæt] *n* piatto(a); *(tyre)* sgonfio(a), a terra; *(battery)* scarico(a); *(denial)* netto(a); *(MUS)* bemolle *inv*; *(: voice)* stonato(a); *(: instrument)* scordato(a) ♦ *n (Brit: rooms)* appartamento; *(MUS)* bemolle *m*; *(AUT)* pneumatico sgonfio ♦ *ad*: **(to work) ~ out** (lavorare) a più non posso; **~ rate of pay** tariffa unica di pagamento.

flat-footed ['flæt'futɪd] *a*: **to be ~** avere i piedi piatti.

flatly ['flætlɪ] *ad* categoricamente, nettamente.

flatmate ['flætmeɪt] *n (Brit)*: **he's my ~** divide l'appartamento con me.

flatness ['flætnɪs] *n (of land)* assenza di rilievi.

flatten ['flætn] *vt (also:* **~ out)** appiattire; *(house, city)* abbattere, radere al suolo.

flatter ['flætə*] *vt* lusingare; *(show to advantage)* donare a.

flatterer ['flætərə*] *n* adulatore/trice.

flattering ['flætərɪŋ] *a* lusinghiero(a); *(clothes etc)* che dona, che abbellisce.

flattery ['flætərɪ] *n* adulazione *f*.

flatulence ['flætjuləns] *n* flatulenza.

flaunt [flɔːnt] *vt* fare mostra di.

flavour, *(US)* **flavor** ['fleɪvə*] *n* gusto, sapore *m* ♦ *vt* insaporire, aggiungere sapore a; **vanilla-~ed** al gusto di vaniglia.

flavo(u)ring ['fleɪvərɪŋ] *n* essenza (artificiale).

flaw [flɔː] *n* difetto.

flawless ['flɔːlɪs] *a* senza difetti.

flax [flæks] *n* lino.

flaxen ['flæksən] *a* biondo(a).

flea [fliː] *n* pulce *f*.

flea market *n* mercato delle pulci.

fleck [flɛk] *n (of mud, paint, colour)* macchiolina; *(of dust)* granello ♦ *vt (with blood, mud etc)* macchiettare; **brown ~ed with white** marrone screziato di bianco.

fled [flɛd] *pt, pp of* **flee**.

fledg(e)ling ['flɛdʒlɪŋ] *n* uccellino.
flee, *pt, pp* **fled** [fli:, flɛd] *vt* fuggire da ♦ *vi* fuggire, scappare.
fleece [fli:s] *n* vello ♦ *vt* (*col*) pelare.
fleecy ['fli:sɪ] *a* (*blanket*) soffice; (*cloud*) come ovatta.
fleet [fli:t] *n* flotta; (*of lorries etc*) convoglio; (*of cars*) parco.
fleeting ['fli:tɪŋ] *a* fugace, fuggitivo(a); (*visit*) volante.
Flemish ['flɛmɪʃ] *a* fiammingo(a) ♦ *n* (*LING*) fiammingo; **the ~** *npl* i Fiamminghi.
flesh [flɛʃ] *n* carne *f*; (*of fruit*) polpa.
flesh wound *n* ferita superficiale.
flew [flu:] *pt of* **fly**.
flex [flɛks] *n* filo (flessibile) ♦ *vt* flettere; (*muscles*) contrarre.
flexibility [flɛksɪ'bɪlɪtɪ] *n* flessibilità.
flexible ['flɛksəbl] *a* flessibile.
flick [flɪk] *n* colpetto; *see also* **flicks**.
flick through *vt fus* sfogliare.
flicker ['flɪkə*] *vi* tremolare ♦ *n* tremolio; **a ~ of light** un breve bagliore.
flick knife *n* (*Brit*) coltello a serramanico.
flicks *npl*: **the ~** (*col*) il cine.
flier ['flaɪə*] *n* aviatore *m*.
flight [flaɪt] *n* volo; (*escape*) fuga; (*also:* **~ of steps**) scalinata; **to take ~** darsi alla fuga; **to put to ~** mettere in fuga.
flight attendant *n* (*US*) steward *m*, hostess *f inv*.
flight crew *n* equipaggio.
flight deck *n* (*AVIAT*) cabina di controllo; (*NAUT*) ponte *m* di comando.
flight recorder *n* registratore *m* di volo.
flimsy ['flɪmzɪ] *a* (*fabric*) inconsistente; (*excuse*) meschino(a).
flinch [flɪntʃ] *vi* ritirarsi; **to ~ from** tirarsi indietro di fronte a.
fling, *pt, pp* **flung** [flɪŋ, flʌŋ] *vt* lanciare, gettare ♦ *n* (*love affair*) avventura.
flint [flɪnt] *n* selce *f*; (*in lighter*) pietrina.
flip [flɪp] *n* colpetto ♦ *vt* dare un colpetto a; (*US: pancake*) far saltare (in aria) ♦ *vi*: **to ~ for sth** (*US*) fare a testa e croce per qc.
flip through *vt fus* (*book, records*) dare una scorsa a.
flippant ['flɪpənt] *a* senza rispetto, irriverente.
flipper ['flɪpə*] *n* pinna.
flip side *n* (*of record*) retro.
flirt [flə:t] *vi* flirtare ♦ *n* civetta.
flirtation [flə:'teɪʃən] *n* flirt *m inv*.
flit [flɪt] *vi* svolazzare.
float [fləut] *n* galleggiante *m*; (*in procession*) carro; (*sum of money*) somma ♦ *vi* galleggiare; (*bather*) fare il morto; (*COMM: currency*) fluttuare ♦ *vt* far galleggiare; (*loan, business*) lanciare; **to ~ an idea** ventilare un'idea.
floating ['fləutɪŋ] *a* a galla; **~ vote** voto oscillante; **~ voter** elettore *m* indeciso.
flock [flɔk] *n* gregge *m*; (*of people*) folla; (*of birds*) stormo.
floe [fləu] *n* (*also:* **ice ~**) banchisa.

flog [flɔg] *vt* flagellare.
flood [flʌd] *n* alluvione *m*; (*of words, tears etc*) diluvio ♦ *vt* inondare, allagare; (*AUT: carburettor*) ingolfare; **in ~** in pieno; **to ~ the market** (*COMM*) inondare il mercato.
flooding ['flʌdɪŋ] *n* inondazione *f*.
floodlight ['flʌdlaɪt] *n* riflettore *m* ♦ *vt* illuminare a giorno.
floodlit ['flʌdlɪt] *pt, pp of* **floodlight** ♦ *a* illuminato(a) a giorno.
flood tide *n* alta marea, marea crescente.
floor [flɔ:*] *n* pavimento; (*storey*) piano; (*of sea, valley*) fondo; (*fig: at meeting*): **the ~** il pubblico ♦ *vt* pavimentare; (*knock down*) atterrare; (*baffle*) confondere; (*silence*) far tacere; **on the ~** sul pavimento, per terra; **ground ~,** (*US*) **first ~** pianterreno; **first ~,** (*US*) **second ~** primo piano; **top ~** ultimo piano; **to have the ~** (*speaker*) prendere la parola.
floorboard ['flɔ:bɔ:d] *n* tavellone *m* di legno.
flooring ['flɔ:rɪŋ] *n* (*floor*) pavimento; (*material*) materiale *m* per pavimentazioni.
floor lamp *n* (*US*) lampada a stelo.
floor show *n* spettacolo di varietà.
floorwalker ['flɔ:wɔ:kə*] *n* (*esp US*) ispettore *m* di reparto.
flop [flɔp] *n* fiasco ♦ *vi* (*fail*) far fiasco.
floppy ['flɔpɪ] *a* floscio(a), molle ♦ *n* (*COMPUT*) = **floppy disk**; **~ hat** cappello floscio.
floppy disk *n* floppy disk *m inv*.
flora ['flɔ:rə] *n* flora.
floral ['flɔ:rl] *a* floreale.
Florence ['flɔrəns] *n* Firenze *f*.
Florentine ['flɔrəntaɪn] *a* fiorentino(a).
florid ['flɔrɪd] *a* (*complexion*) florido(a); (*style*) fiorito(a).
florist ['flɔrɪst] *n* fioraio/a; **at the ~'s (shop)** dal fioraio.
flotation [fləu'teɪʃən] *n* (*COMM*) lancio.
flounce [flauns] *n* balzo.
flounce out *vi* uscire stizzito(a).
flounder ['flaundə*] *vi* annaspare ♦ *n* (*ZOOL*) passera di mare.
flour ['flauə*] *n* farina.
flourish ['flʌrɪʃ] *vi* fiorire ♦ *vt* brandire ♦ *n* abbellimento; svolazzo; (*of trumpets*) fanfara.
flourishing ['flʌrɪʃɪŋ] *a* prosperoso(a), fiorente.
flout [flaut] *vt* (*order*) contravvenire a; (*convention*) sfidare.
flow [fləu] *n* flusso; circolazione *f*; (*of river, also ELEC*) corrente *f* ♦ *vi* fluire; (*traffic, blood in veins*) circolare; (*hair*) scendere.
flow chart *n* schema *m* di flusso.
flow diagram *n* organigramma *m*.
flower ['flauə*] *n* fiore *m* ♦ *vi* fiorire; **in ~** in fiore.
flower bed *n* aiuola.
flowerpot ['flauəpɔt] *n* vaso da fiori.
flowery ['flauərɪ] *a* fiorito(a).
flown [fləun] *pp of* **fly**.

flu [flu:] *n* influenza.
fluctuate ['flʌktjʊeɪt] *vi* fluttuare, oscillare.
fluctuation [flʌktju'eɪʃən] *n* fluttuazione *f*, oscillazione *f*.
flue [flu:] *n* canna fumaria.
fluency ['flu:ənsɪ] *n* facilità, scioltezza; **his ~ in English** la sua scioltezza nel parlare l'inglese.
fluent ['flu:ənt] *a (speech)* facile, sciolto(a); **he's a ~ speaker/reader** si esprime/legge senza difficoltà; **he speaks ~ Italian, he's ~ in Italian** parla l'italiano correntemente.
fluently ['flu:əntlɪ] *ad* con facilità; correntemente.
fluff [flʌf] *n* lanugine *f*.
fluffy ['flʌfɪ] *a* lanuginoso(a); *(toy)* di peluche.
fluid ['flu:ɪd] *a* fluido(a) ♦ *n* fluido; *(in diet)* liquido.
fluid ounce *n (Brit) = 0.028 l; 0.05 pints.*
fluke [flu:k] *n (col)* colpo di fortuna.
flummox ['flʌməks] *vt* rendere perplesso(a).
flung [flʌŋ] *pt, pp of* **fling.**
flunky ['flʌŋkɪ] *n* tirapiedi *m/f inv.*
fluorescent [fluə'resnt] *a* fluorescente.
fluoride ['fluəraɪd] *n* fluoruro.
fluorine ['fluəri:n] *n* fluoro.
flurry ['flʌrɪ] *n (of snow)* tempesta; **a ~ of activity/excitement** una febbre di attività/un'improvvisa agitazione.
flush [flʌʃ] *n* rossore *m*; *(fig)* ebbrezza ♦ *vt* ripulire con un getto d'acqua; *(also:* **~ out:** *birds)* far alzare in volo; *(: animals, fig: criminal)* stanare ♦ *vi* arrossire ♦ *a:* **~ with** a livello di, pari a; **~ against** aderente a; **hot ~es** *(MED)* vampate *fpl* di calore; **to ~ the toilet** tirare l'acqua.
flushed [flʌʃt] *a* tutto(a) rosso(a).
fluster ['flʌstə*] *n* agitazione *f.*
flustered ['flʌstəd] *a* sconvolto(a).
flute [flu:t] *n* flauto.
flutter ['flʌtə*] *n* agitazione *f*; *(of wings)* frullio ♦ *vi (bird)* battere le ali.
flux [flʌks] *n:* **in a state of ~** in continuo mutamento.
fly [flaɪ] *n (insect)* mosca; *(on trousers: also:* **flies)** bracchetta ♦ *vb (pt* **flew,** *pp* **flown** [flu:, fləʊn]) *vt* pilotare; *(passengers, cargo)* trasportare (in aereo); *(distances)* percorrere ♦ *vi* volare; *(passengers)* andare in aereo; *(escape)* fuggire; *(flag)* sventolare; **to ~ open** spalancarsi all'improvviso; **to ~ off the handle** perdere le staffe, uscire dai gangheri.
fly away *vi* volar via.
fly in *vi (plane)* arrivare; *(person)* arrivare in aereo.
fly off *vi* volare via.
fly out *vi (plane)* partire; *(person)* partire in aereo.
fly-fishing ['flaɪfɪʃɪŋ] *n* pesca con la mosca.
flying ['flaɪɪŋ] *n (activity)* aviazione *f*; *(action)* volo ♦ *a:* **~ visit** visita volante; **with ~ colours** con risultati brillanti; **he doesn't like ~** non gli piace viaggiare in aereo.

flying buttress *n* arco rampante.
flying saucer *n* disco volante.
flying start *n:* **to get off to a ~ start** partire come un razzo.
flyleaf ['flaɪli:f] *n* risguardo.
flyover ['flaɪəʊvə*] *n (Brit: bridge)* cavalcavia *m inv.*
flypast ['flaɪpɑ:st] *n* parata aerea.
flysheet ['flaɪʃi:t] *n (for tent)* sopratetto.
flywheel ['flaɪwi:l] *n* volano.
FM *abbr see* **frequency modulation;** *(Brit MIL) see* **Field Marshal.**
FMB *n abbr (US) = Federal Maritime Board.*
FMCS *n abbr (US: = Federal Mediation and Conciliation Services)* organismo di conciliazione in caso di conflitti sul lavoro.
FO *n abbr (Brit) see* **Foreign Office.**
foal [fəʊl] *n* puledro.
foam [fəʊm] *n* schiuma ♦ *vi* schiumare.
foam rubber *n* gommapiuma ®.
FOB *abbr (= free on board)* franco a bordo.
fob [fɔb] *vt:* **to ~ sb off with** appioppare qn con; sbarazzarsi di qn con ♦ *n (also:* **watch ~:** *chain)* catena per orologio; *(: band of cloth)* nastro per orologio.
foc *abbr (Brit)* **= free of charge.**
focal ['fəʊkəl] *a* focale.
focal point *n* punto focale.
focus ['fəʊkəs] *n (pl* **~es)** fuoco; *(of interest)* centro ♦ *vt (field glasses etc)* mettere a fuoco; *(light rays)* far convergere ♦ *vi:* **to ~ on** *(with camera)* mettere a fuoco; *(person)* fissare lo sguardo su; **in ~** a fuoco; **out of ~** sfocato(a).
fodder ['fɔdə*] *n* foraggio.
FOE *n abbr (= Friends of the Earth)* Amici *mpl* della Terra; *(US: = Fraternal Order of Eagles)* organizzazione filantropica.
foe [fəʊ] *n* nemico.
foetus, *(US)* **fetus** ['fi:təs] *n* feto.
fog [fɔg] *n* nebbia.
fogbound ['fɔgbaʊnd] *a* fermo(a) a causa della nebbia.
foggy ['fɔgɪ] *a* nebbioso(a); **it's ~** c'è nebbia.
fog lamp, *(US)* **fog light** *n (AUT)* faro *m* antinebbia *inv.*
foible ['fɔɪbl] *n* debolezza, punto debole.
foil [fɔɪl] *vt* confondere, frustrare ♦ *n* lamina di metallo; *(also:* **kitchen ~)** foglio di alluminio; *(FENCING)* fioretto; **to act as a ~ to** *(fig)* far risaltare.
foist [fɔɪst] *vt:* **to ~ sth on sb** rifilare qc a qn.
fold [fəʊld] *n (bend, crease)* piega; *(AGR)* ovile *m*; *(fig)* gregge *m* ♦ *vt* piegare; **to ~ one's arms** incrociare le braccia.
fold up *vi (map etc)* piegarsi; *(business)* crollare ♦ *vt (map etc)* piegare, ripiegare.
folder ['fəʊldə*] *n (for papers)* cartella; cartellina; *(binder)* raccoglitore *m.*
folding ['fəʊldɪŋ] *a (chair, bed)* pieghevole.
foliage ['fəʊlɪɪdʒ] *n* fogliame *m.*
folk [fəʊk] *npl* gente *f* ♦ *cpd* popolare; **~s** *npl* famiglia.
folklore ['fəʊklɔ:*] *n* folclore *m.*

folk music n musica folk inv.
folk singer n cantante m/f folk inv.
folksong ['fəuksɔŋ] n canto popolare.
follow ['fɔləu] vt seguire ♦ vi seguire; (result) conseguire, risultare; **to ~ sb's advice** seguire il consiglio di qn; **I don't quite ~ you** non ti capisco or seguo affatto; **to ~ in sb's footsteps** seguire le orme di qn; **it ~s that ...** ne consegue che ...; **he ~ed suit** lui ha fatto lo stesso.
  follow on vi (continue): **to ~ on from** seguire.
  follow out vt (implement: idea, plan) eseguire, portare a termine.
  follow through vt = **follow out**.
  follow up vt (victory) sfruttare; (letter, offer) fare seguito a; (case) seguire.
follower ['fɔləuə*] n seguace m/f, discepolo/a.
following ['fɔləuɪŋ] a seguente, successivo(a) ♦ n seguito, discepoli mpl.
follow-up ['fɔləuʌp] n seguito.
folly ['fɔlɪ] n pazzia, follia.
fond [fɔnd] a (memory, look) tenero(a), affettuoso(a); **to be ~ of** volere bene a; **she's ~ of swimming** le piace nuotare.
fondle ['fɔndl] vt accarezzare.
fondly ['fɔndlɪ] ad (lovingly) affettuosamente; (naively): **he ~ believed that ...** ha avuto l'ingenuità di credere che ....
fondness ['fɔndnɪs] n affetto; **~ (for sth)** predilezione f (per qc).
font [fɔnt] n (REL) fonte m (battesimale); (TYP) stile m di carattere.
food [fu:d] n cibo.
food mixer n frullatore m.
food poisoning n intossicazione f alimentare.
food processor n tritatutto m inv elettrico.
foodstuffs ['fu:dstʌfs] npl generi fpl alimentari.
fool [fu:l] n sciocco/a; (HISTORY: of king) buffone m; (CULIN) frullato ♦ vt ingannare ♦ vi (gen: ~ around) fare lo sciocco; **to make a ~ of sb** prendere in giro qn; **to make a ~ of o.s.** coprirsi di ridicolo; **you can't ~ me** non mi inganna.
  fool about, fool around vi (waste time) perdere tempo.
foolhardy ['fu:lha:dɪ] a avventato(a).
foolish ['fu:lɪʃ] a scemo(a), stupido(a); imprudente.
foolishly ['fu:lɪʃlɪ] ad stupidamente.
foolishness ['fu:lɪʃnɪs] n stupidità.
foolproof ['fu:lpru:f] a (plan etc) sicurissimo(a).
foolscap ['fu:lskæp] n carta protocollo.
foot [fut] n (pl feet [fi:t]) piede m; (measure) piede (= 304 mm; 12 inches); (of animal) zampa; (of page, stairs etc) fondo ♦ vt (bill) pagare; **on a ~** a piedi; **to put one's ~ down** (AUT) schiacciare l'accelleratore; (say no) imporsi; **to find one's feet** ambientarsi.
footage ['futɪdʒ] n (CINEMA: length) ≈ metraggio; (: material) sequenza.

foot and mouth (disease) n afta epizootica.
football ['futbɔ:l] n pallone m; (sport: Brit) calcio; (: US) football m americano.
footballer ['futbɔ:lə*] n (Brit) = **football player**.
football ground n campo di calcio.
football match n (Brit) partita di calcio.
football player n (Brit) calciatore m; (US) giocatore m di football americano.
footbrake ['futbreɪk] n freno a pedale.
footbridge ['futbrɪdʒ] n passerella.
foothills ['futhɪlz] npl contrafforti fpl.
foothold ['futhəuld] n punto d'appoggio.
footing ['futɪŋ] n (fig) posizione f; **to lose one's ~** mettere un piede in fallo; **on an equal ~** in condizioni di parità.
footlights ['futlaɪts] npl luci fpl della ribalta.
footman ['futmən] n lacchè m inv.
footnote ['futnəut] n nota (a piè di pagina).
footpath ['futpɑ:θ] n sentiero; (in street) marciapiede m.
footprint ['futprɪnt] n orma, impronta.
footrest ['futrest] n poggiapiedi m inv.
footsore ['futsɔ:*] a coi piedi doloranti or dolenti.
footstep ['futstep] n passo.
footwear ['futweə*] n calzatura.
FOR abbr (= free on rail) franco vagone.
for [fɔ:*] prep per ♦ cj poiché; (in spite of): **~ all that** malgrado ciò; **the train ~ London** il treno per Londra; **it's time ~ lunch** è ora di pranzo; **what ~?** perché?; **what's this button ~?** a cosa serve questo bottone?; **~ all his money/he says ...** nonostante or malgrado tutto il suo denaro/quel che dice ...; **I haven't seen him ~ a week** è una settimana che non lo vedo, non lo vedo da una settimana; **I'll be away ~ 3 weeks** starò via 3 settimane; **he was away ~ 2 years** è stato via per 2 anni; **he went down ~ the paper** è sceso a prendere il giornale; **I sold it ~ £5** l'ho venduto per 5 sterline; **the campaign ~ ...** la campagna a favore di or per ...; **~ sale** da vendere; **there's nothing ~ it but to jump** (Brit) non c'è altro da fare che saltare.
forage ['fɔrɪdʒ] vi foraggiare.
forage cap n bustina.
foray ['fɔreɪ] n incursione f.
forbad(e) [fə'bæd] pt of **forbid**.
forbearing [fɔ:'bɛərɪŋ] a paziente, tollerante.
forbid [fə'bɪd] pt **forbad(e)**, pp **forbidden** [fə'bɪd, -'bæd, -'bɪdn] vt vietare, interdire; **to ~ sb to do sth** proibire a qn di fare qc.
forbidden [fə'bɪdn] a vietato(a).
forbidding [fə'bɪdɪŋ] a arcigno(a), d'aspetto minaccioso.
force [fɔ:s] n forza ♦ vt forzare; (obtain by ~: smile, confession) strappare; **the F~s** npl (Brit) le forze armate; **in ~** (in large numbers) in gran numero; (law) in vigore; **to come into ~** entrare in vigore; **a ~ 5 wind** un vento forza 5; **to join ~s** unire le forze; **the sales ~** (COMM) l'effettivo dei

rappresentanti; **to** ~ **sb to do sth** costringere qn a fare qc.
force back vt (crowd, enemy) respingere;
(tears) ingoiare.
force down vt (food) sforzarsi di
mangiare.
forced [fɔːst] a forzato(a).
force-feed ['fɔːsfiːd] vt sottoporre ad
alimentazione forzata.
forceful ['fɔːsful] a forte, vigoroso(a).
forcemeat ['fɔːsmiːt] n (Brit CULIN) ripieno.
forceps ['fɔːsɪps] npl forcipe m.
forcibly ['fɔːsəblɪ] ad con la forza; (vigorous-
ly) vigorosamente.
ford [fɔːd] n guado ♦ vt guadare.
fore [fɔː*] n: **to the** ~ in prima linea; **to
come to the** ~ mettersi in evidenza.
forearm ['fɔːrɑːm] n avambraccio.
forebear ['fɔːbɛə*] n antenato.
foreboding [fɔː'bəudɪŋ] n presagio di male.
forecast ['fɔːkɑːst] n previsione f; (weather ~)
previsioni fpl del tempo ♦ vt (irg: like **cast**)
prevedere.
foreclose [fɔː'kləuz] vt (LAW: also: ~ **on**)
sequestrare l'immobile ipotecato di.
foreclosure [fɔː'kləuʒə*] n sequestro di
immobile ipotecato.
forecourt ['fɔːkɔːt] n (of garage) corte f
esterna.
forefathers ['fɔːfɑːðəz] npl antenati mpl, avi
mpl.
forefinger ['fɔːfɪŋgə*] n (dito) indice m.
forefront ['fɔːfrʌnt] n: **in the** ~ **of**
all'avanguardia di.
forego [fɔː'gəu] vt = **forgo**.
foregoing ['fɔːgəuɪŋ] a precedente.
foregone ['fɔːgɔn] pp of **forego** ♦ a: **it's a** ~
conclusion è una conclusione scontata.
foreground ['fɔːgraund] n primo piano ♦ cpd
(COMPUT) foreground inv, di primo piano.
forehand ['fɔːhænd] n (TENNIS) diritto.
forehead ['fɔrɪd] n fronte f.
foreign ['fɔrən] a straniero(a); (trade)
estero(a).
foreign body n corpo estraneo.
foreign currency n valuta estera.
foreigner ['fɔrənə*] n straniero/a.
foreign exchange n cambio di valuta;
(currency) valuta estera.
foreign exchange market n mercato delle
valute.
foreign exchange rate n cambio.
foreign investment n investimento
all'estero.
foreign minister n ministro degli Affari
esteri.
Foreign Office (FO) n (Brit) Ministero degli
Esteri.
foreign secretary n (Brit) ministro degli
Affari esteri.
foreleg ['fɔːlɛg] n zampa anteriore.
foreman ['fɔːmən] n caposquadra m; (LAW: of
jury) portavoce m della giuria.
foremost ['fɔːməust] a principale; più in vista

♦ ad: **first and** ~ innanzitutto.
forename ['fɔːneɪm] n nome m di battesimo.
forensic [fə'rɛnsɪk] a: ~ **medicine** medicina
legale; ~ **expert** esperto della (polizia)
scientifica.
forerunner ['fɔːrʌnə*] n precursore m.
foresee, pt **foresaw**, pp **foreseen** [fɔː'siː,
-'sɔː, -'siːn] vt prevedere.
foreseeable [fɔː'siːəbl] a prevedibile.
foreseen [fɔː'siːn] pp of **foresee**.
foreshadow [fɔː'ʃædəu] vt presagire, far
prevedere.
foreshorten [fɔː'ʃɔːtn] vt (figure, scene) rappresentare in scorcio.
foresight ['fɔːsaɪt] n previdenza.
foreskin ['fɔːskɪn] n (ANAT) prepuzio.
forest ['fɔrɪst] n foresta.
forestall [fɔː'stɔːl] vt prevenire.
forestry ['fɔrɪstrɪ] n silvicoltura.
foretaste ['fɔːteɪst] n pregustazione f.
foretell, pt, pp **foretold** [fɔː'tɛl, -'təuld] vt
predire.
forethought ['fɔːθɔːt] n previdenza.
foretold [fɔː'təuld] pt, pp of **foretell**.
forever [fə'rɛvə*] ad per sempre; (fig) sempre, di continuo.
forewarn [fɔː'wɔːn] vt avvisare in precedenza.
forewent [fɔː'wɛnt] pt of **forego**.
foreword ['fɔːwəːd] n prefazione f.
forfeit ['fɔːfɪt] n ammenda, pena ♦ vt perdere;
(one's happiness, health) giocarsi.
forgave [fə'geɪv] pt of **forgive**.
forge [fɔːdʒ] n fucina ♦ vt falsificare; (signature) contraffare, falsificare; (wrought
iron) fucinare, foggiare.
forge ahead vi tirare avanti.
forger ['fɔːdʒə*] n contraffattore m.
forgery ['fɔːdʒərɪ] n falso; (activity) contraffazione f.
forget, pt **forgot**, pp **forgotten** [fə'gɛt, -'gɔt,
-'gɔtn] vt, vi dimenticare.
forgetful [fə'gɛtful] a di corta memoria; ~ **of**
dimentico(a) di.
forgetfulness [fə'gɛtfulnɪs] n smemoratezza;
(oblivion) oblio.
forget-me-not [fə'gɛtmɪnɔt] n nontiscordardimé m inv.
forgive, pt **forgave**, pp **forgiven** [fə'gɪv,
-'geɪv, -'gɪvn] vt perdonare; **to** ~ **sb for sth/
for doing sth** perdonare qc a qn/a qn di aver
fatto qc.
forgiveness [fə'gɪvnɪs] n perdono.
forgiving [fə'gɪvɪŋ] a indulgente.
forgo, pt **forwent**, pp **forgone** [fɔː'gəu,
-'wɛnt, -'gɔn] vt rinunciare a.
forgot [fə'gɔt] pt of **forget**.
forgotten [fə'gɔtn] pp of **forget**.
fork [fɔːk] n (for eating) forchetta; (for
gardening) forca; (of roads) bivio; (of
railways) inforcazione f ♦ vi (road)
biforcarsi.
fork out (col: pay) vt sborsare ♦ vi pagare.
forked [fɔːkt] a (lightning) a zigzag.
fork-lift truck ['fɔːklɪft-] n carrello elevatore.

forlorn [fə'lɔ:n] *a* (*person*) sconsolato(a); (*deserted*: *cottage*) abbandonato(a); (*desperate*: *attempt*) disperato(a).

form [fɔ:m] *n* forma; (*SCOL*) classe *f*; (*questionnaire*) modulo ♦ *vt* formare; (*circle*, *queue etc*) fare; **in the ~ of** a forma di, sotto forma di; **to be in good ~** (*SPORT*, *fig*) essere in forma; **in top ~** in gran forma; **to ~ part of sth** far parte di qc.

formal ['fɔ:məl] *a* (*offer*, *receipt*) vero(a) e proprio(a); (*person*) cerimonioso(a); (*occasion*, *dinner*) formale, ufficiale; (*ART*, *PHILOSOPHY*) formale; **~ dress** abito da cerimonia; (*evening dress*) abito da sera.

formality [fɔ:'mælɪtɪ] *n* formalità *f inv*.

formalize ['fɔ:məlaɪz] *vt* rendere ufficiale.

formally ['fɔ:məlɪ] *ad* ufficialmente; formalmente; cerimoniosamente; **to be ~ invited** ricevere un invito ufficiale.

format ['fɔ:mæt] *n* formato ♦ *vt* (*COMPUT*) formattare.

formation [fɔ:'meɪʃən] *n* formazione *f*.

formative ['fɔ:mətɪv] *a*: **~ years** anni *mpl* formativi.

former ['fɔ:mə*] *a* vecchio(a) (*before n*), ex *inv* (*before n*); **the ~ president** l'ex presidente; **the ~ ... the latter** quello ... questo.

formerly ['fɔ:məlɪ] *ad* in passato.

form feed *n* (*on printer*) alimentazione *f* modulo.

formidable ['fɔ:mɪdəbl] *a* formidabile.

formula ['fɔ:mjulə] *n* formula; **F~ One** (*AUT*) formula uno.

formulate ['fɔ:mjuleɪt] *vt* formulare.

fornicate ['fɔ:nɪkeɪt] *vi* fornicare.

forsake, *pt* forsook, *pp* forsaken [fə'seɪk, -'suk, -'seɪkən] *vt* abbandonare.

fort [fɔ:t] *n* forte *m*; **to hold the ~** (*fig*) prendere le redini (della situazione).

forte ['fɔ:tɪ] *n* forte *m*.

forth [fɔ:θ] *ad* in avanti; **to go back and ~** andare avanti e indietro; **and so ~** e così via.

forthcoming [fɔ:θ'kʌmɪŋ] *a* prossimo(a); (*character*) aperto(a), comunicativo(a).

forthright ['fɔ:θraɪt] *a* franco(a), schietto(a).

forthwith [fɔ:θ'wɪθ] *ad* immediatamente, subito.

fortieth ['fɔ:tɪɪθ] *num* quarantesimo(a).

fortification [fɔ:tɪfɪ'keɪʃən] *n* fortificazione *f*.

fortified wine *n* vino ad alta gradazione alcolica.

fortify ['fɔ:tɪfaɪ] *vt* fortificare.

fortitude ['fɔ:tɪtju:d] *n* forza d'animo.

fortnight ['fɔ:tnaɪt] *n* (*Brit*) quindici giorni *mpl*, due settimane *fpl*; **it's a ~ since ...** sono due settimane da quando ....

fortnightly ['fɔ:tnaɪtlɪ] *a* bimensile ♦ *ad* ogni quindici giorni.

FORTRAN ['fɔ:træn] *n* FORTRAN *m*.

fortress ['fɔ:trɪs] *n* fortezza, rocca.

fortuitous [fɔ:'tju:ɪtəs] *a* fortuito(a).

fortunate ['fɔ:tʃənɪt] *a* fortunato(a); **he is ~**

to have ... ha la fortuna di avere ...; **it is ~ that** è una fortuna che + *sub*.

fortunately ['fɔ:tʃənɪtlɪ] *ad* fortunatamente.

fortune ['fɔ:tʃən] *n* fortuna; **to make a ~** farsi una fortuna.

fortuneteller ['fɔ:tʃəntelə*] *n* indovino/a.

forty ['fɔ:tɪ] *num* quaranta.

forum ['fɔ:rəm] *n* foro; (*fig*) luogo di pubblica discussione.

forward ['fɔ:wəd] *a* (*movement*, *position*) in avanti; (*not shy*) sfacciato(a); (*COMM*: *delivery*, *sales*, *exchange*) a termine ♦ *n* (*SPORT*) avanti *m inv* ♦ *vt* (*letter*) inoltrare; (*parcel*, *goods*) spedire; (*fig*) promuovere, appoggiare; **to move ~** avanzare; **"please ~"** "si prega di inoltrare"; **~ planning** programmazione *f* in anticipo.

forward(s) ['fɔ:wəd(z)] *ad* avanti.

forwent [fɔ:'wɛnt] *pt of* **forgo**.

fossil ['fɔsl] *a*, *n* fossile (*m*); **~ fuel** combustibile *m* fossile.

foster ['fɔstə*] *vt* incoraggiare, nutrire; (*child*) avere in affidamento.

foster brother *n* fratellastro.

foster child *n* bambino(a) preso(a) in affidamento.

foster mother *n* madre *f* affidataria.

fought [fɔ:t] *pt*, *pp of* **fight**.

foul [faul] *a* (*smell*, *food*) cattivo(a); (*weather*) brutto(a), orribile; (*language*) osceno(a); (*deed*) infame ♦ *n* (*FOOTBALL*) fallo ♦ *vt* sporcare; (*football player*) commettere un fallo su; (*entangle*: *anchor*, *propeller*) impigliarsi in.

foul play *n* (*SPORT*) gioco scorretto; **~ is not suspected** si è scartata l'ipotesi del delitto (*or* dell'attentato *etc*).

found [faund] *pt*, *pp of* **find** ♦ *vt* (*establish*) fondare.

foundation [faun'deɪʃən] *n* (*act*) fondazione *f*; (*base*) base *f*; (*also*: **~ cream**) fondo tinta; **~s** *npl* (*of building*) fondamenta *fpl*; **to lay the ~s** gettare le fondamenta.

foundation stone *n* prima pietra.

founder ['faundə*] *n* fondatore/trice ♦ *vi* affondare.

founding ['faundɪŋ] *a*: **~ fathers** (*US*) padri *mpl* fondatori; **~ member** socio fondatore.

foundry ['faundrɪ] *n* fonderia.

fount [faunt] *n* fonte *f*; (*TYP*) stile *m* di carattere.

fountain ['fauntɪn] *n* fontana.

fountain pen *n* penna stilografica.

four [fɔ:*] *num* quattro; **on all ~s** a carponi.

four-poster ['fɔ:'pəustə*] *n* (*also*: **~ bed**) letto a quattro colonne.

foursome ['fɔ:səm] *n* partita a quattro; uscita in quattro.

fourteen ['fɔ:'ti:n] *num* quattordici.

fourth [fɔ:θ] *num* quarto(a) ♦ *n* (*AUT*: *also*: **~ gear**) quarta.

four-wheel drive ['fɔ:wi:l-] *n* (*AUT*): **with ~** con quattro ruote motrici.

fowl [faul] *n* pollame *m*; volatile *m*.

fox [fɔks] *n* volpe *f* ♦ *vt* confondere.
fox fur *n* volpe *f*, pelliccia di volpe.
foxglove ['fɔksglʌv] *n* (*BOT*) digitale *f*.
fox-hunting ['fɔkshʌntɪŋ] *n* caccia alla volpe.
foyer ['fɔɪeɪ] *n* atrio; (*THEATRE*) ridotto.
FP *n abbr* (*Brit*) = *former pupil*; (*US*) = **fire-plug.**
FPA *n abbr* (*Brit*: = *Family Planning Association*) ≈ A.I.E.D. *f* (= *Associazione Italiana Educazione Demografica*).
Fr. *abbr* (*REL*) = **father; friar.**
fr. *abbr* (= *franc*) fr.
fracas ['fræka:] *n* rissa, lite *f*.
fraction ['frækʃən] *n* frazione *f*.
fractionally ['frækʃnəlɪ] *ad* un tantino, minimamente.
fractious ['frækʃəs] *a* irritabile.
fracture ['fræktʃə*] *n* frattura ♦ *vt* fratturare.
fragile ['frædʒaɪl] *a* fragile.
fragment ['frægmənt] *n* frammento.
fragmentary ['frægməntərɪ] *a* frammentario(a).
fragrance ['freɪgrəns] *n* fragranza, profumo.
fragrant ['freɪgrənt] *a* fragrante, profumato(a).
frail [freɪl] *a* debole, delicato(a).
frame [freɪm] *n* (*of building*) armatura; (*of human, animal*) ossatura, corpo; (*of picture*) cornice *f*; (*of door, window*) telaio; (*of spectacles*: *also*: ~**s**) montatura ♦ *vt* (*picture*) incorniciare; **to ~ sb** (*col*) incastrare qn; **~ of mind** stato d'animo.
framework ['freɪmwə:k] *n* struttura.
France [frɑ:ns] *n* Francia.
franchise ['fræntʃaɪz] *n* (*POL*) diritto di voto; (*COMM*) concessione *f*.
franchisee [fræntʃaɪ'zi:] *n* concessionaria.
franchiser ['fræntʃaɪzə*] *n* concedente *m*.
frank [fræŋk] *a* franco(a), aperto(a) ♦ *vt* (*letter*) affrancare.
Frankfurt ['fræŋkfə:t] *n* Francoforte *f*.
frankfurter ['fræŋkfə:tə*] *n* würstel *m inv*.
franking machine ['fræŋkɪŋ-] *n* macchina affrancatrice.
frankly ['fræŋklɪ] *ad* francamente, sinceramente.
frankness ['fræŋknɪs] *n* franchezza.
frantic ['fræntɪk] *a* (*activity, pace*) frenetico(a); (*desperate: need, desire*) pazzo(a), sfrenato(a); (: *search*) affannoso(a); (*person*) fuori di sé.
frantically ['fræntɪklɪ] *ad* freneticamente; affannosamente.
fraternal [frə'tə:nl] *a* fraterno(a).
fraternity [frə'tə:nɪtɪ] *n* (*club*) associazione *f*; (*spirit*) fratellanza.
fraternize ['frætənaɪz] *vi* fraternizzare.
fraud [frɔ:d] *n* truffa; (*LAW*) frode *f*; (*person*) impostore/a.
fraudulent ['frɔ:djulənt] *a* fraudolento(a).
fraught [frɔ:t] *a* (*tense*) teso(a); ~ **with** pieno(a) di, intriso(a) da.
fray [freɪ] *n* baruffa ♦ *vt* logorare ♦ *vi* logorarsi; **to return to the** ~ tornare nella mischia; **tempers were getting** ~**ed**

cominciavano ad innervosirsi; **her nerves were** ~**ed** aveva i nervi a pezzi.
FRB *n abbr* (*US*) = **Federal Reserve Board.**
FRCM *n abbr* (*Brit*) = *Fellow of the Royal College of Music.*
FRCO *n abbr* (*Brit*) = *Fellow of the Royal College of Organists.*
FRCP *n abbr* (*Brit*) = *Fellow of the Royal College of Physicians.*
FRCS *n abbr* (*Brit*) = *Fellow of the Royal College of Surgeons.*
freak [fri:k] *n* fenomeno, mostro; (*col: enthusiast*) fanatico/a ♦ *a* (*storm, conditions*) anormale; (*victory*) inatteso(a).
freak out *vi* (*col*) andare fuori di testa.
freakish ['fri:kɪʃ] *a* (*result, appearance*) strano(a), bizzarro(a); (*weather*) anormale.
freckle ['frɛkl] *n* lentiggine *f*.
free [fri:] *a* libero(a); (*gratis*) gratuito(a); (*liberal*) generoso(a) ♦ *vt* (*prisoner, jammed person*) liberare; (*jammed object*) districare; ~ (**of charge**) gratuitamente; **admission** ~ entrata libera; **to give sb a** ~ **hand** dare carta bianca a qn; ~ **and easy** rilassato.
freebie ['fri:bɪ] *n* (*col*): **it's a** ~ è in omaggio.
freedom ['fri:dəm] *n* libertà.
freedom fighter *n* combattente *m/f* per la libertà.
free enterprise *n* liberalismo economico.
free-for-all ['fri:fərɔ:l] *n* parapiglia *m* generale.
free gift *n* regalo, omaggio.
freehold ['fri:həuld] *n* proprietà assoluta.
free kick *n* (*SPORT*) calcio libero.
freelance ['fri:lɑ:ns] *a* indipendente; ~ **work** collaborazione *f* esterna.
freeloader ['fri:ləudə*] *n* (*pej*) scroccone/a.
freely ['fri:lɪ] *ad* liberamente; (*liberally*) liberalmente.
freemason ['fri:meɪsn] *n* massone *m*.
freemasonry ['fri:meɪsnrɪ] *n* massoneria.
freepost ['fri:pəust] *n* affrancatura a carica del destinatario.
free-range ['fri:'reɪndʒ] *a* (*eggs*) di gallina ruspante.
free sample *n* campione *m* gratuito.
free speech *n* libertà di parola.
freestyle ['fri:staɪl] *n* (*in swimming*) stile *m* libero.
free trade *n* libero scambio.
freeway ['fri:weɪ] *n* (*US*) superstrada.
freewheel [fri:'wi:l] *vi* andare a ruota libera.
freewheeling [fri:'wi:lɪŋ] *a* a ruota libera.
free will *n* libero arbitrio; **of one's own** ~ di spontanea volontà.
freeze [fri:z] *vb* (*pt* **froze,** *pp* **frozen** [frəuz, 'frəuzn]) *vi* gelare ♦ *vt* gelare; (*food*) congelare; (*prices, salaries*) bloccare ♦ *n* gelo; blocco.
freeze over *vi* (*lake, river*) ghiacciarsi; (*windows, windscreen*) coprirsi di ghiaccio.
freeze up *vi* gelarsi.
freeze-dried ['fri:zdraɪd] *a* liofilizzato(a).
freezer ['fri:zə*] *n* congelatore *m*.

freezing ['fri:zɪŋ] *a*: **I'm ~** mi sto congelando ♦ *n* (*also*: **~ point**) punto di congelamento; **3 degrees below ~** 3 gradi sotto zero.

freight [freɪt] *n* (*goods*) merce *f*, merci *fpl*; (*money charged*) spese *fpl* di trasporto; **~ forward** spese a carico del destinatario; **~ inward** spese di trasporto sulla merce in entrata.

freight car *n* (*US*) carro *m* merci *inv*.

freighter ['freɪtə*] *n* (*NAUT*) nave *f* da carico.

freight forwarder [-'fɔ:wədə*] *n* spedizioniere *m*.

freight train *n* (*US*) treno *m* merci *inv*.

French [frɛntʃ] *a* francese ♦ *n* (*LING*) francese *m*; **the ~** *npl* i Francesi.

French bean *n* fagiolino.

French Canadian *a*, *n* franco-canadese (*m/f*).

French dressing *n* (*CULIN*) condimento per insalata.

French fried potatoes, (*US*) **French fries** *npl* patate *fpl* fritte.

French Guiana [-gaɪ'ænə] *n* Guiana francese.

Frenchman ['frɛntʃmən] *n* francese *m*.

French Riviera *n*: **the ~** la Costa Azzurra.

French window *n* portafinestra.

Frenchwoman ['frɛntʃwumən] *n* francese *f*.

frenetic [frə'nɛtɪk] *a* frenetico(a).

frenzy ['frɛnzɪ] *n* frenesia.

frequency ['fri:kwənsɪ] *n* frequenza.

frequency modulation (FM) *n* modulazione *f* di frequenza (F.M.).

frequent *a* ['fri:kwənt] frequente ♦ *vt* [frɪ'kwɛnt] frequentare.

frequently ['fri:kwəntlɪ] *ad* frequentemente, spesso.

fresco ['frɛskəu] *n* affresco.

fresh [frɛʃ] *a* fresco(a); (*new*) nuovo(a); (*cheeky*) sfacciato(a); **to make a ~ start** cominciare da capo.

freshen ['frɛʃən] *vi* (*wind, air*) rinfrescare. **freshen up** *vi* rinfrescarsi.

freshener ['frɛʃnə*] *n*: **skin ~** tonico rinfrescante; **air ~** deodorante *m* per ambienti.

fresher ['frɛʃə*] *n* (*Brit SCOL: col*) = **freshman**.

freshly ['frɛʃlɪ] *ad* di recente, di fresco.

freshman ['frɛʃmən] *n* (*SCOL*) matricola.

freshness ['frɛʃnɪs] *n* freschezza.

freshwater ['frɛʃwɔ:tə*] *a* (*fish*) d'acqua dolce.

fret [frɛt] *vi* agitarsi, affliggersi.

fretful ['frɛtful] *a* (*child*) irritabile.

Freudian ['frɔɪdɪən] *a* freudiano(a); **~ slip** lapsus *m inv* freudiano.

FRG *n abbr see* **Federal Republic of Germany.**

Fri. *abbr* (= *Friday*) ven.

friar ['fraɪə*] *n* frate *m*.

friction ['frɪkʃən] *n* frizione *f*, attrito.

friction feed *n* (*on printer*) trascinamento ad attrito.

Friday ['fraɪdɪ] *n* venerdì *m inv*; *for phrases see also* **Tuesday.**

fridge [frɪdʒ] *n* (*Brit*) frigo, frigorifero.

fried [fraɪd] *pt, pp of* **fry** ♦ *a* fritto(a); **~ egg** uovo fritto.

friend [frɛnd] *n* amico/a; **to make ~s with** fare amicizia con.

friendliness ['frɛndlɪnɪs] *n* amichevolezza.

friendly ['frɛndlɪ] *a* amichevole ♦ *n* (*also*: **~ match**) partita amichevole; **to be ~ with** essere amico di; **to be ~ to** essere cordiale con.

friendly society *n* società *f inv* di mutuo soccorso.

friendship ['frɛndʃɪp] *n* amicizia.

frieze [fri:z] *n* fregio.

frigate ['frɪgɪt] *n* (*NAUT: modern*) fregata.

fright [fraɪt] *n* paura, spavento; **to take ~** spaventarsi; **she looks a ~!** guarda com'è conciata!

frighten ['fraɪtn] *vt* spaventare, far paura a. **frighten away, frighten off** *vt* (*birds, children etc*) scacciare (facendogli paura).

frightened ['fraɪtnd] *a*: **to be ~ (of)** avere paura (di).

frightening ['fraɪtnɪŋ] *a* spaventoso(a), pauroso(a).

frightful ['fraɪtful] *a* orribile.

frightfully ['fraɪtfulɪ] *ad* terribilmente; **I'm ~ sorry** mi dispiace moltissimo.

frigid ['frɪdʒɪd] *a* (*woman*) frigido(a).

frigidity [frɪ'dʒɪdɪtɪ] *n* frigidità.

frill [frɪl] *n* balza; **without ~s** (*fig*) senza fronzoli.

fringe [frɪndʒ] *n* frangia; (*edge: of forest etc*) margine *m*; (*fig*): **on the ~** al margine.

fringe benefits *npl* vantaggi *mpl*.

fringe theatre *n* teatro d'avanguardia.

frisk [frɪsk] *vt* perquisire.

frisky ['frɪskɪ] *a* vivace, vispo(a).

fritter ['frɪtə*] *n* frittella. **fritter away** *vt* sprecare.

frivolity [frɪ'vɔlɪtɪ] *n* frivolezza.

frivolous ['frɪvələs] *a* frivolo(a).

frizzy ['frɪzɪ] *a* crespo(a).

fro [frəu] *ad*: **to and ~** avanti e indietro.

frock [frɔk] *n* vestito.

frog [frɔg] *n* rana; **to have a ~ in one's throat** avere la voce rauca.

frogman ['frɔgmən] *n* uomo *m* rana *inv*.

frogmarch ['frɔgmɑ:tʃ] *vt* (*Brit*): **to ~ sb in/ out** portar qn dentro/fuori con la forza.

frolic ['frɔlɪk] *vi* sgambettare.

from [frɔm] *prep* da; **~ a pound/January** da una sterlina in su/gennaio in poi; **(as) ~ Friday** da *or* a partire da venerdì; **~ what he says** a quanto dice; **where is he ~?** da dove viene?, di dov'è?; **where has he come ~?** da dove arriva?; **a telephone call ~ Mr. Smith** una telefonata dal Signor Smith; **prices range ~ £10 to £50** i prezzi vanno dalle 10 alle 50 sterline.

frond [frɔnd] *n* fronda.

front [frʌnt] *n* (*of house, dress*) davanti *m inv*; (*of train*) testa; (*of book*) copertina; (*promenade: also*: **sea ~**) lungomare *m*; (*MIL, POL, METEOR*) fronte *m*; (*fig*:

appearances) fronte *f* ♦ *a* primo(a); anteriore, davanti *inv* ♦ *vi*: **to ~ onto sth** dare su qc, guardare verso qc; **in ~ (of)** davanti (a).

frontage ['frʌntɪdʒ] *n* facciata.

frontal ['frʌntl] *a* frontale.

front bench *n* (*Brit POL*) banco dei ministri dell'opposizione.

front desk *n* (*US: in hotel*) reception *f inv*; (: *at doctor's*) accettazione *f*.

front door *n* porta d'entrata; (*of car*) sportello anteriore.

frontier ['frʌntɪə*] *n* frontiera.

frontispiece ['frʌntɪspiːs] *n* frontespizio.

front page *n* prima pagina.

front room *n* (*Brit*) salotto.

front runner *n* (*fig*) favorito/a.

front-wheel drive ['frʌntwiːl-] *n* trasmissione *f* anteriore.

frost [frɔst] *n* gelo; (*also:* **hoar~**) brina.

frostbite ['frɔstbaɪt] *n* congelamento.

frosted ['frɔstɪd] *a* (*glass*) smerigliato(a); (*US: cake*) glassato(a).

frosting ['frɔstɪŋ] *n* (*US: on cake*) glassa.

frosty ['frɔstɪ] *a* (*window*) coperto(a) di ghiaccio; (*welcome*) gelido(a).

froth ['frɔθ] *n* spuma; schiuma.

frown [fraun] *n* cipiglio ♦ *vi* accigliarsi.

frown on *vt fus* (*fig*) disapprovare.

froze [frəuz] *pt of* **freeze**.

frozen ['frəuzn] *pp of* **freeze** ♦ *a* (*food*) congelato(a); (*COMM: assets*) bloccato(a).

FRS *n abbr* (*Brit*) = *Fellow of the Royal Society*; (*US: = Federal Reserve System*) sistema bancario degli Stati Uniti.

frugal ['fruːgəl] *a* frugale; (*person*) economo(a).

fruit [fruːt] *n* (*pl inv*) frutto; (*collectively*) frutta.

fruiterer ['fruːtərə*] *n* fruttivendolo; **at the ~'s (shop)** dal fruttivendolo.

fruitful ['fruːtful] *a* fruttuoso(a); (*plant*) fruttifero(a); (*soil*) fertile.

fruition [fruː'ɪʃən] *n*: **to come to ~** realizzarsi.

fruit juice *n* succo di frutta.

fruitless ['fruːtlɪs] *a* (*fig*) vano(a), inutile.

fruit machine *n* (*Brit*) macchina *f* mangiasoldi *inv*.

fruit salad *n* macedonia.

frump [frʌmp] *n*: **to feel a ~** sentirsi infagottato(a).

frustrate [frʌs'treɪt] *vt* frustrare.

frustrated [frʌs'treɪtɪd] *a* frustrato(a).

frustrating [frʌs'treɪtɪŋ] *a* (*job*) frustrante; (*day*) disastroso(a).

frustration [frʌs'treɪʃən] *n* frustrazione *f*.

fry, *pt, pp* **fried** [fraɪ, -d] *vt* friggere ♦ *npl*: **the small ~** i pesci piccoli.

frying pan ['fraɪɪŋ-] *n* padella.

FT *n abbr* (*Brit*: = *Financial Times*) giornale finanziario; **the ~ index** l'indice FT.

ft. *abbr* = **foot, feet**.

FTC *n abbr* (*US*) see **Federal Trade Commission**.

fuchsia ['fjuːʃə] *n* fucsia.

fuck [fʌk] *vt, vi* (*col!*) fottere (*!*); **~ off!** vaffanculo! (*!*).

fuddled ['fʌdld] *a* (*muddled*) confuso(a); (*col: tipsy*) brillo(a).

fuddy-duddy ['fʌdɪdʌdɪ] *n* (*pej*) parruccone *m*.

fudge [fʌdʒ] *n* (*CULIN*) specie di caramella a base di latte, burro e zucchero ♦ *vt* (*issue, problem*) evitare.

fuel [fjuəl] *n* (*for heating*) combustibile *m*; (*for propelling*) carburante *m* ♦ *vt* (*furnace etc*) alimentare; (*aircraft, ship etc*) rifornire di carburante.

fuel oil *n* nafta.

fuel pump *n* (*AUT*) pompa del carburante.

fuel tank *n* deposito *m* nafta *inv*; (*on vehicle*) serbatoio (della benzina).

fug [fʌg] *n* (*Brit*) aria viziata.

fugitive ['fjuːdʒɪtɪv] *n* fuggitivo/a, profugo/a; (*from prison*) evaso/a.

fulfil, (*US*) **fulfill** [ful'fɪl] *vt* (*function*) compiere; (*order*) eseguire; (*wish, desire*) soddisfare, appagare.

fulfilled [ful'fɪld] *a* (*person*) realizzato(a), soddisfatto(a).

fulfil(l)ment [ful'fɪlmənt] *n* (*of wishes*) soddisfazione *f*, appagamento.

full [ful] *a* pieno(a); (*details, skirt*) ampio(a); (*price*) intero(a) ♦ *ad*: **to know ~ well that** sapere benissimo che; **~ (up)** (*hotel etc*) al completo; **I'm ~ (up)** sono pieno; **a ~ two hours** due ore intere; **at ~ speed** a tutta velocità; **in ~** per intero; **to pay in ~** pagare tutto; **~ name** nome *m* e cognome *m*; **~ employment** piena occupazione; **~ fare** tariffa completa.

fullback ['fulbæk] *n* (*RUGBY, FOOTBALL*) terzino.

full-blooded ['ful'blʌdɪd] *a* (*vigorous: attack*) energico(a); (*virile: male*) virile.

full-cream ['ful'kriːm] *a*: **~ milk** (*Brit*) latte *m* intero.

full-grown ['ful'grəun] *a* maturo(a).

full-length ['ful'leŋθ] *a* (*portrait*) in piedi; (*film*) a lungometraggio.

full moon *n* luna piena.

full-scale ['fulskeɪl] *a* (*plan, model*) in grandezza naturale; (*search, retreat*) su vasta scala.

full-sized ['ful'saɪzd] *a* (*portrait etc*) a grandezza naturale.

full stop *n* punto.

full-time ['ful'taɪm] *a, ad* (*work*) a tempo pieno ♦ *n* (*SPORT*) fine *f* partita.

fully ['fulɪ] *ad* interamente, pienamente, completamente; (*at least*): **~ as big** almeno così grosso.

fully-fledged ['fulɪ'fledʒd] *a* (*bird*) adulto(a); (*fig: teacher, member etc*) a tutti gli effetti.

fulsome ['fulsəm] *a* (*pej: praise*) esagerato(a), eccessivo(a); (: *manner*) insincero.

fumble ['fʌmbl] *vi* brancolare, andare a

tentoni ♦ *vt* (*ball*) lasciarsi sfuggire.
fumble with *vt fus* trafficare.
fume [fju:m] *vi* essere furioso(a); ~**s** *npl* esalazioni *fpl*, vapori *mpl*.
fumigate ['fju:mɪɡeɪt] *vt* suffumicare.
fun [fʌn] *n* divertimento, spasso; **to have** ~ divertirsi; **for** ~ per scherzo; **it's not much** ~ non è molto divertente; **to make** ~ **of** prendersi gioco di.
function ['fʌŋkʃən] *n* funzione *f*; cerimonia, ricevimento ♦ *vi* funzionare; **to** ~ **as** fungere da, funzionare da.
functional ['fʌŋkʃənl] *a* funzionale.
function key *n* (*COMPUT*) tasto di funzioni.
fund [fʌnd] *n* fondo, cassa; (*source*) fondo; (*store*) riserva; ~**s** *npl* (*money*) fondi *mpl*.
fundamental [fʌndə'mɛntl] *a* fondamentale; ~**s** *npl* basi *fpl*.
fundamentalist [fʌndə'mɛntəlɪst] *n* fondamentalista *m/f*.
fundamentally [fʌndə'mɛntəlɪ] *ad* essenzialmente, fondamentalmente.
fund-raising ['fʌndreɪzɪŋ] *n* raccolta di fondi.
funeral ['fju:nərəl] *n* funerale *m*.
funeral director *n* impresario di pompe funebri.
funeral parlour *n* impresa di pompe funebri.
funeral service *n* ufficio funebre.
funereal [fju:'nɪərɪəl] *a* funereo(a), lugubre.
fun fair *n* luna park *m inv*.
fungus, *pl* **fungi** ['fʌŋɡəs, -ɡaɪ] *n* fungo; (*mould*) muffa.
funicular [fju:'nɪkjulə*] *a* (*also:* ~ **railway**) funicolare *f*.
funnel ['fʌnl] *n* imbuto; (*of ship*) ciminiera.
funnily ['fʌnɪlɪ] *ad* in modo divertente; (*oddly*) stranamente.
funny ['fʌnɪ] *a* divertente, buffo(a); (*strange*) strano(a), bizzarro(a).
funny bone *n* osso cubitale.
fur [fə:*] *n* pelo; pelliccia; pelle *f*; (*Brit: in kettle etc*) deposito calcare.
fur coat *n* pelliccia.
furious ['fjuərɪəs] *a* furioso(a); (*effort*) accanito(a); (*argument*) violento(a).
furiously ['fjuərɪəslɪ] *ad* furiosamente, accanitamente.
furl [fə:l] *vt* (*sail*) piegare.
furlong ['fə:lɔŋ] *n* = 201.17 m (*termine ippico*).
furlough ['fə:ləu] *n* (*US*) congedo, permesso.
furnace ['fə:nɪs] *n* fornace *f*.
furnish ['fə:nɪʃ] *vt* ammobiliare; (*supply*) fornire; ~**ed flat** *or* (*US*) **apartment** appartamento ammobiliato.
furnishings ['fə:nɪʃɪŋz] *npl* mobili *mpl*, mobilia.
furniture ['fə:nɪtʃə*] *n* mobili *mpl*; **piece of** ~ mobile *m*.
furore [fjuə'rɔ:rɪ] *n* (*protests*) scalpore *m*; (*enthusiasm*) entusiasmo.
furrier ['fʌrɪə*] *n* pellicciaio/a.
furrow ['fʌrəu] *n* solco ♦ *vt* (*forehead*) segnare di rughe.
furry ['fə:rɪ] *a* (*animal*) peloso(a); (*toy*) di peluche.

further ['fə:ðə*] *a* supplementare, altro(a); nuovo(a); più lontano(a) ♦ *ad* più lontano; (*more*) di più; (*moreover*) inoltre ♦ *vt* favorire, promuovere; **until** ~ **notice** fino a nuovo avviso; **how much** ~ **is it?** quanto manca *or* dista?; ~ **to your letter of ...** (*COMM*) con riferimento alla vostra lettera del ...; **to** ~ **one's interests** fare i propri interessi.
further education *n* istruzione *f* superiore.
furthermore [fə:ðə'mɔ:*] *ad* inoltre, per di più.
furthermost ['fə:ðəməust] *a* più lontano(a).
furthest ['fə:ðɪst] *superlative of* **far**.
furtive ['fə:tɪv] *a* furtivo(a).
furtively ['fə:tɪvlɪ] *ad* furtivamente.
fury ['fjuərɪ] *n* furore *m*.
fuse, (*US*) **fuze** [fju:z] *n* fusibile *m*; (*for bomb etc*) miccia, spoletta ♦ *vt* fondere; (*ELEC*): **to** ~ **the lights** far saltare i fusibili ♦ *vi* fondersi; **a** ~ **has blown** è saltato un fusibile.
fuse box *n* cassetta dei fusibili.
fuselage ['fju:zəlɑ:ʒ] *n* fusoliera.
fuse wire *n* filo (di fusibile).
fusillade [fju:zɪ'leɪd] *n* scarica di fucileria; (*fig*) fuoco di fila, serie *f inv* incalzante.
fusion ['fju:ʒən] *n* fusione *f*.
fuss [fʌs] *n* chiasso, trambusto, confusione *f*; (*complaining*) storie *fpl* ♦ *vt* (*person*) infastidire, scocciare ♦ *vi* agitarsi; **to make a** ~ fare delle storie; **to make a** ~ **of sb** coprire qn di attenzioni.
fuss over *vt fus* (*person*) circondare di premure.
fussy ['fʌsɪ] *a* (*person*) puntiglioso(a), esigente; che fa le storie; (*dress*) carico(a) di fronzoli; (*style*) elaborato(a); **I'm not** ~ (*col*) per me è lo stesso.
futile ['fju:taɪl] *a* futile.
futility [fju:'tɪlɪtɪ] *n* futilità *f*.
future ['fju:tʃə*] *a* futuro(a) ♦ *n* futuro, avvenire *m*; (*LING*) futuro; **in** ~ in futuro; **in the near** ~ in un prossimo futuro; **in the immediate** ~ nell'immediato futuro.
futures ['fju:tʃəz] *npl* (*COMM*) operazioni *fpl* a termine.
futuristic [fju:tʃə'rɪstɪk] *a* futuristico(a).
fuze [fju:z] *n*, *vt*, *vi* (*US*) = **fuse**.
fuzzy ['fʌzɪ] *a* (*PHOT*) indistinto(a), sfocato(a); (*hair*) crespo(a).
fwd. *abbr* = **forward**.
fwy *abbr* (*US*) = **freeway**.
FY *abbr* = **fiscal year**.
FYI *abbr* = *for your information*.

G

G, g [dʒi:] n (letter) G, g f or m inv; (MUS): **G** sol m; **G for George** ≈ G come Genova.

G n abbr (Brit SCOL: mark: = good) ≈ buono; (US CINEMA: = general audience) per tutti.

g abbr (= gram; gravity) g.

GA abbr (US POST) = Georgia.

gab [gæb] n (col): **to have the gift of the ~** avere lo scilinguagnolo sciolto.

gabble ['gæbl] vi borbottare; farfugliare.

gaberdine [gæbə'di:n] n gabardine m inv.

gable ['geɪbl] n frontone m.

Gabon [gə'bɔn] n Gabon m.

gad about [gæd-] vi (col) svolazzare (qua e là).

gadget ['gædʒɪt] n aggeggio.

Gaelic ['geɪlɪk] a gaelico(a) ♦ n (language) gaelico.

gaffe [gæf] n gaffe f inv.

gag [gæg] n bavaglio; (joke) facezia, scherzo ♦ vt imbavagliare.

gaga ['gɑ:gɑ:] a: **to go ~** rimbambirsi.

gage [geɪdʒ] n, vt (US) = **gauge**.

gaiety ['geɪtɪ] n gaiezza.

gaily ['geɪlɪ] ad allegramente.

gain [geɪn] n guadagno, profitto ♦ vt guadagnare ♦ vi (watch) andare avanti; **to ~ in/by** aumentare di/con; **to ~ 3lbs (in weight)** aumentare di 3 libbre; **to ~ ground** guadagnare terreno.

gain (up)on vt fus accorciare le distanze da, riprendere.

gainful ['geɪnful] a profittevole, lucrativo(a).

gainsay [geɪn'seɪ] vt irg (like **say**) contraddire; negare.

gait [geɪt] n andatura.

gal. abbr = **gallon**.

gala ['gɑ:lə] n gala; **swimming ~** manifestazione f di nuoto.

Galapagos Islands [gə'læpəgəs-] npl: **the ~** le isole Galapagos.

galaxy ['gæləksɪ] n galassia.

gale [geɪl] n vento forte; burrasca; **~ force 10** vento forza 10.

gall [gɔ:l] n (ANAT) bile f; (fig: impudence) fegato, faccia ♦ vt urtare (i nervi a).

gall. abbr = **gallon**.

gallant ['gælənt] a valoroso(a); (towards ladies) galante, cortese.

gallantry ['gæləntrɪ] n valore m militare; galanteria, cortesia.

gall bladder ['gɔ:l-] n cistifellea.

galleon ['gælɪən] n galeone m.

gallery ['gælərɪ] n galleria; loggia; (for spectators) tribuna; (in theatre) loggione m,

balconata; (also: **art ~**: state-owned) museo; (: private) galleria.

galley ['gælɪ] n (ship's kitchen) cambusa; (ship) galea; (also: **~ proof**) bozza in colonna.

Gallic ['gælɪk] a gallico(a); (French) francese.

galling ['gɔ:lɪŋ] a irritante.

gallon ['gælən] n gallone m (Brit: = 4.543 l; 8 pints; US = 3.785 l).

gallop ['gæləp] n galoppo ♦ vi galoppare; **~ing inflation** inflazione f galoppante.

gallows ['gæləuz] n forca.

gallstone ['gɔ:lstəun] n calcolo biliare.

galore [gə'lɔ:*] ad a iosa, a profusione.

galvanize ['gælvənaɪz] vt galvanizzare; **to ~ sb into action** (fig) galvanizzare qn, spronare qn all'azione.

Gambia ['gæmbɪə] n Gambia m.

gambit ['gæmbɪt] n (fig): (opening) **~** prima mossa.

gamble ['gæmbl] n azzardo, rischio calcolato ♦ vt, vi giocare; **to ~ on** (fig) giocare su; **to ~ on the Stock Exchange** giocare in Borsa.

gambler ['gæmblə*] n giocatore/trice d'azzardo.

gambling ['gæmblɪŋ] n gioco d'azzardo.

gambol ['gæmbəl] vi saltellare.

game [geɪm] n gioco; (event) partita; (HUNTING) selvaggina ♦ a coraggioso(a); (ready): **to be ~ (for sth/to do)** essere pronto(a) (a qc/a fare); **~s** npl (SCOL) attività fpl sportive; **big ~** selvaggina grossa.

game bird n uccello selvatico.

gamekeeper ['geɪmki:pə*] n guardacaccia m inv.

gamely ['geɪmlɪ] ad coraggiosamente.

game reserve n riserva di caccia.

gamesmanship ['geɪmzmənʃɪp] n abilità.

gammon ['gæmən] n (bacon) quarto di maiale; (ham) prosciutto affumicato.

gamut ['gæmət] n gamma.

gang [gæŋ] n banda, squadra ♦ vi: **to ~ up on sb** far combutta contro qn.

Ganges ['gændʒi:z] n: **the ~** il Gange.

gangling ['gæŋglɪŋ] a allampanato(a).

gangplank ['gæŋplæŋk] n passerella.

gangrene ['gæŋgri:n] n cancrena.

gangster ['gæŋstə*] n gangster m inv.

gangway ['gæŋweɪ] n passerella; (Brit: of bus) passaggio.

gantry ['gæntrɪ] n (for crane, railway signal) cavalletto; (for rocket) torre f di lancio.

GAO n abbr (US: = General Accounting Office) ≈ Corte f dei Conti.

gaol [dʒeɪl] n, vt (Brit) = **jail**.

gap [gæp] n buco; (in time) intervallo; (fig) lacuna; vuoto.

gape [geɪp] vi restare a bocca aperta.

gaping ['geɪpɪŋ] a (hole) squarciato(a).

garage ['gærɑ:ʒ] n garage m inv.

garb [gɑ:b] n abiti mpl, veste f.

garbage ['gɑ:bɪdʒ] n immondizie fpl, rifiuti mpl; (fig: film, book) porcheria, robaccia; (: nonsense) fesserie fpl.

garbage can n (US) bidone m della spazzatura.
garbage disposal unit n tritarifiuti m inv.
garbled ['gɑːbld] a deformato(a); ingarbugliato(a).
garden ['gɑːdn] n giardino ♦ vi lavorare nel giardino; ~s npl (public) giardini pubblici; (private) parco.
garden centre n vivaio.
gardener ['gɑːdnə*] n giardiniere/a.
gardening ['gɑːdnɪŋ] n giardinaggio.
gargle ['gɑːgl] vi fare gargarismi ♦ n gargarismo.
gargoyle ['gɑːgɔɪl] n gargouille f inv.
garish ['gɛərɪʃ] a vistoso(a).
garland ['gɑːlənd] n ghirlanda; corona.
garlic ['gɑːlɪk] n aglio.
garment ['gɑːmənt] n indumento.
garner ['gɑːnə*] vt ammucchiare, raccogliere.
garnish ['gɑːnɪʃ] vt guarnire.
garret ['gærɪt] n soffitta.
garrison ['gærɪsn] n guarnigione f ♦ vt guarnire.
garrulous ['gærjuləs] a ciarliero(a), loquace.
garter ['gɑːtə*] n giarrettiera; (US: suspender) gancio (di reggicalze).
garter belt n (US) reggicalze m inv.
gas [gæs] n gas m inv; (used as anaesthetic) etere m; (US: gasoline) benzina ♦ vt asfissiare con il gas; (MIL) gasare.
gas cooker n (Brit) cucina a gas.
gas cylinder n bombola del gas.
gaseous ['gæsɪəs] a gassoso(a).
gas fire n (Brit) radiatore m a gas.
gash [gæʃ] n sfregio ♦ vt sfregiare.
gasket ['gæskɪt] n (AUT) guarnizione f.
gas mask n maschera f antigas inv.
gas meter n contatore m del gas.
gasoline ['gæsəliːn] n (US) benzina.
gasp [gɑːsp] vi ansare, boccheggiare; (in surprise) restare senza fiato.
gasp out vt dire affannosamente.
gas ring n fornello a gas.
gas station n (US) distributore m di benzina.
gas stove n cucina a gas.
gassy ['gæsɪ] a gassoso(a).
gas tank n (US AUT) serbatoio (di benzina).
gas tap n (on cooker) manopola del gas; (on pipe) rubinetto del gas.
gastric ['gæstrɪk] a gastrico(a).
gastric ulcer n ulcera gastrica.
gastroenteritis ['gæstrəuentə'raɪtɪs] n gastroenterite f.
gastronomy [gæs'trɔnəmɪ] n gastronomia.
gasworks ['gæswəːks] n or npl impianto di produzione del gas.
gate [geɪt] n cancello; (of castle, town) porta; (at airport) uscita; (at level crossing) barriera.
gateau, pl ~x ['gætəu, -z] n torta.
gatecrash ['geɪtkræʃ] vt partecipare senza invito a.
gatecrasher ['geɪtkræʃə*] n intruso(a), ospite m/f non invitato(a).

gateway ['geɪtweɪ] n porta.
gather ['gæðə*] vt (flowers, fruit) cogliere; (pick up) raccogliere; (assemble) radunare; raccogliere; (understand) capire ♦ vi (assemble) radunarsi; (dust) accumularsi; (clouds) addensarsi; **to ~ speed** acquistare velocità; **to ~ (from/that)** comprendere (da/che), dedurre (da/che); **as far as I can ~** da quel che ho potuto capire.
gathering ['gæðərɪŋ] n adunanza.
GATT [gæt] n abbr (= General Agreement on Tariffs and Trade) G.A.T.T. m.
gauche [gəuʃ] a goffo(a), maldestro(a).
gaudy ['gɔːdɪ] a vistoso(a).
gauge [geɪdʒ] n (standard measure) calibro; (RAIL) scartamento; (instrument) indicatore m ♦ vt misurare; (fig: sb's capabilities, character) valutare, stimare; **to ~ the right moment** calcolare il momento giusto; **petrol ~,** (US) **gas ~** indicatore m or spia della benzina.
gaunt [gɔːnt] a scarno(a); (grim, desolate) desolato(a).
gauntlet ['gɔːntlɪt] n (fig): **to run the ~ through an angry crowd** passare sotto il fuoco di una folla ostile; **to throw down the ~** gettare il guanto.
gauze [gɔːz] n garza.
gave [geɪv] pt of **give**.
gawky ['gɔːkɪ] a goffo(a), sgraziato(a).
gawp [gɔːp] vi: **to ~ at** guardare a bocca aperta.
gay [geɪ] a (person) gaio(a), allegro(a); (colour) vivace, vivo(a); (col) omosessuale.
gaze [geɪz] n sguardo fisso ♦ vi: **to ~ at** guardare fisso.
gazelle [gə'zɛl] n gazzella.
gazette [gə'zɛt] n (newspaper) gazzetta; (official publication) gazzetta ufficiale.
gazetteer [gæzə'tɪə*] n (book) dizionario dei nomi geografici; (section of book) indice m dei nomi geografici.
gazumping [gə'zʌmpɪŋ] n il fatto di non mantenere una promessa di vendita per accettare un prezzo più alto.
GB abbr (= Great Britain) GB.
GBH n abbr (Brit LAW: col) see **grievous bodily harm**.
GC n abbr (Brit: = George Gross) decorazione al valore.
GCE n abbr (Brit: = General Certificate of Education) ≈ diploma m di maturità.
GCHQ n abbr (Brit: = Government Communications Headquarters) centro per l'intercettazione delle telecomunicazioni straniere.
GCSE n abbr (Brit: = General Certificate of Secondary Education) diploma di istruzione secondaria conseguito a 16 anni in Inghilterra e Galles.
Gdns. abbr = gardens.
GDP n abbr = **gross domestic product**.
GDR n abbr see **German Democratic Republic**.

gear [gɪə*] n attrezzi mpl, equipaggiamento; (belongings) roba; (TECH) ingranaggio; (AUT) marcia ♦ vt (fig: adapt) adattare; **top** or (US) **high/low/bottom** ~ quarta (or quinta)/ seconda/prima; **in** ~ in marcia; **out of** ~ in folle; **our service is** ~**ed to meet the needs of the disabled** la nostra organizzazione risponde espressamente alle esigenze degli handicappati.

gear up vi: **to** ~ **up (to do)** prepararsi (a fare).

gear box n scatola del cambio.

gear lever, (US) **gear shift** n leva del cambio.

GED n abbr (US SCOL) = general educational development.

geese [giːs] npl of **goose**.

Geiger counter ['gaɪgə-] n geiger m inv.

gel [dʒɛl] n gel m inv.

gelatin(e) ['dʒɛləti:n] n gelatina.

gelignite ['dʒɛlɪgnaɪt] n nitroglicerina.

gem [dʒɛm] n gemma.

Gemini ['dʒɛmɪnaɪ] n Gemelli mpl; **to be** ~ essere dei Gemelli.

gen [dʒɛn] n (Brit col): **to give sb the** ~ **on sth** mettere qn al corrente di qc.

Gen. abbr (MIL: = General) Gen.

gen. abbr (= general, generally) gen.

gender ['dʒɛndə*] n genere m.

gene [dʒiːn] n (BIOL) gene m.

genealogy [dʒiːnɪ'ælədʒɪ] n genealogia.

general ['dʒɛnərl] n generale m ♦ a generale; **in** ~ in genere; **the** ~ **public** il grande pubblico.

general anaesthetic n anestesia totale.

general delivery n (US) fermo posta m.

general election n elezioni fpl generali.

generalization ['dʒɛnrəlaɪ'zeɪʃən] n generalizzazione f.

generalize ['dʒɛnrəlaɪz] vi generalizzare.

generally ['dʒɛnrəlɪ] ad generalmente.

general manager n direttore m generale.

general practitioner (GP) n medico generico; **who's your GP?** qual'è il suo medico di fiducia?

general strike n sciopero generale.

generate ['dʒɛnəreɪt] vt generare.

generation [dʒɛnə'reɪʃən] n generazione f; (of electricity etc) produzione f.

generator ['dʒɛnəreɪtə*] n generatore m.

generic [dʒɪ'nɛrɪk] a generico(a).

generosity [dʒɛnə'rɔsɪtɪ] n generosità.

generous ['dʒɛnərəs] a generoso(a); (copious) abbondante.

genesis ['dʒɛnɪsɪs] n genesi f.

genetic [dʒɪ'nɛtɪk] a genetico(a); ~ **engineering** selezione f genetica.

genetics [dʒɪ'nɛtɪks] n genetica.

Geneva [dʒɪ'niːvə] n Ginevra; **Lake** ~ il lago di Ginevra.

genial ['dʒiːnɪəl] a geniale, cordiale.

genitals ['dʒɛnɪtlz] npl genitali mpl.

genitive ['dʒɛnɪtɪv] n genitivo.

genius ['dʒiːnɪəs] n genio.

Genoa ['dʒɛnəuə] n Genova.

genocide ['dʒɛnəusaɪd] n genocidio.

Genoese [dʒɛnəu'iːz] a, n (pl inv) genovese (m/f).

gent [dʒɛnt] n abbr (Brit col) = **gentleman**.

genteel [dʒɛn'tiːl] a raffinato(a), distinto(a).

gentle ['dʒɛntl] a delicato(a); (person) dolce.

gentleman ['dʒɛntlmən] n signore m; (well-bred man) gentiluomo; ~**'s agreement** impegno sulla parola.

gentlemanly ['dʒɛntlmənlɪ] a da gentiluomo.

gentleness ['dʒɛntlnɪs] n delicatezza; dolcezza.

gently ['dʒɛntlɪ] ad delicatamente.

gentry ['dʒɛntrɪ] n nobiltà minore.

gents [dʒɛnts] n W.C. m (per signori).

genuine ['dʒɛnjuɪn] a autentico(a); sincero(a).

genuinely ['dʒɛnjuɪnlɪ] ad genuinamente.

geographer [dʒɪ'ɔgrəfə*] n geografo/a.

geographic(al) [dʒɪə'græfɪk(l)] a geografico(a).

geography [dʒɪ'ɔgrəfɪ] n geografia.

geological [dʒɪə'lɔdʒɪkl] a geologico(a).

geologist [dʒɪ'ɔlədʒɪst] n geologo/a.

geology [dʒɪ'ɔlədʒɪ] n geologia.

geometric(al) [dʒɪə'mɛtrɪk(l)] a geometrico(a).

geometry [dʒɪ'ɔmətrɪ] n geometria.

Geordie ['dʒɔːdɪ] n (col) abitante m/f del Tyneside; originario/a del Tyneside.

geranium [dʒɪ'reɪnɪəm] n geranio.

geriatric [dʒɛrɪ'ætrɪk] a geriatrico(a).

germ [dʒəːm] n (MED) microbo; (BIOL, fig) germe m.

German ['dʒəːmən] a tedesco(a) ♦ n tedesco/a; (LING) tedesco.

German Democratic Republic (GDR) n Repubblica Democratica Tedesca (R.D.T.).

German measles n rosolia.

Germany ['dʒəːmənɪ] n Germania.

germination [dʒəːmɪ'neɪʃən] n germinazione f.

germ warfare n guerra batteriologica.

gerrymandering ['dʒɛrɪmændərɪŋ] n manipolazione f dei distretti elettorali.

gestation [dʒɛs'teɪʃən] n gestazione f.

gesticulate [dʒɛs'tɪkjuleɪt] vi gesticolare.

gesture ['dʒɛstjə*] n gesto; **as a** ~ **of friendship** in segno d'amicizia.

get, pt, pp **got,** (US) pp **gotten** [gɛt, gɔt, 'gɔtn] vt (obtain) avere, ottenere; (receive) ricevere; (find) trovare; (buy) comprare; (catch) acchiappare; (fetch) andare a prendere; (take, move) portare; (understand) comprendere, capire; (have): **to have got** avere; (become): **to** ~ **rich/old** arricchirsi/invecchiare; (col: annoy): **he really** ~**s me** mi dà proprio sui nervi ♦ vi (go): **to** ~ **to** (place) andare a; arrivare a; pervenire a; (modal auxiliary vb): **you've got to do it** deve farlo; **he got across the bridge/under the fence** ha attraversato il ponte/è passato sotto il recinto; **to** ~ **sth for sb** prendere or procurare qc a qn; ~ **me Mr Jones, please** (TEL) mi passi il signor Jones, per favore; **can I ~ you a drink**? ti posso offrire da bere?; **to ~ ready/washed/shaved** *etc* prepararsi/lavarsi/farsi la barba *etc*; **to ~ sth done** (*do*) fare qc; (*have done*) far fare qc; **to ~ sth/sb ready** preparare qc/qn; **to ~ one's hair cut** farsi tagliare i capelli; **to ~ sb to do sth** far fare qc a qn; **to ~ sth through/out of** far passare qc per/uscire qc da; **let's ~ going** *or* **started!** muoviamoci!

get about *vi* muoversi; (*news*) diffondersi.

get across *vt*: **to ~ across (to)** (*message, meaning*) comunicare (a) ♦ *vi*: **to ~ across to** (*subj: speaker*) comunicare con.

get along *vi* (*depart*) andarsene; (*agree*) andare d'accordo; (*manage*) = **to get by**.

get at *vt fus* (*attack*) prendersela con; (*reach*) raggiungere, arrivare a; **what are you ~ting at?** dove vuoi arrivare?

get away *vi* partire, andarsene; (*escape*) scappare.

get away with *vt fus* cavarsela con; farla franca con; **he'll never ~ away with it!** non riuscirà a farla franca!

get back *vi* (*return*) ritornare, tornare ♦ *vt* riottenere, riavere; **to ~ back to** (*start again*) ritornare a; (*contact again*) rimettersi in contatto con.

get back at *vt fus* (*col*): **to ~ back at sb (for sth)** rendere pan per focaccia a qn (per qc).

get by *vi* (*pass*) passare; (*manage*) farcela; **I can ~ by in Dutch** mi arrangio in olandese.

get down *vi, vt fus* scendere ♦ *vt* far scendere; (*depress*) buttare giù.

get down to *vt fus* (*work*) mettersi a; **to ~ down to business** venire al dunque.

get in *vi* entrare; (*train*) arrivare; (*arrive home*) ritornare, tornare ♦ *vt* (*bring in: harvest*) raccogliere; (*: coal, shopping, supplies*) fare provvista di; (*insert*) far entrare, infilare.

get into *vt fus* entrare in; (*vehicle*) salire in, montare in; **to ~ into bed** mettersi a letto; **to ~ into a rage** incavolarsi.

get off *vi* (*from train etc*) scendere; (*depart: person, car*) andare via; (*escape*) cavarsela ♦ *vt* (*remove: clothes, stain*) levare; (*send off*) spedire; (*have as leave: day, time*): **we got 2 days off** abbiamo avuto 2 giorni liberi ♦ *vt fus* (*train, bus*) scendere da; **to ~ off to a good start** (*fig*) cominciare bene.

get on *vi* (*at exam etc*) andare; (*agree*): **to ~ on (with)** andare d'accordo (con) ♦ *vt fus* montare in; (*horse*) montare su; **how are you ~ting on?** come va (la vita)?

get on to *vt fus* (*Brit col: contact: on phone etc*) contattare, rintracciare; (*: deal with*) occuparsi di.

get out *vi* uscire; (*of vehicle*) scendere; (*news etc*) venirsi a sapere, spargersi ♦ *vt* tirar fuori, far uscire; **to ~ out (of)** (*money from bank etc*) ritirare (da).

get out of *vt fus* uscire da; (*duty etc*) evitare ♦ *vt* (*extract: confession, words*) tirare fuori di bocca a; (*gain from: pleasure, benefit*) trarre da.

get over *vt fus* (*illness*) riversi da; (*communicate: idea etc*) comunicare, passare; **let's ~ it over (with)** togliamoci il pensiero.

get round *vi*: **to ~ round to doing sth** trovare il tempo di fare qc ♦ *vt fus* aggirare; (*fig: person*) rigirare.

get through *vi* (*TEL*) avere la linea ♦ *vt fus* (*finish: work*) sbrigare; (*: book*) finire.

get through to *vt fus* (*TEL*) parlare a.

get together *vi* riunirsi ♦ *vt* raccogliere; (*people*) adunare.

get up *vi* (*rise*) alzarsi ♦ *vt fus* salire su per; **to ~ up enthusiasm for sth** entusiasmarsi per qc.

get up to *vt fus* (*reach*) raggiungere; (*Brit: prank etc*) fare.

getaway ['gɛtəweɪ] *n* fuga.

getaway car *n* macchina per la fuga.

get-together ['gɛtləgɛðə*] *n* (piccola) riunione *f*; (*party*) festicciola.

get-up ['gɛtʌp] *n* (*col: outfit*) tenuta.

get-well card [gɛt'wɛl-] *n* cartolina di auguri di pronta guarigione.

geyser ['giːzə*] *n* scaldabagno; (*GEO*) geyser *m inv*.

Ghana ['gɑːnə] *n* Ghana *m*.

Ghanaian [gɑː'neɪən] *a, n* ganaense (*m/f*).

ghastly ['gɑːstlɪ] *a* orribile, orrendo(a).

gherkin ['gəːkɪn] *n* cetriolino.

ghetto ['gɛtəu] *n* ghetto.

ghost [gəust] *n* fantasma *m*, spettro ♦ *vt* (*book*) fare lo scrittore ombra per.

ghostly ['gəustlɪ] *a* spettrale.

ghostwriter ['gəustraɪtə*] *n* scrittore/trice ombra *inv*.

ghoul [guːl] *n* vampiro che si nutre di cadaveri.

ghoulish ['guːlɪʃ] *a* (*tastes etc*) macabro(a).

GHQ *n abbr* (*MIL*: = *general headquarters*) ≈ comando di Stato maggiore.

GI *n abbr* (*US col*: = *government issue*) G.I. *m*, soldato americano.

giant ['dʒaɪənt] *n* gigante/essa ♦ *a* gigante, enorme; **~ (size) packet** confezione *f* gigante.

gibber ['dʒɪbə*] *vi* (*monkey*) squittire confusamente; (*idiot*) farfugliare.

gibberish ['dʒɪbərɪʃ] *n* parole *fpl* senza senso.

gibe [dʒaɪb] *n* frecciata ♦ *vi*: **to ~ at** lanciare frecciate a.

giblets ['dʒɪblɪts] *npl* frattaglie *fpl*.

Gibraltar [dʒɪ'brɔːltə*] *n* Gibilterra.

giddiness ['gɪdɪnɪs] *n* vertigine *f*.

giddy ['gɪdɪ] *a* (*dizzy*): **to be ~** aver le vertigini; (*height*) vertiginoso(a); **I feel ~** mi gira la testa.

gift [gɪft] *n* regalo; (*donation, ability*) dono; (*COMM*: *also*: **free ~**) omaggio; **to have a ~ for sth** (*talent*) avere il dono di qc.

gifted ['gɪftɪd] *a* dotato(a).

gift token, gift voucher *n* buono (acquisto).
gig [gɪg] *n* (*col: of musician*) serata.
gigantic [dʒaɪ'gæntɪk] *a* gigantesco(a).
giggle ['gɪgl] *vi* ridere scioccamente ♦ *n* risolino (sciocco).
GIGO ['gaɪgəu] *abbr* (*COMPUT: col:* = *garbage in, garbage out*) qualità di input = qualità di output.
gild [gɪld] *vt* dorare.
gill [dʒɪl] *n* (*measure*) = *0.25 pints* (*Brit= 0.148 l; US = 0.118 l*).
gills [gɪlz] *npl* (*of fish*) branchie *fpl*.
gilt [gɪlt] *n* doratura ♦ *a* dorato(a).
gilt-edged ['gɪltedʒd] *a* (*stocks, securities*) della massima sicurezza.
gimlet ['gɪmlɪt] *n* succhiello.
gimmick ['gɪmɪk] *n* trucco; **sales** ~ trovata commerciale.
gin [dʒɪn] *n* (*liquor*) gin *m inv.*
ginger ['dʒɪndʒə*] *n* zenzero.
ginger up *vt* scuotere; animare.
ginger ale, ginger beer *n* bibita gassosa allo zenzero.
gingerbread ['dʒɪndʒəbrɛd] *n* pan *m* di zenzero.
ginger group *n* (*Brit*) gruppo di pressione.
ginger-haired ['dʒɪndʒə'hɛəd] *a* rossiccio(a).
gingerly ['dʒɪndʒəlɪ] *ad* cautamente.
gingham ['gɪŋəm] *n* percalle *m* a righe (*or* quadretti).
gipsy ['dʒɪpsɪ] *n* zingaro/a ♦ *a* degli zingari.
giraffe [dʒɪ'rɑːf] *n* giraffa.
girder ['gəːdə*] *n* trave *f*.
girdle ['gəːdl] *n* (*corset*) guaina.
girl [gəːl] *n* ragazza; (*young unmarried woman*) signorina; (*daughter*) figlia, figliola; **a little** ~ una bambina.
girlfriend ['gəːlfrɛnd] *n* (*of girl*) amica; (*of boy*) ragazza.
girlish ['gəːlɪʃ] *a* da ragazza.
Girl Scout *n* (*US*) Giovane Esploratrice *f*.
Giro ['dʒaɪrəu] *n*: **the National** ~ (*Brit*) ≈ la *or* il Bancoposta.
giro ['dʒaɪrəu] *n* (*bank* ~) versamento bancario; (*post office* ~) postagiro.
girth [gəːθ] *n* circonferenza; (*of horse*) cinghia.
gist [dʒɪst] *n* succo.
give [gɪv] *n* (*of fabric*) elasticità ♦ *vb* (*pt* **gave**, *pp* **given** [geɪv, 'gɪvn]) *vt* dare ♦ *vi* cedere; **to** ~ **sb sth,** ~ **sth to sb** dare qc a qn; **to** ~ **a cry/sigh** emettere un grido/ sospiro; **how much did you** ~ **for it?** quanto (l')hai pagato?; **12 o'clock,** ~ **or take a few minutes** mezzogiorno, minuto più minuto meno; **to** ~ **way** *vi* cedere; (*Brit AUT*) dare la precedenza.
give away *vt* dare via; (*give free*) fare dono di; (*betray*) tradire; (*disclose*) rivelare; (*bride*) condurre all'altare.
give back *vt* rendere.
give in *vi* cedere ♦ *vt* consegnare.
give off *vt* emettere.
give out *vt* distribuire; annunciare ♦ *vi* (*be*

exhausted: supplies) esaurirsi, venir meno; (*fail: engine*) fermarsi; (: *strength*) mancare.
give up *vi* rinunciare ♦ *vt* rinunciare a; **to** ~ **up smoking** smettere di fumare; **to** ~ **o.s. up** arrendersi.
give-and-take [gɪvən'teɪk] *n* (*col*) elasticità (da ambo le parti), concessioni *fpl* reciproche.
giveaway ['gɪvəweɪ] *n* (*col*): **her expression was a** ~ le si leggeva tutto in volto; **the exam was a** ~! l'esame è stato uno scherzo! ♦ *cpd*: ~ **prices** prezzi stracciati.
given ['gɪvn] *pp of* **give** ♦ *a* (*fixed: time, amount*) dato(a), determinato(a) ♦ *cj*: ~ **(that)** ... dato che ...; ~ **the circumstances** ... date le circostanze ....
glacial ['gleɪsɪəl] *a* glaciale.
glacier ['glæsɪə*] *n* ghiacciaio.
glad [glæd] *a* lieto(a), contento(a); **to be** ~ **about sth/that** essere contento *or* lieto di qc/ che + *sub*; **I was** ~ **of his help** gli sono stato grato del suo aiuto.
gladden ['glædn] *vt* rallegrare, allietare.
glade [gleɪd] *n* radura.
gladioli [glædɪ'əulaɪ] *npl* gladioli *mpl*.
gladly ['glædlɪ] *ad* volentieri.
glamorous ['glæmərəs] *a* (*gen*) favoloso(a); (*person*) affascinante, seducente; (*occasion*) brillante, elegante.
glamour ['glæmə*] *n* fascino.
glance [glɑːns] *n* occhiata, sguardo ♦ *vi*: **to** ~ **at** dare un'occhiata a.
glance off *vt fus* (*bullet*) rimbalzare su.
glancing ['glɑːnsɪŋ] *a* (*blow*) che colpisce di striscio.
gland [glænd] *n* ghiandola.
glandular ['glændjulə*] *a*: ~ **fever** (*Brit*) mononucleosi *f*.
glare [glɛə*] *n* riverbero, luce *f* abbagliante; (*look*) sguardo furioso ♦ *vi* abbagliare; **to** ~ **at** guardare male.
glaring ['glɛərɪŋ] *a* (*mistake*) madornale.
glass [glɑːs] *n* (*substance*) vetro; (*tumbler*) bicchiere *m*; (*also:* **looking** ~) specchio; *see also* **glasses**.
glass-blowing ['glɑːsbləuɪŋ] *n* soffiatura del vetro.
glasses ['glɑːsɪz] *npl* (*spectacles*) occhiali *mpl*.
glass fibre *n* fibra di vetro.
glasshouse ['glɑːshaus] *n* serra.
glassware ['glɑːswɛə*] *n* vetrame *m*.
glassy ['glɑːsɪ] *a* (*eyes*) vitreo(a).
Glaswegian [glæs'wiːdʒən] *a* di Glasgow ♦ *n* abitante *m/f* di Glasgow; originario/a di Glasgow.
glaze [gleɪz] *vt* (*door*) fornire di vetri; (*pottery*) smaltare; (*CULIN*) glassare ♦ *n* smalto; glassa.
glazed ['gleɪzd] *a* (*eye*) vitreo(a); (*tiles, pottery*) smaltato(a).
glazier ['gleɪzɪə*] *n* vetraio.
GLC *n abbr* (*Brit: old:* = *Greater London Council*) consiglio municipale di *Londra* e

sobborghi.

gleam [gli:m] *n* barlume *m*; raggio ♦ *vi* luccicare; **a ~ of hope** un barlume di speranza.

gleaming ['gli:mɪŋ] *a* lucente.

glean [gli:n] *vt* (*information*) racimolare.

glee [gli:] *n* allegrezza, gioia.

gleeful ['gli:ful] *a* allegro(a), gioioso(a).

glen [glɛn] *n* valletta.

glib [glɪb] *a* dalla parola facile; facile.

glide [glaɪd] *vi* scivolare; (*AVIAT, birds*) planare ♦ *n* scivolata; planata.

glider ['glaɪdə*] *n* (*AVIAT*) aliante *m*.

gliding ['glaɪdɪŋ] *n* (*AVIAT*) volo a vela.

glimmer ['glɪmə*] *vi* luccicare ♦ *n* barlume *m*.

glimpse [glɪmps] *n* impressione *f* fugace ♦ *vt* vedere di sfuggita; **to catch a ~ of** vedere di sfuggita.

glint [glɪnt] *n* luccichio ♦ *vi* luccicare.

glisten ['glɪsn] *vi* luccicare.

glitter ['glɪtə*] *vi* scintillare ♦ *n* scintillio.

glitz [glɪts] *n* (*col*) vistosità, chiassosità.

gloat [gləʊt] *vi:* **to ~ (over)** gongolare di piacere (per).

global ['gləʊbl] *a* globale; (*world-wide*) mondiale.

globe [gləʊb] *n* globo, sfera.

globetrotter ['gləʊbtrɔtə*] *n* giramondo *m/f inv.*

globule ['glɔbju:l] *n* (*ANAT*) globulo; (*of water etc*) gocciolina.

gloom [glu:m] *n* oscurità, buio; (*sadness*) tristezza, malinconia.

gloomy ['glu:mi] *a* fosco(a), triste; **to feel ~** sentirsi giù *or* depresso.

glorification [glɔ:rɪfɪ'keɪʃən] *n* glorificazione *f.*

glorify ['glɔ:rɪfaɪ] *vt* glorificare; celebrare, esaltare.

glorious ['glɔ:rɪəs] *a* glorioso(a); magnifico(a).

glory ['glɔ:rɪ] *n* gloria; splendore *m* ♦ *vi:* **to ~ in** gloriarsi di *or* in.

glory hole *n* (*col*) ripostiglio.

Glos *abbr* (*Brit*) = *Gloucestershire.*

gloss [glɔs] *n* (*shine*) lucentezza; (*also:* ~ **paint**) vernice *f* a olio.

gloss over *vt fus* scivolare su.

glossary ['glɔsərɪ] *n* glossario.

glossy ['glɔsɪ] *a* lucente ♦ *n* (*also:* ~ **magazine**) rivista di lusso.

glove [glʌv] *n* guanto.

glove compartment *n* (*AUT*) vano portaoggetti.

glow [gləʊ] *vi* ardere; (*face*) essere luminoso(a) ♦ *n* bagliore *m*; (*of face*) colorito acceso.

glower ['glaʊə*] *vi:* **to ~ (at sb)** guardare (qn) in cagnesco.

glowing ['gləʊɪŋ] *a* (*fire*) ardente; (*complexion*) luminoso(a); (*fig: report, description etc*) entusiasta.

glow-worm ['gləʊwə:m] *n* lucciola.

glucose ['glu:kəʊs] *n* glucosio.

glue [glu:] *n* colla ♦ *vt* incollare.

glue-sniffing ['glu:snɪfɪŋ] *n* sniffare *m* (colla).

glum [glʌm] *a* abbattuto(a).

glut [glʌt] *n* eccesso ♦ *vt* saziare; (*market*) saturare.

glutinous ['glu:tɪnəs] *a* colloso(a), appiccicoso(a).

glutton ['glʌtn] *n* ghiottone/a; **a ~ for work** un(a) patito(a) del lavoro.

gluttonous ['glʌtənəs] *a* ghiotto(a), goloso(a).

gluttony ['glʌtənɪ] *n* ghiottoneria; (*sin*) gola.

glycerin(e) ['glɪsəri:n] *n* glicerina.

gm *abbr* = **gram.**

GMAT *n abbr* (*US:* = *Graduate Management Admissions Test*) *esame di ammissione all'ultimo biennio di scuola superiore.*

GMT *abbr* (= *Greenwich Mean Time*) T.M.G.

GMWU *n abbr* (*Brit:* = *General and Municipal Workers' Union*) *sindacato degli operai non specializzati e comunali.*

gnarled [nɑ:ld] *a* nodoso(a).

gnash [næʃ] *vt:* **to ~ one's teeth** digrignare i denti.

gnat [næt] *n* moscerino.

gnaw [nɔ:] *vt* rodere.

gnome [nəʊm] *n* gnomo.

GNP *n abbr* = **gross national product.**

go [gəʊ] *vb* (*pt* **went,** *pp* **gone** [wɛnt, gɔn]) *vi* andare; (*depart*) partire, andarsene; (*work*) funzionare; (*break etc*) cedere; (*be sold*): **to ~ for £10** essere venduto per 10 sterline; (*fit, suit*): **to ~ with** andare bene con; (*become*): **to ~ pale** diventare pallido(a); **to ~ mouldy** ammuffire ♦ *n* (*pl* ~**es**): **to have a ~ (at)** provare; **to be on the ~** essere in moto; **whose ~ is it?** a chi tocca?; **to ~ by car/on foot** andare in macchina/a piedi; **he's ~ing to do** sta per fare; **to ~ for a walk** andare a fare una passeggiata; **to ~ dancing/shopping** andare a ballare/fare la spesa; **to ~ looking for sb/sth** andare in cerca di qn/qc; **to ~ to sleep** addormentarsi; **to ~ and see sb, to ~ to see sb** andare a trovare qn; **how is it ~ing?** come va (la vita)?; **how did it ~?** com'è andato?; **to ~ round the back/by the shop** passare da dietro/davanti al negozio; **my voice has gone** m'è andata via la voce; **the cake is all gone** il dolce è finito tutto; **I'll take whatever is ~ing** (*Brit*) prendo quello che c'è; **... to ~** (*US: food*) ... da portar via; **the money will ~ towards our holiday** questi soldi li mettiamo per la vacanza.

go about *vi* (*also:* ~ **around**) aggirarsi; (*rumour*) correre, circolare ♦ *vt fus:* **how do I ~ about this?** qual'è la prassi per questo?; **to ~ about one's business** occuparsi delle proprie faccende.

go after *vt fus* (*pursue*) correr dietro a, rincorrere; (*job, record etc*) mirare a.

go against *vt fus* (*be unfavourable to*) essere contro; (*be contrary to*) andare contro.

go ahead *vi* andare avanti; ~ **ahead!** faccia pure!

go along *vi* andare, avanzare ♦ *vt fus* percorrere; **to ~ along with** (*accompany*) andare con, accompagnare; (*agree with*: *idea*) sottoscrivere, appoggiare.

go away *vi* partire, andarsene.

go back *vi* tornare, ritornare; (*go again*) andare di nuovo.

go back on *vt fus* (*promise*) non mantenere.

go by *vi* (*years, time*) scorrere ♦ *vt fus* attenersi a, seguire (alla lettera); prestar fede a.

go down *vi* scendere; (*ship*) affondare; (*sun*) tramontare ♦ *vt fus* scendere; **that should ~ down well with him** dovrebbe incontrare la sua approvazione.

go for *vt fus* (*fetch*) andare a prendere; (*like*) andar matto(a) per; (*attack*) attaccare; saltare addosso a.

go in *vi* entrare.

go in for *vt fus* (*competition*) iscriversi a; (*be interested in*) interessarsi di.

go into *vt fus* entrare in; (*investigate*) indagare, esaminare; (*embark on*) lanciarsi in.

go off *vi* partire, andar via; (*food*) guastarsi; (*explode*) esplodere, scoppiare; (*lights etc*) spegnersi; (*event*) passare ♦ *vt fus*: **I've gone off chocolate** la cioccolata non mi piace più; **the gun went off** il fucile si scaricò; **the party went off well** la festa è andata *or* è riuscita bene; **to ~ off to sleep** addormentarsi.

go on *vi* continuare; (*happen*) succedere; (*lights*) accendersi ♦ *vt fus* (*be guided by*: *evidence etc*) basarsi su, fondarsi su; **to ~ on doing** continuare a fare; **what's ~ing on here?** che succede *or* che sta succedendo qui?

go on at *vt fus* (*nag*) assillare.

go on with *vt fus* continuare, proseguire.

go out *vi* uscire; (*fire, light*) spegnersi; (*ebb*: *tide*) calare; **to ~ out with sb** uscire con qn.

go over *vi* (*ship*) ribaltarsi ♦ *vt fus* (*check*) esaminare; **to ~ over sth in one's mind** pensare bene a qc.

go round *vi* (*circulate*: *news, rumour*) circolare; (*revolve*) girare; (*visit*): **to ~ round (to sb's)** passare (da qn); (*make a detour*): **to ~ round (by)** passare (per); (*suffice*) bastare (per tutti).

go through *vt fus* (*town etc*) attraversare; (*search through*) frugare in; (*examine*: *list, book*) leggere da capo a fondo; (*perform*) fare.

go through with *vt fus* (*plan, crime*) mettere in atto, eseguire; **I couldn't ~ through with it** non sono riuscito ad andare fino in fondo.

go under *vi* (*sink*: *ship*) affondare, colare a picco; (: *person*) andare sotto; (*fig*: *business, firm*) fallire.

go up *vi* salire ♦ *vt fus* salire su per; **to ~ up in flames** andare in fiamme.

go without *vt fus* fare a meno di.

goad [gəud] *vt* spronare.

go-ahead ['gəuəhɛd] *a* intraprendente ♦ *n*: **to give sb/sth the ~** dare l'okay a qn/qc.

goal [gəul] *n* (*SPORT*) gol *m*, rete *f*; (: *place*) porta; (*fig*: *aim*) fine *m*, scopo.

goalkeeper ['gəulkiːpə*] *n* portiere *m*.

goalpost ['gəulpəust] *n* palo (della porta).

goat [gəut] *n* capra.

gobble ['gɔbl] *vt* (*also*: **~ down**, **~ up**) ingoiare.

go-between ['gəubɪtwiːn] *n* intermediario/a.

Gobi Desert ['gəubɪ-] *n*: **the ~** il Deserto dei Gobi.

goblet ['gɔblɪt] *n* calice *m*, coppa.

goblin ['gɔblɪn] *n* folletto.

go-cart ['gəukɑːt] *n* go-kart *m inv* ♦ *cpd*: **~ racing** *n* kartismo.

god [gɔd] *n* dio; **G~** Dio.

godchild ['gɔdtʃaɪld] *n* figlioccio/a.

goddaughter ['gɔdɔːtə*] *n* figlioccia.

goddess ['gɔdɪs] *n* dea.

godfather ['gɔdfɑːðə*] *n* padrino.

god-forsaken ['gɔdfəseɪkən] *a* desolato(a), sperduto(a).

godmother ['gɔdmʌðə*] *n* madrina.

godparents ['gɔdpɛərənts] *npl*: **the ~** il padrino e la madrina.

godsend ['gɔdsɛnd] *n* dono del cielo.

godson ['gɔdsʌn] *n* figlioccio.

goes [gəuz] *vb see* **go**.

go-getter ['gəugɛtə*] *n* arrivista *m/f*.

goggle ['gɔgl] *vi*: **to ~ (at)** stare con gli occhi incollati *or* appiccicati (a *or* addosso a).

goggles ['gɔglz] *npl* occhiali *mpl* (di protezione).

going ['gəuɪŋ] *n* (*conditions*) andare *m*, stato del terreno ♦ *a*: **the ~ rate** la tariffa in vigore; **a ~ concern** un'azienda avviata; **it was slow ~** si andava a rilento.

goings-on ['gəuɪŋz'ɔn] *npl* (*col*) fatti *mpl* strani, cose *fpl* strane.

go-kart ['gəukɑːt] *n* = **go-cart**.

gold [gəuld] *n* oro ♦ *a* d'oro; (*reserves*) aureo(a).

golden ['gəuldən] *a* (*made of gold*) d'oro; (*gold in colour*) dorato(a).

golden age *n* età d'oro.

golden handshake *n* (*Brit*) gratifica di fine servizio.

golden rule *n* regola principale.

goldfish ['gəuldfɪʃ] *n* pesce *m* dorato *or* rosso.

gold leaf *n* lamina d'oro.

gold medal *n* (*SPORT*) medaglia d'oro.

goldmine ['gəuldmaɪn] *n* miniera d'oro.

gold-plated ['gəuld'pleɪtɪd] *a* placcato(a) oro *inv*.

goldsmith ['gəuldsmɪθ] *n* orefice *m*, orafo.

gold standard *n* tallone *m* aureo.

golf [gɔlf] *n* golf *m*.

golf ball *n* pallina da golf.

golf club *n* circolo di golf; (*stick*) bastone *m or* mazza da golf.

golf course *n* campo di golf.

golfer ['gɔlfə*] n giocatore/trice di golf.
gondola ['gɔndələ] n gondola.
gondolier [gɔndə'lɪə*] n gondoliere m.
gone [gɔn] pp of **go**.
gong [gɔŋ] n gong m inv.
good [gud] a buono(a); (kind) buono(a), gentile; (child) bravo(a) ♦ n bene m; ~! bene!, ottimo!; **to be ~ at** essere bravo(a) in; **it's ~ for you** fa bene; **it's a ~ thing you were there** meno male che c'era; **she is ~ with children/her hands** ci sa fare coi bambini/è abile nei lavori manuali; **to feel ~** sentirsi bene; **it's ~ to see you** che piacere vederla; **he's up to no ~** ne sta combinando qualcuna; **it's no ~ complaining** brontolare non serve a niente; **for the common ~** nell'interesse generale, per il bene comune; **for ~** (for ever) per sempre, definitivamente; **would you be ~ enough to ...?** avrebbe la gentilezza di ...?; **that's very ~ of you** è molto gentile da parte sua; **is this any ~?** (will it do?) va bene questo?; (what's it like?) com'è?; **a ~ deal (of)** molto(a), una buona quantità (di); **a ~ many** molti(e); ~ **morning!** buon giorno!; ~ **afternoon/evening!** buona sera!; ~ **night!** buona notte!; see also **goods**.
goodbye [gud'baɪ] excl arrivederci!; **to say ~ to** (person) salutare.
good faith n buona fede.
good-for-nothing ['gudfənʌθɪŋ] n buono/a a nulla, vagabondo/a.
Good Friday n Venerdì Santo.
good-humoured [gud'hju:məd] a (person) di buon umore; (remark, joke) bonario(a).
good-looking [gud'lukɪŋ] a bello(a).
good-natured [gud'neɪtʃəd] a (person) affabile; (discussion) amichevole, cordiale.
goodness ['gudnɪs] n (of person) bontà; **for ~ sake!** per amor di Dio!; ~ **gracious!** santo cielo!, mamma mia!
goods [gudz] npl (COMM etc) merci fpl, articoli mpl; ~ **and chattels** beni mpl e effetti mpl.
goods train n (Brit) treno m merci inv.
goodwill [gud'wɪl] n amicizia, benevolenza; (COMM) avviamento.
goody-goody ['gudɪgudɪ] n (pej) santarellino/a.
goose, pl geese [gu:s, gi:s] n oca.
gooseberry ['guzbərɪ] n uva spina; **to play ~** (Brit) tenere la candela.
gooseflesh ['gu:sfleʃ] n, **goosepimples** ['gu:spɪmplz] npl pelle f d'oca.
goose step n (MIL) passo dell'oca.
GOP n abbr (US POL: col: = Grand Old Party) partito repubblicano.
gore [gɔ:*] vt incornare ♦ n sangue m (coagulato).
gorge [gɔ:dʒ] n gola ♦ vt: **to ~ o.s. (on)** ingozzarsi (di).
gorgeous ['gɔ:dʒəs] a magnifico(a).
gorilla [gə'rɪlə] n gorilla m inv.
gormless ['gɔ:mlɪs] a (Brit col) tonto(a); (:

stronger) deficiente.
gorse [gɔ:s] n ginestrone m.
gory ['gɔ:rɪ] a sanguinoso(a).
go-slow ['gəu'sləu] n (Brit) rallentamento dei lavori (per agitazione sindacale).
gospel ['gɔspl] n vangelo.
gossamer ['gɔsəmə*] n (cobweb) fili mpl della Madonna or di ragnatela; (light fabric) stoffa sottilissima.
gossip ['gɔsɪp] n chiacchiere fpl; pettegolezzi mpl; (person) pettegolo/a ♦ vi chiacchierare; (maliciously) pettegolare; **a piece of ~** un pettegolezzo.
gossip column n cronaca mondana.
got [gɔt] pt, pp of **get**.
Gothic ['gɔθɪk] a gotico(a).
gotten ['gɔtn] (US) pp of **get**.
gouge [gaudʒ] vt (also: ~ **out**: hole etc) scavare; (: initials) scolpire; (: sb's eyes) cavare.
gourd [guəd] n zucca.
gourmet ['guəmeɪ] n buongustaio/a.
gout [gaut] n gotta.
govern ['gʌvən] vt governare; (LING) reggere.
governess ['gʌvənɪs] n governante f.
governing ['gʌvənɪŋ] a (POL) al potere, al governo; ~ **body** consiglio di amministrazione.
government ['gʌvnmənt] n governo; (Brit: ministers) ministero ♦ cpd statale; **local ~** amministrazione f locale.
governmental [gʌvn'mɛntl] a governativo(a).
government housing n (US) alloggi mpl popolari.
government stock n titoli mpl di stato.
governor ['gʌvənə*] n (of state, bank) governatore m; (of school, hospital) amministratore m; (Brit: of prison) direttore/trice.
Govt abbr = **government**.
gown [gaun] n vestito lungo; (of teacher, judge) toga.
GP n abbr (MED) see **general practitioner**.
GPO n abbr (Brit: old) = General Post Office; (US: = Government Printing Office) ≈ Poligrafici dello Stato.
gr. abbr (COMM) = **gross**.
grab [græb] vt afferrare, arraffare; (property, power) impadronirsi di ♦ vi: **to ~ at** tentare disperatamente di afferrare.
grace [greɪs] n grazia; (graciousness) garbo, cortesia ♦ vt onorare; **5 days' ~** dilazione f di 5 giorni; **to say ~** dire il benedicite; **with a good/bad ~** volentieri/malvolentieri; **his sense of humour is his saving ~** il suo senso dell'umorismo è quello che lo salva.
graceful ['greɪsful] a elegante, aggraziato(a).
gracious ['greɪʃəs] a grazioso(a); misericordioso(a) ♦ excl: **(good) ~!** madonna (mia)!
gradation [grə'deɪʃən] n gradazione f.
grade [greɪd] n (COMM) qualità f inv; classe f; categoria; (in hierarchy) grado; (US SCOL) voto; classe; (gradient) pendenza, gradiente m ♦ vt classificare; ordinare; graduare; **to**

make the ~ (*fig*) farcela.

grade crossing *n* (*US*) passaggio a livello.

grade school *n* (*US*) scuola elementare *or* primaria.

gradient ['greɪdɪənt] *n* pendenza, gradiente *m*.

gradual ['grædjuəl] *a* graduale.

gradually ['grædjuəlɪ] *ad* man mano, a poco a poco.

graduate *n* ['grædjuɪt] laureato/a; (*US SCOL*) diplomato/a, licenziato/a ♦ *vi* ['grædjueɪt] laurearsi.

graduated pension ['grædjueɪtɪd-] *n pensione calcolata sugli ultimi stipendi.*

graduation [grædju'eɪʃən] *n* cerimonia del conferimento della laurea; (*US SCOL*) consegna dei diplomi.

graffiti [grə'fiːtɪ] *npl* graffiti *mpl*.

graft [grɑːft] *n* (*AGR*, *MED*) innesto ♦ *vt* innestare; **hard** ~ (*col*) duro lavoro.

grain [greɪn] *n* (*no pl: cereals*) cereali *mpl*; (*US: corn*) grano; (*of sand*) granello; (*of wood*) venatura; **it goes against the** ~ (*fig*) va contro la mia (*or* la sua *etc*) natura.

gram [græm] *n* grammo.

grammar ['græmə*] *n* grammatica.

grammar school *n* (*Brit*) ≈ liceo.

grammatical [grə'mætɪkl] *a* grammaticale.

gramme [græm] *n* = **gram**.

gramophone ['græməfəun] *n* (*Brit*) grammofono.

granary ['grænərɪ] *n* granaio.

grand [grænd] *a* grande, magnifico(a); grandioso(a) ♦ *n* (*col: thousand*) mille dollari *mpl* (*or* sterline *fpl*).

grandchild, *pl* **-children** ['græntʃaɪld, -tʃɪldrən] *n* nipote *m*.

granddad ['grændæd] *n* (*col*) nonno.

granddaughter ['grændɔːtə*] *n* nipote *f*.

grandeur ['grændjə*] *n* (*of style, house*) splendore *m*; (*of occasion, scenery etc*) grandiosità, maestà.

grandfather ['grændfɑːðə*] *n* nonno.

grandiose ['grændɪəus] *a* grandioso(a); (*pej*) pomposo(a).

grand jury *n* (*US*) giuria (*formata da 12 a 23 membri*).

grandma ['grænmɑː] *n* (*col*) nonna.

grandmother ['grænmʌðə*] *n* nonna.

grandpa ['grænpɑː] *n* (*col*) = **granddad**.

grandparent ['grænpɛərənt] *n* nonno/a.

grand piano *n* pianoforte m a coda.

Grand Prix ['grɑ̃ː'priː] *n* (*AUT*) Gran Premio, Grand Prix *m inv*.

grandson ['grænsʌn] *n* nipote *m*.

grandstand ['grændstænd] *n* (*SPORT*) tribuna.

grand total *n* somma complessiva.

granite ['grænɪt] *n* granito.

granny ['grænɪ] *n* (*col*) nonna.

grant [grɑːnt] *vt* accordare; (*a request*) accogliere; (*admit*) ammettere, concedere ♦ *n* (*SCOL*) borsa; (*ADMIN*) sussidio, sovvenzione *f*; **to take sth for** ~**ed** dare qc per scontato.

granulated ['grænjuleɪtɪd] *a*: ~ **sugar** zucchero cristallizzato.

granule ['grænjuːl] *n* granello.

grape [greɪp] *n* chicco d'uva, acino; **a bunch of** ~**s** un grappolo d'uva.

grapefruit ['greɪpfruːt] *n* pompelmo.

grapevine ['greɪpvaɪn] *n* vite *f*; **I heard it on the** ~ (*fig*) me l'ha detto l'uccellino.

graph [grɑːf] *n* grafico.

graphic ['græfɪk] *a* grafico(a); (*vivid*) vivido(a); *see also* **graphics**.

graphic designer *n* grafico/a.

graphics ['græfɪks] *n* (*art, process*) grafica; (*pl: drawings*) illustrazioni *fpl*.

graphite ['græfaɪt] *n* grafite *f*.

graph paper *n* carta millimetrata.

grapple ['græpl] *vi*: **to** ~ **with** essere alle prese con.

grappling iron ['græplɪŋ-] *n* (*NAUT*) grappino.

grasp [grɑːsp] *vt* afferrare ♦ *n* (*grip*) presa; (*fig*) potere *m*; comprensione *f*; **to have sth within one's** ~ avere qc a portata di mano; **to have a good** ~ **of** (*subject*) avere una buona padronanza di.

grasp at *vt fus* (*rope etc*) afferrarsi a, aggrapparsi a; (*fig: opportunity*) non farsi sfuggire, approfittare di.

grasping ['grɑːspɪŋ] *a* avido(a).

grass [grɑːs] *n* erba; (*pasture*) pascolo, prato; (*Brit col: informer*) informatore/trice; (*ex-terrorist*) pentito/a.

grasshopper ['grɑːshɔpə*] *n* cavalletta.

grassland ['grɑːslænd] *n* prateria.

grass roots *npl* (*fig*) base *f*.

grass snake *n* natrice *f*.

grassy ['grɑːsɪ] *a* erboso(a).

grate [greɪt] *n* graticola (del focolare) ♦ *vi* cigolare, stridere ♦ *vt* (*CULIN*) grattugiare.

grateful ['greɪtful] *a* grato(a), riconoscente.

gratefully ['greɪtfulɪ] *ad* con gratitudine.

grater ['greɪtə*] *n* grattugia.

gratification [grætɪfɪ'keɪʃən] *n* soddisfazione *f*.

gratify ['grætɪfaɪ] *vt* appagare; (*whim*) soddisfare.

gratifying ['grætɪfaɪɪŋ] *a* gradito(a); soddisfacente.

grating ['greɪtɪŋ] *n* (*iron bars*) grata ♦ *a* (*noise*) stridente, stridulo(a).

gratitude ['grætɪtjuːd] *n* gratitudine *f*.

gratuitous [grə'tjuːɪtəs] *a* gratuito(a).

gratuity [grə'tjuːɪtɪ] *n* mancia.

grave [greɪv] *n* tomba ♦ *a* grave, serio(a).

gravedigger ['greɪvdɪgə*] *n* becchino.

gravel ['grævl] *n* ghiaia.

gravely ['greɪvlɪ] *ad* gravemente, solennemente; ~ **ill** in pericolo di vita.

gravestone ['greɪvstəun] *n* pietra tombale.

graveyard ['greɪvjɑːd] *n* cimitero.

gravitate ['grævɪteɪt] *vi* gravitare.

gravity ['grævɪtɪ] *n* (*all senses*) gravità.

gravy ['greɪvɪ] *n* intingolo della carne; salsa.

gravy boat *n* salsiera.

gravy train *n*: **the** ~ (*col*) l'albero della cuccagna.

gray [greɪ] *a* = **grey**.

graze [greɪz] *vi* pascolare, pascere ♦ *vt* (*touch*

lightly) sfiorare; (*scrape*) escoriare ♦ *n* (*MED*) escoriazione *f*.

grazing ['greɪzɪŋ] *n* pascolo.

grease [griːs] *n* (*fat*) grasso; (*lubricant*) lubrificante *m* ♦ *vt* ingrassare; lubrificare; **to** ~ **the skids** (*US: fig*) spianare la strada.

grease gun *n* ingrassatore *m*.

greasepaint ['griːspeɪnt] *n* cerone *m*.

greaseproof paper ['griːspruːf-] *n* (*Brit*) carta oleata.

greasy ['griːsɪ] *a* grasso(a); untuoso(a); (*Brit: road, surface*) scivoloso(a); (*hands, clothes*) unto(a).

great [greɪt] *a* grande; (*pain, heat*) forte, intenso(a); (*col*) magnifico(a), meraviglioso(a); **they're** ~ **friends** sono grandi amici; **the** ~ **thing is that** ... il bello è che ...; **it was** ~! è stato fantastico!; **we had a** ~ **time** ci siamo divertiti un mondo.

Great Barrier Reef *n*: **the** ~ la Grande Barriera Corallina.

Great Britain *n* Gran Bretagna.

great-grandchild, ** *pl* **-children [greɪt-'græntʃaɪld, -tʃɪldrən] *n* pronipote *m/f*.

great-grandfather [greɪt'grændfɑːðə*] *n* bisnonno.

great-grandmother [greɪt'grænmʌðə*] *n* bisnonna.

Great Lakes *npl*: **the** ~ i Grandi Laghi.

greatly ['greɪtlɪ] *ad* molto.

greatness ['greɪtnɪs] *n* grandezza.

Grecian ['griːʃən] *a* greco(a).

Greece [griːs] *n* Grecia.

greed [griːd] *n* (*also*: ~**iness**) avarizia; (*for food*) golosità, ghiottoneria.

greedily ['griːdɪlɪ] *ad* avidamente; golosamente.

greedy ['griːdɪ] *a* avido(a); goloso(a), ghiotto(a).

Greek [griːk] *a* greco(a) ♦ *n* greco/a; (*LING*) greco; **ancient/modern** ~ greco antico/moderno.

green [griːn] *a* verde; (*inexperienced*) inesperto(a), ingenuo(a) ♦ *n* verde *m*; (*stretch of grass*) prato; (*also*: **village** ~) ≈ piazza del paese; ~**s** *npl* (*vegetables*) verdura; (*of golf course*) green *m inv*; **to have** ~ **fingers** *or* (*US*) **a** ~ **thumb** (*fig*) avere il pollice verde.

green belt *n* (*round town*) cintura di verde.

green card *n* (*AUT*) carta verde.

greenery ['griːnərɪ] *n* verde *m*.

greenfly ['griːnflaɪ] *n* afide *f*.

greengage ['griːngeɪdʒ] *n* susina Regina Claudia.

greengrocer ['griːngrəʊsə*] *n* (*Brit*) fruttivendolo/a, erbivendolo/a.

greenhouse ['griːnhaʊs] *n* serra.

greenish ['griːnɪʃ] *a* verdastro(a).

Greenland ['griːnlənd] *n* Groenlandia.

Greenlander ['griːnləndə*] *n* groenlandese *m/f*.

green pepper *n* peperone *m* verde.

greet [griːt] *vt* salutare.

greeting ['griːtɪŋ] *n* saluto; **Christmas/birthday** ~**s** auguri *mpl* di Natale/di compleanno; **Season's** ~**s** Buone Feste.

greeting(s) card *n* cartolina d'auguri.

gregarious [grə'gɛərɪəs] *a* gregario(a); socievole.

grenade [grə'neɪd] *n* (*also*: **hand** ~) granata.

grew [gruː] *pt of* **grow**.

grey [greɪ] *a* grigio(a); **to go** ~ diventar grigio.

grey-haired [greɪ'hɛəd] *a* dai capelli grigi.

greyhound ['greɪhaʊnd] *n* levriere *m*.

grid [grɪd] *n* grata; (*ELEC*) rete *f*; (*US AUT*) area d'incrocio.

griddle ['grɪdl] *n* piastra.

gridiron ['grɪdaɪən] *n* graticola.

grief [griːf] *n* dolore *m*; **to come to** ~ (*plan*) naufragare; (*person*) finire male.

grievance ['griːvəns] *n* doglianza, lagnanza; (*cause for complaint*) motivo di risentimento.

grieve [griːv] *vi* addolorarsi, soffrire ♦ *vt* addolorare; **to** ~ **for sb** compiangere qn; (*dead person*) piangere qn.

grievous bodily harm (GBH) ['griːvəs-] *n* (*LAW*) aggressione *f*.

grill [grɪl] *n* (*on cooker*) griglia ♦ *vt* (*Brit*) cuocere ai ferri; (*question*) interrogare senza sosta; ~**ed meat** carne *f* ai ferri *or* alla griglia.

grille [grɪl] *n* grata; (*AUT*) griglia.

grill(room) ['grɪl(rʊm)] *n* rosticceria.

grim [grɪm] *a* sinistro(a); brutto(a).

grimace [grɪ'meɪs] *n* smorfia ♦ *vi* fare smorfie.

grime [graɪm] *n* sudiciume *m*.

grimy ['graɪmɪ] *a* sudicio(a).

grin [grɪn] *n* sorriso smagliante ♦ *vi*: **to** ~ (**at**) sorridere (a), fare un gran sorriso (a).

grind [graɪnd] *vb* (*pt, pp* **ground** [graʊnd]) *vt* macinare; (*US: meat*) tritare, macinare; (*make sharp*) arrotare; (*polish: gem, lens*) molare ♦ *vi* (*car gears*) grattare ♦ *n* (*work*) sgobbata; **to** ~ **one's teeth** digrignare i denti; **to** ~ **to a halt** (*vehicle*) arrestarsi con uno stridio di freni; (*fig: talks, scheme*) insabbiarsi; (: *work, production*) cessare del tutto; **the daily** ~ (*col*) il trantran quotidiano.

grinder ['graɪndə*] *n* (*machine: for coffee*) macinino.

grindstone ['graɪndstəʊn] *n*: **to keep one's nose to the** ~ darci sotto.

grip [grɪp] *n* presa; (*holdall*) borsa da viaggio ♦ *vt* afferrare; **to come to** ~**s with** affrontare; cercare di risolvere; **to** ~ **the road** (*tyres*) far presa sulla strada; (*car*) tenere bene la strada; **to lose one's** ~ perdere *or* allentare la presa; (*fig*) perdere la grinta.

gripe [graɪp] *n* (*MED*) colica; (*col: complaint*) lagna ♦ *vi* (*col*) brontolare.

gripping ['grɪpɪŋ] *a* avvincente.

grisly ['grɪzlɪ] *a* macabro(a), orrido(a).

grist [grɪst] *n* (*fig*): **it's (all)** ~ **to the mill** tutto aiuta.

gristle ['grɪsl] *n* cartilagine *f*.

grit [grɪt] *n* ghiaia; (*courage*) fegato ♦ *vt* (*road*) coprire di sabbia; **to ~ one's teeth** stringere i denti; **I've got a piece of ~ in my eye** ho un bruscolino nell'occhio.

grits [grɪts] *npl* (*US*) macinato grosso (di avena *etc*).

grizzle ['grɪzl] *vi* (*Brit*) piagnucolare.

grizzly ['grɪzlɪ] *n* (*also*: **~ bear**) orso grigio, grizzly *m inv*.

groan [grəun] *n* gemito ♦ *vi* gemere.

grocer ['grəusə*] *n* negoziante *m* di generi alimentari; **~'s (shop)** negozio di alimentari.

groceries ['grəusərɪz] *npl* provviste *fpl*.

grocery ['grəusərɪ] *n* (*shop*) (negozio di) alimentari.

grog [grɔg] *n* grog *m inv*.

groggy ['grɔgɪ] *a* barcollante.

groin [grɔɪn] *n* inguine *m*.

groom [gru:m] *n* palafreniere *m*; (*also*: **bride~**) sposo ♦ *vt* (*horse*) strigliare; (*fig*): **to ~ sb for** avviare qn a.

groove [gru:v] *n* scanalatura, solco.

grope [grəup] *vi* andare a tentoni; **to ~ for sth** cercare qc a tastoni.

grosgrain ['grəugreɪn] *n* gros-grain *m inv*.

gross [grəus] *a* grossolano(a); (*COMM*) lordo(a) ♦ *n* (*pl inv*) (*twelve dozen*) grossa ♦ *vt* (*COMM*) incassare, avere un incasso lordo di.

gross domestic product (GDP) *n* prodotto interno lordo (P.I.L.).

grossly ['grəuslɪ] *ad* (*greatly*) molto.

gross national product (GNP) *n* prodotto nazionale lordo (P.N.L.).

grotesque [grəu'tɛsk] *a* grottesco(a).

grotto ['grɔtəu] *n* grotta.

grotty ['grɔtɪ] *a* (*Brit col*) squallido(a).

grouch [grautʃ] (*col*) *vi* brontolare ♦ *n* (*person*) brontolone/a.

ground [graund] *pt, pp of* **grind** ♦ *a* (*coffee etc*) macinato(a) ♦ *n* suolo, terra; (*land*) terreno; (*SPORT*) campo; (*reason: gen pl*) ragione *f*; (*US: also*: **~ wire**) (presa a) terra ♦ *vt* (*plane*) tenere a terra; (*US ELEC*) mettere la presa a terra a ♦ *vi* (*ship*) arenarsi; **~s** *npl* (*of coffee etc*) fondi *mpl*; (*gardens etc*) terreno, giardini *mpl*; **on/to the ~** per/a terra; **below ~** sottoterra; **common ~** terreno comune; **to gain/lose ~** guadagnare/perdere terreno; **he covered a lot of ~ in his lecture** ha toccato molti argomenti nel corso della conferenza.

ground cloth *n* (*US*) = **groundsheet**.

ground control *n* (*AVIAT, SPACE*) base *f* di controllo.

ground floor *n* pianterreno.

grounding ['graundɪŋ] *n* (*in education*) basi *fpl*.

groundless ['graundlɪs] *a* infondato(a).

groundnut ['graundnʌt] *n* arachide *f*.

ground rent *n* (*Brit*) canone *m* di affitto di un terreno.

groundsheet ['graundʃi:t] *n* (*Brit*) telone *m* impermeabile.

groundsman ['graundzmən], (*US*) **groundskeeper** ['graundzki:pə*] *n* (*SPORT*) custode *m* (di campo sportivo).

ground staff *n* personale *m* di terra.

groundswell ['graundswɛl] *n* maremoto; (*fig*) movimento.

ground-to-ground ['grauntə'graund] *a*: **~ missile** missile *m* terra-terra.

groundwork ['graundwə:k] *n* preparazione *f*.

group [gru:p] *n* gruppo; (*MUS: pop* **~**) complesso, gruppo ♦ *vt* raggruppare ♦ *vi* raggrupparsi.

grouse [graus] *n* (*pl inv*) (*bird*) tetraone *m* ♦ *vi* (*complain*) brontolare.

grove [grəuv] *n* boschetto.

grovel ['grɔvl] *vi* (*fig*): **to ~ (before)** strisciare (di fronte a).

grow, *pt* **grew**, *pp* **grown** [grəu, gru:, grəun] *vi* crescere; (*increase*) aumentare; (*become*): **to ~ rich/weak** arricchirsi/indebolirsi ♦ *vt* coltivare, far crescere; **to ~ tired of waiting** stancarsi di aspettare.

grow apart *vi* (*fig*) estraniarsi.

grow away from *vt fus* (*fig*) allontanarsi da, staccarsi da.

grow on *vt fus*: **that painting is ~ing on me** quel quadro più lo guardo più mi piace.

grow out of *vt fus* (*clothes*) diventare troppo grande per indossare; (*habit*) perdere (col tempo); **he'll ~ out of it** gli passerà.

grow up *vi* farsi grande, crescere.

grower ['grəuə*] *n* coltivatore/trice.

growing ['grəuɪŋ] *a* (*fear, amount*) crescente; **~ pains** (*also fig*) problemi *mpl* di crescita.

growl [graul] *vi* ringhiare.

grown [grəun] *pp of* **grow** ♦ *a* adulto(a), maturo(a).

grown-up [grəun'ʌp] *n* adulto/a, grande *m/f*.

growth [grəuθ] *n* crescita, sviluppo; (*what has grown*) crescita; (*MED*) escrescenza, tumore *m*.

growth rate *n* tasso di crescita.

GRSM *n abbr* (*Brit*) = *Graduate of the Royal Schools of Music*.

grub [grʌb] *n* larva; (*col: food*) roba (da mangiare).

grubby ['grʌbɪ] *a* sporco(a).

grudge [grʌdʒ] *n* rancore *m* ♦ *vt*: **to ~ sb sth** dare qc a qn di malavoglia; invidiare qc a qn; **to bear sb a ~ (for)** serbar rancore a qn (per).

grudgingly ['grʌdʒɪŋlɪ] *ad* di malavoglia, di malincuore.

gruelling, (*US*) **grueling** ['gruəlɪŋ] *a* estenuante.

gruesome ['gru:səm] *a* orribile.

gruff [grʌf] *a* rozzo(a).

grumble ['grʌmbl] *vi* brontolare, lagnarsi.

grumpy ['grʌmpɪ] *a* stizzito(a).

grunt [grʌnt] *vi* grugnire ♦ *n* grugnito.

G-string ['dʒi:strɪŋ] *n* (*garment*) tanga *m inv*.

GSUSA *n abbr* = *Girl Scouts of the United States of America*.

GT *abbr* (*AUT*: = *gran turismo*) GT.

GU *abbr* (*US POST*) = *Guam*.

guarantee [gærən'tiː] *n* garanzia ♦ *vt* garantire; **he can't ~ (that) he'll come** non può garantire che verrà.

guarantor [gærən'tɔː*] *n* garante *m/f*.

guard [gɑːd] *n* guardia; (*protection*) riparo, protezione *f*; (*BOXING*) difesa; (*one man*) guardia, sentinella; (*Brit RAIL*) capotreno; (*safety device*: *on machine*) schermo protettivo; (*also*: **fire ~**) parafuoco ♦ *vt* fare la guardia a; **to ~ (against** *or* **from)** proteggere (da), salvaguardare (da); **to be on one's ~** (*fig*) stare in guardia.

guard against *vi*: **to ~ against doing sth** guardarsi dal fare qc.

guard dog *n* cane *m* da guardia.

guarded ['gɑːdɪd] *a* (*fig*) cauto(a), guardingo(a).

guardian ['gɑːdɪən] *n* custode *m*; (*of minor*) tutore/trice.

guard's van *n* (*Brit RAIL*) vagone *m* di servizio.

Guatemala [gwɑːtə'mɑːlə] *n* Guatemala *m*.

Guernsey ['gəːnzɪ] *n* Guernesey *f*.

guerrilla [gə'rɪlə] *n* guerrigliero.

guerrilla warfare *n* guerriglia.

guess [gɛs] *vi* indovinare ♦ *vt* indovinare; (*US*) credere, pensare ♦ *n* congettura; **to take** *or* **have a ~** cercare di indovinare; **my ~ is that** ... suppongo che ...; **to keep sb ~ing** tenere qn in sospeso *or* sulla corda; **I ~ you're right** mi sa che hai ragione.

guesstimate ['gɛstɪmɪt] *n* (*col*) stima approssimativa.

guesswork ['gɛswəːk] *n*: **I got the answer by ~** ho azzeccato la risposta.

guest [gɛst] *n* ospite *m/f*; (*in hotel*) cliente *m/f*; **be my ~** (*col*) fai come (se fossi) a casa tua.

guest-house ['gɛsthaus] *n* pensione *f*.

guest room *n* camera degli ospiti.

guffaw [gʌ'fɔː] *n* risata sonora ♦ *vi* scoppiare di una risata sonora.

guidance ['gaɪdəns] *n* guida, direzione *f*; **marriage/vocational ~** consulenza matrimoniale/per l'avviamento professionale.

guide [gaɪd] *n* (*person, book etc*) guida; (*also*: **girl ~**) giovane esploratrice *f* ♦ *vt* guidare; **to be ~d by sb/sth** farsi *or* lasciarsi guidare da qn/qc.

guidebook ['gaɪdbuk] *n* guida.

guided missile *n* missile *m* telecomandato.

guide dog *n* (*Brit*) cane *m* guida *inv*.

guidelines ['gaɪdlaɪnz] *npl* (*fig*) indicazioni *fpl*, linee *fpl* direttive.

guild [gɪld] *n* arte *f*, corporazione *f*; associazione *f*.

guildhall ['gɪldhɔːl] *n* (*Brit*) palazzo municipale.

guile [gaɪl] *n* astuzia.

guileless ['gaɪllɪs] *a* candido(a).

guillotine ['gɪlətiːn] *n* ghigliottina.

guilt [gɪlt] *n* colpevolezza.

guilty ['gɪltɪ] *a* colpevole; **to feel ~ (about)** sentirsi in colpa (per); **to plead ~/not ~** dichiararsi colpevole/innocente.

Guinea ['gɪnɪ] *n*: **Republic of ~** Repubblica di Guinea.

guinea ['gɪnɪ] *n* (*Brit*) ghinea (= *21 shillings: valuta ora fuori uso*).

guinea pig *n* cavia.

guise [gaɪz] *n* maschera.

guitar [gɪ'tɑː*] *n* chitarra.

guitarist [gɪ'tɑːrɪst] *n* chitarrista *m/f*.

gulch [gʌltʃ] *n* (*US*) burrone *m*.

gulf [gʌlf] *n* golfo; (*abyss*) abisso; **the (Persian) G~** il Golfo Persico.

Gulf States *npl*: **the ~** i paesi del Golfo Persico.

Gulf Stream *n*: **the ~** la corrente del Golfo.

gull [gʌl] *n* gabbiano.

gullet ['gʌlɪt] *n* gola.

gullibility [gʌlɪ'bɪlɪtɪ] *n* semplicioneria.

gullible ['gʌlɪbl] *a* credulo(a).

gully ['gʌlɪ] *n* burrone *m*; gola; canale *m*.

gulp [gʌlp] *vi* deglutire; (*from emotion*) avere il nodo in gola ♦ *vt* (*also*: **~ down**) tracannare, inghiottire ♦ *n* (*of liquid*) sorso; (*of food*) boccone *m*; **in** *or* **at one ~** in un sorso, d'un fiato.

gum [gʌm] *n* (*ANAT*) gengiva; (*glue*) colla; (*sweet*) gelatina di frutta; (*also*: **chewing-~**) chewing-gum *m* ♦ *vt* incollare.

gum up *vt*: **to ~ up the works** (*col*) mettere il bastone tra le ruote.

gumboil ['gʌmbɔɪl] *n* ascesso (dentario).

gumboots ['gʌmbuːts] *npl* (*Brit*) stivali *mpl* di gomma.

gumption ['gʌmpʃən] *n* buon senso, senso pratico.

gun [gʌn] *n* fucile *m*; (*small*) pistola, rivoltella; (*rifle*) carabina; (*shotgun*) fucile da caccia; (*cannon*) cannone *m* ♦ *vt* (*also*: **~ down**) abbattere a colpi di pistola *or* fucile; **to stick to one's ~s** (*fig*) tener duro.

gunboat ['gʌnbəut] *n* cannoniera.

gun dog *n* cane *m* da caccia.

gunfire ['gʌnfaɪə*] *n* spari *mpl*.

gung-ho ['gʌŋ'həu] *a* (*col*) stupidamente entusiasta.

gunk [gʌŋk] *n* porcherie *fpl*.

gunman ['gʌnmən] *n* bandito armato.

gunner ['gʌnə*] *n* artigliere *m*.

gunpoint ['gʌnpɔɪnt] *n*: **at ~** sotto minaccia di fucile.

gunpowder ['gʌnpaudə*] *n* polvere *f* da sparo.

gunrunner ['gʌnrʌnə*] *n* contrabbandiere d'armi.

gunrunning ['gʌnrʌnɪŋ] *n* contrabbando d'armi.

gunshot ['gʌnʃɔt] *n* sparo; **within ~** a portata di fucile.

gunsmith ['gʌnsmɪθ] *n* armaiolo.

gurgle ['gəːgl] *n* gorgoglio ♦ *vi* gorgogliare.

guru ['guruː] *n* guru *m inv*.

gush [gʌʃ] *n* fiotto, getto ♦ *vi* sgorgare; (*fig*) abbandonarsi ad effusioni.

gusset ['gʌsɪt] *n* gherone *m; (in tights, pants)* rinforzo.

gust [gʌst] *n (of wind)* raffica; *(of smoke)* buffata.

gusto ['gʌstəu] *n* entusiasmo.

gut [gʌt] *n* intestino, budello; *(MUS etc)* minugia; ~**s** *npl (col: innards)* budella *fpl*; (: *of animals)* interiora *fpl; (courage)* fegato ♦ *vt (poultry, fish)* levare le interiora a, sventrare; *(building)* svuotare; (: *subj: fire)* divorare l'interno di; **to hate sb's ~s** odiare qn a morte.

gut reaction *n* reazione *f* istintiva.

gutter ['gʌtə*] *n (of roof)* grondaia; *(in street)* cunetta.

guttural ['gʌtərl] *a* gutturale.

guy [gaɪ] *n (also: ~rope)* cavo *or* corda di fissaggio; *(col: man)* tipo, elemento; *(figure)* effigie di Guy Fawkes.

Guyana [gaɪ'ænə] *n* Guayana *f*.

guzzle ['gʌzl] *vi* gozzovigliare ♦ *vt* trangugiare.

gym [dʒɪm] *n (also: gymnasium)* palestra; *(also: gymnastics)* ginnastica.

gymkhana [dʒɪm'kɑːnə] *n* gimkana.

gymnasium [dʒɪm'neɪzɪəm] *n* palestra.

gymnast ['dʒɪmnæst] *n* ginnasta *m/f*.

gymnastics [dʒɪm'næstɪks] *n*, *npl* ginnastica.

gym shoes *npl* scarpe *fpl* da ginnastica.

gym slip *n (Brit)* grembiule *m* da scuola *(per ragazze)*.

gynaecologist, *(US)* **gynecologist** [gaɪnɪ'kɔlədʒɪst] *n* ginecologo/a.

gynaecology, *(US)* **gynecology** [gaɪnə'kɔlədʒɪ] *n* ginecologia.

gypsy ['dʒɪpsɪ] *n* = **gipsy**.

gyrate [dʒaɪ'reɪt] *vi* girare.

gyroscope ['dʒaɪərəskəup] *n* giroscopio.

H

H, h [eɪtʃ] *n (letter)* H, h *f or m inv*; **H for Harry,** *(US)* **H for How** ≈ H come hotel.

habeas corpus ['heɪbɪəs'kɔːpəs] *n (LAW)* habeas corpus *m inv*.

haberdashery ['hæbədæʃərɪ] *n* merceria.

habit ['hæbɪt] *n* abitudine *f; (costume)* abito; *(REL)* tonaca; **to get out of/into the ~ of doing sth** perdere/prendere l'abitudine di fare qc.

habitable ['hæbɪtəbl] *a* abitabile.

habitat ['hæbɪtæt] *n* habitat *m inv*.

habitation [hæbɪ'teɪʃən] *n* abitazione *f*.

habitual [hə'bɪtjuəl] *a* abituale; *(drinker, liar)* inveterato(a).

habitually [hə'bɪtjuəlɪ] *ad* abitualmente, di solito.

hack [hæk] *vt* tagliare, fare a pezzi ♦ *n (cut)* taglio; *(blow)* colpo; *(old horse)* ronzino; *(pej: writer)* negro.

hacker ['hækə*] *n (COMPUT)* pirata *m* informatico.

hackles ['hæklz] *npl*: **to make sb's ~ rise** *(fig)* rendere qn furioso.

hackney cab ['hæknɪ-] *n* carrozza a nolo.

hackneyed ['hæknɪd] *a* comune, trito(a).

had [hæd] *pt, pp of* **have**.

haddock ['hædək] *n* eglefino.

hadn't ['hædnt] = **had not**.

haematology, *(US)* **hematology** [hiːmə'tɔlədʒɪ] *n* ematologia.

haemoglobin, *(US)* **hemoglobin** [hiːməu'gləubɪn] *n* emoglobina.

haemophilia, *(US)* **hemophilia** [hiːməu'fɪlɪə] *n* emofilia.

haemorrhage, *(US)* **hemorrhage** ['hemərɪdʒ] *n* emorragia.

haemorrhoids, *(US)* **hemorrhoids** ['hemərɔɪdz] *npl* emorroidi *fpl*.

hag [hæg] *n (ugly)* befana; *(nasty)* megera; *(witch)* strega.

haggard ['hægəd] *a* smunto(a).

haggis ['hægɪs] *n (Scottish)* insaccato a base di frattaglie di pecora e avena.

haggle ['hægl] *vi*: **to ~ (over)** contrattare (su); *(argue)* discutere (su).

haggling ['hæglɪŋ] *n* contrattazioni *fpl*.

Hague [heɪg] *n*: **The ~** L'Aia.

hail [heɪl] *n* grandine *f* ♦ *vt (call)* chiamare; *(greet)* salutare ♦ *vi* grandinare; **to ~ (as)** acclamare (come); **he ~s from Scotland** viene dalla Scozia.

hailstone ['heɪlstəun] *n* chicco di grandine.

hailstorm ['heɪlstɔːm] *n* grandinata.

hair [heə*] *n* capelli *mpl*; *(single hair: on head)* capello; (: *on body)* pelo; **to do one's ~** pettinarsi.

hairbrush ['heəbrʌʃ] *n* spazzola per capelli.

haircut ['heəkʌt] *n* taglio di capelli; **I need a ~** devo tagliarmi i capelli.

hairdo ['heədu:] *n* acconciatura, pettinatura.

hairdresser ['heədresə*] *n* parrucchiere/a.

hair-dryer ['heədraɪə*] *n* asciugacapelli *m inv*.

-haired [heəd] *suffix*: **fair/long~** dai capelli biondi/lunghi.

hairgrip ['heəgrɪp] *n* forcina.

hairline ['heəlaɪn] *n* attaccatura dei capelli.

hairline fracture *n* incrinatura.

hairnet ['heənet] *n* retina (per capelli).

hair oil *n* brillantina.

hairpiece ['heəpi:s] *n* toupet *m inv*.

hairpin ['heəpɪn] *n* forcina.

hairpin bend, *(US)* **hairpin curve** *n* tornante *m*.

hair-raising ['heəreɪzɪŋ] *a* orripilante.

hair remover *n* crema depilatoria.

hair spray *n* lacca per capelli.

hairstyle ['heəstaɪl] *n* pettinatura, acconciatura.

hairy ['heərɪ] *a* irsuto(a); peloso(a); *(col: frightening)* spaventoso(a).

Haiti ['heɪtɪ] n Haiti f.
hake pl ~ or ~s [heɪk] n nasello.
halcyon ['hælsɪən] a sereno(a).
hale [heɪl] a: ~ **and hearty** che scoppia di salute.

half [hɑ:f] n (pl **halves** [hɑ:vz]) mezzo, metà f inv; (SPORT: of match) tempo; (: of ground) metà campo ♦ a mezzo(a) ♦ ad a mezzo, a metà; ~ **an hour** mezz'ora; ~ **a dozen** mezza dozzina; ~ **a pound** mezza libbra; **two and a** ~ due e mezzo; **a week and a** ~ una settimana e mezza; ~ **(of it)** la metà; ~ **(of)** la metà di; ~ **the amount of** la metà di; **to cut sth in** ~ tagliare qc in due; ~ **empty/closed** mezzo vuoto/chiuso, semivuoto/semichiuso; ~ **past 3** le 3 e mezza; **to go halves (with sb)** fare a metà (con qn).

half-back ['hɑ:fbæk] n (SPORT) mediano.
half-baked [hɑ:f'beɪkt] a (fig col: idea, scheme) mal combinato(a), che non sta in piedi.
half-breed ['hɑ:fbri:d] n = **half-caste**.
half-brother ['hɑ:fbrʌðə*] n fratellastro.
half-caste ['hɑ:fkɑ:st] n meticcio/a.
half-hearted [hɑ:f'hɑ:tɪd] a tiepido(a).
half-hour [hɑ:f'auə*] n mezz'ora.
half-mast ['hɑ:f'mɑ:st] n: **at** ~ (flag) a mezz'asta.
halfpenny ['heɪpnɪ] n mezzo penny m inv.
half-price ['hɑ:f'praɪs] a a metà prezzo ♦ ad (also: **at** ~) a metà prezzo.
half term n (Brit SCOL) vacanza a or di metà trimestre.
half-time [hɑ:f'taɪm] n (SPORT) intervallo.
halfway [hɑ:f'weɪ] ad a metà strada; **to meet sb** ~ (fig) arrivare a un compromesso con qn.
half-yearly [hɑ:f'jɪəlɪ] ad semestralmente, ogni sei mesi ♦ a semestrale.
halibut ['hælɪbət] n (pl inv) ippoglosso.
halitosis [hælɪ'təusɪs] n alitosi f.
hall [hɔ:l] n sala, salone m; (entrance way) entrata; (corridor) corridoio; (mansion) grande villa, maniero; ~ **of residence** n (Brit) casa dello studente.
hallmark ['hɔ:lmɑ:k] n marchio di garanzia; (fig) caratteristica.
hallo [hə'ləu] excl = **hello**.
Hallowe'en ['hæləu'i:n] n vigilia d'Ognissanti.
hallucination [həlu:sɪ'neɪʃən] n allucinazione f.
hallway ['hɔ:lweɪ] n ingresso; corridoio.
halo ['heɪləu] n (of saint etc) aureola; (of sun) alone m.
halt [hɔ:lt] n fermata ♦ vt fermare ♦ vi fermarsi; **to call a** ~ **(to sth)** (fig) mettere or porre fine (a qc).
halter ['hɔ:ltə*] n (for horse) cavezza.
halterneck ['hɔ:ltənɛk] a allacciato(a) dietro il collo.
halve [hɑ:v] vt (apple etc) dividere a metà; (expense) ridurre di metà.
halves [hɑ:vz] npl of **half**.

ham [hæm] n prosciutto; (col: also: **radio** ~) radioamatore/trice; (also: ~ **actor**) attore/trice senza talento.
Hamburg ['hæmbə:g] n Amburgo f.
hamburger ['hæmbə:gə*] n hamburger m inv.
ham-fisted ['hæm'fɪstɪd], (US) **ham-handed** ['hæm'hændɪd] a maldestro(a).
hamlet ['hæmlɪt] n paesetto.
hammer ['hæmə*] n martello ♦ vt martellare; (fig) sconfiggere duramente ♦ vi (at door) picchiare; **to** ~ **a point home to sb** cacciare un'idea in testa a qn.
hammer out vt (metal) spianare (a martellate); (fig: solution, agreement) mettere a punto.
hammock ['hæmək] n amaca.
hamper ['hæmpə*] vt impedire ♦ n cesta.
hamster ['hæmstə*] n criceto.
hamstring ['hæmstrɪŋ] n (ANAT) tendine m del ginocchio.
hand [hænd] n mano f; (of clock) lancetta; (handwriting) scrittura; (at cards) mano; (: game) partita; (worker) operaio/a; (measurement: of horse) ≈ dieci centimetri ♦ vt dare, passare; **to give sb a** ~ dare una mano a qn; **at** ~ a portata di mano; **in** ~ a disposizione; (work) in corso; **we have the matter in** ~ ci stiamo occupando della cosa; **we have the situation in** ~ abbiamo la situazione sotto controllo; **to be on** ~ (person) essere disponibile; (emergency services) essere pronto(a) a intervenire; **to** ~ (information etc) a portata di mano; **to force sb's** ~ forzare la mano a qn; **to have a free** ~ avere carta bianca; **to have in one's** ~ (also fig) avere in mano or in pugno; **on the one** ~ ..., **on the other** ~ da un lato ..., dall'altro.
hand down vt passare giù; (tradition, heirloom) tramandare; (US: sentence, verdict) emettere.
hand in vt consegnare.
hand out vt (leaflets) distribuire; (advice) elargire.
hand over vt passare; cedere.
hand round vt (Brit: information, papers) far passare; (distribute: chocolates etc) far girare; (subj: hostess) offrire.
handbag ['hændbæg] n borsetta.
handball ['hændbɔ:l] n pallamano f.
handbasin ['hændbeɪsn] n lavandino.
handbook ['hændbuk] n manuale m.
handbrake ['hændbreɪk] n freno a mano.
hand cream n crema per le mani.
handcuffs ['hændkʌfs] npl manette fpl.
handful ['hændful] n manciata, pugno.
handicap ['hændɪkæp] n handicap m inv ♦ vt handicappare; **to be mentally** ~**ped** essere un handicappato mentale; **to be physically** ~**ped** essere handicappato.
handicraft ['hændɪkrɑ:ft] n lavoro d'artigiano.
handiwork ['hændɪwə:k] n lavorazione f a mano; **this looks like his** ~ (pej) qui c'è il suo zampino.

handkerchief ['hæŋkətʃɪf] *n* fazzoletto.

handle ['hændl] *n* (*of door etc*) maniglia; (*of cup etc*) ansa; (*of knife etc*) impugnatura; (*of saucepan*) manico; (*for winding*) manovella ♦ *vt* toccare, maneggiare; manovrare; (*deal with*) occuparsi di; (*treat: people*) trattare; "~ **with care**" "fragile".

handlebar(s) ['hændlbɑ:(z)] *n*(*pl*) manubrio.

handling charges ['hændlɪŋ-] *npl* commissione *f* per la prestazione; (*for goods*) spese *fpl* di trasporto; (*BANKING*) spese *fpl* bancarie.

hand-luggage ['hændlʌgɪdʒ] *n* bagagli *mpl* a mano.

handmade [hænd'meɪd] *a* fatto(a) a mano; (*biscuits etc*) fatto(a) in casa.

handout ['hændaut] *n* (*leaflet*) volantino; (*press* ~) comunicato stampa.

hand-picked [hænd'pɪkt] *a* (*produce*) scelto(a), selezionato(a); (*staff etc*) scelto(a).

handrail ['hændreɪl] *n* (*on staircase etc*) corrimano.

handshake ['hændʃeɪk] *n* stretta di mano; (*COMPUT*) colloquio.

handsome ['hænsəm] *a* bello(a); (*reward*) generoso(a); (*profit, fortune*) considerevole.

handstand ['hændstænd] *n*: **to do a** ~ fare la verticale.

hand-to-mouth ['hændtə'mauθ] *a* (*existence*) precario(a).

handwriting ['hændraɪtɪŋ] *n* scrittura.

handwritten ['hændrɪtn] *a* scritto(a) a mano, manoscritto(a).

handy ['hændɪ] *a* (*person*) bravo(a); (*close at hand*) a portata di mano; (*convenient*) comodo(a); (*useful: machine etc*) pratico(a), utile; **to come in** ~ servire.

handyman ['hændɪmæn] *n* tuttofare *m inv*; **tools for the** ~ arnesi per il fatelo-da-voi.

hang, pt, pp hung [hæŋ, hʌŋ] *vt* appendere; (*criminal: pt, pp* **hanged**) impiccare ♦ *vi* pendere; (*hair*) scendere; (*drapery*) cadere; **to get the** ~ **of (doing) sth** (*col*) cominiciare a capire (come si fa) qc.

hang about *vi* bighellonare, ciondolare.

hang back *vi* (*hesitate*): **to** ~ **back (from doing)** essere riluttante (a fare).

hang on *vi* (*wait*) aspettare ♦ *vt fus* (*depend on: decision etc*) dipendere da; **to** ~ **on to** (*keep hold of*) aggrapparsi a, attaccarsi a; (*keep*) tenere.

hang out *vt* (*washing*) stendere (fuori); (*col: live*) stare ♦ *vi* penzolare, pendere.

hang together *vi* (*argument etc*) stare in piedi.

hang up *vi* (*TEL*) riattaccare ♦ *vt* appendere; **to** ~ **up on sb** (*TEL*) metter giù il ricevitore a qn.

hangar ['hæŋə*] *n* hangar *m inv*.

hangdog ['hæŋdɔg] *a* (*guilty*: look, expression*) da cane bastonato.

hanger ['hæŋə*] *n* gruccia.

hanger-on [hæŋər'ɔn] *n* parassita *m*.

hang-gliding ['hæŋglaɪdɪŋ] *n* volo col deltaplano.

hanging ['hæŋɪŋ] *n* (*execution*) impiccagione *f*.

hangman ['hæŋmən] *n* boia *m*, carnefice *m*.

hangover ['hæŋəuvə*] *n* (*after drinking*) postumi *mpl* di sbornia.

hang-up ['hæŋʌp] *n* complesso.

hank [hæŋk] *n* matassa.

hanker ['hæŋkə*] *vi*: **to** ~ **after** bramare.

hankie, hanky ['hæŋkɪ] *n abbr* = **handkerchief**.

Hants *abbr* (*Brit*) = *Hampshire*.

haphazard [hæp'hæzəd] *a* a casaccio, alla carlona.

hapless ['hæplɪs] *a* disgraziato(a); (*unfortunate*) sventurato(a).

happen ['hæpən] *vi* accadere, succedere; **she** ~**ed to be free** per caso era libera; **if anything** ~**ed to him** se dovesse succedergli qualcosa; **as it** ~**s** guarda caso; **what's** ~**ing?** cosa succede?, cosa sta succedendo?

happen (up)on *vt fus* capitare su.

happening ['hæpənɪŋ] *n* avvenimento.

happily ['hæpɪlɪ] *ad* felicemente; fortunatamente.

happiness ['hæpɪnɪs] *n* felicità, contentezza.

happy ['hæpɪ] *a* felice, contento(a); ~ **with** (*arrangements etc*) soddisfatto(a) di; **yes, I'd be** ~ **to** (*certo,*) con piacere, (ben) volentieri; ~ **birthday!** buon compleanno!; ~ **Christmas/New Year!** buon Natale/anno!

happy-go-lucky ['hæpɪgəu'lʌkɪ] *a* spensierato(a).

harangue [hə'ræŋ] *vt* arringare.

harass ['hærəs] *vt* molestare.

harassed ['hærəst] *a* assillato(a).

harassment ['hærəsmənt] *n* molestia.

harbour, (*US*) **harbor** ['hɑ:bə*] *n* porto ♦ *vt* dare rifugio a; (*retain: grudge etc*) covare, nutrire.

harbo(u)r dues *npl* diritti *mpl* portuali.

harbo(u)r master *n* capitano di porto.

hard [hɑ:d] *a* duro(a) ♦ *ad* (*work*) sodo; (*think, try*) bene; **to look** ~ **at** guardare fissamente; esaminare attentamente; **to drink** ~ bere forte; ~ **luck!** peccato!; **no** ~ **feelings!** senza rancore!; **to be** ~ **of hearing** essere duro(a) d'orecchio; **to be** ~ **on sb** essere severo con qn; **to be** ~ **done by** essere trattato(a) ingiustamente; **I find it** ~ **to believe that** ... stento *or* faccio fatica a credere che ... + *sub*.

hard-and-fast ['hɑ:dən'fɑ:st] *a* ferreo(a).

hardback ['hɑ:dbæk] *n* libro rilegato.

hardboard ['hɑ:dbɔ:d] *n* legno precompresso.

hard-boiled egg ['hɑ:d'bɔɪld-] *n* uovo sodo.

hard cash *n* denaro in contanti.

hard copy *n* (*COMPUT*) hard copy *f inv*, terminale *m* di stampa.

hard-core ['hɑ:d'kɔ:*] *a* (*pornography*) hardcore *inv*; (*supporters*) irriducibile.

hard court *n* (*TENNIS*) campo in terra battuta.

hard disk n (COMPUT) hard disk m inv, disco rigido.

harden ['hɑ:dn] vt indurire; (steel) temprare; (fig: determination) rafforzare ♦ vi (substance) indurirsi.

hardened ['hɑ:dnd] a (criminal) incallito(a); **to be ~ to sth** essere (diventato) insensibile a qc.

hard graft n: **by sheer ~** lavorando da matti.

hard-headed ['hɑ:d'hɛdɪd] a pratico(a).

hard-hearted ['hɑ:d'hɑ:tɪd] a che non si lascia commuovere, dal cuore duro.

hard labour n lavori forzati mpl.

hardliner [hɑ:d'laɪnə*] n fautore/trice della linea dura.

hardly ['hɑ:dlɪ] ad (scarcely) appena, a mala pena; **it's ~ the case** non è proprio il caso; **~ anyone/anywhere** quasi nessuno/da nessuna parte; **I can ~ believe it** stento a crederci.

hardness ['hɑ:dnɪs] n durezza.

hard sell n (COMM) intensa campagna promozionale.

hardship ['hɑ:dʃɪp] n avversità f inv; privazioni fpl.

hard shoulder n (Brit AUT) corsia d'emergenza.

hard-up [hɑ:d'ʌp] a (col) al verde.

hardware ['hɑ:dwɛə*] n ferramenta fpl; (COMPUT) hardware m.

hardware shop n (negozio di) ferramenta fpl.

hard-wearing [hɑ:d'wɛərɪŋ] a resistente, robusto(a).

hard-working [hɑ:d'wə:kɪŋ] a lavoratore(trice).

hardy ['hɑ:dɪ] a robusto(a); (plant) resistente al gelo.

hare [hɛə*] n lepre f.

hare-brained ['hɛəbreɪnd] a folle; scervellato(a).

harelip ['hɛəlɪp] n (MED) labbro leporino.

harem [hɑ:'ri:m] n harem m inv.

hark back [hɑ:k-] vi: **to ~ back to** (former days) rievocare; (earlier occasion) ritornare a or su.

harm [hɑ:m] n male m; (wrong) danno ♦ vt (person) fare male a; (thing) danneggiare; **to mean no ~** non avere l'intenzione d'offendere; **out of ~'s way** al sicuro; **there's no ~ in trying** tentar non nuoce.

harmful ['hɑ:mful] a dannoso(a).

harmless ['hɑ:mlɪs] a innocuo(a); inoffensivo(a).

harmonic [hɑ:'mɔnɪk] a armonico(a).

harmonica [hɑ:'mɔnɪkə] n armonica.

harmonics [hɑ:'mɔnɪks] npl armonia.

harmonious [hɑ:'məunɪəs] a armonioso(a).

harmonium [hɑ:'məunɪəm] n armonium m inv.

harmonize ['hɑ:mənaɪz] vt, vi armonizzare.

harmony ['hɑ:mənɪ] n armonia.

harness ['hɑ:nɪs] n bardatura, finimenti mpl ♦ vt (horse) bardare; (resources) sfruttare.

harp [hɑ:p] n arpa ♦ vi: **to ~ on about** insistere tediosamente su.

harpist ['hɑ:pɪst] n arpista m/f.

harpoon [hɑ:'pu:n] n arpione m.

harpsichord ['hɑ:psɪkɔ:d] n clavicembalo.

harrow ['hærəu] n (AGR) erpice m.

harrowing ['hærəuɪŋ] a straziante.

harry ['hærɪ] vt (MIL) saccheggiare; (person) assillare.

harsh [hɑ:ʃ] a (hard) duro(a); (severe) severo(a); (unpleasant: sound) rauco(a); (: colour) chiassoso(a); violento(a).

harshly ['hɑ:ʃlɪ] ad duramente; severamente.

harshness ['hɑ:ʃnɪs] n durezza; severità.

harvest ['hɑ:vɪst] n raccolto; (of grapes) vendemmia ♦ vt fare il raccolto di, raccogliere; vendemmiare ♦ vi fare il raccolto; vendemmiare.

harvester ['hɑ:vɪstə*] n (machine) mietitrice f; (also: **combine ~**) mietitrebbia; (person) mietitore/trice.

has [hæz] see have.

has-been ['hæzbi:n] n (col: person): **he's/she's a ~** ha fatto il suo tempo.

hash [hæʃ] n (CULIN) specie di spezzatino fatto con carne già cotta; (fig: mess) pasticcio ♦ n abbr (col) = hashish.

hashish ['hæʃɪʃ] n hascisc m.

hasn't ['hæznt] = has not.

hassle ['hæsl] n (col) sacco di problemi.

haste [heɪst] n fretta.

hasten ['heɪsn] vt affrettare ♦ vi affrettarsi; **I ~ to add that** ... mi preme di aggiungere che ....

hastily ['heɪstɪlɪ] ad in fretta, precipitosamente.

hasty ['heɪstɪ] a affrettato(a), precipitoso(a).

hat [hæt] n cappello.

hatbox ['hætbɔks] n cappelliera.

hatch [hætʃ] n (NAUT: also: **~way**) boccaporto; (Brit: also: **service ~**) portello di servizio ♦ vi schiudersi ♦ vt covare; (fig: scheme, plot) elaborare, mettere a punto.

hatchback ['hætʃbæk] n (AUT) tre (or cinque) porte f inv.

hatchet ['hætʃɪt] n accetta.

hate [heɪt] vt odiare, detestare ♦ n odio; **to ~ to do** or **doing** detestare fare; **I ~ to trouble you, but** ... mi dispiace disturbarla, ma ....

hateful ['heɪtful] a odioso(a), detestabile.

hatred ['heɪtrɪd] n odio.

hat trick n (Brit SPORT, also fig): **to get a ~** segnare tre punti consecutivi (or vincere per tre volte consecutive).

haughty ['hɔ:tɪ] a altero(a), arrogante.

haul [hɔ:l] vt trascinare, tirare ♦ n (of fish) pescata; (of stolen goods etc) bottino.

haulage ['hɔ:lɪdʒ] n trasporto; autotrasporto.

haulage contractor n (Brit: firm) impresa di trasporti; (: person) autotrasportatore m.

haulier ['hɔ:lɪə*], (US) **hauler** ['hɔ:lə*] n autotrasportatore m.

haunch [hɔ:ntʃ] n anca; **a ~ of venison** una coscia di cervo.

haunt [hɔ:nt] vt (subj: fear) pervadere; (: person) frequentare ♦ n rifugio; **a ghost** ~s **this house** questa casa è abitata da un fantasma.

haunted ['hɔ:ntɪd] a (castle etc) abitato(a) dai fantasmi or dagli spiriti; (look) ossessionato(a), tormentato(a).

haunting ['hɔ:ntɪŋ] a (sight, music) ossessionante, che perseguita.

Havana [hə'vænə] n l'Avana.

have pt, pp **had** [hæv, hæd] vt avere; (meal, shower) fare ♦ auxiliary vb avere; **to ~ eaten** aver mangiato; **to ~ arrived** essere arrivato(a); **to ~ breakfast** far colazione; **to ~ lunch** pranzare; **to ~ dinner** cenare; **I'll ~ a coffee** prendo un caffè; **to ~ an operation** avere or subire un'operazione; **to ~ a party** dare una festa; **to ~ sth done** far fare qc; **he had a suit made** si fece fare un abito; **let me ~ a try** fammi or lasciami provare; **she has to do it** lo deve fare; **I had better leave** è meglio che io vada; **I won't ~ it** questo non mi va affatto; **he's been had** (col) c'è cascato dentro; see also **haves**.

have in vt: **to ~ it in for sb** (col) avercela con qn.

have on vt (garment) avere addosso; (be busy with) avere da fare; **I don't ~ any money on me** non ho soldi addosso; ~ **you anything on tomorrow?** (Brit) ha qualcosa in programma per domani?; **to ~ sb on** (Brit col) prendere in giro qn.

have out vt: **to ~ it out with sb** mettere le cose in chiaro con qn.

haven ['heɪvn] n porto; (fig) rifugio.

haversack ['hævəsæk] n zaino.

haves [hævz] npl (col): **the ~ and the have-nots** gli abbienti e i non abbienti.

havoc ['hævək] n caos m.

Hawaii [hə'waɪi:] n le Hawaii.

Hawaiian [hə'waɪjən] a hawaiano(a) ♦ n hawaiano/a; (LING) lingua hawaiana.

hawk [hɔ:k] n falco ♦ vt (goods for sale) vendere per strada.

hawker ['hɔ:kə*] n venditore m ambulante.

hawthorn ['hɔ:θɔ:n] n biancospino.

hay [heɪ] n fieno.

hay fever n febbre f da fieno.

haystack ['heɪstæk] n pagliaio.

haywire ['heɪwaɪə*] a (col): **to go ~** perdere la testa; impazzire.

hazard ['hæzəd] n (chance) azzardo; (risk) pericolo, rischio ♦ vt (one's life) rischiare, mettere a repentaglio; (remark) azzardare; **to be a health/fire ~** essere pericoloso per la salute/in caso d'incendio; **to ~ a guess** tirare a indovinare.

hazardous ['hæzədəs] a pericoloso(a), rischioso(a).

hazard pay n (US) indennità di rischio.

hazard warning lights npl (AUT) luci fpl di emergenza.

haze [heɪz] n foschia.

hazel ['heɪzl] n (tree) nocciolo ♦ a (eyes) (color) nocciola inv.

hazelnut ['heɪzlnʌt] n nocciola.

hazy ['heɪzɪ] a fosco(a); (idea) vago(a); (photograph) indistinto(a).

H-bomb ['eɪtʃbɔm] n bomba H.

h & c abbr (Brit) = hot and cold (water).

HE abbr = high explosive; (REL, DIPLOMACY: = His (or Her) Excellency) S.E.

he [hi:] pronoun lui, egli; **it is ~ who ...** è lui che ...; **here ~ is** eccolo; ~-**bear** etc orso etc maschio.

head [hɛd] n testa, capo; (leader) capo; (on tape recorder, computer etc) testina ♦ vt (list) essere in testa a; (group) essere a capo di; ~**s (or tails)** testa (o croce), pari (o dispari); ~ **first** a capofitto; ~ **over heels in love** pazzamente innamorato(a); **£10 a** or **per ~** 10 sterline a testa; **to sit at the ~ of the table** sedersi a capotavola; **to have a ~ for business** essere tagliato per gli affari; **to have no ~ for heights** soffrire di vertigini; **to lose/keep one's ~** perdere/non perdere la testa; **to come to a ~** (fig: situation etc) precipitare; **to ~ the ball** (SPORT) dare di testa alla palla.

head for vt fus dirigersi verso.

head off vt (threat, danger) sventare.

headache ['hɛdeɪk] n mal m di testa; **to have a ~** aver mal di testa.

head cold n raffreddore m di testa.

headdress ['hɛddrɛs] n (of Indian etc) copricapo; (of bride) acconciatura.

header ['hɛdə*] n (Brit col: FOOTBALL) colpo di testa; (: fall) caduta di testa.

headhunter ['hɛdhʌntə*] n cacciatore m di teste.

heading ['hɛdɪŋ] n titolo; intestazione f.

headlamp ['hɛdlæmp] n (Brit) = headlight.

headland ['hɛdlənd] n promontorio.

headlight ['hɛdlaɪt] n fanale m.

headline ['hɛdlaɪn] n titolo.

headlong ['hɛdlɔŋ] ad (fall) a capofitto; (rush) precipitosamente.

headmaster [hɛd'mɑ:stə*] n preside m.

headmistress [hɛd'mɪstrɪs] n preside f.

head office n sede f (centrale).

head-on [hɛd'ɔn] a (collision) frontale.

headphones ['hɛdfəunz] npl cuffia.

headquarters (HQ) [hɛd'kwɔ:təz] npl ufficio centrale; (MIL) quartiere m generale.

head-rest ['hɛdrɛst] n poggiacapo.

headroom ['hɛdrum] n (in car) altezza dell'abitacolo; (under bridge) altezza limite.

headscarf ['hɛdskɑ:f] n foulard m inv.

headset ['hɛdsɛt] n = headphones.

headstone ['hɛdstəun] n (on grave) lapide f, pietra tombale.

headstrong ['hɛdstrɔŋ] a testardo(a).

head waiter n capocameriere m.

headway ['hɛdweɪ] n: **to make ~** fare progressi or passi avanti.

headwind ['hɛdwɪnd] n controvento.

heady ['hɛdɪ] a che dà alla testa; inebriante.

heal [hi:l] vt, vi guarire.

health [hɛlθ] *n* salute *f*; **Department of H~** ≈ Ministero della Sanità.
health centre *n* (*Brit*) poliambulatorio.
health food(s) *n*(*pl*) alimenti *mpl* integrali.
health hazard *n* pericolo per la salute.
Health Service *n*: **the ~** (*Brit*) ≈ il Servizio Sanitario Statale.
healthy ['hɛlθɪ] *a* (*person*) in buona salute; (*climate*) salubre; (*food*) salutare; (*attitude etc*) sano(a); (*economy*) florido(a); (*bank balance*) solido(a).
heap [hi:p] *n* mucchio ♦ *vt* ammucchiare; **~s (of)** (*col*: *lots*) un sacco (di), un mucchio (di); **to ~ favours/praise/gifts** *etc* **on sb** ricolmare qn di favori/lodi/regali *etc*.
hear, *pt*, *pp* **heard** [hɪə*, hə:d] *vt* sentire; (*news*) ascoltare; (*lecture*) assistere a; (*LAW*: *case*) esaminare ♦ *vi* sentire; **to ~ about** sentire parlare di; (*have news of*) avere notizie di; **did you ~ about the move?** ha sentito del trasloco?; **to ~ from sb** ricevere notizie da qn.
hear out *vt* ascoltare senza interrompere.
hearing ['hɪərɪŋ] *n* (*sense*) udito; (*of witnesses*) audizione *f*; (*of a case*) udienza; **to give sb a ~** dare ascolto a qn.
hearing aid *n* apparecchio acustico.
hearsay ['hɪəseɪ] *n* dicerie *fpl*, chiacchiere *fpl*; **by ~** *ad* per sentito dire.
hearse [hə:s] *n* carro funebre.
heart [hɑ:t] *n* cuore *m*; **~s** *npl* (*CARDS*) cuori *mpl*; **at ~** in fondo; **by ~** (*learn*, *know*) a memoria; **to take ~** farsi coraggio *or* animo; **to lose ~** perdere coraggio, scoraggiarsi; **to have a weak ~** avere il cuore debole; **to set one's ~ on sth/on doing sth** tenere molto a qc/a fare qc; **the ~ of the matter** il nocciolo della questione.
heart attack *n* attacco di cuore.
heartbeat ['hɑ:tbi:t] *n* battito del cuore.
heartbreak ['hɑ:tbreɪk] *n* immenso dolore *m*.
heartbreaking ['hɑ:tbreɪkɪŋ] *a* straziante.
heartbroken ['hɑ:tbrəukən] *a* affranto(a); **to be ~** avere il cuore spezzato.
heartburn ['hɑ:tbə:n] *n* bruciore *m* di stomaco.
-hearted ['hɑ:tɪd] *suffix*: **a kind~ person** una persona molto gentile.
heartening ['hɑ:tnɪŋ] *a* incoraggiante.
heart failure *n* (*MED*) arresto cardiaco.
heartfelt ['hɑ:tfɛlt] *a* sincero(a).
hearth [hɑ:θ] *n* focolare *m*.
heartily ['hɑ:tɪlɪ] *ad* (*laugh*) di cuore; (*eat*) di buon appetito; (*agree*) in pieno, completamente; **to be ~ sick of** (*Brit*) essere veramente stufo di, essere arcistufo di.
heartland ['hɑ:tlænd] *n* zona centrale; **Italy's industrial ~** il cuore dell'industria italiana.
heartless ['hɑ:tlɪs] *a* senza cuore, insensibile; crudele.
heart-to-heart ['hɑ:ttə'hɑ:t] *a*, *ad* a cuore aperto.
heart transplant *n* trapianto del cuore.
heartwarming ['hɑ:twɔ:mɪŋ] *a* confortante,

che scalda il cuore.
hearty ['hɑ:tɪ] *a* caloroso(a); robusto(a), sano(a); vigoroso(a).
heat [hi:t] *n* calore *m*; (*fig*) ardore *m*; fuoco; (*SPORT*: *also*: **qualifying ~**) prova eliminatoria; (*ZOOL*): **in** *or* (*Brit*) **on ~** in calore ♦ *vt* scaldare.
heat up *vi* (*liquids*) scaldarsi; (*room*) riscaldarsi ♦ *vt* riscaldare.
heated ['hi:tɪd] *a* riscaldato(a); (*fig*) appassionato(a); acceso(a), eccitato(a).
heater ['hi:tə*] *n* stufa; radiatore *m*.
heath [hi:θ] *n* (*Brit*) landa.
heathen ['hi:ðn] *a*, *n* pagano(a).
heather ['hɛðə*] *n* erica.
heating ['hi:tɪŋ] *n* riscaldamento.
heat-resistant ['hi:trɪzɪstənt] *a* termoresistente.
heatstroke ['hi:tstrəuk] *n* colpo di sole.
heatwave ['hi:tweɪv] *n* ondata di caldo.
heave [hi:v] *vt* sollevare (con forza) ♦ *vi* sollevarsi ♦ *n* (*push*) grande spinta; **to ~ a sigh** emettere *or* mandare un sospiro.
heave to (*pt*, *pp* **hove**) *vi* (*NAUT*) mettersi in cappa.
heaven ['hɛvn] *n* paradiso, cielo; **~ forbid!** Dio ce ne guardi!; **for ~'s sake!** (*pleading*) per amor del cielo!, per carità!; (*protesting*) santo cielo!, in nome del cielo!; **thank ~!** grazie al cielo!
heavenly ['hɛvnlɪ] *a* divino(a), celeste.
heavily ['hɛvɪlɪ] *ad* pesantemente; (*drink*, *smoke*) molto.
heavy ['hɛvɪ] *a* pesante; (*sea*) grosso(a); (*rain*) forte; (*drinker*, *smoker*) gran (*before noun*); **it's ~ going** è una gran fatica; **~ industry** industria pesante.
heavy cream *n* (*US*) doppia panna.
heavy-duty ['hɛvɪ'dju:tɪ] *a* molto resistente.
heavy goods vehicle (HGV) *n* (*Brit*) veicolo per trasporti pesanti.
heavy-handed ['hɛvɪ'hændɪd] *a* (*clumsy*, *tactless*) pesante.
heavyweight ['hɛvɪweɪt] *n* (*SPORT*) peso massimo.
Hebrew ['hi:bru:] *a* ebreo(a) ♦ *n* (*LING*) ebraico.
Hebrides ['hɛbrɪdi:z] *npl*: **the ~** le Ebridi.
heckle ['hɛkl] *vt* interpellare e dare noia a (*un oratore*).
heckler ['hɛklə*] *n* agitatore/trice.
hectare ['hɛktɑ:*] *n* (*Brit*) ettaro.
hectic ['hɛktɪk] *a* movimentato(a); (*busy*) frenetico(a).
hector ['hɛktə*] *vt* usare le maniere forti con.
he'd [hi:d] = **he would**; **he had**.
hedge [hɛdʒ] *n* siepe *f* ♦ *vi* essere elusivo(a); **as a ~ against inflation** per cautelarsi contro l'inflazione; **to ~ one's bets** (*fig*) coprirsi dai rischi.
hedge in *vt* recintare con una siepe.
hedgehog ['hɛdʒhɔg] *n* riccio.
hedgerow ['hɛdʒrəu] *n* siepe *f*.
hedonism ['hi:dənɪzəm] *n* edonismo.

heed [hi:d] *vt* (*also*: **take ~ of**) badare a, far conto di ♦ *n*: **to pay (no) ~ to, to take (no) ~ of** (non) ascoltare, (non) tener conto di.

heedless ['hi:dlıs] *a* sbadato(a).

heel [hi:l] *n* (*ANAT*) calcagno; (*of shoe*) tacco ♦ *vt* (*shoe*) rifare i tacchi a; **to bring to ~** addomesticare; **to take to one's ~s** (*col*) darsela a gambe, alzare i tacchi.

hefty ['hɛftɪ] *a* (*person*) solido(a); (*parcel*) pesante; (*piece, price*) grosso(a).

heifer ['hɛfə*] *n* giovenca.

height [haɪt] *n* altezza; (*high ground*) altura; (*fig: of glory*) apice *m*; (: *of stupidity*) colmo; **what ~ are you?** quanto sei alto?; **of average ~** di statura media; **to be afraid of ~s** soffrire di vertigini; **it's the ~ of fashion** è l'ultimo grido della moda.

heighten ['haɪtn] *vt* innalzare; (*fig*) accrescere.

heinous ['heɪnəs] *a* nefando(a), atroce.

heir [ɛə*] *n* erede *m*.

heir apparent *n* erede *m/f* legittimo(a).

heiress ['ɛərɛs] *n* erede *f*.

heirloom ['ɛəlu:m] *n* mobile *m* (*or* gioiello *or* quadro) di famiglia.

heist [haɪst] *n* (*US col*) rapina.

held [hɛld] *pt, pp of* **hold**.

helicopter ['hɛlɪkɒptə*] *n* elicottero.

heliport ['hɛlɪpɔ:t] *n* eliporto.

helium ['hi:lɪəm] *n* elio.

hell [hɛl] *n* inferno; **a ~ of a ...** (*col*) un(a) maledetto(a) ...; **oh ~!** (*col*) porca miseria!, accidenti!

he'll [hi:l] = **he will, he shall**.

hellish ['hɛlɪʃ] *a* infernale.

hello [hə'ləu] *excl* buon giorno!; ciao! (*to sb one addresses as "tu"*); (*surprise*) ma guarda!

helm [hɛlm] *n* (*NAUT*) timone *m*.

helmet ['hɛlmɪt] *n* casco.

helmsman ['hɛlmzmən] *n* timoniere *m*.

help [hɛlp] *n* aiuto; (*charwoman*) donna di servizio; (*assistant etc*) impiegato/a ♦ *vt* aiutare; **~!** aiuto!; **with the ~ of** con l'aiuto di; **to be of ~ to sb** essere di aiuto *or* essere utile a qn; **to ~ sb (to) do sth** aiutare qn a far qc; **can I ~ you?** (*in shop*) desidera?; **~ yourself (to bread)** si serva (del pane); **I can't ~ saying** non posso evitare di dire; **he can't ~ it** non ci può far niente.

helper ['hɛlpə*] *n* aiutante *m/f*, assistente *m/f*.

helpful ['hɛlpful] *a* di grande aiuto; (*useful*) utile.

helping ['hɛlpɪŋ] *n* porzione *f*.

helpless ['hɛlplɪs] *a* impotente; debole; (*baby*) indifeso(a).

helplessly ['hɛlplɪslɪ] *ad* (*watch*) senza poter fare nulla.

Helsinki ['hɛlsɪŋkɪ] *n* Helsinki *f*.

helter-skelter ['hɛltə'skɛltə*] *n* (*Brit*: *in funfair*) scivolo (a spirale).

hem [hɛm] *n* orlo ♦ *vt* fare l'orlo a.
  hem in *vt* cingere; **to feel ~med in** (*fig*) sentirsi soffocare.

he-man ['hi:mæn] *n* (*col*) fusto.

hematology [hi:mə'tɒlədʒɪ] *n* (*US*) = **haematology**.

hemisphere ['hɛmɪsfɪə*] *n* emisfero.

hemlock ['hɛmlɒk] *n* cicuta.

hemoglobin [hi:məu'gləubɪn] *n* (*US*) = **haemoglobin**.

hemophilia [hi:məu'fɪlɪə] *n* (*US*) = **haemophilia**.

hemorrhage *n* (*US*) = **haemorrhage**.

hemorrhoids ['hɛmərɔɪdz] *npl* (*US*) = **haemorrhoids**.

hemp [hɛmp] *n* canapa.

hen [hɛn] *n* gallina; (*female bird*) femmina.

hence [hɛns] *ad* (*therefore*) dunque; **2 years ~** di qui a 2 anni.

henceforth [hɛns'fɔ:θ] *ad* d'ora in poi.

henchman ['hɛntʃmən] *n* (*pej*) caudatario.

henna ['hɛnə] *n* henna.

hen party *n* (*col*) festa di sole donne.

henpecked ['hɛnpɛkt] *a* dominato dalla moglie.

hepatitis [hɛpə'taɪtɪs] *n* epatite *f*.

her [hə:*] *pronoun* (*direct*) la, l' + *vowel*; (*indirect*) le; (*stressed, after prep*) lei; *see note at* **she** ♦ *a* il(la) suo(a), i(le) suoi(sue); **I see ~** la vedo; **give ~ a book** le dia un libro; **after ~** dopo (di) lei.

herald ['hɛrəld] *n* araldo ♦ *vt* annunciare.

heraldic [hɛ'rældɪk] *a* araldico(a).

heraldry ['hɛrəldrɪ] *n* araldica.

herb [hə:b] *n* erba; **~s** *npl* (*CULIN*) erbette *fpl*.

herbaceous [hə:'beɪʃəs] *a* erbaceo(a).

herbal ['hə:bəl] *a* di erbe; **~ tea** tisana.

herbicide ['hə:bɪsaɪd] *n* erbicida *m*.

herd [hə:d] *n* mandria; (*of wild animals, swine*) branco ♦ *vt* (*drive, gather: animals*) guidare; (: *people*) radunare; **~ed together** ammassati (come bestie).

here [hɪə*] *ad* qui, qua ♦ *excl* ehi!; **~!** (*at roll call*) presente!; **~ is, ~ are** ecco; **~'s my sister** ecco mia sorella; **~ she is** eccola; **~ she comes** eccola che viene; **come ~!** vieni qui!; **~ and there** qua e là.

hereabouts ['hɪərəbauts] *ad* da queste parti.

hereafter [hɪər'ɑ:ftə*] *ad* in futuro; dopo questo ♦ *n*: **the ~** l'al di là *m*.

hereby [hɪə'baɪ] *ad* (*in letter*) con la presente.

hereditary [hɪ'rɛdɪtrɪ] *a* ereditario(a).

heredity [hɪ'rɛdɪtɪ] *n* eredità.

heresy ['hɛrəsɪ] *n* eresia.

heretic ['hɛrətɪk] *n* eretico/a.

heretical [hɪ'rɛtɪkl] *a* eretico(a).

herewith [hɪə'wɪð] *ad* qui accluso.

heritage ['hɛrɪtɪdʒ] *n* eredità; (*fig*) retaggio; **our national ~** il nostro patrimonio nazionale.

hermetically [hə:'mɛtɪklɪ] *ad* ermeticamente; **~ sealed** ermeticamente chiuso.

hermit ['hə:mɪt] *n* eremita *m*.

hernia ['hə:nɪə] *n* ernia.

hero, ~es ['hɪərəu] *n* eroe *m*.

heroic [hɪ'rəuɪk] *a* eroico(a).

heroin ['hɛrəuɪn] n eroina (droga).
heroin addict n eroinomane m/f.
heroine ['hɛrəuɪn] n eroina (donna).
heroism ['hɛrəuɪzəm] n eroismo.
heron ['hɛrən] n airone m.
hero worship n divismo.
herring ['hɛrɪŋ] n aringa.
hers [hə:z] pronoun il(la) suo(a), i(le) suoi(sue); **a friend of** ~ un suo amico; **this is** ~ questo è (il) suo.
herself [hə:'sɛlf] pronoun (reflexive) si; (emphatic) lei stessa; (after prep) se stessa, sé.
Herts abbr (Brit) = Hertfordshire.
he's [hi:z] = **he is**; **he has**.
hesitant ['hɛzɪtənt] a esitante, indeciso(a); **to be** ~ **about doing sth** esitare a fare qc.
hesitate ['hɛzɪteɪt] vi: **to** ~ **(about/to do)** esitare (su/a fare); **don't** ~ **to ask (me)** non aver timore or paura di chiedermelo.
hesitation [hɛzɪ'teɪʃən] n esitazione f; **I have no** ~ **in saying (that)** ... non esito a dire che ....
hessian ['hɛsɪən] n tela di canapa.
heterogeneous [hɛtərəu'dʒi:nɪəs] a eterogeneo(a).
heterosexual [hɛtərəu'sɛksjuəl] a, n eterosessuale (m/f).
het up [hɛt'ʌp] a agitato(a).
HEW n abbr (US: = Department of Health, Education and Welfare) ministero della sanità, della pubblica istruzione e della previdenza sociale.
hew [hju:] vt tagliare (con l'accetta).
hex [hɛks] (US) n stregoneria ♦ vt stregare.
hexagon ['hɛksəgən] n esagono.
hexagonal [hɛk'sægənl] a esagonale.
hey [heɪ] excl ehi!
heyday ['heɪdeɪ] n: **the** ~ **of** i bei giorni di, l'età d'oro di.
HF n abbr (= high frequency) AF.
HGV n abbr see **heavy goods vehicle**.
HI abbr (US POST) = Hawaii.
hi [haɪ] excl ciao!
hiatus [haɪ'eɪtəs] n vuoto; (LING) iato.
hibernate ['haɪbəneɪt] vi ibernare.
hibernation [haɪbə'neɪʃən] n letargo, ibernazione f.
hiccough, hiccup ['hɪkʌp] vi singhiozzare ♦ n singhiozzo; **to have (the)** ~**s** avere il singhiozzo.
hid [hɪd] pt of **hide**.
hidden ['hɪdn] pp of **hide** ♦ a nascosto(a); **there are no** ~ **extras** è veramente tutto compreso nel prezzo.
hide [haɪd] n (skin) pelle f ♦ vb (pt hid, pp hidden [hɪd, 'hɪdn]) vt: **to** ~ **sth (from sb)** nascondere qc (a qn) ♦ vi: **to** ~ **(from sb)** nascondersi (da qn).
hide-and-seek ['haɪdən'si:k] n rimpiattino.
hideaway ['haɪdəweɪ] n nascondiglio.
hideous ['hɪdɪəs] a laido(a); orribile.
hide-out ['haɪdaut] n nascondiglio.
hiding ['haɪdɪŋ] n (beating) bastonata; **to be**

in ~ (concealed) tenersi nascosto(a).
hiding place n nascondiglio.
hierarchy ['haɪərɑ:kɪ] n gerarchia.
hieroglyphic [haɪərə'glɪfɪk] a geroglifico(a); ~**s** npl geroglifici mpl.
hi-fi ['haɪ'faɪ] a, n abbr (= high fidelity) hi-fi (m) inv.
higgledy-piggledy ['hɪgldɪ'pɪgldɪ] ad alla rinfusa.
high [haɪ] a alto(a); (speed, respect, number) grande; (wind) forte; (Brit CULIN: meat, game) frollato(a); (: spoilt) andato(a) a male; (col: on drugs) fatto(a); (: on drink) su di giri ♦ ad alto, in alto ♦ n: **exports have reached a new** ~ le esportazioni hanno toccato un nuovo record; **20m** ~ alto(a) 20m; **to pay a** ~ **price for sth** pagare (molto) caro qc.
highball ['haɪbɔ:l] n (US: drink) whisky (or brandy) e soda con ghiaccio.
highboy ['haɪbɔɪ] n (US) cassettone m.
highbrow ['haɪbrau] a, n intellettuale (m/f).
highchair ['haɪtʃɛə*] n seggiolone m.
high-class [haɪ'klɑ:s] a (neighbourhood) elegante; (hotel) di prim'ordine; (person) di gran classe; (food) raffinato(a).
high court n (LAW) corte f suprema.
higher ['haɪə*] a (form of life, study etc) superiore ♦ ad più in alto, più in su.
higher education n istruzione f superiore, istruzione universitaria.
high finance n alta finanza.
high-flier [haɪ'flaɪə*] n uno/a che ha delle mire ambiziose.
high-flying [haɪ'flaɪɪŋ] a (fig) ambizioso(a).
high-handed [haɪ'hændɪd] a prepotente.
high-heeled [haɪ'hi:ld] a a tacchi alti.
highjack ['haɪdʒæk] vt, n = **hijack**.
high jump n (SPORT) salto in alto.
highlands ['haɪləndz] npl zona montuosa; **the** H~ le Highlands scozzesi.
high-level ['haɪlɛvl] a (talks etc, COMPUT) ad alto livello.
highlight ['haɪlaɪt] n (fig: of event) momento culminante ♦ vt mettere in evidenza; ~**s** npl (in hair) colpi mpl di sole.
highlighter ['haɪlaɪtə*] n (pen) evidenziatore m.
highly ['haɪlɪ] ad molto; ~ **paid** pagato molto bene; **to speak** ~ **of** parlare molto bene di.
highly-strung ['haɪlɪ'strʌŋ] a teso(a) di nervi, eccitabile.
High Mass n messa cantata or solenne.
highness ['haɪnɪs] n altezza; **Her H**~ Sua Altezza.
high-pitched [haɪ'pɪtʃt] a acuto(a).
high-powered ['haɪ'pauəd] a (engine) molto potente, ad alta potenza; (fig: person) di prestigio.
high-pressure ['haɪprɛʃə*] a ad alta pressione; (fig) aggressivo(a).
high-rise block ['haɪraɪz-] n palazzone m.
high school n (Brit) scuola secondaria; (US) istituto superiore d'istruzione.

high season n (Brit) alta stagione.
high spirits npl buonumore m, euforia; **to be in ~** essere euforico(a).
high street n (Brit) strada principale.
highway ['haɪweɪ] n strada maestra.
Highway Code n (Brit) codice m della strada.
highwayman ['haɪweɪmən] n bandito.
hijack ['haɪdʒæk] vt dirottare ♦ n dirottamento; (also: ~**ing**) pirateria aerea.
hijacker ['haɪdʒækə*] n dirottatore/trice.
hike [haɪk] vi fare un'escursione a piedi ♦ n escursione f a piedi; (col: in prices etc) aumento ♦ vt (col) aumentare.
hiker ['haɪkə*] n escursionista m/f.
hiking ['haɪkɪŋ] n escursioni fpl a piedi.
hilarious [hɪ'lɛərɪəs] a che fa schiantare dal ridere.
hilarity [hɪ'lærɪtɪ] n ilarità.
hill [hɪl] n collina, colle m; (fairly high) montagna; (on road) salita.
hillbilly ['hɪlbɪlɪ] n (US) montanaro/a dal sud degli Stati Uniti; (pej) zotico/a.
hillock ['hɪlək] n collinetta, poggio.
hillside ['hɪlsaɪd] n fianco della collina.
hill start n (AUT) partenza in salita.
hilly ['hɪlɪ] a collinoso(a); montagnoso(a).
hilt [hɪlt] n (of sword) elsa; **to the ~** (fig: support) fino in fondo.
him [hɪm] pronoun (direct) lo, l' + vowel; (indirect) gli; (stressed, after prep) lui; **I see ~** lo vedo; **give ~ a book** gli dia un libro; **after ~** dopo (di) lui.
Himalayas [hɪmə'leɪəz] npl: **the ~** l'Himalaia m.
himself [hɪm'sɛlf] pronoun (reflexive) si; (emphatic) lui stesso; (after prep) se stesso, sé.
hind [haɪnd] a posteriore ♦ n cerva.
hinder ['hɪndə*] vt ostacolare; (delay) tardare; (prevent): **to ~ sb from doing** impedire a qn di fare.
hindquarters ['haɪndkwɔ:təz] npl (ZOOL) posteriore m.
hindrance ['hɪndrəns] n ostacolo, impedimento.
hindsight ['haɪndsaɪt] n senno di poi; **with the benefit of ~** con il senno di poi.
Hindu ['hɪndu:] n indù m/f inv.
hinge [hɪndʒ] n cardine m ♦ vi (fig): **to ~ on** dipendere da.
hint [hɪnt] n accenno, allusione f; (advice) consiglio ♦ vt: **to ~ that** lasciar capire che ♦ vi: **to ~ at** accennare a; **to drop a ~** lasciar capire; **give me a ~** (clue) dammi almeno un'idea, dammi un'indicazione.
hip [hɪp] n anca, fianco; (BOT) frutto della rosa canina.
hip flask n fiaschetta da liquore tascabile.
hippie ['hɪpɪ] n hippy m/f inv.
hip pocket n tasca posteriore dei calzoni.
hippopotamus, pl ~**es** or **hippopòtami** [hɪpə'pɔtəməs, -'pɔtəmaɪ] n ippopotamo.
hippy ['hɪpɪ] n = **hippie**.

hire ['haɪə*] vt (Brit: car, equipment) noleggiare; (worker) assumere, dare lavoro a ♦ n nolo, noleggio; **for ~** da nolo; (taxi) libero(a); **on ~** a nolo.
hire out vt noleggiare, dare a nolo or noleggio, affittare.
hire(d) car n (Brit) macchina a nolo.
hire purchase (HP) n (Brit) acquisto (or vendita) rateale; **to buy sth on ~** comprare qc a rate.
his [hɪz] a, pronoun il(la) suo(sua), i(le) suoi(sue); **this is ~** questo è (il) suo.
hiss [hɪs] vi fischiare; (cat, snake) sibilare ♦ n fischio; sibilo.
histogram ['hɪstəɡræm] n istogramma m.
historian [hɪ'stɔ:rɪən] n storico/a.
historic(al) [hɪ'stɔrɪk(l)] a storico(a).
history ['hɪstərɪ] n storia; **there's a long ~ of that illness in his family** ci sono molti precedenti (della malattia) nella sua famiglia.
histrionics [hɪstrɪ'ɔnɪks] n istrionismo.
hit [hɪt] vt (pt, pp **hit**) colpire, picchiare; (knock against) battere; (reach: target) raggiungere; (collide with: car) urtare contro; (fig: affect) colpire; (find: problem) incontrare ♦ n colpo; (success, song) successo; **to ~ the headlines** far titolo; **to ~ the road** (col) mettersi in cammino; **to ~ it off with sb** andare molto d'accordo con qn.
hit back vi: **to ~ back at sb** restituire il colpo a qn.
hit out at vt fus sferrare dei colpi contro; (fig) attaccare.
hit (up)on vt fus (answer) imbroccare, azzeccare; (solution) trovare (per caso).
hit-and-run driver ['hɪtænd'rʌn-] n pirata m della strada.
hitch [hɪtʃ] vt (fasten) attaccare; (also: ~ up) tirare su ♦ n (difficulty) intoppo, difficoltà f inv; **technical ~** difficoltà tecnica; **to ~ a lift** fare l'autostop.
hitch up vt (horse, cart) attaccare.
hitch-hike ['hɪtʃhaɪk] vi fare l'autostop.
hitch-hiker ['hɪtʃhaɪkə*] n autostoppista m/f.
hi-tech ['haɪ'tɛk] n alta tecnologia ♦ a di alta tecnologia.
hitherto ['hɪðə'tu:] ad finora.
hitman ['hɪtmæn] n sicario.
hit-or-miss ['hɪtə'mɪs] a: **it's ~ whether ...** è in dubbio se ....
hit parade n hit-parade f.
hive [haɪv] n alveare m; **the shop was a ~ of activity** (fig) c'era una grande attività nel negozio.
hive off vt (col) separare.
hl abbr (= hectolitre) hl.
HM abbr (= His (or Her) Majesty) S.M. (= Sua Maestà).
HMG abbr (Brit) = His (or Her) Majesty's Government.
HMI n abbr (Brit SCOL: = His (or Her) Majesty's Inspector) ≈ ispettore m scolastico.
HMO n abbr (US: = health maintenance

organization) organo per la salvaguardia della salute pubblica.

HMS *abbr* (*Brit*) = *His* (*or Her*) *Majesty's Ship*.

HMSO *n abbr* (*Brit*: = *His* (*or Her*) *Majesty's Stationery Office*) ≈ Poligrafici *mpl* dello Stato.

HNC *n abbr* (*Brit*: = *Higher National Certificate*) diploma di istituto tecnico o professionale.

HND *n abbr* (*Brit*: = *Higher National Diploma*) diploma in materie tecniche equivalente ad una laurea.

hoard [hɔːd] *n* (*of food*) provviste *fpl*; (*of money*) gruzzolo ♦ *vt* ammassare.

hoarding ['hɔːdɪŋ] *n* (*Brit*) tabellone *m* per affissioni.

hoarfrost ['hɔːfrɔst] *n* brina.

hoarse [hɔːs] *a* rauco(a).

hoax [həuks] *n* scherzo; falso allarme.

hob [hɔb] *n* piastra (con fornelli).

hobble ['hɔbl] *vi* zoppicare.

hobby ['hɔbɪ] *n* hobby *m inv*, passatempo.

hobby-horse ['hɔbɪhɔːs] *n* cavallo a dondolo; (*fig*) chiodo fisso.

hobnob ['hɔbnɔb] *vi*: **to ~ (with)** mescolarsi (con).

hobo ['həubəu] *n* (*US*) vagabondo.

hock [hɔk] *n* (*Brit*: *wine*) vino del Reno; (*of animal*, *CULIN*) garretto; (*col*): **to be in ~** avere debiti.

hockey ['hɔkɪ] *n* hockey *m*.

hocus-pocus ['həukəs'pəukəs] *n* (*trickery*) trucco; (*words: of magician*) abracadabra *m inv*; (: *jargon*) parolone *fpl*.

hodgepodge ['hɔdʒpɔdʒ] *n* = **hotchpotch**.

hoe [həu] *n* zappa ♦ *vt* (*ground*) zappare.

hog [hɔg] *n* maiale *m* ♦ *vt* (*fig*) arraffare; **to go the whole ~** farlo fino in fondo.

hoist [hɔɪst] *n* paranco ♦ *vt* issare.

hold [həuld] *vb* (*pt, pp* **held** [hɛld]) *vt* tenere; (*contain*) contenere; (*keep back*) trattenere; (*believe*) mantenere; considerare; (*possess*) avere, possedere; detenere ♦ *vi* (*withstand pressure*) tenere; (*be valid*) essere valido(a) ♦ *n* presa; (*fig*) potere *m*; (*NAUT*) stiva; **~ the line!** (*TEL*) resti in linea!; **to ~ office** (*POL*) essere in carica; **to ~ sb responsible for sth** considerare *or* ritenere qn responsabile di qc; **to ~ one's own** (*fig*) difendersi bene; **he ~s the view that ...** è del parere che ...; **to ~ firm** *or* **fast** resistere bene, tenere; **to catch** *or* **get (a) ~ of** afferrare; **to get ~ of** (*fig*) trovare; **to get ~ of o.s.** trattenersi.

hold back *vt* trattenere; (*secret*) tenere celato(a); **to ~ sb back from doing sth** impedire a qn di fare qc.

hold down *vt* (*person*) tenere a terra; (*job*) tenere.

hold forth *vi* fare *or* tenere una concione.

hold off *vt* tener lontano ♦ *vi* (*rain*): **if the rain ~s off** se continua a non piovere.

hold on *vi* tener fermo; (*wait*) aspettare; **~**

on! (*TEL*) resti in linea!

hold on to *vt fus* tenersi stretto(a) a; (*keep*) conservare.

hold out *vt* offrire ♦ *vi* (*resist*): **to ~ out (against)** resistere (a).

hold over *vt* (*meeting etc*) rimandare, rinviare.

hold up *vt* (*raise*) alzare; (*support*) sostenere; (*delay*) ritardare; (*traffic*) rallentare; (*rob*: *bank*) assaltare.

holdall ['həuldɔːl] *n* (*Brit*) borsone *m*.

holder ['həuldə*] *n* (*of ticket, title*) possessore/posseditrice; (*of office etc*) incaricato/a; (*of passport, post*) titolare; (*of record*) detentore/trice.

holding ['həuldɪŋ] *n* (*share*) azioni *fpl*, titoli *mpl*; (*farm*) podere *m*, tenuta.

holding company *n* holding *f inv*.

holdup ['həuldʌp] *n* (*robbery*) rapina a mano armata; (*delay*) ritardo; (*Brit*: *in traffic*) blocco.

hole [həul] *n* buco, buca ♦ *vt* bucare; **~ in the heart** (*MED*) morbo blu; **to pick ~s in** (*fig*) trovare da ridire su.

hole up *vi* nascondersi, rifugiarsi.

holiday ['hɔlədɪ] *n* vacanza; (*from work*) ferie *fpl*; (*day off*) giorno di vacanza; (*public*) giorno festivo; **to be on ~** essere in vacanza; **tomorrow is a ~** domani è festa.

holiday camp *n* (*Brit*: *for children*) colonia (di villeggiatura); (*also*: **holiday centre**) ≈ villaggio (di vacanze).

holiday-maker ['hɔlədɪmeɪkə*] *n* (*Brit*) villeggiante *m/f*.

holiday pay *n* stipendio delle ferie.

holiday resort *n* luogo di villeggiatura.

holiday season *n* stagione *f* delle vacanze.

holiness ['həulɪnɪs] *n* santità.

Holland ['hɔlənd] *n* Olanda.

hollow ['hɔləu] *a* cavo(a), vuoto(a); (*fig*) falso(a); vano(a) ♦ *n* cavità *f inv*; (*in land*) valletta, depressione *f*.

hollow out *vt* scavare.

holly ['hɔlɪ] *n* agrifoglio.

hollyhock ['hɔlɪhɔk] *n* malvone *m*.

holocaust ['hɔləkɔːst] *n* olocausto.

holster ['həulstə*] *n* fondina (di pistola).

holy ['həulɪ] *a* santo(a); (*bread*) benedetto(a), consacrato(a); (*ground*) consacrato(a); **the H~ Father** il Santo Padre.

Holy Communion *n* la Santa Comunione.

Holy Ghost, Holy Spirit *n* Spirito Santo.

Holy Land *n*: **the ~** la Terra Santa.

holy orders *npl* ordini *mpl* (sacri).

homage ['hɔmɪdʒ] *n* omaggio; **to pay ~ to** rendere omaggio a.

home [həum] *n* casa; (*country*) patria; (*institution*) casa, ricovero ♦ *cpd* (*life*) familiare; (*cooking etc*) casalingo(a); (*ECON, POL*) nazionale, interno(a); (*SPORT: team*) di casa; (: *match, win*) in casa ♦ *ad* a casa; in patria; (*right in*: *nail etc*) fino in fondo; **at ~** a casa; **to go** (*or* **come**) **~** tornare a casa (*or* in patria); **it's near my ~**

è vicino a casa mia; **make yourself at** ~ si
metta a suo agio.

home in on vt fus (missiles) dirigersi
(automaticamente) verso.

home address n indirizzo di casa.

home-brew [həum'bru:] n birra or vino
fatto(a) in casa.

homecoming ['həumkʌmɪŋ] n ritorno.

home computer n home computer m inv.

Home Counties npl contee fpl intorno a Londra.

home economics n economia domestica.

home-grown [həum'grəun] a nostrano(a), di
produzione locale.

homeland ['həumlænd] n patria.

homeless ['həumlɪs] a senza tetto; spa-
triato(a); **the** ~ npl i senzatetto.

home loan n prestito con garanzia
immobiliare.

homely ['həumlɪ] a semplice, alla buona;
accogliente.

home-made [həum'meɪd] a casalingo(a).

Home Office n (Brit) ministero degli Interni.

homeopathy etc [həumɪ'ɔpəθɪ] (US) =
homoeopathy etc.

home rule n autogoverno.

Home Secretary n (Brit) ministro degli
Interni.

homesick ['həumsɪk] a: **to be** ~ avere la nostalgia.

homestead ['həumstɛd] n fattoria e terreni.

home town n città f inv natale.

homeward ['həumwəd] a (journey) di ritorno.

homeward(s) ['həumwəd(z)] ad verso casa.

homework ['həumwə:k] n compiti mpl (per
casa).

homicidal [hɔmɪ'saɪdl] a omicida.

homicide ['hɔmɪsaɪd] n (US) omicidio.

homily ['hɔmɪlɪ] n omelia.

homing ['həumɪŋ] a (device, missile)
autocercante; ~ **pigeon** piccione m
viaggiatore.

homoeopath, (US) **homeopath**
['həumɪəupæθ] n omeopatico.

homoeopathic, (US) **homeopathic**
['həumɪəu'pæθɪk] a omeopatico(a).

homoeopathy, (US) **homeopathy**
[həumɪ'ɔpəθɪ] n omeopatia.

homogeneous [hɔməu'dʒi:nɪəs] a
omogeneo(a).

homogenize [hə'mɔdʒənaɪz] vt omogeneizzare.

homosexual [hɔməu'sɛksjuəl] a, n
omosessuale (m/f).

Hon. abbr = **honourable; honorary.**

Honduras [hɔn'djuərəs] n Honduras m.

hone [həun] vt (sharpen) affilare; (fig)
affinare.

honest ['ɔnɪst] a onesto(a); sincero(a); **to be
quite** ~ **with you** ... se devo dirle la verità
....

honestly ['ɔnɪstlɪ] ad onestamente;
sinceramente.

honesty ['ɔnɪstɪ] n onestà.

honey ['hʌnɪ] n miele m; (US col) tesoro,

amore m.

honeycomb ['hʌnɪkəum] n favo ♦ vt (fig):
~**ed with tunnels** etc pieno(a) di gallerie
etc.

honeymoon ['hʌnɪmu:n] n luna di miele,
viaggio di nozze.

honeysuckle ['hʌnɪsʌkl] n caprifoglio.

Hong Kong ['hɔŋ'kɔŋ] n Hong Kong f.

honk [hɔŋk] n (AUT) colpo di clacson ♦ vi
suonare il clacson.

Honolulu [hɔnə'lu:lu:] n Honolulu f.

honorary ['ɔnərərɪ] a onorario(a); (duty, title)
onorifico(a).

honour, (US) **honor** ['ɔnə*] vt onorare ♦ n
onore m; **in** ~ **of** in onore di.

hono(u)rable ['ɔnərəbl] a onorevole.

hono(u)r-bound ['ɔnə'baund] a: **to be** ~ **to
do** dover fare per una questione di onore.

hono(u)rs degree n (SCOL) laurea
specializzata.

Hons. [ɔnz] abbr (SCOL) = **hono(u)rs degree.**

hood [hud] n cappuccio; (Brit AUT) capote f;
(US AUT) cofano; (col) malvivente m/f.

hooded ['hudɪd] a (robber) mascherato(a).

hoodlum ['hu:dləm] n malvivente m/f.

hoodwink ['hudwɪŋk] vt infinocchiare.

hoof, pl ~**s** or **hooves** [hu:f, hu:vz] n zoccolo.

hook [huk] n gancio; (for fishing) amo ♦ vt
uncinare; (dress) agganciare; **to be** ~**ed on**
(col) essere fanatico di; ~**s and eyes**
gancetti; **by** ~ **or by crook** in un modo o
nell'altro.

hook up vt (RADIO, TV etc) allacciare,
collegare.

hooligan ['hu:lɪgən] n giovinastro, teppista m.

hooliganism ['hu:lɪgənɪzəm] n teppismo.

hoop [hu:p] n cerchio.

hoot [hu:t] vi (AUT) suonare il clacson; (owl)
gufare ♦ n colpo di clacson; **to** ~ **with laughter** farsi una gran risata.

hooter ['hu:tə*] n (AUT) clacson m inv;
(NAUT, at factory) sirena.

hoover ® ['hu:və*] n (Brit) aspirapolvere m
inv ♦ vt pulire con l'aspirapolvere.

hooves [hu:vz] npl of **hoof.**

hop [hɔp] vi saltellare, saltare; (on one foot)
saltare su una gamba ♦ n salto; see also
hops.

hope [həup] vt, vi sperare ♦ n speranza; **I** ~
so/not spero di sì/no.

hopeful ['həupful] a (person) pieno(a) di
speranza; (situation) promettente; **I'm** ~
that she'll manage to come ho buone
speranze che venga.

hopefully ['həupfulɪ] ad con speranza; ~ **he
will recover** speriamo che si riprenda.

hopeless ['həuplɪs] a senza speranza, di-
sperato(a); (useless) inutile.

hopelessly ['həuplɪslɪ] ad (live etc) senza
speranza; (involved, complicated) spaventosamente; (late) disperatamente, irrimedia-
bilmente; **I'm** ~ **confused/lost** sono completamente confuso/perso.

hopper ['hɔpə*] n (chute) tramoggia.
hops [hɔps] npl luppoli mpl.
horde [hɔ:d] n orda.
horizon [hə'raɪzn] n orizzonte m.
horizontal [hɔrɪ'zɔntl] a orizzontale.
hormone ['hɔ:məʊn] n ormone m.
horn [hɔ:n] n corno; (AUT) clacson m inv.
horned [hɔ:nd] a (animal) cornuto(a).
hornet ['hɔ:nɪt] n calabrone m.
horny ['hɔ:nɪ] a corneo(a); (hands) calloso(a).
horoscope ['hɔrəskəʊp] n oroscopo.
horrendous [hə'rɛndəs] n orrendo(a).
horrible ['hɔrɪbl] a orribile, tremendo(a).
horrid ['hɔrɪd] a orrido(a); (person) antipatico(a).
horrific [hə'rɪfɪk] a (accident) spaventoso(a); (film) orripilante.
horrify ['hɔrɪfaɪ] vt lasciare inorridito(a).
horrifying ['hɔrɪfaɪɪŋ] a terrificante.
horror ['hɔrə*] n orrore m.
horror film n film m inv dell'orrore.
horror-struck ['hɔrəstrʌk], **horror-stricken** ['hɔrəstrɪkn] a inorridito (a).
hors d'œuvre [ɔ:'də:vrə] n antipasto.
horse [hɔ:s] n cavallo.
horseback ['hɔ:sbæk]: **on ~** a, ad a cavallo.
horsebox ['hɔ:sbɔks] n carro or furgone m per il trasporto dei cavalli.
horse chestnut n ippocastano.
horse-drawn ['hɔ:sdrɔ:n] a tirato(a) da cavallo.
horsefly ['hɔ:sflaɪ] n tafano, mosca cavallina.
horseman ['hɔ:smən] n cavaliere m.
horsemanship ['hɔ:smənʃɪp] n equitazione f.
horseplay ['hɔ:spleɪ] n giochi mpl scatenati.
horsepower (hp) ['hɔ:spauə*] n cavallo (vapore) (c/v).
horse-racing ['hɔ:sreɪsɪŋ] n ippica.
horseradish ['hɔ:srædɪʃ] n rafano.
horseshoe ['hɔ:sʃu:] n ferro di cavallo.
horse show n concorso ippico, gare fpl ippiche.
horse-trading ['hɔ:streɪdɪŋ] n mercanteggiamento.
horse trials npl = **horse show**.
horsewhip ['hɔ:swɪp] vt frustare.
horsewoman ['hɔ:swʊmən] n amazzone f.
horsey ['hɔ:sɪ] a (col: person) che adora i cavalli; (appearance) cavallino(a), da cavallo.
horticulture ['hɔ:tɪkʌltʃə*] n orticoltura.
hose [həʊz] n (also: **~pipe**) tubo; (also: **garden ~**) tubo per annaffiare.
hose down vt lavare con un getto d'acqua.
hosiery ['həʊzɪərɪ] n (in shop) (reparto di) calze fpl e calzini mpl.
hospice ['hɔspɪs] n ricovero, ospizio.
hospitable [hɔ'spɪtəbl] a ospitale.
hospital ['hɔspɪtl] n ospedale m; **in ~**, (US) **in the ~** all'ospedale.
hospitality [hɔspɪ'tælɪtɪ] n ospitalità.
hospitalize ['hɔspɪtəlaɪz] vt ricoverare (in or all'ospedale).
host [həʊst] n ospite m; (TV, RADIO)

presentatore/trice; (REL) ostia; (large number): **a ~ of** una schiera di ♦ vt (TV programme, games) presentare.
hostage ['hɔstɪdʒ] n ostaggio/a.
host country n paese m ospite, paese che ospita.
hostel ['hɔstl] n ostello; (for students, nurses etc) pensionato; (for homeless people) ospizio, ricovero; (also: **youth ~**) ostello della gioventù.
hostelling ['hɔstəlɪŋ] n: **to go (youth) ~** passare le vacanze negli ostelli della gioventù.
hostess ['həʊstɪs] n ospite f; (AVIAT) hostess f inv; (in nightclub) entraineuse f inv.
hostile ['hɔstaɪl] a ostile.
hostility [hɔ'stɪlɪtɪ] n ostilità f inv.
hot [hɔt] a caldo(a); (as opposed to only warm) molto caldo(a); (spicy) piccante; (fig) accanito(a); ardente; violento(a), focoso(a); **to be ~** (person) aver caldo; (thing) essere caldo(a); (METEOR) far caldo.
hot up (Brit col) vi (situation) farsi più teso(a); (party) scaldarsi ♦ vt (pace) affrettare; (engine) truccare.
hot-air balloon [hɔt'ɛə-] n mongolfiera.
hotbed ['hɔtbɛd] n (fig) focolaio.
hotchpotch ['hɔtʃpɔtʃ] n (Brit) pot-pourri m.
hot dog n hot dog m inv.
hotel [həʊ'tɛl] n albergo.
hotelier [həʊ'tɛljeɪ] n albergatore/trice.
hotel industry n industria alberghiera.
hotel room n camera d'albergo.
hotfoot ['hɔtfʊt] ad di gran carriera.
hotheaded [hɔt'hɛdɪd] a focoso(a), eccitabile.
hothouse ['hɔthaʊs] n serra.
hot line n (POL) telefono rosso.
hotly ['hɔtlɪ] ad violentemente.
hotplate ['hɔtpleɪt] n fornello; piastra riscaldante.
hotpot ['hɔtpɔt] n (Brit CULIN) stufato.
hot seat n (fig) posto che scotta.
hot spot n (fig) zona calda.
hot spring n sorgente f termale.
hot-tempered [hɔt'tɛmpəd] a irascibile.
hot-water bottle [hɔt'wɔ:tə-] n borsa dell'acqua calda.
hound [haʊnd] vt perseguitare ♦ n segugio; **the ~s** la muta.
hour ['auə*] n ora; **at 30 miles an ~** a 30 miglia all'ora; **lunch ~** intervallo di pranzo; **to pay sb by the ~** pagare qn a ore.
hourly ['auəlɪ] a (ad) ogni ora; (rate) orario(a) ♦ ad ogni ora; **~ paid** a pagato(a) a ore.
house n [haʊs] (pl **~s** ['haʊzɪz]) (also: firm) casa; (POL) camera; (THEATRE) sala; pubblico; spettacolo ♦ vt [haʊz] (person) ospitare **at** (or **to**) **my ~** a casa mia; **the H~ (of Commons)** (Brit) la Camera dei Comuni; **the H~ (of Representatives)** (US) ≈ la Camera dei Deputati; **on the ~** (fig) offerto(a) dalla casa.
house arrest n arresti mpl domiciliari.

houseboat ['hausbəut] n house boat f inv.
housebound ['hausbaund] a confinato(a) in casa.
housebreaking ['hausbreɪkɪŋ] n furto con scasso.
house-broken ['hausbrəukn] a (US) = **house-trained**.
housecoat ['hauskəut] n vestaglia.
household ['haushəuld] n famiglia, casa.
householder ['haushəuldə•] n padrone/a di casa; (head of house) capofamiglia m/f.
household name n nome m che tutti conoscono.
househunting ['haushʌntɪŋ] n: **to go ~** mettersi a cercar casa.
housekeeper ['hauski:pə•] n governante f.
housekeeping ['hauski:pɪŋ] n (work) governo della casa; (also: ~ **money**) soldi mpl per le spese di casa; (COMPUT) ausilio.
houseman ['hausmən] n (Brit MED) ≈ interno.
house plant n pianta da appartamento.
house-proud ['hauspraud] a che è maniaco(a) della pulizia.
house-to-house ['haustə'haus] a (collection) di porta in porta; (search) casa per casa.
house-trained ['haustreɪnd] a (Brit: animal) che non sporca in casa.
house-warming party ['hauswɔ:mɪŋ-] n festa per inaugurare la casa nuova.
housewife ['hauswaɪf] n massaia, casalinga.
housework ['hauswə:k] n faccende fpl domestiche.
housing ['hauzɪŋ] n alloggio ♦ cpd (problem, shortage) degli alloggi.
housing association n cooperativa edilizia.
housing conditions npl condizioni fpl di abitazione.
housing development, (Brit) **housing estate** n zona residenziale con case popolari e/o private.
hovel ['hɔvl] n casupola.
hover ['hɔvə•] vi (bird) librarsi; (helicopter) volare a punto fisso; **to ~ round sb** aggirarsi intorno a qn.
hovercraft ['hɔvəkrɑ:ft] n hovercraft m inv.
hoverport ['hɔvəpɔ:t] n porto per hovercraft.
how [hau] ad come; **~ are you?** come sta?; **~ do you do?** piacere!, molto lieto!; **~ far is it to ...?** quanto è lontano ...?; **~ long have you been here?** da quanto tempo sta qui?; **~ lovely!** che bello!; **~ many?** quanti(e)?; **~ much?** quanto(a)?; **~ many people/much milk?** quante persone/quanto latte?; **~ old are you?** quanti anni ha?; **~'s life?** (col) come va (la vita)?; **~ about a drink?** che ne diresti di andare a bere qualcosa?; **~ is it that ...?** com'è che ... + sub?
however [hau'evə•] ad in qualsiasi modo or maniera che; (+ adjective) per quanto + sub; (in questions) come ♦ cj comunque, però.
howitzer ['hauɪtsə•] n (MIL) obice m.
howl [haul] n ululato ♦ vi ululare.

howler ['haulə•] n marronata.
HP n abbr (Brit) see **hire purchase**.
hp abbr (AUT) see **horsepower**.
HQ n abbr (= headquarters) Q.G.
HR n abbr (US) = **House of Representatives**.
HRH abbr (= His (or Her) Royal Highness) S.A.R.
hr(s) abbr (= hour(s)) h.
HS abbr (US) = **high school**.
HST abbr (= Hawaiian Standard Time) fuso orario.
HT abbr (= high tension) A.T.
hub [hʌb] n (of wheel) mozzo; (fig) fulcro.
hubbub ['hʌbʌb] n baccano.
hubcap ['hʌbkæp] n (AUT) coprimozzo.
HUD n abbr (US) = Department of Housing and Urban Development.
huddle ['hʌdl] vi: **to ~ together** rannicchiarsi l'uno contro l'altro.
hue [hju:] n tinta; **~ and cry** n clamore m.
huff [hʌf] n: **in a ~** stizzito(a); **to take the ~** mettere il broncio.
hug [hʌg] vt abbracciare; (shore, kerb) stringere ♦ n abbraccio, stretta; **to give sb a ~** abbracciare qn.
huge [hju:dʒ] a enorme, immenso(a).
hulk [hʌlk] n carcassa.
hulking ['hʌlkɪŋ] a: **~ (great)** grosso(a) e goffo(a).
hull [hʌl] n (of ship) scafo.
hullabaloo [hʌləbə'lu:] n (col: noise) fracasso.
hullo [hə'ləu] excl = **hello**.
hum [hʌm] vt (tune) canticchiare ♦ vi canticchiare; (insect, plane, tool) ronzare ♦ n (also ELEC) ronzio; (of traffic, machines) rumore m; (of voices etc) mormorio, brusio.
human ['hju:mən] a umano(a) ♦ n (also: ~ being) essere m umano.
humane [hju:'meɪn] a umanitario(a).
humanism ['hju:mənɪzəm] n umanesimo.
humanitarian [hju:mænɪ'tɛərɪən] a umanitario(a).
humanity [hju:'mænɪtɪ] n umanità; **the humanities** gli studi umanistici.
humanly ['hju:mənlɪ] ad umanamente.
humanoid ['hju:mənɔɪd] a che sembra umano(a) ♦ n umanoide m/f.
humble ['hʌmbl] a umile, modesto(a) ♦ vt umiliare.
humbly ['hʌmblɪ] ad umilmente, modestamente.
humbug ['hʌmbʌg] n inganno; sciocchezze fpl; (Brit: sweet) caramella alla menta.
humdrum ['hʌmdrʌm] a monotono(a), tedioso(a).
humid ['hju:mɪd] a umido(a).
humidifier [hju:'mɪdɪfaɪə•] n umidificatore m.
humidity [hju:'mɪdɪtɪ] n umidità.
humiliate [hju:'mɪlɪeɪt] vt umiliare.
humiliation [hju:mɪlɪ'eɪʃən] n umiliazione f.
humility [hju:'mɪlɪtɪ] n umiltà.
humorist ['hju:mərɪst] n umorista m/f.
humorous ['hju:mərəs] a umoristico(a);

(*person*) buffo(a).

humour, (*US*) **humor** ['hju:mə*] *n* umore *m* ◆ *vt* (*person*) compiacere; (*sb's whims*) assecondare; **sense of** ~ senso dell'umorismo; **to be in a good/bad** ~ essere di buon/cattivo umore.

humo(u)rless ['hju:məlɪs] *a* privo(a) di umorismo.

hump [hʌmp] *n* gobba.

humpback ['hʌmpbæk] *n* schiena d'asino; (*Brit: also:* ~ **bridge**) ponte *m* a schiena d'asino.

humus ['hju:məs] *n* humus *m*.

hunch [hʌntʃ] *n* gobba; (*premonition*) intuizione *f*; **I have a** ~ **that** ho la vaga impressione che.

hunchback ['hʌntʃbæk] *n* gobbo/a.

hunched [hʌntʃt] *a* incurvato(a).

hundred ['hʌndrəd] *num* cento; **about a** ~ **people** un centinaio di persone; ~**s of people** centinaia *fpl* di persone; **I'm a** ~ **per cent sure** sono sicuro al cento per cento.

hundredweight ['hʌndrɪdweɪt] *n* (*Brit*) = 50.8 *kg*; 112 *lb*; (*US*) = 45.3 *kg*; 100 *lb*.

hung [hʌŋ] *pt, pp of* **hang**.

Hungarian [hʌŋ'gɛərɪən] *a* ungherese ◆ *n* ungherese *m/f*; (*LING*) ungherese *m*.

Hungary ['hʌŋgərɪ] *n* Ungheria.

hunger ['hʌŋgə*] *n* fame *f* ◆ *vi:* **to** ~ **for** desiderare ardentemente.

hunger strike *n* sciopero della fame.

hungrily ['hʌŋgrəlɪ] *ad* voracemente; (*fig*) avidamente.

hungry ['hʌŋgrɪ] *a* affamato(a); **to be** ~ aver fame; ~ **for** (*fig*) assetato di.

hung up *a* (*col*) complessato(a).

hunk [hʌŋk] *n* bel pezzo.

hunt [hʌnt] *vt* (*seek*) cercare; (*SPORT*) cacciare ◆ *vi* andare a caccia ◆ *n* caccia.

hunt down *vt* scovare.

hunter ['hʌntə*] *n* cacciatore *m*; (*Brit: horse*) cavallo da caccia.

hunting ['hʌntɪŋ] *n* caccia.

hurdle ['hə:dl] *n* (*SPORT, fig*) ostacolo.

hurl [hə:l] *vt* lanciare con violenza.

hurrah, hurray [hu'rɑ:, hu'reɪ] *excl* urra!, evviva!

hurricane ['hʌrɪkən] *n* uragano.

hurried ['hʌrɪd] *a* affrettato(a); (*work*) fatto(a) in fretta.

hurriedly ['hʌrɪdlɪ] *ad* in fretta.

hurry ['hʌrɪ] *n* fretta ◆ *vi* affrettarsi ◆ *vt* (*person*) affrettare; (*work*) far in fretta; **to be in a** ~ aver fretta; **to do sth in a** ~ fare qc in fretta; **to** ~ **in/out** entrare/uscire in fretta; **to** ~ **back/home** affrettarsi a tornare indietro/a casa.

hurry along *vi* camminare in fretta.

hurry away, hurry off *vi* andarsene in fretta.

hurry up *vi* sbrigarsi.

hurt [hə:t] *vb* (*pt, pp* **hurt**) *vt* (*cause pain to*) far male a; (*injure, fig*) ferire; (*business, interests etc*) colpire, danneggiare ◆ *vi* far

male ◆ *a* ferito(a); **I** ~ **my arm** mi sono fatto male al braccio; **where does it** ~? dove ti fa male?

hurtful ['hə:tful] *a* (*remark*) che ferisce.

hurtle ['hə:tl] *vt* scagliare ◆ *vi:* **to** ~ **past/down** passare/scendere a razzo.

husband ['hʌzbənd] *n* marito.

hush [hʌʃ] *n* silenzio, calma ◆ *vt* zittire; ~! zitto(a)!

hush up *vt* (*fact*) cercare di far passare sotto silenzio.

hush-hush ['hʌʃ'hʌʃ] *a* (*col*) segretissimo(a).

husk [hʌsk] *n* (*of wheat*) cartoccio; (*of rice, maize*) buccia.

husky ['hʌskɪ] *a* roco(a) ◆ *n* cane *m* eschimese.

hustings ['hʌstɪŋz] *npl* (*Brit POL*) comizi *mpl* elettorali.

hustle ['hʌsl] *vt* spingere, incalzare ◆ *n* pigia pigia *m inv*; ~ **and bustle** trambusto.

hut [hʌt] *n* rifugio; (*shed*) ripostiglio.

hutch [hʌtʃ] *n* gabbia.

hyacinth ['haɪəsɪnθ] *n* giacinto.

hybrid ['haɪbrɪd] *a* ibrido(a) ◆ *n* ibrido.

hydrant ['haɪdrənt] *n* (*also:* **fire** ~) idrante *m*.

hydraulic [haɪ'drɒlɪk] *a* idraulico(a).

hydraulics [haɪ'drɒlɪks] *n* idraulica.

hydrochloric [haɪdrə'klɒrɪk] *a:* ~ **acid** acido cloridrico.

hydroelectric [haɪdrəʊɪ'lɛktrɪk] *a* idroelettrico(a).

hydrofoil ['haɪdrəfɔɪl] *n* aliscafo.

hydrogen ['haɪdrədʒən] *n* idrogeno.

hydrogen bomb *n* bomba all'idrogeno.

hydrophobia [haɪdrə'fəʊbɪə] *n* idrofobia.

hydroplane ['haɪdrəʊpleɪn] *n* idrovolante *m*.

hyena [haɪ'i:nə] *n* iena.

hygiene ['haɪdʒi:n] *n* igiene *f*.

hygienic [haɪ'dʒi:nɪk] *a* igienico(a).

hymn [hɪm] *n* inno; cantica.

hype [haɪp] *n* (*col*) clamorosa pubblicità.

hyperactive [haɪpər'æktɪv] *a* iperattivo(a).

hypermarket ['haɪpəmɑ:kɪt] *n* (*Brit*) ipermercato.

hypertension [haɪpə'tɛnʃən] *n* (*MED*) ipertensione *f*.

hyphen ['haɪfn] *n* trattino.

hypnosis [hɪp'nəʊsɪs] *n* ipnosi *f*.

hypnotic [hɪp'nɒtɪk] *a* ipnotico(a).

hypnotism ['hɪpnətɪzəm] *n* ipnotismo.

hypnotist ['hɪpnətɪst] *n* ipnotizzatore/trice.

hypnotize ['hɪpnətaɪz] *vt* ipnotizzare.

hypoallergenic [haɪpəʊæələ'dʒɛnɪk] *a* ipoallergico(a).

hypochondriac [haɪpə'kɒndrɪæk] *n* ipocondriaco/a.

hypocrisy [hɪ'pɒkrɪsɪ] *n* ipocrisia.

hypocrite ['hɪpəkrɪt] *n* ipocrita *m/f*.

hypocritical [hɪpə'krɪtɪkl] *a* ipocrita.

hypodermic [haɪpə'də:mɪk] *a* ipodermico(a) ◆ *n* (*syringe*) siringa ipodermica.

hypothermia [haɪpəʊ'θə:mɪə] *n* ipotermia.

hypothesis, *pl* **hypotheses** [haɪ'pɒθɪsɪs, -si:z] *n* ipotesi *f inv*.

hypothetical [haɪpəʊ'θetɪkl] a ipotetico(a).
hysterectomy [hɪstə'rɛktəmɪ] n isterectomia.
hysteria [hɪ'stɪərɪə] n isteria.
hysterical [hɪ'stɛrɪkl] a isterico(a); **to become** ~ avere una crisi isterica.
hysterics [hɪ'stɛrɪks] npl accesso di isteria; (laughter) attacco di riso; **to have** ~ avere una crisi isterica.
Hz abbr (= hertz) Hz.

I

I, i [aɪ] n (letter) I, i f or m inv; **I for Isaac**, (US) **I for Item** ≈ I come Imola.
I [aɪ] pronoun io ♦ abbr (= island, isle) Is.
IA abbr (US POST) = Iowa.
IAEA n abbr = **International Atomic Energy Agency**).
IBA n abbr (Brit: = Independent Broadcasting Authority) organo di controllo sulle reti televisive.
Iberian [aɪ'bɪərɪən] a iberico(a).
Iberian Peninsula n: **the** ~ la Penisola iberica.
IBEW n abbr (US: = International Brotherhood of Electrical Workers) associazione internazionale degli elettrotecnici.
ib(id). ['ɪb(ɪd)] abbr (= ibidem: from the same source) ibid.
i/c abbr (Brit) = **in charge**.
ICC n abbr (= International Chamber of Commerce) C.C.I. f; (US: = Interstate Commerce Commission) commissione per il commercio tra gli stati degli USA.
ice [aɪs] n ghiaccio; (on road) gelo ♦ vt (cake) glassare; (drink) mettere in fresco ♦ vi (also: ~ **over**) ghiacciare; (also: ~ **up**) gelare; **to keep sth on** ~ (fig: plan, project) mettere da parte (per il momento), accantonare.
Ice Age n era glaciale.
ice axe n piccozza da ghiaccio.
iceberg ['aɪsbəːg] n iceberg m inv; **tip of the** ~ (also fig) punta dell'iceberg.
icebox ['aɪsbɔks] n (US) frigorifero; (Brit) reparto ghiaccio; (insulated box) frigo portatile.
icebreaker ['aɪsbreɪkə*] n rompighiaccio m inv.
ice bucket n secchiello del ghiaccio.
ice-cold [aɪs'kəʊld] a gelato(a).
ice cream n gelato.
ice-cream soda n (gelato) affogato al seltz.
ice cube n cubetto di ghiaccio.
iced [aɪst] a (drink) ghiacciato(a); (coffee, tea) freddo(a); (cake) glassato(a).
ice hockey n hockey m su ghiaccio.

Iceland ['aɪslənd] n Islanda.
Icelander ['aɪsləndə*] n islandese m/f.
Icelandic [aɪs'lændɪk] a islandese ♦ n (LING) islandese m.
ice lolly n (Brit) ghiacciolo.
ice pick n piccone m per ghiaccio.
ice rink n pista di pattinaggio.
ice-skate ['aɪsskeɪt] n pattino da ghiaccio ♦ vi pattinare sul ghiaccio.
ice-skating ['aɪsskeɪtɪŋ] n pattinaggio sul ghiaccio.
icicle ['aɪsɪkl] n ghiacciolo.
icing ['aɪsɪŋ] n (AVIAT etc) patina di ghiaccio; (CULIN) glassa.
icing sugar n zucchero a velo.
ICJ n abbr see **International Court of Justice**.
icon ['aɪkɔn] n icona; (COMPUT) immagine f.
ICR n abbr (US) = Institute for Cancer Research.
ICU n abbr see **intensive care unit**.
icy ['aɪsɪ] a ghiacciato(a); (weather, temperature) gelido(a).
ID abbr (US POST) = Idaho.
I'd [aɪd] = **I would; I had**.
ID card n = **identity card**.
IDD n abbr (Brit TEL: = International direct dialling) teleselezione f internazionale.
idea [aɪ'dɪə] n idea; **good** ~! buon'idea!; **to have an** ~ **that** ... aver l'impressione che ...; **I haven't the least** ~ non ne ho la minima idea.
ideal [aɪ'dɪəl] a, n ideale (m).
idealist [aɪ'dɪəlɪst] n idealista m/f.
ideally [aɪ'dɪəlɪ] ad perfettamente, assolutamente; ~ **the book should have** ... l'ideale sarebbe che il libro avesse ....
identical [aɪ'dɛntɪkl] a identico(a).
identification [aɪdɛntɪfɪ'keɪʃən] n identificazione f; **means of** ~ carta d'identità.
identify [aɪ'dɛntɪfaɪ] vt identificare ♦ vi: **to** ~ **with** identificarsi con.
Identikit ® [aɪ'dɛntɪkɪt] n: ~ (picture) identikit m inv.
identity [aɪ'dɛntɪtɪ] n identità f inv.
identity card n carta d'identità.
identity parade n (Brit) confronto all'americana.
ideological [aɪdɪə'lɔdʒɪkəl] a ideologico(a).
ideology [aɪdɪ'ɔlədʒɪ] n ideologia.
idiocy ['ɪdɪəsɪ] n idiozia.
idiom ['ɪdɪəm] n idioma m; (phrase) espressione f idiomatica.
idiomatic [ɪdɪə'mætɪk] a idiomatico(a).
idiosyncrasy [ɪdɪəʊ'sɪŋkrəsɪ] n idiosincrasia.
idiot ['ɪdɪət] n idiota m/f.
idiotic [ɪdɪ'ɔtɪk] a idiota.
idle ['aɪdl] a inattivo(a); (lazy) pigro(a), ozioso(a); (unemployed) disoccupato(a); (question, pleasures) ozioso(a) ♦ vi (engine) girare al minimo; **to lie** ~ stare fermo, non funzionare.
idle away vt (time) sprecare, buttar via.
idleness ['aɪdlnɪs] n ozio; pigrizia.

idler ['aɪdlə*] n ozioso/a, fannullone/a.
idle time n tempi mpl morti.
idol ['aɪdl] n idolo.
idolize ['aɪdəlaɪz] vt idoleggiare.
idyllic [ɪ'dɪlɪk] a idillico(a).
i.e. abbr (= id est: that is) cioè.
if [ɪf] cj se ♦ n: **there are a lot of ~s and buts** ci sono molti se e ma; **I'd be pleased ~ you could do it** sarei molto contento se potesse farlo; **~ necessary** se (è) necessario; **~ only he were here** se solo fosse qui; **~ only to show him my gratitude** se non altro per esprimergli la mia gratitudine.
igloo ['ɪglu:] n igloo m inv.
ignite [ɪg'naɪt] vt accendere ♦ vi accendersi.
ignition [ɪg'nɪʃən] n (AUT) accensione f; **to switch on/off the ~** accendere/spegnere il motore.
ignition key n (AUT) chiave f dell'accensione.
ignoble [ɪg'nəʊbl] a ignobile.
ignominious [ɪgnə'mɪnɪəs] a vergognoso(a), ignominioso(a).
ignoramus [ɪgnə'reɪməs] n ignorante m/f.
ignorance ['ɪgnərəns] n ignoranza; **to keep sb in ~ of sth** tenere qn all'oscuro di qc.
ignorant ['ɪgnərənt] a ignorante; **to be ~ of** (subject) essere ignorante in; (events) essere ignaro(a) di.
ignore [ɪg'nɔ:*] vt non tener conto di; (person, fact) ignorare.
ikon ['aɪkən] n = **icon**.
IL abbr (US POST) = Illinois.
ILA n abbr (US: = International Longshoremen's Association) associazione internazionale degli scaricatori di porto.
ILEA n abbr (Brit: = Inner London Education Authority) Provveditorato degli Studi per la zona centrale di Londra.
ILGWU n abbr (US: = International Ladies' Garment Workers Union) sindacato internazionale dei lavoratori nell'abbigliamento femminile.
ill [ɪl] a (sick) malato(a); (bad) cattivo(a) ♦ n male m; **to take** or **be taken ~** ammalarsi; **to feel ~** star male; **to speak/think ~ of sb** parlar/pensar male di qn.
I'll [aɪl] = **I will, I shall.**
ill-advised [ɪləd'vaɪzd] a (decision) poco giudizioso(a); (person) mal consigliato(a).
ill-at-ease [ɪlət'i:z] a a disagio.
ill-considered [ɪlkən'sɪdəd] a (plan) avventato(a).
ill-disposed [ɪldɪs'pəʊzd] a: **to be ~ towards sb/sth** essere maldisposto(a) verso qn/qc or nei riguardi di qn/qc.
illegal [ɪ'li:gl] a illegale.
illegally [ɪ'li:gəlɪ] ad illegalmente.
illegible [ɪ'lɛdʒɪbl] a illeggibile.
illegitimate [ɪlɪ'dʒɪtɪmət] a illegittimo(a).
ill-fated [ɪl'feɪtɪd] a nefasto(a).
ill-favoured, (US) **ill-favored** [ɪl'feɪvəd] a sgraziato(a), brutto(a).
ill feeling n rancore m.
ill-gotten ['ɪlgɔtn] a: **~ gains** maltolto.

illicit [ɪ'lɪsɪt] a illecito(a).
ill-informed [ɪlɪn'fɔ:md] a (judgement, speech) pieno(a) di inesattezze; (person) male informato(a).
illiterate [ɪ'lɪtərət] a analfabeta, illetterato(a); (letter) scorretto(a).
ill-mannered [ɪl'mænəd] a maleducato(a), sgarbato(a).
illness ['ɪlnɪs] n malattia.
illogical [ɪ'lɔdʒɪkl] a illogico(a).
ill-suited [ɪl'su:tɪd] a (couple) mal assortito(a); **he is ~ to the job** è inadatto a quel lavoro.
ill-timed [ɪl'taɪmd] a intempestivo(a), inopportuno(a).
ill-treat [ɪl'tri:t] vt maltrattare.
ill-treatment [ɪl'tri:tmənt] n maltrattamenti mpl.
illuminate [ɪ'lu:mɪneɪt] vt illuminare; **~d sign** insegna luminosa.
illuminating [ɪ'lu:mɪneɪtɪŋ] a chiarificatore(trice).
illumination [ɪlu:mɪ'neɪʃən] n illuminazione f.
illusion [ɪ'lu:ʒən] n illusione f; **to be under the ~ that** avere l'impressione che.
illusive [ɪ'lu:sɪv], **illusory** [ɪ'lu:sərɪ] a illusorio(a).
illustrate ['ɪləstreɪt] vt illustrare.
illustration [ɪlə'streɪʃən] n illustrazione f.
illustrator ['ɪləstreɪtə*] n illustratore/trice.
illustrious [ɪ'lʌstrɪəs] a illustre.
ill will n cattiva volontà.
ILO n abbr (= International Labour Organization) OIL f.
ILWU n abbr (US: = International Longshoremen's and Warehousemen's Union) sindacato internazionale degli scaricatori di porto e magazzinieri.
I'm [aɪm] = **I am.**
image ['ɪmɪdʒ] n immagine f; (public face) immagine (pubblica).
imagery ['ɪmɪdʒərɪ] n immagini fpl.
imaginable [ɪ'mædʒɪnəbl] a immaginabile, che si possa immaginare.
imaginary [ɪ'mædʒɪnərɪ] a immaginario(a).
imagination [ɪmædʒɪ'neɪʃən] n immaginazione f, fantasia.
imaginative [ɪ'mædʒɪnətɪv] a immaginoso(a).
imagine [ɪ'mædʒɪn] vt immaginare.
imbalance [ɪm'bæləns] n squilibrio.
imbecile ['ɪmbəsi:l] n imbecille m/f.
imbue [ɪm'bju:] vt: **to ~ sth with** impregnare qc di.
IMF n abbr see **International Monetary Fund.**
imitate ['ɪmɪteɪt] vt imitare.
imitation [ɪmɪ'teɪʃən] n imitazione f.
imitator ['ɪmɪteɪtə*] n imitatore/trice.
immaculate [ɪ'mækjulət] a immacolato(a); (dress, appearance) impeccabile.
immaterial [ɪmə'tɪərɪəl] a immateriale, indifferente; **it is ~ whether** poco importa se or che + sub.
immature [ɪmə'tjuə*] a immaturo(a).

immaturity [ɪmə'tjuərɪtɪ] *n* immaturità, mancanza di maturità.
immeasurable [ɪ'mɛʒərəbl] *a* incommensurabile.
immediacy [ɪ'mi:dɪəsɪ] *n* immediatezza.
immediate [ɪ'mi:dɪət] *a* immediato(a).
immediately [ɪ'mi:dɪətlɪ] *ad* (*at once*) subito, immediatamente; ~ **next to** proprio accanto a.
immense [ɪ'mɛns] *a* immenso(a); enorme.
immensity [ɪ'mɛnsɪtɪ] *n* (*of size, difference*) enormità; (*of problem etc*) vastità.
immerse [ɪ'mə:s] *vt* immergere.
immersion heater [ɪ'mə:ʃən-] *n* (*Brit*) scaldaacqua *m inv* a immersione.
immigrant ['ɪmɪgrənt] *n* immigrante *m/f*; (*already established*) immigrato/a.
immigration [ɪmɪ'greɪʃən] *n* immigrazione *f*.
immigration authorities *npl* ufficio stranieri.
immigration laws *npl* leggi *fpl* relative all'immigrazione.
imminent ['ɪmɪnənt] *a* imminente.
immobile [ɪ'məubaɪl] *a* immobile.
immobilize [ɪ'məubɪlaɪz] *vt* immobilizzare.
immoderate [ɪ'mɔdərɪt] *a* (*person*) smodato(a), sregolato(a); (*opinion, reaction, demand*) eccessivo(a).
immodest [ɪ'mɔdɪst] *a* (*indecent*) indecente, impudico(a); (*boasting*) presuntuoso(a).
immoral [ɪ'mɔrl] *a* immorale.
immorality [ɪmɔ'rælɪtɪ] *n* immoralità.
immortal [ɪ'mɔ:tl] *a, n* immortale (*m/f*).
immortalize [ɪ'mɔ:təlaɪz] *vt* rendere immortale.
immovable [ɪ'mu:vəbl] *a* (*object*) non movibile; (*person*) irremovibile.
immune [ɪ'mju:n] *a*: ~ (**to**) immune (da).
immunity [ɪ'mju:nɪtɪ] *n* (*also fig: of diplomat*) immunità; **diplomatic** ~ immunità diplomatica.
immunization [ɪmjunaɪ'zeɪʃən] *n* immunizzazione *f*.
immunize ['ɪmjunaɪz] *vt* immunizzare.
imp [ɪmp] *n* folletto, diavoletto; (*child*) diavoletto.
impact ['ɪmpækt] *n* impatto.
impair [ɪm'pɛə*] *vt* danneggiare.
impale [ɪm'peɪl] *vt* impalare.
impart [ɪm'pɑ:t] *vt* (*make known*) comunicare; (*bestow*) impartire.
impartial [ɪm'pɑ:ʃl] *a* imparziale.
impartiality [ɪmpɑ:ʃɪ'ælɪtɪ] *n* imparzialità.
impassable [ɪm'pɑ:səbl] *a* insuperabile; (*road*) impraticabile.
impasse [æm'pɑ:s] *n* impasse *f inv*.
impassioned [ɪm'pæʃənd] *a* appassionato(a).
impassive [ɪm'pæsɪv] *a* impassibile.
impatience [ɪm'peɪʃəns] *n* impazienza.
impatient [ɪm'peɪʃənt] *a* impaziente; **to get** *or* **grow** ~ perdere la pazienza.
impeach [ɪm'pi:tʃ] *vt* accusare, attaccare; (*public official*) mettere sotto accusa.
impeachment [ɪm'pi:tʃmənt] *n* (*LAW*)

imputazione *f*.
impeccable [ɪm'pɛkəbl] *a* impeccabile.
impecunious [ɪmpɪ'kju:nɪəs] *a* povero(a).
impede [ɪm'pi:d] *vt* impedire.
impediment [ɪm'pɛdɪmənt] *n* impedimento; (*also*: **speech** ~) difetto di pronuncia.
impel [ɪm'pɛl] *vt* (*force*): **to** ~ **sb** (**to do sth**) costringere *or* obbligare qn (a fare qc).
impending [ɪm'pɛndɪŋ] *a* imminente.
impenetrable [ɪm'pɛnɪtrəbl] *a* impenetrabile.
imperative [ɪm'pɛrətɪv] *a* imperativo(a); necessario(a), urgente; (*voice*) imperioso(a) ♦ *n* (*LING*) imperativo.
imperceptible [ɪmpə'sɛptɪbl] *a* impercettibile.
imperfect [ɪm'pə:fɪkt] *a* imperfetto(a); (*goods etc*) difettoso(a) ♦ *n* (*LING: also*: ~ **tense**) imperfetto.
imperfection [ɪmpə:'fɛkʃən] *n* imperfezione *f*; (*flaw*) difetto.
imperial [ɪm'pɪərɪəl] *a* imperiale; (*measure*) legale.
imperialism [ɪm'pɪərɪəlɪzəm] *n* imperialismo.
imperil [ɪm'pɛrɪl] *vt* mettere in pericolo.
imperious [ɪm'pɪərɪəs] *a* imperioso(a).
impersonal [ɪm'pə:sənl] *a* impersonale.
impersonate [ɪm'pə:səneɪt] *vt* impersonare; (*THEATRE*) imitare.
impersonation [ɪmpə:sə'neɪʃən] *n* (*LAW*) usurpazione *f* d'identità; (*THEATRE*) imitazione *f*.
impersonator [ɪm'pə:səneɪtə*] *n* (*gen, THEATRE*) imitatore/trice.
impertinence [ɪm'pə:tɪnəns] *n* impertinenza.
impertinent [ɪm'pə:tɪnənt] *a* impertinente.
imperturbable [ɪmpə'tə:bəbl] *a* imperturbabile.
impervious [ɪm'pə:vɪəs] *a* impermeabile; (*fig*): ~ **to** insensibile a; impassibile di fronte a.
impetuous [ɪm'pɛtjuəs] *a* impetuoso(a), precipitoso(a).
impetus ['ɪmpətəs] *n* impeto.
impinge [ɪm'pɪndʒ]: **to** ~ **on** *vt fus* (*person*) colpire; (*rights*) ledere.
impish ['ɪmpɪʃ] *a* malizioso(a), birichino(a).
implacable [ɪm'plækəbl] *a* implacabile.
implant [ɪm'plɑ:nt] *vt* (*MED*) innestare; (*fig*: *idea, principle*) inculcare.
implausible [ɪm'plɔ:zɪbl] *a* non plausibile.
implement *n* ['ɪmplɪmənt] attrezzo; (*for cooking*) utensile *m* ♦ *vt* ['ɪmplɪment] effettuare.
implicate ['ɪmplɪkeɪt] *vt* implicare.
implication [ɪmplɪ'keɪʃən] *n* implicazione *f*; **by** ~ implicitamente.
implicit [ɪm'plɪsɪt] *a* implicito(a); (*complete*) completo(a).
implicitly [ɪm'plɪsɪtlɪ] *ad* implicitamente.
implore [ɪm'plɔ:*] *vt* implorare.
imply [ɪm'plaɪ] *vt* insinuare; suggerire.
impolite [ɪmpə'laɪt] *a* scortese.
imponderable [ɪm'pɔndərəbl] *a* imponderabile.
import *vt* [ɪm'pɔ:t] importare ♦ *n* ['ɪmpɔ:t]

(*COMM*) importazione *f*; (*meaning*) significato, senso ♦ *cpd* (*duty, licence etc*) d'importazione.

importance [ɪm'pɔ:tns] *n* importanza; **to be of great/little** ~ importare molto/poco, essere molto/poco importante.

important [ɪm'pɔ:tnt] *a* importante; **it's not** ~ non ha importanza; **it is** ~ **that** è importante che + *sub*.

importantly [ɪm'pɔ:təntlɪ] *ad* (*pej*) con (un'aria d')importanza; **but, more** ~, ... ma, quel che più conta *or* importa, ...

importation [ɪmpɔ:'teɪʃən] *n* importazione *f*.

imported [ɪm'pɔ:tɪd] *a* importato(a).

importer [ɪm'pɔ:tə*] *n* importatore/trice.

impose [ɪm'pəuz] *vt* imporre ♦ *vi*: **to** ~ **on sb** sfruttare la bontà di qn.

imposing [ɪm'pəuzɪŋ] *a* imponente.

imposition [ɪmpə'zɪʃən] *n* imposizione *f*; **to be an** ~ **on** (*person*) abusare della gentilezza di.

impossibility [ɪmpɔsə'bɪlɪtɪ] *n* impossibilità.

impossible [ɪm'pɔsɪbl] *a* impossibile; **it is** ~ **for me to leave now** mi è impossibile venir via adesso.

impostor [ɪm'pɔstə*] *n* impostore/a.

impotence ['ɪmpətns] *n* impotenza.

impotent ['ɪmpətnt] *a* impotente.

impound [ɪm'paund] *vt* confiscare.

impoverished [ɪm'pɔvərɪʃt] *a* impoverito(a).

impracticable [ɪm'præktɪkəbl] *a* impraticabile.

impractical [ɪm'præktɪkl] *a* non pratico(a).

imprecise [ɪmprɪ'saɪs] *a* impreciso(a).

impregnable [ɪm'prɛgnəbl] *a* (*fortress*) inespugnabile; (*fig*) inoppugnabile; irrefutabile.

impregnate ['ɪmprɛgneɪt] *vt* impregnare; (*fertilize*) fecondare.

impresario [ɪmprɪ'sɑ:rɪəu] *n* impresario/a.

impress [ɪm'prɛs] *vt* impressionare; (*mark*) imprimere, stampare; **to** ~ **sth on sb** far capire qc a qn.

impression [ɪm'prɛʃən] *n* impressione *f*; **to be under the** ~ **that** avere l'impressione che; **to make a good/bad** ~ **on sb** fare una buona/ cattiva impressione a *or* su qn.

impressionable [ɪm'prɛʃnəbl] *a* impressionabile.

impressionist [ɪm'prɛʃənɪst] *n* impressionista *m/f*.

impressive [ɪm'presɪv] *a* impressionante.

imprint ['ɪmprɪnt] *n* (*PUBLISHING*) sigla editoriale.

imprinted [ɪm'prɪntɪd] *a*: ~ **on** impresso(a) in.

imprison [ɪm'prɪzn] *vt* imprigionare.

imprisonment [ɪm'prɪznmənt] *n* imprigionamento.

improbable [ɪm'prɔbəbl] *a* improbabile; (*excuse*) inverosimile.

impromptu [ɪm'prɔmptju:] *a* improvvisato(a) ♦ *ad* improvvisando, così su due piedi.

improper [ɪm'prɔpə*] *a* scorretto(a); (*unsuitable*) inadatto(a), improprio(a); sconveniente, indecente.

impropriety [ɪmprə'praɪətɪ] *n* sconvenienza;

(*of expression*) improprietà.

improve [ɪm'pru:v] *vt* migliorare ♦ *vi* migliorare; (*pupil etc*) fare progressi.

improve (up)on *vt fus* (*offer*) aumentare.

improvement [ɪm'pru:vmənt] *n* miglioramento; progresso; **to make** ~**s to** migliorare, apportare dei miglioramenti a.

improvisation [ɪmprəvaɪ'zeɪʃən] *n* improvvisazione *f*.

improvise ['ɪmprəvaɪz] *vt, vi* improvvisare.

imprudence [ɪm'pru:dns] *n* imprudenza.

imprudent [ɪm'pru:dnt] *a* imprudente.

impudence ['ɪmpjudns] *n* impudenza.

impudent ['ɪmpjudnt] *a* impudente, sfacciato(a).

impugn [ɪm'pju:n] *vt* impugnare.

impulse ['ɪmpʌls] *n* impulso; **to act on** ~ agire d'impulso or impulsivamente.

impulse buy *n* acquisto fatto d'impulso.

impulsive [ɪm'pʌlsɪv] *a* impulsivo(a).

impunity [ɪm'pju:nɪtɪ] *n*: **with** ~ impunemente.

impure [ɪm'pjuə*] *a* impuro(a).

impurity [ɪm'pjuərɪtɪ] *n* impurità *f inv*.

IN *abbr* (*US POST*) = Indiana.

in [ɪn] *prep* in; (*with time: during, within*): ~ **May/2 days** in maggio/2 giorni; (: *after*): ~ **2 weeks** entro 2 settimane; (*with town*) a; (*with country*): **it's** ~ **France/the United States** è in Francia/negli Stati Uniti ♦ *ad* entro, dentro; (*fashionable*) alla moda; **is he** ~? lui c'è?; ~ **town/the country** in città/ campagna; ~ **the sun** al sole; ~ **the rain** sotto la pioggia; ~ **1986** nel 1986; ~ **spring/ autumn** in primavera/autunno; ~ **the morning** di *or* alla mattina, la mattina, nella mattinata; ~ **here/there** qui/lì dentro; ~ **French** in francese; ~ **writing** per iscritto; **one man** ~ **10** un uomo su 10; **once** ~ **a hundred years** una volta ogni cento anni; ~ **hundreds** a centinaia; **the best pupil** ~ **the class** il migliore alunno della classe; **a rise** ~ **prices** un aumento dei prezzi; ~ **saying this** nel dire questo; **dressed** ~ **green/a skirt/ trousers** vestito di verde/con una gonna/con i calzoni; **to be** ~ **teaching** fare l'insegnante, insegnare; **to be** ~ **publishing** essere nell'editoria; ~ **that** dal momento che, visto che; **their party is** ~ il loro partito è al potere; **to ask sb** ~ invitare qn a entrare; **to run/limp etc** ~ entrare correndo/zoppicando *etc*; **the** ~**s and outs of** i dettagli di.

in., ins *abbr* = **inch(es)**.

inability [ɪnə'bɪlɪtɪ] *n* inabilità, incapacità; ~ **to pay** impossibilità di pagare.

inaccessible [ɪnək'sɛsɪbl] *a* inaccessibile.

inaccuracy [ɪn'ækjurəsɪ] *n* inaccuratezza; inesattezza; imprecisione *f*.

inaccurate [ɪn'ækjurət] *a* inaccurato(a); (*figures*) inesatto(a); (*translation*) impreciso(a).

inaction [ɪn'ækʃən] *n* inazione *f*.

inactivity [ɪnæk'tɪvɪtɪ] *n* inattività.

inadequacy [ɪn'ædɪkwəsɪ] *n* insufficienza.

inadequate [ɪn'ædɪkwət] *a* insufficiente.
inadmissible [ɪnəd'mɪsəbl] *a* inammissibile.
inadvertent [ɪnəd'vɜːtənt] *a* involontario(a).
inadvertently [ɪnəd'vɜːtntlɪ] *ad* senza volerlo.
inadvisable [ɪnəd'vaɪzəbl] *a* sconsigliabile.
inane [ɪ'neɪn] *a* vacuo(a), stupido(a).
inanimate [ɪn'ænɪmət] *a* inanimato(a).
inapplicable [ɪn'æplɪkəbl] *a* inapplicabile.
inappropriate [ɪnə'prəuprɪət] *a* disadatto(a); (*word, expression*) improprio(a).
inapt [ɪn'æpt] *a* maldestro(a); fuori luogo.
inaptitude [ɪn'æptɪtjuːd] *n* improprietà.
inarticulate [ɪnɑː'tɪkjulət] *a* (*person*) che si esprime male; (*speech*) inarticolato(a).
inasmuch as [ɪnəz'mʌtʃæz] *ad* in quanto che; (*seeing that*) poiché.
inattention [ɪnə'tenʃən] *n* mancanza di attenzione.
inattentive [ɪnə'tentɪv] *a* disattento(a), distratto(a); negligente.
inaudible [ɪn'ɔːdɪbl] *a* che non si riesce a sentire.
inaugural [ɪ'nɔːgjurəl] *a* inaugurale.
inaugurate [ɪ'nɔːgjureɪt] *vt* inaugurare; (*president, official*) insediare.
inauguration [ɪnɔːgju'reɪʃən] *n* inaugurazione *f*; insediamento in carica.
inauspicious [ɪnɔːs'pɪʃəs] *a* poco propizio(a).
in-between [ɪnbɪ'twiːn] *a* fra i (*or* le) due.
inborn [ɪn'bɔːn] *a* (*feeling*) innato(a); (*defect*) congenito(a).
inbred [ɪn'bred] *a* innato(a); (*family*) connaturato(a).
inbreeding [ɪn'briːdɪŋ] *n* incrocio ripetuto di animali consanguinei; unioni *fpl* fra consanguinei.
Inc. *abbr see* **incorporated.**
Inca ['ɪŋkə] *a* (*also:* ~**n**) inca *inv* ♦ *n* inca *m/f inv.*
incalculable [ɪn'kælkjuləbl] *a* incalcolabile.
incapability [ɪnkeɪpə'bɪlɪtɪ] *n* incapacità.
incapable [ɪn'keɪpəbl] *a:* ~ **(of doing sth)** incapace (di fare qc).
incapacitate [ɪnkə'pæsɪteɪt] *vt:* **to** ~ **sb from doing** rendere qn incapace di fare.
incapacitated [ɪnkə'pæsɪteɪtɪd] *a* (*LAW*) inabilitato(a).
incapacity [ɪnkə'pæsɪtɪ] *n* incapacità.
incarcerate [ɪn'kɑːsəreɪt] *vt* imprigionare.
incarnate *a* [ɪn'kɑːnɪt] incarnato(a) ♦ *vt* ['ɪnkɑːneɪt] incarnare.
incarnation [ɪnkɑː'neɪʃən] *n* incarnazione *f*.
incendiary [ɪn'sendɪərɪ] *a* incendiario(a) ♦ *n* (*bomb*) bomba incendiaria.
incense *n* ['ɪnsens] incenso ♦ *vt* [ɪn'sens] (*anger*) infuriare.
incense burner *n* incensiere *m*.
incentive [ɪn'sentɪv] *n* incentivo.
incentive scheme *n* piano di incentivazione.
inception [ɪn'sepʃən] *n* inizio, principio.
incessant [ɪn'sesnt] *a* incessante.
incessantly [ɪn'sesntlɪ] *ad* di continuo, senza sosta.
incest ['ɪnsest] *n* incesto.

inch [ɪntʃ] *n* pollice *m* (= 25 *mm*; 12 *in a foot*); **within an** ~ **of** a un pelo da; **he wouldn't give an** ~ (*fig*) non ha ceduto di un millimetro.
inch forward *vi* avanzare pian piano.
inch tape *n* (*Brit*) metro a nastro (da sarto).
incidence ['ɪnsɪdns] *n* incidenza.
incident ['ɪnsɪdnt] *n* incidente *m*; (*in book*) episodio.
incidental [ɪnsɪ'dentl] *a* accessorio(a), d'accompagnamento; (*unplanned*) incidentale; ~ **to** marginale a; ~ **expenses** *npl* spese *fpl* accessorie.
incidentally [ɪnsɪ'dentəlɪ] *ad* (*by the way*) a proposito.
incidental music *n* sottofondo (musicale), musica di sottofondo.
incinerate [ɪn'sɪnəreɪt] *vt* incenerire.
incinerator [ɪn'sɪnəreɪtə*] *n* inceneritore *m*.
incipient [ɪn'sɪpɪənt] *a* incipiente.
incision [ɪn'sɪʒən] *n* incisione *f*.
incisive [ɪn'saɪsɪv] *a* incisivo(a); tagliante; acuto(a).
incisor [ɪn'saɪzə*] *n* incisivo.
incite [ɪn'saɪt] *vt* incitare.
incl. *abbr* = **including, inclusive (of).**
inclement [ɪn'klemənt] *a* inclemente.
inclination [ɪnklɪ'neɪʃən] *n* inclinazione *f*.
incline *n* ['ɪnklaɪn] pendenza, pendio ♦ *vb* [ɪn'klaɪn] *vt* inclinare ♦ *vi:* **to** ~ **to** tendere a; **to be** ~**d to do** tendere a fare; essere propenso(a) a fare; **to be well** ~**d towards sb** essere ben disposto(a) verso qn.
include [ɪn'kluːd] *vt* includere, comprendere; **the tip is/is not** ~**d** la mancia è compresa/esclusa.
including [ɪn'kluːdɪŋ] *prep* compreso(a), incluso(a); ~ **tip** mancia compresa, compresa la mancia.
inclusion [ɪn'kluːʒən] *n* inclusione *f*.
inclusive [ɪn'kluːsɪv] *a* incluso(a), compreso(a); **£50,** ~ **of all surcharges** 50 sterline, incluse tutte le soprattasse.
inclusive terms *npl* (*Brit*) prezzo tutto compreso.
incognito [ɪnkɔg'niːtəu] *ad* in incognito.
incoherent [ɪnkəu'hɪərənt] *a* incoerente.
income ['ɪnkʌm] *n* reddito; **gross/net** ~ reddito lordo/netto; ~ **and expenditure account** conto entrate ed uscite.
income tax *n* imposta sul reddito.
income tax inspector *n* ispettore *m* delle imposte dirette.
income tax return *n* dichiarazione *f* annuale dei redditi.
incoming ['ɪnkʌmɪŋ] *a* (*passengers*) in arrivo; (*government, tenant*) subentrante; ~ **tide** marea montante.
incommunicado [ɪnkəmjunɪ'kɑːdəu] *a:* **to hold sb** ~ tenere qn in segregazione.
incomparable [ɪn'kɔmpərəbl] *a* incomparabile.
incompatible [ɪnkəm'pætɪbl] *a* incompatibile.
incompetence [ɪn'kɔmpɪtns] *n* incompetenza,

incapacità.
incompetent [ɪn'kɔmpɪtnt] *a* incompetente,
incapace.
incomplete [ɪnkəm'pliːt] *a* incompleto(a).
incomprehensible [ɪnkɔmprɪ'hɛnsɪbl] *a*
incomprensibile.
inconceivable [ɪnkən'siːvəbl] *a*
inimmaginabile.
inconclusive [ɪnkən'kluːsɪv] *a* im-
produttivo(a); (*argument*) poco convincente.
incongruous [ɪn'kɔŋgruəs] *a* poco appro-
priato(a); (*remark, act*) incongruo(a).
inconsequential [ɪnkɔnsɪ'kwɛnʃl] *a* senza
importanza.
inconsiderable [ɪnkən'sɪdərəbl] *a:* **not** ~ non
trascurabile.
inconsiderate [ɪnkən'sɪdərət] *a*
sconsiderato(a).
inconsistency [ɪnkən'sɪstənsɪ] *n* (*of actions
etc*) incongruenza; (*of work*) irregolarità; (*of
statement etc*) contraddizione *f*.
inconsistent [ɪnkən'sɪstnt] *a* incoerente; poco
logico(a); contraddittorio(a); ~ **with** in contraddizione con.
inconsolable [ɪnkən'səuləbl] *a* inconsolabile.
inconspicuous [ɪnkən'spɪkjuəs] *a* inco-
spicuo(a); (*colour*) poco appariscente;
(*dress*) dimesso(a); **to make o.s.** ~ cercare
di passare inosservato(a).
inconstant [ɪn'kɔnstnt] *a* incostante;
mutevole.
incontinence [ɪn'kɔntɪnəns] *n* incontinenza.
incontinent [ɪn'kɔntɪnənt] *a* incontinente.
incontrovertible [ɪnkɔntrə'vəːtəbl] *a* incon-
trovertibile.
inconvenience [ɪnkən'viːnjəns] *n* inconveniente *m*; (*trouble*) disturbo ♦ *vt* disturbare;
to put sb to great ~ creare degli
inconvenienti a qn; **don't** ~ **yourself** non si
disturbi.
inconvenient [ɪnkən'viːnjənt] *a* scomodo(a);
that time is very ~ **for me** quell'ora mi è
molto scomoda, non è un'ora adatta per me.
incorporate [ɪn'kɔːpəreɪt] *vt* incorporare;
(*contain*) contenere.
incorporated [ɪn'kɔːpəraɪtɪd] *a:* ~ **company**
(*US: abbr* **Inc.**) società *f inv* registrata.
incorrect [ɪnkə'rɛkt] *a* scorretto(a);
(*statement*) impreciso(a).
incorrigible [ɪn'kɔrɪdʒəbl] *a* incorreggibile.
incorruptible [ɪnkə'rʌptɪbl] *a* incorruttibile.
increase *n* ['ɪnkriːs] aumento ♦ *vi* [ɪn'kriːs]
aumentare; **to be on the** ~ essere in
aumento; **an** ~ **of £5/10%** un aumento di 5
sterline/del 10%.
increasing [ɪn'kriːsɪŋ] *a* (*number*) crescente.
increasingly [ɪn'kriːsɪŋlɪ] *ad* sempre più.
incredible [ɪn'krɛdɪbl] *a* incredibile.
incredulous [ɪn'krɛdjuləs] *a* incredulo(a).
increment ['ɪnkrɪmənt] *n* aumento, incremento.
incriminate [ɪn'krɪmɪneɪt] *vt* compromettere.
incriminating [ɪn'krɪmɪneɪtɪŋ] *a* incriminante.
incubate ['ɪnkjubeɪt] *vt* (*eggs*) covare ♦ *vi*

(*egg*) essere in incubazione; (*disease*) avere
un'incubazione.
incubation [ɪnkju'beɪʃən] *n* incubazione *f*.
incubation period *n* (periodo di) incubazione
f.
incubator ['ɪnkjubeɪtə*] *n* incubatrice *f*.
inculcate ['ɪnkʌlkeɪt] *vt*: **to** ~ **sth in sb**
inculcare qc a qn, instillare qc a qn.
incumbent [ɪn'kʌmbənt] *a*: **it is** ~ **on him to
do** ... è suo dovere fare ... ♦ *n* titolare *m/f*.
incur [ɪn'kəː*] *vt* (*expenses*) incorrere; (*debt*)
contrarre; (*loss*) subire; (*anger, risk*) esporsi
a.
incurable [ɪn'kjuərəbl] *a* incurabile.
incursion [ɪn'kəːʃən] *n* incursione *f*.
indebted [ɪn'dɛtɪd] *a*: **to be** ~ **to sb** (**for**)
essere obbligato(a) verso qn (per).
indecency [ɪn'diːsnsɪ] *n* indecenza.
indecent [ɪn'diːsnt] *a* indecente.
indecent assault *n* (*Brit*) aggressione *f* a
scopo di violenza sessuale.
indecent exposure *n* atti *mpl* osceni in
luogo pubblico.
indecipherable [ɪndɪ'saɪfərəbl] *a* indecifrabile.
indecision [ɪndɪ'sɪʒən] *n* indecisione *f*.
indecisive [ɪndɪ'saɪsɪv] *a* indeciso(a); (*discussion*) non decisivo(a).
indeed [ɪn'diːd] *ad* infatti; veramente; **yes** ~!
certamente!
indefatigable [ɪndɪ'fætɪgəbl] *a* infaticabile, instancabile.
indefensible [ɪndɪ'fɛnsəbl] *a* (*conduct*) ingiustificabile.
indefinable [ɪndɪ'faɪnəbl] *a* indefinibile.
indefinite [ɪn'dɛfɪnɪt] *a* indefinito(a); (*answer*)
vago(a); (*period, number*) indeterminato(a).
indefinitely [ɪn'dɛfɪnɪtlɪ] *ad* (*wait*)
indefinitamente.
indelible [ɪn'dɛlɪbl] *a* indelebile.
indelicate [ɪn'dɛlɪkɪt] *a* (*tactless*) indelica-
to(a), privo(a) di tatto; (*not polite*)
sconveniente.
indemnify [ɪn'dɛmnɪfaɪ] *vt* indennizzare.
indemnity [ɪn'dɛmnɪtɪ] *n* (*insurance*)
assicurazione *f*; (*compensation*) indennità,
indennizzo.
indent [ɪn'dɛnt] *vt* (*TYP: text*) far rientrare
dal margine.
indentation [ɪndɛn'teɪʃən] *n* dentellatura;
(*TYP*) rientranza; (*dent*) tacca.
indented [ɪn'dɛntɪd] *a* (*TYP*) rientrante.
indenture [ɪn'dɛntʃə*] *n* contratto *m*
formazione *inv*.
independence [ɪndɪ'pɛndns] *n* indipendenza.
independent [ɪndɪ'pɛndnt] *a* indipendente.
independently [ɪndɪ'pɛndntlɪ] *ad*
indipendentemente; separatamente; ~ **of**
indipendentemente da.
indescribable [ɪndɪ'skraɪbəbl] *a* indescrivibile.
indestructible [ɪndɪ'strʌktəbl] *a* indistruttibile.
indeterminate [ɪndɪ'təːmɪnɪt] *a*
indeterminato(a).
index ['ɪndɛks] *n* (*pl* ~**es**: *in book*) indice *m*;
(: *in library etc*) catalogo; (*pl* **indices**

['ɪndɪsi:z]: *ratio, sign*) indice *m*.
index card *n* scheda.
index finger *n* (dito) indice *m*.
index-linked ['ɪndɛks'lɪŋkt], (*US*) **indexed** ['ɪndɛkst] *a* legato(a) al costo della vita.
India ['ɪndɪə] *n* India.
Indian ['ɪndɪən] *a, n* indiano(a).
Indian ink *n* inchiostro di china.
Indian Ocean *n*: **the ~** l'Oceano Indiano.
Indian Summer *n* (*fig*) estate *f* di San Martino.
India paper *n* carta d'India, carta bibbia.
India rubber *n* caucciù *m*.
indicate ['ɪndɪkeɪt] *vt* indicare ♦ *vi* (*Brit AUT*): **to ~ left/right** mettere la freccia a sinistra/a destra.
indication [ɪndɪ'keɪʃən] *n* indicazione *f*, segno.
indicative [ɪn'dɪkətɪv] *a* indicativo(a) ♦ *n* (*LING*) indicativo; **to be ~ of sth** essere indicativo(a) *or* un indice di qc.
indicator ['ɪndɪkeɪtə*] *n* (*sign*) segno; (*AUT*) indicatore *m* di direzione, freccia.
indices ['ɪndɪsi:z] *npl of* **index**.
indict [ɪn'daɪt] *vt* accusare.
indictable [ɪn'daɪtəbl] *a* passibile di pena; **~ offence** atto che costituisce reato.
indictment [ɪn'daɪtmənt] *n* accusa.
indifference [ɪn'dɪfrəns] *n* indifferenza.
indifferent [ɪn'dɪfrənt] *a* indifferente; (*poor*) mediocre.
indigenous [ɪn'dɪdʒɪnəs] *a* indigeno(a).
indigestible [ɪndɪ'dʒɛstɪbl] *a* indigeribile.
indigestion [ɪndɪ'dʒɛstʃən] *n* indigestione *f*.
indignant [ɪn'dɪgnənt] *a*: **~ (at sth/with sb)** indignato(a) (per qc/contro qn).
indignation [ɪndɪg'neɪʃən] *n* indignazione *f*.
indignity [ɪn'dɪgnɪtɪ] *n* umiliazione *f*.
indigo ['ɪndɪgəu] *a, n* indaco (*inv*).
indirect [ɪndɪ'rɛkt] *a* indiretto(a).
indirectly [ɪndɪ'rɛktlɪ] *ad* indirettamente.
indiscreet [ɪndɪ'skri:t] *a* indiscreto(a); (*rash*) imprudente.
indiscretion [ɪndɪ'skrɛʃən] *n* indiscrezione *f*; imprudenza.
indiscriminate [ɪndɪ'skrɪmɪnət] *a* (*person*) che non sa discernere; (*admiration*) cieco(a); (*killings*) indiscriminato(a).
indispensable [ɪndɪ'spɛnsəbl] *a* indispensabile.
indisposed [ɪndɪ'spəuzd] *a* (*unwell*) indisposto(a).
indisposition [ɪndɪspə'zɪʃən] *n* (*illness*) indisposizione *f*.
indisputable [ɪndɪ'spju:təbl] *a* incontestabile, indiscutibile.
indistinct [ɪndɪ'stɪŋkt] *a* indistinto(a); (*memory, noise*) vago(a).
indistinguishable [ɪndɪ'stɪŋgwɪʃəbl] *a* indistinguibile.
individual [ɪndɪ'vɪdjuəl] *n* individuo ♦ *a* individuale; (*characteristic*) particolare, originale.
individualist [ɪndɪ'vɪdjuəlɪst] *n* individualista *m/f*.
individuality [ɪndɪvɪdju'ælɪtɪ] *n* individualità.

individually [ɪndɪ'vɪdjuəlɪ] *ad* singolarmente, uno(a) per uno(a).
indivisible [ɪndɪ'vɪzɪbl] *a* indivisibile.
Indochina ['ɪndəu'tʃaɪnə] *n* Indocina.
indoctrinate [ɪn'dɔktrɪneɪt] *vt* indottrinare.
indoctrination [ɪndɔktrɪ'neɪʃən] *n* indottrinamento.
indolent ['ɪndələnt] *a* indolente.
Indonesia [ɪndəu'ni:zɪə] *n* Indonesia.
Indonesian [ɪndəu'ni:zɪən] *a, n* indonesiano(a).
indoor ['ɪndɔ:*] *a* da interno; (*plant*) d'appartamento; (*swimming pool*) coperto(a); (*sport, games*) fatto(a) al coperto.
indoors [ɪn'dɔ:z] *ad* all'interno; (*at home*) in casa.
indubitable [ɪn'dju:bɪtəbl] *a* indubitabile.
induce [ɪn'dju:s] *vt* persuadere; (*bring about*) provocare; **to ~ sb to do sth** persuadere qn a fare qc.
inducement [ɪn'dju:smənt] *n* incitamento; (*incentive*) stimolo, incentivo.
induct [ɪn'dʌkt] *vt* insediare; (*fig*) iniziare.
induction [ɪn'dʌkʃən] *n* (*MED*: *of birth*) parto indotto.
induction course *n* (*Brit*) corso di avviamento.
indulge [ɪn'dʌldʒ] *vt* (*whim*) compiacere, soddisfare; (*child*) viziare ♦ *vi*: **to ~ in sth** concedersi qc; abbandonarsi a qc.
indulgence [ɪn'dʌldʒəns] *n* lusso (che uno si permette); (*leniency*) indulgenza.
indulgent [ɪn'dʌldʒənt] *a* indulgente.
industrial [ɪn'dʌstrɪəl] *a* industriale; (*injury*) sul lavoro; (*dispute*) di lavoro.
industrial action *n* azione *f* rivendicativa.
industrial estate *n* zona industriale.
industrialist [ɪn'dʌstrɪəlɪst] *n* industriale *m*.
industrialize [ɪn'dʌstrɪəlaɪz] *vt* industrializzare.
industrial park *n* (*US*) zona industriale.
industrial relations *npl* relazioni *fpl* industriali.
industrial tribunal *n* (*Brit*) ≈ Tribunale *m* Amministrativo Regionale.
industrial unrest *n* (*Brit*) agitazione *f* (sindacale).
industrious [ɪn'dʌstrɪəs] *a* industrioso(a), assiduo(a).
industry ['ɪndəstrɪ] *n* industria; (*diligence*) operosità.
inebriated [ɪ'ni:brɪeɪtɪd] *a* ubriaco(a).
inedible [ɪn'edɪbl] *a* immangiabile; non commestibile.
ineffective [ɪnɪ'fɛktɪv] *a* inefficace.
ineffectual [ɪnɪ'fɛktʃuəl] *a* inefficace; incompetente.
inefficiency [ɪnɪ'fɪʃənsɪ] *n* inefficienza.
inefficient [ɪnɪ'fɪʃənt] *a* inefficiente.
inelegant [ɪn'ɛlɪgənt] *a* poco elegante.
ineligible [ɪn'ɛlɪdʒɪbl] *a* (*candidate*) ineleggibile; **to be ~ for sth** non avere il diritto a qc.
inept [ɪ'nɛpt] *a* inetto(a).

ineptitude [ɪ'neptɪtju:d] *n* inettitudine *f*, stupidità.
inequality [ɪnɪ'kwɔlɪtɪ] *n* ineguaglianza.
inequitable [ɪn'ekwɪtəbl] *a* iniquo(a).
ineradicable [ɪnɪ'rædɪkəbl] *a* inestirpabile.
inert [ɪ'nə:t] *a* inerte.
inertia [ɪ'nə:ʃə] *n* inerzia.
inertia-reel seat belt [ɪ'nə:ʃə'ri:l-] *n* cintura di sicurezza con arrotolatore.
inescapable [ɪnɪ'skeɪpəbl] *a* inevitabile.
inessential [ɪnɪ'senʃl] *a* non essenziale.
inestimable [ɪn'estɪməbl] *a* inestimabile, incalcolabile.
inevitable [ɪn'evɪtəbl] *a* inevitabile.
inevitably [ɪn'evɪtəblɪ] *ad* inevitabilmente; **as ~ happens** ... come immancabilmente succede ....
inexact [ɪnɪg'zækt] *a* inesatto(a).
inexcusable [ɪnɪks'kju:zəbl] *a* imperdonabile.
inexhaustible [ɪnɪg'zɔ:stɪbl] *a* inesauribile; (*person*) instancabile.
inexorable [ɪn'eksərəbl] *a* inesorabile.
inexpensive [ɪnɪk'spensɪv] *a* poco costoso(a).
inexperience [ɪnɪk'spɪərɪəns] *n* inesperienza.
inexperienced [ɪnɪk'spɪərɪənst] *a* inesperto(a), senza esperienza; **to be ~ in sth** essere poco pratico di qc.
inexplicable [ɪnɪk'splɪkəbl] *a* inesplicabile.
inexpressible [ɪnɪk'spresəbl] *a* inesprimibile.
inextricable [ɪnɪk'strɪkəbl] *a* inestricabile.
infallibility [ɪnfælə'bɪlɪtɪ] *n* infallibilità.
infallible [ɪn'fælɪbl] *a* infallibile.
infamous ['ɪnfəməs] *a* infame.
infamy ['ɪnfəmɪ] *n* infamia.
infancy ['ɪnfənsɪ] *n* infanzia.
infant ['ɪnfənt] *n* bambino/a.
infantile ['ɪnfəntaɪl] *a* infantile.
infant mortality *n* mortalità infantile.
infantry ['ɪnfəntrɪ] *n* fanteria.
infantryman ['ɪnfəntrɪmən] *n* fante *m*.
infant school *n* (*Brit*) scuola elementare (*per bambini dall'età di 5 a 7 anni*).
infatuated [ɪn'fætjueɪtɪd] *a*: **~ with** infatuato(a) di; **to become ~ (with sb)** infatuarsi (di qn).
infatuation [ɪnfætju'eɪʃən] *n* infatuazione *f*.
infect [ɪn'fekt] *vt* infettare; **~ed with** (*illness*) affetto(a) da; **to become ~ed** (*wound*) infettarsi.
infection [ɪn'fekʃən] *n* infezione *f*.
infectious [ɪn'fekʃəs] *a* (*disease*) infettivo(a); contagioso(a); (*person, laughter*) contagioso(a).
infer [ɪn'fə:*] *vt*: **to ~ (from)** dedurre (da), concludere (da).
inference ['ɪnfərəns] *n* deduzione *f*, conclusione *f*.
inferior [ɪn'fɪərɪə*] *a* inferiore; (*goods*) di qualità scadente ♦ *n* inferiore *m/f*; (*in rank*) subalterno/a; **to feel ~** sentirsi inferiore.
inferiority [ɪnfɪərɪ'ɔrətɪ] *n* inferiorità.
inferiority complex *n* complesso di inferiorità.
infernal [ɪn'fə:nl] *a* infernale.

inferno [ɪn'fə:nəu] *n* inferno.
infertile [ɪn'fə:taɪl] *a* sterile.
infertility [ɪnfə:'tɪlɪtɪ] *n* sterilità.
infested [ɪn'festɪd] *a*: **~ (with)** infestato(a) (di).
infidelity [ɪnfɪ'delɪtɪ] *n* infedeltà.
in-fighting ['ɪnfaɪtɪŋ] *n* lotte *fpl* intestine.
infiltrate ['ɪnfɪltreɪt] *vt* (*troops etc*) far penetrare; (*enemy line etc*) infiltrare ♦ *vi* infiltrarsi.
infinite ['ɪnfɪnɪt] *a* infinito(a); **an ~ amount of time/money** un'illimitata quantità di tempo/denaro.
infinitely ['ɪnfɪnɪtlɪ] *ad* infinitamente.
infinitesimal [ɪnfɪnɪ'tesɪməl] *a* infinitesimale.
infinitive [ɪn'fɪnɪtɪv] *n* infinito.
infinity [ɪn'fɪnɪtɪ] *n* infinità; (*also* MATH) infinito.
infirm [ɪn'fə:m] *a* infermo(a).
infirmary [ɪn'fə:mərɪ] *n* ospedale *m*; (*in school, factory*) infermeria.
infirmity [ɪn'fə:mɪtɪ] *n* infermità *f inv*.
inflamed [ɪn'fleɪmd] *a* infiammato(a).
inflammable [ɪn'flæməbl] *a* infiammabile.
inflammation [ɪnflə'meɪʃən] *n* infiammazione *f*.
inflammatory [ɪn'flæmətərɪ] *a* (*speech*) incendiario(a).
inflatable [ɪn'fleɪtəbl] *a* gonfiabile.
inflate [ɪn'fleɪt] *vt* (*tyre, balloon*) gonfiare; (*fig*) esagerare; gonfiare; **to ~ the currency** far ricorso all'inflazione.
inflated [ɪn'fleɪtɪd] *a* (*style*) gonfio(a); (*value*) esagerato(a).
inflation [ɪn'fleɪʃən] *n* (ECON) inflazione *f*.
inflationary [ɪn'fleɪʃənərɪ] *a* inflazionistico(a).
inflexible [ɪn'fleksɪbl] *a* inflessibile, rigido(a).
inflict [ɪn'flɪkt] *vt*: **to ~ on** infliggere a.
infliction [ɪn'flɪkʃən] *n* inflizione *f*; afflizione *f*.
in-flight ['ɪnflaɪt] *a* a bordo.
inflow ['ɪnfləu] *n* afflusso.
influence ['ɪnfluəns] *n* influenza ♦ *vt* influenzare; **under the ~ of** sotto l'influenza di; **under the ~ of drink** sotto l'influenza *or* l'effetto dell'alcool.
influential [ɪnflu'enʃl] *a* influente.
influenza [ɪnflu'enzə] *n* (MED) influenza.
influx ['ɪnflʌks] *n* afflusso.
inform [ɪn'fə:m] *vt*: **to ~ sb (of)** informare qn (di) ♦ *vi*: **to ~ on sb** denunciare qn; **to ~ sb about** mettere qn al corrente di.
informal [ɪn'fə:ml] *a* (*person, manner*) alla buona, semplice; (*visit, discussion*) informale; (*announcement, invitation*) non ufficiale; **"dress ~"** "non è richiesto l'abito scuro"; **~ language** linguaggio colloquiale.
informality [ɪnfə:'mælɪtɪ] *n* semplicità, informalità; carattere *m* non ufficiale.
informally [ɪn'fə:məlɪ] *ad* senza cerimonie; (*invite*) in modo non ufficiale.
informant [ɪn'fə:mənt] *n* informatore/trice.
informatics [ɪnfə:'mætɪks] *n* informatica.
information [ɪnfə'meɪʃən] *n* informazioni *fpl*; particolari *mpl*; **to get ~ on** informarsi su;

a piece of ~ un'informazione; **for your** ~ a titolo d'informazione, per sua informazione.

information bureau *n* ufficio *m* informazioni *inv*.

information processing *n* elaborazione *f* delle informazioni.

information retrieval *n* ricupero delle informazioni.

information technology (IT) *n* informatica.

informative [ɪn'fɔ:mətɪv] *a* istruttivo(a).

informed [ɪn'fɔ:md] *a* (*observer*) (ben) informato(a); **an ~ guess** un'ipotesi fondata.

informer [ɪn'fɔ:mə*] *n* informatore/trice.

infra dig ['ɪnfrə'dɪg] *a abbr* (*col*: = *infra dignitatem*: *beneath one's dignity*) indecoroso(a).

infra-red [ɪnfrə'rɛd] *a* infrarosso(a).

infrastructure ['ɪnfrəstrʌktʃə*] *n* infrastruttura.

infrequent [ɪn'fri:kwənt] *a* infrequente, raro(a).

infringe [ɪn'frɪndʒ] *vt* infrangere ♦ *vi*: **to ~ on** calpestare.

infringement [ɪn'frɪndʒmənt] *n*: ~ **(of)** infrazione *f* (di).

infuriate [ɪn'fjʊərɪeɪt] *vt* rendere furioso(a).

infuriating [ɪn'fjʊərɪeɪtɪŋ] *a* molto irritante.

infuse [ɪn'fju:z] *vt* (*with courage, enthusiasm*): **to ~ sb with sth** infondere qc a qn, riempire qn di qc.

infusion [ɪn'fju:ʒən] *n* (*tea etc*) infuso, infusione *f*.

ingenious [ɪn'dʒi:njəs] *a* ingegnoso(a).

ingenuity [ɪndʒɪ'nju:ɪtɪ] *n* ingegnosità.

ingenuous [ɪn'dʒɛnjuəs] *a* ingenuo(a).

ingot ['ɪŋgət] *n* lingotto.

ingrained [ɪn'greɪnd] *a* radicato(a).

ingratiate [ɪn'greɪʃɪeɪt] *vt*: **to ~ o.s. with sb** ingraziarsi qn.

ingratiating [ɪn'greɪʃɪeɪtɪŋ] *a* (*smile, speech*) suadente, cattivante; (*person*) compiacente.

ingratitude [ɪn'grætɪtju:d] *n* ingratitudine *f*.

ingredient [ɪn'gri:dɪənt] *n* ingrediente *m*; elemento.

ingrowing ['ɪngrəʊɪŋ], **ingrown** ['ɪngrəʊn] *a*: ~ **(toe)nail** unghia incarnita.

inhabit [ɪn'hæbɪt] *vt* abitare.

inhabitable [ɪn'hæbɪtəbl] *a* abitabile.

inhabitant [ɪn'hæbɪtnt] *n* abitante *m/f*.

inhale [ɪn'heɪl] *vt* inalare ♦ *vi* (*in smoking*) aspirare.

inherent [ɪn'hɪərənt] *a*: ~ **(in or to)** inerente (a).

inherently [ɪn'hɪərəntlɪ] *ad* (*easy, difficult*) di per sé, di per se stesso(a); ~ **lazy** pigro di natura.

inherit [ɪn'hɛrɪt] *vt* ereditare.

inheritance [ɪn'hɛrɪtəns] *n* eredità.

inhibit [ɪn'hɪbɪt] *vt* (*PSYCH*) inibire; **to ~ sb from doing** impedire a qn di fare.

inhibited [ɪn'hɪbɪtɪd] *a* (*person*) inibito(a).

inhibiting [ɪn'hɪbɪtɪŋ] *a* che inibisce.

inhibition [ɪnhɪ'bɪʃən] *n* inibizione *f*.

inhospitable [ɪnhɔs'pɪtəbl] *a* inospitale.

inhuman [ɪn'hju:mən] *a* inumano(a), disumano(a).

inhumane [ɪnhju:'meɪn] *a* inumano(a), disumano(a).

inimitable [ɪ'nɪmɪtəbl] *a* inimitabile.

iniquity [ɪ'nɪkwɪtɪ] *n* iniquità *f inv*.

initial [ɪ'nɪʃl] *a* iniziale ♦ *n* iniziale *f* ♦ *vt* siglare; ~**s** *npl* iniziali *fpl*; (*as signature*) sigla.

initialize [ɪ'nɪʃəlaɪz] *vt* (*COMPUT*) inizializzare.

initially [ɪ'nɪʃəlɪ] *ad* inizialmente, all'inizio.

initiate [ɪ'nɪʃɪeɪt] *vt* (*start*) avviare; intraprendere; iniziare; (*person*) iniziare; **to ~ sb into sth** iniziare qn a qc; **to ~ proceedings against sb** (*LAW*) intentare causa a *or* contro qn.

initiation [ɪnɪʃɪ'eɪʃən] *n* iniziazione *f*.

initiative [ɪ'nɪʃətɪv] *n* iniziativa; **to take the ~** prendere l'iniziativa.

inject [ɪn'dʒɛkt] *vt* (*liquid*) iniettare; (*person*) fare una puntura a; (*fig: money*): **to ~ into** immettere in.

injection [ɪn'dʒɛkʃən] *n* iniezione *f*, puntura; **to have an ~** farsi fare un'iniezione *or* una puntura.

injudicious [ɪndʒu'dɪʃəs] *a* poco saggio(a).

injunction [ɪn'dʒʌŋkʃən] *n* (*LAW*) ingiunzione *f*, intimazione *f*.

injure ['ɪndʒə*] *vt* ferire; (*wrong*) fare male *or* torto a; (*damage: reputation etc*) nuocere a; (*feelings*) offendere; **to ~ o.s.** farsi male.

injured ['ɪndʒəd] *a* (*person, leg etc*) ferito(a); (*tone, feelings*) offeso(a); ~ **party** (*LAW*) parte *f* lesa.

injurious [ɪn'dʒuərɪəs] *a*: ~ **(to)** nocivo(a) (a), pregiudizievole (per).

injury ['ɪndʒərɪ] *n* ferita; (*wrong*) torto; **to escape without** ~ rimanere illeso.

injury time *n* (*SPORT*) tempo di ricupero.

injustice [ɪn'dʒʌstɪs] *n* ingiustizia; **you do me an** ~ mi fa un torto, è ingiusto verso di me.

ink [ɪŋk] *n* inchiostro.

ink-jet printer ['ɪŋkdʒɛt-] *n* stampante *f* a getto d'inchiostro.

inkling ['ɪŋklɪŋ] *n* sentore *m*, vaga idea.

inkpad ['ɪŋkpæd] *n* tampone *m*, cuscinetto per timbri.

inky ['ɪŋkɪ] *a* macchiato(a) *or* sporco(a) d'inchiostro.

inlaid ['ɪnleɪd] *a* incrostato(a); (*table etc*) intarsiato(a).

inland *a* ['ɪnlənd] interno(a) ♦ *ad* [ɪn'lænd] all'interno; ~ **waterways** canali e fiumi *mpl* navigabili.

Inland Revenue *n* (*Brit*) Fisco.

in-laws ['ɪnlɔ:z] *npl* suoceri *mpl*; famiglia del marito (*or* della moglie).

inlet ['ɪnlɛt] *n* (*GEO*) insenatura, baia.

inlet pipe *n* (*TECH*) tubo d'immissione.

inmate ['ɪnmeɪt] *n* (*in prison*) carcerato/a; (*in asylum*) ricoverato/a.

inmost ['ɪnməʊst] *a* più profondo(a), più intimo(a).

inn [ɪn] *n* locanda.

innards ['ɪnədz] *npl* (*col*) interiora *fpl*, budella *fpl*.
innate [ɪ'neɪt] *a* innato(a).
inner ['ɪnə*] *a* interno(a), interiore.
inner city *n* centro di una zona urbana.
innermost ['ɪnəməust] *a* = **inmost**.
inner tube *n* camera d'aria.
innings ['ɪnɪŋz] *n* (*CRICKET*) turno di battuta; (*Brit fig*): **he has had a good ~** ha avuto molto dalla vita.
innocence ['ɪnəsns] *n* innocenza.
innocent ['ɪnəsnt] *a* innocente.
innocuous [ɪ'nɔkjuəs] *a* innocuo(a).
innovation [ɪnəu'veɪʃən] *n* innovazione *f*.
innuendo, **~es** [ɪnju'ɛndəu] *n* insinuazione *f*.
innumerable [ɪ'njuːmrəbl] *a* innumerevole.
inoculate [ɪ'nɔkjuleɪt] *vt*: **to ~ sb with sth/against sth** inoculare qc a qn/qn contro qc.
inoculation [ɪnɔkju'leɪʃən] *n* inoculazione *f*.
inoffensive [ɪnə'fɛnsɪv] *a* inoffensivo(a), innocuo(a).
inopportune [ɪn'ɔpətjuːn] *a* inopportuno(a).
inordinate [ɪ'nɔːdɪnɪt] *a* eccessivo(a).
inordinately [ɪ'nɔːdɪnətlɪ] *ad* smoderatamente.
inorganic [ɪnɔː'gænɪk] *a* inorganico(a).
in-patient ['ɪnpeɪʃənt] *n* ricoverato/a.
input ['ɪnput] *n* (*ELEC*) energia, potenza; (*of machine*) alimentazione *f*; (*of computer*) input *m* ♦ *vt* (*COMPUT*) inserire, introdurre.
inquest ['ɪnkwɛst] *n* inchiesta.
inquire [ɪn'kwaɪə*] *vi* informarsi ♦ *vt* domandare, informarsi di *or* su; **to ~ about** informarsi di *or* su, chiedere informazioni su; **to ~ when/where/whether** informarsi di quando/su dove/se.
  inquire after *vt fus* (*person*) chiedere di; (*sb's health*) informarsi di.
  inquire into *vt fus* indagare su, fare delle indagini *or* ricerche su.
inquiring [ɪn'kwaɪərɪŋ] *a* (*mind*) inquisitivo(a).
inquiry [ɪn'kwaɪərɪ] *n* domanda; (*LAW*) indagine *f*, investigazione *f*; **to hold an ~ into sth** fare un'inchiesta su qc.
inquiry desk *n* (*Brit*) banco delle informazioni.
inquiry office *n* (*Brit*) ufficio *m* informazioni *inv*.
inquisition [ɪnkwɪ'zɪʃən] *n* inquisizione *f*, inchiesta; (*REL*): **the I~** l'Inquisizione.
inquisitive [ɪn'kwɪzɪtɪv] *a* curioso(a).
inroads ['ɪnrəudz] *npl*: **to make ~ into** (*savings*, *supplies*) intaccare (seriamente).
insane [ɪn'seɪn] *a* matto(a), pazzo(a); (*MED*) alienato(a).
insanitary [ɪn'sænɪtərɪ] *a* insalubre.
insanity [ɪn'sænɪtɪ] *n* follia; (*MED*) alienazione *f* mentale.
insatiable [ɪn'seɪʃəbl] *a* insaziabile.
inscribe [ɪn'skraɪb] *vt* iscrivere; (*book etc*): **to ~ (to sb)** dedicare (a qn).
inscription [ɪn'skrɪpʃən] *n* iscrizione *f*; (*in book*) dedica.
inscrutable [ɪn'skruːtəbl] *a* imperscrutabile.

inseam ['ɪnsiːm] *n* (*US*): **~ measurement** lunghezza interna.
insect ['ɪnsɛkt] *n* insetto.
insect bite *n* puntura *or* morsicatura di insetto.
insecticide [ɪn'sɛktɪsaɪd] *n* insetticida *m*.
insect repellent *n* insettifugo.
insecure [ɪnsɪ'kjuə*] *a* malsicuro(a); (*person*) insicuro(a).
insecurity [ɪnsɪ'kjuərɪtɪ] *n* mancanza di sicurezza.
insensible [ɪn'sɛnsɪbl] *a* insensibile; (*unconscious*) privo(a) di sensi.
insensitive [ɪn'sɛnsɪtɪv] *a* insensibile.
insensitivity [ɪnsɛnsɪ'tɪvɪtɪ] *n* mancanza di sensibilità.
inseparable [ɪn'sɛprəbl] *a* inseparabile.
insert *vt* [ɪn'səːt] inserire, introdurre ♦ *n* ['ɪnsəːt] inserto.
insertion [ɪn'səːʃən] *n* inserzione *f*.
in-service ['ɪn'səːvɪs] *a* (*course*, *training*) dopo l'assunzione.
inshore [ɪn'ʃɔː*] *a* costiero(a) ♦ *ad* presso la riva; verso la riva.
inside ['ɪn'saɪd] *n* interno, parte *f* interiore; (*of road*: *Brit*) sinistra; (: *US*, *in Europe etc*) destra ♦ *a* interno(a), interiore ♦ *ad* dentro, all'interno ♦ *prep* dentro, all'interno di; (*of time*): **~ 10 minutes** entro 10 minuti; **~s** *npl* (*col*) ventre *m*; **~ out** *ad* alla rovescia; **to turn sth ~ out** rivoltare qc; **to know sth ~ out** conoscere qc a fondo; **~ information** informazioni *fpl* riservate; **~ story** storia segreta.
inside forward *n* (*SPORT*) mezzala, interno.
inside lane *n* (*AUT*) corsia di marcia.
inside leg measurement *n* (*Brit*) lunghezza interna.
insider [ɪn'saɪdə*] *n* uno(a) che ha le mani in pasta.
insider dealing *n* (*STOCK EXCHANGE*) insider dealing *m*.
insidious [ɪn'sɪdɪəs] *a* insidioso(a).
insight ['ɪnsaɪt] *n* acume *m*, perspicacia; (*glimpse*, *idea*) percezione *f*; **to gain** *or* **get an ~ into sth** potersi render conto di qc.
insignia [ɪn'sɪgnɪə] *npl* insegne *fpl*.
insignificant [ɪnsɪg'nɪfɪknt] *a* insignificante.
insincere [ɪnsɪn'sɪə*] *a* insincero(a).
insincerity [ɪnsɪn'sɛrɪtɪ] *n* falsità, insincerità.
insinuate [ɪn'sɪnjueɪt] *vt* insinuare.
insinuation [ɪnsɪnju'eɪʃən] *n* insinuazione *f*.
insipid [ɪn'sɪpɪd] *a* insipido(a), insulso(a).
insist [ɪn'sɪst] *vi* insistere; **to ~ on doing** insistere per fare; **to ~ that** insistere perché + *sub*; (*claim*) sostenere che.
insistence [ɪn'sɪstəns] *n* insistenza.
insistent [ɪn'sɪstənt] *a* insistente.
insole ['ɪnsəul] *n* soletta; (*fixed part of shoe*) tramezza.
insolence ['ɪnsələns] *n* insolenza.
insolent ['ɪnsələnt] *a* insolente.
insoluble [ɪn'sɔljubl] *a* insolubile.
insolvency [ɪn'sɔlvənsɪ] *n* insolvenza.

insolvent [ɪn'sɔlvənt] *a* insolvente.
insomnia [ɪn'sɔmnɪə] *n* insonnia.
insomniac [ɪn'sɔmnɪæk] *n* chi soffre di insonnia.
inspect [ɪn'spɛkt] *vt* ispezionare; (*Brit: ticket*) controllare.
inspection [ɪn'spɛkʃən] *n* ispezione *f*; controllo.
inspector [ɪn'spɛktə*] *n* ispettore/trice; controllore *m*.
inspiration [ɪnspə'reɪʃən] *n* ispirazione *f*.
inspire [ɪn'spaɪə*] *vt* ispirare.
inspired [ɪn'spaɪəd] *a* (*writer, book etc*) ispirato(a); **in an ~ moment** in un momento d'ispirazione.
inspiring [ɪn'spaɪərɪŋ] *a* stimolante.
inst. [ɪnst] *abbr* (*Brit* COMM: = *instant*) c.m. (*corrente mese*).
instability [ɪnstə'bɪlɪtɪ] *n* instabilità.
install [ɪn'stɔ:l] *vt* installare.
installation [ɪnstə'leɪʃən] *n* installazione *f*.
installment plan *n* (*US*) acquisto a rate.
instalment, (*US*) **installment** [ɪn'stɔ:lmənt] *n* rata; (*of TV serial etc*) puntata; **to pay in ~s** pagare a rate.
instance ['ɪnstəns] *n* esempio, caso; **for ~** per *or* ad esempio; **in that ~** in quel caso; **in the first ~** in primo luogo.
instant ['ɪnstənt] *n* istante *m*, attimo ♦ *a* immediato(a); urgente; (*coffee, food*) in polvere; **the 10th ~** il 10 corrente (mese).
instantaneous [ɪnstən'teɪnɪəs] *a* istantaneo(a).
instantly ['ɪnstəntlɪ] *ad* immediatamente, subito.
instant replay *n* (*US TV*) replay *m inv*.
instead [ɪn'stɛd] *ad* invece; **~ of** invece di; **~ of sb** al posto di qn.
instep ['ɪnstɛp] *n* collo del piede; (*of shoe*) collo della scarpa.
instigate ['ɪnstɪgeɪt] *vt* (*rebellion, strike, crime*) istigare a; (*new ideas etc*) promuovere.
instigation [ɪnstɪ'geɪʃən] *n* istigazione *f*; **at sb's ~** per *or* in seguito al suggerimento di qn.
instil [ɪn'stɪl] *vt*: **to ~ (into)** inculcare (in).
instinct ['ɪnstɪŋkt] *n* istinto.
instinctive [ɪn'stɪŋktɪv] *a* istintivo(a).
instinctively [ɪn'stɪŋktɪvlɪ] *ad* per istinto.
institute ['ɪnstɪtjuːt] *n* istituto ♦ *vt* istituire, stabilire; (*inquiry*) avviare; (*proceedings*) iniziare.
institution [ɪnstɪ'tjuːʃən] *n* istituzione *f*; istituto (d'istruzione); istituto (psichiatrico).
institutional [ɪnstɪ'tjuːʃənl] *a* istituzionale; **~ care** assistenza medica presso un istituto.
instruct [ɪn'strʌkt] *vt* istruire; **to ~ sb in sth** insegnare qc a qn; **to ~ sb to do** dare ordini a qn di fare.
instruction [ɪn'strʌkʃən] *n* istruzione *f*; **~s (for use)** istruzioni per l'uso.
instruction book *n* libretto di istruzioni.
instructive [ɪn'strʌktɪv] *a* istruttivo(a).

instructor [ɪn'strʌktə*] *n* istruttore/trice; (*for skiing*) maestro/a.
instrument ['ɪnstrumənt] *n* strumento.
instrumental [ɪnstru'mɛntl] *a* (MUS) strumentale; **to be ~ in sth/in doing sth** avere un ruolo importante in qc/nel fare qc.
instrumentalist [ɪnstru'mɛntəlɪst] *n* strumentista *m/f*.
instrument panel *n* quadro *m* portastrumenti *inv*.
insubordinate [ɪnsə'bɔːdənɪt] *a* insubordinato(a).
insubordination [ɪnsəbɔːdə'neɪʃən] *n* insubordinazione *f*.
insufferable [ɪn'sʌfrəbl] *a* insopportabile.
insufficient [ɪnsə'fɪʃənt] *a* insufficiente.
insufficiently [ɪnsə'fɪʃəntlɪ] *ad* in modo insufficiente.
insular ['ɪnsjulə*] *a* insulare; (*person*) di mente ristretta.
insulate ['ɪnsjuleɪt] *vt* isolare.
insulating tape ['ɪnsjuleɪtɪŋ-] *n* nastro isolante.
insulation [ɪnsju'leɪʃən] *n* isolamento.
insulin ['ɪnsjulɪn] *n* insulina.
insult *n* ['ɪnsʌlt] insulto, affronto ♦ *vt* [ɪn'sʌlt] insultare.
insulting [ɪn'sʌltɪŋ] *a* offensivo(a), ingiurioso(a).
insuperable [ɪn'sjuːprəbl] *a* insormontabile, insuperabile.
insurance [ɪn'ʃuərəns] *n* assicurazione *f*; **fire/life ~** assicurazione contro gli incendi/sulla vita; **to take out ~ (against)** fare un'assicurazione (contro), assicurarsi (contro).
insurance agent *n* agente *m* d'assicurazioni.
insurance broker *n* broker *m inv* d'assicurazioni.
insurance policy *n* polizza d'assicurazione.
insurance premium *n* premio assicurativo.
insure [ɪn'ʃuə*] *vt* assicurare; **to ~ sb** *or* **sb's life** assicurare qn sulla vita; **to be ~d for £5000** essere assicurato per 5000 sterline.
insured [ɪn'ʃuəd] *n*: **the ~** l'assicurato/a.
insurer [ɪn'ʃuərə*] *n* assicuratore/trice.
insurgent [ɪn'sɜːdʒənt] *a* ribelle ♦ *n* insorto/a, rivoltoso/a.
insurmountable [ɪnsə'mauntəbl] *a* insormontabile.
insurrection [ɪnsə'rɛkʃən] *n* insurrezione *f*.
intact [ɪn'tækt] *a* intatto(a).
intake ['ɪnteɪk] *n* (TECH) immissione *f*; (*of food*) consumo; (*of pupils etc*) afflusso.
intangible [ɪn'tændʒɪbl] *a* intangibile.
integral ['ɪntɪgrəl] *a* integrale; (*part*) integrante.
integrate ['ɪntɪgreɪt] *vt* integrare.
integrated circuit *n* (COMPUT) circuito integrato.
integration [ɪntɪ'greɪʃən] *n* integrazione *f*; **racial ~** integrazione razziale.
integrity [ɪn'tɛgrɪtɪ] *n* integrità.
intellect ['ɪntəlɛkt] *n* intelletto.

intellectual [ɪntə'lɛktjuəl] *a*, *n* intellettuale (*m/f*).

intelligence [ɪn'tɛlɪdʒəns] *n* intelligenza; (*MIL etc*) informazioni *fpl*.

intelligence quotient (IQ) *n* quoziente *m* d'intelligenza (Q.I.).

Intelligence Service *n* servizio segreto.

intelligence test *n* test *m inv* d'intelligenza.

intelligent [ɪn'tɛlɪdʒənt] *a* intelligente.

intelligible [ɪn'tɛlɪdʒɪbl] *a* intelligibile.

intemperate [ɪn'tɛmpərət] *a* immoderato(a); (*drinking too much*) intemperante nel bere.

intend [ɪn'tɛnd] *vt* (*gift etc*): **to ~ sth for** de-stinare qc a; **to ~ to do** aver l'intenzione di fare.

intended [ɪn'tɛndɪd] *a* (*insult*) intenzionale; (*effect*) voluto(a); (*journey*, *route*) progettato(a).

intense [ɪn'tɛns] *a* intenso(a); (*person*) di forti sentimenti.

intensely [ɪn'tɛnslɪ] *ad* intensamente; profondamente.

intensify [ɪn'tɛnsɪfaɪ] *vt* intensificare.

intensity [ɪn'tɛnsɪtɪ] *n* intensità.

intensive [ɪn'tɛnsɪv] *a* intensivo(a).

intensive care *n* terapia intensiva; **~ unit (ICU)** *n* reparto terapia intensiva.

intent [ɪn'tɛnt] *n* intenzione *f* ♦ *a*: **~ (on)** intento(a) (a), immerso(a) (in); **to all ~s and purposes** a tutti gli effetti; **to be ~ on doing sth** essere deciso a fare qc.

intention [ɪn'tɛnʃən] *n* intenzione *f*.

intentional [ɪn'tɛnʃənl] *a* intenzionale, deliberato(a).

intentionally [ɪn'tɛnʃənəlɪ] *ad* apposta.

intently [ɪn'tɛntlɪ] *ad* attentamente.

inter [ɪn'tə:*] *vt* sotterrare.

interact [ɪntər'ækt] *vi* agire reciprocamente, interagire.

interaction [ɪntər'ækʃən] *n* azione *f* reciproca, interazione *f*.

interactive [ɪntər'æktɪv] *a* interattivo(a).

intercede [ɪntə'si:d] *vi*: **to ~ (with sb/on behalf of sb)** intercedere (presso qn/a favore di qn).

intercept [ɪntə'sɛpt] *vt* intercettare; (*person*) fermare.

interception [ɪntə'sɛpʃən] *n* intercettamento.

interchange *n* [ɪntətʃeɪndʒ] (*exchange*) scambio; (*on motorway*) incrocio pluridirezionale ♦ *vt* [ɪntə'tʃeɪndʒ] scambiare; sostituire l'uno(a) per l'altro(a).

interchangeable [ɪntə'tʃeɪndʒəbl] *a* intercambiabile.

intercity [ɪntə'sɪtɪ] *a*: **~ (train)** ≈ (treno) rapido.

intercom ['ɪntəkɔm] *n* interfono.

interconnect [ɪntəkə'nɛkt] *vi* (*rooms*) essere in comunicazione.

intercontinental ['ɪntəkɔntɪ'nɛntl] *a* intercontinentale.

intercourse ['ɪntəkɔ:s] *n* rapporti *mpl*; (*sexual ~*) rapporti sessuali.

interdependent [ɪntədɪ'pɛndənt] *a* interdipendente.

interest ['ɪntrɪst] *n* interesse *m*; (*COMM*: *stake*, *share*) interessi *mpl* ♦ *vt* interessare; **compound/simple ~** interesse composto/ semplice; **business ~s** attività *fpl* commerciali; **British ~s in the Middle East** gli interessi (commerciali) britannici nel Medio Oriente.

interested ['ɪntrɪstɪd] *a* interessato(a); **to be ~ in** interessarsi di.

interest-free ['ɪntrɪst'fri:] *a* senza interesse.

interesting ['ɪntrɪstɪŋ] *a* interessante.

interest rate *n* tasso di interesse.

interface ['ɪntəfeɪs] *n* (*COMPUT*) interfaccia.

interfere [ɪntə'fɪə*] *vi*: **to ~ (in)** (*quarrel*, *other people's business*) immischiarsi (in); **to ~ with** (*object*) toccare; (*plans*) ostacolare; (*duty*) interferire con.

interference [ɪntə'fɪərəns] *n* interferenza.

interfering [ɪntə'fɪərɪŋ] *a* invadente.

interim ['ɪntərɪm] *a* provvisorio(a) ♦ *n*: **in the ~** nel frattempo; **~ dividend** (*COMM*) acconto di dividendo.

interior [ɪn'tɪərɪə*] *n* interno; (*of country*) en-troterra ♦ *a* interiore, interno(a).

interior decorator, interior designer *n* decoratore/trice (d'interni).

interjection [ɪntə'dʒɛkʃən] *n* interiezione *f*.

interlock [ɪntə'lɔk] *vi* ingranarsi ♦ *vt* in-granare.

interloper ['ɪntələupə*] *n* intruso/a.

interlude ['ɪntəlu:d] *n* intervallo; (*THEATRE*) intermezzo.

intermarry [ɪntə'mærɪ] *vi* imparentarsi per mezzo di matrimonio; sposarsi tra parenti.

intermediary [ɪntə'mi:dɪərɪ] *n* intermediario/a.

intermediate [ɪntə'mi:dɪət] *a* intermedio(a); (*SCOL*: *course*, *level*) medio(a).

interminable [ɪn'tə:mɪnəbl] *a* interminabile.

intermission [ɪntə'mɪʃən] *n* pausa; (*THEATRE*, *CINEMA*) intermissione *f*, intervallo.

intermittent [ɪntə'mɪtnt] *a* intermittente.

intermittently [ɪntə'mɪtntlɪ] *ad* a intermittenza.

intern *vt* [ɪn'tə:n] internare ♦ *n* ['ɪntə:n] (*US*) medico interno.

internal [ɪn'tə:nl] *a* interno(a); **~ injuries** lesioni *fpl* interne.

internally [ɪn'tə:nəlɪ] *ad* all'interno; "**not to be taken ~**" "per uso esterno".

Internal Revenue (Service) (IRS) *n* (*US*) Fisco.

international [ɪntə'næʃənl] *a* internazionale ♦ *n* (*Brit SPORT*) partita internazionale.

International Atomic Energy Agency (IAEA) *n* Agenzia Internazionale per l'Energia Atomica (IAEA).

International Court of Justice (ICJ) *n* Corte *f* Internazionale di Giustizia.

international date line *n* linea del cambiamento di data.

internationally [ɪntə'næʃnəlɪ] *ad* a livello internazionale.

International Monetary Fund (IMF) *n*

Fondo monetario internazionale (F.M.I.).
internecine [intəˈniːsaɪn] a sanguinoso(a).
internee [intəːˈniː] n internato/a.
internment [inˈtəːnmənt] n internamento.
interplay [ˈintəpleɪ] n azione e reazione f.
Interpol [ˈintəpɔl] n Interpol f.
interpret [inˈtəːprɪt] vt interpretare ♦ vi fare
da interprete.
interpretation [intəːprɪˈteɪʃən] n interpretazione f.
interpreter [inˈtəːprɪtə*] n interprete m/f.
interpreting [inˈtəːprɪtɪŋ] n (profession) inter-
pretariato.
interrelated [intərɪˈleɪtɪd] a correlato(a).
interrogate [inˈtɛrəugeɪt] vt interrogare.
interrogation [intɛrəuˈgeɪʃən] n interrogazione
f; (of suspect etc) interrogatorio.
interrogative [intəˈrɔgətɪv] a interrogativo(a)
♦ n (LING) interrogativo.
interrogator [inˈtɛrəgeɪtə*] n interrogante m/f.
interrupt [intəˈrʌpt] vt interrompere.
interruption [intəˈrʌpʃən] n interruzione f.
intersect [intəˈsɛkt] vt intersecare ♦ vi (roads)
intersecarsi.
intersection [intəˈsɛkʃən] n intersezione f; (of
roads) incrocio.
intersperse [intəˈspəːs] vt: **to ~ with** co-
stellare di.
intertwine [intəˈtwaɪn] vt intrecciare ♦ vi in-
trecciarsi.
interval [ˈintəvl] n intervallo; (Brit SCOL) ricreazione f, intervallo; **bright ~s** (in
weather) schiarite fpl; **at ~s** a intervalli.
intervene [intəˈviːn] vi (time) intercorrere;
(event, person) intervenire.
intervention [intəˈvɛnʃən] n intervento.
interview [ˈintəvjuː] n (RADIO, TV etc) intervista; (for job) colloquio ♦ vt intervistare;
avere un colloquio con.
interviewer [ˈintəvjuːə*] n intervistatore/trice.
intestate [inˈtɛsteɪt] a intestato(a).
intestinal [inˈtɛstɪnl] a intestinale.
intestine [inˈtɛstɪn] n intestino; **large/small ~**
intestino crasso/tenue.
intimacy [ˈintɪməsɪ] n intimità.
intimate a [ˈintɪmət] intimo(a); (knowledge)
profondo(a) ♦ vt [ˈintɪmeɪt] lasciar capire.
intimately [ˈintɪmɪtlɪ] ad intimamente.
intimation [intɪˈmeɪʃən] n annuncio.
intimidate [inˈtɪmɪdeɪt] vt intimidire,
intimorire.
intimidation [intɪmɪˈdeɪʃən] n intimidazione f.
into [ˈintu] prep dentro, in; **come ~ the house**
vieni dentro la casa; **~ pieces** a pezzi; **~
Italian** in italiano; **to change pounds ~
dollars** cambiare delle sterline in dollari.
intolerable [inˈtɔlərəbl] a intollerabile.
intolerance [inˈtɔlərns] n intolleranza.
intolerant [inˈtɔlərnt] a: **~ (of)** intollerante
(di).
intonation [intəuˈneɪʃən] n intonazione f.
intoxicate [inˈtɔksɪkeɪt] vt inebriare.
intoxicated [inˈtɔksɪkeɪtɪd] a inebriato(a).
intoxication [intɔksɪˈkeɪʃən] n ebbrezza.

intractable [inˈtræktəbl] a intrattabile;
(illness) difficile da curare; (problem)
insolubile.
intransigence [inˈtrænsɪdʒəns] n in-
transigenza.
intransigent [inˈtrænsɪdʒənt] a intransigente.
intransitive [inˈtrænsɪtɪv] a intransitivo(a).
intra-uterine device (IUD) [intrəˈjuːtəraɪn-]
n dispositivo intrauterino (IUD).
intravenous [intrəˈviːnəs] a endovenoso(a).
in-tray [ˈintreɪ] n raccoglitore m per le carte
in arrivo.
intrepid [inˈtrɛpɪd] a intrepido(a).
intricacy [ˈintrɪkəsɪ] n complessità f inv.
intricate [ˈintrɪkət] a intricato(a), com-
plicato(a).
intrigue [inˈtriːg] n intrigo ♦ vt affascinare ♦
vi complottare, tramare.
intriguing [inˈtriːgɪŋ] a affascinante.
intrinsic [inˈtrɪnsɪk] a intrinseco(a).
introduce [intrəˈdjuːs] vt introdurre; **to ~ sb
(to sb)** presentare qn (a qn); **to ~ sb to**
(pastime, technique) iniziare qn a; **may I ~
...?** permette che le presenti ...?
introduction [intrəˈdʌkʃən] n introduzione f;
(of person) presentazione f; **a letter of ~** una
lettera di presentazione.
introductory [intrəˈdʌktərɪ] a introduttivo(a);
an ~ offer un'offerta di lancio; **~ remarks**
osservazioni fpl preliminari.
introspection [intrəuˈspɛkʃən] n introspezione
f.
introspective [intrəuˈspɛktɪv] a intro-
spettivo(a).
introvert [ˈintrəuvəːt] a, n introverso(a).
intrude [inˈtruːd] vi (person) intromettersi; **to
~ on** (person) importunare; **~ on** or **into**
(conversation) intromettersi in; **am I intrud-
ing?** disturbo?
intruder [inˈtruːdə*] n intruso/a.
intrusion [inˈtruːʒən] n intrusione f.
intrusive [inˈtruːsɪv] a importuno(a).
intuition [intjuːˈɪʃən] n intuizione f.
intuitive [inˈtjuːɪtɪv] a intuitivo(a); dotato(a)
di intuito.
inundate [ˈinʌndeɪt] vt: **to ~ with** inondare
di.
inure [inˈjuə*] vt: **to ~ (to)** assuefare (a).
invade [inˈveɪd] vt invadere.
invader [inˈveɪdə*] n invasore m.
invalid n [ˈinvəlɪd] malato/a; (with disability)
invalido/a ♦ a [inˈvælɪd] (not valid)
invalido(a), non valido(a).
invalidate [inˈvælɪdeɪt] vt invalidare.
invalid chair n (Brit) sedia a rotelle.
invaluable [inˈvæljuəbl] a prezioso(a); inestimabile.
invariable [inˈvɛərɪəbl] a costante, invariabile.
invariably [inˈvɛərɪəblɪ] ad invariabilmente;
she is ~ late è immancabilmente in ritardo.
invasion [inˈveɪʒən] n invasione f.
invective [inˈvɛktɪv] n invettiva.
inveigle [inˈviːgl] vt: **to ~ sb into (doing) sth**
circuire qn per (fargli fare) qc.

invent [ɪn'vɛnt] vt inventare.
invention [ɪn'vɛnʃən] n invenzione f.
inventive [ɪn'vɛntɪv] a inventivo(a).
inventiveness [ɪn'vɛntɪvnɪs] n inventiva.
inventor [ɪn'vɛntə*] n inventore m.
inventory ['ɪnvəntrɪ] n inventario.
inventory control n (COMM) controllo delle giacenze.
inverse [ɪn'vəːs] a inverso(a) ♦ n inverso, contrario; **in ~ proportion (to)** in modo inversamente proporzionale (a).
inversely [ɪn'vəːslɪ] ad inversamente.
invert [ɪn'vəːt] vt invertire; (object) rovesciare.
invertebrate [ɪn'vəːtɪbrɪt] n invertebrato.
inverted commas [ɪn'vəːtɪd-] npl (Brit) virgolette fpl.
invest [ɪn'vɛst] vt investire; (fig: time, effort) impiegare; (endow): **to ~ sb with sth** investire qn di qc ♦ vi fare investimenti; **to ~ in** investire in, fare (degli) investimenti in; (acquire) comprarsi.
investigate [ɪn'vɛstɪgeɪt] vt investigare, indagare; (crime) fare indagini su.
investigation [ɪnvɛstɪ'geɪʃən] n investigazione f; (of crime) indagine f.
investigative [ɪn'vɛstɪgətɪv] a: **~ journalism** giornalismo investigativo.
investigator [ɪn'vɛstɪgeɪtə*] n investigatore/trice; **a private ~** un investigatore privato, un detective.
investiture [ɪn'vɛstɪtʃə*] n investitura.
investment [ɪn'vɛstmənt] n investimento.
investment income n reddito da investimenti.
investment trust n fondo comune di investimento.
investor [ɪn'vɛstə*] n investitore/trice; (shareholder) azionista m/f.
inveterate [ɪn'vɛtərət] a inveterato(a).
invidious [ɪn'vɪdɪəs] a odioso(a); (task) spiacevole.
invigilate [ɪn'vɪdʒɪleɪt] vt, vi (Brit SCOL) sorvegliare.
invigilator [ɪn'vɪdʒɪleɪtə*] n (Brit) chi sorveglia agli esami.
invigorating [ɪn'vɪgəreɪtɪŋ] a stimolante; vivificante.
invincible [ɪn'vɪnsɪbl] a invincibile.
inviolate [ɪn'vaɪələt] a inviolato(a).
invisible [ɪn'vɪzɪbl] a invisibile.
invisible assets npl (Brit) beni mpl immateriali.
invisible ink n inchiostro simpatico.
invisible mending n rammendo invisibile.
invitation [ɪnvɪ'teɪʃən] n invito; **by ~ only** esclusivamente su or per invito; **at sb's ~** dietro invito di qn.
invite [ɪn'vaɪt] vt invitare; (opinions etc) sollecitare; (trouble) provocare; **to ~ sb (to do)** invitare qn (a fare); **to ~ sb to dinner** invitare qn a cena.
invite out vt invitare fuori.
invite over vt invitare (a casa).

inviting [ɪn'vaɪtɪŋ] a invitante, attraente.
invoice ['ɪnvɔɪs] n fattura ♦ vt fatturare; **to ~ sb for goods** inviare a qn la fattura per le or delle merci.
invoke [ɪn'vəuk] vt invocare.
involuntary [ɪn'vɔləntrɪ] a involontario(a).
involve [ɪn'vɔlv] vt (entail) richiedere, comportare; (associate): **to ~ sb (in)** implicare qn (in); coinvolgere qn (in); **to involve o.s. in sth** (politics etc) impegnarsi in qc.
involved [ɪn'vɔlvd] a involuto(a), complesso(a); **to feel ~** sentirsi coinvolto(a); **to become ~ with sb** (socially) legarsi a qn; (emotionally) legarsi sentimentalmente a qn.
involvement [ɪn'vɔlvmənt] n implicazione f; coinvolgimento; impegno; partecipazione f.
invulnerable [ɪn'vʌlnərəbl] a invulnerabile.
inward ['ɪnwəd] a (movement) verso l'interno; (thought, feeling) interiore, intimo(a); see also **inward(s).**
inwardly ['ɪnwədlɪ] ad (feel, think etc) nell'intimo, entro di sé.
inward(s) ['ɪnwəd(z)] ad verso l'interno.
I/O abbr (COMPUT: = input/output) I/O.
IOC n abbr (= International Olympic Committee) CIO m (= Comitato Internazionale Olimpico).
iodine ['aɪəudiːn] n iodio.
IOM abbr (Brit) = Isle of Man.
ion ['aɪən] n ione m.
Ionian Sea [aɪ'əunɪən-] n: **the ~** il mare Ionio.
iota [aɪ'əutə] n (fig) briciolo.
IOU n abbr (= I owe you) pagherò m inv.
IOW abbr (Brit) = Isle of Wight.
IPA n abbr (= International Phonetic Alphabet) I.P.A. m.
IQ n abbr = **intelligence quotient.**
IRA n abbr (= Irish Republican Army) I.R.A. f; (US) = individual retirement account.
Iran [ɪ'rɑːn] n Iran m.
Iranian [ɪ'reɪnɪən] a iraniano(a) ♦ n iraniano/a; (LING) iranico.
Iraq [ɪ'rɑːk] n Iraq m.
Iraqi [ɪ'rɑːkɪ] a iracheno(a) ♦ n iracheno/a; (LING) iracheno.
irascible [ɪ'ræsɪbl] a irascibile.
irate [aɪ'reɪt] a irato(a).
Ireland ['aɪələnd] n Irlanda; **Republic of ~** Repubblica d'Irlanda, Eire f.
iris, ~es ['aɪrɪs, -ɪz] n iride f; (BOT) giaggiolo, iride.
Irish ['aɪrɪʃ] a irlandese ♦ npl: **the ~** gli Irlandesi.
Irishman ['aɪrɪʃmən] n irlandese m.
Irish Sea n: **the ~** il mar d'Irlanda.
Irishwoman ['aɪrɪʃwumən] n irlandese f.
irk [əːk] vt seccare.
irksome ['əːksəm] a seccante.
IRN n abbr (= Independent Radio News) agenzia d'informazioni per la radio.
IRO n abbr (US: = International Refugee Organization) O.I.R. f (= Organizzazione

Internazionale per i Rifugiati).

iron ['aɪən] *n* ferro; (*for clothes*) ferro da stiro ♦ *a* di *or* in ferro ♦ *vt* (*clothes*) stirare; *see also* **irons**.

iron out *vt* (*crease*) appianare; (*fig*) spianare; far sparire.

Iron Curtain *n*: **the ~** la cortina di ferro.

iron foundry *n* fonderia.

ironic(al) [aɪ'rɔnɪk(l)] *a* ironico(a).

ironically [aɪ'rɔnɪklɪ] *ad* ironicamente.

ironing ['aɪənɪŋ] *n* (*act*) stirare *m*; (*clothes*) roba da stirare.

ironing board *n* asse *f* da stiro.

iron lung *n* (*MED*) polmone *m* d'acciaio.

ironmonger ['aɪənmʌŋgə*] *n* (*Brit*) negoziante *m* in ferramenta; **~'s (shop)** *n* negozio di ferramenta.

iron ore *n* minerale *m* di ferro.

irons ['aɪənz] *npl* (*chains*) catene *fpl*.

ironworks ['aɪənwə:ks] *n* ferriera.

irony ['aɪrənɪ] *n* ironia.

irrational [ɪ'ræʃənl] *a* irrazionale; irragionevole; illogico(a).

irreconcilable [ɪrɛkən'saɪləbl] *a* irreconciliabile; (*opinion*): **~ with** inconciliabile con.

irredeemable [ɪrɪ'di:məbl] *a* (*COMM*) irredimibile.

irrefutable [ɪrɪ'fju:təbl] *a* irrefutabile.

irregular [ɪ'rɛgjulə*] *a* irregolare.

irregularity [ɪrɛgju'lærɪtɪ] *n* irregolarità *f inv*.

irrelevance [ɪ'rɛləvəns] *n* inappropriatezza.

irrelevant [ɪ'rɛləvənt] *a* non pertinente.

irreligious [ɪrɪ'lɪdʒəs] *a* irreligioso(a).

irreparable [ɪ'rɛprəbl] *a* irreparabile.

irreplaceable [ɪrɪ'pleɪsəbl] *a* insostituibile.

irrepressible [ɪrɪ'prɛsəbl] *a* irrefrenabile.

irreproachable [ɪrɪ'prəutʃəbl] *a* irreprensibile.

irresistible [ɪrɪ'zɪstɪbl] *a* irresistibile.

irresolute [ɪ'rɛzəlu:t] *a* irresoluto(a), indeciso(a).

irrespective [ɪrɪ'spɛktɪv]: **~ of** *prep* senza riguardo a.

irresponsible [ɪrɪ'spɔnsɪbl] *a* irresponsabile.

irretrievable [ɪrɪ'tri:vəbl] *a* (*object*) irrecuperabile; (*loss, damage*) irreparabile.

irreverent [ɪ'rɛvərnt] *a* irriverente.

irrevocable [ɪ'rɛvəkəbl] *a* irrevocabile.

irrigate ['ɪrɪgeɪt] *vt* irrigare.

irrigation [ɪrɪ'geɪʃən] *n* irrigazione *f*.

irritable ['ɪrɪtəbl] *a* irritabile.

irritant ['ɪrɪtənt] *n* sostanza irritante.

irritate ['ɪrɪteɪt] *vt* irritare.

irritation [ɪrɪ'teɪʃən] *n* irritazione *f*.

IRS *n abbr* (*US*) *see* **Internal Revenue Service**.

is [ɪz] *vb see* **be**.

ISBN *n abbr* (= *International Standard Book Number*) I.S.B.N. *m*.

Islam ['ɪzlɑːm] *n* Islam *m*.

island ['aɪlənd] *n* isola; (*also*: **traffic ~**) salvagente *m*.

islander ['aɪləndə*] *n* isolano/a.

isle [aɪl] *n* isola.

isn't ['ɪznt] = **is not**.

isolate ['aɪsəleɪt] *vt* isolare.

isolated ['aɪsəleɪtɪd] *a* isolato(a).

isolation [aɪsə'leɪʃən] *n* isolamento.

isolationism [aɪsə'leɪʃənɪzəm] *n* isolazionismo.

isotope ['aɪsəutəup] *n* isotopo.

Israel ['ɪzreɪl] *n* Israele *m*.

Israeli [ɪz'reɪlɪ] *a, n* israeliano(a).

issue ['ɪʃju:] *n* questione *f*, problema *m*; (*outcome*) esito, risultato; (*of banknotes etc*) emissione *f*; (*of newspaper etc*) numero; (*offspring*) discendenza ♦ *vt* (*rations, equipment*) distribuire; (*orders*) dare; (*book*) pubblicare; (*banknotes, cheques, stamps*) emettere ♦ *vi*: **to ~ (from)** uscire (da), venir fuori (da); **at ~** in gioco, in discussione; **to avoid the ~** evitare la discussione; **to take ~ with sb (over sth)** prendere posizione contro qn (riguardo a qc); **to confuse** *or* **obscure the ~** confondere le cose; **to make an ~ of sth** fare un problema di qc; **to ~ sth to sb, ~ sb with sth** consegnare qc a qn.

Istanbul [ɪstæn'bu:l] *n* Istanbul *f*.

isthmus ['ɪsməs] *n* istmo.

IT *n abbr see* **information technology**.

it [ɪt] *pronoun* (*subject*) esso(a); (*direct object*) lo(la), l'; (*indirect object*) gli(le); **of ~, from ~, about ~, out of ~** *etc* ne; **in ~, to ~, at ~** *etc* ci; **above ~, over ~** (al) di sopra; **below ~, under ~** (al) di sotto; **in front of/behind ~** lì davanti/dietro; **who is ~?** chi è?; **~'s me** sono io; **what is ~?** cosa c'è?; **where is ~?** dov'è?; **~'s Friday tomorrow** domani è venerdì; **~'s raining** piove; **~'s 6 o'clock** sono le 6; **~'s 2 hours on the train** sono *or* ci vogliono 2 ore di treno; **I've come from ~** vengo da lì; **it's on ~** è lì sopra; **he's proud of ~** ne è fiero; **he agreed to ~** ha acconsentito.

ITA *n abbr* (*Brit*: = *initial teaching alphabet*) *alfabeto fonetico semplificato per insegnare a leggere*.

Italian [ɪ'tæljən] *a* italiano(a) ♦ *n* italiano/a; (*LING*) italiano; **the ~s** gli Italiani.

italic [ɪ'tælɪk] *a* corsivo(a); **~s** *npl* corsivo.

Italy ['ɪtəlɪ] *n* Italia.

itch [ɪtʃ] *n* prurito ♦ *vi* (*person*) avere il prurito; (*part of body*) prudere; **to be ~ing to do** non veder l'ora di fare.

itchy ['ɪtʃɪ] *a* che prude; **my back is ~** ho prurito alla schiena.

it'd ['ɪtd] = **it would**; **it had**.

item ['aɪtəm] *n* articolo; (*on agenda*) punto; (*in programme*) numero; (*also*: **news ~**) notizia; **~s of clothing** capi *mpl* di abbigliamento.

itemize ['aɪtəmaɪz] *vt* specificare, dettagliare.

itinerant [ɪ'tɪnərənt] *a* ambulante.

itinerary [aɪ'tɪnərərɪ] *n* itinerario.

it'll ['ɪtl] = **it will**, **it shall**.

ITN *n abbr* (*Brit*: = *Independent Television News*) *agenzia d'informazioni per la televisione*.

its [ɪts] *a, pronoun* il(la) suo(a), i(le)

suoi(sue).

it's [ɪts] = **it is**; **it has**.

itself [ɪt'self] *pronoun (emphatic)* esso(a) stesso(a); *(reflexive)* si.

ITV *n abbr (Brit: = Independent Television)* rete televisiva indipendente.

IUD *n abbr* = **intra-uterine device**.

I've [aɪv] = **I have**.

ivory ['aɪvərɪ] *n* avorio.

Ivory Coast *n* Costa d'Avorio.

ivory tower *n* torre *f* d'avorio.

ivy ['aɪvɪ] *n* edera.

Ivy League *n (US) insieme delle grandi università del Nord-Est degli Stati Uniti.*

J

J, j [dʒeɪ] *n (letter)* J, j *f or m inv*; **J for Jack**, *(US)* **J for Jig** ≈ J come jersey.

JA *n abbr see* **judge advocate**.

J/A *abbr see* **joint account**.

jab [dʒæb] *vt*: **to ~ sth into** affondare *or* piantare qc dentro ♦ *vi*: **to ~ at** dare colpi a ♦ *n* colpo; *(MED: col)* puntura.

jabber ['dʒæbə*] *vt, vi* borbottare.

jack [dʒæk] *n (AUT)* cricco; *(BOWLS)* boccino, pallino; *(CARDS)* fante *m*.

jack in *vt (col)* mollare.

jack up *vt* sollevare sul cricco; *(raise: prices etc)* alzare.

jackal ['dʒækl] *n* sciacallo.

jackass ['dʒækæs] *n (also fig)* asino, somaro.

jackdaw ['dʒækdɔ:] *n* taccola.

jacket ['dʒækɪt] *n* giacca; *(of book)* copertura; **potatoes in their ~s** *(Brit)* patate *fpl* con la buccia.

jack-in-the-box ['dʒækɪnðəbɔks] *n* scatola a sorpresa (con pupazzo a molla).

jack-knife ['dʒæknaɪf] *vi*: **the lorry ~d** l'autotreno si è piegato su se stesso.

jack-of-all-trades [dʒækəv'ɔːltreɪdz] *n* uno che fa un po' di tutto.

jack plug *n (Brit)* jack plug *f inv*.

jackpot ['dʒækpɔt] *n* primo premio (in denaro).

jacuzzi ® [dʒə'kuːzɪ] *n* vasca per idromassaggio Jacuzzi ®.

jade [dʒeɪd] *n (stone)* giada.

jaded ['dʒeɪdɪd] *a* sfinito(a), spossato(a).

JAG *n abbr see* **Judge Advocate General**.

jagged ['dʒægɪd] *a* sboccconcellato(a); *(cliffs etc)* frastagliato(a).

jaguar ['dʒægjuə*] *n* giaguaro.

jail [dʒeɪl] *n* prigione *f* ♦ *vt* mandare in prigione.

jailbird ['dʒeɪlbəːd] *n* avanzo di galera.

jailbreak ['dʒeɪlbreɪk] *n* evasione *f*.

jailer ['dʒeɪlə*] *n* custode *m* del carcere.

jalopy [dʒə'lɔpɪ] *n (col)* macinino.

jam [dʒæm] *n* marmellata; *(of shoppers etc)* ressa; *(also: traffic ~)* ingorgo ♦ *vt (passage etc)* ingombrare, ostacolare; *(mechanism, drawer etc)* bloccare; *(RADIO)* disturbare con interferenze ♦ *vi (mechanism, sliding part)* incepparsi, bloccarsi; *(gun)* incepparsi; **to get sb out of a ~** tirare qn fuori dai pasticci; **to ~ sth into** forzare qc dentro; infilare qc a forza dentro; **the telephone lines are ~med** le linee sono sovraccariche.

Jamaica [dʒə'meɪkə] *n* Giamaica.

Jamaican [dʒə'meɪkən] *a, n* giamaicano(a).

jamb [dʒæm] *n* stipite *m*.

jam-packed [dʒæm'pækt] *a*: **~ (with)** pieno(a) zeppo(a) (di), strapieno(a) (di).

jam session *n* improvvisazione *f* jazzistica.

Jan. *abbr (= January)* gen., genn.

jangle ['dʒæŋgl] *vi* risuonare; *(bracelet)* tintinnare.

janitor ['dʒænɪtə*] *n (caretaker)* portiere *m*; *(SCOL)* bidello.

January ['dʒænjuərɪ] *n* gennaio; *for phrases see also* **July**.

Japan [dʒə'pæn] *n* Giappone *m*.

Japanese [dʒæpə'niːz] *a* giapponese ♦ *n (pl inv)* giapponese *m/f*; *(LING)* giapponese *m*.

jar [dʒɑː*] *n (container)* barattolo, vasetto ♦ *vi (sound)* stridere; *(colours etc)* stonare ♦ *vt (shake)* scuotere.

jargon ['dʒɑːgən] *n* gergo.

jarring ['dʒɑːrɪŋ] *a (sound, colour)* stonato(a).

Jas. *abbr = James*.

jasmin(e) ['dʒæzmɪn] *n* gelsomino.

jaundice ['dʒɔːndɪs] *n* itterizia.

jaundiced ['dʒɔːndɪst] *a (fig)* invidioso(a) e critico(a).

jaunt [dʒɔːnt] *n* gita.

jaunty ['dʒɔːntɪ] *a* vivace; disinvolto(a), spigliato(a).

Java ['dʒɑːvə] *n* Giava.

javelin ['dʒævlɪn] *n* giavellotto.

jaw [dʒɔː] *n* mascella; **~s** *(TECH: of vice etc)* morsa.

jawbone ['dʒɔːbəun] *n* mandibola.

jay [dʒeɪ] *n* ghiandaia.

jaywalker ['dʒeɪwɔːkə*] *n* pedone(a) indisciplinato(a).

jazz [dʒæz] *n* jazz *m*.

jazz up *vt* rendere vivace.

jazz band *n* banda *f* jazz *inv*.

jazzy ['dʒæzɪ] *a* vistoso(a), chiassoso(a).

JCS *n abbr (US) = Joint Chiefs of Staff*.

JD *n abbr (US: = Doctor of Laws)* titolo di studio; *(: = Justice Department)* ministero della Giustizia.

jealous ['dʒeləs] *a* geloso(a).

jealously ['dʒeləslɪ] *ad (enviously)* con gelosia; *(watchfully)* gelosamente.

jealousy ['dʒeləsɪ] *n* gelosia.

jeans [dʒiːnz] *npl* (blue-)jeans *mpl*.

jeep [dʒiːp] *n* jeep *m inv*.

jeer [dʒɪə*] *vi*: **to ~ (at)** fischiare;

beffeggiare; *see also* **jeers.**

jeering ['dʒɪərɪŋ] *a* (*crowd*) che urla e fischia ♦ *n* fischi *mpl*; parole *fpl* di scherno.

jeers ['dʒɪəz] *npl* fischi *mpl*.

jelly ['dʒɛlɪ] *n* gelatina.

jellyfish ['dʒɛlɪfɪʃ] *n* medusa.

jeopardize ['dʒɛpədaɪz] *vt* mettere in pericolo.

jeopardy ['dʒɛpədɪ] *n*: **in ~** in pericolo.

jerk [dʒə:k] *n* sobbalzo, scossa; sussulto; (*col*) povero scemo ♦ *vt* dare una scossa a ♦ *vi* (*vehicles*) sobbalzare.

jerkin ['dʒə:kɪn] *n* giubbotto.

jerky ['dʒə:kɪ] *a* a scatti; a sobbalzi.

jerry-built ['dʒɛrɪbɪlt] *a* fatto(a) di cartapesta.

jerry can ['dʒɛrɪ-] *n* tanica.

Jersey ['dʒə:zɪ] *n* Jersey *m*.

jersey ['dʒə:zɪ] *n* maglia, jersey *m*.

Jerusalem [dʒə'ru:sələm] *n* Gerusalemme *f*.

jest [dʒɛst] *n* scherzo; **in ~** per scherzo.

jester ['dʒɛstə*] *n* (*HISTORY*) buffone *m*.

Jesus ['dʒi:zəs] *n* Gesù *m*; **~ Christ** Gesù Cristo.

jet [dʒɛt] *n* (*of gas, liquid*) getto; (*AUT*) spruzzatore *m*; (*AVIAT*) aviogetto.

jet-black ['dʒɛt'blæk] *a* nero(a) come l'ebano, corvino(a).

jet engine *n* motore *m* a reazione.

jet lag *n* (problemi *mpl* dovuti allo) sbalzo dei fusi orari.

jetsam ['dʒɛtsəm] *n* relitti *mpl* di mare.

jettison ['dʒɛtɪsn] *vt* gettare in mare.

jetty ['dʒɛtɪ] *n* molo.

Jew [dʒu:] *n* ebreo.

jewel ['dʒu:əl] *n* gioiello.

jeweller, (*US*) **jeweler** ['dʒu:ələ*] *n* orefice *m*, gioielliere/a; **~'s** (**shop**) *n* oreficeria, gioielleria.

jewellery, (*US*) **jewelry** ['dʒu:əlrɪ] *n* gioielli *mpl*.

Jewess ['dʒu:ɪs] *n* ebrea.

Jewish ['dʒu:ɪʃ] *a* ebreo(a), ebraico(a).

JFK *n abbr* (*US*) = *John Fitzgerald Kennedy International Airport*.

jib [dʒɪb] *n* (*NAUT*) fiocco; (*of crane*) braccio ♦ *vi* (*horse*) impennarsi; **to ~ at doing sth** essere restio a fare qc.

jibe [dʒaɪb] *n* beffa.

jiffy ['dʒɪfɪ] *n* (*col*): **in a ~** in un batter d'occhio.

jig [dʒɪg] *n* (*dance, tune*) giga.

jigsaw ['dʒɪgsɔ:] *n* (*tool*) sega da traforo; (*also*: **~ puzzle**) puzzle *m inv*.

jilt [dʒɪlt] *vt* piantare in asso.

jingle ['dʒɪŋgl] *n* (*advert*) sigla pubblicitaria ♦ *vi* tintinnare, scampanellare.

jingoism ['dʒɪŋgəuɪzəm] *n* sciovinismo.

jinx [dʒɪŋks] *n* (*col*) iettatura; (*person*) iettatore/trice.

jitters ['dʒɪtəz] *npl* (*col*): **to get the ~** aver fifa.

jittery ['dʒɪtərɪ] *a* (*col*) nervoso(a), agitato(a).

jiujitsu [dʒu:'dʒɪtsu:] *n* jujitsu *m*.

job [dʒɔb] *n* lavoro; (*employment*) impiego, posto; **a part-time/full-time ~** un lavoro a mezza giornata/a tempo pieno; **that's not my ~** non è compito mio; **he's only doing his ~** non fa che il suo dovere; **it's a good ~ that** ... **meno male che ...; just the ~!** proprio quello che ci vuole!

jobber ['dʒɔbə*] *n* (*Brit STOCK EXCHANGE*) intermediario tra agenti di cambio.

jobbing ['dʒɔbɪŋ] *a* (*Brit: workman*) a ore, a giornata.

Jobcentre ['dʒɔbsɛntə*] *n* ufficio di collocamento.

job creation scheme *n* progetto per la creazione di nuovi posti di lavoro.

job description *n* caratteristiche *fpl* (di un lavoro).

jobless ['dʒɔblɪs] *a* senza lavoro, disoccupato(a).

job lot *n* partita di articoli disparati.

job satisfaction *n* soddisfazione *f* nel lavoro.

job security *n* sicurezza del posto di lavoro.

job specification *n* caratteristiche *fpl* (di un lavoro).

jockey ['dʒɔkɪ] *n* fantino, jockey *m inv* ♦ *vi*: **to ~ for position** manovrare per una posizione di vantaggio.

jockey box *n* (*US AUT*) vano portaoggetti.

jocular ['dʒɔkjulə*] *a* gioviale; scherzoso(a).

jog [dʒɔg] *vt* urtare ♦ *vi* (*SPORT*) fare footing, fare jogging; **to ~ along** trottare; (*fig*) andare avanti piano piano; **to ~ sb's memory** stimolare la memoria di qn.

jogger ['dʒɔgə*] *n* persona che fa footing *or* jogging.

jogging ['dʒɔgɪŋ] *n* footing *m*, jogging *m*.

join [dʒɔɪn] *vt* unire, congiungere; (*become member of*) iscriversi a; (*meet*) raggiungere; riunirsi a ♦ *vi* (*roads, rivers*) confluire ♦ *n* giuntura; **to ~ forces (with)** allearsi (con *or* a); (*fig*) mettersi insieme (a); **will you ~ us for dinner?** viene a cena con noi?; **I'll ~ you later** vi raggiungo più tardi.

join in *vt fus* unirsi a, prendere parte a, partecipare a ♦ *vi* partecipare.

join up *vi* arruolarsi.

joiner ['dʒɔɪnə*] *n* falegname *m*.

joinery ['dʒɔɪnərɪ] *n* falegnameria.

joint [dʒɔɪnt] *n* (*TECH*) giuntura; giunto; (*ANAT*) articolazione *f*, giuntura; (*Brit CULIN*) arrosto; (*col: place*) locale *m* ♦ *a* comune; (*responsibility*) collettivo(a); (*committee*) misto(a).

joint account (J/A) *n* (*at bank etc*) conto in comune.

jointly ['dʒɔɪntlɪ] *ad* in comune, insieme.

joint ownership *n* comproprietà.

joint-stock company ['dʒɔɪntstɔk-] *n* società *f inv* per azioni.

joint venture *n* associazione *f* in partecipazione.

joist [dʒɔɪst] *n* trave *f*.

joke [dʒəuk] *n* scherzo; (*funny story*) barzelletta ♦ *vi* scherzare; **to play a ~ on** fare uno scherzo a.

joker ['dʒəukə*] n buffone/a, burlone/a; (CARDS) matta, jolly m inv.

joking ['dʒəukɪŋ] n scherzi mpl.

jollity ['dʒɔlɪtɪ] n allegria.

jolly ['dʒɔlɪ] a allegro(a), gioioso(a) ♦ ad (Brit col) veramente, proprio ♦ vt (Brit): **to ~ sb along** cercare di tenere qn su (di morale); **~ good!** (Brit) benissimo!

jolt [dʒəult] n scossa, sobbalzo ♦ vt urtare.

Jordan ['dʒɔːdən] n (country) Giordania; (river) Giordano.

Jordanian [dʒɔːˈdeɪnɪən] a, n giordano(a).

joss stick ['dʒɔs-] n bastoncino d'incenso.

jostle ['dʒɔsl] vt spingere coi gomiti ♦ vi farsi spazio coi gomiti.

jot [dʒɔt] n: **not one ~** nemmeno un po'.

jot down vt annotare in fretta, buttare giù.

jotter ['dʒɔtə*] n (Brit) quaderno; blocco.

journal ['dʒɔːnl] n (newspaper) giornale m; (periodical) rivista; (diary) diario.

journalese [dʒɔːnəˈliːz] n (pej) stile m giornalistico.

journalism ['dʒɔːnəlɪzəm] n giornalismo.

journalist ['dʒɔːnəlɪst] n giornalista m/f.

journey ['dʒɔːnɪ] n viaggio; (distance covered) tragitto; **a 5-hour ~** un viaggio or un tragitto di 5 ore.

jovial ['dʒəuvɪəl] a gioviale, allegro(a).

jowl [dʒaul] n mandibola; guancia.

joy [dʒɔɪ] n gioia.

joyful ['dʒɔɪful], **joyous** ['dʒɔɪəs] a gioioso(a), allegro(a).

joy ride n gita in automobile (specialmente rubata).

joystick ['dʒɔɪstɪk] n (AVIAT) barra di comando; (COMPUT) joystick m inv.

JP n abbr see **Justice of the Peace.**

Jr. abbr = **junior.**

JTPA n abbr (US: = Job Training Partnership Act) piano governativo di parziale sovvenzione per l'addestramento sul lavoro di apprendisti.

jubilant ['dʒuːbɪlnt] a giubilante; trionfante.

jubilation [dʒuːbɪˈleɪʃən] n giubilo.

jubilee ['dʒuːbɪliː] n giubileo; **silver ~** venticinquesimo anniversario.

judge [dʒʌdʒ] n giudice m/f ♦ vt giudicare; (consider) ritenere; (estimate: weight, size etc) calcolare, valutare ♦ vi: **judging or to ~ by his expression** a giudicare dalla sua espressione; **as far as I can ~** a mio giudizio; **I ~d it necessary to inform him** ho ritenuto necessario informarlo.

judge advocate (JA) n (MIL) magistrato militare.

Judge Advocate General (JAG) n (MIL) consigliere principale in materia di diritto militare.

judg(e)ment ['dʒʌdʒmənt] n giudizio; (punishment) punizione f; **in my ~** a mio giudizio; **to pass ~ (on)** (LAW) pronunciare un giudizio (su); (fig) dare giudizi affrettati (su).

judicial [dʒuːˈdɪʃl] a giudiziale, giudiziario(a).

judiciary [dʒuːˈdɪʃɪərɪ] n magistratura.

judicious [dʒuːˈdɪʃəs] a giudizioso(a).

judo ['dʒuːdəu] n judo.

jug [dʒʌg] n brocca, bricco.

jugged hare [dʒʌgd-] n (Brit) lepre f in salmì.

juggernaut ['dʒʌgənɔːt] n (Brit: huge truck) bestione m.

juggle ['dʒʌgl] vi fare giochi di destrezza.

juggler ['dʒʌglə*] n giocoliere/a.

Jugoslav ['juːgəuslɑːv] a, n = **Yugoslav.**

jugular ['dʒʌgjulə*] a: **~ (vein)** vena giugulare.

juice [dʒuːs] n succo; (of meat) sugo; **we've run out of ~** (col: petrol) siamo rimasti a secco.

juicy ['dʒuːsɪ] a succoso(a).

jukebox ['dʒuːkbɔks] n juke-box m inv.

Jul. abbr (= July) lug., lu.

July [dʒuːˈlaɪ] n luglio; **the first of ~** il primo luglio; **(on) the eleventh of ~** l'undici luglio; **in the month of ~** nel mese di luglio; **at the beginning/end of ~** all'inizio/alla fine di luglio; **in the middle of ~** a metà luglio; **during ~** durante (il mese di) luglio; **in ~ of next year** a luglio dell'anno prossimo; **each or every ~** ogni anno a luglio; **~ was wet this year** ha piovuto molto a luglio quest'anno.

jumble ['dʒʌmbl] n miscuglio ♦ vt (also: ~ up, ~ together) mischiare, mettere alla rinfusa.

jumble sale n (Brit) vendita di oggetti per beneficenza.

jumbo ['dʒʌmbəu] a: **~ jet** jumbo-jet m inv; **~ size** formato gigante.

jump [dʒʌmp] vi saltare, balzare; (start) sobbalzare; (increase) rincarare ♦ vt saltare ♦ n salto, balzo; sobbalzo; (SHOWJUMPING) salto; (fence) ostacolo; **to ~ the queue** (Brit) passare davanti agli altri (in una coda).

jump about vi fare salti, saltellare.

jump at vt fus (fig) cogliere or afferrare al volo; **he ~ed at the offer** si affrettò ad accettare l'offerta.

jump down vi saltare giù.

jump up vi saltare in piedi.

jumped-up ['dʒʌmptʌp] a (Brit pej) presuntuoso(a).

jumper ['dʒʌmpə*] n (Brit: pullover) maglia; (US: pinafore dress) scamiciato; (SPORT) saltatore/trice.

jump leads, (US) **jumper cables** npl cavi mpl per batteria.

jump suit n tuta.

jumpy ['dʒʌmpɪ] a nervoso(a), agitato(a).

Jun. abbr (= June) giu.

Jun., Junr abbr = **junior.**

junction ['dʒʌŋkʃən] n (Brit: of roads) incrocio; (of rails) nodo ferroviario.

juncture ['dʒʌŋktʃə*] n: **at this ~** in questa congiuntura.

June [dʒuːn] n giugno; for phrases see also **July.**

jungle ['dʒʌŋgl] n giungla.
junior ['dʒu:nɪə*] a, n: he's ~ to me (by 2 years), he's my ~ (by 2 years) è più giovane di me (di 2 anni); he's ~ to me (seniority) è al di sotto di me, ho più anzianità di lui.
junior executive n giovane dirigente m.
junior high school n (US) scuola media (da 12 a 15 anni).
junior minister n (Brit POL) ministro che non fa parte del Cabinet.
junior partner n socio meno anziano.
junior school n (Brit) scuola elementare (da 8 a 11 anni).
junior sizes npl (COMM) taglie fpl per ragazzi.
juniper ['dʒu:nɪpə*] n: ~ berry bacca di ginepro.
junk [dʒʌŋk] n (rubbish) chincaglia; (ship) giunca ♦ vt disfarsi di.
junk dealer n rigattiere m.
junket ['dʒʌŋkɪt] n (CULIN) giuncata; (Brit col: also: ~ing): to go on a ~, go ~ing fare bisboccia.
junk foods npl porcherie fpl.
junkie ['dʒʌŋkɪ] n (col) drogato/a.
junk room n (US) ripostiglio.
junk shop n chincaglieria.
junta ['dʒʌntə] n giunta.
Jupiter ['dʒu:pɪtə*] n (planet) Giove m.
jurisdiction [dʒuərɪs'dɪkʃən] n giurisdizione f; **it falls** or **comes within/outside our** ~ è/non è di nostra competenza.
jurisprudence [dʒuərɪs'pru:dəns] n giurisprudenza.
juror ['dʒuərə*] n giurato/a.
jury ['dʒuərɪ] n giuria.
jury box n banco della giuria.
juryman ['dʒuərɪmən] n = juror.
just [dʒʌst] a giusto(a) ♦ ad: he's ~ done it/ left lo ha appena fatto/è appena partito; ~ as I expected proprio come me lo aspettavo; ~ right proprio giusto; ~ 2 o'clock le 2 precise; we were ~ going stavamo uscendo; I was ~ about to phone stavo proprio per telefonare; ~ as he was leaving proprio mentre se ne stava andando; it was ~ before/enough/ here era poco prima/appena assai/proprio qui; it's ~ me sono solo io; it's ~ a mistake non è che uno sbaglio; ~ missed/caught appena perso/preso; ~ listen to this! senta un po' questo!; ~ ask someone the way basta che tu chieda la strada a qualcuno; it's ~ as good è altrettanto buono; it's ~ as well you didn't go per fortuna non ci sei andato; not ~ now non proprio adesso; ~ a minute!, ~ one moment! un attimo!
justice ['dʒʌstɪs] n giustizia; **Lord Chief J~** (Brit) presidente m della Corte d'Appello; **this photo doesn't do you** ~ questa foto non ti fa giustizia.
Justice of the Peace (JP) n giudice m conciliatore.
justifiable [dʒʌstɪ'faɪəbl] a giustificabile.
justifiably [dʒʌstɪ'faɪəblɪ] ad legittimamente,

con ragione.
justification [dʒʌstɪfɪ'keɪʃən] n giustificazione f; (TYP) giustezza.
justify ['dʒʌstɪfaɪ] vt giustificare; (TYP etc) allineare, giustificare; **to be justified in doing sth** avere ragione di fare qc.
justly ['dʒʌstlɪ] ad giustamente.
justness ['dʒʌstnɪs] n giustezza.
jut [dʒʌt] vi (also: ~ out) sporgersi.
jute [dʒu:t] n iuta.
juvenile ['dʒu:vənaɪl] a giovane, giovanile; (court) dei minorenni; (books) per ragazzi ♦ n giovane m/f, minorenne m/f.
juvenile delinquency n delinquenza minorile.
juvenile delinquent n delinquente m/f minorenne.
juxtapose ['dʒʌkstəpəuz] vt giustapporre.
juxtaposition [dʒʌkstəpə'zɪʃən] n giustapposizione f.

K

K, k [keɪ] n (letter) K, k f or m inv; **K for King** ≈ K come Kursaal.
K n abbr (= one thousand) mille ♦ abbr (Brit: = Knight) titolo; (= kilobyte) K.
kaftan ['kæftæn] n caffettano.
Kalahari Desert [kælə'hɑ:rɪ-] n Deserto di Calahari.
kale [keɪl] n cavolo verde.
kaleidoscope [kə'laɪdəskəup] n caleidoscopio.
Kampala [kæm'pɑ:lə] n Kampala f.
Kampuchea [kæmpu'tʃɪə] n Kampuchea f.
kangaroo [kæŋgə'ru:] n canguro.
kaput [kə'put] a (col) kaputt inv.
karate [kə'rɑ:tɪ] n karate m.
Kashmir [kæʃ'mɪə*] n Kashmir m.
KC n abbr (Brit LAW: = King's Counsel) avvocato della Corona.
kd abbr (US: = knocked down) da montare.
kebab [kə'bæb] n spiedino.
keel [ki:l] n chiglia; **on an even** ~ (fig) in uno stato normale.
keel over vi (NAUT) capovolgersi; (person) crollare.
keen [ki:n] a (interest, desire) vivo(a); (eye, intelligence) acuto(a); (competition) serrato(a); (edge) affilato(a); (eager) entusiasta; **to be** ~ **to do** or **on doing sth** avere una gran voglia di fare qc; **to be** ~ **on sth** essere appassionato(a) di qc; **to be** ~ **on sb** avere un debole per qn; **I'm not** ~ **on going** non mi va di andare.
keenly ['ki:nlɪ] ad (enthusiastically) con entusiasmo; (acutely) vivamente; in modo penetrante.

keenness ['ki:nnɪs] *n* (*eagerness*) entusiasmo.
keep [ki:p] *vb* (*pt, pp* **kept** [kɛpt]) *vt* tenere; (*hold back*) trattenere; (*feed: one's family etc*) mantenere, sostentare; (*a promise*) mantenere; (*chickens, bees, pigs etc*) allevare ♦ *vi* (*food*) mantenersi; (*remain: in a certain state or place*) restare ♦ *n* (*of castle*) maschio; (*food etc*): **enough for his ~** abbastanza per vitto e alloggio; **to ~ doing sth** continuare a fare qc; fare qc di continuo; **to ~ sb from doing/sth from happening** impedire a qn di fare/che qc succeda; **to ~ sb busy/a place tidy** tenere qn occupato(a)/un luogo in ordine; **to ~ sb waiting** far aspettare qn; **to ~ an appointment** andare ad un appuntamento; **to ~ a record** *or* **note of sth** prendere nota di qc; **to ~ sth to o.s.** tenere qc per sé; **to ~ sth (back) from sb** celare qc a qn; **to ~ time** (*clock*) andar bene; **~ the change** tenga il resto; *see also* **keeps.**
keep away *vt*: **to ~ sth/sb away from sb** tenere qc/qn lontano da qn ♦ *vi*: **to ~ away (from)** stare lontano (da).
keep back *vt* (*crowds, tears, money*) trattenere ♦ *vi* tenersi indietro.
keep down *vt* (*control: prices, spending*) contenere, ridurre; (*retain: food*) trattenere, ritenere ♦ *vi* tenersi giù, stare giù.
keep in *vt* (*invalid, child*) tenere a casa; (*SCOL*) trattenere a scuola ♦ *vi* (*col*): **to ~ in with sb** tenersi buono qn.
keep off *vt* (*dog, person*) tenere lontano da ♦ *vi* stare alla larga; **~ your hands off!** non toccare!, giù le mani!; **"~ off the grass"** "non calpestare l'erba".
keep on *vi* continuare; **to ~ on doing** continuare a fare.
keep out *vt* tener fuori ♦ *vi* restare fuori; **"~ out"** "vietato l'accesso".
keep up *vi* mantenersi ♦ *vt* continuare, mantenere; **to ~ up with** tener dietro a, andare di pari passo con; (*work etc*) farcela a seguire; **to ~ up with sb** (*in race etc*) mantenersi al passo con qn.
keeper ['ki:pə*] *n* custode *m/f*, guardiano/a.
keep-fit [ki:p'fɪt] *n* ginnastica.
keeping ['ki:pɪŋ] *n* (*care*) custodia; **in ~ with** in armonia con; in accordo con.
keeps [ki:ps] *n*: **for ~** (*col*) per sempre.
keepsake ['ki:pseɪk] *n* ricordo.
keg [kɛg] *n* barilotto *m*.
kennel ['kɛnl] *n* canile *m*.
Kenya ['kɛnjə] *n* Kenia *m*.
Kenyan ['kɛnjən] *a, n* Keniano(a), Keniota (*m/f*).
kept [kɛpt] *pt, pp of* **keep.**
kerb [kə:b] *n* (*Brit*) orlo del marciapiede.
kernel ['kə:nl] *n* nocciolo.
kerosene ['kɛrəsi:n] *n* cherosene *m*.
ketchup ['kɛtʃəp] *n* ketchup *m inv*.
kettle ['kɛtl] *n* bollitore *m*.
kettle drum *n* timpano.
key [ki:] *n* (*gen, MUS*) chiave *f*; (*of piano,*

typewriter) tasto; (*on map*) leg(g)enda ♦ *cpd* (*vital: position, industry etc*) chiave *inv*.
key in *vt* (*text*) introdurre da tastiera.
keyboard ['ki:bɔ:d] *n* tastiera ♦ *vt* (*text*) comporre su tastiera.
keyed up [ki:d'ʌp] *a*: **to be ~** essere agitato(a).
keyhole ['ki:həul] *n* buco della serratura.
keynote ['ki:nəut] *n* (*MUS*) tonica; (*fig*) nota dominante.
keypad ['ki:pæd] *n* tastierino numerico.
key ring *n* portachiavi *m inv*.
keystroke ['ki:strəuk] *n* battuta (di un tasto).
kg *abbr* (= *kilogram*) Kg.
KGB *n abbr* KGB *m*.
khaki ['kɑ:kɪ] *a, n* cachi (*m*).
kibbutz ['kɪ'buts] *n* kibbutz *m inv*.
kick [kɪk] *vt* calciare, dare calci a ♦ *vi* (*horse*) tirar calci ♦ *n* calcio; (*of rifle*) contraccolpo; (*thrill*): **he does it for ~s** lo fa giusto per il piacere di farlo.
kick around *vi* (*col*) essere in giro.
kick off *vi* (*SPORT*) dare il primo calcio.
kick-off ['kɪkɔf] *n* (*SPORT*) calcio d'inizio.
kick-start ['kɪkstɑ:t] *n* (*also*: **~er**) pedale *m* d'avviamento.
kid [kɪd] *n* ragazzino/a; (*animal, leather*) capretto ♦ *vi* (*col*) scherzare ♦ *vt* (*col*) prendere in giro.
kidnap ['kɪdnæp] *vt* rapire, sequestrare.
kidnapper ['kɪdnæpə*] *n* rapitore/trice.
kidnapping ['kɪdnæpɪŋ] *n* sequestro (di persona).
kidney ['kɪdnɪ] *n* (*ANAT*) rene *m*; (*CULIN*) rognone *m*.
kidney bean *n* fagiolo borlotto.
kidney machine *n* rene *m* artificiale.
Kilimanjaro [kɪlɪmənˈdʒɑ:rəu] *n*: **Mount ~** il monte Kilimangiaro.
kill [kɪl] *vt* uccidere, ammazzare; (*fig*) sopprimere; sopraffare; ammazzare ♦ *n* uccisione *f*; **to ~ time** ammazzare il tempo.
kill off *vt* sterminare; (*fig*) eliminare, soffocare.
killer ['kɪlə*] *n* uccisore *m*, killer *m inv*; assassino/a.
killing ['kɪlɪŋ] *n* assassinio; (*massacre*) strage *f*; (*col*): **to make a ~** fare un bel colpo.
kill-joy ['kɪldʒɔɪ] *n* guastafeste *m/f inv*.
kiln [kɪln] *n* forno.
kilo ['ki:ləu] *n abbr* (= *kilogram*) chilo.
kilobyte ['kɪləbaɪt] *n* kilobyte *m inv*.
kilogram(me) ['kɪləugræm] *n* chilogrammo.
kilometre, (*US*) **kilometer** ['kɪləmi:tə*] *n* chilometro.
kilowatt ['kɪləuwɔt] *n* chilowatt *m inv*.
kilt [kɪlt] *n* gonnellino scozzese.
kilter ['kɪltə*] *n*: **out of ~** fuori fase.
kimono [kɪ'məunəu] *n* chimono.
kin [kɪn] *n see* **next of kin, kith.**
kind [kaɪnd] *a* gentile, buono(a) ♦ *n* sorta, specie *f*; (*species*) genere *m*; **to be two of a ~** essere molto simili; **would you be ~ enough to ...?, would you be so ~ as to ...?**

sarebbe così gentile da ...?; **it's very ~ of you (to do)** è molto gentile da parte sua (di fare); **in ~** (*COMM*) in natura; (*fig*): **to repay sb in ~** ripagare qn della stessa moneta.

kindergarten ['kɪndəgɑːtn] *n* giardino d'infanzia.

kind-hearted [kaɪnd'hɑːtɪd] *a* di buon cuore.

kindle ['kɪndl] *vt* accendere, infiammare.

kindling ['kɪndlɪŋ] *n* frasche *fpl*, ramoscelli *mpl*.

kindly ['kaɪndlɪ] *a* pieno(a) di bontà, benevolo(a) ♦ *ad* con bontà, gentilmente; **will you ~ ...** vuole ... per favore; **he didn't take it ~** se l'è presa a male.

kindness ['kaɪndnɪs] *n* bontà, gentilezza.

kindred ['kɪndrɪd] *a* imparentato(a); **~ spirit** spirito affine.

kinetic [kɪ'nɛtɪk] *a* cinetico(a).

king [kɪŋ] *n* re *m inv*.

kingdom ['kɪŋdəm] *n* regno, reame *m*.

kingfisher ['kɪŋfɪʃə*] *n* martin *m inv* pescatore.

kingpin ['kɪŋpɪn] *n* (*TECH*, *fig*) perno.

king-size(d) ['kɪŋsaɪz(d)] *a* super *inv*; gigante; (*cigarette*) extra lungo(a).

kink [kɪŋk] *n* (*of rope*) attorcigliamento; (*in hair*) ondina; (*fig*) aberrazione *f*.

kinky ['kɪŋkɪ] *a* (*fig*) eccentrico(a); dai gusti particolari.

kinship ['kɪnʃɪp] *n* parentela.

kinsman ['kɪnzmən] *n* parente *m*.

kinswoman ['kɪnzwumən] *n* parente *f*.

kiosk ['kiːɔsk] *n* edicola, chiosco; (*Brit*: *also*: **telephone ~**) cabina (telefonica); (: *also*: **newspaper ~**) edicola.

kipper ['kɪpə*] *n* aringa affumicata.

kiss [kɪs] *n* bacio ♦ *vt* baciare; **to ~ (each other)** baciarsi; **to ~ sb goodbye** congedarsi da qn con un bacio; **~ of life** (*Brit*) respirazione *f* bocca a bocca.

kit [kɪt] *n* equipaggiamento, corredo; (*set of tools etc*) attrezzi *mpl*; (*for assembly*) scatola di montaggio; **tool ~** cassetta *or* borsa degli attrezzi.

kit out *vt* (*Brit*) attrezzare, equipaggiare.

kitbag ['kɪtbæg] *n* zaino; sacco militare.

kitchen ['kɪtʃɪn] *n* cucina.

kitchen garden *n* orto.

kitchen sink *n* acquaio.

kitchen unit *n* (*Brit*) elemento da cucina.

kitchenware ['kɪtʃɪnwɛə*] *n* stoviglie *fpl*; utensili *mpl* da cucina.

kite [kaɪt] *n* (*toy*) aquilone *m*; (*ZOOL*) nibbio.

kith [kɪθ] *n*: **~ and kin** amici e parenti *mpl*.

kitten ['kɪtn] *n* gattino/a, micino/a.

kitty ['kɪtɪ] *n* (*money*) fondo comune.

KKK *n abbr* (*US*) = **Ku Klux Klan.**

Kleenex ® ['kliːnɛks] *n* fazzolettino di carta.

kleptomaniac [klɛptəu'meɪnɪæk] *n* cleptomane *m/f*.

km *abbr* (= *kilometre*) km.

km/h *abbr* (= *kilometres per hour*) km/h.

knack [næk] *n*: **to have a ~ (for doing)** avere

una pratica (per fare); **to have the ~ of** avere l'abilità di; **there's a ~ to doing this** c'è un trucco per fare questo.

knapsack ['næpsæk] *n* zaino, sacco da montagna.

knave [neɪv] *n* (*CARDS*) fante *m*.

knead [niːd] *vt* impastare.

knee [niː] *n* ginocchio.

kneecap ['niːkæp] *n* rotula.

knee-deep ['niː'diːp] *a*: **the water was ~** l'acqua ci arrivava alle ginocchia.

kneel [niːl] *vi* (*pt*, *pp* **knelt** [nɛlt]) inginocchiarsi.

kneepad ['niːpæd] *n* ginocchiera.

knell [nɛl] *n* rintocco.

knelt [nɛlt] *pt*, *pp of* **kneel.**

knew [njuː] *pt of* **know.**

knickers ['nɪkəz] *npl* (*Brit*) mutandine *fpl*.

knick-knack ['nɪknæk] *n* ninnolo.

knife [naɪf] *n* (*pl* **knives**) coltello ♦ *vt* accoltellare, dare una coltellata a; **~, fork and spoon** coperto.

knight [naɪt] *n* cavaliere *m*; (*CHESS*) cavallo.

knighthood ['naɪthud] *n* cavalleria; (*title*): **to get a ~** essere fatto cavaliere.

knit [nɪt] *vt* fare a maglia; (*fig*): **to ~ together** unire ♦ *vi* lavorare a maglia; (*broken bones*) saldarsi.

knitted ['nɪtɪd] *a* lavorato(a) a maglia.

knitting ['nɪtɪŋ] *n* lavoro a maglia.

knitting machine *n* macchina per maglieria.

knitting needle *n* ferro (da calza).

knitting pattern *n* modello (per maglia).

knitwear ['nɪtwɛə*] *n* maglieria.

knives [naɪvz] *npl of* **knife.**

knob [nɔb] *n* bottone *m*; manopola; (*Brit*): **a ~ of butter** una noce di burro.

knobbly ['nɔblɪ], (*US*) **knobby** ['nɔbɪ] *a* (*wood*, *surface*) nodoso(a); (*knee*) ossuto(a).

knock [nɔk] *vt* (*strike*) colpire; urtare; (*fig*: *col*) criticare ♦ *vi* (*engine*) battere; (*at door etc*): **to ~ at/on** bussare a ♦ *n* bussata; colpo, botta; **he ~ed at the door** ha bussato alla porta; **to ~ a nail into sth** conficcare un chiodo in qc.

knock down *vt* abbattere; (*pedestrian*) investire; (*price*) abbassare.

knock off *vi* (*col*: *finish*) smettere (di lavorare) ♦ *vt* (*strike off*) far cadere; (*col*: *steal*) sgraffignare, grattare; **to ~ off £10** fare uno sconto di 10 sterline.

knock out *vt* stendere; (*BOXING*) mettere K.O., mettere fuori combattimento.

knock over *vt* (*object*) far cadere; (*pedestrian*) investire.

knockdown ['nɔkdaun] *a* (*price*) fortemente scontato(a).

knocker ['nɔkə*] *n* (*on door*) battente *m*.

knock-for-knock ['nɔkfə'nɔk] *a* (*Brit*): **~ agreement** accordo fra compagnie di assicurazione per il risarcimento dei rispettivi clienti.

knocking ['nɔkɪŋ] *n* colpi *mpl*.

knock-kneed [nɔk'niːd] *a* che ha le gambe ad

x.

knockout ['nɔkaut] n (BOXING) knock out m inv.

knockout competition n (Brit) gara ad eliminazione.

knock-up ['nɔkʌp] n (TENNIS etc) palleggio; **to have a** ~ palleggiare.

knot [nɔt] n nodo ♦ vt annodare; **to tie a** ~ fare un nodo.

knotty ['nɔtɪ] a (fig) spinoso(a).

know [nəu] vt (pt **knew**, pp **known** [nju:, nəun]) sapere; (person, author, place) conoscere ♦ vi sapere; **to** ~ **that** ... sapere che ...; **to** ~ **how to do** sapere fare; **to get to** ~ **sth** venire a sapere qc; **I** ~ **nothing about it** non ne so niente; **I don't** ~ **him** non lo conosco; **to** ~ **right from wrong** distinguere il bene dal male; **as far as I** ~ ... che io sappia ..., per quanto io ne sappia ...; **yes, I** ~ sì, lo so; **I don't** ~ non lo so.

know-all ['nəuɔ:l] n (Brit pej) sapientone/a.

know-how ['nəuhau] n tecnica; pratica.

knowing ['nəuɪŋ] a (look etc) d'intesa.

knowingly ['nəuɪŋlɪ] ad consapevolmente; di complicità.

know-it-all ['nəuɪtɔ:l] n (US) = **know-all**.

knowledge ['nɔlɪdʒ] n consapevolezza; (learning) conoscenza, sapere m; **to have no** ~ **of** ignorare, non sapere; **not to my** ~ che io sappia, no; **to have a working** ~ **of Italian** avere una conoscenza pratica dell'italiano; **without my** ~ a mia insaputa; **it is common** ~ **that** ... è risaputo che ...; **it has come to my** ~ **that** ... sono venuto a sapere che ....

knowledgeable ['nɔlɪdʒəbl] a ben informato(a).

known [nəun] pp of **know** ♦ a (thief, facts) noto(a); (expert) riconosciuto(a).

knuckle ['nʌkl] n nocca.

knuckle under vi (col) cedere.

knuckleduster ['nʌkldʌstə*] n tirapugni m inv.

KO abbr (= knock out) n K.O. m ♦ vt mettere K.O.

koala [kəu'ɑ:lə] n (also: ~ **bear**) koala m inv.

kook [ku:k] n (US col) svitato/a.

Koran [kɔ'rɑ:n] n Corano.

Korea [kə'rɪə] n Corea; **North/South** ~ Corea del Nord/Sud.

Korean [kə'rɪən] a, n coreano(a).

kosher ['kəuʃə*] a kasher inv.

kowtow ['kau'tau] vi: **to** ~ **to sb** mostrarsi ossequioso(a) verso qn.

Kremlin ['krɛmlɪn] n: **the** ~ il Cremlino.

KS abbr (US POST) = Kansas.

Kt abbr (Brit: = Knight) titolo.

Kuala Lumpur ['kwɑ:lə'lumpuə*] n Kuala Lumpur f.

kudos ['kju:dɔs] n gloria, fama.

Kuwait [ku'weɪt] n Kuwait m.

Kuwaiti [ku'weɪtɪ] a, n kuwaitiano(a).

kw abbr (= kilowatt) kw.

KY abbr (US POST) = Kentucky.

L

L, l [ɛl] n (letter) L, l f or m inv; **L for Lucy**, (US) **L for Love** ≈ L come Livorno.

L abbr (= lake) l; (= large) taglia grande; (= left) sin.; (Brit AUT) = **learner**.

l abbr (= litre) l.

LA n abbr (US) = Los Angeles ♦ abbr (US POST) = Louisiana.

lab [læb] n abbr (= laboratory) laboratorio.

label ['leɪbl] n etichetta, cartellino; (brand: of record) casa ♦ vt etichettare; classificare.

labor etc ['leɪbə*] (US) = **labour** etc.

laboratory [lə'bɔrətərɪ] n laboratorio.

Labor Day n (US) festa del lavoro.

laborious [lə'bɔ:rɪəs] a laborioso(a).

labor union n (US) sindacato.

Labour ['leɪbə*] n (Brit POL: also: **the** ~ **Party**) il partito laburista, i laburisti.

labour, (US) **labor** ['leɪbə*] n (task) lavoro; (workmen) manodopera; (MED) travaglio del parto, doglie fpl ♦ vi: **to** ~ **(at)** lavorare duro (a); **to be in** ~ (MED) avere le doglie.

labo(u)r camp n campo dei lavori forzati.

labo(u)r cost n costo del lavoro.

labo(u)r dispute n conflitto tra lavoratori e datori di lavoro.

labo(u)red ['leɪbəd] a (breathing) affaticato(a), affannoso(a); (style) elaborato(a), pesante.

labo(u)rer ['leɪbərə*] n manovale m; (on farm) lavoratore m agricolo.

labo(u)r force n manodopera.

labo(u)r-intensive [leɪbərɪn'tɛnsɪv] a che assorbe molta manodopera.

labo(u)r market n mercato del lavoro.

labo(u)r pains npl doglie fpl.

labo(u)r relations npl relazioni fpl industriali.

labo(u)r-saving ['leɪbəseɪvɪŋ] a che fa risparmiare fatica or lavoro.

labo(u)r unrest n agitazioni fpl degli operai.

labyrinth ['læbɪrɪnθ] n labirinto.

lace [leɪs] n merletto, pizzo; (of shoe etc) laccio ♦ vt (shoe) allacciare; (drink: fortify with spirits) correggere.

lacemaking ['leɪsmeɪkɪŋ] n fabbricazione f dei pizzi or dei merletti.

laceration [læsə'reɪʃən] n lacerazione f.

lace-up ['leɪsʌp] a (shoes etc) con i lacci, con le stringhe.

lack [læk] n mancanza, scarsità ♦ vt mancare di; **through** or **for** ~ **of** per mancanza di; **to be** ~**ing** mancare; **to be** ~**ing in** mancare di.

lackadaisical [lækə'deɪzɪkl] a disinteressato(a), noncurante.

lackey ['lækɪ] n (also fig) lacchè m inv.

lacklustre, (US) **lackluster** ['læklʌstə*] a (surface) opaco(a); (style) scialbo(a); (eyes) spento(a).

laconic [lə'kɔnɪk] a laconico(a).

lacquer ['lækə*] n lacca; **hair** ~ lacca per (i) capelli.

lacy ['leɪsɪ] a (like lace) che sembra un pizzo.

lad [læd] n ragazzo, giovanotto; (Brit: in stable etc) mozzo or garzone m di stalla.

ladder ['lædə*] n scala; (Brit: in tights) smagliatura ♦ vt smagliare ♦ vi smagliarsi.

laden ['leɪdn] a: ~ (**with**) carico(a) or caricato(a) (di); **fully** ~ (truck, ship) a pieno carico.

ladle ['leɪdl] n mestolo.

lady ['leɪdɪ] n signora; **L~ Smith** lady Smith; **the ladies' (toilets)** i gabinetti per signore; **a** ~ **doctor** una dottoressa.

ladybird ['leɪdɪbɜːd], (US) **ladybug** ['leɪdɪbʌg] n coccinella.

lady-in-waiting ['leɪdɪɪn'weɪtɪŋ] n dama di compagnia.

ladykiller ['leɪdɪkɪlə*] n dongiovanni m inv.

ladylike ['leɪdɪlaɪk] a da signora, distinto(a).

ladyship ['leɪdɪʃɪp] n: **your L~** signora contessa etc.

lag [læg] n = **time** ~ ♦ vi (also: ~ **behind**) trascinarsi ♦ vt (pipes) rivestire di materiale isolante.

lager ['lɑːgə*] n lager m inv.

lagging ['lægɪŋ] n rivestimento di materiale isolante.

lagoon [lə'guːn] n laguna.

Lagos ['leɪgɔs] n Lagos f.

laid [leɪd] pt, pp of **lay**.

laid-back [leɪd'bæk] a (col) rilassato(a).

lain [leɪn] pp of **lie**.

lair [lɛə*] n covo, tana.

laissez-faire [lɛseɪ'fɛə*] n liberismo.

laity ['leɪɪtɪ] n laici mpl.

lake [leɪk] n lago.

Lake District n: **the** ~ (Brit) la regione dei laghi.

lamb [læm] n agnello.

lamb chop n cotoletta d'agnello.

lambskin ['læmskɪn] n (pelle f d')agnello.

lambswool ['læmzwʊl] n lamb's wool m.

lame [leɪm] a zoppo(a); ~ **duck** (fig: person) persona inetta; (: firm) azienda traballante.

lamely ['leɪmlɪ] ad (fig) in modo poco convincente.

lament [lə'mɛnt] n lamento ♦ vt lamentare, piangere.

lamentable ['læməntəbl] a doloroso(a); deplorevole.

laminated ['læmɪneɪtɪd] a laminato(a).

lamp [læmp] n lampada.

lamplight ['læmplaɪt] n: **by** ~ a lume della lampada.

lampoon [læm'puːn] n satira.

lamppost ['læmppəʊst] n lampione m.

lampshade ['læmpʃeɪd] n paralume m.

lance [lɑːns] n lancia ♦ vt (MED) incidere.

lance corporal n (Brit) caporale m.

lancet ['lɑːnsɪt] n (MED) bisturi m inv.

Lancs [læŋks] abbr (Brit) = Lancashire.

land [lænd] n (as opposed to sea) terra (ferma); (country) paese m; (soil) terreno; (estate) terreni mpl, terre fpl ♦ vi (from ship) sbarcare; (AVIAT) atterrare; (fig: fall) cadere ♦ vt (obtain) acchiappare; (passengers) sbarcare; (goods) scaricare; **to go/travel by** ~ andare/viaggiare per via di terra; **to own** ~ possedere dei terreni, avere delle proprietà (terriere); **to** ~ **on one's feet** cadere in piedi; (fig: to be lucky) cascar bene.

land up vi andare a finire.

landed gentry ['lændɪd-] n proprietari mpl terrieri.

landing ['lændɪŋ] n (from ship) sbarco; (AVIAT) atterraggio; (of staircase) pianerottolo.

landing card n carta di sbarco.

landing craft n mezzo da sbarco.

landing gear n (AVIAT) carrello d'atterraggio.

landing stage n pontile m da sbarco.

landing strip n pista d'atterraggio.

landlady ['lændleɪdɪ] n padrona or proprietaria di casa.

landlocked ['lændlɔkt] a senza sbocco sul mare.

landlord ['lændlɔːd] n padrone m or proprietario di casa; (of pub etc) oste m.

landlubber ['lændlʌbə*] n marinaio d'acqua dolce.

landmark ['lændmɑːk] n punto di riferimento; (fig) pietra miliare.

landowner ['lændəʊnə*] n proprietario(a) terriero(a).

landscape ['lænskeɪp] n paesaggio.

landscape architect, landscape gardener n paesaggista m/f.

landscape painting n (ART) paesaggistica.

landslide ['lændslaɪd] n (GEO) frana; (fig: POL) valanga.

lane [leɪn] n (in country) viottolo; (in town) stradetta; (AUT, in race) corsia; **shipping** ~ rotta (marittima).

language ['læŋgwɪdʒ] n lingua; (way one speaks) linguaggio; **bad** ~ linguaggio volgare.

language laboratory n laboratorio linguistico.

languid ['læŋgwɪd] a languente; languido(a).

languish ['læŋgwɪʃ] vi languire.

lank [læŋk] a (hair) liscio(a) e opaco(a).

lanky ['læŋkɪ] a allampanato(a).

lanolin(e) ['lænəlɪn] n lanolina.

lantern ['læntn] n lanterna.

Laos [lauz] n Laos m.

lap [læp] n (of track) giro; (of body): **in** or **on one's** ~ in grembo ♦ vt (also: ~ **up**) papparsi, leccare ♦ vi (waves) sciabordare.

lap up vt (fig: compliments, attention)

bearsi di.

La Paz |læ'pæz| n La Paz f.

lapdog ['læpdɔg] n cane m da grembo.

lapel |lə'pɛl| n risvolto.

Lapland ['læplænd] n Lapponia.

Lapp |læp| a lappone ♦ n lappone m/f; (LING) lappone m.

lapse |læps| n lapsus m inv; (longer) caduta; (fault) mancanza; (in behaviour) scorrettezza ♦ vi (law, act) cadere; (ticket, passport) scadere; **to ~ into bad habits** pigliare cattive abitudini; **~ of time** spazio di tempo; **a ~ of memory** un vuoto di memoria.

larceny ['lɑːsənɪ] n furto.

lard |lɑːd| n lardo.

larder ['lɑːdə*] n dispensa.

large |lɑːdʒ| a grande; (person, animal) grosso(a) ♦ ad: **by and ~** generalmente; **at ~** (free) in libertà; (generally) in generale; nell'insieme; **to make ~r** ingrandire; **a ~ number of people** molta gente; **on a ~ scale** su vasta scala.

largely ['lɑːdʒlɪ] ad in gran parte.

large-scale ['lɑːdʒ'skeɪl] a (map, drawing etc) in grande scala; (reforms, business activities) su vasta scala.

lark |lɑːk| n (bird) allodola; (joke) scherzo, gioco.

lark about vi fare lo stupido.

larva, pl **larvae** ['lɑːvə, -iː] n larva.

laryngitis |lærɪn'dʒaɪtɪs| n laringite f.

larynx ['lærɪŋks] n laringe f.

lascivious |lə'sɪvɪəs| a lascivo(a).

laser ['leɪzə*] n laser m.

laser beam n raggio m laser inv.

laser printer n stampante f laser inv.

lash |læʃ| n frustata; (also: **eye~**) ciglio ♦ vt frustare; (tie) legare.

lash down vt assicurare (con corde) ♦ vi (rain) scrosciare.

lash out vi: **to ~ out (at** or **against sb/sth)** attaccare violentemente (qn/qc); **to ~ out (on sth)** (col: spend) spendere un sacco di soldi (per qc).

lashing ['læʃɪŋ] n (beating) frustata, sferzata; **~s of** (Brit col) un mucchio di, una montagna di.

lass |læs| n ragazza.

lasso |læ'suː| n laccio ♦ vt acchiappare con il laccio.

last |lɑːst| a ultimo(a); (week, month, year) scorso(a), passato(a) ♦ ad per ultimo ♦ vi durare; **~ week** la settimana scorsa; **~ night** ieri sera, la notte scorsa; **at ~** finalmente, alla fine; **~ but one** penultimo(a); **the ~ time** l'ultima volta; **it ~s (for) 2 hours** dura 2 ore.

last-ditch ['lɑːst'dɪtʃ] a ultimo(a) e disperato(a).

lasting ['lɑːstɪŋ] a durevole.

lastly ['lɑːstlɪ] ad infine, per finire, per ultimo.

last-minute ['lɑːstmɪnɪt] a fatto(a) (or preso(a) etc) all'ultimo momento.

latch |lætʃ| n serratura a scatto.

latch on to vt fus (cling to: person) attaccarsi a, appiccicarsi a; (: idea) afferrare, capire.

latchkey ['lætʃkiː] n chiave f di casa.

late |leɪt| a (not on time) in ritardo; (far on in day etc) tardi inv; tardo(a); (recent) recente, ultimo(a); (former) ex; (dead) defunto(a) ♦ ad tardi; (behind time, schedule) in ritardo; **to be (10 minutes) ~** essere in ritardo (di 10 minuti); **to work ~** lavorare fino a tardi; **~ in life** in età avanzata; **of ~** di recente; **in the ~ afternoon** nel tardo pomeriggio; **in ~ May** verso la fine di maggio; **the ~ Mr X** il defunto Signor X.

latecomer ['leɪtkʌmə*] n ritardatario/a.

lately ['leɪtlɪ] ad recentemente.

lateness ['leɪtnɪs] n (of person) ritardo; (of event) tardezza, ora tarda.

latent ['leɪtnt] a latente; **~ defect** vizio occulto.

later ['leɪtə*] a (date etc) posteriore; (version etc) successivo(a) ♦ ad più tardi; **~ on today** oggi più tardi.

lateral ['lætərl] a laterale.

latest ['leɪtɪst] a ultimo(a), più recente; **at the ~** al più tardi; **the ~ news** le ultime notizie.

latex ['leɪtɛks] n latice m.

lath, **~s** |læθ, læðz| n assicella.

lathe |leɪð| n tornio.

lather ['lɑːðə*] n schiuma di sapone ♦ vt insaponare ♦ vi far schiuma.

Latin ['lætɪn] n latino ♦ a latino(a).

Latin America n America Latina.

Latin American a sudamericano(a).

latitude ['lætɪtjuːd] n latitudine f; (fig: freedom) libertà d'azione.

latrine |lə'triːn| n latrina.

latter ['lætə*] a secondo(a); più recente ♦ n: **the ~** quest'ultimo, il secondo.

latterly ['lætəlɪ] ad recentemente, negli ultimi tempi.

lattice ['lætɪs] n traliccio; graticolato.

lattice window n finestra con vetrata a losanghe.

Latvia ['lætvɪə] n Lettonia.

laudable ['lɔːdəbl] a lodevole.

laudatory ['lɔːdətrɪ] a elogiativo(a).

laugh |lɑːf| n risata ♦ vi ridere.

laugh at vt fus (misfortune etc) ridere di; **I ~ed at his joke** la sua barzelletta mi fece ridere.

laugh off vt prendere alla leggera.

laughable ['lɑːfəbl] a ridicolo(a).

laughing ['lɑːfɪŋ] a (face) ridente; **this is no ~ matter** non è una cosa da ridere.

laughing gas n gas m esilarante.

laughing stock n: **the ~ of** lo zimbello di.

laughter ['lɑːftə*] n riso; risate fpl.

launch |lɔːntʃ| n (of rocket, product etc) lancio; (of new ship) varo; (boat) scialuppa; (also: **motor ~**) lancia ♦ vt (rocket, product) lanciare; (ship, plan) varare.

launch out vi: **to ~ out (into)** lanciarsi

(in).

launching ['lɔ:ntʃɪŋ] n lancio; varo.

launch(ing) pad n rampa di lancio.

launder ['lɔ:ndə*] vt lavare e stirare.

launderette [lɔ:n'drɛt], (US) **laundromat** ['lɔ:ndrəmæt] n lavanderia (automatica).

laundry ['lɔ:ndrɪ] n lavanderia; (clothes) biancheria; **to do the** ~ fare il bucato.

laureate ['lɔ:rɪət] a see **poet laureate**.

laurel ['lɔrl] n lauro, alloro; **to rest on one's** ~s riposare or dormire sugli allori.

Lausanne [ləu'zæn] n Losanna.

lava ['lɑ:və] n lava.

lavatory ['lævətərɪ] n gabinetto.

lavatory paper n (Brit) carta igienica.

lavender ['lævəndə*] n lavanda.

lavish ['lævɪʃ] a abbondante; sontuoso(a); (giving freely): ~ **with** prodigo(a) di, largo(a) in ♦ vt: **to** ~ **sth on sb/sth** profondere qc a qn/qc.

lavishly ['lævɪʃlɪ] ad (give, spend) generosamente; (furnished) sontuosamente, lussuosamente.

law [lɔ:] n legge f; **against the** ~ contro la legge; **to study** ~ studiare diritto; **to go to** ~ (Brit) ricorrere alle vie legali; **civil/criminal** ~ diritto civile/penale.

law-abiding ['lɔ:əbaɪdɪŋ] a ubbidiente alla legge.

law and order n l'ordine m pubblico.

lawbreaker ['lɔ:breɪkə*] n violatore/trice della legge.

law court n tribunale m, corte f di giustizia.

lawful ['lɔ:ful] a legale.

lawfully ['lɔ:fəlɪ] ad legalmente.

lawless ['lɔ:lɪs] a senza legge; illegale.

lawmaker ['lɔ:meɪkə*] n legislatore m.

lawn [lɔ:n] n tappeto erboso.

lawnmower ['lɔ:nməuə*] n tosaerba m or f inv.

lawn tennis n tennis m su prato.

law school n facoltà f inv di legge.

law student n studente/essa di legge.

lawsuit ['lɔ:su:t] n processo, causa; **to bring a** ~ **against** intentare causa a.

lawyer ['lɔ:jə*] n (consultant, with company) giurista m/f; (for sales, wills etc) ≈ notaio; (partner, in court) ≈ avvocato/essa.

lax [læks] a (conduct) rilassato(a); (person: careless) negligente; (: on discipline) permissivo(a).

laxative ['læksətɪv] n lassativo.

laxity ['læksɪtɪ] n rilassatezza; negligenza.

lay [leɪ] pt of **lie** ♦ a laico(a); secolare ♦ vt (pt, pp **laid** [leɪd]) posare, mettere; (eggs) fare; (trap) tendere; (plans) fare, elaborare; **to** ~ **the table** apparecchiare la tavola; **to** ~ **the facts/one's proposals before sb** presentare i fatti/delle proposte a qn; **to get laid** (col!) scopare (!); essere scopato(a) (!).

lay aside, lay by vt mettere da parte.

lay down vt mettere giù; **to** ~ **down the law** (fig) dettar legge.

lay in vt fare una scorta di.

lay into vt fus (col: attack, scold) aggredire.

lay off vt (workers) licenziare.

lay on vt (water, gas) installare, mettere; (provide: meal etc) fornire; (paint) applicare.

lay out vt (design) progettare; (display) presentare; (spend) sborsare.

lay up vt (to store) accumulare; (ship) mettere in disarmo; (subj: illness) costringere a letto.

layabout ['leɪəbaut] n sfaccendato/a, fannullone/a.

lay-by ['leɪbaɪ] n (Brit) piazzola (di sosta).

lay days npl (NAUT) stallie fpl.

layer ['leɪə*] n strato.

layette [leɪ'ɛt] n corredino (per neonato).

layman ['leɪmən] n laico; profano.

lay-off ['leɪɔf] n sospensione f, licenziamento.

layout ['leɪaut] n lay-out m inv, disposizione f; (PRESS) impaginazione f.

laze [leɪz] vi oziare.

laziness ['leɪzɪnɪs] n pigrizia.

lazy ['leɪzɪ] a pigro(a).

LB abbr (Canada) = Labrador.

lb. abbr (= libra: pound) lb.

lbw abbr (CRICKET: = leg before wicket) fallo dovuto al fatto che il giocatore ha la gamba davanti alla porta.

LC n abbr (US) = Library of Congress.

lc abbr (TYP: = lower case) minuscolo.

L/C abbr = **letter of credit**.

LCD n abbr see **liquid crystal display**.

Ld abbr (Brit: = lord) titolo.

LDS n abbr (= Licentiate in Dental Surgery) specializzazione dopo la laurea; (= Latter-day Saints) Chiesa di Gesù Cristo dei Santi dell'Ultimo Giorno.

LEA n abbr (Brit: = local education authority) ≈ Provveditorato degli Studi.

lead [li:d] n (front position) posizione f di testa; (distance, time ahead) vantaggio; (clue) indizio; (ELEC) filo (elettrico); (for dog) guinzaglio; (THEATRE) parte f principale; [lɛd] (metal) piombo; (in pencil) mina ♦ vb (pt, pp **led** [lɛd]) vt menare, guidare, condurre; (induce) indurre; (be leader of) essere a capo di; (: orchestra: Brit) essere il primo violino di; (: US) dirigere; (SPORT) essere in testa a ♦ vi condurre, essere in testa; **to be in the** ~ (SPORT) essere in testa; **to take the** ~ (SPORT) passare in testa; (fig) prendere l'iniziativa; **to** ~ **to** menare a; condurre a; portare a; **to** ~ **astray** sviare; **to** ~ **sb to believe that ...** far credere a qn che ...; **to** ~ **sb to do sth** portare qn a fare qc.

lead away vt condurre via.

lead back vt riportare, ricondurre.

lead off vt portare ♦ vi partire da.

lead on vt (tease) tenere sulla corda.

lead on to vt (induce) portare a.

lead up to vt fus portare a; (fig) preparare la strada per.

leaded ['lɛdɪd] a: ~ **windows** vetrate fpl (artistiche).

leaden ['lɛdn] a di piombo.

leader ['li:də*] n capo; leader m inv; (in newspaper) articolo di fondo; **they are ~s in their field** (fig) sono all'avanguardia nel loro campo; **the L~ of the House** (Brit) il capo della maggioranza ministeriale.

leadership ['li:dəʃɪp] n direzione f; **under the ~ of** ... sotto la direzione or guida di ...; **qualities of ~** qualità fpl di un capo.

lead-free ['lɛdfri:] a senza piombo.

leading ['li:dɪŋ] a primo(a); principale; **a ~ question** una domanda tendenziosa; **~ role** ruolo principale.

leading lady n (THEATRE) prima attrice.

leading light n (person) personaggio di primo piano.

leading man n (THEATRE) primo attore.

lead pencil n matita con la mina di grafite.

lead poisoning n saturnismo.

lead time n (COMM) tempo di consegna.

lead weight n piombino, piombo.

leaf [li:f] n (pl **leaves**) foglia; (of table) ribalta; **to turn over a new ~** (fig) cambiar vita; **to take a ~ out of sb's book** (fig) prendere esempio da qn.

leaf through vt (book) sfogliare.

leaflet ['li:flɪt] n dépliant m inv; (POL, REL) volantino.

leafy ['li:fɪ] a ricco(a) di foglie.

league [li:g] n lega; (FOOTBALL) campionato; **to be in ~ with** essere in lega con.

leak [li:k] n (out) fuga; (in) infiltrazione f; (fig: of information) fuga di notizie ♦ vi (roof, bucket) perdere; (liquid) uscire; (shoes) lasciar passare l'acqua ♦ vt (liquid) spandere; (information) divulgare.

leak out vi uscire; (information) trapelare.

leakage ['li:kɪdʒ] n (of water, gas etc) perdita.

leaky ['li:kɪ] a (pipe, bucket, roof) che perde; (shoe) che lascia passare l'acqua; (boat) che fa acqua.

lean [li:n] a magro(a) ♦ n (of meat) carne f magra ♦ vb (pt, pp **leaned** or **leant** [lɛnt]) vt: **to ~ sth on** appoggiare qc su ♦ vi (slope) pendere; (rest): **to ~ against** appoggiarsi contro; essere appoggiato(a) a; **to ~ on** appoggiarsi a.

lean back vi sporgersi indietro.

lean forward vi sporgersi in avanti.

lean out vi: **to ~ out (of)** sporgersi (da).

lean over vi inclinarsi.

leaning ['li:nɪŋ] n: ~ **(towards)** propensione f (per) ♦ a inclinato(a), pendente; **the ~ Tower of Pisa** la torre (pendente) di Pisa.

leant [lɛnt] pt, pp of **lean**.

lean-to ['li:ntu:] n (roof) tettoia; (building) edificio con tetto appoggiato ad altro edificio.

leap [li:p] n salto, balzo ♦ vi (pt, pp **leaped** or **leapt** [lɛpt]) saltare, balzare; **to ~ at an offer** afferrare al volo una proposta.

leap up vi (person) alzarsi d'un balzo, balzare su.

leapfrog ['li:pfrɔg] n gioco della cavallina ♦ vi: **to ~ over sb/sth** saltare (alla cavallina) qn/qc.

leapt [lɛpt] pt, pp of **leap**.

leap year n anno bisestile.

learn, pt, pp **learned** or **learnt** [lə:n, -t] vt, vi imparare; **to ~ how to do sth** imparare a fare qc; **to ~ that ...** apprendere che ...; **to ~ about sth** (SCOL) studiare qc; (hear) apprendere qc; **we were sorry to ~ that it was closing down** la notizia della chiusura ci ha fatto dispiacere.

learned ['lə:nɪd] a erudito(a), dotto(a).

learner ['lə:nə*] n principiante m/f; apprendista m/f; **he's a ~ (driver)** (Brit) sta imparando a guidare.

learning ['lə:nɪŋ] n erudizione f, sapienza.

learnt [lə:nt] pt, pp of **learn**.

lease [li:s] n contratto d'affitto ♦ vt affittare; **on ~** in affitto.

lease back vt effettuare un lease-back inv.

leaseback ['li:sbæk] n lease-back m inv.

leasehold ['li:shəuld] n (contract) contratto di affitto (a lungo termine con responsabilità simili a quelle di un proprietario) ♦ a in affitto.

leash [li:ʃ] n guinzaglio.

least [li:st] a: **the ~ + noun** il(la) più piccolo(a), il(la) minimo(a); (smallest amount of) il(la) meno ♦ ad: **the ~ + adjective**: **the ~ beautiful girl** la ragazza meno bella; **the ~ expensive** il(la) meno caro(a); **I have the ~ money** ho meno denaro di tutti; **at ~** almeno; **not in the ~** affatto, per nulla.

leather ['lɛðə*] n (soft) pelle f; (hard) cuoio ♦ cpd di or in pelle; di cuoio; ~ **goods** pelletteria, pelletterie fpl.

leave [li:v] vb (pt, pp **left** [lɛft]) vt lasciare; (go away from) partire da ♦ vi partire, andarsene ♦ n (time off) congedo; (MIL, also: consent) licenza; **to be left** rimanere; **there's some milk left over** c'è rimasto del latte; **to take one's ~ of** congedarsi di; **he's already left for the airport** è già uscito per andare all'aeroporto; **to ~ school** finire la scuola; (~) **it to me!** ci penso io!, lascia fare a me!; **on ~** in congedo; **on ~ of absence** in permesso; (public employee) in congedo; (MIL) in licenza.

leave behind vt (also fig) lasciare indietro; (forget) dimenticare.

leave off vt non mettere; (Brit col: stop): **to ~ off doing sth** smetterla or piantarla di fare qc.

leave on vt lasciare su; (light, fire, cooker) lasciare acceso(a).

leave out vt omettere, tralasciare.

leaves [li:vz] npl of **leaf**.

leavetaking ['li:vteɪkɪŋ] n commiato, addio.

Lebanese [lɛbə'ni:z] a, n (pl inv) libanese (m/f).

Lebanon ['lɛbənən] n Libano.

lecherous ['lɛtʃərəs] a lascivo(a), lubrico(a).

lectern ['lɛktɔːn] *n* leggio.

lecture ['lɛktʃə*] *n* conferenza; (*SCOL*) lezione *f* ♦ *vi* fare conferenze; fare lezioni; (*reprove*) rimproverare, fare una ramanzina a; **to ~ on** fare una conferenza su; **to give a ~ (on)** (*Brit*) fare una conferenza (su); fare lezione (su).

lecture hall *n* aula magna.

lecturer ['lɛktʃɔrə*] *n* (*speaker*) conferenziere/a; (*Brit*: *at university*) professore/essa, docente *m/f*; **assistant ~** (*Brit*) ≈ professore(essa) associato(a); **senior ~** (*Brit*) ≈ professore(essa) ordinario(a).

lecture theatre *n* = **lecture hall**.

LED *n abbr* (*ELEC*: = *light-emitting diode*) diodo a emissione luminosa.

led [lɛd] *pt, pp of* **lead**.

ledge [lɛdʒ] *n* (*of window*) davanzale *m*; (*on wall etc*) sporgenza; (*of mountain*) cornice *f*, cengia.

ledger ['lɛdʒə*] *n* libro maestro, registro.

lee [liː] *n* lato sottovento; **in the ~ of** a ridosso di, al riparo di.

leech [liːtʃ] *n* sanguisuga.

leek [liːk] *n* porro.

leer [lɪə*] *vi*: **to ~ at sb** gettare uno sguardo voglioso (*or* maligno) su qn.

leeward ['liːwəd] *a* sottovento *inv* ♦ *n* lato sottovento; **to ~** sottovento.

leeway ['liːweɪ] *n* (*fig*): **to have some ~** avere una certa libertà di agire.

left [lɛft] *pt, pp of* **leave** ♦ *a* sinistro(a) ♦ *ad* a sinistra ♦ *n* sinistra; **on the ~, to the ~** a sinistra; **the L~** (*POL*) la sinistra.

left-hand drive ['lɛfthænd-] *n* (*Brit*) guida a sinistra.

left-handed [lɛft'hændɪd] *a* mancino(a); **~ scissors** forbici *fpl* per mancini.

left-hand side ['lɛfthænd-] *n* lato *or* fianco sinistro.

leftist ['lɛftɪst] *a* (*POL*) di sinistra.

left-luggage (office) [lɛft'lʌgɪdʒ-] *n* deposito *m* bagagli *inv*.

left-overs ['lɛftəuvəz] *npl* avanzi *mpl*, resti *mpl*.

left wing *n* (*MIL, SPORT*) ala sinistra; (*POL*) sinistra ♦ *a*: **left-wing** (*POL*) di sinistra.

left-winger [lɛft'wɪŋə*] *n* (*POL*) uno/a di sinistra; (*SPORT*) ala sinistra.

leg [lɛg] *n* gamba; (*of animal*) zampa; (*of furniture*) piede *m*; (*CULIN: of chicken*) coscia; (*of journey*) tappa; **1st/2nd ~** (*SPORT*) partita di andata/ritorno; **~ of lamb** (*CULIN*) cosciotto d'agnello; **to stretch one's ~s** sgranchirsi le gambe.

legacy ['lɛgəsɪ] *n* eredità *f inv*; (*fig*) retaggio.

legal ['liːgl] *a* legale; **to take ~ action** *or* **proceedings against sb** intentare un'azione legale contro qn, far causa a qn.

legal adviser *n* consulente *m/f* legale.

legality [lɪ'gælɪtɪ] *n* legalità.

legalize ['liːgəlaɪz] *vt* legalizzare.

legally ['liːgəlɪ] *ad* legalmente; **~ binding**

legalmente vincolante.

legal tender *n* moneta legale.

legation [lɪ'geɪʃən] *n* legazione *f*.

legend ['lɛdʒənd] *n* leggenda.

legendary ['lɛdʒəndərɪ] *a* leggendario(a).

-legged ['lɛgɪd] *suffix*: **two~** a due gambe (*or* zampe), bipede.

leggings ['lɛgɪŋz] *npl* ghette *fpl*.

legibility [lɛdʒɪ'bɪlɪtɪ] *n* leggibilità.

legible ['lɛdʒəbl] *a* leggibile.

legibly ['lɛdʒəblɪ] *ad* in modo leggibile.

legion ['liːdʒən] *n* legione *f*.

legionnaire [liːdʒə'nɛə*] *n* legionario; **~'s disease** morbo del legionario.

legislate ['lɛdʒɪsleɪt] *vi* legiferare.

legislation [lɛdʒɪs'leɪʃən] *n* legislazione *f*; **a piece of ~** una legge.

legislative ['lɛdʒɪslətɪv] *a* legislativo(a).

legislator ['lɛdʒɪsleɪtə*] *n* legislatore/trice.

legislature ['lɛdʒɪslətʃə*] *n* corpo legislativo.

legitimacy [lɪ'dʒɪtɪməsɪ] *n* legittimità.

legitimate [lɪ'dʒɪtɪmət] *a* legittimo(a).

legitimize [lɪ'dʒɪtɪmaɪz] *vt* (*gen*) legalizzare, rendere legale; (*child*) legittimare.

leg-room ['lɛgruːm] *n* spazio per le gambe.

Leics *abbr* (*Brit*) = *Leicestershire*.

leisure ['lɛʒə*] *n* agio, tempo libero; ricreazioni *fpl*; **at ~** all'agio; **a proprio comodo**.

leisure centre *n* centro di ricreazione.

leisurely ['lɛʒəlɪ] *a* tranquillo(a); fatto(a) con comodo *or* senza fretta.

leisure suit *n* (*Brit*) tuta (da ginnastica).

lemon ['lɛmən] *n* limone *m*.

lemonade [lɛmə'neɪd] *n* limonata.

lemon cheese, lemon curd *n* crema di limone (*che si spalma sul pane etc*).

lemon juice *n* succo di limone.

lemon squeezer *n* spremiagrumi *m inv*.

lemon tea *n* tè *m inv* al limone.

lend, *pt, pp* **lent** [lɛnd, lɛnt] *vt*: **to ~ sth (to sb)** prestare qc (a qn); **to ~ a hand** dare una mano.

lender ['lɛndə*] *n* prestatore/trice.

lending library ['lɛndɪŋ-] *n* biblioteca circolante.

length [lɛŋθ] *n* lunghezza; (*section: of road, pipe etc*) pezzo, tratto; **~ of time** periodo (di tempo); **what ~ is it?** quant'è lungo?; **it is 2 metres in ~** è lungo 2 metri; **to fall full ~** cadere lungo disteso; **at ~** (*at last*) finalmente, alla fine; (*lengthily*) a lungo; **to go to any ~(s) to do sth** fare qualsiasi cosa pur di *or* per fare qc.

lengthen ['lɛŋθən] *vt* allungare, prolungare ♦ *vi* allungarsi.

lengthways ['lɛŋθweɪz] *ad* per il lungo.

lengthy ['lɛŋθɪ] *a* molto lungo(a).

leniency ['liːnɪənsɪ] *n* indulgenza, clemenza.

lenient ['liːnɪənt] *a* indulgente, clemente.

leniently ['liːnɪəntlɪ] *ad* con indulgenza.

lens [lɛnz] *n* lente *f*; (*of camera*) obiettivo.

Lent [lɛnt] *n* Quaresima.

lent [lɛnt] *pt, pp of* **lend**.

lentil ['lɛntl] n lenticchia.
Leo ['liːəu] n Leone m; **to be ~** essere del Leone.
leopard ['lɛpəd] n leopardo.
leotard ['liːətɑːd] n calzamaglia.
leper ['lɛpə*] n lebbroso/a.
leper colony n lebbrosario.
leprosy ['lɛprəsɪ] n lebbra.
lesbian ['lɛzbɪən] n lesbica ♦ a lesbico(a).
lesion ['liːʒən] n (MED) lesione f.
Lesotho [lɪ'suːtuː] n Lesotho m.
less [lɛs] a, pronoun, ad meno; **~ than you/ ever** meno di lei/che mai; **~ than half** meno della metà; **~ and ~** sempre meno; **the ~ he works** ... meno lavora ...; **~ than £1/a kilo/3 metres** meno di una sterlina/un chilo/3 metri; **~ 5%** meno il 5%.
lessee [lɛ'siː] n affittuario/a, locatario/a.
lessen ['lɛsn] vi diminuire, attenuarsi ♦ vt diminuire, ridurre.
lesser ['lɛsə*] a minore, più piccolo(a); **to a ~ extent** or **degree** in grado or misura minore.
lesson ['lɛsn] n lezione f; **a maths ~** una lezione di matematica; **to give ~s in** dare or impartire lezioni di; **it taught him a ~** (fig) gli è servito di lezione.
lessor [lɛ'sɔː*] n locatore/trice.
lest [lɛst] cj per paura di + infinitive, per paura che + sub.
let, pt, pp **let** [lɛt] vt lasciare; (Brit: lease) dare in affitto; **to ~ sb do sth** lasciar fare qc a qn, lasciare che qn faccia qc; **to ~ sb know sth** far sapere qc a qn; **to ~ sb have sth** dare qc a qn; **he ~ me go** mi ha lasciato andare; **~ the water boil and** ... fate bollire l'acqua e ...; **~'s go** andiamo; **~ him come** lo lasci venire; "**to ~**" "affittasi".
let down vt (lower) abbassare; (dress) allungare; (hair) sciogliere; (disappoint) deludere; (Brit: tyre) sgonfiare.
let go vi mollare ♦ vt mollare; (allow to go) lasciare andare.
let in vt lasciare entrare; (visitor etc) far entrare; **what have you ~ yourself in for?** in che guai or pasticci sei andato a cacciarti?
let off vt (allow to go) lasciare andare; (firework etc) far partire; (smell etc) emettere; (subj: taxi driver, bus driver) far scendere; **to ~ off steam** (fig col) sfogarsi, scaricarsi.
let on vi (col): **to ~ on that** ... lasciar capire che ....
let out vt lasciare uscire; (dress) allargare; (scream) emettere; (rent out) affittare, dare in affitto.
let up vi diminuire.
let-down ['lɛtdaun] n (disappointment) delusione f.
lethal ['liːθl] a letale, mortale.
lethargic [lɛ'θɑːdʒɪk] a letargico(a).
lethargy ['lɛθədʒɪ] n letargia.
letter ['lɛtə*] n lettera; **~s** npl (LITERATURE) lettere; **small/capital ~** lettera minuscola/ maiuscola; **~ of credit** lettera di credito;

documentary ~ of credit lettera di credito documentata.
letter bomb n lettera esplosiva.
letterbox ['lɛtəbɔks] n buca delle lettere.
letterhead ['lɛtəhɛd] n intestazione f.
lettering ['lɛtərɪŋ] n iscrizione f; caratteri mpl.
letter-opener ['lɛtərəupnə*] n tagliacarte m inv.
letterpress ['lɛtəprɛs] n (method) rilievo-grafia.
letter quality n (of printer) qualità di stampa.
letters patent npl brevetto di invenzione.
lettuce ['lɛtɪs] n lattuga, insalata.
let-up ['lɛtʌp] n (col) interruzione f.
leukaemia, (US) **leukemia** [luː'kiːmɪə] n leucemia.
level ['lɛvl] a piatto(a), piano(a); orizzontale ♦ n livello; (also: **spirit ~**) livella (a bolla d'aria) ♦ vt livellare, spianare; (gun) puntare (verso); (accusation): **to ~** (**against**) lanciare (a or contro) ♦ vi (col): **to ~ with sb** esser franco(a) con qn; **to be ~ with** essere alla pari di; **a ~ spoonful** (CULIN) un cucchiaio raso; **to draw ~ with** (team) mettersi alla pari di; (runner, car) affiancarsi a; **A ~s** npl (Brit) ≈ esami mpl di maturità; **O ~s** npl (Brit) esami fatti in Inghilterra all'età di 16 anni; **on the ~** piatto(a); (fig) onesto(a).
level off, **level out** vi (prices etc) stabilizzarsi; (ground) diventare pianeggiante; (aircraft) volare in quota.
level crossing n (Brit) passaggio a livello.
level-headed [lɛvl'hɛdɪd] a equilibrato(a).
levelling, (US) **leveling** ['lɛvlɪŋ] a (process, effect) di livellamento.
lever ['liːvə*] n leva ♦ vt: **to ~ up/out** sollevare/estrarre con una leva.
leverage ['liːvərɪdʒ] n: **~** (**on** or **with**) ascendente m (su).
levity ['lɛvɪtɪ] n leggerezza, frivolità.
levy ['lɛvɪ] n tassa, imposta ♦ vt imporre.
lewd [luːd] a osceno(a), lascivo(a).
LI abbr (US) = Long Island.
liabilities [laɪə'bɪlətɪz] npl debiti mpl; (on balance sheet) passivo.
liability [laɪə'bɪlətɪ] n responsabilità f inv; (handicap) peso.
liable ['laɪəbl] a (subject): **~ to** soggetto(a) a; passibile di; (responsible): **~** (**for**) responsabile (di); (likely): **~ to do** propenso(a) a fare; **to be ~ to a fine** essere passibile di multa.
liaise [liː'eɪz] vi: **to ~** (**with**) mantenere i contatti (con).
liaison [liː'eɪzɔn] n relazione f; (MIL) collegamento.
liar ['laɪə*] n bugiardo/a.
libel ['laɪbl] n libello, diffamazione f ♦ vt diffamare.
libellous, (US) **libelous** ['laɪbləs] a diffamatorio(a).

liberal ['lɪbərl] *a* liberale; (*generous*): **to be ~ with** distribuire liberalmente ♦ *n* (*POL*): **L~** liberale *m/f.*
liberality [lɪbə'rælɪtɪ] *n* (*generosity*) generosità, liberalità.
liberalize ['lɪbərəlaɪz] *vt* liberalizzare.
liberal-minded [lɪbərl'maɪndɪd] *a* tollerante.
liberate ['lɪbəreɪt] *vt* liberare.
liberation [lɪbə'reɪʃən] *n* liberazione *f.*
Liberia [laɪ'bɪərɪə] *n* Liberia.
Liberian [laɪ'bɪərɪən] *a, n* liberiano(a).
liberty ['lɪbətɪ] *n* libertà *f inv*; **at ~ to do** libero(a) di fare; **to take the ~ of** prendersi la libertà di, permettersi di.
libido [lɪ'biːdəʊ] *n* libido *f.*
Libra ['liːbrə] *n* Bilancia; **to be ~** essere della Bilancia.
librarian [laɪ'breərɪən] *n* bibliotecario/a.
library ['laɪbrərɪ] *n* biblioteca.
library book *n* libro della biblioteca.
libretto [lɪ'bretəʊ] *n* libretto.
Libya ['lɪbɪə] *n* Libia.
Libyan ['lɪbɪən] *a, n* libico(a).
lice [laɪs] *npl of* **louse.**
licence, (*US*) **license** ['laɪsns] *n* autorizzazione *f*, permesso; (*COMM*) licenza; (*RADIO, TV*) canone *m*, abbonamento; (*also*: **driving ~,** (*US*) **driver's ~**) patente *f* di guida; (*excessive freedom*) licenza; **import ~** licenza di importazione; **produced under ~** prodotto su licenza.
licence number *n* (*Brit AUT*) numero di targa.
license ['laɪsns] *n* (*US*) = **licence** ♦ *vt* dare una licenza a; (*car*) pagare la tassa di circolazione *or* il bollo di.
licensed ['laɪsnst] *a* (*for alcohol*) che ha la licenza di vendere bibite alcoliche.
licensed trade *n* commercio di bevande alcoliche con licenza speciale.
licensee [laɪsən'siː] *n* (*Brit*: *of pub*) detentore/ trice di autorizzazione alla vendita di bevande alcoliche.
license plate *n* (*esp US AUT*) targa (automobilistica).
licentious [laɪ'senʃəs] *a* licenzioso(a).
lichen ['laɪkən] *n* lichene *m.*
lick [lɪk] *vt* leccare; (*col*: *defeat*) suonarle a, stracciare ♦ *n* leccata; **a ~ of paint** una passata di vernice.
licorice ['lɪkərɪs] *n* = **liquorice.**
lid [lɪd] *n* coperchio; **to take the ~ off sth** (*fig*) smascherare qc.
lido ['laɪdəʊ] *n* piscina all'aperto; (*part of the beach*) lido, stabilimento balneare.
lie [laɪ] *n* bugia, menzogna ♦ *vi* mentire, dire bugie; (*pt* **lay,** *pp* **lain** [leɪ, leɪn]) (*rest*) giacere, star disteso(a); (*in grave*) giacere, riposare; (*of object: be situated*) trovarsi, essere; **to tell ~s** raccontare *or* dire bugie; **to ~ low** (*fig*) latitare.
lie about, lie around *vi* (*things*) essere in giro; (*person*) bighellonare.
lie back *vi* stendersi.

lie down *vi* stendersi, sdraiarsi.
lie up *vi* (*hide*) nascondersi.
Liechtenstein ['lɪktənstaɪn] *n* Liechtenstein *m.*
lie detector *n* macchina della verità.
lie-down ['laɪdaʊn] *n* (*Brit*): **to have a ~** sdraiarsi, riposarsi.
lie-in ['laɪɪn] *n* (*Brit*): **to have a ~** rimanere a letto.
lieu [luː] *n*: **in ~ of** invece di, al posto di.
Lieut. *abbr* (= *lieutenant*) Ten.
lieutenant [lɛf'tɛnənt, (*US*) luː'tɛnənt] *n* tenente *m.*
lieutenant-colonel [lɛf'tɛnənt'kəːnl, (*US*) luː'tɛnənt'kəːnl] *n* tenente colonnello.
life [laɪf] *n* (*pl* **lives**) vita ♦ *cpd* di vita; della vita; a vita; **country/city ~** vita di campagna/di città; **to be sent to prison for ~** essere condannato all'ergastolo; **true to ~** fedele alla realtà; **to paint from ~** dipingere dal vero.
life annuity *n* rendita vitalizia.
life assurance *n* (*Brit*) = **life insurance.**
lifebelt ['laɪfbɛlt] *n* (*Brit*) salvagente *m.*
lifeblood ['laɪfblʌd] *n* (*fig*) linfa vitale.
lifeboat ['laɪfbəʊt] *n* scialuppa di salvataggio.
life buoy *n* salvagente *m.*
life expectancy *n* durata media della vita.
lifeguard ['laɪfgɑːd] *n* bagnino.
life imprisonment *n* ergastolo.
life insurance *n* assicurazione *f* sulla vita.
life jacket *n* giubbotto di salvataggio.
lifeless ['laɪflɪs] *a* senza vita.
lifelike ['laɪflaɪk] *a* che sembra vero(a); rassomigliante.
lifeline ['laɪflaɪn] *n* cavo di salvataggio.
lifelong ['laɪflɒŋ] *a* per tutta la vita.
life preserver *n* (*US*) salvagente *m*; giubbotto di salvataggio; (*Brit*) sfollagente *m inv.*
life-raft ['laɪfrɑːft] *n* zattera di salvataggio.
life-saver ['laɪfseɪvə*] *n* bagnino.
life sentence *n* (condanna all')ergastolo.
life-sized ['laɪfsaɪzd] *a* a grandezza naturale.
life span *n* (durata della) vita.
life style *n* stile *m* di vita.
life support system *n* (*MED*) respiratore *m* automatico.
lifetime ['laɪftaɪm] *n*: **in his ~** durante la sua vita; **in a ~** nell'arco della vita; in tutta la vita; **the chance of a ~** un'occasione unica.
lift [lɪft] *vt* sollevare, levare; (*steal*) prendere, rubare ♦ *vi* (*fog*) alzarsi ♦ *n* (*Brit: elevator*) ascensore *m*; **to give sb a ~** (*Brit*) dare un passaggio a qn.
lift off *vt* togliere ♦ *vi* (*rocket*) partire; (*helicopter*) decollare.
lift out *vt* tirar fuori; (*troops, evacuees etc*) far evacuare per mezzo di elicotteri (*or* aerei).
lift up *vt* sollevare, alzare.
lift-off ['lɪftɒf] *n* decollo.
ligament ['lɪgəmənt] *n* legamento.
light [laɪt] *n* luce, lume *m*; (*daylight*) luce, giorno; (*lamp*) lampada; (*AUT: rear ~*) luce

di posizione; (: *headlamp*) fanale *m*; (*for cigarette etc*): **have you got a ~?** ha da accendere? ♦ *vt* (*pt, pp* **lighted** *or* **lit** [lɪt]) (*candle, cigarette, fire*) accendere; (*room*) illuminare ♦ *a* (*room, colour*) chiaro(a); (*not heavy, also fig*) leggero(a) ♦ *ad* (*travel*) con poco bagaglio; **~s** *npl* (*AUT: traffic* **~s**) semaforo; **in the ~ of** alla luce di; **to turn the ~ on/off** accendere/spegnere la luce; **to come to ~** venire in luce; **to cast** *or* **shed** *or* **throw ~ on** gettare luce su; **to make ~ of sth** (*fig*) prendere alla leggera qc, non dar peso a qc.

light up *vi* illuminarsi ♦ *vt* illuminare.

light bulb *n* lampadina.

lighten ['laɪtn] *vi* schiarirsi ♦ *vt* (*give light to*) illuminare; (*make lighter*) schiarire; (*make less heavy*) alleggerire.

lighter ['laɪtə*] *n* (*also:* **cigarette ~**) accendino; (*boat*) chiatta.

light-fingered [laɪt'fɪŋgəd] *a* lesto(a) di mano.

light-headed ['laɪt'hɛdɪd] *a* stordito(a).

light-hearted ['laɪt'hɑ:tɪd] *a* gioioso(a), gaio(a).

lighthouse ['laɪthaus] *n* faro.

lighting ['laɪtɪŋ] *n* illuminazione *f*.

lighting-up time ['laɪtɪŋʌp-] *n* (*Brit*) orario per l'accensione delle luci.

lightly ['laɪtlɪ] *ad* leggermente; **to get off ~** cavarsela a buon mercato.

light meter *n* (*PHOT*) esposimetro.

lightness ['laɪtnɪs] *n* chiarezza; (*in weight*) leggerezza.

lightning ['laɪtnɪŋ] *n* lampo, fulmine *m*; **a flash of ~** un lampo, un fulmine.

lightning conductor, (*US*) **lightning rod** *n* parafulmine *m*.

lightning strike *n* (*Brit*) sciopero *m* lampo *inv*.

light pen *n* penna luminosa.

lightship ['laɪtʃɪp] *n* battello *m* faro *inv*.

lightweight ['laɪtweɪt] *a* (*suit*) leggero(a); (*boxer*) peso leggero *inv*.

light year ['laɪtjɪə*] *n* anno *m* luce *inv*.

Ligurian [lɪ'gjuərɪən] *a*, *n* ligure (*m/f*).

like [laɪk] *vt* (*person*) volere bene a; (*activity, object, food*): **I ~ swimming/that book/ chocolate** mi piace nuotare/quel libro/il cioccolato ♦ *prep* come ♦ *a* simile, uguale ♦ *n*: **the ~** uno(a) uguale; **his ~s and dislikes** i suoi gusti; **I would ~, I'd ~** mi piacerebbe, vorrei; **would you ~ a coffee?** gradirebbe un caffè?; **if you ~** se vuoi; **to be/look ~ sb/sth** somigliare a qn/qc; **what's he ~?** che tipo è?, com'è?; **what's the weather ~?** che tempo fa?; **that's just ~ him** è proprio da lui; **something ~ that** qualcosa del genere; **I feel ~ a drink** avrei voglia di bere qualcosa; **there's nothing ~ ...** non c'è niente di meglio di *or* niente come ...

likeable ['laɪkəbl] *a* simpatico(a).

likelihood ['laɪklɪhud] *n* probabilità; **in all ~** con ogni probabilità, molto probabilmente.

likely ['laɪklɪ] *a* probabile; plausibile; **he's ~**

to leave probabilmente partirà, è probabile che parta; **not ~!** (*col*) neanche per sogno!

like-minded ['laɪk'maɪndɪd] *a* che pensa allo stesso modo.

liken ['laɪkən] *vt*: **to ~ sth to** paragonare qc a.

likeness ['laɪknɪs] *n* (*similarity*) somiglianza.

likewise ['laɪkwaɪz] *ad* similmente, nello stesso modo.

liking ['laɪkɪŋ] *n*: **~ (for)** simpatia (per); debole *m* (per); **to be to sb's ~** essere di gusto *or* gradimento di qn; **to take a ~ to sb** prendere qn in simpatia.

lilac ['laɪlək] *n* lilla *m inv* ♦ *a* lilla *inv*.

lilt [lɪlt] *n* cadenza.

lilting ['lɪltɪŋ] *a* melodioso(a).

lily ['lɪlɪ] *n* giglio; **~ of the valley** mughetto.

Lima ['li:mə] *n* Lima.

limb [lɪm] *n* membro; **to be out on a ~** (*fig*) sentirsi spaesato *or* tagliato fuori.

limber ['lɪmbə*]: **to ~ up** *vi* riscaldarsi i muscoli.

limbo ['lɪmbəu] *n*: **to be in ~** (*fig*) essere lasciato(a) nel dimenticatoio.

lime [laɪm] *n* (*tree*) tiglio; (*fruit*) limetta; (*GEO*) calce *f*.

lime juice *n* succo di limetta.

limelight ['laɪmlaɪt] *n*: **in the ~** (*fig*) alla ribalta, in vista.

limerick ['lɪmərɪk] *n* poesiola umoristica di 5 versi.

limestone ['laɪmstəun] *n* pietra calcarea; (*GEO*) calcare *m*.

limit ['lɪmɪt] *n* limite *m* ♦ *vt* limitare; **weight/ speed ~** limite di peso/di velocità; **within ~s** entro certi limiti.

limitation [lɪmɪ'teɪʃən] *n* limitazione *f*, limite *m*.

limited ['lɪmɪtɪd] *a* limitato(a), ristretto(a); **~ edition** edizione *f* a bassa tiratura.

limited (liability) company (Ltd) *n* (*Brit*) ≈ società *f inv* a responsabilità limitata (S.r.l.).

limitless ['lɪmɪtlɪs] *a* illimitato(a).

limousine ['lɪməzi:n] *n* limousine *f inv*.

limp [lɪmp] *n*: **to have a ~** zoppicare ♦ *vi* zoppicare ♦ *a* floscio(a), flaccido(a).

limpet ['lɪmpɪt] *n* patella.

limpid ['lɪmpɪd] *a* (*poet*) limpido(a).

linchpin ['lɪntʃpɪn] *n* acciarino, bietta; (*fig*) perno.

Lincs *abbr* (*Brit*) = Lincolnshire.

line [laɪn] *n* (*gen, COMM*) linea; (*rope*) corda; (*wire*) filo; (*of poem*) verso; (*row, series*) fila, riga; coda ♦ *vt* (*clothes*): **to ~ (with)** foderare (di); (*box*): **to ~ (with)** rivestire *or* foderare (di); (*subj: trees, crowd*) fiancheggiare; **to cut in ~** (*US*) passare avanti; **in his ~ of business** nel suo ramo (di affari); **on the right ~s** sulla buona strada; **a new ~ in cosmetics** una nuova linea di cosmetici; **hold the ~ please** (*Brit TEL*) resti in linea per cortesia; **to be in ~ for sth** (*fig*) essere in lista per qc; **in ~ with** d'accordo

con, in linea con; **to bring sth into** ~ **with sth** mettere qc al passo con qc; **to draw the** ~ **at (doing) sth** (*fig*) rifiutarsi di fare qc; **to take the** ~ **that ...** essere del parere che ....
line up *vi* allinearsi, mettersi in fila ♦ *vt* mettere in fila; **to have sth** ~**d up** avere qc in programma; **to have sb** ~**d up** avere qn in mente.

linear ['lınıə*] *a* lineare.

lined [laınd] *a* (*paper*) a righe, rigato(a); (*face*) rugoso(a); (*clothes*) foderato(a).

line feed *n* (*COMPUT*) avanzamento di una interlinea.

linen ['lının] *n* biancheria, panni *mpl*; (*cloth*) tela di lino.

line printer *n* stampante *f* parallela.

liner ['laınə*] *n* nave *f* di linea; **dustbin** ~ sacchetto per la pattumiera.

linesman ['laınzmən] *n* guardalinee *m inv*, segnalinee *m inv*.

line-up ['laınʌp] *n* allineamento, fila; (*also*: **police** ~) confronto all'americana; (*SPORT*) formazione *f* di gioco.

linger ['lıŋgə*] *vi* attardarsi; indugiare; (*smell, tradition*) persistere.

lingerie ['lænʒəri:] *n* biancheria intima (femminile).

lingering ['lıŋgərıŋ] *a* lungo(a); persistente; (*death*) lento(a).

lingo, ~**es** ['lıŋgəu] *n* (*pej*) gergo.

linguist ['lıŋgwıst] *n* linguista *m/f*; poliglotta *m/f*.

linguistic [lıŋ'gwıstık] *a* linguistico(a).

linguistics [lıŋ'gwıstıks] *n* linguistica.

lining ['laınıŋ] *n* fodera; (*TECH*) rivestimento (interno); (*of brake*) guarnizione *f*.

link [lıŋk] *n* (*of a chain*) anello; (*connection*) legame *m*, collegamento ♦ *vt* collegare, unire, congiungere; **rail** ~ collegamento ferroviario; *see also* **links**.
link up *vt* collegare, unire ♦ *vi* riunirsi; associarsi.

links [lıŋks] *npl* pista *or* terreno da golf.

link-up ['lıŋkʌp] *n* legame *m*; (*of roads*) nodo; (*of spaceships*) aggancio; (*RADIO, TV*) collegamento.

linoleum [lı'nəulıəm] *n* linoleum *m inv*.

linseed oil ['lınsi:d-] *n* olio di semi di lino.

lint [lınt] *n* garza.

lintel ['lıntl] *n* architrave *f*.

lion ['laıən] *n* leone *m*.

lion cub *n* leoncino.

lioness ['laıənıs] *n* leonessa.

lip [lıp] *n* labbro; (*of cup etc*) orlo; (*insolence*) sfacciataggine *f*.

lipread ['lıpri:d] *vi* leggere sulle labbra.

lip salve *n* burro di cacao.

lip service *n*: **to pay** ~ **to sth** essere favorevole a qc solo a parole.

lipstick ['lıpstık] *n* rossetto.

liquefy ['lıkwıfaı] *vt* liquefare ♦ *vi* liquefarsi.

liqueur [lı'kjuə*] *n* liquore *m*.

liquid ['lıkwıd] *n* liquido ♦ *a* liquido(a).

liquid assets *npl* attività *fpl* liquide, crediti

mpl liquidi.

liquidate ['lıkwıdeıt] *vt* liquidare.

liquidation [lıkwı'deıʃən] *n* liquidazione *f*; **to go into** ~ andare in liquidazione.

liquidator ['lıkwıdeıtə*] *n* liquidatore *m*.

liquid crystal display (LCD) *n* visualizzazione *f* a cristalli liquidi.

liquidity [lı'kwıdıtı] *n* (*COMM*) liquidità.

liquidize ['lıkwıdaız] *vt* (*Brit CULIN*) passare al frullatore.

liquidizer ['lıkwıdaızə*] *n* (*Brit CULIN*) frullatore *m* (a brocca).

liquor ['lıkə*] *n* alcool *m*.

liquorice ['lıkərıs] *n* liquirizia.

Lisbon ['lızbən] *n* Lisbona.

lisp [lısp] *n* difetto nel pronunciare le sibilanti.

lissom ['lısəm] *a* leggiadro(a).

list [lıst] *n* lista, elenco; (*of ship*) sbandamento ♦ *vt* (*write down*) mettere in lista; fare una lista di; (*enumerate*) elencare; (*COMPUT*) stampare (un prospetto di) ♦ *vi* (*ship*) sbandare; **shopping** ~ lista *or* nota della spesa.

listed building ['lıstəd-] *n* (*ARCHIT*) edificio sotto la protezione delle Belle Arti.

listed company *n* società quotata in Borsa.

listen ['lısn] *vi* ascoltare; **to** ~ **to** ascoltare.

listener ['lısnə*] *n* ascoltatore/trice.

listing ['lıstıŋ] *n* (*COMPUT*) lista stampata.

listless ['lıstlıs] *a* svogliato(a); apatico(a).

listlessly ['lıstlıslı] *ad* svogliatamente; apaticamente.

list price *n* prezzo di listino.

lit [lıt] *pt, pp of* **light**.

litany ['lıtənı] *n* litania.

liter ['li:tə*] *n* (*US*) = **litre**.

literacy ['lıtərəsı] *n* il sapere leggere e scrivere.

literacy campaign *n* lotta contro l'analfabetismo.

literal ['lıtərl] *a* letterale.

literally ['lıtərəlı] *ad* alla lettera, letteralmente.

literary ['lıtərərı] *a* letterario(a).

literate ['lıtərıt] *a* che sa leggere e scrivere.

literature ['lıtərıtʃə*] *n* letteratura; (*brochures etc*) materiale *m*.

lithe [laıð] *a* agile, snello(a).

lithography [lı'θɔgrəfı] *n* litografia.

Lithuania [lıθju'eınıə] *n* Lituania.

litigate ['lıtıgeıt] *vt* muovere causa a ♦ *vi* litigare.

litigation [lıtı'geıʃən] *n* causa.

litmus ['lıtməs] *n*: ~ **paper** cartina di tornasole.

litre, (*US*) **liter** ['li:tə*] *n* litro.

litter ['lıtə*] *n* (*rubbish*) rifiuti *mpl*; (*young animals*) figliata ♦ *vt* sparpagliare; lasciare rifiuti in; ~**ed with** coperto(a) di.

litter bin *n* (*Brit*) cestino per rifiuti.

litter lout, (*US*) **litterbug** ['lıtəbʌg] *n* persona che butta per terra le cartacce o i rifiuti.

little ['lıtl] *a* (*small*) piccolo(a); (*not much*) poco(a) ♦ *ad* poco; **a** ~ un po' (di); **a** ~ **milk**

un po' di latte; **with** ~ **difficulty** senza fatica *or* difficoltà; ~ **by** ~ a poco a poco; **as** ~ **as possible** il meno possibile; **for a** ~ **while** per un po'; **to make** ~ **of** dare poca importanza a; ~ **finger** mignolo.

liturgy ['lɪtədʒɪ] *n* liturgia.

live *vi* [lɪv] vivere; *(reside)* vivere, abitare ♦ *a* [laɪv] *(animal)* vivo(a); *(issue)* scottante, d'attualità; *(wire)* sotto tensione; *(broadcast)* diretto(a); *(ammunition: not blank)* carico(a); *(unexploded)* inesploso(a); **to** ~ **in London** abitare a Londra; **to** ~ **together** vivere insieme, convivere.

live down *vt* far dimenticare (alla gente).

live in *vi* essere interno(a); avere vitto e alloggio.

live off *vi (land, fish etc)* vivere di; *(pej: parents etc)* vivere alle spalle *or* a spese di.

live on *vt fus (food)* vivere di ♦ *vi* sopravvivere, continuare a vivere; **to** ~ **on £50 a week** vivere con 50 sterline la settimana.

live out *vi (Brit: students)* essere esterno(a) ♦ *vt:* **to** ~ **out one's days** *or* **life** trascorrere gli ultimi anni.

live up *vt:* **to** ~ **it up** *(col)* fare la bella vita.

live up to *vt fus* tener fede a, non venir meno a.

livelihood ['laɪvlɪhud] *n* mezzi *mpl* di sostentamento.

liveliness ['laɪvlɪnəs] *n* vivacità.

lively ['laɪvlɪ] *a* vivace, vivo(a).

liven up ['laɪvn-] *vt (room etc)* ravvivare; *(discussion, evening)* animare.

liver ['lɪvə*] *n* fegato.

liverish ['lɪvərɪʃ] *a* che soffre di mal di fegato; *(fig)* scontroso(a).

Liverpudlian [lɪvə'pʌdlɪən] *a* di Liverpool ♦ *n* abitante *m/f* di Liverpool; originario/a di Liverpool.

livery ['lɪvərɪ] *n* livrea.

lives [laɪvz] *npl of* **life**.

livestock ['laɪvstɔk] *n* bestiame *m*.

livid ['lɪvɪd] *a* livido(a); *(furious)* livido(a) di rabbia, furibondo(a).

living ['lɪvɪŋ] *a* vivo(a), vivente ♦ *n:* **to earn** *or* **make a** ~ guadagnarsi la vita; **cost of** ~ costo della vita, carovita *m*; **within** ~ **memory** a memoria d'uomo.

living conditions *npl* condizioni *fpl* di vita.

living expenses *npl* spese *fpl* di mantenimento.

living room *n* soggiorno.

living standards *npl* tenore *m* di vita.

living wage *n* salario sufficiente per vivere.

lizard ['lɪzəd] *n* lucertola.

llama ['lɑːmə] *n* lama *m inv*.

LLB *n abbr* (= *Bachelor of Laws*) titolo di studio.

LLD *n abbr* (= *Doctor of Laws*) titolo di studio.

LMT *abbr* (*US:* = *Local Mean Time*) tempo medio locale.

load [ləud] *n (weight)* peso; *(ELEC, TECH, thing carried)* carico ♦ *vt:* **to** ~ **(with)**

(lorry, ship) caricare (di); *(gun, camera)* caricare (con); **a** ~ **of**, ~**s of** *(fig)* un sacco di; **to** ~ **a program** *(COMPUT)* caricare un programma.

loaded ['ləudɪd] *a (dice)* falsato(a); *(question, word)* capzioso(a); *(col: rich)* pieno(a) di soldi.

loading bay ['ləudɪŋ-] *n* piazzola di carico.

loaf [ləuf] *n (pl loaves)* pane *m*, pagnotta ♦ *vi (also:* ~ **about,** ~ **around)** bighellonare.

loam [ləum] *n* terra di marna.

loan [ləun] *n* prestito ♦ *vt* dare in prestito; **on** ~ in prestito.

loan account *n* conto dei prestiti.

loan capital *n* capitale *m* di prestito.

loath [ləuθ] *a:* **to be** ~ **to do** essere restio(a) a fare.

loathe [ləuð] *vt* detestare, aborrire.

loathing ['ləuðɪŋ] *n* aborrimento, disgusto.

loathsome ['ləuðsəm] *a (gen)* ripugnante; *(person)* detestabile, odioso(a).

loaves [ləuvz] *npl of* **loaf**.

lob [lɔb] *vt (ball)* lanciare.

lobby ['lɔbɪ] *n* atrio, vestibolo; *(POL: pressure group)* gruppo di pressione ♦ *vt* fare pressione su.

lobbyist ['lɔbɪɪst] *n* appartenente *m/f* ad un gruppo di pressione.

lobe [ləub] *n* lobo.

lobster ['lɔbstə*] *n* aragosta.

lobster pot *n* nassa per aragoste.

local ['ləukl] *a* locale ♦ *n (Brit: pub)* ≈ bar *m inv* all'angolo; **the** ~**s** *npl* la gente della zona.

local anaesthetic *n* anestesia locale.

local authority *n* autorità locale.

local call *n (TEL)* telefonata urbana.

local government *n* amministrazione *f* locale.

locality [ləu'kælɪtɪ] *n* località *f inv*; *(position)* posto, luogo.

localize ['ləukəlaɪz] *vt* localizzare.

locally ['ləukəlɪ] *ad* da queste parti; nel vicinato.

locate [ləu'keɪt] *vt (find)* trovare; *(situate)* collocare.

location [ləu'keɪʃən] *n* posizione *f*; **on** ~ *(CINEMA)* all'esterno.

loch [lɔx] *n* lago.

lock [lɔk] *n (of door, box)* serratura; *(of canal)* chiusa; *(of hair)* ciocca, riccio ♦ *vt (with key)* chiudere a chiave; *(immobilize)* bloccare ♦ *vi (door etc)* chiudersi; *(wheels)* bloccarsi, incepparsi; ~ **stock and barrel** *(fig)* in blocco; **on full** ~ *(Brit AUT)* a tutto sterzo.

lock away *vt (valuables)* tenere (rinchiuso(a)) al sicuro; *(criminal)* metter dentro.

lock out *vt* chiudere fuori; **to** ~ **workers out** fare una serrata.

lock up *vi* chiudere tutto (a chiave).

locker ['lɔkə*] *n* armadietto.

locket ['lɔkɪt] *n* medaglione *m*.

lockjaw ['lɔkdʒɔ:] *n* tetano.
lockout ['lɔkaut] *n* (*INDUSTRY*) serrata.
locksmith ['lɔksmɪθ] *n* magnano.
lock-up ['lɔkʌp] *n* (*prison*) prigione *f*; (*cell*) guardina; (*also*: ~ **garage**) box *m inv*.
locomotive [ləukə'məutɪv] *n* locomotiva.
locum ['ləukəm] *n* (*MED*) medico sostituto.
locust ['ləukəst] *n* locusta.
lodge [lɔdʒ] *n* casetta, portineria; (*FREEMASONRY*) loggia ♦ *vi* (*person*): **to ~ (with)** essere a pensione (presso *or* da) ♦ *vt* (*appeal etc*) presentare, fare; **to ~ a complaint** presentare un reclamo; **to ~ (itself) in/between** piantarsi dentro/fra.
lodger ['lɔdʒə*] *n* affittuario/a; (*with room and meals*) pensionante *m/f*.
lodging ['lɔdʒɪŋ] *n* alloggio; *see also* **board**; **lodgings**.
lodging house *n* (*Brit*) casa con camere in affitto.
lodgings ['lɔdʒɪŋz] *npl* camera d'affitto; camera ammobiliata.
loft [lɔft] *n* soffitta; (*AGR*) granaio; (*US*) appartamento ricavato da solaio (*or* granaio *etc*).
lofty ['lɔftɪ] *a* alto(a); (*haughty*) altezzoso(a); (*sentiments, aims*) nobile.
log [lɔg] *n* (*of wood*) ceppo; (*book*) = **logbook** ♦ *n abbr* (= *logarithm*) log ♦ *vt* registrare.
 log in, log on *vi* (*COMPUT*) aprire una sessione (*con codice di riconoscimento*).
 log off, log out *vi* (*COMPUT*) terminare una sessione.
logarithm ['lɔgərɪðm] *n* logaritmo.
logbook ['lɔgbuk] *n* (*NAUT, AVIAT*) diario di bordo; (*AUT*) libretto di circolazione; (*of lorry driver*) registro di viaggio; (*of events, movement of goods etc*) registro.
log cabin *n* capanna di tronchi.
log fire *n* fuoco di legna.
loggerheads ['lɔgəhɛdz] *npl*: **at ~ (with)** ai ferri corti (con).
logic ['lɔdʒɪk] *n* logica.
logical ['lɔdʒɪkəl] *a* logico(a).
logically ['lɔdʒɪkəlɪ] *ad* logicamente.
logistics [lɔ'dʒɪstɪks] *n* logistica.
logo ['ləugəu] *n* logo *m inv*.
loin [lɔɪn] *n* (*CULIN*) lombata; ~**s** *npl* reni *fpl*.
loin cloth *n* perizoma *m*.
loiter ['lɔɪtə*] *vi* attardarsi; **to ~ (about)** indugiare, bighellonare.
loll [lɔl] *vi* (*also*: ~ **about**) essere stravaccato(a).
lollipop ['lɔlɪpɔp] *n* lecca lecca *m inv*.
lollipop man, lollipop lady *n* (*Brit*) impiegato/a *che aiuta i bambini ad attraversare la strada in vicinanza di scuole*.
lollop ['lɔləp] *vi* (*Brit*) camminare (*or* correre) goffamente.
Lombardy ['lɔmbədɪ] *n* Lombardia.
London ['lʌndən] *n* Londra.
Londoner ['lʌndənə*] *n* londinese *m/f*.
lone [ləun] *a* solitario(a).
loneliness ['ləunlɪnɪs] *n* solitudine *f*,

isolamento.
lonely ['ləunlɪ] *a* solitario(a); (*place*) isolato(a); **to feel ~** sentirsi solo(a).
loner ['ləunə*] *n* solitario/a.
lonesome ['ləunsəm] *a* solo(a).
long [lɔŋ] *a* lungo(a) ♦ *ad* a lungo, per molto tempo ♦ *n*: **the ~ and the short of it is that** ... (*fig*) a farla breve ... ♦ *vi*: **to ~ for sth/to do** desiderare qc/di fare; non veder l'ora di aver qc/di fare; **he had ~ understood that** ... aveva capito da molto tempo che ...; **how ~ is this river/course?** quanto è lungo questo fiume/corso?; **6 metres ~** lungo 6 metri; **6 months ~** che dura 6 mesi, di 6 mesi; **all night ~** tutta la notte; **he no ~er comes** non viene più; **~ before** molto tempo prima; **before ~** (+ *future*) presto, fra poco; (+ *past*) poco tempo dopo; **~ ago** molto tempo fa; **don't be ~!** faccia presto!; **I shan't be ~** non ne avrò per molto; **at ~ last** finalmente; **in the ~ run** alla fin fine; **so** *or* **as ~ as** sempre che + *sub*.
long-distance [lɔŋ'dɪstəns] *a* (*race*) di fondo; (*call*) interurbano(a).
long-haired ['lɔŋ'hɛəd] *a* (*person*) dai capelli lunghi; (*animal*) dal pelo lungo.
longhand ['lɔŋhænd] *n* scrittura normale.
longing ['lɔŋɪŋ] *n* desiderio, voglia, brama ♦ *a* di desiderio; pieno(a) di nostalgia.
longingly ['lɔŋɪŋlɪ] *ad* con desiderio (*or* nostalgia).
longitude ['lɔŋgɪtjuːd] *n* longitudine *f*.
long johns [-dʒɔnz] *npl* mutande *fpl* lunghe.
long jump *n* salto in lungo.
long-lost ['lɔŋlɔst] *a* perduto(a) da tempo.
long-playing ['lɔŋpleɪɪŋ] *a*: ~ **record (LP)** (disco) 33 giri *m inv*.
long-range [lɔŋ'reɪndʒ] *a* a lunga portata; (*weather forecast*) a lungo termine.
longshoreman ['lɔŋʃɔːmən] *n* (*US*) scaricatore *m* (di porto), portuale *m*.
long-sighted [lɔŋ'saɪtɪd] *a* (*Brit*) presbite; (*fig*) lungimirante.
long-standing ['lɔŋstændɪŋ] *a* di vecchia data.
long-suffering [lɔŋ'sʌfərɪŋ] *a* estremamente paziente; infinitamente tollerante.
long-term ['lɔŋtə:m] *a* a lungo termine.
long wave *n* (*RADIO*) onde *fpl* lunghe.
long-winded [lɔŋ'wɪndɪd] *a* prolisso(a), interminabile.
loo [lu:] *n* (*Brit col*) W.C. *m inv*, cesso.
loofah ['lu:fə] *n* luffa.
look [luk] *vi* guardare; (*seem*) sembrare, parere; (*building etc*): **to ~ south/on to the sea** dare a sud/sul mare ♦ *n* sguardo; (*appearance*) aspetto, aria; ~**s** *npl* aspetto; bellezza; **to ~ like** assomigliare a; **to have a ~ at sth** dare un'occhiata a qc; **to have a ~ for sth** cercare qc; **to ~ ahead** guardare avanti; **it ~s about 4 metres long** sarà lungo un 4 metri; **it ~s all right to me** a me pare che vada bene.
look after *vt fus* occuparsi di, prendersi cura di; (*keep an eye on*) guardare, badare

a.

look around *vi* guardarsi intorno.

look at *vt fus* guardare.

look back *vi*: **to ~ back at sth/sb** voltarsi a guardare qc/qn; **to ~ back on** (*event, period*) ripensare a.

look down on *vt fus* (*fig*) guardare dall'alto, disprezzare.

look for *vt fus* cercare.

look forward to *vt fus* non veder l'ora di; **I'm not ~ing forward to it** non ne ho nessuna voglia; **~ing forward to hearing from you** (*in letter*) aspettando tue notizie.

look in *vi*: **to ~ in on sb** (*visit*) fare un salto da qn.

look into *vt fus* (*matter, possibility*) esaminare.

look on *vi* fare da spettatore.

look out *vi* (*beware*): **to ~ out (for)** stare in guardia (per).

look out for *vt fus* cercare; (*watch out for*): **to ~ out for sb/sth** guardare se arriva qn/qc.

look over *vt* (*essay*) dare un'occhiata a, riguardare; (*town, building*) vedere; (*person*) esaminare.

look round *vi* (*turn*) girarsi, voltarsi; (*in shops*) dare un'occhiata; **to ~ round for sth** guardarsi intorno cercando qc.

look through *vt fus* (*papers, book*) scorrere; (*telescope*) guardare attraverso.

look to *vt fus* stare attento(a) a; (*rely on*) contare su.

look up *vi* alzare gli occhi; (*improve*) migliorare ♦ *vt* (*word*) cercare; (*friend*) andare a trovare.

look up to *vt fus* avere rispetto per.

look-out ['lukaut] *n* posto d'osservazione; guardia; **to be on the ~ (for)** stare in guardia (per).

look-up table ['lukʌp-] *n* (*COMPUT*) tabella di consultazione.

LOOM *n abbr* (*US*: = *Loyal Order of Moose*) *organizzazione filantropica*.

loom [lu:m] *n* telaio ♦ *vi* sorgere; (*fig*) minacciare.

loony ['lu:nɪ] *a, n* (*col*) pazzo(a).

loop [lu:p] *n* cappio; (*COMPUT*) anello.

loophole ['lu:phəul] *n* via d'uscita; scappatoia.

loose [lu:s] *a* (*knot*) sciolto(a); (*screw*) allentato(a); (*stone*) cadente; (*clothes*) ampio(a), largo(a); (*animal*) in libertà, scappato(a); (*life, morals*) dissoluto(a); (*discipline*) allentato(a); (*thinking*) poco rigoroso(a), vago(a) ♦ *vt* (*untie*) sciogliere; (*slacken*) allentare; (*free*) liberare; (*Brit: arrow*) scoccare; **~ connection** (*ELEC*) filo che fa contatto; **to be at a ~ end** *or* (*US*) **at ~ ends** (*fig*) non saper che fare; **to tie up ~ ends** (*fig*) avere ancora qualcosa da sistemare.

loose change *n* spiccioli *mpl*, moneta.

loose-fitting ['lu:sfɪtɪŋ] *a* ampio(a).

loose-leaf ['lu:sli:f] *a*: **~ binder** *or* **folder**

raccoglitore *m*.

loose-limbed [lu:s'lɪmd] *a* snodato(a), agile.

loosely ['lu:slɪ] *ad* lentamente; approssimativamente.

loosen ['lu:sn] *vt* sciogliere.

loosen up *vi* (*before game*) sciogliere i muscoli, scaldarsi; (*col: relax*) rilassarsi.

loot [lu:t] *n* bottino ♦ *vt* saccheggiare.

looter ['lu:tə*] *n* saccheggiatore/trice.

looting ['lu:tɪŋ] *n* saccheggio.

lop [lɔp] *vt* (*also*: **~ off**) tagliare via, recidere.

lop-sided ['lɔp'saɪdɪd] *a* non equilibrato(a), asimmetrico(a).

lord [lɔ:d] *n* signore *m*; **L~ Smith** lord Smith; **the L~** (*REL*) il Signore; **the (House of) L~s** (*Brit*) la Camera dei Lord.

lordly ['lɔ:dlɪ] *a* nobile, maestoso(a); (*arrogant*) altero(a).

lordship ['lɔ:dʃɪp] *n* (*Brit*): **your L~** Sua Eccellenza.

lore [lɔ:*] *n* tradizioni *fpl*.

lorry ['lɔrɪ] *n* (*Brit*) camion *m inv*.

lorry driver *n* (*Brit*) camionista *m*.

lose [lu:z], *pt, pp* **lost** [lu:z, lɔst] *vt* perdere; (*pursuers*) distanziare ♦ *vi* perdere; **to ~ (time)** (*clock*) ritardare; **to ~ no time (in doing sth)** non perdere tempo (a fare qc); **to get lost** (*person*) perdersi, smarrirsi; (*object*) andare perso *or* perduto.

loser ['lu:zə*] *n* perdente *m/f*; **to be a good/ bad ~** saper/non saper perdere.

loss [lɔs] *n* perdita; **to cut one's ~es** rimetterci il meno possibile; **to make a ~** subire una perdita; **to sell sth at a ~** vendere qc in perdita; **to be at a ~** essere perplesso(a); **to be at a ~ to explain sth** non saper come fare a spiegare qc.

loss adjuster *n* (*INSURANCE*) responsabile *m/f* della valutazione dei danni.

loss leader *n* (*COMM*) articolo a prezzo ridottissimo per attirare la clientela.

lost [lɔst] *pt, pp of* **lose** ♦ *a* perduto(a); **~ in thought** immerso *or* perso nei propri pensieri; **~ and found property** *n* (*US*) oggetti *mpl* smarriti; **~ and found** *n* (*US*) ufficio oggetti smarriti.

lost property *n* (*Brit*) oggetti *mpl* smarriti; **~ office** *or* **department** ufficio oggetti smarriti.

lot [lɔt] *n* (*at auctions*) lotto; (*destiny*) destino, sorte *f*; **the ~** tutto(a) quanto(a); tutti(e) quanti(e); **a ~** molto; **a ~ of** una gran quantità di, un sacco di; **~s of** molto(a); **to draw ~s (for sth)** tirare a sorte (per qc).

lotion ['ləuʃən] *n* lozione *f*.

lottery ['lɔtərɪ] *n* lotteria.

loud [laud] *a* forte, alto(a); (*gaudy*) vistoso(a), sgargiante ♦ *ad* (*speak etc*) forte; **out ~** ad alta voce.

loudhailer [laud'heɪlə*] *n* (*Brit*) portavoce *m inv*.

loudly ['laudlɪ] *ad* fortemente, ad alta voce.

loudspeaker [laud'spi:kə*] *n* altoparlante *m*.

lounge [laundʒ] *n* salotto, soggiorno; (*of hotel*)

salone m; (of airport) sala d'attesa ♦ vi oziare; starsene colle mani in mano.
lounge bar n bar m inv con servizio a tavolino.
lounge suit n (Brit) completo da uomo.
louse [laus] n (pl lice) pidocchio.
  louse up vt (col) rovinare.
lousy ['lauzɪ] a (fig) orrendo(a), schifoso(a).
lout [laut] n zoticone m.
louvre, (US) **louver** ['luːvə*] a (door, window) con apertura a gelosia.
lovable ['lʌvəbl] a simpatico(a), carino(a); amabile.
love [lʌv] n amore m ♦ vt amare; voler bene a; **to ~ to do: I ~ to do** mi piace fare; **I'd ~ to come** mi piacerebbe molto venire; **to be in ~ with** essere innamorato(a) di; **to fall in ~ with** innamorarsi di; **to make ~** fare l'amore; **~ at first sight** amore a prima vista, colpo di fulmine; **to send one's ~ to sb** mandare i propri saluti a qn; **~ from Anne, ~, Anne** con affetto, Anne; **"15 ~"** (TENNIS) "15 a zero".
love affair n relazione f.
love letter n lettera d'amore.
love life n vita sentimentale.
lovely ['lʌvlɪ] a bello(a); (delicious: smell, meal) buono(a); **we had a ~ time** ci siamo divertiti molto.
lover ['lʌvə*] n amante m/f; (amateur): **a ~ of** un(un')amante di; un(un')appassionato(a) di.
lovesick ['lʌvsɪk] a malato(a) d'amore.
lovesong ['lʌvsɔŋ] n canzone f d'amore.
loving ['lʌvɪŋ] a affettuoso(a), amoroso(a), tenero(a).
low [ləu] a basso(a) ♦ ad in basso ♦ n (METEOR) depressione f ♦ vi (cow) muggire; **to feel ~** sentirsi giù; **he's very ~** (ill) è molto debole; **to reach a new** or **an all-time ~** toccare il livello più basso or il minimo; **to turn (down) ~** vt abbassare.
lowbrow ['ləubrau] a (person) senza pretese intellettuali.
low-calorie ['ləu'kælərɪ] a a basso contenuto calorico.
low-cut ['ləukʌt] a (dress) scollato(a).
low-down ['ləudaun] a (mean) ignobile ♦ n (col): **he gave me the ~ on it** mi ha messo al corrente dei fatti.
lower ['ləuə*] a, ad comparative of **low** ♦ vt (gen) calare; (reduce: price) abbassare, ridurre; (resistance) indebolire ♦ vi ['lauə*] (person): **to ~ (at sb)** dare un'occhiataccia (a qn); (sky) minacciare.
low-fat ['ləu'fæt] a magro(a).
low-key ['ləu'kiː] a moderato(a); (operation) condotto(a) con discrezione.
lowland ['ləulənd] n bassopiano, pianura.
low-level ['ləulɛvl] a a basso livello; (flying) a bassa quota.
low-loader ['ləuləudə*] n camion m a pianale basso.
lowly ['ləulɪ] a umile, modesto(a).

low-lying [ləu'laɪɪŋ] a a basso livello.
low-paid [ləu'peɪd] a mal pagato(a).
loyal ['lɔɪəl] a fedele, leale.
loyalist ['lɔɪəlɪst] n lealista m/f.
loyalty ['lɔɪəltɪ] n fedeltà, lealtà.
lozenge ['lɔzɪndʒ] n (MED) pastiglia; (GEOM) losanga.
LP n abbr (= long-playing record) LP m.
L-plates ['ɛlpleɪts] npl (Brit) cartelli sui veicoli dei guidatori principianti.
LPN n abbr (US: = Licensed Practical Nurse) ≈ infermiera diplomata.
LRAM n abbr (Brit: = Licentiate of the Royal Academy of Music) specializzazione dopo la laurea.
LSAT n abbr (US) = Law School Admission Test.
LSD n abbr (= lysergic acid diethylamide) L.S.D. m; (Brit: = pounds, shillings and pence) sistema monetario in vigore in Gran Bretagna fino al 1971.
LSE n abbr = London School of Economics.
LT abbr (ELEC: = low tension) B.T.
Lt. abbr (= lieutenant) Ten.
Ltd abbr (COMM) = **limited**.
lubricant ['luːbrɪkənt] n lubrificante m.
lubricate ['luːbrɪkeɪt] vt lubrificare.
lucid ['luːsɪd] a lucido(a).
lucidity [luː'sɪdɪtɪ] n lucidità.
luck [lʌk] n fortuna, sorte f; **bad ~** sfortuna, mala sorte; **good ~** (buona) fortuna; **to be in ~** essere fortunato(a); **to be out of ~** essere sfortunato(a).
luckily ['lʌkɪlɪ] ad fortunatamente, per fortuna.
lucky ['lʌkɪ] a fortunato(a); (number etc) che porta fortuna.
lucrative ['luːkrətɪv] a lucrativo(a), lucroso(a), profittevole.
ludicrous ['luːdɪkrəs] a ridicolo(a), assurdo(a).
ludo ['luːdəu] n ≈ gioco dell'oca.
lug [lʌg] vt trascinare.
luggage ['lʌgɪdʒ] n bagagli mpl.
luggage rack n portabagagli m inv.
luggage van, (US) **luggage car** n (RAIL) bagagliaio.
lugubrious [lu'guːbrɪəs] a lugubre.
lukewarm ['luːkwɔːm] a tiepido(a).
lull [lʌl] n intervallo di calma ♦ vt (child) cullare; (person, fear) acquietare, calmare.
lullaby ['lʌləbaɪ] n ninnananna.
lumbago [lʌm'beɪgəu] n lombaggine f.
lumber ['lʌmbə*] n roba vecchia ♦ vt (Brit col): **to ~ sb with sth/sb** affibbiare or rifilare qc/qn a qn ♦ vi (also: **~ about, ~ along**) muoversi pesantemente.
lumberjack ['lʌmbədʒæk] n boscaiolo.
lumber room n (Brit) sgabuzzino.
lumber yard n segheria.
luminous ['luːmɪnəs] a luminoso(a).
lump [lʌmp] n pezzo; (in sauce) grumo; (swelling) gonfiore m ♦ vt (also: **~ together**) riunire, mettere insieme.
lump sum n somma globale.

lumpy ['lʌmpɪ] a (sauce) grumoso(a).
lunacy ['lu:nəsɪ] n demenza, follia, pazzia.
lunar ['lu:nə*] a lunare.
lunatic ['lu:nətɪk] a, n pazzo(a), matto(a).
lunatic asylum n manicomio.
lunch [lʌntʃ] n pranzo, colazione f; **to invite sb to** or **for** ~ invitare qn a pranzo or a colazione.
lunch break n intervallo del pranzo.
luncheon ['lʌntʃən] n pranzo.
luncheon meat n ≈ mortadella.
luncheon voucher n buono m pasto inv.
lunch hour n = **lunch break**.
lunchtime ['lʌntʃtaɪm] n ora di pranzo.
lung [lʌŋ] n polmone m.
lung cancer n cancro del polmone.
lunge [lʌndʒ] vi (also: ~ **forward**) fare un balzo in avanti; **to** ~ **at sb** balzare su qn.
lupin ['lu:pɪn] n lupino.
lurch [lɔ:tʃ] vi vacillare, barcollare ♦ n scatto improvviso; **to leave sb in the** ~ piantare in asso qn.
lure [luə*] n richiamo; lusinga ♦ vt attirare (con l'inganno).
lurid ['luərɪd] a sgargiante; (details etc) impressionante.
lurk [lɔ:k] vi stare in agguato.
luscious ['lʌʃəs] a succulento(a); delizioso(a).
lush [lʌʃ] a lussureggiante.
lust [lʌst] n lussuria; cupidigia; desiderio; (fig): ~ **for** sete f di.
lust after vt fus bramare, desiderare.
luster ['lʌstə*] n (US) = **lustre**.
lustful ['lʌstful] a lascivo(a), voglioso(a).
lustre, (US) **luster** ['lʌstə*] n lustro, splendore m.
lusty ['lʌstɪ] a vigoroso(a), robusto(a).
lute [lu:t] n liuto.
Luxembourg ['lʌksəmbə:g] n (state) Lussemburgo m; (city) Lussemburgo f.
luxuriant [lʌg'zjuərɪənt] a lussureggiante.
luxurious [lʌg'zjuərɪəs] a sontuoso(a), di lusso.
luxury ['lʌkʃərɪ] n lusso ♦ cpd di lusso.
LV n abbr (Brit) = **luncheon voucher**.
LW abbr (RADIO: = long wave) O.L.
lying ['laɪɪŋ] n bugie fpl, menzogne fpl ♦ a (statement, story) falso(a); (person) bugiardo(a).
lynch [lɪntʃ] vt linciare.
lynx [lɪŋks] n lince f.
Lyons ['laɪənz] n Lione f.
lyre ['laɪə*] n lira.
lyric ['lɪrɪk] a lirico(a); ~**s** npl (of song) parole fpl.
lyrical ['lɪrɪkl] a lirico(a).
lyricism ['lɪrɪsɪzəm] n lirismo.

M

M, m [ɛm] n (letter) M, m f or m inv; **M for Mary**, (US) **M for Mike** ≈ M come Milano.
M n abbr (Brit: = motorway): **the M8** ≈ l'A8 ♦ abbr (= medium) taglia media.
m abbr (= metre) m; = **mile**; **million**.
MA n abbr (SCOL) see **Master of Arts**; (US) = military academy ♦ (US POST) = Massachusetts.
mac [mæk] n (Brit) impermeabile m.
macabre [mə'kɑ:brə] a macabro(a).
macaroni [mækə'rəunɪ] n maccheroni mpl.
macaroon [mækə'ru:n] n amaretto (biscotto).
mace [meɪs] n mazza; (spice) macis m or f.
machinations [mækɪ'neɪʃənz] npl macchinazioni fpl, intrighi mpl.
machine [mə'ʃi:n] n macchina ♦ vt (dress etc) cucire a macchina; (TECH) lavorare (a macchina).
machine code n (COMPUT) codice m di macchina, codice assoluto.
machine gun n mitragliatrice f.
machine language n (COMPUT) linguaggio m macchina inv.
machine-readable [mə'ʃi:nri:dəbl] a (COMPUT) leggibile dalla macchina.
machinery [mə'ʃi:nərɪ] n macchinario, macchine fpl; (fig) macchina.
machine shop n officina meccanica.
machine tool n macchina utensile.
machine washable a lavabile in lavatrice.
machinist [mə'ʃi:nɪst] n macchinista m/f.
macho ['mætʃəu] a macho inv.
mackerel ['mækrəl] n (pl inv) sgombro.
mackintosh ['mækɪntəʃ] n impermeabile m.
macro... ['mækrəu] prefix macro....
macroeconomics ['mækrəui:kə'nɔmɪks] n macroeconomia.
mad [mæd] a matto(a), pazzo(a); (foolish) sciocco(a); (angry) furioso(a); **to go** ~ impazzire, diventar matto; ~ **(at** or **with sb)** furibondo(a) (con qn); **to be** ~ **(keen) about** or **on sth** (col) andar pazzo or matto per qc.
madam ['mædəm] n signora; **M**~ **Chairman** Signora Presidentessa.
madden ['mædn] vt fare infuriare.
maddening ['mædnɪŋ] a esasperante.
made [meɪd] pt, pp of **make**.
Madeira [mə'dɪərə] n (GEO) Madera; (wine) madera m.
made-to-measure ['meɪdtə'mɛʒə*] a (Brit) fatto(a) su misura.
madly ['mædlɪ] ad follemente; (love) alla follia.
madman ['mædmən] n pazzo, alienato.

madness ['mædnɪs] n pazzia.
Madrid [mə'drɪd] n Madrid f.
Mafia ['mæfɪə] n mafia f.
mag. [mæg] n abbr (Brit col) = **magazine** (PRESS).
magazine [mægə'zi:n] n (PRESS) rivista; (MIL: store) magazzino, deposito; (of firearm) caricatore m.
maggot ['mægət] n baco, verme m.
magic ['mædʒɪk] n magia ♦ a magico(a).
magical ['mædʒɪkəl] a magico(a).
magician [mə'dʒɪʃən] n mago/a.
magistrate ['mædʒɪstreɪt] n magistrato; giudice m/f.
magnanimous [mæg'nænɪməs] a magnanimo(a).
magnate ['mægneɪt] n magnate m.
magnesium [mæg'ni:zɪəm] n magnesio.
magnet ['mægnɪt] n magnete m, calamita.
magnetic [mæg'nɛtɪk] a magnetico(a).
magnetic disk n (COMPUT) disco magnetico.
magnetic tape n nastro magnetico.
magnetism ['mægnɪtɪzəm] n magnetismo.
magnification [mægnɪfɪ'keɪʃən] n ingrandimento.
magnificence [mæg'nɪfɪsns] n magnificenza.
magnificent [mæg'nɪfɪsnt] a magnifico(a).
magnify ['mægnɪfaɪ] vt ingrandire.
magnifying glass ['mægnɪfaɪɪŋ-] n lente f d'ingrandimento.
magnitude ['mægnɪtju:d] n grandezza; importanza.
magnolia [mæg'nəulɪə] n magnolia.
magpie ['mægpaɪ] n gazza.
mahogany [mə'hɔgənɪ] n mogano ♦ cpd di or in mogano.
maid [meɪd] n domestica; (in hotel) cameriera; **old ~** (pej) vecchia zitella.
maiden ['meɪdn] n fanciulla ♦ a (aunt etc) nubile; (speech, voyage) inaugurale.
maiden name n nome m nubile or da ragazza.
mail [meɪl] n posta ♦ vt spedire (per posta); **by ~** per posta.
mailbox ['meɪlbɔks] n (US) cassetta delle lettere; (COMPUT) mailbox f inv.
mailing list ['meɪlɪŋ-] n elenco d'indirizzi.
mailman ['meɪlmæn] n (US) portalettere m inv, postino.
mail-order ['meɪlɔ:də*] n vendita (or acquisto) per corrispondenza ♦ cpd: **~ firm** or **house** ditta di vendita per corrispondenza.
mailshot ['meɪlʃɔt] n mailing m inv.
mail train n treno postale.
mail truck n (US AUT) = **mail van**.
mail van n (Brit: AUT) furgone m postale; (: RAIL) vagone m postale.
maim [meɪm] vt mutilare.
main [meɪn] a principale ♦ n (pipe) conduttura principale; **the ~s** (ELEC) la linea principale; **~s operated** a che funziona a elettricità; **in the ~** nel complesso, nell'insieme.
main course n (CULIN) piatto principale, piatto forte.
mainframe ['meɪnfreɪm] n (also: **~ computer**) mainframe m inv.
mainland ['meɪnlənd] n continente m.
mainline ['meɪnlaɪn] a (RAIL) della linea principale ♦ vb (drugs slang) vt bucarsi di ♦ vi bucarsi.
main line n (RAIL) linea principale.
mainly ['meɪnlɪ] ad principalmente, soprattutto.
main road n strada principale.
mainstay ['meɪnsteɪ] n (fig) sostegno principale.
mainstream ['meɪnstri:m] n (fig) corrente f principale.
maintain [meɪn'teɪn] vt mantenere; (affirm) sostenere; **to ~ that ...** sostenere che ....
maintenance ['meɪntənəns] n manutenzione f; (alimony) alimenti mpl.
maintenance contract n contratto di manutenzione.
maintenance order n (LAW) obbligo degli alimenti.
maisonette [meɪzə'nɛt] n (Brit) appartamento a due piani.
maize [meɪz] n granturco, mais m.
Maj. abbr (MIL) = **major**.
majestic [mə'dʒɛstɪk] a maestoso(a).
majesty ['mædʒɪstɪ] n maestà f inv.
major ['meɪdʒə*] n (MIL) maggiore m ♦ a (greater, MUS) maggiore; (in importance) principale, importante ♦ vi (US SCOL): **to ~ (in)** specializzarsi (in); **a ~ operation** (MED) una grossa operazione.
Majorca [mə'jɔ:kə] n Maiorca.
major general n (MIL) generale m di divisione.
majority [mə'dʒɔrɪtɪ] n maggioranza ♦ cpd (verdict) maggioritario(a).
majority holding n (COMM): **to have a ~** essere maggiore azionista.
make [meɪk] vt (pt, pp made [meɪd]) fare; (manufacture) fare, fabbricare; (cause to be): **to ~ sb sad** etc rendere qn triste etc; (force): **to ~ sb do sth** costringere qn a fare qc, far fare qc a qn; (equal): **2 and 2 ~ 4** 2 più 2 fa 4 ♦ n fabbricazione f; (brand) marca; **to ~ it** (in time etc) arrivare; (succeed) farcela; **what time do you ~ it?** che ora fai?; **to ~ good** vi (succeed) aver successo ♦ vt (deficit) colmare; (losses) compensare; **to ~ do with** arrangiarsi con.
make for vt fus (place) avviarsi verso.
make off vi svignarsela.
make out vt (write out) scrivere; (understand) capire; (see) distinguere; (: numbers) decifrare; (claim, imply): **to ~ out (that)** voler far credere (che); **to ~ out a case for sth** presentare delle valide ragioni in favore di qc.
make over vt (assign): **to ~ over (to)** passare (a), trasferire (a).
make up vt (invent) inventare; (parcel) fare ♦ vi conciliarsi; (with cosmetics)

truccarsi; **to be made up of** essere composto di *or* formato da.

make up for *vt fus* compensare; ricuperare.

make-believe ['meɪkbɪliːv] *n*: **a world of** ~ un mondo di favole; **it's just** ~ è tutta un'invenzione.

maker ['meɪkə*] *n* fabbricante *m*; creatore/trice, autore/trice.

makeshift ['meɪkʃɪft] *a* improvvisato(a).

make-up ['meɪkʌp] *n* trucco.

make-up bag *n* borsa del trucco.

make-up remover *n* struccatore *m*.

making ['meɪkɪŋ] *n* (*fig*): **in the** ~ in formazione; **he has the** ~s **of an actor** ha la stoffa dell'attore.

maladjusted [mælə'dʒʌstɪd] *a* disadattato(a).

maladroit [mælə'drɔɪt] *a* maldestro(a).

malaise [mæ'leɪz] *n* malessere *m*.

malaria [mə'lɛərɪə] *n* malaria.

Malawi [mə'lɑːwɪ] *n* Malawi *m*.

Malay [mə'leɪ] *a* malese ♦ *n* malese *m/f*; (*LING*) malese *m*.

Malaya [mə'leɪə] *n* Malesia.

Malayan [mə'leɪən] *a*, *n* = **Malay**.

Malaysia [mə'leɪzɪə] *n* Malaysia.

Malaysian [mə'leɪzɪən] *a*, *n* malaysiano(a).

Maldives ['mɔːldaɪvz] *npl*: **the** ~ le (isole) Maldive.

male [meɪl] *n* (*BIO*, *ELEC*) maschio ♦ *a* (*gen*, *sex*) maschile; (*animal*, *child*) maschio(a); ~ **and female students** studenti e studentesse.

male chauvinist *n* maschilista *m*.

male nurse *n* infermiere *m*.

malevolence [mə'lɛvələns] *n* malevolenza.

malevolent [mə'lɛvələnt] *a* malevolo(a).

malfunction [mæl'fʌŋkʃən] *n* funzione *f* difettosa.

malice ['mælɪs] *n* malevolenza.

malicious [mə'lɪʃəs] *a* malevolo(a); (*LAW*) doloso(a).

malign [mə'laɪn] *vt* malignare su; calunniare.

malignant [mə'lɪgnənt] *a* (*MED*) maligno(a).

malingerer [mə'lɪŋgərə*] *n* scansafatiche *m/f inv*.

mall [mɔːl] *n* (*also*: **shopping** ~) centro commerciale.

malleable ['mælɪəbl] *a* malleabile.

mallet ['mælɪt] *n* maglio.

malnutrition [mælnjuː'trɪʃən] *n* denutrizione *f*.

malpractice [mæl'præktɪs] *n* prevaricazione *f*; negligenza.

malt [mɔːlt] *n* malto ♦ *cpd* (*whisky*) di malto.

Malta ['mɔːltə] *n* Malta.

Maltese [mɔːl'tiːz] *a*, *n* (*pl inv*) maltese (*m/f*); (*LING*) maltese *m*.

maltreat [mæl'triːt] *vt* maltrattare.

mammal ['mæml] *n* mammifero.

mammoth ['mæməθ] *n* mammut *m inv* ♦ *a* enorme, gigantesco(a).

man [mæn] *n* (*pl* **men**) uomo; (*CHESS*) pezzo; (*DRAUGHTS*) pedina ♦ *vt* fornire d'uomini; stare a; essere di servizio a.

manacles ['mænəklz] *npl* manette *fpl*.

manage ['mænɪdʒ] *vi* farcela ♦ *vt* (*be in charge of*) occuparsi di; (*shop*, *restaurant*) gestire; **to** ~ **without sth/sb** fare a meno di qc/qn; **to** ~ **to do sth** riuscire a far qc.

manageable ['mænɪdʒəbl] *a* maneggevole; (*task etc*) fattibile.

management ['mænɪdʒmənt] *n* amministrazione *f*, direzione *f*; gestione *f*; (*persons*: *of business*, *firm*) dirigenti *mpl*; (: *of hotel*, *shop*, *theatre*) direzione *f*; **"under new** ~**"** "sotto nuova gestione".

management accounting *n* contabilità di gestione.

management consultant *n* consulente *m/f* aziendale.

manager ['mænɪdʒə*] *n* direttore *m*; (*of shop*, *restaurant*) gerente *m*; (*of artist*) manager *m inv*; **sales** ~ direttore *m* delle vendite.

manageress [mænɪdʒə'rɛs] *n* direttrice *f*; gerente *f*.

managerial [mænə'dʒɪərɪəl] *a* dirigenziale.

managing director (MD) ['mænɪdʒɪŋ-] *n* amministratore *m* delegato.

Mancunian [mæŋ'kjuːnɪən] *a* di Manchester ♦ *n* abitante *m/f* di Manchester; originario/a di Manchester.

mandarin ['mændərɪn] *n* (*person*, *fruit*) mandarino.

mandate ['mændeɪt] *n* mandato.

mandatory ['mændətərɪ] *a* obbligatorio(a); ingiuntivo(a).

mandolin(e) ['mændəlɪn] *n* mandolino.

mane [meɪn] *n* criniera.

maneuver [mə'nuːvə*] *etc* (*US*) = **manoeuvre** *etc*.

manful ['mænful] *a* coraggioso(a), valoroso(a).

manfully ['mænfəlɪ] *ad* valorosamente.

manganese [mæŋgə'niːz] *n* manganese *m*.

mangle ['mæŋgl] *vt* straziare; mutilare ♦ *n* strizzatoio.

mango, ~es ['mæŋgəu] *n* mango.

mangrove ['mæŋgrəuv] *n* mangrovia.

mangy ['meɪndʒɪ] *a* rognoso(a).

manhandle ['mænhændl] *vt* (*treat roughly*) malmenare; (*move by hand*: *goods*) spostare a mano.

manhole ['mænhəul] *n* botola stradale.

manhood ['mænhud] *n* età virile; virilità.

man-hour ['mæn'auə*] *n* ora di lavoro.

manhunt ['mænhʌnt] *n* caccia all'uomo.

mania ['meɪnɪə] *n* mania.

maniac ['meɪnɪæk] *n* maniaco/a.

manic ['mænɪk] *a* maniacale.

manic-depressive ['mænɪkdɪ'prɛsɪv] *a* maniaco-depressivo(a) ♦ *n* persona affetta da mania depressiva.

manicure ['mænɪkjuə*] *n* manicure *f inv*.

manicure set *n* trousse *f inv* della manicure.

manifest ['mænɪfɛst] *vt* manifestare ♦ *a* manifesto(a), palese ♦ *n* (*AVIAT*, *NAUT*) manifesto.

manifestation [mænɪfɛs'teɪʃən] *n* manifestazione *f*.

manifesto [mænɪ'fɛstəu] *n* manifesto.
manifold ['mænɪfəuld] *a* molteplice ♦ *n* (*AUT etc*): **exhaust** ~ collettore *m* di scarico.
Manila [mə'nɪlə] *n* Manila.
manil(l)a [mə'nɪlə] *a* (*paper, envelope*) manilla *inv*.
manipulate [mə'nɪpjuleɪt] *vt* (*tool*) maneggiare; (*controls*) azionare; (*limb, facts*) manipolare.
manipulation [mənɪpju'leɪʃən] *n* maneggiare *m*; capacità di azionare; manipolazione *f*.
mankind [mæn'kaɪnd] *n* umanità, genere *m* umano.
manliness ['mænlɪnɪs] *n* virilità.
manly ['mænlɪ] *a* virile; coraggioso(a).
man-made ['mæn'meɪd] *a* sintetico(a); artificiale.
manna ['mænə] *n* manna.
mannequin ['mænɪkɪn] *n* (*dummy*) manichino; (*fashion model*) indossatrice *f*.
manner ['mænə*] *n* maniera, modo; ~**s** *npl* maniere *fpl*; (**good**) ~**s** buona educazione *f*, buone maniere; **bad** ~**s** maleducazione *f*; **all** ~ **of** ogni sorta di.
mannerism ['mænərɪzəm] *n* vezzo, tic *m inv*.
mannerly ['mænəlɪ] *a* educato(a), civile.
manoeuvrable, (*US*) **maneuverable** [mə'nu:vrəbl] *a* facile da manovrare; (*car*) maneggevole.
manoeuvre, (*US*) **maneuver** [mə'nu:və*] *vt* manovrare ♦ *vi* far manovre ♦ *n* manovra; **to** ~ **sb into doing sth** costringere abilmente qn a fare qc.
manor ['mænə*] *n* (*also*: ~ **house**) maniero.
manpower ['mænpauə*] *n* manodopera.
Manpower Services Commission (MSC) *n* (*Brit*) ente nazionale per l'occupazione.
manservant, *pl* **menservants** ['mænsə:vənt, 'men-] *n* domestico.
mansion ['mænʃən] *n* casa signorile.
manslaughter ['mænslɔ:tə*] *n* omicidio preterintenzionale.
mantelpiece ['mæntlpi:s] *n* mensola del caminetto.
mantle ['mæntl] *n* mantello.
man-to-man ['mæntə'mæn] *a, ad* da uomo a uomo.
Mantua ['mæntjuə] *n* Mantova.
manual ['mænjuəl] *a, n* manuale (*m*).
manual worker *n* manovale *m*.
manufacture [mænju'fæktʃə*] *vt* fabbricare ♦ *n* fabbricazione *f*, manifattura.
manufactured goods *npl* manufatti *mpl*.
manufacturer [mænju'fæktʃərə*] *n* fabbricante *m*.
manufacturing industries [mænju-'fæktʃərɪŋ-] *npl* industrie *fpl* manifatturiere.
manure [mə'njuə*] *n* concime *m*.
manuscript ['mænjuskrɪpt] *n* manoscritto.
many ['mɛnɪ] *a* molti(e) ♦ *pronoun* molti(e), un gran numero; **a great** ~ moltissimi(e), un gran numero (di); ~ **a** ... molti(e) ..., più di un(a) ...; **too** ~ **difficulties** troppe difficoltà; **twice as** ~ due volte tanto; **how** ~**?**

quanti(e)?
map [mæp] *n* carta (geografica) ♦ *vt* fare una carta di.
map out *vt* tracciare un piano di; (*fig*: *career, holiday, essay*) pianificare.
maple ['meɪpl] *n* acero.
mar [ma:*] *vt* sciupare.
Mar. *abbr* (= *March*) mar.
marathon ['mærəθən] *n* maratona ♦ *a*: **a** ~ **session** una seduta fiume.
marathon runner *n* maratoneta *m/f*.
marauder [mə'rɔ:də*] *n* saccheggiatore *m*; predatore *m*.
marble ['ma:bl] *n* marmo; (*toy*) pallina, bilia; ~**s** *n* (*game*) palline, bilie.
March [ma:tʃ] *n* marzo; *for phrases see also* **July**.
march [ma:tʃ] *vi* marciare; sfilare ♦ *n* marcia; (*demonstration*) dimostrazione *f*; **to** ~ **into a room** entrare a passo deciso in una stanza.
marcher ['ma:tʃə*] *n* dimostrante *m/f*.
marching ['ma:tʃɪŋ] *n*: **to give sb his** ~ **orders** (*fig*) dare il benservito a qn.
march-past ['ma:tʃpa:st] *n* sfilata.
mare [mɛə*] *n* giumenta.
marg. [ma:dʒ] *n abbr* (*col*) = **margarine**.
margarine [ma:dʒə'ri:n] *n* margarina.
margin ['ma:dʒɪn] *n* margine *m*.
marginal ['ma:dʒɪnl] *a* marginale; ~ **seat** (*POL*) seggio elettorale ottenuto con una stretta maggioranza.
marginally ['ma:dʒɪnəlɪ] *ad* (*bigger, better*) lievemente, di poco; (*different*) un po'.
marigold ['mærɪgəuld] *n* calendola.
marijuana [mærɪ'wɑ:nə] *n* marijuana.
marina [mə'ri:nə] *n* marina.
marinade *n* [mærɪ'neɪd] marinata ♦ *vt* ['mærɪneɪd] = **marinate**.
marinate ['mærɪneɪt] *vt* marinare.
marine [mə'ri:n] *a* (*animal, plant*) marino(a); (*forces, engineering*) marittimo(a) ♦ *n* fante *m* di marina; (*US*) marine *m inv*.
marine insurance *n* assicurazione *f* marittima.
marital ['mærɪtl] *a* maritale, coniugale; ~ **status** stato coniugale.
maritime ['mærɪtaɪm] *a* marittimo(a).
maritime law *n* diritto marittimo.
marjoram ['ma:dʒərəm] *n* maggiorana.
mark [ma:k] *n* segno; (*stain*) macchia; (*of skid etc*) traccia; (*Brit SCOL*) voto; (*SPORT*) bersaglio; (*currency*) marco; (*Brit TECH*): **M**~ **2/3** 1a/2a serie *f* ♦ *vt* segnare; (*stain*) macchiare; (*Brit SCOL*) dare un voto a; correggere; (*SPORT*: *player*) marcare; **punctuation** ~**s** segni di punteggiatura; **to be quick off the** ~ (**in doing**) (*fig*) non perdere tempo (per fare); **up to the** ~ (*in efficiency*) all'altezza; **to** ~ **time** segnare il passo.
mark down *vt* (*reduce: prices, goods*) ribassare, ridurre.
mark off *vt* (*tick off*) spuntare, cancellare.

mark out vt delimitare.

mark up vt (price) aumentare.

marked ['mɑːkt] a spiccato(a), chiaro(a).

markedly ['mɑːkɪdlɪ] ad visibilmente, notevolmente.

marker ['mɑːkə*] n (sign) segno; (bookmark) segnalibro.

market ['mɑːkɪt] n mercato ♦ vt (COMM) mettere in vendita; (promote) lanciare sul mercato; **to play the ~** giocare or speculare in borsa; **to be on the ~** essere (messo) in vendita or in commercio; **open ~** mercato libero.

marketable ['mɑːkɪtəbl] a commercializzabile.

market analysis n analisi f di mercato.

market day n giorno di mercato.

market demand n domanda del mercato.

market forces npl forze fpl di mercato.

market garden n (Brit) orto industriale.

marketing ['mɑːkɪtɪŋ] n marketing m.

marketplace ['mɑːkɪtpleɪs] n (piazza del) mercato; (world of trade) piazza, mercato.

market price n prezzo di mercato.

market research n indagine f or ricerca di mercato.

market value n valore m di mercato.

marking ['mɑːkɪŋ] n (on animal) marcatura di colore; (on road) segnaletica orizzontale.

marksman ['mɑːksmən] n tiratore m scelto.

marksmanship ['mɑːksmənʃɪp] n abilità nel tiro.

mark-up ['mɑːkʌp] n (COMM: margin) margine m di vendita; (: increase) aumento.

marmalade ['mɑːməleɪd] n marmellata d'arance.

maroon [mə'ruːn] vt (fig): **to be ~ed** (in or at) essere abbandonato(a) (in) ♦ a bordeaux inv.

marquee [mɑː'kiː] n padiglione m.

marquess, marquis ['mɑːkwɪs] n marchese m.

Marrakech, Marrakesh [mærə'keʃ] n Marrakesh f.

marriage ['mærɪdʒ] n matrimonio.

marriage bureau n agenzia matrimoniale.

marriage certificate n certificato di matrimonio.

marriage guidance, (US) **marriage counselling** n consulenza matrimoniale.

married ['mærɪd] a sposato(a); (life, love) coniugale, matrimoniale.

marrow ['mærəu] n midollo; (vegetable) zucca.

marry ['mærɪ] vt sposare, sposarsi con; (subj: father, priest etc) dare in matrimonio ♦ vi (also: **get married**) sposarsi.

Mars [mɑːz] n (planet) Marte m.

Marseilles [mɑː'seɪlz] n Marsiglia.

marsh [mɑːʃ] n palude f.

marshal ['mɑːʃl] n maresciallo; (US: fire ~) capo; (: police ~) capitano; (for demonstration, meeting) membro del servizio d'ordine ♦ vt adunare.

marshalling yard ['mɑːʃlɪŋ-] n scalo smi-

stamento.

marshmallow [mɑːʃ'mæləu] n (BOT) altea; (sweet) caramella soffice e gommosa.

marshy ['mɑːʃɪ] a paludoso(a).

marsupial [mɑː'suːpɪəl] a, n marsupiale (m).

martial ['mɑːʃl] a marziale.

martial law n legge f marziale.

Martian ['mɑːʃən] n marziano/a.

martin ['mɑːtɪn] n (also: **house ~**) balestruccio.

martyr ['mɑːtə*] n martire m/f ♦ vt martirizzare.

martyrdom ['mɑːtədəm] n martirio.

marvel ['mɑːvl] n meraviglia ♦ vi: **to ~ (at)** meravigliarsi (di).

marvellous, (US) **marvelous** ['mɑːvələs] a meraviglioso(a).

Marxism ['mɑːksɪzəm] n marxismo.

Marxist ['mɑːksɪst] a, n marxista (m/f).

marzipan ['mɑːzɪpæn] n marzapane m.

mascara [mæs'kɑːrə] n mascara m inv.

mascot ['mæskət] n mascotte f inv.

masculine ['mæskjulɪn] a maschile ♦ n genere m maschile.

masculinity [mæskju'lɪnɪtɪ] n mascolinità.

MASH [mæʃ] n abbr (US MIL: = mobile army surgical hospital) ospedale di campo di unità mobile dell'esercito.

mash [mæʃ] vt (CULIN) passare, schiacciare.

mashed [mæʃt] a: **~ potatoes** purè m di patate.

mask [mɑːsk] n (gen, ELEC) maschera ♦ vt mascherare.

masochism ['mæsəkɪzəm] n masochismo.

masochist ['mæsəkɪst] n masochista m/f.

mason ['meɪsn] n (also: **stone~**) scalpellino; (also: **free~**) massone m.

masonic [mə'sɔnɪk] a massonico(a).

masonry ['meɪsnrɪ] n muratura.

masquerade [mæskə'reɪd] n ballo in maschera; (fig) mascherata ♦ vi: **to ~ as** farsi passare per.

mass [mæs] n moltitudine f, massa; (PHYSICS) massa; (REL) messa ♦ vi ammassarsi; **the ~es** le masse; **to go to ~** andare a or alla messa.

massacre ['mæsəkə*] n massacro ♦ vt massacrare.

massage ['mæsɑːʒ] n massaggio ♦ vt massaggiare.

masseur [mæ'sɜː*] n massaggiatore m.

masseuse [mæ'sɜːz] n massaggiatrice f.

massive ['mæsɪv] a enorme, massiccio(a).

mass market n mercato di massa.

mass media npl mass media mpl.

mass meeting n (of everyone concerned) riunione f generale; (huge) adunata popolare.

mass-produce ['mæsprə'djuːs] vt produrre in serie.

mass production n produzione f in serie.

mast [mɑːst] n albero; (RADIO, TV) pilone m (a traliccio).

master ['mɑːstə*] n padrone m; (ART etc, teacher: in primary school) maestro;

(: *in secondary school*) professore *m*; (*title for boys*): **M~ X** Signorino X ♦ *vt* domare; (*learn*) imparare a fondo; (*understand*) conoscere a fondo; **M~ of Arts/Science (MA/MSc)** *n* (*detentore di*) *titolo accademico in lettere/scienze superiore alla laurea*; **M~'s degree** *n* titolo accademico superiore alla laurea; **~ of ceremonies (MC)** *n* maestro di cerimonie.

master disk *n* (*COMPUT*) disco master *inv*, disco principale.

masterful ['mɑːstəful] *a* autoritario(a), imperioso(a).

master key *n* chiave *f* maestra.

masterly ['mɑːstəlɪ] *a* magistrale.

mastermind ['mɑːstəmaɪnd] *n* mente *f* superiore ♦ *vt* essere il cervello di.

masterpiece ['mɑːstəpiːs] *n* capolavoro.

master plan *n* piano generale.

master stroke *n* colpo maestro.

mastery ['mɑːstərɪ] *n* dominio; padronanza.

mastiff ['mæstɪf] *n* mastino inglese.

masturbate ['mæstəbeɪt] *vi* masturbare.

masturbation [mæstə'beɪʃən] *n* masturbazione *f*.

mat [mæt] *n* stuoia; (*also*: **door~**) stoino, zerbino ♦ *a* = **matt**.

match [mætʃ] *n* fiammifero; (*game*) partita, incontro; (*fig*) uguale *m/f*; matrimonio; partito ♦ *vt* intonare; (*go well with*) andare benissimo con; (*equal*) uguagliare ♦ *vi* intonarsi; **to be a good ~** andare bene.

match up *vt* intonare.

matchbox ['mætʃbɒks] *n* scatola per fiammiferi.

matching ['mætʃɪŋ] *a* ben assortito(a).

matchless ['mætʃlɪs] *a* senza pari.

mate [meɪt] *n* compagno/a di lavoro; (*col: friend*) amico/a; (*animal*) compagno/a; (*in merchant navy*) secondo ♦ *vi* accoppiarsi ♦ *vt* accoppiare.

material [mə'tɪərɪəl] *n* (*substance*) materiale *m*, materia; (*cloth*) stoffa ♦ *a* materiale; (*important*) essenziale; **~s** *npl* (*equipment etc*) materiali *mpl*; occorrente *m*.

materialistic [mətɪərɪə'lɪstɪk] *a* materialistico(a).

materialize [mə'tɪərɪəlaɪz] *vi* materializzarsi, realizzarsi.

materially [mə'tɪərɪəlɪ] *ad* dal punto di vista materiale; sostanzialmente.

maternal [mə'tɜːnl] *a* materno(a).

maternity [mə'tɜːnɪtɪ] *n* maternità ♦ *cpd* di maternità; (*clothes*) pre-maman *inv*.

maternity benefit *n* sussidio di maternità.

maternity hospital *n* ≈ clinica ostetrica.

matey ['meɪtɪ] *a* (*Brit col*) amicone/a.

math. [mæθ] *n abbr* (*US*) = **mathematics**.

mathematical [mæθə'mætɪkl] *a* matematico(a).

mathematician [mæθəmə'tɪʃən] *n* matematico/a.

mathematics [mæθə'mætɪks] *n* matematica.

maths [mæθs] *n abbr* (*Brit*) = **mathematics**.

matinée ['mætɪneɪ] *n* matinée *f inv*.

mating ['meɪtɪŋ] *n* accoppiamento.

mating call *n* chiamata all'accoppiamento.

mating season *n* stagione *f* degli amori.

matriarchal [meɪtrɪ'ɑːkl] *a* matriarcale.

matrices ['meɪtrɪsiːz] *npl of* **matrix**.

matriculation [mətrɪkju'leɪʃən] *n* immatricolazione *f*.

matrimonial [mætrɪ'məunɪəl] *a* matrimoniale, coniugale.

matrimony ['mætrɪmənɪ] *n* matrimonio.

matrix, pl matrices ['meɪtrɪks, 'meɪtrɪsiːz] *n* matrice *f*.

matron ['meɪtrən] *n* (*in hospital*) capoinfermiera; (*in school*) infermiera.

matronly ['meɪtrənlɪ] *a* da matrona.

matt [mæt] *a* opaco(a).

matted ['mætɪd] *a* ingarbugliato(a).

matter ['mætə*] *n* questione *f*; (*PHYSICS*) materia, sostanza; (*content*) contenuto; (*MED: pus*) pus *m* ♦ *vi* importare; **it doesn't ~** non importa; (*I don't mind*) non fa niente; **what's the ~?** che cosa c'è?; **no ~ what** qualsiasi cosa accada; **that's another ~** quello è un altro affare; **as a ~ of course** come cosa naturale; **as a ~ of fact** in verità; **it's a ~ of habit** è una questione di abitudine; **printed ~** stampe *fpl*; **reading ~** (*Brit*) qualcosa da leggere.

matter-of-fact [mætərəv'fækt] *a* prosaico(a).

matting ['mætɪŋ] *n* stuoia.

mattress ['mætrɪs] *n* materasso.

mature [mə'tjuə*] *a* maturo(a); (*cheese*) stagionato(a) ♦ *vi* maturare; stagionare; (*COMM*) scadere.

maturity [mə'tjuərɪtɪ] *n* maturità.

maudlin ['mɔːdlɪn] *a* lacrimoso(a).

maul [mɔːl] *vt* lacerare.

Mauritania [mɔrɪ'teɪnɪə] *n* Mauritania.

Mauritius [mə'rɪʃəs] *n* Maurizio.

mausoleum [mɔːsə'lɪəm] *n* mausoleo.

mauve [məuv] *a* malva *inv*.

maverick ['mævərɪk] *n* (*fig*) chi sta fuori del branco.

mawkish ['mɔːkɪʃ] *a* sdolcinato(a); insipido(a).

max. *abbr* = **maximum**.

maxim ['mæksɪm] *n* massima.

maxima ['mæksɪmə] *npl of* **maximum**.

maximize ['mæksɪmaɪz] *vt* (*profits etc*) massimizzare; (*chances*) aumentare al massimo.

maximum ['mæksɪməm] *a* massimo(a) ♦ *n* (*pl* **maxima** ['mæksɪmə]) massimo.

May [meɪ] *n* maggio; *for phrases see also* **July**.

may [meɪ] *vi* (*conditional*: **might**) (*indicating possibility*): **he ~ come** può darsi che venga; (*be allowed to*): **~ I smoke?** posso fumare?; **~ I sit here?** le dispiace se mi siedo qua?; (*wishes*): **~ God bless you!** Dio la benedica!; **he might be there** può darsi che ci sia; **he might come** potrebbe venire, può anche darsi che venga; **I might as well go**

potrei anche andarmene; **you might like to try** forse le piacerebbe provare.

maybe ['meɪbɪ] *ad* forse, può darsi; ~ **he'll** ... può darsi che lui ...+*sub*, forse lui ...; ~ **not** forse no, può darsi di no.

mayday ['meɪdeɪ] *n* S.O.S. *m*.

May Day *n* il primo maggio.

mayhem ['meɪhɛm] *n* cagnara.

mayonnaise [meɪə'neɪz] *n* maionese *f*.

mayor [mɛə*] *n* sindaco.

mayoress ['mɛərɛs] *n* sindaco (*donna*); moglie *f* del sindaco.

maypole ['meɪpəʊl] *n* palo ornato di fiori attorno a cui si danza durante la festa di maggio.

maze [meɪz] *n* labirinto, dedalo.

MB *abbr* (*COMPUT*) = megabyte; (*Canada*) = Manitoba.

MBA *n abbr* (= *Master of Business Administration*) titolo di studio.

MBBS, MBChB *n abbr* (*Brit*: = *Bachelor of Medicine and Surgery*) titolo di studio.

MBE *n abbr* (*Brit*: = *Member of the Order of the British Empire*) titolo.

MC *n abbr see* **master of ceremonies**; (*US*: = *Member of Congress*) membro del Congresso.

MCAT *n abbr* (*US*: = *Medical College Admissions Test*) esame di ammissione a studi superiori di medicina.

MCP *n abbr* (*Brit col*: = *male chauvinist pig*) sporco maschilista *m*.

MD *n abbr* (= *Doctor of Medicine*) titolo di studio; (*COMM*) *see* **managing director** ♦ *abbr* (*US POST*) = Maryland.

MDT *abbr* (*US*: = *Mountain Daylight Time*) ora legale delle Montagne Rocciose.

ME *abbr* (*US POST*) = Maine ♦ *n abbr* (*US*) = medical examiner.

me [mi:] *pronoun* mi, m' + *vowel*; (*stressed, after prep*) me; **it's** ~ sono io; **it's for** ~ è per me.

meadow ['mɛdəʊ] *n* prato.

meagre, (*US*) **meager** ['mi:gə*] *a* magro(a).

meal [mi:l] *n* pasto; (*flour*) farina; **to go out for a** ~ mangiare fuori.

mealtime ['mi:ltaɪm] *n* l'ora di mangiare.

mealy-mouthed ['mi:lɪmaʊðd] *a* che parla attraverso eufemismi.

mean [mi:n] *a* (*with money*) avaro(a), gretto(a); (*unkind*) meschino(a), maligno(a); (*US: vicious: animal*) cattivo(a); (: *person*) perfido(a); (*average*) medio(a) ♦ *vt* (*pt, pp* **meant** [mɛnt]) (*signify*) significare, voler dire; (*intend*): **to** ~ **to do** aver l'intenzione di fare ♦ *n* mezzo; (*MATH*) media; **do you** ~ **meant for** essere destinato(a) a; **do you** ~ **it?** dice sul serio?; **what do you** ~? che cosa vuol dire?; *see also* **means**.

meander [mɪ'ændə*] *vi* far meandri; (*fig*) divagare.

meaning ['mi:nɪŋ] *n* significato, senso.

meaningful ['mi:nɪŋfʊl] *a* significativo(a); (*relationship*) valido(a).

meaningless ['mi:nɪŋlɪs] *a* senza senso.

meanness ['mi:nnɪs] *n* avarizia; meschinità.

means [mi:nz] *npl* mezzi *mpl*; **by** ~ **of** per mezzo di; (*person*) a mezzo di; **by all** ~ ma certo, prego.

means test *n* (*ADMIN*) accertamento dei redditi (*per una persona che ha chiesto un aiuto finanziario*).

meant [mɛnt] *pt, pp of* **mean**.

meantime ['mi:ntaɪm], **meanwhile** ['mi:nwaɪl] *ad* (*also*: **in the** ~) nel frattempo.

measles ['mi:zlz] *n* morbillo.

measly ['mi:zlɪ] *a* (*col*) miserabile.

measurable ['mɛʒərəbl] *a* misurabile.

measure ['mɛʒə*] *vt, vi* misurare ♦ *n* misura; (*ruler*) metro; **a litre** ~ una misura da un litro; **some** ~ **of success** un certo successo; **to take** ~**s to do sth** prendere provvedimenti per fare qc.

measure up *vi*: **to** ~ **up (to)** dimostrarsi or essere all'altezza (di).

measured ['mɛʒəd] *a* misurato(a).

measurement ['mɛʒəmənt] *n* (*act*) misurazione *f*; (*measure*) misura; **chest/hip** ~ giro petto/fianchi; **to take sb's** ~**s** prendere le misure di qn.

meat [mi:t] *n* carne *f*; **cold** ~**s** (*Brit*) affettati *mpl*; **crab** ~ polpa di granchio.

meatball ['mi:tbɔ:l] *n* polpetta di carne.

meat pie *n* torta salata in pasta frolla con ripieno di carne.

meaty ['mi:tɪ] *a* che sa di carne; (*fig*) sostanzioso(a).

Mecca ['mɛkə] *n* La Mecca; (*fig*): **a** ~ **(for)** la Mecca (di).

mechanic [mɪ'kænɪk] *n* meccanico; *see also* **mechanics**.

mechanical [mɪ'kænɪkəl] *a* meccanico(a).

mechanical engineering *n* (*science*) ingegneria meccanica; (*industry*) costruzioni *fpl* meccaniche.

mechanics [mə'kænɪks] *n* meccanica ♦ *npl* meccanismo.

mechanism ['mɛkənɪzəm] *n* meccanismo.

mechanization [mɛkənaɪ'zeɪʃən] *n* meccanizzazione *f*.

MEd *n abbr* (= *Master of Education*) titolo di studio.

medal ['mɛdl] *n* medaglia.

medallion [mɪ'dælɪən] *n* medaglione *m*.

medallist, (*US*) **medalist** ['mɛdəlɪst] *n* (*SPORT*) vincitore/trice di medaglia.

meddle ['mɛdl] *vi*: **to** ~ **in** immischiarsi in, mettere le mani in; **to** ~ **with** toccare.

meddlesome ['mɛdlsəm], **meddling** ['mɛdlɪŋ] *a* (*interfering*) che mette il naso dappertutto; (*touching things*) che tocca tutto.

media ['mi:dɪə] *npl* (*PRESS, RADIO, TV*) media *mpl*; (*means*) *pl of* **medium**.

mediaeval [mɛdɪ'i:vl] *a* = **medieval**.

median ['mi:dɪən] *n* (*US: also*: ~ **strip**) banchina *f* spartitraffico *inv*.

media research *n* sondaggio tra gli utenti dei mass media.

mediate ['mi:dɪeɪt] *vi* interporsi; fare da

mediatore/trice.

mediation [miːdɪ'eɪʃən] n mediazione f.

mediator ['miːdɪeɪtə*] n mediatore/trice.

Medicaid ['mɛdɪkeɪd] n (US) assistenza medica ai poveri.

medical ['mɛdɪkl] a medico(a); ~ (**examination**) visita medica.

medical certificate n certificato medico.

medical examiner (ME) n (US) medico incaricato di indagare la causa di morte in circostanze sospette.

medical student n studente/essa di medicina.

Medicare ['mɛdɪkɛə*] n (US) assistenza medica agli anziani.

medicated ['mɛdɪkeɪtɪd] a medicato(a).

medication [mɛdɪ'keɪʃən] n (drugs etc) medicinali mpl, farmaci mpl.

medicinal [me'dɪsɪnl] a medicinale.

medicine ['mɛdsɪn] n medicina.

medicine chest n armadietto farmaceutico.

medicine man n stregone m.

medieval [mɛdɪ'iːvl] a medievale.

mediocre [miːdɪ'əukə*] a mediocre.

mediocrity [miːdɪ'ɔkrɪtɪ] n mediocrità.

meditate ['mɛdɪteɪt] vi: **to ~ (on)** meditare (su).

meditation [mɛdɪ'teɪʃən] n meditazione f.

Mediterranean [mɛdɪtə'reɪnɪən] a mediterraneo(a); **the ~ (Sea)** il (mare) Mediterraneo.

medium ['miːdɪəm] a medio(a) ♦ n (pl **media**: means) mezzo; (pl **mediums**: person) medium m inv; **the happy ~** una giusta via di mezzo; see also **media**.

medium-sized ['miːdɪəmsaɪzd] a (tin etc) di grandezza media; (clothes) di taglia media.

medium wave n (RADIO) onde fpl medie.

medley ['mɛdlɪ] n selezione f.

meek [miːk] a dolce, umile.

meet, pt, pp met [miːt, mɛt] vt incontrare; (for the first time) fare la conoscenza di; (fig) affrontare; far fronte a; soddisfare; raggiungere ♦ vi incontrarsi; (in session) riunirsi; (join: objects) unirsi ♦ n (Brit HUNTING) raduno (dei partecipanti alla caccia alla volpe); (US SPORT) raduno (sportivo); **I'll ~ you at the station** verrò a prenderla alla stazione; **pleased to ~ you!** lieto di conoscerla!, piacere!

meet up vi: **to ~ up with sb** incontrare qn.

meet with vt fus incontrare; **he met with an accident** ha avuto un incidente.

meeting ['miːtɪŋ] n incontro; (session: of club etc) riunione f; (interview) intervista; (formal) colloquio; (SPORT: rally) raduno; **she's at a ~** (COMM) è in riunione; **to call a ~** convocare una riunione.

meeting place n luogo d'incontro.

megabyte ['mɛgəbaɪt] n megabyte m inv.

megalomaniac [mɛgələu'meɪnɪæk] n megalomane m/f.

megaphone ['mɛgəfəun] n megafono.

melancholy ['mɛlənkəlɪ] n malinconia ♦ a malinconico(a).

mellow ['mɛləu] a (wine, sound) ricco(a); (person, light) dolce; (colour) caldo(a); (fruit) maturo(a) ♦ vi (person) addolcirsi.

melodious [mɪ'ləudɪəs] a melodioso(a).

melodrama ['mɛləudrɑːmə] n melodramma m.

melodramatic [mɛlədrə'mætɪk] a melodrammatico(a).

melody ['mɛlədɪ] n melodia.

melon ['mɛlən] n melone m.

melt [mɛlt] vi (gen) sciogliersi, struggersi; (metals) fondersi; (fig) intenerirsi ♦ vt sciogliere, struggere; fondere; (person) commuovere; **~ed butter** burro fuso.

melt away vi sciogliersi completamente.

melt down vt fondere.

meltdown ['mɛltdaun] n melt-down m inv.

melting point ['mɛltɪŋ-] n punto di fusione.

melting pot ['mɛltɪŋ-] n (fig) crogiolo; **to be in the ~** essere ancora in discussione.

member ['mɛmbə*] n membro; (of club) socio/a, iscritto/a; (of political party) iscritto/a; ~ **country/state** n paese m/stato membro; **M~ of Parliament (MP)** n (Brit) deputato; **M~ of the European Parliament (MEP)** n eurodeputato; **M~ of the House of Representatives (MHR)** n (US) membro della Camera dei Rappresentanti.

membership ['mɛmbəʃɪp] n iscrizione f; (numero d')iscritti mpl, membri mpl.

membership card n tessera (di iscrizione).

membrane ['mɛmbreɪn] n membrana.

memento [mə'mɛntəu] n ricordo, souvenir m inv.

memo ['mɛməu] n appunto; (COMM etc) comunicazione f di servizio.

memoir ['mɛmwɑː*] n memoria; ~**s** npl memorie fpl, ricordi mpl.

memo pad n blocchetto per appunti.

memorable ['mɛmərəbl] a memorabile.

memorandum, pl **memoranda** [mɛmə'rændəm, -də] n appunto; (COMM etc) comunicazione f di servizio; (DIPLOMACY) memorandum m inv.

memorial [mɪ'mɔːrɪəl] n monumento commemorativo ♦ a commemorativo(a).

memorize ['mɛməraɪz] vt imparare a memoria.

memory ['mɛmərɪ] n (gen, COMPUT) memoria; (recollection) ricordo; **in ~ of** in memoria di; **to have a good/bad ~** aver buona/cattiva memoria; **loss of ~** amnesia.

men [mɛn] npl of **man**.

menace ['mɛnɪs] n minaccia; (col: nuisance) peste f ♦ vt minacciare; **a public ~** un pericolo pubblico.

menacing ['mɛnɪsɪŋ] a minaccioso(a).

menagerie [mɪ'nædʒərɪ] n serraglio.

mend [mɛnd] vt aggiustare, riparare; (darn) rammendare ♦ n rammendo; **on the ~** in via di guarigione.

mending ['mɛndɪŋ] n rammendo; (items to be

mended) roba da rammendare.

menial ['miːnɪəl] *a* da servo, domestico(a); umile.

meningitis [mɛnɪn'dʒaɪtɪs] *n* meningite *f*.

menopause ['mɛnəupɔːz] *n* menopausa.

menservants ['mɛnsəvənts] *npl of* **manservant**.

menstruate ['mɛnstrueɪt] *vi* mestruare.

menstruation [mɛnstru'eɪʃən] *n* mestruazione *f*.

mental ['mɛntl] *a* mentale; ~ **illness** malattia mentale.

mentality [mɛn'tælɪtɪ] *n* mentalità *f inv*.

mentally ['mɛntlɪ] *ad*: **to be ~ handicapped** essere minorato psichico.

menthol ['mɛnθəl] *n* mentolo.

mention ['mɛnʃən] *n* menzione *f ♦ vt* menzionare, far menzione di; **don't ~ it!** non c'è di che!, prego!; **I need hardly ~ that ...** inutile dire che ...; **not to ~, without** ~**ing** per non parlare di, senza contare.

mentor ['mɛntɔː*] *n* mentore *m*.

menu ['mɛnjuː] *n* (*set* ~, *COMPUT*) menù *m inv*; (*printed*) carta.

menu-driven ['mɛnjuːdrɪvn] *a* (*COMPUT*) guidato(a) da menù.

MEP *n abbr see* **Member of the European Parliament**.

mercantile ['mɜːkəntaɪl] *a* mercantile; (*law*) commerciale.

mercenary ['mɜːsɪnərɪ] *a* venale *♦ n* mercenario.

merchandise ['mɜːtʃəndaɪz] *n* merci *fpl ♦ vt* commercializzare.

merchandiser ['mɜːtʃəndaɪzə*] *n* merchandiser *m inv*.

merchant ['mɜːtʃənt] *n* (*trader*) commerciante *m*; (*shopkeeper*) negoziante *m*; **timber/wine** ~ negoziante di legno/vino.

merchant bank *n* (*Brit*) banca d'affari.

merchantman ['mɜːtʃəntmən] *n* mercantile *m*.

merchant navy, (*US*) **merchant marine** *n* marina mercantile.

merciful ['mɜːsɪful] *a* pietoso(a), clemente.

mercifully ['mɜːsɪflɪ] *ad* con clemenza; (*fortunately*) per fortuna.

merciless ['mɜːsɪlɪs] *a* spietato(a).

mercurial [mɜː'kjuərɪəl] *a* (*unpredictable*) volubile.

mercury ['mɜːkjurɪ] *n* mercurio.

mercy ['mɜːsɪ] *n* pietà; (*REL*) misericordia; **to have ~ on sb** aver pietà di qn; **at the ~ of** alla mercè di.

mercy killing *n* eutanasia.

mere [mɪə*] *a* semplice; **by a ~ chance** per mero caso.

merely ['mɪəlɪ] *ad* semplicemente, non ... che.

merge [mɜːdʒ] *vt* unire; (*COMPUT: files, text*) fondere *♦ vi* fondersi, unirsi; (*COMM*) fondersi.

merger ['mɜːdʒə*] *n* (*COMM*) fusione *f*.

meridian [mə'rɪdɪən] *n* meridiano.

meringue [mə'ræŋ] *n* meringa.

merit ['mɛrɪt] *n* merito, valore *m ♦ vt* meritare.

meritocracy [mɛrɪ'tɔkrəsɪ] *n* meritocrazia.

mermaid ['mɜːmeɪd] *n* sirena.

merriment ['mɛrɪmənt] *n* gaiezza, allegria.

merry ['mɛrɪ] *a* gaio(a), allegro(a); **M~ Christmas!** Buon Natale!

merry-go-round ['mɛrɪgəuraund] *n* carosello.

mesh [mɛʃ] *n* maglia; rete *f ♦ vi* (*gears*) ingranarsi; **wire ~** rete *f* metallica.

mesmerize ['mɛzməraɪz] *vt* ipnotizzare; affascinare.

mess [mɛs] *n* confusione *f*, disordine *m*; (*fig*) pasticcio; (*MIL*) mensa; **to be (in) a ~** (*house, room*) essere in disordine (*or* molto sporco); (*fig: marriage, life*) essere un caos; **to be/get o.s. in a ~** (*fig*) essere/cacciarsi in un pasticcio.

  mess about, mess around *vi* (*col*) trastullarsi.

  mess about *or* **around with** *vt fus* (*col*) gingillarsi con; (*plans*) fare un pasticcio di.

  mess up *vt* sporcare; fare un pasticcio di; rovinare.

message ['mɛsɪdʒ] *n* messaggio; **to get the ~** (*fig col*) capire l'antifona.

message switching *n* (*COMPUT*) smistamento messaggi.

messenger ['mɛsɪndʒə*] *n* messaggero/a.

Messiah [mɪ'saɪə] *n* Messia *m*.

Messrs, Messrs. ['mɛsəz] *abbr* (*on letters:* = *messieurs*) Spett.

messy ['mɛsɪ] *a* sporco(a); disordinato(a); (*confused: situation etc*) ingarbugliato(a).

Met [mɛt] *n abbr* (*US*) = *Metropolitan Opera*.

met [mɛt] *pt, pp of* **meet** *♦ a abbr* (= *meteorological*): **the M~ Office** l'Ufficio Meteorologico.

metabolism [mɛ'tæbəlɪzəm] *n* metabolismo.

metal ['mɛtl] *n* metallo *♦ vt* massicciare.

metallic [mɛ'tælɪk] *a* metallico(a).

metallurgy [mɛ'tælədʒɪ] *n* metallurgia.

metalwork ['mɛtlwɜːk] *n* (*craft*) lavorazione *f* del metallo.

metamorphosis, *pl* **-phoses** [mɛtə'mɔːfəsɪs, -iːz] *n* metamorfosi *f inv*.

metaphor ['mɛtəfə*] *n* metafora.

metaphysics [mɛtə'fɪzɪks] *n* metafisica.

mete [miːt]: **to ~ out** *vt fus* infliggere.

meteor ['miːtɪə*] *n* meteora.

meteoric [miːtɪ'ɔrɪk] *a* (*fig*) fulmineo(a).

meteorite ['miːtɪəraɪt] *n* meteorite *m*.

meteorological [miːtɪərə'lɔdʒɪkl] *a* meteorologico(a).

meteorology [miːtɪə'rɔlədʒɪ] *n* meteorologia.

meter ['miːtə*] *n* (*instrument*) contatore *m*; (*parking* ~) parchimetro; (*US*) = **metre**.

methane ['miːθeɪn] *n* metano.

method ['mɛθəd] *n* metodo; ~ **of payment** modo *or* modalità *f inv* di pagamento.

methodical [mɪ'θɔdɪkl] *a* metodico(a).

Methodist ['mɛθədɪst] *a, n* metodista (*m/f*).

methylated spirits ['mɛθɪleɪtɪd-] *n* (*Brit: also*: **meths**) alcool *m* denaturato.

meticulous [mɛ'tɪkjuləs] *a* meticoloso(a).
metre, *(US)* **meter** ['mi:tə*] *n* metro.
metric ['mɛtrɪk] *a* metrico(a); **to go ~** adottare il sistema metrico decimale.
metrical ['mɛtrɪkl] *a* metrico(a).
metrication [mɛtrɪ'keɪʃən] *n* conversione *f* al sistema metrico.
metric system *n* sistema *m* metrico decimale.
metric ton *n* tonnellata.
metronome ['mɛtrənəum] *n* metronomo.
metropolis [mɪ'trɔpəlɪs] *n* metropoli *f inv*.
metropolitan [mɛtrə'pɔlɪtən] *a* metropolitano(a).
Metropolitan Police *n* (*Brit*): **the ~** la polizia di Londra.
mettle ['mɛtl] *n* coraggio.
mew [mju:] *vi* (*cat*) miagolare.
mews [mju:z] *n* (*Brit*): **~ flat** *appartamentino ricavato da una vecchia scuderia*.
Mexican ['mɛksɪkən] *a, n* messicano(a).
Mexico ['mɛksɪkəu] *n* Messico.
Mexico City *n* Città del Messico.
mezzanine ['mɛtsəni:n] *n* mezzanino.
MFA *n abbr* (*US*: = *Master of Fine Arts*) *titolo di studio.*
mfr *abbr* = **manufacture; manufacturer.**
mg *abbr* (= *milligram*) mg.
Mgr *abbr* (= *Monseigneur, Monsignor*) mons.; (*COMM*) = **manager.**
MHR *n abbr* (*US*) *see* **Member of the House of Representatives.**
MHz *abbr* (= *megahertz*) MHz.
MI *abbr* (*US POST*) = *Michigan.*
MI5 *n abbr* (*Brit*: = *Military Intelligence 5*) *agenzia di controspionaggio.*
MI6 *n abbr* (*Brit*: = *Military Intelligence 6*) *agenzia di spionaggio.*
MIA *abbr* = **missing in action.**
miaow [mi:'au] *vi* miagolare.
mice [maɪs] *npl of* **mouse.**
microbe ['maɪkrəub] *n* microbio.
microbiology [maɪkrəubaɪ'ɔlədʒɪ] *n* microbiologia.
microchip ['maɪkrəutʃɪp] *n* microcircuito integrato, chip *m inv*.
microcomputer [maɪkrəukəm'pju:tə*] *n* microcomputer *m inv*.
microcosm ['maɪkrəukɔzəm] *n* microcosmo.
microeconomics [maɪkrəui:kə'nɔmɪks] *n* microeconomia.
microfiche ['maɪkrəufi:ʃ] *n* microfiche *f inv*.
microfilm ['maɪkrəufɪlm] *n* microfilm *m inv* ♦ *vt* microfilmare.
micrometer [maɪ'krɔmɪtə*] *n* micrometro, palmer *m inv*.
microphone ['maɪkrəfəun] *n* microfono.
microprocessor [maɪkrəu'prəusɛsə*] *n* microprocessore *m*.
microscope ['maɪkrəskəup] *n* microscopio; **under the ~** al microscopio.
microscopic [maɪkrə'skɔpɪk] *a* microscopico(a).
microwave ['maɪkrəuweɪv] *n* (*also:* **~ oven**)

forno a microonde.
mid [mɪd] *a*: **~ May** metà maggio; **~ afternoon** metà pomeriggio; **in ~ air** a mezz'aria; **he's in his ~ thirties** avrà circa trentacinque anni.
midday [mɪd'deɪ] *n* mezzogiorno.
middle ['mɪdl] *n* mezzo; centro; (*waist*) vita ♦ *a* di mezzo; **I'm in the ~ of reading it** sto proprio leggendolo ora; **in the ~ of the night** nel mezzo della notte.
middle age *n* mezza età.
middle-aged [mɪdl'eɪdʒd] *a* di mezza età.
Middle Ages *npl*: **the ~** il Medioevo.
middle class *a* (*also:* **middle-class**) ≈ borghese ♦ *n*: **the ~(es)** ≈ la borghesia.
Middle East *n*: **the ~** il Medio Oriente.
middleman ['mɪdlmæn] *n* intermediario; agente *m* rivenditore.
middle management *n* quadri *mpl* intermedi.
middle name *n* secondo nome *m*.
middle-of-the-road ['mɪdləvðə'rəud] *a* moderato(a).
middleweight ['mɪdlweɪt] *n* (*BOXING*) peso medio.
middling ['mɪdlɪŋ] *a* medio(a).
Middx. *abbr* (*Brit*) = *Middlesex.*
midge [mɪdʒ] *n* moscerino.
midget ['mɪdʒɪt] *n* nano/a.
Midlands ['mɪdləndz] *npl* contee del centro dell'Inghilterra.
midnight ['mɪdnaɪt] *n* mezzanotte *f*; **at ~** a mezzanotte.
midriff ['mɪdrɪf] *n* diaframma *m*.
midst [mɪdst] *n*: **in the ~ of** in mezzo a.
midsummer [mɪd'sʌmə*] *n* mezza *or* piena estate *f*.
midway [mɪd'weɪ] *a, ad*: **~ (between)** a mezza strada (fra).
midweek [mɪd'wi:k] *ad, a* a metà settimana.
midwife, *pl* **midwives** ['mɪdwaɪf, -vz] *n* levatrice *f*.
midwifery ['mɪdwɪfərɪ] *n* ostetrica.
midwinter [mɪd'wɪntə*] *n* pieno inverno.
might [maɪt] *vb see* **may** ♦ *n* potere *m*, forza.
mighty ['maɪtɪ] *a* forte, potente ♦ *ad* (*col*) molto.
migraine ['mi:greɪn] *n* emicrania.
migrant ['maɪgrənt] *n* (*bird, animal*) migratore *m*; (*person*) migrante *m/f*; nomade *m/f* ♦ *a* migratore(trice); nomade; (*worker*) emigrato(a).
migrate [maɪ'greɪt] *vi* migrare.
migration [maɪ'greɪʃən] *n* migrazione *f*.
mike [maɪk] *n abbr* (= *microphone*) microfono.
Milan [mɪ'læn] *n* Milano *f*.
mild [maɪld] *a* mite; (*person, voice*) dolce; (*flavour*) delicato(a); (*illness*) leggero(a) ♦ *n* birra leggera.
mildew ['mɪldju:] *n* muffa.
mildly ['maɪldlɪ] *ad* mitemente; dolcemente; delicatamente; leggermente; **to put it ~** a dire poco.

mildness ['maɪldnɪs] *n* mitezza; dolcezza; delicatezza; non gravità.

mile [maɪl] *n* miglio; **to do 20 ~s per gallon** ≈ usare 14 litri per cento chilometri.

mileage ['maɪlɪdʒ] *n* distanza in miglia, ≈ chilometraggio.

mileage allowance *n* rimborso per miglio.

mileometer [maɪ'lɒmɪtə*] *n* (*Brit*) = **milometer**.

milestone ['maɪlstəun] *n* pietra miliare.

milieu ['miːljəː] *n* ambiente *m*.

militant ['mɪlɪtnt] *a, n* militante (*m/f*).

militarism ['mɪlɪtərɪzəm] *n* militarismo.

militaristic [mɪlɪtə'rɪstɪk] *a* militaristico(a).

military ['mɪlɪtərɪ] *a* militare ♦ *n*: **the ~** i militari, l'esercito.

militate ['mɪlɪteɪt] *vi*: **to ~ against** essere d'ostacolo a.

militia [mɪ'lɪʃə] *n* milizia.

milk [mɪlk] *n* latte *m* ♦ *vt* (*cow*) mungere; (*fig*) sfruttare.

milk chocolate *n* cioccolato al latte.

milk float *n* (*Brit*) furgone *m* del lattaio.

milking ['mɪlkɪŋ] *n* mungitura.

milkman ['mɪlkmən] *n* lattaio.

milk shake *n* frappé *m inv*.

milk tooth *n* dente *m* di latte.

milk truck *n* (*US*) = **milk float**.

milky ['mɪlkɪ] *a* lattiginoso(a); (*colour*) latteo(a).

Milky Way *n* Via Lattea.

mill [mɪl] *n* mulino; (*small: for coffee, pepper etc*) macinino; (*factory*) fabbrica; (*spinning ~*) filatura ♦ *vt* macinare ♦ *vi* (*also: ~ about*) formicolare.

millennium, *pl* **~s** *or* **millennia** [mɪ'lɛnɪəm, -'lɛnɪə] *n* millennio.

miller ['mɪlə*] *n* mugnaio.

millet ['mɪlɪt] *n* miglio.

milli... ['mɪlɪ] *prefix* milli ....

milligram(me) ['mɪlɪgræm] *n* milligrammo.

millilitre, (*US*) **milliliter** ['mɪlɪliːtə*] *n* millilitro.

millimetre, (*US*) **millimeter** ['mɪlɪmiːtə*] *n* millimetro.

milliner ['mɪlɪnə*] *n* modista.

millinery ['mɪlɪnərɪ] *n* modisteria.

million ['mɪljən] *n* milione *m*.

millionaire [mɪljə'nɛə*] *n* milionario, ≈ miliardario.

millipede ['mɪlɪpiːd] *n* millepiedi *m inv*.

millstone ['mɪlstəun] *n* macina.

millwheel ['mɪlwiːl] *n* ruota di mulino.

milometer [maɪ'lɒmɪtə*] *n* ≈ contachilometri *m inv*.

mime [maɪm] *n* mimo ♦ *vt, vi* mimare.

mimic ['mɪmɪk] *n* imitatore/trice ♦ *vt* (*subj: comedian*) imitare; (: *animal, person*) scimmiottare.

mimicry ['mɪmɪkrɪ] *n* imitazioni *fpl*; (*ZOOL*) mimetismo.

Min. *abbr* (*Brit POL*: = *ministry*) Min.

min. *abbr* (= *minute, minimum*) min.

minaret [mɪnə'rɛt] *n* minareto.

mince [mɪns] *vt* tritare, macinare ♦ *vi* (*in walking*) camminare a passettini ♦ *n* (*Brit CULIN*) carne *f* tritata *or* macinata; **he does not ~ (his) words** parla chiaro e tondo.

mincemeat ['mɪnsmiːt] *n* frutta secca tritata per uso in pasticceria.

mince pie *n* specie di torta con frutta secca.

mincer ['mɪnsə*] *n* tritacarne *m inv*.

mincing ['mɪnsɪŋ] *a* lezioso(a).

mind [maɪnd] *n* mente *f* ♦ *vt* (*attend to, look after*) badare a, occuparsi di; (*be careful*) fare attenzione a, stare attento(a) a; (*object to*): **I don't ~ the noise** il rumore non mi dà alcun fastidio; **do you ~ if ...?** le dispiace se ...?; **I don't ~** non m'importa; **~ you, ...** sì, però va detto che ...; **never ~** non importa, non fa niente; **it is on my ~** mi preoccupa; **to change one's ~** cambiare idea; **to be in two ~s about sth** essere incerto su qc; **to my ~** secondo me, a mio parere; **to be out of one's ~** essere uscito(a) di mente; **to keep sth in ~** non dimenticare qc; **to bear sth in ~** tener presente qc; **to have sb/sth in ~** avere in mente qn/qc; **to have in ~ to do** aver l'intenzione di fare; **it went right out of my ~** mi è completamente passato di mente, me ne sono completamente dimenticato; **to bring** *or* **call sth to ~** riportare *or* richiamare qc alla mente; **to make up one's ~** decidersi; **"~ the step"** "attenzione allo scalino".

-minded ['maɪndɪd] *a*: **fair~** imparziale; **an industrially~ nation** una nazione orientata verso l'industria.

minder ['maɪndə*] *n* (*child ~*) bambinaia; (*bodyguard*) guardia del corpo.

mindful ['maɪndful] *a*: **~ of** attento(a) a; memore di.

mindless ['maɪndlɪs] *a* idiota; (*violence, crime*) insensato(a).

mine [maɪn] *pronoun* il(la) mio(a), *pl* i(le) miei(mie); **this book is ~** questo libro è mio ♦ *n* miniera; (*explosive*) mina ♦ *vt* (*coal*) estrarre; (*ship, beach*) minare.

mine detector *n* rivelatore *m* di mine.

minefield ['maɪnfiːld] *n* campo minato.

miner ['maɪnə*] *n* minatore *m*.

mineral ['mɪnərəl] *a* minerale ♦ *n* minerale *m*; **~s** *npl* (*Brit: soft drinks*) bevande *fpl* gasate.

mineralogy [mɪnə'rælədʒɪ] *n* mineralogia.

mineral water *n* acqua minerale.

minesweeper ['maɪnswiːpə*] *n* dragamine *m inv*.

mingle ['mɪŋgl] *vt* mescolare, mischiare ♦ *vi*: **to ~ with** mescolarsi a, mischiarsi con.

mingy ['mɪndʒɪ] *a* (*col: amount*) misero(a); (: *person*) spilorcio(a).

miniature ['mɪnətʃə*] *a* in miniatura ♦ *n* miniatura.

minibus ['mɪnɪbʌs] *n* minibus *m inv*.

minicab ['mɪnɪkæb] *n* (*Brit*) ≈ taxi *m inv*.

minicomputer ['mɪnɪkəm'pjuːtə*] *n* minicomputer *m inv*.

minim ['mɪnɪm] *n* (*MUS*) minima.

minima ['mɪnɪmə] *npl of* **minimum**.

minimal ['mɪnɪml] *a* minimo(a).

minimize ['mɪnɪmaɪz] *vt* minimizzare.

minimum ['mɪnɪməm] *n* (*pl* **minima** ['mɪnɪmə]) minimo ♦ *a* minimo(a); **to reduce to a** ~ ridurre al minimo; ~ **wage** salario minimo garantito.

minimum lending rate (MLR) *n* (*Brit*) ≈ tasso ufficiale di sconto (T.U.S.).

mining ['maɪnɪŋ] *n* industria mineraria ♦ *a* minerario(a); di minatori.

minion ['mɪnjən] *n* (*pej*) caudatario; favorito/a.

miniskirt ['mɪnɪskə:t] *n* minigonna.

minister ['mɪnɪstə*] *n* (*Brit POL*) ministro; (*REL*) pastore *m* ♦ *vi*: **to** ~ **to sb** assistere qn; **to** ~ **to sb's needs** provvedere ai bisogni di qn.

ministerial [mɪnɪs'tɪərɪəl] *a* (*Brit POL*) ministeriale.

ministry ['mɪnɪstrɪ] *n* (*Brit POL*) ministero; (*REL*): **to go into the** ~ diventare pastore.

mink [mɪŋk] *n* visone *m*.

mink coat *n* pelliccia di visone.

minnow ['mɪnəu] *n* pesciolino d'acqua dolce.

minor ['maɪnə*] *a* minore, di poca importanza; (*MUS*) minore ♦ *n* (*LAW*) minorenne *m/f*.

Minorca [mɪ'nɔ:kə] *n* Minorca.

minority [maɪ'nɔrɪtɪ] *n* minoranza; **to be in a** ~ essere in minoranza.

minster ['mɪnstə*] *n* cattedrale *f* (*annessa a monastero*).

minstrel ['mɪnstrəl] *n* giullare *m*, menestrello.

mint [mɪnt] *n* (*plant*) menta; (*sweet*) pasticca di menta ♦ *vt* (*coins*) battere; **the (Royal) M**~, (*US*) **the (US) M**~ la Zecca; **in** ~ **condition** come nuovo(a) di zecca.

mint sauce *n* salsa di menta.

minuet [mɪnju'ɛt] *n* minuetto.

minus ['maɪnəs] *n* (*also*: ~ **sign**) segno meno ♦ *prep* meno.

minute ['mɪnɪt] minuscolo(a); (*detail*) minuzioso(a) ♦ *n* ['mɪnɪt] minuto; (*official record*) processo verbale, resoconto sommario; ~**s** *npl* verbale *m*, verbali *mpl*; **it is 5** ~**s past 3** sono le 3 e 5 (minuti); **wait a** ~! (aspetta) un momento!; **at the last** ~ all'ultimo momento; **up to the** ~ ultimissimo; modernissimo; **in** ~ **detail** minuziosamente.

minute book *n* libro dei verbali.

minute hand *n* lancetta dei minuti.

minutely [maɪ'nju:tlɪ] *ad* (*by a small amount*) di poco; (*in detail*) minuziosamente.

miracle ['mɪrəkl] *n* miracolo.

miraculous [mɪ'rækjuləs] *a* miracoloso(a).

mirage ['mɪrɑ:ʒ] *n* miraggio.

mire ['maɪə*] *n* pantano, melma.

mirror ['mɪrə*] *n* specchio ♦ *vt* rispecchiare, riflettere.

mirror image *n* immagine *f* speculare.

mirth [mə:θ] *n* gaiezza.

misadventure [mɪsəd'vɛntʃə*] *n* disavventura; **death by** ~ (*Brit*) morte *f* accidentale.

misanthropist [mɪ'zænθrəpɪst] *n* misantropo/a.

misapply [mɪsə'plaɪ] *vt* impiegare male.

misapprehension ['mɪsæprɪ'hɛnʃən] *n* malinteso.

misappropriate [mɪsə'prəuprɪeɪt] *vt* appropriarsi indebitamente di.

misappropriation ['mɪsəprəuprɪ'eɪʃən] *n* appropriazione *f* indebita.

misbehave [mɪsbɪ'heɪv] *vi* comportarsi male.

misbehaviour, (*US*) **misbehavior** [mɪsbɪ'heɪvjə*] *n* comportamento scorretto.

misc. *abbr* = **miscellaneous**.

miscalculate [mɪs'kælkjuleɪt] *vt* calcolare male.

miscalculation ['mɪskælkju'leɪʃən] *n* errore *m* di calcolo.

miscarriage ['mɪskærɪdʒ] *n* (*MED*) aborto spontaneo; ~ **of justice** errore *m* giudiziario.

miscarry [mɪs'kærɪ] *vi* (*MED*) abortire; (*fail: plans*) andare a monte, fallire.

miscellaneous [mɪsɪ'leɪnɪəs] *a* (*items*) vario(a); (*selection*) misto(a); ~ **expenses** spese varie.

miscellany [mɪ'sɛlənɪ] *n* raccolta.

mischance [mɪs'tʃɑ:ns] *n*: **by (some)** ~ per sfortuna.

mischief ['mɪstʃɪf] *n* (*naughtiness*) birichineria; (*harm*) male *m*, danno; (*maliciousness*) malizia.

mischievous ['mɪstʃɪvəs] *a* (*naughty*) birichino(a); (*harmful*) dannoso(a).

misconception [mɪskən'sɛpʃən] *n* idea sbagliata.

misconduct [mɪs'kɔndʌkt] *n* cattiva condotta; **professional** ~ reato professionale.

misconstrue [mɪskən'stru:] *vt* interpretare male.

miscount [mɪs'kaunt] *vt*, *vi* contare male.

misdeed [mɪs'di:d] *n* (*old*) misfatto.

misdemeanour, (*US*) **misdemeanor** [mɪsdɪ'mi:nə*] *n* misfatto; infrazione *f*.

misdirect [mɪsdɪ'rɛkt] *vt* mal indirizzare.

miser ['maɪzə*] *n* avaro.

miserable ['mɪzərəbl] *a* infelice; (*wretched*) miserabile; (*weather*) deprimente; **to feel** ~ sentirsi avvilito *or* giù di morale.

miserably ['mɪzərəblɪ] *ad* (*fail, live, pay*) miseramente; (*smile, answer*) tristemente.

miserly ['maɪzəlɪ] *a* avaro(a).

misery ['mɪzərɪ] *n* (*unhappiness*) tristezza; (*pain*) sofferenza; (*wretchedness*) miseria.

misfire [mɪs'faɪə*] *vi* far cilecca; (*car engine*) perdere colpi.

misfit ['mɪsfɪt] *n* (*person*) spostato/a.

misfortune [mɪs'fɔ:tʃən] *n* sfortuna.

misgiving(s) [mɪs'gɪvɪŋ(z)] *n(pl)* dubbi *mpl*, sospetti *mpl*; **to have** ~**s about sth** essere diffidente *or* avere dei dubbi per quanto riguarda qc.

misguided [mɪs'gaɪdɪd] *a* sbagliato(a); poco giudizioso(a).

mishandle [mɪs'hændl] *vt* (*treat roughly*) maltrattare; (*mismanage*) trattare male.

mishap ['mɪshæp] *n* disgrazia.

mishear [mɪs'hɪə*] vt, vi irg capire male.
mishmash ['mɪʃmæʃ] n (col) minestrone m, guazzabuglio.
misinform [mɪsɪn'fɔ:m] vt informare male.
misinterpret [mɪsɪn'tə:prɪt] vt interpretare male.
misinterpretation ['mɪsɪntə:prɪ'teɪʃən] n errata interpretazione f.
misjudge [mɪs'dʒʌdʒ] vt giudicare male.
mislay [mɪs'leɪ] vt irg smarrire.
mislead [mɪs'li:d] vt irg sviare.
misleading [mɪs'li:dɪŋ] a ingannevole.
misled [mɪs'led] pt, pp of **mislead**.
mismanage [mɪs'mænɪdʒ] vt gestire male; trattare male.
mismanagement [mɪs'mænɪdʒmənt] n cattiva amministrazione f.
misnomer [mɪs'nəumə*] n termine m sbagliato or improprio.
misogynist [mɪ'sɔdʒɪnɪst] n misogino.
misplace [mɪs'pleɪs] vt smarrire; collocare fuori posto; **to be ~d** (trust etc) essere malriposto(a).
misprint ['mɪsprɪnt] n errore m di stampa.
mispronounce [mɪsprə'nauns] vt pronunziare male.
misquote [mɪs'kwəut] vt citare erroneamente.
misread [mɪs'ri:d] vt irg leggere male.
misrepresent [mɪsreprɪ'zent] vt travisare.
Miss [mɪs] n Signorina; **Dear ~ Smith** Cara Signorina; (more formal) Gentile Signorina.
miss [mɪs] vt (fail to get) perdere; (appointment, class) mancare a; (escape, avoid) evitare; (notice loss of: money etc) accorgersi di non avere più; (regret the absence of): **I ~ him/it** sento la sua mancanza, lui/esso mi manca ♦ vi mancare ♦ n (shot) colpo mancato; (fig): **that was a near ~** c'è mancato poco; **the bus just ~ed the wall** l'autobus per un pelo non è andato a finire contro il muro; **you're ~ing the point** non capisce.
miss out vt (Brit) omettere.
miss out on vt fus (fun, party) perdersi; (chance, bargain) lasciarsi sfuggire.
missal ['mɪsl] n messale m.
misshapen [mɪs'ʃeɪpən] a deforme.
missile ['mɪsaɪl] n (AVIAT) missile m; (object thrown) proiettile m.
missile base n base f missilistica.
missile launcher n lancia-missili m inv.
missing ['mɪsɪŋ] a perso(a), smarrito(a); **to go ~** sparire; **~ person** scomparso/a, disperso/a; **~ in action** (MIL) disperso/a.
mission ['mɪʃən] n missione f; **on a ~ to sb** in missione da qn.
missionary ['mɪʃənrɪ] n missionario/a.
misspell [mɪs'spel] vt (irg: like **spell**) sbagliare l'ortografia di.
misspent [mɪs'spent] a: **his ~ youth** la sua gioventù sciupata.
mist [mɪst] n nebbia, foschia ♦ vi (also: ~ over, ~ up) annebbiarsi; (Brit: windows) appannarsi.

mistake [mɪs'teɪk] n sbaglio, errore m ♦ vt (irg: like **take**) sbagliarsi di; fraintendere; **to ~ for** prendere per; **by ~** per sbaglio; **to make a ~** (in writing, calculating etc) fare uno sbaglio or un errore; **to make a ~ about sb/sth** sbagliarsi sul conto di qn/su qc.
mistaken [mɪs'teɪkən] pp of **mistake** ♦ a (idea etc) sbagliato(a); **to be ~** sbagliarsi.
mistaken identity n errore m di persona.
mistakenly [mɪs'teɪkənlɪ] ad per errore.
mister ['mɪstə*] n (col) signore m; see **Mr**.
mistletoe ['mɪsltəu] n vischio.
mistook [mɪs'tuk] pt of **mistake**.
mistranslation [mɪstræns'leɪʃən] n traduzione f errata.
mistreat [mɪs'tri:t] vt maltrattare.
mistress ['mɪstrɪs] n padrona; (lover) amante f; (Brit SCOL) insegnante f.
mistrust [mɪs'trʌst] vt diffidare di ♦ n: ~ **(of)** diffidenza (nei confronti di).
mistrustful [mɪs'trʌstful] a: ~ **(of)** diffidente (nei confronti di).
misty ['mɪstɪ] a nebbioso(a), brumoso(a).
misty-eyed ['mɪstɪ'aɪd] a trasognato(a).
misunderstand [mɪsʌndə'stænd] vt, vi irg capire male, fraintendere.
misunderstanding [mɪsʌndə'stændɪŋ] n malinteso, equivoco.
misunderstood [mɪsʌndə'stud] pt, pp of **misunderstand**.
misuse n [mɪs'ju:s] cattivo uso; (of power) abuso ♦ vt [mɪs'ju:z] far cattivo uso di; abusare di.
MIT n abbr (US) = Massachusetts Institute of Technology.
mite [maɪt] n (small quantity) briciolo; (Brit: small child): **poor ~!** povera creaturina!
miter ['maɪtə*] n (US) = **miter**.
mitigate ['mɪtɪgeɪt] vt mitigare; (suffering) alleviare; **mitigating circumstances** circostanze fpl attenuanti.
mitigation [mɪtɪ'geɪʃən] n mitigazione f; alleviamento.
mitre, (US) **miter** ['maɪtə*] n mitra; (CARPENTRY) giunto ad angolo retto.
mitt(en) ['mɪt(n)] n mezzo guanto; manopola.
mix [mɪks] vt mescolare ♦ vi mescolarsi ♦ n mescolanza; preparato; **to ~ sth with sth** mischiare qc a qc; **to ~ business with pleasure** unire l'utile al dilettevole; **cake ~** preparato per torta.
mix in vt (eggs etc) incorporare.
mix up vt mescolare; (confuse) confondere; **to be ~ed up in sth** essere coinvolto in qc.
mixed [mɪkst] a misto(a).
mixed doubles npl (SPORT) doppio misto.
mixed economy n economia mista.
mixed grill n (Brit) misto alla griglia.
mixed-up [mɪkst'ʌp] a (confused) confuso(a).
mixer ['mɪksə*] n (for food: electric) frullatore m; (: hand) frullino; (person): **he is a good ~** è molto socievole.
mixture ['mɪkstʃə*] n mescolanza; (blend: of tobacco etc) miscela; (MED) sciroppo.

mix-up ['mıksʌp] *n* confusione *f*.
MK *abbr* (*Brit TECH*) = **mark**.
mk *abbr* = **mark** (*currency*).
mkt *abbr* = **market**.
MLitt *n abbr* (= *Master of Literature, Master of Letters*) titolo di studio.
MLR *n abbr* (*Brit*) *see* **minimum lending rate**.
mm *abbr* (= *millimetre*) mm.
MN *abbr* (*Brit*) = **Merchant Navy**; (*US POST*) = *Minnesota*.
MO *n abbr* = *medical officer*; (*US col*: = *modus operandi*) modo d'agire ♦ *abbr* (*US POST*) = *Missouri*.
m.o. *abbr* = **money order**.
moan [məun] *n* gemito ♦ *vi* gemere; (*col*: *complain*): **to ~ (about)** lamentarsi (di).
moaning ['məunıŋ] *n* gemiti *mpl*.
moat [məut] *n* fossato.
mob [mɔb] *n* folla; (*disorderly*) calca; (*pej*): **the ~** la plebaglia ♦ *vt* accalcarsi intorno a.
mobile ['məubaıl] *a* mobile ♦ *n* (*ART*) mobile *m inv*; **applicants must be ~** (*Brit*) i candidati devono essere disposti a viaggiare.
mobile home *n* grande roulotte *f inv* (*utilizzata come domicilio*).
mobile shop *n* (*Brit*) negozio ambulante.
mobility [məu'bılıtı] *n* mobilità; (*of applicant*) disponibilità a viaggiare.
mobilize ['məubılaız] *vt* mobilitare ♦ *vi* mobilitarsi.
moccasin ['mɔkəsın] *n* mocassino.
mock [mɔk] *vt* deridere, burlarsi di ♦ *a* falso(a).
mockery ['mɔkərı] *n* derisione *f*; **to make a ~ of** rendere ridicolo.
mocking ['mɔkıŋ] *a* derisorio(a).
mockingbird ['mɔkıŋbə:d] *n* mimo (*uccello*).
mock-up ['mɔkʌp] *n* modello dimostrativo; abbozzo.
MOD *n abbr* (*Brit*) = **Ministry of Defence**; *see* **defence**.
mod cons ['mɔd'kɔnz] *npl abbr* (*Brit*) *see* **modern conveniences**.
mode [məud] *n* modo; (*of transport*) mezzo; (*COMPUT*) modalità *f inv*.
model ['mɔdl] *n* modello; (*person: for fashion*) indossatore/trice; (: *for artist*) modello/a ♦ *vt* modellare ♦ *vi* fare l'indossatore (*or* l'indossatrice) ♦ *a* (*small-scale: railway etc*) in miniatura; (*child, factory*) modello *inv*; **to ~ clothes** presentare degli abiti; **to ~ sb/sth on** modellare qn/qc su.
modem ['məudɛm] *n* modem *m inv*.
moderate ['mɔdərıt] *a* moderato(a) ♦ *n* (*POL*) moderato/a ♦ *vb* ['mɔdərcıt] *vi* moderarsi, placarsi ♦ *vt* moderare.
moderately ['mɔdərıtlı] *ad* (*act*) con moderazione; (*expensive, difficult*) non troppo; (*pleased, happy*) abbastanza, discretamente; **~ priced** a prezzo modico.
moderation [mɔdə'rcıʃən] *n* moderazione *f*, misura; **in ~** in quantità moderata, con moderazione.

modern ['mɔdən] *a* moderno(a); **~ conveniences** comodità *fpl* moderne; **~ languages** lingue *fpl* moderne.
modernization [mɔdənaı'zeıʃən] *n* rimodernamento, modernizzazione *f*.
modernize ['mɔdənaız] *vt* modernizzare.
modest ['mɔdıst] *a* modesto(a).
modesty ['mɔdıstı] *n* modestia.
modicum ['mɔdıkəm] *n*: **a ~ of** un minimo di.
modification [mɔdıfı'keıʃən] *n* modificazione *f*; **to make ~s** fare *or* apportare delle modifiche.
modify ['mɔdıfaı] *vt* modificare.
Mods [mɔdz] *n abbr* (*Brit*: = (*Honour*) *Moderations*) esame all'università di Oxford.
modular ['mɔdjulə*] *a* (*filing, unit*) modulare.
modulate ['mɔdjuleıt] *vt* modulare.
modulation [mɔdju'leıʃən] *n* modulazione *f*.
module ['mɔdju:l] *n* modulo.
Mogadishu [mɔgə'dıʃu:] *n* Mogadiscio *f*.
mogul ['məugl] *n* (*fig*) magnate *m*, pezzo grosso; (*SKI*) cunetta.
MOH *n abbr* (*Brit*: = *Medical Officer of Health*) ≈ ufficiale *m* sanitario.
mohair ['məuhεə*] *n* mohair *m*.
Mohammed [məu'hæmıd] *n* Maometto.
moist [mɔıst] *a* umido(a).
moisten ['mɔısn] *vt* inumidire.
moisture ['mɔıstʃə*] *n* umidità; (*on glass*) goccioline *fpl* di vapore.
moisturize ['mɔıstʃəraız] *vt* (*skin*) idratare.
moisturizer ['mɔıstʃəraızə*] *n* idratante *f*.
molar ['məulə*] *n* molare *m*.
molasses [məu'læsız] *n* molassa.
mold [məuld] *etc* (*US*) = **mould** *etc*.
mole [məul] *n* (*animal*) talpa; (*spot*) neo.
molecule ['mɔlıkju:l] *n* molecola.
molehill ['məulhıl] *n* cumulo di terra sulla tana di una talpa.
molest [məu'lɛst] *vt* molestare.
mollusc, (*US*) **mollusk** ['mɔləsk] *n* mollusco.
mollycoddle ['mɔlıkɔdl] *vt* coccolare, vezzeggiare.
molt [məult] *vi* (*US*) = **moult**.
molten ['məultən] *a* fuso(a).
mom [mɔm] *n* (*US*) = **mum**.
moment ['məumənt] *n* momento, istante *m*; importanza; **at the ~** al momento, in questo momento; **for the ~** per il momento, per ora; **in a ~** tra un momento; **"one ~ please"** (*TEL*) "attenda, prego".
momentarily ['məuməntərılı] *ad* per un momento; (*US: very soon*) da un momento all'altro.
momentary ['məuməntərı] *a* momentaneo(a), passeggero(a).
momentous [məu'mɛntəs] *a* di grande importanza.
momentum [məu'mɛntəm] *n* velocità acquisita, slancio; (*PHYSICS*) momento; **to gather ~** aumentare di velocità; (*fig*) prendere *or* guadagnare terreno.
mommy ['mɔmı] *n* (*US*) = **mummy**.
Mon. *abbr* (= *Monday*) lun.

Monaco ['mɔnəkəu] n Monaco f.

monarch ['mɔnək] n monarca m.

monarchist ['mɔnəkɪst] n monarchico/a.

monarchy ['mɔnəkɪ] n monarchia.

monastery ['mɔnəstərɪ] n monastero.

monastic [mə'næstɪk] a monastico(a).

Monday ['mʌndɪ] n lunedì m inv; for phrases see also **Tuesday**.

Monegasque [mɔnə'gæsk] a, n monegasco(a).

monetarist ['mʌnɪtərɪst] n monetarista m/f.

monetary ['mʌnɪtərɪ] a monetario(a).

money ['mʌnɪ] n denaro, soldi mpl; **to make ~** (person) fare (i) soldi; (business) rendere; **danger ~** (Brit) indennità di rischio; **I've got no ~ left** non ho più neanche una lira.

moneyed ['mʌnɪd] a ricco(a).

moneylender ['mʌnɪlɛndə*] n prestatore m di denaro.

moneymaking ['mʌnɪmeɪkɪŋ] a che rende (bene or molto), lucrativo(a).

money market n mercato monetario.

money order n vaglia m inv.

money-spinner ['mʌnɪspɪnə*] n (col) miniera d'oro (fig).

money supply n liquidità monetaria.

Mongol ['mɔŋgəl] n mongolo/a; (LING) mongolo.

mongol ['mɔŋgəl] a, n (MED) mongoloide (m/f).

Mongolia [mɔŋ'gəulɪə] n Mongolia.

Mongolian [mɔŋ'gəulɪən] a mongolico(a) ♦ n mongolo/a; (LING) mongolo.

mongoose ['mɔŋguːs] n mangusta.

mongrel ['mʌŋgrəl] n (dog) cane m bastardo.

monitor ['mɔnɪtə*] n (Brit SCOL) capoclasse m/f; (US SCOL) chi sorveglia agli esami; (TV, COMPUT) monitor m inv ♦ vt controllare; (foreign station) ascoltare le trasmissioni di.

monk [mʌŋk] n monaco.

monkey ['mʌŋkɪ] n scimmia.

monkey business n (col) scherzi mpl.

monkey nut n (Brit) nocciolina americana.

monkey tricks npl = **monkey business**.

monkey wrench n chiave f a rullino.

mono ['mɔnəu] a mono inv; (broadcast) in mono.

mono... ['mɔnəu] prefix mono....

monochrome ['mɔnəkrəum] a monocromo(a).

monocle ['mɔnəkl] n monocolo.

monogram ['mɔnəgræm] n monogramma m.

monolith ['mɔnəlɪθ] n monolito.

monologue ['mɔnəlɔg] n monologo.

monoplane ['mɔnəupleɪn] n monoplano.

monopolize [mə'nɔpəlaɪz] vt monopolizzare.

monopoly [mə'nɔpəlɪ] n monopolio; **Monopolies and Mergers Commission** (Brit) commissione f antimonopoli.

monorail ['mɔnəureɪl] n monorotaia.

monosodium glutamate (MSG) [mɔnə'səudɪəm'glu:təmeɪt] n glutammato di sodio.

monosyllabic [mɔnəsɪ'læbɪk] a monosillabico(a); (person) che parla a monosillabi.

monosyllable ['mɔnəsɪləbl] n monosillabo.

monotone ['mɔnətəun] n pronunzia (or voce f) monotona; **to speak in a ~** parlare con voce monotona.

monotonous [mə'nɔtənəs] a monotono(a).

monotony [mə'nɔtənɪ] n monotonia.

monoxide [mɔ'nɔksaɪd] n: **carbon ~** ossido di carbonio.

monsoon [mɔn'su:n] n monsone m.

monster ['mɔnstə*] n mostro.

monstrosity [mɔn'strɔsɪtɪ] n mostruosità f inv.

monstrous ['mɔnstrəs] a mostruoso(a).

montage [mɔn'tɑ:ʒ] n montaggio.

Mont Blanc [mɔblɑ̃] n Monte m Bianco.

month [mʌnθ] n mese m; **300 dollars a ~** 300 dollari al mese; **every ~** (happen) tutti i mesi; (pay) mensilmente, ogni mese.

monthly ['mʌnθlɪ] a mensile ♦ ad al mese; ogni mese ♦ n (magazine) rivista mensile; **twice ~** due volte al mese.

monument ['mɔnjumənt] n monumento.

monumental [mɔnju'mentl] a monumentale; (fig) colossale.

monumental mason n lapidario.

moo [mu:] vi muggire, mugghiare.

mood [mu:d] n umore m; **to be in a good/bad ~** essere di buon/cattivo umore; **to be in the ~ for** essere disposto(a) a, aver voglia di.

moody ['mu:dɪ] a (variable) capriccioso(a), lunatico(a); (sullen) imbronciato(a).

moon [mu:n] n luna.

moonbeam ['mu:nbi:m] n raggio di luna.

moon landing n allunaggio.

moonlight ['mu:nlaɪt] n chiaro di luna ♦ vi fare del lavoro nero.

moonlighting ['mu:nlaɪtɪŋ] n lavoro nero.

moonlit ['mu:nlɪt] a illuminato(a) dalla luna; **a ~ night** una notte rischiarata dalla luna.

moonshot ['mu:nʃɔt] n lancio sulla luna.

moonstruck ['mu:nstrʌk] a lunatico(a).

Moor [muə*] n moro/a.

moor [muə*] n brughiera ♦ vt (ship) ormeggiare ♦ vi ormeggiarsi.

moorings ['muərɪŋz] npl (chains) ormeggi mpl; (place) ormeggio.

Moorish ['muərɪʃ] a moresco(a).

moorland ['muələnd] n brughiera.

moose [mu:s] n (pl inv) alce m.

moot [mu:t] vt sollevare ♦ a: **~ point** punto discutibile.

mop [mɔp] n lavapavimenti m inv; (also: **~ of hair**) zazzera ♦ vt lavare con lo straccio; **to ~ one's brow** asciugarsi la fronte.

mop up vt asciugare con uno straccio.

mope [məup] vi fare il broncio.

mope about, mope around vi trascinarsi or aggirarsi con aria avvilita.

moped ['məupɛd] n (Brit) ciclomotore m.

moral ['mɔrəl] a morale ♦ n morale f; **~s** npl moralità.

morale [mɔ'rɑ:l] n morale m.

morality [mə'rælɪtɪ] n moralità.

moralize ['mɔrəlaɪz] vi: **to ~ (about)** fare il

(*or* la) moralista (riguardo), moraleggiare (riguardo).

morally ['mɔrəlɪ] *ad* moralmente.

morass [mə'ræs] *n* palude *f*, pantano.

moratorium [mɔrə'tɔ:rɪəm] *n* moratoria.

morbid ['mɔ:bɪd] *a* morboso(a).

more [mɔ:*] *a* più ♦ *ad* più, di più; ~ **people** più gente; **I want** ~ ne voglio ancora *or* di più; **is there any** ~? ce n'è ancora?; ~ **dangerous than** più pericoloso di (*or* che); ~ **or less** più o meno; ~ **than ever** più che mai; **many/much** ~ molti/molto di più; ~ **and** ~ sempre di più; **and what's** ~ ... e per di più ...; **once** ~ ancora (una volta), un'altra volta; **no** ~, **not any** ~ non ... più.

moreover [mɔ:'rəuvə*] *ad* inoltre, di più.

morgue [mɔ:g] *n* obitorio.

MORI ['mɔ:rɪ] *n abbr* (*Brit*: = *Market & Opinion Research Institute*) istituto di sondaggio.

moribund ['mɔrɪbʌnd] *a* moribondo(a).

morning ['mɔ:nɪŋ] *n* mattina, mattino; (*duration*) mattinata; **in the** ~ la mattina; **this** ~ stamattina; **7 o'clock in the** ~ le 7 di *or* della mattina.

morning sickness *n* nausee *fpl* mattutine.

Moroccan [mə'rɔkən] *a, n* marocchino(a).

Morocco [mə'rɔkəu] *n* Marocco.

moron ['mɔ:rɔn] *n* deficiente *m/f*.

moronic [mə'rɔnɪk] *a* deficiente.

morose [mə'rəus] *a* cupo(a), tetro(a).

morphine ['mɔ:fi:n] *n* morfina.

Morse [mɔ:s] *n* (*also:* ~ **code**) alfabeto Morse.

morsel ['mɔ:sl] *n* boccone *m*.

mortal ['mɔ:tl] *a, n* mortale (*m*).

mortality [mɔ:'tælɪtɪ] *n* mortalità.

mortality rate *n* tasso di mortalità.

mortar ['mɔ:tə*] *n* (*CONSTR*) malta; (*dish*) mortaio.

mortgage ['mɔ:gɪdʒ] *n* ipoteca; (*in house buying*) mutuo ipotecario ♦ *vt* ipotecare; **to take out a** ~ contrarre un mutuo (*or* un'ipoteca).

mortgage company *n* (*US*) società *f inv* immobiliare.

mortgagee [mɔ:gɪ'dʒi:] *n* creditore *m* ipotecario.

mortgagor ['mɔ:gɪdʒə*] *n* debitore *m* ipotecario.

mortician [mɔ:'tɪʃən] *n* (*US*) impresario di pompe funebri.

mortified ['mɔ:tɪfaɪd] *a* umiliato(a).

mortise lock ['mɔ:tɪs-] *n* serratura incastrata.

mortuary ['mɔ:tjuərɪ] *n* camera mortuaria; obitorio.

mosaic [məu'zeɪɪk] *n* mosaico.

Moscow ['mɔskəu] *n* Mosca.

Moslem ['mɔzləm] *a, n* = **Muslim**.

mosque [mɔsk] *n* moschea.

mosquito, ~**es** [mɔs'ki:təu] *n* zanzara.

mosquito net *n* zanzariera.

moss [mɔs] *n* muschio.

mossy ['mɔsɪ] *a* muscoso(a).

most [məust] *a* la maggior parte di; il più di ♦ *pronoun* la maggior parte ♦ *ad* più; (*work, sleep etc*) di più; (*very*) molto, estremamente; **the** ~ (*also:* + *adjective*) il(la) più; ~ **fish** la maggior parte dei pesci; ~ **of** la maggior parte di; ~ **of them** quasi tutti; **I saw** ~ ho visto più io; **at the (very)** ~ al massimo; **to make the** ~ **of** trarre il massimo vantaggio da.

mostly ['məustlɪ] *ad* per lo più.

MOT *n abbr* (*Brit*: = *Ministry of Transport*): **the** ~ **(test)** revisione obbligatoria degli autoveicoli.

motel [məu'tɛl] *n* motel *m inv*.

moth [mɔθ] *n* farfalla notturna; tarma.

mothball ['mɔθbɔ:l] *n* pallina di naftalina.

moth-eaten ['mɔθi:tn] *a* tarmato(a).

mother ['mʌðə*] *n* madre *f* ♦ *vt* (*care for*) fare da madre a.

mother board *n* (*COMPUT*) scheda madre.

motherhood ['mʌðəhud] *n* maternità.

mother-in-law ['mʌðərɪnlɔ:] *n* suocera.

motherly ['mʌðəlɪ] *a* materno(a).

mother-of-pearl [mʌðərəv'pə:l] *n* madreperla.

mother's help *n* bambinaia.

mother-to-be [mʌðətə'bi:] *n* futura mamma.

mother tongue *n* madrelingua.

mothproof ['mɔθpru:f] *a* antitarmico(a).

motif [məu'ti:f] *n* motivo.

motion ['məuʃən] *n* movimento, moto; (*gesture*) gesto; (*at meeting*) mozione *f*; (*Brit*: *also:* **bowel** ~) evacuazione *f* ♦ *vt, vi:* **(to) sb to do** fare cenno a qn di fare; **to be in** ~ (*vehicle*) essere in moto; **to set in** ~ avviare; **to go through the** ~**s of doing sth** (*fig*) fare qc pro forma.

motionless ['məuʃənlɪs] *a* immobile.

motion picture *n* film *m inv*.

motivate ['məutɪveɪt] *vt* (*act, decision*) dare origine a, motivare; (*person*) spingere.

motivated ['məutɪveɪtɪd] *a* motivato(a).

motivation [məutɪ'veɪʃən] *n* motivazione *f*.

motive ['məutɪv] *n* motivo ♦ *a* motore(trice); **from the best** ~**s** con le migliori intenzioni.

motley ['mɔtlɪ] *a* eterogeneo(a), molto vario(a).

motor ['məutə*] *n* motore *m*; (*Brit col: vehicle*) macchina ♦ *a* motore(trice).

motorbike ['məutəbaɪk] *n* moto *f inv*.

motorboat ['məutəbəut] *n* motoscafo.

motorcar ['məutəka:] *n* automobile *f*.

motorcoach ['məutəkəutʃ] *n* (*Brit*) pullman *m inv*.

motorcycle ['məutəsaɪkl] *n* motocicletta.

motorcyclist ['məutəsaɪklɪst] *n* motociclista *m/f*.

motoring ['məutərɪŋ] *n* (*Brit*) turismo automobilistico ♦ *a* (*accident*) d'auto, automobilistico(a); (*offence*) di guida; ~ **holiday** vacanza in macchina.

motorist ['məutərɪst] *n* automobilista *m/f*.

motorize ['məutəraɪz] *vt* motorizzare.

motor oil *n* olio lubrificante.

motor racing *n* (*Brit*) corse *fpl* automobilistiche.

motor scooter n motorscooter m inv.

motor vehicle n autoveicolo.

motorway ['məutəweɪ] n (Brit) autostrada.

mottled ['mɔtld] a chiazzato(a), marezzato(a).

motto, ~es ['mɔtəu] n motto.

mould, (US) **mold** [məuld] n forma, stampo; (mildew) muffa ♦ vt formare; (fig) foggiare.

mo(u)lder ['məuldə*] vi (decay) ammuffire.

mo(u)lding ['məuldɪŋ] n (ARCHIT) modanatura.

mo(u)ldy ['məuldɪ] a ammuffito(a).

moult, (US) **molt** [məult] vi far la muta.

mound [maund] n rialzo, collinetta.

mount [maunt] n monte m, montagna; (horse) cavalcatura; (for jewel etc) montatura ♦ vt montare; (horse) montare a; (exhibition) organizzare; (attack) sferrare, condurre; (picture, stamp) sistemare ♦ vi salire; (get on a horse) montare a cavallo; (also: ~ up) aumentare.

mountain ['mauntɪn] n montagna ♦ cpd di montagna; **to make a ~ out of a molehill** fare di una mosca un elefante.

mountaineer [mauntɪ'nɪə*] n alpinista m/f.

mountaineering [mauntɪ'nɪərɪŋ] n alpinismo; **to go ~** fare dell'alpinismo.

mountainous ['mauntɪnəs] a montagnoso(a).

mountain rescue team n ≈ squadra di soccorso alpino.

mountainside ['mauntɪnsaɪd] n fianco della montagna.

mounted ['mauntɪd] a a cavallo.

mourn [mɔ:n] vt piangere, lamentare ♦ vi: **to ~ (for sb)** piangere (la morte di qn).

mourner ['mɔ:nə*] n parente m/f (or amico/a) del defunto.

mournful ['mɔ:nful] a triste, lugubre.

mourning ['mɔ:nɪŋ] n lutto ♦ cpd (dress) da lutto; **in ~** in lutto.

mouse, pl **mice** [maus, maɪs] n topo; (COMPUT) mouse m inv.

mousetrap ['maustræp] n trappola per i topi.

mousse [mu:s] n mousse f inv.

moustache [məs'tɑ:ʃ] n baffi mpl.

mousy ['mausɪ] a (person) timido(a); (hair) né chiaro(a) né scuro(a).

mouth, ~s [mauθ, -ðz] n bocca; (of river) bocca, foce f; (opening) orifizio.

mouthful ['mauθful] n boccata.

mouth organ n armonica.

mouthpiece ['mauθpi:s] n (MUS) bocchino; (TEL) microfono; (of breathing apparatus) boccaglio; (person) portavoce m/f.

mouth-to-mouth ['mauθtə'mauθ] a: **~ resuscitation** respirazione f bocca a bocca.

mouthwash ['mauθwɔʃ] n collutorio.

mouth-watering ['mauθwɔ:tərɪŋ] a che fa venire l'acquolina in bocca.

movable ['mu:vəbl] a mobile.

move [mu:v] n (movement) movimento; (in game) mossa; (: turn to play) turno; (change of house) trasloco ♦ vt muovere, spostare; (emotionally) commuovere; (POL:

resolution etc) proporre ♦ vi (gen) muoversi, spostarsi; (traffic) circolare; (also: ~ house) cambiar casa, traslocare; **to ~ towards** andare verso; **to ~ sb to do sth** indurre or spingere qn a fare qc; **to get a ~ on** affrettarsi, sbrigarsi; **to be ~d** (emotionally) essere commosso(a).

move about, move around vi (fidget) agitarsi; (travel) viaggiare.

move along vi muoversi avanti.

move away vi allontanarsi, andarsene.

move back vi indietreggiare; (return) ritornare.

move forward vi avanzare ♦ vt avanzare, spostare in avanti; (people) far avanzare.

move in vi (to a house) entrare (in una nuova casa).

move off vi partire.

move on vi riprendere la strada ♦ vt (onlookers) far circolare.

move out vi (of house) sgombrare.

move over vi spostarsi.

move up vi avanzare.

movement ['mu:vmənt] n (gen) movimento; (gesture) gesto; (of stars, water, physical) moto; **~ (of the bowels)** (MED) evacuazione f.

mover ['mu:və*] n proponente m/f.

movie ['mu:vɪ] n film m inv; **the ~s** il cinema.

movie camera n cinepresa.

moviegoer ['mu:vɪgəuə*] n (US) frequentatore/trice di cinema.

moving ['mu:vɪŋ] a mobile; (causing emotion) commovente; (instigating) animatore(trice).

mow, pt **mowed,** pp **mowed** or **mown** [məu, -n] vt falciare; (grass) tagliare.

mow down vt falciare.

mower ['məuə*] n (also: **lawn ~**) tagliaerba m inv.

mown [məun] pp of **mow**.

Mozambique [məuzəm'bi:k] n Mozambico.

MP n abbr = Military Police; (Canada) = Mounted Police; (Brit) see **Member of Parliament**.

mpg n abbr = miles per gallon (30 mpg = 9.4 l. per 100 km).

mph abbr = miles per hour (60 mph = 96 km/h).

MPhil n abbr (US: = Master of Philosophy) titolo di studio.

MPS n abbr (Brit) = Member of the Pharmaceutical Society.

Mr, Mr. ['mɪstə*] n: **~ X** Signor X, Sig. X.

MRC n abbr (Brit: = Medical Research Council) ufficio governativo per la ricerca medica in Gran Bretagna e nel Commonwealth.

MRCP n abbr (Brit) = Member of the Royal College of Physicians.

MRCS n abbr (Brit) = Member of the Royal College of Surgeons.

MRCVS n abbr (Brit) = Member of the Royal College of Veterinary Surgeons.

Mrs, Mrs. ['mɪsɪz] *n*: ~ X Signora X, Sig.ra X.

MS *n abbr* (*US*: = *Master of Science*) *titolo di studio*; (= *manuscript*) ms; (*MED*) = **multiple sclerosis** ♦ *abbr* (*US POST*) = *Mississippi*.

Ms, Ms. [mɪz] *n* (= *Miss or Mrs*): ~ X ≈ Signora X, Sig.ra X.

MSA *n abbr* (*US*: = *Master of Science in Agriculture*) *titolo di studio*.

MSC *n abbr see* **Manpower Services Commission**.

MSc *n abbr see* **Master of Science**.

MSG *abbr see* **monosodium glutamate**.

MST *abbr* (*US*: = *Mountain Standard Time*) *ora invernale delle Montagne Rocciose*.

MSW *n abbr* (*US*: = *Master of Social Work*) *titolo di studio*.

MT *n abbr* = *machine translation* ♦ (*US POST*) = *Montana*.

Mt *abbr* (*GEO*: = *mount*) M.

mth *abbr* (= *month*) m.

much [mʌtʃ] *a* molto(a) ♦ *ad, n or pronoun* molto; ~ **milk** molto latte; **how** ~ **is it?** quanto costa?; **it's not** ~ non è tanto; **too** ~ troppo; **so** ~ così (tanto); **I like it very/so** ~ mi piace moltissimo/così tanto; **thank you very** ~ molte grazie; ~ **to my amazement** con mio grande stupore.

muck [mʌk] *n* (*mud*) fango; (*dirt*) sporcizia.
   muck about, muck around *vi* (*col*) fare lo stupido; (: *waste time*) gingillarsi; (*tinker*) armeggiare.
   muck in *vi* (*Brit col*) mettersi insieme.
   muck out *vt* (*stable*) pulire.
   muck up *vt* (*col: dirty*) sporcare; (: *spoil*) rovinare.

muckraking ['mʌkreɪkɪŋ] *n* (*fig col*) caccia agli scandali ♦ *a* scandalistico(a).

mucky ['mʌkɪ] *a* (*dirty*) sporco(a), lordo(a).

mucus ['mjuːkəs] *n* muco.

mud [mʌd] *n* fango.

muddle ['mʌdl] *n* confusione *f*, disordine *m*; pasticcio ♦ *vt* (*also:* ~ **up**) mettere sottosopra; confondere; **to be in a** ~ (*person*) non riuscire a raccapezzarsi; **to get in a** ~ (*while explaining etc*) imbrogliarsi.
   muddle along *vi* andare avanti a casaccio.
   muddle through *vi* cavarsela alla meno peggio.

muddle-headed [mʌdl'hɛdɪd] *a* (*person*) confusionario(a).

muddy ['mʌdɪ] *a* fangoso(a).

mud flats *npl* distesa fangosa.

mudguard ['mʌdgɑːd] *n* parafango.

mudpack ['mʌdpæk] *n* maschera di fango.

mud-slinging ['mʌdslɪŋɪŋ] *n* (*fig*) infangamento.

muff [mʌf] *n* manicotto ♦ *vt* (*shot, catch etc*) mancare, sbagliare; **to** ~ **it** sbagliare tutto.

muffin ['mʌfɪn] *n* specie di pasticcino soffice da tè.

muffle ['mʌfl] *vt* (*sound*) smorzare, attutire; (*against cold*) imbacuccare.

muffled ['mʌfld] *a* smorzato(a), attutito(a).

muffler ['mʌflə*] *n* (*scarf*) sciarpa (pesante); (*US AUT*) marmitta; (*on motorbike*) silenziatore *m*.

mufti ['mʌftɪ] *n*: **in** ~ in borghese.

mug [mʌg] *n* (*cup*) tazzone *m*; (*for beer*) boccale *m*; (*col: face*) muso; (: *fool*) scemo/a ♦ *vt* (*assault*) assalire; **it's a** ~**'s game** (*Brit*) è proprio (una cosa) da fessi.
   mug up *vt* (*Brit col: also:* ~ **up on**) studiare bene.

mugger ['mʌgə*] *n* aggressore *m*.

mugging ['mʌgɪŋ] *n* aggressione *f* (a scopo di rapina).

muggy ['mʌgɪ] *a* afoso(a).

mulatto, ~es [mjuː'lætəu] *n* mulatto/a.

mulberry ['mʌlbərɪ] *n* (*fruit*) mora (di gelso); (*tree*) gelso, moro.

mule [mjuːl] *n* mulo.

mull [mʌl]: **to** ~ **over** *vt* rimuginare.

mulled [mʌld] *a*: ~ **wine** vino caldo.

multi... ['mʌltɪ] *prefix* multi....

multi-access [mʌltɪ'æksɛs] *a* (*COMPUT*) ad accesso multiplo.

multicoloured, (*US*) **multicolored** ['mʌltɪkʌləd] *a* multicolore, variopinto(a).

multifarious [mʌltɪ'fɛərɪəs] *a* molteplice, svariato(a).

multilateral [mʌltɪ'lætərəl] *a* (*POL*) multilaterale.

multi-level ['mʌltɪlɛvl] *a* (*US*) = **multistorey**.

multimillionaire [mʌltɪmɪljə'nɛə*] *n* multimiliardario/a.

multinational [mʌltɪ'næʃənl] *a*, *n* multinazionale (*f*).

multiple ['mʌltɪpl] *a* multiplo(a); molteplice ♦ *n* multiplo; (*Brit: also:* ~ **store**) *grande magazzino che fa parte di una catena*.

multiple choice *n* esercizi *mpl* a scelta multipla.

multiple crash *n* serie *f inv* di incidenti a catena.

multiple sclerosis *n* sclerosi *f* a placche.

multiplication [mʌltɪplɪ'keɪʃən] *n* moltiplicazione *f*.

multiplication table *n* tavola pitagorica.

multiplicity [mʌltɪ'plɪsɪtɪ] *n* molteplicità.

multiply ['mʌltɪplaɪ] *vt* moltiplicare ♦ *vi* moltiplicarsi.

multiracial [mʌltɪ'reɪʃəl] *a* multirazziale.

multistorey ['mʌltɪ'stɔːrɪ] *a* (*Brit: building, car park*) a più piani.

multitude ['mʌltɪtjuːd] *n* moltitudine *f*.

mum [mʌm] *n* (*Brit*) mamma ♦ *a*: **to keep** ~ non aprire bocca; ~**'s the word!** acqua in bocca!

mumble ['mʌmbl] *vt*, *vi* borbottare.

mummify ['mʌmɪfaɪ] *vt* mummificare.

mummy ['mʌmɪ] *n* (*Brit: mother*) mamma; (*embalmed*) mummia.

mumps [mʌmps] *n* orecchioni *mpl*.

munch [mʌntʃ] *vt*, *vi* sgranocchiare.

mundane [mʌn'deɪn] *a* terra a terra *inv*.

Munich ['mjuːnɪk] *n* Monaco *f* (di Baviera).

municipal [mjuː'nɪsɪpl] *a* municipale.

municipality [mju:nɪsɪ'pælɪtɪ] *n* municipio.
munitions [mju:'nɪʃənz] *npl* munizioni *fpl*.
mural ['mjuərəl] *n* dipinto murale.
murder ['mɜ:də*] *n* assassinio, omicidio ♦ *vt* assassinare; **to commit** ~ commettere un omicidio.
murderer ['mɜ:dərə*] *n* omicida *m*, assassino.
murderess ['mɜ:dərɪs] *n* omicida *f*, assassina.
murderous ['mɜ:dərəs] *a* micidiale.
murk [mɜ:k] *n* oscurità, buio.
murky ['mɜ:kɪ] *a* tenebroso(a), buio(a).
murmur ['mɜ:mə*] *n* mormorio ♦ *vt, vi* mormorare; **heart** ~ (*MED*) soffio al cuore.
MusB(ac) *n abbr* (= *Bachelor of Music*) *titolo di studio*.
muscle ['mʌsl] *n* muscolo.
  muscle in *vi* immischiarsi.
muscular ['mʌskjulə*] *a* muscolare; (*person, arm*) muscoloso(a).
MusD(oc) *n abbr* (= *Doctor of Music*) *titolo di studio*.
muse [mju:z] *vi* meditare, sognare ♦ *n* musa.
museum [mju:'zɪəm] *n* museo.
mush [mʌʃ] *n* pappa.
mushroom ['mʌʃrum] *n* fungo ♦ *vi* (*fig*) svilupparsi rapidamente.
music ['mju:zɪk] *n* musica.
musical ['mju:zɪkəl] *a* musicale ♦ *n* (*show*) commedia musicale.
music(al) box *n* carillon *m inv*.
musical instrument *n* strumento musicale.
music hall *n* teatro di varietà.
musician [mju:'zɪʃən] *n* musicista *m/f*.
music stand *n* leggio.
musk [mʌsk] *n* muschio.
musket ['mʌskɪt] *n* moschetto.
muskrat ['mʌskræt] *n* topo muschiato.
musk rose *n* (*BOT*) rosa muschiata.
Muslim ['mʌzlɪm] *a, n* musulmano(a).
muslin ['mʌzlɪn] *n* mussola.
musquash ['mʌskwɔʃ] *n* (*fur*) rat musqué *m inv*.
mussel ['mʌsl] *n* cozza.
must [mʌst] *auxiliary vb* (*obligation*): **I** ~ **do it** devo farlo; (*probability*): **he** ~ **be there by now** dovrebbe essere arrivato ormai; **I** ~ **have made a mistake** devo essermi sbagliato ♦ *n*: **this programme/trip is a** ~ è un programma/viaggio da non perdersi.
mustache ['mʌstæʃ] *n* (*US*) = **moustache**.
mustard ['mʌstəd] *n* senape *f*, mostarda.
mustard gas *n* iprite *f*.
muster ['mʌstə*] *vt* radunare; (*also:* ~ **up**: *strength, courage*) fare appello a.
mustiness ['mʌstɪnɪs] *n* odor di muffa *or* di stantio.
mustn't ['mʌsnt] = **must not**.
musty ['mʌstɪ] *a* che sa di muffa *or* di rinchiuso.
mutant ['mju:tənt] *a, n* mutante (*m*).
mutate [mju:'teɪt] *vi* subire una mutazione.
mutation [mju:'teɪʃən] *n* mutazione *f*.
mute [mju:t] *a, n* muto(a).
muted ['mju:tɪd] *a* (*noise*) attutito(a),

smorzato(a); (*criticism*) attenuato(a); (*MUS*) in sordina; (: *trumpet*) con sordina.
mutilate ['mju:tɪleɪt] *vt* mutilare.
mutilation [mju:tɪ'leɪʃən] *n* mutilazione *f*.
mutinous ['mju:tɪnəs] *a* (*troops*) ammutinato(a); (*attitude*) ribelle.
mutiny ['mju:tɪnɪ] *n* ammutinamento ♦ *vi* ammutinarsi.
mutter ['mʌtə*] *vt, vi* borbottare, brontolare.
mutton ['mʌtn] *n* carne *f* di montone.
mutual ['mju:tʃuəl] *a* mutuo(a), reciproco(a).
mutually ['mju:tʃuəlɪ] *ad* reciprocamente.
muzzle ['mʌzl] *n* muso; (*protective device*) museruola; (*of gun*) bocca ♦ *vt* mettere la museruola a.
MV *abbr* (= *motor vessel*) M/N, m/n.
MVP *n abbr* (*US SPORT:* = *most valuable player*) titolo ottenuto da sportivo.
MW *abbr* (*RADIO:* = *medium wave*) O.M.
my [maɪ] *a* il(la) mio(a), *pl* i(le) miei(mie).
myopic [maɪ'ɔpɪk] *a* miope.
myriad ['mɪrɪəd] *n* miriade *f*.
myself [maɪ'sɛlf] *pronoun* (*reflexive*) mi; (*emphatic*) io stesso(a); (*after prep*) me.
mysterious [mɪs'tɪərɪəs] *a* misterioso(a).
mystery ['mɪstərɪ] *n* mistero.
mystery story *n* racconto del mistero.
mystic ['mɪstɪk] *a, n* mistico(a).
mystical ['mɪstɪkəl] *a* mistico(a).
mystify ['mɪstɪfaɪ] *vt* mistificare; (*puzzle*) confondere.
mystique [mɪs'ti:k] *n* fascino.
myth [mɪθ] *n* mito.
mythical ['mɪθɪkəl] *a* mitico(a).
mythological [mɪθə'lɔdʒɪkl] *a* mitologico(a).
mythology [mɪ'θɔlədʒɪ] *n* mitologia.

N

N, n [ɛn] *n* (*letter*) N, n *f or m inv;* **N for Nellie,** (*US*) **N for Nan** ≈ N come Napoli.
N *abbr* (= *north*) N.
NA *n abbr* (*US:* = *Narcotics Anonymous*) *associazione in aiuto dei tossicodipendenti;* (*US*) = *National Academy.*
n/a *abbr* (= *not applicable*) non pertinente; (*COMM etc*) = *no account.*
NAACP *n abbr* (*US*) = *National Association for the Advancement of Colored People.*
NAAFI ['næfɪ] *n abbr* (*Brit:* = *Navy, Army & Air Force Institute*) *organizzazione che gestisce negozi, mense ecc. per il personale militare.*
nab [næb] *vt* (*col*) beccare, acchiappare.
NACU *n abbr* (*US*) = *National Association of Colleges and Universities.*
nadir ['neɪdɪə*] *n* (*ASTRONOMY*) nadir *m*; (*fig*)

punto più basso.

nag [næg] *n* (*pej*: *horse*) ronzino; (*person*) brontolone/a ♦ *vt* tormentare ♦ *vi* brontolare in continuazione.

nagging ['nægɪŋ] *a* (*doubt, pain*) persistente ♦ *n* brontolii *mpl*, osservazioni *fpl* continue.

nail [neɪl] *n* (*human*) unghia; (*metal*) chiodo ♦ *vt* inchiodare; **to ~ sb down to a date/price** costringere qn a un appuntamento/ad accettare un prezzo; **to pay cash on the ~** (*Brit*) pagare a tamburo battente.

nailbrush ['neɪlbrʌʃ] *n* spazzolino da *or* per unghie.

nailfile ['neɪlfaɪl] *n* lima da *or* per unghie.

nail polish *n* smalto da *or* per unghie.

nail polish remover *n* acetone *m*, solvente *m*.

nail scissors *npl* forbici *fpl* da *or* per unghie.

nail varnish *n* (*Brit*) = **nail polish.**

Nairobi [naɪˈraubɪ] *n* Nairobi *f*.

naïve [naɪˈiːv] *a* ingenuo(a).

naïveté [nɑːiːvˈteɪ], **naivety** [naɪˈiːvtɪ] *n* ingenuità *f inv*.

naked ['neɪkɪd] *a* nudo(a); **with the ~ eye** a occhio nudo.

nakedness ['neɪkɪdnɪs] *n* nudità.

NALGO ['nælgəu] *n abbr* (*Brit*: = *National and Local Government Officers' Association*) sindacato dei funzionari di governo nazionale e locale.

NAM *n abbr* (*US*) = *National Association of Manufacturers*.

name [neɪm] *n* nome *m*; (*reputation*) nome, reputazione *f* ♦ *vt* (*baby etc*) chiamare; (*person, object*) identificare; (*price, date*) fissare; **by ~** di nome; **she knows them all by ~** li conosce tutti per nome; **in the ~ of** in nome di; **what's your ~?** come si chiama?; **my ~ is Peter** mi chiamo Peter; **to take sb's ~ and address** prendere nome e indirizzo di qn; **to make a ~ for o.s.** farsi un nome; **to get (o.s.) a bad ~** farsi una cattiva fama *or* una brutta reputazione; **to call sb ~s** insultare qn.

name dropping *n menzionare qn o qc per fare bella figura*.

nameless ['neɪmlɪs] *a* senza nome.

namely ['neɪmlɪ] *ad* cioè.

nameplate ['neɪmpleɪt] *n* (*on door etc*) targa.

namesake ['neɪmseɪk] *n* omonimo.

nanny ['nænɪ] *n* bambinaia.

nanny goat *n* capra.

nap [næp] *n* (*sleep*) pisolino; (*of cloth*) peluria ♦ *vi*: **to be caught ~ping** essere preso alla sprovvista; **to have a ~** schiacciare un pisolino.

NAPA *n abbr* (*US*: = *National Association of Performing Artists*) associazione nazionale degli artisti di palcoscenico.

napalm ['neɪpɑːm] *n* napalm *m*.

nape [neɪp] *n*: **~ of the neck** nuca.

napkin ['næpkɪn] *n* tovagliolo; (*Brit*: *for baby*) pannolino.

Naples ['neɪplz] *n* Napoli *f*.

Napoleonic [nəpəulɪˈɔnɪk] *a* napoleonico(a).

nappy ['næpɪ] *n* (*Brit*) pannolino.

nappy liner *n* (*Brit*) fogliettino igienico.

narcissistic [nɑːsɪˈsɪstɪk] *a* narcisistico(a).

narcissus, *pl* **narcissi** [nɑːˈsɪsəs, -saɪ] *n* narciso.

narcotic [nɑːˈkɔtɪk] *n* (*MED*) narcotico; **~s** *npl* (*drugs*) narcotici, stupefacenti *mpl*.

nark [nɑːk] *vt* (*Brit col*) scocciare.

narrate [nəˈreɪt] *vt* raccontare, narrare.

narration [nəˈreɪʃən] *n* narrazione *f*.

narrative ['nærətɪv] *n* narrativa ♦ *a* narrativo(a).

narrator [nəˈreɪtə*] *n* narratore/trice.

narrow ['nærəu] *a* stretto(a); (*resources, means*) limitato(a), modesto(a); (*fig*): **to take a ~ view of** avere una visione limitata di ♦ *vi* restringersi; **to have a ~ escape** farcela per un pelo; **to ~ sth down to** ridurre qc a.

narrow gauge *a* (*RAIL*) a scartamento ridotto.

narrowly ['nærəulɪ] *ad*: **Maria ~ escaped drowning** per un pelo Maria non è affogata; **he ~ missed hitting the cyclist** per poco non ha investito il ciclista.

narrow-minded [nærəuˈmaɪndɪd] *a* meschino(a).

NAS *n abbr* (*US*) = *National Academy of Sciences*.

NASA ['næsə] *n abbr* (*US*: = *National Aeronautics and Space Administration*) N.A.S.A. *f*.

nasal ['neɪzl] *a* nasale.

Nassau ['næsɔ:] *n* Nassau *f*.

nastily ['nɑːstɪlɪ] *ad* con cattiveria.

nastiness ['nɑːstɪnɪs] *n* (*of person, remark*) cattiveria; (: *spitefulness*) malignità.

nasturtium [nəsˈtəːʃəm] *n* cappuccina, nasturzio (indiano).

nasty ['nɑːstɪ] *a* (*person, remark*) cattivo(a); (: *spiteful*) maligno(a); (*smell, wound, situation*) brutto(a); **to turn ~** (*situation*) mettersi male; (*weather*) guastarsi; (*person*) incattivirsi; **it's a ~ business** è una brutta faccenda, è un brutto affare.

NAS/UWT *n abbr* (*Brit*: = *National Association of Schoolmasters/Union of Women Teachers*) sindacato di insegnanti in Inghilterra e Galles.

nation ['neɪʃən] *n* nazione *f*.

national ['næʃənl] *a* nazionale ♦ *n* cittadino/a.

national anthem *n* inno nazionale.

national debt *n* debito pubblico.

national dress *n* costume *m* nazionale.

National Guard *n* (*US*) milizia nazionale (*volontaria, in ogni stato*).

National Health Service (NHS) *n* (*Brit*) servizio nazionale di assistenza sanitaria, ≈ S.A.U.B. *f*.

National Insurance *n* (*Brit*) ≈ Previdenza Sociale.

nationalism ['næʃnəlɪzəm] *n* nazionalismo.

nationalist ['næʃnəlɪst] *a, n* nazionalista (*m/f*).

nationality [næʃəˈnælɪtɪ] *n* nazionalità *f inv*.

nationalization [næʃnəlaɪ'zeɪʃən] *n* nazionalizzazione *f*.
nationalize ['næʃnəlaɪz] *vt* nazionalizzare.
nationally ['næʃnəlɪ] *ad* a livello nazionale.
national park *n* parco nazionale.
national press *n* stampa a diffusione nazionale.
National Security Council *n* (*US*) consiglio nazionale di sicurezza.
national service *n* (*MIL*) servizio militare.
nation-wide ['neɪʃənwaɪd] *a* diffuso(a) in tutto il paese ♦ *ad* in tutto il paese.
native ['neɪtɪv] *n* abitante *m/f* del paese; (*in colonies*) indigeno/a ♦ *a* indigeno(a); (*country*) natio(a); (*ability*) innato(a); **a ~ of Russia** un nativo della Russia; **a ~ speaker of French** una persona di madrelingua francese; **~ language** madrelingua.
Nativity [nə'tɪvɪtɪ] *n* (*REL*): **the ~** la Natività.
NATO ['neɪtəu] *n abbr* (= *North Atlantic Treaty Organization*) N.A.T.O. *f*.
NATSOPA [næt'səupə] *n abbr* (*Brit*: = *National Society of Operative Printers, Graphical and Media Personnel*) *sindacato dei tipografi, grafici e personale dei mass media*.
natter ['nætə*] (*Brit col*) *vi* chiacchierare ♦ *n* chiacchierata.
NATTKE *n abbr* (*Brit*: = *National Association of Television, Theatrical and Kinematographic Employees*) *sindacato dei dipendenti di televisione, teatro e cinema*.
natural ['nætʃrəl] *a* naturale; (*ability*) innato(a); (*manner*) semplice; **death from ~ causes** (*LAW*) morte *f* per cause naturali.
natural childbirth *n* parto indolore.
natural gas *n* gas *m* metano.
naturalist ['nætʃrəlɪst] *n* naturalista *m/f*.
naturalization [nætʃrəlaɪ'zeɪʃən] *n* naturalizzazione *f*; acclimatazione *f*.
naturalize ['nætʃrəlaɪz] *vt*: **to be ~d** (*person*) naturalizzarsi; **to become ~d** (*animal, plant*) acclimatarsi.
naturally ['nætʃrəlɪ] *ad* naturalmente; (*by nature: gifted*) di natura.
naturalness ['nætʃrəlnɪs] *n* naturalezza.
natural resources *npl* risorse *fpl* naturali.
natural wastage *n* (*INDUSTRY*) diminuzione *f* di manodopera (*per pensionamento, decesso etc*).
nature ['neɪtʃə*] *n* natura; (*character*) natura, indole *f*; **by ~** di natura; **documents of a confidential ~** documenti *mpl* di natura privata.
-natured ['neɪtʃəd] *suffix*: **ill~** maldisposto(a).
nature reserve *n* (*Brit*) parco naturale.
nature trail *n* percorso tracciato in parchi nazionali etc con scopi educativi.
naturist ['neɪtʃərɪst] *n* naturista *m/f*, nudista *m/f*.
naught [nɔ:t] *n* = **nought**.
naughtiness ['nɔ:tɪnɪs] *n* cattiveria.
naughty ['nɔ:tɪ] *a* (*child*) birichino(a), cattivello(a); (*story, film*) spinto(a).

nausea ['nɔ:sɪə] *n* (*MED*) nausea; (*fig: disgust*) schifo.
nauseate ['nɔ:sɪeɪt] *vt* nauseare; far schifo a.
nauseating ['nɔ:sɪeɪtɪŋ] *a* nauseante; (*fig*) disgustoso(a).
nauseous ['nɔ:sɪəs] *a* nauseabondo(a); (*feeling sick*): **to be ~** avere la nausea.
nautical ['nɔ:tɪkl] *a* nautico(a).
nautical mile *n* miglio nautico *or* marino.
naval ['neɪvl] *a* navale.
naval officer *n* ufficiale *m* di marina.
nave [neɪv] *n* navata centrale.
navel ['neɪvl] *n* ombelico.
navigable ['nævɪgəbl] *a* navigabile.
navigate ['nævɪgeɪt] *vt* percorrere navigando ♦ *vi* navigare; (*AUT*) fare da navigatore.
navigation [nævɪ'geɪʃən] *n* navigazione *f*.
navigator ['nævɪgeɪtə*] *n* (*NAUT, AVIAT*) ufficiale *m* di rotta; (*explorer*) navigatore *m*; (*AUT*) copilota *m/f*.
navvy ['nævɪ] *n* manovale *m*.
navy ['neɪvɪ] *n* marina; **Department of the N~** (*US*) Ministero della Marina.
navy(-blue) ['neɪvɪ('blu:)] *a* blu scuro *inv*.
Nazareth ['næzərɪθ] *n* Nazareth *f*.
Nazi ['nɑ:tsɪ] *a, n* nazista (*m/f*).
NB *abbr* (= *nota bene*) N.B.; (*Canada*) = *New Brunswick*.
NBA *n abbr* (*US*: = *National Basketball Association*) ≈ F.I.P. *f* (= *Federazione Italiana Pallacanestro*); = *National Boxing Association*.
NBC *n abbr* (*US*: = *National Broadcasting Company*) *compagnia nazionale di radiodiffusione*.
NBS *n abbr* (*US*: = *National Bureau of Standards*) *ufficio per la normalizzazione*.
NC *abbr* (*COMM etc*: = *no charge*) gratis; (*US POST*) = *North Carolina*.
NCB *n abbr* (*Brit*: *old*) = *National Coal Board*.
NCC *n abbr* (= *Nature Conservancy Council*) *organismo di protezione dei beni naturali*; (*US*) = *National Council of Churches*.
NCCL *n abbr* (*Brit*: = *National Council for Civil Liberties*) *associazione per la difesa delle libertà civili*.
NCO *n abbr see* **non-commissioned**.
ND *abbr* (*US POST*) = *North Dakota*.
NE *abbr* (*US POST*) = *Nebraska*; *New England*.
NEA *n abbr* (*US*) = *National Education Association*.
neap [ni:p] *n* (*also*: **~tide**) marea di quadratura.
Neapolitan [nɪə'pɒlɪtən] *a, n* napoletano(a).
near [nɪə*] *a* vicino(a); (*relation*) prossimo(a) ♦ *ad* vicino ♦ *prep* (*also*: **~ to**) vicino a, presso; (*time*) verso ♦ *vt* avvicinarsi a; **to come ~** avvicinarsi; **~ here/there** qui/lì vicino; **£25,000 or ~est offer** (*Brit*) 25.000 sterline trattabili; **in the ~ future** in un prossimo futuro; **the building is ~ing completion** il palazzo è quasi terminato *or* ultimato.

nearby [nɪə'baɪ] *a* vicino(a) ♦ *ad* vicino.

Near East *n*: **the** ~ il Medio Oriente.

nearer ['nɪərə*] *a* più vicino(a) ♦ *ad* più vicino.

nearly ['nɪəlɪ] *ad* quasi; **not** ~ non ... affatto; **I** ~ **lost it** per poco non lo perdevo; **she was** ~ **crying** era lì lì per piangere.

near miss *n*: **that was a** ~ c'è mancato poco.

nearness ['nɪənɪs] *n* vicinanza.

nearside ['nɪəsaɪd] *n* (*right-hand drive*) lato sinistro(a); (*left-hand drive*) lato destro ♦ *a* sinistro(a); destro(a).

near-sighted [nɪə'saɪtɪd] *a* miope.

neat [ni:t] *a* (*person, room*) ordinato(a); (*work*) pulito(a); (*solution, plan*) ben indovinato(a), azzeccato(a); (*spirits*) liscio(a).

neatly ['ni:tlɪ] *ad* con ordine; (*skilfully*) abilmente.

neatness ['ni:tnɪs] *n* (*tidiness*) ordine *m*; (*skilfulness*) abilità.

nebulous ['nɛbjuləs] *a* nebuloso(a); (*fig*) vago(a).

necessarily ['nɛsɪsrɪlɪ] *ad* necessariamente; **not** ~ non è detto, non necessariamente.

necessary ['nɛsɪsrɪ] *a* necessario(a); **if** ~ se necessario.

necessitate [nɪ'sɛsɪteɪt] *vt* rendere necessario(a).

necessity [nɪ'sɛsɪtɪ] *n* necessità *f inv*; **in case of** ~ in caso di necessità.

neck [nɛk] *n* collo; (*of garment*) colletto ♦ *vi* (*col*) pomiciare, sbaciucchiarsi; ~ **and** ~ testa a testa; **to stick one's** ~ **out** (*col*) rischiare (forte).

necklace ['nɛklɪs] *n* collana.

neckline ['nɛklaɪn] *n* scollatura.

necktie ['nɛktaɪ] *n* (*esp US*) cravatta.

nectar ['nɛktə*] *n* nettare *m*.

nectarine ['nɛktərɪn] *n* nocepesca.

NEDC *n abbr* (*Brit*: = *National Economic Development Council*) ≈ C.N.E.L. *m* (= *Consiglio Nazionale dell'Economia e del Lavoro*).

Neddy ['nɛdɪ] *n abbr* (*Brit col*) = **NEDC**.

née [neɪ] *a*: ~ **Scott** nata Scott.

need [ni:d] *n* bisogno ♦ *vt* aver bisogno di; **I** ~ **to do it** lo devo fare, bisogna che io lo faccia; **you don't** ~ **to go** non deve andare, non c'è bisogno che lei vada; **a signature is** ~**ed** occorre *or* ci vuole una firma; **to be in** ~ **of, have** ~ **of** aver bisogno di; **£10 will meet my immediate** ~**s** 10 sterline mi basteranno per le necessità più urgenti; **in case of** ~ in caso di bisogno *or* necessità; **there's no** ~ **for** ... non c'è bisogno *or* non occorre che ...; **there's no** ~ **to do** ... non occorre fare ...; **the** ~**s of industry** le esigenze dell'industria.

needle ['ni:dl] *n* ago; (*on record player*) puntina ♦ *vt* pungere.

needlecord ['ni:dlkɔ:d] *n* (*Brit*) velluto a coste sottili.

needless ['ni:dlɪs] *a* inutile; ~ **to say,** ... inutile dire che ....

needlessly ['ni:dlɪslɪ] *ad* inutilmente.

needlework ['ni:dlwə:k] *n* cucito.

needn't ['ni:dnt] = **need not**.

needy ['ni:dɪ] *a* bisognoso(a).

negation [nɪ'geɪʃən] *n* negazione *f*.

negative ['nɛgətɪv] *n* (*PHOT*) negativa, negativo; (*ELEC*) polo negativo; (*LING*) negazione *f* ♦ *a* negativo(a); **to answer in the** ~ rispondere negativamente *or* di no.

neglect [nɪ'glɛkt] *vt* trascurare ♦ *n* (*of person, duty*) negligenza; **state of** ~ stato di abbandono; **to** ~ **to do sth** trascurare *or* tralasciare di fare qc.

neglected [nɪ'glɛktɪd] *a* trascurato(a).

neglectful [nɪ'glɛktful] *a* (*gen*) negligente; **to be** ~ **of sb/sth** trascurare qn/qc.

negligee ['nɛglɪʒeɪ] *n* négligé *m inv*.

negligence ['nɛglɪdʒəns] *n* negligenza.

negligent ['nɛglɪdʒənt] *a* negligente.

negligently ['nɛglɪdʒəntlɪ] *ad* con negligenza.

negligible ['nɛglɪdʒɪbl] *a* insignificante, trascurabile.

negotiable [nɪ'gəufɪəbl] *a* negoziabile; (*cheque*) trasferibile; (*road*) transitabile.

negotiate [nɪ'gəufɪeɪt] *vi* negoziare ♦ *vt* (*COMM*) negoziare; (*obstacle*) superare; (*bend in road*) prendere; **to** ~ **with sb for sth** trattare con qn per ottenere qc.

negotiation [nɪgəufɪ'eɪʃən] *n* trattativa; (*POL*) negoziato; **to enter into** ~**s with sb** entrare in trattative (*or* intavolare i negoziati) con qn.

negotiator [nɪ'gəufɪeɪtə*] *n* negoziatore/trice.

Negress ['ni:grɪs] *n* negra.

Negro ['ni:grəu] *a, n* (*pl* ~**es**) negro(a).

neigh [neɪ] *vi* nitrire.

neighbour, (*US*) **neighbor** ['neɪbə*] *n* vicino/a.

neighbo(u)rhood ['neɪbəhud] *n* vicinato.

neighbo(u)ring ['neɪbərɪŋ] *a* vicino(a).

neighbo(u)rly ['neɪbəlɪ] *a*: **he is a** ~ **person** è un buon vicino.

neither ['naɪðə*] *a, pronoun* né l'uno(a) né l'altro(a), nessuno(a) dei(delle) due ♦ *cj* neanche, nemmeno, neppure ♦ *ad*: ~ **good nor bad** né buono né cattivo; **I didn't move and** ~ **did Claude** io non mi mossi e nemmeno Claude; ... ~ **did I refuse** ..., ma non ho nemmeno rifiutato.

neo... ['ni:əu] *prefix* neo...

neolithic [ni:əu'lɪθɪk] *a* neolitico(a).

neologism [nɪ'ɔlədʒɪzəm] *n* neologismo.

neon ['ni:ɔn] *n* neon *m*.

neon light *n* luce *f* al neon.

neon sign *n* insegna al neon.

Nepal [nɪ'pɔ:l] *n* Nepal *m*.

nephew ['nɛvju:] *n* nipote *m*.

nepotism ['nɛpətɪzəm] *n* nepotismo.

nerve [nə:v] *n* nervo; (*fig*) coraggio; (*impudence*) faccia tosta; **he gets on my** ~**s** mi dà ai nervi, mi fa venire i nervi; **a fit of** ~**s** una crisi di nervi; **to lose one's** ~ (*self-confidence*) perdere fiducia in se stesso; **I lost my** ~ (*courage*) mi è mancato il coraggio.

nerve centre *n* (*ANAT*) centro nervoso; (*fig*)

cervello, centro vitale.

nerve gas *n* gas *m* nervino.

nerve-racking ['nɔːvrækɪŋ] *a* che spezza i nervi.

nervous ['nɔːvəs] *a* nervoso(a).

nervous breakdown *n* esaurimento nervoso.

nervously ['nɔːvəslɪ] *ad* nervosamente.

nervousness ['nɔːvəsnɪs] *n* nervosismo.

nest [nɛst] *n* nido; ~ **of tables** tavolini *mpl* cicogna *inv*.

nest egg *n* (*fig*) gruzzolo.

nestle ['nɛsl] *vi* accoccolarsi.

nestling ['nɛslɪŋ] *n* uccellino di nido.

net [nɛt] *n* rete *f*; (*fabric*) tulle *m* ♦ *a* netto(a) ♦ *vt* (*subj*: *person*) ricavare un utile netto di; (*deal, sale*) dare un utile netto di; ~ **of tax** netto, al netto di tasse; **he earns £10,000** ~ **per year** guadagna 10.000 sterline nette all'anno.

netball ['nɛtbɔːl] *n* specie di pallacanestro.

net curtains *npl* tende *fpl* di tulle.

Netherlands ['nɛðələndz] *npl*: **the** ~ i Paesi Bassi.

net profit *n* utile *m* netto.

nett [nɛt] *a* = **net**.

netting ['nɛtɪŋ] *n* (*for fence etc*) reticolato; (*fabric*) tulle *m*.

nettle ['nɛtl] *n* ortica.

network ['nɛtwɔːk] *n* rete *f*.

neuralgia [njuə'rældʒə] *n* nevralgia.

neurosis, *pl* **neuroses** [njuə'rəusɪs, -siːz] *n* nevrosi *f inv*.

neurotic [njuə'rɔtɪk] *a*, *n* nevrotico(a).

neuter ['njuːtə*] *a* neutro(a) ♦ *n* neutro ♦ *vt* (*cat etc*) castrare.

neutral ['njuːtrəl] *a* neutro(a); (*person, nation*) neutrale ♦ *n* (*AUT*): **in** ~ in folle.

neutrality [njuː'trælɪtɪ] *n* neutralità.

neutralize ['njuːtrəlaɪz] *vt* neutralizzare.

neutron bomb ['njuːtrɔn-] *n* bomba al neutrone.

never ['nɛvə*] *ad* (non...) mai; ~ **again** mai più; **I'll** ~ **go there again** non ci vado più; ~ **in my life** mai in vita mia; *see also* **mind**.

never-ending [nɛvər'ɛndɪŋ] *a* interminabile.

nevertheless [nɛvəðə'lɛs] *ad* tuttavia, ciò nonostante, ciò nondimeno.

new [njuː] *a* nuovo(a); (*brand new*) nuovo(a) di zecca; **as good as** ~ come nuovo.

newborn ['njuːbɔːn] *a* neonato(a).

newcomer ['njuːkʌmə*] *n* nuovo(a) venuto(a).

new-fangled ['njuːfæŋgld] *a* (*pej*) stramoderno(a).

new-found ['njuːfaund] *a* nuovo(a).

Newfoundland ['njuːfənlənd] *n* Terranova.

New Guinea *n* Nuova Guinea.

newly ['njuːlɪ] *ad* di recente.

newly-weds ['njuːlɪwɛdz] *npl* sposini *mpl*, sposi *mpl* novelli.

new moon *n* luna nuova.

newness ['njuːnɪs] *n* novità.

news [njuːz] *n* notizie *fpl*; (*RADIO*) giornale *m* radio; (*TV*) telegiornale *m*; **a piece of** ~ una notizia; **good/bad** ~ buone/cattive notizie;

financial ~ (*PRESS*) pagina economica e finanziaria; (*RADIO, TV*) notiziario economico.

news agency *n* agenzia di stampa.

newsagent ['njuːzeɪdʒənt] *n* (*Brit*) giornalaio.

news bulletin *n* (*RADIO, TV*) notiziario.

newscaster ['njuːzkɑːstə*] *n* (*RADIO, TV*) annunciatore/trice.

newsdealer ['njuːzdiːlə*] *n* (*US*) = **newsagent**.

newsflash ['njuːzflæʃ] *n* notizia *f* lampo *inv*.

newsletter ['njuːzlɛtə*] *n* bollettino (*di ditta, associazione*).

newspaper ['njuːzpeɪpə*] *n* giornale *m*; **daily** ~ quotidiano; **weekly** ~ settimanale *m*.

newsprint ['njuːzprɪnt] *n* carta da giornale.

newsreader ['njuːzriːdə*] *n* = **newscaster**.

newsreel ['njuːzriːl] *n* cinegiornale *m*.

newsroom ['njuːzrum] *n* (*PRESS*) redazione *f*; (*RADIO, TV*) studio.

news stand *n* edicola.

newt [njuːt] *n* tritone *m*.

New Year *n* Anno Nuovo; **Happy** ~! Buon Anno!; **to wish sb a happy** ~ augurare Buon Anno a qn.

New Year's Day *n* il Capodanno.

New Year's Eve *n* la vigilia di Capodanno.

New York [-'jɔːk] *n* New York *f*, Nuova York *f*; (*also*: ~ **State**) stato di New York.

New Zealand [-'ziːlənd] *n* Nuova Zelanda ♦ *a* neozelandese.

New Zealander [-'ziːləndə*] *n* neozelandese *m/f*.

next [nɛkst] *a* prossimo(a) ♦ *ad* accanto; (*in time*) dopo; ~ **to** *prep* accanto a; ~ **to nothing** quasi niente; ~ **time** *ad* la prossima volta; ~ **week** la settimana prossima; **the** ~ **week** la settimana dopo *or* seguente; **the week after** ~ fra due settimane; **the** ~ **day** il giorno dopo, l'indomani; ~ **year** l'anno prossimo *or* venturo; **"turn to the** ~ **page"** "vedi pagina seguente"; **who's** ~? a chi tocca?; **when do we meet** ~? quando ci rincontriamo?

next door *ad* accanto.

next of kin *n* parente *m/f* prossimo(a).

NF *n abbr* (*Brit POL*: = *National Front*) partito di estrema destra ♦ *abbr* (*Canada*) = **Newfoundland**.

NFL *n abbr* (*US*) = *National Football League*.

NFU *n abbr* (*Brit*: = *National Farmers' Union*) sindacato nazionale degli agricoltori.

NG *abbr* (*US*) = **National Guard**.

NGA *n abbr* (*Brit*: = *National Graphical Association*) sindacato nazionale dei grafici.

NGO *n abbr* (*US*) = *non-governmental organization*.

NH *abbr* (*US POST*) = *New Hampshire*.

NHL *n abbr* (*US*: = *National Hockey League*) ≈ F.I.H.P. *f* (= *Federazione Italiana Hockey e Pattinaggio*).

NHS *n abbr* (*Brit*) *see* **National Health Service**.

NI *abbr* = **Northern Ireland**; (*Brit*) = **National**

Insurance.
Niagara Falls [naɪ'ægərə-] npl: **the** ~ le cascate del Niagara.
nib [nɪb] n (of pen) pennino.
nibble ['nɪbl] vt mordicchiare.
Nicaragua [nɪkə'rægjuə] n Nicaragua m.
Nicaraguan [nɪkə'rægjuən] a, n nicaraguense (m/f).
Nice [ni:s] n Nizza.
nice [naɪs] a (holiday, trip) piacevole; (flat, picture) bello(a); (person) simpatico(a), gentile; (taste, smell, meal) buono(a); (distinction, point) sottile.
nice-looking ['naɪslukɪŋ] a bello(a).
nicely ['naɪslɪ] ad bene; **that will do** ~ andrà benissimo.
niceties ['naɪsɪtɪz] npl finezze fpl.
niche [ni:ʃ] n (ARCHIT) nicchia.
nick [nɪk] n tacca ♦ vt intaccare; tagliare; (col: steal) rubare; (: Brit: arrest) beccare; **in the** ~ **of time** appena in tempo; **in good** ~ (Brit col) decente, in buono stato; **to** ~ **o.s.** farsi un taglietto.
nickel ['nɪkl] n nichel m; (US) moneta da cinque centesimi di dollaro.
nickname ['nɪkneɪm] n soprannome m ♦ vt soprannominare.
Nicosia [nɪkə'si:ə] n Nicosia.
nicotine ['nɪkəti:n] n nicotina.
niece [ni:s] n nipote f.
nifty ['nɪftɪ] a (col: car, jacket) chic inv; (: gadget, tool) ingegnoso(a).
Niger ['naɪdʒə*] n Niger m.
Nigeria [naɪ'dʒɪərɪə] n Nigeria.
Nigerian [naɪ'dʒɪərɪən] a, n nigeriano(a).
niggardly ['nɪgədlɪ] a (person) tirchio(a), spilorcio(a); (allowance, amount) misero(a).
nigger ['nɪgə*] n (col!: highly offensive) negro/a.
niggle ['nɪgl] vt assillare ♦ vi fare il(la) pignolo(a).
niggling ['nɪglɪŋ] a pignolo(a); (detail) insignificante; (doubt, pain) persistente.
night [naɪt] n notte f; (evening) sera; **at** ~ la notte; la sera; **by** ~ di notte; **in the** ~, **during the** ~ durante la notte; **the** ~ **before last** l'altro ieri notte; l'altro ieri sera.
night-bird ['naɪtbə:d] n uccello notturno; (fig) nottambulo/a.
nightcap ['naɪtkæp] n bicchierino prima di andare a letto.
night club n locale m notturno.
nightdress ['naɪtdrɛs] n camicia da notte.
nightfall ['naɪtfɔ:l] n crepuscolo.
nightie ['naɪtɪ] n camicia da notte.
nightingale ['naɪtɪŋgeɪl] n usignolo.
night life n vita notturna.
nightly ['naɪtlɪ] a di ogni notte or sera; (by night) notturno(a) ♦ ad ogni notte or sera.
nightmare ['naɪtmɛə*] n incubo.
night porter n portiere m di notte.
night safe n cassa continua.
night school n scuola serale.
nightshade ['naɪtʃeɪd] n: **deadly** ~ (BOT)

belladonna.
nightshift ['naɪtʃɪft] n turno di notte.
night-time ['naɪttaɪm] n notte f.
night watchman n guardiano notturno.
nihilism ['naɪɪlɪzəm] n nichilismo.
nil [nɪl] n nulla m; (SPORT) zero.
Nile [naɪl] n: **the** ~ il Nilo.
nimble ['nɪmbl] a agile.
nine [naɪn] num nove.
nineteen [naɪn'ti:n] num diciannove.
ninety ['naɪntɪ] num novanta.
ninth [naɪnθ] num nono(a).
nip [nɪp] vt pizzicare ♦ vi (Brit col): **to** ~ **out/down/up** fare un salto fuori/giù/di sopra ♦ n (pinch) pizzico; (drink) goccio, bicchierino.
nipple ['nɪpl] n (ANAT) capezzolo.
nippy ['nɪpɪ] a (weather) pungente; (Brit: car, person) svelto(a).
nit [nɪt] n (of louse) lendine m; (col: idiot) cretino/a, scemo/a.
nit-pick ['nɪtpɪk] vi (col) cercare il pelo nell'uovo.
nitrogen ['naɪtrədʒən] n azoto.
nitroglycerin(e) [naɪtrəu'glɪsəri:n] n nitroglicerina.
nitty-gritty ['nɪtɪ'grɪtɪ] n (col): **to get down to the** ~ venire al sodo.
nitwit ['nɪtwɪt] n (col) scemo/a.
NJ abbr (US POST) = New Jersey.
NLF n abbr (= National Liberation Front) ≈ F.L.N. m.
NLQ abbr (= near letter quality) qualità quasi di corrispondenza.
NLRB n abbr (US: = National Labor Relations Board) organismo per la tutela dei lavoratori.
NM abbr (US POST) = New Mexico.
no [nəu] a nessuno(a), non; **I have** ~ **money** non ho soldi; **there is** ~ **reason to believe ...** non c'è nessuna ragione per credere ...; **I have** ~ **books** non ho libri ♦ ad non; **I have** ~ **more wine** non ho più vino ♦ excl, n no (m inv); **"~ entry"** "vietata l'entrata"; **I won't take** ~ **for an answer** non accetterò un rifiuto; **"~ dogs"** "vietato l'accesso ai cani".
no. abbr (= number) n.
nobble ['nɔbl] vt (Brit col: bribe: person) comprare, corrompere; (: person to speak to, criminal) bloccare, beccare; (RACING: horse, dog) drogare.
Nobel prize [nəu'bɛl-] n premio Nobel.
nobility [nəu'bɪlɪtɪ] n nobiltà.
noble ['nəubl] a, n nobile (m).
nobleman ['nəublmən] n nobile m, nobiluomo.
nobly ['nəublɪ] ad (selflessly) generosamente.
nobody ['nəubədɪ] pronoun nessuno.
no-claims bonus ['nəukleɪmz-] n bonus malus m inv.
nocturnal [nɔk'tə:nl] a notturno(a).
nod [nɔd] vi accennare col capo, fare un cenno; (sleep) sonnecchiare ♦ vt: **to** ~ **one's head** fare di sì col capo ♦ n cenno; **they** ~**ded their agreement** accennarono di sì (col capo).

nod off *vi* assopirsi.
noise [nɔɪz] *n* rumore *m*; (*din, racket*) chiasso.
noiseless ['nɔɪzlɪs] *a* silenzioso(a).
noisily ['nɔɪzɪlɪ] *ad* rumorosamente.
noisy ['nɔɪzɪ] *a* (*street, car*) rumoroso(a); (*person*) chiassoso(a).
nomad ['nəʊmæd] *n* nomade *m/f*.
nomadic [nəʊ'mædɪk] *a* nomade.
no man's land *n* terra di nessuno.
nominal ['nɔmɪnl] *a* nominale.
nominate ['nɔmɪneɪt] *vt* (*propose*) proporre come candidato; (*elect*) nominare.
nomination [nɔmɪ'neɪʃən] *n* nomina; candidatura.
nominee [nɔmɪ'niː] *n* persona nominata; candidato/a.
non... [nɔn] *prefix* non....
non-alcoholic ['nɔnælkə'hɔlɪk] *a* analcolico(a).
non-breakable [nɔn'breɪkəbl] *a* infrangibile.
nonce word ['nɔns-] *n* parola coniata per l'occasione.
nonchalant ['nɔnʃələnt] *a* incurante, indifferente.
non-commissioned [nɔnkə'mɪʃnd] *a*: ~ officer (NCO) sottufficiale *m*.
non-committal [nɔnkə'mɪtl] *a* evasivo(a).
nonconformist [nɔnkən'fɔːmɪst] *n* anticonformista *m/f*; (*Brit REL*) dissidente *m/f* ♦ *a* anticonformista.
non-contributory [nɔnkən'trɪbjutərɪ] *a*: ~ pension scheme *or* (US) plan *sistema di pensionamento con i contributi interamente a carico del datore di lavoro*.
non-cooperation ['nɔnkəʊɔpə'reɪʃən] *n* non cooperazione *f*, non collaborazione *f*.
nondescript ['nɔndɪskrɪpt] *a* qualunque *inv*.
none [nʌn] *pronoun* (*not one thing*) niente; (*not one person*) nessuno(a); ~ of you nessuno(a) di voi; I have ~ non ne ho nemmeno uno; I have ~ left non ne ho più; ~ at all proprio niente; (*not one*) nemmeno uno; he's ~ the worse for it non ne ha risentito.
nonentity [nɔ'nɛntɪtɪ] *n* persona insignificante.
non-essential [nɔnɪ'sɛnʃl] *a* non essenziale ♦ *n*: ~s superfluo, cose *fpl* superflue.
nonetheless ['nʌnðə'lɛs] *ad* nondimeno.
non-executive [nɔnɪg'zɛkjutɪv] *a*: ~ director direttore *m* senza potere esecutivo.
non-existent [nɔnɪg'zɪstənt] *a* inesistente.
non-fiction [nɔn'fɪkʃən] *n* saggistica.
non-flammable [nɔn'flæməbl] *a* ininfiammabile.
non-intervention ['nɔnɪntə'vɛnʃən] *n* non intervento.
non obst. *abbr* (= non obstante: *notwithstanding*) nonostante.
non-payment [nɔn'peɪmənt] *n* mancato pagamento.
nonplussed [nɔn'plʌst] *a* sconcertato(a).
non-profit-making [nɔn'prɔfɪtmeɪkɪŋ] *a* senza scopo di lucro.
nonsense ['nɔnsəns] *n* sciocchezze *fpl*; ~! che

sciocchezze!, che assurdità!; it is ~ to say that ... è un'assurdità *or* non ha senso dire che ....
non-shrink [nɔn'ʃrɪŋk] *a* (*Brit*) irrestringibile.
non-skid [nɔn'skɪd] *a* antisdrucciolo(a).
non-smoker ['nɔn'sməukə*] *n* non fumatore/trice.
non-stick ['nɔn'stɪk] *a* antiaderente, antiadesivo(a).
non-stop ['nɔn'stɔp] *a* continuo(a); (*train, bus*) direttissimo(a) ♦ *ad* senza sosta.
non-taxable [nɔn'tæksəbl] *a*: ~ income reddito non imponibile.
non-U [nɔn'juː] *a abbr* (*Brit col*) = non-upper class.
non-volatile [nɔn'vɔlətaɪl] *a*: ~ memory (*COMPUT*) memoria permanente.
non-voting [nɔn'vəutɪŋ] *a*: ~ shares azioni *fpl* senza diritto di voto.
non-white ['nɔn'waɪt] *a* di colore ♦ *n* persona di colore.
noodles ['nuːdlz] *npl* taglierini *mpl*.
nook [nuk] *n*: ~s and crannies angoli *mpl*.
noon [nuːn] *n* mezzogiorno.
no one ['nəuwʌn] *pronoun* = nobody.
noose [nuːs] *n* nodo scorsoio, cappio; (*hangman's*) cappio.
nor [nɔː*] *cj* = neither ♦ *ad see* neither.
Norf *abbr* (*Brit*) = Norfolk.
norm [nɔːm] *n* norma.
normal ['nɔːml] *a* normale ♦ *n*: to return to ~ tornare alla normalità.
normality [nɔː'mælɪtɪ] *n* normalità.
normally ['nɔːməlɪ] *ad* normalmente.
Normandy ['nɔːməndɪ] *n* Normandia.
north [nɔːθ] *n* nord *m*, settentrione *m* ♦ *a* nord *inv*, del nord, settentrionale ♦ *ad* verso nord.
North Africa *n* Africa del Nord.
North African *a, n* nordafricano(a).
North America *n* America del Nord.
North American *a, n* nordamericano(a).
Northants [nɔː'θænts] *abbr* (*Brit*) = Northamptonshire.
northbound ['nɔːθbaund] *a* (*traffic*) diretto(a) a nord; (*carriageway*) nord *inv*.
Northd *abbr* (*Brit*) = Northumberland.
north-east [nɔːθ'iːst] *n* nord-est *m*.
northerly ['nɔːðəlɪ] *a* (*wind*) del nord; (*direction*) verso nord.
northern ['nɔːðən] *a* del nord, settentrionale.
Northern Ireland *n* Irlanda del Nord.
North Pole *n*: the ~ il Polo Nord.
North Sea *n*: the ~ il mare del Nord.
North Sea oil *n* petrolio del mare del Nord.
northward(s) ['nɔːθwəd(z)] *ad* verso nord.
north-west [nɔːθ'wɛst] *n* nord-ovest *m*.
Norway ['nɔːweɪ] *n* Norvegia.
Norwegian [nɔː'wiːdʒən] *a* norvegese ♦ *n* norvegese *m/f*; (*LING*) norvegese *m*.
nos. *abbr* (= numbers) nn.
nose [nəuz] *n* naso; (*of animal*) muso ♦ *vi* (*also*: ~ one's way) avanzare cautamente; to pay through the ~ (for sth) (*col*) pagare (qc) un occhio della testa.

nose about, nose around *vi* aggirarsi.
nosebleed ['nəuzbli:d] *n* emorragia nasale.
nose-dive ['nəuzdaɪv] *n* picchiata.
nose drops *npl* gocce *fpl* per il naso.
nosey ['nəuzɪ] *a* curioso(a).
nostalgia [nɔs'tældʒɪə] *n* nostalgia.
nostalgic [nɔs'tældʒɪk] *a* nostalgico(a).
nostril ['nɔstrɪl] *n* narice *f*; (*of horse*) frogia.
nosy ['nəuzɪ] *a* = **nosey**.
not [nɔt] *ad* non; ~ **at all** niente affatto; (*after thanks*) prego, s'immagini; **you must** ~ *or* **mustn't do this** non deve fare questo; **he isn't** ... egli non è ...; **I hope** ~ spero di no.
notable ['nəutəbl] *a* notevole.
notably ['nəutəblɪ] *ad* notevolmente; (*in particular*) in particolare.
notary ['nəutərɪ] *n* (*also*: ~ **public**) notaio.
notation [nəu'teɪʃən] *n* notazione *f*.
notch [nɔtʃ] *n* tacca.
  notch up *vt* (*score, victory*) marcare, segnare.
note [nəut] *n* nota; (*letter, banknote*) biglietto ♦ *vt* prendere nota di; **to take** ~ **of** prendere nota di; **to take** ~**s** prendere appunti; **to compare** ~**s** (*fig*) scambiarsi le impressioni; **of** ~ eminente, importante; **just a quick** ~ **to let you know** ... ti scrivo solo due righe per informarti ....
notebook ['nəutbuk] *n* taccuino; (*for shorthand*) bloc-notes *m inv*.
note-case ['nəutkeɪs] *n* (*Brit*) portafoglio.
noted ['nəutɪd] *a* celebre.
notepad ['nəutpæd] *n* bloc-notes *m inv*, blocchetto.
notepaper ['nəutpeɪpə*] *n* carta da lettere.
noteworthy ['nəutwə:ðɪ] *a* degno(a) di nota, importante.
nothing ['nʌθɪŋ] *n* nulla *m*, niente *m*; **he does** ~ non fa niente; ~ **new** niente di nuovo; **for** ~ (*free*) per niente; ~ **at all** proprio niente.
notice ['nəutɪs] *n* avviso; (*of leaving*) preavviso; (*Brit: review: of play etc*) critica, recensione *f* ♦ *vt* notare, accorgersi di; **to take** ~ **of** fare attenzione a; **to bring sth to sb's** ~ far notare qc a qn; **to give sb** ~ **of sth** avvisare qn di qc; **to give** ~, **hand in one's** ~ (*subj: employee*) licenziarsi; **without** ~ senza preavviso; **at short** ~ con un breve preavviso; **until further** ~ fino a nuovo avviso; **advance** ~ preavviso; **to escape** *or* **avoid** ~ passare inosservato; **it has come to my** ~ **that** ... sono venuto a sapere che ....
noticeable ['nəutɪsəbl] *a* evidente.
notice board *n* (*Brit*) tabellone *m* per affissi.
notification [nəutɪfɪ'keɪʃən] *n* annuncio; notifica; denuncia.
notify ['nəutɪfaɪ] *vt*: **to** ~ **sth to sb** notificare qc a qn; **to** ~ **sb of sth** avvisare qn di qc; (*police*) denunciare qc a qn.
notion ['nəuʃən] *n* idea; (*concept*) nozione *f*.
notions ['nəuʃənz] *npl* (*US: haberdashery*) merceria.
notoriety [nəutə'raɪətɪ] *n* notorietà.
notorious [nəu'tɔ:rɪəs] *a* famigerato(a).

notoriously [nəu'tɔ:rɪəslɪ] *ad* notoriamente.
Notts [nɔts] *abbr* (*Brit*) = *Nottinghamshire*.
notwithstanding [nɔtwɪθ'stændɪŋ] *ad* nondimeno ♦ *prep* nonostante, malgrado.
nougat ['nu:gɑ:] *n* torrone *m*.
nought [nɔ:t] *n* zero.
noun [naun] *n* nome *m*, sostantivo.
nourish ['nʌrɪʃ] *vt* nutrire.
nourishing ['nʌrɪʃɪŋ] *a* nutriente.
nourishment ['nʌrɪʃmənt] *n* nutrimento.
Nov. *abbr* (= *November*) nov.
Nova Scotia ['nəuvə'skəuʃə] *n* Nuova Scozia.
novel ['nɔvl] *n* romanzo ♦ *a* nuovo(a).
novelist ['nɔvəlɪst] *n* romanziere/a.
novelty ['nɔvəltɪ] *n* novità *f inv*.
November [nəu'vɛmbə*] *n* novembre *m*; *for phrases see also* **July**.
novice ['nɔvɪs] *n* principiante *m/f*; (*REL*) novizio/a.
NOW [nau] *n abbr* (*US*: = *National Organization for Women*) ≈ U.D.I. *f* (= *Unione Donne Italiane*).
now [nau] *ad* ora, adesso; ♦ *cj*: ~ (**that**) adesso che, ora che; **right** ~ subito; **by** ~ ormai; **just** ~: **that's the fashion just** ~ è la moda del momento; **I saw her just** ~ l'ho vista proprio adesso; **I'll read it just** ~ lo leggo subito; ~ **and then,** ~ **and again** ogni tanto; **from** ~ **on** da ora in poi; **in 3 days from** ~ fra 3 giorni; **between** ~ **and Monday** da qui a lunedì, entro lunedì; **that's all for** ~ per ora basta.
nowadays ['nauədeɪz] *ad* oggidì.
nowhere ['nəuwɛə*] *ad* in nessun luogo, da nessuna parte; ~ **else** in nessun altro posto.
noxious ['nɔkʃəs] *a* nocivo(a).
nozzle ['nɔzl] *n* (*of hose etc*) boccaglio.
NP *n abbr* = **notary public**.
NS *abbr* (*Canada*) = **Nova Scotia**.
NSC *n abbr* (*US*) = **National Security Council**.
NSF *n abbr* (*US*) = *National Science Foundation*.
NSPCC *n abbr* (*Brit*) = *National Society for the Prevention of Cruelty to Children*.
NSW (*Australia*) = *New South Wales*.
NT *n abbr* (= *New Testament*) N.T.
nth [ɛnθ] *a*: **for the** ~ **time** (*col*) per l'ennesima volta.
NUAAW *n abbr* (*Brit*: = *National Union of Agricultural and Allied Workers*) sindacato nazionale dei lavoratori agricoli.
nuance ['nju:ɑ:ns] *n* sfumatura.
NUBE *n abbr* (*Brit*: = *National Union of Bank Employees*) sindacato nazionale dei bancari.
nubile ['nju:baɪl] *a* nubile; (*attractive*) giovane e desiderabile.
nuclear ['nju:klɪə*] *a* nucleare; (*warfare*) atomico(a).
nuclear disarmament *n* disarmo nucleare.
nucleus, pl nuclei ['nju:klɪəs, 'nju:klɪaɪ] *n* nucleo.
nude [nju:d] *a* nudo(a) ♦ *n* (*ART*) nudo; **in the** ~ tutto(a) nudo(a).

nudge [nʌdʒ] *vt* dare una gomitata a.
nudist ['nju:dɪst] *n* nudista *m/f*.
nudist colony *n* colonia di nudisti.
nudity ['nju:dɪtɪ] *n* nudità.
nugget ['nʌgɪt] *n* pepita.
nuisance ['nju:sns] *n*: **it's a** ~ è una seccatura; **he's a** ~ lui dà fastidio; **what a** ~! che seccatura!
NUJ *n abbr* (*Brit*: = *National Union of Journalists*) *sindacato nazionale dei giornalisti*.
nuke [nju:k] *n* (*col*) bomba atomica.
null [nʌl] *a*: ~ **and void** nullo(a).
nullify ['nʌlɪfaɪ] *vt* annullare.
NUM *n abbr* (*Brit*: = *National Union of Mineworkers*) *sindacato nazionale dei minatori*.
numb [nʌm] *a* intorpidito(a) ♦ *vt* intorpidire; ~ **with** (*fear*) paralizzato(a) da; (*grief*) impietrito(a) da; ~ **with cold** intirizzito(a) (dal freddo).
number ['nʌmbə*] *n* numero ♦ *vt* numerare; (*include*) contare; **a** ~ **of** un certo numero di; **telephone** ~ numero di telefono; **wrong** ~ (*TEL*) numero sbagliato; **the staff** ~**s 20** gli impiegati sono in 20.
numbered account ['nʌmbəd-] *n* (*in bank*) conto numerato.
number plate *n* (*Brit AUT*) targa.
Number Ten *n* (*Brit*: = *10 Downing Street*) *residenza del Primo Ministro del Regno Unito*.
numbness ['nʌmnɪs] *n* intorpidimento; (*due to cold*) intirizzimento.
numeral ['nju:mərəl] *n* numero, cifra.
numerate ['nju:mərɪt] *a* (*Brit*): **to be** ~ saper far di conto.
numerical [nju:'mɛrɪkl] *a* numerico(a).
numerous ['nju:mərəs] *a* numeroso(a).
nun [nʌn] *n* suora, monaca.
NUPE ['nju:pɪ] *n abbr* (*Brit*: = *National Union of Public Employees*) *sindacato nazionale dei dipendenti statali*.
nuptial ['nʌpʃəl] *a* nuziale.
NUR *n abbr* (*Brit*: = *National Union of Railwaymen*) *sindacato nazionale dei ferrovieri*.
nurse [nɜ:s] *n* infermiere/a; (*also*: ~**maid**) bambinaia ♦ *vt* (*patient, cold*) curare; (*baby*: *Brit*) cullare; (: *US*) allattare, dare il latte a; (*hope*) nutrire.
nursery ['nɜ:sərɪ] *n* (*room*) camera dei bambini; (*institution*) asilo; (*for plants*) vivaio.
nursery rhyme *n* filastrocca.
nursery school *n* scuola materna.
nursery slope *n* (*Brit SKI*) pista per principianti.
nursing ['nɜ:sɪŋ] *n* (*profession*) professione *f* di infermiere (*or* di infermiera) ♦ *a* (*mother*) che allatta.
nursing home *n* casa di cura.
nurture ['nɜ:tʃə*] *vt* allevare; nutrire.
NUS *n abbr* (*Brit*: = *National Union of Students*) *sindacato nazionale degli studenti*;

(: = *National Union of Seamen*) *sindacato nazionale dei marinai*.
NUT *n abbr* (*Brit*: = *National Union of Teachers*) *sindacato nazionale degli insegnanti*.
nut [nʌt] *n* (*of metal*) dado; (*fruit*) noce *f* (*or* nocciola *or* mandorla *etc*) ♦ *a* (*chocolate etc*) alla nocciola *etc*; **he's** ~**s** (*col*) è matto.
nutcase ['nʌtkeɪs] *n* (*col*) mattarello/a.
nutcrackers ['nʌtkrækəz] *npl* schiaccianoci *m inv*.
nutmeg ['nʌtmɛg] *n* noce *f* moscata.
nutrient ['nju:trɪənt] *a* nutriente ♦ *n* sostanza nutritiva.
nutrition [nju:'trɪʃən] *n* nutrizione *f*.
nutritionist [nju:'trɪʃənɪst] *n* nutrizionista *m/f*.
nutritious [nju:'trɪʃəs] *a* nutriente.
nutshell ['nʌtʃɛl] *n* guscio di noce; **in a** ~ in poche parole.
nuzzle ['nʌzl] *vi*: **to** ~ **up to** strofinare il muso contro.
NV *abbr* (*US POST*) = *Nevada*.
NWT *abbr* (*Canada*) = *Northwest Territories*.
NY *abbr* (*US POST*) = *New York*.
NYC *abbr* (*US POST*) = *New York City*.
nylon ['naɪlɔn] *n* nailon *m*; ~**s** *npl* calze *fpl* di nailon.
nymph [nɪmf] *n* ninfa.
nymphomaniac [nɪmfəu'meɪnɪæk] *a, n* ninfomane (*f*).
NYSE *abbr* (*US*) = *New York Stock Exchange*.
NZ *abbr* = **New Zealand**.

O

O, o [əu] *n* (*letter*) O, o *f or m inv*; (*US SCOL*: = *outstanding*) ≈ ottimo; (*number*: *TEL etc*) zero; **O for Oliver,** (*US*) **O for Oboe** ≈ O come Otranto.
oaf [əuf] *n* zoticone *m*.
oak [əuk] *n* quercia ♦ *cpd* di quercia.
OAP *n abbr* (*Brit*) see **old-age pensioner**.
oar [ɔ:*] *n* remo; **to put** *or* **shove one's** ~ **in** (*fig col*) intromettersi.
oarsman ['ɔ:zmən], **oarswoman** ['ɔ:zwumən] *n* rematore/trice.
OAS *n abbr* (= *Organization of American States*) O.S.A. *f* (= *Organizzazione degli Stati Americani*).
oasis, *pl* **oases** [əu'eɪsɪs, əu'eɪsi:z] *n* oasi *f inv*.
oath [əuθ] *n* giuramento; (*swear word*) bestemmia; **to take the** ~ giurare; **on** ~ (*Brit*) *or* **under** ~ sotto giuramento.
oatmeal ['əutmi:l] *n* farina d'avena.
oats [əuts] *npl* avena.
OAU *n abbr* (= *Organization of African Unity*)

O.A.U. *f.*
obdurate ['ɔbdjurɪt] *a* testardo(a); incallito(a); ostinato(a), irremovibile.
OBE *n abbr* (*Brit*: = *Order of the British Empire*) titolo.
obedience [ə'bi:dɪəns] *n* ubbidienza; **in ~ to** conformemente a.
obedient [ə'bi:dɪənt] *a* ubbidiente; **to be ~ to sb/sth** ubbidire a qn/qc.
obelisk ['ɔbɪlɪsk] *n* obelisco.
obesity [əu'bi:sɪtɪ] *n* obesità.
obey [ə'beɪ] *vt* ubbidire a; (*instructions, regulations*) osservare ♦ *vi* ubbidire.
obituary [ə'bɪtjuərɪ] *n* necrologia.
object *n* ['ɔbdʒɪkt] oggetto; (*purpose*) scopo, intento; (*LING*) complemento oggetto ♦ *vi* [əb'dʒɛkt]: **to ~ to** (*attitude*) disapprovare; (*proposal*) protestare contro, sollevare delle obiezioni contro; **I ~!** mi oppongo!; **he ~ed that** ... obiettò che ...; **do you ~ to my smoking?** la disturba se fumo?; **what's the ~ of doing that?** a che serve farlo?; **expense is no ~** non si bada a spese.
objection [əb'dʒɛkʃən] *n* obiezione *f*; (*drawback*) inconveniente *m*; **if you have no ~** se non ha obiezioni; **to make** *or* **raise an ~** sollevare un'obiezione.
objectionable [əb'dʒɛkʃənəbl] *a* antipatico(a); (*smell*) sgradevole; (*language*) scostumato(a).
objective [əb'dʒɛktɪv] *n* obiettivo ♦ *a* obiettivo(a).
objectivity [ɔbdʒɪk'tɪvɪtɪ] *n* obiettività.
object lesson *n*: ~ **(in)** dimostrazione *f* (di).
objector [əb'dʒɛktə*] *n* oppositore/trice.
obligation [ɔblɪ'geɪʃən] *n* obbligo, dovere *m*; (*debt*) obbligo (di riconoscenza); **"without ~"** "senza impegno"; **to be under an ~ to sb/to do sth** essere in dovere verso qn/di fare qc.
obligatory [ə'blɪɡətərɪ] *a* obbligatorio(a).
oblige [ə'blaɪdʒ] *vt* (*force*): **to ~ sb to do** costringere qn a fare; (*do a favour*) fare una cortesia a; **to be ~d to sb for sth** essere grato a qn per qc; **anything to ~!** (*col*) questo e altro!
obliging [ə'blaɪdʒɪŋ] *a* servizievole, compiacente.
oblique [ə'bli:k] *a* obliquo(a); (*allusion*) indiretto(a) ♦ *n* (*Brit TYP*): ~ **(stroke)** barra.
obliterate [ə'blɪtəreɪt] *vt* cancellare.
oblivion [ə'blɪvɪən] *n* oblio.
oblivious [ə'blɪvɪəs] *a*: ~ **of** incurante di; inconscio(a) di.
oblong ['ɔblɒŋ] *a* oblungo(a) ♦ *n* rettangolo.
obnoxious [əb'nɔkʃəs] *a* odioso(a); (*smell*) disgustoso(a), ripugnante.
o.b.o. *abbr* (*US*: = *or best offer*: *in classified ads*) o al miglior offerente.
oboe ['əubəu] *n* oboe *m*.
obscene [əb'si:n] *a* osceno(a).
obscenity [əb'sɛnɪtɪ] *n* oscenità *f inv*.
obscure [əb'skjuə*] *a* oscuro(a) ♦ *vt* oscurare; (*hide: sun*) nascondere.

obscurity [əb'skjuərɪtɪ] *n* oscurità; (*obscure point*) punto oscuro; (*lack of fame*) anonimato.
obsequious [əb'si:kwɪəs] *a* ossequioso(a).
observable [əb'zɜ:vəbl] *a* osservabile; (*appreciable*) notevole.
observance [əb'zɜ:vns] *n* osservanza; **religious ~s** pratiche *fpl* religiose.
observant [əb'zɜ:vnt] *a* attento(a).
observation [ɔbzə'veɪʃən] *n* osservazione *f*; (*by police etc*) sorveglianza.
observation post *n* (*MIL*) osservatorio.
observatory [əb'zɜ:vətrɪ] *n* osservatorio.
observe [əb'zɜ:v] *vt* osservare.
observer [əb'zɜ:və*] *n* osservatore/trice.
obsess [əb'sɛs] *vt* ossessionare; **to be ~ed by** *or* **with sb/sth** essere ossessionato da qn/qc.
obsession [əb'sɛʃən] *n* ossessione *f*.
obsessive [əb'sɛsɪv] *a* ossessivo(a).
obsolescence [ɔbsə'lɛsns] *n* obsolescenza; **built-in** *or* **planned ~** (*COMM*) obsolescenza programmata.
obsolescent [ɔbsə'lɛsnt] *a* obsolescente.
obsolete ['ɔbsəli:t] *a* obsoleto(a); (*word*) desueto(a).
obstacle ['ɔbstəkl] *n* ostacolo.
obstacle race *n* corsa agli ostacoli.
obstetrics [ɔb'stɛtrɪks] *n* ostetrica.
obstinacy ['ɔbstɪnəsɪ] *n* ostinatezza.
obstinate ['ɔbstɪnɪt] *a* ostinato(a).
obstreperous [əb'strɛpərəs] *a* turbolento(a).
obstruct [əb'strʌkt] *vt* (*block*) ostruire, ostacolare; (*halt*) fermare; (*hinder*) impedire.
obstruction [əb'strʌkʃən] *n* ostruzione *f*; ostacolo.
obstructive [əb'strʌktɪv] *a* ostruttivo(a); che crea impedimenti.
obtain [əb'teɪn] *vt* ottenere ♦ *vi* essere in uso; **to ~ sth (for o.s.)** procurarsi qc.
obtainable [əb'teɪnəbl] *a* ottenibile.
obtrusive [əb'tru:sɪv] *a* (*person*) importuno(a); (*smell*) invadente; (*building etc*) imponente e invadente.
obtuse [əb'tju:s] *a* ottuso(a).
obverse ['ɔbvə:s] *n* opposto, inverso.
obviate ['ɔbvɪeɪt] *vt* ovviare a, evitare.
obvious ['ɔbvɪəs] *a* ovvio(a), evidente.
obviously ['ɔbvɪəslɪ] *ad* ovviamente; **~!** certo!; ~ **not!** certo che no!; **he was ~ not drunk** si vedeva che non era ubriaco; **he was not ~ drunk** non si vedeva che era ubriaco.
OCAS *n abbr* = *Organization of Central American States.*
occasion [ə'keɪʒən] *n* occasione *f*; (*event*) avvenimento ♦ *vt* cagionare; **on that ~** in quell'occasione, quella volta; **to rise to the ~** mostrarsi all'altezza della situazione.
occasional [ə'keɪʒənl] *a* occasionale; **I smoke an ~ cigarette** ogni tanto fumo una sigaretta.
occasionally [ə'keɪʒənəlɪ] *ad* ogni tanto; **very ~** molto raramente.
occasional table *n* tavolino.
occult [ɔ'kʌlt] *a* occulto(a) ♦ *n*: **the ~** l'occulto.

occupancy ['ɔkjupənsɪ] *n* occupazione *f*.

occupant ['ɔkjupənt] *n* occupante *m/f*; (*of boat, car etc*) persona a bordo.

occupation [ɔkju'peɪʃən] *n* occupazione *f*; (*job*) mestiere *m*, professione *f*; **unfit for ~** (*house*) inabitabile.

occupational [ɔkju'peɪʃənl] *a* (*disease*) professionale; (*hazard*) del mestiere; **~ accident** infortunio sul lavoro.

occupational guidance *n* (*Brit*) orientamento professionale.

occupational pension scheme *n* sistema pensionistico programmato dal datore di lavoro.

occupational therapy *n* ergoterapia.

occupier ['ɔkjupaɪə*] *n* occupante *m/f*.

occupy ['ɔkjupaɪ] *vt* occupare; **to ~ o.s. by doing** occuparsi a fare; **to be occupied with sth/in doing sth** essere preso da qc/occupato a fare qc.

occur [ə'kə:*] *vi* accadere; (*difficulty, opportunity*) capitare; (*phenomenon, error*) trovarsi; **to ~ to sb** venire in mente a qn.

occurrence [ə'kʌrəns] *n* caso, fatto; presenza.

ocean ['əuʃən] *n* oceano; **~s of** (*col*) un sacco di.

ocean bed *n* fondale *m* oceanico.

ocean-going ['əuʃəngəuɪŋ] *a* d'alto mare.

Oceania [əuʃɪ'ɑ:nɪə] *n* Oceania.

ocean liner *n* transatlantico.

ochre, (*US*) **ocher** ['əukə*] *a* ocra *inv*.

o'clock [ə'klɔk] *ad*: **it is one ~** è l'una; **it is 5 ~** sono le 5.

OCR *n* abbr *see* **optical character reader**; **optical character recognition**.

Oct. *abbr* (= *October*) ott.

octagonal [ɔk'tægənl] *a* ottagonale.

octane ['ɔkteɪn] *n* ottano; **high-~ petrol** or (*US*) **gas** benzina ad alto numero di ottani.

octave ['ɔktɪv] *n* ottavo.

October [ɔk'təubə*] *n* ottobre *m*; *for phrases see also* **July**.

octogenarian [ɔktəudʒɪ'nɛərɪən] *n* ottuagenario/a.

octopus ['ɔktəpəs] *n* polpo, piovra.

odd [ɔd] *a* (*strange*) strano(a), bizzarro(a); (*number*) dispari *inv*; (*left over*) in più; (*not of a set*) spaiato(a); **60-~** 60 e oltre; **at ~ times** di tanto in tanto; **the ~ one out** l'eccezione *f*.

oddball ['ɔdbɔ:l] *n* (*col*) eccentrico/a.

oddity ['ɔdɪtɪ] *n* bizzarria; (*person*) originale *m/f*.

odd-job man [ɔd'dʒɔb-] *n* tuttofare *m inv*.

odd jobs *npl* lavori *mpl* occasionali.

oddly ['ɔdlɪ] *ad* stranamente.

oddments ['ɔdmənts] *npl* (*Brit COMM*) rimanenze *fpl*.

odds [ɔdz] *npl* (*in betting*) quota; **the ~ are against his coming** c'è poca probabilità che venga; **it makes no ~** non importa; **at ~ in** contesa; **to succeed against all the ~** riuscire contro ogni aspettativa; **~ and ends** avanzi *mpl*.

ode [əud] *n* ode *f*.

odious ['əudɪəs] *a* odioso(a), ripugnante.

odometer [ɔ'dɔmɪtə*] *n* odometro.

odour, (*US*) **odor** ['əudə*] *n* odore *m*.

odo(u)rless ['əudəlɪs] *a* inodoro(a).

OECD *n* abbr (= *Organization for Economic Cooperation and Development*) O.C.S.E. *f* (= *Organizzazione per la Cooperazione e lo Sviluppo Economico*).

oesophagus, (*US*) **esophagus** [i:'sɔfəgəs] *n* esofago.

oestrogen, (*US*) **estrogen** ['i:strəudʒən] *n* estrogeno.

of [ɔv, əv] *prep* di; **a friend ~ ours** un nostro amico; **3 ~ them went** 3 di loro sono andati; **the 5th ~ July** il 5 luglio; **a boy ~ 10** un ragazzo di 10 anni; **made ~ wood** (fatto) di or in legno; **a kilo ~ flour** un chilo di farina; **that was very kind ~ you** è stato molto carino da parte sua; **a quarter ~ 4** (*US*) le 4 meno un quarto.

off [ɔf] *a, ad* (*engine*) spento(a); (*tap*) chiuso(a); (*Brit: food*) andato(a) a male; (*absent*) assente; (*cancelled*) sospeso(a) ♦ *prep* da; a poca distanza di; **to be ~** (*to leave*) partire, andarsene; **to be ~ sick** essere assente per malattia; **a day ~** un giorno di vacanza; **to have an ~ day** non essere in forma; **to be well/badly ~** essere/ non essere benestante; **he had his coat ~** si era tolto il cappotto; **the lid was ~** non c'era il coperchio; **10% ~** (*COMM*) con uno sconto di 10%; **5 km ~ (the road)** a 5 km (dalla strada); **~ the coast** al largo della costa; **a house ~ the main road** una casa fuori della strada maestra; **it's a long way ~** è molto lontano; **I'm ~ meat** la carne non mi va più; non mangio più la carne; **on the ~ chance** a caso; **~ and on, on and ~** di tanto in tanto; **I'm afraid the chicken is ~** (*Brit: not available*) purtroppo il pollo è finito; **that's a bit ~, isn't it?** (*fig col*) non è molto carino, vero?

offal ['ɔfl] *n* (*CULIN*) frattaglie *fpl*.

offbeat ['ɔfbi:t] *a* eccentrico(a).

off-centre, (*US*) **off-center** [ɔf'sɛntə*] *a* storto(a), fuori centro.

off-colour ['ɔf'kʌlə*] *a* (*Brit: ill*) malato(a), indisposto(a); **to feel ~** sentirsi poco bene.

offence, (*US*) **offense** [ə'fɛns] *n* (*LAW*) contravvenzione *f*; (: *more serious*) reato; **to give ~ to** offendere; **to take ~ at** offendersi per; **to commit an ~** commettere un reato.

offend [ə'fɛnd] *vt* (*person*) offendere ♦ *vi*: **to ~ against** (*law, rule*) trasgredire.

offender [ə'fɛndə*] *n* delinquente *m/f*; (*against regulations*) contravventore/trice.

offense [ə'fɛns] *n* (*US*) = **offence**.

offensive [ə'fɛnsɪv] *a* offensivo(a); (*smell etc*) sgradevole, ripugnante ♦ *n* (*MIL*) offensiva.

offer ['ɔfə*] *n* offerta, proposta ♦ *vt* offrire; **"on ~"** (*COMM*) "in offerta speciale"; **to make an ~ for sth** fare un'offerta per qc; **to ~ sth to sb, ~ sb sth** offrire qc a qn; **to ~ to do sth** offrirsi di fare qc.

offering ['ɔfərɪŋ] n offerta.
offhand [ɔf'hænd] a disinvolto(a), noncurante ♦ ad all'improvviso; **I can't tell you** ~ non posso dirglielo su due piedi.
office ['ɔfɪs] n (place) ufficio; (position) carica; **doctor's** ~ (US) ambulatorio; **to take** ~ entrare in carica; **through his good** ~**s** con il suo prezioso aiuto; **O**~ **of Fair Trading** (Brit) organismo di protezione contro le pratiche commerciali abusive.
office automation n automazione f d'ufficio, burotica.
office bearer n (of club etc) membro dell'amministrazione.
office block, (US) **office building** n complesso di uffici.
office boy n garzone m.
office hours npl orario d'ufficio; (US MED) orario di visite.
office manager n capoufficio m/f.
officer ['ɔfɪsə*] n (MIL etc) ufficiale m; (of organization) funzionario; (also: **police** ~) agente m di polizia.
office work n lavoro d'ufficio.
office worker n impiegato/a d'ufficio.
official [ə'fɪʃl] a (authorized) ufficiale ♦ n ufficiale m; (civil servant) impiegato/a statale; funzionario.
officialdom [ə'fɪʃəldəm] n burocrazia.
officially [ə'fɪʃəlɪ] ad ufficialmente.
official receiver n curatore m fallimentare.
officiate [ə'fɪʃɪeɪt] vi (REL) ufficiare; **to** ~ **as Mayor** esplicare le funzioni di sindaco; **to** ~ **at a marriage** celebrare un matrimonio.
officious [ə'fɪʃəs] a invadente.
offing ['ɔfɪŋ] n: **in the** ~ (fig) in vista.
off-key [ɔf'kiː] a stonato(a) ♦ ad fuori tono.
off-licence ['ɔflaɪsns] n (Brit) spaccio di bevande alcoliche.
off-limits [ɔf'lɪmɪts] a (esp US) in cui vige il divieto d'accesso.
off line a, ad (COMPUT) off line inv, fuori linea; (: switched off) spento(a).
off-load ['ɔflaud] vt scaricare.
off-peak ['ɔf'piːk] a (ticket etc) a tariffa ridotta; (time) non di punta.
off-putting ['ɔfputɪŋ] a (Brit) un po' scostante.
off-season ['ɔfsiːzn] a, ad fuori stagione.
offset ['ɔfsɛt] vt irg (counteract) controbilanciare, compensare ♦ n (also: ~ **printing**) offset m.
offshoot ['ɔfʃuːt] n (fig) diramazione f.
offshore [ɔf'ʃɔː*] a (breeze) di terra; (island) vicino alla costa; (fishing) costiero(a); ~ **oilfield** giacimento petrolifero in mare aperto.
offside ['ɔf'saɪd] a (SPORT) fuori gioco; (AUT: with right-hand drive) destro(a); (: with left-hand drive) sinistro(a) ♦ n destra; sinistra.
offspring ['ɔfsprɪŋ] n prole f, discendenza.
offstage [ɔf'steɪdʒ] ad dietro le quinte.
off-the-cuff [ɔfðə'kʌf] ad improvvisando.
off-the-job ['ɔfðə'dʒɔb] a: ~ **training** addestramento fuori sede.

off-the-peg ['ɔfðə'pɛg], (US) **off-the-rack** ['ɔfðə'ræk] ad prêt-à-porter.
off-white ['ɔfwaɪt] a bianco sporco inv.
often ['ɔfn] ad spesso; **how** ~ **do you go?** quanto spesso ci va?; **as** ~ **as not** quasi sempre.
ogle ['əugl] vt occhieggiare.
ogre ['əugə*] n orco.
OH abbr (US POST) = Ohio.
oh [əu] excl oh!
OHMS abbr (Brit) = On His (or Her) Majesty's Service.
oil [ɔɪl] n olio; (petroleum) petrolio; (for central heating) nafta ♦ vt (machine) lubrificare.
oilcan ['ɔɪlkæn] n oliatore m a mano; (for storing) latta da olio.
oil change n cambio dell'olio.
oilfield ['ɔɪlfiːld] n giacimento petrolifero.
oil filter n (AUT) filtro dell'olio.
oil-fired ['ɔɪlfaɪəd] a a nafta.
oil gauge n indicatore m del livello dell'olio.
oil industry n industria del petrolio.
oil level n livello dell'olio.
oil painting n quadro a olio.
oil refinery n raffineria di petrolio.
oil rig n derrick m inv; (at sea) piattaforma per trivellazioni subacquee.
oilskins ['ɔɪlskɪnz] npl indumenti mpl di tela cerata.
oil slick n chiazza d'olio.
oil tanker n petroliera.
oil well n pozzo petrolifero.
oily ['ɔɪlɪ] a unto(a), oleoso(a); (food) untuoso(a).
ointment ['ɔɪntmənt] n unguento.
OK abbr (US POST) = Oklahoma.
O.K., okay [əu'keɪ] excl d'accordo! ♦ vt approvare ♦ n: **to give sth one's** ~ approvare qc ♦ a: **is it** ~**?, are you** ~**?** tutto bene?; **it's** ~ **with** or **by me** per me va bene; **are you** ~ **for money?** sei a posto coi soldi?
old [əuld] a vecchio(a); (ancient) antico(a), vecchio(a); (person) vecchio(a), anziano(a); **how** ~ **are you?** quanti anni ha?; **he's 10 years** ~ ha 10 anni; ~**er brother/sister** fratello/sorella maggiore; **any** ~ **thing will do** va bene qualsiasi cosa.
old age n vecchiaia.
old-age pensioner (OAP) ['əuldeɪdʒ-] n (Brit) pensionato/a.
old-fashioned ['əuld'fæʃnd] a antiquato(a), fuori moda; (person) all'antica.
old maid n zitella.
old people's home n ricovero per anziani.
old-time ['əuldtaɪm] a di una volta.
old-timer [əuld'taɪmə*] n veterano/a.
old wives' tale n vecchia superstizione f.
olive ['ɔlɪv] n (fruit) oliva; (tree) olivo ♦ a (also: ~**-green**) verde oliva inv.
olive oil n olio d'oliva.
Olympic [əu'lɪmpɪk] a olimpico(a); **the** ~ **Games, the** ~**s** i giochi olimpici, le Olimpiadi.

OM *n abbr* (*Brit:* = *Order of Merit*) titolo.

O & M *abbr* = *organization and method.*

Oman [əu'ma:n] *n* Oman *m*.

OMB *n abbr* (*US:* = *Office of Management and Budget*) servizio di consulenza al Presidente in materia di bilancio.

omelet(te) ['ɔmlɪt] *n* omelette *f inv;* **ham/cheese** ~ omelette al prosciutto/al formaggio.

omen ['əumən] *n* presagio, augurio.

ominous ['ɔmɪnəs] *a* minaccioso(a); (*event*) di malaugurio.

omission [əu'mɪʃən] *n* omissione *f.*

omit [əu'mɪt] *vt* omettere; **to** ~ **to do sth** tralasciare *or* trascurare di fare qc.

omnivorous [ɔm'nɪvərəs] *a* onnivoro(a).

ON *abbr* (*Canada*) = *Ontario.*

on [ɔn] *prep* su; (*on top of*) sopra ♦ *a, ad* (*machine*) in moto; (*light, radio*) acceso(a); (*tap*) aperto(a); **is the meeting still** ~? avrà sempre luogo la riunione?; la riunione è ancora in corso?; **when is this film** ~? quando c'è questo film?; ~ **the train** in treno; ~ **the wall** sul *or* al muro; ~ **television** alla televisione; ~ **the Continent** nell'Europa continentale; **a book** ~ **physics** un libro di *or* sulla fisica; ~ **learning this** imparando questo; ~ **arrival** all'arrivo; ~ **the left** sulla *or* a sinistra; ~ **Friday** venerdì; ~ **Fridays** di *or* il venerdì; **a week** ~ **Friday** venerdì fra otto giorni; **to be** ~ **holiday** *or* (*US*) ~ **vacation** essere in vacanza; **I haven't any money** ~ **me** non ho soldi con me; **he's** ~ **£6000 a year** guadagna 6000 sterline all'anno; **this round's** ~ **me** questo giro lo offro io; **put your coat** ~ mettiti il cappotto; **to walk** *etc* ~ continuare a camminare *etc;* **from that day** ~ da quel giorno in poi; **it was well** ~ **in the evening** era sera inoltrata; **my father's always** ~ **at me to get a job** (*col*) mio padre mi sta sempre addosso perché trovi un lavoro; **that's not** ~! (*not acceptable*) non si fa così!; (*not possible*) non se ne parla neanche!; ~ **and off** ogni tanto.

ONC *n abbr* (*Brit:* = *Ordinary National Certificate*) diploma in materie tecniche a livello di maturità.

once [wʌns] *ad* una volta ♦ *cj* non appena, quando; ~ **he had left/it was done** dopo che se n'era andato/fu fatto; **at** ~ subito; (*simultaneously*) a un tempo; **all at** ~ (tutto) ad un tratto; ~ **a week** una volta alla settimana; ~ **more** ancora una volta; **I knew him** ~ un tempo *or* in passato lo conoscevo; ~ **and for all** una volta per sempre; ~ **upon a time there was** ... c'era una volta ....

oncoming ['ɔnkʌmɪŋ] *a* (*traffic*) che viene in senso opposto.

OND *n abbr* (*Brit:* = *Ordinary National Diploma*) diploma in materie tecniche conseguito dopo un corso biennale.

one [wʌn] *a, num* un(uno) *m*, una(un') *f* ♦ *pronoun* uno(a); (*impersonal*) si; **this** ~ questo(a) qui; **that** ~ quello(a) là; **the** ~ **book which** ... l'unico libro che ...; ~ **by** ~ a

uno(a) a uno(a); ~ **never knows** non si sa mai; **to express** ~'s **opinion** esprimere la propria opinione; ~ **another** l'un(a) l'altro(a); **it's** ~ (**o'clock**) è l'una; **which** ~ **do you want?** quale vuole?; **to be** ~ **up on sb** essere avvantaggiato rispetto a qn; **to be at** ~ (**with sb**) andare d'accordo (con qn).

one-armed bandit ['wʌnɑ:md-] *n* slot-machine *f inv.*

one-day excursion ['wʌndeɪ-] *n* (*US*) biglietto giornaliero di andata e ritorno.

one-man ['wʌn'mæn] *a* (*business*) diretto(a) *etc* da un solo uomo.

one-man band *n* suonatore ambulante con vari strumenti.

one-off [wʌn'ɔf] (*Brit col*) *n* fatto eccezionale ♦ *a* eccezionale.

one-piece ['wʌnpi:s] *a* (*bathing suit*) intero(a).

onerous ['ɔnərəs] *a* (*task, duty*) gravoso(a); (*responsibility*) pesante.

oneself [wʌn'sɛlf] *pronoun* si; (*after prep*) sé, se stesso(a); **to do sth (by)** ~ fare qc da sé.

one-shot [wʌn'ʃɔt] *n* (*US*) = **one-off.**

one-sided [wʌn'saɪdɪd] *a* (*decision, view*) unilaterale; (*judgement, account*) parziale; (*game, contest*) impari *inv.*

one-time ['wʌntaɪm] *a* ex *inv.*

one-to-one ['wʌntəwʌn] *a* (*relationship*) univoco(a).

one-upmanship [wʌn'ʌpmənʃɪp] *n:* **the art of** ~ l'arte *f* di primeggiare.

one-way ['wʌnweɪ] *a* (*street, traffic*) a senso unico.

ongoing ['ɔngəuɪŋ] *a* in corso; in attuazione.

onion ['ʌnjən] *n* cipolla.

on line *a* (*COMPUT*) on line *inv*, in linea; (*: switched on*) acceso(a).

onlooker ['ɔnlukə*] *n* spettatore/trice.

only ['əunlɪ] *ad* solo, soltanto ♦ *a* solo(a), unico(a) ♦ *cj* solo che, ma; **an** ~ **child** un figlio unico; **not** ~ non solo; **I** ~ **took one** ne ho preso soltanto uno, non ne ho preso che uno; **I saw her** ~ **yesterday** l'ho vista appena ieri; **I'd be** ~ **too pleased to help** sarei proprio felice di essere d'aiuto; **I would come,** ~ **I'm very busy** verrei volentieri, solo che sono molto occupato.

ono *abbr* = **or nearest offer;** *see* **near.**

onset ['ɔnsɛt] *n* inizio; (*of winter*) arrivo.

onshore ['ɔnʃɔ:*] *a* (*wind*) di mare.

onslaught ['ɔnslɔ:t] *n* attacco, assalto.

on-the-job ['ɔnðə'dʒɔb] *a:* ~ **training** addestramento in sede.

onto ['ɔntu] *prep* su, sopra.

onus ['əunəs] *n* onere *m*, peso; **the** ~ **is upon him to prove it** sta a lui dimostrarlo.

onward(s) ['ɔnwəd(z)] *ad* (*move*) in avanti; **from this time** ~ d'ora in poi.

onyx ['ɔnɪks] *n* onice *f.*

ooze [u:z] *vi* stillare.

opacity [əu'pæsɪtɪ] *n* opacità.

opal ['əupl] *n* opale *m or f.*

opaque [əu'peɪk] *a* opaco(a).

OPEC ['əupɛk] *n abbr* (= *Organization of Petroleum-Exporting Countries*) O.P.E.C. *f.*

open ['əupn] *a* aperto(a); (*road*) libero(a); (*meeting*) pubblico(a); (*admiration*) evidente, franco(a); (*question*) insoluto(a); (*enemy*) dichiarato(a) ♦ *vt* aprire ♦ *vi* (*eyes, door, debate*) aprirsi; (*flower*) sbocciare; (*shop, bank, museum*) aprire; (*book etc*: *commence*) cominciare; **in the ~ (air)** all'aperto; **the ~ sea** il mare aperto, l'alto mare; **~ ground** (*among trees*) radura; (*waste ground*) terreno non edificato; **to have an ~ mind (on sth)** non avere ancora deciso (su qc).
  open on to *vt fus* (*subj: room, door*) dare su.
  open out *vt* aprire ♦ *vi* aprirsi.
  open up *vt* aprire; (*blocked road*) sgombrare ♦ *vi* aprirsi.

open-air |əupn'ɛə*| *a* all'aperto.

open-and-shut ['əupnən'ʃʌt] *a*: **~ case** caso indubbio.

open day *n* (*Brit*) giornata di apertura al pubblico.

open-ended [əupn'ɛndɪd] *a* (*fig*) aperto(a), senza limiti.

opener ['əupnə*] *n* (*also*: **can ~, tin ~**) apriscatole *m inv.*

open-heart [əupn'hɑ:t] *a*: **~ surgery** chirurgia a cuore aperto.

opening ['əupnɪŋ] *n* apertura; (*opportunity*) occasione *f,* opportunità *f inv*; sbocco; (*job*) posto vacante.

opening night *n* (*THEATRE*) prima.

openly ['əupnlɪ] *ad* apertamente.

open-minded [əupn'maɪndɪd] *a* che ha la mente aperta.

open-necked ['əupnnɛkt] *a* col collo slacciato.

openness ['əupnnɪs] *n* (*frankness*) franchezza, sincerità.

open-plan ['əupn'plæn] *a* senza pareti divisorie.

open sandwich *n* canapè *m inv.*

open shop *n* fabbrica o ditta dove sono accolti anche operai non iscritti ai sindacati.

Open University (OU) *n* (*Brit*) corsi universitari per corrispondenza.

opera ['ɔpərə] *n* opera.

opera glasses *npl* binocolo da teatro.

opera house *n* opera.

opera singer *n* cantante *m/f* d'opera *or* lirico(a).

operate ['ɔpəreɪt] *vt* (*machine*) azionare, far funzionare; (*system*) usare ♦ *vi* funzionare; (*drug, person*) agire; **to ~ on sb (for)** (*MED*) operare qn (di).

operatic [ɔpə'rætɪk] *a* dell'opera, lirico(a).

operating ['ɔpəreɪtɪŋ] *a* (*COMM*: *costs etc*) di gestione; (*MED*) operatorio(a).

operating system *n* (*COMPUT*) sistema *m* operativo.

operating theatre *n* (*MED*) sala operatoria.

operation [ɔpə'reɪʃən] *n* operazione *f*; **to be in ~** (*machine*) essere in azione *or*

funzionamento; (*system*) essere in vigore; **to have an ~ (for)** (*MED*) essere operato(a) (di).

operational [ɔpə'reɪʃənl] *a* operativo(a); (*COMM*) di gestione, d'esercizio; (*ready for use or action*) in attività, in funzione; **when the service is fully ~** quando il servizio sarà completamente in funzione.

operative ['ɔpərətɪv] *a* (*measure*) operativo(a) ♦ *n* (*in factory*) operaio/a; **the ~ word** la parola chiave.

operator ['ɔpəreɪtə*] *n* (*of machine*) operatore/trice; (*TEL*) centralinista *m/f.*

operetta [ɔpə'rɛtə] *n* operetta.

ophthalmologist [ɔfθæl'mɔlədʒɪst] *n* oftalmologo/a.

opinion [ə'pɪnjən] *n* opinione *f,* parere *m*; **in my ~** secondo me, a mio avviso; **to seek a second ~** (*MED etc*) consultarsi con un altro medico *etc.*

opinionated [ə'pɪnjəneɪtɪd] *a* dogmatico(a).

opinion poll *n* sondaggio di opinioni.

opium ['əupɪəm] *n* oppio.

opponent [ə'pəunənt] *n* avversario/a.

opportune ['ɔpətju:n] *a* opportuno(a).

opportunist [ɔpə'tju:nɪst] *n* opportunista *m/f.*

opportunity [ɔpə'tju:nɪtɪ] *n* opportunità *f inv*, occasione *f*; **to take the ~ to do** *or* **of doing** cogliere l'occasione per fare.

oppose [ə'pəuz] *vt* opporsi a; **~d to** contrario(a) a; **as ~d to** in contrasto con.

opposing [ə'pəuzɪŋ] *a* opposto(a); (*team*) avversario/a.

opposite ['ɔpəzɪt] *a* opposto(a); (*house etc*) di fronte ♦ *ad* di fronte, dirimpetto ♦ *prep* di fronte a ♦ *n* opposto, contrario; (*of word*) contrario; **"see ~ page"** "vedere pagina a fronte".

opposite number *n* controparte *f,* corrispondente *m/f.*

opposite sex *n*: **the ~** l'altro sesso.

opposition [ɔpə'zɪʃən] *n* opposizione *f.*

oppress [ə'prɛs] *vt* opprimere.

oppression [ə'prɛʃən] *n* oppressione *f.*

oppressive [ə'prɛsɪv] *a* oppressivo(a).

opprobrium [ə'prəubrɪəm] *n* (*formal*) obbrobrio.

opt [ɔpt] *vi*: **to ~ for** optare per; **to ~ to do** scegliere di fare; **to ~ out of** ritirarsi da.

optical ['ɔptɪkl] *a* ottico(a).

optical character reader/recognition (OCR) *n* lettore *m* ottico/lettura ottica di caratteri.

optical fibre *n* fibra ottica.

optician [ɔp'tɪʃən] *n* ottico.

optics ['ɔptɪks] *n* ottica.

optimism ['ɔptɪmɪzəm] *n* ottimismo.

optimist ['ɔptɪmɪst] *n* ottimista *m/f.*

optimistic [ɔptɪ'mɪstɪk] *a* ottimistico(a).

optimum ['ɔptɪməm] *a* ottimale.

option ['ɔpʃən] *n* scelta; (*SCOL*) materia facoltativa; (*COMM*) opzione *f*; **to keep one's ~s open** (*fig*) non impegnarsi; **I have no ~** non ho scelta.

optional ['ɔpʃənl] *a* facoltativo(a); (*COMM*) a scelta; ~ **extra** optional *m inv*.
opulence ['ɔpjuləns] *n* opulenza.
opulent ['ɔpjulənt] *a* opulento(a).
OR *abbr* (*US POST*) = *Oregon*.
or [ɔ:*] *cj* o, oppure; (*with negative*): **he hasn't seen** ~ **heard anything** non ha visto né sentito niente; ~ **else** se no, altrimenti; oppure.
oracle ['ɔrəkl] *n* oracolo.
oral ['ɔ:rəl] *a* orale ♦ *n* esame *m* orale.
orange ['ɔrɪndʒ] *n* (*fruit*) arancia ♦ *a* arancione.
orangeade [ɔrɪndʒ'eɪd] *n* aranciata.
oration [ɔ:'reɪʃən] *n* orazione *f*.
orator ['ɔrətə*] *n* oratore/trice.
oratorio [ɔrə'tɔ:rɪəu] *n* oratorio.
orb [ɔ:b] *n* orbe *m*.
orbit ['ɔ:bɪt] *n* orbita ♦ *vt* orbitare intorno a; **to be in/go into** ~ (**round**) essere/entrare in orbita (attorno a).
orchard ['ɔ:tʃəd] *n* frutteto; **apple** ~ meleto.
orchestra ['ɔ:kɪstrə] *n* orchestra; (*US: seating*) platea.
orchestral [ɔ:'kɛstrəl] *a* orchestrale; (*concert*) sinfonico(a).
orchestrate ['ɔ:kɪstreɪt] *vt* (*MUS, fig*) orchestrare.
orchid ['ɔ:kɪd] *n* orchidea.
ordain [ɔ:'deɪn] *vt* (*REL*) ordinare; (*decide*) decretare.
ordeal [ɔ:'di:l] *n* prova, travaglio.
order ['ɔ:də*] *n* ordine *m*; (*COMM*) ordinazione *f* ♦ *vt* ordinare; **to** ~ **sb to do** ordinare a qn di fare; **in** ~ in ordine; (*of document*) in regola; **in** ~ **of size** in ordine di grandezza; **in** ~ **to do** per fare; **in** ~ **that** affinché +*sub*; **a machine in working** ~ una macchina che funziona bene; **to be out of** ~ (*machine*, *toilets*) essere guasto(a); (*telephone*) essere fuori servizio; **to place an** ~ **for sth with sb** ordinare qc a qn; **to the** ~ **of** (*BANKING*) all'ordine di; **to be under** ~**s to do sth** avere l'ordine di fare qc; **a point of** ~ una questione di procedura; **to be on** ~ essere stato ordinato; **made to** ~ fatto su commissione; **the lower** ~**s** (*pej*) i ceti inferiori.
order book *n* copiacommissioni *m inv*.
order form *n* modulo d'ordinazione.
orderly ['ɔ:dəlɪ] *n* (*MIL*) attendente *m* ♦ *a* (*room*) in ordine; (*mind*) metodico(a); (*person*) ordinato(a), metodico(a).
order number *n* numero di ordinazione.
ordinal ['ɔ:dɪnl] *a* (*number*) ordinale.
ordinary ['ɔ:dnrɪ] *a* normale, comune; (*pej*) mediocre ♦ *n*: **out of the** ~ diverso dal solito, fuori dell'ordinario.
ordinary seaman (OS) *n* (*Brit*) marinaio semplice.
ordinary shares *npl* azioni *fpl* ordinarie.
ordination [ɔ:dɪ'neɪʃən] *n* ordinazione *f*.
ordnance ['ɔ:dnəns] *n* (*MIL*: *unit*) (reparto di) sussistenza.

Ordnance Survey map *n* (*Brit*) ≈ carta topografica dell'IGM.
ore [ɔ:*] *n* minerale *m* grezzo.
organ ['ɔ:gən] *n* organo.
organic [ɔ:'gænɪk] *a* organico(a).
organism ['ɔ:gənɪzəm] *n* organismo.
organist ['ɔ:gənɪst] *n* organista *m/f*.
organization [ɔ:gənaɪ'zeɪʃən] *n* organizzazione *f*.
organization chart *n* organigramma *m*.
organize ['ɔ:gənaɪz] *vt* organizzare; **to get** ~**d** organizzarsi.
organized labour *n* manodopera organizzata.
organizer ['ɔ:gənaɪzə*] *n* organizzatore/trice.
orgasm ['ɔ:gæzəm] *n* orgasmo.
orgy ['ɔ:dʒɪ] *n* orgia.
Orient ['ɔ:rɪənt] *n*: **the** ~ l'Oriente *m*.
oriental [ɔ:rɪ'ɛntl] *a*, *n* orientale (*m/f*).
orientate ['ɔ:rɪənteɪt] *vt* orientare.
orifice ['ɔrɪfɪs] *n* orifizio.
origin ['ɔrɪdʒɪn] *n* origine *f*; **country of** ~ paese *m* d'origine.
original [ə'rɪdʒɪnl] *a* originale; (*earliest*) originario(a) ♦ *n* originale *m*.
originality [ərɪdʒɪ'nælɪtɪ] *n* originalità.
originally [ə'rɪdʒɪnəlɪ] *ad* (*at first*) all'inizio.
originate [ə'rɪdʒɪneɪt] *vi*: **to** ~ **from** venire da, essere originario(a) di; (*suggestion*) provenire da; **to** ~ **in** nascere in; (*custom*) avere origine in.
originator [ə'rɪdʒɪneɪtə*] *n* iniziatore/trice.
Orkneys ['ɔ:knɪz] *npl*: **the** ~ (*also*: **the Orkney Islands**) le (isole) Orcadi.
ornament ['ɔ:nəmənt] *n* ornamento; (*trinket*) ninnolo.
ornamental [ɔ:nə'mɛntl] *a* ornamentale.
ornamentation [ɔ:nəmɛn'teɪʃən] *n* decorazione *f*, ornamento.
ornate [ɔ:'neɪt] *a* molto ornato(a).
ornithologist [ɔ:nɪ'θɔlədʒɪst] *n* ornitologo/a.
ornithology [ɔ:nɪ'θɔlədʒɪ] *n* ornitologia.
orphan ['ɔ:fn] *n* orfano/a ♦ *vt*: **to be** ~**ed** diventare orfano.
orphanage ['ɔ:fənɪdʒ] *n* orfanotrofio.
orthodox ['ɔ:θədɔks] *a* ortodosso(a).
orthopaedic, (*US*) **orthopedic** [ɔ:θə'pi:dɪk] *a* ortopedico(a).
OS *abbr* (*Brit*: = *Ordnance Survey*) ≈ IGM *m* (= *Istituto Geografico Militare*); (: *NAUT*) *see* **ordinary seaman**; (: *DRESS*) = **outsize**.
O/S *abbr* = **out of stock**.
oscillate ['ɔsɪleɪt] *vi* oscillare.
OSHA *n abbr* (*US*: = *Occupational Safety and Health Administration*) Amministrazione per la sicurezza e la salute sul lavoro.
Oslo ['ɔzləu] *n* Oslo *f*.
ostensible [ɔs'tɛnsɪbl] *a* preteso(a); apparente.
ostensibly [ɔs'tɛnsɪblɪ] *ad* all'apparenza.
ostentation [ɔstɛn'teɪʃən] *n* ostentazione *f*.
ostentatious [ɔstɛn'teɪʃəs] *a* pretenzioso(a); ostentato(a).
osteopath ['ɔstɪəpæθ] *n* specialista *m/f* di osteopatia.

ostracize ['ɔstrəsaɪz] *vt* dare l'ostracismo a.
ostrich ['ɔstrɪtʃ] *n* struzzo.
OT *abbr* (= *Old Testament*) V.T.
OTB *n abbr* (*US*: = *off-track betting*) puntate *effettuate fuori dagli ippodromi*.
OTE *abbr* (= *on-target earnings*) stipendio *compreso le commissioni*.
other ['ʌðə*] *a* altro(a) ♦ *pronoun*: **the ~** l'altro(a); **the ~s** gli altri; **the ~ day** l'altro giorno; **some ~ people have still to arrive** (alcuni) altri devono ancora arrivare; **some actor or ~** un certo attore; **somebody or ~** qualcuno; **~ than** altro che; a parte; **the car was none ~ than Roberta's** la macchina era proprio di Roberta.
otherwise ['ʌðəwaɪz] *ad*, *cj* altrimenti; **an ~ good piece of work** un lavoro comunque buono.
OTT *abbr* (*col*) = **over the top**; *see* **top.**
otter ['ɔtə*] *n* lontra.
OU *n abbr* (*Brit*) *see* **Open University.**
ouch [autʃ] *excl* ohi!, ahi!
ought, *pt* **ought** [ɔːt] *auxiliary vb*: **I ~ to do it** dovrei farlo; **this ~ to have been corrected** questo avrebbe dovuto essere corretto; **he ~ to win** dovrebbe vincere; **you ~ to go and see it** dovreste andare a vederlo, fareste bene ad andarlo a vedere.
ounce [auns] *n* oncia (= *28.35 g*; *16 in a pound*).
our [auə*] *a* il(la) nostro(a), *pl* i(le) nostri(e).
ours [auəz] *pronoun* il(la) nostro(a), *pl* i(le) nostri(e).
ourselves [auə'sɛlvz] *pronoun pl* (*reflexive*) ci; (*after preposition*) noi; (*emphatic*) noi stessi(e); **we did it (all) by ~** l'abbiamo fatto (tutto) da soli.
oust [aust] *vt* cacciare, espellere.
out [aut] *ad* fuori; (*published, not at home etc*) uscito(a); (*light, fire*) spento(a); (*on strike*) in sciopero; **~ here** qui fuori; **~ there** là fuori; **he's ~** è uscito; (*unconscious*) ha perso conoscenza; **to be ~ in one's calculations** essersi sbagliato nei calcoli; **to run/ back** *etc* **~** uscire di corsa/a marcia indietro *etc*; **to be ~ and about** *or* (*US*) **around again** essere di nuovo in piedi; **the journey ~** l'andata; **the boat was 10 km ~** la barca era a 10 km dalla costa; **before the week was ~** entro la fine della settimana; **he's ~ for all he can get** sta cercando di trarne il massimo profitto; **~ of** (*outside*) fuori di; (*because of*: *anger etc*) per; (*from among*): **~ of 10** su 10; (*without*): **~ of petrol** senza benzina, a corto di benzina; **made ~ of wood** (fatto) di or in legno; **it's ~ of stock** (*COMM*) non è disponibile.
outage ['autɪdʒ] *n* (*esp US*: *power failure*) interruzione *f or* mancanza di corrente elettrica.
out-and-out ['autəndaut] *a* vero(a) e proprio(a).
outback ['autbæk] *n* zona isolata; (*in Australia*) interno, entroterra.

outbid, *pt*, *pp* **outbid** [aut'bɪd] *vt* fare un'offerta più alta di.
outboard ['autbɔːd] *n*: **~ (motor)** (motore *m*) fuoribordo.
outbreak ['autbreɪk] *n* scoppio; epidemia.
outbuilding ['autbɪldɪŋ] *n* dipendenza.
outburst ['autbəːst] *n* scoppio.
outcast ['autkɑːst] *n* esule *m/f*; (*socially*) paria *m inv*.
outclass [aut'klɑːs] *vt* surclassare.
outcome ['autkʌm] *n* esito, risultato.
outcrop ['autkrɔp] *n* affioramento.
outcry ['autkraɪ] *n* protesta, clamore *m*.
outdated [aut'deɪtɪd] *a* (*custom, clothes*) fuori moda; (*idea*) sorpassato(a).
outdistance [aut'dɪstəns] *vt* distanziare.
outdo [aut'duː] *vt irg* sorpassare.
outdoor [aut'dɔː*] *a* all'aperto.
outdoors [aut'dɔːz] *ad* fuori; all'aria aperta.
outer ['autə*] *a* esteriore; **~ suburbs** estrema periferia.
outer space *n* spazio cosmico.
outfit ['autfɪt] *n* equipaggiamento; (*clothes*) abito; (*col*: *organization*) organizzazione *f*.
outfitter ['autfɪtə*] *n* (*Brit*): **"(gent's) ~s"** "confezioni da uomo".
outgoing ['autgəuɪŋ] *a* (*president, tenant*) uscente; (*means of transport*) in partenza; (*character*) socievole.
outgoings ['autgəuɪŋz] *npl* (*Brit*: *expenses*) spese *fpl*.
outgrow [aut'grəu] *vt irg* (*clothes*) diventare troppo grande per.
outhouse ['authaus] *n* costruzione *f* annessa.
outing ['autɪŋ] *n* gita; escursione *f*.
outlandish [aut'lændɪʃ] *a* strano(a).
outlast [aut'lɑːst] *vt* sopravvivere a.
outlaw ['autlɔː] *n* fuorilegge *m/f* ♦ *vt* (*person*) mettere fuori della legge; (*practice*) proscrivere.
outlay ['autleɪ] *n* spesa.
outlet ['autlet] *n* (*for liquid etc*) sbocco, scarico; (*for emotion*) sfogo; (*for goods*) sbocco, mercato; (*also*: **retail ~**) punto di vendita; (*US ELEC*) presa di corrente.
outline ['autlaɪn] *n* contorno, profilo; (*summary*) abbozzo, grandi linee *fpl*.
outlive [aut'lɪv] *vt* sopravvivere a.
outlook ['autluk] *n* prospettiva, vista.
outlying ['autlaɪŋ] *a* periferico(a).
outmanoeuvre, (*US*) **outmaneuver** [autmə'nuːvə*] *vt* (*rival etc*) superare in strategia.
outmoded [aut'məudɪd] *a* passato(a) di moda; antiquato(a).
outnumber [aut'nʌmbə*] *vt* superare in numero.
out-of-date [autəv'deɪt] *a* (*passport, ticket*) scaduto(a); (*theory, idea*) sorpassato(a), superato(a); (*custom*) antiquato(a); (*clothes*) fuori moda.
out-of-the-way ['autəvðə'weɪ] *a* (*remote*) fuori mano; (*unusual*) originale, insolito(a).
outpatient ['autpeɪʃənt] *n* paziente *m/f*

esterno(a).

outpost ['autpəust] *n* avamposto.

output ['autput] *n* produzione *f*; *(COMPUT)* output *m inv* ♦ *vt* emettere.

outrage ['autreɪdʒ] *n* oltraggio; scandalo ♦ *vt* oltraggiare.

outrageous [aut'reɪdʒəs] *a* oltraggioso(a); scandaloso(a).

outrider ['autraɪdə*] *n* *(on motorcycle)* battistrada *m inv*.

outright *ad* [aut'raɪt] completamente; schiettamente; apertamente; sul colpo ♦ *a* ['autraɪt] completo(a); schietto(a) e netto(a).

outrun [aut'rʌn] *vt irg* superare (nella corsa).

outset ['autsɛt] *n* inizio.

outshine [aut'ʃaɪn] *vt irg* *(fig)* eclissare.

outside [aut'saɪd] *n* esterno, esteriore *m* ♦ *a* esterno(a), esteriore; *(remote, unlikely)*: **an ~ chance** una vaga possibilità ♦ *ad* fuori, all'esterno ♦ *prep* fuori di, all'esterno di; **at the ~** *(fig)* al massimo; **~ left/right** *n* *(FOOTBALL)* ala sinistra/destra.

outside broadcast *n* *(RADIO, TV)* trasmissione *f* in esterno.

outside lane *n* *(AUT)* corsia di sorpasso.

outside line *n* *(TEL)* linea esterna.

outsider [aut'saɪdə*] *n* *(in race etc)* outsider *m inv*; *(stranger)* straniero/a.

outsize ['autsaɪz] *a* enorme; *(clothes)* per taglie forti.

outskirts ['autskə:ts] *npl* sobborghi *mpl*.

outsmart [aut'sma:t] *vt* superare in astuzia.

outspoken [aut'spəukən] *a* molto franco(a).

outspread ['autsprɛd] *a* *(wings)* aperto(a), spiegato(a).

outstanding [aut'stændɪŋ] *a* eccezionale, di rilievo; *(unfinished)* non completo(a); non evaso(a); non regolato(a); **your account is still ~** deve ancora saldare il conto.

outstay [aut'steɪ] *vt*: **to ~ one's welcome** diventare un ospite sgradito.

outstretched [aut'strɛtʃt] *a* *(hand)* teso(a); *(body)* disteso(a).

outstrip [aut'strɪp] *vt* *(also fig)* superare.

out-tray ['auttreɪ] *n* raccoglitore *m* per le carte da spedire.

outvote [aut'vəut] *vt*: **to ~ sb (by)** avere la maggioranza rispetto a qn (per); **to ~ sth (by)** respingere qc (per).

outward ['autwəd] *a* *(sign, appearances)* esteriore; *(journey)* d'andata.

outwardly ['autwədlɪ] *ad* esteriormente; in apparenza.

outweigh [aut'weɪ] *vt* avere maggior peso di.

outwit [aut'wɪt] *vt* superare in astuzia.

oval ['əuvl] *a*, *n* ovale (*m*).

ovary ['əuvərɪ] *n* ovaia.

ovation [əu'veɪʃən] *n* ovazione *f*.

oven ['ʌvn] *n* forno.

ovenproof ['ʌvnpru:f] *a* da forno.

oven-ready ['ʌvnrɛdɪ] *a* pronto(a) da infornare.

ovenware ['ʌvnwɛə*] *n* vasellame *m* da mettere in forno.

over ['əuvə*] *ad* al di sopra; *(excessively)* molto, troppo ♦ *a* *(or ad)* *(finished)* finito(a), terminato(a); *(too much)* troppo; *(remaining)* che avanza ♦ *prep* su; sopra; *(above)* al di sopra di; *(on the other side of)* di là di; *(more than)* più di; *(during)* durante; **~ here** qui; **~ there** là; **all ~** *(everywhere)* dappertutto; *(finished)* tutto(a) finito(a); **~ and ~ (again)** più e più volte; **~ and above** oltre (a); **to ask sb ~** invitare qn (a passare); **now ~ to our Paris correspondent** diamo ora la linea al nostro corrispondente da Parigi; **the world ~** in tutto il mondo; **she's not ~ intelligent** *(Brit)* non è troppo intelligente; **they fell out ~ money** litigarono per una questione di denaro.

over... ['əuvə*] *prefix*: **~abundant** sovrabbondante.

overact [əuvər'ækt] *vi* *(THEATRE)* esagerare *or* strafare la propria parte.

overall *a*, *n* ['əuvərɔ:l] *a* totale ♦ *n* *(Brit)* grembiule *m* ♦ *ad* [əuvər'ɔ:l] nell'insieme, complessivamente; **~s** *npl* tuta (da lavoro).

overanxious [əuvər'æŋkʃəs] *a* troppo ansioso(a).

overawe [əuvər'ɔ:] *vt* intimidire.

overbalance [əuvə'bæləns] *vi* perdere l'equilibrio.

overbearing [əuvə'bɛərɪŋ] *a* imperioso(a), prepotente.

overboard ['əuvəbɔ:d] *ad* *(NAUT)* fuori bordo, in mare; **to go ~ for sth** *(fig)* impazzire per qc.

overbook [əuvə'buk] *vt* sovrapprenotare.

overcapitalize [əuvə'kæpɪtəlaɪz] *vt* sovraccapitalizzare.

overcast ['əuvəka:st] *a* coperto(a).

overcharge [əuvə'tʃa:dʒ] *vt*: **to ~ sb for sth** far pagare troppo caro a qn per qc.

overcoat ['əuvəkəut] *n* soprabito, cappotto.

overcome [əuvə'kʌm] *vt irg* superare; sopraffare; **~ with grief** sopraffatto(a) dal dolore.

overconfident [əuvə'kɒnfɪdənt] *a* troppo sicuro(a) (di sé), presuntuoso(a).

overcrowded [əuvə'kraudɪd] *a* sovraffollato(a).

overcrowding [əuvə'kraudɪŋ] *n* sovraffollamento; *(in bus)* calca.

overdo [əuvə'du:] *vt irg* esagerare; *(overcook)* cuocere troppo; **to ~ it, to ~ things** *(work too hard)* lavorare troppo.

overdose ['əuvədəus] *n* dose *f* eccessiva.

overdraft ['əuvədra:ft] *n* scoperto (di conto).

overdrawn [əuvə'drɔ:n] *a* *(account)* scoperto(a).

overdrive ['əuvədraɪv] *n* *(AUT)* overdrive *m inv*.

overdue [əuvə'dju:] *a* in ritardo; *(recognition)* tardivo(a); *(bill)* insoluto(a); **that change was long ~** quel cambiamento ci voleva da tempo.

overestimate [əuvər'ɛstɪmeɪt] *vt* sopravvalutare.

overexcited [əuvərɪk'saɪtɪd] *a* sovraeccitato(a).

overexertion [əuvərɪg'zə:ʃən] *n* logorio (fisico).

overexpose [əuvərɪk'spəuz] *vt* (*PHOT*) sovraesporre.

overflow *vi* [əuvə'fləu] traboccare ♦ *n* ['əuvəfləu] eccesso; (*also:* ~ **pipe**) troppopieno.

overfly [əuvə'flaɪ] *vt irg* sorvolare.

overgenerous [əuvə'dʒənərəs] *a* troppo generoso(a).

overgrown [əuvə'grəun] *a* (*garden*) ricoperto(a) di vegetazione; **he's just an** ~ **schoolboy** è proprio un bambinone.

overhang [əuvə'hæŋ] *vt irg* sporgere da ♦ *vi* sporgere.

overhaul *vt* [əuvə'hɔ:l] revisionare ♦ *n* ['əuvəhɔ:l] revisione *f*.

overhead *ad* [əuvə'hɛd] di sopra ♦ *a* ['əuvəhɛd] aereo(a); (*lighting*) verticale ♦ *n* (*US*) = **overheads**.

overheads ['əuvəhɛdz] *npl* (*Brit*) spese *fpl* generali.

overhear [əuvə'hɪə*] *vt irg* sentire (per caso).

overheat [əuvə'hi:t] *vi* surriscaldarsi.

overjoyed [əuvə'dʒɔɪd] *a* pazzo(a) di gioia.

overkill ['əuvəkɪl] *n* (*fig*) strafare *m*.

overland ['əuvələnd] *a, ad* per via di terra.

overlap *vi* [əuvə'læp] sovrapporsi ♦ *n* ['əuvəlæp] sovrapposizione *f*.

overleaf [əuvə'li:f] *ad* a tergo.

overload [əuvə'ləud] *vt* sovraccaricare.

overlook [əuvə'luk] *vt* (*have view of*) dare su; (*miss*) trascurare; (*forgive*) passare sopra a.

overlord ['əuvəlɔ:d] *n* capo supremo.

overmanning [əuvə'mænɪŋ] *n* eccedenza di manodopera.

overnight *ad* [əuvə'naɪt] (*happen*) durante la notte; (*fig*) tutto ad un tratto ♦ *a* ['əuvənaɪt] di notte; fulmineo(a); **he stayed there** ~ ci ha passato la notte; **if you travel** ~ ... se viaggia di notte ...; **he'll be away** ~ passerà la notte fuori.

overpass ['əuvəpɑ:s] *n* cavalcavia *m inv*.

overpay [əuvə'peɪ] *vt*: **to** ~ **sb by £50** pagare 50 sterline in più a qn.

overpower [əuvə'pauə*] *vt* sopraffare.

overpowering [əuvə'pauərɪŋ] *a* irresistibile; (*heat, stench*) soffocante.

overproduction ['əuvəprə'dʌkʃən] *n* sovrapproduzione *f*.

overrate [əuvə'reɪt] *vt* sopravvalutare.

overreach [əuvə'ri:tʃ] *vt*: **to** ~ **o.s.** volere strafare.

overreact [əuvəri:'ækt] *vi* reagire in modo esagerato.

override [əuvə'raɪd] *vt* (*irg: like* **ride**) (*order, objection*) passar sopra a; (*decision*) annullare.

overriding [əuvə'raɪdɪŋ] *a* preponderante.

overrule [əuvə'ru:l] *vt* (*decision*) annullare; (*claim*) respingere.

overrun [əuvə'rʌn] *vt irg* (*MIL*: *country etc*) invadere; (*time limit etc*) superare, andare al di là di ♦ *vi* protrarsi; **the town is** ~ **with tourists** la città è invasa dai turisti.

overseas [əuvə'si:z] *ad* oltremare; (*abroad*) all'estero ♦ *a* (*trade*) estero(a); (*visitor*) straniero(a).

overseer ['əuvəsɪə*] *n* (*in factory*) caposquadra *m*.

overshadow [əuvə'ʃædəu] *vt* (*fig*) eclissare.

overshoot [əuvə'ʃu:t] *vt irg* superare.

oversight ['əuvəsaɪt] *n* omissione *f*, svista; **due to an** ~ per una svista.

oversimplify [əuvə'sɪmplɪfaɪ] *vt* rendere troppo semplice.

oversleep [əuvə'sli:p] *vi irg* dormire troppo a lungo.

overspend [əuvə'spɛnd] *vi irg* spendere troppo; **we have overspent by 5000 dollars** abbiamo speso 5000 dollari di troppo.

overspill ['əuvəspɪl] *n* eccedenza di popolazione.

overstaffed [əuvə'stɑ:ft] *a*: **to be** ~ avere troppo personale.

overstate [əuvə'steɪt] *vt* esagerare.

overstatement [əuvə'steɪtmənt] *n* esagerazione *f*.

overstep [əuvə'stɛp] *vt*: **to** ~ **the mark** superare ogni limite.

overstock [əuvə'stɔk] *vt* sovrapprovvigionare, sovraimmagazzinare.

overstrike *n* ['əuvəstraɪk] (*on printer*) sovrapposizione *f* (di caratteri) ♦ *vt irg* [əuvə'straɪk] sovrapporre.

overt [əu'və:t] *a* palese.

overtake [əuvə'teɪk] *vt irg* sorpassare.

overtaking [əuvə'teɪkɪŋ] *n* (*AUT*) sorpasso.

overtax [əuvə'tæks] *vt* (*ECON*) imporre tasse eccessive a, tassare eccessivamente; (*fig: strength, patience*) mettere alla prova, abusare di; **to** ~ **o.s.** chiedere troppo alle proprie forze.

overthrow [əuvə'θrəu] *vt irg* (*government*) rovesciare.

overtime ['əuvətaɪm] *n* (lavoro) straordinario; **to do** *or* **work** ~ fare lo straordinario.

overtime ban *n* rifiuto sindacale a fare gli straordinari.

overtone ['əuvətəun] *n* (*also:* ~**s**) sfumatura.

overture ['əuvətʃuə*] *n* (*MUS*) ouverture *f inv*; (*fig*) approccio.

overturn [əuvə'tə:n] *vt* rovesciare ♦ *vi* rovesciarsi.

overweight [əuvə'weɪt] *a* (*person*) troppo grasso(a); (*luggage*) troppo pesante.

overwhelm [əuvə'wɛlm] *vt* sopraffare; sommergere; schiacciare.

overwhelming [əuvə'wɛlmɪŋ] *a* (*victory, defeat*) schiacciante; (*desire*) irresistibile; **one's** ~ **impression is of heat** l'impressione dominante è quella di caldo.

overwhelmingly [əuvə'wɛlmɪŋlɪ] *ad* in massa.

overwork [əuvə'wə:k] *vt* far lavorare troppo ♦ *vi* lavorare troppo, strapazzarsi.

overwrite [əuvə'raɪt] *vt* (*COMPUT*) ricoprire.
overwrought [əuvə'rɔːt] *a* molto agitato(a).
ovulation [ɔvju'leɪʃən] *n* ovulazione *f*.
owe [əu] *vt* dovere; **to ~ sb sth, to ~ sth to sb** dovere qc a qn.
owing to ['əuɪŋtuː] *prep* a causa di.
owl [aul] *n* gufo.
own [əun] *a* proprio(a) ♦ *vt* possedere ♦ *vi* (*Brit*): **to ~ to sth** ammettere qc; **to ~ to having done sth** ammettere di aver fatto qc; **a room of my ~** la mia propria camera; **to get one's ~ back** vendicarsi; **on one's ~** tutto(a) solo(a); **can I have it for my (very) ~?** posso averlo tutto per me?; **to come into one's ~** mostrare le proprie qualità.
   own up *vi* confessare.
own brand *n* (*COMM*) etichetta propria.
owner ['əunə*] *n* proprietario/a.
owner-occupier ['əunər'ɔkjupaɪə*] *n* proprietario/a della casa in cui abita.
ownership ['əunəʃɪp] *n* possesso; **it's under new ~** ha un nuovo proprietario.
ox, *pl* **oxen** [ɔks, 'ɔksn] *n* bue *m*.
Oxfam ['ɔksfæm] *n* abbr (*Brit*: = *Oxford Committee for Famine Relief*) organizzazione per aiuti al terzo mondo.
oxide ['ɔksaɪd] *n* ossido.
Oxon. ['ɔksn] abbr (*Brit*: = *Oxoniensis*) = *of Oxford*.
oxtail ['ɔksteɪl] *n*: **~ soup** minestra di coda di bue.
oxyacetylene ['ɔksɪə'sɛtɪliːn] *a* ossiacetilenico(a); **~ burner, ~ lamp** cannello ossiacetilenico.
oxygen ['ɔksɪdʒən] *n* ossigeno.
oxygen mask *n* maschera ad ossigeno.
oxygen tent *n* tenda ad ossigeno.
oyster ['ɔɪstə*] *n* ostrica.
oz. abbr = **ounce**.
ozone ['əuzəun] *n* ozono.
ozone layer *n* strato di ozono.

P

P, p [piː] *n* (*letter*) P, p *f or m inv*; **P for Peter** ≈ P come Padova.
P abbr = **president; prince.**
p abbr (= *page*) p; (*Brit*) = **penny, pence.**
PA *n* abbr see **personal assistant; public address system** ♦ abbr (*US POST*) = *Pennsylvania*.
pa [pɑː] *n* (*col*) papà *m inv*, babbo.
p.a. abbr = **per annum.**
PAC *n* abbr (*US*) = *political action committee*.
pace [peɪs] *n* passo; (*speed*) passo; velocità ♦ *vi*: **to ~ up and down** camminare su e giù; **to keep ~ with** camminare di pari passo a;

(*events*) tenersi al corrente di; **to put sb through his ~s** (*fig*) mettere qn alla prova; **to set the ~** (*running*) fare l'andatura; (*fig*) dare il la *or* il tono.
pacemaker ['peɪsmeɪkə*] *n* (*MED*) pacemaker *m inv*, stimolatore *m* cardiaco; (*SPORT*) chi fa l'andatura.
pacific [pə'sɪfɪk] *a* pacifico(a) ♦ *n*: **the P~ (Ocean)** il Pacifico, l'Oceano Pacifico.
pacification [pæsɪfɪ'keɪʃən] *n* pacificazione *f*.
pacifier ['pæsɪfaɪə*] *n* (*US*: *dummy*) succhiotto, ciuccio (*col*).
pacifist ['pæsɪfɪst] *n* pacifista *m/f*.
pacify ['pæsɪfaɪ] *vt* pacificare; (*soothe*) calmare.
pack [pæk] *n* (*packet*) pacco; (*COMM*) confezione *f*; (*US*: *of cigarettes*) pacchetto; (*of goods*) balla; (*of hounds*) muta; (*of wolves*) branco; (*of thieves etc*) banda; (*of cards*) mazzo ♦ *vt* (*goods*) impaccare, imballare; (*in suitcase etc*) mettere; (*box*) riempire; (*cram*) stipare, pigiare; (*press down*) tamponare; turare; (*COMPUT*) comprimere, impaccare ♦ *vi*: **to ~** (**one's bags**) fare la valigia; **to send sb ~ing** (*col*) spedire via qn.
   pack in (*Brit col*) *vi* (*watch, car*) guastarsi ♦ *vt* mollare, piantare; **~ it in!** piantala!
   pack off *vt* (*person*) spedire.
   pack up *vi* (*Brit col*: *machine*) guastarsi; (: *person*) far fagotto ♦ *vt* (*belongings, clothes*) mettere in una valigia; (*goods, presents*) imballare.
package ['pækɪdʒ] *n* pacco; balla; (*also*: **~ deal**) pacchetto; forfait *m inv* ♦ *vt* (*goods*) confezionare.
package holiday *n* (*Brit*) vacanza organizzata.
package tour *n* viaggio organizzato.
packaging ['pækɪdʒɪŋ] *n* confezione *f*, imballo.
packed [pækt] *a* (*crowded*) affollato(a); **~ lunch** (*Brit*) pranzo al sacco.
packer ['pækə*] *n* (*person*) imballatore/trice.
packet ['pækɪt] *n* pacchetto.
packet switching *n* (*COMPUT*) commutazione *f* di pacchetto.
pack ice ['pækaɪs] *n* banchisa.
packing ['pækɪŋ] *n* imballaggio.
packing case *n* cassa da imballaggio.
pact [pækt] *n* patto, accordo; trattato.
pad [pæd] *n* blocco; (*for inking*) tampone *m*; (*col*: *flat*) appartamentino ♦ *vt* imbottire ♦ *vi*: **to ~ about/in** *etc* camminare/entrare *etc* a passi felpati.
padding ['pædɪŋ] *n* imbottitura; (*fig*) riempitivo.
paddle ['pædl] *n* (*oar*) pagaia ♦ *vi* sguazzare ♦ *vt* (*boat*) fare andare a colpi di pagaia.
paddle steamer *n* battello a ruote.
paddling pool ['pædlɪŋ-] *n* piscina per bambini.
paddock ['pædək] *n* recinto; paddock *m inv*.
paddy ['pædɪ] *n* (*also*: **~ field**) risaia.
padlock ['pædlɔk] *n* lucchetto ♦ *vt* chiudere

con il lucchetto.

padre ['pɑ:drɪ] *n* cappellano.

Padua ['pædʒuə] *n* Padova.

paediatrics, *(US)* **pediatrics** [pi:dɪ'ætrɪks] *n* pediatria.

pagan ['peɪgən] *a*, *n* pagano(a).

page [peɪdʒ] *n* pagina; *(also:* ~ **boy)** fattorino; *(: at wedding)* paggio ♦ *vt (in hotel etc)* (far) chiamare.

pageant ['pædʒənt] *n* spettacolo storico; grande cerimonia.

pageantry ['pædʒəntrɪ] *n* pompa.

page break *n* interruzione *f* di pagina.

pager ['peɪdʒə*] *n* cicalino.

paginate ['pædʒɪneɪt] *vt* impaginare.

pagination [pædʒɪ'neɪʃən] *n* impaginazione *f*.

pagoda [pə'gəudə] *n* pagoda.

paid [peɪd] *pt, pp of* **pay** ♦ *a (work, official)* rimunerato(a); **to put** ~ **to** *(Brit)* mettere fine a.

paid-up ['peɪdʌp], *(US)* **paid in** ['peɪdɪn] *a (member)* che ha pagato la sua quota; *(share)* interamente pagato(a); ~ **capital** capitale *m* interamente versato.

pail [peɪl] *n* secchio.

pain [peɪn] *n* dolore *m*; **to be in** ~ soffrire, aver male; **to have a** ~ **in** aver male *or* un dolore a; **to take** ~**s to do** mettercela tutta per fare; **on** ~ **of death** sotto pena di morte.

pained [peɪnd] *a* addolorato(a), afflitto(a).

painful ['peɪnful] *a* doloroso(a), che fa male; *(difficult)* difficile, penoso(a).

painfully ['peɪnfəlɪ] *ad (fig: very)* fin troppo.

painkiller ['peɪnkɪlə*] *n* antalgico, antidolorifico.

painless ['peɪnlɪs] *a* indolore.

painstaking ['peɪnzteɪkɪŋ] *a* sollecito(a).

paint [peɪnt] *n (for house etc)* tinta, vernice *f*; *(ART)* colore *m* ♦ *vt (ART, walls)* dipingere; *(door etc)* verniciare; **a tin of** ~ un barattolo di tinta *or* vernice; **to** ~ **the door blue** verniciare la porta di azzurro; **to** ~ **in oils** dipingere a olio.

paintbox ['peɪntbɔks] *n* scatola di colori.

paintbrush ['peɪntbrʌʃ] *n* pennello.

painter ['peɪntə*] *n (artist)* pittore *m*; *(decorator)* imbianchino.

painting ['peɪntɪŋ] *n (activity: of artist)* pittura; *(: of decorator)* imbiancatura; verniciatura; *(picture)* dipinto, quadro.

paint-stripper ['peɪntstrɪpə*] *n* prodotto sverniciante.

paintwork ['peɪntwɔ:k] *n (Brit)* tinta; *(: of car)* vernice *f*.

pair [pɛə*] *n (of shoes, gloves etc)* paio; *(of people)* coppia; duo *m inv*; **a** ~ **of scissors/ trousers** un paio di forbici/pantaloni.
pair off *vi*: **to** ~ **off (with sb)** fare coppia (con qn).

pajamas [pə'dʒɑ:məz] *npl (US)* pigiama *m*.

Pakistan [pɑ:kɪ'stɑ:n] *n* Pakistan *m*.

Pakistani [pɑ:kɪ'stɑ:nɪ] *a*, *n* pakistano(a).

PAL [pæl] *n abbr (TV:* = *phase alternation line)* PAL *m*.

pal [pæl] *n (col)* amico/a, compagno/a.

palace ['pæləs] *n* palazzo.

palatable ['pælɪtəbl] *a* gustoso(a).

palate ['pælɪt] *n* palato.

palatial [pə'leɪʃəl] *a* sontuoso(a), sfarzoso(a).

palaver [pə'lɑ:və*] *n* chiacchiere *fpl*; storie *fpl*.

pale [peɪl] *a* pallido(a) ♦ *vi* impallidire ♦ *n*: **to be beyond the** ~ aver oltrepassato ogni limite; **to grow** *or* **turn** ~ *(person)* diventare pallido(a), impallidire; **to** ~ **into in- significance (beside)** perdere d'importanza (nei confronti di); ~ **blue** azzurro *or* blu pallido *inv*.

paleness ['peɪlnɪs] *n* pallore *m*.

Palestine ['pælɪstaɪn] *n* Palestina.

Palestinian [pælɪs'tɪnɪən] *a*, *n* palestinese *(m/f)*.

palette ['pælɪt] *n* tavolozza.

paling ['peɪlɪŋ] *n (stake)* palo; *(fence)* palizzata.

palisade [pælɪ'seɪd] *n* palizzata.

pall [pɔ:l] *n (of smoke)* cappa ♦ *vi*: **to** ~ **(on)** diventare noioso(a) (a).

pallet ['pælɪt] *n (for goods)* paletta.

pallid ['pælɪd] *a* pallido(a), smorto(a).

pallor ['pælə*] *n* pallore *m*.

pally ['pælɪ] *a (col)* amichevole.

palm [pɑ:m] *n (ANAT)* palma, palmo; *(also:* ~ **tree)** palma ♦ *vt*: **to** ~ **sth off on sb** *(col)* rifilare qc a qn.

palmist ['pɑ:mɪst] *n* chiromante *m/f*.

Palm Sunday *n* Domenica delle Palme.

palpable ['pælpəbl] *a* palpabile.

palpitation [pælpɪ'teɪʃən] *n* palpitazione *f*; **to have** ~**s** avere le palpitazioni.

paltry ['pɔ:ltrɪ] *a* derisorio(a); insignificante.

pamper ['pæmpə*] *vt* viziare, accarezzare.

pamphlet ['pæmflət] *n* dépliant *m inv*; *(political etc)* volantino, manifestino.

pan [pæn] *n (also:* **sauce~)** casseruola; *(also:* **frying** ~) padella ♦ *vi (CINEMA)* fare una panoramica; **to** ~ **for gold** (lavare le sabbie aurifere per) cercare l'oro.

panacea [pænə'sɪə] *n* panacea.

panache [pə'næʃ] *n* stile *m*.

Panama ['pænəmɑ:] *n* Panama *m*.

Panama Canal *n* canale *m* di Panama.

Panamanian [pænə'meɪnɪən] *a*, *n* panamense *(m/f)*.

pancake ['pænkeɪk] *n* frittella.

Pancake Day *n (Brit)* martedì *m* grasso.

pancreas ['pæŋkrɪəs] *n* pancreas *m inv*.

panda ['pændə] *n* panda *m inv*.

panda car *n (Brit)* auto *f* della polizia.

pandemonium [pændɪ'məunɪəm] *n* pandemonio.

pander ['pændə*] *vi*: **to** ~ **to** lusingare; concedere tutto a.

pane [peɪn] *n* vetro.

panel ['pænl] *n (of wood, cloth etc)* pannello; *(RADIO, TV)* giuria.

panel game *n (Brit)* quiz *m inv* a squadre.

panelling, *(US)* **paneling** ['pænəlɪŋ] *n* rivestimento a pannelli.

panellist, (US) **panelist** ['pænəlıst] n partecipante m/f (al quiz, alla tavola rotonda etc).

pang [pæŋ] n: **to feel ~s of remorse** essere torturato(a) dal rimorso; **~s of hunger** spasimi mpl della fame; **~s of conscience** morsi mpl di coscienza.

panic ['pænık] n panico ♦ vi perdere il sangue freddo.

panicky ['pænıkı] a (person) pauroso(a).

panic-stricken ['pænıkstrıkən] a (person) preso(a) dal panico, in preda al panico; (look) terrorizzato(a).

pannier ['pænıə*] n (on animal) bisaccia; (on bicycle) borsa.

panorama [pænə'rɑːmə] n panorama m.

panoramic [pænə'ræmık] a panoramico(a).

pansy ['pænzı] n (BOT) viola del pensiero, pensée f inv; (col) femminuccia.

pant [pænt] vi ansare.

pantechnicon [pæn'tɛknıkən] n (Brit) grosso furgone m per traslochi.

panther ['pænθə*] n pantera.

panties ['pæntız] npl slip m, mutandine fpl.

pantihose ['pæntıhəuz] n (US) collant m inv.

pantomime ['pæntəmaım] n pantomima; (Brit: at Christmas) spettacolo natalizio (sulla falsariga delle favole per bambini).

pantry ['pæntrı] n dispensa.

pants [pænts] npl (Brit) mutande fpl, slip m; (US: trousers) pantaloni mpl.

pantsuit ['pæntsuːt] n (US) completo m or tailleur m inv pantalone inv.

papacy ['peɪpəsı] n papato.

papal ['peɪpəl] a papale, pontificio(a).

paper ['peɪpə*] n carta; (also: **wall~**) carta da parati, tappezzeria; (also: **news~**) giornale m; (study, article) saggio; (exam) prova scritta ♦ a di carta ♦ vt tappezzare; **a piece of ~** (odd bit) un pezzo di carta; (sheet) un foglio (di carta); **to put sth down on ~** mettere qc per iscritto; see also **papers**.

paper advance n (on printer) avanzamento della carta.

paperback ['peɪpəbæk] n tascabile m; edizione f economica ♦ a: **~ edition** edizione f tascabile.

paper bag n sacchetto di carta.

paperboy ['peɪpəbɔɪ] n (selling) strillone m; (delivering) ragazzo che recapita i giornali.

paper clip n graffetta, clip f inv.

paper handkerchief n fazzolettino di carta.

paper mill n cartiera.

paper money n cartamoneta, moneta cartacea.

paper profit n utile m teorico.

papers ['peɪpəz] npl (also: **identity ~**) carte fpl, documenti mpl.

paperweight ['peɪpəweɪt] n fermacarte m inv.

paperwork ['peɪpəwɜːk] n lavoro amministrativo.

papier-mâché ['pæpɪeɪ'mæʃeɪ] n cartapesta.

paprika ['pæprıkə] n paprica.

Pap test, Pap smear ['pæp-] n (MED) pap-test m inv.

par [pɑː*] n parità, pari f; (GOLF) norma; **on a ~ with** alla pari con; **at/above/below ~** (COMM) alla/sopra la/sotto la pari; **above/below ~** (gen, GOLF) al di sopra/al di sotto della norma; **to feel below** or **under** or **not up to ~** non sentirsi in forma.

parable ['pærəbl] n parabola (REL).

parabola [pə'ræbələ] n parabola (MATH).

parachute ['pærəʃuːt] n paracadute m inv ♦ vi scendere col paracadute.

parachute jump n lancio col paracadute.

parachutist ['pærəʃuːtıst] n paracadutista m/f.

parade [pə'reɪd] n parata; (inspection) rivista, rassegna ♦ vt (fig) fare sfoggio di ♦ vi sfilare in parata; **a fashion ~** (Brit) una sfilata di moda.

parade ground n piazza d'armi.

paradise ['pærədaıs] n paradiso.

paradox ['pærədɔks] n paradosso.

paradoxical [pærə'dɔksıkl] a paradossale.

paradoxically [pærə'dɔksıklı] ad paradossalmente.

paraffin ['pærəfın] n (Brit): **~ (oil)** paraffina; **liquid ~** olio di paraffina.

paraffin heater n (Brit) stufa al cherosene.

paraffin lamp n (Brit) lampada al cherosene.

paragon ['pærəgən] n modello di perfezione or di virtù.

paragraph ['pærəgrɑːf] n paragrafo; **to begin a new ~** andare a capo.

Paraguay ['pærəgwaı] n Paraguay m.

Paraguayan [pærə'gwaıən] a, n paraguaiano(a).

parallel ['pærəlɛl] a (also COMPUT) parallelo(a); (fig) analogo(a) ♦ n (line) parallela; (fig, GEO) parallelo; **~ (with** or **to)** parallelo(a) (a).

paralysis, pl **paralyses** [pə'rælısıs, -siːz] n paralisi f inv.

paralytic [pærə'lıtık] a paralitico(a); (Brit col: drunk) ubriaco(a) fradicio(a).

paralyze ['pærəlaız] vt paralizzare.

parameter [pə'ræmıtə*] n parametro.

paramilitary [pærə'mılıtərı] a paramilitare.

paramount ['pærəmaunt] a: **of ~ importance** di capitale importanza.

paranoia [pærə'nɔıə] n paranoia.

paranoid ['pærənɔıd] a paranoico(a).

paranormal [pærə'nɔːml] a paranormale.

paraphernalia [pærəfə'neılıə] n attrezzi mpl, roba.

paraphrase ['pærəfreız] vt parafrasare.

paraplegic [pærə'pliːdʒık] n paraplegico(a).

parapsychology [pærəsaı'kɔlədʒı] n parapsicologia.

parasite ['pærəsaıt] n parassita m.

parasol ['pærəsɔl] n parasole m inv.

paratrooper ['pærətruːpə*] n paracadutista m (soldato).

parcel ['pɑːsl] n pacco, pacchetto ♦ vt (also: ~ up) impaccare.

parcel out *vt* spartire.
parcel bomb *n* (*Brit*) pacchetto esplosivo.
parcel post *n* servizio pacchi.
parch [pɑːtʃ] *vt* riardere.
parched ['pɑːtʃt] *a* (*person*) assetato(a).
parchment ['pɑːtʃmənt] *n* pergamena.
pardon ['pɑːdn] *n* perdono; grazia ♦ *vt* perdonare; (*LAW*) graziare; ~! scusi!; ~ me! mi scusi!; **I beg your** ~! scusi!; **(I beg your)** ~?, (*US*) ~ **me?** prego?
pare [pɛə*] *vt* (*Brit*: *nails*) tagliarsi; (: *fruit etc*) sbucciare, pelare.
parent ['pɛərənt] *n* padre *m* (*or* madre *f*); ~**s** *npl* genitori *mpl*.
parentage ['pɛərəntɪdʒ] *n* natali *mpl*; **of unknown** ~ di genitori sconosciuti.
parental [pə'rɛntl] *a* dei genitori.
parent company *n* società madre *f inv*.
parenthesis, *pl* **parentheses** [pə'rɛnθɪsɪs, -siːz] *n* parentesi *f inv*; **in parentheses** fra parentesi.
parenthood ['pɛərənthud] *n* paternità *or* maternità.
parenting ['pɛərəntɪŋ] *n* mestiere *m* di genitore.
Paris ['pærɪs] *n* Parigi *f*.
parish ['pærɪʃ] *n* parrocchia; (*civil*) ≈ municipio ♦ *a* parrocchiale.
parish council *n* (*Brit*) ≈ consiglio comunale.
parishioner [pə'rɪʃənə*] *n* parrocchiano/a.
Parisian [pə'rɪzɪən] *a*, *n* parigino(a).
parity ['pærɪtɪ] *n* parità.
park [pɑːk] *n* parco; (*public*) giardino pubblico ♦ *vt*, *vi* parcheggiare.
parka ['pɑːkə] *n* eskimo.
parking ['pɑːkɪŋ] *n* parcheggio; **"no** ~**"** "sosta vietata".
parking lights *npl* luci *fpl* di posizione.
parking lot *n* (*US*) posteggio, parcheggio.
parking meter *n* parchimetro.
parking offence *n* (*Brit*) infrazione *f* al divieto di sosta.
parking place *n* posto di parcheggio.
parking ticket *n* multa per sosta vietata.
parking violation *n* (*US*) = **parking offence**.
parkway ['pɑːkweɪ] *n* (*US*) viale *m*.
parlance ['pɑːləns] *n*: **in common/modern** ~ nel gergo *or* linguaggio comune/moderno.
parliament ['pɑːləmənt] *n* parlamento.
parliamentary [pɑːlə'mɛntərɪ] *a* parlamentare.
parlour, (*US*) **parlor** ['pɑːlə*] *n* salotto.
parlous ['pɑːləs] *a* periglioso(a).
Parmesan [pɑːmɪ'zæn] *n* (*also*: ~ **cheese**) parmigiano.
parochial [pə'rəukɪəl] *a* parrocchiale; (*pej*) provinciale.
parody ['pærədɪ] *n* parodia.
parole [pə'rəul] *n*: **on** ~ in libertà per buona condotta.
paroxysm ['pærəksɪzəm] *n* (*MED*) parossismo; (*of anger, laughter, coughing*) convulso; (*of grief*) attacco.

parquet ['pɑːkeɪ] *n*: ~ **floor(ing)** parquet *m*.
parrot ['pærət] *n* pappagallo.
parrot fashion *ad* in modo pappagallesco.
parry ['pærɪ] *vt* parare.
parsimonious [pɑːsɪ'məunɪəs] *a* parsimonioso(a).
parsley ['pɑːslɪ] *n* prezzemolo.
parsnip ['pɑːsnɪp] *n* pastinaca.
parson ['pɑːsn] *n* prete *m*; (*Church of England*) parroco.
part [pɑːt] *n* parte *f*; (*of machine*) pezzo; (*THEATRE etc*) parte, ruolo; (*MUS*) voce *f*; parte ♦ *a* in parte ♦ *ad* = **partly** ♦ *vt* separare ♦ *vi* (*people*) separarsi; (*roads*) dividersi; **to take** ~ **in** prendere parte a; **to take sb's** ~ parteggiare per qn, prendere le parti di qn; **on his** ~ da parte sua; **for my** ~ per parte mia; **for the most** ~ in generale; nella maggior parte dei casi; **for the better** ~ **of the day** per la maggior parte della giornata; **to be** ~ **and parcel of** essere parte integrante di; **to take sth in good/bad** ~ prendere bene/male qc; ~ **of speech** (*LING*) parte del discorso.
part with *vt fus* separarsi da; rinunciare a.
partake [pɑː'teɪk] *vi irg* (*formal*): **to** ~ **of sth** consumare qc, prendere qc.
part exchange *n* (*Brit*): **in** ~ in pagamento parziale.
partial ['pɑːʃl] *a* parziale; **to be** ~ **to** avere un debole per.
partially ['pɑːʃəlɪ] *ad* in parte, parzialmente.
participant [pɑː'tɪsɪpənt] *n*: ~ **(in)** partecipante *m/f* (a).
participate [pɑː'tɪsɪpeɪt] *vi*: **to** ~ **(in)** prendere parte (a), partecipare (a).
participation [pɑːtɪsɪ'peɪʃən] *n* partecipazione *f*.
participle ['pɑːtɪsɪpl] *n* participio.
particle ['pɑːtɪkl] *n* particella.
particular [pə'tɪkjulə*] *a* particolare; speciale; (*fussy*) difficile; meticoloso(a); ~**s** *npl* particolari *mpl*, dettagli *mpl*; (*information*) informazioni *fpl*; **in** ~ in particolare, particolarmente; **to be very** ~ **about** essere molto pignolo(a) su; **I'm not** ~ per me va bene tutto.
particularly [pə'tɪkjulələɪ] *ad* particolarmente; in particolare.
parting ['pɑːtɪŋ] *n* separazione *f*; (*Brit*: *in hair*) scriminatura ♦ *a* d'addio; ~ **shot** (*fig*) battuta finale.
partisan [pɑːtɪ'zæn] *n* partigiano/a ♦ *a* partigiano(a); di parte.
partition [pɑː'tɪʃən] *n* (*POL*) partizione *f*; (*wall*) tramezzo.
partly ['pɑːtlɪ] *ad* parzialmente; in parte.
partner ['pɑːtnə*] *n* (*COMM*) socio/a; (*SPORT*) compagno/a; (*at dance*) cavaliere/dama.
partnership ['pɑːtnəʃɪp] *n* associazione *f*; (*COMM*) società *f inv*; **to go into** ~ **(with)**, **form a** ~ **(with)** mettersi in società (con), associarsi (a).
part payment *n* acconto.

partridge ['pɑ:trɪdʒ] *n* pernice *f.*
part-time ['pɑ:t'taɪm] *a*, *ad* a orario ridotto, part-time (*inv*).
part-timer ['pɑ:t'taɪmə*] *n* (*also:* **part-time worker**) lavoratore/trice part-time.
party ['pɑ:tɪ] *n* (*POL*) partito; (*team*) squadra; gruppo; (*LAW*) parte *f;* (*celebration*) ricevimento; serata; festa; **dinner ~** cena; **to give** *or* **throw a ~** dare una festa *or* un party; **to be a ~ to a crime** essere coinvolto in un reato.
party line *n* (*POL*) linea del partito; (*TEL*) duplex *m inv.*
par value *n* (*of share, bond*) valore *m* nominale.
pass [pɑ:s] *vt* (*gen*) passare; (*place*) passare davanti a; (*exam*) passare, superare; (*candidate*) promuovere; (*overtake, surpass*) sorpassare, superare; (*approve*) approvare ♦ *vi* passare; (*SCOL*) essere promosso(a) ♦ *n* (*permit*) lasciapassare *m inv*; permesso; (*in mountains*) passo, gola; (*SPORT*) passaggio; (*SCOL: also:* **~ mark**): **to get a ~** prendere la sufficienza; **to ~ for** passare per; **could you ~ the vegetables round?** potrebbe far passare i contorni?; **to make a ~ at sb** (*col*) fare delle proposte *or* delle avances a qn; **things have come to a pretty ~** (*Brit*) ecco a cosa siamo arrivati.
pass away *vi* morire.
pass by *vi* passare ♦ *vt* trascurare.
pass down *vt* (*customs, inheritance*) tramandare, trasmettere.
pass on *vi* (*die*) spegnersi, mancare ♦ *vt* (*hand on*): **to ~ on (to)** (*news, information, object*) passare (a); (*cold, illness*) attaccare (a); (*benefits*) trasmettere (a); (*price rises*) riversare (su).
pass out *vi* svenire; (*Brit MIL*) uscire dall'accademia.
pass over *vi* (*die*) spirare ♦ *vt* lasciare da parte.
pass up *vt* (*opportunity*) lasciarsi sfuggire, perdere.
passable ['pɑ:səbl] *a* (*road*) praticabile; (*work*) accettabile.
passage ['pæsɪdʒ] *n* (*gen*) passaggio; (*also:* **~way**) corridoio; (*in book*) brano, passo; (*by boat*) traversata.
passbook ['pɑ:sbuk] *n* libretto di risparmio.
passenger ['pæsɪndʒə*] *n* passeggero/a.
passer-by [pɑ:sə'baɪ] *n* passante *m/f.*
passing ['pɑ:sɪŋ] *a* (*fig*) fuggevole; **to mention sth in ~** accennare a qc di sfuggita.
passing place *n* (*AUT*) piazzola (di sosta).
passion ['pæʃən] *n* passione *f*; amore *m*; **to have a ~ for sth** aver la passione di *or* per qc.
passionate ['pæʃənɪt] *a* appassionato(a).
passive ['pæsɪv] *a* (*also LING*) passivo(a).
passkey ['pɑ:ski:] *n* passe-partout *m inv.*
Passover ['pɑ:səʊvə*] *n* Pasqua ebraica.
passport ['pɑ:spɔ:t] *n* passaporto.
passport control *n* controllo *m* passaporti

inv.
password ['pɑ:swə:d] *n* parola d'ordine.
past [pɑ:st] *prep* (*further than*) oltre, di là di; dopo; (*later than*) dopo ♦ *ad*: **to run ~** passare di corsa; **to walk ~** passare ♦ *a* passato(a); (*president etc*) ex *inv* ♦ *n* passato; **quarter/half ~ four** le quattro e un quarto/e mezzo; **ten/twenty ~ four** le quattro e dieci/venti; **he's ~ forty** ha più di quarant'anni; **it's ~ midnight** è mezzanotte passata; **for the ~ few days** da qualche giorno; in questi ultimi giorni; **for the ~ 3 days** negli ultimi 3 giorni; **in the ~** in *or* nel passato; (*LING*) al passato; **I'm ~ caring** non me ne importa più nulla; **to be ~ it** (*Brit col: person*) essere finito(a).
pasta ['pæstə] *n* pasta.
paste [peɪst] *n* (*glue*) colla; (*CULIN*) pâté *m inv*; pasta ♦ *vt* collare; **tomato ~** concentrato di pomodoro.
pastel ['pæstl] *a* pastello *inv.*
pasteurized ['pæstəraɪzd] *a* pastorizzato(a).
pastille ['pæstl] *n* pastiglia.
pastime ['pɑ:staɪm] *n* passatempo.
past master *n* (*Brit*): **to be a ~ at** essere molto esperto(a) in.
pastor ['pɑ:stə*] *n* pastore *m.*
pastoral ['pɑ:stərl] *a* pastorale.
pastry ['peɪstrɪ] *n* pasta.
pasture ['pɑ:stʃə*] *n* pascolo.
pasty *n* ['pæstɪ] pasticcio di carne ♦ *a* ['peɪstɪ] pastoso(a); (*complexion*) pallido(a).
pat [pæt] *vt* accarezzare, dare un colpetto (affettuoso) a ♦ *n*: **a ~ of butter** un panetto di burro; **to give sb/o.s. a ~ on the back** (*fig*) congratularsi *or* compiacersi con qn/se stesso; **he knows it (off) ~**, (*US*) **he has it down ~** lo conosce *or* sa a menadito.
patch [pætʃ] *n* (*of material*) toppa; (*spot*) macchia; (*of land*) pezzo ♦ *vt* (*clothes*) rattoppare; **a bad ~** (*Brit*) un brutto periodo.
patch up *vt* rappezzare.
patchwork ['pætʃwə:k] *n* patchwork *m.*
patchy ['pætʃɪ] *a* irregolare.
pate [peɪt] *n*: **a bald ~** una testa pelata.
pâté ['pæteɪ] *n* pâté *m inv.*
patent ['peɪtnt] *n* brevetto ♦ *vt* brevettare ♦ *a* patente, manifesto(a).
patent leather *n* cuoio verniciato.
patently ['peɪtntlɪ] *ad* palesemente.
patent medicine *n* specialità *f inv* medicinale.
patent office *n* ufficio brevetti.
paternal [pə'tə:nl] *a* paterno(a).
paternity [pə'tə:nɪtɪ] *n* paternità.
paternity suit *n* (*LAW*) causa di riconoscimento della paternità.
path [pɑ:θ] *n* sentiero, viottolo; viale *m*; (*fig*) via, strada; (*of planet, missile*) traiettoria.
pathetic [pə'θetɪk] *a* (*pitiful*) patetico(a); (*very bad*) penoso(a).
pathological [pæθə'lɒdʒɪkl] *a* patologico(a).
pathologist [pə'θɒlədʒɪst] *n* patologo/a.
pathology [pə'θɒlədʒɪ] *n* patologia.

pathos ['peɪθɔs] n pathos m.
pathway ['pɑːθweɪ] n sentiero, viottolo.
patience ['peɪʃns] n pazienza; (Brit CARDS) solitario; **to lose one's ~** spazientirsi.
patient ['peɪʃnt] n paziente m/f; malato/a ♦ a paziente; **to be ~ with sb** essere paziente or aver pazienza con qn.
patiently ['peɪʃntlɪ] ad pazientemente.
patio ['pætɪəu] n terrazza.
patriot ['peɪtrɪət] n patriota m/f.
patriotic [pætrɪ'ɔtɪk] a patriottico(a).
patriotism ['pætrɪətɪzəm] n patriottismo.
patrol [pə'trəul] n pattuglia ♦ vt pattugliare; **to be on ~** fare la ronda; essere in ricognizione; essere in perlustrazione.
patrol boat n guardacoste m inv.
patrol car n autoradio f inv (della polizia).
patrolman [pə'trəulmən] n (US) poliziotto.
patron ['peɪtrən] n (in shop) cliente m/f; (of charity) benefattore/trice; **~ of the arts** mecenate m/f.
patronage ['pætrənɪdʒ] n patronato.
patronize ['pætrənaɪz] vt essere cliente abituale di; (fig) trattare con condiscendenza.
patronizing ['pætrənaɪzɪŋ] a condiscendente.
patron saint n patrono.
patter ['pætə*] n picchiettio; (sales talk) propaganda di vendita ♦ vi picchiettare.
pattern ['pætən] n modello; (SEWING etc) modello (di carta), cartamodello; (design) disegno, motivo; (sample) campione m; **behaviour ~s** tipi mpl di comportamento.
patterned ['pætənd] a a disegni, a motivi; (material) fantasia inv.
paucity ['pɔːsɪtɪ] n scarsità.
paunch [pɔːntʃ] n pancione m.
pauper ['pɔːpə*] n indigente m/f; **~'s grave** fossa comune.
pause [pɔːz] n pausa ♦ vi fare una pausa, arrestarsi; **to ~ for breath** fermarsi un attimo per riprender fiato.
pave [peɪv] vt pavimentare; **to ~ the way for** aprire la via a.
pavement ['peɪvmənt] n (Brit) marciapiede m; (US) pavimentazione f stradale.
pavilion [pə'vɪlɪən] n padiglione m; tendone m; (SPORT) edificio annesso ad un campo sportivo.
paving ['peɪvɪŋ] n pavimentazione f.
paving stone n lastra di pietra.
paw [pɔː] n zampa ♦ vt dare una zampata a; (subj: person: pej) palpare.
pawn [pɔːn] n pegno; (CHESS) pedone m; (fig) pedina ♦ vt dare in pegno.
pawnbroker ['pɔːnbrəukə*] n prestatore m su pegno.
pawnshop ['pɔːnʃɔp] n monte m di pietà.
pay [peɪ] n (gen) paga ♦ vb (pt, pp paid [peɪd]) vt pagare; (be profitable to: also fig) convenire a ♦ vi pagare; (be profitable) rendere; **to ~ attention (to)** fare attenzione (a); **I paid £5 for that record** quel disco l'ho pagato 5 sterline; **how much did you ~ for it?** quanto l'ha pagato?; **to ~ one's way**

pagare la propria parte; (company) coprire le spese; **to ~ dividends** (fig) dare buoni frutti.
pay back vt rimborsare.
pay for vt fus pagare.
pay in vt versare.
pay off vt (debts) saldare; (creditor) pagare; (mortgage) estinguere; (workers) licenziare ♦ vi (scheme) funzionare; (patience) dare dei frutti; **to ~ sth off in instalments** pagare qc a rate.
pay out vt (money) sborsare, tirar fuori; (rope) far allentare.
pay up vt saldare.
payable ['peɪəbl] a pagabile; **to make a cheque ~ to sb** intestare un assegno a (nome di) qn.
pay day n giorno di paga.
PAYE n abbr (Brit: = pay as you earn) pagamento di imposte tramite ritenute alla fonte.
payee [peɪ'iː] n beneficiario/a.
pay envelope n (US) busta f paga inv.
paying ['peɪɪŋ] a: **~ guest** ospite m/f pagante, pensionante m/f.
payload ['peɪləud] n carico utile.
payment ['peɪmənt] n pagamento; **advance ~** (part sum) anticipo, acconto; (total sum) pagamento anticipato; **deferred ~, ~ by instalments** pagamento dilazionato or a rate; **in ~ for, in ~ of** in pagamento di; **on ~ of £5** dietro pagamento di 5 sterline.
pay packet n (Brit) busta f paga inv.
payphone ['peɪfəun] n cabina telefonica.
payroll ['peɪrəul] n ruolo (organico); **to be on a firm's ~** far parte del personale di una ditta.
pay slip n (Brit) foglio m paga inv.
pay station n (US) cabina telefonica.
PBS n abbr (US: = Public Broadcasting Service) servizio che collabora alla realizzazione di programmi per la rete televisiva nazionale.
PBX abbr (= private branch exchange) sistema telefonico con centralino.
PC n abbr see **personal computer**; (Brit) see **police constable** ♦ abbr (Brit) = **Privy Councillor**.
pc abbr = **per cent**; (= postcard) C.P.
p/c abbr = **petty cash**.
PCB n abbr see **printed circuit board**.
pcm abbr = **per calendar month**.
PD n abbr (US) = **police department**.
pd abbr = **paid**.
PDQ abbr (col) = **pretty damn quick**.
PDSA n abbr (Brit: = People's Dispensary for Sick Animals) assistenza veterinaria gratuita.
PDT abbr (US: = Pacific Daylight Time) ora legale del Pacifico.
PE n abbr (= physical education) ed. fisica ♦ abbr (Canada) = **Prince Edward Island**.
pea [piː] n pisello.
peace [piːs] n pace f; (calm) calma, tranquillità; **to be at ~ with sb/sth** essere

in pace con qn/qc; **to keep the ~** (*subj*: *policeman*) mantenere l'ordine pubblico; (: *citizen*) rispettare l'ordine pubblico.

peaceable ['piːsəbl] *a* pacifico(a).

peaceful ['piːsful] *a* pacifico(a), calmo(a).

peace-keeping ['piːskiːpɪŋ] *n* mantenimento della pace.

peace offering *n* (*fig*) dono in segno di riconciliazione.

peach [piːtʃ] *n* pesca.

peacock ['piːkɔk] *n* pavone *m*.

peak [piːk] *n* (*of mountain*) cima, vetta; (*mountain itself*) picco; (*fig*) massimo; (: *of career*) acme *f*.

peak-hour ['piːkauə*] *a* (*traffic etc*) delle ore di punta.

peak hours *npl* ore *fpl* di punta.

peak period *n* periodo di punta.

peaky ['piːkɪ] *a* (*Brit col*) sbattuto(a).

peal [piːl] *n* (*of bells*) scampanio, carillon *m inv*; **~s of laughter** scoppi *mpl* di risa.

peanut ['piːnʌt] *n* arachide *f*, nocciolina americana.

peanut butter *n* burro di arachidi.

pear [pɛə*] *n* pera.

pearl [pəːl] *n* perla.

peasant ['pɛznt] *n* contadino/a.

peat [piːt] *n* torba.

pebble ['pɛbl] *n* ciottolo.

peck [pɛk] *vt* (*also*: **~ at**) beccare; (: *food*) mangiucchiare ♦ *n* colpo di becco; (*kiss*) bacetto.

pecking order ['pɛkɪŋ-] *n* (*fig*) ordine *m* gerarchico.

peckish ['pɛkɪʃ] *a* (*Brit col*): **I feel ~** ho un languorino.

peculiar [pɪ'kjuːlɪə*] *a* strano(a), bizzarro(a); (*particular*: *importance*, *qualities*) particolare; **~ to** tipico(a) di, caratteristico(a) di.

peculiarity [pɪkjuːlɪ'ærɪtɪ] *n* peculiarità *f inv*; (*oddity*) bizzarria.

pecuniary [pɪ'kjuːnɪərɪ] *a* pecuniario(a).

pedal ['pɛdl] *n* pedale *m* ♦ *vi* pedalare.

pedal bin *n* (*Brit*) pattumiera a pedale.

pedantic [pɪ'dæntɪk] *a* pedantesco(a).

peddle ['pɛdl] *vt* (*goods*) andare in giro a vendere; (*drugs*) spacciare; (*gossip*) mettere in giro.

peddler ['pɛdlə*] *n* venditore *m* ambulante.

pedestal ['pɛdəstl] *n* piedestallo.

pedestrian [pɪ'dɛstrɪən] *n* pedone/a ♦ *a* pedonale; (*fig*) prosaico(a), pedestre.

pedestrian crossing *n* (*Brit*) passaggio pedonale.

pedestrian precinct *n* (*Brit*) zona pedonale.

pediatrics [piːdɪ'ætrɪks] *n* (*US*) = **paediatrics**.

pedigree ['pɛdɪgriː] *n* stirpe *f*; (*of animal*) pedigree *m inv* ♦ *cpd* (*animal*) di razza.

pedlar ['pɛdlə*] *n* = **peddler**.

pee [piː] *vi* (*col*) pisciare.

peek [piːk] *vi* guardare furtivamente.

peel [piːl] *n* buccia; (*of orange, lemon*) scorza ♦ *vt* sbucciare ♦ *vi* (*paint etc*) staccarsi.

peel back *vt* togliere, levare.

peeler [piːlə*] *n*: **potato ~** sbucciapatate *m inv*.

peelings ['piːlɪŋz] *npl* bucce *fpl*.

peep [piːp] *n* (*Brit*: *look*) sguardo furtivo, sbirciata; (*sound*) pigolio ♦ *vi* (*Brit*) guardare furtivamente.

peep out *vi* (*Brit*) mostrarsi furtivamente.

peephole ['piːphəul] *n* spioncino.

peer [pɪə*] *vi*: **to ~ at** scrutare ♦ *n* (*noble*) pari *m inv*; (*equal*) pari *m/f inv*, uguale *m/f*.

peerage ['pɪərɪdʒ] *n* dignità di pari; pari *mpl*.

peerless ['pɪəlɪs] *a* impareggiabile, senza pari.

peeved [piːvd] *a* stizzito(a).

peevish ['piːvɪʃ] *a* stizzoso(a).

peg [pɛg] *n* (*tent* ~) picchetto; (*for coat etc*) attaccapanni *m inv*; (*Brit*: *also*: **clothes ~**) molletta ♦ *vt* (*clothes*) appendere con le mollette; (*Brit*: *groundsheet*) fissare con i picchetti; (*fig*: *prices*, *wages*) fissare, stabilizzare; **off the ~** confezionato(a).

pejorative [pɪ'dʒɔrətɪv] *a* peggiorativo(a).

Pekin [piː'kɪn], **Peking** [piː'kɪŋ] *n* Pechino *f*.

pekin(g)ese [piːkɪ'niːz] *n* pechinese *m*.

pelican ['pɛlɪkən] *n* pellicano.

pelican crossing *n* (*Brit AUT*) attraversamento pedonale con semaforo a controllo manuale.

pellet ['pɛlɪt] *n* pallottola, pallina.

pell-mell ['pɛl'mɛl] *ad* disordinatamente, alla rinfusa.

pelmet ['pɛlmɪt] *n* mantovana; cassonetto.

pelt [pɛlt] *vt*: **to ~ sb (with)** bombardare qn (con) ♦ *vi* (*rain*) piovere a dirotto ♦ *n* pelle *f*.

pelvis ['pɛlvɪs] *n* pelvi *f inv*, bacino.

pen [pɛn] *n* penna; (*for sheep*) recinto; (*US col*: *prison*) galera; **to put ~ to paper** prendere la penna in mano.

penal ['piːnl] *a* penale.

penalize ['piːnəlaɪz] *vt* punire; (*SPORT*) penalizzare; (*fig*) svantaggiare.

penal servitude [-'səːvɪtjuːd] *n* lavori *mpl* forzati.

penalty ['pɛnltɪ] *n* penalità *f inv*; sanzione *f* penale; (*fine*) ammenda; (*SPORT*) penalizzazione *f*; (*FOOTBALL*: *also*: **~ kick**) calcio di rigore.

penalty area *n* (*Brit SPORT*) area di rigore.

penalty clause *n* penale *f*.

penalty kick *n* (*FOOTBALL*) calcio di rigore.

penance ['pɛnəns] *n* penitenza.

pence [pɛns] *npl* (*Brit*) of **penny**.

penchant ['pɑ̃ːʃɑ̃ːŋ] *n* debole *m*.

pencil ['pɛnsl] *n* matita ♦ *vt* (*also*: **~ in**) scrivere a matita.

pencil case *n* astuccio per matite.

pencil sharpener *n* temperamatite *m inv*.

pendant ['pɛndnt] *n* pendaglio.

pending ['pɛndɪŋ] *prep* in attesa di ♦ *a* in sospeso.

pendulum ['pɛndjuləm] *n* pendolo.

penetrate ['pɛnɪtreɪt] *vt* penetrare.

penetrating ['pɛnɪtreɪtɪŋ] *a* penetrante.

penfriend ['pɛnfrɛnd] n (Brit) corrispondente m/f.

penguin ['pɛŋgwɪn] n pinguino.

penicillin [pɛnɪ'sɪlɪn] n penicillina.

peninsula [pə'nɪnsjulə] n penisola.

penis ['pi:nɪs] n pene m.

penitence ['pɛnɪtns] n penitenza.

penitent ['pɛnɪtnt] a penitente.

penitentiary [pɛnɪ'tɛnʃərɪ] n (US) carcere m.

penknife ['pɛnnaɪf] n temperino.

pen name n pseudonimo.

pennant ['pɛnənt] n banderuola.

penniless ['pɛnɪlɪs] a senza un soldo.

Pennines ['pɛnaɪnz] npl: **the** ~ i Pennini.

penny, pl **pennies** or **pence** ['pɛnɪ, 'pɛnɪz, pɛns] n penny m (pl pence); (US) centesimo.

penpal ['pɛnpæl] n corrispondente m/f.

pension ['pɛnʃən] n pensione f.

pension off vt mandare in pensione.

pensionable ['pɛnʃənəbl] a che ha diritto a una pensione.

pensioner ['pɛnʃənə*] n (Brit) pensionato/a.

pension fund n fondo pensioni.

pensive ['pɛnsɪv] a pensoso(a).

pentagon ['pɛntəgən] n pentagono.

Pentecost ['pɛntɪkɔst] n Pentecoste f.

penthouse ['pɛnthaus] n appartamento (di lusso) nell'attico.

pent-up ['pɛntʌp] a (feelings) represso(a).

penultimate [pɪ'nʌltɪmət] a penultimo(a).

penury ['pɛnjurɪ] n indigenza.

people ['pi:pl] npl gente f; persone fpl; (citizens) popolo ♦ n (nation, race) popolo ♦ vt popolare; **old** ~ i vecchi; **young** ~ i giovani; ~ **at large** il grande pubblico; **a man of the** ~ un uomo del popolo; **4/several** ~ **came** 4/parecchie persone sono venute; **the room was full of** ~ la stanza era piena di gente; ~ **say that** ... si dice or la gente dice che ....

pep [pɛp] n (col) dinamismo.

pep up vt vivacizzare; (food) rendere più gustoso(a).

pepper ['pɛpə*] n pepe m; (vegetable) peperone m ♦ vt pepare.

peppermint ['pɛpəmɪnt] n (plant) menta peperita; (sweet) pasticca di menta.

pepperpot ['pɛpəpɔt] n pepaiola.

peptalk ['pɛptɔ:k] n (col) discorso di incoraggiamento.

per [pə:*] prep per; a; ~ **hour** all'ora; ~ **kilo** etc il chilo etc; ~ **day** al giorno; ~ **week** alla settimana; ~ **person** a testa, a or per persona; **as** ~ **your instructions** secondo le vostre istruzioni.

per annum ad all'anno.

per capita a, ad pro capite.

perceive [pə'si:v] vt percepire; (notice) accorgersi di.

per cent ad per cento; **a 20** ~ **discount** uno sconto del 20 per cento.

percentage [pə'sɛntɪdʒ] n percentuale f; **on a** ~ **basis** a percentuale.

perceptible [pə'sɛptɪbl] a percettibile.

perception [pə'sɛpʃən] n percezione f; sensibilità; perspicacia.

perceptive [pə'sɛptɪv] a percettivo(a); perspicace.

perch [pə:tʃ] n (fish) pesce m persico; (for bird) sostegno, ramo ♦ vi appollaiarsi.

percolate ['pə:kəleɪt] vt filtrare.

percolator ['pə:kəleɪtə*] n caffettiera a pressione; caffettiera elettrica.

percussion [pə'kʌʃən] n percussione f; (MUS) strumenti mpl a percussione.

peremptory [pə'rɛmptərɪ] a perentorio(a).

perennial [pə'rɛnɪəl] a perenne ♦ n pianta perenne.

perfect a, n ['pə:fɪkt] a perfetto(a) ♦ n (also: ~ **tense**) perfetto, passato prossimo ♦ vt [pə'fɛkt] perfezionare; mettere a punto; **he's a** ~ **stranger to me** mi è completamente sconosciuto.

perfection [pə'fɛkʃən] n perfezione f.

perfectionist [pə'fɛkʃənɪst] n perfezionista m/f.

perfectly ['pə:fɪktlɪ] ad perfettamente; **I'm** ~ **happy with the situation** sono completamente soddisfatta della situazione; **you know** ~ **well** sa benissimo.

perforate ['pə:fəreɪt] vt perforare.

perforated ulcer n (MED) ulcera perforata.

perforation [pə:fə'reɪʃən] n perforazione f; (line of holes) dentellatura.

perform [pə'fɔ:m] vt (carry out) eseguire, fare; (symphony etc) suonare; (play, ballet) dare; (opera) fare ♦ vi suonare; recitare.

performance [pə'fɔ:məns] n esecuzione f; (at theatre etc) rappresentazione f, spettacolo; (of an artist) interpretazione f; (of player etc) performance f; (of car, engine) prestazione f; **the team put up a good** ~ la squadra ha giocato una bella partita.

performer [pə'fɔ:mə*] n artista m/f.

performing [pə'fɔ:mɪŋ] a (animal) ammaestrato(a).

perfume ['pə:fju:m] n profumo ♦ vt profumare.

perfunctory [pə'fʌŋktərɪ] a superficiale, per la forma.

perhaps [pə'hæps] ad forse; ~ **he'll come** forse verrà, può darsi che venga; ~ **so/not** forse sì/no, può darsi di sì/di no.

peril ['pɛrɪl] n pericolo.

perilous ['pɛrɪləs] a pericoloso(a).

perilously ['pɛrɪləslɪ] ad: **they came** ~ **close to being caught** sono stati a un pelo dall'esser presi.

perimeter [pə'rɪmɪtə*] n perimetro.

perimeter wall n muro di cinta.

period ['pɪərɪəd] n periodo; (HISTORY) epoca; (SCOL) lezione f; (full stop) punto; (US FOOTBALL) tempo; (MED) mestruazioni fpl ♦ a (costume, furniture) d'epoca; **for a** ~ **of three weeks** per un periodo di or per la durata di tre settimane; **the holiday** ~ (Brit) il periodo delle vacanze.

periodic [pɪərɪ'ɔdɪk] a periodico(a).

periodical [pɪərɪ'ɔdɪkl] *a* periodico(a) ♦ *n* periodico.

periodically [pɪərɪ'ɔdɪklɪ] *ad* periodicamente.

period pains *npl* (*Brit*) dolori *mpl* mestruali.

peripatetic [perɪpə'tetɪk] *a* (*salesman*) ambulante; (*Brit: teacher*) peripatetico(a).

peripheral [pə'rɪfərəl] *a* periferico(a) ♦ *n* (*COMPUT*) unità *f inv* periferica.

periphery [pə'rɪfərɪ] *n* periferia.

periscope ['perɪskəʊp] *n* periscopio.

perish ['perɪʃ] *vi* perire, morire; (*decay*) deteriorarsi.

perishable ['perɪʃəbl] *a* deperibile.

perishables ['perɪʃəblz] *npl* merci *fpl* deperibili.

perishing ['perɪʃɪŋ] *a* (*Brit col*): **it's ~ (cold)** fa un freddo da morire.

peritonitis [perɪtə'naɪtɪs] *n* peritonite *f*.

perjure ['pə:dʒə*] *vt*: **to ~ o.s.** spergiurare.

perjury ['pə:dʒərɪ] *n* (*LAW: in court*) falso giuramento; (*breach of oath*) spergiuro.

perk [pə:k] *n* vantaggio.

perk up *vi* (*cheer up*) rianimarsi.

perky ['pə:kɪ] *a* (*cheerful*) vivace, allegro(a).

perm [pə:m] *n* (*for hair*) permanente *f* ♦ *vt*: **to have one's hair ~ed** farsi fare la permanente.

permanence ['pə:mənəns] *n* permanenza.

permanent ['pə:mənənt] *a* permanente; (*job, position*) fisso(a); (*dye, ink*) indelebile; **~ address** residenza fissa; **I'm not ~ here** non sono fisso qui.

permanently ['pə:mənəntlɪ] *ad* definitivamente.

permeable ['pə:mɪəbl] *a* permeabile.

permeate ['pə:mɪeɪt] *vi* penetrare ♦ *vt* permeare.

permissible [pə'mɪsɪbl] *a* permissibile, ammissibile.

permission [pə'mɪʃən] *n* permesso; **to give sb ~ to do sth** dare a qn il permesso di fare qc.

permissive [pə'mɪsɪv] *a* tollerante; **the ~ society** la società permissiva.

permit *n* ['pə:mɪt] permesso; (*entrance pass*) lasciapassare *m* ♦ *vt, vi* [pə'mɪt] permettere; **fishing ~** licenza di pesca; **to ~ sb to do** permettere a qn di fare, dare il permesso a qn di fare; **weather ~ting** tempo permettendo.

permutation [pə:mju'teɪʃən] *n* permutazione *f*.

pernicious [pə:'nɪʃəs] *a* pernicioso(a), nocivo(a).

pernickety [pə'nɪkɪtɪ] *a* (*col: person*) pignolo(a); (*: task*) da certosino.

perpendicular [pə:pən'dɪkjʊlə*] *a, n* perpendicolare (*f*).

perpetrate ['pə:pɪtreɪt] *vt* perpetrare, commettere.

perpetual [pə'petjʊəl] *a* perpetuo(a).

perpetuate [pə'petjʊeɪt] *vt* perpetuare.

perpetuity [pə:pɪ'tju:ɪtɪ] *n*: **in ~** in perpetuo.

perplex [pə'pleks] *vt* lasciare perplesso(a).

perplexing [pə'pleksɪŋ] *a* che lascia perplesso(a).

perquisites ['pə:kwɪzɪts] *npl* (*also*: **perks**) benefici *mpl* collaterali.

persecute ['pə:sɪkju:t] *vt* perseguitare.

persecution [pə:sɪ'kju:ʃən] *n* persecuzione *f*.

perseverance [pə:sɪ'vɪərəns] *n* perseveranza.

persevere [pə:sɪ'vɪə*] *vi* perseverare.

Persia ['pə:ʃə] *n* Persia.

Persian ['pə:ʃən] *a* persiano(a) ♦ *n* (*LING*) persiano; **the (~) Gulf** il Golfo Persico.

persist [pə'sɪst] *vi*: **to ~ (in doing)** persistere (nel fare); ostinarsi (a fare).

persistence [pə'sɪstəns] *n* persistenza; ostinazione *f*.

persistent [pə'sɪstənt] *a* persistente; ostinato(a); (*lateness, rain*) continuo(a); **~ offender** (*LAW*) delinquente *m/f* abituale.

persnickety [pə'snɪkɪtɪ] *a* (*US col*) = **pernickety**.

person ['pə:sn] *n* persona; **in ~** di *or* in persona, personalmente; **on** *or* **about one's ~** (*weapon*) su di sé; (*money*) con sé; **a ~ to ~ call** (*TEL*) una chiamata con preavviso.

personable ['pə:snəbl] *a* di bell'aspetto.

personal ['pə:snl] *a* personale; individuale; **~ belongings, ~ effects** oggetti *mpl* d'uso personale; **a ~ interview** un incontro privato.

personal allowance *n* (*TAX*) quota del reddito non imponibile.

personal assistant (PA) *n* segretaria personale.

personal call *n* (*TEL*) chiamata con preavviso.

personal column *n* messaggi *mpl* personali.

personal computer (PC) *n* personal computer *m inv*.

personal details *npl* dati *mpl* personali.

personal identification number (PIN) *n* (*COMPUT, BANKING*) numero di codice segreto.

personality [pə:sə'nælɪtɪ] *n* personalità *f inv*.

personally ['pə:snəlɪ] *ad* personalmente.

personal property *n* beni *mpl* personali.

personify [pə:'sɔnɪfaɪ] *vt* personificare.

personnel [pə:sə'nel] *n* personale *m*.

personnel department *n* ufficio del personale.

personnel manager *n* direttore/trice del personale.

perspective [pə'spektɪv] *n* prospettiva; **to get sth into ~** ridimensionare qc.

Perspex ® ['pə:speks] *n* (*Brit*) *tipo di resina termoplastica*.

perspicacity [pə:spɪ'kæsɪtɪ] *n* perspicacia.

perspiration [pə:spɪ'reɪʃən] *n* traspirazione *f*, sudore *m*.

perspire [pə'spaɪə*] *vi* traspirare.

persuade [pə'sweɪd] *vt*: **to ~ sb to do sth** persuadere qn a fare qc; **to ~ sb of sth/that** persuadere qn di qc/che.

persuasion [pə'sweɪʒən] *n* persuasione *f*; (*creed*) convinzione *f*, credo.

persuasive [pə'sweɪsɪv] *a* persuasivo(a).

pert [pə:t] *a* (*bold*) sfacciato(a), impertinente; (*hat*) spiritoso(a).

pertaining [pə'teɪnɪŋ]: ~ **to** *prep* che riguarda.

pertinent ['pɜːtɪnənt] *a* pertinente.

perturb [pə'tɜːb] *vt* turbare.

perturbing [pə'tɜːbɪŋ] *a* inquietante.

Peru [pə'ruː] *n* Perù *m*.

perusal [pə'ruːzl] *n* attenta lettura.

Peruvian [pə'ruːvjən] *a*, *n* peruviano(a).

pervade [pə'veɪd] *vt* pervadere.

pervasive [pə:'veɪsɪv] *a* (*smell*) penetrante; (*influence*) dilagante; (*gloom*, *feelings*) diffuso(a).

perverse [pə'vɜːs] *a* perverso(a).

perversion [pə'vɜːʃən] *n* pervertimento, perversione *f*.

perversity [pə'vɜːsɪtɪ] *n* perversità.

pervert *n* ['pɜːvɜːt] pervertito/a ♦ *vt* [pə'vɜːt] pervertire.

pessimism ['pesɪmɪzəm] *n* pessimismo.

pessimist ['pesɪmɪst] *n* pessimista *m/f*.

pessimistic [pesɪ'mɪstɪk] *a* pessimistico(a).

pest [pest] *n* animale *m* (*or* insetto) pestifero; (*fig*) peste *f*.

pest control *n* disinfestazione *f*.

pester ['pestə*] *vt* tormentare, molestare.

pesticide ['pestɪsaɪd] *n* pesticida *m*.

pestilent ['pestɪlənt], **pestilential** [pestɪ'lenʃəl] *a* (*col*: *exasperating*) pestifero(a).

pestle ['pesl] *n* pestello.

pet [pet] *n* animale *m* domestico; (*favourite*) favorito/a ♦ *vt* accarezzare ♦ *vi* (*col*) fare il petting; ~ **lion** *etc* leone *m etc* ammaestrato.

petal ['petl] *n* petalo.

peter ['piːtə*]: **to** ~ **out** *vi* esaurirsi; estinguersi.

petite [pə'tiːt] *a* piccolo(a) e aggraziato(a).

petition [pə'tɪʃən] *n* petizione *f* ♦ *vi* richiedere; **to** ~ **for divorce** presentare un'istanza di divorzio.

pet name *n* (*Brit*) nomignolo.

petrified ['petrɪfaɪd] *a* (*fig*) morto(a) di paura.

petrify ['petrɪfaɪ] *vt* pietrificare; (*fig*) terrorizzare.

petrochemical [petrə'kemɪkl] *a* petrol-chimico(a).

petrodollars ['petrəudɔləz] *npl* petrodollari *mpl*.

petrol ['petrəl] *n* (*Brit*) benzina.

petrol can *n* (*Brit*) tanica per benzina.

petrol engine *n* (*Brit*) motore *m* a benzina.

petroleum [pə'trəuliəm] *n* petrolio.

petroleum jelly *n* vaselina.

petrol pump *n* (*Brit*: *in car*, *at garage*) pompa di benzina.

petrol station *n* (*Brit*) stazione *f* di rifornimento.

petrol tank *n* (*Brit*) serbatoio della benzina.

petticoat ['petɪkəut] *n* sottana.

pettifogging ['petɪfɔgɪŋ] *a* cavilloso(a).

pettiness ['petɪnɪs] *n* meschinità.

petty ['petɪ] *a* (*mean*) meschino(a); (*unimportant*) insignificante.

petty cash *n* piccola cassa.

petty officer *n* sottufficiale *m* di marina.

petulant ['petjulənt] *a* irritabile.

pew [pjuː] *n* panca (di chiesa).

pewter ['pjuːtə*] *n* peltro.

Pfc *abbr* (*US MIL*) = *private first class*.

PG *n* *abbr* (*CINEMA*: = *parental guidance*) consenso dei genitori richiesto.

PGA *n* *abbr* (= *Professional Golfers Association*) associazione dei giocatori di golf professionisti.

PH *n* *abbr* (*US MIL*: = *Purple Heart*) decorazione per ferite riportate in guerra.

p&h *abbr* (*US*: = *postage and handling*) affrancatura e trasporto.

PHA *n* *abbr* (*US*: = *Public Housing Administration*) amministrazione per l'edilizia pubblica.

phallic ['fælɪk] *a* fallico(a).

phantom ['fæntəm] *n* fantasma *m*.

Pharaoh ['feərəu] *n* faraone *m*.

pharmaceutical [fɑːmə'sjuːtɪkl] *a* farmaceutico(a) ♦ *n*: ~**s** prodotti *mpl* farmaceutici.

pharmacist ['fɑːməsɪst] *n* farmacista *m/f*.

pharmacy ['fɑːməsɪ] *n* farmacia.

phase [feɪz] *n* fase *f*, periodo ♦ *vt*: **to** ~ **sth in/out** introdurre/eliminare qc progressivamente.

PhD *n* *abbr* = **Doctor of Philosophy**.

pheasant ['feznt] *n* fagiano.

phenomenon, pl phenomena [fə'nɔmɪnən, -nə] *n* fenomeno.

phew [fjuː] *excl* uff!

phial ['faɪəl] *n* fiala.

philanderer [fɪ'lændərə*] *n* donnaiolo.

philanthropic [fɪlən'θrɔpɪk] *a* filantropico(a).

philanthropist [fɪ'lænθrəpɪst] *n* filantropo.

philatelist [fɪ'lætəlɪst] *n* filatelico/a.

philately [fɪ'lætəlɪ] *n* filatelia.

Philippines ['fɪlɪpiːnz] *npl* (*also*: **Philippine Islands**): **the** ~ le Filippine.

philosopher [fɪ'lɔsəfə*] *n* filosofo/a.

philosophical [fɪlə'sɔfɪkl] *a* filosofico(a).

philosophy [fɪ'lɔsəfɪ] *n* filosofia.

phlegm [flem] *n* flemma.

phlegmatic [fleg'mætɪk] *a* flemmatico(a).

phobia ['fəubjə] *n* fobia.

phone [fəun] *n* telefono ♦ *vt* telefonare a ♦ *vi* telefonare; **to be on the** ~ avere il telefono; (*be calling*) essere al telefono.
    phone back *vt*, *vi* richiamare.

phone book *n* guida del telefono, elenco telefonico.

phone box, phone booth *n* cabina telefonica.

phone call *n* telefonata.

phone-in *n* ['fəunɪn] *n* (*Brit RADIO, TV*) trasmissione radiofonica o televisiva con intervento telefonico degli ascoltatori.

phonetics [fə'netɪks] *n* fonetica.

phoney ['fəunɪ] *a* falso(a), fasullo(a) ♦ *n* (*person*) ciarlatano.

phonograph ['fəunəgrɑːf] *n* (*US*) giradischi *m inv*.

phony ['fəunɪ] *a*, *n* = **phoney**

phosphate ['fɔsfeɪt] *n* fosfato.
phosphorus ['fɔsfərəs] *n* fosforo.
photo ['fəutəu] *n* foto *f inv*.
photo... ['fəutəu] *prefix* foto....
photocopier ['fəutəukɔpɪə*] *n* fotocopiatrice *f*.
photocopy ['fəutəukɔpɪ] *n* fotocopia ♦ *vt* fotocopiare.
photoelectric [fəutəuɪ'lɛktrɪk] *a*: ~ **cell** cellula fotoelettrica.
photogenic [fəutəu'dʒɛnɪk] *a* fotogenico(a).
photograph ['fəutəgræf] *n* fotografia ♦ *vt* fotografare; **to take a ~ of sb** fare una fotografia a *or* fotografare qn.
photographer [fə'tɔgrəfə*] *n* fotografo.
photographic [fəutə'græfɪk] *a* fotografico(a).
photography [fə'tɔgrəfɪ] *n* fotografia.
photostat ® ['fəutəustæt] *n* fotocopia.
photosynthesis [fəutəu'sɪnθəsɪs] *n* fotosintesi *f*.
phrase [freɪz] *n* espressione *f*; (*LING*) locuzione *f*; (*MUS*) frase *f* ♦ *vt* esprimere; (*letter*) redigere.
phrasebook ['freɪzbuk[*n* vocabolarietto.
physical ['fɪzɪkl] *a* fisico(a); ~ **examination** visita medica; ~ **education** educazione *f* fisica; ~ **exercises** ginnastica.
physically [fɪzɪklɪ] *ad* fisicamente.
physician [fɪ'zɪʃən] *n* medico.
physicist ['fɪzɪsɪst] *n* fisico.
physics ['fɪzɪks] *n* fisica.
physiological [fɪzɪə'lɔdʒɪkəl] *a* fisiologico(a).
physiology [fɪzɪ'ɔlədʒɪ] *n* fisiologia.
physiotherapist [fɪzɪəu'θɛrəpɪst] *n* fisioterapista *m/f*.
physiotherapy [fɪzɪəu'θɛrəpɪ] *n* fisioterapia.
physique [fɪ'ziːk] *n* fisico.
pianist ['piːənɪst] *n* pianista *m/f*.
piano [pɪ'ænəu] *n* pianoforte *m*.
piano accordion *n* (*Brit*) fisarmonica (a tastiera).
piccolo ['pɪkələu] *n* ottavino.
pick [pɪk] *n* (*tool*: *also*: ~-**axe**) piccone *m* ♦ *vt* scegliere; (*gather*) cogliere; (*scab, spot*) grattarsi ♦ *vi*: **to ~ and choose** scegliere con cura; **take your** ~ scelga; **the** ~ **of** il fior fiore di; **to ~ one's nose** mettersi le dita nel naso; **to ~ one's teeth** stuzzicarsi i denti; **to ~ sb's brains** farsi dare dei suggerimenti da qn; **to ~ pockets** borseggiare; **to ~ a fight/quarrel with sb** attaccar rissa/briga con qn; **to ~ one's way through** attraversare stando ben attento a dove mettere i piedi.
pick off *vt* (*kill*) abbattere.
pick on *vt fus* (*person*) avercela con.
pick out *vt* scegliere; (*distinguish*) distinguere.
pick up *vi* (*improve*) migliorarsi ♦ *vt* raccogliere; (*collect*) passare a prendere; (*AUT*: *give lift to*) far salire; (*learn*) imparare; (*RADIO, TV, TEL*) captare; **to ~ o.s. up** rialzarsi; **to ~ up where one left off** riprendere dal punto in cui ci si era fermati; **to ~ up speed** acquistare velocità.

pickaxe, (*US*) **pickax** ['pɪkæks] *n* piccone *m*.
picket ['pɪkɪt] *n* (*in strike*) scioperante *m/f* che fa parte di un picchetto; picchetto ♦ *vt* picchettare.
picket line *n* cordone *m* degli scioperanti.
pickings ['pɪkɪŋz] *npl* (*pilferings*): **there are good ~ to be had here** qui ci sono buone possibilità di intascare qualcosa sottobanco.
pickle ['pɪkl] *n* (*also*: ~**s**: *as condiment*) sottaceti *mpl*; (*fig*): **in a ~** nei pasticci ♦ *vt* mettere sottaceto; mettere in salamoia.
pick-me-up ['pɪkmiːʌp] *n* tiramisù *m inv*.
pickpocket ['pɪkpɔkɪt] *n* borsaiolo.
pickup ['pɪkʌp] *n* (*Brit*: *on record player*) pick-up *m inv*; (*small truck*: *also*: ~ **truck,** ~ **van**) camioncino.
picnic ['pɪknɪk] *n* picnic *m inv* ♦ *vi* fare un picnic.
picnicker ['pɪknɪkə*] *n* chi partecipa a un picnic.
pictorial [pɪk'tɔːrɪəl] *a* illustrato(a).
picture ['pɪktʃə*] *n* quadro; (*painting*) pittura; (*photograph*) foto(grafia); (*drawing*) disegno; (*TV*) immagine *f*; (*film*) film *m inv* ♦ *vt* raffigurarsi; **the ~s** (*Brit*) il cinema; **to take a ~ of sb/sth** fare una foto a qn/di qc; **we get a good ~ here** (*TV*) la ricezione qui è buona; **the overall ~** il quadro generale; **to put sb in the ~** mettere qn al corrente.
picture book *n* libro illustrato.
picturesque [pɪktʃə'rɛsk] *a* pittoresco(a).
picture window *n* finestra panoramica.
piddling ['pɪdlɪŋ] *a* (*col*) insignificante.
pidgin English ['pɪdʒɪn-] *n* inglese semplificato misto ad elementi indigeni.
pie [paɪ] *n* torta; (*of meat*) pasticcio.
piebald ['paɪbɔːld] *a* pezzato(a).
piece [piːs] *n* pezzo; (*of land*) appezzamento; (*DRAUGHTS etc*) pedina; (*item*): **a ~ of furniture/advice** un mobile/consiglio ♦ *vt*: **to ~ together** mettere insieme; **in ~s** (*broken*) in pezzi; (*not yet assembled*) smontato(a); **to take to ~s** smontare; ~ **by** ~ poco alla volta; **a 10p** ~ (*Brit*) una moneta da 10 pence; **a six-~ band** un complesso di sei strumentisti; **in one** ~ (*object*) intatto; **to get back all in one** ~ (*person*) tornare a casa incolume *or* sano e salvo; **to say one's** ~ dire la propria.
piecemeal ['piːsmiːl] *ad* pezzo a pezzo, a spizzico.
piece rate *n* tariffa a cottimo.
piecework ['piːswəːk] *n* (lavoro a) cottimo.
pie chart *n* grafico a torta.
Piedmont ['piːdmɔnt] *n* Piemonte *m*.
pier [pɪə*] *n* molo; (*of bridge etc*) pila.
pierce [pɪəs] *vt* forare; (*with arrow etc*) trafiggere; **to have one's ears ~d** farsi fare i buchi per gli orecchini.
piercing ['pɪəsɪŋ] *a* (*cry*) acuto(a).
piety ['paɪətɪ] *n* pietà, devozione *f*.
piffling ['pɪflɪŋ] *a* insignificante.
pig [pɪg] *n* maiale *m*, porco.
pigeon ['pɪdʒən] *n* piccione *m*.

pigeonhole ['pɪdʒənhəul] *n* casella ♦ *vt* classificare.

pigeon-toed ['pɪdʒən'təud] *a* che cammina con i piedi in dentro.

piggy bank ['pɪgɪ-] *n* salvadanaio.

pigheaded ['pɪg'hɛdɪd] *a* caparbio(a), cocciuto(a).

piglet ['pɪglɪt] *n* porcellino.

pigment ['pɪgmənt] *n* pigmento.

pigmentation [pɪgmən'teɪʃən] *n* pigmentazione *f*.

pigmy ['pɪgmɪ] *n* = **pygmy**.

pigskin ['pɪgskɪn] *n* cinghiale *m*.

pigsty ['pɪgstaɪ] *n* porcile *m*.

pigtail ['pɪgteɪl] *n* treccina.

pike [paɪk] *n* (*spear*) picca; (*fish*) luccio.

pilchard ['pɪltʃəd] *n* specie di sardina.

pile [paɪl] *n* (*pillar, of books*) pila; (*heap*) mucchio; (*of carpet*) pelo ♦ *vb* (*also:* ~ **up**) *vt* ammucchiare ♦ *vi* ammucchiarsi; **in a** ~ ammucchiato; *see also* **piles**.
   pile on *vt:* **to** ~ **it on** (*col*) esagerare, drammatizzare.

piles [paɪlz] *npl* (*MED*) emorroidi *fpl*.

pileup ['paɪlʌp] *n* (*AUT*) tamponamento a catena.

pilfer ['pɪlfə*] *vt* rubacchiare ♦ *vi* fare dei furtarelli.

pilfering ['pɪlfərɪŋ] *n* rubacchiare *m*.

pilgrim ['pɪlgrɪm] *n* pellegrino/a.

pilgrimage ['pɪlgrɪmɪdʒ] *n* pellegrinaggio.

pill [pɪl] *n* pillola; **to be on the** ~ prendere la pillola.

pillage ['pɪlɪdʒ] *vt* saccheggiare.

pillar ['pɪlə*] *n* colonna.

pillar box *n* (*Brit*) cassetta delle lettere (a colonnina).

pillion ['pɪljən] *n* (*of motor cycle*) sellino posteriore; **to ride** ~ viaggiare dietro.

pillory ['pɪlərɪ] *n* berlina ♦ *vt* mettere alla berlina.

pillow ['pɪləu] *n* guanciale *m*.

pillowcase ['pɪləukeɪs], **pillowslip** ['pɪləuslɪp] *n* federa.

pilot ['paɪlət] *n* pilota *m/f* ♦ *cpd* (*scheme etc*) pilota *inv* ♦ *vt* pilotare.

pilot boat *n* pilotina.

pilot light *n* fiammella di sicurezza.

pimento [pɪ'mɛntəu] *n* peperoncino.

pimp [pɪmp] *n* mezzano.

pimple ['pɪmpl] *n* foruncolo.

pimply ['pɪmplɪ] *a* foruncoloso(a).

PIN *n* *abbr see* **personal identification number**.

pin [pɪn] *n* spillo; (*TECH*) perno; (*Brit: drawing* ~) puntina da disegno; (*Brit ELEC: of plug*) spinotto ♦ *vt* attaccare con uno spillo; ~**s and needles** formicolio; **to** ~ **sb against/to** inchiodare qn contro/a; **to** ~ **sth on sb** (*fig*) addossare la colpa di qc a qn.
   pin down *vt* (*fig*): **to** ~ **sb down** obbligare qn a pronunziarsi; **there's something strange here but I can't quite** ~ **it down** c'è qualcosa di strano qua ma non riesco a capire cos'è.

pinafore ['pɪnəfɔ:*] *n* grembiule *m* (senza maniche).

pinafore dress *n* scamiciato.

pinball ['pɪnbɔ:l] *n* flipper *m inv*.

pincers ['pɪnsəz] *npl* pinzette *fpl*.

pinch [pɪntʃ] *n* pizzicotto, pizzico ♦ *vt* pizzicare; (*col: steal*) grattare ♦ *vi* (*shoe*) stringere; **at a** ~ in caso di bisogno; **to feel the** ~ (*fig*) trovarsi nelle ristrettezze.

pinched [pɪntʃt] *a* (*drawn*) dai lineamenti tirati; (*short*): ~ **for money/space** a corto di soldi/di spazio; ~ **with cold** raggrinzito dal freddo.

pincushion ['pɪnkuʃən] *n* puntaspilli *m inv*.

pine [paɪn] *n* (*also:* ~ **tree**) pino ♦ *vi:* **to** ~ **for** struggersi dal desiderio di.
   pine away *vi* languire.

pineapple ['paɪnæpl] *n* ananas *m inv*.

pine nut, (*Brit*) **pine kernel** *n* pinolo.

ping [pɪŋ] *n* (*noise*) tintinnio.

ping-pong ® ['pɪŋpɔŋ] *n* ping-pong ® *m*.

pink [pɪŋk] *a* rosa *inv* ♦ *n* (*colour*) rosa *m inv*; (*BOT*) garofano.

pinking shears, pinking scissors ['pɪŋkɪŋ-] *n* forbici *fpl* a zigzag.

pin money *n* (*Brit*) denaro per le piccole spese.

pinnacle ['pɪnəkl] *n* pinnacolo.

pinpoint ['pɪnpɔɪnt] *vt* indicare con precisione.

pinstripe ['pɪnstraɪp] *n* stoffa gessata; (*also:* ~ **suit**) gessato.

pint [paɪnt] *n* pinta (*Brit = 0.57 l; US = 0.47 l*); (*Brit col: of beer*) ≈ birra piccola.

pinup ['pɪnʌp] *n* pin-up girl *f inv*.

pioneer [paɪə'nɪə*] *n* pioniere/a ♦ *vt* essere un pioniere in.

pious ['paɪəs] *a* pio(a).

pip [pɪp] *n* (*seed*) seme *m*; (*time signal on radio*) segnale *m* orario.

pipe [paɪp] *n* tubo; (*for smoking*) pipa; (*MUS*) piffero ♦ *vt* portare per mezzo di tubazione; ~**s** *npl* (*also:* **bag**~**s**) cornamusa (scozzese).
   pipe down *vi* (*col*) calmarsi.

pipe cleaner *n* scovolino.

piped music *n* musica di sottofondo.

pipe dream *n* vana speranza.

pipeline ['paɪplaɪn] *n* conduttura; (*for oil*) oleodotto; (*for natural gas*) metanodotto; **it is in the** ~ (*fig*) è in arrivo.

piper ['paɪpə*] *n* piffero; suonatore/trice di cornamusa.

pipe tobacco *n* tabacco da pipa.

piping ['paɪpɪŋ] *ad:* ~ **hot** bollente.

piquant ['pi:kənt] *a* (*sauce*) piccante; (*conversation*) stimolante.

pique [pi:k] *n* picca.

piracy ['paɪərəsɪ] *n* pirateria.

pirate ['paɪərət] *n* pirata *m* ♦ *vt* (*record, video, book*) riprodurre abusivamente.

pirate radio *n* (*Brit*) radio pirata *f inv*.

pirouette [pɪru'ɛt] *n* piroetta ♦ *vi* piroettare.

Pisces ['paɪsi:z] *n* Pesci *mpl*; **to be** ~ essere dei Pesci.

piss [pɪs] *vi* (*col!*) pisciare; ~ **off!** vaffanculo! (*!*).

pissed [pɪst] *a* (*Brit col*: *drunk*) ubriaco(a) fradicio(a).

pistol ['pɪstl] *n* pistola.

piston ['pɪstən] *n* pistone *m*.

pit [pɪt] *n* buca, fossa; (*also*: *coal* ~) miniera; (*also*: *orchestra* ~) orchestra ♦ *vt*: **to** ~ **sb against sb** opporre qn a qn; ~**s** *npl* (*AUT*) box *m*; **to** ~ **o.s. against** opporsi a.

pitapat ['pɪtə'pæt] *ad* (*Brit*): **to go** ~ (*heart*) palpitare, battere forte; (*rain*) picchiettare.

pitch [pɪtʃ] *n* (*throw*) lancia; (*MUS*) tono; (*of voice*) altezza; (*fig*: *degree*) grado, punto; (*also*: *sales* ~) discorso di vendita, imbonimento; (*Brit SPORT*) campo; (*NAUT*) beccheggio; (*tar*) pece *f* ♦ *vt* (*throw*) lanciare ♦ *vi* (*fall*) cascare; (*NAUT*) beccheggiare; **to** ~ **a tent** piantare una tenda; **at this** ~ a questo ritmo.

pitch-black [pɪtʃ'blæk] *a* nero(a) come la pece.

pitched battle [pɪtʃt-] *n* battaglia campale.

pitcher ['pɪtʃə*] *n* brocca.

pitchfork ['pɪtʃfɔːk] *n* forcone *m*.

piteous ['pɪtɪəs] *a* pietoso(a).

pitfall ['pɪtfɔːl] *n* trappola.

pith [pɪθ] *n* (*of plant*) midollo; (*of orange*) parte *f* interna della scorza; (*fig*) essenza, succo; vigore *m*.

pithead ['pɪthɛd] *n* (*Brit*) imbocco della miniera.

pithy ['pɪθɪ] *a* conciso(a); vigoroso(a).

pitiable ['pɪtɪəbl] *a* pietoso(a).

pitiful ['pɪtɪfʊl] *a* (*touching*) pietoso(a); (*contemptible*) miserabile.

pitifully ['pɪtɪfəlɪ] *ad* pietosamente; **it's** ~ **obvious** è penosamente chiaro.

pitiless ['pɪtɪlɪs] *a* spietato(a).

pittance ['pɪtns] *n* miseria, magro salario.

pitted ['pɪtɪd] *a*: ~ **with** (*potholes*) pieno(a) di; (*chickenpox*) butterato(a) da.

pity ['pɪtɪ] *n* pietà ♦ *vt* aver pietà di, compatire, commiserare; **to have** *or* **take** ~ **on sb** aver pietà di qn; **it is a** ~ **that you can't come** è un peccato che non possa venire; **what a** ~**!** che peccato!

pitying ['pɪtɪɪŋ] *a* compassionevole.

pivot ['pɪvət] *n* perno ♦ *vi* imperniarsi.

pixel ['pɪksl] *n* (*COMPUT*) pixel *m inv*.

pixie ['pɪksɪ] *n* folletto.

pizza ['piːtsə] *n* pizza.

P&L *abbr* (= *profit and loss*) P.P.

placard ['plækɑːd] *n* affisso.

placate [plə'keɪt] *vt* placare, calmare.

placatory [plə'keɪtərɪ] *a* conciliante.

place [pleɪs] *n* posto, luogo; (*proper position, rank, seat*) posto; (*house*) casa, alloggio; (*home*): **at/to his** ~ a casa sua; (*in street names*): **Laurel P~** via dei Lauri ♦ *vt* (*object*) posare, mettere; (*identify*) riconoscere; individuare; (*goods*) piazzare; **to take** ~ aver luogo; succedere; **out of** ~ (*not suitable*) inopportuno(a); **I feel rather out of**

~ **here** qui mi sento un po' fuori posto; **in the first** ~ in primo luogo; **to change** ~**s with sb** scambiare il posto con qn; **to put sb in his** ~ (*fig*) mettere a posto qn, mettere qn al suo posto; **from** ~ **to** ~ da un posto all'altro; **all over the** ~ dappertutto; **he's going** ~**s** (*fig col*) si sta facendo strada; **it is not my** ~ **to do it** non sta a me farlo; **how are you** ~**d next week?** com'è messo la settimana prossima?; **to** ~ **an order with sb** (*for*) (*COMM*) fare un'ordinazione a qn (di).

placebo [plə'siːbəʊ] *n* placebo *m inv*.

place mat *n* sottopiatto; (*in linen etc*) tovaglietta.

placement ['pleɪsmənt] *n* collocamento; (*job*) lavoro.

place name *n* toponimo.

placenta [plə'sɛntə] *n* placenta.

placid ['plæsɪd] *a* placido(a), calmo(a).

placidity [plə'sɪdɪtɪ] *n* placidità.

plagiarism ['pleɪdʒjərɪzəm] *n* plagio.

plagiarist ['pleɪdʒjərɪst] *n* plagiario/a.

plagiarize ['pleɪdʒjəraɪz] *vt* plagiare.

plague [pleɪg] *n* peste *f* ♦ *vt* tormentare; **to** ~ **sb with questions** assillare qn di domande.

plaice [pleɪs] *n* (*pl inv*) pianuzza.

plaid [plæd] *n* plaid *m inv*.

plain [pleɪn] *a* (*clear*) chiaro(a), palese; (*simple*) semplice; (*frank*) franco(a), aperto(a); (*not handsome*) bruttino(a); (*without seasoning etc*) scondito(a); naturale; (*in one colour*) tinta unita *inv* ♦ *ad* francamente, chiaramente ♦ *n* pianura; **to make sth** ~ **to sb** far capire chiaramente qc a qn; **in** ~ **clothes** (*police*) in borghese.

plain chocolate *n* cioccolato fondente.

plainly ['pleɪnlɪ] *ad* chiaramente; (*frankly*) francamente.

plainness ['pleɪnnɪs] *n* semplicità.

plaintiff ['pleɪntɪf] *n* attore/trice.

plaintive ['pleɪntɪv] *a* (*voice, song*) lamentoso(a); (*look*) struggente.

plait [plæt] *n* treccia ♦ *vt* intrecciare; **to** ~ **one's hair** farsi una treccia (*or* le trecce).

plan [plæn] *n* pianta; (*scheme*) progetto, piano ♦ *vt* (*think in advance*) progettare; (*prepare*) organizzare; (*intend*) avere in progetto ♦ *vi*: **to** ~ (**for**) far piani *or* progetti (per); **to** ~ **to do** progettare di fare, avere l'intenzione di fare; **how long do you** ~ **to stay?** quanto conta di restare?

plane [pleɪn] *n* (*AVIAT*) aereo; (*tree*) platano; (*tool*) pialla; (*ART, MATH etc*) piano ♦ *a* piano(a), piatto(a) ♦ *vt* (*with tool*) piallare.

planet ['plænɪt] *n* pianeta *m*.

planetarium [plænɪ'tɛərɪəm] *n* planetario.

plank [plæŋk] *n* tavola, asse *f*.

plankton ['plæŋktən] *n* plancton *m*.

planner ['plænə*] *n* pianificatore/trice; (*chart*) calendario; **town** *or* (*US*) **city** ~ urbanista *m/f*.

planning ['plænɪŋ] *n* progettazione *f*; (*POL, ECON*) pianificazione *f*; **family** ~ pianificazione delle nascite.

planning permission *n* (*Brit*) permesso di costruzione.

plant [plɑːnt] *n* pianta; (*machinery*) impianto; (*factory*) fabbrica ♦ *vt* piantare; (*bomb*) mettere.

plantation [plæn'teɪʃən] *n* piantagione *f*.

plant pot *n* (*Brit*) vaso (di fiori).

plaque [plæk] *n* placca.

plasma ['plæzmə] *n* plasma *m*.

plaster ['plɑːstə*] *n* intonaco; (*also*: ~ **of Paris**) gesso; (*Brit*: *also*: **sticking** ~) cerotto ♦ *vt* intonacare; ingessare; (*cover*): **to** ~ **with** coprire di; (*col*: *mud etc*) impiastricciare; **in** ~ (*Brit*: *leg etc*) ingessato(a).

plaster cast *n* (*MED*) ingessatura, gesso; (*model, statue*) modello in gesso.

plastered ['plɑːstəd] *a* (*col*) ubriaco(a) fradicio(a).

plasterer ['plɑːstərə*] *n* intonacatore *m*.

plastic ['plæstɪk] *n* plastica ♦ *a* (*made of plastic*) di *or* in plastica; (*flexible*) plastico(a), malleabile; (*art*) plastico(a).

plastic bag *n* sacchetto di plastica.

plasticine ® ['plæstɪsiːn] *n* plastilina ®.

plastic surgery *n* chirurgia plastica.

plate [pleɪt] *n* (*dish*) piatto; (*sheet of metal*) lamiera; (*PHOT*) lastra; (*TYP*) cliché *m inv*; (*in book*) tavola; (*on door*) targa, targhetta; (*AUT*: *number* ~) targa; (*dishes*): **gold** ~ vasellame *m* d'oro; **silver** ~ argenteria.

plateau, ~**s** *or* ~**x** ['plætəu, -z] *n* altipiano.

plateful ['pleɪtful] *n* piatto.

plate glass *n* vetro piano.

platelayer ['pleɪtleɪə*] *n* (*Brit RAIL*) armatore *m*.

platen ['plætən] *n* (*on typewriter, printer*) rullo.

plate rack *n* scolapiatti *m inv*.

platform ['plætfɔːm] *n* (*stage, at meeting*) palco; (*Brit*: *on bus*) piattaforma; (*RAIL*) marciapiede *m*; **the train leaves from** ~ **7** il treno parte dal binario 7.

platform ticket *n* (*Brit*) biglietto d'ingresso ai binari.

platinum ['plætɪnəm] *n* platino.

platitude ['plætɪtjuːd] *n* luogo comune.

platoon [plə'tuːn] *n* plotone *m*.

platter ['plætə*] *n* piatto.

plaudits ['plɔːdɪts] *npl* plauso.

plausible ['plɔːzɪbl] *a* plausibile, credibile; (*person*) convincente.

play [pleɪ] *n* gioco; (*THEATRE*) commedia ♦ *vt* (*game*) giocare a; (*team, opponent*) giocare contro; (*instrument, piece of music*) suonare; (*play, part*) interpretare ♦ *vi* giocare; suonare; recitare; **to bring** *or* **call into** ~ (*plan*) mettere in azione; (*emotions*) esprimere; ~ **on words** gioco di parole; **to** ~ **a trick on sb** fare uno scherzo a qn; **they're** ~**ing at soldiers** stanno giocando ai soldati; **to** ~ **for time** (*fig*) cercare di guadagnar tempo; **to** ~ **into sb's hands** (*fig*) fare il gioco di qn.

play about, play around *vi* (*person*)

divertirsi; **to** ~ **about** *or* **around with** (*fiddle with*) giocherellare con; (*idea*) accarezzare.

play along *vi*: **to** ~ **along with** (*fig*: *person*) stare al gioco di; (: *plan, idea*) fingere di assecondare ♦ *vt* (*fig*): **to** ~ **sb along** tenere qn in sospeso.

play back *vt* riascoltare, risentire.

play down *vt* minimizzare.

play on *vt fus* (*sb's feelings, credulity*) giocare su; **to** ~ **on sb's nerves** dare sui nervi a qn.

play up *vi* (*cause trouble*) fare i capricci.

playact ['pleɪækt] *vi* fare la commedia.

playboy ['pleɪbɔɪ] *n* playboy *m inv*.

played-out ['pleɪd'aut] *a* spossato(a).

player ['pleɪə*] *n* giocatore/trice; (*THEATRE*) attore/trice; (*MUS*) musicista *m/f*.

playful ['pleɪful] *a* giocoso(a).

playgoer ['pleɪɡəuə*] *n* assiduo(a) frequentatore(trice) di teatri.

playground ['pleɪɡraund] *n* (*in school*) cortile *m* per la ricreazione; (*in park*) parco *m* giochi *inv*.

playgroup ['pleɪɡruːp] *n* giardino d'infanzia.

playing card ['pleɪɪŋ-] *n* carta da gioco.

playing field *n* campo sportivo.

playmate ['pleɪmeɪt] *n* compagno/a di gioco.

play-off ['pleɪɔf] *n* (*SPORT*) bella.

playpen ['pleɪpɛn] *n* box *m inv*.

playroom ['pleɪruːm] *n* stanza dei giochi.

plaything ['pleɪθɪŋ] *n* giocattolo.

playtime ['pleɪtaɪm] *n* (*SCOL*) ricreazione *f*.

playwright ['pleɪraɪt] *n* drammaturgo/a.

plc *abbr* (*Brit*) *see* **public limited company**.

plea [pliː] *n* (*request*) preghiera, domanda; (*excuse*) scusa; (*LAW*) (argomento di) difesa.

plead [pliːd] *vt* patrocinare; (*give as excuse*) addurre a pretesto ♦ *vi* (*LAW*) perorare la causa; (*beg*): **to** ~ **with sb** implorare qn; **to** ~ **for sth** implorare qc; **to** ~ **guilty/not guilty** (*defendant*) dichiararsi colpevole/innocente.

pleasant ['plɛznt] *a* piacevole, gradevole.

pleasantly ['plɛzntlɪ] *ad* piacevolmente.

pleasantness ['plɛzntnɪs] *n* (*of person*) amabilità; (*of place*) amenità.

pleasantry ['plɛzntrɪ] *n* (*joke*) scherzo; (*polite remark*): **to exchange pleasantries** scambiarsi i convenevoli.

please [pliːz] *vt* piacere a ♦ *vi* (*think fit*): **do as you** ~ faccia come le pare; ~**!** per piacere!; **my bill,** ~ il conto, per piacere; ~ **yourself!** come ti (*or* le) pare!; ~ **don't cry!** ti prego, non piangere!

pleased [pliːzd] *a* (*happy*) felice, lieto(a); ~ (**with**) (*satisfied*) contento(a) (di); **we are** ~ **to inform you that** ... abbiamo il piacere di informarla che ...; ~ **to meet you!** piacere!

pleasing ['pliːzɪŋ] *a* piacevole, che fa piacere.

pleasurable ['plɛʒərəbl] *a* molto piacevole, molto gradevole.

pleasure ['plɛʒə*] *n* piacere *m*; **with** ~ con piacere, volentieri; "**it's a** ~" "prego"; **is**

this trip for business or ~? è un viaggio d'affari o di piacere?

pleasure steamer n vapore m da diporto.

pleat [pli:t] n piega.

plebiscite ['plɛbɪsɪt] n plebiscito.

plebs [plɛbz] npl (pej) plebe f.

plectrum ['plɛktrəm] n plettro.

pledge [plɛdʒ] n pegno; (promise) promessa ♦ vt impegnare; promettere; **to ~ support for sb** impegnarsi a sostenere qn; **to ~ sb to secrecy** far promettere a qn di mantenere il segreto.

plenary ['pli:nərɪ] a plenario(a); **in ~ session** in seduta plenaria.

plentiful ['plɛntɪful] a abbondante, copioso(a).

plenty ['plɛntɪ] n abbondanza; **~ of** tanto(a), molto(a); un'abbondanza di; **we've got ~ of time to get there** abbiamo un sacco di tempo per arrivarci.

pleurisy ['pluərɪsɪ] n pleurite f.

Plexiglas ® ['plɛksɪglɑ:s] n (US) plexiglas ® m.

pliable ['plaɪəbl] a flessibile; (person) malleabile.

pliers ['plaɪəz] npl pinza.

plight [plaɪt] n situazione f critica.

plimsolls ['plɪmsəlz] npl (Brit) scarpe fpl da tennis.

plinth [plɪnθ] n plinto; piedistallo.

PLO n abbr (= Palestine Liberation Organization) O.L.P. f.

plod [plɔd] vi camminare a stento; (fig) sgobbare.

plodder ['plɔdə*] n sgobbone m.

plodding ['plɔdɪŋ] a lento(a) e pesante.

plonk [plɔŋk] (col) n (Brit: wine) vino da poco ♦ vt: **to ~ sth down** buttare giù qc bruscamente.

plot [plɔt] n congiura, cospirazione f; (of story, play) trama; (of land) lotto ♦ vt (mark out) fare la pianta di; rilevare; (: diagram etc) tracciare; (conspire) congiurare, cospirare ♦ vi congiurare; **a vegetable ~** (Brit) un orticello.

plotter ['plɔtə*] n cospiratore/trice; (COMPUT) plotter m inv, tracciatore m di curve.

plough, (US) **plow** [plau] n aratro ♦ vt (earth) arare.
  plough back vt (COMM) reinvestire.
  plough through vt fus (snow etc) procedere a fatica in.

ploughing, (US) **plowing** ['plauɪŋ] n aratura.

ploughman, (US) **plowman** ['plaumən] n aratore m; **~'s lunch** (Brit) semplice pasto a base di pane e formaggio.

ploy [plɔɪ] n stratagemma m.

pluck [plʌk] vt (fruit) cogliere; (musical instrument) pizzicare; (bird) spennare ♦ n coraggio, fegato; **to ~ one's eyebrows** depilarsi le sopracciglia; **to ~ up courage** farsi coraggio.

plucky ['plʌkɪ] a coraggioso(a).

plug [plʌg] n tappo; (ELEC) spina; (AUT: also: **spark(ing) ~**) candela ♦ vt (hole) tappare; (col: advertise) spingere; **to give sb/sth a ~**

fare pubblicità a qn/qc.
  plug in (ELEC) vi inserire la spina ♦ vt attaccare a una presa.

plughole ['plʌghəul] n (Brit) scarico.

plum [plʌm] n (fruit) susina ♦ cpd: **~ job** (col) impiego ottimo or favoloso.

plumage ['plu:mɪdʒ] n piume fpl, piumaggio.

plumb [plʌm] a verticale ♦ n piombo ♦ ad (exactly) esattamente ♦ vt sondare.
  plumb in vt (washing machine) collegare all'impianto idraulico.

plumber ['plʌmə*] n idraulico.

plumbing ['plʌmɪŋ] n (trade) lavoro di idraulico; (piping) tubature fpl.

plumbline ['plʌmlaɪn] n filo a piombo.

plume [plu:m] n piuma, penna; (decorative) pennacchio.

plummet ['plʌmɪt] vi cadere a piombo.

plump [plʌmp] a grassoccio(a) ♦ vt: **to ~ sth (down) on** lasciar cadere qc di peso su.
  plump for vt fus (col) decidersi per.
  plump up vt sprimacciare.

plunder ['plʌndə*] n saccheggio ♦ vt saccheggiare.

plunge [plʌndʒ] n tuffo ♦ vt immergere ♦ vi (dive) tuffarsi; (fall) cadere, precipitare; **to take the ~** (fig) saltare il fosso; **to ~ a room into darkness** far piombare una stanza nel buio.

plunger ['plʌndʒə*] n (for blocked sink) sturalavandini m inv.

plunging ['plʌndʒɪŋ] a (neckline) profondo(a).

pluperfect [plu:'pə:fɪkt] n piuccheperfetto.

plural ['pluərl] a, n plurale (m).

plus [plʌs] n (also: **~ sign**) segno più ♦ prep più ♦ a (MATH, ELEC) positivo(a); **ten/ twenty ~** più di dieci/venti; **it's a ~** (fig) è un vantaggio.

plus fours npl calzoni mpl alla zuava.

plush [plʌʃ] a lussuoso(a) ♦ n felpa.

plutonium [plu:'təunɪəm] n plutonio.

ply [plaɪ] n (of wool) capo; (of wood) strato ♦ vt (tool) maneggiare; (a trade) esercitare ♦ vi (ship) fare il servizio; **three ~ (wool)** lana a tre capi; **to ~ sb with drink** dare da bere continuamente a qn.

plywood ['plaɪwud] n legno compensato.

PM n abbr (Brit) see **prime minister**.

p.m. ad abbr (= post meridiem) del pomeriggio.

pneumatic [nju:'mætɪk] a pneumatico(a); **~ drill** martello pneumatico.

pneumonia [nju:'məunɪə] n polmonite f.

PO n abbr (= Post Office) ≈ P.T. (= Poste e Telegrafi) ♦ abbr (NAUT) = **petty officer**.

po abbr = **postal order**.

POA n abbr (Brit: = Prison Officers' Association) sindacato delle guardie carcerarie.

poach [pəutʃ] vt (cook) affogare; (steal) cacciare (or pescare) di frodo ♦ vi fare il bracconiere.

poached [pəutʃt] a (egg) affogato(a).

poacher ['pəutʃə*] n bracconiere m.

poaching ['pəutʃɪŋ] *n* caccia (*or* pesca) di frodo.

PO Box *n abbr see* **Post Office Box.**

pocket ['pɔkɪt] *n* tasca ♦ *vt* intascare; **to be out of ~** rimetterci; **to be £5 in/out of ~** (*Brit*) trovarsi con 5 sterline in più/in meno; **air ~** vuoto d'aria.

pocketbook ['pɔkɪtbuk] *n* (*wallet*) portafoglio; (*notebook*) taccuino; (*US: handbag*) busta.

pocket knife *n* temperino.

pocket money *n* paghetta, settimana.

pockmarked ['pɔkmɑːkt] *a* (*face*) butterato(a).

pod [pɔd] *n* guscio ♦ *vt* sgusciare.

podgy ['pɔdʒɪ] *a* grassoccio(a).

podiatrist [pɔ'diːɪtrɪst] *n* (*US*) callista *m/f*, pedicure *m/f*.

podiatry [pɔ'diːətrɪ] *n* (*US*) mestiere *m* di callista.

podium ['pəudɪəm] *n* podio.

POE *n abbr* = *port of embarkation*; *port of entry.*

poem ['pəuɪm] *n* poesia.

poet ['pəuɪt] *n* poeta/essa.

poetic [pəu'ɛtɪk] *a* poetico(a).

poet laureate *n* (*Brit*) poeta *m* laureato (*nominato dalla Corte Reale*).

poetry ['pəuɪtrɪ] *n* poesia.

POEU *n abbr* (*Brit*: = *Post Office Engineering Union*) sindacato del personale tecnico delle Poste.

poignant ['pɔɪnjənt] *a* struggente.

point [pɔɪnt] *n* (*gen*) punto; (*tip: of needle etc*) punta; (*Brit ELEC: also:* **power ~**) presa (di corrente); (*in time*) punto, momento; (*SCOL*) voto; (*main idea, important part*) nocciolo; (*also:* **decimal ~**): **2 ~ 3 (2.3)** 2 virgola 3 (2,3) ♦ *vt* (*show*) indicare; (*gun etc*): **to ~ sth at** puntare qc contro ♦ *vi* mostrare a dito; **~s** *npl* (*AUT*) puntine *fpl*; (*RAIL*) scambio; **to ~ to** indicare; (*fig*) dimostrare; **to make a ~** fare un'osservazione; **to get the ~** capire; **to come to the ~** venire al fatto; **when it comes to the ~** quando si arriva al dunque; **to be on the ~ of doing sth** essere sul punto di *or* stare (proprio) per fare qc; **to be beside the ~** non entrarci; **to make a ~ of doing sth** non mancare di fare qc; **there's no ~ (in doing)** è inutile (fare); **in ~ of fact** a dire il vero; **that's the whole ~!** precisamente!, sta tutto lì!; **you've got a ~ there!** giusto!, ha ragione!; **the train stops at Carlisle and all ~s south** il treno ferma a Carlisle e in tutte le stazioni a sud di Carlisle; **good ~s** vantaggi *mpl*; (*of person*) qualità *fpl*; **~ of departure** (*also fig*) punto di partenza; **~ of order** mozione *f* d'ordine; **~ of sale** (*COMM*) punto di vendita; **~ of view** punto di vista.

point out *vt* far notare.

point-blank ['pɔɪnt'blæŋk] *ad* (*also:* **at ~ range**) a bruciapelo; (*fig*) categoricamente.

point duty *n* (*Brit*): **to be on ~** dirigere il traffico.

pointed ['pɔɪntɪd] *a* (*shape*) aguzzo(a), appuntito(a); (*remark*) specifico(a).

pointedly ['pɔɪntɪdlɪ] *ad* in maniera inequivocabile.

pointer ['pɔɪntə*] *n* (*stick*) bacchetta; (*needle*) lancetta; (*clue*) indizio; (*advice*) consiglio; (*dog*) pointer *m*, cane *m* da punta.

pointless ['pɔɪntlɪs] *a* inutile, vano(a).

poise [pɔɪz] *n* (*balance*) equilibrio; (*of head, body*) portamento; (*calmness*) calma ♦ *vt* tenere in equilibrio; **to be ~d for** (*fig*) essere pronto(a) a.

poison ['pɔɪzn] *n* veleno ♦ *vt* avvelenare.

poisoning ['pɔɪznɪŋ] *n* avvelenamento.

poisonous ['pɔɪznəs] *a* velenoso(a); (*fumes*) venefico(a), tossico(a); (*ideas, literature*) pernicioso(a); (*rumours, individual*) perfido(a).

poke [pəuk] *vt* (*fire*) attizzare; (*jab with finger, stick etc*) punzecchiare; (*put*): **to ~ sth in(to)** spingere qc dentro ♦ *n* (*jab*) colpetto; (*with elbow*) gomitata; **to ~ one's head out of the window** mettere la testa fuori dalla finestra; **to ~ fun at sb** prendere in giro qn.

poke about *vi* frugare.

poker ['pəukə*] *n* attizzatoio; (*CARDS*) poker *m*.

poker-faced ['pəukə'feɪst] *a* dal viso impassibile.

poky ['pəukɪ] *a* piccolo(a) e stretto(a).

Poland ['pəulənd] *n* Polonia.

polar ['pəulə*] *a* polare.

polar bear *n* orso bianco.

polarize ['pəuləraɪz] *vt* polarizzare.

Pole [pəul] *n* polacco/a.

pole [pəul] *n* (*of wood*) palo; (*ELEC, GEO*) polo.

pole bean *n* (*US*) fagiolino.

polecat ['pəulkæt] *n* puzzola; (*US*) moffetta.

Pol. Econ. ['pɔlɪkɔn] *n abbr* = *political economy.*

polemic [pɔ'lɛmɪk] *n* polemica.

pole star *n* stella polare.

pole vault *n* salto con l'asta.

police [pə'liːs] *n* polizia ♦ *vt* mantenere l'ordine in; (*streets, city, frontier*) presidiare; **a large number of ~ were hurt** molti poliziotti sono rimasti feriti.

police car *n* macchina della polizia.

police constable (PC) *n* (*Brit*) agente *m* di polizia.

police department *n* (*US*) dipartimento di polizia.

police force *n* corpo di polizia, polizia.

policeman [pə'liːsmən] *n* poliziotto, agente *m* di polizia.

police officer *n* = **police constable.**

police record *n*: **to have a ~** avere precedenti penali.

police state *n* stato di polizia.

police station *n* posto di polizia.

policewoman [pə'li:swumən] *n* donna *f* poliziotto *inv*.

policy ['pɒlɪsɪ] *n* politica; (*of newspaper, company*) linea di condotta, prassi *f inv*; (*also*: **insurance** ~) polizza (d'assicurazione); **to take out a ~** (*INSURANCE*) stipulare una polizza di assicurazione.

policy holder *n* assicurato/a.

polio ['pəulɪəu] *n* polio *f*.

Polish ['pəulɪʃ] *a* polacco(a) ♦ *n* (*LING*) polacco.

polish ['pɒlɪʃ] *n* (*for shoes*) lucido; (*for floor*) cera; (*for nails*) smalto; (*shine*) lucentezza, lustro; (*fig*: *refinement*) raffinatezza ♦ *vt* lucidare; (*fig*: *improve*) raffinare.

polish off *vt* (*work*) sbrigare; (*food*) mangiarsi.

polished ['pɒlɪʃt] *a* (*fig*) raffinato(a).

polite [pə'laɪt] *a* cortese; **it's not ~ to do that** non è educato *or* buona educazione fare questo.

politely [pə'laɪtlɪ] *ad* cortesemente.

politeness [pə'laɪtnɪs] *n* cortesia.

politic ['pɒlɪtɪk] *a* diplomatico(a).

political [pə'lɪtɪkl] *a* politico(a).

political asylum *n* asilo politico.

politically [pə'lɪtɪklɪ] *ad* politicamente.

politician [pɒlɪ'tɪʃən] *n* politico.

politics ['pɒlɪtɪks] *n* politica ♦ *npl* idee *fpl* politiche.

polka ['pɒlkə] *n* polca.

polka dot *n* pois *m inv*.

poll [pəul] *n* scrutinio; (*votes cast*) voti *mpl*; (*also*: **opinion** ~) sondaggio (d'opinioni) ♦ *vt* ottenere; **to go to the ~s** (*voters*) andare alle urne; (*government*) indire le elezioni.

pollen ['pɒlən] *n* polline *m*.

pollen count *n* tasso di polline nell'aria.

pollination [pɒlɪ'neɪʃən] *n* impollinazione *f*.

polling ['pəulɪŋ] *n* (*Brit POL*) votazione *f*, votazioni *fpl*; (*TEL*) interrogazione *f* ciclica.

polling booth *n* (*Brit*) cabina elettorale.

polling day *n* (*Brit*) giorno delle elezioni.

polling station *n* (*Brit*) sezione *f* elettorale.

pollute [pə'lu:t] *vt* inquinare.

pollution [pə'lu:ʃən] *n* inquinamento.

polo ['pəuləu] *n* polo.

polo neck *n* collo alto; (*also*: ~ **sweater**) dolcevita ♦ *a* a collo alto.

poly ['pɒlɪ] *n abbr* (*Brit*) = **polytechnic**.

polyester [pɒlɪ'estə*] *n* poliestere *m*.

polygamy [pə'lɪgəmɪ] *n* poligamia.

Polynesia [pɒlɪ'ni:zɪə] *n* Polinesia.

Polynesian [pɒlɪ'ni:zɪən] *a, n* polinesiano(a).

polyp ['pɒlɪp] *n* (*MED*) polipo.

polystyrene [pɒlɪ'staɪri:n] *n* polistirolo.

polytechnic [pɒlɪ'teknɪk] *n* (*college*) istituto superiore ad indirizzo tecnologico.

polythene ['pɒlɪθi:n] *n* politene *m*.

polythene bag *n* sacco di plastica.

polyurethane [pɒlɪ'juərɪθeɪn] *n* poliuretano.

pomegranate ['pɒmɪgrænɪt] *n* melagrana.

pommel ['pɒml] *n* pomo ♦ *vt* = **pummel**.

pomp [pɒmp] *n* pompa, fasto.

pompom ['pɒmpɒm], **pompon** ['pɒmpɒn] *n* pompon *m inv*.

pompous ['pɒmpəs] *a* pomposo(a); (*person*) pieno(a) di boria.

pond [pɒnd] *n* stagno; (*in park*) laghetto.

ponder ['pɒndə*] *vi* riflettere, meditare ♦ *vt* ponderare, riflettere su.

ponderous ['pɒndərəs] *a* ponderoso(a), pesante.

pong [pɒŋ] (*Brit col*) *n* puzzo ♦ *vi* puzzare.

pontiff ['pɒntɪf] *n* pontefice *m*.

pontificate [pɒn'tɪfɪkeɪt] *vi* (*fig*): **to ~ (about)** pontificare (su).

pontoon [pɒn'tu:n] *n* pontone *m*; (*Brit CARDS*) ventuno.

pony ['pəunɪ] *n* pony *m inv*.

ponytail ['pəunɪteɪl] *n* coda di cavallo.

pony trekking *n* (*Brit*) escursione *f* a cavallo.

poodle ['pu:dl] *n* barboncino, barbone *m*.

pooh-pooh [pu:'pu:] *vt* deridere.

pool [pu:l] *n* (*of rain*) pozza; (*pond*) stagno; (*artificial*) vasca; (*also*: **swimming** ~) piscina; (*sth shared*) fondo comune; (*COMM*: *consortium*) pool *m inv*; (*US*: *monopoly trust*) trust *m inv*; (*billiards*) specie di biliardo a buca ♦ *vt* mettere in comune; **typing** ~, (*US*) **secretary** ~ servizio comune di dattilografia; **to do the (football) ~s** ≈ fare la schedina, giocare al totocalcio.

poor [puə*] *a* povero(a); (*mediocre*) mediocre, cattivo(a) ♦ *npl*: **the** ~ i poveri.

poorly ['puəlɪ] *ad* poveramente; (*badly*) male ♦ *a* indisposto(a), malato(a).

pop [pɒp] *n* (*noise*) schiocco; (*MUS*) musica pop; (*US col*: *father*) babbo; (*col*: *drink*) bevanda gasata ♦ *vt* (*put*) mettere (in fretta) ♦ *vi* scoppiare; (*cork*) schioccare; **she ~ped her head out** (*of the window*) sporse fuori la testa.

pop in *vi* passare.

pop out *vi* fare un salto fuori.

pop up *vi* apparire, sorgere.

pop concert *n* concerto *m* pop *inv*.

popcorn ['pɒpkɔ:n] *n* pop-corn *m*.

pope [pəup] *n* papa *m*.

poplar ['pɒplə*] *n* pioppo.

poplin ['pɒplɪn] *n* popeline *f*.

popper ['pɒpə*] *n* (*Brit*) bottone *m* automatico, bottone a pressione.

poppy ['pɒpɪ] *n* papavero.

poppycock ['pɒpɪkɒk] *n* (*col*) scempiaggini *fpl*.

popsicle ® ['pɒpsɪkl] *n* (*US*) ghiacciolo.

populace ['pɒpjuləs] *n* popolo.

popular ['pɒpjulə*] *a* popolare; (*fashionable*) in voga; **to be ~ (with)** (*person*) essere benvoluto(a) *or* ben visto(a) (da); (*decision*) essere gradito(a) (a); **a ~ song** una canzone di successo.

popularity [pɒpju'lærɪtɪ] *n* popolarità.

popularize ['pɒpjuləraɪz] *vt* divulgare; (*science*) volgarizzare.

populate ['pɒpjuleɪt] *vt* popolare.

population [pɔpju'leɪʃən] n popolazione f.
population explosion n forte espansione f demografica.
populous ['pɔpjuləs] a popolato(a).
porcelain ['pɔ:slɪn] n porcellana.
porch [pɔ:tʃ] n veranda.
porcupine ['pɔ:kjupaɪn] n porcospino.
pore [pɔ:*] n poro ♦ vi: **to ~ over** essere immerso(a) in.
pork [pɔ:k] n carne f di maiale.
pork chop n braciola or costoletta di maiale.
pornographic [pɔ:nə'græfɪk] a pornografico(a).
pornography [pɔ:'nɔgrəfɪ] n pornografia.
porous ['pɔ:rəs] a poroso(a).
porpoise ['pɔ:pəs] n focena.
porridge ['pɔrɪdʒ] n porridge m.
port [pɔ:t] n porto; (opening in ship) portello; (NAUT: left side) babordo; (COMPUT) porta; (wine) porto; **to ~** (NAUT) a babordo; **~ of call** (porto di) scalo.
portable ['pɔ:təbl] a portatile.
portal ['pɔ:tl] n portale m.
portcullis [pɔ:'tkʌlɪs] n saracinesca.
portent ['pɔ:tent] n presagio.
porter ['pɔ:tə*] n (for luggage) facchino, portabagagli m inv; (doorkeeper) portiere m, portinaio; (US RAIL) addetto ai vagoni letto.
portfolio [pɔ:t'fəuliəu] n (POL: office; ECON) portafoglio; (of artist) raccolta dei propri lavori.
porthole ['pɔ:thəul] n oblò m inv.
portico ['pɔ:tɪkəu] n portico.
portion ['pɔ:ʃən] n porzione f.
portly ['pɔ:tlɪ] a corpulento(a).
portrait ['pɔ:treɪt] n ritratto.
portray [pɔ:'treɪ] vt fare il ritratto di; (character on stage) rappresentare; (in writing) ritrarre.
portrayal ['pɔ:treɪəl] n ritratto; rappresentazione f.
Portugal ['pɔ:tjugl] n Portogallo.
Portuguese [pɔ:tju'gi:z] a portoghese ♦ n (pl inv) portoghese m/f; (LING) portoghese m.
Portuguese man-of-war [-mænəv'wɔ:*] n (jellyfish) medusa.
pose [pəuz] n posa ♦ vi posare; (pretend): **to ~ as** atteggiarsi a, posare a ♦ vt porre; **to strike a ~** mettersi in posa.
poser ['pəuzə*] n domanda difficile; (person) = **poseur**.
poseur [pəu'zə:*] n (pej) persona affettata.
posh [pɔʃ] a (col) elegante; (family) per bene ♦ ad (col): **to talk ~** parlare in modo snob.
position [pə'zɪʃən] n posizione f; (job) posto ♦ vt mettere in posizione, collocare; **to be in a ~ to do sth** essere nella posizione di fare qc.
positive ['pɔzɪtɪv] a positivo(a); (certain) sicuro(a), certo(a); (definite) preciso(a); definitivo(a).
posse ['pɔsɪ] n (US) drappello.
possess [pə'zes] vt possedere; **like one ~ed** come un ossesso; **whatever can have ~ed you?** cosa ti ha preso?

possession [pə'zeʃən] n possesso; (object) bene m; **to take ~ of sth** impossessarsi di, impadronirsi di qc.
possessive [pə'zesɪv] a possessivo(a).
possessively [pə'zesɪvlɪ] ad in modo possessivo.
possessor [pə'zesə*] n possessore/posseditrice.
possibility [pɔsɪ'bɪlɪtɪ] n possibilità f inv; **he's a ~ for the part** è uno dei candidati per la parte.
possible ['pɔsɪbl] a possibile; **it is ~ to do it** è possibile farlo; **if ~** se possibile; **as big as ~** il più grande possibile; **as far as ~** nei limiti del possibile.
possibly ['pɔsɪblɪ] ad (perhaps) forse; **if you ~ can** se le è possibile; **I cannot ~ come** proprio non posso venire.
post [pəust] n (Brit: mail, letters, delivery) posta; (: collection) levata; (job, situation) posto; (pole) palo; (trading ~) stazione f commerciale ♦ vt (Brit: send by post) impostare; (MIL) appostare; (notice) affiggere; (Brit: appoint): **to ~ to** assegnare a; **by ~** (Brit) per posta; **by return of ~** (Brit) a giro di posta; **to keep sb ~ed** tenere qn al corrente.
post... [pəust] prefix post...; **~-1990** dopo il 1990.
postage ['pəustɪdʒ] n affrancatura.
postage stamp n francobollo.
postal ['pəustəl] a postale.
postal order n vaglia m inv postale.
postbag ['pəustbæg] n (Brit) sacco postale, sacco della posta.
postbox ['pəustbɔks] n cassetta delle lettere.
postcard ['pəustkɑ:d] n cartolina.
postcode ['pəustkəud] n (Brit) codice m (di avviamento) postale.
postdate ['pəust'deɪt] vt (cheque) postdatare.
poster ['pəustə*] n manifesto, affisso.
poste restante [pəust'restɑ:nt] n (Brit) fermo posta m.
posterior [pɔs'tɪərɪə*] n (col) deretano, didietro.
posterity [pɔs'terɪtɪ] n posterità.
poster paint n tempera.
post exchange (PX) n (US MIL) spaccio militare.
post-free [pəust'fri:] a, ad (Brit) franco di porto.
postgraduate ['pəust'grædjuət] n laureato/a che continua gli studi.
posthumous ['pɔstjuməs] a postumo(a).
posthumously ['pɔstjuməslɪ] ad dopo la mia (or sua etc) morte.
posting ['pəustɪŋ] n (Brit) incarico.
postman ['pəustmən] n postino.
postmark ['pəustmɑ:k] n bollo or timbro postale.
postmaster ['pəustmɑ:stə*] n direttore m di un ufficio postale.
Postmaster General n ≈ ministro delle Poste.
postmistress ['pəustmɪstrɪs] n direttrice f di

un ufficio postale.

post-mortem [pəust'mɔːtəm] *n* autopsia; *(fig)* analisi *f inv* a posteriori.

postnatal ['pəust'neɪtl] *a* post-parto *inv*.

post office *n* *(building)* ufficio postale; *(organization)* poste *fpl*.

post office box (PO box) *n* casella postale (C.P.).

post-paid ['pəust'peɪd] *a* già affrancato(a).

postpone [pəust'pəun] *vt* rinviare.

postponement [pəust'pəunmənt] *n* rinvio.

postscript ['pəustskrɪpt] *n* poscritto.

postulate ['pɒstjuleɪt] *vt* postulare.

posture ['pɒstʃə*] *n* portamento; *(pose)* posa, atteggiamento ♦ *vi* posare.

postwar ['pəust'wɔː*] *a* del dopoguerra.

posy ['pəuzɪ] *n* mazzetto di fiori.

pot [pɒt] *n* *(for cooking)* pentola; casseruola; *(for plants, jam)* vaso; *(piece of pottery)* ceramica; *(col: marijuana)* erba ♦ *vt* *(plant)* piantare in vaso; **to go to ~** *(col)* andare in malora; **~s of** *(Brit col)* un sacco di.

potash ['pɒtæʃ] *n* potassa.

potassium [pə'tæsɪəm] *n* potassio.

potato, ~es [pə'teɪtəu] *n* patata.

potato crisps, *(US)* **potato chips** *npl* patatine *fpl*.

potato flour *n* fecola di patate.

potato peeler *n* sbucciapatate *m inv*.

potbellied ['pɒtbelɪd] *a* *(from overeating)* panciuto(a); *(from malnutrition)* dal ventre gonfio.

potency ['pəutnsɪ] *n* potenza; *(of drink)* forza.

potent ['pəutnt] *a* potente, forte.

potentate ['pəutnteɪt] *n* potentato.

potential [pə'tenʃl] *a* potenziale ♦ *n* possibilità *fpl*; **to have ~** essere promettente.

potentially [pə'tenʃəlɪ] *ad* potenzialmente.

pothole ['pɒthəul] *n* *(in road)* buca; *(Brit: underground)* marmitta.

potholer ['pɒthəulə*] *n* *(Brit)* speleologo/a.

potholing ['pɒthəulɪŋ] *n* *(Brit)*: **to go ~** fare la speleologia.

potion ['pəuʃən] *n* pozione *f*.

potluck [pɒt'lʌk] *n*: **to take ~** tentare la sorte.

potpourri [pəu'puri:] *n* *(dried petals etc)* miscuglio di petali essiccati profumati; *(fig)* pot-pourri *m inv*.

pot roast *n* brasato.

potshot ['pɒtʃɒt] *n*: **to take ~s at** tirare a casaccio contro.

potted ['pɒtɪd] *a* *(food)* in conserva; *(plant)* in vaso; *(fig: shortened)* condensato(a).

potter ['pɒtə*] *n* vasaio ♦ *vi* *(Brit)*: **to ~ around, ~ about** lavoracchiare; **to ~ round the house** sbrigare con calma le faccende di casa; **~'s wheel** tornio (da vasaio).

pottery ['pɒtərɪ] *n* ceramiche *fpl*; **a piece of ~** una ceramica.

potty ['pɒtɪ] *a* *(Brit col: mad)* tocco(a) ♦ *n* *(child's)* vasino.

potty-trained ['pɒtɪtreɪnd] *a* che ha imparato a farla nel vasino.

pouch [pautʃ] *n* borsa; *(ZOOL)* marsupio.

pouf(fe) [pu:f] *n* *(stool)* pouf *m inv*.

poultice ['pəultɪs] *n* impiastro, cataplasma *m*.

poultry ['pəultrɪ] *n* pollame *m*.

poultry farm *n* azienda avicola.

poultry farmer *n* pollicoltore/trice.

pounce [pauns] *vi*: **to ~ (on)** balzare addosso (a), piombare (su) ♦ *n* balzo.

pound [paund] *n* *(weight = 453g, 16 ounces)* libbra; *(money = 100 pence)* (lira) sterlina; *(for dogs)* canile *m* municipale ♦ *vt* *(beat)* battere; *(crush)* pestare, polverizzare ♦ *vi* *(beat)* battere, martellare; **half a ~** mezza libbra; **a five-~ note** una banconota da cinque sterline.

pounding ['paundɪŋ] *n*: **to take a ~** *(fig)* prendere una batosta.

pound sterling *n* sterlina.

pour [pɔː*] *vt* versare ♦ *vi* riversarsi; *(rain)* piovere a dirotto.

pour away, pour off *vt* vuotare.

pour in *vi* *(people)* entrare in fiotto; **to come ~ing in** *(water)* entrare a fiotti; *(letters)* arrivare a valanghe; *(cars, people)* affluire in gran quantità.

pour out *vi* *(people)* riversarsi fuori ♦ *vt* vuotare; versare.

pouring ['pɔːrɪŋ] *a*: **~ rain** pioggia torrenziale.

pout [paut] *vi* sporgere le labbra; fare il broncio.

poverty ['pɒvətɪ] *n* povertà, miseria.

poverty-stricken ['pɒvətɪstrɪkən] *a* molto povero(a), misero(a).

poverty trap *n* *(Brit)* circolo vizioso della povertà.

POW *n abbr* = **prisoner of war**.

powder ['paudə*] *n* polvere *f* ♦ *vt* spolverizzare; *(face)* incipriare; **~ed milk** latte *m* in polvere; **to ~ one's nose** incipriarsi il naso; *(euphemism)* andare alla toilette.

powder compact *n* portacipria *m inv*.

powder puff *n* piumino della cipria.

powder room *n* toilette *f inv* (per signore).

powdery ['paudərɪ] *a* polveroso(a).

power ['pauə*] *n* *(strength)* potenza, forza; *(ability, POL: of party, leader)* potere *m*; *(MATH)* potenza; *(ELEC)* corrente *f* ♦ *vt* fornire di energia; azionare; **to be in ~** essere al potere; **to do all in one's ~ to help sb** fare tutto quello che si può per aiutare qn; **the world ~s** le grandi potenze; **mental ~s** capacità *fpl* mentali.

powerboat ['pauəbəut] *n* *(Brit)* motobarca, imbarcazione *f* a motore.

power cut *n* *(Brit)* interruzione *f* or mancanza di corrente.

power-driven ['pauədrɪvn] *a* a motore; *(ELEC)* elettrico(a).

powered ['pauəd] *a*: **~ by** azionato(a) da; **nuclear-~ submarine** sottomarino a propulsione atomica.

power failure *n* guasto alla linea elettrica.

powerful ['pauəful] *a* potente, forte.

powerhouse ['pauəhaus] *n* *(fig: person)*

persona molto dinamica; **a ~ of ideas** una miniera di idee.

powerless ['pauəlıs] *a* impotente, senza potere.

power line *n* linea elettrica.

power point *n* (*Brit*) presa di corrente.

power station *n* centrale *f* elettrica.

power steering *n* (*AUT*: *also:* **power-assisted steering**) servosterzo.

powwow ['pauwau] *n* riunione *f*.

pp *abbr* (= *pages*) pp.; (= *per procurationem*: *by proxy*): **~ J. Smith** per il Signor J. Smith.

p&p *abbr* (*Brit*: = *postage and packing*) affrancatura ed imballaggio.

PPE *n abbr* (*Brit SCOL*: = *philosophy, politics and economics*) corso di laurea.

PPS *n abbr* (*Brit*: = *parliamentary private secretary*) parlamentare che assiste un ministro; = *post postscriptum*.

PQ *abbr* (*Canada*) = *Province of Quebec*.

PR *n abbr see* proportional representation; **public relations ♦** *abbr* (*US POST*) = *Puerto Rico*.

Pr. *abbr* = **prince**.

practicability [præktıkə'bılıtı] *n* praticabilità.

practicable ['præktıkəbl] *a* (*scheme*) praticabile.

practical ['præktıkl] *a* pratico(a).

practicality [præktı'kælıtı] *n* (*of plan*) fattibilità; (*of person*) senso pratico; **practicalities** dettagli *mpl* pratici.

practical joke *n* beffa.

practically ['præktıklı] *ad* (*almost*) quasi, praticamente.

practice ['præktıs] *n* pratica; (*of profession*) esercizio; (*at football etc*) allenamento; (*business*) gabinetto; clientela **♦** *vt, vi* (*US*) = **practise**; **in ~** (*in reality*) in pratica; **out of ~** fuori esercizio; **2 hours' piano ~** 2 ore di esercizio al pianoforte; **it's common ~** è d'uso; **to put sth into ~** mettere qc in pratica; **target ~** pratica di tiro.

practice match *n* partita di allenamento.

practise, (*US*) **practice** ['præktıs] *vt* (*work at: piano, one's backhand etc*) allenarsi a; (*train for: skiing, running etc*) allenarsi a; (*a sport, religion*) praticare; (*method*) usare; (*profession*) esercitare **♦** *vi* esercitarsi; (*train*) allenarsi; **to ~ for a match** allenarsi per una partita.

practised ['præktıst] *a* (*Brit*: *person*) esperto(a); (*: performance*) da virtuoso(a); (*: liar*) matricolato(a); **with a ~ eye** con occhio esperto.

practising ['præktısıŋ] *a* (*Christian etc*) praticante; (*lawyer*) che esercita la professione; (*homosexual*) attivo(a).

practitioner [præk'tıʃənə*] *n* professionista *m/f*; (*MED*) medico.

pragmatic [præg'mætık] *a* prammatico(a).

Prague [prɑːg] *n* Praga.

prairie ['prɛərı] *n* prateria.

praise [preız] *n* elogio, lode *f* **♦** *vt* elogiare, lodare.

praiseworthy ['preızwə:ðı] *a* lodevole.

pram [præm] *n* (*Brit*) carrozzina.

prance [prɑːns] *vi* (*horse*) impennarsi.

prank [præŋk] *n* burla.

prattle ['prætl] *vi* cinguettare.

prawn [prɔːn] *n* gamberetto.

pray [preı] *vi* pregare.

prayer [prɛə*] *n* preghiera.

prayer book *n* libro di preghiere.

pre... [priː] *prefix* pre...; **~-1970** prima del 1970.

preach [priːtʃ] *vt, vi* predicare; **to ~ at sb** fare la predica a qn.

preacher ['priːtʃə*] *n* predicatore/trice; (*US*: *minister*) pastore *m*.

preamble [priː'æmbl] *n* preambolo.

prearranged [priːə'reındʒd] *a* organizzato(a) in anticipo.

precarious [prı'kɛərıəs] *a* precario(a).

precaution [prı'kɔːʃən] *n* precauzione *f*.

precautionary [prı'kɔːʃənərı] *a* (*measure*) precauzionale.

precede [prı'siːd] *vt, vi* precedere.

precedence ['presıdəns] *n* precedenza; **to take ~ over** avere la precedenza su.

precedent ['presıdənt] *n* precedente *m*; **to establish** *or* **set a ~** creare un precedente.

preceding [prı'siːdıŋ] *a* precedente.

precept ['priːsept] *n* precetto.

precinct ['priːsıŋkt] *n* (*round cathedral*) recinto; (*US*: *district*) circoscrizione *f*; **~s** *npl* (*neighbourhood*) dintorni *mpl*, vicinanze *fpl*; **pedestrian ~** zona pedonale; **shopping ~** (*Brit*) centro commerciale.

precious ['preʃəs] *a* prezioso(a) **♦** *ad* (*col*): **~ little/few** ben poco/pochi; **your ~ dog** (*ironic*) il suo amatissimo cane.

precipice ['presıpıs] *n* precipizio.

precipitate *a* [prı'sıpıtıt] (*hasty*) precipitoso(a) **♦** *vt* [prı'sıpıteıt] accelerare.

precipitation [prısıpı'teıʃən] *n* precipitazione *f*.

precipitous [prı'sıpıtəs] *a* (*steep*) erto(a), ripido(a).

précis, *pl* **précis** ['preısiː, -z] *n* riassunto.

precise [prı'saıs] *a* preciso(a).

precisely [prı'saıslı] *ad* precisamente; **~!** appunto!

precision [prı'sıʒən] *n* precisione *f*.

preclude [prı'kluːd] *vt* precludere, impedire; **to ~ sb from doing** impedire a qn di fare.

precocious [prı'kəuʃəs] *a* precoce.

preconceived [priːkən'siːvd] *a* (*idea*) preconcetto(a).

preconception [priːkən'sepʃən] *n* preconcetto.

precondition [priːkən'dıʃən] *n* condizione *f* necessaria.

precursor [priː'kəːsə*] *n* precursore *m*.

predate [priː'deıt] *vt* (*precede*) precedere.

predator ['predətə*] *n* predatore *m*.

predatory ['predətərı] *a* predatore(trice).

predecessor ['priːdısesə*] *n* predecessore/a.

predestination [priːdestı'neıʃən] *n* predestinazione *f*.

predetermine [pri:dɪ'tə:mɪn] *vt* predeterminare.

predicament [prɪ'dɪkəmənt] *n* situazione *f* difficile.

predicate ['prɛdɪkɪt] *n* (*LING*) predicativo.

predict [prɪ'dɪkt] *vt* predire.

predictable [prɪ'dɪktəbl] *a* prevedibile.

predictably [prɪ'dɪktəblɪ] *ad* (*behave*, *react*) in modo prevedibile; ~ **she didn't arrive** come era da prevedere, non è arrivata.

prediction [prɪ'dɪkʃən] *n* predizione *f*.

predispose [pri:dɪs'pəuz] *vt* predisporre.

predominance [prɪ'dɔmɪnəns] *n* predominanza.

predominant [prɪ'dɔmɪnənt] *a* predominante.

predominantly [prɪ'dɔmɪnəntlɪ] *ad* in maggior parte; soprattutto.

predominate [prɪ'dɔmɪneɪt] *vi* predominare.

pre-eminent [pri:'emɪnənt] *a* preminente.

pre-empt [prɪ'empt] *vt* acquistare per diritto di prelazione; (*fig*) anticipare.

pre-emptive [prɪ'emptɪv] *a*: ~ **strike** azione *f* preventiva.

preen [pri:n] *vt*: **to** ~ **itself** (*bird*) lisciarsi le penne; **to** ~ **o.s.** agghindarsi.

prefab ['pri:fæb] *n* casa prefabbricata.

prefabricated [pri:'fæbrɪkeɪtɪd] *a* prefabbricato(a).

preface ['prɛfəs] *n* prefazione *f*.

prefect ['pri:fɛkt] *n* (*Brit: in school*) *studente/ essa con funzioni disciplinari*; (*in Italy*) prefetto.

prefer [prɪ'fə:*] *vt* preferire; (*LAW: charges*, *complaint*) sporgere; (*: action*) intentare; **to** ~ **coffee to tea** preferire il caffè al tè.

preferable ['prɛfrəbl] *a* preferibile.

preferably ['prɛfrəblɪ] *ad* preferibilmente.

preference ['prɛfrəns] *n* preferenza; **in** ~ **to sth** piuttosto che qc.

preference shares *npl* (*Brit*) azioni *fpl* privilegiate.

preferential [prɛfə'rɛnʃəl] *a* preferenziale; ~ **treatment** trattamento di favore.

preferred stock *npl* (*US*) = **preference shares**.

prefix ['pri:fɪks] *n* prefisso.

pregnancy ['prɛgnənsɪ] *n* gravidanza.

pregnant ['prɛgnənt] *a* incinta *af*; (*animal*) gravido(a); (*fig: remark*, *pause*) significativo(a); **3 months** ~ incinta di 3 mesi.

prehistoric ['pri:hɪs'tɔrɪk] *a* preistorico(a).

prehistory [pri:'hɪstərɪ] *n* preistoria.

prejudge [pri:'dʒʌdʒ] *vt* pregiudicare.

prejudice ['prɛdʒudɪs] *n* pregiudizio; (*harm*) torto, danno ♦ *vt* pregiudicare, ledere; (*bias*): **to** ~ **sb in favour of/against** disporre bene/male qn verso.

prejudiced ['prɛdʒudɪst] *a* (*person*) pieno(a) di pregiudizi; (*view*) prevenuto(a); **to be** ~ **against sb/sth** essere prevenuto contro qn/qc.

prelate ['prɛlət] *n* prelato.

preliminaries [prɪ'lɪmɪnərɪz] *npl* preliminari *mpl*.

preliminary [prɪ'lɪmɪnərɪ] *a* preliminare.

prelude ['prɛlju:d] *n* preludio.

premarital ['pri:'mærɪtl] *a* prematrimoniale.

premature ['prɛmətʃuə*] *a* prematuro(a); (*arrival*) (molto) anticipato(a); **you are being a little** ~ è un po' troppo precipitoso.

premeditated [pri:'mɛdɪteɪtɪd] *a* premeditato(a).

premeditation [pri:mɛdɪ'teɪʃən] *n* premeditazione *f*.

premenstrual tension [pri:'mɛnstruəl-] *n* (*MED*) tensione *f* premestruale.

premier ['prɛmɪə*] *a* primo(a) ♦ *n* (*POL*) primo ministro.

première ['prɛmɪɛə*] *n* prima.

premise ['prɛmɪs] *n* premessa.

premises ['prɛmɪsɪz] *npl* locale *m*; **on the** ~ sul posto; **business** ~ locali commerciali.

premium ['pri:mɪəm] *n* premio; **to be at a** ~ (*fig: housing etc*) essere ricercatissimo; **to sell at a** ~ (*shares*) vendere sopra la pari.

premium bond *n* (*Brit*) obbligazione *f* a premio.

premium deal *n* (*COMM*) offerta speciale.

premium gasoline *n* (*US*) super *f*.

premonition [prɛmə'nɪʃən] *n* premonizione *f*.

preoccupation [pri:ɔkju'peɪʃən] *n* preoccupazione *f*.

preoccupied [pri:'ɔkjupaɪd] *a* preoccupato(a).

prep [prɛp] *n abbr* (*SCOL*: = *preparation*) studio ♦ *a abbr*: ~ **school** = **preparatory school**.

prepackaged [pri:'pækɪdʒd] *a* già impacchettato(a).

prepaid [pri:'peɪd] *a* pagato(a) in anticipo; (*envelope*) affrancato(a).

preparation [prɛpə'reɪʃən] *n* preparazione *f*; ~**s** *npl* (*for trip*, *war*) preparativi *mpl*; **in** ~ **for sth** in vista di qc.

preparatory [prɪ'pærətərɪ] *a* preparatorio(a); ~ **to sth/to doing sth** prima di qc/di fare qc.

preparatory school *n* (*Brit*) scuola elementare privata; (*US*) *scuola superiore privata in preparazione al college*.

prepare [prɪ'pɛə*] *vt* preparare ♦ *vi*: **to** ~ **for** prepararsi a.

prepared [prɪ'pɛəd] *a*: ~ **for** preparato(a) a; ~ **to** pronto(a) a; **to be** ~ **to help sb** (*willing*) essere disposto *or* pronto ad aiutare qn.

preponderance [prɪ'pɔndərns] *n* preponderanza.

preposition [prɛpə'zɪʃən] *n* preposizione *f*.

prepossessing [pri:pə'zɛsɪŋ] *a* simpatico(a), attraente.

preposterous [prɪ'pɔstərəs] *a* assurdo(a).

prerecord ['pri:rɪ'kɔ:d] *vt* registrare in anticipo; ~**ed broadcast** trasmissione *f* registrata; ~**ed cassette** (*musi*)cassetta.

prerequisite [pri:'rɛkwɪzɪt] *n* requisito indispensabile.

prerogative [prɪ'rɔgətɪv] *n* prerogativa.

presbyterian [prɛzbɪ'tɪərɪən] *a*, *n* presbiteriano(a).

presbytery ['prɛzbɪtərɪ] *n* presbiterio.

preschool ['pri:'sku:l] *a* (*age*) prescolastico(a); (*child*) in età prescolastica.

prescribe [prɪ'skraɪb] *vt* prescrivere; (*MED*) ordinare; ~**d books** (*Brit SCOL*) testi *mpl* in programma.

prescription [prɪ'skrɪpʃən] *n* prescrizione *f*; (*MED*) ricetta; **to make up** *or* (*US*) **fill a ~** preparare *or* fare una ricetta; **"only available on ~"** "ottenibile solo dietro presentazione di ricetta medica".

prescription charges *npl* (*Brit*) ticket *m inv*.

prescriptive [prɪ'skrɪptɪv] *a* normativo(a).

presence ['prɛzns] *n* presenza; **~ of mind** presenza di spirito.

present ['prɛznt] *a* presente; (*wife, residence, job*) attuale ♦ *n* regalo; (*also*: **~ tense**) tempo presente ♦ *vt* [prɪ'zɛnt] presentare; (*give*): **to ~ sb with sth** offrire qc a qn; **to be ~ at** essere presente a; **those ~** i presenti; **at ~** al momento; **to make sb a ~ of sth** regalare qc a qn.

presentable [prɪ'zɛntəbl] *a* presentabile.

presentation [prɛzn'teɪʃən] *n* presentazione *f*; (*gift*) regalo, dono; (*ceremony*) consegna ufficiale; **on ~ of the voucher** dietro presentazione del buono.

present-day ['prɛzntdeɪ] *a* attuale, d'oggigiorno.

presenter [prɪ'zɛntə*] *n* (*Brit RADIO, TV*) presentatore/trice.

presently ['prɛzntlɪ] *ad* (*soon*) fra poco, presto; (*at present*) al momento; (*US: now*) adesso, ora.

preservation [prɛzə'veɪʃən] *n* preservazione *f*, conservazione *f*.

preservative [prɪ'zə:vətɪv] *n* conservante *m*.

preserve [prɪ'zə:v] *vt* (*keep safe*) preservare, proteggere; (*maintain*) conservare; (*food*) mettere in conserva ♦ *n* (*for game, fish*) riserva; (*often pl: jam*) marmellata; (: *fruit*) frutta sciroppata.

preshrunk [pri:'ʃrʌŋk] *a* irrestringibile.

preside [prɪ'zaɪd] *vi* presiedere.

presidency ['prɛzɪdənsɪ] *n* presidenza; (*US: of company*) direzione *f*.

president ['prɛzɪdənt] *n* presidente *m*; (*US: of company*) direttore/trice generale.

presidential [prɛzɪ'dɛnʃl] *a* presidenziale.

press [prɛs] *n* (*tool, machine*) pressa; (*for wine*) torchio; (*newspapers*) stampa; (*crowd*) folla ♦ *vt* (*push*) premere, pigiare; (*doorbell*) suonare; (*squeeze*) spremere; (: *hand*) stringere; (*clothes: iron*) stirare; (*pursue*) incalzare; (*insist*): **to ~ sth on sb** far accettare qc da qn; (*urge, entreat*): **to ~ sb to do** *or* **into doing sth** fare pressione su qn affinché faccia qc ♦ *vi* premere; accalcare; **to go to ~** (*newspaper*) andare in macchina; **to be in the ~** (*in the newspapers*) essere sui giornali; **we are ~ed for time** ci manca il tempo; **to ~ for sth** insistere per avere qc; **to ~ sb for an answer** insistere perché qn risponda; **to ~ charges**

against sb (*LAW*) sporgere una denuncia contro qn.

press on *vi* continuare.

press agency *n* agenzia di stampa.

press clipping *n* ritaglio di giornale.

press conference *n* conferenza stampa.

press cutting *n* = **press clipping**.

press-gang ['prɛsgæŋ] *vt*: **to ~ sb into doing sth** costringere qn a viva forza a fare qc.

pressing ['prɛsɪŋ] *a* urgente ♦ *n* stiratura.

press release *n* comunicato stampa.

press stud *n* (*Brit*) bottone *m* a pressione.

press-up ['prɛsʌp] *n* (*Brit*) flessione *f* sulle braccia.

pressure ['prɛʃə*] *n* pressione *f* ♦ *vt* = **to put ~ on**; **high/low ~** alta/bassa pressione; **to put ~ on sb** fare pressione su qn.

pressure cooker *n* pentola a pressione.

pressure gauge *n* manometro.

pressure group *n* gruppo di pressione.

pressurize ['prɛʃəraɪz] *vt* pressurizzare; (*fig*): **to ~ sb (into doing sth)** fare delle pressioni su qn (per costringerlo a fare qc).

pressurized ['prɛʃəraɪzd] *a* pressurizzato(a).

Prestel ® ['prɛstɛl] *n* Videotel ® *m inv*.

prestige [prɛs'ti:ʒ] *n* prestigio.

prestigious [prɛs'tɪdʒəs] *a* prestigioso(a).

presumably [prɪ'zju:məblɪ] *ad* presumibilmente; **~ he did it** penso *or* presumo che l'abbia fatto.

presume [prɪ'zju:m] *vt* supporre; **to ~ to do** (*dare*) permettersi di fare.

presumption [prɪ'zʌmpʃən] *n* presunzione *f*; (*boldness*) audacia.

presumptuous [prɪ'zʌmpʃəs] *a* presuntuoso(a).

presuppose [pri:sə'pəuz] *vt* presupporre.

pre-tax [pri:'tæks] *a* al lordo d'imposta.

pretence, (*US*) **pretense** [prɪ'tɛns] *n* (*claim*) pretesa; (*pretext*) pretesto, scusa; **to make a ~ of doing** far finta di fare; **on** *or* **under the ~ of doing sth** con il pretesto *or* la scusa di fare qc; **she is devoid of all ~** non si nasconde dietro false apparenze.

pretend [prɪ'tɛnd] *vt* (*feign*) fingere ♦ *vi* far finta; (*claim*): **to ~ to sth** pretendere a qc; **to ~ to do** far finta di fare.

pretense [prɪ'tɛns] *n* (*US*) = **pretence**.

pretension [prɪ'tɛnʃən] *n* (*claim*) pretesa; **to have no ~s to sth/to being sth** non avere la pretesa di avere qc/di essere qc.

pretentious [prɪ'tɛnʃəs] *a* pretenzioso(a).

preterite ['prɛtərɪt] *n* preterito.

pretext ['pri:tɛkst] *n* pretesto; **on** *or* **under the ~ of doing sth** col pretesto di fare qc.

pretty ['prɪtɪ] *a* grazioso(a), carino(a) ♦ *ad* abbastanza, assai.

prevail [prɪ'veɪl] *vi* (*win, be usual*) prevalere; (*persuade*): **to ~ (up)on sb to do** persuadere qn a fare.

prevailing [prɪ'veɪlɪŋ] *a* dominante.

prevalent ['prɛvələnt] *a* (*belief*) predominante; (*customs*) diffuso(a); (*fashion*) corrente; (*disease*) comune.

prevarication [prɪværɪ'keɪʃən] n tergiversazione f.

prevent [prɪ'vɛnt] vt prevenire; **to ~ sb from doing** impedire a qn di fare.

preventable [prɪ'vɛntəbl] a evitabile.

preventative [prɪ'vɛntətɪv] a preventivo(a).

prevention [prɪ'vɛnʃən] n prevenzione f.

preventive [prɪ'vɛntɪv] a preventivo(a).

preview ['priːvjuː] n (of film) anteprima.

previous ['priːvɪəs] a precedente; anteriore; **I have a ~ engagement** ho già (preso) un impegno; **~ to doing** prima di fare.

previously ['priːvɪəslɪ] ad prima.

prewar ['priːˈwɔː*] a anteguerra inv.

prey [preɪ] n preda ♦ vi: **to ~ on** far preda di; **it was ~ing on his mind** gli rodeva la mente.

price [praɪs] n prezzo; (BETTING: odds) quotazione f ♦ vt (goods) fissare il prezzo di; valutare; **what is the ~ of ...?** quanto costa ...?; **to go up** or **rise in ~** salire or aumentare di prezzo; **to put a ~ on sth** valutare or stimare qc; **he regained his freedom, but at a ~** ha riconquistato la sua libertà, ma a caro prezzo; **what ~ his promises now?** (Brit) a che valgono ora le sue promesse?; **to be ~d out of the market** (article) essere così caro da diventare invendibile; (producer, nation) non poter sostenere la concorrenza.

price control n controllo dei prezzi.

price-cutting ['praɪskʌtɪŋ] n riduzione f dei prezzi.

priceless ['praɪslɪs] a di valore inestimabile; (col: amusing) impagabile, spassosissimo(a).

price list n listino (dei) prezzi.

price range n gamma di prezzi; **it's within my ~** rientra nelle mie possibilità.

price tag n cartellino del prezzo.

price war n guerra dei prezzi.

pricey ['praɪsɪ] a (col) caruccio(a).

prick [prɪk] n puntura ♦ vt pungere; **to ~ up one's ears** drizzare gli orecchi.

prickle ['prɪkl] n (of plant) spina; (sensation) pizzicore m.

prickly ['prɪklɪ] a spinoso(a); (fig: person) permaloso(a).

prickly heat n sudamina.

prickly pear n fico d'India.

pride [praɪd] n orgoglio; superbia ♦ vt: **to ~ o.s. on** essere orgoglioso(a) di; vantarsi di; **to take (a) ~ in** tenere molto a; essere orgoglioso di; **to take a ~ in doing** andare orgoglioso di fare; **to have ~ of place** (Brit) essere al primo posto.

priest [priːst] n prete m, sacerdote m.

priestess ['priːstɪs] n sacerdotessa.

priesthood ['priːsthud] n sacerdozio.

prig [prɪg] n: **he's a ~** è compiaciuto di se stesso.

prim [prɪm] a pudico(a); contegnoso(a).

prima facie ['praɪmə'feɪʃɪ] a: **to have a ~ case** (LAW) presentare una causa in apparenza fondata.

primarily ['praɪmərɪlɪ] ad principalmente, essenzialmente.

primary ['praɪmərɪ] a primario(a); (first in importance) primo(a); (US: election) primarie fpl.

primary colour n colore m fondamentale.

primary products npl prodotti mpl di base.

primary school n (Brit) scuola elementare.

primate n (REL: ['praɪmɪt], ZOOL: ['praɪmeɪt]) primate m.

prime [praɪm] a primario(a), fondamentale; (excellent) di prima qualità ♦ n: **in the ~ of life** nel fiore della vita ♦ vt (gun) innescare; (pump) adescare; (fig) mettere al corrente.

prime minister (PM) n primo ministro.

primer ['praɪmə*] n (book) testo elementare; (paint) mano f preparatoria.

prime time n (RADIO, TV) fascia di massimo ascolto.

primeval [praɪ'miːvl] a primitivo(a).

primitive ['prɪmɪtɪv] a primitivo(a).

primrose ['prɪmrəuz] n primavera.

primus (stove) ® ['praɪməs-] n (Brit) fornello a petrolio.

prince [prɪns] n principe m.

prince charming n principe m azzurro.

princess [prɪn'sɛs] n principessa.

principal ['prɪnsɪpl] a principale ♦ n (of school, college etc) preside m/f; (money) capitale m; (in play) protagonista m/f.

principality [prɪnsɪ'pælɪtɪ] n principato.

principally ['prɪnsɪplɪ] ad principalmente.

principle ['prɪnsɪpl] n principio; **in ~** in linea di principio; **on ~** per principio.

print [prɪnt] n (mark) impronta; (letters) caratteri mpl; (fabric) tessuto stampato; (ART, PHOT) stampa ♦ vt imprimere; (publish) stampare, pubblicare; (write in capitals) scrivere in stampatello; **out of ~** esaurito(a).

print out vt (COMPUT) stampare.

printed circuit board (PCB) n circuito stampato.

printed matter n stampe fpl.

printer ['prɪntə*] n tipografo; (machine) stampante m.

printhead ['prɪnthɛd] n testa di stampa.

printing ['prɪntɪŋ] n stampa.

printing press n macchina tipografica.

print-out ['prɪntaut] n tabulato.

print wheel n margherita.

prior ['praɪə*] a precedente ♦ n (REL) priore m; **~ to doing** prima di fare; **without ~ notice** senza preavviso; **to have a ~ claim to sth** avere un diritto di precedenza su qc.

priority [praɪ'ɔrɪtɪ] n priorità f inv, precedenza; **to have** or **take ~ over sth** avere la precedenza su qc.

priory ['praɪərɪ] n monastero.

prise [praɪz] vt: **to ~ open** forzare.

prism ['prɪzəm] n prisma m.

prison ['prɪzn] n prigione f.

prison camp n campo di prigionia.

prisoner ['prɪznə*] n prigioniero/a; **to take sb**

~ far prigioniero qn; **the ~ at the bar**
l'accusato, l'imputato; ~ **of war** prigioniero/a
di guerra.

prissy ['prɪsɪ] *a* per benino.

pristine ['prɪstiːn] *a* originario(a); intatto(a);
puro(a).

privacy ['prɪvəsɪ] *n* solitudine *f*, intimità.

private ['praɪvɪt] *a* privato(a); personale ♦ *n*
soldato semplice; "*~*" (*on envelope*)
"riservata"; **in ~** in privato; **in (his) ~ life**
nella vita privata; **he is a very ~ person** è
una persona molto riservata; **~ hearing**
(*LAW*) udienza a porte chiuse; **to be in ~**
practice essere medico non convenzionato
(con la mutua).

private enterprise *n* iniziativa privata.

private eye *n* investigatore *m* privato.

private limited company *n* (*Brit*) società
per azioni non quotata in Borsa.

privately ['praɪvɪtlɪ] *ad* in privato; (*within
o.s.*) dentro di sé.

private parts *npl* (*ANAT*) parti *fpl* intime.

private property *n* proprietà privata.

private school *n* scuola privata.

privation [praɪ'veɪʃən] *n* (*state*) privazione *f*;
(*hardship*) privazioni *fpl*, stenti *mpl*.

privatize ['praɪvɪtaɪz] *vt* privatizzare.

privet ['prɪvɪt] *n* ligustro.

privilege ['prɪvɪlɪdʒ] *n* privilegio.

privileged ['prɪvɪlɪdʒd] *a* privilegiato(a); **to
be ~ to do sth** avere il privilegio *or* l'onore
di fare qc.

privy ['prɪvɪ] *a*: **to be ~ to** essere al corrente
di.

Privy Council *n* (*Brit*) Consiglio della Corona.

Privy Councillor *n* (*Brit*) Consigliere *m* della
Corona.

prize [praɪz] *n* premio ♦ *a* (*example, idiot*)
perfetto(a); (*bull, novel*) premiato(a) ♦ *vt*
apprezzare, pregiare.

prize fight *n* incontro di pugilato tra
professionisti.

prize giving *n* premiazione *f*.

prize money *n* soldi *mpl* del premio.

prizewinner ['praɪzwɪnə*] *n* premiato/a.

prizewinning ['praɪzwɪnɪŋ] *a* vincente; (*novel,
essay etc*) premiato(a).

PRO *n abbr* = **public relations officer.**

pro [prəu] *n* (*SPORT*) professionista *m/f*; **the
~s and cons** il pro e il contro.

pro- [prəu] *prefix* (*in favour of*) filo...; **~Soviet**
a filosovietico(a).

probability [prɔbə'bɪlɪtɪ] *n* probabilità *f inv*; **in
all ~** con ogni probabilità.

probable ['prɔbəbl] *a* probabile; **it is ~/hardly
~ that** ... è probabile/poco probabile che ... +
sub.

probably ['prɔbəblɪ] *ad* probabilmente.

probate ['prəubɪt] *n* (*LAW*) omologazione *f* (di
un testamento).

probation [prə'beɪʃən] *n* (*in employment*)
periodo di prova; (*LAW*) libertà vigilata;
(*REL*) probandato; **on ~** (*employee*) in
prova; (*LAW*) in libertà vigilata.

probationary [prəu'beɪʃənərɪ] *a*: ~ **period**
periodo di prova.

probe [prəub] *n* (*MED, SPACE*) sonda;
(*enquiry*) indagine *f*, investigazione *f* ♦ *vt*
sondare, esplorare; indagare.

probity ['prəubɪtɪ] *n* probità.

problem ['prɔbləm] *n* problema *m*; **to have
~s with the car** avere dei problemi con la
macchina; **what's the ~?** che cosa c'è?; **I
had no ~ in finding her** non mi è stato
difficile trovarla; **no ~!** ma certamente!, non
c'è problema!

problematic [prɔblə'mætɪk] *a* pro-
blematico(a).

procedure [prə'siːdʒə*] *n* (*ADMIN, LAW*)
procedura; (*method*) metodo, procedimento.

proceed [prə'siːd] *vi* (*go forward*) avanzare,
andare avanti; (*go about it*) procedere;
(*continue*): **to ~ (with)** continuare; **to ~ to**
andare a; passare a; **to ~ to do** mettersi a
fare; **to ~ against sb** (*LAW*) procedere contro qn; **I am not sure how to ~** non so bene
come fare.

proceeding [prə'siːdɪŋ] *n* procedimento, modo
d'agire.

proceedings [prə'siːdɪŋz] *npl* misure *fpl*;
(*LAW*) procedimento; (*meeting*) riunione *f*;
(*records*) rendiconti *mpl*; atti *mpl*.

proceeds ['prəusiːdz] *npl* profitto, incasso.

process ['prəusɛs] *n* processo; (*method*)
metodo, sistema *m* ♦ *vt* trattare;
(*information*) elaborare ♦ *vi* [prə'sɛs] (*Brit
formal: go in procession*) sfilare, procedere in
corteo; **we are in the ~ of moving to** ...
stiamo per trasferirci a ....

processed cheese, (*US*) **process cheese** *n*
formaggio fuso.

processing ['prəusɛsɪŋ] *n* trattamento;
elaborazione *f*.

procession [prə'sɛʃən] *n* processione *f*, corteo;
funeral ~ corteo funebre.

proclaim [prə'kleɪm] *vt* proclamare, dichiarare.

proclamation [prɔklə'meɪʃən] *n* pro-
clamazione *f*.

proclivity [prə'klɪvɪtɪ] *n* tendenza, propensione
f.

procrastination [prəukræstɪ'neɪʃən] *n* procra-
stinazione *f*.

procreation [prəukrɪ'eɪʃən] *n* procreazione *f*.

procure [prə'kjuə*] *vt* (*for o.s.*) procurarsi;
(*for sb*) procurare.

procurement [prə'kjuəmənt] *n* approvvigionamento.

prod [prɔd] *vt* dare un colpetto a ♦ *n* (*push,
jab*) colpetto.

prodigal ['prɔdɪgl] *a* prodigo(a).

prodigious [prə'dɪdʒəs] *a* prodigioso(a).

prodigy ['prɔdɪdʒɪ] *n* prodigio.

produce *n* ['prɔdjuːs] (*AGR*) prodotto, prodotti
mpl ♦ *vt* [prə'djuːs] produrre; (*to show*)
esibire, mostrare; (*proof of identity*)
produrre, fornire; (*cause*) cagionare,
causare; (*THEATRE*) mettere in scena.

producer [prə'dju:sə*] *n* (*THEATRE*) direttore/trice; (*AGR*, *CINEMA*) produttore *m*.

product ['prɒdʌkt] *n* prodotto.

production [prə'dʌkʃən] *n* produzione *f*; (*THEATRE*) messa in scena; **to put into** ~ mettere in produzione.

production agreement *n* (*US*) accordo sui tempi di produzione.

production control *n* controllo di produzione.

production line *n* catena di lavorazione.

production manager *n* production manager *m inv*, direttore *m* della produzione.

productive [prə'dʌktɪv] *a* produttivo(a).

productivity [prɒdʌk'tɪvɪtɪ] *n* produttività.

productivity agreement *n* (*Brit*) accordo sui tempi di produzione.

productivity bonus *n* premio di produzione.

Prof. *abbr* (= *professor*) Prof.

profane [prə'feɪn] *a* profano(a); (*language*) empio(a).

profess [prə'fɛs] *vt* professare; **I do not** ~ **to be an expert** non pretendo di essere un esperto.

professed [prə'fɛst] *a* (*self-declared*) dichiarato(a).

profession [prə'fɛʃən] *n* professione *f*; **the** ~**s** le professioni liberali.

professional [prə'fɛʃənl] *n* (*SPORT*) professionista *m/f* ♦ *a* professionale; (*work*) da professionista; **he's a** ~ **man** è un professionista; **to take** ~ **advice** consultare un esperto.

professionalism [prə'fɛʃnəlɪzəm] *n* professionismo.

professionally [prə'fɛʃnəlɪ] *ad* professionalmente, in modo professionale; (*SPORT*: *play*) come professionista; **I only know him** ~ con lui ho solo rapporti di lavoro.

professor [prə'fɛsə*] *n* professore *m* (*titolare di una cattedra*); (*US*: *teacher*) professore/essa.

professorship [prə'fɛsəʃɪp] *n* cattedra.

proffer ['prɒfə*] *vt* (*remark*) profferire; (*apologies*) porgere, presentare; (*one's hand*) porgere.

proficiency [prə'fɪʃənsɪ] *n* competenza, abilità.

proficient [prə'fɪʃənt] *a* competente, abile.

profile ['prəufaɪl] *n* profilo; **to keep a low** ~ (*fig*) cercare di passare inosservato *or* di non farsi notare troppo; **to maintain a high** ~ mettersi in mostra.

profit ['prɒfɪt] *n* profitto; beneficio ♦ *vi*: **to** ~ (**by** *or* **from**) approfittare (di); ~ **and loss account** conto perdite e profitti; **to make a** ~ realizzare un profitto; **to sell sth at a** ~ vendere qc con un utile.

profitability [prɒfɪtə'bɪlɪtɪ] *n* redditività.

profitable ['prɒfɪtəbl] *a* redditizio(a); (*fig*: *beneficial*) vantaggioso(a); (: *meeting*, *visit*) fruttuoso(a).

profit centre *n* centro di profitto.

profiteering [prɒfɪ'tɪərɪŋ] *n* (*pej*) affarismo.

profit-making ['prɒfɪtmeɪkɪŋ] *a* a scopo di lucro.

profit margin *n* margine *m* di profitto.

profit-sharing ['prɒfɪtʃɛərɪŋ] *n* compartecipazione *f* agli utili.

profits tax *n* (*Brit*) imposta sugli utili.

profligate ['prɒflɪgɪt] *a* (*dissolute*: *behaviour*) dissipato(a); (: *person*) debosciato(a); (*extravagant*): **he's very** ~ **with his money** è uno che sperpera i suoi soldi.

pro forma ['prəu'fɔ:mə] *ad*: ~ **invoice** fattura proforma.

profound [prə'faund] *a* profondo(a).

profuse [prə'fju:s] *a* infinito(a), abbondante.

profusely [prə'fju:slɪ] *ad* con grande effusione.

profusion [prə'fju:ʒən] *n* profusione *f*, abbondanza.

progeny ['prɒdʒɪnɪ] *n* progenie *f*; discendenti *mpl*.

programme, (*US*) **program** ['prəugræm] *n* programma *m* ♦ *vt* programmare.

program(m)er ['prəugræmə*] *n* programmatore/trice.

program(m)ing ['prəugræmɪŋ] *n* programmazione *f*.

program(m)ing language *n* linguaggio di programmazione.

progress *n* ['prəugrɛs] progresso ♦ *vi* [prə'grɛs] (*go forward*) avanzare, procedere; (*in time*) procedere; (*also*: **make** ~) far progressi; **in** ~ in corso.

progression [prə'grɛʃən] *n* progressione *f*.

progressive [prə'grɛsɪv] *a* progressivo(a); (*person*) progressista.

progressively [prə'grɛsɪvlɪ] *ad* progressivamente.

progress report *n* (*MED*) bollettino medico; (*ADMIN*) rendiconto dei lavori.

prohibit [prə'hɪbɪt] *vt* proibire, vietare; **to** ~ **sb from doing sth** vietare *or* proibire a qn di fare qc; "**smoking** ~**ed**" "vietato fumare".

prohibition [prəuɪ'bɪʃən] *n* (*US*) proibizionismo.

prohibitive [prə'hɪbɪtɪv] *a* (*price etc*) proibitivo(a).

project *n* ['prɒdʒɛkt] (*plan*) piano; (*venture*) progetto; (*SCOL*) studio, ricerca ♦ *vb* [prə'dʒɛkt] *vt* proiettare ♦ *vi* (*stick out*) sporgere.

projectile [prə'dʒɛktaɪl] *n* proiettile *m*.

projection [prə'dʒɛkʃən] *n* proiezione *f*; sporgenza.

projectionist [prə'dʒɛkʃənɪst] *n* (*CINEMA*) proiezionista *m/f*.

projection room *n* (*CINEMA*) cabina *or* sala di proiezione.

projector [prə'dʒɛktə*] *n* proiettore *m*.

proletarian [prəulɪ'tɛərɪən] *a*, *n* proletario(a).

proletariat [prəulɪ'tɛərɪət] *n* proletariato.

proliferate [prə'lɪfəreɪt] *vi* proliferare.

proliferation [prəlɪfə'reɪʃən] *n* proliferazione *f*.

prolific [prə'lɪfɪk] *a* prolifico(a).

prologue, (*US*) **prolog** ['prəulɒg] *n* prologo.

prolong [prə'lɒŋ] *vt* prolungare.

prom [prɔm] *n abbr* = **promenade, promenade concert;** (*US:* *ball*) ballo studentesco.

promenade [prɔmə'nɑːd] *n* (*by sea*) lungomare *m*.

promenade concert *n* concerto (*con posti in piedi*).

promenade deck *n* (*NAUT*) ponte *m* di passeggiata.

prominence ['prɔmɪnəns] *n* prominenza; importanza.

prominent ['prɔmɪnənt] *a* (*standing out*) prominente; (*important*) importante; **he is ~ in the field of** ... è un'autorità nel campo di ....

prominently ['prɔmɪnəntlɪ] *ad* (*display, set*) ben in vista; **he figured ~ in the case** ha avuto una parte di primo piano nella faccenda.

promiscuity [prɔmɪs'kjuːɪtɪ] *n* (*sexual*) rapporti *mpl* multipli.

promiscuous [prə'mɪskjuəs] *a* (*sexually*) di facili costumi.

promise ['prɔmɪs] *n* promessa ♦ *vt, vi* promettere; **to make sb a ~** fare una promessa a qn; **a young man of ~** un giovane promettente; **to ~ (sb) to do sth** promettere (a qn) di fare qc.

promising ['prɔmɪsɪŋ] *a* promettente.

promissory note ['prɔmɪsərɪ-] *n* pagherò *m inv*.

promontory ['prɔməntrɪ] *n* promontorio.

promote [prə'məut] *vt* promuovere; (*venture, event*) organizzare; (*product*) lanciare, reclamizzare; **the team was ~d to the second division** (*Brit FOOTBALL*) la squadra è stata promossa in serie B.

promoter [prə'məutə*] *n* (*of sporting event*) organizzatore/trice; (*of cause etc*) sostenitore/trice.

promotion [prə'məuʃən] *n* promozione *f*.

prompt [prɔmpt] *a* rapido(a), svelto(a); puntuale; (*reply*) sollecito(a) ♦ *ad* (*punctually*) in punto ♦ *n* (*COMPUT*) guida ♦ *vt* incitare; provocare; (*THEATRE*) suggerire a; **at 8 o'clock ~** alle 8 in punto; **to be ~ to do sth** essere sollecito nel fare qc; **to ~ sb to do** spingere qn a fare.

prompter ['prɔmptə*] *n* (*THEATRE*) suggeritore *m*.

promptly ['prɔmptlɪ] *ad* prontamente; puntualmente.

promptness ['prɔmptnɪs] *n* prontezza; puntualità.

prone [prəun] *a* (*lying*) prono(a); **~ to** propenso(a) a, incline a; **to be ~ to illness** essere soggetto(a) a malattie; **she is ~ to burst into tears if** ... può facilmente scoppiare in lacrime se ....

prong [prɔŋ] *n* rebbio, punta.

pronoun ['prəunaun] *n* pronome *m*.

pronounce [prə'nauns] *vt* pronunziare ♦ *vi:* **to ~ (up)on** pronunziare su; **they ~d him unfit to drive** lo hanno dichiarato inabile alla guida.

pronounced [prə'naunst] *a* (*marked*) spiccato(a).

pronouncement [prə'naunsmənt] *n* dichiarazione *f*.

pronunciation [prənʌnsɪ'eɪʃən] *n* pronunzia.

proof [pruːf] *n* prova; (*of book*) bozza; (*PHOT*) provino; (*of alcohol*): **70% ~** ≈ 40° in volume ♦ *vt* (*tent, anorak*) impermeabilizzare ♦ *a:* **~ against** a prova di.

proofreader ['pruːfriːdə*] *n* correttore/trice di bozze.

prop [prɔp] *n* sostegno, appoggio ♦ *vt* (*also:* **~ up**) sostenere, appoggiare; (*lean*): **to ~ sth against** appoggiare qc contro *or* a.

Prop. *abbr* (*COMM*) = **proprietor.**

propaganda [prɔpə'gændə] *n* propaganda.

propagation [prɔpə'geɪʃən] *n* propagazione *f*.

propel [prə'pɛl] *vt* spingere (in avanti), muovere.

propeller [prə'pɛlə*] *n* elica.

propelling pencil [prə'pɛlɪŋ-] *n* (*Brit*) matita a mina.

propensity [prə'pɛnsɪtɪ] *n* tendenza.

proper ['prɔpə*] *a* (*suited, right*) adatto(a), appropriato(a); (*seemly*) decente; (*authentic*) vero(a); (*col: real*) *n* + vero(a) e proprio(a); **to go through the ~ channels** (*ADMIN*) seguire la regolare procedura.

properly ['prɔpəlɪ] *ad* decentemente; (*really, thoroughly*) veramente.

proper noun *n* nome *m* proprio.

property ['prɔpətɪ] *n* (*things owned*) beni *mpl*; (*land, building, CHEM etc*) proprietà *f inv*.

property developer *n* (*Brit*) costruttore *m* edile.

property owner *n* proprietario/a.

property tax *n* imposta patrimoniale.

prophecy ['prɔfɪsɪ] *n* profezia.

prophesy ['prɔfɪsaɪ] *vt* predire, profetizzare.

prophet ['prɔfɪt] *n* profeta *m*.

prophetic [prə'fɛtɪk] *a* profetico(a).

proportion [prə'pɔːʃən] *n* proporzione *f*; (*share*) parte *f* ♦ *vt* proporzionare, commisurare; **to be in/out of ~ to** *or* **with sth** essere in proporzione/sproporzionato rispetto a qc; **to see sth in ~** (*fig*) dare il giusto peso a qc.

proportional [prə'pɔːʃənl] *a* proporzionale.

proportional representation (PR) *n* rappresentanza proporzionale.

proportionate [prə'pɔːʃənɪt] *a* proporzionato(a).

proposal [prə'pəuzl] *n* proposta; (*plan*) progetto; (*of marriage*) proposta di matrimonio.

propose [prə'pəuz] *vt* proporre, suggerire ♦ *vi* fare una proposta di matrimonio; **to ~ to do** proporsi di fare, aver l'intenzione di fare.

proposer [prə'pəuzə*] *n* (*Brit: of motion*) proponente *m/f*.

proposition [prɔpə'zɪʃən] *n* proposizione *f*; (*proposal*) proposta; **to make sb a ~** proporre qualcosa a qn.

propound [prə'paund] *vt* proporre, presentare.

proprietary [prə'praɪətərɪ] *a*: ~ **article** prodotto con marchio depositato; ~ **brand** marchio di fabbrica.

proprietor [prə'praɪətə*] *n* proprietario/a.

propriety [prə'praɪətɪ] *n* (*seemliness*) decoro, rispetto delle convenienze sociali.

propulsion [prə'pʌlʃən] *n* propulsione *f*.

pro rata [prəʊ'rɑːtə] *ad* in proporzione.

prosaic [prəʊ'zeɪɪk] *a* prosaico(a).

Pros. Atty. *abbr* (*US*) = **prosecuting attorney.**

proscribe [prə'skraɪb] *vt* proscrivere.

prose [prəʊz] *n* prosa; (*SCOL: translation*) traduzione *f* dalla madrelingua.

prosecute ['prɔsɪkjuːt] *vt* intentare azione contro.

prosecuting attorney ['prɔsɪkjuːtɪŋ-] *n* (*US*) ≈ procuratore *m*.

prosecution [prɔsɪ'kjuːʃən] *n* (*LAW*) azione *f* giudiziaria; (*accusing side*) accusa.

prosecutor ['prɔsɪkjuːtə*] *n* (*also:* **public** ~) ≈ procuratore *m* della Repubblica.

prospect *n* ['prɔspekt] prospettiva; (*hope*) speranza ♦ *vb* [prə'spekt] *vt* esplorare ♦ *vi*: **to** ~ **for gold** cercare l'oro; **there is every** ~ **of an early victory** tutto lascia prevedere una rapida vittoria; *see also* **prospects.**

prospecting [prə'spektɪŋ] *n* prospezione *f*.

prospective [prə'spektɪv] *a* (*buyer*) probabile; (*legislation, son-in-law*) futuro(a).

prospector [prə'spektə*] *n* prospettore *m*; **gold** ~ cercatore *m* d'oro.

prospects ['prɔspekts] *npl* (*for work etc*) prospettive *fpl*.

prospectus [prə'spektəs] *n* prospetto, programma *m*.

prosper ['prɔspə*] *vi* prosperare.

prosperity [prɔ'sperɪtɪ] *n* prosperità.

prosperous ['prɔspərəs] *a* prospero(a).

prostate ['prɔsteɪt] *n* (*also:* ~ **gland**) prostata, ghiandola prostatica.

prostitute ['prɔstɪtjuːt] *n* prostituta; **male** ~ uomo che si prostituisce.

prostitution [prɔstɪ'tjuːʃən] *n* prostituzione *f*.

prostrate *a* ['prɔstreɪt] prostrato(a) ♦ *vt* [prɔ'streɪt]: **to** ~ **o.s.** (*before sb*) prostrarsi.

protagonist [prə'tægənɪst] *n* protagonista *m/f*.

protect [prə'tekt] *vt* proteggere, salvaguardare.

protection [prə'tekʃən] *n* protezione *f*; **to be under sb's** ~ essere sotto la protezione di qn.

protectionism [prə'tekʃənɪzəm] *n* protezionismo.

protection racket *n* racket *m inv*.

protective [prə'tektɪv] *a* protettivo(a); ~ **custody** (*LAW*) protezione *f*.

protector [prə'tektə*] *n* protettore/trice.

protégé ['prəʊtɪʒeɪ] *n* protetto.

protégée ['prəʊtɪʒeɪ] *n* protetta.

protein ['prəʊtiːn] *n* proteina.

pro tem [prəʊ'tem] *ad abbr* (= *pro tempore*: *for the time being*) pro tempore.

protest *n* ['prəʊtest] protesta ♦ *vt, vi* [prə'test]

protestare; **to do sth under** ~ fare qc protestando; **to** ~ **against/about** protestare contro/per.

Protestant ['prɔtɪstənt] *a, n* protestante (*m/f*).

protester, protestor [prə'testə*] *n* (*in demonstration*) dimostrante *m/f*.

protest march *n* marcia di protesta.

protocol ['prəʊtəkɔl] *n* protocollo.

prototype ['prəʊtətaɪp] *n* prototipo.

protracted [prə'træktɪd] *a* tirato(a) per le lunghe.

protractor [prə'træktə*] *n* (*GEOM*) goniometro.

protrude [prə'truːd] *vi* sporgere.

protuberance [prə'tjuːbərəns] *n* sporgenza.

proud [praud] *a* fiero(a), orgoglioso(a); (*pej*) superbo(a); **to be** ~ **to do sth** essere onorato(a) di fare qc; **to do sb** ~ non far mancare nulla a qn; **to do o.s.** ~ trattarsi bene.

proudly ['praudlɪ] *ad* con orgoglio, fieramente.

prove [pruːv] *vt* provare, dimostrare ♦ *vi*: **to** ~ **correct** *etc* risultare vero(a) *etc*; **to** ~ **o.s.** mostrare le proprie capacità; **to** ~ **o.s./itself (to be) useful** *etc* mostrarsi *or* rivelarsi utile *etc*; **he was** ~**d right in the end** alla fine i fatti gli hanno dato ragione.

Provence [prɔvɑ̃s] *n* Provenza.

proverb ['prɔvɔːb] *n* proverbio.

proverbial [prə'vɔːbɪəl] *a* proverbiale.

provide [prə'vaɪd] *vt* fornire, provvedere; **to** ~ **sb with** fornire *or* provvedere qn di qc; **to be** ~**d with** essere dotato *or* munito di.

provide for *vt fus* provvedere a.

provided [prə'vaɪdɪd] *cj*: ~ **that** purché + *sub*, a condizione che + *sub*.

Providence ['prɔvɪdəns] *n* Provvidenza.

providing [prə'vaɪdɪŋ] *cj* purché + *sub*, a condizione che + *sub*.

province ['prɔvɪns] *n* provincia.

provincial [prə'vɪnʃəl] *a* provinciale.

provision [prə'vɪʒən] *n* (*supply*) riserva; (*supplying*) provvista; rifornimento; (*stipulation*) condizione *f*; ~**s** *npl* (*food*) provviste *fpl*; **to make** ~ **for** (*one's family, future*) pensare a; **there's no** ~ **for this in the contract** il contratto non lo prevede.

provisional [prə'vɪʒənl] *a* provvisorio(a) ♦ *n*: **P**~ (*Irish POL*) provisional *m inv*.

provisional licence *n* (*Brit AUT*) ≈ foglio *m* rosa *inv*.

provisionally [prə'vɪʒnəlɪ] *ad* provvisoriamente; (*appoint*) a titolo provvisorio.

proviso [prə'vaɪzəʊ] *n* condizione *f*; **with the** ~ **that** a condizione che + *sub*, a patto che + *sub*.

Provo ['prɔvəʊ] *n abbr* (*col*) = **Provisional.**

provocation [prɔvə'keɪʃən] *n* provocazione *f*.

provocative [prə'vɔkətɪv] *a* (*aggressive*) provocatorio(a); (*thought-provoking*) stimolante; (*seductive*) provocante.

provoke [prə'vəʊk] *vt* provocare; incitare; **to** ~ **sb to sth/to do** *or* **into doing sth** spingere qn a qc/a fare qc.

provoking [prə'vəʊkɪŋ] a irritante, esasperante.

provost ['prɔvəst] n (Brit: of university) rettore m; (Scottish) sindaco.

prow [praʊ] n prua.

prowess ['praʊɪs] n prodezza; **his ~ as a footballer** le sue capacità di calciatore.

prowl [praʊl] vi (also: ~ **about**, ~ **around**) aggirarsi furtivamente; **on the ~** in cerca di preda.

prowler ['praʊlə*] n tipo sospetto (che s'aggira con l'intenzione di rubare, aggredire etc).

proximity [prɔk'sɪmɪtɪ] n prossimità.

proxy ['prɔksɪ] n procura; **by ~** per procura.

prude [pru:d] n puritano/a.

prudence ['pru:dns] n prudenza.

prudent ['pru:dnt] a prudente.

prudish ['pru:dɪʃ] a puritano(a).

prune [pru:n] n prugna secca ♦ vt potare.

pry [praɪ] vi: **to ~ into** ficcare il naso in.

PS n abbr (= postscript) P.S.

psalm [sɑ:m] n salmo.

PSAT n abbr (US) = Preliminary Scholastic Aptitude Test.

PSBR n abbr (Brit: = public sector borrowing requirement) fabbisogno di prestiti per il settore pubblico.

pseud ['sju:d] n (Brit col: intellectually) intellettualoide m/f; (: socially) snob m/f inv.

pseudo- ['sju:dəʊ] prefix pseudo....

pseudonym ['sju:dənɪm] n pseudonimo.

PST abbr (US: = Pacific Standard Time) ora invernale del Pacifico.

PSV n abbr (Brit) see **public service vehicle**.

psyche ['saɪkɪ] n psiche f.

psychedelic [saɪkɪ'dɛlɪk] a psichedelico(a).

psychiatric [saɪkɪ'ætrɪk] a psichiatrico(a).

psychiatrist [saɪ'kaɪətrɪst] n psichiatra m/f.

psychiatry [saɪ'kaɪətrɪ] n psichiatria.

psychic ['saɪkɪk] a (also: ~**al**) psichico(a); (person) dotato(a) di qualità telepatiche.

psychoanalyse [saɪkəʊ'ænəlaɪz] vt psicanalizzare.

psychoanalysis, pl **-lyses** [saɪkəʊə'nælɪsɪs, -sɪz] n psicanalisi f inv.

psychoanalyst [saɪkəʊ'ænəlɪst] n psicanalista m/f.

psychological [saɪkə'lɔdʒɪkl] a psicologico(a).

psychologist [saɪ'kɔlədʒɪst] n psicologo/a.

psychology [saɪ'kɔlədʒɪ] n psicologia.

psychopath ['saɪkəʊpæθ] n psicopatico/a.

psychosis, pl **psychoses** [saɪ'kəʊsɪs, -sɪz] n psicosi f inv.

psychosomatic [saɪkəʊsə'mætɪk] a psicosomatico(a).

psychotherapy [saɪkəʊ'θɛrəpɪ] n psicoterapia.

psychotic [saɪ'kɔtɪk] a, n psicotico(a).

PT n abbr (Brit: = physical training) ed. fisica.

pt abbr (= pint; point) pt.

Pt. abbr (in place names: = Point) Pt.

PTA n abbr (= Parent-Teacher Association) associazione genitori e insegnanti.

Pte. abbr (Brit MIL) = **private**.

PTO abbr (= please turn over) v.r. (= vedi retro).

PTV n abbr (US) = pay television, public television.

pub [pʌb] n abbr (= public house) pub m inv.

puberty ['pju:bətɪ] n pubertà.

pubic ['pju:bɪk] a pubico(a), del pube.

public ['pʌblɪk] a pubblico(a) ♦ n pubblico; **in ~** in pubblico; **the general ~** il pubblico; **to make sth ~** render noto or di pubblico dominio qc; **to be ~ knowledge** essere di dominio pubblico; **to go ~** (COMM) emettere le azioni sul mercato.

public address system (PA) n impianto di amplificazione.

publican ['pʌblɪkən] n (Brit) gestore m (or proprietario) di un pub.

publication [pʌblɪ'keɪʃən] n pubblicazione f.

public company n ≈ società f inv per azioni (costituita tramite pubblica sottoscrizione).

public convenience n (Brit) gabinetti mpl.

public holiday n (Brit) giorno festivo, festa nazionale.

public house n (Brit) pub m inv.

publicity [pʌb'lɪsɪtɪ] n pubblicità.

publicize ['pʌblɪsaɪz] vt fare (della) pubblicità a, reclamizzare.

public limited company (plc) n ≈ società per azioni a responsabilità limitata (quotata in Borsa).

publicly ['pʌblɪklɪ] ad pubblicamente.

public opinion n opinione f pubblica.

public ownership n proprietà pubblica or sociale; **to be taken into ~** essere statalizzato(a).

public relations n pubbliche relazioni fpl.

public relations officer n addetto/a alle pubbliche relazioni.

public school n (Brit) scuola privata; (US) scuola statale.

public sector n settore m pubblico.

public service vehicle (PSV) n (Brit) mezzo pubblico.

public-spirited [pʌblɪk'spɪrɪtɪd] a che ha senso civico.

public transport, (US) **public transportation** n mezzi mpl pubblici.

public utility n servizio pubblico.

public works npl lavori mpl pubblici.

publish ['pʌblɪʃ] vt pubblicare.

publisher ['pʌblɪʃə*] n editore m; (firm) casa editrice.

publishing ['pʌblɪʃɪŋ] n (industry) editoria; (of a book) pubblicazione f.

publishing company n casa or società editrice.

puce [pju:s] a color pulce inv.

puck [pʌk] n (ICE HOCKEY) disco.

pucker ['pʌkə*] vt corrugare.

pudding ['pʊdɪŋ] n budino; (dessert) dolce m; **black ~**, (US) **blood ~** sanguinaccio; **rice ~** budino di riso.

puddle ['pʌdl] n pozza, pozzanghera.

puerile ['pjuəraɪl] a puerile.
Puerto Rico ['pwɜːtəu'riːkəu] n Portorico.
puff [pʌf] n sbuffo; (also: powder ~) piumino ♦ vt (also: ~ out: sails, cheeks) gonfiare ♦ vi uscire a sbuffi; (pant) ansare; **to ~ out smoke** mandar fuori sbuffi di fumo; **to ~ one's pipe** tirare sboccate di fumo.
puffed [pʌft] a (col: out of breath) senza fiato.
puffin ['pʌfɪn] n puffino.
puff paste, (US) **puff paste** n pasta sfoglia.
puffy ['pʌfɪ] a gonfio(a).
pugnacious [pʌg'neɪʃəs] a combattivo(a).
pull [pul] n (tug) strattone m, tirata; (of moon, magnet, the sea etc) attrazione f; (fig) influenza ♦ vt tirare; (muscle) strappare, farsi uno strappo a ♦ vi tirare; **to give sth a ~** tirare su qc; **to ~ a face** fare una smorfia; **to ~ to pieces** fare a pezzi; **to ~ one's punches** (BOXING) risparmiare l'avversario; **not to ~ one's punches** (fig) non avere peli sulla lingua; **to ~ one's weight** dare il proprio contributo; **to ~ o.s. together** ricomporsi, riprendersi; **to ~ sb's leg** prendere in giro qn; **to ~ strings (for sb)** muovere qualche pedina (per qn).
pull about vt (Brit: handle roughly: object) strapazzare; (: person) malmenare.
pull apart vt (break) fare a pezzi.
pull down vt (house) demolire; (tree) abbattere.
pull in vi (AUT: at the kerb) accostarsi; (RAIL) entrare in stazione.
pull off vt (deal etc) portare a compimento.
pull out vi partire; (withdraw) ritirarsi; (AUT: come out of line) spostarsi sulla mezzeria ♦ vt staccare; far uscire; (withdraw) ritirare.
pull over vi (AUT) accostare.
pull round vi (unconscious person) rinvenire; (sick person) ristabilirsi.
pull through vi farcela.
pull up vi (stop) fermarsi ♦ vt (uproot) sradicare; (stop) fermare.
pulley ['pulɪ] n puleggia, carrucola.
pull-out ['pulaut] n inserto ♦ cpd staccabile.
pullover ['puləuvə*] n pullover m inv.
pulp [pʌlp] n (of fruit) polpa; (for paper) pasta per carta; (magazines, books) stampa di qualità e di tono scadenti; **to reduce sth to ~** spappolare qc.
pulpit ['pulpɪt] n pulpito.
pulsate [pʌl'seɪt] vi battere, palpitare.
pulse [pʌls] n polso; **to feel or take sb's ~** sentire or tastare il polso a qn.
pulses ['pʌlsəz] npl (CULIN) legumi mpl.
pulverize ['pʌlvəraɪz] vt polverizzare.
puma ['pjuːmə] n puma m inv.
pumice (stone) ['pʌmɪs-] n (pietra) pomice f.
pummel ['pʌml] vt dare pugni a.
pump [pʌmp] n pompa; (shoe) scarpetta ♦ vt pompare; (fig: col) far parlare; **to ~ sb for information** cercare di strappare delle informazioni a qn.
pump up vt gonfiare.

pumpkin ['pʌmpkɪn] n zucca.
pun [pʌn] n gioco di parole.
punch [pʌntʃ] n (blow) pugno; (fig: force) forza; (tool) punzone m; (drink) ponce m ♦ vt (hit): **to ~ sb/sth** dare un pugno a qn/qc; **to ~ a hole (in)** fare un buco (in).
punch in vi (US) timbrare il cartellino (all'entrata).
punch out vi (US) timbrare il cartellino (all'uscita).
punch-drunk ['pʌntʃdrʌŋk] a (Brit) stordito(a).
punch(ed) card n scheda perforata.
punch line n (of joke) battuta finale.
punch-up ['pʌntʃʌp] n (Brit col) rissa.
punctual ['pʌŋktjuəl] a puntuale.
punctuality [pʌŋktju'ælɪtɪ] n puntualità.
punctually [pʌŋktjuəlɪ] ad puntualmente; **it will start ~ at 6** comincerà alle 6 precise or in punto.
punctuate ['pʌŋktjueɪt] vt punteggiare.
punctuation [pʌŋktju'eɪʃən] n interpunzione f, punteggiatura.
punctuation mark n segno d'interpunzione.
puncture ['pʌŋktʃə*] n (Brit) foratura ♦ vt forare; **to have a ~** (AUT) forare (una gomma).
pundit ['pʌndɪt] n sapientone/a.
pungent ['pʌndʒənt] a piccante; (fig) mordace, caustico(a).
punish ['pʌnɪʃ] vt punire; **to ~ sb for sth/for doing sth** punire qn per qc/per aver fatto qc.
punishable ['pʌnɪʃəbl] a punibile.
punishing ['pʌnɪʃɪŋ] a (fig: exhausting) sfiancante.
punishment ['pʌnɪʃmənt] n punizione f; (fig col): **to take a lot of ~** (boxer) incassare parecchi colpi; (car) essere messo(a) a dura prova.
punk [pʌŋk] n (person: also: ~ rocker) punk m/f inv; (music: also: ~ rock) musica punk, punk rock m; (US col: hoodlum) teppista m.
punt [pʌnt] n (boat) barchino; (FOOTBALL) colpo a volo ♦ vi (Brit: bet) scommettere.
punter ['pʌntə*] n (Brit: gambler) scommettitore/trice.
puny ['pjuːnɪ] a gracile.
pup [pʌp] n cucciolo/a.
pupil ['pjuːpl] n allievo/a; (ANAT) pupilla.
puppet ['pʌpɪt] n burattino.
puppet government n governo fantoccio.
puppy ['pʌpɪ] n cucciolo/a, cagnolino/a.
purchase ['pɜːtʃɪs] n acquisto, compera; (grip) presa ♦ vt comprare; **to get a ~ on** (grip) trovare un appoggio su.
purchase order n ordine m d'acquisto, ordinazione f.
purchase price n prezzo d'acquisto.
purchaser ['pɜːtʃɪsə*] n compratore/trice.
purchase tax n (Brit) tassa d'acquisto.
purchasing power ['pɜːtʃɪsɪŋ-] n potere m d'acquisto.
pure [pjuə*] a puro(a); **a ~ wool jumper** un golf di pura lana; **it's laziness ~ and simple**

è pura pigrizia.
purebred ['pjuəbred] *a* di razza pura.
purée ['pjuəreɪ] *n* purè *m inv*.
purely ['pjuəlɪ] *ad* puramente.
purge [pə:dʒ] *n* (*MED*) purga; (*POL*) epurazione *f* ♦ *vt* purgare; (*fig*) epurare.
purification [pjuərɪfɪ'keɪʃən] *n* purificazione *f*.
purify ['pjuərɪfaɪ] *vt* purificare.
purist ['pjuərɪst] *n* purista *m/f*.
puritan ['pjuərɪtən] *a*, *n* puritano(a).
puritanical [pjuərɪ'tænɪkl] *a* puritano(a).
purity ['pjuərɪtɪ] *n* purità.
purl [pə:l] *n* punto rovescio ♦ *vt* lavorare a rovescio.
purloin [pə:'lɔɪn] *vt* rubare.
purple ['pə:pl] *a* di porpora; viola *inv*.
purport [pə:'pɔ:t] *vi*: **to ~ to be/do** pretendere di essere/fare.
purpose ['pə:pəs] *n* intenzione *f*, scopo; **on ~** apposta, di proposito; **for illustrative ~s** a titolo illustrativo; **for teaching ~s** per l'insegnamento; **for the ~s of this meeting** agli effetti di questa riunione; **to no ~** senza nessun risultato, inutilmente.
purpose-built ['pə:pəs'bɪlt] *a* (*Brit*) costruito(a) allo scopo.
purposeful ['pə:pəsful] *a* deciso(a), risoluto(a).
purposely ['pə:pəslɪ] *ad* apposta.
purr [pə:*] *n* fusa *fpl* ♦ *vi* fare le fusa.
purse [pə:s] *n* borsellino; (*US: handbag*) borsetta, borsa ♦ *vt* contrarre.
purser ['pə:sə*] *n* (*NAUT*) commissario di bordo.
purse snatcher [-'snætʃə*] *n* (*US*) scippatore *m*.
pursue [pə'sju:] *vt* inseguire; essere alla ricerca di; (*inquiry, matter*) approfondire.
pursuer [pə'sju:ə*] *n* inseguitore/trice.
pursuit [pə'sju:t] *n* inseguimento; (*occupation*) occupazione *f*, attività *f inv*; **in (the) ~ of sth** alla ricerca di qc; **scientific ~s** ricerche *fpl* scientifiche.
purveyor [pə'veɪə*] *n* fornitore/trice.
pus [pʌs] *n* pus *m*.
push [puʃ] *n* spinta; (*effort*) grande sforzo; (*drive*) energia ♦ *vt* spingere; (*button*) premere; (*thrust*): **to ~ sth (into)** ficcare qc (in); (*fig*) fare pubblicità a ♦ *vi* spingere; premere; **to ~ a door open/shut** aprire/chiudere una porta con una spinta *or* spingendola; **to be ~ed for time/money** essere a corto di tempo/soldi; **she is ~ing 50** (*col*) va per i 50; **to ~ for** (*better pay, conditions etc*) fare pressione per ottenere; **"~"** (*on door*) "spingere"; (*on bell*) "suonare"; **at a ~** (*Brit col*) in caso di necessità.
push aside *vt* scostare.
push in *vi* introdursi a forza.
push off *vi* (*col*) filare.
push on *vi* (*continue*) continuare.
push over *vt* far cadere.
push through ♦ *vt* (*measure*) far approvare.
push up *vt* (*total, prices*) far salire.

push-bike ['puʃbaɪk] *n* (*Brit*) bicicletta.
push-button ['puʃbʌtn] *a* a pulsante.
pushchair ['puʃtʃɛə*] *n* passeggino.
pusher ['puʃə*] *n* (*also*: **drug ~**) spacciatore/trice (di droga).
pushing ['puʃɪŋ] *a* (*pej*) troppo intraprendente.
pushover ['puʃəuvə*] *n* (*col*): **it's a ~** è un lavoro da bambini.
push-up ['puʃʌp] *n* (*US*) flessione *f* sulle braccia.
pushy ['puʃɪ] *a* (*pej*) troppo intraprendente.
puss, pussy(-cat) [pus, 'pusɪ(kæt)] *n* micio.
put, *pt*, *pp* **put** [put] *vt* mettere, porre; (*say*) dire, esprimere; (*a question*) fare; (*estimate*) stimare ♦ *ad*: **to stay ~** non muoversi; **to ~ sb to bed** mettere qn a letto; **to ~ sb in a good/bad mood** mettere qn di buon/cattivo umore; **to ~ sb to a lot of trouble** scomodare qn; **to ~ a lot of time into sth** dedicare molto tempo a qc; **to ~ money on a horse** scommettere su un cavallo; **how shall I ~ it?** come dire?; **I ~ it to you that ...** (*Brit*) io sostengo che ....
put about *vi* (*NAUT*) virare di bordo ♦ *vt* (*rumour*) diffondere.
put across *vt* (*ideas etc*) comunicare, far capire.
put aside *vt* (*lay down: book etc*) mettere da una parte, posare; (*save*) mettere da parte; (*in shop*) tenere da parte.
put away *vt* (*clothes, toys etc*) mettere via.
put back *vt* (*replace*) rimettere (a posto); (*postpone*) rinviare; (*delay*) ritardare; (*set back: watch, clock*) mettere indietro; **this will ~ us back 10 years** questo ci farà tornare indietro di 10 anni.
put by *vt* (*money*) mettere da parte.
put down *vt* (*parcel etc*) posare, mettere giù; (*pay*) versare; (*in writing*) mettere per iscritto; (*suppress: revolt etc*) reprimere, sopprimere; (*attribute*) attribuire.
put forward *vt* (*ideas*) avanzare, proporre; (*date*) anticipare.
put in *vt* (*application, complaint*) presentare.
put in for *vt fus* (*job*) far domanda per; (*promotion*) far domanda di.
put off *vt* (*postpone*) rimandare, rinviare; (*discourage*) dissuadere.
put on *vt* (*clothes, lipstick etc*) mettere; (*light etc*) accendere; (*play etc*) mettere in scena; (*concert, exhibition etc*) allestire, organizzare; (*extra bus, train etc*) mettere in servizio; (*food, meal*) servire; (*brake*) mettere; (*assume: accent, manner*) affettare; (*col: tease*) prendere in giro; (*inform, indicate*): **to ~ sb on to sb/sth** indicare qn/qc a qn; **to ~ on weight** ingrassare; **to ~ on airs** darsi delle arie.
put out *vt* mettere fuori; (*one's hand*) porgere; (*light etc*) spegnere; (*person: inconvenience*) scomodare; (*dislocate: shoulder, knee*) lussarsi; (*: back*) farsi uno

strappo a ♦ *vi* (*NAUT*): **to** ~ **out to sea** prendere il largo; **to** ~ **out from Plymouth** partire da Plymouth.

put through *vt* (*caller*) mettere in comunicazione; (*call*) passare; ~ **me through to Miss Blair** mi passi la signorina Blair.

put together *vt* mettere insieme, riunire; (*assemble: furniture*) montare; (*: meal*) improvvisare.

put up *vt* (*raise*) sollevare, alzare; (*pin up*) affiggere; (*hang*) appendere; (*build*) costruire, erigere; (*increase*) aumentare; (*accommodate*) alloggiare; (*incite*): **to** ~ **sb up to doing sth** istigare qn a fare qc; **to** ~ **sth up for sale** mettere in vendita qc.

put upon *vt fus*: **to be** ~ **upon** (*imposed on*) farsi mettere sotto i piedi.

put up with *vt fus* sopportare.

putrid ['pju:trɪd] *a* putrido(a).

putt [pʌt] *vt* (*ball*) colpire leggermente ♦ *n* colpo leggero.

putter ['pʌtə*] *n* (*GOLF*) putter *m inv* ♦ *vi* (*US*) = **potter**.

putting green ['pʌtɪŋ-] *n* green *m inv*; campo da putting.

putty ['pʌtɪ] *n* stucco.

put-up ['putʌp] *a*: ~ **job** montatura.

puzzle ['pʌzl] *n* enigma *m*, mistero; (*jigsaw*) puzzle *m* ♦ *vt* confondere, rendere perplesso(a) ♦ *vi* scervellarsi; **to be** ~**d about sth** domandarsi il perché di qc; **to** ~ **over** (*sb's actions*) cercare di capire; (*mystery, problem*) cercare di risolvere.

puzzling ['pʌzlɪŋ] *a* (*question*) poco chiaro(a); (*attitude, set of instructions*) incomprensibile.

PVC *n abbr* (= *polyvinyl chloride*) P.V.C. *m*.

Pvt. *abbr* (*US MIL*) = **private**.

PW *n abbr* (*US*) = **prisoner of war**.

pw *abbr* = *per week*.

PX *n abbr* (*US MIL*) *see* **post exchange**.

pygmy ['pɪgmɪ] *n* pigmeo/a.

pyjamas, (*US*) **pajamas** [pə'dʒɑːməz] *npl* pigiama *m*; **a pair of** ~ un pigiama.

pylon ['paɪlən] *n* pilone *m*.

pyramid ['pɪrəmɪd] *n* piramide *f*.

Pyrenean [pɪrə'niːən] *a* pirenaico(a).

Pyrenees [pɪrə'niːz] *npl*: **the** ~ i Pirenei.

Pyrex ® ['paɪrɛks] *n* Pirex ® *m inv* ♦ *cpd*: ~ **dish** pirofila.

python ['paɪθən] *n* pitone *m*.

QC *n abbr* (*Brit*: = *Queen's Counsel*) avvocato della Corona.

QED *abbr* (= *quod erat demonstrandum*) qed.

QM *n abbr see* **quartermaster**.

q.t. *n abbr* (*col*: = *quiet*): **on the** ~ di nascosto.

qty *abbr* = **quantity**.

quack [kwæk] *n* (*of duck*) qua qua *m inv*; (*pej: doctor*) ciarlatano/a.

quad [kwɔd] *n abbr* = **quadrangle; quadruple; quadruplet**.

quadrangle ['kwɔdræŋgl] *n* (*MATH*) quadrilatero; (*courtyard: abbr* **quad**) cortile *m*.

quadruped ['kwɔdruped] *n* quadrupede *m*.

quadruple [kwɔ'drupl] *a* quadruplo(a) ♦ *n* quadruplo ♦ *vt* quadruplicare ♦ *vi* quadruplicarsi.

quadruplet [kwɔ'druːplɪt] *n* uno/a di quattro gemelli.

quagmire ['kwægmaɪə*] *n* pantano.

quail [kweɪl] *n* (*ZOOL*) quaglia ♦ *vi*: **to** ~ **at** *or* **before** perdersi d'animo davanti a.

quaint [kweɪnt] *a* bizzarro(a); (*old-fashioned*) antiquato(a) e pittoresco(a).

quake [kweɪk] *vi* tremare ♦ *n abbr* = **earthquake**.

Quaker ['kweɪkə*] *n* quacchero/a.

qualification [kwɔlɪfɪ'keɪʃən] *n* (*degree etc*) qualifica, titolo; (*ability*) competenza, qualificazione *f*; (*limitation*) riserva, restrizione *f*; **what are your** ~**s?** quali sono le sue qualifiche?

qualified ['kwɔlɪfaɪd] *a* qualificato(a); (*able*) competente, qualificato(a); (*limited*) condizionato(a); ~ **for/to do** qualificato(a) per/per fare; **he's not** ~ **for the job** non ha i requisiti necessari per questo lavoro; **it was a** ~ **success** è stato un successo parziale.

qualify ['kwɔlɪfaɪ] *vt* abilitare; (*limit: statement*) modificare, precisare ♦ *vi*: **to** ~ (**as**) qualificarsi (come); **to** ~ (**for**) acquistare i requisiti necessari (per); (*SPORT*) qualificarsi (per *or* a); **to** ~ **as an engineer** diventare un perito tecnico.

qualifying ['kwɔlɪfaɪɪŋ] *a* (*exam*) di ammissione; (*round*) eliminatorio(a).

qualitative ['kwɔlɪtətɪv] *a* qualitativo(a).

quality ['kwɔlɪtɪ] *n* qualità *f inv* ♦ *cpd* di qualità; **of good** ~ di buona qualità; **of poor** ~ scadente.

quality control *n* controllo di qualità.

quality papers *npl* (*Brit*): **the** ~ la stampa d'informazione.

qualm [kwɑːm] *n* dubbio; scrupolo; **to have** ~**s about sth** avere degli scrupoli per qc.

quandary ['kwɔndrɪ] *n*: **in a** ~ in un dilemma.

quango ['kwæŋgəu] *n abbr* (*Brit*: = *quasi-autonomous non-governmental organization*) commissione consultiva di nomina governativa.

quantitative ['kwɔntɪtətɪv] *a* quantitativo(a).

quantity ['kwɔntɪtɪ] *n* quantità *f inv*; **in** ~ in grande quantità.

quantity surveyor *n* (*Brit*) geometra *m*

Q

Q, q [kju:] *n* (*letter*) Q, q *f or m inv*; **Q for Queen** ≈ Q come Quarto.

Qatar [kæ'tɑ:*] *n* Qatar *m*.

(*specializzato nel calcolare la quantità e il costo del materiale da costruzione*).

quarantine ['kwɔrntiːn] *n* quarantena.

quarrel ['kwɔrl] *n* lite *f*, disputa ♦ *vi* litigare; **to have a ~ with sb** litigare con qn; **I've no ~ with him** non ho niente contro di lui; **I can't ~ with that** non ho niente da ridire su questo.

quarrelsome ['kwɔrəlsəm] *a* litigioso(a).

quarry ['kwɔrɪ] *n* (*for stone*) cava; (*animal*) preda ♦ *vt* (*marble etc*) estrarre.

quart [kwɔːt] *n* ≈ litro.

quarter ['kwɔːtə*] *n* quarto; (*of year*) trimestre *m*; (*district*) quartiere *m*; (*US, Canada: 25 cents*) quarto di dollaro, 25 centesimi ♦ *vt* dividere in quattro; (*MIL*) alloggiare; **~s** *npl* alloggio; (*MIL*) alloggi *mpl*, quadrato; **to pay by the ~** pagare trimestralmente; **a ~ of an hour** un quarto d'ora; **it's a ~ to 3**, (*US*) **it's a ~ of 3** sono le 3 meno un quarto, manca un quarto alle 3; **it's a ~ past 3**, (*US*) **it's a ~ after 3** sono le 3 e un quarto; **from all ~s** da tutte le parti *or* direzioni; **at close ~s** a distanza ravvicinata.

quarter-deck ['kwɔːtədɛk] *n* (*NAUT*) cassero.

quarter final *n* quarto di finale.

quarterly ['kwɔːtəlɪ] *a* trimestrale ♦ *ad* trimestralmente ♦ *n* periodico trimestrale.

quartermaster (QM) ['kwɔːtəmɑːstə*] *n* (*MIL*) furiere *m*.

quartet(te) [kwɔːˈtɛt] *n* quartetto.

quarto ['kwɔːtəu] *a*, *n* in quarto (*m*) *inv*.

quartz [kwɔːts] *n* quarzo ♦ *cpd* di quarzo; (*watch, clock*) al quarzo.

quash [kwɔʃ] *vt* (*verdict*) annullare.

quasi- ['kweɪzaɪ] *prefix* quasi + *noun*; quasi, pressoché + *adjective*.

quaver ['kweɪvə*] *n* (*Brit MUS*) croma ♦ *vi* tremolare.

quay [kiː] *n* (*also:* **~side**) banchina.

queasy ['kwiːzɪ] *a* (*stomach*) delicato(a); **to feel ~** aver la nausea.

Quebec [kwɪˈbɛk] *n* Quebec *m*.

queen [kwiːn] *n* (*gen*) regina; (*CARDS etc*) regina, donna.

queen mother *n* regina madre.

queer [kwɪə*] *a* strano(a), curioso(a); (*suspicious*) dubbio(a), sospetto(a); (*Brit: sick*): **I feel ~** mi sento poco bene ♦ *n* (*col*) finocchio.

quell [kwɛl] *vt* domare.

quench [kwɛntʃ] *vt* (*flames*) spegnere; **to ~ one's thirst** dissetarsi.

querulous ['kwɛruləs] *a* querulo(a).

query ['kwɪərɪ] *n* domanda, questione *f*; (*doubt*) dubbio ♦ *vt* mettere in questione; (*disagree with, dispute*) contestare.

quest [kwɛst] *n* cerca, ricerca.

question ['kwɛstʃən] *n* domanda, questione *f* ♦ *vt* (*person*) interrogare; (*plan, idea*) mettere in questione *or* in dubbio; **to ask sb a ~, put a ~ to sb** fare una domanda a qn; **to bring** *or* **call sth into ~** mettere in dubbio qc; **the ~ is ...** il problema è ...; **it's a ~ of doing** si

tratta di fare; **there's some ~ of doing** c'è chi suggerisce di fare; **beyond ~** fuori di dubbio; **out of the ~** fuori discussione, impossibile.

questionable ['kwɛstʃənəbl] *a* discutibile.

questioner ['kwɛstʃənə*] *n* interrogante *m/f*.

questioning ['kwɛstʃənɪŋ] *a* interrogativo(a) ♦ *n* interrogatorio.

question mark *n* punto interrogativo.

questionnaire [kwɛstʃəˈnɛə*] *n* questionario.

queue [kjuː] *n* coda, fila ♦ *vi* fare la coda; **to jump the ~** passare davanti agli altri (in una coda).

quibble ['kwɪbl] *vi* cavillare.

quick [kwɪk] *a* rapido(a), veloce; (*reply*) pronto(a); (*mind*) pronto(a), acuto(a) ♦ *ad* rapidamente, presto ♦ *n*: **cut to the ~** (*fig*) toccato(a) sul vivo; **be ~!** fa presto!; **to be ~ to act** agire prontamente; **she was ~ to see that ...** ha visto subito che ....

quicken ['kwɪkn] *vt* accelerare, affrettare; (*rouse*) animare, stimolare ♦ *vi* accelerarsi, affrettarsi.

quicklime ['kwɪklaɪm] *n* calce *f* viva.

quickly ['kwɪklɪ] *ad* rapidamente, velocemente; **we must act ~** dobbiamo agire tempestivamente.

quickness ['kwɪknɪs] *n* rapidità; prontezza; acutezza.

quicksand ['kwɪksænd] *n* sabbie *fpl* mobili.

quickstep ['kwɪkstɛp] *n* (*dance*) fox-trot *m inv*.

quick-tempered [kwɪkˈtɛmpəd] *a* che si arrabbia facilmente.

quick-witted [kwɪkˈwɪtɪd] *a* pronto(a) d'ingegno.

quid [kwɪd] *n* (*pl inv*) (*Brit col*) sterlina.

quid pro quo ['kwɪdprəuˈkwəu] *n* contraccambio.

quiet ['kwaɪət] *a* tranquillo(a), quieto(a); (*reserved*) quieto(a), taciturno(a); (*ceremony*) semplice; (*not noisy: engine*) silenzioso(a); (*not busy: day*) calmo(a), tranquillo(a); (*colour*) discreto(a) ♦ *n* tranquillità, calma ♦ *vt*, *vi* (*US*) = **quieten**; **keep ~!** sta zitto!; **on the ~** di nascosto; **I'll have a ~ word with him** gli dirò due parole in privato; **business is ~ at this time of year** questa è la stagione morta.

quieten ['kwaɪətn] (*Brit: also*: **~ down**) *vi* calmarsi, chetarsi ♦ *vt* calmare, chetare.

quietly ['kwaɪətlɪ] *ad* tranquillamente, calmamente; silenziosamente.

quietness ['kwaɪətnɪs] *n* tranquillità, calma; silenzio.

quill [kwɪl] *n* penna d'oca.

quilt [kwɪlt] *n* trapunta; **continental ~** piumino.

quilting ['kwɪltɪŋ] *n* stoffa per trapunta; trapunto.

quin [kwɪn] *n abbr* = **quintuplet**.

quince [kwɪns] *n* (mela) cotogna; (*tree*) cotogno.

quinine [kwɪˈniːn] *n* chinino.

quintet(te) [kwɪn'tɛt] n quintetto.
quintuplet [kwɪn'tju:plɪt] n uno/a di cinque gemelli.
quip [kwɪp] n battuta di spirito.
quire ['kwaɪə*] n ventesima parte di una risma.
quirk [kwɜ:k] n ghiribizzo; **by some ~ of fate** per un capriccio della sorte.
quit, pt, pp quit or quitted [kwɪt] vt lasciare, partire da ♦ vi (give up) mollare; (resign) dimettersi; **to ~ doing** smettere di fare; **~ stalling!** (US col) non tirarla per le lunghe!; **notice to ~** (Brit) preavviso (dato all'inquilino).
quite [kwaɪt] ad (rather) assai; (entirely) completamente, del tutto; **I ~ understand** capisco perfettamente; **~ a few of them** non pochi di loro; **~ (so)!** esatto!; **~ new** proprio nuovo; **that's not ~ right** non è proprio esatto; **she's ~ pretty** è piuttosto carina.
Quito ['ki:təu] n Quito m.
quits [kwɪts] a: **~ (with)** pari (con); **let's call it ~** adesso siamo pari.
quiver ['kwɪvə*] vi tremare, fremere ♦ n (for arrows) faretra.
quiz [kwɪz] n (game) quiz m inv; indovinello ♦ vt interrogare.
quizzical ['kwɪzɪkəl] a enigmatico(a).
quoits [kwɔɪts] npl gioco degli anelli.
quorum ['kwɔ:rəm] n quorum m.
quota ['kwəutə] n quota.
quotation [kwəu'teɪʃən] n citazione f; (of shares etc) quotazione f; (estimate) preventivo.
quotation marks npl virgolette fpl.
quote [kwəut] n citazione f ♦ vt (sentence) citare; (price) dare, indicare, fissare; (shares) quotare ♦ vi: **to ~ from** citare; **to ~ for a job** dare un preventivo per un lavoro; **~s** npl (col) = **quotation marks**; **in ~s** tra virgolette; **~ ... unquote** (in dictation) aprire le virgolette ... chiudere le virgolette.
quotient ['kwəuʃənt] n quoziente m.
qv abbr (= quod vide: which see) v.
qwerty keyboard ['kwə:tɪ-] n tastiera qwerty inv.

R

R, r [ɑ:*] n (letter) R, r f or m inv; **R for Robert,** (US) **R for Roger** ≈ R come Roma.
R abbr (= Réaumur (scale)) R; (= river) F; (= right) D; (US CINEMA: = restricted) ≈ vietato; (US POL) = **republican**; (Brit) ≈ Rex, Regina.
RA n abbr (Brit) = Royal Academy, Royal

Academician ♦ abbr = **rear admiral.**
RAAF n abbr = Royal Australian Air Force.
Rabat [rə'bɑ:t] n Rabat f.
rabbi ['ræbaɪ] n rabbino.
rabbit ['ræbɪt] n coniglio ♦ vi: **to ~ (on)** (Brit) blaterare.
rabbit hole n tana di coniglio.
rabbit hutch n conigliera.
rabble ['ræbl] n (pej) canaglia, plebaglia.
rabid ['ræbɪd] a rabbioso(a); (fig) fanatico(a).
rabies ['reɪbi:z] n rabbia.
RAC n abbr (Brit: = Royal Automobile Club) ≈ A.C.I. m (= Automobile Club d'Italia).
raccoon [rə'ku:n] n procione m.
race [reɪs] n razza; (competition, rush) corsa ♦ vt (person) gareggiare (in corsa) con; (horse) far correre; (engine) imballare ♦ vi correre; **the human ~** la razza umana; **he ~d across the road** ha attraversato la strada di corsa; **to ~ in/out** etc precipitarsi dentro/ fuori etc.
race car n (US) = **racing car.**
race car driver n (US) = **racing driver.**
racecourse ['reɪskɔ:s] n campo di corse, ippodromo.
racehorse ['reɪshɔ:s] n cavallo da corsa.
race relations npl rapporti razziali.
racetrack ['reɪstræk] n pista.
racial ['reɪʃəl] a razziale.
racial discrimination n discriminazione f razziale.
racialism ['reɪʃəlɪzəm] n razzismo.
racialist ['reɪʃəlɪst] a, n razzista (m/f).
racing ['reɪsɪŋ] n corsa.
racing car n (Brit) macchina da corsa.
racing driver n (Brit) corridore m automobilista.
racism ['reɪsɪzəm] n razzismo.
racist ['reɪsɪst] a, n (pej) razzista (m/f).
rack [ræk] n rastrelliera; (also: **luggage ~**) rete f, portabagagli m inv; (also: **roof ~**) portabagagli ♦ vt torturare, tormentare; **magazine ~** portariviste m inv; **shoe ~** scarpiera; **toast ~** portatoast m inv; **to ~ one's brains** scervellarsi; **to go to ~ and ruin** (building) andare in rovina; (business) andare in malora or a catafascio.
rack up vt accumulare.
rack-and-pinion ['rækənd'pɪnjən] n (TECH) rocchetto-cremagliera m.
racket ['rækɪt] n (for tennis) racchetta; (noise) fracasso, baccano; (swindle) imbroglio, truffa; (organized crime) racket m inv.
racketeer [rækɪ'tɪə*] n (US) trafficante m/f.
racoon [rə'ku:n] n = **raccoon.**
racquet ['rækɪt] n racchetta.
racy ['reɪsɪ] a brioso(a); piccante.
RADA ['rɑ:də] n abbr (Brit) = Royal Academy of Dramatic Art.
radar ['reɪdɑ:*] n radar m ♦ cpd radar inv.
radar trap n controllo della velocità con radar.
radial ['reɪdɪəl] a (also: **~-ply**) radiale.
radiance ['reɪdɪəns] n splendore m, radiosità.

radiant ['reɪdɪənt] *a* raggiante; (*PHYSICS*) radiante.

radiate ['reɪdɪeɪt] *vt* (*heat*) irraggiare, irradiare ♦ *vi* (*lines*) irradiarsi.

radiation [reɪdɪ'eɪʃən] *n* irradiamento; (*radioactive*) radiazione *f*.

radiation sickness *n* malattia da radiazioni.

radiator ['reɪdɪeɪtə*] *n* radiatore *m*.

radiator cap *n* tappo del radiatore.

radiator grill *n* (*AUT*) mascherina, calandra.

radical ['rædɪkl] *a* radicale.

radii ['reɪdɪaɪ] *npl of* **radius**.

radio ['reɪdɪəu] *n* radio *f inv* ♦ *vt* (*information*) trasmettere per radio; (*one's position*) comunicare via radio; (*person*) chiamare via radio ♦ *vi*: **to ~ to sb** comunicare via radio con qn; **on the ~** alla radio.

radio... ['reɪdɪəu] *prefix* radio....

radioactive ['reɪdɪəu'æktɪv] *a* radioattivo(a).

radioactivity ['reɪdɪəuæk'tɪvɪtɪ] *n* radioattività.

radio announcer *n* annunciatore/trice della radio.

radio-controlled ['reɪdɪəukən'trəuld] *a* radiocomandato(a), radioguidato(a).

radiographer [reɪdɪ'ɔgrəfə*] *n* radiologo/a (*tecnico*).

radiography [reɪdɪ'ɔgrəfɪ] *n* radiografia.

radiologist [reɪdɪ'ɔlədʒɪst] *n* radiologo/a (*medico*).

radiology [reɪdɪ'ɔlədʒɪ] *n* radiologia.

radio station *n* stazione *f* radio *inv*.

radio taxi *n* radiotaxi *m inv*.

radiotelephone ['reɪdɪəu'telɪfəun] *n* radiotelefono.

radiotherapist ['reɪdɪəu'θerəpɪst] *n* radioterapista *m/f*.

radiotherapy ['reɪdɪəu'θerəpɪ] *n* radioterapia.

radish ['rædɪʃ] *n* ravanello.

radium ['reɪdɪəm] *n* radio.

radius, *pl* **radii** ['reɪdɪəs, -ɪaɪ] *n* raggio; (*ANAT*) radio; **within a ~ of 50 miles** in un raggio di 50 miglia.

RAF *n abbr* (*Brit*) *see* **Royal Air Force**.

raffia ['ræfɪə] *n* rafia.

raffish ['ræfɪʃ] *a* dal look trasandato.

raffle ['ræfl] *n* lotteria ♦ *vt* (*object*) mettere in palio.

raft [rɑːft] *n* zattera.

rafter ['rɑːftə*] *n* trave *f*.

rag [ræg] *n* straccio, cencio; (*pej: newspaper*) giornalaccio; (*for charity*) iniziativa studentesca a scopo benefico ♦ *vt* (*Brit*) prendere in giro; **~s** *npl* stracci *mpl*, brandelli *mpl*; **in ~s** stracciato.

rag-and-bone man ['rægən'bəun-] *n* straccivendolo.

ragbag ['rægbæg] *n* (*fig*) guazzabuglio.

rag doll *n* bambola di pezza.

rage [reɪdʒ] *n* (*fury*) collera, furia ♦ *vi* (*person*) andare su tutte le furie; (*storm*) infuriare; **it's all the ~** fa furore; **to fly into a ~** andare *or* montare su tutte le furie.

ragged ['rægɪd] *a* (*edge*) irregolare; (*cuff*) logoro(a); (*appearance*) pezzente.

raging ['reɪdʒɪŋ] *a* (*all senses*) furioso(a); **in a ~ temper** su tutte le furie.

ragman ['rægmæn] *n* straccivendolo.

rag trade *n* (*col*): **the ~** l'abbigliamento.

raid [reɪd] *n* (*MIL*) incursione *f*; (*criminal*) rapina; (*by police*) irruzione *f* ♦ *vt* fare un'incursione in; rapinare; fare irruzione in.

raider ['reɪdə*] *n* rapinatore/trice; (*plane*) aeroplano da incursione.

rail [reɪl] *n* (*on stair*) ringhiera; (*on bridge, balcony*) parapetto; (*of ship*) battagliola; (*for train*) rotaia; **~s** *npl* binario, rotaie *fpl*; **by ~** per ferrovia, in treno.

railing(s) ['reɪlɪŋ(z)] *n(pl)* ringhiere *fpl*.

railway ['reɪlweɪ], (*US*) **railroad** ['reɪlrəud] *n* ferrovia.

railway engine *n* (*Brit*) locomotiva.

railway line *n* (*Brit*) linea ferroviaria.

railwayman ['reɪlweɪmən] *n* (*Brit*) ferroviere *m*.

railway station *n* (*Brit*) stazione *f* ferroviaria.

rain [reɪn] *n* pioggia ♦ *vi* piovere; **in the ~** sotto la pioggia; **it's ~ing** piove; **it's ~ing cats and dogs** piove a catinelle.

rainbow ['reɪnbəu] *n* arcobaleno.

raincoat ['reɪnkəut] *n* impermeabile *m*.

raindrop ['reɪndrɔp] *n* goccia di pioggia.

rainfall ['reɪnfɔːl] *n* pioggia; (*measurement*) piovosità.

rainproof ['reɪnpruːf] *a* impermeabile.

rainstorm ['reɪnstɔːm] *n* pioggia torrenziale.

rainwater ['reɪnwɔːtə*] *n* acqua piovana.

rainy ['reɪnɪ] *a* piovoso(a).

raise [reɪz] *n* aumento ♦ *vt* (*lift*) alzare, sollevare; (*build*) erigere; (*increase*) aumentare; (*a protest, doubt, question*) sollevare; (*cattle, family*) allevare; (*crop*) coltivare; (*army, funds*) raccogliere; (*loan*) ottenere; (*end: siege, embargo*) togliere; **to ~ one's voice** alzare la voce; **to ~ sb's hopes** accendere le speranze di qn; **to ~ one's glass to sb/sth** brindare a qn/qc; **to ~ a laugh/a smile** far ridere/sorridere.

raisin ['reɪzn] *n* uva secca.

Raj [rɑːdʒ] *n*: **the ~** l'impero britannico (*in India*).

rajah ['rɑːdʒə] *n* ragià *m inv*.

rake [reɪk] *n* (*tool*) rastrello; (*person*) libertino ♦ *vt* (*garden*) rastrellare; (*with machine gun*) spazzare ♦ *vi*: **to ~ through** (*fig: search*) frugare tra.

rake-off ['reɪkɔf] *n* (*col*) parte *f* percentuale, fetta.

rakish ['reɪkɪʃ] *a* dissoluto(a); disinvolto(a).

rally ['rælɪ] *n* (*POL etc*) riunione *f*; (*AUT*) rally *m inv*; (*TENNIS*) scambio ♦ *vt* riunire, radunare ♦ *vi* raccogliersi, radunarsi; (*sick person, STOCK EXCHANGE*) riprendersi.

rally round *vt fus* raggrupparsi intorno a; venire in aiuto di.

rallying point ['rælɪŋ-] *n* (*POL, MIL*) punto di riunione, punto di raduno.

RAM [ræm] *n abbr* (*COMPUT: = random access*

memory) RAM *f*.

ram [ræm] *n* montone *m*, ariete *m*; *(device)* ariete ♦ *vt* conficcare; *(crash into)* cozzare, sbattere contro; percuotere; speronare.

ramble ['ræmbl] *n* escursione *f* ♦ *vi* (*pej: also:* ~ **on**) divagare.

rambler ['ræmblə*] *n* escursionista *m/f*; *(BOT)* rosa rampicante.

rambling ['ræmblɪŋ] *a* *(speech)* sconnesso(a); *(BOT)* rampicante; *(house)* tutto(a) nicchie e corridoi.

rambunctious [ræm'bʌŋkʃəs] *a* *(US)* = **rumbustious**.

RAMC *n abbr (Brit)* = *Royal Army Medical Corps*.

ramification [ræmɪfɪ'keɪʃən] *n* ramificazione *f*.

ramp [ræmp] *n* rampa; "~" *(AUT)* "fondo stradale in rifacimento".

rampage [ræm'peɪdʒ] *n*: **to go on the** ~ scatenarsi in modo violento ♦ *vi*: **they went rampaging through the town** si sono scatenati in modo violento per la città.

rampant ['ræmpənt] *a (disease etc)* che infierisce.

rampart ['ræmpɑ:t] *n* bastione *m*.

ramshackle ['ræmʃækl] *a (house)* cadente; *(car etc)* sgangherato(a).

RAN *n abbr* = *Royal Australian Navy*.

ran [ræn] *pt of* **run**.

ranch [rɑ:ntʃ] *n* ranch *m inv*.

rancher ['rɑ:ntʃə*] *n (owner)* proprietario di un ranch; *(ranch hand)* cowboy *m inv*.

rancid ['rænsɪd] *a* rancido(a).

rancour, (US) rancor ['ræŋkə*] *n* rancore *m*.

random ['rændəm] *a* fatto(a) *or* detto(a) per caso; *(COMPUT, MATH)* casuale ♦ *n*: **at** ~ a casaccio.

random access *n (COMPUT)* accesso casuale.

randy ['rændɪ] *a (col)* arrapato(a); lascivo(a).

rang [ræŋ] *pt of* **ring**.

range [reɪndʒ] *n (of mountains)* catena; *(of missile, voice)* portata; *(of products)* gamma; *(MIL: also:* **shooting** ~) campo di tiro; *(also:* **kitchen** ~) fornello, cucina economica ♦ *vt (place)* disporre, allineare; *(roam)* vagare per ♦ *vi*: **to** ~ **over** coprire; **to** ~ **from** ... **to** andare da ... a; **price** ~ gamma di prezzi; **do you have anything else in this price** ~**?** ha nient'altro su *or* di questo prezzo?; **within** *(firing)* ~ a portata di tiro; ~**d left/right** *(text)* allineato(a) a destra/sinistra.

ranger ['reɪndʒə*] *n* guardia forestale.

Rangoon [ræŋ'gu:n] *n* Rangun *f*.

rank [ræŋk] *n* fila; *(MIL)* grado; *(Brit: also:* **taxi** ~) posteggio di taxi ♦ *vi*: **to** ~ **among** essere nel numero di ♦ *a (smell)* puzzolente; *(hypocrisy, injustice)* vero(a) e proprio(a); **the** ~**s** *(MIL)* la truppa; **the** ~ **and file** *(fig)* la gran massa; **to close** ~**s** *(MIL, fig)* serrare i ranghi; **I** ~ **him 6th** gli do il sesto posto, lo metto al sesto posto.

rankle ['ræŋkl] *vi*: **to** ~ **(with sb)** bruciare (a qn).

ransack ['rænsæk] *vt* rovistare; *(plunder)* saccheggiare.

ransom ['rænsəm] *n* riscatto; **to hold sb to** ~ *(fig)* esercitare pressione su qn.

rant [rænt] *vi* vociare.

ranting ['ræntɪŋ] *n* vociare *m*.

rap [ræp] *n (noise)* colpetti *mpl*; *(at a door)* bussata ♦ *vt* dare dei colpetti a; bussare a.

rape [reɪp] *n* violenza carnale, stupro ♦ *vt* violentare.

rape(seed) oil ['reɪp(si:d)-] *n* olio di ravizzone.

rapid ['ræpɪd] *a* rapido(a).

rapidity [rə'pɪdɪtɪ] *n* rapidità.

rapidly ['ræpɪdlɪ] *ad* rapidamente.

rapids ['ræpɪdz] *npl (GEO)* rapida.

rapist ['reɪpɪst] *n* violentatore *m*.

rapport [ræ'pɔ:*] *n* rapporto.

rapt [ræpt] *a (attention)* rapito(a), profondo(a); **to be** ~ **in contemplation** essere in estatica contemplazione.

rapture ['ræptʃə*] *n* estasi *f inv*; **to go into** ~**s over** andare in sollucchero per.

rapturous ['ræptʃərəs] *a* estatico(a).

rare [rɛə*] *a* raro(a); *(CULIN: steak)* al sangue; **it is** ~ **to find that ...** capita di rado *or* raramente che ... + *sub*.

rarebit ['rɛəbɪt] *n see* **Welsh rarebit**.

rarefied ['rɛərɪfaɪd] *a (air, atmosphere)* rarefatto(a).

rarely ['rɛəlɪ] *ad* raramente.

raring ['rɛərɪŋ] *a*: **to be** ~ **to go** *(col)* non veder l'ora di cominciare.

rarity ['rɛərɪtɪ] *n* rarità *f inv*.

rascal ['rɑ:skl] *n* mascalzone *m*.

rash [ræʃ] *a* imprudente, sconsiderato(a) ♦ *n (MED)* eruzione *f*; **to come out in a** ~ avere uno sfogo.

rasher ['ræʃə*] *n* fetta sottile (di lardo *or* prosciutto).

rasp [rɑ:sp] *n (tool)* lima ♦ *vt (speak: also:* ~ **out)** gracchiare.

raspberry ['rɑ:zbərɪ] *n* lampone *m*.

raspberry bush *n* lampone *m (pianta)*.

rasping ['rɑ:spɪŋ] *a* stridulo(a).

rat [ræt] *n* ratto.

ratable ['reɪtəbl] *a* = **rateable**.

ratchet ['rætʃɪt] *n*: ~ **wheel** ruota dentata.

rate [reɪt] *n (proportion)* tasso, percentuale *f*; *(speed)* velocità *f inv*; *(price)* tariffa ♦ *vt* valutare; stimare; **to** ~ **sb/sth as** valutare qn/qc come; **to** ~ **sb/sth among** annoverare qn/qc tra; **to** ~ **sb/sth highly** stimare molto qn/qc; **at a** ~ **of 60 kph** alla velocità di 60 km all'ora; ~ **of exchange** tasso di cambio; ~ **of flow** flusso medio; ~ **of growth** tasso di crescita; ~ **of return** tasso di rendimento; **pulse** ~ frequenza delle pulsazioni; *see also* **rates**.

rateable value ['reɪtəbl-] *n (Brit)* valore *m* imponibile (agli effetti delle imposte comunali).

ratepayer ['reɪtpeɪə*] *n (Brit)* contribuente *m/f* (che paga le imposte comunali).

rates [reɪts] *npl* (*Brit*) imposte *fpl* comunali.

rather ['rɑ:ðə*] *ad* piuttosto; (*somewhat*) abbastanza; (*to some extent*) un po'; **it's ~ expensive** è piuttosto caro; (*too much*) è un po' caro; **there's ~ a lot** ce n'è parecchio; **I would** *or* **I'd ~ go** preferirei andare; **I had ~ go** farei meglio ad andare; **I'd ~ not leave** preferirei non partire; **or ~** (*more accurately*) anzi, per essere (più) precisi; **I ~ think he won't come** credo proprio che non verrà.

ratification [rætɪfɪ'keɪʃən] *n* ratificazione *f*.

ratify ['rætɪfaɪ] *vt* ratificare.

rating ['reɪtɪŋ] *n* classificazione *f*; punteggio di merito; (*NAUT: category*) classe *f*; (*: sailor: Brit*) marinaio semplice.

ratings ['reɪtɪŋz] *npl* (*RADIO, TV*) indice *m* di ascolto.

ratio ['reɪʃɪəu] *n* proporzione *f*; **in the ~ of 2 to 1** in rapporto di 2 a 1.

ration ['ræʃən] *n* razione *f* ♦ *vt* razionare.

rational ['ræʃənl] *a* razionale, ragionevole; (*solution, reasoning*) logico(a).

rationale [ræʃə'nɑ:l] *n* fondamento logico; giustificazione *f*.

rationalization [ræʃnəlaɪ'zeɪʃən] *n* razionalizzazione *f*.

rationalize ['ræʃnəlaɪz] *vt* razionalizzare.

rationally ['ræʃnəlɪ] *ad* razionalmente; logicamente.

rationing ['ræʃnɪŋ] *n* razionamento *m*.

rat poison *n* veleno per topi.

rat race *n* carrierismo, corsa al successo.

rattan [ræ'tæn] *n* malacca.

rattle ['rætl] *n* tintinnio; (*louder*) rumore *m* di ferraglia; (*object: of baby*) sonaglio; (*: of sports fan*) raganella ♦ *vi* risuonare, tintinnare; fare un rumore di ferraglia ♦ *vt* agitare; far tintinnare; (*col: disconcert*) sconcertare.

rattlesnake ['rætlsneɪk] *n* serpente *m* a sonagli.

ratty ['rætɪ] *a* (*col*) incavolato(a).

raucous ['rɔːkəs] *a* sguaiato(a).

raucously ['rɔːkəslɪ] *ad* sguaiatamente.

ravage ['rævɪdʒ] *vt* devastare.

ravages ['rævɪdʒɪz] *npl* danni *mpl*.

rave [reɪv] *vi* (*in anger*) infuriarsi; (*with enthusiasm*) andare in estasi; (*MED*) delirare ♦ *cpd*: **~ review** (*col*) critica entusiastica.

raven ['reɪvən] *n* corvo.

ravenous ['rævənəs] *a* affamato(a).

ravine [rə'viːn] *n* burrone *m*.

raving ['reɪvɪŋ] *a*: **~ lunatic** pazzo(a) furioso(a).

ravings ['reɪvɪŋz] *npl* vaneggiamenti *mpl*.

ravioli [rævɪ'əulɪ] *n* ravioli *mpl*.

ravish ['rævɪʃ] *vt* (*delight*) estasiare.

ravishing ['rævɪʃɪŋ] *a* incantevole.

raw [rɔː] *a* (*uncooked*) crudo(a); (*not processed*) greggio(a); (*sore*) vivo(a); (*inexperienced*) inesperto(a); **to get a ~ deal** (*col: bad bargain*) prendere un bidone; (*: harsh treatment*) venire trattato ingiu-

stamente.

Rawalpindi [rɔːl'pɪndɪ] *n* Rawalpindi *f*.

raw material *n* materia prima.

ray [reɪ] *n* raggio.

rayon ['reɪɔn] *n* raion *m*.

raze [reɪz] *vt* radere, distruggere; (*also*: **~ to the ground**) radere al suolo.

razor ['reɪzə*] *n* rasoio.

razor blade *n* lama di rasoio.

razzle(-dazzle) ['ræzl('dæzl)] *n* (*Brit col*): **to be/go on the ~** darsi alla pazza gioia.

razzmatazz ['ræzmə'tæz] *n* (*col*) clamore *m*.

R&B *n abbr* = *rhythm and blues*.

RC *abbr* = **Roman Catholic**.

RCAF *n abbr* = *Royal Canadian Air Force*.

RCMP *n abbr* = *Royal Canadian Mounted Police*.

RCN *n abbr* = *Royal Canadian Navy*.

RD *abbr* (*US POST*) = *rural delivery*.

Rd *abbr* = **road**.

R&D *n abbr see* **research and development**.

RDC *n abbr* (*Brit*) *see* **rural district council**.

RE *n abbr* (*Brit MIL*: = *Royal Engineers*) ≈ G.M. (= *Genio Militare*); (*Brit*) = *religious education*.

re [riː] *prep* con riferimento a.

reach [riːtʃ] *n* portata; (*of river etc*) tratto ♦ *vt* raggiungere; arrivare a ♦ *vi* stendersi; (*stretch out hand: also*: **~ down**, **~ over**, **~ across** *etc*) allungare una mano; **out of/ within ~** (*object*) fuori/a portata di mano; **within easy ~ (of)** (*place*) a breve distanza (di), vicino (a); **to ~ sb by phone** contattare qn per telefono; **can I ~ you at your hotel?** posso trovarla al suo albergo?

reach out *vi*: **to ~ out for** stendere la mano per prendere.

react [riː'ækt] *vi* reagire.

reaction [riː'ækʃən] *n* reazione *f*.

reactionary [riː'ækʃənrɪ] *a, n* reazionario(a).

reactor [riː'æktə*] *n* reattore *m*.

read, *pt, pp* **read** [riːd, rɛd] *vi* leggere ♦ *vt* leggere; (*understand*) intendere, interpretare; (*study*) studiare; **do you ~ me?** (*TEL*) mi ricevete?; **to take sth as read** (*fig*) dare qc per scontato.

read out *vt* leggere ad alta voce.

read over *vt* rileggere attentamente.

read through *vt* (*quickly*) dare una scorsa a; (*thoroughly*) leggere da cima a fondo.

read up *vt*, **read up on** *vt fus* studiare bene.

readable ['riːdəbl] *a* leggibile; che si legge volentieri.

reader ['riːdə*] *n* lettore/trice; (*book*) libro di lettura; (*Brit: at university*) professore con funzioni preminenti di ricerca.

readership ['riːdəʃɪp] *n* (*of paper etc*) numero di lettori.

readily ['rɛdɪlɪ] *ad* volentieri; (*easily*) facilmente.

readiness ['rɛdɪnɪs] *n* prontezza; **in ~** (*prepared*) pronto(a).

reading ['riːdɪŋ] *n* lettura; (*understanding*)

interpretazione *f*; (*on instrument*) indicazione *f*.

reading lamp *n* lampada da studio.

reading room *n* sala di lettura.

readjust [ri:ə'dʒʌst] *vt* raggiustare ♦ *vi* (*person*): **to ~ (to)** riadattarsi (a).

ready ['rɛdɪ] *a* pronto(a); (*willing*) pronto(a), disposto(a); (*quick*) rapido(a); (*available*) disponibile ♦ *n*: **at the ~** (*MIL*) pronto a sparare; (*fig*) tutto(a) pronto(a); **~ for use** pronto per l'uso; **to be ~ to do sth** essere pronto a fare qc; **to get ~** *vi* prepararsi ♦ *vt* preparare.

ready cash *n* denaro in contanti.

ready-cooked [rɛdɪ'kukt] *a* già cotto(a).

ready-made [rɛdɪ'meɪd] *a* prefabbricato(a); (*clothes*) confezionato(a).

ready reckoner [-'rɛkənə*] *n* (*Brit*) prontuario di calcolo.

ready-to-wear [rɛdɪtə'wɛə*] *a* prêt-à-porter *inv*.

reagent [ri:'eɪdʒənt] *n*: **chemical ~** reagente *m* chimico.

real [rɪəl] *a* reale; vero(a) ♦ *ad* (*US col*: *very*) veramente, proprio; **in ~ terms** in realtà; **in ~ life** nella realtà.

real estate *n* beni *mpl* immobili.

realism ['rɪəlɪzəm] *n* (*also ART*) realismo.

realist ['rɪəlɪst] *n* realista *m/f*.

realistic [rɪə'lɪstɪk] *a* realistico(a).

reality [ri:'ælɪtɪ] *n* realtà *f inv*; **in ~** in realtà, in effetti.

realization [rɪəlaɪ'zeɪʃən] *n* (*awareness*) presa di coscienza; (*of hopes, project etc*) realizzazione *f*.

realize ['rɪəlaɪz] *vt* (*understand*) rendersi conto di; (*a project, COMM: asset*) realizzare; **I ~ that ...** mi rendo conto *or* capisco che ....

really ['rɪəlɪ] *ad* veramente, davvero.

realm [rɛlm] *n* reame *m*, regno.

real time *n* (*COMPUT*) tempo reale.

realtor ['rɪəltɔ:*] *n* (*US*) agente *m* immobiliare.

ream [ri:m] *n* risma; **~s** (*fig col*) pagine e pagine *fpl*.

reap [ri:p] *vt* mietere; (*fig*) raccogliere.

reaper ['ri:pə*] *n* (*machine*) mietitrice *f*.

reappear [ri:ə'pɪə*] *vi* ricomparire, riapparire.

reappearance [ri:ə'pɪərəns] *n* riapparizione *f*.

reapply [ri:ə'plaɪ] *vi*: **to ~ for** fare un'altra domanda per.

reappraisal [ri:ə'preɪzl] *n* riesame *m*.

rear [rɪə*] *a* di dietro; (*AUT*: *wheel etc*) posteriore ♦ *n* didietro, parte *f* posteriore ♦ *vt* (*cattle, family*) allevare ♦ *vi* (*also: ~ up*: *animal*) impennarsi.

rear admiral *n* contrammiraglio.

rear-engined ['rɪər'ɛndʒɪnd] *a* (*AUT*) con motore posteriore.

rearguard ['rɪəgɑ:d] *n* retroguardia.

rearm [ri:'ɑ:m] *vt*, *vi* riarmare.

rearmament [ri:'ɑ:məmənt] *n* riarmo.

rearrange [ri:ə'reɪndʒ] *vt* riordinare.

rear-view mirror ['rɪəvju:-] *n* (*AUT*) specchio

retrovisivo.

reason ['ri:zn] *n* ragione *f*; (*cause, motive*) ragione, motivo ♦ *vi*: **to ~ with sb** far ragionare qn; **to have ~ to think** avere motivi per pensare; **it stands to ~ that** è ovvio che; **the ~ for/why** la ragione *or* il motivo di/per cui; **with good ~** a ragione; **all the more ~ why you should not sell it** ragione di più per non venderlo.

reasonable ['ri:znəbl] *a* ragionevole; (*not bad*) accettabile.

reasonably ['ri:znəblɪ] *ad* ragionevolmente; **one can ~ assume that ...** uno può facilmente supporre che ....

reasoned ['ri:znd] *a* (*argument*) ponderato(a).

reasoning ['ri:znɪŋ] *n* ragionamento.

reassemble [ri:ə'sɛmbl] *vt* riunire; (*machine*) rimontare.

reassert [ri:ə'sə:t] *vt* riaffermare.

reassurance [ri:ə'ʃuərəns] *n* rassicurazione *f*.

reassure [ri:ə'ʃuə*] *vt* rassicurare; **to ~ sb of** rassicurare qn di *or* su.

reassuring [ri:ə'ʃuərɪŋ] *a* rassicurante.

reawakening [ri:ə'weɪknɪŋ] *n* risveglio.

rebate ['ri:beɪt] *n* rimborso.

rebel *n* ['rɛbl] ribelle *m/f* ♦ *vi* [rɪ'bɛl] ribellarsi.

rebellion [rɪ'bɛljən] *n* ribellione *f*.

rebellious [rɪ'bɛljəs] *a* ribelle.

rebirth [ri:'bə:θ] *n* rinascita.

rebound *vi* [rɪ'baund] (*ball*) rimbalzare ♦ *n* ['ri:baund] rimbalzo.

rebuff [rɪ'bʌf] *n* secco rifiuto ♦ *vt* respingere.

rebuild [ri:'bɪld] *vt irg* ricostruire.

rebuke [rɪ'bju:k] *n* rimprovero ♦ *vt* rimproverare.

rebut [rɪ'bʌt] *vt* rifiutare.

rebuttal [rɪ'bʌtl] *n* rifiuto.

recalcitrant [rɪ'kælsɪtrənt] *a* recalcitrante.

recall [rɪ'kɔ:l] *vt* (*gen, COMPUT*) richiamare; (*remember*) ricordare, richiamare alla mente ♦ *n* richiamo; **beyond ~** irrevocabile.

recant [rɪ'kænt] *vi* ritrattarsi; (*REL*) fare abiura.

recap ['ri:kæp] *n* ricapitolazione *f* ♦ *vt* ricapitolare ♦ *vi* riassumere.

recapture [ri:'kæptʃə*] *vt* riprendere; (*atmosphere*) ricreare.

recd. *abbr* = **received**.

recede [rɪ'si:d] *vi* allontanarsi; ritirarsi; calare.

receding [rɪ'si:dɪŋ] *a* (*forehead, chin*) sfuggente; **he's got a ~ hairline** è stempiato.

receipt [rɪ'si:t] *n* (*document*) ricevuta; (*act of receiving*) ricevimento; **to acknowledge ~ of** accusare ricevuta di; **we are in ~ of ...** abbiamo ricevuto ....

receipts *npl* (*COMM*) introiti *mpl*.

receivable [rɪ'si:vəbl] *a* (*COMM*) esigibile; (: *owed*) dovuto(a).

receive [rɪ'si:v] *vt* ricevere; (*guest*) ricevere, accogliere; **"~d with thanks"** (*COMM*) "per quietanza".

receiver [rɪ'si:və*] *n* (*TEL*) ricevitore *m*; (*RADIO*) apparecchio ricevente; (*of stolen* *goods*) ricettatore/trice; (*LAW*) curatore *m* fallimentare.

recent ['ri:snt] *a* recente; **in ~ years** negli ultimi anni.

recently ['ri:sntlɪ] *ad* recentemente; **as ~ as** ... soltanto ...; **until ~** fino a poco tempo fa.

receptacle [rɪ'sɛptɪkl] *n* recipiente *m*.

reception [rɪ'sɛpʃən] *n* (*gen*) ricevimento; (*welcome*) accoglienza; (*TV etc*) ricezione *f*.

reception centre *n* (*Brit*) centro di raccolta.

reception desk *n* (*in hotel*) reception *f inv*; (*in hospital, at doctor's*) accettazione *f*; (*in large building, offices*) portineria.

receptionist [rɪ'sɛpʃənɪst] *n* receptionist *m/f inv*.

receptive [rɪ'sɛptɪv] *a* ricettivo(a).

recess [rɪ'sɛs] *n* (*in room*) alcova; (*POL etc: holiday*) vacanze *fpl*; (*US LAW: short break*) sospensione *f*; (*US SCOL*) intervallo.

recession [rɪ'sɛʃən] *n* (*ECON*) recessione *f*.

recharge [ri:'tʃɑ:dʒ] *vt* (*battery*) ricaricare.

rechargeable ['ri:'tʃɑ:dʒəbl] *a* ricaricabile.

recipe ['rɛsɪpɪ] *n* ricetta.

recipient [rɪ'sɪpɪənt] *n* beneficiario/a; (*of letter*) destinatario/a.

reciprocal [rɪ'sɪprəkl] *a* reciproco(a).

reciprocate [rɪ'sɪprəkeɪt] *vt* ricambiare, contraccambiare.

recital [rɪ'saɪtl] *n* recital *m inv*; concerto (di solista).

recite [rɪ'saɪt] *vt* (*poem*) recitare.

reckless ['rɛkləs] *a* (*driver etc*) spericolato(a); (*spender*) incosciente.

recklessly ['rɛkləslɪ] *ad* in modo spericolato; da incosciente.

reckon ['rɛkən] *vt* (*count*) calcolare; (*consider*) considerare, stimare; (*think*): **I ~ that** ... penso che ... ♦ *vi* contare, calcolare; **to ~ without sb/sth** non tener conto di qn/qc; **he is somebody to be ~ed with** è uno da non sottovalutare.

reckon on *vt fus* contare su.

reckoning ['rɛknɪŋ] *n* conto; stima; **the day of ~** il giorno del giudizio.

reclaim [rɪ'kleɪm] *vt* (*land*) bonificare; (*demand back*) richiedere, reclamare.

reclamation [rɛklə'meɪʃən] *n* bonifica.

recline [rɪ'klaɪn] *vi* stare sdraiato(a).

reclining [rɪ'klaɪnɪŋ] *a* (*seat*) ribaltabile.

recluse [rɪ'klu:s] *n* eremita *m*, recluso/a.

recognition [rɛkəg'nɪʃən] *n* riconoscimento; **to gain ~** essere riconosciuto(a); **in ~ of** in *or* come segno di riconoscimento per; **transformed beyond ~** irriconoscibile.

recognizable ['rɛkəgnaɪzəbl] *a*: **~ (by)** riconoscibile (a *or* da).

recognize ['rɛkəgnaɪz] *vt*: **to ~ (by/as)** riconoscere (a *or* da/come).

recoil [rɪ'kɔɪl] *vi* (*gun*) rinculare; (*spring*) balzare indietro; (*person*): **to ~ (from)** indietreggiare (davanti a) ♦ *n* (*of gun*) rinculo.

recollect [rɛkə'lɛkt] *vt* ricordare.

recollection [rɛkə'lɛkʃən] *n* ricordo; **to the best of my ~** per quello che mi ricordo.

recommend [rɛkə'mɛnd] *vt* raccomandare; (*advise*) consigliare; **she has a lot to ~ her** ha molti elementi a suo favore.

recommendation [rɛkəmɛn'deɪʃən] *n* raccomandazione *f*; consiglio.

recommended retail price (RRP) *n* (*Brit*) prezzo raccomandato al dettaglio.

recompense ['rɛkəmpɛns] *vt* ricompensare; (*compensate*) risarcire ♦ *n* ricompensa; risarcimento.

reconcilable ['rɛkənsaɪləbl] *a* conciliabile.

reconcile ['rɛkənsaɪl] *vt* (*two people*) riconciliare; (*two facts*) conciliare, quadrare; **to ~ o.s. to** rassegnarsi a.

reconciliation [rɛkənsɪlɪ'eɪʃən] *n* riconciliazione *f*; conciliazione *f*.

recondite [rɪ'kɔndaɪt] *a* recondito(a).

recondition [ri:kən'dɪʃən] *vt* rimettere a nuovo; rifare.

reconnaissance [rɪ'kɔnɪsns] *n* (*MIL*) ricognizione *f*.

reconnoitre, (US) reconnoiter [rɛkə'nɔɪtə*] (*MIL*) *vt* fare una ricognizione di ♦ *vi* fare una ricognizione.

reconsider [ri:kən'sɪdə*] *vt* riconsiderare.

reconstitute [ri:'kɔnstɪtju:t] *vt* ricostituire.

reconstruct [ri:kən'strʌkt] *vt* ricostruire.

reconstruction [ri:kən'strʌkʃən] *n* ricostruzione *f*.

record *n* ['rɛkɔ:d] ricordo, documento; (*of meeting etc*) nota, verbale *m*; (*register*) registro; (*file*) pratica, dossier *m inv*; (*COMPUT*) record *m inv*, registrazione *f*; (*also*: **police ~**) fedina penale sporca; (*MUS: disc*) disco; (*SPORT*) record *m inv*, primato ♦ *vt* [rɪ'kɔ:d] (*set down*) prendere nota di, registrare; (*relate*) raccontare; (*COMPUT, MUS: song etc*) registrare; **public ~s** archivi *mpl*; **Italy's excellent ~** i brillanti successi italiani; **in ~ time** a tempo di record; **to keep a ~ of** tener nota di; **to set the ~ straight** mettere le cose in chiaro; **off the ~** *a* ufficioso(a) ♦ *ad* ufficiosamente; **he is on ~ as saying that** ... ha dichiarato pubblicamente che ....

record card *n* (*in file*) scheda.

recorded delivery letter *n* (*Brit POST*) lettera raccomandata.

recorder [rɪ'kɔ:də*] *n* (*LAW*) avvocato *che funge da giudice*; (*MUS*) flauto diritto.

record holder *n* (*SPORT*) primatista *m/f*.

recording [rɪ'kɔ:dɪŋ] *n* (*MUS*) registrazione *f*.

recording studio *n* studio di registrazione.

record library *n* discoteca.

record player *n* giradischi *m inv*.

recount [rɪ'kaunt] *vt* raccontare, narrare.

re-count *n* ['ri:kaunt] (*POL: of votes*) nuovo conteggio ♦ *vt* [ri:'kaunt] ricontare.

recoup [rɪ'ku:p] *vt* ricuperare; **to ~ one's losses** ricuperare le perdite, rifarsi.

recourse [rɪ'kɔ:s] *n*: **to have ~ to** ricorrere a.

recover [rɪ'kʌvə*] *vt* ricuperare ♦ *vi* (*from illness*) rimettersi (in salute), ristabilirsi; (*country, person: from shock*) riprendersi.

re-cover [riː'kʌvə*] vt (chair etc) ricoprire.

recovery [rɪ'kʌvərɪ] n ricupero; ristabilimento; ripresa.

recreate [riː'kriːeɪt] vt ricreare.

recreation [rɛkrɪ'eɪʃən] n ricreazione f; svago.

recreational [rɛkrɪ'eɪʃənəl] a ricreativo(a).

recreational vehicle (RV) n (US) camper m inv.

recrimination [rɪkrɪmɪ'neɪʃən] n recriminazione f.

recruit [rɪ'kruːt] n recluta ♦ vt reclutare.

recruiting office [rɪ'kruːtɪŋ-] n ufficio di reclutamento.

recruitment [rɪ'kruːtmənt] n reclutamento.

rectangle ['rɛktæŋgl] n rettangolo.

rectangular [rɛk'tæŋgjulə*] a rettangolare.

rectify ['rɛktɪfaɪ] vt (error) rettificare; (omission) riparare.

rector ['rɛktə*] n (REL) parroco (anglicano); (in Scottish universities) personalità eletta dagli studenti per rappresentarli.

rectory ['rɛktərɪ] n presbiterio.

rectum ['rɛktəm] n (ANAT) retto.

recuperate [rɪ'kjuːpəreɪt] vi ristabilirsi.

recur [rɪ'kə:*] vi riaccadere; (idea, opportunity) riapparire; (symptoms) ripresentarsi.

recurrence [rɪ'kʌrəns] n ripresentarsi m; riapparizione f.

recurrent [rɪ'kʌrənt] a ricorrente, periodico(a).

recurring [rɪ'kʌrɪŋ] a (MATH) periodico(a).

red [rɛd] n rosso; (POL: pej) rosso/a ♦ a rosso(a); **in the ~** (account) scoperto; (business) in deficit.

red carpet treatment n cerimonia col gran pavese.

Red Cross n Croce f Rossa.

redcurrant ['rɛdkʌrənt] n ribes m inv.

redden ['rɛdn] vt arrossare ♦ vi arrossire.

reddish ['rɛdɪʃ] a rossiccio(a).

redecorate [riː'dɛkəreɪt] vt tinteggiare (e tappezzare) di nuovo.

redeem [rɪ'diːm] vt (debt) riscattare; (sth in pawn) ritirare; (fig, also REL) redimere.

redeemable [rɪ'diːməbl] a con diritto di riscatto; redimibile.

redeeming [rɪ'diːmɪŋ] a (feature) che salva.

redeploy [riːdɪ'plɔɪ] vt (MIL) riorganizzare lo schieramento di; (resources) riorganizzare.

redeployment [riːdɪ'plɔɪmənt] n riorganizzazione f.

redevelop [riːdɪ'vɛləp] vt ristrutturare.

redevelopment [riːdɪ'vɛləpmənt] n ristrutturazione f.

red-haired [rɛd'hɛəd] a dai capelli rossi.

red-handed [rɛd'hændɪd] a: **to be caught ~** essere preso(a) in flagrante or con le mani nel sacco.

redhead ['rɛdhɛd] n rosso/a.

red herring n (fig) falsa pista.

red-hot [rɛd'hɔt] a arroventato(a).

redirect [riːdaɪ'rɛkt] vt (mail) far seguire.

redistribute [riːdɪ'strɪbjuːt] vt ridistribuire.

red-letter day ['rɛdlɛtə-] n giorno memorabile.

red light n: **to go through a ~** (AUT) passare col rosso.

red-light district [rɛd'laɪt-] n quartiere m luce rossa inv.

redness ['rɛdnɪs] n rossore m; (of hair) rosso.

redo [riː'duː] vt irg rifare.

redolent ['rɛdələnt] a: **~ of** che sa di; (fig) che ricorda.

redouble [riː'dʌbl] vt: **to ~ one's efforts** raddoppiare gli sforzi.

redraft [riː'drɑːft] vt fare una nuova stesura di.

redress [rɪ'drɛs] n riparazione f ♦ vt riparare; **to ~ the balance** ristabilire l'equilibrio.

Red Sea n: **the ~** il mar Rosso.

redskin ['rɛdskɪn] n pellerossa m/f.

red tape n (fig) burocrazia.

reduce [rɪ'djuːs] vt ridurre; (lower) ridurre, abbassare; **"~ speed now"** (AUT) "rallentare"; **to ~ sth by/to** ridurre qc di/a; **to ~ sb to silence/despair/tears** ridurre qn al silenzio/alla disperazione/in lacrime.

reduced [rɪ'djuːst] a (decreased) ridotto(a); **at a ~ price** a prezzo ribassato or ridotto; **"greatly ~ prices"** "grandi ribassi".

reduction [rɪ'dʌkʃən] n riduzione f; (of price) ribasso; (discount) sconto.

redundancy [rɪ'dʌndənsɪ] n licenziamento (per eccesso di personale); **compulsory ~** licenziamento; **voluntary ~** forma di cassa integrazione volontaria.

redundancy payment n (Brit) indennità f inv di licenziamento.

redundant [rɪ'dʌndnt] a (Brit: worker) licenziato(a); (detail, object) superfluo(a); **to make ~** (Brit) licenziare (per eccesso di personale).

reed [riːd] n (BOT) canna; (MUS: of clarinet etc) ancia.

reedy ['riːdɪ] a (voice, instrument) acuto(a).

reef [riːf] n (at sea) scogliera; **coral ~** barriera corallina.

reek [riːk] vi: **to ~ (of)** puzzare (di).

reel [riːl] n bobina, rocchetto; (TECH) aspo; (FISHING) mulinello; (CINEMA) rotolo ♦ vt (TECH) annaspare; (also: **~ up**) avvolgere ♦ vi (sway) barcollare, vacillare; **my head is ~ing** mi gira la testa.

reel off vt snocciolare.

re-election [riːɪ'lɛkʃən] n rielezione f.

re-enter [riː'ɛntə*] vt rientrare in.

re-entry [riː'ɛntrɪ] n rientro.

re-export vt [riːɪk'spɔːt] riesportare ♦ n [riː'ɛkspɔːt] merce f riesportata, riesportazione f.

ref [rɛf] n abbr (col: = referee) arbitro.

ref. abbr (Comm: = with reference to) sogg.

refectory [rɪ'fɛktərɪ] n refettorio.

refer [rɪ'fəː*] vt: **to ~ sth to** (dispute, decision) deferire qc a; **to ~ sb to** (inquirer: for information) indirizzare qn a; (reader: to text) rimandare qn a; **he ~red me to the manager** mi ha detto di rivolgermi al direttore.

refer to vt fus (allude to) accennare a; (apply to) riferire a; (consult) rivolgersi a; ~**ring to your letter** (COMM) in riferimento alla Vostra lettera.

referee [rɛfə'ri:] n arbitro; (TENNIS) giudice m di gara; (Brit: for job application) referenza ♦ vt arbitrare.

reference ['rɛfrəns] n riferimento; (mention) menzione f, allusione f; (for job application: letter) referenza; lettera di raccomandazione; (: person) referenza; (in book) rimando; **with** ~ **to** riguardo a; (COMM: in letter) in or con riferimento a; **"please quote this** ~**"** (COMM) "si prega di far riferimento al numero di protocollo".

reference book n libro di consultazione.

reference number n (COMM) numero di riferimento.

referendum, pl referenda [rɛfə'rɛndəm, -də] n referendum m inv.

refill vt [ri:'fɪl] riempire di nuovo; (pen, lighter etc) ricaricare ♦ n ['ri:fɪl] (for pen etc) ricambio.

refine [rɪ'faɪn] vt raffinare.

refined [rɪ'faɪnd] a raffinato(a).

refinement [rɪ'faɪnmənt] n (of person) raffinatezza.

refinery [rɪ'faɪnəri] n raffineria.

refit n ['ri:fɪt] (NAUT) raddobbo ♦ vt [ri:'fɪt] (ship) raddobbare.

reflate [ri:'fleɪt] vt (economy) rilanciare.

reflation [ri:'fleɪʃən] n rilancio.

reflationary [ri:'fleɪʃənərɪ] a nuovamente inflazionario(a).

reflect [rɪ'flɛkt] vt (light, image) riflettere; (fig) rispecchiare ♦ vi (think) riflettere, considerare.

reflect on vt fus (discredit) rispecchiarsi su.

reflection [rɪ'flɛkʃən] n riflessione f; (image) riflesso; (criticism): ~ **on** giudizio su; attacco a; **on** ~ pensandoci sopra.

reflector [rɪ'flɛktə*] n (also AUT) catarifrangente m.

reflex ['ri:flɛks] a riflesso(a) ♦ n riflesso.

reflexive [rɪ'flɛksɪv] a (LING) riflessivo(a).

reform [rɪ'fɔ:m] n riforma ♦ vt riformare.

reformat [rɪ'fɔ:mæt] vt (COMPUT) riformattare.

Reformation [rɛfə'meɪʃən] n: **the** ~ la Riforma.

reformatory [rɪ'fɔ:mətərɪ] n (US) riformatorio.

reformed [rɪ'fɔ:md] a cambiato(a) (per il meglio).

reformer [rɪ'fɔ:mə*] n riformatore/trice.

refrain [rɪ'freɪn] vi: **to** ~ **from doing** trattenersi dal fare ♦ n ritornello.

refresh [rɪ'frɛʃ] vt rinfrescare; (subj: food, sleep) ristorare.

refresher course [rɪ'frɛʃə-] n (Brit) corso di aggiornamento.

refreshing [rɪ'frɛʃɪŋ] a (drink) rinfrescante;

(sleep) riposante, ristoratore(trice); (change etc) piacevole; (idea, point of view) originale.

refreshment [rɪ'frɛʃmənt] n (eating, resting etc) ristoro; ~**(s)** rinfreschi mpl.

refreshment room n posto di ristoro.

refrigeration [rɪfrɪdʒə'reɪʃən] n refrigerazione f.

refrigerator [rɪ'frɪdʒəreɪtə*] n frigorifero.

refuel [ri:'fjuəl] vt rifornire (di carburante) ♦ vi far rifornimento (di carburante).

refuge ['rɛfju:dʒ] n rifugio; **to take** ~ **in** rifugiarsi in.

refugee [rɛfju'dʒi:] n rifugiato/a, profugo/a.

refugee camp n campo (di) profughi.

refund n ['ri:fʌnd] rimborso ♦ vt [rɪ'fʌnd] rimborsare.

refurbish [ri:'fə:bɪʃ] vt rimettere a nuovo.

refurnish [ri:'fə:nɪʃ] vt ammobiliare di nuovo.

refusal [rɪ'fju:zəl] n rifiuto; **to have first** ~ **on sth** avere il diritto d'opzione su qc.

refuse n ['rɛfju:s] rifiuti mpl ♦ vt, vi [rɪ'fju:z] rifiutare; **to** ~ **to do sth** rifiutare or rifiutarsi di fare qc.

refuse collection n raccolta di rifiuti.

refuse collector n netturbino.

refuse disposal n sistema m di scarico dei rifiuti.

refute [rɪ'fju:t] vt confutare.

regain [rɪ'geɪn] vt riguadagnare; riacquistare, ricuperare.

regal ['ri:gl] a regale.

regale [rɪ'geɪl] vt: **to** ~ **sb with sth** intrattenere qn con qc.

regalia [rɪ'geɪlɪə] n insegne fpl reali.

regard [rɪ'gɑ:d] n riguardo, stima ♦ vt considerare, stimare; **to give one's** ~**s to** porgere i suoi saluti a; **(kind)** ~**s** cordiali saluti; **as** ~**s, with** ~ **to** riguardo a.

regarding [rɪ'gɑ:dɪŋ] prep riguardo a, per quanto riguarda.

regardless [rɪ'gɑ:dlɪs] ad lo stesso; ~ **of** a dispetto di, nonostante.

regatta [rɪ'gætə] n regata.

regency ['ri:dʒənsɪ] n reggenza.

regenerate [rɪ'dʒɛnəreɪt] vt rigenerare; (feelings, enthusiasm) far rinascere ♦ vi rigenerarsi; rinascere.

regent ['ri:dʒənt] n reggente m.

régime [reɪ'ʒi:m] n regime m.

regiment n ['rɛdʒɪmənt] reggimento ♦ vt ['rɛdʒɪment] irreggimentare.

regimental [rɛdʒɪ'mentl] a reggimentale.

regimentation [rɛdʒɪmɛn'teɪʃən] n irreggimentazione f.

region ['ri:dʒən] n regione f; **in the** ~ **of** (fig) all'incirca di.

regional ['ri:dʒənl] a regionale.

regional development n sviluppo regionale.

register ['rɛdʒɪstə*] n registro; (also: **electoral** ~) lista elettorale ♦ vt registrare; (vehicle) immatricolare; (luggage) spedire assicurato(a); (letter) assicurare; (subj: instrument) segnare ♦ vi iscriversi; (at hotel) firmare il registro; (*make impression*) entrare in testa; **to ~ a protest** fare un esposto; **to ~ for a course** iscriversi a un corso.

registered ['rɛdʒɪstəd] *a* (*design*) depositato(a); (*Brit: letter*) assicurato(a); (*student, voter*) iscritto(a).

registered company *n* società iscritta al registro.

registered nurse *n* (*US*) infermiere(a) diplomato(a).

registered office *n* sede *f* legale.

registered trademark *n* marchio depositato.

registrar ['rɛdʒɪstrɑ:*] *n* ufficiale *m* di stato civile; segretario.

registration [rɛdʒɪs'treɪʃən] *n* (*act*) registrazione *f*; iscrizione *f*; (*AUT: also:* ~ **number**) numero di targa.

registry ['rɛdʒɪstrɪ] *n* ufficio del registro.

registry office *n* (*Brit*) anagrafe *f*; **to get married in a ~** ≈ sposarsi in municipio.

regret [rɪ'grɛt] *n* rimpianto, rincrescimento ♦ *vt* rimpiangere; **I ~ that I/he cannot help** mi rincresce di non poter aiutare/che lui non possa aiutare; **we ~ to inform you that** ... siamo spiacenti di informarla che ....

regretfully [rɪ'grɛtfəlɪ] *ad* con rincrescimento.

regrettable [rɪ'grɛtəbl] *a* deplorevole.

regrettably [rɪ'grɛtəblɪ] *ad* purtroppo, sfortunatamente.

regroup [ri:'gru:p] *vt* raggruppare ♦ *vi* raggrupparsi.

regt *abbr* (= *regiment*) Reg.

regular ['rɛgjulə*] *a* regolare; (*usual*) abituale, normale; (*listener, reader*) fedele; (*soldier*) dell'esercito regolare; (*COMM: size*) normale ♦ *n* (*client etc*) cliente *m/f* abituale.

regularity [rɛgju'lærɪtɪ] *n* regolarità *f inv*.

regularly ['rɛgjuləlɪ] *ad* regolarmente.

regulate ['rɛgjuleɪt] *vt* regolare.

regulation [rɛgju'leɪʃən] *n* (*rule*) regola, regolamento; (*adjustment*) regolazione *f* ♦ *cpd* (*MIL*) di ordinanza.

rehabilitation ['ri:əbɪlɪ'teɪʃən] *n* (*of offender*) riabilitazione *f*; (*of disabled*) riadattamento.

rehash [ri:'hæʃ] *vt* (*col*) rimaneggiare.

rehearsal [rɪ'hə:səl] *n* prova; **dress ~** prova generale.

rehearse [rɪ'hə:s] *vt* provare.

rehouse [ri:'hauz] *vt* rialloggiare.

reign [reɪn] *n* regno ♦ *vi* regnare.

reigning ['reɪnɪŋ] *a* (*monarch*) regnante; (*champion*) attuale.

reimburse [ri:ɪm'bə:s] *vt* rimborsare.

rein [reɪn] *n* (*for horse*) briglia; **to give sb free ~** (*fig*) lasciare completa libertà a qn.

reincarnation [ri:ɪnkɑ:'neɪʃən] *n* reincarnazione *f*.

reindeer ['reɪndɪə*] *n* (*pl inv*) renna.

reinforce [ri:ɪn'fɔ:s] *vt* rinforzare.

reinforced concrete *n* cemento armato.

reinforcement [ri:ɪn'fɔ:smənt] *n* (*action*) rinforzamento; **~s** *npl* (*MIL*) rinforzi *mpl*.

reinstate [ri:ɪn'steɪt] *vt* reintegrare.

reinstatement [ri:ɪn'steɪtmənt] *n* reinte-

grazione *f*.

reissue [ri:'ɪʃju:] *vt* (*book*) ristampare, ripubblicare; (*film*) distribuire di nuovo.

reiterate [ri:'ɪtəreɪt] *vt* reiterare, ripetere.

reject *n* ['ri:dʒɛkt] (*COMM*) scarto ♦ *vt* [rɪ'dʒɛkt] rifiutare, respingere; (*COMM: goods*) scartare.

rejection [rɪ'dʒɛkʃən] *n* rifiuto.

rejoice [rɪ'dʒɔɪs] *vi*: **to ~ (at** *or* **over)** provare diletto (in).

rejoinder [rɪ'dʒɔɪndə*] *n* (*retort*) replica.

rejuvenate [rɪ'dʒu:vəneɪt] *vt* ringiovanire.

rekindle [ri:'kɪndl] *vt* riaccendere.

relapse [rɪ'læps] *n* (*MED*) ricaduta.

relate [rɪ'leɪt] *vt* (*tell*) raccontare; (*connect*) collegare ♦ *vi*: **to ~ to** (*refer to*) riferirsi a; (*get on with*) stabilire un rapporto con.

related [rɪ'leɪtɪd] *a* imparentato(a); collegato(a), connesso(a); **~ to** imparentato(a) con; collegato(a) *or* connesso(a) con.

relating [rɪ'leɪtɪŋ]: **~ to** *prep* che riguarda, rispetto a.

relation [rɪ'leɪʃən] *n* (*person*) parente *m/f*; (*link*) rapporto, relazione *f*; **in ~ to** con riferimento a; **diplomatic/international ~s** rapporti diplomatici/internazionali; **to bear a ~ to** corrispondere a.

relationship [rɪ'leɪʃənʃɪp] *n* rapporto; (*personal ties*) rapporti *mpl*, relazioni *fpl*; (*also:* **family ~**) legami *mpl* di parentela; (*affair*) relazione *f*; **they have a good ~** vanno molto d'accordo.

relative ['rɛlətɪv] *n* parente *m/f* ♦ *a* relativo(a); (*respective*) rispettivo(a).

relatively ['rɛlətɪvlɪ] *ad* relativamente; (*fairly, rather*) abbastanza.

relax [rɪ'læks] *vi* rilasciarsi; (*person: unwind*) rilassarsi ♦ *vt* rilasciare; (*mind, person*) rilassare; **~!** (*calm down*) calma!

relaxation [ri:læk'seɪʃən] *n* rilasciamento; rilassamento; (*entertainment*) ricreazione *f*, svago.

relaxed [rɪ'lækst] *a* rilasciato(a); rilassato(a).

relaxing [rɪ'læksɪŋ] *a* rilassante.

relay ['ri:leɪ] *n* (*SPORT*) corsa a staffetta ♦ *vt* (*message*) trasmettere.

release [rɪ'li:s] *n* (*from prison*) rilascio; (*from obligation*) liberazione *f*; (*of gas etc*) emissione *f*; (*of film etc*) distribuzione *f*; (*record*) disco; (*device*) disinnesto ♦ *vt* (*prisoner*) rilasciare; (*from obligation, wreckage etc*) liberare; (*book, film*) fare uscire; (*news*) rendere pubblico(a); (*gas etc*) emettere; (*TECH: catch, spring etc*) disinnestare; (*let go*) rilasciare; lasciar andare; sciogliere; **to ~ one's grip** mollare la presa; **to ~ the clutch** (*AUT*) staccare la frizione.

relegate ['rɛləgeɪt] *vt* relegare; (*SPORT*): **to be ~d** essere retrocesso(a).

relent [rɪ'lɛnt] *vi* cedere.

relentless [rɪ'lɛntlɪs] *a* implacabile.

relevance ['rɛləvəns] *n* pertinenza; **~ of sth to sth** rapporto tra qc e qc.

relevant ['rɛləvənt] *a* pertinente; (*chapter*) in questione; ~ **to** pertinente a.
reliability [rɪlaɪə'bɪlɪtɪ] *n* (*of person*) serietà; (*of machine*) affidabilità.
reliable [rɪ'laɪəbl] *a* (*person, firm*) fidato(a), che dà affidamento; (*method*) sicuro(a); (*machine*) affidabile.
reliably [rɪ'laɪəblɪ] *ad*: **to be** ~ **informed** sapere da fonti sicure.
reliance [rɪ'laɪəns] *n*: ~ **(on)** dipendenza (da).
reliant [rɪ'laɪənt] *a*: **to be** ~ **on sth/sb** dipendere da qc/qn.
relic ['rɛlɪk] *n* (*REL*) reliquia; (*of the past*) resto.
relief [rɪ'li:f] *n* (*from pain, anxiety*) sollievo; (*help, supplies*) soccorsi *mpl*; (*of guard*) cambio; (*ART, GEO*) rilievo; **by way of light** ~ come diversivo.
relief map *n* carta in rilievo.
relief road *n* (*Brit*) circonvallazione *f*.
relieve [rɪ'li:v] *vt* (*pain, patient*) sollevare; (*bring help*) soccorrere; (*take over from:* *gen*) sostituire; (: *guard*) rilevare; **to** ~ **sb of sth** (*load*) alleggerire qn di qc; **to** ~ **sb of his command** (*MIL*) esonerare qn dal comando; **to** ~ **o.s.** (*euphemism*) fare i propri bisogni.
religion [rɪ'lɪdʒən] *n* religione *f*.
religious [rɪ'lɪdʒəs] *a* religioso(a).
reline [ri:'laɪn] *vt* (*brakes*) sostituire le guarnizioni di.
relinquish [rɪ'lɪŋkwɪʃ] *vt* abbandonare; (*plan, habit*) rinunziare a.
relish ['rɛlɪʃ] *n* (*CULIN*) condimento; (*enjoyment*) gran piacere *m* ♦ *vt* (*food etc*) godere; **to** ~ **doing** adorare fare.
relive [ri:'lɪv] *vt* rivivere.
reload [ri:'ləud] *vt* ricaricare.
relocate [ri:ləu'keɪt] *vt* (*business*) trasferire ♦ *vi*: **to** ~ **in** trasferire la propria sede a.
reluctance [rɪ'lʌktəns] *n* riluttanza.
reluctant [rɪ'lʌktənt] *a* riluttante, mal disposto(a); **to be** ~ **to do sth** essere restio a fare qc.
reluctantly [rɪ'lʌktəntlɪ] *ad* di mala voglia, a malincuore.
rely [rɪ'laɪ]: **to** ~ **on** *vt fus* contare su; (*be dependent*) dipendere da.
remain [rɪ'meɪn] *vi* restare, rimanere; **to** ~ **silent** restare in silenzio; **I** ~, **yours faithfully** (*Brit: in letters*) distinti saluti.
remainder [rɪ'meɪndə*] *n* resto; (*COMM*) rimanenza.
remaining [rɪ'meɪnɪŋ] *a* che rimane.
remains [rɪ'meɪnz] *npl* resti *mpl*.
remand [rɪ'mɑ:nd] *n*: **on** ~ **in** detenzione preventiva ♦ *vt*: **to** ~ **in custody** rinviare in carcere; trattenere a disposizione della legge.
remand home *n* (*Brit*) riformatorio, casa di correzione.
remark [rɪ'mɑ:k] *n* osservazione *f* ♦ *vt* osservare, dire; (*notice*) notare ♦ *vi*: **to** ~ **on sth** fare dei commenti su qc.
remarkable [rɪ'mɑ:kəbl] *a* notevole;

eccezionale.
remarry [ri:'mærɪ] *vi* risposarsi.
remedial [rɪ'mi:dɪəl] *a* (*tuition, classes*) di riparazione.
remedy ['rɛmədɪ] *n*: ~ **(for)** rimedio (per) ♦ *vt* rimediare a.
remember [rɪ'mɛmbə*] *vt* ricordare, ricordarsi di; **I** ~ **seeing it, I** ~ **having seen it** (mi) ricordo di averlo visto; **she** ~**ed to do it** si è ricordata di farlo; ~ **me to your wife and children!** saluti sua moglie e i bambini da parte mia!
remembrance [rɪ'mɛmbrəns] *n* memoria; ricordo.
remind [rɪ'maɪnd] *vt*: **to** ~ **sb of sth** ricordare qc a qn; **to** ~ **sb to do** ricordare a qn di fare; **that** ~**s me!** a proposito!
reminder [rɪ'maɪndə*] *n* richiamo; (*note etc*) promemoria *m inv*.
reminisce [rɛmɪ'nɪs] *vi*: **to** ~ **(about)** abbandonarsi ai ricordi (di).
reminiscences [rɛmɪ'nɪsnsɪz] *npl* reminiscenze *fpl*, memorie *fpl*.
reminiscent [rɛmɪ'nɪsnt] *a*: ~ **of** che fa pensare a, che richiama.
remiss [rɪ'mɪs] *a* negligente; **it was** ~ **of me** è stata una negligenza da parte mia.
remission [rɪ'mɪʃən] *n* remissione *f*; (*of fee*) esonero.
remit [rɪ'mɪt] *vt* rimettere.
remittance [rɪ'mɪtəns] *n* rimessa.
remnant ['rɛmnənt] *n* resto, avanzo; ~**s** *npl* (*COMM*) scampoli *mpl*; fine *f* serie.
remonstrate ['rɛmənstreɪt] *vi* protestare; **to** ~ **with sb about sth** fare le proprie rimostranze a qn circa qc.
remorse [rɪ'mɔ:s] *n* rimorso.
remorseful [rɪ'mɔ:sful] *a* pieno(a) di rimorsi.
remorseless [rɪ'mɔ:slɪs] *a* (*fig*) spietato(a).
remote [rɪ'məut] *a* remoto(a), lontano(a); (*person*) distaccato(a); **there is a** ~ **possibility that ...** c'è una vaga possibilità che ... + *sub*.
remote control *n* telecomando.
remote-controlled [rɪ'məutkən'trəuld] *a* telecomandato(a).
remotely [rɪ'məutlɪ] *ad* remotamente; (*slightly*) vagamente.
remoteness [rɪ'məutnɪs] *n* lontananza.
remould ['ri:məuld] *n* (*Brit: tyre*) gomma rivestita.
removable [rɪ'mu:vəbl] *a* (*detachable*) staccabile.
removal [rɪ'mu:vəl] *n* (*taking away*) rimozione *f*; soppressione *f*; (*from house*) trasloco; (*from office: sacking*) destituzione *f*; (*MED*) ablazione *f*.
removal man *n* (*Brit*) addetto ai traslochi.
removal van *n* (*Brit*) furgone *m* per traslochi.
remove [rɪ'mu:v] *vt* togliere, rimuovere; (*employee*) destituire; (*stain*) far sparire; (*doubt, abuse*) sopprimere, eliminare; **first cousin once** ~**d** cugino di secondo grado.

remover |rɪ'muː:vəˈ| n (for paint) prodotto sverniciante; (for varnish) solvente m; **make-up** ~ struccatore m; **~s** npl (Brit: company) ditta or impresa di traslochi.

remunerate |rɪ'mjuːnəreɪt| vt rimunerare.

remuneration |rɪmjuːnə'reɪʃən| n rimunerazione f.

Renaissance |rə'neɪsəns| n: **the** ~ il Rinascimento.

rename |riː'neɪm| vt ribattezzare.

rend, pt, pp **rent** |rɛnd, rɛnt| vt lacerare.

render |'rɛndəˈ| vt rendere; (CULIN: fat) struggere.

rendering |'rɛndərɪŋ| n (MUS etc) interpretazione f.

rendez-vous |'rɔndɪvuː| n appuntamento; (place) luogo d'incontro; (meeting) incontro ♦ vi ritrovarsi; (spaceship) effettuare un rendez-vous.

rendition |rɛn'dɪʃən| n (MUS) interpretazione f.

renegade |'rɛnɪgeɪd| n rinnegato/a.

renew |rɪ'njuː| vt rinnovare; (negotiations) riprendere.

renewal |rɪ'njuːəl| n rinnovamento; ripresa.

renounce |rɪ'naʊns| vt rinunziare a; (disown) ripudiare.

renovate |'rɛnəveɪt| vt rinnovare; (art work) restaurare.

renovation |rɛnə'veɪʃən| n rinnovamento; restauro.

renown |rɪ'naʊn| n rinomanza.

renowned |rɪ'naʊnd| a rinomato(a).

rent |rɛnt| pt, pp of **rend** ♦ n affitto ♦ vt (take for rent) prendere in affitto; (car, TV) noleggiare, prendere a noleggio; (also: ~ **out**) dare in affitto; (car, TV) noleggiare, dare a noleggio.

rental |'rɛntl| n (cost: on TV, telephone) abbonamento; (: on car) nolo, noleggio.

renunciation |rɪnʌnsɪ'eɪʃən| n rinnegamento; (self-denial) rinunzia.

reopen |riː'əʊpən| vt riaprire.

reopening |riː'əʊpnɪŋ| n riapertura.

reorder |riː'ɔːdəˈ| vt ordinare di nuovo; (rearrange) riorganizzare.

reorganize |riː'ɔːgənaɪz| vt riorganizzare.

Rep abbr (US POL) = **representative**; **republican**.

rep |rɛp| n abbr (COMM: = representative) rappresentante m/f; (THEATRE: = repertory) teatro di repertorio.

repair |rɪ'pɛəˈ| n riparazione f ♦ vt riparare; **in good/bad** ~ in buona/cattiva condizione; **under** ~ in riparazione.

repair kit n corredo per riparazioni.

repair man n riparatore m.

repair shop n (AUT etc) officina.

repartee |rɛpɑː'tiː| n risposta pronta.

repast |rɪ'pɑːst| n (formal) pranzo.

repatriate |riː'pætrɪeɪt| vt rimpatriare.

repay |riː'peɪ| vt irg (money, creditor) rimborsare, ripagare; (sb's efforts) ricompensare.

repayment |riː'peɪmənt| n rimborsamento; ricompensa.

repeal |rɪ'piːl| n (of law) abrogazione f; (of sentence) annullamento ♦ vt abrogare; annullare.

repeat |rɪ'piːt| n (RADIO, TV) replica ♦ vt ripetere; (pattern) riprodurre; (promise, attack, also COMM: order) rinnovare ♦ vi ripetere.

repeatedly |rɪ'piːtɪdlɪ| ad ripetutamente, spesso.

repeat order n (COMM): **to place a** ~ **(for)** rinnovare l'ordinazione (di).

repel |rɪ'pɛl| vt respingere.

repellent |rɪ'pɛlənt| a repellente ♦ n: **insect** ~ prodotto m anti-insetti inv; **moth** ~ antitarmico.

repent |rɪ'pɛnt| vi: **to** ~ **(of)** pentirsi (di).

repentance |rɪ'pɛntəns| n pentimento.

repercussion |riː:pə'kʌʃən| n (consequence) ripercussione f.

repertoire |'rɛpətwɑːˈ| n repertorio.

repertory |'rɛpətərɪ| n (also: ~ **theatre**) teatro di repertorio.

repertory company n compagnia di repertorio.

repetition |rɛpɪ'tɪʃən| n ripetizione f; (COMM: of order etc) rinnovo.

repetitious |rɛpɪ'tɪʃəs| a (speech) pieno(a) di ripetizioni.

repetitive |rɪ'pɛtɪtɪv| a (movement) che si ripete; (work) monotono(a); (speech) pieno(a) di ripetizioni.

replace |rɪ'pleɪs| vt (put back) rimettere a posto; (take the place of) sostituire; (TEL): "**~ the receiver**" "riattaccare".

replacement |rɪ'pleɪsmənt| n rimessa; sostituzione f; (person) sostituto/a.

replacement part n pezzo di ricambio.

replay |'riː:pleɪ| n (of match) partita ripetuta; (of tape, film) replay m inv.

replenish |rɪ'plɛnɪʃ| vt (glass) riempire; (stock etc) rifornire.

replete |rɪ'pliːt| a: ~ **(with)** ripieno(a) (di); (well-fed) sazio(a) (di).

replica |'rɛplɪkə| n replica, copia.

reply |rɪ'plaɪ| n risposta ♦ vi rispondere; **in** ~ in risposta; **there's no** ~ (TEL) non risponde (nessuno).

reply coupon n buono di risposta.

report |rɪ'pɔːt| n rapporto; (PRESS etc) cronaca; (Brit: also: **school** ~) pagella ♦ vt riportare; (PRESS etc) fare una cronaca su; (bring to notice: occurrence) segnalare; (: person) denunciare ♦ vi (make a report) fare un rapporto (or una cronaca); (present o.s.): **to** ~ **(to sb)** presentarsi (a qn); **to** ~ **(on)** fare un rapporto (su); **it is ~ed that** si dice che; **it is ~ed from Berlin that** ... ci è stato riferito da Berlino che ....

report card n (US, Scottish) pagella.

reportedly |rɪ'pɔːtɪdlɪ| ad: **she is** ~ **living in Spain** si dice che vive in Spagna.

reported speech n (LING) discorso indiretto.

reporter [rɪ'pɔːtə*] n (PRESS) cronista m/f, reporter m inv; (RADIO) radiocronista m/f; (TV) telecronista m/f.

repose [rɪ'pəuz] n: in ~ in riposo.

repossess [riːpə'zɛs] vt rientrare in possesso di.

reprehensible [rɛprɪ'hɛnsɪbl] a riprensibile.

represent [rɛprɪ'zɛnt] vt rappresentare.

representation [rɛprɪzɛn'teɪʃən] n rappresentazione f; ~s npl (protest) protesta.

representative [rɛprɪ'zɛntətɪv] n rappresentativo/a; (COMM) rappresentante m (di commercio); (US: POL) deputato/a ♦ a: ~ (of) rappresentativo(a) (di).

repress [rɪ'prɛs] vt reprimere.

repression [rɪ'prɛʃən] n repressione f.

repressive [rɪ'prɛsɪv] a repressivo(a).

reprieve [rɪ'priːv] n (LAW) sospensione f dell'esecuzione della condanna; (fig) dilazione f ♦ vt sospendere l'esecuzione della condanna a; accordare una dilazione a.

reprimand ['rɛprɪmɑːnd] n rimprovero ♦ vt rimproverare, redarguire.

reprint ['riːprɪnt] n ristampa ♦ vt ristampare.

reprisal [rɪ'praɪzl] n rappresaglia; to take ~s fare delle rappresaglie.

reproach [rɪ'prəutʃ] n rimprovero ♦ vt: to ~ sb with sth rimproverare qn di qc; beyond ~ irreprensibile.

reproachful [rɪ'prəutʃful] a di rimprovero.

reproduce [riːprə'djuːs] vt riprodurre ♦ vi riprodursi.

reproduction [riːprə'dʌkʃən] n riproduzione f.

reproductive [riːprə'dʌktɪv] a riproduttore(trice); riproduttivo(a).

reproof [rɪ'pruːf] n riprovazione f.

reprove [rɪ'pruːv] vt (action) disapprovare; (person): to ~ (for) biasimare (per).

reproving [rɪ'pruːvɪŋ] a di disapprovazione.

reptile ['rɛptaɪl] n rettile m.

Repub. abbr (US POL) = republican.

republic [rɪ'pʌblɪk] n repubblica.

republican [rɪ'pʌblɪkən] a, n repubblicano(a).

repudiate [rɪ'pjuːdɪeɪt] vt ripudiare.

repugnant [rɪ'pʌɡnənt] a ripugnante.

repulse [rɪ'pʌls] vt respingere.

repulsion [rɪ'pʌlʃən] n ripulsione f.

repulsive [rɪ'pʌlsɪv] a ripugnante, ripulsivo(a).

reputable ['rɛpjutəbl] a di buona reputazione; (occupation) rispettabile.

reputation [rɛpju'teɪʃən] n reputazione f; he has a ~ for being awkward ha la fama di essere un tipo difficile.

repute [rɪ'pjuːt] n reputazione f.

reputed [rɪ'pjuːtɪd] a reputato(a); to be ~ to be rich/intelligent etc essere ritenuto(a) ricco(a)/intelligente etc.

reputedly [rɪ'pjuːtɪdlɪ] ad secondo quanto si dice.

request [rɪ'kwɛst] n domanda; (formal) richiesta ♦ vt: to ~ (of or from sb) chiedere (a qn); at the ~ of su richiesta di; "you are ~ed not to smoke" "si prega di non fumare".

request stop n (Brit: for bus) fermata facoltativa or a richiesta.

requiem ['rɛkwɪəm] n requiem m or f inv.

require [rɪ'kwaɪə*] vt (need: subj: person) aver bisogno di; (: thing, situation) richiedere; (want) volere; esigere; (order) obbligare; to ~ sb to do sth/sth of sb esigere che qn faccia qc/qc da qn; what qualifications are ~d? che requisiti ci vogliono?; ~d by law prescritto dalla legge; if ~d in caso di bisogno.

required [rɪ'kwaɪəd] a richiesto(a).

requirement [rɪ'kwaɪəmənt] n (need) esigenza; (condition) requisito; to meet sb's ~s soddisfare le esigenze di qn.

requisite ['rɛkwɪzɪt] n cosa necessaria ♦ a necessario(a); toilet ~s articoli mpl da toletta.

requisition [rɛkwɪ'zɪʃən] n: ~ (for) richiesta (di) ♦ vt (MIL) requisire.

reroute [riː'ruːt] vt (train etc) deviare.

resale ['riː'seɪl] n rivendita.

resale price maintenance (RPM) n prezzo minimo da vendita imposto.

rescind [rɪ'sɪnd] vt annullare; (law) abrogare; (judgement) rescindere.

rescue ['rɛskjuː] n salvataggio; (help) soccorso ♦ vt salvare; to come/go to sb's ~ venire/andare in aiuto a or di qn.

rescue party n squadra di salvataggio.

rescuer ['rɛskjuə*] n salvatore/trice.

research [rɪ'sɜːtʃ] n ricerca, ricerche fpl ♦ vt fare ricerche su ♦ vi: to ~ (into sth) fare ricerca (su qc); a piece of ~ un lavoro di ricerca; ~ and development (R&D) ricerca e sviluppo.

researcher [rɪ'sɜːtʃə*] n ricercatore/trice.

research work n ricerche fpl.

resell [riː'sɛl] vt irg rivendere.

resemblance [rɪ'zɛmbləns] n somiglianza; to bear a strong ~ to somigliare moltissimo a.

resemble [rɪ'zɛmbl] vt assomigliare a.

resent [rɪ'zɛnt] vt risentirsi di.

resentful [rɪ'zɛntful] a pieno(a) di risentimento.

resentment [rɪ'zɛntmənt] n risentimento.

reservation [rɛzə'veɪʃən] n (booking) prenotazione f; (doubt) dubbio; (protected area) riserva; (Brit AUT: also: central ~) spartitraffico m inv; to make a ~ (in an hotel/a restaurant/on a plane) prenotare (una camera/una tavola/un posto); with ~s (doubts) con le dovute riserve.

reservation desk n (US: in hotel) reception f inv.

reserve [rɪ'zɜːv] n riserva ♦ vt (seats etc) prenotare; ~s npl (MIL) riserve fpl; in ~ in serbo.

reserve currency n valuta di riserva.

reserved [rɪ'zɜːvd] a (shy) riservato(a); (seat) prenotato(a).

reserve price n (Brit) prezzo di riserva, prezzo m base inv.

reserve team n (Brit SPORT) seconda squadra.

reservist [rɪ'zɜːvɪst] n (*MIL*) riservista m.

reservoir ['rezəvwɑː*] n serbatoio; (*artificial lake*) bacino idrico.

reset [riː'sɛt] vt (*COMPUT*) azzerare.

reshape [riː'ʃeɪp] vt (*policy*) ristrutturare.

reshuffle [riː'ʃʌfl] n: **Cabinet ~** (*POL*) rimpasto governativo.

reside [rɪ'zaɪd] vi risiedere.

residence ['rezɪdəns] n residenza; **to take up ~** prendere residenza; **in ~** (*queen etc*) in sede; (*doctor*) fisso.

residence permit n (*Brit*) permesso di soggiorno.

resident ['rezɪdənt] n (*gen, COMPUT*) residente m/f; (*in hotel*) cliente m/f fisso(a) ♦ a residente.

residential [rezɪ'dɛnʃəl] a di residenza; (*area*) residenziale.

residue ['rezɪdjuː] n resto; (*CHEM, PHYSICS*) residuo.

resign [rɪ'zaɪn] vt (*one's post*) dimettersi da ♦ vi: **to ~ (from)** dimettersi (da), dare le dimissioni (da); **to ~ o.s.** to rassegnarsi a.

resignation [rezɪg'neɪʃən] n dimissioni fpl; rassegnazione f; **to tender one's ~** dare le dimissioni.

resigned [rɪ'zaɪnd] a rassegnato(a).

resilience [rɪ'zɪlɪəns] n (*of material*) elasticità, resilienza; (*of person*) capacità di recupero.

resilient [rɪ'zɪlɪənt] a elastico(a); (*person*) che si riprende facilmente.

resin ['rezɪn] n resina.

resist [rɪ'zɪst] vt resistere a.

resistance [rɪ'zɪstəns] n resistenza.

resistant [rɪ'zɪstənt] a: **~ (to)** resistente (a).

resolute ['rezəluːt] a risoluto(a).

resolution [rezə'luːʃən] n (*resolve*) fermo proposito, risoluzione f; (*determination*) risolutezza; (*on screen*) risoluzione f; **to make a ~** fare un proposito.

resolve [rɪ'zɒlv] n risoluzione f ♦ vi (*decide*): **to ~ to do** decidere di fare ♦ vt (*problem*) risolvere.

resolved [rɪ'zɒlvd] a risoluto(a).

resonance ['rezənəns] n risonanza.

resonant ['rezənənt] a risonante.

resort [rɪ'zɔːt] n (*town*) stazione f; (*place*) località f inv; (*recourse*) ricorso ♦ vi: **to ~ to** far ricorso a; **seaside/winter sports ~** stazione f balneare/di sport invernali; **as a last ~** come ultima risorsa.

resound [rɪ'zaund] vi: **to ~ (with)** risonare (di).

resounding [rɪ'zaundɪŋ] a risonante.

resource [rɪ'sɔːs] n risorsa; **~s** npl risorse fpl; **natural ~s** risorse naturali; **to leave sb to his (or her) own ~s** (*fig*) lasciare che qn si arrangi (per conto suo).

resourceful [rɪ'sɔːsful] a pieno(a) di risorse, intraprendente.

resourcefulness [rɪ'sɔːsfəlnɪs] n intraprendenza.

respect [rɪs'pɛkt] n rispetto; (*point, detail*): **in**

some ~s sotto certi aspetti ♦ vt rispettare; **~s** npl ossequi mpl; **to have** or **show ~ for** aver rispetto per; **out of ~ for** per rispetto or riguardo a; **with ~ to** rispetto a, riguardo a; **in ~ of** quanto a; **in this ~** per questo riguardo; **with (all) due ~ I ...** con rispetto parlando, io ....

respectability [rɪspɛktə'bɪlɪtɪ] n rispettabilità.

respectable [rɪs'pɛktəbl] a rispettabile; (*quite big*: amount etc) considerevole; (*quite good*: player, result etc) niente male inv.

respectful [rɪs'pɛktful] a rispettoso(a).

respective [rɪs'pɛktɪv] a rispettivo(a).

respectively [rɪs'pɛktɪvlɪ] ad rispettivamente.

respiration [rɛspɪ'reɪʃən] n respirazione f.

respirator ['rɛspɪreɪtə*] n respiratore m.

respiratory ['rɛspərətərɪ] a respiratorio(a).

respite ['rɛspaɪt] n respiro, tregua.

resplendent [rɪs'plɛndənt] a risplendente.

respond [rɪs'pɒnd] vi rispondere.

respondent [rɪs'pɒndənt] n (*LAW*) convenuto/a.

response [rɪs'pɒns] n risposta; **in ~ to** in risposta a.

responsibility [rɪspɒnsɪ'bɪlɪtɪ] n responsabilità f inv; **to take ~ for sth/sb** assumersi or prendersi la responsabilità di qc/per qn.

responsible [rɪs'pɒnsɪbl] a (*liable*): **~ (for)** responsabile (di); (*trustworthy*) fidato(a); (*job*) di (grande) responsabilità; **to be ~ to sb (for sth)** dover rispondere a qn (di qc).

responsibly [rɪs'pɒnsəblɪ] ad responsabilmente.

responsive [rɪs'pɒnsɪv] a che reagisce.

rest [rɛst] n riposo; (*stop*) sosta, pausa; (*MUS*) pausa; (*support*) appoggio, sostegno; (*remainder*) resto, avanzi mpl ♦ vi riposarsi; (*remain*) rimanere, restare; (*be supported*): **to ~ on** appoggiarsi su ♦ vt (*lean*): **to ~ sth on/against** appoggiare qc su/contro; **to set sb's mind at ~** tranquillizzare qn; **the ~ of them** gli altri; **to ~ one's eyes** or **gaze on** posare lo sguardo su; **~ assured that ...** stia tranquillo che ...; **it ~s with him to decide** sta a lui decidere.

restart [riː'stɑːt] vt (*engine*) rimettere in marcia; (*work*) ricominciare.

restaurant ['rɛstərɒŋ] n ristorante m.

restaurant car n (*Brit*) vagone m ristorante.

rest cure n cura del riposo.

restful ['rɛstful] a riposante.

rest home n casa di riposo.

restitution [rɛstɪ'tjuːʃən] n (*act*) restituzione f; (*reparation*) riparazione f.

restive ['rɛstɪv] a agitato(a), impaziente; (*horse*) restio(a).

restless ['rɛstlɪs] a agitato(a), irrequieto(a); **to get ~** spazientirsi.

restlessly ['rɛstlɪslɪ] ad in preda all'agitazione.

restock [riː'stɒk] vt rifornire.

restoration [rɛstə'reɪʃən] n restauro; restituzione f.

restorative [rɪ'stɔrətɪv] a corroborante, ristorativo(a) ♦ n ricostituente m.

restore [rɪ'stɔː*] vt (building) restaurare; (sth stolen) restituire; (peace, health) ristorare.
restorer [rɪs'tɔːrə*] n (ART etc) restauratore/trice.
restrain [rɪs'treɪn] vt (feeling) contenere, frenare; (person): **to ~ (from doing)** trattenere (dal fare).
restrained [rɪs'treɪnd] a (style) contenuto(a), sobrio(a); (manner) riservato(a).
restraint [rɪs'treɪnt] n (restriction) limitazione f; (moderation) ritegno; **wage ~** restrizioni fpl salariali.
restrict [rɪs'trɪkt] vt restringere, limitare.
restricted area n (AUT) zona a velocità limitata.
restriction [rɪs'trɪkʃən] n restrizione f, limitazione f.
restrictive [rɪs'trɪktɪv] a restrittivo(a).
restrictive practices npl (INDUSTRY) pratiche restrittive di produzione.
rest room n (US) toletta.
restructure [riː'strʌktʃə*] vt ristrutturare.
result [rɪ'zʌlt] n risultato ♦ vi: **to ~ in** avere per risultato; **as a ~ (of)** in or di conseguenza (a), in seguito (a); **to ~ (from)** essere una conseguenza (di), essere causato(a) (da).
resultant [rɪ'zʌltənt] a risultante, conseguente.
resume [rɪ'zjuːm] vt, vi (work, journey) riprendere; (sum up) riassumere.
résumé ['reɪzjuːmeɪ] n riassunto; (US: curriculum vitae) curriculum vitae m inv.
resumption [rɪ'zʌmpʃən] n ripresa.
resurgence [rɪ'sɜːdʒəns] n rinascita.
resurrection [rezə'rekʃən] n risurrezione f.
resuscitate [rɪ'sʌsɪteɪt] vt (MED) risuscitare.
resuscitation [rɪsʌsɪ'teɪʃən] n rianimazione f.
retail ['riːteɪl] n (vendita al) minuto ♦ cpd al minuto ♦ vt vendere al minuto ♦ vi: **to ~ at** essere in vendita al pubblico al prezzo di.
retailer ['riːteɪlə*] n commerciante m/f al minuto, dettagliante m/f.
retail outlet n punto di vendita al dettaglio.
retail price n prezzo al minuto.
retail price index n indice m dei prezzi al consumo.
retain [rɪ'teɪn] vt (keep) tenere, serbare.
retainer [rɪ'teɪnə*] n (servant) servitore m; (fee) onorario.
retaliate [rɪ'tælɪeɪt] vi: **to ~ (against)** vendicarsi (di); **to ~ on sb** fare una rappresaglia contro qn.
retaliation [rɪtælɪ'eɪʃən] n rappresaglie fpl; **in ~ for** per vendicarsi di.
retaliatory [rɪ'tælɪətərɪ] a di rappresaglia, di ritorsione.
retarded [rɪ'tɑːdɪd] a ritardato(a); (also: **mentally ~**) tardo(a) (di mente).
retch [retʃ] vi aver conati di vomito.
retentive [rɪ'tentɪv] a ritentivo(a).
rethink ['riː'θɪŋk] vt ripensare.
reticence ['retɪsns] n reticenza.
reticent ['retɪsnt] a reticente.
retina ['retɪnə] n retina.

retinue ['retɪnjuː] n seguito, scorta.
retire [rɪ'taɪə*] vi (give up work) andare in pensione; (withdraw) ritirarsi, andarsene; (go to bed) andare a letto, ritirarsi.
retired [rɪ'taɪəd] a (person) pensionato(a).
retirement [rɪ'taɪəmənt] n pensione f.
retirement age n età del pensionamento.
retiring [rɪ'taɪərɪŋ] a (person) riservato(a); (departing: chairman) uscente.
retort [rɪ'tɔːt] n (reply) rimbecco; (container) storta ♦ vi rimbeccare.
retrace [riː'treɪs] vt ricostruire; **to ~ one's steps** tornare sui propri passi.
retract [rɪ'trækt] vt (statement) ritrattare; (claws, undercarriage, aerial) ritrarre, ritirare ♦ vi ritrarsi.
retractable [rɪ'træktəbl] a retrattile.
retrain [riː'treɪn] vt (worker) riaddestrare.
retraining [rɪ'treɪnɪŋ] n riaddestramento.
retread vt [riː'tred] (AUT: tyre) rigenerare ♦ n ['riːtred] gomma rigenerata.
retreat [rɪ'triːt] n ritirata; (place) rifugio ♦ vi battere in ritirata; (flood) ritirarsi; **to beat a hasty ~** (fig) battersela.
retrial [riː'traɪəl] n nuovo processo.
retribution [retrɪ'bjuːʃən] n castigo.
retrieval [rɪ'triːvəl] n ricupero.
retrieve [rɪ'triːv] vt (sth lost) ricuperare, ritrovare; (situation, honour) salvare; (COMPUT) ricuperare.
retriever [rɪ'triːvə*] n cane m da riporto.
retroactive [retrəʊ'æktɪv] a retroattivo(a).
retrograde ['retrəʊgreɪd] a retrogrado(a).
retrospect ['retrəspekt] n: **in ~** guardando indietro.
retrospective [retrə'spektɪv] a retrospettivo(a); (law) retroattivo(a) ♦ n (ART) retrospettiva.
return [rɪ'tɜːn] n (going or coming back) ritorno; (of sth stolen etc) restituzione f; (COMM: from land, shares) profitto, reddito; (: of merchandise) resa; (report) rapporto; (reward): **in ~ (for)** in cambio (di) ♦ cpd (journey, match) di ritorno; (Brit: ticket) di andata e ritorno ♦ vi tornare, ritornare ♦ vt rendere, restituire; (bring back) riportare; (send back) mandare indietro; (put back) rimettere; (POL: candidate) eleggere; **~s** npl (COMM) incassi mpl; profitti mpl; **by ~ of post** a stretto giro di posta; **many happy ~s (of the day)!** auguri!, buon compleanno!
returnable [rɪ'tɜːnəbl] a: **~ bottle** vuoto a rendere.
return key n (COMPUT) tasto di ritorno.
reunion [riː'juːnɪən] n riunione f.
reunite [riːjuː'naɪt] vt riunire.
rev [rev] n abbr (= revolution: AUT) giro ♦ vb (also: **~ up**) vt imballare ♦ vi imballarsi.
revaluation [riːvæljʊ'eɪʃən] n rivalutazione f.
revamp ['riː'væmp] vt rinnovare; riorganizzare.
rev counter n contagiri m inv.
Rev(d). abbr = **reverend**.
reveal [rɪ'viːl] vt (make known) rivelare,

svelare; (*display*) rivelare, mostrare.
revealing [rɪ'viːlɪŋ] *a* rivelatore(trice); (*dress*) scollato(a).
reveille [rɪ'vælɪ] *n* (*MIL*) sveglia.
revel ['rɛvl] *vi*: **to ~ in sth/in doing** dilettarsi di qc/a fare.
revelation [rɛvə'leɪʃən] *n* rivelazione *f*.
reveller ['rɛvlə*] *n* festaiolo/a.
revelry ['rɛvlrɪ] *n* baldoria.
revenge [rɪ'vɛndʒ] *n* vendetta; (*in game etc*) rivincita ♦ *vt* vendicare; **to take ~** vendicarsi; **to get one's ~ (for sth)** vendicarsi (di qc).
revengeful [rɪ'vɛndʒful] *a* vendicatore(trice); vendicativo(a).
revenue ['rɛvənjuː] *n* reddito.
reverberate [rɪ'vəːbəreɪt] *vi* (*sound*) rimbombare; (*light*) riverberarsi.
reverberation [rɪvəːbə'reɪʃən] *n* (*of light, sound*) riverberazione *f*.
revere [rɪ'vɪə*] *vt* venerare.
reverence ['rɛvərəns] *n* venerazione *f*, riverenza.
Reverend ['rɛvərənd] *a* (*in titles*) reverendo(a).
reverent ['rɛvərənt] *a* riverente.
reverie ['rɛvərɪ] *n* fantasticheria.
reversal [rɪ'vəːsl] *n* capovolgimento.
reverse [rɪ'vəːs] *n* contrario, opposto; (*back*) rovescio; (*AUT: also*: **~ gear**) marcia indietro ♦ *a* (*order*) inverso(a); (*direction*) opposto(a) ♦ *vt* (*turn*) invertire, rivoltare; (*change*) capovolgere, rovesciare; (*LAW: judgement*) cassare ♦ *vi* (*Brit AUT*) fare marcia indietro; **in ~ order** in ordine inverso; **to go into ~** fare marcia indietro.
reversed charge call *n* (*Brit TEL*) telefonata con addebito al ricevente.
reverse video *n* reverse video *m*.
reversible [rɪ'vəːsəbl] *a* (*garment*) double-face *inv*; (*procedure*) reversibile.
reversing lights [rɪ'vəːsɪŋ-] *npl* (*Brit AUT*) luci *fpl* per la retromarcia.
reversion [rɪ'vəːʃən] *n* ritorno.
revert [rɪ'vəːt] *vi*: **to ~ to** tornare a.
review [rɪ'vjuː] *n* rivista; (*of book, film*) recensione *f* ♦ *vt* passare in rivista; fare la recensione di; **to come under ~** essere preso in esame.
reviewer [rɪ'vjuːə*] *n* recensore/a.
revile [rɪ'vaɪl] *vt* insultare.
revise [rɪ'vaɪz] *vt* (*manuscript*) rivedere, correggere; (*opinion*) emendare, modificare; (*study: subject, notes*) ripassare; **~d edition** edizione riveduta.
revision [rɪ'vɪʒən] *n* revisione *f*; ripasso; (*revised version*) versione *f* riveduta e corretta.
revitalize [riː'vaɪtəlaɪz] *vt* ravvivare.
revival [rɪ'vaɪvəl] *n* ripresa; ristabilimento; (*of faith*) risveglio.
revive [rɪ'vaɪv] *vt* (*person*) rianimare; (*custom*) far rivivere; (*hope, courage*) ravvivare; (*play, fashion*) riesumare ♦ *vi* (*person*)

rianimarsi; (*hope*) ravvivarsi; (*activity*) riprendersi.
revoke [rɪ'vəuk] *vt* revocare; (*promise, decision*) rinvenire su.
revolt [rɪ'vəult] *n* rivolta, ribellione *f* ♦ *vi* rivoltarsi, ribellarsi; **to ~ (against sb/sth)** ribellarsi (a qn/qc).
revolting [rɪ'vəultɪŋ] *a* ripugnante.
revolution [rɛvə'luːʃən] *n* rivoluzione *f*; (*of wheel etc*) rivoluzione, giro.
revolutionary [rɛvə'luːʃənrɪ] *a*, *n* rivoluzionario(a).
revolutionize [rɛvə'luːʃənaɪz] *vt* rivoluzionare.
revolve [rɪ'vɔlv] *vi* girare.
revolver [rɪ'vɔlvə*] *n* rivoltella.
revolving [rɪ'vɔlvɪŋ] *a* girevole.
revolving credit *n* credito a termine rinnovabile automaticamente.
revolving door *n* porta girevole.
revue [rɪ'vjuː] *n* (*THEATRE*) rivista.
revulsion [rɪ'vʌlʃən] *n* ripugnanza.
reward [rɪ'wɔːd] *n* ricompensa, premio ♦ *vt*: **to ~ (for)** ricompensare (per).
rewarding [rɪ'wɔːdɪŋ] *a* (*fig*) soddisfacente; **financially ~** conveniente dal punto di vista economico.
rewind [riː'waɪnd] *vt irg* (*watch*) ricaricare; (*ribbon etc*) riavvolgere.
rewire [riː'waɪə*] *vt* (*house*) rifare l'impianto elettrico di.
reword [riː'wəːd] *vt* formulare *or* esprimere con altre parole.
rewrite [riː'raɪt] *vt irg* riscrivere.
Reykjavik ['reɪkjəviːk] *n* Reykjavik *f*.
RFD *abbr* (*US POST*) = *rural free delivery*.
Rh *abbr* (= *rhesus*) Rh.
rhapsody ['ræpsədɪ] *n* (*MUS*) rapsodia; (*fig*) elogio stravagante.
rhesus factor ['riːsəs-] *n* (*MED*) fattore *m* Rh.
rhetoric ['rɛtərɪk] *n* retorica.
rhetorical [rɪ'tɔrɪkl] *a* retorico(a).
rheumatic [ruː'mætɪk] *a* reumatico(a).
rheumatism ['ruːmətɪzəm] *n* reumatismo.
rheumatoid arthritis ['ruːmətɔɪd-] *n* artrite *f* reumatoide.
Rhine [raɪn] *n*: **the ~** il Reno.
rhinestone ['raɪnstəun] *n* diamante *m* falso.
rhinoceros [raɪ'nɔsərəs] *n* rinoceronte *m*.
Rhodes [rəudz] *n* Rodi *f*.
Rhodesia [rəu'diːʒə] *n* Rhodesia.
Rhodesian [rəu'diːʒən] *a*, *n* Rhodesiano(a).
rhododendron [rəudə'dɛndrn] *n* rododendro.
Rhone [rəun] *n*: **the ~** il Rodano.
rhubarb ['ruːbɑːb] *n* rabarbaro.
rhyme [raɪm] *n* rima; (*verse*) poesia ♦ *vi*: **to ~ (with)** fare rima (con); **without ~ or reason** senza capo né coda.
rhythm ['rɪðm] *n* ritmo.
rhythmic(al) ['rɪðmɪk(əl)] *a* ritmico(a).
rhythmically ['rɪðmɪkəlɪ] *ad* con ritmo.
RI *abbr* (*US POST*) = *Rhode Island* ♦ *n abbr* (*Brit*) = *religious instruction*.
rib [rɪb] *n* (*ANAT*) costola ♦ *vt* (*tease*) punzecchiare.

ribald ['rɪbəld] *a* licenzioso(a), volgare.
ribbed [rɪbd] *a* (*knitting*) a coste.
ribbon ['rɪbən] *n* nastro; **in** ~**s** (*torn*) a brandelli.
rice [raɪs] *n* riso.
ricefield ['raɪsfiːld] *n* risaia.
rice pudding *n* budino di riso.
rich [rɪtʃ] *a* ricco(a); (*clothes*) sontuoso(a); **the** ~ *npl* i ricchi; ~**es** *npl* ricchezze *fpl*; **to be** ~ **in sth** essere ricco di qc.
richly ['rɪtʃlɪ] *ad* riccamente; (*dressed*) sontuosamente; (*deserved*) pienamente.
richness ['rɪtʃnɪs] *n* ricchezza.
rickets ['rɪkɪts] *n* rachitismo.
rickety ['rɪkɪtɪ] *a* zoppicante.
rickshaw ['rɪkʃɔː] *n* risciò *m inv*.
ricochet ['rɪkəʃeɪ] *n* rimbalzo ♦ *vi* rimbalzare.
rid, *pt*, *pp* **rid** [rɪd] *vt*: **to** ~ **sb of** sbarazzare *or* liberare qn di; **to get** ~ **of** sbarazzarsi di.
riddance ['rɪdns] *n*: **good** ~! che liberazione!
ridden ['rɪdn] *pp of* **ride.**
riddle ['rɪdl] *n* (*puzzle*) indovinello ♦ *vt*: **to be** ~**d with** essere crivellato(a) di.
ride [raɪd] *n* (*on horse*) cavalcata; (*outing*) passeggiata; (*distance covered*) cavalcata; corsa ♦ *vb* (*pt* **rode**, *pp* **ridden** [raʊd, 'rɪdn]) *vi* (*as sport*) cavalcare; (*go somewhere: on horse, bicycle*) andare (a cavallo *or* in bicicletta *etc*); (*journey: on bicycle, motorcycle, bus*) andare, viaggiare ♦ *vt* (*a horse*) montare, cavalcare; **to go for a** ~ andare a fare una cavalcata; andare a fare un giro; **can you** ~ **a bike?** sai andare in bicicletta?; **we rode all day/all the way** abbiamo cavalcato tutto il giorno/per tutto il tragitto; **to** ~ **a horse/bicycle/camel** montare a cavallo/in bicicletta/in groppa a un cammello; **to** ~ **at anchor** (*NAUT*) essere alla fonda; **horse** ~ cavalcata; **car** ~ passeggiata in macchina; **to take sb for a** ~ (*fig*) prendere in giro qn; fregare qn.
ride out *vt*: **to** ~ **out the storm** (*fig*) mantenersi a galla.
rider ['raɪdə*] *n* cavalcatore/trice; (*jockey*) fantino; (*on bicycle*) ciclista *m/f*; (*on motorcycle*) motociclista *m/f*; (*in document*) clausola addizionale, aggiunta.
ridge [rɪdʒ] *n* (*of hill*) cresta; (*of roof*) colmo; (*of mountain*) giogo; (*on object*) riga (in rilievo).
ridicule ['rɪdɪkjuːl] *n* ridicolo ♦ *vt* mettere in ridicolo; **to hold sb/sth up to** ~ mettere in ridicolo qn/qc.
ridiculous [rɪ'dɪkjuləs] *a* ridicolo(a).
riding ['raɪdɪŋ] *n* equitazione *f*.
riding school *n* scuola d'equitazione.
rife [raɪf] *a* diffuso(a); **to be** ~ **with** abbondare di.
riffraff ['rɪfræf] *n* canaglia, gentaglia.
rifle ['raɪfl] *n* carabina ♦ *vt* vuotare.
rifle through *vt fus* frugare.
rifle range *n* campo di tiro; (*at fair*) tiro a segno.
rift [rɪft] *n* fessura, crepatura; (*fig: dis-*

agreement) incrinatura.
rig [rɪg] *n* (*also:* **oil** ~: **on land**) derrick *m inv*; (: *at sea*) piattaforma di trivellazione ♦ *vt* (*election etc*) truccare.
rig out *vt* (*Brit*) attrezzare; (*pej*) abbigliare, agghindare.
rig up *vt* allestire.
rigging ['rɪgɪŋ] *n* (*NAUT*) attrezzatura.
right [raɪt] *a* giusto(a); (*suitable*) appropriato(a); (*not left*) destro(a) ♦ *n* (*title, claim*) diritto; (*not left*) destra ♦ *ad* (*answer*) correttamente; (*not on the left*) a destra ♦ *vt* raddrizzare; (*fig*) riparare ♦ *excl* bene!; **the** ~ **time** l'ora esatta; **to be** ~ (*person*) aver ragione; (*answer*) essere giusto(a) *or* corretto(a); **to get sth** ~ far giusto qc; **you did the** ~ **thing** ha fatto bene; **let's get it** ~ **this time!** cerchiamo di farlo bene stavolta!; **to put a mistake** ~ (*Brit*) correggere un errore; ~ **now** proprio adesso; subito; ~ **away** subito; ~ **before/after** subito prima/dopo; **to go** ~ **to the end of sth** andare fino in fondo a qc; ~ **against the wall** proprio contro il muro; ~ **ahead** sempre diritto; proprio davanti; ~ **in the middle** proprio nel mezzo; **by** ~**s** di diritto; **on the** ~, **to the** ~ a destra; ~ **and wrong** il bene e il male; **to have a** ~ **to sth** aver diritto a qc; **film** ~**s** diritti di riproduzione cinematografica; ~ **of way** diritto di passaggio; (*AUT*) precedenza.
right angle *n* angolo retto.
righteous ['raɪtʃəs] *a* retto(a), virtuoso(a); (*anger*) giusto(a), giustificato(a).
righteousness ['raɪtʃəsnɪs] *n* rettitudine *f*, virtù *f*.
rightful ['raɪtful] *a* (*heir*) legittimo(a).
rightfully ['raɪtfəlɪ] *ad* legittimamente.
right-handed [raɪt'hændɪd] *a* (*person*) che adopera la mano destra.
right-hand man ['raɪthænd-] *n* braccio destro (*fig*).
right-hand side *n* lato destro.
rightly ['raɪtlɪ] *ad* bene, correttamente; (*with reason*) a ragione; **if I remember** ~ se mi ricordo bene.
right-minded [raɪt'maɪndɪd] *a* sensato(a).
rights issue *n* (*STOCK EXCHANGE*) emissione *f* di azioni riservate agli azionisti.
right wing *n* (*MIL, SPORT*) ala destra; (*POL*) destra ♦ *a*: **right-wing** (*POL*) di destra.
right-winger [raɪt'wɪŋə*] *n* (*POL*) uno/a di destra; (*SPORT*) ala destra.
rigid ['rɪdʒɪd] *a* rigido(a); (*principle*) rigoroso(a).
rigidity [rɪ'dʒɪdɪtɪ] *n* rigidità.
rigidly ['rɪdʒɪdlɪ] *ad* rigidamente.
rigmarole ['rɪgmərəul] *n* tiritera; commedia.
rigor ['rɪgə*] *n* (*US*) = **rigour.**
rigor mortis ['rɪgə'mɔːtɪs] *n* rigidità cadaverica.
rigorous ['rɪgərəs] *a* rigoroso(a).
rigorously ['rɪgərəslɪ] *ad* rigorosamente.
rigour, (*US*) **rigor** ['rɪgə*] *n* rigore *m*.
rig-out ['rɪgaut] *n* (*Brit col*) tenuta.

rile [raɪl] *vt* irritare, seccare.

rim [rɪm] *n* orlo; (*of spectacles*) montatura; (*of wheel*) cerchione *m*.

rimless ['rɪmlɪs] *a* (*spectacles*) senza montatura.

rimmed [rɪmd] *a* bordato(a); cerchiato(a).

rind [raɪnd] *n* (*of bacon*) cotenna; (*of lemon etc*) scorza.

ring [rɪŋ] *n* anello; (*also*: **wedding** ~) fede *f*; (*of people, objects*) cerchio; (*of spies*) giro; (*of smoke etc*) spirale *m*; (*arena*) pista, arena; (*for boxing*) ring *m inv*; (*sound of bell*) scampanio; (*telephone call*) colpo di telefono ♦ *vb* (*pt* **rang**, *pp* **rung** [ræŋ, rʌŋ]) *vi* (*person, bell, telephone*) suonare; (*also*: ~ **out**: *voice, words*) risuonare; (*TEL*) telefonare ♦ *vt* (*Brit TEL*: *also*: ~ **up**) telefonare a; **to ~ the bell** suonare il campanello; **to give sb a ~** (*TEL*) dare un colpo di telefono a qn; **that has the ~ of truth about it** questo ha l'aria d'essere vero; **the name doesn't ~ a bell (with me)** questo nome non mi dice niente.

  ring back *vt, vi* (*Brit TEL*) richiamare.

  ring off *vi* (*Brit TEL*) mettere giù, riattaccare.

ring binder *n* classificatore *m* a anelli.

ring finger *n* anulare *m*.

ringing ['rɪŋɪŋ] *n* (*of bell*) scampanio; (: *louder*) scampanellata; (*of telephone*) squillo; (*in ears*) fischio, ronzio.

ringing tone *n* (*Brit TEL*) segnale *m* di libero.

ringleader ['rɪŋliːdə*] *n* (*of gang*) capobanda *m*.

ringlets ['rɪŋlɪts] *npl* boccoli *mpl*.

ring road *n* (*Brit*) raccordo anulare.

rink [rɪŋk] *n* (*also*: **ice** ~) pista di pattinaggio; (*for roller-skating*) pista di pattinaggio (a rotelle).

rinse [rɪns] *n* risciacquatura; (*hair tint*) cachet *m inv* ♦ *vt* sciacquare.

Rio (de Janeiro) ['riːəu(dədʒə'nɪərəu)] *n* Rio de Janeiro *f*.

riot ['raɪət] *n* sommossa, tumulto ♦ *vi* tumultuare; **a ~ of colours** un'orgia di colori; **to run ~** creare disordine.

rioter ['raɪətə*] *n* dimostrante *m/f* (*durante dei disordini*).

riotous ['raɪətəs] *a* tumultuoso(a); che fa crepare dal ridere.

riotously ['raɪətəslɪ] *ad*: ~ **funny** che fa crepare dal ridere.

riot police *n* ≈ la Celere.

RIP *abbr* (= *rest in peace*) R.I.P.

rip [rɪp] *n* strappo ♦ *vt* strappare ♦ *vi* strapparsi.

  rip up *vt* stracciare.

ripcord ['rɪpkɔːd] *n* cavo di spiegamento.

ripe [raɪp] *a* (*fruit*) maturo(a); (*cheese*) stagionato(a).

ripen ['raɪpən] *vt* maturare ♦ *vi* maturarsi; stagionarsi.

ripeness ['raɪpnɪs] *n* maturità.

rip-off ['rɪpɔf] *n* (*col*): **it's a ~!** è un furto!

riposte [rɪ'pɔst] *n* risposta per le rime.

ripple ['rɪpl] *n* increspamento, ondulazione *f*; mormorio ♦ *vi* incresparsi ♦ *vt* increspare.

rise [raɪz] *n* (*slope*) salita, pendio; (*hill*) altura; (*increase*: *in wages*) aumento; (: *in prices, temperature*) rialzo, aumento; (*fig*: *to power etc*) ascesa ♦ *vi* (*pt* **rose**, *pp* **risen** [rəuz, 'rɪzn]) alzarsi, levarsi; (*prices*) aumentare; (*waters, river*) crescere; (*sun, wind*) levarsi; (*also*: ~ **up**: *rebel*) insorgere; ribellarsi; **to give ~ to** provocare, dare origine a; **to ~ to the occasion** dimostrarsi all'altezza della situazione.

rising ['raɪzɪŋ] *a* (*increasing*: *number*) sempre crescente; (*prices*) in aumento; (*tide*) montante; (*sun, moon*) nascente, che sorge ♦ *n* (*uprising*) sommossa.

rising damp *n* infiltrazioni *fpl* d'umidità.

risk [rɪsk] *n* rischio ♦ *vt* rischiare; **to take** *or* **run the ~ of doing** correre il rischio di fare; **at ~** in pericolo; **at one's own ~** a proprio rischio e pericolo; **fire/health ~** rischio d'incendio/per la salute; **I'll ~ it** ci proverò lo stesso.

risk capital *n* capitale *m* di rischio.

risky ['rɪskɪ] *a* rischioso(a).

risqué ['riːskeɪ] *a* (*joke*) spinto(a).

rissole ['rɪsəul] *n* crocchetta.

rite [raɪt] *n* rito; **last ~s** l'estrema unzione.

ritual ['rɪtjuəl] *a, n* rituale (*m*).

rival ['raɪvl] *n* rivale *m/f*; (*in business*) concorrente *m/f* ♦ *a* rivale; che fa concorrenza ♦ *vt* essere in concorrenza con; **to ~ sb/sth in** competere con qn/qc in.

rivalry ['raɪvlrɪ] *n* rivalità; concorrenza.

river ['rɪvə*] *n* fiume *m* ♦ *cpd* (*port, traffic*) fluviale; **up/down ~** a monte/valle.

riverbank ['rɪvəbæŋk] *n* argine *m*.

riverbed ['rɪvəbed] *n* alveo (fluviale).

riverside ['rɪvəsaɪd] *n* sponda del fiume.

rivet ['rɪvɪt] *n* ribattino, rivetto ♦ *vt* ribadire; (*fig*) concentrare, fissare.

riveting ['rɪvɪtɪŋ] *a* (*fig*) avvincente.

Riviera [rɪvɪ'eərə] *n*: **the (French) ~** la Costa Azzurra; **the Italian ~** la Riviera.

Riyadh [rɪ'jɑːd] *n* Riad *f*.

RN *n abbr* (*Brit*) = **Royal Navy**; (*US*) = **registered nurse**.

RNA *n abbr* (= *ribonucleic acid*) R.N.A. *m*.

RNLI *n abbr* (*Brit*: = *Royal National Lifeboat Institution*) associazione volontaria che organizza e dispone di scialuppe di salvataggio.

RNZAF *n abbr* = *Royal New Zealand Air Force*.

RNZN *n abbr* = *Royal New Zealand Navy*.

road [rəud] *n* strada; (*small*) cammino; (*in town*) via; **main ~** strada principale; **major/minor ~** strada con/senza diritto di precedenza; **it takes 4 hours by ~** sono 4 ore di macchina (*or* in camion *etc*); **on the ~ to success** sulla via del successo; **"~ up"** (*Brit*) "attenzione: lavori in corso".

roadblock ['rəudblɔk] *n* blocco stradale.

road haulage n autotrasporti mpl.
roadhog ['rəudhɔg] n pirata m della strada.
road map n carta stradale.
road safety n sicurezza sulle strade.
roadside ['rəudsaɪd] n margine m della strada; **by the** ~ a lato della strada.
roadsign ['rəudsaɪn] n cartello stradale.
roadsweeper ['rəudswiːpə*] n (Brit: person) spazzino.
road transport n autotrasporti mpl.
road user n utente m/f della strada.
roadway ['rəudweɪ] n carreggiata.
roadworks ['rəudwə:ks] npl lavori mpl stradali.
roadworthy ['rəudwə:ðɪ] a in buono stato di marcia.
roam [rəum] vi errare, vagabondare ♦ vt vagare per.
roar [rɔ:*] n ruggito; (of crowd) tumulto; (of thunder, storm) muggito ♦ vi ruggire; tumultuare; muggire; **to** ~ **with laughter** scoppiare dalle risa.
roaring ['rɔ:rɪŋ] a: **a** ~ **fire** un bel fuoco; **to do a** ~ **trade** fare affari d'oro; **a** ~ **success** un successo strepitoso.
roast [rəust] n arrosto ♦ vt (meat) arrostire.
roast beef n arrosto di manzo.
rob [rɔb] vt (person) rubare; (bank) svaligiare; **to** ~ **sb of sth** derubare qn di qc; (fig: deprive) privare qn di qc.
robber ['rɔbə*] n ladro; (armed) rapinatore m.
robbery ['rɔbərɪ] n furto; rapina.
robe [rəub] n (for ceremony etc) abito; (also: **bath**~) accappatoio ♦ vt vestire.
robin ['rɔbɪn] n pettirosso.
robot ['rəubɔt] n robot m inv.
robotics ['rəubɔtɪks] n robotica.
robust [rəu'bʌst] a robusto(a); (material) solido(a).
rock [rɔk] n (substance) roccia; (boulder) masso; roccia; (in sea) scoglio; (Brit: sweet) zucchero candito ♦ vt (swing gently: cradle) dondolare; (: child) cullare; (shake) scrollare, far tremare ♦ vi dondolarsi; oscillare; **on the** ~**s** (drink) col ghiaccio; (ship) sugli scogli; (marriage etc) in crisi; **to** ~ **the boat** (fig) piantare grane.
rock and roll n rock and roll m.
rock-bottom ['rɔk'bɔtəm] n (fig) stremo; **to reach** or **touch** ~ (price) raggiungere il livello più basso; (person) toccare il fondo.
rock climber n rocciatore/trice, scalatore/trice.
rock climbing n roccia.
rockery ['rɔkərɪ] n giardino roccioso.
rocket ['rɔkɪt] n razzo; (MIL) razzo, missile m ♦ vi (prices) salire alle stelle.
rocket launcher n lanciarazzi m inv.
rock face n parete f della roccia.
rock fall n caduta di massi.
rocking chair ['rɔkɪŋ-] n sedia a dondolo.
rocking horse n cavallo a dondolo.
rocky ['rɔkɪ] a (hill) roccioso(a); (path) sassoso(a); (unsteady: table) traballante.
Rocky Mountains npl: **the** ~ le Montagne Rocciose.
rod [rɔd] n (metallic, TECH) asta; (wooden) bacchetta; (also: **fishing** ~) canna da pesca.
rode [rəud] pt of **ride**.
rodent ['rəudnt] n roditore m.
rodeo ['rəudɪəu] n rodeo.
roe [rəu] n (species: also: ~ **deer**) capriolo; (of fish: also: **hard** ~) uova fpl di pesce; **soft** ~ latte m di pesce.
roe deer n (species) capriolo; (female deer: pl inv) capriolo femmina.
rogue [rəug] n mascalzone m.
roguish ['rəugɪʃ] a birbantesco(a).
role [rəul] n ruolo.
roll [rəul] n rotolo; (of banknotes) mazzo; (also: **bread** ~) panino; (register) lista; (sound: of drums etc) rullo; (movement: of ship) rullio ♦ vt rotolare; (also: ~ **up:** string) aggomitolare; (also: ~ **out:** pastry) stendere ♦ vi rotolare; (wheel) girare; **cheese** ~ panino al formaggio.
roll about, roll around vi rotolare qua e là; (person) rotolarsi.
roll by vi (time) passare.
roll in vi (mail, cash) arrivare a bizzeffe.
roll over vi rivoltarsi.
roll up vi (col: arrive) arrivare ♦ vt (carpet, cloth, map) arrotolare; (sleeves) rimboccare; **to** ~ **o.s. up into a ball** raggomitolarsi.
roll call n appello.
rolled gold [rəuld-] a d'oro laminato.
roller ['rəulə*] n rullo; (wheel) rotella.
roller blind n (Brit) avvolgibile m.
roller coaster n montagne fpl russe.
roller skates npl pattini mpl a rotelle.
rollicking ['rɔlɪkɪŋ] a allegro(a) e chiassoso(a); **to have a** ~ **time** divertirsi pazzamente.
rolling ['rəulɪŋ] a (landscape) ondulato(a).
rolling mill n fabbrica di laminati.
rolling pin n matterello.
rolling stock n (RAIL) materiale m rotabile.
roll-on-roll-off ['rəulɔn'rəulɔf] a (Brit: ferry) roll-on roll-off inv.
roly-poly ['rəulɪ'pəulɪ] n (Brit CULIN) rotolo di pasta con ripieno di marmellata.
ROM [rɔm] n abbr (COMPUT: = read-only memory) ROM f.
Roman ['rəumən] a, n romano(a).
Roman Catholic a, n cattolico(a).
romance [rə'mæns] n storia (or avventura or film m inv) romantico(a); (charm) poesia; (love affair) idillio.
Romanesque [rəumə'nɛsk] a romanico(a).
Romania [rəu'meɪnɪə] n Romania.
Romanian [rəu'meɪnɪən] a romeno(a) ♦ n romeno/a; (LING) romeno.
Roman numeral n numero romano.
romantic [rə'mæntɪk] a romantico(a); sentimentale.
romanticism [rə'mæntɪsɪzəm] n romanticismo.

Romany ['rɒmənı] *a* zingaresco(a) ♦ *n* (*person*) zingaro/a; (*LING*) lingua degli zingari.

Rome [rəum] *n* Roma.

romp [rɒmp] *n* gioco chiassoso ♦ *vi* (*also*: ~ **about**) giocare chiassosamente; **to ~ home** (*horse*) vincere senza difficoltà, stravincere.

rompers ['rɒmpəz] *npl* pagliaccetto.

rondo ['rɒndəu] *n* (*MUS*) rondò *m inv.*

roof [ru:f] *n* tetto; (*of tunnel, cave*) volta ♦ *vt* coprire (con un tetto); ~ **of the mouth** palato.

roof garden *n* giardino pensile.

roofing ['ru:fıŋ] *n* materiale *m* per copertura.

roof rack *n* (*AUT*) portabagagli *m inv.*

rook [ruk] *n* (*bird*) corvo nero; (*CHESS*) torre *f* ♦ *vt* (*cheat*) truffare, spennare.

room [ru:m] *n* (*in house*) stanza, camera; (*in school etc*) sala; (*space*) posto, spazio; ~**s** *npl* (*lodging*) alloggio; "~**s to let**", (*US*) "~**s for rent**" "si affittano camere"; **is there ~ for this?** c'è spazio per questo?, ci sta anche questo?; **to make ~ for sb** far posto a qn; **there is ~ for improvement** si potrebbe migliorare.

rooming house ['ru:mıŋ-] *n* (*US*) casa in cui si affittano camere o appartamentini ammobiliati.

roommate ['ru:mmeɪt] *n* compagno/a di stanza.

room service *n* servizio da camera.

room temperature *n* temperatura ambiente.

roomy ['ru:mı] *a* spazioso(a); (*garment*) ampio(a).

roost [ru:st] *n* appollaiato ♦ *vi* appollaiarsi.

rooster ['ru:stə*] *n* gallo.

root [ru:t] *n* radice *f* ♦ *vt* (*plant, belief*) far radicare; **to take ~** (*plant*) attecchire, prendere; (*idea*) far presa; **the ~ of the problem is that** ... il problema deriva dal fatto che ....

 root about *vi* (*fig*) frugare.

 root for *vt fus* (*col*) fare il tifo per.

 root out *vt* estirpare.

rope [rəup] *n* corda, fune *f*; (*NAUT*) cavo ♦ *vt* (*box*) legare; (*climbers*) legare in cordata; **to ~ sb in** (*fig*) coinvolgere qn; **to know the ~s** (*fig*) conoscere i trucchi del mestiere.

rope ladder *n* scala di corda.

rosary ['rəuzərı] *n* rosario; roseto.

rose [rəuz] *pt of* **rise** ♦ *n* rosa; (*also*: ~ **bush** rosaio; (*on watering can*) rosetta ♦ *a* rosa *inv.*

rosé ['rəuzeı] *n* vino rosato.

rosebed ['rəuzbed] *n* roseto.

rosebud ['rəuzbʌd] *n* bocciolo di rosa.

rosebush ['rəuzbuʃ] *n* rosaio.

rosemary ['rəuzmərı] *n* rosmarino.

rosette [rəu'zɛt] *n* coccarda.

ROSPA ['rɒspə] *n abbr* (*Brit*: = *Royal Society for the Prevention of Accidents*) ≈ E.N.P.I. *m* (= *Ente Nazionale Prevenzione Infortuni*).

roster ['rɒstə*] *n*: **duty ~** ruolino di servizio.

rostrum ['rɒstrəm] *n* tribuna.

rosy ['rəuzı] *a* roseo(a).

rot [rɒt] *n* (*decay*) putrefazione *f*; (*col: nonsense*) stupidaggini *fpl* ♦ *vt, vi* imputridire, marcire; **dry/wet ~** funghi parassiti del legno; **to stop the ~** (*Brit fig*) salvare la situazione.

rota ['rəutə] *n* tabella dei turni; **on a ~ basis** a turno.

rotary ['rəutərı] *a* rotante.

rotate [rəu'teıt] *vt* (*revolve*) far girare; (*change round: crops*) avvicendare; (: *jobs*) fare a turno ♦ *vi* (*revolve*) girare.

rotating [rəu'teıtıŋ] *a* (*movement*) rotante.

rotation [rəu'teıʃən] *n* rotazione *f*; **in ~** a turno, in rotazione.

rote [rəut] *n*: **to learn sth by ~** imparare qc a memoria.

rotor ['rəutə*] *n* rotore *m.*

rotten ['rɒtn] *a* (*decayed*) putrido(a), marcio(a); (: *teeth*) cariato(a); (*dishonest*) corrotto(a); (*col: bad*) brutto(a); (: *action*) vigliacco(a); **to feel ~** (*ill*) sentirsi proprio male.

rotting ['rɒtıŋ] *a* in putrefazione.

rotund [rəu'tʌnd] *a* grassoccio(a); tondo(a).

rouble, (*US*) **ruble** ['ru:bl] *n* rublo.

rouge [ru:ʒ] *n* belletto.

rough [rʌf] *a* aspro(a); (*person, manner: coarse*) rozzo(a), aspro(a); (: *violent*) brutale; (*district*) malfamato(a); (*weather*) cattivo(a); (*plan*) abbozzato(a); (*guess*) approssimativo(a) ♦ *n* (*GOLF*) macchia; ~ **estimate** approssimazione *f*; **to ~ it** far vita dura; **to play ~** far il gioco pesante; **to sleep ~** (*Brit*) dormire all'addiaccio; **to feel ~** (*Brit*) sentirsi male; **to have a ~ time (of it)** passare un periodaccio; **the sea is ~ today** c'è mare grosso oggi.

 rough out *vt* (*draft*) abbozzare.

roughage ['rʌfıdʒ] *n* alimenti *mpl* ricchi di cellulosa.

rough-and-ready ['rʌfən'rɛdı] *a* rudimentale.

rough-and-tumble ['rʌfən'tʌmbl] *n* zuffa.

roughcast ['rʌfkɑ:st] *n* intonaco grezzo.

rough copy, rough draft *n* brutta copia.

roughen ['rʌfn] *vt* (*a surface*) rendere ruvido(a).

rough justice *n* giustizia sommaria.

roughly ['rʌflı] *ad* (*handle*) rudemente, brutalmente; (*make*) grossolanamente; (*approximately*) approssimativamente; ~ **speaking** grosso modo, ad occhio e croce.

roughness ['rʌfnıs] *n* asprezza; rozzezza; brutalità.

roughshod ['rʌfʃɔd] *ad*: **to ride ~ over** (*person*) mettere sotto i piedi; (*objection*) passare sopra a.

rough work *n* (*at school etc*) brutta copia.

roulette [ru:'lɛt] *n* roulette *f.*

Roumania *etc* [ru:'meınıə] = **Romania** *etc.*

round [raund] *a* rotondo(a) ♦ *n* tondo, cerchio; (*Brit: of toast*) fetta; (*duty: of policeman, milkman etc*) giro; (: *of doctor*) visite *fpl*; (*game: of cards, in competition*) partita;

(*BOXING*) round *m inv*; (*of talks*) serie *f inv* ♦ *vt* (*corner*) girare; (*bend*) prendere; (*cape*) doppiare ♦ *prep* intorno a ♦ *ad*: **right ~, all** ~ tutt'attorno; **the long way** ~ il giro più lungo; **all the year** ~ tutto l'anno; **in** ~ **figures** in cifra tonda; **it's just** ~ **the corner** (*also fig*) è dietro l'angolo; **to ask sb** ~ invitare qn (a casa propria); **I'll be** ~ **at 6 o'clock** ci sarò alle 6; **to go** ~ fare il giro; **to go** ~ **to sb's (house)** andare da qn; **to go** ~ **an obstacle** aggirare un ostacolo; **go** ~ **the back** passi da dietro; **to go** ~ **a house** visitare una casa; **enough to go** ~ abbastanza per tutti; **she arrived** ~ (**about**) **noon** è arrivata intorno a mezzogiorno; ~ **the clock** 24 ore su 24; **to go the ~s** (*illness*) diffondersi; (*story*) circolare, passare di bocca in bocca; **the daily** ~ (*fig*) la routine quotidiana; ~ **of ammunition** cartuccia; ~ **of applause** applausi *mpl*; ~ **of drinks** giro di bibite; ~ **of sandwiches** (*Brit*) sandwich *m inv*.

round off *vt* (*speech etc*) finire.

round up *vt* radunare; (*criminals*) fare una retata di; (*prices*) arrotondare.

roundabout ['raundəbaut] *n* (*Brit AUT*) rotatoria; (*at fair*) giostra ♦ *a* (*route, means*) indiretto(a).

rounded ['raundɪd] *a* arrotondato(a); (*style*) armonioso(a).

rounders ['raundəz] *npl* (*game*) gioco simile al baseball.

roundly ['raundlɪ] *ad* (*fig*) chiaro e tondo.

round-shouldered [raund'ʃəuldəd] *a* dalle spalle tonde.

roundsman ['raundzmən] *n* (*Brit*) fattorino.

round trip *n* (viaggio di) andata e ritorno.

roundup ['raundʌp] *n* raduno; (*of criminals*) retata; **a** ~ **of the latest news** un sommario *or* riepilogo delle ultime notizie.

rouse [rauz] *vt* (*wake up*) svegliare; (*stir up*) destare; provocare; risvegliare.

rousing ['rauzɪŋ] *a* (*speech, applause*) entusiastico(a).

rout [raut] *n* (*MIL*) rotta ♦ *vt* mettere in rotta.

route [ruːt] *n* itinerario; (*of bus*) percorso; (*of trade, shipping*) rotta; **"all ~s"** (*AUT*) "tutte le direzioni"; **the best** ~ **to London** la strada migliore per andare a Londra; **en** ~ **for** in viaggio verso; **en** ~ **from ... to** viaggiando da ... a.

route map *n* (*Brit: for journey*) cartina di itinerario; (*for trains etc*) pianta dei collegamenti.

routine [ruː'tiːn] *a* (*work*) corrente, abituale; (*procedure*) solito(a) ♦ *n* (*pej*) routine *f*, tran tran *m*; (*THEATRE*) numero; (*COMPUT*) sottoprogramma *m*; **daily** ~ orario quotidiano; ~ **procedure** prassi *f*.

roving ['rəuvɪŋ] *a* (*life*) itinerante.

roving reporter *n* reporter *m inv* volante.

row [rəu] *n* (*line*) riga, fila; (*KNITTING*) ferro; (*behind one another: of cars, people*) fila; [rau] (*noise*) baccano, chiasso; (*dispute*) lite *f*

♦ *vi* (*in boat*) remare; (*as sport*) vogare; [rau] litigare ♦ *vt* (*boat*) manovrare a remi; **in a** ~ (*fig*) di fila; **to make a** ~ far baccano; **to have a** ~ litigare.

rowboat ['rəubəut] *n* (*US*) barca a remi.

rowdiness ['raudɪnɪs] *n* baccano; (*fighting*) zuffa.

rowdy ['raudɪ] *a* chiassoso(a); turbolento(a) ♦ *n* teppista *m/f*.

rowdyism ['raudɪɪzəm] *n* teppismo.

rowing ['rəuɪŋ] *n* canottaggio.

rowing boat *n* (*Brit*) barca a remi.

rowlock ['rɔlək] *n* scalmo.

royal ['rɔɪəl] *a* reale.

Royal Air Force (RAF) *n* (*Brit*) aeronautica militare britannica.

royal blue *a* blu reale *inv*.

royalist ['rɔɪəlɪst] *a, n* realista (*m/f*).

Royal Navy (RN) *n* (*Brit*) marina militare britannica.

royalty ['rɔɪəltɪ] *n* (*royal persons*) (membri *mpl* della) famiglia reale; (*payment: to author*) diritti *mpl* d'autore; (: *to inventor*) diritti di brevetto.

RP *n abbr* (*Brit*: = *received pronunciation*) pronuncia standard.

RPM *abbr* = **resale price maintenance.**

rpm *abbr* (= *revolutions per minute*) giri/min.

RR *abbr* (*US* = *railroad*) Ferr.

R&R *n abbr* (*US MIL*: = *rest and recreation*) permesso per militari.

RRP *n abbr* (*Brit*) *see* **recommended retail price.**

RSA *n abbr* (*Brit*) = *Royal Society of Arts*; *Royal Scottish Academy*.

RSPB *n abbr* (*Brit*: = *Royal Society for the Protection of Birds*) ≈ L.I.P.U. *f* (= *Lega Italiana Protezione Uccelli*).

RSPCA *n abbr* (*Brit*: = *Royal Society for the Prevention of Cruelty to Animals*) ≈ E.N.P.A. *m* (= *Ente Nazionale per la Protezione degli Animali*).

RSVP *abbr* (= *répondez s'il vous plaît*) R.S.V.P.

Rt Hon. *abbr* (*Brit*: = *Right Honourable*) ≈ On. (= *Onorevole*).

Rt Rev. *abbr* (= *Right Reverend*) Rev.

rub [rʌb] *n* (*with cloth*) fregata, strofinata; (*on person*) frizione *f*, massaggio ♦ *vt* fregare, strofinare; frizionare; **to** ~ **sb up** *or* (*US*) ~ **sb the wrong way** lisciare qn contro pelo.

rub down *vt* (*body*) strofinare, frizionare; (*horse*) strigliare.

rub in *vt* (*ointment*) far penetrare (massaggiando *or* frizionando).

rub off *vi* andare via; **to** ~ **off on** lasciare una traccia su.

rub out *vt* cancellare ♦ *vi* cancellarsi.

rubber ['rʌbə*] *n* gomma.

rubber band *n* elastico.

rubber plant *n* ficus *m inv*.

rubber ring *n* (*for swimming*) ciambella.

rubber stamp *n* timbro di gomma.

rubber-stamp [rʌbə'stæmp] *vt* (*fig*) approvare

senza discussione.

rubbery ['rʌbərɪ] *a* gommoso(a).

rubbish ['rʌbɪʃ] *n* (*from household*) immondizie *fpl*, rifiuti *mpl*; (*fig: pej*) cose *fpl* senza valore; robaccia; (*nonsense*) sciocchezze *fpl* ♦ *vt* (*col*) sputtanare; **what you've just said is** ~ quello che ha appena detto è una sciocchezza.

rubbish bin *n* (*Brit*) pattumiera.

rubbish dump *n* luogo di scarico.

rubbishy ['rʌbɪʃɪ] *a* (*Brit col*) scadente, che non vale niente.

rubble ['rʌbl] *n* macerie *fpl*; (*smaller*) pietrisco.

ruble ['ruːbl] *n* (*US*) = **rouble**.

ruby ['ruːbɪ] *n* rubino.

RUC *n abbr* (*Brit*: = *Royal Ulster Constabulary*) forza di polizia dell'Irlanda del Nord.

rucksack ['rʌksæk] *n* zaino.

ructions ['rʌkʃənz] *npl* putiferio, finimondo.

rudder ['rʌdə*] *n* timone *m*.

ruddy ['rʌdɪ] *a* (*face*) fresco(a); (*col: damned*) maledetto(a).

rude [ruːd] *a* (*impolite: person*) scortese, rozzo(a); (: *word, manners*) grossolano(a), rozzo(a); (*shocking*) indecente; **to be ~ to sb** essere maleducato con qn.

rudely ['ruːdlɪ] *ad* scortesemente, grossolanamente.

rudeness ['ruːdnɪs] *n* scortesia; grossolanità.

rudiment ['ruːdɪmənt] *n* rudimento.

rudimentary [ruːdɪ'mɛntərɪ] *a* rudimentale.

rueful ['ruːful] *a* mesto(a), triste.

ruff [rʌf] *n* gorgiera.

ruffian ['rʌfɪən] *n* briccone *m*, furfante *m*.

ruffle ['rʌfl] *vt* (*hair*) scompigliare; (*clothes, water*) increspare; (*fig: person*) turbare.

rug [rʌg] *n* tappeto; (*Brit: for knees*) coperta.

rugby ['rʌgbɪ] *n* (*also*: ~ **football**) rugby *m*.

rugged ['rʌgɪd] *a* (*landscape*) aspro(a); (*features, determination*) duro(a); (*character*) brusco(a).

rugger ['rʌgə*] *n* (*col*) rugby *m*.

ruin ['ruːɪn] *n* rovina ♦ *vt* rovinare; (*spoil: clothes*) sciupare; ~**s** *npl* rovine *fpl*, ruderi *mpl*; **in** ~**s** in rovina.

ruination [ruːɪ'neɪʃən] *n* rovina.

ruinous ['ruːɪnəs] *a* rovinoso(a); (*expenditure*) inverosimile.

rule [ruːl] *n* (*gen*) regola; (*regulation*) regolamento, regola; (*government*) governo; (*dominion etc*): **under British** ~ sotto la sovranità britannica ♦ *vt* (*country*) governare; (*person*) dominare; (*decide*) decidere ♦ *vi* regnare; decidere; (*LAW*) dichiarare; **to** ~ **against/in favour of/on** (*LAW*) pronunciarsi a sfavore di/in favore di/su; **it's against the** ~**s** è contro le regole *or* il regolamento; **by** ~ **of thumb** a lume di naso; **as a** ~ normalmente, di regola.

rule out *vt* escludere; **murder cannot be** ~**d out** non si esclude che si tratti di omicidio.

ruled [ruːld] *a* (*paper*) vergato(a).

ruler ['ruːlə*] *n* (*sovereign*) sovrano/a; (*leader*) capo (dello Stato); (*for measuring*) regolo, riga.

ruling ['ruːlɪŋ] *a* (*party*) al potere; (*class*) dirigente ♦ *n* (*LAW*) decisione *f*.

rum [rʌm] *n* rum *m* ♦ *a* (*Brit col*) strano(a).

Rumania *etc* [ruː'meɪnɪə] = **Romania** *etc*.

rumble ['rʌmbl] *n* rimbombo; brontolio ♦ *vi* rimbombare; (*stomach, pipe*) brontolare.

rumbustious [rʌm'bʌstʃəs] *a* (*person*): **to be** ~ essere un terremoto.

rummage ['rʌmɪdʒ] *vi* frugare.

rumour, (*US*) **rumor** ['ruːmə*] *n* voce *f* ♦ *vt*: **it is** ~**ed that** corre voce che.

rump [rʌmp] *n* (*of animal*) groppa.

rumple ['rʌmpl] *vt* (*hair*) arruffare, scompigliare; (*clothes*) spiegazzare, sgualcire.

rump steak *n* bistecca di girello.

rumpus ['rʌmpəs] *n* (*col*) baccano; (: *quarrel*) rissa; **to kick up a** ~ fare un putiferio.

run [rʌn] *n* corsa; (*outing*) gita (in macchina); (*distance travelled*) percorso, tragitto; (*series*) serie *f inv*; (*THEATRE*) periodo di rappresentazione; (*SKI*) pista ♦ *vb* (*pt* **ran**, *pp* **run** [ræn, rʌn]) *vt* (*operate: business*) gestire, dirigere; (: *competition, course*) organizzare; (: *hotel*) gestire; (: *house*) governare; (*COMPUT: program*) eseguire; (*water, bath*) far scorrere; (*force through: rope, pipe*): **to** ~ **sth through** far passare qc attraverso; (*to pass: hand, finger*): **to** ~ **sth over** passare qc su ♦ *vi* correre; (*pass: road etc*) passare; (*work: machine, factory*) funzionare, andare; (*bus, train: operate*) far servizio; (: *travel*) circolare; (*continue: play, contract*) durare; (*slide: drawer; flow: river, bath*) scorrere; (*colours, washing*) stemperarsi; (*in election*) presentarsi come candidato; **to go for a** ~ andare a correre; (*in car*) fare un giro (in macchina); **to break into a** ~ mettersi a correre; **a** ~ **of luck** un periodo di fortuna; **to have the** ~ **of sb's house** essere libero di andare e venire in casa di qn; **there was a** ~ **on ...** c'era una corsa a ...; **in the long** ~ alla lunga; in fin dei conti; **in the short** ~ sulle prime; **on the** ~ in fuga; **to make a** ~ **for it** scappare, tagliare la corda; **I'll** ~ **you to the station** la porto alla stazione; **to** ~ **a risk** correre un rischio; **to** ~ **errands** andare a fare commissioni; **the train** ~**s between Gatwick and Victoria** il treno collega Gatwick alla stazione Victoria; **the bus** ~**s every 20 minutes** c'è un autobus ogni 20 minuti; **it's very cheap to** ~ comporta poche spese; **to** ~ **on petrol** *or* (*US*) **gas/on diesel/off batteries** andare a benzina/a diesel/a batterie; **to** ~ **for the bus** fare una corsa per prendere l'autobus; **to** ~ **for president** presentarsi come candidato per la presidenza; **their losses ran into millions** le loro perdite hanno raggiunto i milioni; **to be** ~ **off one's feet** (*Brit*) doversi fare in quattro.

run about vi (children) correre qua e là.

run across vt fus (find) trovare per caso.

run away vi fuggire.

run down vi (clock) scaricarsi ♦ vt (AUT) investire; (criticize) criticare; (Brit: reduce: production) ridurre gradualmente; (: factory, shop) rallentare l'attività di; **to be ~ down** (battery) essere scarico(a); (person) essere giù (di corda).

run in vt (Brit: car) rodare, fare il rodaggio di.

run into vt fus (meet: person) incontrare per caso; (: trouble) incontrare, trovare; (collide with) andare a sbattere contro; **to ~ into debt** trovarsi nei debiti.

run off vi fuggire ♦ vt (water) far defluire; (copies) fare.

run out vi (person) uscire di corsa; (liquid) colare; (lease) scadere; (money) esaurirsi.

run out of vt fus rimanere a corto di; **I've ~ out of petrol** or (US) **gas** sono rimasto senza benzina.

run over vt (AUT) investire, mettere sotto ♦ vt fus (revise) rivedere.

run through vt fus (instructions) dare una scorsa a.

run up vt (debt) lasciar accumulare; **to ~ up against** (difficulties) incontrare.

runaway ['rʌnəweɪ] a (person) fuggiasco(a); (horse) in libertà; (truck) fuori controllo; (inflation) galoppante.

rundown ['rʌndaun] n (Brit: of industry etc) riduzione f graduale dell'attività di.

rung [rʌŋ] pp of **ring** ♦ n (of ladder) piolo.

run-in ['rʌnɪn] n (col) scontro.

runner ['rʌnə*] n (in race) corridore m; (on sledge) pattino; (for drawer etc, carpet) guida.

runner bean n (Brit) fagiolino.

runner-up [rʌnər'ʌp] n secondo(a) arrivato(a).

running ['rʌnɪŋ] n corsa; direzione f; organizzazione f; funzionamento ♦ a (water) corrente; (commentary) simultaneo(a); **6 days ~** 6 giorni di seguito; **to be in/out of the ~ for sth** essere/non essere più in lizza per qc.

running costs npl (of business) costi mpl d'esercizio; (of car) spese fpl di mantenimento.

running head n (TYP, WORD PROCESSING) testata, titolo corrente.

running mate n (US POL) candidato alla vicepresidenza.

runny ['rʌnɪ] a che cola.

run-off ['rʌnɔf] n (in contest, election) confronto definitivo; (extra race) spareggio.

run-of-the-mill ['rʌnəvðə'mɪl] a solito(a), banale.

runt [rʌnt] n (also pej) omuncolo; (ZOOL) animale m più piccolo del normale.

run-through ['rʌnθru:] n prova.

run-up ['rʌnʌp] n (Brit): **~ to sth** periodo che precede qc.

runway ['rʌnweɪ] n (AVIAT) pista (di decollo).

rupee [ru:'pi:] n rupia.

rupture ['rʌptʃə*] n (MED) ernia ♦ vt: **to ~ o.s.** farsi venire un'ernia.

rural ['ruərl] a rurale.

rural district council (RDC) n (Brit) consiglio (amministrativo) di distretto rurale.

ruse [ru:z] n trucco.

rush [rʌʃ] n corsa precipitosa; (of crowd) afflusso; (hurry) furia, fretta; (current) flusso; (BOT) giunco ♦ vt mandare or spedire velocemente; (attack: town etc) prendere d'assalto ♦ vi precipitarsi; **is there any ~ for this?** è urgente?; **we've had a ~ of orders** abbiamo avuto una valanga di ordinazioni; **I'm in a ~ (to do)** ho fretta or premura (di fare); **gold ~** corsa all'oro; **to ~ sth off** spedire con urgenza qc; **don't ~ me!** non farmi fretta!

rush through vt (meal) mangiare in fretta; (book) dare una scorsa frettolosa a; (town) attraversare in fretta; (COMM: order) eseguire d'urgenza ♦ vt fus (work) sbrigare frettolosamente.

rush hour n ora di punta.

rush job n (urgent) lavoro urgente.

rush matting n stuoia.

rusk [rʌsk] n fetta biscottata.

Russia ['rʌʃə] n Russia.

Russian ['rʌʃən] a russo(a) ♦ n russo/a; (LING) russo.

rust [rʌst] n ruggine f ♦ vi arrugginirsi.

rustic ['rʌstɪk] a rustico(a) ♦ n (pej) cafone/a.

rustle ['rʌsl] vi frusciare ♦ vt (paper) far frusciare; (US: cattle) rubare.

rustproof ['rʌstpru:f] a inossidabile.

rustproofing ['rʌstpru:fɪŋ] n trattamento antiruggine.

rusty ['rʌstɪ] a arrugginito(a).

rut [rʌt] n solco; (ZOOL) fregola; **to be in a ~** (fig) essersi fossilizzato(a).

rutabaga [ru:tə'beɪgə] n (US) rapa svedese.

ruthless ['ru:θlɪs] a spietato(a).

ruthlessness ['ru:θlɪsnɪs] n spietatezza.

RV abbr (= revised version) versione riveduta della Bibbia Anglicana ♦ n abbr (US) see **recreational vehicle**.

rye [raɪ] n segale f.

rye bread n pane m di segale.

S

S, s [ɛs] n (letter) S, s f or m inv; (US SCOL: = satisfactory) ≈ sufficiente; **S for Sugar** ≈ S come Savona.

S abbr (= saint) S.; (= south) S; (on clothes) = small.

SA *abbr* = **South Africa; South America.**
Sabbath ['sæbəθ] *n* (*Jewish*) sabato; (*Christian*) domenica.
sabbatical [sə'bætɪkl] *a*: ~ **year** anno sabbatico.
sabotage ['sæbətɑ:ʒ] *n* sabotaggio ♦ *vt* sabotare.
saccharin(e) ['sækərɪn] *n* saccarina.
sachet ['sæʃeɪ] *n* bustina.
sack [sæk] *n* (*bag*) sacco ♦ *vt* (*dismiss*) licenziare, mandare a spasso; (*plunder*) saccheggiare; **to get the** ~ essere mandato a spasso; **to give sb the** ~ licenziare qn, mandare qn a spasso.
sackful ['sækful] *n*: **a** ~ **of** un sacco di.
sacking ['sækɪŋ] *n* tela di sacco; (*dismissal*) licenziamento.
sacrament ['sækrəmənt] *n* sacramento.
sacred ['seɪkrɪd] *a* sacro(a).
sacrifice ['sækrɪfaɪs] *n* sacrificio ♦ *vt* sacrificare; **to make** ~**s** (**for sb**) fare (dei) sacrifici (per qn).
sacrilege ['sækrɪlɪdʒ] *n* sacrilegio.
sacrosanct ['sækrəusæŋkt] *a* sacrosanto(a).
sad [sæd] *a* triste; (*deplorable*) deplorevole.
sadden ['sædn] *vt* rattristare.
saddle ['sædl] *n* sella ♦ *vt* (*horse*) sellare; **to be** ~**d with sth** (*col*) avere qc sulle spalle.
saddlebag ['sædlbæg] *n* bisaccia; (*on bicycle*) borsa.
sadism ['seɪdɪzəm] *n* sadismo.
sadist ['seɪdɪst] *n* sadico/a.
sadistic [sə'dɪstɪk] *a* sadico(a).
sadly ['sædlɪ] *ad* tristemente; (*regrettably*) sfortunatamente; ~ **lacking in** penosamente privo di.
sadness ['sædnɪs] *n* tristezza.
sae *abbr* (*Brit*) = **stamped addressed envelope;** *see* **stamp.**
safari [sə'fɑ:rɪ] *n* safari *m inv*.
safari park *n* zoosafari *m inv*.
safe [seɪf] *a* sicuro(a); (*out of danger*) salvo(a), al sicuro; (*cautious*) prudente ♦ *n* cassaforte *f*; ~ **from** al sicuro da; ~ **and sound** sano(a) e salvo(a); ~ **journey!** buon viaggio!; **(just) to be on the** ~ **side** per non correre rischi; **to play** ~ giocare sul sicuro; **it is** ~ **to say that** ... si può affermare con sicurezza che ....
safe-breaker ['seɪfbreɪkə*] *n* (*Brit*) scassinatore *m*.
safe-conduct [seɪf'kɔndʌkt] *n* salvacondotto.
safe-cracker ['seɪfkrækə*] *n* = **safe-breaker.**
safe-deposit ['seɪfdɪpɔzɪt] *n* (*vault*) caveau *m inv*; (*box*) cassetta di sicurezza.
safeguard ['seɪfgɑ:d] *n* salvaguardia ♦ *vt* salvaguardare.
safekeeping ['seɪf'ki:pɪŋ] *n* custodia.
safely ['seɪflɪ] *ad* sicuramente; sano(a) e salvo(a); prudentemente; **I can** ~ **say** ... posso tranquillamente asserire ....
safety ['seɪftɪ] *n* sicurezza; ~ **first!** la prudenza innanzitutto!
safety belt *n* cintura di sicurezza.

safety curtain *n* telone *m*.
safety net *n* rete *f* di protezione.
safety pin *n* spilla di sicurezza.
safety valve *n* valvola di sicurezza.
saffron ['sæfrən] *n* zafferano.
sag [sæg] *vi* incurvarsi; afflosciarsi.
saga ['sɑ:gə] *n* saga; (*fig*) odissea.
sage [seɪdʒ] *n* (*herb*) salvia; (*man*) saggio.
Sagittarius [sædʒɪ'tɛərɪəs] *n* Sagittario; **to be** ~ essere del Sagittario.
sago ['seɪgəu] *n* sagù *m*.
Sahara [sə'hɑ:rə] *n*: **the** ~ **Desert** il Deserto del Sahara.
Sahel [sæ'hɛl] *n* Sahel *m*.
said [sɛd] *pt, pp of* **say.**
Saigon [saɪ'gɔn] *n* Saigon *f*.
sail [seɪl] *n* (*on boat*) vela; (*trip*): **to go for a** ~ fare un giro in barca a vela ♦ *vt* (*boat*) condurre, governare ♦ *vi* (*travel: ship*) navigare; (*: passenger*) viaggiare per mare; (*set off*) salpare; (*SPORT*) fare della vela; **they** ~**ed into Genoa** entrarono nel porto di Genova.
sail through *vt fus* (*fig*) superare senza difficoltà ♦ *vi* farcela senza difficoltà.
sailboat ['seɪlbəut] *n* (*US*) barca a vela.
sailing ['seɪlɪŋ] *n* (*sport*) vela; **to go** ~ fare della vela.
sailing boat *n* barca a vela.
sailing ship *n* veliero.
sailor ['seɪlə*] *n* marinaio.
saint [seɪnt] *n* santo/a.
saintly ['seɪntlɪ] *a* da santo(a); santo(a).
sake [seɪk] *n*: **for the** ~ **of** per, per amore di; **for pity's** ~ per pietà; **for the** ~ **of argument** tanto per fare un esempio; **art for art's** ~ l'arte per l'arte.
salad ['sæləd] *n* insalata; **tomato** ~ insalata di pomodori.
salad bowl *n* insalatiera.
salad cream *n* (*Brit*) (tipo di) maionese *f*.
salad dressing *n* condimento per insalata.
salad oil *n* olio da tavola.
salami [sə'lɑ:mɪ] *n* salame *m*.
salaried ['sælərɪd] *a* stipendiato(a).
salary ['sælərɪ] *n* stipendio.
salary scale *n* scala dei salari.
sale [seɪl] *n* vendita; (*at reduced prices*) svendita, liquidazione *f*; **"for** ~**"** "in vendita"; **on** ~ in vendita; **on** ~ **or return** da vendere o rimandare; **a closing-down** *or* (*US*) **liquidation** ~ una liquidazione; ~ **and lease back** *n* lease back *m inv*.
saleroom ['seɪlrum] *n* sala delle aste.
sales assistant *n* (*Brit*) commesso/a.
sales clerk *n* (*US*) commesso/a.
sales conference *n* riunione *f* marketing e vendite.
sales drive *n* campagna di vendita, sforzo promozionale.
sales force *n* personale *m* addetto alle vendite.
salesman ['seɪlzmən] *n* commesso; (*representative*) rappresentante *m*.

sales manager n direttore m commerciale.
salesmanship ['seɪlzmənʃɪp] n arte f del vendere.
sales tax n (US) imposta sulle vendite.
saleswoman ['seɪlzwumən] n commessa.
salient ['seɪlɪənt] a saliente.
saline ['seɪlaɪn] a salino(a).
saliva [sə'laɪvə] n saliva.
sallow ['sæləu] a giallastro(a).
sally forth, sally out ['sælɪ-] vi uscire di gran carriera.
salmon ['sæmən] n (pl inv) salmone m.
salmon trout n trota (di mare).
saloon [sə'lu:n] n (US) saloon m inv, bar m inv; (Brit AUT) berlina; (ship's lounge) salone m.
Salop ['sæləp] n abbr (Brit) = Shropshire.
SALT [sɔ:lt] n abbr (= Strategic Arms Limitation Talks/Treaty) S.A.L.T. m.
salt [sɔ:lt] n sale m ♦ vt salare ♦ cpd di sale; (CULIN) salato(a); **an old ~** un lupo di mare.
salt away vt ammucchiare, mettere via.
salt cellar n saliera.
salt-free ['sɔ:lt'fri:] a senza sale.
saltwater ['sɔ:ltwɔ:tə*] a (fish etc) di mare.
salty ['sɔ:ltɪ] a salato(a).
salubrious [sə'lu:brɪəs] a salubre; (fig: district etc) raccomandabile.
salutary ['sæljutərɪ] a salutare.
salute [sə'lu:t] n saluto ♦ vt salutare.
salvage ['sælvɪdʒ] n (saving) salvataggio; (things saved) beni mpl salvati or recuperati ♦ vt salvare, mettere in salvo.
salvage vessel n scialuppa di salvataggio.
salvation [sæl'veɪʃən] n salvezza.
Salvation Army n Esercito della Salvezza.
salver ['sælvə*] n vassoio.
salvo, ~es ['sælvəu] n salva.
Samaritan [sə'mærɪtən] n: **the ~s** (organization) ≈ telefono amico.
same [seɪm] a stesso(a), medesimo(a) ♦ pronoun: **the ~** lo(la) stesso(a), gli(le) stessi(e); **the ~ book as** lo stesso libro di (or che); **on the ~ day** lo stesso giorno; **at the ~ time** allo stesso tempo; **all** or **just the ~** tuttavia; **to do the ~** fare la stessa cosa; **to do the ~ as sb** fare come qn; **the ~ again** (in bar etc) un altro; **they're one and the ~** (person/thing) sono la stessa persona/cosa; **and the ~ to you!** altrettanto a lei!; **~ here!** anch'io!
sample ['sɑ:mpl] n campione m ♦ vt (food) assaggiare; (wine) degustare; **to take a ~** prelevare un campione; **free ~** campione omaggio.
sanatorium, pl **sanatoria** [sænə'tɔ:rɪəm, -rɪə] n sanatorio.
sanctify ['sæŋktɪfaɪ] vt santificare.
sanctimonious [sæŋktɪ'məunɪəs] a bigotto(a), bacchettone(a).
sanction ['sæŋkʃən] n sanzione f ♦ vt sancire, sanzionare; **to impose economic ~s on** or **against** adottare sanzioni economiche contro.
sanctity ['sæŋktɪtɪ] n santità.

sanctuary ['sæŋktjuərɪ] n (holy place) santuario; (refuge) rifugio; (for wildlife) riserva.
sand [sænd] n sabbia ♦ vt cospargere di sabbia; (also: ~ **down**: wood etc) cartavetrare; see also **sands**.
sandal ['sændl] n sandalo.
sandbag ['sændbæg] n sacco di sabbia.
sandblast ['sændblɑ:st] vt sabbiare.
sandbox ['sændbɒks] n (US: for children) buca di sabbia.
sandcastle ['sændkɑ:sl] n castello di sabbia.
sand dune n duna di sabbia.
sandpaper ['sændpeɪpə*] n carta vetrata.
sandpit ['sændpɪt] n (Brit: for children) buca di sabbia.
sands [sændz] npl spiaggia.
sandstone ['sændstəun] n arenaria.
sandstorm ['sændstɔ:m] n tempesta di sabbia.
sandwich ['sændwɪtʃ] n tramezzino, panino, sandwich m inv ♦ vt (also: ~ **in**) infilare; **cheese/ham ~** sandwich al formaggio/ prosciutto; **to be ~ed between** essere incastrato(a) fra.
sandwich board n cartello pubblicitario (portato da un uomo sandwich).
sandwich course n (Brit) corso di formazione professionale.
sandwich man n uomo m sandwich inv.
sandy ['sændɪ] a sabbioso(a); (colour) color sabbia inv, biondo(a) rossiccio(a).
sane [seɪn] a (person) sano(a) di mente; (outlook) sensato(a).
sang [sæŋ] pt of **sing**.
sanguine ['sæŋgwɪn] a ottimista.
sanitarium, pl **sanitaria** [sænɪ'tɛərɪəm, -rɪə] n (US) = **sanatorium**.
sanitary ['sænɪtərɪ] a (system, arrangements) sanitario(a); (clean) igienico(a).
sanitary towel, (US) **sanitary napkin** n assorbente m (igienico).
sanitation [sænɪ'teɪʃən] n (in house) impianti mpl sanitari; (in town) fognature fpl.
sanitation department n (US) nettezza urbana.
sanity ['sænɪtɪ] n sanità mentale; (common sense) buon senso.
sank [sæŋk] pt of **sink**.
San Marino [sænmə'ri:nəu] n San Marino f.
Santa Claus [sæntə'klɔ:z] n Babbo Natale.
Santiago [sæntɪ'ɑ:gəu] n (also: ~ **de Chile**) Santiago (del Cile) f.
sap [sæp] n (of plants) linfa ♦ vt (strength) fiaccare.
sapling ['sæplɪŋ] n alberello.
sapphire ['sæfaɪə*] n zaffiro.
sarcasm ['sɑ:kæzm] n sarcasmo.
sarcastic [sɑ:'kæstɪk] a sarcastico(a); **to be ~** fare del sarcasmo.
sarcophagus, pl **sarcophagi** [sɑ:'kɒfəgəs, -gaɪ] n sarcofago.
sardine [sɑ:'di:n] n sardina.
Sardinia [sɑ:'dɪnɪə] n Sardegna.
Sardinian [sɑ:'dɪnɪən] a, n sardo(a).

sardonic [sɑːˈdɒnɪk] *a* sardonico(a).

sari [ˈsɑːrɪ] *n* sari *m inv*.

sartorial [sɑːˈtɔːrɪəl] *a* di sartoria.

SAS *n abbr* (*Brit MIL:* = *Special Air Service*) *reparto dell'esercito britannico specializzato in operazioni clandestine.*

SASE *n abbr* (*US:* = *self-addressed stamped envelope*) *lettera affrancata e con indirizzo.*

sash [sæʃ] *n* fascia.

sash window *n* finestra a ghigliottina.

SAT *n abbr* (*US*) = *Scholastic Aptitude Test.*

Sat. *abbr* (= *Saturday*) sab.

sat [sæt] *pt, pp of* **sit.**

Satan [ˈseɪtən] *n* Satana *m*.

satanic [səˈtænɪk] *a* satanico(a).

satchel [ˈsætʃl] *n* cartella.

sated [ˈseɪtɪd] *a* soddisfatto(a); sazio(a).

satellite [ˈsætəlaɪt] *a, n* satellite (*m*).

satiate [ˈseɪʃɪeɪt] *vt* saziare.

satin [ˈsætɪn] *n* satin *m* ♦ *a* di *or* in satin; **with a ~ finish** satinato(a).

satire [ˈsætaɪə*] *n* satira.

satirical [səˈtɪrɪkl] *a* satirico(a).

satirist [ˈsætərɪst] *n* (*writer etc*) scrittore(trice) *etc* satirico(a); (*cartoonist*) caricaturista *m/f*.

satirize [ˈsætɪraɪz] *vt* satireggiare.

satisfaction [sætɪsˈfækʃən] *n* soddisfazione *f*; **has it been done to your ~?** ne è rimasto soddisfatto?

satisfactory [sætɪsˈfæktərɪ] *a* soddisfacente.

satisfy [ˈsætɪsfaɪ] *vt* soddisfare; (*convince*) convincere; **to ~ the requirements** rispondere ai requisiti; **to ~ sb (that)** convincere qn (che), persuadere qn (che); **to ~ o.s. of sth** accertarsi di qc.

satisfying [ˈsætɪsfaɪɪŋ] *a* soddisfacente.

saturate [ˈsætʃəreɪt] *vt*: **to ~ (with)** saturare (di).

saturation [sætʃəˈreɪʃən] *n* saturazione *f*.

Saturday [ˈsætədɪ] *n* sabato; *for phrases see also* **Tuesday.**

sauce [sɔːs] *n* salsa; (*containing meat, fish*) sugo.

saucepan [ˈsɔːspən] *n* casseruola.

saucer [ˈsɔːsə*] *n* piattino.

saucy [ˈsɔːsɪ] *a* impertinente.

Saudi Arabia [ˈsaʊdɪ-] *n* Arabia Saudita.

Saudi (Arabian) *a, n* saudita (*m/f*).

sauna [ˈsɔːnə] *n* sauna.

saunter [ˈsɔːntə*] *vi* andare a zonzo, bighellonare.

sausage [ˈsɒsɪdʒ] *n* salsiccia; (*salami etc*) salame *m*.

sausage roll *n* rotolo di pasta sfoglia ripieno di salsiccia.

sauté [ˈsəʊteɪ] *a* (*CULIN: potatoes*) saltato(a); (: *onions*) soffritto(a) ♦ *vt* far saltare; far soffriggere.

savage [ˈsævɪdʒ] *a* (*cruel, fierce*) selvaggio(a), feroce; (*primitive*) primitivo(a) ♦ *n* selvaggio/a ♦ *vt* attaccare selvaggiamente.

savagery [ˈsævɪdʒrɪ] *n* crudeltà, ferocia.

save [seɪv] *vt* (*person, belongings, COMPUT*)

salvare; (*money*) risparmiare, mettere da parte; (*time*) risparmiare; (*food*) conservare; (*avoid: trouble*) evitare ♦ *vi* (*also:* **~ up**) economizzare ♦ *n* (*SPORT*) parata ♦ *prep* salvo, a eccezione di; **it will ~ me an hour** mi farà risparmiare un'ora; **to ~ face** salvare la faccia; **God ~ the Queen!** Dio salvi la Regina!

saving [ˈseɪvɪŋ] *n* risparmio ♦ *a*: **the ~ grace of** l'unica cosa buona di; **~s** *npl* risparmi *mpl*; **to make ~s** fare economia.

savings account *n* libretto di risparmio.

savings bank *n* cassa di risparmio.

saviour, (*US*) **savior** [ˈseɪvjə*] *n* salvatore *m*.

savour, (*US*) **savor** [ˈseɪvə*] *n* sapore *m*, gusto ♦ *vt* gustare.

savoury, (*US*) **savory** [ˈseɪvərɪ] *a* saporito(a); (*dish: not sweet*) salato(a).

savvy [ˈsævɪ] *n* (*col*) arguzia.

saw [sɔː] *pt of* **see** ♦ *n* (*tool*) sega ♦ *vt* (*pt* **sawed**, *pp* **sawed** *or* **sawn** [sɔːn]) segare; **to ~ sth up** fare a pezzi qc con la sega.

sawdust [ˈsɔːdʌst] *n* segatura.

sawmill [ˈsɔːmɪl] *n* segheria.

sawn [sɔːn] *pp of* **saw.**

sawn-off [ˈsɔːnɔf], (*US*) **sawed-off** [ˈsɔːdɔf] *a*: **~ shotgun** fucile *m* a canne mozze.

saxophone [ˈsæksəfəʊn] *n* sassofono.

say [seɪ] *n*: **to have one's ~** fare sentire il proprio parere; **to have a** *or* **some ~** avere voce in capitolo ♦ *vt* (*pt, pp* **said** [sɛd]) dire; **could you ~ that again?** potrebbe ripeterlo?; **to ~ yes/no** dire di sì/di no; **she said (that) I was to give you this** ha detto di darle questo; **my watch ~s 3 o'clock** il mio orologio fa le 3; **shall we ~ Tuesday?** facciamo martedì?; **that doesn't ~ much for him** non torna a suo credito; **when all is said and done** a conti fatti; **there is something** *or* **a lot to be said for it** ha i suoi lati positivi; **that is to ~** cioè, vale a dire; **to ~ nothing of** per non parlare di; **~ that ...** mettiamo *or* diciamo che ...; **that goes without ~ing** va da sé.

saying [ˈseɪɪŋ] *n* proverbio, detto.

SBA *n abbr* (*US:* = *Small Business Administration*) *organismo ausiliario per piccole imprese.*

SC *n abbr* (*US*) = **supreme court** ♦ *abbr* (*US POST*) = *South Carolina.*

s/c *abbr* (= *self-contained*) indipendente.

scab [skæb] *n* crosta; (*pej*) crumiro/a.

scabby [ˈskæbɪ] *a* crostoso(a).

scaffold [ˈskæfəʊld] *n* impalcatura; (*gallows*) patibolo.

scaffolding [ˈskæfəldɪŋ] *n* impalcatura.

scald [skɔːld] *n* scottatura ♦ *vt* scottare.

scalding [ˈskɔːldɪŋ] *a* (*also:* **~ hot**) bollente.

scale [skeɪl] *n* scala; (*of fish*) squama ♦ *vt* (*mountain*) scalare; **pay ~** scala dei salari; **~ of charges** tariffa; **on a large ~** su vasta scala; **to draw sth to ~** disegnare qc in scala; **small-~ model** modello in scala ridotta; *see also* **scales.**

scale down *vt* ridurre (proporzionalmente).
scale drawing *n* disegno in scala.
scale model *n* modello in scala.
scales [skeɪlz] *npl* bilancia.
scallion ['skæljən] *n* cipolla; (*US: shallot*) scalogna; (: *leek*) porro.
scallop ['skɔləp] *n* pettine *m*.
scalp [skælp] *n* cuoio capelluto ♦ *vt* scotennare.
scalpel ['skælpl] *n* bisturi *m inv.*
scalper ['skælpə*] *n* (*US   col: of tickets*) bagarino.
scamp [skæmp] *n* (*col: child*) peste *f*.
scamper ['skæmpə*] *vi:* **to ~ away, ~ off** darsela a gambe.
scampi ['skæmpɪ] *npl* scampi *mpl*.
scan [skæn] *vt* scrutare; (*glance at quickly*) scorrere, dare un'occhiata a; (*poetry*) scandire; (*TV*) analizzare; (*RADAR*) esplorare ♦ *n* (*MED*) ecografia.
scandal ['skændl] *n* scandalo; (*gossip*) pettegolezzi *mpl*.
scandalize ['skændəlaɪz] *vt* scandalizzare.
scandalous ['skændələs] *a* scandaloso(a).
Scandinavia [skændɪ'neɪvɪə] *n* Scandinavia.
Scandinavian [skændɪ'neɪvɪən] *a, n* scandinavo(a).
scanner ['skænə*] *n* (*RADAR, MED*) scanner *m inv.*
scant [skænt] *a* scarso(a).
scantily ['skæntɪlɪ] *ad:* **~ clad** *or* **dressed** succintamente vestito(a).
scanty ['skæntɪ] *a* insufficiente; (*swimsuit*) ridotto(a).
scapegoat ['skeɪpgəut] *n* capro espiatorio.
scar [skɑ:*] *n* cicatrice *f* ♦ *vt* sfregiare.
scarce [skɛəs] *a* scarso(a); (*copy, edition*) raro(a).
scarcely ['skɛəslɪ] *ad* appena; **~ anybody** quasi nessuno; **I can ~ believe it** faccio fatica a crederci.
scarcity ['skɛəsɪtɪ] *n* scarsità, mancanza.
scarcity value *n* valore *m* di rarità.
scare [skɛə*] *n* spavento, paura ♦ *vt* spaventare, atterrire; **to ~ sb stiff** spaventare a morte qn; **bomb ~** evacuazione *f* per sospetta presenza di un ordigno esplosivo.
scare away, scare off *vt* mettere in fuga.
scarecrow ['skɛəkrəu] *n* spaventapasseri *m inv.*
scared [skɛəd] *a:* **to be ~** aver paura.
scaremonger ['skɛəmʌŋgə*] *n* allarmista *m/f*.
scarf, *pl* **scarves** [skɑ:f, skɑ:vz] *n* (*long*) sciarpa; (*square*) fazzoletto da testa, foulard *m inv.*
scarlet ['skɑ:lɪt] *a* scarlatto(a).
scarlet fever *n* scarlattina.
scarves [skɑ:vz] *npl of* **scarf**.
scary ['skɛərɪ] *a* (*col*) che fa paura.
scathing ['skeɪðɪŋ] *a* aspro(a); **to be ~ about sth** essere molto critico rispetto a qc.
scatter ['skætə*] *vt* spargere; (*crowd*) disperdere ♦ *vi* disperdersi.
scatterbrained ['skætəbreɪnd] *a*

scervellato(a), sbadato(a).
scattered ['skætəd] *a* sparso(a), sparpagliato(a).
scatty ['skætɪ] *a* (*col*) scervellato(a), sbadato(a).
scavenge ['skævɪndʒ] *vi* (*person*): **to ~ (for)** frugare tra i rifiuti (alla ricerca di); (*hyenas etc*) nutrirsi di carogne.
scavenger ['skævəndʒə*] *n* spazzino.
SCE *n abbr* = *Scottish Certificate of Education*.
scenario [sɪ'nɑ:rɪəu] *n* (*THEATRE, CINEMA*) copione *m*; (*fig*) situazione *f*.
scene [si:n] *n* (*THEATRE, fig etc*) scena; (*of crime, accident*) scena, luogo; (*sight, view*) vista, veduta; **behind the ~s** (*also fig*) dietro le quinte; **to appear** *or* **come on the ~** (*also fig*) entrare in scena; **the political ~ in Italy** il quadro politico in Italia; **to make a ~** (*col: fuss*) fare una scenata.
scenery ['si:nərɪ] *n* (*THEATRE*) scenario; (*landscape*) panorama *m*.
scenic ['si:nɪk] *a* scenico(a); panoramico(a).
scent [sɛnt] *n* odore *m*, profumo; (*sense of smell*) olfatto, odorato; (*fig: track*) pista; **to put** *or* **throw sb off the ~** (*fig*) far perdere le tracce a qn, sviare qn.
sceptic, (*US*) **skeptic** ['skɛptɪk] *n* scettico/a.
sceptical, (*US*) **skeptical** ['skɛptɪkl] *a* scettico(a).
scepticism, (*US*) **skepticism** ['skɛptɪsɪzm] *n* scetticismo.
sceptre, (*US*) **scepter** ['sɛptə*] *n* scettro.
schedule ['ʃɛdju:l, (*US*) 'skɛdju:l] *n* programma *m*, piano; (*of trains*) orario; (*of prices etc*) lista, tabella ♦ *vt* fissare; **as ~d** come stabilito; **on ~** in orario; **to be ahead of/behind ~** essere in anticipo/ritardo sul previsto; **we are working to a very tight ~** il nostro programma di lavoro è molto intenso; **everything went according to ~** tutto è andato secondo i piani *or* secondo il previsto.
scheduled ['ʃɛdju:ld, (*US*) 'skɛdju:ld] *a* (*date, time*) fissato(a); (*visit, event*) programmato(a); (*train, bus, stop*) previsto(a) (sull'orario); **~ flight** volo di linea.
schematic [skɪ'mætɪk] *a* schematico(a).
scheme [ski:m] *n* piano, progetto; (*method*) sistema *m*; (*dishonest plan, plot*) intrigo, trama; (*arrangement*) disposizione *f*, sistemazione *f* ♦ *vt* progettare; (*plot*) ordire ♦ *vi* fare progetti; (*intrigue*) complottare; **colour ~** combinazione *f* di colori.
scheming ['ski:mɪŋ] *a* intrigante ♦ *n* intrighi *mpl*, macchinazioni *fpl*.
schism ['skɪzəm] *n* scisma *m*.
schizophrenia [skɪtsə'fri:nɪə] *n* schizofrenia.
schizophrenic [skɪtsə'frɛnɪk] *a, n* schizofrenico(a).
scholar ['skɔlə*] *n* erudito/a.
scholarly ['skɔləlɪ] *a* dotto(a), erudito(a).
scholarship ['skɔləʃɪp] *n* erudizione *f*; (*grant*) borsa di studio.

school [sku:l] *n* scuola; (*in university*) scuola, facoltà *f inv* ♦ *cpd* scolare, scolastico(a) ♦ *vt* (*animal*) addestrare.

school age *n* età scolare.

schoolbook ['sku:lbuk] *n* libro scolastico.

schoolboy ['sku:lbɔɪ] *n* scolaro.

schoolchild, *pl* **-children** ['sku:ltʃaɪld, -'tʃɪldrən] *n* scolaro/a.

schooldays ['sku:ldeɪz] *npl* giorni *mpl* di scuola.

schoolgirl ['sku:lgə:l] *n* scolara.

schooling ['sku:lɪŋ] *n* istruzione *f*.

school-leaving age [sku:l'li:vɪŋ-] *n* limite *m* d'età della scuola dell'obbligo.

schoolmaster ['sku:lmɑ:stə*] *n* (*primary*) maestro; (*secondary*) insegnante *m*.

schoolmistress ['sku:lmɪstrɪs] *n* (*primary*) maestra; (*secondary*) insegnante *f*.

school report *n* (*Brit*) pagella.

schoolroom ['sku:lru:m] *n* classe *f*, aula.

schoolteacher ['sku:lti:tʃə*] *n* insegnante *m/f*, docente *m/f*; (*primary*) maestro/a.

schooner ['sku:nə*] *n* (*ship*) goletta, schooner *m inv*; (*glass*) bicchiere *m* alto da sherry.

sciatica [saɪ'ætɪkə] *n* sciatica.

science ['saɪəns] *n* scienza; **the ~s** le scienze; (*SCOL*) le materie scientifiche.

science fiction *n* fantascienza.

scientific [saɪən'tɪfɪk] *a* scientifico(a).

scientist ['saɪəntɪst] *n* scienziato/a.

sci-fi ['saɪfaɪ] *n abbr* (*col*) = **science fiction**.

Scilly Isles ['sɪlɪ'aɪlz] *npl*, **Scillies** ['sɪlɪz] *npl*: **the ~** le isole Scilly.

scintillating ['sɪntɪleɪtɪŋ] *a* scintillante; (*wit, conversation, company*) brillante.

scissors ['sɪzəz] *npl* forbici *fpl*; **a pair of ~** un paio di forbici.

sclerosis [sklɪ'rəʊsɪs] *n* sclerosi *f*.

scoff [skɔf] *vt* (*Brit col: eat*) trangugiare, ingozzare ♦ *vi*: **to ~ (at)** (*mock*) farsi beffe (di).

scold [skəʊld] *vt* rimproverare.

scolding ['skəʊldɪŋ] *n* lavata di capo, sgridata.

scone [skɔn] *n* focaccina da tè.

scoop [sku:p] *n* mestolo; (*for ice cream*) cucchiaio dosatore; (*PRESS*) colpo giornalistico, notizia (in) esclusiva.

scoop out *vt* scavare.

scoop up *vt* tirare su, sollevare.

scooter ['sku:tə*] *n* (*motor cycle*) motoretta, scooter *m inv*; (*toy*) monopattino.

scope [skəʊp] *n* (*capacity: of plan, undertaking*) portata; (: *of person*) capacità *fpl*; (*opportunity*) possibilità *fpl*; **to be with-in the ~ of** rientrare nei limiti di; **it's well within his ~ to ...** è perfettamente in grado di ...; **there is plenty of ~ for improvement** (*Brit*) ci sono notevoli possibilità di miglioramento.

scorch [skɔ:tʃ] *vt* (*clothes*) strinare, bruciacchiare; (*earth, grass*) seccare, bruciare.

scorched earth policy *n* tattica della terra bruciata.

scorcher ['skɔ:tʃə*] *n* (*col: hot day*) giornata torrida.

scorching ['skɔ:tʃɪŋ] *a* cocente, scottante.

score [skɔ:*] *n* punti *mpl*, punteggio; (*MUS*) partitura, spartito; (*twenty*): **a ~** venti ♦ *vt* (*goal, point*) segnare, fare; (*success*) ottenere; (*cut: leather, wood, card*) incidere ♦ *vi* segnare; (*FOOTBALL*) fare un goal; (*keep score*) segnare i punti; **on that ~** a questo riguardo; **to have an old ~ to settle with sb** (*fig*) avere un vecchio conto da saldare con qn; **~s of people** (*fig*) un sacco di gente; **to ~ 6 out of 10** prendere 6 su 10.

score out *vt* cancellare con un segno.

scoreboard ['skɔ:bɔ:d] *n* tabellone *m* segnapunti.

scorecard ['skɔ:kɑ:d] *n* cartoncino segnapunti.

scorer ['skɔ:rə*] *n* marcatore/trice; (*keeping score*) segnapunti *m inv*.

scorn [skɔ:n] *n* disprezzo ♦ *vt* disprezzare.

scornful ['skɔ:nful] *a* sprezzante.

Scorpio ['skɔ:pɪəʊ] *n* Scorpione *m*; **to be ~** essere dello Scorpione.

scorpion ['skɔ:pɪən] *n* scorpione *m*.

Scot [skɔt] *n* scozzese *m/f*.

Scotch [skɔtʃ] *n* whisky *m* scozzese, scotch *m*.

scotch [skɔtʃ] *vt* (*rumour etc*) soffocare.

Scotch tape ® *n* scotch ® *m*.

scot-free ['skɔt'fri:] *a* impunito(a); **to get off ~** (*unpunished*) farla franca; (*unhurt*) uscire illeso(a).

Scotland ['skɔtlənd] *n* Scozia.

Scots [skɔts] *a* scozzese.

Scotsman ['skɔtsmən] *n* scozzese *m*.

Scotswoman ['skɔtswumən] *n* scozzese *f*.

Scottish ['skɔtɪʃ] *a* scozzese.

scoundrel ['skaundrl] *n* farabutto/a; (*child*) furfantello/a.

scour ['skauə*] *vt* (*clean*) pulire strofinando; raschiare via; ripulire; (*search*) battere, perlustrare.

scourer ['skauərə*] *n* (*pad*) paglietta; (*powder*) (detersivo) abrasivo.

scourge [skə:dʒ] *n* flagello.

scout [skaut] *n* (*MIL*) esploratore *m*; (*also:* **boy ~**) giovane esploratore, scout *m inv*.

scout around *vi* cercare in giro.

scowl [skaul] *vi* accigliarsi, aggrottare le sopracciglia; **to ~ at** guardare torvo.

scrabble ['skræbl] *vi* (*claw*): **to ~ (at)** graffiare, grattare; **to ~ about** *or* **around for sth** cercare affannosamente qc ♦ *n*: **S~** ® Scarabeo ®.

scraggy ['skrægɪ] *a* scarno(a), molto magro(a).

scram [skræm] *vi* (*col*) filare via.

scramble ['skræmbl] *n* arrampicata ♦ *vi* inerpicarsi; **to ~ out** *etc* uscire *etc* in fretta; **to ~ for** azzuffarsi per; **to go scrambling** (*SPORT*) fare il motocross.

scrambled eggs *npl* uova *fpl* strapazzate.

scrap [skræp] *n* pezzo, pezzetto; (*fight*) zuffa; (*also:* **~ iron**) rottami *mpl* di ferro, ferraglia ♦ *vt* demolire; (*fig*) scartare; **~s** *npl* (*waste*) scarti *mpl*; **to sell sth for ~** vendere qc come ferro vecchio.

scrapbook ['skræpbuk] *n* album *m inv* di ritagli.

scrap dealer *n* commerciante *m* di ferraglia.

scrape [skreɪp] *vt, vi* raschiare, grattare ♦ *n*: **to get into a** ~ cacciarsi in un guaio.

scrape through *vi* (*succeed*) farcela per un pelo, cavarsela ♦ *vt fus* (*exam*) passare per miracolo, passare per il rotto della cuffia.

scraper ['skreɪpə*] *n* raschietto.

scrap heap *n* mucchio di rottami; **to throw sth on the** ~ (*fig*) mettere qc nel dimenticatoio.

scrap merchant *n* (*Brit*) commerciante *m* di ferraglia.

scrap metal *n* ferraglia.

scrap paper *n* cartaccia.

scrappy ['skræpɪ] *a* frammentario(a), sconnesso(a).

scrap yard *n* deposito di rottami; (*for cars*) cimitero delle macchine.

scratch [skrætʃ] *n* graffio ♦ *cpd*: ~ **team** squadra raccogliticcia ♦ *vt* graffiare, rigare; (*COMPUT*) cancellare ♦ *vi* grattare, graffiare; **to start from** ~ cominciare *or* partire da zero; **to be up to** ~ essere all'altezza.

scratch pad *n* (*US*) notes *m inv*, blocchetto.

scrawl [skrɔ:l] *n* scarabocchio ♦ *vi* scarabocchiare.

scrawny ['skrɔ:nɪ] *a* scarno(a), pelle e ossa *inv*.

scream [skri:m] *n* grido, urlo ♦ *vi* urlare, gridare; **to** ~ **at sb (to do sth)** gridare a qn (di fare qc); **it was a** ~ (*fig col*) era da crepar dal ridere; **he's a** ~ (*fig col*) è una sagoma, è uno spasso.

scree [skri:] *n* ghiaione *m*.

screech [skri:tʃ] *n* strido; (*of tyres, brakes*) stridore *m* ♦ *vi* stridere.

screen [skri:n] *n* schermo; (*fig*) muro, cortina, velo ♦ *vt* schermare, fare schermo a; (*from the wind etc*) riparare; (*film*) proiettare; (*book*) adattare per lo schermo; (*candidates etc*) passare al vaglio; (*for illness*) sottoporre a controlli medici.

screen editing *n* (*COMPUT*) correzione *f* e modifica su schermo.

screening ['skri:nɪŋ] *n* (*MED*) dépistage *m inv*; (*of film*) proiezione *f*; (*for security*) controlli *mpl* (di sicurezza).

screen memory *n* (*COMPUT*) memoria di schermo.

screenplay ['skri:npleɪ] *n* sceneggiatura.

screen test *n* provino (cinematografico).

screw [skru:] *n* vite *f*; (*propeller*) elica ♦ *vt* avvitare; **to** ~ **sth to the wall** fissare qc al muro con viti.

screw up *vt* (*paper, material*) spiegazzare; (*col: ruin*) mandare a monte; **to** ~ **up one's face** fare una smorfia.

screwdriver ['skru:draɪvə*] *n* cacciavite *m*.

screwy ['skru:ɪ] *a* (*col*) svitato(a).

scribble ['skrɪbl] *n* scarabocchio ♦ *vt* scribacchiare ♦ *vi* scarabocchiare; **to** ~ **sth down**

scribacchiare qc.

scribe [skraɪb] *n* scriba *m*.

script [skrɪpt] *n* (*CINEMA etc*) copione *m*; (*in exam*) elaborato *or* compito d'esame; (*writing*) scrittura.

scripted ['skrɪptɪd] *a* (*RADIO, TV*) preparato(a).

Scripture ['skrɪptʃə*] *n* Sacre Scritture *fpl*.

scriptwriter ['skrɪptraɪtə*] *n* soggettista *m/f*.

scroll [skrəul] *n* rotolo di carta ♦ *vt* (*COMPUT*) scorrere.

scrotum ['skrəutəm] *n* scroto.

scrounge [skraundʒ] *vt* (*col*): **to** ~ **sth (off** *or* **from sb)** scroccare qc (a qn) ♦ *vi*: **to** ~ **on sb** vivere alle spalle di qn.

scrounger ['skraundʒə*] *n* scroccone/a.

scrub [skrʌb] *n* (*clean*) strofinata; (*land*) boscaglia ♦ *vt* pulire strofinando; (*reject*) annullare.

scrubbing brush ['skrʌbɪŋ-] *n* spazzolone *m*.

scruff [skrʌf] *n*: **by the** ~ **of the neck** per la collottola.

scruffy ['skrʌfɪ] *a* sciatto(a).

scrum(mage) ['skrʌm(ɪdʒ)] *n* mischia.

scruple ['skru:pl] *n* scrupolo; **to have no** ~s **about doing sth** non avere scrupoli a fare qc.

scrupulous ['skru:pjuləs] *a* scrupoloso(a).

scrupulously ['skru:pjuləslɪ] *ad* scrupolosamente; **he tries to be** ~ **fair/honest** cerca di essere più imparziale/onesto che può.

scrutinize ['skru:tɪnaɪz] *vt* scrutare, esaminare attentamente.

scrutiny ['skru:tɪnɪ] *n* esame *m* accurato; **under the** ~ **of sb** sotto la sorveglianza di qn.

scuba ['sku:bə] *n* autorespiratore *m*.

scuba diving *n* immersioni *fpl* subacquee.

scuff [skʌf] *vt* (*shoes*) consumare strascicando.

scuffle ['skʌfl] *n* baruffa, tafferuglio.

scullery ['skʌlərɪ] *n* retrocucina *m or f*.

sculptor ['skʌlptə*] *n* scultore *m*.

sculpture ['skʌlptʃə*] *n* scultura.

scum [skʌm] *n* schiuma; (*pej: people*) feccia.

scupper ['skʌpə*] *vt* (*Brit*) autoaffondare; (*fig*) far naufragare.

scurrilous ['skʌrɪləs] *a* scurrile, volgare.

scurry ['skʌrɪ] *vi* sgambare, affrettarsi.

scurvy ['skə:vɪ] *n* scorbuto.

scuttle ['skʌtl] *n* (*NAUT*) portellino; (*also*: **coal** ~) secchio del carbone ♦ *vt* (*ship*) autoaffondare ♦ *vi* (*scamper*): **to** ~ **away,** ~ **off** darsela a gambe, scappare.

scythe [saɪð] *n* falce *f*.

SD *abbr* (*US POST*) = **South Dakota.**

SDI *n abbr* (= *Strategic Defense Initiative*) S.D.I. *f*.

SDLP *n abbr* (*Brit POL*) = **Social Democratic and Labour Party.**

SDP *n abbr* (*Brit POL*) = **Social Democratic Party.**

sea [si:] *n* mare *m* ♦ *cpd* marino(a), del mare; (*ship, port*) marittimo(a), di mare; **on the** ~ (*boat*) in mare; (*town*) di mare; **to go by** ~

andare per mare; **by** *or* **beside the ~**
(*holiday*) al mare; (*village*) sul mare; **to
look out to ~** guardare il mare; **(out) at ~**
al largo; **heavy** *or* **rough ~(s)** mare grosso
or agitato; **a ~ of faces** (*fig*) una marea di
gente; **to be all at ~** (*fig*) non sapere che pesci pigliare.

sea bed *n* fondo marino.

sea bird *n* uccello di mare.

seaboard ['si:bɔ:d] *n* costa.

sea breeze *n* brezza di mare.

seafarer ['si:fɛərə*] *n* navigante *m*.

seafaring   ['si:fɛərɪŋ]   *a*   (*community*)
marinaro(a); (*life*) da marinaio.

seafood ['si:fu:d] *n* frutti *mpl* di mare.

sea front *n* lungomare *m*.

seagoing ['si:gəuɪŋ] *a* (*ship*) d'alto mare.

seagull ['si:gʌl] *n* gabbiano.

seal [si:l] *n* (*animal*) foca; (*stamp*) sigillo;
(*impression*)   impronta   del   sigillo   ♦ *vt*
sigillare; (*decide: sb's fate*) segnare; (*:
bargain*) concludere; **~ of approval** bene-
placito.

seal off *vt* (*close*) sigillare; (*forbid entry
to*) bloccare l'accesso a.

sea level *n* livello del mare.

sealing wax ['si:lɪŋ-] *n* ceralacca.

sea lion *n* leone *m* marino.

sealskin ['si:lskɪn] *n* pelle *f* di foca.

seam [si:m] *n* cucitura; (*of coal*) filone *m*; **the
hall was bursting at the ~s** l'aula era piena
zeppa.

seaman ['si:mən] *n* marinaio.

seamanship   ['si:mənʃɪp]   *n*   tecnica   di
navigazione.

seamless ['si:mlɪs] *a* senza cucitura.

seamy ['si:mɪ] *a* malfamato(a); squallido(a).

seance ['seɪɔns] *n* seduta spiritica.

seaplane ['si:pleɪn] *n* idrovolante *m*.

seaport ['si:pɔ:t] *n* porto di mare.

search [sə:tʃ] *n* (*for person, thing*) ricerca; (*of
drawer, pockets*) esame *m* accurato; (*LAW:
at sb's home*) perquisizione *f* ♦ *vt* perlustrare,
frugare; (*scan, examine*) esaminare minuziosamente; (*COMPUT*) ricercare ♦ *vi*: **to ~ for**
ricercare; **in ~ of** alla ricerca di; "**~ and replace**" (*COMPUT*) "ricercare e sostituire".

search through *vt fus* frugare.

searcher ['sə:tʃə*] *n* chi cerca.

searching ['sə:tʃɪŋ] *a* minuzioso(a); penetrante; (*question*) pressante.

searchlight ['sə:tʃlaɪt] *n* proiettore *m*.

search party *n* squadra di soccorso.

search warrant *n* mandato di perquisizione.

searing ['sɪərɪŋ] *a* (*heat*) rovente; (*pain*)
acuto(a).

seashore ['si:ʃɔ:*] *n* spiaggia; **on the ~** sulla
riva del mare.

seasick ['si:sɪk] *a* che soffre il mal di mare; **to
be ~** avere il mal di mare.

seaside ['si:saɪd] *n* spiaggia; **to go to the ~**
andare al mare.

seaside resort *n* stazione *f* balneare.

season ['si:zn] *n* stagione *f* ♦ *vt* condire,

insaporire; **to be in/out of ~** essere di/fuori
stagione; **the busy ~** (*for shops*) il periodo di
punta; (*for hotels etc*) l'alta stagione; **the
open ~** (*HUNTING*) la stagione della caccia.

seasonal ['si:zənl] *a* stagionale.

seasoned ['si:znd] *a* (*wood*) stagionato(a);
(*fig: worker, actor, troops*) con esperienza; **a
~ campaigner** un veterano.

seasoning ['si:znɪŋ] *n* condimento.

season ticket *n* abbonamento.

seat [si:t] *n* sedile *m*; (*in bus, train: place*) posto; (*PARLIAMENT*) seggio; (*centre: of
government etc, of infection*) sede *f*;
(*buttocks*) didietro; (*of trousers*) fondo ♦ *vt*
far sedere; (*have room for*) avere *or* essere
fornito(a) di posti a sedere per; **are there
any ~s left?** ci sono posti?; **to take one's ~**
prendere posto; **to be ~ed** essere seduto(a);
please be ~ed accomodatevi per favore.

seat belt *n* cintura di sicurezza.

seating arrangements ['si:tɪŋ-] *npl* sistemazione *f or* disposizione *f* dei posti.

seating capacity *n* posti *mpl* a sedere.

SEATO ['si:təu] *n abbr* (= *Southeast Asia
Treaty Organization*) SEATO *f*.

sea water *n* acqua di mare.

seaweed ['si:wi:d] *n* alghe *fpl*.

seaworthy ['si:wə:ðɪ] *a* atto(a) alla
navigazione.

SEC *n abbr* (*US*: = *Securities and Exchange
Commission*) commissione di controllo sulle
operazioni in Borsa.

sec. *abbr* = **second**.

secateurs [sɛkə'tə:z] *npl* forbici *fpl* per potare.

secede [sɪ'si:d] *vi*: **to ~ (from)** ritirarsi (da).

secluded   [sɪ'klu:dɪd]   *a*   isolato(a),
appartato(a).

seclusion [sɪ'klu:ʒən] *n* isolamento.

second ['sɛkənd] *num* secondo(a) ♦ *ad* (*in
race etc*) al secondo posto; (*RAIL*) in seconda
♦ *n* (*unit of time*) secondo; (*in series,
position*) secondo/a; (*Brit SCOL*) laurea con
punteggio discreto; (*AUT*: also: **~ gear**)
seconda; (*COMM: imperfect*) scarto ♦ *vt*
(*motion*) appoggiare; [sɪ'kɔnd] (*employee*) distaccare; **Charles the S~** Carlo Secondo;
just a ~! un attimo!; **~ floor** (*Brit*) secondo
piano; (*US*) primo piano; **to ask for a ~
opinion** (*MED*) chiedere un altro *or* ulteriore
parere; **to have ~ thoughts (about doing
sth)** avere dei ripensamenti (quanto a fare
qc); **on ~ thoughts** *or* (*US*) **thought** ci
ripensarci, ripensandoci bene.

secondary ['sɛkəndərɪ] *a* secondario(a).

secondary picket *n* picchetto di solidarietà.

secondary school *n* scuola secondaria.

second-best [sɛkənd'bɛst] *n* ripiego; **as a ~**
in mancanza di meglio.

second-class [sɛkənd'klɑ:s] *a* di seconda
classe ♦ *ad*: **to travel ~** viaggiare in seconda
(classe); **to send sth ~** spedire qc per posta
ordinaria; **~ citizen** cittadino di
second'ordine.

second cousin *n* cugino di secondo grado.

seconder ['sɛkəndə*] n sostenitore/trice.
second hand n (on clock) lancetta dei secondi.
second-hand [sɛkənd'hænd] a di seconda mano, usato(a) ♦ ad (buy) di seconda mano; **to hear sth** ~ venire a sapere qc da terze persone.
second-in-command ['sɛkəndɪnkə'mɑ:nd] n (MIL) comandante m in seconda; (ADMIN) aggiunto.
secondly ['sɛkəndlɪ] ad in secondo luogo.
secondment [sɪ'kɔndmənt] n (Brit) distaccamento.
second-rate [sɛkənd'reɪt] a scadente.
secrecy ['si:krəsɪ] n segretezza.
secret ['si:krɪt] a segreto(a) ♦ n segreto; **in** ~ in segreto, segretamente; **to keep sth** ~ **(from sb)** tenere qc segreto (a qn), tenere qc nascosto (a qn); **keep it** ~ che rimanga un segreto; **to make no** ~ **of sth** non far mistero di qc.
secret agent n agente m segreto.
secretarial [sɛkrɪ'tɛərɪəl] a (work) da segretario/a; (college, course) di segretariato.
secretariat [sɛkrɪ'tɛərɪət] n segretariato.
secretary ['sɛkrətrɪ] n segretario/a; **S~ of State** (US POL) ≈ Ministro degli Esteri; (Brit POL): **S~ of State (for)** ministro (di).
secrete [sɪ'kri:t] vt (MED, ANAT, BIOL) secernere; (hide) nascondere.
secretion [sɪ'kri:ʃən] n secrezione f.
secretive ['si:krətɪv] a riservato(a).
secretly ['si:krɪtlɪ] ad in segreto, segretamente.
sect [sɛkt] n setta.
sectarian [sɛk'tɛərɪən] a settario(a).
section ['sɛkʃən] n sezione f; (of document) articolo ♦ vt sezionare, dividere in sezioni; **the business** ~ (PRESS) la pagina economica.
sector ['sɛktə*] n settore m.
secular ['sɛkjuə*] a secolare.
secure [sɪ'kjuə*] a (free from anxiety) sicuro(a); (firmly fixed) assicurato(a), ben fermato(a); (in safe place) al sicuro ♦ vt (fix) fissare, assicurare; (get) ottenere, assicurarsi; (COMM: loan) garantire; **to make sth** ~ fissare bene qc; **to** ~ **sth for sb** procurare qc per or a qn.
secured creditor [sɪ'kjuəd-] n creditore m privilegiato.
security [sɪ'kjuərɪtɪ] n sicurezza; (for loan) garanzia; **securities** npl (STOCK EXCHANGE) titoli mpl; **to increase/tighten** ~ aumentare/intensificare la sorveglianza; ~ **of tenure** garanzia del posto di lavoro, garanzia di titolo or di godimento.
security forces npl forze fpl dell'ordine.
security guard n guardia giurata.
security risk n rischio per la sicurezza.
secy. abbr = **secretary**.
sedan [sə'dæn] n (US AUT) berlina.
sedate [sɪ'deɪt] a posato(a); calmo(a) ♦ vt calmare.

sedation [sɪ'deɪʃən] n (MED): **to be under** ~ essere sotto l'azione di sedativi.
sedative ['sɛdɪtɪv] n sedativo, calmante m.
sedentary ['sɛdntrɪ] a sedentario(a).
sediment ['sɛdɪmənt] n sedimento.
sedition [sɪ'dɪʃən] n sedizione f.
seduce [sɪ'dju:s] vt sedurre.
seduction [sɪ'dʌkʃən] n seduzione f.
seductive [sɪ'dʌktɪv] a seducente.
see [si:] vb (pt **saw**, pp **seen** [sɔ:, si:n]) vt vedere; (accompany): **to** ~ **sb to the door** accompagnare qn alla porta ♦ vi vedere; (understand) capire ♦ n sede f vescovile; **to** ~ **that** (ensure) badare che + sub, fare in modo che + sub; **to go and** ~ **sb** andare a trovare qn; ~ **you soon/later/tomorrow!** a presto/più tardi/domani!; **as far as I can** ~ da quanto posso vedere; **there was nobody to be** ~**n** non c'era anima viva; **let me** ~ (show me) fammi vedere; (let me think) vediamo (un po'); ~ **for yourself** vai a vedere con i tuoi occhi; **I don't know what she** ~**s in him** non so che cosa ci trovi in lui.
see about vt fus (deal with) occuparsi di.
see off vt salutare alla partenza.
see through vt portare a termine ♦ vt fus non lasciarsi ingannare da.
see to vt fus occuparsi di.
seed [si:d] n seme m; (fig) germe m; (TENNIS) testa di serie; **to go to** ~ fare seme; (fig) scadere.
seedless ['si:dlɪs] a senza semi.
seedling ['si:dlɪŋ] n piantina di semenzaio.
seedy ['si:dɪ] a (shabby: person) sciatto(a); (: place) cadente.
seeing ['si:ɪŋ] cj: ~ **(that)** visto che.
seek [si:k], pt, pp **sought** vt cercare; **to** ~ **advice/help from sb** chiedere consiglio/aiuto a qn.
seek out vt (person) andare a cercare.
seem [si:m] vi sembrare, parere; **there** ~**s to be** ... sembra che ci sia ...; **it** ~**s (that)** ... sembra or pare che ... + sub; **what** ~**s to be the trouble?** cosa c'è che non va?
seemingly ['si:mɪŋlɪ] ad apparentemente.
seen [si:n] pp of **see**.
seep [si:p] vi filtrare, trapelare.
seer [sɪə*] n profeta/essa, veggente m/f.
seersucker ['sɪəsʌkə*] n cotone m indiano.
seesaw ['si:sɔ:] n altalena a bilico.
seethe [si:ð] vi ribollire; **to** ~ **with anger** fremere di rabbia.
see-through ['si:θru:] a trasparente.
segment ['sɛgmənt] n segmento.
segregate ['sɛgrɪgeɪt] vt segregare, isolare.
segregation [sɛgrɪ'geɪʃən] n segregazione f.
Seine [seɪn] n Senna.
seismic ['saɪzmɪk] a sismico(a).
seize [si:z] vt (grasp) afferrare; (take possession of) impadronirsi di; (LAW) sequestrare.
seize up vi (TECH) grippare.
seize (up)on vt fus ricorrere a.
seizure ['si:ʒə*] n (MED) attacco; (LAW) confisca, sequestro.

seldom ['sɛldəm] *ad* raramente.
select [sɪ'lɛkt] *a* scelto(a); *(hotel, restaurant)* chic *inv*; *(club)* esclusivo(a) ♦ *vt* scegliere, selezionare; **a ~ few** pochi eletti *mpl*.
selection [sɪ'lɛkʃən] *n* selezione *f*, scelta.
selection committee *n* comitato di selezione.
selective [sɪ'lɛktɪv] *a* selettivo(a).
selector [sɪ'lɛktə*] *n* *(person)* selezionatore/trice; *(TECH)* selettore *m*.
self [sɛlf] *n* (*pl* **selves** [sɛlvz]): **the ~** l'io *m* ♦ *prefix* auto....
self-addressed ['sɛlfə'drɛst] *a*: **~ envelope** busta col proprio nome e indirizzo.
self-adhesive [sɛlfəd'hi:zɪv] *a* autoadesivo(a).
self-assertive [sɛlfə'sə:tɪv] *a* autoritario(a).
self-assurance [sɛlfə'ʃuərəns] *n* sicurezza di sé.
self-assured [sɛlfə'ʃuəd] *a* sicuro(a) di sé.
self-catering [sɛlf'keɪtərɪŋ] *a* *(Brit)* in cui ci si cucina da sé; **~ apartment** appartamento (per le vacanze).
self-centred, *(US)* **self-centered** [sɛlf'sɛntəd] *a* egocentrico(a).
self-cleaning [sɛlf'kli:nɪŋ] *a* autopulente.
self-coloured, *(US)* **self-colored** [sɛlf'kʌləd] *a* monocolore.
self-confessed [sɛlfkən'fɛst] *a* *(alcoholic etc)* dichiarato(a).
self-confidence [sɛlf'kɔnfɪdəns] *n* sicurezza di sé.
self-conscious [sɛlf'kɔnʃəs] *a* timido(a).
self-contained [sɛlfkən'teɪnd] *a* *(Brit: flat)* indipendente.
self-control [sɛlfkən'trəul] *n* autocontrollo.
self-defeating [sɛlfdɪ'fi:tɪŋ] *a* futile.
self-defence, *(US)* **self-defense** [sɛlfdɪ'fɛns] *n* autodifesa; *(LAW)* legittima difesa.
self-discipline [sɛlf'dɪsɪplɪn] *n* autodisciplina.
self-employed [sɛlfɪm'plɔɪd] *a* che lavora in proprio.
self-esteem [sɛlfɪ'sti:m] *n* amor proprio *m*.
self-evident [sɛlf'ɛvɪdənt] *a* evidente.
self-explanatory [sɛlfɪk'splænətərɪ] *a* ovvio(a).
self-governing [sɛlf'gʌvənɪŋ] *a* autonomo(a).
self-help ['sɛlf'hɛlp] *n* iniziativa individuale.
self-importance [sɛlfɪm'pɔ:tns] *n* sufficienza.
self-indulgent [sɛlfɪn'dʌldʒənt] *a* indulgente verso se stesso(a).
self-inflicted [sɛlfɪn'flɪktɪd] *a* autoinflitto(a).
self-interest [sɛlf'ɪntrɪst] *n* interesse *m* personale.
selfish ['sɛlfɪʃ] *a* egoista.
selfishly ['sɛlfɪʃlɪ] *ad* egoisticamente.
selfishness ['sɛlfɪʃnɪs] *n* egoismo.
selfless ['sɛlflɪs] *a* altruista.
selflessly ['sɛlflɪslɪ] *ad* altruisticamente.
selflessness ['sɛlflɪsnɪs] *n* altruismo.
self-made man ['sɛlfmeɪd-] *n* self-made man *m inv*, uomo che si è fatto da sé.
self-pity [sɛlf'pɪtɪ] *n* autocommiserazione *f*.
self-portrait [sɛlf'pɔ:trɪt] *n* autoritratto.
self-possessed [sɛlfpə'zɛst] *a* controllato(a).

self-preservation ['sɛlfprɛzə'veɪʃən] *n* istinto di conservazione.
self-raising [sɛlf'reɪzɪŋ], *(US)* **self-rising** [sɛlf'raɪzɪŋ] *a*: **~ flour** miscela di farina e lievito.
self-reliant [sɛlfrɪ'laɪənt] *a* indipendente.
self-respect [sɛlfrɪs'pɛkt] *n* rispetto di sé, amor proprio.
self-respecting [sɛlfrɪs'pɛktɪŋ] *a* che ha rispetto di sé.
self-righteous [sɛlf'raɪtʃəs] *a* soddisfatto(a) di sé.
self-rising [sɛlf'raɪzɪŋ] *a* *(US)* = **self-raising.**
self-sacrifice [sɛlf'sækrɪfaɪs] *n* abnegazione *f*.
self-same ['sɛlfsɛm] *a* stesso(a).
self-satisfied [sɛlf'sætɪsfaɪd] *a* compiaciuto(a) di sé.
self-sealing [sɛlf'si:lɪŋ] *a* autosigillante.
self-service [sɛlf'sə:vɪs] *n* autoservizio, self-service *m*.
self-styled [sɛlf'staɪld] *a* sedicente.
self-sufficient [sɛlfsə'fɪʃənt] *a* autosufficiente.
self-supporting [sɛlfsə'pɔ:tɪŋ] *a* economicamente indipendente.
self-taught [sɛlf'tɔ:t] *a* autodidatta.
self-test ['sɛlftɛst] *n* *(COMPUT)* autoverifica.
sell, *pt, pp* **sold** [sɛl, səuld] *vt* vendere ♦ *vi* vendersi; **to ~ at** *or* **for 1000 lire** essere in vendita a 1000 lire; **to ~ sb an idea** *(fig)* far accettare un'idea a qn.
sell off *vt* svendere, liquidare.
sell out *vi*: **to ~ out (to sb/sth)** *(COMM)* vendere (tutto) (a qn/qc) ♦ *vt* esaurire; **the tickets are all sold out** i biglietti sono esauriti.
sell up *vi* vendere (tutto).
sell-by date ['sɛlbaɪ-] *n* scadenza.
seller ['sɛlə*] *n* venditore/trice; **~'s market** mercato favorevole ai venditori.
selling price ['sɛlɪŋ-] *n* prezzo di vendita.
sellotape ® ['sɛləuteɪp] *n* *(Brit)* nastro adesivo, scotch ® *m*.
sellout ['sɛlaut] *n* *(betrayal)* tradimento; *(of tickets)*: **it was a ~** registrò un tutto esaurito.
selves [sɛlvz] *npl of* **self.**
semantic [sɪ'mæntɪk] *a* semantico(a).
semantics [sɪ'mæntɪks] *n* semantica.
semaphore ['sɛməfɔ:*] *n* segnali *mpl* con bandiere; *(RAIL)* semaforo.
semblance ['sɛmbləns] *n* parvenza, apparenza.
semen ['si:mən] *n* sperma *m*.
semester [sɪ'mɛstə*] *n* *(US)* semestre *m*.
semi... ['sɛmɪ] *prefix* semi... ♦ *n*: **semi =** **semidetached (house).**
semi-breve ['sɛmɪbri:v] *n* *(Brit)* semibreve *f*.
semicircle ['sɛmɪsə:kl] *n* semicerchio.
semicircular ['sɛmɪ'sə:kjulə*] *a* semicircolare.
semicolon [sɛmɪ'kəulən] *n* punto e virgola.
semiconductor [sɛmɪkən'dʌktə*] *n* semiconduttore *m*.
semiconscious [sɛmɪ'kɔnʃəs] *a* parzialmente cosciente.
semidetached (house) [sɛmɪdɪ'tætʃt-] *n*

(*Brit*) casa gemella.
semifinal [sɛmɪ'faɪnl] *n* semifinale *f*.
seminar ['sɛmɪnɑː*] *n* seminario.
seminary ['sɛmɪnərɪ] *n* (*REL*: *for priests*) seminario.
semiprecious [sɛmɪ'prɛʃəs] *a* semiprezioso(a).
semiquaver ['sɛmɪkweɪvə*] *n* (*Brit*) semicroma.
semiskilled ['sɛmɪ'skɪld] *a*: ~ **worker** operaio(a) non specializzato(a).
semitone ['sɛmɪtəun] *n* (*MUS*) semitono.
semolina [sɛmə'liːnə] *n* semolino.
SEN *n abbr* (*Brit*: = *State Enrolled Nurse*) *infermiera diplomata* (*dopo corso biennale*).
Sen., sen. *abbr* = **senator; senior.**
senate ['sɛnɪt] *n* senato.
senator ['sɛnɪtə*] *n* senatore/trice.
send [sɛnd], *pt, pp* **sent** *vt* mandare; **to ~ by post** *or* (*US*) **mail** spedire per posta; **to ~ sb for sth** mandare qn a prendere qc; **to ~ word that** ... mandare a dire che ...; **she ~s (you) her love** ti saluta affettuosamente; **to ~ sb to Coventry** (*Brit*) dare l'ostracismo a qn; **to ~ sb to sleep/into fits of laughter** far addormentare/scoppiare dal ridere qn; **to ~ sth flying** far volare via qc.
send away *vt* (*letter, goods*) spedire; (*person*) mandare via.
send away for *vt fus* richiedere per posta, farsi spedire.
send back *vt* rimandare.
send for *vt fus* mandare a chiamare, far venire; (*by post*) ordinare per posta.
send in *vt* (*report, application, resignation*) presentare.
send off *vt* (*goods*) spedire; (*Brit SPORT*: *player*) espellere.
send on *vt* (*Brit*: *letter*) inoltrare; (*luggage etc*: *in advance*) spedire in anticipo.
send out *vt* (*invitation*) diramare; (*emit*: *light, heat*) mandare, emanare; (: *signals*) emettere.
send round *vt* (*letter, document etc*) far circolare.
send up *vt* (*person, price*) far salire; (*Brit*: *parody*) mettere in ridicolo.
sender ['sɛndə*] *n* mittente *m/f*.
send-off ['sɛndɔf] *n*: **to give sb a good ~** festeggiare la partenza di qn.
Senegal [sɛnɪ'gɔːl] *n* Senegal *m*.
Senegalese [sɛnɪgə'liːz] *a, n* senegalese (*m/f*).
senile ['siːnaɪl] *a* senile.
senility [sɪ'nɪlɪtɪ] *n* senilità *f*.
senior ['siːnɪə*] *a* (*older*) più vecchio(a); (*of higher rank*) di grado più elevato ♦ *n* persona più anziana; (*in service*) persona con maggiore anzianità; **P. Jones ~** P. Jones senior, P. Jones padre.
senior citizen *n* anziano/a.
senior high school *n* (*US*) ≈ liceo.
seniority [siːnɪ'ɔrɪtɪ] *n* anzianità; (*in rank*) superiorità.
sensation [sɛn'seɪʃən] *n* sensazione *f*; **to create a ~** fare scalpore.

sensational [sɛn'seɪʃənl] *a* sensazionale; (*marvellous*) eccezionale.
sense [sɛns] *n* senso; (*feeling*) sensazione *f*, senso; (*meaning*) senso, significato; (*wisdom*) buonsenso ♦ *vt* sentire, percepire; **~s** *npl* (*sanity*) ragione *f*; **it makes ~** ha senso; **there is no ~ in (doing) that** non ha senso (farlo); **~ of humour** (*senso dell'*)umorismo; **to come to one's ~s** (*regain consciousness*) riprendere i sensi; (*become reasonable*) tornare in sé; **to take leave of one's ~s** perdere il lume *or* l'uso della ragione.
senseless ['sɛnslɪs] *a* sciocco(a); (*unconscious*) privo(a) di sensi.
sensibilities [sɛnsɪ'bɪlɪtɪz] *npl* sensibilità *fsg*.
sensible ['sɛnsɪbl] *a* sensato(a), ragionevole.
sensitive ['sɛnsɪtɪv] *a*: ~ (**to**) sensibile (a); **he is very ~ about it** è un tasto che è meglio non toccare con lui.
sensitivity [sɛnsɪ'tɪvɪtɪ] *n* sensibilità.
sensual ['sɛnsjuəl] *a* sensuale.
sensuous ['sɛnsjuəs] *a* sensuale.
sent [sɛnt] *pt, pp of* **send**.
sentence ['sɛntns] *n* (*LING*) frase *f*; (*LAW*: *judgement*) sentenza; (: *punishment*) condanna ♦ *vt*: **to ~ sb to death/to 5 years** condannare qn a morte/a 5 anni; **to pass ~ on sb** condannare qn.
sentiment ['sɛntɪmənt] *n* sentimento; (*opinion*) opinione *f*.
sentimental [sɛntɪ'mɛntl] *a* sentimentale.
sentimentality [sɛntɪmɛn'tælɪtɪ] *n* sentimentalità, sentimentalismo.
sentry ['sɛntrɪ] *n* sentinella.
sentry duty *n*: **to be on ~** essere di sentinella.
Seoul [səul] *n* Seul *f*.
separable ['sɛprəbl] *a* separabile.
separate *a* ['sɛprɪt] separato(a) ♦ *vb* ['sɛpəreɪt] *vt* separare ♦ *vi* separarsi; ~ **from** separato da; **under ~ cover** (*COMM*) in plico a parte; **to ~ into** dividere in; *see also* **separates**.
separately ['sɛprɪtlɪ] *ad* separatamente.
separates ['sɛprɪts] *npl* (*clothes*) coordinati *mpl*.
separation [sɛpə'reɪʃən] *n* separazione *f*.
Sept. *abbr* (= *September*) sett., set.
September [sɛp'tɛmbə*] *n* settembre *m*; *for phrases see also* **July.**
septic ['sɛptɪk] *a* settico(a); (*wound*) infettato(a); **to go ~** infettarsi.
septicaemia, (*US*) **septicemia** [sɛptɪ'siːmɪə] *n* setticemia.
septic tank *n* fossa settica.
sequel ['siːkwl] *n* conseguenza; (*of story*) seguito.
sequence ['siːkwəns] *n* (*series*) serie *f inv*; (*order*) ordine *m*; **in ~** in ordine, di seguito; **~ of tenses** concordanza dei tempi.
sequential [sɪ'kwɛnʃəl] *a*: ~ **access** (*COMPUT*) accesso sequenziale.
sequin ['siːkwɪn] *n* lustrino, paillette *f inv*.
Serbo-Croat ['səːbəu'krəuæt] *n* (*LING*) serbocroato.

serenade [sɛrə'neɪd] n serenata ♦ vt fare la serenata a.

serene [sɪ'riːn] a sereno(a), calmo(a).

serenity [sɪ'rɛnɪtɪ] n serenità, tranquillità.

sergeant ['sɑːdʒənt] n sergente m; (POLICE) brigadiere m.

sergeant major n maresciallo.

serial ['sɪərɪəl] n (PRESS) romanzo a puntate; (RADIO, TV) trasmissione f a puntate ♦ cpd (number) di serie; (COMPUT) seriale.

serialize ['sɪərɪəlaɪz] vt pubblicare a puntate; trasmettere a puntate.

serial number n numero di serie.

series ['sɪəriːz] n (pl inv) serie f inv; (PUBLISHING) collana.

serious ['sɪərɪəs] a serio(a), grave; **are you ~ (about it)?** parla sul serio?

seriously ['sɪərɪəslɪ] ad seriamente; **to take sth/sb ~** prendere qc/qn sul serio.

seriousness ['sɪərɪəsnɪs] n serietà, gravità.

sermon ['sɜːmən] n sermone m.

serrated [sɪ'reɪtɪd] a seghettato(a).

serum ['sɪərəm] n siero.

servant ['sɜːvənt] n domestico/a.

serve [sɜːv] vt (employer etc) servire, essere a servizio di; (purpose) servire a; (customer, food, meal) servire; (apprenticeship) fare; (prison term) scontare ♦ vi (also TENNIS) servire; (soldier etc) prestare servizio; (be useful): **to ~ as/for/to do** servire da/per/per fare ♦ n (TENNIS) servizio; **are you being ~d?** la stanno servendo?; **to ~ on a committee/jury** far parte di un comitato/una giuria; **it ~s him right** ben gli sta, se l'è meritata; **it ~s my purpose** fa al caso mio, serve al mio scopo.

serve out, serve up vt (food) servire.

service ['sɜːvɪs] n servizio; (AUT: maintenance) revisione f; (REL) funzione f ♦ vt (car, washing machine) revisionare; **the S~s** npl le forze armate; **to be of ~ to sb, to do sb a ~** essere d'aiuto a qn; **to put one's car in for (a) ~** portare la macchina in officina per una revisione; **dinner ~** servizio da tavola.

serviceable ['sɜːvɪsəbl] a pratico(a), utile; (usable, working) usabile.

service area n (on motorway) area di servizio.

service charge n (Brit) servizio.

service industries npl settore m terziario.

serviceman ['sɜːvɪsmən] n militare m.

service station n stazione f di servizio.

serviette [sɜːvɪ'ɛt] n (Brit) tovagliolo.

servile ['sɜːvaɪl] a servile.

session ['sɛʃən] n (sitting) seduta, sessione f; (SCOL) anno scolastico (or accademico); **to be in ~** essere in seduta.

set [sɛt] n serie f inv; (RADIO, TV) apparecchio; (TENNIS) set m inv; (group of people) mondo, ambiente m; (CINEMA) scenario; (THEATRE: stage) scene fpl; (: scenery) scenario; (MATH) insieme m; (HAIRDRESSING) messa in piega ♦ a (fixed)

stabilito(a), determinato(a); (ready) pronto(a) ♦ vb (pt, pp set) (place) posare, mettere; (fix) fissare; (assign: task, homework) dare, assegnare; (adjust) regolare; (decide: rules etc) stabilire, fissare; (TYP) comporre ♦ vi (sun) tramontare; (jam, jelly) rapprendersi; (concrete) fare presa; **to be ~ on doing** essere deciso a fare; **to be all ~ to do sth** essere pronto fare qc; **to be (dead) ~ against** essere completamente contrario a; **~ in one's ways** abitudinario; **a novel ~ in Rome** un romanzo ambientato a Roma; **to ~ to music** mettere in musica; **to ~ on fire** dare fuoco a; **to ~ free** liberare; **to ~ sth going** mettere in moto qc; **to ~ sail** prendere il mare; **a ~ phrase** una frase fatta; **a ~ of false teeth** una dentiera; **a ~ of dining-room furniture** una camera da pranzo.

set about vt fus (task) intraprendere, mettersi a; **to ~ about doing sth** mettersi a fare qc.

set aside vt mettere da parte.

set back vt (progress) ritardare; **to ~ back (by)** (in time) mettere indietro (di); **a house ~ back from the road** una casa a una certa distanza dalla strada.

set in vi (infection) svilupparsi; (complications) intervenire; **the rain has ~ in for the day** ormai pioverà tutto il giorno.

set off vi partire ♦ vt (bomb) far scoppiare; (cause to start) mettere in moto; (show up well) dare risalto a.

set out vi partire; (aim): **to ~ out to do** proporsi di fare ♦ vt (arrange) disporre; (state) esporre, presentare.

set up vt (organization) fondare, costituire; (record) stabilire; (monument) innalzare.

setback ['sɛtbæk] n (hitch) contrattempo, inconveniente m; (in health) ricaduta.

set menu n menù m inv fisso.

set square n squadra.

settee [sɛ'tiː] n divano, sofà m inv.

setting ['sɛtɪŋ] n ambiente m; (scenery) sfondo; (of jewel) montatura.

setting lotion n fissatore m.

settle ['sɛtl] vt (argument, matter) appianare; (problem) risolvere; (pay: bill, account) regolare, saldare; (MED: calm) calmare; (colonize: land) colonizzare ♦ vi (bird, dust etc) posarsi; (sediment) depositarsi; (also: ~ down) sistemarsi, stabilirsi; (become calmer) calmarsi; **to ~ to sth** applicarsi a qc; **to ~ for sth** accontentarsi di qc; **to ~ on sth** decidersi per qc; **that's ~d then** allora è deciso; **to ~ one's stomach** calmare il mal di stomaco.

settle in vi sistemarsi.

settle up vi: **to ~ up with sb** regolare i conti con qn.

settlement ['sɛtlmənt] n (payment) pagamento, saldo; (agreement) accordo; (colony) colonia; (village etc) villaggio, comunità f inv; **in ~ of our account** (COMM)

a saldo del nostro conto.
settler ['sɛtlə*] n colonizzatore/trice.
setup ['sɛtʌp] n (arrangement) sistemazione f; (situation) situazione f.
seven ['sɛvn] num sette.
seventeen [sɛvn'tiːn] num diciassette.
seventh ['sɛvnθ] num settimo(a).
seventy ['sɛvntɪ] num settanta.
sever ['sɛvə*] vt recidere, tagliare; (relations) troncare.
several ['sɛvərl] a, pronoun alcuni(e), diversi(e); ~ of us alcuni di noi; ~ times diverse volte.
severance ['sɛvərəns] n (of relations) rottura.
severance pay n indennità di licenziamento.
severe [sɪ'vɪə*] a severo(a); (serious) serio(a), grave; (hard) duro(a); (plain) semplice, sobrio(a).
severely [sɪ'vɪəlɪ] ad (gen) severamente; (wounded, ill) gravemente.
severity [sɪ'vɛrɪtɪ] n severità; gravità; (of weather) rigore m.
sew, pt **sewed**, pp **sewn** [səu, səud, səun] vt, vi cucire.
   sew up vt ricucire; **it is all sewn up** (fig) è tutto apposto.
sewage ['suːɪdʒ] n acque fpl di scolo.
sewer ['suːə*] n fogna.
sewing ['səuɪŋ] n cucito.
sewing machine n macchina da cucire.
sewn [səun] pp of **sew**.
sex [sɛks] n sesso; **to have ~ with** avere rapporti sessuali con.
sex act n atto sessuale.
sexism ['sɛksɪzəm] n sessismo.
sexist ['sɛksɪst] a sessista.
sextet [sɛks'tɛt] n sestetto.
sexual ['sɛksjuəl] a sessuale; ~ **assault** violenza carnale; ~ **intercourse** rapporti mpl sessuali.
sexy ['sɛksɪ] a provocante, sexy inv.
Seychelles [seɪ'ʃɛlz] npl: **the ~** le Seicelle.
SF n abbr = **science fiction**.
SG n abbr (US) = **Surgeon General**.
Sgt. abbr (= sergeant) serg.
shabbiness ['ʃæbɪnɪs] n trasandatezza; squallore m; meschinità.
shabby ['ʃæbɪ] a trasandato(a); (building) squallido(a), malandato(a); (behaviour) meschino(a).
shack [ʃæk] n baracca, capanna.
shackles ['ʃæklz] npl ferri mpl, catene fpl.
shade [ʃeɪd] n ombra; (for lamp) paralume m; (of colour) tonalità f inv; (US: window ~) veneziana; (small quantity): **a ~ of** un po' or un'ombra di ♦ vt ombreggiare, fare ombra a; **~s** npl (US: sunglasses) occhiali mpl da sole; **in the ~** all'ombra; **a ~ smaller** un tantino più piccolo.
shadow ['ʃædəu] n ombra ♦ vt (follow) pedinare; **without** or **beyond a ~ of doubt** senz'ombra di dubbio.
shadow cabinet n (Brit POL) governo m ombra inv.

shadowy ['ʃædəuɪ] a ombreggiato(a), ombroso(a); (dim) vago(a), indistinto(a).
shady ['ʃeɪdɪ] a ombroso(a); (fig: dishonest) losco(a), equivoco(a).
shaft [ʃɑːft] n (of arrow, spear) asta; (AUT, TECH) albero; (of mine) pozzo; (of lift) tromba; (of light) raggio; **ventilator ~** condotto di ventilazione.
shaggy ['ʃægɪ] a ispido(a).
shake [ʃeɪk] vb (pt **shook**, pp **shaken** [ʃuk, 'ʃeɪkn]) vt scuotere; (bottle, cocktail) agitare ♦ vi tremare ♦ n scossa; **to ~ one's head** scuotere la testa; **to ~ hands with sb** stringere or dare la mano a qn.
   shake off vt scrollare (via); (fig) sbarazzarsi di.
   shake up vt scuotere.
shake-up ['ʃeɪkʌp] n riorganizzazione f drastica.
shakily ['ʃeɪkɪlɪ] ad (reply) con voce tremante; (walk) con passo malfermo; (write) con mano tremante.
shaky ['ʃeɪkɪ] a (hand, voice) tremante; (memory) labile; (knowledge) incerto(a); (building) traballante.
shale [ʃeɪl] n roccia scistosa.
shall [ʃæl] auxiliary vb: **I ~ go** andrò.
shallot [ʃə'lɔt] n (Brit) scalogna.
shallow ['ʃæləu] a poco profondo(a); (fig) superficiale.
sham [ʃæm] n finzione f, messinscena; (jewellery, furniture) imitazione f ♦ a finto(a) ♦ vt fingere, simulare.
shambles ['ʃæmblz] n confusione f, baraonda, scompiglio; **the economy is (in) a complete ~** l'economia è nel caos più totale.
shame [ʃeɪm] n vergogna ♦ vt far vergognare; **it is a ~ (that/to do)** è un peccato (che + sub/fare); **what a ~!** che peccato!; **to put sb/sth to ~** (fig) far sfigurare qn/qc.
shamefaced ['ʃeɪmfeɪst] a vergognoso(a).
shameful ['ʃeɪmful] a vergognoso(a).
shameless ['ʃeɪmlɪs] a sfrontato(a); (immodest) spudorato(a).
shampoo [ʃæm'puː] n shampoo m inv ♦ vt fare lo shampoo a; ~ **and set** shampoo e messa in piega.
shamrock ['ʃæmrɔk] n trifoglio (simbolo nazionale dell'Irlanda).
shandy ['ʃændɪ] n birra con gassosa.
shan't [ʃɑːnt] = **shall not**.
shanty town ['ʃæntɪ-] n bidonville f inv.
SHAPE [ʃeɪp] n abbr (= Supreme Headquarters Allied Powers, Europe) supremo quartier generale delle Potenze Alleate in Europa.
shape [ʃeɪp] n forma ♦ vt (clay, stone) dar forma a; (fig: ideas, character) formare; (: course of events) determinare, condizionare; (statement) formulare; (sb's ideas) condizionare ♦ vi (also: ~ **up**: events) andare, mettersi; (: person) cavarsela; **to take ~** prendere forma; **in the ~ of a heart** a forma di cuore; **to get o.s. into ~**

rimettersi in forma; **I can't bear gardening in any ~ or form** detesto il giardinaggio d'ogni genere e specie.

-shaped [ʃeɪpt] *suffix*: **heart-~** a forma di cuore.

shapeless ['ʃeɪplɪs] *a* senza forma, informe.

shapely ['ʃeɪplɪ] *a* ben proporzionato(a).

share [ʃeə*] *n* (*thing received*, *contribution*) parte *f*; (COMM) azione *f* ♦ *vt* dividere; (*have in common*) condividere, avere in comune; **to ~ out (among or between)** dividere (tra); **to ~ in** partecipare a.

share capital *n* capitale *m* azionario.

share certificate *n* certificato azionario.

shareholder ['ʃɛəhəʊldə*] *n* azionista *m/f*.

share index *n* listino di Borsa.

shark [ʃɑːk] *n* squalo, pescecane *m*.

sharp [ʃɑːp] *a* (*razor*, *knife*) affilato(a); (*point*) acuto(a), acuminato(a); (*nose*, *chin*) aguzzo(a); (*outline*) netto(a); (*curve*, *bend*) stretto(a), accentuato(a); (*cold*, *pain*) pungente; (*voice*) stridulo(a); (*person: quick-witted*) sveglio(a); (: *unscrupulous*) disonesto(a); (MUS): **C ~** do diesis ♦ *n* (MUS) diesis *m inv* ♦ *ad*: **at 2 o'clock ~** alle due in punto; **turn ~ left** giri tutto a sinistra; **to be ~ with sb** rimproverare qn; **look ~!** sbrigati!

sharpen ['ʃɑːpən] *vt* affilare; (*pencil*) fare la punta a; (*fig*) aguzzare.

sharpener ['ʃɑːpnə*] *n* (*also*: **pencil ~**) temperamatite *m inv*; (*also*: **knife ~**) affilacoltelli *m inv*.

sharp-eyed [ʃɑːp'aɪd] *a* dalla vista acuta.

sharply ['ʃɑːplɪ] *ad* (*abruptly*) bruscamente; (*clearly*) nettamente; (*harshly*) duramente, aspramente.

sharp-tempered [ʃɑːp'tɛmpəd] *a* irascibile.

shatter ['ʃætə*] *vt* mandare in frantumi, frantumare; (*fig*: *upset*) distruggere; (: *ruin*) rovinare ♦ *vi* frantumarsi, andare in pezzi.

shattered ['ʃætəd] *a* (*grief-stricken*) sconvolto(a); (*exhausted*) a pezzi, distrutto(a).

shatterproof ['ʃætəpruːf] *a* infrangibile.

shave [ʃeɪv] *vt* radere, rasare ♦ *vi* radersi, farsi la barba ♦ *n*: **to have a ~** farsi la barba.

shaven ['ʃeɪvn] *a* (*head*) rasato(a), tonsurato(a).

shaver ['ʃeɪvə*] *n* (*also*: **electric ~**) rasoio elettrico.

shaving ['ʃeɪvɪŋ] *n* (*action*) rasatura; **~s** *npl* (*of wood etc*) trucioli *mpl*.

shaving brush *n* pennello da barba.

shaving cream *n* crema da barba.

shaving soap *n* sapone *m* da barba.

shawl [ʃɔːl] *n* scialle *m*.

she [ʃiː] *pronoun* ella, lei; **there ~ is** eccola; **~-bear** orsa; **~-elephant** elefantessa; NB: *for ships, countries follow the gender of your translation.*

sheaf, *pl* **sheaves** [ʃiːf, ʃiːvz] *n* covone *m*.

shear [ʃɪə*] *vt* (*pt* **~ed**, *pp* **~ed** *or* **shorn**

[ʃɔːn]) (*sheep*) tosare.

shear off *vi* (*break off*) spezzarsi.

shears ['ʃɪəz] *npl* (*for hedge*) cesoie *fpl*.

sheath [ʃiːθ] *n* fodero, guaina; (*contraceptive*) preservativo.

sheathe [ʃiːð] *vt* rivestire; (*sword*) rinfoderare.

sheath knife *n* coltello (con fodero).

sheaves [ʃiːvz] *npl of* **sheaf**.

shed [ʃɛd] *n* capannone *m* ♦ *vt* (*pt*, *pp* **shed**) (*leaves*, *fur etc*) perdere; (*tears*) versare; **to ~ light on** (*problem*, *mystery*) far luce su.

she'd [ʃiːd] = **she had**; **she would**.

sheen [ʃiːn] *n* lucentezza.

sheep [ʃiːp] *n* (*pl inv*) pecora.

sheepdog ['ʃiːpdɔg] *n* cane *m* da pastore.

sheep farmer *n* allevatore *m* di pecore.

sheepish ['ʃiːpɪʃ] *a* vergognoso(a), timido(a).

sheepskin ['ʃiːpskɪn] *n* pelle *f* di pecora.

sheepskin jacket *n* (giacca di) montone *m*.

sheer [ʃɪə*] *a* (*utter*) vero(a) (e proprio(a)); (*steep*) a picco, perpendicolare; (*transparent*) trasparente ♦ *ad* a picco; **by ~ chance** per puro caso.

sheet [ʃiːt] *n* (*on bed*) lenzuolo; (*of paper*) foglio; (*of glass*) lastra; (*of metal*) foglio, lamina.

sheet feed *n* (*on printer*) alimentazione *f* di fogli.

sheet lightning *n* lampo diffuso.

sheet metal *n* lamiera.

sheet music *n* fogli *mpl* di musica.

sheik(h) [ʃeɪk] *n* sceicco.

shelf, *pl* **shelves** [ʃɛlf, ʃɛlvz] *n* scaffale *m*, mensola.

shelf life *n* (COMM) durata di conservazione.

shell [ʃɛl] *n* (*on beach*) conchiglia; (*of egg, nut etc*) guscio; (*explosive*) granata; (*of building*) scheletro, struttura ♦ *vt* (*peas*) sgranare; (MIL) bombardare, cannoneggiare.

shell out *vi* (*col*): **to ~ out (for)** sganciare soldi (per).

she'll [ʃiːl] = **she will**; **she shall**.

shellfish ['ʃɛlfɪʃ] *n* (*pl inv*) (*crab etc*) crostaceo; (*scallop etc*) mollusco; (*pl: as food*) crostacei; molluschi.

shelter ['ʃɛltə*] *n* riparo, rifugio ♦ *vt* riparare, proteggere; (*give lodging to*) dare rifugio *or* asilo a ♦ *vi* ripararsi, mettersi al riparo; **to take ~ (from)** mettersi al riparo (da).

sheltered ['ʃɛltəd] *a* (*life*) ritirato(a); (*spot*) riparato(a), protetto(a).

shelve [ʃɛlv] *vt* (*fig*) accantonare, rimandare.

shelves [ʃɛlvz] *npl of* **shelf**.

shelving ['ʃɛlvɪŋ] *n* scaffalature *fpl*.

shepherd ['ʃɛpəd] *n* pastore *m* ♦ *vt* (*guide*) guidare.

shepherdess ['ʃɛpədɪs] *n* pastora.

shepherd's pie *n* timballo di carne macinata e purè di patate.

sherbet ['ʃɜːbət] *n* (*Brit*: *powder*) polvere effervescente al gusto di frutta; (US: *water ice*) sorbetto.

sheriff ['ʃɛrɪf] *n* sceriffo.

sherry ['ʃɛrɪ] *n* sherry *m inv*.
she's [ʃiːz] = **she is; she has**.
Shetland ['ʃɛtlənd] *n* (*also*: **the ~s, the ~ Isles**) le (isole) Shetland.
shield [ʃiːld] *n* scudo ♦ *vt*: **to ~ (from)** riparare (da), proteggere (da *or* contro).
shift [ʃɪft] *n* (*change*) cambiamento; (*of workers*) turno ♦ *vt* spostare, muovere; (*remove*) rimuovere ♦ *vi* spostarsi, muoversi; **~ in demand** (*COMM*) variazione *f* della domanda; **the wind has ~ed to the south** il vento si è girato e soffia da sud.
shift key *n* (*on typewriter*) tasto delle maiuscole.
shiftless ['ʃɪftlɪs] *a* fannullone(a).
shift work *n* lavoro a squadre; **to do ~** fare i turni.
shifty ['ʃɪftɪ] *a* ambiguo(a); (*eyes*) sfuggente.
shilling ['ʃɪlɪŋ] *n* (*Brit*) scellino (= *12 old pence; 20 in a pound*).
shilly-shally ['ʃɪlɪʃælɪ] *vi* tentennare, esitare.
shimmer ['ʃɪmə*] *vi* brillare, luccicare.
shimmering ['ʃɪmərɪŋ] *a* (*gen*) luccicante, scintillante; (*haze*) tremolante; (*satin etc*) cangiante.
shin [ʃɪn] *n* tibia ♦ *vi*: **to ~ up/down a tree** arrampicarsi in cima a/scivolare giù da un albero.
shindig ['ʃɪndɪg] *n* (*col*) festa chiassosa.
shine [ʃaɪn] *n* splendore *m*, lucentezza ♦ *vb* (*pt, pp* **shone** [ʃɔn]) *vi* (ri)splendere, brillare ♦ *vt* far brillare, far risplendere; (*torch*): **to ~ sth on** puntare qc verso.
shingle ['ʃɪŋgl] *n* (*on beach*) ciottoli *mpl*; (*on roof*) assicella di copertura.
shingles ['ʃɪŋglz] *n* (*MED*) herpes zoster *m*.
shining ['ʃaɪnɪŋ] *a* (*surface, hair*) lucente; (*light*) brillante.
shiny ['ʃaɪnɪ] *a* lucente, lucido(a).
ship [ʃɪp] *n* nave *f* ♦ *vt* trasportare (via mare); (*send*) spedire (via mare); (*load*) imbarcare, caricare; **on board ~** a bordo.
shipbuilder ['ʃɪpbɪldə*] *n* costruttore *m* navale.
shipbuilding ['ʃɪpbɪldɪŋ] *n* costruzione *f* navale.
ship chandler [-'tʃɑːndlə*] *n* fornitore *m* marittimo.
shipment ['ʃɪpmənt] *n* carico.
shipowner ['ʃɪpəunə*] *n* armatore *m*.
shipper ['ʃɪpə*] *n* spedizioniere *m* (marittimo).
shipping ['ʃɪpɪŋ] *n* (*ships*) naviglio; (*traffic*) navigazione *f*.
shipping agent *n* agente *m* marittimo.
shipping company *n* compagnia di navigazione.
shipping lane *n* rotta (di navigazione).
shipping line *n* = **shipping company**.
shipshape ['ʃɪpʃeɪp] *a* in perfetto ordine.
shipwreck ['ʃɪprɛk] *n* relitto; (*event*) naufragio ♦ *vt*: **to be ~ed** naufragare, fare naufragio.
shipyard ['ʃɪpjɑːd] *n* cantiere *m* navale.

shire ['ʃaɪə*] *n* (*Brit*) contea.
shirk [ʃəːk] *vt* sottrarsi a, evitare.
shirt [ʃəːt] *n* (*man's*) camicia; **in ~ sleeves** in maniche di camicia.
shirty ['ʃəːtɪ] *a* (*Brit col*) incavolato(a).
shit [ʃɪt] *excl* (*col!*) merda(!).
shiver ['ʃɪvə*] *n* brivido ♦ *vi* rabbrividire, tremare.
shoal [ʃəul] *n* (*of fish*) banco.
shock [ʃɔk] *n* (*impact*) urto, colpo; (*ELEC*) scossa; (*emotional*) colpo, shock *m inv*; (*MED*) shock ♦ *vt* colpire, scioccare; scandalizzare; **to give sb a ~** far venire un colpo a qn; **to be suffering from ~** essere in stato di shock; **it came as a ~ to hear that** ... è stata una grossa sorpresa sentire che ....
shock absorber *n* ammortizzatore *m*.
shocking ['ʃɔkɪŋ] *a* scioccante, traumatizzante; (*scandalous*) scandaloso(a); (*very bad: weather, handwriting*) orribile; (: *results*) disastroso(a).
shockproof ['ʃɔkpruːf] *a* antiurto *inv*.
shock therapy, shock treatment *n* (*MED*) shockterapia.
shod [ʃɔd] *pt, pp of* **shoe**.
shoddy ['ʃɔdɪ] *a* scadente.
shoe [ʃuː] *n* scarpa; (*also*: **horse~**) ferro di cavallo; (*brake ~*) ganascia (del freno) ♦ *vt* (*pt, pp* **shod** [ʃɔd]) (*horse*) ferrare.
shoebrush ['ʃuːbrʌʃ] *n* spazzola per le scarpe.
shoehorn ['ʃuːhɔːn] *n* calzante *m*.
shoelace ['ʃuːleɪs] *n* stringa.
shoemaker ['ʃuːmeɪkə*] *n* calzolaio.
shoe polish *n* lucido per scarpe.
shoeshop ['ʃuːʃɔp] *n* calzoleria.
shoestring ['ʃuːstrɪŋ] *n* stringa (delle scarpe); **on a ~** (*fig: do sth*) con quattro soldi.
shoetree ['ʃuːtriː] *n* forma per scarpe.
shone [ʃɔn] *pt, pp of* **shine**.
shoo [ʃuː] *excl* sciò!, via! ♦ *vt* (*also*: **~ away, ~ off**) cacciare (via).
shook [ʃuk] *pt of* **shake**.
shoot [ʃuːt] *n* (*on branch, seedling*) germoglio; (*shooting party*) partita di caccia; (*competition*) gara di tiro ♦ *vb* (*pt, pp* **shot** [ʃɔt]) *vt* (*game: Brit*) cacciare, andare a caccia di; (*person*) sparare a; (*execute*) fucilare; (*film*) girare ♦ *vi* (*with gun*): **to ~ (at)** sparare (a), fare fuoco (su); (*with bow*): **to ~ (at)** tirare (su); (*FOOTBALL*) sparare, tirare (forte); **to ~ past sb** passare vicino a qn come un fulmine; **to ~ in/out** entrare/ uscire come una freccia.
shoot down *vt* (*plane*) abbattere.
shoot up *vi* (*fig*) salire alle stelle.
shooting ['ʃuːtɪŋ] *n* (*shots*) sparatoria; (*murder*) uccisione *f* (a colpi d'arma da fuoco); (*HUNTING*) caccia; (*CINEMA*) riprese *fpl*.
shooting range *n* poligono (di tiro), tirassegno.
shooting star *n* stella cadente.
shop [ʃɔp] *n* negozio; (*workshop*) officina ♦ *vi* (*also*: **go ~ping**) fare spese; **repair ~**

officina di riparazione; **to talk ~** (*fig*) parlare di lavoro.

shop around *vi* fare il giro dei negozi.

shop assistant *n* (*Brit*) commesso/a.

shop floor *n* (*Brit*: *fig*) operai *mpl*, maestranze *fpl*.

shopkeeper ['ʃɔpkiːpəˈ] *n* negoziante *m/f*, bottegaio/a.

shoplift ['ʃɔplɪft] *vi* taccheggiare.

shoplifter ['ʃɔplɪftəˈ] *n* taccheggiatore/trice.

shoplifting ['ʃɔplɪftɪŋ] *n* taccheggio.

shopper ['ʃɔpəˈ] *n* compratore/trice.

shopping ['ʃɔpɪŋ] *n* (*goods*) spesa, acquisti *mpl*.

shopping bag *n* borsa per la spesa.

shopping centre *n* centro commerciale.

shop-soiled ['ʃɔpsɔɪld] *a* sciupato(a) a forza di stare in vetrina.

shop steward *n* (*Brit INDUSTRY*) rappresentante *m* sindacale.

shop window *n* vetrina.

shore [ʃɔːˈ] *n* (*of sea*) riva, spiaggia; (*of lake*) riva ♦ *vt*: **to ~ (up)** puntellare; **on ~** a terra.

shore leave *n* (*NAUT*) franchigia.

shorn [ʃɔːn] *pp of* **shear**.

short [ʃɔːt] *a* (*not long*) corto(a); (*soon finished*) breve; (*person*) basso(a); (*curt*) brusco(a), secco(a); (*insufficient*) insufficiente ♦ *n* (*also*: **~ film**) cortometraggio; **it is ~ for** è l'abbreviazione *or* il diminutivo di; **a ~ time ago** poco tempo fa; **in the ~ term** nell'immediato futuro; **to be ~ of sth** essere a corto di *or* mancare di qc; **to run ~ of sth** rimanere senza qc; **to be in ~ supply** scarseggiare; **I'm 3 ~** me ne mancano 3; **in ~** in breve; **~ of doing** a meno che non si faccia; **everything ~ of** tutto fuorché; **to cut ~** (*speech, visit*) accorciare, abbreviare; (*person*) interrompere; **to fall ~ of** venire meno a; non soddisfare; **to stop ~** fermarsi di colpo; **to stop ~ of** non arrivare fino a; *see also* **shorts**.

shortage ['ʃɔːtɪdʒ] *n* scarsezza, carenza.

shortbread ['ʃɔːtbrɛd] *n* biscotto di pasta frolla.

short-change [ʃɔːt'tʃeɪndʒ] *vt*: **to ~ sb** imbrogliare qn sul resto.

short-circuit [ʃɔːt'səːkɪt] *n* cortocircuito ♦ *vt* cortocircuitare ♦ *vi* fare cortocircuito.

shortcoming ['ʃɔːtkʌmɪŋ] *n* difetto.

short(crust) pastry ['ʃɔːt(krʌst)-] *n* (*Brit*) pasta frolla.

shortcut ['ʃɔːtkʌt] *n* scorciatoia.

shorten ['ʃɔːtn] *vt* accorciare, ridurre.

shortening ['ʃɔːtnɪŋ] *n* grasso per pasticceria.

shortfall ['ʃɔːtfɔːl] *n* deficienza.

shorthand ['ʃɔːthænd] *n* (*Brit*) stenografia; **to take sth down in ~** stenografare qc.

shorthand notebook *n* (*Brit*) bloc-notes *m inv* per stenografia.

shorthand typist *n* (*Brit*) stenodattilografo/a.

short list *n* (*Brit*: *for job*) rosa dei candidati.

short-lived ['ʃɔːt'lɪvd] *a* effimero(a), di breve durata.

shortly ['ʃɔːtlɪ] *ad* fra poco.

shortness ['ʃɔːtnɪs] *n* brevità; insufficienza.

shorts [ʃɔːts] *npl* (*also*: **a pair of ~**) i calzoncini.

short-sighted [ʃɔːt'saɪtɪd] *a* (*Brit*) miope; (*fig*) poco avveduto(a).

short-staffed [ʃɔːt'stɑːft] *a* a corto di personale.

short story *n* racconto, novella.

short-tempered [ʃɔːt'tɛmpəd] *a* irascibile.

short-term ['ʃɔːtːəːm] *a* (*effect*) di *or* a breve durata.

short time *n* (*INDUSTRY*): **to work ~, be on ~** essere *or* lavorare a orario ridotto.

short wave *n* (*RADIO*) onde *fpl* corte.

shot [ʃɔt] *pt, pp of* **shoot** ♦ *n* sparo, colpo; (*shotgun pellets*) pallottole *fpl*; (*person*) tiratore *m*; (*try*) prova; (*injection*) iniezione *f*; (*PHOT*) foto *f inv*; **like a ~** come un razzo; (*very readily*) immediatamente; **to fire a ~ at sb/sth** sparare un colpo a qn/qc; **to have a ~ at sth/doing sth** provarci con qc/a fare qc; **a big ~** (*col*) un pezzo grosso, un papavero; **to get ~ of sb/sth** (*col*) sbarazzarsi di qn/qc.

shotgun ['ʃɔtgʌn] *n* fucile *m* da caccia.

should [ʃud] *auxiliary vb*: **I ~ go now** dovrei andare ora; **he ~ be there now** dovrebbe essere arrivato ora; **I ~ go if I were you** se fossi in lei andrei; **I ~ like to** mi piacerebbe; **~ he phone ...** se telefonasse ....

shoulder ['ʃəuldəˈ] *n* spalla; (*Brit*: *of road*): **hard ~** corsia d'emergenza ♦ *vt* (*fig*) addossarsi, prendere sulle proprie spalle; **to look over one's ~** guardarsi alle spalle; **to rub ~s with sb** (*fig*) essere a contatto con qn; **to give sb the cold ~** (*fig*) trattare qn con freddezza.

shoulder bag *n* borsa a tracolla.

shoulder blade *n* scapola.

shoulder strap *n* bretella, spallina.

shouldn't ['ʃudnt] = **should not**.

shout [ʃaut] *n* urlo, grido ♦ *vt* gridare ♦ *vi* urlare, gridare; **to give sb a ~** chiamare qn gridando.

shout down *vt* zittire gridando.

shouting ['ʃautɪŋ] *n* urli *mpl*.

shove [ʃʌv] *vt* spingere; (*col*: *put*): **to ~ sth in** ficcare qc in ♦ *n* spintone *m*; **he ~d me out of the way** mi ha spinto da parte.

shove off *vi* (*NAUT*) scostarsi.

shovel ['ʃʌvl] *n* pala ♦ *vt* spalare.

show [ʃəu] *n* (*of emotion*) dimostrazione *f*, manifestazione *f*; (*semblance*) apparenza; (*exhibition*) mostra, esposizione *f*; (*THEATRE, CINEMA*) spettacolo; (*COMM, TECH*) salone *m*, fiera ♦ *vb* (*pt* **~ed**, *pp* **shown** [ʃəun]) *vt* far vedere, mostrare; (*courage etc*) dimostrare, dar prova di; (*exhibit*) esporre ♦ *vi* vedersi, essere visibile; **to ~ sb to his seat/ to the door** accompagnare qn al suo posto/ alla porta; **to ~ a profit/loss** (*COMM*) registrare un utile/una perdita; **it just goes to ~ that** ... il che sta a dimostrare che ...; **to ask for a ~ of hands** chiedere che si voti per alzata di mano; **to be on ~** essere esposto; **it's just for ~** è solo per far scena; **who's running the ~ here?** (col) chi è il padrone qui?

show in vt far entrare.

show off vi (pej) esibirsi, mettersi in mostra ♦ vt (display) mettere in risalto; (pej) mettere in mostra.

show out vt accompagnare alla porta.

show up vi (stand out) essere ben visibile; (col: turn up) farsi vedere ♦ vt mettere in risalto; (unmask) smascherare.

show business n industria dello spettacolo.

showcase ['ʃəukeıs] n vetrina, bacheca.

showdown ['ʃəudaun] n prova di forza.

shower ['ʃauə*] n (also: ~ bath) doccia; (rain) acquazzone m; (of stones etc) pioggia; (US: party) festa (di fidanzamento etc) in cui si fanno regali alla persona festeggiata ♦ vi fare la doccia ♦ vt: **to ~ sb with** (gifts, abuse etc) coprire qn di; (missiles) lanciare contro qn una pioggia di; **to have** or **take a ~** fare la doccia.

shower cap n cuffia da doccia.

showerproof ['ʃauəpru:f] a impermeabile.

showery ['ʃauərı] a (weather) con piogge intermittenti.

showground ['ʃəugraund] n terreno d'esposizione.

showing ['ʃəuıŋ] n (of film) proiezione f.

show jumping n concorso ippico (di salto ad ostacoli).

showman ['ʃəumən] n (at fair, circus) impresario; (fig) attore m.

showmanship ['ʃəumənʃıp] n abilità d'impresario.

shown [ʃəun] pp of **show**.

show-off ['ʃəuɔf] n (col: person) esibizionista m/f.

showpiece ['ʃəupi:s] n (of exhibition) pezzo forte; **that hospital is a ~** è un ospedale modello.

showroom ['ʃəurum] n sala d'esposizione.

showy ['ʃəuı] a vistoso(a), appariscente.

shrank [ʃræŋk] pt of **shrink**.

shrapnel ['ʃræpnl] n shrapnel m.

shred [ʃred] n (gen pl) brandello; (fig: of truth, evidence) briciola ♦ vt fare a brandelli; (CULIN) sminuzzare, tagliuzzare; (documents) distruggere, sminuzzare.

shredder ['ʃredə*] n (for documents, papers) distruttore m di documenti, sminuzzatrice f.

shrew [ʃru:] n (ZOOL) toporagno; (fig: pej: woman) strega.

shrewd [ʃru:d] a astuto(a), scaltro(a).

shrewdness ['ʃru:dnıs] n astuzia.

shriek [ʃri:k] n strillo ♦ vt, vi strillare.

shrift [ʃrıft] n: **to give sb short ~** sbrigare qn.

shrill [ʃrıl] a acuto(a), stridulo(a), stridente.

shrimp [ʃrımp] n gamberetto.

shrine [ʃraın] n reliquario; (place) santuario.

shrink [ʃrıŋk] vb (pt **shrank**, pp **shrunk** [ʃræŋk, ʃrʌŋk]) vi restringersi; (fig) ridursi ♦ vt (wool) far restringere ♦ n (col: pej) psicanalista m/f; **to ~ from doing sth** rifuggire dal fare qc.

shrinkage ['ʃrıŋkıdʒ] n restringimento.

shrink-wrap ['ʃrıŋkræp] vt confezionare con plastica sottile.

shrivel ['ʃrıvl] (also: ~ up) vt raggrinzare, avvizzire ♦ vi raggrinzirsi, avvizzire.

shroud [ʃraud] n sudario ♦ vt: **~ed in mystery** avvolto(a) nel mistero.

Shrove Tuesday ['ʃrəuv-] n martedì m grasso.

shrub [ʃrʌb] n arbusto.

shrubbery ['ʃrʌbərı] n arbusti mpl.

shrug [ʃrʌg] n scrollata di spalle ♦ vt, vi: **to ~ (one's shoulders)** alzare le spalle, fare spallucce.

shrug off vt passare sopra a; (cold, illness) sbarazzarsi di.

shrunk [ʃrʌŋk] pp of **shrink**.

shrunken ['ʃrʌŋkən] a rattrappito(a).

shudder ['ʃʌdə*] n brivido ♦ vi rabbrividire.

shuffle ['ʃʌfl] vt (cards) mescolare; **to ~ (one's feet)** strascicare i piedi.

shun [ʃʌn] vt sfuggire, evitare.

shunt [ʃʌnt] vt (RAIL: direct) smistare; (: divert) deviare ♦ vi: **to ~ (to and fro)** fare la spola.

shunting ['ʃʌntıŋ] n (RAIL) smistamento.

shunting yard n fascio di smistamento.

shush [ʃuʃ] excl zitto(a)!

shut, pt, pp **shut** [ʃʌt] vt chiudere ♦ vi chiudersi, chiudere.

shut down vt, vi chiudere definitivamente.

shut off vt (stop: power) staccare; (: water) chiudere; (: engine) spegnere; (isolate) isolare.

shut out vt (person, noise, cold) non far entrare; (block: view) impedire, bloccare; (: memory) scacciare.

shut up vi (col: keep quiet) stare zitto(a) ♦ vt (close) chiudere; (silence) far tacere.

shutdown ['ʃʌtdaun] n chiusura.

shutter ['ʃʌtə*] n imposta; (PHOT) otturatore m.

shuttle ['ʃʌtl] n spola, navetta; (also: ~ service) servizio m navetta inv ♦ vi (subj: vehicle, person) fare la spola ♦ vt (to and fro: passengers) portare (avanti e indietro).

shuttlecock ['ʃʌtlkɔk] n volano.

shy [ʃaı] a timido(a) ♦ vi: **to ~ away from doing sth** (fig) rifuggire dal fare qc; **to fight ~ of** tenersi alla larga da; **to be ~ of doing sth** essere restio a fare qc.

shyness ['ʃaınıs] n timidezza.

Siam [saı'æm] n Siam m.

Siamese [saıə'mi:z] a: **~ cat** gatto siamese; **~ twins** fratelli mpl (or sorelle fpl) siamesi.

Siberia [saı'bıərıə] n Siberia.

sibling ['sıblıŋ] n (formal) fratello/sorella.

Sicilian [sı'sılıən] a, n siciliano(a).

Sicily ['sɪsɪlɪ] *n* Sicilia.

sick [sɪk] *a* (*ill*) malato(a); (*vomiting*): **to be ~** vomitare; (*humour*) macabro(a); **to feel ~** avere la nausea; **to be ~ of** (*fig*) averne abbastanza di; **a ~ person** un malato; **to be (off) ~** essere assente perché malato; **to fall** *or* **take ~** ammalarsi.

sick bay *n* infermeria.

sicken ['sɪkn] *vt* nauseare ♦ *vi*: **to be ~ing for sth** (*cold, flu etc*) covare qc.

sickening ['sɪknɪŋ] *a* (*fig*) disgustoso(a), rivoltante.

sickle ['sɪkl] *n* falcetto.

sick leave *n* congedo per malattia.

sickly ['sɪklɪ] *a* malaticcio(a); (*causing nausea*) nauseante.

sickness ['sɪknɪs] *n* malattia; (*vomiting*) vomito.

sickness benefit *n* indennità di malattia.

sick pay *n* sussidio per malattia.

sickroom ['sɪkruːm] *n* stanza di malato.

side [saɪd] *n* (*gen*) lato; (*of person, animal*) fianco; (*of lake*) riva; (*face, surface: gen*) faccia; (*: of paper*) facciata; (*fig: aspect*) aspetto, lato; (*team: SPORT*) squadra; (*: POL etc*) parte *f* ♦ *cpd* (*door, entrance*) laterale ♦ *vi*: **to ~ with sb** parteggiare per qn, prendere le parti di qn; **by the ~ of** a fianco di; (*road*) sul ciglio di; **~ by ~** fianco a fianco; **to take ~s (with)** schierarsi (con); **the right/wrong ~** il dritto/rovescio; **from ~ to ~** da una parte all'altra; **~ of beef** quarto di bue.

sideboard ['saɪdbɔːd] *n* credenza.

sideboards ['saɪdbɔːdz] (*Brit*), **sideburns** ['saɪdbəːnz] *npl* (*whiskers*) basette *fpl*.

sidecar ['saɪdkɑː*] *n* sidecar *m inv.*

side dish *n* contorno.

side drum *n* (*MUS*) piccolo tamburo.

side effect *n* (*MED*) effetto collaterale.

sidekick ['saɪdkɪk] *n* (*col*) compagno/a.

sidelight ['saɪdlaɪt] *n* (*AUT*) luce *f* di posizione.

sideline ['saɪdlaɪn] *n* (*SPORT*) linea laterale; (*fig*) attività secondaria.

sidelong ['saɪdlɔŋ] *a* obliquo(a); **to give a ~ glance at sth** guardare qc con la coda dell'occhio.

side plate *n* piattino.

side road *n* strada secondaria.

sidesaddle ['saɪdsædl] *ad* all'amazzone.

side show *n* attrazione *f.*

sidestep ['saɪdstɛp] *vt* (*question*) eludere; (*problem*) scavalcare ♦ *vi* (*BOXING etc*) spostarsi di lato.

side street *n* traversa.

sidetrack ['saɪdtræk] *vt* (*fig*) distrarre.

sidewalk ['saɪdwɔːk] *n* (*US*) marciapiede *m.*

sideways ['saɪdweɪz] *ad* (*move*) di lato, di fianco; (*look*) con la coda dell'occhio.

siding ['saɪdɪŋ] *n* (*RAIL*) binario di raccordo.

sidle ['saɪdl] *vi*: **to ~ up (to)** avvicinarsi furtivamente (a).

siege [siːdʒ] *n* assedio; **to lay ~ to** porre l'assedio a.

siege economy *n* economia da stato d'assedio.

Sierra Leone [sɪ'ɛrəlɪ'əun] *n* Sierra Leone *f.*

sieve [sɪv] *n* setaccio ♦ *vt* setacciare.

sift [sɪft] *vt* passare al crivello; (*fig*) vagliare ♦ *vi*: **to ~ through** esaminare minuziosamente.

sigh [saɪ] *n* sospiro ♦ *vi* sospirare.

sight [saɪt] *n* (*faculty*) vista; (*spectacle*) spettacolo; (*on gun*) mira ♦ *vt* avvistare; **in ~** in vista; **out of ~** non visibile; **at first ~** a prima vista; **to catch ~ of sth/sb** scorgere qc/qn; **to lose ~ of sb/sth** perdere di vista qn/qc; **to set one's ~s on sth/on doing sth** mirare a qc/a fare qc; **at ~** a vista; **I know her by ~** la conosco di vista.

sighted ['saɪtɪd] *a* che ha il dono della vista; **partially ~** parzialmente cieco.

sightseeing ['saɪtsiːɪŋ] *n* turismo; **to go ~** visitare una località.

sightseer ['saɪtsiːə*] *n* turista *m/f.*

sign [saɪn] *n* segno; (*with hand etc*) segno, gesto; (*notice*) insegna, cartello; (*road ~*) segnale *m* ♦ *vt* firmare; **as a ~ of** in segno di; **it's a good/bad ~** è buon/brutto segno; **to show ~s/no ~ of doing sth** accennare/non accennare a fare qc; **plus/minus ~** segno del più/meno; **to ~ one's name** firmare, apporre la propria firma.

sign away *vt* (*rights etc*) cedere (con una firma).

sign in *vi* firmare il registro (all'arrivo).

sign off *vi* (*RADIO, TV*) chiudere le trasmissioni.

sign on *vi* (*MIL etc: enlist*) arruolarsi; (*as unemployed*) iscriversi sulla lista (dell'ufficio di collocamento); (*begin work*) prendere servizio; (*enrol*): **to ~ on for a course** iscriversi a un corso.

sign out *vi* firmare il registro (alla partenza).

sign over *vt*: **to ~ sth over to sb** cedere qc con scrittura legale a qn.

sign up (*MIL*) *vt* arruolare ♦ *vi* arruolarsi.

signal ['sɪgnl] *n* segnale *m* ♦ *vt* (*person*) fare segno a; (*message*) comunicare per mezzo di segnali ♦ *vi*: **to ~ to sb (to do sth)** far segno a qn (di fare qc); **to ~ a left/right turn** (*AUT*) segnalare un cambiamento di direzione a sinistra/destra.

signal box *n* (*RAIL*) cabina di manovra.

signalman ['sɪgnlmən] *n* (*RAIL*) deviatore *m.*

signatory ['sɪgnətərɪ] *n* firmatario/a.

signature ['sɪgnətʃə*] *n* firma.

signature tune *n* sigla musicale.

signet ring ['sɪgnət-] *n* anello con sigillo.

significance [sɪg'nɪfɪkəns] *n* (*of remark*) significato; (*of event*) importanza; **that is of no ~** ciò non ha importanza.

significant [sɪg'nɪfɪkənt] *a* (*improvement, amount*) notevole; (*discovery, event*) importante; (*evidence, smile*) significativo(a); **it is ~ that ...** è significativo che ....

significantly [sɪg'nɪfɪkəntlɪ] *ad* (*smile*) in

modo eloquente; *(improve, increase)* considerevolmente, decisamente.

signify ['sɪgnɪfaɪ] *vt* significare.

sign language *n* linguaggio dei muti.

signpost ['saɪnpəʊst] *n* cartello indicatore.

silage ['saɪlɪdʒ] *n* insilato.

silence ['saɪlns] *n* silenzio ♦ *vt* far tacere, ridurre al silenzio.

silencer ['saɪlənsə*] *n* *(on gun, Brit AUT)* silenziatore *m*.

silent ['saɪlnt] *a* silenzioso(a); *(film)* muto(a); **to keep** *or* **remain** ~ tacere, stare zitto(a).

silently ['saɪlntlɪ] *ad* silenziosamente, in silenzio.

silent partner *n* *(COMM)* socio accomandante.

silhouette [sɪlu:'ɛt] *n* silhouette *f inv* ♦ *vt*: **to be ~d against** stagliarsi contro.

silicon ['sɪlɪkən] *n* silicio.

silicon chip *n* piastrina di silicio.

silicone ['sɪlɪkəʊn] *n* silicone *m*.

silk [sɪlk] *n* seta ♦ *cpd* di seta.

silky ['sɪlkɪ] *a* di seta, come la seta.

sill [sɪl] *n* *(window~)* davanzale *m*; *(AUT)* predellino.

silly ['sɪlɪ] *a* stupido(a), sciocco(a); **to do something** ~ fare una sciocchezza.

silo ['saɪləʊ] *n* silo.

silt [sɪlt] *n* limo.

silver ['sɪlvə*] *n* argento; *(money)* monete da 5, 10 o 50 pence; *(also:* ~**ware**) argenteria ♦ *cpd* d'argento.

silver foil, *(Brit)* **silver paper** *n* carta argentata, (carta) stagnola.

silver-plated [sɪlvə'pleɪtɪd] *a* argentato(a).

silversmith ['sɪlvəsmɪθ] *n* argentiere *m*.

silverware ['sɪlvəweə*] *n* argenteria, argento.

silvery ['sɪlvərɪ] *a* *(colour)* argenteo(a); *(sound)* argentino(a).

similar ['sɪmɪlə*] *a*: ~ **(to)** simile (a).

similarity [sɪmɪ'lærɪtɪ] *n* somiglianza, rassomiglianza.

similarly ['sɪmɪləlɪ] *ad* *(in a similar way)* allo stesso modo; *(as is similar)* così pure.

simile ['sɪmɪlɪ] *n* similitudine *f*.

simmer ['sɪmə*] *vi* cuocere a fuoco lento.
simmer down *vi* *(fig col)* calmarsi.

simper ['sɪmpə*] *vi* fare lo(la) smorfioso(a).

simpering ['sɪmpərɪŋ] *a* lezioso(a), smorfioso(a).

simple ['sɪmpl] *a* semplice; **the** ~ **truth** la pura verità.

simple interest *n* *(MATH, COMM)* interesse *m* semplice.

simple-minded [sɪmpl'maɪndɪd] *a* sempliciotto(a).

simpleton ['sɪmpltən] *n* semplicione/a, sempliciotto/a.

simplicity [sɪm'plɪsɪtɪ] *n* semplicità.

simplification [sɪmplɪfɪ'keɪʃən] *n* semplificazione *f*.

simplify ['sɪmplɪfaɪ] *vt* semplificare.

simply ['sɪmplɪ] *ad* semplicemente.

simulate ['sɪmjuleɪt] *vt* fingere, simulare.

simulation [sɪmju'leɪʃən] *n* simulazione *f*.

simultaneous [sɪməl'teɪnɪəs] *a* simultaneo(a).

simultaneously [sɪməl'teɪnɪəslɪ] *ad* simultaneamente, contemporaneamente.

sin [sɪn] *n* peccato ♦ *vi* peccare.

Sinai ['saɪnaɪ] *n* Sinai *m*.

since [sɪns] *ad* da allora ♦ *prep* da ♦ *cj* *(time)* da quando; *(because)* poiché, dato che; ~ **then** da allora; ~ **Monday** da lunedì; **(ever)** ~ **I arrived** (fin) da quando sono arrivato.

sincere [sɪn'sɪə*] *a* sincero(a).

sincerely [sɪn'sɪəlɪ] *ad* sinceramente; **Yours** ~ *(at end of letter)* distinti saluti.

sincerity [sɪn'sɛrɪtɪ] *n* sincerità.

sine [saɪn] *n* *(MATH)* seno.

sinew ['sɪnju:] *n* tendine *m*; ~**s** *npl (muscles)* muscoli *mpl*.

sinful ['sɪnful] *a* peccaminoso(a).

sing, *pt* **sang**, *pp* **sung** [sɪŋ, sæŋ, sʌŋ] *vt, vi* cantare.

Singapore [sɪŋgə'pɔ:*] *n* Singapore *f*.

singe [sɪndʒ] *vt* bruciacchiare.

singer ['sɪŋə*] *n* cantante *m/f*.

Singhalese [sɪŋə'li:z] *a* = **Sinhalese**.

singing ['sɪŋɪŋ] *n* *(of person, bird)* canto; *(of kettle, bullet, in ears)* fischio.

single ['sɪŋgl] *a* solo(a), unico(a); *(unmarried: man)* celibe; *(: woman)* nubile; *(not double)* semplice ♦ *n* *(Brit: also:* ~ **ticket)** biglietto di (sola) andata; *(record)* 45 giri *m inv*; **not a** ~ **one was left** non ne è rimasto nemmeno uno; **every** ~ **day** tutti i santi giorni; *see also* **singles**.
single out *vt* scegliere; *(distinguish)* distinguere.

single bed *n* letto a una piazza.

single-breasted ['sɪŋglbrɛstɪd] *a* a un petto.

single file *n*: **in** ~ in fila indiana.

single-handed [sɪŋgl'hændɪd] *ad* senza aiuto, da solo(a).

single-minded [sɪŋgl'maɪndɪd] *a* tenace, risoluto(a).

single parent *n* ragazzo padre/ragazza madre; genitore *m* separato.

single room *n* camera singola.

singles ['sɪŋglz] *npl* *(TENNIS)* singolo; *(US: single people)* single *m/fpl*.

singlet ['sɪŋglɪt] *n* canottiera.

singly ['sɪŋglɪ] *ad* separatamente.

singsong ['sɪŋsɔŋ] *a* *(tone)* cantilenante ♦ *n* *(songs)*: **to have a** ~ farsi una cantata.

singular ['sɪŋgjulə*] *a* *(LING)* singolare; *(unusual)* strano(a), singolare ♦ *n* *(LING)* singolare *m;* **in the feminine** ~ al femminile singolare.

singularly ['sɪŋgjuləlɪ] *ad* stranamente.

Sinhalese [sɪnhə'li:z] *a* singalese.

sinister ['sɪnɪstə*] *a* sinistro(a).

sink [sɪŋk] *n* lavandino, acquaio ♦ *vb* *(pt* **sank**, *pp* **sunk** [sæŋk, sʌŋk]) *vt* *(ship)* (fare) affondare, colare a picco; *(foundations)* scavare; *(piles etc)*: **to** ~ **sth into** conficcare qc in ♦ *vi* affondare, andare a fondo; *(ground etc)* cedere, avvallarsi; **he sank into a**

chair/the mud sprofondò in una poltrona/nel fango.

sink in vi penetrare; **it took a long time to ~ in** ci ho (or ha etc) messo molto a capirlo.

sinking fund ['sɪŋkɪŋ-] n (COMM) fondo d'ammortamento.

sink unit n blocco lavello.

sinner ['sɪnə*] n peccatore/trice.

sinuous ['sɪnjuəs] a sinuoso(a).

sinus ['saɪnəs] n (ANAT) seno.

sip [sɪp] n sorso ♦ vt sorseggiare.

siphon ['saɪfən] n sifone m ♦ vt (funds) trasferire.

siphon off vt travasare (con un sifone).

sir [sə*] n signore m; **S~ John Smith** Sir John Smith; **yes ~** sì, signore; **Dear S~** (in letter) Egregio signor (followed by name); **Dear S~s** Spettabile ditta.

siren ['saɪərn] n sirena.

sirloin ['sə:lɔɪn] n controfiletto.

sirloin steak n bistecca di controfiletto.

sirocco [sɪ'rɔkəu] n scirocco.

sisal ['saɪsəl] n sisal f inv.

sissy ['sɪsɪ] n (col) femminuccia.

sister ['sɪstə*] n sorella; (nun) suora; (nurse) infermiera f caposala inv ♦ cpd: ~ **organization** organizzazione f affine; ~ **ship** nave f gemella.

sister-in-law ['sɪstərɪnlɔ:] n cognata.

sit, pt, pp **sat** [sɪt, sæt] vi sedere, sedersi; (dress etc) cadere; (assembly) essere in seduta ♦ vt (exam) sostenere, dare; **to ~ on a committee** far parte di una commissione.

sit about, sit around vi star seduto(a) (senza far nulla).

sit back vi (in seat) appoggiarsi allo schienale.

sit down vi sedersi; **to be ~ting down** essere seduto(a).

sit in vi: **to ~ in on a discussion** assistere ad una discussione.

sit up vi tirarsi su a sedere; (not go to bed) stare alzato(a) fino a tardi.

sitcom ['sɪtkɔm] n abbr (TV: = situation comedy) sceneggiato a episodi (comico).

sit-down ['sɪtdaun] a: ~ **strike** sciopero bianco (con occupazione della fabbrica); **a ~ meal** un pranzo.

site [saɪt] n posto; (also: **building** ~) cantiere m ♦ vt situare.

sit-in ['sɪtɪn] n (demonstration) sit-in m inv.

siting ['saɪtɪŋ] n ubicazione f.

sitter ['sɪtə*] n (for painter) modello/a; (also: **baby** ~) babysitter m/f inv.

sitting ['sɪtɪŋ] n (of assembly etc) seduta; (in canteen) turno.

sitting member n (POL) deputato/a in carica.

sitting room n soggiorno.

sitting tenant n (Brit) attuale affittuario.

situate ['sɪtjueɪt] vt collocare.

situated ['sɪtjueɪtɪd] a situato(a).

situation [sɪtju'eɪʃən] n situazione f; "~s vacant/wanted" (Brit) "offerte/domande di impiego".

situation comedy n (THEATRE) commedia di situazione.

six [sɪks] num sei.

sixteen [sɪks'ti:n] num sedici.

sixth [sɪksθ] num sesto(a) ♦ n: **the upper/lower ~** (Brit SCOL) l'ultimo/il penultimo anno di scuola superiore.

sixty ['sɪkstɪ] num sessanta.

size [saɪz] n dimensioni fpl; (of clothing) taglia, misura; (of shoes) numero; (glue) colla; **I take ~ 14 in a dress** ≈ porto la 44 di vestiti; **I'd like the small/large ~** (of soap powder etc) vorrei la confezione piccola/grande.

size up vt giudicare, farsi un'idea di.

sizeable ['saɪzəbl] a considerevole.

sizzle ['sɪzl] vi sfrigolare.

SK abbr (Canada) = Saskatchewan.

skate [skeɪt] n pattino; (fish: pl inv) razza ♦ vi pattinare.

skate over, skate around vi (problem, issue) prendere alla leggera, prendere sottogamba.

skateboard ['skeɪtbɔ:d] n skateboard m inv.

skater ['skeɪtə*] n pattinatore/trice.

skating ['skeɪtɪŋ] n pattinaggio.

skating rink n pista di pattinaggio.

skeleton ['skelɪtn] n scheletro.

skeleton key n passe-partout m inv.

skeleton staff n personale m ridotto.

skeptic etc ['skeptɪk] (US) = **sceptic** etc.

sketch [sketʃ] n (drawing) schizzo, abbozzo; (THEATRE etc) scenetta comica, sketch m inv ♦ vt abbozzare, schizzare.

sketch book n album m inv per schizzi.

sketch pad n blocco per schizzi.

sketchy ['sketʃɪ] a incompleto(a), lacunoso(a).

skew [skju:] n (Brit): **on the ~** di traverso.

skewer ['skju:ə*] n spiedo.

ski [ski:] n sci m inv ♦ vi sciare.

ski boot n scarpone m da sci.

skid [skɪd] n slittamento; (sideways slip) sbandamento ♦ vi slittare; sbandare; **to go into a ~** slittare; sbandare.

skid mark n segno della frenata.

skier ['ski:ə*] n sciatore/trice.

skiing ['ski:ɪŋ] n sci m.

ski instructor n maestro/a di sci.

ski jump n (ramp) trampolino; (event) salto con gli sci.

skilful, (US) skillful ['skɪlful] a abile.

ski lift n sciovia.

skill [skɪl] n abilità f inv, capacità f inv; (technique) tecnica.

skilled [skɪld] a esperto(a); (worker) qualificato(a), specializzato(a).

skillet ['skɪlɪt] n padella.

skillful etc ['skɪlful] (US) = **skilful** etc.

skil(l)fully ['skɪlfəlɪ] ad abilmente.

skim [skɪm] vt (milk) scremare; (soup) schiumare; (glide over) sfiorare ♦ vi: **to ~ through** (fig) scorrere, dare una scorsa a.

skimmed milk n latte m scremato.

skimp [skɪmp] *vi*: **to ~ on**, *vt* (*work*) fare alla carlona; (*cloth etc*) lesinare.

skimpy ['skɪmpɪ] *a* misero(a); striminzito(a); frugale.

skin [skɪn] *n* pelle *f*; (*of fruit, vegetable*) buccia; (*on pudding, paint*) crosta ♦ *vt* (*fruit etc*) sbucciare; (*animal*) scuoiare, spellare; **wet** *or* **soaked to the ~** bagnato fino al midollo.

skin-deep [skɪn'diːp] *a* superficiale.

skin diver *n* subacqueo.

skin diving *n* nuoto subacqueo.

skinflint ['skɪnflɪnt] *n* taccagno/a, tirchio/a.

skin graft *n* innesto epidermico.

skinny ['skɪnɪ] *a* molto magro(a), pelle e ossa *inv*.

skin test *n* prova di reazione cutanea.

skintight ['skɪntaɪt] *a* aderente.

skip [skɪp] *n* saltello, balzo; (*container*) benna ♦ *vi* saltare; (*with rope*) saltare la corda ♦ *vt* (*pass over*) saltare; **to ~ school** (*US*) marinare la scuola.

ski pants *npl* pantaloni *mpl* da sci.

ski pole *n* racchetta (da sci).

skipper ['skɪpə*] *n* (*NAUT, SPORT*) capitano.

skipping rope ['skɪpɪŋ-] *n* (*Brit*) corda per saltare.

ski resort *n* località *f inv* sciistica.

skirmish ['skɜːmɪʃ] *n* scaramuccia.

skirt [skɜːt] *n* gonna, sottana ♦ *vt* fiancheggiare, costeggiare.

skirting board ['skɜːtɪŋ-] *n* (*Brit*) zoccolo.

ski run *n* pista da sci.

ski suit *n* tuta da sci.

skit [skɪt] *n* parodia; scenetta satirica.

ski tow *n* = **ski lift**.

skittle ['skɪtl] *n* birillo; **~s** *n* (*game*) (gioco dei) birilli *mpl*.

skive [skaɪv] *vi* (*Brit col*) fare il lavativo.

skulk [skʌlk] *vi* muoversi furtivamente.

skull [skʌl] *n* cranio, teschio.

skullcap ['skʌlkæp] *n* (*worn by Jews*) zucchetto; (*worn by Pope*) papalina.

skunk [skʌŋk] *n* moffetta.

sky [skaɪ] *n* cielo; **to praise sb to the skies** portare alle stelle qn.

sky-blue [skaɪ'bluː] *a* azzurro(a), celeste.

sky-high [skaɪ'haɪ] *ad* (*throw*) molto in alto; **prices have gone ~** i prezzi sono saliti alle stelle.

skylark ['skaɪlɑːk] *n* allodola.

skylight ['skaɪlaɪt] *n* lucernario.

skyline ['skaɪlaɪn] *n* (*horizon*) orizzonte *m*; (*of city*) profilo.

skyscraper ['skaɪskreɪpə*] *n* grattacielo.

slab [slæb] *n* lastra; (*of wood*) tavola; (*of meat, cheese*) pezzo.

slack [slæk] *a* (*loose*) allentato(a); (*slow*) lento(a); (*careless*) negligente; (*COMM: market*) stagnante; (: *demand*) scarso(a); (*period*) morto(a) ♦ *n* (*in rope etc*) parte *f* non tesa; **business is ~** l'attività commerciale è scarsa; *see also* **slacks**.

slacken ['slækn] (*also*: **~ off**) *vi* rallentare,

diminuire ♦ *vt* allentare; (*pressure*) diminuire.

slacks [slæks] *npl* pantaloni *mpl*.

slag [slæg] *n* scorie *fpl*.

slag heap *n* ammasso di scorie.

slain [sleɪn] *pp of* **slay**.

slake [sleɪk] *vt* (*one's thirst*) spegnere.

slalom ['slɑːləm] *n* slalom *m*.

slam [slæm] *vt* (*door*) sbattere; (*throw*) scaraventare; (*criticize*) stroncare ♦ *vi* sbattere.

slander ['slɑːndə*] *n* calunnia; (*LAW*) diffamazione *f* ♦ *vt* calunniare; diffamare.

slanderous ['slɑːndrəs] *a* calunnioso(a); diffamatorio(a).

slang [slæŋ] *n* gergo, slang *m*.

slant [slɑːnt] *n* pendenza, inclinazione *f*; (*fig*) angolazione *f*, punto di vista.

slanted ['slɑːntɪd] *a* tendenzioso(a).

slanting ['slɑːntɪŋ] *a* in pendenza, inclinato(a).

slap [slæp] *n* manata, pacca; (*on face*) schiaffo ♦ *vt* dare una manata a; schiaffeggiare ♦ *ad* (*directly*) in pieno; **it fell ~ in the middle** cadde proprio nel mezzo.

slapdash ['slæpdæʃ] *a* abborracciato(a).

slapstick ['slæpstɪk] *n* (*comedy*) farsa grossolana.

slap-up ['slæpʌp] *a* (*Brit*): **a ~ meal** un pranzo (*or* una cena) coi fiocchi.

slash [slæʃ] *vt* squarciare; (*face*) sfregiare; (*fig: prices*) ridurre drasticamente, tagliare.

slat [slæt] *n* (*of wood*) stecca.

slate [sleɪt] *n* ardesia ♦ *vt* (*fig: criticize*) stroncare, distruggere.

slaughter ['slɔːtə*] *n* (*of animals*) macellazione *f*; (*of people*) strage *f*, massacro ♦ *vt* macellare; trucidare, massacrare.

slaughterhouse ['slɔːtəhaus] *n* macello, mattatoio.

Slav [slɑːv] *a*, *n* slavo(a).

slave [sleɪv] *n* schiavo/a ♦ *vi* (*also*: **~ away**) lavorare come uno schiavo; **to ~ (away) at sth/at doing sth** ammazzarsi di fatica *or* sgobbare per qc/per fare qc.

slave labour *n* lavoro degli schiavi; (*fig*): **we're just ~ here** siamo solamente sfruttati qui dentro.

slaver ['slævə*] *vi* (*dribble*) sbavare.

slavery ['sleɪvərɪ] *n* schiavitù *f*.

Slavic ['slævɪk] *a* slavo(a).

slavish ['sleɪvɪʃ] *a* servile; pedissequo(a).

Slavonic [slə'vɔnɪk] *a* slavo(a).

slay [sleɪ], *pt* **slew**, *pp* **slain** [sleɪ, sluː, sleɪn] *vt* (*formal*) uccidere.

SLD *n abbr* (*Brit*) = *Social and Liberal Democrats*.

sleazy ['sliːzɪ] *a* trasandato(a).

sledge [sledʒ] *n* slitta.

sledgehammer ['sledʒhæmə*] *n* martello da fabbro.

sleek [sliːk] *a* (*hair, fur*) lucido(a), lucente; (*car, boat*) slanciato(a), affusolato(a).

sleep [sliːp] *n* sonno ♦ *vi* (*pt, pp* **slept** [slept]) dormire ♦ *vt*: **we can ~ 4** abbiamo 4 posti letto, possiamo alloggiare 4 persone; **to have a good night's** ~ farsi una bella dormita; **to go to** ~ addormentarsi; **to** ~ **lightly** avere il sonno leggero; **to put to** ~ (*patient*) far addormentare; (*animal: euphemistic: kill*) abbattere; **to** ~ **with sb** (*euphemistic: have sex*) andare a letto con qn.

sleep in *vi* (*lie late*) alzarsi tardi; (*over-sleep*) dormire fino a tardi.

sleeper ['sli:pə*] *n* (*person*) dormiente *m/f*; (*Brit RAIL: on track*) traversina; (: *train*) treno di vagoni letto.

sleepily ['sli:pɪlɪ] *ad* con aria assonnata.

sleeping ['sli:pɪŋ] *a* addormentato(a).

sleeping bag *n* sacco a pelo.

sleeping car *n* vagone *m* letto *inv*, carrozza *f* letto *inv*.

sleeping partner *n* (*Brit COMM*) = **silent partner**.

sleeping pill *n* sonnifero.

sleepless ['sli:plɪs] *a* (*person*) insonne; **a** ~ **night** una notte in bianco.

sleeplessness ['sli:plɪsnɪs] *n* insonnia.

sleepwalker ['sli:pwɔ:kə*] *n* sonnambulo/a.

sleepy ['sli:pɪ] *a* assonnato(a), sonnolento(a); (*fig*) addormentato(a); **to be** *or* **feel** ~ avere sonno.

sleet [sli:t] *n* nevischio.

sleeve [sli:v] *n* manica; (*of record*) copertina.

sleeveless ['sli:vlɪs] *a* (*garment*) senza maniche.

sleigh [sleɪ] *n* slitta.

sleight [slaɪt] *n*: ~ **of hand** gioco di destrezza.

slender ['slendə*] *a* snello(a), sottile; (*not enough*) scarso(a), esiguo(a).

slept [slɛpt] *pt, pp of* **sleep**.

sleuth [slu:θ] *n* (*col*) segugio.

slew [slu:] *vi* (*also*: ~ **round**) girare ♦ *pt of* **slay**.

slice [slaɪs] *n* fetta ♦ *vt* affettare, tagliare a fette; **~d bread** pane *m* a cassetta.

slick [slɪk] *a* (*clever*) brillante; (*insincere*) untuoso(a), falso(a) ♦ *n* (*also*: **oil** ~) chiazza di petrolio.

slid [slɪd] *pt, pp of* **slide**.

slide [slaɪd] *n* (*in playground*) scivolo; (*PHOT*) diapositiva; (*microscope* ~) vetrino; (*Brit: also*: **hair** ~) fermaglio (per capelli); (*in prices*) caduta ♦ *vb* (*pt, pp* **slid** [slɪd]) *vt* far scivolare ♦ *vi* scivolare; **to let things** ~ (*fig*) lasciare andare tutto, trascurare tutto.

slide projector *n* proiettore *m* per diapositive.

slide rule *n* regolo calcolatore.

sliding ['slaɪdɪŋ] *a* (*door*) scorrevole; ~ **roof** (*AUT*) capotte *f inv*.

sliding scale *n* scala mobile.

slight [slaɪt] *a* (*slim*) snello(a), sottile; (*frail*) delicato(a), fragile; (*trivial*) insignificante; (*small*) piccolo(a) ♦ *n* offesa, affronto ♦ *vt* (*offend*) offendere, fare un affronto a; **the ~est** il minimo (*or* la minima); **not in the ~est** affatto, neppure per sogno.

slightly ['slaɪtlɪ] *ad* lievemente, un po'; ~ **built**

esile.

slim [slɪm] *a* magro(a), snello(a) ♦ *vi* dimagrire, fare (*or* seguire) una dieta dimagrante.

slime [slaɪm] *n* limo, melma; viscidume *m*.

slimming ['slɪmɪŋ] *a* (*diet, pills*) dimagrante.

slimy ['slaɪmɪ] *a* (*also fig: person*) viscido(a); (*covered with mud*) melmoso(a).

sling [slɪŋ] *n* (*MED*) benda al collo ♦ *vt* (*pt, pp* **slung** [slʌŋ]) lanciare, tirare; **to have one's arm in a** ~ avere un braccio al collo.

slink, *pt, pp* **slunk** [slɪŋk, slʌŋk] *vi*: **to** ~ **away**, ~ **off** svignarsela.

slip [slɪp] *n* scivolata, scivolone *m*; (*mistake*) errore *m*, sbaglio; (*underskirt*) sottoveste *f*; (*paper*) bigliettino, talloncino ♦ *vt* (*slide*) far scivolare ♦ *vi* (*slide*) scivolare; (*move smoothly*): **to** ~ **into/out of** scivolare in/via da; (*decline*) declinare; **to give sb the** ~ sfuggire qn; **a** ~ **of paper** un foglietto; **a** ~ **of the tongue** un lapsus linguae; **to** ~ **sth on/off** infilarsi/togliersi qc; **to let a chance** ~ **by** lasciarsi scappare un'occasione; **it** ~**ped from her hand** le sfuggì di mano.

slip away *vi* svignarsela.

slip in *vt* introdurre casualmente.

slip out *vi* uscire furtivamente.

slip-on ['slɪpɔn] *a* (*gen*) comodo(a) da mettere; (*shoes*) senza allacciatura.

slipped disc ['slɪpt-] *n* spostamento delle vertebre.

slipper ['slɪpə*] *n* pantofola.

slippery ['slɪpərɪ] *a* scivoloso(a).

slip road *n* (*Brit: to motorway*) rampa di accesso.

slipshod ['slɪpʃɔd] *a* sciatto(a), trasandato(a).

slip-up ['slɪpʌp] *n* granchio (*fig*).

slipway ['slɪpweɪ] *n* scalo di costruzione.

slit [slɪt] *n* fessura, fenditura; (*cut*) taglio; (*tear*) strappo ♦ *vt* (*pt, pp* **slit**) tagliare; **to** ~ **sb's throat** tagliare la gola a qn.

slither ['slɪðə*] *vi* scivolare, sdrucciolare.

sliver ['slɪvə*] *n* (*of glass, wood*) scheggia; (*of cheese, sausage*) fettina.

slob [slɔb] *n* (*col*) sciattone/a.

slog [slɔg] (*Brit*) *n* faticata ♦ *vi* lavorare con accanimento, sgobbare.

slogan ['sləugən] *n* motto, slogan *m inv*.

slop [slɔp] *vi* (*also*: ~ **over**) traboccare; versarsi ♦ *vt* spandere; versare ♦ *npl*: ~**s** acqua sporca; sbobba.

slope [sləup] *n* pendio; (*side of mountain*) versante *m*; (*of roof*) pendenza; (*of floor*) inclinazione *f* ♦ *vi*: **to** ~ **down** declinare; **to** ~ **up** essere in salita.

sloping ['sləupɪŋ] *a* inclinato(a).

sloppy ['slɔpɪ] *a* (*work*) fatto(a) via; (*appearance*) sciatto(a); (*film etc*) sdolcinato(a).

slosh [slɔʃ] *vi* (*col*): **to** ~ **about** *or* **around** (*person*) sguazzare; (*liquid*) guazzare.

sloshed [slɔʃt] *a* (*col: drunk*) sbronzo(a).

slot [slɔt] *n* fessura; (*fig: in timetable, RADIO, TV*) spazio ♦ *vt*: **to** ~ **into** introdurre in una fessura.

sloth [sləuθ] *n* (*vice*) pigrizia, accidia; (*ZOOL*)

bradipo.

slot machine n (Brit: vending machine) distributore m automatico; (for amusement) slot-machine f inv.

slot meter n contatore m a gettoni.

slouch [slautʃ] vi (when walking) camminare dinoccolato(a); **she was ~ed in a chair** era sprofondata in una poltrona.

slouch about, slouch around vi (laze) oziare.

slovenly ['slʌvənlɪ] a sciatto(a), trasandato(a).

slow [sləu] a lento(a); (watch): **to be ~** essere indietro ♦ ad lentamente ♦ vt, vi (also: **~ down, ~ up**) rallentare; **"~"** (road sign) "rallentare"; **at a ~ speed** a bassa velocità; **to be ~ to act/decide** essere lento ad agire/a decidere; **my watch is 20 minutes ~** il mio orologio è indietro di 20 minuti; **business is ~** (COMM) gli affari procedono a rilento; **to go ~** (driver) andare piano; (in industrial dispute) fare uno sciopero bianco.

slow-acting ['sləu'æktɪŋ] a che agisce lentamente, ad azione lenta.

slowly ['sləulɪ] ad lentamente; **to drive ~** andare piano.

slow motion n: **in ~** al rallentatore.

slowness ['sləunɪs] n lentezza.

sludge [slʌdʒ] n fanghiglia.

slug [slʌg] n lumaca; (bullet) pallottola.

sluggish ['slʌgɪʃ] a lento(a); (business, market, sales) stagnante, fiacco(a).

sluice [slu:s] n chiusa ♦ vt: **to ~ down** or **out** lavare (con abbondante acqua).

slum [slʌm] n catapecchia.

slumber ['slʌmbə*] n sonno.

slump [slʌmp] n crollo, caduta; (economic) depressione f, crisi f inv ♦ vi crollare; **he was ~ed over the wheel** era curvo sul volante.

slung [slʌŋ] pt, pp of **sling**.

slunk [slʌŋk] pt, pp of **slink**.

slur [slɔ:*] n pronuncia indistinta; (stigma) diffamazione f, calunnia; (MUS) legatura; (smear): **~ (on)** macchia (su) ♦ vt pronunciare in modo indistinto; **to cast a ~ on sb** calunniare qn.

slurred [slɔ:d] a (pronunciation) inarticolato(a), disarticolato(a).

slush [slʌʃ] n neve f mista a fango.

slush fund n fondi mpl neri.

slushy ['slʌʃɪ] a (snow) che si scioglie; (Brit: fig) sdolcinato(a).

slut [slʌt] n donna trasandata, sciattona.

sly [slaɪ] a furbo(a), scaltro(a); **on the ~** di soppiatto.

smack [smæk] n (slap) pacca; (on face) schiaffo ♦ vt schiaffeggiare; (child) picchiare ♦ vi: **to ~ of** puzzare di; **to ~ one's lips** fare uno schiocco con le labbra.

smacker ['smækə*] n (col: kiss) bacio; (: Brit: pound note) sterlina; (: US: dollar bill) dollaro.

small [smɔ:l] a piccolo(a); (in height) basso(a); (letter) minuscolo(a) ♦ n: **the ~ of**

the back le reni; **to get** or **grow ~er** (stain, town) rimpicciolire; (debt, organization, numbers) ridursi; **to make ~er** (amount, income) ridurre; (garden, object, garment) rimpicciolire; **in the ~ hours** alle ore piccole; **a ~ shopkeeper** un piccolo negoziante.

small ads npl (Brit) piccoli annunci mpl.

small arms npl armi fpl portatili or leggere.

small change n moneta, spiccioli mpl.

smallholder ['smɔ:lhəuldə*] n (Brit) piccolo proprietario.

smallholding ['smɔ:lhəuldɪŋ] n (Brit) piccola tenuta.

smallish ['smɔ:lɪʃ] a piccolino(a).

small-minded [smɔ:l'maɪndɪd] a meschino(a).

smallpox ['smɔ:lpɔks] n vaiolo.

small print n caratteri mpl piccoli; (on document) parte scritta in piccolo.

small-scale ['smɔ:lskeɪl] a (map, model) in scala ridotta; (business, farming) modesto(a).

small talk n chiacchiere fpl.

small-time ['smɔ:ltaɪm] a (col) da poco; **a ~ thief** un ladro di polli.

smarmy ['smɑ:mɪ] a (Brit pej) untuoso(a), strisciante.

smart [smɑ:t] a elegante; (clever) intelligente; (quick) sveglio(a) ♦ vi bruciare; **the ~ set** il bel mondo; **to look ~** essere elegante; **my eyes are ~ing** mi bruciano gli occhi.

smarten up ['smɑ:tn-] vi farsi bello(a) ♦ vt (people) fare bello(a); (things) abbellire.

smash [smæʃ] n (also: **~-up**) scontro, collisione f; (sound) fracasso ♦ vt frantumare, fracassare; (opponent) annientare, schiacciare; (hopes) distruggere; (SPORT: record) battere ♦ vi frantumarsi, andare in pezzi.

smash up vt (car) sfasciare; (room) distruggere.

smash-hit [smæʃ'hɪt] n successone m.

smashing ['smæʃɪŋ] a (col) favoloso(a), formidabile.

smattering ['smætərɪŋ] n: **a ~ of** un'infarinatura di.

smear [smɪə*] n macchia; (MED) striscio; (insult) calunnia ♦ vt ungere; (fig) denigrare, diffamare; **his hands were ~ed with oil/ink** aveva le mani sporche di olio/inchiostro.

smear campaign n campagna diffamatoria.

smear test n (Brit MED) Pap-test m inv.

smell [smɛl] n odore m; (sense) olfatto, odorato ♦ vb (pt, pp smelt or smelled [smɛlt, smɛld]) vt sentire (l')odore di ♦ vi (food etc): **to ~ (of)** avere odore (di); (pej) puzzare, avere un cattivo odore; **it ~s good** ha un buon odore.

smelly ['smɛlɪ] a puzzolente.

smelt [smɛlt] pt, pp of **smell** ♦ vt (ore) fondere.

smile [smaɪl] n sorriso ♦ vi sorridere.

smiling ['smaɪlɪŋ] a sorridente.

smirk [smɜ:k] n sorriso furbo; sorriso

compiaciuto.

smith [smɪθ] *n* fabbro.

smithy ['smɪðɪ] *n* fucina.

smitten ['smɪtn] *a*: ~ **with** colpito(a) da.

smock [smɔk] *n* grembiule *m*, camice *m*.

smog [smɔg] *n* smog *m*.

smoke [sməuk] *n* fumo ♦ *vt*, *vi* fumare; **to have a** ~ fumarsi una sigaretta; **do you** ~? fumi?; **to go up in** ~ (*house etc*) bruciare, andare distrutto dalle fiamme; (*fig*) andare in fumo.

smoked [sməukt] *a* (*bacon*, *glass*) affumicato(a).

smokeless fuel ['sməuklɪs-] *n* carburante *m* che non da fumo.

smokeless zone *n* (*Brit*) zona dove sono vietati gli scarichi di fumo.

smoker ['sməukə*] *n* (*person*) fumatore/trice; (*RAIL*) carrozza per fumatori.

smoke screen *n* cortina fumogena *or* di fumo; (*fig*) copertura.

smoke shop *n* (*US*) tabaccheria.

smoking ['sməukɪŋ] *n* fumo; "**no** ~" (*sign*) "vietato fumare"; **he's given up** ~ ha smesso di fumare.

smoking compartment, (*US*) **smoking car** *n* carrozza (per) fumatori.

smoky ['sməukɪ] *a* fumoso(a); (*surface*) affumicato(a).

smolder ['sməuldə*] *vi* (*US*) = **smoulder**.

smooth [smu:ð] *a* liscio(a); (*sauce*) omogeneo(a); (*flavour*, *whisky*) amabile; (*cigarette*) leggero(a); (*movement*) regolare; (*person*) mellifluo(a); (*landing*, *take-off*, *flight*) senza scosse ♦ *vt* lisciare, spianare; (*also*: ~ **out**: *difficulties*) appianare.

smooth over *vt*: **to** ~ **things over** (*fig*) sistemare le cose.

smoothly ['smu:ðlɪ] *ad* (*easily*) liscio; **everything went** ~ tutto andò liscio.

smother ['smʌðə*] *vt* soffocare.

smoulder, (*US*) **smolder** ['sməuldə*] *vi* covare sotto la cenere.

smudge [smʌdʒ] *n* macchia; sbavatura ♦ *vt* imbrattare, sporcare.

smug [smʌg] *a* soddisfatto(a), compiaciuto(a).

smuggle ['smʌgl] *vt* contrabbandare; **to** ~ **in/out** (*goods etc*) far entrare/uscire di contrabbando.

smuggler ['smʌglə*] *n* contrabbandiere/a.

smuggling ['smʌglɪŋ] *n* contrabbando.

smut [smʌt] *n* (*grain of soot*) granello di fuliggine; (*mark*) segno nero; (*in conversation etc*) sconcezze *fpl*.

smutty ['smʌtɪ] *a* (*fig*) osceno(a), indecente.

snack [snæk] *n* spuntino; **to have a** ~ fare uno spuntino.

snack bar *n* tavola calda, snack bar *m inv*.

snag [snæg] *n* intoppo, ostacolo imprevisto.

snail [sneɪl] *n* chiocciola.

snake [sneɪk] *n* serpente *m*.

snap [snæp] *n* (*sound*) schianto, colpo secco; (*photograph*) istantanea; (*game*) rubamazzo ♦ *a* improvviso(a) ♦ *vt* (*far*) schioccare;

(*break*) spezzare di netto; (*photograph*) scattare un'istantanea di ♦ *vi* spezzarsi con un rumore secco; (*fig*: *person*) crollare; **to** ~ **at sb** rivolgersi a qn con tono brusco; (*subj*: *dog*) cercare di mordere qn; **to** ~ **open/shut** aprirsi/chiudersi di scatto; **to** ~ **one's fingers at** (*fig*) infischiarsi di; **a cold** ~ (*of weather*) un'improvvisa ondata di freddo.

snap off *vt* (*break*) schiantare.

snap up *vt* afferrare.

snap fastener *n* bottone *m* automatico.

snappy ['snæpɪ] *a* rapido(a); **make it** ~! (*col*: *hurry up*) sbrigati!, svelto!

snapshot ['snæpʃɔt] *n* istantanea.

snare [snɛə*] *n* trappola.

snarl [snɑ:l] *vi* ringhiare ♦ *vt*: **to get** ~**ed up** (*wool*, *plans*) ingarbugliarsi; (*traffic*) intasarsi.

snatch [snætʃ] *n* (*fig*) furto; (*Brit*: *small amount*): ~**es of** frammenti *mpl* di ♦ *vt* strappare (con violenza); (*steal*) rubare ♦ *vi*: **don't** ~! non strappare le cose di mano!; **to** ~ **a sandwich** mangiarsi in fretta un panino; **to** ~ **some sleep** riuscire a dormire un po'.

snatch up *vt* raccogliere in fretta.

sneak [sni:k] *vi*: **to** ~ **in/out** entrare/uscire di nascosto ♦ *vt*: **to** ~ **a look at sth** guardare di sottecchi qc.

sneakers ['sni:kəz] *npl* scarpe *fpl* da ginnastica.

sneaking ['sni:kɪŋ] *a*: **to have a** ~ **feeling/ suspicion that ...** avere la vaga impressione/ il vago sospetto che ....

sneaky ['sni:kɪ] *a* falso(a), disonesto(a).

sneer [snɪə*] *n* ghigno, sogghigno ♦ *vi* ghignare, sogghignare; **to** ~ **at sb/sth** farsi beffe di qn/qc.

sneeze [sni:z] *n* starnuto ♦ *vi* starnutire.

snide [snaɪd] *a* maligno(a).

sniff [snɪf] *n* fiutata, annusata ♦ *vi* fiutare, annusare; tirare su col naso; (*in contempt*) arricciare il naso ♦ *vt* fiutare, annusare; (*glue*, *drug*) sniffare.

sniff at *vt fus*: **it's not to be** ~**ed at** non è da disprezzare.

snigger ['snɪgə*] *n* riso represso ♦ *vi* ridacchiare, ridere sotto i baffi.

snip [snɪp] *n* pezzetto; (*bargain*) (buon) affare *m*, occasione *f* ♦ *vt* tagliare.

sniper ['snaɪpə*] *n* franco tiratore *m*, cecchino.

snippet ['snɪpɪt] *n* frammento.

snivelling ['snɪvlɪŋ] *a* piagnucoloso(a).

snob [snɔb] *n* snob *m/f inv*.

snobbery ['snɔbərɪ] *n* snobismo.

snobbish ['snɔbɪʃ] *a* snob *inv*.

snooker ['snu:kə*] *n* tipo di gioco del biliardo.

snoop [snu:p] *vi*: **to** ~ **on sb** spiare qn; **to** ~ **about** curiosare.

snooper ['snu:pə*] *n* ficcanaso *m/f*.

snooty ['snu:tɪ] *a* borioso(a), snob *inv*.

snooze [snu:z] *n* sonnellino, pisolino ♦ *vi* fare un sonnellino.

snore [snɔ:*] *vi* russare.

snoring ['snɔ:rɪŋ] *n* russare *m*.

snorkel ['snɔːkl] n (of swimmer) respiratore m a tubo.

snort [snɔːt] n sbuffo ♦ vi sbuffare ♦ vt (drugs slang) sniffare.

snotty ['snɔtɪ] a moccioso(a).

snout [snaut] n muso.

snow [snəu] n neve f ♦ vi nevicare ♦ vt: **to be ~ed under with work** essere sommerso di lavoro.

snowball ['snəubɔːl] n palla di neve.

snowbound ['snəubaund] a bloccato(a) dalla neve.

snow-capped ['snəukæpt] a (mountain) con la cima coperta di neve; (peak) coperto(a) di neve.

snowdrift ['snəudrɪft] n cumulo di neve (ammucchiato dal vento).

snowdrop ['snəudrɔp] n bucaneve m inv.

snowfall ['snəufɔːl] n nevicata.

snowflake ['snəuflɛɪk] n fiocco di neve.

snowman ['snəumæn] n pupazzo di neve.

snowplough, (US) **snowplow** ['snəuplau] n spazzaneve m inv.

snowshoe ['snəuʃuː] n racchetta da neve.

snowstorm ['snəustɔːm] n tormenta.

snowy ['snəuɪ] a nevoso(a).

SNP n abbr (Brit POL) = Scottish National Party.

snub [snʌb] vt snobbare ♦ n offesa, affronto.

snub-nosed [snʌb'nəuzd] a dal naso camuso.

snuff [snʌf] n tabacco da fiuto ♦ vt (also: ~ out: candle) spegnere.

snug [snʌg] a comodo(a); (room, house) accogliente, comodo(a); **it's a ~ fit** è attillato.

snuggle ['snʌgl] vi: **to ~ down in bed** accovacciarsi a letto; **to ~ up to sb** stringersi a qn.

snugly ['snʌglɪ] ad comodamente; **it fits ~** (object in pocket etc) entra giusto giusto; (garment) sta ben attillato.

SO abbr (BANKING) = **standing order**.

so [səu] ad (degree) così, tanto; (manner: thus) così, in questo modo ♦ cj perciò; **~ as to do** in modo da or così da fare; **~ that** (purpose) affinché + sub; (result) così che; **~ that's the reason!** allora è questo il motivo!, ecco perché!; **~ do I, ~ am I** etc anch'io etc; **~ it is!, ~ it does!** davvero!; if **~ se è così; I hope ~** spero di sì; **10 or ~** circa 10; **quite ~!** esattamente!; **even ~** comunque; **~ far** fin qui, finora; (in past) fino ad allora; **~ long!** arrivederci!; **~ many** tanti(e); **~ much** ad tanto ♦ det tanto(a); **~ to speak** per così dire; **~ (what)?** (col) e allora?, e con questo?

soak [səuk] vt inzuppare; (clothes) mettere a mollo ♦ vi inzupparsi; (clothes) essere a mollo; **to be ~ed through** essere fradicio.

soak in vi penetrare.

soak up vt assorbire.

soaking ['səukɪŋ] a (also: ~ **wet**) fradicio(a).

so-and-so ['səuənsəu] n (somebody) un tale; **Mr/Mrs ~** signor/signora tal dei tali.

soap [səup] n sapone m.

soapflakes ['səupfleɪks] npl sapone m in scaglie.

soap opera n soap opera f inv.

soap powder n detersivo.

soapsuds ['səupsʌdz] npl saponata.

soapy ['səupɪ] a insaponato(a).

soar [sɔː*] vi volare in alto; (price, morale, spirits) salire alle stelle.

sob [sɔb] n singhiozzo ♦ vi singhiozzare.

s.o.b. n abbr (US col!: = son of a bitch) figlio di puttana (!).

sober ['səubə*] a non ubriaco(a); (sedate) serio(a); (moderate) moderato(a); (colour, style) sobrio(a).

sober up vt far passare la sbornia a ♦ vi farsi passare la sbornia.

sobriety [səu'braɪətɪ] n (not being drunk) sobrietà; (seriousness, sedateness) sobrietà, pacatezza.

Soc. abbr (= society) Soc.

so-called ['səu'kɔːld] a cosiddetto(a).

soccer ['sɔkə*] n calcio.

soccer pitch n campo di calcio.

soccer player n calciatore m.

sociable ['səuʃəbl] a socievole.

social ['səuʃl] a sociale ♦ n festa, serata.

social climber n arrampicatore/trice sociale, arrivista m/f.

social club n club m inv sociale.

Social Democrat n socialdemocratico/a.

social insurance n (US) assicurazione f sociale.

socialism ['səuʃəlɪzəm] n socialismo.

socialist ['səuʃəlɪst] a, n socialista (m/f).

socialite ['səuʃəlaɪt] n persona in vista nel bel mondo.

socialize ['səuʃəlaɪz] vi frequentare la gente; farsi degli amici; **to ~ with** socializzare con.

socially ['səuʃəlɪ] ad socialmente, in società.

social science n scienze fpl sociali.

social security n previdenza sociale; **Department of S~ S~ (DSS)** (Brit) ≈ Istituto di Previdenza Sociale.

social welfare n assistenza sociale.

social work n servizio sociale.

social worker n assistente m/f sociale.

society [sə'saɪətɪ] n società f inv; (club) società, associazione f; (also: **high ~**) alta società ♦ cpd (party, column) mondano(a).

socioeconomic ['səusɪəuiːkə'nɔmɪk] a socioeconomico(a).

sociological [səusɪə'lɔdʒɪkl] a sociologico(a).

sociologist [səusɪ'ɔlədʒɪst] n sociologo/a.

sociology [səusɪ'ɔlədʒɪ] n sociologia.

sock [sɔk] n calzino ♦ vt (hit) dare un pugno a; **to pull one's ~s up** (fig) darsi una regolata.

socket ['sɔkɪt] n cavità f inv; (of eye) orbita; (ELEC: also: **wall ~**) presa di corrente; (: for light bulb) portalampada m inv.

sod [sɔd] n (of earth) zolla erbosa; (Brit col!) bastardo/a (!).

soda ['səudə] n (CHEM) soda; (also: ~ **water**) acqua di seltz; (US: also: ~ **pop**) gassosa.

sodden ['sɔdn] a fradicio(a).
sodium ['səudiəm] n sodio.
sodium chloride n cloruro di sodio.
sofa ['səufə] n sofà m inv.
Sofia ['səufiə] n Sofia.
soft [sɔft] a (not rough) morbido(a); (not hard) soffice; (not loud) sommesso(a); (kind) gentile; (: look, smile) dolce; (not strict) indulgente; (weak) debole; (stupid) stupido(a).
soft-boiled ['sɔftbɔild] a (egg) alla coque.
soft drink n analcolico.
soft drugs npl droghe fpl leggere.
soften ['sɔfn] vt ammorbidire; addolcire; attenuare ♦ vi ammorbidirsi; addolcirsi; attenuarsi.
softener ['sɔfnə*] n ammorbidente m.
soft fruit n (Brit) ≈ frutta rossa.
soft furnishings npl tessuti mpl d'arredo.
soft-hearted [sɔft'hɑ:tid] a sensibile.
softly ['sɔftli] ad dolcemente; morbidamente.
softness ['sɔftnis] n dolcezza; morbidezza.
soft sell n persuasione f all'acquisto.
soft toy n giocattolo di peluche.
software ['sɔftwɛə*] n software m.
software package n pacchetto di software.
soft water n acqua non calcarea.
SOGAT ['səugæt] n abbr (Brit: = Society of Graphical and Allied Trades) sindacato dei dipendenti dell'industria della stampa.
soggy ['sɔgi] a inzuppato(a).
soil [sɔil] n (earth) terreno, suolo ♦ vt sporcare; (fig) macchiare.
soiled [sɔild] a sporco(a), sudicio(a).
sojourn ['sɔdʒə:n] n (formal) soggiorno.
solace ['sɔlis] n consolazione f.
solar ['səulə*] a solare.
solarium, pl **solaria** [sə'lɛəriəm, -riə] n solarium m inv.
solar plexus [-'plɛksəs] n (ANAT) plesso solare.
sold [səuld] pt, pp of **sell**.
solder ['səuldə*] vt saldare ♦ n saldatura.
soldier ['səuldʒə*] n soldato, militare m ♦ vi: to ~ on perseverare; **toy** ~ soldatino.
sold out a (COMM) esaurito(a).
sole [səul] n (of foot) pianta (del piede); (of shoe) suola; (fish: pl inv) sogliola ♦ a solo(a), unico(a); (exclusive) esclusivo(a).
solely ['səulli] ad solamente, unicamente; **I will hold you** ~ **responsible** la considererò il solo responsabile.
solemn ['sɔləm] a solenne; grave; serio(a).
sole trader n (COMM) commerciante m in proprio.
solicit [sə'lisit] vt (request) richiedere, sollecitare ♦ vi (prostitute) adescare i passanti.
solicitor [sə'lisitə*] n (Brit: for wills etc) ≈ notaio; (in court) ≈ avvocato.
solid ['sɔlid] a (not hollow) pieno(a); (strong, sound, reliable, not liquid) solido(a); (meal) sostanzioso(a); (line) ininterrotto(a); (vote) unanime ♦ n solido; **to be on** ~ **ground**

essere su terraferma; (fig) muoversi su terreno sicuro; **we waited 2** ~ **hours** abbiamo aspettato due ore buone.
solidarity [sɔli'dæriti] n solidarietà.
solidify [sə'lidifai] vi solidificarsi ♦ vt solidificare.
solidity [sə'liditi] n solidità.
solid-state ['sɔlidsteit] a (ELEC) a transistor.
soliloquy [sə'liləkwi] n soliloquio.
solitaire [sɔli'tɛə*] n (game, gem) solitario.
solitary ['sɔlitəri] a solitario(a).
solitary confinement n (LAW): **to be in** ~ essere in cella d'isolamento.
solitude ['sɔlitju:d] n solitudine f.
solo ['səuləu] n (MUS) assolo.
soloist ['səuləuist] n solista m/f.
Solomon Islands ['sɔləmən-] n: **the** ~ le isole Salomone.
solstice ['sɔlstis] n solstizio.
soluble ['sɔljubl] a solubile.
solution [sə'lu:ʃən] n soluzione f.
solve [sɔlv] vt risolvere.
solvency ['sɔlvənsi] n (COMM) solvenza, solvibilità.
solvent ['sɔlvənt] a (COMM) solvibile ♦ n (CHEM) solvente m.
solvent abuse n abuso di solventi.
Som. abbr (Brit) = **Somerset**.
Somali [sə'mɑ:li] a somalo(a).
Somalia [səu'mɑ:liə] n Somalia.
sombre, (US) **somber** ['sɔmbə*] a scuro(a); (mood, person) triste.
some [sʌm] a (a few) alcuni(e), qualche; (certain) certi(e); (a certain number or amount) see phrases below; (unspecified) un(a) ... qualunque ♦ pronoun alcuni(e); un po' ♦ ad: ~ **10 people** circa 10 persone; ~ **children came** sono venuti dei bambini; have ~ **tea/ice-cream/water** prendi un po' di tè/gelato/acqua; **there's** ~ **milk in the fridge** c'è un po' di latte nel frigo; ~ **people say that** ... certa gente dice che ...; **I have** ~ **books** ho qualche libro o alcuni libri; ~ (of it) **was left** ne è rimasto un po'; **could I have** ~ **of that cheese?** potrei avere un po' di quel formaggio?; **I've got** ~ (i.e. books etc) ne ho alcuni; (i.e. milk, money etc) ne ho un po'; **after** ~ **time** dopo un po'; **at** ~ **length** a lungo; **in** ~ **form or other** in una forma o nell'altra.
somebody ['sʌmbədi] pronoun qualcuno; ~ **or other** qualcuno.
someday ['sʌmdei] ad uno di questi giorni, un giorno o l'altro.
somehow ['sʌmhau] ad in un modo o nell'altro, in qualche modo; (for some reason) per qualche ragione.
someone ['sʌmwʌn] pronoun = **somebody**.
someplace ['sʌmpleis] ad (US) = **somewhere**.
somersault ['sʌməsɔ:lt] n capriola; (in air) salto mortale ♦ vi fare una capriola (or un salto mortale); (car) cappottare.
something ['sʌmθiŋ] pronoun qualcosa; ~

interesting qualcosa di interessante; ~ **to do** qualcosa da fare; **he's** ~ **last month** durante il mese scorso; **I'll finish it** ~ lo finirò prima o poi.

sometime ['sʌmtaɪm] *ad* (*in future*) una volta o l'altra; (*in past*): ~ **last month** durante il mese scorso; **I'll finish it** ~ lo finirò prima o poi.

sometimes ['sʌmtaɪmz] *ad* qualche volta.

somewhat ['sʌmwɔt] *ad* piuttosto.

somewhere ['sʌmwɛə*] *ad* in *or* da qualche parte; ~ **else** da qualche altra parte.

son [sʌn] *n* figlio.

sonar ['səʊnɑ:*] *n* sonar *m*.

sonata [sə'nɑ:tə] *n* sonata.

song [sɔŋ] *n* canzone *f*.

songbook ['sɔŋbʊk] *n* canzoniere *m*.

songwriter ['sɔŋraɪtə*] *n* compositore/trice di canzoni.

sonic ['sɔnɪk] *a* (*boom*) sonico(a).

son-in-law ['sʌnɪnlɔ:] *n* genero.

sonnet ['sɔnɪt] *n* sonetto.

sonny ['sʌnɪ] *n* (*col*) ragazzo mio.

soon [su:n] *ad* presto, fra poco; (*early*) presto; ~ **afterwards** poco dopo; **very/quite** ~ molto/abbastanza presto; **as** ~ **as possible** prima possibile; **I'll do it as** ~ **as I can** lo farò appena posso; **how** ~ **can you be ready?** fra quanto tempo sarà pronto?; **see you** ~! a presto!

sooner ['su:nə*] *ad* (*time*) prima; (*preference*): **I would** ~ **do** preferirei fare; ~ **or later** prima o poi; **no** ~ **said than done** detto fatto; **the** ~ **the better** prima è meglio è; **no** ~ **had we left than ...** eravamo appena partiti, quando ....

soot [sʊt] *n* fuliggine *f*.

soothe [su:ð] *vt* calmare.

soothing ['su:ðɪŋ] *a* (*ointment etc*) calmante; (*tone, words etc*) rassicurante.

SOP *n abbr* = *standard operating procedure*.

sop [sɔp] *n*: **that's only a** ~ è soltanto un contentino.

sophisticated [sə'fɪstɪkeɪtɪd] *a* sofisticato(a); raffinato(a); (*film, mind*) sottile.

sophistication [səfɪstɪ'keɪʃən] *n* raffinatezza; (*of machine*) complessità; (*of argument etc*) sottigliezza.

sophomore ['sɔfəmɔ:*] *n* (*US*) studente/essa del secondo anno.

soporific [sɔpə'rɪfɪk] *a* soporifero(a).

sopping ['sɔpɪŋ] *a* (*also*: ~ **wet**) bagnato(a) fradicio(a).

soppy ['sɔpɪ] *a* (*pej*) sentimentale.

soprano [sə'prɑ:nəʊ] *n* (*voice*) soprano *m*; (*singer*) soprano *m/f*.

sorbet ['sɔ:beɪ] *n* sorbetto.

sorcerer ['sɔ:sərə*] *n* stregone *m*, mago.

sordid ['sɔ:dɪd] *a* sordido(a).

sore [sɔ:*] *a* (*painful*) dolorante; (*col: offended*) offeso(a) ♦ *n* piaga; **my eyes are** ~, **I have** ~ **eyes** mi fanno male gli occhi; ~ **throat** mal *m* di gola; **it's a** ~ **point** (*fig*) è un punto delicato.

sorely ['sɔ:lɪ] *ad* (*tempted*) fortemente.

sorrel ['sɔrəl] *n* acetosa.

sorrow ['sɔrəʊ] *n* dolore *m*.

sorrowful ['sɔrəʊful] *a* triste.

sorry ['sɔrɪ] *a* spiacente; (*condition, excuse*) misero(a), pietoso(a); (*sight, failure*) triste; ~! scusa! (*or* scusi! *or* scusate!); **to feel** ~ **for sb** rincrescersi per qn; **I'm** ~ **to hear that ...** mi dispiace (sentire) che ...; **to be** ~ **about sth** essere dispiaciuto *or* spiacente di qc.

sort [sɔ:t] *n* specie *f*, genere *m*; (*make: of coffee, car etc*) tipo ♦ *vt* (*also*: ~ **out**: *papers*) classificare; ordinare; (: *letters etc*) smistare; (: *problems*) risolvere; (*COMPUT*) ordinare; **what** ~ **of car?** che tipo di macchina?; **I shall do nothing of the** ~! nemmeno per sogno!; **it's** ~ **of awkward** (*col*) è piuttosto difficile.

sortie ['sɔ:tɪ] *n* sortita.

sorting office ['sɔ:tɪŋ-] *n* ufficio *m* smistamento *inv*.

SOS *n abbr* (= *save our souls*) S.O.S. *m inv*.

so-so ['səʊsəʊ] *ad* così così.

soufflé ['su:fleɪ] *n* soufflé *m inv*.

sought [sɔ:t] *pt, pp of* **seek**.

sought-after ['sɔ:tɑ:ftə*] *a* richiesto(a).

soul [səʊl] *n* anima; **the poor** ~ **had nowhere to sleep** il poveraccio non aveva dove dormire; **I didn't see a** ~ non ho visto anima viva.

soul-destroying ['səʊldɪ'strɔɪɪŋ] *a* demoralizzante.

soulful ['səʊlful] *a* pieno(a) di sentimento.

soulless ['səʊllɪs] *a* senz'anima, inumano(a).

soul mate *n* anima gemella.

soul-searching ['səʊlsə:tʃɪŋ] *n*: **after much** ~ dopo un profondo esame di coscienza.

sound [saʊnd] *a* (*healthy*) sano(a); (*safe, not damaged*) solido(a), in buono stato; (*reliable, not superficial*) solido(a); (*sensible*) giudizioso(a), di buon senso; (*valid: argument, policy, claim*) valido(a) ♦ *ad*: ~ **asleep** profondamente addormentato ♦ *n* (*noise*) suono; rumore *m*; (*GEO*) stretto ♦ *vt* (*alarm*) suonare; (*also*: ~ **out**: *opinions*) sondare ♦ *vi* suonare; (*fig: seem*) sembrare; **to be of** ~ **mind** essere sano di mente; **I don't like the** ~ **of it** (*fig: of film etc*) non mi dice niente; (: *of news*) è preoccupante; **it** ~**s as if ...** ho l'impressione che ...; **it** ~**s like French** somiglia al francese; **that** ~**s like them arriving** mi sembra di sentirli arrivare.

sound off *vi* (*col*): **to** ~ **off (about)** (*give one's opinions*) fare dei grandi discorsi (su).

sound barrier *n* muro del suono.

sound effects *npl* effetti *mpl* sonori.

sound engineer *n* tecnico del suono.

sounding ['saʊndɪŋ] *n* (*NAUT etc*) scandagliamento.

sounding board *n* (*MUS*) cassa di risonanza; (*fig*): **to use sb as a** ~ **for one's ideas** provare le proprie idee su qn.

soundly ['saʊndlɪ] *ad* (*sleep*) profondamente;

(*beat*) duramente.

soundproof ['saundpru:f] *vt* insonorizzare, isolare acusticamente ♦ *a* insonorizzato(a), isolato(a) acusticamente.

soundtrack ['saundtræk] *n* (*of film*) colonna sonora.

sound wave *n* (*PHYSICS*) onda sonora.

soup [su:p] *n* minestra; (*clear*) brodo; (*thick*) zuppa; **in the ~** (*fig*) nei guai.

soup course *n* minestra.

soup kitchen *n* mensa per i poveri.

soup plate *n* piatto fondo.

soupspoon ['su:pspu:n] *n* cucchiaio da minestra.

sour ['sauə*] *a* aspro(a); (*fruit*) acerbo(a); (*milk*) acido(a), fermentato(a); (*fig*) acido(a); **to go** *or* **turn ~** (*milk, wine*) inacidirsi; (*fig: relationship, plans*) guastarsi; **it's ~ grapes** (*fig*) è soltanto invidia.

source [sɔ:s] *n* fonte *f*, sorgente *f*; (*fig*) fonte; **I have it from a reliable ~ that** ... ho saputo da fonte sicura che ....

south [sauθ] *n* sud *m*, meridione *m*, mezzogiorno ♦ *a* del sud, sud *inv*, meridionale ♦ *ad* verso sud; (**to the**) **~ of** a sud di; **the S~ of France** il sud della Francia; **to travel ~** viaggiare verso sud.

South Africa *n* Sudafrica *m*.

South African *a*, *n* sudafricano(a).

South America *n* Sudamerica *m*, America del sud.

South American *a*, *n* sudamericano(a).

southbound ['sauθbaund] *a* (*gen*) diretto(a) a sud; (*carriageway*) sud *inv*.

south-east [sauθ'i:st] *n* sud-est *m*.

South-East Asia *n* Asia sudorientale.

southerly ['sʌðəlɪ] *a* del sud.

southern ['sʌðən] *a* del sud, meridionale; (*wall*) esposto(a) a sud; **the ~ hemisphere** l'emisfero australe.

South Pole *n* Polo Sud.

South Sea Islands *npl*: **the ~** le isole dei Mari del Sud.

South Seas *npl*: **the ~** i Mari del Sud.

southward(s) ['sauθwəd(z)] *ad* verso sud.

south-west [sauθ'west] *n* sud-ovest *m*.

souvenir [su:və'nɪə*] *n* ricordo, souvenir *m inv*.

sovereign ['sɔvrɪn] *a*, *n* sovrano(a).

sovereignty ['sɔvrəntɪ] *n* sovranità.

soviet ['səuvɪət] *a* sovietico(a).

Soviet Union *n*: **the ~** l'Unione *f* Sovietica.

sow *n* [sau] scrofa ♦ *vt* [səu] (*pt ~ed, pp* **sown** [səun]) seminare.

soya ['sɔɪə], (*US*) **soy** [sɔɪ] *n*: **~ bean** seme *m* di soia; **~ sauce** salsa di soia.

spa [spa:] *n* (*resort*) stazione *f* termale; (*US: also:* **health ~**) centro di cure estetiche.

space [speɪs] *n* spazio; (*room*) posto; spazio; (*length of time*) intervallo ♦ *cpd* spaziale ♦ *vt* (*also:* **~ out**) distanziare; **in a confined ~** in un luogo chiuso; **to clear a ~ for sth** fare posto per qc; **in a short ~ of time** in breve tempo; **(with)in the ~ of an hour/three gen-**

erations nell'arco di un'ora/di tre generazioni.

space bar *n* (*on typewriter*) barra spaziatrice.

spacecraft ['speɪskrɑ:ft] *n* (*pl inv*) veicolo spaziale.

spaceman ['speɪsmæn] *n* astronauta *m*, cosmonauta *m*.

spaceship ['speɪsʃɪp] *n* astronave *f*, navicella spaziale.

space shuttle *n* shuttle *m inv*.

spacesuit ['speɪssu:t] *n* tuta spaziale.

spacewoman ['speɪswumən] *n* astronauta *f*, cosmonauta *f*.

spacing ['speɪsɪŋ] *n* spaziatura; **single/double ~** (*TYP etc*) spaziatura singola/doppia.

spacious ['speɪʃəs] *a* spazioso(a), ampio(a).

spade [speɪd] *n* (*tool*) vanga; pala; (*child's*) paletta; **~s** *npl* (*CARDS*) picche *fpl*.

spadework ['speɪdwə:k] *n* (*fig*) duro lavoro preparatorio.

spaghetti [spə'getɪ] *n* spaghetti *mpl*.

Spain [speɪn] *n* Spagna.

span [spæn] *pt of* **spin** ♦ *n* (*of bird, plane*) apertura alare; (*of arch*) campata; (*in time*) periodo; durata ♦ *vt* attraversare; (*fig*) abbracciare.

Spaniard ['spænjəd] *n* spagnolo/a.

spaniel ['spænjəl] *n* spaniel *m inv*.

Spanish ['spænɪʃ] *a* spagnolo(a) ♦ *n* (*LING*) spagnolo; **the ~** *npl* gli Spagnoli; **~ omelette** *frittata di cipolle, pomodori e peperoni*.

spank [spæŋk] *vt* sculacciare.

spanner ['spænə*] *n* (*Brit*) chiave *f* inglese.

spar [spa:*] *n* asta, palo ♦ *vi* (*BOXING*) allenarsi.

spare [spɛə*] *a* di riserva, di scorta; (*surplus*) in più, d'avanzo ♦ *n* (*part*) pezzo di ricambio ♦ *vt* (*do without*) fare a meno di; (*afford to give*) concedere; (*refrain from hurting, using*) risparmiare; **to ~** (*surplus*) d'avanzo; **there are 2 going ~** (*Brit*) ce ne sono 2 in più; **to ~ no expense** non badare a spese; **can you ~ the time?** ha tempo?; **I've a few minutes to ~** ho un attimo di tempo; **there is no time to ~** non c'è tempo da perdere; **can you ~ (me) £10?** puoi prestarmi 10 sterline?

spare part *n* pezzo di ricambio.

spare room *n* stanza degli ospiti.

spare time *n* tempo libero.

spare tyre *n* (*AUT*) gomma di scorta.

spare wheel *n* (*AUT*) ruota di scorta.

sparing ['spɛərɪŋ] *a* (*amount*) scarso(a); (*use*) parsimonioso(a); **to be ~ with** essere avaro(a) di.

sparingly ['spɛərɪŋlɪ] *ad* moderatamente.

spark [spa:k] *n* scintilla.

spark(ing) plug ['spa:k(ɪŋ)-] *n* candela.

sparkle ['spa:kl] *n* scintillio, sfavillio ♦ *vi* scintillare, sfavillare; (*bubble*) spumeggiare, frizzare.

sparkling ['spa:klɪŋ] *a* scintillante, sfavillante; (*wine*) spumante.

sparrow ['spærəu] *n* passero.
sparse [spɑ:s] *a* sparso(a), rado(a).
spartan ['spɑ:tən] *a* (*fig*) spartano(a).
spasm ['spæzəm] *n* (*MED*) spasmo; (*fig*) accesso, attacco.
spasmodic [spæz'mɔdɪk] *a* spasmodico(a); (*fig*) intermittente.
spastic ['spæstɪk] *n* spastico/a.
spat [spæt] *pt, pp of* **spit ♦** *n* (*US*) battibecco.
spate [speɪt] *n* (*fig*): ~ **of** diluvio *or* fiume *m* di; **in** ~ (*river*) in piena.
spatial ['speɪʃəl] *a* spaziale.
spatter ['spætə*] *vt, vi* schizzare.
spatula ['spætjulə] *n* spatola.
spawn [spɔ:n] *vt* deporre; (*pej*) produrre ♦ *vi* deporre le uova ♦ *n* uova *fpl*.
SPCA *n abbr* (*US*: = *Society for the Prevention of Cruelty to Animals*) ≈ E.N.P.A. *m* (= *Ente Nazionale per la Protezione degli Animali*).
SPCC *n abbr* (*US*) = *Society for the Prevention of Cruelty to Children*.
speak, *pt* **spoke,** *pp* **spoken** [spi:k, spəuk, 'spəukn] *vt* (*language*) parlare; (*truth*) dire ♦ *vi* parlare; **to** ~ **to sb/of** *or* **about sth** parlare a qn/di qc; ~ **up!** parli più forte!; **to** ~ **at a conference/in a debate** partecipare ad una conferenza/ad un dibattito; ~**ing!** (*on telephone*) sono io!; **to** ~ **one's mind** dire quello che si pensa; **he has no money to** ~ **of** non si può proprio dire che sia ricco.
  speak for *vt fus*: **to** ~ **for sb** parlare a nome di qn; **that picture is already spoken for** (*in shop*) quel quadro è già stato venduto.
speaker ['spi:kə*] *n* (*in public*) oratore/trice; (*also*: **loud**~) altoparlante *m*; (*POL*): **the S**~ *il presidente della Camera dei Comuni* (*Brit*) *or dei Rappresentanti* (*US*); **are you a Welsh** ~**?** parla gallese?
speaking ['spi:kɪŋ] *a* parlante; **Italian-**~ **people** persone che parlano italiano; **to be on** ~ **terms** parlarsi.
spear [spɪə*] *n* lancia.
spearhead ['spɪəhɛd] *n* punta di lancia; (*MIL*) reparto d'assalto ♦ *vt* (*attack etc*) condurre.
spearmint ['spɪəmɪnt] *n* (*BOT etc*) menta verde.
spec [spɛk] *n* (*Brit col*): **on** ~ sperando bene; **to buy sth on** ~ comprare qc sperando di fare un affare.
special ['spɛʃl] *a* speciale ♦ *n* (*train*) treno supplementare; **nothing** ~ niente di speciale; **take** ~ **care** siate particolarmente prudenti.
special agent *n* agente *m* segreto.
special correspondent *n* inviato speciale.
special delivery *n* (*POST*): **by** ~ per espresso.
specialist ['spɛʃəlɪst] *n* specialista *m/f*; **a heart** ~ (*MED*) un cardiologo.
speciality [spɛʃɪ'ælɪtɪ], (*esp US*) **specialty** specialità *f inv*.
specialize ['spɛʃəlaɪz] *vi*: **to** ~ **(in)** specializzarsi (in).
specially ['spɛʃəlɪ] *ad* specialmente,

particolarmente.
special offer *n* (*COMM*) offerta speciale.
specialty ['spɛʃəltɪ] *n* (*esp US*) = **speciality**.
species ['spi:ʃi:z] *n* (*pl inv*) specie *f inv*.
specific [spə'sɪfɪk] *a* specifico(a); preciso(a); **to be** ~ **to** avere un legame specifico con.
specifically [spə'sɪfɪklɪ] *ad* (*explicitly*: *state*, *warn*) chiaramente, esplicitamente; (*especially*: *design*, *intend*) appositamente.
specification [spɛsɪfɪ'keɪʃən] *n* specificazione *f*; ~**s** *npl* (*of car, machine*) dati *mpl* caratteristici; (*for building*) dettagli *mpl*.
specify ['spɛsɪfaɪ] *vt* specificare, precisare; **unless otherwise specified** salvo indicazioni contrarie.
specimen ['spɛsɪmən] *n* esemplare *m*, modello; (*MED*) campione *m*.
specimen copy *n* campione *m*.
specimen signature *n* firma depositata.
speck [spɛk] *n* puntino, macchiolina; (*particle*) granello.
speckled ['spɛkld] *a* macchiettato(a).
specs [spɛks] *npl* (*col*) occhiali *mpl*.
spectacle ['spɛktəkl] *n* spettacolo; *see also* **spectacles.**
spectacle case *n* (*Brit*) fodero per gli occhiali.
spectacles ['spɛktəklz] *npl* (*Brit*) occhiali *mpl*.
spectacular [spɛk'tækjulə*] *a* spettacolare ♦ *n* (*CINEMA etc*) film *m inv etc* spettacolare.
spectator [spɛk'teɪtə*] *n* spettatore/trice.
spectra ['spɛktrə] *npl of* **spectrum.**
spectre, (*US*) **specter** ['spɛktə*] *n* spettro.
spectrum, *pl* **spectra** ['spɛktrəm, -rə] *n* spettro; (*fig*) gamma.
speculate ['spɛkjuleɪt] *vi* speculare; (*try to guess*): **to** ~ **about** fare ipotesi su.
speculation [spɛkju'leɪʃən] *n* speculazione *f*; congetture *fpl*.
speculative ['spɛkjulətɪv] *a* speculativo(a).
speculator ['spɛkjuleɪtə*] *n* speculatore/trice.
sped [spɛd] *pt, pp of* **speed.**
speech [spi:tʃ] *n* (*faculty*) parola; (*talk*) discorso; (*manner of speaking*) parlata; (*language*) linguaggio; (*enunciation*) elocuzione *f*.
speech day *n* (*Brit SCOL*) giorno della premiazione.
speech impediment *n* difetto di pronuncia.
speechless ['spi:tʃlɪs] *a* ammutolito(a), muto(a).
speech therapy *n* cura dei disturbi del linguaggio.
speed [spi:d] *n* velocità *f inv*; (*promptness*) prontezza; (*AUT*: *gear*) marcia ♦ *vi* (*pt, pp* **sped** [spɛd]): **to** ~ **along** procedere velocemente; **the years sped by** gli anni sono volati; (*AUT*: *exceed* ~ *limit*) andare a velocità eccessiva; **at** ~ (*Brit*) velocemente; **at full** *or* **top** ~ a tutta velocità; **at a** ~ **of 70 km/h** a una velocità di 70 km l'ora; **shorthand/typing** ~**s** numero di parole al minuto in stenografia/dattilografia; **a five-**~ **gearbox** un cambio a cinque marce.

speed up, *pt, pp* ~**ed up** *vi, vt* accelerare.

speedboat ['spi:dbəut] *n* motoscafo; fuoribordo *m inv*.

speedily ['spi:dılı] *ad* velocemente; prontamente.

speeding ['spi:dıŋ] *n* (*AUT*) eccesso di velocità.

speed limit *n* limite *m* di velocità.

speedometer [spı'dɔmıtə*] *n* tachimetro.

speed trap *n* (*AUT*) *tratto di strada sul quale la polizia controlla la velocità dei veicoli*.

speedway ['spi:dweı] *n* (*SPORT*) pista per motociclismo.

speedy ['spi:dı] *a* veloce, rapido(a); (*reply*) pronto(a).

speleologist [spɛlı'ɔlədʒıst] *n* speleologo/a.

spell [spɛl] *n* (*also:* **magic** ~) incantesimo; (*period of time*) (*breve*) periodo ♦ *vt* (*pt, pp* **spelt** *or* ~**ed** [spɛlt, spɛld]) (*in writing*) scrivere (lettera per lettera); (*aloud*) dire lettera per lettera; (*fig*) significare; **to cast a** ~ **on sb** fare un incantesimo a qn; **he can't** ~ fa errori di ortografia; **how do you** ~ **your name?** come si scrive il suo nome?; **can you** ~ **it for me?** me lo può dettare lettera per lettera?

spellbound ['spɛlbaund] *a* incantato(a), affascinato(a).

spelling ['spɛlıŋ] *n* ortografia.

spelt [spɛlt] *pt, pp of* **spell**.

spend, *pt, pp* **spent** [spɛnd, spɛnt] *vt* (*money*) spendere; (*time, life*) passare; **to** ~ **time/money/effort on sth** dedicare tempo/soldi/energie a qc.

spending ['spɛndıŋ] *n*: **government** ~ spesa pubblica.

spending money *n* denaro per le piccole spese.

spending power *n* potere *m* d'acquisto.

spendthrift ['spɛndθrıft] *n* spendaccione/a.

spent [spɛnt] *pt, pp of* **spend** ♦ *a* (*patience*) esaurito(a); (*cartridge, bullets, match*) usato(a).

sperm [spə:m] *n* sperma *m*.

sperm whale *n* capodoglio.

spew [spju:] *vt* vomitare.

sphere [sfıə*] *n* sfera.

spherical ['sfɛrıkl] *a* sferico(a).

sphinx [sfıŋks] *n* sfinge *f*.

spice [spaıs] *n* spezia ♦ *vt* aromatizzare.

spick-and-span ['spıkən'spæn] *a* impeccabile.

spicy ['spaısı] *a* piccante.

spider ['spaıdə*] *n* ragno; ~'**s web** ragnatela.

spiel [spi:l] *n* (*col*) tiritera.

spike [spaık] *n* punta; ~**s** *npl* (*SPORT*) scarpe *fpl* chiodate.

spike heel *n* (*US*) tacco a spillo.

spiky ['spaıkı] *a* (*bush, branch*) spinoso(a); (*animal*) ricoperto(a) di aculei.

spill, *pt, pp* **spilt** *or* ~**ed** [spıl, -t, -d] *vt* versare, rovesciare ♦ *vi* versarsi, rovesciarsi; **to** ~ **the beans** (*col*) vuotare il sacco.

spill out *vi* riversarsi fuori.

spill over *vi*: **to** ~ **over (into)** (*liquid*)

versarsi (in); (*crowd*) riversarsi (in).

spin [spın] *n* (*revolution of wheel*) rotazione *f*; (*AVIAT*) avvitamento; (*trip in car*) giretto ♦ *vb* (*pt* **spun, span**, *pp* **spun** [spʌn, spæn]) *vt* (*wool etc*) filare; (*wheel*) far girare; (*Brit: clothes*) mettere nella centrifuga ♦ *vi* girare; **to** ~ **a yarn** raccontare una storia; **to** ~ **a coin** (*Brit*) lanciare in aria una moneta.

spin out *vt* far durare.

spinach ['spınıtʃ] *n* spinacio; (*as food*) spinaci *mpl*.

spinal ['spaınl] *a* spinale.

spinal column *n* colonna vertebrale, spina dorsale.

spinal cord *n* midollo spinale.

spindly ['spındlı] *a* lungo(a) e sottile, filiforme.

spin-dry ['spın'draı] *vt* asciugare con la centrifuga.

spin-dryer [spın'draıə*] *n* (*Brit*) centrifuga.

spine [spaın] *n* spina dorsale; (*thorn*) spina.

spine-chilling ['spaıntʃılıŋ] *a* agghiacciante.

spineless ['spaınlıs] *a* invertebrato(a), senza spina dorsale; (*fig*) smidollato(a).

spinner ['spınə*] *n* (*of thread*) tessitore/trice.

spinning ['spınıŋ] *n* filatura.

spinning top *n* trottola.

spinning wheel *n* filatoio.

spin-off ['spınɔf] *n* applicazione *f* secondaria.

spinster ['spınstə*] *n* nubile *f*; zitella.

spiral ['spaıərl] *n* spirale *f* ♦ *a* a spirale ♦ *vi* (*prices*) ~ salire vertiginosamente; **the inflationary** ~ la spirale dell'inflazione.

spiral staircase *n* scala a chiocciola.

spire ['spaıə*] *n* guglia.

spirit ['spırıt] *n* (*soul*) spirito, anima; (*ghost*) spirito, fantasma *m*; (*mood*) stato d'animo, umore *m*; (*courage*) coraggio; ~**s** *npl* (*drink*) alcolici *mpl*; **in good** ~**s** di buon umore; **in low** ~**s** triste, abbattuto(a); **community** ~, **public** ~ senso civico.

spirit duplicator *n* duplicatore *m* a spirito.

spirited ['spırıtıd] *a* vivace, vigoroso(a); (*horse*) focoso(a).

spirit level *n* livella a bolla (d'aria).

spiritual ['spırıtjuəl] *a* spirituale ♦ *n* (*also:* **Negro** ~) spiritual *m inv*.

spiritualism ['spırıtjuəlızəm] *n* spiritismo.

spit [spıt] *n* (*for roasting*) spiedo; (*spittle*) sputo; (*saliva*) saliva ♦ *vi* (*pt, pp* **spat** [spæt]) sputare; (*fire, fat*) scoppiettare.

spite [spaıt] *n* dispetto ♦ *vt* contrariare, far dispetto a; **in** ~ **of** nonostante, malgrado.

spiteful ['spaıtful] *a* dispettoso(a); (*tongue, remark*) maligno(a), velenoso(a).

spitroast ['spıt'rəust] *vt* cuocere allo spiedo.

spitting ['spıtıŋ] *n*: "~ **prohibited**" "vietato sputare" ♦ *a*: **to be the** ~ **image of sb** essere il ritratto vivente *or* sputato di qn.

spittle ['spıtl] *n* saliva; sputo.

spiv [spıv] *n* (*Brit col*) imbroglione *m*.

splash [splæʃ] *n* spruzzo; (*sound*) tonfo; (*of colour*) schizzo ♦ *vt* spruzzare ♦ *vi* (*also:* ~ **about**) sguazzare; **to** ~ **paint on the floor** schizzare il pavimento di vernice.

splashdown ['splæʃdaun] n ammaraggio.
splay [spleɪ] a: ~ **footed** che ha i piedi piatti.
spleen [spli:n] n (ANAT) milza.
splendid ['splɛndɪd] a splendido(a), magnifico(a).
splendour, (US) **splendor** ['splɛndə*] n splendore m.
splice [splaɪs] vt (rope) impiombare; (wood) calettare.
splint [splɪnt] n (MED) stecca.
splinter ['splɪntə*] n scheggia ♦ vi scheggiarsi.
splinter group n gruppo dissidente.
split [splɪt] n spaccatura; (fig: division, quarrel) scissione f ♦ vb (pt, pp **split**) vt spaccare; (party) dividere; (work, profits) spartire, ripartire ♦ vi (divide) dividersi; **to do the ~s** fare la spaccata; **to ~ the difference** dividersi la differenza.
split up vi (couple) separarsi, rompere; (meeting) sciogliersi.
split-level ['splɪtlɛvl] a (house) a piani sfalsati.
split peas npl piselli mpl secchi spaccati.
split personality n doppia personalità.
split second n frazione f di secondo.
splitting ['splɪtɪŋ] a: **a ~ headache** un mal di testa da impazzire.
splutter ['splʌtə*] vi farfugliare; sputacchiare.
spoil, pt, pp **spoilt** or **~ed** [spɔɪl, -t, -d] vt (damage) rovinare, guastare; (mar) sciupare; (child) viziare; (ballot paper) rendere nullo(a), invalidare; **to be ~ing for a fight** morire dalla voglia di litigare.
spoils [spɔɪlz] npl bottino.
spoilsport ['spɔɪlspɔ:t] n guastafeste m/f inv.
spoilt [spɔɪlt] pt, pp of **spoil** ♦ a (child) viziato(a); (ballot paper) nullo(a).
spoke [spəuk] pt of **speak** ♦ n raggio.
spoken ['spəukn] pp of **speak.**
spokesman ['spəuksmən], **spokeswoman** [-wumən] n portavoce m/f inv.
sponge [spʌndʒ] n spugna; (CULIN: also: ~ **cake**) pan m di Spagna ♦ vt spugnare, pulire con una spugna ♦ vi: **to ~ on** or (US) **off of** scroccare a.
sponge bag n (Brit) nécessaire m inv.
sponge cake n pan m di Spagna.
sponger ['spʌndʒə*] n (pej) parassita m/f, scroccone/a.
spongy ['spʌndʒɪ] a spugnoso(a).
sponsor ['spɔnsə*] n (RADIO, TV, SPORT etc) sponsor m inv; (of enterprise, bill, for fund-raising) promotore/trice ♦ vt sponsorizzare; patrocinare; (POL: bill) presentare; **I ~ed him at 3p a mile** (in fund-raising race) ho offerto in beneficenza 3 penny per ogni miglio che fa.
sponsorship ['spɔnsəʃɪp] n sponsorizzazione f; patrocinio.
spontaneity [spɔntə'neɪɪtɪ] n spontaneità.
spontaneous [spɔn'teɪnɪəs] a spontaneo(a).
spooky ['spu:kɪ] a che fa accapponare la pelle.
spool [spu:l] n bobina.
spoon [spu:n] n cucchiaio.
spoon-feed ['spu:nfi:d] vt nutrire con il cuc-

chiaio; (fig) imboccare.
spoonful ['spu:nful] n cucchiaiata.
sporadic [spə'rædɪk] a sporadico(a).
sport [spɔ:t] n sport m inv; (person) persona di spirito; (amusement) divertimento ♦ vt sfoggiare; **indoor/outdoor ~s** sport mpl al chiuso/all'aria aperta; **to say sth in ~** dire qc per scherzo.
sporting ['spɔ:tɪŋ] a sportivo(a); **to give sb a ~ chance** dare a qn una possibilità (di vincere).
sport jacket n (US) = **sports jacket.**
sports car n automobile f sportiva.
sports ground n campo sportivo.
sports jacket n giacca sportiva.
sportsman ['spɔ:tsmən] n sportivo.
sportsmanship ['spɔ:tsmənʃɪp] n spirito sportivo.
sports page n pagina sportiva.
sportswear ['spɔ:tswɛə*] n abiti mpl sportivi.
sportswoman ['spɔ:tswumən] n sportiva.
sporty ['spɔ:tɪ] a sportivo(a).
spot [spɔt] n punto; (mark) macchia; (dot: on pattern) pallino; (pimple) foruncolo; (place) posto; (also: ~ **advertisement**) spot m inv; (small amount): **a ~ of** un po' di ♦ vt (notice) individuare, distinguere; **on the ~** sul posto; **to do sth on the ~** fare qc immediatamente or lì per lì; **to put sb on the ~** mettere qn in difficoltà; **to come out in ~s** coprirsi di foruncoli.
spot check n controllo senza preavviso.
spotless ['spɔtlɪs] a immacolato(a).
spotlight ['spɔtlaɪt] n proiettore m; (AUT) faro ausiliario.
spot-on [spɔt'ɔn] a (Brit) esatto(a).
spot price n (COMM) prezzo del pronto.
spotted ['spɔtɪd] a macchiato(a); a puntini, pallini; ~ **with** punteggiato(a) di.
spotty ['spɔtɪ] a (face) foruncoloso(a).
spouse [spauz] n sposo/a.
spout [spaut] n (of jug) beccuccio; (of liquid) zampillo, getto ♦ vi zampillare.
sprain [spreɪn] n storta, distorsione f ♦ vt: **to ~ one's ankle** storcersi una caviglia.
sprang [spræŋ] pt of **spring.**
sprawl [sprɔ:l] vi sdraiarsi (in modo scomposto) ♦ n: **urban ~** sviluppo urbanistico incontrollato; **to send sb ~ing** mandare qn a gambe all'aria.
spray [spreɪ] n spruzzo; (container) nebulizzatore m, spray m inv; (of flowers) mazzetto ♦ cpd (deodorant) spray inv ♦ vt spruzzare; (crops) irrorare.
spread [sprɛd] n diffusione f; (distribution) distribuzione f; (PRESS, TYP: two pages) doppia pagina; (: across columns) articolo a più colonne; (CULIN) pasta (da spalmare) ♦ vb (pt, pp **spread**) vt (cloth) stendere, distendere; (butter etc) spalmare; (disease, knowledge) propagare, diffondere ♦ vi stendersi, distendersi; spalmarsi; propagarsi, diffondersi; **middle-age ~** pancetta; **repayments will be ~ over 18 months** i

versamenti saranno scaglionati lungo un periodo di 18 mesi.

spread-eagled ['sprɛdi:gld] *a*: **to be** *or* **lie** ~ essere disteso(a) a gambe e braccia aperte.

spreadsheet ['sprɛdʃi:t] *n* (*COMPUT*) foglio elettronico.

spree [spri:] *n*: **to go on a** ~ fare baldoria.

sprig [sprɪg] *n* ramoscello.

sprightly ['spraɪtlɪ] *a* vivace.

spring [sprɪŋ] *n* (*leap*) salto, balzo; (*bounciness*) elasticità; (*coiled metal*) molla; (*season*) primavera; (*of water*) sorgente *f* ♦ *vi* (*pt* **sprang**, *pp* **sprung** [spræŋ, sprʌŋ]) saltare, balzare ♦ *vt*: **to** ~ **a leak** (*pipe etc*) cominciare a perdere; **to walk with a** ~ **in one's step** camminare con passo elastico; **in** ~, **in the** ~ in primavera; **to** ~ **from** provenire da; **to** ~ **into action** entrare (rapidamente) in azione; **he sprang the news on me** mi ha sorpreso con quella notizia.

spring up *vi* (*problem*) presentarsi.

springboard ['sprɪŋbɔ:d] *n* trampolino.

spring-clean [sprɪŋ'kli:n] *n* (*also*: ~**ing**) grandi pulizie *fpl* di primavera.

spring onion *n* (*Brit*) cipollina.

springtime ['sprɪŋtaɪm] *n* primavera.

springy ['sprɪŋɪ] *a* elastico(a).

sprinkle ['sprɪŋkl] *vt* spruzzare; spargere; **to** ~ **water** *etc* **on**, ~ **with water** *etc* spruzzare dell'acqua *etc* su; **to** ~ **sugar** *etc* **on**, ~ **with sugar** *etc* spolverizzare di zucchero *etc*; ~**d with** (*fig*) cosparso(a) di.

sprinkler ['sprɪŋklə*] *n* (*for lawn etc*) irrigatore *m*; (*for fire-fighting*) sprinkler *m inv*.

sprinkling ['sprɪŋklɪŋ] *n* (*of water*) qualche goccia; (*of salt, sugar*) pizzico.

sprint [sprɪnt] *n* scatto ♦ *vi* scattare; **the 200-metres** ~ i 200 metri piani.

sprinter ['sprɪntə*] *n* velocista *m/f*.

sprite [spraɪt] *n* elfo, folletto.

sprocket ['sprɔkɪt] *n* (*on printer etc*) dente *m*, rocchetto.

sprout [spraut] *vi* germogliare.

sprouts [sprauts] *npl* (*also*: **Brussels** ~) cavolini *mpl* di Bruxelles.

spruce [spru:s] *n* abete *m* rosso ♦ *a* lindo(a); azzimato(a).

spruce up *vt* (*tidy*) mettere in ordine; (*smarten up: room etc*) abbellire; **to** ~ **o.s. up** farsi bello(a).

sprung [sprʌŋ] *pp of* **spring**.

spry [spraɪ] *a* arzillo(a), sveglio(a).

SPUC *n abbr* (= *Society for the Protection of Unborn Children*) associazione anti-abortista.

spun [spʌn] *pt, pp of* **spin**.

spur [spə:*] *n* sperone *m*; (*fig*) sprone *m*, incentivo ♦ *vt* (*also*: ~ **on**) spronare; **on the** ~ **of the moment** lì per lì.

spurious ['spjuərɪəs] *a* falso(a).

spurn [spə:n] *vt* rifiutare con disprezzo, sdegnare.

spurt [spə:t] *n* getto; (*of energy*) esplosione *f* ♦

vi sgorgare; zampillare; **to put in** *or* **on a** ~ (*runner*) fare uno scatto; (*fig*: *in work etc*) affrettarsi, sbrigarsi.

sputter ['spʌtə*] *vi* = **splutter**.

spy [spaɪ] *n* spia ♦ *cpd* (*film, story*) di spionaggio ♦ *vi*: **to** ~ **on** spiare ♦ *vt* (*see*) scorgere.

spying ['spaɪɪŋ] *n* spionaggio.

Sq. *abbr* (*in address*) = **square**.

sq. *abbr* (*MATH etc*) = **square**.

squabble ['skwɔbl] *n* battibecco ♦ *vi* bisticciarsi.

squad [skwɔd] *n* (*MIL*) plotone *m*; (*POLICE*) squadra; **flying** ~ (*POLICE*) volante *f*.

squad car *n* (*Brit POLICE*) automobile *f* della polizia.

squadron ['skwɔdrn] *n* (*MIL*) squadrone *m*; (*AVIAT, NAUT*) squadriglia.

squalid ['skwɔlɪd] *a* sordido(a).

squall [skwɔ:l] *n* burrasca.

squalor ['skwɔlə*] *n* squallore *m*.

squander ['skwɔndə*] *vt* dissipare.

square [skwɛə*] *n* quadrato; (*in town*) piazza; (*US: block of houses*) blocco, isolato; (*instrument*) squadra ♦ *a* quadrato(a); (*honest*) onesto(a); (*col: ideas, person*) di vecchio stampo ♦ *vt* (*arrange*) regolare; (*MATH*) elevare al quadrato ♦ *vi* (*agree*) accordarsi; **a** ~ **meal** un pasto abbondante; **2 metres** ~ di 2 metri per 2; **1** ~ **metre** 1 metro quadrato; **we're back to** ~ **one** (*fig*) siamo al punto di partenza; **all** ~ pari; **to get one's accounts** ~ mettere in ordine i propri conti; **I'll** ~ **it with him** (*col*) sistemo io le cose con lui; **can you** ~ **it with your conscience?** (*reconcile*) puoi conciliarlo con la tua coscienza?

square up *vi* (*Brit: settle*) saldare, pagare; **to** ~ **up with sb** regolare i conti con qn.

square bracket *n* (*TYP*) parentesi *f inv* quadra.

squarely ['skwɛəlɪ] *ad* (*directly*) direttamente; (*honestly, fairly*) onestamente.

square root *n* radice *f* quadrata.

squash [skwɔʃ] *n* (*Brit: drink*): **lemon/orange** ~ sciroppo di limone/arancia; (*vegetable*) zucca; (*SPORT*) squash *m* ♦ *vt* schiacciare.

squat [skwɔt] *a* tarchiato(a), tozzo(a) ♦ *vi* accovacciarsi; (*on property*) occupare abusivamente.

squatter ['skwɔtə*] *n* occupante *m/f* abusivo(a).

squawk [skwɔ:k] *vi* emettere strida rauche.

squeak [skwi:k] *vi* squittire ♦ *n* (*of hinge, wheel etc*) cigolio; (*of shoes*) scricchiolio; (*of mouse etc*) squittio.

squeal [skwi:l] *vi* strillare.

squeamish ['skwi:mɪʃ] *a* schizzinoso(a); disgustato(a).

squeeze [skwi:z] *n* pressione *f*; (*also ECON*) stretta; (*credit* ~) stretta creditizia ♦ *vt* premere; (*hand, arm*) stringere ♦ *vi*: **to** ~ **in** infilarsi; **to** ~ **past/under sth** passare vicino/sotto a qc con difficoltà; **a** ~ **of lemon**

una spruzzata di limone.

squeeze out *vt* spremere.

squelch [skwɛltʃ] *vi* fare ciac; sguazzare.

squib [skwɪb] *n* petardo.

squid [skwɪd] *n* calamaro.

squint [skwɪnt] *vi* essere strabico(a); (*in the sunlight*) strizzare gli occhi ♦ *n*: **he has a ~** è strabico; **to ~ at sth** guardare qc di traverso; (*quickly*) dare un'occhiata a qc.

squire ['skwaɪə*] *n* (*Brit*) proprietario terriero.

squirm [skwə:m] *vi* contorcersi.

squirrel ['skwɪrəl] *n* scoiattolo.

squirt [skwə:t] *n* schizzo ♦ *vi* schizzare; zampillare.

Sr *abbr* = **senior; sister** (*REL*).

SRC *n abbr* (*Brit:* = *Students' Representative Council*) comitato di rappresentanza studenti.

Sri Lanka [srɪ'læŋkə] *n* Sri Lanka *m*.

SRN *n abbr* (*Brit:* = *State Registered Nurse*) infermiera diplomata (*dopo corso triennale*).

SRO *abbr* (*US:* = *standing room only*) solo posti in piedi.

SS *abbr* = **steamship**.

SSA *n abbr* (*US:* = *Social Security Administration*) ≈ Previdenza Sociale.

SST *n abbr* (*US*) = *supersonic transport*.

ST *abbr* (*US:* = *Standard Time*) ora ufficiale.

St *abbr* = **saint; street**.

stab [stæb] *n* (*with knife etc*) pugnalata; (*col: try*): **to have a ~ at (doing) sth** provare a fare qc ♦ *vt* pugnalare; **to ~ sb to death** uccidere qn a coltellate.

stabbing ['stæbɪŋ] *n*: **there's been a ~** qualcuno è stato pugnalato ♦ *a* (*pain, ache*) lancinante.

stability [stə'bɪlɪtɪ] *n* stabilità.

stabilization [steɪbəlaɪ'zeɪʃən] *n* stabilizzazione *f*.

stabilize ['steɪbəlaɪz] *vt* stabilizzare ♦ *vi* stabilizzarsi.

stabilizer ['steɪbəlaɪzə*] *n* (*AVIAT, NAUT*) stabilizzatore *m*.

stable ['steɪbl] *n* (*for horses*) scuderia; (*for cattle*) stalla ♦ *a* stabile; **riding ~s** maneggio.

staccato [stə'kɑ:təu] *ad* in modo staccato ♦ *a* (*MUS*) staccato(a); (*sound*) scandito(a).

stack [stæk] *n* catasta, pila; (*col*) mucchio, sacco ♦ *vt* accatastare, ammucchiare; **there's ~s of time to finish it** (*Brit col*) abbiamo un sacco di tempo per finirlo.

stadium ['steɪdɪəm] *n* stadio.

staff [stɑ:f] *n* (*work force: gen*) personale *m*; (: *Brit: SCOL*) personale insegnante; (: *servants*) personale di servizio; (*MIL*) stato maggiore; (*stick*) bastone *m* ♦ *vt* fornire di personale.

staffroom ['stɑ:fru:m] *n* sala dei professori.

Staffs *abbr* (*Brit*) = **Staffordshire**.

stag [stæg] *n* cervo; (*Brit STOCK EXCHANGE*) rialzista *m/f* su nuove emissioni.

stage [steɪdʒ] *n* (*platform*) palco; (*in theatre*) palcoscenico; (*profession*): **the ~** il teatro, la scena; (*point*) fase *f*, stadio ♦ *vt* (*play*) alle-

stire, mettere in scena; (*demonstration*) organizzare; (*fig: perform: recovery etc*) effettuare; **in ~s** per gradi; a tappe; **in the early/final ~s** negli stadi iniziali/finali; **to go through a difficult ~** attraversare un periodo difficile.

stagecoach ['steɪdʒkəutʃ] *n* diligenza.

stage door *n* ingresso degli artisti.

stage fright *n* paura del pubblico.

stagehand ['steɪdʒhænd] *n* macchinista *m*.

stage-manage ['steɪdʒmænɪdʒ] *vt* allestire le scene per; montare.

stage manager *n* direttore *m* di scena.

stagger ['stægə*] *vi* barcollare ♦ *vt* (*person*) sbalordire; (*hours, holidays*) scaglionare.

staggering ['stægərɪŋ] *a* (*amazing*) incredibile, sbalorditivo(a).

stagnant ['stægnənt] *a* stagnante.

stagnate [stæg'neɪt] *vi* (*also fig*) stagnare.

stagnation [stæg'neɪʃən] *n* stagnazione *f*, ristagno.

stag party *n* festa di addio al celibato.

staid [steɪd] *a* posato(a), serio(a).

stain [steɪn] *n* macchia; (*colouring*) colorante *m* ♦ *vt* macchiare; (*wood*) tingere.

stained glass window ['steɪnd-] *n* vetrata.

stainless ['steɪnlɪs] *a* (*steel*) inossidabile.

stain remover *n* smacchiatore *m*.

stair [stɛə*] *n* (*step*) gradino; **~s** *npl* (*flight of ~s*) scale *fpl*, scala.

staircase ['stɛəkeɪs], **stairway** ['stɛəweɪ] *n* scale *fpl*, scala.

stairwell ['stɛəwɛl] *n* tromba delle scale.

stake [steɪk] *n* palo, piolo; (*BETTING*) puntata, scommessa ♦ *vt* (*bet*) scommettere; (*risk*) rischiare; (*also:* **~ out:** *area*) delimitare con paletti; **to be at ~** essere in gioco; **to have a ~ in sth** avere un interesse in qc; **to ~ a claim (to sth)** rivendicare (qc).

stalactite ['stæləktaɪt] *n* stalattite *f*.

stalagmite ['stæləgmaɪt] *n* stalagmite *f*.

stale [steɪl] *a* (*bread*) raffermo(a), stantio(a); (*beer*) svaporato(a); (*smell*) di chiuso.

stalemate ['steɪlmeɪt] *n* stallo; (*fig*) punto morto.

stalk [stɔ:k] *n* gambo, stelo ♦ *vt* inseguire ♦ *vi* camminare impettito(a).

stall [stɔ:l] *n* (*Brit: in street, market etc*) bancarella; (*in stable*) box *m inv* di stalla ♦ *vt* (*AUT*) far spegnere ♦ *vi* (*AUT*) spegnersi, fermarsi; (*fig*) temporeggiare; **~s** *npl* (*Brit: in cinema, theatre*) platea; **newspaper/flower ~** chiosco del giornalaio/del fioraio.

stallholder ['stɔ:lhəuldə*] *n* (*Brit*) bancarellista *m/f*.

stallion ['stæljən] *n* stallone *m*.

stalwart ['stɔ:lwət] *n* membro fidato.

stamen ['steɪmɛn] *n* stame *m*.

stamina ['stæmɪnə] *n* vigore *m*, resistenza.

stammer ['stæmə*] *n* balbuzie *f* ♦ *vi* balbettare.

stamp [stæmp] *n* (*postage ~*) francobollo; (*implement*) timbro; (*mark, also fig*) marchio, impronta; (*on document*) bollo; timbro ♦ *vi* *(also:* ~ **one's foot**) battere il piede ♦ *vt* battere; *(letter)* affrancare; *(mark with a ~)* timbrare; **~ed addressed envelope (sae)** busta affrancata per la risposta.

stamp out *vt (fire)* estinguere; *(crime)* eliminare; *(opposition)* soffocare.

stamp album *n* album *m inv* per francobolli.

stamp collecting *n* filatelia.

stamp duty *n (Brit)* bollo.

stampede [stæm'pi:d] *n* fuggi fuggi *m inv; (of cattle)* fuga precipitosa.

stamp machine *n* distributore *m* automatico di francobolli.

stance [stæns] *n* posizione *f.*

stand [stænd] *n (position)* posizione *f;* (MIL) resistenza; *(structure)* supporto, sostegno; *(at exhibition)* stand *m inv; (at market)* bancarella; *(booth)* chiosco; *(SPORT)* tribuna; *(also:* **music** ~) leggio *m* ♦ *vb (pt, pp* **stood** [stud]) *vi* stare in piedi; *(rise)* alzarsi in piedi; *(be placed)* trovarsi ♦ *vt (place)* mettere, porre; *(tolerate, withstand)* resistere, sopportare; **to make a** ~ prendere posizione; **to take a** ~ **on an issue** prendere posizione su un problema; **to** ~ **for parliament** *(Brit)* presentarsi come candidato (per il parlamento); **to** ~ **guard** *or* **watch** (MIL) essere di guardia; **it** ~**s to reason** è logico; **as things** ~ stando così le cose; **to** ~ **sb a drink/meal** offrire da bere/un pranzo a qn; **I can't** ~ **him** non lo sopporto.

stand aside *vi* farsi da parte, scostarsi.

stand by *vi (be ready)* tenersi pronto(a) ♦ *vt fus (opinion)* sostenere.

stand down *vi (withdraw)* ritirarsi; *(LAW)* lasciare il banco dei testimoni.

stand for *vt fus (signify)* rappresentare, significare; *(tolerate)* sopportare, tollerare.

stand in for *vt fus* sostituire.

stand out *vi (be prominent)* spiccare.

stand up *vi (rise)* alzarsi in piedi.

stand up for *vt fus* difendere.

stand up to *vt fus* tener testa a, resistere a.

stand-alone ['stændələun] *a* (COMPUT) standalone *inv.*

standard ['stændəd] *n* modello, standard *m inv; (level)* livello; *(flag)* stendardo ♦ *a (size etc)* normale, standard *inv; (practice)* normale; *(model)* di serie; ~**s** *npl (morals)* principi *mpl,* valori *mpl;* **to be** *or* **come up to** ~ rispondere ai requisiti; **below** *or* **not up to** ~ *(work)* mediocre; **to apply a double** ~ usare metri diversi (nel giudicare *or* fare *etc);* ~ **of living** livello di vita.

standardization [stændədaɪ'zeɪʃən] *n* standardizzazione *f.*

standardize ['stændədaɪz] *vt* normalizzare, standardizzare.

standard lamp *n (Brit)* lampada a stelo.

standard time *n* ora ufficiale.

stand-by ['stændbaɪ] *n* riserva, sostituto; **to be on** ~ *(gen)* tenersi pronto(a); *(doctor)* essere di guardia.

stand-by generator *n* generatore *m* d'emergenza.

stand-by passenger *n* (AVIAT) passeggero/a in lista d'attesa.

stand-by ticket *n* (AVIAT) biglietto senza garanzia.

stand-in ['stændɪn] *n* sostituto/a; (CINEMA) controfigura.

standing ['stændɪŋ] *a* diritto(a), in piedi; *(permanent: committee)* permanente; (: *rule)* fisso(a); (: *army)* regolare; *(grievance)* continuo(a); *(duration):* **of 6 months'** ~ che dura da 6 mesi ♦ *n* rango, condizione *f,* posizione *f;* **it's a** ~ **joke** è diventato proverbiale; **he was given a** ~ **ovation** tutti si alzarono per applaudirlo; **a man of some** ~ un uomo di una certa importanza.

standing committee *n* commissione *f* permanente.

standing order *n (Brit: at bank)* ordine *m* di pagamento (permanente); ~**s** *npl* (MIL) regolamento.

standing room *n* posto all'impiedi.

standoffish [stænd'ɔfɪʃ] *a* scostante, freddo(a).

standpat ['stændpæt] *a (US)* irremovibile.

standpipe ['stændpaɪp] *n* fontanella.

standpoint ['stændpɔɪnt] *n* punto di vista.

standstill ['stændstɪl] *n:* **at a** ~ fermo(a); *(fig)* a un punto morto; **to come to a** ~ fermarsi; giungere a un punto morto.

stank [stæŋk] *pt of* **stink.**

stanza ['stænzə] *n* stanza *(poesia).*

staple ['steɪpl] *n (for papers)* graffetta; *(chief product)* prodotto principale ♦ *a (food etc)* di base; *(crop, industry)* principale ♦ *vt* cucire.

stapler ['steɪplə*] *n* cucitrice *f.*

star [stɑ:*] *n* stella; *(celebrity)* divo/a; *(principal actor)* vedette *f inv* ♦ *vi:* **to** ~ **(in)** essere il *(or* la) protagonista (di) ♦ *vt* (CINEMA) essere interpretato(a) da; **four-**~ **hotel** ≈ albergo di prima categoria; **2-**~ **petrol** *(Brit)* ≈ benzina normale; **4-**~ **petrol** *(Brit)* ≈ super *f.*

star attraction *n* numero principale.

starboard ['stɑ:bəd] *n* dritta; **to** ~ a dritta.

starch [stɑ:tʃ] *n* amido.

starched ['stɑ:tʃt] *a (collar)* inamidato(a).

starchy ['stɑ:tʃɪ] *a (food)* ricco(a) di amido.

stardom ['stɑ:dəm] *n* celebrità.

stare [stɛə*] *n* sguardo fisso ♦ *vi:* **to** ~ **at** fissare.

starfish ['stɑ:fɪʃ] *n* stella di mare.

stark [stɑ:k] *a (bleak)* desolato(a); *(simplicity, colour)* austero(a); *(reality, poverty, truth)* crudo(a) ♦ *ad:* ~ **naked** completamente nudo(a).

starlet ['stɑ:lɪt] *n* (CINEMA) stellina.

starlight ['stɑ:laɪt] *n:* **by** ~ alla luce delle stelle.

starling ['stɑ:lɪŋ] *n* storno.

starlit ['stɑ:lɪt] *a* stellato(a).

starry ['stɑ:rɪ] *a* stellato(a).

starry-eyed [stɑ:rɪ'aɪd] *a (idealistic, gullible)*

ingenuo(a); (*from wonder*) meravigliato(a).

star-studded ['stɑː:stʌdɪd] *a*: **a ~ cast** un cast di attori famosi.

start [stɑː:t] *n* inizio; (*of race*) partenza; (*sudden movement*) sobbalzo; (*advantage*) vantaggio ♦ *vt* cominciare, iniziare; (*found: business, newspaper*) fondare, creare ♦ *vi* cominciare; (*on journey*) partire, mettersi in viaggio; (*jump*) sobbalzare; **to ~ doing sth** (in)cominciare a fare qc; **at the ~** all'inizio; **for a ~** tanto per cominciare; **to make an early ~** partire di buon'ora; **to ~ (off) with** ... (*firstly*) per prima cosa ...; (*at the beginning*) all'inizio; **to ~ a fire** provocare un incendio.

start off *vi* cominciare; (*leave*) partire.

start over *vi* (*US*) ricominciare.

start up *vi* cominciare; (*car*) avviarsi ♦ *vt* iniziare; (*car*) avviare.

starter ['stɑː:tə*] *n* (*AUT*) motorino d'avviamento; (*SPORT: official*) starter *m inv*; (: *runner, horse*) partente *m/f*; (*Brit CULIN*) primo piatto.

starting handle ['stɑː:tɪŋ-] *n* (*Brit*) manovella d'avviamento.

starting point *n* punto di partenza.

starting price *n* prezzo *m* base *inv*.

startle ['stɑː:tl] *vt* far trasalire.

startling ['stɑː:tlɪŋ] *a* sorprendente, sbalorditivo(a).

star turn *n* (*Brit*) attrazione *f* principale.

starvation [stɑː:'veɪʃən] *n* fame *f*, inedia; **to die of ~** morire d'inedia.

starve [stɑː:v] *vi* morire di fame; soffrire la fame ♦ *vt* far morire di fame, affamare; **I'm starving** muoio di fame.

state [steɪt] *n* stato; (*pomp*): **in ~** in pompa ♦ *vt* dichiarare, affermare; annunciare; **to be in a ~** essere agitato(a); **the ~ of the art** il livello di tecnologia (*or* cultura *etc*); **~ of emergency** stato di emergenza; **~ of mind** stato d'animo.

state control *n* controllo statale.

stated ['steɪtɪd] *a* fissato(a), stabilito(a).

State Department *n* (*US*) Dipartimento di Stato, ≈ Ministero degli Esteri.

state education *n* (*Brit*) istruzione *f* pubblica *or* statale.

stateless ['steɪtlɪs] *a* apolide.

stately ['steɪtlɪ] *a* maestoso(a), imponente.

statement ['steɪtmənt] *n* dichiarazione *f*; (*LAW*) deposizione *f*; (*FINANCE*) rendiconto; **official ~** comunicato ufficiale; **~ of account, bank ~** estratto conto.

state-owned ['steɪt'əund] *a* statalizzato(a).

States [steɪts] *npl*: **the ~** (*USA*) gli Stati Uniti.

statesman ['steɪtsmən] *n* statista *m*.

statesmanship ['steɪtsmənʃɪp] *n* abilità politica.

static ['stætɪk] *n* (*RADIO*) scariche *fpl* ♦ *a* statico(a); **~ electricity** elettricità statica.

station ['steɪʃən] *n* stazione *f*; (*rank*) rango, condizione *f* ♦ *vt* collocare, disporre; **action**

~s posti *mpl* di combattimento; **to be ~ed in** (*MIL*) essere di stanza in.

stationary ['steɪʃənərɪ] *a* fermo(a), immobile.

stationer ['steɪʃənə*] *n* cartolaio/a; **~'s shop** cartoleria.

stationery ['steɪʃənərɪ] *n* articoli *mpl* di cancelleria; (*writing paper*) carta da lettere.

station master *n* (*RAIL*) capostazione *m*.

station wagon *n* (*US*) giardinetta.

statistic [stə'tɪstɪk] *n* statistica; *see also* **statistics**.

statistical [stə'tɪstɪkəl] *a* statistico(a).

statistics [stə'tɪstɪks] *n* (*science*) statistica.

statue ['stætjuː] *n* statua.

statuesque [stætju'ɛsk] *a* statuario(a).

statuette [stætju'ɛt] *n* statuetta.

stature ['stætʃə*] *n* statura.

status ['steɪtəs] *n* posizione *f*, condizione *f* sociale; (*prestige*) prestigio; (*legal, marital*) stato.

status quo [-'kwəu] *n*: **the ~** lo statu quo.

status symbol *n* simbolo di prestigio.

statute ['stætjuːt] *n* legge *f*; **~s** *npl* (*of club etc*) statuto.

statute book *n* codice *m*.

statutory ['stætjutərɪ] *a* stabilito(a) dalla legge, statutario(a); **~ meeting** (*COMM*) assemblea ordinaria.

staunch [stɔː:ntʃ] *a* fidato(a), leale ♦ *vt* (*flow*) arrestare; (*blood*) arrestare il flusso di.

stave [steɪv] *n* (*MUS*) rigo ♦ *vt*: **to ~ off** (*attack*) respingere; (*threat*) evitare.

stay [steɪ] *n* (*period of time*) soggiorno, permanenza ♦ *vi* rimanere; (*reside*) alloggiare, stare; (*spend some time*) trattenersi, soggiornare; **~ of execution** (*LAW*) sospensione *f* dell'esecuzione; **to ~ put** non muoversi; **to ~ with friends** stare presso amici; **to ~ the night** passare la notte.

stay behind *vi* restare indietro.

stay in *vi* (*at home*) stare in casa.

stay on *vi* restare, rimanere.

stay out *vi* (*of house*) rimanere fuori (di casa); (*strikers*) continuare lo sciopero.

stay up *vi* (*at night*) rimanere alzato(a).

staying power ['steɪŋ-] *n* capacità di resistenza.

STD *n abbr* (*Brit*: = *subscriber trunk dialling*) teleselezione *f*; (= *sexually transmitted disease*) malattia venerea.

stead [stɛd] *n* (*Brit*): **in sb's ~** al posto di qn; **to stand sb in good ~** essere utile a qn.

steadfast ['stɛdfɑː:st] *a* fermo(a), risoluto(a).

steadily ['stɛdɪlɪ] *ad* continuamente; (*walk*) con passo sicuro.

steady ['stɛdɪ] *a* stabile, solido(a), fermo(a); (*regular*) costante; (*boyfriend etc*) fisso(a); (*person*) calmo(a), tranquillo(a) ♦ *vt* stabilizzare; calmare; **to ~ o.s.** ritrovare l'equilibrio.

steak [steɪk] *n* (*meat*) bistecca; (*fish*) trancia.

steakhouse ['steɪkhaus] *n* ristorante specializzato in bistecche.

steal, *pt* **stole**, *pp* **stolen** [sti:l, stəul, 'stəuln] *vt* rubare ♦ *vi* (*thieve*) rubare.
steal away, steal off *vi* svignarsela, andarsene alla chetichella.
stealth [stɛlθ] *n*: **by** ~ furtivamente.
stealthy ['stɛlθɪ] *a* furtivo(a).
steam [sti:m] *n* vapore *m* ♦ *vt* trattare con vapore; (*CULIN*) cuocere a vapore ♦ *vi* fumare; (*ship*): **to** ~ **along** filare; **to let off** ~ (*fig*) sfogarsi; **under one's own** ~ (*fig*) da solo, con i propri mezzi; **to run out of** ~ (*fig: person*) non farcela più.
steam up *vi* (*window*) appannarsi; **to get** ~**ed up about sth** (*fig*) andare in bestia per qc.
steam engine *n* macchina a vapore; (*RAIL*) locomotiva a vapore.
steamer ['sti:mə*] *n* piroscafo, vapore *m*; (*CULIN*) pentola a vapore.
steam iron *n* ferro a vapore.
steamroller ['sti:mrəulə*] *n* rullo compressore.
steamship ['sti:mʃɪp] *n* piroscafo, vapore *m*.
steamy ['sti:mɪ] *a* pieno(a) di vapore; (*window*) appannato(a).
steed [sti:d] *n* (*literary*) corsiero, destriero.
steel [sti:l] *n* acciaio ♦ *cpd* di acciaio.
steel band *n* banda di strumenti a percussione (*tipica dei Caribi*).
steel industry *n* industria dell'acciaio.
steel mill *n* acciaieria.
steelworks ['sti:lwə:ks] *n* acciaieria.
steely ['sti:lɪ] *a* (*determination*) inflessibile; (*gaze*) duro(a); (*eyes*) freddo(a) come l'acciaio.
steep [sti:p] *a* ripido(a), scosceso(a); (*price*) eccessivo(a) ♦ *vt* inzuppare; (*washing*) mettere a mollo.
steeple ['sti:pl] *n* campanile *m*.
steeplechase ['sti:pltʃeɪs] *n* corsa a ostacoli, steeplechase *m inv*.
steeplejack ['sti:pldʒæk] *n* chi ripara campanili e ciminiere.
steer [stɪə*] *n* manzo ♦ *vt* (*ship*) governare; (*car*) guidare ♦ *vi* (*NAUT: person*) governare; (: *ship*) rispondere al timone; (*car*) guidarsi; **to** ~ **clear of sb/sth** (*fig*) tenersi alla larga da qn/qc.
steering ['stɪərɪŋ] *n* (*AUT*) sterzo.
steering column *n* piantone *m* dello sterzo.
steering committee *n* comitato direttivo.
steering wheel *n* volante *m*.
stem [stɛm] *n* (*of flower, plant*) stelo; (*of tree*) fusto; (*of glass*) gambo; (*of fruit, leaf*) picciolo ♦ *vt* contenere, arginare.
stem from *vt fus* provenire da, derivare da.
stench [stɛntʃ] *n* puzzo, fetore *m*.
stencil ['stɛnsl] *n* (*of metal, cardboard*) stampino, mascherina; (*in typing*) matrice *f*.
stenographer [stɛ'nɔgrəfə*] *n* (*US*) stenografo/a.
stenography [stɛ'nɔgrəfɪ] *n* (*US*) stenografia.
step [stɛp] *n* passo; (*stair*) gradino, scalino; (*action*) mossa, azione *f* ♦ *vi*: **to** ~ **forward** fare un passo avanti; ~**s** *npl* (*Brit*) =

stepladder; ~ **by** ~ un passo dietro l'altro; (*fig*) poco a poco; **to be in/out of** ~ **with** (*also fig*) stare/non stare al passo con.
step down *vi* (*fig*) ritirarsi.
step in *vi* fare il proprio ingresso.
step off *vt fus* scendere da.
step over *vt fus* scavalcare.
step up *vt* aumentare; intensificare.
stepbrother ['stɛpbrʌðə*] *n* fratellastro.
stepchild ['stɛptʃaɪld] *n* figliastro/a.
stepdaughter ['stɛpdɔːtə*] *n* figliastra.
stepfather ['stɛpfɑːðə*] *n* patrigno.
stepladder ['stɛplædə*] *n* scala a libretto.
stepmother ['stɛpmʌðə*] *n* matrigna.
stepping stone ['stɛpɪŋ-] *n* pietra di un guado; (*fig*) trampolino.
stepsister ['stɛpsɪstə*] *n* sorellastra.
stepson ['stɛpsʌn] *n* figliastro.
stereo ['stɛrɪəu] *n* (*system*) sistema *m* stereofonico; (*record player*) stereo *m inv* ♦ *a* (*also*: ~**phonic**) stereofonico(a); **in** ~ in stereofonia.
stereotype ['stɪərɪətaɪp] *n* stereotipo.
sterile ['stɛraɪl] *a* sterile.
sterility [stɛ'rɪlɪtɪ] *n* sterilità.
sterilization [stɛrɪlaɪ'zeɪʃən] *n* sterilizzazione *f*.
sterilize ['stɛrɪlaɪz] *vt* sterilizzare.
sterling ['stə:lɪŋ] *a* (*gold, silver*) di buona lega; (*fig*) autentico(a), genuino(a) ♦ *n* (*ECON*) (*lira*) sterlina; **a pound** ~ una lira sterlina.
sterling area *n* area della sterlina.
stern [stə:n] *a* severo(a) ♦ *n* (*NAUT*) poppa.
sternum ['stə:nəm] *n* sterno.
steroid ['stɪərɔɪd] *n* steroide *m*.
stethoscope ['stɛθəskəup] *n* stetoscopio.
stevedore ['sti:vɪdɔ:*] *n* scaricatore *m* di porto.
stew [stju:] *n* stufato ♦ *vt, vi* cuocere in umido; ~**ed tea** *tè lasciato troppo in infusione*; ~**ed fruit** frutta cotta.
steward ['stju:əd] *n* (*AVIAT, NAUT, RAIL*) steward *m inv*; (*in club etc*) dispensiere *m*; (*shop* ~) rappresentante *m/f* sindacale.
stewardess ['stju:ədɛs] *n* assistente *f* di volo, hostess *f inv*.
stewing steak ['stju:ɪŋ-], (*US*) **stew meat** *n* carne *f* (di manzo) per stufato.
St. Ex. *abbr* = **stock exchange**.
stg *abbr* = **sterling**.
stick [stɪk] *n* bastone *m*; (*of rhubarb, celery*) gambo ♦ *vb* (*pt, pp* **stuck** [stʌk]) *vt* (*glue*) attaccare; (*thrust*): **to** ~ **sth into** conficcare *or* piantare *or* infiggere qc in; (*col: put*) ficcare; (: *tolerate*) sopportare ♦ *vi* conficcarsi; tenere; (*remain*) restare, rimanere; (*get jammed: door, lift*) bloccarsi; **to** ~ **to** (*one's word, promise*) mantenere; (*principles*) tener fede a; **to get hold of the wrong end of the** ~ (*fig*) capire male; **it stuck in my mind** mi è rimasto in mente.
stick around *vi* (*col*) restare, fermarsi.
stick out, stick up *vi* sporgere, spuntare ♦ *vt*: **to** ~ **it out** (*col*) tener duro.

stick up for *vt fus* difendere.
sticker ['stɪkə*] *n* cartellino adesivo.
sticking plaster ['stɪkɪŋ-] *n* cerotto adesivo.
stickleback ['stɪklbæk] *n* spinarello.
stickler ['stɪklə*] *n*: **to be a ~ for** essere pignolo(a) su, tenere molto a.
stick-on ['stɪkɔn] *a (label)* adesivo(a).
stick-up ['stɪkʌp] *n (col)* rapina a mano armata.
sticky ['stɪkɪ] *a* attaccaticcio(a), vischioso(a); *(label)* adesivo(a).
stiff [stɪf] *a* rigido(a), duro(a); *(muscle)* legato(a), indolenzito(a); *(difficult)* difficile, arduo(a); *(cold: manner etc)* freddo(a), formale; *(strong)* forte; *(high: price)* molto alto(a); **to be** *or* **feel ~** *(person)* essere *or* sentirsi indolenzito; **to have a ~ neck/back** avere il torcicollo/mal di schiena; **to keep a ~ upper lip** *(Brit fig)* conservare il sangue freddo.
stiffen ['stɪfn] *vt* irrigidire; rinforzare ♦ *vi* irrigidirsi; indurirsi.
stiffness ['stɪfnɪs] *n* rigidità; indolenzimento; difficoltà; freddezza.
stifle ['staɪfl] *vt* soffocare.
stifling ['staɪflɪŋ] *a (heat)* soffocante.
stigma, *pl (BOT, MED)* ~**ta**, *(fig)* ~**s** ['stɪgmə, stɪg'mɑːtə] *n* stigma *m*.
stigmata [stig'mɑːtə] *npl (REL)* stigmate *fpl*.
stile [staɪl] *n* cavalcasiepe *m*; cavalcasteccato.
stiletto [stɪ'lɛtəu] *n (also: ~ **heel**)* tacco a spillo.
still [stɪl] *a* fermo(a); *(quiet)* silenzioso(a); *(orange juice etc)* non gassato(a) ♦ *ad (up to this time, even)* ancora; *(nonetheless)* tuttavia, ciò nonostante ♦ *n (CINEMA)* fotogramma *m*; **keep ~!** stai fermo!; **he ~ hasn't arrived** non è ancora arrivato.
stillborn ['stɪlbɔːn] *a* nato(a) morto(a).
still life *n* natura morta.
stilt [stɪlt] *n* trampolo; *(pile)* palo.
stilted ['stɪltɪd] *a* freddo(a), formale; artificiale.
stimulant ['stɪmjulənt] *n* stimolante *m*.
stimulate ['stɪmjuleɪt] *vt* stimolare.
stimulating ['stɪmjuleɪtɪŋ] *a* stimolante.
stimulation [stɪmju'leɪʃən] *n* stimolazione *f*.
stimulus, *pl* **stimuli** ['stɪmjuləs, 'stɪmjulaɪ] *n* stimolo.
sting [stɪŋ] *n* puntura; *(organ)* pungiglione *m*; *(col)* trucco ♦ *vt (pt, pp* **stung** [stʌŋ]) pungere ♦ *vi* bruciare; **my eyes are ~ing** mi bruciano gli occhi.
stingy ['stɪndʒɪ] *a* spilorcio(a), tirchio(a).
stink [stɪŋk] *n* fetore *m*, puzzo ♦ *vi (pt* **stank**, *pp* **stunk** [stæŋk, stʌŋk]) puzzare.
stinker ['stɪŋkə*] *n (col)* porcheria; *(person)* fetente *m/f*.
stinking ['stɪŋkɪŋ] *a (col)*: **a ~** ... uno schifo di ..., un(a) maledetto(a) ...; **~ rich** ricco(a) da far paura.
stint [stɪnt] *n* lavoro, compito ♦ *vi*: **to ~ on** lesinare su.
stipend ['staɪpɛnd] *n* stipendio, congrua.

stipendiary [staɪ'pɛndɪərɪ] *a*: **~ magistrate** magistrato stipendiato.
stipulate ['stɪpjuleɪt] *vt* stipulare.
stipulation [stɪpju'leɪʃən] *n* stipulazione *f*.
stir [stəː*] *n* agitazione *f*, clamore *m* ♦ *vt* rimescolare; *(move)* smuovere, agitare ♦ *vi* muoversi; **to give sth a ~** mescolare qc; **to cause a ~** fare scalpore.
stir up *vt* provocare, suscitare.
stirring ['stəːrɪŋ] *a* eccitante; commovente.
stirrup ['stɪrəp] *n* staffa.
stitch [stɪtʃ] *n (SEWING)* punto; *(KNITTING)* maglia; *(MED)* punto (di sutura); *(pain)* fitta ♦ *vt* cucire, attaccare; suturare.
stoat [stəut] *n* ermellino.
stock [stɔk] *n* riserva, provvista; *(COMM)* giacenza, stock *m inv*; *(AGR)* bestiame *m*; *(CULIN)* brodo; *(FINANCE)* titoli *mpl*, azioni *fpl*; *(RAIL: also:* **rolling ~**) materiale *m* rotabile; *(descent, origin)* stirpe *f* ♦ *a (fig: reply etc)* consueto(a); solito(a), classico(a); *(greeting)* usuale; *(COMM: goods, size)* standard *inv* ♦ *vt (have in stock)* avere, vendere; **well-~ed** ben fornito(a); **to have sth in ~** avere qc in magazzino; **out of ~** esaurito(a); **to take ~** *(fig)* fare il punto; **~s and shares** valori *mpl* di borsa; **government ~** titoli di Stato.
stock up *vi*: **to ~ up (with)** fare provvista (di).
stockade [stɔ'keɪd] *n* palizzata.
stockbroker ['stɔkbrəukə*] *n* agente *m* di cambio.
stock control *n* gestione *f* magazzino.
stock cube *n (Brit CULIN)* dado.
stock exchange *n* Borsa (valori).
stockholder ['stɔkhəuldə*] *n (FINANCE)* azionista *m/f*.
Stockholm ['stɔkhəum] *n* Stoccolma.
stocking ['stɔkɪŋ] *n* calza.
stock-in-trade ['stɔkɪn'treɪd] *n (fig)*: **it's his ~** è la sua specialità.
stockist ['stɔkɪst] *n (Brit)* fornitore *m*.
stock market *n (Brit)* Borsa, mercato finanziario.
stock phrase *n* cliché *m inv*.
stockpile ['stɔkpaɪl] *n* riserva ♦ *vt* accumulare riserve di.
stockroom ['stɔkrum] *n* magazzino.
stocktaking ['stɔkteɪkɪŋ] *n (Brit COMM)* inventario.
stocky ['stɔkɪ] *a* tarchiato(a), tozzo(a).
stodgy ['stɔdʒɪ] *a* pesante, indigesto(a).
stoic ['stəuɪk] *n* stoico/a.
stoical ['stəuɪkəl] *a* stoico(a).
stoke [stəuk] *vt* alimentare.
stoker ['stəukə*] *n* fochista *m*.
stole [stəul] *pt of* **steal** ♦ *n* stola.
stolen ['stəuln] *pp of* **steal**.
stolid ['stɔlɪd] *a* impassibile.
stomach ['stʌmək] *n* stomaco; *(abdomen)* ventre *m* ♦ *vt* sopportare, digerire.
stomach ache *n* mal *m* di stomaco.
stomach pump *n* pompa gastrica.

stomach ulcer *n* ulcera allo stomaco.

stomp [stɔmp] *vi*: **to ~ in/out** *etc* entrare/ uscire *etc* con passo pesante.

stone [stəun] *n* pietra; (*pebble*) sasso, ciottolo; (*in fruit*) nocciolo; (*MED*) calcolo; (*Brit: weight*) = *6.348 kg.*; *14 libbre* ♦ *cpd* di pietra ♦ *vt* lapidare; **within a ~'s throw of the station** a due passi dalla stazione.

Stone Age *n*: **the ~** l'età della pietra.

stone-cold [stəun'kəuld] *a* gelido(a).

stoned [stəund] *a* (*col: drunk*) sbronzo(a); (*on drugs*) fuori *inv*.

stone-deaf [stəun'dɛf] *a* sordo(a) come una campana.

stonemason ['stəunmeisn] *n* scalpellino.

stonework ['stəunwə:k] *n* muratura.

stony ['stəunɪ] *a* pietroso(a), sassoso(a).

stood [stud] *pt*, *pp* of **stand**.

stool [stu:l] *n* sgabello.

stoop [stu:p] *vi* (*also*: **have a ~**) avere una curvatura; (*bend*) chinarsi, curvarsi; **to ~ to sth/doing sth** abbassarsi a qc/a fare qc.

stop [stɔp] *n* arresto; (*stopping place*) fermata; (*in punctuation*) punto ♦ *vt* arrestare, fermare; (*break off*) interrompere; (*also*: **put a ~ to**) porre fine a; (*prevent*) impedire ♦ *vi* fermarsi; (*rain, noise etc*) cessare, finire; **to ~ doing sth** cessare *or* finire di fare qc; **to ~ sb (from) doing sth** impedire a qn di fare qc; **to ~ dead** fermarsi di colpo; **~ it!** smettila!, basta!

stop by *vi* passare, fare un salto.

stop off *vi* sostare brevemente.

stop up *vt* (*hole*) chiudere, turare.

stopcock ['stɔpkɔk] *n* rubinetto di arresto.

stopgap ['stɔpgæp] *n* (*person*) tappabuchi *m/f inv*; (*measure*) ripiego ♦ *cpd* (*measures, solution*) di fortuna.

stoplights ['stɔplaɪts] *npl* (*AUT*) stop *mpl*.

stopover ['stɔpəuvə*] *n* breve sosta; (*AVIAT*) scalo.

stoppage ['stɔpɪdʒ] *n* arresto, fermata; (*of pay*) trattenuta; (*strike*) interruzione *f* del lavoro.

stopper ['stɔpə*] *n* tappo.

stop press *n* ultimissime *fpl*.

stopwatch ['stɔpwɔtʃ] *n* cronometro.

storage ['stɔ:rɪdʒ] *n* immagazzinamento; (*COMPUT*) memoria.

storage heater *n* (*Brit*) radiatore *m* elettrico che accumula calore.

store [stɔ:*] *n* provvista, riserva; (*depot*) deposito; (*Brit: department ~*) grande magazzino; (*US: shop*) negozio ♦ *vt* mettere da parte; conservare; (*grain, goods*) immagazzinare; (*COMPUT*) registrare; **to set great/little ~ by sth** dare molta/poca importanza a qc; **who knows what is in ~ for us?** chissà cosa ci riserva il futuro?

store up *vt* mettere in serbo, conservare.

storehouse ['stɔ:haus] *n* magazzino, deposito.

storekeeper ['stɔ:ki:pə*] *n* (*US*) negoziante *m/f*.

storeroom ['stɔ:rum] *n* dispensa.

storey, (*US*) **story** ['stɔ:rɪ] *n* piano.

stork [stɔ:k] *n* cicogna.

storm [stɔ:m] *n* tempesta; (*also*: **thunder~**) temporale *m* ♦ *vi* (*fig*) infuriarsi ♦ *vt* prendere d'assalto.

storm cloud *n* nube *f* temporalesca.

storm door *n* controporta.

stormy ['stɔ:mɪ] *a* tempestoso(a), burrascoso(a).

story ['stɔ:rɪ] *n* storia; racconto; (*PRESS*) articolo; (*US*) = **storey**.

storybook ['stɔ:rɪbuk] *n* libro di racconti.

storyteller ['stɔ:rɪtɛlə*] *n* narratore/trice.

stout [staut] *a* solido(a), robusto(a); (*brave*) coraggioso(a); (*fat*) corpulento(a), grasso(a) ♦ *n* birra scura.

stove [stəuv] *n* (*for cooking*) fornello; (: *small*) fornelletto; (*for heating*) stufa; **gas/ electric ~** cucina a gas/elettrica.

stow [stəu] *vt* mettere via.

stowaway ['stəuəwei] *n* passeggero(a) clandestino(a).

straddle ['strædl] *vt* stare a cavalcioni di.

strafe [strɑ:f] *vt* mitragliare.

straggle ['strægl] *vi* crescere (*or* estendersi) disordinatamente; trascinarsi; rimanere indietro; **~d along the coast** disseminati(e) lungo la costa.

straggler ['stræglə*] *n* sbandato/a.

straggling ['stræglɪŋ], **straggly** ['strægli] *a* (*hair*) in disordine.

straight [streit] *a* (*continuous, direct*) dritto(a); (*frank*) onesto(a), franco(a); (*plain, uncomplicated*) semplice; (*THEATRE: part, play*) serio(a); (*col: heterosexual*) eterosessuale ♦ *ad* diritto; (*drink*) liscio ♦ *n*: **the ~** la linea retta; (*RAIL*) il rettilineo; (*SPORT*) la dirittura d'arrivo; **to put** *or* **get ~** mettere in ordine, mettere ordine in; **to be (all) ~** (*tidy*) essere a posto, essere sistemato; (*clarified*) essere chiaro; **ten ~ wins** dieci vittorie di fila; **~ away, ~ off** (*at once*) immediatamente; **~ off, ~ out** senza esitare; **I went ~ home** sono andato direttamente a casa.

straighten ['streitn] *vt* (*also*: **~ out**) raddrizzare; **to ~ things out** mettere le cose a posto.

straight-faced [streit'feist] *a* impassibile, imperturbabile ♦ *ad* con il viso serio.

straightforward [streit'fɔ:wəd] *a* semplice; (*frank*) onesto(a), franco(a).

strain [strein] *n* (*TECH*) sollecitazione *f*; (*physical*) sforzo; (*mental*) tensione *f*; (*MED*) strappo; (*streak, trace*) tendenza; elemento; (*breed*) razza; (*of virus*) tipo ♦ *vt* tendere; (*muscle*) slogare; (*ankle*) storcere; (*friendship, marriage*) mettere a dura prova; (*filter*) colare, filtrare ♦ *vi* sforzarsi; **~s** *npl* (*MUS*) note *fpl*; **she's under a lot of ~** è molto tesa, è sotto pressione.

strained [streind] *a* (*laugh etc*) forzato(a); (*relations*) teso(a).

strainer ['streinə*] *n* passino, colino.

strait [streɪt] n (GEO) stretto; **to be in dire ~s** (fig) essere nei guai.

straitjacket ['streɪtdʒækɪt] n camicia di forza.

strait-laced [streɪt'leɪst] a puritano(a).

strand [strænd] n (of thread) filo.

stranded ['strændɪd] a nei guai; senza mezzi di trasporto.

strange [streɪndʒ] a (not known) sconosciuto(a); (odd) strano(a), bizzarro(a).

strangely ['streɪndʒlɪ] ad stranamente.

stranger ['streɪndʒə*] n (unknown) sconosciuto/a; (from another place) estraneo/a; **I'm a ~ here** non sono del posto.

strangle ['stræŋgl] vt strangolare.

stranglehold ['stræŋglhəʊld] n (fig) stretta (mortale).

strangulation [stræŋgju'leɪʃən] n strangolamento.

strap [stræp] n cinghia; (of slip, dress) spallina, bretella ♦ vt legare con una cinghia; (child etc) punire (con una cinghia).

straphanging ['stræphæŋɪŋ] n viaggiare m in piedi (su mezzi pubblici reggendosi a un sostegno).

strapless ['stræplɪs] a (bra, dress) senza spalline.

strapping ['stræpɪŋ] a ben piantato(a).

Strasbourg ['stræzbə:g] n Strasburgo f.

strata ['strɑːtə] npl of **stratum**.

stratagem ['strætɪdʒəm] n stratagemma m.

strategic [strə'tiːdʒɪk] a strategico(a).

strategist ['strætɪdʒɪst] n stratega m.

strategy ['strætɪdʒɪ] n strategia.

stratosphere ['strætəsfɪə*] n stratosfera.

stratum, pl **strata** ['strɑːtəm, 'strɑːtə] n strato.

straw [strɔː] n paglia; (drinking ~) cannuccia; **that's the last ~!** è la goccia che fa traboccare il vaso!

strawberry ['strɔːbərɪ] n fragola.

stray [streɪ] a (animal) randagio(a) ♦ vi perdersi; allontanarsi, staccarsi (dal gruppo); **~ bullet** proiettile m vagante.

streak [striːk] n striscia; (fig: of madness etc): **a ~ of** una vena di ♦ vt striare, screziare ♦ vi: **to ~ past** passare come un fulmine; **to have ~s in one's hair** avere le mèche nei capelli; **a winning/losing ~** un periodo fortunato/sfortunato.

streaky ['striːkɪ] a screziato(a), striato(a).

streaky bacon n (Brit) ≈ pancetta.

stream [striːm] n ruscello; corrente f; (of people) fiume m ♦ vt (SCOL) dividere in livelli di rendimento ♦ vi scorrere; (of people): **to ~ in/out** entrare/uscire a fiotti; **against the ~** controcorrente; **on ~** (new power plant etc) in funzione, in produzione.

streamer ['striːmə*] n (of paper) stella filante.

stream feed n (on photocopier etc) alimentazione f continua.

streamline ['striːmlaɪn] vt dare una linea aerodinamica a; (fig) razionalizzare.

streamlined ['striːmlaɪnd] a aerodinamico(a), affusolato(a); (fig) razionalizzato(a).

street [striːt] n strada, via; **the back ~s** le strade secondarie; **to be on the ~s** (homeless) essere senza tetto; (as prostitute) battere il marciapiede.

streetcar ['striːtkɑː*] n (US) tram m inv.

street lamp n lampione m.

street lighting n illuminazione f stradale.

street map, street plan n pianta (di una città).

street market n mercato all'aperto.

streetwise ['striːtwaɪz] a (col) esperto(a) dei bassifondi.

strength [streŋθ] n forza; (of girder, knot etc) resistenza, solidità; (of chemical solution) concentrazione f; (of wine) gradazione f alcolica; **on the ~ of** sulla base di, in virtù di; **below/at full ~** con gli effettivi ridotti/al completo.

strengthen ['streŋθən] vt rinforzare; (muscles) irrobustire; (economy, currency) consolidare.

strenuous ['strenjuəs] a vigoroso(a), energico(a); (tiring) duro(a), pesante.

stress [stres] n (force, pressure) pressione f; (mental strain) tensione f; (accent) accento; (emphasis) enfasi f ♦ vt insistere su, sottolineare; **to be under ~** essere sotto tensione; **to lay great ~ on sth** dare grande importanza a qc.

stressful ['stresful] a (job) difficile, stressante.

stretch [stretʃ] n (of sand etc) distesa; (of time) periodo ♦ vi stirarsi; (extend): **to ~ to** or **as far as** estendersi fino a; (be enough: money, food): **to ~ (to)** bastare (per) ♦ vt tendere, allungare; (spread) distendere; (fig) spingere (al massimo); **at a ~** ininterrottamente; **to ~ a muscle** tendere un muscolo; **to ~ one's legs** sgranchirsi le gambe.

stretch out vi allungarsi, estendersi ♦ vt (arm etc) allungare, tendere; (to spread) distendere; **to ~ out for sth** allungare la mano per prendere qc.

stretcher ['stretʃə*] n barella, lettiga.

stretcher-bearer ['stretʃəbɛərə*] n barelliere m.

stretch marks npl smagliature fpl.

strewn [struːn] a: **~ with** cosparso(a) di.

stricken ['strɪkən] a provato(a); affranto(a); **~ with** colpito(a) da.

strict [strɪkt] a (severe) rigido(a), severo(a); (: order, rule) rigoroso(a); (: supervision) stretto(a); (precise) preciso(a), stretto(a); **in ~ confidence** in assoluta confidenza.

strictly ['strɪktlɪ] ad severamente; rigorosamente; strettamente; **~ confidential** strettamente confidenziale; **~ speaking** a rigor di termini; **~ between ourselves ...** detto fra noi ....

stride [straɪd] n passo lungo ♦ vi (pt **strode**, pp **stridden** [strəʊd, 'strɪdn]) camminare a grandi passi; **to take in one's ~** (fig: changes etc) prendere con tranquillità.

strident ['straɪdnt] a stridente.

strife [straɪf] n conflitto; litigi mpl.

strike [straɪk] n sciopero; (of oil etc) scoperta; (attack) attacco ♦ vb (pt, pp **struck** [strʌk]) vt colpire; (oil etc) scoprire, trovare; (produce, make: coin, medal) coniare; (: agreement, deal) concludere ♦ vi far sciopero, scioperare; (attack) attaccare; (clock) suonare; **to go on** or **come out on ~** mettersi in sciopero; **to ~ a match** accendere un fiammifero; **to ~ a balance** (fig) trovare il giusto mezzo.
  strike back vi (MIL) fare rappresaglie; (fig) reagire.
  strike down vt (fig) atterrare.
  strike off vt (from list) cancellare; (: doctor etc) radiare.
  strike out vt depennare.
  strike up vt (MUS) attaccare; **to ~ up a friendship with** fare amicizia con.
strikebreaker ['straɪkbreɪkə*] n crumiro/a.
striker ['straɪkə*] n scioperante m/f; (SPORT) attaccante m.
striking ['straɪkɪŋ] a impressionante.
string [strɪŋ] n spago; (row) fila; sequenza; catena; (COMPUT) stringa, sequenza; (MUS) corda ♦ vt (pt, pp **strung** [strʌŋ]): **to ~ out** disporre di fianco; **to ~ together** mettere insieme; **the ~s** npl (MUS) gli archi; **~ of pearls** filo di perle; **with no ~s attached** (fig) senza vincoli, senza obblighi; **to get a job by pulling ~s** ottenere un lavoro a forza di raccomandazioni.
string bean n fagiolino.
string(ed) instrument n (MUS) strumento a corda.
stringent ['strɪndʒənt] a rigoroso(a); (reasons, arguments) stringente, impellente.
string quartet n quartetto d'archi.
strip [strɪp] n striscia; (SPORT): **wearing the Celtic ~** con la divisa del Celtic ♦ vt spogliare; (also: **~ down**: machine) smontare ♦ vi spogliarsi.
strip cartoon n fumetto.
stripe [straɪp] n striscia, riga.
striped ['straɪpt] a a strisce or righe.
strip light n (Brit) tubo al neon.
stripper ['strɪpə*] n spogliarellista.
striptease ['strɪptiːz] n spogliarello.
strive, pt **strove**, pp **striven** [straɪv, strəuv, 'strɪvn] vi: **to ~ to do** sforzarsi di fare.
strode [strəud] pt of **stride**.
stroke [strəuk] n colpo; (of piston) corsa; (MED) colpo apoplettico; (SWIMMING: style) nuoto; (caress) carezza ♦ vt accarezzare; **at a ~** in un attimo; **on the ~ of 5** alle 5 in punto, allo scoccare delle 5; **a ~ of luck** un colpo di fortuna; **two-~ engine** motore a due tempi.
stroll [strəul] n giretto, passeggiatina ♦ vi andare a spasso; **to go for a ~, have** or **take a ~** andare a fare un giretto or due passi.
stroller ['strəulə*] n (US) passeggino.
strong [strɔŋ] a (gen) forte; (sturdy: table, fabric etc) solido(a); (concentrated, intense: bleach, acid) concentrato(a); (protest,

letter, measures) energico(a) ♦ ad: **to be going ~** (company) andare a gonfie vele; (person) essere attivo(a); **they are 50 ~** sono in 50; **~ language** (swearing) linguaggio volgare.
strong-arm ['strɔŋɑːm] a (tactics, methods) energico(a).
strongbox ['strɔŋbɔks] n cassaforte f.
strong drink n alcolici mpl.
stronghold ['strɔŋhəuld] n fortezza, roccaforte f.
strongly ['strɔŋlɪ] ad fortemente, con forza; solidamente; energicamente; **to feel ~ about sth** avere molto a cuore qc.
strongman ['strɔŋmæn] n personaggio di spicco.
strongroom ['strɔŋrum] n camera di sicurezza.
strove [strəuv] pt of **strive**.
struck [strʌk] pt, pp of **strike**.
structural ['strʌktʃərəl] a strutturale; (CONSTR) di costruzione; di struttura.
structurally ['strʌktʃrəlɪ] ad dal punto di vista della struttura.
structure ['strʌktʃə*] n struttura; (building) costruzione f, fabbricato.
struggle ['strʌgl] n lotta ♦ vi lottare; **to have a ~ to do sth** avere dei problemi per fare qc.
strum [strʌm] vt (guitar) strimpellare.
strung [strʌŋ] pt, pp of **string**.
strut [strʌt] n sostegno, supporto ♦ vi pavoneggiarsi.
strychnine ['strɪkniːn] n stricnina.
stub [stʌb] n mozzicone m; (of ticket etc) matrice f, talloncino ♦ vt: **to ~ one's toe (on sth)** urtare or sbattere il dito del piede (contro qc).
  stub out vt: **to ~ out a cigarette** spegnere una sigaretta.
stubble ['stʌbl] n stoppia; (on chin) barba ispida.
stubborn ['stʌbən] a testardo(a), ostinato(a).
stubby ['stʌbɪ] a tozzo(a).
stucco ['stʌkəu] n stucco.
stuck [stʌk] pt, pp of **stick** ♦ a (jammed) bloccato(a); **to get ~** bloccarsi.
stuck-up [stʌk'ʌp] a presuntuoso(a).
stud [stʌd] n bottoncino; borchia; (of horses) scuderia, allevamento di cavalli; (also: **~ horse**) stallone m ♦ vt (fig): **~ded with** tempestato(a) di.
student ['stjuːdənt] n studente/essa ♦ cpd studentesco(a); universitario(a); degli studenti; **a law/medical ~** uno studente di legge/di medicina.
student driver n (US) conducente m/f principiante.
students' union n (Brit: association) circolo universitario; (: building) sede f del circolo universitario.
studied ['stʌdɪd] a studiato(a), calcolato(a).
studio ['stjuːdɪəu] n studio.
studio flat, (US) **studio apartment** n

appartamento monolocale.

studious ['stju:dɪəs] *a* studioso(a); (*studied*) studiato(a), voluto(a).

studiously ['stju:dɪəslɪ] *ad* (*carefully*) deliberatamente, di proposito.

study ['stʌdɪ] *n* studio ♦ *vt* studiare; esaminare ♦ *vi* studiare; **to make a ~ of sth** fare uno studio su qc; **to ~ for an exam** prepararsi a un esame.

stuff [stʌf] *n* (*substance*) roba; (*belongings*) cose *fpl*, roba ♦ *vt* imbottire; (*animal: for exhibition*) impagliare; (*CULIN*) farcire; **my nose is ~ed up** ho il naso chiuso; **get ~ed!** (*col!*) va' a farti fottere! (*!*); **~ed toy** giocattolo di peluche.

stuffing ['stʌfɪŋ] *n* imbottitura; (*CULIN*) ripieno.

stuffy ['stʌfɪ] *a* (*room*) mal ventilato(a), senz'aria; (*ideas*) antiquato(a).

stumble ['stʌmbl] *vi* inciampare; **to ~ across** (*fig*) imbattersi in.

stumbling block ['stʌmblɪŋ-] *n* ostacolo, scoglio.

stump [stʌmp] *n* ceppo; (*of limb*) moncone *m* ♦ *vt*: **to be ~ed for an answer** essere incapace di rispondere.

stun [stʌn] *vt* stordire; (*amaze*) sbalordire.

stung [stʌŋ] *pt, pp of* **sting**.

stunk [stʌŋk] *pp of* **stink**.

stunning ['stʌnɪŋ] *a* (*piece of news etc*) sbalorditivo(a); (*girl, dress*) favoloso(a), stupendo(a).

stunt [stʌnt] *n* bravata; trucco pubblicitario; (*AVIAT*) acrobazia ♦ *vt* arrestare.

stunted ['stʌntɪd] *a* stentato(a), rachitico(a).

stuntman ['stʌntmæn] *n* cascatore *m*.

stupefaction [stju:pɪ'fækʃən] *n* stupefazione *f*, stupore *m*.

stupefy ['stju:pɪfaɪ] *vt* stordire; intontire; (*fig*) stupire.

stupendous [stju:'pendəs] *a* stupendo(a), meraviglioso(a).

stupid ['stju:pɪd] *a* stupido(a).

stupidity [stju:'pɪdɪtɪ] *n* stupidità.

stupidly ['stju:pɪdlɪ] *ad* stupidamente.

stupor ['stju:pə*] *n* torpore *m*.

sturdy ['stə:dɪ] *a* robusto(a), vigoroso(a); solido(a).

sturgeon ['stə:dʒən] *n* storione *m*.

stutter ['stʌtə*] *n* balbuzie *f* ♦ *vi* balbettare.

Stuttgart ['ʃtutgart] *n* Stoccarda.

sty [staɪ] *n* (*of pigs*) porcile *m*.

stye [staɪ] *n* (*MED*) orzaiolo.

style [staɪl] *n* stile m; (*distinction*) eleganza, classe *f*; (*hair ~*) pettinatura; (*of dress etc*) modello, linea; **in the latest ~** all'ultima moda.

styli ['staɪlaɪ] *npl of* **stylus**.

stylish ['staɪlɪʃ] *a* elegante.

stylist ['staɪlɪst] *n*: **hair ~** parrucchiere/a.

stylized ['staɪlaɪzd] *a* stilizzato(a).

stylus, *pl* **styli** *or* **styluses** ['staɪləs, -laɪ] *n* (*of record player*) puntina.

suave [swɑ:v] *a* untuoso(a).

sub [sʌb] *n abbr* = **submarine**; **subscription**.

sub... [sʌb] *prefix* sub..., sotto....

subcommittee ['sʌbkəmɪtɪ] *n* sottocomitato.

subconscious [sʌb'kɔnʃəs] *a, n* subcosciente (*m*).

subcontinent [sʌb'kɔntɪnənt] *n*: **the (Indian) ~** il subcontinente (indiano).

subcontract *n* [sʌb'kɔntrækt] subappalto ♦ *vt* [sʌbkən'trækt] subappaltare.

subcontractor ['sʌbkən'træktə*] *n* subappaltatore/trice.

subdivide [sʌbdɪ'vaɪd] *vt* suddividere.

subdivision ['sʌbdɪvɪʒən] *n* suddivisione *f*.

subdue [səb'dju:] *vt* sottomettere, soggiogare.

subdued [səb'dju:d] *a* pacato(a); (*light*) attenuato(a); (*person*) poco esuberante.

sub-editor ['sʌb'edɪtə*] *n* (*Brit*) redattore(trice) aggiunto(a).

subject ['sʌbdʒɪkt] *n* soggetto; (*citizen etc*) cittadino/a; (*SCOL*) materia ♦ *a* (*liable*): **~ to** soggetto(a) a ♦ *vt* [səb'dʒɛkt]: **to ~ to** sottomettere a; esporre a; **~ to confirmation in writing** a condizione di ricevere conferma scritta; **to change the ~** cambiare discorso.

subjection [səb'dʒɛkʃən] *n* sottomissione *f*, soggezione *f*.

subjective [səb'dʒɛktɪv] *a* soggettivo(a).

subject matter *n* argomento; contenuto.

sub judice [sʌb'dʒu:dɪsɪ] *a* (*LAW*) sub iudice.

subjugate ['sʌbdʒugeɪt] *vt* sottomettere, soggiogare.

subjunctive [səb'dʒʌŋktɪv] *a* congiuntivo(a) ♦ *n* congiuntivo.

sublet [sʌb'let] *vt, vi irg* subaffittare.

sublime [sə'blaɪm] *a* sublime.

subliminal [sʌb'lɪmɪnl] *a* subliminale.

submachine gun ['sʌbmə'ʃi:n-] *n* mitra *m* *inv*.

submarine [sʌbmə'ri:n] *n* sommergibile *m*.

submerge [səb'mə:dʒ] *vt* sommergere; immergere ♦ *vi* immergersi.

submersion [səb'mə:ʃən] *n* sommersione *f*; immersione *f*.

submission [səb'mɪʃən] *n* sottomissione *f*; (*to committee etc*) richiesta, domanda.

submissive [səb'mɪsɪv] *a* remissivo(a).

submit [səb'mɪt] *vt* sottomettere; (*proposal, claim*) presentare ♦ *vi* sottomettersi.

subnormal [sʌb'nɔ:məl] *a* subnormale.

subordinate [sə'bɔ:dɪnət] *a, n* subordinato(a).

subpoena [səb'pi:nə] *n* (*LAW*) citazione *f*, mandato di comparizione ♦ *vt* (*LAW*) citare in giudizio.

subroutine ['sʌbru:ti:n] *n* (*COMPUT*) sottoprogramma *m*.

subscribe [səb'skraɪb] *vi* contribuire; **to ~ to** (*opinion*) approvare, condividere; (*fund*) sottoscrivere; (*newspaper*) abbonarsi a; essere abbonato(a) a.

subscriber [səb'skraɪbə*] *n* (*to periodical, telephone*) abbonato/a.

subscript ['sʌbskrɪpt] *n* deponente *m*.

subscription [səb'skrɪpʃən] *n* sottoscrizione *f*; abbonamento; **to take out a ~ to** abbonarsi

a.

subsequent ['sʌbsɪkwənt] *a* (*later*) successivo(a); (*further*) ulteriore; ~ **to** in seguito a.

subsequently ['sʌbsɪkwəntlɪ] *ad* in seguito, successivamente.

subservient [səb'sə:vɪənt] *a*: ~ **(to)** remissivo(a) (a), sottomesso(a) (a).

subside [səb'saɪd] *vi* cedere, abbassarsi; (*flood*) decrescere; (*wind*) calmarsi.

subsidence [səb'saɪdns] *n* cedimento, abbassamento.

subsidiary [səb'sɪdɪərɪ] *a* sussidiario(a); accessorio(a); (*Brit SCOL*: *subject*) complementare ♦ *n* filiale *f*.

subsidize ['sʌbsɪdaɪz] *vt* sovvenzionare.

subsidy ['sʌbsɪdɪ] *n* sovvenzione *f*.

subsist [səb'sɪst] *vi*: **to** ~ **on sth** vivere di qc.

subsistence [səb'sɪstəns] *n* esistenza; mezzi *mpl* di sostentamento.

subsistence allowance *n* indennità *f inv* di trasferta.

subsistence level *n* livello minimo di vita.

substance ['sʌbstəns] *n* sostanza; (*fig*) essenza; **to lack** ~ (*argument*) essere debole.

substandard [sʌb'stændəd] *a* (*goods, housing*) di qualità scadente.

substantial [səb'stænʃl] *a* solido(a); (*amount, progress etc*) notevole; (*meal*) sostanzioso(a).

substantially [səb'stænʃəlɪ] *ad* sostanzialmente; ~ **bigger** molto più grande.

substantiate [səb'stænʃɪeɪt] *vt* comprovare.

substitute ['sʌbstɪtju:t] *n* (*person*) sostituto/a; (*thing*) succedaneo, surrogato ♦ *vt*: **to** ~ **sth/sb for** sostituire qc/qn a.

substitute teacher *n* (*US*) supplente *m/f*.

substitution [sʌbstɪ'tju:ʃən] *n* sostituzione *f*.

subterfuge ['sʌbtəfju:dʒ] *n* sotterfugio.

subterranean [sʌbtə'reɪnɪən] *a* sotterraneo(a).

subtitle ['sʌbtaɪtl] *n* (*CINEMA*) sottotitolo.

subtle ['sʌtl] *a* sottile; (*flavour, perfume*) delicato(a).

subtlety ['sʌtltɪ] *n* sottigliezza.

subtly ['sʌtlɪ] *ad* sottilmente; delicatamente.

subtotal [sʌb'təutl] *n* somma parziale.

subtract [səb'trækt] *vt* sottrarre.

subtraction [səb'trækʃən] *n* sottrazione *f*.

suburb ['sʌbə:b] *n* sobborgo; **the** ~**s** la periferia.

suburban [sə'bə:bən] *a* suburbano(a).

suburbia [sə'bə:bɪə] *n* periferia, sobborghi *mpl*.

subversion [səb'və:ʃən] *n* sovversione *f*.

subversive [səb'və:sɪv] *a* sovversivo(a).

subway ['sʌbweɪ] *n* (*US*: *underground*) metropolitana; (*Brit*: *underpass*) sottopassaggio.

subzero [sʌb'zɪərəu] *a*: ~ **temperatures** temperature *fpl* sotto zero.

succeed [sək'si:d] *vi* riuscire, avere successo ♦ *vt* succedere a; **to** ~ **in doing** riuscire a fare.

succeeding [sək'si:dɪŋ] *a* (*following*) successivo(a); ~ **generations** generazioni *fpl*

future.

success [sək'sɛs] *n* successo.

successful [sək'sɛsful] *a* (*venture*) coronato(a) da successo, riuscito(a); **to be** ~ **(in doing)** riuscire (a fare).

successfully [sək'sɛsfəlɪ] *ad* con successo.

succession [sək'sɛʃən] *n* successione *f*; **in** ~ di seguito.

successive [sək'sɛsɪv] *a* successivo(a); consecutivo(a); **on 3** ~ **days** per 3 giorni consecutivi *or* di seguito.

successor [sək'sɛsə*] *n* successore *m*.

succinct [sək'sɪŋkt] *a* succinto(a), breve.

succulent ['sʌkjulənt] *a* succulento(a) ♦ *n* (*BOT*): ~**s** piante *fpl* grasse.

succumb [sə'kʌm] *vi* soccombere.

such [sʌtʃ] *a* tale; (*of that kind*): ~ **a book** un tale libro, un libro del genere; ~ **books** tali libri, libri del genere; (*so much*): ~ **courage** tanto coraggio ♦ *ad*: ~ **a long trip** un viaggio così lungo; ~ **good books** libri così buoni; ~ **a lot of** talmente *or* così tanto(a); **making** ~ **a noise that** facendo un rumore tale che; ~ **a long time ago** tanto tempo fa; ~ **as** (*like*) come; **a noise** ~ **as to** un rumore tale da; ~ **books as I have** quei pochi libri che ho; **as** ~ come *or* in quanto tale; **I said no** ~ **thing** non ho detto niente del genere.

such-and-such ['sʌtʃənsʌtʃ] *a* tale (*after noun*).

suchlike ['sʌtʃlaɪk] *pronoun* (*col*): **and** ~ e così via.

suck [sʌk] *vt* succhiare; (*subj*: *baby*) poppare; (: *pump, machine*) aspirare.

sucker ['sʌkə*] *n* (*ZOOL, TECH*) ventosa; (*BOT*) pollone *m*; (*col*) gonzo/a, babbeo/a.

suckle ['sʌkl] *vt* allattare.

suction ['sʌkʃən] *n* succhiamento; (*TECH*) aspirazione *f*.

suction pump *n* pompa aspirante.

Sudan [su:'dɑ:n] *n* Sudan *m*.

Sudanese [su:də'ni:z] *a*, *n* sudanese (*m/f*).

sudden ['sʌdn] *a* improvviso(a); **all of a** ~ improvvisamente, all'improvviso.

suddenly ['sʌdnlɪ] *ad* bruscamente, improvvisamente, di colpo.

suds [sʌdz] *npl* schiuma (di sapone).

sue [su:] *vt* citare in giudizio ♦ *vi*: **to** ~ **(for)** intentare causa (per); **to** ~ **for divorce** intentare causa di divorzio; **to** ~ **sb for damages** citare qn per danni.

suede [sweɪd] *n* pelle *f* scamosciata ♦ *cpd* scamosciato(a).

suet ['suɪt] *n* grasso di rognone.

Suez ['su:ɪz] *n*: **the** ~ **Canal** il Canale di Suez.

Suff. *abbr* (*Brit*) = Suffolk.

suffer ['sʌfə*] *vt* soffrire, patire; (*bear*) sopportare, tollerare; (*undergo*: *loss, setback*) subire ♦ *vi* soffrire; **to** ~ **from** soffrire di; **to** ~ **from the effects of alcohol/a fall** risentire degli effetti dell'alcool/di una caduta.

sufferance ['sʌfərəns] *n*: **he was only there on** ~ era più che altro sopportato lì.

sufferer ['sʌfərə*] n (MED): ~ **(from)** malato/a (di).

suffering ['sʌfərɪŋ] n sofferenza; (hardship, deprivation) privazione f.

suffice [sə'faɪs] vi essere sufficiente, bastare.

sufficient [sə'fɪʃənt] a sufficiente; ~ **money** abbastanza soldi.

sufficiently [sə'fɪʃəntlɪ] ad sufficientemente, abbastanza.

suffix ['sʌfɪks] n suffisso.

suffocate ['sʌfəkeɪt] vi (have difficulty breathing) soffocare; (die through lack of air) asfissiare.

suffocation [sʌfə'keɪʃən] n soffocamento; (MED) asfissia.

suffrage ['sʌfrɪdʒ] n suffragio.

suffuse [sə'fjuːz] vt: **to ~ (with)** (colour) tingere (di); (light) soffondere (di); **her face was ~d with joy** la gioia si dipingeva sul suo volto.

sugar ['ʃugə*] n zucchero ♦ vt zuccherare.

sugar beet n barbabietola da zucchero.

sugar bowl n zuccheriera.

sugar cane n canna da zucchero.

sugar-coated ['ʃugəkəutɪd] a ricoperto(a) di zucchero.

sugar lump n zolletta di zucchero.

sugar refinery n raffineria di zucchero.

sugary ['ʃugərɪ] a zuccherino(a), dolce; (fig) sdolcinato(a).

suggest [sə'dʒɛst] vt proporre, suggerire; (indicate) indicare; **what do you ~ I do?** cosa mi suggerisce di fare?

suggestion [sə'dʒɛstʃən] n suggerimento, proposta.

suggestive [sə'dʒɛstɪv] a suggestivo(a); (indecent) spinto(a), indecente.

suicidal [suɪ'saɪdl] a suicida inv; (fig) fatale, disastroso(a).

suicide ['suɪsaɪd] n (person) suicida m/f; (act) suicidio; **to commit ~** suicidarsi.

suicide attempt, suicide bid n tentato suicidio.

suit [suːt] n (man's) completo; (woman's) completo, tailleur m inv; (law~) causa; (CARDS) seme m, colore m ♦ vt andar bene a or per; essere adatto(a) a or per; (adapt): **to ~ sth to** adattare qc a; **to be ~ed to sth** (suitable for) essere adatto a qc; **well ~ed** (couple) fatti l'uno per l'altro; **to bring a ~ against sb** intentare causa a qn; **to follow ~** (fig) fare altrettanto.

suitable ['suːtəbl] a adatto(a); appropriato(a); **would tomorrow be ~?** andrebbe bene domani?; **we found somebody ~** abbiamo trovato la persona adatta.

suitably ['suːtəblɪ] ad (dress) in modo adatto; (thank) adeguatamente.

suitcase ['suːtkeɪs] n valigia.

suite [swiːt] n (of rooms) appartamento; (MUS) suite f inv; (furniture): **bedroom/ dining room ~** arredo or mobilia per la camera da letto/sala da pranzo; **a three-piece ~** un salotto comprendente un divano e due poltrone.

suitor ['suːtə*] n corteggiatore m, spasimante m.

sulfate ['sʌlfeɪt] n (US) = **sulphate**.

sulfur etc ['sʌlfə*] (US) = **sulphur** etc.

sulk [sʌlk] vi fare il broncio.

sulky ['sʌlkɪ] a imbronciato(a).

sullen ['sʌlən] a scontroso(a); cupo(a).

sulphate, (US) **sulfate** ['sʌlfeɪt] n solfato; **copper ~** solfato di rame.

sulphur, (US) **sulfur** ['sʌlfə*] n zolfo.

sulphuric, (US) **sulfuric** [sʌl'fjuərɪk] a: ~ **acid** acido solforico.

sultan ['sʌltən] n sultano.

sultana [sʌl'tɑːnə] n (fruit) uva (secca) sultanina.

sultry ['sʌltrɪ] a afoso(a).

sum [sʌm] n somma; (SCOL etc) addizione f.

sum up vt riassumere; (evaluate rapidly) valutare, giudicare ♦ vi riassumere.

Sumatra [su'mɑːtrə] n Sumatra.

summarize ['sʌməraɪz] vt riassumere, riepilogare.

summary ['sʌmərɪ] n riassunto ♦ a (justice) sommario(a).

summer ['sʌmə*] n estate f ♦ cpd d'estate, estivo(a); **in (the) ~** d'estate.

summer camp n (US) colonia (estiva).

summerhouse ['sʌməhaus] n (in garden) padiglione m.

summertime ['sʌmətaɪm] n (season) estate f.

summer time n (by clock) ora legale (estiva).

summery ['sʌmərɪ] a estivo(a).

summing-up [sʌmɪŋ'ʌp] n (LAW) ricapitolazione f del processo.

summit ['sʌmɪt] n cima, sommità; (POL) vertice m.

summit conference n conferenza al vertice.

summon ['sʌmən] vt chiamare, convocare; **to ~ a witness** citare un testimone.

summon up vt raccogliere, fare appello a.

summons n ordine m di comparizione ♦ vt citare; **to serve a ~ on sb** notificare una citazione a qn.

sump [sʌmp] n (AUT) coppa dell'olio.

sumptuous ['sʌmptjuəs] a sontuoso(a).

Sun. abbr (= Sunday) dom.

sun [sʌn] n sole m; **in the ~** al sole; **to catch the ~** prendere sole; **they have everything under the ~** hanno tutto ciò che possono desiderare.

sunbathe ['sʌnbeɪð] vi prendere un bagno di sole.

sunbeam ['sʌnbiːm] n raggio di sole.

sunbed ['sʌnbɛd] n lettino solare.

sunburn ['sʌnbəːn] n (tan) abbronzatura; (painful) scottatura.

sunburnt ['sʌnbəːnt], **sunburned** ['sʌnbəːnd] a abbronzato(a); (painfully) scottato(a) dal sole.

sun cream n crema solare.

sundae ['sʌndeɪ] n coppa di gelato guarnita.

Sunday ['sʌndɪ] n domenica; for phrases see

also **Tuesday**.

Sunday school *n* ≈ scuola di catechismo.

sundial ['sʌndaɪəl] *n* meridiana.

sundown ['sʌndaun] *n* tramonto.

sundries ['sʌndrɪz] *npl* articoli diversi, cose diverse.

sundry ['sʌndrɪ] *a* vari(e), diversi(e); **all and ~** tutti quanti.

sunflower ['sʌnflauə*] *n* girasole *m*.

sung [sʌŋ] *pp of* **sing**.

sunglasses ['sʌnglɑːsɪz] *npl* occhiali *mpl* da sole.

sunk [sʌŋk] *pp of* **sink**.

sunken ['sʌŋkən] *a* sommerso(a); (*eyes, cheeks*) infossato(a); (*bath*) incassato(a).

sunlamp ['sʌnlæmp] *n* lampada a raggi ultravioletti.

sunlight ['sʌnlaɪt] *n* (luce *f* del) sole *m*.

sunlit ['sʌnlɪt] *a* assolato(a), soleggiato(a).

sunny ['sʌnɪ] *a* assolato(a), soleggiato(a); (*fig*) allegro(a), felice; **it is ~** c'è il sole.

sunrise ['sʌnraɪz] *n* levata del sole, alba.

sunroof ['sʌnruːf] *n* (*on building*) tetto a terrazzo; (*AUT*) tetto apribile.

sunset ['sʌnsɛt] *n* tramonto.

sunshade ['sʌnʃeɪd] *n* parasole *m*.

sunshine ['sʌnʃaɪn] *n* (luce *f* del) sole *m*.

sunspot ['sʌnspɔt] *n* macchia solare.

sunstroke ['sʌnstrəuk] *n* insolazione *f*, colpo di sole.

suntan ['sʌntæn] *n* abbronzatura.

suntanned ['sʌntænd] *a* abbronzato(a).

suntan oil *n* olio solare.

suntrap ['sʌntræp] *n* luogo molto assolato, angolo pieno di sole.

super ['suːpə*] *a* (*col*) fantastico(a).

superannuation [suːpərænju'eɪʃən] *n* contributi *mpl* pensionistici; pensione *f*.

superb [suː'pəːb] *a* magnifico(a).

supercilious [suːpə'sɪlɪəs] *a* sprezzante, sdegnoso(a).

superficial [suːpə'fɪʃəl] *a* superficiale.

superficially [suːpə'fɪʃəlɪ] *ad* superficialmente.

superfluous [suː'pəːfluəs] *a* superfluo(a).

superhuman [suːpə'hjuːmən] *a* sovrumano(a).

superimpose ['suːpərɪm'pəuz] *vt* sovrapporre.

superintend [suːpərɪn'tɛnd] *vt* dirigere, sovraintendere.

superintendent [suːpərɪn'tɛndənt] *n* direttore/trice; (*POLICE*) ≈ commissario (capo).

superior [suː'pɪərɪə*] *a* superiore; (*COMM: goods, quality*) di prim'ordine, superiore; (*smug: person*) che fa il superiore ♦ *n* superiore *m/f*; **Mother S~** (*REL*) Madre *f* Superiora, Superiora.

superiority [supɪərɪ'ɔrɪtɪ] *n* superiorità.

superlative [suː'pəːlətɪv] *a* superlativo(a), supremo(a) ♦ *n* (*LING*) superlativo.

superman ['suːpəmæn] *n* superuomo.

supermarket ['suːpəmɑːkɪt] *n* supermercato.

supernatural [suːpə'nætʃərəl] *a* soprannaturale.

superpower ['suːpəpauə*] *n* (*POL*) superpotenza.

superscript ['suːpəskrɪpt] *n* esponente *m*.

supersede [suːpə'siːd] *vt* sostituire, soppiantare.

supersonic ['suːpə'sɔnɪk] *a* supersonico(a).

superstition [suːpə'stɪʃən] *n* superstizione *f*.

superstitious [suːpə'stɪʃəs] *a* superstizioso(a).

superstore ['suːpəstɔː*] *n* (*Brit*) grande supermercato.

supertanker ['suːpətæŋkə*] *n* superpetroliera.

supertax ['suːpətæks] *n* soprattassa.

supervise ['suːpəvaɪz] *vt* (*person etc*) sorvegliare; (*organization*) soprintendere a.

supervision [suːpə'vɪʒən] *n* sorveglianza, supervisione *f*; **under medical ~** sotto controllo medico.

supervisor ['suːpəvaɪzə*] *n* sorvegliante *m/f*, soprintendente *m/f*; (*in shop*) capocommesso/a; (*at university*) relatore/trice.

supervisory ['suːpəvaɪzərɪ] *a* di sorveglianza.

supine ['suːpaɪn] *a* supino(a).

supper ['sʌpə*] *n* cena; **to have ~** cenare.

supplant [sə'plɑːnt] *vt* soppiantare.

supple ['sʌpl] *a* flessibile; agile.

supplement *n* ['sʌplɪmənt] supplemento ♦ *vt* [sʌplɪ'mɛnt] completare, integrare.

supplementary [sʌplɪ'mɛntərɪ] *a* supplementare.

supplementary benefit *n* (*Brit*) *forma di indennità assistenziale*.

supplier [sə'plaɪə*] *n* fornitore *m*.

supply [sə'plaɪ] *vt* (*goods*): **to ~ sth (to sb)** fornire qc (a qn); (*people, organization*): **to ~ sb (with sth)** fornire a qn (qc); (*system, machine*): **to ~ sth (with sth)** alimentare qc (con qc); (*a need*) soddisfare ♦ *n* riserva, provvista; (*supplying*) approvvigionamento; (*TECH*) alimentazione *f*; **supplies** *npl* (*food*) viveri *mpl*; (*MIL*) sussistenza; **office supplies** forniture *fpl* per ufficio; **to be in short ~** scarseggiare, essere scarso(a); **the electricity/water/gas ~** l'erogazione *f* di corrente/d'acqua/di gas; **~ and demand** la domanda e l'offerta; **the car comes supplied with a radio** l'auto viene fornita completa di radio.

supply teacher *n* (*Brit*) supplente *m/f*.

support [sə'pɔːt] *n* (*moral, financial etc*) sostegno, appoggio; (*TECH*) supporto ♦ *vt* sostenere; (*financially*) mantenere; (*uphold*) sostenere, difendere; (*SPORT: team*) fare il tifo per; **they stopped work in ~ (of)** hanno smesso di lavorare per solidarietà (con); **to ~ o.s.** (*financially*) mantenersi.

supporter [sə'pɔːtə*] *n* (*POL etc*) sostenitore/trice, fautore/trice; (*SPORT*) tifoso/a.

supporting [sə'pɔːtɪŋ] *a* (*THEATRE: role*) secondario(a), di secondo piano; (: *actor*) che ha un ruolo secondario.

suppose [sə'pəuz] *vt*, *vi* supporre; immaginare; **to be ~d to do** essere tenuto(a) a fare; **always supposing (that) he comes** ammesso e non concesso che venga; **I don't ~ she'll come** non credo che venga;

he's ~d to be an expert dicono che sia un esperto, passa per un esperto.

supposedly [sə'pəuzɪdlɪ] *ad* presumibilmente; (*seemingly*) apparentemente.

supposing [sə'pəuzɪŋ] *cj* se, ammesso che + *sub*.

supposition [sʌpə'zɪʃən] *n* supposizione *f*, ipotesi *f inv*.

suppository [sə'pɔzɪtərɪ] *n* supposta, suppositorio.

suppress [sə'prɛs] *vt* reprimere; sopprimere; tenere segreto(a).

suppression [sə'prɛʃən] *n* repressione *f*; soppressione *f*.

suppressor [sə'prɛsə*] *n* (*ELEC etc*) soppressore *m*.

supremacy [su'prɛməsɪ] *n* supremazia.

supreme [su'priːm] *a* supremo(a).

Supreme Court *n* (*US*) Corte *f* suprema.

Supt. *abbr* (*POLICE*) = **superintendent**.

surcharge ['sɜːtʃɑːdʒ] *n* supplemento; (*extra tax*) soprattassa.

sure [ʃuə*] *a* sicuro(a); (*definite, convinced*) sicuro(a), certo(a) ♦ *ad* (*col: US*): **that ~ is pretty, that's ~ pretty** è veramente *or* davvero carino; **~!** (*of course*) senz'altro!, certo!; **~ enough** infatti; **to make ~ of** assicurarsi di; **to be ~ of sth** essere sicuro di qc; **to be ~ of o.s.** essere sicuro di sé; **I'm not ~ how/why/when** non so bene come/perché/quando + *sub*.

sure-footed [ʃuə'futɪd] *a* dal passo sicuro.

surely ['ʃuəlɪ] *ad* sicuramente; certamente; **~ you don't mean that!** non parlerà sul serio!

surety ['ʃuərətɪ] *n* garanzia; **to go** *or* **stand ~ for sb** farsi garante per qn.

surf [sɜːf] *n* (*waves*) cavalloni *mpl*; (*foam*) spuma.

surface ['sɜːfɪs] *n* superficie *f* ♦ *vt* (*road*) asfaltare ♦ *vi* risalire alla superficie; (*fig: person*) venire a galla, farsi vivo(a); **on the ~ it seems that ...** (*fig*) superficialmente sembra che ....

surface area *n* superficie *f*.

surface mail *n* posta ordinaria.

surfboard ['sɜːfbɔːd] *n* tavola per surfing.

surfeit ['sɜːfɪt] *n*: **a ~ of** un eccesso di; un'indigestione di.

surfer ['sɜːfə*] *n* chi pratica il surfing.

surfing ['sɜːfɪŋ] *n* surfing *m*.

surge [sɜːdʒ] *n* (*strong movement*) ondata; (*of feeling*) impeto; (*ELEC*) sovracorrente *f* transitoria ♦ *vi* (*waves*) gonfiarsi; (*ELEC: power*) aumentare improvvisamente; **to ~ forward** buttarsi avanti.

surgeon ['sɜːdʒən] *n* chirurgo.

Surgeon General *n* (*US*) ≈ Ministro della Sanità.

surgery ['sɜːdʒərɪ] *n* chirurgia; (*Brit MED: room*) studio *or* gabinetto medico, ambulatorio; (: *session*) visita ambulatoriale; (*Brit: of MP etc*) incontri *mpl* con gli elettori; **to undergo ~** subire un intervento chirurgico.

surgery hours *npl* (*Brit*) orario delle visite *or* di consultazione.

surgical ['sɜːdʒɪkl] *a* chirurgico(a).

surgical spirit *n* (*Brit*) alcool denaturato.

surly ['sɜːlɪ] *a* scontroso(a), burbero(a).

surmise [sɜː'maɪz] *vt* supporre, congetturare.

surmount [sɜː'maunt] *vt* sormontare.

surname ['sɜːneɪm] *n* cognome *m*.

surpass [sɜː'pɑːs] *vt* superare.

surplus ['sɜːpləs] *n* eccedenza; (*ECON*) surplus *m inv* ♦ *a* eccedente, d'avanzo; **it is ~ to our requirements** eccede i nostri bisogni; **~ stock** merce *f* in sovrappiù.

surprise [sə'praɪz] *n* sorpresa; (*astonishment*) stupore *m* ♦ *vt* sorprendere; stupire; **to take by ~** (*person*) cogliere di sorpresa; (*MIL: town, fort*) attaccare di sorpresa.

surprising [sə'praɪzɪŋ] *a* sorprendente, stupefacente.

surprisingly [se'praɪzɪŋlɪ] *ad* sorprendentemente; (*somewhat*) **~, he agreed** cosa (alquanto) sorprendente, ha accettato.

surrealism [sə'rɪəlɪzəm] *n* surrealismo.

surrealist [sə'rɪəlɪst] *a*, *n* surrealista (*m/f*).

surrender [sə'rɛndə*] *n* resa, capitolazione *f* ♦ *vi* arrendersi ♦ *vt* (*claim, right*) rinunciare a.

surrender value *n* (*COMM*) valore *m* di riscatto.

surreptitious [sʌrəp'tɪʃəs] *a* furtivo(a).

surrogate ['sʌrəgɪt] *n* (*Brit: substitute*) surrogato ♦ *a* surrogato(a).

surrogate mother *n* madre *f* sostitutiva.

surround [sə'raund] *vt* circondare; (*MIL etc*) accerchiare.

surrounding [sə'raundɪŋ] *a* circostante.

surroundings [sə'raundɪŋz] *npl* dintorni *mpl*; (*fig*) ambiente *m*.

surtax ['sɜːtæks] *n* soprattassa.

surveillance [sɜː'veɪləns] *n* sorveglianza, controllo.

survey *n* ['sɜːveɪ] (*comprehensive view: of situation, development*) quadro generale; (*study*) indagine *f*, studio; (*in housebuying etc*) perizia; (*of land*) rilevamento, rilievo topografico ♦ *vt* [sɜː'veɪ] osservare; esaminare; (*SURVEYING: building*) fare una perizia di; (: *land*) fare il rilevamento di.

surveying [sɜː'veɪɪŋ] *n* (*of land*) agrimensura.

surveyor [sɜː'veɪə*] *n* perito; (*of land*) agrimensore *m*.

survival [sə'vaɪvl] *n* sopravvivenza; (*relic*) reliquia, vestigio.

survival course *n* corso di sopravvivenza.

survival kit *n* equipaggiamento di prima necessità.

survive [sə'vaɪv] *vi* sopravvivere ♦ *vt* sopravvivere a.

survivor [sə'vaɪvə*] *n* superstite *m/f*, sopravvissuto/a.

susceptible [sə'sɛptəbl] *a*: **~ (to)** sensibile (a); (*disease*) predisposto(a) (a).

suspect *a*, *n* ['sʌspɛkt] *a* sospetto(a) ♦ *n* persona sospetta ♦ *vt* [səs'pɛkt] sospettare; (*think likely*) supporre; (*doubt*) dubitare di.

suspend [səs'pɛnd] vt sospendere.
suspended sentence n condanna con la condizionale.
suspender belt [səs'pɛndə*-] n (Brit) reggicalze m inv.
suspenders [sə'spɛndəz] npl (Brit) giarrettiere fpl; (US) bretelle fpl.
suspense [səs'pɛns] n apprensione f; (in film etc) suspense m.
suspense account n (COMM) conto in sospeso.
suspension [səs'pɛnʃən] n (gen, AUT) sospensione f; (of driving licence) ritiro temporaneo.
suspension bridge n ponte m sospeso.
suspicion [səs'pɪʃən] n sospetto; **to be under ~** essere sospettato; **arrested on ~ of murder** arrestato come presunto omicida.
suspicious [səs'pɪʃəs] a (suspecting) sospettoso(a); (causing suspicion) sospetto(a); **to be ~ of or about sb/sth** nutrire sospetti nei riguardi di qn/qc.
suss out vt (Brit col): **I've ~ed it/him out** ho capito come stanno le cose/che tipo è.
sustain [səs'teɪn] vt sostenere; sopportare; (suffer) subire.
sustained [sə'steɪnd] a (effort) prolungato(a).
sustenance ['sʌstɪnəns] n nutrimento; mezzi mpl di sostentamento.
suture ['su:tʃə*] n sutura.
SW abbr (RADIO: = short wave) O.C.
swab [swɔb] n (MED) tampone m ♦ vt (NAUT: also: ~ **down**) radazzare.
swagger ['swægə*] vi pavoneggiarsi.
swallow ['swɔləu] n (bird) rondine f; (of food) boccone m; (of drink) sorso ♦ vt inghiottire; (fig: story) bere.
swallow up vt inghiottire.
swam [swæm] pt of **swim**.
swamp [swɔmp] n palude f ♦ vt sommergere.
swampy ['swɔmpɪ] a palludoso(a), pantanoso(a).
swan [swɔn] n cigno.
swank [swæŋk] vi (col: talk boastfully) fare lo spaccone; (: show off) mettersi in mostra.
swan song n (fig) canto del cigno.
swap [swɔp] n scambio ♦ vt: **to ~ (for)** scambiare (con).
swarm [swɔ:m] n sciame m ♦ vi formicolare; (bees) sciamare.
swarthy ['swɔ:ðɪ] a di carnagione scura.
swashbuckling ['swɔʃbʌklɪŋ] a (role, hero) spericolato(a).
swastika ['swɔstɪkə] n croce f uncinata, svastica.
swat [swɔt] vt schiacciare ♦ n (Brit: also: **fly ~**) ammazzamosche m inv.
swathe [sweɪð] n fascio ♦ vt: **to ~ in** (bandages, blankets) avvolgere in.
swatter ['swɔtə*] n (also: **fly ~**) ammazzamosche m inv.
sway [sweɪ] vi (building) oscillare; (tree) ondeggiare; (person) barcollare ♦ vt (influence) influenzare ♦ n (rule, power): ~

(over) influenza (su); **to hold ~ over sb** dominare qn.
Swaziland ['swɑ:zɪlænd] n Swaziland m.
swear [swɛə*], pt **swore**, pp **sworn** [swɛə*, swɔ:*, swɔ:n] vi (witness etc) giurare; (curse) bestemmiare, imprecare ♦ vt: **to ~ an oath** prestare giuramento; **to ~ to sth** giurare qc.
swear in vt prestare giuramento a.
swearword ['swɛəwə:d] n parolaccia.
sweat [swɛt] n sudore m, traspirazione f ♦ vi sudare; **in a ~** in un bagno di sudore.
sweatband ['swɛtbænd] n (SPORT) fascia elastica (per assorbire il sudore).
sweater ['swɛtə*] n maglione m.
sweatshirt ['swɛtʃə:t] n maglione m in cotone felpato.
sweatshop ['swɛtʃɔp] n azienda o fabbrica dove i dipendenti sono sfruttati.
sweaty ['swɛtɪ] a sudato(a); bagnato(a) di sudore.
Swede [swi:d] n svedese m/f.
swede [swi:d] n (Brit) rapa svedese.
Sweden ['swi:dn] n Svezia.
Swedish ['swi:dɪʃ] a svedese ♦ n (LING) svedese m.
sweep [swi:p] n spazzata; (curve) curva; (expanse) distesa; (range) portata; (also: **chimney ~**) spazzacamino ♦ vb (pt, pp **swept** [swɛpt]) vt spazzare, scopare; (subj: fashion, craze) invadere ♦ vi camminare maestosamente; precipitarsi, lanciarsi; (e)stendersi.
sweep away vt spazzare via; trascinare via.
sweep past vi sfrecciare accanto; passare accanto maestosamente.
sweep up vt, vi spazzare.
sweeping ['swi:pɪŋ] a (gesture) ampio(a); (changes, reforms) ampio(a), radicale; **a ~ statement** un'affermazione generica.
sweepstake ['swi:psteɪk] n lotteria (spesso abbinata alle corse dei cavalli).
sweet [swi:t] n (Brit) dolce m; (candy) caramella ♦ a dolce; (fresh) fresco(a); (kind) gentile; (cute) carino(a) ♦ ad: **to smell/taste ~** avere un odore/sapore dolce; ~ **and sour** a agrodolce.
sweetbread ['swi:tbrɛd] n animella.
sweetcorn ['swi:tkɔ:n] n granturco dolce.
sweeten ['swi:tn] vt addolcire; zuccherare.
sweetener ['swi:tnə*] n (CULIN) dolcificante m.
sweetheart ['swi:thɑ:t] n innamorato/a.
sweetly ['swi:tlɪ] ad dolcemente.
sweetness ['swi:tnɪs] n sapore m dolce; dolcezza.
sweet pea n pisello odoroso.
sweet potato n patata americana, patata dolce.
sweetshop ['swi:tʃɔp] n (Brit) ≈ pasticceria.
sweet tooth n: **to have a ~** avere un debole per i dolci.
swell [swɛl] n (of sea) mare m lungo ♦ a (col: excellent) favoloso(a) ♦ vb (pt ~**ed**, pp

swollen, ~**ed** ['swəulən]) *vt* gonfiare, ingrossare; (*numbers, sales etc*) aumentare ♦ *vi* gonfiarsi, ingrossarsi; (*sound*) crescere; (*MED*) gonfiarsi.

swelling ['swɛlɪŋ] *n* (*MED*) tumefazione *f*, gonfiore *m*.

sweltering ['swɛltərɪŋ] *a* soffocante.

swept [swɛpt] *pt, pp of* **sweep.**

swerve [swəːv] *vi* deviare; (*driver*) sterzare; (*boxer*) scartare.

swift [swɪft] *n* (*bird*) rondone *m* ♦ *a* rapido(a), veloce.

swiftly ['swɪftlɪ] *ad* rapidamente, velocemente.

swiftness ['swɪftnɪs] *n* rapidità, velocità.

swig [swɪg] *n* (*col: drink*) sorsata.

swill [swɪl] *n* broda ♦ *vt* (*also:* ~ **out,** ~ **down**) risciacquare.

swim [swɪm] *n*: **to go for a** ~ andare a fare una nuotata ♦ *vb* (*pt* **swam,** *pp* **swum** [swæm, swʌm]) *vi* nuotare; (*SPORT*) fare del nuoto; (*head, room*) girare ♦ *vt* (*river, channel*) attraversare *or* percorrere a nuoto; **to go** ~**ming** andare a nuotare; **to** ~ **a length** fare una vasca (a nuoto).

swimmer ['swɪmə*] *n* nuotatore/trice.

swimming ['swɪmɪŋ] *n* nuoto.

swimming baths *npl* (*Brit*) piscina.

swimming cap *n* cuffia.

swimming costume *n* (*Brit*) costume *m* da bagno.

swimming pool *n* piscina.

swimming trunks *npl* costume *m* da bagno (per uomo).

swimsuit ['swɪmsuːt] *n* costume *m* da bagno.

swindle ['swɪndl] *n* truffa ♦ *vt* truffare.

swindler ['swɪndlə*] *n* truffatore/trice.

swine [swaɪn] *n* (*pl inv*) maiale *m*, porco; (*col!*) porco (*!*).

swing [swɪŋ] *n* altalena; (*movement*) oscillazione *f*; (*MUS*) ritmo; (*also:* ~ **music**) swing *m* ♦ *vb* (*pt, pp* **swung** [swʌŋ]) *vt* dondolare, far oscillare; (*also:* ~ **round**) far girare ♦ *vi* oscillare, dondolare; (*also:* ~ **round:** *object*) roteare; (: *person*) girarsi, voltarsi; **to be in full** ~ (*activity*) essere in piena attività; (*party etc*) essere nel pieno; **a** ~ **to the left** (*POL*) una svolta a sinistra; **to get into the** ~ **of things** entrare nel pieno delle cose; **the road** ~**s south** la strada prende la direzione sud.

swing bridge *n* ponte *m* girevole.

swing door *n* (*Brit*) porta battente.

swingeing ['swɪndʒɪŋ] *a* (*Brit: defeat*) violento(a); (: *price increase*) enorme.

swinging ['swɪŋɪŋ] *a* (*step*) cadenzato(a), ritmico(a); (*rhythm, music*) trascinante; ~ **door** (*US*) porta battente.

swipe [swaɪp] *n* forte colpo; schiaffo ♦ *vt* (*hit*) colpire con forza; dare uno schiaffo a; (*col: steal*) sgraffignare.

swirl [swəːl] *n* turbine *m*, mulinello ♦ *vi* turbinare, far mulinello.

swish [swɪʃ] *a* (*col: smart*) all'ultimo grido, alla moda ♦ *n* (*sound: of whip*) sibilo; (: *of skirts, grass*) fruscio ♦ *vi* sibilare.

Swiss [swɪs] *a, n* (*pl inv*) svizzero(a).

Swiss French *a* svizzero(a) francese.

Swiss German *a* svizzero(a) tedesco(a).

switch [swɪtʃ] *n* (*for light, radio etc*) interruttore *m*; (*change*) cambiamento ♦ *vt* (*also:* ~ **round,** ~ **over**) cambiare; scambiare.

switch off *vt* spegnere.

switch on *vt* accendere; (*engine, machine*) mettere in moto, avviare; (*AUT: ignition*) inserire; (*Brit: water supply*) aprire.

switchback ['swɪtʃbæk] *n* (*Brit*) montagne *fpl* russe.

switchblade ['swɪtʃbleɪd] *n* (*also:* ~ **knife**) coltello a scatto.

switchboard ['swɪtʃbɔːd] *n* centralino.

switchboard operator *n* centralinista *m/f*.

Switzerland ['swɪtsələnd] *n* Svizzera.

swivel ['swɪvl] *vi* (*also:* ~ **round**) girare.

swollen ['swəulən] *pp of* **swell** ♦ *a* (*ankle etc*) gonfio(a).

swoon [swuːn] *vi* svenire.

swoop [swuːp] *n* (*by police etc*) incursione *f*; (*of bird etc*) picchiata ♦ *vi* (*also:* ~ **down**) scendere in picchiata; (*police*): **to** ~ **(on)** fare un'incursione (in).

swop [swɔp] *n, vt* = **swap.**

sword [sɔːd] *n* spada.

swordfish ['sɔːdfɪʃ] *n* pesce *m* spada *inv.*

swore [swɔː*] *pt of* **swear.**

sworn [swɔːn] *pp of* **swear.**

swot [swɔt] *vt* sgobbare su ♦ *vi* sgobbare.

swum [swʌm] *pp of* **swim.**

swung [swʌŋ] *pt, pp of* **swing.**

sycamore ['sɪkəmɔː*] *n* sicomoro.

sycophant ['sɪkəfənt] *n* leccapiedi *m/f*.

sycophantic [sɪkə'fæntɪk] *a* ossequioso(a), adulatore(trice).

Sydney ['sɪdnɪ] *n* Sydney *f*.

syllable ['sɪləbl] *n* sillaba.

syllabus ['sɪləbəs] *n* programma *m; on the* ~ in programma d'esame.

symbol ['sɪmbl] *n* simbolo.

symbolic(al) [sɪm'bɔlɪk(l)] *a* simbolico(a); **to be** ~ **of sth** simboleggiare qc.

symbolism ['sɪmbəlɪzəm] *n* simbolismo.

symbolize ['sɪmbəlaɪz] *vt* simbolizzare.

symmetrical [sɪ'mɛtrɪkl] *a* simmetrico(a).

symmetry ['sɪmɪtrɪ] *n* simmetria.

sympathetic [sɪmpə'θɛtɪk] *a* (*showing pity*) compassionevole; (*kind*) comprensivo(a); ~ **towards** ben disposto(a) verso; **to be** ~ **to a cause** (*well-disposed*) simpatizzare per una causa.

sympathetically [sɪmpə'θɛtɪklɪ] *ad* in modo compassionevole; con comprensione.

sympathize ['sɪmpəθaɪz] *vi*: **to** ~ **with sb** compatire qn; partecipare al dolore di qn; (*understand*) capire qn.

sympathizer ['sɪmpəθaɪzə*] *n* (*POL*) simpatizzante *m/f*.

sympathy ['sɪmpəθɪ] *n* compassione *f*; **in** ~ **with** d'accordo con; (*strike*) per solidarietà

con; **with our deepest** ~ con le nostre più sincere condoglianze.
symphonic [sɪm'fɔnɪk] *a* sinfonico(a).
symphony ['sɪmfənɪ] *n* sinfonia.
symphony orchestra *n* orchestra sinfonica.
symposium [sɪm'pəuzɪəm] *n* simposio.
symptom ['sɪmptəm] *n* sintomo; indizio.
symptomatic [sɪmptə'mætɪk] *a*: ~ **(of)** sintomatico(a) (di).
synagogue ['sɪnəgɔg] *n* sinagoga.
synchromesh [sɪŋkrəu'mɛʃ] *n* cambio sincronizzato.
synchronize ['sɪŋkrənaɪz] *vt* sincronizzare ♦ *vi*: **to** ~ **with** essere contemporaneo(a) a.
syncopated ['sɪŋkəpeɪtɪd] *a* sincopato(a).
syndicate ['sɪndɪkɪt] *n* sindacato; (*PRESS*) agenzia di stampa.
syndrome ['sɪndrəum] *n* sindrome *f*.
synonym ['sɪnənɪm] *n* sinonimo.
synonymous [sɪ'nɔnɪməs] *a*: ~ **(with)** sinonimo(a) (di).
synopsis, *pl* **synopses** [sɪ'nɔpsɪs, -si:z] *n* sommario, sinossi *f inv*.
syntax ['sɪntæks] *n* sintassi *f inv*.
synthesis, *pl* **syntheses** ['sɪnθəsɪs, -si:z] *n* sintesi *f inv*.
synthesizer ['sɪnθəsaɪzə*] *n* (*MUS*) sintetizzatore *m*.
synthetic [sɪn'θɛtɪk] *a* sintetico(a) ♦ *n* prodotto sintetico; (*TEXTILES*) fibra sintetica.
syphilis ['sɪfɪlɪs] *n* sifilide *f*.
syphon ['saɪfən] *n*, *vb* = **siphon**.
Syria ['sɪrɪə] *n* Siria.
Syrian ['sɪrɪən] *a*, *n* siriano(a).
syringe [sɪ'rɪndʒ] *n* siringa.
syrup ['sɪrəp] *n* sciroppo; (*also*: **golden** ~) melassa raffinata.
syrupy ['sɪrəpɪ] *a* sciropposo(a).
system ['sɪstəm] *n* sistema *m*; (*network*) rete *f*; (*ANAT*) apparato; **it was a shock to his** ~ è stato uno shock per il suo organismo.
systematic [sɪstə'mætɪk] *a* sistematico(a).
system disk *n* (*COMPUT*) disco del sistema.
systems analyst *n* analista *m/f* di sistemi.

T

T, t [ti:] *n* (*letter*) T, t *m or f inv*; **T for Tommy** ≈ T come Taranto.
TA *n abbr* (*Brit*) = *Territorial Army*.
ta [tɑ:] *excl* (*Brit col*) grazie!
tab [tæb] *n abbr* = **tabulator** ♦ *n* (*loop on coat etc*) laccetto; (*label*) etichetta; **to keep ~s on** (*fig*) tenere d'occhio.
tabby ['tæbɪ] *n* (*also*: ~ **cat**) (gatto) soriano, gatto tigrato.
tabernacle ['tæbənækl] *n* tabernacolo.

table ['teɪbl] *n* tavolo, tavola; (*chart*) tabella ♦ *vt* (*motion etc*) presentare; **to lay** *or* **set the** ~ apparecchiare *or* preparare la tavola; **to clear the** ~ sparecchiare; **league** ~ (*FOOTBALL*, *RUGBY*) classifica; ~ **of contents** indice *m*.
tablecloth ['teɪblklɔθ] *n* tovaglia.
table d'hôte [tɑ:bl'dəut] *a* (*meal*) a prezzo fisso.
table lamp *n* lampada da tavolo.
tableland ['teɪbllænd] *n* tavolato, altopiano.
tablemat ['teɪblmæt] *n* sottopiatto.
table salt *n* sale *m* fino or da tavola.
tablespoon ['teɪblspu:n] *n* cucchiaio da tavola; (*also*: ~**ful**: *as measurement*) cucchiaiata.
tablet ['tæblɪt] *n* (*MED*) compressa; (: *for sucking*) pastiglia; (*for writing*) blocco; (*of stone*) targa; ~ **of soap** (*Brit*) saponetta.
table tennis *n* tennis *m* da tavolo, ping-pong ® *m*.
table wine *n* vino da tavola.
tabloid ['tæblɔɪd] *n* (*newspaper*) tabloid *m inv* (*giornale illustrato di formato ridotto*); **the** ~**s** i giornali popolari.
taboo [tə'bu:] *a*, *n* tabù (*m inv*).
tabulate ['tæbjuleɪt] *vt* (*data*, *figures*) tabulare, disporre in tabelle.
tabulator ['tæbjuleɪtə*] *n* tabulatore *m*.
tachograph ['tækəgrɑ:f] *n* tachigrafo.
tachometer [tæ'kɔmɪtə*] *n* tachimetro.
tacit ['tæsɪt] *a* tacito(a).
taciturn ['tæsɪtə:n] *a* taciturno(a).
tack [tæk] *n* (*nail*) bulletta; (*stitch*) punto d'imbastitura; (*NAUT*) bordo, bordata ♦ *vt* imbullettare; imbastire ♦ *vi* bordeggiare; **to change** ~ virare di bordo; **on the wrong** ~ (*fig*) sulla strada sbagliata; **to** ~ **sth on to (the end of) sth** (*of letter*, *book*) aggiungere qc alla fine di qc.
tackle ['tækl] *n* (*equipment*) attrezzatura, equipaggiamento; (*for lifting*) paranco; (*RUGBY*) placcaggio; (*FOOTBALL*) contrasto ♦ *vt* (*difficulty*) affrontare; (*RUGBY*) placcare; (*FOOTBALL*) contrastare.
tacky ['tækɪ] *a* colloso(a), appiccicaticcio(a); ancora bagnato(a); (*col*: *shabby*) scadente.
tact [tækt] *n* tatto.
tactful ['tæktful] *a* delicato(a), discreto(a); **to be** ~ avere tatto.
tactfully ['tæktfəlɪ] *ad* con tatto.
tactical ['tæktɪkl] *a* tattico(a).
tactics ['tæktɪks] *n*, *npl* tattica.
tactless ['tæktlɪs] *a* che manca di tatto.
tactlessly ['tæktlɪslɪ] *ad* senza tatto.
tadpole ['tædpəul] *n* girino.
taffy ['tæfɪ] *n* (*US*) caramella *f* mou *inv*.
tag [tæg] *n* etichetta; **price/name** ~ etichetta del prezzo/con il nome.
tag along *vi* seguire.
Tahiti [tə'hi:ti] *n* Tahiti *f*.
tail [teɪl] *n* coda; (*of shirt*) falda ♦ *vt* (*follow*) seguire, pedinare; **to turn** ~ voltare la schiena; *see also* **head**.

tail away, tail off vi (*in size, quality etc*) diminuire gradatamente.

tailback ['teɪlbæk] n (*Brit*) ingorgo.

tail coat n marsina.

tail end n (*of train, procession etc*) coda; (*of meeting etc*) fine f.

tailgate ['teɪlgeɪt] n (*AUT*) portellone m posteriore.

tail light n (*AUT*) fanalino di coda.

tailor ['teɪlə*] n sarto ♦ vt: **to ~ sth (to)** adattare qc (alle esigenze di); **~'s (shop)** sartoria (da uomo).

tailoring ['teɪlərɪŋ] n (*cut*) taglio.

tailor-made ['teɪlə'meɪd] a (*also fig*) fatto(a) su misura.

tailwind ['teɪlwɪnd] n vento di coda.

taint [teɪnt] vt (*meat, food*) far avariare; (*fig: reputation*) infangare.

tainted ['teɪntɪd] a (*food*) guasto(a); (*water, air*) infetto(a); (*fig*) corrotto(a).

Taiwan [taɪ'wɑːn] n Taiwan m.

take [teɪk] vb (*pt* **took**, *pp* **taken** [tʊk, 'teɪkn]) vt prendere; (*gain: prize*) ottenere, vincere; (*require: effort, courage*) occorrere, volerci; (*tolerate*) accettare, sopportare; (*hold: passengers etc*) contenere; (*accompany*) accompagnare; (*bring, carry*) portare; (*conduct: meeting*) condurre; (*exam*) sostenere, presentarsi a ♦ vi (*dye, fire etc*) prendere; (*injection*) fare effetto; (*plant*) attecchire ♦ n (*CINEMA*) ripresa; **I ~ it that** suppongo che; **to ~ for a walk** (*child, dog*) portare a fare una passeggiata; **to ~ sb's hand** prendere qn per mano; **to ~ it upon o.s. to do sth** prendersi la responsabilità di fare qc; **to be ~n ill** avere un malore; **to be ~n with sb/sth** (*attracted*) essere tutto preso da qn/qc; **it won't ~ long** non ci vorrà molto tempo; **it ~s a lot of time/courage** occorre *or* ci vuole molto tempo/coraggio; **it will ~ at least 5 litres** contiene almeno 5 litri; **~ the first on the left** prenda la prima a sinistra; **to ~ Russian at university** fare russo all'università; **I took him for a doctor** l'ho preso per un dottore.

take after vt fus assomigliare a.

take apart vt smontare.

take away vt portare via; togliere; **to ~ away (from)** sottrarre (da).

take back vt (*return*) restituire; riportare; (*one's words*) ritirare.

take down vt (*building*) demolire; (*dismantle: scaffolding*) smontare; (*letter etc*) scrivere.

take in vt (*lodger*) prendere, ospitare; (*orphan*) accogliere; (*stray dog*) raccogliere; (*SEWING*) stringere; (*deceive*) imbrogliare, abbindolare; (*understand*) capire; (*include*) comprendere, includere.

take off vi (*AVIAT*) decollare ♦ vt (*remove*) togliere; (*imitate*) imitare.

take on vt (*work*) accettare, intraprendere; (*employee*) assumere; (*opponent*) sfidare, affrontare.

take out vt portare fuori; (*remove*) togliere; (*licence*) prendere, ottenere; **to ~ sth out of** tirare qc fuori da; estrarre qc da; **don't ~ it out on me!** non prendertela con me!

take over vt (*business*) rilevare ♦ vi: **to ~ over from sb** prendere le consegne *or* il controllo da qn.

take to vt fus (*person*) prendere in simpatia; (*activity*) prendere gusto a; (*form habit of*): **to ~ to doing sth** prendere *or* cominciare a fare qc.

take up vt (*one's story*) riprendere; (*dress*) accorciare; (*absorb: liquids*) assorbire; (*accept: offer, challenge*) accettare; (*occupy: time, space*) occupare; (*engage in: hobby etc*) mettersi a; **to ~ up with sb** fare amicizia con qn.

takeaway ['teɪkəweɪ] a (*Brit: food*) da portar via.

take-home pay ['teɪkhəum-] n stipendio netto.

taken ['teɪkn] pp of **take**.

takeoff ['teɪkɔf] n (*AVIAT*) decollo.

takeout ['teɪkaut] a (*US*) = **takeaway**.

takeover ['teɪkəuvə*] n (*COMM*) assorbimento.

takeover bid n offerta di assorbimento.

takings ['teɪkɪŋz] npl (*COMM*) incasso.

talc [tælk] n (*also*: **~um powder**) talco.

tale [teɪl] n racconto, storia; (*pej*) fandonia; **to tell ~s** fare la spia.

talent ['tælənt] n talento.

talented ['tæləntɪd] a di talento.

talent scout n talent scout m/f inv.

talk [tɔːk] n discorso; (*gossip*) chiacchiere fpl; (*conversation*) conversazione f; (*interview*) discussione f ♦ vi parlare; (*chatter*) chiacchierare; **to give a ~** tenere una conferenza; **to ~ about** parlare di; (*converse*) discorrere *or* conversare su; **to ~ sb out of/into doing** dissuadere qn da/convincere qn a fare; **to ~ shop** parlare del lavoro *or* degli affari; **~ing of films, have you seen ...?** a proposito di film, ha visto ...?

talk over vt discutere.

talkative ['tɔːkətɪv] a loquace, ciarliero(a).

talking point ['tɔːkɪŋ-] n argomento di conversazione.

talking-to ['tɔːkɪŋtuː] n: **to give sb a good ~** fare una bella paternale a qn.

talk show n (*TV, RADIO*) intervista (informale), talk show m inv.

tall [tɔːl] a alto(a); **to be 6 feet ~** ≈ essere alto 1 metro e 80; **how ~ are you?** quanto è alto?

tallboy ['tɔːlbɔɪ] n (*Brit*) cassettone m alto.

tallness ['tɔːlnɪs] n altezza.

tall story n panzana, frottola.

tally ['tælɪ] n conto, conteggio ♦ vi: **to ~ (with)** corrispondere (a); **to keep a ~ of sth** tener il conto di qc.

talon ['tælən] n artiglio.

tambourine [tæmbə'riːn] n tamburello.

tame [teɪm] a addomesticato(a); (*fig: story,*

style) insipido(a), scialbo(a).

tamper ['tæmpə*] *vi*: **to ~ with** manomettere.

tampon ['tæmpɔn] *n* tampone *m*.

tan [tæn] *n* (*also*: **sun~**) abbronzatura ♦ *vt* abbronzare ♦ *vi* abbronzarsi ♦ *a* (*colour*) marrone rossiccio *inv*; **to get a ~** abbronzarsi.

tandem ['tændəm] *n* tandem *m inv*.

tang [tæŋ] *n* odore *m* penetrante; sapore *m* piccante.

tangent ['tændʒənt] *n* (*MATH*) tangente *f*; **to go off at a ~** (*fig*) partire per la tangente.

tangerine [tændʒə'riːn] *n* mandarino.

tangible ['tændʒəbl] *a* tangibile; **~ assets** patrimonio reale.

Tangier [tæn'dʒɪə*] *n* Tangeri *f*.

tangle ['tæŋgl] *n* groviglio ♦ *vt* aggrovigliare; **to get in(to) a ~** finire in un groviglio.

tango ['tæŋgəu] *n* tango.

tank [tæŋk] *n* serbatoio; (*for processing*) vasca; (*for fish*) acquario; (*MIL*) carro armato.

tankard ['tæŋkəd] *n* boccale *m*.

tanker ['tæŋkə*] *n* (*ship*) nave *f* cisterna *inv*; (*for oil*) petroliera; (*truck*) autobotte *f*, autocisterna.

tanned [tænd] *a* abbronzato(a).

tannin ['tænɪn] *n* tannino.

tanning ['tænɪŋ] *n* (*of leather*) conciatura.

tannoy ® ['tænɔɪ] *n* (*Brit*) altoparlante *m*; **over the ~** per altoparlante.

tantalizing ['tæntəlaɪzɪŋ] *a* allettante.

tantamount ['tæntəmaunt] *a*: **~ to** equivalente a.

tantrum ['tæntrəm] *n* accesso di collera; **to throw a ~** fare le bizze.

Tanzania [tænzə'nɪə] *n* Tanzania.

Tanzanian [tænzə'nɪən] *a, n* tanzaniano(a).

tap [tæp] *n* (*on sink etc*) rubinetto; (*gentle blow*) colpetto ♦ *vt* dare un colpetto a; (*resources*) sfruttare, utilizzare; (*telephone conversation*) intercettare; (*telephone*) mettere sotto controllo; **on ~** (*beer*) alla spina; (*fig: resources*) a disposizione.

tap-dancing ['tæpdɑːnsɪŋ] *n* tip tap *m*.

tape [teɪp] *n* nastro; (*also*: **magnetic ~**) nastro (magnetico) ♦ *vt* (*record*) registrare (su nastro); **on ~** (*song etc*) su nastro.

tape deck *n* piastra di registrazione.

tape measure *n* metro a nastro.

taper ['teɪpə*] *n* candelina ♦ *vi* assottigliarsi.

tape-record ['teɪprɪkɔːd] *vt* registrare (su nastro).

tape recorder *n* registratore *m* (a nastro).

tape recording *n* registrazione *f*.

tapered ['teɪpəd], **tapering** ['teɪpərɪŋ] *a* affusolato(a).

tapestry ['tæpɪstrɪ] *n* arazzo; tappezzeria.

tape-worm ['teɪpwəːm] *n* tenia, verme *m* solitario.

tapioca [tæpɪ'əukə] *n* tapioca.

tappet ['tæpɪt] *n* punteria.

tar [tɑː*] *n* catrame *m*; **low-/middle-~ cigarettes** sigarette a basso/medio contenuto di nicotina.

tarantula [tə'ræntjulə] *n* tarantola.

tardy ['tɑːdɪ] *a* tardo(a); tardivo(a).

target ['tɑːgɪt] *n* bersaglio; (*fig: objective*) obiettivo; **to be on ~** (*project*) essere nei tempi (di lavorazione).

target practice *n* tiro al bersaglio.

tariff ['tærɪf] *n* tariffa.

tariff barrier *n* barriera tariffaria.

tarmac ['tɑːmæk] *n* (*Brit: on road*) macadam *m* al catrame; (*AVIAT*) pista di decollo ♦ *vt* (*Brit*) macadamizzare.

tarnish ['tɑːnɪʃ] *vt* offuscare, annerire; (*fig*) macchiare.

tarpaulin [tɑː'pɔːlɪn] *n* tela incatramata.

tarragon ['tærəgən] *n* dragoncello.

tart [tɑːt] *n* (*CULIN*) crostata; (*Brit col: pej: woman*) sgualdrina ♦ *a* (*flavour*) aspro(a), agro(a).

tart up *vt* (*col*): **to ~ o.s. up** farsi bello(a); (*pej*) agghindarsi.

tartan ['tɑːtn] *n* tartan *m inv*.

tartar ['tɑːtə*] *n* (*on teeth*) tartaro.

tartar sauce *n* salsa tartara.

task [tɑːsk] *n* compito; **to take to ~** rimproverare.

task force *n* (*MIL, POLICE*) unità operativa.

taskmaster ['tɑːskmɑːstə*] *n*: **he's a hard ~** è un vero tiranno.

Tasmania [tæz'meɪnɪə] *n* Tasmania.

tassel ['tæsl] *n* fiocco.

taste [teɪst] *n* gusto; (*flavour*) sapore *m*, gusto; (*fig: glimpse, idea*) idea ♦ *vt* gustare; (*sample*) assaggiare ♦ *vi*: **to ~ of** (*fish etc*) sapere di, avere sapore di; **what does it ~ like?** che sapore *or* gusto ha?; **it ~s like fish** sa di pesce; **you can ~ the garlic (in it)** (ci) si sente il sapore dell'aglio; **can I have a ~ of this wine?** posso assaggiare un po' di questo vino?; **to have a ~ of sth** assaggiare qc; **to have a ~ for sth** avere un'inclinazione per qc; **to be in bad** *or* **poor ~** essere di cattivo gusto.

taste bud *n* papilla gustativa.

tasteful ['teɪstful] *a* di buon gusto.

tastefully ['teɪstfəlɪ] *ad* con gusto.

tasteless ['teɪstlɪs] *a* (*food*) insipido(a); (*remark*) di cattivo gusto.

tasty ['teɪstɪ] *a* saporito(a), gustoso(a).

tattered ['tætəd] *a* see **tatters**.

tatters ['tætəz] *npl*: **in ~** (*also*: **tattered**) a brandelli, sbrindellato(a).

tattoo [tə'tuː] *n* tatuaggio; (*spectacle*) parata militare ♦ *vt* tatuare.

tatty ['tætɪ] *a* (*Brit col*) malandato(a).

taught [tɔːt] *pt, pp* of **teach**.

taunt [tɔːnt] *n* scherno ♦ *vt* schernire.

Taurus ['tɔːrəs] *n* Toro; **to be ~** essere del Toro.

taut [tɔːt] *a* teso(a).

tavern ['tævən] *n* taverna.

tawdry ['tɔːdrɪ] *a* pacchiano(a).

tawny ['tɔːnɪ] *a* fulvo(a).

tax [tæks] *n* imposta, tassa; (*on income*) imposte *fpl*, tasse *fpl* ♦ *vt* tassare; (*fig: strain*:

patience etc) mettere alla prova; **free of ~** esentasse *inv*, esente da imposte; **before/ after ~** al lordo/netto delle tasse.

taxable ['tæksəbl] *a* imponibile.

tax allowance *n* detrazione *f* d'imposta.

taxation [tæk'seɪʃən] *n* tassazione *f*; tasse *fpl*, imposte *fpl*; **system of ~** sistema *m* fiscale.

tax avoidance *n* l'evitare legalmente il pagamento di imposte.

tax collector *n* esattore *m* delle imposte.

tax disc *n* (*Brit AUT*) ≈ bollo.

tax evasion *n* evasione *f* fiscale.

tax exemption *n* esenzione *f* fiscale.

tax exile *n* chi ripara all'estero per evadere le imposte.

tax-free [tæks'fri:] *a* esente da imposte.

tax haven *n* paradiso fiscale.

taxi ['tæksɪ] *n* taxi *m inv* ♦ *vi* (*AVIAT*) rullare.

taxidermist ['tæksɪdə:mɪst] *n* tassidermista *m/f*.

taxi driver *n* tassista *m/f*.

tax inspector *n* (*Brit*) ispettore *m* delle tasse.

taximeter ['tæksɪmi:tə*] *n* tassametro *m*.

taxi rank, (*US*) **taxi stand** *n* posteggio dei taxi.

tax payer *n* contribuente *m/f*.

tax rebate *n* rimborso fiscale.

tax relief *n* sgravio fiscale.

tax return *n* dichiarazione *f* dei redditi.

tax shelter *n* paradiso fiscale.

tax year *n* anno fiscale.

TB *n abbr* (= *tuberculosis*) TBC *f*.

TD *n abbr* (*US*) = **Treasury Department**; (: *FOOTBALL*) = **touchdown.**

tea [ti:] *n* tè *m inv*; (*Brit: snack: for children*) merenda; **high ~** (*Brit*) cena leggera (*presa nel tardo pomeriggio*).

tea bag *n* bustina di tè.

tea break *n* (*Brit*) intervallo per il tè.

teacake ['ti:keɪk] *n* (*Brit*) panino dolce all'uva.

teach, *pt, pp* **taught** [ti:tʃ, tɔ:t] *vt*: **to ~ sb sth, ~ sth to sb** insegnare qc a qn ♦ *vi* insegnare; **it taught him a lesson** (*fig*) gli è servito da lezione.

teacher ['ti:tʃə*] *n* (*gen*) insegnante *m/f*; (*in secondary school*) professore/essa; (*in primary school*) maestro/a; **French ~** insegnante di francese.

teacher training college *n* (*for primary schools*) ≈ istituto magistrale; (*for secondary schools*) scuola universitaria per l'abilitazione all'insegnamento nelle medie superiori.

teaching ['ti:tʃɪŋ] *n* insegnamento.

teaching aids *npl* materiali *mpl* per l'insegnamento.

teaching hospital *n* (*Brit*) clinica universitaria.

teaching staff *n* (*Brit*) insegnanti *mpl*, personale *m* insegnante.

tea cosy *n* copriteiera *m inv*.

teacup ['ti:kʌp] *n* tazza da tè.

teak [ti:k] *n* teak *m*.

tea leaves *npl* foglie *fpl* di tè.

team [ti:m] *n* squadra; (*of animals*) tiro.

team up *vi*: **to ~ up (with)** mettersi insieme (a).

team games *npl* giochi *mpl* di squadra.

teamwork ['ti:mwə:k] *n* lavoro di squadra.

tea party *n* tè *m inv* (*ricevimento*).

teapot ['ti:pɔt] *n* teiera.

tear *n* [tɛə*] strappo; [tɪə*] lacrima ♦ *vb* [tɛə*] (*pt* tore, *pp* torn [tɔ:*, tɔ:n]) *vt* strappare ♦ *vi* strapparsi; **in ~s** in lacrime; **to burst into ~s** scoppiare in lacrime; **to ~ to pieces** *or* **to bits** *or* **to shreds** (*also fig*) fare a pezzi *or* a brandelli.

tear along *vi* (*rush*) correre all'impazzata.

tear apart *vt* (*also fig*) distruggere.

tear away *vt*: **to ~ o.s. away (from sth)** (*fig*) staccarsi (da qc).

tear out *vt* (*sheet of paper, cheque*) staccare.

tear up *vt* (*sheet of paper etc*) strappare.

tearaway ['tɛərəweɪ] *n* (*col*) monello/a.

teardrop ['tɪədrɔp] *n* lacrima.

tearful ['tɪəful] *a* piangente, lacrimoso(a).

tear gas *n* gas *m* lacrimogeno.

tearoom ['ti:ru:m] *n* sala da tè.

tease [ti:z] *vt* canzonare; (*unkindly*) tormentare.

tea set *n* servizio da tè.

teashop ['ti:ʃɔp] *n* (*Brit*) sala da tè.

teaspoon ['ti:spu:n] *n* cucchiaino da tè; (*also: ~ful: as measurement*) cucchiaino.

tea strainer *n* colino da tè.

teat [ti:t] *n* capezzolo; (*of bottle*) tettarella.

teatime ['ti:taɪm] *n* ora del tè.

tea towel *n* (*Brit*) strofinaccio (per i piatti).

tea urn *n* bollitore *m* per il tè.

tech [tɛk] *n abbr* (*col*) = **technical college**; **technology.**

technical ['tɛknɪkl] *a* tecnico(a).

technical college *n* ≈ istituto tecnico.

technicality [tɛknɪ'kælɪtɪ] *n* tecnicità; (*detail*) dettaglio tecnico; **on a legal ~** grazie a un cavillo legale.

technically ['tɛknɪklɪ] *ad* dal punto di vista tecnico.

technician [tɛk'nɪʃən] *n* tecnico/a.

technique [tɛk'ni:k] *n* tecnica.

technocrat ['tɛknəkræt] *n* tecnocrate *m/f*.

technological [tɛknə'lɔdʒɪkl] *a* tecnologico(a).

technologist [tɛk'nɔlədʒɪst] *n* tecnologo/a.

technology [tɛk'nɔlədʒɪ] *n* tecnologia.

teddy (bear) ['tɛdɪ-] *n* orsacchiotto.

tedious ['ti:dɪəs] *a* noioso(a), tedioso(a).

tedium ['ti:dɪəm] *n* noia, tedio.

tee [ti:] *n* (*GOLF*) tee *m inv*.

teem [ti:m] *vi* abbondare, brulicare; **to ~ with** brulicare di; **it is ~ing (with rain)** piove a dirotto.

teenage ['ti:neɪdʒ] *a* (*fashions etc*) per giovani, per adolescenti.

teenager ['ti:neɪdʒə*] *n* adolescente *m/f*.

teens [ti:nz] *npl*: **to be in one's ~** essere adolescente.

tee-shirt ['ti:ʃə:t] *n* = **T-shirt.**

teeter ['ti:tə•] *vi* barcollare, vacillare.
teeth [ti:θ] *npl of* **tooth**.
teethe [ti:ð] *vi* mettere i denti.
teething ring ['ti:ðɪŋ-] *n* dentaruolo.
teething troubles *npl* (*fig*) difficoltà *fpl* iniziali.
teetotal ['ti:'təutl] *a* astemio(a).
teetotaller, (*US*) **teetotaler** ['ti:'təutlə•] *n* astemio/a.
TEFL ['tefl] *n abbr* = *Teaching of English as a Foreign Language.*
Tehran [tɛə'rɑːn] *n* Tehran *f.*
tel. *abbr* (= *telephone*) tel.
Tel Aviv ['tɛlə'vi:v] *n* Tel Aviv *f.*
telecast ['tɛlɪkɑ:st] *vt, vi* teletrasmettere.
telecommunications ['tɛlɪkəmju:nɪ'keɪʃənz] *n* telecomunicazioni *fpl.*
telegram ['tɛlɪgræm] *n* telegramma *m.*
telegraph ['tɛlɪgrɑ:f] *n* telegrafo.
telegraphic [tɛlɪ'græfɪk] *a* telegrafico(a).
telegraph pole *n* palo del telegrafo.
telegraph wire *n* filo del telegrafo.
telepathic [tɛlɪ'pæθɪk] *a* telepatico(a).
telepathy [tə'lɛpəθɪ] *n* telepatia.
telephone ['tɛlɪfəun] *n* telefono ♦ *vt* (*person*) telefonare a; (*message*) telefonare; **to have a** ∼, (*Brit*) **to be on the** ∼ (*subscriber*) avere il telefono; **to be on the** ∼ (*be speaking*) essere al telefono.
telephone booth, (*Brit*) **telephone box** *n* cabina telefonica.
telephone call *n* telefonata.
telephone directory *n* elenco telefonico.
telephone exchange *n* centralino telefonico.
telephone kiosk *n* (*Brit*) cabina telefonica.
telephone number *n* numero di telefono.
telephone operator *n* centralinista *m/f.*
telephone tapping *n* intercettazione *f* telefonica.
telephonist [tə'lɛfənɪst] *n* (*Brit*) telefonista *m/f.*
telephoto lens ['tɛlɪfəutəu-] *n* teleobiettivo.
teleprinter ['tɛlɪprɪntə•] *n* telescrivente *f.*
Teleprompter ® ['tɛlɪprɔmptə•] *n* (*US*) gobbo.
telescope ['tɛlɪskəup] *n* telescopio ♦ *vi* chiudersi a telescopio; (*fig: vehicles*) accartocciarsi.
telescopic [tɛlɪs'kɔpɪk] *a* telescopico(a); (*umbrella*) pieghevole.
teletext ['tɛlɪtɛks] *n* (*TEL*) Teletex *m.*
televiewer ['tɛlɪvju:ə•] *n* telespettatore/trice.
televise ['tɛlɪvaɪz] *vt* teletrasmettere.
television ['tɛlɪvɪʒən] *n* televisione *f*; **on** ∼ alla televisione.
television licence *n* (*Brit*) abbonamento alla televisione.
television programme *n* programma *m* televisivo.
television set *n* televisore *m.*
telex ['tɛlɛks] *n* telex *m inv* ♦ *vt* trasmettere per telex ♦ *vi* mandare un telex; **to** ∼ **sb (about sth)** informare qn via telex (di qc).
tell, *pt, pp* **told** [tɛl, təuld] *vt* dire; (*relate: story*) raccontare; (*distinguish*): **to** ∼ **sth**

from distinguere qc da ♦ *vi* (*have effect*) farsi sentire, avere effetto; **to** ∼ **sb to do** dire a qn di fare; **to** ∼ **sb about sth** dire a qn di qc; raccontare qc a qn; **to** ∼ **the time** leggere l'ora; **can you** ∼ **me the time?** può dirmi l'ora?; **(I)** ∼ **you what** ... so io che cosa fare ...; **I couldn't** ∼ **them apart** non riuscivo a distinguerli.
tell off *vt* rimproverare, sgridare.
tell on *vt fus* (*inform against*) denunciare.
teller ['tɛlə•] *n* (*in bank*) cassiere/a.
telling ['tɛlɪŋ] *a* (*remark, detail*) rivelatore(trice).
telltale ['tɛlteɪl] *a* (*sign*) rivelatore(trice) ♦ *n* malalingua, pettegolo/a.
telly ['tɛlɪ] *n abbr* (*Brit col: = television*) tivù *f inv.*
temerity [tə'mɛrɪtɪ] *n* temerarietà.
temp [tɛmp] *abbr* (*Brit col: = temporary*) *n* impiegato(a) straordinario(a) ♦ *vi* lavorare come impiegato(a) straordinario(a).
temper ['tɛmpə•] *n* (*nature*) carattere *m*; (*mood*) umore *m*; (*fit of anger*) collera ♦ *vt* (*moderate*) temperare, moderare; **to be in a** ∼ essere in collera; **to keep one's** ∼ restare calmo; **to lose one's** ∼ andare in collera.
temperament ['tɛmprəmənt] *n* temperamento.
temperamental [tɛmprə'mɛntl] *a* capriccioso(a).
temperance ['tɛmpərns] *n* moderazione *f*; (*in drinking*) temperanza nel bere.
temperate ['tɛmprət] *a* moderato(a); (*climate*) temperato(a).
temperature ['tɛmprətʃə•] *n* temperatura; **to have** *or* **run a** ∼ avere la febbre.
tempered ['tɛmpəd] *a* (*steel*) temprato(a).
tempest ['tɛmpɪst] *n* tempesta.
tempestuous [tɛm'pɛstjuəs] *a* (*relationship, meeting*) burrascoso(a).
tempi ['tɛmpi:] *npl of* **tempo.**
template, (*US*) **templet** ['tɛmplɪt] *n* sagoma.
temple ['tɛmpl] *n* (*building*) tempio; (*ANAT*) tempia.
templet ['tɛmplɪt] *n* (*US*) = **template.**
tempo, ∼s *or* **tempi** ['tɛmpəu, 'tɛmpi:] *n* tempo; (*fig: of life etc*) ritmo.
temporal ['tɛmpərl] *a* temporale.
temporarily ['tɛmpərərɪlɪ] *ad* temporaneamente.
temporary ['tɛmpərərɪ] *a* temporaneo(a); (*job, worker*) avventizio(a), temporaneo(a); ∼ **secretary** segretaria temporanea; ∼ **teacher** supplente *m/f.*
temporize ['tɛmpəraɪz] *vi* temporeggiare.
tempt [tɛmpt] *vt* tentare; **to** ∼ **sb into doing** indurre qn a fare; **to be** ∼**ed to do sth** essere tentato di fare qc.
temptation [tɛmp'teɪʃən] *n* tentazione *f.*
tempting ['tɛmptɪŋ] *a* allettante, seducente.
ten [tɛn] *num dieci* ♦ *n* dieci; ∼**s of thousands** decine di migliaia.
tenable ['tɛnəbl] *a* sostenibile.
tenacious [tə'neɪʃəs] *a* tenace.
tenacity [tə'næsɪtɪ] *n* tenacia.

tenancy ['tɛnənsɪ] n affitto; condizione f di inquilino.

tenant ['tɛnənt] n inquilino/a.

tend [tɛnd] vt badare a, occuparsi di; (sick etc) prendersi cura di ♦ vi: **to ~ to do** tendere a fare; (colour): **to ~ to** tendere a.

tendency ['tɛndənsɪ] n tendenza.

tender ['tɛndə*] a tenero(a); (sore) sensibile; (fig: subject) delicato(a) ♦ n (COMM: offer) offerta; (money): **legal ~** valuta (a corso legale) ♦ vt offrire; **to put in a ~ (for)** fare un'offerta (per); **to put work out to ~** (Brit) dare lavoro in appalto; **to ~ one's resignation** presentare le proprie dimissioni.

tenderize ['tɛndəraɪz] vt (CULIN) far intenerire.

tenderly ['tɛndəlɪ] ad teneramente.

tenderness ['tɛndənɪs] n tenerezza; sensibilità.

tendon ['tɛndən] n tendine m.

tenement ['tɛnəmənt] n casamento.

Tenerife [tɛnə'riːf] n Tenerife f.

tenet ['tɛnət] n principio.

tenner ['tɛnə*] n (Brit col) (banconota da) dieci sterline fpl.

tennis ['tɛnɪs] n tennis m.

tennis ball n palla da tennis.

tennis court n campo da tennis.

tennis elbow n (MED) gomito del tennista.

tennis match n partita di tennis.

tennis player n tennista m/f.

tennis racket n racchetta da tennis.

tennis shoes npl scarpe fpl da tennis.

tenor ['tɛnə*] n (MUS, of speech etc) tenore m.

tenpin bowling ['tɛnpɪn-] n (Brit) bowling m.

tense [tɛns] a teso(a) ♦ n (LING) tempo ♦ vt (tighten: muscles) tendere.

tenseness ['tɛnsnɪs] n tensione f.

tension ['tɛnʃən] n tensione f.

tent [tɛnt] n tenda.

tentacle ['tɛntəkl] n tentacolo.

tentative ['tɛntətɪv] a esitante, incerto(a); (conclusion) provvisorio(a).

tenterhooks ['tɛntəhuks] npl: **on ~** sulle spine.

tenth [tɛnθ] num decimo(a).

tent peg n picchetto da tenda.

tent pole n palo da tenda, montante m.

tenuous ['tɛnjuəs] a tenue.

tenure ['tɛnjuə*] n (of property) possesso; (of job) incarico; (guaranteed employment): **to have ~** essere di ruolo.

tepid ['tɛpɪd] a tiepido(a).

term [tə:m] n (limit) termine m; (word) vocabolo, termine; (SCOL) trimestre m; (LAW) sessione f ♦ vt chiamare, definire; **~s** npl (conditions) condizioni fpl; (COMM) prezzi mpl, tariffe fpl; **~ of imprisonment** periodo di prigionia; **during his ~ of office** durante il suo incarico; **in the short/long ~** a breve/lunga scadenza; **"easy ~s"** (COMM) "facilitazioni di pagamento"; **to be on good ~s with** essere in buoni rapporti con; **to come to ~s with** (person) arrivare a un accordo con; (problem) affrontare.

terminal ['tə:mɪnl] a finale, terminale; (disease) nella fase terminale ♦ n (ELEC, COMPUT) terminale m; (AVIAT, for oil, ore etc) terminal m inv; (Brit: also: **coach ~**) capolinea m.

terminate ['tə:mɪneɪt] vt mettere fine a ♦ vi: **to ~ in** finire in or con.

termination [tə:mɪ'neɪʃən] n fine f; (of contract) rescissione f; **~ of pregnancy** (MED) interruzione f della gravidanza.

termini ['tə:mɪnaɪ] npl of **terminus**.

terminology [tə:mɪ'nɔlədʒɪ] n terminologia.

terminus, pl **termini** ['tə:mɪnəs, 'tə:mɪnaɪ] n (for buses) capolinea m; (for trains) stazione f terminale.

termite ['tə:maɪt] n termite f.

Ter(r). abbr = **terrace**.

terrace ['tɛrəs] n terrazza; (Brit: row of houses) fila di case a schiera; **the ~s** npl (Brit SPORT) le gradinate.

terraced ['tɛrɪst] a (garden) a terrazze; (in a row: house, cottage etc) a schiera.

terrain [tɛ'reɪn] n terreno.

terrible ['tɛrɪbl] a terribile; (weather) bruttissimo(a); (performance, report) pessimo(a).

terribly ['tɛrəblɪ] ad terribilmente; (very badly) malissimo.

terrier ['tɛrɪə*] n terrier m inv.

terrific [tə'rɪfɪk] a incredibile, fantastico(a); (wonderful) formidabile, eccezionale.

terrify ['tɛrɪfaɪ] vt terrorizzare; **to be terrified** essere atterrito(a).

territorial [tɛrɪ'tɔ:rɪəl] a territoriale.

territorial waters npl acque fpl territoriali.

territory ['tɛrɪtərɪ] n territorio.

terror ['tɛrə*] n terrore m.

terrorism ['tɛrərɪzəm] n terrorismo.

terrorist ['tɛrərɪst] n terrorista m/f.

terrorize ['tɛrəraɪz] vt terrorizzare.

terse [tə:s] a (style) conciso(a); (reply) laconico(a).

tertiary ['tə:ʃərɪ] a (gen) terziario(a); **~ education** (Brit) educazione f superiore post-scolastica.

Terylene ® ['tɛrɪliːn] n (Brit) terital ® m, terilene ® m.

TESL ['tɛsl] n abbr = Teaching of English as a Second Language.

test [tɛst] n (trial, check) prova; (: of goods in factory) controllo, collaudo; (MED) esame m; (CHEM) analisi f inv; (exam: of intelligence etc) test m inv; (: in school) compito in classe; (also: **driving ~**) esame m di guida ♦ vt provare; controllare, collaudare; esaminare; analizzare; sottoporre a esame; **to put sth to the ~** mettere qc alla prova; **to ~ sth for sth** analizzare qc alla ricerca di qc; **to ~ sb in history** esaminare qn in storia.

testament ['tɛstəmənt] n testamento; **the Old/New T~** il Vecchio/Nuovo testamento.

test ban n (also: **nuclear ~**) divieto di

esperimenti nucleari.

test case n (LAW, fig) caso che farà testo.

test flight n volo di prova.

testicle ['tɛstɪkl] n testicolo.

testify ['tɛstɪfaɪ] vi (LAW) testimoniare, deporre; **to ~ to sth** (LAW) testimoniare qc; (gen) comprovare or dimostrare qc; (be sign of) essere una prova di qc.

testimonial [tɛstɪ'məʊnɪəl] n (Brit: reference) benservito; (gift) testimonianza di stima.

testimony ['tɛstɪmənɪ] n (LAW) testimonianza, deposizione f.

testing ['tɛstɪŋ] a (difficult: time) duro(a).

testing ground n terreno di prova.

test match n (CRICKET, RUGBY) partita internazionale.

test paper n (SCOL) interrogazione f scritta.

test pilot n pilota m collaudatore.

test tube n provetta.

test-tube baby ['tɛsttjuː-b] n bambino(a) concepito(a) in provetta.

testy ['tɛstɪ] a irritabile.

tetanus ['tɛtənəs] n tetano.

tetchy ['tɛtʃɪ] a irritabile, irascibile.

tether ['tɛðə*] vt legare ♦ n: **at the end of one's ~** al limite (della pazienza).

text [tɛkst] n testo.

textbook ['tɛkstbʊk] n libro di testo.

textile ['tɛkstaɪl] n tessile m; **~s** npl tessuti mpl.

texture ['tɛkstʃə*] n tessitura; (of skin, paper etc) struttura.

TGIF abbr (col) = thank God it's Friday.

TGWU n abbr (Brit: = Transport and General Workers' Union) sindacato degli operai dei trasporti e non specializzati.

Thai [taɪ] a tailandese ♦ n tailandese m/f; (LING) tailandese m.

Thailand ['taɪlænd] n Tailandia.

thalidomide ® [θə'lɪdəmaɪd] n talidomide ® m.

Thames [tɛmz] n: **the ~** il Tamigi.

than [ðæn, ðən] cj che; (with numerals, pronouns, proper names): **more ~ 10/me/Maria** più di 10/me/Maria; **you know her better ~ I do** la conosce meglio di me or di quanto non la conosca io; **she has more apples ~ pears** ha più mele che pere; **it is better to phone ~ to write** è meglio telefonare che scrivere; **no sooner did he leave ~ the phone rang** non appena uscì il telefono suonò.

thank [θæŋk] vt ringraziare; **~ you (very much)** grazie (tante); **~ heavens/God!** grazie al cielo/a Dio!; see also **thanks**.

thankful ['θæŋkfʊl] a: **~ (for)** riconoscente (per); **~ for/that** (relieved) sollevato(a) da/dal fatto che.

thankfully ['θæŋkfəlɪ] ad con riconoscenza; con sollievo; **~ there were few victims** grazie al cielo ci sono state poche vittime.

thankless ['θæŋklɪs] a ingrato(a).

thanks [θæŋks] npl ringraziamenti mpl, grazie fpl ♦ excl grazie!; **~ to** prep grazie a.

Thanksgiving (Day) ['θæŋksgɪvɪŋ-] n giorno

del ringraziamento.

that [ðæt, ðət] cj che ♦ a (pl **those**) quel(quell', quello) m; quella(quell') f ♦ pronoun ciò; (the one, not "this one") quello(a); (relative) che; prep + il(la) quale: (with time): **on the day ~ he came** il giorno in cui or quando venne ♦ ad: **~ high** così alto; alto così; **it's about ~ high** è alto circa così; **~ one** quello(a) (là); **~ one over there** quello là; **after ~** dopo; **what's ~?** cos'è?; **who's ~?** chi è?; **is ~ you?** sei tu?; **~'s what he said** questo è ciò che ha detto; **~ is ... cioè ...**, vale a dire ...; **at or with ~ she ...** con ciò lei ...; **do it like ~** fallo così; **not ~ I know of** non che io sappia; **I can't work ~ much** non posso lavorare così tanto.

thatched [θætʃt] a (roof) di paglia; **~ cottage** cottage m inv col tetto di paglia.

thaw [θɔː] n disgelo ♦ vi (ice) sciogliersi; (food) scongelarsi ♦ vt (food) (fare) scongelare; **it's ~ing** (weather) sta sgelando.

the [ðiː, ðə] definite article il(lo, l') m; la(l') f; i(gli) mpl; le fpl; (in titles): **Richard ~ Second** Riccardo secondo ♦ ad: **~ more he works ~ more he earns** più lavora più guadagna; **700 lire to ~ dollar** 700 lire per un dollaro; **paid by ~ hour** pagato a ore; **~ sooner ~ better** prima è, meglio è.

theatre, (US) **theater** ['θɪətə*] n teatro.

theatre-goer ['θɪətəgəʊə*] n frequentatore/trice di teatri.

theatrical [θɪ'ætrɪkl] a teatrale.

theft [θɛft] n furto.

their [ðɛə*] a il(la) loro, pl i(le) loro.

theirs [ðɛəz] pronoun il(la) loro, pl i(le) loro; **it is ~** è loro; **a friend of ~** un loro amico.

them [ðɛm, ðəm] pronoun (direct) li(le); (indirect) gli, loro (after vb); (stressed, after prep: people) loro; (: people, things) essi(e); **I see ~** li vedo; **give ~ the book** dà loro or dagli il libro; **give me a few of ~** dammene un po' or qualcuno.

theme [θiːm] n tema m.

theme song, **theme tune** n tema musicale.

themselves [ðəm'sɛlvz] pl pronoun (reflexive) si; (emphatic) loro stessi(e); (after prep) se stessi(e); **between ~** tra (di) loro.

then [ðɛn] ad (at that time) allora; (next) poi, dopo; (and also) e poi ♦ cj (therefore) perciò, dunque, quindi ♦ a: **the ~ president** il presidente di allora; **from ~ on** da allora in poi; **until ~** fino ad allora; **and ~ what?** e poi?, e allora?; **what do you want me to do ~?** allora cosa vuole che faccia?

theologian [θɪə'ləʊdʒən] n teologo/a.

theological [θɪə'lɒdʒɪkl] a teologico(a).

theology [θɪ'ɒlədʒɪ] n teologia.

theorem ['θɪərəm] n teorema m.

theoretical [θɪə'rɛtɪkl] a teorico(a).

theorize ['θɪəraɪz] vi teorizzare.

theory ['θɪərɪ] n teoria; **in ~** in teoria.

therapeutic(al) [θɛrə'pjuːtɪk(l)] a terapeutico(a).

therapist ['θɛrəpɪst] n terapista m/f.

therapy ['θerəpɪ] n terapia.

there [ðɛə*] ad là, lì; ~, ~! su, su!; **it's ~** è lì; **he went ~** ci è andato; **~ is** c'è; **~ are** ci sono; **~ has been** c'è stato; **~ he is** eccolo (là); **back ~** là dietro; **down ~** laggiù; **in ~** là dentro; **on ~** lassù; **over ~** là; **through ~** di là; **to go ~ and back** andarci e ritornare.

thereabouts ['ðɛərəbauts] ad (place) nei pressi, da quelle parti; (amount) giù di lì, all'incirca.

thereafter [ðɛər'ɑ:ftə*] ad da allora in poi.

thereby [ðɛə'baɪ] ad con ciò.

therefore ['ðɛəfɔ:*] ad perciò, quindi.

there's [ðɛəz] = **there is; there has.**

thereupon [ðɛərə'pɒn] ad (at that point) a quel punto; (formal: on that subject) in merito.

thermal ['θə:ml] a (currents, spring) termale; (underwear, printer) termico(a); (paper) termosensibile.

thermodynamics [θə:məudaɪ'næmɪks] n termodinamica.

thermometer [θə'mɒmɪtə*] n termometro.

thermonuclear ['θə:məu'nju:klɪə*] a termonucleare.

Thermos ® ['θə:məs] n (also: ~ **flask**) thermos ® m inv.

thermostat ['θə:məstæt] n termostato.

thesaurus [θɪ'sɔ:rəs] n dizionario dei sinonimi.

these [ði:z] pl pronoun, a questi(e).

thesis, pl **theses** ['θi:sɪs, 'θi:si:z] n tesi f inv.

they [ðeɪ] pl pronoun essi(esse); (people only) loro; **~ say that** ... (it is said that) si dice che ....

they'd [ðeɪd] = **they would; they had.**

they'll [ðeɪl] = **they will; they shall.**

they're [ðɛə*] = **they are.**

they've [ðeɪv] = **they have.**

thick [θɪk] a spesso(a); (crowd) compatto(a); (stupid) ottuso(a), lento(a) ♦ n: **in the ~ of** nel folto di; **it's 20 cm ~** ha uno spessore di 20 cm.

thicken ['θɪkən] vi ispessire ♦ vt (sauce etc) ispessire, rendere più denso(a).

thicket ['θɪkɪt] n boscaglia.

thickly ['θɪklɪ] ad (spread) a strati spessi; (cut) a fette grosse; (populated) densamente.

thickness ['θɪknɪs] n spessore m.

thickset [θɪk'sɛt] a tarchiato(a), tozzo(a).

thickskinned [θɪk'skɪnd] a (fig) insensibile.

thief, pl **thieves** [θi:f, θi:vz] n ladro/a.

thieving ['θi:vɪŋ] n furti mpl.

thigh [θaɪ] n coscia.

thighbone ['θaɪbəun] n femore m.

thimble ['θɪmbl] n ditale m.

thin [θɪn] a sottile; (person) magro(a); (soup) poco denso(a); (hair, crowd) rado(a); (fog) leggero(a) ♦ vt (hair) sfoltire ♦ vi (fog) diradarsi; (also: ~ **out**: crowd) disperdersi; **to ~ (down)** (sauce, paint) diluire; **his hair is ~ning** sta perdendo i capelli.

thing [θɪŋ] n cosa; (object) oggetto; (contraption) aggeggio; **~s** npl (belongings) cose fpl; **for one ~** tanto per cominciare; **the**

best ~ would be to la cosa migliore sarebbe di; **the ~ is** ... il fatto è che ...; **the main ~ is to** ... la cosa più importante è di ...; **first ~ (in the morning)** come or per prima cosa (di mattina); **last ~ (at night)** come or per ultima cosa (di sera); **poor ~** poveretto/a; **she's got a ~ about mice** è terrorizzata dai topi; **how are ~s?** come va?

think, pt, pp **thought** [θɪŋk, θɔ:t] vi pensare, riflettere ♦ vt pensare, credere; (imagine) immaginare; **to ~ of** pensare a; **what did you ~ of them?** cosa ne ha pensato?; **to ~ about sth/sb** pensare a qc/qn; **I'll ~ about it** ci penserò; **to ~ of doing** pensare di fare; **I ~ so** penso or credo di sì; **to ~ well of** avere una buona opinione di; **to ~ aloud** pensare ad alta voce; **~ again!** rifletti!, pensaci su!

think out vt (plan) elaborare; (solution) trovare.

think over vt riflettere su; **I'd like to ~ things over** vorrei pensarci su.

think through vt riflettere a fondo su.

think up vt ideare.

thinking ['θɪŋkɪŋ] n: **to my (way of) ~** a mio parere.

think tank n gruppo di esperti.

thinly ['θɪnlɪ] ad (cut) a fette sottili; (spread) in uno strato sottile.

thinness ['θɪnnɪs] n sottigliezza; magrezza.

third [θə:d] num terzo(a) ♦ n terzo/a; (fraction) terzo, terza parte f; (Brit SCOL: degree) laurea col minimo dei voti.

third-degree burns ['θə:ddɪ'gri:-] npl ustioni fpl di terzo grado.

thirdly ['θə:dlɪ] ad in terzo luogo.

third party insurance n (Brit) assicurazione f contro terzi.

third-rate [θə:d'reɪt] a di qualità scadente.

Third World n: **the ~** il Terzo Mondo.

thirst [θə:st] n sete f.

thirsty ['θə:stɪ] a (person) assetato(a), che ha sete; **to be ~** aver sete.

thirteen [θə:'ti:n] num tredici.

thirtieth ['θə:tɪɪθ] num trentesimo(a).

thirty ['θə:tɪ] num trenta.

this [ðɪs] a, pronoun (pl **these**) questo(a) ♦ ad: **~ high** alto così; così alto; **it's about ~ high** è alto circa così; **~ one** questo(a) (qui); **~ is what he said** questo è ciò che ha detto; **who/what is ~?** chi è/che cos'è questo?; **~ is Mr Brown** (in introductions, in photo) questo è il signor Brown; (on telephone) sono il signor Brown; **~ time** questa volta; **~ time last year** l'anno scorso in questo periodo; **~ way** (in this direction) da questa parte; (in this fashion) così; **they were talking of ~ and that** stavano parlando del più e del meno.

thistle ['θɪsl] n cardo.

thong [θɒŋ] n cinghia.

thorn [θɔ:n] n spina.

thorny ['θɔ:nɪ] a spinoso(a).

thorough ['θʌrə] a (person) preciso(a),

accurato(a); (*search*) minuzioso(a); (*knowledge, research*) approfondito(a), profondo(a); (*cleaning*) a fondo.

thoroughbred ['θʌrəbrɛd] *n* (*horse*) purosangue *m/f inv*.

thoroughfare ['θʌrəfɛə*] *n* strada transitabile; **"no ~"** (*Brit*) "divieto di transito".

thoroughly ['θʌrəlɪ] *ad* accuratamente; minuziosamente; in profondità; a fondo; **he ~ agreed** fu completamente d'accordo.

thoroughness ['θʌrənɪs] *n* precisione *f*.

those [ðəuz] *pl pronoun* quelli(e) ♦ *pl a* quei(quegli) *mpl*; quelle *fpl*.

though [ðəu] *cj* benché, sebbene ♦ *ad* comunque, tuttavia; **even ~** anche se; **it's not so easy, ~** tuttavia non è così facile.

thought [θɔːt] *pt, pp of* think ♦ *n* pensiero; (*opinion*) opinione *f*; (*intention*) intenzione *f*; **after much ~** dopo molti ripensamenti; **I've just had a ~** mi è appena venuta un'idea; **to give sth some ~** prendere qc in considerazione, riflettere su qc.

thoughtful ['θɔːtful] *a* pensieroso(a), pensoso(a); ponderato(a); (*considerate*) premuroso(a).

thoughtfully ['θɔːtfəlɪ] *ad* (*pensively*) con aria pensierosa.

thoughtless ['θɔːtlɪs] *a* sconsiderato(a); (*behaviour*) scortese.

thoughtlessly ['θɔːtlɪslɪ] *ad* sconsideratamente; scortesemente.

thousand ['θauzənd] *num* mille; **one ~** mille; **~s of** migliaia di.

thousandth ['θauzəntθ] *num* millesimo(a).

thrash [θræʃ] *vt* picchiare; bastonare; (*defeat*) battere.

thrash about *vi* dibattersi.

thrash out *vt* dibattere, sviscerare.

thrashing ['θræʃɪŋ] *n*: **to give sb a ~** = to thrash sb.

thread [θrɛd] *n* filo; (*of screw*) filetto ♦ *vt* (*needle*) infilare; **to ~ one's way between** infilarsi tra.

threadbare ['θrɛdbɛə*] *a* consumato(a), logoro(a).

threat [θrɛt] *n* minaccia; **to be under ~ of** (*closure, extinction*) rischiare di; (*exposure*) essere minacciato(a) di.

threaten ['θrɛtn] *vi* (*storm*) minacciare ♦ *vt*: **to ~ sb with sth/to do** minacciare qn con qc/di fare.

threatening ['θrɛtnɪŋ] *a* minaccioso(a).

three [θriː] *num* tre.

three-dimensional [θriːdaɪ'mɛnʃənl] *a* tridimensionale.

three-piece ['θriːpiːs]: **~ suit** *n* completo (con gilè); **~ suite** *n* salotto comprendente un divano e due poltrone.

three-ply [θriː'plaɪ] *a* (*wood*) a tre strati; (*wool*) a tre fili.

three-quarters [θriː'kwɔːtəz] *npl* tre quarti *mpl*; **~ full** pieno per tre quarti.

three-wheeler [θriː'wiːlə*] *n* (*car*) veicolo a tre ruote.

thresh [θrɛʃ] *vt* (*AGR*) trebbiare.

threshing machine ['θrɛʃɪŋ-] *n* trebbiatrice *f*.

threshold ['θrɛʃhəuld] *n* soglia; **to be on the ~ of** (*fig*) essere sulla soglia di.

threshold agreement *n* (*ECON*) ≈ scala mobile.

threw [θruː] *pt of* **throw**.

thrift [θrɪft] *n* parsimonia.

thrifty ['θrɪftɪ] *a* economico(a), parsimonioso(a).

thrill [θrɪl] *n* brivido ♦ *vi* eccitarsi, tremare ♦ *vt* (*audience*) elettrizzare; **I was ~ed to get your letter** la tua lettera mi ha fatto veramente piacere.

thriller ['θrɪlə*] *n* film *m inv* (*or* dramma *m or* libro) del brivido.

thrilling ['θrɪlɪŋ] *a* (*book, play etc*) pieno(a) di suspense; (*news, discovery*) entusiasmante.

thrive, *pt* **thrived, throve**, *pp* **thrived, thriven** [θraɪv, θrəuv, 'θrɪvn] *vi* crescere *or* svilupparsi bene; (*business*) prosperare; **he ~s on it** gli fa bene, ne gode.

thriving ['θraɪvɪŋ] *a* (*industry etc*) fiorente.

throat [θrəut] *n* gola; **to have a sore ~** avere (un *or* il) mal di gola.

throb [θrɔb] *n* (*of heart*) battito; (*of engine*) vibrazione *f*; (*of pain*) fitta ♦ *vi* (*heart*) palpitare; (*engine*) vibrare; (*with pain*) pulsare; **my head is ~bing** mi martellano le tempie.

throes [θrəuz] *npl*: **in the ~ of** alle prese con; in preda a; **in the ~ of death** in agonia.

thrombosis [θrɔm'bəusɪs] *n* trombosi *f*.

throne [θrəun] *n* trono.

throng [θrɔŋ] *n* moltitudine *f* ♦ *vt* affollare.

throttle ['θrɔtl] *n* (*AUT*) valvola a farfalla; (*on motorcycle*) (manopola del) gas ♦ *vt* strangolare.

through [θruː] *prep* attraverso; (*time*) per, durante; (*by means of*) per mezzo di; (*owing to*) a causa di ♦ *a* (*ticket, train, passage*) diretto(a) ♦ *ad* attraverso; **(from) Monday ~ Friday** (*US*) da lunedì a venerdì; **I am half-way ~ the book** sono a metà libro; **to let sb ~** lasciar passare qn; **to put sb ~ to sb** (*TEL*) passare qn a qn; **to be ~** (*TEL*) ottenere la comunicazione; (*have finished*) avere finito; **"no ~ traffic"** (*US*) "divieto d'accesso"; **"no ~ road"** (*Brit*) "strada senza sbocco".

throughout [θruː'aut] *prep* (*place*) dappertutto in; (*time*) per *or* durante tutto(a) ♦ *ad* dappertutto; sempre.

throughput ['θruːput] *n* (*of goods, materials*) materiale *m* in lavorazione; (*COMPUT*) volume *m* di dati immessi.

throve [θrəuv] *pt of* **thrive**.

throw [θrəu] *n* tiro, getto; (*SPORT*) lancio ♦ *vt* (*pt* **threw**, *pp* **thrown** [θruː, θrəun]) tirare, gettare; (*SPORT*) lanciare; (*rider*) disarcionare; (*fig*) confondere; (*pottery*) formare al tornio; **to ~ a party** dare una fe-

sta; **to ~ open** (*doors, windows*) spalancare;
(*house, gardens etc*) aprire al pubblico;
(*competition, race*) aprire a tutti.
throw about, throw around *vt* (*litter etc*) spargere.
throw away *vt* gettare *or* buttare via.
throw off *vt* sbarazzarsi di.
throw out *vt* buttare fuori; (*reject*) respingere.
throw together *vt* (*clothes, meal etc*) mettere insieme; (*essay*) buttar giù.
throw up *vi* vomitare.
throwaway ['θrəυəweɪ] *a* da buttare.
throwback ['θrəυbæk] *n*: **it's a ~ to** (*fig*) ciò risale a.
throw-in ['θrəυɪn] *n* (*SPORT*) rimessa in gioco.
thrown [θrəυn] *pp of* **throw.**
thru [θruː] *prep, a, ad* (*US*) = **through.**
thrush [θrʌʃ] *n* (*ZOOL*) tordo; (*MED: esp in children*) mughetto; (: *Brit: in women*) candida.
thrust [θrʌst] *n* (*TECH*) spinta ♦ *vt* (*pt, pp* **thrust**) spingere con forza; (*push in*) conficcare.
thrusting ['θrʌstɪŋ] *a* (troppo) intraprendente.
thud [θʌd] *n* tonfo.
thug [θʌg] *n* delinquente *m*.
thumb [θʌm] *n* (*ANAT*) pollice *m* ♦ *vt* (*book*) sfogliare; **to ~ a lift** fare l'autostop; **to give sb/sth the ~s up** dare la propria approvazione a qn/qc.
thumb index *n* indice *m* a rubrica.
thumbnail ['θʌmneɪl] *n* unghia del pollice.
thumbnail sketch *n* descrizione *f* breve.
thumbtack ['θʌmtæk] *n* (*US*) puntina da disegno.
thump [θʌmp] *n* colpo forte; (*sound*) tonfo ♦ *vt* battere su ♦ *vi* picchiare, battere.
thunder ['θʌndə*] *n* tuono ♦ *vi* tuonare; (*train etc*): **to ~ past** passare con un rombo.
thunderbolt ['θʌndəbəʊlt] *n* fulmine *m*.
thunderclap ['θʌndəklæp] *n* rombo di tuono.
thunderous ['θʌndərəs] *a* fragoroso(a).
thunderstorm ['θʌndəstɔːm] *n* temporale *m*.
thunderstruck ['θʌndəstrʌk] *a* (*fig*) sbigottito(a).
thundery ['θʌndərɪ] *a* temporalesco(a).
Thur(s). *abbr* (= *Thursday*) gio.
Thursday ['θɜːzdɪ] *n* giovedì *m inv*; *for phrases see also* **Tuesday.**
thus [ðʌs] *ad* così.
thwart [θwɔːt] *vt* contrastare.
thyme [taɪm] *n* timo.
thyroid ['θaɪrɔɪd] *n* tiroide *f*.
tiara [tɪ'ɑːrə] *n* (*woman's*) diadema *m*.
Tiber ['taɪbə*] *n*: **the ~** il Tevere.
Tibet [tɪ'bet] *n* Tibet *m*.
Tibetan [tɪ'betən] *a* tibetano(a) ♦ *n* tibetano/a; (*LING*) tibetano.
tibia ['tɪbɪə] *n* tibia.
tic [tɪk] *n* tic *m inv*.
tick [tɪk] *n* (*sound: of clock*) tic tac *m inv*; (*mark*) segno; spunta; (*ZOOL*) zecca; (*Brit col*): **in a ~** in un attimo; (*Brit col: credit*):

to buy sth on ~ comprare qc a credito ♦ *vi* fare tic tac ♦ *vt* spuntare; **to put a ~ against sth** fare un segno di fianco a qc.
tick off *vt* spuntare; (*person*) sgridare.
tick over *vi* (*Brit: engine*) andare al minimo.
ticker tape ['tɪkə-] *n* nastro di telescrivente; (*US: in celebrations*) stelle *fpl* filanti.
ticket ['tɪkɪt] *n* biglietto; (*in shop: on goods*) etichetta; (: *from cash register*) scontrino; (*for library*) scheda; (*US POL*) lista dei candidati; **to get a (parking) ~** (*AUT*) prendere una multa (per sosta vietata).
ticket agency *n* (*THEATRE*) agenzia di vendita di biglietti.
ticket collector *n* bigliettaio.
ticket holder *n* persona munita di biglietto.
ticket inspector *n* controllore *m*.
ticket office *n* biglietteria.
tickle ['tɪkl] *n* solletico ♦ *vt* fare il solletico a, solleticare; (*fig*) stuzzicare; piacere a; far ridere.
ticklish ['tɪklɪʃ] *a* che soffre il solletico; (*which tickles: blanket, cough*) che provoca prurito.
tidal ['taɪdl] *a* di marea.
tidal wave *n* onda anomala.
tidbit ['tɪdbɪt] *n* (*US*) = **titbit.**
tiddlywinks ['tɪdlɪwɪŋks] *n* gioco della pulce.
tide [taɪd] *n* marea; (*fig: of events*) corso ♦ *vt*: **will £20 ~ you over till Monday?** ti basteranno 20 sterline fino a lunedì?; **high/low ~** alta/bassa marea; **the ~ of public opinion** l'orientamento dell'opinione pubblica.
tidily ['taɪdɪlɪ] *ad* in modo ordinato; **to arrange ~** sistemare; **to dress ~** vestirsi per benino.
tidiness ['taɪdɪnɪs] *n* ordine *m*.
tidy ['taɪdɪ] *a* (*room*) ordinato(a), lindo(a); (*dress, work*) curato(a), in ordine; (*person*) ordinato(a); (*mind*) organizzato(a) ♦ *vt* (*also: ~ up*) riordinare, mettere in ordine; **to ~ o.s. up** rassettarsi.
tie [taɪ] *n* (*string etc*) legaccio; (*Brit: also:* **neck~**) cravatta; (*fig: link*) legame *m*; (*SPORT: draw*) pareggio (: *match*) incontro; (*US RAIL*) traversina ♦ *vt* (*parcel*) legare; (*ribbon*) annodare ♦ *vi* (*SPORT*) pareggiare; **"black/white ~"** "smoking/abito di rigore"; **family ~s** legami familiari; **to ~ sth in a bow** annodare qc; **to ~ a knot in sth** fare un nodo a qc.
tie down *vt* fissare con una corda; (*fig*): **to ~ sb down to** costringere qn ad accettare.
tie in *vi*: **to ~ in (with)** (*correspond*) corrispondere (a).
tie on *vt* (*Brit: label etc*) attaccare.
tie up *vt* (*parcel, dog*) legare; (*boat*) ormeggiare; (*arrangements*) concludere; **to be ~d up** (*busy*) essere occupato *or* preso.
tie-break(er) ['taɪbreɪk(ə*)] *n* (*TENNIS*) tie-break *m inv*; (*in quiz*) spareggio.
tie-on ['taɪɒn] *a* (*Brit: label*) volante.
tie-pin ['taɪpɪn] *n* (*Brit*) fermacravatta *m inv*.
tier [tɪə*] *n* fila; (*of cake*) piano, strato.
Tierra del Fuego [tɪ'erədɛl'fweɪgəʊ] *n* Terra

del Fuoco.

tie tack *n* (*US*) fermacravatta *m inv*.

tiff [tɪf] *n* battibecco.

tiger ['taɪgə*] *n* tigre *f*.

tight [taɪt] *a* (*rope*) teso(a), tirato(a); (*clothes*) stretto(a); (*budget, programme, bend*) stretto(a); (*control*) severo(a), fermo(a); (*col: drunk*) sbronzo(a) ♦ *ad* (*squeeze*) fortemente; (*shut*) ermeticamente; **to be packed** ~ (*suitcase*) essere pieno zeppo; (*people*) essere pigiati; **everybody hold** ~! tenetevi stretti!; *see also* **tights**.

tighten ['taɪtn] *vt* (*rope*) tendere; (*screw*) stringere; (*control*) rinforzare ♦ *vi* tendersi; stringersi.

tight-fisted [taɪt'fɪstɪd] *a* avaro(a).

tightly ['taɪtlɪ] *ad* (*grasp*) bene, saldamente.

tightrope ['taɪtrəup] *n* corda (da acrobata).

tightrope walker *n* funambolo/a.

tights [taɪts] *npl* (*Brit*) collant *m inv*.

tigress ['taɪgrɪs] *n* tigre *f* (femmina).

tilde ['tɪldə] *n* tilde *f*.

tile [taɪl] *n* (*on roof*) tegola; (*on floor*) mattonella; (*on wall*) piastrella ♦ *vt* (*floor, bathroom etc*) piastrellare.

tiled [taɪld] *a* rivestito(a) di tegole; a mattonelle; a piastrelle.

till [tɪl] *n* registratore *m* di cassa ♦ *vt* (*land*) coltivare ♦ *prep, cj* = **until**.

tiller ['tɪlə*] *n* (*NAUT*) barra del timone.

tilt [tɪlt] *vt* inclinare, far pendere ♦ *vi* inclinarsi, pendere ♦ *n* (*slope*) pendio; **to wear one's hat at a** ~ portare il cappello sulle ventitré; **(at) full** ~ a tutta velocità.

timber ['tɪmbə*] *n* (*material*) legname *m*; (*trees*) alberi *mpl* da legname.

time [taɪm] *n* tempo; (*epoch: often pl*) epoca, tempo; (*by clock*) ora; (*moment*) momento; (*occasion, also MATH*) volta; (*MUS*) tempo ♦ *vt* (*race*) cronometrare; (*programme*) calcolare la durata di; (*remark etc*): **to ~ sth well/badly** scegliere il momento più/meno opportuno per qc; **a long** ~ molto tempo; **for the** ~ **being** per il momento; **from** ~ **to** ~ ogni tanto; ~ **after** ~, ~ **and again** mille volte; **in** ~ (*soon enough*) in tempo; (*after some time*) col tempo; (*MUS*) a tempo; **at** ~**s** a volte; **to take one's** ~ prenderla con calma; **in a week's** ~ fra una settimana; **in no** ~ in un attimo; **on** ~ puntualmente; **to be 30 minutes behind/ahead of** ~ avere 30 minuti di ritardo/anticipo; **by the** ~ **he arrived** quando è arrivato; **5** ~**s 5** 5 volte 5, 5 per 5; **what** ~ **is it?** che ora è?, che ore sono?; **what** ~ **do you make it?** che ora fa?; **to have a good** ~ divertirsi; **they had a hard** ~ **of it** è stato duro per loro; ~**'s up!** è (l')ora!; **to be behind the** ~**s** vivere nel passato; **I've no** ~ **for it** (*fig*) non ho tempo da perdere con cose del genere; **he'll do it in his own (good)** ~ (*without being hurried*) lo farà quando avrà (un minuto di) tempo; **he'll do it in** *or* (*US*) **on his own** ~ (*out of working hours*) lo farà nel suo tempo libero; **the**

bomb was ~**d to explode 5 minutes later** la bomba era stata regolata in modo da esplodere 5 minuti più tardi.

time-and-motion study ['taɪmənd'məuʃən-] *n* analisi *f inv* dei tempi e dei movimenti.

time bomb *n* bomba a orologeria.

time card *n* cartellino (da timbrare).

time clock *n* orologio *m* marcatempo *inv*.

time-consuming ['taɪmkənsju:mɪŋ] *a* che richiede molto tempo.

time difference *n* differenza di fuso orario.

time-honoured, (*US*) **time-honored** ['taɪmɒnəd] *a* consacrato(a) dal tempo.

timekeeper ['taɪmki:pə*] *n* (*SPORT*) cronometrista *m/f*.

time lag *n* intervallo, ritardo; (*in travel*) differenza di fuso orario.

timeless ['taɪmlɪs] *a* eterno(a).

time limit *n* limite *m* di tempo.

timely ['taɪmlɪ] *a* opportuno(a).

time off *n* tempo libero.

timer ['taɪmə*] *n* (*in kitchen*) contaminuti *m inv*; (*TECH*) timer *m inv*, temporizzatore *m*.

time-saving ['taɪmseɪvɪŋ] *a* che fa risparmiare tempo.

time scale *n* tempi *mpl* d'esecuzione.

time-sharing ['taɪmʃɛərɪŋ] *n* (*COMPUT*) divisione *f* di tempo.

time sheet *n* = **time card.**

time signal *n* segnale *m* orario.

time switch *n* interruttore *m* a tempo.

timetable ['taɪmteɪbl] *n* orario; (*programme of events etc*) programma *m*.

time zone *n* fuso orario.

timid ['tɪmɪd] *a* timido(a); (*easily scared*) pauroso(a).

timidity [tɪ'mɪdɪtɪ] *n* timidezza.

timing ['taɪmɪŋ] *n* sincronizzazione *f*; (*fig*) scelta del momento opportuno, tempismo; (*SPORT*) cronometraggio.

timing device *n* (*on bomb*) timer *m inv*.

timpani ['tɪmpənɪ] *npl* timpani *mpl*.

tin [tɪn] *n* stagno; (*also*: ~ **plate**) latta; (*Brit: can*) barattolo (di latta), lattina, scatola; (*for baking*) teglia; **a** ~ **of paint** un barattolo di tinta *or* vernice.

tin foil *n* stagnola.

tinge [tɪndʒ] *n* sfumatura ♦ *vt*: ~**d with** tinto(a) di.

tingle ['tɪŋgl] *vi* (*cheeks, skin: from cold*) pungere, pizzicare; (: *from bad circulation*) formicolare.

tinker ['tɪŋkə*] *n* stagnino ambulante; (*gipsy*) zingaro/a.

  tinker with *vt fus* armeggiare intorno a; cercare di riparare.

tinkle ['tɪŋkl] *vi* tintinnare ♦ *n* (*col*): **to give sb a** ~ dare un colpo di telefono a qn.

tin mine *n* miniera di stagno.

tinned [tɪnd] *a* (*Brit: food*) in scatola.

tinny ['tɪnɪ] *a* metallico(a).

tin-opener ['tɪnəupnə*] *n* (*Brit*) apriscatole *m inv*.

tinsel ['tɪnsl] *n* decorazioni *fpl* natalizie

(*argentate*).

tint [tɪnt] *n* tinta; (*for hair*) shampoo *m inv* colorante ♦ *vt* (*hair*) fare uno shampoo colorante a.

tinted ['tɪntɪd] *a* (*hair*) tinto(a); (*spectacles, glass*) colorato(a).

tiny ['taɪnɪ] *a* minuscolo(a).

tip [tɪp] *n* (*end*) punta; (*protective: on umbrella etc*) puntale *m*; (*gratuity*) mancia; (*for coal*) discarica; (*for rubbish*) immondezzaio; (*advice*) suggerimento ♦ *vt* (*waiter*) dare la mancia a; (*tilt*) inclinare; (*overturn: also:* ~ **over**) capovolgere; (*empty: also:* ~ **out**) scaricare; (*predict: winner*) pronosticare; (: *horse*) dare vincente; **he ~ped out the contents of the box** ha rovesciato il contenuto della scatola.

tip off *vt* fare una soffiata a.

tip-off ['tɪpɔf] *n* (*hint*) soffiata.

tipped ['tɪpt] *a* (*Brit: cigarette*) col filtro; **steel-~** con la punta d'acciaio.

Tipp-Ex ® ['tɪpɛks] *n* (*Brit*) liquido correttore.

tipple ['tɪpl] (*Brit*) *vi* sbevazzare ♦ *n*: **to have a ~** prendere un bicchierino.

tipsy ['tɪpsɪ] *a* brillo(a).

tiptoe ['tɪptəʊ] *n*: **on ~** in punta di piedi.

tiptop ['tɪptɔp] *a*: **in ~ condition** in ottime condizioni.

tire ['taɪə*] *vt* stancare ♦ *vi* stancarsi ♦ *n* (*US*) = **tyre**.

tire out *vt* sfinire, spossare.

tired ['taɪəd] *a* stanco(a); **to be/feel/look ~** essere/sentirsi/sembrare stanco; **to be ~ of** essere stanco *or* stufo di.

tiredness ['taɪədnɪs] *n* stanchezza.

tireless ['taɪəlɪs] *a* instancabile.

tiresome ['taɪəsəm] *a* noioso(a).

tiring ['taɪərɪŋ] *a* faticoso(a).

tissue ['tɪʃuː] *n* tessuto; (*paper handkerchief*) fazzolettino di carta.

tissue paper *n* carta velina.

tit [tɪt] *n* (*bird*) cinciallegra; (*col: breast*) tetta; **to give ~ for tat** rendere pan per focaccia.

titanium [tɪ'teɪnɪəm] *n* titanio.

titbit ['tɪtbɪt], (*US*) **tidbit** ['tɪdbɪt] *n* (*food*) leccornia; (*news*) notizia ghiotta.

titillate ['tɪtɪleɪt] *vt* titillare.

titivate ['tɪtɪveɪt] *vt* agghindare.

title ['taɪtl] *n* titolo; (*LAW: right*): ~ **(to)** diritto (a).

title deed *n* (*LAW*) titolo di proprietà.

title page *n* frontespizio.

title role *n* ruolo *or* parte *f* principale.

titter ['tɪtə*] *vi* ridere scioccamente.

tittle-tattle ['tɪtltætl] *n* chiacchiere *fpl*, pettegolezzi *mpl*.

titular ['tɪtjʊlə*] *a* (*in name only*) nominale.

tizzy ['tɪzɪ] *n* (*col*): **to be in a ~** essere in agitazione.

T-junction ['tiː'dʒʌŋkʃən] *n* incrocio a T.

TM *n abbr* (= *transcendental meditation*) M.T. *f*; (*COMM*) = **trademark**.

TN *abbr* (*US POST*) = *Tennessee*.

TNT *n abbr* (= *trinitrotoluene*) T.N.T. *m*.

to [tuː, tə] *prep* (*gen, with expressions of time*) a; (*towards*) verso ♦ *with vb* (*simple infinitive*): ~ **go/eat** andare/mangiare; (*following another vb*): **to want** ~ **do** voler fare; **to try** ~ **do** cercare di fare; (*purpose, result*) per; **to give sth** ~ **sb** dare qc a qn; **give it** ~ **me** dammelo; **the key** ~ **the front door** la chiave della porta d'ingresso; **it belongs** ~ **him** gli appartiene, è suo; **to go** ~ **France/Portugal** andare in Francia/Portogallo; **the road** ~ **Edinburgh** la strada per Edimburgo; **I went** ~ **Claudia's** sono andato da Claudia; **to go** ~ **town/school** andare in città/a scuola; **8 apples** ~ **the kilo** 8 mele in un chilo; **it's twenty-five** ~ **3** sono *or* mancano venticinque minuti alle 3, sono le 2 e trentacinque; **to pull/push the door** ~ tirare/spingere la porta; **to go** ~ **and fro** andare e tornare; **I don't want** ~ non voglio (farlo); **I have things** ~ **do** ho (delle cose) da fare; **ready** ~ **go** pronto a partire; **he did it** ~ **help you** l'ha fatto per aiutarti.

toad [təʊd] *n* rospo.

toadstool ['təʊdstuːl] *n* fungo (velenoso).

toady ['təʊdɪ] *vi* adulare.

toast [təʊst] *n* (*CULIN*) toast *m*, pane *m* abbrustolito; (*drink, speech*) brindisi *m inv* ♦ *vt* (*CULIN*) abbrustolire; (*drink to*) brindare a; **a piece** *or* **slice of** ~ una fetta di pane abbrustolito.

toaster ['təʊstə*] *n* tostapane *m inv*.

toastmaster ['təʊstmɑːstə*] *n* direttore *m* dei brindisi.

toast rack *n* portatoast *m inv*.

tobacco [tə'bækəʊ] *n* tabacco; **pipe** ~ tabacco da pipa.

tobacconist [tə'bækənɪst] *n* tabaccaio/a; ~**'s (shop)** tabaccheria.

Tobago [tə'beɪgəʊ] *n see* **Trinidad**.

toboggan [tə'bɔgən] *n* toboga *m inv*; (*child's*) slitta.

today [tə'deɪ] *ad, n* (*also fig*) oggi (*m inv*); **what day is it** ~**?** che giorno è oggi?; **what date is it** ~**?** quanti ne abbiamo oggi?; ~ **is the 4th of March** (oggi) è il 4 di marzo; ~**'s paper** il giornale di oggi; **a fortnight** ~ quindici giorni a oggi.

toddler ['tɔdlə*] *n* bambino/a che impara a camminare.

toddy ['tɔdɪ] *n* grog *m inv*.

to-do [tə'duː] *n* (*fuss*) storie *fpl*.

toe [təʊ] *n* dito del piede; (*of shoe*) punta ♦ *vt*: **to** ~ **the line** (*fig*) stare in riga, conformarsi; **big** ~ alluce *m*; **little** ~ mignolino.

toehold ['təʊhəʊld] *n* punto d'appoggio.

toenail ['təʊneɪl] *n* unghia del piede.

toffee ['tɔfɪ] *n* caramella.

toffee apple *n* (*Brit*) mela caramellata.

toga ['təʊgə] *n* toga.

together [tə'gɛðə*] *ad* insieme; (*at same time*) allo stesso tempo; ~ **with** insieme a.

togetherness [tə'gɛðənɪs] *n* solidarietà;

intimità.

toggle switch ['tɔgl-] n (COMPUT) tasto bi-
stabile.

Togo ['təugəu] n Togo.

togs [tɔgz] npl (col: clothes) vestiti mpl.

toil [tɔil] n travaglio, fatica ♦ vi affannarsi;
sgobbare.

toilet ['tɔilət] n (Brit: lavatory) gabinetto ♦
cpd (bag, soap etc) da toletta; **to go to the**
~ andare al gabinetto or al bagno.

toilet bag n (Brit) nécessaire m inv da
toilette.

toilet bowl n vaso or tazza del gabinetto.

toilet paper n carta igienica.

toiletries ['tɔilitriz] npl articoli mpl da toletta.

toilet roll n rotolo di carta igienica.

toilet water n acqua di colonia.

to-ing and fro-ing ['tu:iŋən'frəuiŋ] n (Brit)
andirivieni m inv.

token ['təukən] n (sign) segno; (voucher)
buono ♦ cpd (fee, strike) simbolico(a);
book/record ~ (Brit) buono-libro/-disco; **by
the same** ~ (fig) per lo stesso motivo.

Tokyo ['təukjəu] n Tokyo f.

told [təuld] pt, pp of **tell**.

tolerable ['tɔlərəbl] a (bearable) tollerabile;
(fairly good) passabile.

tolerably ['tɔlərəbli] ad (good, comfortable)
abbastanza.

tolerance ['tɔlərns] n (also TECH) tolleranza.

tolerant ['tɔlərnt] a: ~ (of) tollerante (nei confronti di).

tolerate ['tɔləreit] vt sopportare; (MED, TECH)
tollerare.

toleration [tɔlə'reifən] n tolleranza.

toll [təul] n (tax, charge) pedaggio ♦ vi (bell)
suonare; **the accident** ~ **on the roads** il
numero delle vittime della strada.

tollbridge ['təulbridʒ] n ponte m a pedaggio.

tomato, ~es [tə'mɑ:təu] n pomodoro.

tomb [tu:m] n tomba.

tombola [tɔm'bəulə] n tombola.

tomboy ['tɔmbɔi] n maschiaccio.

tombstone ['tu:mstəun] n pietra tombale.

tomcat ['tɔmkæt] n gatto.

tomorrow [tə'mɔrəu] ad, n (also fig) domani
(m inv); **the day after** ~ dopodomani; **a
week** ~ domani a otto; ~ **morning** domani
mattina.

ton [tʌn] n tonnellata (Brit: = 1016 kg; 20 cwt;
US = 907 kg; metric = 1000 kg); (NAUT:
also: **register** ~) tonnellata di stazza (= 2.83
cu.m; 100 cu. ft); ~**s of** (col) un mucchio or
sacco di.

tonal ['təunl] a tonale.

tone [təun] n tono; (of musical instrument)
timbro ♦ vi intonarsi.
  tone down vt (colour, criticism, sound)
attenuare.
  tone up vt (muscles) tonificare.

tone-deaf [təun'dɛf] a che non ha orecchio
(musicale).

toner ['təunə*] n (for photocopier) colorante m
organico, toner m.

Tonga ['tɔŋgə] n isole fpl Tonga.

tongs [tɔŋz] npl tenaglie fpl; (for coal) molle
fpl; (for hair) arricciacapelli m inv.

tongue [tʌŋ] n lingua; ~ **in cheek** (fig)
ironicamente.

tongue-tied ['tʌŋtaid] a (fig) muto(a).

tongue-twister ['tʌŋtwistə*] n scioglilingua m
inv.

tonic ['tɔnik] n (MED) ricostituente m; (skin
~) tonico; (MUS) nota tonica; (also: ~
water) acqua tonica.

tonight [tə'nait] ad stanotte; (this evening)
stasera ♦ n questa notte; questa sera; **I'll see
you** ~ ci vediamo stasera.

tonnage ['tʌnidʒ] n (NAUT) tonnellaggio,
stazza.

tonne [tʌn] n (Brit: metric ton) tonnellata.

tonsil ['tɔnsl] n tonsilla; **to have one's** ~**s out**
farsi operare di tonsille.

tonsillitis [tɔnsi'laitis] n tonsillite f; **to have** ~
avere la tonsillite.

too [tu:] ad (excessively) troppo; (also) anche; **it's** ~ **sweet** è troppo dolce; **I went** ~
ci sono andato anch'io; ~ **much** ad troppo ♦
a troppo(a); ~ **many** a troppi(e); ~ **bad!**
tanto peggio!; peggio così!

took [tuk] pt of **take**.

tool [tu:l] n utensile m, attrezzo; (fig: person)
strumento ♦ vt lavorare con un attrezzo.

tool box n cassetta f portautensili inv.

tool kit n cassetta di attrezzi.

toot [tu:t] vi suonare; (with car horn) suonare
il clacson.

tooth, pl **teeth** [tu:θ, ti:θ] n (ANAT, TECH)
dente m; **to clean one's teeth** lavarsi i
denti; **to have a** ~ **out** or (US) **pulled** farsi
togliere un dente; **by the skin of one's teeth**
per il rotto della cuffia.

toothache ['tu:θeik] n mal m di denti; **to
have** ~ avere il mal di denti.

toothbrush ['tu:θbrʌʃ] n spazzolino da denti.

toothpaste ['tu:θpeist] n dentifricio.

toothpick ['tu:θpik] n stuzzicadenti m inv.

tooth powder n dentifricio in polvere.

top [tɔp] n (of mountain, page, ladder) cima;
(of box, cupboard, table) sopra m inv, parte f
superiore; (lid: of box, jar) coperchio; (: of
bottle) tappo; (toy) trottola; (DRESS: blouse
etc) camicia (or maglietta etc); (of pyjamas)
giacca ♦ a più alto(a); (in rank) primo(a);
(best) migliore ♦ vt (exceed) superare; (be
first in) essere in testa a; **on** ~ **of** sopra, in
cima a; (in addition to) oltre a; **from** ~ **to
toe** (Brit) dalla testa ai piedi; **at the** ~ **of
the stairs/page/street** in cima alle scale/alla
pagina/alla strada; **the** ~ **of the milk** (Brit)
la panna; **at** ~ **speed** a tutta velocità; **at the**
~ **of one's voice** (fig) a squarciagola; **over
the** ~ (col: behaviour etc) eccessivo(a); **to
go over the** ~ esagerare.
  top up, (US) **top off** vt riempire.

topaz ['təupæz] n topazio.

topcoat ['tɔpkəut] n soprabito.

topflight ['tɔpflait] a di primaria importanza.

top floor n ultimo piano.
top hat n cilindro.
top-heavy [tɔp'hɛvɪ] a (object) con la parte superiore troppo pesante.
topic ['tɔpɪk] n argomento.
topical ['tɔpɪkəl] a d'attualità.
topless ['tɔplɪs] a (bather etc) col seno scoperto; ~ **swimsuit** topless m inv.
top-level ['tɔplɛvl] a (talks) ad alto livello.
topmost ['tɔpməust] a il(la) più alto(a).
topography [tə'pɔgrəfɪ] n topografia.
topping ['tɔpɪŋ] n (CULIN) guarnizione f.
topple ['tɔpl] vt rovesciare, far cadere ♦ vi cadere; traballare.
top-ranking ['tɔp'ræŋkɪŋ] a di massimo grado.
TOPS [tɔps] n abbr (Brit: = Training Opportunities Scheme) corsi di addestramento professionale per chi ha più di 19 anni.
top-secret ['tɔp'si:krɪt] a segretissimo(a).
top-security ['tɔpsɪ'kjuərɪtɪ] a (Brit) di massima sicurezza.
topsy-turvy ['tɔpsɪ'tə:vɪ] a, ad sottosopra (inv).
top-up ['tɔpʌp] n: would you like a ~? vuole che le riempia il bicchiere (or la tazza etc)?
torch [tɔ:tʃ] n torcia; (Brit: electric) lampadina tascabile.
tore [tɔ:*] pt of tear.
torment n ['tɔ:mɛnt] tormento ♦ vt [tɔ:'mɛnt] tormentare; (fig: annoy) infastidire.
torn [tɔ:n] pp of tear ♦ a: ~ **between** (fig) combattuto(a) tra.
tornado, ~es [tɔ:'neɪdəu] n tornado.
torpedo, ~es [tɔ:'pi:dəu] n siluro.
torpedo boat n motosilurante f.
torpor ['tɔ:pə*] n torpore m.
torque [tɔ:k] n coppia di torsione.
torrent ['tɔrnt] n torrente m.
torrential [tɔ'rɛnʃl] a torrenziale.
torrid ['tɔrɪd] a torrido(a); (fig) denso(a) di passione.
torso ['tɔ:səu] n torso.
tortoise ['tɔ:təs] n tartaruga.
tortoiseshell ['tɔ:təʃɛl] a di tartaruga.
tortuous ['tɔ:tjuəs] a tortuoso(a).
torture ['tɔ:tʃə*] n tortura ♦ vt torturare.
torturer ['tɔ:tʃərə*] n torturatore/trice.
Tory ['tɔ:rɪ] a tory inv, conservatore(trice) ♦ n tory m/f inv, conservatore/trice.
toss [tɔs] vt gettare, lanciare; (Brit: pancake) far saltare; (head) scuotere ♦ n (movement: of head etc) movimento brusco; (of coin) lancio; **to win/lose the** ~ vincere/perdere a testa o croce; (SPORT) vincere/perdere il sorteggio; **to** ~ **a coin** fare a testa o croce; **to** ~ **up for sth** fare a testa o croce per qc; **to** ~ **and turn** (in bed) girarsi e rigirarsi.
tot [tɔt] n (Brit: drink) bicchierino; (child) bimbo/a.
tot up vt (Brit: figures) sommare.
total ['təutl] a totale ♦ n totale m ♦ vt (add up) sommare; (amount to) ammontare a; **in** ~ in tutto.

totalitarian [təutælɪ'tɛərɪən] a totalitario(a).
totality [təu'tælɪtɪ] n totalità.
totally ['təutəlɪ] ad completamente.
tote bag ['təut-] n sporta.
totem pole ['təutəm-] n totem m inv.
totter ['tɔtə*] vi barcollare; (object, government) vacillare.
touch [tʌtʃ] n tocco; (sense) tatto; (contact) contatto; (FOOTBALL) fuori gioco m ♦ vt toccare; **a** ~ **of** (fig) un tocco di; un pizzico di; **to get in** ~ **with** mettersi in contatto con; **to lose** ~ (friends) perdersi di vista; **I'll be in** ~ mi farò sentire; **to be out of** ~ **with events** essere tagliato fuori; **the personal** ~ una nota personale; **to put the finishing** ~**es to sth** dare gli ultimi ritocchi a qc.
touch on vt fus (topic) sfiorare, accennare a.
touch up vt (improve) ritoccare.
touch-and-go ['tʌtʃən'gəu] a incerto(a); **it was** ~ **with the sick man** il malato era tra la vita e la morte.
touchdown ['tʌtʃdaun] n atterraggio; (on sea) ammaraggio; (US FOOTBALL) meta.
touched [tʌtʃt] a commosso(a); (col) tocco(a), toccato(a).
touching ['tʌtʃɪŋ] a commovente.
touchline ['tʌtʃlaɪn] n (SPORT) linea laterale.
touch-type ['tʌtʃtaɪp] vi dattilografare (senza guardare i tasti).
touchy ['tʌtʃɪ] a (person) suscettibile.
tough [tʌf] a duro(a); (resistant) resistente; (meat) duro(a), tiglioso(a); (journey) faticoso(a), duro(a); (person: rough) violento(a), brutale ♦ n (gangster etc) delinquente m/f; ~ **luck!** che sfortuna!
toughen ['tʌfn] vt indurire, rendere più resistente.
toughness ['tʌfnɪs] n durezza; resistenza.
toupee ['tu:peɪ] n parrucchino.
tour [tuə*] n viaggio; (also: package ~) viaggio organizzato or tutto compreso; (of town, museum) visita; (by artist) tournée f inv ♦ vt visitare; **to go on a** ~ **of** (region, country) fare il giro di; (museum, castle) visitare; **to go on** ~ andare in tournée.
touring ['tuərɪŋ] n turismo.
tourism ['tuərɪzəm] n turismo.
tourist ['tuərɪst] n turista m/f ♦ ad (travel) in classe turistica ♦ cpd turistico(a); **the** ~ **trade** il turismo.
tourist office n pro loco f inv.
tournament ['tuənəmənt] n torneo.
tourniquet ['tuənɪkeɪ] n (MED) laccio emostatico, pinza emostatica.
tour operator n (Brit) operatore m turistico.
tousled ['tauzld] a (hair) arruffato(a).
tout [taut] vi: **to** ~ **for** procacciare, raccogliere; cercare clienti per ♦ n (Brit: also: ticket ~) bagarino; **to** ~ **sth (around)** (Brit) cercare di (ri)vendere qc.
tow [təu] vt rimorchiare ♦ n rimorchio; "on ~", (US) "in ~" (AUT) "veicolo rimorchiato"; **to give sb a** ~ rimorchiare qn.

toward(s) [təˈwɔːd(z)] *prep* verso; (*of attitude*) nei confronti di; (*of purpose*) per; ~ **noon/the end of the year** verso mezzogiorno/la fine dell'anno; **to feel friendly** ~ **sb** provare un sentimento d'amicizia per qn.

towel [ˈtauəl] *n* asciugamano; (*also*: **tea** ~) strofinaccio; **to throw in the** ~ (*fig*) gettare la spugna.

towelling [ˈtauəlɪŋ] *n* (*fabric*) spugna.

towel rail, (*US*) **towel rack** *n* portasciugamano.

tower [ˈtauə*] *n* torre *f* ♦ *vi* (*building*, *mountain*) innalzarsi; **to** ~ **above** *or* **over sb/sth** sovrastare qn/qc.

tower block *n* (*Brit*) palazzone *m*.

towering [ˈtauərɪŋ] *a* altissimo(a), imponente.

towline [ˈtəulaɪn] *n* (cavo da) rimorchio.

town [taun] *n* città *f inv*; **to go to** ~ andare in città; (*fig*) mettercela tutta; **in (the)** ~ in città; **to be out of** ~ essere fuori città.

town centre *n* centro (città).

town clerk *n* segretario comunale.

town council *n* consiglio comunale.

town hall *n* ≈ municipio.

town plan *n* pianta della città.

town planner *n* urbanista *m/f*.

town planning *n* urbanistica.

townspeople [ˈtaunzpiːpl] *npl* cittadinanza, cittadini *mpl*.

towpath [ˈtəupɑːθ] *n* alzaia.

towrope [ˈtəurəup] *n* (cavo da) rimorchio.

tow truck *n* (*US*) carro m'attrezzi *inv*.

toxic [ˈtɔksɪk] *a* tossico(a).

toxin [ˈtɔksɪn] *n* tossina.

toy [tɔɪ] *n* giocattolo.

toy with *vt fus* giocare con; (*idea*) accarezzare, trastullarsi con.

toyshop [ˈtɔɪʃɔp] *n* negozio di giocattoli.

trace [treɪs] *n* traccia ♦ *vt* (*draw*) tracciare; (*follow*) seguire; (*locate*) rintracciare; **without** ~ (*disappear*) senza lasciare traccia; **there was no** ~ **of it** non ne restava traccia.

trace element *n* oligoelemento.

trachea [trəˈkɪə] *n* (*ANAT*) trachea.

tracing paper [ˈtreɪsɪŋ-] *n* carta da ricalco.

track [træk] *n* (*mark*: *of person*, *animal*) traccia; (*on tape*, *SPORT*; *path*: *gen*) pista; (: *of bullet etc*) traiettoria; (: *of suspect*, *animal*) pista, tracce *fpl*; (*RAIL*) binario, rotaie *fpl*; (*COMPUT*) traccia, pista ♦ *vt* seguire le tracce di; **to keep** ~ **of** seguire; **to be on the right** ~ (*fig*) essere sulla buona strada.

track down *vt* (*prey*) scovare; snidare; (*sth lost*) rintracciare.

tracker dog [ˈtrækə-] *n* (*Brit*) cane *m* poliziotto *inv*.

track events *npl* (*SPORT*) prove *fpl* su pista.

tracking station [ˈtrækɪŋ-] *n* (*SPACE*) osservatorio spaziale.

track record *n*: **to have a good** ~ (*fig*) avere un buon curriculum.

tracksuit [ˈtræksuːt] *n* tuta sportiva.

tract [trækt] *n* (*GEO*) tratto, estensione *f*;

(*pamphlet*) opuscolo, libretto; **respiratory** ~ (*ANAT*) apparato respiratorio.

traction [ˈtrækʃən] *n* trazione *f*.

tractor [ˈtræktə*] *n* trattore *m*.

tractor feed *n* (*on printer*) trascinamento a trattore.

trade [treɪd] *n* commercio; (*skill*, *job*) mestiere *m*; (*industry*) industria, settore *m* ♦ *vi* commerciare; **to** ~ **with/in** commerciare con/in; **foreign** ~ commercio estero; **Department of T**~ **and Industry** (**DTI**) (*Brit*) ≈ Ministero del Commercio.

trade in *vt* (*old car etc*) dare come pagamento parziale.

trade barrier *n* barriera commerciale.

trade deficit *n* bilancio commerciale in deficit.

Trade Descriptions Act *n* (*Brit*) legge *f* a tutela del consumatore.

trade discount *n* sconto sul listino.

trade fair *n* fiera campionaria.

trade-in [ˈtreɪdɪn] *n*: **to take as a** ~ accettare in permuta.

trade-in price *n* prezzo di permuta.

trademark [ˈtreɪdmɑːk] *n* marchio di fabbrica.

trade mission *n* missione *f* commerciale.

trade name *n* marca, nome *m* depositato.

trader [ˈtreɪdə*] *n* commerciante *m/f*.

trade secret *n* segreto di fabbricazione.

tradesman [ˈtreɪdzmən] *n* fornitore *m*; (*shopkeeper*) negoziante *m*.

trade union *n* sindacato.

trade unionist [-ˈjuːnjənɪst] *n* sindacalista *m/f*.

trade wind *n* aliseo.

trading [ˈtreɪdɪŋ] *n* commercio.

trading estate *n* (*Brit*) zona industriale.

trading stamp *n* bollo premio.

tradition [trəˈdɪʃən] *n* tradizione *f*; ~**s** *npl* tradizioni, usanze *fpl*.

traditional [trəˈdɪʃənl] *a* tradizionale.

traffic [ˈtræfɪk] *n* traffico ♦ *vi*: **to** ~ **in** (*pej*: *liquor*, *drugs*) trafficare in.

traffic circle *n* (*US*) isola rotatoria.

traffic island *n* salvagente *m*, isola *f* spartitraffico *inv*.

traffic jam *n* ingorgo (del traffico).

trafficker [ˈtræfɪkə*] *n* trafficante *m/f*.

traffic lights *npl* semaforo.

traffic offence *n* (*Brit*) infrazione *f* al codice stradale.

traffic sign *n* cartello stradale.

traffic violation *n* (*US*) = **traffic offence**.

traffic warden *n* addetto/a al controllo del traffico e del parcheggio.

tragedy [ˈtrædʒədɪ] *n* tragedia.

tragic [ˈtrædʒɪk] *a* tragico(a).

trail [treɪl] *n* (*tracks*) tracce *fpl*, pista; (*path*) sentiero; (*of smoke etc*) scia ♦ *vt* trascinare, strascicare; (*follow*) seguire ♦ *vi* essere al traino; (*dress etc*) strusciare; (*plant*) arrampicarsi; strisciare; **to be on sb's** ~ essere sulle orme di qn.

trail away, **trail off** *vi* (*sound*) affievolirsi;

(interest, voice) spegnersi a poco a poco.
trail behind *vi* essere al traino.
trailer ['treɪlə*] *n* *(AUT)* rimorchio; *(US)* roulotte *f inv*; *(CINEMA)* prossimamente *m inv*.
trailer truck *n* *(US)* autoarticolato.
train [treɪn] *n* treno; *(of dress)* coda, strascico; *(Brit: series)*: **~ of events** serie *f* di avvenimenti a catena ♦ *vt* *(apprentice, doctor etc)* formare; *(sportsman)* allenare; *(dog)* addestrare; *(memory)* esercitare; *(point: gun etc)*: **to ~ sth on** puntare qc contro ♦ *vi* formarsi; allenarsi; *(learn a skill)* fare pratica, fare tirocinio; **to go by ~** andare in or col treno; **one's ~ of thought** il filo dei propri pensieri; **to ~ sb to do sth** preparare qn a fare qc.
train attendant *n* *(US)* addetto/a ai vagoni letto.
trained [treɪnd] *a* qualificato(a); allenato(a); addestrato(a).
trainee [treɪ'ni:] *n* allievo/a; *(in trade)* apprendista *m/f*; **he's a ~ teacher** sta facendo tirocinio come insegnante.
trainer ['treɪnə*] *n* *(SPORT)* allenatore/trice; *(of dogs etc)* addestratore/trice; **~s** *npl* *(shoes)* scarpe *fpl* da ginnastica.
training ['treɪnɪŋ] *n* formazione *f*; allenamento; addestramento; **in ~** *(SPORT)* in allenamento; *(fit)* in forma.
training college *n* istituto professionale.
training course *n* corso di formazione professionale.
training shoes *npl* scarpe *fpl* da ginnastica.
traipse [treɪps] *vi*: **to ~ in/out** *etc* entrare/uscire *etc* trascinandosi.
trait [treɪt] *n* tratto.
traitor ['treɪtə*] *n* traditore *m*.
trajectory [trə'dʒɛktərɪ] *n* traiettoria.
tram [træm] *n* *(Brit: also: **~car**)* tram *m inv*.
tramline ['træmlaɪn] *n* linea tranviaria.
tramp [træmp] *n* *(person)* vagabondo/a; *(col: pej: woman)* sgualdrina ♦ *vi* camminare con passo pesante ♦ *vt* *(walk through: town, streets)* percorrere a piedi.
trample ['træmpl] *vt*: **to ~ (underfoot)** calpestare.
trampoline ['træmpəli:n] *n* trampolino.
trance [trɑ:ns] *n* trance *f inv*; *(MED)* catalessi *f inv*; **to go into a ~** cadere in trance.
tranquil ['træŋkwɪl] *a* tranquillo(a).
tranquillity, *(US)* **tranquility** [træŋ'kwɪlɪtɪ] *n* tranquillità.
tranquillizer, *(US)* **tranquilizer** ['træŋkwɪlaɪzə*] *n* *(MED)* tranquillante *m*.
transact [træn'zækt] *vt* *(business)* trattare.
transaction [træn'zækʃən] *n* transazione *f*; **~s** *npl* *(minutes)* atti *mpl*; **cash ~** operazione *f* in contanti.
transatlantic ['trænzət'læntɪk] *a* transatlantico(a).
transcend [træn'sɛnd] *vt* trascendere; *(excel over)* superare.
transcendental [trænsɛn'dɛntl] *a*: **~ medita-**

tion meditazione *f* trascendentale.
transcribe [træn'skraɪb] *vt* trascrivere.
transcript ['trænskrɪpt] *n* trascrizione *f*.
transcription [træn'skrɪpʃən] *n* trascrizione *f*.
transept ['trænsɛpt] *n* transetto.
transfer *n* ['trænsfə*] *(gen, also SPORT)* trasferimento; *(POL: of power)* passaggio; *(picture, design)* decalcomania; *(: stick-on)* autoadesivo ♦ *vt* [træns'fə:*] trasferire; passare; decalcare; **by bank ~** tramite trasferimento bancario; **to ~ the charges** *(Brit TEL)* telefonare con addebito al ricevente.
transferable [træns'fə:rəbl] *a* trasferibile; **not ~** non cedibile, personale.
transfix [træns'fɪks] *vt* trafiggere; *(fig)*: **~ed with fear** paralizzato dalla paura.
transform [træns'fɔ:m] *vt* trasformare.
transformation [trænsfə'meɪʃən] *n* trasformazione *f*.
transformer [træns'fɔ:mə*] *n* *(ELEC)* trasformatore *m*.
transfusion [træns'fju:ʒən] *n* trasfusione *f*.
transgress [træns'grɛs] *vt* *(go beyond)* infrangere; *(violate)* trasgredire, infrangere.
tranship [træn'ʃɪp] *vt* = **transship**.
transient ['trænzɪənt] *a* transitorio(a), fugace.
transistor [træn'zɪstə*] *n* *(ELEC)* transistor *m inv*; *(also: **~ radio**)* radio *f inv* a transistor.
transit ['trænzɪt] *n*: **in ~** in transito.
transit camp *n* campo (di raccolta) profughi.
transition [træn'zɪʃən] *n* passaggio, transizione *f*.
transitional [træn'zɪʃənl] *a* di transizione.
transitive ['trænzɪtɪv] *a* *(LING)* transitivo(a).
transit lounge *n* *(AVIAT)* sala di transito.
transitory ['trænzɪtərɪ] *a* transitorio(a).
translate [trænz'leɪt] *vt* tradurre; **to ~ (from/into)** tradurre (da/in).
translation [trænz'leɪʃən] *n* traduzione *f*; *(SCOL: as opposed to prose)* versione *f*.
translator [trænz'leɪtə*] *n* traduttore/trice.
translucent [trænz'lu:snt] *a* traslucido(a).
transmission [trænz'mɪʃən] *n* trasmissione *f*.
transmit [trænz'mɪt] *vt* trasmettere.
transmitter [trænz'mɪtə*] *n* trasmettitore *m*.
transparency [træns'pɛərnsɪ] *n* *(PHOT)* diapositiva.
transparent [træns'pærnt] *a* trasparente.
transpire [træns'paɪə*] *vi* *(happen)* succedere; **it finally ~d that ...** alla fine si è venuto a sapere che ....
transplant *vt* [træns'plɑ:nt] trapiantare ♦ *n* ['trænsplɑ:nt] trapianto; **to have a heart ~** subire un trapianto cardiaco.
transport *n* ['trænspɔ:t] trasporto ♦ *vt* [træns'pɔ:t] trasportare; **public ~** mezzi *mpl* pubblici; **Department of T~** *(Brit)* Ministero dei Trasporti.
transportation ['trænspɔ:'teɪʃən] *n* (mezzo di) trasporto; *(of prisoners)* deportazione *f*; **Department of T~** *(US)* Ministero dei Trasporti.
transport café *n* *(Brit)* trattoria per camionisti.

transpose [træns'pəuz] *vt* trasporre.
transship [træns'ʃɪp] *vt* trasbordare.
transverse ['trænzvə:s] *a* trasversale.
transvestite [trænz'vɛstaɪt] *n* travestito/a.

trap [træp] *n* (*snare*, *trick*) trappola; (*carriage*) calesse *m* ♦ *vt* prendere in trappola, intrappolare; (*immobilize*) bloccare; (*jam*) chiudere, schiacciare; **to set** *or* **lay a** ~ **(for sb)** tendere una trappola (a qn); **to** ~ **one's finger in the door** chiudersi il dito nella porta; **shut your** ~! (*col*) chiudi quella boccaccia!
trap door *n* botola.
trapeze [trə'pi:z] *n* trapezio.
trapper ['træpə*] *n* cacciatore *m* di animali da pelliccia.
trappings ['træpɪŋz] *npl* ornamenti *mpl*; indoratura, sfarzo.
trash [træʃ] *n* (*pej: goods*) ciarpame *m*; (: *nonsense*) sciocchezze *fpl*; (*US: rubbish*) rifiuti *mpl*, spazzatura.
trash can *n* (*US*) secchio della spazzatura.
trauma ['trɔ:mə] *n* trauma *m*.
traumatic [trɔ:'mætɪk] *a* (*PSYCH*, *fig*) traumatico(a), traumatizzante.
travel ['trævl] *n* viaggio; viaggi *mpl* ♦ *vi* viaggiare; (*move*) andare, spostarsi ♦ *vt* (*distance*) percorrere; **this wine doesn't** ~ **well** questo vino non resiste agli spostamenti.
travel agency *n* agenzia (di) viaggi.
travel agent *n* agente *m* di viaggio.
travel brochure *n* dépliant *m* di viaggi.
traveller, (*US*) **traveler** ['trævlə*] *n* viaggiatore/trice; (*COMM*) commesso viaggiatore.
traveller's cheque, (*US*) **traveler's check** *n* assegno turistico.
travelling, (*US*) **traveling** ['trævlɪŋ] *n* viaggi *mpl* ♦ *a* (*circus*, *exhibition*) itinerante ♦ *cpd* (*bag*, *clock*) da viaggio; (*expenses*) di viaggio.
travel(l)ing salesman *n* commesso viaggiatore.
travelogue ['trævəlɔg] *n* (*book*, *film*) diario *or* documentario di viaggio; (*talk*) conferenza sui viaggi.
travel sickness *n* mal *m* d'auto (*or* di mare *or* d'aria).
traverse ['trævəs] *vt* traversare, attraversare.
travesty ['trævɪstɪ] *n* parodia.
trawler ['trɔ:lə*] *n* peschereccio (a strascico).
tray [treɪ] *n* (*for carrying*) vassoio; (*on desk*) vaschetta.
treacherous ['trɛtʃərəs] *a* traditore(trice); **road conditions today are** ~ oggi il fondo stradale è pericoloso.
treachery ['trɛtʃərɪ] *n* tradimento.
treacle ['tri:kl] *n* melassa.
tread [trɛd] *n* passo; (*sound*) rumore *m* di passi; (*of tyre*) battistrada *m inv* ♦ *vi* (*pt trod*, *pp* **trodden** [trɔd, 'trɔdn]) camminare.
tread on *vt fus* calpestare.
treadle ['trɛdl] *n* pedale *m*.
treas. *abbr* = **treasurer**.
treason ['tri:zn] *n* tradimento.

treasure ['trɛʒə*] *n* tesoro ♦ *vt* (*value*) tenere in gran conto, apprezzare molto; (*store*) custodire gelosamente.
treasure hunt *n* caccia al tesoro.
treasurer [trɛʒərə*] *n* tesoriere/a.
treasury ['trɛʒərɪ] *n* tesoreria; (*POL*): **the T~**, (*US*) **the T~ Department** ≈ il Ministero del Tesoro.
treasury bill *n* buono del tesoro.
treat [tri:t] *n* regalo ♦ *vt* trattare; (*MED*) curare; (*consider*) considerare; **it was a** ~ **mi** (*or* ci *etc*) ha fatto veramente piacere; **to** ~ **sb to sth** offrire qc a qn; **to** ~ **sth as a joke** considerare qc uno scherzo.
treatise ['tri:tɪz] *n* trattato.
treatment ['tri:tmənt] *n* trattamento; **to have** ~ **for sth** (*MED*) farsi curare qc.
treaty ['tri:tɪ] *n* patto, trattato.
treble [trɛbl] *a* triplo(a), triplice ♦ *n* (*MUS*) soprano *m/f* ♦ *vt* triplicare ♦ *vi* triplicarsi.
treble clef *n* chiave *f* di violino.
tree [tri:] *n* albero.
tree-lined ['tri:laɪnd] *a* fiancheggiato(a) da alberi.
treetop ['tri:tɔp] *n* cima di un albero.
tree trunk *n* tronco d'albero.
trek [trɛk] *n* (*hike*) spedizione *f*; (*tiring walk*) camminata sfiancante ♦ *vi* (*as holiday*) fare dell'escursionismo.
trellis ['trɛlɪs] *n* graticcio, pergola.
tremble ['trɛmbl] *vi* tremare; (*machine*) vibrare.
trembling ['trɛmblɪŋ] *n* tremito ♦ *a* tremante.
tremendous [trɪ'mɛndəs] *a* (*enormous*) enorme; (*excellent*) meraviglioso(a), formidabile.
tremendously [trɪ'mɛndəslɪ] *ad* incredibilmente; **he enjoyed it** ~ gli è piaciuto da morire.
tremor [trɛmə*] *n* tremore *m*, tremito; (*also: earth* ~) scossa sismica.
trench [trɛntʃ] *n* trincea.
trench coat *n* trench *m inv*.
trench warfare *n* guerra di trincea.
trend [trɛnd] *n* (*tendency*) tendenza; (*of events*) corso; (*fashion*) moda; ~ **towards/ away from** tendenza a/ad allontanarsi da; **to set the** ~ essere all'avanguardia; **to set a** ~ lanciare una moda.
trendy ['trɛndɪ] *a* (*idea*) di moda; (*clothes*) all'ultima moda.
trepidation [trɛpɪ'deɪʃən] *n* trepidazione *f*, agitazione *f*.
trespass ['trɛspəs] *vi*: **to** ~ **on** entrare abusivamente in; (*fig*) abusare di; "**no** ~**ing**" "proprietà privata", "vietato l'accesso".
trespasser ['trɛspəsə*] *n* trasgressore *m*; "~**s will be prosecuted**" "i trasgressori saranno puniti secondo i termini di legge".
tress [trɛs] *n* ciocca di capelli.
trestle ['trɛsl] *n* cavalletto.
trestle table *n* tavola su cavalletti.
trial ['traɪəl] *n* (*LAW*) processo; (*test: of*

machine etc) collaudo; (*hardship*) prova, difficoltà *f inv*; (*worry*) cruccio; **~s** *npl* (*ATHLETICS*) prove *fpl* di qualificazione; **horse ~s** concorso ippico; **to be on ~** essere sotto processo; **~ by jury** processo penale con giuria; **to be sent for ~** essere rinviato a giudizio; **to bring sb to ~ (for a crime)** portare qn in giudizio (per un reato); **by ~ and error** a tentoni.

trial balance *n* (*COMM*) bilancio di verifica.

trial basis *n*: **on a ~** in prova.

trial run *n* periodo di prova.

triangle ['traɪæŋgl] *n* (*MATH, MUS*) triangolo.

triangular [traɪ'æŋgjulə*] *a* triangolare.

tribal ['traɪbəl] *a* tribale.

tribe [traɪb] *n* tribù *f inv*.

tribesman ['traɪbzmən] *n* membro della tribù.

tribulation [trɪbju'leɪʃən] *n* tribolazione *f*.

tribunal [traɪ'bju:nl] *n* tribunale *m*.

tributary ['trɪbju:tərɪ] *n* (*river*) tributario, affluente *m*.

tribute ['trɪbju:t] *n* tributo, omaggio; **to pay ~ to** rendere omaggio a.

trice [traɪs] *n*: **in a ~** in un attimo.

trick [trɪk] *n* trucco; (*clever act*) stratagemma *m*; (*joke*) tiro; (*CARDS*) presa ♦ *vt* imbrogliare, ingannare; **to play a ~ on sb** giocare un tiro a qn; **it's a ~ of the light** è un effetto ottico; **that should do the ~** (*col*) vedrai che funziona; **to ~ sb into doing sth** convincere qn a fare qc con l'inganno; **to ~ sb out of sth** fregare qc a qn.

trickery ['trɪkərɪ] *n* inganno.

trickle ['trɪkl] *n* (*of water etc*) rivolo; gocciolio ♦ *vi* gocciolare; **to ~ in/out** (*people*) entrare/uscire alla spicciolata.

trick question *n* domanda *f* trabocchetto *inv*.

trickster ['trɪkstə*] *n* imbroglione/a.

tricky ['trɪkɪ] *a* difficile, delicato(a).

tricycle ['traɪsɪkl] *n* triciclo.

trifle ['traɪfl] *n* sciocchezza; (*Brit CULIN*) ≈ zuppa inglese ♦ *ad*: **a ~ long** un po' lungo ♦ *vi*: **to ~ with** prendere alla leggera.

trifling ['traɪflɪŋ] *a* insignificante.

trigger ['trɪgə*] *n* (*of gun*) grilletto.

trigger off *vt* dare l'avvio a.

trigonometry [trɪgə'nɔmətrɪ] *n* trigonometria.

trilby ['trɪlbɪ] *n* (*Brit: also:* **~ hat**) cappello floscio di feltro.

trill [trɪl] *n* (*of bird, MUS*) trillo.

trilogy ['trɪlədʒɪ] *n* trilogia.

trim [trɪm] *a* ordinato(a); (*house, garden*) ben tenuto(a); (*figure*) snello(a) ♦ *n* (*haircut etc*) spuntata, regolata; (*embellishment*) finiture *fpl*; (*on car*) guarnizioni *fpl* ♦ *vt* spuntare; (*decorate*): **to ~ (with)** decorare (con); (*NAUT: a sail*) orientare; **to keep in (good) ~** mantenersi in forma.

trimmings ['trɪmɪŋz] *npl* decorazioni *fpl*; (*extras: gen CULIN*) guarnizione *f*.

Trinidad and Tobago ['trɪnɪdæd-] *n* Trinidad e Tobago *m*.

Trinity ['trɪnɪtɪ] *n*: **the ~** la Trinità.

trinket ['trɪŋkɪt] *n* gingillo; (*piece of*

jewellery) ciondolo.

trio ['tri:əu] *n* trio.

trip [trɪp] *n* viaggio; (*excursion*) gita, escursione *f*; (*stumble*) passo falso ♦ *vi* inciampare; (*go lightly*) camminare con passo leggero; **on a ~** in viaggio.

trip up *vi* inciampare ♦ *vt* fare lo sgambetto a.

tripartite [traɪ'pɑ:taɪt] *a* (*agreement*) tripartito(a); (*talks*) a tre.

tripe [traɪp] *n* (*CULIN*) trippa; (*pej: rubbish*) sciocchezze *fpl*, fesserie *fpl*.

triple ['trɪpl] *a* triplo(a) ♦ *ad*: **~ the distance/the speed** tre volte più lontano/più veloce.

triplets ['trɪplɪts] *npl* bambini(e) trigemini(e).

triplicate ['trɪplɪkət] *n*: **in ~** in triplice copia.

tripod ['traɪpɔd] *n* treppiede *m*.

Tripoli ['trɪpəlɪ] *n* Tripoli *f*.

tripper ['trɪpə*] *n* (*Brit*) gitante *m/f*.

tripwire ['trɪpwaɪə*] *n* filo in tensione che fa scattare una trappola, allarme etc.

trite [traɪt] *a* banale, trito(a).

triumph ['traɪʌmf] *n* trionfo ♦ *vi*: **to ~ (over)** trionfare (su).

triumphal [traɪ'ʌmfl] *a* trionfale.

triumphant [traɪ'ʌmfənt] *a* trionfante.

trivia ['trɪvɪə] *npl* banalità *fpl*.

trivial ['trɪvɪəl] *a* (*matter*) futile; (*excuse, comment*) banale; (*amount*) irrisorio(a); (*mistake*) di poco conto.

triviality [trɪvɪ'ælɪtɪ] *n* frivolezza; (*trivial detail*) futilità.

trivialize ['trɪvɪəlaɪz] *vt* sminuire.

trod [trɔd] *pt of* **tread.**

trodden ['trɔdn] *pp of* **tread.**

trolley ['trɔlɪ] *n* carrello; (*in hospital*) lettiga.

trolley bus *n* filobus *m inv*.

trollop ['trɔləp] *n* prostituta.

trombone [trɔm'bəun] *n* trombone *m*.

troop [tru:p] *n* gruppo; (*MIL*) squadrone *m*; **~s** *npl* (*MIL*) truppe *fpl*; **~ing the colour** (*Brit: ceremony*) sfilata della bandiera.

troop in *vi* entrare a frotte.

troop out *vi* uscire a frotte.

troop carrier *n* (*plane*) aereo per il trasporto (di) truppe; (*NAUT: also:* **troopship**) nave *f* per il trasporto (di) truppe.

trooper ['tru:pə*] *n* (*MIL*) soldato di cavalleria; (*US: policeman*) poliziotto (della polizia di stato).

troopship ['tru:pʃɪp] *n* nave *f* per il trasporto (di) truppe.

trophy ['trəufɪ] *n* trofeo.

tropic ['trɔpɪk] *n* tropico; **in the ~s** ai tropici; **T~ of Cancer/Capricorn** tropico del Cancro/Capricorno.

tropical ['trɔpɪkəl] *a* tropicale.

trot [trɔt] *n* trotto ♦ *vi* trottare; **on the ~** (*Brit fig*) di fila, uno(a) dopo l'altro(a).

trot out *vt* (*excuse, reason*) tirar fuori; (*names, facts*) recitare di fila.

trouble ['trʌbl] *n* (*problems*) difficoltà *fpl*, problemi *mpl*; (*worry*) preoccupazione *f*; (*bother, effort*) sforzo; (*with sth mechanical*) noie *fpl*; (*POL*) conflitti *mpl*, disordine *m*; (*MED*): **stomach** *etc* ~ disturbi *mpl* gastrici *etc* ♦ *vt* disturbare; (*worry*) preoccupare ♦ *vi*: **to ~ to do** disturbarsi a fare; **~s** *npl* (*POL etc*) disordini *mpl*; **to be in ~** avere dei problemi; (*for doing wrong*) essere nei guai; **to go to the ~ of doing** darsi la pena di fare; **it's no ~**! di niente!; **what's the ~?** cosa c'è che non va?; **the ~ is ...** c'è che ..., il guaio è che ...; **to have ~ doing sth** avere delle difficoltà a fare qc; **please don't ~ yourself** non si disturbi.

troubled ['trʌbld] *a* (*person*) preoccupato(a), inquieto(a); (*epoch, life*) agitato(a), difficile.

trouble-free ['trʌblfri:] *a* senza problemi.

troublemaker ['trʌblmeɪkə*] *n* elemento disturbatore, agitatore/trice.

troubleshooter ['trʌblʃu:tə*] *n* (*in conflict*) conciliatore *m*.

troublesome ['trʌblsəm] *a* fastidioso(a), seccante.

trouble spot *n* zona calda.

trough [trɔf] *n* (*also*: **drinking ~**) abbeveratoio; (*also*: **feeding ~**) trogolo, mangiatoia; (*channel*) canale *m*; **~ of low pressure** (*METEOROLOGY*) depressione *f*.

trounce [trauns] *vt* (*defeat*) sgominare.

troupe [tru:p] *n* troupe *f inv*.

trouser press *n* stirapantaloni *m inv*.

trousers ['trauzəz] *npl* pantaloni *mpl*, calzoni *mpl*; **short ~** (*Brit*) calzoncini *mpl*.

trouser suit *n* (*Brit*) completo *m or* tailleur *m inv* pantalone *inv*.

trousseau, *pl* **~x** *or* **~s** ['tru:səu, -z] *n* corredo da sposa.

trout [traut] *n* (*pl inv*) trota.

trowel ['trauəl] *n* cazzuola.

truant ['truənt] *n*: **to play ~** (*Brit*) marinare la scuola.

truce [tru:s] *n* tregua.

truck [trʌk] *n* autocarro, camion *m inv*; (*RAIL*) carro merci aperto; (*for luggage*) carrello *m* portabagagli *inv*.

truck driver, (*US*) **trucker** ['trʌkə*] *n* camionista *m/f*.

truck farm *n* (*US*) orto industriale.

trucking ['trʌkɪŋ] *n* (*esp US*) autotrasporto.

trucking company *n* (*esp US*) impresa di trasporti.

truculent ['trʌkjulənt] *a* aggressivo(a), brutale.

trudge [trʌdʒ] *vi* trascinarsi pesantemente.

true [tru:] *a* vero(a); (*accurate*) accurato(a), esatto(a); (*genuine*) reale; (*faithful*) fedele; (*wall, beam*) a piombo; (*wheel*) centrato(a); **to come ~** avverarsi; **~ to life** verosimile.

truffle ['trʌfl] *n* tartufo.

truly ['tru:lɪ] *ad* veramente; (*truthfully*) sinceramente; (*faithfully*) fedelmente; **yours ~** (*in letter-writing*) distinti saluti.

trump [trʌmp] *n* (*CARDS*) atout *m inv*; **to turn up ~s** (*fig*) fare miracoli.

trump card *n* atout *m inv*; (*fig*) asso nella manica.

trumped-up [trʌmp'ʌp] *a* inventato(a).

trumpet ['trʌmpɪt] *n* tromba.

truncated [trʌŋ'keɪtɪd] *a* tronco(a).

truncheon ['trʌntʃən] *n* sfollagente *m inv*.

trundle ['trʌndl] *vt*, *vi*: **to ~ along** rotolare rumorosamente.

trunk [trʌŋk] *n* (*of tree, person*) tronco; (*of elephant*) proboscide *f*; (*case*) baule *m*; (*US AUT*) bagagliaio.

trunk call *n* (*Brit TEL*) (telefonata) interurbana.

trunk road *n* (*Brit*) strada principale.

trunks [trʌŋks] *npl* (*also*: **swimming ~**) calzoncini *mpl* da bagno.

truss [trʌs] *n* (*MED*) cinto erniario ♦ *vt*: **to ~ (up)** (*CULIN*) legare.

trust [trʌst] *n* fiducia; (*LAW*) amministrazione *f* fiduciaria; (*COMM*) trust *m inv* ♦ *vt* (*have confidence in*) fidarsi di; (*rely on*) contare su; (*entrust*): **to ~ sth to sb** affidare qc a qn; (*hope*): **to ~ (that)** sperare (che); **you'll have to take it on ~** deve credermi sulla parola; **in ~** (*LAW*) in amministrazione fiduciaria.

trust company *n* trust *m inv*.

trusted ['trʌstɪd] *a* fidato(a).

trustee [trʌs'ti:] *n* (*LAW*) amministratore(trice) fiduciario(a); (*of school etc*) amministratore/trice.

trustful ['trʌstful] *a* fiducioso(a).

trust fund *n* fondo fiduciario.

trusting ['trʌstɪŋ] *a* = **trustful**.

trustworthy ['trʌstwə:ðɪ] *a* fidato(a), degno(a) di fiducia.

trusty ['trʌstɪ] *a* fidato(a).

truth, **~s** [tru:θ, tru:ðz] *n* verità *f inv*.

truthful ['tru:θful] *a* (*person*) sincero(a); (*description*) veritiero(a), esatto(a).

truthfully ['tru:θfəlɪ] *ad* sinceramente.

truthfulness ['tru:θfəlnɪs] *n* veracità.

try [traɪ] *n* prova, tentativo; (*RUGBY*) meta ♦ *vt* (*LAW*) giudicare; (*test: sth new*) provare; (*strain: patience, person*) mettere alla prova ♦ *vi* provare; **to ~ to do** provare a fare; (*seek*) cercare di fare; **to give sth a ~** provare qc; **to ~ one's (very) best** *or* **one's (very) hardest** mettercela tutta.

try on *vt* (*clothes*) provare, mettere alla prova; **to ~ it on** (*fig*) cercare di farla.

try out *vt* provare, mettere alla prova.

trying ['traɪŋ] *a* (*day, experience*) logorante, pesante; (*child*) difficile, insopportabile.

tsar [zɑ:*] *n* zar *m inv*.

T-shirt ['ti:ʃə:t] *n* maglietta.

T-square ['ti:skwɛə*] *n* riga a T.

TT *a abbr* (*Brit col*) = **teetotal** ♦ *abbr* (*US POST*) = Trust Territory.

tub [tʌb] *n* tinozza; mastello; (*bath*) bagno.

tuba ['tju:bə] *n* tuba.

tubby ['tʌbɪ] *a* grassoccio(a).

tube [tju:b] *n* tubo; (*Brit*: *underground*) metropolitana; (*for tyre*) camera d'aria; (*col*: *television*): **the ~** la tele.

tubeless ['tju:blɪs] *a* (*tyre*) senza camera

d'aria.

tuber ['tju:bə*] n (BOT) tubero.
tuberculosis (TB) [tjubə:kju'ləusɪs] n tubercolosi f.
tube station n (Brit) stazione f del metrò.
tubing ['tju:bɪŋ] n tubazione f; **a piece of** ~ un tubo.
tubular ['tju:bjulə*] a tubolare.
TUC n abbr (Brit: = Trades Union Congress) confederazione f dei sindacati britannici.
tuck [tʌk] n (SEWING) piega ♦ vt (put) mettere.
   tuck away vt riporre.
   tuck in vt mettere dentro; (child) rimboccare ♦ vi (eat) mangiare di buon appetito; abbuffarsi.
   tuck up vt (child) rimboccare.
   tuck shop n negozio di pasticceria (in una scuola).
Tue(s). abbr (= Tuesday) mar.
Tuesday ['tju:zdɪ] n martedì m inv; **(the date) today is** ~ **23rd March** oggi è martedì 23 marzo; **on** ~ martedì; **on** ~**s** di martedì; **every** ~ tutti i martedì; **every other** ~ ogni due martedì; **last/next** ~ martedì scorso/ prossimo; ~ **next** martedì prossimo; **the following** ~ (in past) il martedì successivo; (in future) il martedì dopo; **a week/fortnight on** ~, ~ **week/fortnight** martedì fra una settimana/quindici giorni; **the** ~ **before last** martedì di due settimane fa; **the** ~ **after next** non questo martedì ma il prossimo; ~ **morning/lunchtime/afternoon/evening** martedì mattina/all'ora di pranzo/pomeriggio/ sera; ~ **night** martedì sera; (overnight) martedì notte; ~**'s newspaper** il giornale di martedì.
tuft [tʌft] n ciuffo.
tug [tʌg] n (ship) rimorchiatore m ♦ vt tirare con forza.
tug-of-war [tʌgəv'wɔ:*] n tiro alla fune.
tuition [tju:'ɪʃən] n (Brit: lessons) lezioni fpl; (US: fees) tasse fpl scolastiche (or universitarie).
tulip ['tju:lɪp] n tulipano.
tumble ['tʌmbl] n (fall) capitombolo ♦ vi capitombolare, ruzzolare; (somersault) fare capriole ♦ vt far cadere; **to** ~ **to sth** (col) realizzare qc.
tumbledown ['tʌmbldaun] n cadente, diroccato(a).
tumble dryer n (Brit) asciugatrice f.
tumbler ['tʌmblə*] n bicchiere m (senza stelo).
tummy ['tʌmɪ] n (col) pancia.
tumour, (US) **tumor** ['tju:mə*] n tumore m.
tumult ['tju:mʌlt] n tumulto.
tumultuous [tju:'mʌltjuəs] a tumultuoso(a).
tuna ['tju:nə] n (pl inv) (also: ~ **fish**) tonno.
tune [tju:n] n (melody) melodia, aria ♦ vt (MUS) accordare; (RADIO, TV, AUT) regolare, mettere a punto; **to be in/out of** ~ (instrument) essere accordato(a)/scordato(a); (singer) essere intonato(a)/stonato(a); **to the**

~ **of** (fig: amount) per la modesta somma di; **in** ~ **with** (fig) in accordo con.
   tune in vi (RADIO, TV): **to** ~ **in (to)** sintonizzarsi (su).
   tune up vi (musician) accordare lo strumento.
tuneful ['tju:nful] a melodioso(a).
tuner ['tju:nə*] n (radio set) sintonizzatore m; **piano** ~ accordatore/trice di pianoforte.
tuner amplifier n amplificatore m di sintonia.
tungsten ['tʌŋstn] n tungsteno.
tunic ['tju:nɪk] n tunica.
tuning ['tju:nɪŋ] n messa a punto.
tuning fork n diapason m inv.
Tunis ['tju:nɪs] n Tunisi f.
Tunisia [tju:'nɪzɪə] n Tunisia.
Tunisian [tju:'nɪzɪən] a, n tunisino(a).
tunnel ['tʌnl] n galleria ♦ vi scavare una galleria.
tunny ['tʌnɪ] n tonno.
turban ['tə:bən] n turbante m.
turbid ['tə:bɪd] a torbido(a).
turbine ['tə:baɪn] n turbina.
turbojet ['tə:bəu'dʒɛt] n turboreattore m.
turboprop ['tə:bəu'prɔp] n turboelica m inv.
turbot ['tə:bət] n (pl inv) rombo gigante.
turbulence ['tə:bjuləns] n turbolenza.
turbulent ['tə:bjulənt] a turbolento(a); (sea) agitato(a).
tureen [tə'ri:n] n zuppiera.
turf [tə:f] n terreno erboso; (clod) zolla ♦ vt coprire di zolle erbose; **the T**~ l'ippodromo.
   turf out vt (col) buttar fuori.
turf accountant n (Brit) allibratore m.
turgid ['tə:dʒɪd] a (speech) ampolloso(a), pomposo(a).
Turin [tjuə'rɪn] n Torino f.
Turk [tə:k] n turco/a.
Turkey ['tə:kɪ] n Turchia.
turkey ['tə:kɪ] n tacchino.
Turkish ['tə:kɪʃ] a turco(a) ♦ n (LING) turco.
Turkish bath n bagno turco.
Turkish delight n gelatine ricoperte di zucchero a velo.
turmeric ['tə:mərɪk] n curcuma.
turmoil ['tə:mɔɪl] n confusione f, tumulto.
turn [tə:n] n giro; (in road) curva; (tendency: of mind, events) tendenza; (performance) numero; (MED) crisi f inv, attacco ♦ vt girare, voltare; (milk) far andare a male; (shape: wood, metal) tornire; (change): **to** ~ **sth into** trasformare qc in ♦ vi girare; (person: look back) girarsi, voltarsi; (reverse direction) girarsi indietro; (change) cambiare; (become) diventare; **to** ~ **into** trasformarsi in; **a good** ~ un buon servizio; **a bad** ~ un brutto tiro; **it gave me quite a** ~ mi ha fatto prendere un bello spavento; **"no left** ~" (AUT) "divieto di svolta a sinistra"; **it's your** ~ tocca a lei; **in** ~ a sua volta; a turno; **to take** ~**s (at sth)** fare (qc) a turno; **at the** ~ **of the year/century** alla fine dell'anno/del secolo; **to take a** ~ **for the worse** (situation, events) volgere al peggio;

(*patient, health*) peggiorare; **to ~ left/right** girare a sinistra/destra.

turn about *vi* girarsi indietro.

turn away *vi* girarsi (dall'altra parte) ♦ *vt* (*reject: person*) mandar via; (*: business*) rifiutare.

turn back *vi* ritornare, tornare indietro.

turn down *vt* (*refuse*) rifiutare; (*reduce*) abbassare; (*fold*) ripiegare.

turn in (*col: go to bed*) andare a letto ♦ *vt* (*fold*) voltare in dentro.

turn off *vi* (*from road*) girare, voltare ♦ *vt* (*light, radio, engine etc*) spegnere.

turn on *vt* (*light, radio etc*) accendere; (*engine*) avviare.

turn out *vt* (*light, gas*) chiudere, spegnere; (*produce: goods*) produrre; (*: novel, good pupils*) creare ♦ *vi* (*appear, attend: troops, doctor etc*) presentarsi; **to ~ out to be ...** rivelarsi ..., risultare ....

turn over *vi* (*person*) girarsi; (*car etc*) capovolgersi ♦ *vt* girare.

turn round *vi* girare; (*person*) girarsi.

turn up *vi* (*person*) arrivare, presentarsi; (*lost object*) saltar fuori ♦ *vt* (*collar, sound, gas etc*) alzare.

turnabout ['tə:nəbaut], **turnaround** ['tə:nəraund] *n* (*fig*) dietrofront *m inv*.

turncoat ['tə:nkəut] *n* voltagabbana *m/f inv*.

turned-up ['tə:ndʌp] *a* (*nose*) all'insù.

turning ['tə:nɪŋ] *n* (*in road*) curva; (*side road*) strada laterale; **the first ~ on the right** la prima a destra.

turning circle *n* (*Brit*) diametro di sterzata.

turning point *n* (*fig*) svolta decisiva.

turning radius *n* (*US*) = **turning circle**.

turnip ['tə:nɪp] *n* rapa.

turnout ['tə:naut] *n* presenza, affluenza.

turnover ['tə:nəuvə*] *n* (*COMM: amount of money*) giro di affari; (*: of goods*) smercio; (*CULIN*): **apple** *etc* ~ sfogliatella alle mele *etc*; **there is a rapid ~ in staff** c'è un ricambio molto rapido di personale.

turnpike ['tə:npaɪk] *n* (*US*) autostrada a pedaggio.

turnstile ['tə:nstaɪl] *n* tornella.

turntable ['tə:nteɪbl] *n* (*on record player*) piatto.

turn-up ['tə:nʌp] *n* (*Brit: on trousers*) risvolto.

turpentine ['tə:pəntaɪn] *n* (*also:* **turps**) acqua ragia.

turquoise [tə:kwɔɪz] *n* (*stone*) turchese *m* ♦ *a* color turchese; di turchese.

turret ['tʌrɪt] *n* torretta.

turtle ['tə:tl] *n* testuggine *f*.

turtleneck (sweater) ['tə:tlnɛk-] *n* maglione *m* con il collo alto.

Tuscan ['tʌskən] *a, n* toscano(a).

Tuscany ['tʌskənɪ] *n* Toscana.

tusk [tʌsk] *n* zanna.

tussle ['tʌsl] *n* baruffa, mischia.

tutor ['tju:tə*] *n* (*in college*) docente *m/f* (*responsabile di un gruppo di studenti*); (*private teacher*) precettore *m*.

tutorial [tju:'tɔ:rɪəl] *n* (*SCOL*) lezione *f* con discussione (*a un gruppo limitato*).

tuxedo [tʌk'si:dəu] *n* (*US*) smoking *m inv*.

TV [ti:'vi:] *n abbr* (= *television*) tivù *f inv*.

twaddle ['twɔdl] *n* scemenze *fpl*.

twang [twæŋ] *n* (*of instrument*) suono vibrante; (*of voice*) accento nasale ♦ *vi* vibrare ♦ *vt* (*guitar*) pizzicare le corde di.

tweak [twi:k] *vt* (*nose*) pizzicare; (*ear, hair*) tirare.

tweed [twi:d] *n* tweed *m inv*.

tweezers ['twi:zəz] *npl* pinzette *fpl*.

twelfth [twɛlfθ] *num* dodicesimo(a).

Twelfth Night *n* la notte dell'Epifania.

twelve [twɛlv] *num* dodici; **at ~** alle dodici, a mezzogiorno; (*midnight*) a mezzanotte.

twentieth ['twɛntɪɪθ] *num* ventesimo(a).

twenty ['twɛntɪ] *num* venti.

twerp [twə:p] *n* (*col*) idiota *m/f*.

twice [twaɪs] *ad* due volte; **~ as much** due volte tanto; **~ a week** due volte alla settimana; **she is ~ your age** ha il doppio dei suoi anni.

twiddle ['twɪdl] *vt, vi:* **to ~ (with) sth** giocherellare con qc; **to ~ one's thumbs** (*fig*) girarsi i pollici.

twig [twɪg] *n* ramoscello ♦ *vt, vi* (*col*) capire.

twilight ['twaɪlaɪt] *n* (*evening*) crepuscolo; (*morning*) alba; **in the ~** nella penombra.

twill [twɪl] *n* spigato.

twin [twɪn] *a, n* gemello(a).

twin(-bedded) room ['twɪn('bɛdɪd)-] *n* stanza con letti gemelli.

twin beds *npl* letti *mpl* gemelli.

twin-carburettor ['twɪnka:bju'rɛtə*] *a* a doppio carburatore.

twine [twaɪn] *n* spago, cordicella ♦ *vi* (*plant*) attorcigliarsi; (*road*) serpeggiare.

twin-engined [twɪn'ɛndʒɪnd] *a* a due motori; **~ aircraft** bimotore *m*.

twinge [twɪndʒ] *n* (*of pain*) fitta; **a ~ of conscience/regret** un rimorso/rimpianto.

twinkle ['twɪŋkl] *n* scintillio ♦ *vi* scintillare; (*eyes*) brillare.

twin town *n* città *f inv* gemella.

twirl [twə:l] *n* piroetta ♦ *vt* far roteare ♦ *vi* roteare.

twist [twɪst] *n* torsione *f*; (*in wire, flex*) storta; (*in story*) colpo di scena; (*bend*) svolta, piega ♦ *vt* attorcigliare; (*weave*) intrecciare; (*roll around*) arrotolare; (*fig*) deformare ♦ *vi* attorcigliarsi; arrotolarsi; (*road*) serpeggiare; **to ~ one's ankle/wrist** (*MED*) slogarsi la caviglia/il polso.

twisted ['twɪstɪd] *a* (*wire, rope*) attorcigliato(a); (*ankle, wrist*) slogato(a); (*fig: logic, mind*) contorto(a).

twit [twɪt] *n* (*col*) minchione/a.

twitch [twɪtʃ] *n* tiratina; (*nervous*) tic *m inv* ♦ *vi* contrarsi; avere un tic.

two [tu:] *num* due; **~ by ~**, **in ~s** a due a due; **to put ~ and ~ together** (*fig*) trarre le conclusioni.

two-door [tu:'dɔ:*] *a* (*AUT*) a due porte.

two-faced ['tu:'feɪst] a (pej: person) falso(a).
twofold ['tu:fəuld] ad: **to increase** ~ aumentare del doppio ♦ a (increase) doppio(a); (reply) in due punti.
two-piece ['tu:'pi:s] n (also: ~ **suit**) due pezzi m inv; (also: ~ **swimsuit**) (costume m da bagno a) due pezzi m inv.
two-seater ['tu:'si:tə*] n (plane) biposto; (car) macchina a due posti.
twosome ['tu:səm] n (people) coppia.
two-stroke ['tu:strəuk] n (engine) due tempi m inv ♦ a a due tempi.
two-tone ['tu:təun] a (colour) bicolore.
two-way ['tu:weɪ] a (traffic) a due sensi; ~ **radio** radio f inv ricetrasmittente.
TX abbr (US POST) = Texas.
tycoon [taɪ'ku:n] n: (business) ~ magnate m.
type [taɪp] n (category) genere m; (model) modello; (example) tipo; (TYP) tipo, carattere m ♦ vt (letter etc) battere (a macchina), dattilografare; **what** ~ **do you want?** che tipo vuole?; **in bold/italic** ~ in grassetto/corsivo.
type-cast ['taɪpkɑ:st] a (actor) a ruolo fisso.
typeface ['taɪpfeɪs] n carattere m tipografico.
typescript ['taɪpskrɪpt] n dattiloscritto.
typeset ['taɪpsɛt] vt comporre.
typesetter ['taɪpsɛtə*] n compositore m.
typewriter ['taɪpraɪtə*] n macchina da scrivere.
typewritten ['taɪprɪtn] a dattiloscritto(a), battuto(a) a macchina.
typhoid ['taɪfɔɪd] n tifoidea.
typhoon [taɪ'fu:n] n tifone m.
typhus ['taɪfəs] n tifo.
typical ['tɪpɪkl] a tipico(a).
typify ['tɪpɪfaɪ] vt essere tipico(a) di.
typing ['taɪpɪŋ] n dattilografia.
typing error n errore m di battitura.
typing pool n ufficio m dattilografia inv.
typist ['taɪpɪst] n dattilografo/a.
typo ['taɪpəu] n abbr (col: = typographical error) refuso.
typography [taɪ'pɒgrəfɪ] n tipografia.
tyranny ['tɪrənɪ] n tirannia.
tyrant ['taɪərnt] n tiranno.
tyre, (US) **tire** ['taɪə*] n pneumatico, gomma.
tyre pressure n pressione f (delle gomme).
Tyrol [tɪ'rəul] n Tirolo.
Tyrolean [tɪrə'li:ən], **Tyrolese** [tɪrə'li:z] a, n tirolese (m/f).
Tyrrhenian Sea [tɪ'ri:nɪən-] n: **the** ~ il mar Tirreno.
tzar [zɑ:*] n = **tsar**.

U

U, u [ju:] n (letter) U, u m or f inv; **U for Uncle** ≈ U come Udine.
U n abbr (Brit CINEMA: = universal) per tutti.
UAW n abbr (US: = United Automobile Workers) sindacato degli operai automobilistici.
UB40 n abbr (Brit: = unemployment benefit form 40) modulo per la richiesta del sussidio di disoccupazione.
U-bend ['ju:bɛnd] n (in pipe) sifone m.
ubiquitous [ju:'bɪkwɪtəs] a onnipresente.
UCCA ['ʌkə] n abbr (Brit: = Universities Central Council on Admissions) organo centrale per la registrazione delle iscrizioni universitarie.
UDA n abbr (Brit: = Ulster Defence Association) organizzazione paramilitare protestante.
UDC n abbr (Brit) = Urban District Council.
udder ['ʌdə*] n mammella.
UDI abbr (Brit POL) = unilateral declaration of independence.
UDR n abbr (Brit: = Ulster Defence Regiment) reggimento dell'esercito britannico in Irlanda del Nord.
UEFA [ju:'eɪfə] n abbr (= Union of European Football Associations) U.E.F.A. f.
UFO ['ju:fəu] n abbr (= unidentified flying object) UFO m inv.
Uganda [ju:'gændə] n Uganda.
Ugandan [ju:'gændən] a, n ugandese (m/f).
UGC n abbr (Brit: = University Grants Committee) organo che autorizza sovvenzioni alle università.
ugh [ə:h] excl puah!
ugliness ['ʌglɪnɪs] n bruttezza.
ugly ['ʌglɪ] a brutto(a).
UHF abbr = ultra-high frequency.
UHT a abbr (= ultra-heat treated): ~ **milk** n latte m UHT.
UK n abbr see **United Kingdom**.
ulcer ['ʌlsə*] n ulcera; **mouth** ~ afta.
Ulster ['ʌlstə*] n Ulster m.
ulterior [ʌl'tɪərɪə*] a ulteriore; ~ **motive** secondo fine m.
ultimata [ʌltɪ'meɪtə] npl of **ultimatum**.
ultimate ['ʌltɪmɪt] a ultimo(a), finale; (authority) massimo(a), supremo(a) ♦ n: **the** ~ **in luxury** il non plus ultra del lusso.
ultimately ['ʌltɪmɪtlɪ] ad alla fine; in definitiva, in fin dei conti.
ultimatum, pl ~**s** or **ultimata** [ʌltɪ'meɪtəm, -tə] n ultimatum m inv.
ultrasonic [ʌltrə'sɒnɪk] a ultrasonico(a).

ultrasound [ˈʌltrəˈsaund] *n* (*MED*) ecografia.
ultraviolet [ˈʌltrəˈvaiəlit] *a* ultravioletto(a).
umbilical [ʌmˈbilikl] *a*: ~ **cord** cordone *m* ombelicale.
umbrage [ˈʌmbridʒ] *n*: **to take** ~ offendersi, impermalirsi.
umbrella [ʌmˈbrɛlə] *n* ombrello; **under the** ~ **of** (*fig*) sotto l'egida di.
umpire [ˈʌmpaiə*] *n* arbitro.
umpteen [ʌmpˈtiːn] *a* non so quanti(e); **for the** ~**th time** per l'ennesima volta.
UMW *n abbr* (= *United Mineworkers of America*) *unione dei minatori d'America*.
UN *n abbr see* **United Nations**.
unabashed [ʌnəˈbæʃt] *a* imperturbato(a).
unabated [ʌnəˈbeitid] *a* non diminuito(a).
unable [ʌnˈeibl] *a*: **to be** ~ **to** non potere, essere nell'impossibilità di; (*not to know how to*) essere incapace di, non sapere.
unabridged [ʌnəˈbridʒd] *a* integrale.
unacceptable [ʌnəkˈsɛptəbl] *a* (*proposal, behaviour*) inaccettabile; (*price*) impossibile.
unaccompanied [ʌnəˈkʌmpənid] *a* (*child, lady*) non accompagnato(a); (*singing, song*) senza accompagnamento.
unaccountably [ʌnəˈkauntəbli] *ad* inesplicabilmente.
unaccounted [ʌnəˈkauntid] *a*: **two passengers are** ~ **for** due passeggeri mancano all'appello.
unaccustomed [ʌnəˈkʌstəmd] *a* insolito(a); **to be** ~ **to sth** non essere abituato(a) a qc.
unacquainted [ʌnəˈkweintid] *a*: **to be** ~ **with** (*facts*) ignorare, non essere al corrente di.
unadulterated [ʌnəˈdʌltəreitid] *a* (*gen*) puro(a); (*wine*) non sofisticato(a).
unaffected [ʌnəˈfɛktid] *a* (*person, behaviour*) naturale, spontaneo(a); (*emotionally*): **to be** ~ **by** non essere toccato(a) da.
unafraid [ʌnəˈfreid] *a*: **to be** ~ non aver paura.
unaided [ʌnˈeidid] *ad* senza aiuto.
unanimity [juːnəˈnimiti] *n* unanimità.
unanimous [juːˈnæniməs] *a* unanime.
unanimously [juːˈnæniməsli] *ad* all'unanimità.
unanswered [ʌnˈɑːnsəd] *a* (*question, letter*) senza risposta; (*criticism*) non confutato(a).
unappetizing [ʌnˈæpitaiziŋ] *a* poco appetitoso(a).
unappreciative [ʌnəˈpriːʃiətiv] *a* che non apprezza.
unarmed [ʌnˈɑːmd] *a* (*person*) disarmato(a); (*combat*) senz'armi.
unashamed [ʌnəˈʃeimd] *a* sfacciato(a); senza vergogna.
unassisted [ʌnəˈsistid] *a, ad* senza nessun aiuto.
unassuming [ʌnəˈsjuːmiŋ] *a* modesto(a), senza pretese.
unattached [ʌnəˈtætʃt] *a* senza legami, libero(a).
unattended [ʌnəˈtɛndid] *a* (*car, child, luggage*) incustodito(a).
unattractive [ʌnəˈtræktiv] *a* privo(a) di at-

trattiva, poco attraente.
unauthorized [ʌnˈɔːθəraizd] *a* non autorizzato(a).
unavailable [ʌnəˈveiləbl] *a* (*article, room, book*) non disponibile; (*person*) impegnato(a).
unavoidable [ʌnəˈvɔidəbl] *a* inevitabile.
unavoidably [ʌnəˈvɔidəbli] *ad* (*detained*) per cause di forza maggiore.
unaware [ʌnəˈwɛə*] *a*: **to be** ~ **of** non sapere, ignorare.
unawares [ʌnəˈwɛəz] *ad* di sorpresa, alla sprovvista.
unbalanced [ʌnˈbælənst] *a* squilibrato(a).
unbearable [ʌnˈbɛərəbl] *a* insopportabile.
unbeatable [ʌnˈbiːtəbl] *a* imbattibile.
unbeaten [ʌnˈbiːtn] *a* (*team, army*) imbattuto(a); (*record*) insuperato(a).
unbecoming [ʌnbiˈkʌmiŋ] *a* (*unseemly: language, behaviour*) sconveniente; (*unflattering: garment*) che non dona.
unbeknown(st) [ʌnbiˈnəun(st)] *ad*: ~ **to** all'insaputa di.
unbelief [ʌnbiˈliːf] *n* incredulità.
unbelievable [ʌnbiˈliːvəbl] *a* incredibile.
unbelievingly [ʌnbiˈliːviŋli] *ad* con aria incredula.
unbend [ʌnˈbɛnd] *vb* (*irg*) *vi* distendersi ♦ *vt* (*wire*) raddrizzare.
unbending [ʌnˈbɛndiŋ] *a* (*fig*) inflessibile, rigido(a).
unbias(s)ed [ʌnˈbaiəst] *a* obiettivo(a), imparziale.
unblemished [ʌnˈblɛmiʃt] *a* senza macchia.
unblock [ʌnˈblɔk] *vt* (*pipe, road*) sbloccare.
unborn [ʌnˈbɔːn] *a* non ancora nato(a).
unbounded [ʌnˈbaundid] *a* sconfinato(a), senza limite.
unbreakable [ʌnˈbreikəbl] *a* infrangibile.
unbridled [ʌnˈbraidld] *a* sbrigliato(a).
unbroken [ʌnˈbrəukən] *a* (*intact*) intero(a); (*continuous*) continuo(a); (*record*) insuperato(a).
unbuckle [ʌnˈbʌkl] *vt* slacciare.
unburden [ʌnˈbəːdn] *vt*: **to** ~ **o.s.** sfogarsi.
unbutton [ʌnˈbʌtn] *vt* sbottonare.
uncalled-for [ʌnˈkɔːldfɔː*] *a* (*remark*) fuori luogo *inv*; (*action*) ingiustificato(a).
uncanny [ʌnˈkæni] *a* misterioso(a), strano(a).
unceasing [ʌnˈsiːsiŋ] *a* incessante.
unceremonious [ʌnsɛriˈməuniəs] *a* (*abrupt, rude*) senza tante cerimonie.
uncertain [ʌnˈsəːtn] *a* incerto(a); **it's** ~ **whether ...** non è sicuro se ...; **in no** ~ **terms** chiaro e tondo, senza mezzi termini.
uncertainty [ʌnˈsəːtnti] *n* incertezza.
unchallenged [ʌnˈtʃælindʒd] *a* incontestato(a); **to go** ~ non venire contestato, non trovare opposizione.
unchanged [ʌnˈtʃeindʒd] *a* immutato(a).
uncharitable [ʌnˈtʃæritəbl] *a* duro(a), severo(a).
uncharted [ʌnˈtʃɑːtid] *a* inesplorato(a).
unchecked [ʌnˈtʃɛkt] *a* incontrollato(a).

uncivilized [ʌn'sɪvɪlaɪzd] *a* (*gen*) selvaggio(a); (*fig*) incivile, barbaro(a).

uncle ['ʌŋkl] *n* zio.

unclear [ʌn'klɪə*] *a* non chiaro(a); **I'm still ~ about what I'm supposed to do** non ho ancora ben capito cosa dovrei fare.

uncoil [ʌn'kɔɪl] *vt* srotolare ♦ *vi* srotolarsi, svolgersi.

uncomfortable [ʌn'kʌmfətəbl] *a* scomodo(a); (*uneasy*) a disagio, agitato(a); (*situation*) sgradevole.

uncomfortably [ʌn'kʌmfətəblɪ] *ad* scomodamente; (*uneasily*: *say*) con voce inquieta; (: *think*) con inquietudine.

uncommitted [ʌnkə'mɪtɪd] *a* (*attitude*, *country*) neutrale.

uncommon [ʌn'kɔmən] *a* raro(a), insolito(a), non comune.

uncommunicative [ʌnkə'mjuːnɪkətɪv] *a* poco comunicativo(a), chiuso(a).

uncomplicated [ʌn'kɔmplɪkeɪtɪd] *a* semplice, poco complicato(a).

uncompromising [ʌn'kɔmprəmaɪzɪŋ] *a* intransigente, inflessibile.

unconcerned [ʌnkən'səːnd] *a* (*unworried*) tranquillo(a); **to be ~ about** non darsi pensiero di, non preoccuparsi di *or* per.

unconditional [ʌn'kən'dɪʃənl] *a* incondizionato(a), senza condizioni.

uncongenial [ʌnkən'dʒiːnɪəl] *a* (*work*, *surroundings*) poco piacevole.

unconnected [ʌnkə'nɛktɪd] *a* (*unrelated*) senza connessione, senza rapporto; **to be ~ with** essere estraneo(a) a.

unconscious [ʌn'kɔnʃəs] *a* privo(a) di sensi, svenuto(a); (*unaware*) inconsapevole, inconscio(a) ♦ *n*: **the ~** l'inconscio; **to knock sb ~** far perdere i sensi a qn con un pugno.

unconsciously [ʌn'kɔnʃəslɪ] *ad* inconsciamente.

unconstitutional ['ʌnkɔnstɪ'tjuːʃənl] *a* incostituzionale.

uncontested [ʌnkən'tɛstɪd] *a* (*champion*) incontestato(a); (*POL*: *seat*) non disputato(a).

uncontrollable [ʌnkən'trəuləbl] *a* incontrollabile, indisciplinato(a).

uncontrolled [ʌnkən'trəuld] *a* (*child*, *dog*, *emotion*) sfrenato(a); (*inflation*, *price rises*) che sfugge al controllo.

unconventional [ʌnkən'vɛnʃənl] *a* poco convenzionale.

unconvinced [ʌnkən'vɪnst] *a*: **to be** *or* **remain ~** non essere convinto(a).

unconvincing [ʌnkən'vɪnsɪŋ] *a* non convincente, poco persuasivo(a).

uncork [ʌn'kɔːk] *vt* stappare.

uncorroborated [ʌnkə'rɔbəreɪtɪd] *a* non convalidato(a).

uncouth [ʌn'kuːθ] *a* maleducato(a), grossolano(a).

uncover [ʌn'kʌvə*] *vt* scoprire.

unctuous ['ʌŋktjuəs] *a* untuoso(a).

undamaged [ʌn'dæmɪdʒd] *a* (*goods*) in buono stato; (*fig*: *reputation*) intatto(a).

undaunted [ʌn'dɔːntɪd] *a* intrepido(a).

undecided [ʌndɪ'saɪdɪd] *a* indeciso(a).

undelivered [ʌndɪ'lɪvəd] *a* non recapitato(a); **if ~ return to sender** in caso di mancato recapito rispedire al mittente.

undeniable [ʌndɪ'naɪəbl] *a* innegabile, indiscutibile.

under ['ʌndə*] *prep* sotto; (*less than*) meno di; al disotto di; (*according to*) secondo, in conformità a ♦ *ad* (al) disotto; **from ~ sth** da sotto a *or* dal disotto di qc; **~ there** là sotto; **in ~ 2 hours** in meno di 2 ore; **~ anaesthetic** sotto anestesia; **~ discussion** in discussione; **~ repair** in riparazione; **~ the circumstances** date le circostanze.

under... ['ʌndə*] *prefix* sotto..., sub....

under-age [ʌndər'eɪdʒ] *a* minorenne.

underarm ['ʌndərɑːm] *n* ascella ♦ *a* ascellare ♦ *ad* da sotto in su.

undercapitalized [ʌndə'kæpɪtəlaɪzd] *a* carente di capitali.

undercarriage ['ʌndəkærɪdʒ] *n* (*Brit AVIAT*) carrello (d'atterraggio).

undercharge [ʌndə'tʃɑːdʒ] *vt* far pagare di meno a.

underclothes ['ʌndəkləuðz] *npl* biancheria (intima).

undercoat ['ʌndəkəut] *n* (*paint*) mano *f* di fondo.

undercover ['ʌndəkʌvə*] *a* segreto(a), clandestino(a).

undercurrent ['ʌndəkʌrənt] *n* corrente *f* sottomarina.

undercut [ʌndə'kʌt] *vt irg* vendere a prezzo minore di.

underdeveloped ['ʌndədɪ'vɛləpt] *a* sottosviluppato(a).

underdog ['ʌndədɔg] *n* oppresso/a.

underdone [ʌndə'dʌn] *a* (*CULIN*) poco cotto(a).

under-employment ['ʌndərɪm'plɔɪmənt] *n* sottoccupazione *f*.

underestimate [ʌndər'ɛstɪmeɪt] *vt* sottovalutare.

underexposed [ʌndərɪks'pəuzd] *a* (*PHOT*) sottoesposto(a).

underfed [ʌndə'fɛd] *a* denutrito(a).

underfoot [ʌndə'fut] *ad* sotto i piedi.

undergo [ʌndə'gəu] *vt irg* subire; (*treatment*) sottoporsi a; **the car is ~ing repairs** la macchina è in riparazione.

undergraduate [ʌndə'grædjuɪt] *n* studente(essa) universitario(a) ♦ *cpd*: **~ courses** corsi *mpl* di laurea.

underground ['ʌndəgraund] *n* metropolitana; (*POL*) movimento clandestino ♦ *a* sotterraneo(a); (*fig*) clandestino(a); (*ART*, *CINEMA*) underground *inv* ♦ *ad* sottoterra; clandestinamente.

undergrowth ['ʌndəgrəuθ] *n* sottobosco.

underhand(ed) [ʌndə'hænd(ɪd)] *a* (*fig*) furtivo(a), subdolo(a).

underinsured [ʌndərɪn'ʃuəd] *a* non

sufficientemente assicurato(a).

underlie [ʌndə'laɪ] vt irg essere alla base di; **the underlying cause** il motivo di fondo.

underline [ʌndə'laɪn] vt sottolineare.

underling ['ʌndəlɪŋ] n (pej) subalterno/a, tirapiedi m/f inv.

undermanning [ʌndə'mænɪŋ] n carenza di personale.

undermentioned [ʌndə'menʃənd] a (riportato(a)) qui sotto or qui di seguito.

undermine [ʌndə'maɪn] vt minare.

underneath [ʌndə'niːθ] ad sotto, disotto ♦ prep sotto, al di sotto di.

undernourished [ʌndə'nʌrɪʃt] a denutrito(a).

underpaid [ʌndə'peɪd] a mal pagato(a).

underpants ['ʌndəpænts] npl (Brit) mutande fpl, slip m inv.

underpass ['ʌndəpɑːs] n (Brit) sottopassaggio.

underpin [ʌndə'pɪn] vt puntellare; (argument, case) corroborare.

underplay [ʌndə'pleɪ] vt minimizzare.

underpopulated [ʌndə'pɒpjuleɪtɪd] a scarsamente popolato(a), sottopopolato(a).

underprice [ʌndə'praɪs] vt vendere a un prezzo inferiore al dovuto.

underprivileged [ʌndə'prɪvɪlɪdʒd] a svantaggiato(a).

underrate [ʌndə'reɪt] vt sottovalutare.

underscore [ʌndə'skɔː*] vt sottolineare.

underseal ['ʌndəsiːl] vt rendere stagno il fondo di.

undersecretary [ʌndə'sekrətrɪ] n sottosegretario.

undersell ['ʌndə'sel] vt irg (competitors) vendere a prezzi più bassi di.

undershirt ['ʌndəʃəːt] n (US) maglietta.

undershorts ['ʌndəʃɔːts] npl (US) mutande fpl, slip m inv.

underside ['ʌndəsaɪd] n disotto.

undersigned ['ʌndəsaɪnd] a, n sottoscritto(a).

underskirt ['ʌndəskəːt] n sottoveste f.

understaffed [ʌndə'stɑːft] a a corto di personale.

understand [ʌndə'stænd] vb (irg: like **stand**) vt, vi capire, comprendere; **I ~ that** ... sento che ...; credo di capire che ...; **to make o.s. understood** farsi capire.

understandable [ʌndə'stændəbl] a comprensibile.

understanding [ʌndə'stændɪŋ] a comprensivo(a) ♦ n comprensione f; (agreement) accordo; **on the ~ that** ... a patto che or a condizione che ...; **to come to an ~ with sb** giungere ad un accordo con qn.

understate [ʌndə'steɪt] vt minimizzare, sminuire.

understatement [ʌndə'steɪtmənt] n: **that's an ~!** a dire poco!

understood [ʌndə'stʊd] pt, pp of **understand** ♦ a inteso(a); (implied) sottinteso(a).

understudy ['ʌndəstʌdɪ] n sostituto/a, attore/trice supplente.

undertake [ʌndə'teɪk] vt irg intraprendere; **to ~ to do sth** impegnarsi a fare qc.

undertaker ['ʌndəteɪkə*] n impresario di pompe funebri.

undertaking [ʌndə'teɪkɪŋ] n impresa; (promise) promessa.

undertone ['ʌndətəun] n (low voice) tono sommesso; (of criticism etc) vena, sottofondo; **in an ~** sottovoce.

undervalue [ʌndə'væljuː] vt svalutare sottovalutare.

underwater [ʌndə'wɔːtə*] ad sott'acqua ♦ a subacqueo(a).

underwear ['ʌndəwɛə*] n biancheria (intima).

underweight [ʌndə'weɪt] a al di sotto del giusto peso; (person) sottopeso inv.

underworld ['ʌndəwəːld] n (of crime) malavita.

underwrite ['ʌndəraɪt] vt (FINANCE) sottoscrivere; (INSURANCE) assicurare.

underwriter ['ʌndəraɪtə*] n sottoscrittore trice; assicuratore/trice.

undeserving [ʌndɪ'zəːvɪŋ] a: **to be ~ of** non meritare, non essere degno di.

undesirable [ʌndɪ'zaɪərəbl] a indesiderabile sgradito(a).

undeveloped [ʌndɪ'veləpt] a (land, resources) non sfruttato(a).

undies ['ʌndɪz] npl (col) robina, biancheria intima da donna.

undiluted [ʌndaɪ'luːtɪd] a non diluito(a).

undiplomatic [ʌndɪplə'mætɪk] a poco diplomatico(a).

undischarged ['ʌndɪs'tʃɑːdʒd] a: **~ bankrupt** fallito non riabilitato.

undisciplined [ʌn'dɪsɪplɪnd] a indisciplinato(a).

undisguised [ʌndɪs'gaɪzd] a (dislike, amusement etc) palese.

undisputed [ʌndɪs'pjuːtɪd] a indiscusso(a).

undistinguished [ʌndɪs'tɪŋgwɪʃt] a mediocre qualunque.

undisturbed [ʌndɪs'təːbd] a tranquillo(a); **to leave sth ~** lasciare qc così com'è.

undivided [ʌndɪ'vaɪdɪd] a: **I want your ~ attention** esigo tutta la sua attenzione.

undo [ʌn'duː] vt irg disfare.

undoing [ʌn'duːɪŋ] n rovina, perdita.

undone [ʌn'dʌn] pp of **undo**; **to come ~** slacciarsi.

undoubted [ʌn'dautɪd] a sicuro(a), certo(a).

undoubtedly [ʌn'dautɪdlɪ] ad senza alcun dubbio.

undress [ʌn'dres] vi spogliarsi.

undrinkable [ʌn'drɪŋkəbl] a (unpalatable) imbevibile; (poisonous) non potabile.

undue [ʌn'djuː] a eccessivo(a).

undulating ['ʌndjuleɪtɪŋ] a ondeggiante ondulato(a).

unduly [ʌn'djuːlɪ] ad eccessivamente.

undying [ʌn'daɪɪŋ] a imperituro(a).

unearned [ʌn'əːnd] a (praise, respect) immeritato(a); **~ income** rendita.

unearth [ʌn'əːθ] vt dissotterrare; (fig) scoprire.

unearthly [ʌn'əːθlɪ] a soprannaturale; (hour

impossibile.

uneasy [ʌn'iːzɪ] *a* a disagio; (*worried*) preoccupato(a); **to feel ~ about doing sth** non sentirsela di fare qc.

uneconomic(al) ['ʌniːkə'nɔmɪk(l)] *a* non economico(a), antieconomico(a).

uneducated [ʌn'ɛdjukeɪtɪd] *a* senza istruzione, incolto(a).

unemployed [ʌnɪm'plɔɪd] *a* disoccupato(a) ♦ *npl*: **the ~** i disoccupati.

unemployment [ʌnɪm'plɔɪmənt] *n* disoccupazione *f*.

unemployment benefit, (*US*) **unemployment compensation** *n* sussidio di disoccupazione.

unending [ʌn'ɛndɪŋ] *a* senza fine.

unenviable [ʌn'ɛnvɪəbl] *a* poco invidiabile.

unequal [ʌn'iːkwəl] *a* (*length, objects*) disuguale; (*amounts*) diverso(a); (*division of labour*) ineguale.

unequalled, (*US*) **unequaled** [ʌn'iːkwəld] *a* senza pari, insuperato(a).

unequivocal [ʌnɪ'kwɪvəkəl] *a* (*answer*) inequivocabile; (*person*) esplicito(a), chiaro(a).

unerring [ʌn'əːrɪŋ] *a* infallibile.

UNESCO [juː'nɛskəu] *n abbr* (= *United Nations Educational, Scientific and Cultural Organization*) U.N.E.S.C.O. *f*.

unethical [ʌn'ɛθɪkəl] *a* (*methods*) poco ortodosso(a), non moralmente accettabile; (*doctor's behaviour*) contrario(a) all'etica professionale.

uneven [ʌn'iːvn] *a* ineguale; (*ground*) disuguale, accidentato(a); (*heartbeat*) irregolare.

uneventful [ʌnɪ'vɛntful] *a* senza sorprese, tranquillo(a).

unexceptional [ʌnɪk'sɛpʃənl] *a* che non ha niente d'eccezionale.

unexciting [ʌnɪk'saɪtɪŋ] *a* (*news*) poco emozionante; (*film, evening*) poco interessante.

unexpected [ʌnɪk'spɛktɪd] *a* inatteso(a), imprevisto(a).

unexpectedly [ʌnɪk'spɛktɪdlɪ] *ad* inaspettatamente.

unexplained [ʌnɪk'spleɪnd] *a* inspiegato(a).

unexploded [ʌnɪk'spləudɪd] *a* inesploso(a).

unfailing [ʌn'feɪlɪŋ] *a* (*supply, energy*) inesauribile; (*remedy*) infallibile.

unfair [ʌn'fɛə*] *a*: **~ (to)** ingiusto(a) (nei confronti di); **it's ~ that ...** non è giusto che ... + *sub*.

unfair dismissal *n* licenziamento ingiustificato.

unfairly [ʌn'fɛəlɪ] *ad* ingiustamente.

unfaithful [ʌn'feɪθful] *a* infedele.

unfamiliar [ʌnfə'mɪlɪə*] *a* sconosciuto(a), strano(a); **to be ~ with sth** non essere pratico di qc, non avere familiarità con qc.

unfashionable [ʌn'fæʃnəbl] *a* (*clothes*) fuori moda *inv*; (*district*) non alla moda.

unfasten [ʌn'fɑːsn] *vt* slacciare; sciogliere.

unfathomable [ʌn'fæðəmabl] *a* insondabile.

unfavourable, (*US*) **unfavorable** [ʌn'feɪvərəbl] *a* sfavorevole.

unfavo(u)rably [ʌn'feɪvərəblɪ] *ad*: **to look ~ upon** vedere di malocchio.

unfeeling [ʌn'fiːlɪŋ] *a* insensibile, duro(a).

unfinished [ʌn'fɪnɪʃt] *a* incompiuto(a).

unfit [ʌn'fɪt] *a* inadatto(a); (*ill*) non in forma; (*incompetent*): **~ (for)** incompetente (in); (: *work, MIL*) inabile (a); **~ for habitation** inabitabile.

unflagging [ʌn'flægɪŋ] *a* instancabile.

unflappable [ʌn'flæpəbl] *a* calmo(a), composto(a).

unflattering [ʌn'flætərɪŋ] *a* (*dress, hairstyle*) che non dona.

unflinching [ʌn'flɪntʃɪŋ] *a* che non indietreggia, risoluto(a).

unfold [ʌn'fəuld] *vt* spiegare; (*fig*) rivelare ♦ *vi* (*view*) distendersi; (*story*) svelarsi.

unforeseeable ['ʌnfɔː'siːəbl] *a* imprevedibile.

unforeseen [ʌnfɔː'siːn] *a* imprevisto(a).

unforgettable [ʌnfə'gɛtəbl] *a* indimenticabile.

unforgivable [ʌnfə'gɪvəbl] *a* imperdonabile.

unformatted [ʌn'fɔːmætɪd] *a* (*disk, text*) non formattato(a).

unfortunate [ʌn'fɔːtʃnɪt] *a* sfortunato(a); (*event, remark*) infelice.

unfortunately [ʌn'fɔːtʃnɪtlɪ] *ad* sfortunatamente, purtroppo.

unfounded [ʌn'faundɪd] *a* infondato(a).

unfriendly [ʌn'frɛndlɪ] *a* poco amichevole, freddo(a).

unfulfilled [ʌnful'fɪld] *a* (*ambition*) non realizzato(a); (*prophecy*) che non si è avverato(a); (*desire*) insoddisfatto(a); (*promise*) non mantenuto(a); (*terms of contract*) non rispettato(a); (*person*) frustrato(a).

unfurl [ʌn'fɔːl] *vt* spiegare.

unfurnished [ʌn'fɔːnɪʃt] *a* non ammobiliato(a).

ungainly [ʌn'geɪnlɪ] *a* goffo(a), impacciato(a).

ungodly [ʌn'gɔdlɪ] *a* empio(a); **at an ~ hour** a un'ora impossibile.

ungrateful [ʌn'greɪtful] *a* ingrato(a).

unguarded [ʌn'gɑːdɪd] *a*: **in an ~ moment** in un momento di distrazione.

unhappily [ʌn'hæpɪlɪ] *ad* (*unfortunately*) purtroppo, sfortunatamente.

unhappiness [ʌn'hæpɪnɪs] *n* infelicità.

unhappy [ʌn'hæpɪ] *a* infelice; **~ with** (*arrangements etc*) insoddisfatto(a) di.

unharmed [ʌn'hɑːmd] *a* incolume, sano(a) e salvo(a).

unhealthy [ʌn'hɛlθɪ] *a* (*gen*) malsano(a); (*person*) malaticcio(a).

unheard-of [ʌn'hɔːdɔv] *a* inaudito(a), senza precedenti.

unhelpful [ʌn'hɛlpful] *a* poco disponibile.

unhesitating [ʌn'hɛzɪteɪtɪŋ] *a* (*loyalty*) che non vacilla; (*reply, offer*) pronto(a), immediato(a).

unhook [ʌn'huk] *vt* sganciare; sfibbiare.

unhurt [ʌn'hɔːt] *a* incolume, sano(a) e

salvo(a).

unhygienic [ʌnhaɪˈdʒiːnɪk] a non igienico(a).

UNICEF [ˈjuːnɪsɛf] n abbr (= United Nations International Children's Emergency Fund) U.N.I.C.E.F. m.

unicorn [ˈjuːnɪkɔːn] n unicorno.

unidentified [ʌnaɪˈdɛntɪfaɪd] a non identificato(a).

uniform [ˈjuːnɪfɔːm] n uniforme f, divisa ♦ a uniforme.

uniformity [juːnɪˈfɔːmɪtɪ] n uniformità.

unify [ˈjuːnɪfaɪ] vt unificare.

unilateral [junɪˈlætərəl] a unilaterale.

unimaginable [ʌnɪˈmædʒɪnəbl] a inimmaginabile, inconcepibile.

unimaginative [ʌnɪˈmædʒɪnətɪv] a privo(a) di fantasia, a corto di idee.

unimpaired [ʌnɪmˈpɛəd] a intatto(a), non danneggiato(a).

unimportant [ʌnɪmˈpɔːtənt] a senza importanza, di scarsa importanza.

unimpressed [ʌnɪmˈprɛst] a niente affatto impressionato(a).

uninhabited [ʌnɪnˈhæbɪtɪd] a disabitato(a).

uninhibited [ʌnɪnˈhɪbɪtɪd] a senza inibizioni; senza ritegno.

uninjured [ʌnˈɪndʒəd] a incolume.

unintelligent [ʌnɪnˈtɛlɪdʒənt] a poco intelligente.

unintentional [ʌnɪnˈtɛnʃənəl] a involontario(a).

unintentionally [ʌnɪnˈtɛnʃnəlɪ] ad senza volerlo, involontariamente.

uninvited [ʌnɪnˈvaɪtɪd] a non invitato(a).

uninviting [ʌnɪnˈvaɪtɪŋ] a (place, food) non invitante, poco invitante; (offer) poco allettante.

union [ˈjuːnjən] n unione f; (also: trade ~) sindacato ♦ cpd sindacale; the U~ (US) gli stati dell'Unione.

unionize [ˈjuːnjənaɪz] vt sindacalizzare, organizzare in sindacato.

Union Jack n bandiera nazionale britannica.

Union of Soviet Socialist Republics (USSR) n Unione f delle Repubbliche Socialiste Sovietiche (U.R.S.S.).

union shop n stabilimento in cui tutti gli operai sono tenuti ad aderire ad un sindacato.

unique [juːˈniːk] a unico(a).

unisex [ˈjuːnɪsɛks] a unisex inv.

unison [ˈjuːnɪsn] n: **in ~** all'unisono.

unit [ˈjuːnɪt] n unità f inv; (section: of furniture etc) elemento; (team, squad) reparto, squadra; **production ~** reparto m produzione inv; **sink ~** blocco m lavello inv.

unit cost n costo unitario.

unite [juːˈnaɪt] vt unire ♦ vi unirsi.

united [juːˈnaɪtɪd] a unito(a); (efforts) congiunto(a).

United Arab Emirates npl Emirati mpl Arabi Uniti.

United Kingdom (UK) n Regno Unito.

United Nations (Organization) (UN, UNO) n (Organizzazione f delle) Nazioni

Unite (O.N.U.).

United States (of America) (US, USA) n Stati mpl Uniti (d'America) (USA).

unit price n prezzo unitario.

unit trust n (Brit COMM) fondo d'investimento.

unity [ˈjuːnɪtɪ] n unità.

Univ. abbr = **university**.

universal [juːnɪˈvɔːsl] a universale.

universe [ˈjuːnɪvɔːs] n universo.

university [juːnɪˈvɔːsɪtɪ] n università f inv ♦ cpd (student, professor, education) universitario(a); (year) accademico(a).

university degree n laurea.

unjust [ʌnˈdʒʌst] a ingiusto(a).

unjustifiable [ˈʌndʒʌstɪˈfaɪəbl] a ingiustificabile.

unjustified [ʌnˈdʒʌstɪfaɪd] a ingiustificato(a); (TYP) non allineato(a).

unkempt [ʌnˈkɛmpt] a trasandato(a); spettinato(a).

unkind [ʌnˈkaɪnd] a poco gentile, villano(a).

unkindly [ʌnˈkaɪndlɪ] ad (speak) in modo sgarbato; (treat) male.

unknown [ʌnˈnəun] a sconosciuto(a); **~ to me …** a mia insaputa …; **~ quantity** (MATH, fig) incognita.

unladen [ʌnˈleɪdn] a (ship, weight) a vuoto.

unlawful [ʌnˈlɔːful] a illecito(a), illegale.

unleash [ʌnˈliːʃ] vt sguinzagliare; (fig) scatenare.

unleavened [ʌnˈlɛvnd] a non lievitato(a), azzimo(a).

unless [ʌnˈlɛs] cj a meno che (non) + sub; **~ otherwise stated** salvo indicazione contraria; **~ I am mistaken** se non mi sbaglio.

unlicensed [ʌnˈlaɪsənst] a (Brit) senza licenza per la vendita di alcolici.

unlike [ʌnˈlaɪk] a diverso(a) ♦ prep a differenza di, contrariamente a.

unlikelihood [ʌnˈlaɪklɪhud] a improbabilità.

unlikely [ʌnˈlaɪklɪ] a improbabile; (explanation) inverosimile.

unlimited [ʌnˈlɪmɪtɪd] a illimitato(a).

unlisted [ʌnˈlɪstɪd] a (US TEL): **to be ~** non essere sull'elenco; (STOCK EXCHANGE) non quotato(a).

unlit [ʌnˈlɪt] a (room) senza luce; (road) non illuminato(a).

unload [ʌnˈləud] vt scaricare.

unlock [ʌnˈlɔk] vt aprire.

unlucky [ʌnˈlʌkɪ] a sfortunato(a); (object, number) che porta sfortuna, di malaugurio; **to be ~** (person) essere sfortunato, non avere fortuna.

unmanageable [ʌnˈmænɪdʒəbl] a (tool, vehicle) poco maneggevole; (situation) impossibile.

unmanned [ʌnˈmænd] a (spacecraft) senza equipaggio.

unmannerly [ʌnˈmænəlɪ] a maleducato(a).

unmarked [ʌnˈmɑːkt] a (unstained) pulito(a), senza macchie; **~ police car** civetta della polizia.

unmarried [ʌn'mærɪd] *a* non sposato(a); (*man only*) scapolo, celibe; (*woman only*) nubile.
unmarried mother *n* ragazza *f* madre *inv*.
unmask [ʌn'mɑːsk] *vt* smascherare.
unmatched [ʌn'mætʃt] *a* senza uguali.
unmentionable [ʌn'menʃnəbl] *a* (*vice, topic*) innominabile; (*word*) irripetibile.
unmerciful [ʌn'mɔːsɪful] *a* spietato(a).
unmistakable [ʌnmɪs'teɪkəbl] *a* indubbio(a); facilmente riconoscibile.
unmitigated [ʌn'mɪtɪgeɪtɪd] *a* (*disaster etc*) totale, assoluto(a).
unnamed [ʌn'neɪmd] *a* (*nameless*) senza nome; (*anonymous*) anonimo(a).
unnatural [ʌn'nætʃrəl] *a* innaturale; contro natura.
unnecessary [ʌn'nesəsərɪ] *a* inutile, superfluo(a).
unnerve [ʌn'nɔːv] *vt* (*subj: accident*) sgomentare; (*: hostile attitude*) bloccare; (*: long wait, interview*) snervare.
unnoticed [ʌn'nəutɪst] *a*: **to go** *or* **pass ~** passare inosservato(a).
UNO ['juːnəu] *n abbr see* **United Nations Organization**.
unobservant [ʌnəb'zɔːvənt] *a*: **to be ~** non avere spirito di osservazione.
unobtainable [ʌnəb'teɪnəbl] *a* (*TEL*) non ottenibile.
unobtrusive [ʌnəb'truːsɪv] *a* discreto(a).
unoccupied [ʌn'ɔkjupaɪd] *a* (*house*) vuoto(a); (*seat, MIL: zone*) libero(a), non occupato(a).
unofficial [ʌnə'fɪʃl] *a* non ufficiale; (*strike*) non dichiarato(a) dal sindacato.
unopened [ʌn'əupənd] *a* (*letter*) non aperto(a); (*present*) ancora incartato(a).
unopposed [ʌnə'pəuzd] *a* senza incontrare opposizione.
unorthodox [ʌn'ɔːθədɔks] *a* non ortodosso(a).
unpack [ʌn'pæk] *vi* disfare la valigia (*or* le valigie).
unpaid [ʌn'peɪd] *a* (*holiday*) non pagato(a); (*work*) non retribuito(a); (*bill, debt*) da pagare.
unpalatable [ʌn'pælətəbl] *a* (*food*) immangiabile; (*drink*) imbevibile; (*truth*) sgradevole.
unparalleled [ʌn'pærəleld] *a* incomparabile, impareggiabile.
unpatriotic ['ʌnpætrɪ'ɔtɪk] *a* (*person*) poco patriottico(a); (*speech, attitude*) antipatriottico(a).
unplanned [ʌn'plænd] *a* (*visit*) imprevisto(a); (*baby*) non previsto(a).
unpleasant [ʌn'pleznt] *a* spiacevole; (*person, remark*) antipatico(a); (*day, experience*) brutto(a).
unplug [ʌn'plʌg] *vt* staccare.
unpolluted [ʌnpə'luːtɪd] *a* non inquinato(a).
unpopular [ʌn'pɔpjulə*] *a* impopolare; **to make o.s. ~ (with)** rendersi antipatico (a); (*subj: politician etc*) alienarsi le simpatie (di).
unprecedented [ʌn'presɪdəntɪd] *a* senza precedenti.
unpredictable [ʌnprɪ'dɪktəbl] *a* imprevedibile.
unprejudiced [ʌn'predʒudɪst] *a* (*not biased*) obiettivo(a), imparziale; (*having no prejudices*) senza pregiudizi.
unprepared [ʌnprɪ'peəd] *a* (*person*) impreparato(a); (*speech*) improvvisato(a).
unprepossessing [ʌnpriːpə'zesɪŋ] *a* insulso(a).
unpretentious [ʌnprɪ'tenʃəs] *a* senza pretese.
unprincipled [ʌn'prɪnsɪpld] *a* senza scrupoli.
unproductive [ʌnprə'dʌktɪv] *a* improduttivo(a); (*discussion*) sterile.
unprofessional ['ʌnprə'feʃənl] *a*: **~ conduct** scorrettezza professionale.
unprofitable [ʌn'prɔfɪtəbl] *a* (*financially*) non redditizio(a); (*job, deal*) poco lucrativo(a).
unprovoked [ʌnprə'vəukt] *a* non provocato(a).
unpunished [ʌn'pʌnɪʃt] *a*: **to go ~** restare impunito(a).
unqualified [ʌn'kwɔlɪfaɪd] *a* (*worker*) non qualificato(a); (*in professions*) non abilitato(a); (*success*) assoluto(a), senza riserve.
unquestionably [ʌn'kwestʃənəblɪ] *ad* indiscutibilmente.
unquestioning [ʌn'kwestʃənɪŋ] *a* (*obedience, acceptance*) cieco(a).
unravel [ʌn'rævl] *vt* dipanare, districare.
unreal [ʌn'rɪəl] *a* irreale.
unrealistic [ʌnrɪə'lɪstɪk] *a* (*idea*) illusorio(a); (*estimate*) non realistico(a).
unreasonable [ʌn'riːznəbl] *a* irragionevole; **to make ~ demands on sb** voler troppo da qn.
unrecognizable [ʌn'rekəgnaɪzəbl] *a* irriconoscibile.
unrecognized [ʌn'rekəgnaɪzd] *a* (*talent, genius*) misconosciuto(a); (*POL: regime*) non ufficialmente riconosciuto(a).
unrecorded [ʌnrɪ'kɔːdɪd] *a* non documentato(a), non registrato(a).
unrefined [ʌnrɪ'faɪnd] *a* (*sugar, petroleum*) greggio(a); (*person*) rozzo(a).
unrehearsed [ʌnrɪ'hɔːst] *a* (*THEATRE etc*) improvvisato(a); (*spontaneous*) improvviso(a).
unrelated [ʌnrɪ'leɪtɪd] *a*: **~ (to)** senza rapporto (con); (*by family*) non imparentato(a) (con).
unrelenting [ʌnrɪ'lentɪŋ] *a* implacabile; accanito(a).
unreliable [ʌnrɪ'laɪəbl] *a* (*person, machine*) che non dà affidamento; (*news, source of information*) inattendibile.
unrelieved [ʌnrɪ'liːvd] *a* (*monotony*) uniforme.
unremitting [ʌnrɪ'mɪtɪŋ] *a* incessante, infaticabile.
unrepeatable [ʌnrɪ'piːtəbl] *a* (*offer*) unico(a).
unrepentant [ʌnrɪ'pentənt] *a* impenitente.
unrepresentative [ʌnreprɪ'zentətɪv] *a* atipico(a), poco rappresentativo(a).
unreserved [ʌnrɪ'zɔːvd] *a* (*seat*) non prenotato(a), non riservato(a); (*approval, admiration*) senza riserve.

unresponsive [ʌnrɪs'pɔnsɪv] *a* che non reagisce.

unrest [ʌn'rɛst] *n* agitazione *f*.

unrestricted [ʌnrɪ'strɪktɪd] *a* (*power*, *time*) illimitato(a); (*access*) libero(a).

unrewarded [ʌnrɪ'wɔ:dɪd] *a* non ricompensato(a).

unripe [ʌn'raɪp] *a* acerbo(a).

unrivalled, (*US*) **unrivaled** [ʌn'raɪvəld] *a* senza pari.

unroll [ʌn'rəul] *vt* srotolare.

unruffled [ʌn'rʌfld] *a* (*person*) calmo(a) e tranquillo(a), imperturbato(a); (*hair*) a posto.

unruly [ʌn'ru:lɪ] *a* indisciplinato(a).

unsafe [ʌn'seɪf] *a* pericoloso(a), rischioso(a); ~ **to drink** non potabile; ~ **to eat** non commestibile.

unsaid [ʌn'sɛd] *a*: **to leave sth** ~ passare qc sotto silenzio.

unsaleable, (*US*) **unsalable** [ʌn'seɪləbl] *a* invendibile.

unsatisfactory ['ʌnsætɪs'fæktərɪ] *a* che lascia a desiderare, insufficiente.

unsavoury, (*US*) **unsavory** [ʌn'seɪvərɪ] *a* (*fig*: *person*) losco(a); (: *reputation*, *subject*) disgustoso(a), ripugnante.

unscathed [ʌn'skeɪðd] *a* incolume.

unscientific ['ʌnsaɪən'tɪfɪk] *a* poco scientifico(a).

unscrew [ʌn'skru:] *vt* svitare.

unscrupulous [ʌn'skru:pjuləs] *a* senza scrupoli.

unsecured [ʌnsɪ'kjuəd] *a*: ~ **creditor** creditore *m* chirografario.

unseemly [ʌn'si:mlɪ] *a* sconveniente.

unseen [ʌn'si:n] *a* (*person*) inosservato(a); (*danger*) nascosto(a).

unselfish [ʌn'sɛlfɪʃ] *a* (*person*) altruista; (*act*) disinteressato(a).

unsettled [ʌn'sɛtld] *a* (*person*, *future*) incerto(a); (*question*) non risolto(a); (*weather*, *market*) instabile; **to feel** ~ sentirsi disorientato(a).

unsettling [ʌn'sɛtlɪŋ] *a* inquietante.

unshak(e)able [ʌn'ʃeɪkəbl] *a* irremovibile.

unshaven [ʌn'ʃeɪvn] *a* non rasato(a).

unsightly [ʌn'saɪtlɪ] *a* brutto(a), sgradevole a vedersi.

unskilled [ʌn'skɪld] *a*: ~ **worker** manovale *m*.

unsociable [ʌn'səuʃəbl] *a* (*person*) poco socievole; (*behaviour*) antipatico(a).

unsocial [ʌn'səuʃəl] *a*: ~ **hours** orario sconveniente.

unsold [ʌn'səuld] *a* invenduto(a).

unsolicited [ʌnsə'lɪsɪtɪd] *a* non richiesto(a).

unsophisticated [ʌnsə'fɪstɪkeɪtɪd] *a* semplice, naturale.

unsound [ʌn'saund] *a* (*health*) debole, cagionevole; (*in construction*: *floor*, *foundations*) debole, malsicuro(a); (*policy*, *advice*) poco sensato(a); (*judgment*, *investment*) poco sicuro(a).

unspeakable [ʌn'spi:kəbl] *a* (*bad*) abominevole.

unspoken [ʌn'spəukən] *a* (*words*) non detto(a); (*agreement*, *approval*) tacito(a).

unsteady [ʌn'stɛdɪ] *a* instabile, malsicuro(a).

unstinting [ʌn'stɪntɪŋ] *a* (*support*) incondizionato(a); (*generosity*) illimitato(a); (*praise*) senza riserve.

unstuck [ʌn'stʌk] *a*: **to come** ~ scollarsi; (*fig*) fare fiasco.

unsubstantiated [ʌnsəb'stænʃɪeɪtɪd] *a* (*rumour*, *accusation*) infondato(a).

unsuccessful [ʌnsək'sɛsful] *a* (*writer*, *proposal*) che non ha successo; (*marriage*, *attempt*) mal riuscito(a), fallito(a); **to be** ~ (*in attempting sth*) non riuscire; non avere successo; (*application*) non essere considerato(a).

unsuccessfully [ʌnsək'sɛsfəlɪ] *ad* senza successo.

unsuitable [ʌn'su:təbl] *a* inadatto(a); (*moment*) inopportuno(a).

unsuited [ʌn'su:tɪd] *a*: **to be** ~ **for** *or* **to** non essere fatto(a) per.

unsupported [ʌnsə'pɔ:tɪd] *a* (*claim*) senza fondamento; (*theory*) non dimostrato(a).

unsure [ʌn'ʃuə*] *a*: ~ (**of** *or* **about**) incerto(a) (su); **to be** ~ **of o.s.** essere insicuro(a).

unsuspecting [ʌnsə'spɛktɪŋ] *a* che non sospetta niente.

unsweetened [ʌn'swi:tnd] *a* senza zucchero.

unswerving [ʌn'swɜ:vɪŋ] *a* fermo(a).

unsympathetic ['ʌnsɪmpə'θɛtɪk] *a* (*attitude*) poco incoraggiante; (*person*) antipatico(a); ~ (**to**) non solidale (verso).

untangle [ʌn'tæŋgl] *vt* sbrogliare.

untapped [ʌn'tæpt] *a* (*resources*) non sfruttato(a).

untaxed [ʌn'tækst] *a* (*goods*) esente da imposte; (*income*) non imponibile.

unthinkable [ʌn'θɪŋkəbl] *a* impensabile, inconcepibile.

untidy [ʌn'taɪdɪ] *a* (*room*) in disordine; (*appearance*, *work*) trascurato(a); (*person*, *writing*) disordinato(a).

untie [ʌn'taɪ] *vt* (*knot*, *parcel*) disfare; (*prisoner*, *dog*) slegare.

until [ʌn'tɪl] *prep* fino a; (*after negative*) prima di ♦ *cj* finché, fino a quando; (*in past after negative*) prima che + *sub*, prima di ~ *infinitive*; ~ **now** finora; ~ **then** fino a allora; **from morning** ~ **night** dalla mattina alla sera.

untimely [ʌn'taɪmlɪ] *a* intempestivo(a), inopportuno(a); (*death*) prematuro(a).

untold [ʌn'təuld] *a* incalcolabile; indescrivibile.

untouched [ʌn'tʌtʃt] *a* (*not used etc*) non toccato(a), intatto(a); (*safe*: *person*) incolume; (*unaffected*): ~ **by** insensibile a.

untoward [ʌntə'wɔ:d] *a* sfortunato(a), sconveniente.

untrammelled [ʌn'træmld] *a* illimitato(a).

untranslatable [ʌntrænz'leɪtəbl] *a* intraducibile.

untrue [ʌn'tru:] *a* (*statement*) falso(a), non vero(a).

untrustworthy [ʌn'trʌstwə:ðɪ] *a* di cui non ci si può fidare.

unusable [ʌn'ju:zəbl] *a* inservibile, inutilizzabile.

unused [ʌn'ju:zd] *a* (*new*) nuovo(a); (*not made use of*) non usato(a), non utilizzato(a); **to be ~ to sth/to doing sth** non essere abituato(a) a qc/a fare qc.

unusual [ʌn'ju:ʒuəl] *a* insolito(a), eccezionale, raro(a).

unusually [ʌn'ju:ʒuəlɪ] *ad* insolitamente.

unveil [ʌn'veɪl] *vt* scoprire, svelare.

unwanted [ʌn'wɔntɪd] *a* non desiderato(a).

unwarranted [ʌn'wɔrəntɪd] *a* ingiustificato(a).

unwary [ʌn'wεərɪ] *a* incauto(a).

unwavering [ʌn'weɪvərɪŋ] *a* fermo(a), incrollabile.

unwelcome [ʌn'wεlkəm] *a* (*gen*) non gradito(a); **to feel ~** sentire che la propria presenza non è gradita.

unwell [ʌn'wεl] *a* indisposto(a); **to feel ~** non sentirsi bene.

unwieldy [ʌn'wi:ldɪ] *a* poco maneggevole.

unwilling [ʌn'wɪlɪŋ] *a*: **to be ~ to do** non voler fare.

unwillingly [ʌn'wɪlɪŋlɪ] *ad* malvolentieri.

unwind [ʌn'waɪnd] *vb* (*irg*) *vt* svolgere, srotolare ♦ *vi* (*relax*) rilassarsi.

unwise [ʌn'waɪz] *a* (*decision, act*) avventato(a).

unwitting [ʌn'wɪtɪŋ] *a* involontario(a).

unworkable [ʌn'wə:kəbl] *a* (*plan etc*) inattuabile.

unworthy [ʌn'wə:ðɪ] *a* indegno(a); **to be ~ of sth/to do sth** non essere degno di qc/di fare qc.

unwrap [ʌn'ræp] *vt* disfare; (*present*) aprire.

unwritten [ʌn'rɪtn] *a* (*agreement*) tacito(a).

unzip [ʌn'zɪp] *vt* aprire (la chiusura lampo di).

up [ʌp] *prep*: **to go/be ~ sth** salire/essere su qc ♦ *ad* su, (di) sopra; in alto ♦ *vt* (*col: price*) alzare ♦ *vi* (*col*): **she ~ped and left** improvvisamente se ne andò; **~ there** lassù; **~ above** al di sopra; **~ to** fino a; **to be ~** (*out of bed*) essere alzato(a); (*building*) essere terminato(a); (*tent*) essere piantato(a); (*curtains, shutters, wallpaper*) essere su; **"this side ~"** "alto"; **to be ~ (by)** (*in price, value*) essere andato(a) su (di); **when the year was ~** (*finished*) finito l'anno; **time's ~** il tempo è scaduto; **it is ~ to you** tocca a lei decidere; **what's ~?** (*col: wrong*) che c'è?; **what's ~ with him?** che ha?, che gli prende?; **what is he ~ to?** cosa sta tramando?; **he is not ~ to it** non ne è capace; **he's well ~ in** *or* **on politics** (*Brit: knowledgeable*) è informatissimo di *or* sulla politica; **~ with Leeds United!** viva il Leeds United!; **~s and downs** *npl* (*fig*) alti e bassi *mpl*.

up-and-coming [ʌpənd'kʌmɪŋ] *a* pieno(a) di promesse, promettente.

upbeat ['ʌpbi:t] *n* (*MUS*) tempo in levare; (*in economy, prosperity*) incremento ♦ *a* (*col*) ottimistico(a).

upbraid [ʌp'breɪd] *vt* rimproverare.

upbringing ['ʌpbrɪŋɪŋ] *n* educazione *f*.

update [ʌp'deɪt] *vt* aggiornare.

upend [ʌp'εnd] *vt* rovesciare.

upgrade [ʌp'greɪd] *vt* promuovere; (*job*) rivalutare; (*COMPUT*) far passare a potenza superiore.

upheaval [ʌp'hi:vl] *n* sconvolgimento; tumulto.

uphill [ʌp'hɪl] *a* in salita; (*fig: task*) difficile ♦ *ad*: **to go ~** andare in salita, salire.

uphold [ʌp'həuld] *vt irg* approvare; sostenere.

upholstery [ʌp'həulstərɪ] *n* tappezzeria.

upkeep ['ʌpki:p] *n* manutenzione *f*.

up-market [ʌp'mɑ:kɪt] *a* (*product*) che si rivolge ad una fascia di mercato superiore.

upon [ə'pɔn] *prep* su.

upper ['ʌpə*] *a* superiore ♦ *n* (*of shoe*) tomaia; **the ~ class** ≈ l'alta borghesia.

upper-class [ʌpə'klɑ:s] *a* dell'alta borghesia; (*district*) signorile; (*accent*) aristocratico(a); (*attitude*) snob *inv*.

upper hand *n*: **to have the ~** avere il coltello dalla parte del manico.

uppermost ['ʌpəməust] *a* il(la) più alto(a); predominante; **it was ~ in my mind** è stata la mia prima preoccupazione.

Upper Volta [-'vɔltə] *n* Alto Volta *m*.

upright ['ʌpraɪt] *a* diritto(a); verticale; (*fig*) diritto(a), onesto(a) ♦ *n* montante *m*.

uprising ['ʌpraɪzɪŋ] *n* insurrezione *f*, rivolta.

uproar ['ʌprɔ:*] *n* tumulto, clamore *m*.

uproot [ʌp'ru:t] *vt* sradicare.

upset *n* ['ʌpsεt] turbamento ♦ *vt* [ʌp'sεt] (*irg: like* **set**) (*glass etc*) rovesciare; (*plan, stomach*) scombussolare; (*person: offend*) contrariare; (: *grieve*) addolorare; sconvolgere ♦ *a* [ʌp'sεt] contrariato(a); addolorato(a); (*stomach*) scombussolato(a), disturbato(a); **to have a stomach ~** (*Brit*) avere lo stomaco in disordine *or* scombussolato; **to get ~** contrariarsi; addolorarsi.

upset price *n* (*US, Scottish*) prezzo di riserva.

upsetting [ʌp'sεtɪŋ] *a* (*saddening*) sconvolgente; (*offending*) offensivo(a); (*annoying*) fastidioso(a).

upshot ['ʌpʃɔt] *n* risultato; **the ~ of it all was that ...** la conclusione è stata che ....

upside down ['ʌpsaɪd-] *ad* sottosopra; **to turn ~** capovolgere; (*fig*) mettere sottosopra.

upstairs [ʌp'stεəz] *ad*, *a* di sopra, al piano superiore ♦ *n* piano di sopra.

upstart ['ʌpstɑ:t] *n* parvenu *m inv*.

upstream [ʌp'stri:m] *ad* a monte.

upsurge ['ʌpsə:dʒ] *n* (*of enthusiasm etc*) ondata.

uptake ['ʌpteɪk] *n*: **he is quick/slow on the ~** è pronto/lento di comprendonio.

uptight [ʌp'taɪt] *a* (*col*) teso(a).

up-to-date [ˈʌptəˈdeɪt] *a* moderno(a); aggiornato(a).

upturn [ˈʌptəːn] *n* (*in luck*) svolta favorevole; (*in value of currency*) rialzo.

upturned [ˈʌptəːnd] *a* (*nose*) all'insù.

upward [ˈʌpwəd] *a* ascendente; verso l'alto.

upward(s) [ˈʌpwəd(z)] *ad* in su, verso l'alto.

URA *n abbr* (*US:* = *Urban Renewal Administration*) amministrazione per il rinnovamento urbano.

Ural Mountains [ˈjuərəl-] *npl*: **the ~** (*also*: **the Urals**) gli Urali, i Monti Urali.

uranium [juəˈreɪnɪəm] *n* uranio.

Uranus [juəˈreɪnəs] *n* (*planet*) Urano.

urban [ˈəːbən] *a* urbano(a).

urbane [əːˈbeɪn] *a* civile, urbano(a), educato(a).

urbanization [əːbənaɪˈzeɪʃən] *n* urbanizzazione *f*.

urchin [ˈəːtʃɪn] *n* monello; **sea ~** riccio di mare.

urge [əːdʒ] *n* impulso, stimolo ♦ *vt* (*caution etc*) raccomandare vivamente; **to ~ sb to do** esortare qn a fare, spingere qn a fare; raccomandare a qn di fare.

urge on *vt* spronare.

urgency [ˈəːdʒənsɪ] *n* urgenza; (*of tone*) insistenza.

urgent [ˈəːdʒənt] *a* urgente; (*earnest, persistent: plea*) pressante; (: *tone*) insistente, incalzante.

urgently [ˈəːdʒəntlɪ] *ad* d'urgenza, urgentemente; con insistenza.

urinal [ˈjuərɪnl] *n* (*Brit: building*) vespasiano; (: *vessel*) orinale *m*, pappagallo.

urinate [ˈjuərɪneɪt] *vi* orinare.

urine [ˈjuərɪn] *n* orina.

urn [əːn] *n* urna; (*also*: **tea ~**) bollitore *m* per il tè.

Uruguay [ˈjuərəgwaɪ] *n* Uruguay *m*.

Uruguayan [juərəˈgwaɪən] *a*, *n* uruguaiano(a).

US *n abbr see* **United States**.

us [ʌs] *pronoun* ci; (*stressed, after prep*) noi.

USA *n abbr* (*GEO*) *see* **United States (of America)**; (*MIL*) = *United States Army*.

usable [ˈjuːzəbl] *a* utilizzabile, usabile.

USAF *n abbr* = *United States Air Force*.

usage [ˈjuːzɪdʒ] *n* uso.

USCG *n abbr* = *United States Coast Guard*.

USDA *n abbr* = *United States Department of Agriculture*.

USDAW [ˈʌzdɔː] *n abbr* (*Brit:* = *Union of Shop, Distributive and Allied Workers*) sindacato dei dipendenti di negozi, reti di distribuzione e simili.

USDI *n abbr* = *United States Department of the Interior*.

use *n* [juːs] uso; impiego, utilizzazione *f* ♦ *vt* [juːz] usare, utilizzare, servirsi di; **she ~d to do it** lo faceva (una volta), era solita farlo; **in ~** in uso; **out of ~** fuori uso; **to be of ~** essere utile, servire; **to make ~ of sth** far uso di qc, utilizzare qc; **ready for ~** pronto per l'uso; **it's no ~** non serve, è inutile; **to**

have the ~ of poter usare; **what's this ~d for?** a che serve?; **to be ~d to** avere l'abitudine di; **to get ~d to** abituarsi a, fare l'abitudine.

use up *vt* finire; (*supplies*) dare fondo a; (*left-overs*) utilizzare.

used [juːzd] *a* (*car*) d'occasione.

useful [ˈjuːsful] *a* utile; **to come in ~** fare comodo, tornare utile.

usefulness [ˈjuːsfəlnɪs] *n* utilità.

useless [ˈjuːslɪs] *a* inutile; (*unusable: object*) inservibile.

user [ˈjuːzə*] *n* utente *m/f*; (*of petrol, gas etc*) consumatore/trice.

user-friendly [ˈjuːzəˈfrɛndlɪ] *a* orientato(a) all'utente.

USES *n abbr* = *United States Employment Service*.

usher [ˈʌʃə*] *n* usciere *m*; (*in cinema*) maschera ♦ *vt*: **to ~ sb in** far entrare qn.

usherette [ʌʃəˈrɛt] *n* (*in cinema*) maschera.

USIA *n abbr* = *United States Information Agency*.

USM *n abbr* = *United States Mint*; *United States Mail*.

USN *n abbr* = *United States Navy*.

USPHS *n abbr* = *United States Public Health Service*.

USPO *n abbr* = *United States Post Office*.

USS *abbr* = *United States Ship* (*or Steamer*).

USSR *n abbr see* **Union of Soviet Socialist Republics**.

usu. *abbr* = **usually**.

usual [ˈjuːʒuəl] *a* solito(a); **as ~** come a solito, come d'abitudine.

usually [ˈjuːʒuəlɪ] *ad* di solito.

usurer [ˈjuːʒərə*] *a* usuraio/a.

usurp [juːˈzəːp] *vt* usurpare.

UT *abbr* (*US POST*) = *Utah*.

utensil [juːˈtɛnsl] *n* utensile *m*.

uterus [ˈjuːtərəs] *n* utero.

utilitarian [juːtɪlɪˈtɛərɪən] *a* utilitario(a).

utility [juːˈtɪlɪtɪ] *n* utilità; (*also*: **public ~**) servizio pubblico.

utility room *n* locale adibito alla stiratura dei panni etc.

utilization [juːtɪlaɪˈzeɪʃən] *n* utilizzazione *f*.

utilize [ˈjuːtɪlaɪz] *vt* utilizzare; sfruttare.

utmost [ˈʌtməust] *a* estremo(a) ♦ *n*: **to do one's ~** fare il possibile *or* di tutto; **of the ~ importance** della massima importanza; **it is of the ~ importance that ...** è estremamente importante che ... + *sub*.

utter [ˈʌtə*] *a* assoluto(a), totale ♦ *vt* pronunciare, proferire; emettere.

utterance [ˈʌtərəns] *n* espressione *f*; parole *fpl*.

utterly [ˈʌtəlɪ] *ad* completamente, del tutto.

U-turn [ˈjuːtəːn] *n* inversione *f* a U; (*fig*) voltafaccia *m inv*.

V

V, v [vi:] *n* (*letter*) V, *v* *m or f inv*; **V for Victor** ≈ V come Venezia.

v *abbr* (= *verse*) = *vide*: see) v.; (= *volt*) V.; (= *versus*) contro.

VA *abbr* (*US POST*) = *Virginia*.

vac [væk] *n* *abbr* (*Brit col*) = **vacation**.

vacancy ['veɪkənsɪ] *n* (*job*) posto libero; (*room*) stanza libera; **"no vacancies"** "completo"; **have you any vacancies?** (*office*) avete bisogno di personale?; (*hotel*) avete una stanza?

vacant ['veɪkənt] *a* (*job*, *seat etc*) libero(a); (*expression*) assente.

vacant lot *n* terreno non occupato; (*for sale*) terreno in vendita.

vacate [və'keɪt] *vt* lasciare libero(a).

vacation [və'keɪʃən] *n* (*esp US*) vacanze *fpl*; **to take a ~** prendere una vacanza, prendere le ferie; **on ~** in vacanza, in ferie.

vacation course *n* corso estivo.

vaccinate ['væksɪneɪt] *vt* vaccinare.

vaccination [væksɪ'neɪʃən] *n* vaccinazione *f*.

vaccine ['væksiːn] *n* vaccino.

vacuum ['vækjum] *n* vuoto.

vacuum bottle *n* (*US*) = **vacuum flask**.

vacuum cleaner *n* aspirapolvere *m inv*.

vacuum flask *n* (*Brit*) thermos ® *m inv*.

vacuum-packed ['vækjum'pækt] *a* confezionato(a) sottovuoto.

vagabond ['vægəbɔnd] *n* vagabondo/a.

vagary ['veɪgərɪ] *n* capriccio.

vagina [və'dʒaɪnə] *n* vagina.

vagrancy ['veɪgrənsɪ] *n* vagabondaggio.

vagrant ['veɪgrənt] *n* vagabondo/a.

vague [veɪg] *a* vago(a); (*blurred*: *photo*, *memory*) sfocato(a); **I haven't the ~st idea** non ho la minima *or* più pallida idea.

vaguely ['veɪglɪ] *ad* vagamente.

vain [veɪn] *a* (*useless*) inutile, vano(a); (*conceited*) vanitoso(a); **in ~** inutilmente, invano.

valance ['væləns] *n* volant *m inv*, balza.

valedictory [vælɪ'dɪktərɪ] *a* di commiato.

valentine ['væləntaɪn] *n* (*also*: **~ card**) cartolina *or* biglietto di San Valentino.

valet ['vælɪt] *n* cameriere *m* personale.

valet parking *n* parcheggio effettuato da un dipendente (*dell'albergo etc*).

valet service *n* (*for clothes*) servizio di lavanderia; (*for car*) servizio completo di lavaggio.

valiant ['vælɪənt] *a* valoroso(a), coraggioso(a).

valid ['vælɪd] *a* valido(a), valevole; (*excuse*) valido(a).

validate ['vælɪdeɪt] *vt* (*contract*, *document*) convalidare; (*argument*, *claim*) comprovare.

validity [və'lɪdɪtɪ] *n* validità.

valise [və'liːz] *n* borsa da viaggio.

valley ['vælɪ] *n* valle *f*.

valour, (*US*) **valor** ['vælə*] *n* valore *m*.

valuable ['væljuəbl] *a* (*jewel*) di (grande) valore; (*time*) prezioso(a); **~s** *npl* oggetti *mpl* di valore.

valuation [vælju'eɪʃən] *n* valutazione *f*, stima.

value ['væljuː] *n* valore *m* ♦ *vt* (*fix price*) valutare, dare un prezzo a; (*cherish*) apprezzare, tenere a; **to be of great ~ to sb** avere molta importanza per qn; **to lose (in) ~** (*currency*) svalutarsi; (*property*) perdere (di) valore; **to gain (in) ~** (*currency*) guadagnare; (*property*) aumentare di valore; **you get good ~ (for money) in that shop** si compra bene in quel negozio.

value added tax (VAT) *n* (*Brit*) imposta sul valore aggiunto (I.V.A.).

valued ['væluːd] *a* (*appreciated*) stimato(a), apprezzato(a).

valuer ['væljuə*] *n* stimatore/trice.

valve [vælv] *n* valvola.

vampire ['væmpaɪə*] *n* vampiro.

van [væn] *n* (*AUT*) furgone *m*; (*Brit RAIL*) vagone *m*.

V and A *n* *abbr* (*Brit*) = *Victoria and Albert Museum*.

vandal ['vændl] *n* vandalo/a.

vandalism ['vændəlɪzəm] *n* vandalismo.

vandalize ['vændəlaɪz] *vt* vandalizzare.

vanguard ['vænɡɑːd] *n* avanguardia.

vanilla [və'nɪlə] *n* vaniglia ♦ *cpd* (*ice cream*) alla vaniglia.

vanish ['vænɪʃ] *vi* svanire, scomparire.

vanity ['vænɪtɪ] *n* vanità.

vanity case *n* valigetta per cosmetici.

vantage ['vɑːntɪdʒ] *n*: **~ point** posizione *f or* punto di osservazione; (*fig*) posizione vantaggiosa.

vaporize ['veɪpəraɪz] *vt* vaporizzare ♦ *vi* vaporizzarsi.

vapour, (*US*) **vapor** ['veɪpə*] *n* vapore *m*.

vapo(u)r trail *n* (*AVIAT*) scia.

variable ['vɛərɪəbl] *a* variabile; (*mood*) mutevole ♦ *n* fattore *m* variabile, variabile *f*.

variance ['vɛərɪəns] *n*: **to be at ~ (with)** essere in disaccordo (con); (*facts*) essere in contraddizione (con).

variant ['vɛərɪənt] *n* variante *f*.

variation [vɛərɪ'eɪʃən] *n* variazione *f*; (*in opinion*) cambiamento.

varicose ['værɪkəus] *a*: **~ veins** varici *fpl*.

varied ['vɛərɪd] *a* vario(a), diverso(a).

variety [və'raɪətɪ] *n* varietà *f inv*; (*quantity*): **a wide ~ of ...** una vasta gamma di ...; **for a ~ of reasons** per una serie di motivi.

variety show *n* spettacolo di varietà.

various ['vɛərɪəs] *a* vario(a), diverso(a); (*several*) parecchi(e), molti(e); **at ~ times** in momenti diversi; (*several*) diverse volte.

varnish ['vɑːnɪʃ] *n* vernice *f*; (*for nails*)

smalto ♦ *vt* verniciare; **to ~ one's nails** mettersi lo smalto sulle unghie.

vary ['vɛərɪ] *vt, vi* variare, mutare; **to ~ (with** *or* **according to)** variare (con *or* a seconda di).

varying ['vɛərɪŋ] *a* variabile.

vase [vɑːz] *n* vaso.

vasectomy [væ'sɛktəmɪ] *n* vasectomia.

vaseline ® ['væsɪliːn] *n* vaselina.

vast [vɑːst] *a* vasto(a); (*amount, success*) enorme.

vastly ['vɑːstlɪ] *ad* enormemente.

vastness ['vɑːstnɪs] *n* vastità.

VAT [væt] *n abbr (Brit) see* **value added tax.**

vat [væt] *n* tino.

Vatican ['vætɪkən] *n*: **the ~** il Vaticano.

vault [vɔːlt] *n* (*of roof*) volta; (*tomb*) tomba; (*in bank*) camera blindata; (*jump*) salto ♦ *vt* (*also*: **~ over**) saltare (d'un balzo).

vaunted ['vɔːntɪd] *a*: **much~** tanto celebrato(a).

VC *n abbr* (*Brit*: = *Victoria Cross*) *medaglia al coraggio*; = **vice-chairman.**

VCR *n abbr see* **video cassette recorder.**

VD *n abbr see* **venereal disease.**

VDU *n abbr see* **visual display unit.**

veal [viːl] *n* vitello.

veer [vɪə*] *vi* girare; virare.

veg. [vɛdʒ] *n abbr* (*Brit col*: = *vegetable(s)*) ≈ contorno.

vegetable ['vɛdʒtəbl] *n* verdura, ortaggio ♦ *a* vegetale.

vegetable garden *n* orto.

vegetarian [vɛdʒɪ'tɛərɪən] *a, n* vegetariano(a).

vegetate ['vɛdʒɪteɪt] *vi* vegetare.

vegetation [vɛdʒɪ'teɪʃən] *n* vegetazione *f*.

vehemence ['viːɪməns] *n* veemenza, violenza.

vehement ['viːɪmənt] *a* veemente, violento(a); profondo(a).

vehicle ['viːɪkl] *n* veicolo; (*fig*) mezzo.

vehicular [vɪ'hɪkjulə*] *a*: **"no ~ traffic"** "chiuso al traffico di veicoli".

veil [veɪl] *n* velo ♦ *vt* velare; **under a ~ of secrecy** (*fig*) protetto da una cortina di segretezza.

veiled [veɪld] *a* (*also fig*) velato(a).

vein [veɪn] *n* vena; (*on leaf*) nervatura; (*fig: mood*) vena, umore *m*.

vellum ['vɛləm] *n* (*writing paper*) carta patinata.

velocity [vɪ'lɔsɪtɪ] *n* velocità *f inv*.

velvet ['vɛlvɪt] *n* velluto.

vending machine ['vɛndɪŋ-] *n* distributore *m* automatico.

vendor ['vɛndə*] *n* venditore/trice; **street ~** venditore ambulante.

veneer [və'nɪə*] *n* impiallacciatura; (*fig*) vernice *f*.

venerable ['vɛnərəbl] *a* venerabile.

venereal disease (VD) [vɪ'nɪərɪəl-] *n* malattia venerea.

Venetian [vɪ'niːʃən] *a, n* veneziano(a).

Venetian blind *n* (tenda alla) veneziana.

Venezuela [vɛnɪ'zweɪlə] *n* Venezuela *m*.

Venezuelan [vɛnɪ'zweɪlən] *a, n* venezuelano(a).

vengeance ['vɛndʒəns] *n* vendetta; **with a ~** (*fig*) davvero; furiosamente.

vengeful ['vɛndʒful] *a* vendicativo(a).

Venice ['vɛnɪs] *n* Venezia.

venison ['vɛnɪsn] *n* carne *f* di cervo.

venom ['vɛnəm] *n* veleno.

venomous ['vɛnəməs] *a* velenoso(a).

vent [vɛnt] *n* foro, apertura; (*in dress, jacket*) spacco ♦ *vt* (*fig: one's feelings*) sfogare, dare sfogo a.

ventilate ['vɛntɪleɪt] *vt* (*room*) dare aria a, arieggiare.

ventilation [vɛntɪ'leɪʃən] *n* ventilazione *f*.

ventilation shaft *n* condotto di aerazione.

ventilator ['vɛntɪleɪtə*] *n* ventilatore *m*.

ventriloquist [vɛn'trɪləkwɪst] *n* ventriloquo/a.

venture ['vɛntʃə*] *n* impresa (rischiosa) ♦ *vt* rischiare, azzardare ♦ *vi* arrischiarsi, azzardarsi; **a business ~** un'iniziativa commerciale; **to ~ to do sth** azzardarsi a fare qc.

venture capital *n* capitale *m* di rischio.

venue ['vɛnjuː] *n* luogo di incontro; (*SPORT*) luogo (designato) per l'incontro.

Venus ['viːnəs] *n* (*planet*) Venere *m*.

veracity [və'ræsɪtɪ] *n* veridicità.

veranda(h) [və'rændə] *n* veranda.

verb [vɜːb] *n* verbo.

verbal ['vɜːbəl] *a* verbale; (*translation*) letterale.

verbally ['vɜːbəlɪ] *ad* a voce.

verbatim [vɜː'beɪtɪm] *ad, a* parola per parola.

verbose [vɜː'bəus] *a* verboso(a).

verdict ['vɜːdɪkt] *n* verdetto; (*opinion*) giudizio, parere *m*; **~ of guilty/not guilty** verdetto di colpevolezza/non colpevolezza.

verge [vɜːdʒ] *n* bordo, orlo; **"soft ~s"** (*Brit*) "banchina cedevole"; **on the ~ of doing** sul punto di fare.

verge on *vt fus* rasentare.

verger ['vɜːdʒə*] *n* (*REL*) sagrestano.

verification [vɛrɪfɪ'keɪʃən] *n* verifica.

verify ['vɛrɪfaɪ] *vt* verificare; (*prove the truth of*) confermare.

veritable ['vɛrɪtəbl] *a* vero(a).

vermin ['vɜːmɪn] *npl* animali *mpl* nocivi; (*insects*) insetti *mpl* parassiti.

vermouth ['vɜːməθ] *n* vermut *m inv*.

vernacular [və'nækjulə*] *n* vernacolo.

versatile ['vɜːsətaɪl] *a* (*person*) versatile; (*machine, tool etc*) (che si presta) a molti usi.

verse [vɜːs] *n* (*of poem*) verso; (*stanza*) stanza, strofa; (*in bible*) versetto; (*no pl: poetry*) versi *mpl*; **in ~** in versi.

versed [vɜːst] *a*: **(well-)~ in** versato(a) in.

version ['vɜːʃən] *n* versione *f*.

versus ['vɜːsəs] *prep* contro.

vertebra, pl ~e ['vɜːtɪbrə, -briː] *n* vertebra.

vertebrate ['vɜːtɪbrɪt] *n* vertebrato.

vertebrae ['vɜːtɪbriː] *npl of* **vertebra.**

vertical ['vɜːtɪkl] *a, n* verticale (*m*).

vertically ['vəːtɪklɪ] *ad* verticalmente.

vertigo ['vəːtɪgəu] *n* vertigine *f;* **to suffer from** ~ soffrire di vertigini.

verve [vəːv] *n* brio; entusiasmo.

very ['vɛrɪ] *ad* molto ♦ *a:* **the ~ book which** proprio il libro che; ~ **much** moltissimo; ~ **well** molto bene; ~ **little** molto poco; **at the** ~ **end** proprio alla fine; **the** ~ **last** proprio l'ultimo; **at the** ~ **least** almeno; **the** ~ **thought (of it) alarms me** il solo pensiero mi spaventa, sono spaventato solo al pensiero.

vespers ['vɛspəz] *npl* vespro.

vessel ['vɛsl] *n* (*ANAT*) vaso; (*NAUT*) nave *f;* (*container*) recipiente *m*.

vest [vɛst] *n* (*Brit*) maglia; (: *sleeveless*) canottiera; (*US: waistcoat*) gilè *m inv* ♦ *vt:* **to** ~ **sb with sth, to** ~ **sth in sb** conferire qc a qn.

vested interest *n:* **to have a** ~ **in doing** avere tutto l'interesse a fare; ~**s** *npl* (*COMM*) diritti *mpl* acquisiti.

vestibule ['vɛstɪbjuːl] *n* vestibolo.

vestige ['vɛstɪdʒ] *n* vestigio.

vestment ['vɛstmənt] *n* (*REL*) paramento liturgico.

vestry ['vɛstrɪ] *n* sagrestia.

Vesuvius [vɪ'suːvɪəs] *n* Vesuvio.

vet [vɛt] *n* *abbr* (= *veterinary surgeon*) veterinario ♦ *vt* esaminare minuziosamente; (*text*) rivedere; **to** ~ **sb for a job** raccogliere delle informazioni dettagliate su qn prima di offrirgli un posto.

veteran ['vɛtərn] *n* veterano; (*also:* **war** ~) reduce *m* ♦ *a:* **she's a** ~ **campaigner for** ... lotta da sempre per ....

veteran car *n* auto *f inv* d'epoca (*anteriore al 1919*).

veterinarian [vɛtrɪ'nɛərɪən] *n* (*US*) = **veterinary surgeon**.

veterinary ['vɛtrɪnərɪ] *a* veterinario(a).

veterinary surgeon *n* (*Brit*) veterinario.

veto ['viːtəu] *n* (*pl* ~**es**) veto ♦ *vt* opporre il veto a; **to put a** ~ **on** opporre il veto a.

vex [vɛks] *vt* irritare, contrariare.

vexed [vɛkst] *a* (*question*) controverso(a), dibattuto(a).

VFD *n abbr* (*US*) = *voluntary fire department*.

VG *abbr* (*Brit: SCOL etc* = *very good*) ottimo.

VHF *abbr* (= *very high frequency*) VHF.

VI *abbr* (*US POST*) = *Virgin Islands*.

via ['vaɪə] *prep* (*by way of*) via; (*by means of*) tramite.

viability [vaɪə'bɪlɪtɪ] *n* attuabilità.

viable ['vaɪəbl] *a* attuabile; vitale.

viaduct ['vaɪədʌkt] *n* viadotto.

vibrant ['vaɪbrənt] *a* (*sound*) vibrante; (*colour*) vivace, vivo(a).

vibrate [vaɪ'breɪt] *vi:* **to** ~ **(with)** vibrare (di); (*resound*) risonare (di).

vibration [vaɪ'breɪʃən] *n* vibrazione *f*.

vicar ['vɪkə*] *n* pastore *m*.

vicarage ['vɪkərɪdʒ] *n* presbiterio.

vicarious [vɪ'kɛərɪəs] *a* sofferto(a) al posto di un altro; **to get** ~ **pleasure out of sth** trarre piacere indirettamente da qc.

vice [vaɪs] *n* (*evil*) vizio; (*TECH*) morsa.

vice- [vaɪs] *prefix* vice....

vice-chairman [vaɪs'tʃɛəmən] *n* vicepresidente *m*.

vice-chancellor [vaɪs'tʃɑːnsələ*] *n* (*Brit SCOL*) rettore *m* (*per elezione*).

vice-president [vaɪs'prɛzɪdənt] *n* vice-presidente *m*.

vice squad *n* (squadra del) buon costume *f*.

vice versa ['vaɪsɪ'vəːsə] *ad* viceversa.

vicinity [vɪ'sɪnɪtɪ] *n* vicinanze *fpl*.

vicious ['vɪʃəs] *a* (*remark*) maligno(a), cattivo(a); (*blow*) violento(a); **a** ~ **circle** un circolo vizioso.

viciousness ['vɪʃəsnɪs] *n* malignità, cattiveria; ferocia.

vicissitudes [vɪ'sɪsɪtjuːdz] *npl* vicissitudini *fpl*.

victim ['vɪktɪm] *n* vittima; **to be the** ~ **of** essere vittima di.

victimization [vɪktɪmaɪ'zeɪʃən] *n* persecuzione *f;* rappresaglie *fpl*.

victimize ['vɪktɪmaɪz] *vt* perseguitare; compiere delle rappresaglie contro.

victor ['vɪktə*] *n* vincitore *m*.

Victorian [vɪk'tɔːrɪən] *a* vittoriano(a).

victorious [vɪk'tɔːrɪəs] *a* vittorioso(a).

victory ['vɪktərɪ] *n* vittoria; **to win a** ~ **over sb** riportare una vittoria su qn.

video ['vɪdɪəu] *cpd* video... ♦ *n* (~ *film*) video *m inv*; (*also:* ~ **cassette**) videocassetta; (*also:* ~ **cassette recorder**) videoregistratore *m*.

video cassette *n* videocassetta.

video cassette recorder (VCR) *n* videoregistratore *m*.

video recording *n* registrazione *f* su video.

video tape *n* videotape *m inv*.

vie [vaɪ] *vi:* **to** ~ **with** competere con, rivaleggiare con.

Vienna [vɪ'ɛnə] *n* Vienna.

Vietnam, Viet Nam [vjɛt'næm] *n* Vietnam *m*.

Vietnamese [vjɛtnə'miːz] *a* vietnamita ♦ *n* vietnamita *m/f;* (*LING*) vietnamita *m*.

view [vjuː] *n* vista, veduta; (*opinion*) opinione *f* ♦ *vt* (*situation*) considerare; (*house*) visitare; **on** ~ (*in museum etc*) esposto(a); **to be in** *or* **within** ~ **(of sth)** essere in vista (di qc); **in full** ~ **of sb** sotto gli occhi di qn; **an overall** ~ **of the situation** una visione globale della situazione; **in my** ~ a mio avviso, secondo me; **in** ~ **of the fact that** considerato che; **to take** *or* **hold the** ~ **that** ... essere dell'opinione che ...; **with a** ~ **to doing sth** con l'intenzione di fare qc.

viewdata ['vjuːdeɪtə] *n* (*Brit*) sistema di tele-video.

viewer ['vjuːə*] *n* (*viewfinder*) mirino; (*small projector*) visore *m;* (*TV*) telespettatore/trice.

viewfinder ['vjuːfaɪndə*] *n* mirino.

viewpoint ['vjuːpɔɪnt] *n* punto di vista.

vigil ['vɪdʒɪl] *n* veglia; **to keep** ~ vegliare.

vigilance ['vɪdʒɪləns] *n* vigilanza.

vigilant ['vɪdʒɪlənt] *a* vigile.
vigorous ['vɪgərəs] *a* vigoroso(a).
vigour, *(US)* **vigor** [vɪgə*] *n* vigore *m*.
vile [vaɪl] *a* *(action)* vile; *(smell)* disgustoso(a), nauseante; *(temper)* pessimo(a).
vilify ['vɪlɪfaɪ] *vt* diffamare.
villa ['vɪlə] *n* villa.
village ['vɪlɪdʒ] *n* villaggio.
villager ['vɪlɪdʒə*] *n* abitante *m/f* di villaggio.
villain ['vɪlən] *n* *(scoundrel)* canaglia; *(criminal)* criminale *m*; *(in novel etc)* cattivo.
VIN *n abbr (US)* = *vehicle identification number*.
vindicate ['vɪndɪkeɪt] *vt* comprovare; giustificare.
vindication [vɪndɪ'keɪʃən] *n*: **in ~ of** per giustificare; a discolpa di.
vindictive [vɪn'dɪktɪv] *a* vendicativo(a).
vine [vaɪn] *n* vite *f*; *(climbing plant)* rampicante *m*.
vinegar ['vɪnɪgə*] *n* aceto.
vine grower *n* viticoltore *m*.
vine-growing ['vaɪngrəʊɪŋ] *a* viticolo(a) ♦ *n* viticoltura.
vineyard ['vɪnjɑ:d] *n* vigna, vigneto.
vintage ['vɪntɪdʒ] *n* *(year)* annata, produzione *f*; **the 1970 ~** il vino del 1970.
vintage car *n* auto *f inv* d'epoca.
vintage wine *n* vino d'annata.
vinyl ['vaɪnl] *n* vinile *m*.
viola [vɪ'əʊlə] *n* viola.
violate ['vaɪəleɪt] *vt* violare.
violation [vaɪə'leɪʃən] *n* violazione *f*; **in ~ of** **sth** violando qc.
violence ['vaɪələns] *n* violenza; *(POL etc)* incidenti *mpl* violenti.
violent [vaɪələnt] *a* violento(a); **a ~ dislike of** **sb/sth** una violenta avversione per qn/qc.
violently ['vaɪələntlɪ] *ad* violentemente; *(ill, angry)* terribilmente.
violet ['vaɪələt] *a* *(colour)* viola *inv*, violetto(a) ♦ *n (plant)* violetta.
violin [vaɪə'lɪn] *n* violino.
violinist [vaɪə'lɪnɪst] *n* violinista *m/f*.
VIP *n abbr* (= *very important person*) V.I.P. *m/f inv*.
viper ['vaɪpə*] *n* vipera.
virgin ['və:dʒɪn] *n* vergine *f* ♦ *a* vergine *inv*; **she is a ~** lei è vergine; **the Blessed V~** la Beatissima Vergine.
virginity [və:'dʒɪnɪtɪ] *n* verginità.
Virgo ['və:gəʊ] *n (sign)* Vergine *f*; **to be ~** essere della Vergine.
virile ['vɪraɪl] *a* virile.
virility [vɪ'rɪlɪtɪ] *n* virilità.
virtual ['və:tjuəl] *a* effettivo(a), vero(a); *(COMPUT, PHYSICS)* virtuale; *(in effect)*: **it's** **a ~ impossibility** è praticamente impossibile; **the ~ leader** il capo all'atto pratico.
virtually ['və:tjuəlɪ] *ad (almost)* praticamente; **it is ~ impossible** è praticamente impossibile.

virtue ['və:tju:] *n* virtù *f inv*; *(advantage)* pregio, vantaggio; **by ~ of** grazie a.
virtuoso [və:tju'əʊzəu] *n* virtuoso.
virtuous ['və:tjuəs] *a* virtuoso(a).
virulent ['vɪrulənt] *a* virulento(a).
virus ['vaɪərəs] *n* virus *m inv*.
visa ['vi:zə] *n* visto.
vis-à-vis [vi:zə'vi:] *prep* rispetto a, nei riguardi di.
viscount ['vaɪkaunt] *n* visconte *m*.
viscous ['vɪskəs] *a* viscoso(a).
vise [vaɪs] *n (US TECH)* = **vice**.
visibility [vɪzɪ'bɪlɪtɪ] *n* visibilità.
visible ['vɪzəbl] *a* visibile; **~ exports/imports** esportazioni *fpl*/importazioni *fpl* visibili.
visibly ['vɪzəblɪ] *ad* visibilmente.
vision ['vɪʒən] *n (sight)* vista; *(foresight, in dream)* visione *f*.
visionary ['vɪʒənərɪ] *n* visionario/a.
visit ['vɪzɪt] *n* visita; *(stay)* soggiorno ♦ *vt* *(person)* andare a trovare; *(place)* visitare; **to pay a ~ to** *(person)* fare una visita a; *(place)* andare a visitare; **on a private/** **official ~** in visita privata/ufficiale.
visiting ['vɪzɪtɪŋ] *a (speaker, professor, team)* ospite.
visiting card *n* biglietto da visita.
visiting hours *npl* orario delle visite.
visitor ['vɪzɪtə*] *n* visitatore/trice; *(guest)* ospite *m/f*.
visitors' book *n* libro d'oro; *(in hotel)* registro.
visor ['vaɪzə*] *n* visiera.
VISTA ['vɪstə] *n abbr* (= *Volunteers in Service to America*) volontariato in zone depresse degli Stati Uniti.
vista ['vɪstə] *n* vista, prospettiva.
visual ['vɪzjuəl] *a* visivo(a); visuale; ottico(a).
visual aid *n* sussidio visivo.
visual display unit (VDU) *n* unità *f inv* di visualizzazione.
visualize ['vɪzjuəlaɪz] *vt* immaginare, figurarsi; *(foresee)* prevedere.
visually ['vɪzjuəlɪ] *ad*: **~ appealing** piacevole a vedersi; **~ handicapped** con una menomazione della vista.
vital ['vaɪtl] *a* vitale; **of ~ importance (to sb/** **sth)** di vitale importanza (per qn/qc).
vitality [vaɪ'tælɪtɪ] *n* vitalità.
vitally ['vaɪtəlɪ] *ad* estremamente.
vital statistics *npl (of population)* statistica demografica; *(col: woman's)* misure *fpl*.
vitamin ['vɪtəmɪn] *n* vitamina.
vitiate ['vɪʃɪeɪt] *vt* viziare.
vitreous ['vɪtrɪəs] *a (rock)* vetroso(a); *(china, enamel)* vetrificato(a).
vitriolic [vɪtrɪ'ɔlɪk] *a (fig)* caustico(a).
viva ['vaɪvə] *n (also: ~ voce)* (esame *m*) orale.
vivacious [vɪ'veɪʃəs] *a* vivace.
vivacity [vɪ'væsɪtɪ] *n* vivacità.
vivid ['vɪvɪd] *a* vivido(a).
vividly ['vɪvɪdlɪ] *ad (describe)* vividamente; *(remember)* con precisione.

vivisection [vɪvɪ'sɛkʃən] *n* vivisezione *f*.
vixen ['vɪksn] *n* volpe *f* femmina; (*pej*: *woman*) bisbetica.
viz *abbr* (= *vide licet*: *namely*) cioè.
VLF *abbr* (= *very low frequency*) bassissima frequenza.
V-neck ['viːnɛk] *n* maglione *m* con lo scollo a V.
VOA *n abbr* (= *Voice of America*) voce *f* dell'America (*alla radio*).
vocabulary [vəu'kæbjuləri] *n* vocabolario.
vocal ['vəukl] *a* (*MUS*) vocale; (*communication*) verbale; (*noisy*) rumoroso(a).
vocal chords *npl* corde *fpl* vocali.
vocalist ['vəukəlɪst] *n* cantante *m/f* (*in un gruppo*).
vocation [vəu'keɪʃən] *n* vocazione *f*.
vocational [vəu'keɪʃənl] *a* professionale; ~ **guidance** orientamento professionale; ~ **training** formazione *f* professionale.
vociferous [və'sɪfərəs] *a* rumoroso(a).
vodka ['vɔdkə] *n* vodka *f inv*.
vogue [vəug] *n* moda; (*popularity*) popolarità, voga; **to be in ~, be the ~** essere di moda.
voice [vɔɪs] *n* voce *f* ♦ *vt* (*opinion*) esprimere; **in a loud/soft ~** a voce alta/bassa; **to give ~ to** esprimere.
void [vɔɪd] *n* vuoto ♦ *a*: ~ **of** privo(a) di.
voile [vɔɪl] *n* voile *m*.
vol. *abbr* (= *volume*) vol.
volatile ['vɔlətaɪl] *a* volatile; (*fig*) volubile.
volcanic [vɔl'kænɪk] *a* vulcanico(a).
volcano, ~es [vɔl'keɪnəu] *n* vulcano.
volition [və'lɪʃən] *n*: **of one's own ~** di propria volontà.
volley ['vɔlɪ] *n* (*of gunfire*) salva; (*of stones etc*) raffica, gragnola; (*TENNIS etc*) volata.
volleyball ['vɔlɪbɔːl] *n* pallavolo *f*.
volt [vəult] *n* volt *m inv*.
voltage ['vəultɪdʒ] *n* tensione *f*, voltaggio; **high/low ~** alta/bassa tensione.
voluble ['vɔljubl] *a* loquace, ciarliero(a).
volume ['vɔljuːm] *n* volume *m*; (*of tank*) capacità *f inv*; ~ **one/two** (*of book*) volume primo/secondo; **his expression spoke ~s** la sua espressione lasciava capire tutto.
volume control *n* (*RADIO, TV*) regolatore *m or* manopola del volume.
volume discount *n* (*COMM*) vantaggio sul volume di vendita.
voluminous [və'luːmɪnəs] *a* voluminoso(a); (*notes etc*) abbondante.
voluntarily ['vɔləntrɪlɪ] *ad* volontariamente; gratuitamente.
voluntary ['vɔləntərɪ] *a* volontario(a); (*unpaid*) gratuito(a), non retribuito(a).
voluntary liquidation *n* (*COMM*) liquidazione *f* volontaria.
volunteer [vɔlən'tɪə*] *n* volontario/a ♦ *vi* (*MIL*) arruolarsi volontario; **to ~ to do** offrire (volontariamente) di fare.
voluptuous [və'lʌptjuəs] *a* voluttuoso(a).
vomit ['vɔmɪt] *n* vomito ♦ *vt, vi* vomitare.
vote [vəut] *n* voto, suffragio; (*cast*) voto;

(*franchise*) diritto di voto ♦ *vi* votare ♦ *vt* (*gen*) votare; (*sum of money etc*) votare a favore di; **to ~ to do sth** votare a favore di fare qc; **he was ~d secretary** è stato eletto segretario; **to put sth to the ~, to take a ~ on sth** mettere qc ai voti; ~ **for/against** voto a favore/contrario; **to pass a ~ of confidence/no confidence** dare il voto di fiducia/sfiducia; ~ **of thanks** discorso di ringraziamento.
voter ['vəutə*] *n* elettore/trice.
voting ['vəutɪŋ] *n* scrutinio.
voting paper *n* (*Brit*) scheda elettorale.
voting right *n* diritto di voto.
vouch [vautʃ]: **to ~ for** *vt fus* farsi garante di.
voucher ['vautʃə*] *n* (*for meal, petrol*) buono; (*receipt*) ricevuta; **travel ~** voucher *m inv*, tagliando.
vow [vau] *n* voto, promessa solenne ♦ *vi* giurare; **to take *or* make a ~ to do sth** fare voto di fare qc.
vowel ['vauəl] *n* vocale *f*.
voyage ['vɔɪdʒ] *n* viaggio per mare, traversata.
VP *n abbr* (= *vice-president*) V.P.
vs *abbr* (= *versus*) contro.
VSO *n abbr* (*Brit*: = *Voluntary Service Overseas*) servizio volontario in paesi sottosviluppati.
VT *abbr* (*US POST*) = *Vermont*.
vulgar ['vʌlgə*] *a* volgare.
vulgarity [vʌl'gærɪtɪ] *n* volgarità.
vulnerability [vʌlnərə'bɪlɪtɪ] *n* vulnerabilità.
vulnerable ['vʌlnərəbl] *a* vulnerabile.
vulture ['vʌltʃə*] *n* avvoltoio.

W

W, w ['dʌblju:] *n* (*letter*) W, w *m or f inv*; **W for William** ≈ W come Washington.
W *abbr* (= *west*) O; (*ELEC*: = *watt*) w.
WA *abbr* (*US POST*) = *Washington*.
wad [wɔd] *n* (*of cotton wool, paper*) tampone *m*; (*of banknotes etc*) fascio.
wadding ['wɔdɪŋ] *n* imbottitura.
waddle ['wɔdl] *vi* camminare come una papera.
wade [weɪd] *vi*: **to ~ through** camminare a stento in ♦ *vt* guadare.
wafer ['weɪfə*] *n* (*CULIN*) cialda; (*REL*) ostia; (*COMPUT*) wafer *m inv*.
wafer-thin ['weɪfə'θɪn] *a* molto sottile.
waffle ['wɔfl] *n* (*CULIN*) cialda; (*col*) ciance *fpl*; riempitivo ♦ *vi* cianciare; parlare a vuoto.
waffle iron *n* stampo per cialde.
waft [wɔft] *vt* portare ♦ *vi* diffondersi.

wag [wæg] *vt* agitare, muovere ♦ *vi* agitarsi; **the dog ~ged its tail** il cane scodinzolò.

wage [weɪdʒ] *n* (*also:* **~s**) salario, paga ♦ *vt*: **to ~ war** fare la guerra; **a day's ~s** un giorno di paga.

wage claim *n* rivendicazione *f* salariale.

wage differential *n* differenza di salario.

wage earner *n* salariato/a.

wage freeze *n* blocco dei salari.

wage packet *n* (*Brit*) busta *f* paga *inv*.

wager ['weɪdʒə*] *n* scommessa.

waggle ['wægl] *vt* dimenare, agitare ♦ *vi* dimenarsi, agitarsi.

wag(g)on ['wægən] *n* (*horse-drawn*) carro; (*truck*) furgone *m*; (*Brit RAIL*) vagone *m* (merci).

wail [weɪl] *n* gemito; (*of siren*) urlo ♦ *vi* gemere; urlare.

waist [weɪst] *n* vita, cintola.

waistcoat ['weɪskəut] *n* panciotto, gilè *m inv*.

waistline ['weɪstlaɪn] *n* (giro di) vita.

wait [weɪt] *n* attesa ♦ *vi* aspettare, attendere; **to ~ for** aspettare; **to keep sb ~ing** far aspettare qn; **~ a moment!** (aspetti) un momento!; **"repairs while you ~"** "riparazioni lampo"; **I can't ~ to ...** (*fig*) non vedo l'ora di ...; **to lie in ~ for** stare in agguato a.

  wait behind *vi* rimanere (ad aspettare).

  wait on *vt fus* servire.

  wait up *vi* restare alzato(a) (ad aspettare); **don't ~ up for me** non rimanere alzato per me.

waiter ['weɪtə*] *n* cameriere *m*.

waiting ['weɪtɪŋ] *n*: **"no ~"** (*Brit AUT*) "divieto di sosta".

waiting list *n* lista d'attesa.

waiting room *n* sala d'aspetto *or* d'attesa.

waitress ['weɪtrɪs] *n* cameriera.

waive [weɪv] *vt* rinunciare a, abbandonare.

waiver ['weɪvə*] *n* rinuncia.

wake [weɪk] *vb* (*pt* **woke**, **~d** [wəuk, 'wəukn]) *vt* (*also:* **~ up**) svegliare ♦ *vi* (*also:* **~ up**) svegliarsi ♦ *n* (*for dead person*) veglia funebre; (*NAUT*) scia; **to ~ up to sth** (*fig*) rendersi conto di qc; **in the ~ of** sulla scia di; **to follow in sb's ~** (*fig*) seguire le tracce di qn.

waken ['weɪkn] *vt*, *vi* = **wake**.

Wales [weɪlz] *n* Galles *m*.

walk [wɔːk] *n* passeggiata; (*short*) giretto; (*gait*) passo, andatura; (*path*) sentiero; (*in park etc*) sentiero, vialetto ♦ *vi* camminare; (*for pleasure, exercise*) passeggiare ♦ *vt* (*distance*) fare *or* percorrere a piedi; (*dog*) accompagnare, portare a passeggiare; **10 minutes' ~ from** 10 minuti di cammino *or* a piedi da; **to go for a ~** andare a fare quattro passi; andare a fare una passeggiata; **from all ~s of life** di tutte le condizioni sociali; **to ~ in one's sleep** essere sonnambulo(a); **I'll ~ you home** ti accompagno a casa.

  walk out *vi* (*go out*) uscire; (*as protest*) uscire (in segno di protesta); (*strike*)

scendere in sciopero; **to ~ out on sb** piantare in asso qn.

walker ['wɔːkə*] *n* (*person*) camminatore/ trice.

walkie-talkie ['wɔːkɪ'tɔːkɪ] *n* walkie-talkie *m inv*.

walking ['wɔːkɪŋ] *n* camminare *m*; **it's within ~ distance** ci si arriva a piedi.

walking holiday *n* vacanza fatta di lunghe camminate.

walking shoes *npl* scarpe *fpl* da passeggio.

walking stick *n* bastone *m* da passeggio.

walk-on ['wɔːkɔn] *a* (*THEATRE*: *part*) da comparsa.

walkout ['wɔːkaut] *n* (*of workers*) sciopero senza preavviso *or* a sorpresa.

walkover ['wɔːkəuvə*] *n* (*col*) vittoria facile, gioco da ragazzi.

walkway ['wɔːkweɪ] *n* passaggio pedonale.

wall [wɔːl] *n* muro; (*internal, of tunnel, cave*) parete *f*; **to go to the ~** (*fig*: *firm etc*) fallire.

  wall in *vt* (*garden etc*) circondare con un muro.

wall cupboard *n* pensile *m*.

walled [wɔːld] *a* (*city*) fortificato(a).

wallet ['wɔlɪt] *n* portafoglio.

wallflower ['wɔːlflauə*] *n* violacciocca; **to be a ~** (*fig*) fare da tappezzeria.

wall hanging *n* tappezzeria.

wallop ['wɔləp] *vt* (*col*) pestare.

wallow ['wɔləu] *vi* sguazzare, rotolarsi; **to ~ in one's grief** crogiolarsi nel proprio dolore.

wallpaper ['wɔːlpeɪpə*] *n* carta da parati.

wall-to-wall ['wɔːltə'wɔːl] *a*: **~ carpeting** moquette *f*.

wally ['wɔlɪ] *n* (*col*) scemo/a.

walnut ['wɔːlnʌt] *n* noce *f*; (*tree*) noce *m*.

walrus, *pl* **~** *or* **~es** ['wɔːlrəs] *n* tricheco.

waltz [wɔːlts] *n* valzer *m inv* ♦ *vi* ballare il valzer.

wan [wɔn] *a* pallido(a), smorto(a); triste.

wand [wɔnd] *n* (*also:* **magic ~**) bacchetta (magica).

wander ['wɔndə*] *vi* (*person*) girare senza meta, girovagare; (*thoughts*) vagare; (*river*) serpeggiare.

wanderer ['wɔndərə*] *n* vagabondo/a.

wandering ['wɔndrɪŋ] *a* (*tribe*) nomade; (*minstrel, actor*) girovago(a); (*path, river*) tortuoso(a); (*glance, mind*) distratto(a).

wane [weɪn] *vi* (*moon*) calare; (*reputation*) declinare.

wangle ['wæŋgl] (*Brit col*) *vt* procurare (con l'astuzia) ♦ *n* astuzia.

want [wɔnt] *vt* volere; (*need*) aver bisogno di; (*lack*) mancare di ♦ *n* (*poverty*) miseria, povertà; **~s** *npl* (*needs*) bisogni *mpl*; **for ~ of** per mancanza di; **to ~ to do** volere fare; **to ~ sb to do** volere che qn faccia; **you're ~ed on the phone** la vogliono al telefono; **"cook ~ed"** "cercasi cuoco".

want ads *npl* (*US*) piccoli annunci *mpl*.

wanting ['wɔntɪŋ] *a*: **to be ~ (in)** mancare

(di); **to be found** ~ non risultare all'altezza.
wanton ['wɔntn] a sfrenato(a); senza motivo.
war [wɔ:*] n guerra; **to go to** ~ entrare in
guerra.
warble ['wɔ:bl] n (of bird) trillo ♦ vi trillare.
war cry n grido di guerra.
ward [wɔ:d] n (in hospital: room) corsia; (:
section) reparto; (POL) circoscrizione f;
(LAW: child) pupillo/a.
ward off vt parare, schivare.
warden ['wɔ:dn] n (of institution) direttore/
trice; (of park, game reserve) guardiano/a;
(Brit: also: **traffic** ~) addetto/a al controllo
del traffico e del parcheggio.
warder ['wɔ:də*] n (Brit) guardia carceraria.
wardrobe ['wɔ:drəub] n (cupboard)
guardaroba m inv, armadio; (clothes)
guardaroba; (THEATRE) costumi mpl.
warehouse ['wɛəhaus] n magazzino.
wares [wɛəz] npl merci fpl.
warfare ['wɔ:fɛə*] n guerra.
war game n war game m inv.
warhead ['wɔ:hɛd] n (MIL) testata, ogiva.
warily ['wɛərɪlɪ] ad cautamente, con prudenza.
warlike ['wɔ:laɪk] a guerriero(a).
warm [wɔ:m] a caldo(a); (welcome, applause)
caloroso(a); (person, greeting) cordiale;
(heart) d'oro; (supporter) convinto(a); **it's** ~
fa caldo; **I'm** ~ ho caldo; **to keep sth** ~
tenere qc al caldo; **with my** ~**est thanks** con
i miei più sentiti ringraziamenti.
warm up vi scaldarsi, riscaldarsi; (athlete,
discussion) riscaldarsi ♦ vt scaldare, riscaldare; (engine) far scaldare.
warm-blooded ['wɔ:m'blʌdɪd] a a sangue
caldo.
war memorial n monumento ai caduti.
warm-hearted [wɔ:m'hɑ:tɪd] a affettuoso(a).
warmly ['wɔ:mlɪ] ad caldamente; calorosa-
mente; vivamente.
warmonger ['wɔ:mʌŋgə*] n guerrafondaio.
warmongering ['wɔ:mʌŋgrɪŋ] n bellicismo.
warmth [wɔ:mθ] n calore m.
warm-up ['wɔ:mʌp] n (SPORT) riscaldamento.
warn [wɔ:n] vt avvertire, avvisare; **to** ~ **sb
not to do sth** or **against doing sth** avvertire
qn di non fare qc.
warning ['wɔ:nɪŋ] n avvertimento; (notice)
avviso; **without** (any) ~ senza preavviso;
gale ~ avviso di burrasca.
warning light n spia luminosa.
warning triangle n (AUT) triangolo.
warp [wɔ:p] n (TEXTILES) ordito ♦ vi
deformarsi ♦ vt deformare; (fig) corrompere.
warpath ['wɔ:pɑ:θ] n: **to be on the** ~ (fig)
essere sul sentiero di guerra.
warped [wɔ:pt] a (wood) curvo(a); (fig:
character, sense of humour etc) contorto(a).
warrant ['wɔrnt] n (LAW: to arrest) mandato
di cattura; (: to search) mandato di
perquisizione ♦ vt (justify, merit) giustificare.
warrant officer (WO) n sottufficiale m.
warranty ['wɔrəntɪ] n garanzia; **under** ~
(COMM) in garanzia.

warren ['wɔrən] n (of rabbits) tana.
warring ['wɔ:rɪŋ] a (interests etc) opposto(a),
in lotta; (nations) in guerra.
warrior ['wɔrɪə*] n guerriero/a.
Warsaw ['wɔ:sɔ:] n Varsavia.
warship ['wɔ:ʃɪp] n nave f da guerra.
wart [wɔ:t] n verruca.
wartime ['wɔ:taɪm] n: **in** ~ in tempo di
guerra.
wary ['wɛərɪ] a prudente; **to be** ~ **about** or of
doing sth andare cauto nel fare qc.
was [wɔz] pt of **be**.
wash [wɔʃ] vt lavare; (sweep, carry: sea etc)
portare, trascinare ♦ vi lavarsi ♦ n: **to give
sth a** ~ lavare qc, dare una lavata a qc; **to
have a** ~ lavarsi; **he was** ~**ed overboard** fu
trascinato in mare (dalle onde).
wash away vt (stain) togliere lavando;
(subj: river etc) trascinare via.
wash down vt lavare.
wash off vi andare via con il lavaggio.
wash up vi lavare i piatti; (US: have a
wash) lavarsi.
washable ['wɔʃəbl] a lavabile.
washbasin ['wɔʃbeɪsn] n lavabo.
washcloth ['wɔʃklɔθ] n (US) pezzuola (per
lavarsi).
washer ['wɔʃə*] n (TECH) rondella.
wash-hand basin ['wɔʃhænd-] n (Brit)
lavabo.
washing ['wɔʃɪŋ] n (Brit: linen etc) bucato;
dirty ~ biancheria da lavare.
washing line n (Brit) corda del bucato.
washing machine n lavatrice f.
washing powder n (Brit) detersivo (in
polvere).
Washington ['wɔʃɪŋtən] n Washington f.
washing-up [wɔʃɪŋ'ʌp] n (dishes) piatti mpl
sporchi; **to do the** ~ lavare i piatti,
rigovernare.
washing-up liquid n (Brit) detersivo liquido
(per stoviglie).
wash-out ['wɔʃaut] n (col) disastro.
washroom ['wɔʃrum] n gabinetto.
wasn't ['wɔznt] = **was not**.
Wasp, WASP [wɔsp] n abbr (US: = White
Anglo-Saxon Protestant) W.A.S.P. m
(protestante bianco anglosassone).
wasp [wɔsp] n vespa.
waspish ['wɔspɪʃ] a litigioso(a).
wastage ['weɪstɪdʒ] n spreco; (in
manufacturing) scarti mpl.
waste [weɪst] n spreco; (of time) perdita;
(rubbish) rifiuti mpl ♦ a (material) di scarto;
(food) avanzato(a); (energy, heat) spreca-
to(a); (land, ground: in city) abbandona-
to(a); (: in country) incolto(a) ♦ vt sprecare;
(time, opportunity) perdere; ~**s** npl distesa
desolata; **it's a** ~ **of money** sono soldi
sprecati; **to go to** ~ andare sprecato; **to lay**
~ devastare.
waste away vi deperire.
wastebin ['weɪstbɪn] n (Brit) bidone m or secchio della spazzatura.

waste disposal (unit) *n* (*Brit*) eliminatore *m* di rifiuti.

wasteful ['weistful] *a* sprecone(a); (*process*) dispendioso(a).

waste ground *n* (*Brit*) terreno incolto *or* abbandonato.

wasteland ['weistlænd] *n* terra desolata.

wastepaper basket ['weistpeipə-] *n* cestino per la carta straccia.

waste pipe *n* tubo di scarico.

waste products *n* (*INDUSTRY*) materiali *mpl* di scarto.

watch [wɔtʃ] *n* (*wrist~*) orologio; (*act of watching*) sorveglianza; (*guard*: MIL, NAUT) guardia; (*NAUT*: *spell of duty*) quarto ♦ *vt* (*look at*) osservare; (*: match, programme*) guardare; (*spy on, guard*) sorvegliare, tenere d'occhio; (*be careful of*) fare attenzione a ♦ *vi* osservare, guardare; (*keep guard*) fare *or* montare la guardia; **to keep a close ~ on sb/sth** tener bene d'occhio qn/qc; **~ how you drive/what you're doing** attento a come guidi/quel che fai.

watch out *vi* fare attenzione.

watchband ['wɔtʃbænd] *n* (*US*) cinturino da orologio.

watchdog ['wɔtʃdɔg] *n* cane *m* da guardia; (*fig*) sorvegliante *m/f*.

watchful ['wɔtʃful] *a* attento(a), vigile.

watchmaker ['wɔtʃmeikə*] *n* orologiaio/a.

watchman ['wɔtʃmən] *n* guardiano *m*; (*also*: **night ~**) guardiano notturno.

watch stem *n* (*US*) corona di carica.

watch strap *n* cinturino da orologio.

watchword ['wɔtʃwɔːd] *n* parola d'ordine.

water [wɔːtə*] *n* acqua ♦ *vt* (*plant*) annaffiare ♦ *vi* (*eyes*) piangere; **in British ~s** acque territoriali britanniche; **I'd like a drink of ~** vorrei un bicchier d'acqua; **to pass ~** orinare; **to make sb's mouth ~** far venire l'acquolina in bocca a qn.

water down *vt* (*milk*) diluire; (*fig*: *story*) edulcorare.

water closet *n* (*Brit*) W.C. *m inv*, gabinetto.

watercolour, (*US*) **watercolor** ['wɔːtəkʌlə*] *n* (*picture*) acquerello; **~s** *npl* colori *mpl* per acquerelli.

water-cooled ['wɔːtəkuːld] *a* raffreddato(a) ad acqua.

watercress ['wɔːtəkrɛs] *n* crescione *m*.

waterfall ['wɔːtəfɔːl] *n* cascata.

waterfront ['wɔːtəfrʌnt] *n* (*seafront*) lungomare *m*; (*at docks*) banchina.

water heater *n* scaldabagno.

water hole *n* pozza d'acqua.

water ice *n* (*Brit*) sorbetto.

watering can ['wɔːtərɪŋ-] *n* annaffiatoio.

water level *n* livello dell'acqua; (*of flood*) livello delle acque.

water lily *n* ninfea.

waterline ['wɔːtəlaɪn] *n* (*NAUT*) linea di galleggiamento.

waterlogged ['wɔːtəlɔgd] *a* saturo(a) d'acqua; imbevuto(a) d'acqua; (*football pitch etc*) allagato(a).

water main *n* conduttura dell'acqua.

watermark ['wɔːtəmɑːk] *n* (*on paper*) filigrana.

watermelon ['wɔːtəmɛlən] *n* anguria, cocomero.

water polo *n* pallanuoto *f*.

waterproof ['wɔːtəpruːf] *a* impermeabile.

water-repellent ['wɔːtərɪ'pɛlənt] *a* idrorepellente.

watershed ['wɔːtəʃɛd] *n* (*GEO, fig*) spartiacque *m*.

water-skiing ['wɔːtəskiːɪŋ] *n* sci *m* acquatico.

water softener *n* addolcitore *m*; (*substance*) anti-calcare *m*.

water tank *n* serbatoio d'acqua.

watertight ['wɔːtətaɪt] *a* stagno(a).

water vapour *n* vapore *m* acqueo.

waterway ['wɔːtəweɪ] *n* corso d'acqua navigabile.

waterworks ['wɔːtəwɔːks] *npl* impianto idrico.

watery ['wɔːtərɪ] *a* (*colour*) slavato(a); (*coffee*) acquoso(a).

watt [wɔt] *n* watt *m inv*.

wattage ['wɔtɪdʒ] *n* wattaggio.

wattle ['wɔtl] *n* graticcio.

wave [weɪv] *n* onda; (*of hand*) gesto, segno; (*in hair*) ondulazione *f*; (*fig*: *of enthusiasm, strikes etc*) ondata ♦ *vi* fare un cenno con la mano; (*flag*) sventolare ♦ *vt* (*handkerchief*) sventolare; (*stick*) brandire; (*hair*) ondulare; **short/medium/long ~** (*RADIO*) onde corte/medie/lunghe; **the new ~** (*CINEMA, MUS*) la new wave; **to ~ sb goodbye, to ~ goodbye to sb** fare un cenno d'addio a qn; **he ~d us over to his table** ci invitò con un cenno al suo tavolo.

wave aside, wave away *vt* (*person*): **to ~ sb aside** fare cenno a qn di spostarsi; (*fig*: *suggestion, objection*) respingere, rifiutare; (*: doubts*) scacciare.

waveband ['weɪvbænd] *n* gamma di lunghezze d'onda.

wavelength ['weɪvlɛŋθ] *n* lunghezza d'onda.

waver ['weɪvə*] *vi* vacillare; (*voice*) tremolare.

wavy ['weɪvɪ] *a* ondulato(a); ondeggiante.

wax [wæks] *n* cera ♦ *vt* dare la cera a; (*car*) lucidare ♦ *vi* (*moon*) crescere.

waxworks ['wækswɔːks] *npl* cere *fpl*; museo delle cere.

way [weɪ] *n* via, strada; (*path, access*) passaggio; (*distance*) distanza; (*direction*) parte *f*, direzione *f*; (*manner*) modo, stile *m*; (*habit*) abitudine *f*; (*condition*) condizione *f*; **which ~?** — **this ~** da che parte *or* in quale direzione? — da questa parte *or* per di qua; **to crawl one's ~ to ...** raggiungere ... strisciando; **he lied his ~ out of it** se l'è cavata mentendo; **to lose one's ~** perdere la strada; **on the ~** (*en route*) per strada; (*expected*) in arrivo; **you pass it on your ~ home** ci passi davanti andando a casa; **to be on one's ~** essere in cammino *or* sulla strada; **to be in the** ~ bloccare il passaggio; (*fig*) essere tra i piedi *or* d'impiccio; **to keep out of sb's** ~ evitare qn; **it's a long** ~ **away** è molto lontano da qui; **the village is rather out of the** ~ il villaggio è abbastanza fuori mano; **to go out of one's** ~ **to do** (*fig*) mettercela tutta *or* fare di tutto per fare; **to be under** ~ (*work, project*) essere in corso; **to make** ~ **(for sb/sth)** far strada (a qn/qc); (*fig*) lasciare il posto *or* far largo (a qn/qc); **to get one's own** ~ fare come si vuole; **put it the right** ~ **up** (*Brit*) mettilo in piedi dalla parte giusta; **to be the wrong** ~ **round** essere al contrario; **he's in a bad** ~ è ridotto male; **in a** ~ in un certo senso; **in some** ~**s** sotto certi aspetti; **in the** ~ **of** come; **by** ~ **of** (*through*) attraverso; **"**~ **in"** "entrata", "ingresso"; **"**~ **out"** "uscita"; **the** ~ **back** la via del ritorno; **this** ~ **and that** di qua e di là; **"give** ~**"** (*Brit AUT*) "dare la precedenza"; **no** ~! (*col*) assolutamente no!

waybill ['weɪbɪl] *n* (*COMM*) bolla di accompagnamento.

waylay [weɪ'leɪ] *vt irg* tendere un agguato a; attendere al passaggio; (*fig*): **I got waylaid** ho avuto un contrattempo.

wayside ['weɪsaɪd] *n* bordo della strada; **to fall by the** ~ (*fig*) perdersi lungo la strada.

way station *n* (*US RAIL*) stazione *f* secondaria; (*fig*) tappa.

wayward ['weɪwəd] *a* capriccioso(a); testardo(a).

WC *n abbr* (*Brit*: = *water closet*) W.C. *m inv*, gabinetto.

WCC *n abbr* (= *World Council of Churches*) Consiglio Ecumenico delle Chiese.

we [wiː] *pl pronoun* noi; **here** ~ **are** eccoci.

weak [wiːk] *a* debole; (*health*) precario(a); (*beam etc*) fragile; (*tea, coffee*) leggero(a); **to grow** ~**(er)** come;

weaken ['wiːkən] *vi* indebolirsi ♦ *vt* indebolire.

weak-kneed ['wiːk'niːd] *a* (*fig*) debole, codardo(a).

weakling ['wiːklɪŋ] *n* smidollato/a; debole *m/f*.

weakly ['wiːklɪ] *a* deboluccio(a), gracile ♦ *ad* debolmente.

weakness ['wiːknɪs] *n* debolezza; (*fault*) punto debole, difetto.

wealth [wɛlθ] *n* (*money, resources*) ricchezza, richezze *fpl*; (*of details*) abbondanza, profusione *f*.

wealth tax *n* imposta sul patrimonio.

wealthy ['wɛlθɪ] *a* ricco(a).

wean [wiːn] *vt* svezzare.

weapon ['wɛpən] *n* arma.

wear [wɛə*] *n* (*use*) uso; (*deterioration through use*) logorio, usura; (*clothing*): **sports/baby** ~ abbigliamento sportivo/per neonati ♦ *vb* (*pt* **wore**, *pp* **worn** [wɔː*, wɔːn]) *vt* (*clothes*) portare; mettersi; (*look, smile, beard etc*) avere; (*damage: through use*) consumare ♦ *vi* (*last*) durare; (*rub etc through*) consumarsi; ~ **and tear** usura,

consumo; **to:vn/evening** ~ abiti *mpl or* tenuta da città/sera; **to** ~ **a hole in sth** bucare qc a furia di usarlo.

wear away *vt* consumare; erodere ♦ *vi* consumarsi; essere eroso(a).

wear down *vt* consumare; (*strength*) esaurire.

wear off *vi* sparire lentamente.

wear on *vi* passare.

wear out *vt* consumare; (*person, strength*) esaurire.

wearable ['wɛərəbl] *a* indossabile.

wearily ['wɪərɪlɪ] *ad* stancamente.

weariness ['wɪərɪnɪs] *n* stanchezza.

wearisome ['wɪərɪsəm] *a* (*tiring*) estenuante; (*boring*) noioso(a).

weary ['wɪərɪ] *a* stanco(a); (*tiring*) faticoso(a) ♦ *vt* stancare ♦ *vi*: **to** ~ **of** stancarsi di.

weasel ['wiːzl] *n* (*ZOOL*) donnola.

weather ['wɛðə*] *n* tempo // *vt* (*wood*) stagionare; (*storm, crisis*) superare; **what's the** ~ **like?** che tempo fa?; **under the** ~ (*fig: ill*) poco bene.

weather-beaten ['wɛðəbiːtn] *a* (*person*) segnato(a) dalle intemperie; (*building*) logorato(a) dalle intemperie.

weather cock *n* banderuola.

weather forecast *n* previsioni *fpl* del tempo, bollettino meteorologico.

weatherman ['wɛðəmæn] *n* meteorologo.

weatherproof ['wɛðəpruːf] *a* (*garment*) impermeabile.

weather report *n* bollettino meteorologico.

weather vane *n* = **weather cock**.

weave *pt* **wove**, *pp* **woven** [wiːv, wəuv, 'wəuvn] *vt* (*cloth*) tessere; (*basket*) intrecciare ♦ *vi* (*fig: pt, pp* ~**d**: *move in and out*) zigzagare.

weaver ['wiːvə*] *n* tessitore/trice.

weaving ['wiːvɪŋ] *n* tessitura.

web [wɛb] *n* (*of spider*) ragnatela; (*on foot*) palma; (*fabric, also fig*) tessuto.

webbed [wɛbd] *a* (*foot*) palmato(a).

webbing ['wɛbɪŋ] *n* (*on chair*) cinghie *fpl*.

wed [wɛd] *vt* (*pt, pp* **wedded**) sposare ♦ *n*: **the newly-**~**s** gli sposi novelli.

Wed. *abbr* (= *Wednesday*) mer.

we'd [wiːd] = **we had; we would**.

wedded ['wɛdɪd] *pt, pp of* **wed**.

wedding ['wɛdɪŋ] *n* matrimonio; **silver/golden** ~ nozze *fpl* d'argento/d'oro.

wedding anniversary *n* anniversario di matrimonio.

wedding day *n* giorno delle nozze *or* del matrimonio.

wedding dress *n* abito nuziale.

wedding present *n* regalo di nozze.

wedding ring *n* fede *f*.

wedge [wɛdʒ] *n* (*of wood etc*) cuneo; (*under door etc*) zeppa; (*of cake*) spicchio, fetta ♦ *vt* mettere una zeppa sotto (*or* in); **to** ~ **a door open** tenere aperta una porta con un fermo.

wedge-heeled shoes ['wɛdʒhiːld-] *npl* scarpe *fpl* con tacco a zeppa.

wedlock ['wɛdlɔk] n vincolo matrimoniale.
Wednesday ['wɛdnzdɪ] n mercoledì m inv; for phrases see also **Tuesday**.
wee [wi:] a (Scottish) piccolo(a).
weed [wi:d] n erbaccia ♦ vt diserbare.
weed-killer ['wi:dkɪlə*] n diserbante m.
weedy ['wi:dɪ] a (man) allampanato.
week [wi:k] n settimana; **once/twice a** ~ una volta/due volte alla settimana; **in 2** ~**s' time** fra 2 settimane, fra 15 giorni; **Tuesday** ~, **a** ~ **on Tuesday** martedì a otto.
weekday ['wi:kdeɪ] n giorno feriale; (COMM) giornata lavorativa; **on** ~**s** durante la settimana.
weekend [wi:k'ɛnd] n fine settimana m or f inv, weekend m inv.
weekend case n borsa da viaggio.
weekly ['wi:klɪ] ad ogni settimana, settimanalmente ♦ a, n settimanale (m).
weep, pt, pp **wept** [wi:p, wɛpt] vi (person) piangere; (MED: wound etc) essudare.
weeping willow ['wi:pɪŋ-] n salice m piangente.
weft [wɛft] n (TEXTILES) trama.
weigh [weɪ] vt, vi pesare; **to** ~ **anchor** salpare or levare l'ancora; **to** ~ **the pros and cons** valutare i pro e i contro.
  weigh down vt (branch) piegare; (fig: with worry) opprimere, caricare.
  weigh out vt (goods) pesare.
  weigh up vt valutare.
weighbridge ['weɪbrɪdʒ] n bascula.
weighing machine ['weɪɪŋ-] n pesa.
weight [weɪt] n peso; **sold by** ~ venduto(a) a peso; ~**s and measures** pesi e misure; **to put on/lose** ~ ingrassare/dimagrire.
weighting ['weɪtɪŋ] n: ~ **allowance** indennità f inv speciale (per carovita etc).
weightlessness ['weɪtlɪsnɪs] n mancanza di peso.
weightlifter ['weɪtlɪftə*] n pesista m.
weighty ['weɪtɪ] a pesante; (fig) importante, grave.
weir [wɪə*] n diga.
weird [wɪəd] a strano(a), bizzarro(a); (eerie) soprannaturale.
welcome ['wɛlkəm] a benvenuto(a) ♦ n accoglienza, benvenuto ♦ vt accogliere cordialmente; (also: **bid** ~) dare il benvenuto a; (be glad of) rallegrarsi di; **to be** ~ essere il(la) benvenuto(a); **to make sb** ~ accogliere bene qn; **you're** ~ (after thanks) prego; **you're** ~ **to try** provi pure.
welcoming ['wɛlkəmɪŋ] a accogliente.
weld [wɛld] n saldatura ♦ vt saldare.
welder ['wɛldə*] n (person) saldatore m.
welding ['wɛldɪŋ] n saldatura (autogena).
welfare ['wɛlfɛə*] n benessere m.
welfare state n stato assistenziale.
welfare work n assistenza sociale.
well [wɛl] n pozzo ♦ ad bene ♦ a: **to be** ~ (person) stare bene ♦ excl allora!; ma!; ebbene!; ~ **done!** bravo(a)!; **get** ~ **soon!** guarisci presto!; **to do** ~ **in sth** riuscire in

qc; **to be doing** ~ stare bene; **to think** ~ **of sb** avere una buona opinione di qn; **I don't feel** ~ non mi sento bene; **as** ~ (in addition) anche; **X as** ~ **as Y** sia X che Y; **he did as** ~ **as he could** ha fatto come meglio poteva; **you might as** ~ **tell me** potresti anche dirmelo; **it would be as** ~ **to ask** sarebbe bene chiedere; ~, **as I was saying** ... dunque, come stavo dicendo ....
  well up vi (tears, emotions) sgorgare.
we'll [wi:l] = **we will, we shall**.
well-behaved ['wɛlbɪ'heɪvd] a ubbidiente.
well-being ['wɛl'bi:ɪŋ] n benessere m.
well-bred ['wɛl'brɛd] a educato(a), beneducato(a).
well-built ['wɛl'bɪlt] a (person) ben fatto(a).
well-chosen ['wɛl'tʃəuzn] a (remarks, words) ben scelto(a), appropriato(a).
well-developed ['wɛldɪ'vɛləpt] a sviluppato(a).
well-disposed ['wɛldɪs'pəuzd] a: ~ **to(wards)** bendisposto(a) verso.
well-dressed ['wɛl'drɛst] a ben vestito(a), vestito(a) bene.
well-earned ['wɛl'ə:nd] a (rest) meritato(a).
well-groomed ['wɛl'gru:md] a curato(a), azzimato(a).
well-heeled ['wɛl'hi:ld] a (col: wealthy) agiato(a), facoltoso(a).
well-informed ['welɪn'fɔ:md] a ben informato(a).
Wellington ['wɛlɪŋtən] n Wellington f.
wellingtons ['wɛlɪŋtənz] npl (also: **wellington boots**) stivali mpl di gomma.
well-kept ['wɛl'kɛpt] a (house, grounds, secret) ben tenuto(a); (hair, hands) ben curato(a).
well-known ['wɛl'nəun] a noto(a), famoso(a).
well-mannered ['wɛl'mænəd] a ben educato(a).
well-meaning ['wɛl'mi:nɪŋ] a ben intenzionato(a).
well-nigh ['wɛl'naɪ] ad: ~ **impossible** quasi impossibile.
well-off ['wɛl'ɔf] a benestante, danaroso(a).
well-read ['wɛl'rɛd] a colto(a).
well-spoken ['wɛl'spəukn] a che parla bene.
well-stocked ['wɛl'stɔkt] a (shop, larder) ben fornito(a).
well-timed ['wɛl'taɪmd] a opportuno(a).
well-to-do ['wɛltə'du:] a abbiente, benestante.
well-wisher ['wɛlwɪʃə*] n ammiratore/trice; **letters from** ~**s** lettere fpl di incoraggiamento.
Welsh [wɛlʃ] a gallese ♦ n (LING) gallese m; **the** ~ npl i gallesi.
Welshman, Welshwoman ['wɛlʃmən, -wumən] n gallese m/f.
Welsh rarebit n crostino al formaggio.
welter ['wɛltə*] n massa, mucchio.
went [wɛnt] pt of **go**.
wept [wɛpt] pt, pp of **weep**.
were [wə:*] pt of **be**.
we're [wɪə*] = **we are**.

weren't [wɔ:nt] = **were not.**

werewolf, *pl* **-wolves** ['wɪəwulf, -wulvz] *n* licantropo, lupo mannaro (*col*).

west [wɛst] *n* ovest *m*, occidente *m*, ponente *m* ♦ *a* (a) ovest *inv*, occidentale ♦ *ad* verso ovest; **the W~** l'Occidente.

westbound ['wɛstbaund] *a* (*traffic*) diretto(a) a ovest; (*carriageway*) ovest *inv*.

West Country *n*: **the ~** il sud-ovest dell'Inghilterra.

westerly ['wɛstəlɪ] *a* (*wind*) occidentale, da ovest.

western ['wɛstən] *a* occidentale, dell'ovest ♦ *n* (*CINEMA*) western *m inv*.

westernized ['wɛstənaɪzd] *a* occidentalizzato(a).

West German *a, n* tedesco(a) occidentale.

West Germany *n* Germania Occidentale.

West Indian *a* delle Indie Occidentali ♦ *n* abitante *m/f* (*or* originario/a) delle Indie Occidentali.

West Indies [-'ɪndɪz] *npl*: **the ~** le Indie Occidentali.

westward(s) ['wɛstwəd(z)] *ad* verso ovest.

wet [wɛt] *a* umido(a), bagnato(a); (*soaked*) fradicio(a); (*rainy*) piovoso(a) ♦ *vt*: **to ~ one's pants** *or* **o.s.** farsi la pipì addosso; **to get ~** bagnarsi; **"~ paint"** "vernice fresca".

wet blanket *n* (*fig*) guastafeste *m/f inv*.

wetness ['wɛtnɪs] *n* umidità.

wet suit *n* tuta da sub.

we've [wi:v] = **we have.**

whack [wæk] *vt* picchiare, battere.

whacked [wækt] *a* (*col*: *tired*) sfinito(a), a pezzi.

whale [weɪl] *n* (*ZOOL*) balena.

whaler ['weɪlə*] *n* (*ship*) baleniera.

wharf, *pl* **wharves** [wɔ:f, wɔ:vz] *n* banchina.

what [wɔt] *excl* cosa!, come! ♦ *a* quale ♦ *pronoun* (*interrogative*) che cosa, cosa, che; (*relative*) quello che, ciò che; **~ are you doing?** che *or* (che) cosa fa?; **~'s happening?** che *or* (che) cosa succede?; **~'s in there?** cosa c'è lì dentro?; **for ~ reason?** per quale motivo?; **I saw ~ you did/was on the table** ho visto quello che ha fatto/quello che era sul tavolo; **I don't know ~ to do** non so cosa fare; **~ a mess!** che disordine!; **~ is his address?** qual'è il suo indirizzo?; **~ will it cost?** quanto sarà *or* costerà?; **~ is it called?** come si chiama?; **~ I want is a cup of tea** ciò che voglio adesso è una tazza di tè; **~ about doing ...?** cosa ne diresti di fare ...; **~ about me?** e io?

whatever [wɔt'ɛvə*] *a*: **~ book** qualunque *or* qualsiasi libro + *sub* ♦ *pronoun*: **do ~ is necessary/you want** faccia qualunque *or* qualsiasi cosa sia necessaria/lei voglia, **~ happens** qualunque cosa accada; **no reason ~** *or* **whatsoever** nessuna ragione affatto *or* al mondo; **~ it costs** costi quello che costi.

whatsoever [wɔtsəu'ɛvə*] = **whatever.**

wheat [wi:t] *n* grano, frumento.

wheatgerm ['wi:tdʒə:m] *n* germe *m* di grano.

wheatmeal ['wi:tmi:l] *n* farina integrale di frumento.

wheedle ['wi:dl] *vt*: **to ~ sb into doing sth** convincere qn a fare qc (con lusinghe); **to ~ sth out of sb** ottenere qc da qn (con lusinghe).

wheel [wi:l] *n* ruota; (*AUT*: *also*: **steering ~**) volante *m*; (*NAUT*) (ruota del) timone *m* ♦ *vt* spingere ♦ *vi* (*also*: **~ round**) girare.

wheelbarrow ['wi:lbærəu] *n* carriola.

wheelbase ['wi:lbeɪs] *n* interasse *m*.

wheelchair ['wi:ltʃɛə*] *n* sedia a rotelle.

wheel clamp *n* (*AUT*) morsetto *m* bloccaruota *inv*.

wheeler-dealer ['wi:lə'di:lə*] *n* trafficone *m*, maneggione *m*.

wheeling ['wi:lɪŋ] *n*: **~ and dealing** maneggi *mpl*.

wheeze [wi:z] *n* respiro affannoso ♦ *vi* ansimare.

when [wɛn] *ad* quando ♦ *cj* quando, nel momento in cui; (*whereas*) mentre; **on the day ~** il giorno in cui.

whenever [wɛn'ɛvə*] *ad* quando mai ♦ *cj* quando; (*every time that*) ogni volta che; **I go ~ I can** ci vado ogni volta che posso.

where [wɛə*] *ad, cj* dove; **this is ~** è qui che; **~ are you from?** di dov'è?; **~ possible** quando è possibile, se possibile.

whereabouts ['wɛərəbauts] *ad* dove ♦ *n*: **sb's ~** luogo dove qn si trova.

whereas [wɛər'æz] *cj* mentre.

whereby [wɛə'baɪ] *ad* (*formal*) per cui.

whereupon [wɛərə'pɔn] *ad* al che.

wherever [wɛər'ɛvə*] *ad* dove mai ♦ *cj* dovunque + *sub*; **sit ~ you like** si sieda dove vuole.

wherewithal ['wɛəwɪðɔ:l] *n*: **the ~ (to do sth)** i mezzi (per fare qc).

whet [wɛt] *vt* (*tool*) affilare; (*appetite etc*) stimolare.

whether ['wɛðə*] *cj* se; **I don't know ~ to accept or not** non so se accettare o no; **it's doubtful ~** è poco probabile che; **~ you go or not** che lei vada o no.

whey [weɪ] *n* siero.

which [wɪtʃ] *a* (*interrogative*) che, quale; **~ one of you?** chi di voi?; **tell me ~ one you want** mi dica quale vuole ♦ *pronoun* (*interrogative, indirect*) quale; (*relative: subject*) che; (: *object*) che, *prep* + cui, il(la) quale; **I don't mind ~** non mi importa quale; **the apple ~ you ate/~ is on the table** la mela che ha mangiato/che è sul tavolo; **the chair on ~** la sedia sulla quale *or* su cui; **the book of ~** il libro del quale *or* di cui; **he said he knew, ~ is true/I feared** disse che lo sapeva, il che è vero/ciò che temevo; **after ~** dopo di che; **in ~ case** nel qual caso; **by ~ time** e a quel punto.

whichever [wɪtʃ'ɛvə*] *a*: **take ~ book you prefer** prenda qualsiasi libro che preferisce; **~ book you take** qualsiasi libro prenda; **~ way you ...** in qualunque modo lei ... + *sub*.

whiff [wɪf] n odore m; **to catch a ~ of sth** sentire l'odore di qc.

while [waɪl] n momento ♦ cj mentre; (as long as) finché; (although) sebbene + sub; **for a ~** per un po'; **in a ~** tra poco; **all the ~** tutto il tempo; **we'll make it worth your ~** faremo in modo che le valga la pena.
 while away vt (time) far passare.

whilst [waɪlst] cj = **while**.

whim [wɪm] n capriccio.

whimper ['wɪmpə*] n piagnucolio ♦ vi piagnucolare.

whimsical ['wɪmzɪkl] a (person) capriccioso(a); (look) strano(a).

whine [waɪn] n gemito ♦ vi gemere; uggiolare; piagnucolare.

whip [wɪp] n frusta; (for riding) frustino; (POL: person) capogruppo (che sovrintende alla disciplina dei colleghi di partito) ♦ vt frustare; (CULIN: cream etc) sbattere; (snatch) sollevare (or estrarre) bruscamente.
 whip up vt (cream) montare, sbattere; (col: meal) improvvisare; (: stir up: support, feeling) suscitare, stimolare.

whiplash ['wɪplæʃ] n (MED: also: ~ **injury**) colpo di frusta.

whipped cream ['wɪpt-] n panna montata.

whipping boy ['wɪpɪŋ-] n (fig) capro espiatorio.

whip-round ['wɪpraund] n (Brit) colletta.

whirl [wə:l] n turbine m ♦ vt (far) girare rapidamente; (far) turbinare ♦ vi turbinare; (dancers) volteggiare; (leaves, dust) sollevarsi in un vortice.

whirlpool ['wə:lpu:l] n mulinello.

whirlwind ['wə:lwɪnd] n turbine m.

whirr [wə:*] vi ronzare.

whisk [wɪsk] n (CULIN) frusta; frullino ♦ vt sbattere, frullare; **to ~ sb away** or **off** portar via qn a tutta velocità.

whiskers ['wɪskəz] npl (of animal) baffi mpl; (of man) favoriti mpl.

whisky, (Irish, US) **whiskey** ['wɪskɪ] n whisky m inv.

whisper ['wɪspə*] n bisbiglio, sussurro; (rumour) voce f ♦ vt, vi bisbigliare, sussurrare; **to ~ sth to sb** bisbigliare qc a qn.

whispering ['wɪspərɪŋ] n bisbiglio.

whist [wɪst] n (Brit) whist m.

whistle ['wɪsl] n (sound) fischio; (object) fischietto ♦ vi fischiare ♦ vt fischiare; **to ~ a tune** fischiettare un motivetto.

whistle-stop ['wɪslstɔp] a: ~ **tour** (POL, fig) rapido giro.

Whit [wɪt] n Pentecoste f.

white [waɪt] a bianco(a); (with fear) pallido(a) ♦ n bianco; (person) bianco/a; **to turn** or **go ~** (person) sbiancare; (hair) diventare bianco; **the ~s** (washing) i capi bianchi; **tennis ~s** completo da tennis.

whitebait ['waɪtbeɪt] n bianchetti mpl.

white coffee n (Brit) caffellatte m inv.

white-collar worker ['waɪtkɔlə-] n impiegato/a.

white elephant n (fig) oggetto (or progetto) costoso ma inutile.

white goods npl (appliances) elettrodomestici mpl; (linens) biancheria per la casa.

white-hot [waɪt'hɔt] a (metal) incandescente.

white lie n bugia pietosa.

whiteness ['waɪtnɪs] n bianchezza.

white noise n rumore m bianco.

white paper n (POL) libro bianco.

whitewash ['waɪtwɔʃ] n (paint) bianco di calce ♦ vt imbiancare; (fig) coprire.

whiting ['waɪtɪŋ] n (pl inv) merlango.

Whit Monday n lunedì m inv di Pentecoste.

Whitsun ['wɪtsn] n Pentecoste f.

whittle ['wɪtl] vt: **to ~ away, ~ down** ridurre, tagliare.

whizz [wɪz] vi passare sfrecciando.

whizz kid n (col) prodigio.

WHO n abbr (= World Health Organization) O.M.S. f (= Organizzazione mondiale della sanità).

who [hu:] pronoun (interrogative) chi; (relative) che.

whodunit [hu:'dʌnɪt] n (col) giallo.

whoever [hu:'ɛvə*] pronoun: ~ **finds it** chiunque lo trovi; **ask ~ you like** lo chieda a chiunque vuole; ~ **told you that?** chi mai gliel'ha detto?

whole [həul] a (complete) tutto(a), completo(a); (not broken) intero(a), intatto(a) ♦ n (total) totale m; (sth not broken) tutto; **the ~ lot (of it)** tutto; **the ~ lot (of them)** tutti; **the ~ of the time** tutto il tempo; **the ~ of the town** la città intera; **on the ~, as a ~** nel complesso, nell'insieme; ~ **villages were destroyed** interi paesi furono distrutti.

wholehearted [həul'hɑ:tɪd] a sincero(a).

wholemeal ['həulmi:l] a (Brit: flour, bread) integrale.

whole note n (US) semibreve f.

wholesale ['həulseɪl] n commercio or vendita all'ingrosso ♦ a all'ingrosso; (destruction) totale.

wholesaler ['həulseɪlə*] n grossista m/f.

wholesome ['həulsəm] a sano(a); (climate) salubre.

wholewheat ['həulwi:t] a = **wholemeal**.

wholly ['həulɪ] ad completamente, del tutto.

whom [hu:m] pronoun che, prep + il(la) quale; (interrogative) chi; **those to ~ I spoke** le persone con le quali ho parlato.

whooping cough ['hu:pɪŋ-] n pertosse f.

whoosh [wuʃ] n: **it came out with a ~** (sauce etc) è uscito di getto; (air) è uscito con un sibilo.

whopper ['wɔpə*] n (col: lie) balla; (: large thing) cosa enorme.

whopping ['wɔpɪŋ] a (col: big) enorme.

whore [hɔ:*] n (pej) puttana.

whose [hu:z] a: ~ **book is this?** di chi è questo libro?; ~ **pencil have you taken?** di chi è la matita che ha preso?; **the man ~ son you rescued** l'uomo di cui or del quale ha salvato il figlio; **the girl ~ sister you were speaking to** la ragazza alla cui sorella *or* alla sorella della quale stava parlando ♦ *pronoun*: **~ is this?** di chi è questo?; **I know ~ it is** so di chi è.

Who's Who ['huːz'huː] *n* elenco di personalità.

why [waɪ] *ad, cj* perché ♦ *excl* (*surprise*) ma guarda un po'!; (*remonstrating*) ma (via)!; (*explaining*) ebbene!; **~ not?** perché no?; **~ not do it now?** perché non farlo adesso?; **the reason ~** il motivo per cui.

whyever [waɪ'ɛvə*] *ad* perché mai.

WI *n abbr* (*Brit*: = *Women's Institute*) circolo femminile ♦ *abbr* (*GEO*) = **West Indies**; (*US POST*) = *Wisconsin*.

wick [wɪk] *n* lucignolo, stoppino.

wicked ['wɪkɪd] *a* cattivo(a), malvagio(a); (*mischievous*) malizioso(a); (*terrible: prices, weather*) terribile.

wicker ['wɪkə*] *n* vimine *m*; (*also*: **~work**) articoli *mpl* di vimini.

wicket ['wɪkɪt] *n* (*CRICKET*) porta; area tra le due porte.

wicket keeper *n* (*CRICKET*) ≈ portiere *m*.

wide [waɪd] *a* largo(a); (*region, knowledge*) vasto(a); (*choice*) ampio(a) ♦ *ad*: **to open ~** spalancare; **to shoot ~** tirare a vuoto *or* fuori bersaglio; **it is 3 metres ~** è largo 3 metri.

wide-angle lens ['waɪdæŋgl-] *n* grandangolare *m*.

wide-awake [waɪdə'weɪk] *a* completamente sveglio(a).

wide-eyed [waɪd'aɪd] *a* con gli occhi spalancati.

widely ['waɪdlɪ] *ad* (*different*) molto, completamente; (*believed*) generalmente; **~ spaced** molto distanziati(e); **to be ~ read** (*author*) essere molto letto; (*reader*) essere molto colto.

widen ['waɪdn] *vt* allargare, ampliare.

wideness ['waɪdnɪs] *n* larghezza; vastità; ampiezza.

wide open *a* spalancato(a).

wide-ranging [waɪd'reɪndʒɪŋ] *a* (*survey, report*) vasto(a); (*interests*) svariato(a).

widespread ['waɪdsprɛd] *a* (*belief etc*) molto *or* assai diffuso(a).

widow ['wɪdəu] *n* vedova.

widowed ['wɪdəud] *a* (che è rimasto(a)) vedovo(a).

widower ['wɪdəuə*] *n* vedovo.

width [wɪdθ] *n* larghezza; **it's 7 metres in ~** è largo 7 metri.

widthways ['wɪdθweɪz] *ad* trasversalmente.

wield [wiːld] *vt* (*sword*) maneggiare; (*power*) esercitare.

wife, *pl* **wives** [waɪf, waɪvz] *n* moglie *f*.

wig [wɪg] *n* parrucca.

wigging ['wɪgɪŋ] *n* (*Brit col*) lavata di capo.

wiggle ['wɪgl] *vt* dimenare, agitare ♦ *vi* (*loose screw etc*) traballare; (*worm*) torcersi.

wiggly ['wɪglɪ] *a* (*line*) ondulato(a),

sinuoso(a).

wild [waɪld] *a* (*animal, plant*) selvatico(a); (*countryside, appearance*) selvaggio(a); (*sea*) tempestoso(a); (*idea, life*) folle; (*col: angry*) arrabbiato(a), furibondo(a); (*enthusiastic*): **to be ~ about** andar pazzo(a) per ♦ *n*: **the ~** la natura; **~s** *npl* regione *f* selvaggia.

wild card *n* (*COMPUT*) wild card *m inv*.

wildcat ['waɪldkæt] *n* gatto(a) selvatico(a).

wildcat strike *n* ≈ sciopero selvaggio.

wilderness ['wɪldənɪs] *n* deserto.

wildfire ['waɪldfaɪə*] *n*: **to spread like ~** propagarsi rapidamente.

wild-goose chase [waɪld'guːs-] *n* (*fig*) pista falsa.

wildlife ['waɪldlaɪf] *n* natura.

wildly ['waɪldlɪ] *ad* (*applaud*) freneticamente; (*hit, guess*) a casaccio; (*happy*) follemente.

wiles [waɪlz] *npl* astuzie *fpl*.

wilful, (*US*) **willful** ['wɪlful] *a* (*person*) testardo(a); ostinato(a); (*action*) intenzionale; (*crime*) premeditato(a).

will [wɪl] *auxiliary vb*: **he ~ come** verrà ♦ *vt* (*pt, pp* **~ed**): **to ~ sb to do** pregare (tra sé) perché qn faccia; **he ~ed himself to go on** continuò grazie a un grande sforzo di volontà ♦ *n* volontà; (*LAW*) testamento; **you won't lose it, ~ you?** non lo perderai, vero?; **that ~ be the postman** (*in conjectures*) sarà il postino; **~ you sit down** (*politely*) prego, si accomodi; (*angrily*) vuoi metterti seduto!; **the car won't start** la macchina non parte; **against sb's ~** contro la volontà *or* il volere di qn; **to do sth of one's own free ~** fare qc di propria volontà.

willful ['wɪlful] *a* (*US*) = **wilful**.

willing ['wɪlɪŋ] *a* volenteroso(a) ♦ *n*: **to show ~** dare prova di buona volontà; **~ to do** disposto(a) a fare.

willingly ['wɪlɪŋlɪ] *ad* volentieri.

willingness ['wɪlɪŋnɪs] *n* buona volontà.

will-o'-the-wisp [wɪləðə'wɪsp] *n* (*also fig*) fuoco fatuo.

willow ['wɪləu] *n* salice *m*.

will power *n* forza di volontà.

willy-nilly ['wɪlɪ'nɪlɪ] *ad* volente o nolente.

wilt [wɪlt] *vi* appassire.

Wilts [wɪlts] *abbr* (*Brit*) = *Wiltshire*.

wily ['waɪlɪ] *a* furbo(a).

wimp [wɪmp] *n* (*col*) mezza calzetta.

win [wɪn] *n* (*in sports etc*) vittoria ♦ *vb* (*pt, pp* **won** [wʌn]) *vt* (*battle, prize*) vincere; (*money*) guadagnare; (*popularity*) conquistare; (*contract*) aggiudicarsi ♦ *vi* vincere.

win over, (*Brit*) **win round** *vt* convincere.

wince [wɪns] *n* trasalimento, sussulto ♦ *vi* trasalire.

winch [wɪntʃ] *n* verricello, argano.

Winchester disk ['wɪntʃɪstə-] *n* (*COMPUT*) disco Winchester.

wind *n* [wɪnd] vento; (*MED*) flatulenza, ventosità ♦ *vb* [waɪnd] (*pt, pp* **wound** [waund]) *vt* attorcigliare; (*wrap*) avvolgere;

(*clock*, *toy*) caricare; (*take breath away*: [wɪnd]) far restare senza fiato ♦ *vi* (*road*, *river*) serpeggiare; **the ~(s)** (*MUS*) i fiati; **into** *or* **against the ~** controvento; **to get ~ of sth** venire a sapere qc; **to break ~** scoreggiare (*col*).

wind down *vt* (*car window*) abbassare; (*fig*: *production*, *business*) diminuire.

wind up *vt* (*clock*) caricare; (*debate*) concludere.

windbreak ['wɪndbreɪk] *n* frangivento.

windcheater ['wɪndtʃiːtə*], (*US*) **windbreaker** ['wɪndbreɪkə*] *n* giacca a vento.

winder ['waɪndə*] *n* (*Brit*: *on watch*) corona di carica.

windfall ['wɪndfɔːl] *n* colpo di fortuna.

winding ['waɪndɪŋ] *a* (*road*) serpeggiante; (*staircase*) a chiocciola.

wind instrument *n* (*MUS*) strumento a fiato.

windmill ['wɪndmɪl] *n* mulino a vento.

window ['wɪndəu] *n* (*gen*, *COMPUT*) finestra; (*in car*, *train*) finestrino; (*in shop etc*) vetrina; (*also*: **~ pane**) vetro.

window box *n* cassetta da fiori.

window cleaner *n* (*person*) pulitore *m* di finestre.

window dressing *n* allestimento della vetrina.

window envelope *n* busta a finestra.

window frame *n* telaio di finestra.

window ledge *n* davanzale *m*.

window pane *n* vetro.

window-shopping ['wɪndəuʃɔpɪŋ] *n*: **to go ~** andare a vedere le vetrine.

windowsill ['wɪndəusɪl] *n* davanzale *m*.

windpipe ['wɪndpaɪp] *n* trachea.

windscreen ['wɪndskriːn], (*US*) **windshield** ['wɪndʃiːld] *n* parabrezza *m inv*.

windscreen washer *n* lavacristallo.

windscreen wiper *n* tergicristallo.

windshield ['wɪndʃiːld] *n* (*US*) = **windscreen**.

windswept ['wɪndswɛpt] *a* spazzato(a) dal vento.

wind tunnel *n* galleria aerodinamica *or* del vento.

windy ['wɪndɪ] *a* ventoso(a); **it's ~** c'è vento.

wine [waɪn] *n* vino ♦ *vt*: **to ~ and dine sb** offrire un ottimo pranzo a qn.

wine cellar *n* cantina.

wine glass *n* bicchiere *m* da vino.

wine list *n* lista dei vini.

wine merchant *n* commerciante *m* di vino.

wine tasting *n* degustazione *f* dei vini.

wine waiter *n* sommelier *m inv*.

wing [wɪŋ] *n* ala; **~s** *npl* (*THEATRE*) quinte *fpl*.

winger ['wɪŋə*] *n* (*SPORT*) ala.

wing mirror *n* (*Brit*) specchietto retrovisore esterno.

wing nut *n* galletto.

wingspan ['wɪŋspæn], **wingspread** ['wɪŋsprɛd] *n* apertura alare, apertura d'ali.

wink [wɪŋk] *n* occhiolino, strizzatina d'occhi ♦

vi ammiccare, fare l'occhiolino.

winkle ['wɪŋkl] *n* litorina.

winner ['wɪnə*] *n* vincitore/trice.

winning ['wɪnɪŋ] *a* (*team*) vincente; (*goal*) decisivo(a); (*charming*) affascinante; *see also* **winnings**.

winning post *n* traguardo.

winnings ['wɪnɪŋz] *npl* vincite *fpl*.

winsome ['wɪnsəm] *a* accattivante.

winter ['wɪntə*] *n* inverno; **in ~** d'inverno, in inverno.

winter sports *npl* sport *mpl* invernali.

wintry ['wɪntrɪ] *a* invernale.

wipe [waɪp] *n* pulita, passata ♦ *vt* pulire (strofinando); (*dishes*) asciugare; **to give sth a ~** dare una pulita *or* una passata a qc; **to ~ one's nose** soffiarsi il naso.

wipe off *vt* cancellare; (*stains*) togliere strofinando.

wipe out *vt* (*debt*) pagare, liquidare; (*memory*) cancellare; (*destroy*) annientare.

wipe up *vt* asciugare.

wire ['waɪə*] *n* filo; (*ELEC*) filo elettrico; (*TEL*) telegramma *m* ♦ *vt* (*ELEC*: *house*) fare l'impianto elettrico di; (: *circuit*) installare; (*also*: **~ up**) collegare, allacciare.

wire brush *n* spazzola metallica.

wire cutters [-kʌtəz] *npl* tronchese *m or f*.

wireless ['waɪəlɪs] *n* (*Brit*) telegrafia senza fili; (*set*) (apparecchio *m*) radio *f inv*.

wire netting *n* rete *f* metallica.

wire-tapping ['waɪə'tæpɪŋ] *n* intercettazione *f* telefonica.

wiring ['waɪərɪŋ] *n* (*ELEC*) impianto elettrico.

wiry ['waɪərɪ] *a* magro(a) e nerboruto(a).

wisdom ['wɪzdəm] *n* saggezza; (*of action*) prudenza.

wisdom tooth *n* dente *m* del giudizio.

wise [waɪz] *a* saggio(a); (*advice*, *remark*) prudente; **I'm none the ~r** ne so come prima.

wise up *vi* (*col*): **to ~ up to** divenire più consapevole di.

...wise [waɪz] *suffix*: **time~** per quanto riguarda il tempo, in termini di tempo.

wisecrack ['waɪzkræk] *n* battuta spiritosa.

wish [wɪʃ] *n* (*desire*) desiderio; (*specific desire*) richiesta ♦ *vt* desiderare, volere; **best ~es** (*on birthday etc*) i migliori auguri; **with best ~es** (*in letter*) cordiali saluti, con i migliori saluti; **give her my best ~es** le faccia i migliori auguri da parte mia; **to ~ sb goodbye** dire arrivederci a qn; **he ~ed me well** mi augurò di riuscire; **to ~ to do/sb to do** desiderare *or* volere fare/che qn faccia; **to ~ for** desiderare; **to ~ sth on sb** rifilare qc a qn.

wishful ['wɪʃful] *a*: **it's ~ thinking** è prendere i desideri per realtà.

wishy-washy ['wɪʃɪ'wɔʃɪ] *a* insulso(a).

wisp [wɪsp] *n* ciuffo, ciocca; (*of smoke*, *straw*) filo.

wistful ['wɪstful] *a* malinconico(a); (*nostalgic*) nostalgico(a).

wit [wɪt] n (gen pl) intelligenza; presenza di spirito; (wittiness) spirito, arguzia; (person) bello spirito; **to be at one's ~s' end** (fig) non sapere più cosa fare; **to have** or **keep one's ~s about one** avere presenza di spirito; **to ~** ad cioè.

witch [wɪtʃ] n strega.

witchcraft ['wɪtʃkrɑːft] n stregoneria.

witch doctor n stregone m.

witch-hunt ['wɪtʃhʌnt] n (fig) caccia alle streghe.

with [wɪð, wɪθ] prep con; **red ~ anger** rosso dalla or per la rabbia; **covered ~ snow** coperto di neve; **the man ~ the grey hat** l'uomo dal cappello grigio; **to shake ~ fear** tremare di paura; **to stay overnight ~ friends** passare la notte da amici; **to be ~ it** (fig) essere al corrente; essere sveglio(a); **I am ~ you** (I understand) la seguo.

withdraw [wɪθ'drɔː] vb (irg) vt ritirare; (money from bank) ritirare, prelevare ♦ vi ritirarsi; **to ~ into o.s.** chiudersi in se stesso.

withdrawal [wɪθ'drɔːəl] n ritiro; prelievo; (of army) ritirata; (MED) stato di privazione.

withdrawal symptoms npl crisi f di astinenza.

withdrawn [wɪθ'drɔːn] pp of **withdraw** ♦ a distaccato(a).

wither ['wɪðə*] vi appassire.

withered ['wɪðəd] a appassito(a); (limb) atrofizzato(a).

withhold [wɪθ'həuld] vt irg (money) trattenere; (permission): **to ~ (from)** rifiutare (a); (information): **to ~ (from)** nascondere (a).

within [wɪð'ɪn] prep all'interno di; (in time, distances) entro ♦ ad all'interno, dentro; **~ sight of** in vista di; **~ a mile of** entro un miglio da; **~ the week** prima della fine della settimana; **~ an hour from now** da qui a un'ora; **to be ~ the law** restare nei limiti della legge.

without [wɪð'aut] prep senza; **to go** or **do ~ sth** fare a meno di qc; **~ anybody knowing** senza che nessuno lo sappia.

withstand [wɪθ'stænd] vt irg resistere a.

witness ['wɪtnɪs] n (person) testimone m/f ♦ vt (event) essere testimone di; (document) attestare l'autenticità di ♦ vi: **to ~ to sth/having seen sth** testimoniare qc/di aver visto qc; **to bear ~ to sth** testimoniare qc; **~ for the prosecution/defence** testimone a carico/discarico.

witness box, (US) **witness stand** n banco dei testimoni.

witticism ['wɪtɪsɪzəm] n spiritosaggine f.

witty ['wɪtɪ] a spiritoso(a).

wives [waɪvz] npl of **wife**.

wizard ['wɪzəd] n mago.

wizened ['wɪznd] a raggrinzito(a).

wk abbr = **week**.

Wm. abbr = **William**.

WO n abbr see **warrant officer**.

wobble ['wɔbl] vi tremare; (chair) traballare.

wobbly ['wɔblɪ] a (hand, voice) tremante; (table, chair) traballante; (object about to fall) che oscilla pericolosamente.

woe [wəu] n dolore m; disgrazia.

woke [wəuk] pt of **wake**.

woken ['wəukn] pp of **wake**.

wolf, pl **wolves** [wulf, wulvz] n lupo.

woman, pl **women** ['wumən, 'wɪmɪn] n donna ♦ cpd: **~ doctor** n dottoressa; **~ friend** n amica; **~ teacher** n insegnante f; **women's page** n (PRESS) rubrica femminile.

womanize ['wumənaɪz] vi essere un donnaiolo.

womanly ['wumənlɪ] a femminile.

womb [wuːm] n (ANAT) utero.

women ['wɪmɪn] npl of **woman**.

Women's (Liberation) Movement n (also: **Women's Lib**) Movimento per la Liberazione della Donna.

won [wʌn] pt, pp of **win**.

wonder ['wʌndə*] n meraviglia ♦ vi: **to ~ whether** domandarsi se; **to ~ at** essere sorpreso(a) di; meravigliarsi di; **to ~ about** domandarsi di; pensare a; **it's no ~ that** c'è poco or non c'è da meravigliarsi che + sub.

wonderful ['wʌndəful] a meraviglioso(a).

wonderfully ['wʌndəfəlɪ] ad (+ adjective) meravigliosamente; (+ verb) a meraviglia.

wonky ['wɔŋkɪ] a (Brit col) traballante.

won't [wəunt] = **will not**.

woo [wuː] vt (woman) fare la corte a.

wood [wud] n legno; (timber) legname m; (forest) bosco ♦ cpd di bosco, silvestre.

wood carving n scultura in legno, intaglio.

wooded ['wudɪd] a boschivo(a); boscoso(a).

wooden ['wudn] a di legno; (fig) rigido(a); inespressivo(a).

woodland ['wudlənd] n zona boscosa.

woodpecker ['wudpɛkə*] n picchio.

wood pigeon n colombaccio, palomba.

woodwind ['wudwɪnd] npl (MUS): **the ~** i legni.

woodwork ['wudwəːk] n parti fpl in legno; (craft, subject) falegnameria.

woodworm ['wudwɔːm] n tarlo del legno.

woof [wuf] n (of dog) bau bau m ♦ vi abbaiare; **~, ~!** bau bau!

wool [wul] n lana; **to pull the ~ over sb's eyes** (fig) fargliela a qn.

woollen, (US) **woolen** ['wulən] a di lana ♦ n: **~s** indumenti mpl di lana.

woolly, (US) **wooly** ['wulɪ] a lanoso(a); (fig: ideas) confuso(a).

word [wəːd] n parola; (news) notizie fpl ♦ vt esprimere, formulare; **~ for ~** parola per parola, testualmente; **what's the ~ for "pen" in Italian?** come si dice "pen" in italiano?; **to put sth into ~s** esprimere qc a parole; **in other ~s** in altre parole; **to have a ~ with sb** scambiare due parole con qn; **to have ~s with sb** (quarrel with) avere un diverbio con qn; **to break/keep one's ~** non mantenere/mantenere la propria parola; **I'll take your ~ for it** la crederò sulla parola; **to**

send ~ **of** avvisare di; **to leave ~ (with** *or* **for sb) that** ... lasciare detto (a qn) che ....

wording ['wɔ:dɪŋ] *n* formulazione *f*.

word-perfect ['wɔ:d'pɔfɪkt] *a* (*speech etc*) imparato(a) a memoria.

word processing *n* word processing *m*, elaborazione *f* testi.

word processor *n* word processor *m inv*.

wordwrap ['wɔ:dræp] *n* (*COMPUT*) ritorno carrello automatico.

wordy ['wɔ:dɪ] *a* verboso(a), prolisso(a).

wore [wɔ:*] *pt of* wear.

work [wɔ:k] *n* lavoro; (*ART, LITERATURE*) opera ♦ *vi* lavorare; (*mechanism, plan etc*) funzionare; (*medicine*) essere efficace ♦ *vt* (*clay, wood etc*) lavorare; (*mine etc*) sfruttare; (*machine*) far funzionare; **to be at ~ (on sth)** lavorare (a qc); **to set to ~, to start ~** mettersi all'opera; **to go to ~** andare al lavoro; **to be out of ~** essere disoccupato(a); **to ~ one's way through a book** riuscire a leggersi tutto un libro; **to ~ one's way through college** lavorare per pagarsi gli studi; **to ~ hard** lavorare sodo; **to ~ loose** allentarsi; *see also* **works**.

work on *vt fus* lavorare a; (*principle*) basarsi su; **he's ~ing on the car** sta facendo dei lavori alla macchina.

work out *vi* (*plans etc*) riuscire, andare bene; (*SPORT*) allenarsi ♦ *vt* (*problem*) risolvere; (*plan*) elaborare; **it ~s out at £100** fa 100 sterline.

workable ['wɔ:kəbl] *a* (*solution*) realizzabile.

workaholic [wɔ:kə'hɔlɪk] *n* stacanovista *m/f*.

workbench ['wɔ:kbɛntʃ] *n* banco (da lavoro).

worked up *a*: **to get ~** andare su tutte le furie; eccitarsi.

worker ['wɔ:kə*] *n* lavoratore/trice; (*esp AGR, INDUSTRY*) operaio/a; **office ~** impiegato/a.

work force *n* forza lavoro.

work-in ['wɔ:kɪn] *n* (*Brit*) sciopero alla rovescia.

working ['wɔ:kɪŋ] *a* (*day*) feriale; (*tools, conditions*) di lavoro; (*clothes*) da lavoro; (*wife*) che lavora; (*partner*) attivo(a); **in ~ order** funzionante; **~ knowledge** conoscenza pratica.

working capital *n* (*COMM*) capitale *m* d'esercizio.

working class *n* classe *f* operaia *or* lavoratrice ♦ *a*: **working-class** operaio(a).

working man *n* lavoratore *m*.

working model *n* modello operativo.

working party *n* (*Brit*) commissione *f*.

working week *n* settimana lavorativa.

work-in-progress ['wɔ:kɪn'prəugrɛs] *n* (*products*) lavoro in corso; (*value*) valore *m* del manufatto in lavorazione.

workload ['wɔ:kləud] *n* carico di lavoro.

workman ['wɔ:kmən] *n* operaio.

workmanship ['wɔ:kmənʃɪp] *n* (*of worker*) abilità; (*of thing*) fattura.

workmate ['wɔ:kmeɪt] *n* collega *m/f*.

workout ['wɔ:kaut] *n* (*SPORT*) allenamento.

work permit *n* permesso di lavoro.

works [wɔ:ks] *n* (*Brit: factory*) fabbrica ♦ *npl* (*of clock, machine*) meccanismo; **road ~** opere stradali.

works council *n* consiglio aziendale.

work sheet *n* (*COMPUT*) foglio col programma di lavoro.

workshop ['wɔ:kʃɔp] *n* officina.

work station *n* stazione *f* di lavoro.

work study *n* studio di organizzazione del lavoro.

work-to-rule ['wɔ:ktə'ru:l] *n* (*Brit*) sciopero bianco.

world [wɔ:ld] *n* mondo ♦ *cpd* (*tour*) del mondo; (*record, power, war*) mondiale; **all over the ~** in tutto il mondo; **to think the ~ of sb** pensare un gran bene di qn; **out of this ~** (*fig*) formidabile; **what in the ~ is he doing?** che cavolo sta facendo?; **to do sb a ~ of good** fare un gran bene a qn; **W~ War One/Two** la prima/seconda guerra mondiale.

world champion *n* campione/essa mondiale.

World Cup *n* (*FOOTBALL*) Coppa del Mondo.

world-famous [wɔ:ld'feɪməs] *a* di fama mondiale.

worldly ['wɔ:ldlɪ] *a* di questo mondo.

world-wide ['wɔ:ld'waɪd] *a* universale.

worm [wɔ:m] *n* verme *m*.

worn [wɔ:n] *pp of* wear ♦ *a* usato(a).

worn-out ['wɔ:naut] *a* (*object*) consumato(a), logoro(a); (*person*) sfinito(a).

worried ['wʌrɪd] *a* preoccupato(a); **to be ~ about sth** essere preoccupato per qc.

worrier ['wʌrɪə*] *n* ansioso/a.

worrisome ['wʌrɪsəm] *a* preoccupante.

worry ['wʌrɪ] *n* preoccupazione *f* ♦ *vt* preoccupare ♦ *vi* preoccuparsi; **to ~ about** *or* **over sth/sb** preoccuparsi di qc/per qn.

worrying ['wʌrɪɪŋ] *a* preoccupante.

worse [wɔ:s] *a* peggiore ♦ *ad, n* peggio; **a change for the ~** un peggioramento; **to get ~, to grow ~** peggiorare; **he is none the ~ for it** non ha avuto brutte conseguenze; **so much the ~ for you!** tanto peggio per te!

worsen ['wɔ:sn] *vt, vi* peggiorare.

worse off *a* in condizioni (economiche) peggiori; (*fig*): **you'll be ~ this way** così sarà peggio per lei; **he is now ~ than before** ora è in condizioni peggiori di prima.

worship ['wɔ:ʃɪp] *n* culto ♦ *vt* (*God*) adorare, venerare; (*person*) adorare; **Your W~** (*to mayor*) signor sindaco; (*to judge*) signor giudice.

worshipper ['wɔ:ʃɪpə*] *n* adoratore/trice; (*in church*) fedele *m/f*, devoto/a.

worst [wɔ:st] *a* il(la) peggiore ♦ *ad, n* peggio; **at ~** al peggio, per male che vada; **to come off ~** avere la peggio; **if the ~ comes to the ~** nel peggior dei casi.

worsted ['wustɪd] *n*: (**wool**) ~ lana pettinata.

worth [wɔ:θ] *n* valore *m* ♦ *a*: **to be ~** valere; **how much is it ~?** quanto vale?; **it's ~ it** ne vale la pena; **it's not ~ the trouble** non ne vale la pena; **50 pence ~ of apples** 50 pence di mele.

worthless ['wə:θlɪs] *a* di nessun valore.

worthwhile ['wə:θ'waɪl] *a* (*activity*) utile; (*cause*) lodevole; **a ~ book** un libro che vale la pena leggere.

worthy ['wə:ðɪ] *a* (*person*) degno(a); (*motive*) lodevole; **~ of** degno di.

would [wud] *auxiliary vb*: **she ~ come** verrebbe; **he ~ have come** sarebbe venuto; **~ you like a biscuit?** vuole *or* vorrebbe un biscotto?; **~ you close the door, please** chiuda la porta per favore; **he ~ go there on Mondays** ci andava il lunedì; **you** *WOULD* **say that, ~n't you!** (*emphatic*) doveva dirlo, vero!; **he ~n't behave** (*insistence*) non ha voluto comportarsi bene.

would-be ['wudbi:] *a* (*pej*) sedicente.

wound *vb* [waund] *pt, pp of* **wind ♦** *n, vt* [wu:nd] *n* ferita ♦ *vt* ferire; **~ed in the leg** ferito(a) alla gamba.

wove [wəuv] *pt of* **weave**.

woven ['wəuvən] *pp of* **weave**.

WP *abbr* (*Brit col*: = *weather permitting*) tempo permettendo ♦ *n abbr* = **word processing; word processor**.

WPC *n abbr* (*Brit*: = *woman police constable*) donna poliziotto.

wpm *abbr* (= *words per minute*) p.p.m.

WRAC *n abbr* (*Brit*: = *Women's Royal Army Corps*) ausiliarie dell'esercito.

WRAF *n abbr* (*Brit*: = *Women's Royal Air Force*) ausiliarie dell'aeronautica militare.

wrangle ['ræŋgl] *n* litigio ♦ *vi* litigare.

wrap [ræp] *n* (*stole*) scialle *m*; (*cape*) mantellina ♦ *vt* (*also*: ~ **up**) avvolgere; (*parcel*) incartare; **under ~s** segreto.

wrapper ['ræpə*] *n* (*of book*) copertina; (*on chocolate*) carta.

wrapping paper ['ræpɪŋ-] *n* carta da pacchi; (*for gift*) carta da regali.

wrath [rɔθ] *n* collera, ira.

wreak [ri:k] *vt* (*destruction*) portare, causare; **to ~ vengeance on** vendicarsi su; **to ~ havoc on** portare scompiglio in.

wreath, ~s [ri:θ, ri:ðz] *n* corona.

wreck [rɛk] *n* (*sea disaster*) naufragio; (*ship*) relitto; (*pej: person*) rottame *m* ♦ *vt* demolire; (*ship*) far naufragare; (*fig*) rovinare.

wreckage ['rɛkɪdʒ] *n* rottami *mpl*; (*of building*) macerie *fpl*; (*of ship*) relitti *mpl*.

wrecker ['rɛkə*] *n* (*US: breakdown van*) carro *m* attrezzi *inv*.

WREN [rɛn] *n abbr* (*Brit*) membro del *WRNS*.

wren [rɛn] *n* (*ZOOL*) scricciolo.

wrench [rɛntʃ] *n* (*TECH*) chiave *f*; (*tug*) torsione *f* brusca; (*fig*) strazio ♦ *vt* strappare; storcere; **to ~ sth from** strappare qc a *or* da.

wrest [rɛst] *vt*: **to ~ sth from sb** strappare qc a qn.

wrestle ['rɛsl] *vi*: **to ~ (with sb)** lottare (con qn); **to ~ with** (*fig*) combattere *or* lottare contro.

wrestler ['rɛslə*] *n* lottatore/trice.

wrestling ['rɛslɪŋ] *n* lotta; (*also*: **all-in ~**: *Brit*) catch *m*, lotta libera.

wrestling match *n* incontro di lotta (*or* lotta libera).

wretch [rɛtʃ] *n* disgraziato/a, sciagurato/a; **little ~!** (*often humorous*) birbante!

wretched ['rɛtʃɪd] *a* disgraziato(a); (*col: weather, holiday*) orrendo(a), orribile; (: *child, dog*) pestifero(a).

wriggle ['rɪgl] *n* contorsione *f* ♦ *vi* dimenarsi; (*snake, worm*) serpeggiare, muoversi serpeggiando.

wring *pt, pp* **wrung** [rɪŋ, rʌŋ] *vt* torcere; (*wet clothes*) strizzare; (*fig*): **to ~ sth out of** strappare qc a.

wringer ['rɪŋə*] *n* strizzatoio (manuale).

wringing ['rɪŋɪŋ] *a* (*also*: ~ **wet**) bagnato(a) fradicio(a).

wrinkle ['rɪŋkl] *n* (*on skin*) ruga; (*on paper etc*) grinza ♦ *vt* corrugare; raggrinzire ♦ *vi* corrugarsi; raggrinzirsi.

wrinkled ['rɪŋkld], **wrinkly** ['rɪŋklɪ] *a* (*fabric, paper*) stropicciato(a); (*surface*) corrugato(a), increspato(a); (*skin*) rugoso(a).

wrist [rɪst] *n* polso.

wristband ['rɪstbænd] *n* (*of shirt*) polsino; (*of watch*) cinturino.

wrist watch *n* orologio da polso.

writ [rɪt] *n* ordine *m*; mandato; **to issue a ~ against sb, serve a ~ on sb** notificare un mandato di comparizione a qn.

write, *pt* **wrote**, *pp* **written** [raɪt, rəut, 'rɪtn] *vt, vi* scrivere; **to ~ sb a letter** scrivere una lettera a qn.

write away *vi*: **to ~ away for** (*information*) richiedere per posta; (*goods*) ordinare per posta.

write down *vt* annotare; (*put in writing*) mettere per iscritto.

write off *vt* (*debt*) cancellare; (*depreciate*) deprezzare; (*smash up: car*) distruggere.

write out *vt* scrivere; (*copy*) ricopiare.

write up *vt* redigere.

write-off ['raɪtɔf] *n* perdita completa; **the car is a ~** la macchina va bene per il demolitore.

write-protect ['raɪtprə'tɛkt] *vt* (*COMPUT*) proteggere contro scrittura.

writer ['raɪtə*] *n* autore/trice, scrittore/trice.

write-up ['raɪtʌp] *n* (*review*) recensione *f*.

writhe [raɪð] *vi* contorcersi.

writing ['raɪtɪŋ] *n* scrittura; (*of author*) scritto, opera; **in ~** per iscritto; **in my own ~** scritto di mio pugno.

writing case *n* nécessaire *m inv* per la corrispondenza.

writing desk *n* scrivania, scrittoio.

writing paper *n* carta da scrivere.

written ['rɪtn] *pp of* **write**.

WRNS *n abbr* (*Brit*: = *Women's Royal Naval Service*) ausiliarie della marina militare.

wrong [rɔŋ] *a* sbagliato(a); (*not suitable*)

inadatto(a); (wicked) cattivo(a); (unfair) ingiusto(a) ♦ ad in modo sbagliato, erroneamente ♦ n (evil) male m; (injustice) torto ♦ vt fare torto a; **to be ~** (answer) essere sbagliato; (in doing, saying) avere torto; **you are ~ to do it** ha torto a farlo; **you are ~ about that, you've got it ~** si sbaglia; **to be in the ~** avere torto; **what's ~?** cosa c'è che non va?; **there's nothing ~** va tutto bene; **what's ~ with the car?** cos'ha la macchina che non va?; **to go ~** (person) sbagliarsi; (plan) fallire, non riuscire; (machine) guastarsi; **it's ~ to steal, stealing is ~** è male rubare.

wrongful ['rɔŋful] a illegittimo(a); ingiusto(a); **~ dismissal** licenziamento ingiustificato.

wrongly ['rɔŋli] ad (accuse, dismiss) a torto; (answer, do, count) erroneamente; (treat) ingiustamente.

wrong number n: **you have the ~** (TEL) ha sbagliato numero.

wrong side n (of cloth) rovescio.

wrote [rəut] pt of **write**.

wrought [rɔːt] a: **~ iron** ferro battuto.

wrung [rʌŋ] pt, pp of **wring**.

WRVS n abbr (Brit) = Women's Royal Voluntary Service.

wry [rai] a storto(a).

wt. abbr = **weight**.

WV abbr (US POST) = West Virginia.

WY abbr (US POST) = Wyoming.

WYSIWYG ['wiziwig] abbr (COMPUT) = what you see is what you get.

X

X, x [ɛks] n (letter) X, x f or m inv; (Brit CINEMA: old) ≈ film vietato ai minori di 18 anni; **X for Xmas** ≈ X come Xeres.

Xerox ® ['ziərɔks] n (also: **~ machine**) fotocopiatrice f; (photocopy) fotocopia ♦ vt fotocopiare.

XL abbr = extra large.

Xmas ['ɛksməs] n abbr = **Christmas**.

X-rated ['ɛks'reitid] a (US: film) ≈ vietato ai minori di 18 anni.

X-ray ['ɛks'rei] n raggio X; (photograph) radiografia ♦ vt radiografare; **to have an ~** farsi fare una radiografia.

xylophone ['zailəfəun] n xilofono.

Y

Y, y [wai] n (letter) Y, y f or m inv; **Y for Yellow**, (US) **Y for Yoke** ≈ Y come Yacht.

yacht [jɔt] n panfilo, yacht m inv.

yachting ['jɔtiŋ] n yachting m, sport m della vela.

yachtsman ['jɔtsmən] n yachtsman m inv.

yam [jæm] n igname m; (sweet potato) patata dolce.

Yank [jæŋk], **Yankee** ['jæŋki] n (pej) yankee m/f inv, nordamericano/a.

yank [jæŋk] n strattone m ♦ vt tirare, dare uno strattone a.

yap [jæp] vi (dog) guaire.

yard [jɑːd] n (of house etc) cortile m; (US: garden) giardino; (measure) iarda (= 914 mm; 3 feet); **builder's ~** deposito di materiale da costruzione.

yardstick ['jɑːdstik] n (fig) misura, criterio.

yarn [jɑːn] n filato; (tale) lunga storia.

yawn [jɔːn] n sbadiglio ♦ vi sbadigliare.

yawning ['jɔːniŋ] a (gap) spalancato(a).

yd. abbr = **yard**.

yeah [jɛə] ad (col) sì.

year [jiə*] n (gen, SCOL) anno; (referring to harvest, wine etc) annata; **every ~** ogni anno, tutti gli anni; **this ~** quest'anno; **~ in, ~ out** anno dopo anno; **she's three ~s old** ha tre anni; **a or per ~** all'anno.

yearbook ['jiəbuk] n annuario.

yearly ['jiəli] a annuale ♦ ad annualmente; **twice-~** semestrale.

yearn [jəːn] vi: **to ~ for sth/to do** desiderare ardentemente qc/di fare.

yearning ['jəːniŋ] n desiderio intenso.

yeast [jiːst] n lievito.

yell [jɛl] n urlo ♦ vi urlare.

yellow ['jɛləu] a giallo(a).

yellow fever n febbre f gialla.

yellowish ['jɛləuiʃ] a giallastro(a), giallognolo(a).

Yellow Sea n: **the ~** il mar Giallo.

yelp [jɛlp] n guaito, uggiolio ♦ vi guaire, uggiolare.

Yemen ['jɛmən] n Yemen m.

yen [jɛn] n (currency) yen m inv; (craving): **~ for/to do** gran voglia di/di fare.

yeoman ['jəumən] n: **Y~ of the Guard** guardiano della Torre di Londra.

yes [jɛs] ad, n sì (m inv); **to say ~ (to)** dire di sì (a), acconsentire (a).

yesterday ['jɛstədi] ad, n ieri (m inv); **~ morning/evening** ieri mattina/sera; **the day before ~** l'altro ieri; **all day ~** ieri tutto il giorno.

yet [jɛt] *ad* ancora; già ♦ *cj* ma, tuttavia; **it is not finished** ~ non è ancora finito; **the best** ~ il migliore finora; **as** ~ finora; ~ **again** di nuovo; **must you go just** ~? deve andarsene di già?; **a few days** ~ ancora qualche giorno.

yew [ju:] *n* tasso (*albero*).

YHA *n abbr* (*Brit*: = *Youth Hostels Association*) Y.H.A. *f*.

Yiddish ['jɪdɪʃ] *n* yiddish *m*.

yield [ji:ld] *n* resa; (*of crops etc*) raccolto ♦ *vt* produrre, rendere; (*surrender*) cedere ♦ *vi* cedere; (*US AUT*) dare la precedenza; **a** ~ **of 5%** un profitto *or* un interesse del 5%.

YMCA *n abbr* (= *Young Men's Christian Association*) Y.M.C.A. *m*.

yob(bo) ['jɔb(əu)] *n* (*Brit col*) bullo.

yodel ['jəudl] *vi* cantare lo jodel *or* alla tirolese.

yoga ['jəugə] *n* yoga *m*.

yog(h)ourt, yog(h)urt ['jəugət] *n* iogurt *m inv*.

yoke [jəuk] *n* giogo ♦ *vt* (*also*: ~ **together**: *oxen*) aggiogare.

yolk [jəuk] *n* tuorlo, rosso d'uovo.

yonder ['jɔndə*] *ad* là.

Yorks [jɔ:ks] *abbr* (*Brit*) = *Yorkshire*.

you [ju:] *pronoun* tu; (*polite form*) lei; (*pl*) voi; (: *very formal*) loro; (*complement*: *direct*) ti; la; vi; li; (: *indirect*) ti; le; vi; gli; (*stressed*) te; lei; voi; loro; (*one*) si; **fresh air does** ~ **good** l'aria fresca fa bene; ~ **never know** non si sa mai; **I'll see** ~ **tomorrow** ti (*or* la *etc*) vedrò domani; **if I was** *or* **were** ~ se fossi in te (*or* lei *etc*).

you'd [ju:d] = **you had; you would**.

you'll [ju:l] = **you will; you shall**.

young [jʌŋ] *a* giovane ♦ *npl* (*of animal*) piccoli *mpl*; (*people*): **the** ~ i giovani, la gioventù; **a** ~ **man** un giovanotto; **a** ~ **lady** una signorina; **a** ~ **woman** una giovane donna; **the** ~**er generation** la nuova generazione; **my** ~**er brother** il mio fratello minore.

youngish ['jʌŋɪʃ] *a* abbastanza giovane.

youngster ['jʌŋstə*] *n* giovanotto/a; (*child*) bambino/a.

your [jɔ:*] *a* il(la) tuo(a), *pl* i(le) tuoi(tue); (*polite form*) il(la) suo(a), *pl* i(le) suoi(sue); (*pl*) il(la) vostro(a), *pl* i(le) vostri(e); (: *very formal*) il(la) loro, *pl* i(le) loro.

you're [juə*] = **you are**.

yours [jɔ:z] *pronoun* il(la) tuo(a), *pl* i(le) tuoi(tue); (*polite form*) il(la) suo(a), *pl* i(le) suoi(sue); (*pl*) il(la) vostro(a), *pl* i(le) vostri(e); (: *very formal*) il(la) loro, *pl* i(le) loro; ~ **sincerely/faithfully** (*in letter*) cordiali/distinti saluti; **a friend of** ~ un tuo (*or* suo *etc*) amico; **is it** ~? è tuo (*or* suo *etc*)?

yourself [jɔ:'sɛlf] *pronoun* (*reflexive*) ti; (: *polite form*) si; (*after prep*) te; se; (*emphatic*) tu stesso(a); lei stesso(a); **you** ~ **told me** me l'hai detto proprio tu, tu stesso

me l'hai detto.

yourselves [jɔ:'sɛlvz] *pl pronoun* (*reflexive*) vi; (: *polite form*) si; (*after prep*) voi; loro; (*emphatic*) voi stessi(e); loro stessi(e).

youth [ju:θ] *n* gioventù *f*; (*young man: pl* ~**s** [ju:ðz]) giovane *m*, ragazzo; **in my** ~ da giovane, quando ero giovane.

youth club *n* centro giovanile.

youthful ['ju:θful] *a* giovane; da giovane; giovanile.

youthfulness ['ju:θfəlnɪs] *n* giovinezza.

youth hostel *n* ostello della gioventù.

youth movement *n* movimento giovanile.

you've [ju:v] = **you have**.

yowl [jaul] *n* (*of dog, person*) urlo; (*of cat*) miagolio ♦ *vi* urlare; miagolare.

yr *abbr* = **year**.

YT *abbr* (*Canada*) = *Yukon Territory*.

YTS *n abbr* (*Brit*: = *Youth Training Scheme*) *programma di tirocinio per giovani tramite sovvenzioni al datore di lavoro*.

Yugoslav ['ju:gəuslɑ:v] *a*, *n* jugoslavo(a).

Yugoslavia [ju:gəu'slɑ:vɪə] *n* Jugoslavia.

Yugoslavian [ju:gəu'slɑ:vɪən] *a*, *n* jugoslavo(a).

Yule log [ju:l-] *n* ceppo nel caminetto a Natale.

yuppie ['jʌpɪ] *a*, *n* (*col*) yuppie (*m/f*) *inv*.

YWCA *n abbr* (= *Young Women's Christian Association*) Y.W.C.A. *m*.

Z

Z, z [zɛd, (*US*) zi:] *n* (*letter*) Z, z *f or m inv*; **Z for Zebra** ≈ Z come Zara.

Zaire [zɑ:'ɪə*] *n* Zaire *m*.

Zambia ['zæmbɪə] *n* Zambia *m*.

Zambian ['zæmbɪən] *a*, *n* zambiano(a).

zany ['zeɪnɪ] *a* un po' pazzo(a).

zap [zæp] *vt* (*COMPUT*) cancellare.

zeal [zi:l] *n* zelo; entusiasmo.

zealot ['zɛlət] *n* zelota *m/f*.

zealous ['zɛləs] *a* zelante; premuroso(a).

zebra ['zi:brə] *n* zebra.

zebra crossing *n* (*Brit*) (passaggio pedonale a) strisce *fpl*, zebre *fpl*.

zenith ['zɛnɪθ] *n* zenit *m inv*; (*fig*) culmine *m*.

zero ['zɪərəu] *n* zero; **5° below** ~ 5° sotto zero.

zero hour *n* l'ora zero.

zero-rated ['zɪərəu'reɪtd] *a* (*Brit*) ad aliquota zero.

zest [zɛst] *n* gusto; (*CULIN*) buccia.

zigzag ['zɪgzæg] *n* zigzag *m inv* ♦ *vi* zigzagare.

Zimbabwe [zɪm'bɑ:bwɪ] *n* Zimbabwe *m*.

Zimbabwean [zɪm'bɑ:bwɪən] *a* dello Zimbabwe.

zinc [zɪŋk] *n* zinco.

Zionism ['zaɪənɪzəm] *n* sionismo.
Zionist ['zaɪənɪst] *a* sionistico(a) ♦ *n* sionista *m/f*.
zip [zɪp] *n* (*also:* ~ **fastener,** (*US*) ~**per**) chiusura *f or* cerniera *f* lampo *inv*; (*energy*) energia, forza ♦ *vt* (*also:* ~ **up**) chiudere con una cerniera lampo.
zip code *n* (*US*) codice *m* di avviamento postale.
zither ['zɪðə*] *n* cetra.
zodiac ['zəudɪæk] *n* zodiaco.
zombie ['zɔmbɪ] *n* (*fig*): **like a** ~ come un morto che cammina.

zone [zəun] *n* zona.
zoo [zuː] *n* zoo *m inv*.
zoological [zuə'lɔdʒɪkl] *a* zoologico(a).
zoologist [zuː'ɔlədʒɪst] *n* zoologo/a.
zoology [zuː'ɔlədʒɪ] *n* zoologia.
zoom [zuːm] *vi*: **to** ~ **past** sfrecciare; **to** ~ **in (on sb/sth)** (*PHOT, CINEMA*) zumare (su qn/qc).
zoom lens *n* zoom *m inv*, obiettivo a focale variabile.
zucchini [zuː'kiːnɪ] *n* (*pl inv*) (*US*) zucchina.
Zulu ['zuːluː] *a, n* zulù (*m/f*) *inv*.
Zürich ['zjuərɪk] *n* Zurigo *f*.